*"Value-packed, accur...
comprehensive..."*

—*Los Angeles Times*

"Unbeatable..."

—*The Washington Post*

Let's Go
USA & CANADA

is the best book for anyone traveling on a budget. Here's why:

■ No other guidebook has as many budget listings.

Take New York City, for example. We list 10 accommodations for under $30. In San Francisco we found 8 hostels and hotels for less than $19. We tell you how to get there the cheapest way, whether by bus, plane, or bike, and where to get an inexpensive and satisfying meal once you've arrived. We give hundreds of money-saving tips that anyone can use, plus invaluable advice on discounts and deals for students, children, families, and senior travelers.

■ Let's Go researchers have to make it on their own.

Our Harvard-Radcliffe researcher-writers travel on budgets as tight as your own—no expense accounts, no free hotel rooms.

■ Let's Go is completely revised each year.

We don't just update the prices, we go back to the place. If a charming cafe has become an overpriced tourist trap, we'll replace the listing with a new and better one.

■ No other guidebook includes all this:

Honest, engaging coverage of both the cities and the countryside; up-to-the-minute prices, directions, addresses, phone numbers, and opening hours; in-depth essays on local culture, history, and politics; comprehensive listings on transportation between and within regions and cities; straight advice on work and study, budget accommodations, sights, nightlife, and food; detailed city and regional maps; and much more.

■ Let's Go is for anyone who wants to see the USA and Canada on a budget.

Books by Let's Go, Inc.

EUROPE

Let's Go: Europe

Let's Go: Austria

Let's Go: Britain & Ireland

Let's Go: France

Let's Go: Germany & Switzerland

Let's Go: Greece & Turkey

Let's Go: Ireland

Let's Go: Italy

Let's Go: London

Let's Go: Paris

Let's Go: Rome

Let's Go: Spain & Portugal

NORTH & CENTRAL AMERICA

Let's Go: USA & Canada

Let's Go: Alaska & The Pacific Northwest

Let's Go: California & Hawaii

Let's Go: New York City

Let's Go: Washington, D.C.

Let's Go: Mexico

MIDDLE EAST & ASIA

Let's Go: Israel & Egypt

Let's Go: Thailand

Let's Go

The Budget Guide to the

USA & CANADA
1994

Mark D. Moody
Editor

Maia A. Gemmill
Assistant Editor

John D. Ruark
Assistant Editor

Written by
Let's Go, Inc.
A subsidiary of
Harvard Student Agencies, Inc.

M
Macmillan Reference

HELPING LET'S GO

If you have suggestions or corrections, or just want to share your discoveries, drop us a line. We read every piece of correspondence, whether a 10-page letter, a velveteen Elvis postcard, or, as in one case, a collage. All suggestions are passed along to our researcher-writers. Please note that mail received after May 5, 1994 will probably be too late for the 1995 book, but will be retained for the following edition. Address mail to:

Let's Go: USA & Canada
Let's Go, Inc.
1 Story Street
Cambridge, MA 02138
USA

In addition to the invaluable travel advice our readers share with us, many are kind enough to offer their services as researchers or editors. Unfortunately, the charter of Let's Go, Inc. and Harvard Student Agencies, Inc. enables us to employ only currently enrolled Harvard students.

Published in Great Britain 1994 by Pan Macmillan Ltd., Cavaye Place, London SW10 9PG.

10 9 8 7 6 5 4 3 2 1

Maps by David Lindroth, copyright © 1994, 1993, 1992, 1991, 1990, 1989 by St. Martin's Press, Inc.

Published in the United States of America by St. Martin's Press, Inc.

ISBN: 0 333 61153 5

Let's Go: **USA & Canada** is written by the Publishing Division of Let's Go, Inc., 1 Story Street, Cambridge, MA 02138.

Editor	Mark D. Moody
Assistant Editors	Maia Anastasia Gemmill
	John D. Ruark
Managing Editor	Peter Jon Lindberg
Publishing Director	Mark N. Templeton
Production Manager	Edward Owen
Office Coordinator	Susan P. Krause
Assistant General Manager	Anne E. Chisholm

Researcher-Writers

Connecticut (except New Haven), Kentucky, Massachusetts (Berkshires), Michigan, New York (Albany, Catskills, Cooperstown, Finger Lakes, Niagara Falls), Ohio, Ontario (except Ottawa), Pennsylvania (western half), West Virginia (Monongahela National Forest)	John Aboud III
New Jersey (Atlantic City), New York (New York City and Long Island)	Allen Baler
Maine, Massachusetts (Cape Cod, Martha's Vineyard, Nantucket, Plymouth), New Brunswick, Newfoundland (except Labrador), New Hampshire, New York (Adirondacks, Thousand Island Seaway), Nova Scotia, Ontario (Ottawa), Prince Edward Island, Québec, Vermont	Natalie Boutin
Arizona (Grand Canyon North Rim), Colorado, Nevada (Las Vegas), Utah, Wyoming (Casper and Cheyenne)	Carrie Busch
California (Lake Tahoe, Marin County, Mono Lake, Northern California, Yosemite), Nevada (Reno and Carson City), Oregon (Klamath Falls and Crater Lake)	Sergio Camacho
Maryland, Washington, D.C.	Caralee Caplan
Connecticut (New Haven), New York (New York City)	Danielle Do
California (Berkeley, San Francisco, Santa Cruz)	Michael Echenberg
California (The Desert, Kings Canyon and Sequoia National Parks, Mammoth Lakes, Orange County)	Brian Ericson
Oregon (except Klamath Falls and Crater Lake), Washington	Jen Etter
Hawaii	David Filippi
Massachusetts (Boston Area)	Maia Anastasia Gemmill
Alabama, Arkansas, Georgia (Atlanta), Louisiana, Mississippi, North Carolina (Carolina Mountains), Tennessee	Risa Goluboff
Alaska (The Panhandle, Southcentral Alaska except Wrangell-St. Elias National Park)	Seth Harkness
Alaska (Denali National Park, Fairbanks, Wrangell-St. Elias National Park), Yukon Territory	Matthew Heid
Virginia (Williamsburg and Virginia Beach), Washington, D.C., West Virginia (Harper's Ferry)	Sam Hilton

Acknowledgments

RESEARCHER-WRITERS

John Aboud III is Ma Lampy's boy, and his eye for kitsch and laugh-a-minute headers (fourteen-ninety-food, indeed!) filled his Rust Belt route with chortles. Not afraid to tell it like it is, the drab and drear withered under his pen ("a city so boring they set *Howard the Duck* here") while he exposed the American Midwest.

Natalie Boutin survived a startlingly long itinerary—from Cape Cod, Massachusetts to Cape Breton, Nova Scotia and Cape St. Francis, Newfoundland—and despite the public transportation horrors of the rural northeast, piled us with absolutely amazing coverage. Our own *Parisienne*, Natalie filled Montréal with *élan*, and brought us "The Rock" with always funky, ever-upbeat prose. *Merci.*

Carrie Busch blitzed through the West on a grand tour of some grand country and the Grand Canyon, expanding our listings beyond our wildest dreams. Visiting some of the highest points in the U.S., the quality of Carrie's prose was as great as her altitudes.

Risa Goluboff was this year's Southern Belle, taking in N'awlins, North Carolina, and the Ozarks, praising their virtues while exposing their frequently tragic past. Her evenhanded discourse on an often denigrated region brought a breath of Southern warmth to 1 Story St., and a kinder, better coverage of the Southland.

Amelia Kaplan held in her trust the heartland, and delivered, finding hipness in Iowa City and echoing the call of the Prairie Buffalo in her glowing intros. Initially wary, Amelia was a convert to the lure of the plains by midsummer, rhapsodizing about the vibrancy of small-town America.

Ann Kennon ranged through the southwest, facing auto rental disaster (twice) and grueling stretches of dusty highway. Stranded in Phoenix for days, Ann got back on the road in a modern Conestoga and quickly lasooed Texas for us.

Jason Nolan battled mosquitoes in the Everglades and traffic cops in Palm Beach to bring Florida and the Atlantic seaboard the wryest coverage it had ever seen. Discovering the secret to world peace in Key West, his marginalia left us gasping for air for all the laughter as his Texan charm bucked Harvard's establishment grip.

Stephanie Stein drove through the wild and wooly north, facing blizzards in Jackson Hole and new ground in Canada, eh?; her incredibly compact copy squeezed lotsoffactsintoalittlespace and thrilled us with adventure ("today I got to pet a burro!"). Stephanie's "ice cream" itinerary kept us entertained for weeks.

Thanks are also due to the numerous people and organizations who have helped us this year. Chief among these are: Tom Little and Matilda Bosanac of **VIA Rail Canada,** Robin Kelleher of **Voyageur Colonial Limitée,** and Jennifer Chiles of **Greyhound.** Their encouragement and generosity are much appreciated.

—MDM, MAG, JDR

I have to start by thanking my RWs—without you all, this book would be nothing. Back in Cambridge, John and Maia deserve all my platitudes and more for putting up with my loose definition of working hours and an aborted attempt to escape to Latvia prematurely. Maia's bubbly enthusiasm spurred me on even when the things I hated most reared their heads (CRUNCH!), while John's computer wizardry and attention to detail more than made up for my grand designs foiled by reality. You guys are the greatest. Managing Editor Peter Lindroth...er, Lindberg gets praise for his support of the bloodsport GI Axe-o-Rama, and for more all-nighters than I can imagine. And for never making me turn in a Book Plan. And for Snausages.

More in-office thanks go to: Lynne, our fabulous substitute mommy; Ed, master of format, maps, and microchips; Mark Templeton, for his crisis-brokering; Anne, for level-headed influence; Justin "Chitterlings" Bernold for Espresso; Sue Krause for holding the office together; Mira for *letting* me hire a few good people and for

Spree; Liz (the *other* Big Book); UGH (for Boston, and for feeding me); NYWAS; Ben and Dov; and Amy and Nina and Steve and the rest for help on the last night. I've *also got to thank* Rebecca (C&H '93) for sending me to California to begin with. More *appreciation flows out* to Howard Blossom and George Barhorst for instilling my love of *rural wandering*. To Mom, Dad, Greg, Grandma, and the rest of the family, who have *supported me always*, even in running away to the other side of the world—I love you. Pittsburgh is *my birthday gift* to Adam—you're one helluva roommate. To Sue W., I owe the SW, my sanity, *and my senior year*: you're wonderful—what should I cook next? And kudos, of course, to *Bosun*. **—MDM**

Way back in June I didn't think this was possible. But we did it. Mark, you *didn't* know what you were getting into when you hired me, but I hope you're glad you did; I know I am. John's hyper-organization kept my scatterbrainedness under control; where would we have been without those damned colored dots!?!? Peter L put his all into his ME group—and inspired us to do the same. (SNAUSAGES!!!) Peter, you were there for us. Lynne "Canada is *too* a cool place" Echenberg proofread through the long night; thanks for helping me get through everything. Steve B., whose insightful proofing helped us to trim that fatty prose, lent his hand even though he still had to cut his book by 24 pages. Liz S. turned her veteran pen to our copy, while Justin and Marc zelanked through a few batches, too—our book is too *big*, guys; we try to *conserve* space. Even B&I (Mike and Tracey) pitched in—and their deadline was the same day as ours. Credit is also due to those who helped before the crunch—I know I wouldn't have made it through the summer without the bottomless patience of Ed O., computer-master extraordinaire, who answered all my stupid questions intelligently. And Ben and Mira—A&P is a beautiful book; it was a joy to crunch. Thanks for all your help. Nor would our tome be so wonderful without the tireless work of Sue Walther—you really saved us from possible disaster. Ben Wizner, you are, and will always be, my hero. The credit for my sanity lies with the witty e-mail of *gossip—what a relief it was to be able to sound off. Dov, you're the best. Pete, if I was the purple squash at the end of the tunnel, then you were certainly the blue, furry G. Thanks for everything; it's been wonderful. And of course my parents, who have made everything possible. I love you all. **—MAG**

I know right where to start, or, perhaps, end. Thanks to my four RWs: Natalie, Amelia, Jason, and Stephanie. Great job; I had fun typing your copy. Back at the ranch I must begin with my partner in format-o-mania, Maia Gemmill. Never at a loss for conversation, she remained chipper throughout, always optimistic and boundlessly exuberant. Peter "Lindy Lindroth" Lindberg has been, is, and always shall be, far too hip to be working on USA and Canada; B&I still seems more his calling. Also, AE thanks to those who hopped on board for the tough times; Lynne, Adina, Daniel, Ben, Mira, Dov, Ed (the in-house calm computer-guy), and all who proofed. Also to Phantom Regiment and Suncoast Sound '89, my fresh aire this summer. Sooperdooperlooper kudos to my boss and fellow St. Louisian Mark Moody, who landed me here in the first place. Ultimately, I owe my presence here in this office and this book to his eleventh-hour (11th-hr.? 11th hr.?) decision to bring me aboard. When I got crazy he was there to get me crazier, and, as such, budget travel to Labrador was born. Great indexing and 7am email, too (elvis and Moody's...). May you always find cheap and soft food in Latvia and St. Louis. Finally, to Liz, who inspired me to apply to LG to begin with. She helped me move, relax, do crosswords, learn, and deal with all sorts of problems, including moving again and a dreadful cabaret. Liz, everything will be, I believe, okay, no matter what happens or where you go. Mwah.

Let me not forget my brother Marcus, who has landed me tickets for DCI'94 (I may see you yet, Phantom), and my parents, who got me tickets for Boston and Harvard, and pretty much everything else in my life, including Tiger (mraowl). Thanks mom and dad. With that, I bid a fond farewell to Fair Harvard and head down to the mighty Institute, towards a PhD. *Illigetimum non carborundum.* **—JDR**

About Let's Go

Back in 1960, a few students at Harvard got together to produce a 20-page pamphlet offering a collection of tips on budget travel in Europe. For three years, Harvard Student Agencies, a student-run nonprofit corporation, had been doing a brisk business booking charter flights to Europe; this modest, mimeographed packet was offered to passengers as an extra. The following year, students traveling to Europe researched the first full-fledged edition of *Let's Go: Europe*, a pocket-sized book featuring advice on shoestring travel, irreverent write-ups of sights, and a decidedly youthful slant.

Throughout the 60s, the guides reflected the times: one section of the 1968 *Let's Go: Europe* talked about "Street Singing in Europe on No Dollars a Day." During the 70s, *Let's Go* gradually became a large-scale operation, adding regional European guides and expanding coverage into North Africa and Asia. The 80s saw the arrival of *Let's Go: USA & Canada* and *Let's Go: Mexico*, as well as regional North American guides; in the 90s we introduced five in-depth city guides to Paris, London, Rome, New York, and Washington, DC.

This year we're proud to announce three new guides: *Let's Go: Austria* (including Prague and Budapest), *Let's Go: Ireland*, and *Let's Go: Thailand* (including Honolulu, Tokyo, and Singapore), bringing our total number of titles up to twenty.

We've seen a lot in thirty-four years. *Let's Go: Europe* is now the world's #1 best selling international guide, translated into seven languages. And our guides are still researched, written, and produced entirely by students who know firsthand how to see the world on the cheap.

Every spring, we recruit nearly 100 researchers and an editorial team of 50 to write our books anew. Come summertime, after several months of training, researchers hit the road for seven weeks of exploration, from Bangkok to Budapest, Anchorage to Ankara. With pen and notebook in hand, a few changes of underwear stuffed in our backpacks, and a budget as tight as yours, we visit every *pensione*, *palapa*, pizzeria, café, club, campground, or castle we can find to make sure you'll get the most out of *your* trip.

We've put the best of our discoveries into the book you're now holding. A brand-new edition of each guide hits the shelves every year, only months after it was researched, so you know you're getting the most reliable, up-to-date, and comprehensive information available. And even as you read this, work on next year's editions is well underway.

At *Let's Go*, we think of budget travel not only as a means of cutting down on costs, but as a way of breaking down a few walls as well. Living cheap and simple on the road brings you closer to the real people and places you've been saving up to visit. This book will ease your anxieties and answer your questions about the basics—to help *you* get off the beaten track and explore. We encourage you to put *Let's Go* away now and then and strike out on your own. As any seasoned traveler will tell you, the best discoveries are often those you make yourself. If you find something worth sharing, drop us a line and let us know. We're at Let's Go, Inc., 1 Story Street, Cambridge, MA, 02138, USA.

Happy travels!

Contents

xi

Maps

How To Use This Book

Let's Go: USA & Canada, like Gaul, is divided into three parts. The opening section, **Essentials,** will tell you where to turn for all your pre-travel preparations, with tips on acquiring passports, visas, and other important documents, packing, how to save on the cost of transportation to North America, and the budget travel options once you're there. We also include information for travelers with specific concerns, such as women, gays and lesbians, and senior citizens.

In the second portion of the book, the **United States,** we divide the country into 12 geographic regions, presented roughly east to west and north to south. These regions contain travel information on all 50 states. Some of these regions are groups of states (such as New England), while others are single states (such as California). Each region is intended to present information on travel within an area of the country with geographical and historical similiarities. Within each region, the states are presented alphabetically; popular cities, parks, and other attractions that we cover are presented alphabetically within each state. The **USA Essentials** and **American Culture** sections contain travel information specific to the U.S. as well as brilliant monographs on U.S. history, architecture, and art.

Canada, the third section, is organized much like the U.S. The 11 provinces are presented east to west; important destinations are arranged alphabetically by province. **Canadian Essentials** provides information specific to travel in Canada, and **Canadian Culture** contains groundbreaking tracts on history, literature, and music.

For all of the destinations within Canada and the United States, whether a single city such as Montréal, or a large area like Cape Cod, we normally provide information on **Accommodations, Food, Camping, Sights,** and **Entertainment.** We also tell you all the **Practical Information** you will need as a budgeteer, including how to get there, how to get mail there, and where to seek aid, transportation, and welcome faces. Occasionally, we list excursionary trips.

Although our researchers beat an "annual trail across the nation," there are parts of the U.S. and Canada as yet undiscovered. Always keep an eye out for attractions that *Let's Go* doesn't list, and follow your spirit and imagination. If you intend to travel for an extended period, you may want to consider one of our regional guides, *Let's Go: Alaska & The Pacific Northwest* and *Let's Go:California & Hawaii,* or either of our city guides, *Let's Go: New York City* and *Let's Go: Washington, D.C.*

A NOTE TO OUR READERS

The information for this book is gathered by *Let's Go*'s researchers during the late spring and summer months. Each listing is derived from the assigned researcher's opinion based upon his or her visit at a particular time. The opinions are expressed in a candid and forthright manner. Other travelers might disagree. Those traveling at a different time may have different experiences since prices, dates, hours, and conditions are always subject to change. You are urged to check beforehand to avoid inconvenience and surprises. Travel always involves a certain degree of risk, especially in low-cost areas. When traveling, especially on a budget, you should always take particular care to ensure your safety.

EXPLORE THE EAST COAST WITH HOSTELLING INTERNATIONAL

New York   **Washington, DC**   **Miami Beach**

With Hostelling International you can visit some of America's exciting East Coast for a budget price. They're priced to fit a student's budget and are great places to meet people from all over the world. You can stay at a landmark building on the trendy Upper West Side of Manhattan, a highrise in the heart of the Nation's Capital or a historic masterpiece in Miami's Art Deco district just two blocks from the ocean. For reservations call:

New York City...................... (212) 932-2300
Washington, DC .... (202) 737-2333
Miami Beach .... (305) 534-2988

HOSTELLING INTERNATIONAL

The new seal of approval of the International Youth Hostel Federation.

HOSTELLING INTERNATIONAL®

■ ESSENTIALS

■ Planning Your Trip

When do you want to go? In every season it's tourist season someplace in the U.S. Some places are more pleasant in summer, others have primarily winter or fall draws. If you have a particular destination in mind, write to the chamber of commerce or visitors bureau to find out about local festivals and celebrations which you might want to attend (or avoid if you're looking for a quiet vacation). Traveling during the off-season has its advantages as well—transportation and accommodations may be cheaper, and sights won't be crawling with other tourists, but be sure to call ahead. They call it the off-season for a reason and the sights you traveled so far to see might be closed. Also take the weather into consideration when planning your vacation. Getting trapped in a blizzard in the Rockies in December or having to beat off swarms of helicopter-sized mosquitoes in the summer-time Everglades might be a less than pleasant experience.

Holidays

Official holidays may mean extended hours at some tourist attractions, but many banks and offices will close for the day.

U.S. holidays in 1994 are: **New Year's Day,** Sat. Jan. 1; **Martin Luther King, Jr.'s Birthday,** Mon. Jan. 17 (observed); **Presidents Day,** Mon. Feb. 21 (observed); **Memorial Day,** Mon. May 30; **Independence Day,** Sun. July 4; **Labor Day,** Mon. Sept. 5; **Columbus Day,** Mon. Oct. 10; **Veterans Day (Armistice Day),** Fri. Nov. 11 (observed); **Thanksgiving,** Thurs. Nov. 24; **Christmas Day,** Sun. Dec. 25.

In **Canada,** official holidays for 1994 fall on: **New Year's Day,** Sat. Jan.1; **Easter Monday,** Mon. April 4; **Victoria Day,** Mon. May 23; **Canada Day,** Fri. July 1; **Thanksgiving,** Mon. Oct. 10; **Remembrance Day,** Fri. Nov. 11; **Christmas Day,** Sun. Dec. 25; **Boxing Day,** Mon. Dec. 26.

U.S. Festivals

It can never be said the U.S. has passed up an opportunity to throw a party. There are lots of them here. Really smashing ones. The important thing to remember when trying to attend a classic American celebration is what city you need to be in.

New Year's Day (Jan. 1): Rose Bowl, Pasadena, CA; Orange Bowl, Miami, FL
St. Patrick's Day (Mar. 17): St. Pat's Day Parade, New York City, NY
Mardi Gras (Feb. 8-15): New Orleans, LA
Independence Day (July 4): celebrations in St. Louis, Boston, Washington, DC
Labor Day (Sept. 5): wherever the tourists are not
Thanksgiving (Nov. 24): Macy's Parade, New York City, NY
New Year's Eve (Dec. 31): Times Square, New York City, NY

■■■ USEFUL ORGANIZATIONS AND PUBLICATIONS

As you plan your itinerary, read the section of the book which covers that region. Write to the local chambers of commerce and visitors bureaus, who will happily pile you up with brochures, pamphlets, and other sorts of helpful info. They're out there to help you; take advantage of them. There are also many organizations catering directly to the needs of the budget traveler. Check 'em out; it can't hurt.

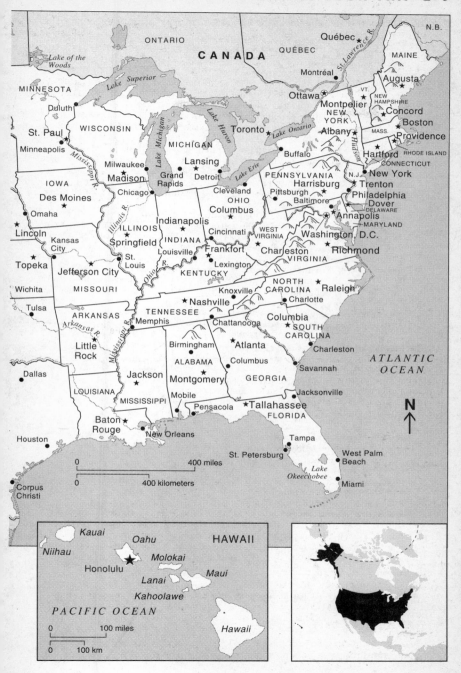

■ Budget Travel Services

Council on International Educational Exchange (CIEE/Council Travel/Council Charter): Low-cost travel arrangements, books (including *Let's Go* and *Where to Stay U.S.A.)* and gear. 43 U.S. offices, including Boston, Los Angeles, Chicago, Seattle, and the main office in **New York,** 205 E. 42nd St., NY 10017 (212-661-1450). In **Australia,** contact SSA/STA Swap Program, P.O. Box 399 (1st Floor), 220 Faraday St., Carlton South, Melbourne, Victoria 3053 (03 347 69 11). In the **United Kingdom,** contact London Student Travel, 52 Grosvenor Gardens, London WC1 ((071) 730 3402). In **Canada** write to Travel CUTS (see below). If you can't locate an affiliated office in your country, contact CIEE's office in New York.

STA Travel, 17 E. 45th St., New York, NY 10017 (800-777-0112 or 212-986-9470) operates 10 offices in the U.S. and over 100 offices around the world. Offers discount airfares for travelers under 26 and full-time students under 32. Main office in **Boston,** 273 Newbury St., MA 02116 (617-266-6014). In the **U.K.,** the main offices are at 86 Old Brompton Rd., London SW7 3LQ and 117 Euston Rd., London NW1 2SX (071) 937 9962 for North American travel). In **New Zealand,** 10 High St., Auckland ((09) 309 9995).

Travel CUTS, 187 College St., Toronto, Ont. M5T 1P7 (416-979-2406). In Britain, 295-A Regent St., London W1R 7YA ((071) 637 31 61). Does many wonderful, wonderful things, including offering discounted transatlantic and domestic flights with special student fares. Sells the ISIC, FIYTO and HI/IYHF hostel cards, and discount travel passes. Has 35 offices in Canada.

Campus Travel, 52 Grosvenor Gardens, London SW1W 0AG ((071) 730 88 32; fax (071) 730 57 39). A new travel service; offers special student and youth fares on travel by plane, train, boat and bus, as well as flexible airline tickets, so that you can change your date of travel on short notice without incurring big expenses. Also provides discount and ID cards for youths, special travel insurance for students and those under 35, and maps and guides.

■ Publications and Maps

Planning ahead includes reading up on your destinations. Look for relevant publications in bookstores or peruse the following listings for useful stuff. If you're planning to drive in the U.S., good road maps are essential. The maps in *Let's Go: USA and Canada* are intended for general orientation only; you will probably get hopelessly lost if you try to drive around in a major city without a real map.

Michelin Maps and Guides. Exquisite maps. Use their famous Green Guides as a companion to your trusty *Let's Go* for excellent supplemental coverage of Canada and parts of the U.S. In bookstores everywhere.

Travelling Books, PO Box 77114, Seattle, WA 98177, publishes a catalogue of travel guides which will make the armchair traveler weep with wanderlust.

Rand McNally publishes one of the most comprehensive road atlases of the U.S., available in most bookstores for around $8.

Hippocrene Books, Inc., 171 Madison Ave., New York NY 10016 (212-685-4371; orders 718-454-2360, fax 718-454-1391). Free catalog. Publishes travel reference books, travel guides, maps, and foreign language dictionaries.

Superintendent of Documents, U.S. Government Printing Office, Washington, DC 20402 (202-783-3238). Publishes the helpful, regionally specific publication, *Tips for Travelers,* available for $1 from the address above.

■■■ DOCUMENTS & FORMALITIES

■ Passports

As a precaution in case your passport is lost or stolen, be sure *before you leave* to photocopy the page of your passport that contains your photograph and identifying information. Especially important is your passport number. This information will facilitate the issuing of a new passport if your old one is lost or stolen.

If it is lost or stolen, immediately notify the local police and the nearest embassy or consulate of your government. Some consulates can issue new passports within two days if you give them proof of citizenship. In an emergency, ask for immediate temporary traveling papers that will permit you to return to your home country.

American citizens do not need a passport to travel in the U.S. (duh) or Canada. Likewise, **Canadian citizens** are not required to have a passport to travel in Canada (duh, again) or the U.S.

British citizens can obtain either a full passport or a more restricted Visitor's Passport. For a **full passport** valid for 10 years (5 yrs. if under 16), apply in person or by mail to a passport office. There is an £18 fee. Children under 16 may be included on a parent's passport. Processing usually takes 4-6 weeks. The London office offers same-day walk-in rush service; arrive early.

Irish citizens can apply for a passport by mail to the Department of Foreign Affairs, Passport Office, Setanta Centre, Molesworth St., Dublin 2 ((01) 671 1633). Passports cost £45 and are valid for 10 years. Citizens younger than 18 and older than 65 can request a 3 year passport that costs £10.

Australian citizens must apply for a passport in person at a local post office, a passport office, or an Australian diplomatic mission overseas. A parent may file an application for a child who is under 18 and unmarried. Application fees are adjusted every three months; call the toll free info service for current details (13 12 32).

New Zealanders must contact their local Link Centre, travel agent, or New Zealand Representative for an application form, which they must complete and mail to the New Zealand Passport Office, Documents of National Identity Division, Department of Internal Affairs, Box 10-526, Wellington ((04) 474 81 00). The application fee is NZ$56 (if under age 16, NZ$25.30).

South African citizens can apply for a passport at any Home Affairs Office. Two photos, either a birth certificate or an identity book, and the R30 fee must accompany a completed application.

■ U.S. and Canadian Entrance Requirements

Foreign visitors to the United States and Canada are required to have a **passport, visa,** and **proof of intent to leave** (for example, an exiting plane ticket). To visit Canada, you must be healthy and law-abiding, and demonstrate ability to support yourself financially during your stay. To work or study in the U.S. or Canada, you must obtain special documents (see Work and Study).

VISAS FOR THE U.S.

To acquire a visa for entrance to the U.S., you will need your passport and proof of intent to leave. Visitors from certain nations (including Japan and most of Western Europe) may enter the U.S. without visas through the **Visa Waiver Pilot Program.** Travelers qualify as long as they are traveling for business or pleasure, are staying for 90 days or less, have proof of intent to leave, and enter aboard particular air or sea carriers. Contact the nearest U.S. consulate for more information on visas.

VISAS FOR CANADA

To acquire a visa for entrance to Canada, you will need your passport and proof of intent to leave. Visitors from certain nations may enter Canada without visas. Travelers qualify if they are staying for 90 days or less, have proof of intent to leave, and are citizens of Australia, the Bahamas, Barbados, Costa Rica, Dominica, the EC., Singapore, Swaziland, the U.K., the U.S., Venezuela, Western Samoa, or Zimbabwe. Contact the nearest Canadian consulate for more information.

DOCUMENTS & FORMALITIES

■ Customs

Unless you plan to import a BMW or a barnyard beast, you will probably pass right over the customs barrier and into the arms of relieved relations with minimal ado. The many rules and regulations of customs and duties hardly pose a threat to the budget traveler. To avoid problems when you transport prescription drugs, ensure that the bottles are clearly marked, and carry a copy of the prescription to show the customs officer. In addition, officials may seize articles made from protected species, such as certain reptiles and the big cats.

You may bring the following into the U.S. duty free: 200 cigarettes, 50 cigars, or 2 kg of smoking tobacco; $100 in gifts; and personal belongings such as clothes and jewelry. Travelers ages 21 and over may also bring up to one liter of alcohol, although state laws may further restrict the amount of alcohol you can carry.

You can bring any amount of currency, but if you carry over $10,000, you'll need to report it. In general, customs officers ask how much money you're carrying and your planned departure date in order to ensure that you'll be able to support yourself while here. In some cases they may ask about traveling companions and political affiliation. For more information, including the helpful pamphlet *U.S. Customs Hints for Visitors (nonresidents),* contact the nearest U.S. Embassy.

■ Hostel Membership

Hosteling can be one of the most fun and inexpensive ways to travel. Some American hostels are independent, but many belong to the American Youth Hostels Association, which is associated with Hosteling International.

Hosteling International (HI) is the new and universal trademark name adopted by the former International Youth Hostel Federation (IYHF). The 6000 official youth hostels worldwide will normally display the new HI logo (a blue triangle) alongside the symbol of one of the 70 national hostel associations.

A one-year Hosteling International (HI) membership permits you to stay at youth hostels throughout the U.S. and Canada at unbeatable prices. Membership in AYH can save you money, as beds are often cheaper for members, and some hostels are members-only. And, despite the name, you need not be a youth; travelers over 25 pay only a slight surcharge for a bed. You can save yourself potential trouble by procuring a membership card before you leave home, as some hostels do not sell them on the spot. For more information, contact HI/AYH or the affiliate in your country (listed below). For more information on hosteling, see Accommodations.

Hosteling International Headquarters, 9 Guessens Rd., Welwyn Garden City, Hertfordshire, AL8 6QW, England ((0707) 33 24 87).
American Youth Hostels (AYH), 733 15th St. NW, Suite 840, Washington, D.C., 20005 (202-783-6161, fax 202-783-6171); also dozens of regional offices across the U.S. Fee $25, under 18 $10, over 54 $15. AYH is the U.S. chapter of HI. Contact AYH for ISICs, student and charter flights, travel equipment, literature on budget travel, and information on summer positions as a group leader for domestic outings; to lead, you must first complete a seven day, $350 course.
Hosteling International—Canada (HI-C), National Office, 1600 James Naismith Dr., #608, Gloucester, Ontario K1B 5N4, Canada (613-748-5638). One-year membership fee CDN$26.75, under 18 CDN$12.84, two-year CDN$37.45.
Youth Hostels Ass'n of England and Wales (YHA), Trevelyan House, 8 St. Stephen's Hill, St. Albans, Herts, AL1 2DY ((0727) 855 215). Fee £9, under 18 £3.
An Oíge (Irish Youth Hostel Association), 61 Mountjoy Sq., Dublin 7, Ireland ((01) 304 555, fax (01) 305 808). Fee £9, under 18 £3.
Australian Youth Hostels Association (AYHA), Level 3, 10 Mallett St., Camperdown, NSW, 2050 Australia ((02) 565 16 99, fax (02) 565 13 25). Fee AUS$40.
Youth Hostels Association of New Zealand, P.O. Box 436, Christchurch 1, New Zealand (64 3 379 99 70, fax 64 3 379 44 76). Fee NZ$24.

HI has recently instituted an **International Booking Network.** To reserve space in high season, obtain an International Booking Voucher from any national youth hostel association and send it to a participating hostel 4-8 weeks in advance of your stay, along with $2 in local currency. Hostel locations throughout the U.S. and Canada are listed under Accommodations in individual cities and towns.

■ Youth and Student Identification

In the world of budget travel, youth has its privileges. Two main forms of student and youth identification are accepted worldwide; they are extremely useful, especially for the insurance packages that accompany them.

The **International Student Identity Card (ISIC)** is the most widely accepted form of student identification. Flashing this card can garner you discounts for sights, theaters, museums, accommodations, train, ferry, and airplane travel, and other services throughout the U.S. and Canada. Present the card wherever you go, and ask about discounts even when none are advertised. It also provides accident insurance of up to $3,000 as well as $100 per day of in-hospital care for up to 60 days. In addition, cardholders have access to a toll-free Traveler's Assistance hotline whose multilingual staff can provide help in medical, legal, and financial emergencies overseas. In many cases, establishments will also honor an ordinary student ID from your university for student discounts. Many student travel offices issue ISICs (see Useful Organizations, above). When you apply for the card, procure a copy of the *International Student Identity Card Handbook,* which lists some available discounts.

To apply, supply in person or by mail: (1) current, dated proof of your degree-seeking student status (a letter on school stationery signed and sealed by the registrar or a photocopied grade report); (2) a 1½" x 2" photo (vending machine-size) with your name printed and signed on the back; (3) proof of your birthdate and nationality; and (4) the name, address, and phone number of a beneficiary; in the event of the insured's death, payment will be made to the beneficiary. Applicants must be at least 12 years old and must be a student at a secondary or post-secondary school. The 1994 card is valid Sept. 1993-Dec. 1994. The fee is $15.

Federation of International Youth Travel Organisations (FIYTO) issues its own discount card to travelers under 26. Also known as the **International Youth Discount Travel Card** or the **GO 25 Card,** this one-year card offers many of the same benefits as the ISIC, and most organizations that sell the ISIC also sell the Go 25 Card. A brochure that lists discounts is free when you purchase the card. To apply, bring: (1) proof of birthdate (copy of birth certificate or passport or a valid driver's license); and (2) a passport-sized photo (with your name printed on the back). The fee is $10, CDN$12, or £4. For more information, contact FIYTO at Bredgage 25H, DK-1260, Copenhagen K, Denmark (33 33 96 00; fax 33 93 96 76).

■ International Driving Permit

Although not required in United States or Canada, the International Driving Permit is almost a necessity if you intend to see the countryside by car. The IDP can smooth out difficulties with American and Canadian police officers, and serves as an additional piece of identification. A valid driver's license from your home country must always accompany the IDP.

Your IDP must be issued in your own country before you depart (you can't get one here); check with your national automobile association. Also make sure you have proper insurance (required by law). Some foreign driver's licenses will be valid in the U.S. for up to one year (check before you leave). Members of national automobile associations affiliated with the American Automobile Association can receive services from the AAA while they're in the U.S. Automobile associations in 19 countries have full reciprocity agreements with the AAA. Check your club for details.

Don't forget to write.

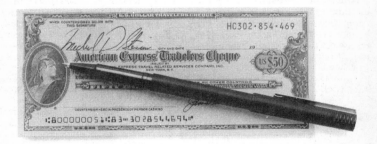

Now that you've said, "Let's go," it's time to say
"Let's get American Express® Travelers Cheques." If they are lost or
stolen, you can get a fast and full refund virtually anywhere you
travel. So before you leave be sure and write.

Travelers Cheques

■■■ MONEY

Remember that it is usually more expensive to buy foreign currency than it is to buy domestic. Converting a small amount of money before you go, however, will allow you to breeze through the airport while others languish in exchange counter lines. This is also a good practice in case you find yourself stuck with no money after banking hours or on a holiday, or if your flight arrives late in the evening. Observe commission rates closely when abroad; check newspapers to get the standard rate of exchange. Bank rates are generally preferable. Since you lose money with every transaction, it's wise to convert in large sums (provided the exchange rate is either staying constant or deteriorating), but not more than you will need. For information on U.S. currency and on Canadian currency, see the Currency and Exchange sections in the introductions to the U.S. and to Canada.

■ Traveler's Checks

Traveler's checks are the safest way to carry large sums of money. They are refundable if lost or stolen, and many issuing agencies offer additional services such as refund hotlines, message relaying, travel insurance, and emergency assistance. Most tourist establishments will accept traveler's checks and almost any bank will cash them. Usually banks sell traveler's checks for a 1-2% commission, although your own bank may waive the surcharge. The **American Automobile Association (AAA)** offers commission-free American Express travelers cheques to its members. Buying checks in small denominations ($20 checks rather than $50 ones or higher) is safer and more convenient. Call any of the numbers below to find out the advantages of a particular type of check and the name of an selling agency near you.

Always keep your traveler's check receipts, a list of their serial numbers, and a record of which ones you've cashed separate from the checks themselves; this speeds up replacement if they are lost or stolen. Never countersign checks until you're prepared to cash them.

American Express (800-221-7282 in the U.S. and Canada; (0800) 52 13 13 in the U.K.; (02) 886 0689 in Australia, New Zealand, and the South Pacific. Elsewhere, call U.S. collect 801-964-6665). AmEx Travelers Cheques are the most widely recognized worldwide and easiest to replace if lost or stolen. AmEx offices cash their own Cheques commission-free. AAA members can obtain AmEx Travelers Cheques commission-free at AAA offices.

Citicorp sells Visa traveler's checks. (800-645-6556 in the U.S. and Canada; from abroad call collect 813-623-1709.) Commission is 1-2% on check purchases. Check holders are automatically enrolled in **Travel Assist Hotline** (800-523-1199) for 45 days after checks are bought. This service provides travelers with English-speaking doctor, lawyer, and interpreter referrals as well as traveler's check refund assistance. Citicorp also has a World Courier Service which guarantees hand-delivery of traveler's checks anywhere in the world.

Mastercard International (800-223-9920 in the U.S. and Canada; from abroad call collect 609-987-7300). Commission varies from 1-2% for purchases depending on the bank. Issued in U.S. dollars only.

Thomas Cook: Thomas Cook and Mastercard International have formed a "global alliance." In contrast to MC International, Thomas Cook handles the distribution of checks in U.S. dollars as well as ten other currencies. Call 800-223-4030 for orders in the U.S. From elsewhere, call collect 212-974-5696. Some Thomas Cook Currency Services offices (located in major cities around the globe) do not charge any fee for purchase of checks. You can buy Mastercard travelers checks from Thomas Cook at any bank displaying a Mastercard sign.

MONEY

■ Credit Cards

Credit cards are not always useful to the budget traveler—many smaller establishments will not accept them, and those enticing, pricier establishments accept them all too willingly—but they can prove invaluable in a financial emergency. Visa and Mastercard are the most common, followed by American Express and Diner's Club. Note that the British "Barclaycard" and "Access" are equivalent to Visa and Mastercard, respectively. Foreign visitors can often reduce conversion fees by charging a purchase instead of changing traveler's checks. With credit cards such as **American Express, Visa,** and **Mastercard,** associated banks will give you an instant cash advance in the local currency as large as your remaining credit line. Unfortunately, in most cases you will pay mortifying rates of interest for such an advance.

■ Electronic Banking

Automatic Teller Machines (frequently abbreviated as ATMs; operated by bank cards) offer 24-hour service in banks, groceries, gas stations, and even in telephone booths across the U.S. Before you can use your bank card, be sure that your bank belongs to a network which has machines in the region you're headed for. The two largest networks are **PLUS** (800-THE-PLUS) and **CIRRUS** (800-4-CIRRUS). PLUS is also the most widely accepted ATM card in Canada. Keep in mind that ATMs often give one of the best rates of currency "exchange," because they get the wholesale rate which is generally 5% better than the retail rate most banks use.

■ Sending Money

If you run out of money on the road, you can have more mailed to you in the form of **traveler's checks** bought in your name, a **certified check,** or through **postal money orders,** available at post offices (orders under $25, 75¢ fee; $700 limit per order; cash only). Certified checks are redeemable at any bank, while postal money orders can be cashed at post offices upon display of two IDs (1 of which must be photo). Keep receipts since money orders are refundable if lost.

Money can be **wired** directly from bank to bank for about $30 for amounts less than $1000, plus the commission charged by your home bank. Once you've found a bank that will accept a wire, write or telegram your home bank with your account number, the name and address of the bank to receive the wire, and a routing number. Also notify the bank of the form of ID that the second bank should accept before paying the money. **Bank drafts** or **international money orders** are cheaper but slower. As a *last, last* resort, **consulates** will wire home for you and deduct the cost from the money you receive. But they will not be very happy about it.

Another alternative is **cabling money.** Through **Bank of America** (800-346-7693), money can be sent to any affiliated bank. Have someone bring cash, a credit card, or a cashier's check to the sending bank—you need not have an account. You can pick up the money one to three working days later with ID, and it will be paid out to you in U.S. currency. If you do not have a Bank of America account, there is a $40 fee for domestic cabling, $45 for international. Other fees apply depending on the bank at which you receive the money.

To take advantage of a classic, time-honored, and expensive service, use **Western Union** (800-325-6000). You or someone else can phone in a credit card number, or else someone can bring cash to a Western Union office. As always, you need ID to pick up your money. Their charge is $50 for $500, $60 for $1000. Money sent from Europe to the U.S. will usually be available within two working days, but there is an additional surcharge.

■■■ HEALTH

In many places in the United States and Canada, **you can call 911 toll free in case of medical emergencies.** In many rural areas, however, the 911 system has not yet been introduced; if 911 doesn't work, dial the **operator (0),** who will contact the appropriate emergency service.

■ Before You Go

While it is rather difficult to lead a normal life while living out of a backpack, several tips will make preventative care easier. If you're going to be doing a lot of walking, take along some quick-energy foods to keep your strength up. You will need plenty of protein (for sustained energy) and fluids (to prevent dehydration and constipation, two of the most common health problems for travelers). Carry a canteen or water bottle and make sure to drink frequently. If you are prone to sunburn, be sure to bring a potent sunscreen with you from home, cover up with long sleeves and a hat, and drink plenty of fluids. Finally, remember to treat your most valuable resource well: lavish your feet with attention.

For minor health problems on the road, a compact **first-aid kit** should suffice. Some hardware stores carry ready-made kits, but it's just as easy to assemble your own. Items you might want to include are bandages, aspirin, antiseptic soap or antibiotic cream, a thermometer in a sturdy case, a Swiss Army knife with tweezers, moleskin, a decongestant (to clear your ears if you fly with a cold), motion sickness remedy, medicine for diarrhea and stomach problems, sunscreen, insect repellent, burn ointment, and an elastic bandage.

Always go prepared with any **medication** you may need while away as well as a copy of the prescription and/or a statement from your doctor, especially if you will be bringing insulin, syringes, or any narcotics into the United States or Canada. Make sure you have a supply sufficient for the duration of your trip; getting refills on the road is inconvenient, and pharmacies can be few and far between in rural areas. Be aware also that matching prescriptions with foreign equivalents may be difficult. If you wear **glasses** or **contact lenses,** take an extra prescription and make arrangements with someone at home to send you a replacement pair in an emergency.

Any traveler with a medical condition that cannot be easily recognized (i.e. diabetes, epilepsy, heart conditions, allergies to antibiotics) may want to obtain a **Medic Alert Identification Tag.** In an emergency, their internationally recognized tag indicates the nature of the bearer's problem and provides the number of Medic Alert's 24-hr. hotline. Attending medical personnel can call this number to obtain information about the member's medical history. Lifetime membership (tag, annually-updated wallet card, and 24-hr. hotline access) begins at $35. Contact Medic Alert Foundation, P.O. Box 1009, Turlock, CA 95381-1009 (800-432-5378).

Reliable **contraception** may be difficult to come by while traveling. Women on the pill should bring enough to allow for possible loss or extended stays. Condoms are widely available in the U.S. and Canada, but you may also want to stock up before you go to save yourself the inconvenience of purchasing them on the road. **Abortion** is legal in the U.S. and Canada. Some states restrict availability through waiting periods and parental consent requirements for minors. The **National Abortion Federation's hotline** (800-772-9100, Mon.-Fri. 9:30am-5:30pm) refers its callers to U.S. clinics that perform abortions.

Before you leave, check and see whether your insurance policy (if you have one) covers medical costs incurred while traveling. Familiarity with your insurance policy can save you headaches and speed paperwork in cases of emergency.

■ On the Road

When traveling in the summer, if you are going to be spending any time outside, especially in the middle of the day, be sure to apply **sunscreen** often and liberally.

SPF 15 is usually sufficient, but if your skin is really fair, you might want to use SPF 30 or 45. **Heatstroke** is another danger associated with warm weather travel. Heatstroke can begin without direct exposure to the sun; it results from continuous heat stress, lack of fitness, or overactivity following heat exhaustion. In the early stages of heatstroke, sweating stops, body temperature rises, and an intense headache develops, soon followed by mental confusion. To treat heatstroke, cool the victim off immediately with fruit juice or salted water, wet towels, and shade. Rush the victim to the hospital.

Extreme cold is no less dangerous—it brings risks of hypothermia and frostbite. **Hypothermia** is a result of exposure to cold and can occur even in the middle of the summer, especially in rainy or windy conditions. The signs are easy to detect: body temperature drops rapidly, resulting in the failure to produce body heat. Other possible symptoms are uncontrollable shivering, poor coordination, and exhaustion followed by slurred speech, sleepiness, hallucinations, and amnesia. *Do not* let victims fall asleep if they are in advanced stages—if they lose consciousness, they might die. To avoid hypothermia, always keep dry. Wear wool, *especially* in soggy weather—it retains its insulating properties even when wet. Dress in layers, and stay out of the wind. Remember that most loss of body heat is through your head, so always carry a wool hat with you. **Frostbite** occurs in freezing temperatures. The affected skin will turn white, then waxy and cold. To counteract the problem, the victim should drink warm beverages, stay or get dry, and gently and slowly warm the frostbitten are in dry fabric or with steady body contact. NEVER rub frostbite—the skin is easily damaged. Take serious cases to a doctor or medic as soon as possible.

Travelers in **high altitudes** should allow their body a couple of days to adjust to the lower atmospheric oxygen levels before engaging in any strenuous activity. This particularly applies to those intent on setting out on long alpine hikes. Those new to high-altitude areas may feel drowsy, and one alcoholic beverage may have the same effect as three at a lower altitude.

One of the most common symptoms associated with eating and drinking in another country is **diarrhea.** Known variously as *turista, Montezuma's revenge,* and "what a way to spend my vacation," diarrhea has unmistakable symptoms but also, thankfully, some means of relief. Many people take with them over-the-counter remedies (such as Pepto-Bismol). Since dehydration is the most common side effect of diarrhea, those suffering should drink plenty of fruit juice and pure water. The simplest anti-dehydration formula is still the most effective: 8oz. of water with a 1/2 tsp. of sugar or honey and a pinch of salt. Down several of these a day, rest and let the heinous disease run its course.

If you become ill on the road, seek medical advice. If you are not a U.S. citizen, check with your embassy for help in finding treatment. Be aware that the current health care system can be fickle; if you lack insurance, you may have trouble getting treated for conditions which are not emergencies. If you are traveling without insurance, there is some recourse. In an emergency, call the local hotline or crisis center listed in *Let's Go* under Practical Information for each area. Operators at these organizations have the numbers of public health organizations and clinics that treat patients without demanding proof of solvency. Such centers charge low fees. University teaching hospitals usually run inexpensive clinics as well. In Canada, contact your embassy or consulate for help.

DESERT SURVIVAL

In the desert, water, not bread, is the staff of life. The body loses at least a gallon of liquid per day in the desert (two gallons during strenuous activity such as hiking), so keep drinking even when you're not thirsty. If you're using sweet beverages, dilute them with water to avoid overreacting to high sugar content.

If you arrive from a cooler climate, allow yourself a couple of days to adjust to the heat, especially if you're planning a hike or other strenuous activity. Keep clothing on (light colors reflect heat). Thick-soled shoes and socks can help to keep feet com-

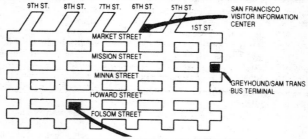

fortable on a hike during the summer as the sand can reach scorching temperatures. Whether you are driving or hiking, tote *two gallons of water per person per day.*

Before driving in the desert, make sure that your car has been recently serviced and is in good running condition. Carry water for drinking and for the radiator, and make sure your car is equipped with a spare tire and necessary tools. For any trips off major roads, a board and shovel are useful in case your car gets stuck in sand. Although settlements are sometimes sparse, enough traffic usually passes on the roads to help you if you have trouble. The isolated areas of the big parks pose more of a threat, especially in summer, when few tourists visit. *Stay with your vehicle if it breaks down;* it is easier to spot than a person. Never pour water over the engine to cool it; you can crack the engine block. In an absolute emergency, turn the heater on full force to help cool the engine.

■■■ ALCOHOL AND DRUGS

The minimum drinking age in the U.S. is 21. In Canada, the minimum age is 19, except in Alberta, Manitoba, and Quebec, where it is 18. In each country, the law is strictly enforced. Particularly in the U.S., be prepared to show a photo ID (preferably some government document—driver's license or passport) if you look under 30. Some areas of the country are "dry," meaning they do not permit the sale of alcohol at all, while other places do not allow it to be sold on Sundays. Furthermore, some states require possession of a *liquor license.*

If you carry prescription drugs while you travel, it is vital to have a copy of the prescriptions itself readily accessible at country borders. In general, possession of illicit drugs during travel is a remarkably bad idea. Dealing with marijuana, cocaine, and most opiate derivatives are federal crimes in both the U.S. and Canada.

■■■ WORK AND STUDY

■ Work

Finding a job far from home is often a matter of luck and timing. Your best leads in the job hunt often come from local residents, hostels, employment offices, and Chambers of Commerce. Temporary agencies often hire for non-secretarial placement as well as for standard typing assignments. Marketable skills, i.e. touch-typing, dictation, computer knowledge, and experience with children will prove very helpful (even necessary) in your search for a temporary job. Consult local newspapers and bulletin boards on local college campuses.

In The U.S.

Volunteer jobs are readily available almost everywhere in the U.S. Some jobs provide rooms and board in exchange for labor. Write to **CIEE** (see Useful Organizations) for *Volunteer! The Comprehensive Guide to Voluntary service in the U.S. and Abroad* ($11, postage $1.50). CIEE also administers the **International Voluntary Service Program,** an international workcamp program which places young people interested in short-term voluntary service with organizations conducting projects including restoring historical sights, working with children, and taking part in nature conservation. Room and board are provided.

Foreign university-level students can get on-the-job technical training in fields such as engineering, computer science, agriculture, and natural and physical sciences from the **Association for International Practical Training,** which is the U.S. member of the **International Association for the Exchange of Students for Technical Experience (IAESTE).** You must apply through the IAESTE office at home; application deadlines vary. For more information, contact the local IAESTE committee or write to IAESTE, c/o AIPT, 10 Corporate Center, Suite 250, 10400 Little Patuxent Pkwy., Columbia, MD (410-997-2200).

Another organization to contact is **SCI-International Voluntary Service,** Route 2, Box 506B, Crozet, VA 22932 (804-823-1826). SCI arranges placement in work-camps in the U.S. for people over 16. Registration fees range from $40 (U.S.) to $200 (former USSR).

In Canada

Most of the organizations and the literature discussed above is not aimed solely at those interested in working in the U.S. Accordingly, many of the same programs which arrange volunteer and work programs in the U.S. are also active in Canada. Write for the publications and contact the individual organizations which interest you most. **Travel CUTS** (see Budget Travel Services) may also help you out.

■ Study

If you are interested in studying in the U.S. or in Canada, there are a number of different paths you can take. One possibility is to enroll in a language education program, particularly if you are interested in a short-term stay. Contact **World Learning, Inc.,** which runs the **International Students of English** program, offering intensive language courses at select U.S. campuses. The price of a four-week program averages $1800. For more information, write to World Learning, PO Box 676, Brattleboro, VT 05302-0676 (802-257-7751).

An excellent source of information on studying in the U.S., Canada, and abroad is the **Institute of International Education (IIE),** which administers many exchange programs. IIE publishes *Academic Year Abroad,* which describes over 2100 semester and academic-year programs offered in the Canada, the U.S., and overseas ($43 plus $4 shipping), and *Vacation Study Abroad,* with information on 1500 short-term programs ($37, shipping $4).

■ Visa Requirements for Work or Study

If you want to work or study in the U.S. or Canada, you need to obtain the appropriate visas and other documentation. Failure to do so can have very unpleasant consequences–including deportation. Read this section carefully and contact the U.S. or Canadian Embassy at home for more information.

In The U.S.

Working or studying in the U.S. with only a B-2 (tourist) visa is grounds for deportation. Before an appropriate visa can be issued to you, you must—depending on the visa category you are seeking—join a USIA-authorized Exchange Visitor Program (J-1 visa) or locate an employer who will sponsor you (usually an H-2B visa) and file the necessary paperwork with the Immigration and Naturalization Service (INS) in the United Sates on your behalf. In order to apply to the U.S. Embassy or Consulate for a J-1 visa you must obtain an IAP-66 eligibility form, issued by a U.S. academic institution or a private organization involved in U.S. exchanges. The H-2 visa is difficult to obtain, as your employer must prove that there are no other American or foreign permanent residents already residing in the U.S. with your job skills. For more specific information on visa categories and requirements, contact the nearest U.S. embassy or consulate.

Foreign students who wish to study in the U.S. must apply for either a J-1 visa (for exchange students) or a F-1 visas (for full-time students enrolled in an academic or language program). Neither the F-1 nor the J-1 visa specifies any expiration date; instead they are both valid for the duration of stay, which includes the length of your particular program and a brief grace period thereafter. Requests to extend a visa must be submitted 15-60 days before the original departure date.

In Canada

If you intend to work in Canada, you will need an **Employment Authorization,** which must be obtained before you enter the country; visitors ordinarily are not

allowed to change status once they have arrived. There is a $100 processing fee. Employment authorizations are only issued after it has been determined that qualified Canadian citizens and residents will not be adversely affected by the admission of a foreign worker. Your potential employer must contact the nearest **Canadian Employment Centre (CEC)** for approval of the employment offer. For more information, contact the consulate or embassy in your home country.

To study in Canada you will need a Student Authorization in addition to any entry visa you may need (see Documents and Formalities). To obtain one, contact the nearest Canadian Consulate or Embassy. Be sure to apply well ahead of time; it can take up to six months, and there is a fee of $75. You will also need to prove to the Canadian government that you are able to support yourself financially. A student authorization is good for one year. If you plan to stay longer, it is extremely important that you do not let it expire before you apply for renewal. Canadian immigration laws do permit full-time students to seek on campus employment, but you will need to apply for an Employment Authorization. For specifics on official documentation, contact a Canadian Immigration Center (CIC) or consulate.

Residents of the U.S., Greenland, and St. Pierre/Miquelon may apply for employment authorization or Student Authorization at a port of entry.

■■■ PACKING

Your backpack or suitcase may be light as a feather when you buy it or drag it out of storage, but as soon as you leave home, it will magically transform itself into a hot, itchy monster. Before you leave, pack your bag and take it for a walk. Try to convince it that you're on the road already. At the slightest sign of heaviness, curb vanity and hedonism and unpack something. A good general rule is to set out what you think you'll need, then take half of it and more money.

If you plan to cover a lot of ground by foot, a sturdy **backpack** with several external compartments is hard to beat. Internal frames stand up to airline baggage handlers and can often be converted to shoulder bags; external frames distribute weight more evenly and lift the pack off your back. Whichever style you choose to buy, avoid extremely low economy prices (good packs usually cost at least $100). If checking a backpack on your flight, tape down loose straps, which can catch in the conveyer belt. A plastic bag packed inside your luggage will be useful for dirty laundry, as well as one to cover your knapsack when it rains. Wrap sharper items in clothing so they won't stab you or puncture your luggage, and pack heavy items along the inside wall if you're carrying a backpack. A small **daypack** is also indispensable for plane flights, sight-seeing, carrying a camera and/or keeping some of your valuables with you. For more information on purchasing a backpack, see Camping and the Outdoors.

The **clothing** you bring will, of course, depend on where in the U.S. you're planning on traveling, and during what time of year you plan to be there. There really is no need to worry about looking too informal. America, compared to Europe, is a very casual place, clothing-wise. In the summer t-shirts and shorts are the rule; in the winter sweatshirts and jeans. Anyplace formal enough to require a jacket and tie will likely be too expensive for a budget traveler anyhow. Weather more often than style will determine your mode of dress. The "layer concept" covers most of the bases. Start with several t-shirts, which take up virtually no space and over which you can wear a sweatshirt or sweater in cold or wet weather. Remember that wool retains its insulating ability, even when wet. Then pack a few pairs of shorts and jeans. Add underwear and socks, and you've got your essential wardrobe. For winter you will probably want a few heavier layers as well, especially if you're headed up north. Natural fibers and lightweight cottons are the best materials for hot weather. It's a good idea to have at least one layer that will insulate while wet, such as polypropylene, polarfleece or wool. Make sure your clothing can be washed in a sink and will survive a spin in the dryer. And don't forget a towel and swimwear.

PACKING

IF YOU CAN'T AFFORD TO TRAVEL, JOIN THE CLUB.

Traveling doesn't have to mean snobby hotels that cost $200 a night. With a Hostelling International card you can stay in Paris for just $16, New York for $19 or Tokyo for $23. Hostels even offer special discounts on everything from museum fees and ski lifts to air, rail and ferry tickets. Plus they have fully equipped do-it-yourself kitchens, which not only save you money but also are great for meeting fellow world travelers. So if you're looking for a less expensive way to travel, join the club. Call (202) 783-6161.

HOSTELLING INTERNATIONAL

The new seal of approval of the International Youth Hostel Federation.

HOSTELLING
INTERNATIONAL®

Comfortable **shoes** are essential. In sunny climates, sandals or other light shoes serve well. It is often a good idea to bring an extra pair of walking shoes in case your first gets wet. For heavy-duty hiking, sturdy lace-up walking boots are necessary. Make sure they have good ventilation. Leather-reinforced nylon hiking boots are particularly good for hiking and for walking in general: they're lightweight, rugged and dry quickly. A double pair of socks—light absorbent cotton inside and thick wool outside—will cushion feet, keep them dry and help prevent blisters. Bring a pair of light flip-flops for protection against the fungal floors of some stations and hostels.

In most parts of the U.S. and Canada, **rain gear** is essential; a rain poncho is cumbersome but lightweight.

In addition to all the stuff above, there are many other useful items which you may not think you would need or might easily forget, including: all your documents (i.e. your passport, visa, traveler's checks), first-aid kit (see Health), flashlight, pens and paper, perhaps a travel journal, travel alarm, canteen or water bottle, your child's bottle or juice container, Ziplock bags (for isolating damp or dirty clothing), garbage bags, sewing kit, string, safety pins, tweezers, a pencil with some electrical tape wound around it for patching tears, rubber bands, sturdy plastic containers (for soap and detergent, for example), a padlock, a pocketknife, earplugs for noisy hostels, waterproof matches, clothespins and a length of cord, sunglasses, sunscreen, toilet paper (not all bathrooms come so well-equipped!), and the other essential toiletries. A rubber squash ball or a golf ball is a universal sink stopper, and either liquid soap or shampoo will do for handwashing clothes. Don't forget to bring along your prescription medicine, and copies of the prescription in case you run out. You should also bring a copy of your glasses/contact lens prescription.

■■■ SPECIFIC CONCERNS

■ Women and Travel

Women exploring any area on their own inevitably face additional safety concerns. In all situations it is best to trust your instincts: if you'd feel better somewhere else, don't hesitate to move on. You may want to consider staying in hostels which offer single rooms which lock from the inside, YWCAs, or religious organizations that offer rooms for women only. Stick to centrally-located accommodations and avoid late-night treks or subway rides. Remember that hitching is *never* safe for lone women, or even for two women traveling together. Choose train compartments occupied by other women or couples.

The less you look like a tourist, the better off you'll be. In general, dress conservatively, especially in more rural areas. If you spend time in cities, you may be harassed no matter how you're dressed. Look as if you know where you're going (even when you don't) and ask women or couples for directions if you're lost or if you feel uncomfortable. Your best answer to verbal harassment is no answer at all (a reaction is what the harasser wants); wearing a conspicuous wedding band may help prevent such incidents. Don't hesitate to seek out a police officer or a passerby if you are being harassed. *Let's Go* lists emergency numbers (including rape crisis lines) and women's centers in the Practical Information section of most cities. Always carry change for the phone and extra money for a bus or taxi. Carry a whistle or an airhorn on your keychain, and don't hesitate to use it in an emergency. All of these warnings and suggestions should not discourage women from traveling alone. Don't take unnecessary risks, but don't lose your spirit of adventure either.

■ Older Travelers and Senior Citizens

Seniors are eligible for a wide range of discounts on transportation, museums, movies, theater, concerts, restaurants, and accommodations. Proof of age is usually

required (e.g., a driver's license, Medicare card, or membership card from a recognized society of retired persons). Resources include:

AARP (American Association of Retired Persons), 601 E St. NW, Washington, DC 20049 (202-434-2277). U.S. residents over 50 and their spouses receive benefits which include travel programs and discounts for groups and individuals, as well as discounts on lodging, car and RV rental, air arrangements and sight-seeing. $8 annual fee. Call 800-927-0111 or write to the above address for information on membership and programs.

Golden Age Passport ($20 at park entrances). Available to adults 62 and over. Entitles you to free entry into all national parks and a 50% discount on recreational activities.

National Council of Senior Citizens, 1331 F St. NW, Washington, DC 20004 (202-347-8800). For $12 a year an individual or couple of any age can receive hotel and auto rental discounts, a senior citizen newspaper, use of a discount travel agency, and supplemental Medicare insurance (if you're over 65).

■ Travelers with Disabilities

Planning a trip presents extra challenges to individuals with disabilities, but the difficulties are by no means insurmountable. Hotels and motels have become more and more accessible to disabled persons (see Hotels and Motels under Accommodations below), and exploring the outdoors is often feasible. If you research areas ahead of time, your trip will go more smoothly. You can call restaurants, hotels, parks, and other facilities to find out about the existence of ramps, the widths of doors, the dimensions of elevators, etc. There may also be restrictions on motorized wheelchairs which are worth discovering beforehand.

Arrange transportation well in advance. **Hertz, Avis,** and **National** car rental agencies have hand-controlled vehicles at some locations (see By Car). **Amtrak** trains and all **airlines** can better serve disabled passengers if notified in advance; tell the ticket agent when making reservations which services you'll need. **Greyhound** allows a traveler with disabilities and a companion to ride for the price of a single fare with a doctor's statement confirming that a companion is necessary. Wheelchairs, seeing-eye dogs, and oxygen tanks are not deducted from your luggage allowance. A booklet entitled, *Access travel: Airports,* replete with info on the accessibility of airports across the globe, is available from Federal Consumer Information Center, Pueblo, CO 81009. (Free.)

If you're planning to visit a national park, get a **Golden Access Passport** ($20) at the park entrance. This exempts disabled travelers and their families from the entrance fee and allows a 50% discount on recreational activity fees.

Directions Unlimited, 720 North Bedford Rd., Bedford Hills, NY 10507 (800-533-5343 or 914-241-1700). Specializes in arranging individual and group vacations, tours, and cruises for those with disabilities. Organizes tours for individuals rather than for groups.

Evergreen Travel Service, 4114 198th St. SW, Suite #13, Lynnwood, WA 98036 (800-435-2288 or 206-776-1184). Arranges wheelchair-accessible tours and individual travel worldwide. Other services include tours for the blind, the deaf and tours for those not wanting a fast-paced itinerary.

Society for the Advancement of Travel for the Handicapped, 347 Fifth Ave., Suite 610, New York, NY 10016 (212-447-7284; fax 212-725-8253). Publishes quarterly travel newsletter *SATH News* and information booklets (free for members, $3 each for nonmembers). Advice on trip planning for people with disabilities. Annual membership is $45, students and seniors $25.

Twin Peaks Press, P.O. Box 129, Vancouver, WA 98666 (206-694-2462, orders only 800-637-2256). *Travel for the Disabled* lists tips and resources for disabled travelers ($20). Also available are the *Directory for Travel Agencies of the Dis-*

abled ($20) and *Wheelchair Vagabond* ($15). Postage $2 for first book, $1 for each additional.

■ Bisexual, Gay, and Lesbian Travelers

Prejudice against bisexuals, gays and lesbians still exists in many areas of the U.S. and Canada. In many areas, public displays of homosexual affection are illegal. Colorado became the site of much controversy recently, when leaders of the bisexual, gay, and lesbian communities called for a tourist boycott of Colorado in protest of a law passed by the state legislature stating that sexual orientation was not a category which could receive equal protection under the law. Aspen, Boulder, and Denver city governments have passed resolutions protesting the state law, in hopes of protecting their stake in the lucrative tourism industry.

On the other hand, acceptance is growing. San Francisco, Los Angeles, New York, New Orleans, Atlanta, and Montréal have large, active gay and lesbian communities. Legislation to make discrimination on the basis of sexual orientation (in hiring, for example) a civil rights violation is being debated in several states.

Whenever available, *Let's Go* lists local gay and lesbian hotline numbers, which can provide counseling and crisis and social information for bisexual, gay and lesbian visitors. *Let's Go* also lists local gay and lesbian hotspots whenever possible.

Ferrari Publications, P.O. Box 37887, Phoenix, AZ 85069 (602-863-2408). Publishes *Ferrari's Places of Interest* ($15), *Ferrari's for Men* ($14), *Ferrari's for Women* ($12), and *Inn Places: US and Worldwide Gay Accommodations* ($15).

Damron, P.O. Box 422458, San Francisco, CA 94142 (800-462-6654 or 415-255-0404). The *Damron Address Book* ($14) lists over 8000 bars, restaurants, guest houses, and services catering to the gay male community. Covers the U.S., Canada, and Mexico. *The Damron Road Atlas* ($13) includes color maps of 56 major U.S. and Canadian cities and gay and lesbian resorts, and listings of bars and accommodations. *The Women's Traveller* ($10) is a guide for the lesbian community, including maps of 50 major U.S. cities; lists bars, restaurants, accommodations, bookstores, and services. Shipping is $4 per book in the United States.

Gayellow Pages, available from Renaissance House, P.O. Box 533, Village Station, New York, NY 10014 (212-674-0120). USA/Canada edition $12. Lists accommodations, resorts, hotlines, and other items of interest to gay travelers.

Giovanni's Room, 345 S. 12th St., Philadelphia, PA 19107 (215-923-2960; fax 215-923-0813). International feminist, lesbian, and gay bookstore with mail-order service which carries many of the publications listed here.

■ Kosher and Vegetarian Travelers

Travelers who keep **kosher** should contact synagogues in the larger cities for information on kosher restaurants; your own synagogue or college Hillel should have access to lists of Jewish institutions across the nation. If you are strict in your observance, consider preparing your own food. *The Jewish Travel Guide* lists Jewish institutions, synagogues, and kosher restaurants in over 80 countries and is available in the U.S. from Sepher-Hermon Press, 1265 46th St., Brooklyn, NY 11219 (718-972-9010) for $12 plus $1.75 shipping, and in the U.K. from Jewish Chronicle Publications, 25 Furnival St., London EC4A England.

You should have no problem finding vegetarian cuisine in North America. Most restaurants have vegetarian selections on their menus, and some cater specifically to the needs of vegetarians. *Let's Go* notes restaurants with good vegetarian selections in the appropriate city listings. Contact the **North American Vegetarian Society** at P.O. Box 72, Dolgeville, NY 13329 (518-568-7970) for information.

Getting There and Getting Around

■■■ BY AIR

■ Commercial Airlines

When dealing with any commercial airline, buying in advance is always the best bet. The commercial carriers' lowest regular offer is the **Advanced Purchase Excursion Fare (APEX);** specials advertised in newspapers may be cheaper, but have correspondingly more restrictions and fewer available seats. APEX fares provide you with confirmed reservations and often allow "open-jaw" tickets (landing and returning from different cities). APEX tickets must usually be purchased two to three weeks ahead of the departure date. Be sure to inquire about any restrictions on length of stay (the minimum is most often seven days, the maximum two months; shorter or longer stays usually mean more money).

To obtain the cheapest fare, buy a round-trip ticket and stay over at least one Saturday; traveling on off-peak days (Mon.-Thurs. morning) is usually $30-40 cheaper than traveling on the weekends. Any change in plans incurs a fee of between $25 (for some domestic flights) and $150 (for many international flights), even if only to change the date of departure or return. Since travel peaks June-Aug. and around holidays, reserve a seat several months in advance for these times.

It is not wise to buy "free" tickets (i.e. **"frequent-flyer" coupons** given by airlines allowing the passenger named on them to fly a stated number of miles) from other people—it is standard policy on most commercial airlines to check a photo ID, and you could find yourself paying for a new, full-fare ticket.

Getting Bumped: Airlines often overbook. If your travel plans are flexible, consider giving up your seat when the airline asks for volunteers—you will probably leave on the next flight and receive either a free ticket or a cash bonus.

Be sure to check with your travel agent for system-wide air passes and excursion fares, especially since these generally have fewer advance-purchase requirements than standard tickets. Consider **discount travel agencies** (see Useful Organizations, above), which sometimes have special deals that regular travel agents can't offer.

WITHIN NORTH AMERICA

Given the long distances between points within the United States and Canada, North Americans rely on buses and trains for travel much less than everyone else in the world. Buses and trains take considerably longer, and, especially over larger distances, do not always confer a savings equal to the added trouble (a cross-country trip will take three or four days, compared with 6 hr. by plane). Expect, then, to use these forms of transportation less than you would at home. A few of the major carriers serving the U.S. and Canada are listed below, together with sample fares:

Air Canada, P.O. Box 14000, St. Laurent, Québec H4Y1H4 (800-776-3000). Ask about special discounts for youths ages 12-24 on stand-by tickets for flights within Canada. Discounts can be substantial, but youth tickets can be more expensive than advance purchase fares. In summer 1993, round-trip fares included Montréal to Seattle $486; Montréal to Halifax $293; Montréal to Vancouver $524. All tickets 14-day advance purchase with a max. stay of 1 year.

America West, 222 S. Mill Ave., Tempe, AZ 85281 (800-235-9292). In summer 1993, fares included NYC to LA $380 round-trip, flying mid-week with a 7 day advance purchase.

Northwest Airlines, Customer Relations M.S. SC 5270, 5101 Northwest Dr., St. Paul, MN 55111 (800-225-2525). In summer 1993, round-trip fares included NYC to Los Angeles $550 with max. stay of 30 days, $610 with max. stay of 1 year; Los Angeles to Toronto $335-400 with no max. stay. Tickets must be purchased either 7 or 14 days in advance.

Air Passes

Many major U.S. airlines offer special **"Visit USA"** air passes and fares to international travelers. You must purchase these passes outside the U.S., paying one price for a certain number of "flight coupons." Each coupon is good for one flight segment on an airline's domestic system within a certain time period; typically, all travel must be completed within 30-60 days. Some cross-country trips may require two segments. The point of departure and the destination must be specified for each coupon at the time of purchase, and once in the States, any change in route will incur a fee of between $50 and $75. Dates of travel may be changed once travel has begun at no extra charge. **United** offers three vouchers for $305, and additional vouchers (up to 5 more) sell for $97 apiece. **USAir** offers three vouchers for $409 from July-Sept., and for $349 off-season. Additional vouchers (up to 5 more) run $80 apiece year round. **Continental**, **Delta,** and **TWA** all offer programs as well.

Hitching Airplanes

If all you need is a short flight, scout local airfields for prospective rides on private, non-commercial planes. Some airfields have ride boards. If not, a good place to begin is the operations counter, where pilots file their flight plans. Private pilots in general are very kind people. Ask where they are headed and if they'd like a passenger. Offer to pay something towards the gasoline costs. A pilot would often rather fly with someone than by himself. And it's great fun. However, keep in mind that propeller planes have a higher accident rate than commercial jets; if the pilots seem concerned about the weather, think about staying earthbound. The above is not meant to imply that *Let's Go* encourages or supports hitchhiking—we don't.

FROM EUROPE

Travelers from Europe will face the least competition for inexpensive seats during the off-season; but "off-season" need not mean the dead of winter. Peak season rates generally take effect in mid-May or early June and run until mid-Sept. Take advantage of cheap off-season flights within Europe to reach an advantageous point of departure for North America. (London is a major connecting point for budget flights to the U.S.; New York City is often the destination.) Once in the States, catch a coast-to-coast flight to make your way out West; see Within North America above for details.

If you decide to fly with a commercial airline rather than through a charter agency or ticket consolidator (see below), you'll be purchasing greater reliability, security, and flexibility. Many major airlines offer reduced-fare options, such as three-day advance purchase fares: these tickets can only be purchased within 72 hours of the time of the departure, and are restricted to youths under a certain age (often 24). Check with a travel agent for availability. **TWA** and **British Airways** both offer these fares on many international flights. Seat availability is known only a few days before the flight, although airlines will sometimes issue predictions. The worst crunch leaving Europe takes place from mid-June to early July, while August is uniformly tight for returning flights; at no time can you count on getting a seat right away.

Another reduced-fare option is the **APEX,** described at the beginning of this section. APEX normally requires a minimum stay of seven to 14 days and a maximum stay of 60 to 90 days. You must purchase your ticket between seven and 21 days in advance and it is almost always non-refundable. For summer travel, book APEX fares early; by June you may have difficulty getting the departure date you want. **American,** 15 Berkeley St., London, W1A 6ND, often has good fares from London: 1993 rates included London to NYC for US$593 peak-season and $357 off-season, with a maximum stay of one year. Tickets must be purchased 21 days in advance, and flights leave mid-week. **British Airways,** P.O. Box 10, Heathrow Airport (London), Hounslow TW6 2JA, England, has extensive service from London to North America. 1993 fares included London to NYC for US$609 peak-season and $395 off-season; London to Seattle $736/517; London to Montreal $731/456. All fares are 14-day advance purchase, leaving mid-week with a Saturday stop-over.

Smaller, budget airlines often undercut major carriers by offering bargain fares on regularly scheduled flights. Competition for seats on these smaller carriers during peak season is fierce—book early. Discount trans-Atlantic airlines include **Virgin Atlantic Airways** and **Icelandair.** Virgin Atlantic's fares from London to NYC range between $430-645, depending on the season, and prices to Boston are equivalent. Tickets require a 21-day advance purchase with mid-week travel and a Saturday stop-over. Icelandair flies heavily into and out of Luxembourg; all trans-Atlantic flights connect via Iceland.

FROM AUSTRALIA AND NEW ZEALAND

A good place to start searching for tickets is the local branch of one of the budget travel agencies listed under Useful Organizations. STA Travel is probably the largest international agency you will find: they have offices in Sydney, Melbourne, and in Auckland. **Qantas, Air New Zealand, United,** and **Northwest** fly between Australia or New Zealand and the United States, and both **Canadian Pacific Airlines** and **Northwest** fly to Canada. Prices are roughly equivalent among the five (American carriers tend to be a bit less), but the cities they serve differ. A typical fare from Sydney to Los Angeles ranges $1250-1400 peak-season, and $1000-1200 off-season. A typical fare from Sydney to Toronto ranges $100-150 more. Advance purchase fares from Australia have extremely tough restrictions. If you are uncertain about your plans, pay extra for an advance purchase ticket that has only a 50% penalty for cancellation. Travelers from Australia and New Zealand might also consider taking Singapore Air or another Far-East based carrier during the initial leg of their trip. Check with STA or another budget agency for more comprehensive information.

■ Charter Flights

Charter flights can save you a lot of money if you can afford to be flexible. Many charters book passengers up to the last minute—some will not even sell tickets more than 30 days in advance. However, many flights fill up well before their departure date. You must choose your departure and return dates when you book, and you will lose all or most of your money if you cancel your ticket. Charter companies themselves reserve the right to change the dates of your flight or even cancel the flight a mere 48 hours in advance. Delays are not uncommon. To be safe, get your ticket as early as possible, and arrive at the airport several hours before departure time. Many of the smaller charter companies work by contracting service with commercial airlines, and the length of your stay is often limited by the length of the company's contract. Prices and destinations can change (sometimes markedly) from season to season, so be sure to contact as many organizations as possible in order to get the best deal. For more information, contact the charter companies listed below:

CIEE Travel Services (see Budget Travel Services).
Travel CUTS (see Budget Travel Services).
Unitravel, 1177 N. Warson Rd., St. Louis, MO 63132 (800-325-2222; fax 314-569-2503). Specializes in trans-continental and long distance flights within the U.S. 6-day advance purchase with a Saturday stop-over required. Max. stay varies.
Travac, 989 6th Ave., New York, NY 10016 (800-872-8800 or 212-563-3303; fax 212-563-3631). In 1993, Travac ran flights between NYC and either LA or San Francisco—any ticket $403 round-trip. Prices and destinations vary with changing contracts, as do the maximum lengths of stay. Phones open Mon.-Fri. 8:30am-8:30pm, Sat. 9am-4pm.

■ Ticket Consolidators

Ticket consolidators sell unbooked commercial and charter airline seats; tickets gained through them are both less expensive and more risky than those on charter flights. Companies work on a space-available basis which does not guarantee a seat; you get priority over those flying stand-by but below that of regularly-booked passengers. Although consolidators which originate flights in Europe, Australia, or Asia are scarce, the market for flights within North America is a good one, and growing. Consolidators tend to be reliable on these domestic flights, both in getting you on the flight and in getting you exactly where you want to go. Flexibility is often necessary, but all companies guarantee that they will put you on a flight or refund your money. On the day of the flight, the earlier you arrive at the airport the better, since ticket agents seat passengers in the order that they've checked them in.

Now Voyager, 74 Varick St. #307, New York, NY 10013 (212-431-1616), boasts reliability which rivals that of most charter companies (97% of customers get on their flights the first time), while its prices are still considerably less. NYC to LA runs $125 each way; NYC to Chicago $75; NYC to Honolulu $225; and Los Angeles to Honolulu $115. Flights, except LA to Honolulu, run exclusively out of and into NYC. (Phones open Mon.-Fri. 10am-5:30pm and Sat. noon-4:30pm, EST.)

Airhitch, 2790 Broadway #100, New York, NY 10025 (212-864-2000 on the East Coast; 310-394-0550 on the West Coast), works through more cities and to a greater number of destinations, although their prices are slightly higher and flights are less destination-specific (meaning that often you must list two or three cities within a given region which you are willing to fly to; Airhitch guarantees only that you will get to one of them). For most flights you must give a range of three to five days within which you are willing to travel. Be sure to read *all* the fine print. The aptly named "Calhitch" program connects NYC with LA and San Francisco for $129; "Hawaiihitch" connects LA with Oahu and Maui for $129; "USAhitch" connects NYC with Miami ($99), Chicago ($79), San Juan ($119), Dallas ($79), and Orlando ($99). All fares are one way in either direction.

■■■ BY TRAIN

Locomotion is still one of the cheapest and most comfortable ways to tour the U.S. and Canada. You can walk from car to car to stretch your legs, buy overpriced edibles in the snack bar, and shut out the sun to sleep in a reclining chair (avoid paying unnecessarily for a roomette or bedroom). It is essential to travel light; not all stations will check your baggage and not all trains carry large amounts.

Amtrak, 60 Massachusetts Ave. N.E., Washington D.C. 20002 (800-872-7245) offers a discount **All-Aboard America** fare which divides the Continental U.S. into three regions—Eastern, Central, and Western. Amtrak charges the same rate for one-way and round-trip travel, with three stopovers permitted and a maximum trip duration of 45 days. During the summer, rates are $199 within one region, $299 within and between two regions, and $399 among three (Sept.-mid-Dec. and Jan.-May, rates are $179, $229, and $259). Drawing a line from Chicago south roughly divides the first region from the second; drawing a north-south line through Denver roughly divides regions two and three. Your itinerary, including both cities and dates, must be set at the time the passes are purchased; the route may not be changed once travel has begun, although times and dates may be changed at no cost. All-Aboard fares subject to availability, and Amtrak recommends reserving two to three months in advance for summer travel.

Another discount option, available only to those who aren't citizens of North America, is the **USA Rail Pass** which allows unlimited travel and unlimited stops over a period of either 15 or 30 days. As with the All-Aboard America program, the cost of this pass depends on the number of regions within which you wish to travel. The pass allowing 30 days of travel nationwide sells for $389 peak season, and $308 off-season; the 15-day nationwide pass sells for $309/208. The 30-day pass which limits travel to the western region only (as far east as Denver) sells for $229/178; the 15-day pass for the western region sells for $178/158. The 30-day pass which limits travel to the eastern region (as far west as Chicago) sells for $229/209; the 15-day pass for the eastern region sells for $178/158.

A final discount option on Amtrak is the **Air-Rail Travel Plan,** offered in conjunction with United Airlines, which allows you to travel in one direction by train and then fly home, or to fly to a distant point and then return home by train. The train-portion of the journey allows up to three stopovers, and you have 180 days to complete your travel. The transcontinental plan, which allows coast-to-coast travel originating in either coast, sells for $549 peak season and for $459 off-season. The East Coast plan, which allows travel roughly as far west as Atlanta, is $379/339. The West Coast plan, allowing travel roughly as far east as Tucson, AZ, sells for $389/339. A multitude of variations on these plans are available as well; call for details.

Amtrak offers several **discounts** off its full fares: children under 15 accompanied by a parent (½-fare); children under age two (free); senior citizens (15% off for travel Mon.-Thurs.) and travelers with disabilities (25% off); current members of the U.S. armed forces and active-duty veterans (25% discount) and their dependents (12.5% discount). Circle trips and special holiday packages can save you money as well. Keep in mind that discounted air travel, particularly for longer distances, may be cheaper than train travel. For up-to-date information and reservations, contact your local Amtrak office or call 800-872-7245 (use a touch-tone phone).

For information on traveling by train in **Canada,** see Getting Around in Canada in the Canada Essentials.

■■■ BY BUS

Buses generally offer the most frequent and complete service between the cities and towns of the U.S. and Canada. Often they are the only way to reach smaller locales without a car. The exceptions are some rural areas and more open spaces where bus lines tend to be equally sparse. Your biggest challenge when you travel by bus is scheduling. *Russell's Official National Motor Coach Guide* ($12.80 including postage) is an indispensable tool for constructing an itinerary. Updated each month, *Russell's Guide* contains schedules of literally every bus route (except Greyhound) between any two towns in the United States and Canada. Russell's also publishes a semiannual *Supplement,* which includes a Directory of Bus Lines, Bus Stations, and Route Maps ($5 each). To order any of the above, write Russell's Guides, Inc., P.O. Box 278, Cedar Rapids, IA 52406 (319-364-6138).

Greyhound, P.O. Box 660362, Dallas TX 75266-0362 (800-231-2222 in the U.S.), operates the largest number of routes in both the U.S. and Canada. Within specific regions, other bus companies may provide more exhaustive services. A number of **discounts** are available on Greyhound's standard-fare tickets (restrictions apply): senior citizens (Mon.-Thurs. 10%, Fri.-Sat. 5% off); children ages two to 11 (50% off); travelers with disabilities and their companions together ride for the price of one; active and retired U.S. military personnel and National Guard Reserves, and their spouses and dependents, may (with valid ID) take a round-trip between any two points in the U.S. for $169.

Greyhound allows passengers to carry two pieces of luggage (up to 45 lbs. total) and to check two pieces of luggage (up to 100 lbs.). Whatever you stow in compartments underneath the bus should be clearly marked; be sure to get a claim check for it, and watch to make sure your luggage is on the same bus as you.

If you plan to tour a great deal by bus within the U.S., you may save money with the **Ameripass,** which entitles you to unlimited travel for seven days ($250), 15 days ($350), or 30 days ($450); extensions for the seven- and 15-day passes cost $15 per day. The pass takes effect the first day used, so make sure you have a pretty good idea of your itinerary before you start. Before you purchase an Ameripass, total up

the separate bus fares between towns to make sure that the pass is indeed more economical, or at least worth the unlimited flexibility it provides. **TNM&D Coaches, Vermont Transit,** and **Adirondack Trailways** are actually Greyhound subsidiaries, and as such will honor Ameripasses. Check with the companies for specifics. Greyhound also offers an **International Ameripass** for those from outside North America. These are primarily peddled in foreign countries, but they can also be purchased in either of Greyhound's International Offices, located in New York City (212-971-0492) and Los Angeles (213-629-840). A seven-day pass sells for $175, a 15-day pass for $250, and a 30-day pass for $325.

Greyhound schedule information can be obtained from any Greyhound terminal, or from the reservation center at the new toll-free number (800-231-2222). Greyhound is implementing a reservation system much like the airlines, which will allow you to call and reserve a seat or purchase a ticket by mail. If you call seven days or more in advance and want to purchase your ticket with a credit card, reservations can be made and the ticket mailed to you. Otherwise, you may make a reservation up to 24 hours in advance. You can also buy your ticket at the terminal, but arrive early. If you are boarding at a remote "flag stop," be sure you know exactly where the bus stops. It's a good idea to call the nearest agency and let them know you'll be waiting at the flag-stop for the bus and at what time. Catch the driver's attention by standing on the side of the road and flailing your arms wildly—better to be embarrassed than stranded. If the bus speeds on by (usually because of over-crowding), the next less-crowded bus should stop.

For a more unusual and social trip, consider **Green Tortoise,** P.O. Box 24459, San Francisco, CA 94124 (800-227-4766, in CA 415-821-0803). These funky "hostels on wheels" are remodeled diesel buses done up with foam mattresses, sofa seats, stereos, and dinettes; meals are prepared communally. Bus drivers operate in teams so that one can drive and the other can point out sites and chat with passengers. Prices include transportation, sleeping space on the bus, and tours of the regions through which you pass. Deposits ($100 most trips) are generally required since space is tight and economy is important for the group.

Green Tortoise can get you to San Francisco from Boston or New York in 10-14 days for $299-349 (plus $75-85 for food); from Seattle for $69; or from Los Angeles for $30. For the vacation-oriented, Green Tortoise also operates a series of round-trip "loops" which start and finish in San Francisco and travel to Yosemite National Park, Northern California, Baja California, the Grand Canyon, and Alaska. The Baja trip (9 days, $249, plus $51 for food) includes several days on the beach, with sea-kayaking provided for a fee. Much of Green Tortoise's charm lies in its low price and the departure it offers from the impersonality of Greyhound service. Beyond San Francisco, there are regional agents in Boston, New York, Los Angeles, Santa Barbara, Santa Cruz, Vancouver, Seattle, Portland, and Eugene, OR. To be assured of a reservation, book one to two months in advance; however, many trips have space available at departure.

■■■ BY AUTOMOBILE

Getting Revved Up

If you'll be relying heavily on car travel, you might do well to join an automobile club. For $15-70 per year (depending on where you live and how many benefits you choose) the **American Automobile Association (AAA),** 100 AAA Drive, Heathrow, FL 32746-5080 (800-222-4357), offers free trip-planning services, roadmaps and guidebooks, discounts on car rentals, emergency road service anywhere in the U.S., free towing, and commission-free traveler's cheques from American Express. Your membership card doubles as a $5000 bail bond (if you find yourself in jail) or a $1000 arrest bond certificate (which you can use in lieu of being arrested for any motor vehicle offense except drunk driving, driving without a valid license, or fail-

AUTOMOBILE TRAVEL

ure to appear in court on a prior motor-vehicle arrest). If someone in your household already owns a membership, you may be added on as an associate with full benefits for a cost of about $20-25 per year. AAA has reciprocal agreements with the auto associations of many other countries which often provide you with full benefits while in the U.S.

Other automobile travel service organizations include:

AMOCO Motor Club, P.O Box 9041, Des Moines, IA 50368 (800-334-3300). $50 annual membership enrolls you, your spouse, and your car. Services include 24-hr. towing (5 mi. free or free back to the tower's garage) and emergency road service. Premier membership ($75) brings 50 mi. free towing.

Mobil Auto Club, 200 N. Martingale Rd., Schaumburg, IL 60174 (800-621-5581). $45 annual membership covers you and one other person of your choice. Benefits include locksmith, free towing (up to 10 mi.) and other roadside services, as well as car-rental discounts with Hertz, Avis, and National.

Montgomery Ward Auto Club, 200 N. Martingale Rd., Schaumbourg, IL 60173-2096 (800-621-5151). $52 annual membership includes you and your spouse in any car. Children (ages 16-23) $1.50 a month.

If you'll be driving during your trip, make sure that your insurance is up-to-date and that you are completely covered. Car rental companies often offer additional insurance coverage, as does American Express if you use them to rent the car. *In Canada, automobile insurance with coverage of CDN$200,000 is mandatory.* If you are involved in a car accident and you don't have insurance, the stiff fine will not improve the experience. U.S. motorists are advised to carry the **Canadian Non-Resident Inter-Provincial Motor Vehicle Liability Card,** which is proof of coverage. The cards are available only through U.S. insurers. For information on the International Driver's License, see Documents and Formalities.

Let's Go lists U.S. highways in this format: "I" (as in "I-90") refers to Interstate highways, "U.S." (as in "U.S. 1") to United States Highways, and "Rte." (as in "Rte. 7") to state and local highways. For Canadian highways, "TCH" refers to the Trans-Canada Highway, "Hwy." or "autoroute" refers to standard autoroutes.

On The Road

Learn a bit about minor automobile maintenance and repair before you leave, and pack an easy-to-read manual—it may at the very least help you keep your car alive long enough to reach a reputable garage. Your trunk should contain the following bare **necessities:** a spare tire and jack, jumper cables, extra oil, flares, a blanket (several, if you're traveling in winter), extra water (if you're traveling in summer or through the desert), and a flashlight. If there's a chance you may be stranded in a remote area, bring an emergency food and water supply. Always have plenty of gas and check road conditions ahead of time when possible, particularly during the winter. Carry a good **map** with you at all times. Rand McNally publishes a comprehensive road atlas of the U.S. and Canada, available in bookstores for around $8.

Gas is generally cheaper in towns than at interstate service stops. When planning your budget, remember that the enormous travel distances of North America will require you to spend more on gas than you might expect. Burn less money by burning less fuel. Tune up the car, make sure the tires are in good repair, check the oil, and avoid running the air-conditioner unnecessarily.

Sleeping in a car or van parked in the city is extremely dangerous—even the most dedicated budget traveler should not consider it an option.

Be sure to **buckle up**—it's the law in most of the regions in the U.S. and Canada. Before you hit the road, check rental cars to make sure that the seatbelts work properly. In general, the speed limit in the U.S. is 55mph, but rural sections of major interstates may well be 65mph (when posted). Heed the limit; not only does it save gas, but most local police forces and state troopers make frequent use of radar to catch speed demons. The speed limit in Canada is 100kph.

FREE
USE OF OUR
CARS
VANS, RVs, TRUCKS

If you need a vehicle for traveling to another state, you will find, as many other thousands of happy travelers have, that we provide a very exciting economical way to travel.

WE OFFER

- **FREE** Use of vehicle with time to sightsee
- First tank of gas **FREE** on most cars (some cars all gas paid plus bonuses).
- All vehicles are insured.
- Cars leave daily to California, Arizona, NY, Texas, Florida, Illinois, Washington State, Washington D.C., etc.
- Passengers allowed.

No gimmicks, our corporation is in the transportation industry delivering newer vehicles nationwide.

Requirements
21yrs or over - Valid Driver License or International Drivers License - Passport or U.S. Citizen

One Call Does It All
219-852-0134 (Chicagoland, Illinois Location)

We Provide A **FREE** Shuttle Service To Our Location.

800-77-TEXAS (Dallas, Texas Location)

310-798-3374 (Los Angeles , California Location)

We Are Located In Hermosa Beach, 7-Minutes South Of LAX, 1-Block from the Ocean.

Across America Driveaway

Division of

SCHULTZ INTERNATIONAL

In the 1950s, President Dwight D. Eisenhower envisioned an **interstate system,** a federally funded network of highways designed primarily to increase military mobility and subsidize American commerce. Eisenhower's asphalt dream gradually has been realized, although Toyotas far outnumber tanks on the federally funded roads. Believe it or not, there is actually an easily comprehensible, consistent system for numbering interstates. Even-numbered interstates run east-west and odd ones run north-south, decreasing in number the further north or west they are. If the interstate has a three-digit number, it is a branch of another interstate (i.e., I-285 is a branch of I-85), often a bypass skirting around a large city. An *even* digit in the *hundred's* place means the branch will eventually return to the main interstate; an *odd* digit means it won't. North-south routes begin on the West Coast with I-5 and end with I-95 on the East Coast. The southernmost east-west route is I-4 in Florida. The northernmost east-west route is I-94, stretching from Montana to Wisconsin.

Renting

Although the cost of renting a car for long distances is often prohibitive, renting for local trips may be reasonable. **Auto rental agencies** fall into two categories: national companies with thousands of branches, and local agencies that serve only one city or region. The former usually allow cars to be picked up in one city and dropped off in another (for a hefty charge). By calling a toll-free number you can reserve a reliable car anywhere in the country. Drawbacks include steep prices and high minimum ages for rentals (usually 25). If you're 21 or older and have a major credit card in your name, you may be able to rent where the minimum age would otherwise rule you out. Try **Alamo** (800-327-9633), **Avis** (800-331-1212), **Budget** (800-527-0700), **Dollar** (800-800-4000), **Hertz** (800-654-3131), **National** (800-328-4567), or **Thrifty** (800-367-2277). Dollar, Thrifty, and Alamo rent to those 21 to 25; expect to pay an additional charge of $10-20 per day, even when renting for a week or more.

Local companies are often more flexible and cheaper than major companies, but you'll generally have to return the car to its point of origin. Some local companies will accept a cash deposit ($50-100) in lieu of a credit card. Companies such as **Rent-A-Wreck** (800-421-7253) supply cars that are long past their prime. Sporting dents and purely decorative radios, the cars sometimes get very poor mileage, but they run and they're cheap. *Let's Go* lists the addresses and phone numbers of local rental agencies in most towns.

Most packages allow you a certain number of miles free before the usual charge of 30-40¢ a mile takes effect; if you'll be driving a long distance (a few hundred miles or more), ask for an unlimited-mileage package. For rentals longer than a week, look into **automobile leasing,** which costs less than renting. Make sure, however, that your car is covered by a service plan to avoid outrageous repair bills.

Auto Transport Companies

Automobile transport companies match drivers with car owners who need cars moved from one city to another. Would-be travelers give the company their desired destination; the company finds the car. The only expenses are gas, food, tolls, and lodging. A security deposit covers any breakdowns or damage. You must be at least 21, have a valid license, and agree to drive about 400 mi. per day on a fairly direct route. Companies regularly inspect current and past job references, take your fingerprints, and require a cash bond. Cars are available between most points, although it's easiest to find cars for traveling from coast to coast; New York and Los Angeles are popular transfer points.

If offered a car, look it over first. Think twice about accepting a gas guzzler since you'll be paying for the gas. With the company's approval, however, you may be able to share the cost with several companions. For more information, contact **Auto Driveaway,** 310 S. Michigan Ave., Chicago, IL 60604 (800-346-2277). Also try **A Anthony's Driveaway,** P.O. Box 502, 62 Railroad Ave., East Rutherford, NJ 07073 (201-935-8030; fax 201-935-2567).

■■■ BY BICYCLE

Get in touch with a local biking club if you don't know a great deal about bicycle equipment and repair. Make your first investment in an issue of *Bicycling* magazine (published by Rodale Press; see below), which advertises low sale prices. When you shop around, compare knowledgeable local retailers to mail-order firms. If the disparity in price is modest, buy locally. Otherwise, order by phone or mail and make sure you have a local reference to consult. **Bike Nashbar,** 4111 Simon Rd., Youngstown, OH 44512 (800-627-4227; fax 216-782-2856), is the leading mail-order catalog for cycling equipment. They will beat any nationally-advertised price by 5¢, and will ship anywhere in the U.S. and Canada, and to overseas military addresses. They also have a hotline (216-788-6464) to answer questions about repairs and maintenance. Another exceptional mail-order firm which specializes in mountain bikes is **Bikecology,** P.O. Box 3900, Santa Monica, CA 90403 (800-326-2453).

There are also a number of good books about bicycle touring and repair in general. **Rodale Press,** 33 E. Minor St., Emmaus, PA 18908 (215-967-5171) publishes *Mountain Biking Skills* and *Basic Maintenance and Repair* ($7 apiece) and other general publications on prepping yourself and your bike for an excursion. *Bike Touring* ($11, **Sierra Club**) and *Bicycle Touring in the 90s* ($7, Rodale Press) both discuss how to equip and plan a bicycle trip. *Bicycle Gearing: A Practical Guide* ($9) is available from **The Mountaineers Books,** 1011 SW Klickitat Way #107, Seattle, WA 98134 (800-553-4453), and discusses in lay terms how bicycle gears work, covering everything you need to know in order to shift properly and get the maximum propulsion from the minimum exertion. *The Bike Bag Book* ($5 plus $2.50 shipping), available from **10-Speed Press,** Box 7123, Berkeley, CA 94707 (800-841-2665 or 415-845-8414), is a bite-sized manual with broad utility.

■■■ BY THUMB

Let's Go urges you to consider the large risks and disadvantages of hitchhiking before thumbing it. Hitching means entrusting your life to a randomly selected person who happens to stop beside you on the road. While this may be comparatively safe in some areas of Europe and Australia, it is generally *not* so in the United States. We do NOT recommend it. We strongly urge you to find other means of transportation.

In general, hitching in the United States is less safe the farther south or east one goes, and the more urban the area in which one travels. Near metropolises like New York City and Los Angeles, hitching is tantamount to suicide. In areas like rural Alaska and some island communities, hitching is reportedly less unsafe. All states prohibit hitchhiking while standing on the roadway itself or behind a posted freeway entrance sign.

■ Once There

■■■ ACCOMMODATIONS

The U.S. and Canada have a pleasant variety of inexpensive alternatives to hotels and motels. Before you set out, try to locate places to stay along your route and make reservations, especially if you plan to travel during peak tourist seasons. If you don't have the money for lodgings, call the **Traveler's Aid Society**, listed in *Let's Go*

under Practical Information wherever it exists. The local crisis center hotline may also have a list of persons or groups who will house you in such an emergency.

■ Hotels and Motels

The United States is owner and master of the budget motel paradigm and its proliferation. Many budget motels preserve single digits in their names (e.g. Motel 6), but the cellar-level price of a single has matured to just about $27. Nevertheless, budget chain motels still cost significantly less than the chains catering to the next-pricier market, such as Holiday Inn. Chains usually adhere more consistently to a level of cleanliness and comfort than locally operated budget competitors; some budget motels even feature heated pools and cable TV. In bigger cities, budget motels are just off the highway, often inconveniently far from the downtown area, so if you don't have a car, you may well spend the difference between a budget motel and one downtown on transportation. Contact these chains for free directories:

Motel 6, 3391 S. Blvd., Rio Rancho, NM 87124 (505-891-6161).
Super 8 Motels, Inc., 1910 8th Ave. NE, P.O. Box 4090, Aberdeen, SD 57402-4090 (800-800-8000).
Choice Hotels International, 10750 Columbia Pike, Silver Springs, MD 20901-4494 (800-453-4511).
Best Western, P.O. Box 10203, Phoenix, AZ 85064-0203 (800-528-1234).

You may also want to consult an omnibus directory, like the *State by State Guide to Budget Motels* ($11) from **Marlor Press, Inc.,** 4304 Brigadoon Drive, St. Paul, MN 55126 (800-669-4908), or the *National Directory of Budget Motels* ($6, shipping included), from **Pilot Books,** 103 Cooper St., Babylon, NY 11702 (516-422-2225). If you are excessively addicted to Hiltons and Marriots, consider joining **Discount Travel International,** 114 Forrest Ave., Narbeth, PA 19072 (215-668-7184). For an annual membership fee of $45, you and your household can have access to a clear-

ACCOMODATIONS

ing house of unsold hotel rooms (as well as airline tickets, cruises, car rentals, and the like) which can save you as much as 50%.

■ Youth Hostels

Youth hostels offer unbeatable deals on indoor lodging, and they are great places to meet traveling companions from all over the world; many hostels even have ride boards to help you hook up with other hostelers going your way. As a rule, hostels are dorm-style accommodations where the sexes sleep apart, often in large rooms with bunk beds. (Some hostels allow families and couples to have private rooms.) Hostels often have kitchens and utensils for your use, and some have storage areas and laundry facilities. Many also require you to perform a communal chore, usually lasting no more than 15 min.

Hosteling International/American Youth Hostels (HI/AYH) maintains over 300 hostels in the U.S. and Canada. Basic HI/AYH rules (with some local variation): check-in between 5-8pm, check-out by 9:30am, maximum stay three days, no pets or alcohol allowed on the premises. All ages are welcome. Fees range from $7-14 per night. Hostels are graded according to the number of facilities they offer and their overall level of quality—consult *Let's Go* evaluations for each town. The **International Youth Hostel Federation (IYHF)** recently changed its name to **Hosteling International (HI).** HI memberships are valid at all HI/AYH hostels. For more info, contact HI/AYH (see Hostel Membership under Documents and Formalities).

There are also a number of non-HI/AYH affiliated hostels across the country. A number of these are members of **Rucksackers North America,** PO Box 28038, Washington, DC 28038, formerly the American Association of Independent Hostels (AAIH). For only the cost of a self-addressed stamped envelope, they'll send you a free guidebook to RNA hostels. If you send an additional $5.00, they will include a validation sticker, good for a year, entitling you to a dollar discount on the first night at any participating RNA hostel.

■ Bed and Breakfasts

As alternatives to impersonal hotel rooms, bed and breakfasts (private homes with spare rooms available to travelers) range from the acceptable to the sublime. B&Bs may provide an excellent way to explore an area with the help of a host who knows it well, and some go out of their way to be accommodating, by accepting travelers with pets or giving personalized tours. The best part of your stay will often be a home-cooked breakfast (and occasionally dinner). However, many B&Bs do not provide phones, TVs, or private showers with your room.

For information on B&Bs, contact **Bed and Breakfast International,** P.O. Box 282910, San Francisco, CA 94128-2910 (800-872-4500 or 415-696-1690, fax 415-696-1699) or CIEE's (212-661-1414) *Where to Stay USA* ($14) which includes listings for hostels, YMCAs and dorms, along with B&Bs with singles under $30 and doubles under $35. Two useful guidebooks on the subject are *Bed & Breakfast, USA,* ($14) by Betty R. Rundback and Nancy Kramer, available in bookstores or through Tourist House Associates, Inc., RD 2, Box 355-A, Greentown, PA 18426 (717-676-3222), and *The Complete Guide to Bed and Breakfasts, Inns and Guesthouses in the U.S. and Canada,* by Pamela Lanier, from Ten Speed Press, available in book stores.

■ YMCAs and YWCAs

Not all Young Men's Christian Associations (YMCAs) offer lodging; those that do are often located in urban downtowns, which can be convenient though a little gritty. Rates in YMCAs are usually lower than a hotel but higher than the local hostel and include use of the showers (often communal), libraries, pools, and other facilities. Economy packages that include lodging, some meals, and excursions are available in New York, New Orleans, and Hollywood. Many YMCAs accept women and families, but some (e.g., the Los Angeles chapters) will not accept ages under 18 without parental permission. Reservations (strongly recommended) are $3 in the U.S. and Canada, except Hawaii ($5), and key deposits are $5. Payment for reservations must

be made in advance, with a traveler's check (signed top and bottom), U.S. money order, certified check, Visa, or Mastercard. For information and reservations, write the **Y's Way to Travel,** 224 East 47th St., New York, NY 10017. Send a self-addressed envelope with a 65¢ stamp for a free catalogue.

Most Young Women's Christian Associations (YWCAs) accommodate only women. Non-members are usually required to join when lodging. For more information, write **YWCA-USA,** 726 Broadway, New York, NY 10003 (212-614-2700).

■ Alternative Accommodations

Many **colleges and universities** open their residence halls to travelers when school is not in session—some do so even during term-time. No general policy covers all of these institutions, but rates tend to be low, and many schools require that you to express at least a vague interest in attending their institution. Since college dorms are popular with many travelers, you should call or write ahead for reservations.

Students traveling through a college or university town while school is in session might try introducing themselves to friendly looking local students. At worst you'll receive a cold reception; at best, a good conversation might lead to an offer of a place to crash. International visitors may have especially good luck here. In general, college campuses are some of the best sources for information on things to do, places to stay, and possible rides out of town. In addition, dining halls often serve reasonably priced, reasonably edible all-you-can-stomach meals.

Another alternative is **Servas,** an international cooperative system devoted to promoting peace and understanding by providing opportunities for more personal contacts among people of diverse cultures. Travelers are invited to share life in hosts' homes in over 100 countries. You are asked to contact hosts in advance, and you must be willing to fit into the household routine. Homestays are two nights. Prospective travelers must submit an application with references, have an interview, and pay a membership fee of $55, plus a $25 deposit for up to five host lists which

provide a short description of each host member. Servas is non-profit organization and no money passes between traveler and host. Write to U.S. Servas Committee, 11 John St. #407, New York, NY 10038 (212-267-0252).

■ ■ ■ CAMPING & THE OUTDOORS

■ Useful Publications

For information about camping, hiking, and biking, write or call the publishers listed below to receive a free catalog.

Sierra Club Bookstore, 730 Polk St., San Francisco, CA 94109 (415-923-5500). Books on many national parks, as well as *The Best About Backpacking* ($11), *Cooking for Camp and Trail* ($12), *Learning to Rock Climb* ($14), and *Wildwater* ($12). Shipping $3.

The Mountaineers Books, 1011 Klickitat Way, Suite 107, Seattle, WA 98134 (800-553-4453 or 206-223-6303). Numerous titles on hiking (the *100 Hikes* series), biking, mountaineering, natural history, and environmental conservation.

Wilderness Press, 2440 Bancroft Way, Berkeley, CA 94704-1676 (800-443-7227 or 510-543-8080). Specializes in hiking guides and maps for the Western U.S. Also publishes *Backpacking Basics* ($9, including postage) and *Backpacking with Babies and Small Children* ($10).

Take advantage of *Woodall's Campground Directory* (Western and Eastern editions, $11 USA/$13 Canada. Shipping $2.75) and *Woodall's Plan-It, Pack-It, Go...!: Great Places to Tent, Fun Things to Do* (North American edition, $12 USA/$14 Canada. Shipping $3.25). If you can't find a copy locally, contact Woodall Publishing Company, P.O. Box 5000, 28167 N. Keith Dr., Lake Forest, IL 60045 (800-323-9076 or 708-362-6700). For topographical maps, write the U.S. Geological Survey, Map

CAMPING & THE OUTDOORS

Distribution, Box 25286, Denver, CO 80225 (303-236-7477) or the Canada Map Office, 615 Booth St., Ottawa, Ont., K1A 0E9 (613-952-7000), which distributes geographical and topographical maps as well as aeronautical charts.

■ Parks and Forests

At the turn of the century it may have seemed unnecessary to set aside parts of the vast American and Canadian wilderness for conservation, but today that act is recognized as a stroke of genius. National parks protect some of the most spectacular scenery throughout North America. Though their primary purpose is preservation, the parks also make room for recreational activities such as ranger talks, guided hikes, skiing, and snowshoe expeditions. Most national parks have backcountry with developed tent camping; others welcome RVs, and a few offer opulent living in grand lodges. Internal road systems allow you to reach the interior and major sights even if you are not a long-distance hiker. For information on camping, accommodations, and regulations, write the National Park Service, Office of Public Inquiries, P.O. Box 37127, Washington, D.C. 20013-7127.

Entry fees vary from park to park. The larger and more popular national parks charge a $3-5 entry fee for vehicles and sometimes a nominal one for pedestrians and cyclists. Most national parks sell the annual **Golden Eagle Passport** ($25), which allows the bearer and family free entry into all parks. Visitors ages 62 and over qualify for the **Golden Age Passport,** entitling them to free entry and a 50% discount on recreational fees; travelers with disabilities enjoy the same privileges with the Golden Access Passport. Both the Golden Age and Golden Access Passports are free. These passports are also valid at national monuments.

Many states and provinces have parks of their own, which are smaller than the national parks but offer some of the best camping around—handsome surroundings, elaborate facilities, and plenty of space. In contrast to national parks, the primary function of state parks is recreation. Prices for camping at public sites are almost always better than those at private campgrounds.

At the more popular parks in the U.S. and Canada, reservations are absolutely essential; make them through **MISTIX** (800-365-2267). Lodges and indoor accommodations are generally in the shortest supply and should be reserved months in advance. However, most campgrounds are strictly first-come, first-camped. Arrive early: many campgrounds, public and private, fill up by late morning. Some limit your stay and/or the number of people in a group (usually no more than 25).

If the national parks are too developed for your tastes, national forests provide a purist's alternative. While some have recreation facilities, most are equipped only for primitive camping—pit toilets and no water are the rule. Fees are nominal or nonexistent. Forests are generally less accessible than the parks, but are consequentially less crowded. Backpackers can take advantage of specially designated wilderness areas, which are even less accessible due to regulations barring all vehicles. Wilderness permits, required for backcountry hiking, can usually be obtained (sometimes for free) at parks; check ahead. Adventurers who plan to explore some real wilderness should always check in at a U.S. Forest Service field office before heading out. Many of the wilderness areas are difficult to find (a reason they are under-utilized), so write ahead for detailed, accurate maps. Contact a U.S. Forest Service field office for further information.

The **U.S. Department of the Interior's** Bureau of Land Management (BLM) offers a wide variety of outdoor recreation opportunities—including camping, hiking, mountain biking, rock climbing, river rafting and wildlife viewing—on the 270 million acres it oversees in ten Western states and Alaska. These lands also contain hundreds of archaeological artifacts, such as ancient Indian cliff dwellings and rock art, and historic sites like ghost towns. For more information, write or call BLM Public Affairs, Washington D.C. 20240 (202-208-5717).

■ Tent Camping and Hiking

EQUIPMENT

At the core of your equipment is the **sleeping bag.** Sleeping bags are rated according to the lowest outdoor temperature at which they will still keep you warm. If a bag's rating is not a temperature but a seasonal description, keep in mind that "summer" translates to a rating of 30-40°F, "three-season" can be anywhere from 5-30°F, and "four-season" means below 0°F. Bags are made either of down (warmer and lighter) or of synthetic material (cheaper, heavier, more durable, and warmer when wet). Lowest prices for good sleeping bags: $60-70 for a summer synthetic, $150 for a three-season synthetic, $150-180 for a three-season down bag, and upwards of $250-300 for a down sleeping bag you can use in the winter.

When you select a **tent,** your major considerations should be shape and size. A-frame tents are the best all-around. When they are pitched, their internal space is almost entirely usable; this means little unnecessary bulk. Dome and umbrella shapes offer more spacious living, but tend to be bulkier to carry. For especially small and lightweight models, contact **Sierra Design,** 2039 4th St., Berkeley, CA 94710, which sells a two-person tent that weighs less than 1.4 kg (3 lbs.) Be sure your tent has a rain fly. Good two-person tents start at about $100; $150 for a four-person. You can, however, often find last year's version for half the price.

If you intend to do a lot of hiking or biking, you should have a **frame backpack.** Buy a backpack with an internal frame if you'll be hiking on difficult trails that require a lot of bending and maneuvering—internal-frame packs mould better to your back, keep a lower center of gravity, and have enough give to follow you through your contortions. An internal-frame backpack is also good as an all-around travel pack, something you can carry by hand when you return to civilization. External-frame packs are more comfortable for long hikes over even terrain; since they keep the weight higher, walking upright will not cost you additional exertion. The size of a backpack is measured in cubic inches. Any serious backpacking requires at least 3300 of them, while longer trips require around 4000. Add an additional 500 cubic inches for internal-frame packs, since you'll have to pack your sleeping bag inside, rather than strap it on the outside as you do with an external-frame pack. Backpacks with many compartments generally turn a large space into many unusable small spaces. Packs that load from the front rather than the top allow you access to your gear more easily (see Packing for more hints). Sturdy backpacks start anywhere from $75-125. This is one area where it doesn't pay to economize—cheaper packs may be less comfortable, and the straps are more likely to fray or rip quickly. Test-drive a backpack for comfort before you buy it.

WILDERNESS CONCERNS

The first thing to preserve in the wilderness is you—health, safety, and food should be your primary concerns when you camp. See Health for information about basic medical concerns and first-aid. A comprehensive guide to outdoor survival is *How to Stay Alive in the Woods*, by Bradford Angier (Macmillan, $8). Many rivers, streams, and lakes are contaminated with bacteria such as giardia, which causes gas, cramps, loss of appetite, and violent diarrhea. To protect yourself from the effects of this invisible trip-wrecker, always boil your water vigorously before drinking it, or use an iodine solution made for purification. *Never go camping or hiking by yourself for any significant time or distance.* If you're going into an area that is not well-traveled or well-marked, let someone know where you're hiking and how long you intend to be out. If you fail to return on schedule or if you need to be reached for some reason, searchers will at least know where to look for you.

The second thing to protect while you are outdoors is the wilderness. The thousands of outdoor enthusiasts that pour into the parks every year threaten to trample the land to death. Because firewood is scarce in popular parks, campers are asked to make small fires using only dead branches or brush; using a campstove is the more

cautious way to cook. Check ahead to see if the park prohibits campfires altogether. To avoid digging a rain trench for your tent, pitch it on high, dry ground. Don't cut vegetation, and don't clear campsites. If there are no toilet facilities, bury human waste at least four inches deep and 100 feet or more from any water supplies and campsites. Always pack up your trash in a plastic bag and carry it with you until you reach the next trash can; burning and burying pollute the environment.

BEAR NECESSITIES

No matter how tame a bear appears, don't be fooled—they're wild and dangerous animals who are simply not impressed or intimidated by humans. A basic rule of thumb to follow is that if you're close enough for a bear to be observing you, you're too close. To avoid a grizzly experience, never feed a bear, or tempt it with such delectables as open trash cans. They will come back to demand seconds as a right. Keep your camp clean. Do not cook near where you sleep. Do not leave trash or food lying around camp.

When you sleep, don't even think about leaving food or other scented items (trash, toiletries) near your tent. The best way to keep your toothpaste from becoming a condiment is to **bear-bag**. This amounts to hanging your delectables from a tree, out of reach of hungry paws. Ask a salesperson at a wilderness store to show you how. Food and waste should be sealed in airtight plastic bags, all of which should be placed in duffel bags and hung in a tree ten feet from the ground and five feet from the trunk. Also avoid indulging in greasy foods, especially bacon and ham.

Park rangers can tell you how to identify bear trails (don't camp on them!). Bears are attracted to perfume smells; do without cologne, scented soap, and hairspray while camping. Leave your packs empty and open on the ground so that a bear can nose through them without ripping them to shreds.

If you see a bear at a distance, calmly walk (don't run) in the other direction. If it seems interested, some suggest waving your arms or a long stick above your head and talking loudly; the general flailing creates the impression in the bear's eyes that

TIME & MEASUREMENT

you're much taller than a person, and it may decide that you are the menacing High Lord of the Forest. Always shine a flashlight when walking at night: the bears will clear out before you arrive given sufficient warning. If you stumble upon a sweet-looking bear cub, leave immediately, lest its over-protective mother stumble upon you. If you are attacked by a bear, get in a fetal position to protect yourself, put your arms over the back of your neck, and play dead. The aggressiveness of bears varies from region to region. Always ask local rangers for details.

■■■ TIME AND MEASUREMENT

U.S. residents tell time on a 12-hour clock cycle. Hours before noon are *ante meridiem,* or "am." Hours after noon are *post meridiem,* or "pm." Due to the confusions of 12pm and 12am, *Let's Go* uses "noon" and "midnight" instead. The continental U.S. divides into four time zones (east to west): Eastern, Central, Mountain, and Pacific. Canada contains these four, plus Newfoundland and Atlantic to the east. Alaska, and Hawaii and the Aleutian Islands have their own time zones as well. When it's noon Eastern time, it's 1:30pm Newfoundland, 1pm Atlantic, 11am Central, 10am Mountain, 9am Pacific, 7am Alaska, and 6am Hawaii and Aleutian. Most of the U.S. and all of Canada observe **daylight saving time** from the last Sunday in April (April 24th in 1994) to the last Sunday in October (October 30 in 1994) by advancing clocks ahead one hour. Arizona, Hawaii, and parts of Indiana are exempt from daylight saving and do not advance their clocks. Upstarts.

Although the metric system has made considerable inroads into American business and science, the English system of weights and measures continues to prevail in the U.S. (now the only country in the world not on the metric system). The following is a list of U.S. units and their metric equivalents:

1 inch (in.) = 25.4 millimeters (mm)
1 foot (ft.) = 0.30 meter (m)
1 yard (yd.) = 0.91 meter (m)
1 mile (mi.) = 1.61 kilometers (km)
1 ounce (oz.; mass) = 28.4 grams (g)
1 fluid ounce (fl. oz.; volume) = 29.6 milliliters (ml)
1 pound (lb.) = 0.45 kilogram (kg)
1 liquid quart (qt.) = 0.95 liter (L)
1 gallon (gal.) = 3.78 liter (L)

It should be noted that gallons in the U.S. are not identical to those in Canada; one U.S. gallon equals .83 Imperial gallons. Electric outlets throughout the U.S., Canada, and Mexico provide current at 117 volts, 60 cycles (Hertz). Appliances designed for the European electrical system (220 volts) will not operate without a transformer and a plug adapter (this includes electric systems for disinfecting contact lenses). Transformers are sold to convert specific wattages (e.g. 0-50 watt transformers for razors and radios; larger watt transformers for hair dryers and other appliances).

The U.S. uses the Fahrenheit temperature scale rather than the Centigrade (Celsius) scale. To convert Fahrenheit to Centigrade temperatures, subtract 32, then multiply by 5/9.

■ UNITED STATES

The cause of America is in great measure the cause of all mankind.
—Thomas Paine

American culture is omnipresent; but what is America? Is it the rocky, tumultuous shores of Maine, the granite magnificence of Yosemite, or the skyscraping canyons of Manhattan? From the frontier tundra of Alaska to the languid Florida Gulf Coast, the people of the United States of America have inhabited and flourished in the best and worst of environments. The United States is a country supported by every breed of individual; while Armani-clad brokers keep the money moving in the metropoli, blue-collar America wrestles with the soil and within the factories to keep the wheels of this mighty juggernaut turning, moving ever forward.

Born in the tempest of revolution, America emerged in July of 1776 as a union representing and protecting high philosophical ideals such as freedom of religion and speech. Over the next hundred years, the United States grew westward to encompass a vast continent, tilling and taming the land, sowing the seeds of industrial might. In spirit and at its heart, the country's ideal is to remain fair and provide equal opportunity to all. It is the individual chance to follow—and achieve—a dream, to make it, to become succesful, rich, or happy, that has driven millions of immigrants to the American shores. Often, they come looking for paradise, only to find despair. This is the hurdle which remains to America: to live up to the ideals it set over two centuries ago.

Whatever it is the traveler seeks—the cool jazz of New Orleans, the hot swamps of the Everglades, or the mellow, rolling hills of the Ozarks—it can be found in the U.S. In many places the city blocks stretch on and on for endless miles, suburbs in search of a city, and in others forests drift to the horizon in a sea of green haze. Occasionally, some of the most solitary, beautiful vistas can be found just miles from cities packed with vibrant millions. Reaching from below the Tropic of Cancer to above the Arctic Circle, America encompasses a vast region which defies instant description and instant understanding. Just as one cannot know New York City from seeing the Statue of Liberty, one cannot understand the U.S. from touring only the largest cities. To get to know America, get out beyond the cities and see it.

American Culture

HISTORY

In the Beginning

It is not known exactly when the first people set foot in the Americas. The earliest inhabitants were probably intrepid travelers who trekked from the region now called Siberia in search of more hospitable living space. Until recently, scientists estimated that the first Americans crossed the Bering Sea on a land bridge which arose during the last Ice Age, about 25,000 years ago, and has since disappeared. New archaeological finds, however, show evidence of even earlier habitation, leading experts to theorize two waves of immigration. Whenever they may have arrived, these people multiplied, and their descendants spread to populate the entire continent. Little is known about the culture of the original tribes, since they possessed an oral rather than a written tradition. Even those few who recorded their presence in writing did so only in petroglyphs on rocks and cliffs, primarily in the Southwest,

HISTORY

which have not yet been deciphered. Nevertheless, the heritage of these people has not been entirely lost—it reverberates still in the culture of the modern Native American tribes scattered throughout the United States and Canada.

European Exploration

The exact date of the arrival of the first Europeans in the Americas is also unknown. It is likely that the earliest Europeans to alight upon the "New World" were sea voyagers blown off course by storms, but the first deliberate European visitors were probably Scandinavians—Vikings led by Leif Erikson explored the Atlantic coast around the year 1000, but left little trace of their visit. The Irish may argue with this point; an Irish legend asserts that a monk named Brendan (later St. Brendan) sailed across the Atlantic sometime in the 6th century, but unfortunately, there is no evidence to back this legend up. Europeans next stumbled upon the Americas in 1492 when Christopher Columbus found his trip around the world blocked by Hispaniola in the Caribbean Sea. Thinking he had reached the spice islands of the East Indies, he dubbed the inhabitants "Indians." In recent years, a spate of revisionism has transformed Columbus from a much celebrated hero who brought civilization and religion to the Americas to a rapacious, greedy exploiter who ruthlessly destroyed the natives' paradise. The truth most likely lies somewhere in between, but we won't attempt to sort it out here. Whatever one may say about Columbus, those who followed him—such as the Spanish *conquistadore* Hernando Cortez, who demolished the Aztec Empire in 1519—did indeed exploit the local peoples.

Colonization

Most of the Europeans who came to the Americas in search of immediate wealth were unsuccessful. Instead of giving up and going home, however, many chose to settle down. They were followed by a second wave of immigrants whose primary purpose was colonization—English religious dissenters headed for New England, French fur trappers traipsed the bountiful woods of eastern Canada, and Spanish missionaries and conquistadores claimed California, the Southwest, Florida, and Mexico. The Spaniards were the earliest European power to establish permanent colonies; St. Augustine, founded in Florida in 1565, was the first permanent European settlement in the United States. Of all these groups, however, it was the English who concentrated the most on settling the vast New World. After a few unsuccessful attempts, like the "lost colony" at Roanoke, Virginia, the English finally managed, with the help of some friendly natives, to establish a colony at Jamestown in 1607. Facing a labor shortage, it was not long before the English discovered the profitability of slave labor, and the first black slaves were imported to Jamestown in 1619. Virginia thrived as an increasing number of Europeans became addicted to tobacco, its main cash crop. As Britain expanded its colonial empire, Virginia tobacco became an important aspect of a lucrative mercantile economy.

Not all English colonists sought wealth. Pilgrims, the followers of a Puritan Anglican sect not tolerated in England, sailed to the New World in search of a place where they could practice their religion in peace. They landed at Plymouth Rock in what is now Massachusetts in 1620, and their struggle to survive in a harsh land inspired one of the most treasured and overdone holidays in modern American culture: Thanksgiving. The English crown largely ignored the Puritan colonists of New England until the late 17th and early 18th century, when it realized that they were a potential source of tax revenue and sent a viceroy to collect.

Consolidation and Revolution

If history were only the high flown drama of kings and princes, then the first part of 18th century would be fairly uninteresting. The English colonies expanded and grew as people moved outward into unsettled regions in search of more land to cultivate. Fields were plowed, babies born, and valleys settled. This peaceful existence was disturbed by the advent of a world war, known in Europe as the "Seven Years War" but locally as the "French and Indian War." From 1756-1763, the English colonists and British troops fought the French and their Native American allies. The British emerged victorious, and the 1763 Treaty of Paris ceded French Canada to King George III, securing the colonies' western boundaries from French incursion.

However, enormous debts accompanied Britain's victory. Bound and determined to make the colonists help pay the debts incurred in assuring their safety, the British government levied a number of taxes on a variety of products in the 1760s and early 1770s. Two of the most hated were the Stamp Act, which placed a tax on paper products, and the tax on tea. A movement arose to protest these taxes and the colonists, led by the Sons of Liberty (a semi-secret society which originated in Boston), boycotted many English goods. The colonists' anger at what they termed "taxation without representation" was met with general indifference from the British government, which only added more taxes. The straw that broke the camel's back was the Boston Tea Party, when in December of 1774, a group of colonists dressed as Native Americans dumped several shiploads of English tea into Boston Harbor. The British response, known as the Intolerable Acts, was swift and harsh. Boston was effectively cut off from the rest of the colonies and filled to the brim with red-coated British soldiers. Armed rebellion ensued. On July 4, 1776, the Continental Congress formally issued the Declaration of Independence, officially announcing the thirteen colonies' desire to be free of British rule. Though initially a guerilla army composed of home-spun militia known as Minutemen, the Continental forces eventually grew into an effective army under the leadership of George Washington. Despite many hardships on the way, the Continental forces prevailed, sealing their victory by vanquishing British forces at Yorktown, VA in 1781 with the help of the French fleet. Until 1787, the newly independent states were governed by a loose confederation. This proved unstable and problematic, so a Constitutional Convention was convened in Philadelphia to draw up a new plan of government. The fruit of the work of the "Founding Fathers" is still the law of the land, although the states refused to ratify it without a number of immediate amendments. These first ten amendments are known as the Bill of Rights and delineate the rights of all American citizens on which the government may not infringe. The original Constitution in itself is a landmark political document, putting the principles of the French Enlightenment philosophers to work. It creates three separate branches of government—legislative, executive, and judicial—and a system of checks and balances which safeguard against both dictatorship and anarchy. It has been amended a total of twenty-six times to include issues which could not even have been dreamed of in 18th century, as its authors intended it to be flexible and grow with the nation.

Onward and Outward

With the original thirteen states under stable, federal rule, America turned westward and began to expand. In 1803, President Thomas Jefferson purchased the Louisiana Territory, one-fourth of the present day United States, from Napoleon for the bargain price of three cents an acre. Curious about what lay in this tract and eager to tap the northwest fur trade, Jefferson sent explorers Merriwether Lewis and William Clark to trek all the way to the Pacific coast. With the aid of a Native American woman called Sacajawea, they reached Seaside, Oregon, in October, 1805.

After the historical hiccup known as the War of 1812 (an offshoot of the Napoleonic Wars fought between the new United States and Great Britain), the westward movement gained momentum. The doctrine of "Manifest Destiny," a belief that the United States was destined by God to rule the continent, gathered a large following at this time. People moved west in droves in search of cheap, fertile land and a new life. The discovery of gold in California in 1848 also motivated a mass migration. Friction between American settlers in Texas and the Mexican government led to a war which ultimately concluded with Mexico selling Texas and much of the southwest to the United States for a song. Some Americans took their Manifest Destiny far too seriously—in 1855 William Walker and a band of 53 mercenaries known as his

"Immortals" conquered Nicaragua for Cornelius Vanderbilt's steamship company, and ruled the country for two bloody and turbulent years.

As white settlers moved west, enduring incredible hardships, they came into conflict with the Native Americans on whose lands they were intruding. Much of the legend of the Wild West revolves around the stories of brave white settlers and stoic cowboys fending off attacks by marauding Indians. Unfortunately, these stories are largely distortions, created to justify the actions of the government in exploiting and displacing Native Americans, and to sell books, newspapers, and, much later, movie tickets and television advertising. Nevertheless, a desire for expansion into wild, unknown territory retains its significance in the American mind.

Division and Reconstruction

As the United States approached its adolescence in the mid-19th century, it became increasingly difficult to subsume the tensions created by the existence of slavery within its borders. Although the Declaration of Independence nobly asserted that "all men are created equal," slavery remained the basis of Southern agriculture. Many in the industrialized North, weaned from their dependence on slave labor by the mid-18th century, clamored for the end of this "peculiar institution." This hybrid nation, half-free, half-slave, was the fruit of compromises made in drawing up the Constitution, creating a festering division between North and South. As the nation grew, it had to decide whether new territories would become free or slave states. Ad-hoc decisions like the "Missouri Compromise" of 1821 and bloody local conflicts like that in Kansas in the 1850s, eventually gave way to nationwide conflict.

In 1861, the Southern states, outraged by the growing federal government, decided to secede from the Union and form a Confederacy which would permit the states greater autonomy and allow the South to pursue its agrarian, slave-based economy unmolested by Northern abolitionists. From 1861-1865, the country endured a vicious and bloody war, fought by the North to restore the Union, and by the South to be free of the North and establish greater states' rights. The Civil War (alternately called the "War Between the States" or even the "Great War of Northern Aggression" depending on the speaker's sympathies) killed more men than any other war in which the U.S. has been involved. Although the North emerged victorious and brought the South back into the Union, wartime promises of equality for blacks went unfulfilled; the push for Southern industrialization during Reconstruction tied the emancipated slaves to new, more subtle, forms of bondage.

Industrialization

After the end of the Reconstruction in the 1870s, the nation entered a period of tremendous industrial growth and technological innovation. Rapid investment spurred by the Social Darwinist "captains of industry" such as Vanderbilt, Carnegie, and Rockefeller boosted the American economy and increased American influence abroad. This rapid industrial expansion occurred at great cost to workers and farmers, and trade unions grew in response to poor working conditions and low wages. The 19th-century form of unabashed "free market" capitalism soon began to collapse under its own weight, as witnessed by the cyclical recessions of the 1870s, the 1890s, and particularly, the 1930s. Nevertheless, the false high which the U.S. rode during this time has lent the period around the turn of the century the moniker "Gilded Age."

On the agricultural side, the Homestead Act of 1862, which distributed tracts of government land to settlers who developed and lived on that land, prompted the first large-scale cultivation of the Great Plains, which soon became the bread basket of America. Poor land-management techniques, however, depleted the topsoil at an alarming pace.

Politically, the United States was coming of age. Through victory in the Spanish-American War in 1898, the United States acquired colonies in the Philippines, Puerto Rico, and Cuba to become an empire. Tardy but serious involvement in World War I further boosted the international and economic status of the U.S.

Boom, Bust, and Boom!

The decade following World War I, known as the "Roaring Twenties," brought many changes to American society. Women were granted the right to vote by the 19th Amendment to Constitution, while the 21st Amendment banned alcohol. Flappers danced the Charleston, mobsters were lionized in the cinema, and the wealthy consumed conspicuously. The economic euphoria of the 20s, however, was largely inflated by credit. It came tumbling down on "Black Thursday," October 24, 1929, when the New York Stock Exchange crashed to the ground, taking with it countless suicidal financiers, and heralding the start of the Great Depression. Compounding the industrial collapse, American agriculture suffered as the abused soil of the Great Plains blew away, leaving a "dust bowl" and ruining thousands of farmers.

Under the firm hand of President Franklin D. Roosevelt, the United States began a slow recovery. His "New Deal" program created work for hundreds of thousands of the unemployed, building monuments, bridges and parks with public funds. Out-of-work artists created paintings, sculptures, mosaics, and written and photographic records of the impoverished South and West under federal patronage. The New Deal also laid the ground-work for the modern system of social legislation. Unfortunately, all of this good work initiated a stultifying level of bureaucracy which still plagues the U.S. government today. Final recovery from the Depression was aided by the economic boost provided by the war economy of the 1940s.

Cold War and the New Frontier

Spared the war-time devastation of Europe and Japan, the U.S. economy boomed domestically and internationally in the post-war era, building the United States into the world's foremost economic and military power. At the same time, fears of Soviet expansion led to the "Red Scare" of the 1950s, when Congressional committees saw communists behind every tree and thousands of artists, writers, actors, and academics were blacklisted. Suspicion of communism had grown in the U.S. since the Russian Revolution in 1917, but the feverish intensity it gained during the Cold War ultimately led to American involvement in wars in Korea and Vietnam. At the same time, the nuclear arsenals built after World War II by the U.S. and the USSR made their strained relations potentially apocalyptic, culminating in 1962, when President Kennedy and Nikita Khrushchev brought the world to the brink of nuclear war in their showdown over the deployment of Soviet nuclear missiles in Cuba.

Despite the nuclear shadow, the early 1960s were characterized domestically by an optimism engendered by the President himself. Kennedy launched the Peace Corps to bring technology to developing countries through youthful volunteers, NASA's program to place Americans on the moon, and the New Frontier to eliminate the poverty and racism which still plagued American society. This mood eroded on account of Kennedy's escalation of the Vietnam conflict, and was shattered by Kennedy's assassination in Dallas in 1963. The latter part of the decade was marked by increasing social unrest, with extensive public protests against involvement in Vietnam and against the continuing discrimination directed towards African-Americans. Dr. Martin Luther King, Jr. led the non-violent campaign for civil rights, which was marked by peaceful demonstrations, marches, and sit-ins. Unfortunately, they were often met with violence; civil rights activists were drenched with fire hoses, arrested, and sometimes even killed. Dr. King himself was eventually felled by an assassin's bullet in Memphis in 1968.

Accompanying the civil rights movement was the second wave of the women's movement. Sparked by Betty Friedan's landmark text, *The Feminine Mystique,* American women sought to change the delineation between men's and women's roles in society, demanding access to male-dominated professions and equal pay. The sexual revolution, fueled by the development of the birth control pill, brought a woman's right to control her body to the forefront of national debate; the 1973 Supreme Court decision *Roe v. Wade* legalized abortion and engendered a fierce battle between pro-life and pro-choice advocates which continues to be a major national divisor today.

Recent Times

Surprisingly, in the late 1970s and the 1980s, it was the younger generation who most chafed against the dramatic social changes of the 1960s. College campuses became quieter and more conservative as graduates flocked to Wall Street to become investment bankers. Materialism and conspicuous consumption reigned, as convicted insider trader Ivan Boesky declared "greed is good." In 1980, former California governor Ronald Reagan was elected to the White House on a tidal wave of conservatism that crested in 1988 when his vice-president, George Bush, was elected as his successor. The 90s, however, look to be a new era, as activists have again taken up the banner of change on such issues as abortion, AIDS, ecology, women's rights, gay and lesbian rights, homelessness, and racism. In 1992, a faltering economy, no longer able to absorb a surfeit of young urban professionals, led Americans to elect Democrat Bill Clinton president from a three-horse race also featuring the populist billionaire Ross Perot, who claimed to be the voice of the little man. Clinton's campaign focused on attracting the adherents of the new activism. Although it remains to be seen how Clinton will fulfill many of his campaign promises, he has adhered to his promise to make his administration "look like America"— nominees to high government positions have included a number of women, African-Americans, and members of other minority groups.

LITERATURE

If American literature were reduced to one image, it would depict a rugged American donning a backpack filled not with an abundant supply of food, but rather with ideas and dreams, trudging at sunrise through a rustling field; the colossus of European tradition looming overhead, casting a shadow across the field, jungles, and mountains that await. American fiction is the ongoing saga of the neotenic, sincere, and uncorrupted—but not necessarily incorruptible—individual who struggles for freedom at all costs.

Dawn broke with the birth of the new nation. Starting in the mid-1800s, there was an array of works that told the tale of the strong, semi-innocent American individual: Herman Melville's *Moby Dick,* Walt Whitman's *Leaves of Grass,* Nathaniel Hawthorne's *Scarlet Letter.* Accompanying these fictional works were soaring philosophical works like Henry David Thoreau's *Walden* and Ralph Waldo Emerson's *Self Reliance* which sang of independence and the wisdom of common sense. New England culture sought to separate itself from the European culture from which it arose. In the Midwest, humorists attempted to define the American soul in rollicking stories and tall tales set in the natural and human landscapes of the new continent. Their captain in spirit was Mark Twain, whose best-known work, *The Adventures of Huckleberry Finn,* explores American naivete and coming-of-age along the mighty Mississippi.

Early 20th-century literature marked a reflective, self-examining midmorn. No longer were the virtues of the frontier celebrated; instead, the vices of the Gilded Age were attacked. The Industrial Revolution inspired talk of the allure of corruption—Upton Sinclair's muckraking in *The Jungle* left an entire generation unable to eat sausage. Even those who ostensibly succeeded led lives of misery: Sinclair Lewis's *Main Street* and F. Scott Fitzgerald's *Great Gatsby* both tell the tales of people who've "made it" but live in silent desperation. Women writers, meantime, were acutely examining societal roles in novels of self-discovery, such as Kate Chopin's *The Awakening* and the world of Willa Cather and Edith Wharton.

Evening set in with the 1950s, when the Beatniks, spearheaded by cult heroes Jack Kerouac and Allen Ginsberg, raved wildly through postwar America's dull conformity with soulful bursts of jazz-like poetry and prose—Kerouac's *On the Road* (1955), though quite dated by now, nonetheless makes a fine companion to this guidebook for the contemporary road scholar. For other appropriate roadside reads, consider William Least Heat Moon's meditative, transcontinental travelogue *Blue Highways*, John Steinbeck's *Travels With Charley* (your dog will approve), expatriate Bill Bryson's hilarious *The Lost Continent*, or Jonathan Raban's *Old Glory*.

Over the last few decades there has been an intense scrutiny of the tensions of American life not only in literature itself but in the study and reception of literature as well. The rising debate over multiculturalism in American schools has provoked some revisionists to renounce Hemingway and Faulkner without mercy while equally vociferous intellectuals scramble to defend this rather homogeneous legacy. However one-sided America's canon has proven in the past, a great deal of remarkable literature has been produced by writers of varying backgrounds. Ralph Ellison's searing narrative of life as a black man, *Invisible Man,* Piri Thomson's examination of the life in Spanish Harlem, *Down These Mean Streets,* and Oliver LaFarge's portrayal of a Navajo youth's coming of age, *Laughin' Boy*, all reflect this ongoing examination.

MOVIES AND TELEVISION

From the days when viewers were amazed by Thomas Edison's 30-second film of a galloping horse through the Great Depression when Hollywood became the great escape, to today, when stunning computer-generated special effects like those of Disney's *Alladin* and *Jurassic Park* are the norm, Americans have always been fascinated by moving pictures. The big screen more frequently makes an effort to bring art into the picture. The success of that endeavor may be in the eye of the beholder, but the success of the movie industry and its bastard offspring, the movie-star-watching industry, is undisputed. The genres themselves are unqualified Americana: sci-fi (*Star Wars, 2001: A Space Odyssey, Blade Runner*), thriller (*Raiders of the Lost Ark, Silence of the Lambs*), drama (*Casablanca, The Godfather*), and the most American of them all, the western (*Unforgiven, The Magnifcent Seven*).

There are television sets in almost 98% of U.S. homes, and the competition between the four national networks (ABC, CBS, Fox, and NBC) and cable television has led to an exponential growth in TV culture over the last few years. During prime time (8-11pm EST) find the most popular shows of American entertainment: *In Living Color, L.A. Law, Beverly Hills, 90210,* and *The Simpsons,* the smartest, most hysterical show ever to leave Springfield. Over cable you'll discover around-the-clock channels offering news, sports, movies, kid shows, or weather exclusively. Then there's the music video of MTV, whose dazzling display of calculatedly random visceral images affords a disconcerting glimpse into the psyche of the American under-30 set.

MUSIC

The impact of broadcast and recording technology on the American music scene cannot be overstated. No longer do you have to lilt to the nearest concert hall to hear the classics, or journey to New Orleans or St. Louis to hear true blues. Today, the full panoply of music is available at your fingertips, in the form of compact dics and radio waves. The power to create, re-create, or just over-power is in the hands of anyone with a sufficiently large instrument—be it pen, orchestra, or stereo. As such, American music is universal, open to and experienced by all. Defining American music today is akin to determining the key of John Cage's *4:33*. But, we try.

American music must be considered as the music written, performed, and heard in America. Its foundation rests upon the bedrock of the European classical tradition and the roots of jazz and blues. The music of the American soul has been sounded by jazz greats like Louis Armstrong, Ella Fitzgerald, Miles Davis, Billie Holiday, Charlie Parker, John Coltrane, Glen Miller, Wynton Marsalis, David Sanborn, among many others. An extension of the blues, rock n' roll and its derivative siblings—from metal to punk to rap to pop—are the mainstream of American popular music today. The motto to remember, in the words of Nicholas Brown: "60s rock is a million and disco is zero; pop music is a combination of 60s rock and disco, which just goes to show that a million times zero is still zero."

Yet it is not enough to extol the virtues of jazz and blues, and similar forms which are the classic American music, or even the people who brought this music to life. To hear some American music first hand and make if part of you, head to the halls, clubs, and stadiums of any American city, particularly the following:

For classical: New York, Philadelphia, Cleveland, Chicago, Boston, and St. Louis
For jazz or blues: New Orleans, St. Louis, Chicago, and New York.
For country/western: Nashville, Memphis, Dallas, and Houston.
For rock and roll: New York, Boston, Chapel Hill, NC, Seattle, Olympia, WA.
For rap: New York, Los Angeles, and Oakland.

THEATER

Ah, the art of the American stage. Nowhere else has the simple premise of pretense taken on so many varied perversions as in the U.S. You cannot escape actors and actor-wanna-bes here. From rural summer stock to New York City's Broadway, there's a stage in almost every town, performing the smallest, shortest plays and "visual pieces" to gargantuan operas like *Nixon in China* and musicals (a U.S. original) like remakes of Cole Porter, Rogers and Hammerstein (and Hart), Stephen Sondheim, and George and Ira Gershwin, as well as all the great hits from London. But that's not all. You'll also encounter countless people on the streets and in stores who clearly think it's their personal calling to become famous actors; yet these often un-talented performers provide the U.S. with a street theater which cannot be overlooked, no matter how hard you try.

VISUAL ART

American art is as diverse and multifaceted as the American experience it depicts. The works of artists such as Edward Hopper and Thomas Hart Benton explore the innocence and mythic values of the United States before its emergence as a superpower. The vigorous Abstract Expressionism of Arshile Gorky and Jackson Pollock displays both the swaggering confidence and frenetic insecurity of cold-war America. Pop Art, popularized by Jasper Johns, Robert Rauschenberg, Roy Lichtenstein, and Andy Warhol, uses as its subject matter the icons and motifs of contemporary American life and pop culture, satirizing and exposing what has become since World War II the *de facto* world culture. Cindy Sherman and Robert Mapplethorpe have exposed Americans to personal-as-political photography, despite efforts of self-styled guardians of morality to censor their work. Contemporary American art is often a highly experimental, mixed-media pastiche of audio, video, and performance art which acknowledges and incorporates technology.

ARCHITECTURE

The story of American architecture is its own tall tale. This country is by far best remembered architecturally as the land where buildings soar into the heavens from monstrous pedestals grounded on measured city blocks. The U.S. is the home of the skyscraper; Louis Sullivan catalyzed it all in the late 19th century in Chicago. Since then, architects and builders have realized and developed the notion that the future of building is up, not out or away. It may be claimed that architecture in the U.S. is much more than just tall buildings; there are also the villages and cities of the Native Americans, and the Colonial period, the birth and growth of Pierre l'Enfant's Washington, DC, American city planning, neo-Georgianism, neo-Classicism, Modernism, post-modernism, and the international style. But all of these are just that—international. The U.S. can truly call its own only the unique distinction of its love for and fascination with skyscrapers and the provincial architectural styles which dot and litter the country.

To get a taste of any local style, it is best to visit different cities and take numerous walking tours in city blocks. Locales have had a way of greatly altering classic forms by changing materials, shapes, or functions of houses and buildings. Most buildings in the southwest are made of clay-brick, while those of New England follow traditional patterns of ornamentation, down to the smallest cornice moulding or frame designs. Wrought-iron was extremely popular in the south, especially on old plantation houses, for its stability, availability, and appearance. Many of the minor aspects of architecture that go into a building are distinctly American. The basic forms—house, church, public building—have not changed in hundreds of years.

The skyscraper is where the U.S. truly shines. It is, as Philip Johnson said, "the great American gift to the art of building." The skyscrapers have gone from following the current styles to leading them; they are now often the pinnacle of an architect's career, the chance to really make a statement. And statements are made; far too many, it seems. From the austere Seagram's Building by Mies van de Rohe in New York, a classic example of modern, functional construction which served as *the* model for skyscrapers of the 1960s and 70s, to the sleek glass and metal rail-stations of Helmut Jahn in Chicago, which seem to shift with the sun and melt away into their own corners and curves, the skyscraper always speaks for the architect and the builder, and often for the community which it oversees. The skyscraper is America's quest for heaven, for the unattainable, for perfect engineering, and for absolute beauty, visually and structurally.

USA Essentials

■■■ CURRENCY AND EXCHANGE

CDN$1 = US$0.76	US$1 = CDN$1.31
UK£1 = US$1.52	US$1 = UK£0.66
IR£1 = US$1.40	US$1 = IR£0.72
AUS$1 = US$0.67	US$1 = AUS$1.49
NZ$1 = US$0.56	US$1 = NZ$1.80

U.S. currency uses a decimal system based on the **dollar ($)**. Paper money ("bills") comes in six denominations, all the same size, shape, and dull green color. The bills now issued are $1, $5, $10, $20, $50, and $100. You may occasionally see denominations of $2, which are no longer printed but are still acceptable as currency. Some restaurants and retail stores may not accept $50 bills and higher. The dollar divides into 100 cents (¢); fractions such as 35 cents are represented as 35¢. The penny (1¢), the nickel (5¢), the dime (10¢), and the quarter (25¢) are the most common coins. The half-dollar (50¢) and one-dollar coins are rare but valid currency.

It is nearly impossible to use foreign currency in the U.S., although in some regions near the Canadian border, shops may accept Canadian money at a very unfavorable rate of exchange. In some parts of the country you may even have trouble **exchanging your currency** for U.S. dollars. Convert your currency infrequently and in large amounts to minimize fees. Buy U.S. traveler's checks, which can be used in lieu of cash (when an establishment specifies "no checks accepted" this usually refers to checks drawn on a bank account). **Personal checks** can be very difficult to cash in the U.S.; most banks require that you have an account with them to cash one. You may want to bring a U.S.-affiliated credit card such as Interbank (Master-Card), Barclay Card (Visa), or American Express. For more information see Traveler's checks and Credit Cards, in Essentials, at the front of this book.

KEEPING IN TOUCH

Sales tax is the U.S. equivalent of the Value Added Tax. Expect to pay 4-10% depending on the item and place. See the state introductions for information on local taxes. Some areas charge a hotel tax; ask in advance. In addition, a **tip** of 15% is expected by restaurant servers and taxi drivers, although restaurants sometimes include this service charge in the bill. Tip bellhops $1 per bag. It is also customary to tip barkeeps 25¢ to $1 for a drink.

■■■ KEEPING IN TOUCH

■ Mail

Individual offices of the U.S. Postal Service are usually open Mon.-Fri. 9am-5pm and sometimes on Sat. until about noon; branches in many larger cities open earlier and close later. All are closed on national holidays. **Postcards** mailed within the U.S. cost 19¢ and **letters** cost 29¢ for the first ounce and 23¢ for each additional ounce. To Canada, it costs 30¢ to mail a postcard, and 40¢ to mail a letter for the first ounce and 23¢ for each additional ounce. Postcards mailed to any other nation cost 40¢, and letters are 50¢ for a half-ounce, 95¢ for an ounce, and 39¢ for each additional half-ounce up to 64 ounces. **Aerogrammes** are available at post offices for 45¢. Domestic mail takes from two to five days to reach its destination. Mail to northern Europe, Canada, and Mexico takes a week to ten days; to Southern Europe, North Africa, and the Middle East, two weeks; and to South America or Asia, a week to ten days. Of course, all of the above estimated times of arrival are dependent on the particular foreign country's mail service as well. Be sure to write "Air Mail" on the front of the envelope for the speediest delivery.

The U.S. is divided into postal zones, each with a five-digit ZIP code particular to a region, city, or part of a city. Writing this code on letters is essential for delivery. Some addresses have nine-digit ZIP codes, used primarily for business mailings to speed up delivery. The normal form of an address is as follows:

P. J. Lindberg (name)
Ruark Publishing (name of organization, optional)
1792 Gemmill Drive, #42 (address, apartment number)
Moody, MO 32284 (city, state abbreviation, ZIP)
USA (country, if mailing internationally)

Depending on how neurotic your family is, consider making arrangements for them to get in touch with you. Mail can be sent **General Delivery** (a.k.a. Poste Restante) to a city's main post office. Once a letter arrives it will be held for about 30 days; it can be held for longer at the discretion of the Postmaster if such a request is clearly indicated on the envelope. General delivery letters should be labeled like this:

Captain James T. Kirk (underline last name for accurate filing)
c/o General Delivery
Main Post Office
USS-Enterprise Building
1701 NCC Drive
San Francisco, CA 36803

Alternately, **American Express** offices throughout the U.S. and Canada will act as a mail service for cardholders, *if* you contact them in advance. Under this free "Client Letter Service," they will hold mail for 30 days, forward upon request, and accept telegrams. For a complete list of offices and instructions on how to use the service, call 800-528-4800.

■ Telephones

Telephone numbers in the U.S. consist of a three-digit area code, a three-digit exchange, and a four-digit number, written as 123-456-7890. Only the last seven digits are used in a **local call**. **Non-local calls** *within* the area code from which you are dialing require a "1" before the last seven digits, while **long-distance calls** *outside* the area code from which you are dialing require a "1" and the area code. For example, to call Harvard University in Cambridge, MA from Las Vegas, NV, you would dial 1-617-495-1000. Canada and much of Mexico share the same system. Generally, **discount rates** apply after 5pm on weekdays and Sunday and **economy rates** every day between 11pm and 8am; on Saturday and on Sunday until 5pm, economy rates are also in effect.

Pay phones are plentiful, often stationed on street corners and in public areas. Put your coins (10-25¢ for a local call depending on the region) into the slot and listen for a dial tone before dialing. If there is no answer or if you get a busy signal, you will get your money back after hanging up; if you connect with an answering machine, you won't. To make a long-distance direct call, dial the number. An operator will tell you the cost for the first three minutes; deposit that amount in the coin slot. The operator or a recording will cut in when you must deposit more money. A second, rarer variety of pay phone can be found in some large train stations and charges 25¢ for a one-minute call to any place in the continental U.S.

If you are at an ordinary telephone and don't have barrels of change, you may want to make a collect call (i.e., charge the call to the recipient). First dial "0" and then the area code and number you wish to reach. An operator will cut in and ask to help you. Tell him or her that you wish to place a **collect call** from Blackie Onassis, or whatever your name happens to be; anyone who answers may accept or refuse the call. If you tell the operator you are placing a **person-to-person collect call** (more expensive than a regular, station-to-station collect call), you must give both your name and the receiving person's name; the benefit is that a charge appears only if the person with whom you wish to speak is there (and accepts the charges, of course). The cheapest method of reversing the charges is MCI's new 1-800-COLLECT service: just dial 1-800-COLLECT, tell the operator what number you want to engage (it can be anywhere in the world), and receive a 20-44% discount off normal rates; discounts are greatest when the rates are cheapest. Note that in some areas, particularly rural ones, you may have to dial "0" alone for any operator-assisted call.

You can place **international calls** from any telephone. To call direct, dial the international access code (011) followed the country code, the city code, and the local number. Country codes and city codes may sometimes be listed with a zero in front (e.g. 033), but when using 011, drop succeeding zeros (e.g., 011-33). In some areas you will have to give the operator the number and he or she will place the call.

■■■ ETIQUETTE

American etiquette exists in the form of several conventions which more invite your awareness than demand your adherence. In the U.S., a brief shaking of hands is the most prevalent form of greeting among acquaintances. In social relationships, people often refer to one another by first name from the moment they are introduced, although younger people should use titles (Mr. or Mrs.) and last names to address their elders. Prevalent in America's larger cities is the practice of "civil inattention," or the purposeful ignorance of every person one sees, as well as the illegal practice of jaywalking (crossing streets against lit signals or outside of painted crosswalks).

Waiters and waitresses in America's restaurants are usually not addressed as Sir and Miss; make eye contact with them and say, "Excuse me." In many restaurants, your check will be delivered before you ask for it; you should not consider this a personal affront or even a subtle hint that it's time to leave.

NEW ENGLAND

New England, with its centuries-old commitment to education and its fascination with government, has been an intellectual and political center for the entire nation since before the States were even officially United. Students and scholars from across the country funnel into New England's colleges each fall, and town meetings still take place in many rural villages. Yet this region is an unlikely cradle for any sort of civilization: the soil is barren, the climate is harsh, the coast is rocky and treacherous, and the land is wrinkled with mountains.

Though the terrain gave the region's early settlers a tough time, it is kind to today's visitors. New England's dramatic coastline is a popular destination for summer vacationers; the slopes of the Green and White Mountains, with their many rivers and lakes, inspire skiers, hikers, cyclists, and canoers. In the fall, the "changing of the leaves" transforms the entire region into a giant kaleidoscope as the nation's most brilliant foliage bleeds and burns. Though largely rural, very little of New England (inland Maine excepted) is wild. Many vacation sites here are calculated to give you loads of human history—semi-old buildings, museums, battlegrounds, ubiquitous quaint inns, and famous-people sculptures dot the hillside hamlets. However, groups such as the Appalachian Mountain Club battle developers and tour promoters in their quest to preserve the privately owned backcountry.

Mark Twain once said if you don't like the weather in New England, wait 10 minutes. Unpredictable at best, the region's climate can be particularly dismal in November and March. Watch out for black flies and swarming greenhead flies in summer, especially in Maine, and be warned that everything from rivers and state camprounds to tourist attractions may slow down or freeze up during the winter.

 # Connecticut

Although it's hard to imagine, Connecticut was once a rugged frontier. The European colonists' westward movement began with the settlement of the Connecticut Valley by Massachusetts Puritans in the 1630s. Their state motto *Qui Transtulit Sustinet* (He who is transplanted still sustains) refers to the state's origin as a haven for Puritan divine Thomas Hooker and his loyal flock. From the very beginning, "Nutmeggers" were independent—their democratic state constitution gave rise to the state's other nickname, the "Constitution State." The citizens of Connecticut have not lost their Yankee roots, yet they also have tendrils reaching out to modern pop culture. Both the lollipop and the pay phone were born here. Today, Connecticut's traditional style mingles with urbanity in cities like Hartford and New Haven, where glass skyscrapers reflect small brick churches and historical landmarks.

PRACTICAL INFORMATION

Capital: Hartford.
Tourist Information Line: 800-282-6863. Call for vacation guides. **Bureau of State Parks and Forests,** 165 Capitol Ave. #265, Hartford 06106 (566-2304). Will mail you an application for a permit to camp in the state parks and forests; also sends brochures describing sites. **Connecticut Forest and Park Association,** 16 Meriden Rd., Rockfall 06481 (346-2372). Outdoor activities information.
Time Zone: Eastern. **Postal Abbreviation:** CT
Sales Tax: 6.5%

New England

QUÉBEC

St. Lawrence River

Québec

Montréal

Sherbrooke

10

Lake Champlain

Plattsburgh

Burlington

St. Johnsbury

Montpelier

Barre

91

Middlebury

89

VERMONT

Lebanon

Rutland

91

7

Franklin

Concord

Dover

Manchester

Bennington

Keene

Brattleboro

Nashua

2

91

MASSACHUSETTS

Pittsburg

Cambridge

90

Worcester

Salem

Springfield

Sturbridge

Boston

495

95

Hartford

Providence

Brockton

84

7

CONNECTICUT

R.I.

New Haven

Norwich

95

New Bedford

95

Bridgeport

New London

Newport

Stamford

495

Block Island

Martha's Vineyard

Nantucket Island

Long Island Sound

Long Island

Caribou

Presque Isle

1

NEW BRUNSWICK

Houlton

95

East Millinocket

Millinocket

Lincoln

Calais

MAINE

Penobscot River

Bangor

Ellsworth

Waterville

Belfast

Augusta

Bar Harbor

ACADIA NAT'L. PARK

Lewiston

Auburn

1

Brunswick

Portland

Laconia

Berlin

Littleton

93

NEW HAMPSHIRE

Kennebunk

Kittery

Portsmouth

95

ATLANTIC OCEAN

Provincetown

Cape Cod

6

N

↑

| 0 | | 100 miles |
| 0 | | 100 kilometers |

■■■ HARTFORD

Although Bridgeport is Connecticut's largest city, Hartford—home to both the state government and the nation's insurance headquarters—is the most prominent.

Practical Information Hartford lies at the intersection of **I-91** and **I-84.** The **Greater Hartford Convention and Visitors Bureau** is located on Main St. in the Pavilion (open Mon.-Fri. 10am-6pm, Sat. 10am-5pm). The other branch of the Convention and Visitors Bureau is located a short distance away at the **Hartford Civic Center** (728-6789), One Civic Center Plaza. Both offer dozens of maps, booklets, and guides to the state's resorts, campgrounds, and historical sights. Just in front of the old State House, **Connecticut Transit's Information Center** (525-9181) can answer questions concerning the city's public transportation (basic fare 85¢) and can also give a helpful map of the downtown area. Hartford's **area code** is 203.

Food There are a number of reasonably priced places to eat in Hartford—scope out food courts in malls, hot dog stands at Bushnell, and restaurants around local schools like **Trinity College** and the **University of Hartford**. The food court on the second level of the **Pavilion** offers the standard, inexpensive variety of ethnic food court fare (open Mon.-Fri. 10am-6pm, Sat. 10am-5pm). The **Municipal Cafe,** 485 Main St. (278-4844), at Elm, is a popular and friendly place to catch a good breakfast or lunch. (Sandwiches under $4, hot dinners $6.) At night, the "Muni" is big, big, big on the local music scene. (Open daily 7am-2:30pm with breakfast and lunch menu and from 7pm with bar menu under $5; bands usually Wed.-Sat.)

Sights The gold-domed **Old State House,** 800 Main St., is at the heart of the city. Designed by Charles Bullfinch in 1796, this building housed the state government until 1914 (it will be closed for renovations Nov. 1994). In its stead, **Renovation Headquarters** (522-6766), located just across the plaza in the **Pavilion,** has taken in the State House's historical exhibits (open Mon.-Fri. 10am-6pm, Sat. 10am-5pm).

Thomas Hooker once preached across Main Street, at the **Center Church and Ancient Burying Grounds,** 675 Main St., and you can see the centuries-old tombstones of his descendants in the graveyard. A block or so west, park n' ride at **Bushnell Park,** bordered by Jewell, Trinity, and Elm St., on one of the country's few extant hand-crafted merry-go-rounds. The **Bushnell Park Carousel,** built in 1914, spins 48 horses and two lovers' chariots to the tunes of a 1925 Wurlitzer Organ. (Open April Sat.-Sun. 11am-5pm; May-Sept. 2 Tues.-Sun. 11am-5pm. Admission 50¢.) The **State Capitol,** 210 Capitol Ave., overlooks the park. Also gold-domed, this beautiful building houses Lafayette's camp bed and a war-ravaged tree trunk from the Civil War's Battle of Chicamauga, among other historic exhibits. Free 1-hr. tours begin at the West entrance of the neighboring **Legislative Office Building,** behind which is free parking. (Tours Mon.-Fri. 9:15am-1:15pm, Sat. 10:15am-2:15pm. See the Capitol's Room 101 or call 240-0224 for more info.)

Lovers of American literature won't want to miss engaging tours of the **Mark Twain** and **Harriet Beecher Stowe Houses** (525-9317), both located just west of the city center on Farmington Ave.; from the Old State House take any east Farmington Ave. bus. The gaudy Victorian Mark Twain Mansion housed the Missouri-born author for 17 years. Twain composed his controversial masterpiece *Huckleberry Finn* here. Harriet Beecher Stowe lived next door on Nook Farm after the publication of *Uncle Tom's Cabin,* from 1873 until her death. (Both houses open Tues.-Sat. 9:30am-4pm. Admission $6.50 for Twain house, $5 for Stowe, $10 for both.)

Farther out Farmington Ave. in the colonial village of **Farmington** lies the **Hill-Stead Museum** (677-4787). Hill-Stead is a completely Colonial Revival "country house" built by Alfred Pope around 1900 to house his French Impressionist Collection. Pieces by Manet, Monet and Degas, as well as works by the Americans Cassat and Whistler, are on display. Hill-Stead is one of the very few places in the country where Impressionist masterpieces are shown in a domestic setting, as was originally intended. (Guided tour only. Open Tues.-Sun. noon-4pm. Tours every ½ hr. Admission $6, seniors and students $5, kids 6-12 $3.)

Another must-see for the aesthetically inclined is the **Wadsworth Atheneum,** 600 Main St. (278-2670), the oldest public art museum in the country. The museum has absorbing collections of contemporary and Baroque art, including one of only three Caravaggios in the United States. (Open Tues.-Sun. 11am-5pm. Galleries 2 and 3 close at 2pm Tues.-Thurs. $5, seniors and students $2, under 13 free. Free all day Thurs., and on Sat. from 11am-1pm. Tours Thurs. at 1pm and Sat.-Sun. 2pm.)

■■■ NEW HAVEN

Today New Haven is simultaneously university town and depressed city. Academic types and a working-class population live somewhat uneasily side by side—bumper stickers proclaiming "Tax Yale, Not Us" embellish a number of street signs downtown. But there is more than mere political tension here. New Haven has a reputation as something of a battleground, and Yalies tend to stick to areas on or near campus, further widening the rift between town and gown. The difference between the controlled, wealthy academic environment and the rest of the town is apparent in every facet of the city, from architecture to safety.

Practical Information The **Greater New Haven Convention and Visitors Bureau,** 1 Long Wharf Dr. (777-8550 or 800-332-STAY/332-7829) provides free maps and information on current events in town. For recorded events information, updated weekly, call 498-5050, ext. 1310. (Open Mon.-Fri. 9am-5pm.) For free campus maps, head to the **Yale Information Center,** Phelps Gateway, 344 College St. (432-2300), facing the Green. Pick up a 75¢ walking guide and *The Yale,* a guide to undergraduate life ($3). Bus maps and a New Haven bookstore guide available. (Open daily 10am-3:30pm. Free one-hour tours Mon.-Fri. at 10:30am and 2pm, Sat.-Sun. at 1:30pm.) **Amtrak** (800-872-7245), Union Station, Union Ave., runs out of a newly renovated station, but the area is unsafe at night. Trains to New York ($22), Boston ($36), and Washington, D.C ($73). Also at Union Station is **Greyhound** (547-1500). Frequent service to New York ($13.50), Boston ($24), and Providence ($19). (Ticket office open daily 7:30am-7:30pm.) New Haven's **area code** is 203.

New Haven is a cinch to get to by car. The city lies at the intersection of I-95 and I-91, 40 mi. from Hartford. At night, don't wander too freely out of the immediate downtown and campus areas, as surrounding sections are notably less safe. New Haven is laid out in nine squares. The central one is the **Green,** which, despite the fact that it lies between **Yale University** and City Hall, is a pleasant escape from the hassles of city life. A small but thriving business district borders the Green, consisting mostly of bookstores, boutiques, cheap sandwich places, and other services catering to students and professors.

Accommodations and Food Inexpensive accommodations are sparse in New Haven. The hunt is especially difficult around Yale Parents Weekend (mid-Oct.) and commencement (early June). Two decent places are **Hotel Duncan,** 1151 Chapel St. (787-1273) with the oldest elevator in CT (singles $40, doubles $55; reservations recommended on weekends), and **Nutmeg Bed & Breakfast,** 222 Girard Ave. (236-6698), Hartford (doubles $35-45; open Mon.-Fri. 9am-5pm). The nearest parks for camping are **Cattletown** (264-5678; sites $10), 40 minutes away, and **Hammonasset Beach** (245-2755; sites $12), 20 minutes away.

Food in New Haven is reasonably cheap, catering to the student population. The primary distinction is the superb pizza, understandably the pride of New Haven. Started by an Eli Alum, the **Daily Caffe,** 376 Elm St. (776-5063), is quickly becoming the haunt of the university's coffee-and-cigarette set. (Open Mon.-Sat. 8am-1am, Sun. 8am-midnight.) A Yale tradition, and understandably student-infested, **Naples**

Pizza, 90 Wall St. (776-9021 or 776-6214), serves up interesting pizzas with broccoli, pineapple, or white clams ($7.25). Pitcher of beer $5.50. (Open Mon.-Wed. 7-10pm, Thurs.-Fri. 7-11pm; Sept.-May Sun.-Thurs. 7pm-1am, Fri.-Sat. 7pm-2am.)

Sights and Entertainment James Gambel Rodgers, a firm believer in the sanctity of printed material, designed **Sterling Memorial Library,** 120 High St. (432-1775). The building looks so much like a monastery that even the telephone booths are shaped like confessionals. Rodgers spared no expense in making Yale's library look "authentic," even decapitating the figurines on the library's exterior to replicate those at Oxford, which, because of decay, often fall to the ground and shatter. (Open in summer Mon.-Wed. and Fri. 8:30am-5pm, Thurs. 8:30am-10pm, Sat. 10am-5pm; during academic year Mon.-Thurs. 8:30am-midnight, Fri. 8:30am-5pm, Sat. 10am-5am, Sun. 1pm-midnight.)

The massive **Beinecke Rare Book and Manuscript Library,** 121 Wall St. (432-2977), has no windows. Instead this intriguing modern structure is paneled with Vermont marble cut thin enough to be translucent; supposedly its volumes (including one Gutenberg Bible and an extensive collection of William Carlos Williams's writings) can survive a nuclear war. (Open Mon.-Fri. 8:30am-5pm, Sat. 10am-5pm.) Along New Haven's own Wall St., between High and Yale St., the Neo-Gothic gargoyles perched on the **Law School** building are in fact cops and robbers.

Most of New Haven's museums are on the Yale campus. The **Yale University Art Gallery,** 1111 Chapel St. (432-0600), open since 1832, claims to be the oldest university art museum in the Western Hemisphere. Its collections of John Trumbull paintings and Italian Renaissance works are especially notable. (Open Tues.-Sat. 10am-5pm, Sun. 2-5pm. Closed Aug. Suggested donation $3.) The **Yale Center for British Art,** 1080 Chapel St. (432-2800), sponsors some thought-provoking exhibits—two years ago they displayed a collection of snuff boxes. A must for Anglophiles. (Open Tues.-Sat. 10am-5pm, Sun. noon-5pm. Free.) The **Peabody Museum of Natural History,** 170 Whitney Ave. (recorded message 432-5050), houses Rudolf F. Zallinger's Pulitzer Prize-winning mural, which portrays the North American continent as it appeared 70 to 350 million years ago. Other exhibits range from Central American cultural artifacts to a dinosaur hall displaying the skeleton of a *brontosaurus.* (Open Mon.-Sat. 10am-5pm, Sun. noon-5pm. Admission $3.50, seniors $2.50, children 3-15 $2. Free Mon.-Fri. 3-5pm.)

New Haven offers plenty of late-night entertainment. Check **Toad's Place,** 300 York St. (562-5589, recorded information 624-8623), to see if one of your favorite bands is in town. Toad's has hosted impromptu gigs by everyone from Dylan to the Stones. While you get tickets, grab a draft beer ($1) at the bar. (Box office open daily 11am-6pm; tickets available at the bar after 8pm. Bar open Sun.-Thurs. 8pm-1am, Fri.-Sat. 8pm-2am.) The **Anchor Bar,** 272 College St. (865-1512), just off the Green, is the kind of place that serves Corona and St. Pauli Girl Dark; a local paper rated its jukebox the best in the region, though we're skeptical. Harrumph. (Open Mon.-Thurs. 11am-1am, Fri.-Sat. 10am-2am.)

Once a famous testing ground for Broadway-bound plays, New Haven's thespian community carries on today on a lesser scale. The **Schubert Theater,** 247 College St. (526-5666, 800-228-6622), a significant part of the town's on-stage tradition, still mounts shows. (Box office open Mon.-Fri. 10am-5pm, Sat. 11am-3pm.) New Haven's **Long Wharf Theater,** 222 Sargent Dr. (787-4282), received a special Tony Award for Achievement in Regional Theater in 1978. (Tickets $21-26, student rush $5. Season June-late Sept.) Yale itself accounts for an impressive portion of the theater activity in the city. The **Yale Repertory Theater** (432-1234) has turned out such illustrious alums as Meryl Streep, Glenn Close, and James Earl Jones, and it continues to produce excellent shows (open Oct.-May). In summer, the Green is the site of free **New Haven Symphony** concerts (865-0831), the **New Haven Jazz Festival** (787-8228), and other free musical series. The **Department of Cultural Affairs** (787-8956), 770 Chapel St., can answer questions about concerts on the

Green. On the banks of the Housatonic River south of New Haven, the smaller town of Stratford is home to the **American Shakespeare Theater,** 1850 Elm St. (375-5000), exit 32 off I-95; tickets $19-29. At the summer Shakespeare Festival, some of the country's ablest actors and directors stage the Bard's plays while strolling minstrels, musicians, and artists grace the grounds.

■■■ NEW LONDON AND MYSTIC

Connecticut's coastal towns along the Long Island Sound were busy seaports in the days of Melville and Richard Henry Dana, but the dark, musty inns filled with tattooed sailors swapping sea journeys have been consigned to history. Today, the coast is important mainly as a resort and sailing base, and maritime enthusiasts in particular will enjoy these two former whaling ports, New London and nearby Mystic. **New London** sits proudly on a hillside overlooking the majestic **Thames River.** You'll recognize **Union Station** (designed by H. H. Richardson) by the flock of cabs in front of it and the flock of seagulls on the city pier behind. The **Coast Guard Academy** (444-8270), a five-minute drive up Rte. 32, offers free tours through the Coast Guard Museum (444-8511; open May-Oct. Mon.-Fri. 9am-4:30pm, Sat. 10am-5pm, Sun. noon-5pm) and the beautiful cadet-training vessel *U.S.S. Eagle* when it is in port. (Best chance to catch the Eagle is on Sunday. Call for winter hours.)

The town of **Mystic** is a short way up I-95 (exit 90). The **Tourist and Information Center,** Building 1d, Olde Mysticke Village, 06355 (536-1641) in **Olde Mysticke Village,** provides a list of local accommodations and can make same-day reservations (open Mon.-Sat. 9am-6:30pm, Sun. 9am-6pm). **Mystic Seaport Museum** (572-0711) is a restored 19th-century whaling port. The museum's docks hold three boats: a fishing schooner, a military training vessel, and most impressive of all, the three-masted whaling ship **Charles W. Morgan**, on which reenactments of the whaling life are held daily. Although prices are steep and the area is essentially a maritime tourist trap, fans of Melville and Conrad will thoroughly enjoy it. (Seaport open daily 9am-5pm. Admission $14.50, kids 6-15 $8.75. Take I-95 5 mi. east from Union Station to Groton, then bus #10 to Mystic; $1.15 total.)

The **area code** for New London and Mystic is 203.

Maine

A sprawling evergreen wilderness pocked with lakes, swollen with mountains, and defined by a tattered shore, Maine protrudes from the neat stack of New England states below. The Maine "Downeaster" is known for reticent humor, rugged pragmatism, and disdain for urban pretension. Maine's landscape is renowned for its deep wilderness and for rocky coastlines strewn with lighthouses and lobster shacks. It's also a bastion of New England preppiness. Even urban refugees cannot resist swathing themselves in plaid flannel.

The state lives by its waters and forests. Fishing communities along the coast and logging companies inland support the state's economy, and fresh-water fishing is a major Maine stream sport. The rapids of the Allagash Waterway challenge canoeists, and the remote backwood lakes are perfect for hikers, bicyclists, and campers.

PRACTICAL INFORMATION

Capital: Augusta.
Maine Publicity Bureau, 209 Maine Ave., Farmingdale (582-9300). Send mail to P.O. Box 2300, Hallowell 04347. **Bureau of Parks and Recreation,** State House Station #22 (1st floor Harlow Bldg.), Augusta 04333 (289-3821). **Maine Forest**

Service, Bureau of Forestry, State House Station #22 (2nd floor Harlow Bldg.), Augusta 04333 (289-2791). All 3 agencies open Mon.-Fri. 8am-5pm.
Time Zone: Eastern. **Postal Abbreviation:** ME
Sales Tax: 6%.

■■■ BANGOR

Bangor has fallen from its former glory as the nation's largest lumber port; today the city trafficks more in traffic, funneling visitors in from points south and sending them out into the beautiful northern nether regions of Maine. Get a good night's sleep, stock up on provisions and get the hell out of town and into the bush. I-95 runs north-south through the city, parallel to the Penobscot River; about half-a-dozen minor highways also meet there, notably U.S. 1A, which runs east to Bar Harbor and Acadia National Park and south to Penobscot Bay and U.S. 2, which runs southwest across the width of the state and into New Hampshire.

Practical Information For maps, local accommodation and restaurant lists, and brochures detailing almost every activity, sight, lodging, and eatery in the city, check the **Chamber of Commerce,** 519 Main St. (947-0307; open mid-May-mid-Aug. daily 9am-6pm; mid-Aug.-mid-Oct. Mon.-Fri. 8am-5pm.) Two main bus lines can take you out of Bangor. **Concord Trailways,** 1039 Union St. (945-4000 or 800-639-5150), at the corner of Main St., offers 3 buses daily to Boston ($30) and Portland ($20). Concord rides are much quicker, more comfortable, and show a movie (woo!). (Station open daily 6:45am-6:45pm.) **Greyhound,** 158 Main St. (945-3000 or 942-1700), near downtown, runs three buses daily to Boston ($29), New York ($49), and Portland ($17.75). Greyhound will also take you to Bar Harbor daily ($8.50, June-Labor Day only). (Open daily 5-6am and 7:30am-5:30pm.) From the greyhound station, **Cyr Bus Line** (827-2335 or 800-244-2335) runs once daily to Medway ($10.50) and Caribo ($25). From the same station, **Seacoast Connections** (546-7548 or 800-339-9422) departs daily at 3:30pm to Calais ($18). It is possible to reach **Canada** from Bangor; be willing to face an uncertain and mysterious journey though. The Canadian line **SMT** runs from the Concord Trailways Terminal to Fredericton, NB, on Sat. and Mon. mornings ($28; call for departure time which can be early). Otherwise, take Cyr Bus Line to Calais, and catch the SMT bus in St. Stephen the next morning. Calais and St. Stephen are separated by a walkable bridge.

Bangor's **post office** (941-2016) sits at 202 Harlow. (Open Mon.-Thurs. 7:30am-5pm, Fri. 7:30am-noon, Sat. 8am-noon.) The **ZIP code** is 04401; the **area code** 207.

Accommodations and Food Highway culture dominates lodging and food; Bangor specializes in budget roadside motels, most of which lie just off I-95 and charge identical rates for nearly identical rooms. The **Scottish Inn,** 1476 Hammond St. extension (945-2934), has even lower rates because of its distance from the interstate. Take exit 45B from I-95, go straight at the lights and 1½ mi. ahead on the left. It also has clean rooms with showers, TV, and phone. Just remember: if it's not Scottish, it's craaap! (Singles $25, doubles $35. Weekends $30/$40.) The **Riverview Motel,** 810 State St. (947-0125), offers clean and fairly large rooms with TV but no phone (July-Aug. singles $43, doubles $52; off-season $33/$39). The **Budget Traveler,** 327 Odlin Rd. (945-0111), off exit 45B and right at the lights, is decorated with groovy earth tones and blond wood, and furniture with buffed corners—totally 70s. (Singles or doubles $40. 10% discount for AAA members. Breakfast included weekdays.) **Pleasant Hill Campground** (848-5127) lies near town on Rte. 222 and offers swimming, laundry, and free showers. (Sites $12, with varying degrees of hookup $16-19. $3 per additional person after 2. Reservations suggested.)

MAINE COAST

As the seagull flies, the length of the Maine coast from Kittery to Lubec measures 228 mi., but if you untangled all of the convoluted inlets and rocky promontories, the distance would be a whopping 3478 mi. Fishing was the earliest business here, later augmented by a vigorous shipbuilding industry; both traditions retain visibility today. Lobster pounds are ubiquitous in coastal Maine; stop under one of the innumerable makeshift red wooden lobster signs which speckle the roadsides, set yourself down on a grey wooden bench and chow, but keep in mind that lobsters are tastier before July, when most start to molt. Also be forewarned that lobster-poaching is treated seriously here; the color codings and designs on the buoy markers are as distinct as a cattle rancher's brand and serve the same purpose.

U.S. 1 hugs the coastline and strings the port towns together. Lesser roads and small ferry lines connect the remote villages and offshore islands. The best place for info is the **Maine Information Center** in Kittery (439-1319; P.O. Box 396, Kittery 03904), 3 mi. north of the Maine-New Hampshire bridge (open Mon.-Sat. 8am-9pm, Sun. 8am-6pm, off-season daily 9am-5pm). **Greyhound** serves points between Portland and Bangor along I-95, the coastal town of Brunswick as well as connecting routes to Boston. Reaching most coastal points of interest is virtually impossible by bus and a car or bike is necessary.

■■■ SOUTH OF PORTLAND

Driving south on U.S. 1 out of Portland, you'll encounter nothing but traffic and stores until the town of **Kennebunk,** and, several miles east on Rte. 35, its coastal counterpart **Kennebunkport.** If you want to bypass busy U.S. 1, take the Maine Turnpike south of Portland to exit 3 and take Fletcher St. east into Kennebunk.

Both of these towns are popular hideaways for wealthy authors and artists. A number of rare and used bookstores line U.S. 1 just south of Kennebunk, while art galleries fill the town itself. Recently the blue-haired resort of Kennebunkport has grown reluctantly famous as the summer home of former President Bush, who owns a sprawling estate on Walker's Point. The **Kennebunk-Kennebunkport Chamber of Commerce** (967-0857), at the intersection of Rte. 9 and 35 in Kennebunkport, has a free guide to area sights (open Mon.-Fri. 8:30am-8pm, Sat. 10am-8pm, Sun. 11am-pm; off season Mon.-Fri. 8:30am-5:30pm, Sat.-Sun. 10am-4pm).

Biking provides a graceful ride on the road past rocky shores and spares visitors the aggravation of fighting thick summer traffic. In nearby **Biddeford,** a few minutes north on U.S. 1, **Quinn's Bike and Fitness,** 140 U.S. 1 (284-4632), rents 10, 5, and 3-speeds ($10 per day, $30 per week), and mountain bikes ($18.50/$59). (Open Sat.-Thurs. 9am-5:30pm, Fri. 9am-8pm.) You can get a copy of *25 Bicycle Tours in Maine* ($15) from the Portland Chamber of Commerce (see above).

A visit to Kennebunkport will cost you a pretty penny. Buy groceries. The **Lobster Deck Restaurant** (967-5535), on Rte. 9 overlooking Kennebunk Harbor, serves lobster dinners, though they cost $14-18 (open Memorial Day-Columbus Day Mon.-Thurs. 11am-10pm, Fri.-Sun. 11am-11:30pm; Columbus Day-Dec. and mid-April-Memorial Day Fri.-Sat. 11am-10pm). For affordable lodging, camp. **Salty Acres Campground** (967-8623), 4½ mi. northeast of Kennebunkport on Rte. 9, offers swimming, a grocery store, laundry and a convenient location about 1 mi. from the beaches. (Sites $14, with electricity and water $20, full hookup $22, $7 per additional adult after 2; $2 per additional child after 2. RVs $20. Open mid-May to mid-Oct.) A little farther out is the **Mousam River Campground** (985-2507), on Alfred Rd. just west of exit 3 off I-95 in West Kennebunk (sites $16; free showers, open mid-May to mid-Oct.).

To escape the tourist throngs, head west to the **Rachel Carson National Wildlife Refuge** (646-9226), on Rte. 9 near U.S. 1. A self-guided trail takes you through the salt marsh home of over 200 species of shorebirds and waterfowl, a moving tribute to the naturalist/author of *Silent Spring,* which publicized the perils of chemical pollution and environment waste. (Open daily sunrise to sunset.)

South of Kennebunk, **Ogunquit's** long, sandy strip of beach is the best on the coast, and nearby **Perkins Cove** charms the polo-shirt crowd with boutiques hawking sandshell sculptures and delicious lobster rolls from **Barnacle Billy's** restaurant, on the water. **Moody,** just south of Ogunquit, has some of the less expensive lodgings in the region. Ogunquit is summer home to a vibrant gay community.

■■■ PORTLAND

For a relatively tourist-free taste of the New England coast, go to Portland. Destroyed by a fire in 1866, the city rebuilt only to decline again in the 1960s. Lately, Portland profits from a downtown area advantageously located along the ocean and its revitalized microclime. Stroll down the attractive Old Port Exchange, whose restaurants, taverns and craft shops occupy former warehouses and 19th-century buildings. The reasonable location and low cost of living in Maine's largest city makes it an ideal base for sight-seeing and daytrips to the surrounding coastal areas, such as Casco Bay and the Casco Bay Islands. Nearby Sebago Lake provides ample opportunities for sunning and waterskiing.

PRACTICAL INFORMATION

Emergency: 911.

Visitor Information Bureau, 305 Commercial St. (772-5800), at the corner of Center St. Open Mon.-Sat. 9am-6pm, Sun. 9am-3pm; Oct. 15-May 15 Mon.-Sat. 9am-5pm. Offers comprehensive *Portland Visitor's Guide.*

Buses: Concord Trailways, 161 Marginal Way (828-1151 or 800-639-3317), a 15-min. walk from downtown. Office open daily 7am-8:30pm. To: Boston (6 per day, $15); Bangor (2 per day, $19). A local Metro Bus (#8) will transport you from the station to downtown, but you must call. **Greyhound,** 950 Congress St. (772-6587 or 800-231-2222), on the western outskirts of town. Don't go there at night. Take the #1 Congress St. bus to downtown. Office open daily 6am-6pm. To: Boston (5 per day, $14); Bangor (3 per day, $18); also to other points north.

Prince of Fundy Cruises: P.O. Box 4216, 468 Commercial St. (800-341-7540; 800-482-0955 in ME). Ferries to Yarmouth in southern Nova Scotia leave from the Portland Marine Terminal, on Commercial St. near Million Dollar Bridge, May-late Oct. at 9pm. Fare mid-June-mid-Sept. $75, ages 5-14 $37.50; off-season $55 and $27.50. Cars $98; off-season $80. Reservations required. Specials up to 50% off car fare, especially on Tues. and Wed. during high season.

Help Lines: Rape Crisis, 774-3613.

Post Office: 125 Forest Ave. (871-8410). Open Mon.-Fri. 7:30am-7pm, Sat. 7:30am-5pm. Self-service lobby open until 11pm. **ZIP code:** 04101.

Area Code: 207.

The downtown area sits along Congress St. towards the bay; a few blocks south lies the Old Port on Commercial and Fore St. These two districts contain most of the city's sights and attractions. I-295 veers off I-95 to form the western boundary of the downtown area. Several offshore islands are served by regular ferries. Get a map.

ACCOMMODATIONS AND CAMPING

Portland has some inexpensive accommodations, but prices jump during the summer season. You can always try exit 8 off I-95, where **Super 8** (854-1881) and other similar budget staples (singles around $36) proliferate.

Portland Youth Hostel, 645 Congress St. (874-3281). Centrally located in a university dorm. 48 beds in college-like, clean doubles with bath and shower. Poor lighting and no locks. Kitchen, lounge with giant cable TV, laundry facilities. An eager-to-help staff will store your stuff 10am-5pm. $14, nonmembers $17. Linen $2. Locks (bike locks will do) $2. Check in 5pm-1:30am. Check out 7am-10am. 5 day max. stay. Reservations recommended.

YWCA, 87 Spring St. (874-1130), downtown near the Civic Center. Women only. Small rooms verge on sterile, but an amiable atmosphere more than compensates. Fills up in summer. Lounge, pool, and kitchen (bring utensils). Check-out by 11am. Singles $25, doubles $40. Phone in reservations with a credit card.

YMCA, 70 Forest Ave. (874-1111), north side of Congress St., 1 block from the post office. Cash only. Men only. Check-in 11am-10pm. Access to pool and exercise facilities. Singles $21.50 per night, $81 per week. Key deposit $10.

Hotel Everett, 51A Oak St. (773-7882), off Congress St. Central location; carefully carpeted rooms. Singles $35, with bath $45; doubles $45/$49. Off-season rates 20% less. Weekly rates available. Reservations are recommended in summer.

Wassamki Springs, 855 Saco St. (839-4276), in Westbrook. Closest campground (15 min.) to Portland. Drive west down Congress St. (becomes Rte. 22, then County Rd.) about 6 mi., turn right on Saco St. Full facilities plus a sandy beach. Flocks of migrant Winnebagos nest here. Sites $21 for 2 people, $4 per additional person. Hook-up $23. Shower 25¢. Open May-mid-Oct. Reservations recommended 4-6 weeks in advance, with $10 deposit per day, especially July-Aug.

FOOD AND NIGHTLIFE

Diners, delis and cafes abound in Portland. Check out the active port on Commercial St., lined with sheds peddling fresh clams, fish, and lobsters.

Raffles Cafe Bookstore, 555 Congress St. (761-3930), in the heart of downtown. Exotic gourmet coffees (try the Tanzanian Peaberry, $1.50) and "breakfast things" (muffins 50-85¢) in an intellectual setting. Enjoy breakfast, a light lunch (soups made from scratch $2, sandwiches $3-4) or scrumptious desserts ($1-2.50) while doing heavy reading. Open Mon.-Tues. and Fri. 8am-5:30pm, Wed.-Thurs. 8am-8pm, Sat. 9:30am-5:30pm, Sun. noon-5pm.

The Pepperclub, 78 Middle St. (772-0531). A colorful, casual cafe that features a diverse but always excellent selection of mostly vegetarian dishes—some chicken, fish and organic beef items listed. The entree menu ($6-10) somehow includes the words Maine, Tunisian, Indonesian, Mexican, Bulgarian, and Italian. Open Sun.-Wed. 5-9pm, Thurs.-Sat. 5-10pm. Ample parking across the street.

Carbur's, 123 Middle St. (772-7794), near the Old Port. Over 50 whimsical sandwiches for $4-10. If you try the quintuple sandwich ($10), the servers and cooks will parade around the dining room chanting "Down East Feast," and they guarantee "free medical attention" if you hurt yourself trying to finish it. Open Mon.-Fri. 11am-10pm, Sat. 11am-11pm, Sun. noon-10pm.

Seamen's Club, 375 Fore St. (773-3333), at Exchange St. in the Old Port with a harbor view. Top-notch seafood dining steeped in briny lore. Lunch entrees $6-11, dinner $10 and up. Fresh lobster year-round. Open Sun.-Thurs. 11am-10pm, Fri.-Sat. 11am-11pm.

Ruby's Choice, 116 Free St. (772-7311), near downtown. Fresh, homemade buns for thick burgers you dress yourself ($2.50-4.50). Seats 250. Open Mon.-Wed. 11:30am-5:30pm, Thurs.-Fri. 11:30am-7:30pm, Sat. 11:30am-5:30pm.

Portland's Old Port area with its numerous restaurants and bars is more active at night than the rest of the day. **Gritty MacDuff's,** 396 Fore St. (772-2739), brews its own sweet beer for an adoring local crowd. Even the mayor drinks here. Tasty pints a bargain at $2.50. Open Mon.-Sat. 11:30am-1am, Sun. noon-1am. **Three Dollar Dewey's** (722-3310), down the block at 446 Fore St., re-creates the atmosphere of an English pub, serving over 65 varieties of beer and ale along with great chili and free popcorn to an eclectic clientele (open Mon.-Sat. 11am-1am, Sun. noon-1am). **Cafe No,** 20 Danforth St. (772-8114), Maine's self-proclaimed "only real jazz club" features jazz jams Thurs., Fri., and Sat. evenings, poetry readings the second Tues. of every month, and Lebanese delicacies or imaginative sandwiches all the time (open Tues.-Sat. 11am-9pm, Sun. 2-8pm; jazz Thurs.-Sat. after sunset and Sun. 4:30-8pm).

SIGHTS

Many of Portland's most spectacular sights are to be found outside the city proper, along the rugged coast or on the beautiful, secluded islands a short ferry ride off-shore. **Two Lights State Park** (799-5871), across the million Dollar Bridge on State St. and south along Rte. 77 to Cape Elizabeth, is a wonderful place to picnic and relax along the rocky shoreline in view of two (count 'em, two) lighthouses. (Open Memorial Day-Labor Day daily 9am-sunset. $2, ages 5-11 50¢, seniors and under 5 free.) **Casco Bay Lines,** on State Pier near the corner of Commercial and Franklin (774-7871), America's oldest ferry service, runs year-round to the nearby islands. Daily ferries depart approximately every hr. (5:45am-11:30pm) for nearby **Peaks Island** ($4.50) where you can rent a bike at **Brad's Recycled Bike Shop,** 115 Island Ave. (766-5631), for $10 per day, $6 per 4 hr. If your feet aren't up to pedaling, try the quiet and unpopulated beach on **Long Island.** (Departures daily 6am-9pm. $8.75-17.50, seniors and kids ½-price. Bikes $4-6 extra.) The sea may beckon from the instant you arrive in Portland, but the city does have a full slate of non-aquatic activities. The **Portland Museum of Art,** 7 Congress Sq. (775-6148), at the intersection of Congress, High, and Free St., collects U.S. art by notables such as John Singer Sargent and Winslow Homer. (Open Tues.-Wed. and Fri.-Sat. 10am-5pm, Thurs. 10am-9pm, Sun. noon-5pm. $6, seniors and students $5, under 12 $1. May-Oct. 1st Sat. of month 10am-2pm and Nov.-April 1st Thurs. of month 6-9pm free.) Down the street at 487 Congress St., the **Wadsworth-Longfellow House** (879-0427), a museum of social history and U.S. literature, zeroes in on late 18th- and 19th-century antiques as well as at the life of the poet. (Open June-Oct. Tues.-Sat. 10am-4pm. Tours every ½ hr. $3, under 12 $1. Purchase tickets at 489 Congress St.)

While the history of Portland's **Old Port Exchange** began in the 17th century, the area's shops, stores and homes were rebuilt in Victorian style after the fire of 1866. The **Portland Observatory,** 138 Congress St. (772-5547), set atop a promontory east of downtown, went up in 1807. Climb 102 steps for a panoramic view of Casco Bay and the city. (Open July-Aug. Wed.-Fri. and Sun. 1-5pm, Sat. 10am-5pm; June Fri.-Sun. 1-5pm; Sept.-Oct. Sat.-Sun. 1-5pm. Closed if raining. $1.50, kids 50¢.)

The **Old Port Festival** (772-6828) begins the summer season with a bang in early June, spanning several blocks from Federal to Commercial St. and drawing as many as 50,000 people. On summer afternoons, enjoy the **Noontime Performance Series** (774-6364), in which bands from ragtime to Dixieland perform in Portland's Monument Square. (Late June-early July Mon.-Fri. noon-1:15pm.) The **6-Alive Sidewalk Arts Festival** (828-6666) lines Congress St. with booths featuring artists from all over the country, and is generally held around mid-August. Weather permitting, take the ferry out to **Cushings Island** for the annual **croquet tournament.** Event listings can be found within the free guide distributed by the visitors information bureau (see Practical Information).

■■■ NORTH OF PORTLAND

Much like the coastal region south of Portland, the north offers the traveler sunny beaches and cool breezes—for a price. Lodgings are never cheap, but if you're either outfitted for camping or just passing through, you'll find fun and interesting shopping as well as ample access to the ocean. Much of the region is unserviced by public transportation; driving is rewarding, however. U.S. 1, running north along the coast, offers motorists a charming glimpse of woods and small towns.

Freeport About 20 mi. north of Portland on I-95, Freeport once garnered glory as the "birthplace of Maine": the 1820 signing of documents declaring the state's independence from Massachusetts took place at the historic **Jameson Tavern,** at 115 Main St. Now the town finds fame as the factory outlet capital of the world, offering over 100 downtown stores. The grandaddy of them all, **L.L. Bean,** began manufacturing Maine Hunting Shoes in Freeport in 1912. The hunting shoe hasn't

changed much since then, but now Bean sells diverse products from clothes epitomizing preppy *haute couture* to sturdy tenting gear. The factory outlet on Depot St.
has pretty decent bargains. The retail store on Main St. (865-4767 or 800-221-4221)
stays open 24 hrs., 365 days a year. Legend has it the store has closed only once,
when its founder, Leon Leonwood (no wonder he called himself L.L.) Bean, died.

Heading up to **Penobscot Bay** (not to be confused with the town of Penobscot)
from factory-outlet purgatory, be sure to stop at **Moody's Diner** (832-7785) off U.S.
1 in Waldoboro. It seems like nothing has changed since business started in 1927;
tourists and old salts rub shoulders here over fantastic food. Try the homemade
strawberry-rhubarb pie à la mode ($2.25). (Open Sun. 7am-Thurs. midnight, Fri.-Sat.
5am-11:30pm.)

Camden   In summer, preppies flock to friendly Camden, 100 mi. north of Portland, to dock their yachts alongside the eight tall masted schooners in Penobscot
Bay. Many of the cruises, like the neighboring yachts, are out of the budget traveler's
price range, but the Rockport-Camden-Lincolnville **Chamber of Commerce** (236-
4404), on the public landing in Camden behind Cappy's Chowder House, can tell
you which are affordable. They also have information on a few rooms in local private homes for $12-30. (Open Mon.-Fri. 9am-5pm, Sat. 10am-5pm, Sun. noon-5pm,
mid-Oct.-mid-May Mon.-Fri. 9am-5pm, Sat. 10am-5pm.) Cheaper still, the **Camden
Hills State Park** (287-3824 out of state, 800-332-1501 in ME), 1¼ mi. north of town
on U.S. 1, is almost always full in July and August, but you're fairly certain to get a
site if you arrive before 2pm. This coastal retreat offers more than 25 mi. of trails;
one leads up to Mt. Battie with a harbor view. Make reservations by phone with a
credit card Mon.-Fri. 9am-3pm. Showers and toilets available. (Open May 15-Oct. 15.
Day use $1.50. Sites $13, ME residents $10.50.)

Affordable to all and in the heart of downtown Camden is **Cappy's Chowder
House,** 1 Main St. (236-2254), a kindly, comfortable hangout where the great seafood draws tourists and townspeople alike. Try the seafood pie ($8), made with scal-
lops, shrimp, mussels and clams. (Open daily 7:30am-midnight.)

The **Maine State Ferry Service** (596-2202), 5 mi. north of Camden in Lincoln-
ville, takes you through the Bay to Isleboro Island (5-9 per day; fare $1.75, kids $1,
auto $6.25). The ferry also has an agency in Rockland on U.S. 1, running boats to
North Haven, Vinalhaven, and Matinicus. Always call the ferry service to confirm;
rates and schedules change with the weather.

Deer Isle   South of Blue Hill on the other side of Penobscot Bay lies Deer Isle, a
picturesque forested island with rocky coasts accessible by bridge from the mainland (the bridge has been under construction for 7 years; prepare for a 30 min.
wait). Off Main St. in Stonington, at the southern tip of Deer Isle, a mailboat (367-
5193; mid-June-early Sept. Mon.-Sat. 2 per day) leaves for **Isle au Haut,** part of Acadia National Park. (Fare $9, kids $4.50.) Island exploration is done by foot or bike
(no rental bikes available on the island). The only accommodations are five lean-tos,
each of which can accommodate up to six people, at **Duck Harbor Campground**
(no showers; sites $5; reservations necessary; open mid-May-mid-Oct.). Contact Aca-
dia Park Headquarters (288-3338) or write P.O. Box 177, Bar Harbor 04609.

■■■ MOUNT DESERT ISLAND

In spite of its name, Mt. Desert (de-ZERT) is not barren. In summer, campers and
tourists abound, drawn by mountains, rocky beaches, and spruce and birch forests.
The Atlantic waters—calm in summer but stormy in winter—are too cold for all but
the hardiest of souls. Wind-swept **Acadia National Park** features rugged headlands, fine beaches, plenty of tidal-pool critters, and a variety of naturalist activities.
Bar Harbor is a lively but crowded town packed with over 2400 guest rooms. The

island's other towns, such as Seal and Northeast Harbors, are more relaxed but more expensive.

PRACTICAL INFORMATION

Emergency: Acadia National Park, 288-3369. **Bar Harbor Police, Fire Department, and Ambulance,** 911. **Mt. Desert Police,** 276-5111.

Acadia National Park Visitors Center (288-4932 or 288-5262), 3 mi. north of Bar Harbor on Rte. 3. Maps, park info, and over 100 weekly naturalist programs. Browse through the mighty *Beaver Log,* the park's info newspaper. Open May-June and mid-Sept.-Oct. daily 8am-4:30pm, July-mid-Sept. daily 8am-6pm. **Park Headquarters** (288-3338), 3 mi. west of Bar Harbor on Rte. 233. Open Oct.-May Mon.-Fri. 8am-4:30pm. **Mount Desert Island Joint Chamber of Commerce** (288-3411), on Rte. 3 at the entrance to Thompson Island. Information on the whole island and Frenton. Open July-Aug. daily 10am-8pm, May-June and Sept.-Oct. daily 10am-6pm. In the same building is an **Acadia National Park Information Center** (288-9702). Open June-Sept. daily 9:30am-2:30pm.

Ferries: Beal & Bunker, from Northeast Harbor on the town dock (244-3575) To: Cranberry Islands (5-7 per day, 45 min., $8, under 12 $4). **Marine Atlantic,** Bar Harbor (288-3395 or 800-341-7981). To: Yarmouth, Nova Scotia (1 per day, 6 hr.; $39, seniors $29, kids $20, with car $51, with bike $8.50; mid-Sept.-late June $22, $20, $13, $47, $6, respectively; $3 port tax per person).

Buses: Greyhound (800-231-2222) leaves for Bangor daily at 7am in front of the Post Office on Cottage St. ($8.50 June-Labor Day).

Bike Rental: Bar Harbor Bicycle Shop, 141 Cottage St. (288-3886). Mountain bikes $9 per 4 hr., $14 per day, $79 per week. Rentals include helmet, lock, and map. Driver's license, cash deposit, or credit card required. Open Jun-mid-Sept. daily 8am-8pm, off-season daily 8am-6pm.

National Park Canoe Rentals (244-5854), north end of Long Pond off Rte. 102. Canoes $20 per 4 hr., $27 per day. Open May-Labor Day daily 8:30am-5pm.

Crisis Lines: Downeast Sexual Assault Helpline, 800-228-2470; **abused women crisis line,** 667-9489; **mental health crisis line,** 800-245-8889. All 24 hrs.

Post Office: 55 Cottage St. (288-3122), near downtown. Open Mon.-Fri. 8am-4:45pm, Sat. 9am-noon. **ZIP code:** 04609.

Area Code: 207.

Rte. 3 runs through Bar Harbor, becoming Mt. Desert Street; it and Cottage Street are the major east-west arteries. Rte. 102 circuits the western half of the island.

ACCOMMODATIONS AND CAMPING

Grand hotels with grand prices remain from Rockefeller's day, and you still have to be a Rockefeller to afford them. Nevertheless, a few reasonable establishments can be found, particularly on Rte. 3 north of Bar Harbor. Camping exists throughout the island; most campgrounds line Rte. 198 and 102, well west of the city.

Mt. Desert Island Hostel (HI/AYH), 27 Kennebec St., Bar Harbor (288-5587), behind the Episcopal Church. Adjacent to the bus stop. Two large dorm rooms which can accommodate 24 in cheery red bunks, common room, full kitchen, and a perfect location. Curfew 11pm. Lockout 9:30am-4:30pm. $9, nonmembers $12. Linen $1.50. Reservations essential July-Aug. Open mid-June-Aug. 31.

Mt. Desert Island YWCA, 36 Mt. Desert St. (288-5008), near downtown. Extensive common space, full kitchen, laundry facilities. Women only. Dorm-style singles in summer only with bath on hall $25 per night, $80 per week; doubles $18/$70; solarium with 7 beds $15/$60. $25 security deposit for stays of 1 week and longer. Fills in summer; make reservations early. Office open Mon.-Fri. 9am-11pm, Sat.-Sun. 3-11pm.

Acadia Hotel, 20 Mt. Desert St., Bar Harbor (288-5721). Sweet, homey place overlooking park. TV, private bath. Breakfast served on charming patio late June-early

Sept. Late June-early Sept. room for 1 or 2 people $45-68; May-late June and early Sept.-Oct. $35-50.

Mt. Desert Campground, off Rte. 198 (244-3710). Tent sites, platforms in a woodsy location overlooking the Somes Sound. Boat dock, swimming for the hearty, and free blueberry picking. Open June-Sept. Sites $18-23, Memorial Day-June 21 and Labor Day-late Sept. $15-20. Hookup $1 extra. $5 per additional adult, child $2.

Acadia National Park Campgrounds: Blackwoods, 5 mi. south of Bar Harbor on Rte. 3. Over 300 sites mid-May-mid-June and mid-Sept.-mid-Oct. $10, mid-June-mid-Sept. $12, free other times. Reservations up to 8 weeks in advance; call 800-365-2267. **Seawall,** Rte. 102A on the western side of the island, 4 mi. south of Southwest Harbor. Station open May-Sept., 8am-8pm, first come, first served. Walk-in sites $7, drive-in $10. Both campgrounds are within a 10-min. walk of the ocean and have toilets but no showers or hookups. Privately owned public-access showers available nearby for a fee. No reservations.

FOOD AND ENTERTAINMENT

Seafood is all the rage on the island. "Lobster pounds" sell the underwater crustaceans for little money; cooking them is the only problem.

Beals's, Southwest Harbor (244-7178 or 244-3202), at the end of Clark Point Rd. The best price for lobster in an appropriate setting. Pick your own live lobster from a tank; Beals's does the rest ($7-8). Dining on the dock. A nearby stand sells munchies and beverages. Open daily 9am-8pm; off-season daily 9am-5pm.

The Lighthouse Restaurant (276-3958), in Seal Harbor. Fairly upscale; a nice way to escape from the crowds at Bar Harbor. Sandwiches $4-9, entrees $9-15, lobster dinner $14. Open May-Nov. daily 8:30am-9pm, July-Aug. daily 9am-11pm.

Cottage St. Bakery and Deli, 59 Cottage St., Bar Harbor (288-3010). Memorably delicious muffins (75¢), pancakes ($2.45), and breads (loaf $2.25-3.50) baked fresh on the premises. Blueberry lovers will go nuts here. Open May-Oct. Mon.-Sat. 6:30am-10pm, Sun. 7am-10pm.

Most after-dinner pleasures on the island are simple ones. For a treat, try **Ben and Bill's Chocolate Emporium,** 80 Main St. (288-3281), near Cottage, which boasts 24 flavors of homemade ice cream and a huge selection of fresh chocolates which will make you gasp (open March-Dec. daily 9am-11pm). **Benbow's Espresso Bar** (288-5271), at the Alternative Market, 99 Main Street, features over 30 coffees roasted in house ($.75-2.50). Try the German Chocolate Nut Cream for a change. Or, caramel mocha latte ($1.50), mocha ($1.75), espresso (75¢). Their seating is very limited and rather uncomfortable, but the waterfront and park are one block away. **Geddy's,** 19 Main St. (288-5077), is a self-proclaimed three-tier entertainment complex with bar, sporadic live music, and dancing. Most bands are free; the more popular ones charge a $2 cover. (Fri.-Sat. DJ nights. Open April-Oct. daily noon-1am.) **The Lompoc Café & Brew Pub,** 36 Rodick St. (288-9392), off Cottage St., features an eclectic selection of live music nightly. Locals prefer it to Geddy's because it's not as geared towards tourists. Jazz, blues, celtic, rock, folk. (Shows June-Sept. at 9pm, $1-2 cover charge.) *Bar Harbor Real Ale* brewed on location. (Open May-Oct. 11:30am-1am, Nov. 11:30am-9pm.) The art-deco **Criterion Theatre** (288-3441), on Cottage St., was recently declared a national landmark and continues to show movies in the summer Mon.-Thurs. at 8pm and Fri.-Sun. at 7:30 and 9:30pm. Matinees are scheduled on rainy days; a new film arrives every few days. Don't be discouraged by interminable lines; the theater seats 891. Programs are available at the desk.

SIGHTS

Mt. Desert Island is shaped roughly like a lobster claw. To the east on Rte. 3 lie Bar Harbor and Seal Harbor. South on Rte. 198 near the cleft is **Northeast Harbor,** and across Somes Sound on Rte. 102 is the **Southwest Harbor. Bar Harbor** is by far the most crowded part of the large island, sandwiched by the Blue Hill and French-men Bays. Once a summer hamlet for the very wealthy, the town now harbors a motley melange of R&R-seekers. The wealthy have fled to the quieter and more secluded Northeast and Seal Harbors. Anyone desiring a taste of coastal Maine life purged of wealth and kitsch should head west to Southwest Harbor, where fishing and shipbuilding still thrive. **Little Cranberry Island,** out in the Atlantic Ocean south of Mt. Desert, offers a spectacular view of Acadia as well as the cheapest uncooked lobster in the area at the fishers' co-op.

On the Sea The staff at the **Mt. Desert Oceanarium** (244-7330), at the end of Clark Pt. Rd. in Southwest Harbor, can teach you about the sea at each of their three facilities (the lobster hatchery and Salt Marsh Walk are located near Bar Harbor). The main museum—though resembling a grammar-school science fair—fascinates onlookers. (Open mid-May-late Oct. Mon.-Sat. 9am-5pm. Tickets for all 3 facilities $9, kids $6.) Cruises head out to sea from a number of points on the island. In Bar Harbor, the **Frenchman Bay Co.,** 1 West St., Harbor Place (288-3322), offers sailing trips (2 hr., $16.75, under 12 $10.75), lobster fishing and seal-watching trips (1½ hr., $16.75, ages 5-12 $10.75, under 5 free), and whale watching (4 hr., $30, ages 5-12 $18, under 5 free). (Open May-Oct. Reservations recommended, especially for whale watching. Call for details or schedule.) The **Acadian Whale Watcher,** Golden Anchor Pier, West St. (288-9794, 288-9776, or 800-421-3307), has slightly lower prices, guarantees sightings or you go again free, and has food and a full bar on board. Sunset ($12.50, ages 9-15 $7.50) and whale-watching cruises ($29, seniors $21, ages 9-14 $19, ages 6-8 $16; open June-Oct.) leave 2-3 times a day. Bring extra clothing—the temperature can drop dramatically on the water.

From Northeast Harbor, the **Sea Princess Islesford Historical and Naturalist Cruise** (276-5352) brings you past an osprey nesting site and lobster buoys to Little Cranberry Island. You may be lucky enough to see harbor seals, cormorants, or pilot whales on the cruise. The crew takes you to the **Islesford Historical Museum** in sight of the fjord-like Somes Sound. (Four cruises per day July-Aug., 1-3 per day May-June and Sept.-Columbus Day; $10, ages 4-12 $8, under 4 free.)

Acadia National Park The 33,000 acres that comprise **Acadia National Park** are a landlubber's dream, offering easy trails and challenging hikes which allow for an intimate exploration of Mt. Desert Island. More acres are available on the nearby **Schoodic Peninsula** and **Isle au Haut** to the west. Millionaire and expert horseman John D. Rockefeller funded half of the park's 120 mi. of trails out of fear that the park would someday be overrun by cars. These **carriage roads** make for easy walking, fun mountain biking, and pleasant horseback riding and are accessible to disabled persons. **Precipice Trail** and others offer more advanced hiking. Be realistic about your abilities here; the majority of injuries in the park occur in hiking accidents. Swim in the relatively warm **Echo Lake,** which has on-duty life-guards in summer. **The Eagle Lake Loop Road** is graded for bicyclists. At the park visitors center, pick up the handy *Biking Guide* (50¢), which offers invaluable safety advice. Some of these paths are accessible only by mountain bike and can be dangerously desertic and labyrinthine without a map. Touring the park by auto will cost a little more. ($5 per day private vehicle, $2 per pedestrian or cyclist; permit is good for 7 consecutive days. Seniors and disabled admitted free.) About 4 mi. south of Bar Harbor on Rte. 3, take the **Park Loop Road** running along the shore of the island where great waves roll up against steep granite cliffs. The sea comes into **Thunder Hole** at half-tide with a bang, sending plumes of spray high into the air and onto tourists. To the right just before the Loop Rd. turns back to the visitors center stands **Cadillac Mountain,** the highest Atlantic headland north of Brazil. A 5-mi. hiking trail to the summit starts at Blackwoods campground, 2 mi. east of Seal Harbor. The top of Mt. Cadillac, the very first place sunlight touches the U.S., makes a great place for an early morning (or late night—the sun rises between 4 and 4:30am in the summer) breakfast (Grape Nuts, of course).

Tourists also can explore the island by horse, the way Rockefeller intended. **Wildwood Stables** (276-3622), along the Park Loop Rd. in Seal Harbor, runs one-and two-hour carriage tours through the park (1 hr.: $10.50, seniors $9.50, ages 6-12 $6, under 5 $3.50; 2 hr.: $13.50/$12.50/$7/$4.50 respectively). Reservations are strongly suggested. No horses are available for rental on the island.

Massachusetts

Massachusetts considers itself the cerebral cortex of the national body, and the state certainly has the credentials. Harvard, the oldest university in America, was founded in Cambridge in 1636. The nation's first public school was established soon after, in 1647. Countless literati have hocked their wares in this intellectual marketplace, from Hawthorne, Dickinson, Melville, Wharton, and the Jameses to Sylvia Plath, Robert Lowell, and Jack Kerouac. Myriad colleges and universities congregate in Massachusetts, drawing scholars from around the world and lending parts of this relatively small state a quirkily cosmopolitan flavor—where espresso bars and leftist bookstores join Paul Revere statues and whitewashed churches on Main Street.

But there's more beyond the pale of academia in Massachusetts. A needlepoint charm blesses the rolling hills of the Berkshires in the west, resplendent during the fall foliage season. Boston, one of the most idiosyncratic cities in America (and one of the oldest, which may explain something), attracts visitors with colonial legends, an Old World face, and an impressive array of cultural offerings. And on the Atlantic coast, from Newburyport to Nantucket, the great shipping ports and whaling centers of bygone days now lure tourists and leisured locals to summer homes and beachfront B&Bs.

PRACTICAL INFORMATION

Capital: Boston.
Massachusetts Division of Tourism, Department of Commerce and Development, 100 Cambridge St., Boston 02202 (727-3201; 800-632-8038 for guides). Can send you a complimentary, comprehensive *Spirit of Massachusetts Guidebook* and direct you to regional resources. Open Mon.-Fri. 9am-5pm.
Time Zone: Eastern. **Postal Abbreviation:** MA
Sales Tax: 5%.

■■■ THE BERKSHIRES

The swelling urban centers of Boston and New York have long sent their upwardly mobile to the Berkshire Mountains in search of a less taxing, more relaxing country escape. Today a host of affordable B&Bs, restaurants, and campgrounds make this sub-range of the Appalachians accessible to budget travelers who seek the "deep greens and blues" of its forests and lakes. The slower pace of life and the open friendliness of the townspeople will erase the words "rush hour" from any weary urbanite's mind.

■ Berkshire County

Practical Information Just about everything in Berkshire County runs north-south: the mountain range giving the county its name (a southern extension of the Green Mountains of Vermont); the 80 mi. of the **Appalachian Trail** that wind through Massachusetts; the Hoosac and the Housatonic rivers; and **U.S. 7**, the region's main artery. To see sights located far from the town centers, you'll have to drive. The roads are slow and often pocked with potholes, but certainly scenic. **Pete's Rent-a-Car** (445-5795), on the corner of Fenn and East St., offers some of the lowest local prices ($26 per day; 100 free mi., 26¢ each additional mi.; must be at least 23). **Berkshire Regional Transit Association** (499-2782), known as "the B," spans the Berkshires from Great Barrington to Williamstown. Buses run every hour at some bus stops (Mon.-Sat. 6am-6pm); fares (60¢-$6) depend on the route you take. System schedules are available on the bus and at some bus stops. The **information booth** on the east side of **Pittsfield's** rotary circle can give more information on restaurants and accommodations in Pittsfield and the surrounding cities along U.S. 7 (open mid-June-Oct 10am-6pm). The Berkshires' **area code** is 413.

Accommodations, Sights, and Activities Berkshire county's dozen state parks and forests cover 100,000 acres and offer numerous campsites (with hookup $18) and cabins. For info about the parks, stop by the **Region 5 Headquarters,** 740 South St. (442-8928), or write to P.O. Box 1433, Pittsfield 01202.

One of the Berkshires' greatest treasures is **Tanglewood**, the famed summer home of the **Boston Symphony Orchestra,** a short distance west of Lenox Center on Rte. 183 (West St.). Although its offerings are primarily classical, Tanglewood concerts show off a variety of music, from Ray Charles to Wynton Marsalis to James Taylor. Buy a lawn ticket, bring a picnic dinner, and listen to your favorites under the stars or in the Sunday afternoon sunshine. (Tickets $18-65. Sat. rehearsals $11. Summer info. 413-637-1940, recorded concert line 413-637-1666. Schedules available through the mail from the BSO, Symphony Hall, Boston, 02115.)

The Berkshire's rich literary history can be sampled at Herman Melville's home **Arrowhead,** 780 Holmes Rd. (442-1793). The headquarters of the Berkshire County Historical Society has displays on 19th century country life and the role of women on the farm. (Open Mon.-Sat. 10am-4:30pm, Sun. 11am-3:30pm. Tours of the house are conducted every ½-hour. Admission $3.50, seniors $3, kids 6-16 $2.)

■ The Mohawk Trail

The best way to see the beauty of the Berkshires by car is to follow the **Mohawk Trail** (Rte. 2). Perhaps the most famous highway in the state, its awe-inspiring view of the surrounding mountains draws crowds during fall foliage weekends. Millers Falls, MA is the trail's eastern terminus. Other than the forests, the first real tourist attraction as you travel west is actually off the Trail, in **Historic Deerfield** (774-5581), 5 mi. south of Greenfield on U.S. 5. This idyllic, 19th-century village contains 11 fully restored buildings. You can wander around outside them for free, or you can pay admission to go inside. Each building conducts its own ½-hr. guided tour; admission is good for two consecutive days. (Open Mon.-Sat. 9:30am-4:30pm. $10, ages 6-17 $5, under 6 free.)

The Trail is dotted with affordable campgrounds and lodgings. Six mi. west of Greenfield at **Highland Springs Guests** (625-2648) in Shelburne, the elderly Mrs. Sauter rents clean rooms with comfortable beds and a shared bath for $30 to an occasionally international clientele. Further west on the trail lies **Mohawk Trail State Forest** (339-5504), which offers campsites without hookups along a river ($12) and rents cabins (no electricity; large $20, small $16). (Bathrooms and showers available. July-Aug. min. stay 1 week, other times 2 nights. Call for reservations.)

Continuing west on Rte. 2, you'll find **North Adams,** home to the **Western Gateway** (663-6312), on Furnace St. Bypass of Rte. 8 N, a railroad museum and one of Massachusetts' five Heritage State Parks, housed in an old Boston and Maine Railroad building (open daily 10am-4:30pm; Labor Day-Memorial Day Thurs.-Mon. 10am-4:30pm; free, donations encouraged).

Mt. Greylock, the highest peak in Massachusetts (3491 ft.), is south of the Mohawk Trail, accessible by Rte. 2 to the north and U.S. 7 to the west. By car, take Notch Rd. from Rte. 2 between North Adams and Williamstown, or take Rockwell

Rd. from Lanesboro on U.S. 7. Hiking trails begin from nearly all the towns aro
the mountain; get maps at the **Mount Greylock Visitors Information Cen**
Rockwell Rd. (499-4262; open mid-May to mid-Oct. daily 9am-4pm). Once at
top, climb the **War Memorial** for a breathtaking view. Sleep high in nearby **Bas-com Lodge** (743-1591), built from the rock excavated for the monument (bunks
for members of the Appalachian Mountain Club $21, nonmembers $28, member
children under 12 $12, nonmember kids $15; no member discount in Aug.). The
lodge offers breakfast ($5) and dinner ($10) to guests (snackbar open daily 9am-5pm).

The Mohawk Trail ends in **Williamstown** at its junction with U.S. 7; here, an
information booth (458-4922) provides an abundance of free local maps and sea-sonal brochures, and can help you find a place to stay in one of Williamstown's
many reasonably-priced **B&Bs** (open 24 hrs., staffed by volunteers daily mid-May-Oct. 10am-6pm). At **Williams College**, the second oldest in Massachusetts (est.
1793), lecturers compete with the beautiful scenery of surrounding mountains for
their students' attention. Campus maps are available from the **Admissions Office**,
988 Main St. (597-2211; open Mon.-Fri. 8:30am-4:30pm; tours at 10am, 11:15am,
1:15pm, 3:30pm, and in Aug. at 9am). First among the college's many cultural
resources, **Chapin Library** (597-2462) displays a number of rare U.S. manuscripts,
including early copies of the *Declaration of Independence, Articles of Confedera-tion, Constitution,* and *Bill of Rights* (open Mon.-Fri. 10am-noon and 1-4:30pm;
free). The small but impressive **Williams College Museum of Art** (597-2429) mer-its a visit; rotating exhibits have included pop art and Impressionist works (open
Mon.-Sat. 10am-5pm, Sun. 1-5pm; free).

A good place to eat near campus is **Pappa Charlie's Deli,** 28 Spring St. (458-5969), a popular, well-lit deli offering sandwiches ranging from the "Dick Cavett" to
the "Dr. Johnny Fever." (Under $4; open Mon.-Sat. 8am-11pm, Sun. 9am-11pm.)

Try not to spend too much time indoors in Williamstown; the surrounding
wooded hills beckon from the moment you arrive. The **Hopkins Memorial Forest,**
owned and run by Williams' Center for Environmental Study (597-2346), has over
2250 acres open to the public for hiking and cross-country skiing. Take U.S. 7 north,
turn left on Bulkley St., go to the end and turn right onto Northwest Hill Rd. **Spoke
Bicycles and Repairs,** 618 Main St. (458-3456), rents 10-speed bikes ($10 per day)
and can give you advice on good rides in the area.

BOSTON AREA ✳

■■■ BOSTON

America has often been called a "melting pot" in which different cultures mesh to
create a homogeneous, all-American alloy. Not Boston. If anything, Beantown is a
salad bowl in which the diverse ingredients comprising the city are linked only by
their relative proximity. The several communities of Boston—the Brahmins, the
working classes, the college kids, and the ethnic communities—rarely interact in
more than a perfunctory manner, imbuing the town with a dynamic tension
unmatched within New England. At its best, the relative isolation of each of these
groups preserves distinctive cultural flavors and gives Boston a cosmopolitan feel in
an otherwise provincial area of the country. At its worst, however, these divisions
result in xenophobia, snobbery, racism, and violence.

Many first-time visitors to Boston—even many residents—mistakenly see the city
from only one angle, sticking to the familiar landmarks of the Freedom Trail, the
blue-blood and brownstone neighborhoods of Beacon Hill and Back Bay, or the san-itized commercialism of Faneuil Hall Marketplace. Charming as cobblestones and
colonial cannons can be, Boston deserves more than this narrow glimpse. Step off

the Freedom Trail to explore Boston's less-touristed neighborhoods, from the Irish enclave of South Boston to small-yet-vital Chinatown. The city's population *is* remarkably diverse, if incohesive, with large numbers of Southeast Asians, Portuguese, Italians, Irish, West Indians, and African-Americans dominating particular neighborhoods. Plunked down in the middle of this sometimes uneasy mosaic are over 100,000 college students—drawn to "The Hub" in search of the $80,000 keg party, or enlightenment, whichever comes first. Gown often overwhelms town in Boston and nearby Cambridge (see below), and the strong student presence means plenty of cheap eats, bookstores, and great (high or low) entertainment for the budget traveler to scavenge. It also means you'll have to do a little searching to find it, as many student haunts are well-kept secrets: all the more reason to explore.

PRACTICAL INFORMATION

Emergency: 911.

Visitor Information: Boston Common Information Center, 147 Tremont St., Boston Common. T: Park St. The main office is at the Prudential Building (536-4100). A good first stop on a tour of downtown. Free maps of downtown Boston. Also sells The Official Guidebook to Boston ($5; comes with free coupon book) and Freedom Trail maps. Informational pamphlets and telephone numbers galore, postcards, and posted daily schedules of tours and events. **Greater Boston Convention and Tourist Bureau,** Prudential Plaza West, P.O. Box 490, Boston 02199 (536-4100). T: Prudential. Open Mon.-Fri. 8:30am-6pm, Sat. 9am-6pm, Sun. 9am-5pm. **National Historical Park Tourist Bureau,** 15 State St. (242-5642). T: State. Info on historical sights and 8-min. slide shows on the Freedom Trail narrated by the avuncular Sam Adams. Some rangers speak French or German. Open daily 9am-5pm; summer Mon.-Fri. 8am-6pm, Sat.-Sun. 9am-6pm, except holidays.

Airport: Logan International Airport (567-5400), in East Boston. Easily accessible by public transport. The free **Massport Shuttle** connects all terminals with the "Airport" T-stop. **Airways Transportation Company** (267-2981) runs shuttle buses between Logan and major downtown hotels (service daily every 30 min. 7am-7pm, every hr. on the hr. until 10pm. Fare $7.50-8.50, one way.)

Amtrak: South Station, Atlantic Ave. and Summer St. (482-3660 or 800-872-7245). T: South Station. Frequent daily service to: New York City (5 hr., $52); Philadelphia (6 hr., $68); Washington, D.C. (8 hr., $101).

Buses: Greyhound, South Station (800-231-2222). T: South Station. To: New York City ($24); Philadelphia ($39); Washington, D.C. ($42). Also the station for **Vermont Transit.** To: Burlington ($42). **Bonanza** (720-4110) lines operate out of the Back Bay Railroad Station on Dartmouth (T: Back Bay), with frequent daily service to: Providence ($7.75); Fall River ($8); Newport ($12); Falmouth ($12); Woods Hole ($12). Open 24 hrs. **Peter Pan Lines** (426-7838), across from South Station on Atlantic Ave. (T: South Station), runs to Western Massachusetts and Albany, NY ($25). Connections to New York City via Springfield ($22). Open daily 5:30am-midnight.

Public Transport: Massachusetts Bay Transportation Authority (MBTA). The subway system, known as the "T," consists of the Red, Green, Blue, and Orange lines. Green and Red Lines run daily 5:30am-12:30am. Fare 85¢, kids 5-11 40¢, seniors 20¢. Some automated T entrances in outlying areas require tokens although they are not sold on location; buy several tokens at a time and have them handy. Bus service reaches more of the city and suburbs; fare generally 60¢, but may vary depending on destination. Bus schedules available at Park St. or Harvard Sq. T-stations. A "T passport" offers discounts at local businesses and unlimited travel on all subway and bus lines and some commuter rail zones. (1-day pass $5, 3-day $9; 7-day $18.) **MBTA Commuter Rail:** Lines to suburbs and the North Shore leave from North Station, Porter Square, and South Station T-stops. For more information on any of these services call 722-3200 or 800-392-6100.

Taxi: Red Cab, 734-5000. **Checker Taxi,** 536-7000. **Yellow Cab,** 876-5000. A taxi from downtown to Logan $10-12, more if there's heavy traffic.

Car Rental: Dollar Rent-a-Car, 110 Mt. Auburn St. (354-6410), in the Harvard Manor House, Harvard Sq. T: Harvard. Sub-compact with unlimited mi. $37 per

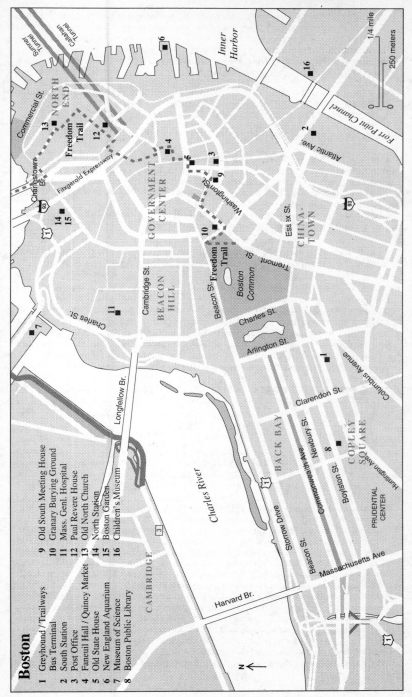

Boston

1 Greyhound / Trailways
  Bus Terminal
2 South Station
3 Post Office
4 Faneuil Hall / Quincy Market
5 Old State House
6 New England Aquarium
7 Museum of Science
8 Boston Public Library

9 Old South Meeting House
10 Granary Burying Ground
11 Mass. Genl. Hospital
12 Paul Revere House
13 Old North Church
14 North Station
15 Boston Garden
16 Children's Museum

day; must stay within New England. Open Mon.-Thurs. 7:30am-6pm, Fri. 7:30am-7pm, Sat.-Sun. 8am-4pm. $20 extra per day for renters under 25. Must have credit card. 10% discount for AAA members. Other offices at many locations in Boston, including the Sheraton Hotel (523-5098) and Logan Airport (569-5300).

Bike Rental: Community Bike Shop, 490 Tremont St. (542-8623), near the Common. $20 per day. Open Mon.-Wed. 9:30am-7pm, Thurs.-Fri. 9:30am-8pm, Sat. 9:30am-6pm., Sun. noon-5pm (summer only). Must have major credit card.

Help Lines: Rape Hotline, 492-7273; open 24 hrs. **Gay and Lesbian Helpline,** 267-9001; open Mon.-Fri. 4pm-11pm, Sat.-Sun. 6pm-11pm.

Post Office: 24 Dorchester Ave. (654-5327). Open Mon.-Fri. 8am-midnight, Sat. 8am-5pm, Sun. noon-5pm. **ZIP code:** 02205.

Area Code: 617.

The hub of the Hub is the 48-acre **Boston Common,** bounded by Tremont, Boylston, Charles, Beacon, and Park St. The **Freedom Trail,** a walking path that leads you past several historical sights in the city, begins in the Common, winds northeast to **Government Center** and **Faneuil Hall,** jogs through the **North End** and then heads north to **Charlestown** and **Bunker Hill.**

Leave your car near your lodgings and take to the sidewalks and subways—the public transportation system here is excellent, parking is expensive, and Boston drivers have a somewhat-deserved reputation for maniacal driving. Several outlying T stations offer **park-and-ride** services. Boston is very compact and is best explored on foot. If you *do* choose to drive around the city, be defensive and alert; Boston's pedestrians can be as aggressive as its drivers. Don't contribute to the coffers of the Boston Police Department by illegally parking.

Boston was not a planned city. Its mishmash of urban thoroughfares and semi-rural paths were designed by meandering colonial-era cows rather than civic planners. Many street names (e.g. Harvard St.) are repeated within the city as well as in neighboring towns. Get a map at the visitors center and ask for detailed directions wherever you go. The best directions will use landmarks, not road names, to steer you; the most frustrating thing about driving in Boston is that street signs almost *never* tell you the name of the thoroughfare on which you are traveling.

ACCOMMODATIONS AND CAMPING

Cheap accommodations do not thrive in Boston. Early September, when students and their parents arrive for the beginning of the school year, is especially tight; likewise the first week in June, when families with graduating seniors pack into hotel rooms reserved six months to a year in advance. Those with cars should investigate the motels along highways in outlying areas. **Boston Reservations,** 1643 Beacon St., #23, Waban MA 02168 (332-4199), presides over 100 accommodations around the Boston area. Access to private membership clubs, small inns, and apartments. (Singles $60-70. Doubles $70-95. Open Mon.-Fri. 9am-5pm.)

Boston International Hostel (HI/AYH), 12 Hemenway St. (536-9455), in the Fenway. T: Hynes/ICA. This cheery, colorful hostel in a great location has clean and slightly crowded but liveable rooms, some with sinks. Hall bathrooms, some recently renovated. Lockers, common rooms, cafeteria, kitchens and laundry. 190 beds in summer, 140 in winter. Planned activities nightly; ask about discounts. Check-in 24hrs. Check-out 10:30am. No lockout. $14, non-members $17; under 14 ½-price. Membership required in summer. $5 deposit for sheets. Linens $2. Wheelchair-accessible. Reservations highly recommended.

Berkeley Residence Club (YWCA), 40 Berkeley St. (482-8850). T: Arlington. Solid, industrial, clean. Men are not allowed above the lobby. Grand piano, patio, pool, TV room, sun deck, laundry, library. Hall baths. Some doubles with sinks (extra charge). Cafeteria ($2 breakfast, $5.25 dinner). Members $30, nonmembers $35; ask for the recession rates. Two weeks $110. Checkout 11am.

Greater Boston YMCA, 316 Huntington Ave. (536-7800). T: Northeastern. Down the street from Symphony Hall on Mass. Ave. Must be 18. Women accepted. Hall

bathrooms. Elegant lobby, friendly atmosphere, partially used as overflow housing for Northeastern University students. Cafeteria, pool, and recreational facilities. Breakfast included. Key deposit $5. ID and luggage required for check-in.
Check-out 11am. Singles $36. Doubles $52. Office staffed 24 hrs.

Anthony's Town House, 1085 Beacon St. (566-3972), Brookline. T: Take Green C
train and get off at second surface stop after Kenmore. Very convenient to the T-
stop. Nicely furnished: TV in every room, some with A/C and cable TV. 14 rooms
for 20 guests, who range from trim professionals to scruffy backpackers. Singles
$40-50. Doubles $65, $72 for 3 people. Winter and off-season $5 less. Ask about
weekly rates; mention *Let's Go* for 5% off the in-season rate. Noon check-out.

Garden Halls Residences, 164 Marlborough St. (267-0079), Back Bay. T: Copley.
Rents only to students. Excellent location. Spartan dorms with bed, dresser, and
desk. Singles, doubles, triples, and quads available. No cooking, no meals served.
Must bring own linen. $30 per person, 3-night min. stay. Reservations required;
book early. Open June-Aug. 15. Office open daily 9am-4pm.

The Farrington Inn, 23 Farrington Ave. (787-1860 or 800-767-5337), Allston Station. T: Green Line-B, or #66 bus. Call for driving directions. Not fancy, but pleasant; prices include local phone, parking, and breakfast. Most rooms have TVs.
Shared baths. Singles $35-45. Doubles from $45.

The Irving House, 24 Irving St. (547-4600), in Cambridge near Cambridge St., in a
residential neighborhood near the university and the Square. T: Harvard. Unique
rooms, libraries, comfortable fishtanked lounge, spacious wood floors. Singles
$35-45, with bath $60. Doubles $48-65, with bath $80. Includes breakfast. Discounts for groups of 16 or more and for longer stays. Reservations required.

FOOD

Besides baked beans, Boston's most familiar crop is seafood; lobsters and clam
chowder are the local faves. The former are always expensive and usually delicious
(and best before July, when lobsters molt); the latter can be sampled in virtually
every local restaurant and inspires fierce debate over whose concoction is the best
in town. Most locals would give that honor to **Legal Seafood,** whose remarkable
clam chowder ($4) has been served at several U.S. Presidential Inaugurations. The
rest of their menu is likewise excellent (but not cheap). They're at the Park Plaza
Hotel (T: Arlington; 426-4444.)

Seafood is only one option in a city with many; Boston dishes out an impressive
variety of international cuisines, from Ethiopian to Vietnamese, often at reasonable
prices. The scent of garlic wafts from the **North End** (T: Haymarket), home to an
endless array of Italian groceries, bakeries, caffès, and restaurants. Hanover and
Salem St. are lined with fine eateries. You haven't really sipped until you've sipped
cappuccino at **Caffe Vittoria,** 294 Hanover St. (open daily 8am-midnight). **Chinatown** crowds a bevy of delectable restaurants in all price ranges into its several narrow blocks (T: Chinatown; be careful here at night). Wander through the open-air
stalls at **Haymarket** and pick up produce, fresh fish, cheeses, and pigs' eyes for well
below supermarket prices. Try to get here early, especially during summer. (Indoor
stores open daily dawn-dusk; outdoor stalls Fri.-Sat. only. T: Government Center or
Haymarket.) Just up Congress St. from Haymarket, the mobbed food stands at
Faneuil Hall and **Quincy Market** offer the culinary equivalent of EPCOT Center to
indiscriminating tourists (T: Government Center, or just skip it).

Addis Red Sea, 544 Tremont St. (426-8727). T: Back Bay. From the station, walk 5
blocks south on Clarendon St., then turn left on Tremont (about a 10-min. walk).
The best Ethiopian food in Boston, served on *mesobs,* woven tables which support a communal platter. Entrees $8-9, but if you like variety go for the combina-
tion platters, which let you sample five different dishes for $10-12 (the Winnie
Mandela Combination Platter commemorates her visit to the restaurant). Open
Mon.-Thurs. 5-11pm, Fri.-Sat. 5pm-midnight, Sat. noon-3pm, Sun. noon-11pm.

Giorgio's Pizzeria, 69 Salem St. (523-1373). T: Haymarket. Walk under the bridge;
Salem St. is to the left of Martignetti's Liquors. The finest pizza in town, bar none.

From the portrait of founder Gramma Giorgio to the cheerful relatives behind the counter, Giorgio's is the quintessential family-run pizzeria. Using Gramma's original recipe from Sicily, the cooks create 15 varieties of garden-fresh, preservative-free pizza. Huge slices from $1.50. Entrees $4-7. Open daily 11am-11pm.

Ruby's, 280 Cambridge St. (367-3224) T: Charles. Walk toward the Holiday Inn from the T-stop; Ruby's is on your right about four blocks down. Locals stop into this small Beacon Hill dive before 10am weekdays and "Beat the House" for 75¢—two eggs, home fries, and toast for less than a subway ride. Hearty sandwiches ($4.50) and deli fare served all day, but breakfast is the star attraction. Open Mon.-Thurs. 7am-9pm, Fri.-Sun. 8am-11pm.

Bob the Chef's, 604 Columbus Ave. (536-6204). T: Symphony or Mass. Ave. From either stop, exit onto Mass. Ave. and walk away from the Symphony and turn right onto Columbus Ave. Best (and damn near only) soul food in Boston. Fried fish, chicken livers, pigs feet, corn bread, and the famed "glorifried chicken" keep devotees clamoring for more. Die-hard tripe fans have not lived until they have experienced Bob's chitterlings. Vegetarians take caution! Entrees $7-10. Open Mon.-Sat. 8am-9pm, Sun. 9am-6pm.

Chau Chow, 52 Beach St. (426-6266). T: South Station. Follow Atlantic Ave. south to Beach St. No messing around here; you arrive, you wait in line, you sit down, you eat, you pay, and you leave. But you eat top-quality, award-winning Chinese food. Their seafood dishes are renowned, or try the chicken with cashews or the vegetarian Buddha's Delight. Most dishes on the encyclopedic menu hover around $6, and portions are huge. Open Mon.-Thurs. 10am-2am, Fri.-Sat. 10am-4am, Sun 10am-1am.

Thai Cuisine, 14a Westland Ave. (262-1485), near Mass. Ave. behind Symphony Hall. T: Symphony. Cheap, yummy, spicy Thai food. The Masaman Curry and Pad Thai are amazingly good. Entrees $6-10. Open Mon.-Sat.11:30am-3pm, 5-10pm, Sun. 5-10pm.

La Famiglia, 112 Salem St. (367-6711), in the North End. T: Haymarket. Be prepared for two full-sized meals: the one you eat in the restaurant and the one you take home. Portions are enormous at this noisy and popular establishment. Plenty of vegetarian options, including a towering tribute to eggplant, aptly named pasta with eggplant. No reservations; expect to wait, especially on weekends. Entrees $6-15. Open daily 11am-11pm.

Tangiers Cafe, 37 Bowdoin St. (367-0273), around the corner from the State House. T: Park or Government Center. Much of the menu is generic Mediterranean: hummus, tabouleh, kebab, grape leaves, and ever-flowing pita, but for truer Moroccan fare, try the daily specials. A wonderful selection of coffees, leaf-brewed teas, and iced drinks. Entrees $6.25-13.

Kebab-n-Kurry, 30 Mass. Ave. (536-9835), between Marlborough and Beacon St. T: Hynes/ICA. From the T-stop, walk 3 blocks right (towards the river). Savory North Indian cuisine in a semi-subterranean, yet jovial and potentially intimate setting. Numerous chicken and vegetarian dishes, kebabs, curries, and excellent appetizer combo platters. Entrees $7-14, saffroned rice or bread included. Open Mon.-Sat. noon-3pm, 5-10:30pm, Sun. 5-10:30pm.

SIGHTS

At two lofty locations, you can map out the zones you want to visit or simply zone out as you take in the city skyline. The **Prudential Skywalk,** on the 50th floor of the Prudential Center, 800 Boylston St., Back Bay (236-3318), grants a full 360° view from New Hampshire to the Cape. (T: Prudential. Open Mon.-Sat. 10am-10pm, Sun. noon-10pm. $2.75, seniors, students with ID, and kids $1.75.) The **John Hancock Observatory,** 200 Clarendon St. (247-1977 recorded, 572-6429 live), refuses to be outdone, with 60 beefy floors and the distinction of being the highest building in New England (740 ft.). On good days, you can see New Hampshire. (T: Copley. Open Mon.-Sat. 9am-10pm, Sun. 10am-10pm. $3, age 5-15 and seniors $2.25.)

The **Freedom Trail** (536-4100) leads pedestrians along a clearly marked red brick or painted line through the **Boston National Historical Park,** really a scattering of buildings and sites beginning at the **Boston Visitor Information Center** (see

Practical Information above). Most of the sites are free, but a few charge $2.50 to $3 for admission. Don't bother buying the map ($1) to the country's most famous footpath since you can pick up free ones at almost any brochure rack. The trail makes two loops. The easier Downtown Loop passes the **Old North Church**, the **Boston Massacre Sight**, the **Granary Burial Ground**, the **Old Corner Bookstore**, and **Paul Revere's House**, among 11 other sights, and takes only an afternoon. The fascinating **Black Heritage Trail** makes 14 stops of its own, each marked by a redblack-and-green logo. The tour begins at the **Boston African-American National Historic Site**, 46 Joy St. (T: Park Street), where you can pick up a free map before visiting the museum inside (742-1854; open daily 10am-4pm). The trail covers sights of particular importance to the development of Boston's African-American community, including: the **African Meeting House** (1805), the earliest black church in North America; the **Robert Gould Shaw and 54th Regiment Memorial** on the Common, dedicated to black soldiers who fought in the Union Army and (more prominently) to their white Boston leader memorialized in the movie *Glory*; and the **Lewis and Harriet Hayden House**, a station on the Underground Railroad.

The Common, Fenway, Beacon Hill, and Back Bay

The areas immediately northwest of the **Boston Common** (T: Park Street) are brahmin heaven: some quaint streets seem frozen in time, and the more contemporary sections are gilded with chic.

Early inhabitants established the Common, the oldest park in the nation, as a place to graze their cattle in 1634. Now street vendors, not cows, live off the fat of the land. While the frisbee players, drug dealers, street musicians, students, families, cops, and government employees all stake equal claim to it in the daytime, the Common is dangerous at night—don't go here alone after dark. Across Charles St. from the Common waddle the title characters from the children's book *Make Way for Ducklings*. The ducklings point the way to the **Swan Boats** (522-1966) in the fragrant and lovely **Public Gardens**. These pedal-powered boats glide around a quiet pond lined with shady willows. (T: Arlington. Boats open mid-April-mid-June daily 10am-4pm; mid-June-Labor Day daily 10am-5pm; Labor Day-mid-Sept. Mon.-Fri. noon-4pm, Sat.-Sun. 10am-4pm. $1.45, seniors $1.20, under 12 95¢.)

Residential since its settlement by the Puritans, **Beacon Hill** has always pulsed with blueblood. Several buildings, including the gold-domed **State House** (727-3676) designed by Charles Bulfinch, offer exhibits of Massachusetts and colonial history and government. There are free tours of the Hall of Flags, House of Representatives, and Senate Chamber. (Visitor info: Doric Hall, 2nd floor. Open Mon.-Fri. 9am-5pm; tours Mon.-Fri. 10am-4pm.) The **Harrison Gray Otis House**, 141 Cambridge St. (227-3956), another Bulfinch original, headquarters the Society for the Preservation of New England Antiquities. (Tours on the hr. Tues.-Fri. noon-4pm, Sat. 10am-4pm. $4, seniors $3.50, under 12 $2.) The Society hoards info about historical sights. The nearby **Boston Athenaeum**, 10½ Beacon St. (227-0270), houses over 700,000 books and offers tours of its library, art gallery, and print room. (Open Mon.-Fri. 9am-5:30pm, Sat. 9am-4pm; no Sat. hrs. in summer. Free tours Tues. and Thurs. at 3pm; reservations required.)

Charles Street serves as the Hill's front door. This exclusive residential bastion of Boston brahminism now shares its brick sidewalks with the fashionable contingent of Boston's gay community. The art galleries, cafes, antique stores, and other small shops with hanging wooden signs make this a fine avenue for a stroll.

In the **Back Bay**, southwest of Beacon Hill, three-story brownstone row houses line the only gridded streets in Boston. Originally the marshy, uninhabitable "back bay" of Boston Harbor, the area was filled in during the last century. Back Bay was filled in gradually, as reflected in its architectural styles, which run the gamut of 19th-century designs as you travel from east to west. **Commonwealth Avenue** ("Comm. Ave.") is a European-style boulevard with statuary and benches punctuating its large and grassy median. **Newbury Street** is Boston's most flamboyant promenade; dye your poodle, pierce your navel, and just vogue, Katya. The dozens of small art galleries, boutiques, bookstores, and cafes that line the stage are a bastion of exclusivity. (T: Arlington, Copley, or Hynes/ICA.)

The handsome **Copley Square** area extends the whole length of Back Bay on commercial Boylston St. Renovated and officially reopened in June 1989, the square (T: Copley) accommodates a range of seasonal activities, including summertime concerts (1993 saw Roseanne Cash and Mark Cohn, among others), folk dancing, a food pavilion, and people-watching. A permanent feature is the **Boston Public Library,** 666 Boylston St. (536-5400), a massive, spartan, Orwellian building, liberally inscribed with the names of literally hundreds of literati. Benches and window seats inside overlook a tranquil courtyard with fountain and garden. Relax here or in the vaulted reading room. The auditorium gives a program of lectures and films. The library is undergoing renovations until 1995, but it's still open and you can still get to everything. (Open Mon.-Thurs. 9am-9pm, Fri.-Sat. 9am-5pm.) Across the square, H.H. Richardson's Romanesque fantasy, **Trinity Church,** gazes at its reflection in I.M. Pei's mirrored **Hancock Tower.** Many consider Trinity, built in 1877, a masterpiece of U.S. church architecture—the interior explains this opinion. (T: Copley. Open daily 8am-6pm.) **Copley Place,** a gaudy complex containing two hotels and a ritzy mall in the corner next to the library, attracts a steady stream of local high school students with big hair. The partially gentrified **South End,** south of Copley, makes for good brownstone viewing and casual dining.

Two blocks down Massachusetts Ave. from Copley sits the Mother Church of the **First Church of Christ, Scientist,** One Norway St. (450-2000), at Mass. Ave. and Huntington, founded in Boston by Mary Baker Eddy. The lovely **Mother Church** is the world headquarters of the Christian Science movement, and its complex of buildings is appropriately vast and imposing. Both the Mother Church and the smaller, older church out back can be seen by guided tour only; the guides do not proselytize. (Tours every ½ hr. Tues.-Fri. 10am-4pm, Sun. 11:15am-2pm.) In the Christian Science Publishing Society next door, use the catwalk to pass through the **Mapparium,** a 30-ft.-wide stained-glass globe with funky acoustics. Whisper in the ear of Pakistan while standing next to Surinam. (Tours Tues.-Fri. 9:30am-4pm. Free.)

Back Bay loses some of its formality on the riverside **Esplanade** (T: Charles), a park extending from the Longfellow Bridge to the Harvard Bridge. Boston's quasi-pseudo-beach on the Charles, the Esplanade fills in the summer with sun-seekers and sail-boaters; but don't go in the water unless you *like* tetanus shots. Bikers and rollerbladers, upholding Boston's tradition of good road manners, try to mow down pedestrians on the walkway. The bike path, which follows the river to the posh suburb of **Wellesley,** makes a terrific afternoon's ride. The Esplanade also hosts some of Boston's best-loved cultural events—the concerts of the **Boston Pops Orchestra** (266-1492) at the mauve **Hatch Shell** (727-9547). Until December, 1993, the Pops were conducted by John Williams, who composed the score for such movie spectacles as *Jaws, Star Wars, Indiana Jones,* and *Jurassic Park.* The Pops play here during the first week of July. Concerts are free and begin at 8pm; arrive early so you can sit within earshot of the orchestra. On the **4th of July,** nearly 100,000 patriotic thrill-seekers pack the Esplanade to hear the Pops concert (broadcast by loudspeaker throughout the area) and watch the ensuing terrific fireworks display. Arrive before noon for a seat on the Esplanade, although you can watch the fireworks from basically anywhere along the river. The regular Pops season at **Symphony Hall,** 301 Mass. Ave. (266-2378 box office and concert info; 266-2378, recorded message), runs mid-May through July. (Tickets $10-45. Box office open Mon.-Sat. 10am-6pm, Sun. 1pm-6pm on concert days, but the best way to get tickets is to call 266-1200.)

Beyond the Back Bay, west on Commonwealth Ave., glows **Kenmore Square** (T: Kenmore), watched over by the landmark **Citgo sign** (familiar to anyone who's watched a Red Sox game). The area around Kenmore Sq. has more than its share of neon, containing many of the city's most popular nightclubs (see Nightlife below).

Below Kenmore Sq., the **Fenway** comprises a large area of the city, containing some of its best museums. Ubiquitous landscaper Frederick Olmsted of Central Park fame designed the **Fens** area at the center of the Fenway as part of his "Emerald Necklace" vision for Boston—a necklace he fortunately never completed. A gem nonetheless, the park's fragrant rose gardens and neighborhood vegetable patches make perfect picnic turf. Bring your own vegetables. Just north of the Fens, **Fenway Park,** home of the "Green Monster," is the nation's oldest Major League ballpark and center stage for the perennially heart-rending **Boston Red Sox** baseball club, which if given a chicken filet, would find a bone to choke on—don't ask Bostonians about the most recent Choke in 1986 to the New York Mets. (Box office 267-8661; open Mon.-Fri. 9am-5pm, Sat. 9:30am-2pm, or until game time if the team's in town. T: Kenmore.) Tickets sell out far in advance, but they can usually be procured from a scalper; those who wait until game-time for procurement can haggle the price down. West still of Fenway along T: Green lines C and D sits suburban **Brookline,** with its slightly upper-crust charm; curfewed-but-defiant **Boston University** shuts out the lights along Commonwealth Ave. on Green line B.

Downtown, the North End, and the Waterfront

A fluke of commerce and neighborhood politics made historic **Quincy Market** in the West End (T: Government Center) an unfortunate focal point of contemporary Boston. City officials and developers, desperate to lure shoppers and tourists back downtown after years of exodus and an economic slump, finally settled on a modest (and ill-prophesied) shopping-mall complex to be built next to the old Faneuil Hall. Upon completion in 1976, the red-brick and cobblestone "marketplace" became a lucrative model for urban revitalization, inspiring other *faux-downtown* projects such as South St. Seaport in New York. Though pricey and crowded, the market and its clientele can be amusing. The info center in the market's South Canopy (523-3886) can provide direction. At night, tourists come back again for the lively bar scene and fascinating street performances. In 1742, Peter Faneuil (FAN-yul) donated **Faneuil Hall,** the gateway to the market, to serve as a marketplace and community hall. Sometimes called the "cradle of American Liberty," it served as quarters for British Redcoats as well as a gathering spot for Bostonians pissed at King George III. Occasionally, free concerts are given outside the Hall; call 523-1300 for details about the **Summer Nights** concert series featuring blues, calypso, and rock. (Info line Mon.-Fri. 9am-5pm.) The hall has been recently renovated.

Across Congress St. from the market, the red brick plaza of **Government Center,** as its name indicates, proves a trifle less picturesque. The monstrous concrete **City Hall** (725-4000), designed by I.M. "Everywhere" Pei, opens to the public Monday through Friday (T: Government Center). A few blocks south, its more aesthetically pleasing precursor, the **Old State House,** 206 Washington St. (720-1713 or -3290), built in 1713, once rocked with revolutionary fervor. The State House has also just been renovated (T: State).

Downtown Crossing, south of City Hall at Washington St. (T: Downtown Crossing), is a wonderful pedestrian mall set amidst Boston's business district. **Filene's Basement,** 426 Washington St., jives here as the world's oldest bargain store, in business since 1908. The area shuts down after business hours. Directly southwest of the Common, Boston's engaging **Chinatown** (T: Chinatown) demarcates itself with pagoda-style telephone booths and streetlamps and an arch at its Beach St. entrance. Within this small area cluster many restaurants, food stores, and novelty shops where you can buy Chinese slippers and 1000-year-old eggs. Chinatown has two big celebrations each year. The first, **New Year,** usually falls on a Sunday in February, and festivities include lion dances, fireworks and Kung Fu exhibitions. The **August Moon Festival** honors a mythological pair of lovers at the time of the full moon. Watch for listings in *Where Boston.*

The eastern tip of Boston contains the historic **North End** (T: Haymarket). The city's oldest residential district, now an Italian neighborhood, overflows with windowboxes, Italian flags, fragrant pastry shops, crèches, Sicilian restaurants, and Catholic churches. The most famous of the latter, **Old St. Stephens Church,** 401 Hanover St. (523-1230), is the classically colonial brainchild of Charles Bulfinch (open 8:30am-5pm daily). Down the street, the brilliant and sweet-smelling **Peace Gardens** try to drown out the honking horns of the North End with beautiful flora. The **Old North Church** has seen over 200 years of religious service since April 18, 1775 when it did its military duty of signaling to Paul Revere that the British were coming across Back Bay. Nearby, **Paul Revere's Home** contains displays on the silversmith-*cum*-patriot's domestic life.

The **waterfront area,** bounded by Atlantic and Commercial St., runs along Boston Harbor from South Station to the North End Park. Stroll down Commercial, Lewis, or Museum Wharf for a slurp of briny air. At the excellent **New England Aquarium** (973-5200; T: Aquarium), Central Wharf on the Waterfront, giant sea turtles, sharks, and their scaly friends swim tranquilly as visitors peer into their cylindrical 187,000-gallon tank. Penguins cavort in a mini-archipelago around the base of the tank. Dolphins and sea lions perform in the ship *Discovery,* moored alongside. On weekends lines tend to be long. (Open Mon.-Tues. and Fri. 9am-5pm, Thurs. 9am-8pm, Sat.-Sun. and holidays 9am-7pm, Sept.-June Mon.-Wed. and Fri. 9am-5pm, Thurs. 9am-8pm, Sat.-Sun. and holidays 9am-6pm. $7.50, seniors and students $6.50, ages 3-11 $3.50. Thurs. after 4pm $1 discount.) The aquarium also offers **whale-watching cruises** (973-5277) from April to October. (Generally 1 trip each before and after noon; call for times. $23, seniors and students $18.50, ages 12-18 $17, ages 3-11 $16, under 36 in. not allowed. Reservations suggested.) **Boston Harbor Cruises** (227-4320) leave from Long Wharf, adjacent to the aquarium, for 90-minute tours of the harbor from roughly March to October. (Departs hourly 10am-4pm and 7pm. $8, seniors $6, under 12 $4.) They also have 45-minute cruises ($5, seniors $4, kids $3).

Across Fort Point Channel from the waterfront, predominantly Irish-American **South Boston** has a unique accent. (T: South Station). "Southie" has great seafood, two beaches, and a pub on every corner.

Museums

Boston's intellectual and artistic community supports a higher concentration of museums than anywhere else in New England. Check the free *Guide to Museums of Boston* for details on the museums not mentioned here.

Museum of Fine Arts (MFA), 465 Huntington Ave. (267-9300; T: Ruggles/ Museum, Green line E train), near the intersection with Massachusetts Ave. The most famous of Boston's museums. It gathers one of the world's finest collections of Asian ceramics, outstanding Egyptian art, a good showing of Impressionists, and superb Americana. Worth a gander are the two famous unfinished portraits of George and Martha Washington, painted by (who else?) Gilbert Stuart in 1796. Open Tues. and Thurs.-Sun. 10am-4:45pm, Wed. 10am-9:45pm. West Wing only open Thurs.-Fri. 5-10pm. $7, seniors and students $6, kids $3. West Wing only, $5. Both free Wed. 4-10pm.

Isabella Stewart Gardner Museum, 280 Fenway (566-1401), a few hundred yards from the MFA. The eccentric "Mrs. Jack" Gardner built the small, Venetian-style palace with a stunning courtyard seeking surcease from sorrow at the loss of her only child. She scandalized Boston with her excesses, but left posterity a superb art collection. Unfortunately—in what has been termed the greatest art heist in history—a 1989 break-in relieved the museum of works by Rembrandt, Verñeer, Dégas, and others. Many masterpieces still remain, and the courtyard garden is worth a thousand pictures. Open Tues.-Sun. 11am-5pm. Chamber music on 1st floor Sept.-June Sat. and Sun. afternoons. $5, seniors and students $2.50, kids free. Wed. students free.

Museum of Science, Science Park (723-2500; T: Science Park), at the far eastern end of the Esplanade on the Charles River Dam. Contains, among other wonders, the largest "lightning machine" in the world. A multi-story roller-coaster for small metal balls purports to explain energy states, but is just fun to watch. Within the museum, the **Hayden Planetarium** features models, lectures, films, and laser and star shows; the **Mugar Omni Theatre** shows popular films of scientific interest on a gee-whiz-four-story-domed screen. Museum open Sat.-Thurs. 9am-5pm (until 7pm in summer), Fri. 9am-9pm. Admission to museum and Omni (separate fees) $7, seniors, students, and ages 4-14 $5. Planetarium and laser show $6/4. Any 2 events $11/8, all 3 $15/11. Free Wed. afternoons Sept.-May.

Children's Museum, 300 Congress St. (426-8855), in southern Boston on Museum Wharf. T: South Station. Follow the signs with the milk bottles on them. Here kids of all ages toy with way-cool hands-on exhibits. Open July-Sept. Sat.-Thurs. 10am-5pm, Fri. 10am-9pm; closed Mon. during off-season. $7, seniors and ages 2-15 $6, kids age 1 $2, under 1 free; Fri. 5-9pm $1.

John F. Kennedy Presidential Library (929-4567), on Morrissey Blvd., Dorchester (T: JFK/UMass; free MBTA shuttle to the U Mass campus, a short walk from the library). Dedicated "to all those who through the art of politics seek a new and better world." Designed by I.M. Pei, the white cuboid oceanside edifice contains fascinating, sometimes trivial exhibits that employ photographs, documents, audio-visual presentation, and mementos to document the careers of JFK and his brother, RFK. Open daily 9am-5pm. $5, seniors $3, under 16 free.

Institute of Contemporary Art (ICA), 955 Boylston St. (266-5151 recorded message arts information line, 266-5152 operator; T: Hynes/ICA). Boston's lone outpost of the avant-garde attracts major contemporary artists while aggressively promoting lesser-known work. Their innovative, sometimes controversial exhibits change every 8 weeks. The museum also presents experimental theater, music, dance, and film. Open Wed.-Thurs. noon-9pm, Fri.-Sun. noon-5pm. $5, students with ID $3, seniors and under 16 $2. Free Thurs. 5-9pm.

NIGHTLIFE

Boston's nightlife, while occasionally top-notch, is tempered somewhat by the city's obstinate "Blue laws" (forbidding the sale of liquor after certain hours) and the dearth of public transportation after midnight. Nearly all bars and most clubs close between 1 and 2am, and bar admittance for anyone under 21 is hard-won. Those qualifications aside, you'll find a great variety of bars and pubs throughout the city, several compelling dance clubs, and some *excellent* live-music venues, as well as a number of quality comedy clubs. Boston's local music scene runs the gamut from folk to funk; Beantown natives-gone-national include the Pixies, Dinosaur Jr., Lemonheads, Mission of Burma, Aerosmith, Bobby Brown, Mighty Mighty Bosstones, and the J. Geils Band. National acts usually check in at the Orpheum, the Paradise, Avalon, the cavernous Boston Garden, or at one of the local colleges' theaters and arenas. By all means, peruse the weekly *Boston Phoenix* for its comprehensive "Boston-After-Dark" club and concert listings ($1.50, out on Thursdays).

Avalon; Axis; Venus de Milo, 7-13 Lansdowne St. T: Kenmore. Upscale 80s-style pre-yuppie (262-24-24); neo-punk/industrial (262-2437); relentlessly techno and outrageously attired (421-9595), respectively. All three clubs are open on weekends 10pm-2am; exact hours for each club vary, as do cover charges.

Ryles, 212 Hampshire St. (876-9330), in Inman Square. Take the #69 Lechmere bus. A Boston jazz-scene standby, with nightly live music and a jazz brunch on Sun. noon-4pm. Open Sun.-Thurs. 5pm-1am, Fri.-Sat. 5pm-2am.

The Black Rose, 160 State St., Faneuil Hall (742-2286). T: Government Center. This raucous Irish bar features live, traditional Irish music (daily 9pm-1:30am) in a rollicking, convivial atmosphere. Wear your claddagh ring. $5 cover. Open Mon.-Sat. 11:30am-1:30am, Sun. noon-1:30am.

Plough and Stars, 912 Mass. Ave. (492-9653). T: Central. Enjoy literature, liquor, and song in the very place where the literary journal *Ploughshares* was conceived. A mellow crowd of locals and aficionados pack the tiny Plough nightly for live folk, blues, c&w, rock and roll, and reggae. SometimestheytintolerablypacktthePlough. Open Mon.-Fri. 11:30am-1am, Sat.-Sun. noon-1am.

Rathskeller, 528 Commonwealth Ave., Kenmore Sq. (536-2750). T: Kenmore. A somewhat faded legend on the Boston scene (Talking Heads, Mission of Burma, and the Police all played here on the upswing), the "Rat" still cultivates a grungy atmosphere to accompany its excellent program of grungy bands. Mosh pit. Watch your head on the ceiling pipes. Open daily 6pm-2am. Cover varies.

A few places cater to a gay and lesbian clientele at all times or on specific nights. **Indigo's** clientele is predominantly women, and **Chaps, Club Café,** and **Sporters** are all gay clubs. Club Café, 209 Columbus Ave. (536-0966; T: Back Bay) has a largely yuppie clientele, live music nightly, and no cover. If you're feeling more adventurous, try the **Boston Ramrod,** 1254 Boylston St. (266-2986; T: Kenmore), behind Fenway Park on Boylston St., where Thursday and Friday are official leather nights, in keeping with the bar's biker theme. **Campus/Manray,** 21 Brookline St. (864-0406; T: Central), Central Sq., features top-40 and progressive music for women on Sundays and is open to a mixed crowd the rest of the week. Check the *Bay Windows* listings for more information.

ARTS AND ENTERTAINMENT

Musicians, dancers, actors, and *artistes* of every description fill Boston. Worth special mention is the large community of **street performers** ("buskers") who juggle steak knives, swallow torches, wax poetic, and sing folk tunes in the subways and squares of Boston and Cambridge. Though enthusiastic crowds may be incentives in themselves, these artists earn very little in an average day; show your support with a donation as well as applause.

The *Boston Phoenix* and the "Calendar" section of Thursday's *Boston Globe* list activities for the coming week. Also check the *Where Boston* booklet available at the visitors center. What Boston doesn't have, Cambridge does (see Cambridge below). **Bostix,** a Ticketron outlet in Faneuil Hall (723-5181), sells half-price tickets to performing arts events on the day of performance. (Service charge $1.50-2.50 per ticket. Cash and travelers checks only. Open Tues.-Sat. 11am-6pm, Sun. 11am-4pm.)

Actors in town cluster around Washington St. and Harrison Ave., in the **Theater District** (T: Boylston). The famous **Wang Center for the Performing Arts,** 268 Tremont St. (482-9393), produces theater, classical music, and opera in its modern complex. The **Shubert Theater,** 265 Tremont St. (426-4520), and the **Wilbur Theater,** 246 Tremont St. (423-4008), host Broadway hits breezing through Boston. Tickets for these and for shows at the **Charles Playhouse,** 74 Warrenton St. (426-6912), are costly (around $30). The area's professional companies are cheaper, and may provide a more interesting evening. The **New Ehrlich Theater,** 539 Tremont St. (247-7388), and **Huntington Theater Co.,** 264 Huntington Ave. (266-7900; 266-0800 for box office), at Boston University have solid artistic reputations. (Tickets $10-24.) More affordable college theater is also available; during term-time, watch students thesp at **Tufts Theater-Arena** (628-5000), the **BU Theatre** (353-3320), the **MIT Drama Shop** (253-2908), and the **MIT Shakespeare Ensemble** (253-2903).

The renowned **Boston Ballet** (695-6950), in neighboring Newton, annually brings to life such classics as the *Nutcracker* and *Swan Lake*. The **Boston Symphony Orchestra,** 201 Mass. Ave. (266-1492; T: Symphony), at Huntington, holds its concert season from October to April. Rush seats go on sale three hours before concerts (tickets for 8pm concerts available at 5pm; Fri. 2pm concert tickets available at 9am). Open Wednesday rehearsals cost under $10; bargain tickets are also available Friday at noon for that evening's show. In summer, when the BSO retreats to Tanglewood, the **Boston Pops Orchestra** sets up at Symphony Hall or the Esplanade and plays classics and pop on weekend evenings. The **Berklee Performance Center,** 136 Mass. Ave. (266-7455), an adjunct of the Berklee School of Music, holds concerts featuring students, faculty, and jazz and classical luminaries.

Despite its ostensible air of refinement, Boston goes ape for sports. Long known for fans as committed as Charles Manson, Beantown always seems to be in some seasonal basketball, baseball, or hockey frenzy. On summer nights, thousands of base-ball fans pour out of **Fenway Park** (see above) and clog Kenmore Sq. traffic for an hour. **Boston Garden** (T: North Station), located off the JFK Expressway between the West and North Ends, hosts the illustrious **Boston Celtics** basketball team (season Oct.-May; 523-3030 for info) and **Boston Bruins** hockey team (season Oct.-April; call 227-3200 for more info). A fair distance outside Boston, **Sullivan Stadium** hosts the perennially lackluster **New England Patriots** football franchise.

In October, the **Head of the Charles** regatta, the largest such single-day event in the U.S., attracts rowing clubs, white baseball caps, and beer-stained college sweatshirts from across the country. The 3-mi. boat races begin at Boston University Bridge; the best vantage points are on the Weeks footbridge and Anderson Bridge near Harvard University. On April 19, the 10,000 runners competing in the **Boston Marathon** tread memories of the "Head" underfoot. Call the Massachusetts Division of Tourism for details (617-727-3201).

For info on other special events, such as the **St. Patrick's Day Parade** (March 17), **Patriot's Day** celebrations (April 19), the week-long **Boston Common Dairy Festival** (June), the **Boston Harbor Fest** (early July), and the North End's **Festival of St. Anthony** (mid-August), see the *Boston Phoenix* or *Globe* calendars.

■■■ CAMBRIDGE

The binary intellectual stars of Harvard and MIT dominate this city on the Charles River. Each school believes itself to be the center of the universe (you be the judge). Harvard (est. 1636) is the oldest university in the United States. Its alumni include countless luminaries in the American intellectual and political firmament; Emerson, Thoreau, Santayana, Franklin D. Roosevelt, John F. Kennedy and Albert Gore all have Harvard degrees. MIT, Harvard's younger and somewhat nerdier kin, takes the lead in technology. It was hardware developed in the radar laboratory at MIT which enabled the Allies to dominate the skies in WWII. Rumor has it that an MIT-owned nuclear reactor is hidden somewhere beneath the city streets. MIT's computer and biology labs continue to define and then redesign the cutting edge and have taken the lead in the burgeoning bio-technology industry.

The city takes on the character of both of these universities. Around MIT radiate concentric rings of bio-technology and computer science buildings. Harvard, on the other hand, clusters stellar bookstores and pretentious coffee houses around its Georgian brick buildings. When Harvard Square's turbo-gentrification and MIT's techno-terrors get you down, escape to Central Square (conveniently located between the two) for inexpensive restaurants and clubs in a vibrant ethnic enclave.

PRACTICAL INFORMATION

See Boston: Practical Information, above, for a complete listing. The **Cambridge Discovery Booth** (497-1630), in Harvard Sq., has the best and most comprehensive information about Cambridge, as well as MBTA bus and subway schedules. Pick up the *Old Cambridge Walking Guide,* an excellent self-guided tour ($1). Walking tours of Harvard and the surrounding area are given in summer. (Open summer Mon.-Sat. 9am-6pm, Sun. 1-5pm; off-season Mon.-Sat. 9am-5pm, Sun. 1-5pm.) **Out-Of-Town News** (354-7777), right next to the Discovery Booth, has no official status as a tourist resource, but sells a large number of excellent maps and guides to the area. (Open daily 6am-11:30pm.) The **Harvard University Information Center,** Holyoke Center, in Harvard Sq. (495-1573), has free guides to the university museums, and offers tours of the university Mon.-Fri. at 10am and 2pm; two additional tours per day Mon.-Fri. and one Sat. in summer. (Open Mon.-Sat. 9am-4:45pm)

Let's Go's compendium **The Unofficial Guide to Life at Harvard** ($8), has the inside scoop and up-to-date listings of area restaurants, entertainment, sights, transportation and services as well as a fine chapter on beer and its uses. It's available in Square bookstores and the Discovery Booth.

Cambridge's general delivery **post office** (876-0620) is in Central Square, T: Central. General Delivery hours are Mon.-Fri. 7:30am-6:45pm, Sat. 7:30am-noon. The **ZIP code** is 02139; the **area code** is 617.

Massachusetts Avenue ("Mass. Ave.") is Cambridge's major artery. Most of the action takes place in "squares" (that is, commercial areas which are of every geometric shape *except* square) along Mass. Ave. and the Red Line of the T. **MIT (The Massachusetts Institute of Technology)** is just across the Mass. Ave. Bridge from Boston at **Kendall Square,** on the Red Line. The Red Line continues outbound one T-stop at a time through: **Central Square,** the heart of urban Cambridge; frenetic, eclectic **Harvard Square;** and more suburban **Porter Square.** Cambridge is a 10-min. T ride from the heart of Boston.

FOOD

Nightly, thousands of college students renounce cafeteria fare and head to the funky eateries of Harvard Square. Ask a student where to go. For quick food you might try **The Garage** at 36 Kennedy St., a mall of restaurants offering everything from hummus to gourmet coffee to sushi. Pick up the weekly *Square Deal,* usually shoved in your face by distributors near the T-stop, for coupons and discounts on local fare.

Tandoor House, 991 Mass. Ave. (661-9001), between Harvard and Central. Not only the best Indian restaurant in Cambridge (which it is, resoundingly), but one of Cambridge's finest restaurants, period. The green carpeting running half-way up the walls, the eerie sitar music wafting across the twin domes of everybody's poori bread, and owner Shantoo make dining at Tandoor House a constant source of delight. All dishes are exquisite; vegetarians should not miss the Shahi Baingan Bharta, a miracle made with a little eggplant and a lot of love. Entrees $6-12; lunch specials from $3.25. Open daily 11:30am-2:30pm, 5-10:30pm.

The Middle East, 472 Mass. Ave. (354-8238), beyond Tandoor House in Central Sq.. Although the service is erratic in this pink restaurant, the food is the best and most innovative Middle Eastern cuisine around. Huge sandwiches $3-4, dinner entrees $7-10. An especially good deal if you go early with a two-for-one coupon from the *Square Deal* (mentioned above). Live alternative music in the evenings. Open Sun.-Wed. 11am-1am, Thurs.-Sun. 11:30am-2am.

Boca Grande, 1728 Mass. Ave. (354-7400), between Harvard and Porter, the opposite direction on Mass. Ave. from Tandoor House. Award-winning Mexican food you can eat-in or take-out. All food is made to order, including enchiladas ($5), spicy tamales ($4), and burritos grandes ($4.15), and the salsa and guacamole are fresh and delicious. The burritos grandes are certainly *grande,* but your bill here will be *muy poco.* Open Sun.-Wed. 10am-9pm, Thurs. 10am-9:30pm, Fri.-Sat. 10am-10pm.

Jake and Earl's Dixie BBQ, 1273 Cambridge St., Inman Sq., nowhere near Tandoor House; take the #69 Lechmere bus from Harvard Sq.; look for the laughing pigs and the Elvis bust in the window (491-7427; for delivery call Vidi-Go at 547-0000). Next door to the East Coast Grill. They slop up masterfully spiced barbecue plates, all of which include coleslaw, baked beans, and a slice of watermelon, here at this tiny, award-winning BBQ joint. Mostly take-out, with a few stools for in-house pigging out. Entrees $4-7.50, no plastic. Open daily 11:30am-11pm.

Tasty Sandwich Shop, 2a JFK St., Harvard Sq. (354-9016). T: Harvard. More than just a 12-seater, fluorescent lit, formica-countered, all-night diner, The Tasty (est. 1916) is all things good in America, having provided generations of street-roamers, students, and suits with red meat and bottomless mugs of coffee in their hours of most dire need. The Tasty is there for you. Tonight and forever. Entrees $1-7. Open 24 hrs.

A meal in the vicinity of Harvard Square would not be complete without dessert afterwards. Dens of sin abound, like **Herrell's,** 15 Dunster St., Harvard Sq. (497-2179), whose ice cream, fro-yo and no-moo selections range from classic vanilla to eggnog, peanut butter, and their famous (but lethal) chocolate pudding, the "Best

Chocolate Ice Cream in Boston." Drown in lusciousness inside a vault painted to resemble the watery depths. (Open daily noon-midnight, extended hrs. in summer.) If you prefer your chocolate in squares (other than Harvard), go to Inman Square, to **Rosie's Bakery,** 243 Hampshire St., for a "chocolate orgasm" (open Mon.-Wed. 7:30am-10pm, Thurs.-Fri. 7:30am-11pm, Sat. 8:30am-10pm).

NIGHTLIFE AND ENTERTAINMENT

In warm weather, Cambridge entertainment is free. Street musicians ranging from Andean folk singers to jazz trios staff every streetcorner of Harvard Square. Cafes crowd at all times of year for lunch or after-hours coffee. The low-ceilinged, smoke-and-Heidegger-filled **Café Pamplona** (a.k.a. Café Pompous) 12 Bow St., might be too angst-ridden for you; in summer escape to their outdoor tables. (Open Mon.-Sat. 11am-1am, Sun. 2pm-1am.) The **Coffee Connection,** 36 JFK St. (492-4881), in the Garage, proffers almost blasphemously high-caliber-low-viscosity coffees. The smell is fantastic; try the *café con panna* ($1.50) or the addictive frappuccino. (Open Mon.-Thurs. 7am-11pm, Fri. 7am-midnight, Sat. 9am-midnight, Sun. 9am-11pm.) **Café Algiers,** 40 Brattle St. (492-1557), has 2 beautiful floors of airy, wood-latticed seating (open Mon.-Thurs. 8am-midnight, Fri.-Sat. 8am-1am, Sun. 9am-midnight).

Rich cultural offerings keep Cambridge vital. Harvard sponsors any number of readings and lectures each week; check the kiosks that fill Harvard Yard for posters about the events that most students are too busy to attend. Also look at the windows of one of the over 25 bookstores in the Square to see if any literary luminaries will appear during your visit. Theater, both undergraduate and professional, thrives here. The renowned **American Repertory Theater,** 64 Brattle St., produces shows from Sept.-June. (Tickets $17-38.) Purchase tickets for undergraduate and ART productions through the ticket office at the Loeb Drama Center (547-8300; box office open daily 10am-5:30pm).

Cambridge can also accommodate those whose idea of nightlife is something other than an evening with Umberto Eco: both the **Middle East** (a three-stage nirvana for the musically adventurous; see Food above) and **Johnny D's,** 17 Holland St. (776-9667), in neighboring Somerville (T: Davis), are fine venues for live music. The recent opening of the **House of Blues** in Harvard Square (a blues club-*cum*-theme park masterminded by Isaac "Hard Rock Cafe" Tigrett and Blues "Brother" Dan Aykroyd) has at least brought local and national blues *musicians* to deserved attention (the music *is* stellar); the pre-packaged "wear-and-tear" of the club's interior deserves skeptical consideration, however. (The graffiti in the bathroom was there opening night—you be the judge.) Still, it's blue.

T.T. The Bear's Place, 10 Brookline St., Central Sq. (492-0082). Brings really live, really loud rock bands to its intimate, seemingly makeshift stage. Paul Westerberg began a national tour here incognito in July 1993. Open Mon.-Thurs. 8pm-1am, Fri.-Sun. noon-1am. Cover rarely exceeds $6. Really.

Cantab Lounge, 738 Mass. Ave., Central Sq. (354-2684). For over 10 years, Little Joe Cook and his blues band have been packing the place with local fans and recently enlightened college students. Cover Thurs. $3, Fri.-Sat. $5. Open Mon.-Wed. 8am-1am, Thurs.-Sat. 8am-2am, Sun. noon-1am.

Passim, 47 Palmer St., Harvard Sq. (492-9653). Just off Church St. across from the Border Cafe. This legendary basement coffeehouse has sung along to the likes of Suzanne Vega and Shawn Colvin and still carries the folk-music torch proudly. National and local acts (mainly acoustic) usually check into Passim (pass-EEM) for a full weekend of shows, often two per night; during the week, Bob and Rae Ann tend a gift shop and restaurant. No alcohol, but you can feast on breadsticks and cream cheese. Cover $6-9. Open Tues.-Sat. noon-5:30pm, evening hours vary.

Shays, 58 JFK St., Harvard Sq. A cozy, mahogany-and-brass interior, a choice selection of beers and wines, and an outdoor patio makes this pub/wine bar a popular hangout for Anglophilic Harvard students. Guinness, Bass, Newcastle, Woodpecker Cider, and Boston's own Sam Adams all on tap ($3.25 for a pint). Open daily 11am-1am.

SIGHTS

People-watching—the favorite Cantabrigian pastime aside from reading—may account for the number of cafes. But if you can tear yourself away from staring at balding professors, yuppies, hippies, street punks, and slumming high-schoolers, you might see some interesting buildings as well.

The Massachusetts Institute of Technology (MIT) is as much a tribute to, as an institute of, technology. The campus buildings are a huge slice in the I.M. Pei; it also contains an impressive collection of modern outdoor sculpture, and an "infinite corridor" ¼-mi. long, second only to the Pentagon's. Tours are available weekdays at 10am and 2pm from the Rogers Building, or "Building Number 7" as the ultra-efficient students here term it. Contact MIT Information at 77 Mass. Ave. (253-1000; open Mon.-Fri. 9am-5pm). The **MIT Museum**, 265 Mass. Ave. (253-4444), contains a slide rule collection and wonderful photography exhibits, including the famous stop-action photos of Harold Edgerton. (Open Tues.-Fri. 9am-5pm, Sat-Sun. 1-5pm. $2, seniors and kids under 12 free.)

Up Mass. Ave., the other university seems to shun such futuristic delights for glories of the past, especially its own. **Harvard University** is the oldest university in the country and won't let anyone forget it. Ask at the info center about self-guided, self-gratifying walking tours (see Practical Information above). **Radcliffe College,** founded in 1879 and once its own all-female entity, "merged" with Harvard College in 1971. Now female undergraduates attend Harvard-Radcliffe College, and, as such, go to class, eat, sleep, and brush their teeth with the male undergraduates. Radcliffe has its own buildings northwest of Harvard Yard in a garden oasis, known as Radcliffe Yard, between Brattle St. and Garden St.

The university, if not the universe, revolves around **Harvard Yard.** Step into the Yard and shut out the rest of the world. One moment you'll be dodging an Iveco truck in the square, trying to think straight amidst the cacophonic din of caterwauling street-singers and mendicants, the next you'll be in the Yard listening to the chirping of a cricket while being attacked by aggressive squirrels. In the western half ("The Old Yard"), some of the school's first buildings still stand. Today all Harvard students live in the Yard during their first year of study; John F. Kennedy lived in Weld, while Emerson and Thoreau resided in Hollis. Besides classroom buildings, the Yard's eastern half holds **Memorial Church** and **Widener Library** (495-2413), the largest academic library in the world, containing a significant portion of the collection's 10.5 million volumes. While visitors can't browse among Widener's shelves, they are welcome to examine Harvard's reproduction-copy of the Gutenberg Bible and other rare books in the Harry Elkins Widener Memorial Reading Room, or to take in the tacky John Singer Sargent murals.

The oldest of Harvard's museums, the **Fogg Art Museum,** 32 Quincy St., gathers a considerable collection of works ranging from ancient Chinese jade to contemporary photography, as well as the largest Ingres collection outside of France. The limited display space around its uplifting Italian Renaissance courtyard frequently rotates well-planned exhibits. Across the street, the post-modern exterior of the **Arthur M. Sackler Museum,** 485 Broadway (495-9400), belies a rich collection of ancient Asian and Islamic art. (Both museums open Tues.-Sun. 10am-5pm. Admission to each $4, students and seniors $2.50. Free Sat. mornings.) Hawking over the Fogg, Le Corbusier's guitar-shaped **Carpenter Center,** 24 Quincy St. (495-3251), shows student and professional work with especially strong photo exhibits, not to mention a great film series at the **Harvard Film Archive.** The only building in the U.S. designed by the great architect, the Center is testament to the logic and power of modernism. (Open Mon.-Fri. 9am-11pm, Sat. 9am-6pm, Sun. noon-10pm.) Included in the **Museums of Natural History** at 24 Oxford St. (495-3045), are the **Peabody Museum of Archaeology and Ethnology,** which houses treasures from prehistoric and Native American cultures, and the **Mineralogical and Geological Museums,** containing gems, minerals, ores, and meteorites. But the overhyped "glass flowers" at the **Botanical Museum** draw the largest crowds. A German glass-blower and his son created these remarkably accurate but not at all aesthetic enlarged reproductions of over 840 plant species. (Open Mon.-Sat. 9am-4:30pm, Sun. 1-4:30pm. $3, students and seniors $2, ages 5-15 $1.)

Washington worshiped at **Christ Church** on Garden St., the oldest church in Cambridge, which had its organ pipes melted down for Revolutionary bullets. Soldiers felled in the struggle are buried in the 17th-century **Old Burying Ground** or "God's Acre" on Garden St., also the final resting place of colonial settlers and early Harvard presidents. Behind Garden St., on 105 Brattle St., is the restored **Longfellow House** (876-4491), home of the poet Henry Wadsworth Longfellow and a National Historic Site. Headquarters of the Continental Army in olden days, the site now sponsors garden concerts and poetry readings in the summer; the staff can give you info on local historic sights. Rumor has it that in the summer the occasionally-stressed *Let's Go:Europe* editor Liz Stein may be spotted in the garden. (Tours daily 10:45am-4pm. Admission $2, seniors and under 17 free.) The **Mt. Auburn Cemetery** lies about 1 mi. up the road at the end of Brattle St. This first botanical-garden/cemetery in the U.S. has 170 acres of beautifully landscaped grounds fertilized by Louis Agassiz, Charles Bulfinch, Dorothea Dix, Mary Baker Eddy, and H.W. Longfellow among others. About 1 mi. in the other direction, on Mt. Auburn St. 2 blocks east of JFK St., sits **Lowell House,** where toll the only authentic **Russian Bells** in this hemisphere. On Sundays at 1pm, climb up seven flights into the tower for magnificent views of Boston and a chance to pound away at the 26-ton *zvon* of bells brought from Russia after the Revolution. They say that the *Let's Go: USA and Canada* editor supervises the ringing of these historic bells.

■■■ LEXINGTON AND CONCORD

> Listen, my children and you shall hear/ Of the midnight ride of Paul Revere/ On the 18th of April in '75/ Hardly a man is now alive/ Who remembers that famous day and year.
> —Henry Wadsworth Longfellow, "The Midnight Ride of Paul Revere"

Lexington Inhabitants will constantly remind you that the Minutemen skirmished with advancing British troops on the **Lexington Battle Green,** falling back to the **Old North Bridge** in Concord where colonial troops first officially received orders to fire upon the Redcoats. On the Lexington Green, the **Minuteman Statue** of Captain John Parker—one of the first American casualties—looks back to Boston, still watching for the Redcoats. The surrounding houses seem nearly as historic as the land; the **Hancock-Clarke House,** 36 Hancock St., sheltered John Hancock and Samuel Adams and was Paul Revere's destination the night of his ride. The **Buckman Tavern,** on Hancock St. opposite the Green, had already slung ale for 65 years before it headquartered the Minutemen. The Lexington Historical Society carefully restored the interior to its 1775 appearance. The society also did a number on **Munroe Tavern,** 1332 Mass Ave., 1 mi. from the Green, which served as a field hospital for wounded British. (House and Taverns open mid-April to late Oct. Mon.-Sat. 10am-5pm, Sun. 1-5pm. $2.50 per house, ages 6-16 50¢, under 6 free. All three $5.) Along with a walking map of the area, the **visitors center,** 1875 Mass. Ave. (862-1450), behind the Buckman Tavern, displays a 50-year-old, painstakingly detailed diorama of the Battle of Lexington. (Open daily 9am-5pm; Nov.-May 10am-3pm.)

The easiest access to Lexington is by bike. Take Mass Ave. up from Cambridge or, better yet, the **Minuteman Trail** path which charges from Concord to Bedford (access off Mass Ave. in Arlington) and has access points at key revolutionary spots, including the Lexington visitors center. Bikes are so prevalent in downtown Lexington—an upscale, gorgeous planned community—that they are often not locked.

The **Battle Road** winds 6 mi. from the Lexington Green to Concord and is now part of **Minuteman National Historical Park;** the **Battle Road Visitors Center** (862-7753) on Rte. 2A in Lexington distributes maps of the park and shows a 22-min. film detailing events precipitating the Revolutionary War. (Open mid-April to Nov. 1 daily 9am-5:30pm.) At the **North Bridge Visitors Center,** 174 Liberty St. (508-369-6944), park rangers lead 20-min. interpretive talks at the Old North Bridge over the Concord River, site of "the shot heard 'round the world." (Open daily 9am-5:30pm; mid-Nov.-late April 8:30am-4pm.) The **area code** for Lexington is 617.

Concord   Concord garnered fame not only for its military history but as a U.S. literary capital of the 19th century as well. The Alcotts and Hawthornes once inhabited **Wayside,** 455 Lexington Rd. (369-6975), while Emerson himself lived down the road for the latter part of the century. Now a part of the **Minute Man National Historical Park,** the house is open for public viewing. (Open April-Oct. Tues.-Sun. 9:30am-5pm. $1, under 17 and over 61 free.) The **Concord Museum** (369-9763), directly across the street from the house, houses a reconstruction of Emerson's study alongside Paul Revere's lantern and items from Henry David Thoreau's cabin. (Open Thurs.-Sat. 10am-5pm, Sun. 1-5pm.; May-Dec. Mon.-Sat. 10am-5pm, Sun. 1-5pm. $5, seniors $4, students $3, under 5 $2.) Emerson, Hawthorne, Alcott, and Thoreau all wait for Ichabod Crane on "Author's Ridge" in the **Sleepy Hollow Cemetery** on Rte. 62, three blocks from the center of town.

While alive, Thoreau retreated to **Walden Pond,** 1½ mi. south of Concord on Rte. 126, in 1845 "to live deliberately, to front only the essential facts of life." His pre-hippie handbook *Walden* contains observations about his two-year habitation there. The **Thoreau Lyceum,** 156 Belknap St. (369-5912), national headquarters of the Thoreau Society, will answer questions about this naturalist-philosopher. The Lyceum sponsors the society's convention in July, and has a replica of Thoreau's cabin in its backyard. (Open April-Dec. Mon.-Sat. 10am-5pm, Sun. 2-5pm; early Feb.-March Thurs.-Sat. 10am-5pm, Sun. 2-5pm. $2, students $1.50, kids 50¢.) **Walden Pond State Reservation** (369-3254) is popular with picnickers, swimmers, and boaters. Don't come expecting the same divine solitude Thoreau enjoyed. Granite posts at the far end of the pond mark the site of Thoreau's cabin. (Open April-Oct. daily dawn-dusk. Parking $5.) The Pond only holds 1000 visitors; rangers will turn you away, so call before coming out. When Walden Pond swarms with crowds, head down Rte. 62 east from Concord center to **Great Meadows National Wildlife Refuge** (443-4661), another of Thoreau's haunts (open daily dawn-dusk).

Concord and Lexington make easy daytrips from Boston. Concord, just 20 mi. north, is served by **MBTA** trains from North Station ($2.75). MBTA buses from Alewife station in Cambridge run several times daily to Lexington (60¢). (See Boston: Practical Information.) The **area code** for Concord is 508.

■■■ SALEM

On one hand, Salem seems to resent the hullabaloo about the "witch stuff." Instead, they'll try to tell you how the town was once the sixth-largest city in the United States—a trading center with a fleet so vast that merchants in faraway lands believed "Salem" was an independent country. They will point you towards the many historic homes in the city center and the excellent museums and entreat you (usually with success) to gain an appreciation of Salem's sea-faring days.

On the other hand, Salem realizes that most of its tourists come here for its more occult offerings. In 1992, local authorities brewed up a year-long Witch Trials Tercentenary, which created a flap among witches in the area who resented their beliefs being concocted into a tourist gimmick. The city has had a long-standing practice of capitalizing on the sensationalized **witch trials** of the summer of 1692, when a volatile combination of superstition, small-town jealousy, boredom, and fermented wheat exploded in one of the ugliest incidents in American history. Today, the witch-on-a-broomstick motif appears just about everywhere—on the daily newspaper, on the police uniforms, on the shops and bars, and even on the garbage cans.

Salem's most substantive sight, the **Peabody Museum,** in East India Sq. (745-1876, for recorded info 745-9500), recalls the port's former leading role in Atlantic whaling and merchant shipping. (Daily guided tour at 2pm; in summer also at 11am. Open Mon.-Sat. 10am-5pm, Sun. noon-5pm. $6, seniors and students $5, ages 6-18 $3.) Down by the waterfront, the National Park Service administers the **Salem Maritime National Historic Site,** a collection of three wharves and several historic buildings along Derby St. which are definitely worth exploring. Federal officials, including Nathaniel Hawthorne, collected import duties until 1917 at the **Customs House,** 178 Derby St. (744-4323), where the narrator of Hawthorne's novel claims to find *The Scarlet Letter.* (Open daily 9am-6pm; off-season 9am-5pm. No import duty is charged for the self-guided tour.) Hawthorne lost his desk job here thanks to the spoils system; he later took them to task in his writing.

If you succumb to your baser touristic instincts, start at the gothic **Witch Museum** (744-1692—notice the numerology), witch presents a melodramatic but informative multi-media presentation that fleshes out the history of the trials. (Open Mon.-Fri. 10am-5pm, Sat.-Sun. 10am-7pm; Sept.-June daily 10am-5pm; shows on the ½ hr. $4, seniors $3.50, ages 6-14 $2.50.) Never actually a dungeon, the **Witch Dungeon,** 16 Lynde St. (741-3570), has actresses present skits about the trials which amplify the toil and trouble of the proceedings. (Open early May-early Nov. daily 10am-5pm. $3.75, seniors $3.25, ages 6-14 $2.25.) The child in you will like the spooky atmosphere of the dungeon tour; the adult in you will enjoy the cynical commentary that accompanies it.

Salem boasts the "second most famous house in America," the **House of Seven Gables,** 54 Turner St. (744-0991), built in 1668 and made famous by Nathaniel Hawthorne's Gothic romance of the same name. Tourists who've most likely never read the book tromp through the place where Hawthorne's aunt once lived. Prices are steeper than the famed roof. (Open daily 10am-4:30pm; July-Aug. Fri.-Wed. 9:30am-5:30pm, Thurs. 9:30am-8:30pm. Tour $6.50, ages 6-17 $4, access to grounds $1, although you can see all 7 gables from the street for free.)

From the T-station on Bridge St., head down Washington to Essex; on your left will be a pedestrian-only road to the **Museum Place mall.** The National Park Service runs two **information centers:** one in the mall (741-3648; open daily 9am-6pm, off-season 9am-5pm) and one at Derby Wharf (745-1470; open daily 8:30am-5pm). Both provide a free map of historic Salem. A 1.3-mi. **Heritage Trail** traces an easy footpath past all the main sights in town, marked clearly by a painted red line (blood?) on the pavement. The **Essex Institute,** 132 Essex St., is an important archive of materials relating to New England history which also contains a museum crammed to the rafters with silver, furniture, portraits, toys, and other oddities. Three old houses on the same block under the institute's care are open to visitors during frequent tours. Due to a consolidation, the name of the Institute may change soon; details are unavailable as we go to press. (Museum and houses open Mon.-Wed. and Fri.-Sat. 9am-5pm, Thurs. 9am-9pm, Sun. noon-5pm; Nov.-May Tues.-Sat. 9am-5pm, Sun. noon-5pm. Admission to all $6, ages 6-16 $3.50.)

Salem is packed to the belfries during Halloween with a week-long festival called **Haunted Happenings,** which includes costume balls, ghost stories, and a parade. Book months in advance if you plan to be in town for Halloween.

Food is about the only inexpensive commodity in Salem; cheap subs ping at **Red's Sandwich Shop,** 15 Central St., which serves breakfast (55¢-$3.50) and sandwiches ($1.25-3.50) at small tables and a cozy counter. (Open Mon.-Sat. 5:30am-3pm, Sun. 6am-1pm.) The restaurants on Derby St. close to the wharfside attractions serve a range of American fare which is only slightly overpriced.

Salem hexes 20 mi. northeast of Boston; take the Rockport/Ipswich commuter train from North Station (1 per hr.; ½ hr.; $2.50). The **area code** for Salem is 508.

CAPE COD

> The time must come when this coast will be a place of resort for those New Englanders who really wish to visit the sea-side. At present it is wholly unknown to the fashionable world, and probably it will never be agreeable to them.
>
> —Henry David Thoreau

Yeah, right, Henry. Think again. In 1602, when English navigator and Jamestown colonist Bartholomew Gosnold landed on this peninsula in southeastern Massachusetts, he named it in honor of all the codfish he caught in the surrounding waters. In recent decades, tourism—not fishing—has sustained the Cape. Within this small strip of land you can find a great diversity of delicate landscapes—long unbroken stretches of beach, salt marshes, hardwood forests, deep freshwater ponds carved by glaciers, and desert-like dunes constantly being sculpted by the wind. The fragility of the environment is palpable; every year chunks of the Cape's delicate ecosystem wash away into the ocean and sand dunes visibly recede under tourists' careless trampling. When the Cape's forests were destroyed for lumber to build houses and fences, the peninsula began to wash away into the sea. Local authorities then required citizens to plant beach grass in the early 1800s. President Kennedy established the Cape Cod National Seashore in 1961 to protect less developed areas from the tide of rampant commercialism. Blessed with an excellent hostel system, Cape Cod is an ideal budget seaside getaway and is used by many cross-country travelers as a place to rest and relax after cramming in the cultural sights of urban America. It also serves as the gateway to Martha's Vineyard and Nantucket.

In a bit of confusing terminology, the part of Cape Cod closer to the mainland is called the **Upper Cape**, which is suburbanized and the most developed area on the Cape. As you proceed away from the mainland, you travel "down Cape" until you get to the **Lower Cape; the National Seashore** encompasses much of this area. Cape Cod resembles a bent arm, with **Wood's Hole** at its armpit, **Chatham** at the elbow, and **Provincetown** at its clenched fist. Accordingly, Cape Codders often use their arms to give directions.

Cycling is the best way to travel the Cape's gentle slopes. The park service can give you a free map of the trails or sell you the detailed **Cape Cod Bike Book** ($3.50; also available at most of the Cape's bookstores). The 135-mi. **Boston-Cape Cod Bikeway** connects Boston to Provincetown at land's end. Some of the most scenic bike trails in the country line either side of the **Cape Cod Canal** in the National Seashore, and the 14-mi. **Cape Cod Rail Trail** from Dennis to Eastham.

The **area code** for the Cape is 508.

■■■ CAPE COD NATIONAL SEASHORE

As early as 1825, the Cape was so heavily damaged by the hand of man that the town of Truro mandated local residents to plant beach grass and keep their cows off the dunes; the sea was threatening to wash the sandy town away and make Provincetown an island. This fragile environment is easily disturbed, and conservation efforts culminated in 1961 with the creation of the Cape Cod National Seashore, which includes much of the Lower Cape from Provincetown south to Chatham.

Most visitors are simply not prepared for the beauty of this landscape, one of the country's greatest treasures. Here you'll find over 30 mi. of soft, wide, uninterrupted sandy beaches, tucked under tall clay cliffs spotted with 19th-century lighthouses. You can also explore salt marshes, home to migrating and native waterfowl, or go galumphing through the great Sand Dunes near Provincetown. You can squintingly contemplate both a sunrise and a sunset reflecting off broad expanses of water.

There are even warm, fresh-water ponds where you can escape for a dip when the waves or the crowds at the beach become too intense; try Gull or Long Pond in Wellfleet or Pilgrim Lake in Truro.

Thanks to conservationism, this area largely has escaped the condo-strip board-walk commercialism that afflicts most seacoasts in America. Although some of the beaches are crowded in the summer, it is surprisingly easy to escape the crush of humanity; a 20-min. walk away from the lifeguards can take you away from the hordes of umbrella- and cooler-luggers. Or hike one of the underused nature trails, and you'll be impressed by the wide variety of habitats that huddle together on this narrow slice of land.

Beachgoers face one eternal question: ocean or bay. The ocean beaches attract with whispering winds and singing surf; the water on the bay side is calmer, a bit warmer, and better for swimming. The National Seashore overseas six beaches: **Coast Guard** and **Nauset Light** in Eastham, **Marconi** in Wellfleet, **Head of the Meadow** in Truro, and **Race Point** and **Herring Cove** in Provincetown. Parking costs $5 per day and $15 per season. Walkers and riders are supposed to pay a $2 entrance fee, but this is rarely collected.

To park at any other beach, you'll need a town permit. Each town has a different beach-parking policy, but permits usually cost $25-30 per week, $75 per season, or $10 per day. To avoid a parking fiasco (beaches can be miles from any other legal parking and police with tow trucks roam the area like vultures), call Town Hall before heading for the waves. On sunny days, parking lots usually fill up by 11am or earlier. If sitting in a metal box under the scorching sun is not your idea of a good time, rent a bike and ride in. Most town beaches do not require bikers and walkers to pay an entrance fee. All ocean beaches are worth the visit, but at Wellfleet and Truro you are more likely to experience the Cape's famous, endangered sand dunes. **Cahoon Hollow Beach** in Wellfleet stands out with its spectacular, cliff-like dunes, particularly young crowd, and day parking availability.

Nine self-guiding **nature trails** wind through an extraordinary range of beautiful landscapes. One of the best walks is the **Great Island Trail** in Wellfleet, an 8-mi. loop taking you through pine forests, grassy marshes, and a ridge with a view of the bay and Provincetown. A shorter and less strenuous walk starts from the visitors center at **Salt Pond**—a 1-mi. loop which gives a good vantage of the Salt Pond, where shore birds flock to feed on the rich influx of vegetation the tide brings in. Also inquire at the visitors center about the three bike trails maintained by the park.

Camping is illegal on the public lands of the national seashore. See Lower Cape for accommodations in the area.

Start your exploration at the **National Seashore's Salt Pond Visitors Center** (255-3421), at Salt Pond, off U.S. 6 in Eastham (open daily 9am-6pm, Sept.-June 9am-4:30pm). The center offers info and advice on the whole seashore, as well as free 10-min. films on the half-hour and a free museum which has excellent exhibits on the human and natural history of the Cape.

■■■ UPPER CAPE

■ Hyannis

JFK spent his summers in nearby Hyannisport, and though the Kennedy Compound still houses his family, you can't get anywhere near it. Though Hyannis itself has a handful of tourist attractions such as an art museum and a stage with big-name sing-ers, it's really a transportation hub; most travelers stop here on their way to the true jewels of the Cape. Go through and get out as quickly as possible; the Kennedys *aren't* going to meet you at the bus station.

Accommodations If you need a place to stay the night before moving on, the **HyLand Hostel (HI/AYH)**, 465 Falmouth Rd. (775-2970), situated among three acres of pine trees, offers the 40 most affordable beds in Hyannis. 1½ mi. from the bus station, go west to Bearses Way, then north to Falmouth Rd. (Rte. 28) and turn left. The hostel is a few hundred yards from the traffic light. You can park in their lot for $2 per day if you aren't sleeping there—a good deal if you're planning a trip to the islands. (Mountain bikes available to members for $8.50-10.50 per day. Linen $2. Check in 7:30-9am and 5-10pm. Reservations essential June-Aug. $10, nonmembers $13. Open March-Nov.)

Practical Information Hyannis is tattooed midway across the Cape's upper arm, 3 mi. south of U.S. 6 on Nantucket Sound. The **Hyannis Area Chamber of Commerce**, 1481 Route 132 (775-2201), about 3 mi. up the road from the bus station, can help and hands out the *Hyannis Guidebook*. (Open Mon.-Thurs. 9am-5pm, Fri. 9am-7pm, Sat. 9am-4:30pm, Sun. 11am-3pm. Closed Sundays Sept.-May.)

   Plymouth & Brockton (746-0378) runs a Boston-to-Provincetown bus four times a day which makes a ½-hr. layover at the **Hyannis Bus Station**, 17 Elm St. (775-5524), and also stops in Plymouth, Sagamore, Yarmouth, Orleans, Wellfleet, and Truro, among others. (Boston to Hyannis: 3½ hr., $19. Hyannis to Provincetown: 1½ hr., $9.) **Bonanza Bus Lines** (800-556-3815) operates a line to New York City (6 per day, 6 hr., $39, with stop in Providence). **Amtrak**, 252 Main St. (800-872-7245), sends a direct train from New York City to Hyannis on Fri., and one from Hyannis to New York on Sun. (6 hr., $61). For info on **ferries** to Martha's Vineyard and Nantucket, see the listings for those islands. Hyannis's **ZIP code** is 02601.

■ Sandwich

The oldest town on the Cape, Sandwich cultivates a charm unmatched by its neighbors in the Upper Cape. Sandwich glass became famous for its beauty and workmanship when the Boston & Sandwich Glass Company was founded here in 1825. The original company is gone, but you can still see master glassblowers shaping their works of art from blobs of molten sand at **Pairpoint Crystal** on Rte. 6-A, just across the town border in Sagamore (888-2344; open daily 8:30am-6pm, glass blowing Mon.-Fri. 8:30am-4:30pm; free).

Practical Information and Camping Sandwich lies at the intersection of Rte. 6A and 130, about 13 mi. from Hyannis. The Plymouth and Brockton bus makes its closest stop in Sagamore, 3 mi. west. You can also reach Sandwich from Hyannis via the **Cape Cod Railroad** (771-3788), a scenic 1-hr. ride through cranberry bogs and marshes (3 per day from Main and Center St. in Hyannis; $10.50 round-trip).

   Across the Sagamore Bridge, **Scusset Beach** (888-0859), right on the canal near the junction of U.S. 6 and Rte. 3, offers fishing and camping. (Sites—mostly for RVs—$12, hookup $18, day use $5 per carload.) The **Shawme-Crowell State Forest** (888-0351), on Rte. 130 and U.S. 6, has 280 wooded campsites with showers and campfires but no hookups. (Open mid-March-late Nov.; $12, including parking at Scusset Beach.) **Peters Pond Park Campground,** Cotuit Rd. (477-1775), in south Sandwich, offers aquatic activities, a grocery store, showers, and a few prime waterside sites ($18-31, open mid-April to mid-Oct).

Sights The **Sandwich Glass Museum** (888-0251), on Tupper Rd. in Sandwich Center, preserves many 19th-century products with a coherence and quality unusual in a small town museum (open daily 9:30am-4:30pm; Nov.-March Wed.-Sun. 9:30am-4pm; $3, under 12 50¢). The **Thornton W. Burgess Museum** (888-6870) on Water St. pays tribute to the Sandwich-born naturalist who wrote tales about Peter Rabbit and the "dear old briar patch" (free). Ask for directions to the actual briar patch, **The Green Briar Nature Center and Jam Kitchen,** 6 Discovery Rd. Wander through trails and wildflower gardens, or watch jam-making in the center kitchen Wed. and Sat. (Open Mon.-Sat. 10am-4pm, Sun. 1-4pm; Jan.-March Tues.-Sat. 10am-4pm. Free.) **Sandy Neck Beach,** 3 mi. east of Sandwich on Sandy

Neck Rd. off Rte. 6-A, is the best beach on the Upper Cape. Stroll 6 mi. along Cape Cod Bay on beautifully polished egg-sized granite pebbles, or hike out through the verdant dunes (only on the marked trails; the plants are very fragile).

■■■ LOWER CAPE

Much less suburbanized than the Upper Cape, the Lower Cape preserves the weathered-shingle, dirt-road atmosphere of yore. In some towns, the majority of the land belongs to the National Seashore. On a whole, development here has mercifully been restrained, leaving an unsullied paradise for generations of vacationers to discover anew. Hop in a bike or a car, wander aimlessly to a picturesque vista, and meditate on life, love, and lighthouses.

■ Truro, Wellfleet, Eastham, and Orleans

From Orleans to Truro the Lower Cape shines thanks to its development-free beaches, blueberry- and pine-scented beaches, and unique impressionistic light. Go there to experience the dazzling natural setting which has inspired countless artists. When searching for night activities, head to Provincetown.

Accommodations, Camping, and Food There are two hostels in or near the national seashore. The **Little America Hostel (HI/AYH),** at the far end of North Pamet Rd., Truro 02666 (349-3889), 1 mi. from a bus stop, is one of the best hostels in the country. You can see the ocean through the big picture windows in the large, wood-paneled kitchen and eating area; it's just a 100-yd. walk to the beach. (Office open 7:30-9:30am and 5-10pm. $10, nonmembers $13. Reservations essential. Open early June-early Sept.) The **Mid-Cape HI/AYH Hostel** (255-2785) sleeps many bikers from the Cape Cod Rail Trail in its half-dozen cabins. The location is wooded, and quiet...until the local girl scouts troop by. Ask to be let off the Plymouth-Brockton bus to Provincetown at the traffic circle in Orleans (*not* the Eastham stop), walk out on the exit to Rock Harbor, turn right on Bridge Rd., and take a right onto Goody Hallet Rd., ½-mi. from U.S. 6. (Office open 7:30-9:30am and 5-10:30pm. $10, nonmembers $13. Reservations essential July-Aug. Open mid-May-mid-Sept.) See also accommodations in Provincetown.

There are seven private campgrounds on the Lower Cape; pick up a free campground directory at the **Cape Cod Chamber of Commerce** in Hyannis. One of the best places to pitch a tent is **Nickerson State Park** (896-3491) on Rte. 6A in Brewster, on the Cape Cod Rail Trail bike path. There are two large ponds with a boat rental on the waterfront, showers, flush toilets, but no hookups. (Sites $12. No reservations. The 418 sites fill quickly.) About 7 mi. southeast of Provincetown on U.S. 6, several popular campgrounds nestle among the dwarf pines by the dunelands of the villages of North Truro and Truro. **North Truro Camping Area,** on Highland Rd. (487-1847), ½-mi. east of U.S. 6., has small sandy sites. ($15 for 2-people, hookup $20. Each additional person $7.)

Located right at the oceanfront at the end of Cahoon Hollow Rd. off U.S. 6, the **Beachcomber** (349-6055) serves up large baskets of fish and chips ($6), burgers and fries ($5), and attracts a young crowd of bathing-suit clad beach mongers (open in summer daily noon-1am). The **Bayside Lobster Hutt** (349-6333), on Commercial St., Wellfleet, offers the cheapest lobster dinners ($12) in the area in a very casual, usually crowded setting, where you can bring your own booze (open July-Aug. noon-10pm, June and Sept. 4:30-9pm).

Sights and Activities Cape Cod is dotted with historical houses and buildings, most of which are older than the United States. The **First Congregation Parish of Truro** (United Church of Christ) will transport you back to the 19th century. The church, built in 1827, has changed little since its construction; electricity was installed just 30 years ago, and the outhouse (painted church-white) still serves in place of new-fangled toilets. Take the Bridge Rd. exit off U.S. 6 and turn right onto Town Hall Rd. (Sunday morning services at 10am.)

Without streams to provide power, Cape Codders built windmills to grind corn and pump seawater into their saltworks. On U.S. 6 at Samoset Rd., the **Eastham Windmill** was built in 1680 to grind corn—a crop grown here by Native Americans long before newcomers from Europe arrived. The windmill still functions, and its interior is open to the public. The guide explains how the roof can be swiveled on rollers to face the wind. (Open July-Aug. Mon.-Sat. 10am-5pm, Sun. 1-5pm. Free.)

The **Wellfleet Bay Wildlife Sanctuary,** off U.S. 6 in Wellfleet (349-2615), maintains a large nature preserve with daily organized programs such as bird walks, canoe trips, night-time walks and lectures. (Open daily 8am-dusk. Admission $3.) A $1.25 booklet identifies over 70 species of plants and birds on the 1-mi. **Goose Pond Trail.** The sanctuary, run by the Massachusetts Audubon Society, also guides tours of the **Monomoy National Wildlife Refuge.** The tours (3-7 hr., $30-50) leave several times a week from Chatham. Call the sanctuary for more details.

People don't usually associate Cape Cod with fresh water, but melting glaciers left behind deep "kettle ponds" which are warmer and less crowded than the salty beaches. One of the best spots to paddle is **Gull Pond,** off Gull Pond Rd. in Wellfleet, which connects by a series of shallow channels to three more secluded ponds. From Higgins Pond you can see the home of the Wellfleet Oysterman, where Thoreau stayed and about which he wrote a chapter in *Cape Cod.* **Jack's Boat Rentals** (349-9808) has a "u-pick-up" location on U.S. 6 in Wellfleet, where you can rent a canoe ($35 per 4 hr., $55 per day) or kayak ($32 per 4 hr., $45 per day). At their waterfront locations on Gull Pond, Beach Point in North Truro, and Flax Pond in Nickerson State Park, you can rent sailboats, as well.

■■■ PROVINCETOWN

Provincetown is the end of the road—where Cape Cod ends and the wide Atlantic begins. Two-thirds of "P-Town" is conservation land protected by the national seashore; the inhabited sliver snuggles up against the harbor on the south side of town. Once a busy whale port, today artists and not sailors fill the major thoroughfare—Commercial Street—where numerous Portuguese bakeries and gay and lesbian bookstores happily coexist. Browsing strollers clog the narrow width of pavement to the exclusion of automobiles.

For over a century, Provincetown has been known for its broad acceptance of many different lifestyles, and a widely known gay and lesbian community has flowered here. Over half the couples on the street are same-sex, and a walk here makes it quietly plain that sexual orientation does not adhere to any stereotype of size, shape, color, or dress.

Practical Information Provincetown rests in the cupped hand at the end of the Cape Cod arm, 123 mi. away from Boston as the crow drives, or 3 hr. by ferry across Massachusetts Bay. Parking spots are always rare and virtually cease to exist on grey days when the Cape's frustrated sun-worshippers flock to Provincetown, its funky stores, and fascinating people-watching scene. **Bradford Street** is the town's auto-friendly thoroughfare; follow the parking signs to dock your car for $5-7 per day. **MacMillan Wharf** is at the center of town, just down the hill from the Pilgrim Monument. Whale-watching boats, the Boston ferry, and the bus all leave from here.

Emergency is 911. The **Provincetown Chamber of Commerce** sits at 307 Commercial St. (487-3424), MacMillan Wharf (open mid-June-late Sept. daily 9am-5pm; April-mid-June and late Sept.-Nov. Mon.-Fri. 10am-4pm). Acquire info on the national seashore and free guides to the nature and bike trails at **Province Lands Visitors Center,** Race Point Rd. (487-1256; open July-Aug. daily 9am-6pm; mid-April-June and Sept.-Nov. daily 9am-4:30pm). Instead of Greyhound hop **Plymouth**

and **Brockton Bus** (1-746-0378), which stops at MacMillan Wharf, behind Provincetown Chamber of Commerce (with schedules and information). 4 buses per day in summer to Boston ($19, 3½ hr.). Also at the Chamber of Commerce is **Bay State Cruises** (487-9284), 67 Long Wharf, Boston. (Operates May 27-mid-June and Labor Day-Columbus Day weekends only; summer daily.) Ferries to Boston (1 per day, 3 hr., $15, same-day round-trip $25). To get around in Provincetown and Herring Cove Beach, take the **Provincetown Shuttle Bus** (487-3353). 1 route travels the length of Bradford St., the other from MacMillan Wharf to Herring Cove Beach. (Operates late June-early Sept. daily 8am-midnight; 10am-6pm for the beach. Fare $1.25, seniors 75¢. 1 bus per hr.) Or, rent a bike at **Arnold's,** 329 Commercial St. (487-0844). 3-speeds, 10-speeds, and mountain bikes ($2.75-4 per hr., $7-12 per day, deposit and ID required; credit cards accepted; open daily 8:30am-5:30pm). The **post office** (487-0163) hangs at 211 Commercial St. (open Mon.-Fri. 8:30am-5pm, Sat. 9:30-11:30am). The **ZIP code** is 02657.

Accommodations and Camping Provincetown is known for old clap-board houses lining narrow roads—fortunately, guesthouses are a part of that tradition, although not all are affordable. One of the best hostels in America is only 10 mi. away, secluded in nearby Truro (see Lower Cape). The cheapest bed in town is at **The Outermost House,** 28 Winslow St. (487-4378), barely 100 yds. from the Pilgrim monument. $14 gets you a bed in one of the cottages, a kitchen, free parking, and no curfew. There are no lockers here and the cottages are often left vulnerably unlocked. (Office open 8-10am and 6-10pm. Reservations recommended for weekends.) In the quiet east end of town, the **Cape Codder,** 570 Commercial St. (487-0131, call 9am-3pm or 9-11pm), welcomes you back with archetypical Cape Cod decor, right down to the wicker furniture. Offers access to a private beach. (Mid-June to mid-Sept. singles $26-52, doubles $36-52; off-season about $10 less. Light continental breakfast included. Open May-Oct.)

Camping is expensive here. The western part of **Coastal Acres Camping Court** (487-1700), a 1-mi. walk from the center of town west on Bradford or Commercial St. and right on West Vine St., has crowded sites; try to snag one on the waterside. (3-day min. stay. Sites $19, with electricity and water $25.) For more accommodations in the area see Truro, Wellfleet, Eastham, and Orleans, on the Lower Cape.

Food Sit-down meals in Provincetown will cost you a pretty penny. Grab a bite at one of the Portuguese bakeries on Commercial St., or at a seafood shack on Mac-Millan Wharf. The **Mayflower Family Dining** restaurant, 300 Commercial St. (487-0121), established in 1921, has walls lined with ancient caricatures. Choose from Portuguese ($6-8.50) and Italian ($5-8) entrees, or Puritan seafood meals ($7-10). (Open daily 11:30am-10pm.) **George's Pizza,** 275 Commercial St. (487-3744), serves up scrumptious deep-dish pizza ($5-7.50). Devour while sitting at the outside deck. (Open daily 11am-1am.) If you are staying in the hostel in Truro, make use of its excellent kitchen. The **A&P** super- and seafood market on Shank Painter Rd. will fill your grocery bag more cheaply than will the smaller groceries in Truro.

Sights Provincetown has long been a refuge for artists and craftsmen; you can look but not touch (to say *nothing* of buying!) at any of the over 20 galleries—most are free and can be found east of **MacMillan Wharf** on Commercial St. (Most are open in the afternoon and evening until 11pm, but take a 2-hr. break for dinner. Get the free *Provincetown Gallery Guide* for complete details.) The kingpin of the artsy district is the **Provincetown Art Association and Museum,** 460 Commercial St. (487-1750), established in 1914. Alongside the permanent 500-piece collection, it exhibits works by new Provincetown artists. (Open late June-Sept. daily noon-5pm and 9-10pm. $2, seniors and kids $1.)

Contrary to popular belief, the Pilgrims first landed at Provincetown, not Plymouth. They moved on two weeks later in search of better farmland. The **Pilgrim**

Monument (487-1310) on High Pole Hill commemorates that 17-day Puritan lay-over, and as the nation's tallest granite structure (255 ft.) serves as a dandy navigation aid to mariners. It also affords a gorgeous panorama of the Cape and, on clear days, a glimpse of Boston's skyscrapers. The **Provincetown Museum** at its base exhibits a broad swath of Cape history, from whaling artifacts to dollhouses.

Activities and Entertainment Whales are still hunted by Provincetown seamen, but telephoto lenses and not harpoons are used today to shoot these mighty mammals. **Whale-watch cruises** are some of P-town's most popular attractions, and several companies offer essentially the same service. The ride out to the feeding waters takes 40 min., and you will cruise around them for about 2 hrs. The companies claim that whales are sighted on 99% of the journeys. Tickets cost about $16, but there are many discounts, and since competition is fierce you may be able to successfully haggle the price down. Three of your options are **Dolphin Fleet** (255-3857 or 800-826-9300), **Portuguese Princess** (487-2651 or 800-442-3188), and **Provincetown Whale-Watch** (487-3322 or 800-992-9333). All leave from and operate ticket booths on MacMillan Wharf.

Back on *terra firma*, one of Provincetown's most entertaining attractions can be found sporadically at the corner of Commercial and Standish St. There, police officer extraordinaire Donald Thomas directs traffic to the rhythm of his whistle, hurling arms, and dancing feet. Dozens stop wide-eyed to watch this unusual ballet.

Provincetown has a nightlife with no holds barred; a local bumper sticker reads "Your place, then mine." The scene is almost totally gay- and lesbian-oriented but open to all. Most places have cover charges and shut down at 1am. Frantic, funky, and uninhibited dancing shakes the ground nightly for a mixed crowd at the **Back-room,** 247 Commercial St. (487-1430; 10pm-1am, $5 cover). The **Atlantic House,** 6 Masonic Ave. (487–3821), offers dancing and two bars to a predominantly gay crowd, and is proud to be the "oldest gay bar on the oldest seacoast" (dancing cover $3-5; open daily 9pm-1am; bars open daily noon-1am).

■■■ MARTHA'S VINEYARD

In 1606, British explorer Bartholomew Gosnold named Martha's Vineyard after his daughter and the wild grapes that grew here. In the 18th century, the Vineyard prospered as a port, with shepherding the main home trade. Try to visit the Vineyard in fall, when the tourist season wanes, weather turns crisp, leaves turn color, and prices drop. If you simply *must* visit in summer, try to avoid weekends.

Martha's Vineyard poses as the most famous island off the New England Coast with "quaintness" as its undeniable unifying theme—from the dunes of the wide sandy beaches to the dark, beautiful inland woods. The landscape captivates even the most frequent of visitors, converting many to semi-residents. In August, 1993, this captivating island won out over all other quaint summer resorts as the destination for President Bill Clinton's vacation. Walter Cronkite, Billy Joel, Spike Lee, and Jackie Onassis all hobnob on the island (probably not together); however, unlike many of its continental counterparts, "the Vineyard" is as welcoming budgetarily as it is scenically. Seven different communities comprise Martha's Vineyard, behaving in many ways as islands unto themselves:

Oak Bluffs, 3 mi. west of Vineyard Haven on State Rd., is the most youth-oriented of the Vineyard villages. Tour **Trinity Park,** near the harbor, and see the famous "Gingerbread Houses" (minutely detailed, elaborately pastel Victorian cottages) or Oak Bluffs' **Flying Horses Carousel,** on Circuit Ave. Ext., the oldest in the nation (built in 1876), containing 20 handcrafted horses with real horsehair tails and manes. (Open daily 10am-10pm. Fare $1.)

Edgartown, 7 mi. south of Oak Bluffs, displays a waterfront cluster of stately Federal-style homes built for whaling captains; skip the shops and stores here and visit the town's historic sights maintained by **Dukes County Historical Society,** School and Cooke St. (627-4441).

West Tisbury, 12 mi. west of Edgartown on the West Tisbury-Edgartown Rd., hosts the only vineyard on the Vineyard, the **Chicama Vineyards,** on Stoney Hill Rd. (693-0309), off State Rd. Free tasting follows the tour. (Open Jan.-April Fri.-Sat. 1-4pm; May Mon.-Sat. noon-5pm; June-Oct. Mon.-Sat. 11am-5pm, Sun. 1-5pm. Free.) The town supplies a well-stocked general store, providing sustenance for the trip "up-island."

Gay Head, 12 mi. off West Tisbury, offers just about the best view in all of New England. The local Wampanoog frequently saved sailors whose ships wrecked on the breath-absconding **Gay Head Cliffs.** The 100-million-year-old precipice contains a collage of brilliant colors with 1 of 5 lighthouses on the island.

Menemsha and Chilmark, a little northeast of Gay Head, gives good coastline, claiming the only working fishing town on the island, where tourists can fish off the pier or purchase fresh lobster.

Vineyard Haven has more tacky t-shirt shops and fewer charming old homes than other towns.

The western end of the island is called "up island," from the nautical days when sailors had to tack upwind to get there. The three largest towns of Oak Bluffs, Vineyard Haven, and Edgartown are "down island" and have flatter terrain.

Practical Information Though only about 30 mi. across at its widest point, the Vineyard is heavy with the fruit of 15 beaches and one state forest. A good free map, as well as brochures and advice, is available at the **Martha's Vineyard Chamber of Commerce,** Beach Rd., Vineyard Haven (693-0085; open Mon.-Fri. 9am-5pm, Sat. 10am-2pm; Sept.-May Mon.-Fri. 9am-5pm; mailing address: P.O. Box 1698, Vineyard Haven 02568).

Ferries serve the island from Hyannis (778-2600); New Bedford (997-1688); Falmouth (548-4800); Montauk, NY (516-668-5709); and Nantucket (778-2600), but the shortest and cheapest ride, as well as the only one to transport cars, leaves from Wood's Hole on Cape Cod. From there, **Steamship Authority** (548-3788) sends 10 boats per day on the 45-min. ride. (One way $4.50, bike $2.75, kid $2.25.) The ferry company has three parking lots ($7 per day) and provide a shuttle service to the dock. **Bonanza** buses (800-556-3815) stop at the Ferry Terminal in Wood's Hole and depart, via Bowrne, for Boston (11 per day, 1¾ hr., $12) and New York (6 per day, 6 hr., $39), with a stop in Providence, RI.

Transporting a car can cost $38-48, and the island isn't designed for them anyway. Bring a bike or rent one at **Martha's Vineyard Scooter and Bike** (693-0782), at the Steamship Authority Dock in Vineyard Haven (open daily 8am-8pm); **Vineyard Bike and Moped,** Circuit Ave. Ext. in Oak Bluffs (693-4498; open daily 9am-6pm); or **R.W. Cutler,** Main St., Edgartown (627-4052; open April 7-Oct. 15 daily 9am-5pm). All three charge $10-12 per day for a three-speed, $15-18 per day for a mountain bike or hybrid. Trail maps are available at R.W. Cutler. Most **taxis** are vans and fares are negotiable; set a price before you get in. In Oak Bluffs, call 693-0037; in Edgartown 627-4677, in Vineyard Haven 693-3705. The **Down-Island Shuttle bus** (693-1589) connects Vineyard Haven (Union St.), Oak Bluffs (Ocean Park), and Edgartown (Church St.) every 15 min. from 10am-6pm, and every 30 min. from 8-10am and 6pm-midnight ($1.50). Buses run July-Aug.

The **area code** for Martha's Vineyard is 508.

Accommodations and Camping The most deluxe youth hostel you may ever encounter also offers the least expensive beds on the island. The lovely **Manter Memorial Youth Hostel (HI/AYH),** Edgartown Rd., West Tisbury (693-2665), 7 mi. south of Vineyard Haven, 5 mi. inland from Edgartown on the bike route, is quite crowded in summer. (Check in 7:30-9:30am and 5-10:30pm. $10, nonmembers $13. Linen $1. Open April-Nov. Reservations required.) The Chamber of Commerce provides a list of inns and guest houses; all recommend reservations in July and August, especially for packed weekends. For relatively inexpensive rooms, the century-old **Nashua House** (693-0043), on Kennebec Ave. in Oak Bluffs, sits across from the post office. Some rooms overlook the ocean; all are brightly painted and cheerful. (Singles $25, doubles $49; on weekends $40/$65. Off-season $20/$29.)

Campers have two options. **Martha's Vineyard Family Campground,** 1 mi. from Vineyard Haven on Edgartown Rd. (693-3772), has 180 sites. Groceries are available nearby. Metered showers. (Sites $23 for 2 people. Each additional person $8. Open mid-May-mid-Oct.) **Webb's Camping Area,** Barnes Rd., Oak Bluffs (693-0233), is more spacious, with 150 shaded sites. (Sites $23-25, depending on degree of privacy, for 2 people. Each additional person $8. Open mid-May-mid-Sept.)

Food and Entertainment Cheap sandwich and lunch places speckle the Vineyard—the traveler who watches the wallet rather than the waistline may have the best luck in Vineyard Haven and Oak Bluffs. Fried-food shacks across the island sell clams, shrimp, and potatoes. Sit-down dinners generally cost at least $15. A glorious exception is **Louis',** State Rd., Vineyard Haven (693-3255), serving Italian food in a country-style atmosphere with unlimited bread and salad bar. (Lunch $4-5. Dinner $9-15. Open Mon.-Thurs. 11am-9pm, Fri.-Sat. 11am-9:30pm, Sun. 4-9pm.) **Shindigs,** 32 Kennebec Ave. (696-7727), in Oak Bluffs, serves generous portions of tasty BBQ ($6-7) and sandwiches ($4-7). (Open daily 10am-10pm.) Prospective revelers should note that Edgartown and Oak Bluffs are the only "wet" towns on the Vineyard. Bar owners here are notoriously strict about ID. Given Teddy Kennedy's drunken escapades in nearby Chappaquiddick, you can hardly fault them.

A number of good take-out places freckle the island, and with the beauty of the surrounding landscape you just might want to grab food and run. You can buy yet another frigging sweatshirt at the **Black Dog Bakery** (693-9223), on Beach St. Ext. in Vineyard Haven, which is also filled with sumptuous breads and pastries (75¢-$3.50). (Open daily 5:30am-9pm.) An island legend and institution, **Mad Martha's** scoops out 26 homemade flavors of sinfully rich ice cream (including the limited editions made with genuine booze) and frrrrrozen yogurt. The main store (693-9151) is on Circuit Ave. in Oak Bluffs (open daily 11am-midnight), but there are seven other locations throughout the island (two more are in Oak Bluffs). Several **farm stands** on the island sell inexpensive produce; the free chamber of commerce map shows their locations.

Sights Exploring the Vineyard should involve much more than hamlet-hopping. Five walking trails will take you through widely different habitats—a salt marsh, a beach dune, and a forest—at **Felix Neck Wildlife Sanctuary** (627-4850) on the Edgartown-Vineyard Haven Rd. (open until 7pm; admission $3, under 12 $2, seniors $1). **Cedar Tree Neck** on the western shore provides trails across 250 acres of headland off Indian Hill Rd., while the **Long Point** park in West Tisbury preserves 550 acres and a shore on the Tisbury Great Pond. **Camp Pogue Wildlife Refuge and Wasque Reservation** on Chappaquiddick is the largest conservation area on the island. One of the most awe-inspiring, natural beaches on the island which is accessible to the public is **South Beach,** at the end of Katama Rd. 3 mi. south of Edgartown. The big waves alternately licking and slapping the shore attract quite a crowd. A narrow spit of land between Oak Bluffs and Edgartown divides Sengekontacket Pond from Nantucket Sound. A bike path bordering Beach Rd. follows this sandy strip, and the whole 4 mi. is a glorious state beach. All public beaches are free.

■■■ NANTUCKET

Melville wrote about Nantucket in *Moby Dick* without ever visiting the island; many of today's travelers also form their judgments—too pretentious, too expensive, too difficult to get to—without bothering to take the ferry ride over. See it for yourself.

Bike the dirt roads through the heaths, catch a bluefish on the beach, go sea-kayaking, explore Nantucket Town's cobblestone streets and weathered fishing shacks, or sit on the docks which once were the scene of the busiest whaling port in the world. If possible, visit during the last weeks of the tourist season when prices drop. Only a few places stay open during the cold, rainy winter months, when awesome storms churn the slate-blue seas.

Practical Information The visitor services center is on 25 Federal St. (228-0925; open Mon.-Sat. 9am-10pm, Sun. 9am-6pm). It has a full complement of brochures and can help you find a place to stay. **Hyline** (778-2600) provides ferry service to Nantucket from Hyannis (6 per day, $10.75) and from Martha's Vineyard (3 per day, $10.75). **Steamship Authority** (540-2022) runs ferries from Hyannis only (6 per day, $9.75). Both charge $4.50 for bikes and take about 2 hr. The Hyannis docks are near South and Pleasant St.

Rent bikes at **Young's Bicycle Shop,** Steamboat Wharf (228-1151). Three-speeds are $10 per day, mountain bikes $18 (its worth the extra dough to get the mountain bike—you'll want to travel dirt roads through the heath). Young's distributes free, decent maps of the island, but for an extended stay buy the *Complete Map of Nantucket* ($3). (Open daily 8am-8pm.) Alternatively, **Barrett's Bus Lines,** 20 Federal St. (228-0174), opposite the visitors center, runs buses on sunny days only to Jetty's Beach (every ½-hr. 10am-5pm, $1), and Sconset (every hr. 10:10am-4:10pm, $5). Nantucket's regular **ZIP code** is 02554; the **area code** is 508.

Accommodations and Food Wake up to the sound of surf at the **Star of the Sea Youth Hostel (HI/AYH)** (228-0433) at Surfside Beach, 3 mi. from the town of Nantucket (a 45-min. walk from town on Surfside Rd.). This former Coast Guard Station is a stellar hostel. ($10, nonmembers $13. Open 7-9:30am and 5-10:30pm. Reservations essential.) Apart from the Star, accommodation prices on the island are astronomical, with guest houses starting at $85 per night.

Restaurants on Nantucket are expensive; most entrees cost $3-5 more than they would on the mainland. **The Elegant Dump Lobster Pot,** 56 Union St. (228-4634), is your best bet for a sit-down dinner, with a witty owner and one meal actually under $10: linguini for $7.25. (Open daily 6-10pm.) For a hearty breakfast at reasonable prices, take **Two Steps Up,** at 10 India St. (Open daily 5am-1pm; the only place to chow before catching the morning ferry.) To avoid restaurant prices altogether, buy groceries at the **A&P,** on Commercial St. at Washington St. (Open Mon.-Sat. 7am-midnight, Sun. 8am-8pm.)

Sights and Activities Nantucket is an island of incredible beauty; enjoy it now before developers consign it to the subdivided fate of Cape Cod. For a great **bike trip,** head east from Nantucket Town on Milestone Rd. and turn left onto a path that looks promising. Head across beautiful moors of heather, huckleberries, bayberries and wild roses. Those who want adventure in the water should go to **Sea Nantucket,** at the end of Washington St., at the waterfront (228-7499), and rent a **sea kayak** ($25 for 4½ hrs.; open daily 9am-7pm). It is easy to learn how to maneuver the kayaks, and they are not too physically demanding; take one out to a nearby salt marsh, or head across the harbor to one of the isolated beaches on the Coatue peninsula and enjoy a picnic undisturbed by other beachgoers. If you prefer to stand on the strand between land and sea, rent **surf fishing** equipment from **Barry Thurston's** (228-9595), at Harbor Square near the A&P, for $15 per day. (Open Mon.-Sat. 8am-9pm, Sun. 9am-1am.)

The excellent **Nantucket Whaling Museum** (228-1736), in Nantucket Town, recreates the old whaling community with exhibits on whales and whaling methods. The museums' collection of scrimshaw (etched whale ivory) includes some pieces carved by sailors for their sweethearts. The **Museum of Nantucket History** (228-3889), in the Thomas Macy Warehouse, will help you appreciate the island's boom years as a whaling port and also describes other island industries such as candlemaking and sheep raising. (Both museums open summer daily 10am-5pm.) Pick up a free copy of *Yesterday's Island* for listings of nature walks, concerts, lectures, art exhibitions, and more.

■■■ PLYMOUTH

Despite what American high school textbooks say, the Pilgrims did *not* first step ashore onto the New World at Plymouth—they first stopped at Provincetown but left because the soil was inadequate. **Plymouth Rock** itself was just one more stone in the sea until 1741, when a 95-year-old man identified it as the one where the Pilgrims disembarked. Since then, the rock has served as a symbol of liberty during the American Revolution, been moved three times, and been chipped away by tourists before landing at its current home on Water St. at the foot of North St. Go to Plymouth to experience a town steeped in history, and, particularly, the brilliant performances of Plimoth Plantation's actors. But considering the proximity of Cape Cod's soft sand beaches, you won't want to spend more than a day here.

Camping and Sights Camping comes cheaper than the area's overpriced hotels; majestic **Myles Standish Forest** (866-2526), 7 myles south of Plymouth via Rte. 3., offers wooded ground (sites $10 for 2 people, with showers $12).

Plimoth Plantation, Warren Ave. (746-1622 for recording), superbly re-creates the early settlement. In the **Pilgrim Village** costumed actors impersonate actual villagers; they feign ignorance of all events after the 1630s. Each day at the Plantation corresponds to a day in William Bradford's record of the first year of the settlement: if you arrive on August 2, 1993, you'll see a recreation of what was happening on August 2, 1620. The nearby **Wampanoag Summer Encampment** recreates a Native American village of the same period. Admission to the plantation includes entry to the **Mayflower II,** built in the 1950s to recapture the atmosphere of the original ship. (Ship docked off Water St., 4 blocks south of the info center. Open June-Aug. daily 9am-6:30pm, April-May and Sept.-Nov. 9am-5pm. Separate admission $5.75, kids $3.75. Plantation open April-Nov. daily 9am-5pm. Admission for village and encampment $18.50, kids $11.)

Less fanfare surrounds the sights in town. The nation's oldest museum in continuous existence, the **Pilgrim Hall Museum,** 75 Court St. (746-1620), houses Puritan crafts, furniture, books, paintings, and weapons (open daily 9:30am-4:30pm; admission $5, seniors $4 ages 6-15 $2.50). An unexpected pleasure, **Cranberry World,** 225 Water St. (747-2350), glorifies one of the only four indigenous American fruits (the others are the tomato, the blueberry and the Concord grape). Exhibits show how cranberries are grown, harvested, sorted, and sold and include a small cranberry bog in front of the museum. (Open May-Nov. 9:30am-5pm. Free.)

▨ New Hampshire

New Hampshire's farmers have struggled for over two centuries with the state's rugged landscape, but a cultivator's *inferno* is a hiker's *paradiso*. The White Mountains dominate the central and northern regions, and nearly every part of the state identifies with some towering crag. Rising above them all, Mt. Washington is the highest point in the Appalachians (6288 ft.); from its summit you can see the Atlantic and five states. Besides the stony beaches of the shortest shore of any seaboard state (15 mi.), much of the southeastern region of the state has mutated into a suburb of the

Boston megalopolis. Although the state motto and license-plate blazon "Live Free or Die," "Live Well or Die" may be more appropriate in these parts.

PRACTICAL INFORMATION

Capital: Concord.

Office of Travel and Tourism, Box 856 Concord 03302 (271-2666, 800-262-6660 or 800-258-3608). With a touch-tone phone these numbers provide fall foliage reports, daily ski conditions, weekly snowmobile conditions and weekly special events. Operators available Mon.-Fri. 8am-4pm. **Fish and Game Department,** 2 Hazen Dr., Concord 03301 (271-3421) can provide info on hunting and fishing regulations and license fees. **U.S. Forest Service,** 719 Main St., mail to P.O. Box 638, Laconia 03247 (528-8721). Open Mon.-Fri. 8am-4:30pm.

Time Zone: Eastern. **Postal abbreviation:** NH

Sales Tax: 0%. Live Tax-Free or Die.

■■■ WHITE MOUNTAINS

In the late 19th century, the White Mountains became an immensely popular summer retreat for wealthy New Englanders. Grand hotels peppered the rolling green landscape and as many as 50 trains per day chugged through the region, filling hotel rooms with tourists marveling at nature. The mountains are not quite so busy or posh these days, but the valleys, forests and gnarled granite peaks still attract upwardly mobile travelers, recast today as outdoorsy hikers and skiers. Unfortunately, the mountains still shun budget travelers; affordable lodgings here are rustic at best, public transportation scarce and weather unpredictable.

Useful Organizations The **White Mountain Attraction Center** (745-8720), on Rte. 112 in North Woodstock east of I-93 (exit 32), can give you information on just about anything in the area. (Write P.O. Box 10, N. Woodstock 03262. Open daily 8:30am-6pm; Columbus Day-Memorial Day daily 8:30am-5pm.) Local Chambers of Commerce are also good sources of information. Those looking to bypass cities will have a much more relaxing time of it thanks to two superb organizations which help visitors camp in and preserve the forests. One is the **U.S. Forest Service** (528-8721), whose main information station lies south of the mountains at 719 Main St., Laconia 03246. **Forest service ranger stations,** dotting the main highways through the forest, can also answer questions about trail locations and conditions: **Androscoggin** (466-2713), on Rte. 16, ½-mi. south of the U.S. 2 junction in Gorham (open Mon.-Fri. 7am-4:30pm); **Amoosuc** (869-2626), on Trudeau Rd. in Bethlehem west of U.S. 3 on U.S. 302 (open Mon.-Fri. 7am-4:30pm); **Saco** (447-5448), on the Kancamangus Hwy. in Conway 100 yd. off Rte. 16 (open daily 8am-4:30pm); and **Pemigewasset** (536-1310), on Rte. 175 in Plymouth (open Mon-Fri 8am-4:30pm). Each station provides a guide to the **backcountry facilities** in its area.

The other organization is the **Appalachian Mountains Club (AMC),** whose main base in the mountains is the Pinkham Notch Visitors Center on Rte. 16 between Gorham and Jackson (see Pinkham Notch below). The AMC is the area's primary supplier of hiking and camping equipment, information, lodging and food. The club's main car-accessible lodge is the Joe Dodge Lodge, adjoining the Pinkham visitors center (again, see Pinkham Notch). The AMC's other car-accessible lodging is the **Shapleigh Hostel** (846-7774), adjoining the **Crawford Notch Depot,** east of Bretton Woods on U.S. 302. The hostel has room for 20 people and provides toilets, metered showers and a full kitchen. Bring your own sleeping bag and food. Reservations recommended. (AMC members $10, nonmembers $15.) The Depot sells trail guides, maps, food, and film, and has restrooms. (Open late May-Labor Day daily 9am-5pm.) The AMC also has a system of eight **huts,** none of which is accessible by car; they are spaced about a day's hike apart along the Appalachian Trail. Either breakfast or dinner must be taken with each night's lodging, and guests must provide their own sleeping bags or sheets. (Bunk with 2 meals for member $47, child members $20, nonmember $53/$26; with only dinner $41/$17 and $47/$23; with only breakfast $37/$15 and $43/$21.) All huts are open for **full service** May-Sept.; **self-service rates** (caretaker in residence but no meals provided) are available at other times. (AMC member $10, nonmember $15.) For all AMC info, consult the AMC's *The Guide,* available at either visitors center.

Camping, Hiking, and Biking Camping is free in a number of areas throughout the **White Mountains National Forest** (WMNF). No camping is allowed above the tree line (approximately 4000 ft.), within 200 ft. of a trail, or within ¼ mi. of roads, huts, shelters, tent platforms, lakes, or streams; the same rules apply to building a wood or charcoal fire. Since these rules often vary depending on forest conditions, call the U.S. Forest Service before pitching a tent. The forest also holds 22 designated **campgrounds** (sites $8-12, bathrooms and firewood usually available). Call 528-8727 to find out which is closest to your destination or to reserve (800-283-2267), especially in July and Aug.

If you plan to do much **hiking**, invest in the invaluable *AMC White Mountain Guide,* available in most bookstores and huts ($16), which includes full maps and descriptions of all trails in the mountains; with these, you can pinpoint precisely where you are on the trail at any given time. *Never* drink untreated water from a stream or lake; all AMC outposts sell water-purification kits. Also, be prepared for sudden weather changes. Though often peaceful, the peaks can prove treacherous.

Next to hiking, **bicycling** offers the best way to see the mountains close up. The approach to the WMNF from the north is slightly less steep, according to some bikers. Check the guide/map *New Hampshire Bicycle,* available at information centers, or *25 Bicycle Tours in New Hampshire* ($7), available in local bookstores and outdoor equipment stores. (For bike rental suggestions, see North Conway below.)

Getting There and Getting Around While getting to the general vicinity poses little difficulty, getting around the White Mountains can be very problematic. **Concord Trailways** (228-3300 or 639-3317) runs north-south and connects the Boston Peter Pan bus station at 555 Atlantic Ave. (617-426-7838) with Concord ($11), Conway ($25), and Franconia ($26). **Vermont Transit** (800-451-3292) runs buses from Boston's Greyhound terminal, 10 St. James Ave. (617-423-5810), to Concord ($11) on the way to Vermont. The AMC runs a **shuttle service** (466-2727) connecting points within the mountains. For a complete map of routes and times consult *The Guide.* Reservations are recommended for all stops and required for some. (Runs late May-early Sept. 8:45am-4pm, tickets $4.75-11.75.)

Trail and Weather Information can be obtained by calling the Pinkham Notch Visitors Center (466-2725). Regional **zip codes** include: Franconia, 03580; Jackson, 03846 and Gorham, 03587. The **area code** here is 603.

■ Franconia Notch Area

About 400 million years old, Franconia Notch in the northern White Mountains has developed some interesting wrinkles. Sheer and dramatic granite cliffs, waterfalls, endless woodlands, and one very famous rocky profile attract droves of summer campers. The nearest town is Lincoln, just off I-93. From Lincoln, the Kancamangus Hwy. (Rte. 112) branches east for a scenic 35 mi. through the **Pemigewasset Wilderness** to Conway. The large basin is rimmed by 4000-ft. peaks and attracts many backpackers and skiers. South of the highway, trails head into the **Sandwich Ranges,** whose **Mount Chocorua,** south along Rte. 16 near Ossipee, is a dramatic and steep exposed peak, and a favorite of 19th-century naturalist painters

Sights and Activities Before you begin your exploration of this geological wonder, ask about the Franconia Notch State Park at the **Flume Visitors Center** (745-8391), off I-93 north of Lincoln. Their excellent free 15-min. film acquaints visitors with the landscape. (Open May-Oct. daily 9am-4:30pm, July-Aug. until 5pm.) While at the center, purchase tickets to **The Flume,** a 2-mi. nature walk over hills, through a covered bridge to a boardwalk above a fantastic gorge with 90-ft.-high granite cliffs. (Tickets $5.50, ages 6-12 $2.50.)

The westernmost of the three great notches, Franconia is best known for the **Old Man of the Mountains,** a 40-ft.-high human profile formed by three ledges of stone atop a 1200-ft. cliff north of The Flume on the parkway. Hawthorne addressed this geological Rorschach Test in his 1850 story "The Great Stone Face," and P.T. Barnum once offered to buy the rock. Today the Old Man is really doddering; his forehead is now supported by cables and turnbuckles. The best view of the man, both at high noon and in the moonlight, is from **Profile Lake,** a 10-min. walk from Lafayette Place in the park.

West of the Old Man, off I-93 exit 2, **Great Cannon Cliff,** a 1000-ft. sheer drop into the cleft between **Mount Lafayette** and **Cannon Mountain,** is not just for onlookers—many test their technical skill and climb the "Sticky Fingers" or "Meat Grinder" route; the 80-passenger **Cannon Mountain Aerial Tramway** (823-5563; open daily 9am-4:30pm; Nov.-mid-April Sat.-Sun. 9am-4:30pm; $8, ages 6-12 $4, $6 for one-way hikers) will do the work for you. The Flume and the Tramway may be purchased as a package. ($11, ages 6-12 $5.)

Myriad trails lead up into the mountains on both sides of the notch, providing excellent day hikes and spectacular views. Be prepared for severe weather, especially above 4000 ft. The **Lake Trail,** a relatively easy hike, wends its way from Lafayette Place in the park 1½ mi. to **Lonesome Lake,** where the AMC operates its westernmost summer hut (see White Mountains AMC huts above). The **Greenleaf Trail** (2½ mi.), which starts at the Cannon Tramway parking lot, and the **Old Bridle Path** (3 mi.), which starts at Lafayette Place, are much more ambitious; both lead up to the AMC's Greenleaf Hut near the summit of Mt. Lafayette overlooking Eagle Lake, a favorite destination for sunset photographers. From Greenleaf, you can trudge the next 7½ mi. east along **Garfield Ridge** to the AMC's most remote hut, the Galehead. Dayhikes from this base can keep you occupied for days. (Sites at the Garfield Ridge campsite $4.) A number of other campsites, mainly lean-tos and tent platforms with no showers or toilets, are dispersed throughout the mountains. Most run $4 per night on a first-come, first-served basis, but many are free. Contact the U.S. Forest Service or consult the AMC's two-page, free photocopied handout *Backpacker Shelters, Tentsites, Campsites and Cabins in the White Mountains.*

Those who find hiking anathema can take advantage of the 9 mi. of **bike paths** that begin off U.S. 3 and run through the White Mountain National Forest. After any exertion, cool off at the lifeguard-protected beach on the northern shore of **Echo Lake State Park** (356-2672), west off Rte. 16/U.S. 302 in North Conway. (Open daily mid-June-Sept. 9am-8pm. $2.50, under 12 and over 65 free.)

Camping At reasonable altitudes, you can camp at the **Lafayette Campground** (823-9513), in Franconia Notch State Park. (Open mid-May to mid-Oct., weather permitting; sites $15 for 2 people, $7 per extra person, showers available.) If Lafayette is full, try the more suburban **Fransted Campground** (823-5675), 1 mi. south of the village and 3 mi. north of the notch. (Sites $13 for 1 person, $16 on river. Each additional person $1. Showers and bathrooms available. Open May-Columbus Day.)

■ North Conway and Skiing

Located along the lengthy stretch shared by Routes 16 and 302, North Conway differs from the region's other small towns in that it doesn't exploit the beauty of its natural surroundings, but instead lures tourists seeking frenzied factory-outlet shopping. Nearly every major clothing label, from L.L. Bean to Ralph Lauren, has a sizeable store on the main road. While North Conway clearly shows the strain of being the area's largest city, it also enjoys some of the benefits. You'll find many affordable places to eat, the region's best outdoor equipment stores, and, within a short drive, a number of very good cross-country and downhill ski centers.

Skiing Though close to many ski areas, North Conway is proudest of its own local mountain, **Cranmore** (800-543-9206), which boasts the oldest ski train in the country. On winter Wednesdays, the slopes host a ski racing series; local teams also compete in the nationally known **Mountain Meisters,** open to the public. You can ski day ($33) or night ($15). Mid-week rates are 1/3 less. Students receive a $3 discount with ID. The other two major downhill ski areas in the Mt. Washington valley are **Attitash** (800-223-7669) and **Wildcat** (466-3326). Attitash, on U.S. 302 west of its intersection with Rte. 16, offers snowmaking on nearly 100% of its trails. (Lift tickets Mon.-Fri. $27, Sat.-Sun. $34.) With both the largest vertical drop and the largest lift capacity in the valley, Wildcat guarantees that if you wait more than 10 min. for a chairlift you'll get $5 off your next lift ticket. (Located near the AMC Pinkham Notch Camp on Rte. 16. Lift tickets Sun.-Fri. $27, Sat. $33.)

A number of stores in the North Conway area rent quality skis and other outdoor equipment. For downhill skis, try **Joe Jones** in North Conway on Main St. at Mechanic (356-9411; skis, boots and poles $15 per day, $25 per 2 days; open July-Aug and Dec.-March daily 9am-9pm; off-season Sun.-Thurs. 10am-6pm, Fri.-Sat. 10am-9pm). **Eastern Mountain Sports (EMS),** Main St. (356-5433), on the premises of the Eastern Slope Inn, has free mountaineering pamphlets and excellent books on the area, including *25 Bicycle Tours in New Hampshire*. EMS rents tents ($15 per night for a 2-person, $20 for 4-person), sleeping bags ($10-15), and sells other camping equipment. (Open June-Sept. daily 9am-9pm; off-season daily 9am-6pm, Fri.-Sat. until 9pm.) In Jackson, next to the Jack Frost Ski Shop, at **David's Bike Shop** (383-4563), the extremely amiable Dave Miller rents mountain bikes ($20 per day, $10 per ½-day; open May-Oct. Tues.-Sun. 9am-5pm.)

Outside the Mt. Washington valley, the major downhill ski areas cluster along I-93. Collectively known as **Ski-93** (745-8101 or write P.O. Box 517 Lincoln 13251), these mountains offer quick access and lift-ticket packages for multiple areas. **Loon Mountain** (745-8111), 3 mi. east of I-93 at Lincoln, avoids overcrowding by limiting lift-ticket sales, and also has a free beginners' tow (9 lifts, 41 trails). **Waterville Valley** (236-8311) offers great downhill as well as cross-country skiing (12 lifts, 53 trails). **Cannon Mountain** (823-5563; 800-552-1234 in New England), north of Franconia Notch, offers decent slopes off a large tram.

Accommodations and Food The **Maple Leaf Motel** (356-5388), on Main St., south of the North Conway city park, has clean, spacious rooms for reasonable rates. (Singles $55, doubles $65; mid-Oct.-late June $36/$48.) Farther south on Main St., the **Yankee Clipper** (356-5736 or 800-343-5900) offers similar rooms for similar prices (room with 1 double bed $55, 2 double beds $75; mid-Oct.-July $40/$50).

Sandwich and pizza places line North Conway's Main St. The hotspot for the *après ski* crowd is **Jackson Square,** on the premises of the Eastern Slope Inn, with a DJ and dancing every Thurs.-Sat. (Most entrees $10, Thurs. has 2-for-1 entrees, Fri.-Sat. all-u-can-eat buffet $10. Happy hours Sun.-Fri. 4-7pm. Open daily 7:30am-10pm.) **Studebakers** (356-3011), on Rte. 16 south of town, is a 50s-style drive-in diner. Sandwiches $3-5. (Open Sun.-Thurs. 11:30am-9pm, Fri.-Sat. 11:30am-10pm.)

■ Pinkham Notch

Practical Information Easternmost of the New Hampshire notches, Pinkham Notch skirts the eastern edge of the base of Mt. Washington. Stretching from Gorham to Jackson along Rte. 16, the notch is most notable as the home of the AMC's main visitors and information center in the White Mountains, the **Pinkham Notch Visitors Center** (466-2725, 466-2727 for reservations). The visitors center, the New England hiker's mecca, lies about halfway between Gorham and Jackson on Rte. 16, less than 15 mi. from each. From I-93, the best route is to take exit 42 to

U.S. 302 east, then take Rte. 16 north to U.S. 2 east to Rte. 16 south. Open daily 7am-10pm, it's the best source for weather and trail conditions in the area. The center can also make reservations at any of the AMC huts and hostels, as well as at the adjoining Joe Dodge Lodge. The center also sells the complete line of AMC books, trail maps ($3, weatherproofed $5), and all types of camping and hiking necessities.

Mt. Washington Beginning just behind the center, and leading all the way to the top of Mt. Washington, **Tuckerman's Ravine Trail** is a steep climb taking 4 to 5 hr. each way. For Pete's sake, be careful. Every year, Mt. Washington claims at least one life. A gorgeous day can suddenly transmute into a chilling storm, with wind kicking up over 100 mph and thunderclouds ominously rumbling. It has never been warmer than 72°F atop Mt. Washington, and the *average* temperature on the peak is a bone-chilling 26.7°F. All risks aside, the climb *is* stellar, and the view well worth it. Non-climbers with cars can take the **Mount Washington Auto Road** (466-3988), a paved and dirt road that leads motorists 8 mi. to the summit. There they can get bumper stickers boasting "This Car Climbed Mt. Washington" and cruise around impressing easily awed folks. The road begins at Glen House, a short distance north of the visitors center on Rte. 16. ($12 per driver, $5 per passenger, ages 5-12 $3. Road open mid-May-mid-Oct. daily 7:30am-6pm.) Guided van tours which give a 30-min. presentation on the mountain's natural and human history and then take a 30-min. trip back down are also available. ($17, kids 5-12 $12.) On the summit you'll find an information center, a snack bar, a museum (466-3347), strong wind and the Mt. Washington Observatory (466-3388).

Accommodations Just 1½ mi. from Mt. Washington's summit sits the **Lakes of the Clouds** AMC hut; the largest, highest and most popular of the AMC's huts. There is also sleeping space here in a **Refuge Room** for eight backpackers at $6 per night. Backpackers' reservations can be made from any hut, no more than 48 hrs. in advance. For those who fancy a more leisurely climb, the **Hermit's Lake Shelter** skulks about 2 hr. up the trail. The shelter, which has bathrooms but no shower, gives access to lean-tos and tent platforms ($7 per night; make reservations at the visitors center). **Carter Notch Hut** lies to the east of the visitors center, a 4-mi. hike up the Nineteen Mile Brook Trail. At the **Joe Dodge Lodge,** immediately behind the visitors center, get a comfy bunk with a delicious and sizeable breakfast and dinner for $38 (nonmembers $44). A bunk with only supper is $5 less; with only breakfast $10 less, and if you plead, they might let you off without any meals for $14 less.

If all the AMC facilities are booked, head to the **Berkshire Manor** in Gorham, 133 Main St. (466-2186). The rooms here are large, if oddly decorated, and guests have access to a full kitchen and living room. (Hall bathroom. Singles $20, doubles $32.) Much more rustic is **Bowman's Base Camp (HI/AYH)** (466-5130), 7 mi. west of Gorham on U.S. 2. An unfinished log cabin, the Base Camp has a kitchen and a phone. And mice. ($11, nonmembers $12; open Memorial Day-Columbus Day.).

Rhode Island

Although Rhode Island—the "biggest little state in the Union"—is indeed smaller than some ranches in Texas and some icebergs in Antarctica, some parks in Wyoming, and some dogs in Newfoundland (notably Bosun), most Rhode Islanders are nonetheless proud of their non-conformist heritage. From founder Roger Williams, a religious outcast during colonial days, to Buddy Cianci, convicted felon and two-time mayor of Providence, spirited Rhode Island has always lured a different crowd.

NEWPORT

Outside the two main cities, coastal Rhode Island and Providence Plantations (the official state name, the longest in the Union) is eminently explorable. Numerous small and provincial spots dot the shores down to Connecticut, while the inland roads are quiet, unpaved thoroughfares lined with family fruit stands, marshes, or ponds. Working ports derive their lifeblood from the fishblood of Narragansett Bay and Block Island Sound, and Block Island itself is a must-see.

PRACTICAL INFORMATION

Capital: Providence.
Rhode Island Division of Tourism, 7 Jackson Walkway, Providence 02903 (800-556-2484 or 277-2601). Open Mon.-Fri. 8:30am-4:30pm. **Department of Environmental Management** (State Parks), 9 Hayes St., Providence 02908 (277-2771). Open Mon.-Fri. 8:30am-4pm.
Time Zone: Eastern. **Postal Abbreviation:** RI
Sales Tax: 7%.

■■■ NEWPORT

Before the American Revolution, Newport was one of the five largest towns in the American colonies, a thriving seaport grown fat on the spoils of the triangle trade of rum, slaves, and molasses. Sugar purchased in the West Indies was here converted to rum in one of Newport's 21 distilleries. Affluent vacationers of the mid-19th century made Newport a hoity-toity resort, where Mrs. Astor felt money had the stench of newness until it was four generations old. The elite employed the country's best architects to confect elaborate neoclassical and baroque "summer cottages," huge mansions occupied for eight weeks or less per year. Crammed to the rafters with *objets d'art*, these "white elephants," as Henry James called them, signified the desperation of the *arrivistes* to purchase as much culture as money could buy.

Today, 40-foot racing yachts have replaced fishing boats, and fish comes swathed in sauce with a soupçon of something. There is a 25-year waiting period to get a slip at the marina in Newport, so plan ahead. Visit in the off-season or you will battle large crowds which funnel in during the summer for world-famous music festivals, national tennis competitions, and yachting.

PRACTICAL INFORMATION

Emergency: 911.
Newport County Convention and Visitors Bureau, 23 America's Cup Ave. (849-8048 or 800-326-6030), in the Newport Gateway Center. Free maps. Open Sun.-Thurs. 9am-6pm, Fri.-Sat. 9am-7pm; early Sept.-mid-May daily 9am-5pm. Pick up *Best-Read Guide Newport* and *Newport this Week* for current listings.
Bonanza Buses: 23 America's Cup Ave. (846-1820), at the visitors center. To: Boston (6 per day, $12); New York (5 per day via Fall River, $34).
Rhode Island Public Transit Authority (RIPTA): 1547 W. Main Rd. (847-0209 or 800-221-3797). Buses leave from the Newport Gateway Center daily 7am-7pm. Fare 85¢. Ride free on most routes Mon.-Fri. 9am-3pm and 6-7pm, all day Sat.-Sun. Frequent service to Providence (1 hr., $2.50) and points between on Rte. 114. Office open daily 6am-7pm.
Bike Rental: Ten Speed Spokes, 18 Elm St. (847-5609). Surprisingly, no 10-speeds. Mountain bikes $5 per hr., $25 per day. Must have credit card and photo ID. Open daily 9:30am-6pm.
Post Office: 320 Thames St. (847-2329), opposite Perry Hill Market. Window service open Mon.-Fri. 8:30am-5pm, Sat. 9am-1pm. **ZIP code:** 02840.
Area Code: 401.

ACCOMMODATIONS, CAMPING, AND FOOD

When staying in town, head for the visitors bureau for guest house brochures and free phones to call them. Guest houses offer bed and continental breakfast with colonial intimacy. Those not fussy about sharing a bathroom or foregoing a sea view might find a double for $60. Singles are practically nonexistent. Be warned that many hotels and guest houses are booked solid two months in advance for summer weekends. **Bed and Breakfasts of Rhode Island, Inc.** (941-0444) can make a reservation for you in Newport at an average rate of $65 per night.

Camping is actually available at **Fort Getty Recreation Area** (423-7264), on Conanicut Island, walking distance from the Fox Hill Salt Marsh, a good spot for birdwatching. 125 sites. (Showers and beach access; tent sites $15, hookup $20.)

Seafood is the recurring dream here, high prices the recurrent nightmare. Even though eating downtown generally means helping restaurant owners meet their high rents, a number of delis, cafes, and bakeries provide affordable meals. The young crowd favors the **Corner Store and Deli,** 372 Thames St. (847-1978), a restaurant-deli-grocery store with sandwiches ($3-5), salads, and Italian specialties to go (open Sun.-Thurs. 7am-9pm, Fri.-Sat. 7am-10pm). Along the waterfront and wharves, sandwiches, salads, and pasta dishes make good deals. Sit at a booth and try Linda's breakfast special ($2) or Tish's Pea Soup ($2.50) at the **Franklin Spa,** 229 Franklin St. (open Mon.-Sat. 7am-3pm, Sun. 7am-2pm). Pull into a slip at **Dry Dock Seafood,** 448 Thames St. (847-3974), a few blocks south of the wharves, a small, cheap, homey seafood joint frequented by locals. Munch on big, crispy fish and chips ($6), or indulge in the lobster special ($8). (Open Sun.-Thurs. 11am-10pm, Fri.-Sat. 11am-11pm.) Most of the town's restaurants grill and thrill on **Thames St.**

SIGHTS

In 1839, George Noble Jones of Savannah, GA, seeking to avoid the summer heat of the South, had a "summer cottage" built in Newport. Soon, Newport attracted the wealthiest families in the country, and each one had to build a bigger mansion than the last, thus originating the expression keeping up with the Joneses." Many of these ostentatious displays of wealth are still occupied, but seven of the gaudiest are operated by the **Preservation Society of Newport** (847-1000). The **Newport Mansions** are the biggest draw here, and any visit to town should include a tour of at least one of them. The 172-room **The Breakers,** modeled on an Italian palace, is the largest cottage, built for Cornelius Vanderbilt in 1895. **Marble House** and **Rosecliff,** both on Bellevue Ave., furnished settings for the movie *The Great Gatsby.* The mansions open to the public are on the eastern edge of Newport, a 2-mi. walk from Gateway center. You must pay admission just to get on the grounds; from the street you can't see much. (Most cottages open April-Nov. daily 10am-5pm, some open year-round. Tours leave every 10 min. at each house. Admission to The Breakers $7.50, others $6-7, kids 6-11 $3.50.) For a windswept view of the mansions and a rose-framed panorama of the ocean, hike the **Cliff Walk,** a 3.5-mi. trail along the ocean (right off the east end of Memorial Blvd.; entrance is near Easton's Beach).

The colonial buildings downtown are more unassuming than the mansions, but provide wonderful windows on that epoch. The 1765 **Wanton-Lyman Hazard House,** 17 Broadway (846-3622), the oldest standing house in Newport, has been restored in different period styles (open mid-June-early Aug. and late Aug.-late Sept. Fri.-Sat. 10am-4pm, early Aug.-late Aug. Thurs.-Sat. 10am-4pm, Sun. 1-4pm; admission $4). The **White Horse Tavern,** on Marlborough St. (849-3600), the oldest drinking establishment in the country, dates from 1673, but the father of William Mayes, a notorious Red Sea pirate, first opened it as a tavern in 1687 (beer $2-4). The **Touro Synagogue,** 85 Touro St. (847-4794), a beautifully restored Georgian building and the oldest synagogue in the U.S., dates back to 1763. It was to the Newport congregation that George Washington wrote his famous letter promising the U.S. would give "to bigotry no sanction, to persecution no assistance." (Must visit in free tour; every ½-hr. in summer. Open late June-Sept. Sun.-Fri. 10am-5pm; spring and fall Sun.-Fri. 1-3pm; winter Sun. 1-3pm and by appointment.)

After a few hours of touring Newport, you might think of escaping to the shore; unfortunately, the beaches crowd as frequently as the streets. The most popular of the shores is **First Beach** (call the Recreational Department at 846-1398 for info), or Easton's Beach, on Memorial Blvd., with its wonderful old beach houses and carousel. (Open Memorial Day-Labor Day Mon.-Fri. 9am-9pm, Sat.-Sun. 10am-9pm. Parking $5, weekends $10.) Those who prefer hiking over dunes to building sandcastles should try **Fort Adams State Park** (847-2400), south of town on Ocean Dr., 2½ mi. from Gateway Center, with showers, picnic areas, and two fishing piers (entrance booth open daily 9am-4pm, park open sunrise to sunset; parking $4). Other good beaches line Little Compton, Narragansett, and the shore between Watch Hill and Point Judith. For more details, consult the free *Ocean State Beach Guide,* available at the visitors center (see Practical Information above).

ENTERTAINMENT

In July and August, lovers of classical, folk, and jazz each have a festival to call their own. The **Newport Jazz Festival** is the oldest and best-known jazz festival in the world; Duke Ellington, Count Basie, and many other young jazz noblemen made their break here. Bring your beach chairs and coolers to **Fort Adams State Park** in mid-Aug. For info, write JVC Jazz Festival, P.O. Box 605, Newport 02840 (after May, 847-3700). The **Newport Music Festival** (849-0700) in mid-July attracts pianists, violinists, and other classical musicians from around the world, presenting them in the ballrooms and on the lawns of the mansions for two weeks of concerts. For info write Newport Music Festival, P.O. Box 3300, Newport 02840. Tickets are available through Ticketron (800-382-8080). In August, you might chorus with folksingers Joan Baez and the Indigo Girls at the legendary **Newport Folk Festival** (June-Aug. 847-3709), which runs two days, noon to dusk, rain or shine (tickets $23 per day).

Newport's nightlife is easy to find but relatively subdued. Down by the water at **Pelham East** (849-9460), at the corner of Thames and Pelham, they tend to play straight rock 'n' roll. (Live music nightly. Open daily noon-1am. Weekend cover $5.) Those longing for disco should visit **Maximillian's,** 108 William St., 2nd floor (849-4747), a popular video-enhanced dance club across from the Tennis Hall of Fame (open Tues.-Sun. 9pm-1am; cover Sun. and Tues.-Thurs. $3, Fri.-Sat. $5). The **Black Pearl Pub** (846-5264) (and cafe in good weather) on Bannister's Wharf is reserved and elegant (open daily 11:30am-1am).

■ Near Newport

Block Island Ten mi. southeast of Newport in the Atlantic, sand-blown **Block Island** has become an increasingly popular daytrip as tourists saturate Nantucket and Martha's Vineyard. The island is endowed with weathered shingles, quaint buildings, and serenity. One quarter of the island is protected open space; local conservationists hope to increase that to 50%. You can bike or hike 4 mi. north from Old Harbor to the **National Wildlife Refuge,** or bring a picnic, head due south from Old Harbor where the ferry lets you off, and hike 2 mi. south to the **Mohegan Bluffs.** Those who are adventurous, careful, and strong enough can wind their way down to the Atlantic waters 200 ft. below. The **Southeast Lighthouse,** high in the cliffs, has warned *Downeaster Alexas* since 1875; its beacon shines the brightest of any on the Atlantic coast.

No camping is allowed on the island, so make it a daytrip unless you're willing to shell out $50 or more for a room in a guest house. Most restaurants are close to the ferry dock in Old Harbor; several cluster at New Harbor 1 mi. inland.

The **Block Island Chamber of Commerce** (466-2982) advises at the ferry dock in Old Harbor Drawer D, Block Island 02807 (open Mon.-Fri. 9am-3pm, Sat. 9am-1pm; mid-Oct.-mid-May Mon.-Fri. approximately 10am-2pm). Rest stop information centers operated by the state of Rhode Island supply the free *Block Island Travel Planner.* Cycling is the ideal way to explore the tiny (7 mi. by 3 mi.) island. Try the **Old Harbor Bike Shop** (466-2029), to the left of where you exit the ferry. (10-speeds and mountain bikes $3 per hr., $15 per day; single mopeds $12/$40 weekdays, $15/$50 weekends; license required. Car rentals $60 per day, 20¢ per mi. Must be 21 with credit card. Open daily 9am-7pm.)

The **Interstate Navigation Co.** (783-4613) provides year-round ferry service to Block Island from Point Judith, RI (8 per day in summer, 1-4 per day in winter, 1¼ hr., $6.60, under 12 $3, cars by reservation $20.25, bikes $1.75), and summer service from Newport, RI (1 per day, 2 hr., $6.45), New London, CT (1 per day, 2 hr., $13.50), Providence, RI, and Montauk, NY. Leave from Galilee State Pier in Point Judith if possible; it's the most frequent, cheapest, and shortest ride. The **police** can be reached at 466-2622, the **Coast Guard** at 466-2086. Block Island's **post office** sorts on Ocean Ave.; the **ZIP code** is 02807.

■■■ PROVIDENCE

Like Rome, Providence sits aloft seven hills. Unlike Rome, its residents are Ivy Leaguers, starving artists, and smartly suited business types. This state capital has more of a college-town identity, with cobbled sidewalks, colonial buildings, and more than its share of bookstores and cafés—even those who aren't students look like they should be. But Providence has more on its horizon than a constellation of BAs. Prescient *Newsweek* recently voted Providence one of the country's most liveable cities, with an urban renaissance in the cards. The city last boomed in the 18th century as a thriving seaport.

Practical Information The state capitol and the downtown business district cluster just east of the intersection of I-95 and I-195. **Brown University** and the **Rhode Island School of Design (RISD)** (pronounced RIZZ-dee) pose on top of a steep hill, a 10-min. walk east of downtown. **Providence College** tucks into the northwestern corner of town, about 2 mi. from the city center out Douglas Pike.

Emergency is 911. For a self-guided walking tour and the usual maps and tourist literature head to the **Greater Providence Convention and Visitors Bureau,** 30 Exchange Terrace (274-1636 or 800-233-1636), on the first floor, near North Main St. next to City Hall (open Mon.-Fri. 8:30am-5pm). The **Providence Preservation Society,** 21 Meeting St. (831-7440), at the foot of College Hill off Main St. in the 1772 Shakespeare's Head, hawks detailed info on historic Providence. Self-guided tour instructions for the city's historic neighborhoods are $1 each, and an audio-cassette tour is $5 (open Mon.-Fri. 9am-5pm).

Amtrak thinks it can from a gleaming white structure behind the state capitol at 100 Gaspee St. (800-872-7245; open daily 5am-11:15pm), a 10-min. walk to Brown or downtown. To Boston ($14) and New York ($46). **Greyhound** and **Bonanza,** 1 Bonanza Way (751-8800), off exit 29 of I-95, have very frequent service to Boston (1 hr., $7.75) and New York (4 hr., $29). Bonanza accepts Ameripass. All buses make a stop at the Kennedy Plaza downtown, where Bonanza also has a ticket office (open daily 7am-6pm). **Rhode Island Public Transit Authority (RIPTA),** 776 Elmwood Ave. (781-9400 or 800-221-3797, from Newport 847-0209), has an **information booth** on Kennedy Plaza across from the visitors center which provides in-person route and schedule assistance, as well as free maps of the bus system, which has service to points south, including Newport ($2.50). The fare ranges from 25¢ to $2.50; within Providence, fares are generally 85¢. Senior citizens ride free on weekends 9am-3pm, weekdays all day. Buses operate daily 4:30am-midnight. You can also catch the **FreeBee,** a bus unmistakably painted with bees, for free. It loops by Capitol Hill and the Kennedy Plaza. (Office open Mon.-Sat. 8:30am-6pm. Info booth open Mon.-Fri. 8am-4:30pm.) For help contact **Traveler's Aid** (521-2255; 24 hrs.). Providence's **post office** posts from 2 Exchange Terrace (421-4360; open Mon.-Fri. 7am-5:30pm, Sat. 8am-noon). The **ZIP code** is 02903; the **area code** 401.

Accommodations and Camping The lack of a youth hostel combined with the high rates of motels downtown make Providence an expensive overnight

PROVIDENCE

stay, unless you have a friend at one of the local universities. Rooms are booked far in advance for the graduation season in May and early June; don't expect vacancy signs to be lit during that time. The friendly **International House,** 8 Stimson Ave. (421-7181), near the Brown campus, has two comfortable rooms that usually book up. (Singles $45, students $30; doubles $50/$35. If staying at least 5 nights, discount $5 off every price. Reservations required.) The cheapest room around is at the **New Yorker Motor Lodge,** 400 Newport Ave., East Providence (434-8000; single $35, double $38). A 30-min. drive from downtown reaches over a dozen campgrounds, but none are closer than that. **Colwell's Campground** (397-4614) is one of the closest; from Providence, take I-95 south to exit 10, then head west 8.5 mi. on Rte. 117 to Coventry. The campground has showers and hookups, and is on the shore of the Flat River Reservoir. (Tent sites $9-14 depending on waterfront proximity.) For an out-in-the-open good time, try **Dyer Woods Nudist Campground,** 114 Johnson Rd. (397-3007), 3 mi. south of U.S. 6. Provides athletic facilities (volleyball, badminton, and swings) at 14 sites ($20 per day, $10 per night; open May-Sept.).

Food Good food in Providence emanates from three areas: on Atwells Ave. in the Italian district, on Federal Hill just west of downtown; the student hangouts on Thayer St., on College Hill to the east; and the city's beautiful old diners near downtown. **Louis' Family Restaurant,** 286 Brook St. (861-5225), is a friendly venue that has made the entire community its family. Students swear by its prices, donating the artwork on the walls in return. Try the famous #1 special (2 eggs, homefries, toast, coffee) for $2.30. (Lunches $1-4.50, dinners $2.75-5.50. Open daily 5:30am-3pm.) Thayer St. is densely populated with bookstores, New Age stores, and restaurants (from Indian to Thai to Middle Eastern). You'll find **Geoff's,** 178 Angel St. (751-9214), there, where students bite into more than 60 types of generic or superlative sandwiches ($3-9). (Open Mon.-Fri. 8am-10pm, Sat.-Sun. 10am-10pm.) You'll also find **Spats,** 230 Thayer St. (331-3435), the most clubby, Ivy-League joint on College Hill, decorated with brass handrails and dark wood furniture. Burgers and sandwiches are $5-7. (Open Mon.-Fri. 11am-1am, Sat.-Sun. 11am-2am.)

Sights and Entertainment Providence's most notable historic sights cluster on **College Hill,** a 350-year-old neighborhood. **Brown University,** established in 1764, claims several 18th-century buildings and provides the best info about the area. The Office of Admissions, housed in the historic Carliss-Brackett House at 45 Prospect St. (863-2378), gives a free walking tours of the campus daily at 10 and 11am, and 1, 3 and 4pm. (Open Mon.-Fri. 8am-4pm.) In addition to founding Rhode Island, Roger Williams created the Baptist Church; the *first* **First Baptist Church of America,** built in 1775, stands at 75 N. Main St. Looking down from the hill, you'll see the **Rhode Island State Capitol** (277-2357), crowned with one of the only three freestanding marble domes in the world. (Free guided tours Mon., Tues., Thurs. at 10 and 11am; free self-guide booklets available in room 218. Building open Mon.-Fri. 8:30am-4:30pm.)

The nearby **RISD Museum of Art,** 224 Benefit St. (454-6100), gathers a fine collection of Greek, Roman, Asian, and Impressionist art and a gigantic, 10th-century Japanese Buddha. (Open Tues.-Sat. noon-5pm; Sept.-mid-June Tues.-Wed. and Fri.-Sat. 10:30am-5pm, Thurs. noon-6pm, Sun. 2-5pm. $2, seniors and under 18 $1. Free on Sat.) The New England textile industry was born in 1793 when Samuel Slater built the first water-powered factory in America, from plans smuggled out of Britain. The **Slater Mill Historic Site** (725-8638) on Roosevelt Ave. in Pawtucket preserves this fiber heritage with operating machinery. ($4, kids 6-14 $2. Open June-Aug. Tues.-Sat. 10am-5pm, Sun. 1-5pm; spring and fall weekends only.)

Other attractions particular to Providence and places in proximity include the nationally acclaimed **Trinity Repertory Company,** 201 Washington St., Providence (351-4242), the AAA-level **Pawtucket Red Sox** (724-7300), who play at McCoy Stadium in Pawtucket, the stock-car races at the **Seekonk Speedway**

(336-8488), a few miles east on Rte. 6 in Massachusetts (1756 Fall River Ave.), and the **Providence Performing Arts Center,** 220 Weybosset St. (421-2787), which hosts a variety of concerts and Broadway musicals. The **Cable Car Cinema,** 204 S. Main St., Providence (272-3970), with an attached cafe, shows art and foreign films in an unusual setting—patrons recline on couches instead of regular seats. Read the *New Paper,* distributed free Thurs. or check the "Weekend" section of the *Friday Providence Journal* for theater and nightlife listings.

Vermont

Though insulated and isolated by the luxuriant Green Mountain range that dominates the state, Vermonters from every sparsely settled hollow have never shied from public dissent. They voice their opinions loudly and proudly, from conservatism (only Vermont and Maine voted against Franklin Roosevelt in all four elections) to liberalism (Burlington's socialist mayor Bernie Sanders has taken his views all the way to an Independent seat in the U.S. House of Representatives).

Several decades ago, many dissatisfied young urbanites headed to Vermont seeking its promise of peace and serenity. Needing a way to support themselves, these ex-urbanites-cum-granolas chose to live off nature by packaging and marketing it: organic food stores and mountaineering shops shot up faster than you can say "Ben and Jerry's." But Vermonters have responded to the influx of BMWs with anti-littering legislation and prohibition of billboards. Should tourism continue to threaten this pristine landscape, the protest of Vermonters, no doubt, will be heard.

PRACTICAL INFORMATION

Capital: Montpelier.
Vermont Travel Division, 134 State St., Montpelier 05602 (828-3236; open Mon.-Fri. 8am-4:30pm; longer hours during fall foliage). **Department of Forests, Parks and Recreation,** 103 S. Main St., Waterbury 05676 (244-8711; open Mon.-Fri. 8am-4:30pm). **Travel Division Fall Foliage Hotline** for fall colors info (828-3239). **Vermont Snowline** (229-0531), all day Nov.-May on snow conditions.
Time Zone: Eastern. **Postal Abbreviation:** VT
Sales Tax: 5%.

SKIING

Twenty-four downhill resorts and 47 cross-country trail systems lace Vermont. For a free winter attractions packet, call the Vermont Travel Division (see Practical Information above), or write **Ski Vermont,** 134 State St., Montpelier 05602. Ask about the "Ski Vermont Classics" program and the "Vermont Sunday Take-Off" package. Also contact **Vermont Ski Areas Association,** 26 State St., Montpelier 05601 (223-2439; open Mon.-Fri. 8am-4:30pm).

Vermont's famous downhill ski resorts offer a great range of terrain and accommodations, including cheap dorms. Some better resorts include: Killington (773-1300 or 800-621-6867; 107 trails, 18 lifts, 6 mountains, and the most extensive snowmaking system in the world); Stratton (297-2200 or 800-843-6867; area lodging 824-6915; 92 trails, 12 lifts); Sugarbush (583-2381; lodging 800-537-8427; 80 trails, 16 lifts, 2 mountains); Stowe (253-8521; lodging 800-247-8693; 44 trails, 10 lifts); and Jay Peak (800-451-4449; 37 trails, 6 lifts). Cross-country resorts include the Trapp Family Lodge, Stowe (253-8511; lodging 800-826-7000; 60 mi. of trails); Mountain Meadows, Killington (757-7077; 25 mi.); Woodstock (457-2114; 47 mi.); and Sugarbush-Rossignol (583-2301 or 800-451-4320; 30 mi. of trails.).

■■■ BRATTLEBORO

Southeastern Vermont is often accused of living too much in its colonial past, but Brattleboro, a favorite destination for peregrinating hippies, seems to be more a captive of the Age of Aquarius than the War for Independence. Indian prints are ubiquitous. The smell of patchouli wafts through the air. Craft and food cooperatives abound. The biggest sign in the window of the shoe store on Main St. reads "Birkenstock Repair." Nature-worship peaks in the fall when the city swells with an influx of tourists and when residents and visitors alike head for the hills to rollick in the resplendent foliage.

Practical Information The **Chamber of Commerce,** 180 Main St. (254-4565) will barrage you with countless brochures, among them the *Brattleboro Main Street Walking Tour.* Seasonal events are also posted. (Open Mon.-Fri. 8am-5pm.) In summer, information booths are open on the **Town Common** off Putney Rd. (257-1112), and on Western Ave. (257-4801), just beyond the historic **Creamery Bridge** built in 1879. (Putney Rd. booth open summer Mon.-Fri. 9am-6pm. During fall foliage and peak summer months open weekends 9am-6pm. Western Ave. booth open summer Thurs.-Sun. 10am-6pm.)

Amtrak's (800-835-8725) "Montrealer" train from New York City and Springfield stops in Brattleboro behind the museum. Trains go once daily to Montréal ($46), New York ($44), and Washington D.C. ($85). Arrange tickets and reservations at **Lyon Travel,** 10 Elliot St. (254-6033; open Mon.-Fri. 9am-5pm). **Greyhound** and **Vermont Transit** (254-6066) stop in the parking lot behind the Citgo station at the junction of U.S. 5, Rte. 9, and I-91 on Putney Rd. (Open Mon.-Fri. 8am-5pm, Sat. 8am-12:15pm, Sun. 10:30am-12:15pm, 2-3:30pm, and 6-7pm.) Brattleboro is on Vermont Transit's Burlington-New York City route (3 per day, $37.50). Other destinations include Springfield, MA (3 per day, $13) and White River Junction (3 per day, $11), with connections to Montpelier, Waterbury, Burlington, and Montréal. To get downtown from the Vermont Transit station, take the **Brattleboro Town Bus** (257-1761). Buses stop in front of the station and run on Putney Rd. to Main St. and then up High St. to West Brattleboro. (Buses Mon.-Fri. 7am-5pm. Fare 75¢, students 25¢.)

Brattleboro's **ZIP code** is 05301; the **area code** is 802.

Accommodations and Camping Next door to the Latchis Grille (see Food below), the renovated Art-Deco **Latchis Hotel** (254-6300), on the corner of Flat and Main St. downtown, has nice rooms at decent prices. (Singles $38-52, doubles $46-62.) The **West Village,** 480 Western Ave. (254-5610), is about three mi. out of town on Rte. 9 in West Brattleboro. Although happy to have one-night guests, West Village caters to the weekly client, taking reservations no more than one week in advance. (Singles with kitchenette and microwave $35. Doubles with kitchenette and microwave $40, weekly $160.) Somewhat closer to town is the newly renovated **Days Inn** (254-4583) on Putney Rd. past the Marina. (Double-bed $39, 2 double beds $55. $6 each additional adult, roll-away bed $6. Free continental breakfast.) Ramble north on Rte. 30 half an hour to find the **Vagabond Hostel (HI/AYH)** (874-4096) outside the town of East Jamaica. The Vagabond is very close to the summer offerings of the Stratton, Mt. Snow, and Bromley ski areas. (Open May 15-Nov. 16. $12 , nonmembers $15.) **Fort Dummer State Park,** (254-2610; 2 mi. south on U.S. 5, turn left on Fairground Ave. just before the I-91 interchange, and follow it around to South Main St.), has campsites with fireplaces, picnic tables, and bathroom facilities, and one lean-to with disabled access. (Tentsites $10. Lean-tos $14. Firewood $2 per armload. Hot showers 25¢. Reservations accepted up to 21 days in advance; $3, non-refundable, min. stay 2 nights. Open May 21-Labor Day.) **Molly Stark State Park** (464-5460) is 15 mi. west of town on Rte. 9. (24 tentsites, $10 each; 11 lean-

tos, $14 each; 9 motor home sites without hookups, $10 each. Hot showers 25¢.
Reservations $3, min. of 3 days in advance. Open Memorial Day-Columbus Day.)

Food Just across Putney Rd. from the Connecticut River Safari is the **Marina Restaurant** (257-7563). The Marina overlooks the West River, offering a cool breeze
and a beautiful view. Try the chicken with fusilli ($7.75) or the eggplant parmesan
($6.75). (Open Wed.-Sat. 4-10pm, Sun. 11am-2pm. Summer lunch Fri.-Sat. 11:30am-
3pm.) The **Common Ground,** 25 Eliot St. (257-0855), where the town's laid-back
"granolas" cluster, supports organic farmers and cottage industries. It features a
wide range of affordable veggie dishes. You can get a people's meal (soup, salad,
bread, and beverage) for $4.25, good ol' PB&J for $3. For dinner, try a square meal
in a round bowl. (Open Mon. and Wed.-Sat. 11:30am-9pm, Sun. 10:30am-9pm.) The
Backside Cafe, 24 High St. (257-5056), serves delicious food in an artsy loft with
rooftop dining. For dinner, create your own burrito ($5.25) or *chile rellenos* (2 for
$5.50). (Open Mon.-Fri. 7:30am-4pm, Sat. 8am-3pm, Sun. 10am-3pm; for dinner
Mon.-Fri. 5-9pm. In winter, no lunch on Fri.) For locally grown fruits, vegetables,
and cider, go to the **farmers markets** (254-9657) on the Town Common, Main St.
(June 12-Sept. 11 Wed. 10am-2pm), or on Western Ave. near Creamery Bridge (May
11-Oct. 12 Sat. 9am-2pm, Wed. 3-6pm). Visit the **Latchis Grille,** 6 Flat St. (254-
4747), and sample some beer made by the **Windham Brewery** right on the premises (7 oz. sampler $1.75, 12 oz. Pilsner $2.20). Free tours of the brewery Thursdays at 6pm. (Grille open daily 11:30am-midnight.) **Mole's Eye Cafe** (257-0771), at
the corner of High and Main St., has rock, R&B, blues, and reggae bands on Wed.,
Fri., and Sat. nights at 9pm. (Open daily 11:30am-midnight or 1am; in summer open
Mon.-Fri. 11:30am-midnight or 1am, Sat. 4pm-midnight or 1am. Light meals about
$5. Cover Fri.-Sat. $3. Open mike Thurs. 8:30pm.)

Sights Brattleboro chills at the confluence of the West and Connecticut Rivers,
both of which can be explored by **canoe.** Rentals are available at **Connecticut
River Safari** (257-5008 or 254-3908) on Putney Rd. just across the West River
Bridge. They will also transport canoes to other rivers in New England. (Open May
1-Oct. 31 daily 8am-6pm, 2-hr. minimum $8; $12 per ½-day, $18 per day. 2 days—
not necessarily consecutive—$28; longer packages available.)

The **Windham Gallery,** 69 Main St. (257-1881), hosts local art openings the first
Friday of every month as well as poetry readings and discussions by artists about
their work. (Open Fri.-Sat. noon-8pm, Sun. and Wed.-Thurs. noon-4pm, $1 sug-
gested donation.) For a bit of local color, visit the **Brightside Boutique,** 24 High St.
(258-4536), which sells tie-dye shirts, imported Guatemalan and Indian clothing,
and politically correct bumper stickers. (Open Mon.-Thurs. 10am-5:30pm, Fri.
10am-8pm, Sun. noon-5pm.)

Foliage mavens shouldn't miss **Brattleboro's New England Bach Festival** (257-
4523). Internationally renowned, the festival runs annually from early October
through early November, featuring vocal and instrumental soloists. Thousands cram
the common for **Village Days,** the last weekend in July, and **Apple Days,** the last
weekend in September, to browse through displays of local arts and crafts. Village
Days also features **Riff-Raft Regatta** where man-made, non-motorized rafts (two
kegs strung together will do) race against each other.

■■■ BURLINGTON

Burlington has taken the oxymoronic expression "middle-class hippie" and made it
not just a reality but a way of life. Familiar 60s platitudes such as "Arms are for Hug-
ging," once the rallying-cries of sit-ins, have become slogans for "stuck-ons," the
ubiquitous bumperstickers on Hondas and Volvos. In downtown Burlington tie-dye
and Grateful Dead-esque stores coexist peacefully with elegant art galleries and
designer clothing boutiques. Local colleges—the University of Vermont (UVM) and

Champlain College, among others—endow the city with the swank and smarm of youth. Burlington's ideal location, tucked between Lake Champlain and the Green Mountains, quaint village-like atmosphere, and young, cultural vibrancy make it a pleasant, peaceful destination.

PRACTICAL INFORMATION

Emergency: 911.

Tourist Information: Lake Champlain Regional Chamber of Commerce, 209 Battery St. (863-3489), right next to the ferry pier. Provides free maps of the Burlington Bike Path and parks, as well as numerous other brochures on local attractions, B&Bs, and restaurants. Open Mon.-Fri. 8:30am-5pm, Sat.-Sun. 10am-2pm; late Oct.-early June Mon.-Fri. 8:30am-5pm. More centrally located is the **Church St. Marketplace Information Gallery,** on the corner of Church and Bank St. Open May 15-June Mon.-Sat. 11am-4pm, July-mid-Oct. daily 11am-5pm.

Amtrak: 29 Railroad Ave., Essex Jct. (800-872-7245 or 879-7298), 5 mi. east of Rte. 15 from the center of Burlington. To: Montréal ($19); New York ($60). Open daily 6am-9pm. Bus downtown every ½ hr., 75¢.

Buses: Vermont Transit, 135 Saint Paul St. (864-6811), at Main St. Connections to: Boston ($42); Montréal ($23); White River Junction ($14); Middlebury ($7); Bennington ($18); Montpelier ($7); Albany ($29). Connections made with Greyhound. Mid-Sept.-early June 25% discount for students with ID. Ameripasses accepted. Open daily 7am-8pm.

Public Transport: Chittenden County Transit Authority (CCTA), (864-0211). Frequent, reliable service. Downtown hub at Cherry and Church St. Connections with Shelburne and other outlying areas. Buses operate every ½ hr. Mon.-Sat. 5:45am-10:30pm, depending on routes. Fare 75¢, seniors and disabled 35¢, under 18 50¢, under 5 free. **Special Services Transportation Agency** (658-5817),supplies information and advice about disabled travel.

Bike Rental: Ski Rack, 85 Main St. (658-3313). Road bike ($5 per hr., $18 per day, $66 per week), mountain bike ($6/22/100), cross bike ($5/20/85). Helmet and lock included. Bike repairs guaranteed 48 hrs. or less; minor repairs while you wait. Also rent in-line skates ($6 per 3 hr., $10 per day), helmet and pads included. Open Mon.-Fri. 9am-8pm, Sat. 9am-6pm, Sun. 11am-5pm.

Help Lines: Women's Rape Crisis Center, 863-1236. **Crises Services of Chittenden County,** 656-3587. Both open 24 hrs.

Post Office: 11 Elmwood Ave. (863-6033), at Pearl St. Open Mon.-Fri. 8am-5pm, Sat. 9am-noon. **ZIP code:** 05401.

Area Code: 802.

ACCOMMODATIONS, CAMPING, AND FOOD

The Chamber of Commerce has complete accommodations listings for the area. Bed & Breakfasts are generally found in the outlying suburbs. Reasonably priced hotels and guest houses pepper Shelburne Rd. south of downtown. Three mi. from downtown, **Mrs. Farrell's Home Hostel (HI/AYH),** 27 Arlington (865-3730), off Heineburg, has six beds: four in a clean, comfortable basement, and two on a screened-in porch amidst her garden's flowers. Ubiquitous yet socially-conscious signs remind you of the do's and don'ts of the place. (Members $15, nonmembers $17. Accessible by public transport.) The curfew is 10pm. Reservations are necessary and drop-ins cannot be accommodated. Getting hold of the owner is difficult—try calling around 7-8am or 5-7pm. Close to downtown is **Howden Cottage,** 32 N. Champlain (864-7198). A local artist will rent you a slope-ceilinged room and bake muffins for your continental breakfast in this lovely B&B. (Mid-May-mid-Oct. singles $39, doubles $49; off-season singles $35, doubles $45. Reservations strongly recommended by credit card.) **North Beach Campsites,** Institute Rd. (862-0942), is only 1½ mi. north of town on North Ave., along Lake Champlain. (Open mid-May-mid-Sept. Sites $13, $15 with electricity, $18 with full hookup. Showers 25¢, beach free, but closes at 9pm.) Take the CCTA North Ave. bus leaving from the main city terminal on Saint Paul St. **Shelburne Campground,** Shelburne Rd. (985-2540), 1 mi.

north of Shelburne and 5 mi. south of Burlington, offers a pool, laundry facilities, and free showers. Buses *en route* to Shelburne South stop right next to the campground. (Open May-Oct. Sites for 2 people $16, $18 with hookup, $2 each additional person.)

Freddy's, 171 Church St. (863-7171), sums up Burlington's character by offering rempeh- and seitan-based all-veggie burgers cooked in the fast-food spirit which will appeal to hippies, yuppies, and any combination of the two. (Veggie burgers $2.40-3.30. Open Mon.-Thurs. 11am-9pm, Fri.-Sat. 11am-10pm, Sun. noon-8pm.) **Henry's Diner,** 155 Bank St. (862-9010), has offered the ultimate American diner experience since 1925. (Sandwiches $2-4, full meals $5-10, breakfast offered all day. Open Mon. 6:30am-2:30pm, Tues.-Thurs. 6:30am-4pm, Fri. 6:30am-8pm, Sat. 6:30am-4pm, Sun. 8am-2pm.) A must-visit is **Noonies Deli,** at 131 Main St. (658-3354; also at 294 N. Winooski, 658-4888). Fill up on their huge sandwiches, including the delicious vegetarian on home-made bread ($4-5). (Open Mon.-Thurs.8am-8pm, Fri. 8am-9pm, Sat. 9am-9pm.) Catch their coffee house (Sept.-May Fri.-Sat. 8pm-midnight). Loads of booze and fun can be found at the **Vermont Pub and Brewery,** 144 College St. (865-0500), at Saint Paul's, which offers affordable sandwiches, delicious home-made beers, and English pub favorites like cornish *pasties*—similar to a pot pie ($5). Should you want to learn more about Original Vermont Lager, the brewers and publicans would be happy to escort you on a brewery tour. (Open daily 11:30-1am. Free tours Wed. at 8pm and Sat. at 4pm. Others by appointment. Live entertainment Fri.-Sat.9:30pm.) A fine wine and cheese feast can be purchased at the **Cheese Outlet,** 400 Pine St. (863-3968 or 800-447-1205). Purchase wine for as little as $4 in this strong-smelling warehouse. (Open Mon.-Sat. 9am-7pm, Sun. 11am-5pm.) Just next door, the **Olive Branch Bakery,** 398 Pine St. (658-1882), serves up outstanding peaces of bread and pastries. Try the Vermont Cheddar Bread ($2.25), a calzone ($2.25), or a thick slice of scrumptious poppy seed bread (95¢). No seating. (Open Mon.-Sat. 9am-6pm, Sun. noon-5pm.)

Here's where the whole adventure began. This is the place. Savor the ultimate Vermont experience in the company of mural cows at the original **Ben and Jerry's,** 69 Cherry St. (862-9620). (Cherry Garcia or Cookie Dough cone $2. Open Mon.-Thurs. 10:30am-11:30pm, Fri.-Sat. 10:30am-12:30am, Sun. 11am-11:30pm.)

SIGHTS AND ENTERTAINMENT

With its sprawling, low-lying suburbs, Burlington might not look like a cultural mecca. However, the city still manages to take advantage of its scenic location along Lake Champlain, its artistic community, and its status as the largest city in the midst of ruralia. **Church Street Marketplace** downtown is a popular pedestrian mall; besides being a haven for tie-dye and ice-cream lovers, this historic district serves as a shopping center for modern northern Vermont and displays and sells the works of local artists. The history-inclined also should stroll through Victorian **South Willard Street,** which now houses Champlain College, and the campus of the **University of Vermont** (656-3480), founded in 1797. **City Hall Park,** in the heart of downtown, and **Battery Street Park,** in the pancreas of downtown on Lake Champlain, are beautiful places to relax and study the scenery.

Summer culture vultures won't want to miss the many festivities Burlington offers: the **Vermont Mozart Festival** (862-7352 or 800-639-9097) which sends Bach, Beethoven, and Mozart to barns, farms, and meadows in July and early August, the **Discover Jazz Festival** (863-7992) featuring over 200 international and Vermont musicians in early to mid-June, and the **Champlain Valley Folk Festival** (796-3048) in August. The Flynn Theatre Box Office, 153 Main St. (863-5966), handles sales for the Mozart and jazz performances. (Open Mon.-Fri. 10am-5pm, Sat. 10am-1pm.) The **Burlington Community Boathouse,** at the base of College St. at Lake Champlain (865-3377), is a good place to go if you're looking to get onto the water. The Boathouse rents 13-ft. laser sailboats ($15 per hr., $40 per 4 hr., $65 per 8 hr., Sat.-Sun. rates are $20/50/60) as well as 19 ft. Rhodes sailboats ($25/60/95; Sat.-Sun.

$30/75/120), and rowboats ($5 per hr.). Classes in sailing throughout the summer (Tues.-Sun. 9am-5pm) by appointment. (Open Memorial Day-early Oct. Mon.-Fri. 11am-7pm, Sat.-Sun. 9am-7pm.)

■ Near Burlington

Seven mi. south of Burlington, in **Shelburne,** is the **Shelburne Museum** (985-3346), which houses one of the best collections of Americana in the country. Beside 35 buildings transported from all over New England, 45-acre Shelburne has a covered bridge from Cambridge, a steamboat and a lighthouse from Lake Champlain, and a bit of a local railroad. Don't miss the Degas, Cassatt, Manet, Monet, Rembrandt, and Whistler paintings. Tickets are valid for two days; you'll need both to cover the mile-long exhibit. (Open mid-May-mid-Oct. daily 9am-5pm, mid-Oct.-mid-May Sat. only by reservation; $15, students $9, ages 6-14 $6.50, under 6 free.) 5 mi. farther south on U.S. 7, the **Vermont Wildflower Farm** (425-3500), has a seed shop and 6½ acres of wildflower gardens. (Open April-late Oct. daily 10am-5pm. Admission April-May free; July-Oct. $3, seniors and AAA members $2.50, under 12 free.)

Northeast of Burlington on Rte. 127 is the **Ethan Allen Homestead** (865-4556). In the 1780s, Allen, who forced the surrender of Fort Ticonderoga and helped establish the state of Vermont, built his cabin in what is now the Winooski Valley Park. A multi-media show and tour give insight into the hero and his era. (Open Tues.-Sun. 1-5pm; mid-June-Labor Day Mon.-Sat. 10am-5pm, Sun. 1-5pm; Labor Day-late Oct. daily 1-5pm; $3.50, seniors $3, kids 5-17 $2, under 5 free.)

Ferries crisscross **Lake Champlain,** a 100-mi.-long lake between Vermont's Green Mountains and New York's Adirondacks, often referred to as "Vermont's West Coast." The **Lake Champlain Ferry** (864-9804), at the bottom of King St., will ship you across the lake and back from Burlington's King St. Dock to Port Kent, NY. (Mid-June-early Sept. daily 7:15am-7:45pm, 14 per day; mid-May-mid-June 8am-5:30pm, 8 per day; Sept.-mid-Oct. 8am-5:30pm, 8-11 per day; $3, ages 6-12 $1, with car $12. Crossing time 1 hr.) You can also take a ferry from Grand Isle to Plattsburg, NY, or go 14 mi. south of Burlington and take one from Charlotte, VT, to Essex, NY (either fare $1.75, ages 6-12 50¢, with car $6.75). The Grand Isle Ferry is the only one of the three to run year-round. The **Spirit of Ethan Allen** scenic cruise (862-9685) departs from Burlington's Perkins Pier at the bottom of Maple St. The boat cruises along the Vermont coast, giving passengers a close-up view of the famous Thrust Fault, invisible from land. (Late May-mid-Oct. daily at 10am, noon, 2pm, and 4pm. $7.50, ages 5-11 $3.50. Call about the more costly Captain's Dinner and Sunset Cruises.) The campsite near the peak of nearby **Mt. Philo State Park** (425-2390) affords great views of the environs. (Open Memorial Day-Columbus Day daily 10am-sunset. Campsites $10. Lean-tos $14. Admission $1.50, ages 4-13 $1.) Take the **Vermont Transit** bus from Burlington heading south along U.S. 7 toward Vergennes. There's a sign on the left for the park before you're out of Charlotte. Twisting U.S. 2 cuts through the center of the lake by hopping from the mainland to Grand Isle, then north to North Hero Island and up into Québec.

Several state campgrounds speckle the islands, and much of the surrounding land is wilderness. The marsh to the north is protected in the **Missiquoi National Wildlife Refuge.** Camp at **Burton Island State Park** (524-6353), accessible only by ferry (8:30am-6:30pm) from Kill Kare State Park, 35 mi. north of Burlington and 3½ mi. southwest of St. Albans off U.S. 7. The camp has 46 lean-to and tent sites ($15.50 and $11 respectively, $3 per additional person in tent, $4 in lean-to). **Grand Isle** also has a state park with camping (372-4300), just off U.S. 2 north of Keeler Bay. (Sites $12, $3 each additional person after 4, lean-tos $16, $4 each additional person after 4. Open late May-mid-Oct.)

■■■ MONTPELIER

Montpelier (pop. 8200), the smallest state capital in the union, allows the maintenance of an intimate small-town timbre (the town shuts down on Sat.).

Practical Information The **Central Vermont Chamber of Commerce** (229-5711; open Mon.-Fri. 9am-5pm) is located on Stewart St. in Berlin, 1½ mi. from Montpelier, and can provide you with a list of restaurants and accommodations in the area, a helpful town map, and info about the whole state. Consult their yellow info booth in Barre in the summer when the Chamber is closed (open late June-Labor Day Mon.-Sat. 10am-5pm, Sun. 10am-1pm). **Vermont Transit** is behind Chittenden Bank at 112 State St. (223-7112). Daily buses go to: Boston ($37); New York City ($55); White River Junction ($10); Waterbury ($3); Burlington ($7). VT also serves Montréal and Portland, ME. (Open Mon.-Fri. 8am-6:30pm, Sat. 8am-4pm, Sun. noon-4pm.) Montpelier's **ZIP code** is 05602; the **area code** is 802.

Food and Sights The city is the proud home of the **New England Culinary Institute,** 250 Main St. (223-6324); sample first-year students' innovations (such as roast loin of pork with maple mustard glaze and cranapple compote) at the **Elm Street Cafe,** 38 Elm St. (223-3188). (Dinner entrees $9-11, lunch specials under $5. Open Mon.-Fri. 7-10am, 11:30am-1:30pm and 5:30-9pm, Sat. 8am-1:30pm and 5:30-9pm.) **Tubbs Restaurant,** 24 Elm St. (229-9202), features the French cuisine of second-year students in the now-elegant confines of the original Montpelier jailhouse. (Lunch entrees $6-8. Dinner entrees $12-18. Open Mon.-Fri. 11:30am-2pm and 6-9:30pm, Sat. 6-9:30pm.) The school's bakery/café, **La Brioche** (229-0443), now at the City Center on the corner of State and Main, offers delicious pastries and cakes, as well as fresh-baked bread and homemade pâtés. (Open Mon.-Fri. 7:30am-7pm, Sat. 8am-5:30pm, Sun. 8am-3pm.)

Up Main St. on County Rd. oozes the **Morse Farm** (223-2740 or 800-242-2740), a working maple syrup farm that offers free samples of multicolored syrups. Maples are tapped and the sugarhouse operates in early spring. The farm gives a splendid panoramic view of the hills during foliage. (Open daily 8am-8pm, Labor Day-June 15 9am-5pm.) **The Green Mountain Club** (244-7037) headquarters used to be in Montpelier, but they've since moved to Waterbury Center, near Stowe along Rte. 100. Founded in 1910, the GMC built and maintains the **Long Trail,** the oldest long-distance hiking trail in the U.S. Call or write for info on hiking and outdoor activities in all of Vermont RR1: Box 650, Rte. 100 Waterbury Center VT 05677.

■■■ STOWE

Between Montpelier and Burlington lies **Stowe,** like its namesake gardens in England, beautiful and serene in summer. But the gardens offer no slopes, whereas Stowe, VT, bustles among the blizzards in winter as one of the east's ski capitals, with four fine downhill skiing areas (see Skiing below).

Practical Information The ski areas all lie northwest of Stowe on Rte. 108. Stowe is 12 mi. north of I-89s exit 10, which is 27 mi. southwest of Burlington. Getting to and around Stowe without a car is virtually impossible as there is no public transportation. **Vermont Transit** will only take you to **Vincent's Drug and Variety Store,** off Park Row in Waterbury, 10 mi. from Stowe. (Open Mon.-Fri. 8:30am-7pm, Sat. 8:30am-6pm, Sun. 9am-3pm.) To explore and get a good workout, rent a **bike**. You can also take the less strenuous route and rent a **car** from **Stowe Auto Service** on Mountain Rd. (253-7608). ($30 per day, 50 free mi., 20¢ per extra mi.; $10 insurance. Package deal of $57 with unlimited mileage; must be 21 with credit card. Open 7am-6pm daily.) The **Stowe Trolley** (253-7585) will take you up the mountain from Main Street (every hr., 10am-4pm; winter every ½ hr. 7:30am-

STOWE

4:30pm; $1). If you're trying to get back to Waterbury, **Lamoille County Taxi** (253-9433 or 800-252-0204) will charge $17.

Contact the **Stowe Area Association** (253-7321 or 800-247-8693), on Main St., in the center of the village, for free booking service and summer info on the area's lodging, restaurants, and activities, including skiing. (Open Mon.-Fri. 9am-5pm, Sat. 10am-5pm, Sun. 10am-4pm; winter Mon.-Fri. 9am-9pm, Sat.-Sun. 10am-6pm.) Stowe's **post office** (253-2571) is at 105 Depot St., off Main St. (Open Mon.-Fri. 8:30am-5pm, Sat. 9am-noon.) The **ZIP code** is 05672; the **area code** is 802.

Food, Accommodations, and Camping For a filling meal try the **Sunset Grille and Tap Room** (253-9281), on Cottage Club Rd. off Mountain Rd., a friendly, down-home barbecue place with a vast selection of domestic beers and generous meals ($5-15). (Open daily 11:30am-midnight.) At the **Depot Street Malt Shoppe,** 57 Depot St. (253-4269), step back in time for a taste of the American '50s. Sit at the counter as they used to and delight in a Lumberjack Burger ($3.80) or a Fountain Treat (vanilla coke $1, malted milk $2). Open daily 11am-9pm, Nov.-May Mon. 11am-4pm, Tues.-Sun. 11am-9pm.

The best lodging bargain in town by far, **the Vermont State Ski Dorm** (253-4010), up 7 mi. into Mountain Rd., doubles as a hostel from April-Dec. ($10 per night, breakfast $3.25, dinner $3.50; kitchen available), while the rest of the year, manager Jim Sanderson, who happens to be a trained chef, serves two meals a day and charges $27.50. This austere and all-wooden cabin will accommodate 48 people in a serene plot of forest which sits by a sparkling stream. Make sure to reserve by phone far in advance for ski and foliage seasons. The friendly, eccentric host of the **Golden Kitz,** Mountain Rd. (253-4217 or 800-548-7568), offers her "lovie" travelers a relaxed atmosphere, great stories, and kitschy theme bedrooms. (Singles with shared bath $36-40 in highest season; $30-36 midwinter weekends; $24-26 in early and late ski season; off-season and summer $20-28. Doubles $52-70 highest season; $46-50 midwinter weekends; $38-56 early and late ski season; $36-56 off-season and summer. Multi-day packages available.) The (soon-to-be) committed budget traveler should ask if "dungeon" doubles are available ($30). Situated on a real brook, the **Gold Brook Campground** (253-7683 or 253-8147) babbles 1½ mi. south of the town center on Rte. 100. (Open year-round. Hot showers, laundry, volleyball, badminton, horseshoes. Tent sites for 2 people $12, with varying degrees of hookup $16, $18, and $21; $3 per each additional person.) **Smuggler's Notch State Park** (253-4014) offers hot showers, lean-tos ($15 for 4 people, $4 per additional person to max. of 8) and tent sites ($11 for 4 people, $3 per each additional person to max. of 8). (Open Queen Victoria Day-Columbus Day; reservations suggested.)

Skiing and Activities Stowe Mountain Resort (253-3000 or 800-253-4754), formerly Mount Mansfield (the highest peak in Vermont, at 4393 ft.), **Smuggler's Notch** (664-8851 or 800-451-8752), **Bolton Valley** (434-2131), and **Sugarbush** (583-2381). The **Trapp Family Lodge** (yes, *the* Trapp family of *Sound of Music* fame) Luce Hill Rd. (253-8511), offers the area's best cross-country skiing. Skiing is expensive; a one-day lift ticket at any of these areas costs nearly $45. A better bet might be the **Ski Vermont's Classics** program. A three-day $106 lift ticket (available at participating slopes) allows you to ski at any number of resorts in the area; for more info contact the **Stowe Area Association** (see Practical Information above). **AJ's Ski and Sports** (253-4593), at the base of Mountain Rd., rents virtually brand new ski and snow equipment (skis, boots, and poles: downhill $16 per day, 2 days $28; cross country $12/20; snowboards with boots: $20 per day). Reserve equipment five days in advance for 20% off. (Open Nov.-April daily 8am-6pm; off-season 10am-6pm.)

In summer, Stowe's frenetic pace drops off—as do its prices. Rent **mountain bikes** at **Stowe Mountain Sports,** 1056 Mountain Rd. (253-4896; $6 for first hr., $4 for second hr., and $2 for each additional hr.; open daily 9am-6pm), and **in-line skates** at **Front Four Sports,** 430 Mountain Rd. (253-9690; $7 per hr., $12 for 3 hr., $18 per day; open summer 9am-5:30pm daily). Stowe's 5½-mi. asphalt recreation path, which starts behind the Community Church and roughly parallels Mountain Rd.'s ascent into, well, the mountain, is smoothly suited for cross-country skiing in the winter, and biking, skating, or strolling in the summer.

Those interested in checking out the area's excellent **fly-fishing** should head to the **Fly Rod Shop** (253-7347), 3 mi. south of Stowe on Rte. 100. The shop rents fly rods and reels ($12 per day), and rods with spinning reels ($6 per day). Watch the owner tie a fly or two, or call about fly-tying classes in winter. Free fly-fishing classes are offered on the shop's own new pond (April-Oct.). Fishing licenses are available (non-residents $18 per 3 days, $35 for season; residents $18 for season). If you're looking to canoe on the nearby Lamoille River, **Umiak,** 1880 Mountain Rd. (253-2317), in Gale Farm Center, is the place to go. The store (its name is the Inuit word for "kayak") rents *umiaks* and canoes in the summer ($20 per ½-day, $28 per day) and offers a full day river trip for $18 (rental and transportation to the river included). In the winter try on a pair of snowshoes ($14 per day, $9 per ½-day), or their metal-edged cross-country skis for off-trail use ($12 per day, $8 per ½-day). (Open daily 10am-6pm; Dec.-March Sat.-Wed. 10am-6pm, Thurs.-Fri. 10am-8pm.) Summer horseback riding is available at **Topnotch Stowe,** on Mountain Rd. (253-8585). Gallop or trot into the woods for $20 per hr. (tours are guided and available thrice daily, summer only).

Sights and Entertainment The socially conscious and fun-loving **Ben and Jerry's Ice Cream Factory** (244-5641) lies north on Rte. 100, a couple miles off I-89 in Waterbury. Having Started in 1978 in a converted gas station through a Penn State correspondence course in ice-cream making, Ben and Jerry have since developed some of the best ice cream in the world. After the October, 1988 stock market crash, this caloric duo made the trek to Wall Street to serve up free scoops of two made-for-the-occasion flavors: "Economic Crunch" and "That's Life." You can sample other celebrated flavors such as Rainforest Crunch, White Russian, and Cherry Garcia. ($1 tours daily 9am-5pm every ½ hr., July-Aug. every ¼ hr.)

Ski resorts have culture too. After a long day hiking, unwind at a performance of the **Stowe Stage Company,** the Playhouse, Mountain Rd. (253-7944; performances 8pm June-Oct.). The sound of music fills the Trapp Family Concert Meadow, Sundays at 7pm, for Stowe Performing Arts **Music in the Meadow.** (253-7321; Tickets $12, $10 in advance, under 19 $5.) **Noon Music in May** each Wed. at the Stowe Community Church, and the **Gazebo Lawn Concert Series** at 7pm on the library lawn in Aug. are free (donations welcome). (Call 253-7321 for info on all three.)

In 1994, Stowe will celebrate its **bicentennial** with a plethora of special events. Call the Stowe Area Association for information (see Practical Info. above).

■■■ WOODSTOCK AND WHITE RIVER JUNCTION

White River Junction Taking its name from its location at the confluence of the White and Connecticut rivers, today the Junction receives more visitors as a result of the nearby intersection of I-89 and I-91. Central Vermont is graced with quiet winding back roads and grazing cows in quiet green pastures; if you enjoy rural rubbernecking, plan an east-west trip along U.S. 4, or a north-south trip on Rte. 100. The roads are best reached from U.S. 5 or I-89, at the Connecticut River.

An **information booth** across Sykes Ave. from the bus station (intersection of Sykes and U.S. 5 off I-89 and 91) can fill your pockets with brochures on Vermont. (Open May 27-Oct. 15 daily 10am-5pm.) In town, the **Chamber of Commerce,** 12 Gates St. (295-6200), just off S. Main, can also supply you with information. (Open Mon.-Fri. 9am-noon and sporadically in the afternoons, especially on Wed.) Once the hub of railroad transportation in the northeastern U.S., White River Junction now serves as the major bus center for central and eastern Vermont. **Vermont Transit** (295-3011), on U.S. 5 adjoining the Wm. Tally House Restaurant, has connections across New Hampshire and up and down the Connecticut River. (Students with ID 25% discount May-Sept. Office open Sun.-Fri. 7am-9:30pm, Sat. 7am-5pm.) **Amtrak's** *Montrealer* train running south to New York City and Washington D.C., and north to Essex Junction (near Burlington) and Montréal chugs through here daily (800-872-7245; station on Railroad Rd. off N. Main St.; open daily 9:15am-6pm).

For a quick bite to eat, stop at the local favorite, the **Polkadot Restaurant,** 1 N. Main St. (295-9722), a classic and remarkably good diner. (Sandwiches $1.15-4.15, 2 pork chops, applesauce, mashed potatoes, veggie, soup, rolls, and coffee $5.50. Open daily 5am-8pm.) The best—and pretty much the only—bet for lodging is the old-style **Hotel Coolidge,** 17 S. Main St. (295-3118 or 800-622-1124), across the road from the retired Boston and Maine steam engine. From the bus station, walk to the right along U.S. 5, down the hill past two stop lights (about 1 mi.) into town. Renamed in honor of "Silent Cal" Coolidge's pop, a frequent guest at the railroad hotel, the Coolidge boasts neatly kept rooms at fair prices and a housekeeping manager with a keen sense of humor. (Singles from $22, doubles from $28. For the cheapest rates, ask for the hostel rooms. A good bargain is the deal on 2 adjoining rooms sharing a full bath: $55 for 2 plus $10 per extra person.)

Also in the Junction you'll find the **Catamount Brewery,** 58 S. Main St. (296-2248), where you can sample, among other things, delicious, unpasteurized amber ale produced in strict accordance with British brewing methods. (Tours Mon.-Thurs. 11am, and 1 and 3pm, Sat. 1 and 3pm, Nov.-June Sat. 11am, and 1 and 3pm. Tours are apt to vary seasonally; call for details.)

Woodstock A Vermont-village-cum-wealthy-tourist-hangout, Woodstock is 14 mi. west of White River Junction on U.S. 4. The Woodstock **Chamber of Commerce** (457-3555; open Mon.-Fri. 10am-2pm), upstairs at 18 Central St., provides maps of trails for nearby mountains Peg and Tom (a ½-hour walk up Mt. Tom will afford a good view of the town), as well as complete lists of local B&Bs, restaurants, and stores. It is also helpful for finding the limited hiking and skiing in the area. The chamber also sponsors an **information booth** (457-1042) in the middle of the village green. (Open late June-mid-Oct. Mon.-Fri. 10am-4pm, Sat.-Sun. 10am-5pm.) In addition there is the **Woodstock Town Crier,** a chalkboard with local listings on the corner of Elm and Church St. The **Vermont Transit** (457-1325) agency in Woodstock, at the Whippletree Shop, 4 Central St., provides schedules and timetables of Vermont transit buses. Buses travel to: White River Junction (1 per day, $4); Rutland (1 per day, $7). Students with ID receive 25% discount Sept.-May.

Woodstock is home to a number of **Bed and Breakfasts.** Consult the *Woodstock Guide to Lodgings,* available at the Chamber of Commerce and the info booth. **Quechee State Park** (295-2990), off U.S. 4 between Woodstock and White River, has hiking trails around **Quechee Gorge,** a spectacular 163-ft. drop from cliffs to the Ottauquechee River below. A bridge connecting the trails to the park's picnic grounds offers a view that makes you feel small and quite mortal; on the eastern side of the bridge an **info booth** can answer questions. (Open May-Oct. day use $1.50, under 14 $1. Tent sites $11 for 4 people, $3 each additional person up to 8. Lean-tos $15 per person, $4 each additional person up to 8. Disabled-accessible tent site and lean-tos. Metered showers. Reservations minimum 3 nights in advance $3.)

MID-ATLANTIC STATES

Ranging from the sleepy, almost-Southern slave state of Maryland, home to Edgar-Allen Poe, through the experiment in Federal Democracy that is the District of Columbia, up to the vast melting pot of New York City, the diverse and densely populated states along the Eastern seaboard tell the story of the nation's creation and development. Constitutional democracy and free speech are still celebrated in Philadelphia, the nation's first capital, and the search for religious freedom persists as Mennonites and Amish cling to their Old-World ways and shun materialism. The presence of some of the nation's oldest and finest universities alongside large rural areas reflect the origins of the U.S. in an educated yeomanry. During the Civil War, theis area witnessed the troops of North and South forever alter the American agenda. Around the turn of the century, the coal of Appalachia and the steel of Pittsburgh transformed the United States into a global economic power. The polyglot populations of the Mid-Atlantic demonstrate how differences can contribute to the vitality of national identity or mire it in hopeless conflict.

In spite of the concentration of urban centers in the Mid-Atlantic, there is plenty of outdoor fun. The celebrated Appalachian Trail treks through the area; in northern New York the Adirondack reign as the largest park in the U.S. outside of Alaska. The wilds of Pennsylvania's Allegheny Mountains provide a setting where you can raft, backpack, and even be chased by bears in truly remote areas. Wildlife refuges scattered along the Atlantic coast and its bays protect birdlife and wild ponies alike.

▩ Delaware

Delawareans strive to make up for their state's small size with a fierce pride in its historical past and geography. They adopted "First State" as their slightly misleading nickname—they were the first to ratify the U.S. Constitution in 1787. Most of Delaware's population sleeps in the northern industrial region, on the strip between Wilmington and Newark. Tourists usually associate the state with chemical industry and big corporations: here, in 1938, nylon first shimmered and ran. But Delaware offers its tourist pleasures in the less synthetic regions of the seacoast; Lewes and Rehoboth Beach have the natural charm of southern resort towns, while the Delaware Dunes stretch across more than 2000 acres of accessible seashore.

PRACTICAL INFORMATION

Capital: Dover.
Visitor Information: State Visitors Service, P.O. Box 1401, 99 King's Hwy., Dover 19903 (800-441-8846 outside DE). Open Mon.-Fri. 8am-4:30pm. **Division of Fish and Wildlife,** William Penn St., Dover 19901 (739-4431).
Time Zone: Eastern. **Postal Abbreviation:** DE
Sales Tax: 0%.

■■■ REHOBOTH BEACH

Lewes The reserved atmosphere of these seaside retreats spells relief from the usual boardwalk fare. The beaches remain clean, the air stays salty, and the people, particularly in Lewes (LOO-iss), keep to themselves. Founded in 1613 by the Zwaanendael colony from Hoorn, Holland, **Lewes** rightly touts itself as Delaware's first town. The **Lighthouse Restaurant,** on Fisherman's Wharf (645-6271) just over the drawbridge in Lewes, flashes with occasionally brilliant food. Try the grilled swordfish ($14) with homemade bread. (Open Sun.-Fri. 5am-9pm, Sat. 4am-10pm.) East of Lewes, on the Atlantic Ocean, lurks the secluded **Cape Henlopen State Park** (645-8983), home to a seabird nesting colony, sparkling white "walking dunes," and campsites (645-2103) available on a first-come, first-served basis (sites $14; open April-Oct.). To learn more about Lewes, stop by the **Lewes Chamber of Commerce** (645-8073), in the Fisher Martin House on King's Hwy. (Open Mon.-Sat. 10am-5pm.)

Rehoboth Beach With a minimum of planning, you can join the committees of vacationing bureaucrats from Washington, DC who convene at the sand reefs of gay hotspot **Rehoboth Beach** on summer weekends to mix and mingle. At the **Country Squire,** 17 Rehoboth Ave. (227-3985), talk with locals over one of the complete dinner specials (about $7). The breakfast special ($3) is served at all times, and the cheesesteak is a county and city favorite ($4.50). (Open daily 7am-1am.) **Thrasher's** has served fries and only fries, in enormous paper tubs ($3.50-6), for over 60 years. Bite too hastily into one of the tangy peanut-oil-soaked potato treats and understand how the place was named. Locations on both sides of the main drag, at 7 and 10 Rehoboth Ave., make it easy to find. (Open daily 11am-11pm.)

For inexpensive lodging, walk one block from the boardwalk to **The Lord Baltimore,** 16 Baltimore Ave. (227-2855), which has clean, antiquated, practically beachfront rooms. (Singles and doubles $35-65. Call ahead; it's popular.) Or walk a little farther from the beach to the cluster of guest houses on the side lanes off First St., just north of Rehoboth Ave. **The Abbey Inn,** 31 Maryland Ave. (227-7023), is what the proprietress calls an "old-fashioned tourist home." A decorous and friendly inn, there's always a local and a conversation on the front porch. Call for reservations at least one week in advance, especially in the summer. (2-day minimum stay. Doubles from $37, weekends $42.) The **Big Oaks Family Campground,** P.O. Box 53 (645-6838), sprawls at the intersection of Rte. 1 and 270. (Sites with hookup $19.50.)

The **Rehoboth Beach Chamber of Commerce,** in the restored train station at 501 Rehoboth Ave. (800-441-1329 or 227-2233 for information), provides brochures. (Open Mon.-Fri. 9am-4:30pm, Sat. 9am-1pm.)

Practical Information Greyhound serves Lewes (no phone; flag stop at the parking lot for Tom Best's on Rte. 1) and Rehoboth Beach (227-7223; small station at 251 Rehoboth Ave.). Buses run to: Washington, DC (3½ hr., $28), Baltimore (3½ hr., $26), and Philadelphia (4 hr., $30). Lewes makes up one end of the 70-minute **Cape May NJ/Lewes DE Ferry** route (Lewes terminal 645-6313; for schedule and fare info., see Cape May, NJ). Grab a cab ($15) from the pier to reach Rehoboth. To get around within Rehoboth, use free shuttle transportation run by **Ruddertowne Complex** (227-3888; May 27-Sept. 2 daily 3pm-midnight every hr.), which serves points between Rehoboth and Dewey Beaches, including a stop at Rehoboth Ave.

The **post office** in Rehoboth stamps your postcards at 179 Rehoboth Ave. (227-8406; open Mon.-Fri. 9am-5pm, Sat. 9am-noon). The **ZIP code** for Lewes and Rehoboth Beach is 19971; the **area code** is 302.

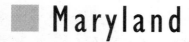

Maryland

Used to be everyone knew what Maryland was about. There was the Chesapeake Bay, a picturesque, shellfish-rich estuary running straight through from the ocean

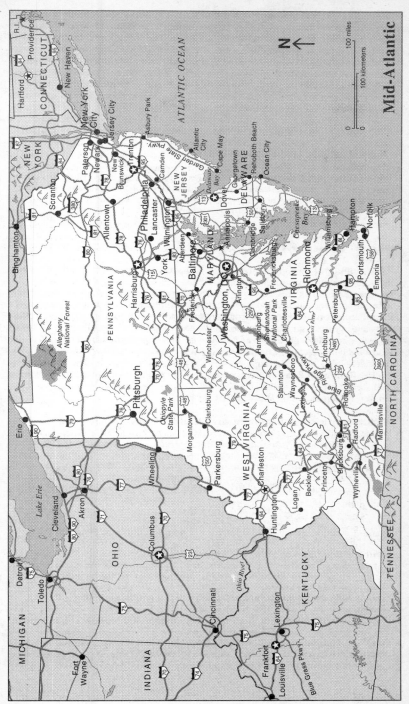

Mid-Atlantic

north to Pennsylvania. On the rural eastern shore, small-town Marylanders captured crabs and raised tobacco. Across the bay in Baltimore, workers ate the crabs, loaded the ships, ran the factories, and joined the club of blue-collar port cities from Cleveland to Providence. Then the federal government expanded, industry shrank, and Maryland had a new, slenderer core: not the bay, but the Baltimore-Washington Parkway. Suburbs grew up and down the corridor, Baltimore cleaned up its smokestack act and the Old Line State acquired a new, liberal urbanity. As D.C.'s homogenized commuter suburbs break the limits of Maryland's Montgomery and Prince Georges counties, Baltimore revels in its polyglot immensity and Annapolis, the capital, stays small-town. The mountains and mines of the state's western panhandle— geographic and cultural kin to West Virginia—are still ignored after all these years.

PRACTICAL INFORMATION

Capital: Annapolis.
Office of Tourist Development, 217 E. Redwood St., Baltimore 21202 (333-6611) or 800-543-1036). **Forest and Parks Service,** Dept. of Natural Resources, Tawes State Office Building, Annapolis 21401 (974-3771).
Time Zone: Eastern. **Postal Abbreviation:** MD
Sales Tax: 5%.

■■■ BALTIMORE

Once a center of East Coast shipping and industry, "Bawlmer" (pop. 751,000) declined structurally and economically from the late 1950s to the mid-'70s. Its renaissance began as then-mayor Donald Schaefer launched a program to clean up pollution, restore old buildings, and convert the Inner Harbor into a tourist playground. Run by the articulate Mayor Kurt Schmoke, modern Baltimore still serves as Maryland's urban core, and old-time, shirtsleeve Bawlmer endures in the quiet limelight of Anne Tyler's novels. Near the downtown skyscrapers, old ethnic neighborhoods like Little Italy front Baltimore's signature rowhouses, whose unique facades are microcosms of the larger city—polished marble stoops represent the shiny Inner Harbor, while straightforward brick fits the proud and gritty urban environs.

PRACTICAL INFORMATION

Emergency: 911.
Visitor Information: Baltimore Area Visitors Centers, 300 W. Pratt St. (837-INFO or 800-282-6632), at S. Howard St. 4 blocks from Harborplace. Pick up a map, an *MTA Ride Guide,* and a *Quick City Guide,* a quarterly glossy with excellent maps and events listings. Open daily 9am-5:30pm.
Airport: Baltimore-Washington International Airport (BWI), 859-7100. On I-195 off the Baltimore-Washington Expressway (I-295), about 10 mi. south of the city center. Take MTA bus #230 downtown. Airport shuttles to hotels (859-0800) run daily every ½ hr. 7am-midnight ($8 to downtown Baltimore). For D.C., shuttles leave every 1½ hrs. between 7am-10pm and drop passengers off at 16th and K St. NW ($14). Trains from BWI Airport run to Baltimore ($5); MARC trains are considerably cheaper ($2.75) but also slower and only run Mon.-Fri. Trains to Washington, D.C. ($10); MARC ($4.25). BWI train office 410-672-6167.
Amtrak: Penn Station, 1500 N. Charles St. (800-872-7245), at Mt. Royal Ave. Easily accessible by bus #3, 11, or 18 from Charles Station downtown. Trains run about every ½ hour to: New York ($62, Metroliner $88); Washington D.C. ($12, Metroliner $17); Philadelphia ($28, Metroliner $42). Ticket window open daily 5:30am-9:30pm, self-serve machines open 24 hrs. (credit card only).
Greyhound: (800-231-2222). Two locations: downtown at 210 W. Fayette St. (752-0868), near N. Howard St.; and at 5625 O'Donnell St. (744-9311), 3 mi. east of downtown near I-95. Frequent buses to: New York ($31); Washington, D.C. ($8.50); Philadelphia ($19). Open 24 hrs.
Public Transport: Mass Transit Administration (MTA), 300 W. Lexington St. (recorded bus and Metro info. 539-5000, main office 333-3434), near N. Howard

St. Bus and rapid-rail service to most major sights in the city; service to outlying areas is more complicated. Bus #230 serves the airport. Free *MTA Ride Guide* available at any visitor information center. Some buses run 24 hrs. **Metro** operates Mon.-Fri. 5am-midnight, Sat. 8am-midnight. Bus fare $1.25, transfers 10¢; Metro base rate $1.25. The **Water Taxi,** makes stops every 8-18 min. at the harbor museums, Harborplace, Fell's Point, and more. An easy and pleasant way to travel to the main sights of Baltimore, especially in summer when service continues until 11pm. Full-day pass $2-3. For info call Harbor Boating (547-0090).

Help Lines: Sexual Assault and Domestic Violence Center (828-6390). **Gay and Lesbian Information** (837-8888).

Post Office: 900 E. Fayette St. (655-9832). **ZIP code:** 21233.

Area Code: 410.

Baltimore dangles in central Maryland, 100 mi. south of Philadelphia and about 150 mi. up the Chesapeake Bay from the Atlantic Ocean. The Jones Falls Expressway (I-83) halves the city with its southern end at the Inner Harbor, while the Baltimore Beltway (I-695) circles it. I-95 cuts across the southwest corner of the city.

Baltimore is plagued by one-way streets. Pratt Street (which runs east across the Inner Harbor) and Charles Street (running north from the west side of the Harbor) divide the city into quarters. Streets parallel to Pratt St. get "West" or "East" tacked onto their names, depending on which side of Charles St. a given block is on. North-south streets are dubbed "North" or "South" according to their relation to Pratt St.

ACCOMMODATIONS AND CAMPING

Baltimore International Youth Hostel (HI/AYH), 17 W. Mulberry St. (576-8880), at Cathedral St. Near bus and Amtrak terminals. Take MTA bus #3, 11, or 18. Elegant, centrally located 19th-century brownstone provides 48 beds in dorms, kitchen, laundry, and lounge with baby grand piano. Friendly managers are a great source of information about Baltimore. Max. stay 3 nights, longer with manager's approval. Lockout 10am-5pm. Curfew 11pm, but house keys available for rent ($2). Chores required. Members $10, non-members $13. Sheet rental $2. Reservations recommended, especially in the summer.

Duke's Motel, 7905 Pulaski Highway (686-0400), in Rosedale off the Beltway. Don't worry about the bulletproof glass in the front office—all the motels around here have them. Simple, clean rooms and probably the best deal on the Pulaski Hwy. motel strip, though slightly more expensive. Suitable only for people with cars. Cable TV. Singles $36, doubles $41. $2 key deposit and ID required.

Abbey Schaefer Hotel, 722 St. Paul St. (332-0405), near E. Madison St. Right on the bus route from Penn Station. Slightly decrepit but functional rooms with working bathrooms. Great location. Room keys are held at the desk when you are out; exercise caution with your belongings as at any time when others may have access to them. Suites with "the works"—attached bathroom and air conditioning—are $44 and good for 2 people. For extras, roll-out bed $8. Rooms without attached bath $39; without A/C are even cheaper. $2 key deposit required.

FOOD

Virginia may be for lovers, but Maryland is for crabs—every eatery here serves crab cakes. The Light Street Pavilion at **Harborplace,** Pratt and Light St. (332-4191), has multifarious foodstuffs to suit every tourist, but expect long lines. **Phillips'** serves some of the best crabcakes in Baltimore; buy them cheaper from the cafeteria-style Phillips' Express line. (Harborplace open Mon.-Sat. 10am-9:30pm, Sun. noon-8pm.) **Lexington Market,** 400 W. Lexington at Eutaw St., provides an endless variety of produce, fresh meat, and seafood, often at cheaper prices (open Mon.-Sat. 8am-6pm; take the subway to Lexington Station or bus #7).

Bertha's Dining Room, 734 S. Broadway (327-5795), at Lancaster. Obey the bumper stickers and "Eat Bertha's Mussels." Gorge yourself on the black-shelled bivalves ($7.50) while sitting at butcher-block tables, and don't miss the chunky vegetable mussel chowder (cup $1.75). Come for afternoon tea (make a reservation): share a platter of scones and assorted tarts with homemade whipped cream for only $7.50. Locals of all ages crowd in to hear jazz bands play Mon.-Wed. and Fri.-Sat. nights. Twelve kinds of beer and ale ($1.50-6). Kitchen open Sun.-Thurs. 11:30am-11pm, Fri.-Sat. 11:30am-midnight. Bar until 2am.

Obrycki's, 1727 E. Pratt St. (732-6399), near Broadway; take bus #7 or 10. Some of Balto's best crabs served every and any way—steamed, broiled, sauteed, or in crab cakes. Sandwiches $5.50-8.50. Steamed hard-shell crabs $20-46 per dozen depending on size. Expect lines on weekends. Don't walk here alone at night. Open Mon.-Sat. noon-11pm, Sun. noon-9:30pm.

Buddies, 313 N. Charles St. (332-4200). Extensive salad bar with over 80 items ($3 per lb.; open Mon.-Fri. 11am-2:30pm) and pile-driving sandwiches ($5-7). Jazz quartet draws in loyal locals and visitors of all ages (Thurs.-Sat. 9:30pm-1am). Happy hour 4-7pm with an assortment of free foodstuffs and 2-for-1 drinks. Ladies night on Tues. features 2-for-1 drinks. Brunch served Sun. 11am-4pm). Open Sun.-Wed. 11am-1am, Thurs.-Sat. 11am-2am. Food served daily until 12:30am.

Haussner's, 3242 Eastern Ave. (410-327-8365), at S. Clinton; take bus #10. An East Baltimore institution. 700 original oil paintings crowd the huge dining room, including some copies of Rembrandt, Gainsborough, Whistler, and Homer. Central European cuisine like fresh pig knuckle and *sauerbraten* (meat stewed in vinegar and juices) $9.30, sandwiches $4 and up; big portions. Try the famous strawberry pie ($3.65), or get other freshly baked goods to go. Long pants preferred after 3pm; lines for dinner on weekends. Open Tues.-Sat. 11am-10pm.

SIGHTS

Most tourists start at the Inner Harbor; all too many finish there. The harbor ends in a five-square block of water bounded by the National Aquarium, Harborplace, the Science Museum, and a fleet of boardable ships; visitors roam the horseshoe-shaped perimeter and neglect the *real* neighborhoods to the east and north.

The **National Aquarium,** Pier 3, 501 E. Pratt St. (576-3800), makes the whole Inner Harbor worthwhile. Multi-level exhibits and tanks show off rare fish, big fish, red fish, and blue fish along with the biology and ecology of oceans, rivers, and rainforests. The Children's Cove (level 4) lets visitors handle intertidal marine animals. (Open Mon.-Thurs. 9am-5pm, Fri.-Sun. 9am-8pm; Sept.-May Sat.-Thurs. 10am-5pm, Fri. 10am-8pm. Admission $11.50 (Sept.-May Fri. 5-8pm, $3.50), kids 3-11 $7.50.)

Several ships bob in the harbor, among them the frigate **U.S.S. Constellation,** the first commissioned U.S. Navy ship, which sailed from 1797 until 1945, serving in the War of 1812, the Civil War, and as flagship of the Pacific Fleet during WWII. Go below decks to see (and aim) the cannons. (Open daily 10am-8pm; May-June and Sept.-Oct. 10am-6pm; Nov.-April 10am-4pm. $3.50, seniors $2.50, kids 6-15 $1.50, active military $1.) Also moored in the harbor are the submarine *U.S.S. Torsk* and the lightship *Chesapeake.* These vessels make up the **Baltimore Maritime Museum** at Piers 3 and 4 (open Mon.-Thurs. 9:30am-6pm, Fri.-Sat. 9:30am-8pm; winter Fri.-Sun. 9:30am-5pm; $4, seniors $3, kids $1.50, active military free).

At the Inner Harbor's far edge lurks the **Maryland Science Center,** 601 Light St. (685-5225), where kids can learn basic principles of chemistry and physics through displays cleverly disguised as hands-on games and activities. The IMAX Theater's 5-story screen stuns audiences. On summer weekends, come in the morning while lines are short. (Open Mon.-Thurs. 10am-6pm, Fri.-Sun. 10am-8pm; Sept.-May Mon.-Fri. 10am-5pm, Sat.-Sun. 10am-6pm. $8.50, kids 4-17, seniors and military $6.50, under 3 free. Separate IMAX shows Mon.-Thurs. on the hr. and Fri.-Sat. evenings $6.)

The **Baltimore Museum of Art,** N. Charles and 31st St. (396-7100 or 396-7101), exhibits a fine collection of modern art (including pieces by Andy Warhol), and paintings and sculpture by Matisse, Picasso, Renoir and Van Gogh. Two adjacent sculpture gardens highlight 20th-century works and make wonderful picnic grounds. The museum's **Baltimore Film Forum** shows classic and current American, foreign, and independent films (Thurs.-Fri. 8pm, $5); get schedules at the museum or call 889-1993. (Open Wed.-Fri. 10am-4pm, Sat.-Sun. 11am-6pm. $5.50, seniors and students $3.50, kids 7-18 $1.50, under 7 free; Thurs. free.)

Baltimore's best museum, the **Walters Art Gallery,** 600 N. Charles St. (547-9000), at Centre, keeps one of the largest private collections in the world, spanning 50 centuries. The museum's apex is the Ancient Art collection (level 2); its seven marble sarcophagi with intricate relief carvings are of a type found in only two known collections (the other is the National Museum in Rome). Other high points are the Italian works and Impressionists, including Manet's *At the Café* and Monet's *Springtime,* as well as rare early Buddhist sculptures from China and Japanese decorative arts of the late 18th and 19th century. (Open Tues.-Sun. 11am-5pm. $4, seniors $3, students and kids under 18 free; Sat. free. Tours Wed. 12:30pm and Sun. 2pm.)

Druid Hill Park (396-6106) off Jones Falls Parkway on Druid Park Lake Drive, contains the **Baltimore Zoo** (366-5466 or 396-7102), featuring elephants in a simulated savannah, Siberian tigers, and a waterfall. The Children's Zoo imports animals (otters and crafty woodchucks) from the Maryland wilds. (Open Mon.-Fri. 10am-4pm, Sat.-Sun. 10am-5:30pm; winter daily 10am-4pm. $6.50, seniors and kids 2-15 $3.50, under 2 free. Kids under 15 free on the first Sat. of each month 10am-noon.)
Fort McHenry National Monument (962-4290) at the foot of E. Fort Ave. off Rte. 2 (Hanover St.) and Lawrence Ave. (take bus #1), commemorates the victory against the British in the War of 1812. This famous battle inspired Francis Scott Key to write the "Star Spangled Banner," but the flag isn't still there (it's in the Smithsonian now). Admission ($2, seniors and under 17 free) includes entrance to the museum, a way-too-long film, and a fort tour. (Open daily 8am-8pm; Sept.-May 8am-5pm.)

Itself once a station for the Baltimore & Ohio Railroad, the **B&O Railroad Museum,** 901 W. Pratt St. (752-2388; take bus #31), looks out on train tracks where dining cars, Pullman sleepers, and mail cars park themselves for your touring frenzy. The Roundhouse captures historic trains and a replica of the 1829 "Tom Thumb," the first American steam-driven locomotive. Don't miss the extensive model-train display. (Open daily 10am-5pm. $5, seniors $4, kids 5-12 $3, under 5 free. Train rides on weekends $2, kids $1, under 3 free.)

Baltimore also holds a few historic houses and birthplaces: **Edgar Allen Poe's House,** 203 N. Amity St. (378-7228; open Wed.-Sat. noon-3:45pm; $3, under 13 $1), and the **Babe Ruth Birthplace and Baltimore Orioles Museum,** 216 Emory St. (727-1539; open daily 10am-5pm; $4.50, seniors $3, kids 5-16 $2). To get a feel for Baltimore's historic districts, take bus #7 or 10 from Pratt St. to Abermarle St. and see **Little Italy,** or ride the same buses to Broadway and walk four blocks to **Fells Point.** The neighborhood around Abermarle, Fawn, and High St. is still predominantly Italian, even if the restaurant clientele no longer are; many of the brownstones have been in the same family for generations. Fell's Point imitates the past with cobblestone streets, quaint shops and historic pubs.

ENTERTAINMENT AND NIGHTLIFE

The **Showcase of Nations Ethnic Festivals** (752-8632, 800-282-6632) celebrates Baltimore's ethnic neighborhoods with a different culture each week June-Sept. Though somewhat generic, the fairs are fun, vending international fare and the inescapable crab cakes and beer. Most events are at **Festival Hall,** W. Pratt and Sharp St.

The **Pier Six Concert Pavilion** (625-4230) at—where else?—Pier 6 at the Inner Harbor presents big-name musical acts at 8pm from late July-Sept. Get tickets at the Mechanic Theatre Box Office between Oct.-May, and at the pavilion or through TeleCharge (625-1400, 800-638-2444) during the summer ($10-28). Sit on Pier 5, near Harborplace, and overhear the music for free. The **Baltimore Arts United (BAU) House** (659-5520) hosts frequent jazz concerts, poetry readings, local art shows, chamber music, and rock and roll (tickets $4-7; call for showtimes and locations). The **Left Bank Jazz Society** (945-2266) can tell you what's happening jazz-wise every week. For alternative rock, country, R&B, reggae, and world beat, **Max's** on **Broadway,** 735 S. Broadway (276-2850, concert schedule 675-6297), at Lancaster St. in Fell's Point, is the place to be. Most shows start around 9:30pm on weekends, 7pm weekdays; doors open at least an hour before. Get tickets at the club, or through Ticketmaster (800-481-7328).

The beloved **Baltimore Orioles** now play at their new stadium at **Camden Yards,** just a few blocks from the Inner Harbor at the corner of Russell and Camden St. Bawlmer holds its breath for the yearly ups and downs of the O's with an attention very few cities could equal.

■■■ CHESAPEAKE BAY

The Chesapeake Bay—long scraggly arm of Atlantic Ocean reaching from the Virginia coast up through Maryland—nearly halves the state. Originally, the water's shallowness and salinity (Native Americans worshiped the bay as the "Great Salt River") made it one of the world's best oyster and blue crab breeding grounds. Centuries of exploitation, however, have damaged the waters. Despite recent conservation measures, fish, oysters, and crabs are slowly disappearing. Sedimentation is already filling and shortening many tributaries. Within 10,000 years, the Chesapeake Bay may be a flat piece of tidewater swamp.

Three states and the District of Columbia share the bay waters and divvy-up the tourism. For info, write or call the Virginia Division of Tourism, the Maryland Office of Tourist Development, the Delaware State Visitors Center, or the Washington, D.C. Convention and Visitors Association. (Addresses and phone numbers given in respective state or district Practical Information sections.)

The region's public transport is underdeveloped. **Carolina Trailways** buses service Salisbury, Princess Anne, Westover Junction, and Pocomoke City from the NYC Greyhound terminal. Make connections with D.C., Baltimore, or Philadelphia via Greyhound bus #127. **Greyhound** covers the east shores of the Chesapeake and Annapolis. The bay is bounded on the west by I-95; on the south by I-64; on the east by U.S. 9, 13, and 50; and on the north by U.S. 40.

Assateague and Chincoteague Islands Sometime in the 1820s, the Spanish frigate *San Lorenzo* foundered off the Maryland coast. All lives were lost, but a few horses struggled ashore. More than a century and a half later, the Chincoteague ponies, descendants of those survivors, roam the unspoiled beaches of Assateague Island.

Assateague Island is divided into three parts. The **Assateague State Park** (301-641-2120), off U.S. 113 in southeast Maryland, is a 2-mi. stretch of picnic areas, beaches, hot-water bathhouses, and campsites ($18). The **Assateague Island National Seashore** (301-641-1441), claims most of the long sandbar north and south of the park, and has its own campground (sites $10, winter $8), beaches, and ranger station providing free backcountry camping permits (301-641-3030). Fire rings illuminate some relatively challenging (4- to 13-mi.) hikes; otherwise it's just you and nature. Bring plenty of insect repellent; six-legged unkindnesses swarm.

The **Chincoteague National Wildlife Refuge** (804-336-6122; open Mon.-Fri. 7:30am-4:30pm), stretches south of the island on the Virginia side of the Maryland/Virginia border. The refuge provides a temporary home for the threatened migratory peregrine falcon, a half million Canadian and snow geese, and beautiful Chincoteague ponies. At low tide, on the last Thursday in July, the wild ponies are herded together and made to swim from Assateague, MD, to Chincoteague, VA, where the local fire department auctions off the foals. The adults swim back to Assateague and reproduce, providing next year's crop.

To get to Assateague Island, take **Carolina Trailways** to **Ocean City,** via daily express and local routes from Greyhound Stations in Baltimore ($22), Washington, DC ($35), Norfolk, VA ($38), and Philadelphia ($35.) The Ocean City station idles at Philadelphia and 2nd St. (410-213-0552; open daily 7:30-8am and 10am-5pm).

Ocean City Chamber of Commerce, 1320 Ocean Gateway, Ocean City 21842 (289-8559), on Rte. 50 at the south of town, has accommodations info. (Open Mon.-Sat. 9am-4:30pm, Sun. 10am-4pm.) To get to Assateague Island from Ocean City, take a taxi (289-8164; about $12). Carolina Trailways buses from Salisbury, MD, and Norfolk, VA, make a stop on U.S. 13 at T's Corner (804-824-5935), 11 mi. from Chincoteague. For more area info, call or write to **Chincoteague Chamber of Commerce,** P.O. Box 258 (Maddox Blvd.), Chincoteague, VA 23336 (804-336-6161; open daily 9am-5pm during the summer, Mon.-Sat. 9am-4:30pm after Labor Day).

■ New Jersey

Listen, let's get one thing straight right now: New Jersey (rhymes with "noisy") is *not* just a giant roadway, and if you ask a native what exit they're from, they have, under a new state statute, the *right* to belt you in the gut until you hemorrhage. Much maligned by myopic Northeasterners who never take the trouble to leave the Garden State Parkway or the New Jersey Turnpike, the state—home to one of America's finest state universities (Rutgers) and one of the world's finest universities (Princeton)—offers hundreds of miles of beautiful boardwalked beaches. And the water is *not* polluted (at least, no more than anywhere else on the northeast coast). Got that? Now we can continue.

While Cape May and the tragicomic gambling mecca Atlantic City—both at the extreme southern end of the state—are the only coastal resorts listed here, beach-loving travelers also might want to look into areas such as Asbury Park and Long Beach Island on their own. If reputation were reality, New Jersey would be an American wasteland; but it's not, and the Garden State is a fine place to visit.

PRACTICAL INFORMATION

Capital: Trenton.
Visitor Information: State Division of Tourism, CN 826, Trenton 08625 (609-292-2470).
Time Zone: Eastern. **Postal Abbreviation:** NJ
Sales Tax: 6%.

■■■ ATLANTIC CITY

The riches-to-rags-to-riches tale of Atlantic City began half a century ago when the beachside hotspot was tops among resort towns. Vanderbilts and Girards graced the boardwalk that inspired *Monopoly,* the Depression-era board game for coffee-table high rollers. Fans of the game will enjoy seeing the real Boardwalk and Park Place they've squabbled over for years. But the opulence has faded. With the rise of competition from Florida resorts, the community chest closed. Atlantic City suffered decades of decline, unemployment, and virtual abandonment.

In 1976, state voters gave Atlantic City a reprieve by legalizing gambling. Casinos soon rose out of the rubble of Boardwalk. Those who enter soon forget the dirt and dank outside, especially since the managers see to it that you need never leave. Each velvet-lined temple of tackiness has a dozen restaurants, big-name entertainment, even skyways connecting it to other casinos. Notice the one-way "moving side-walks" that whisk gamblers into the casinos; neither big winners nor the newly penniless receive such convenience when they leave. The chance to win big draws everyone to Atlantic City, from international jet-setters to seniors clutching plastic coin cups. One-third of the U.S. population lives within 300 mi. of Atlantic City, and fortune-seeking foreigners flock to its shore to toss the dice. Budgeteers can even

ATLANTIC CITY

take a casino-sponsored bus from Manhattan—pay $15 for the trip and get it all back in quarters upon arrival. How can you lose?

PRACTICAL INFORMATION

Emergency: 911.

Visitor Information: Atlantic City Convention and Visitors Bureau, 2314 Pacific Ave. (348-7130, 800-262-7395; they play "Under the Boardwalk" while you sit on hold), home of the Miss America pageant. There is also a booth on the Boardwalk at Mississippi Ave. Personal assistance daily 10am-6pm; leaflets available 24 hrs. Open Mon.-Fri. 9am-5pm.

Amtrak: (800-872-7245) at Kirkman Blvd. near Michigan Ave. Follow Kirkman to its end, bear right, and follow the signs. To: New York City (1 per day, 2½ hr., $28); Philadelphia (2 per day, 1½ hr., $15); Washington, D.C. (2 per day, 3½ hr., $40). Open Sun.-Fri. 9:30am-7:40pm, Sat. 9:30am-10pm.

Buses: Greyhound (345-6617). Buses every hr. to New York (2½ hr., $19) and Philadelphia (1¼ hr., $9). **New Jersey Transit** (800-582-5946). Runs 6am-10pm. Hourly service to New York City ($21) and Philadelphia ($10) with connections to Ocean City ($2.05), Cape May ($3.45), and Hammonton ($3.15). Also runs along Atlantic Ave. (base fare $1). Both lines operate from **Atlantic City Municipal Bus Terminal,** Arkansas and Arctic Ave. Both offer casino-sponsored round-trip discounts, including cash back on arrival in Atlantic City. In Manhattan, go to a local pharmacy and ask where you can buy bus tickets to Atlantic City. **Bally's** has a particularly good deal—you get your full fare ($15) back in quarters upon arrival. Terminal open 24 hrs.

Help Line: Rape and Abuse Hotline (646-6767). 24-hr. counseling, referrals, and accompaniment.

Post Office: (345-4212) at Martin Luther King and Pacific Ave. Open Mon.-Fri. 8:30am-5pm, Sat. 10am-noon. **ZIP code:** 08401.

Area Code: 609.

Atlantic City lies about half-way down New Jersey's coast, accessible via the **Garden State Parkway** and the **Atlantic City Expressway,** and easily reached by train from Philadelphia and New York. Hitching is not recommended—in fact, in these parts, it's exceptionally stupid.

Gamblers' specials make bus travel a cheap, efficient way to get to Atlantic City. Many casinos will give the bearer of a bus ticket receipt $10 in cash and sometimes a free meal. Specials change frequently, depending on business and season, although Trump seems unusually generous these days. Deals are hard to miss at any bus station, tourist info center, or casino lobby. Look for deals in the Yellow Pages under "Bus Charters" in New Jersey, New York, Pennsylvania, Delaware, and Washington, D.C. Also check the Arts and Entertainment section of the *New York Times.*

Getting around Atlantic City is easy on foot. The casinos pack tightly together on the Boardwalk along the beach. When your winnings become too heavy to carry, you can hail a **Rolling Chair,** quite common along the Boardwalk. Though a bit of an investment ($1 per block for 2 people, 5-block min.), Atlantic City locals or erudite foreign exchange students chat with you while they push.

ACCOMMODATIONS, CAMPING, AND FOOD

Large, red-carpeted beachfront hotels have bumped smaller operators out of the game. Expect to pay a hundred bucks for a single, although you should check New York newspapers for occasional specials from the large casino-hotels. Smaller hotels along **Pacific Avenue,** a block from the Boardwalk, have rooms for less than $60, and rooms in the city's guest houses are reasonably priced, though facilities there can be dismal. Reserve ahead, especially on weekends. Many hotels lower their rates mid-week. Winter is also slow in Atlantic City, as water temperature, gambling fervor, and hotel rates all drop significantly. Campsites closest to the action cost the most; the majority close Sept.-April. Reserve a site if you plan to visit in July-Aug.

Irish Pub and Inn, 164 St. James Pl. (344-9063), near the Boardwalk, directly north of Sands Casino. Clean, cheap rooms fully decorated with antiques. Victorian sitting rooms open onto sprawling porch lined with large rocking chairs. Laundry in basement. Singles $25, doubles $40, with private shower $60. Quads $60. Cot in room $10. Key deposit $5. Breakfast and dinner $10, children $8. Open Feb.-Nov.

Hotel Cassino, 28 S. Georgia Ave. (344-0747), at Pacific Ave. Named after a *cassino* in the Italian hometown of kindly proprietors Felix and Mina. Multi-cultural atmosphere. A little run-down, but no sleaze. Strictly a family business. Rates negotiable depending on specific room, day, time of year, and number of people. Singles $30-45, doubles $35-50. Key deposit $10. Open May-Oct.

Birch Grove Park Campground (641-3778), Mill Rd. in Northfield. About 6 mi. from Atlantic City. 50 sites. Attractive and secluded. Sites $15 for 2 people, with hookup $18.

Pleasantville Campground, 408 N. Mill Rd. (641-3176). About 7 mi. from the casinos. 70 sites. Sites $24 for four people with full hookup.

After cashing in your chips, visit a cheap **casino buffet.** Most casinos offer all-you-can-eat lunch/dinner deals for $10-12; sometimes you can catch a $5 special.

Pacific Avenue is cramped with steak, sub, and pizza shops. Since 1946, the **White House Sub Shop** (345-1564, 345-8599), Mississippi and Arctic Ave., has served world-famous subs and sandwiches. Celebrity supporters include Bill Cosby, Johnny Mathis, and Frank Sinatra, who is rumored to have subs flown to him while he's on tour ($6-8, half-subs $3-4). (Open Mon.-Sat. 10am-midnight, Sun. 11am-midnight.) The **Inn of the Irish Pub,** 164 St. James Pl. (345-9613), serves hearty, modestly priced dishes like deep-fried crab cakes ($4.25), honey-dipped chicken ($4.25), and Dublin beef stew ($5). This oaky, inviting pub has a century's worth of Joycean élan and Irish memorabilia draped on the walls. (Open 24 hrs.) For a traditional and toothsome oceanside dessert, try custard ice cream or saltwater taffy, both available at vendors along the Boardwalk.

CASINOS

Inside, thousands of square feet of flashing lights and plush carpet stupefy the gaping crowds; everyone pretends not to notice the one-way ceiling mirrors concealing big-brother gambling monitors. Chumps in formalwear yearn in vain to re-live Atlantic City's glamorous past. Winnebago pioneers in matching tees easily outnumber the dipsticks in butterfly bowties. The luring rattle of chips and clicking of slot machines never stop. Occasionally these are joined by the clacking of coins.

The casinos on the Boardwalk all fall within a dice toss of one another. Even if you tried, you couldn't miss the newest beanstalk on the block, the **Taj Mahal** (449-1000), Donald Trump's meditation on sacred Indian art and architecture. Trump has two other casinos, each screaming out his name in humongous, lighted letters—the **Trump Castle** (441-2000) and **Trump Plaza** (441-6000). Other peacocks include **Bally's Park Place** (340-2000) and **Resorts International** (344-6000). **Caesar's Boardwalk Regency** (348-4411) and **Harrah's Marina Hotel** (441-5000) are hot clubs. Rounding out the list are the **Claridge** (340-3400), at Indiana Ave. and the Boardwalk, and **Showboat** (343-4000), at States Ave. and the Boardwalk. The **Sands** (441-4000), at Indiana Ave. and the Boardwalk, and **TropWorld Casino** (340-4000), at Iowa Ave. and the Boardwalk, have facilities that include golf and tennis.

Open nearly all the time (Mon.-Fri. 10am-4am, Sat.-Sun. 10am-6am), casinos lack windows and clocks, denying you the cues that signal the hours slipping away. Free drinks and bathrooms at every turn keep you stupid and satisfied. To curb inevitable losses, stick to the cheaper games: blackjack, slot machines, and the low bets in roulette and craps. The minimum gambling age of 21 is strictly enforced.

BEACHES AND BOARDWALK

Atlantic City squats on the northern end of long, narrow **Absecon Island,** which has seven miles of beaches—some pure white, some lumpy gray. The **Atlantic City**

Beach is free and often crowded. Adjacent **Ventnor City's** sands are nicer. The legendary **Boardwalk** of Atlantic City has given itself over to junk-food stands, souvenir shops, and carnival amusements. Take a walk, jog, or bike ride in Ventnor City, where Boardwalk development tapers off.

■■■ CAPE MAY

Good Atlantic beaches bless all the towns on the Jersey shore. While Atlantic City chose gambling and cheap pizza joints, Cape May decided to accentuate different attributes. Century-old cottage inns stretch from shore to pedestrian mall. Tree-lined boulevards make for a nice afternoon stroll. No matter where you are in Cape May, the beach never lies more than two or three blocks away.

Practical Information Despite its geographic isolation, Cape May is easily accessible. By car from the north, Cape May is literally the end of the road—follow the **Garden State Parkway** south as far as it goes, watch for signs to Center City, and you'll end up on Lafayette St. From the south, take a 70-minute **ferry** from Lewes, DE (terminal 302-645-6346) to Cape May (886-9699; for recorded schedule info 800-643-3779). In summer months, 13-16 ferries cross daily; in the off-season 5-9. (Toll $18 for vehicle and driver, passengers $4.50, pedestrians $4.50, motorcyclists $15, bicyclists $8.) From Cape May, take **bus** #552 (16 per day, $1.40) from the depot to north Cape May and walk one mi. to the ferry.

The **Welcome Center,** 405 Lafayette St. (884-9562), provides a wagonload of friendly info about Cape May and free hotlines to B&Bs (open daily 9am-4pm). As its name indicates, the **Chamber of Commerce and Bus Depot,** 609 Lafayette St. (884-5508), near Ocean St. across from the Acme, provides tourist info and a local stop for **New Jersey Transit** (800-582-5946; northern NJ 800-772-2222). Buses to: Atlantic City (2 hr., $3.50), Philadelphia (3 hr., $13.50), and New York City (4½ hr., $27). (Terminal open July-Sept. daily 9am-8pm; off-season Mon.-Fri. 9am-8pm, Sat. 10am-8pm.) Try your hand at polo at the **Village Bike Shop** (884-8500), Washington and Ocean St., right off the mall. Also ask about the four-person tandem bike. (Bikes $3.50 per hr., $9 per day. Open daily 7am-6pm.) But no riding on the beach!

The **post office** in Cape May is located at 700 Washington St. (884-3578; open Mon.-Fri. 9am-5pm, Sat. 9am-noon.) The **ZIP code** is 08204. The **area code** is 609.

Accommodations and Camping Many of the well-preserved seaside mansions now take in nightly guests, but cater to the well-heeled *New York Times* B&B set. Still, several inns with reasonable rates fly in the thick of the action. The **Hotel Clinton,** 202 Perry St. (844-3993), at Lafayette St., has decent-sized singles ($25) and doubles ($35) with shared bath. Add $5 for weekend rates. (Open mid-June-early Sept. Call 516-799-8889 for off-season reservations.) **Paris Inn,** 204 Perry St. (884-8015), near Lafayette St., has old but decent rooms, some with private baths (singles $45, doubles $55; weekends add $10, ask about the student discount). Clinton and Paris are the two cheapest accommodations near the action, but if they are full try looking for specials at one of the many hotels which line Beach Drive.

Campgrounds line U.S. 9 from Atlantic City to the Cape. The two closest to town are **Cold Springs Campground,** 541 New England Rd. (884-8717; sites $14, with hookup $16.50), and **Cape Island Campground,** 709 U.S. 9 (884-5777; sites with water and electricity $25, with full hookup $30).

Food There are plenty of places to sample the day's catch or a sandwich in Cape May. **The Ugly Mug,** 426 Washington St. (884-3459), a bar/restaurant in the mall, serves a dozen ugly clams for half as many dollars. (Open Mon.-Sat. 11am-2am, Sun. noon-2am. Food served until 11pm.) **Carney's,** 401 Beach Ave. (884-4424), is the self-proclaimed "best bar in town" with live bands nightly. A mug of beer costs $1.75, sandwiches $5. (Open Mon.-Sat. 11:30-10pm, Sun. noon-10pm, last call daily

2am.) The **Ocean View Restaurant** (884-3772), at Beach and Grant Ave., offers fine fresh seafood, to the tuna of $10-15. (Open daily 7am-10pm.)

Hitting the Beach In 1988, the Jersey shore gained notoriety for the garbage and syringes which washed up on its shore. A very successful clean-up effort ensued. Today, the sand at Cape May literally glistens, dotted with some of the famous Cape May diamonds (actually quartz pebbles that glow when cut and polished). When you unroll your beach towel on a city-protected beach (off Beach Ave.), make sure you have the **beach tag** which beachgoers over 12 must wear June-Sept. 10am-5pm. Pick up a tag (daily $3, weekly $8, seasonal $15) from the vendors roaming the shore. For more info, call the Beach Tag Office at 884-9520.

The **Mid-Atlantic Center for the Arts,** 1048 Washington St. (884-5404), offers a multitude of tours and activities. Pick up *This Week in Cape May* in any of the public buildings or stores for a detailed listing. (Guided walking and trolley tours $4. 2-hr. guided cruises $8.) The **Cape May Light House** in **Cape May Point State Park** (884-2159) west of town at the end of the point, guides tourists, not ships. Built in 1859, the lighthouse offers a magnificent panorama of the New Jersey and Delaware coasts at the top of a 199-step staircase. ($3.50 adults, $1 kids.) Free summer concerts enliven the town's bandstand.

■ New York

The beauty and tranquility of upstate New York may prompt one to ask, "This is the Empire State?" Well, yes, it is, but Nature is the Emperor here. The smell of rotting apples wafting up from the south? That's the Big Apple—New York City. For those who want to escape the fresh air, the City is a welcome oasis of traffic and steel. The rest of us will stay in the idyllic Finger Lakes, peaceful Catskills, and overwhelming Niagara Falls.

PRACTICAL INFORMATION

Capital: Albany.
Tourist Information: 800-225-5697 or 474-4116. Operators available Mon.-Fri. 8:30am-5pm; voice mail system all other times. Write to **Division of Tourism**, 1 Commerce Plaza, Albany 12245. Excellent, comprehensive *I Love NY Travel Guide* includes disabled access and resource information. **New York State Office of Parks and Recreation,** Agency Bldg. 1, Empire State Plaza, Albany 12238 (518-474-0456), has literature on camping and biking. **Division of Lands and Forests** (518-457-7432) has information on hiking and canoeing.
Time Zone: Eastern. **Postal Abbreviation:** NY
Sales Tax: 4-8.25%, depending on county ordinance.

■■■ ALBANY

With millions of dollars spent on urban renewal, Albany has undergone what many residents term a "renaissance." This may be an overstatement, but recent efforts to stimulate tourism have made the state capital more than just a soapbox for Governor Mario Cuomo or a transportation hub for passers-through. Although the English took Albany in 1664, the city was actually founded in 1614 as a trading post for the Dutch West Indies Company, and is the oldest continuous settlement in the original 13 colonies (established six years before the Pilgrims landed on the rocky New England shore). Albany (once named Fort Orange) became New York's state capital in 1797, but never matched the growth of its southern sibling, the Big Apple. Today, juxtaposing the two cities would be like comparing...well, oh, never mind.

Practical Information The **Albany Visitors Center,** 25 Quackenbush Sq. 12207 (434-5132), at Clinton Ave. and Broadway, runs trolley/walking tours on Thurs.-Fri. **Amtrak,** East St., Rensselaer (800-872-7245 or 462-5763), across the Hudson from downtown Albany, runs to: New York (9-10 per day, 2½ hr., $46); Boston (1 per day, 4¾ hr., $42); Montréal (1 per day, 7¼ hr. $48). (Station open Mon.-Fri. 5:30am-11pm, Sat.-Sun. 6am-midnight.) **Greyhound,** 34 Hamilton St. (434-8095), offers service to: New York (7 per day, 3 hr., $23); Montréal (6 per day, 5 hr., $45); Boston (4 per day, 4-5 hr., $46); Syracuse (6 per day, 3 hr., $18). Students receive discounts on selected routes. (Station open 24 hrs., but in an unsafe area.) **Adirondack Trailways** (436-9651), one block away at 360 Broadway, connects to other upstate locales: Lake George (5 per day, in winter 4 per day, 1 hr., $9); Lake Placid (2 per day, in winter 1 per day, 4 hr., $22); Tupper Lake (1 per day, 4 hr., $26). Senior and college-student discounts are available for both routes on certain lines. (Open daily 5:30am-midnight.) For local travel, the **Capitol District Transit Authority (CDTA)** (482-8822) serves Albany, Troy, and Schenectady. CDTA has a confusing schedule and often patchy coverage; a quick call to the main office will set you straight (fare 75¢). The **post office** (452-2499) is located at 30 Old Karner Rd. Albany's **ZIP code** is 12201; the **area code** is 518.

Accommodations and Food If you're spending more than a day in Albany, treat yourself to the hospitality of **Pine Haven (HI/AYH),** 531 Western Ave. 482-1574, where Janice Tricarico runs a hostel and a B&B. From the bus station, walk by the State University of New York offices on Broadway and turn left on State St. From the stop in front of the Hilton, take the #10 bus up Western Ave. and get off at N. Allen St. Pine Haven is on your right, at the convergence of Madison and Western Ave. Parking in rear. (B&B singles $49, doubles $64. Hostel $12. Reservations recommended; call ahead.) If Pine Haven is full in summertime, try the nearby **College of Saint Rose,** Lima Hall, 366 Western Ave. (For reservations contact Tonita Nagle at Student Affairs, Box 114, 432 Western Ave., 454-5171, after hours 454-5100. Open May 15-Aug. 15 Mon.-Fri. 8:30am-4:30pm.) You'll find large rooms and impeccable bathrooms in student dorms on a safe campus. The dining hall is open for use. (Singles $35. Doubles $50.)

Food is sparse in the heart of downtown. Inexpensive sub shops and cafes line **Lark St.** between Madison and Western. Gourmet muffins (90¢) and Mexican platters ($3.50) are served at **MMM! Muffins and More,** 200 Lark St. (432-4616; open daily 8am-4pm). **Next Door,** 142 Washington St. (434-1616), has a half-sandwich special with soup and salad ($4) and great chocolate chip cookies (55¢). (Open Mon.-Fri. 7am-9pm.) If you're further away from downtown, try **Dahlia's,** 858 Madison Ave. (482-0931), and have a scoop of their "hot" yet cold ginger ice cream ($1.31) and a bowl of black bean chili. All food is vegetarian and kosher. (Open Sun.-Thurs. noon-10pm, Fri.-Sat. noon-midnight.)

Sights Albany offers about a day's worth of sight-seeing activity. The **Rockefeller Empire State Plaza,** State St., is a $1.9 billion towering modernist Stonehenge. It houses, aside from state offices, the **New York State Museum** (474-5877; open daily 10am-5pm; free). The huge flying saucer is the **New York State Performing Arts Center** (473-1845). The museum's exhibits depict the history of the state's different regions, including Manhattan; displays range from Native American arrowheads to an original set for "Sesame Street." For a bird's-eye view of Albany, visit the observation deck on the 44th floor of the Corning Tower, the tallest skyscraper in the plaza (open daily 9am-4pm). Look, but please don't touch the "art for the public" **Empire State Collection** (473-7521). Scattered throughout the plaza, the collection features work by innovative New York School artists such as Jackson Pollock, Mark Rothko, and David Smith (open daily, tours by appointment; free).

The modern plaza provides a striking contrast to the more traditional architectural landscape of the rest of the city. Within walking distance on Washington Ave. are **City Hall,** an earthy Romanesque edifice, and the **Capitol Building** (474-2418), a Gothic marvel, both worked on by H. H. Richardson (free tours on the hour Mon.-Fri. 9am-4pm). The **Schuyler** (SKY-ler) **Mansion,** 32 Catherine St. (434-0834), gives a sense of Albany's rich history. Colonial statesman and general Philip Schuyler owned the elegant Georgian home, built in 1761. Here George Washington and Benjamin Franklin dined, and here Alexander Hamilton married Schuyler's daughter. (Open April-Oct. Wed.-Sat. 10am-5pm, Sun. 1-5pm. Free.) The **First Church in Albany** (463-4449), on the corner of Orange and N. Pearl, was founded in 1642. Its present building was constructed in 1798, and houses the oldest known pulpit and weather vane in America. (Open Mon.-Fri. 8:30am-3:30pm.)

Albany blossoms in a colorful rainbow of music, dancing, food, and street-scrubbing in May during the **Tulip Festival** (434-2032). The state sponsors free concerts at the plaza every other Wednesday night in July and August (call 473-0559 for info). **Washington Park,** bounded by State St. and Madison Ave. north of downtown, has tennis courts, paddle boats, and verdant fields. From mid-July to mid-August, the **Park Playhouse** (434-2035) stages free theater (Tues.-Sun. 8pm). On Monday at 8pm, a musical production under the title **Dark Nights** takes place at the lake house. Come **Alive at Five** on Thursdays during the summer, to the sound of free concerts at the **Tercentennial Plaza** across from Norstar on Broadway.

■ ■ ■ CATSKILLS

These lovely mountains have captivated city-dwellers since long before Washington Irving celebrated them in his short stories. The Ashokan reservoir, one of the nation's purest, supplies the Big Apple with much of its water. It also supplied the inspiration for Jay Ungar's haunting "Ashokan Farewell," the theme music of PBS's *The Civil War.* In the late 1940s and 1950s, lakeside resorts here featured the stars of stand-up comedy, creating the legend of "Borscht Belt" humor. Aside from the resorts, visitors can find peace and natural beauty in the state-managed Catskill Preserve, home to quiet villages, sparkling streams, and miles of hiking and skiing trails.

Practical Information **Adirondack Pine Hill Trailways** provides excellent service through the Catskills. The main stop is **Kingston,** 400 Washington Ave. (914-331-0744 or 800-225-6815). To: New York City (10 per day, 2 hr., $18.50, Ameripass accepted). Other stops in the area include Woodstock, Pine Hill, Saugerties, and Hunter; each connects with New York City, Albany, and Utica.

■ Catskill Forest Preserve

Outdoors Activities The 250,000-acre Catskill Forest Preserve contains many small towns ready to host and equip the travelers who come here to enjoy the outdoors. The slow-moving town of **Phoenicia,** accessible by bus from Kingston, marks a good place to anchor your trip. The **Esopus River,** just to the west, is great for trout fishing and for late-summer inner-tubing in the Phoenicia area. Rent tubes at **The Town Tinker** (914-688-5553), on Bridge St. in Phoenicia. (Inner tubes $7 per day, with a seat $10. Driver's license or $15 required as a deposit. Transportation $3. Life jackets available. Open May-Sept. daily 9am-6pm, last rental 4:30pm.) Take a dive at the 65-ft. **Sundance Rappel Tower,** Rte. 214, Phoenicia 12464 (914-688-5640). Four levels of lessons available: beginner $20 for 3-4 hr. Reservations required. Lessons are only given when a group of four is available. If you plan to go fishing, you must buy a **fishing permit** (5 days, non-NY resident $16), available in any sporting goods store. To camp in the backcountry for more than three days, you must obtain a permit from the nearest ranger station. Trails are maintained year-round; available lean-tos are sometimes dilapidated and crowded. Boil or treat water with chemicals, and pack your garbage. To reach the head of your chosen trail, take an **Adirondack Trailways** bus from Kingston—drivers will let you out anywhere along the bus routes. (Call 914-331-0744 for info on routes and fares.) The **Ulster County Public Information Office**, 244 Fair St. 5th Floor (914-331-9500, ext. 336 or 800-342-5826), six blocks from the Kingston bus station, has a helpful travel guide and a list of Catskill trails.

Camping and Accommodations One of the many **state campgrounds** can serve as a base for your adventures. Reservations (800-456-2267) are vital during the summer, especially Thurs.-Sun. (Sites $7-13. Open May-Sept.) Call the rangers at the individual campgrounds for the best info on sites in the area, or for brochures on state campgrounds call the Office of Parks (518-474-0456). **North Lake**, Rte. 23A (518-589-5058), 3 mi. northeast of Haines Falls in Greene County, rents canoes and has showers and good hiking trails. **Kenneth L. Wilson** (914-679-7020), a 4-mi. hike from Bearsville bus stop, has showers, a pond-front beach, and a family atmosphere ($9 per site). **Woodland Valley** (914-688-7647), 5 mi. southeast of Phoenicia, has no showers, but sits on a good 16-mi. hiking trail.

If you prefer sleeping in civilization, go to the **Super 8 Motel**, 487 Washington Ave. (914-338-3078), 2 blocks from the Kingston bus station (singles from $49, doubles from $55; make reservations for summer weekends). Those seeking peace with nature can join in meditation at the **Zen Mountain Monastery**, S. Plank Rd. P.O. Box 197PC, Mt. Tremper, NY 12457 (914-688-2228), a short walk from Mt. Tremper. (Free meditation sessions Wed. 7:30pm and Sun. 9am. Weekend retreats $165.)

■■■ COOPERSTOWN

Cooperstown is a village rich in American mythology. In fact, few cities could claim a more prominent place in the nation's collective idea of how America used to be. Two former residents are responsible—author James Fenimore Cooper and soldier Abner Doubleday. Cooper's novels of the American frontier, collectively known as the Leatherstocking Tales, are perhaps the first true pieces of American folklore. Civil War hero Doubleday was the inventor of baseball according to myth; the 1905 Mills Commission finally settled the matter. Tourists invade every summer to visit the Baseball Hall of Fame, buy memorabilia from over a dozen shops, eat in baseball-themed restaurants, and sleep in baseball themed motels.

Practical Information Cooperstown is accessible from I-90 and I-88 via Rte. 28. Street parking barely exists in Cooperstown; your best bet is the free parking lots just outside town near the Fenimore House, on Rte. 28 south of Cooperstown, and on Glen Ave. From there, take a trolley (really a school bus with an attitude). (Trolley runs daily July-Sept. 8:30am-8pm. All-day pass $1.) **Adirondack Trailways** (800-225-6815) runs two buses per day from New York City (4½-5 hr., $40), Greyhound Ameripasses honored. The **Cooperstown Area Chamber of Commerce**, 31 Chestnut St. (547-9983), on Rte. 80 near Main St., has maps, brochures, and hotel and B&B listings; it also can make reservations for you (open daily 9am-7pm).

Cooperstown's **post office** (225-6815) is at 40 Main St. (open Mon.-Fri. 8:30am-5pm, Sat. 9:30am-1pm). **ZIP code:** 13326. Cooperstown's **area code** is 607.

Accommodations and Food Camping is the way to go in Cooperstown; lodging in the summertime is hideously expensive and generally full, although the Chamber of Commerce (see above) can help out in a pinch. **Glimmerglass State Park**, RD2 Box 580 (547-8662 or 800-456-2267), on Otsego County Rte. 31 on the east side of Ostego Lake, 8 mi. north of Cooperstown, has 36 pristine campsites in a gorgeous lakeside park. Swimming, fishing, and boating 11am-7pm. (Sites $10 for 6 people with 2 night min.; showers, dumping station, no hookups.) **Cooperstown Beaver Valley Campground,** Box 704 Cooperstown (293-7324 or 800-726-7314), take Rte. 28 south 4 mi., turn right on Seminary Rd., never fills up, even in high season. Two **bunkhouses** available (bring your own linen), 110 sites, three ponds, and laundry facilities. On Fri.-Sun., the owner personally buses campers into town. (Bunkhouse $12, tent site for 4 $18, tenting without site $15, RV site with hookup $20, paddleboat rental $5 per hr. Open mid-May to mid-Sept.) **The Phoenix Bed and Breakfast,** R.D. 4, Box 360 (547-8250), on River Rd. (Rte. 33), is both sumptuous and affordable (singles $50). Take Rte. 52 off Chestnut St. to River Rd. (just past the metal bridge). The Phoenix is 3 mi. down on the left. Reservations greatly urged.

For decent food, an amusing baseball atmosphere, and a souvenir shop, check out **T.J.'s Place** (547-4040), on Main St. across from Doubleday Field. (Dinners $5-10. Open daily 7am-9pm.) The **Pioneer Patio,** on Pioneer Alley off Pioneer St. (547-5601), is an affordable cafe with traditional American and German food (lunch $2-6, dinner $7-9; open Mon.-Thurs. 11am-8pm, Fri.-Sat. 8am-10pm). **Sal's Pizzeria,** 139 Main St., has good pizza for $1.25 a slice (open Mon.-Thurs. 11am-9pm, Fri.-Sun. 11am-10pm).

Sights and Activities The **National Baseball Hall of Fame and Museum** (547-9988) on Main St. is an enormous paean to baseball. Among the bats, balls, uniforms, and plaques are exhibits on women and minorities in baseball, how a baseball is made, and a wooden statue of Babe Ruth. The annual ceremonies for new inductees are held in Cooper Park, next to the building (usually late July-early Aug.; call ahead). There are special exhibits for hearing and visually impaired fans. (Open daily 9am-9pm; Nov.-April 9am-5pm. $6, ages 7-15 $2.50, under 7 free. Combination tickets with the Farmers' Museum and Fenimore House $13, $10 for 2 sites.)

Just as the Hall of Fame emphasizes Baseball's roots, so too the **Farmers' Museum and Village Crossroads** (547-2593), 1 mi. from town on Rte. 80 and accessible from the trolley, celebrates the heritage of farming. The museum is a living microcosm of life in upstate New York's "homespun" era of the early 1800s. See blacksmithing, horseshoeing, and P.T. Barnum's famous fossil hoax, the Cardiff Giant. (Open daily May-Oct. 9am-6pm. $6, 7-15 $2.50, under 7 free.) Those with a curiosity about American folk art will be intrigued by **Fenimore House** (547-2533), on Rte. 80 across from the Farmers' Museum. 18th- and 19th-century American paintings and sculptures dot the corners of the vast period rooms overlooking Otsego Lake. (Open daily May-Oct. 9am-6pm. $5, 7-15 $2, under 7 free.) You can tour the lake with a cruise on **Classic Boat Tours,** P.O. Box 664 (547-5295; 1-hr. cruises depart hourly 10-11am, 1-4pm, and 6pm; $8.50, kids 3-12 $5).

■■■ THE FINGER LAKES

According to Iroquois legend, the Great Spirit laid his hand upon the earth, and the impression of his fingers made the Finger Lakes: Canandaigua, Keuka, Seneca, Cayuga, Owasco, and Skaneateles, among others. Many fingers has the Great Spirit. The double attraction of superlative scenery and acclaimed regional wineries make spending time here sublime.

PRACTICAL INFORMATION

Emergency: Fire and Ambulance, 273-8000. **Tompkins Cty. Sheriff,** 272-2444.
Visitor Information: Tompkins County Convention and Visitors Bureau, 904 E. Shore Dr., Ithaca 14850 (272-1313 or 800-284-8422). Tremendous number of brochures on Ithaca, the Finger Lakes, and every other county in upstate New York. Hotel and B&B listings. Best map of the area ($3). Open Mon.-Fri. 9am-5pm, Sat.-Sun. 10am-5pm; Labor Day-Memorial Day Mon.-Fri. 9am-5pm.

Buses: Ithaca Bus Terminal (272-7930), W. State and N. Fulton St., for **Short Line** and **Greyhound.** To: New York City (8 per day); Philadelphia (3 per day); Buffalo (3 per day). Call for frequently-changing fares. Open daily 7:30am-6:30pm.

Public Transport: Tomtran (Tompkins County Transportation Services Project), 274-5370. Covers a wider area than Ithaca Transit, including Trumansburg and Ulysses, both northwest of Ithaca on Rte. 96, and Cayuga Heights and Lansing Village, both north of Ithaca on Rte. 13. Only choice for getting out to the Finger Lakes. Buses stop at Ithaca Commons, westbound on Seneca St., and eastbound on Green. 60¢, $1.25 for more distant zones. Mon.-Fri. only.

Bike Rental: Pedal Away, 700 W. Buffalo St. (272-5425), near the commons. $20 per day, $18 per day for 3-day rentals. Take Ithaca Transit to the Tompkins County Trust, west end branch. Open daily 10am-8pm.

Car Rental: Chuck John's Auto Rental, 652 Spencer Rd.(272-2222), 3 mi. south on Rte. 13, . $21 per day with 50 free mi., 18¢ per additional mi. Under 25, add $5 per day. Credit card required. (Open Mon.-Fri. 8am-5pm, Sat. 8am-noon.)

Post Office, 213 N. Tioga St. (272-5454), at E. Buffalo. Open Mon.-Fri. 8:30am-5:30pm, Sat. 8:30am-1pm. **ZIP code:** 14850.

Area code: 607.

ACCOMMODATIONS AND CAMPING

The Tompkins County Visitors Bureau (see Practical Information above) has full Ithaca area B&B listings.

Podunk House Hostel (HI/AYH), Podunk Rd. (387-9277), in Trumansburg about 8 mi. northwest of Ithaca. Greyhound has eliminated its Trumansburg flag stop, and you can only take the Tomtran Mon.-Fri. Venture into the land of Oz, friendly owner of the hostel. He's happy to talk philosophy or architecture or let you soak up the silence of his 30-acre farm. Finnish sauna fired up twice a week. Hiking trails and cross-country skiing accessible. Beds in the loft of a homestead barn. No kitchen. Members only, $6. Linen $1.50. Open April-Oct. Call ahead, before 9pm.

Elmshade Guest House, 402 S. Albany St. (273-1707), at Center St. 3 blocks from the Ithaca Commons. From the bus station, walk up State St. and turn right onto Albany. Impeccably clean, well-decorated, good-sized rooms with shared bath. You'll feel like a guest at a rich relative's house. TV in every room, refrigerator, microwave on hall. Singles $35. Doubles $45; prices may rise. Morning coffee, rolls, fruit included. Reservations recommended.

Camping options in this area are virtually endless. Fifteen of the 20 state parks in the Finger Lakes region have campsites, and nine have cabins. The brochure *Finger Lakes State Parks* contains a description of each park's location, services, and environs; pick it up from any tourist office, park, or the **Finger Lakes State Park Region,** 2221 Taughannock Park Rd., RD 3, Trumansburg 14886 (607-387-7041). (Sites $5-12.) Whatever your plans, reserve ahead. The Winnebagos are rolling in to steal your spot even as you read this. Summer weekends almost always fill up.

FOOD AND NIGHTLIFE

Restaurants cluster in Ithaca along Aurora St. and Ithaca Commons. Pick up the *Ithaca Dining Guide* pamphlet at the Tompkins County Visitors Center (see above) for more options.

Moosewood Restaurant (273-9610), Seneca and Cayuga St., in Ithaca. Legendary! The *Moosewood Cookbook* originated here. Creative, well-prepared vegetarian, fish, and pasta dishes. Menu changes daily. Lunches $5-6, dinners around $9-11. Open Mon.-Sat. 11:30am-2pm and 5:30-9pm, Sun. 5:30-9pm; in winter Sun.-Thurs. 5:30-8:30pm.

Joe's Restaurant, 602 W. Buffalo St. (273-2693), at Rte. 13 (Meadow St.), 10 min. walk from Ithaca Commons. Italian and American food; their specialty is veal (they serve the equivalent of one calf per day). Original art-deco interior dates from 1932; this is a *big* student spot. Entrees $7-15. Open 4-10pm.

Just a Taste, 116 N. Aurora (272-9463), near Ithaca Common. The place to taste fine wines (2½ oz. $1.75-3.75) and savor *tapas,* the Spanish "little dishes" ($3.50-5.50). Individual pizzas from $3.50. Open Sun.-Wed. 11:30am-10pm, Thurs.-Sat. 11:30am-midnight. Bar open Mon.-Wed. until midnight, Thurs.-Sat. until 1am, Sun. until 11pm.

Rongovian Embassy to the USA, Rte. 96 (387-3334), in the main strip of Trumansburg about 10 mi. out of Ithaca. Worth the drive. Amazing Mexican entrees in a classic restaurant/bar. Plot your next trip to "Beefree", "Nearvarna", or "Freelonch" on their huge wall map. Tacos $2.50. Dinners about $8. Mug of beer $1-1.50. Live bands on weekends, cover $4-5. Food served Tues.-Thurs. and Sun. 5-9pm, Fri.-Sat. 5-10pm. Open until 1am.

SIGHTS

The fertile soil of the Finger Lakes area makes this region the heart of New York's wine industry. Wine tasting and touring at one of the small local vineyards is a relaxing way to pass a day. All of the vineyards on the Cayuga Wine Trail (P.O. Box 123, Fayette, NY 13065; write for their brochure) offer picnic facilities and free tastings, though some require purchase of a glass ($1.50-2). **Americana Vineyards Winery,** 4367 East Covert Rd., Interlaken (387-6801), ferments 1 mi. or so from Trumansburg, accessible by Greyhound and Tomtran. A family of four operates this winery from grape-picking to bottle-corking; one will give you a personal tour and free tasting. Pick up a bottle for about $5. (Open May-Oct. Mon.-Sat. 10am-5pm, Sun. noon-5pm, April and Nov.-Dec. weekends only; if you're driving, take Rte. 96 or 89 north of Trumansburg to E. Covert Rd.)

Cornell University, youngest of the Ivy League schools, sits atop a hill in downtown Ithaca. Its campus contains impressive works of stone masonry and the newest scientific facilities. A stroll along Fall Creek and Beebe Lake makes for a fine weekend afternoon. The **Information and Referral Center** is located in the Day Hall Lobby (254-INFO; open Mon.-Sat. 8am-5pm).

Considered the birthplace of the women's rights movement, **Seneca Falls** hosted the 1848 Seneca Falls Convention. Elizabeth Cady Stanton and Amelia Bloomer, two leading suffragists who lived here, organized a meeting of those seeking the vote for women. Visit the **National Women's Hall of Fame,** 76 Fall St. (315-568-8060), where photographs and biographies commemorate 38 outstanding U.S. women (open Mon.-Sat. 10am-4pm, Sun. noon-4pm; donation requested).

The town of **Corning** bakes 40 mi. out of Ithaca on Rte. 17 West off Rte. 13 South, home to the Corning Glass Works. The **Corning Glass Center,** Centerway, Corning 14831 (607-974-8271), built in honor of the Glass Works' Centenary in 1951, chronicles the 3500-year history of glass-making in a display of over 20,000 pieces (open daily 9am-5pm; $6, over 60 $5, under 18 $4). The nearby **Rockwell Museum,** 111 Cedar St. Rte. 17 (607-937-5386), displays glass pieces by Frederick Carder, founder of the Steuben Glass Works and an excellent collection of American Western art. (Open Mon.-Sat. 9am-5pm, Sun. noon-5pm; July-Aug. Mon.-Sat. until 7pm, Sun. noon-5pm. $3, seniors $2.50, under 18 free.)

In the Lakes region, a car provides the easiest transportation, but biking and hiking allow more intimate contact with this beautiful country. Reach out and touch the **Finger Lakes State Park Region** (see Practical Information above) for free maps and tips. Write the **Finger Lakes Trail Conference,** P.O. Box 18048, Rochester 14618 (716-288-7191), for free maps of the **Finger Lakes Trail,** an east-west footpath from the Catskills westward to the Allegheny Mountains. This 350-mi. trail and its 300 mi. of branch trails link several state parks, most with camping facilities. Bicyclers can buy *25 Bicycle Tours in the Finger Lakes* ($9) or write to the publisher: The Countryman Press, Inc., P.O. Box 175, Woodstock, VT 05091.

■■■ NEW YORK CITY

This rural America thing. It's a joke.
—Edward I. Koch, former mayor of New York

Most people, upon entering The City, are simply not prepared for the *immensity* of the place. Neck-breaking skyscrapers line bullet-straight avenues seemingly to infinity. Nowhere in America is the metronomic rhythm of urban life more pronounced and syncopated than in New York City. Cramped into tiny spaces, millions of people find themselves confronting each other every day in a vast sea of humanity. Despite this (or, perhaps, *because* of the crush of the populace), people here are some of the coldest, loudest, most neurotic and loneliest in the world. But don't fault New Yorkers. Much that is unique, attractive, and repulsive about the Big Apple is merely a function of its incomprehensible scale. The city is just too goddamn big, too heterogeneous, too jumbled, too exciting.

Since New York's early days, outsiders have regarded it with wonder and alarm. The city has a history of dramatic and often ungainly growth; services and infrastructures have rarely kept pace with the rapid rate of expansion. For the city's long-term residents, however, the magic produced by that stunning growth compensates for its drawbacks. New York's much-vaunted self-sufficiency—a startlingly high percentage of New Yorkers do not have drivers licenses—began very early. The colony was founded in 1624 by the Dutch West Indies Company as a trading post. England soon asserted rival claims, but the colonists here went about their daily grind oblivious to far-off political haggling. In 1626, in a particularly shrewd transaction, Peter Minuit bought Manhattan for 60 guilders, or just under 24 bucks.

Left to its own devices, the city continued to grow. By the late 1770s the city had become an active port with a population of 20,000. New York's primary concern was maintaining that prosperity, and it reacted apathetically to the first whiffs of revolution; British rule was good for business, so... The new American Army—understandably—made no great efforts to protect the city. New York fell to the British in September of 1776 and remained in their hands until late November 1783. All the while, New York merchants conducted business as usual.

New York emerged as the nation's pre-eminent city in the 19th century. The Randal Plan simplified the organization of the city streets in 1811, establishing Manhattan's grid scheme. Administration and services lagged behind—pigs, dogs, and chickens continued to run freely. The world-famous corruption of Tammany Hall, a political machine set in motion in the 1850s and operative for nearly a century, exacerbated an already desperate situation. New York continued to ignore national concerns in favor of local interests. The city initially opposed the Civil War, its desire to protect trade with the South contravening abolitionist ideals. After the war, New York entered a half-century of peace and prosperity during which the seeds of recognizable modernity were sown. Manhattan went vertical to house the growing population streaming in from Western Europe. Escaping famine, persecution, and political unrest, immigrants faced the perils of the sea for the promise of America.

Booming construction and burgeoning culture helped to generate a sort of urban bliss. Mayor Fiorello LaGuardia navigated the city safely past the shoals of the Great Depression, and post-WWII prosperity brought still more immigrants, especially African-Americans from the rural South, and businesses into the city. However, cracks in the city's infrastructure became increasingly evident. By the 60s, crises in public transportation, education, and housing fanned the flames of ethnic tensions and fostered the rise of a criminal element. City officials raised taxes to improve services, but in the process drove away middle-class residents and corporations.

In the 80s, New York rebounded. Large manufacturing industries were superseded by fresh money from finance and infotech. Wall Street in the 80s was a tragically hip place to be, as evidenced by films and novels like *Bonfire of the Vanities* and *Bright Lights, Big City*. As the rosy blush of the 80s fades to grey 90s malaise,

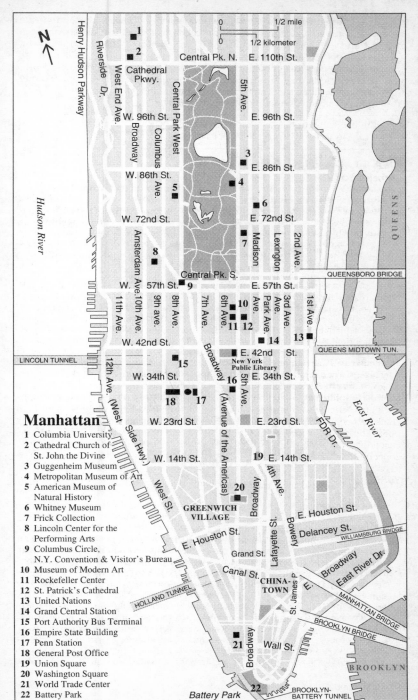

N

1/2 mile
1/2 kilometer

Henry Hudson Parkway
Riverside Dr.
West End Ave.
Cathedral Pkwy.
Central Park West
Broadway
Columbus Ave.
Amsterdam Ave.
10th Ave.
11th Ave.
9th ave.
8th Ave.
7th Ave.
6th Ave.
Park Ave.
Madison Ave.
Lexington Ave.
3rd Ave.
2nd Ave.
1st Ave.
5th Ave.
4th Ave.
12th Ave. (West Side Hwy.)
West St.
Broadway (Avenue of the Americas)
Broadway
Lafayette St.
Bowery
St. James P.
E.
FDR Dr.

Hudson River
East River

Central Pk. N.   E. 110th St.
W. 96th St.   E. 96th St.
W. 86th St.   E. 86th St.
W. 72nd St.   E. 72nd St.
Central Pk. S.   E. 57th St.
W. 57th St.
W. 42nd St.
W. 34th St.   E. 34th St.
W. 23rd St.   E. 23rd St.
W. 14th St.   E. 14th St.
E. 42nd St.
E. 57th St.

New York Public Library

1 Columbia University
2 Cathedral Church of
   St. John the Divine
3 Guggenheim Museum
4 Metropolitan Museum of Art
5 American Museum of
   Natural History
6 Whitney Museum
7 Frick Collection
8 Lincoln Center for the
   Performing Arts
9 Columbus Circle,
   N.Y. Convention & Visitor's Bureau
10 Museum of Modern Art
11 Rockefeller Center
12 St. Patrick's Cathedral
13 United Nations
14 Grand Central Station
15 Port Authority Bus Terminal
16 Empire State Building
17 Penn Station
18 General Post Office
19 Union Square
20 Washington Square
21 World Trade Center
22 Battery Park

Manhattan

GREENWICH VILLAGE
CHINA-TOWN
BROOKLYN

QUEENS

QUEENSBORO BRIDGE
QUEENS MIDTOWN TUN.
LINCOLN TUNNEL
HOLLAND TUNNEL
WILLIAMSBURG BRIDGE
MANHATTAN BRIDGE
BROOKLYN BRIDGE
BROOKLYN-BATTERY TUNNEL

E. Houston St.
Delancey St.
Grand St.
Canal St.
Wall St.
Broadway
East River Dr.

Battery Park

the city is confronted once again with old problems—too many people, too little money, and not enough consideration for each other. The first African-American mayor, David Dinkins, was elected in 1988 on a platform of harmonious growth, this "melting pot" of New York continues to burn, smolder and belch. Still, there are signs of life and renewed commitment in the urban blightscape; a recent resurgence of community activism and do-it-yourself politics is a glimmer of hope. Former Mayor Ed Koch echoed the sentiments of generations in his inaugural speech. "New York is not a problem. New York is a stroke of genius."

For the ultimate coverage of New York City, see our city guide, *Let's Go: New York City*, available wherever fine books are sold.

PRACTICAL INFORMATION

Emergency: 911.

Police: 212-374-5000. Use this for inquiries that are not urgent. Open 24 hrs.

Visitor Information: New York Convention and Visitors Bureau, 2 Columbus Circle (397-8222 or 484-1200), 59th St. and Broadway. Subway: #1, 9 or A, B, C, D to Columbus Circle/59th St. Multilingual staff will help you with directions, hotel listings, entertainment ideas, safety tips, and "insiders'" descriptions of New York's neighborhoods. Request two invaluable maps: the *MTA Manhattan Bus Map,* and the *MTA New York City Subway Map.* Try to show up in person; the phone lines tend to be busy, the maps and brochures worthwhile. Open Mon.-Fri. 9am-6pm, Sat.-Sun. and holidays 10am-6pm.

Travelers' Aid Society: 1481 Broadway (944-0013), near 42nd St.; and at JFK International Airport (718-656-4870), in the International Arrivals Building. JFK office provides general counseling and referral to travelers, as well as emergency assistance (open Mon.-Thurs. 10am-7pm, Fri. 10am-6pm, Sat.-Sun. 11am-6pm). Times Square branch specializes in crisis intervention services for stranded travelers or crime victims. Open Mon.-Tues. and Thurs.-Fri. 9am-5pm, Wed. 9am-noon; closed for lunch Mon.-Fri. 1-2pm. Subway: #1, 2, 3, 7, 9 or N, R, S to 42nd St.

Consulates: Australian, 636 Fifth Ave. (245-4000). **British,** 845 Third Ave. (745-0202). **Canadian,** 1251 Sixth Ave. (768-2400). **German,** 460 Park Ave. (308-8700). **South African,** 326 E. 48th St. (213-4880).

American Express: Multi-task agency providing gift and travelers' cheques, cashing services, and other financial assistance. Branches throughout Manhattan include: **American Express Tower,** 200 Vesey St. (640-2000), near the World Financial Center (open Mon.-Fri. 8am-5:30pm); **Macy's Herald Square,** 151 W. 34th St. (695-8075), at Seventh Ave. inside Macy's (open Mon.-Sat. 10am-6pm); in **Bloomingdale's** (705-3171), 59th St. and Lexington Ave. (open Mon.-Wed. and Fri.-Sat. 10am-6pm, Thurs. 10am-8pm); **822 Lexington Ave.** (758-6510), between 63rd and 64th St. (open Mon.-Fri. 9am-6pm, Sat. 10-4).

Taxis: Radio-dispatched taxis 718-361-7270, (or see Yellow Pages under "Taxicabs"). Yellow (licensed) cabs can be hailed on the street: $1.50 base, 25¢ each additional one-fifth mi; 25¢ is tacked on for every 75 seconds spent in slow or stopped traffic; passengers pay for all tolls. Don't forget to tip. Ask for a receipt, which will have the taxi's ID number. This is necessary to trace lost articles or to make a complaint to the **Taxi Commission,** 221 W. 41st St. (221-TAXI/8294).

Car Rental: All agencies have min. age requirements and ask for deposits. Call in advance to reserve, especially near the weekend. **Thrifty,** 330 W. 58th St. (867-1234), between Eighth and Ninth Ave., and 213 E. 43rd St. (867-1234), between Second and Third Ave. Large, reputable nationwide rental chain. Mid-sized domestic sedan $59 per day, $289 per week, with unlimited mileage. Open Mon.-Fri. 7am-7pm, Sat. 7am-5pm, Sun. 8am-4pm. Must be 23 with a major credit card.

Auto Transport Companies: New York serves as one of their major departure points. The length of time for application processing varies from place to place; these 2 process immediately. Nearly all agencies require references and a refundable cash deposit. **Dependable Car Services,** 801 E. Edgar Rd., Linden, NJ (840-6262 or 908-474-8080). Must be 21, have 3 personal references, and a valid license without major violations. $150-200 deposit. Open Mon.-Fri. 8:30am-4:30pm, Sat. 9am-1pm. **Auto Driveaway,** 264 W. 35th St., Suite 500 (967-2344); 33-70 Prince St., Flushing, Queens (718-762-3800). Must be 21 years old, with 2 local references and a valid driver's license. $250 deposit, $10 application fee. Open Mon.-Fri. 9am-5pm.

Bicycle Rentals: May-Oct. weekdays 10am-3pm and 7-10pm and from Fri. 7pm to Mon. 6am, Central Park closes to cars, allowing bicycles to rule its roads. **Pedal Pushers,** 1306 Second Ave. (288-5594), between 68th and 69th St. Rents 10-speeds for $5/$14; mountain bikes for $6/$17. Overnight rentals $25. Passport, driver's license, or a major credit card required. Open daily 10am-6pm. **Gene's,** 242 E. 79th St. (249-9344), near Second Ave. This discount bike shop rents 3-speeds for $3 per hr., $10.50 per day; mountain bikes for $6/$21. Deposit of $20-40 required, as well as a driver's license or major credit card. Open Mon.-Fri. 9:30am-8pm, Sat.-Sun. 9am-7pm.

Help Lines: Crime Victim's Hotline, 577-7777; 24-hr. counseling and referrals. **Sex Crimes Report Line,** New York Police Dept., 267-7273; 24-hr. help, counseling, and referrals.

Walk-in Medical Clinic, 57 E. 34th St. (683-1010), between Park and Madison. Open Mon.-Fri. 8am-6pm, Sat. 10am-2pm. Affiliated with Beth Israel Hospital.

24-Hr. Medical Assistance: Beth Israel Medical Center Emergency Room, (420-2840), First Ave. and 16th St. **Mount Sinai Medical Center Emergency Room** (241-7171), 100th St. and First Ave.

Post Office: Central branch, 421 Eighth Ave. (967-8585 Mon.-Fri. 8:30am-5pm), across from Madison Square Garden (open 24 hrs.). For General Delivery, mail to and use the entrance at 390 Ninth Ave. C.O.D.s, money orders, and passport applications are also processed at some branches. **ZIP code:** 10001.

Area Codes: 212 (Manhattan, the Bronx); 718 (Brooklyn, Queens, Staten Island.)

GETTING THERE

By Plane

Three airports service the New York Metro Region. **John F. Kennedy Airport (JFK)** (718-656-4520), 12 mi. from Midtown in southern Queens, is the largest, handling most international flights. **LaGuardia Airport** (718-476-5072), 6 mi. from midtown in northwestern Queens, is the smallest, offering domestic flights and air shuttles. **Newark International Airport** (201-961-2000), 12 mi. from Midtown in Newark, NJ, offers both domestic and international flights at budget fares often unavailable at other airports (though getting to and from Newark can be expensive).

To and From the Airports

Public transport can get you easily from **JFK** to midtown Manhattan. Catch a brown and white JFK long-term parking lot bus (718-330-1234) from any airport terminal (every 15 min.) to the **Howard Beach-JFK subway station,** where you can take the A train to the city (1 hr.). Or you can take one of the city buses (Q10 or Q3; $1.25, exact change required) into Queens. The Q10 and Q3 connect with subway lines to Manhattan. Ask the bus driver where to get off, and make sure you know which subway line you want. Those willing to pay more can take the **Carey Airport Express** (718-632-0500), a private line that runs between JFK and Grand Central Station and the Port Authority Terminal (leaves every 30 min. from 5am-1am, 1 hr., $11).

You have two options to get into Manhattan from **LaGuardia.** If you have extra time and light luggage, you can take the MTA Q33 bus ($1.25 exact change or token) to the 74th St./Broadway/Roosevelt Ave./Jackson Hts. subway stop in Queens, and from there, take the #7, E, F, G or R train into Manhattan ($1.25). Allow at least 90 min. travel time. The second option, the Carey bus, stops at Grand Central Station and the Port Authority Terminal (30 min., $8.50).

The trip from **Newark Airport** to Manhattan takes about as long as from JFK. **New Jersey Transit (NJTA)** (201-460-8444) runs a fast, efficient bus (NJTA #300) between the airport and Port Authority every 15 minutes during the day, less often at night ($7). For the same fare, the **Olympia Trails Coach** (212-964-6233) travels between the airport and either Grand Central or the World Trade Center (every 20 min. Mon.-Fri. 6am-1am, Sat.-Sun. 7am-8pm; ¾-1 hr. depending on traffic; $7).

By Bus or Train

Bus: Greyhound (971-0492 or 800-231-2222) is the titan, wandering through the hub of their northeastern bus network, the **Port Authority Terminal,** 41st. and Eighth Ave. (435-7000; Subway: A, C, or E to 42nd St.-Port Authority). Port Authority has good information and security services, but the surrounding neighborhood is somewhat deserted at night. Avoid the terminal's bathrooms at all times. To: Boston (5 hr., $24); Philadelphia (2½ hr., Mon.-Thurs. $15, Fri.-Sun. $16); Washington, DC (5 hr., $25); Montréal (8 hr., $65).

Train Train service in New York is primarily through two stations. **Grand Central Station,** 42nd St. and Park Ave. (Subway: #4, 5, 6, 7, or S to 42nd St./Grand Central), handles **Metro-North** (800-638-7646, 532-4900) commuter lines to Connecticut and New York suburbs. Longer routes run from the smaller **Penn Station,** 33rd St. and Eighth Ave. (Subway: #1, 2, 3, 9, A, C, or E to 34th St./Penn Station). **Amtrak** (800-872-7245 or 582-6875) trains rumble out of Penn, serving most major cities in the U.S., especially in the Northeast. To: Washington, DC (3½ hr., $68); (4 hr., $57). Penn Station also handles the **Long Island Railroad (LIRR)** (718-217-5477) and **PATH** service to New Jersey (466-7649, Mon.-Fri. 9am-5pm).

By Car

Driving into New York there are several major approaches. From New Jersey there are three choices. The **Holland Tunnel** connects to lower Manhattan, exiting into the SoHo and TriBeCa area. From the New Jersey turnpike you'll probably end up at the **Lincoln Tunnel,** which exits in midtown in the West 40s. The third option is the **George Washington Bridge,** which crosses the Hudson River into northern Manhattan, giving fairly easy access to either Harlem River Drive or the West Side Highway. Coming from New England or Connecticut on I-95, follow signs for the **Triboro Bridge.** From there get onto the FDR Drive, which runs along the east side of Manhattan and exits onto city streets every 10 blocks or so. Another option is to look for the Willis Avenue Bridge exit on I-95 to avoid the toll, and enter Manhattan farther north on FDR Drive.

Hitchhiking is illegal in New York state and cops strictly enforce the law within NYC. Hitching in and around New York City is suicidal. Don't do it.

ORIENTATION

Five **boroughs** comprise New York City: Brooklyn, the Bronx, Queens, Staten Island, and Manhattan. **Manhattan** island's length is only half that of a marathon; 13 mi. long and 2.5 mi. wide. For all its notoriety, Manhattan houses only the third largest population of the five boroughs, after Brooklyn and the Bronx. Though small, Manhattan has all the advantages—surrounded by water and adjacent to the other four boroughs. **Queens,** the largest and most ethnically diverse of the boroughs, is located to the east of midtown Manhattan. **Brooklyn** lies due south of Queens and is even older than Manhattan. **Staten Island,** to the south of Manhattan, has remained defiantly residential, similar to the suburban bedroom communities of outer Long Island. North of Manhattan nests the **Bronx,** the only borough connected by land to the rest of the U.S., home of the lovely suburb Riverdale as well as New York's most depressed area, the South Bronx.

Districts of Manhattan

Glimpsed from the window of an approaching plane, New York City can seem a monolithic jungle of urbania. But up close, New York breaks down into manageable neighborhoods, each with a history and personality of its own. As a result of city zoning ordinances, quirks of history, and random forces of urban evolution, boundaries between these neighborhoods can often be abrupt.

The city began at the southern tip of Manhattan, in the area around **Battery Park** where the first Dutch settlers made their homes. The nearby harbor, now jazzed up with the **South Street Seaport** tourist magnet, provided the growing city with the commercial opportunities that helped it succeed. Historic Manhattan, however, lies in the shadows of the imposing financial buildings around **Wall Street** and the civic offices around **City Hall.** A little farther north, neighborhoods rich in the cultures brought by late 19th-century immigrants rub elbows below Houston Street—**Little Italy, Chinatown,** and the southern blocks of the **Lower East Side.** Formerly the home of Russian Jews, Delancey and Elizabeth Streets now offer pasta and silks. To the west lies the newly fashionable **TriBeCa** ("Triangle Below Canal St."). **SoHo** (for "South of Houston"), a former warehouse district west of Little Italy, has transformed into a pocket of gleaming art studios and galleries. Above SoHo huddles **Greenwich Village,** an actual village of lower buildings, jumbled streets, and neon glitz that has for decades been home to intense political and artistic activity.

A few blocks north of Greenwich Village, stretching across the West teens and twenties, lies **Chelsea,** the late artist Andy Warhol's favorite hangout and former home of Dylan Thomas and Arthur Miller. East of Chelsea, presiding over the East River, is **Gramercy Park,** a pastoral collection of elegant brownstones immortalized in Edith Wharton's *Age of Innocence.* **Midtown Manhattan** towers from 34th to 59th St., where traditional and controversial new skyscrapers share the skies, supporting over a million elevated offices. Here department stores outfit New York while the nearby **Theater District** attempts to entertain the world, or at least people who like musicals. North of Midtown, **Central Park** slices Manhattan into East and West. On the **Upper West Side,** the gracious museums and residences of Central Park West neighbor the chic boutiques and sidewalk cafes of Columbus Ave. On the **Upper East Side,** the galleries and museums scattered among the elegant apartments of Fifth and Park Ave. create an even more rarefied atmosphere.

Above 97th St., the Upper East Side's opulence ends with a whimper where commuter trains emerge from the tunnel and the *barrio* begins. Above 110th St. on the Upper West Side sits majestic **Columbia University** (founded as King's College in 1754), an urban member of the Ivy League. The communities of **Harlem** and **Morningside Heights** produced the Harlem Renaissance of black artists and writers in the 1920s and the revolutionary Black Power movement of the 1960s. Although torn by crime, **Washington Heights,** just north of St. Nicholas Park, is nevertheless somewhat safer and more attractive than much of Harlem and is home to Fort Tryon Park, the Met's Medieval Cloisters museum, and a quiet community of Old World immigrants. Still farther north, the island ends in a rural patch of wooded land with caves inhabited at various times by the Algonquin and homeless New Yorkers.

Manhattan's Street Plan

New York's east/west division refers to an address's location in relation to the two borders of Central Park—**Fifth Avenue** along the east side and **Central Park West** along the west. Below 59th St. where the park ends, the West Side begins at the western half of Fifth Ave. **Midtown** is between 34th and 59th St. **Uptown** (59th St. and *up*) refers to the area north of Midtown. **Downtown** (34th St. and *down*) means the area south of Midtown.

When given the street number of an address (e.g. #250 E. 52nd St.), find the avenue closest to the address by thinking of Fifth Ave. as point zero on the given street. Address numbers increase as you move east or west of Fifth Ave. On the East Side, address numbers are 1 at Fifth Ave., 100 at Park Ave., 200 at Third Ave., 300 at Second Ave., 400 at First Ave., 500 at York Ave. (uptown) or Avenue A (in the Village). On the West Side, address numbers are 1 at Fifth Ave., 100 at the Ave. of the Americas (Sixth Ave.), 200 at Seventh Ave., 300 at Eighth Ave., 400 at Ninth Ave., 500 at Tenth Ave., and 600 at Eleventh Ave. In general, numbers increase from south to north along the avenues, but you always should ask for a cross street when you getting an avenue address.

GETTING AROUND

(For info on **Taxis** and **Biking,** see Practical Information.)

Get a free subway map from station token booths or the visitors bureau, which also has a free street map (see Practical Information above). For a more detailed program of interborough travel, find a Manhattan Yellow Pages, which contains detailed subway, PATH, and bus maps. In the city, round-the-clock staff at the **Transit Authority Information Bureau** (718-330-1234) dispenses subway and bus info.

Subways and Buses

The fare for **Metropolitan Transit Authority (MTA)** subways and buses is a hefty $1.25; groups of four or more may find cabs cheaper for short rides. Once inside you may transfer to any train without restrictions. Most buses have access ramps, but steep stairs make subway transit more difficult for disabled people. Call the Transit Authority Information Bureau for specific info on public transport.

In crowded stations (notably those around 42nd St.), pickpockets find plenty of work; in deserted stations, more violent crimes can occur. Always watch yourself and your belongings, and try to stay in lit areas near a transit cop or token clerk. Many stations have clearly marked "off-hours" waiting areas under observation that are significantly safer. Boarding the train, make sure to pick a car with a number of other passengers on it.

For safety, try to avoid riding the subways between 11pm and 7am, especially above E. 96th St. and W. 120th St. and outside Manhattan. Try also to avoid rush-hour crowds, where you'll be fortunate to find air, let alone seating—on an average morning, more commuters take the E and the F than use the entire rapid-transit system of Chicago (the nation's second-largest system). Buy a bunch of tokens at once at the booth or, preferably, at the new and more efficient token-vending machines now at most stations: you'll not only avoid a long line, but you'll be able to use all the entrances to a station (some lack token clerks).

Buses

Because **buses** sit in traffic, during the day they often take twice as long as subways, but they also stay relatively safe, clean—and always windowed. They'll also probably get you closer to your destination, since they stop roughly every two blocks and run crosstown (east-west), as well as uptown and downtown (north-south), unlike the subway which mostly travels north-south. The MTA transfer system provides north-south bus riders with a slip good for a free east-west bus ride, or vice-versa. Just ask the driver for a transfer when you pay. Ring when you want to get off. A yellow-painted curb indicates bus stops, but you're better off looking for the blue signpost announcing the bus number or for a glass-walled shelter displaying a map of the bus's route and a schedule (often unreliable) of arrival times. Either exact change or a subway token is required; drivers will not accept dollar bills.

ETIQUETTE

Like the French and the Visigoths, New Yorkers have a widespread reputation for rudeness. For most of them, lack of politeness is not a matter of principle; it's a strategy for survival. Nowhere is the anonymous rhythm of urban life more pounding than in New York City. Cramped into tiny spaces, millions of people find themselves confronting one another every day, rudderless in a vast sea of humanity. If the comfort of strangers seems overshadowed by the confusion, keep in mind that it's partly a question of scale. The city, by the most fundamental human standards, is just too big and heterogeneous and jumbled. And people react by keeping to themselves, especially in public. But if you feel that the city is intolerably unfriendly, try to note the small humanitarian gestures that appear in unlikely places.

ACCOMMODATIONS

If you know someone who knows someone who lives in New York—get that person's phone number. The cost of living in New York can rip the seams off your wallet. Don't expect to fall into a hotel; if you do, odds are it will be a pit. At true full-service establishments, a night will cost you around $125 plus the hefty 14.25% hotel tax. However, many reasonable choices are available for under $60 a night; it depends on your priorities. People traveling alone may want to spend more to stay in a safer neighborhood. The young and the outgoing may prefer a budget-style place crowded with students. Honeymooning couples will not.

Hostels and Student Organizations

New York International HI/AYH Hostel-CIEE Student Center, 891 Amsterdam Ave. (932-2300; Student Center 666-3619), at 103rd St. Subway: #1, 9, B, or C to 102nd St. Located in a block-long, landmark building designed by Richard Morris Hunt, this is the largest hostel in the U.S., with 90 dorm-style rooms and 480 beds. Spiffy new soft carpets, bunks, spotless bathrooms. Kitchens, dining rooms, coin-operated laundry machines, lounges, and a large outdoor garden. Secure storage area and individual lockers. No curfew. Max. stay 29 days, 7 in summer. Open 24 hrs. Check out 11am (late fee $5). Members $20, $22 in summer. Non-members $23/$25. Family room $60. Groups of 4-12 may get rooms to themselves; call ahead. Linen rental $3. Towel $2.50. Excellent disabled access.

International Student Hospice, 154 E. 33rd St. (228-7470), between Lexington and Third. Subway: #6 to 33rd St. Inconspicuous converted brownstone with a brass plaque saying "I.S.H." 20 very small rooms with bunk beds bursting with crusty bric-a-brac. Preference for internationals and students. Strict midnight curfew. $30 per night, with some weekly discounts.

International Student Center, 38 W. 88th St. (787-7706). Subway: B or C to 86th St. Between Central Park West and Columbus Ave. Open only to foreigners (except Canadians) aged 18-30; you must show a foreign passport to be admitted. A once-gracious, welcoming brownstone on a cheerful, tree-lined street noted for frequent celebrity sightings. Single-sex no-frills bunk rooms. Large basement TV lounge. No curfew. 7-day max. stay when full. Open daily 8am-11pm (guests can get key for $5 deposit). $12 a night. No reservations; call by 10pm for a bed.

International House, 500 Riverside Dr. (316-8436), at 123rd St. Subway: #1 or 9 to 116th St. or 125th St. Very large hostel fairly close to Columbia University with culturally diverse student residents. Great facilities: gymnasium, TV lounge, cafeteria, music practice rooms, library, coin-op laundry. 24-hr. security. Singles $25 per night, $18 per night for a stay of 2 weeks or longer. Communal bath for each sex. Make reservations 8am-10pm. Often vacancies, but try to call in advance. They try to keep at least 15 rooms for short-term visitors available year-round.

Sugar Hill International House, 722 Saint Nicholas Ave. (926-7030), at 146th St. in Harlem. Subway A, B, C, or D to 145th St. Located on Sugar Hill, right across from the subway station. 30-person occupancy with 2-10 people per room in standard bunkbeds. A hostel with few rules, no curfew, no chores, and no lockout. Staff is incredibly friendly and helpful, with a vast knowledge of NYC which they are more than willing to share. Kitchens, TV, stereo, paperback library. Beautiful garden in back. All-female room available. International travelers preferred, but well-traveled Americans accepted; passport required. Check in 9-11am, or call. $12 per person per night. Call in advance. Expect the **Blue Rabbit Hostel** (491-3892), their new 4-floor hostel next door, to be fully operational by 1994.

Big Apple Hostel, 109th W. 45th St. (302-2603), between 6th and 7th Ave., in same building as St. James Hotel. Centrally located, offering new beds in clean, comfortable, carpeted rooms. Passport required. Double bed with desk and small, clean bathroom $45. Dorm-style beds with shared bathroom $17. Lockers. Free coffee. Reservations recommended. Reception open daily 8am-3am.

Mid-City Hostel, 608 Eighth Ave. (704-0562), between 39th and 40th St. on the 3rd and 4th floors. No sign; just look for the narrow yellow building toward the middle of the block, across the street from Burger King. Don't be intimidated by the lively neighborhood and busy streets that surround this comfortable, homey hostel. Skylights, brick walls, and old wooden beams make it feel like a friend's apartment. Charismatic owner attracts primarily international backpackers: passport, backpack, and ticket out of the country required. Lockout noon-6pm. Curfew Sun.-Thurs. midnight, Fri.-Sat. 1am. 15 dorm-style beds ($15, $18 during peak season, including a light breakfast). 5 day max. stay in summer. Call in advance.

YMCA—West Side, 5 W. 63rd St. (787-4400). Subway: #1, 9, A, B, C, or D to 59th St./Columbus Circle. Small, well-maintained rooms but dilapidated halls in a big, popular Y whose impressive, Islamic-inspired facade is undergoing renovations. Free access to 2 pools, indoor track, racquet courts, and Nautilus equipment. Shower on every floor with spotless bathrooms. A/C and cable TV in every room. Check out noon; lockout at 11pm. Singles $42, doubles $52.

YMCA, 138-46 Northern Blvd. (718-961-6880), in Flushing, Queens. Subway: #7 to Main St.; the "Y" is two blocks down. About ½ hr. from Manhattan. Walk north on Main St. and turn right onto Northern Blvd. Men only. The area between the "Y" and Flushing's nearby shopping district is lively and well-populated, but the neighborhood quickly deteriorates past Northern Blvd. Gym, Nautilus, squash, and swimming facilities. $25 per person, $120 per week, 28-day maximum stay. Key deposit $20. Passport or driver's license required.

Chelsea Center Hostel, 313 W. 29th St. (643-0214), between Eighth and Ninth Ave. Subway: #1, 2, 3, 9, A, C, E to 34th St. Gregarious, knowledgeable staff will help you out with New York tips in multiple languages (including Gaelic). Twenty-five bunks in a low-ceilinged room make for a slightly cramped setup; the decor and lighting are currently being renovated. The owners' pride and joy is the tiny backdoor garden, replete with ivy and a picnic table. Check in anytime, but lockout 11am-5pm. Dorm beds $20 in summer, $18 in winter, light breakfast included. Be sure to call ahead.

Hotels

Carlton Arms Hotel, 160 E. 25th St. (679-0680), at Third Ave. Subway: #6 to 23rd St. The funkiest hotel in Manhattan and possibly the world. Stay inside a submarine and peer through windows at the lost city of Atlantis, travel to Renaissance Venice, or stow your clothes in a dresser suspended on an astroturf wall. Each room has been designed by a different avant-garde artist. Discounts for students and foreign tourists. Singles $44 (with discount $37). Doubles $57 ($53), with private bath $65 ($59). Triples $69 ($64), with private bath $77 ($69). Pay for six nights up front and get the seventh free. Confirm reservations 10 days in advance.

Pickwick Arms Hotel, 230 E. 51st St. (355-0300 or 800-742-5945), between Second and Third Ave. Subway: #6 to 51st St. or E, F to Lexington/Third Ave. Business types congregate in this extremely well-located and well-priced mid-sized hotel. Chandeliered marble lobby filled with the silken strains of "Unforgettable You" contrasts with disenchantingly dark and minuscule rooms and equally microscopic bathrooms. Even with nearly 400 rooms to fill, the Pickwick Arms gets very busy, so make reservations. Check in 2pm; check out 1pm. Singles $40, with shared bathrooms $50, doubles $85. Studios (up to four people) $99.50.

Portland Square Hotel, 132 W. 47th St. (382-0600), between Sixth and Seventh Ave. Subway: B, D, F, Q to 50th St.-Sixth Ave. Pleasant lobby painted dusty rose lures guests up to carpeted rooms with firm beds, TVs, A/C, and bathrooms big enough to turn around in. Keycard entry to individual rooms. Attracts mostly foreigners. Singles $40, with bath $60, doubles $85, triples $90, quads $95.

Herald Square Hotel, 19 W. 31st St. (279-4017 or 800-727-1888), at Fifth Ave. Quartered in the original Beaux Arts home of *Life* magazine (built in 1893); today, the reception desk is shielded in glass while sirens blare in the crowded streets outside. Above the entrance note the reading cherub carved by Philip Martiny entitled "Winged Life." The sculpture was a frequent presence on the pages of early *Life* magazines. Work by some of America's most noted illustrators adorns the lobby, halls, and rooms. Immaculate, renovated rooms with color TV and A/C. Singles (1 person only) $55, doubles $70, single or double (1 bed) with bath $90.

Mansfield Hotel, 12 W. 44th St. (944-6050 or 800-255-5167), at Fifth Ave. A dignified establishment housed in a turn-of-the-century building with comfortable leather couches in the lobby and beautiful oak doors in the hallways. Rooms in process of renovation: new lighting, new paint, and sauna whirlpool. Get one of the fixed-up ones. A bar/restaurant is conveniently located in the lobby. Check out at noon. Singles $65, doubles $75, triples $85, quads $118. Large suites $120 for 5 people, $140 for 6. Reservations and one night's deposit required.

Martha Washington, 30 E. 30th St. (689-1900), near Madison. Subway: #6 to 28th St. Women-only dormitory with 400 reasonably sized rooms. Somewhat dingy lobby and questionable security measures make the place less a good deal than it appears. Private bath may be worth money. Doors locked midnight-7am, but residents get keys. Singles $35, with private bath $54. Doubles $50/$69. Weekly: singles $140/$175, with bath and kitchenette $210; doubles $224/$245/$273.

FOOD

This city takes its food seriously. In New York, delis war. Brunch rules. Trendy dining has caught on. Supermarkets haven't—with so many bakeries, bistros, butcher shops, and greengrocers, who needs to stop and shop in a food mall? Don't be confused by the conflation of food and art. Certain eateries think they are galleries, while select delis look like museums. Assorted gourmet cooks pose as pushcart vendors. Sidewalk gourmands can stick with the old roving standbys on wheels (hot dogs, pretzels, roasted chestnuts), or try something more adventurous (shish kebabs, felafel, hot knishes).

New York's restaurants do more than the United Nations to promote international goodwill and cross-cultural exchanges. City dining spans the globe, with eateries ranging from relatively tame sushi bars to wild combinations like Afghani/Italian, or Mexican/Lebanese. In a city where the melting pot is sometimes less than tranquil, one can still peacefully sample Chinese pizza and Cajun knishes. Be openminded: you won't get very far in New York if you eat only what you can pronounce.

East Midtown

New York has six "four-star" restaurants, four of them (La Grenouille, Hatsuhana, Lutèce, and The Quilted Giraffe) in this area. Tycoons dine here among skyscraping office buildings, Art Deco monuments, and high rents. But it's possible to eat here without the company card. East Midtown hosts many sidewalk food vendors and fast-food peddlers. You can drop by the **Food Emporium,** 969 Second Ave. (593-2224), between 51st and 52nd, or **D'Agostino,** Third Ave. (684-3133), between 35th and 36th. These upscale supermarket chains, with branches scattered throughout Manhattan, feature reliable, well-stocked delis, fresh fruit and salad bars, ice cold drinks, gourmet ice cream, tons of munchies, and lots more—all at reasonable prices. After you've stocked up, picnicking is free in the area's green cloisters: try **Greenacre Park,** 51st St. between Second and Third; **Paley Park,** 53rd St. between Fifth and Madison; or the **United Nations Plaza,** 8th St. at First Ave.

Royal Canadian Pancake House, 1004 Second Ave. (219-3038), at 53rd St. "Pancakes make people happy," screams the slogan above the door, and at this benevolent institution, one pancake can make up to three people happy. Pancakes the size of Saskatchewan saturated with syrup, plunked with berries, titillated by exotic toppings, and spiked with Grand Marnier. Most around $8 but still quite a deal. Sharing costs $5. Another location in the Village. Open daily 7am-10pm.

Dosanko, 135 E. 45th St. (697-2967), between Lexington and Third Ave. Japanese fast food, very cheap and very fast. Don't come looking for a *sashimi* dinner: the main dish here is *lo mein* $4.90. Six pork dumplings with rice and salad $5.70. Fried and marinated chicken, served with green salad and sauteed vegetables, only $6. Open daily 11am-9:30pm.

Coldwaters, 988 Second Ave. (888-2122), between 52nd and 53rd St. Seafood ($6-11) served under nautical paraphernalia and stained-glass lamps. Lunch is a bargain: two drinks (alcoholic or non), choice of entree, salad, and fries for $7 (daily

NEW YORK CITY

11:30am-4pm). The yuppie midtown crowd gathers here for after-work cocktails, and parties into the wee hours. Open 11:30am-3:30am.

West Midtown

Around Times Square and the Port Authority Terminal, the number of fast-food chains nearly approaches the combined tally of tourists, pushers, pimps, and prostitutes—quite an achievement. In the Theater District, the stretch of Broadway from Times Square to 52nd St., you'll run into plenty of first-rate, ethnically diverse restaurants, from French to Japanese to Thai and back to Italian. While the food in these places can be mouthwatering, your check will probably be harder to swallow.

Celebrities occasionally drift over to **Sardi's,** 234 W. 44th St., and take a seat on the plush, red leather, surrounded by caricatures of themselves and their best friends. Traditionally, on the opening night of a major Broadway play, the main star makes an exalted entrance following the show—to hearty cheers for a superb performance or polite applause for a bomb. Farther uptown, near Carnegie Hall, lies the **Russian Tea Room,** 150 W. 57th St., a New York institution where dancers, musicians, and businessmen meet to down caviar and vodka.

Ariana Afghan Kebab, 787 Ninth Ave. (262-2323), between 52nd and 53rd St. Bedecked with embroidered textiles, Arabic calligraphy, and, oddly, slick reproductions of Alpine snow scenes. Try the *Bandinjah Burani,* a spicy eggplant dish served with sour cream and bread ($2.50). Selection of entrees mocks the indecisive ($5-8). The default choice is *lamb tikka kebab,* with chunks of marinated meat cooked in a wooden charcoal oven, served on a bed of brown rice with bread and salad ($6.75). BYOB. Open Mon.-Sat. 11:30am-3pm and 5-11pm.

Little Italy Pizza Parlour, 72 W. 45th St. (730-7575), corner of 45th St. and Sixth Ave. All of the pizzerias on 45th St. claim to be world famous, but this one takes the pie. Walls shine with the usual studio glossies, including the autographed color photo of a daring blonde: "Love ya pizza—Madonna." Hot crispy slice with plenty of mozzarella $1.65. Large Neapolitan pie $12.65, pie with the works $21. Calzones around $3.75. Open Mon.-Fri. 9:30am-7:30pm, Sat. 10:30am-6:30pm.

Carnegie Delicatessen, 854 Seventh Ave. (757-2245), at 55th St. *One of New York's great delis.* Ceiling fans whir gently overhead as photos of illustrious dead people stare out from the walls. Eat elbow-to-elbow at long tables. The "Woody Allen," an incredible pastrami and corned beef sandwich could easily stuff two people ($12.45), but sharing incurs a $3 penalty. First-timers shouldn't leave without trying the sinfully rich cheesecake topped with strawberries, blueberries, or cherries ($5.45). Open daily 6:30am-4am.

Uncle Vanya Café, 315 W. 54th St. (262-0542), between Eighth and Ninth Ave. Marionettes hang from the ceiling and the samovar reigns in this cheerful yellow cafe. Delicacies of czarist Russia include borscht ($3), *teftley,* Russian meatballs in sour cream sauce ($4.50), and caviar (market price—a concession to capitalism). Undiscovered, homey, and very good. Open Mon.-Sat. noon-11pm.

Lower East Midtown

This slightly gentrified, ethnically diverse neighborhood features many places where an honest meal is wed to reasonable prices. On Lexington, Pakistani and Indian restaurants battle for customers. Liberally sprinkled throughout are Korean corner shops. You can often fill up on prepared pastas, salads, and hot entrees, paying for them by the pound. Small Cuban restaurants offer cheap and filling fare.

Ray's Famous Original Pizza, 77 Lexington Ave. (795-1186), at 26th St. One of the 22 "Original" Ray's Pizzas in NYC. Lovely grease-dripping, cheese-laden, crusty-doughed pizza that tastes especially good after a few beers at the bar next door. Don't look for atmosphere here—just pizza at small fiberglass tables, serve-yourself-please-style. Slice $1.55, large pie $11. Open Mon.-Thurs. 10am-midnight, Fri.-Sat. 10am-1am, Sun. 11am-midnight.

Daphne's Hibiscus, 243 E. 14th St. (505-1180), at Second Ave. Large Day-Glo fish hover in the window; inside, Caribbean art adorns the walls of this spacious Jamaican restaurant. Try the chicken cooked in coconut milk or the special meat-filled pastries called "patties." Hibiscus colada (made with grapefruit juice) for the adventurous. Entrees $8-17. Sometimes music at night. Many drinks half-price at afternoon happy hour (4:30-6pm). Open Tues.-Thurs. 11am-11pm, Fri. 11am-midnight, Sat. 4pm-midnight, Sun noon-10pm.

Swagat, 110 Lexington Ave. (683-1900), at 28th St. One of the best Indian restaurants downtown, Swagat thankfully replaces ordinary Indian-restaurant decor (i.e., mirrors and reds) with California-influenced pink and teal. The tandoori specialties are especially good. The all-you-can-eat lunch is a steal at $10 (includes breads, dessert, and a salad; served daily 11:30am-3pm). Sun.-Thurs. noon-3pm and 5-10pm, Fri.-Sat. noon-3pm and 5-11pm.

Upper East Side

Unless you feel like eating a large bronze sculpture or an Armani suit, you won't find many dining opportunities on Museum Mile along Fifth and Madison Ave., aside from some charming cappuccino haunts, brunch breweries, and near-invisible ritzy restaurants. For less glamorous and more affordable dining, head east of Park Ave. Costs descend as you venture toward the lower-numbered avenues, though many do not escape the Madison pricing orbit. Hot dog hounds shouldn't miss the 100% beef "better than filet mignon" $1.50 franks at **Papaya King,** 179 E. 86th St. (369-0648), off Third Ave. (open Sun.-Thurs. 8am-1am, Fri.-Sat. 9am-3am). Don't feel confined to restaurant dining; grocery stores, delis, and bakeries speckle every block. You can buy your provisions here and picnic in honor of frugality in Central Park.

Afghanistan Kebab House, 1345 Second Ave. (517-2776), between 70th and 71st St. Behind an inconspicuous sign lurks one of the most rewarding restaurants in New York. Tender meats are broiled to perfection in a charcoal oven. Rich smells waft, subdued hues of Afghani rugs soothe, and soft Middle Eastern music drifts in from an invisible source. Bring your own booze. Ask the owner about the establishment's fleeting first incarnation as New York's sole Afghani pizzeria. Youngish crowd, casual atmosphere, irresistible kebab. All kebab dishes $9-11, vegetarian entrees $8. Take-out and free delivery ($10 min.). Open Sun.-Thurs. 4pm-10pm, Fri.-Sat. 4pm-11pm.

Zucchini, 1336 First Ave. (249-0559), between 71st and 72nd St. A nutrition-conscious triathlete runs this healthy establishment. No red meat, but fresh seafood, salads, pasta, and chicken dishes should satiate even militant carnivores. A steaming loaf of whole-wheat bread precedes dinner. Rough brick walls covered with naturalistic renderings of fresh fruits and veggies. Lunch $7, most pasta and vegetable entrees (soup included) about $12. Before 7pm try the Early Bird Special for only $9. Open daily 10:30am-10:30pm, brunch Sat.-Sun. 11am-4:30pm.

Mimi's Pizza and Ristorante, 1248 Lexington Ave. (861-3363), at 84th St. Pizza the way it should be: thin, crispy crust, spicy sauce, and the perfect amount of not-too-greasy cheese. Craved by New Yorkers, copied without success by impersonators (Mimmo's and Mimma's), and the favorite of at least one Englishman in New York—Paul McCartney. Large pie $11.75, slice, $1.50, spaghetti with meatballs $6, veal parmigiana $7.50. If the pizzeria seems impersonal, dine in the cozy *ristorante*. Take-out and free delivery. Open daily 11am-11pm.

Sesumi, 222 E. 86th St. (879-1024), between Second and Third Ave. Small, romantic, and Japanese. One of New York's best-kept secrets. Inconspicuous outside but a blizzard of ornate silk tapestries, paper lanterns, and winding greens inside, topped off by a full suit of samurai armor. Fresh food presented with a keen aesthetic sense. Entrees $9-14, sushi from $7.50. Dine early and take advantage of the generous 4-course Early Bird Special (5:30pm-7pm; $8). Open Mon.-Fri. noon-2:30pm and 5:30-11pm, Sat. 5:30-11:30pm, Sun. 5-10:30pm.

Upper West Side

The Upper West Side stays up later than its austere counterpart to the east. Monthly rents are heading up, "in" bars are going out, and high-fashion boutiques multiply—but here, gentrification does not make for boredom. Old New York charms endure: fancy Central Park West buildings with refined names, outdoor Columbus cafes with fried zucchini and gleaming chrome, dollar-a-book Broadway peddlers, Riverside views of sunset on the Hudson. If browsing in Laura Ashley or Charivari makes you tired, go haggle at the Columbus Avenue Street Fair, happen on a hidden gallery, or wander down the tempting aisles of **Zabar's,** 2245 Broadway (787-2002), the deli-cum-grocery that never ends.

Café Lalo, 201 83rd St. (496-6031), at Amsterdam Ave. Fabulously popular and new-looking dessert cafe attracts struggling artists, young people, and loaded professionals; it's worth the short wait to join them all at their high tables and antique chairs amid the strains of the Baroque top 40. More than 60 different pastry and cake desserts, most of them excellent, $3-6; try any fruit tart. Not the best value for your café dollar, but probably the best food. Cappuccino $1.75. Peach, pear, or apricot nectar $1.25. Wine and beer from $2.75. Open Sun.-Thurs. noon-2am, Fri.-Sat. 11am-4am.

La Caridad, 2199 Broadway (874-2780), at 78th St. One of New York's most successful Chinese-Spanish hybrids. Feed yourself and a pack of burros with one entree. *Arroz con pollo* (¼ chicken with yellow rice) $5.55. Other entrees of the Americas, including *Chop suey de cerdo ahumada,* $5-7. Fast-food ambience, but so what? Diverse crowd; beware of lines during dinner-time rush. Open Mon.-Sat. 11:30am-1am, Sun. 11:30am-10:30pm.

Diane's Uptown, 251 Columbus Ave. (799-6750), near 71st St. Large portions and reasonable prices make this popular, brass-railed, inexplicably dark cafe a student hangout. Spice up a 7-oz. burger ($4) with chili, chutney, or your choice of seven cheeses (85¢ per topping). Sandwiches $3-5, omelettes $3.90, onion rings and lots of fries $3. Open daily 11am-2am.

Mingala West, 325 Amsterdam Ave. (873-0787), at 75th St. Burmese cooking involves rice noodles, peanut sauces, coconuts, and curries, yet tastes nothing like Thai or Indonesian food. This place, with its lavender walls and ebony elephants, makes for a friendly introduction to a new cuisine. Mon.-Fri. noon-4pm lunch specials $5, "light meal" samplers 5-7pm $6. Or try glass noodles and beef dishes from the main menu ($7-13). Open Mon.-Thurs. noon-11pm, Fri.-Sat. noon-midnight.

Greenwich Village

Whatever your take on the West Village's bohemian authenticity, it's undeniable that all the free-floating artistic angst does result in many creative (and inexpensive) food venues. Aggressive and entertaining street life makes stumbling around, deciding where to go, almost as much fun as eating. Try the major avenues for cheap, decent food. Wander by the posh row houses around Jane and Bank St. for classier fare. The European-style bistros of **Bleecker Street** and **MacDougal Street,** south of Washington Square Park, have perfected the homey "antique" look.

Late night in the Village is a unique New York treat: as the sky grows dark, the streets quicken. Don't let a mob at the door make you hesitant about sitting over your coffee for hours and watching the spectacle—especially if the coffee is good. Explore twisting side streets and alleyways where you can drop into a jazz club or join Off-Broadway theater-goers as they settle down over a burger and a beer to write their own reviews. Or ditch the high life and slump down 8th St. to Sixth Ave. to join the freak scene and find some of the most respectable pizzerias in the city.

Ray's Pizza, 465 Sixth Ave. (243-2253), at 11th St. Half of the uptown pizza joints claim to be the "Original Ray's," but any New Yorker will tell you that this is the real McCoy. People fly here from Europe just to bring back a few pies—it's the best pizza in town. Well worth braving the lines and paying upwards of $1.75 for a slice. Open Sun.-Thurs. 11am-2am, Fri.-Sat. 11am-3am.

Olive Tree Cafe, 117 MacDougal St. (254-3630), north of Bleecker St. Standard Middle Eastern food offset by seemingly endless stimulation. If you get bored by the old movies on the wide screen, rent chess, backgammon, and Scrabble sets ($1), or doodle with colored chalk on the slate tables. Felafel $2.50, chicken kebab platter with salad, rice pilaf, and vegetable $7.50. Delicious egg creams only $1.75. Open Sun.-Thurs. 11am-3am, Fri.-Sat. 11am-5am.

Villa Florence, 9 Jones St. (989-1220), north of Bleecker St. A quiet, friendly spot with brick walls, checked tablecloths, and excellent food. The owner also runs the butcher shop next door; meat dishes are especially good. Pasta $6-12. Newport steak $9. Rainbow salad (arugula, endive, and radicchio), which is big enough for two, $3.50. *Maria tiramisu,* a trifle-like Sicilian dessert, $3. Open Tues.-Thurs. 5-11pm, Fri.-Sat. 5pm-midnight, Sun. 4-11pm.

The Pink Teacup, 42 Grove St. (925-3065), between Bleecker and Bedford. Soul food in a small, pink, and friendly environment. The $6 lunch special includes fried chicken, stew, or barbecued anything; soup or salad; two vegetables; and dessert (served 11am-2pm). Coffee, eggs, and fritters can feed two well for under $10. BYOB. Open Sun.-Thurs. 8am-midnight, Fri.-Sat. 8am-1am.

SoHo and TriBeCa

In SoHo, food, like life, is art. Down with the diner: food here comes in a variety of exquisite and pricey forms, with long and often unpronounceable names. Most of the restaurants in SoHo demonstrate an occasionally distracting preoccupation with art (some are practically indistinguishable from their neighboring galleries). With art, of course, comes money, so don't be surprised if you find it hard to get a cheap meal. Often the best deal in SoHo is brunch, when the neighborhood shows its most cozy and good-natured front. Dining in TriBeCa means dinner. Many of New York's highest-priced restaurants hide behind closed curtains; inexpensive places are few and far between.

Elephant and Castle, 183 Prince St. (260-3600), at Sullivan St.; also at 68 Greenwich Ave. Popular with locals for its excellent coffee and creative light food. Perfect for brunch. Prepare to wait for a table. Dinner around $10, brunch around $8. Open Mon.-Thurs. 8:30am-midnight, Fri.-Sat. 9am-1am, Sun. 10am-midnight.

SoHo Kitchen and Bar, 103 Greene St. (925-1866), near Prince St. A quintessential SoHo hangout: sky-high ceiling, gigantic artwork, scores of wines by the glass, and casual (but still calculated and hip) dress: the very definition of bourgeois tastefulness. Rich art crowd poses and struts while hapless tourists ogle. Chic pizza (topped with wild mushroom, roasted pepper, and grilled eggplant) $10, sandwiches $8. Open Mon.-Thurs. 11:30am-2am, kitchen closes 12:45am; Fri.-Sat. 11:30am-4am, kitchen closes 1:45am; Sun. noon-11pm.

East Village, Lower East Side, and Alphabet City

Culinary cultures clash on the lower end of the East Side, where pasty-faced punks and starving artists dine alongside an older generation conversing in Polish, Hungarian, and Yiddish. Observant Jews and Slavophiles reach nirvana in the delis and restaurants here. The Eastern European eateries distributed along First and Second avenues serve up some of the best deals in Manhattan. The **9th St. Bakery,** 350 E. 9th St. (open daily 8:30am-7pm), and **Kossar's Hot Bialys,** 367 Grand St. at Essex St. (473-4810; open 24 hrs.), sell cheap and unsurpassable bagels and bialys.

Dojo Restaurant, 24 St. Mark's Place (674-9821), between Second and Third Ave. One of the most popular restaurants and hangouts in the East Village, and rightly so. Offers an incredible variety of healthful, delicious, and inexplicably inexpensive food in a comfortable brick and darkwood interior. Tasty soyburgers with brown rice and salad $3.20. Spinach and pita sandwich with assorted veggies $2.15. Outdoor tables. Open Sun.-Thurs. 11am-1am, Fri.-Sat. 11am-2am.

Odessa, 117 Ave. A (473-8916), at 7th St. Beware of ordinary-looking coffee shops with Slavic names. Lurking beneath the title may be an excellent and inexpensive restaurant serving Eastern European specialties. Choose your favorites from a huge assortment of *pirogi*, stuffed cabbage, *kielbasa,* sauerkraut, potato pancakes, and other delicacies for the combination dinner ($6.70). Spinach pie and small Greek salad $4.50. Bargain breakfast special includes eggs, toast, potatoes, coffee, and juice ($1.75). Open daily 7am-midnight.

Veselka, 144 Second Ave. (228-9682), at 9th St. Down-to-earth soup-and-bread Polish-Ukrainian joint. Enormous menu includes about 10 varieties of soups, as well as salads, blintzes, meats, and other Eastern European fare. Blintzes $3.25, soup $1.75 a cup. Combination special gets you soup, salad, stuffed cabbage, and 4 melt-in-your-mouth *pirogi* ($7.25). Open 24 hrs.

Second Ave. Delicatessen, 156 Second Ave. (677-0606), at 10th St. The definitive New York deli since 1954; people come into the city just to be snubbed by the waiters here. Have pastrami (reputed to be the best in the city) or tongue on rye bread for $7, a fabulous burger deluxe for $6.50, or chicken soup for $3. Note the Hollywood-style star plaques embedded in the sidewalk outside: this was once the heart of the Yiddish theater district. Open Sun.-Thurs. 8am-midnight, Fri.-Sat. 8am-2am.

Kiev, 117 Second Ave. (674-4040), at E. 7th St. Unparalleled *pirogi* and tons of heavy foods laced with sour cream and butter (around $6). Upscale deli decor. A popular late-night and early-morning pit stop for East Village club hoppers with the munchies or a craving for borscht (small $3, large $5.50). Open 24 hrs.

Seekers of kosher food won't find much *traif* east of First Ave., especially south of East Houston St., where there has been a Jewish community since turn-of-the-century immigrant days.

Ratner's Restaurant, 138 Delancey St. (677-5588), just west of the Manhattan Bridge. The most famous of the kosher restaurants, partly because of its frozen-food line. Despite the run-down surroundings, this place is large, shiny, and popular. Jewish dietary laws are strictly followed and only dairy food is served; you will have to go elsewhere for a pastrami sandwich with Swiss and mayo. But there's no better place to feast on fruit blintzes and sour cream ($8.75) or simmering vegetarian soups ($4). Potato pancake to go $6. Open Sun.-Thurs. 6am-midnight, Fri. 6am-3pm, Sat. sundown-2am.

Katz's Delicatessen, 205 E. Houston St. (254-2246), near Orchard. Classic informal deli established in 1888. The fake-orgasm scene in *When Harry Met Sally* took place here. You'd better know what you want, because the staff here doesn't fool around. Have an overstuffed corned beef sandwich with a pickle for $6.45. Mail-order department enables you to send a salami to a loved one. With testimonial letters from both Carter and Reagan, how could it be bad? Open Sun.-Wed. 8am-9pm, Thurs. 8am-10pm, Fri.-Sat. 8am-11pm.

Chinatown

If you're looking for cheap and authentic Asian fare, join the crowds that push through the narrow, chaotic streets of one of the oldest Chinatowns in the U.S. New Yorkers have long thrived on the delectable food in this area, whether dining in, taking out, or picking and choosing in grocery stores and spillover stalls. The neighborhood's 200-plus restaurants cook up some of the best Chinese, Thai, and Vietnamese cooking around. Competition has been a boon for palates; once-predominantly Cantonese cooking has now burgeoned into different cuisines from the various regions of China: hot and spicy Hunan or Szechuan food; the sweet and mildly spiced seafood of Soochow; or the hearty and filling fare of Beijing. This competition has not diminished the popularity of Cantonese *dim sum,* however. In this Sunday afternoon tradition, waiters roll carts filled with assorted dishes of bite-sized goodies up and down the aisles. To partake, you simply point at what you want (beware of "Chinese Bubblegum," a euphemism for tripe). At the end of the meal, the number of empty dishes on your table is tallied up.

Hunan Joy's, 48 Mott St. (267-4421), on the 2nd floor, near Bayard St. Good and inexpensive Szechuan and Hunan food. Try the spicy hot and sour soup ($1.50) and shredded beef in garlic sauce ($7). Take advantage of the lunch special (Mon.-Fri. 11:30am-3pm): choice of 16 possible entrees served with soup and fried rice for $4.25-5. Open daily 11:30am-2am.

Mueng Thai Restaurant, 23 Pell St. (406-4259), near Mott St. The curry comes in 4 different colors—good luck to those who choose hot green. Try the Matsuman curry ($9) or the coconut chicken soup ($3). Lunch special weekdays 11:30am-3pm: rice and your choice of curry for $5. Open Sun., Tues.-Thurs. 11:30am-10pm, Fri.-Sat. 11:30am-11pm.

House of Vegetarian, 68 Mott St. (226-6572), at Bayard St. Faux chicken, faux beef, faux lamb, and faux fish comprise the huge menu: all the animals are ersatz here, made from soy and wheat by-products. Try *lo mein* (with 3 kinds of mushrooms, $5) or seaweed fish ($9). An ice-cold lotus seed or *lychee* drink ($2) really hits the spot on hot summer days. Open daily 11:30am-11pm.

Nha Trang Vietnamese Restaurant, 87 Baxter St. (233-5948), between Bayard and Canal. Authentic Vietnamese food in a quiet, unassuming setting. Most dishes average around $6.50 for dinner, $3.50 for lunch. Try the *bún* (rice vermicelli soup), which starts at $3.50, and the excellent iced coffee ($1.50). Open daily 10am-10pm.

Little Italy

A chunk of Naples seems to have migrated to this lively quarter roughly bounded by Canal, Lafayette, Houston St., and the Bowery. Mulberry Street is the main drag and the appetite avenue of Little Italy. Stroll here after 7pm to catch street life but arrive earlier to get one of the better tables. For the sake of variety and thrift, dine at a restaurant but get your just desserts at a cafe.

Luna, 112 Mulberry St. (226-8657), between Hester and Canal St. Enter through the small kitchen—where a halo of steam surrounds a generous platter of clams—to emerge into a narrow, somewhat haphazard dining room furnished with stray photos. Don't be afraid to ask for translations and advice; waiters give honest appraisals of the vast menu. Spaghetti with white clam sauce $7.50, tumbler of wine $3, fish from $9. Open daily noon-midnight.

Paolucci's, 149 Mulberry St. (226-9653 or 925-2288). Family-owned restaurant with a penchant for heaping portions. The boss watches you from the front wall. Chicken *cacciatore* with salad and spaghetti $11, pasta from $8, daily lunch specials (until 4pm) $5-9.50. Open Sun. 11:30am-9:30pm, Mon.-Thurs. 11:30am-10:30pm, Fri.-Sat. 11:30am-11:30pm.

Caffè Roma, 385 Broome St. (226-8413), at Mulberry St. A good *caffè* gets better with time. A full-fledged saloon in the 1890s, Roma has kept its original furnishings intact: dark green walls with polished brass ornaments, chandeliers, and darkwood cabinets. Since its saloon days, Roma has removed the imbibery and installed several elegant Tuscan landscapes. The pastries and coffee, Roma's *raison d'etre*, prove as refined as the setting. Try the neapolitan *cannoli* or the *baba au rhum* ($1.30 to take out, $2 to eat in). Potent espresso $1.50; obligatory cappuccino, with a tiara of foamed milk, $2.35. Open daily 8am-midnight.

Caffè Biondo, 141 Mulberry St. (226-9285). Don't mistake the glass front and polished black-and-white checkered floor for a gallery. Sip espresso ($1.50) while surrounded by cornucopias and diabolical grimaces. Or try *caffè corretto* (espresso with Sambuca, $2.50), *caffè alla panna* (with whipped cream, $1.75). *Cannoli* $2.50. Open Sun.-Thurs. noon-12:30am, Fri.-Sat. noon-1:30am.

Financial District

Bargain-basement cafeterias here can fill you up with everything from gazpacho to Italian sausages. Fast-food joints pepper Broadway between Dey and John St. just a few feet from the overpriced offerings of the Main Concourse of the World Trade Center. In the summer, food pushcarts form a solid wall along Broadway between Cedar and Liberty St., wheeling and dealing in a realm beyond hot dogs. Vendors sell felafel and eggplant plates ($2.75), cheese nachos ($3), and chilled gazpacho with an onion roll ($3). You can sup in Liberty Park, across the street.

Broadway Farm, 181 Broadway (587-1105 or 227-0701), between John and Cortlandt St. A salad bar the size of Guam—choose your favorite greens, pasta, and fruit ($4 per lb.). Seating in rear. Open 24 hrs.

Wolf's Delicatessen, 42 Broadway (422-4141). A deli untainted by any trend in cuisine or decor that hit after the early '60s. Formica, pickles, no pretensions. Burgers start at $2.65, bacon burger $3.65, turkey burgers 20¢ extra. Open Mon.-Fri. 6am-7:45pm, Sat. 6am-3:45pm.

Brooklyn

Ethnic flavor changes every 2 blocks in Brooklyn. Brooklyn Heights offers nouvelle cuisine, but specializes in pita bread and *baba ghanoush*. Williamsburg seems submerged in kosher and cheap Italian restaurants, while Greenpoint is a borscht-lover's paradise. And for those who didn't get enough in Manhattan, Brooklyn now has its own Chinatown in Sunset.

Downtown And North Brooklyn

Junior's, 986 Flatbush Ave. Extension (718-852-5257), across the Manhattan Bridge at De Kalb St. Subway: #2, 3, 4, 5, B, D, M, N, Q, or R to Atlantic Ave. Lit up like a jukebox, Junior's feeds classic roast beef and brisket to hordes of loyals. Brisket sandwich $6.25, dinner specials $10. Suburbanites drive for hours to satisfy their cheesecake cravings here (plain slice $3.50). Amy loves the pudding, too. Open Sun.-Thurs. 6:30am-1:30am, Fri.-Sat. 6:30am-3am.

Moroccan Star, 205 Atlantic Ave. (718-643-0800), in Brooklyn Heights. Subway: #2, 3, 4, 5, M, or R to Borough Hall, then down 4 blocks on Court St. Ensconced in the local Arab community, this restaurant serves delicious and reasonably cheap food. Try the *pastello,* a delicate semi-sweet pigeon pie with almonds ($8.75, lunch $6). Open Sun. noon-10pm, Tues.-Thurs. 10am-11pm, Fri.-Sat. 11am-11pm.

Central Brooklyn

El Gran Castillo de Jagua, 345 Flatbush Ave. (718-622-8700), at Carlton St. near Grand Army Plaza. Subway: D or Q to 7th Ave. A terrific place for cheap, authentic Spanish food. Meat dinners with rice and beans or plantains and salad $5-7, exotic fruit drinks $1. Try the *mofungo* (crushed green plantains with roast pork and gravy), $3.50. Open daily 7am-midnight.

Aunt Sonia's, 1123 Eighth Ave. (718-965-9526), at 12th St. near Park Slope. Subway: F to Seventh Ave./Park Slope. A tiny, very classy haven for the budget gourmand. Besides providing daily specials, the chef unveils a new menu every two months to loyal crowds. Entrees $8-10. Open Mon.-Thurs. 5:30-10pm, Fri.-Sat. 5:30-11pm, Sun. 11am-3:30pm, 5:30-10pm.

South Brooklyn

Primorski Restaurant, 282 Brighton Beach Ave. (718-891-3111). Subway: D or Q to Brighton Beach. Populated by Russian-speaking Brooklynites, this red-and-blue restaurant serves the best Ukrainian borscht ($1.70) in the Western hemisphere. Menu is pot-luck, as many of the waiters struggle with English. (That's okay—every dish is tasty.) Eminently affordable lunch special ($4) available weekdays 11am-5pm, weekends 11am-4pm. At night, prices rise as the disco ball begins to spin. You pay for entertainment, too. Open daily 11am-2am.

Queens

With nearly every ethnic group represented in Queens, this often overlooked borough offers visitors authentic and reasonably priced international cuisine away from

Manhattan's urban neighborhoods. **Astoria** specializes in discount shopping and cheap eats. The number of Greek and Italian restaurants increases right around the elevated station at Broadway and 31st St. In **Flushing**, you can find excellent Chinese, Japanese, and Korean restaurants, but always check the prices. An identical dish may cost half as much only a few doors away. **Bell Boulevard** in Bayside, out east near the Nassau border, is the center of Queens night life, and on most weekends you can find crowds of young natives bar-hopping here. In **Jamaica** and the other West Indian neighborhoods to its southeast, you can try food like Jamaican beef pattie or West Indian *rito* (flour tortilla filled with potatoes, meat, and spices).

Waterfront Crabhouse, 2-03 Borden Ave. Long Island City (718-729-4862). Subway: #7 to Vernon Blvd./Jackson Ave., then south on Vernon; walk all the way to the river on Borden Ave. Former home of the turn-of-the-century "Miller's Hotel," through which the rich and famous passed as they escaped to Long Island by ferry. Today the likes of Paul Newman and Ed Asner dine in the Crabhouse's wooden booths, which are decorated with the requisite antiques and touches of stained glass. Kindle a romance with the "Loveboat," a stuffed lobster floating in an ocean of shrimp scampi ($19). Beef steaks $7-14. Daily entertainment. Reservations recommended. Open Mon.-Wed. noon-10pm, Thurs. noon-11pm, Fri.-Sat. noon-midnight, Sun. 1-10pm.

Woo Chon Restaurant, 41-19 Kissena Blvd., Flushing (718-463-0803). Subway: #7 to Main St., then walk south two blocks. Duck behind the waterfall for some of the finest Korean food in Flushing. Abandon the safety of Korean-style "barbecue" ($15) and experiment with selections like *chun jou gob dol bibim bab* ($10), an obscure and ancient rice dish served in a superheated stone vessel; mix immediately, or the rice will be scorched by the bowl. For lunch, try a filling bowl of *seollung-tang* ($6.50), fine rice noodles in a beef broth with assorted Oriental veggies. An unlimited supply of *kim-chi* (spicy marinated vegetables) accompanies every meal. Open 24 hrs.

Uncle George's, 33-19 Broadway, Astoria (718-626-0593). Subway: G or R to Steinway St., then four blocks west, or N to Broadway, then two blocks east. This popular Greek restaurant, known as "Barba Yiogis O Ksenihtis" to the locals, serves inexpensive and hearty delicacies around the clock. Almost all entrees are under $10; try the goat soup ($6), rabbit stew, or lamb and potatoes (both $7). The hanging plants and flowers on the table lend the diner a cheery greenhouse effect. Open 24 hrs.

Bronx

When Italian immigrants settled the Bronx, they brought their recipes and tradition of hearty communal dining with them. While much of the Bronx is a culinary disaster zone, the New York cognoscenti soon discovered the few oases along Arthur Avenue and in Westchester where the fare is as robust and the patrons as rambunctious as their counterparts in Naples. Established in 1910, **Ruggieri Pastry Shop,** under the dynamic leadership of Sam and Lurdes, produces mountains of classic Italian pastries, though they're especially proud of their *sfogliatella*, a flaky Neapolitan pastry stuffed with ricotta. Those nostalgic for the groovy golden 50s will be glad to know that Ruggieri operates one of the last authentic ice cream fountains in New York. Ruggieri blends and bakes at 2373 Prospect Ave., at E. 187th St. (open daily 8am-10pm).

Mario's, 2342 Arthur Ave. (584-1188). Five generations of the Migliucci *famiglia* have worked the kitchen of this celebrated southern Italian *trattoria*. The original clan left Naples in the early 1900s and opened the first Italian restaurant in Egypt, then came to the U.S. and cooked themselves into local lore: Mario's appears in the pages of Puzo's *Godfather*. Celebrities pass through, among them the starting lineups for the Yankees and the Giants. A room-length couch embraces patrons with familial arms. Try *spiedini alla romana*, a deep-fried sandwich made with anchovy sauce and mozzarella ($8). Notorious for pizza too. Traditional pasta $9-

11, *antipasto* $5.50, eggplant stuffed with ricotta $6.25. Open Sun. and Tues.-Thurs. noon-10:30pm, Fri.-Sat. noon-midnight.

Caffè Margherita, 689 E. 187 St., near Arthur Ave. In the late 70s the *New York Times* called Margherita's cappuccino the "best in the world." On hot summer nights, retreat from the city into the fantasies offered by this *caffè,* complete with an outdoor jukebox with tunes ranging from Sinatra and Madonna to Italian folk music. Also serves pizza. "Cold" espresso $2. Alcohol served but no desserts. Open daily 8am-midnight.

SIGHTS

The classic sightseeing quandary experienced by New York tourists is finding the Empire State Building. They've seen it in dozens of pictures and drawings, captured in sharp silhouettes or against a steamy pink sky as a monument of dreams. They've seen it towering over the grey landscape as their plane descends onto the runway, or in perspective down long avenues, or from a river tour. But they can't see it when they're standing right next to it.

This optical illusion may explain why many New Yorkers have never visited some of the major sights in their hometown. When you're smack in the middle of them, the tallest skyscrapers seem like a casual part of the scenery. Not all sights are as glaringly green and obvious as the Statue of Liberty. Sometimes you'll enter a modest doorway to find treasures inside. If it's your first time in the big city, you'll notice even more subtle attractions—the neighborhoods and personalities jumbled together on shared turf, the frenzy of throngs at rush hour, the metropolitan murmur at dusk. And if it's your hundredth time in the city, there will still be areas you don't know too well, architectural quirks you've never noticed, and plain old doorways you have yet to discover and enter. Seeing New York takes a lifetime.

East Midtown

The massive Beaux Arts **Grand Central Terminal,** 42nd to 45th St. between Vanderbilt Pl. and Madison Ave., served as the gateway to New York for millions of travelers in the early 20th century. Fewer trains roll into and out of its depots today; nonetheless, it remains a starkly powerful symbol. Near the Vanderbilt entrance, you can see the famous 13-ft.-wide clock mounted on the southern facade and surrounded by a statuary group designed by Jules Alexis Coutan. This is an excellent spot for people-watching, as specimens of all descriptions hobble, stride, meander, and dash across the marble floor. Keep your eyes peeled for the bag-snatchers and pickpockets who also roam the halls. The Municipal Art Society leads popular (and free) guided tours of the terminal every Wednesday at 12:30pm, departing from the Chemical Commuter Bank in the Main Concourse.

The New York skyline would be incomplete without the familiar Art Deco headdress of the **Chrysler Building,** at 42nd and Lexington, built by William Van Allen as a series of rectangular boxes and topped by a spire modeled on a radiator grille. Other details evoke the romance of the automobile in the Golden Age of the Chrysler Automobile Company: a frieze of idealized cars in white and gray brick on the 26th floor; flared gargoyles at the fourth setback styled after 1929 hood ornaments and hubcaps; and stylized lightning-bolt designs symbolizing the energy of the new machine. When completed in 1929, this elegantly seductive building stood as the world's tallest. The Empire State topped it a year later.

42nd St. also delivers the **Daily News Building,** home to the country's first successful tabloid. Inside, an immense globe rotates at the center, enveloped by a black glass dome representing the night sky. A brass analog clock keeps time for 17 major cities worldwide, and frequent exhibitions breeze in and out. In 1990, the paper became entangled in a bitter and drawn-out battle with its union workers that threatened to shut the presses down permanently. Now-dead multimedia mogul Robert Maxwell purchased the rag in March 1991, and Mortimer Zuckerman finally settled it with big money in 1992.

The **United Nations** (963-7713) overlooks the East River between 42nd and 48th St. Designed in the early 50s by an international committee including Le Corbusier, Oscar Niemeyer, and Wallace Harrison (whose ideas won out in the end), the complex itself makes a diplomatic statement—part bravura, part compromise. Outside the U.N., enjoy the delightful promenade above the riverbank. Visitors can take a 1-hr. guided tour of the **General Assembly (G.A.)** and the **Security Council;** the tour starts in the main lobby of the G.A. every half-hour from 9:15am to 4:45pm. (Open daily 9am-6pm. $5.50, students $3.50. Visitor's Entrance at First Ave. and 46th.) Sept.-Dec., free tickets to G.A. meetings can be obtained in the main lobby about ½-hr. before sessions, which usually begin at 10:30am and 3pm Mon.-Fri.

St. Patrick's Cathedral (753-2261), New York's most famous church and the largest Catholic cathedral in America, stands at 51st St. and Fifth Ave. Designed by James Renwick, the structure captures the essence of great European cathedrals like Reims and Cologne yet retains its own spirit. The twin spires on the Fifth Ave. facade streak 330 ft. into the air. Today High Society intermarries at the cathedral.

Back at 375 Park Ave., between 52nd and 53rd, is Van der Rohe's innovative masterpiece, the dark and gracious **Seagram Building.** Completed in 1958, it remains a paragon of the International Style. Van der Rohe envisioned it as an oasis from the tight canyon of skyscrapers on Park Avenue. He set the tower back 90 ft. from the plaza and put two great fountains in the foreground. The public approved; in 1961 the city altered its building code to encourage further construction of tall box buildings with plazas; unfortunately this incentive resulted in a slew of trashy imitations.

The shiny, slanted **Citicorp Center** stands on four 10-story stilts in order to accommodate Saint Peter's Church, 619 Lexington Ave. (935-2200), at 53rd St. The 45-degree-angled roof was originally intended for use as a solar collector. Now, however, the roof supports an intriguing gadget, the so-called TMD, or Tuned Mass Damper, which senses the tremors of the earth and warns of earthquakes.

Philip Johnson's postmodern **AT&T Building** stands farther west, on Madison Ave. between 55th and 56th St. Most connoisseurs of Manhattan architecture agree that this black-striped building, with its pinkish marble (resembling a crystallized salmon mousse spread), doesn't quite succeed. The cross-vaulted arcade underneath (open Mon.-Fri. 8am-6pm) features open cafes and the ritzy four-star **Quilted Giraffe,** ranked as one of New York's five best restaurants. Tabs here can quite easily skyrocket up to $150 per person. One block uptown, fellow blue-chipper IBM sits in the green granite **IBM Building** at 590 Madison Ave. between 56th and 57th St. The **IBM Gallery of Science and Art** is contained here, worth a look.

Even a fanatical architect will feel like a kid again inside **F.A.O. Schwarz,** 767 Fifth Ave. (644-9400), at 58th St., the Godzilla of toy stores. Six-foot-high dolls of your favorite nursery heroes greet you at the entrance ($2000). Check out the gold Monopoly game ($1 million—not Monopoly money, either). (Open Mon.-Wed. and Fri.-Sat. 10am-6pm, Thurs. 10am-8pm, Sun. noon-6pm.)

West Midtown

The **Empire State Building** (slurred together by any self-respecting New Yorker into "Empire Statebuilding"), on Fifth Ave. between 33rd and 34th St. (736-3100), has style. It retains its place in the hearts and minds of New Yorkers even though it is no longer the tallest building in the U.S., or even the tallest building in New York (now the upstart twin towers of the World Trade Center). It doesn't even have the best looks (the Chrysler building is more delicate, the Woolworth more ornate). But the Empire State remains New York's best-known and best-loved landmark and dominates the postcards, the movies, and the skyline. The limestone and granite structure, with glistening mullions of stainless steel, stretches 1454 ft. into the sky; its 73 elevators run on 2 mi. of shafts. The nighttime view will leave you gasping. High winds can bend the entire structure up to a ¼-in. off-center. The Empire State was among the first of the truly spectacular skyscrapers, benefiting from innovations like Eiffel's pioneering work with steel frames and Otis's perfection of the "safety elevator." In Midtown it towers in relative solitude, away from the forest of monoliths that has grown around Wall St. (Admission $3.75, children and seniors $1.75; observatory open daily 9:30am-midnight, tickets sold until 11:30pm.) It's within walking distance of Penn and Grand Central Stations. The nearest subway stations are at 34th St. (subway: B, D, F, N, Q, and R), 33rd St. (#6), and 28th St. (R).

Pennsylvania Station crouches sadly at the bottom of west Midtown. The original Penn Station, a classical marble building modeled on the Roman Baths of Caracalla, was gratuitously demolished in the 60s. The railway tracks were depressed and covered by the dreadfully depressing **Madison Square Garden** complex. Facing the Garden at 421 Eighth Ave., New York's immense main post office, the **James A. Farley Building,** luxuriates in its primary 10001 ZIP code. A lengthy swath of Corinthian columns shoulders broadly across the front, and a 280-ft. frieze on top of the broad portico bears the bold, Cliff Clavenesque-motto of the U.S. Postal Service: "Neither snow nor rain nor heat nor gloom of night stays these couriers from the swift completion of their appointed rounds." Few realize that the motto was lifted from Herodotus's description of Persian messengers in the 6th century BC.

The **New York Public Library** (661-7220) reposes on the west side of Fifth Ave. between 40th and 42nd St., near Bryant Park. On sunny afternoons, throngs of people perch on the marble steps, which are dutifully guarded by the mighty lions Patience and Fortitude. This is the world's seventh-largest research library; witness the immense third floor reading room. They don't lend books. Free tours Tues.-Sat. at 11am and 2pm. (Open Tues.-Wed. 11am-7:30pm, Thurs.-Sat. 10am-6pm.)

Swing westward, and you'll soon find yourself in the flickering streets of **Times Square,** at the intersection of 42nd St. and Broadway. If any place deserves to be called the dark and seedy core of the Big Apple, this is it. Big-name Broadway stages and first-run movie houses compete with flashing neon, street performers, peep shows, and porn palaces. Teens in search of fake IDs wait on street corners, while hustlers scrounge the streets for suckers. The carnival excitement here is unique, and perhaps endangered. Women often find the area especially unnerving, although police presence is considerable. The entire area is currently undergoing a multi-year, $2.5 billion demolition and reconstruction program. A plethora of subway lines stop in Times Square (#1, 2, 3, 7, and 9, and A, C, E, N, R, and S).

On 42nd St. between Ninth and Tenth Ave. lies **Theater Row,** a block of renovated Broadway theaters. The adjacent **Theater District** stretches from 41st to 57th St. Approximately 40 theaters remain active, most of them grouped around 45th St.

Between 48th and 51st St. and Fifth and Sixth Ave. stretches **Rockefeller Center,** a monument to the conjunction of business and art. Raymond Hood and his cohorts did an admirable job of glorifying business through architecture. On Fifth Ave., between 49th and 50th St., the famous gold-leaf statue of Prometheus sprawls out on a ledge of the sunken **Tower Plaza** while jet streams of water pulse around it. The Plaza serves as an overpriced open-air cafe in the spring and summer and as an ice-skating rink in the winter. The 70-story **RCA Building,** seated at Sixth Ave., remains the most accomplished artistic creation in this complex. Every chair in the building sits less than 28 feet from natural light. Nothing quite matches watching a sunset from the 65th floor as a coral burnish fills the room. The **NBC Television Network** makes its headquarters here, allowing you to take a behind-the-scenes look at their operations. (Open daily 9:30am-4:30pm. Tours leave every 15 min.; maximum 17 per group; tickets are first come, first served, so buy in advance. $7.75, children under 6 not admitted. Call 664-4000 for information.)

Despite possessing an illustrious history and a wealth of Art Deco treasures, **Radio City Music Hall** (632-4041) was almost demolished in 1979 to make way for new office high-rises. However, the public rallied and the music hall was declared a national landmark. First opened in 1932, at the corner of Sixth Ave. and 51st St., the 5874-seat theater remains the largest in the world. The brainchild of Roxy Rothafel (originator of the Rockettes), it was originally intended as a variety showcase. Yet the hall functioned primarily as a movie theater; over 650 feature films debuted here from 1933 to 1979, including *King Kong, Breakfast at Tiffany's,* and *Doctor Zhivago.* The Rockettes, Radio City's chorus line, still dance on. Tours of the great hall are given daily 10am-4:45pm. ($8, children 6 and under $4.)

At 25 W. 52nd St., the **Museum of Television and Radio** (621-6600) broadcasts changing exhibits of artifacts and documents related to television and radio. Continue over a block down W. 53rd St. towards Sixth Ave. and take in a handful of masterpieces in the windows of the **American Craft Museum** and the **Museum of Modern Art** (see Museums). Rest your tired feet with a visit to the sculpture garden of the MoMA, featuring the works of Rodin, Renoir, Miró, Lipschitz, and Picasso.

On Fifth Ave. and 59th St., at the southeast corner of Central Park, sits the legendary **Plaza Hotel,** built in 1907 by Henry J. Hardenberg. Its 18-story, 800-room French Renaissance interior flaunts five marble staircases, and a two-story Grand Ballroom. Past guests and residents have included Frank Lloyd Wright, the Beatles, and F. Scott Fitzgerald. *Let's Go* recommends the $15,000-per-night suite.

How do you get to **Carnegie Hall?** Practice. This venerable institution at 57th St. and Seventh Ave. was founded in 1891 and remains New York's foremost soundstage. During its illustrious existence, the likes of Tchaikovsky, Caruso, Toscanini, and Bernstein have played Carnegie; as have the Beatles and the Rolling Stones. Other notable events from Carnegie's playlist include the world premiere of Dvořák's *Symphony No. 9 (From the New World)* on December 16, 1893, and an energetic lecture by Albert Einstein in 1934. Carnegie Hall was facing the wrecking ball in the 1950s. Outraged citizens managed to stop the impending destruction through special legislation in 1960. Tours are given Mon., Tues., and Thurs. at 11:30am, 2pm, and 3pm ($6, students $5). Carnegie Hall's **museum** displays artifacts and memorabilia from its illustrious century of existence (open daily 10am-4:30pm; free).

Lower Midtown

In the **Pierpont Morgan Library,** 29 E. 36th St. (685-0610), a Low Renaissance-style palazzo, you can see a stunning collection of rare books, sculpture, and paintings gathered by the banker and his son, J.P. Morgan, Jr. (Subway: #6 to 33rd St. Open Tues.-Sat. 10:30am-5pm, Sun. 1-5pm. Suggested contribution $5, seniors and students $3. Free tours on various topics Tues.-Fri. 2:30pm.) **Macy's,** the largest department store in the world, stands on 34th St. and Broadway in Herald Square. With some two million sq. ft. of merchandise, it occupies an entire city block. Macy's has a separate Visitors Center, located on the first-floor balcony, where the concierge service (560-3827) will assist anyone looking for anything. (Open Mon. and Thurs.-Fri. 10am-8:30pm, Tues.-Wed. and Sat. 10am-7pm, Sun. 11am-6pm. Subway: #1, 2, 3, or 9 to Penn Station, or B, D, F, N, Q, or R to 34th St.)

Yet another distinguished club member is the eminently photogenic **Flatiron Building;** originally named the Fuller Building, its dramatic wedge shape, imposed by the intersection of Broadway, Fifth Ave., and 23rd St., quickly earned it its *nom de plume.* St. Martin's Press currently occupies some of its floors, and will soon occupy roughly half the building's space. The building's old-fashioned electrical and hydraulic systems are too outdated for most contemporary enterprises, so publishers (who don't need many modern conveniences) have taken over.

The **Palladium,** at 126 E. 14th St. between Third and Fourth Ave., a former movie palace converted into a disco in 1985 by Japanese designer Arata Isozaki, contains a staircase with 2400 round lights. The nightclub hosts huge parties and special events and boasts the world's largest dance floor.

Upper East Side

The Golden Age of the East Side society epic began in the 1860s and progressed until the outbreak of World War I. Scores of wealthy people moved into the area and refused to budge, even during the Great Depression when armies of the unemployed pitched their tents across the way in Central Park. So it was that select hotels, mansions, and churches first colonized the primordial wilderness of the Upper East Side. The lawns of Central Park covered the land where squatters had dwelt; **Fifth Avenue** rolled over a stretch once grazed by pigs. These days parades, millionaires, and unbearably slow buses share Fifth Avenue. Its **Museum Mile** includes the Metropolitan, the Guggenheim, the International Center of Photography, the Cooper-Hewitt, the Museum of the City of New York, and the Jewish Museum, among others (for more information see Museums and Galleries).

Gracie Mansion, at the northern end of Carl Schurz Park, in the far east between 84th and 90th St. along East End Ave., has been the residence of every New York mayor since Fiorello LaGuardia moved in during World War II. David Dinkins occupies this hottest of hot seats. To make a reservation for a tour of the colonial mansion, call 570-4751 (tours Wed. only; suggested admission $3, seniors $1.)

Central Park

Central Park rolls from Grand Army Plaza all the way up to 110th between Fifth and Eighth Ave. Twenty years of construction turned these 843 acres, laid out by Brookliner Frederick Law Olmsted and Calvert Vaux in 1850-60, into a compressed sequence of landscapes of nearly infinite variety. The park contains lakes, ponds, fountains, skating rinks, ball fields, tennis courts, a castle, an outdoor theater, a bandshell, two zoos, and one of the most prestigious museums in the U.S., the **Metropolitan Museum of Art** (see Museums).

The Park may be roughly divided between north and south at the main reservoir; the southern section affords more intimate settings, serene lakes, and graceful promenades, while the northern end has a few ragged edges. Nearly 1400 species of trees, shrubs, and flowers grow here, the work of distinguished horticulturist Ignaz Anton Pilat. When you wander amidst the shrubbery, you can't get lost. Look to the nearest lamppost for guidance, and check the small metal four-digit plaque bolted to it. The first two digits tell you what street you're nearest (e.g., 89), and the second two whether you're on the east or west side of the Park (even numbers mean east, an odd west). In an emergency, call the 24-hr. Park telephone line (800-834-3832).

At the renovated **Central Park Zoo** (439-6500), Fifth Ave. at 64th St., the monkeys effortlessly ape their visitors. ($2.50, seniors $1.25, children 3-12 50¢. Open Mon.-Fri. 10am-5pm, Sat.-Sun. 11:30am-5:30pm, last entry ½-hr. before closing.) The **Wollman Skating Rink** (517-4800) doubles as a **miniature golf course** in late spring. (Ice- or roller-skating $6, kids and seniors $3, plus $3.25 skate rental or $6.50 rollerblade rental; 9-hole mini-golf $6, kids $3; bankshot $5, kids $2.50; discounts for combining activities. Whole megillah open Mon. 10am-5pm, Tues. 10am-9:30pm, Wed.-Thurs. 10am-6pm and 7:30-9:30pm, Fri.-Sat. 10am-11pm, Sun. 10am-9:30pm.) The best thing about the roller rink is the railed ledge overlooking it, from which an unparalleled view of midtown can be had free of charge.

In summer the park hosts **free concerts** from Paul Simon to the Metropolitan Opera, and excellent free drama (for the first 1936 lucky souls) during the **Shakespeare in the Park** festival (see Theater). Full info on recreational activities fills a handy booklet, *Green Pages,* available at all info centers.

Upper West Side

Broadway leads uptown to **Columbus Circle,** 59th St. and Broadway, the symbolic entrance to the Upper West Side and the end of Midtown—with a statue of Christopher himself. One of the Circle's landmarks, the **New York Coliseum,** was replaced by the **Javits Center** in 1990.

Broadway intersects Columbus Ave. at **Lincoln Center,** the cultural hub of the city, between 62nd and 66th St. The seven facilities that constitute Lincoln Center—Avery Fisher Hall, the New York State Theater, the Metropolitan Opera House, the Library and Museum of Performing Arts, the Vivian Beaumont Theater, The Walter

Reade Theater, and the Juilliard School of Music—accommodate over 13,000 spectators at a time. At night, the Metropolitan Opera House lights up, making its chandeliers and huge Chagall murals visible through its glass-panel facade. The Metropolitan Opera shop sells gift books, posters, libretti, and boxes of cough drops used and autographed by Caruso. Mmm. The shop also broadcasts performances live on house monitors; sneaky budgeteers can get a quick opera fix just browsing in the shop at performance time. (Open Mon.-Sat. 10am-5:30pm or until 2nd intermission of performance; Sun. noon-6pm.)

As Manhattan's urbanization peaked in the late 19th century, wealthy residents sought tranquility in the elegant **Dakota Apartments,** at 1 W. 72nd St. on Central Park West. Built in 1884, the apartment house was named for its remote location. John Lennon's streetside murder here in 1981 brought new notoriety to the mammoth building.

Harlem

Half a million people are packed into the 3 sq. mi. of Harlem's two neighborhoods. On the East Side above 96th St. lies Spanish Harlem, known as *El Barrio,* and on the West Side lies Harlem proper. It begins at 110th St. in the region known as **Morningside Heights** and stretches up to 155th. Both poverty-ridden neighborhoods heat up with street activity, not always of the wholesome variety; visit Harlem during the day or go there with someone who knows the area. If you lack the street wisdom or can't find your own guide opt for a commercial tour.

It is a colossal misconception that Harlem is merely a crime-ridden slum. Although an extremely poor neighborhood, it is culturally rich; and, contrary to popular opinion, much of it is relatively safe. Known as the "city within the City," Harlem is considered by many to be the black capital of the Western world. Over the years Harlem has often been viewed as the archetype of America's frayed cities—you won't believe that hype after you've visited. The 1920s were Harlem's Renaissance; a thriving scene of artists, writers, and scholars lived fast and loose, producing cultural masterworks in the process. The Cotton Club and the Apollo Theater, along with numerous other jazz clubs, were on the musical vanguard.

New York's member of the Ivy League, **Columbia University,** chartered in 1754, is tucked between Morningside Dr. and Broadway, and 114th and 121st St. Now co-ed, Columbia also has cross-registration with all-female **Barnard College** across Broadway. Suggestively, this urban campus occupies the former site of the Bloomingdale Insane Asylum. The silver dome of the **Masjid Malcolm Shabazz,** where Malcolm X was once a minister, glitters on 116th St. and Lenox Ave. (visit Fri. at 1pm and Sun. at 10am for services and information, or call 662-2200).

The **Cathedral of St. John the Divine,** between 110th and 113th, promises to be the world's largest cathedral when finished. Construction, begun in 1812, is still going on and is not expected to be completed for another century or two.

125th Street, also known as Martin Luther King Jr. Boulevard, spans the heart of traditional Harlem. Fast-food joints, jazz bars, and the **Apollo Theater** (222-0992, box office 749-5838) keep the street humming day and night. 125th has recently resurged as a center of urban life; small shops, families with children, and an increasing vogue have combined to make this part of Harlem a lively community center.

Off 125th St., at 328 Lenox Ave., **Sylvia's** (966-0660) has magnetized New York for 22 years with enticing soul-food dishes (open Mon.-Sat. 7am-10pm, Sun. 1-7pm). Live music (Wed.-Fri. 7-9pm; no cover) features jazz and R&B.

In Washington Heights, north of 155th St., the **George Washington Bridge,** a 1931 construction by Othmar Amman, is a 14-lane suspension bridge once pronounced "the most beautiful bridge in the world" by Le Corbusier.

Greenwich Village

In "The Village," bordered by 14th St. to the north and Houston to the south, bohemian cool meets New York neurosis, resulting in the "downtown" approach to life.

NEW YORK CITY

The buildings here do not scrape the skies, the street grid dissolves into geometric whimsy, and the residents revel in countercultural logic. Pop culture and P.C. politics thrive here, but both are the secret slaves to the real arbiter of cool: fashion. "Greenwich Village" or "The Village" actually refers, these days, to the West Village, the area west of Broadway, as well as Washington Square Park and its environs. The East Village, on the cutting edge of Boho authenticity, is actually part of the Lower East Side (see below). An ongoing yuppification campaign has purged the Village of most of its aspiring artists, although the Christopher St. neighborhood is home to a vibrant (and upscale) gay and lesbian scene. The Villages of the city stay lively all day and most of the night. Those seeking propriety should head uptown immediately. Everyone else should revel in the funky atmosphere, stores, and people-watching.

Washington Square Park Area

Washington Square Park has been the universally acknowledged heart of the Village since the district's days as a suburb. The marshland here served first as a colonial cemetery (around 15,000 bodies lie buried there), but in the 1820s the area was converted into a park and parade ground. Soon high-toned residences made the area the center of New York's social scene. Society has long since gone north, and **New York University** has moved in. The country's largest private university and one of the city's biggest landowners (along with the city government, the Catholic Church, and Columbia University), NYU has dispersed its administrative buildings, affiliated housing, and eccentric students throughout the Village.

In the late 1970s and early 80s Washington Square Park became a base for low-level drug dealers, and a rough resident scene. The mid-80s saw a noisy clean-up campaign that has made the park fairly safe and allowed a more diverse cast of characters to return. A lot of people still buy drugs here, but it's not a good idea; you'll likely end up with oregano or supermarket-variety mushrooms. You will also encounter several dozen of New York's homeless; try to keep your distance, particularly at night. (Subway: A, B, C, D, E, F, or Q to W. 4th St./Washington Sq.)

On the south side of Washington Square Park, at 133 MacDougal St., is the **Provincetown Playhouse,** a theatrical landmark. Originally based on Cape Cod, the Provincetown Players were joined by the young Eugene O'Neill in 1916 and went on to premiere many of his works. Farther south on MacDougal are the Village's finest coffeehouses, which had their glory days in the 1950s when Beatnik heroes and coffee-bean connoisseurs Jack Kerouac and Allen Ginsberg attended jazz-accompanied poetry readings at **Le Figaro** and **Café Borgia.** These sidewalk cafes still provide some of the best coffee and people-watching in the city.

The north side of the park, called **The Row,** showcases some of the most renowned architecture in the city. Built largely in the 1830s, this stretch of elegant Federal-style brick residences soon became an urban center roamed by 19th-century professionals, dandies, and novelists.

Up Fifth Ave., at the corner of 10th St., rises the **Church of the Ascension,** a fine 1841 Gothic church with a notable altar and stained-glass windows (open daily noon-2pm and 5-7pm). Many consider the block down 10th St. between Fifth and Sixth Ave. the most beautiful residential stretch in the city. This short strip plays out innumerable variations in brick and stucco, layered with wood and iron detailing. Ivy clothes the facades of many buildings, while window boxes brighten others.

Back on the other side of Sixth Ave., at 18 W. 11th St., a striking new building replaces the house destroyed in 1970 by a bomb-making mishap of the Weathermen, a radical group residing in the basement. Farther east at 47 Fifth Ave. is **The Salmagundi Club,** New York's oldest club for artists. Founded in 1870, the club's building is the only remaining mansion from the area's heyday at the pinnacle of New York society. (Open during exhibitions. Call 255-7740 for details.)

West Village

The bulk of Greenwich Village lies west of Sixth Ave., thriving on the new and different. In spite of rising property prices, the West Village still boasts an eclectic summer street life and excellent nightlife. The West Village has a large and very visible gay community based around Sheridan Square. This is the native territory of the Guppie (Gay Urban Professional), although all kinds of gay males and lesbians shop, eat, and live here. Same-sex couples can walk together openly. **Christopher Street,** the main byway to the south, swims in novelty restaurants and specialty shops. (Subway: #1 or 9 to Christopher St./Sheridan Sq.) A few street signs refer to Christopher St. as "Stonewall Place," alluding to the **Stonewall Inn,** the club where police raids in 1969 prompted the riots that sparked the U.S. Gay Rights Movement.

SoHo and TriBeCa

SoHo is bounded by Houston St. (pronounced HOW-ston), Canal, Lafayette, and Sullivan St. The architecture here is American Industrial (1860-1890), notable for its cast-iron facades. SoHo has become the high-priced home of New York's artistic community. Here, art is nothing if not for sale; while museums populate the rest of the city, the gallery reigns supreme in SoHo. Don't be put off by snooty gallery-owners; unless you're interrupting a private showing to a visiting head of state, visitors short on cash are always allowed, if not entirely welcome, in SoHo galleries.

Greene Street offers the best of SoHo's lofty architecture. Once architects here made sweatshops look like iron palaces; now artists have converted factory lofts into studios. More than just a place for galleries, the street is filled with experimental theaters and designer clothing stores. This is a great place for star-gazing, too, so bring your autograph book and a bright flash for your camera. Celebrities like that.

A mind-twisting mural by Richard Haas covers the southeast corner of Prince and Greene St. Try to pick out which windows are real and which are painted. To the south, on a lot at Wooster and Spring St., a daily fair sets up shop. Flea market devotees should check out Sunday's market on the corner of Broadway and Grand St.

If you're looking for genuine starving artists, you probably won't find them in SoHo. But you may find a few in young SoHo, called **TriBeCa** ("Triangle Below Canal St."), an area bounded by Chambers St., Broadway, Canal St., and the West Side Highway. Admire the cast-iron edifices lining White Street, Thomas Street, and Broadway, the 19th-century Federal-style buildings on Harrison Street, and the shops, galleries, and bars on Church and Reade streets.

The avant-garde art world has migrated south from SoHo. Art lovers should look to **Artists Space,** at 223 West Broadway, and to the **Franklin Furnace,** at 112 Franklin St., which battle fire regulations in their continuing quest to display the most alternative of alternative art.

Lower East Side

The old Lower East Side, once home to Eastern European immigrants, extended from Hester to 14th St. Now this area has developed a three-way split personality, encompassing the part south of Houston and east of the Bowery (now considered the whole Lower East Side), the section east of Broadway and north of Houston (known as the "East Village"), and the part of the East Village east of First Ave. (known as "Alphabet City").

Down below Houston in the somewhat deserted Lower East Side you can still find some excellent kosher delis and a few old-timers who remember the time when the Second Ave. El ran from the power station at Allen and Pike St. On the **Bowery,** you can haggle for lamps; on **Allen Street,** shirts and ties. Check out Stanford White's **Bowery Savings Bank,** at Grand St., a repository of wealth now surrounded by lots of homeless people. You'd probably feel safe leaving your money here, but don't go wandering around down here at night with a full wallet.

East Village

The East Village, a comparatively new creation, was carved out of the Bowery and the Lower East Side as rents in the West Village soared and its residents sought accommodations elsewhere. Allen Ginsberg, Jack Kerouac, and William Burroughs all eschewed the Village establishment to develop their junked-up "beat" sensibility east of Washington Square Park. A fun stretch of Broadway runs through the Village, marking the western boundary of the East Village. Everyone and their grandmother know about this browser's paradise.

Grace Church, constructed in 1845, asserts its powerful Gothic presence at 800 Broadway between 10th and 11th. The church used to be *the* place for weddings. The dark interior has a distinctly Medieval feel. (Open Mon.-Fri. 10am-5:45pm, Sat. noon-4pm.) One of the world's most famous bookstores is the **Strand,** at the corner of 12th St. and Broadway, which bills itself as the "largest used bookstore in the world" with over two million books on eight miles of shelves. At Broadway and 4th St., you'll find another of the Village's spiritual landmarks, **Tower Records,** not only a popular hangout, but also a bonding ground for people of similar musical taste. Lots of models have been "discovered" here.

Walk one block east of Broadway on E. 4th to reach Lafayette St. To your right will be **Colonnade Row,** with the Public Theater across the street. Colonnade Row consists of four magnificently columned houses, built in 1833, once the homes of New York's most famous 19th-century millionaires: John Jacob Astor and Cornelius "Commodore" Vanderbilt.

Across from a church at 156 Second Ave. stands a famous Jewish landmark, the **Second Avenue Deli** (677-0606). This is all that remains of the "Yiddish Rialto," the stretch of Second Ave. between Houston and 14th St. that comprised the Yiddish theater district in the early part of this century. The Stars of David embedded in the sidewalk in front of the restaurant contain the names of some of the great actors and actresses who spent their lives entertaining the poor Jewish immigrants of the city.

St. Mark's Place, running from Third Avenue at 8th Street down to Tompkins Square Park, is the geographical and spiritual center of the East Village. In the 1960s, the street was the Haight-Ashbury of the East Coast, full of pot-smoking flower children waiting for the next concert at the Electric Circus. In the late 1970s it became the King's Road of New York, as mohawked youths hassled the passers-by from the brownstone steps off Astor Place. Today things are changing again: a Gap store sells its conventional color-me-matching combos across the street from a shop stocking "You Make Me Sick" T-shirts. Though many "Village types" now shun the commercialized and crowded street, St. Mark's is still central to life in this part of town and a good place to start a tour of the neighborhood.

Alphabet City

East of First Ave., south of 14th St., and north of Houston, the avenues run out of numbers and take on letters. This part of the East Village has so far escaped the escalating yuppification campaign that has claimed much of St. Mark's Place; in the area's heyday in the 60s, Jimi Hendrix and the Fugs would play open-air shows to bright-eyed Love Children. There has been a great deal of drug-related crime in the recent past, although the community has done an admirable job of making the area livable again. Alphabet City is generally safe during the day, and the addictive nightlife on Avenue A ensures some protection there, but try to avoid straying east of Avenue B at night. Alphabet City's extremist Boho activism has made the neighborhood chronically ungovernable in the last several years, a little kernel of Amsterdam or old West Berlin set deep in the bowels of Manhattan. A few years ago, police officers set off a riot when they attempted to forcibly evict a band of the homeless and their supporters in **Tompkins Square Park,** at E. 7th St. and Ave. A. Today, the park is no longer a glum testament to the progress of gentrification—it has just reopened after a two-year hiatus, and officials have high hopes for the area. The park still serves as a psycho-geographical epicenter for many a churlish misfit.

Lower Manhattan

Many of the city's superlatives congregate at the southern tip of Manhattan. The Wall Street area is the densest in all New York. Wall Street itself measures less than a

½-mile long. Along with density comes history: lower Manhattan was the first part of the island to be settled. Touring here won't cost much. Parks, churches, and temperature-controlled cathedrals of commerce such as the New York Stock Exchange and City Hall charge no admission. Visit during the work week.

Wall Street and the Financial District

Battery Park, named for a battery of guns the British stored there from 1683 to 1687, is now a chaotic chunk of green on the southernmost toenail of Manhattan Island. The #1 and 9 trains to South Ferry terminate at the southern tip of the park; the #4 and 5 stop at Bowling Green, just off the northern tip. On their way to the Statue of Liberty Ferry, mobs often descend upon the park and become prey for parasitic peddlers. Try not to talk to strangers here.

Once the northern border of the New Amsterdam settlement, **Wall Street** takes its name from the wall built in 1653 to shield the Dutch colony from a British invasion from the north. By the early 19th century, it had already become the financial capital of the United States.

Just a bit farther down Wall St., meet **Federal Hall** (264-8711), the original City Hall, where the trial of John Peter Zenger helped to establish freedom of the press in 1735. On the southwestern corner of Wall and Broad St. stands the current home of the **New York Stock Exchange** (656-5168; open to the public Mon.-Fri. 9:15am-2:45pm). The Stock Exchange was first created as a marketplace for handling the $80 million in U.S. bonds that were issued in 1789 and 1790 to pay Revolutionary War debts. Arrive early in the morning, preferably before 9am, to ensure a convenient admission time. Tickets usually run out by around 1pm. The real draw is the observation gallery that overlooks the zoo-like main trading floor of the exchange.

Around the corner, at the end of Wall St., rises the seemingly ancient **Trinity Church** (602-0800). Its Gothic spire was the tallest structure in the city when first erected in 1846. The vaulted interior feels positively medieval, especially in contrast to the neighborhood temples of Mammon. Behind the altar is a small **museum** (open Mon.-Fri. 9-11:45am and 1-3:45pm, Sat. 10am-3:45pm, Sun. 1-3:45pm; daily tours given at 2pm).

World Trade Center and Battery Park City

Walk up Broadway to Liberty Park, and in the distance you'll see the twin towers of the city's tallest buildings, the **World Trade Center.** Two World Trade Center has an **observation deck** (435-7397) on the 107th floor, and a banner indicating as much hangs outside. (Open daily June-Sept. 9:30am-11:30pm, Oct.-May 9:30am-9:30pm. $4, seniors $2.25, children $2.)

To the west glimmers Cesar Pelli's golden-hued **World Financial Center,** towering with geometric shapes, and obviously designed to be seen from above. Its crisp, glinting angles and smooth curves look more like an architect's model than a real building. Each of its 40-story towers is more spacious than the 102-story Empire State Building because the buildings were built for computers requiring huge windowless rooms—not people who need a view to survive.

Across Chambers St. on the northern edge of City Hall Park is **City Hall** itself, which still serves as the focus of the city's administration. The Colonial chateau-style structure, completed in 1811, may be the finest piece of architecture in the city.

Towering at 233 Broadway, off the southern tip of the park, is the Gothic **Woolworth Building,** one of the most sublime and ornate commercial buildings in the world. Erected in 1913 by F.W. Woolworth to house the offices of his corner-store empire, it stood as the world's tallest until the Chrysler Building opened in 1930. The lobby of this five-and-dime Versailles is littered with Gothic arches and flourishes, including caricatures of Woolworth himself counting change and of architect Cass Gilbert holding a model of the building.

A block and a half farther south on Broadway, **St. Paul's Chapel** was inspired by London's St. Martin-in-the-Fields. St. Paul's is Manhattan's oldest public building in continuous use. For information on the chapel, call the office of the Trinity Museum (602-0800; open Mon.-Fri. 8am-3pm, Sun. 7am-3pm).

Fulton St. is one block farther along William St. Turn right onto Fulton and head to the **South Street Seaport.** New York's shipping industry thrived here for most of the 19th century. At the end of Fulton St., you can watch as the river comes suddenly into view—and smell as the spirits of dead fish pass through your nostrils. The stench comes from the **Fulton Fish Market,** the largest fresh-fish mart in the country, hidden right on South St. on the other side of the overpass. Those who can stomach wriggling scaly things might be interested in the behind-the-scenes tour of the market given some Thurs. mornings June-Oct. (market opens at 4am).

The Pier 16 kiosk, the main ticket booth for the seaport, stays open 10am-7pm (open 1 hr. later on summer weekends). The **Seaport Line** offers 90-minute day cruises, one-hour cocktail cruises, and evening cruises with live music.

The Statue of Liberty and Ellis Island

Another ferry will take you to the renovated **Statue of Liberty** (363-3200), landmark of a century of immigrant crossings. From its conception the Statue of Liberty has been a repository for America's promise, an oversized icon of the wonder of "The American Dream." There are only two reasons to go to the crown: 1) like Mt. Everest, because it's there, or 2) because you dig engineering. The **American Museum of Immigration,** located under the green lady's bathrobe, enshrines the dreams of all those who have come to look for America. Chaotic **Ellis Island,** represents the disillusionment of 15 million Europeans who first experienced the U.S. through the New York Harbor's people-processing facilities. Two ferries bring you to and from Liberty and Ellis islands. One runs Battery Park-Manhattan-Liberty-Ellis, and the other Liberty State Park-Jersey City, NJ-Ellis-Liberty. Both run daily every ½-hr., 9:15am-4:30pm. (Ferry information 269-5755. $6, seniors $5, children 2-17 $3.)

Brooklyn

When romantics ponder Brooklyn, they conjure up images of the rough stickball players who grew up to become the Brooklyn Dodgers. What goes on in Brooklyn tends to happen on the streets and out of doors, whether it's neighborhood banter, baseball games in the park, ethnic festivals, or gang violence. The Dutch originally settled the borough in the 17th century. When asked to join New York in 1833, Brooklyn refused, saying that the two cities shared no interests except common waterways. Not until 1898 did Brooklyn decide, in a close vote, to become a borough of New York City. The visitors bureau publishes an excellent free guide to Brooklyn's rich historical past that outlines 10 walking tours of the borough.

Head south on Henry St. after the bridge, then turn right on Clark St. toward the river for a synapse-shorting view of Manhattan. Many prize-winning photographs have been taken here from the **Brooklyn Promenade,** overlooking the southern tip of Manhattan and New York Harbor. George Washington's headquarters during the Battle of Long Island, now-posh **Brooklyn Heights** has advertised itself to many authors, from Walt Whitman to Norman Mailer, with its beautiful old brownstones, tree-lined streets, and proximity to Manhattan. Continuing south, soon you'll be at **Atlantic Avenue,** home to a large Arab community, with second-hand stores and inexpensive Middle Eastern bakeries and grocery stores. Atlantic runs from the river to Flatbush Ave. At the Flatbush Ave. Extension, pick up **Fulton Street,** the center of downtown Brooklyn, recently transformed into a pedestrian mall.

Williamsburg, several blocks north of downtown Brooklyn, has retained its Hasidic Jewish culture more overtly than Manhattan's Lower East Side. The quarter encloses Broadway, Bedford, and Union Avenues. It closes on *shabbat* (Saturday), the Jewish holy day.

Prospect Park, designed by Frederick Law Olmsted in the mid-1800s, was supposedly his favorite creation. He was even more pleased with it than with his Manhattan project—Central Park. Because crime has given Prospect's ambience a sinister twist, exercise caution in touring the grounds. At the corner of the park stands **Grand Army Plaza,** an island in the midst of the borough's busiest thoroughfares, designed by Olmsted to shield surrounding apartment buildings from traffic. (Subway: 2 or 3 to Grand Army Plaza.) The nearby **Botanic Gardens** seem more secluded, and include a lovely rose garden, behind the **Brooklyn Museum.**

Sheepshead Bay lies on the southern edge of Brooklyn, name to both a body of water (really part of the Atlantic) and a mass of land. The seafood here comes fresh and cheap (clams $5 per dozen along the water). Walk along Restaurant Row from E. 21st to E. 29th St. on Emmons Ave., and peruse menus for daily seafood specials. Nearby **Brighton Beach,** nicknamed "Little Odessa by the Sea," has been homeland to Russian emigrés since the turn of the century. (Subway: D, M, QB.)

Once a resort for the City's elite, made accessible to the rest of the Apple because of the subway, fading **Coney Island** still warrants a visit. The **Boardwalk,** once one of the most seductive of Brooklyn's charms, now squeaks nostalgically as tourists are jostled by roughnecks. Enjoy a hot dog and crinkle-cut fries at historic **Nathan's,** Surf and Sitwell. The **Cyclone,** 834 Surf Ave. (718-266-3434), at W. 10th St., built in 1927, remains the most terrifying roller coaster ride in the world (open daily mid-June to Labor Day noon-midnight; Easter weekend to mid-June Fri.-Sun. noon-midnight). Enter its 100-second-long screaming battle over nine hills of rickety wooden tracks—the ride's well worth $3. Go meet a walrus, dolphin, sea lion, shark, or other ocean critter in the tanks of the **New York Aquarium,** Surf and West 8th (718-265-3400; open daily 10am-4:45pm, holidays and summer weekends 10am-7pm; $5.75, children and seniors.) Look for the house beneath the roller coaster, which inspired a hilarious scene in Woody Allen's *Annie Hall.*

The Brooklyn Bridge

Uptown a few blocks looms the **Brooklyn Bridge.** Built in 1883, the bridge was one of the greatest engineering feats of the 19th century, second only to the Eads Bridge in St. Louis. The 1-mi. walk along the pedestrian path (make sure to walk on the left side, as the right is reserved for bicycles) will show you why every New York poet feels compelled to write at least one verse about it, why photographers snap the bridge's airy spider-web cables, and why people jump off. Once on the bridge, you can do what you've always wanted to do while driving, but couldn't for fear of careening out of control—look straight up at the cables and Gothic arches. To get to the entrance on Park Row, walk a couple of blocks west from the East River to the city hall area. Plaques on the bridge towers commemorate John Augustus Roebling, its builder, who, along with 20 of his workers, died during its construction.

Queens

Archie and Edith Bunker-types (and the employees of the Steinway Piano Factory) now share the brick houses and clipped hedges of their "bedroom borough" with immigrants from Korea, China, India, and the West Indies. In this urban suburbia, the American melting pot bubbles away with a more than 30% foreign-born population. Immigrant groups rapidly sort themselves out into neighborhoods where they try to maintain the memory of their homeland while living "the American Dream."

Queens is easily New York's largest borough, covering over a third of the city's total area. To understand Queens' kaleidoscope of communities is to understand the borough. If you visit only one place in Queens, let it be **Flushing.** Here you will find some of the most important colonial neighborhood landmarks, a bustling downtown, and the largest rose garden in the Northeast. Transportation could not be easier: the #7 Flushing line runs straight from Times Square. Just get on and sit back for about half an hour, until you reach the last stop (Main St., Flushing) in the northeastern part of the borough. Manhattan it isn't, but the streets usually are congested. Walk past the restaurants, discount stores, and businesses, and soak in Main St.'s crush of people and cultures.

Bronx

While the media presents the Bronx as a crime-ravaged husk, the borough offers its few tourists over 2000 acres of parkland, a great zoo, turn-of-the-century riverfront mansions, grand boulevards more evocative of Europe than of late 20th-century America, and thriving ethnic neighborhoods, including a Little Italy to shame its counterpart to the south. If you're not heading for Yankee Stadium, stay out of the South Bronx unless you're in a car and with someone who knows the area.

The most obvious reason to come to the Bronx is the **Bronx Zoo,** also known as the New York Zoological Society. The largest urban zoo in the United States, it houses over 4000 animals. You can explore the zoo on foot or ride like the king of the jungle aboard the Safari Train, which runs between the elephant house and Wild Asia (one-way $1, children 75¢). Soar into the air for a funky cool view of the zoo from the **Skyfari** aerial tramway that runs between Wild Asia and the Children's Zoo (one-way $1.50, children $1). The **Bengali Express Monorail** glides round Wild Asia (20 min.; $1.50, children $1). If you find the pace too hurried, saddle up a camel in the Wild Asia area ($2). **Walking tours** are given on weekends by the Friends of the Zoo; call 220-5142 three weeks in advance to reserve a place. Pamphlets containing self-guided tours are available at the Zoo Center for 75¢. Parts of the zoo close down during the winter (Nov.-April); call 367-1010 or 220-5100 for more information. (Open Mon.-Fri. 10am-5pm, Sat.-Sun. 10am-5:30pm; Nov.-Jan. daily 10am-4:30pm. Tues.-Thurs. free; Fri.-Mon. $5.75, seniors and children $2. For disabled-access information, call 220-5188.)

North across East Fordham Rd. from the zoo sprawls the labyrinthine **New York Botanical Garden** (817-8705). Snatches of forest and virgin waterways allow you to imagine the area's original landscape. (Garden grounds open Tues.-Sun. 10am-7pm; Nov.-March 10am-6pm. Suggested donation $5, seniors, students, and children $3. Parking $4. Call 817-8705 for information.)

Wave Hill, 675 W. 252nd St., a pastoral estate in Riverdale, commands an astonishing view of the Hudson and the Palisades. Samuel Clemens (a.k.a. Mark Twain), Arturo Toscanini, and Teddy Roosevelt all resided here. Picnic on the splendid lawns. (Gardens open Wed.-Sun. 9am-5:30pm. Estate open Wed.-Sun. 10am-4:30pm. $4, seniors and students $2. Call 549-2055 for information.)

Staten Island

Getting there is half the fun. At 50¢ (round-trip), the half-hour ferry ride from Manhattan's Battery Park to Staten Island is as unforgettable as it is inexpensive. Or you can drive from Brooklyn over the **Verrazzano-Narrows Bridge,** the world's second-longest (4260 ft.) suspension span. Because of the hills and the distances (and some very dangerous neighborhoods in between), it's a bad idea to walk from one site to the next. Make sure to plan your excursion with the bus schedule in mind.

The most concentrated number of sights on the island cluster around the beautiful 19th-century **Sailor's Snug Harbour Cultural Center,** at 1000 Richmond Terrace. Picnic and see its catch: the **Newhouse Center for Contemporary Art** (718-448-2500), a small gallery displaying American art with an indoor/outdoor sculpture show in the summer (open Wed.-Sun. noon-5pm; free); the **Staten Island Children's Museum** (718-273-2060), with participation exhibits for the five- to 12-year-old in you (open Tues.-Sun. noon-5pm; $3, children under 2 free); and the **Staten Island Botanical Gardens.**

MUSEUMS AND GALLERIES

For museum and gallery listings consult the following publications: *New Yorker* (the most accurate and extensive listing), *New York,* the Friday *New York Times* (in the Weekend section), the *Quarterly Calendar,* (available free at any visitors bureau) and *Gallery Guide,* found in local galleries. Most museums and all galleries close on Mondays, and are jam-packed on the weekends. Many museums require a "donation" in place of an admission fee—but no one will throw large, rotting papayas at you if you give less than the suggested amounts. Call ahead to find out about free times which usually occur on a weeknight.

Major Collections

Metropolitan Museum of Art, Fifth Ave. (879-5500), at 82nd St. Subway: 4, 5, 6 to 86th St. If you see only one, see this. The largest in the Western Hemisphere, the Met's art collection encompasses 3.3 million works from almost every period through Impressionism; particularly strong in Egyptian and non-Western sculpture and European painting. Contemplate infinity in the secluded Japanese Rock Garden. When blockbuster exhibits tour the world they usually stop at the Met— get tickets in advance through Ticketron. Open Sun. and Tues.-Thurs. 9:30am-5:15pm, Fri.-Sat. 9:30am-8:45pm. Donation $6, students and seniors $3.

Museum of Modern Art (MoMA), 11 W. 53rd St. (708-9400), off Fifth Ave. in Midtown. Subway: E, F to Fifth Ave./53rd St. One of the most extensive contemporary (post-Impressionist) collections in the world, founded in 1929 by scholar Alfred Barr in response to the Met's reluctance to embrace modern art. Cesar Pelli's recent structural glass additions flood the masterpieces with natural light. See Monet's sublime *Water Lily* room, Ross's *Engulfed Cathedral,* and a virtual Picasso warehouse. Sculpture garden good for resting and people-watching. Open Fri.-Tues. 11am-6pm, Thurs. 11am-9pm. $7.50, seniors and students $4.50, under 16 free. Films require free tickets in advance. Free Thurs. after 5pm.

The Frick Collection, 1 E. 70th St. (288-0700), at Fifth Ave. Subway: #6 to 68th St. Robber baron Henry Clay Frick left his house and art collection to the city, and the museum retains the elegance of his French "Classic Eclectic" château. Impressive grounds. The Living Hall displays 17th-century furniture, Persian rugs, Holbein portraits, and paintings by El Greco, Rembrandt, Velázquez, and Titian. After exploring what may be NYC's least exhausting museum, relax in a courtyard inhabited by elegant statues surrounding the garden pool and fountain. Open Tues.-Sat. 10am-6pm, Sun. 1-6pm. $3, students and seniors $1.50. Ages under 10 not allowed, under 16 must be accompanied by an adult.

Guggenheim Museum, 1071 Fifth Ave. and 89th St. (recording 423-3500, human being 423-3600, TDD 423-3607). Many have called this controversial construction a giant turnip, Frank Lloyd Wright's joke on the Big Apple. The museum closed from 1990-92 while a ten-story "tower gallery" sprouted behind the original structure, allowing the museum to show more of its permanent collection. Currently, most of the museum's space will be devoted to touring and temporary exhibits: "Abstraction in the 20th Century" begins in Sept. 1993. Open Fri.-Wed. 10am-8pm. $7, seniors and students $4, under 12 free. Pay what you wish Tues. 5-8pm. Two-day pass to this museum and **Guggenheim Museum SoHo** $10, seniors and students $6.

Whitney Museum of American Art, 945 Madison Ave. (570-3676), at 75th St. Subway: #6 to 77th St. Futuristic fortress featuring the largest collection of 20th-century American art in the world, with works by Hopper, Soyer, de Kooning, Motherwell, Warhol, and Calder. Controversial political art has infiltrated what was once a bastion of high-modernist aestheticism, and exhibitions have become increasingly puzzling as food, trash, and video have become the accepted media. Open Wed. 11am-6pm, Thurs. 1pm-8pm, Fri.-Sun. 11am-6pm. $6, students and seniors $4, under 12 free. Thurs. 6pm-8pm free.

Cooper-Hewitt Museum, 2 E. 91st St. (860-6868), at Fifth Ave. Subway: #4, 5, 6 to 86th St. Andrew Carnegie's majestic, Georgian mansion now houses the Smithsonian Institution's National Museum of Design. The playful special exhibits have considerable flair, focusing on such topics as doghouses and the history of the pop-up book. Open Tues. 10am-9pm, Wed.-Sat. 10am-5pm, Sun. noon-5pm. Admission $3, seniors and students $1.50, under 12 free. Free Tues. 5-9pm.

American Museum of Natural History, Central Park West (769-5100), at 79th to 81st St. Subway: B or C to 81st St. The largest science museum in the world, in a suitably imposing Romanesque structure guarded by a statue of Teddy Roosevelt on horseback. Teddy's distant ancestors can be seen in the Ocean Life display, while J.P. Morgan's Indian emeralds blaze in the Hall of Minerals and Gems. Open

Sun.-Thurs. 10am-5:45pm, Fri.-Sat. 10am-8:45pm. Donation $5, seniors and students $3, kids $2.50. Free Fri.-Sat. 5-8:45pm. The museum also houses **Naturemax** (769-5650), a cinematic extravaganza on New York's largest (4 stories) movie screen. Admission for museum visitors $5, students and seniors $4, kids $2.50, Fri.-Sat. double features $7, kids $3.50. The **Hayden Planetarium** (769-5920) offers outstanding multi-media presentations. Seasonal celestial light shows twinkle in the dome of the **Theater of the Stars,** accompanied by astronomy lectures. Admission $5, seniors and students $4, kids $2.50. Electrify your senses with **Laser Rock** (769-5921) Fri.-Sat. nights, $6.

Smaller and Specialized Collections

American Craft Museum, 40 W. 53rd St. (956-3535), across from MoMA. Subway: E, F to Fifth Ave.-53rd St. Offering more than quilts, this museum revises the notion of crafts with its modern media, including metal and plastic. Open Tues. 10am-8pm, Wed.-Sun. 10am-5pm. $4.50, seniors and students $2.

The Cloisters (923-3700), Fort Tryon Park, upper Manhattan. Subway: A through Harlem to 190th St. This monastery, built from pieces of 12th- and 13th-century French and Spanish cloisters, was assembled at John D. Rockefeller's behest by Charles Collens in 1938 as a setting for the Met's medieval art collection. Highlights include the Unicorn Tapestries, the Cuxa Cloister, and the Treasury, with 15th century playing cards. Open Tues.-Sun. 9:30am-5:15pm. Museum tours daily at 3pm, in winter Wed. at 3pm. Donation $6, students and seniors $3. (Includes admission to the Metropolitan Museum of Art main building.)

New Museum of Contemporary Art, 583 Broadway (219-1222), between Prince and Houston St. Subway: R to Prince, #6 to Bleecker, or B, D, F to Broadway/Lafayette. Dedicated to the destruction of the canon and of conventional ideas of "art," the New Museum supports the hottest, the newest, and the most controversial. Many works deal with fashionable politics of identity—sexual, racial, and ethnic. Once a month, an artist sits in the front window and converses with passersby. Open Wed.-Thurs. and Sun. noon-6pm, Fri.-Sat. noon-8pm. $3.50, artists, seniors, and students $2.50, children under 12 free.

International Center of Photography, 1130 Fifth Ave. (860-1778), at 94th St. Subway: #6 to 96th St. Housed in a landmark townhouse built in 1914 for *New Republic* founder Willard Straight. The foremost exhibitor of photography in the city, and a gathering-place for its practitioners. Historical, thematic, contemporary, and experimental works, running from fine art to photo-journalism. Midtown branch at 1133 Sixth Ave. (768-4680), at 43rd St. Both open Tues. 11am-8pm, Wed.-Sun. 11am-6pm. $3.50, seniors and students $2.

Jacques Marchais Center of Tibetan Art, 338 Lighthouse Ave., Staten Island (718-987-3478). Take bus S74 from Staten Island Ferry to Lighthouse Ave., turn right and walk up the hill. One of the finest Tibetan collections in the U.S., but the real attractions are the gardens, set on beautifully landscaped cliffs. Exuding serenity, the center itself is a replica of a Tibetan temple set amid dramatic cliffs. Open April-Nov. Wed.-Sun. 1-5pm; $3, seniors $2.50, children $1.

Museum of Television and Radio, 25 W. 52nd St. (621-6600), between Fifth and Sixth Ave. Subway: B, D, F, Q to Rockefeller Center, or E, F to 53rd St. Boob tube relics and memorabilia, as well as over 50,000 programs in the museum's permanent collection. You can watch or listen to anything from a 1935 broadcast of *La Traviata* to a 1976 *Saturday Night Live.* Special screenings can be arranged for large groups. Open Tues.-Wed. and Fri.-Sun. noon-6pm, Thurs. noon-8pm. Suggested admission $5, students $4, seniors and children $3.

ENTERTAINMENT AND NIGHTLIFE

New York's incomparable nightlife presents the traveler with a welcome problem: finding the "right show" from among the city's dizzyingly broad selection of entertainment. Unlike in other cities, New York's cultural activity does not revolve around a nuclear institution; instead, hundreds of independent venues compete for attention and credibility, each claiming greater artistry than the others but all equally (well, nearly equally) responsible for New York's cultural hegemony over the rest of the country. **Publications** with especially noteworthy sections on nightlife include *New York* magazine, the *Village Voice,* and the Sunday edition of the *New York Times.* The most comprehensive survey of the current theater scene can be found in *The New Yorker.* An all-purpose **entertainment hotline** (360-3456; 24 hrs.) runs down the events of the week by both borough and kind.

Theater

Broadway is currently undergoing a revival—ticket sales are booming, and mainstream musicals are receiving more than their fair share of attention. Dorky, old-fashioned productions such as *Crazy For You* and *Guys and Dolls* are very popular, and tickets can be hard to get. Broadway tickets cost about $50 apiece when purchased through regular channels. **TKTS** (768-1818 for recorded info) sells half-priced tickets to many Broadway shows on the same day of the performance. TKTS has a booth in the middle of Duffy Square (the northern part of Times Square, at 47th and Broadway). TKTS tickets are usually about $25 each plus a $2.50 service charge per ticket. (Tickets are sold Mon.-Sat. 3-8pm for evening performances, Wed. and Sat. 10am-2pm for matinees, and Sun. noon-8pm for matinees and evening performances.) For information on shows and ticket availability, call the **NYC/ON STAGE hotline** at 768-1818, **Ticket Central** between 1 and 8pm at 279-4200, or the **New York City Department of Cultural Affairs hotline** at 956-2787. **Ticketmaster** (307-7171) deals in everything from Broadway shows to mud-truck races; they charge at least $2 more than other outlets, but take most major credit cards. *Listings,* a weekly guide to entertainment in Manhattan ($1), has listings of Broadway, Off-Broadway, and Off-Off-Broadway shows.

Off-Broadway theaters have between 100 and 499 seats; only Broadway houses have over 500. Off-Broadway houses frequently offer more offbeat or quirky shows, with shorter runs. Occasionally these shows have long runs or jump to Broadway houses. Tickets cost $10-20. The best of the Off-Broadway houses huddle in the Sheridan Square area of the West Village. TKTS also sells tickets for the larger Off-Broadway houses. **Off-Off-Broadway** is not a comical designation but an actual category of cheaper, younger theaters.

For years, the **Joseph Papp Public Theater,** 425 Lafayette St. (598-7150), was inextricably linked with its namesake founder, one of the city's leading producers and favorite sons. The theater recently produced an exhaustive and exhausting Shakespeare Marathon, which includes every single one of the Bard's plays down to *Timon of Athens.* Ticket prices $15-35. About one quarter of the seats are sold at **Quixtix** for $10 on the day of performance (starting at 6pm for evening performances and 1pm for matinees). Papp also founded **Shakespeare in the Park,** a New York summer tradition that practically everyone in the city has attended (or attempted to). From June through August, two Shakespeare plays are presented at the **Delacorte Theater** in Central Park, near the 81st St. entrance on the Upper West Side, just north of the main road (861-7277). Top-notch productions attract the most important actors around. Tickets are free.

Movies

If Hollywood is *the* place to make films, New York City is *the* place to see them. Most movies open in New York weeks before they're distributed across the country, and the response of Manhattan audiences and critics can shape a film's success or failure nationwide. Dozens of revival houses show motion picture classics year round. And independent filmmakers from around the reel world come to New York to flaunt their work. Big-screen fanatics should check out the cavernous **Ziegfeld,** 141 W. 54th St. (765-7600), one of the largest screens left in America, which shows first-run films of interest. Consult local newspapers for complete listings. **Tele Ticket** (777-FILM/3456) allows you to reserve tickets for most major movie-houses and pick them up at showtime from the theater's automated ticket dispenser; you charge the ticket price plus a small fee over the phone. Top revival and independent film houses include **Revolution Books,** 13 E. 16th St. (691-3345), home of films, videos, lectures ($2), and subversive activities transpiring unsuspected and on auspicious nights; **The Kitchen,** 512 W. 19th St. (255-5793), between Tenth and Eleventh Ave., subway C or E to 23rd St., a world-renowned showcase for the off-beat from New York-based struggling artists (prices vary); and **Theater 80,** 80 Mark Pl. (254-7400), between First and Second Ave., subway #6 to Astor Pl.,a great revival house running a nightly double bill of all your favorite chisel-nosed actresses ($7).

Opera and Dance

Lincoln Center (875-5000) is New York's one-stop shopping mall for high-culture consumers; there's usually opera or dance at one of its many venues. Write Lincoln Center Plaza, NYC 10023, or drop by its Performing Arts Library (870-1930) for a full schedule and a press kit as long as the *Ring* cycle. The **Metropolitan Opera Company** (362-6000), opera's premier outfit, plays on a Lincoln Center stage as big as a football field. Regular tickets run as high as $100—go for the upper balcony (around $15; the cheapest seats have an obstructed view) unless you're prone to vertigo. You can stand in the orchestra ($12) along with the opera freakazoids who've brought along the score, or all the way back in the Family Circle ($9). (Regular season runs Sept.-May Mon.-Sat.; box office open Mon.-Sat. 10am-8pm, Sun. noon-6pm.) In the summer, watch for free concerts in city parks (362-6000). The Met also plays host to dance companies like the Kirov Ballet.

At right angles to the Met, the **New York City Opera** (870-5570) has a new sound under the direction of Christopher Keene. Now offering a summer season (July-Nov.), "City" keeps its ticket prices low year-round ($10-62). For rush tickets, call the night before and wait in line the morning of. In July, look for free performances by the **New York Grand Opera** (360-2777) at Central Park Summerstage every Wednesday night. Check the papers for performances of the old warhorses by the **Amato Opera Company,** 319 Bowery (228-8200; Sept.-May; tickets $16, seniors $13). Music schools often stage opera as well; see Music for further details.

The New York State Theater (870-5570) is home to the late, great George Balanchine's **New York City Ballet,** the country's oldest and most famous dance company. Decent tickets for the *Nutcracker* in December sell out almost immediately. (Performances Nov.-Feb. and April-June. Tickets $11-55, standing room $8.) The **American Ballet Theater** (477-3030), under Mikhail Baryshnikov's guidance, dances at the Met every May and June (tickets $12-65). The **Alvin Ailey American Dance Theater** (767-0940) bases its repertoire of modern dance on jazz, spirituals, and contemporary music. Often on the road, it always performs at the **City Center** in December. Tickets ($15-40) can be difficult to obtain. Write or call the City Center, 131 W. 55th St. (581-7907), weeks in advance, if possible. Look for ½-price tickets at the Bryant Park ticket booth (see below).

Other companies include the **Martha Graham Dance Co.,** 316 E. 63rd St. (838-5886), performing original Graham pieces during its October New York season; **Anna Sokolov's Players' Project,** dancing the acclaimed Russian choreographer's modern pieces to the sounds of Erik Satie, Kurt Weill, and Jelly Roll Morton; and the **Merce Cunningham Dance Company** (718-255-8240), of John Cage fame. Half-price tickets for many music and dance events can be purchased on the day of performance at the **Bryant Park** ticket booth, 42nd St. (382-2323), between Fifth and Sixth Ave. (Open Tues.-Sun. noon-2pm and 3-7pm; cash and traveler's checks only.) Concert tickets to Monday shows are available on the Sunday prior to the performance. Call for daily listings.

Music

Classical Music

Musicians advertise themselves vigorously; you should have no trouble finding the notes. Begin with the ample listings in the *New York Times, The New Yorker,* or *New York* magazine. Remember that many events, like outdoor music, are seasonal.

The **Lincoln Center Halls** have a wide, year-round selection of concerts. The **Great Performers Series,** featuring famous and foreign musicians, packs the Avery Fisher and Alice Tully Halls and the Walter Reade Theater, from October until May (call 721-6500; tickets from $11). **Avery Fisher Hall** (875-5030; wheelchair accessible) paints the town ecstatic with its annual Mostly Mozart Festival. Show up early; there are usually pre-concert recitals beginning one hour before the main concert and free to ticketholders. The festival runs July-Aug., with tickets to individual events $12-25. The **New York Philharmonic** (875-5700) begins its regular season in mid-September. (Call CenterCharge for tickets, ranging $10-50, at 721-6500 Mon.-Sat. 10am-8pm, Sun. noon-8pm.) Students and seniors can sometimes get **$5 tickets;** call ahead for availability (Tues.-Thurs. only). Anyone can get $5 tickets for the odd morning rehearsal; again, call ahead. In late June for a couple of weeks, Kurt Masur and friends lead the posse at **free concerts** (875-5709) on the Great Lawn in Central Park, in Prospect Park in Brooklyn, in Van Cortland Park in the Bronx, and around the city.

Saved from demolition in the 1960s by Isaac Stern, **Carnegie Hall** (247-7800), Seventh Ave. at 57th St., is still the favorite coming-out locale of musical debutantes. Open Sept.-June daily 11am-8pm; tickets $10-40. One of the best ways for the budget traveler to absorb New York musical culture is to visit a **music school.** Except for opera and ballet productions ($5- 12), concerts at the following schools are free and frequent: The **Juilliard School of Music,** Lincoln Center (see above), the **Mannes School of Music** (580-0210), the **Manhattan School of Music** (749-2802).

Jazz

The **JVC Jazz Festival** (787-2020) blows into the city in June. All-star performances in the 1993 series included Wynton Marsalis, Joshua Redman, and Clark Terry. Tickets go on sale in early May.

Augie's, 2751 Broadway (864-9834), between 105th and 106th St. Subway: #1 or 9 to 103rd St. Small and woody. Jazz until 3am. The saxophonist sits on your lap and the bass rests on your table. Quality musicians and a cool, unpretentious crowd. No cover; $3 drink min. Sets start around 10pm. Open daily 8pm-3am.

Blue Note, 131 W. 3rd St. (475-8592), near MacDougal St. Subway: A, B, C, D, E, F, or Q to Washington Sq. The Carnegie Hall of jazz clubs. Now a commercialized concert space with crowded tables and a sedate audience. Often books top performers. Sets Sun.-Thurs. 9pm and 11:30pm, Fri.-Sat. 9pm, 11:30pm, and 1:30am.

Village Gate, 160 Bleecker St. (475-5120), near Thompson St. Subway: #6 to Bleecker. This landmark entertainment complex houses three bars, a jazz terrace, and two theaters staging concerts, Off-Broadway shows, musical revues, and nightly jazz music. Dark, old village hangout. Every Sun. salsa meets jazz downstairs in the big room 9pm-2am. Jazz regulars play Wed.-Sun. nights. Open mike for college jazz prodigies Mon.-Fri. 7:30-10pm. Original plays $20-33 (call 777-7100 for information). Jazz on the terrace free with a $7.50 drink min. Open daily 6pm-2am.

Birdland, 2745 Broadway (749-2228), at 105th St. Subway: #1 or 9 to 103rd St. Reasonably good food and top jazz. Feels Upper West-nouveau but the music is smoked-out-and-splendid 52nd St. Blue Note Records records them here. Appetizers $7, entrees $12-16, sandwiches $8-10. Sun. jazz brunch. Cover Fri.-Sat $5 plus $5 min. per set at bar, $10/$15 at tables; Sun.-Thurs. $5 plus $5 min. per set at tables; no cover at bar. No cover for brunch Sun. noon-4pm. Open Mon.-Sat. 4pm-4am, Sun. noon-4pm and 5pm-4am. First set nightly at 9pm.

Rock & Pop Clubs

In addition to the two venues listed below, check the *Village Voice* for shows at the **Bottom Line,** the **Ritz,** the **Knitting Factory,** and the **Lone Star Roadhouse,** all in Manhattan and all fine clubs for live music of all varieties.

CBGB/OMFUG (CBGB's), 313 Bowery (982-4052), at Bleecker St. Subway: #6 to Bleecker St. The initials stand for "country, bluegrass, blues, and other music for uplifting gourmandizers," but everyone knows that since 1976 this club has been all about punk rock. Blondie and the Talking Heads got their starts here, and the club continues to be *the* place to see great alternative rock. Shows nightly at around 8pm, Sun. (often hardcore) matinee at 3pm. Cover $5-10.

Maxwell's, 1039 Washington St. (201-798-4064), in Hoboken, NJ. Subway: B, D, F, N, Q, or R to 34th St., then PATH train ($1), or simply take the PATH train ($1) to the Hoboken stop; walk down Washington to 11th St. High-quality underground rockers from America and abroad have plied their trade in the back room of a Hoboken restaurant for going-on-15 years. Cover $5-10; shows occasionally sell out, so get tix in advance from Maxwell's, Pier Platters in Hoboken, or Ticketmaster. Restaurant (sandwiches $6, entrees $7-9) open Tues.-Sun. 2pm-midnight.

Dance Clubs

Building, 51 W. 26th St. (576-1890), near Broadway. Subway: R to 28th St. One of the foundations of the New York club scene. Converted power plant with 50-ft. ceilings and a great crowd. If it's empty there is no place worse to be, but a full house is quite a party. Friday is Industrial Alternative. Open Thurs.-Sun. 9pm-4am.

Nell's, 246 W. 14th St. (675-1567), between Seventh and Eighth Ave. Subway: #1, 2, 3, or 9 to 14th St. A legendary hotspot; some faithful admirers hang on even through its decline. Dingy neighborhood belies the opulence of the huge Victorian-style sitting room inside. Overstuffed chairs, chandeliers, and bejeweled Beautiful People upstairs. Angular dance floor downstairs. Not a gay club, but a popular gay spot. Cover Mon.-Wed. $7, Thurs.-Sun. $15. Open daily 10pm-4am.

Au Bar, 41 E. 58th St. (308-9455), between Park and Madison Ave. Subway: #4, 5, 6 to 59th St., or N, R to Lexington Ave. Au dear. Très Euro. Gypsy Kings music on the dance floor. Lots of thirtysomething men in Armani suits, cigars in hand, put the moves on willing women. Serves "supper" to the refined and "breakfast" to the diehards. Open daily 9pm-4am. Cover Sun.-Wed. $10, Thurs.-Sat. $15.

Sounds of Brazil (SOBs), 204 Varick St. (243-4940), at Houston. Subway: #1 or 9 to Houston. Books great world beat, reggae, and rap acts nightly. Most shows Sun.-Thurs. 9:30pm and 11:30pm, Fri.-Sat. 10:30pm and 1am, or 10pm, midnight, and 2am. Cover $10-16, depending on the act.

Bars

Automatic Slims, 733 Washington St. (645-8660), at Bank St. Subway: A, C, or E to 14th St. Simple bar in the West Village; best selection of blues and screamin' soul. Twentysomething Villagers sit at tables with classic 45s under the glass top. More diverse crowd packs on weekends. American cooking 6pm-midnight. Entrees $7.50-14. Open Sun.-Mon. 5:30pm-2:30am, Tues.-Sat. 5:30pm-4:30am.

Downtown Beirut, 158 First Ave. (260-4248). Subway: L to First Ave. Hardcore but friendly East Village crowd gathers under a large inflatable man to listen to the jukebox belt out hits by Mudhoney and the Clash. Perfect for relaxed, cheap boozing. Draft beer $1. Mon.-Fri. mixed-drink specials $2. Open daily noon-4am.

King Tut's Wah Wah Hut, 112 Ave. A (254-7772), in the East Village. Subway: #6 to Astor Pl. In the middle of the scene a few years ago; now only a vestigial East Village crowd remains. Play pool with the punkish crowd here and avoid the long waits at many other pool spots. Immediate surroundings are safer than a few blocks away. Antique couches melt into surreal psychedelic walls, platinum hair, and wrinkled tattoos. Draft $2, hot dog $1.50. Open daily 4pm-4am.

10th Street Lounge, 212 E. 10th St. (473-5252), between Second and Third Ave. A chic, new East Village hotspot where the artsy twentysomething set sips $4 beers on over-stuffed couches or around the circular bar. Dim red lighting and all kinds of music from reggae to hip-hop lure all types to this inconspicuous, unmarked hole-in-the-wall. Open daily until 3:30am.

The Shark Bar, 307 Amsterdam Ave. (496-6600), at 75th. High-class and enjoyable bar and soul-food restaurant; possibly the only truly interracial establishment on the Upper West Side below 110th St. Well-dressed after-work crowd nurses stiff drinks. Live jazz on Tues. with a $5 cover; "gospel brunch" Sat. 12:30pm and 2pm (no cover). Reasonable drink prices (bottled beer from $3). Entrees from $11. Open Mon.-Fri. 11:30am-2am, Sat.-Sun. 11:30am-4:30pm and 6:30pm-4am.

Gay and Lesbian

DTs Fat Cat (243-9041), at W. 4th St. and W. 12th St. Subway: A, C, E, or L to 14th St. Yes, these two streets do intersect in the non-Euclidean West Village, near Eighth Ave. Piano bar with a large straight clientele; relaxed scene for lesbians. No cover. Open daily until 4am.

Pandora's Box, 70 Grove St., on Seventh Ave. South. Dark bar with older lesbian scene. Crowded on weekends, popular hangout and meeting place. Dyke dance club some nights. Beer starts at $3.50. Cover $5-7. Ages 21 and over; two picture proofs of ID required. Open daily 4pm-4am.

The Pyramid, 101 Ave. A (420-1590), at 6th St. Subway: #6 to Astor Pl. Also known by its street address, this dance club mixes gay, lesbian, and straight folks. Vibrant drag scene. Continues to push the limits of exotic with the freshest mixes. Fri. is straight night. Cover $5-10. Open daily 9pm-4am.

Comedy Clubs

The Original Improvisation, 358 W. 44th St. (765-8268). Subway: A, C, or E to 42nd St. A quarter-century of comedy—acts from Saturday Night Live, Johnny Carson, and David Letterman. Richard Pryor and Robin Williams got started here. Shows Sun.-Thurs. 9pm, Fri.-Sat. 9pm and 11:15pm. Cover: Mon.-Tues. $8 and $8 min. on drinks, Wed.-Thurs. and Sun. $11 and $9, Fri.-Sat. $12 and $9.

Comedy Cellar, 117 MacDougal St. (254-3630), near Bleecker St. Subway: A, B, C, D, E, F, or Q to W. 4th St. Subterranean annex of the artsy Olive Tree Cafe. Dark, intimate, atmospheric. Features rising comics like John Manfrellott and drop-ins by superstars like Robin Williams. Cover Sun.-Thurs. $5 plus 2-drink min., Fri.-Sat. $10 plus $5 drink min. Shows Sun.-Thurs. 9pm-2am, Fri. 9pm and 11pm, Sat. 9pm, 10:45pm, and 12:30am. Make reservations on weekends.

Chicago City Limits, 351 E. 74th St. (772-8707). Subway: #6 to 77th St. For something a little different, check out New York's longest running theater-style comedy revue. Shows are careful syntheses of cabaret, scripted comedy sketches, and improvisation, often with a political bent. Extemporaneous skits allow the crowd to get into the act. No alcohol. Shows Mon. and Wed.-Thurs. 8:30pm, Fri.-Sat. 8pm and 10:30pm. Cover Mon. $10, Wed.-Thurs. $15, Fri.-Sat. $20.

Sports

While most cities would be content to field a major-league team in each big-time sport, New York opts for the Noah's Ark approach: two baseball teams, two hockey teams, and two NFL football teams. In addition to local teams' regularly scheduled games, New York hosts a number of celebrated world-class events. Get tickets 3 months in advance for the prestigious **United States Open** (718-271-5100; tickets from $12), held in late Aug. and early Sept. at the USTA Tennis Center in Flushing Meadows, Queens. On the third Sunday in Oct., two million spectators witness the 22,000 runners of the **New York City Marathon** (only 16,000 finish). The race begins on the Verrazzano Bridge and ends at Central Park's Tavern on the Green.

Baseball been berry berry good to me: The **New York Mets** bat at **Shea Stadium** in Queens (718-507-8499; tickets $6.50-15). The legendary but mortal **New York Yankees** play ball at Yankee Stadium in the Bronx (293-6000; tickets $5.50-16).

Football: Both the **New York Giants** (201-935-3900) and the **Jets** (526-538-7200) play across the river at **Giants Stadium** in East Rutherford, NJ. Tickets from $12.

Basketball: The **New York Knickerbockers** (that's the Knicks to you) dribble at **Madison Square Garden** (465-6751, 751-6130 off-season; tickets from $12).

Hockey: The **New York Rangers** skate at **Madison Square Garden** (465-6741 or 308-6977); the **New York Islanders** hang their skates at the **Nassau Coliseum** (516-794-9300), Uniondale, Long Island. Tickets from $12 and $14, respectively.

■ Near New York City: Long Island

Long Island is easy to stereotype but difficult to grasp. For some, the Island evokes images of sprawling suburbia dotted with malls and office parks; others see it as the privileged retreat of New York WASPs, a summer refuge of white sand and open spaces. What few notice about the Island are its decidedly urban qualities: somewhere between the malls and beaches lie vital cultural centers as well as pockets of poverty. While in theory "Long Island" includes the entire 120-mi.-long fish-shaped landmass, in practice the term excludes the westernmost sections, Brooklyn and Queens. The residents of these two boroughs at the head of the "fish" will readily remind you that they are officially part of the City. This leaves Nassau and Suffolk Counties to constitute the real Long Island. East of the Queens-Nassau line, people back the Islanders, not the Rangers, and they enjoy their role as neighbor to, rather than part of, the great metropolis.

Practical Information Get Long Island info at the **Long Island Convention and Visitors Bureau** (794-4222), Eisenhower Park (off Hempstead Turnpike, in East Meadow) or on the LIE South between Exits 51 and 52 in Commack. The Island's main public-transportation, **Long Island Railroad (LIRR)** (822-5477), has four central lines. Depending on how far you want to go, peak fares range from $4.25-14, and off-peak fares range from $3-9.50. Daytime bus service is provided by **Metropolitan Suburban Bus Authority (MSBA)** in Queens, Nassau, and western Suffolk (542-0100, bus information 766-6722). The routes are complex and irregular—make sure you confirm your destination with the driver. (Fare $1.50, crossing into Queens an additional 50¢, transfers 25¢. Disabled travelers and senior citizens pay ½-fare.) The MSBA has daily service to and from Jones Beach during the summer months. The S-92 bus of **Suffolk Transit** (852-5200; open Mon.-Fri. 8am-4:30pm) loop-de-loops back and forth between the tips of the north and south forks, with nine runs daily, most of them between East Hampton and Orient Point. Call to confirm stops and schedules. The route also connects with the LIRR at Riverhead, where the forks meet. (No service Sun. Fare $1.50, senior and the disabled 50¢, under 5 free. Transfers 25¢.) Long Island's **area code** is 516.

Accommodations Finding a place to stay on the island can be daunting. Daytrippers in Nassau do best to return to the city. Suffolk County provides a wider variety of mostly touristy accommodations. In Montauk, sleep at **Montauket,** Tuthill Rd. (668-5992). Follow the Montauk Hwy. to Montauk; at the traffic circle take Edgemere, then left onto Fleming, then another left. The Island's best bargain. From March-May and Oct.-Nov. 15, only four rooms are open; every room open for the summer. Make reservations for summer weekends starting March 1st—it fills up quickly. Almost always full on weekends. (Doubles $35, with private bath $40.) For camping, dig your trenches at **Battle Row** (293-7120), in Bethpage, Nassau. Eight tent sites, and 50 trailer sites available on first come, first served basis. Electricity, restrooms, showers, grills, and a playground. (Tent sites $5 for Nassau residents, $7 for visitors. Trailer sites $8 for residents, $12 for visitors.)

SIGHTS

Nassau At **Old Westbury Gardens** (333-0048), on Old Westbury Rd., nature overwhelms architecture. The elegant house, modeled after 19th-century English country manors, sits in the shadow of its surroundings of gardens and tall evergreens. A vast rose garden adjoins a number of theme gardens (such as the Grey Garden, which contains only plants in shades of silver and deep purple). (Open Wed.-Mon. 10am-5pm. House and garden $8, seniors $5, children $4. Take LIE to Exit 39S (Glen Cove Rd.), turn right on Old Westbury Rd., and continue a ¼ mi.)

Jones Beach State Park (785-1600) is the best compromise between convenience and crowd for city daytrippers. There are nearly 2500 acres of beachfront here and the parking area accommodates 23,000 cars. Only 40 min. from the city,

Jones Beach packs in the crowds during the summer months; the beach becomes a sea of umbrellas and blankets with barely a patch of sand showing. Along the 1½-mi. boardwalk you can find deck games, roller-skating, miniature golf, basketball, and nightly dancing. The **Marine Theater** in the park hosts rock concerts. There are eight different bathing areas on the rough Atlantic Ocean and the calmer Zachs Bay, plus a number of beaches restricted to residents of certain towns in Nassau County. In the summer you can take the LIRR to Freeport or Wantaugh, where you can get a bus to the beach. Call 212-739-4200 or 212-526-0900 for information. **Recreation Lines** (718-788-8000) provides bus service straight from mid-Manhattan. If you are driving, take the LIE east to the Northern State Pkwy., go east to the Meadowbrook (or Wantaugh) Pkwy., and then south to Jones Beach.

Suffolk   The peaceful villages of Suffolk County, only a few hours' drive from Manhattan, are New York's version of the tradition-steeped towns of New England. Many of Suffolk's colonial roots have been successfully preserved, and the county offers some fine colonial house-museums. Salty old towns, full of shady streets—refreshing retreats from the din of New York—line the lazy coast.

After shopping at the **Walt Whitman Mall,** the nearby **Walt Whitman's Birthplace,** 246 Old Walt Whitman Rd. (427-5240), will seem a more appropriate memorial to the great American poet whose 1855 *Leaves of Grass* innovated a democratic free-verse style that revolutionized poetry. (Open Wed.-Fri. 1-4pm, Sat.-Sun. 10am-4pm. Suggested donation $3, seniors and students $2. Take LIE to Exit 49N, drive 1¾ mi. on Rte. 110, and turn left onto Old Walt Whitman Rd.)

Wine Country   Long Island does not readily conjure up images of plump wine-grapes just waiting to be plucked by epicurean Islanders. But a visit to one of the North Fork's 40 vineyards can be a pleasant and interesting surprise. Twelve wineries and 40 vineyards produce the best Chardonnay, Cabernet Sauvignon, Merlot, Pinot Noir, and Riesling in New York State. Many of the Island wineries offer free tours and tastings. To get to there, take the LIE to its end (Exit 73), then Rte. 58, which becomes Rte. 25 (Main Rd.). North of and parallel to Rte. 25 is Rte. 48 (North Rd. or Middle Rd.), which claims a number of wineries. Road signs announce tours and tastings. Of note is **Palmer Vineyards,** 108 Sound Ave. (722-9463), in Riverhead. Take a self-guided tour of the most advanced equipment on the Island and see a tasting room with an interior assembled from two 18th-century English pubs.

Sag Harbor   Out on the South Fork's north shore droops Sag Harbor, one of the best-kept secrets of Long Island. Founded in 1707, this port used to be more important than New York Harbor since its deep shore made for easy navigation. The legacy of Sag Harbor's former grandeur survives in the second-largest collection of Colonial buildings in the U.S., and in the cemeteries lined with the gravestones of Revolutionary soldiers and sailors. Check out the **Sag Harbor Whaling Museum** (725-0770). Enter the museum through the jawbones of a whale. Note the antique 1864 washing-machine and the excellent scrimshaw collection. (Open May-Sept. Mon.-Sat. 10am-5pm, Sun. 1-5pm. $3, children $1. Call for tours.)

Montauk   At the easternmost tip of the south fork, Montauk is one of the most popular destinations on Long Island. And with good reason, considering the thrill of looking out at the Atlantic Ocean and realizing that you have reached the end and there is nothing but water and some sharks between you and Limerick. Many tourists are lured to Montauk by the image of its famous lighthouse, a symbol of Long Island. Though the trip from Manhattan takes 4 hr. by car, the peaceful, salty air of Montauk Point makes the drive well worth it. Take the LIE to Exit 70 (Manorville), then go south to Sunrise Hwy. (Rte. 27), which becomes Montauk Hwy., and drive east. You will know you've arrived when water sloshes around your brake pedal.

The **Montauk Point Lighthouse and Museum** (668-2544) is the real high point of a trip here. This lighthouse is exactly as it should be, set on the rocky edge of the water, its sloping white sides adorned by a single wide band of brown. The bulky, solid form rises with a utilitarian elegance from a cluster of smaller, flimsier buildings. The 86-ft. structure went up by special order of President George Washington. On a clear day, you should climb the 138 spiralling steps to the top, where you can look out over the seascape, across the Long Island Sound to Connecticut and Rhode Island. The best seasons for viewing are spring and fall, when the sea has scarcely a stain on it; the thick summer air, on the other hand, can haze over the view. But even on a foggy day, you may want to climb up to see if you can spot the *Will o' the Wisp,* a clipper ship sometimes sighted on hazy days under full sail with a lantern hanging from its mast. Experts claim that the ship is a mirage resulting from the presence of phosphorus in the atmosphere, but what do they know? (Open May-June and Oct.-Nov. Sat.-Sun. 10:30am-4pm; June-Sept. daily 10:30am-6pm; Sept.-Oct. Fri.-Mon. 10:30am-5pm. $2.50, children $1, plus $3 to park a car.)

Try **Viking** (668-5700) or **Lazybones'** (668-5671) for half-day fishing cruises ($20-25). **Okeanos Whale Watch Cruise** (728-4522) offers excellent six-hour trips for spotting fin, minke, and humpback whales ($30 and up).

Fire and Shelter Islands The **Fire Island National Seashore** is the main draw here, and in summer it offers fishing, clamming, and guided nature walks. The facilities at **Sailor's Haven** include a marina, a nature trail, and a famous beach. Similar facilities at **Watch Hill** include a 20-unit campground, where reservations are required. **Smith Point West** has a small visitor-information center and a nature trail with disabled access (289-4810). Here spot horseshoe crabs, whitetail deer, and monarch butterflies, which flit across country each year to winter in Baja California.

Shelter Island bobs in the protected body of water between the north and south forks. Accessible by ferry or by private boat, this island offers wonderful beaches and a serene sense of removal from the intrusions of the city. But that doesn't mean you'll have to rough it here; the island has virtually everything that you could possibly need, including a coalyard, four insurance agencies, and a real-estate attorney.

■■■ NIAGARA FALLS

The "Honeymoon Capital of the World" is actually like a honeymoon itself—a spectacle framed by constant preoccupation with money before and after. The otherworldly falls are without a doubt among the most moving sights nature has created. Hydroelectric companies think so—the falls move turbines fast enough to generate a minimum of 2 million kilowatts. An increased environmental consciousness has stopped the practice of dumping chemical waste into the Niagara River, making the area is healthier than it has been in years. Also, the work of hydroelectricians to regulate water flow has slowed the erosion which was eating away at the falls at an alarming rate. It is believed that the falls now move back at a rate of 1 ft. per decade, down from 6 ft. per year.

PRACTICAL INFORMATION

Emergency: 911.

Visitor Information: Niagara Falls Convention and Visitors Bureau, 310 3rd St., Niagara Falls, NY (285-2400 or 800-421-5223; 24 hr. Niagara Cty. Events Line 285-8711) will send you the excellent *Niagara USA* travel guide. Open daily 9am-5pm. In Niagara, the **information center** that adjoins the bus station on 4th and Niagara is the place to visit. It's a 10-min. walk from the Falls, with 1-hr. parking. Open daily 9am-9pm; Oct.-April Mon.-Fri. 9am-5pm. The state runs a **Niagara Reservation Visitors Center** (278-1796) right in front of the Falls' observation deck. Open summer daily 9am-9:30pm, winter 10am-6:30pm. The **Niagara Falls Canada Visitor and Convention Bureau,** 5433 Victoria Ave., Niagara Falls, Ont. L2E 3L1 (416-356-6061), will send info on the Canadian side. Also, the

Ontario Travel Information Center at 5355 Stanley Ave. (416-358-6441) can help with tourism questions on the entire province.

Amtrak: 27th St. and Lockport, Niagara Falls, 1 block east of Hyde Park Blvd. Take #52 bus to get to the Falls/downtown. (800-872-7245, 683-8440 for baggage problems). To: New York City (2 per day, 9 hr., $85); Boston (14 hr., $124).

Greyhound: Niagara Falls Bus Terminal (282-1331), 4th St. and Niagara St. (open Mon.-Fri. 8am-4pm) only sells tickets for use in Buffalo, NY. To get to the Buffalo bus station, take bus #40 from the Niagara Falls bus terminal (18 per day, 1 hr., $1.75) to the **Buffalo Transportation Center,** 181 Ellicott St. (855-7511; open daily 3am-1am). To: New York City (9 per day, 8 hr., $51); Boston (4 per day, 12 hr., $72); Chicago (6 per day, 12 hr., $77); Rochester (8 per day, 2 hr., $8); Syracuse (9 per day, 4 hr., $15); and Albany (5 per day, 7 hr., $29).

Public Transport: Niagara Frontier Metro Transit System (285-9369). Provides local city transit and free map of bus routes. **ITA Buffalo Shuttle,** 800-551-9369. Service from Niagara Falls info center and major hotels to Buffalo Airport ($14.50). A **taxi** from Buffalo Airport to Niagara costs about $40, so take this bus.

Taxi: Rainbow Taxicab, 282-3221; **United Cab,** 285-9331. Both are $1.50 base fare, $1.10 per mi.

Post Office: Niagara Falls, 615 Main St. (285-7561), in Niagara Falls, NY. Open Mon.-Fri. 8:30am-5pm, Sat. 9am-noon. **ZIP code:** 14302.

Area Code: 716 (New York), 416 (Ontario). It costs 24¢ first min., 17¢ each additional min. to call from metro area to metro area.

Niagara St. is the main east-west drag in town; it ends on the western side in Rainbow Bridge, which crosses to Canada. Outside town, Rte. 62 (Niagara Falls Blvd.) is lined with stores, restaurants, and motels. Falls Park is at the western edge of the city. North-south streets are numbered; numbers increase going east. Parking in the city is plentiful. Most lots near the Falls charge $3, but you can park in an equivalent spot for less on streets bordering the park. A free parking lot on Goat Island fills up early in the day.

ACCOMMODATIONS AND CAMPING

Niagara Falls International HI/AYH-Hostel, 1101 Ferry Ave., Niagara Falls, NY 14301 (282-3700). From station, walk east on Niagara St., turn left on Memorial Pkwy.; hostel is at corner of Ferry Ave. Good facilities, with kitchen, TV lounge. 46 beds. Travelers without cars given first priority; nonmembers turned away when space is short, as it usually is in summer. Owners will shuttle you to airport or train or bus station on request; rate depends on size of group going. Limited parking available. Bike rental $10 per day. Check-in 7:30-9:30am and 5-11pm. Lockout 9:30am-5pm. Curfew 11:30pm. Lights out midnight. $10, non-members $13. Required sheet sacks $1. Reservations essential. Open Jan. 4-Dec. 16.

Niagara Falls International Hostel (HI-C), 4699 Zimmerman Ave., Niagara Falls, Ontario (416-357-0770). Pleasant brick Tudor building 2½ mi. from the Falls, about 2 blocks from the Canada bus station and VIA Rail. Beautiful kitchen, dining room, lounge, peaceful backyard. 58 beds; can be cramped when full. Young, friendly manager will conduct bike trips and day hikes along the Niagara gorge. Bike rentals $10 per day. Laundry facilities and plentiful parking. Open 9-11am and 5pm-midnight. CDN$12, non-members CDN$16.28. 50¢ returned for performing morning chore. Linen $1. Reservations recommended.

YMCA, 1317 Portage Rd., Niagara Falls, NY (285-8491), a 15-min. walk from Falls; at night take a bus from Main St. Six standard dorm rooms available. 24-hr. check-in, no laundry. Fee includes use of full YMCA facilities. Dorm rooms men only (single $20, $10 key deposit). Men and women can sleep on mats in gym ($10).

Henri's Motel, 4671 River Road, Niagara Falls, Ontario (416-358-6573). The first motel in Niagara Falls (est. 1938) is still run by the same friendly family. Clean rooms with a variety of arrangements to accommodate families or couples. Rooms start at CDN$17. Owners run a store featuring handmade Canadian arts and crafts. Call for reservations. Open April-Sept.

NIAGARA FALLS

Niagara Falls Motel and Campsite, 2405 Niagara Falls Blvd., Wheatfield, NY (731-3434), 7 mi. from downtown. Nice-sized doubles with A/C, color TV, private bath $40-55, off-season $35-40; cheapest double in high season is $55. Sites $16, with hookup $21. Free pool.

Niagara Glen-View Tent & Trailer Park, 3950 Victoria Ave., Niagara Falls, Ontario (800-263-2570). Closest camp to the Falls; hiking trail across the street. Ice, showers, laundry available. Shuttle runs from driveway to bottom of Clifton Hill during the day every ½ hr. Sites US$19, with hookup $21. Open May-mid-Oct., reception 8am-11pm.

FOOD

Ferraro's, on the corner of 7th and Niagara St. (282-7020), has belly-filling Italian food. Pasta dishes, with salad and bread, $5 (open Mon.-Wed. 11:30am-8pm, Thurs.-Fri. 11:30am-10pm, Sat. 4-10pm). Decidedly more upscale (and expensive) are the flagship restaurants of Niagara Falls's vibrant Little Italy. **The Como,** 2220 Pine Ave. (285-9341), has hosted a galaxy of stars and has the photographs to prove it. Entrees run $8-11. **Mackri's Palace,** 755 W. Market St. (282-4707), has an equally wide array of Italian specialties. Prices are in the $6-11 range, but, as at the Como, portions are hefty. (Both restaurants open Mon.-Thurs. 11:30am-11pm, Fri.-Sat. until midnight.) Food on the run can be found at the food court of the **Rainbow Centre Factory Outlet Mall,** 302 Rainbow Blvd., just one block from the falls (free parking; shops open Mon.-Sat. 10am-9pm, Sun. noon-5pm). Or stroll through **Tops International Grocery Store,** 7200 Niagara Falls Blvd. (283-3100), one of the largest in the nation (open 24 hrs.). **The Press Box Bar,** 324 Niagara St. (284-5447), between 3rd and 4th St., is a popular spot; add a dollar bill to the several thousand taped to the wall. Every winter the owner takes them down and gives them to a cancer-fighting charity. (Burgers $1.50; food served Sun.-Thurs. 11:30am-midnight, Fri.-Sat. until 1am.) For a bite on the Canadian side, there's **Simon's Newsstand Restaurant,** 4116 Bridge St., Niagara Falls, Ontario (416-356-5310), directly across from the whirlpool bridge. Enjoy hearty diner fare and big breakfasts, but the real attraction is the home-made giant muffins (CDN90¢). (Open Mon.-Sat. 6am-8pm.)

SIGHTS AND ENTERTAINMENT

The American side of the Falls can easily be done in an afternoon. The **gardens** near the U.S. Falls (est. 1885) are one of the nation's oldest parks. The **Caves of the Wind Tour** on Goat Island will outfit you with a yellow raincoat and take you to the gardens by elevator. (Open May 15-Oct. 20. $3.50, ages 5-11 $3, under 4 free.) From the base of the **Observation Deck** (75¢), U.S. side, catch the **Maid of the Mist Tour** (284-8897), a boat ride to the foot of both Falls. Don't bring anything that isn't waterproof; you'll get wet. (Tours every 15 min. May-Oct. 24 daily 10am-6pm, longer hours in height of summer. $6.75, ages 6-12 $3.40, under 6 free.) The Falls are illuminated for three hours every night, starting one hour after sunset.

The park runs **Niagara Wonders** (278-1792), an interesting show on the falls, in the info center. (Shown on the hr. in the summer daily 10am-8pm; in the fall and early spring, daily 10am-6pm. $2, seniors $1.50, ages 6-12 $1.) The **Master Pass,** available in the park visitors center, is only worth the price if you plan to visit every single sight. One pass provides admission to the observation tower, the Cave of the Wind, the theater and the geological museum, plus discounts on Maid of the Mist tours and free parking. (Pass $13, kids $8.) The highest view of the Falls (775 ft. up) is from the **Skylon Tower,** 5200 Robinson St. (356-2651), in Canada. On a clear day you can see Toronto as well. (CDN$6, kids CDN$3.50.) Brunch daily in summer in revolving dining room (CDN$13).

Away from the Falls, tourist snares abound—some good, some for which the English language lacks words to express their...their...*inanity*. Browse through an impressive collection of regional Iroquois arts and crafts and watch performances of Iroquois dancing at **The Turtle,** 25 Rainbow Mall, Niagara Falls, NY (284-2427), between Winter Garden and the river. (Open daily 9am-6pm; Oct.-April Tues.-Fri.

9am-5pm, Sat.-Sun. noon-5pm. $3.50, seniors $3, kids and students $2.) Wander into the peaceful **Artisans Alley,** 10 Rainbow Blvd. (282-0196), at 1st St., to see works by over 600 American craftsmen. (Open Mon.-Fri. 10am-6pm, Sat.-Sun. 10am-9pm.) **Schoellkopf's Geological Museum** (SHULL-koffs) (278-1780) depicts the birth of the Falls with slide shows every half hour. (Open daily 9:30am-7pm; Labor Day-Oct. daily 10am-5pm; Nov.-Memorial Day Wed.-Sun. 10am-5pm. 50¢.)

From late Nov. to early Jan., Niagara Falls holds the annual **Festival of Lights.** Bright bulbs line the trees and create brilliant animated and outdoor scenes. Illumination of the Falls caps the spectacle. (Animated display areas open Sun.-Thurs. 5-10pm, Fri.-Sat. 5-11pm; exterior display areas nightly 5-11pm.)

On the Canada side (across the Rainbow Bridge) **Queen Victoria Park** provides the best view of the Horseshoe Falls. Parking costs CDN$8, however. To beat this misery system, park in the **free lot** across from the **Minolta Tower,** 6732 Oakes Dr., and take the **Incline,** directly behind the tower, for CDN75¢. Just minutes from the Falls, on **Clifton Hill,** the rule is *cave crapem*—let the tourist beware! "The Hill" is home to Ripley's Believe It or Not Museum, the Guinness Museum of World Records, the Super Star Recording Studio, and many other exhibitions of vacuous offal. If you pay the average CDN$6 these people want, put this book down and have a long look at yourself in the mirror. Okay, let's try to move on.

Three different flags (French, British, and U.S.) have flown over **Old Fort Niagara** (716-745-7611), which once guarded the entrance to the Niagara River. Its French Castle was built in 1726. (Box 169, Youngstown, NY 14174; follow Robert Moses Pkwy. north from Niagara Falls. Open July-Labor Day 9am-7:30pm; hours vary off-season. Call for rates.)

NORTHERN NEW YORK

■ ■ ■ THE ADIRONDACKS

One hundred and two years ago the New York State legislature, demonstrating uncommon foresight, established the **Adirondacks State Park**—the largest U.S. park outside Alaska. Unfortunately, in recent years the twin pressures of pollution and development have left a harsh imprint. Acid rain has damaged many tree and fish populations, especially in the fragile high-altitude environments, and tourist meccas like **Lake George** have continued to rapidly expand. Despite these urban intrusions, much of the area retains the beauty it had a century ago.

Of the six million acres in the Adirondacks Park, 40% is open to the public. Two thousand miles of trails traverse the forest and provide the best access to the spectacular mountain scenery, whether you're hiking, snow-shoeing, or cross-country skiing. An interlocking network of lakes and streams makes the gentle Adirondack wilds a perennial favorite of canoeists. Mountain-climbers may wish to surmount **Mt. Marcy,** the state's highest peak (5344 ft.), at the base of the Adirondacks, and skiers can choose from any of a dozen well-known alpine ski centers. **Lake Placid** hosted the winter Olympics in 1932 and 1980, and frequently welcomes national and international sports competitions (see Lake Placid below). **Saranac Lake** hosts the **International Dog Sledding Championship** at the end of January. **Tupper Lake** and **Lake George** also have carnivals every January and February, and Tupper hosts the **Tin Man Triathlon** in July. In September, the hot air balloons of the **Adirondack Balloon Festival** in Glens Falls race the trees to be the first to provide fall color.

Practical Information The best source of information on hiking and other outdoor activities in the region is the **Adirondack Mountain Club (ADK).** The ADK is in its 72nd year, has over 19,000 members, with offices at RR3, Box 3055,

Lake George 12845 (668-4447) and at Adirondack Loj Rd., P.O. Box 867, Lake Placid 12946 (523-3441). The club sponsors outdoors skills classes such as canoeing, rock climbing, fly fishing, and white water kayaking. The ADK's **High Peaks Information Center,** off Rte. 73 outside Lake Placid, near the sign for the Adirondack Loj, has the latest in backcountry info, sells basic outdoor equipment and trail snacks, and has washrooms (open daily 8am-8pm). Those interested in rock climbing should consult the **Mountaineer** (576-2281; halfway between I-87 and Lake Placid on Rte. 73). All employees here are experienced mountaineers, and the store is a good source of weather forecasts. Rent snowshoes for $10 per day, and ice-climbing equipment (boots and crampons) for $15 per day. And if you're planning to stay on a glacier for two months (to research), the Mountaineer promises much better rates.

Traveling in the backwoods is tough during the muddy spring thaw (March-April). Contact the **State Office of Parks and Recreation** (see New York Practical Information) in Albany for more information on the region. For trails in the Lake Placid area, try ADK's particularly good *Guide to the High Peaks* ($18).

The Adirondacks are served by **Adirondacks Trailways,** with frequent stops along I-87. From Albany buses go to Lake Placid, Tupper Lake, and Lake George. From the Lake George bus stop, at the Mobil station, 320 Canada St. (668-9511; 800-225-6815 for bus info), buses reach Lake Placid (1 per day, $12.45), Albany (1 per day, $9.30), and New York City ($36.30). (Open June-Sept. daily 7am-midnight, Oct.-May daily 7am-10pm.) The Adirondacks' **area code** is 518.

Accommodations and Camping

Two lodges near Lake Placid are also run by the ADK. The **Adirondack Loj** (523-3441), eight mi. east of Lake Placid off Rte. 73, is a beautiful log cabin on Heart Lake with comfortable bunk facilities and a family atmosphere. Guests can swim, fish, canoe, and use rowboats on the premises (canoe or boat rental $3). In winter, explore the wilderness trails on rented snowshoes ($15 per day) or cross-country skis ($20 per day). (B&B $30, with dinner $41. Linen included. Campsites $13. Lean-tos $16.) Call ahead for weekends and during peak holiday seaons. For an even better mix of rustic comfort and wilderness experience, hike 3½ mi. from the closest trailhead to the **John's Brook Lodge,** in Keene Valley 16 mi. southeast of Lake Placid off Rte. 73 (call the Adirondack Loj for reservations). From Placid, follow Rte. 73 15 mi. through Keene to Keene Valley, turning right at the Ausable Inn. The hike is slightly uphill, and the food is well worth the exertion; the staff packs in groceries every day and cooks on a gas stove. A great place to meet friendly New Yorkers, John's Brook is no secret; beds fill completely on weekends. Make reservations at least one day in advance for dinner, longer for a weekend. Bring sheets or a sleeping bag. (B&B $24, with dinner $35. Lean-tos $7. Open mid-June-early Sept.) From Memorial Day-June 12 and Labor Day-Columbus Day, rent a bunk for $9 weekdays, $10 weekends, with full access to the kitchen.

If ADK facilities are too pricey, try the **High Peaks Base Camp,** P.O. Box 91, Upper Jay 12987 (946-2133), a charming restaurant/lodge/campground just a 20-minute drive from Lake Placid. Take Rte. 86 N. to Wilmington, turn right at the Mobil station, then go right 3½ mi. on Springfield Rd.; $12 (Sun.-Thurs.) or $15 (Fri.-Sat.) buys you a bed for the night and a huge breakfast. (Check-in until 10pm, later with reservations. Sites $3 per person. Cabins $30 for 4 people.) Transportation is tough without a car but sometimes rides can be arranged from Keene; call ahead. **Free camping** abounds; in the forest, you can use the free shelters by the trails. Always inquire about their location before you plan a hike. Better still, camp for free in the **backcountry** anywhere on public land, as long as you are at least 150 ft. away from a trail, road, water source or campground and stay below 4000 ft. altitude.

The **Lake George Youth Hostel** is located in the basement of **St. James Episcopal Church Hall,** P.O. Box 176, Lake George (668-2634), on Montcalm St. at Ottawa, several blocks from the lake. From the bus terminal, walk south one block to Montcalm, turn right and go one block to Ottawa for the slightly musty bunk-room with a decent kitchen. (Check-in 5-9pm, later only with reservations. Curfew 10pm. $10, nonmembers $13. Open late May-early Sept.)

■■■ LAKE PLACID

Lake Placid is strewn with reminders of its Olympic status—it has twice hosted the Winter Games (in 1932 and 1980). Not only do international flags adorn Main Street, but the post office still sells 1980 Olympic badges, and Team-USA shirts are still available in local stores. The town's sporting facilities finely attest to its Olympic tradition. Unmatched by many of the world's metropoli, they attract world-class athletes year round, while Lake Placid's inviting village atmosphere and grandiose natural setting lure crowds of more casual visitors. Temperatures can plummet to minus 40°F and more than 200 inches of snow may fall in any given Adirondack winter, but well-plowed main roads keep the region open year-round.

Practical Information The Olympic spirit clearly makes its presence felt in Lake Placid, with a number of venues scattered in and just outside the town. The **Olympic Regional Development Authority,** Olympic Ctr. (523-1655 or 800-462-6236), operates the facilities. The **Lake Placid Convention and Visitors Bureau** (523-2999), also in Olympic Ctr., just above the hockey rink, gives price info and directions (open daily 8am-5pm).

To explore Lake Placid by **bike**, rent mountain bikes at **High Peak Cyclery,** 18 Saranac Ave. (523-3764; $15 per ½-day, $20 per day). The shop also rents downhill skis ($10 per day), and roller blades ($8 per ½-day, $12 per day). (Must have ID. Open Mon.-Thurs. 10am-6pm, Fri.-Sat. 10am-8pm, Sun. 11am-5pm.)

Adirondack Trailways has extensive service in the area, stopping at the **326 Main St. Deli** in Lake Placid (523-1527; 523-4309 for bus info). Buses run to New York City (1 per day, $45.60) and Lake George (1 per day, $12.45). By car, Lake Placid is at the intersection of Rte. 86 and Rte. 73.

For **weather** information call 523-1363 or 523-3518. Lake Placid has a **post office** at 201 Main St. (523-3071; open Mon.-Fri. 6:30am-5:15pm, Sat. 7am-3:30pm). Lake Placid's **ZIP code** is 12946; the **area code** is 518.

Accommodations and Camping Most accommodations in the area are expensive. The **White Sled** (523-9314; on Rte. 73 between the Sports Complex and the ski jumps) is the best bargain around: for $15 you get a comfortable, clean bed in the bunkhouse, which includes a full kitchen, living room, and entertainment by the friendly, Francophone hosts. Bus travelers should ask the driver to be dropped off at the level of the ski jumps to avoid the three mi. walk from downtown. The **Hotel St. Moritz,** 31 Saranac Ave. (523-9240), one block from Main St., offers "Old World Charm at an Affordable Price." For $30 you get a decent single and a full breakfast (7-9am). Doubles $35. Prices hiked up for weekends and seasonal holidays. Chain motels litter the area, including **Holly Hill,** 215 Saranac Ave. (523-9231), about 2 mi. out of Lake Placid, with two beds and private bath for $35. **Lysek's Inn,** 50 Hillcrest Ave. (523-1700), rents beds and serves a buffet breakfast for $21 (mid-Sept.-May). Call ahead; Lysek's fills up quickly with athletes. (From Main St. go uphill on Marcy St. and turn left on Hillcrest.) The closest campgrounds to Lake Placid are **Meadowbrook State Park** (891-4351; 5 mi. west on Rte. 86 in Ray Brook), and **Wilmington Notch State Campground** (946-7172; off Rte. 86 between Wilmington and Lake Placid). Both offer sites without hookups ($10.50 first night, $9 each additional night) which can accommodate two tents and up to six people.

Food **Main Street** in Lake Placid Village offers pickings to suit any palate, and prices are generally reasonable. Lunch buffet (Mon.-Sat. noon-2pm) at the **Hilton Hotel,** 1 Mirror Lake Dr. (523-4411), buys a sandwich and all-you-can-eat soup and

NORTHERN NEW YORK: THOUSAND ISLANDS

salad ($4.75). At the **Black Bear Restaurant,** 157 Main St. (523-9886), enjoy a $4 lunch special and a $2.75 Saranac lager (the Adirondack's own beer) in the company of a stuffed bobcat, an otter, a fox, and three deer heads (open Sun.-Thurs. 6:30am-9pm, Fri.-Sat. 24 hrs.). **The Cottage,** 5 Mirror Lake Dr. (523-9845), has relatively inexpensive meals (sandwiches and salads $4-6) with scrumptious views of Mirror Lake; watch the U.S. canoe and kayaking teams practice on the water. (Meals served daily 11:30am-9pm. Bar open daily 11:30am-1am.) **Mud Puddles,** 3 School St. (523-4446), below the speed skating rink, is popular with disco throwbacks and the pop music crowd (open Wed.-Sun. 9pm-3am; cover $1.50).

Sights You can't miss the 70 and 90m runs of the Olympic ski jumps, which, with the **Kodak Sports Park,** make up the **Olympic Jumping Complex,** just outside of town on Rte. 73. The $5 admission fee includes a chairlift and elevator ride to the top of the spectator towers, where you might catch summer (June-mid-Oct.) jumpers flipping and sailing into a swimming pool. (Open daily 9am-5pm, Sept.-May 9am-4pm.) Three mi. farther along Rte. 73, the **Olympic Sports Complex** (523-4436) at Mt. Van Hoevenberg has a summer trolley coasting to the top of the bobsled run ($3, mid-June-mid-Oct.). In the winter (Dec.-March Tues.-Sun. 1-3pm) you can bobsled down the Olympic run ($25), or try the luge ($10). The park is open for self-guided tours ($3) daily 9am-4pm June-Columbus Day, and has 35 mi. of well-groomed cross-country ski trails ($9).

In addition to fantastic ski slopes, **Whiteface Mountain,** near Lake Placid, provides a panoramic view of the Adirondacks. You can surmount the summit via the **Whiteface Memorial Highway** ($5 toll, cars only) or a chairlift (446-2223; $5, seniors and kids $4). (Road open mid-May-mid-Oct.; lift open mid-June-mid-Oct.) The extensive **Whiteface Mountain Ski Center** (523-1655) has the largest vertical drop in the Northeast U.S. (3216 ft.). Don't bother with the $4 tour of the waterfalls at **High Falls Gorge** (946-2278) on Rte. 86 near Whiteface; hike below the road to see the same scenery for free, and laugh at all the people who paid. **Ice fishing** on the lakes is popular with locals, as is **ice skating** (Olympic speed-skating rink $3; open daily 7-9pm, Mon.-Fri. 1-3pm weather permitting).

History buffs will enjoy a quick visit to the **farm and grave** of the militant abolitionist traitor **John Brown** (hung in 1859 for his role in an attack on the U.S. arsenal at Harpers Ferry, VA), off Rte. 73, 2 mi. southeast of Lake Placid (523-3900; open late May-late Oct. Wed.-Sat. 10am-5pm, Sun. 1-5pm; free). The west branch of the **Ausable River,** just east of Lake Placid, lures anglers to its shores. **Fishing licenses** for non-New Yorkers are $16 for five days (season $28); for residents $6 for three days (season $14) at Town Hall, 301 Main St. (523-2162), or Jones Outfitters, 37 Main St. (523-3468). Call the "Fishing Hotline" (891-5413) for an in-depth recording of the hot fresh-water fishing spots. The **Lake Placid Center for the Arts,** on Saranac Ave. just outside town at Fawn Ridge (523-2512), houses a local art gallery and hosts theater, dance, and musical performances. (Open daily 1-5pm; winter Mon.-Fri. 1-5pm. Gallery free; call for prices and listings of performances.)

■■■ THOUSAND ISLAND SEAWAY REGION

The Thousand Island-St. Lawrence Seaway spans 100 mi. from the mouth of Lake Ontario to the first of the giant man-made locks on the St. Lawrence River. Some 1800 islands splatter throughout the waterway, and are accessible both by small pleasure-boats and huge ocean-bound freighters. The Thousand Island Region boasts a number of attractions to lure visitors, from the extravagant homes of millionaires who once idled here to the plentiful stock of bass and muskellunge (the world's largest—69lb. 5oz.—was caught here in 1957) to the proud fact that it's the only region in the U.S. to have an eponymous salad dressing.

Practical Information The three main cities of the region are **Clayton, Alexandria Bay,** and **Cape Vincent.** Write the **Clayton Chamber of Commerce,** 403 Riverside Dr., Clayton 13624 (686-3771), for the *Clayton Vacation Guide* and the *Thousand Islands Seaway Region Travel Guide.* The **Alexandria Bay Chamber of Commerce** (482-9531) is on Market St. just off James St., Alexandria Bay 13607. The **Cape Vincent Chamber of Commerce** (654-2481) is down James St. Access the region by bus through **Greyhound,** 540 State St., Watertown (788-8110). Hounds trot to New York City (1 per day, 8 hr., $49), Syracuse (2 per day, 1¾ hr., $11.50), and Albany (1 per day, 5½ hr., $31). From the same station, **Thousand Islands Bus Lines** runs to Alexandria Bay and Clayton at 1pm (Sun.-Fri., $5.60 to Alexandria, $3.55 to Clayton); return trips leave from Clayton at the Nutshell Florist, 234 James St. (686-5791), at 8:45am, and from Alexandria at the Dockside Cafe, 17 Market St. (482-9819), at 8:30am. (Station open 9:30am-2:30pm and 4:30-8pm.)

Clayton and the Thousand Islands region are just two hours from Syracuse by way of I-81 N. For Welleslet Island, Alexandria Bay, and the eastern 500 islands, stay on I-81 until you reach Rte. 12 E. For Clayton and points west, take exit 47 and follow Rte. 12 until you reach 12 E.

The Clayton **post office** (686-3311) is at 236 John St. The Alexandria Bay **post office** (482-9321) is at 13 Bethune St. The Cape Vincent **post office** (654-2424) is at 360 Broadway St. Clayton's **ZIP code** is 13624; Alexandria Bay's **ZIP code** is 13607; Cape Vincent's **ZIP code** is 13618. The region's **area code** is 315.

Accommodations and Camping Cape Vincent, on the western edge of the seaway, keeps one of the most idyllic youth hostels in the country. **Tibbetts Point Lighthouse Hostel (HI/AYH),** RR1 Box 330 (654-3450), strategically and scenically situated where Lake Ontario meets the St. Lawrence, has two houses with 31 beds; choose between a riverfront or a lakefront view, and watch the ships glide past spectacular sunsets. A large, full kitchen with microwave is available, and the hosts George and Jean Cougler are like certified grandparents. Take Rte. 12 E. into town, turn left on Broadway, and follow the river until it ends. There is no public transportation to Cape Vincent, but if warned far enough in advance, George or Jean will come get you in Clayton. (Curfew 10pm. Check-in 5-9:30pm. $10, nonmembers $13. Open May 15-Sept. 30.) **Burnham Point State Park** (654-2324) on Rte. 12 E. between Cape Vincent and Clayton, sports 50 tent sites that can accommodate two tents and up to six people. Boat docking facilities available. (No showers. $10.50 first night, $9 each additional night. Hookup $2 extra. Open Memorial Day weekend to Labor Day, 8am-9pm daily.) **Keewaydin State Park** (482-3331), just north of Alexandria Bay, has 41 campsites along the St. Lawrence River. An Olympic-size swimming pool is free for campers. (Open Memorial Day-Labor Day, $11.50 first night, $10 each additional night. Showers available. No hookups or dumping stations.)

Exploring the Seaway Any of the small towns dotting Rte. 12 can serve as a good base for exploring the region, though Clayton and Cape Vincent tend to be less expensive than Alexandria Bay. For $11 (ages 6-12 $6), **Uncle Sam Boat Tours** in **Clayton,** 604 Riverside Dr. (686-3511), or in **Alexandria Bay** (482-2611), on James St., gives a good look at most of the islands and the plush estates that bask atop them. Look for both the shortest and the longest international bridges linking Canada and the U.S. Tours highlight **Heart Island** and its famous **Boldt Castle** (482-9724) but do not cover the price of admission to the castle. George Boldt, former owner of New York City's elegant Waldorf-Astoria Hotel, financed this six-story replica of a Rhineland castle as a gift for his wife, who died before its completion. The originally planned 365 bedrooms, 52 bathrooms, and one power house were never completed, and Boldt's project now remains as the tragic reminder of a dream that never was. (Open May-Oct. $3.25, ages 6-12, $1.75.) **Rental boats** are available in Clayton, Alexandria Bay, and Cape Vincent. In Clayton, **French Creek Marina,** 98

Wahl St. (686-3621), rents 14-ft. fishing boats ($45 per day) and pontoon boats ($110 per day); launches boats ($5); and provides overnight docking ($15 per night). In Alexandria Bay, **O'Brien's U-Drive Boat Rentals,** 51 Walton St. (482-9548), rents 16-ft. fishing boats ($50 per day) and 18-ft. runabouts ($150 per day). (Open May-Oct.; mechanic on duty daily.) **Aqua Mania** (482-4678), across from the information center on Rte. 12, rents jet skis, although at $70 per hr. you might think you were renting a jet airplane. In Cape Vincent, the **Sunset Trailer Park** (654-2482), 2 mi. beyond town on 12 E., rents motor boats for $38 per day. This location is especially convenient if staying at the nearby Tibbets Point Hostel.

    Fishing licenses (non-NY residents: season $28, 5 days $16; NY residents: season $14, 3 days $6) are available at a number of sporting goods stores, as well as at the **Town Clerk's Office,** 405 Riverside Dr., Clayton (686-3512; open Mon.-Fri. 9am-noon and 1-4pm). No local store rents equipment, so bring your own rods and reels or plan to buy them. **The Skipper Shop,** 430 Riverside Dr., Clayton (686-4067), sells fishing rods for $6-26.

■ Pennsylvania

Driven by the persecution of his fellow Quakers, William Penn, Jr. petitioned the British Crown for a slice of North America in 1680. In 1681, Charles II assented, granting to the Quakers a vast tract of land between what is now Maryland and New York. Arriving in 1682, Penn attracted all types of settlers by making his colony a bastion of religious tolerance; the rapid growth of its cities made Pennsylvania seem destined to become the most prominent state in the new nation. The emerging colonies signed the *Declaration of Independence* in Philadelphia, the country's original capital and site of the First Continental Congress. However, other cities soon overshadowed it—New York City rapidly grew into the nation's most important commercial center, and Washington, D.C. usurped the role of national capital.

    But Pennsylvania, a state accustomed to revolution, has rallied in the face of adversity. In 1976, Philadelphia groomed its historic shrines for the nation's bicentennial celebration, and they have remained immaculate ever since. Even Pittsburgh, a city once dirty enough to fool streetlights into burning during the day, has initiated a cultural renaissance. Between the two cities, Pennsylvania's landscape, from the farms of Lancaster County to the deep river gorges of the Allegheny Plateau, retains much of the sylvanism that drew Penn here over 300 years ago.

PRACTICAL INFORMATION

Capital: Harrisburg.
Visitor Information: Bureau of Travel Development, 453 Forum Bldg., Harrisburg 17120 (717-787-5453 or 800-237-4363). Information on hotels, restaurants, and sights. **Bureau of State Parks,** P.O. Box 1467, Harrisburg 17120 (800-631-7105). The detailed *Recreational Guide* is available at no charge from all visitors information centers.
Time Zone: Eastern. **Postal Abbreviation:** PA
Sales Tax: 6%.

■■■ ALLEGHENEY NATIONAL FOREST

Containing half a million acres of woodland stretching 40 mi. south of the New York state border, the Allegheny National Forest offers year-round recreational opportunities such as hunting, fishing, trail-biking, and cross-country skiing. The forest makes an excellent stopover on a cross-state jaunt; its southern border is only 20 miles from I-80, and the park is never as crowded as the more ballyhooed Poconos or Catskills.

Practical Information The forest divides into four quadrants, each with its own ranger station providing maps and information about activities and facilities within its region. **SW: Marienville Ranger District** (927-6628), on Rte. 66 (open Mon.-Sat. 7am-5pm). **SE: Ridgeway Ranger District** (776-6172), on Montmorenci Rd. (open Mon.-Fri. 7:30am-4pm). **NW: Sheffield Ranger District** (968-3232), on U.S. 6 (open Mon.-Fri. 8am-4pm). **NE: Bradford Ranger District** (362-4613), on Rte. 59 west of Marshburg (open Mon.-Fri. 7am-5:30pm, Sat.-Sun. 7am-8pm). The Bradford ranger station, at the junction of Rte. 59 and Rte. 321, has extended its hours to fill in for the temporarily-closed Kinzua Point Information Center. The Devil's Elbow bridge on Rte. 59 is being rebuilt as of this writing but is scheduled to reopen in January 1994. Meanwhile, the Kinzua and Allegheny Dams are still accessible via Rte. 6, which dips south of the bridge. For park information call the Bradford ranger station or write to **Forest Service, USDA,** P.O. Box 847, Warren, PA 16365. **Greyhound** no longer serves the area. When driving in the forest, be very careful during wet weather; about half the region is served only by dirt roads. Get good maps of the area ($2) at any ranger station. The **area code** for this area is 814.

Accommodations and Camping From whatever direction you approach the Allegheny Forest, you'll encounter a small, rustic community near the park that offers groceries and accommodations. **Ridgeway,** 25 mi. from I-80 (exit 16) at the southeast corner, and **Warren,** on the northeastern fringe of the forest where U.S. 6 and 62 meet, have comparable services. There are 13 **campgrounds** in the park (7 are open May-Oct., 3 open April-Dec.). Sites cost $5-12, depending on the location and the time of year. **Tracy Ridge** in the Bradford district and **Heart's Content** in the Sheffield district are particularly pretty. You can call 800-283-2267 to reserve sites ($6 fee), but the park keeps 50% of them on a first-come, first-served basis. You don't need a site to camp in the Allegheny; stay 1500 ft. from a major road or body of water, and you can pitch a tent anywhere.

Sights and Activities Each summer, the **Allegheny Reservoir,** located in the northern section of the forest, is stocked with fish and tourists. Here you can enjoy fishing, boating, swimming, or grab a tour of the **Kinzua Dam,** operated by the U.S. Corps of Engineers. The six boat-accessible camping sites along the 95-mile shore of the reservoir are free and do not require reservations or a permit (fresh water, toilets, no showers). Anglers should dial the 24-hr. fishing hotline for tips (726-0164). **Hikers** should pick up the free 14-page pamphlet describing the 10 trails in the forest. **Buzzard Swamp,** near Marienville, has 8 mi. of trails through a wildlife refuge where no motor vehicles are permitted. **Kinzua Boat Rentals and Marina** (726-1650), on Rte. 59 4 mi. east of Kinzua Dam, rents canoes ($5 per hr., $18 per day), rowboats ($5.50 per hr., $20 per day), and motorboats ($12 per hr., $50 per day). **Allegheny Outfitters** (723-1203) at Market St. Plaza in Warren provides canoe livery service for the reservoir and the Allegheny River.

■■■ GETTYSBURG

In November 1863, four months after 7000 men had died in the Civil War's bloodiest battle, President Abraham Lincoln arrived in Gettysburg to dedicate a national cemetery and give "a few appropriate remarks." In a two-minute speech, Lincoln urged preservation of the union in one of the greatest orations in U.S. history. Lincoln's *Gettysburg Address* and the sheer enormity of the battle which prompted him to write it have entrenched Gettysburg as the most famous battlefield in U.S.

history. Each year thousands of visitors head for these Pennsylvania fields, heeding Honest Abe's call to "resolve that these dead shall not have died in vain."

Practical Information Before attacking Gettysburg's phalanx of Civil War memorabilia, get your bearings at the **National Military Park Visitors Information Center** (334-1124), 1 mi. south of town on Washington St. (open daily 8am-6pm, Labor Day-Memorial Day 8am-5pm.) Go on your own, letting the free map navigate your bike or car tour, or pay a park guide to show you the sights ($20 for a 2-hr. tour). The same building houses a 750-square-foot **electric map.** This representation of the area as it was in 1863 lights up in coordination with a taped narration and is a must when trying to bring the great sweep of the battle into brighter focus. ($2, seniors $1.50, under 15 free.) The **Cyclorama Center** next door has a facsimile of Lincoln's speech and a huge painting (356x26 ft.) of the turning point of the Civil War. Stand in the middle and you're back in 1863. (Open daily 9am-5pm. $2, seniors $1.50, under 15 free.) For an excellent perspective of the area, walk over to the **National Tower** (334-6754), where high-speed elevators whisk you up 300 ft. for a spectacular view. (Open daily 9am-5:30pm. Admission $4, kids $2.)

Gettysburg orates in south-central Pennsylvania, off U.S. 15 about 30 mi. south of Harrisburg. Unfortunately, when the Union and Confederacy decided to lock horns here, they didn't have the traveler's convenience in mind. Neither Greyhound nor Amtrak services Gettysburg. The **post office** (337-3781) is at 115 Buford Ave. (open Mon.-Fri. 8am-4:30pm, Sat. 9am-noon); the **ZIP code** is 17325; the **area code** is 717.

Food, Accommodations, and Camping Gettysburg's eateries are classy and affordable. The **Dutch Cupboard,** 523 Baltimore (334-6227), serves up Pennsylvania Dutch specialties like *schnitz un knepp* (dried apples cooked with dumplings, $7.50) and the famous shoo fly pie (brown sugar, flour, special spices, and 2 kinds of molasses; $1.75). (Open daily 11am-9pm.) The candle-lit **Springhouse Tavern,** 89 Steinwehr Ave. (334-2100), lies in the basement of the **Dobben House,** Gettysburg's first building (c. 1776) once an Underground Railroad shelter for runaway slaves during the Civil War. Try the "Mason's Mile High" sandwich ($5.75) or create your own grilled burger ($6).

The best place to sleep in Gettysburg remains the roomy and cheerful **Gettysburg International Hostel (HI/AYH),** 27 Chambersburg St. (334-1020), on U.S. 30 just west of Lincoln Sq. in the center of town. Kitchen, stereo, living room, laundry, library, piano. (Check-in 7-9am and 5-9pm. Check-out 9:30am. $8, nonmembers $11. Sleepsack rental $1.) This remarkably friendly hostel usually has space, but when you're lusting for a motel, the **Gettysburg Travel Council,** 35 Carlisle St., Lincoln Sq. (334-6274), stocks a full line of brochures, as well as maps and information on local sights (open daily 9am-5pm). There are also **campgrounds** in the area. One mi. south on Rte. 134 is **Artillery Ridge,** 610 Tarrytown Rd. (334-1288). Showers, riding stable, laundry, pool (sites $12.50 for 2 people, with hookup $16-19). Further down the road, the **Round Top Campground,** (334-9565) has everything Artillery Ridge does—plus a mini golf course ($10 for 2 people, with hookup $15).

■■■ LANCASTER COUNTY

When persecuted flocks of German Anabaptists fled to William Penn's bastion of religious freedom, locals quickly and wrongly labeled them the Pennsylvania Dutch. A misunderstanding of the word *Deutschland* for "Germany," the name stuck. Since the late 1700s, three distinct families of Anabaptists have lived in Lancaster County: **Brethren, Mennonite,** and **Amish.** The latter, and the Old Order Amish in particular, are famed for their idiosyncratic and anachronistic lifestyle. Emphatically rejecting modern technology and fashion, the Amish worship at home, educate their children at home, and discourage association with outsiders. Quite ironically, the modest Lancaster Amish community of 22,000 draws many times that many visitors each year, who are eager to glimpse the secluded country lifestyle of horse-drawn carriages, home-style dining, and old-fashioned dress. In contrast to the Amish, some of the Mennonites embrace modern conveniences like cars and electricity. Many sell their farm goods at roadside stands or operate bed and breakfasts and craft shops. As a result, Lancaster County today has evolved into an odd hybrid of time-capsule austerity and modern consumerism.

PRACTICAL INFORMATION

Visitor Information: Lancaster Chamber of Commerce and Industry, 100 Queen St. (397-3531), in the Southern Market Center. Pick up guided walking tours of Lancaster City (April-Oct. Mon.-Sat. 10am and 1:30pm, Sun. and holidays 10am, 11am, 1:30pm; $4 adults, $3 kids) or buy a worthwhile self-guided booklet ($1.50). To reserve a tour off-season call 653-8225 or 394-2339. (Open April-Oct. Mon.-Fri. 8:30am-5pm; open 1 hr. later off-season.) **Pennsylvania Dutch Visitors Bureau Information Center,** 501 Greenfield Rd. (299-8901), on the east side of Lancaster City just off Rte. 30. The bureau has walls of brochures and free phone lines to most area inns and campsites. (Open mid-May-early Sept. Sun.-Thurs. 8am-6pm, Fri.-Sat. 8am-7pm.) **Mennonite Information Center,** 2209 Millstream Rd. (299-0954; open Mon.-Sat. 8am-5pm), just off Rte. 30. guides for $8.50 per hr.; call for times. **Alverta Moore** (626-2421) offers to guide for about $5 per hr.

Amtrak: 53 McGovern Ave. (291-508 or 800-872-7245; reservations 24 hrs.), in Lancaster City. Eight trains per day to Philadelphia (1 hr., $12).

Greyhound: 22 W. Clay St. (397-4861 or 800-231-2222). 3 buses per day between Lancaster City and Philadelphia (2 hr., $12). Open daily 7am-5:15pm.

Public Transportation: Red Rose Transit, 45 Erick Rd. (397-4246), serves Lancaster and the surrounding countryside. Pick up route maps at the office. Base fare 90¢, seniors free during off-peak hrs. and weekends.

Post Office: 1400 Harrisburg Pike (396-6900). **ZIP code:** Lancaster City, 17604 **Area Code:** 717.

Lancaster County—even the concentrated spots of interest to tourists—covers a huge area. Cars are the vehicle of choice for most visitors. You can pay a guide to hop in and show you around. If you'd rather go it alone, pick up maps at Lancaster City or Pennsylvania Dutch visitors bureaus (see above), veer off U.S. 30, and explore the winding roads. Pick up a free *Map of Amish Farmlands* at any tourist spot in Lancaster County, or write to 340-23 Club, P.O. Box 239, Intercourse 17534.

ACCOMMODATIONS

Hundreds of hotels, B&Bs, and campgrounds cluster in this area. Don't search for accommodations without stopping by the **Pennsylvania Dutch Visitors Bureau Information Center** (see Practical Information above). There seem to be as many **campgrounds** as cows in this lush countryside, all of which (the campgrounds, not the cows) have laundry and shower facilities.

Marsh Creek State Park Hostel (HI/AYH), P.O. Box 376, E. Reeds Rd., Lyndell 19354 (215-458-5881), in Marsh Creek State Park. This old farmhouse proves a challenge to find and to contact, but it is well-kept and lies on a gorgeous lake. Check out 9:30am, 11pm curfew. Each of its 30 beds goes for $9, $12 nonmembers. $1 linen fee. **Amtrak** stops in Downington, 5 mi. away on its Philadelphia-Lancaster route. **Downington Cab** (269-3000) charges about $12 to get there.

Shirey's Youth Hostel (HI/AYH), P.O. Box 49, Geigertown 19523 (215-286-9537; open March 2-Nov. 30). 15 mi. east of Marsh Creek, near French Creek State Park off Rte. 82. Though the area is beautiful, the hostel's remote location may not merit the trip. Transportation from Reading, 15 mi. away, might be arranged if you call ahead. Check out 9:30am, curfew 11pm. $9, $12 nonmembers, sleepsack rental $1.

Old Millstream Camping Manor, 2249 U.S. 30 E. (Lincoln Hwy.) (299-2314). The closest year-round facility, 4 mi. east of Lancaster City. Office open daily 8am-9pm. Sites $16, with hookup $19. Reservations recommended.

Roamers Retreat, 5005 Lincoln Hwy. (442-4287 or 800-525-5605), off U.S. 30, 7½ mi. east of Rte. 896, opens only April-Oct. For reservations, call or write RD #1, P.O. Box 41B, Kinzers 17535. Sites $17, with hookup $19.

Shady Grove, P.O. Box 28, Adamstown 19501 (215-484-4225), on Rte. 272 at Rte. 897, 264 W. Swartzville Rd. 80 sites, with electricity ($16, full hookup $18).

FOOD

Just about everyone passing through Lancaster County expects a taste of real Dutch cuisine—and a flock of high priced "family-style" restaurants, have sprouted up to please them. If you have the cash (all-you-can-eat meals $12-16) try any of the huge restaurants such as **The Amish Barn** (768-8886) which spread thick on Rte. 340 in Bird-in-Hand. **Dell's Family Restaurant,** 213 E. Main St. (445-9233), in Terre Hill off Rte. 897 about 20 mi. north of Lancaster City serves scrapple with vegetables and salad bar for $6 (open Mon-Sat. 6am-8pm). More varied fare can be found in Lancaster City. Don't miss the **Central Market,** in the northwest corner of Penn Sq., a huge food bazaar vending inexpensive meats, cheeses, vegetables, and sandwiches since 1899. (Open Tues. and Fri. 6am-4pm, Sat. 6am-2pm.) There are many fun, interesting and inexpensive restaurants surrounding the market. If you try nothing else in Lancaster County, at least sample a **whoopie pie** (75¢).

SIGHTS

A good place to start is the **People's Place** (768-7171), on Main St./Rte. 340, in Intercourse, 11 mi. east of Lancaster City. The film *Who Are the Amish* shows every half hour 9:30am-5pm. The Place spans an entire block with bookstores, craft shops, and an art gallery. (Open Mon.-Sat. 9:30am-9:30pm; Nov.-March 9:30am-4:30pm.) If you have specific questions, seek out friendly locals at the Mennonite Information Center (see above), which also shows the film *Portraits of Our Heritage and Faith*. Memorial Day-Labor Day, People's Place also shows another film titled *Hazel's People* ($5, under 12 $3). **Amish World,** also in Intercourse, has charming hands-on exhibits on Amish and Mennonite life, from barn-raising to hatstyles. (Admission to one $3, kids $1.50. To both $5.50, kids $2.75.) A quiet metropolis in the heart of Dutch country, county seat **Lancaster City** reflects the area's character well—clean, red-brick row houses huddle around historic **Penn Square** in the city center.

■ Candyland

Milton S. Hershey, a Mennonite resident of eastern Pennsylvania farms, failed in his first several jaunts into the confectionery world. Then he found chocolate. Today the company that bears his name has become the world's largest chocolate factory in **Hershey** just across the northeastern border of Lancaster. Here, street lights are shaped like candy kisses, and the streets are named Chocolate and Cocoa. East of town at **Hershey Park** (800-437-7439), the **Chocolate World Visitors Center** (534-4900) presents a free, automated tour through a simulated chocolate factory. After viewing the processing of the cacao bean from tropical forests past the Oompa-Loompas of Willy Wonka fame to final packaging, visitors emerge with two free Hershey Kisses in hand into a pavilion full of chocolate cookies, discounted chocolate candy, chocolate milk, and fashionable Hershey sportswear—all for a small fee, of course. (Open Sept. to mid-June 9am-4:45pm, mid-June-Labor Day 9am-7:45pm.)

Amusement park fans will love Hershey Park's **amusement center** for its short lines and heart-stopping rides. Don't miss Sidewinder or the Comet. The **Sooper-dooperLooper** is also a must. (Open late May-early Sept. daily 10:30am-10pm. $23, ages 3-8 and over 55 $15.) Camp 8 mi. from Hershey and 15 mi. from Lancaster City at **Ridge Run Campground,** 867 Schwanger Rd., Elizabethtown 17022 (367-3454). Schwanger Rd. connects Rte. 230 and Rte. 283. (Sites $17, with water and electricity $18, full hookup $19.) **Greyhound** (397-4861) goes to Hershey from Lancaster City (1 per day, 3 hr., $19), stopping at 337 W. Chocolate St.

■■■ OHIOPYLE STATE PARK

In southwestern Pennsylvania lie some of the loveliest forests in the East, lifted by steep hills and cut by cascading rivers. Native Americans dubbed this part of the state "Ohiopehhle" ("white frothy water"), because of the grand Youghiogheny River Gorge (pronounced yock-a-gay-nee; "The Yock" to locals). The river provides the focal point of Pennsylvania's Ohiopyle State Park. The park's 18,000 acres offer hiking, fishing, hunting, whitewater rafting, and a complete range of winter activities. The latest addition to the banks of the Yock is a gravelled bike trail. Converted from a riverside railroad bed, the trail winds 28 mi. north from the town of Confluence to Connellsville. When this ingenious "rails to trails" project is complete, a bicycle trail will extend from Pittsburgh to Washington, DC.

Practical Information, Accommodations, and Food In order to do just about anything in the river you'll need a launch permit ($2.50). The **Park Information Center** (329-8591), just off Rte. 381 on Dinnerbell Rd., P.O. Box 105 (open daily 8am-4pm; Nov.-April Mon.-Fri. 8am-4pm) recommends calling at least 30 days in advance. You must also purchase a $2 token for the park's shuttle bus to return you to the launch area. Fishing licenses ($20) are required in the park and are available at Falls Market (see below). The 223 **campsites** in Ohiopyle also require advanced booking—especially for summer weekends (Pennsylvania residents $9, out-of-staters $11, $3 reservation fee.).

Motels around Ohiopyle are sparse but the excellent **Ohiopyle State Park Hostel (HI/AYH),** P.O. Box 99 (329-4476) sits right in the center of town off Rte. 381. Sue Moore has 24 bunks, a kitchen, a great yard, 4 cats, and 2 dogs, eieio. ($8, non-members $11. Check-in 6-9pm.) Just down the street, **Falls Market and Overnight Rooms** (329-4973), on Rte. 381 in the center of town, rents singles ($22) and doubles ($30) with shared baths. Washer, dryer, TV, and the classic arcade game "Frogger" available. The downstairs store has a decent selection of groceries and a snackbar/restaurant. Burgers $1.25, pancakes $2.25. (Open Mon.-Sat. 7am-9pm, Sun. 7am-6:30pm.)

Ohiopyle is on Rte. 381, 64 mi. southeast of Pittsburgh via Rte. 51 and U.S. 41. The closest public transport is to **Uniontown,** a large town 20 mi. to the west on U.S. 40. **Greyhound** serves Uniontown from Pittsburgh (3 per day, 1½ hr., $10). The **post office** (329-8650) is open Mon.-Fri. 7:30am-4:30pm, Sat. 7:30-11:30am. The **ZIP code** is 15470. The **area code** for the Ohiopyle area is 412.

Sights and Activities Ohiopyle's white water rafting is reputably the best in the East and draws throngs of tourists yearly. The rapids are 8 mi. long, class three, and take about five hours to conquer. Lined up in a row on Rte. 381 in "downtown" Ohiopyle are four outfitters: **White Water Adventurers** (P.O. Box 31, 329-8850 or 800-992-7238); **Wilderness Voyageurs** (P.O. Box 97, 329-5517 or 800-272-4141); **Laurel Highlands River Tours** (P.O. Box 107, 329-8531 or 800-472-3846); and **Mountain Streams and Trails** (P.O. Box 106, 329-8810 or 800-245-4090). Guided trips on the Yock vary dramatically in price ($20-70 per person per day), depending on season, day of week, and difficulty. If you're an experienced river rat (or if you just happen to *enjoy* flipping boats) any of the above companies will rent you equipment. (Rafts about $9 per person, canoes $15, "duckies"—inflatable kayaks—about $15.) Bike rentals vary with bike styles ($3 per hr. to $14 per day, max. 8 hrs.). **Youghiogheny Outfitters** (P.O. Box 21, 329-4549) may be a bit cheaper since they do rental business only.

Near Ohiopyle **Fort Necessity National Battlefield,** on U.S. 40 near Rte. 381 (329-5512), was built by founding father George Washington. Young George, then of the British army, was trounced in a sneak attack that left commanding officer General Braddock dead, and started the French and Indian War. The fort has been rebuilt and features a half-hour talk (8 per day) by historians dressed up as English and French soldiers as well as a musket-firing demonstration. Chop down the door of the **Visitors Information Center** (open daily 8:30am-5pm; Labor Day-Memorial Day 10:30am-5pm; admission $1, families $3). **Braddock's Grave** is 2 mi. northwest of the fort on U.S. 40.

Fallingwater (329-8501), 8 mi. north of Ohiopyle on Rte. 381, is the cantilevered masterpiece by the father of modern architecture, Frank Lloyd Wright. Designed in 1936 for the wealthy Kaufmann family, Fallingwater is perched over a waterfall. The stunning effect this yields has made this home "the most famous private residence ever built." (Open Tues.-Sun. 10am-4pm; Dec.-March weekends only. Admission Tues.-Fri $6, Sat.-Sun. $8.)

■■■ PHILADELPHIA

Philadelphia has the rare distinction of having a name before it was founded. From the start, founder William Penn, Jr. had noble aspirations for the city which was to be the keystone of his new colony. An avid classics scholar, Penn chose the name from the Greek word meaning "being kindly and affectionate to one another with brotherly love." As it grew, the city of "brotherly love" became one of the most important cities in American history. Both the **Declaration of Independence** and the **United States Constitution** were drafted in Philadelphia's Independence Hall, the former home of the Liberty Bell. Today, Philadelphia remains one of America's safest cities. Most of Philly's historic sights, as well as its very hip South Street, are within easy walking distance of each other and the brand new Bank Street Hostel.

PRACTICAL INFORMATION

Emergency: 911.

Visitors Center, 1525 John F. Kennedy Blvd. (636-1666), at 16th St. Pick up a free *Philadelphia Visitor's Guide* and the *Philadelphia Quarterly Calendar of Events.* Open Labor Day-Memorial Day daily 9am-6pm; off-season daily 9am-5pm. **Directory Events Hotline,** 377-7777, ext. 2540. **National Park Service Visitors Center,** 3rd and Chestnut (597-8974; 627-1776 for recording). Info on Independence Park, including maps, schedules, and the film *Independence.* Also distributes the *Visitor's Guide* and the *Quarterly Calendar of Events.* Open Sept.-June daily 9am-5pm; July-Aug. 9am-6pm. Film shown 9:30am-4pm. Tour assistance for non-English-speaking and disabled travelers.

Airport: Philadelphia International Airport, 8 mi. SW of Center City on I-76 (info line 937-1930, 24 hrs.). The 27-min. **SEPTA Airport Rail Line** runs from Center City to the airport. Trains leave daily 5:30am-11:52pm from 30th St. Station, Suburban Station, and Market East ($5.75). Last train from airport 12:10am. Cab fare downtown $21, but **Airport Limelight Limousine** (342-5557) will deliver you to a hotel ($8) or a specific address downtown.

Amtrak: 30th St. Station (349-2153 or 800-872-7245), at 30th and Market St., in University City. To: New York City (39 per day, 2 hr., $31), Washington, DC (36 per day, 2 hr., $35), Boston (8 per day, 8 hr., $68), Chicago (2 per day, 17 hr., $121), and points in PA. Office open Mon.-Fri. 5:10am-10:45pm, Sat.-Sun. 6:10am-10:45pm. Station open 24 hrs. Take the SEPTA commuter train to Trenton, NJ ($4-5), then hop on a New Jersey Transit train to NYC through Newark ($7.75).

Buses: Greyhound, 10th and Filbert St. (931-4014), 1 block north of Market near the 10th and Market St. subway/commuter rail stop in the heart of Philadelphia. To: New York City (18 per day, 2½ hr., $16), Washington, DC (9 per day, 3½ hr., Mon.-Thurs. $19, Fri.-Sun. $21), Atlantic City (17 per day, 1½ hr., $10). **New Jer-**

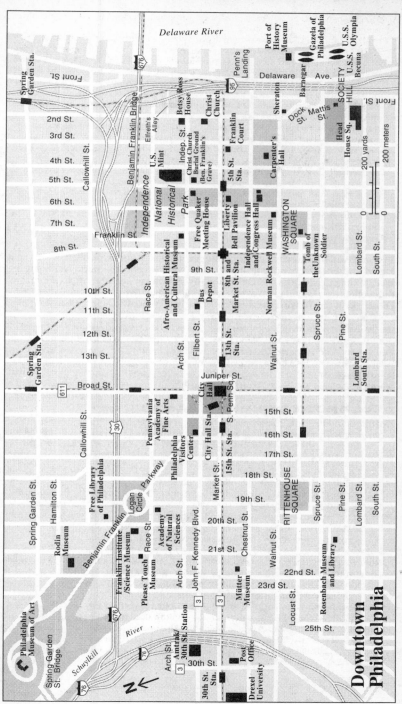

Downtown
Philadelphia

PHILADELPHIA

sey Transit, 800-582-5946. To: Atlantic City ($6), Ocean City ($12), and other points on the New Jersey Shore.

Public Transport: Southeastern Pennsylvania Transportation Authority (SEPTA), (580-7800). Most buses operate 6:30am-1am, some all night. Extensive bus and rail service to suburbs. Two major subway routes: the **Market St. line** running east-west (including 30th St. Station and the historic area) and the **Broad St. line** running north-south (including the stadium complex in south Philadelphia). Subway is unsafe after dark, but buses are usually okay. Buses serve the 5-county area. Subway connects with commuter rails—the Main Line Local runs through the western suburb of Paoli ($3.50), and SEPTA runs north as far as Trenton, NJ ($4-5). Pick up a SEPTA system map ($1.50), and a good street map at any subway stop. Fare $1.50, 2 tokens for $2.10, transfers 40¢.

Taxi: Yellow Cab, 922-8400. **United Cab,** 238-9500. $1.50 base plus $1.25 each additional mi.

Car Rental: Courtesy Rent-a-Car, (446-6200), near the hostel downtown. $17 per day, unlimited mileage. Must be 21 with $100 deposit or major credit card.

Help Lines: Gay Switchboard, 546-7100; **Suicide and Crisis Intervention,** 686-4420; **Youth Crisis Line,** 800-827-7571.

Post Office: 30th and Market St. (895-8000), across from the Amtrak station. Open 24 hrs. **ZIP code:** 19104.

Area Code: 215.

William Penn, Jr., a survivor of London's great fire in the 1660s, planned his city as a logical and easily accessible grid pattern of wide streets. The north-south streets ascend numerically from the **Delaware River,** flowing near **Penn's Landing** and **Independence Hall** on the east side, to the **Schuylkill River** (pronounced SKOOL-kill) on the west. The first street is **Front,** the others follow consecutively from 2 to 69. **Center City** runs from 8th Street to the Schuylkill River. From north to south, the primary streets are Race, Arch, JFK, Market, Chestnut, and South. The intersection of Broad (14th St.) and Market, location of City Hall, marks the focal point of Center City. The **Historic District** stretches from Front to 8th Street and from Vine to South Street. The **University of Pennsylvania** sprawls on the far side of the Schuylkill River, about 1 mi. west of Center City. **University City** includes the Penn/Drexel area west of the Schuylkill River.

ACCOMMODATIONS AND CAMPING

Downtown Philadelphia is saturated with luxury hotels, so anything inexpensive is popular. But if you make arrangements even a few days in advance, you should be able to find comfortable lodging close to Center City for under $40. **Bed and Breakfast Center City,** 1804 Pine St., Philadelphia 19103 (735-1137 or 800-354-8401) will find you a room in a private home; it's your best chance to stay in a real colonial building. No sign on the outside. (Singles $40-75, doubles $45-80. Check-in 3-7pm, make reservations a week ahead. Best to call 9am-9pm.) The **Philadelphia Naturist and Work Camp Center,** P.O. Box 4755, Philadelphia 19134 (634-7057), rents beds to foreign students ($5 with light breakfast) and will arrange free room and board on a nearby farm in exchange for daily chores. Camping is available to the north and west of the city, but you must travel at least 15 mi.

Bank Street Hostel, 32 S. Bank St. (922-0222 or 800-392-4678), is by far the best deal in town. Located in the historic district, it has A/C, TV, free coffee and tea, laundry facilities, kitchen, and a free pool table. Lockout 10am-4:30pm. Curfew Sun.-Thurs. midnight, Fri.-Sat. 1am. $14. Linen $2.

Chamounix Mansion International Youth Hostel (HI/AYH), West Fairmount Park (878-3676). Take bus #38 from JFK Blvd. to Ford and Cranston Rd., walk in the direction of the bus to Chamounix St., then turn left and follow the road to the hostel (about a 20-min. walk). Former country estate built in 1802. Clean and beautifully furnished, with 50 beds, showers, kitchen, and coin-operated laundry. Some basic groceries for sale. Extraordinarily friendly and helpful staff. Check-in

4:30pm-midnight. Lockout 11am-4:30pm. Curfew midnight. $10, nonmembers $13. Linen $2.

Old First Reformed Church (922-4566), 4th and Race St., in Center City 1 block from the Independence Mall and 4 blocks from Penn's Landing. Historic church that converts its social hall to a youth hostel sleeping 20. Mattresses on the floor, showers. 3-night max. stay. Check-in 5-10pm. Curfew 11pm. $10. Breakfast included. Open early July-late Aug.

The Divine Tracy Hotel, 20 S. 36th St. (382-4310), near Market St. in University City. Immaculately clean, quiet, and well-maintained rooms, though no bright Dick Tracy colors. Women must wear skirts and stockings at all times in the public areas of the hotel; men, long pants and socks with their shirts tucked in. Strictly single-sex floors. No smoking, vulgarity, obscenity, or blasphemy. Fans and TVs for rent. Check-in 7am-11pm. Singles $20, with private bath $23-26. Shared doubles $17-19 per person. The management does not permit alcohol or food (except small snacks) in the rooms, but the **Keyflower Dining Room** (386-2207) offers incredibly cheap and healthful, although bland, food. Entrees $2-4. Open to the public Mon.-Fri. 11:30am-2pm and 5-8pm.

The closest camping is across the Delaware River in New Jersey. Check out **Timberline Campground,** 117 Timber Lane, Clarksboro, NJ 08020 (609-423-6677), 15 mi. from Center City. Take 295 S. to exit 18A, Clarksboro, turn left and then right at the first stop sign, Cohawkin Rd. Go ½-mi. and turn right on Friendship Rd. Timber Lane is 1 block on the right. (Sites $16, with full hookup $18.) In Pennsylvania, try the **Baker Park Campground,** 400 East Pothoure Rd. (933-5865), 45 min. to 76 west to 23 through Valley Forge Park. (Sites $14, with electricity $16.)

FOOD

More than 500 new restaurants have opened their doors in Philadelphia in the past decade, making the city one of the most exciting dining spots in the U.S. Inexpensive food abounds on **Sansom St.** between 17th and 18th, on **South St.** between 2nd and 7th, and on **2nd St.** between Chestnut and Market. Numerous new places are opening up in **Penn's Landing,** on the Delaware River between **Locust** and **Market St.** Philadelphia's **Chinatown** is a short wok from downtown action, bounded by 8th, 11th, Vine, and Race St. In **University City,** the University of Pennsylvania (UPenn) and Drexel University collide on the west side of the Schuylkill River, making cheap student eateries easy to find. Try the famous **hoagie** and **cheesesteak,** two local specialties. You may grow attached to the renowned **Philly soft pretzel;** have one for about 50¢ at a street-side vendor.

To stock up on staples, visit the **Italian Market** at 9th and Christian St. (open daily dawn-dusk). The **Reading Terminal Market** (922-2317), at 12th and Arch St., is the place to go for picnic-packing, grocering, or a quick lunch. Since 1893, food stands have clustered together in this huge indoor market—selling fresh meats, produce, and delicious alternatives to fast-food courts. (Open Mon.-Sat. 8am-6pm.)

Historic District

Jim's Steaks, 400 South St. (928-1911). Take 4th St. trolley or bus #10 down Locust St. A Philadelphia institution since 1939, serving some of the best steak sandwiches in town ($3.80-4.25). Eat to beat Jim's current record holder—11 steaks in 90 minutes. Open Mon.-Thurs. 10am-1am, Fri.-Sat. 10am-3am, Sun. noon-10pm.

Dickens Inn (928-9307), Head House Sq., on 2nd St. between Pine and Lombard. Restaurant upstairs upscale but excellent food. British country cooking served at the bakery—try a cornish pastie ($5.50) or shepherd's pie ($5). Open Mon.-Tues. 8am-9pm, Wed.-Thurs. 8am-10pm, Fri. 8am-11pm, Sat. 8am-midnight, Sun. 11am-9pm. Pay slightly more at the bar, open daily 11:30am-1:30am.

Pizza at 4th and South Inc., 347 South St. (928-1942). Personal pizzas ($2.75-3.25) and strombolie ($3.25) hot and ready to go. Open daily 11am-3am.

Center City

Charlie's Waterwheel Restaurant, 1526 Sansom St. (563-4155), between 15th and 16th St., downstairs. First hoagie steak shop in Center City—their subs will sink you for days. Sandwiches and steaks with fresh fruit and vegetables ($5.75). Munch on free meatballs, pickles, and fried mushrooms at the counter while you wait. Open daily 11am-4pm.

Lee's Hoagie House, 1334 Walnut St. (735-8809), near 2nd St. Authentic hoagies ($3.75-6) since 1953. The 3-ft. hoagie challenges even ravenous appetites. Open Tues.-Thurs. 10am-11pm, Fri.-Sat. 10am-2am, Sun. 10am-10pm.

Seafood Unlimited, 270 S. 20th St. (732-3663), began as a fish store and evolved into a "you buy it and we'll cook it!" Now the cheapest seafood around, lunch or dinner ($5-10). Open Mon.-Thurs. 11am-9pm, Fri.-Sat. 11am-10pm.

Saladalley, 1720 Sansom St. (564-0767), between 17th and 18th. Huge salad bar featuring truly innovative combinations of fresh fruits, vegetables, and homemade muffins ($6). Try the pasta bows in walnut zucchini sauce ($8). Open Mon.-Fri. 11am-9pm, Sat. 11:30am-10pm.

University City

Smoky Joe's, 208-10 S. 40th St. (222-0770), between Locust and Walnut. Call it "smokes" like the college kids have for fifty years. Try Rosie's Homemade Chili ($4) or a 10-oz. burger ($4.25). Open daily 11am-2am; live music occasionally.

Tandoor India Restaurant, 106 S. 40th St. (222-7122). Northern Indian cuisine cooked in a clay oven. All-you-can-eat lunch buffet ($6), dinner buffet ($9). Open daily noon-3pm lunch; Mon.-Thurs. 4:30-10pm dinner.

Palladium, 3601 Locust Walk (387-3463), the on-campus eatery and watering hole, right across from the Wharton school. Enjoy a classy lunch or dinner ($7-12). Open Mon.-Sat. 11:30am-2:30pm and 5-9pm, bar open Mon.-Sat. till 1am.

SIGHTS

Independence Hall and The Historic District

The buildings of the **Independence National Historical Park** (open daily 9am-5pm; in summer 9am-9pm, all free) witnessed events that have since passed into U.S. history textbooks. The park **visitors center** (see Practical Information above) makes a good starting point. Site of the signing of the *Declaration of Independence* in 1776, and the drafting and signing of the Constitution in 1787, **Independence Hall** lies between 5th and 6th St. on Chestnut. Engraved with a half-sun, George Washington's chair at the head of the assembly room prompted Ben Franklin to remark after the ratification of the Constitution that "Now at length I have the happiness to know that it is a rising and not a setting sun." (Free guided tours daily every 15-20 min., arrive before 11am in summer to avoid an hr.-long line.) The U.S. Congress first assembled in nearby **Congress Hall** (free self-guided tour), while its predecessor, the First Continental Congress, convened in **Carpenters' Hall,** two blocks away at 4th and Chestnut St. (Open Tues.-Sun. 10am-4pm.) North of Independence Hall lies the **Liberty Bell Pavilion.** The cracked **Liberty Bell** itself, one of the most famous U.S. symbols, refuses to toll even when vigorously prodded.

The remainder of the park contains preserved residential and commercial buildings of the Revolutionary era. Ben Franklin's home lies in **Franklin Court** to the north, on Market between 3rd and 4th St., and includes an underground museum, a 20-minute movie and an architectural archeology exhibit. (Open daily 9am-5pm. Free.) At nearby **Washington Square,** a flame burns eternally commemorating the **Tomb of the Unknown Soldier.** Across from Independence Hall is Philadelphia's branch of the **U.S. Mint** (597-7350). A self-paced guided tour explains the mechanized coin-making procedure. No free samples here. (Open May-June Mon.-Sat. 9am-4:30pm; July-Aug. daily 9am-4:30pm; off-season Mon.-Fri. 9am-4:30pm. Free.)

Tucked away near 2nd and Arch St. is the quiet, residential **Elfreth's Alley,** allegedly "the oldest street in America," along which a penniless Ben Franklin walked when he arrived in town in 1723. On Arch near 3rd St. sits the tiny **Betsy Ross**

House (627-5343), where Ross supposedly sewed the first flag of the original 13 states. (Open Tues.-Sun. 10am-5pm, $1 donation requested.) **Christ Church,** on 2nd near Market, hosted the Quakers who sought a more fashionable way of life in colonial Philadelphia. Ben Franklin lies buried in the nearby **Christ Church ceme-tery** at 5th and Arch St. Also see the Quaker meeting houses: the original **Free Quaker Meeting House** at 5th and Arch St., and a new and larger one at 4th and Arch St.

Mikveh Israel, the first Jewish congregation of Philadelphia, has a burial ground on Spruce near 8th St. The **Afro-American Historical and Cultural Museum** (574-0380), 7th and Arch St., stands as the first U.S. museum devoted solely to the history of African-Americans. (Open Tues.-Sat. 10am-5pm, Sun. noon-6pm. Admission $3.50, seniors, handicapped, and children $1.75.)

Society Hill proper begins where the park ends, on Walnut St. between Front and 7th St. Now Philadelphia's most distinguished residential neighborhood, housing both old-timers and a new yuppie crowd, the area was originally a tract of land owned by the Free Society of Traders, a company formed to help William Penn, Jr. consolidate Pennsylvania. Federal-style townhouses dating back 300 years line picturesque cobblestone walks, illuminated by old-fashioned streetlights. **Head House Square,** 2nd and Pine St., held a marketplace in 1745 and now houses restaurants, boutiques, and craft shops. An outdoor flea market occurs here summer weekends.

Located on the Delaware River, **Penn's Landing** (923-8181) is the largest freshwater port in the world. Among other vessels it holds the *Gazela,* a three-masted, 178-ft. Portuguese square rigger built in 1883; the *U.S.S. Olympia,* Commodore Dewey's flagship during the Spanish-American War (922-1898; tours daily 10am-5pm; admission $5, children $2); and the *U.S.S. Becuna,* a WWII submarine (tours in conjunction with the *Olympia.*) The **Port of History,** Delaware Ave. and Walnut St. (925-3804), has frequently changing exhibits (open Wed.-Sun. 10am-4pm; admission $2, ages 5-12 $1). The Delaware Landing is a great spot to soak up sun on a nice day. For $1.50 you can jump on **Penn's Landing Trolley** (627-0807), Delaware Ave., between Catharine and Race St., which rolls along the waterfront giving guided tours (Thurs.-Sun. from 11am till dusk).

Center City

Center City, the area bounded by 12th, 23rd, Vine, and Pine St., whirls with activity. **City Hall** (686-1776), Broad and Market St., an ornate structure of granite and marble with 20-ft.-thick foundation walls, is the nation's largest municipal building. Until 1908, it also held the record for tallest building in the U.S., with the help of the 37-ft. statue of William Penn, Jr. on top. A municipal statute prohibited building higher than the top of Penn's hat until entrepreneurs in the mid-80s overturned it, finally launching Philadelphia into the skyscraper era. (Open Mon.-Fri. 7am-6pm. Free guided tours Mon.-Fri. at 12:30pm; meet in room 201.) The **Pennsylvania Academy of Fine Arts** (972-7600), Broad and Cherry St., the country's first art school and one of its first museums, has an extensive collection of U.S. and British art, including works by Charles Wilson Peale, Thomas Eakins, Winslow Homer, and some contemporary artists. (Open Tues.-Sat. 10am-5pm, Sun. 11am-5pm. Tours daily 12:30 and 2pm. $5, seniors $3, students $2, under 5 free. Free Sat. 10am-1pm.)

Just south of **Rittenhouse Square,** 2010 Delancey St., the **Rosenbach Museum and Library** (732-1600) houses rare manuscripts and paintings, including some of the earliest-known copies of Cervantes' *Don Quixote,* the original manuscript of James Joyce's *Ulysses,* and the original *Yankee Doodle Dandy.* (Open Sept.-July Tues.-Sun. 11am-4pm. Guided tours $3.50, seniors, students, and kids $2.50. Exhibitions only, $2.) The nearby **Mütter Museum** (563-3737) of Philadelphia's College of Physicians displays gory medical paraphernalia including a death cast of Siamese twins and a tumor removed from President Cleveland's jaw. (Open Tues.-Fri. 10am-4pm. $1 suggested donation.) Ben Franklin founded the **Library Company of Philadelphia,** 1314 Locust St. (546-3181), near 13th St., over 250 years ago, as a club whose members' dues paid for books from England. A weather-worn statue of Franklin stands outside its headquarters. (Open Mon.-Fri. 9am-4:45pm. Free.) Next door, the **Historical Society of Pennsylvania,** 1300 Locust St. (732-6201), has frequently changing exhibits and its own library (open Tues.-Sat. 10am-5pm; galleries $2.50, libraries $5, both $2 each for students). The **Norman Rockwell Museum** (922-4345), 6th and Sansom St., houses all of the artist's *Saturday Evening Post* cover works. (Open Mon.-Sat. 10am-4pm, Sun. 11am-4pm; $2, kids $1.50.)

Benjamin Franklin Parkway

Nicknamed "America's Champs-Elysées," the Benjamin Franklin Parkway is a wide, diagonal deviation from William Penn's original grid pattern of city streets. Built in the 1920s, this tree- and flag-lined street connects Center City with Fairmount Park and the Schuylkill River. Admire the elegant architecture of the twin buildings at Logan Square, 19th and Parkway, that house the **Free Library of Philadelphia** and the **Municipal Court.**

At 20th and Parkway, visit the **Franklin Institute** (448-1200), whose **Science Center** amazes visitors with four floors of gadgets and games depicting the intricacies of space, time, motion, and the human body. A 20-ft. **Benjamin Franklin National Memorial** statue divines lightening at the entrance. In 1990, to commemorate the 200th anniversary of Franklin's death, the Institute unveiled the **Futures Center;** glimpses of life in the 21st century including simulated zero gravity and a timely set of exhibits on the changing global environment. (Futures Center open Mon.-Wed. 9:30am-5pm, Thurs.-Sun. 9:30am-9pm. Science Center daily 9am-5pm. Admission to both $9.50, seniors and kids $8.50.) The **Omniverse Theater** provides 180° and 4½ stories of optical ooohs and aaahs. (shows daily on the hr., Mon.-Fri. 10am-4pm, Sat.-Sun. 10am-5pm; also Thurs. 7-8pm, Fri. and Sat. 7-9pm. $7, seniors and kids $6.) **Fels Planetarium** boasts an advanced computer-driven system that projects a simulation of life billions of years beyond. (Shows daily at 12:15 and 2:15pm, Sat. and Sun. also at 4:15pm. $7, seniors and kids $6.) See all the sights for $14 (seniors and kids $12) or check out any two for $12 (seniors and kids $10.50).

A ubiquitous casting of the *Gates of Hell* outside the **Rodin Museum** (684-7788), 22nd St., guards the portal of the most complete collection of the artist's works outside of Paris, including one of the gazillion versions of *The Thinker* (Open Tues.-Sun. 10am-5pm; donation). Try your hand at the sensual **Please Touch Museum,** 210 N. 21st St. (963-0666), designed specifically for grabby kids under eight (open daily 9am-4:30pm; $6).

The exhibit of precious gems and the 65-million-year-old dinosaur skeleton at the **Academy of Natural Sciences** (299-1000), 19th and Parkway, excite even the basest of human desires (open Mon.-Fri. 10am-4:30pm, Sat.-Sun. and holidays 10am-5pm; admission $6, kids $5). Further down 26th St., the **Philadelphia Museum of Art** (763-8100) protects one of the world's major art collections, including Rubens's *Prometheus Bound,* Picasso's *Three Musicians,* and Duchamp's *Nude Descending a Staircase,* as well as extensive Asian, Egyptian, and decorative arts collections. (Open Tues.-Sun. 10am-5pm. $6, seniors and students under 18 $3. Free Sun. 10am-1pm.) The **Free Library of Philadelphia** (686-5322) has a tremendous library of orchestral music, and one of the nation's largest rare book collections (open Mon.-Wed. 9am-9pm, Thurs.-Fri. 9am-6pm, Sat. 9am-5pm, Sun. 1-5pm).

Fairmount Park sprawls behind the Philadelphia Museum of Art on both sides of the Schuylkill River. Bike trails and picnic areas abound, and the famous **Philadelphia Zoo** (243-1100) at 34th St. and Girard Ave., the oldest in the U.S., houses 1500 species in one corner of the park (open daily 9:30am-5pm; admission $7, seniors and kids $5). **Boathouse Row,** which houses the shells of local crew teams, is particularly beautiful at night. During the day, hikers and non-hikers alike may wish to venture out to the northernmost arm of Fairmount Park, where trails leave the Schuylkill River and wind along secluded Wissahickon Creek for five mi. The **Horti-**

cultural **Center** (879-4062), off Belmont Ave. (open daily 9am-3pm) blooms with greenhouses, Japanese gardens and periodic flower shows ($2 suggested donation).

West Philadelphia (University City)

West Philly is home to both the **University of Pennsylvania** and **Drexel University,** located across the Schuylkill from Center City, within easy walking distance of the 30th St. Station. Benjamin Franklin founded UPenn in 1740. Fifteen years later the country's first medical school came to life, and students have been pulling all-nighters ever since. The Penn campus provides a cloistered retreat of green lawns, red-brick quadrangles, and rarefied air. Ritzy shops line Chestnut St. and boisterous fraternities line Spruce; warm weather brings out a variety of street vendors along the Drexel and Penn borders.

Penn's **University Museum of Archeology and Anthropology** (898-4000), 33rd and Spruce St., houses one of the finest archeological collections in the world. (Open Tues.-Sat. 10am-4:30pm, Sun. 1-5pm. Admission $5, seniors and students $2.50.) In 1965, Andy Warhol had his first one-man show at the **Institute of Contemporary Art** (898-7108), 34th and Walnut St. Today, the gallery remains cutting edge. (Open Thurs.-Sun. 10am-5pm, Wed. 10am-7pm. Admission $3, seniors and students $2. Free Sun. 10am-noon.)

ENTERTAINMENT

Check Friday's weekend magazine section in the Philadelphia *Inquirer* for entertainment listings. *City Paper,* distributed on Fridays for free at newsstands and markets, has weekly listings of city events. *Au Courant,* a gay and lesbian weekly newspaper, lists and advertises events throughout the Delaware Valley region. The bar scene enlivens University City with a younger crowd. Along South Street, there is a wide variety of live music on weekends. Stop by **Dobbs,** 304 South St. (928-1943), between 3rd and 4th, a mixed-menu restaurant (entrees $6-8.50) with live rock nightly. (Open daily 6pm-2am.) Nearby **Penn's Landing** (923-8181) has free concerts in summer. Formerly under the direction of the late Eugene Ormandy, and now under Ricardo Muti, the **Philadelphia Academy of Music** (893-1930), Broad and Locust St., houses the **Philadelphia Orchestra,** rated by many as the best in the U.S. The academy was modeled after Milan's *La Scala.* The season runs Sept.-May. General admission tickets ($2) go on sale at the Locust St. entrance 45 minutes before Friday and Saturday concerts. Check with the box office for availability. The **Mann Music Center,** George's Hill (878-7707), near 52nd St. and Parkside Ave. in Fairmount Park, has 5000 seats under cover, 10,000 on outdoor benches and lawns—and hosts summer Philadelphia Orchestra, ballet, jazz, and rock events. Pick up free lawn tickets June-Aug. on the day of performance from the visitors center at 16th St. and JFK Blvd. (See Practical Information above.) For the big-name shows, sit just outside the theater and soak in the sounds gratis. The **Robin Hood Dell East,** Strawberry Mansion Dr. (686-1776 or 477-8810 in summer), in Fairmount Park, brings in top names in pop, jazz, gospel, and ethnic dance in July and August. The Philadelphia Orchestra holds several free performances here in summer, and as many as 30,000 people gather on the lawn. Inquire at the visitors center (636-1666) about upcoming events. **Merriam Theater,** 250 S. Broad St., Center City (732-5446), stages a variety of dance, musical, and comedy performances year-round.

Philly has four professional sports franchises. The Phillies (baseball; 463-1000) and Eagles (football; 463-5500) play at **Veterans Stadium,** while the **Spectrum** houses the 76ers (basketball; 339-7676) and the Flyers (hockey; 755-9700). Baseball and hockey general admission tickets run $5-20 while football and basketball tickets go for more, $15-50.

■ Near Philadelphia: Valley Forge

Neither rockets red glare nor bombs bursting in air took place here, but during the winter of 1777-78, the 12,000 men under General George Washington spent agonizing months fighting starvation, bitter cold, and disease. Only 8000 survived. Nonetheless, inspired by Washington's fierce spirit and the news of a American alliance with France, the troops left Valley Forge stronger and better trained, going on to victories in New Jersey and eventually reoccupying Philadelphia.

The park today encompasses over 3600 acres. (Open daily 9am-5pm.) Self-guided tours begin at the **visitors center** (783-1077), which also has a museum and film (twice per hr. 9am-4:30pm, 15 min.). (Center open daily 9am-5pm.) The tour features Washington's headquarters, reconstructed soldier huts and fortifications, and the Grand Parade Ground where the army drilled. Admission to the park costs $2, and includes all historic sights and buildings. Audio tapes can be rented for $7. The park has three picnic areas; although there is no camping within the park, campgrounds thrive nearby. A 5-mi. bike trail winds up and down the hills of the park.

To get to Valley Forge, take the Schuylkill Expressway westbound from Philadelphia for about 12 mi. Get off at the Valley Forge exit, then take Rte. 202 S. for one mi. and Rte. 422 W. for 1½ mi. to another Valley Forge exit. SEPTA runs buses to the visitors center Monday through Friday only. Catch #125 at 16th and JFK ($3.10).

■■■ PITTSBURGH

Charles Dickens called this city "Hell with the lid off" for a reason. As late as the 1950s, smoke from area steel mills made street lamps essential even during the day. However, the decline of the steel industry means clean air and sparkling rivers. A similar renaissance has occurred in Pittsburgh's economy. Private-public partnerships have produced some shiny urban architecture, like Phillip Johnson's Pittsburgh Plate Glass Building, a gothic black-glass cathedral. Admittedly, some of the character of old, sooty Pittsburgh has retreated to the suburbs. Most of the city's small neighborhoods have maintained strong identities however, constants in a city of monumental change. One need but view downtown from atop Mount Washington, accessible via the Duquene Incline, to see how thoroughly Pittsburgh has entered a new age.

PRACTICAL INFORMATION

Visitor Information: Pittsburgh Convention and Visitors Bureau, 4 Gateway Ctr. (281-7711), downtown in a little glass building on Liberty Ave., across from the Hilton. Their city maps won't get you past downtown. Open Mon.-Fri. 9:30am-5pm, Sat.-Sun. 9:30am-3pm; Nov.-April Mon.-Fri. 9:30am-5pm, Sat. 9:30am-3pm.

Travelers Aid: two locations: **Greyhound Bus Terminal** (281-5474), 11th St. and Liberty Ave., and the **airport** (472-3599). Good maps, advice, and help for stranded travelers. Open Mon.-Fri. 8am-10pm, Sat. 9am-5pm, Sun. 9am-9pm.

Airport: Pittsburgh International Airport, (472-3525), 15 mi. west of downtown by I-279 and Rte. 60 in Findlay Township. Serves most major airlines. **Airline Transportation Company** (471-2250) serves downtown (daily, every 30 min., 6am-1pm; every 20 min., 1-7pm; every hr., 7-10pm, $17 round-trip), Oakland (Mon.-Fri., every hr., 9am-9pm; every 2 hr. Sat.-Sun., $18 round-trip), and Monroeville (daily, every 2 hr., 6am-2pm, every hr., 2pm-7pm, $15 round-trip).

Amtrak: Liberty and Grant Ave. (800-872-7245 for reservations; 471-6170 for station info), on the northern edge of downtown next to Greyhound and the post office. Safe and very clean inside, but be cautious about walking from here to the city center at night. Open 24 hrs. Ticket office open daily 8:30am-5:15pm and 11pm-4am. To: Philadelphia (2 per day, 7½ hr., $64); New York (2 per day, 9 hr., $88); Chicago (2 per day, 9 hr., $81).

Greyhound: (391-2300), 11th St. and Liberty Ave. near Amtrak. Large and fairly clean with police on duty. Station and ticket office open 24 hrs. To: Philadelphia (9 per day, 7 hr., $44); New York (11 per day, 9-11 hr., $67); Chicago (11 per day, 9-14 hr., $59).

Public Transport: Port Authority of Allegheny County (PAT): General office 237-7000; bus info 442-2000. Bus rides free within the Golden Triangle until 7pm, 75¢ after 7pm. For the rest of the city and inner suburbs, $1.25; weekend daily pass $3. The **subway's** 3 downtown stops are free. Taking the subway beyond the confines of the Triangle $1.60-1.95. Schedules and maps at most department stores and in the Community Interest section of the yellow pages.
Taxi: Yellow Cab, 665-8100.
Car Rental: Rent-A-Wreck, 1200 Liberty Ave. (488-3440), one block up from Liberty tunnels. $28 per day; 50 free mi., 18¢ each additional mi. Must be 21 with major credit card or $150 cash deposit. Open daily 8am-6pm.
Help Lines: General Help Line, 255-1155. **Rape Action Hotline,** 765-2731. **Persad Center, Inc.,** a counseling service for the gay community. 441-0857, emergencies 392-2472. All three open 24 hrs. **Pittsburgh Office for International Visitors,** 624-7800. Open Mon. Fri. 9am-5pm, Sat. 9am-1pm. Aid for non-English speakers.
Post Office: 7th and Grant St. (642-4472; general delivery 642-4478). Open Mon.-Fri. 7am-6pm, Sat. 7am-2:30pm. **ZIP code:** 15219.
Area Code: 412.

The downtown area is the **Golden Triangle** formed by two rivers—the Allegheny on the north and the Monongahela to the south—flowing together to form a third, the Ohio. Parallel to the Monongahela, streets in the downtown triangle number 1 through 7. The **Hill District** just northeast of downtown has the reputation of being rather rough. **Oakland,** east of the Triangle, is home to the University of Pittsburgh and Carnegie-Mellon University.

ACCOMMODATIONS AND CAMPING

Reasonable accommodations aren't very easy to find in Pittsburgh, but downtown is fairly safe, even at night; Pittsburgh has one of the lowest crime rates for a city of its size in the country.

Point Park College, 201 Wood St. (392-3824), eight blocks from the Greyhound Station, corner of Blvd. of the Allies and Wood St. Closer to a hotel than a hostel; clean rooms, some with private baths. Office hours 8am-4pm. Check-in until 11pm (tell the guards you're a hosteler). 3-day max. stay; members only, $7.50. No kitchen but all-you-can-eat breakfast ($2.50) served in the third-floor cafeteria 7-9:30am. Reservations recommended. Open May 15-Aug. 15.
Red Roof Inn, 6404 Stubenville Pike (787-7870), south on I-279, past Rte. 22-Rte. 30 junction, at the Moon Run exit. From the Greyhound station, take bus #26F. Clean and quiet. Check in before 6pm or call before 6pm with a major credit card number. Check out by noon. (Singles $40, doubles $45.) Call more than a week in advance in the summer.
Pittsburgh North Campground, 6610 Mars Rd., Evans City 16033 (776-1150). The nearest camping—still 20 mi. from downtown. Take I-79 to the Mars exit. Facilities include tents and swimming. (Sites $17 for 2 people, $3 per extra adult, $2 per extra kid. Hookup $3.50.)

FOOD

Aside from the pizza joint/bars downtown, **Oakland** is your best bet for a good inexpensive meal. **Forbes Ave.,** around the University of Pittsburgh, is packed with collegiate watering holes and cafes. Walnut St. in Shadyside and East Carson St. on the Southside are also lined with colorful eateries and shops. The **Strip District** on Penn Ave. between 16th and 22nd Street (north of downtown along the Allegheny) bustles with Italian, Greek, and Asian cuisine, vendors, grocers and craftsmen. Saturday mornings are busiest as fresh produce, fresh fish, and street performers vie for attention.

Original Hot Dog Shops, Inc., 3901 Forbes Ave., at Bouquet St. in Oakland. A rowdy (actually, very rowdy), greasy Pittsburgh institution with lots and lots of fries, burgers, dogs and pizza. Call it "the O" like a local. 16" pizza $3.49 Open Sun.-Thurs. 9am-4:30pm, Fri.-Sat. 9am-6am.

Hot Licks, 5520 Walnut St. (683-2583), in the Theater Mall. Take bus #71B or D down 5th Ave., get off at Aiken, and walk north 2 blocks to Walnut. Ribs and chicken are mesquite-grilled here. Sandwiches $5.75-6.50. Open Mon.-Thurs. 11:30am-11pm, Fri.-Sat. 11:30am-midnight, Sun. 3-9pm.

The Elbow Room, 5744 Ellsworth Ave. (441-5222). Relaxed clientele take advantage of the garden seating, free refills, and crayolas for the tablecloths. Spicy chicken sandwiches ($6) and combination southwest/front parlor decoration worth the trip. Open daily 11am-1am.

Harris' Grill-A Cafe is across the street at 5747 Ellsworth Ave. (363-0833). Inexpensive Greek specialties ($3-$9) on an outdoor deck. Open daily 11:30am-2am.

Pittsburgh is also home to several chain restaurants which are rapidly catching on. **Arabica Caffe,** 1501 East Carson and two other locations, is an oak-paneled, brass-trimmed coffee house with ambiance to spare. Small coffee 80¢, cappuccino $1.60. **Brown Bag Deli,** 411 Wood St. and nine other locations, was named best quick lunch by *In Pittsburgh* magazine. Many weekly specials.

SIGHTS

The **Golden Triangle,** formed by the Allegheny and Monongahela rivers, is home to **Point State Park** and its famous 200-ft. fountain. A ride on the **Duquene Incline,** 1220 Grandview Ave. on the Southside (381-1665), affords a spectacular view of the city. Fare $2, children 6-11 $1, under 6 free. The **Fort Pitt Blockhouse and Museum** (281-9285) in the park dates back to the French and Indian War. (Open Tues.-Sat. 10am-4:30pm, Sun. noon-4:30pm. Admission $4, seniors $3, kids $2.) The **Phipps Conservatory** (622-6915) conserves 2½ acres of happiness for the flower fanatic, about 3 mi. east along the Blvd. of the Allies in Schenley Park. (Open daily 9am-5pm. Admission $3, seniors and kids $1, $1 more for shows. Reserve tours at 622-6958.) Founded in 1787, the **University of Pittsburgh** (624-4141; for tours call 624-7488) now stands in the shadow of the 42-story **Cathedral of Learning** (624-6000) at Bigelow Blvd. between Forbes and 5th Ave. The "cathedral," an academic building dedicated in 1934, features 23 "nationality classrooms" designed and decorated by artisans from each of Pittsburgh's ethnic traditions. **Carnegie-Mellon University** (268-2000) hyphenates right down the street.

Other city sights lie across the three rivers from the Golden Triangle. Northward, across the Allegheny, steal a look at **Three Rivers Stadium,** where the Steelers and Pirates play ball. To the west of Allegheny Sq. soars the tropical **Pittsburgh Aviary** (323-7234; open daily 9am-4:30pm; admission $3, seniors and kids under 12 $1; take bus #16D or the Ft. Duquesne bridge).

Two of America's greatest financial legends, Andrew Carnegie and Henry Clay Frick, made their fortunes in Pittsburgh. Their bequests to the city have enriched its cultural scene. The most spectacular of Carnegie's gifts are the art and natural history museums, together called **The Carnegie,** 4400 Forbes Ave. (622-3328; 622-3289 for guided tours), across the street from the Cathedral of Learning. The natural history section is famous for its 500 dinosaur specimens, including an 84-ft. giant named for the philanthropist himself—**Diplodocus Carnegii.** The modern wing hosts a strong collection of Impressionist, Post-Impressionist, and 20th-century works. (Open Tues.-Sat. 10am-5pm, Sun. 1-5pm. Take any bus to Oakland and get off at the Cathedral of Learning.)

While most know Henry Clay Frick for his art collection in New York, the **Frick Art Museum,** 7227 Reynolds St., Point Breeze (371-0600), displays some of his early, less famous acquisitions. The permanent collection contains Italian, Flemish, and French works from the 13th-18th centuries. Chamber music concerts monthly, Oct.-April.

ENTERTAINMENT

Pittsburgh's metamorphosis from industrial to corporate town has erased Carnegie's occupation—steel baron—and strengthened his avocation—juicy grants for the arts. Most restaurants and shops carry the weekly *In Pittsburgh*, a great source for free up-to-date entertainment listings and racy personals. The internationally-acclaimed **Pittsburgh Symphony Orchestra** performs October through May at **Heinz Hall**, 600 Penn Ave. downtown, and gives free summer evening concerts outdoors at Point State Park (392-4835 for tickets and information). The **Pittsburgh Public Theater** (323-8200) is widely renowned, and tickets cost a pretty penny ($12 and up). Visitors with thin wallets should check out the **Three Rivers Shakespeare Festival** (624-0933), at University of Pittsburgh's Steven Foster Memorial Theater, near Forbes Ave. and Bigelow Blvd. downtown. The troupe, consisting of students and professionals, performs from late May to mid-August. Seniors and students can line up a half hour before show time for half-price tickets. Box office (624-7529) open 10am-show time and Monday 10am-4pm. (Tickets Tues.-Thurs. $15, Fri.-Sat. $18.) All-student casts perform with the **Young Company** at City Theater (tickets $9).

 # Washington, D.C.

Washington, D.C.'s strange experiment—an infant nation building a capital city from scratch—has matured into one of America's most influential, most interesting, and most visited cities. Monuments, museums, and politicos draw visitors from around the world for a gander at lunar landers and a glimpse of the president.

After winning independence from Great Britain in 1783, the United States was faced with the challenge of finding a home for its fledgling government. Both Northern and Southern states wanted the capital on their turf. The final location—100 sq. mi. pinched between Virginia and Maryland—was a compromise resulting in what President Kennedy later termed "a city of Northern charm and Southern efficiency."

Nineteenth-century Washington was a "city of magnificent distances"—a smattering of slave markets, elegant government buildings, and boarding houses along the absurdly large-scale avenues designed by French engineer Pierre L'Enfant. The city had the awkward feel of a child wearing clothes far too large for its age in the expectation that they would someday fit. As the capital grew, so did its problems—a port city squeezed between two plantation states, the district made a logical first stop for slave traders, whose shackled cargo awaited sale in crowded pens on the Mall and near the White House. Foreign diplomats were disgusted, deeming DC to be unequivocally "Southern." The War Between the States altered this forever, changing Washington from the Union's embarrassing appendix to its jugular vein.

The city grew slowly until the Great Depression, when Franklin Delano Roosevelt founded his alphabet soup of federal agencies staffed by liberal out-of-towners; by the end of World War II, D.C. had become the cynosure of the free world and a genuine metropolis to boot. During the 1960s Washington was the nation's "March Central," hosting a concatenation of demonstrations advocating civil rights and condemning America's role in Vietnam. The 1963 March on Washington brought 250,000 people of all colors to the Mall to hear Martin Luther King, Jr.'s "I Have a Dream" speech. In 1968, an anti-war gathering ringed the Pentagon with chants and shouts. In the same year, riots touched off by King's assassination torched parts of the city; some blocks still await rebuilding.

Though government institutions are its economic and geographic mainstay, Washington isn't just a government town—tourists who merely breeze through the Mall and the monuments have hardly begun to see the city. The arts thrive in

Dupont Circle, while youngsters spar for turf and great budget meals in Adams-Morgan. The Kennedy Center bows and pirouettes with high culture almost every night, while indigenous music scenes pump out high-quality, honest tunes. Of course, there are neighborhoods a tourist would rather not stumble upon: some parts of D.C. justify the media stereotype of Washington's low-income areas—poor tenements devastated by crack, guns, and institutional neglect. Still, you'll be rewarded for venturing beyond the conventional grade-school-tour-group attractions; Washington is a city that has matured gracefully and wears its leadership well.

For the ultimate in Washington, D.C. budget coverage, see *Let's Go: Washington, D.C.,* available from discerning booksellers everywhere.

PRACTICAL INFORMATION

Emergency: 911

Visitor Information: Visitor Information Center, 1455 Pennsylvania Ave. NW (789-7038), is a very helpful first stop. Ask for the *Washington Visitor Map,* which shows Metro stops near points of interest, and *Washington's Attractions.* Language-bank service in over 20 tongues. Open Mon.-Sat. 9am-5pm. **International Visitors Information Service (IVIS),** 1630 Crescent Pl. NW (667-6800). Info in over 50 languages (6am-11pm). Office open Mon.-Fri. 9am-5pm.

Traveler's Aid: 512 C St. NE (546-3120). Helpful in emergencies. Open Mon.-Fri. 9am-5pm. Other desks at Union Station (546-3120; open Mon.-Fri. 9:30am-5:30pm, Sat.-Sun. 12:30-5:30pm), National Airport (684-3472; open Sun.-Fri. 9am-9pm, Sat. 9am-6pm), and Dulles International Airport (703-661-8636; open Mon.-Fri. 10am-9pm, Sat.-Sun. 10am-6pm). **24-hr. emergency aid** 546-3120.

Embassies: Australia, 1601 Massachusetts Ave. NW (797-3000); **Canada,** 501 Pennsylvania Ave. NW (682-1740); **Ireland,** 2234 Massachusetts Ave. NW (462-3939); **Latvia,** 4325 17th St. NW (726-8213); **New Zealand,** 37 Observatory Circle NW (328-4800); **Great Britain,** 3100 Massachusetts Ave. NW (462-1340).

Airport: National Airport (703-685-8000). It's best to fly here from within the U.S., since National is on the Metro and close to Washington by car. Metro: National Airport; the terminals are a short walk or shuttle ride away. Cabs run $10-15 from downtown. **Dulles International Airport** (703-661-2700) is Washington's international airport and much further away, though some domestic flights also land here. Taxis to Dulles cost over $40. There's no Metro near the airport, but the **Dulles Express Bus** (703-685-1400) runs from the West Falls Church Metro every 20-30 min. ($8 one-way). Mon.-Fri. 6am-10:30pm, Sat-Sun. 8am-10:30pm; last bus from Metro 11pm. The **Washington Flyer Express,** (703-685-1400) shuttles between National, Dulles, and their station at 1517 K St. NW. Buses run roughly every ½-hr. 6am-10:30pm Mon.-Fri., every hr. 6am-1pm Sat.-Sun. National one-way $8, round-trip $14; Dulles one-way $16, round-trip $26.

Trains: Amtrak, Union Station, 50 Massachusetts Ave. NE (484-7540 or 800-872-8720; 800-523-8720 for Metroliner). Frequent daily service to: New York City (Metroliner: 3hr., $93; regular: 3½hr., $68); Baltimore (Metroliner: 30min., $17; regular: 40min., $12); Philadelphia (Metroliner: 1½hr., $53; regular: 2hr., $35); Boston (8hr., $101). Less frequent service to: Richmond ($21); Williamsburg ($29); Virginia Beach ($42). **MARC** (800-325-7245), Maryland's commuter rail, also leaves Union Station for Baltimore ($5), Harpers Ferry, and Martinsburg, WV.

Greyhound: 1005 1st St. NE (800-231-2222) at L St. The modern station rises over a rather decrepit neighborhood. Buses to: Philadelphia ($21); New York City ($25); Baltimore ($8.50).

Public Transportation: Metrorail, main office, 600 5th St. NW, (637-7000; open daily 6am-11:30pm). Clean, quiet, carpeted trains with A/C; the system is nearly crime-free. Computerized fare card must be bought from machines. If you plan to use the Metro several times, buy a $10 or more farecard; you will get a 5% bonus. Trains run daily 6:30am-11:30pm. Fare $1-2, depending on distance traveled; during peak-hour $1.05-$3.15. **Flash Pass** allows unlimited bus (and sometimes Metro) rides for 2-weeks ($20-34, depending on the zone it's good for). 1-day

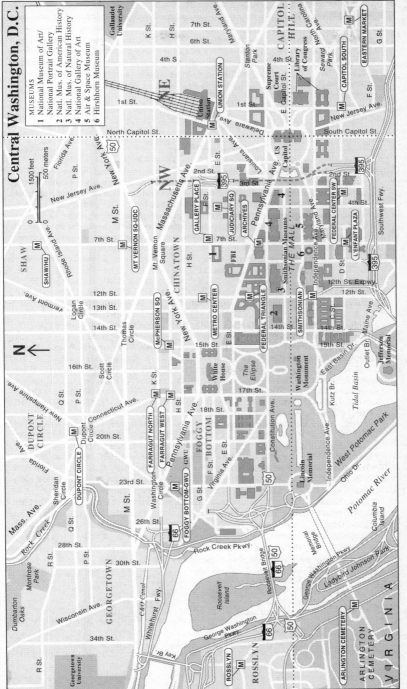

Central Washington, D.C.

MUSEUMS
1 National Museum of Art/
  National Portrait Gallery
2 Natl. Mus. of American History
3 Natl. Mus. of Natural History
4 National Gallery of Art
5 Air & Space Museum
6 Hirshhorn Museum

Metro pass $5. To make a bus transfer, get a pass from machines on the platform *before* boarding the train. The extensive **Metrobus** (same address, phone, and hours as Metrorail) system reliably serves Georgetown, downtown, and the suburbs. Fare $1. A comprehensive bus map is available from the main Metro office.

Taxi: Yellow Cab (544-1212). Fares are not based on a meter but on a map which splits the city into five zones and 27 subzones. Zone prices are fixed; ask how much the fare will be at the beginning of your trip. Max. fare within D.C. $10.20.

Car Rental: Easi Car Rentals, 2480 S. Glebe Rd. (703-521-0188), in Arlington. From $20 per day, 10¢ per mi. Weekly rates from $125, with 300 free mi. Must be 21 or older with major credit card or $300 cash deposit. Reservations advised. Open Mon.-Fri. 9am-7pm, Sat. 9am-2pm. **Bargain Buggies Rent-a-Car,** 6461 Gasall Rd. (703-522-4141), in Alexandria. $20 per day or 10¢ per mi.; $110 per week (local rental) with 200 free mi. Must be 18 or older with major credit card or cash deposit of $300. Those under 21 need full insurance coverage of their own. Open Mon.-Fri. 8am-7pm, Sat.-Sun. 8am-5pm.

Bike Rental: Thompson Boat Center, 2900 Virginia Ave. NW (333-4861), between Rock Creek Pkwy. and Virginia Ave. near Watergate. 18-speed mountain bikes $6 per hr. or $22 per day, locks strongly recommended at 50¢ a day. Thompson also rents tandems and single-speeders. Open Mon.-Fri. 7am-6pm, Sat.-Sun. 8am-5pm. **Big Wheel Bikes,** 315 7th St. SE (543-1600). Regular bikes as low as $5 per hr., $25 per business day; 3-hr. min. charge. For an extra $5, you can keep the bike overnight. Major credit card, driver's license, or $150 cash deposit per bike rental. Open Tues.-Fri. 11am-7pm, Sat. 10am-6pm.

Helplines: Gay and Lesbian Hotline: 833-3234. 7am-11pm. **Rape Crisis Center:** 333-7273. **Disabled Persons Services:** 703-841-2531.

Post Office: General delivery indescribably inconvenient at 900 Brentwood Rd. NE (682-9595). Open Mon.-Fri. 8am-8pm, Sat. 10am-6pm. **ZIP code:** 20066. **Area Code:** 202

D.C. is ringed by the **Capital Beltway,** or I-495 (except where it's part of I-95); the Beltway is bisected by **U.S. 1,** which incorporates several local thoroughfares, and is intruded upon via Virginia by **I-395. I-95** shoots up from Florida, links Richmond, VA, to Washington and Baltimore, then rockets up the East Coast past Boston. The high-speed **Baltimore-Washington Parkway** also connects D.C. to Baltimore. **I-595** trickles off the Capital Beltway and scenically east and south to Annapolis. **I-66** heads west through Virginia.

ORIENTATION

Pierre L'Enfant's street design operates with a simple and understandable logic (at least in the downtown). The city is roughly diamond-shaped, with the four tips of the diamond pointed at the four compass directions, and the street names and addresses split up into four quadrants: NW, NE, SE, and SW, as defined by their relation to the U.S. Capitol. The names of the four quadrants distinguish otherwise identical addresses. Pay attention to it; those two little letters can make a lot of difference. The basic plan is a rectilinear grid. Streets running from east to west are named in alphabetical order running north and south from the Capitol, from two A Streets two blocks apart (nearest the Capitol) out to two W Streets dozens of blocks apart. After W St., east-west streets take on two-syllable names, then three-syllable names, then (at the north end of NW) names of trees and flowers in alphabetical order. Streets running north-south get numbers (1st St., 2nd St., etc.). Numbered and lettered streets sometimes disappear for a block, then keep going as if nothing happened. Addresses on lettered streets indicate the numbered cross street (1100 D St. SE will be between 11th and 12th St.). L'Enfant's plan also included a sheaf of state avenues radiating outward from the U.S. Capitol or the White House or otherwise crossing downtown. The U.S. added space as the city added streets, which thus acquired avenues named for all 50 states.

Some **major roads** are **Pennsylvania Ave.,** which runs SE-NE from Anacostia to Capitol Hill to the Capitol, through downtown, past the White House, and ends finally at 28th and M St. NW in Georgetown; **Connecticut Ave.,** which runs north-northwest from the White House through Dupont Circle and past the Zoo; **Wisconsin Ave.,** north from Georgetown past the Cathedral to Friendship Heights; **16th St. NW,** which zooms from the White House north through offices, townhouses, Adams-Morgan, and Mt. Pleasant; **K St. NW,** a major artery downtown; **Constitution and Independence Ave.,** just north and south of the Mall; **Massachusetts Ave.,** from American University past the Cathedral, then through Dupont and the old downtown to Capitol Hill; **New York Ave.,** whose principal arm runs from the White House through NE; and **North Capitol St.**

D.C. isn't just for cigar-smoking congressmen. Over 600,000 residents inhabit the federal city; rich and poor and black, white, Asian and Latino are all well-repre-sented. Escape the Mall to get a true feel for the city. **Capitol Hill** extends east from the Capitol; its townhouses and bars mix white- and blue-collar locals with legisla-tion-minded pols. The **Southwest** quadrant of the city, south of the Mall, begins as federal offices, then passes under I-395 and becomes a low-income neighborhood (to the east) and the waterfront area (to the west). North of the Mall, the **Old Downtown** goes about its business accompanied by **Foggy Bottom** (sometimes called the "West End") on the other side of the White House and the **New Downtown** around K St. west of 15th St. NW. **Georgetown** draws crowds and sucks away bucks nightly from its center at Wisconsin and M St. NW. Business and plea-sure, embassies and streetlife, straight and gay converge around **Dupont Circle;** east of 16th St. the Dupont Circle character changes to struggling **Logan Circle,** then to rundown **Shaw,** and then to Howard University and **LeDroit Park,** an early residence for Washington's African-American elite. A strong Hispanic community coexists with black, white, and cool in **Adams-Morgan,** north of Dupont and east of Rock Creek Park. West of the park begins **upper Northwest,** a big stretch of spread-out territory that includes the National Zoo, and the Cathedral. Across the Anacostia River, the **Southeast** (including **Anacostia**), has been damaged and fur-ther isolated by poverty, crack, and guns.

Though D.C. is the "Murder Capital of the U.S.," almost all of the killings take place in areas most visitors do not frequent, such as NE, SE, and NW (east of 14th St.). All the same, use common sense: avoid public parks after dark, walk on busy, well-lit streets whenever possible, and don't go out alone at night.

ACCOMMODATIONS

Business travelers desert D.C. during the summer months, leaving business hotels to discount deeply and swell with tourists on summer weekends. No less busy during the summer are the hostels, guest houses, and university dormitories that round out the selection of D.C.'s temporary residences. If you're lucky enough to hit the District without a car and you don't want a hostel, the guest houses around Dupont Cir-cle and Adams-Morgan should be your first try. Check the *New York Times* Sunday Travel section for summer weekend deals before you go and feel free to bargain. D.C. automatically adds an 11% occupancy surcharge and another $3 per room per night to your bill. **Bed & Breakfast of Washington, D.C.,** P.O. Box 12011, Wash-ington, D.C. 20005 (328-3510), reserves rooms in private home with an interesting array of hosts (singles start at $45, doubles at $55; $15 per additional person).

Washington International Hostel (HI/AYH), 1009 11 St. NW 20001 (737-2333). Metro: Metro Center; take the 11th St. exit, then walk 3 blocks north. Interna-tional travelers appreciate the college-aged staff, bunk beds, bulletin boards, kitchen, and common rooms. Rooms with A/C hold 4-12 beds, accessible by ele-vator. Lockers, game room, and laundry facilities. No alcohol or drugs. Relatively safe neighborhood, but less so to the northeast. Open 24 hrs. $15 per night; non-members $3 extra on the 1st night. Call at least 48 hrs. in advance; written reser-vations must be received 3 weeks in advance. MC & Visa. Wheelchair accessible.

Washington International Student Center, 2452 18th St. NW (265-6555), near Columbia Rd. (on "restaurant row") in the heart of Adams-Morgan. Metro: Woodley Park-Zoo, then a 10-min. walk along Calvert St. This hostel accommodates out-of-state and international visitors in 3 very clean but somewhat cramped rooms. The friendly managers are helpful and eager to please newcomers to D.C. for only $13 per night. Free linen, A/C, kitchen facilities. Laundromat nearby on Columbia Road. Alcohol permitted, smoking on balcony. No curfew.

Kalorama Guest House at Kalorama Park, 1854 Mintwood Place NW (667-6369) and **at Woodley Park,** 2700 Cathedral Ave. NW (328-0860). Metro (both): Woodley Park-Zoo. Well-run, impeccably decorated guest rooms in Victorian townhouses; the first is in the upscale western slice of Adams-Morgan near Rock Creek Park, the second in a high-class neighborhood near the zoo. Enjoy evening sherry or lemonade among the oriental rugs. All rooms have A/C and a clock/radio. Both have laundry facilities and free local calls. Free continental breakfast. Mintwood location also has a fireplace and refrigerator space. Rooms with shared bath $40-70, $5 per additional person (all but 2 rooms come with private sink). Rooms with private baths $75-105. Reserve 1-2 weeks in advance; office open Mon.-Fri. 7:30am-9pm, Sat.-Sun. 8am-7pm.

Davis House, 1822 R St. NW (232-3196), near 19th St. Metro: Dupont Circle. Charming and spacious wood-floored building equipped with common living room, sun room, patio, fridge, and microwave. Accepts international visitors, staff of Quaker organizations, and "those working on peace and justice concerns." Other visitors occasionally accepted on a same-day, space-available basis. No smoking or alcohol. Max. stay 2 weeks. Open daily 8am-10pm. Singles $35, doubles $60 (both with hall bath). One night's deposit required. Reserve early.

Allen Lee Hotel, 2224 F St. NW (331-1224, 800-462-0128), near 23rd St. and George Washington University. Metro: Foggy Bottom-GWU. Large, rickety, blue hallways. Rooms vary widely in size, furnishings, and state of repair, so look at several before accepting one. Bedrooms and bathrooms old but clean. Singles $32, with private bath $40. Doubles $40, with private bath $51. Twins $42, with private bath $55. Reserve in advance in summer.

2005 Columbia Guest House, 2005 Columbia Rd. NW (265-4006), near 20th St., ½-block from the Washington Hilton Hotel. An old senator's house southwest of central Adams-Morgan, with a creaky central staircase and 7 rooms featuring faded decor and sometimes lumpy beds. Clean, quiet rooms with unmatchable rates. Tennis courts and 2 free pools within walking distance. No alcohol. Call ahead. Singles $19-26, doubles $28-39. Weekly rates available. Summertime discounts for students and youth hostel members.

Adams Inn, 1744 Lanier Place NW (745-3600 or 800-578-6807), behind the Columbia Rd. Safeway supermarket, 2 blocks from the center of Adams-Morgan. Metro: Woodley Park-Zoo, then a 12-min. walk; or #42 bus to Columbia Rd. from Dupont Circle. Elegant Victorian townhouses smothered in Persian rugs. Sinks in all shared-bath rooms. Patio, coin laundry facilities, pay phones, and eating facilities. TV in common living room. Free breakfast. Office open Mon.-Sat. 8am-9pm, Sun. 1-9pm. Singles with shared bath $45, with private bath $60. Doubles with shared bath $55, with private bath $70. Weekly rates available.

Brickskeller Inn, 1523 22nd St. NW (293-1885), between P and Q St. Metro: Dupont Circle. Small, clean, linoleum-floored rooms, most with private sinks and shared baths down the hall. Some rooms come with private bath, A/C, and TV. Singles $35-65, doubles $60-80.

Swiss Inn, 1204 Massachusetts Ave. NW (371-1816 or 800-955-7947). Metro: Metro Center. 4 blocks from Metro Center; close to downtown. Clean, quiet studio apartments with fridge, private bath, high ceilings, kitchenettes, and A/C. Free local calls and free laundry (!). Once-a-summer cookout, all on the house. French-speaking managers (one speaks Swiss-German also) welcome an international crowd. Singles $98, with 20% discount for travel club members (including HI/AYH) and seniors. Weekly rates: singles $58, doubles $68 per night.

University Dorms: Georgetown University Summer Housing: available only for summer educational pursuits; they gladly take college-aged interns but cannot house self-declared tourists. Housing is single-sex. 3-week min. stay. Singles $18, with A/C $19. Doubles with A/C $16, with bath $17. Available June 1-Aug.8. Woe to those stranded without A/C. Contact G.U. Office of Housing and Conferences

Services 20057 (687-3999). **American University Summer Housing:** Write to 4400 Massachusetts Ave. NW 20016-8039, attn.: Housing Management (885-2598). Metro: Tenleytown-AU. Simple dorm rooms with A/C for students and interns (late May-mid-Aug). Double rooms only with hall bathrooms $91 per week per person; come with a friend or they'll find one for you. 3-week min. stay. Valid ID from any university and full payment for stay must be presented at check-in. Reserve early for check-in dates in early June; after that you can call 24 hrs. ahead.

Cherry Hill Park, 9800 Cherry Hill Rd. (301-937-7116). Metrobus from the Metrorail runs to and from the grounds every 30 min., every 15 min. during rush hour. Call for directions by car. The closest campground to Washington. Most of the 400 sites are for RVs. Cable hookup available; coin-operated laundry; heated swimming pool with whirlpool and sauna. Pets allowed. Tent site $25; RV site with electricity, water, and sewer $32. Extra person $2. $25 deposit required. Reserve at least 5 days ahead (call 9am-8pm).

FOOD

D.C. makes up for its days as a "sleepy Southern town" with a kaleidoscope of international restaurants. Haughty European dining rooms strive to impress the expense-account crowd, while bargains from Africa, Southeast Asia, and the Americas feed a melange of immigrants from all over. Smithsonian-goers should plan to eat dinner far away from the triceratops and the biplanes: visitors to the Mall get stuffed at mediocre cafeterias, only blocks from the respectable food on Capitol Hill. You can eat for $4 or eat well for $7 at many places in D.C.; while Adams-Morgan is famous for budget restaurants, Dupont Circle and the Hill are worth the Metro rides as well.

It's an open secret among interns that **happy hours** provide the cheapest dinners in Washington. Bars desperate to attract early-evening drinkers set up plates, platters, and tables of free appetizers; the trick is to drop by and munch but drink little or nothing. The best seem to concentrate, along with the interns, on Capitol Hill or south of Dupont.

Capitol Hill

The Hill's residential character means neighborhood establishments outnumber obnoxious chains. Food vendors do their thing in the block-long red-brick bustle of **Eastern Market** on 7th St. SE (Metro: Eastern Market; open Sat.-Sun. 7am-5pm). Over 50 eateries inhabit the lower level of **Union Station** (Metro: Union Station), serving burgers, pizza, sushi, bagels, and fruit shakes for under $4.

Chicken and Steak, 320 D St. NE (543-4633). Metro: Union Station. Ignore the spare decor and fall for the succulent chicken and steak, cooked Peruvian-style *à la brasa* (grilled) at bargain prices. Delicious ¼ chicken with plenty of fried *yucca* and salad $3.50; ½ chicken with *yucca* and salad $5.25. *Chorizo* sandwich $4.25. Open Mon.-Sat. 11am-9:30pm.

Hawk 'n Dove, 329 Pennsylvania Ave. SE (543-3300). Metro: Capitol South. A good bar with good bar food, which interns, regulars, and powerful politicians eagerly consume. Full menu. Sandwiches $4-6.50; 14 kinds of bottled beer and 11 drafts available ($1.75 and up). Midnight breakfast served Mon.-Thurs. 11pm-1am, Fri.-Sat. 11pm-2am ($7-9). Open Sun.-Thurs. 10am-2am, Fri.-Sat. 10am-3am.

Kelley's "The Irish Times," 14 F St. NW (543-5433). Metro: Union Station. Irish street signs, the *Irish Times,* Joyce on the wall and Yeats and Keats on the menu make this more than just another Irish pub (don't tell them Keats wasn't Irish). Live music Wed.-Sat. starting at 8:30pm. Lunch special $5, sandwiches around $5.25, soup $2. Beer from $2.50, Irish whiskey from $4. Big deals on weekends. Open Sun.-Thurs. 10:30am-1:30am, Fri.-Sat. 10:30am-2:30am.

Neil's Outrageous Deli, 208 Massachusetts Ave. NE (546-6970). Metro: Union Station. Combination deli and liquor store offers creative sandwiches to go. Try the "Crazy Louie," sour-dough rye topped with Dijon mustard, pastrami, turkey, and Thousand Island dressing ($4). A bristling array of sandwiches (over 23) range in price from $3-4. Cold soda 55¢, or free with a sandwich purchase after 4pm Mon.-Fri. Frozen yogurt 25¢ per oz. Open Mon.-Tues. 9am-7:30pm, Wed.-Sat. 9am-9pm.

Thai Roma, 313 Pennsylvania Ave. SE (544-2338/2339). Metro: Capitol South. A wild combination of Italian pastas and tomato sauces with the zest and spice of Thai food that makes area reviewers rave. A favorite spot for Hill denizens and homestead gourmands. Try the Italian linguine with peanut sauce ($7). Lunch entrees under $8. Reservations advised for lunch. Takeout available. Open Mon.-Fri. 11:30am-10:30pm, Sat. 11:30am-11pm, Sun. 4-10pm.

2 Quail, 320 Massachusetts Ave. NE (543-8030). Metro: Union Station. Three restored Victorian townhouses get cutely sumptuous with flowered curtains, cozy armchairs and plush, fluffy pillows. Uncategorizable and consistently excellent cuisine changes every season. Might be crowded at lunchtime. Try the delicious cream of broccoli soup ($3.50) or the tortellini with crab meat ($10.50). Big appetizers $4-7; entrees $10-18, with average damage at $14. Check the *Washington Blade* for coupons. Open Mon.-Thurs. 11:30am-2:30pm and 5:30-10:30pm, Fri. 11:30am-2:30pm and 5:30-11:15pm, Sat. 5:30-11:15pm, Sun. 5-10pm.

Old Downtown

A.V. Ristorante, 607 New York Ave. NW (737-0550). Metro: Mt. Vernon Sq.-UDC. Quite a few blocks away from the hubbub of commercial old downtown, though still frequented by suits on lunch break. Chianti bottles top-heavy with melted wax, lamps turned so low they flicker on and off, huge plates of expert pasta ($6-10), and pizza (starting at $8 for a pie). Open Mon.-Thurs. 11:30am-11pm, Fri. 11:30am-midnight, Sat. 5pm-midnight. Plenty of free parking for patrons.

Chun King Gourmet Inn, 1010 15th St. NW (347-2098). Metro: McPherson Sq. One of the many Chinese fast-food establishments that dot the city. Look for the sign outside that advertises the day's special (always $3.25). Decent food, good-sized portions, and low prices. Open Mon.-Sat. 10am-10pm, Sun. noon-10pm.

Chinatown

You don't have to dig a hole to China to find authentic Chinese food and groceries. Don't be turned off by a decrepit-seeming exterior; a restaurant's appearance will have little relation to its quality; apparent dives often serve wonderful food.

Burma Restaurant, 740 6th St. NW (393-3453), upstairs. The owner, a retired Burmese diplomat and former United Nations delegate, loves to talk about Burma's rare cuisine, which replaces soy sauce with pickles, mild curries, and unique spices. Make it your mission at Burma to try the rice noodles with dried shrimp, fried onion, coriander, garlic, and lemon juice ($6) or the bean curd and chopped shrimp cooked in Tabasco ($7). Open Mon.-Thurs. 11am-3pm and 6-9:30pm, Fri. 11am-3pm and 6-10:30pm, Sat. noon-3pm and 6-10:30pm, Sun. 6-9:30pm.

Szechuan Restaurant, 615 I St. NW (393-0130). One block from the main drag, the 2nd-floor Szechuan sizzles. For lunch, crispy orange beef ($8), *kung pao* chicken ($7), and crispy whole fish are old favorites (price and fish vary by season). Dinner $9-15. Owner shows off pictures of himself posing with 4 U.S. Presidents and his invitation to Clinton's inauguration. Open Mon.-Fri. 11am-11pm, Sat. 11am-midnight, Sun. 11am-10pm.

Tony Cheng's Mongolian Barbecue, 619 H St. NW (842-8669). Load your bowl with beef, leeks, mushrooms, sprouts, and such, then watch the cooks make it sizzle and shrink (1 serving $6, all-you-can-eat $14). Two or more people can stir up their own feast in charcoal hotpots. Base platter $5 per person; more meat costs extra. Open Sun.-Thurs. 11am-11pm, Fri.-Sat. 11am-midnight.

White House Area/Foggy Bottom

The Art Gallery Grille, 1712 I St. NW (298-6658), near 17th St. Metro: Farragut West. Art Deco interior and jukebox. Original Erté serigraphs, professional clientele. Breakfasts are traditional and inviting—Belgian waffles, creative granola, and various omelettes ($5). DJ Wed.-Fri. nights. Lots of fresh seafood; try the crab cake platter ($15) or sandwich ($11). Happy hour 5:30-7:30pm: drink specials and free food, like chicken wings, tacos, nachos, and fried rice. Open Mon.-Tues. 6:30pm-midnight, Wed.-Fri. 6:30pm-2am.

Lindy's Bon Apétit, 2040 I St. NW (452-0055), near Pennsylvania Ave. and Tower Records. Metro: Foggy Bottom-GWU. Ronald Reagan once said that life at George Washington University was not complete without a bone burger from this carry-out deli. Grab a bacon cheeseburger ($3.20), a Monterey sandwich with refried beans, raw onions, and American cheese ($2.85), or a 6-in. sub ($2.75-3.75). All breakfast sandwiches under $1.85. Open Mon.-Fri. 7am-8pm, Sat.-Sun. 11am-4pm.

Milo's, 2142 Pennsylvania Ave. NW (338-3000). GW students enjoy Euro-chic decor and Italian food—pasta ($5-8), fried mozzarella ($3), *calamari* ($5), and pizza (small pizza $5.70-$7.50). All-you-can-eat pizza and salad Mon.-Tues. 11:30am-2:30pm ($5, children $2.50); Wed.-Fri. $6 buffet at the same hrs. Happy hour Mon.-Fri. 4-7pm in the Foggy Bottom Pub downstairs. Open Mon.-Wed. 11:30am-11pm, Thurs.-Fri. 11:30am-midnight, Sat. 11:30am-2am, Sun. 5-10pm.

Georgetown

Georgetown's restaurants have got pretension if you want it: tourists can feed with the powerful and boring at inflated prices amid brass rails and autographed photos. On the other hand, some of the best food comes from the smaller ethnic restaurants: Indian, Ethiopian, Thai, and Vietnamese are well-established in Georgetown.

Au Pied du Cochon/Aux Fruits de Mer, 1335 Wisconsin Ave. NW (333-5440 and 333-2333), near Dumbarton St. Two sister restaurants, one serving casual French fare like salads and crepes and decorated with rustic copper pots and photos, the other serving fish and seafood in a maritime setting with an aquarium. Come by for a late snack ($3-3.75) and a cappuccino ($2.45) or a *café au lait* ($1.25). Watch passers-by in the glass-enclosed café. Open daily 24 hrs.

Booeymonger, 3265 Prospect St. NW (333-4810), at Potomac St. Georgetown students and residents stop by for breakfast ($2.75 for the special) or a quick, giant sandwich, each of which seems a specialty (all under $5). Highlights include California-style vegetarian pita pockets, Booey's cheesesteak, and kosher beef frankfurters. Create your own sandwich from 15 fillings, 8 breads, and 13 condiments. At peak lunch hours, the tables are packed. Open daily 8am-midnight.

Nakeysa, 1564 Wisconsin Ave. NW (337-6500), near Q St. Small, elegant Persian restaurant with salmon-colored tablecloths and napkins and fragrant flowers on every table. Salads and kebab sandwiches $5. Good vegetarian dishes too. Everything on the lunch menu under $6. Beef, cornish hen, game hen, and chicken kebabs $7-12. Take-out available. Open Mon. and Wed.-Thurs. noon-10pm, Tues. 5-10pm, Fri.-Sat. noon-11pm, Sun. noon-9pm.

Quick Pita, 1210 Potomac St. NW (338-PITA or 338-7482), near M St. Good, cheap Middle Eastern fare, perfect for a Quick Snack or take-out. All sandwiches under $4. Felafel $2.75. Free delivery in the Georgetown area after 6pm ($12 min. order). Open Mon.-Sun. 11:30am-6am.

Saigon Inn, 2928 M St. NW (337-5588), at 30th St. Slightly cheaper and more intimate than next-door Vietnam-Georgetown, its much older rival. Go for the lunch special: 4 dishes for $4, served daily 11am-3pm. Dinner $7-13. The Saigon pancake is their specialty ($7). Open Mon.-Sat. 11am-11pm, Sun. noon-11pm.

Sushi-Ko, 2309 Wisconsin Ave. NW (333-4187), below Calvert St. Authentic, no-frills Japanese food prepared before your eyes. Try the affordable *Maki-sushi* or *Temaki* (over 20 kinds to choose from), under $5. Fish offerings include the customary trout, flounder, and tuna, as well as the more exotic *Uzara* (with quail eggs). Order of sushi (2 rolls per serving) $2-4.50. Open Mon. 6-10:30pm, Tues.-Fri. noon-2:30pm and 6-10:30pm, Sat. 5-10:30pm, Sun. 5-10pm.

Thomas Sweet, 3214 P St. NW (337-0616), at Wisconsin Ave. All the ice cream, yogurt, muffins, and bagels made daily in the store. The best ice cream in D.C. by a light-year. Single-scoop cup/cone $1.70. Hefty helpings of yogurt or ice cream mixed with fruit or candy $3.44. Open Mon.-Thurs. 9:30am-midnight, Fri.-Sat. 9:30am-1am, Sun. 11am-midnight; Sept.-May closes 1 hr. earlier every night.

New Downtown

Sholl's Colonial Cafeteria, 1990 K St. NW (296-3065), in the Esplanade Mall. Metro: Farragut West. Good cooking at exceptionally low prices: chopped steak ($1.70) and plain roast beef ($1.85). These guys have been around forever; so have dozens of their patrons. Fresh food and generous portions, plus daily specials. Try the homemade pies. Open Mon.-Sat. 7am-2:30pm and 4-8pm.

The Star of Siam, 1136 19th St. NW (785-2839), near L St. Metro: Farragut West or North. Delights its diners with spicy curry dishes and unobtrusively fried foods. Dinner entrees from $6.25. Awesome desserts include sticky rice with coconut milk and sliced mango ($3). Open Mon.-Sat. 11:30am-11pm, Sun. 4-10pm.

Tokyo Terrace, 1025 Vermont Ave. NW (628-7304), near K St. Join every other sushi-lover in the new downtown for an inexpensive Japanese lunch served fast-food-style inside or out. The "Sushi Deluxe" (6 California rolls, 2 *futomaki*, and 2 *inari*) is only $5.25 on Sat. Just $10 buys all-you-can-eat sushi rolls plus 1 entree, salad, shrimp roll, and soup. Open Mon.-Fri. 7:30am-7pm, Sat. 11am-7pm.

Dupont Circle

Bua, 1635 P St. NW (265-0828, delivery 546-8646), near 17th St. Award-winning Thai cuisine in a cool, spacious dining room or on the patio. Entrees $7-13, with most meals hovering around $8. Happy hour Thurs.-Fri. 5-7pm: margaritas $1.50. Open Mon.-Thurs. 11:30am-2:30pm and 5-10:30pm, Fri. 11:30am-2:30pm and 5-11pm, Sat. noon-2:30pm and 5-11pm, Sun. 5-10:30pm.

Dante's, 1522 14th St. NW (667-7260), near Church St. Not to be missed after midnight, when punk rockers and actors jam the place with hipness and hair. Teal and black decor complements heavenly-healthful pita sandwiches ($5-6.50) and devilish cheesecake ($2.50). Try the delicious white-pizza appetizer: melted provolone cheese on pita bread with Italian spices for $3.50. Don't come around here alone at night. Happy hour Mon.-Fri. 3-5pm: $1 off drinks. Open Sun.-Mon. 5pm-3am, Tues.-Thurs. 11:30am-3am, Fri. 11:30am-4:30am, Sat. 5pm-4:30am.

Dupont Italian Kitchen, 1641 17th St. NW (328-3222), at R St. Delicious, no-frills Italian food at excellent prices. Pasta $4.50-7, hot sandwiches $3-4, small pizza with cheese $4.50. Two floors of indoor seating plus a sidewalk cafe. Free delivery in Dupont Circle area. Open Mon.-Sat. noon-midnight, Sun. 10:30am-11pm.

Food for Thought, 1738 Connecticut Ave. NW (797-1095), two blocks from Dupont Circle. Veggie-hippie-folknik mecca with good, healthy food in a 60s atmosphere. 10 different vegetable and fruit salads, plus sandwiches and daily hot specials. Local musicians strum in the evenings, open mike every Mon. 9-11:30pm. Blues jam last Sun. of every month. Bulletin boards announce everything from rallies to beach parties to rides to L.A. Great chunky gazpacho ($2.95 a cup). Lunch $6-8, lunch combos with soup or salad $4.75-6.75 (Mon.-Fri. until 4:30pm), dinner $6-10. Open Mon. 11:30am-2:30pm and 5pm-12:30am; Tues.-Thurs. 11:30am-12:30am, Fri. 11:30am-2am, Sat. noon-2am, Sun. 4pm-12:30am.

Kramerbooks & Afterwords Cafe, 1517 Connecticut Ave. NW (387-3825), near Q St. Late-night sweets behind a very good bookshop. Some expensive *nouvelle* entrees, but Washington's best cakes, pies, and mousses ($3-6) are rich rewards for living the literary life. Cappuccino freaks should head here too. Live music Fri.-Sun. after 10pm. Open Sun.-Thurs. 7:30am-1am, Fri.-Sat. 24 hrs.

Shaw

The immediate vicinity of 14th and U St. NW, on the area's edge near the U St.-Cardozo Metro stop, is a safe source for supreme soul food, a uniquely Southern cuisine. Come during the day. Metro: U St.-Cardozo, for all of the following.

Ben's Chili Bowl, 1213 U St. NW (667-0909), at 13th St. The self-declared "Home of the Famous Chili Dog," this venerable (30-year-old) neighborhood hangout now has a facelift, with a new jukebox, smooth new counters, and a molded ceiling. Spicy homemade chili—on a chili dog (served with onion, mustard, and potato chips, $1.85), on a half-smoke ($2.75), or on a ¼-lb. burger ($2.10). Diehards eat it plain: small bowl $1.90, large bowl $2.55. Open Mon.-Thurs. 6am-2am, Fri.-Sat. 6am-3am, Sun. noon-8pm.

Florida Avenue Grill, 1100 Florida Ave. NW (265-1586), at 11th St. Small, enduring (since 1944) diner once fed black leaders and entertainers. Now their framed famed faces beam down at the hordes of locals who frequent the place. Don't miss the article in the first booth about a 32-year veteran Grill server: "I'd love to serve [President Reagan] chitlins," she says. "It might straighten his head out." Awesome Southern-style food: breakfast with salmon cakes or spicy sausage, eggs, grits, hotcakes, or biscuits ($2.75-7). Lunch and dinner dishes served with choice of 2 vegetables ($6-9). Take-out available. Open Tues.-Sat. 6am-9pm.

Hogs on the Hill, 14th and U St. NW (332-1817). Plain decor offsets enticing smells from the kitchen. You'll get big portions, too. Half chickens $4.25, whole chickens $7.50. Platters, served with corn bread and 2 side orders, are $5-9. Choices include pork ribs, chopped BBQ beef, or chicken. Sides include collard greens, potato salad, cole slaw, red beans and rice, and fries. Open Mon.-Thurs. 11am-10pm, Fri.-Sat. 10am-11pm, Sun. noon-9pm.

Adams-Morgan

The word is out. Adams-Morgan's jambalaya of cultures can satisfy all sorts of unusual tastes, from Latin American to Ethiopian to Caribbean—all for around $7. Adams-Morgan has justifiably become D.C.'s preferred locale for budget dining.

Calvert Cafe, 1967 Calvert St. NW (232-5431), right across the Duke Ellington Bridge. Metro: Woodley Park-Zoo. Look for the brown and gold tiles; though it looks boarded-up, this landmark has lasted 30 years. Huge, unadorned platters of Middle Eastern food. Appetizers $2-3.50, dinner entrees $6-8.50. Half a broiled chicken with salad $6. Shish kebab with rice and salad $8.50. Open daily 11:30am-11:30pm.

The Islander, 1762 Columbia Rd. NW (234-4955), above a shoe store. Small Trinidadian and Caribbean restaurant is more than 15 years old. Consider curried goat or Calypso chicken (each $8.50). Nine kinds of *roti* (thin pancakes stuffed with vegetables and meat) are a bargain for $3.25-6. Platters $6.50-9.75, appetizers $1.75-3. Open Mon. 5-10pm, Tues.-Thurs. noon-10pm, Fri.-Sat. noon-11pm.

Meskerem, 2434 18th St. NW (462-4100), near Columbia Rd. Another fine Ethiopian place and certainly the best-looking one in Adams-Morgan. Cheery yellow 3-level interior incorporates an upstairs gallery with Ethiopian woven tables and a view of the diners below. Appetizers $2.50-4.75, meat entrees $8.75-11, vegetarian entrees $7-8.75. A combination of 5 vegetable dishes and 2 salads $9.45 for one person, $17.50 for two. Try the *meskerem tibbs* (lamb with vegetables, $11) or *yemisir watt* (lentils in hot sauce, $8.50). Open daily noon-midnight.

Mixtec, 1792 Columbia Rd. NW (332-1011), near 18th St. Popular, well-known Mexican restaurant. Two bright rooms wear neat paper lanterns and wooden Mexican chairs. Neon window-sign flashes the specialty, *tacos al carbon*. The $3 version consists of 2 small tortillas filled with delicious beef and served with 3 kinds of garnish. Mixtec makes a mind-bending chicken *mole*, too. Lunch entrees, served with salad and beans, $6-9. Appetizers $2.25-4.25. Entrees $4.50-9.95. Open Sun.-Thurs. 11am-11:30pm, Fri.-Sat. 11am-12:30am.

El Pollo Primo, 2471 18th St. NW (588-9551), near Columbia Rd. By their awning shall ye know them. Second-story beige and brown rotisserie produces moist, flavorful, tender, greaseless, cheap chicken on a big grill behind the counter. Two-piece chicken dinner with tortillas, salsa, and 2 side orders $3.65, 3-piece dinner $4.60. Side orders include beans and rice ($2 each a la carte). Open Sun.-Thurs. 10:30am-9:30pm, Fri.-Sat. 10:30am-10:30pm.

Red Sea, 2463 18th St. NW (483-5000), near Columbia Rd. The first of Adams-Morgan's famous Ethiopian restaurants and still among the best. The red-painted exterior is weatherbeaten but enticing (and scheduled for re-painting in Sept. 1993). Placemats describe Ethiopian cuisine and climate. Use the traditional pancake bread, *injera*, to eat spicy lamb, beef, chicken, and vegetable *wats* (stews). Lunch entrees $4.50-8.75, dinners $6-10. Open daily 11:30am-midnight.

WASHINGTON, D.C.

SIGHTS

Of course every first-time visitor has to go to the Capitol and the Smithsonian. But the rest of Washington also deserves your time. D.C. is a veritable thicket of art museums, public events, ethnic communities, parks, and streets to delight and educate the attentive tourist. Adams-Morgan, Dupont Circle, Connecticut Ave., and Georgetown are all good bets for those sick of the Mall.

If you like to do the tourist thang, **Tourmobile Sight-seeing,** 1000 Ohio Drive SW (554-7950 or 554-7020 for recorded info), near the Washington Monument offers one of the most popular standard tours (9am-6:30pm, mid-Sept.-mid-June 9:30am-4:30pm; standard 18-sight loop $8.50, kids 3-11 $4; buy tickets by 1pm from booth or drivers). Other companies run specialized, thematic tours, such as **Scandal Tours** (783-7212), which steers tourists from one place of infamy to the next, including Gary Hart's townhouse, Watergate, and the Vista Hotel, where Mayor Barry was caught with his pants down (75 min., $27). Capitol Entertainment Services (636-9203) specializes in a **Black History Tour** through Lincoln Park, Anacostia, and the Frederick Douglass home. (Tours begin at area hotels. 3 hr. $15, children 5-12 $10.)

Capitol Hill

The **U.S. Capitol** (House 225-3121, Senate 224-3121) may no longer be America's most beautiful building, but its scale and style still evoke the power of the republic. (Metro: Capitol South.) The **East Front** faces the Supreme Court; from Jackson (1829) to Carter (1977), most Presidents were inaugurated here. Reagan moved the ceremony to the newly-fixed-up **West Front,** overlooking the Mall. Nothing built in Washington can be taller than the tip of the cast-iron dome, and if there's light in the dome at night, Congress is still meeting. The public East Front entrance brings you into the 180-ft.-high **rotunda;** statesmen from Lincoln to JFK have lain in state in its center. You can get a map from the tour desk (free guided tours begin here daily every 20 min. 9am-3:45pm). Downstairs, ceremony and confusion reign in the **crypt** area; most of the functioning rooms are upstairs. For a spectacle, but little insight, climb to the **House and Senate visitors galleries.** Americans should request a gallery pass (valid for the whole 2-year session of Congress) from the office of their representative, delegate, or senator. Foreign nationals should ask for a pass from the Office of the House Doorkeeper or the Senate Sergeant at Arms. Expect to see a few bored-looking elected officials failing to listen to the person on the podium who is probably speaking only for benefit of home-district cable TV viewers. The real business of Congress is conducted in **committee hearings.** Most are open to the public; look in the *Washington Post's* "Today in Congress" box for times and locations. The **Senate Cafeteria** on the second floor is also open to the public. The free **Capitol subway** travels between the basement of the Capitol and the House and Senate office buildings; a buzzer and flashing red lights signals an imminent vote. (Open daily 9am-4:30pm, Memorial Day-Labor Day daily 9am-8pm.)

The nine justices of the **Supreme Court,** 1 1st St. NE (479-3000), across from the East Front of the Capitol building, are the final interpreters of the U.S. Constitution (Metro: Capitol South or Union Station). Oral arguments are open to the public; show up early to be seated or walk through the standing gallery to hear 5 min. of the argument. (Court is in session Oct.-June Mon.-Wed. 10am-3pm for 2 weeks each month.) The *Washington Post's* A-section can tell you what case is up. You can still view the courtroom when the Justices are on vacation. Brief lectures cover the history, operations, duties and architecture of the court and its building (July-Aug. every hr. on the ½-hr. 9:30am-3:30pm). (Open Mon.-Fri. 9am-4:30pm. Free.)

The **Library of Congress,** 1st St. SE (707-5000; recorded events schedule 707-8000), between East Capitol and Independence Ave. (Metro: Capitol South), is the world's largest library, with 20 million books and over 60 million other holdings occupying three buildings: the 1897 Beaux Arts Jefferson Building; the 1939 Adams Building across 2nd St.; and the 1980 Madison Building. The entire collection, including rare items, is open to those of college age or older with a legitimate research purpose, but anyone can take the tour, which starts in the Madison Building lobby across from the sales shop. After a brief talk, the tour scuttles through tunnels to the Jefferson Building, which is otherwise closed for renovations. The octagonal Main Reading Room spreads out under a spectacular dome. (Most reading rooms open Mon.-Fri. 8:30am-9:30pm, Sat. 8:30am-5pm, Sun. 1-5pm.)

Although the **Folger Shakespeare Library,** 201 East Capitol St. SE (544-4600), houses the world's largest collection of Shakespeareana (about 275,000 books and manuscripts), most of it is closed to the public. You can, however, see the Great Hall exhibition gallery and the theater, which imitates the Elizabethan Inns of Court indoor theaters where Shakespeare's company performed. The Folger also sponsors readings, lectures, and concerts such as the PEN/Faulkner poetry and fiction readings and the Folger Consort, a chamber music group specializing in Renaissance music. (Exhibits open Mon.-Sat. 10am-4pm; library open Mon.-Sat. 8:45am-4:45pm.)

The trains run on time at **Union Station,** 50 Massachusetts Ave. NE (general information 371-9441), 2 blocks north of the Capitol (Metro: Union Station). Daniel Burnham's much-admired, monumental Beaux Arts design took four years (1905-1908) to erect. Colonnades, archways, and huge domed ceilings equate Burnham's Washington with imperial Rome and the then-dominant train network with Roman roads. Today it is a spotless ornament in the crown of capitalism, with a food court, chic stores, and mall rats aplenty (shops open Mon.-Sat. 10am-9pm, Sun. noon-6pm).

Directly west of Union Station is the new **National Postal Museum,** 1st St. and Massachusetts Ave. NE (357-2700), on the lower level of the City Post Office (Metro: Union Station). The Smithsonian's collection of stamps and other philatelic materials was relocated here in July 1993. The collection includes such artifacts of American postal history as airmail planes hung from the ceiling in the 90-ft.-high atrium, half of a fake mustache used by a train robber, funky mail boxes, and the letter-carrier uniform worn by Cliff Claven in the television series "Cheers." (Open daily 10am-5pm. Free.) Northeast of Union Station is the red-brick **Capital Children's Museum,** 800 3rd St. NE (675-4127; Metro: Union Station). Touch and feel every exhibit in this huge interactive experiment of a museum; walk through the life-sized cave, make a simple Zoetrope cartoon movie, learn how a printing press works, make your own tortillas, or wander through the room-sized maze. (Open daily 10am-5pm. $7, children under 2 free. All kids must be accompanied by an adult.)

The **Sewall-Belmont House,** 144 Constitution Ave. NE (546-3989; Metro: Union Station), one of the oldest houses in Washington and the former headquarters of the National Woman's Party, is now a museum of the U.S. women's movement (open Tues.-Fri. 11am-3pm, Sat.-Sun. noon-4pm; ring the bell, as tours are unscheduled).

Southeast

Several museums and a destroyer you can board stay ship-shape among the booms at the **Washington Navy Yard,** at 9th and M St. SE (Metro: Navy Yard). Use caution in this neighborhood. The best of the lot, the **Navy Museum,** Building 76 (433-4882), should buoy anyone let down by the admire-but-don't-touch Air & Space Museum on the Mall. Climb inside the space capsule, play human cannonball inside huge ship guns, jam yourself into a bathysphere used to explore the sea floor, or give orders on the bridge. (Open Mon.-Fri. 9am-5pm, Sat.-Sun. 10am-5pm; Sept.-May Mon.-Fri. 9am-4pm, Sat.-Sun. 10am-5pm.) Tour the **U.S.S. Barry,** a decommissioned destroyer, docked a few steps from the Navy Museum (open daily 10am-5pm). The **Marine Corps Historical Museum,** Building 58 (433-3534), marches through Marine Corps time from the American Revolution to the present, touting the actions, guns, uniforms, swords, and other memorabilia of marines from the halls of Montezuma to the shores of Kuwait (open Mon.-Thurs. and Sat. 10am-4pm, Fri. 10am-8pm, Sun. noon-5pm; Sept.-May Mon.-Sat. 10am-4pm, Sun. noon-5pm).

After the Civil War, one-acre plots sold by the Freedmen's Bureau drew freed slaves to **Anacostia.** Despite the opening of the Anacostia Metro, this neglected neighborhood remains largely unattractive to tourists, despite community struggles to overcome drug-related violence. If you prefer exploring on foot, do so here only during the day and with a friend or two. The **Anacostia Museum,** 1901 Fort Place SE (287-3369, Sat.-Sun. 357-2700), focuses on African-American history and culture. (Take the W-1 or W-2 bus from Howard Rd. near the Metro Station to Fort Place.) This former "neighborhood museum," now run by the Smithsonian, holds temporary exhibits on African-American culture and history. Pick up a flyer at the Smithsonian Castle to see what's showing at the museum. (Open daily 10am-5pm; free.) Cedar Hill, the **Frederick Douglass Home,** 1411 W St. SE (426-5960), was the final residence of Abolitionist statesman, orator, and autobiographer Frederick Douglass, who escaped from slavery in 1838, published the *North Star* newspaper in the 1840s, and served in the 1880s as a D.C. official and as the U.S. Ambassador to Haiti. (Take the B-1 from Howard Rd. near the Metro station to the home.) Cedar Hill remains as Douglass furnished it. Tours (every ½-hr. 9am-4pm) begin with a ½-hr. movie. (Open daily 9am-5pm; Nov.-March 9am-4pm. Free.)

Museums on the Mall

The **Smithsonian** is the catalogued attic of the United States. The world's largest museum complex (11 buildings) stretches out along Washington's longest lawn, the Mall. **Constitution Ave.** (on the north) and **Independence Ave.** (on the south) fence the double row of museums. All Smithsonian museums are free and wheelchair-accessible; all offer written guides in various languages. Allow no less than three days to see the Smithsonian—they'd take a lifetime to "finish." For museum info, call 357-2700; for info on tours, concerts, lectures, and films, call 357-2020.

The **National Mall,** the U.S.'s taxpayer-supported national backyard, is a sight in itself. On any sunny day hundreds of natives and out-of-towners sunbathe and lounge, play frisbee or football, knock down their little brothers, go fly a kite, or just get high. The **Smithsonian Castle,** 1000 Jefferson Dr. SW (357-2700, recording 357-2020), holds no real exhibits, but it does have info desks, a thorough but tedious 20-min. movie, and James Smithson's body (open daily 9am-5:30pm).

The National Museum of American History: Though Henry Ford said "History is bunk," this museum's premise is that history is junk—several centuries' worth of machines, textiles, photographs, vehicles, harmonicas, hats, and uncategorizable American detritus reside here. The Smithsonian's quirky artifacts of popular history, like Dorothy's slippers from *The Wizard of Oz,* are here. On the second floor, a Foucault's Pendulum demonstrates the Earth's rotation by knocking over pegs in a circular pattern. The flag that inspired the "Star Spangled Banner" hangs behind the pendulum, shielded from light by an opaque cover (lifted every hr. on the ½hr.). Open daily 10am-6:30pm; Sept.-May daily 10am-5:30pm.

The Museum of Natural History, at 10th and Constitution Ave. This golden-domed, neoclassical museum considers the earth and its life in 2½ big, crowded floors of exhibits. Corridors, cases, dioramas, and hanging specimens reflect the Victorian mania to collect, catalogue, and display. Inside, the largest African elephant ever captured stands under dome-filtered sunshine. Dinosaur skeletons dwarf it in a nearby gallery, dwarfed in turn by a blue whale suspended from the ceiling in the "Ancient Seas and Sea Life" exhibit. Upstairs, cases of naturally-occurring crystals (including glow-the-dark rocks) make the final plush room of cut gems anticlimactic, despite the famous Hope Diamond. The Insect Zoo pleases with an array of live creepy-crawlies, from cockroaches to walking sticks. Open daily 10am-6:30pm; Sept.-May daily 10am-5:30pm.

The National Gallery of Art: West Building (737-4215), at 6th and Constitution Ave. NW, houses and hangs its jumble of pre-1900 art in a domed marble temple to Western Tradition, including important works by El Greco, Raphael, Rembrandt, Vermeer, and Monet. Leonardo da Vinci's earliest surviving portrait, the only da Vinci in the U.S., hangs amongst a fine collection of Italian Renaissance Art. Other highlights include: a bevy of French Impressionist pieces, a hall of

Dutch masters, and works by John Singer Sargent, George Bellows, and Winslow Homer. Open Mon.-Sat. 10am-5pm, Sun. 11am-6pm.

The National Gallery Of Art: East Building (737-4215), houses the museum's plentiful 20th-century collection. I. M. Pei's celebrated design is a logical outcome of the idea that a building itself should be a work of art. The National Gallery owns works by a veritable parade of modern artists, including Picasso, Matisse, Mondrian, Miró, Magritte, Pollock, Warhol, Lichtenstein, and Rothko. Don't expect to see all of them, however; the East Building constantly rearranges, closes, opens, and remodels parts of itself for temporary exhibits. Open Mon.-Sat. 10am-5pm, Sun. 11am-6pm; in summer Fri. 10am-8pm.

The National Air and Space Museum (357-2700), on the south side of the Mall between 4th and 7th St. SW, is the world's most popular museum, with 7.5 million visitors per year. Airplanes and space vehicles dangle from the ceiling; the Wright brothers' biplane in the entrance gallery looks intimidated by all its younger kin. The space-age atrium holds a moon rock, worn smooth by two decades of tourists' fingertips. Walk through the Skylab space station, the Apollo XI command module, and the DC-7. A full-scale lunar lander has touched down outside the cafeteria. A new exhibit in the museum entitled "Where Next, Columbus?" brings a historical perspective to issues dealing with space-exploration, while another gallery test-flies the *U.S.S. Enterprise* from *Star Trek.* The gift shop is a blast. IMAX movies on Langley Theater's 5-story screen are so realistic that some viewers suffer motion sickness. Films 9:30am-6:45pm. Tickets $3.25, kids, students, and seniors $2; available at the box office on the ground floor. Open daily 10am-6:30pm; Sept.-June daily 10am-5:30pm.

Hirshhorn Museum and Sculpture Garden (357-2700), 8th St. and Independence Ave. SW. This four-story, slide-carousel-shaped brown building has outraged traditionalists since 1966. Each floor consists of 2 concentric circles, an outer ring of rooms and paintings, and an inner corridor of sculptures. The Hirshhorn's best shows feature art since 1960; no other gallery or museum in Washington even pretends to keep up with the Hirshhorn's avant-garde paintings, mind-bending sculptures, and mixed-media installations. The museum claims the world's most comprehensive set of 19th- and 20th-century Western sculpture, including works by Rodin and Giacometti. Outdoor sculpture shines in the museum's courtyard. Museum open daily 10am-5:30pm. Sculpture Garden open daily 7:30am-dusk.

The Arts and Industries Building, between the castle and the Hirshhorn, is an exhibition of an exhibition, the 1876 Centennial Exhibition of American technology in Philadelphia. Pause for the exterior: a polychromatic, multi-style chaos of gables, arches, rails, shingles, and bricks. Inside, furniture and candy-making equipment congregate near the Mall entrance; further back, heavy machinery will delight advocates of steam power. Open daily 10am-5:30pm.

The National Museum of African Art, 950 Independence Ave. SW (357-4600). This underground museum displays artifacts from Sub-Saharan Africa. Art objects include masks, textiles, ceremonial figures, and fascinating musical instruments like a harp made partly of pangolin scales. A permanent display contains sophisticated bronze works from Benin, in modern Nigeria. Open daily 10am-5:30pm.

The Arthur M. Sackler Gallery, 1050 Independence Ave. SW (357-4880), showcases an extensive collection of art from China, South and Southeast Asia, and Persia, including illuminated manuscripts, Chinese and Japanese painting, carvings and friezes from Egypt, Phoenicia, and Sumeria, Hindu gods, and other works. Also underground. Open daily 10am-5:30pm.

The Freer Gallery of Art, at Jefferson Dr. and 12th St. SW, reopened in May 1993 with a marble and limestone stairway that connects the Freer to the Sackler via a new shared exhibition gallery. The Freer collects Asian art, including Chinese bronzes, precious manuscripts, and jade carvings, as well as American art, much of which shows Eastern influences. Open daily 10am-5:30pm.

South of the Mall

Exotic foliage from all continents and climates vegetates inside and outside the **U.S. Botanical Garden** (225-7099), 1st St. and Maryland Ave. SW (Metro: Federal Center SW). Cactuses, bromeliads, and other odd-climate plants flourish indoors. (Open daily 9am-8pm; Sept.-May daily 9am-5pm. 40 min. guided tours at 10am and 2pm; call ahead.) Further west, the Mint, or the **Bureau of Engraving and Printing** (662-2000), 14th St. and C St. SW, offers tours of the presses that annually print over $20 billion worth of money and stamps. So atrophied is the American species-being that tourists have made this the area's longest line; arrive early or expect a 2-hr. wait. (Open Mon.-Fri. 9am-2pm; free.)

The **U.S. Holocaust Memorial Museum,** 100 Raoul Wallenberg Place SW (653-9220; Metro: Smithsonian), opened in April 1993, is a self-conscious but earnest attempt to involve modern Americans in the memory of atrocities that, even as they were happening, were far removed from the American consciousness. The **permanent exhibit** is a three-story presentation of the Holocaust in chronological order, utilizing graphic black-and-white movies, still photographs, victims' personal items, and survivors' tape-recorded accounts of their experiences in the camps. Visitors can light memorial candles in the **Hall of Remembrance.** This museum suffers from over-popularity, despite the strict entry-by-ticket system. (Open daily 10am-5:30pm. Tickets available at the 14th St. entrance starting at 9am the same day; arrive early and expect long lines. Free.)

Monuments and West of the Mall

The **Washington Monument** (Metro: Smithsonian) is a vertical altar to America's first president. During the Civil War the half-finished obelisk was nicknamed the "Beef Depot Monument" in honor of the cattle that Army quartermasters herded on the grounds. The stairs up the monument were a famous (and strenuous) tourist exercise until the Park Service closed them after heart attacks (on the way up) and vandalism (on the way down). The elevator line takes 45 min. to circle the monument. At the top, tiny windows offer lookout points. People with disabilities can bypass the long lines. (Open daily 8am-midnight; Sept.-March daily 9am-5pm. Free.)

Maya Ying Lin, who designed the **Vietnam Veterans Memorial,** south of Constitution Ave. at 22nd St. NW (Metro: Smithsonian or Foggy Bottom/GWU), called it "a rift in the earth—a long, polished black stone wall, emerging from and receding into the earth." While still an undergraduate at Yale, Lin beat 1400 contestants with her design. The "meaning of the memorial" lies in its lists of names: 58,132 Americans died in Vietnam, and the memorial's slabs bear each one's name, arranged in chronological order. Families and veterans visit the memorial to ponder and to mourn; many make rubbings of their loved ones' names from the walls. (Open 24 hrs.)

Anyone with a penny already knows what the **Lincoln Memorial** looks like, at the west end of the Mall (Metro: Smithsonian or Foggy Bottom/GWU); the design copies the rectangular grandeur of Athens' Parthenon. A massive layer of stone atop the columns lends the building the watchful solemnity of a crypt. From these steps, Martin Luther King Jr. gave his "I Have a Dream" speech to the 1963 March on Washington. Daniel Chester French's seated Lincoln presides over the memorial from the inside, keeping watch over protesters and Fourth of July fireworks. You can read his Gettysburg address on the wall to the left of the statue. (Open 24 hrs.) The **Reflecting Pool,** between the Washington Monument and the Lincoln Memorial, contains 7 million gallons of water.

The **Jefferson Memorial's** rotunda-centric design pays tribute to Jefferson's home, Monticello, which he himself designed. A 19-ft. hollow bronze statue of President Jefferson rules the rotunda, and the interior walls quote from Jefferson's writings: the *Declaration of Independence,* the *Virginia Statute of Religious Freedom, Notes on Virginia,* and an 1815 letter. The *Declaration of Independence* extract contains 11 discrepancies with the original, several committed to shorten the quote so it would fit on the wall. The sentence around the top of the dome rebukes those who wrongly called Jefferson an atheist. (Open 24 hrs.) The memorial overlooks the **Tidal Basin,** where pedalboats ripple in and out of the memorial's shadow.

Downtown/North of the Mall

It's only proper that an architectural marvel should house the **National Building Museum,** which towers above F St. NW between 4th and 5th St. (Metro: Judiciary Square). Montgomery Meigs's Italian-inspired edifice remains one of Washington's most beautiful; the Great Hall is big enough to hold a 15-story building. "Washington: Symbol and City," one of the NBM's first permanent exhibits, covers D.C. architecture. Other highlights include rejected designs for the Washington Monument and the chance to design your own Capitol Hill rowhouse. (Open Mon.-Sat. 10am-4pm, Sun. noon-4pm. Tours Mon.-Fri. 12:30pm, Sat.-Sun. 12:30pm, 1:30pm. Free.)

The **National Museum of American Art** and the **National Portrait Gallery** (357-2700) share the Old Patent Office Building, a neoclassical edifice 2 blocks long (American Art entrance at 8th and G St., Portrait Gallery entrance at 8th and F; Metro: Gallery Place-Chinatown). The NMAA's corridors contain a diverse collection of major 19th- and 20th-century painters, as well as folk and ethnic artists. D.C. janitor James Hampton stayed up nights in an unheated garage for 15 years to create the *Throne of the Third Heaven of the Nations' Millennium General Assembly,* to the right of the main entrance. George Caitlin's studies of Native Americans put the U.S.'s westward expansion in perspective, while Edward Hopper competes with the abstractions of Franz Kline on the third floor. (Open daily 10am-5:30pm; tours Mon.-Fri. noon, Sat.-Sun. 2pm. Free.) The wide range of media, periods, styles, and people represented make the National Portrait Gallery a museum of the American character (open daily 10am-5:30pm; tours Mon.-Fri. 10am-3pm by request, Sat.-Sun. 11am-2pm; free).

The U.S.'s founding documents can still be found at the **National Archives** (501-5000, guided tours 501-5205), 8th St. and Constitution Ave. NW (Metro: Archives-Navy Memorial). Visitors line up outside to view the original *Declaration of Independence, U.S. Constitution,* and *Bill of Rights.* Humidity-controlled, helium-filled glass cases preserve and exhibit all three documents in the central rotunda. (Exhibit area open daily 10am-9pm, Sept.-March 10am-5:30pm. Free.) The **Federal Bureau of Investigation** (324-3000) still keeps the nation safe by hunting Commies, freaks, druggies, and interstate felons with undiminished vigor. Tour lines form on the beige-but-brutal J. Edgar Hoover building's outdoor plaza (tour entrance from 10th St. NW at Pennsylvania Ave.; Metro: Federal Triangle or Archives-Navy Memorial). Real FBI agents sport walkie-talkies as they speed you through gangster paraphernalia and photos, relics of crime bosses, confiscated drugs, gun displays, and mugshots of the nation's 10 most wanted criminals. John Dillinger's death mask hangs alongside his machine gun. At the tour's end, a marksman shreds cardboard evildoers; most of the audience applauds vigorously. (Tours Mon.-Fri 8:45am-4:15pm; free.)

"Sic semper tyrannis!" muttered assassin John Wilkes Booth after shooting President Abraham Lincoln during a performance at **Ford's Theatre,** 511 10th St. NW (426-6924; Metro: Metro Center). National Park rangers narrate the events of the April 14, 1865 assassination. (Open daily 9am-5pm; talks every hr. 9am-noon and 2-5pm; Feb.-June every 30 min. Free.) Lincoln passed away the next day at the **Petersen House,** 526 10th St. NW (426-6830; open daily 9am-5pm). The **Old Post Office** (523-5691), at Pennsylvania Ave. and 12th St. NW, sheathes a shopping mall in architectural wonder (Metro: Federal Triangle). Its arched windows, conical turrets, and 315-ft. clock tower are a rebuke to its sleeker contemporary neighbors. The National Park Service can show you around the clock tower (523-5691; tours meet at the elevators in the patio area). The view from the top may be D.C.'s best. (Tower open 8am-11pm; mid-Sept.-mid-April 10am-6pm. Shops open Mon.-Sat. 10am-8pm, Sun. noon-6pm.) The **National Museum of Women in the Arts,** 1250 New York Ave. NW (783-5000; Metro: Metro Center), unwittingly imitates the experience of women in the art world: you'll have a hard time making it to the top. The

hunt for the museum's permanent collection, which begins on the third floor, is something like an initiation rite. Women artists have come into their own in the last 100 years, and the permanent collection proves it with works by Mary Cassatt, Georgia O'Keeffe, Isabel Bishop, Frida Kahlo, and Alma Thomas. (Open Mon.-Sat. 10am-5pm, Sun. noon-5pm. Requested donation $3, seniors, students, and kids $2.)

White House and Foggy Bottom

The **White House**, 1600 Pennsylvania Ave. NW (456-7041), isn't Versailles; the President's house, with its simple columns and expansive lawns, seems a compromise between patrician lavishness and democratic simplicity. The President's personal staff works in the West Wing, while the First Lady's cohort occupies the East Wing. Get a free ticket for a short tour at the ticket booth on the **Ellipse,** the park due south of the White House. Expect a 2½ hr. wait after you have your ticket. (Tours Tues.-Sat. 10am-noon; tickets distributed starting at 8am.) American citizens can arrange a better tour of the White House through their Congressmen. Sometimes it's hard to tell the homeless, the political demonstrators, and the statues apart in **Lafayette Park,** across Pennsylvania Ave. from the White House. All three are more-or-less permanent presences.

At 17th St. and Pennsylvania Ave. NW, the **Renwick Gallery** (357-1718) is filled with "American craft" (Metro: Farragut West). The first floor's temporary exhibits often show fascinating mixed-media sculptures and constructions by important contemporary artists. Stare for hours at *Gamefish,* a sculpture made of sailfish parts, rhinestones, poker chips, and badminton birdies. (Open daily 10am-5:30pm. Free.) Once housed in the Renwick's mansion, the **Corcoran Gallery** (638-3211) is now in much larger quarters on 17th St. between E St. and New York Ave. NW (Metro: Farragut West). The Corcoran shows off American artists like John Singer Sargent, Mary Cassatt, and Winslow Homer. Frederic Church's huge *Niagara Falls* drenches you just looking at it. The gallery's temporary exhibits seek the cutting edge of contemporary art. (Open Mon., Wed. and Fri.-Sun. 10am-5pm, Thurs. 10am-9pm. Suggested donation $3, families $5, students and seniors $1, under 12 free.)

The **Organization of American States** (458-3000, museum 458-6016), 17th St. and Constitution Ave. NW, is a Latin American extravaganza (Metro: Farragut West). The second-floor art gallery displays 20th-century art from Central and South America. Next door is the OAS meeting room, which holds formal sessions. The meetings, held largely in Spanish, welcome tourists; they even have translation machines. Outside, the path through the Aztec Garden leads to the Museum of the Americas, a collection of art from the member states. (Open Tues.-Sat. 10am-5pm. Free.) The **National Academy of Sciences** (334-2000), 21st and C St. NW, holds scientific and medical exhibits. It's customary to get your picture taken while sitting in the lap of the statue of Albert Einstein outside. (Open Mon.-Fri. 8:30am-5pm.)

Above Rock Creek Parkway, the **John F. Kennedy Center for the Performing Arts** (tickets and info 467-4600; entrance off 25th St. and New Hampshire Ave. NW) rises like a marble sarcophagus (Metro: Foggy Bottom-GWU). Built in the late 60s, the center boasts four major stages and a film theater. The flag-decked Hall of States and Hall of Nations lead to the Grand Foyer, which could swallow the Washington Monument with room to spare. A 7-ft. bronze bust of JFK stares up and away at 18 Swedish chandeliers. In the Opera House, snowflake-shaped chandeliers require 1735 electric light bulbs. The terrace has an unbeatable view of the Potomac. (Open daily 10am-11pm. Tours 10am-1pm. Free.)

Georgetown

Oh so painfully hip. The best sights in Georgetown are the people, an odd mixture of funky and preppy, all of them wealthy.

The inside of **Dumbarton Oaks,** 1703 32nd St. NW (recorded info 338-8278, tour info 342-3212), between R and S St., holds Byzantine and pre-Columbian art; outside are magnificent terraced gardens. Philip Johnson's 1963 gallery holds a collection of pre-Columbian art, including carvings and tools from the Aztec and Mayan civilizations. In 1944, the Dumbarton Oaks Conference, held in the Music Room, helped write the United Nations charter. (Collections open Tues.-Sun. 2-5pm; free.) Save at least an hour for the Edenic gardens (open daily 2-6pm, Nov.-March 2-5pm; $2, seniors and kids $1; seniors free each Wed.).

When Archbishop John Carroll learned where the new capital would be built, he rushed to found **Georgetown University** (main entrance at 37th and O St.), which opened in 1789 as the U.S.'s first Catholic institution of higher learning. Students live, study, and party together in the townhouses lining the streets near the university. Georgetown's basketball team, the Hoyas, are perennial contenders for the national college championship. Buy tickets through the Capital Centre (301-350-3400), the campus Ticket Office (687-4692), or Athletic Department (687-2449).

Retired from commercial use since the 1800s, the **Chesapeake & Ohio Canal** (301-299-3613) extends 185 mi. from Georgetown to Cumberland, MD. The benches under the trees around 30th St. make a prime city lunch spot.

Dupont Circle and New Downtown

Dupont Circle used to be called Washington's most diverse neighborhood; then it turned expensive and Adams-Morgan turned cool. Nevertheless, the circle and its environs remain a haven for Washington's artsy, international, and gay communities. Unless otherwise stated, the closest Metro to these sites is Dupont Circle. Massachusetts Ave. between Dupont Circle and Observatory Circle is also called **Embassy Row.** Identify an embassy by the national coat-of-arms or flag out front.

The **Phillips Collection,** 1600-1612 21st St. (387-2151), at Q St. NW, was the first museum of modern art in the U.S. Everyone gapes at Auguste Renoir's masterpiece *Luncheon of the Boating Party* at the landing of the second floor. Van Goghs and Picassos inhabit the rest of the floor. The collection also includes works by Mondrian, Rothko, O'Keeffe, Kandinsky, Klee, and Braque. (Open Mon.-Sat. 10am-5pm, Sun. noon-7pm. Sat.-Sun. Admission $6.50, students and seniors $3.25, required Sat.-Sun. and suggested Mon.-Fri. Under 18 free.

Anderson House, 2118 Massachusetts Ave. NW (785-2040), retains the robber-baron decadence of U.S. ambassador Larz Anderson, who built it in 1902-5; in the two-story ballroom, visitors can marvel at the marble and feel the gilt Anderson must have felt. The Society of the Cincinnati makes this mansion its home base. (Open Tues.-Sat. 1-4pm. Free.) The **Textile Museum,** 2320 S St. NW (667-0441), houses exhibits of rare or intricate textiles; ethnographic displays alternate with shows of individual artists (open Mon.-Sat. 10am-5pm, Sun. 1-5pm; admission by contribution). Flags line the entrance to the **Islamic Center,** 2551 Massachusetts Ave. NW (332-8343), a brilliant white building whose stunning designs stretch to the tips of its spired ceilings. No shorts; women must cover their heads and wear sleeved clothing (no short dresses). (Open daily 10am-5pm. Donation requested.)

Past M St. on 17th St. NW, the **National Geographic Society Explorer's Hall** conquers the first floor of its black-and-white pin-striped building. (857-7588, group tours 857-7689, N.G. Society 857-7000; Metro: Farragut North). The museum proffers working display screens, a short film, a live parrot, a huge globe, and fascinating changing exhibits, often by *National Geographic* magazine's crack photographers. (Open Mon.-Sat. 9am-5pm, Sun. 10am-5pm.) Picnic to the summer sounds of flute duets and jazz sax players in **Farragut Square,** 3 blocks south of Connecticut Ave. on 17th St. between I and K St. NW.

Elsewhere

In the late 80s, the mantle of multicultural hipness passed to **Adams-Morgan,** when cool kids and the cool at heart arrived alongside immigrants from Mexico and El Salvador. A wreath of awesome ethnic food circles 18th, Columbia, and Calvert St. NW, and street carts and secondhand stores lines Columbia Rd. east of 18th St. From the Woodley Park-Zoo Metro, walk to Calvert St., turn left, and hoof east. Don't go to Adams-Morgan in search of a specific establishment; do go to wander around. The neighborhood is a jambalaya of Hispanic, Caribbean, and hipness any city would envy. From the central intersection, walk south along 18th or east along Columbia to soak in the flavor and eat well. Stay west of 16th St. (bring a friend at night), and safety should require only common sense.

Legend has it that "pandemonium" entered the vernacular when the first giant pandas left China for **Washington's National Zoological Park** (673-4800 or 673-4717) as a gift from Mao to Nixon. But after years of unsuccessful attempts to birth a baby panda in captivity, Ling-Ling recently died. Her life-mate Hsing-Hsing remains in the Panda House. The zoo spreads east from Connecticut Ave. a few blocks uphill from the Woodley Park-Zoo Metro; follow the crowds to the entrance at 3000 Connecticut Ave. NW. Forested paths—sometimes very steep—and flat walks near the entrance pass plenty of outdoor exhibits in fields and cages, which visitors seeking the big attractions often ignore. Valley Trail (marked with blue bird tracks) connects the bird and sealife exhibits, while the red Olmsted Walk (marked with elephant feet) links land-animal houses. (Grounds open daily 8am-8pm, Oct. 16-April 14 8am-6pm; buildings open daily 9am-6pm, Sept. 16-April 9am-4:30pm. Free.)

The **Cathedral Church of Saint Peter and Saint Paul,** also called the **Washington National Cathedral** (537-6207; recording 364-6616), at Massachusetts and Wisconsin Ave. NW (Metro: Tenleytown, then take the #30, 32, 34 or 36 bus toward Georgetown; or walk up Cathedral Ave. from the equidistant Woodley Park-Zoo Metro), took over 80 years (1907-90) to build, though the cathedral's interior spaces have been in use for decades. Rev. Martin Luther King Jr. preached his last Sunday sermon from the Canterbury pulpit; more recently, the Dalai Lama spoke here. Take the elevator to the Pilgrim Observation Gallery and see Washington from the highest vantage point in the city (open daily 9:30am-5pm). Angels, gargoyles, and grotesques loom outside. (Open daily 10am-9pm; Sept.-April 10am-4:30pm. Free.) The **National Arboretum** (544-8733), 24th and R St. NE (Metro: Stadium-Armory, take #B2, B3, or B4 bus), is the U.S.'s living library of trees and flowers. Experts go berserk over the arboretum's world-class stock of *bonsai* (dwarf trees). Azaleas and azalea-watchers clog the place each spring. Use caution in the surrounding area. (Open Mon.-Fri. 8am-5pm, Sat.-Sun. 10am-5pm; *bonsai* collection 10am-3:30pm. Free.)

The silence of **Arlington National Cemetery** (Metro: Arlington Cemetery) honors those who sacrificed their lives in war. The 612 acres of hills and tree-lined avenues hold the bodies of U.S. military veterans from five-star generals to unknown soldiers. Before you enter the main gate, get a map from the visitors center. The Kennedy Gravesites hold both President John F. Kennedy and his brother, Robert F. Kennedy. The Eternal Flame flickers above JFK's simple memorial stone. The Tomb of the Unknowns honors all servicemen who died fighting for the United States and is guarded by delegations from the Army's Third Infantry (changing of the guard every ½-hr., Oct.-March every hr. on the hr.). Robert E. Lee's home, **Arlington House,** overlooks the cemetery. Enter the pastel-peach mansion at the front door; tours are self-guided. Head down Custis Walk in front of Arlington House and exit the cemetery through Weitzel Gate to get to the **Iwo Jima Memorial,** based on Joe Rosenthal's Pulitzer Prize-winning photograph of six Marines straining to raise the U.S. flag on Mount Suribachi. (Open daily 8am-7pm, Oct.-March daily 8am-5pm.)

The **Pentagon,** the world's largest office building, shows just how huge a military bureaucracy can get (Metro: Pentagon). To take the guided tour, sign in, walk through a metal detector, get X-rayed, and show proper identification. The guide keeps the pace of the tour so brisk that it's like a military music video. (Tours every ½-hr. Mon.-Fri. 9:30am-3:30pm, Oct.-May no tours at 10:30am, 1:30, and 3pm. Non-U.S. citizens should bring their passports for the security check. Free.)

The tours, exhibits, and restorations at **Mount Vernon** (703-780-2000), George Washington's Fairfax County estate, are staid and worshipful even by Virginia standards. (Metro: Huntington, then take the 11P bus. To drive, take the Beltway (I-495) to the George Washington Parkway and follow it to Mount Vernon.) A key to the

Bastille, a gift from the Marquis de Lafayette, is on display in the hallway. Upstairs, see the bedroom of George and Martha Washington. A gravel path outside leads to their tomb. Don't expect to get too close to the Founder of His Country; George and Martha rest in a mausoleum behind a sturdy iron gate. The graveless "slave burial ground" is nearby. The estate also has 18th-century gardens to view; its fields once grew corn, wheat, tobacco, and marijuana. (Open daily 8am-5pm, Sept.-Oct. and March 9am-5pm, Nov.-Feb. 9am-4pm. $7, seniors $6, kids 6-11 $3.)

ENTERTAINMENT AND NIGHTLIFE

Though Washington cannot boast a world-class compilation of nocturnal delights on the scale of London or New York, just about everyone should be able to find a play, performance, concert, club, or flick to suit their taste among D.C.'s variegated scenes. Major culture purveyors, especially the Kennedy Center, make up for high ticket prices with student discounts and frequent low-cost or free events.

It's also hip to just hang out. Cruise around **Georgetown**, and watch all the beautiful people. In the early evening, most of the excitement is outside; throngs of students, interns, and young professionals share the sidewalk with street performers. Stroll down to **Washington Harbor** and watch those harbor lights at twilight time.

Theater and Film

At 25th St. and New Hampshire Ave., the **Kennedy Center's** (416-8000) zillions of performing-arts spaces include two theaters. Though tickets get expensive (many range from $10-60), all Kennedy Center productions offer ½-price tickets on the day of performance to students, seniors, military personnel, and handicapped persons; call 467-4600 about discount tickets. Free events also dot the Kennedy calendar.

The prestigious **Shakespeare Theater,** 450 7th St. NW (box office 393-2700; Metro: Archives-Navy Memorial), at the Lansburgh on Pennsylvania Ave., puts on Shakespeare for the most part. Call for ticket prices, show times, and discounts for students and seniors. Standing-room tickets ($10) are available 2 hr. before curtain.

Thespians thrive in Washington's **14th St. theater district,** where tiny repertory companies explore and experiment with truly enjoyable results. *City Paper* provides very good coverage of this scene. **Woolly Mammoth,** 1401 Church St. NW (393-3939), **Studio Theater,** 1333 P St. NW (332-3300), and **The Source Theater,** 1835 14th St. NW (462-1073), all hang out in this borderline dangerous neighborhood near Dupont Circle (tickets $16-29; call for info on student discounts).

The excellent **American Film Institute** (828-4000), at the Kennedy Center, shows classic American, foreign, and avant-garde films, usually two per night. **Biograph,** 2819 M St. NW (333-2696), in Georgetown, shows first-run independents, foreign films, and classics. Film festivals are frequent; the eclectic is the norm. ($6, seniors and kids $3.) **Key Theatre,** 1222 Wisconsin Ave. NW (333-5100), near Prospect St. (1 block north of M St.) features first-run art films. Subtitled films offer plenty of chances to polish up your French. ($6.50, seniors $4, matinees $3.50.)

Classical Music

D.C. is home to the well-respected **National Symphony Orchestra,** which performs in the **Kennedy Center** (416-8000), 25th St. and New Hampshire Ave. NW. Tickets are normally expensive ($18-45), but ½-price tickets are available (see above). The NSO also gives concerts in celebration of Memorial Day, the Fourth of July, and Labor Day. The **Washington Opera** (416-7890) also calls the Kennedy Center home. For a schedule of free events, call 467-4600.

The **Library of Congress,** 1st St. SE (concert line 707-5502), sponsors concerts in the Coolidge Auditorium, one of the finest chamber music performance spaces in the world. Concerts are currently being held elsewhere while the auditorium is being renovated. The **Phillips Collection,** 1600-1612 21st St. (387-2151), at Q St. NW, provides an appropriate setting for chamber music and classical piano concerts

(Sept.-May Sun. 5pm; free with museum admission). Check the *Washington Post's* Weekend section for information.

Jazz

A free lunchtime summer jazz series takes place downtown at the **Corcoran Gallery** (638-3211), 17th St. between E St. and New York Ave. NW, in the Hammer Auditorium every Wed. at 12:30pm. (Metro: Farragut West.)

Blues Alley, 1073 Rear Wisconsin Ave. NW (337-4141), in an actual alley, below M St. Cool jazz in an intimate supper club dedicated to the art. Past performers include Mary Wilson of the Supremes and Wynton Marsalis. Tickets $13-30. $7 food-or-drink min. Creole cuisine (entrees $14-19) served from 6pm, snacks ($2-9) served after 9:30pm. Upscale casual dress; some sport tuxes on big nights. Call for reservations and showtimes.

One Step Down, 2517 Pennsylvania Ave. NW (331-8863), near M St. More casual and less expensive than Blues Alley. Jukebox well-stocked with jazz. Local jazz Sun., Mon., and Thurs.; out-of-town talent Fri.-Sat. Free jam-sessions Sat.-Sun. 3:30-7:30pm. Cover $5, up to $17 for out-of-towners. Beers start at $3 and sandwiches $3.50-6. Showtimes vary. Open Mon.-Fri. 10:30am-2am, Sat.-Sun. noon-3am.

Rock, Punk, R&B, Dance, and Bars, all for $19.95. But wait...there's more!

If you don't mind a young crowd, squeeze into a *local* rock-and-roll show; the D.C. punk scene is, or at least was, one of the nation's finest. To see what's up with local bands, just look at *City Paper*. George Washington University sponsors shows in **Lisner Auditorium** (994-1500), 21st and H St. NW, which hosts plays and rock concerts by well-known "alternative" acts. Tickets are sometimes free and never cost more than $25. Call in advance for prices and purchase locations.

In summer on Sat. and Sun., jazz and R&B shows occupy the outdoor **Carter-Barron Amphitheater** (426-0486), in Rock Creek Park up 16th St. and Colorado Ave. NW (tickets about $13.50). From late June-Aug., rock, punk, and metal pre-empt soccer-playing at **Fort Reno Park** (282-0018 or 619-7225), at Chesapeake and Belt St. NW above Wisconsin Ave. (Metro: Tenley Circle.)

9:30 club, 930 F St. NW (393-0930 or 638-2008). Metro: Metro Center. D.C.'s best local and alternative rock since the legendary d.c. space closed down. $3 to see 3 local bands; $7-14 for nationally known acts, which often sell out weeks in advance. Box office open Mon.-Fri. 1-6pm, as well as door time (Sun.-Thurs. 8-11:30pm, Fri.-Sat. 9-11:30pm). Under 21 admitted and hand-stamped.

Kilimanjaro, 1724 California St. NW (328-3839), between Florida Ave. and 18th St. Dimly lit, big-deal club for international music—African, Latin, and Caribbean groups; ju-ju, reggae, and salsa DJs (reggae on Sun.). Caribbean food (restaurant open Tues.-Sun. 5-11pm). No sneakers, shorts, sweats, torn jeans, or tank tops on weekends. No cover Tues.-Thurs.; $5 Fri.-Sat. before 10pm, $10 after 10pm. Up to $20 for live bands. Open Tues.-Thurs. 5pm-2am, Fri. 5pm-4am, Sat. 8pm-4am.

Fifth Colvmn, 915 F St. NW (393-3632), near 9th St. Metro: Gallery Place-China-town. Euro-crowd brings serious disco into the trendy 90s. Splashy "underwater" decor in a converted bank, with fish tanks, fast-paced dizzying films, and lights. House music shakes the basement; quieter bar upstairs. Look for the 4 stone columns outside: the line to get in is the 5th. Cover $5-8 for anything from hip-hip and alternative industrial to acid jazz and New York freestyle. Open Mon. 9pm-2am, Tues.-Thurs. 10pm-2am, Fri.-Sat. 10pm-3am.

Brickskeller, 1523 22nd St. NW (293-1885), between P and Q St. Metro: Dupont Circle. Deserves its reputation for "the world's largest selection of beer"—over 500 brands from such locales as the Ivory Coast, Togo, Belgium, and South America. Bi-monthly beer-tasting events ($22 for the night; Sept.-June, usually on Tues. or Wed.; call ahead for reservations). Read the menu for beer listings "from Aass to Zywiece." DJ upstairs Fri.-Sat. Must be 21 after 10pm. Open Mon.-Thurs. 11:30am-2am, Fri. 11:30am-3am, Sat. 6pm-3am, Sun. 6pm-2am.

The Front Page, 1333 New Hampshire Ave. NW (296-6500). Metro: Dupont Circle. Well-known among the intern crowd for its generous happy hours, which include chicken wings or taco bar (Mon.-Fri. 4-7pm). Open daily 11:30am-1:30am; bar closes earlier if business slows.

Cities, 2424 18th St. NW (328-7194). This packed restaurant n' bar stays hip, or tries to, by changing decor and menu every 8 months or so to mimic a different city. The chic decor hints at out-of-budget-range entrees, but the menu's low end satisfies too. (Appetizers $3.50-6). Upstairs at the bar, funky wooden tables brawl with leopard skin benches beside a spectacular, view-from-the-'copter-style full-length window. Beer from $3.75. No cover. Open Mon.-Fri. 5pm-2am, Sat. 5pm-3am, Sun. 11am-2am. Restaurant closes at 11pm.

Club Heaven and **Club Hell,** 2327 18th St. NW (667-4355), near Columbia Rd. Hell's downstairs, Heaven's upstairs, so the ground-floor Italian restaurant must be Purgatory. In Hell, smoke blurs the funky gold tables and loud music emanates from spooky, yellow-backlit masks. Heaven looks rather like an old townhouse: scuffed wood floor, comfy couches, a small bar, and TVs, but the dance floor throbs to pounding beats. No cover unless a band is playing. Domestic beer $3, imports $3.75. Dancing starts about 10pm. Heaven open Sun.-Thurs. 10pm-2am, Fri.-Sat. 10pm-3am. Hell open Sun.-Thurs. 6pm-2am, Fri.-Sat. 6pm-3am.

Chief Ikes Mambo Room, Chaos, and Pandemonium, 1725 Columbia Rd. (Chief Ikes 332-2211, Chaos and Pandemonium 797-4637), near Ontario Rd., about 2½ blocks from 18th St. Downstairs at Chief Ikes, diner-style American food ($5.25-10) accompanied by live jazz (Sun.), rock, and R&B (other days). Up a long red staircase are Chaos and Pandemonium, 2 tumultuous rooms featuring alternative music and pseudo-Japanese decor. Pool table in Pandemonium. In Chaos, Psychotronic Film Festival with free popcorn and cheesy horror movies every Mon. (admission $2). Usually no cover. Live bands Mon.-Tues.; must be 21. Chief Ikes open Mon.-Thurs. and Sun. 4pm-2am, Fri.-Sat. 4pm-3am. Chaos and Pandemonium open Mon.-Thurs. and Sun. 6pm-2am, Fri.-Sat. 6pm-3am.

J.R.'s, 1519 17th St. NW (328-0090). Metro: Dupont Circle. An upscale but down-home brick and varnished-wood bar, with wood floors, stained-glass windows, and a DJ in a choir stall overlooking the tank of "guppies" (gay urban professionals). Open Sun.-Thurs. 11am-2am, Fri.-Sat. 11am-3am.

Sports

Opportunities for sports addicts abound in the D.C. area. The Georgetown Hoyas (basketball) pack the USAir Arena (formerly the Capital Centre). The Hoyas won it all in 1987. Their professional counterparts, the Bullets, also fire away here, as do the Capitals (hockey). (Call USAir Arena at 301-350-3400. It is located between Landover Rd. and Central Ave. in Landover, MD. Take the Beltway (I-95) to exits 15 or 17 and follow signs.) The Redskins won the Super Bowl in 1982, 1987, and 1992, and fans flock religiously to Robert F. Kennedy Stadium to see them. (For tickets, call RFK Stadium, 2001 E. Capitol St. SE, at 547-9077; expect to wait a few years.)

Festivals and Annual Events

In its role as a national capital, D.C. plays host to dozens of annual festivals celebrating the nation's heritage, various ethnic cultures, all genres of music, folk art, and famous authors; honoring veterans and civil rights activists; tossing frisbees and flying kites; and oh so much more. The most fanfare accompanies the **4th of July** celebrations, which commemorate the signing of the *Declaration of Independence* and the nation's birthday with a big ole parade and fireworks on the Mall—get there early or you won't get a seat with a decent view. For a complete listing of annual events, consult the **D.C. Committee to Promote Washington,** 1212 New York Ave., #200 (724-4091).

THE SOUTH

The American South has always fought to maintain a unique identity in the face of the economically more powerful North. The culture battle isn't fought with guns anymore (they tried that), but with stereotypes and conventional wisdom. Today's South has adopted the industry and urbanity of the North while retaining notions of hospitality, an easy-going pace, and a carpe diem philosophy. Northern stereotypes of rednecks, racists, and impoverished hayseeds are being countered by the rapid economic growth of the southern metropoli—Atlanta, Nashville, Little Rock, and New Orleans—infusing much of the region with a modern flavor. But the past lingers on both in the division of wealth beneath the white and black and in the genuine warmth of southern hospitality.

This region's history and culture, a melange of Anglo, African, French, and Spanish, are reflected in its architecture, cuisine, geography, language, and people. From time immemorial—before people began creating their rich histories here—nature blessed the region with overwhelming mountains, lush marshlands, and sparkling beaches. From the Atlantic's Sea Islands to the rolling Ozarks, the Gulf's bayous to the Mississippi Delta, the South's beauty will awe, entice, and enchant you.

 ## Alabama

The "Heart of Dixie" has matured since the 1960s and 1970s when Governor George Wallace fought a vicious campaign opposing African-American advancement. During decades of internal racial strife, Alabama was the home to bigotry but also to dynamic Civil Rights leaders like Reverend Dr. Martin Luther King, Jr., whose amazing patience and fortitude helped spawn the first real changes in race relations.

Today, Alabama's larger cities attract a cosmopolitan populace as art museums, concerts, and ethnic restaurants appear. A coastal city, Mobile has grown from one of the Gulf's first settlements to one of the busiest ports in the nation. Though plantation estates endure throughout the countryside, King Cotton now shares his throne with mineral ores and one of the largest beds of white marble in the world.

While these modern attractions are enough to keep you busy, the most compelling reasons to visit Alabama remain the monuments and legacies of a divided past. From the poignant statues in Birmingham's Kelly Ingram Park commemorating the struggles of the 1950s to Booker T. Washington's pioneering Tuskegee Institute (now University), Alabama's history is both tragic and enlightening.

PRACTICAL INFORMATION

Capital: Montgomery.
Visitor Information: Alabama Bureau of Tourism and Travel, 401 Adams Ave. (242-4670; 800-252-2262 outside AL). Open Mon.-Fri. 8am-5pm. **Travel Council,** 702 Oliver Rd. #254, Montgomery 36117 (271-0050). **Division of Parks,** 64 N. Union St., Montgomery 36130 (800-252-7275).
Time Zone: Central (1 hr. behind Eastern). **Postal Abbreviation:** AL
Sales Tax: 4%.

■■■ BIRMINGHAM

This city literally sprung up from the ground. Like its English namesake, Birmingham sits on soil rich in coal, iron ore, and limestone—responsible for its lightning transformation into a premier steel industry center. No longer an industrial town, the city's largest employer is now the University of Alabama, home to one of the best cardiology hospitals in the world. With an urban version of Southern charm and hospitality, arts festivals and museums may suffice in drawing visitors, but the most compelling sights of the area hark back to less idyllic times. Birmingham has been "A Place of Revolution and Reconciliation," trying in recent decades to heal the wounds left by Eugene "Bull" Connor, firehoses, bombings, and police dogs, whose images were spread all over the American news media during the civil rights protests of the early 1960s.

PRACTICAL INFORMATION

Emergency: 911.

Visitor Information: Birmingham Visitors Center, 1200 University Blvd. (254-1654), I-65 exit 259. Maps, calendars, and coupons for accommodations. Open Mon.-Sat. 8:30am-5pm, Sun. 1-5pm. Another location on the lower level of **Birmingham Municipal Airport** (254-1640). Open daily 8:30am-8pm. **Greater Birmingham Convention and Visitors Bureau,** 2027 1st Ave. N., 3rd floor (252-9825), downtown. Open Mon.-Fri. 8:30am-5pm.

Amtrak: 1819 Morris Ave. (324-3033 or 800-872-7245), downtown. To: Montgomery ($12); Atlanta ($32); and Mobile ($54). Open daily 8:30am-4:30pm.

Greyhound: 618 N. 19th St. (800-231-2222). To: Montgomery ($16); Atlanta ($23.50); and Mobile ($37.50). Open 24 hrs.

Public Transport: Metropolitan Area Express (MAX), 252-0101. Runs Mon.-Sat. 7am-6pm. Fare 80¢. **Downtown Area Runabout Transit (DART),** 252-0101. Runs Mon.-Fri. 10am-4pm. Fare 25¢.

Taxi: Yellow Cab, 252-1131. Base fare $2.95, $1.20 each additional mi.

Help Lines: Crisis Center, 323-7777. Open 24 hrs.

Post Office: 351 24th St. N. (521-0209). Open Mon.-Fri. 7:30am-7pm. **ZIP code:** 35203.

Area Code: 205.

The downtown area grid system has avenues running east-west and streets running north-south. Each numbered avenue has a north and a south. Major cultural and government buildings surround **Linn Park,** located between 19th and 21st St. N. on 7th Ave. N. The **University of Alabama in Birmingham (UAB)** extends along University Blvd. (8th Ave. S.) from 11th to 20th St.

ACCOMMODATIONS AND CAMPING

Passport Inn, 821 20th St. S. (252-8041), 2 blocks from UAB. Large, clean rooms, tasteful decor in a convenient location. Pool. Singles and doubles $30.

Ranch House, 2127 7th Ave. S. (322-0691). Near busy bars and restaurants. Pleasant rooms with cable TV and wood paneling. Check out the cowboy tiling in each bathroom. Local calls 25¢ each. Singles and doubles $28.

Economy Inn, 2224 5th Ave. N. (324-6688). Near some run-down buildings in the middle of downtown. Ample, tidy rooms. Laundry room. Singles and doubles $24.

Oak Mountain State Park (663-3061), 15 mi. south of Birmingham off I-65 in Pelham. Heavily forested area with 85-acre recreational lake. Sites $9 for 1-4 people, with electricity $12.

FOOD

Barbecue remains the local specialty, although more ethnic variations have sprung up downtown. The best places to eat cheaply (and meet young people) are at **Five Points South,** located at the intersection of Highland Ave. and 20th St. South. Choose from pesto pizza with sun-dried tomatoes ($2 per slice) at **Cosmo's Pizza,**

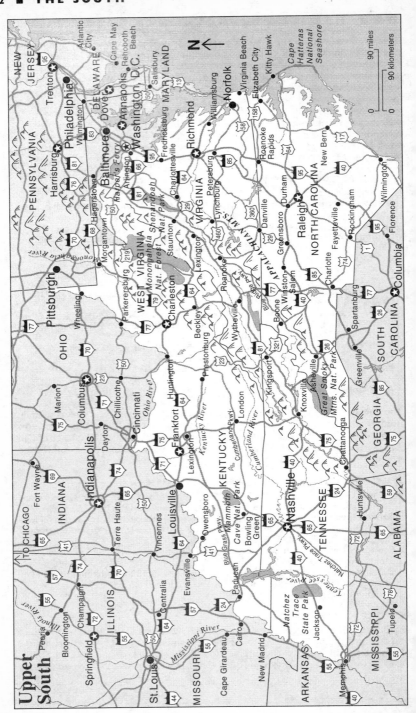

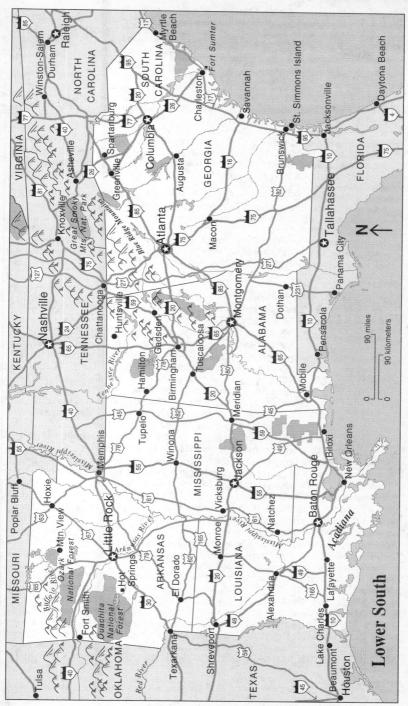

Lower South

2012 Magnolia Ave. (930-9971; open Mon.-Thurs. 11am-11pm, Fri.-Sat. 11am-midnight, Sun. noon-10pm), or health-conscious veggie lunches and groceries at **The Golden Temple,** 1901 11th Ave. S. (933-6333; open Mon.-Fri. 8:30am-7:30pm, Sat. 9:30am-5:30pm, Sun. noon-5:30pm; kitchen open daily 11:30am-2pm, 5-7pm).

The Mill, 1035 20th St. S. (939-3001), sits at the center of Five Points South, serving tasty and health-conscious pizzas ($4-7), sandwiches ($4-6), and other treats, complete with fat, calorie, and sodium counts next to each entree. Microbrewery, bakery, and restaurant in one, this sidewalk cafe/restaurant/bar is the perfect place for any gastronomic need. Live entertainment Wed.-Sun. (cover $2). Open Sun.-Thurs. 6:30am-midnight, Wed.-Sat. 6:30-2am.

Café Bottega, 2240 Highland Ave. S. (939-1000). High-ceilinged and sophisticated, this cafe serves fresh bread to dip in olive oil and Italian specialties brimming with fresh vegetables and herbs. Marinated pasta with sweet peas and mint $5.25. Entrees $5-12. Open Mon.-Fri. 11am-11pm, Sat. 5-11pm. Bar open until "everyone goes home."

Bogue's, 3028 Clairmont Ave. (254-9780). A short-order diner with true delicious Southern fare (cheese omelette and biscuit $3). Always busy weekend mornings. Open Mon.-Fri. 6am-2pm, Sat.-Sun. 6-11:30am.

Ollie's, 515 University Blvd. (324-9485), near Green Springs Hwy. Bible Belt dining in an enormous circular 50s-style building. Pamphlets shout "Is there really a Hell?" while you lustfully consume your beef. BBQ sandwich $2, homemade pie $1.50. Diet plates available. Open Mon.-Sat. 9:30am-8pm.

SIGHTS

A prominent part of Birmingham's efforts towards reconciliation has culminated in the **Black Heritage Tour** of the downtown area. The newly finished **Birmingham Civil Rights Institute,** 520 16th St. N. (328-9696), at 6th Ave. N., rivals the museum in Memphis (see Memphis, TN) in thoroughness, and surpasses it in visual and audio evocations, depictions, and footage of African-American history and the turbulent events of the Civil Rights Movement. In addition to commemorating and educating, the Institute intends to display exhibits on human rights across the globe, and to serves as a research facility open to the public. A trip to Birmingham would be incomplete without a more than cursory tour. (Open Tues.-Sat. 10am-6pm, Sun. 1-5pm.) Other significant sights include the **Sixteenth Street Baptist Church,** 1530 6th Ave. N. (251-9402), at 16th St. N. (in the lower level), where four African-American girls died in a September 1963 bombing by white segregationists after a protest push which culminated in Dr. Martin Luther King's "Letter From a Birmingham Jail." The deaths spurred many protests in nearby **Kelly-Ingram Park,** corner of 6th Ave. and 16th St., where a bronze statue of Dr. Martin Luther King, Jr. and granite representations of oppression, revolution, and reconciliation grace the green lawns.

Remnants of Birmingham's steel industry are best viewed at the gigantic **Sloss Furnaces National Historic Landmark** (324-1911), adjacent to the 1st Ave. N. viaduct off 32nd St. downtown. Though the blast furnaces closed 20 years ago, they stand as the only preserved example of 20th-century iron-smelting in the world. Ballet and drama performances and music concerts are often held here at night. (Open Tues.-Sat. 10am-4pm, Sun. noon-4pm; free guided tours Sat.-Sun. at 1, 2, and 3pm.) To anthropomorphize the steel industry, Birmingham cast the **Vulcan** (Roman god of the forge) who overwhelms the city skyline as the largest cast-iron statue in the world. Visitors can watch over the city from its observation deck. The Vulcan's glowing torch burns red when a car fatality has occurred that day, green when none occur. (Open daily 8am-10:30pm. $1, kids 6 and under free.)

The **Alabama Sports Hall of Fame** (323-6665), corner of Civic Center Blvd. and 22nd St. North, honors the careers of outstanding sportsmen like Jesse Owens, Joe Louis, and Willie Mays (open Mon.-Sat. 9am-5pm, Sun 1-5pm). A few blocks down from the Hall of Fame blooms the refreshing **Linn Park,** across from the **Birmingham Museum of Art,** 2000 8th Ave. N. (254-2565). The museum displays U.S. paintings and English Wedgewood ceramics, as well as a superb collection of African textiles and sculptures (free).

For a breather from the downtown scene, revel in the marvelously sculpted grounds of the **Birmingham Botanical Gardens,** 2612 Lane Park Rd. (879-1227), whose spectacular floral displays, elegant Japanese gardens, and enormous greenhouse vegetate on 68 acres (open daily dawn-dusk; free).

Antebellum **Arlington,** 331 Cotton Ave. (780-5656), southwest of downtown, houses a fine array of Southern decorative arts from the 19th century. Go west on 1st Ave. N., which becomes Cotton Ave., to reach the stately white Greek Revival building, which also hosts craft fairs throughout the year. (Open Tues.-Sat. 10am-4pm, Sun. 1-4pm. $3, ages 6-18 $2.)

To learn more about the geology of the area, visit the **Red Mountain Museum and Cut,** 1421 22nd St. S. (933-4104). You can wander a walkway above the highway to see different levels of rock formation inside Red Mountain. The museum indoors has various exhibits on the prehistoric inhabitants of Alabama. The **Discovery Place** next door, 1320 22nd St. S (939-1176), invites children of all ages to explore body mechanics, the ins and outs of cities, brainteasers, channels of communication, and much more. (Both sites open Mon.-Fri. 9am-3pm, Sat. 10am-4pm, Sun. 1-4pm. Museum free, admission to Discovery Place $2, kids $1.50)

Music lovers lucky or smart enough to visit Birmingham in the middle of June for **City Stages** (251-1272) will hear everything from country to gospel to big name rock groups, with headliners like James Brown and George Jones. The three-day festival also includes food, crafts, and children's activities. (Weekend pass $10.)

ENTERTAINMENT AND NIGHTLIFE

Historic **Alabama Theater,** 1817 3rd Ave. N. (251-0418), shows old movies on occasional weekends throughout the year. Their organ, the "Mighty Wurlitzer," entertains the audience before each showing. ($4, seniors $3, under 12 $2.) Pick up a free copy of *Fun and Stuff* or see the "Kudzu" in the Friday edition of *The Birmingham Post Herald* for listings of all movies, plays, and clubs in the area.

The **Five Points South (Southside)** has a high concentration of nightclubs. On cool summer nights many people grab outdoor tables in front of their favorite bars or hang out by the fountain. Use caution here, and avoid parking or walking in dark alleys near the square. For the hippest licks year-round check out **The Nick,** 2514 10th Ave. S. (322-7550). The poster-covered exterior asserts "the Nick...rocks." (Open Mon.-Sat. Live music nightly. Cover $2-5.) **The Burly Earl,** 2109 7th Ave. S. (322-5848), specializes in fried finger-foods and local acoustic, blues, and sometimes rock sounds. Sandwiches $3-5. (Restaurant open Mon.-Thurs. 10am-11pm, bar open until midnight; Fri.-Sat. 10am-1am, bar open until 2am. Live music Wed.-Thurs. 8:30pm-midnight, Fri.-Sat. 9:30pm-2am.)

■■■ MOBILE

Situated on the Gulf of Mexico, Mobile (mo-BEEL) reflects its checkered past under English, French, and Spanish dominion through its distinctive and diverse architectural styles. Antebellum mansions, Italianate dwellings, Spanish and French historical forts, and Victorian homes line the azalea-edged streets of this, Alabama's oldest major city. Mobile is also awash with museums and gardens that further enhance its color. Site of the first U.S. Mardi Gras, Mobile resembles New Orleans and the Mississippi Coast more than it does the rest of Alabama. Mobile's coastal location proves a nice lagniappe for tourists by offering a moderate climate, fresh seafood, and nearby beautiful white sandy beaches.

PRACTICAL INFORMATION

Emergency: 911.

Visitor Information: Fort Condé Information Center, 150 S. Royal St. (434-7304), in a reconstructed French near Government St. Open daily 8am-5pm.
Mobile Convention and Visitors Bureau, 1 St. Louis Center #2002 (433-5100; 800-662-6282 outside AL). Provides friendly, eager info. Open Mon.-Fri. 8am-5pm.
Traveler's Aid: 438-1625. Operated by the Salvation Army; ask for Travelers Services. Lines open Mon.-Fri. 9-11am, 1-3pm.
Amtrak: 11 Government St. (432-4052 or 800-872-7245). The "Gulf Breeze" blows from Mobile to New York via Birmingham ($56); Atlanta ($74); Greenville, S.C. ($116); Washington, DC ($155). All require advance reservations.
Greyhound: 2545 Government St. (432-9793), at S. Conception downtown. To: Montgomery (8 per day, 4 hr., $27); New Orleans (15 per day, 3 hr., $26); Birmingham (6 per day, 6 hr., $38). Open 24 hrs.
Public Transport: Mobile Transit Authority (MTA), 344-5656. Major depots are at Bienville Sq., St. Joseph, and Dauphin St. Operates Mon.-Sat. 5am-7pm. Fare 75¢, seniors and disabled 35¢, transfers 10¢.
Taxi: Yellow Cab, 476-7711. Base fare $1.30, $1.20 each additional mi.
Help Lines: Rape Crisis, 473-7273. **Crisis Counseling,** 666-7900. Both 24 hrs.
Post Office: 250 Saint Joseph St. (694-5917). Open Mon.-Fri. 7am-5pm, Sat. 9am-4pm. **ZIP code:** 36601.
Area Code: 205.

The downtown district fronts the Mobile River. **Dauphin Street** and **Government Boulevard** (U.S. 90), which becomes Government Street downtown, are the major east-west routes. **Royal Street** and **St. Joseph Street** are the north-south byways. Some of Mobile's major attractions lie outside downtown. The *U.S.S. Alabama* is off the causeway leading out of the city; **Dauphin Island** is 30 mi. south.

ACCOMMODATIONS AND CAMPING

Accommodations are both reasonable and accessible, but stop at the Fort Condé Information Center (see Practical Information) first; they can make reservations for you at a 10-15% discount. The MTA runs a "Government St." bus regularly which reaches the Government St. motels listed below, but they are all within a 15-min. walk of downtown.

Economy Inn, 1119 Government St. (433-8800). Big beds, clean sheets, a pool, and dark-panelled walls. Singles and doubles $30. Key deposit $5.
Motel 6, 400 Beltline Hwy. (343-8448). Small, dark rooms with tidy furnishings. Free movie channel and local calls. $27 for 1 person, $6 per additional person.
Family Inns, 900 S. Beltline Rd. (344-5500), I-65 at Airport Blvd., sports new carpets, firm beds, and general comfort. Singles $27; doubles $35.
I-10 Kampground, 6430 Theodore Dawes Rd. E. (653-9816), 7½ mi. west on I-10 (exit 13 and turn south). No public transportation. Pool, kids' playground, laundry, and bath facilities. Sites $12, $1 per additional person.

FOOD

Mobile's proximity to the Gulf makes both seafood and Southern cookin' regional specialties. As well-known for its atmosphere as for its seafood, **Wintzels,** 605 Dauphin St., (433-1004) six blocks west of downtown, offers a dozen oysters on the half shell "fried, stewed, and nude" for $6 (open Mon.-Thurs. and Sat. 11am-9pm, Fri. 11am-9:45pm). Farther out from downtown, **The Lumber Yard Cafe,** 2617 Dauphin St. (471-1241), serves seafood gumbo for $4 and sandwiches ($5-7). Live bands sometimes blare on weekends, and the big-screen TV entertains during the week. (Open daily 11am-about 3am.) **Argiro's,** 1320 Battleship Pkwy. (626-1060), is a quick-stop deli that provides businessmen and sailors with cheap hot dogs and sandwiches ($2-5) and Southern specialties such as red beans and rice next to the *U.S.S. Alabama* (open Mon.-Tues. and Sat. 8am-3:45pm, Wed.-Fri. 8am-4:45pm).

SIGHTS AND ENTERTAINMENT

Mobile encompasses four historic districts: **Church Street, DeToni Square, Old Dauphin Way,** and **Oakleigh Garden.** Each offers a unique array of architectural styles. The Information Center (see Practical Information) provides maps for walking or driving tours of these former residences of cotton brokers and river pilots as well as the "shotgun" cottages of their servants. Package tour admission prices are available at the center, $10 for four house museums.

Church St. divides into east and west subdistricts. The homes in the venerable **Church St. East District,** showcase popular U.S. architectural styles of the mid- to late-19th century, including Federal, Greek Revival, Queen Anne, and Victorian. While on Church St., be sure and pass through the **Spanish Plaza,** Hamilton and Government St., which honors Mobile's sibling city—Málaga, Spain—while recalling Spain's early presence in Mobile. Also of interest in this area is the **Christ Episcopal Church,** 115 S. Conception St. (433-1842), opposite the tourist office at Fort Condé. Dedicated in 1842, the church contains beautiful German, Italian, and Tiffany stained glass windows. Call the office (8am-4pm weekdays) or wander in when the church is open on weekends.

In the **DeToni Historical District,** north of downtown, tour the tastefully restored **Richards-DAR House,** 256 North Joachim St. (434-7320), whose red Bohemian stained glass and rococo chandeliers blend beautifully with its antebellum Italianate architecture and ornate "Iron Lace." On slow days, the staff may invite you in for tea and cookies. (Open Tues.-Sat. 10am-4pm, Sun. 1-4pm. Tours $3, kids $1.) Brick townhouses with wrought-iron balconies fill the rest of the district.

The restored Victorian buildings of the **Old Dauphin Way** are today settings for homes and businesses. Attempts at revitalization, with new restaurants and club opening in the Victorian buildings, will hopefully bring new life to the area that has become rather quiet over the years.

One of the most elegant buildings in Mobile is **Oakleigh,** 350 Oakleigh Place (432-1281) off Government St., with a cantilevered staircase and enormous windows that open onto all the balconies upstairs. Inside, a museum contains furnishings of the early Victorian, Empire, and Regency periods. (Tours every ½ hr.; last tour at 3:30pm. $4, seniors $3, students $2, kids 6-18 $1; tickets sold next door at the simple **Cox-Deasy House.**) Also part of the museum system is the **Carlen House** (470-7768), Carlen St. off Dauphin St., a six-room restored Creole cottage with period furnishings. The **Phoenix Fire Museum,** 203 S. Claiborne St., displays several antique fire engines including an 1898 steam-powered fire engine. (All open Tues.-Sat. 10am-5pm, Sun. 1-5pm. Free.)

The fascinating African-American artists' works on display merit a trip to the famous **Fine Arts Museum of the South (FAMOS),** 4850 Museum Dr. (343-2667; open Tues.-Sun. 10am-5pm; free). The **Exploreum,** 1906 Springhill Ave. (476-6873), offers scientific diversions geared to children with hands-on investigations and experiments (open Tues.-Fri. 9am-5pm, Sat.-Sun. 1-5pm; $3, kids 2-17 $2).

The battleship *U.S.S. Alabama,* permanently moored at **Battleship Park** (433-2703), took part in every major World War II Pacific battle. The park is at the entrance of the Bankhead Tunnel, 2½ mi. east of town on I-10. Berthed along the port side of this intriguing ship is one of the most famous submarines of the war, the *U.S.S. Drum.* (Open daily 8am-sunset. Admission to both vessels $5, kids 6-11 $2.50. Parking $2.)

Gray Line of Mobile (432-2228) leads interesting one to two-hour sight-seeing tours of the downtown historic areas, **Battleship Park,** and **Bellingrath Gardens** from the Fort Condé Information Center; see Practical Information. (Tours of downtown, Mon.-Sat. 10:30am and 2pm, Sun. 2pm. $8, kids 4-14 $4; of Battleship Park 10:30am and 2pm daily, $12, kids $6.50; of the Gardens 8:30 daily, $20, kids $10, admission to home $7.50) For a lengthier excursion, travel south on Rte. 193 to **Dauphin Island** where you can fish, dive, or just lounge around. No beach though.

For nighttime entertainment, stop in at **Trinity's Downtown,** 456 Civic Center Dr. (433-3333), across from the Civic Center, where bands play rock and reggae Wednesday through Saturday nights (open Mon.-Wed. 11:30am-midnight, Thurs.-Sat. 11am-2am). There's more rock and reggae at **G.T. Henry's,** 462 Dauphin St. (432-0300), on a multi-tiered stage, with crawfish boils on Sundays to boot (open Wed-Sun. 5:30pm until everyone leaves; cover $2-5).

■■■ MONTGOMERY

A look into Montgomery's history unveils a concatenation of firsts and beginnings: the first capital of the Confederacy, the first operating electric streetcar in 1886, and the first Wright Brothers' flight school in 1910. This is also the city where Dr. Martin Luther King, Jr. began his ministry. In late 1955, King went on to lead bus boycotts here that introduced the nation to his nonviolent approach to gaining equal rights for African-Americans. With its nationally acclaimed Alabama Shakespeare Festival and the recently completed Arts Museum, Montgomery lures culture-seekers. Retaining an ambiance of easygoing lifestyles, the capital of Alabama celebrates its rural past alongside a busy, diverse present.

PRACTICAL INFORMATION

Emergency: 911.
Visitor Information: Visitor Information Center, 401 Madison Ave. (262-0013). Open Mon.-Fri. 8:30am-5pm, Sat.-Sun. 9am-4pm. **Chamber of Commerce,** 401 Adams Ave. (242-4670). Open Mon.-Fri. 8:30am-5pm.
Traveler's Aid: 265-0568. Operated by Salvation Army. Open Mon.-Fri. 9am-5pm.
Greyhound: 210 S. Court St. (800-231-2222). To: Tuskegee (7 per day, 1 hr., $8); Birmingham (7 per day, 3 hr., $16); Mobile (8 per day, 4 hr., $26.50); and Atlanta ($27.50). Open 24 hrs.
Amtrak: 335 Coosa St. (262-4103), in Riverfront Park. To: Birmingham ($12); Mobile ($46); Atlanta ($41), and Washington, DC ($147).
Public Transport: Montgomery Area Transit System (MATS), 701 N. McDonough St. (262-7321). Operates throughout the metropolitan area Mon.-Sat. 6am-6pm. Fare $1, transfers 10¢.
Taxi: Yellow Cab, 262-5225. $2.60 first mi., $1 each additional mi.
Help Lines: Council Against Rape, 286-5987. **Help-A-Crisis,** 279-7837. Both open 24 hrs.
Post Office: 135 Catoma St. (244-7576). Open Mon.-Fri. 7:30am-5:30pm, Sat. 8am-noon. **ZIP code:** 36104.
Area Code: 205.

Downtown Montgomery follows a grid pattern: **Madison Avenue** and **Dexter Avenue** are the major east-west routes; **Perry Street** and **Lawrence Street** run north-south.

ACCOMMODATIONS AND FOOD

Those with a car will find it easy to procure accommodations; I-65 at the Southern Blvd. exit overflows with cheap beds. Two well-maintained budget motels centrally located downtown are the **Capitol Inn,** 205 N. Goldthwaite St. (265-0541), at Heron St., with spacious, clean, and comfortable rooms and a pool (and free continental breakfast), near the bus station on a hill overlooking the city (singles $30, doubles $32) and the venerable, somewhat comfortable **Town Plaza,** 743 Madison Ave. (269-1561), at N. Ripley St. (singles $20, doubles $22). The Plaza, actually closer to the capitol, absolutely prohibits pets. Off exit 168 on I-65 sleep a slew of budget motels. **Budget Inn,** 995 W. South Blvd. (284-4004), has a pool, clean, big rooms, and lots of funky light switches ($25 for 1-4 people). **The Inn South,** 4243 Inn South Ave. (288-7999), has very nicely decorated rooms and a lobby with a grand double staircase and chandelier (singles $29, doubles $33). For an alternative to these inns, contact **Bed and Breakfast Montgomery,** P.O. Box 1026, Montgomery, AL 36101 (264-0056). **KOA Campground** (288-0728), ¼ mi. south of Hope Hull exit, 4 mi. from town, has a pool, laundry, and showers (tent sites $11, with water and electricity $16, with A/C add $2.50 (but if you have A/C it's not really camping, is it?)).

Martha's Place, 458 Sayre St. (263-9135), is a new but soon-to-be-legendary, family-run, down-home restaurant with a daily country-style buffet ($5.50). Read the articles on the wall and discover a real-life American dream come true (which you can eat!). (Open Mon.-Fri. 11am-3pm, Sun. 11am-4pm.) **Chris's Hot Dogs,** 138 Dexter Ave. (265-6850), with over 70 years under its belt, is an established Montgomery institution. This small diner serves gourmet hot dogs (under $2) and thick Brunswick stew ($1.65). (Open Mon.-Thurs. 8:30am-7pm, Fri. 8:30am-8pm, Sat. 10am-7pm.) At **The China Bowl,** 701 Madison Ave. (832-4004), 2 blocks from the Town Plaza Motel, large portions include a daily special of one entree, fried rice, egg roll, chicken wing, and a fried wonton for $4.20; take-out available (open Mon.-Thurs. 11am-9pm, Fri. 11am-9:30pm). For a great snack, make your way over to the **Montgomery State Farmers Market** (242-5350), at the corner of Federal Dr. (U.S. 231) and Coliseum Blvd., and snag a bag of peaches for $1 (open spring and summer daily 7am-8pm). For a more filling meal, right next door there is nary an empty seat for the Southern cooking at **The Farmer's Market Cafeteria,** 315 N. McDonough St. Free iced tea with every inexpensive meal ($4-5). (Open Mon.-Fri. 5am-2pm.)

SIGHTS AND ENTERTAINMENT

Montgomery's newest sight is the **Civil Rights Memorial,** 400 Washington Ave. at Hull St. Maya Lin, the architect who designed the Vietnam Memorial in Washington, D.C., also designed this dramatically minimalist tribute to 40 of the men, women, and children who died fighting for civil rights. The outdoor monument bears names and dates of significant events on a circular black marble table over which water and flowers of remembrance continuously flow; a wall frames the table with Martin Luther King's words, "...Until Justice rolls down like waters and righteousness like a mighty stream." (Open daily.) The legacy and life of African-American activism and faith can also be seen one block away at the **Dexter Avenue King Memorial Baptist Church,** 454 Dexter Ave. (263-3970), where King preached. At this 112-year-old church, Reverend King and other Civil Rights leaders organized the 1955 Montgomery bus boycott; 10 years later, King led a nationwide Civil Rights march past the church to the Montgomery capitol. The basement mural chronicles King's role in the nation's struggle during the 1950s and 1960s. (Tours Mon.-Fri. 10am and 2pm, Sat. every 45 min. beginning at 10:30am. Free.)

Three blocks north is **Old Alabama Town,** 310 N. Hull St. (263-4355), at Madison, an artfully maintained historic district of 19th-century buildings. The complex includes a pioneer homestead, an 1892 grocery, a schoolhouse, and an early African-American church. While the restored buildings accurately reflect a variety of living conditions, the tour's narrative belies an appallingly 19th century attitude toward slavery, sharecropping, and race relations. (Open Mon.-Sat. 9:30am-3:30pm, last tour at 3:30pm; Sun. 1:30-3:30pm. $5, kids 5-18 $1.50.)

After years (and years and years) of restoration, the **State Capitol** (242-3750), Bainbridge St. at Dexter Ave., is once again open for public viewing (open Mon.-Fri. 8am-5pm for free, self-guided tours; make an appointment for a guide; free). You can also visit the nearby **Alabama State History Museum and State Archives,** 624 Washington Ave. (242-4363). On exhibit are many Native American artifacts along with early military swords and medals. Stop by "Grandma's Attic" where you can try on antique furs and play with antique sewing machines and typewriters in a wooden-frame attic replica. (Open Mon.-Fri. 8am-5pm, Sat. 9am-5pm. Free.) Next door to the Archives is the elegant **First White House of the Confederacy,** 644 Washington Ave. (242-1861), which contains many original furnishings from Jeff Davis's presidency (open Mon.-Fri. 8am-4:30pm, Sat.-Sun. 9am-4:30pm; free). Another restored home of interest is the **F. Scott and Zelda Fitzgerald Museum,**

919 Felder Ave. (264-4222), off Carter Hill Rd. Zelda, originally from Montgomery, lived here with Scott from October 1931 to April 1932. The museum contains a few of her paintings and some of his original manuscripts, as well as their strangely monogrammed bath towels. (Open Wed.-Fri. 10am-2pm, Sat.-Sun. 1-5pm.)

Country music fans might want to join the hundreds who make daily pilgrimages to the **Hank Williams Memorial,** located in the Oakwood Cemetery Annex off Upper Wetumpka Rd. Oversize music notes flank the gravestone upon which rests a stone cowboy hat and engravings of guitars, cowboy boots, and titles of his most famous hits. Green astro-turf carpets the holy ground. (Open daily 7am-sunset.) For more live entertainment, turn to the renowned **Alabama Shakespeare Festival,** (800-841-4ASF) staged at the remarkable $22 million **Wynton M. Blount Cultural Park,** 15 min. southeast of the downtown area. In addition to Shakespeare, Broadway shows and other plays are staged. Nearby, off Woodmere Blvd., is the **Montgomery Museum of Fine Arts,** 1 Museum Dr. (244-5700). This attractive museum houses a substantial collection of 19th- and 20th-century paintings and graphics, as well as ARTWORKS, a hands-on gallery and art studio for children. (Open Tues.-Wed. and Fri-Sat. 10am-5pm, Thurs. 10am-9pm, Sun. noon-5pm. Free.)

Montgomery shuts down fairly early, but if you're in the mood for some blues and beers, try **1048,** 1048 E. Fairview Ave. (834-1048), near Woodley Ave. (open Mon.-Fri. 4pm-until and Sat. 6pm-until). For further information on events in the city, call the Chamber of Commerce's 24-hr. **FunPhone** (240-9447).

■ Near Montgomery: Tuskegee

Late in the 19th century after Reconstruction, Southern states still segregated and disenfranchised "emancipated" African-Americans. Booker T. Washington, a former slave, believed that blacks could best combat repression and racism by educating themselves and learning a trade, as opposed to pursuing the classical, more erudite education which W.E.B. Dubois proposed. Therefore, the curriculum at the college Washington founded, **Tuskegee Institute,** revolved around such practical endeavors as agriculture and carpentry, with students constructing almost all of the campus buildings. Washington raised money for the college by giving lectures on social structure across the country. Artist, teacher, and scientist George Washington Carver became head of the Agricultural Department at Tuskegee, where he discovered many practical uses for the peanut, including axle grease and peanut butter.

Today, a more academically oriented Tuskegee University covers over 260 acres and a wide range of subjects; the buildings of Washington's original institute also comprise a national historical site. A walking tour of the campus begins at the **Carver Museum,** with the **Visitor Orientation Center** (727-3200) inside (both open daily 9am-5pm; free). Down the street from the museum on old Montgomery Rd. is **The Oaks,** a restored version of Washington's home. Free tours from the museum begin on the hour.

For a filling, delicious, and inexpensive meal after your touring, just cross the street from campus to **Thomas Reed's Chicken Coop,** 527 Old Montgomery Rd. (727-3841). Chicken sold by the piece or as a full dinner (all under $5). And you *will* lick your fingers. (Open daily 9am-5pm.)

To get to Tuskegee, take I-85 toward Atlanta and exit at Rte. 81 south. Turn right at the intersection of Rte. 81 and Old Montgomery Rd. onto Rte. 126. **Greyhound** also runs frequently from Montgomery (1 hr., $8). Tuskegee's **ZIP code** is 36083; the **area code** is 205.

Arkansas

Most Americans have probably heard by now of a place called Hope, birthplace of a man called Clinton. Arkansas' offerings, however, hardly end with the nation's latest president. Even as you zip over the Mississippi River from the east, you can feel nature's expanse widen, the landscape transform into green fields that sparkle with the last rain. "The Natural State," as its license plate proclaims, certainly lives up to its boast, encompassing the ascents of the Ozarks, the clear waters of Hot Springs, and the very natural friendliness of its people.

PRACTICAL INFORMATION

Capital: Little Rock.
Visitor Information: Arkansas Dept. of Parks and Tourism, 1 Capitol Mall, Little Rock 72201 (501-682-7777 or 800-643-8383). Open Mon.-Fri. 8am-5pm.
Nickname: "Land of Opportunity." **State Bird:** Mockingbird.
Time Zone: Central (1 hr. behind Eastern). **Postal Abbreviation:** AR
Sales Tax: 5.5%.

■■■ HOT SPRINGS NATIONAL PARK

Don't let the alligator farms, gift shops, wax museums, and amphibious tour-buses/boats turn you away. Despite the ubiquitous commercialism, Hot Springs delivers precisely what it advertises: cleansing, soothing relaxation. Previous consumers—from early Native Americans to Hernando de Soto to the frontiersmen of the last century—expected far more from these very pure waters; their healing and medicinal powers were legendary. Today they are simply legend. But once you've bathed in one of the many coils of these 143° springs and dined in one of several fine and friendly eateries, don't be surprised if you find yourself floating past the stores to stare into the park itself, or collect water (be careful; it *is* hot) from the public faucets, or merely stare blankly and dreamily recall the whirling water of the baths.

Practical Information Before touring Hot Springs, stop by the **visitors center** (321-2277), downtown at the corner of Central and Reserve St., and pick up their valuable coupon packets for many attractions and restaurants (open Mon.-Sat. 9:30am-5pm, Sun. 1-5pm). Hot Springs is especially crowded during the horse racing season at nearby **Oaklawn** (Feb.-April; admission $1; 623-4411 or 800-722-3652 for racetrack information). For more information on food, lodging, and current area attractions, call the visitor's bureau at 800-543-2284 or 800-772-2489, or pick up a copy of *Hot Springs Pipeline,* available for free at the visitors center.

Hot Springs's **Post Office** is at the corner of Central and Reserve in the Federal Reserve Building. The **ZIP code** is 71901; the **area code** is 501.

Accommodations and Food Walk into a fairy tale at the **Best Motel,** 630 Ouachita (624-5736), which has gingerbread-like cabins, a storybook pool, and relaxing chairs. (Singles $20. Doubles $30.) The **Margarete Motel,** 217 Fountain St., offers an excellent deal with large rooms, each with kitchen. (Singles $24-26. Doubles $26-30.) For no frills, no phones (yes, there is cable TV), rooms at the **Parkway Motel,** 815 Park Ave. (624-2551), start at $18. The motels clustered along Rtes. 7 and 88 have similar prices, although rates rise during the tourist season (Feb.-Aug.); camping is far cheaper (see State Parks below). For the budget traveler who has a little stashed away in the ol' moneybelt, the **Arlington Resort Hotel and Spa** (623-7771 or 800-643-1502), at Fountain and Central St., is a lavish, bordering on gaudy, resort of yesteryear (Capone used to stay here)—at very reasonable rates. (Singles from $40. Doubles $50. Family rates with 2 double beds from $56.)

Hot Springs has a number of small, inexpensive restaurants. Snack on *beignets* (doughnuts without the hole; 3 for 90¢) and *café au lait* (75¢) at **Café New Orleans,** 210 Central Ave. (624-3200), or try their deliciously filling breakfasts, especially the fruited crepes (3 for $3). Dinner is also divine, with mouth-watering seafood selections ($5-10). (Open Sun.-Thurs. 7am-9pm, Fri.-Sat. 7am-10pm.) For good ol' country food, try **Granny's Kitchen,** 322 Central Ave. (624-9201), with full dinners and veggie plates under $4, and a damn good blackberry cobbler for only $2 (open daily 6:30am-8pm). Also try **Ma's Cafe,** 362 Central (623-4091), which costs a bit more ($5-8), but serves a fabulous chicken-fried steak ($7); be sure to have the Mississippi mud pie ($2) for dessert (open daily 9am-9pm).

Sights and Entertainment The **Fordyce Bathhouse Visitors Center,** 300 Central Ave. (623-1433), offers information and fascinating tours on the surrounding wilderness areas and on the bathhouse itself, both of which are part of the Hot Springs National Park. As Hot Springs was the "boyhood home" of Bill Clinton, Fordyce has recently constructed an exhibit of his rise to fame. (Open daily 9am-5pm.) The **Buckstaff** (623-2308), in "Bathhouse Row" on Central, retains the dignity and elegance of Hot Spring's heyday in the 1920s. Baths are $11.50, massages $11.75. (Open Mon.-Fri. 7-11:45am and 1:30-3pm, Sat. 7-11:45am.) Around the corner is the rather unconventional **Hot Springs Health Spa,** N. 500 Reserve (321-9664). Not only does the spa allow the only coed baths in town (mandatory bathing suits are very conventional) but you can bring your children, stay as long as you like, and meander among the many baths. Note the late hours. (Bath $10, massage $10-13; open daily 9am-9pm.) The **Downtowner,** at Central and Park, gives the cheapest hands-on, full treatment baths with no difference in quality. (Bath $9.50, massage $10. Open Mon.-Fri. 7-11:30am and 1:30-3:30pm, Sat. 7-11:30am and 2-4:30pm, closed Wed. afternoons.) The handy guide at the visitor's center (above) lists all the hours and prices around town.

There is more to Hot Springs than bathing, as any number of tours demonstrate for you. Try cruising Lake Hamilton on the **Belle of Hot Springs** (525-4438), with 1-hr. narrated tours alongside the Ouachita Mountains and Lake Hamilton mansions ($8, kids $4). If you prefer to waddle some when you aren't swimming, the **White and Yellow Duck Tours** (623-1111 or 800-934-0374) cruise through both city streets and serene waterways ($8.50, seniors $8, kids $5.50). In town, the **Mountain Valley Spring Water Company,** 150 Central Ave. (623-6671 or 800-643-1501), offers free samples and tours of its national headquarters (open Mon.-Fri. 9am-5pm, Sat.-Sun. 10am-4pm). From the **Hot Springs Mountain Observatory Tower** (623-6035), located in the national park (turn off Central Ave. to Rte. 7), you can view the beautiful panorama of the surrounding mountains and lakes (open daily May 16-Labor Day 9am-9pm, Nov.-Feb. 9am-5pm, March-Oct. 9am-6pm; $2.75, kids $1.75). A more horizontal escape from the bustling town center is **Whittington Park,** on Whittington off Central, where shops and animal farms quickly give way to an expanse of trees, grass, and shaded picnic tables.

Nighttime family entertainment percolates throughout Hot Springs. You may simply want to marvel at the well-lit architecture on Central Ave. For a more active evening, **The Famous Bath House Show,** 701 Central Ave. (623-1415), performs a smattering of every possible type of music (well, perhaps not industrial-funk-hip-hop) around (shows nightly 8pm, May-Sept. $8.45, children $4. Reservations recommended). A short drive out of town is the **Music Mountain Jamboree,** 2720 Albert Pike (767-3841) (also called U.S. 270 W). Family-style country music shows take place nightly during the summer, and at various times throughout the rest of the year (shows at 8pm; $9, kids $4.50; reservations recommended).

■ Nearby Parks

The closest campgrounds can be found at **Gulpha Gorge** (part of Hot Springs National Park); follow Rte. 70 to 70B, about 3 mi. N.E. of town (sites $6, seniors $3, no hookups).

The 48,000-acre **Lake Ouachita Park** (767-9366) encompasses the largest of three clear, beautiful, artificial lakes near Hot Springs. Travel 3 mi. west of Hot Springs on U.S. 270, then 12 mi. north on Rte. 227. Numerous islands float offshore promising an escape from civilization in quiet coves and rocky beaches. Fishing abounds, and camping is available from $6-14 per day, depending on the beauty of the site and the facilities available; fishing boats rent for $10 per day.

By car from Hot Springs you can easily reach **Lake Catherine Park** (844-4176), which covers over 2000 acres of Ouachita Mountain, and stretches along the shores of beautiful Lake Catherine. Campsites start at $12 per day. Take exit 97 off I-30 at Malvern and go 12 mi. north on Rte. 171. (Canoe rentals $3.50 per hr., power boats $18 per ½ day, $25 per day.) **Shore Line Campground,** 5321 Central Ave. (525-1902), just south of town on Lake Hamilton, has full RV hookup, a pool, restrooms, showers, and laundry facilities ($12 per day, $72 per week). Call for reservations. Tents and houseboats are permitted.

■■■ LITTLE ROCK

Once upon a time, a little rock jutting into the Arkansas River served as an important landmark for boats pushing their way upstream. Over time, that rock was overshadowed by the big city that grew up around it. Soon that city became the most important in the state, forgetting in its bustle the namesake pebble. Trouble swept this burgeoning metropolis in 1957 when Little Rock became the focus of a nationwide civil rights controversy. Governor Orval Faubus led a violent segregationist movement, using troops to prevent nine black students from enrolling in Central High School; they entered only under National Guard protection. As years passed, this hotbed of racial tension cooled to become the integrated cultural center that it is today. The little rock on the mighty Arkansas river was finally remembered and given a happy green park in which to live. It lived there happily ever after. The End.

PRACTICAL INFOMATION

Emergency: 911.

Visitor Information: Arkansas Dept. of Parks and Tourism, 1 Capitol Mall (800-643-8383 or 682-7777 in-state), in a complex directly behind the capitol building, has any map or brochure that you could possibly need. Open Mon.-Fri. 8am-5pm. **Little Rock Bureau for Conventions and Visitors** (376-4781 or 800-844-4781), at Markham and Main St. next door to the Excelsior Hotel. Also dispenses useful information. Open Mon.-Fri. 8:30am-5pm; closed for lunch about 11:30am-12:30pm.

Airport: Little Rock Regional Airport (372-3430), 5 mi. east of downtown off I-440. Easily accessible to downtown (taxi $5-10, bus 80¢).

Amtrak: Union Station, 1400 W. Markham (372-6841 or 800-872-7245), at Victory St. downtown. One train per day to: St. Louis (7 hr., $72); Dallas (7 hr., $79); Malvern, 20 mi. east of Hot Springs (40 min., $11). Open daily 6:15-11am, noon-9pm.

Greyhound: 118 E. Washington St. (372-1861), across the river in North Little Rock. Use the walkway over the bridge to get downtown. To: St. Louis ($60); New Orleans ($69); Memphis ($18.50). Tickets are more expensive weekends, but 14-day advance purchases come with a 25% discount.

Public Transportation: Central Arkansas Rapid Transit (375-1163). Little Rock has a fairly comprehensive local transport system (although no evening hours), with 21 bus routes running through the city from 6am-6pm.

Taxi: Black and White Cabs, 374-0333. $1 per mi.

Car Rental: Budget Car and Truck Rental, 3701 E. Roosevelt St. at the airport (375-5521 or 800-527-0700), does its thing for $37.50 per day, 150 free mi., 25¢

per mi. over 150; $175 per week, 700 free mi.; 25¢ over 700. No extra charge for 21-25. Open Mon.-Sat. 6am-midnight, Sun. 7am-10pm.
Help Lines: Rape Crisis, 663-3334. Open 24 hrs. **First Call for Help,** 376-4567.
Post Office: 600 W. Capitol (377-6470), at 5th St. Open Mon.-Fri. 7am-5:15pm.
ZIP code: 72201.
Area Code: 501.

Most of Little Rock's streets were "planned" with no apparent pattern in mind, although downtown is relatively grid-like. **Broadway** and **Main** are the major north-south arteries running to and from the river. **Markham** and all streets numbered one to 36 run east-west. **Third St.** turns into **W. Markham St.** as it moves west.

ACCOMMODATIONS

Inexpensive accommodations in Little Rock tend to cluster around **I-30,** which is right next to downtown, and **University Ave.** at the intersection of I-630 and I-430, both of which are a good 5-10 min drive from downtown. The few motels in town that cost less are generally unkempt.

Master's Inn Economy (372-4392 or 800-633-3434), I-30 (exit 140) and 9th St., *almost* in downtown. Locations in North Little Rock as well. Spacious, well-lit, newly furnished rooms with a lovely pool, restaurant, and even room service; this chain is unbeatable. Singles $20, $6 per extra person; under 18 free with adult.
Little Rock Inn (376-8301), 6th and Center St., tenants half of a block downtown and includes a pool, saloon, laundry room, and spacious but worn rooms without TV and telephone. $30 per night for 1-2 people, $70 per week with $20 security deposit. Booked solid.
Mark 4000 Motel, 4000 W. Markham (664-0950). Don't be fooled by the dingy exterior—recently renovated rooms boast comfortable and attractive decor. Be careful at night in the surrounding neighborhood. Singles $25, doubles $28.

If you prefer the great outdoors, you can "rough it" at the **KOA Campground** (758-4598), on Crystal Hill Rd. in North Little Rock, 7 mi. from downtown between exit 12 on I-430 and exit 148 on I-48, and its pool (sites from $16, with hookups $23), or at the **Sands RV Park** (565-7491), on Chicot Rd. at I-30 (full hookup $12).

FOOD AND NIGHTLIFE

Many of Little Rock's restaurants and cafes serve up an artsy and casual atmosphere along with good deals. Though never neglectful of native southern cooking, the Arkansian palate also savors and serves food from around the globe.There are a few fast-food joints downtown, but most lie along I-30 closer to the university.

Solar Cafe, 1706 W. 3rd (375-4747), across from Capitol, radiates from inside a former gas station. This mellow, laid-back eatery shines with sun-sational lunches for under $4 and dinners under $7 (try the Rainbow Salad or the Sunburger), and has nightly live entertainment. Good vegetarian options. Open Mon.-Fri. 8:30am-9:30pm, Sat. brunch 9am-2pm.
Vino's, 923 W. 7th (375-8466), at Chester, the only micro-brewery in Little Rock, gives Italian food a good name and a good price (pizza 95¢ a slice, sandwiches $3-4, calzones $5). This youthful hangout is also a mecca for the night owl—week-ends mean live music, poetry, plays, and film showings. The owner has a knack for names, so you'll feel like a regular your first time in. Open Mon.-Wed. 11am-10pm. Thurs.-Fri. 11am-midnight, Sat. noon-midnight.
Juanita's, 1300 S. Main (372-1228), at 13th. Fragrant Mexican food on the pricey side (dinner $8-12), but wonderfully prepared. If it's beyond your budget, the live nightly music may not be; call or stop by for a jam-packed schedule. Open daily 11am-2:30pm, Mon.-Sat. 5:30pm-1am, Sun. 5:30-9pm. Cover $1-6.
The Oyster Bar, 3003 W. Markham St. (666-7100). The good-naturedly disgruntled staff serves reasonably priced seafood and "Po'Boy" sandwiches ($4-5). It has

a big screen TV, pool tables, cheap draft beer, and a decidedly laid-back atmosphere where paper towel rolls take the place of napkins. Open Mon.-Thurs. 11am-9:30pm, Fri.-Sat. noon-10:30pm. Happy Hour Mon.-Fri. 3-6:30pm.

Hungry's Cafe, 1001 W. 7th St. (372-9720), is a popular, lively joint that proves that hillbillies and yuppies alike know good food. Tasty, filling sandwiches, country chicken, and veggie plates are under $5. Tip your hat to the impressive cap collection. Open Mon.-Fri. 6am-2pm, Sat. 7am-12:30pm, Sun. 9:30am-2pm.

Back Street, 1021 Jessie Rd. (664-2744), near Riverfront Rd. and Cantrell Rd., is a popular gay bar for both men and women complete with a fully stocked and fully fun game room. Open daily 7pm-5am.

SIGHTS

Tourists can visit the legendary "Little Rock" which jutted into the Arkansas River and spurred the development of this big city, at **Riverfront Park,** a pleasant place for a walk and a painless history lesson. Pay close attention; the rock has had a hard life and is (oddly enough) *little* and easy to miss. For the best access, cut through the back of the Excelsior Hotel at Markham and Center St. The town celebrates the waterway annually at **Riverfest,** on Memorial Day weekend, with arts and crafts, a number of bands, lots of food, and a firework display the last evening.

One block from the visitors bureau resides the refined **Old State House,** 300 W. Markham St. (324-9685), which served as the capitol from 1836 until the ceiling collapsed in 1899 while the legislature was in session. The restored building now houses exhibits of the gowns of the first ladies, and provides a good starting point for a downtown tour. (Open Mon.-Sat. 9am-5pm, Sun. 1-5pm. Free.) The functioning **state capitol** (682-5080) at the west end of Capitol St. may look very familiar—it's actually a replica of the U.S. Capitol in Washington, DC (which meant no big adjustment for President Clinton). Take a free self-guided tour or one of the 45-min. group tours given on the hour. (Open Mon.-Fri. 9am-4pm, Sat. 10am-5pm, Sun. 1-5pm. Call in advance on weekends.) To glimpse President Clinton's previous life, you might want to swing by the **Governor's Mansion,** at S. Center and 18th, in the middle of a gorgeous historic district. For a look at the history of the townspeople of 19th-century Little Rock, visit the **Arkansas Territorial Restoration,** 214 E. Third St. (324-9351). Tours of four restored buildings include an old grog shop and a typical old-fashioned print shop. Though long, the tours are varied and fascinating. Pick the tour guides' brains; they've done all the research themselves and are not merely hired robots. (Open Mon.-Sat. 9am-5pm, Sun. 1-5pm. 1-hr. tours every hr. on the hr. $2, seniors $1, kids 50¢. Free first Sun. of each month.)

On the eastern edge of town lounges **MacArthur Park,** elegant home to the **Museum of Science and History** (324-9231). Particularly suited to kids, the museum houses exhibits on Arkansas history, including a walk-through bear cave and an entire room of stuffed birds. (Open Mon.-Sat. 9am-9:30pm, Sun. 1-4:30pm; $1, kids under 12 and seniors 50¢, free on Mon.) Next door poses the **Arkansas Art Center** (372-4000), featuring outstanding collections by both the old European masters and contemporary artists (open Mon.-Sat. 10am-5pm, Sun. noon-5pm; free). Just a block or so north of the park furbishes the **Decorative Arts Museum** (372-4000), 7th and Rock St., where innovative silverware and furniture designs demonstrate that art can be functional. Look for the Civil War in the fireplaces. (Tours given Wed. at noon, Sun. at 1:30. Open Mon.-Sat. 10am-5pm, Sun. noon-5pm. Free.) The **War Memorial Park,** northwest of the state capitol off I-30 at Fair Park Blvd. houses the 40-acre **Little Rock Zoo,** 1 Jonesboro Dr. (666-2406), which simulates the animals' natural habitats (open daily 9am-5pm; $2, kids under 12 $1).

The opening scene of *Gone With the Wind* features **Old Mill Park** (758-2445), Lakeshore Dr. at Fairway Ave. in North Little Rock, one of the city's most treasured attractions. The WPA constructed this water-powered grist mill during the Depression. (Open daily. Free.) The opening scene of the TV show "Designing Women" also features a Little Rock location—**The Villa Marre,** 1321 Scott (374-9979), a restored 19th-century house and museum (open Sun. 1-5pm, Mon.-Fri. 9am-1pm; $3, seniors and kids $2).

Archaeologists are uncovering part of Arkansas' past that goes back much farther than the historic homes and parks—all the way to the year 700AD. More than 1000 years ago, the **Toltec Mounds State Park** (961-9442), 15 mi. east of North Little Rock on Rte. 386, was the political and religious center of the Plum Bayou people (open Tues.-Sat. 8am-5pm, Sun. noon-5pm; 1hr. guided tours at 9:30 and 11am, 12:30, 2, and 3:30pm; $2, kids 6-15 $1).

■■■ THE OZARKS

Their name taken from the French "Aux Arcs," the **Ozark Mountains** have lorded over the fertile resplendence of southern Missouri and northern Arkansas for many a moon. Not towering or jagged, they gently ripple over the land. The roads along the range are less docile, twisting and tying a knot of pavement through the ridges and valleys. These inroads are relatively recent; the natural boundaries that isolated the lives and customs of highland natives buffered unique crafts, music, and oral traditions from the vagaries of modern American consumer culture. Arkansas' frontier motto—"I've never seen nothin', I don't know nothin', I hain't got nothin', and I don't want nothin'"—is belied by the scenic views, the myriad crafts, and the easy and consistent camaraderie of the people of these verdant ridges.

In past decades, the "homespun" quality of life here was often denigrated and mocked, but in the 60s, students began to "discover" and glorify the "simple living" of American mountain culture. Today, this appreciation has extended beyond anthropological awe to the casual tourist, the ardent nature-lover, and the serious hunter of dusty antiques.

Few buses venture into the area, and hitching is *not* recommended. Drivers should follow U.S. 71, or Rtes. 7 or 23 for best access and jaw-dropping views. Eureka Springs to Huntsville on Rte. 23 south is a scenic 1-hr. drive. Also head east or west on U.S. 62 from Eureka Springs for attractive stretches. The **Arkansas Department of Parks and Tourism** (800-643-8383; see Arkansas Practical Information) can help with your trip. For hiking, the **Ozark National Forest** presents myriad opportunities. If you want to paddle a portion of the **Buffalo National River,** call the ranger station for camping and canoe rental info (449-4311; canoe rental $22 per day, cabin $46 per day), or contact Buffalo Point Concessions, HCR, P.O. Box 388, Yellville 72687 (449-6206). The **Arkansas Bikeways Commission,** 1200 Worthen Bank Bldg., Little Rock 72201, dispenses a bike trail map for the Ozark region. The **Eureka Springs Chamber of Commerce** (253-8737; 800-643-3546 outside AR), also has helpful vacation-planning material.

■ Mountain View

Although this petite village (pop. 2439) traces its name to a paper slip drawn from a hat in 1878, the town holds its own, refusing to kowtow to the surrounding beauty. The town sprawls around a picturesque courthouse square, interspersed with clusters of people engaged in animated discussion and merry-making.

Practical Information Mountain View's **Chamber of Commerce** (269-8068), is located on Main St. (open Mon.-Fri. 8am-4:30pm, Sat. 9am-4pm). Pick up one of their essential and easy-to-read maps. **Rental cars** are available at **Lackey Motors Car Rental** (269-3211), at the corner of Main St. and Peabody Ave. ($25 per day plus 25¢ per mi.; open Mon.-Sat. 8am-5:30pm). 1993 witnessed the creation of a brand-new "vintage" shuttle bus reminiscent of a 1935 Ford with service to and from all the major sites and downtown (269-4423; every hr. 8am-6pm; fare $1). The **Mental Health and Rape Crisis Hotline** (800-592-9503) and **Crisis Intervention** (800-542-

1031) are both open 24 hours. In **emergencies** dial 911. Mountain View's **post office** is located in courthouse square; the **ZIP code** is 72560; the **area code** is 501.

Accommodations and Food Mountain View is one small town with enough lodgings for the traveler with a budget. Sprinkled throughout the area are lodgings such as the **Mountain View Motel,** 407 East Main St. (269-3209), whose rustic but clean rooms come with hot pots of free coffee. (Singles $26. Doubles $28.) The charming bed and country breakfast **Inn at Mountain View,** P.O. Box 812 Washington St. (269-4200 or 800-535-1301), a Victorian home with white trim and flower-lined stone paths, settles elegantly just off the town square. The reasonable price of its plushly decorated rooms and suites (all with private baths) includes a seven-course homemade breakfast. (Rooms and suites $44-91, with 20% discounts in the winter off-season.) **The Hearthstone Bakery** (269-3297) next door provides culinary delights which include cookies and danishes for under $1, and loaves of home-made bread for $2. Specialty diet breads are also available. Visitors who choose to sleep at the **Ozark Folk Lodge** (269-3871 or 800-264-3655) will enjoy a cottage with simple country furnishings and convenience to the folk center ($45 plus $5 per additional person, 13 and under free with an adult). Right on Main St., at the junction of Rtes. 9, 5, and 14 (a central corner), you can find a "home away from home" at the **Scottish Inns** (269-3287 or 800-252-1962) with a pool, clean rooms, and new furniture. (Singles $22, Doubles $26.)

Because Mountain View lies only 5-10 mi. south of the Ozark National Forest, the cheapest way to stay in the area is free: **camping.** Pitching a tent anywhere is free and legal (and usually safe) as long as the campsite does not block any road, path, or thoroughfare. Campgrounds around the Blanchard Springs caverns include **Blanchard Springs Recreation Area** (sites $8), **Gunner Pool Recreation Area** (sites $5), and **Barkshed Recreation Area** (free). Barkshed has recently become the latest hotspot for teenage roving, so if you're looking for a quiet evening of camping, don't be swayed by the (non)price. For more information about the caverns, camping, and the fabulous hiking trails through the Ozark Forest, consult the **Ozark National Sylamore Ranger District** at P.O. Box 1279, Mountain View (757-2211).

While Mountain View is refreshingly unfettered by strings of fast-food restaurants (it only has 2), inexpensive food still abounds in local cafes and diners. The **Catfish House** (269-3820), from Rte. 14 take School Dr. to Senior Dr., runs out of the gym of an old school complex and dishes up Mountain View's "Best Food in the Worst Location" for $5-8 as well as nightly hoedowns with banjo and fiddle music, clogging, and "Ozark humor" (open Thurs.-Sat. 11am-9pm, Sun.-Wed. 11am-8pm). **Joshua's Mountain View** (269-4136) is a simple diner serving daily lunch specials and several different daily buffets, including a seafood and a vegetable buffet (sandwiches $2-3, dinner $6-8; open Mon.-Sat. 5:30am-9pm, Sun. 5:30am-2pm).

Sights and Entertainment A melisma of mountain music has long found its home in this region: the dulcimer, a stringed instrument distinguished by a fret that extends the instrument's length, is native to the Ozarks. Mountain View boasts one of the finest dulcimer shops in the world, **McSpadden Dulcimers and Crafts,** P.O. Box 1230 (269-4313), on Rte. 9N, where observers can watch craftsmen fashion this mellow music maker and can even hammer a few strings themselves (open Mon.-Fri. 9am-5pm, Sat. 10am-5pm). The annual **October Beanfest** draws cooks from all over Arkansas, and guarantees free samples from cast-iron pots full of beans. Cold winter nights find the town wrapped around a **community bonfire,** while during March and April, thousands of people from around the world arrive to celebrate spring with parades, square and jig dancing, clogging, and musical tributes. These annual occasions both sustain local traditions and initiate outsiders into the idiosyncrasies of Ozark culture. In the meantime, visitors can revel in the musical charisma of triple Grammy Award winner Jimmy Driftwood, the quintessential Ozark artist.

His music emanates from the **Jimmy Driftwood Barn and Folk Museum** (269-8042), also on Rte. 9N. (shows Fri. and Sun., 7:30pm until whenever; free).

To catch some slightly different sounds, check out the **Old Mill** (269-4514), on Main St. This renovated 1914 grist mill still grinds some very fine flour for its museum visitors. (Open April-Oct. Wed.-Sun. 9am-5pm. Free.)

Ozark culture survives most undiluted on the lush grounds of the **Ozark Folk Center** (269-3851), just minutes north of Mountain View off Rte. 9N. The center recreates a mountain village and is a living museum of the cabin crafts, music, and lore of the Ozarks. For those who shudder at the steep walk to the center, a tram transports visitors from the central parking lot (free). Among the artisans practicing their trades in the **Crafts Forum** are a blacksmith, a basket weaver, a potter, a gunsmith, and a furniture maker. Visitors can taste freshly baked biscuits prepared by a cook in an antique kitchen for free, or for 50¢ dip their own candles in the chandler's shop. A wood carver sculpts faces from dried apples and a local herbalist concocts medicines from a garden beside the cottage. Musicians fiddle, pluck, and strum daily at lunchtime and nightly in the auditorium (shows at 7:30pm) while dancers implore the audience to jig and clog along. The activities inspire both respect for the settlers' ingenuity as well as a reverent appreciation and understanding of nature. All year long you can expect concerts and workshops galore. Seasonal events at the center include the **Arkansas Folk Festival** and the **Mountain and Hammered Dulcimer Championships** in late April, the **Banjo Weekend** in late May, the **Arkansas Old-Time Fiddlers Association State Championship** in late September, and the **SPBGMA National Fiddle Championships** in mid-November. The Fiddlers Championships in particular are quite a sight; hundreds of experienced fiddlers, young and old, play the authentic music of the Ozarks. (Open May-Oct. daily 10am-5pm. Crafts area $5.50, ages 6-12 $3.25. Evening musical performances $6, kids 6-12 $4. Combination tickets and family rates are available.)

The areas around Mountain View abound with recreational activities. Fishing and rafting on the **White River** are popular diversions; fishing licenses can be purchased at the Wal-Mart (269-4395) in Mountain View for around $10. If your legs ache from hiking, climb atop a horse and experience the Ozarks from a saddle for $10 per hour at either **Sylamore Trail Rides**, P.O. Box 210, Mountain View (585-2231; open Tues.-Sun. from 9am) or the **OK Trading Post** (585-2217), on Rte. 14 approximately 3½ mi. from the entrance to Blanchard Spring Caverns. Both places offer overnight trips and all-day rides by reservation. If you have your own horse, Sylamore horse trail loop maps are available at the Sylamore Ranger Station.

Daytrips from Mountain View to Buffalo River (about 45 min. northwest) add the option of **canoeing** down the river for about $25 per day. Concessionaires permitted by the National Park Services to rent equipment include **Dodd's Float Service** (800-423-8731) and **Bennett's Canoe Rental** (449-6431). Such businesses also provide paddles, life jackets, and shuttle services to Take-Out Point. For the adventurous hiker, the town of **Rush**, part of the Buffalo National Park River District, slowly decays about 30 mi. northwest of Mountain View off Rte. 14. Now a ghost town, it was formerly a zinc ore mining hub. Rush dates back to the 1880s and still has buildings and foundations standing. Primitive camping areas with vault toilet, fire grates, and drinking water are available year-round; the town also has river access.

Blanchard Springs Caverns (757-2291), on the southern border of the Ozark Forest, glow and drip with exquisite cave formations and glassy, cool springs. Two guided trails navigate the caverns (open daily 9am-6pm, in winter Mon.-Fri. 9am-6pm; $7, seniors and kids 6-15 $3.50).

■ Eureka Springs

In the early 19th century, the Osage spread reports of a wonderful spring with magical healing powers. White settlers flocked to the site and quickly established a small town from which they sold bottles of the miraculous water. Tourists still flock to this tiny town in northwest Arkansas, but the spring is hardly the main attraction; in fact, it is easily overlooked—now the Passion Play's the thing.

Practical Information For extra help in planning your time in Eureka Springs, call the **Chamber of Commerce** (800-643-3546 or 253-8737), located on U.S. 62 just north of Rte. 23 (open Mon.-Sat. 9am-5:30pm, Sun. 9am-5pm; Nov.-April Mon.-Fri. 9am-5pm). The **post office** (253-9850) is located on the historic loop (open Mon.-Fri. 8:15am-4:15 pm). The **ZIP code** is 72632; the **area code** is 501.

Accommodations and Food Accommodations in Eureka Springs are not difficult to find, as the town has more hotel beds than it does residents, yet prices are impossible to foresee. Daily fluctuations in supply and demand determine the price of a room. The clean but plain rooms of the **Frontier Motel** (253-9508), Rte. 62 East are standard fare for the area. (Singles and doubles $32, two beds $38.) Prices generally drop on Mondays and Thursdays, when Passion Players take a break. For the best deal, call Richard Keller of **Keller's Country Dorm** (253-8418), to make reservations for a dorm bed, breakfast, dinner, and a reserved ticket to the Passion Play, all at $29 per night, for groups of 12 or more. (Open May-Oct.) **Pinehaven Campsites** (253-9052), on U.S. 62, 2 mi. east of town, has tent sites ($10) and full hookup ($14). **Kettle Campgrounds** (253-9100), on the eastern edge of town on Rte. 62, also provides tent and hookup sites ($9/14). They also give great advice to travelers.

The town is filled with tourist-oriented restaurants. Get away from the usual tourist glitz at the **Wagon Wheel,** 84 S. Main St. (253-9934), a country-western bar decorated with antiques (open Mon.-Fri. 10am-2am, Sat. 10am-midnight).

Sights and Entertainment Built on piety, holy water, and slick marketing, the **Great Passion Play** (253-9200 or 800-882-PLAY), a production modeled after Germany's *Oberammergau* Passion Play, has begun to draw crowds, at times hordes, to its depiction of Jesus Christ's life and death. (Performances April-Oct. Tues.-Wed. and Fri.-Sun. 8:30pm. Tickets $9-12, kids 4-11 ½-price. For reservations, ask where you're staying, or write P.O. Box 471, Eureka Springs 72632.) The amphitheater is off U.S. 62, on Rte. 23 just outside of town. **Gray Line Bus Tours** (253-9540) provides transportation to and from the play ($3 per person round-trip). They pick you up and drop you off at your hotel, motel, or campground. The theater is wheelchair-accessible. The **Eureka Springs Chamber of Commerce** (253-8737) also operates a trolley service which runs to the play, local churches, and the downtown historic loop ($2.50 for any one of the 5 routes for the entire day, 9am-6pm; kids 6 and under free). The loop is chock full with what might once have been charming old-style buildings but are now crammed with trinkets and souvenirs.

■ Fayetteville

Fayetteville, one of America's top 10 places to live, merits distinction not only as the largest city in this part of the state (pop. 42,099), but also perhaps as the only one in which residents outnumber tourists. This is a real city where people live and work which just happens to be situated in the beautiful Ozarks and entertains a number of attractions worth seeing. **Prairie Grove Battlefield State Park** (846-2990), a 130-acre historic park located 8 mi. west of Fayetteville off Rte. 62, evokes the Civil War history of Fayetteville—the battle, the manner of life, the buildings in which it all occurred (open daily 8am-10pm; free). For more modern history, the **Arkansas Air Museum** (521-4947), Northwest Hangar, Drake Field, will lift your spirits with its soaring exhibits of aviation history (open daily 10am-5pm; free). Check out the cultural goings-on at the **Walton Arts Center,** P.O. Box 3547 72702 (443-9216). For more info, call the **Fayetteville Chamber of Commerce** (800-766-4626).

■ Florida

Ponce de León landed on the Florida coast in 1513, near what would soon be St. Augustine, in search of the elusive Fountain of Youth. Although the multitudes who flock to Florida today aren't desperately seeking fountains, many find their youth restored in the Sunshine State—whether they're dazzled by Orlando's fantasia Disney World or bronzed by the sun on the state's seductive beaches. Droves of senior citizens also migrate to Florida, where they thrive in comfortable retirement communities, leaving one to wonder whether the unpolluted, sun-warmed air isn't just as good as Ponce de León's fabled magical elixir.

But a dark shadow hangs over this land of the winter sun. Anything as attractive as Florida is bound to draw hordes of *people,* the nemesis of natural beauty. Florida's population boom is straining the state's resources; commercial strips and tremendous development in some areas have turned pristine beaches into tourist traps. Nevertheless, it is possible to find a deserted strand on this peninsula. Sit yourself down, grease yourself up, and pay homage to the sun.

In August, 1992, Hurricane Andrew ripped through southern Florida, causing over $30 billion in damage and claiming more than 40 lives. Most tourist facilities and attractions have been restored, but much of Florida's plant life remains damaged and will take years to recover from the bout with Andrew.

PRACTICAL INFORMATION

Capital: Tallahassee.
Visitor Information: Florida Division of Tourism, 126 W. Van Buren St., Tallahassee 32301 (487-1462). **Department of Natural Resources—Division of Recreation and Parks,** 3900 Commonwealth Blvd. #506, Tallahassee 32399-2000 (488-9872).
Time Zones: Eastern and Central (westernmost part). **Postal Abbreviation:** FL
Sales Tax: 6%.

■■■ COCOA BEACH AND CAPE CANAVERAL

Known primarily for its rocket launches, space shuttle blast-offs, and enormous **NASA** space center complex, the "Space Coast" also has uncrowded golden sand beaches and vast wildlife preserves. Even during spring break the place remains placid because most vacationers and sunbathers are neighborly Florida or Space Coast residents.

Practical Information The Cocoa Beach area, 50 mi. east of Orlando, consists of mainland towns Cocoa and Rockledge, oceanfront towns Cocoa Beach and Cape Canaveral, plus Merritt Island in between. **Route A1A** runs through Cocoa Beach and Cape Canaveral, and **North Atlantic Avenue** runs parallel to the beach. Inaccessible by bus, Cocoa Beach also lacks local public transport. But Cocoa, 8 mi. inland, is serviced by **Greyhound,** 302 Main St. (636-3917), from Orlando ($11.50). From the bus station, **taxi** fare to Cocoa Beach is about $14 (call 783-8294). A **shuttle** service (784-3831) connects Cocoa Beach with Orlando International Airport, Disney World (round-trip $75 for 1 or 2 people), and the Kennedy Space Center (round-trip only $45, 1 or 2 people). Make reservations one day in advance and ask about special rates for groups of five or more.

Try the **Cocoa Beach Chamber of Commerce,** 400 Fortenberry Rd. (459-2200), Merritt Island, or the **Brevard County Tourist Development Council** (453-0823 or

Florida Peninsula

GEORGIA

TO TALLAHASSEE

Jacksonville

St. Augustine

Osceola National Forest

Gainesville

Ocala

Ocala National Forest

Daytona Beach

ATLANTIC OCEAN

Cedar Keys

NASA Kennedy Space Center

Walt Disney World

Orlando

Cape Canaveral

Florida's Turnpike

Tampa

St. Petersburg

Sarasota

Manatee R.

Peace R.

Kissimmee R.

Fort Pierce

Lake Okeechobee

West Palm Beach

Palm Beach

Caloosahatchee R.

Fort Myers

Loxahatchee Nat. Wildlife Refuge

Seminole Indian Reservation

Naples

Big Cypress National Preserve

Fort Lauderdale

Miami

Miami Beach

GULF OF MEXICO

Biscayne Bay

Everglades National Park

Florida City

Key Largo

Florida Bay

Florida Keys

Key West

N

0   100 miles

0   100 kilometers

800-872-1969), at Kennedy Space Center, for area info. Cocoa Beach's **post office** is at 25 N. Brevard Ave. (783-2544); the **ZIP code** is 32931; **area code** is 407.

Food and Lodging For a bite to eat, try **Herbie K's Diner,** 2080 N. Atlantic Ave. (783-6740), south of Motel 6. A shiny chrome reproduction of a 50s diner, Herbie K's serves mac and cheese, chicken pot pie, "happy haw" (apple sauce), great malts, and hamburgers ($5-7). (Open Sun.-Thurs. 6am-10pm, Fri.-Sat. 24 hrs.) At the beach, **Motel 6,** 3701 N. Atlantic Ave. (783-3103), has a pool and large, clean rooms with cable TV and A/C. (Singles $34, Jan.-March $38. Each additional person $4. Reservations required.) If Motel 6 is full, try farther down N. Atlantic Ave. at the **Sunrise Motel,** 3185 N. Atlantic Ave. (783-0500 or 800-348-0348), where singles are $30, Jan.-March $50 (each additional person $6). If you get stuck in Cocoa or need a place to spend the night between bus connections, walk right behind the Greyhound station to the **Dixie Motel,** 301 Forrest Ave. (632-1600), one block east of U.S. 1. For big clean rooms, a swimming pool, A/C, and friendly service. (Singles $28. Doubles $32.) Or pitch your tent at scenic **Jetty Park Campgrounds,** 400 East Jetty Rd. (783-4001), Cape Canaveral. (Sites $18, with hookup $22. Reservations necessary six months in advance.)

Sights The **Kennedy Space Center,** 8 mi. north of Cocoa Beach, is the site of all of NASA's shuttle flights. The Kennedy Center's **Spaceport USA** (452-2121 for reservations) provides a huge welcoming center for visitors. There are two different two-hour bus tours of the complex. The **red tour** takes you around the space sites, the **blue tour** to the Air Force Station. There are also two IMAX films projected on a 5½-story screen: *The Dream is Alive* is about the space shuttle, and *The Blue Planet* is about environmental issues. Tours depart from Spaceport USA daily from 9:45am to 6pm every 15 min. ($7, ages 3-11 $4. Movie tickets $4, ages 3-11 $2). Buy tickets to both immediately upon arrival at the complex to avoid a long line. The center itself is free, as are the five movies in the Galaxy Theater and the half-hour walking tours of the exhibits. The NASA Parkway, site of the visitors center, is accessible only by car via State Rd. 405. From Cocoa Beach, take Rte. A1A north until it turns west into Rte. 528, then follow Rte. 3 north to the Spaceport. With NASA's ambitious launch schedules, you may have a chance to watch the space shuttles *Endeavor, Columbia, Atlantis,* or *Discovery* thunder off into the blue skies above the cape. In Florida, call 800-KSC-INFO (800-572-4636) for **launch information.**

Surrounding the NASA complex, the marshy **Merritt Island Wildlife Refuge** (861-0667) stirs with deer, sea turtles, alligators, and eagles (open daily 8am-sunset). Just north of Merritt Island is **Canaveral National Seashore** (867-2805), 67,000 acres of undeveloped beach and dunes, home to more than 300 species of birds and mammals. (Take Rte. 406 east off U.S. 1 in Titusville; open daily 6am-sunset.) Closed 3 days before and 1 day after NASA launches.

■■■ THE EVERGLADES

■ Everglades National Park

Near Miami, the **Everglades National Park** teems with exotic life. Visit the park in winter or spring, when heat, humidity, storms, and bugs are at a minimum and when wildlife congregates around the water. *Always* bring mosquito repellent to the Everglades. **Shark Valley** (15 mile loop) is accessible on the northern boundary of the park via the **Tamiami Trail (U.S. 41),** but the best way to tour the largely inaccessible park is to take the main park road **(Rte. 9336)** out of Florida City. Rte. 9336 runs 40 mi. through the flat grasslands to Flamingo, on Florida Bay, stopping at the various nature trails and pullouts along the way. Park entrance fee $5. Stop at the **Visitors center,** 40001 State Rd. 9336, Homestead 33034 (305-242-7700), by the park headquarters just inside the entrance, to pick up maps and info. (Open daily

8am-5pm.) The Visitors center also sponsors a variety of hikes, canoe trips, and amphitheater programs. To get face-to-snout with an alligator, try the **Anhinga Trail,** at **Royal Palm,** 4 mi. beyond the entrance. The **Mahogany Hammock** trail boasts the largest living mahogany tree in the U.S. **Pa-hay-okee Overlook** affords a terrific view of the "river of grass" for which the Park is named.

There are a number of options for campers in the Everglades. The park **campgrounds** at **Long Pine Key** and **Flamingo** have drinking water, grills, and restrooms. The Flamingo site has showers, but neither site has RV hookups. These sites are free during the summer, and only a small fee is charged in the winter. The park also has lots of primitive backcountry campsites, accessible by boat, foot, or bicycle. Free permits for backcountry camping are available at ranger stations. Canoe rental ($7 per hr., $25 per day) is available at the **Flamingo Marina** (305-253-2241) in Flamingo, and at the **Gulf Coast Visitors Center** (813-695-3311), near Everglades City.

The National Park Service doesn't give airboat tours, but dozens of airboat concessionaires line the northern and eastern park borders, especially along the Tamiami Trail. Cruises into Florida Bay offered daily at the Flamingo Marina ($8, ages 6-12 $4, under 6 free). Catch the **Sunset Cruise** (1½ hr.) for a gorgeous end to the day.

The **Park Headquarters** and after hours **emergency** number is 305-242-7700. If you would like to tune into park info on the radio, turn your dial to AM1610. If you're not a camper, or just grow weary of swatting mosquitos in a tent, the **Flaming Lodge** (305-253-2241) offers hip rooms with A/C, TV, private baths, and a pool. (May-Oct. singles and doubles $50, Nov.-Dec. $70, Jan.-Mar. $80.) Other accommodations can easily be found in Everglades City, Homestead, and Florida City.

■ Big Cypress National Preserve

Adjacent to the Everglades lies **Big Cypress National Preserve.** Information can be obtained at the **Preserve Headquarters** (HCR 61, Box 11, Ochopee, FL 33943, 813-695-4111) on the Tamiami Trail near Everglades City. There is no entrance fee at Big Cypress, and several free primitive campgrounds line U.S. 41. The campground at **Dona Drive** boasts potable water and picnic tables, and most campgrounds have a portajon and dumpster from Dec. to April. **Burns Lake** and **Monument Lake** campgrounds surround small lakes with good fishing and abundant wildlife. For hotel accommodations just outside the preserve, or other sights near the preserve, check with the **Everglades City Chamber of Commerce** (813-695-3941).

THE FLORIDA KEYS

The coral rock islands, mangrove trees, and relaxed attitude of the residents make the Florida Keys pleasant places to visit and live. With a character quite different from anywhere else in the U.S., these islands off the coast are a nation unto themselves. The Keys are more Caribbean than Floridian, with cool breezes at night, wild tropical rainstorms, and a vertical sun hot enough to roast a turkey. When the sun *does* set, clouds, heat lightning, and the surrounding ocean provide an incredible accompaniment. Approximately 6 mi. offshore from these islands, a 100-yd. wide chain of barrier reef parallel to the Keys runs from Key Largo south to Key West. Adored by divers, these reefs harbor some of the ocean's most diverse and colorful marine life as well as hundreds of wrecked ships and legendary lost treasure. Contrary to popular belief, there are very few sharks.

The Keys run southwest into the ocean from the southern tip of Florida, accessible by the **Overseas Highway (U.S. 1). Mile markers** divide the highway into sections and replace street addresses to indicate the location of homes and businesses. They begin with Mile 126 in Florida City and count down to zero on the corner of Whitehead and Fleming St. in Key West.

Greyhound runs three buses per day to Key West from Miami ($26), stopping in Perrine, Homestead (247-2040), Key Largo (451-2908), Marathon (743-3488), Big Pine Key (872-4022), and Key West (296-9072). If there's a particular mile marker where you need to get off, most drivers can be convinced to stop at the side of the road. Biking along U.S. 1 across the swamps between Florida City and Key Largo is impossible because the road lacks shoulders. Bring your bike on the bus.

■■■ KEY LARGO

After traversing the thick swamps and crocodile marshland of Upper Florida Bay, Key Largo opens the door to the islands. Without a car it can be difficult to get around, although everything of importance lies within a 6-mi. range.

Practical Information The **Florida Upper Keys Chamber of Commerce,** Mile 105.5 (451-1414), at Rte. 905, has maps and brochures on local attractions, including scenes from the film *Key Largo.* Also offers free phone calls to many hotels, restaurants, and attractions. (Open daily 9am-6pm.) The dramatic mailroom scene from *Key Largo* was filmed at the **post office,** Mile 100 (451-3155; open Mon.-Fri. 8am-4:30pm). Key Largo's **ZIP** code is 33037; the **area code** is 305.

Accommodations and Food After the state park's campsites fill up (see below), try crowded but well-run **Kings Kamp Marina,** Mile 103.5 (451-0010; sites by the bay $20). Look for the concealed entrance on the northwest (Gulf) side of U.S. 1. The **Hungry Pelican,** Mile 99.5 (451-3576), boasts beautiful bougainvillea vines in the trees and friendly managers Larry and Dana. Stuff your beak full in a clean, cozy trailer or room with a double bed ($40-55).

The Italian Fisherman, Mile 104 (451-4471), has it all—fine food and a spectacular view of Florida Bay. Formerly an illegal gambling casino, this restaurant was the locale for some scenes from Bogart and Bacall's movie *Key Largo.* (Dinners $7-17. Open daily 11am-10pm.) The seafood and 99-beer selection at **Crack'd Conch,** Mile 105 (451-0732), is superb. Try the "sorry Charlie" tuna fish sandwich ($4.50) or an entire key lime pie ($7.50), once called "the secret to world peace and the alignment of the planets." (Open Thurs.-Tues. noon-10pm.) With two locations, **Perry's** serves fresh local seafood and charbroiled steaks at Mile 102 (451-1834); and the most famous location at Key West, 3800 N. Roosevelt Blvd. (294-8472). Lunch $4-10, dinner $10-23. (Open daily 9am-10:30pm.) They also offer a "you hook 'em, we cook 'em" service for $3.50. Other scenes from *Key Largo* were filmed at the **Caribbean Club,** Mile 104 (451-9970), a friendly local bar. The in-house band Blackwater Sound plays a wide variety of rock for the locals Thurs.-Sun. evenings; snapshots of Bogart and Bacall grace the walls. Beer $1.50, drinks $2. (Open daily 7am-4am.)

Camping and Sights Largo's **John Pennecamp State Park,** Mile 102.5 (451-1202), 60 mi. from Miami, provides the visitor with a rare though somewhat murky view from glass-bottomed boats of the living reef off the Keys. (3 trips per day at 9:15am, 12:15pm and 3pm. $14, under 13 $7.50.) Mostly off-shore, the beautiful state park encompasses the largest uninterrupted stretch of the barrier reef in the Keys, the only underwater park in the country, and the only underwater Christ statue in the world. (Admission $3.75 for vehicle operator, each additional person 50¢. Campsites $24, with hookup $26.) The **Coral Reef Company** (451-1621) sails visitors 6 mi. past mangrove swamps to the reef. (Snorkeling tours daily at 9am, noon, and 3pm. 1½ hrs. of water time and quick lesson including gear $25, under 19, $20.)

■■■ KEY WEST

This is the end of the road. When searching for a tropical paradise, you can do no better than Key West. The island's pastel clapboard houses, hibiscus and bougainvillea vines, year-round tropical climate, and gin-clear waters make it a beautiful spot to visit in summer or winter.

Like most of this region, the city of Key West has a relaxed atmosphere, hot sunshine, and spectacular sunsets. Over the years, it has attracted travelers and famous authors like Tennessee Williams, Ernest Hemingway, Elizabeth Bishop, and Robert Frost. Today, an easygoing diversity still attracts a new generation of writers, artists, gays, recluses, adventurers, and eccentrics.

One note before you off and throw yourself into the Key West sun—the island lies as far south as the Bahamas, and the tropical sun will scald you if you don't take precautions. Especially if you're getting to the farthest key via the Overseas Highway, the sun reflecting off the water is powerful.

PRACTICAL INFORMATION

Emergency: 911.

Visitor Information: Key West Chamber of Commerce, 402 Wall St. (294-2587), in old Mallory Sq. Useful *Guide to the Florida Keys* available here. Accommodations list of guest houses popular with gays. **Key West Welcome Center,** 3840 N. Roosevelt Blvd. (296-4444 or 800-284-4482), just north of the intersection of U.S. 1 and Roosevelt Blvd. Arranges accommodations, theater tickets, weddings, and reef trips if you call in advance. Both sites open daily 9am-5pm.

Airport: Key West International Airport: (296-5439) on the southeast corner of the island. Serviced by **Eastern, American Eagle, U.S. Air Express,** and **Vintage** airlines. No public bus service.

Greyhound: 615½ Duval St. (296-9072). Obscure location in an alley behind Antonio's restaurant. To Miami, stopping along all the Keys (3 per day, 4 hr., $26). Open Mon.-Fri. 7am-12:30pm and 2:30-5pm, Sat. 7-noon.

Public Transport: Key West Port and Transit Authority, City Hall (292-8161). One bus ("Old Town") runs clockwise around the island and Stock Island; the other ("Mallory St.") runs counterclockwise. Pick up a clear and helpful free map from the Chamber of Commerce (see above) or any bus driver. Service Mon.-Sat. 6:10am-10:35pm, Sun. 6:40am-6:40pm. Fare 75¢, seniors and students 35¢. **Handicapped Transportation,** 292-3515.

Taxi: Keys Taxi, 296-6666, $1.40 plus $1.75 per mi.

Car Rental: Alamo, Ramada Inn, 3420 N. Roosevelt Blvd. (294-6675 or 800-327-9633), near the airport. $30 per day, $115 per week. Under 25 $15 extra. Must be 21 with major credit card or $50 deposit. Miami drop-off costs a prohibitive $55.

Bike Rental: Key West Hostel, 718 South St. (296-5719). $6 per day, $30 per week. Open daily 8-11am. Credit card and deposit required.

Help Line: 296-4357. Everything from General Info. to Crises. 24 hr.

Post Office: 400 Whitehead St. (294-2557), 1 block west of Duval at Eaton. Open Mon.-Fri. 8:30am-5pm. **ZIP code:** 33040.

Area Code: 305.

Just five miles long and three wide, Key West resides at the southernmost point of the continental U.S. and at the end of Rte. 1, 160 miles southwest of Miami. Only 90 miles north of Cuba, Key West dips farther south than much of the Bahamas.

Divided into two sectors, the eastern part of the island, called "Des Moines" or "America" by some, harbors the tract houses, chain motels, shopping malls, and the airport. **Old Town,** the west side of town below White St., is cluttered with beautiful old conch houses. **Duval Street** is the main north-south thoroughfare in Old Town, **Truman Avenue** the major east-west route. Key West is cooler than mainland Florida in summer, and much warmer in winter.

On the way to, and in, the city of Key West, driving is slow; most of the highway is a two-lane road with only an occasional passing lane. Bikers beware: police enforce traffic laws. Use hand signals, stop at signs, and watch for one-way streets.

ACCOMMODATIONS AND CAMPING

Beautiful weather resides year-round in Key West alongside beautiful tourists. As a result, good rooms at the nicer hotels go for up to $400 per day, especially during the winter holidays. There is no "off-season." Key West remains packed virtually year-round, with a lull of sorts from mid-September to mid-December; even then, don't expect to find a room for less than $40.

Try to bed down in **Old Key West;** the beautiful, 19th-century clapboard houses capture the flavor of the Keys. Some of the guest houses in the Old Town offer complimentary breakfasts and some are for gay men exclusively. Do *not* park overnight on the bridges—this is illegal and dangerous.

Key West Hostel, 718 South St. (296-5719), at Sea Shell Motel in Old Key West, 3 blocks east of Duval St. Call for airport or bus station pickup. Rooms with 4-6 beds, shared bath. A/C at night. Famous $1 dinners and $2 breakfasts. Kitchen open until 9pm. No curfew. Office open daily 8am-10pm. Members $13, non-members $16. Key deposit $5. Motel rooms in summer $45, in winter $50-100. Call ahead to check availability; also call for late arrival. 24 hr. check-in.

Eden House, 1015 Fleming St. (296-6868 or 800-533-5397). Bright, clean, friendly hotel with very nice rooms, just 5 short blocks from downtown. Cooool rooms with private or shared bath, some with balconies. Pool, jacuzzi. In-season $75-105, summer $50-70.

Caribbean House, 226 Petronia St. (296-1600 or 800-543-4518), at Thomas St. in Bahama Village. Brand-new, Caribbean-style rooms with cool tile floors, A/C, TV, fridge, and ceiling fans. Comfy double beds. Free continental breakfast. Norman, the friendly manager, may be able to place you in a completely furnished Caribbean Cottage (sleeps 6) or an unfurnished low-rent apartment for comfortable summer living. Rooms $69, cottage $98. In summer: rooms $39, cottage $59.

Tilton Hilton, 511 Angela St. (294-8697), next to the Greyhound station near downtown. Plain rhyming rooms, as cheap as you'll find. Color TV, some rooms with A/C and fridge, shared baths. Singles in season $75-100, summer $40-55.

Boyd's Campground, 6401 Maloney Ave. (294-1465), on Stock Island. Take bus to Maloney Ave. from Stock Island. 12 acres on the ocean. Full facilities, including showers. Primitive sites $22. Water and electricity $5 extra, A/C or heat $5 extra. Waterfront sites $3 extra.

FOOD

Expensive restaurants line festive Duval Street. Side streets offer lower prices and fewer crowds. Sell your soul and stock up on supplies at **Fausto's Food Palace,** 522 Fleming St. (296-5663), the best darn grocery store in Old Town. (Open Mon.-Sat. 8am-8pm, Sun. 8am-6pm.) Although the genuine article with a tangy yellow filling is hard to come by (key limes are not green), don't leave Key West without having a sliver of (or even a whole) **key lime pie.**

Half-Shell Raw Bar, Land's End Village (294-7496), at the foot of Margaret St. on the waterfront 5 blocks east of Duval. Rowdy and popular with tourists. Great variety of seafood dinners $10-14. Famed for its spring conch chowder ($2.95). Open daily 11am-11pm.

El Cacique, 125 Duval St. (294-4000). Cuban food at reasonable prices. Homey and colorful. Filling lunch specials, with pork or local fish, black beans, and rice for $6-10, dinner $11-15. Try fried plantains, conch chowder, or bread pudding as side dishes and flan for dessert. Open daily 8am-10pm.

Blue Heaven Fruit Market, 729 Thomas St. (296-8666), 1 block from the Caribbean House. Hemingway used to drink beer and referee boxing matches here when it was a pool hall. Dinners $8-12. Open Mon.-Sat. 3-11pm.

SIGHTS

Biking is a good way to see Key West, but you might want to take the **Conch Tour Train** (294-5161), a narrated ride through Old Town, leaving from Mallory Sq. This touristy one-and-a-half-hour trip costs $12 (kids $6), but guides provide a fascinating history of the area. (Operates daily 9am-4:30pm.) **Old Town Trolley** (296-6688) runs a similar tour, but you can get on and off throughout the day ($14, kids $6).

The glass-bottomed boat *Fireball* takes two-hr. cruises to the reefs and back (296-6293; tickets $16, ages 3-12 $8). One of a few cruise specialists, the **Coral Princess Fleet,** 700 Front St. (296-3287), offers snorkeling trips with free instruction for beginners (1 per day, leaves 1:30pm returns 5:30pm, $20; open daily 8:30am-6:30pm). For a landlubber's view of the fish of Key West, the **Key West Aquarium,** #1 Whitehead St. (296-2051), in Mallory Square, offers a 50,000 gallon Atlantic shore exhibit as well as a touch pool and shark feedings. Adults $6, seniors, students, and military $5, children 8-15 $3. Open daily 9am-6pm.

Long a mecca to artists and writers, the **Hemingway House,** 907 Whitehead St. (294-1575), off Olivia St., is where "Papa" wrote *For Whom the Bell Tolls* and *A Farewell to Arms.* Tour guides at the houses are rumored to be notoriously awful; grin and bear it, or traipse through the house on your own. About 50 cats (descendants of Hemingway's cats) make their home on the grounds; ask their names from the tour guides and be mildly amused. (House open daily 9am-5pm. Admission $6, kids $1.50.) The **Audubon House,** 205 Whitehead St. (294-2116), built in the early 1800s, houses some fine antiques and a private collection of the works of ornithologist John James Audubon. (Open daily 9:30am-5pm. Admission $5, ages 6-12 $1.)

Down Whitehead St., past Hemingway House, you'll come to the **southernmost point** in the continental U.S. and the adjacent **Southernmost Beach.** A small, conical monument and a few conchshell hawkers mark the spot. The **Monroe County Beach,** off Atlantic Ave., has an old pier allowing access past the weed line. The **Old U.S. Naval Air Station** offers deep water swimming on Truman Beach ($1). **Mel Fisher's Treasure Exhibit,** 200 Greene St. (294-2633), will dazzle you with glorious gold. Fisher discovered the sunken treasures from the shipwrecked Spanish vessel, *Atocha.* A *National Geographic* film is included in the entrance fee. (Open daily 9:30am-5pm. Admission $5, under 12, $1.50.)

The **San Carlos Institute,** 516 Duval St., built in 1871, is a freshly restored paragon of Cuban architecture that shines with majorca tiles from Spain and houses a research center for Hispanic studies. The **Haitian Art Company,** 600 Frances St. (296-8932), six blocks east of Duval St., is crammed full of vivid Caribbean artworks. (Open daily 10am-6pm. Free.)

Watching a sunset from the **Mallory Square Dock** is always a treat. Magicians, street entertainers, and hawkers of tacky wares work the crowd, while swimmers and speedboaters show off; the crowd always cheers when the sun slips into the Gulf with a blazing red farewell.

Every October, Key West holds a week-long celebration known as **Fantasy Fest,** culminating in an extravagant parade. The entire population of the area turns out for the event in costumes that stretch the imagination. In April, the **Conch Republic** celebration is highlighted by a bed race, and the Jan.-March **Old Island Days** features art exhibits, a conch shell-blowing contest, and the blessing of the shrimp fleet.

ENTERTAINMENT

The daily *Key West Citizen* (sold in front of the post office), monthly *Solares Hill,* and *The Conch Republic* (available at the Key West Chamber of Commerce—see Practical Information—and in lobbies and waiting rooms) all cover events on the island. Nightlife in Key West revs up at 11pm and runs down very late.

> **Rick's,** 208 Duval St. (296-4890). This place rocks, especially when the **Terry Cassidy Band** plays (Tues.-Sat. 5-11pm). Ask bartender Mike about the house specials, including the $1.50 draft. Open daily 11am-4am.

Sloppy Joe's, 201 Duval St. (294-5717), at Greene. Reputedly one of "Papa" Hemingway's preferred watering holes; the decor and rowdy tourists would probably now send him packing. Originally located in Havana but moved to "Cayo Hueso" (i.e. Key West) when Castro rose to power. The bar's usual frenzy heightens during the Hemingway Days Festival in mid-July. Drafts $2.25. R&B day and night. Open daily 9am-4am.

Captain Tony's Saloon, 428 Greene St. (294-1838). The oldest bar in Key West. Tony Tarracino, the owner, usually shows up at 9pm. Open Mon.-Thurs. 10am-1am, Fri.-Sat. 10am-2am, Sun. noon-1am.

■■■ FORT LAUDERDALE

Every spring, thousands of pale, lust-crazed college students flock to Fort Lauderdale, the official spring-break party capital. In recent years, open-container laws have been passed, and there have been crack-downs on drunk driving, fake IDs, and indecent exposure. This has caused the spring-break crowds largely to fizzle and head to less restrictive places. When the testosteroned hordes finally do leave each year, Fort Lauderdale breathes a huge sigh of relief. In the off-season, tourists less preoccupied with inebriated and anonymous carnal fulfillment can peacefully stroll along the wide beach. Broad-sailed boats and luxury yachts frame the seascape as they cruise the coast or anchor at the city's canals and ports.

PRACTICAL INFORMATION

Emergency: 911.

Visitor Information: Chamber of Commerce, 512 NE 3rd Ave. (462-6000), 3 blocks off Federal Hwy. at 5th St. Pick up the helpful *Visitor's Guide.* Open Mon.-Fri. 8am-5pm.

Airport: Fort Lauderdale/Hollywood International Airport, 359-6100. 3½ mi. south of downtown on U.S. 1, at exits 26 and 27 on I-95. **American, Continental, Delta, TWA, Northwest, United,** and **USAir** all serve this airport.

Amtrak: 200 SW 21st Terrace (463-8251 or 800-872-7245), just west of I-95, ¼-mi. south of Broward Blvd. Take bus #9, 10, or 81 from downtown. Daily service on "The Floridian" to: Miami (2 per day, 45 min., $6); Orlando (1 per day, 4 hr., $44); Jacksonville (2-3 per day, 7 hr., $68). Open daily 7am-6:15pm.

Greyhound: 513 NE 3rd St. (764-6551), 3 blocks north of Broward Blvd., downtown. Unsavory location, especially unfriendly at night. To: Orlando (9 per day, 4½ hr., $35); Daytona Beach (6 per day, 6 hr., $28); Miami (14 per day, 1 hr., $6). Open 6am-midnight daily.

Public Transport: Broward County Transit (BCT), 357-8400 (call Mon.-Fri. 7am-8:30pm, Sat. 7am-8pm, Sun. 8:30am-5pm). Extensive regional coverage. Most routes go to the terminal at the corner of 1st St. NW and 1st Ave. NW, downtown. Operates daily 6am-9pm every ½-hr. on most routes. Fare 85¢, seniors 40¢, students with ID 40¢, transfers 10¢. 7-day passes $8, available at beachfront hotels. Pick up a handy system map at the terminal. **Tri-Rail** (800-874-7245 or 728-8445) connects West Palm Beach, Ft. Lauderdale, and Miami. Trains run Mon.-Sat. 5am-9:30pm. Pick up schedules at the airport or at Tri-Rail stops. Fare $3, students and seniors with ID $1.50.

Car Rental: Alamo, 2601 S. Federal Hwy. (525-4715 or 800-327-9633). Cheapest cars $18 per day, $70 per week. Unlimited mileage, free drop-off in Daytona and Miami. Shuttle to airport $3. Must be 21 with credit card or deposit of $50 per day or $200 per week for out-of-state renters. Under 25 surcharge $15.

Bike Rentals: International Bicycle Shop, 1900 E. Sunrise Blvd. at N. Federal Hwy. (764-8800). Take bus #10 from downtown or bus #36 from A1A north of Sunrise. $10 per day, $35 per week. $100 deposit. Open Mon.-Fri. 10am-9pm, Sat. 9am-9pm, Sun. 11am-5pm. Must be 18. Avoid the expensive joints on the beach.

Taxi: Yellow Cab (565-5400) and **Public Service Taxi** (587-9090), both $2.45 plus $1.75 per mi.

Help Line: Crisis Hotline, 746-2756. 24 hrs.

Post Office: 1900 W. Oakland Park Blvd. (527-2028). Open Mon.-Fri. 7:30am-7pm, Sat. 8:30am-2pm. **ZIP code:** 33310.
Area Code: 305.

I-95 runs north-south, connecting W. Palm Beach, Ft. Lauderdale, and Miami. Rte. 84/I-75 (Alligator Alley) slithers 100 mi. west from Ft. Lauderdale across the Everglades to Naples and other small cities on the Gulf Coast of Southern Florida. It is currently under construction; delays are possible, but the road provides a good opportunity to view alligators. Ft. Lauderdale is bigger than it looks. The place is huge. The city extends westward from its 23 mi. of beach to encompass nearly 450 sq. mi. of land area. Most of the maps show distances deceptively; when traveling from the beach to downtown, take a bus. Roads are divided into two categories: streets and boulevards (east-west) and avenues (north-south). All are labeled NW, NE, SW, or SE according to the quadrant. **Broward Boulevard** divides the city east-west, **Andrews Avenue** north-south. The unpleasant downtown centers around the intersection of **Federal Highway (U.S. 1)** and **Las Olas Boulevard,** about 2 mi. west of the oceanfront. Between downtown and the waterfront, yachts fill the ritzy inlets of the **Intracoastal Waterway.** The strip (variously called Rte. A1A, N. Atlantic Blvd., 17th St. Causeway, Ocean Blvd., and Seabreeze Blvd.) runs along the beach for 4 mi. between **Oakland Park Boulevard** to the north and Las Olas Blvd. to the south. Las Olas Blvd. is the pricey shopping street; **Sunrise Boulevard** has most shopping malls. Both degenerate into ugly commercial strips west of downtown.

ACCOMMODATIONS AND CAMPING

Hotel prices vary from slightly unreasonable to absolutely ridiculous, increasing exponentially as you approach prime beachfront and spring break. High season runs from mid-February to early April. Investigate package deals at the slightly worse-for-wear hotels along the strip in Ft. Lauderdale. Many hotels offer off-season deals for under $35.

Small motels crowd each other one or two blocks off the beach area; many offer small kitchenettes. Look along **Birch Rd.,** one block back from Rte. A1A. **The Broward County Hotel and Motel Association** (462-0409) provides a free directory of area hotels (open Mon.-Fri. 9am-5pm). Scan the *Ft. Lauderdale News* and the Broward Section of the *Miami Herald* for occasional listings of local residents who rent rooms to tourists in spring. Sleeping on the well-patrolled beaches is impossible between 9pm and sunrise.

International House, 3811 N. Ocean Blvd. (568-1615). Take bus #10 to Coral Ridge. Walk 3 blocks south of Commercial Blvd. on the Strip. Pick up at bus station available. Shuttle service throughout Florida. Rooms with 6 beds, showers, A/C, cable TV, kitchen. Pool. Members $12, nonmembers $15. $5 key deposit. $2 linen fee. One block from beach. Private rooms $26.

Estoril Apartments, 2648 NE 32nd St. (563-3840; 800-548-9398 reservations only). From downtown, take bus #20, 10, 55, or 72 to Coral Ridge Shopping Center and walk 2 blocks east on Oakland. Students can probably persuade the proprietors to pick them up from the bus station or airport. A 10-min. walk to the beach. Very clean rooms with A/C, TV, and small kitchenette. Pool and barbecue. Students with *Let's Go* receive 10% discount. Office closes about 11pm. Singles $26, doubles $28; Jan.-April singles $38, doubles $40. Additional person $6 off-season, $10 in season. Reservations recommended.

Motel 6, 1801 State Rd. 84 (760-7999), 3 blocks east of I-95 and 3 mi. southwest of downtown. Take bus #14 to Rte. 84 and SW 15th Ave. and walk 3 blocks west. Far from the action. Clean. A/C, HBO. Singles $30, doubles $36; Nov.-April singles $38, doubles $44.

Budget Inn, 300 S. Ocean Blvd. (942-2030), Pompano Beach near the Ft. Lauderdale border on A1A. From downtown, take bus #11 north up A1A. Clean, attractive rooms on the beach. Cable TV, A/C. Singles $29-35, doubles $35-39; Jan.-April singles $48-66, doubles $54-72.

Easterlin County Park, 1000 NW 38th St. (938-0610), Oakland Park, less than 4 mi. west of the strip and 3 mi. north of downtown. Take bus #14 to NW 38th St. or #72 along Oakland Park to Powerline Rd. By car take Oakland Park exit from I-95. 2-week max. stay. Registration open 24 hrs. Sites with electricity, barbecue pits, and picnic table $17.

Quiet Waters County Park, 6601 N. Powerline Rd. (NW 9th Ave.) (360-1315), Pompano Beach, 10 mi. north of Oakland Park Blvd. I-95 exit 37B. Take Hillsboro Blvd. west to Powerline Rd. From downtown, take bus #14. Cramped, commercialized, but friendly. Bizarre 8-person "boatless water skiing" at the end of a cable and other water sports. No electricity. Check-in 2-6pm. Fully equipped campsites (tent, mattresses, cooler, grill, canoe) for up to 6 people, Sun.-Thurs. $17, Fri.-Sat. $25 plus $20 refundable deposit.

FOOD

The clubs along the strip offer massive quantities of free grub during happy hour: surfboard-sized platters of wieners, chips, and hors d'oeuvres, or all-you-can-eat pizza and buffets. However, these bars have hefty cover charges (from $5) and expect you to buy a drink once you're there (from $2). In addition, these bars are nightclubs, not restaurants, and the quality of their cuisine proves it. In contrast, the restaurants listed below serve "real" food.

La Spada's, 4346 Seagrape Drive (776-7893). Two blocks from the beach, off Commercial Blvd. Best, and biggest, subs in southern Florida. The foot-long Italian sub ($6.50) is an absolute must. Open Mon.-Sat. 10am-8pm, Sun. 11am-8pm.

Golden Chopsticks, 4350 N. Federal Hwy. (776-0953). Some of the best Chinese food in town. For a treat, try the steak kew ($12). Most of the uniformly delicious food is more reasonably priced. Open Mon.-Thurs. 11:30am-midnight, Fri. 11:30am-1am, Sat. 1pm-1am, Sun.1pm-11pm.

Southport Raw Bar, 1536 Cordova Rd. (525-2526), by the 17th St. Causeway behind the Southport Mall on the Intracoastal Waterway. Take bus #40 from the strip or #30 from downtown. Aggressively marine decor. Spicy conch chowder $2.25, fried shrimp $5.25. Open Mon.-Sat. 11am-2am, Sun. noon-2am.

Tina's Spaghetti House, 2110 S. Federal Hwy. (522-9943), just south of 17th St. Take bus #1 from downtown. Authentic red-checkered tablecloths, hefty oak furniture, and bibs. Popular with locals since 1951. Lunch specials $4-5. Spaghetti dinner $6-7. Open Mon.-Thurs. 11:30am-10pm, Fri. 11:30am-11pm, Sat. 4-11pm, Sun. 4-10pm.

SIN

Ft. Lauderdale offers all kinds of licit and illicit entertainment by night. (Mostly illicit.) Planes flying over the beach hawk hedonistic happy hours at local watering holes. Students frequent the night spots on the A1A strip along the beach, with an emphasis on "strip." When going out, bring a driver's license or a passport as proof of age; most bars and nightclubs don't accept college IDs. Be warned that this is *not* the place for cappuccino and conversation but for nude jello wrestling and similarly lubricated entertainment.

For those who prefer garbed service, several popular nightspots line N. Atlantic Blvd. next to the beach. **The Candy Store,** 1 N. Atlantic Blvd. (761-1888), was once at the pinnacle of Ft. Lauderdale nightlife. It's still a great hangout for drinking and people-watching; rowdy sailors on leave have been known to liven up the place. Get their the all-you-can-eat afternoon pizza. (Open Mon.-Fri. 11am-2am, Sat. 11am-3am. Cover $5.) Also try **Banana Joe's on the Beach,** 837 N. Atlantic Blvd. (565-4446), at Sunrise and A1A. (Open Mon.-Fri. 7am-2am, Sat. 7am-3am, Sun. noon-2am. Kitchen open 11:30am-7pm.) For off-the-beach entertainment, Ft. Lauderdale's new hotspot is **Crocco's World Class Sports Bar,** 3339 N. Federal Hwy. (566-2406). Built in an old movie theater, this gargantuan club has lines out the door almost every night. (Open Sun.-Fri 11am-2am, Sat. 11am-3am.) **Mombasa Bay,** 3051 NE 32nd Ave. (561-8220), is a new club on the Intracoastal Waterway. Live R&B

Thurs., live Reggae Fri.-Mon. (Open Sun.-Fri. 11:30am-2am, Sat. 11:30am-3am. Concerts start at 9:30pm.)

SIGHTS AND ACTIVITIES

Besides sun and sin, Ft. Lauderdale is pretty low on activities. To see why Ft. Lauderdale is called the "Venice of America," take a tour of its waterways aboard the **Jungle Queen,** located at the **Bahia Mar Yacht Center** (462-5596), on Rte. A1A three blocks south of Las Olas Blvd. (3-hr. tours daily at 10am, 2pm, and 7pm. Fare $7.50, kids $5.) For more intimate acquaintance with the ocean, **Water Sports Unlimited,** 301 Seabreeze Blvd. (467-1316), offers equipment for a variety of water sports. Located on the beach, Water Sports offers wave runners ($35 per ½-hr., $55 per hr.), motor boats ($40 per hour, $220 per day), and parasailing trips ($42 per ride).

■■■ MIAMI

Hard hit by Hurricane Andrew in August 1992, Miami has made an excellent comeback. Today, about the only scars left by Andrew are visible in the foliage, which will probably take years to recuperate. Many areas appear untouched by Andrew, especially Miami Beach, where tourists flock to lie-and-fry by day, then move inland about 400 meters to dance the night away. The rest of Miami is relatively residential and made up of many smaller cultures: Little Havana, a well-established Cuban community; Coconut Grove, with its village-in-the-swampland bohemianism; placid, well-to-do Coral Gables, one of the country's earliest planned cities; and the African-American communities of Liberty City and Overtown. Wherever you find yourself in Miami, a knowledge of Spanish is always helpful and sometimes necessary.

PRACTICAL INFORMATION

Emergency: 911.

Visitor Information: Greater Miami Convention and Visitors Bureau, 701 Brickell Ave. (539-3000 or 800-283-2707 outside Miami), 27th floor of the Barnett Bank building downtown. Open Mon.-Fri. 8:30am-5pm. **Coconut Grove Chamber of Commerce,** 2820 McFarlane Rd. (444-7270). Mountains of maps and advice. Open Mon.-Fri. 9am-5pm. The **Miami Beach Resort Hotel Association,** 407 Lincoln Rd. #10G (531-3553), can help you find a place on the beach. Open Mon.-Fri. 9am-5pm.

Airport: Miami International Airport, 7 mi. northwest of downtown (876-7000). Bus #20 is the most direct public transportation into downtown (bus #3 is also usable); from there, take bus C, K, or S to South Miami Beach. Helpful maps of Miami and the Public Transportation systems available at the **Information** booth for free.

Amtrak: 8303 NW 37th Ave. (835-1221 or 800-872-7245), not far from the Northside station of Metrorail. Bus L goes directly to Lincoln Rd. Mall in South Miami Beach. Open Tues., Thurs., Sat., and Sun. 6:15am-7:15pm; Mon., Wed., and Fri. 6:15pm-midnight. To: Orlando (1 per day, 5 hr., $50); Jacksonville (2-3 per day, 8 hr., $76); and Washington, DC (2 per day, 22 hr., $153).

Greyhound: Miami Beach Station, 7101 Harding Ave. (538-0381 for fare and schedule info). To: Orlando (4 per day, 6 hr., $37); Jacksonville (4 per day, 8 hr., $39); and Atlanta (4 per day,19 hr., $79). Ticket window open daily 5am-midnight.

Public Transport: Metro Dade Transportation (638-6700; 6am-11pm for info). Complex system; buses tend to be quite tardy. The extensive **Metrobus** network converges downtown; most long bus trips transfer in this area. Lettered bus routes A through X serve Miami Beach. After dark, some stops are patrolled by police (indicated with a sign). Service daily 6am-8pm; major routes until 11pm or midnight. Fare $1.25. Pick up a *Map Manual* at the visitors bureau or at information stands at the corner of W. Flagler and NW 1st Ave. and at the Lincoln Rd. Mall in Miami Beach. Both open Mon.-Fri. 8am-5pm. Warning: it is illegal to carry car batteries on the bus. Futuristic **Metrorail** elevated train service downtown. Fare $1.25, rail to bus transfers 25¢. The **Metromover** loop downtown, which runs

MIAMI

6:30am-7pm, is linked to the Metrorail stations. **Tri-Rail** (800-874-7245) connects Miami, Ft. Lauderdale, and West Palm Beach. Trains run Mon.-Sat. 5am-9:30pm. Fare $3, students and seniors $1.50.

Taxis: Yellow Cab, 444-4444 (easy enough). **Metro Taxi,** 888-8888 (really easy). **Central Cab,** 532-5555 (not too hard). $1.75 per minute.

Car Rental: Value Rent-a-Car, 1620 Collins Ave. (532-8257), Miami Beach. $27 per day, $129 per week. Drivers under 25 pay $12 additional daily charge. Open daily 8am-6pm. Must be 21 with credit card.

Auto Transport Company: Dependable Car Travel, 162 Sunny Isles Blvd. (945-4104). Open Mon.-Fri. 8:30am-5pm, Sat. 8:30am-noon. Must be 18 with credit card or $150 deposit and passport and foreign license. This is a free service.

Bike Rental: Miami Beach Bicycle Center, 923 W. 39th St. (531-4161), Miami Beach. $5 per hr., $12 per day, $40 per week. Open Mon.-Fri. 9:30am-6pm, Sat. 9:30am-5pm. Must be 18 with credit card or $40 deposit. **Dade Cycle Shop,** 3216 Grand Ave., Coconut Grove (443-6075). $5.50 per hr., $15-22 per day. Open daily 9:30am-5:30pm. Must have $100 deposit or driver's license or credit card.

Help Lines: Crisis Hotline, 358-4357. **Rape Treatment Center and Hotline,** 1611 NW 12th Ave. (585-7273). **Gay Community Hotline,** 759-3661.

Post Office: 500 NW 2nd Ave. (371-2911). Open Mon.-Fri. 8:30am-5pm, Sat. 8:30am-12:30pm. **ZIP code:** 33101.

Area Code: 305.

ORIENTATION

Three highways criss-cross the Miami area. Just south of downtown, I-95, the most direct route north-south, runs into **U.S. I (Dixie Highway).** U.S. 1 goes as far as the Everglades entrance at Florida City and then all the way out to Key West as the Overseas Highway. **Route 836,** a major east-west artery through town, connects I-95 with the **Florida Turnpike,** passing the airport in between. Take Rte. 836 and the Turnpike to Florida City to avoid the traffic on Rte. 1.

When looking for street addresses, pay careful attention to the systematic street layout; it's *very* easy to confuse North Miami Beach, West Miami, Miami Beach, and Miami addresses. Streets in Miami run east-west, avenues north-south, and numbers into the hundreds refer to both. Miami divides into NE, NW, SE, and SW sections; the dividing lines (downtown) are **Flagler Street** (east-west) and **Miami Avenue** (north-south). Some numbered streets and avenues also have names—i.e., Le Jeune Rd. is SW 42nd Ave., and SW 40th St. is called Bird Rd. Try to get a map with both numbers and names in order to solve this conundrum.

Several four-lane causeways connect Miami to **Miami Beach.** The most useful is **MacArthur Causeway,** which feeds onto 5th St. in Miami Beach. Numbered streets run across the island, with numbers increasing as you go north; the main north-south drag is **Collins Avenue.** In South Miami Beach, **Washington Avenue,** one block to the west, is the main commercial strip, while **Ocean Avenue,** actually on the waterfront, lies one block east. The **Rickenbacker Causeway** is the only connection to Key Biscayne.

Spanish-speakers will have an advantage getting around Miami. The city has a large Spanish-speaking community; the *Miami Herald* now even puts out a Spanish edition. You may even run into problems on buses without speaking Spanish, since many drivers only speak Spanish.

ACCOMMODATIONS AND CAMPING

Finding cheap rooms in Miami should never pose a problem. Several hundred art-deco hotels in South Miami Beach stand at your service. For safety, convenience, and security, stay north of 5th St. A "pullmanette" (in 1940s lingo) is a room with a refrigerator, stove, and sink; getting one and some groceries allows you to save money on food. In South Florida, since any hotel room short of the Fontainebleau Hilton is likely to have two- to three-inch cockroaches ("palmetto bugs"), try not to

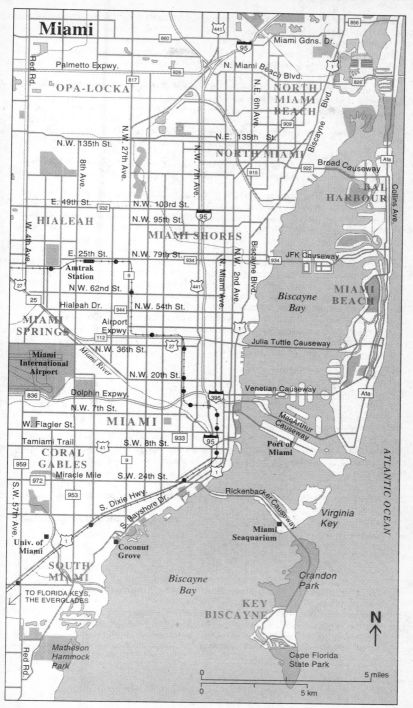

Miami

MIAMI

860
856
441
95
Miami Gdns. Dr.
Palmetto Expwy.
826
1
N. Miami Beach Blvd.
817
Red Rd.
826
OPA-LOCKA
N.E. 6th Ave.
NORTH MIAMI BEACH
909
N.W. 135th St.
N.W. 27th Ave.
N.E. 135th St.
Biscayne Blvd.
8th Ave.
NORTH MIAMI
922
Broad Causeway
915
A1a
E. 49th St.
N.W. 7th Ave.
BAL HARBOUR
332
N.W. 103rd St.
Collins Ave.
HIALEAH
95
N.W. 95th St.
27
W. 4th Ave.
N.W. 2nd Ave.
MIAMI SHORES
N. Miami Ave.
Biscayne Blvd.
E. 25th St.
N.W. 79th St.
934
JFK Causeway
934
Amtrak Station
9
N. W. 62nd St.
441
MIAMI BEACH
25
Hialeah Dr.
944
N.W. 54th St.
Biscayne Bay
MIAMI SPRINGS
Airport Expwy.
112
Miami River
N.W. 36th St.
27
1
Julia Tuttle Causeway
Miami International Airport
N.W. 20th St.
836
Dolphin Expwy.
395
Venetian Causeway
A1a
N.W. 7th St.
MacArthur Causeway
W. Flagler St.
MIAMI
933
95
Tamiami Trail
41
S.W. 8th St.
Port of Miami
CORAL GABLES
9
959
S.W. 24th St.
972
Miracle Mile
953
S. Dixie Hwy.
Rickenbacker Causeway
S.W. 57th Ave.
S. Bayshore Dr.
Virginia Key
1
Miami Seaquarium
Univ. of Miami
Coconut Grove
ATLANTIC OCEAN
SOUTH MIAMI
Crandon Park
Biscayne Bay
TO FLORIDA KEYS, THE EVERGLADES
KEY BISCAYNE
N
Red Rd.
Matheson Hammock Park
Cape Florida State Park
0   5 miles
0   5 km

take them as absolute indicators of quality. In general, the peak season for Miami Beach runs late Dec. to mid-March.

Camping is not allowed in Miami, and the nearest campgrounds are north or west of the city. Those who can't bear to put their tents aside for a night or two should head on to one of the nearby national parks.

Miami Beach International Travelers Hostel (9th Street Hostel), 236 9th St. (534-0268), at the intersection with Washington Ave. From the airport, take J bus to 41st and Indian Creek, then transfer to bus C to 9th and Washington. From downtown, take bus C, K, or S or call for directions. Has a relaxed international atmosphere and central location, kitchen, laundry, common room. No curfew. 29 rooms, all with A/C and private bath. Hostel rooms $12 (max. 4 people). Private rooms $28 single or double.

The Tropics, 1550 Collins Ave. (531-0361). Across the street from the beach, clean hostel rooms with 4-8 beds, A/C, private baths. $12. No curfew. Private rooms $30 single or double.

The Clay Hotel (HI/AYH), 1438 Washington Ave. (534-2988). Take bus C or K from downtown. Cheerful chaos reigns in the 7 buildings. Kitchen, laundry facilities, and a useful ride board. Very international crowd. Most rooms have 4 beds; 2 rooms share a bathroom. A/C. No curfew. Members $10, winter $11. Nonmembers $13, winter $14. Hotel singles $26. Doubles $29. Key deposit $5.

Kent Hotel, 1131 Collins Ave. (531-6771), one block from the beach. Beautifully renovated rooms and friendly staff. TV, A/C, fridge, kitchen and breakfast. Singles or doubles May 1-Oct. 15 $45-50, Oct. 15-May 1 $65-70. Ocean view $10 more.

Tudor Hotel, 1111 Collins Ave. (534-2934). Beautiful renovations make this one of the nicest hotels in Miami Beach, in all pastels with flamingo murals and deco-period lighting. Rooms have refrigerator, microwave, cable TV, A/C, phone. Singles/doubles May 1-Oct. 15 $50, weekly $210. Oct. 15-May 1 $70, weekly $390.

Miami Airways Motel, 5001 36th St. (883-4700). Will pick you up at nearby airport for free. Clean, small rooms, breakfast, A/C, pool, HBO, but pretty far from the action. Singles $36. Doubles $42.

Larry & Penny Thompson Memorial Campground, 12451 SW 184th St. (232-1049), a long way from anywhere. By car, drive 20-30 min. south along Dixie Hwy. Pretty grounds in a grove of mango trees. Laundry, store, and all facilities, plus artificial lake with swimming beach, beautiful park, and even water slides. For further lake info, call 255-8251. Office open daily 8am-7pm but takes late arrivals. Lake open daily 10am-5pm. Sites with hookup $17, $90 weekly.

FOOD

If you eat nothing else in Miami, be sure to try Cuban food. Specialties include *media noche* sandwiches (a sort of Cuban club sandwich on a soft roll, heated and compressed); *mamey,* a bright red ice cream concoction; rich *frijoles negros* (black beans); and *picadillo* (shredded beef and peas in tomato sauce, served with white rice). For Cuban sweets, seek out a *dulcería,* and punctuate your rambles around town with thimble-sized shots of strong, sweet *café cubano* (25¢).

Cheap restaurants are not common in Miami Beach, but an array of fresh bakeries and fruit stands can sustain you with melons, mangoes, papayas, tomatoes, and carrots for under $3 a day.

Irish House (534-5667), 14th St. and Alton Rd., Miami Beach. A favorite hangout for local journalists, politicos and beach-goers. Noted for its buffalo wings ($3.50) and cheeseburgers ($4.50). Open Mon.-Sat. 11am-2am, Sun. 2am-2am—this place never closes on Sat. night.

Renaissance Cafe, 410 Española Way (672-5539), attached to the Clay Hotel. Try the big burgers ($3.95) or the pizza ($5.95). Open 8am-2am daily.

La Rumba, 2008 Collins Ave. (538-8998), Miami Beach, between 20th and 21st St. Good, cheap Cuban food and noisy fun. Try their *arroz con pollo* (chicken with yellow rice, $6) or a banana milkshake ($1.75). Open Fri.-Wed. 7:30am-midnight.

Flamingo Restaurant, 1454 Washington Ave. (673-4302), right down the street from the hostel. Friendly service, all in Spanish. Peck at the grilled chicken with pinto beans and rice ($5.50). Open Mon.-Sat. 7am-7:30pm.

Our Place Natural Foods Eatery, 830 Washington Ave. (674-1322), Miami Beach. All vegetarian fare. New Age books mingle with juices, salads, pita, tofutti, etc. Lunch $3-6, dinner $5-10. Great daily specials with soup ($6). Open Mon.-Thurs. 11am-9pm, Fri.-Sat 11am-11pm, Sun. 1pm-8pm.

King's Ice Cream, 1831 SW 8th St. (643-1842), on Calle Ocho. Tropical fruit *helado* (ice cream, $2) flavors include coconut (served in its own shell), *mamey,* and banana. Also try *churros* (thin Spanish donuts, 10 for $1) or *café cubano* (10¢). Open Mon.-Sat. 10am-11pm, Sun. 2pm-11pm.

SIGHTS

The best sight in Miami is the beach. When you get too burned or dazed and are in need of some shade, try the **Seaquarium,** 4400 Rickenbacker Causeway (361-5703), Virginia Key, just minutes from downtown. While not on par with Sea World in Orlando, it has an impressive array of shows, including obligatory dolphins, hungry sharks, and Lolita, the killer whale. The aquarium also displays tropical fish. (Open daily 9:30am-6:00pm; ticket office closes 4:30pm. $18, kids $12.)

South Miami Beach or **South Beach,** the swath of town between 6th and 23rd St., teems with hundreds of hotels and apartments whose sun-faded pastel facades recall what sun-thirsty northerners of the 1920s thought a tropical paradise should look like. The art-deco palaces constitute the country's largest national historic district and the only one which has preserved 20th-century buildings. A fascinating mixture of people populates the area, including large retired and first-generation Latin communities; knowing Spanish is a big advantage here. **Walking tours** of the historic district are offered Saturdays at 10:30am ($6). **Bike tours** available Sundays at 10:30am ($5, rental $5 extra). Call 672-2014 to find out the point of departure.

On the waterfront downtown is Miami's newest attraction, the **Bayside** shopping complex, with fancy shops (many beyond the realm of the budget traveler), exotic food booths, and live reggae or *salsa* on Friday and Saturday nights. Near Bayside, visit the **Police Hall of Fame and Museum,** 3801 Biscayne Blvd. (891-1700), and learn more than you ever wanted to know about the police. Watch in your rearview mirror for the police car suspended alongside the building. (Open daily 10am-5:30pm. Admission $6, seniors and kids $3.)

Little Havana lies between SW 12th and SW 27th Ave. (Take bus #3, 11, 14, 15, 17, 25, or 37.) The street scenes of **Calle Ocho** (SW 8th St.) lie at the heart of this district; the corresponding section of W. Flagler St. is a center of Cuban business. The changing exhibits at the **Cuban Museum of Arts and Culture,** 1300 SW 12th Ave. (858-8006), reflect the bright colors and rhythms of Cuban art. Take bus #27. (Open Wed.-Sun. 1-5pm. Admission by donation.)

An entirely different atmosphere prevails on the bay south of downtown in self-consciously rustic **Coconut Grove** (take bus #1 or Metrorail from downtown). The grove centers around the intersection of Grand Ave. and Main Hwy. Drop into a watering hole like **Señor Frog's,** 3008 Grand Ave. (448-0999), home of bang-up tables and phenomenal *salsa.* Be prepared to speak Spanish! (Open Sun.-Thurs. 10:30am-1am, Fri.-Sat. 10:30am-2am.)

On the bayfront between the Grove and downtown stands **Vizcaya,** 3251 S. Miami Ave. (579-2708), set in acres of elaborately landscaped grounds. Built in 1916 by International Harvester heir James Deering, the four facades of this 70-room Italianate mansion hide a hodgepodge of European antiques. (Open daily 9:30am-5pm; last admission 4:30pm. $8, ages 6-12 $4. Take bus #1 or Metrorail to Vizcaya.) Across the street from Vizcaya, the **Museum of Science** and its **Planetarium,** 3280 S. Miami Ave. (854-4247; show info 854-2222), offer laser shows and their ilk. Both congest with kids. (Open daily 10am-6pm. $6, ages 3-12 and seniors $4. Shows $6 extra.)

ENTERTAINMENT

The art-deco district in South Miami Beach is filled with clubs; Ocean Blvd., on the beach, is crowded with a young, rowdy set nearly every night of the week. Any club will do, just wander down and take your pick. For blues, try the **Peacock Cafe,** 2977 McFarlane Rd. (442-8877), Coconut Grove (open Tues.-Sun. 11:30am-5am). After the money's gone, head for **Friday Night Live** (673-7224 for info; Mon.-Fri. 8:30am-5pm), at South Point Park, the very southern tip of Miami Beach, which features free city-sponsored concerts 8-11pm. Down Washington Ave. at Española Way, the **Cameo Theater** (532-0922 for showtimes and prices) hosts live punk and other rock bands about once per week. For gay nightlife, check out **Uncle Charlie's,** 3673 Bird Ave. (442-8687), just off Dixie Hwy. (cover $3 Mon.-Wed., $4 Thurs.-Sun.).

Performing Arts and Community Education (PACE) (681-1470; open Mon.-Fri. 9am-5pm) offers more than 1000 concerts each year (jazz, rock, soul, dixieland, reggae, *salsa,* and bluegrass), most of which are free. For more info on what's happening in Miami, check *Miami-South Florida Magazine,* or the "Living Today," "Lively Arts," and Friday "Weekend" sections of the *Miami Herald.* Guides to what's happening may be found at all kinds of shops and restaurants in Miami Beach.

■■■ ORLANDO & DISNEY WORLD

Though Orlando likes to tout itself as "the world's vacation center" and one of the country's fastest-growing cities, millions annually descend on this central Florida city for just one reason: **Disney World,** the world's most popular tourist attraction. Walt Disney selected the area south of Orlando as the place for his sequel to California's Disneyland. Disney has since augmented the Magic Kingdom with the Epcot Center and the new Disney-MGM Studios theme park.

A number of parasitic attractions, such as expensive water parks, abound in the area to scavenge the left-overs of Disney tourism. Be warned: of the many ways to blow your dough in this land of illusions, usually you are best off spending your time and money at Disney first. Two exceptions to this rule are Sea World and the spanking new Universal Studios Florida. With fun and exciting exhibits and rides, both are well worth their admission prices.

PRACTICAL INFORMATION

Emergency: 911.

Visitor Information: Orlando-Orange County Visitors and Convention Bureau, 8445 International Dr. (363-5871), several mi. southwest of downtown at the Mercado (Spanish-style mall). Take bus #8, and ask the bus driver to drop you off at the Mercado. Maps and info on nearly all of the amusement park attractions in the area. Pick up a free bus system map. Open daily 8am-8pm.

Amtrak: 1400 Sligh Blvd. (843-7611 or 800-872-7245). Three blocks east of I-4. Take S. Orange Ave., turn west on Columbia, then right on Sligh. To: Tampa (2 per day, 2 hr., $18); Jacksonville (2 per day, 3½ hr., $28); Miami (1 per day, 5½ hr., $46). Open daily 6am-8:30pm.

Greyhound: 300 W. Amelia St. (843-7720 for 24-hr. fare and ticket info), at Hughy Ave. downtown near Sunshine Park. To: Tampa (8 per day, 2½ hr., $15); Jacksonville (8 per day, 3 hr., $28); Miami (7 per day, 5 hr., $46). Open 24 hrs.

Public Transport: LYNX, 438 Woods Ave. (841-8240 for info Mon.-Fri. 6:30am-6:30pm, Sat. 7:30am-6pm, Sun. 8am-4pm). Downtown terminal between Central and Pine St., 1 block west of Orange Ave. and 1 block east of I-4. Schedules available at most shopping malls, banks, and at the downtown terminal. Serves the airport (bus #11 at "B" terminal luggage claim), Sea World, and Wet 'n' Wild. Buses operate daily 6am-9pm. Fare 75¢, under 18 25¢, transfers 10¢.

Mears Motor Shuttle, 324 W. Gore St. (423-5566). Has a booth at the airport for transportation to most hotels, including the Airport Hostel (see Accommodations below). Cheapest transport besides city bus #11 if you're alone and can't split taxi

fare. Also runs from most hotels to Disney ($14 round-trip). Open 24 hrs. Call day in advance to reserve seat to Disney.
Taxi: Yellowcab, 422-4455. $2.45 first mi., $1.40 each additional mi.
Car Rental: Alamo, 8200 McCoy Rd. (857-8200 or 800-327-9633), near the airport. $25 per day, $122 per week. Under 25 $10 extra per day. Open 24 hrs. Must have major credit card or a $50 deposit and book through travel agent.
Help Lines: Rape Hotline, 740-5408. **Crisis Information:** 648-3028. Both 24 hrs.
Post Office: 46 E. Robinson St. (843-5673), at Magnolia downtown. Open Mon.-Fri. 8am-5pm, Sat. 9am-noon. **ZIP code:** 32801.
Area Code: 407.

Orlando proper lies at the center of hundreds of small lakes and amusement parks. **Lake Eola** reclines at the center of the city, east of I-4 and south of Colonial Dr. Streets divide north-south by **Route 17-92 (Orange Blossom Trail)** and east-west by **Colonial Drive.** I-4, supposedly an east-west expressway, actually runs north-south through the center of town. To reach either downtown youth hostel (see Accommodations) by car, take the Robinson St. exit and turn right. **Disney World** and **Sea World** are 15-20 mi. south of downtown on I-4; **Cypress Gardens** is 30 mi. south of Disney off U.S. 27 near Winter Haven. Transportation out to the parks is simple—most hotels offer a shuttle service to Disney, but you can take a city bus or call Mears Motor Shuttle (see above).

ACCOMMODATIONS AND CAMPING

Orlando does not cater to the budget traveler. Prices for hotel rooms rise exponentially as you approach Disney World; plan to stay in a hostel or in downtown Orlando. Reservations are a good idea Dec.-Jan., March-April, and on holidays. Or try **Kissimmee,** a few mi. east of Disney World along U.S. 192, which has some of the cheapest places around to camp. One city park and four Orange County parks have campsites ($11, with hookup $14). Contact **Orange County Parks & Recreation Department,** 118 W. Kaley St. (836-4290), and **Orlando Parks Department,** 1206 W. Columbia (246-2283), for more info. (Both open Mon.-Fri. 8am-8pm.)

Orlando International Youth Hostel at Plantation Manor (HI/AYH), 227 N. Eola Dr. (843-8888), at E. Robinson, downtown on the east shore of Lake Eola. Usually full July-Oct., so make reservations. Porch, TV room, kitchen facilities, A/C in most rooms, (negotiable) midnight curfew Mon.-Wed. Rooms sleep 4-8. Hostel beds $11, nonmembers $13. Private rooms $28. Breakfast $2, linen $2, key deposit $5. The friendly managers will take you to the theme park of your choice for $10 round-trip.
Airport Hostel, 3500 McCoy Rd. (859-3165 or 851-1612), off Daetwiler Rd. behind the La Quinta Motel. Take "Airport" bus #11 from the airport or downtown. Little glamour, but very homey, with tropical fruit trees out back. Kitchen facilities, pool access, no curfew. Check-in by 10pm. $10 per night, $60 per week. Breakfast and linen included.
Women's Residential Counseling Center (HI/AYH), 107 E. Hillcrest St. (425-1076), at Magnolia, 4 blocks from Plantation Manor right behind the Orlando Sentinel. Take bus #10 or 12; staff recommends a taxi. Women aged 18-54 only. Clean, safe, and friendly. Pool. Flexible 3-night max. stay. $10. Linen $2. Good breakfast $2, dinner $4.50. No reservations. No curfew.
Sun Motel, 5020 W. Irlo Bronson Memorial Hwy. (396-6666 or 800-541-2674), in Kissimmee. Very reasonable considering proximity to Disney World (4 mi.). Cable TV, phone, pool, A/C. Singles $45, doubles $55. Off-season: singles $22, doubles $25.
KOA, U.S. 192 (396-2400; 800-331-1453), down the road from Twin Lakes. Kamping kabins $38. Pool, tennis, store (open 7am-11pm). Even in season you're bound to get a site, but arrive early. Free buses twice per day to Disney. Office open 24 hrs. Tent sites with hookup $25.

Stage Stop Campground, 700 W. Rte. 50 (656-8000), 8 mi. north of Disney in Winter Garden. Take exit 80 off the Florida Turnpike N., then left on Rte. 50. Office open daily 8am-8:30pm. Sites with full hookup $17. Weekly: $112, A/C $1.50 per day.

FOOD

Lilia's Grilled Delight, 3150 S. Orange Ave. (351-9087), 2 blocks south of Michigan St., 5 min. from the downtown business district. Small, modestly decorated Philippine restaurant—one of the best-kept secrets in town. Don't pass up *lumpia,* a tantalizing combination of sauteed meat, shrimp, vegetables, and peanut butter in a fried dough or the *adobo,* the Philippine national dish. Lunch $4-6, dinner $5-9. Open Mon.-Fri. 11am-2:30pm.

Numero Uno, 2499 S. Orange Ave. (841-3840). A #1 local favorite serving tasty Cuban specialties in a casual setting. Roast pork dinner with rice, plantains, and salad about $8. Open Mon.-Wed. 11am-3pm, Thurs.-Fri. 11am-3pm and 5-10pm, Sat. 1-10pm.

Deter's Restaurant and Pub, 17 W. Pine St.(839-5975), just up from Orange St. near the Church Street Mall. German-American cuisine in an after-work-let's-have-a-beer-touch-my-monkey atmosphere. Try the amazing chicken in *reisling* sauce ($10). Live entertainment Fri.-Sat. nights. Open Mon.-Sat. 11am-1am.

Ronnie's Restaurant, 2702 Colonial Plaza (894-2943), at Bumby St. just past the Colonial Plaza mall. Art-deco booths and counters from the 50s. Mix of Jewish, Cuban, and American cuisine. The famous breakfast special (eggs, rolls, juice, coffee, and more) may fill you up for a few days ($5). Steak dinner $11, fresh breads, swell pancakes. Open Sun.-Thurs. 7am-11pm, Fri.-Sat. 7am-1am.

Nature's Table, 8001 South Orange Blossom Trail (857-5496). Vegetarian and healthful specialties. Delicious fruit and protein powder shakes ($1-2), yogurt, juice. Excellent, thick sandwiches under $4. Open Mon.-Fri. 9am-5pm.

ENTERTAINMENT

The **Church Street Station,** 129 W. Church St. (422-2434), downtown between South and Garland St., is a slick, block-long entertainment, shopping, and restaurant complex. Get 89¢ beef tacos at **NACO'S,** or the $3 dinner platter at the **Chinese Cafe.** Listen to free folk and bluegrass music at **Apple Annie's Courtyard.** Boogie down (and enjoy 5¢ beers on Wed.) at **Phineas Phogg's Balloon Works** (enforced 21 age restriction). Or pay $15 to go to the three theme shows. **Rosie O'Grady's** is the most popular show, featuring Dixieland and can-can girls. **Cheyenne Saloon and Opera House** has a country and western show, while rock and roll rules at the **Orchid Garden Ballroom.** For less expensive nightlife, explore **Orange Avenue** downtown. Several good bars and clubs have live music and dancing at very reasonable prices. The **Beach Club Cafe,** 68 N. Orange Ave. (839-0457), at Washington St., hosts DJ dancing or live reggae nightly.

■ Disney World

Admit it: you came here to see Disney, the mother of all amusement parks, a sprawling three-park labyrinth of kiddie rides, movie sets, and futuristic world displays. If bigger is better, Disney World certainly wins the prize for best park in the U.S. (824-4321 for info daily 8am-10pm). Like Gaul, Disney World is divided into three parts: the **Magic Kingdom,** with seven theme regions; the **Epcot Center,** part science fair, part World's Fair; and the newly completed **Disney-MGM Studios,** a pseudo movie and TV studio with Magic Kingdom-style rides. All are located a few mi. from each other in the town of **Lake Buena Vista,** 20 mi. west of Orlando via I-4.

A one-day entrance fee of $35 (ages 3-9 $28) admits you to *one* of the three parks; it also allows you to leave and return to the same park later in the day. A four-day **Super Pass** ($125, ages 3-9 $98) admits you to all three, including unlimited transportation between attractions on the Disney monorail, boats, buses, and trains. You can opt for a five-day **Super Duper Pass** ($170, ages 3-9 $135), which also admits you to all other Disney attractions. Multi-day passes need not be used on consecutive days, and they are valid forever and ever. Those Disney attractions that charge separate admissions (unless you have the five-day Super Duper Pass) are: **River Country** ($13.25, ages 3-9 $10.50); **Discovery Island** ($8.50, ages 3-9 $4.75); **Typhoon Lagoon** ($20.50, ages 3-9 $16.50); and **Pleasure Island** ($14, over 18 only unless with adult). For descriptions, see Other Disney Attractions below.

Gray Line Tours (422-0744) and **Mears Motor Shuttle** (423-5566) offer transport from most hotels to Disney (depart hotel at 9am, depart Disney at 7pm; $14 roundtrip). Major hotels and some campgrounds provide their own shuttles for guests. **Cyclists** are stopped at the main gate and driven by security guards to the inner entrance where they can stash their bikes free of charge.

Disney World opens its gates 365 days per year, but hours fluctuate according to season. It's busy during the summer when school is out, but "peak times" during Christmas, Thanksgiving, spring break, and the month around Easter also pack in the crowds. More people visit between Christmas and New Year's than at any other time of year. Since the crowd hits the main gates at 10am, arrive before the 9am opening time and seek out your favorite rides or exhibits before noon. During peak period (and perhaps the rest of the year), the Disney parks actually open earlier than the stated time. Begin the day at the rear of a park and work your way to the front. You'll have mondo fun at the distant attractions while lines for those near the entrance are jammed. Persevere through dinner time (5:30-8pm), when a lot of cranky kids head home. Regardless of tactics, you'll often have to wait anywhere from 45 minutes to two hours at big attractions.

Magic Kingdom Seven "lands" comprise the Magic Kingdom. You enter on **Main Street, USA,** meant to capture the essence of turn-of-the-century hometown U.S. In a potpourri of styles, architects employed "forced perspective" here, building the ground floor of the shops 9/10 of the normal size, while the second and third stories get progressively smaller. Walt describes his vision in the "Walt Disney Movie" at the Hospitality House, to the right as you emerge from under the railroad station. The Main Street Cinema shows some great old silent films. Late afternoons on Main Street turn gruesome when the not-so-impressive "All America Parade" marches through at 3pm; take this chance to ride some of the more crowded attractions. Near the entrance, you'll find a steam train that huffs and puffs its way across the seven different lands.

Tomorrowland has rides and early-70s exhibits of space travel and possible future lifestyles. Tease the workers who have to wear hideous blue-and-orange polyester jumpsuits. The indoor roller coaster **Space Mountain** proves the high point of this section, if not the high point of the park, and is worth the extensive wait.

The golden-spired Cinderella Castle marks the gateway to **Fantasyland,** where you'll find Dumbo the Elephant and a twirling teacup ride. **20,000 Leagues Under the Sea** sinks to new depths of brilliant premise but flawed implementation. The chilly temperatures in **It's A Small World** are the ride's only redeeming feature. Don't ride this until the end of the day. You may never, ever, get the evil tune out of your head, and you may be forced to learn first-hand about those damn unwanted thoughts—it's a small world after all. Catch "Magic Journeys," a plotless 3-D movie with extraordinary effects.

Liberty Square and **Frontierland** devote their resources to U.S. history and a celebration of Mark Twain. History buffs will enjoy the Hall of Presidents, and adventurers should catch the rickety, runaway Big Thunder Mountain Railroad rollercoaster. Haunted Mansion is both spooky and dorky. A steamboat ride or a canoe trip both rest your feet from the seemingly endless trek. Also be sure to stop and watch the entertaining animatronics at the Country Bear Jamboree.

Adventureland is a home away from home for those who feel the White Man's Burden. The Jungle Cruise takes a tongue-in-cheek tour through tropical waterways populated by not-so-authentic-looking wildlife. Pirates of the Caribbean explores caves where animated buccaneers battle, drink, and sing. The Swiss Family Robinson tree house, a replica of the shipwrecked family's home, provides more mental than adrenal excitement.

Epcot Center In 1966, Walt dreamed up an "Experimental Prototype Community Of Tomorrow" (EPCOT) that would evolve constantly, never be completed, and incorporate new ideas from U.S. technology—functioning as a self-sufficient, futuristic utopia. At present, Epcot splits into **Future World** and **World Showcase.** For smaller crowds, visit the former in the evening and the latter in the morning.

The 180-ft.-high trademark geosphere forms the entrance to Future World and houses the **Spaceship Earth** attraction, where visitors board a "time machine" for a tour through the evolution of communications. The **CommuniCore** highlights new technologies and offers several "hands-on" displays. The **World of Motion** traces the evolution of transportation, and the **Universe of Energy** traces (in a somewhat outdated fashion, since it glorifies the Alaskan port of Valdez—site of the 1989 Exxon oil spill) the history of energy. The **Wonders of Life** takes its visitors on a tour of the human body (with the help of a simulator) and tells us all where babies come from. **Horizons** lamely presents the lifestyles of the 21st century, but has a fabulous movie sequence on a huge screen extending above and below you, only ten feet away. **The Land** has a thought-provoking film about people's relationship with the land, and takes visitors on a tour of futuristic agrarian methods. **The Living Seas** fails to recreate an underwater research station. Finally, the ever-popular **Journey Into Imagination** pavilion features the 3-D "Captain Eo" (starring moon-walking, sequin-sporting rock star Michael Jackson).

The rest of Epcot is the **World Showcase** series of international pavilions surrounding an artificial lake. An architectural style or monument, as well as typical food, represents each country. People in costumes from past and present perform dances, theatrical skits, and other "cultural" entertainment at each pavilion. Before setting out around the lake, pick up a schedule of daily events at **Epcot Center Information** in Earth Station. Three of the best attractions are the two 360° films made in China and Canada and the 180° film made in France. They all include spectacular landscapes, some national history, and an inside look at the people of the respective countries. **The American Adventure** gives a very enthusiastic and patriotic interpretation of American history. Save your pesos by shopping at your local Pier 1 store rather than the marked-up Mexican marketplace. Norwegian life must be more exciting than the fishing, sailing, and oil exploring shown by the boat ride in the Norway Pavilion. Every summer night at 9pm, Sat. 10pm (off-season Sat. only), Epcot has a magnificent show called **Illuminations,** which features music from the represented nations accompanied by dancing, lights, and fireworks.

The World Showcase pavilions also offer regional cuisine. Make reservations first thing in the morning at the Earth Station World Key Terminal, behind Spaceship Earth. At the **Restaurant Marrakesh** in the Moroccan Pavilion, for example, head chef Lahsen Abrache cooks delicious *brewat* (spicy minced beef fried in pastry) and *bastilla* (sweet and slightly spicy pie). A belly dancer performs in the restaurant every evening. (Lunch $10-15. Dinner $15-20.) The Mexican, French, and Italian pavilions also serve up excellent food at similar prices.

Disney-MGM Studios Disney-MGM Studios has successfully created a "living movie set." Many familiar Disney characters stroll through the park, as do a host of characters dressed as directors, starlets, gossip columnists, and fans. A different has-been movie star leads a parade across Hollywood Boulevard every day. Events such as stunt shows and mini-theatricals take place continually throughout the park.

The Great Movie Ride, inside the Chinese Theater, takes you on a simple but nostalgic trip through old and favorite films; the interactive ride varies by your selection of the first or second set of cars. **Superstar Television** projects members of the audience alongside TV stars, and the **Monster Sound Show** requires volunteers to add special effects to a short movie. The biggest attractions at this park are the **Indiana Jones Epic Stunt Spectacular,** in which you watch stuntmen and audience volunteers pull off amazing moves, and the **Star Tours** Star Wars ride, in which you feel the jerk of your space cargo ship dodging laser blasts.

Other Disney Attractions For those who did not get enough amusement at the three main parks, Disney also offers several other attractions on its grounds with different themes and separate admissions (see Disney World above). The newest is **Typhoon Lagoon,** a 50-acre water park centered around the world's largest wave-making pool. Surf the 7-ft. waves that occasionally appear out of nowhere, or snorkel in a salt water coral reef stocked with tropical fish and harmless sharks. Besides eight water slides, the lagoon has a wonderful creek on which you can take a relaxing inner-tube ride, an anomaly at Disney. Built to resemble a swimming hole, **River Country** offers water slides, rope swings, and plenty of room to swim. Both parks fill up early on hot days, and you might get turned away. Across Bay Lake from River Country is **Discovery Island,** a zoological park. Those seeking more (relatively) sinful excitations should head at night to **Pleasure Island,** Disney's attempt to draw students and the thirtysomething set. Those over 17 can roam freely between the theme nightclubs; those under 18 can enter if they remain with their guardians.

■ Near Orlando: Sea World, Cypress Gardens, and Universal Studios Florida

Sea World One of the country's largest marine parks, **Sea World** (407-351-3600 for operator; 407-351-0021 for recording), 19 mi. southwest of Orlando off I-4 at Rte. 528, requires about six hours to see everything. Shows feature marine mammals such as whales, dolphins, sea lions, seals, and otters. Though the Seal and Otter Show and the USO waterski show are enjoyable, the killer whales Baby Shamu and Baby Namu are the big stars. Not only do they share the stage (or pool) with two beautiful white whales and two Orcas, the trainers actually mix it up with the huge creatures and take rides on their snouts. People in the park gravitate towards Shamu Stadium before the show; arrive early to get a seat. After your brow gets sweaty, visit the air-conditioned **Fantasy Theater,** an educational show with live characters in costume. The smallest crowds cling in Feb. and Sept.-Oct. Most hotel brochure counters and hostels have coupons for $2-3 off regular admission prices. (Open daily 8:30am-10pm; off-season daily 9am-10pm. Admission $33, ages 3-9 $29. Sky Tower ride $3 extra. Guided tours $6, kids $5. Take bus #8.)

Cypress Gardens (813-324-2111), in Winter Haven, is a botanical garden with over 8000 varieties of plants and flowers (open daily 9:30am-5:30pm; in winter daily 9am-7pm. $23, ages 3-9 $16.50). Take I-4 southwest to Rte. 27 south, then Rte. 540 west. The "Gardens of the World" features plants, flowers, and sculptured mini-gardens depicting the horticultural styles of many countries and periods. Winding walkways and electric boat rides take you through the foliage. The main attraction is a water-ski show performed daily at 10am, noon, 2pm, and 4pm. **Greyhound** stops here once a day on its Tampa-West Palm Beach schedule ($20 from Tampa to Cypress Gardens). Look for coupons at motels and visitors centers.

Universal Studios Florida, 435 N. State Rd. (363-8000), and Vineland Rd., opened in 1990 and is a two-in-one park containing a number of amazing theme rides: **Kongfrontation,** where King Kong will roughhouse your cable car; the **E.T. Adventure** bike ride; and **Jaws,** a boat trip where you can see the shark used in the movie. Also look for the **Back to the Future...The Ride,** with seven-story high OMNI-MAX surround screens and spectacular special effects.

Since the park serves as a working studio making films, stars abound. Recently, Steve Martin played a dad in *Parenthood* here, and John Goodman starred in *Mati-*

nee. Nickelodeon TV programs are in continuous production. Universal also has a number of back-lot locations that you may have seen before in the movies—displaying Hollywood, Central Park, and Beverly Hills, as well as the infamous Bates Motel from *Psycho.* $35, ages 3-9 $28. Open Mon.-Sat. 9am-10pm, Sun. 9am-9pm, off-season daily 9am-7pm.

■■■ PALM BEACH / WEST PALM

Palm Beach is the best known of the 37 municipalities that constitute Palm Beach County. Like a moat, the Intracoastal Waterway separates the Mediterranean Fantasyland of Palm Beach from the banal urban problems of its ragged sibling, West Palm. Similar to young Confucius who was shielded from the harsh reality outside his princely poshness, Palm Beach is blinded to the unpleasantness of real life; the city forbids hospitals, funerals parlors and even plumbers from setting up shop on the island. One of the first resort communities in the United States, vital Palm Beach owes much of its original appeal to hundreds of picturesque coconut palms. It owes these palms, in turn, entirely to the *Providencia,* the Spanish brigatine that wrecked on Palm Beach's shores in 1878, spilling its cargo of 20,000 non-native coconuts.

Practical Information If you would like to learn more about Palm Beach, contact the **Town of Palm Beach Chamber of Commerce,** 45 Coconut Row (655-3282). Pick up Co-Tran bus maps and pamphlets on attractions in Palm Beach proper. (Open Mon.-Fri. 9am-5pm, summer 10am-4:30pm.) Also try **Discover Palm Beach County, Inc.,** 1555 Palm Beach Lakes Blvd., Suite 204 (471-3995), across from the baseball stadium. They have bags of free maps, visitors guides, and info on events. (Open Mon.-Fri. 8:30am-5pm.)

Amtrak serves Palm Beach county from 201 S. Tamarind Ave. (832-6164), W. Palm Beach, in the pink building at the corner of Tamarind and Clematis St. To: Miami (2 per day, $12); Ft. Lauderdale (2 per day, $9); Tampa (1 per day, $35); Orlando (1 per day, $32). (Open daily 8am-5:45pm.) **Greyhound** stalls at 100 Banyan Blvd. (833-0825), West Palm Beach, on the Intracoastal Waterway. To: Orlando (8 per day, $35); Tampa (6 per day, $32); Miami W. Station (10 per day, $13); Ft. Lauderdale (10 per day, $6). **Co-Tran Bus System** is the public transportation in the area, covering all of Palm Beach and West Palm Beach with three circular bus routes. Fare: 90¢. Buses run Mon.-Sat. 7am-9pm. The main office is at Palm Beach International Airport, Building 5-1440 (233-1111). You can also try the **Tri-Rail System** (800-874-7245) that connects W. Palm Beach with Miami and Ft. Lauderdale at the Amtrak stop, 201 S. Tamarind Ave. Trains run Mon.-Sat. 5am-9:30pm. Pick up schedules at the stop in Palm Beach. (Fare $3, students and seniors with ID $1.50.) **Yellow Cab Co.** (689-2222) charges $1.25 base fare plus $1.50 per mi. If you'd rather do the driving yourself, try **BEST Car Rental,** 470 S. Congress Ave. (697-1753). Cars are $20 per day with unlimited mileage. (Must be 25 with major card.)

In an **emergency,** call 911. The **Rape Crisis and Sexual Abuse** line is at 833-7273, and the **Abuse Registry** is at 800-962-2873. All are 24 hrs. The **post office** sorts at 355 S. County Rd. (655-4321), in Palm Beach. Open Mon.-Fri. 8:30am-5pm. The **ZIP code** is 33480. The **area code** is 407.

Accommodations and Camping Like nearly everything else in the island-paradise of Palm Beach or West Palm Beach, hotels are stylish and expensive. There are no hostels in either town, but many of the slightly run-down motels along South Dixie Hwy. offer rooms in the off-season for under $35. You are best off lodging in one of the reasonably-priced motels in West Palm. **Parkview Motor Lodge,** 4710 S. Dixie Hwy. (833-4644), West Palm Beach, is newer and cleaner than most of the neighboring hotels. Take a northbound bus to the corner of S. Dixie and Murray, walk one block north along S. Dixie. (Reception 7am-midnight, with 24-hr. security. Continental breakfast included. Singles $38-50, doubles $40-55; Jan.-March singles

$60-68, doubles $70-78.) Right across the street from the Palm Coast Shopping Center and its bus stop is **Aqua Motel,** S. Dixie Hwy. (582-7459). The Aqua has a pool, patio, and friendly proprietor. Old, clean, pastel rooms. Singles $36, doubles $38; May-Dec. singles $26, doubles $28. Make reservations a week ahead in-season. **KOA Campground** (793-9797), off Southern Blvd. West, P.O. Box 16066, W. Palm Beach 33416, 18 mi. from I-95, is the closest campground to Palm Beach. Wooded sites adjacent to Safari Park; lions may wake campers. ($21 for two with hookup, each additional person $2. Tent sites with electricity $19. Laundry, convenience store, showers, 10pm quiet time. Make reservations a few days ahead in season.)

Food Palm Beach brims with chic cafes where lunch can cost more than a good bicycle. Travelers staying in Palm Beach proper can buy groceries (especially fruit—Florida fruit prices are very reasonable) at **Publix Supermarket,** 265 Sunrise Blvd., across from the Palm Beach Hotel. (Open Mon.-Sat. 7am-10pm, Sun. 7am-9pm.) There are also some reasonable restaurants in the area: **Champs-Elysées,** 229 Sunrise Blvd. (833-1949), near County Rd. and Sunrise Blvd. intersection. This tiny French-style mère 'n' père bakery serves breakfast and lunch with an accent. For breakfast, the gigantic fruit-filled croissants ($1.75) are wonderful. "Yesterday's" croissants are a bargain at $3.50 for a bag of five. Also try the quiche ($1.50) and assorted sandwiches with a drink ($4.25). (Open Mon.-Sat. 7am-5pm.) For style and stucco, skulk into **E.R. Bradley's Saloon,** 111 Bradley Place (833-3520), right across County Rd. from Bradley Park. Funky pink-stuccoed restaurant/bar with loud music, a young clientele, and reasonable prices for Palm Beach. The widely varied menu offering big portions is supported by very quick service. Snail fanciers will want to try the *escargot* ($6). Specialties include chicken sauteed with lots of vegetables ($13). The salads ($6) are huge. (Open Mon.-Fri. 11am-3am, Sat.-Sun. 10am-3am.)

Sights and Entertainment The best way to see the pink stucco mansions of Palm Beach is by bicycle. Pick up a map of established trails at **Palm Beach Bicycle Trail Shop,** 223 Sunrise Ave. (659-4583; bikes for $6 per hr., $15 per ½-day; open Mon.-Sat. 9am-5pm, Sun. 10am-5pm). When they're not sunbathing or golfing, Palm Beach's visitors and residents enjoy shopping. Arguably the most famous shopping street east of Rodeo Drive, **Worth Avenue** overflows with galleries, designer shops, and Jaguars. Worth Ave. owes much of its fame to the pretty *faux*-Mediterranean buildings that house its stores. Addison Minzer, the playboy/architect commissioned to renovate Worth Ave. in the early 1920s, is often credited with introducing stucco pastels to South Florida with his Worth Ave. designs.

If you prefer the conspicuous consumption of earlier times to that of today, you may want to visit **Whitehall** (665-2833), the Palm Beach home of Florida railroad magnate Henry Flagler, off Coconut Row, across from the Chamber of Commerce. Built at the turn of the century, this palatial house contains hundreds of paintings, sculptures, and tapestries, all unlabeled and decaying in humid, air-condition-less splendor. (Open Tues.-Sat 10am-5pm, Sun. noon-5pm. $5.) If you're looking for the beach in Palm Beach, try **Phipps Ocean Park,** on S. Ocean Blvd. (free admission but metered parking). Those in town for the first weekend of May should not miss **Sun-Fest,** a two-day bash featuring free concerts by big names in jazz and blues.

■■■ SAINT AUGUSTINE

Spanish adventurer Juan Ponce de León founded St. Augustine in 1565, making it the first European colony in North America and the oldest city in the U.S. Although he never found the legendary Fountain of Youth, de León did live to age 61, twice the expected life span at that time. Much of St. Augustine's original Spanish flavor remains intact, thanks to the town's efforts at preservation. Today in its dotage, the town is fairly quiet; its brick, palm-lined streets see few cars, and during the summer months the heat slows everything and everyone. Yet historic sights, good food, and friendly people make St. Augustine well worth a few rejuvenating days.

PRACTICAL INFORMATION

Emergency: 911.

Visitor Information: Visitors Center, 10 Castillo (825-1000), at San Marco Ave. From the Greyhound station, walk north on Ribeira, then right on Orange. Pick up hotel coupons and the free *Chamber of Commerce Map*, a comprehensive city guide. A free 20-min. video plays continuously. Open daily 8:30am-5:30pm, summer 8am-7:30pm.

Greyhound: 100 Malaga St. (829-6401). To: Jacksonville (5 per day, 1 hr., $6.50); Daytona Beach (6 per day, 1 hr., $8). Open Mon.-Fri. 8am-5:30pm, Sat. 8am-4pm.

Taxi: Ancient City Taxi, 824-8161. From the bus station to motels on San Marco about $2.

Help Lines: Rape Crisis, 355-7273.

Post Office: King St. (829-8716), at Martin Luther King Ave. Open Mon.-Fri. 8:30am-5pm, Sat. 10am-1pm. **ZIP code:** 32084.

Area Code: 904.

Unfortunately, the city has no public transportation, though most points of interest are within walking distance of one another. Historic St. Augustine, concentrated in the area between the **San Sebastian River** and the **Matanzas Bay** to the east, is easily covered on foot. **King Street,** running along the river, is the major east-west axis and crosses the bay to the beaches. **St. George Street,** also east-west, is closed to vehicular traffic and contains most of the shops and many sights in St. Augustine. **San Marco Avenue** and **Cordova Street** travel north-south. Winter brings a surge of activity to nearby **Vilano, Anastasia,** and **St. Augustine Beaches.**

ACCOMMODATIONS AND CAMPING

Beyond the often full youth hostel, you'll find several clusters of cheap motels in St. Augustine—one is a short walk north of town on San Marco Ave.; another is directly to the east of the historic district, over the Bridge of Lions along Anastasia Blvd.; and a third is near Vilano Beach. Several inns in the historic district offer nice rooms, but rates start at about $49 per night. Those traveling by car should consider the excellent seaside camping facilities at **Anastasia State Park.**

St. Augustine Hostel (HI/AYH), 32 Treasury St. (829-6163), at Charlotte, 6 blocks from the Greyhound station. Large, dormitory-style rooms with shower and fans. Kitchen available. Singles $10, nonmembers $13. Doubles $20, nonmembers $26. Guest bike rental $5 per day. Reservation must be made in advance. Open for reservations 8-10am and 5-10pm. 10am-5pm lockout.

American Inn, 42 San Marco Ave. (829-2292), near the visitors center. Owner won't take your money until you've inspected your room. He also provides transportation to and from the bus station when a car is available. Big, clean singles and doubles $29-36, weekends $38-49. Check visitors center (see Practical Information) for coupons.

Seabreeze Motel, 208 Anastasia Blvd. (829-8122), just over the Bridge of Lions east of the historic district. Clean rooms with A/C, TV. Pool. Good restaurants nearby. Singles $25. Doubles $28.

The St. Francis Inn, 279 Saint George St. (824-6068), at Saint Francis St., 2 doors down from the Oldest House. Built in 1791, it's a charming 10-room inn with a jungle of flowers and a tucked-away pool. Much of its original 18th-century interior has been preserved. Iced tea and juice served all day. Free bike use. Rooms $49-89. Cottage on premises with full kitchen and living room $140 for 4 people, $10 each additional person. Continental breakfast included.

Anastasia State Recreation Area (461-2033), on Rte. A1A 4 mi. south of the historic district. From town, cross the Bridge of Lions, and bear left just beyond the

Alligator Farm. Open daily 8am-8pm. Sites $19, with electricity $21. Make weekend reservations.

FOOD

The flood of daytime tourists and abundance of budget eateries make lunch in St. Augustine's historic district a delight. Stroll **St. George St.** to check the daily specials scrawled on blackboards outside each restaurant; locals prefer those clustered at the southern end of St. George near King St. Finding a budget dinner in St. Augustine is trickier, since the downtown is deserted after 5pm. However, an expedition along Anastasia Blvd. should unearth good meals for under $6. The seafood-wise will seek out the surf 'n' turf dinners ($15) at **Captain Jack's,** 410 Anastasia Blvd. (829-6846; open Mon.-Fri. 11:30am-9pm, Sat.-Sun. noon-9pm). Those with wheels interested in mass quantities of food should try the all-you-can-eat buffet at the **Quincey Family Steakhouse** (797-5677), 2 mi. south of town on Rte. A1A at Ponce de León Mall. Lunch $5, dinner $6. (Open Sun.-Thurs. 11am-10pm, Fri.-Sat. 11am-11pm.)

St. George Pharmacy and Restaurant, 121 Saint George St. (829-5929). Museum, luncheonette, and bookstore. Cheap sandwiches from $1.50; dinners from $3. Try the grilled cheese with a thick chocolate malt ($4). Breakfast special (egg, bacon, grits, toast or biscuit, and jelly) $2. Open Mon.-Fri. 7am-5pm, Sat.-Sun. 7:30am-5pm.

Cafe Camacho, 11-C Aviles St. (824-7030), at Charlotte St., 1 block from Saint George St. in the historic district. Part vintage clothes shop, part cafe. Serves delicious fruit shakes, soups, sandwiches, breakfast specials, vegetarian dishes, and an all-you-can-eat lunch bar from 11am-3pm ($5). Open Wed.-Mon. 7:30am-5pm.

El Toro Con Sombrero, 10 Anastasia Blvd. (824-9682), on the left just over the Bridge of Lions from downtown. Look carefully because the sign is hidden by a sign for the adjoining sports bar. If you like Mexican food and 50s music, this is the place. Open daily 11am-1am.

A New Dawn, 110 Anastasia Blvd. (824-1337). A health-conscious grocery store with a sandwich and juice counter. Delicious vegetarian sandwiches; try the tofu salad surprise ($3.25). Banana smoothies $2.25. Open Mon.-Sat. 9am-5:30pm.

SIGHTS AND ENTERTAINMENT

Saint George St. is the center of the **historic district,** which begins at the Gates of the City near the visitors center and runs south past Cadiz St. and the Oldest Store. Visit **San Agustín Antiguo** (825-6830), Gallegos House, Saint George St., St. Augustine's authentically restored 18th-century neighborhood, where artisans and villagers in period costumes describe the customs, crafts, and highlights of the Spanish New World. (Open daily 9am-5pm. $5, seniors $3.75, students and ages 6-18 $2.50.) The oldest masonry fortress in the continental U.S., **Castillo de San Marcos,** 1 Castillo Dr. (829-6506), off San Marco Ave., has 14-ft. thick walls built of coquina, the local shellrock. The fort itself is a four-pointed star complete with drawbridge and a murky moat. Inside you'll find a museum, a large courtyard surrounded by guardrooms, livery quarters for the garrison, a jail, a chapel, and the original cannon brought overseas by the Spanish. A cannon-firing ceremony occurs four times per day on the weekend. (Open daily 8:45am-4:45pm. $2, over 62 and under 16 free.)

St. Augustine has several old stores and museums. The self-descriptive **Oldest House,** 14 Saint Francis St. (824-2872), has been occupied continuously since its construction in the 1600s. (Open daily 9am-5pm. $5, seniors $4.50, students $2.50.) The **Oldest Store Museum,** 4 Artillery Lane (829-9729), has over 100,000 odds and ends from the 18th and 19th centuries. (Open Mon.-Sat. 9am-5pm, Sun. 10am-5pm. $3.50, ages 6-12 $1.50.) Also in the old part of the city is the coquina **Cathedral of St. Augustine,** begun in 1793. Although several fires destroyed parts of the cathedral, the walls and facade are original.

Six blocks north of the info center is the **Mission of Nombre de Dios,** 27 Ocean St. (824-2809), a moss- and vine-covered mission which held the first Catholic service in the U.S. on September 8, 1565. Soaring over the structure is a 208-ft. steel cross commemorating the city's founding. (Open Mon.-Fri. 8am-6pm, Sat.-Sun. 9am-8pm. Mass Mon.-Fri. at 8:30am, Sat. at 6pm, Sun. at 8am. Admission by donation.) No trip to St. Augustine would be complete without a trek to the **Fountain of Youth,** 155 Magnolia Ave. (829-3168). Go right on Williams St. from San Marco Ave. and continue a few blocks past Nombre de Dios. (Open daily 9am-5pm. $4, seniors $3, ages 6-12 $1.50.) In addition to drinking from the spring that Ponce de León mistakenly thought would give him eternal youth, you can see a statue of the explorer that does not age.

Though oil and water don't usually mix, Henry Flagler, co-founder of Standard Oil and a good friend of the Rockefellers, retired to St. Augustine. He built two hotels in the downtown area that the rich and famous once frequented, making St. Augustine the "Newport of the South" (that's Newport, Rhode Island). The former Ponce de León Hotel, at King and Cordova St., is now **Flagler College.** In summer the college is deserted, but during the school year students liven the town. In 1947, Chicago publisher and lover *objets d'art* Otto Lightner converted the Alcazar Hotel into the **Lightner Museum** (824-2874), with an impressive collection of cut, blown, and burnished glass. (Open daily 9am-5pm. $4, ages 12-18 and college students with ID $1.)

Visitors can tour St. Augustine by land or by sea. **St. Augustine Sight-Seeing Trains,** 170 San Marcos Ave. (829-6545), offers a variety of city tours (1-8 hr.; open daily 8:30am-5pm). The one-hour tour ($9, ages 6-12 $4), a good introduction to the city, starts at the front of the visitors center (see Practical Information). **Colée Sight-Seeing Carriage Tours** (829-2818) begin near the entrance to the fort, take about an hour, and cover the historic area of St. Augustine. ($9, ages 4-11 $4; open daily 9am-10pm.) The **Victory II Scenic Cruise Ships** (824-1806) navigate the emerald Matanzas River. Catch the boat at the City Yacht Pier, a block south of the Bridge of Lions (leaves at 11am and 1, 2:45, 4:30, 6:45, and 8:30pm; $7.50, under 12 $3).

On Anastasia Island, at **Anastasia State Park,** you can see Paul Green's *Cross and Sword,* Florida's official state play, telling the story of St. Augustine with the help of a large cast, booming cannon, and swordfights. (Admission $8, ages 6-12 and students $4; seniors, AAA members, and large groups $8.)

With a penchant for loudness and liquid, St. Augustine has an impressive array of bars. **Scarlett O'Hara's,** 70 Hypolita St. (824-6535), at Cordova St., is popular with locals. The barbecue chicken sandwiches ($4) are filling and juicy, the drinks hefty and cool. Live entertainment begins at 9pm nightly. (Open daily 11:30am-1am.) Try the **Milltop,** 19½ Saint George St. (829-2329), a tiny bar situated above an old mill in the restored area. Local string musicians play on the tiny stage (daily 11am-midnight). On St. Augustine Beach, **Panama Hattie's,** 361 A1A Beach Blvd. (471-2255), caters to the post-college crowd (open daily 11am-midnight). Pick up a copy of the *Today Tonight* newspaper, available at most grocery and convenience stores, for a complete listing of current concerts, events, and dinner specials.

■■■ TAMPA AND ST. PETERSBURG

The Gulf Coast communities of Tampa and St. Petersburg have a less raucous style than Florida's Atlantic Coast vacation destinations. The two cities offer quiet beaches, beautiful harbors, and perfect weather year-round unpoisoned by droves of tourists. One of the nation's fastest-growing cities and largest ports, Tampa contains thriving financial, industrial, and artistic communities. Across the bay, St. Petersburg caters to a relaxed, attractive retirement community, with oodles of health-food shops and pharmacies. Meanwhile, the town's beaches beckon with 28 miles of soft white sand, emerald water, and beautiful sunsets. The high season on the Gulf Coast runs from October to April.

PRACTICAL INFORMATION

Emergency: 911.

Visitor Information: Tampa/Hillsborough Convention and Visitors Associa- **tion,** 111 Madison St. (223-1111 or 800-826-8358). Open Mon.-Fri. 9am-8pm. **St. Petersburg C.O.C.,** 100 2nd Ave. N. (821-4069). Open Mon.-Fri. 9am-5pm.

Traveler's Aid: Tampa, 273-5936. St. Pete, 823-4891. Mon.-Fri. 8:30am-4:30pm.

Airport: Tampa International Airport: (870-8700), 5 mi. west of downtown. HARTline bus #30 runs between the airport and downtown Tampa. **St. Peters-** **burg Clearwater International Airport** (539-7491) sits right across the bay. **The Limo** (822-3333) offers 24-hr. service from both airports to the cities and to all the beaches between Ft. De Soto and Clearwater ($9.25 from St. Pete, $11.75 from Tampa). Make reservations 6 hr. in advance.

Amtrak: In Tampa, 601 Nebraska Ave. (221-7600 or 800-872-7245), at Twiggs St. 1 block north of Kennedy. Two trains per day to: Orlando (2 hr., $17); Jacksonville (5 hr., $45); Savannah (8 hr., $77). Open daily 7:30am-8pm. No trains go south of Tampa—no service to St. Pete. In St. Pete, 3601 31st St. N. (522-9475). Amtrak will transport you to Tampa by bus ($7).

Greyhound: In Tampa, 610 E. Polk St. (229-1501), next to Burger King downtown. To Miami (6 per day, 10 hr., $34) and Orlando (9 per day, 1½ hr., $12). In St. Pete, 180 9th St. N. (895-4455) downtown. To Miami (12 per day, 9 hr., $40) and Orlando (10 per day, 2 hr., $13).

Public Transport: In Tampa, **Hillsborough Area Regional Transit (HARTline),** 254-4278. Fare 85¢, transfers 10¢. To reach St. Pete, take bus #100 express from downtown to the Gateway Mall ($1.50). In St. Pete, **St. Petersburg Municipal Transit System,** 530-9911. Most routes depart from Williams Park at 1st Ave. N. and 3rd St. N. Get directions at the info booth there. Fare 75¢, transfers 10¢.

Help Lines: In Tampa, **Rape Crisis,** 238-8821. **Gay/Lesbian Crisis Line,** 229-8839. In St. Petersburg, **Rape Crisis,** 530-7233.

ZIP codes: Tampa 33601, St. Pete 33731.

Area Code: 813.

Tampa divides into quarters with **Florida Avenue** running east-west and **Kennedy Boulevard,** which becomes **Frank Adams Drive** (Rte. 60), running north-south. Numbered avenues run east-west and numbered streets run north-south. You can reach Tampa on I-75 from the north, or I-4 from the east.

In St. Petersburg, 22 mi. south, **Central Avenue** runs east-west. **34th Street** (U.S. 19) cuts north-south through the city and links up with the new **Sunshine-Skyway Bridge,** connecting St. Pete with the Bradenton-Sarasota area to the south. Avenues run east-west, streets north-south. The St. Pete beachfront is a chain of barrier islands accessible by bridges on the far west side of town, and extends from Clearwater Beach in the north to Pass-a-Grille Beach in the south. Many towns on the islands offer quiet beaches and reasonably priced hotels and restaurants. From north to south, these towns include: **Clearwater Beach, Indian Rocks Beach, Madiera Beach, Treasure Island,** and **St. Petersburg Beach.** The stretch of beach past the Don Cesar Hotel (a pink monstrosity recently declared a historical landmark) in St. Petersburg Beach and Pass-a-Grille Beach has the best sand, a devoted following, and the least pedestrian and motor traffic.

ACCOMMODATIONS AND CAMPING

Inexpensive, convenient lodgings are rare in Tampa, but St. Petersburg has two youth hostels as well as many cheap motels lining 4th St. N. and U.S. 19. Some establishments advertise singles for as little as $16, but these tend to be ancient and dirty. To avoid the worst neighborhoods, stay on the north end of 4th St. and the south end of U.S. 19. Several inexpensive motels also line the St. Pete beach. In Tampa, you can try to contact the Overseas Information Center at the **University of South Florida** (974-3104) for help in finding accommodations.

Tampa

Motel 6, 333 E. Fowler Ave. (932-4948), off I-275 near Busch Gardens and the Tom Bodett Memorial. On the northern outskirts of Tampa, 30 mi. from the beach. Clean, small rooms. Singles $24. Each additional person $6.

Holiday Inn, 2708 N. 50th St. (621-2081). From I-4, take Exit #3. Pool, whirlpool, spa, HBO and cable. Breakfast buffet $5, lunch buffet $7. 1-4 people $58.

St. Petersburg

St. Petersburg Youth Hostel, 326 1st Ave. N. (822-4141), downtown. Small, clean singles, doubles, and quads, all with private showers. Common room with kitchen, TV, A/C $11, nonmembers $13, not including $2 linen fee. 11pm curfew. If staying here Thurs.-Sat., check out **Janus Landing** a block away (corner of 1st Ave.N. and 1st St.) for some great live music or a $2 draft.

Clearwater Beach International Hostel, 606 Bay Esplande Ave. (443-1211), 20 mi. out of town, but just 2 blocks from a superb white-sand beach. Bunk in shared room $11, nonmembers $13. Private rooms available (call for rates).

Kentucky Motel, 4246 4th St. N. (526-7373). Large, clean rooms with friendly owners, cable TV, refrigerator in each room, and free postcards. Singles $24. Doubles $26. Dec.-April rooms $10 more.

Grant Motel, 9046 4th St. (576-1369), 4 mi. north of town on U.S. 92. Pool. Clean rooms with A/C; most have a fridge. Singles $28, doubles $30. Jan. 1-April 15 singles $39, doubles $43.

Treasure Island Motel, 10315 Gulf Blvd. (367-3055). Across the street from beach, big rooms with A/C, fridges, and color TV. Pool. Singles $28, doubles $29. Jan.-Feb. $52/$53 respectively. Each additional person $4. Pirates not allowed.

Fort De Soto State Park (866-2662), composed of five islands at the southern end of a long chain of keys and islands, has the best camping. A wildlife sanctuary, the park makes a great oceanside picnic spot (2-day min. stay; curfew 10pm; no alcohol; sites $16.50). Disregard the "no vacancy" sign at the toll booth (85¢) by the Pinellas Bayway exit. However, from January to April, you may want to make a reservation in person at the St. Petersburg County Building, 150 5th St. N. #146, or at least call ahead. In Tampa, try the **Busch Travel Park,** 10001 Malcolm McKinley Dr. (971-0008), ¼ mi. north of Busch Gardens, with a pool, store, recreation room, and train service to Busch Gardens and Adventure Island. (Tent sites $9. RV sites $15.)

FOOD

Prices for food leap high in Tampa, but cheap Cuban and Spanish establishments dot the city. Black bean soup, gazpacho, and Cuban bread usually yield the best bargains. For Cuban food, **Ybor City** definitely has superior prices and atmosphere.

St. Petersburg's cheap, health-conscious restaurants cater to its retired population—and generally close by 8 or 9pm. Those hungry later should try St. Pete Beach and 4th St.

Tampa

JD's, 2029 E. 7th Ave. (247-9683), in Ybor City. Take bus #12. Soups, sandwiches, and Cuban food in a roomy, low-key restaurant. Breakfast $2.50. Lunch $3-5. Open Mon.-Fri. 9am-3pm.

The Loading Dock, 100 Madison St., downtown. Sandwiches $3-5. Try the "flatbed" or the "forklift" for a filling diesel-fueled meal. Open Mon.-Fri. 8am-8pm, Sat. 10:30am-2:30pm.

Cepha's, 1701 E. 4th Ave. (247-9022), has cheap Jamaican specialties. Red snapper or curry chicken $4-7. Colorful garden in back and reggae shows throughout the summer. Open Mon.-Wed. 11:30am-10pm, Thurs. 11:30am-1am, Fri.-Sat. 11:30am-3am.

Ybor Square, 1901 13th St., offers several mid-priced restaurants, including **The Spaghetti Warehouse** (248-1720). Lunch or dinner $7, in a cool, relaxing atmosphere. Open Sun.-Thurs. 11am-10pm, Fri.-Sat. noon-11pm.

St. Pete

Crabby Bills, 412 1st St. N. (593-4825), Indian Rocks Beach. Cheap, extensive menu. Ultra-casual atmosphere. Six blue crabs $5.50. Open Mon.-Thurs. 11am-10pm, Fri.-Sat. 11am-11pm. Arrive before 5pm to avoid substantial wait.

Tangelo's Bar and Grille, 226 1st Ave. NE (894-1695), St. Pete. Try a carb burger ($4.50) or cold gazpacho soup ($2). Open Mon.-Sat. 11am-9pm.

Beach Nutts, 9600 W. Gulf Blvd., Treasure Island. Not much selection, but Oh! what an atmosphere. Right on the beach. Live reggae most nights next door. Open 9am-2am.

Russo's Pizza, 103-104th Ave. (367-2874), Treasure Island. A local joint connected to an arcade. Try the tasty, filling stromboli ($3.85). Open 11am-midnight.

SIGHTS AND ACTIVITIES

Tampa

Bounded roughly by 22nd Street, Nebraska Avenue, 5th Avenue, and Columbus Drive, **Ybor City** is Tampa's Latin Quarter. The area expanded rapidly after Vincent Martínez Ybor moved his cigar factories here from Key West in 1886. Although cigar manufacturing has since been mechanized, some people still roll cigars by hand and sell them for $1 in **Ybor Square,** 1901 13th St. (247-4497), a 19th-century cigar factory converted into an upscale retail complex. (Open Mon.-Sat. 9:30am-5:30pm, Sun. noon-5:30pm.) **Ybor City State Museum,** 1818 9th Ave. (247-6323), at 21st St., traces the development of Ybor City, Tampa, the cigar industry, and Cuban migration (open Tues.-Sat. 9am-noon and 1-5pm; 50¢). The **Three Birds Bookstore and Coffee Room,** 1518 7th Ave. (247-7041), contributes artsily to Ybor City. Sip orange zinger tea or get a slice of black forest cheesecake while you read the latest Paris Review. (Open Mon.-Thurs. 11am-6pm, Fri.-Sat. 11am-10pm.) Aside from the square, the Ybor City area has remained relatively unsullied by the rapid urban growth that typifies the rest of Tampa; **East 7th Avenue** still resembles an old neighborhood. Keep an ear out for jazz and a nose out for Cuban cuisine. Be careful not to stray more than two blocks north or south of 7th Ave. since the area can be extremely dangerous, even during the daytime. Buses #5, 12, and 18 run to Ybor City from downtown.

Now part of the University of Tampa, the Moorish **Tampa Bay Hotel,** 401 W. Kennedy Blvd., once epitomized fashionable Florida coast hotels. Teddy Roosevelt trained his Rough Riders in the backyard before the Spanish-American War. The small **Henry B. Plant Museum** (254-1891), in a wing of the University of Tampa building, is an orgy of rococo craftsmanship and architecture; the exhibits themselves, which include Victorian furniture and Wedgewood pottery, pale in comparison. (Guided tours at 1:30pm. Open Tues.-Sat. 10am-4pm. Admission by donation.)

Downtown, the **Tampa Museum of Art,** 601 Doyle Carlton Dr. (223-8130), houses the Joseph Veach Nobre collection of classical and modern works. (Open Tues.-Sat. 10am-5pm, Sun. 1-5pm. Free.) Across from the University of South Florida, north of downtown, the **Museum of Science and Industry,** 4801 E. Fowler Ave. (985-5531), features a simulated hurricane. (Open Sun.-Thurs. 9am-4:30pm, Fri.-Sat. 9am-9pm. $4, ages 5-15 $2.) The **Museum of African American Art,** 1308 N. Marion St. (292-2466), features the art history and culture of the classical Barnett-Aden collection. (Open Tues.-Sat. 10am-4pm and Sun. 1-4:30pm. $2 donation requested.)

The **waterfront** provides much of Tampa's atmosphere. *"Day-O! Day-O! Daylight come and me wanna go home."* Banana boats from South and Central America unload and tally their cargo every day at the docks on 139 Twiggs St., near 13th St. and Kennedy Blvd. Every year in February the *Jose Gasparilla,* a fully rigged pirate ship loaded with hundreds of exuberant "pirates," "invades" Tampa and kicks off a month of parades and festivals, such as the **Gasparilla Sidewalk Art Festival.** (Pick up a copy of the visitors guide, for current info on various events and festivals.)

Enjoy everything from bumper cars to corkscrew rollercoasters at Tampa's **Busch Gardens—The Dark Continent** (971-8282), E. 3000 Busch Blvd. and NE 40th St.

Take I-275 to Busch Blvd., or take bus #5 from downtown. Not only are people confined to trains, boats, and walkways while giraffes, zebras, ostriches, and antelope roam freely across the park's 60-acre plain, but Busch Gardens has two of only 50 white Bengal tigers in existence. (Open daily 9am-8pm; off-season daily 9:30am-6pm. Admission $29, infants free. Parking $3.) A visit to the **Anheuser-Busch Hospitality House** inside the park provides a sure-fire way to make your afternoon more enjoyable. You must stand in line for each beer, with a three-drink limit.

About ¼ mi. northeast of Busch Gardens at 4500 Bougainvillea Ave. is **Adventure Island** (971-7978), a 13-acre water theme park. (Admission $15. For those under 48 in. $12. Open 10am-5pm with extended hours in summer.)

St. Petersburg

St. Petersburg's main attraction is its coastline. **Pass-a-Grille Beach** may be the nicest, but with parking meters, it exacts a toll. The **Municipal Beach** at Treasure Island, accessible from Rte. 699 via Treasure Island Causeway, offers free parking. When you're too sunburned to spend another day on the sand, head for **Sunken Gardens,** 1825 4th St. N. (896-3186), home of over 7000 varieties of exotic flowers and plants. (Open daily 9am-5:30pm. $7, ages 3-11 $4.)

Well, hello Dalí! The **Salvador Dalí Museum,** 1000 3rd St. S. (823-3767), in Poynter Park on the Bayboro Harbor waterfront, contains the world's largest collection of Dalí works and memorabilia—93 oil paintings, 1300 graphics, and even works from a 14-year-old Dalí. (Tours available. Open Tues.-Sat. 10am-5pm, Sun. noon-5pm. $5, seniors and students $3.50, under 9 free.) **Great Explorations,** 1120 4th St. S. (821-8992), is a museum with six areas of exhibits to fondle. Test your strength at the Body Shop, where you can compare your muscles with scores taken from around the country. (Open Mon.-Sat. 10am-5pm, Sun. 1-5pm. $4.50, seniors $4, ages 4-17 $3.50.) **The Pier** (821-6164), at the end of 2nd Ave. NE, downtown, extends out into Tampa Bay from St. Pete, ending in a five-story inverted pyramid complex that contains a shopping center, aquarium, and restaurant. (Closed Tues.)

Georgia

Where else can you find great state roads, restaurants serving pre-sweetened iced tea, TV programs on how to fish and an indigenous population that speaks two languages (English and Suthun)? From the North Georgia mountains to the coastal plains and swamps, Georgia thrives on such alliterative industries as paper products, peanuts, pecans, peaches, poultry, and politicians. President Jimmy Carter's hometown and the only house ever owned by President Franklin D. Roosevelt both stand on red Georgia clay. Coca-Cola was invented here in 1886; since then, it has gone on to carbonate and caffeinate the rest of the world. As 1996 nears, the leading industry will be tourism when the Olympic Games alight in Atlanta and are shared by coastal Savannah, a city with stately, romantic antebellum homes and colonial city blocks. The state blooms in the spring, glistens in the summer, and mellows in the autumn, all the while welcoming y'all with peachy Southern hospitality. Stay here long and you'll *never* be able to shake Georgia from your mind.

PRACTICAL INFORMATION

Capital: Atlanta.
Visitor Information: Department of Industry and Trade, Tourist Division, 230 Peachtree St., Atlanta 30301 (656-3590), across from **Atlanta Convention and Visitors Bureau.** Write for or pick up a comprehensive *Georgia Travel Guide.* Open Mon.-Fri. 8am-5pm. **Department of Natural Resources,** 270 Washington St. SW, Atlanta 30334 (800-542-7275; 404-656-3530 in GA). **U.S. For-**

est Service, 1720 Peachtree Rd. NW, Atlanta 30367 (347-2385). Info on the Chattahoochee and Oconee National Forests. Open Mon.-Fri. 10am-5pm.
Time Zone: Eastern. **Postal Abbreviation:** GA
Sales Tax: 4-6%.

■■■ ATLANTA

Unlike other southern cities which are defined by their Civil War past, Atlanta defines itself in terms of its ever-expanding present. Not even Union General Sherman's "scorched earth" burning of Atlanta to the ground in 1864 could quench its spirit which—like its seal (the phoenix) and its motto *resurgens*—arose from the ashes to soar today as the largest metropolis in the Southeast and a nationwide economic powerhouse. The city contains the world's largest airport complex, the headquarters of Coca-Cola and CNN, and offices of 400 of the Fortune 500 corporations. Nineteen institutions of higher learning, including Georgia Tech, Morehouse College, Spelman College, and Emory University, call "Hotlanta" home, as does "America's team," the Atlanta Braves.

Not surprisingly, fame and prosperity have diluted Atlanta's Old South flavor. An influx of transplanted Northerners and Californians, the third-largest gay population in the U.S., and a host of ethnic groups contribute to the city's cosmopolitan air. This birthplace of Martin Luther King, Jr. witnessed unrest and activism during the 1960s; deeply impressed by lessons learned in the Civil Rights struggle, Atlanta elected one of the nation's first African-American mayors, Maynard Jackson, in 1974. Sleek and upbeat, Atlantans are already burning with Olympic fever; the city is besieged by new construction at nearly every turn.

PRACTICAL INFORMATION

Emergency: 911.
Visitor Information: Atlanta Convention and Visitors Bureau, 231 Peachtree St. #200 (551-6600), Peachtree Center, Harris Tower, downtown. Caters more to conventions; stop by to pick up a free copy of *Atlanta and Georgia Visitors' Guide* ($3 at newsstands). Open Mon.-Fri. 9am-5pm. Also at **Underground Atlanta** (577-2148), Peachtree St. and Martin Luther King, Jr. Dr. Open Mon.-Sat. 10am-9pm, Sun. noon-6pm.
Airport: Hartsfield International Airport, (530-6600 for general info; international services and flight info 530-2081), south of the city. Headquarters of **Delta Airlines** (756-5000 or 800-221-1212). International travelers can get phone assistance in 6 languages at the **Calling Assistance Center,** a computerized telephone system in the international terminal. MARTA (see Public Transport below) is the easiest way to get downtown, with 15-min. rides departing every 8 min., daily 5am-1am with baggage space available. **Atlanta Airport Shuttle** (525-2177) runs vans from the airport to midtown, downtown, Emory, and Lenox Sq. ($8-12). **Northside Airport Express** (768-7600) serves Stone Mountain, Marietta, and Dunwoody. Buses run daily 5am-midnight ($15-30).
Amtrak: 1688 Peachtree St. NW (872-9815), 3 mi. north of downtown at I-85. Take bus #23 to and from the "Arts Center" MARTA station. To: New Orleans (1 per day, 11 hr., $95); Washington, DC (1 per day, 14 hr., $119); Charlotte (1 per day, 5 hr., $52). Open daily 6:30am-9:30pm.
Greyhound: 81 International Blvd. (522-6300), 1 block from Peachtree Center. MARTA: Peachtree Center. To: New Orleans (7 per day, 9 hr., $55); Washington, DC (8 per day, 16 hr., $82); Chattanooga (8 per day, 2½ hr., $24). Open 24 hrs.
Public Transport: Metropolitan Atlanta Rapid Transit Authority (MARTA), 848-4711; schedule info Mon.-Fri. 6am-10pm, Sat.-Sun. 8am-4pm. Combined rail and bus system serves virtually all area attractions and hotels. Operates Mon.-Sat. 5am-1:30am, Sun. 6am-12:30am in most areas. Fare $1.25 exact change or buy a token at station machines; transfers free. Unlimited weekly pass $11. Pick up a system map at the **MARTA Ride Store,** Five Points Station downtown, or at one

of the satellite visitors bureaus. If you get confused, just find the nearest MARTA courtesy phone in each rail station.

Taxi: Checker, 351-1111. **Rapid,** 681-2280. Base fare $1.50, $1.20 per mi.

Car Rental: Atlanta Rent-a-Car, 3185 Camp Creek Pkwy. (763-1160), just inside I-285, 3 mi. east of the airport. 9 other locations in the area including Cheshire Bridge Rd. and I-85, 1 mi. west of the Liddberg Center Railstop. Rates from $20 per day. 100 free mi., 19¢ each additional mi. Must be 21 with major credit card.

Help Lines: Rape Crisis Counseling, 659-7273. Open 24 hrs. **Gay/Lesbian Help Line,** 892-0661. Open daily 6-11pm. Center located at 63 12th St. (876-5372).

Post Office: 3900 Crown Rd. (768-4126). Open 24 hrs. **ZIP code:** 30321.

Area Code: 404.

Atlanta sprawls and drawls across the northwest quadrant of the state, 150 mi. east of Birmingham, AL and 113 mi. south of Chattanooga, TN, at the junctures of I-75, I-85, and I-20, and is circumscribed by I-285 ("the perimeter").

Getting around is confusing—*everything* seems to be named Peachtree. However, of the 40-odd roads bearing that name, only one, **Peachtree Street,** is a major north-south thoroughfare, as are **Spring Street** and **Piedmont Avenue. Ponce De León Avenue** and **North Avenue** are major east-west routes. In the heart of downtown, the area to the west of I-75/85, south of International Blvd. and north of the capitol, where angled streets and shopping plazas run amok, navigation is difficult.

ACCOMMODATIONS AND CAMPING

When planning to stay in Atlanta for more than a few days, check with the **International Youth Travel Program (IYTP).** The convention and visitors bureau (see Practical Information), will try to locate a single for a reasonable price. The IYTP is your cheapest bet besides the YMCA and the hostels. Unfortunately, some options are not available to women from the U.S. **Bed and Breakfast Atlanta,** 1801 Piedmont Ave. NE (875-0525; call Mon.-Fri. 9am-noon or 2-5pm), offers singles from $45, doubles from $48-60.

Atlanta Dream Hostel, 222 E. Howard Ave. (370-0380; MARTA: Decatur), is located in a safe enclave near the heart of the city. The proprietor of this aptly named hostel envisions Japanese gardens, extensive landscaping, and an international treehouse village to create the ultimate in funky, communal comfort. Judging by the already materialized creative common room, the shaded outdoor patio, and the cool collection of antique cars, his dreams are more than likely to come true. $10 per night with kitchen, laundry, and showers and free linen.

The Woodruff HI/AYH-Hostel, 223 Ponce de León Ave. (875-9449). Reach it by MARTA: North Ave. station, exit onto Ponce de León, about 3½ blocks east. Part of a B&B in a Victorian home with stained glass windows. Kitchen and showers at no charge. Bike rentals $1. Linens $1. Sleep sack $2 (no sleeping bags). A/C. Free local calls. Luggage storage $1. Free city magazine and map, and occasional free passes to city attractions. No alcohol allowed. Free coffee and doughnuts 8-10am. Lockout noon-5pm and midnight-8am but key rentals available at small charge. 3-day max. stay. Members $13.25, nonmembers $16.25.

Motel 6, 4427 Commerce Dr. (762-5201), off Washington in East Point, exit 2 off the Perimeter Rd. I-285, has a small earth-toned rooms and a pool. Four other perimeter locations: 3585 Chamblee Tucker Rd. in Chamblee exit 27 (455-8000); 6015 Oakbridge Pkwy. (446-2311), in Norcross exit 37; 4100 Wendell Dr. SW (696-0757), exit 14; and 2565 Weseley Chapel Rd. (288-6911), in Decatur exit 36. All locations $24-25 for 1 person, $6 per additional person. Each location offers free movie channel, free local calls, and kids under 18 stay free with their parents.

Villages Lodge, 144 14th St. NW (873-4171). A fence separates you from the highway. Tidy rooms in a dark decor. Chinese restaurant. Optional phone ($10 deposit); local calls 30¢. Laundry facilities. Friendly management. Mexican restaurant. Pool. Singles $35. Doubles $40. Key deposit $5.

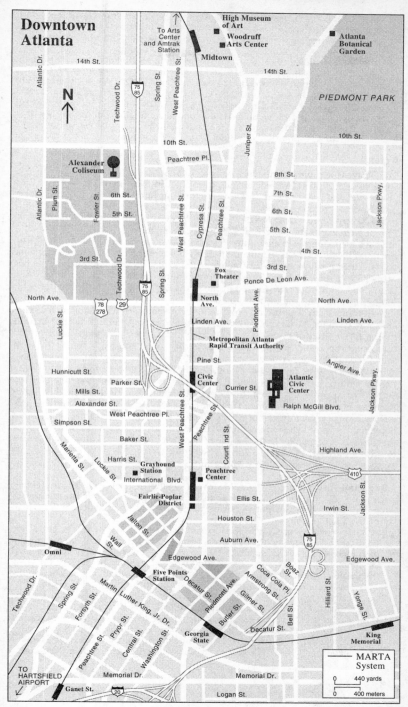

Downtown Atlanta

N

To Arts Center and Amtrak Station

High Museum of Art
Woodruff Arts Center
Atlanta Botanical Garden
Midtown

14th St.
Atlantic Dr.
Techwood Dr.
Spring St.
West Peachtree St.
14th St.

PIEDMONT PARK

Juniper St.
10th St.
10th St.
Peachtree Pl.

Alexander Coliseum

Plum St.
Fowler St.
6th St.
5th St.

West Peachtree St.
Cypress St.
Peachtree St.
8th St.
7th St.
6th St.
5th St.
4th St.

Jackson Pkwy.

Atlantic Dr.
3rd St.
Techwood Dr.

Fox Theater
3rd St.
Ponce De Leon Ave.

North Ave.
Spring St.
North Ave.
78 278
75 85
29

North Ave.
Luckie St.
Linden Ave.
Piedmont Ave.
North Ave.
Linden Ave.

Metropolitan Atlanta Rapid Transit Authority

Pine St.

Angier Ave.

Hunnicutt St.
Parker St.
Civic Center
Currier St.
Atlantic Civic Center
Mills St.
Alexander St.
West Peachtree Pl.
Ralph McGill Blvd.
Jackson Pkwy.

Simpson St.

West Peachtree St.
Peachtree St.
Courtland St.

Baker St.
Highland Ave.

Marietta St.
Luckie St.
Harris St.
Grayhound Station
International Blvd.
410

Fairlie-Poplar District

Peachtree Center
Ellis St.
Jackson St.

Houston St.

Jalton St.
Wall St.
Auburn Ave.
75 85

Omni
Edgewood Ave.
Boaz St.
Edgewood Ave.

Five Points Station
Coca Cola Pl.
Hilliard St.
Yonge St.

Techwood Dr.
Spring St.
Forsyth St.
Martin Luther King, Jr. Dr.
Decatur St.
Piedmont Ave.
Armstrong St.
Gilmer St.
Bell St.

Peachtree St.
Pryor St.
Central St.
Washington St.
Georgia State
Butler St.
Decatur St.

King Memorial

TO HARTSFIELD AIRPORT

Memorial Dr.
Memorial Dr.

MARTA System

Ganet St.
20
Logan St.

0 ___ 440 yards
0 ___ 400 meters

Red Roof Inn, 1960 Druid Hills (321-1653), exit 31 off I-85, offers rooms with clean, modern decor and pleasant tree-cloistered location. Convenient to downtown. Look carefully for the sign, it's partially hidden by branches. Singles $37. Doubles $40.

KOA South Atlanta (957-2610), Mt. Olive Rd. in McDonough exit 72 off I-75, offers tent sites with water for $15, add $2 for electricity. Showers, pool, laundry, and fishing pond on the premises. You can also try **KOA West Atlanta,** 2420 Old Alabama Rd. in Austell (941-7485), 3 mi. west of Six Flags Amusement Park.

Stone Mountain Family Campground (498-5710), on U.S. 78 16 mi. east of town. Exit 30-B off I-285 or subway to Avondale then "Stone Mountain" bus. Part of state park system. Tent sites $12. RV sites $13 with water and electricity and $1 for dump. Reservations not accepted. Entrance fee $5 per car.

FOOD

You'll have to scrounge to find inexpensive home-style Southern cooking in Atlanta. Some favorite dishes to sample include fried chicken, black-eyed peas, okra, sweet-potato pie, and mustard greens. Dip a hunk of cornbread into "pot likker," water used to cook greens, and enjoy. For a cheap breakfast, you can't beat the Atlanta-based **Krispy Kreme Doughnuts** whose baked delights are a Southern institution. The original company store is at 295 Ponce de León Ave. NE (876-7307). Savor Atlanta's many European and ethnic restaurants which, from Russian to Ethiopian, provide a torrent of treats to tantalize tourists' tastebuds. A flock of these foreign flavors fly at **Little Five Points,** at the intersection of Moreland and Euclid Ave. NE, Atlanta's bohemian "village" of quirky shops crammed with crystals, rare books, and beads, second-hand stores dressed to the nines in grunge, and a plethora of cafes run by both true and wanna-be hippies.

Do-it-yourself-ers can procure produce and regionally popular items such as chitlins, pork cracklin', sugar cane, collards, and yams at the **Atlanta Municipal Market** (659-1665), corner of Butler St. and Edgewood Ave. Pick up a guide to Georgia's markets at the info center to find a list of what's ripe and ready while you're in town. Serving downtown Atlantans since 1923, this market also houses inexpensive deli stalls such as the **Snack Bar** where the adventurous visitor can munch on a hot pig ear sandwich ($1.25). For a more international arena, shoppers should take the subway to Arondale and then the "Stone Mountain" bus to the **Dekalb County Farmers Market,** 3000 E. Ponce De León Ave. (377-6400), where world-wide specialties run the gustatory gamut from Chinese to Middle Eastern and everything in between. For those who wouldn't mind finding themselves sifting through heaps of fresh fruit and vegetables in the middle of nowhere, head for the 80 acres of **Atlanta's State Farmers Market,** 16 Forest Pkwy. (366-6910), exit 78 off I-75 south. (No MARTA service; open Mon.-Fri. 10am-10pm, Sat.-Sun. 9am-9pm.)

Beautiful Restaurant, 397 Auburn Ave. (505-0271), heartily feeds the "Sweet Auburn" district, locals and visitors alike. This is "down-home" as in *real* down-home. And cheap, as country-cookin' should always. Dinner under $5, vegetarian platter $2.50. Open daily 7am-8:30pm.

Eat Your Vegetables Cafe, 438 Moreland Ave. NE (523-2671), in the Little Five Points area. A friendly corner eatery serving vegetarian entrees $7-8, including a daily macrobiotic dinner special. Chicken and seafood entrees $8-9. Also vegetarian lunches (hummus, soyburgers, and salads) at cheaper prices. Try the zesty BBQ Tofu sandwich ($3.75). Your mother would be proud. Open Mon.-Thurs. 11:30am-10pm, Fri. 11:30am-10:30pm, Sat. 11am-10:30pm, Sun. 11am-3pm.

The Varsity, 61 North Ave. NW (881-1706), at I-85. Take MARTA to North Ave. station. Order at the world's largest drive-in or brave the local masses to eat inside this local institution since 1928. Best known for chili dogs ($1-2) and the greasiest onion rings (90¢) in the South. Heaping ice cream cones a bargain at 80¢. Employees have a language all their own. Eat in one of the giant TV rooms—1 room for each channel and vice-versa. Open Sun.-Thurs. 7am-12:30am, Fri.-Sat. 7am-2am.

Touch of India, 962 Peachtree St. (876-7777) and 2065 Piedmont Rd. (876-7775). 3-course lunch specials $4. Popular with locals. Atmosphere and service worthy of a much more expensive restaurant. Dinners $6-10. Open Mon.-Sat. 11:30am-2:30pm and 5:30-10:30pm.

Mary Mac's Tea Room, 224 Ponce De León Ave. (875-4337). NE Take the "Georgia Tech" bus north. Famous for its amazing home-made cornbread and array of real Southern vegetables. A bit like cafeteria food, but home-cooked and very filling. Order by writing your own ticket. Waiters tend to rush you. Lunches $5-7, dinners $6-10. Students with ID receive 10% discount at dinner. Open Mon.-Fri. 11am-3pm. New branches opening in late '93 in Buckhead and Tucker with longer hours. Call for info.

Nicola's, 1602 Lavista Rd. NE (325-2524), cooks, bakes, and dishes up the most savory and authentic Lebanese cuisine in Atlanta. Try the meza combination platter ($25) that can satisfy 4. Probably the best bet for individuals is to order among the appetizers, forget the silverware, and scoop the flavorful food with the warm pita that comes with the meal. Look for raw kibby, a Lebanese delicacy, on Sat. nights. Open daily 5:30-10:30pm.

SIGHTS

Atlanta's sights may seem scattered, but the effort it takes to find them usually pays off. The **Atlanta Preservation Center,** The De Soto # 3, 156 7th St. NE (876-2040), offers eight walking tours of popular areas: Fox Theatre District, West End and the Wren's Nest, Historic Downtown, Miss Daisy's Druid Hills, Inman Park, Underground and Capitol area, Ansley Park, and Sweet Auburn—from April through November. The Fox Theater tour is given year-round. All tours last about two hours. ($5, students $4, seniors $3. Call for exact times and starting points.)

Hopping on MARTA and taking in the sites on your own is the cheapest and most rewarding tour option. An intimate part of southern history can be explored at the **Martin Luther King, Jr. National Historic Site** at the Church, birthplace, burial place, and museum of the youngest man (at 35 years old) ever to be awarded a Nobel Peace Prize. Stop by the **National Park Service Visitors Center,** 522 Auburn Ave. NE (331-3920; open daily 9am-5pm), for helpful and informative maps, pamphlets, and a video about the **Sweet Auburn District** and the life of King. **Ebenezer Baptist Church,** 407 Auburn Ave. (688-7263), where King was pastor from 1960 to 1968, is now open to the public, as are its Sunday worship services. In the coming year, however, the church will be transformed into a visitors center for the National Park Service and a new church for the local congregation will be built across the street. (Open Mon.-Fri. 9am-5:30pm. Call for weekend hours.) The 23½-acre area encompassed by the park also includes the restored Victorian **birthplace of King,** 501 Auburn Ave. NE (331-3920; open daily 10am-5pm, hours extended April-Sept.; free, but arrive early in the morning as very few visitors get to tour the inside). Plaques line Sweet Auburn (once called the humbler Wheat St.), pointing out the Queen Anne architecture and eminent past residents of this historically African-American neighborhood. King is buried at the **Martin Luther King Center for Non-violent Social Exchange,** 449 Auburn Ave. NE (524-1956), which also holds a collection of King's personal effects and a film about his life. Take bus #3 from Five Points or Edgewood/Candler Park Stations. (Open daily 9am-5pm, later in the summer months. Film $1.)

Other fine reflections of African-American history are mounted in the galleries of **Hammonds House,** 503 Peeples St. SW (752-8730), which display a fantastic collection of African-American art. Take bus #71 from West End Station South to the corner of Oak and Peeples. (Open Tues.-Fri. 10am-5pm, Sat.-Sun. 1-6pm; $1, 17 and under free.) Also in the **West End**—Atlanta's oldest neighborhood, dating from 1835—hover the **Wren's Nest,** 1050 Ralph D. Abernathy Blvd. (753-5835), home to Joel Chandler Harris who popularized the African folktale trickster Br'er Rabbit through stereotypical slave character Uncle Remus. Take bus #71 from West End station South. (Open Tues.-Sat. 10am-5pm, Sun. 1-5pm. Tours $3, teens and seniors

$2, ages 4-12 $1, storytelling $1 extra.) Visit also the **Herndon Home,** 587 University Place NW (581-9813), a 1910 Beaux Arts Classical mansion built by slave-born Alonzo F. Herndon who was a prominent barber before becoming Atlanta's wealthiest African-American in the early 1900s. Herndon amassed his fortune by founding Atlanta Life Insurance Company, the country's largest black insurance company. Take bus #3 from Five Points station to the corner of Martin Luther King, Jr. Drive and Maple, walk one block north. (Open Tues.-Sat. 10am-4pm. Free.)

A drive through **Buckhead** (north of midtown off Peachtree near W. Paces Ferry Rd.) uncovers the "Beverly Hills of Atlanta"—the sprawling mansions and manicured lawns of Coca-Cola CEOs and sports-team owners. It is also a hub of local grub and grog (see Entertainment below). Buckhead shows off one of the most beautiful residences in the Southeast. The Greek Revival **Governor's Mansion,** 391 West Paces Ferry Rd. (261-1776; take bus #40 "West Paces Ferry" from Lenox Station), has elaborate gardens and furniture from the Federal period. (Tours Tues.-Thurs. 10-11:30am. Free.) In the same neighborhood, discover the **Atlanta History Society,** 3101 Andrew Dr. NW (261-1837). On the grounds are the **Swan House,** a lavish Anglo-Palladian Revival home, and the **Tullie Smith House,** an antebellum farmhouse. Don't miss the intriguing *"Atlanta Resurgens"* exhibit, in which famous and not-so-famous Atlantans praise the city. Look also for the late 1993 opening of the **New Museum of Atlanta History** on the grounds, featuring a Civil War Gallery with one of the finest collections in the country. (Tours every ½ hr. Open Mon.-Sat. 9am-5:30pm, Sun. noon-5pm. Admission $6, seniors and students $4.50, kids $3.)

North of mid-town but south of Buckhead sprawls **Piedmont Park,** home to the 60-acre **Atlanta Botanical Garden** (876-5858), Piedmont Ave. at the Prado. Stroll through five acres of landscaped gardens, a 15-acre hardwood forest with walking trails, and an exhibition hall. The **Dorothy Chapman Fuqua Conservatory** houses hundreds of species of rare tropical plants. Take bus #36 "North Decatur" from the Arts Center subway stop. (Open Tues.-Sat. 9am-8pm during Daylight Savings Time, until 6pm at other times of the year. $4.50, seniors and kids $2.25. Thurs. free.) Just to the west of the park, the **Woodruff Arts Center,** 1280 Peachtree St. (892-3600; take the subway to Arts Center), houses the **High Museum** (892-HIGH), Richard Meier's award-winning building of glass, steel, and white porcelain. The museum includes American and European decorative arts, paintings, photography, and a variety of contemporary art exhibits. (Open Tues.-Thurs. and Sat. 10am-5pm, Fri. 10am-9pm, Sun. noon-5pm. $5, seniors and students with ID $3, kids $1. Free Thurs. 1-5pm.) The museum branch at **Georgia-Pacific Center** (577-6939), one block south of Peachtree Center Station, is free (open Mon.-Fri. 11am-5pm).

A different mode of culture prances at the **Center for Puppetry Arts,** 1404 Soring St. NW (873-3089 or 874-0398), at 18th St., whose museum features Wayland Flower's "Madame," traditional Punch and Judy figures, Asian hand-carved puppets, and some of Jim Henson's original Muppets. Attend one of the center's highly popular productions given at a variety of times throughout the year. Call for current info and reservations. (Museum open Mon.-Sat. 9am-4pm. $3, ages 2-13 $2.)

Further downtown but directly below Piedmont Park lie Atlanta's two other major spots of greenery. **Oakland Cemetery,** 248 Oakland Ave. SE (577-8163), pushes up daisies with the graves of golfer Bobby Jones and *Gone With the Wind* author Margaret Mitchell. (Open daily sunrise-sunset. Information Center open Mon.-Fri. 9am-5pm. Free. Take bus #3.) True fans of Rhett Butler and Scarlett O'Hara can visit the Margaret Mitchell Room in the **Atlanta Public Library,** 1 Margaret Mitchell (730-1700), to peruse memorabilia such as autographed copies of her famous novel (open Mon and Fri. 9am-6pm, Tues.-Thurs. 9am-8pm, Sat. 10am-6pm, Sun. 2-6pm), or they can drive by the dilapidated three-story house on the corner of 10th and Crescent where Mitchell used to live.

Directly south, in **Grant Park,** between Cherokee Ave. and Boulevard, revolves the **Cyclorama** (758-7625), a massive panoramic painting (42 ft. high and 900 ft. around) recreating the 1864 Battle of Atlanta with 3-D features and light and sound effects. (Open daily 9:30am-5:30pm, Oct.-May daily 9:30am-4:30pm. $3.50, students and seniors $3, ages 6-12 $2.) Next door growls **Zoo Atlanta,** 800 Cherokee Ave. (624-5600), whose entertaining animal displays stress conservation and environmental awareness. Among the special exhibits are the Masai Mara, Mzima Springs and the Ford African Rain Forest. (Open daily 10am-4:30pm, until 5:30pm on weekends during Daylight Savings Time. $7.50, ages 3-11 $5, under 3 free.)

Outside of these historical and culture-preserving sights, high-tech "Hotlanta" reigns with multinational business powerhouses situated in business-oriented **Five Points District** downtown. Influential **Turner Broadcasting System** offers an insider's peek with its **Cable News Network (CNN) Studio Tour** (827-2300), corner of Techwood Dr. and Marietta St., that reveals the day-to-day workings of a 24-hr. cable news station. Witness anchorpeople broadcasting live while writers toil in the background. (Open daily 9am-5:30pm; 50-min. tours given on the ½-hr. $5, kids 5-12 and seniors $2.50. Take MARTA west to the Omni/Dome/GWCC Station at W1.)

Redeveloped **Underground Atlanta** gets down with six subterranean blocks filled with over 120 shops, restaurants, and night spots in 19th century Victorian-style storefronts. Descend the entrance beside the Five Points subway station. In the summer, live musicians often play in and around Underground. (Shops open Mon.-Sat. 10am-9:30pm, Sun. noon-6pm. Bars and restaurants open later.) **Atlanta Heritage Row,** 55 Upper Alabama St. (584-7879), Underground, documents the city's past and looks into the future with exhibits and films (open Tues.-Sat. 10am-5pm, Sun. 1-5pm; $3, seniors and students over 12 $2.50, kids $2). Adjacent to the shopping complex is the **World of Coca-Cola Pavilion,** 55 Martin Luther King, Jr. Dr. (676-5151), clearly recognizable with its Times-Square-style neon Coca-Cola sign stretching 26 ft. across. The $15 million facility highlights "the real thing's" humble beginnings in Atlanta with over 1000 artifacts and interactive displays. (Open Mon.-Sat. 10am-9:30pm, Sun. noon-6pm. $2.50, seniors $2, ages 6-12 $1.50. The lines around the block suggest you make reservations.)

While Coca Cola tries to rule the soft-drink world, **Georgia State Capitol** (656-2844; MARTA: Georgia State), Capitol Hill at Washington St., is content to govern the state of Georgia. The gold that gilds the dome was mined nearby in Dahlonega, GA. (Tours Mon.-Fri. on the hr. 10am-2pm except noon. Open Mon.-Fri. 8am-5pm. Free.) The **Carter Presidential Center,** 1 Copenhill (331-0296), north of Little Five Points, documents the Carter Administration (1977-1981) through exhibits and films; surrounded by lovely landscaped grounds, the center also houses a Japanese garden and cafe. Take bus #16 to Cleburne Ave. (Open Mon.-Sat. 9am-4:45pm, Sun. noon-4:45pm. $2.50, seniors $1.50, under 16 free.)

A respite from the city is available at **Stone Mountain Park** (498-5600), 16 mi. east on U.S. 78, where a fabulous bas-relief monument to the Confederacy is carved into the world's largest mass of granite. The "Mount Rushmore of the South" features Jefferson Davis, Robert E. Lee, and Stonewall Jackson and measures 90 by 190 ft. Surrounded by a 3200-acre recreational area, the mountain dwarfs the enormous statue. Check out the dazzling laser show on the side of the mountain each summer night at 9:30pm (free). Take bus #120 "Stone Mountain" from the Avondale subway stop (buses leave Mon.-Fri. only at 4:30 and 7:50pm). (Park gates open daily 6am-midnight; attractions open daily 10am-9pm, off-season 10am-5:30pm. $5 per car.)

A jaunt eastward will open up new horizons with the discovery of the **Fernbank Museum of Natural History,** 767 Clifton Rd. NE (378-0127). With the forest, the museum, and the science center, there's more than a day's adventure to be found (open Mon.-Sat. 9am-6pm, Sun. noon-6pm; $5.50, students and seniors $4.50).

ENTERTAINMENT

For sure-fire fun in Atlanta, buy a MARTA pass (see Practical Information above) and pick up one of the city's free publications on music and events. *Creative Loafing, Music Atlanta,* the *Hudspeth Report,* or "Leisure" in the Friday edition of the *Atlanta Journal* will all help you "eat the peach." *Southern Voice* also has complete

BRUNSWICK & ENVIRONS

listings on gay and lesbian news and nightclubs throughout Atlanta. Stop by **Charls,** 419 Moreland Ave., NE (524-0304), for your free copy (open Mon.-Sat. 10:30am-6:30pm, Sun. 1-6pm). Look for free summer concerts in Atlanta's parks.

The outstanding **Woodruff Arts Center,** 1280 Peachtree St. NE (892-3600), houses the Atlanta Symphony and the Alliance Theater Company. For more plays and movies check the Moorish and Egyptian Revival Movie Palace, the **Fox,** 660 Peachtree St. (249-6400), or the **Atlanta Civic Center,** 395 Piedmont St. (523-6275).

Atlanta's nightlife ripens into a frenetic, sweet, and inexpensive fuzziness. Hotspots center in Little Five Points, **Virginia Highlands,** a neighborhood east of downtown with trendy shops and a hip atmosphere, Buckhead, and Underground Atlanta. A college-age crowd usually fills Little Five Points heading for **The Point,** 420 Moreland Ave. (577-6468); there's always live music (open Mon.-Fri. 4pm-4am, Sat. 1pm-3am, Sun. 1pm-4am; cover $4-5). For blues, go to **Blind Willie's,** 828 N. Highland Ave. (873-2583), a dim, usually packed club with Cajun food and occasional big name acts (live music 10pm-2am; open daily at 8pm; cover $5-8).

Rub elbows and hob-nob with the Buckhead hoi polloi near Peachtree and Lenox Rd. Try the **Good Old Boys,** 3013 Peachtree Rd. (266-2597), for light fare and relaxed hanging out (open Tues.-Fri. 5pm-until, Sat. 11-3am, Sun. 11am-until). A street called **Kenny's Alley** is composed solely of bars—a blues club, a dance emporium, a jazz bar, a country/western place, a New Orleans-style daiquiri bar, and an oldies dancing spot. Towards downtown, **Masquerade,** 695 North Ave. NE (577-8178), is housed in an original turn-of-the-century mill. The bar has three different levels: heaven, with live hard-core music; purgatory, a more laid-back coffee house; and hell, offering progressive dance music. (Open Wed.-Sun. 9pm-4am. Cover $5-7 or more, depending on band. 18 and over.) **Backstreet,** 845 Peachtree St. NE (873-1986), a hot gay dance spot which prides itself on being straight-friendly, stays open all night. (Thurs.-Sun. at 11:30pm plays an extra-special hoppin' cabaret. Cover Sun.-Thurs. $2 after midnight; Fri.-Sat. $5.)

Six Flags, 7561 Flags Rd. SW (948-9290), at I-20 W., is one of the largest theme amusement parks in the nation, and includes several rollercoasters, a free-fall machine, live shows, and white-water rides. On summer weekends, the park is packed to the gills. Take bus #201 ("Six Flags") from Hightower Station. (Open summer Sun.-Thurs. 10am-10pm, Fri.-Sat. 10am-midnight. 1-day admission $24, kids under 48 in. $18; be sure to check local grocery stores and soda cans for discounts.)

■■■ BRUNSWICK AND ENVIRONS

Beyond its hostel and the nearby beaches, laid-back Brunswick is of little interest to the traveler except as a relaxing layover between destinations.

Practical Information The **Greyhound** station, at 1101 Glouster St. (265-2800; open Mon.-Sat. 8am-1pm and 2-7pm), offers service to Jacksonville (6 per day, 1½ hr., $16) and Savannah (6 per day, 1½ hr., $13). The **area code** is 912.

Accommodations and Food The **Hostel in the Forest (HI/AYH)** (264-9738, 265-0220, or 638-2623) is located 9 mi. west of Brunswick on U.S. 82, just past a small convenience store. Take I-95 to exit 6 and travel west on U.S. 82 (a.k.a. 84) about 1½ mi. from the interchange until you see the white-lettered wooden sign set back in the trees along the eastbound lane. The hostel itself is of low-impact construction ½ mi. back from the highway; every effort is made to keep the area surrounding the complex of geodesic domes and treehouses as natural as possible. No lock-out, no curfew, and few rules. The low-key managers will shuttle you to the Brunswick Greyhound station for $2. The manager can usually be convinced to use the pickup to make daytrips to Savannah, the Okefenokee Swamp, and the coastal islands. If possible, arrange to stay in one of the three treehouses at the hostel, each complete with a 25-square-ft. picture window and a spacious double bed. Bring insect repellent if you plan to stay in the summertime since mosquitos and yellow biting flies abound. In addition to a peahen named Cleopatra and numerous chickens, the hostel has an extensive patch of blueberry bushes; you can pick and eat as many berries as you wish May-June. ($8, nonmembers $10.)

Twin Oaks Pit Barbecue, 2618 Norwick St. (265-3131), eight blocks from downtown Brunswick across from the Southern Bell building, features a chicken-and-pork combination ($6). The breaded french fries ($1) are deep fried and deeeeelicious. (Open Mon.-Thurs. 10am-8:30pm, Fri.-Sat. 10am-10pm.)

Sights The nearby **Golden Isles,** which include **St. Simon's Island, Jekyll Island,** and **Sea Island,** have miles of white sand beaches. Near the isles, **Cumberland Island National Seashore** is 16 mi. of salt marsh, live-oak forest, and sand dunes laced with a network of trails and disturbed only by a few decaying mansions. Reservations (882-4335) are necessary for overnight visits, but the effort is often rewarded; you can walk all day on the beaches without seeing another person. (Reservations by phone only: call daily 10am-2pm.) Sites are available on a stand-by basis 15 minutes before the twice-daily ferry departures to Cumberland Island. The **ferry** (45 min., $10, children $6) leaves from St. Mary's on the mainland at the terminus of Rte. 40, at the Florida border. Daily departures are at 9am and 11:45am, returning at 10:15am and 4:45pm; off-season Thurs.-Mon. only.

■■■ SAVANNAH

In February of 1733, General James Oglethorpe and his rag-tag band of 120 colonists founded the state of Georgia at Tamacraw Bluff on the Savannah River. Since then the city has had a stint as the capital of Georgia, housed the first girl scout troop in the U.S., and provided enough inspiration for Eli Whitney, longtime Savannah resident, to invent the cotton gin.

When the price of cotton crashed at the turn of the century, many of the homes and warehouses along River Street fell into disrepair, and the townhouses and mansions that lined Savannah's boulevards became boarding houses or rubble. In the mid-1950s, a group of concerned citizens mobilized to restore the downtown area, preserving the numerous Federalist and English Regency houses as historic monuments. Today four historic forts, broad streets, and trees hung with Spanish moss enhance the city's classic Southern aura. This beautiful backdrop will serve as the site for the boating and yachting events during the 1996 Olympic Summer Games.

PRACTICAL INFORMATION

Emergency: 911.

Visitor Information: Savannah Visitors Center, 301 Martin Luther King, Jr. Blvd. (944-0456), at Liberty St. in a lavish former train station. Excellent free maps and guides. Open Mon.-Fri. 8:30am-5pm, Sat.-Sun. 9am-5pm. The **Savannah History Museum,** in the same building, has photographs, exhibits, and films depicting the city's history. Open daily 8:30am-5pm. $3, seniors $2.50, ages 6-12 $1.75.

Amtrak: 2611 Seaboard Coastline Dr. (234-2611 or 800-872-7245), 4 mi. outside the city. Taxi fare to city about $6. To: Charleston, SC (2 per day; 2 hr.; $22); Washington, DC (4 per day; 11 hr.; $112). Open 24 hrs.

Greyhound: 610 E. Oglethorpe Ave. (232-2135), convenient to downtown. To: Jacksonville (11 per day; 3 hr.; $27); Charleston, SC (4 per day; 3 hr.; $28); Washington, DC (6 per day; 14 hr.; $98). Open 24 hrs.

Public Transport: Chatham Area Transit (CAT), 233-5767. Buses operate daily 6am-11pm. Fare 75¢, transfers 5¢. **C&H Bus,** 530 Montgomery St. (232-7099). The only public transportation to Tybee Beach. Buses leave from the civic center in summer at 8:15am, 1:30pm, and 3:30pm, returning from the beach at 9:25am, 2:30pm, and 4:30pm. Fare $1.75.

Help Line: Rape Crisis Center, 233-7273. 24 hrs.

S A V A N N A H

Post Office: 2 N. Fahm St. (235-4646). Open Mon.-Fri. 8:30am-5pm. **ZIP code:** 31402.
Area Code: 912.

Savannah smiles on the coast of Georgia at the mouth of the **Savannah River,** which runs along the border with South Carolina. Charleston, SC, lies 100 mi. up the coast; Brunswick, GA lies 90 mi. to the south. The city stretches south from bluffs overlooking the river. The restored 2½-sq.-mi. **downtown historic district** is bordered by **East Broad, Martin Luther King, Jr. Blvd., Gaston Street,** and the river. Best explored on foot. **Tybee Island,** Savannah's beach, is 18 mi. east on U.S. 80 and Rte. 26. Try to visit at the beginning of spring, the most beautiful season in Savannah.

ACCOMMODATIONS AND CAMPING

Make your first stop in Savannah the visitors center (see Practical Information), where a wide array of coupons offer 15-20% discounts on area hotels. The downtown motels cluster near the historic area, visitors center, and Greyhound station. Do not stray south of Gwinnett St., where the historic district quickly deteriorates into an unsafe and seedy area. For those with cars, Ogeechee Rd. (U.S. 17) has several independently owned budget options.

Savannah International Youth Hostel (HI/AYH), 304 E. Hall St. (236-7744), far and away the best deal in town. Two blocks from the historic district. 7:30-10am and 5-10pm check-in. Call the friendly manager, Brian, for late check-in. $11, non-members $13. A/C, kitchen, laundry facilities, located in a restored Victorian mansion. No curfew, 10am-5pm lockout. Private rooms $22, nonmembers $26. Flexible 3 night max. stay.

Bed and Breakfast Inn, 117 Gordon St. (238-0518), on Chatham Sq. in the historic district. Pretty little rooms have TV, A/C, and shared bath. Singles $45, doubles $59. Add $10 on weekends. Reservations required.

Budget Inn, 3702 Ogeechee Rd. (233-3633), a 10-min. drive from the historic district. Take bus #25B ("Towers and Ogeechee"). Comfortable rooms with TV and A/C. Pool. Singles and doubles $29, cheaper with coupons. Reservations recommended; call collect.

Sanddollar Motel, 11 16th St. (786-5362), at Tybee Island 1½ mi. south on Butler Ave. A small, family-run motel practically on the beach. Most rooms rented weekly for $125. Singles may be available for $30, Fri.-Sat. $45.

Skidaway Island State Park (598-2300), 13 mi. southeast of downtown off Diamond Causeway. Inaccessible by public transportation. Follow Liberty St. east out of downtown; soon after it becomes Wheaton St., turn right on Waters Ave. and follow it to the Diamond Causeway. Bathrooms and heated showers. Sites $10. Parking $2. Check-in before 10pm.

Richmond Hill State Park (727-2339), off Rte. 144 ½ hr. south of downtown; take exit 15 off I-95. Quieter than Skidaway and usually less crowded. Sites $10. Parking $2. Check-in before 10pm. Registration office open daily 8am-5pm.

FOOD

In Savannah cheap food is easy to come by. Try the waterfront area for budget meals in a pub-like atmosphere. The early-bird dinner specials at **Corky's,** 407 E. River St. (234-0113), range from $4-6. **Kevin Barry's Irish Pub,** 117 W. River St. (233-9626), has live Irish folk music Wednesday to Sunday after 9pm, as well as cheap drinks during happy hour.

Jack's Food World, 30 Barnard St. (223-2552). It doesn't look like much from the outside, but the food is truly good. Sandwiches $3-5, 6-in. individual pizza $1.50. Open Mon.-Thurs. 11am-6pm, Fri. 11am-8pm, Sat.-Sun. 7:30am-8pm.

Olympic Cafe, 5 E. River St. (233-3131). On the river, great Greek specialities. Lunch or dinner $6-10. Open Sun.-Thurs. 10am-10pm, Fri.-Sat. 10am-midnight.

Morrison's Family Dining, 15 Bull St. (232-5264), near Johnson Sq. downtown. Traditional U.S. and Southern cooking, multi-item menu. Full meals $4-6. Whole pies $2. The food is guaranteed—if you don't like it, you don't pay for it. Open daily 7:30am-8pm.

SIGHTS AND EVENTS

In addition to restored antebellum houses, the downtown area includes over 20 small parks and gardens. The **Historic Savannah Foundation,** 210 Broughton St. (233-7703; call 233-3597 for reservations; 24-hrs.), offers a variety of guided one- and two-hour tours ($7-14). You can also catch any number of bus and van tours ($7-12) leaving about every 10-15 minutes from outside the visitors center (see Practical Information above). Ask inside for details.

The best-known historic houses in Savannah are the **Owens-Thomas House,** 124 Abercorn St. (233-9743), on Oglethorpe Sq., and the **Davenport House,** 324 E. State St. (236-8097), a block away on Columbia Sq. The Owens-Thomas House is one of the best examples of English Regency architecture in the U.S. (Open Feb.-Dec. Sun.-Mon. 2-5pm., Tues.-Sat. 10am-5pm. Last tour at 4:30pm. Admission $5, students $3, under 13 $2.) The Davenport House typifies the Federalist style and contains an excellent collection of Davenport china. Earmarked to be razed for a parking lot, its salvation in 1955 marked the birth of the Historical Savannah Foundation and the effort to restore the city. There are guided tours of the first floor every 15 minutes; explore the second and third floors at your leisure. (Open Mon.-Sat. 10am-4:30pm, Sun. 1:30-4:30pm. Closed Thurs. Last tour at 4pm. Admission $5.)

Lovers of Thin Mints, Scot-teas, and, of course, Savannahs should make a pilgrimage to the **Juliette Gordon Low Girl Scout National Center,** 142 Bull St. (233-4501), near Wright Square. The association's founder was born here on Halloween of 1860, possibly explaining the Girl Scouts' door-to-door treat-selling technique. The center's "cookie shrine," in one of the most beautiful houses in Savannah, contains an interesting collection of Girl Scout memorabilia. (Open Mon.-Sat. 10am-4pm, Sun. 12:30pm-4:30pm, closed Wed. $4, ages under 18 $3, group and Girl Scout discount rates.) One block down in **Johnson Square,** at the intersection of Bull and E. Saint Julian St., is the burial obelisk of Revolutionary War hero Nathaniel Green; a plaque contains an epitaph by the Marquis de Lafayette.

For a less conventional view of Savannah's history, follow the **Negro Heritage Trail,** visiting African-American historic sights from early slave times to the present. Three different tours are available on request from the Savannah branch of the **Association for the Study of Afro-American Life and History,** King-Tisdell Cottage, Negro Heritage Trail, 520 E. Harris St. (234-8000). Tours originate at visitors center Mon.-Sat. at 10am and 1pm. One day's notice is necessary; $10, children $5.

Savannah's four forts once protected the city's port from Spanish, British, and other invaders. The most interesting of these is **Fort Pulaski National Monument** (786-5787), 15 mi. east of Savannah on U.S. 80 and Rte. 26. (Open daily 8:30am-5:15pm, summer 8:30am-6:45pm. $2, over 62 and under 16 free.) Fort Pulaski marks the Civil War battle site where walls were first pummeled by rifled cannon, instantly making Pulaski and similar forts obsolete. Built in the early 1800s **Fort Jackson** (232-3945), also along U.S. 80 and Rte. 26, contains exhibits on the Revolution, the War of 1812, and the Civil War. Together with Fort Pulaski, it makes for a quick detour on a daytrip to Tybee Beach. (Open daily 9am-5pm; July and Aug. 9am-7pm. $2, seniors and students $1.50.)

Special events in Savannah include the **Hidden Garden of the Nogs Tour** (238-0248), in mid-April, when private walled gardens are opened to the public, and the **Tybee Island Beach Bum's Parade** (234-5884), with a beach music festival and other island activities in mid-June. The **St. Patrick's Day Weekend Music Fest** (232-4903), is a three-day free musical festival organized in City Market. Jazz, blues, and rock and roll blare from noon-midnight, Fri.-Sun.

Kentucky

Kentucky's intermediary position between the North and South and between the East and Midwest lends the state more than its share of paradoxes. Although Kentucky is renowned for its bourbon distilleries, most of the counties in the state are dry. Much of the countryside is genuine Appalachia, with problems lingering from mining and 19th-century industrialization; gracious Southern-style mansions rise amidst this crushing penury. Despite borders on seven different states, about 75% of Kentucky's residents were born in-state. Even its signature city, Louisville, has a complex identity. It hosts the aristocratic, eminently Southern Kentucky Derby but is also an important site for labor historians—the legacy of the coal boom during World War I.

PRACTICAL INFORMATION

Capital: Frankfort.
Visitor Information: Kentucky Department of Travel Development, 500 Metro St., #2200, Frankfort 40601 (502-564-4930 or 800-225-8747). **Department of Parks,** 500 Metro St., #1000, Frankfort 40601-1974 (800-255-7275).
Time Zones: Eastern and Central. **Postal Abbreviation:** KY
Sales Tax: 6%.

■■■ LEXINGTON

With Louisville's eyes turned northward, Lexington, Kentucky's second-largest city, has assumed the responsibility of giving the state a focal point. Lexington is rich in Southern heritage, and even recent growth spurts have not changed its atmosphere from *town* to *city,* nor have they divorced it from the rest of the largely rural state. Historic mansions downtown aren't too heavily overshadowed by skyscrapers, and a 20-minute drive from the city will set you squarely in bluegrass countryside.

Like the rest of Kentucky and almost every 10-year-old girl, Lexington is horse-crazy—the Kentucky Horse Park is heavily advertised, and the shopping complexes and "lite" industries whose presence clutters the outskirts of town still share space with quaint, green, rolling horse farms. The 150-odd farms gracing the Lexington area have nurtured such equine greats as Citation, Lucky Debonair, Majestic Prince, and Whirlaway.

PRACTICAL INFORMATION

Emergency: 911.
Visitor Information: Greater Lexington Convention and Visitors Bureau, # 363, 430 W. Vine St. (800-848-1224 or 233-1221), in the civic center. Brochures and maps. Open Mon.-Fri. 8:30am-5pm, Sat. 10am-5pm. Information centers also grace I-75 north and south of Lexington.
Airport: Blue Grass Field, 4000 Versailles Rd. (255-7218). Serves regional airlines/flights; often easier to fly to Louisville's Standiford Field (see Louisville: Practical Information).
Greyhound: 477 New Circle Rd. N.W. (255-4261). Lets passengers off north of Main St. Take Lex-Tran bus #6 downtown. Open daily 6:45am-11:30pm. To: Louisville (1 per day, 1½ hr., $16); Cincinnati (5 per day, 1½ hr., $18); Knoxville (4 per day, 3 hr., $41).
Public Transport: Lex-Tran, 109 W. London Ave. (253-4636). Modest system serving the university and city outskirts. Buses leave from the **Transit Center,** 220 W. Vine St. between Limestone and Quality. Fare 80¢, transfers free. Buses operate Mon.-Fri. 6am-6pm, Sat. 9am-6pm; some routes have evening schedules.
Taxi: Lexington Yellow Cab, 231-8294. Base fare $1.90 plus $1.35 per mi.

Transportation for People with Disabilities: WHEELS, 233-3433. Daily, 7am-6pm. 24-hr. notice required. After hours call 231-8294.
Help Line: Rape Crisis, 253-2511. Open 24 hrs. **GLSO Gayline,** 231-0335.
Time Zone: Eastern.
Post Office: 1088 Nandino Blvd. (231-6700). Take bus #2. Open Mon.-Fri. 8:30am-5pm, Sat. 9am-1pm. **ZIP code:** 40511. General Delivery is handled through the downtown branch at Barr and Limestone.
Area Code: 606.

New Circle Road highway (Rte. 4/U.S. 60 bypass), which is intersected by many roads that connect the downtown district to the surrounding towns, corrals the city. **High, Vine,** and **Main Streets** are the major east-west routes downtown; **Limestone Street** and **Broadway** the north-south thoroughfares.

ACCOMMODATIONS AND CAMPING

The concentration of horse-related wealth in the Lexington area tends to push accommodation prices up. The cheapest places are outside of the city beyond New Circle Rd. If you're having trouble on your own, **Dial-A-Accommodations,** 430. W. Vine St. #363 (233-7299), will locate and reserve a room free of charge in a requested area of town and a specific price range. (Open Mon.-Fri. 8:30am-5pm.)

Kimball House Motel, 267 S. Limestone St. (252-9565), between downtown and the university. The grungy sign conceals a collection of clean, quiet rooms, friendly management, and monkeys in the backyard. Some singles (1st floor, no A/C, shared bath) $20. Ask for them specifically; they often fill by late afternoon. Otherwise, cheapest singles $25. Doubles $28. Key deposit $5. Parking in back.
University of Kentucky, Apartment Housing, 700 Woodland Ave. (257-3721). Full kitchen and private bathroom. Fold-out sleeper. Rooms also available during the school year, space permitting. 14-day max. stay. Singles $21, doubles $26. Call ahead on a weekday. Available June-Aug. Explain that you only want a short stay; longer-term rentals are for U of K affiliates only.
Microtel, 2240 Buena Vista Dr. (299-9600), near I-75 and Winchester Rd. New, light motel rooms. Singles $27, each extra adult $3.
Bryan Station Inn, 273 New Circle Rd. (299-4162). Take bus #4 or Limestone St. north from downtown and turn right onto Rte. 4. Clean, pleasant rooms in the middle of a motel/fast-food strip. No phones. Singles or doubles $28. Rates decrease the longer you stay. Must be 21.

Good, cheap **campgrounds** can be found around Lexington; unfortunately, you'll need a car to reach them. The **Kentucky Horse Park Campground,** 4089 Ironworks Pike (233-4303), 10 mi. north off I-75, has laundry, showers, tennis, basketball and volleyball courts, swimming pool, more lawn than shade, and a free shuttle to the KY Horse Park and Museum (see Horses and Seasonal Events). (2-week max. stay. Sites $10, with hookup $14.50.)

FOOD

Lexington specializes in good, down-home feed-bags, and the lefty (college) side of town contributes some vegetarian and other wholesome options.

Alfalfa Restaurant, 557 S. Limestone St. (253-0014), across from Memorial Hall at the university. Take bus #2A. Fantastic international and veggie meals. Complete dinners with salad and bread under $10. Excellent, filling soups and exotic salads from $2. Live music nightly. Open Tues.-Thurs. 5:30-9pm, in summer until 9:30pm, Fri. 5:30-10pm, Sat. 10am-2pm and 5:30-10pm, Sun. 10am-2pm.
Ramsey's Diner, 49 E. High St. (259-2708). Real classy Southern grease. Vegetarians beware: authenticity means that even the vegetables are cooked with pork parts. Sandwiches under $5, entrees around $8, 4 vegetables for $6. Open Mon.-Sat. 11am-1am, Sun. 11am-11pm.

Everybody's Natural Foods and Deli, 503 Euclid Ave. (255-4162). This pleasant health-food store has a few tables where they serve excellent gazpacho, sandwiches ($2.50-3.50), and a daily lunch special ($3.75). Open Mon.-Fri. 8am-8pm, Sat. 10am-6pm, Sun. noon-5pm.

Park-N-Eat, 1216 New Circle Rd. (254-8723). 50s style drive-up eatery. No roller-skates on the waitresses, though, as they bring out your "Poor Boy" ($2.40) or chicken boxed lunch (Open Mon.-Thurs. 5-11pm. Fri.-Sat. 6pm-1am).

SIGHTS AND NIGHTLIFE

To escape the stifling swamp conditions farther south, antebellum plantation owners built beautiful summer retreats in milder Lexington. The most attractive of these stately houses preen only a few blocks northeast of the town center in the **Gratz Park** area near the public library. In addition to their past, the wrap-around porches, wooden minarets, stone foundations, and rose-covered trellises distinguish these estates from the neighborhood's newer homes.

The **Hunt Morgan House,** 201 N. Mill St. (253-0362), hunkers down at the end of the park across from the library. Built in 1814 by John Wesley Hunt, the first millionaire west of the Alleghenies, the house later witnessed the birth of Thomas Hunt Morgan, who won a Nobel Prize in 1933 for proving the existence of the gene. The house's most colorful inhabitant, however, was Confederate General John Hunt Morgan. Chased by Union troops, the general rode his horse up the front steps and into the house, leaned down to kiss his mother, and rode out the back door. What a guy. (Tours Tues.-Sat. 10am-4pm, Sun. 2-5pm. $4, kids $2.)

Kentucky's loyalties divided sharply in the Civil War. Mary Todd, who grew up five blocks from the Hunt-Morgan House, later married Abraham Lincoln. The **Mary Todd Lincoln House** is at 578 W. Main St. (233-9999; open April 1-Dec. 15 Tues.-Sat. 10am-4pm; $4, kids 6-12 $1).

In Victorian Square on the west side of downtown, the **Lexington Children's Museum,** 401 W. Main St. (258-3255), puts kids in a variety of simulated contexts for fun and undercover education. (Open Mon.-Sat. 10am-5pm, Sun. 1-5pm; early Sept.-late May closed Mon. Kids $1.50, grown-ups $2.50.) The **Lexington Cemetery,** 833 W. Main St. (255-5522), serves another stage in the life cycle. Henry Clay and John Hunt Morgan are buried here. (Open daily 8am-5pm. Free.) At the corner of Sycamore and Richmond Rd., you can admire **Ashland** (266-8581), the 20-acre homestead where statesman Henry Clay lived before he moved to the cemetery. The mansion's carved ash interior came from trees grown on the property. (Open Mon.-Sat. 10am-4:30pm, Sun. 1-4:30pm. $5, kids $2. Take bus #4A.)

The sprawling **University of Kentucky** (257-7173) gives free campus tours in "Old Blue," an English double-decker bus, at 10am and 2pm weekdays and on Saturday mornings (call 257-3595). The university's specialties include architecture and (surprise!) equine medicine. For updates of U of K's arts calendar, call 257-7173; for more info about campus attractions, call 257-3595.

Lexington's nightlife is pretty good for a town its size. **Breeding's** showcases lively times and music for the breeding set at 509 W. Main St. (255-2822). **The Brewery** is a friendly country-Western bar (both open daily 8am-1am). **Comedy on Broadway,** 144 N. Broadway (259-0013), features stand-up comics most nights. **The Bar,** 224 E. Main St. (255-1551), is a disco popular with gays and lesbians. (Open Sun.-Fri. until 1:30am, Sat. until 3:30am. Cover $3 on weekends.) **The Wrocklage,** 361 W. Short St. (231-7655), serves up alternative and punkish rock, and **Lynagh's** (259-9944), in University Plaza at Woodland and Euclid St., is a great neighborhood pub with superlative burgers ($4.35). Meet fraternity-sorority types at **Two Keys Tavern,** 333 S. Limestone (254-5000). *Ace* magazine gives info on stuff to do in the area; *GLSO News,* published monthly and available free at Alfalfa's (see Food), and The Bar, is a key to events in Lexington's substantial gay and lesbian community. The "Weekender" section of Friday's *Heraldleader* is filled with useful leisure notes.

HORSES AND SEASONAL EVENTS

A visit to Lexington is not complete without a close encounter with its quadruped citizenry. Try **Spendthrift Farm,** 884 Ironworks Pike (299-5271), 8 mi. northeast of downtown. (Free tours Feb.-July Mon.-Sat. 10am-noon; Aug.-Jan. Mon.-Sat. 10am-2pm. Take Broadway until it becomes Paris Pike, turn left onto Ironworks.)

The **Kentucky Horse Park,** 4089 Ironworks Pike (233-4303), exit 120 10 mi. north on I-75, is a highly touristy state park with full facilities for equestrians, a museum, two films, and the Man O' War Monument. (Open mid-March-Oct. daily 9am-5pm; times vary Nov.-Feb. $8, ages 7-12 $4. Horse-drawn vehicle tours included.) The **American Saddle Horse Museum** (259-2746), on the park grounds, continues the celebration of Lexington's favorite animal. (Open daily 9am-6pm; Labor Day-Memorial Day reduced hrs. $2, seniors $1.50, ages 7-12 $1.)

If horse racing is more your style, visit **Keeneland Race Track,** 4201 Versailles Rd. (254-3412; 800-354-9092), west on U.S. 60. (Races Oct. and April; post time 1pm. $2.) Morning workouts open to the public (April-Oct. daily 6-10am). The final prep race for the Kentucky Derby occurs here in April. The **Red Mile Harness Track,** 847 S. Broadway (255-0752; take bus #3 on S. Broadway), has racing April-June and also late Sept.-early Oct. (Post time 7pm.) The crowds run the gamut from wholesome families to seasoned gamblers. ($3, programs $2; parking free. Seniors free Thurs.) Morning workouts (7:30am-noon) are open to the public in racing season.

In June, the **Festival of the Bluegrass** (846-4995), at the Kentucky Horse Park, attracts thousands. Camping at the festival grounds is free. The **Lexington Junior League Horse Show** (mid-July; 252-1893), the largest outdoor show in the nation, unfolds its pageantry at the Red Mile (see above).

■ Near Lexington

The Shakers, a 19th-century celibate religious sect, practiced the simple life between Harrodsburg and Lexington, about 25 mi. southwest on U.S. 68, at the **Shaker Village** (734-5411). The 5000-acre farm features 27 restored Shaker buildings. A tour includes demonstrations of everything from apple-butter-making to coopering (barrel-making). (Open daily 9:30am-6pm. $8, $4 for students 12-17, ages 6-11 $2.) Although the last Shaker to live here died in 1923, you can still eat and sleep in original though somewhat altered Shaker buildings. (Dinner $12-14. Singles $30-55. Doubles $45-65. All rooms have A/C and private bath. Reservations required.) Greyhound bus #350 runs to Harrodsburg, seven mi. from the village (see Lexington: Practical Information). Outside Lexington, in **Richmond,** exit 90 off I-75, is **White Hall** (623-9178), home of the abolitionist (not the boxer) Cassius M. Clay, Senator Henry Clay's cousin. This elegant mansion really consists of two houses, one Georgian and one Italianate. The 45-min. tour covers seven different living levels. (Open April-Labor Day daily 9am-4:30pm; Labor Day-Oct. 31 Wed.-Sun; open briefly in winter for a Christmas celebration. Guided tours only. $3, under 13 $2, under 6 free.) The Richmond pre-packaged tourism experience also includes **Fort Boonesborough** (527-3328), a re-creation of one of Daniel Boone's forts. The park has samples of 18th-century crafts, a small museum, and films about the pioneers. (Open April-Aug. daily 9am-5:30pm; Sept.-Oct. Wed.-Sun. 9am-5:30pm. $4, ages 6-12 $2.50, under 6 free. Combination White Hall/Boonesborough tickets available.)

The **Red River Gorge,** in the northern section of the Daniel Boone National Forest, approximately 50 mi. southeast of Lexington, draws visitors from around the country. A day outing from Lexington will show why song and square dance have immortalized this spacious land of sandstone cliffs and stone arches. **Natural Bridge State Park** (663-2214), 2 mi. south of Slade, highlights the major attraction of the upper valley. The Red River Gorge highlights the lower valley. Greyhound bus #296 (see Lexington: Practical Information) will get you to Stanton (10 mi. west of Slade) and a **U.S. Forest Service Office** (663-2853). If you're driving, take the Mountain Parkway (south off I-64) straight to Slade, and explore the region bounded by the scenic loop road, Rte. 715. Camp at **Natural Bridge State Resort Park** (800-325-1710). The campground, complete with pool, facilities for disabled people, and organized square dances, hosts the **National Mountain Style Square Dance and Clogging Festival,** a celebration of Appalachian folk dances. (Square dance tickets $1-3. Tent sites $8.50, with hookup $10.50.)

■ ■ ■ LOUISVILLE

Perched on the Ohio River, hovering between the North and the South, Louisville (LOU-uh-vul) has its own way of doing things. An immigrant town imbued with Southern grace and architecture, Louisville's beautiful Victorian neighborhoods surround smokestacks and the enormous meat-packing district of Butchertown. The splayed, laid-back city has riverfront parks and excellent cultural attractions fostered by the University of Louisville. The year's main event is undoubtedly the Kentucky Derby (see below). The nation's most prestigious horse race ends a week-long extravaganza, luring over half a million visitors who pay through the teeth for a week-long carnival, fashion display, and equestrian show, which culminates in a two-minute gallop that you'll miss if you're standing in line for mint juleps. The $15 million wagered on Derby Day alone proves that Kentuckians are deadly serious about their racing—the winning horse earns studding privileges with hundreds of hot fillies, the winning jockey earns the congratulations of the state, and the winning owner earns $800,000, enough to make any stable stable.

PRACTICAL INFORMATION

Emergency: 911.

Visitor Information: Louisville Convention and Visitors Bureau, 400 S. First St. (584-2121; 800-633-3384 outside Louisville; 800-626-5646 outside KY), at Liberty downtown. The standard goodies, including some bus schedules. Open Mon.-Fri. 8:30am-5pm, Sat. 9am-4pm, Sun. 11am-4pm. Visitors centers also in Standiford Field airport and in the Galleria Mall at 4th and Liberty St. downtown.

Traveler's Aid: 584-8186. Open Mon.-Fri. 9am-5pm.

Airport: Standiford Field (367-4636), 15 min. south of downtown on I-65. Take bus #2 into the city.

Greyhound: 720 W. Muhammad Ali Blvd. (800-231-2222), at 7th St. To: Indianapolis (8 per day, 2 hr., $21); Cincinnati (6 per day, 2 hr., $18); Chicago (8 per day, 6 hr., $57; $29 special); Nashville (12 per day, 3 hr., $29); Lexington (1 per day, 2 hr., $13.50). Storage lockers $1 first day, $3 per additional day (call 561-2870 for locker and storage info). Open 24 hrs.

Public Transport: Transit Authority River City (TARC), 585-1234. Extensive system of thoroughly air-conditioned buses serves most of the metro area; buses run daily, some 4am-1am. Fare 60¢ during peak hours (6:30-8:30am and 3:30-5:30pm), 35¢ other times. Disabled access. Also runs a trolley on 4th Ave. from River Rd. to Broadway (free).

Taxi: Yellow Cab, 636-5511. Base fare $1.50 plus $1.50 per mi.

Car Rental: Dollar Rent-a-Car (366-6944), in Standiford Field airport. Weekends from $27 per day, weekdays $45. Must be 21 with credit card. Additional $6 per day for ages under 25. Open daily 6am-midnight. **Budget Rent-a-Car,** 4330 Crittenden Dr. (363-4300). From $40 per day, from $27 on weekends. Must be 21 with a major credit card or 25 without one. Open daily 6:30am-9pm.

Help Lines: Rape Hot Line, 581-7273. **Crisis Center,** 589-4313. Both 24 hrs. **Gay/Lesbian Hotline,** 589-3316. Open Sun.-Thurs. 6-10pm, Fri.-Sat. 6pm-1am.

Time Zone: Eastern.

Post Office: 1420 Gardner Lane (454-1650). Take the Louisville Zoo exit off I-264. Open Mon.-Fri. 7:30am-7pm, Sat. 7:30am-1pm. **ZIP code:** 40231.

Area Code: 502.

Major highways through the city include I-65 (north-south expressway), I-71, and I-64. The **Henry Watterson Expressway,** also called I-264, is an easily accessible freeway that reins in the city. The central downtown area is defined north-south by **Main Street** and **Broadway,** and east-west by **Preston** and **19th Street.**

Aside from theater and riverfront attractions, much activity in Louisville takes place outside the central city, but the fairly extensive bus system goes to all major areas. Call TARC (see above) for help since written schedules are incomplete and sometimes confusing.

ACCOMMODATIONS

Though easy to find, accommodations in Louisville are not particularly cheap. If you want a bed during Derby Week, make a reservation at least six months to a year in advance; be prepared to pay high prices. The visitors center (see Practical Information above) will help after March 13. If you don't choose one of the few affordable downtown options, try one of the many cheap motels that line the roads just outside town. **Kentucky Homes Bed and Breakfast** (635-7341) offers stays in private homes from $65. Call 7-10 days ahead. **Newburg** (6 mi. away) and **Bardstown** (39 mi. away) are also likely spots for budget accommodations.

Collier's Motor Court, 4812 Bardstown Rd. (499-1238), south of I-264. 30 min. from downtown by car, or take bus #17. Inconvenient, but well-maintained and cheap. Singles $33. Doubles $37.

Travelodge, 2nd and Liberty St. (583-2841), downtown behind the visitors center. Big, clean, and oh-so-convenient. Singles $39. Doubles $43.

Motel 6, 3304 Bardstown Rd. (456-2861), is in the middle of the heavy traffic zone near the junction of Bardstown and 264. Noisy, but they do leave that light on for you. Prices start at a hard-to-beat $25.

KOA, 900 Marriot Dr., Clarksville, IN (812-282-4474), across the bridge from downtown beside I-65; take the Stansifer Ave. exit. Grocery, playground, mini-golf and a fishing lake across the street. Sites $15 for 2 people. Each additional person $3, under 18 $2. Kamping kabins (for 2) $26. RV sites $16.50.

FOOD

Louisville's chefs whip up a wide variety of cuisines, though prices can be steep. Butchertown and the Churchill Downs area have several cheap delis and pizza places. Bardstown Rd. near Eastern Pkwy. offers budget pizzas and more expensive French cuisine.

The Rudyard Kipling, 422 W. Oak St. (636-1311), just south of downtown. Take bus #4. Eclectic menu includes French, Mexican and vegetarian entrees, Kentucky burgoo (a regional stew), and other creative fare ($5-13). Half-jungle, half-back porch. Fun and easy-going. Weekend nights feature piano music or rock n' roll; weeknights range from Celtic to bluegrass or folk music. Free Louisville Songwriters Cooperative acoustic music show each Mon. at 9pm. Open Mon.-Thurs. 11:30am-2pm and 5:30pm-midnight, Fri. 11:30am-around midnight, Sat. 5:30pm-midnight. Call for events calendar. Wheelchair accessible.

Miller's Cafeteria, 429 S. 2nd St. (582-9129), downtown. Serve yourself a full breakfast or lunch (entree, pie, 2 vegetables, and drink) for $3-4. Big, comfortable dining room built in 1826 is barely older than most of the customers. Open Mon.-Fri. 7am-2:30pm, Sun. 10am-2:30pm.

Ditto's, 1114 Bardstown Rd. (581-9129). Large burgers ($4-5.50), pastas ($5-5.50) and delicious pizzas ($6). Open Mon.-Thurs. 11am-11pm, Fri.-Sat. 11am-midnight, Sun. 9am-10pm.

Smoothie Shop and Deli, 1293 Bardstown Rd. (454-6890). Large, tasty blended-fruit shakes with honey and brewers yeast ($3), named after streets in the area to help you learn your Louisville geography by food association.

Old Spaghetti Factory, 235 W. Market St. (581-1070). Elegant brass decor doesn't mean elegant brass prices. Entrees $4.25-7. Touristy, but an attractive value; great for families.

IN THE NEIGH-BORHOOD

Even if you miss the Kentucky Derby, you can still visit **Churchill Downs,** 700 Central Ave. (636-4400), 3 mi. south of downtown. Take bus #4 (4th St.) to Central Ave. Bet, watch a race, or just admire the twin spires, colonial columns, gardens, and sheer scale of the track. (Grounds open in racing season daily 10am-4pm. Races April-June Tues.-Fri. 3:30-7:30pm, Sat.-Sun. 1-6pm; Oct.-Nov. Tues.-Sun. 1-6pm. Grandstand seats $1.50, clubhouse $3, reserved clubhouse $5. Parking $2-3.)

The **Kentucky Derby Festival** commences the week before the Derby and climaxes with the prestigious **Run for the Roses** the first Saturday in May. Balloon and steamboat races, concerts, and parades fill the week. Tickets for the Derby have a five-year waiting list. On Derby morning tickets are sold for standing-room-only spots in the grandstand or infield. Get in line early lest the other 80,000 spectators get there first. And you thought seeing *Phantom* was tough.

The **Kentucky Derby Museum** (637-1111) at Churchill Downs offers a slide presentation on a 360° screen, tours of the stadium, profiles of famous stables and trainers (including the African-Americans who dominated racing early on), a simulated horse-race for betting practice, and tips on exactly what makes a horse a "sure thing." (Open daily 9am-5pm. $3.50, seniors $2.50, ages 5-12 $1.50, under 5 free.)

The **Louisville Downs,** 4520 Poplar Level Rd. (964-6415), south of I-264, hosts harness racing most of the year. There are three meets: July-Sept. Mon.-Sat., Sept.-Oct. and Dec.-April Tues.-Sat. Post time 7:30pm; 10-12 races per night. ($3.50 clubhouse, $2.50 grandstand. Minimum bet $2. Parking $2. Take bus #43 from downtown.)

If you're tired of spectating, go on a trail ride at **Iroquois Riding Stable,** 5216 New Cut Rd. (363-9159; $10 per hr.). Take 3rd St. south to Southern Parkway or ride bus #4 or 6 to Iroquois Park.

NOT JUST A ONE-HORSE TOWN

Book, antique, and second-hand shops line **Bardstown Road** north and south of Eastern Pkwy. The grandaddy of all antique shops is **Joe Ley's Antiques, Inc.,** 615 E. Market St. (583-4014), downtown. Over two acres of spellbinding relics from all over the world are spread over four floors of a renovated schoolhouse. (Open Tues.-Sat. 8:30am-5pm. One-time entrance fee $1.) Between downtown and the university, **Old Louisville** harbors interesting Victorian architecture and a high crime rate. Farther south, in University of Louisville territory, the **J.B. Speed Art Museum,** 2035 S. 3rd St. (636-2893), has an impressive collection of Dutch paintings and tapestries, Renaissance and contemporary art, and a sculpture court. The museum also has a touch-to-see gallery for visually-impaired visitors. (Open Tues.-Sat. 10am-4pm, Sun. 12-5pm. Free. Parking $2. Nominal fee for special exhibitions. Take bus #4.)

The **Kentucky Center for the Arts,** 5 Riverfront Plaza (information and tickets 584-7777 or 800-283-7777), off Main St. is Louisville's newest entertainment complex. The KCA hosts the **Louisville Orchestra** and other major productions. The **Lonesome Pines** series showcases indigenous Kentucky music, including bluegrass. Ticket prices vary as wildly as the music, but student discounts are available.

Down a few stairs waits the **Belle of Louisville** (625-2355), an authentic sternwheeler. Ohio River cruises leave from Riverfront Plaza at the foot of 4th St. (Departs May 27-Sept. 2 Tues.-Sun. at 2pm. Sunset cruises Tues. and Thurs. 7-9pm; nighttime dance cruise Sat. 8:30-11:30pm. Boarding begins 1 hr. before the ship leaves; arrive early especially in July. $7, seniors $6, under 13 $3. Dance cruise $12.)

The **Museum of History and Science,** 727 W. Main St. (561-6100), downtown, emphasizes hands-on exhibits. Press your face against the window of an Apollo space capsule, then settle back and enjoy the four-story screen at the new IMAX theater. (Open Mon.-Thurs. 9am-5pm, Fri.-Sat. 9am-9pm, Sun. noon-5pm. $4, kids $3; $6/$5 with IMAX tickets.) At the **Louisville Zoo,** 1100 Trevilian Way (459-2181), between Newbury and Poplar Level Rd. across I-264 from Louisville Downs (take bus #18 or 43), the animals are exhibited in neo-natural settings. Ride on an elephant's back or on the tiny train that circles the zoo. (Open Fri.-Tues. 10am-5pm,

Wed.-Thurs. 10am-8pm; Sept.-April Tues.-Sun. 10am-4pm. Last entry 1 hr. before closing. $4.50, seniors $2.50, kids $2.)

Downtown is the **Actors Theater,** 316 W. Main St. (584-1265), a Tony award-winning repertory company, giving performances Sept.-mid-June at 8pm and some matinees. Call for details. Tickets start at $15, with $7 student rush tickets available 15 minutes before each show. Bring a picnic dinner to **Shakespeare in the Park** (634-8237), in Central Park, weekends June 19-August 4. (Performances at 8:30pm.) Call the **Louisville Visual Arts Association,** 3005 Upper River Rd. (896-2146), for information on local artists' shows and events.

Hillerich and Bradsby Co., 1525 Charleston-New Albany Rd., Jeffersonville, IN (585-5226), 6 mi. north of Louisville, manufactures the famous "Louisville Slugger" baseball bat. (Go north on I-65 to exit for Rte. 131, then turn east. Tours Mon.-Fri. 8-10am and 1-2pm on the hr. except on national holidays and Good Friday. Free.)

The free weekly *Leo,* available at many businesses, has event calendars and night-life ideas. **Uncle Pleasant's,** 2126 S. Preston (634-4804), one block north of Eastern Pkwy., features local bands ($2-5 cover) and sells every kind of beer. The best place in town for dancing is the gay bar **The Connection,** 130 S. Floyd St. **Dietrich's,** 2868 Frankfort Ave. (897-6076), is a hip bar in an old movie theater. (Open Mon.-Thurs. 4:30–11pm, Fri.-Sat. 4:30pm-midnight.)

■ Near Louisville

Ninety percent of the nation's bourbon hails from Kentucky, and 60% of that is distilled in Nelson and Bullitt Counties, close to Louisville. At **Jim Beam's American Outpost** (543-9877), in Clermont, 15 mi. west of Bardstown, Booker Noe, Jim Beam's grandson and current "master distiller," narrates a film about bourbon. Don't miss the free lemonade and sampler bourbon candies. From Louisville, take I-65 south to exit 112, then Rte. 245 south for 2½ mi. (Open Mon.-Sat. 9am-4:30pm, Sun. 1-4pm. Free.) You can't actually tour Beam's huge distillery, but you can visit the **Maker's Mark Distillery** (865-2099), in Loretto, 19 mi. southeast of Bardstown, for an investigation of 19th-century bourbon production. Take Rte. 49 S. to Rte. 52 E. (Tours Mon.-Sat. every hr. on the ½-hr. 10:30am-3:30pm; Jan.-Feb. Mon.-Fri. only. Free.) Neither site has a license to sell its liquors.

Hundreds of enormous caves and narrow passageways wind through **Mammoth Cave National Park** (758-2328), 80 mi. south of Louisville off I-65, west on Rte. 70. Mammoth Cave comprises the world's longest network of cavern corridors—over 325 mi. in length. Devoted spelunkers (ages 16 and over) will want to try the 6-hr. "Wild Cave Tour" in summer ($25); also available are 2-hr., 2-mi. historical walking tours ($3.50, seniors and kids $1.75) and 90-minute tours for people with disabilities ($4). Since the caves stay at 54°F year-round, bring a sweater. (**Visitors center** open daily 7:30am-7:30pm; off-season 7:30am-5:30pm.) **Greyhound** serves **Cave City,** just east of I-65 on Rte. 70, but the national park still lies miles away. **Gray Line** (637-6511; ask for the Gray Line) gives tours for groups of more than five people ($30 per person) and bus rides to the caves; call a few days ahead (tours April 10-Labor Day).

Bardstown proper hosts **The Stephen Foster Story** (800-626-1563 or 348-5971), a mawkish, heavily promoted outdoor musical about America's first major song-writer, the author of "My Old Kentucky Home." (Performances mid-June-Labor Day Tues.-Sun. at 8:30pm, plus Sat. at 3pm. $10, $5 for ages 12 and under).

Now a national historic site, **Abraham Lincoln's birthplace** (358-3874) bulges 45 mi. south of Louisville near Hodgenville on U.S. 31E. From Louisville, take I-65 down to Rte. 61; public transportation does not serve the area. Fifty-six steps representing the 56 years of Lincoln's tragically foreshortened life lead up to a stone monument sheltering the small log cabin that was the scene of his birth. Only a few of the Lincoln logs that you see are believed to be original. A plodding film describes Lincoln's ties to Kentucky. (Open June-Aug. daily 8am-6:45pm; Labor Day-Oct. and May 8am-5:45pm; Nov.-April 8am-4:45pm. Free.)

Louisiana

Cross the Mississippi into Louisiana and you'll enter a state markedly different from its Southern neighbors. Here empires, races, and cultures mix in a unique and spicy jambalaya. The battlefields and old forts that liberally pepper the state—some dating back to the original French and Spanish settlers—illustrate the bloody succession of Native American, French, Spanish and American acquisition. The devout Catholicism of early settlers spawned the annual celebrations of Mardi Gras which flavor every February with festivity and parades throughout the state. Louisiana also cooks with Acadians ("Cajuns"), descendants of French Nova Scotians. Exiled by the British in 1755, Cajuns created a culture that contributes the Creole dialect, zydeco music, swampy folklore, and spicy cuisine that enliven the simmering, lazy Southern atmosphere. The African-Americans imported as plantation laborers became an integral part of this most diverse culture. The cosmopolitan ambience and French tolerance in antebellum southern Louisiana combined to produce a black aristocracy unique in the South of the time. Thomas Jefferson struck quite a bargain when he ordered up the Louisiana Territory from Napoleon in 1803 for a cool $15 million, tip included.

PRACTICAL INFORMATION

Capital: Baton Rouge.
Visitor Information: State Travel Office, P.O. Box 94291, Capitol Station, Baton Rouge 70804 (342-7317 or 800-334-8626). Open daily 8am-4pm. **Office of State Parks,** P.O. Box 1111, Baton Rouge 70821. Open Mon.-Fri. 9am-5pm.
Time Zone: Central (1 hr. behind Eastern). **Postal Abbreviation:** LA
Sales Tax: 4%.

ACADIANA

In 1755, the English government expelled French settlers from their homes in New Brunswick. Migrating down the Atlantic coastline and into the Caribbean, the so-called Acadians received a hostile reception; people in Massachusetts, Georgia, and South Carolina made them indentured servants. The Acadians (Cajuns) soon realized that their only hope for freedom lay in reaching the French territory of Louisiana and settling on the Gulf Coast. Many of the present-day inhabitants of St. Martin, Lafayette, Iberia, and St. Mary parishes are descended from these settlers.

Since their exodus began, many factors have threatened Acadian culture with extinction. Louisiana passed laws in the 1920s forcing Acadian schoolchildren to speak English. The oil boom of the past few decades has also endangered the survival of Acadian culture. Oil executives and developers envisioned Lafayette—a center of Acadian life—as the Houston of Louisiana, threatening to flood this small town and its neighbors with mass culture. However, the proud people of southern Louisiana have resisted homogenization, making the state officially bilingual and establishing a state agency to preserve Acadian French in schools and in the media.

Today "Cajun Country" spans the southern portion of the state, from Houma in the east to the Texas border. Mostly bayou and swampland, this unique natural environment has intertwined with Cajun culture. The music and the cuisine especially symbolize the ruggedness of this traditional, family-centered society. This is the place to try some crawfish or to dance the two-step to a fiddle and an accordion.

■■■ LAFAYETTE

The official capital of Acadiana, Lafayette is a perfect place to sample the zydeco music, boiled crawfish, and *pirogues* (carved cypress boats) that characterize Cajun culture. With all of its homey culture and small-town atmosphere, Lafayette is still a sizeable city of almost 100,000. And in addition to the Acadian sites, historical villages, and museums, you can find all the amenities—from natural history museums and zoos to racetracks and chain motels.

Practical Information Lafayette stands at Louisiana's major crossroad. I-10 leads east to New Orleans (130 mi.) and west to Lake Charles (76 mi.); U.S. 90 heads south to New Iberia (20 mi.) and the bayou country; U.S. 167 runs north into central Louisiana. Lafayette also provides a railroad stop for **Amtrak's** "Sunset Limited," linking the city with New Orleans (3 per week, 3 hr., $28), Houston (3 per week, 5 hr., $51), and Los Angeles ($206). The unstaffed station is at 133 E. Grant St., near the bus station; tickets must be purchased in advance through a travel agent. **Greyhound**, 315 Lee Ave. (235-1541), connects Lafayette to New Orleans (7 per day, 3½ hr., $22.50) and Baton Rouge (7 per day, 1 hr., $10), as well as to small towns such as New Iberia (2 per day, ½ hr., $4). Open 24 hrs. The **Lafayette Bus System,** 400 Dorset Rd. (261-8570), runs infrequently and not on Sundays (fare 45¢). You'll need a car to really explore Acadiana and the Gulf Coast bayou country. **Thrifty Rent-a-Car,** 401 E. Pinhook Rd. (237-1282), usually has the best deals ($25 per day for a compact, 100 free mi.; must be 25 with major credit card).

The **post office** is at 1105 Moss St. (269-4800; open Mon.-Fri. 8am-5:30pm, Sat. 8am-12:30pm). Lafayette's **ZIP code** is 70501; the **area code** is 318.

Accommodations and Camping Several motels are a $3 cab fare from the bus station. The close **Travelodge Lafayette,** 1101 W. Pinhook Rd. (234-7402 or 800-255-3050) has large, attractive rooms, cable TV, and a pool. (Singles $35, doubles $38.) Inexpensive chain and local hotels line the **Evangeline Thruway,** just off I-10, including the clean and Taco Bell-convenient **Gateway Motor Inn,** 1314 N.E. Evangeline Thruway (233-2090 or 800-677-1466; singles $24, doubles $26). The **Super 8,** 2224 N. Evangeline Thruway (232-8826 or 800-800-8000), just off I-10, has ample, plain-looking rooms, a pool, and a stunning view of the highway. (Singles $28. Doubles $31.)

Campgrounds include the lakeside **KOA Lafayette** (235-2739), 5 mi. west of town on I-10 (exit 97), with a komplete store and a pool. (Sites $14.50, a few small cabins $25.) Closer to town is **Acadiana Park Campground,** 11201 E. Alexander off Louisiana (234-3838) with shaded grounds, tennis courts, a football/soccer field, and a **nature station** (261-8348) offering trail guides and maps. (Sites $8. Office open Fri. 3-10pm, Sat. 7-11am and 3-7pm, Sun. 7am-noon and 2-5pm.)

Food and Nightlife Cajun restaurants with live music and dancing have popped up all over Lafayette, but tend to be expensive since they cater to the tourist crowd. **Mulates,** 325 Mills Ave. (332-4648), Beaux Bridge, calls itself the most famous Cajun restaurant in the world, and the autographs on the door corroborate its claim. Try the house specialty, Catfish Mulate's, featured on the Euro-Disney World American Cuisine Restaurant in France. Cajun seafood dinners ($10-15). (Open Mon.-Sat. 7am-10:30pm, Sun. 11am-11pm. Music noon-2pm and 7:30-10pm.) In downtown Lafayette, visit **Chris' Po'Boys,** 4 locations including 1941 Moss St. (237-1095) and 631 Jefferson St. (234-1696), which (not surprisingly) offers po'boys ($4-5) and seafood platters (open Mon.-Fri. 11am-6pm). **Prejeans,** 3480 U.S. 167 N. (896-3247), dances in as another Cajun restaurant (dinners $8-12) with savory food and nightly Acadian entertainment at 7pm. Check out the 14-ft. alligator by the entrance. (Open Mon.-Thurs. 11am-9:30pm, Fri.-Sat. 11am-11pm, Sun. 11am-10pm.)

ACADIANA: NEW IBERIA

Pick up a copy of *The Times,* available at restaurants and gas stations all over town or at the **Lafayette Parish Tourist Information bureau,** 1400 Evangeline Thruway, to find out about what's going down this week (open Mon.-Fri. 8:30am-5pm, Sat.-Sun. 9am-5pm). Considering its size and location, Lafayette has a surprising variety of after-hours entertainment, including **Randol's,** 2320 Kaliste Saloon Rd. (981-7080), which romps with live music nightly. Doubles as a restaurant. (Open Sun.-Thurs. 5-10pm, Fri.-Sat. 5-10:30pm.) Lafayette kicks off spring and fall weekends with **Downtown Alive!,** a series of free concerts featuring everything from new wave to Cajun and zydeco (all concerts Fri. at 5:30pm; call 268-5566 for info). The **Festival International de Louisiane** (232-8086) in late April blends the music, visual arts, and cuisine of this region into a francophone tribute to southwestern Louisiana.

Sights and Activities Full of music, crafts, and food, **Vermilionville,** 1600 Surrey St. (233-4077 or 800-992-2968), is an historic bayou attraction that educates as it entertains. This re-creation of an Acadian settlement invites guests to dance the two-step, ride an Acadian skiff, make a cornhusk doll, and more. (Open daily 9am-5pm. $8, seniors $6.50, ages 6-18 $5.) A folk-life museum of restored 19th-century homes, **Acadian Village,** 200 Greenleaf Rd. (981-2364 or 800-962-9133), 10 mi. from the tourist center, offers another view of Cajun life. Take U.S. 167 north, turn right on Ridge Rd., left on Mouton, and then follow the signs. (Open daily 10am-5pm. $5, seniors $4, kids $2.50.) The **Lafayette Museum,** 1122 Lafayette St. (234-2208), exhibits heirlooms, antiques, and Mardi Gras costumes. (Open Tues.-Sat. 9am-5pm, Sun. 3-5pm. $3, seniors $2, students and kids $1.)

Built on the edge of the Atchafalaya Swamp, Lafayette links up with Baton Rouge via a triumph of modern engineering. The **Atchafalaya Freeway** is a 32-mi. long bridge over the bayous. Get closer to the elements by embarking upon one of the **Atchafalaya Basin Swamp Tours** (228-8567), in the nearby town of Henderson. The captain explains the harvesting of crawfish and the construction of the inter-state on quavering swamp mud. (Tours in English and French at 10am, and 1, 3, and 5pm. $7, kids $4.) Alternately, the **Acadiana Park Nature Station and Trails,** E. Alexander St. (235-6181), snakes through 50 acres of bottomland forest. At the station itself find demonstrations on the environment, lectures, and slide shows. (Open Mon.-Fri. 9am-5pm, Sat.-Sun. 11am-3pm. Free, as nature should be.)

Don't lose sight of the trees for the forest. Be sure not to miss **St. John's Cathedral Oak,** in the yard of St. John's Cathedral, 914 St. John St. This 450 yr. old tree—one of the largest in the U.S.—shades the entire lawn with its gargantuan, spidery limbs that create a spread of 210 ft. The weight of a single limb is estimated at 72 tons. When that bough breaks, boy, does that cradle fall. Free. Climb it.

If you can't quite swing the tree-climbing thing, you can watch the experts at the **Zoo of Acadiana** (837-4325), 4 mi. south of Broussard on Rte. 182, known locally as "the little zoo that could." (Open daily 9am-5pm. $4, kids $2.) While the zoo tends to its live animals, the **Lafayette Natural History Museum and Planetar-ium,** 637 Girard Park Dr. (268-5544), pays homage to their ancestors, their environ-ments, and the cosmos itself (open Mon., Wed., Fri. 9am-5pm, Tues. 9am-9pm, Sat.-Sun. 1pm-5pm; $2.50, kids $1, families $5).

The newest addition to Lafayette races to the top with fast-paced thorough-bred racing. **New Evangeline Downs** (896-7223 or 800-256-1234), on I-49, U.S. 167N, opens its gates Mon.-Fri. at 7pm (admission $1, clubhouse $2). Call for more info.

■■■ NEW IBERIA AND SOUTHCENTRAL LOUISIANA

While oil magnates invaded Lafayette in the '70s and '80s, trying to build the town into a Louisiana oil-business center, New Iberia kept right on about its daily busi-ness. Although its attractions are less numerous, this small bayou town with pictur-esque streets and quiet neighborhoods is a gem worth discovering.

Practical Information New Iberia crouches 21 mi. southeast of Lafayette on U.S. 90. **Amtrak** (800-872-7245) serves New Iberia between New Orleans and Lafayette. To: Lafayette ($6); New Orleans ($27). **Greyhound** (364-8571) pulls into town at 101 Perry St. Buses wander to: Morgan City ($10), New Orleans ($20), and Lafayette ($3) three times per day. The **Iberia Parish Tourist Commission**, 2690 Center St. at the intersection with Rte. 14 (365-8246), offers city maps for $1 and free pamphlets (open daily 9am-5pm). The **post office** is at 817 E. Dale St. (364-4568; open daily 8am-4:30pm). The **ZIP code** is 70560; the **area code** is 318.

Sights and Activities While other plantations made their fortunes off cotton, most plantations in southern Louisiana grew sugarcane. Today most of these stay in private hands, but **Shadows on the Teche**, 317 E. Main St. (369-6446), is open to the public. A Southern aristocrat saved the crumbling mansion, built in 1831, from neglect after the Civil War. (Open daily 9am-4:30pm. $4, kids $3.)

Seven mi. away is **Avery Island**, on Rte. 329 off Rte. 90, actually a salt dome. Avery houses the world-famous **Tabasco Pepper Sauce factory**, where the McIlhenny family has produced the famous condiment for nearly a century. Guided tours include a sample taste. *OOOOOeeeeeee!!!!* (Open Mon.-Fri. 9am-4pm, Sat. 9am-noon. Free. 50¢ toll to enter the island.) Nearby crawl the **Jungle Gardens** (369-6243), 250 acres developed in the 19th century that include waterways, a lovely wisteria arch, camellia gardens, Chinese bamboo, alligators, and an 800-year-old statue of the Buddha. The jungle's sanctuary for herons and egrets helped to save the snowy egret from extinction. This elegant bird, once hunted for the long plumes it grows during mating season, now nests in the gardens from February to mid-summer. (Open daily 9am-6pm. $5, kids $3.50.) For a unique look at swamp and bayou wildlife, take an **Airboat Tour** (229-4457) of Lake Fausse Point and the surrounding area. (Tickets $10.)

Live Oak Gardens, 5505 Rip Van Winkle Rd. (365-3332), may seem like just another ancient Victorian house with sprawling colorful gardens, but its beauty shrouds a mysterious and bizarre history. Little more than a decade ago, while drilling for oil, a rig apparently ruptured a 1300-ft.-deep salt mine which subsequently devoured the entire lake, several barges, numerous buildings, and historic gardens in a whirlpool ¼-mi. in diameter. Miraculously, no one was killed. A canal which flowed from the lake to the Gulf of Mexico reversed its course and Gulf waters filled the rest of the mine and the lake. Remarkably, several barges resurfaced shortly thereafter. Today the peaceful gardens and scenic boat tours belie this hectic past. (Open daily 9am-5pm. Admission $8.50, kids $5.)

The best stuff to see in this region, however, is Acadiana's lush wilderness, a subtropical environment of marsh, bottomland hardwoods, and stagnant backwater bayous. The **Atchafalaya Delta Wildlife Area** lies at the mouth of the Atchafalaya River in St. Mary Parish. The preserve encompasses bayous, potholes, low and high marsh, and dry ground. Rails, snipes, coot, and gallinules thrive here. Access it by boat launch from Morgan City near the Bayou Boeuf locks. Primitive **campsites** are available. **Attakapas Wildlife Area,** in southern St. Martin and Iberia Parishes, lies 20 mi. northwest of Morgan City and 10 mi. northeast of Franklin. Flat swampland comprises most of this hauntingly beautiful area, which includes a large amount of raised land used as a refuge by animals during flooding. In Attakapas cypress, tupelo, oak, maple, and hackberry grow on the high ground, and a cornucopia of swamp plants and animals slog about in the wetlands. Squirrel, deer, and rabbit hunting is popular here. The area can be reached by boat; public launches leave from Morgan City on Rte. 70. No camping allowed. Bring a LOT of bug repellent.

■■■ BATON ROUGE

Owing its name to Native Americans who, as early as 8000BC delineated their tribal hunting boundaries with a "red stick," Baton Rouge later hosted French explorers and Acadian communities. But until the 1800s, Baton Rouge was little more than a backwoods, (red-)stick-in-the-mud village; at that time, New Orleans was Louisiana's capital. But a group of evangelical North Louisiana politicians, concerned that the state government was wallowing in a hotbed of debauchery in the "Big Easy," stuck a provision in the new state constitution mandating that the state capital be at least 60 mi. from New Orleans. Fun-loving legislators responded by drawing a 60-mi. circle on their state map in order to find the nearest legal human settlement that could serve as the capital city, and picked Baton Rouge.

Caught between two traditions, Baton Rouge fuses its aggressive Mississippi River industry with a quieter plantation country, yielding a hybrid culture alive with trade, historical museums and homes. Its research university, a progressive music scene and a thriving gay community in Spanish Town attest to a cosmopolitan temperament enriched by eclectic city architecture and a rambunctious and fascinating political history. Baton Rouge served as the home of "Kingfish" Huey P. Long—a Depression-era populist demagogue who, until his assassination, was considered Franklin D. Roosevelt's biggest political threat. Current governor Edwin Edwards, a flamboyant Cajun Democrat, survived two federal indictments and regained the governorship for a third time by defeating "ex-"Ku Klux Klansman David Duke.

PRACTICAL INFORMATION

Emergency: 911.

Visitor Information: Baton Rouge Area Visitors Center (382-3595), 1st floor of the State Capitol, off I-110 on U.S. 61, west to 3rd St. and north to the sky-scraping capitol. Pick up info here not only on Baton Rouge, but the rest of Louisiana as well.

Greyhound: 1253 Florida Blvd. (343-4891), at 13th St. A short walk from downtown. Unsafe area at night. To: New Orleans (11 per day, 2 hr., $14) and Lafayette (7 per day, 1 hr., $10). Open 24 hrs.

Public Transport: Capital City Transportation, 336-0821. Terminal at 22nd and Florida Blvd. Buses run Mon.-Sat. 6:30am-6:30pm. Service to LSU decent, otherwise unreliable and/or infrequent. Fare $1, transfers 25¢.

Help Lines: Crisis Intervention/Suicide Prevention Center, 924-3900. **Rape Crisis,** 383-7273. Both open 24 hrs.

Post Office: 750 Florida Blvd. (381-0713), off River Rd. Open Mon.-Fri. 8:30am-4:30pm, Sat. 9-11am. **ZIP code:** 70821.

Area Code: 504.

The state capitol sits on the east bank of the river; the city spreads eastward. The heart of downtown, directly south of the capitol, runs until **Government Street. Highland Road** leads south from downtown directly into Louisiana State University.

ACCOMMODATIONS, FOOD, AND NIGHTLIFE

Most budget accommodations snuggle and cuddle outside of town along east-west Florida Blvd., (U.S. 190), or north-south Airline Hwy. (U.S. 61). **Louisiana State University (LSU)** provides cheap accommodations at their on-campus hotel run out of Pleasant Hall (387-0297). Take bus #7 ("University") from North Blvd. behind the Old State Capitol. There is a flat rate of $38 for standard rooms that cover the heads of about four people; for more room try the concierge ($45) or the suite ($55). **Motel 6,** 9901 Airport Hwy. (924-2130) has cookie-cutter rooms. (Singles $28, doubles $38.) The **Alamo Plaza Hotel Courts,** 4243 Florida Blvd. (924-7231), has spacious rooms (some with kitchenettes) in the less safe downtown area. Take bus #6 ("Sherwood Forest") east on Florida Blvd. from the Greyhound station. (Singles $20-24. Doubles $25-28.) The **KOA Campground,** 7628 Vincent Rd. (664-7281), is 12 mi. east of Baton Rouge (Denham Springs exit off I-12). Well-maintained sites include clean facilities and pool. (Sites $12.50 for 2 people, with hookup $14.)

Near LSU on (and off) **Highland Rd.,** you can find all the sustenance you need: food, coffee, and the occasional beer. **Louie's Café,** 209 W. State (246-8221), is a 24-hr. grill that has been lauded in *Rolling Stone;* it's famous for stir-fried vegetable omelettes served all the time ($5). On the corner of Chimes and Highland behind Louie's, is local favorite **The Bayou** (346-1765), the site of the bar scene in *Sex, Lies, and Videotape.* Free pool 5-8pm and drink select longnecks for 99¢. (Open Mon.-Sat. 2pm-2am.) **Highland Coffees,** 3350 Highland (336-9773), will pick you up with its roasted-on-the-premises coffees and chill you out with its free reading material.

Downtown, you can't miss the **Frostop Drive-In,** 402 Government (344-1179); a giant frothy root beer mug spinning on a post outside welcomes diners, and a Wurlitzer jukebox entertains them. Try the delicious root beer floats ($2) and sandwiches ($1-3). (Open Mon.-Fri. 9am-4pm, Sat. 10am-4pm.) For a power breakfast or lunch at a grassroots price, join the state lawmakers at the **House of Representatives Dining Hall,** outside the state capitol. Entrees $2-3. (Open daily 7-10:30am and 11am-2pm.)

SIGHTS

The most prominent building in Baton Rouge is also the first sight you should visit. In a move reminiscent of Ramses II, Huey Long ordered the unique **Louisiana State Capitol** (342-7317), a magnificent modern skyscraper, built in a mere 14 months in 1931-32. The front lobby alone merits a visit, but visitors should also go to the free 27th-floor observation deck. (Open daily 8am-4pm.) One of the most interesting in the U.S., the building attests to the staying power of Long's monumental personality. Look for the bullet holes in a back corridor near the plaque indicating the site of his assassination, the display case full of newspaper clippings, and graphic paintings and photos; the place of his burial is under the statue in front. (½-hr. tours every hr. on the ½ hr.) Right across the lawn fires the **Old Arsenal Museum,** whose smoky smell originates from the powder barrels and other wartime equipment on display. (Open Mon.-Sat. 10am-4pm, Sun. 1-4pm. $1, kids 50¢, seniors free.) You can also tour the great white **Governor's Mansion** by appointment; call Betty George at 342-5855 between 8am and 4pm. The **Old State Capitol,** at River Rd. and North Blvd., an eccentric Gothic Revival castle, is closed until spring 1994 for renovations. Check at the visitors center for opening date. (Open Tues.-Sat. 9am-4:30pm.) Just south of downtown, the **Beauregard District** boasts typically ornate antebellum homes. Walk down North Blvd. from the Old State Capitol to the visitors center to take in the beauty of this neighborhood.

Just a block away from the Old State Capitol on River Rd. floats the **Riverside Museum** of the Louisiana Arts and Science Center, 100 S. River Rd. (344-LASC). Climb on the old steam engine and train cars parked next door. The museum also has a varied collection of sculpture, photographs, and paintings by contemporary Louisiana artists. (Open Tues.-Fri. 10am-3pm, Sat. 10am-4pm, Sun. 1-4pm. $2, seniors, students, and kids 75¢.) The museum runs the **Old Governor's Mansion,** the chief executive's residence from 1930-1963, at North Blvd. and St. Charles St. The mansion houses a planetarium and various art exhibits. (Open Sat. 10am-4pm, Sun. 1-4pm. $2, seniors, students, and kids $1.)

The **LSU Rural Life Museum,** 6200 Burden Lane (765-2437), off Perkins Rd., re-creates everyday rural life in pre-industrial Louisiana. The authentically furnished shops, cabins, and storage houses adjoin meticulously kept rose and azalea gardens. (Open Mon.-Fri. 8:30am-4pm. $3, kids $2. $1 donation for a guide book.)

Tour the harbor in the **Samuel Clemens** steamboat (381-9606), which departs from Florida Blvd. at the river for one-hour cruises. (Tours April-Aug. daily at 10am, noon, and 2pm; Sept.-Dec., March Wed.-Sun. at 10am, noon, and 2pm. $6, kids $4.) Open for inspection, the *U.S.S. Kidd* (342-1942), a World War II destroyer, throws militant tantrums on the river just outside the **Louisiana Naval War Memorial**

Museum featuring ship models and the Louisiana Military Veterans Hall of Honor. (Open daily 9am-5pm. Ship and museum admission $5, kids $3.50. Ship only $3, kids $2.) Alongside the ship museum, the **Louisiana Memorial Plaza** commemorates the deaths of Louisianians from the Revolutionary War to the Persian Gulf. Baton Rouge commemorates life as well as death with the annual **Blues Festival** (800-LA-ROUGE) on Labor Day weekend.

Within the varied cultural centers of the state, the Baton Rouge region is known as "Plantation Country." For a taste of these stately old homes in the downtown area, visit the well-restored **Magnolia Mound Plantation,** 2161 Nicholson Dr. (343-4955), the only plantation on the regular bus line. (Open Tues.-Sat. 10am-4pm, Sun. 1-4pm; last tour at 3:30pm. $3.50, seniors $2.50, students $1.50, children 75¢.) If just one plantation isn't enough to satisfy your thirst for 19th century luxury, **St. Francisville** is a mere 25 mi. to the north on U.S. 61. Among its notable estates is the **Oakley House,** where John Audubon painted his famous depictions of nature, on LA Rte. 965. Call the **West Feliciana Historical Society Museum** (504-635-6330) for more info and perfect maps (open Mon.-Sat. 9am-4pm, Sun. 1-4pm).

■■■ NEW ORLEANS

New Orleans is a country unto itself. Once ruled by France and Spain and drawing settlers from all over the world to its rich port, the "Crescent City" displays a multicultural heritage in which Spanish courtyards, Victorian verandas, Acadian jambalaya, Caribbean Gumbo and French beignets mingle, mix and are juxtaposed. Don't try to place the accent of its people—it's a singular combination found nowhere else. Similarly unique to the city, New Orleans jazz fuses traditional African rhythms with modern brass, achieving international fame. Architectural styles ranging from old Spanish and French to ultra- and post-modern rub shoulders downtown.

In the 19th century, the red-light district known as "Storyville" flared. Today, New Orleans is still a city that loves to party. Come late February there's no escaping the month-long celebration of Mardi Gras, the apotheosis of the city's already festive atmosphere. Anxious to accrue as much sin as spirit and flesh will allow before Lent, the "city that care forgot" promenades, shuffles, sings, and swigs until midnight of Mardi Gras itself. Afterwards, the soulful melodies of jazz play on, comforting those who have forsaken drunken cavorting for the next 40 long and Lenten days.

PRACTICAL INFORMATION

Emergency: 911.

Visitor Information: To plan your vacation before you leave home, write or call the very helpful **New Orleans/Louisiana Tourist Center,** 529 St. Ann, Jackson Square (568-5661), in the French Quarter. Free city and walking tour maps. Open daily 10am-6pm. **New Orleans Tourist Convention Commission,** 1520 Sugar Bowl Dr., New Orleans, LA 70112 (566-5033), on the main floor of the Superdome. Open Mon.-Fri. 8:30am-5pm. **Tourist Information Service,** 525-5000.

Traveler's Aid: 846 Barone St. (525-8726), at the **YMCA.** Assists stranded people by providing temporary shelter, food, and counseling. Open Mon.-Fri. 8am-4pm.

Airport: Moisant International Airport (464-0831), 15 mi. west of the city. Served by the major domestic airlines as well as larger Latin American carriers. **Louisiana Transit Authority** (737-9611; office open 4am-6pm) runs between the airport and downtown at Elk and Tulane every 15-25 min. for $1.10 in exact change (travel time approx. 45 min. to downtown). Pick-up in front of Hertz. Airport limousine to downtown hotels $8, cab $21.

Amtrak: (528-1610 or 800-872-7245) at Union Passenger Terminal, 1001 Loyola Ave., a 10-min. walk to Canal St. via Elk. To: Memphis (1 per day, 8 hr., $75) and Houston (3 per week, 8 hr., $72). Open 24 hrs.

Greyhound: (525-9371), also at Union Passenger Terminal. To: Baton Rouge (2 hr., $14, $9.50 with college ID); Memphis (11 hr., $57); Houston (9 hr., $44); and Atlanta ($61). Tickets cheaper if bought two weeks in advance. Open 24 hrs.

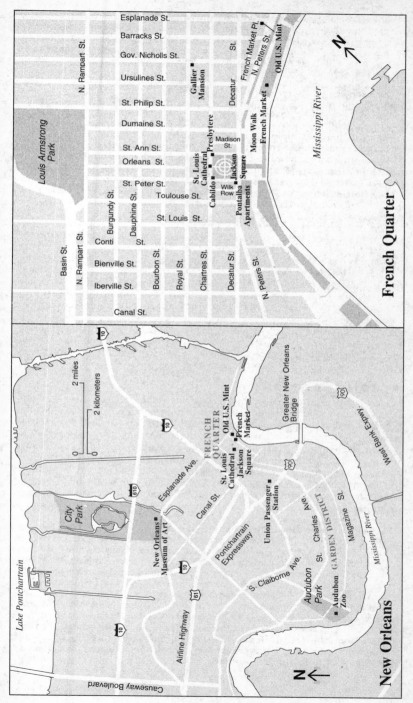

NEW ORLEANS

French Quarter

Esplanade St.
Barracks St.
Gov. Nicholls St.
Ursulines St.
St. Philip St.
Dumaine St.
St. Ann St.
Orleans St.
St. Peter St.
Toulouse St.
St. Louis St.
Conti St.
Bienville St.
Iberville St.
Canal St.

N. Rampart St.
Basin St.
N. Rampart St.
Burgundy St.
Dauphine St.
Bourbon St.
Royal St.
Chartres St.
Decatur St.
N. Peters St.

Louis Armstrong Park

Gallier Mansion
Decatur St.
French Market Pl.
N. Peters St.
Old U.S. Mint
Presbytere
Madison St.
Moon Walk
French Market
St. Louis Cathedral
Cabildo
Jackson Square
Wilk Row
Pontalba Apartments

Mississippi River

New Orleans

N

Lake Pontchartrain

City Park

New Orleans Museum of Art

Esplanade Ave.

Canal St.

Pontchartrain Expressway

Union Passenger Station

S. Claiborne Ave.

Airline Highway

Causeway Boulevard

FRENCH QUARTER
Old U.S. Mint
French Market
St. Louis Cathedral
Jackson Square

Greater New Orleans Bridge

West Bank Expwy.

St. Charles Ave.
GARDEN DISTRICT
Magazine St.

Audubon Park
Audubon Zoo

Mississippi River

2 miles
2 kilometers

NEW ORLEANS

Public Transport: Regional Transit Authority (RTA), Plaza Tower, 101 Dauphin St., 4th floor (569-2700), at Canal St. Bus schedules and transit info. Office open Mon.-Fri. 8:30am-5pm. Phone line provides 24-hr. route information. All buses pass by Canal St., at the edge of the French Quarter. Major buses and street-cars run 24 hrs. Fare $1, transfers 10¢, disabled and elderly 40¢ and 2¢. 1- and 3-day passes are also available.

Taxi: United Cabs (522-9771). **Checker Yellow Cabs** (943-2411). **Classic Cabs** (835-CABS). Base fare $1.70, each additional mi. $1.

Car Rental: Budget Car Rental, 1317 Canal (467-2277), and 6 other locations. $37 per day, $33 weekends. 100 free mi. Open daily 7:30am-5:30pm. Airport branch only closed 1-5am. Must be 25 with credit card. Reservations suggested.

Bike Rental: Michael's, 618 Frenchman (945-9505), a few blocks west of the Quarter. $3.50 per hr., $12.50 per day. Weekly rates. Open Mon.-Sat. 10am-7pm, Sun. 10am-5pm. Must have major credit card for deposit.

Help Lines: Gay Counseling Line, 522-5815. Usually operates 5-11pm. **Crisis Line,** 523-2673. Open 24 hrs. **Rape Hotline,** 483-8888.

Post Office: 701 Loyola Ave. (589-1111 or 589-1112), near the Union Passenger Terminal. Open Mon.-Fri. 8:30am-4:30pm, Sat. 8:30am-noon. **ZIP code:** 70113.

Area Code: 504.

It's easy to get lost in New Orleans even though it is fairly small. The main streets of the city follow the curve in the river. There are many one-way streets, and drivers must sometimes make U-turns to cross intersections. The major tourist area is the small **French Quarter (Vieux Carré),** bounded by the Mississippi River, **Canal Street, Esplanade Avenue,** and **Rampart Street.** Streets in the French Quarter follow a grid pattern; traveling there on foot is easy. The **Garden District** is west of downtown. Buses to all parts of the city pass by Canal St. at the edge of the Quarter.

Parts of New Orleans are unsafe, particularly the tenement areas directly to the north of the French Quarter and those directly northwest of Lee Circle. Even quaint-looking side streets in the Quarter can be dangerous at night—stick to busy, well-lit thoroughfares and try to look as little like a tourist as possible. Take a cab back to your lodgings when returning late at night from the Quarter.

ACCOMMODATIONS

Finding inexpensive yet decent accommodations in the French Quarter is as difficult as finding a sober citizen on Mardi Gras. But then, the French Quarter is the only happenin' place in the city. Several **hostels** dot the area, as do **bed and breakfasts** near the Garden District, which often cater to the young and almost penniless.

About the only way to get accommodations for Mardi Gras is to reserve them a year in advance. **Jazzfest** in late April also makes budget rooms scarce. Pay close attention to warnings under individual lodgings regarding the safety of its location; avoid areas where you feel at all uncomfortable, and do not walk around alone at night, anywhere in this city. During these peak times, proprietors will rent out any extra space—be sure you know what you're paying for.

Marquette House New Orleans International Hostel (HI/AYH), 2253 Carondelet St. (523-3014), is actually several smaller houses congregating around a large, well-lit Victorian home with two dining rooms, a fully equipped kitchen, locker room, and a couple of study lounges. Very clean, nice furnishings and bathrooms. Laundry room open 11am-11pm. No alcohol permitted; smoking only in the courtyard; no curfew. Exceptionally quiet for a hostel. $12, nonmembers $15. Private doubles $27-30. Private apartments $39-45. Linens $2.50. Key deposit $5.

India House, 124 S. Lopez St. (821-1904), entertains as it accommodates. The artistically decorated rooms may lack luxury and order, but if you've come to New Orleans for its bawdy reputation, this bohemian haunt is party central. The common room, kitchen, and dining areas are supplemented with a bar/coffee shop and homemade pool. $10 per night. Key deposit $5, free linens, no curfew or lockout. Best to walk in groups at night.

Longpre House (RNA), 1726 Prytania St. (501-4440), a block off the streetcar route, a 20-min. walk from the Quarter, attracts travelers because of its relaxed atmosphere in a 150-year-old house. Free coffee. Check-in 8am-10pm. Dorm rooms $10 per person. Singles $35. Doubles $50.

Cairo Pete's, 4220 Canal St. (488-0341 or 484-7749), offers the cheapest accommodations in New Orleans. TV room, kitchen, patio. No curfew. $8 per night.

Prytania Inn, 1415 Prytania St. (566-1515), includes 3 restored 19th century homes about 5 blocks from each other. The owners/proprietors have lovingly furnished each room with antiques, including an elegant and airy breakfast room (breakfast $5, served Mon.-Fri. 8-10am, Sat.-Sun. until 10:30am). The more than reasonable prices, the multilingual staff (German, French, Italian, Spanish, and Japanese), and the historic beauty attract the young and old, international and local travelers. Singles $30-50, doubles $40-69; rooms are discounted in off-season. Book in advance for the peaks.

St. Charles Guest House, 1748 Prytania St. (523-6556), in a serene neighborhood near the Garden District and St. Charles streetcar. Free breakfast. Lovely pool and grounds. Backpackers' singles $25; doubles $35; 2 double beds $65. Ask about $12.50 student rate for groups of 3 or more.

Hotel LaSalle, 1113 Canal St. (523-5831 or 800-521-9450), 4 blocks from Bourbon St. downtown. Attractive lobby with coffee around the clock on an antique sideboard. Ample rooms and free movies. Laundry 50-75¢. Singles $28, with bath $44. Doubles $32, with bath $47. Reservations recommended.

Old World Inn, 1330 Prytania St. (566-1330). Multi-colored carpeting and walls covered with paintings create a slightly tacky but homey atmosphere. Complimentary continental breakfast. Singles from $30. Doubles from $40.

Cheap motels line the seedy and sometimes scary Tulane Ave. off I-10. Public buses run along the length of the street, but a car is recommended for safety. One of the best choices is **Rose Inn,** 3522 Tulane Ave. (484-7611), exit 232 off I-10, 4 blocks from S. Carrollton, with older but spacious rooms. Lone travelers and women may feel uncomfortable. Pool. Extra charge for phone. (Singles $25. Doubles $28.)

CAMPING

The several campgrounds near New Orleans are tough to reach via public transportation. Try to enjoy Louisiana's beautiful forests, lakes, and bayous anyway, if only to escape the French Quarter crowds. Bring insect repellent and baking soda (for a poultice); the mosquitoes are voracious. Check out the **Golden Pelican passes** available at state parks, which allow you to stay in state campgrounds for $6 per night ($30 for Louisianians, $50 for others).

Bayou Segnette State Park (736-7140), Westbank Expressway at Drake (flashing yellow light), 7 mi. from the French Quarter. RTA transport available. Cabins on the bayou $65 for up to 8 people. Campsites with water, electricity $12.

KOA West, 11129 Jefferson Hwy., River Ridge 70123 (467-1792), off I-10. RTA bus transport available. Pool, laundry facilities. Full-hookup sites $26 for 2 people. Shuttle to French Quarter $3 each way.

St. Bernard State Park, P.O. Box 534, Violet 70092 (682-2101), 14 mi. southeast of New Orleans. Take Rte. 47 south and go right on Rte. 39. Nearest public transport to New Orleans ½ mi. away. Registration to 8pm, weekends 10pm. Sites $12.

Parc d'Orleans II, 10910 Chef Menteur Hwy. (242-6176; 800-535-2598 outside LA), 3 mi. east of the junction of I-10 and U.S. 90 (Chef Menteur Hwy.). Near public transport into the city. Pool, showers, and laundry facilities. Sites from $17.

FOOD

You will find more restaurants per capita in New Orleans than in any major city in the world outside of Paris. Acadian refugees, Spaniards, Italians, ex-slaves and Native Americans have all contributed to the hot, spicy, Cajun culinary style that—like a good stew—has a bit of everything thrown in. Here, Cajun cult members gather to worship the "holy trinity": bell peppers, onions, and celery. **Jambalaya**—a jumble of rice, shrimp, oysters, and ham or chicken mixed with spices—and the African stew-like gumbo grace practically every menu in New Orleans. A southern breakfast of grits, eggs, bacon, and corn bread will satisfy even the biggest of eaters. Also, sample the regional delights: red beans and rice, seafood **po'boys** (a french-bread sandwich filled with fried oysters and shrimp), and shrimp or crawfish **étouffé**. And you may *not* leave New Orleans without dining on **beignets** and **café au lait** at the world-famous, 1862 **Café du Monde** (see below).

If the eats in the Quarter prove too trendy, touristy, or tough on your budget, take a jaunt down **Magazine St.**, where coffee shops, antique stores, and book fairs abound, or hop on the St. Charles streetcar to the **Tulane** area for some late-night grub and collegiate character.

Cool off in the summer months and "air condition your tummy" with a snow-blitz sundae from **Hansen's Snow-Blitz Sweet Shop**, 481 Tchoupitoulas St. (891-9788) where if the 50¢- or $1-size cups can't quench your need for a "Hansen's fix," then trash-can-size servings are available for only $200. Always expect a line. (Open Tues.-Fri. and Sun. 3-9pm.) Indulge in **Creole pralines** (90¢); some of the best and cheapest bake at **Laura's Candies**, 600 Conti (525-3880) and 155 Royal St. (525-3886; open daily 9am-7pm). The **French Market,** between Decatur and N. Peters St. on the east side of the French Quarter, sells fresh vegetables. The grocery stores on Decatur St. have the rest of the fixings you'll need for a picnic.

French Quarter

Acme Oyster House, 724 Iberville (522-5973). Slurp fresh oysters shucked before your eyes (6 for $3.75, 12 for $6.50) or sit at the red checkered tables for a good ol' po'boy. Open Mon.-Sat. 11am-10pm, Sun. noon-7pm.

Croissant d'Or, 617 Ursuline St. (524-4663). In an historic building that was the first ice cream parlor in New Orleans. Delicious, reasonably-priced French pastries (75¢-$2) that locals swear by. Courtyard seating. Open daily 7am-5pm.

Mama Rosa's, 616 N. Rampart (523-5546), on the edge of the French Quarter. Reputed to be the best pizza in New Orleans (10" cheese $7.25, with everything, $10.50). Also serves heaping salads and gumbo ($3-5). Open Tues.-Thurs. 10:30am-10:30pm, Fri.-Sun. 10:30am-11:30pm.

Quarter Scene Restaurant, 900 Dumaine (522-6533). This elegant cornerside cafe serves delicious salads and seafood and pasta entrees ($6-13). A tasty surprise is the *Dumaine* ($4), a peanut butter and banana sandwich topped with nuts and honey. Open 24 hrs., except Tues. closes at 11:30pm, reopening Wed. at 8:30am.

Café du Monde (587-0835), French Market at the intersection of Decatur and St. Ann St. The consummate people-watching paradise since 1862. Drink *café au lait* and down perfectly prepared hot *beignets* with powdered sugar (3 for $.75). Open 24 hrs.

Outside The Quarter

Mother's Restaurant, 401 Poydras (523-9656), 4 blocks southwest of Bourbon St. Yo Mama has been serving up unparalleled crawfish *étouffé* ($7.50) and seafood po'boys ($5-8) to locals for almost half a century. Be daring and try the crawfish or shrimp *étouffé* omelette ($8). Tremendous entrees $4.25-15. Open Mon.-Sat. 5am-10pm, Sun. 7am-10pm.

All Natural, 5517 Magazine St. (891-2651). This friendly neighborhood health store cooks up fabulous and healthy sandwiches, pizzas, and hot specials ($3-5). Munch on the garlic pita pizza or the Live Food Sandwich at an outdoor table and chat with the young staff about the local music scene, et al. Probably the only place in the world serving vegetarian jambalaya ($5 with salad). Open Mon.-Sat. 10am-7pm, Sun. 10am-5pm.

P.J.'s (482-6437), across the street, soothes the throat and the spirit. Sit, read, drink coffee, sit, have a pastry, sit. Pastries under $2. Open Mon.-Fri. 7am-11pm, Sat.-Sun. 8am-11pm. Sit.

Mais Oui, 5908 Magazine (897-1540). But yes! This is home cooking at its best. Delicious corn bread and gumbo. Entrees run $5-10. Menu changes daily. Bring your own wine; $1 corkage fee. No credit cards or personal checks accepted. Open Mon.-Fri. 11:30am-2:45pm and 5:30-8:45pm, Sat. 5:30-8:45pm.

Franky and Johnny's, 321 Arabella (899-9146), southwest of downtown towards Tulane off Tchoupitoulas. Good seafood and po'boys served in a fun and lively atmosphere. Try the excellent gumbo ($2.50-4). Open Mon.-Thurs. 11am-11pm, Fri.-Sat. 11am-midnight, Sun. 11am-10pm.

Camellia Grill, 626 S. Carrollton Ave. (866-9573). Take the St. Charles streetcar away from the Quarter to the Tulane area. One of the finest diners in America, complete with friendly napkins and cloth servers, or vice-versa. Try the chef's special omelette ($5.50) or partake of the tasty pecan pie. Expect a wait on weekend mornings. Open Sun.-Wed. 8am-1am, Thurs.-Sat. 8am-2am.

O'Henry's, 634 S. Carrollton, next door to Camellia Grill (866-9741), serves food and spirits in a darker, bar-like atmosphere complete with peanut shells on the floor. The nachos are huge and delicious ($5). Most items under $6. Open Sun.-Wed. 11am-midnight, Thurs.-Sat. 11am-2am.

SIGHTS

French Quarter

Allow yourself *at least* a full day (some take a lifetime) in the Quarter. The oldest section of the city, it is famous for its ornate wrought-iron balconies, French, Spanish, and uniquely New Orleans architectures and joyous atmosphere. Known as the **Vieux Carré,** meaning Old Square, the historic district of New Orleans offers interesting used book and record stores, museums, and shops that pawn off ceramic masks and cheap t-shirts to innocent tourists. Walk through the residential section down **Dumaine Street** to escape the more crowded area near the river. Stop in at a neighborhood bar. Tourists are taken in stride here, and you should feel welcome.

North of the Quarter, one block past the **Esplanade** in the **Marigny,** New Orleans' large gay community lives, eats, parties, and reads. Stop in at **Faubourg Marigny Books** to find out what's happening and where to go. (Open Mon.-Fri. 11am-8pm, Sat.10am-6pm., Sun noon-6pm.)

The heart of the Quarter beats at **Jackson Square** whose center boasts a bronze equestrian statue of General Andrew Jackson, victor of the Battle of New Orleans. While the square boogies with artists, mimes, musicians, psychics, and magicians, the **St. Louis Cathedral** presides at its head. Across the street, the **Jackson Brewery Rivermarket** (586-8021; open Sun.-Thurs. 10am-9pm, Fri.-Sat. 10am-10pm) offers fast food and a modern shopping complex, which, though very nice, doesn't hold a candle to the bundles of flea market paraphernalia, jewelry, and leather goods amassed at the **French Market** (522-2621).

The rich cultural history of the French Quarter has made it a National Historic Park, and free tours and interpretive programs are given by the **Jean Lafitte National Historical Park,** 916-918 North Peters (589-2636), located in the back section of the French Market at Decatur and St. Phillip St. Free 90-min. tours at 10:30am, 11:30am, and 2:30pm emphasize various aspects of New Orleans' cultural, ethnic, and environmental history. Because some tours require reservations and fill up quickly, call ahead for specific info.

The Park Service no longer conducts tours of the city cemeteries—these areas have been deemed too unsafe. Ironically, visitors who are interested in touring in the dark graveyards are left with no guide except the **New Orleans Historic Voodoo Museum,** 724 Dumaine St. (523-7685), which offers tour packages including graveyards ($10-28) and haunted plantations ($38) as well as other tours of the Atchafalaya Swamp ($58). (Open daily 10am-dusk. Museum admission $5.) Be careful here; ghosts may not bother you, but other shady characters might.

Outside The Quarter

The French Quarter is certainly not the only interesting area of New Orleans. In the southernmost corner of the Quarter at the "foot of Canal St." where the riverboats dock, stands the **World Trade Center** (525-2185), where you can take in New Orleans from 31 flights up ($2, ages 6-12 $1, seniors $1.50; open 9am-5pm daily) and then grab a snack at Riverview Cafeteria on the third floor (open 7am-2:30pm). In this same area ambles the **Riverwalk,** a multi-million dollar conglomeration of overpriced shops overlooking the port. For entertainment and an unbeatable meal, let the **Cookin' Cajun New Orleans Cooking School,** 116 Riverwalk (586-8832), prepare a Cajun or Creole meal before your eyes. Call ahead for the menu of the day. ($15 for 2 hrs, Mon.-Sat. 11am-1pm.) You can take the free **Canal Street Ferry** to Algiers Point until about 9pm for a 25-minute view of the Mississippi River.

Relatively new in the downtown area, the **Warehouse Arts District,** on Julia St. between Commerce and Baronne, contains historic architecture and contemporary art galleries housed in revitalized warehouse buildings. Exhibits range from Southern folk art to experimental sculpture. Maps of the area are available in each gallery. Be sure to check out the **Contemporary Arts Center,** 900 Camp St. (523-1216), an old brick building with a modern glass and chrome facade. The exhibits range from cryptic to puzzling, but you will always enjoy the amazing artsy architecture that flourishes within. (Open Wed.-Sun. 11am-5pm. $3, kids, students, and seniors $2, ages 1-12 free; everyone free on Thurs.)

Though much of the Crescent City's fame derives from the riverfront, as you move "uptown" (called that for an apparent reason), you certainly don't move away from the beauty or the action. The streetcar named "Desire" was derailed long ago, but you can take the **St. Charles Streetcar** to the west of the French Quarter to view some of the city's finest buildings, including the elegant, mint-condition 19th-century homes along **St. Charles Avenue.** The old-fashioned train takes you through some of New Orleans' most beautiful neighborhoods at a leisurely pace for a mere $1. Be sure to disembark at the **Garden District,** an opulent neighborhood between Jackson and Louisiana Ave. The legacies of French, Italian, Spanish, and American architecture create an extraordinary combination of magnificent structures, rich colors, ironworks, and, of course, exquisite gardens. Many are raised several feet above the ground as protection from the swamp on which New Orleans was built. The wet foundation of the city even troubles the dead—all the city's cemeteries must be elevated to let the deceased rest in (dry) peace.

The St. Charles Street Car runs all the way to **Audubon Park,** across from Tulane University. Designed by Frederick Law Olmsted—the same architect who planned New York City's Central Park—Audubon contains lagoons, statues, stables, and the delightful **Audubon Zoo** (861-2537), with its re-created Louisiana swamp harboring alligators and all. A free museum shuttle glides from the Audubon Park entrance (streetcar stop #36) to the zoo. (Zoo open daily 9:30am-4:30pm. $7, seniors and ages 2-12 $3.25.) The steamboat **John Audubon** shuttles four round-trips a day between the aquarium on Canal Street and the zoo (10am-4pm; fare round-trip cruise $11.50, $5.75 kids; one-way cruise $9.50, kids $4.75; package tours include cruise, zoo, and aquarium range from $17-25, kids $9-13).

If animals, fish, and much water don't quench your thirst for nature, a 10-min. drive north of the Quarter will lead you to **City Park** (482-4888), at the corner of City Park Ave. and Marconie Dr., accessible by the Esplanade or City Park bus. This 1500-acre park is one of the five largest city parks in the U.S. In addition to the **Museum of Art** (see Museums below), it contains a botanical garden, golf courses, tennis courts, 800-year-old oak trees, lagoons, and a miniature train.

One of the most unique sights near New Orleans, the coastal wetlands that line Lake Salvador make up another segment of the **Jean Lafitte National Historical Park** called the **Barataria Unit** (589-2330). Unfortunately, the park can only be reached with a car, but the free park service swamp tours almost warrant renting one. The park is off the West Bank Expressway across the Mississippi River down Barataria Blvd. (Rte. 45).

For one of the best swamp tours around, **Nielson's** (241-5994 or 531-7884), Rte. 90 at East Pearl River Bridge in Slidell off I-10 E, won't just show you alligators, birds, and trees (which they will do), but will explain it to you. Birdwatcher, fisherman, geologist, and above all, environmentalist, John Nielson knows his nature and will share it with you. (Adults $20, kids under 12 $10; double the price for round-trip transportation. Ask for the 10% *Let's Go* discount as well as group discounts.)

MUSEUMS

Louisiana State Museum, P.O. Box 2448 (568-6972), oversees eight separate museums, ranging from the **Old U.S. Mint,** 400 Esplanade, to historic homes like the **Cabildo, Presbytère,** and **1850 House.** They contain artifacts, papers, and other changing exhibits on the history of Louisiana and New Orleans. The Cabildo is not open for viewing. All open Tues.-Sun. 10am-5pm. $3, students and seniors $1.50, ages 12 and under free.

New Orleans Museum of Art (488-2631), City Park. Take the Esplanade bus from Canal and Rampart. Recently expanded to a space of 130,000 sq. ft., this magnificent museum houses the arts of North and South America, a small collection of local decorative arts, opulent works by the jeweler Fabergé, and a strong collection of French paintings including works by Degas. Guided tours available. Open Tues.-Sun. 10am-5pm. $6, seniors and kids ages 2-17 $3.

Historic New Orleans Collection, 533 Royal St. (523-4662) boasts extensive facilities and offers 2 guided tours ($2 each). The History Tour explores New Orleans' past, while the interesting Williams Residence Tour showcases the eclectic ethnic furnishings of the home of the collection founders, General and Mrs. L. Kemper Williams. The downstairs gallery displays varying exhibitions. Open Tues.-Sat. 10am-4:45pm; tours at 10 and 11am, 2 and 3pm. Free; guided tours $2.

K&B Plaza, 1055 St. Charles Ave. on Lee Circle, houses the Virlane Foundation collection of art and sculpture surrounding the building and in the hallways and lobbies on six of its seven floors. Among the creative displays of this outstanding contemporary collection: sculpture by Henry Moore, mobiles by Alexander Calder, and a bust by Renoir. Open 24 hrs. Free.

Musée Conti Wax Museum, 917 Conti St. (525-2605). One of the world's finest houses of wax. The voodoo display and haunted dungeon are perennial favorites. Open 10am-5:30pm daily, except Mardi Gras. $5, under 17 $3.25, seniors $4.50.

Confederate Museum, 929 Camp St. (523-4522). An extensive collection of Civil War records and artifacts. Located just west of Lee Circle in an ivy-covered stone building. Open Mon.-Sat. 10am-4pm. $3, seniors and students $2, kids $1.

Louisiana Children's Museum, 428 Julia St. (523-STAR). Invites kids to star on their own news show, shop at a mini-mart, pretend to be a streetcar driver, and much, much more. They'll never know they're learning at the same time. Kids under 12 must be accompanied by an adult. Open Tues.-Sun. 9:30-4:30pm. $3.

Louisiana Nature and Science Center, 11000 Lake Forest Blvd. (246-5672), in Joe Brown Memorial Park. Hard to reach without a car, but a wonderful escape from the frivolity of the French Quarter. Trail walks, exhibits, planetarium shows, laser shows, and 86 acres of natural wildlife preserve. Open Tues.-Fri. 9am-5pm; $2, seniors and kids $1, Sat.-Sun. noon-5pm; $3, seniors and kids $2.

NASA Michoud Assembly Facility, 13800 Old Gentilly Rd. (257-1310) Fascinating tours of the facility that builds Space Shuttle External Tanks. Walk the factory and gape at the 154-ft. long, 28-ft. diameter tanks. Reservations must be made and several restrictions apply; you must be a US citizen to visit the museum. Call for an appointment.

HISTORIC HOMES AND PLANTATIONS

Called the "Great Showplace of New Orleans," **Longue Vue House and Gardens,** 7 Bamboo Rd. (488-5488), off Metairie Rd., epitomizes the grand Southern estate with lavish furnishings and opulent decor. The sculpted gardens are startlingly beautiful. The Old South is preserved here (in a jar on the second floor). Tours available in

English, French, Spanish, Italian, and Japanese. (Open Mon.-Sat. 10am-4:30 pm, Sun. 1-5pm. House and garden $6, students $3; gardens only $3, students $1.) **River Road,** a winding street that follows the Mississippi River, holds several preserved plantations from the 19th century. Pick up a copy of *Great River Road Plantation Parade: A River of Riches* at the New Orleans or Baton Rouge visitors centers for a good map and descriptions of the houses. Free and frequent ferries cross the Mississippi at Plaquemines, White Castle, and between Lutcher and Vacherie. A tour of all the plantations would be quite expensive. Those below are listed in order from New Orleans to Baton Rouge.

Hermann-Grima Historic House, 820 St. Louis St. (525-5661), exemplifies early American architecture and features the only working 1830s Creole kitchen and private stable in the area. Also has period garden and interior restorations. Open Mon.-Sat. 10am-3:30pm. $4, students $3.

Gallier House Museum, 1118-1132 Royal St. (523-6722), French Quarter. This elegant restored residence brings alive the taste and life-style of mid-19th century New Orleans. Tours every ½ hr., last tour at 3:45pm. Open Mon.-Sat. 10am-4:30pm. $4, seniors and students $3, kids $2.25.

San Francisco Plantation House (535-2341), Rte. 44 2 mi. north of Reserve, 23 mi. from New Orleans on the north bank of the Mississippi. Beautifully restored plantation built in 1856. Galleried in the old Creole style with the main living room on the 2nd floor. Exterior painted 3 different colors with many colorfully decorated ceilings. Tours daily 10am-4pm. $6.50, students $3.75, kids free.

Houmas House (473-7841), River Rd., Burnside, just over halfway to Baton Rouge on the northern bank of the Mississippi. Setting for the movie *Hush, Hush, Sweet Charlotte,* starring Bette Davis and Olivia DeHavilland. Built in two sections, the rear constructed in the last quarter of the 18th century, the Greek Revival mansion in front in 1840. Beautiful gardens and furnishings. Open Feb.-Oct. daily 10am-5pm; Nov.-Jan. 10am-4pm. $7, ages 13-17 $5, ages 6-12 $3.50.

Nottoway (545-2730), Rte. 405, between Bayou Goula and White Castle, 20 mi. south of Baton Rouge on the southern bank of the Mississippi. Largest plantation home in the South; often called the "White Castle of Louisiana." An incredible 64-room mansion with 22 columns, a large ballroom, and a 3-story stairway. The first choice of David O. Selznick for filming *Gone with the Wind,* but the owners didn't give a damn and simply wouldn't allow it. Open daily 9am-5pm. Admission and 1-hr. guided tour $8, kids $3.

ENTERTAINMENT AND NIGHTLIFE

On any night of the week, at any time of year, multitudes of people join the constant fete of the French Quarter. After exploring the more traditional jazz, blues, and brass sound of the Quarter, assay the rest of the city for less tourist-oriented bands playing to a more local clientele. Check *Off Beat* for maps of the clubs; try opening *Gambit,* the free weekly entertainment newspaper, or the Friday edition of the *Times-Picayune's* entertainment guide *Lagniappe* to find out who's playing where. There's a large gay community here; check out local newsletters *Impact* and *Ambush* for more information on gay events and nightlife.

Traditional New Orleans jazz, born here at the turn of the century in **Armstrong Park,** can still be enjoyed at tiny, dimly lit, historic **Preservation Hall,** 726 Saint Peter St. (523-8939). This is jazz in its most fundamental and visceral element. If you don't arrive before the doors open, be prepared for a lengthy wait in line, poor visibility and sweaty standing-room only ($3). Beverages not sold. Doors open at 8pm; music begins at 8:30pm and goes on until midnight.

Keep your ears open for **Cajun** and **zydeco** bands. Using accordions, washboards, triangles and drums, they perform hot dance tunes (to which locals expertly two-step) and exuberantly sappy waltzes. Their traditional fare is the *fais do-do,* a lengthy, wonderfully sweaty dance. Anyone who thinks couple-dancing went out in the '50s should try one of these; just grab a partner and throw yourself into the rhythm. The locally based **Radiators** do it up real spicy like.

The annual **New Orleans Jazz Festival** (522-4786), held at the fairgrounds in late April, features music played simultaneously on six stages. The entertainment also includes a Cajun food and crafts festival. Though exhilaratingly fun, the festival grows more zoo-like each year. Book a room early.

French Quarter

New Orleans bars stay open late, and few bars adhere to a strict schedule. In general, they open around 11am and close around 3am. Many bars in the area are very expensive, charging $3-5 for drinks. Yet on most blocks, you can find cheap draft beer and "Hurricanes," sweet drinks made of juice and rum; visitors can totter around the streets, get pleasantly soused, and listen to great music without going broke. A walk down Bourbon St. after midnight is so crowded it feels like noon. Music pours out of the bars, and bouncers beckon you inside. Beware of con-men and always bring ID—the party's fun, but the law is enforced.

The Napoleon House, 500 Chartres St. (524-9752, is one of the world's great watering holes. Located on the ground floor of the Old Girod House, it was built as an exile home for Napoleon in a plan to spirit him away from St. Helena. Setting for the opening scene of Oliver Stone's lamentable *JFK*. New Orleans fare ($3-9). Open Mon.-Thurs. 11am-1am, Fri.-Sat. 11am-2am. Sun. 11am-7pm.

The Absinthe Bar, 400 Bourbon St. (525-8108). Reasonably-priced drinks for the French Quarter, with a blues band sometimes led by Bryan Lee. Has irrigated the likes of Mark Twain, Franklin D. Roosevelt, the Rolling Stones, and Humphrey Bogart. Bet you've never heard those four names together in the same sentence! Open daily noon-3am, since 1806. Music begins at 5:30pm.

Pat O'Brien's, 718 Saint Peter St. (525-4823). The busiest bar in the French Quarter, bursting with happy (read: drunk) tourists. You can listen to the pianos in one room, mix with local students in another, or lounge beneath huge fans near a fountain in the courtyard. Home of the original Hurricane; purchase your first in a souvenir glass ($6.75). Open daily 10:30am-4am, weekends until 5am.

Bourbon Pub/Parade, 801 Bourbon St. (529-2107). This gay dance bar sponsors a "tea dance" on Sun. with all the beer you can drink for $5. Open 24 hrs. Dancing nightly 9pm-4am.

Old Absinthe House, 240 Bourbon St. (523-3181). The marble absinthe fountain inside has been dry since absinthe was outlawed. The Absinthe Frappe is a re-invention of the infamous drink with anisette or Pernod liqueur ($4.75). Reputed to be the oldest bar in the U.S., having opened in 1807; the Absinthe Bar right down the street (est. 1806) shows up its story. Open daily 10am-2am.

Storyville Jazz Hall, 1104 Decatur St. (525-8199). This large music hall opens onto the street and hosts a variety of bands from Southern metal to cool jazz. Generally a concert hall; call for times and ticket information.

Outside The Quarter

Many great bars frolic outside the French Quarter—those below are grouped according to nearby landmarks. Most cluster near the **University.**

Mid City Lanes, 4133 S. Carrolton Ave. (482-3133), at Tulane, is "Home of Rock n' Bowl," bowling alley by day, dance club by night. (Don't worry, you can bowl at night too.) Featuring local zydeco, blues, and rock n' roll, this is where the locals go to party. Every Thursday is zydeco night—and is it a blast! Music starts at 9:30 or 10pm. Cover $3-5. Pick up a *Rock n' Bowlletin* for specific band info (and a list of the regulars' birthdays).

Café Brasil, 541 Frenchman St., plays some serious jazz in an airy, sparse room decorated with funky but tasteful neon art. Open daily 5pm until...

Checkpoint Charlie's, 501 Esplanade (947-0979), in the Marigny, grunges it up like the best of Seattle. Do your laundry while you listen to live rockin' music seven nights a week. No cover. Open 24 hrs.

Tipitina's, 501 Napoleon Ave. (897-3943 concert line; 895-8477 regular line). This locally renowned establishment attracts the best local bands and even some big names. Favorite bar of late jazz pianist and scholar Professor Longhair; his bust now graces the front hall. Though the prof's pedagogy is no longer, the club books a wide variety of music. A Neville Brothers show at Tip's is an essential New Orleans experience. Call ahead for times and prices. Cover $4-15.

Michaul's, 701 Magazine St. (522-5517), at Girnod. A huge floor for Cajun dancing; they'll even teach you how. Open Mon.-Thurs. 6-11pm, Fri.-Sat. 6pm-midnight.

Maple Leaf Bar, 8316 Oak St. (866-9359), near Tulane University. The best local dance bar offers zydeco and Cajun music; everyone does the two-step. Poetry readings Sun. at 3pm. Open Mon.-Sat. 11am-4am, Sun. 1pm-4am. The party begins Sun.-Thurs. at 10pm, Fri.-Sat. at 10:30pm. Cover $3-5.

Muddy Water's, 8301 Oak St. (966-7174), near Tulane. Live music every night, mostly blues. Burgers and seafood ($3-10); cover $4-5. Open Mon.-Thurs. 3pm-4am, Fri.-Sun. noon-6am.

Snug Harbor, 626 Frenchman St. (949-0696), just east of the Quarter near Decatur. Blues vocalists Charmaine Neville and Amasa Miller sing here regularly, giving 2 shows per night. Ellis Marsalis also performs here. The cover is no bargain ($6-14), but Mon. evening with Ms. Neville is worth it. You can also hear, but not see, the soulful music from the bar in the front room. Open daily 11am-3am.

Mississippi

Understandably known as the "Magnolia State," Mississippi grows grass so green around magnolias and oaks so leafy that the flora seems to defy the humid, wilting heat for which the South is so famous. When traveling here, steer off the interstate to explore lush forests, swamps, and countryside. A major passageway for hundreds of years, the Natchez Trace winds gracefully through the shade from Natchez, MS to Nashville, TN, passing through a beautiful national park and many historic landmarks. The park's strictly-enforced 50 mph speed limit encourages travelers to amble at a leisurely pace.

The beauty of this roadway and the Mississippi River contrasts with the many disturbing years of racial conflicts and appalling economic conditions for which the state is notorious. When Vicksburg witnessed a major Civil War battle won by the Union in 1863, the battle for Civil Rights had only just begun—the state would see many more years of turbulent racial strife. Mississippi's culture is strongly influenced by its African-American heritage; the blues, born in Mississippi, derived from African slave songs, and Mississippians Robert Johnson and B.B. King are responsible for popularizing this great art form.

PRACTICAL INFORMATION

Capital: Jackson.

Visitor Information: Division of Tourism, 1301 Walter Siller Bldg., 550 High St. (359-3414 or 800-647-2290). Open Mon.-Fri. 8am-5pm. **Bureau of Parks and Recreation,** P.O. Box 10600, Jackson 39209.

Time Zone: Central (1 hr. behind Eastern). **Postal Abbreviation:** MS

Sales Tax: 6%.

■■■ BILOXI AND THE MISSISSIPPI COAST

For more than a century, Biloxi's shores have served it well—providing sustenance first through the thriving seafood and canning industries and now as "America's Riviera." Today, the gambling industry expands quicker than the roll of the dice, both reinvigorating the local economy and drawing record numbers of fortune-seeking tourists to its flashy floating casinos. The picturesque small-town charm still resonates with sun-drenched history; the fine, sandy shores still soothe bathers and swarm with scrumptious seafood, but as Biloxi surfs into the 21st century, it is likely to become famed for its 24-hr. entertainment.

Practical Information The **Biloxi Chamber of Commerce,** 1048 Beach Blvd. (374-2717), across from the lighthouse, eagerly aids tourists (open Mon.-Fri. 8:30am-noon, 1-5pm). The **Biloxi Tourist Information Center,** 710 Beach Blvd. (374-3105), down the street from the bus station, distributes brochures (open Mon.-Fri. 8am-5pm, Sat. 9am-5pm, Sun. noon-5pm). For more info contact the **Mississippi Gulf Coast Convention and Visitor's Bureau,** 135 Courthouse Rd. (896-6699 or 800-237-9493), or tune your radio to 1490 AM for beach and tourist info.

Getting into and out of Biloxi is rarely problematic because buses service the town well. **Greyhound,** 322 Main St. (436-4335; open daily 6:30am-10pm), offers frequent service to New Orleans (8 per day, 2½ hr., $19) and Jackson (2 per day, 4 hr., $26). **Amtrak** (800-872-7245) is located on Reynoir St. a few blocks from U.S. 90. Trains run 3 times per week to New Orleans ($31) and Los Angeles ($206). Unstaffed station; call to reserve tickets. **Coast Area Transit** (896-8080) operates buses (marked "Beach") along the beach on U.S. 90 (Beach Blvd.) from Biloxi to Gulfport. Nine other lines serve the entire gulf coast area. (Buses operate Mon.-Sat. every 70 min. Board at any intersection. Fare 75¢, students 50¢, seniors 35¢.)

The **post office** is at 135 Main St. (432-0311), near the bus station (open Mon.-Fri. 8:30am-5pm, Sat. 9am-noon). Biloxi's **ZIP code** is 39530; **area code: 601.**

Accommodations and Food Rooms with a pretty coastal view will cost you a pretty penny, but just a few blocks from the beach (and the casinos, and the bus, the train, restaurants, bars, and stores), the brand new **Biloxi International Hostel,** 128 Fayard St., 2 blocks north of Beach Blvd. and east of I-10 (435-2666), welcomes travelers with literally open doors. The spotless and homey accommodations are surpassed only by the incredible warmth of proprietors J.D. and Julie. Comfy living room, kitchen, laundry. ($11 per person. Key deposit $2.) Since hotel/motel prices fluctuate according to complex laws which we won't go into, your best bet to find cheap rates is to ask at the Visitors Center or flip through a current copy of *Traveler Discount Guide* distributed there. Sun.-Thurs. is cheaper, as is the off-season which runs from Labor Day to January-February. **Camping** is an inexpensive alternative; rates vary from $10-15 depending on the season. The most convenient site is the **Biloxi Beach Campground,** 1816 W. Beach Blvd. (432-2755; $10 per primitive site, $12 full hookup, for 2 people; $2 per additional person). Farther from town are **Martin's Lake and Campground,** 14605 Parker Rd. (875-9157; $12 per site for 2 people plus $2 each additional person), 1 mi. north of I-10 at exit 50 in Ocean Springs, and the campground at **Gulf Islands National Seashore, Davis Bayou** (875-0823), on Hanley Rd. off U.S. 90 also in Ocean Springs ($10 per site).

Biloxi swims with seafood restaurants, but they're often pricey. **Mary Mahoney's** (432-0349), a sidewalk cafe at the Magnolia Mall on Beach Blvd., offers reasonable and filling po'boys ($4-6) and sandwiches ($3-5), 24 hrs. a day. For a treat to beat the heat, try **Anna-Lisa's Yogurt and Dessert Shoppe,** 271 E. Beauvoir Rd. (385-1464; open Mon.-Thurs. 10am-10pm, Fri.-Sat. 10am-11pm, Sun. 11am-10pm).

Sights and Activities Although the 26-mi. snow-white, sandy **Gulf Islands National Seashore** today sports a few too many souvenir shops, the natural beauty of this—the longest man-made beach in the world—still attracts throngs of sun worshipers and beachcombers. If jetskis and sand volleyball sound too hectic, travel west on I-90 toward **Gulfport's** sparsely populated beaches with views only of lovely historic homes. The Spanish moss hanging from the oak trees along the road (actually neither Spanish nor moss, but a relative of the pineapple plant) and old **antebellum mansions** in the **historic district** also merit more than a glance.

Between Biloxi and Gulfport you'll find the garden and grounds of **Beauvoir,** 2244 Beach Blvd. (388-1313), at Beauvoir Rd. Jefferson Davis's last home, it is now a shrine in his honor, containing a Confederate Museum, a Davis Family Museum, and a Confederate Veterans Cemetery with the tomb of the Unknown Confederate Soldier. Each October, Beauvoir is also the site of a Confederate boot camp simulation, complete with drills. (Open daily 9am-5pm. $4.75, kids $2.50.) Also along the shoreline is the **Biloxi Lighthouse** (435-6293), which legend claims was painted black after President Lincoln's assassination; *actually* the rusty edifice just needed a paint job. Today the South's first cast-metal lighthouse is snowy white and seasonally open for tours. (Open March-Oct. Mon.-Fri. 8am-noon. Donations accepted.) For a city tour take the **Ole Biloxi Train Tour,** a 1½-hr. ride beginning at the lighthouse; the first tour leaves at 9:30am (374-8687; tour $6, kids $3).

The **Visitors Center** (see above) offers a more athletic and less expensive alternative with its free, self-guided **Historic Heart of Biloxi Walking Tour** (about 1 hr.). Amble through quiet streets to the **Tullis-Toledano Manor,** 360 Beach Blvd. (435-6293), a summer retreat for wealthy New Orleans cotton merchants in the 19th century (open Mon.-Fri. 10am-noon, and 1-5pm).

Take a spin through the **Mississippi Museum of Art, Gulf Coast,** 136 George E. Ohr St. (374-5547), off Beach Blvd., and check out the bizarre yet functional pottery of Ohr, the Mad Potter of Biloxi (open Tues.-Sat. 10am-5pm, Sun. 1-5pm; free).

To learn more about Biloxi's fishy past, visit the **Seafood Industry Museum** (435-6320), at Point Cadet Plaza, turn off U.S. 90 onto Myrtle Rd. at the foot of the Biloxi-Ocean Springs Bridge. The museum traces Biloxi's growth from a French colony to its current "Seafood Capital" status. (Open Mon.-Sat. 9am-5pm. $2.50, seniors and kids 6-16 $1.50.) Drop by the **Farmer's Market** next door (open Tues.-Thurs. 6am-6pm) or try to catch your own shrimp, horseshoe crabs, and other marine life in the "touch tank" at the **J.L. Scott Marine Education Center and Aquarium,** 115 Beach Blvd. (374-5550), next to the **Isle of Capri Casino.** The largest public aquarium in the state, the center's cynosure is a 42,000-gallon Gulf of Mexico tank in which sharks, sea turtles, eels and larger residents frolic and feed. (Open Mon.-Sat. 9am-4pm, $3, seniors $2, kids 3-17 $1.50.)

Ship Island floats 12 mi. off the Mississippi Coast, far enough out to sea to exempt it from federal bans on liquor and gambling in the 1920s. Crystal blue waters and white sandy beaches are the lures today, as visitors swim, fish, and explore. Defending the island is **Fort Massachusetts** (875-0821), which served as both a Confederate and Union command center at different points during the Civil War (free). Ship Island has had two parts, East and West, since it was sliced in two by Hurricane Camille in 1969. To get to West Ship Island, where overnight camping is prohibited, take the Skrmetta-family **ferry service** that leaves from Biloxi's **Point Cadet Marina,** Beach Blvd. near Isle of Capri (432-2197; 2 ferries per day leave for the island at 9am and noon; arrive back in Biloxi 4 and 7pm; 70min.; round-trip $12, kids $6). A different kind of 70-minute cruise is the **Biloxi Shrimping Trip,** U.S. 90E (374-5718)**.** The *Sailfish* departs from the Biloxi Small Craft Harbor several times a day, giving passengers an opportunity to see what trawling between the Biloxi shore and nearby Deer Island will yield ($9, kids $5). Call for reservations.

Evening brings cool breezes off the gulf and beaches ripe for moonlit strolls. New destinations now sporadically interrupt the sand: recently legalized "floating" casinos. Starting with the **Grand Casino** in Gulfport, these gaming hotspots moved east along Beach Blvd. with the **Presidents** next, then **Biloxi Belle, Casino Magic,** and the **Isle of Capri.** All are open 24 hrs. to those 21 and over. A little tamer, and a lot easier on the pocket, the **Silver Screen,** 2650 Beach Blvd., shows second-run films for $1, $2 after 6pm, and even offers a movie and all-you-can-eat pizza for $5. For show times call 388-9200.

■■■ JACKSON

A sleepy Deep South town the size of a sunbelt city, Jackson offers travelers a glimpse into southern life without overwhelming them with the usual plastic and pricey tourist traps. The lush homes and posh country clubs of North Jackson root Mississippi's commercial and political capital in its southern heritage. Jackson has shaded campsites, cool reservoirs, national forests, and Native American burial mounds only minutes away. Combining history with natural beauty, the Natchez Trace Parkway can lead you north to Nashville or south to Natchez.

PRACTICAL INFORMATION

Emergency: 911.

Visitor Information: Visitor Information Center, 1100 Lakeland Dr. (960-1800), off I-55 Lakeland East exit. Open Mon.-Sun. 8:30am-2pm. Chock full of guides, brochures, and helpful hints. **Convention and Visitors Bureau,** 921 N. President St. (960-1891), downtown. Open Mon.-Fri. 8:30am-5pm.

Airport: Allen C. Thompson Municipal Airport, (932-2859); east of downtown, off I-20. Cab fare to downtown about $13-14.

Amtrak: 300 W. Capitol St. (355-6350). Neighborhood is deserted at night. To Memphis (1 per day, 4 hr., $46) and New Orleans (1 per day, 4 hr., $42). Open Mon.-Fri. 7:30am-1pm and 2-7pm, Sat.-Sun. 7:30-10:30am and 4:30-7pm.

Greyhound: 201 S. Jefferson (353-6342). Be cautious walking in the area at night. To: Dallas (5 per day, 10 hr., $72); Montgomery (3 per day, 7 hr., $46); Memphis (5 per day, 4½ hr., $37); New Orleans (4 per day, 4½ hr., $36). Open 24 hrs.

Public Transport: Jackson Transit System (JATRAN) (948-3840), in the Federal Bldg. downtown. Limited service. Bus schedules and maps posted at most bus stops. Buses run Mon.-Fri. 5am-7pm, Sat. 7am-6pm. Fare 75¢, transfers 10¢.

Help Lines: First Call for Help, 352-4357; referrals. **Rape Hotline,** 982-7273.

Taxi: Veterans Cab, 355-8319. Base fare $1.10, $1 per mi.

Post Office: 401 E. South St. (968-1612). Open Mon.-Fri. 7am-7pm, Sat. 8am-noon. **ZIP code:** 39201.

Area Code: 601.

The downtown area, just west of I-55, is bordered on the north by **High St.,** the south by **Pascagoula,** and the west by **Farish St. State St.,** running north-south, cuts it in half.

ACCOMMODATIONS

There are few motels downtown, but with a car you easily can find rooms along I-20 and I-55; price is directly related to proximity and comfort.

Sun n' Sand Motel, 401 N. Lamar St. (354-2501), downtown. Large, newly-renovated rooms with 50s orange n' aqua—even a Polynesian room. Cable TV. Pool. Lounge/restaurant in motel serves $5 lunch buffet. Singles $30, $5 each additional person.

Admiral Benbow Inn, 905 N. State St. (948-4161), downtown. Large, comfortable rooms, pool, remote control TV. Singles/doubles $36-48. Frequent $29 specials.

Motel 6, (two locations) 970 I-20 Frontage Rd. (969-3423). Tidy, small, white-walled rooms with spotless bathrooms. Pool. Free local calls. Movie channel. Singles $23. Doubles $28. Also 61455 I-55N, exit 103 (956-8848). Similar rooms closer to downtown. Singles $27.50. Doubles $34.

Parkside Inn, 3720 I-55N, exit 98B (982-1122), close to downtown. Drab, worn rooms with full amenities: pool, cable TV, restaurant/lounge, free local calls. Singles $25. Doubles $30.

The most inexpensive, not to mention aesthetically pleasing, accommodations option in Jackson is camping. Overlooking the massive Ross Barnett Reservoir, the

JACKSON

Timberland Campgrounds (992-9100), off Old Fanon Rd., stays busy throughout the summer. (Pool, video games, pool tables. Tent sites $7.50; full hookup $12.)

FOOD

Jackson eateries specialize in catfish and plate lunch specials, catering to the young professional crowd and older regulars. Most are inexpensive and lively. As in any American town, fast-food chains scatter along the east end of High St.

The Iron Horse Grill, 320 W. Pearl St. (355-8419), at Gallatin. A huge converted smokehouse with a waterfall cascading from the 2nd floor. A young happening place to hang. Checks not accepted. Primarily Tex-Mex ($7-10); steak and seafood entrees more expensive. A pianist accompanies lunch and dinner. Open Mon.-Thurs. 11am-10pm, Fri.-Sat. 11am-11pm.

Primo's, 1016 N. State St. (948-4343). A Jackson tradition; in fact, the decor hasn't changed in 40 years. Excellent, cheap Southern food; breakfasts with creamy grits and huge omelettes under $4 (breakfast served till 11:30am). Lunch specials $5. Vegetable plates, with country-style dinners $6-8. Open Mon.-Fri. 7am-9pm, Sat.-Sun. 8am-9pm.

The Elite Cafe, 141 E. Capitol (352-5606). Egalitarian lunch spot with great home-made cornbread, rolls, and steaks. Plate lunch specials with two vegetables and bread under $4.50. Be prepared to wait in line during lunch rush. Dinner slightly pricier. Open Mon.-Fri. 7am-9:30pm, Sat. 5-9:30pm.

SIGHTS AND ENTERTAINMENT

Rich in history (and proud of it), Jackson hardly neglects the wonders of the present (and the future). Built in 1840, the Old State Capitol (359-6920), at the intersection of Capitol and State St., houses an excellent, lucid museum of Mississippi's often tur-bulent history, including artifacts from original Native American settlements and documentaries on the Civil Rights Movement. Frequently changing contemporary exhibits spice up the past. (Open Mon.-Fri. 8am-5pm, Sat. 9:30am-4:30pm, Sun. 12:30-4:30pm. Free.) The War Memorial Building, 120 S. State St. (354-7207), depicts an often gruesome narrative of American wars and the Mississippians who fought, were honored, and often died in them. (Open Mon.-Fri. 8am-4:30pm. Free.) For a more upbeat and family-pleasing presentation of nature and wildlife try the Mississippi Museum of Natural Science on Jefferson St. (354-7303), across from the fairground (open Tues.-Fri. 8am-5pm, Sat. 9:30am-4:30pm; free). Don't miss the Greek Revival Governor's Mansion, 300 E. Capitol St. (359-3175), a national historic landmark. The tours (every ½ hr.) are an enlightening introduction to Mississippi politics. (Open Mon.-Fri. 9:30-11am.) For a more in-depth look at some fine architec-ture, visit the Manship House, 420 E. Fortification (961-4724), a short walk north from the New Capitol. Charles Henry Manship, Jackson's Civil War mayor, built this Gothic Revival "cottage villa," now restored to its 19th-century condition. (Open Tues.-Fri. 9am-4pm, Sat. 1-4pm.) Sherman occupied both Manship and Jackson's oldest house, The Oaks, 823 N. Jefferson St. (353-9339), built in 1746, during the siege of the city in 1863. Enjoy a delightful tour by the current loquacious tenant. (Open Tues.-Sat. 10am-4pm, Sun. 1:30-4pm. $2, students $1.)

Moving into the present once again, the state legislature's current home is the beautiful New State Capitol (359-3114), at Mississippi and Congress St., completed in 1903. A huge restoration project preserved the *beaux arts* grandeur of the build-ing, complete with a gold-leaf-covered eagle perched on the capitol dome, carnival-like colors, and strings of light which brighten the spacious inside. (Open Mon.-Fri. 8am-5pm. Guided 45-min. tours Mon.-Fri. at 9, 10, and 11am, and 1:30, 2:30, and 3:30pm. Free.) For less functional but more priceless beauty, The Mississippi Museum of Art, 201 E. Pascagoula (960-1515 or 800-423-4971), at Lamar St., has a fabulous collection of Americana and a fun participatory Impression Gallery for kids. (Open Mon.-Fri. 10am-5pm, Sat.-Sun. noon-5pm. $3, kids $2, students free Tues. and Thurs.) Next door is the Russell C. Davis Planetarium (960-1550), considered one of the most stellar worldwide. (Galactic and musical shows Mon.-Fri. at noon, Tues.-Sat. at 8pm, Sat.-Sun. at 2 and 4pm. $4, seniors and kids $2.50.)

Don't keep your eyes glued to the stars or you'll miss the trees and crops that have been the basis for Mississippi's prosperity; if you do miss them, they're highlighted at the **Agriculture and Forestry Museum/National Agricultural Aviation Museum,** 1150 Lakeland Dr. (354-6113), near the Visitors Center. (Open Mon.-Sat. 9am-5pm. Sun. 1-5pm. $3, seniors $2.75, children $1.)

African-Americans have been some of the main contributors to agricultural progress in this Deep South state since the 18th century. Witness the struggles and achievements of Mississippi's African-Americans at the **Smith-Robertson Museum and Cultural Center,** 528 Bloom St. (960-1457), directly behind the Sun n' Sand Motel. This large, expanding museum once housed the state's first black public school, which *Native Son* author Richard Wright attended until the eighth grade. Now it displays folk art, photographs, and excellent exhibits on the Civil Rights Movement, particularly the role of African-American women in Mississippi history. (Open Mon.-Fri. 9am-5pm, Sat.-Sun. 9am-noon. $1, kids 50¢.) Every Labor Day, the surrounding neighborhood celebrates African-American culture through art, theater, crafts, and great food at the **Farish Street Festival** (355-ARTS). For another, very different perspective on southern history and culture, take a trip to the **Museum of the Southern Jewish Experience** (362-6357 or 885-6042), on the grounds of the UAHC Henry S. Jacobs Camp (open for tours by appointment; $3, seniors and children $1.50).

The **New Jackson Zoo,** 2918 W. Capitol St. (352-2582), has a fair-sized collection of spots and stripes and teeth and shells and paws and wings and heads and tails. (Open daily 9am-6pm; Labor Day-Memorial Day 9am-5pm. Admission $3.50, seniors and children $1.75.) The ever-blooming **Mynelle Gardens,** 4736 Clinton Blvd. (960-1894 or 960-1814), relaxes the eyes and the mind with its fragrant and colorful beauty. Picnic tables (open 9am-5:15pm; $2, kids 50¢.)

After soaking in the history of life and politics in Jackson, soak up some music and fun at **Hal & Mal's Restaurant and Oyster Bar,** 200 Commerce St. (948-0888), which entertains in a converted warehouse. Everything from reggae to innovative rock bands play Thursday through Saturday nights. (Restaurant open Mon.-Sat. 11am-10pm; bar open until 1am. Cover $3-12.) If you'd rather mellow out with the art crowd or some college students, stop by **cups,** 2757 Old Canton Rd. (362-7422), for a cappuccino and conversation.

■■■ NATCHEZ

Talk about squattin' in high cotton—just before the Civil war, Natchez preened as one of the wealthiest settlements on the Mississippi. Of the thirteen millionaires in Mississippi at the time, eleven built their cotton plantation estates here, as did several other well-to-do farmers. The custom then was to fashion the home on one side of the River and till the soil on the Louisiana side. Although the cotton-based agricultural economy began to wane, Natchez waxed and matured on the plantation side of Ol' Man River where 40 mansions continue to preside.

Practical Information The **Mississippi Welcome Center,** 370 Seargent Prentiss Dr. (442-5849), housed in an antique-filled home, does its thing southern style—no comfort is missed. Pick up maps, discount books, suggested tours, and even have them book your hotel! (Open daily 8am-6:30pm; in winter daily 8am-5pm.)

Make connections to Vicksburg ($13.50) and Baton Rouge ($19.50) at the **Natchez Bus Station,** 103 Lower Woodville Rd. (445-5291). In-town transportation is available at the **Natchez Ford Rental** (445-0076), with rates of $38 per day plus 20¢ per mi. ($250 deposit or major credit card required, must be at least 21 years old). The **Natchez Bicycling Center,** 334 Main St. (446-7794), will rent you wheels at $7.50 for 1-3 hours, $10 for 3-5 hours. and $14 for all day. (Must be at least 14 years old accompanied by an adult or 18 unaccompanied. Open Mon.-Fri. 10am-5:30pm, Sat. 10am-4pm. Other times by appointment.) Natchez's **post office** (442-4361) delivers from 214 Canal St. (open Mon.-Fri. 8:30am-5pm, Sat. 10am-noon), and its **ZIP code** is 39120.

Accommodations and Food The most economical way to visit Natchez is as a daytrip from either Vicksburg, MS, or Baton Rouge, LA. If you prefer to stay in Natchez, **Scottish Inns** (442-9141 or 800-251-1962), on U.S. 61, has fully furnished rooms in newly painted facilities with a refreshing pool. (Singles $26, doubles $35.) **Days Inn** (800-524-4892), occasionally has specials at $35 for one to four people, though regular rates are $40-45. Call for current info on possible discounts. If you want to go whole hog and stay in a plantation home, dig deep in your pockets—$75 is the cheapest rate for a night in one of the homes that doubles as a bed and breakfast. Make B&B reservations through the tour facility (see above).

If you'd prefer a secluded **campground,** head for **Natchez State Park** (442-2658), less than 10 mi. north of Natchez on U.S. 61 in Stanton. Full hookups are $10, primitive camping $6. Watch closely; signs are rare.

Satisfying your stomach is less costly; inexpensive cafes and diners abound in Natchez. **Cock of the Walk,** 200 N. Broadway (446-8920), has certainly earned its title and stature with spicy catfish and smooth baked potatoes. Plate lunch $5. (Open daily 11:30am-1:30pm, 5-9pm.) **Nothin' Fancee Delicatessen,** 112 N. Commerce St. (442-6886), has tastee specials and sandwiches for $2 to $3 and a full breakfast for under $3. At **Fat Mama's Tamales,** 500 S. Canal St. (442-4548), Cajun boudin, chili, and peanut butter pie are served in a log cabin (open Mon.-Wed. 11am-7pm, Thurs.-Sat. 11am-9pm, Sun. noon-5pm). Several local seafood eateries bake, grill, and broil fresh fish. Try the **Main Street Steamery,** 326 Main St. (445-0608), which prepares absolutely *no* fried foods and has seafood sandwiches, salads, and entrees ($5-7). (Open Fri.-Sat. 11am-10pm, Sun. 11am-3pm.)

Sights Open for public tours, the manorial restorations of the "white gold" days are under the supervision of the efficient **Natchez Pilgrimage Tours,** on the corner of Canal St. and State St., P.O. Box 347 (446-6631 or 800-647-6742). Pick up free tour schedules, maps, miscellaneous pamphlets, and an interesting and informative guidebook about the homes and their histories ($5). (Open daily 8:30am-5pm.) Visitors can marvel at the unbelievable opulence which cotton tycoons were often able to acquire as early as their 13th birthdays. Although tickets can be purchased at individual houses for $4.50, Pilgrimage Tours offers packages of 3 houses for $12, 4 houses for $15, and 5 houses for $18 (children always ½ price). They can also book rooms at many of these homes which double as B&Bs, starting at $75.

The largest octagonal house in America, **Longwood,** 140 Lower Woodville Rd. (442-5193), astounds visitors with its creative and elaborate decor and imaginative floor plan designed to be an "Arabian palace." The six-story edifice remains unfinished because the builders, hired from the North, abandoned work at the beginning of the Civil War so that they could fight for the Union. They never returned; their discarded tools and undisturbed crates still lie as they were left. **Stanton Hall,** 401 High St. (442-6282), on the other hand, arose under the direction of local Natchez architects and artisans. Completed in 1857, this mansion regales with almost ostentatious splendor; French mirrors, Italian marble mantels, and specially-cut chandeliers drip with magnificence in this estate.

For centuries before the rise of such opulence, the Natchez Indians created their own riches on this fertile land. The arrival of the French incited warfare in the late 1720s and 1730s; French military successes caused the death of the Natchez as a flourishing community. Their culture lives on it the town's name and at the **Grand Village of the Natchez Indians,** 400 Jefferson Davis Blvd. (446-6502), where stupendously large burial mounds dominate green, grassy fields. According to historical documentation, when the Great Sun, or chief, of the tribe died, his wife and others who so desired were strangled and buried also. The house of the chief's successor was supposed to sit atop the mound. A museum documenting the history and culture of the Natchez sits there now. (Open Mon.-Sat. 9am-5pm, Sun. 1:30-5pm. Free.)

Historic **Jefferson College** (442-2901), off U.S. 61 near U.S. 84E, stands 6 mi. east of Natchez as the first educational institution in the Mississippi Territory. Incorporated in 1802, the peaceful grounds and buildings are the site where Aaron Burr, Vice-President under Thomas Jefferson, was tried for treason in 1807. Fortunately for Burr, the judges couldn't be found for sentencing, and Burr escaped in the night. (He was later acquitted in Virginia, if your curiosity is killing you.) (Grounds open sunrise-sunset, buildings open Mon.-Sat. 9am-5pm, Sun 1-5pm. Free.)

■■■ VICKSBURG

Started as a mission by Rev. Newit Vick in 1814, Vicksburg is best known for its role in the Civil War. President Abraham Lincoln called this town the "key," and maintained that the war "can never be brought to a close until that key is in our pocket." Its verdant hills and prime Mississippi River location proved extremely strategic for the Confederate forces, though not strategic enough; the "Gibraltar of the South" fell to Union forces on July 4, 1863, after valiant resistance to a 47-day bombardment. The loss of this critical river city augured death for the Confederacy; the city proved more buoyant. Although the siege devastated the area, today Vicksburg has put its trying history to good use, welcoming visitors to recapture and relive the battle through historic homes, salvaged ships, and restored battlefields.

Practical Information For more information about Vicksburg, visit the **Tourist Information Center** (636-9421), across the street from the park. Pick up one of the many pamphlets with discount coupons for area hostels and restaurants, as well as copies of *The Newcomer's Guide* and *Southland Explorer*. (Open daily 8am-5:30pm.) Unfortunately, you'll need a car to see most of Vicksburg: the bus station, the information center, downtown, and the far end of the sprawling military park are at the city's four extremes. The **Greyhound** station (636-1230) is inconveniently located at 3324 Hall's Ferry Rd., off Frontage Rd. Buses lope to Jackson (4 per day, 1 hr., $9.50). The **Rape and Sexual Assault Service** (638-0031) answers calls all day.

Vicksburg's **post office** is on U.S. 61 at Pemberton Blvd. (636-1822; open Mon.-Fri. 8:30am-5pm, Sat. 9am-noon). The **ZIP code** is 39180; the **area code** is 601.

Accommodations, Food, and Nightlife Inexpensive accommodations are easily found in Vicksburg, except over the July Fourth weekend, when the military park's war reenactment brings thousands of tourists and inflated hotel rates. The **Hillcrest Motel**, 4503 Rte. 80 E. (638-1491), has a pool and spacious, ground-floor singles for $19, doubles $22. Most hotels are near the park; don't expect to stay in town, unless you choose the **Dixiana Motel**, 4033 Washington St. (636-9876), where you pay for a bed and all you get is a bed (and TV, of course). Note the antique bathrooms. (Rooms $20.) The **Beachwood Motel**, 4449 Rte. 80E (636-2271), has no pool but has cable and newly furnished orange rooms. (Bed $25, 2 beds $30.) **The Vicksburg Battlefield Kampground**, 4407 I-20 Frontage Rd. (636-9946), has a pool and laundry accompanying smallish sites. (Sites $10-12 for 2 people.) If you're willing to drive 30 mi. out of town, the **Leisure Living Campground** (279-4259), on 465 West, on Eagle Lake, sprawls along a quiet lake ($10 per site).

While downtown, chow down at the **Burger Village**, 1220 Washington St. (638-0202), home of the happy community of ground chuck on buns and other sandwiches, all under $3 (open Mon.-Thurs. 9am-6pm, Fri.-Sat. 9am-7pm). The **New Orleans Café**, 1100 Washington St. (638-8182), serves mouth-watering sandwiches for under $6, delectable Cajun specialties, seafood, and more. Popular with the locals. (Open Mon.-Thurs. 11am-10pm, Fri.-Sat. 11am-2am.) On the weekends, the café's **Other Side Lounge** is a popular nightspot (open Fri.-Sat. 5:30pm-2am).

Across the street is **Miller's Still Lounge** (638-8661), a real Southern watering hole with live entertainment and popcorn nightly (open Mon.-Sat. 3pm-2am).

Sights Markers of combat sites and prominent memorials riddle the grass-covered 1700-acre **Vicksburg National Military Park** (636-0583 or 800-221-3536 out-of-state) that blockades the eastern and northern edges of the city. If possible, drive to the battlefield, museums, and cemetery east of town on Clay St. at exit 4B off I-20. ($4 per car, $2 per person on bus, seniors and kids free; tickets are valid for 7 days.) The visitors center at the entrance provides maps that detail a brief history as well as prominent sights along the 16-mi. loop. Take a guide with you on a two-hour driving tour ($20) of the military park, or drive the trail yourself. (Open summer daily 8am-sunset; visitors center closes at 5pm.) Within the park, visit the **National Cemetery** and the **U.S.S. Cairo Museum** (636-2199). The museum's centerpiece is the restored Union iron-clad gunboat *U.S.S. Cairo* (KAY-ro), the first vessel sunk by an electronically detonated mine (*Goooo* Rebels!!). The museum displays a fascinating array of artifacts preserved for over a century since the ship sank in the Yazoo River. (Open daily 9:30am-6pm; off-season 8am-5pm. Free with park admission.) Learn more about the battle at Vicksburg by catching **"Vanishing Glory,"** 717 Clay St. (634-1863), a multi-media theatrical panorama. (Shows daily on the hr. 10am-5pm; $3.50, ages 6-18 $2.) Preserving a more comprehensive history of the time when this house was divided, the **Old Courthouse Museum,** 1008 Cherry St. (636-0741), presides over the town center, 3 mi. from the park's entrance. Many consider it one of the South's finest Civil War museums, with everything from newspapers printed on wallpaper to Jefferson Davis's tie to an interpretation of Klan activities. (Open Mon.-Sat. 8:30am-5pm, Sun. 1:30-5pm. $2, seniors $1.50, ages under 18 $1.) Next door, continuing the martial theme, is **Toys and Soldiers, A Museum,** 1100 Cherry St. (638-1986), where 32,000 toy soldiers from all over the world await. (Open Mon.-Sat. 9am-4:30pm, Sun. 1:30-4:30pm. $2, kids $1.50, families $5.)

The Battle of Vicksburg was not alone in focusing its energies on the magnificent Mississippi River. A free tour, either by yourself or guided, of the **U.S. Army Engineer Waterways Experiment Station** (the largest in the nation) explains the role of the Mississippi River in urban and rural development and the functions of locks and dams. The entire floor of one room is a scale model of the dam system of Niagara Falls. (Open daily 7:45am-4:15pm, guided tours at 10am and 2pm. Free.)

For a taste of the lighter side of Vicksburg history, two blocks away lie the **Museum of Coca-Cola History and Memorabilia** and the **Biedenharn Candy Company,** 1107 Washington St. (638-6514), which first bottled Coca-Cola. Though the two-room museum displays Coke memorabilia from as far back as 1894, the admission fee seems a bit steep for the brief 10 minutes it takes to admire the artifacts. Coke floats and over 100 different Coca-Cola items are sold. (Open Mon.-Sat. 9am-5pm, Sun. 1:30-4:30pm. $1.75, kids $1.25. Disabled access.)

Escape from the downtown heat during a walk along the well-preserved tree-lined streets showing off several fine antebellum homes. The **Duff Green Mansion,** 1114 First East St. (638-6968), hosted numerous social events before it was converted into a war-time hospital during the siege of Vicksburg. (Open daily 9am-5pm. $5, kids $4.) Many of the restored Vicksburg estates double as B&Bs (ask for more information at the visitors center). The **Martha Vick House,** 1300 Grove St. (638-7036), was the home of an unmarried daughter of Reverend Vick, founder of the city. The restored building contains many elegant French paintings. (Open daily 9am-5pm. $5, ages 12-18 $2.) Slightly farther away, **McRaven,** 1445 Harrison St. (636-1663), is a popular historic home, and was featured in *National Geographic* as a "time capsule of the South" (open daily 9am-5pm, Sun. 10am-5pm; 1½-hr. guided tours $5, ages 12-18 $3, ages 6-11 $2.50).

Drive south on Washington St. to the **Louisiana Circle,** a secluded overview serving truly breathtaking vistas of the great Mississippi River. For a glimpse of Americana, visit **Holidays Washateria and Lanes** (636-9682), near the park entrance on

Rte. 80 across from the KFC. It's a bowling alley, pool room, and laundromat, all in one! Enjoy yourself and clean your socks at the same time! (Open Sun.-Thurs. 3-11pm, Fri. 3pm-midnight, Sat. 10am-2am.)

If billiards don't get your juices, maybe riverboat gambling will (watch your pockets, budget travelers!). Part of a growing national fad, Vicksburg is home to the **Isle of Capri,** 3990 Washington Blvd. (800-THE ISLE), a "player's paradise" open 24 hrs.

North Carolina

North Carolina splits neatly into thirds: the west's down-to-earth mountain culture, the mellow sophistication of the Raleigh/Durham/Chapel Hill Research Triangle in the state's center, and the lonely placidity of the eastern coast and the Outer Banks. Whatever their cultural differences, these three regions share one similarity—an unmatched North Carolinian beauty apparent the moment you cross the state border. Even the occasional urban veneer complements Carolina's fertile resplendence. The streets are unlittered, the buildings well-spaced, the businesses clean, and the universities spacious. North Carolinian mud turtles know how best to enjoy their state: slowly, warmly and quietly.

PRACTICAL INFORMATION

Capital: Raleigh.
Visitor Information: Travel and Tourism Division, 430 N. Salisbury St., Raleigh 27611 (919-733-4171 or 800-847-4862). **Department of Natural Resources and Community Development,** Division of Parks and Recreation, P.O. Box 27287, Raleigh 27611 (919-733-4181).
Time Zone: Eastern. **Postal Abbreviation:** NC
Sales Tax: 6%.

THE CAROLINA MOUNTAINS

The sharp ridges and endless rolling slopes of the southern Appalachian ranges create some of the most spectacular scenery in the Southeast. At one time, North Carolina's verdant highlands provided an exclusive refuge for the country's rich and famous. The Vanderbilts owned a large portion of the 500,000-acre Pisgah National Forest, which they subsequently willed to the U.S. government. Today the Blue Ridge, Great Smoky, Black, Craggy, Pisgah, and Balsam Mountains that comprise the western half of North Carolina beckon budget travelers, not billionaires. Campsites blanket the region, coexisting with elusive but inexpensive youth hostels and ski lodges. Enjoy the area's rugged wilderness while backpacking, canoeing, whitewater rafting, or cross-country skiing. Motorists and cyclists can follow the **Blue Ridge Parkway** to some unforgettable views (see Blue Ridge Parkway, VA).

The Blue Ridge Mountains bifurcate into two areas. The northern area is the **High Country,** which includes the territory between the town of Boone and the town of Asheville, 100 mi. to the southwest. The second area comprises the **Great Smoky Mountains National Park** (see Great Smoky Mountains National Park, TN) and **Nanatahala National Forest**.

■■■ BOONE

Named for famous frontiersman Daniel Boone, who built a cabin here in the 1760s on his journey into the western wilderness, the town continues to evoke (and profit from) its pioneer past through shops such as the Mast General Store and the Candy Barrel. Boone is not just a tourist town, though, and Appalachian State University's sprawling campus and youthful inhabitants lend a relaxed and funky atmosphere, bookshops, coffee houses, and hole-in-the-wall restaurants.

PRACTICAL INFORMATION

Emergency: 911. **National Park Service/Blue Ridge Parkway Emergency,** 259-0701 or 800-727-5928.

Visitor Information: Boone Area Chamber of Commerce, 112 W. Howard St. (264-2225), turn from Rte. 321 onto River St., drive behind the university, turn right onto Depot St. then take the first left onto W. Howard St. Info on accommodations and sights. Open Mon.-Fri. 9am-5pm. **North Carolina High Country Host,** 701 Blowing Rock Rd. (264-1299; 800-438-7500). Pick up copies of the *High Country Host Area Travel Guide*, an informative and detailed map of the area, and the *Blue Ridge Parkway Directory*, a mile-by-mile description of all services and attractions located on or near the Parkway. Open daily 9am-5pm.

Greyhound: (262-0501). At the AppalCart station on Winkler's Creek Rd., off Rte. 321. Flag stop in Blowing Rock. One per day to most points east, south, and west. To: Charlotte (2½ hr., $28). Open Mon.-Fri. 8am-5pm, Sat.-Sun. 10am-4:30pm.

Public Transport: Boone AppalCart (264-2278), on Winkler's Creek Rd.. Local bus and van service; 3 routes. The Red Route links downtown Boone with ASU and the motels and restaurants on Blowing Rock Rd. The Green Route serves Rte. 421. Crosstown route between the campus and the new marketplace. The Red Route operates Mon.-Fri. every hr. 7am-7pm; Green Mon.-Fri. every hr. 7am-6pm; crosstown Mon.-Fri. 7am-11pm, Sat. 8am-6pm. Fare 50¢ in town, charged by zones for the rest of the county (25-75¢).

Post Office: 637 Blowing Rock Rd. (264-3813), and 103 W. King St. (262-1171). Open Mon.-Fri. 9am-5pm, Sat. 9am-noon. Lobby sells stamps until 10pm. **ZIP code:** 28607.

Area Code: 704.

ACCOMMODATIONS, CAMPING AND FOOD

Catering primarily to wealthy visitors, the area fields more than its share of expensive motels and B&Bs. Scratch the lodging surface, however, and you will also find enough inexpensive motels, hostels and campsites to answer one's financial woes.

Blowing Rock Assembly Grounds, P.O. Box 2530, Blowing Rock (295-7813), near the Blue Ridge Parkway, has clean rooms, communal bathrooms, sports facilities, and a cheap cafeteria, all in a gorgeous setting with access to hiking trails. Ask the bus driver to let you off at Blowing Rock Town Hall or at the Rte. 321 bypass and Sunset Dr., depending on the direction you're traveling—it's about 2 mi. from both points. Call the hostel for a pick-up, or stay on Rte. 321 and drive south to Goforth Rd. on the left, near a huge white building; follow along the golf course until you see the "BRAG" signs. Primarily a retreat for religious groups. (Check in after 4pm, check out before 1pm. Desk open daily 9am-5pm. Package rates available. No laundry facilities. $14; price subject to change early 1994. Reservations required.)

Most inexpensive hotels are concentrated along Blowing Rock Rd. (Rte. 321), or Rte. 105. The red-brick **Red Carpet Inn** (264-2457) has spacious rooms that come with remote TV, a playground, and a pool. Prices may vary with seasonal availability. Some holiday weekends have 2-night minimum stay, e.g. July 4. All credit cards accepted; reservations not required. No laundry facilities. (Singles and doubles $43. Weekend singles and doubles $63.) The **High Country Inn** (264-1000 or 800334-5605), Rte. 105 also has a pool, jacuzzi, sauna and exercise room. They even boast a watermill. Standard-sized, comfortable rooms. Check in 4pm, check out 11am (Mid-range prices: Singles $37. Doubles $42. Weekend rates $10 more. Ask about seasonal prices. Breakfast and dinner packages available.)

Boone and **Pisgah National Forest** offer developed and well-equipped **campsites** as well as **primitive camping** options for those who are looking to rough it. Along the Blue Ridge Pkwy., spectacular sites without hookups are available for $8 at the **Julian Price Campground,** Mile 297 (963-5911); **Linville Falls,** Mile 316 (963-5911); and **Crabtree Meadows,** Mile 340 (675-4444; open May-Oct. only). Cabins in **Roan Mountain State Park** (772-3314) comfortably sleep 6 and are furnished with linens and cooking utensils (Sun.-Thurs. $62, Fri.-Sat. $85, weekly $419). The state park offers pool and tennis facilities and tends to attract smaller crowds than the campgrounds on the parkway. May-Sept. visitors can unwind from a day of hiking at the park's "Summer in the Park" festival featuring cloggers and storytellers. For more info call the **Roan Mountain Visitors Center** at 772-3314 or 772-3303.

Fast food restaurants deep-fat fry on both sides of Rte. 321. Try the **Daniel Boone Inn** (264-8657), Jct. Rtes. 321 and 421, for a hefty country sit-down meal served family style, all-you-can-eat. Dinner includes dessert. (Open Mon.-Sun., dinner 11am-9pm, $10; breakfast Sat.-Sun. only, $6.) For an Italian flavor, dine at **Piccadeli's,** 818 Blowing Rock Rd. (704-262-3500). Appetizers from 95¢, with homemade soups and sandwiches $3-5. Italian specialties like spaghetti from $5. (Open Mon.-Sun, 11am-10pm). College hangouts (for students and professors alike) line **King St.** (U.S. 441/U.S. 221). **Our Daily Bread,** 109 King St. (264-0173), serves sandwiches, salads, and super vegetarian specials for $3-5 (open Mon.-Fri. 8am-6:30pm, Sat. 9am-5pm). Down the block, the **Appalachian Soda Shop,** 213 King St. (262-1500), lays the grease on thicker, but the prices are lower. Huge, juicy burgers for under $2, "famous" BBQ for $3-5 (open Mon.-Sat. 8:30am-5pm).

SIGHTS AND ACTIVITIES

In an open air amphitheater, **Horn in the West** (264-2120), located near Boone off Rte. 105, presents an outdoor drama of the American Revolution as it was fought in the southern Appalachians. (Shows Tues.-Sun. at 8:30pm. Admission $8-12, children under 13 ½-price. Group rates upon request. Reservations recommended.) Adjacent to the theater the **Daniel Boone Native Gardens** celebrate mountain foliage, while the **Hickory Ridge Homestead** documents 18th-century mountain life. **An Appalachian Summer** (262-6084) is a month-long, high-caliber festival of music, art, theater, and dance sponsored by Appalachian State University.

Use Boone as a base from which to explore the mountain towns to the west and south. The community of **Blowing Rock,** 7 mi. south at the entrance to the Blue Ridge Pkwy., is a folk artists' colony. Its namesake overhangs **Johns River Gorge;** chuck a piece of paper (biodegradable, of course) over the edge and the wind will blow it back in your face. AppalCart goes to the Blowing Rock Town Hall from Boone twice daily. The town hall also houses the **Blowing Rock Chamber of Commerce** (295-7851;open Mon.-Sat. 9am-5pm). Stop by **Parkway Craft Center** Mile 294 (295-7938), 2 mi. south of Blowing Rock Village, where members of the Southern Highland Handicraft Guild demonstrate their skills and sell their crafts. The craft center is in the Cone Manor House on the grounds of the **Moses H. Cone Memorial Park,** 3500 acres of shaded walking trails and magnificent views including a picture-postcard view of Bass Lake. Check out the National Park Service desk in the center for a copy of "This Week's Activities." (Open May-Oct. daily 9am-5:30pm; free.) To see the magnificence of the Moses H. Cone Park from another perspective, take the $15 per hr. guided horseback ride. Tours leave the **Blowing Rock Stables** from the **L.M. Tate Showgrounds,** "Home of the oldest continuous horse show in America." Get off the Blue Ridge Pkwy. at the Blowing Rock sign, turn left onto Yonahlossee Rd. and look for the "Blowing Rock Stables" sign on the right; call a day in advance for reservations (295-7847; open April-Dec. Mon.-Sun.).

For physical and aesthetic nourishment in Blowing Rock, the **Cosmic Coffee House** (295-4762), N. Main St., brews wonderful coffee, shows the artwork of local artists in its mezzanine gallery, and hosts local bands several nights a week (open Mon. and Wed.-Sat. 8am-11pm, Tues. and Sun. 8am-9pm).

Hikers should arm themselves with the invaluable large-scale map *100 Favorite Trails* ($3.50). Consider joining one of the guided expeditions led by the staff of **Edge of the World**, P.O. Box 1137, Banner Elk (898-9550), on Rte. 184 downtown. A complete outdoor equipment/clothing store, the Edge rents equipment and gives regional hiking information. They also lead day-long backpacking, whitewater canoeing, spelunking and rock climbing trips throughout the High Country for about $65. (Open Mon.-Sat. 9am-6pm, until 10pm in the summer; Sun. 9am-1pm.)

Downhill skiers can enjoy the Southeast's largest concentration of alpine resorts. Four converge on the Boone/Blowing Rock/Banner Elk area: **Appalachian Ski Mountain**, P.O. Box 106, Blowing Rock, 28604 (800-322-2373; lift tickets weekends $26, weekdays $18, with full rental $27); **Ski Beech**, P.O. Box 1118, Beech Mountain 28605 (387-2011; lift tickets weekends $26, weekdays $21, with rentals $38 and $28 respectively); **Ski Hawknest**, Town of Seven Devils, 1605 Skyland Dr., Banner Elk (963-6561; lift tickets weekends $20, weekdays $10, with rentals $30 and $16); and **Sugar Mountain**, P.O. Box 369, Banner Elk (898-4521; lift tickets weekends $35, weekdays $25, with rentals $47 and $35). AppalCart (264-2278) runs a daily shuttle in winter to Sugar Mountain and 4 times per week to Ski Beech. Call the High Country Host (264-1299) for ski reports. It is best to call ahead to the resort for specific prices of ski packages.

Traveled by car, the 5-mi. access road to **Grandfather Mountain** (800-468-7325) reveals an unparalleled view of the entire High Country area. At the top you'll find a private park featuring a 1 mi.-high suspension bridge, a nature museum with minerals, bird and plant life indigenous to NC, and a small zoo. ($9, kids $5, under 4 free.) To hike or camp on Grandfather Mt. you need a permit ($4 per day, $8 per night for camping—available at the Grandfather Mountain Country Store on Rte. 221 or at the entrance to the park). To learn which trails are available for overnight use, be sure to pick up a trail map at the entrance. (Contact the Backcountry Manager, Grandfather Mt., Linville 28646 for more info. Mountain open daily 8am-7pm; Dec.-March 9am-4pm, weather permitting.)

■■■ ASHEVILLE

A drive along the winding Blue Ridge Parkway reveals the scenic vistas of Asheville's hazy blue mountains, deep valleys, spectacular waterfalls, and plunging gorges. The people of this Appalachian Mountain hub rival nature in their diversity and excitement. Students at UNC-Asheville and naturelovers, a thriving gay and lesbian community, artisans and artists make the city itself as intriguing as the mountains that surround it. The sheer number of attractions—the Vanderbilt's Biltmore Estate, campgrounds and trails, Cherokee museums and cultural exhibitions less than an hour to the south, and almost continuous year-round festivals—disperses tourists and leaves the streets relatively uncluttered.

PRACTICAL INFORMATION

Emergency: 911

Visitor Information: Chamber of Commerce, 151 Haywood St. (258-3858; 800-257-1300 in NC), off I-240 on the northwest end of downtown; just follow the frequent signs. Ask at the desk for a detailed city and trasit route and a comprehensive sight-seeing guide. Open Mon.-Fri. 8:30am-5:30pm, Sat.-Sun. 9am-5pm.

Greyhound: 2 Tunnel Rd. (253-5353), 2 mi. east of downtown, near the Beaucatcher Tunnel. Asheville Transit bus #13 or 14 runs to and from downtown every ½-hr. Last bus at 5:50pm. To: Charlotte (5 per day, 3 hr., $22); Knoxville (7 per day, 3 hr., $24.50); Atlanta ($44). Open daily 8am-10pm.

Public Transport: Asheville Transit, 360 W. Haywood (253-5691). Service within city limits. All routes converge on Pritchard Park downtown. Buses oper-

ate Mon.-Fri. (and some Sat.) 5:30am-7pm, most at ½-hr. intervals. Fare 60¢, transfers 10¢. Special fares for seniors, disabled, and multi-fare tickets.
Post Office: 33 Coxe Ave. (257-4112), at Patton Ave. Open Mon.-Fri. 8am-5pm, Sat. 9am-noon. **ZIP code:** 28802.
Area Code: 704.

ACCOMMODATIONS AND CAMPING

Asheville's many reasonably priced motels cluster in two spots—several independent motels lie on **Merrimon Ave.** near downtown (take bus #2), while **Tunnel Rd.** (east of downtown; take buses #4 and 12) also sports major chains like Holiday Inn, Days Inn, and Econo Lodge near the Folk Art Center and two major malls. The **American Court Motel**, 85 Merrimon Ave. (253-4427 or 800-233-3582 for reservation desk only), has bright, cozy and well-kept rooms with cable, A/C, pool, and laundromat. (Ask for *Let's Go* discount of 10%, 15% for non-smoking rooms. No pets. All credit cards accepted. A little pricier than most with singles for $36, doubles $54.) The **Down Town Motel**, 65 Merrimon Ave. (253-9841), on Merrimon St. just north of the I-240 expressway, is a 10-min. walk from downtown (or take bus #2), with cable, A/C, renovated rooms, new furniture and bathrooms. Prices are seasonal, starting at $25. Ask about long-term (several days) discounts. As of press time, the Down Town was still being renovated, and on-season rates may rise. Travelers with *Let's Go* are warmly welcomed. **In Town Motor Lodge**, 100 Tunnel Rd. (252-1811), provides clean rooms with cable, A/C, pool, and free local calls. (Singles $26, doubles $32; weekends $36; Nov.-May singles $24, doubles $29.) The **Skyway Motel**, 131 Tunnel Rd. (253-2631), dazzles with its daintily painted walls and decorative prints in simple rooms. (Off-season rooms start at $20. In-season singles $25, doubles $27; weekend rates are higher. Group and long-term rates available.)

With the Blue Ridge Pkwy., Pisgah National Forest, and the Great Smokies easily accessible by car, you can find a campsite to suit any taste. Close to town is **Bear Creek RV Park and Campground**, 81 S. Bear Creek Rd. (253-0798). Take I-40 exit 47, and look for the sign at the top of the hill. (Pool, laundry, groceries, and game room. Tent sites $16.50. RV sites with hookup $22.) In Pisgah National Forest, the nearest campground is **Powhatan**, off Rte. 191, 12 mi. southwest of Asheville. (All sites along the Pkwy $8. Open May-Sept.)

FOOD

You'll find greasy links in most major fast-food chains on **Tunnel Road** and **Biltmore Avenue**. The **Western North Carolina Farmers Market** (253-1691), at the intersection of I-40 and Rte. 191, near I-26, hawks fresh produce and crafts. Take bus #16 to I-40, then walk ½-mi. (Open daily 8am-6pm.)

Stone Soup (252-7687), at Broadway and Walnut St. Also on Wall St. (254-0844), downtown (open daily 8am-3pm). A cooperative that bakes its own bread and cookies and serves nitrate-free sausage. Soup and sandwiches from $2.75. Try the Hungarian Peasant Bread. Packed noon-2pm and for Sun. brunch. Open Mon.-Sat. 7am-4pm, Sun. 9:30am-1:30pm, Thurs.-Sat. 5-9pm.

Malaprops Bookstore/Cafe, 61 Haywood St. (254-6734), downtown in the basement of the bookstore. Gourmet coffees, bagels, and great smells that emanate throughout the store. Cerebral readings, great book curriculum, and walking staff. Large gay and lesbian (especially lesbian) literature section. Check out the Malaprops staff art on the walls. Open Mon.-Thurs. 9am-8pm, Fri.-Sat. 9am-10pm, Sun. noon-5pm.

Five Points Restaurant, 258 Broadway (252-8030), at the corner of Chestnut two blocks from Merrimon. For home cookin' close to several motels, this unremarkable-looking diner cannot be beat. So inexpensive it's almost unbelievable. You can get a full dinner (entree, salad, and two veggies) for $3-5 and sandwiches from $1.70. Open Mon.-Sat. 6am-8:30pm.

Superette, 78 Patton Ave. (254-0255), in the heart of the downtown, serves out Middle Eastern food good, fast, and cheap. The felafel, hummus, and gyros are complemented nicely by jewelry and knickknacks, moon pies, and chips. Salads from $1.50, sandwiches $2.50-$3.50. Open daily 9am-6pm.

SIGHTS AND FESTIVALS

Elvis's Southern mansion, Graceland, has nothing on the Vanderbilt family's **Biltmore Estate,** 1 North Pack Sq. (255-1700 or 800-543-2961). Take exit 50 off I-40, and go 3 blocks north. A tour of this true French Renaissance-style castle can take all day if it's crowded; try to arrive early in the morning. The not-so-humble abode was built in the 1890s and is the largest private home in America. The self-guided tour winds through a portion of the 250 rooms, enabling one to view an indoor pool, a bowling alley, rooms lined with Sargent paintings and Dürer prints, and immense rare-book libraries. Tours of the surrounding gardens, designed by Central Park planner Frederick Law Olmsted, and the Biltmore winery (with sour-wine tasting for those over 21) are included in the hefty admission price. (Open daily 9am-5pm. Winery open Mon.-Sat. at 11am, Sun. at 1pm. $23, ages 10-16 $17.25, disabled $13, under 9 free. Ticket prices rise $2-3 in Nov.-Dec. in order to defray the cost of Christmas decorations.) Be sure to get your ticket validated—if you decide to return the next day, your visit will be free. Also, pay a visit to **Biltmore Village,** the quaint shopping district that George Vanderbilt had built right outside the gates of his chateau. It contains craft galleries, antique stores, and a music shop. On Memorial Day, July 4th, and Labor Day weekends, the Village hosts outdoor jazz, and September always brings the International Exposition overflowing with food, crafts, and music from around the world and grown at home.

Past travelers like Henry Ford, Thomas Edison, and F. Scott Fitzgerald all stayed in the towering **Grove Park Inn** (252-2711), on Macon St. off Charlotte St.; look for the bright red tile roof peeking through the trees. Made of stone quarried from the surrounding mountains, the still-operating hotel has many pieces of original early-20th-century furniture and fireplaces so immense you can walk into them. Walk to the right wing of the inn and you will happen upon the **Biltmore Industrial Museum** (253-7651) where looms loom large and homespun handicrafts used on the Biltmore Estate gather dust (open 10am-6pm). Next door is the **Estes-Winn Memorial Museum** which houses about 20 vintage automobiles ranging from a Model T Ford to a 1959 Edsel. Check out the 1922 candy red America La France fire engine. On the way out, peruse the door engraving: "Doing a common thing uncommonly well often brings success." Mr. Vanderbilt must have been pretty darn uncommonly common. (Open Mon.-Sat. 10am-5pm, Sun. 1-5pm for both museums. Free.) Trod on your favorite author at the **Riverside Cemetery,** Birch St. off Montford Ave., north of I-240, where writers Thomas Wolfe and O. Henry are buried. The **Thomas Wolfe Memorial,** 48 Spruce St. (253-8304), between Woodfin and Walnut St., site of the novelist's boyhood home, was a boarding house run by his mother. Wolfe depicted the "Old Kentucky Home" as "Dixieland" in his first novel, *Look Homeward, Angel.* (Open Mon.-Sat. 9am-5pm, Sun. 1-5pm; hours vary in winter. Tours given every ½-hr. Admission $1, students and kids 50¢.)

Asheville's artistic tradition remains as strong as its literary one; visit the **Folk Art Center** (704-298-7928), east of Asheville at mile 382 on the Blue Ridge Pkwy., north of U.S. 70, to see outstanding work of the **Southern Highland Handicraft Guild.** (Open daily 9am-6pm. Free.) Each year around mid-July the Folk Art Center sponsors a **Guild Fair** (298-7928), at the Asheville Civic Center, off I-240 on Haywood St. Both the Folk Art Center and the chamber of commerce have more info on this weekend of craft demonstrations, dancing, and music.

A well-rounded city, Asheville offers **McCormick Field** (258-0428), at the intersection of Biltmore Ave. and S. Charlotte St., to baseball enthusiasts. This stadium is home to "the greatest show on dirt" where the farm team for the Houston Astros plays. Scrutinizing observers may catch the next rising baseball star for the Astros. ($3.75, students with ID $3, ages 3-12 $2.)

■■■ OUTER BANKS

England's first attempt to colonize North America took place on the shores of North Carolina in 1587. This ill-fated adventure ended when Sir Walter Raleigh's Roanoke Island settlement inexplicably vanished. Since then, a succession of pirates, patriots, and secessionists have brought adventure to the North Carolina coast. Blackbeard called Ocracoke home in the early 18th century until a savvy serviceman struck down the buccaneer at Pamlico Sound. Most seafarers didn't fare well here; over 600 ships have foundered on the shoals of the Banks' southern shores. Though they were the site of the deaths of countless sailors, the Outer Banks also saw the birth of powered flight—the Wright Brothers flew the first airplane at Kitty Hawk in 1903.

The Outer Banks descend from touristy beach towns southward into heavenly wilderness. Highly developed Bodie Island, on the Outer Banks' northern end, holds the towns of Nags Head, Kitty Hawk, and Kill Devil Hills. In order to get far, far away from the madding crowd, travel south on Rte. 12 through magnificent wildlife preserves and across Hatteras Inlet to Ocracoke island—where you will find the Outer Banks' isolated beaches.

PRACTICAL INFORMATION

Emergency: 911, north of the Oregon Inlet. In **Ocracoke,** 928-4831.
Visitor Information: Aycock Brown Visitors Center (261-4644), off U.S. 158, after the Wright Memorial Bridge, Bodie Island. Info on accommodations, picnic areas, and National Park Service schedules. Open Mon.-Thurs. 8:30am-6:30pm, Fri.-Sun. 8:30am-7:30pm; in winter Mon.-Fri. 9am-5pm.
Cape Hatteras National Seashore Information Centers: Bodie Island (441-5711), Rte. 12 at Bodie Island Lighthouse. Info and special programs. Open Memorial Day to Labor Day daily 10am-4pm. **Hatteras Island** (995-4474), Rte. 12 at Cape Hatteras. Camping info, demonstrations, and special programs. Open daily 9am-6pm; off-season daily 9am-5pm. **Ocracoke Island** (928-4531), next to the ferry terminal at the south end of the island. Info on ferries, camping, lighthouses, and wild ponies. Open daily 9am-5pm, mid-June to Aug. daily 9am-6pm.
Ferries: Toll ferries operate to Ocracoke from **Cedar Island,** east of New Bern on U.S. 70 (4-8 per day, 2¼ hr.), and **Swan Quarter,** on the northern side of Pamlico Sound off U.S. 264/Rte. 45 (2 per day, 2½ hr.), both on the mainland. $10 per car (reserve in advance), $2 per biker, $1 on foot. (Cedar Island 225-3551, Swan Quarter 926-1111, Ocracoke 928-3841. All open daily 5:30am-8:30pm.) Free ferry across Hatteras Inlet between Hatteras and Ocracoke (daily 5am-11pm, 40 min.).
Taxi: Beach Cab, 441-2500. Serves Bodie Island and Manteo. $1.50 first mi., $1.20 each additional mi.
Car Rental: National, Mile 6, Beach Rd. (800-328-4567 or 441-5488), Kill Devil Hills. $55 per day. 75 free mi., 30¢ each additional mi. Must be 25 with major credit card. Open Mon.-Fri. 9am-5pm, Sat. 9am-3pm.
Bike Rental: Pony Island Motel (928-4411) and the **Slushy Stand** on Rte. 12, both on Ocracoke Island. $1 per hr., $7 per day. Open daily 8am-dusk.
ZIP Codes: Manteo 27954, Nags Head 27959, Ocracoke 27960.
Area Code: 919.

Four narrow islands strung north-to-south along half the length of the North Carolina coast comprise the Outer Banks. **Bodie Island** includes the towns of **Kitty Hawk, Kill Devil Hills,** and **Nags Head,** connecting to Elizabeth, NC, and Norfolk, VA, by U.S. 158. **Roanoke Island** swims between Bodie and the mainland on U.S. 64, and includes the town of **Manteo. Hatteras Island,** connected to Bodie by a bridge, stretches like a great sandy elbow. **Ocracoke Island,** the southernmost, is linked by free ferry to Hatteras Island, and by toll ferry to towns on the mainland. **Cape Hat-**

teras **National Seashore** encompasses Hatteras, Ocracoke, and the southern end of Bodie Island. On Bodie Island, U.S. 158 and Rte. 12 run parallel to each other until the beginning of the preserve. After that Rte. 12 (also called Beach Rd.) continues south, stringing Bodie, Hatteras, and Ocracoke together with free bridges and ferries. Addresses on Bodie Island are determined by their distance in miles from the Wright Memorial Bridge.

Nags Head and Ocracoke lie 76 mi. apart, and public transportation is virtually nonexistent. Hitching, though common, is not recommended, and may require lengthy waits. The flat terrain makes hiking and biking pleasant, but the Outer Banks' ferocious traffic calls for extra caution.

ACCOMMODATIONS AND CAMPING

Most motels cling to Rte. 12 in the costly town of Nags Head. For budget accommodations, try **Ocracoke.** On all three islands the "in season" usually lasts from mid-June to Labor Day, when rates are much higher. Reserve seven to ten days ahead for weekday stays and up to a month for weekends. Rangers advise campers to bring extra-long tent spikes because of the loose dirt as well as tents with extra-fine screens to keep out the flea-sized, biting "no-see-ums." Strong insect repellent is also helpful. Crashing on the beach is illegal.

Nags Head/Kill Devil Hills

Olde London Inn, Mile 12, Beach Rd. (441-7115), Nags Head oceanfront. Oceanfronte location, golfe privileges, recreationale facilities. Huge picture windowes offset drab decor in cleane, spacious roomes. More powerful than a silent "e". Cable TV, A/C, refrigerator. Singles/doubles $49; off-season $29. Open Apr.-Oct.

The Ebbtide, Mile 10, Beach Rd. (441-4913), Kill Devil Hills. A family place with spruce, wholesome rooms. Cable TV, A/C, pool. Offers "inside track" on local activities. Singles or doubles $49-57; off-season $29-35. Open Apr.-Oct.

Nettlewood Motel, Mile 7, Beach Rd. (441-5039), Kill Devil Hills, on both sides of the highway. Imagine that. Private beach access. Don't let the uninviting exterior prevent you from enjoying this clean, comfortable motel. TV, A/C, pool, refrigerator. 4-day min. stay on weekends. Singles or doubles $42; off-season: rooms $27-33. Free day for week-long stays.

Ocracoke

Sand Dollar Motel (928-5571), off Rte. 12. South on Rte. 12, turn right at the Pony Island Inn, right at the Back Porch Restaurant, and left at the Edwards Motel. Accommodating owners make you feel at home in this breezy, quiet, immaculate motel. Singles $43, doubles $53. Off-season: $32/37. (Sand dollars not accepted in payment.)

Beach House (928-4271), just off Rte. 12, behind the Slushy Stand. B&B with 4 charming, clean, antiques-filled rooms. Rooms $45; spring and fall $40.

Edwards Motel (928-4801), off Rte. 12, by the Back Porch Restaurant. Fish-cleaning facilities on premises. Bright assortment of accommodations, all with A/C and TV. Rooms with 2 double beds $44, with 2 double beds and 1 single bed $49; efficiencies $58; cottages $75-85. Off-season $37, $42, $53, and $65-70, respectively.

Oscar's House (928-1311), on the ocean side of Rte. 12, 1 block from Silver Lake harbor. Charming B&B with 4 rooms, shared baths. Memorial Day-June singles $45, doubles $55; July-Labor Day singles $50, doubles $60; off-season: singles $40, doubles $50. Full vegetarian breakfast included.

The four oceanside **campgrounds** on Cape Hatteras National Seashore are all open mid-April to mid-October. **Oregon Inlet** squats on the southern tip of Bodie Island; **Cape Point** (in Buxton), and **Frisco** near the elbow of Hatteras Island; and **Ocracoke** in the middle of Ocracoke Island. All have restrooms, cold running water, and grills. All sites (except Ocracoke's) cost $11, and are rented on a first-come, first-served basis. Reserve Ocracoke sites ($12) through **MISTIX** (800-365-2267). For info, contact Cape Hatteras National Seashore, Rte. 1, P.O. Box 675, Manteo, NC 27954 (473-2111).

SIGHTS AND ACTIVITIES

The **Wright Brothers National Memorial,** Mile 8, U.S. 158 (441-7430), marks the spot in Kill Devil Hills where Orville and Wilbur Wright made the world's first sustained, controlled power flight in 1903. You can see models of their planes, hear a detailed account of the day of the first flight, chat with the flight attendants, and view the dramatic monument the U.S. government dedicated to the brothers in 1932. (Open daily 9am-6pm; winter 9am-5pm. Presentations every hr. 10am-5pm. Admission $2, $4 per car, free with seniors.) In nearby **Jockey's Ridge State Park,** home of the East Coast's largest sand dunes, hang-gliders soar in the wind that Orville and Wilbur first broke.

On **Roanoke Island,** the **Fort Raleigh National Historic Site,** off U.S. 64, offers separately run attractions in one park. In the **Elizabeth Gardens** (473-3234), antique statues and fountains punctuate a beautiful display of flowers, herbs, and trees. (Open daily 9am-8pm; off-season 9am-5pm. $2.50, under 12 free.) Behind door number two lies the theater where *The Lost Colony,* the longest-running 3outdoor drama in the U.S., has been performing since 1937 (473-3414; performed Mon.-Sat. mid-June-late Aug. at 8:30pm; $10, seniors and disabled people $9, under 12 $5; bring insect repellent). **Fort Raleigh** (473-5772) is a reconstructed 1585 battery—basically a pile of dirt. The nearby **visitors center** contains a tiny museum and plays Elizabethan music as part of its losing battle to recall the earliest days of English activity in North America. (Open Mon.-Sat. 9am-8pm, Sun. 9am-6pm.) Lay your hands on a horseshoe crab and make faces at marine monsters in the Shark, Skate, and Ray Gallery at the **North Carolina Aquarium** (473-3493), 1 mi. west of U.S. 64. A full slate of educational programs keeps things lively. (Open Mon.-Sat. 9am-5pm, Sun. 1-5pm. Free, donations accepted.)

On **Ocracoke Island,** historical sights give way to the incessant, soothing surf. With the exception of the town of Ocracoke on the southern tip, the island remains an undeveloped national seashore. Speedy walkers or meandering cyclists can cover the town in less than an hour. Pick up a walking tour pamphlet at the visitors center (see Practical Information above). Better yet, stroll or swim along the waters that lick the pristine shore. At the **Soundside Snorkel,** park rangers teach visitors to snorkel. Bring tennis shoes and a swimsuit. (Wed. and Fri. at 2:30pm. Equipment rental $1. Make reservations at the Ocracoke Visitors Center from 9am the day before until 2:30pm the day of program.)

■■■ RALEIGH, DURHAM, AND CHAPEL HILL

The Research Triangle, a region embracing Raleigh, Durham, and Chapel Hill, contains more PhDs per capita that any other part of the nation. Durham, the former tobacco mecca of the world, is now, ironically, a city devoted to medicine, sprinkled with hospitals and diet clinics. It also houses Duke University, one of the greenest and most prestigious universities in the nation. Chapel Hill, just 20 mi. down the road, holds its own in education as the home of the nation's first public university, the University of North Carolina. Raleigh, the state capital, is an easygoing, historic town, as well as the home of North Carolina State University.

PRACTICAL INFORMATION

Emergency: 911.
Visitor Information: Raleigh Capitol Area Visitors Center, 301 N. Blount St. (733-3456). Focuses on buildings in the capitol area. Open Mon.-Fri. 8am-5pm, Sat. 9am-5pm, Sun. 1-5pm. **Durham Chamber of Commerce,** People's Security Building, 14th floor, 300 W. Morgan St. (682-2133). *Not* geared to the budget trav-

eler. Complimentary maps and a great view of Durham. Open Mon.-Fri. 8:30am-5pm. **Chapel Hill Chamber of Commerce,** 104 S. Estes Dr. (967-7075). Open Mon.-Fri. 9am-5pm.

Airport: Raleigh-Durham Airport: 15 mi. northwest of Raleigh on U.S. 70 (829-1477). Many hotels and rental car agencies provide free airport limousine service (596-2361) if you have reservations. Pick up helpful complimentary maps of Raleigh and Durham at the **information counter** on the airport's lower level.

Amtrak: 320 W. Cabarrus, Raleigh (833-7594 or 800-872-7245). To: Miami (1 per day, 16 hr., $148), Washington, DC (2 per day, 6 hr., $46), and Richmond (2 per day, 4 hr., $34). Open daily 6:30am-8:30pm.

Greyhound: In Raleigh: 314 W. Jones St. (828-2567). To: Durham (6 per day, 40 min., $6), Chapel Hill (5 per day, 80 min., $7), Richmond (6 per day, 3½ hr., $34), North Charleston (2 per day, 8 hr., $36 if reservations made 7 days in advance). Open 24 hrs. **In Durham:** 820 Morgan St. (687-4800), 1 block off Chapel Hill St. downtown, 2½ mi. northeast of Duke University. To: Chapel Hill (5 per day, ½ hr., $4), Washington, DC (4 per day, 7 hr., $40). Open daily 7am-11:30pm. **In Chapel Hill:** 311 W. Franklin St. (942-3356), 4 blocks from the UNC campus. Open Mon.-Fri. 9am-4pm, Sat.-Sun. 8am-3:30pm.

Public Transport: Capital Area Transit, Raleigh (828-7228). Operates Mon.-Fri., fewer buses on Sat. Fare 50¢. **Duke Power Company Transit Service,** Durham (688-4587). Most routes start at the 1st Federal Bldg. at Main St. on the loop, downtown. Buses run daily 6am-6pm, some to 10:30pm. Fare 50¢, transfers 10¢.

Taxi: Safety Taxi, 832-8800, and **Cardinal Cab,** 828-3228. Both $2.85 plus $1.50 each mi., 24-hr. service.

Help Lines: Rape Crisis, 828-3005, 24 hrs.

Post Office: Raleigh: 310 New Bern Ave. (831-3661). Open Mon.-Fri. 7am-6pm, Sat. 8am-noon. **ZIP code:** 27611. **Durham:** 323 E. Chapel Hill St. (683-1976). Open Mon.-Fri. 8am-5pm. **ZIP code:** 27701. **Chapel Hill:** 179 E. Franklin St. (967-6297). Open Mon.-Fri. 8:30am-5pm, Sat. 8:30am-noon. **ZIP code:** 27514.

Area Code: 919.

ACCOMMODATIONS AND CAMPING

YMCA, 1601 Hillsborough St. (832-6601), Raleigh, 5 blocks from Greyhound station. Comfortable rooms in a communal atmosphere. Free recreational facilities. Singles $17, with bath $20. Key deposit $2. Call ahead for reservations.

YWCA, 1012 Oberlin Rd. (828-3205), Raleigh, ½ mi. north of Cameron Village Shopping Center. Women only. Large, luxurious facility. Hall bath. Free recreational facilities. Singles $15, weekly $55. Must have an informal interview with the director to stay here.

Carolina-Duke Motor Inn (286-0771), I-85 at Guess Rd., Durham. Clean rooms, with duck pics on the walls. Free Movie Channel, swimming pool. Free shuttle to Duke University Medical Center on the main campus. 10% discount for *Let's Go* users, seniors, and AAA cardholders. Singles $28, doubles $34. $3 for each additional person. The **Wabash Express** (286-0020) next door serves cheap and filling breakfasts (6 pancakes $2.75) Sat.-Sun.

Motel 6, 3921 Arrow Dr. (782-7071), Raleigh. U.S. 70 at Crabtree Valley Exit. Same as the last one you stayed in: pool, A/C, movie channel. Single $28, double $32.

Umstead State Park (787-3033), U.S. 70, 2 mi. northwest of Raleigh. Tent and trailer sites. Large lake for fishing and hiking. Open June-Aug. 8am-9pm; Sept.-May shorter hrs. Sites $9. Closed to camping Mon.-Wed.

FOOD

The restaurants near the universities are suited to the budget traveler. In Raleigh, **Hillsborough Street,** across from North Carolina State University, has a wide array of inexpensive restaurants and bakeries staffed, for the most part, by students. The same can be said of **9th Street** in Durham and **Franklin Street** in Chapel Hill.

Ramshead Rath-Skellar, 157-A E. Franklin St., Chapel Hill (942-5158), directly across from the campus. A student hang-out featuring pizza, sandwiches, and hot apple pie Louise. Ship mastheads, German beer steins, and old Italian wine bottles decorate 8 different dining rooms with names such as "Rat Trap Lounge." "Flukey" Hayes, here since 1963, may cook your steak. Full meals $7-8. Open Mon.-Sat. 11am-2:30pm and 5-10:30pm, Sun. 11am-11pm.

The Ninth Street Bakery Shop, 754 9th St., Durham (286-0303). More than a bakery; sandwiches from $2.50. Try the dense bran or blueberry muffins. Live music nightly. Open Mon.-Thurs. 8am-7pm, Fri.-Sat. 8am-11pm, Sun. 8am-5pm.

Skylight Exchange, 405½ W. Rosemary St., Chapel Hill (933-5550). A sandwich restaurant with a huge brass espresso machine. Doubles as a used book and record store. Sandwiches $2-3. Live music on weekends. Open Mon.-Thurs. 10am-11pm, Fri.-Sat. 11am-midnight, Sun. 1-11pm.

Side Street, 225 N. Bloodworth St., Raleigh (828-4927), at E. Lane St. 3 blocks from the capitol. A classy place with antique furniture, flower table settings, and huge sandwiches with exotic names. Salads too. All selections under $6. Open Mon.-Fri. 11am-3pm and 5-9pm, Sat. 11am-3pm.

Clyde Cooper's Barbeque, 109 E. Davie, Raleigh (832-7614), 1 block east of the Fayetteville Street Mall downtown. If you like BBQ, this is the place to try it NC-style. The local favorites are the baby back ribs ($5 per lb.) or the barbeque chicken ($3.50). Open Mon.-Sat. 10am-6pm.

Well Spring Grocery, 1002 9th St., Durham (286-2290). A health food grocery with a wide variety of inexpensive fruits, vegetables, and whole grains. Open Mon.-Sat. 9am-8pm, Sun. 10am-7pm.

SIGHTS AND ENTERTAINMENT

While the triangle's main attractions are universities, Raleigh has its share of histori-cal sights. The **capitol building,** in Union Square at Edenton and Salisbury, was built in 1840. (Open Mon.-Fri. 8am-5pm, Sat. 9am-5pm. Tours available for large groups. Free.) Across the street and around the corner at Bicentennial Square is the **Museum of Natural Sciences** (733-7450), which has fossils, gems, and animal exhibits includ-ing a live 17-ft. Burmese python named George. (Open Mon.-Sat. 9am-5pm, Sun. 1-5pm. Free.) Just down the way at 109 E. Jones St., the **North Carolina Museum of History** (733-3894) exhibits memorabilia from the state's Roanoke days to the present. (Open Tues.-Sat. 9am-5pm, Sun. 1-6pm. Free.) Pick up a brochure at the vis-itors center for a self-guided tour of the renovated 19th-century homes of **Historic Oakwood,** where eight North Carolina governors are buried. The **North Carolina Museum of Art,** 2110 Blue Ridge Blvd. (833-1935), off I-40 (Wade Ave. exit), has eight galleries, including works by Raphael (the painter, not the turtle), Botticelli, Rubens, Monet, Wyeth, and O'Keeffe, as well as some ancient Egyptian artifacts. (Tours Tues.-Sun. at 1:30pm. Open Tues.-Sat. 9am-5pm, Fri. 9am-9pm, Sun. 11am-6pm. Free.) A tour of **North Carolina State University** on Hillsborough St. (737-3276), includes the **Pulstar Nuclear Reactor.** (Free tours during the semester Mon.-Fri. at noon, leaving from the Bell Tower on Hillsborough St.) Barring a nuclear acci-dent, none of these sights is all that glowing.

For less urban entertainment, visit Chapel Hill where the **University of North Carolina** (962-2211), the oldest state university in the country, sprawls over 729 acres. Astronauts practiced celestial navigation until 1975 at the university's **More-head Planetarium** (962-1236), which houses one of twelve $2.2 million Zeiss Star projectors. The planetarium puts up six different shows yearly, each involving a combination of films and Zeiss projections. These shows are conceived and pro-duced while you watch. The best part is the staff of friendly UNC students, some of whom are Zeissmeisters; they will give advice to travelers—celestial and otherwise. (Open Sun.-Fri. 12:30-5pm and 6:30-9:30pm, Sat. noon-5pm and 6:30-9:30pm. $3, seniors, students, and kids $2.50.) Call the university (962-2211) for info on sporting events and concerts at the Smith Center (a.k.a. the Dean Dome).

In Durham, **Duke University** is the major attraction. The **admissions office,** at 2138 Campus Dr. (684-3214), doubles as a visitors center (open 8am-5pm). The **Duke Chapel** (tours and info 684-2572) at the center of the university has more than a million pieces of stained glass in 77 windows depicting almost 900 figures. The Duke Memorial Organ inside has 5000 pipes; its music may send shivers up the back of your neck—beauty that transcends mathematics. Show up around lunchtime and you might catch a free personal concert. (Open daily Sept.-June 8am-8pm.)

To the left is the walkway to the **Bryan Center,** Duke's labyrinthine student center, with a gift shop, a cafe, and a small art gallery; the info desk has brochures on activities, concerts and local buses, as well as free campus maps. Near West Campus on Anderson St. are the **Sarah Duke Gardens** (684-3698), with over 15 acres of landscaped gardens and tiered flower beds. Giant goldfish swim in a small pond near a vined gazebo good for shaded picnics. (Open daily 8am-dusk.) Take the free Duke campus shuttle bus to East Campus, where the **Duke Museum of Art** (684-5135), hangs with a small but impressive collection. (Open Tues.-Fri. 9am-5pm, Sat. 11am-2pm, Sun. 2-5pm. Free.) Also take time to enjoy Duke's 7700-acre **forest,** and its more than 30 mi. of trails and drivable roads.

On the other side of Durham, up Guess Rd., is the **Duke Homestead,** 2828 Duke Homestead Rd. (477-5498). Washington Duke first started in the tobacco business here, and went on, with the help of his sons, to fund what would become Duke University. The beautiful estate is still a small working farm. (Open April-Oct. Mon.-Sat. 9am-5pm, Sun. 1-5pm; Nov.-March Tues.-Sat. 10am-4pm, Sun. 1-4pm. Free.)

At night, students frequent bars along **Franklin Street** in Chapel Hill, and **9th Street** in Durham. Before doing the same, you can catch a **Durham Bulls** (688-8211) baseball game. The Bulls, a class A farm team for the Atlanta Braves, became famous after the 1988 movie *Bull Durham* was filmed in their ballpark. (Reserved tickets $6, general admission and under 18 $3, students and seniors $2.50.)

The Research Triangle area always offers something to do, whether it's a concert, guest lecture, exhibit or going to a bar and getting super-trashed. For a complete listing, pick up free copies of both the *Spectator* and *Independent* weekly magazines, available at most restaurants, bookstores, and hotels.

■ South Carolina

The first state to secede from the Union in 1860, South Carolina takes great pride in its Confederate history, with Civil War monuments dotting virtually every public green or city square. A strange mix of progressive and reactionary, South Carolina houses Harley-riding traditionalists who descend upon the statehouse when legislation is drafted to remove the Confederate flag, while it also prepares for its third reasonably well-attended gay pride parade. The capital, Columbia, is slow-paced with little to ogle—Sherman ruined its future-tourist-town potential by burning it to the ground—but Charleston, despite a recent hurricane, still boasts beautiful, stately, antebellum charm. You'll want to do the Charleston for a few days and take in the city's favors and flavors.

PRACTICAL INFORMATION

Capital: Columbia.
Visitor Information: Department of Parks, Recreation, and Tourism, Edgar A. Brown Bldg., 1205 Pendleton St. #106, Columbia 29201 (734-0122). **U.S. Forest Service,** P.O. Box 970, Columbia 29202 (765-5222).
Time Zone: Eastern. **Postal Abbreviation:** SC
Sales Tax: 6%.

■■■ CHARLESTON

It seems that natural disasters gravitate to Charleston like tornadoes to trailer parks. In recent years this town has withstood five fires and ten hurricanes, along with the occasional earthquake. The reconstruction after the most recent unkindness—Hurricane Hugo's rampage in September, 1989—is nearly complete; fresh paint, new storefronts, and tree stumps mix with beautifully refurbished antebellum homes, old churches, and hidden gardens. Dukes, barons, and earls once presided over Charleston's great coastal plantations, leaving in their wake an extensive historic downtown district. The Charleston area also offers visitors the resources of the nearby Atlantic coastal islands. Most noticeably, the people of Charleston are some of the friendliest people you will meet on your journeys in the South. They survive and flourish with a smile.

PRACTICAL INFORMATION

Emergency: 911.

Visitor Information: Charleston Visitors Center, 375 Meeting St. (853-8000), by the Municipal Auditorium. Walking tour map (50¢) has historical information and good directions. The film *Forever Charleston* gives an overview of Charleston's past and present. Tickets $3, children $1.50. Open daily 8:30am-5:30pm.

Amtrak: 4565 Gaynor Ave. (744-8263), 8 mi. west of downtown. The "Durant Ave." bus will take you from the station to the historic district. Trains to: Richmond (1 per day, 7 hr., $83), Savannah (1 per day, 2 hr., $24), and Washington, DC (1 per day, 9 hr., $107). Open daily 4:15am-9:30pm.

Greyhound: 3610 Dorchester Rd. (722-7721), in N. Charleston near I-26. Because the downtown bus station is closed, this is the only one available—try to avoid the area at night. To: Myrtle Beach (2 per day, 2 hr., $23), Savannah (2 per day, 3 hr., $28), and Washington, DC (2 per day, 14 hr., $83). To get into town, take the **South Carolina Electric and Gas** bus marked "Broad St." or "South Battery" that stops right in front of the station, and get off at the intersection of Meeting St. and Calhoun St. To get back to the station from town, pick up the bus marked "Navy Yard: 5 Mile Dorchester Rd." at the same intersection. There are two "Navy Yard" buses, so be sure to take this one; it's the only one that stops in front of the station. Open daily 6am-10pm.

Public Transport: South Carolina Electric and Gas Company (SCE&G) City Bus Service, 2469 Leeds Ave. (747-0922). Operates Mon.-Sat. 5:10am-1am. Fare 75¢. **Downtown Area Shuttle (DASH)** also operates Mon.-Fri. 8am-5pm. Fare 75¢, transfers to other SCE&G buses free.

Car Rental: Thrifty Car Rental, 3565 W. Montague Ave. (552-7531 or 800-367-2277). $32 per day with unlimited mileage. Must be 25 with major credit card. Open daily 5:45am-11:30pm.

Bike Rental: The Bicycle Shoppe, 283 Meeting St. (722-8168). $3 per hr., $15 per day. Open Mon.-Sat. 9am-8pm, Sun. 1-5pm.

Taxi: North Area Taxi, 554-7575. Base fare $1.

Help Lines: Hotline, 744-4357. Open 24 hrs. General counseling and information on transient accommodations. **People Against Rape,** 722-7273. Open 24 hrs.

Post Office: 83 Broad St. Open Mon.-Fri. 8:30am-5pm, Sat. 8:30am-noon. **ZIP code:** 29402.

Area Code: 803.

Old Charleston is confined to the southernmost point of the mile-wide peninsula below **Calhoun Street. Meeting, King,** and **East Bay Streets** are major north-south routes through the city. North of Calhoun St. runs the **Savannah Hwy. (U.S. 17).**

ACCOMMODATIONS AND CAMPING

Motel rooms in historic downtown Charleston are expensive. All the cheap motels are far out and not a practical option for those without cars. Investigate the tiny accommodations just across the Ashley River on U.S. 17 South; several offer $15-20

CHARLESTON

rooms. The best budget option in town is the **Rutledge Victoria Inn,** 114 Rutledge Ave. (722-7551), a beautiful historic home with shared rooms and free coffee or tea. ($20 per person first day, $15 additional days.) The friendly manager will not let you set foot in Charleston until she's given you a full orientation. Lockout 10:30am-4:30pm. If she can't house you, try **Charleston East Bed and Breakfast,** 1031 Tall Pine Rd. (884-8208), in Mt. Pleasant east of Charleston off U.S. 701; they will try to place you in one of 15 private homes. (Rooms $20-80. Prior reservations recommended—call 9am-10pm.) **Motel 6,** 2058 Savannah Hwy. (556-5144), 4 mi. out at 7th Ave., is clean and pleasant but far from downtown and frequently filled. (Singles $28, additional person $6. Call ahead; fills up quickly in summer months.)

There are several inexpensive campgrounds in the Charleston area, but none are near downtown. Eight mi. south on U.S. 17, try **Oak Plantation Campground** (766-5936; sites $8, with hookup $11.50. Office open 7:30am-9pm.). Also look for **Pelican's Cove,** 97 Center St. (588-2072), at Folly Beach (sites with full hookup $17; office open 8am-9pm).

FOOD AND NIGHTLIFE

Most restaurants in the revamped downtown area are also expensive. If you choose to eat out, eat lunch, since most restaurants serve their dinner selections at noonday at discounted prices.

Craig Cafeteria (953-5539), corner of St. Philip and George St., the place to chow in Chaz. Serves all-you-can-eat buffets for breakfast (7-9am, $3.75), lunch (11am-2pm, $4), and dinner (4:30-6:30pm, $4.25). Open daily.

Marina Variety Store/City Marina, 17 Lockwood Blvd. (723-6325). Pleasant view of the Ashley River from an otherwise unremarkable dining room. Good shellfish and great nightly specials under $7. Open daily 6:30am-3pm and 5-10pm.

Henry's, 54 N. Market St. (723-4363), at Anson. A local favorite. Not cheap, but the food is good, especially the grilled shrimp ($8). On weekends, live jazz upstairs starts at 9pm, followed by a late-night breakfast. Open Mon.-Wed. 11:30am-10:30pm, Thurs.-Sun. 11:30am-1am.

T-Bonz, 80 N. Market St. (517-2511). Typical steak and seafood in an atypical atmosphere. Live music on Tues. nights is a local favorite. Lunch or dinner $5-12. Open daily 11am-midnight.

Hyman's Seafood Company, 215 Meeting St. (723-0233). Kudos to the proprietor, who manages to serve about 15 different kinds of fresh fish daily ($8). If you like shellfish, the snow crabs ($10) are a must. Open daily 11am-11pm.

Before going out in Charleston, pick up a free copy of *Poor Richard's Omnibus,* available at grocery stores and street corners all over town; the *PRO* lists concerts and other events. Locals rarely dance the *Charleston* anymore, and the city's nightlife has suffered accordingly. Most bars and clubs are in the **Market Street** area. **Cafe 99,** 99 S. Market St. (577-4499), has nightly live entertainment, strong drinks ($2-4), and reasonably priced dinners ($5-10). (Open daily 11:30am-2am. No cover.) For the best bands go to **Myskyns Tavern,** 5 Faber St. (577-5595), near Market St., and have a drink ($1-3) at the enormous mahogany bar. Hang out with the locals on Friday and Saturday nights in front of **San Miguel's Mexican Restaurant** (723-9745), off Market St., or sit on the roof at **The Colony House** on East Bay St. and watch the ships sail into the harbor.

SIGHTS AND EVENTS

Saturated with ancient homes, historical monuments, churches, galleries, and gardens, Charleston gives a tourist something to chew on. A multitude of organized tours allow you to see the city by foot, car, bus, boat, trolley, or carriage. Information on these tours can be obtained at the visitors center. **Gray Line Water Tours** (722-1112) gives you your money's worth. Their two-hour boat rides leave daily at 10am, 12:30pm, and 3pm ($9, ages 6-11 $4; reservations recommended). The bus tours, however, provide the best overview of the city. **Talk of the Towne** (795-8199) has tours thrice a day and will even pick you up from your hotel (75 min. tour $11, 2 hr. tour $17.50). **Trolley Tours** (795-3000) mix the charm and nostalgia of historic Charleston by touring the narrow streets in real trolley cars. 75 min. tours depart from the City Market at "Quarter Hill" every hour and from the visitors center on the hour 9am-5pm. ($11, children $6.) The **Gibbes Gallery,** 135 Meeting St. (722-2706), has a fine collection of portraits by prominent American artists. (Open Sun.-Mon. 1-5pm, Tues.-Sat. 10am-5pm. $3, seniors and students $2, under 13 50¢.)

The **Nathanial Russell House,** 51 Meeting St. (723-1623), features a magnificent staircase that spirals without support from floor to floor. The house gives an idea of how Charleston's wealthy merchant class lived in the early 19th century. The **Edmonston-Allston House,** 21 E. Battery St. (722-7171), looks out over Charleston Harbor. (Both open Mon.-Sat. 10am-5pm, Sun. 2-5pm. Admission to one house $4, to both $6. Get tickets to both homes at 52 Meeting St.) Founded in 1773, the **Charleston Museum,** 360 Meeting St. (722-2996), maintains a collection of bric-a-brac ranging from natural history specimens to old sheet music (open Mon.-Sat. 9am-5pm, Sun. 1-5pm). The museum also offers combination tickets for the museum itself and the three historic homes within easy walking distance: the **Aiken-Rhett Mansion** built in 1817; the 18th-century **Heyward-Washington House,** 87 Church St.; and the **Joseph Manigault House,** 350 Meeting St. (for info on all three tours call 722-2996). The Washington House includes the only 18th-century kitchen open to the public in Charleston. Hope they hide those dirty dishes. (Aiken-Rhett, Washington, and Manigault homes open Mon.-Sat. 10am-5pm, Sun. 1-5pm. Admission to museum and three homes $10, children $5.)

A visit to Charleston just wouldn't be complete without a **boat tour** to **Fort Sumter** (722-1691) in the harbor. The Civil War was touched off when rebel forces in South Carolina, the first state to secede, attacked this Federal fortress on April 12, 1861. Over seven million pounds of metal were fired against the fort before those inside finally fled in February 1865. Tours ($8.50, ages 6-12 $4.25) leave several times daily from the Municipal Marina, at the foot of Calhoun St. and Lockwood Blvd. **Fort Sumter Tours,** a company that runs the tour boats to the fort, also offers tours to **Patriots' Point,** the world's largest naval and maritime museum. Here you can walk the decks of the retired U.S. aircraft carrier *Yorktown,* or stroke the destroyer *Laffey's* huge fore and aft cannon.

If you are feeling a tad gun-shy, visit the **City Market,** downtown at Meeting St., which vends everything from porcelain sea lions to handwoven sweetgrass baskets in the open air daily from 9:30am to sunset.

Magnolia Gardens, (571-1266), 10 mi. out of town on Rte. 61 off U.S. 17, is the 300-year-old ancestral home of the Drayton family, and treats visitors to 50 acres of gorgeous gardens with 900 varieties of camelia and 250 varieties of azalea. Get lost in the hedge maze. You'll probably want to skip the manor house, but do consider renting bicycles ($2 per hr.) to explore the neighboring swamp and bird sanctuary. (Open daily 9:30am-5pm. $8, seniors $7, teens $6, kids $4.)

From mid-March to mid-April, the **Festival of Houses** (723-1623) celebrates Charleston's architecture and traditions as many private homes open their doors to the public. Music, theater, dance, and opera converge on the city during **Spoleto Festival U.S.A.** (722-2764) in late May and early June. During **Christmas in Charleston** (853-8000), tours of many private homes and buildings are given, and many motels offer special reduced rates.

■■■ COLUMBIA

This quiet, unassuming city sprung up in 1786 when bureaucrats in Charleston decided that their territory needed a proper capital. Surveyors found some land near the Congaree River, cleared it, and within two decades, over 1000 people had poured into one of America's first planned cities. President Woodrow Wilson called

Columbia home during his boyhood; now thousands of University of South Carolina (USC) students do the same, providing most of the city's excitement and nightlife. In many ways, the pervasive college-town flavor overshadows state politics here.

Practical Information Emergency is 911. The **Greater Columbia Convention and Visitors Bureau,** 1012 Gervais St. (254-0479), is not budget-oriented, but provides a free street map with all the historical sights marked and a free coupon book for discounts at area hotels and restaurants. (Open Mon.-Fri. 9am-5pm, Sat. 10am-4pm.) The **University of South Carolina Information Desk,** Russell House Student Center, 2nd floor (777-7000), on Green at Sumter St., stocks campus maps, shuttle schedules, advice on budget accommodations, and the low-down on campus life and events. If you get stranded in the area and/or need transportation in a hurry, contact **Traveler's Aid,** 1924 Taylor St. (343-7071; open Mon.-Fri. 9am-5pm).

Most buses running along the East Coast stop here. The **Congaree River** marks the western edge of the city. **Assembly Street** and **Sumter Street** are downtown's major north-south arteries; **Gervais Street** and **Calhoun Street** cut east-west. **Columbia Metropolitan Airport,** 3000 Aviation Way (822-5000), is serviced by **Delta, American, United, USAir,** and others. **Amtrak,** 850 Pulaski St. (252-8246 or 800-872-7245), has trains once per day to Washington, DC (10 hr., $89), Miami (13 hr., $123), and Savannah (2 hr., $31). The northbound train leaves daily at 5:31am, the southbound at 10:43pm. (Station open Mon.-Sat. 8:30am-4:30pm and 10:30pm-6:30am, Sun. 10:30pm-6:30am.) **Greyhound,** 2015 Gervais St. (779-0650 or 800-231-2222), is near the intersection of Harden and Gervais St., about 1 mi. east of the capitol. Buses to: Charlotte (3 per day, 2 hr., $20), Charleston (4 per day, 2 hr., $20), Atlanta (9 per day, 6 hr., $45). Open 24 hrs. **South Carolina Electric and Gas** (748-3019) operates local buses. Most routes start from the transfer depot at the corner of Assembly and Gervais St. (fare 75¢). Local **help lines** are **Helpline of the Midlands** (790-4357) and **Rape Crisis** (771-7273), both 24 hrs. The **Richland Memorial Hospital,** 5 Richland Medical Park (434-7000), has emergency services and a walk-in clinic. The **post office,** 1601 Assembly St. (733-4647), is open Mon.-Fri. 7:30am-5pm. Columbia's **ZIP code** is 29201; the **area code** is 803.

Accommodations and Food The only budget option downtown is the **Heart of Columbia,** 1011 Assembly St. (799-1140), with a shabby-looking exterior but clean chambers. (Singles $31, doubles $34.) Just west of downtown across the Congaree River, a number of inexpensive motels line Knox Abbot Dr. **Econo Lodge** (731-4060), at I-26 and Piney Grove Rd., has bright rooms, a swimming pool, A/C, and a movie channel. (Singles $29, doubles $34.) The **Sesquicentennial State Park** (788-2706) has sites with electricity and water ($11). Take the "State Park" bus from downtown. By car, take I-20 to Two Notch Rd. (Rte. 1) exit, and head northeast four mi. Gate locked at 9pm.

Sights Columbia's 18th-century aristocratic elegance has been preserved by the Historic Columbia Foundation in the **Robert Mills House,** 1616 Blanding St. (252-3964), three blocks east of Sumter St. (tours Tues.-Sat. 10:15am-3:15pm, Sun. 1:15-4:15pm; $3, students $1.50). Mills, one of America's first federal architects, designed the Washington Monument and 30 of South Carolina's public buildings. Across the street is the **Hampton-Preston Mansion** (252-0935), once used by Union forces as headquarters during the Civil War. (Open Tues.-Sat. 10:15am-3:15pm, Sun. 1:15-4:15pm. Tours $3, students $1.50, under 6 free.) Stroll through USC's **Horseshoe,** at the junction of College and Sumter St., which holds the university's oldest buildings, dating from the beginning of the 19th century. The **McKissick Museum** (777-7251), at the top of the Horseshoe, showcases scientific, folk, and pottery exhibits, as well as selections from the university's extensive collection of Twentieth Century-Fox newsreels. (Open Mon.-Fri. 9am-4pm, Sat. 10am-5pm, Sun. 1-5pm. Free.) Columbia's award-winning **Riverbanks Zoo** (779-8730), on I-26 at Greystone Blvd. northwest of downtown, is home to more than 2000 animals. See frogs, sharks, cobras, and tigers before stopping at the concessions stand for a sno cone. (Open daily 9am-4pm. Admission $4, seniors $2.50, students $3, ages 3-12 $1.75.)

The **South Carolina State Museum,** 301 Gervais St. (737-4921), beside the Bridge, is inside the historic Columbia Mills building. Exhibits include replicas of two denizens of the deep—a great white shark and a Confederate submarine—the first submarine ever to sink an enemy ship. (Open Mon.-Sat. 10am-5pm, Sun. 1-5pm. $4, seniors and students with ID $3, ages 6-17 $1.50, under 6 free.)

The **Five Points** business district, at the junction of Harden, Devine, and Blossom St. (from downtown, take the "Veterans Hospital" bus), caters to Columbia's large student population. **Groucho's,** 611 Harden St. (799-5708), in the heart of Five Points, is a Columbia institution and anomaly: a New York-style Jewish deli (large sandwiches $4-6). (Open Mon.-Wed. 11am-4:30pm, Thurs.-Fri. 11am-9pm, Sat. 11am-4pm.) **Eddie's Restaurant,** 1301 Assembly St. (799-6222), serves huge sandwiches ($4) from 11am-6pm, and has a bar with $1.50 drafts open until 9pm. (Closed Sat.-Sun.) **Kinch's Restaurant,** 1115 Assembly St. (256-3843), across the street from the State House, has an early-bird breakfast special for $1.90. (Open daily 7am-4pm.) **The Columbia State Farmers Market** (253-4041), Bluff Rd. across from the USC Football Stadium, is a good place to stock up on fresh Carolina produce.

Tennessee

Tennessee, the last state to secede from the Union and the first to rejoin, reveals a landscape noticeably free of the antebellum plantations that seem to blanket every other Southern state. Interestingly enough, industry has been the moving force in this state rather than agriculture—the state leads the South in production of commercial machinery, chemicals, and electronics. Tennessee defies other regional stereotypes. In 1920, it provided the final vote needed to engrave women's suffrage in the Constitution, and Oak Ridge—pivotal in the development of the A-bomb—still houses one of the world's most sophisticated military laboratories. Tennessee has added to the culture of the world; country music twangs from Nashville, and the blues wail from Memphis. Both cities offer a veritable treasure trove of modern diversions for the tourist. Balance seems to be the rule in Tennessee—home to the famous original Jack Daniels whiskey distillery as well as the largest Bible producing business in the world. After a spell here, you too will be singin' "There ain't no place I'd rather be than the grand ol' state of Tennessee."

PRACTICAL INFORMATION

Capital: Nashville.
Visitor Information: Tennessee Dept. of Tourist Development, P.O. Box 23170, Nashville 37202 (741-2158). Open Mon.-Fri. 8am-4:30pm. **Tennessee State Parks Information,** 701 Broadway, Nashville 37203 (742-6667).
Time Zones: Central and Eastern. **Postal Abbreviation:** TN
Sales Tax: 5.5-8.25%.

■■■ GREAT SMOKY MOUNTAINS NATIONAL PARK

The largest wilderness area in the eastern U.S., Great Smoky Mountains National Park encompasses a half-million acres of gray-green Appalachian peaks bounded on either side by misty North Carolina and Tennessee valleys. Bears, wild hogs, white-tailed deer, groundhogs, wild turkeys, and more than 1500 species of flowering

GREAT SMOKY MOUNTAINS NATIONAL PARK

plants make their homes here. Whispering conifer forests line the mountain ridges at elevations of over 6000 ft. Rhododendrons burst into their full glory in June and July, and by mid-October the sloping mountains become a giant crazy-quilt of color, reminiscent of the area's well-preserved crafts tradition.

Practical Information Start any exploration of the area with a visit to one of the park's three visitors centers. **Sugarlands** (436-1200), on Newfound Gap Rd., 2 mi. south of Gatlinburg, TN, is next to the park's headquarters (open daily 8am-7pm; spring and fall 8am-6pm; winter 8am-4:30pm). **Cades Cove** (436-1275) is in the park's western valley, 15 mi. southwest of Sugarlands on Little River Rd., 7 mi. southwest of Townsend, TN (open in summer daily 9am-7pm; fall and spring 9am-6pm). The **Oconaluftee Visitors Center** (704-497-9147), 4 mi. north of Cherokee, NC, serves travelers entering the park from the Blue Ridge Parkway and all points south and east (open April 1-15 8am-4:30pm, April 16-May 8am-6pm, summer 8am-7pm, fall 8am-6pm). The park's **information line** (615-436-1200; open daily 8:30am-4:30pm) telelinks all three visitors centers. The rangers can answer travel questions, field emergency message calls, and trace lost equipment.

At each visitors center you'll find displays amplifying the park's natural and cultural resources, bulletin boards displaying emergency messages or public information, brochures and films, and comfort stations. Be sure to ask for *The Smokies Guide*, a newspaper offering a comprehensive explanation of the park's changing natural graces. The helpful journal also includes info on tours, lectures, and other activities, such as rafting or horseback riding. The standard park service brochure provides the best driving map in the region. Hikers should ask the visitors center staff for assistance in locating an appropriately detailed backcountry map. You can also tune your car radio to 1610 AM at various marked points for information.

Sleeping and Eating After a Long Day of Hiking There are 10 campgrounds in the park, each with tent sites, limited trailer space, water, tables, and comfort stations (no showers or hookups). **Smokemont, Elkmont,** and **Cades Cove** accept reservations; the rest are first-come, first-served. (Sites $11.) For those hauling a trailer or staying at one of the campgrounds near the main roads during the summer, reservations are a must. Obtain them at least eight weeks in advance by writing to Ticketron, P.O. Box 617516, Chicago, IL 60661 (800-452-1111).

Both Cherokee and Gatlinburg have many small motels. The prices vary widely depending on the season and the economy. In general, the cheaper motels are in Cherokee, and the nicer ones are in Gatlinburg, where the best deals are off Main St., especially by street light #6. Expect to pay at least $35 in Cherokee ($10 more on weekends) and at least $40-45 in Gatlinburg (again weekends are more expensive). The **Mountaineer Motel** (497-2453), U.S. 441 1 mi. south of Cherokee, provides newly refinished, clean rooms with a lovely pool. (Singles and doubles $35, $10 more on weekends, as low as $25 off-season.)

Three youth hostels are located in the area around the park. The closest is **Bell's Wa-Floy Retreat (HI/AYH)**, 3610 East Pkwy (615-436-5575), 10 mi. east of Gatlinburg on Rte. 321, at mile marker 21. From the center of Gatlinburg catch the eastbound trolley (25¢) to the end of the line. From there, it's a 5-mi. walk to Wa-Floy. Located centrally in the Wa-Floy Retreat (which doubles as the Steiner-Bell Center for Physical and Spiritual Rejuvenation), the hostel is no more than a rustic cabin divided into a few apartments with kitchenettes. The shabby interior is clean, though the showers may be unpleasant. If driving, be careful not to hit the ducks and peacocks, which roam the lovely grounds complete with a pool, tennis courts, meditation area, chapel, and bubbling brook. The friendly proprietor, Mrs. Floy Steiner-Bell loves to chat and may welcome you warmly with her poetry. ($10, nonmembers $12, linens $1. Call for reservations at least 1 day ahead. Check-in before 10pm. Midnight curfew. Poetry free.) On the other side of the park, about 35 mi. away on a slow, winding road in North Carolina, you can vegetate after a hike or river ride in the spacious communal living room of Louise Phillip's **Smokeseege Lodge (HI/AYH)**, P.O. Box 179, Dillsboro on U.S. 441, 11 mi. south of Cherokee. Walk from the nearest Greyhound stop, nearly 3 mi. away in Sylva. If you're driving from the Smokies, watch carefully on the right-hand side of U.S. 441 for a brick community center and a mailbox with "TV servicing" written on it by the 2nd dirt road—the hostel is at the end of the gravel road. This hostel is beautiful and serene but very isolated, a good distance from the road and any area towns, and operates under a self-help system; women and those traveling alone may feel uneasy going to this hostel. Kitchen facilities are available; no smoking or drinking permitted. (Lockout 9am-5pm. Curfew 11pm. $7. Open April-Oct.)

Further south, near Wesser, NC in the **Nantahala National Forest,** the bustling **Nantahala Outdoor Center (NOC)**, U.S. 19 W., P.O. Box 41, Bryson City (704-488-2175), 80 mi. from Gatlinburg and 13 mi. from downtown Bryson City, offers cheap beds. Bunks occupy simple wooden cabins at "base camp" on the far side of the river and fairly large-sized motel rooms with kitchenettes. Showers, kitchen, and laundry facilities included. ($8. Call ahead.) Keep in mind the center is not at all convenient to the GSM park or Gatlinburg. Staying at the NOC is a good idea when planning a whitewater rafting trip. The NOC's rates for 2½-hr. whitewater rafting expeditions are pricey, but you can rent your own raft for a self-designed trip down the Nantahala River. (Sun.-Fri. $14, Sat. $16. 1-person inflatable "duckies" $27 per day. Group rates available. Look out for higher prices on "premium Saturdays," July-Aug.) The NOC also rents canoes and kayaks and offers instruction for the novice. Most trips have minimum age or weight limits; daycare service is available at the center. Trip prices include transportation to the put-in site and all necessary equipment. Don't let *Deliverance* steer you clear. For further information, call 800-232-7238. Hike on the **Appalachian Trail** to explore some of the old forest service roads. The NOC staff will gladly assist if you need help charting an appropriate daytrip. The NOC also maintains seasonal "outposts" on the **Ocoee, Nolichucky, Chattoga,** and **French Broad Rivers;** a rafting expedition on any of these rivers makes a satisfying daytrip if you have a car. Be sure to look into NOC's 20% discounts March-April.

After your stomach has settled following a full day of rafting, try **Maxwell's Bakery** (586-5046), Dillsboro exit off U.S. 74. Relish the heavenly smell of freshly baked bread while munching on a delectable sandwich in this country cafe. Sandwiches $3-4, biscuits $1, cookies 50¢. Large portions and convenient to GSM. (Open Mon.-Sat. 6am-6pm, Sun. 9am-5pm year-round.) In Cherokee, **My Grandma's** (497-9801), U.S. 19 and U.S. 441, serves up real home-cookin' at down-low prices ($2-4). (Open daily 7am-2pm, sometimes later.)

Sights and Activities Over 900 mi. of hiking trails and 170 mi. of road traverse the park. Ask the rangers at the visitors centers to help you devise a trip appropriate to your time and physical ability. Driving and walking routes are clearly charted. To hike off the marked trails, you must ask for a free backcountry camping permit. Otherwise, just choose a route, bring water, and DON'T FEED THE BEARS. Some of the most popular trails are the 5 mi. to **Rainbow Falls,** the 4 mi. to **Chimney Tops,** and the 21½ mi. to **Laurel Falls.** For a splendid drive with beautiful scenery, visitors can enjoy **Cades Cove loop,** which lassoes the last vestiges of a mountain community that occupied the area from the 1850s to the 1920s when the GSM national park materialized. What was once a living, breathing settlement today displays splendid grassy, open fields against peaceful mountain backdrop. Deep green contemplative forests enhance the pastoral aura of Cades Cove as do the horses, deer, bears, and other animals. The 50¢ tour guide available at the entrance to the 11-mi. loop shares detailed, well-written descriptions of the old churches and homesteads as well as the history. In the summer months, visit **Mingus Mill** located 1 mi. north of the Oconaluftee visitors center along Newfound Gap Rd. This 1876 Turbine mill boasts 107-year-old wooden tools and machinery which still operate. Watch corn and wheat being ground, or browse through the book of old photos to see the last miller, John Jones, hard at work. The **Pioneer Farmstead,** next door to the Oconaluftee center, recreates a turn of the century settlement including a blacksmith shop and a corncrib. The 25¢ pamphlets give informative illustrations of the grounds. (Both sights are free and open the same hours as the visitors center.)

Great Smoky Mountains National Park straddles the Tennessee/North Carolina border. On the Tennessee side, the city of **Gatlinburg** just 2 mi. from Sugarlands, appears and vanishes within the blink of a driver's eye, but is jam-packed enough to keep you dizzy with amazement for an evening or a day. Touristic hordes occupy its kitschy corners, ranging from a theme park devoted to Dolly Parton (Dollywood) to a wax museum dedicated to President Bush. Also in Gatlinburg, Christus Gardens bills itself as America's #1 religious attraction, and **Ober Gatlinburg** has America's largest cable car. Between all these attractions are endless rows of hotels and motor inns. For more guidance and specific listings of accommodations and campgrounds, stop in at the **Tourist Information Center,** 520 Pkwy. (615-436-4178; open Mon.-Sat. 8am-8pm, Sun. 9am-5pm; Nov.-April Mon.-Sat. 8am-6pm, Sun. 9am-5pm).

On the N.C. side of the Mountains (a scenic 1 hr. drive south on U.S. 441), 1 mi. from the Oconaluftee Visitors Center is the **Cherokee Indian Reservation,** replete with a guided tour of a re-created 1750-ish Indian village, an outdoor drama about the Cherokee tribe, and an informative museum. Invest your time and money for a ticket to "Unto these Hills," an outdoor drama that retells the story of the Cherokees and climaxes with a moving re-enactment of the Trail of Tears. (Evening shows Jun.-Aug., Mon.-Sat. $8, children 12 and under $5.) At the **Museum of the Cherokee Indian** (704-497-3481), on Drama Rd. off U.S. 441, you can hear the Cherokee language spoken, view artifacts and films, and learn about the past and the present of the Cherokee. Fascinating and well worth a visit. (Open Mon.-Sat. 9am-8pm, Sun. 9am-5pm; Sept.-mid-June daily 9am-5pm. $3.50, under 13 $1.75.) The **Cherokee Visitors Center** (800-438-1601), on U.S. 19, provides brochures, maps, and helpful hints about the town and the culture (open daily 9am-5pm).

■■■ MEMPHIS

In the southwestern corner of Tennessee, follow the sound of soulful melodies to Memphis, home of the blues and the birthplace of rock n' roll. Decades after W.C. Handy published the first blues piece on legendary Beale Street in 1912, Elvis Presley (also a Memphean) became the "King of Rock n' Roll" with the help of his scandalously gyrating pelvis and amazingly versatile voice. Beyond music, Memphis stimulates each of the other four senses, as well. Visitors can feast their eyes on both national and local history in the many museums around town, or focus instead on a live performance given by one of the city's increasingly sophisticated theaters. Noses and taste buds will be tempted by barbecue, a Memphis specialty. Though travelers' feet may feel sore after trekking to all of these recreations, the feelings of friendliness and genuine geniality evinced by residents are sure to impress even the most jaded tourist.

PRACTICAL INFORMATION

Emergency: 911.
Visitor Information: Visitor Information Center, 340 Beale St. (543-5333), 2 blocks south on 2nd St. and 2 blocks east on Beale from the Greyhound station. Quite helpful, with everything from bus maps to restaurant menus and guides. Open Mon.-Sat. 9am-6pm, Sun. noon-6pm.
Airport: Memphis International Airport (922-8000), just south of the southern loop of I-240. Taxi fare to the city $15—negotiate in advance. Public transport to and from the airport only $1.25, but sporadically available and a long, difficult trip for a traveler unfamiliar with the area.
Amtrak: 545 S. Main St. (526-0052 or 800-872-7245), at Calhoun on the southern edge of downtown. *Very* unsafe area even during the day, downright hellish at night. To: New Orleans (1 per day, 7½ hr., $75); Chicago (1 per day, 11 hr., $95);

Atlanta ($170, via New Orleans with forced overnight stay). Open Mon.-Sat. 8am-12:30pm, 1:30-5pm and 9pm-6am, Sun. 9pm-6am.

Greyhound: 203 Union Ave. (523-7676), at 4th St. downtown. Unsafe area at night, but it beats the Amtrak station. To: Nashville ($33); New Orleans ($55); Atlanta ($62). Open 24 hrs.

Public Transport: Memphis Area Transit Authority (MATA), 1370 Levee Rd. (274-6282). Extensive bus routes cover most suburbs, but buses take their own sweet time and don't run very frequently. The two major downtown stops are at Front and Jefferson St. and at 2nd St. and Madison Ave. Operates Mon.-Fri. 6am-7pm, Sat.10am-6pm, Sun. 11am-4pm. Fare $1, transfers 10¢. MATA recently refurbished original Portuguese trolley cars from the 19th century. They cruise Main St. Mon.-Thurs. 6:30am-9pm. Fri. 6:30am-11pm. Sat. 9:30am-11pm, Sun. 10am-6pm. A bargain at 50¢.

Taxi: Yellow Cab, 526-2121. $2.35 first mi., $1.10 each additional mi.

Crisis Line: 458-8772. Open 24 hrs. Also refers to other numbers.

Time Zone: Central (1 hr. behind Eastern).

Post Office: 555 S. 3rd St. (521-2140), at Calhoun St. Take bus #13. Open Mon.-Fri. 8:30am-5:30pm, Sat. 10am-noon. **ZIP code:** 38101.

Area Code: 901.

Downtown, named avenues run east-west and numbered ones north-south. **Madison** (and several other early presidents) bifurcates north and south addresses. Two main thoroughfares, **Poplar** and **Union** Avenues, pierce the heart of the city from the east; 2nd and 3rd Streets arrive from the south. **Bellevue** becomes **Elvis Presley Blvd.** and leads you straight to Graceland. If traveling by car, take advantage of the free, unmetered parking along the river.

ACCOMMODATIONS

Two hostels and a handful of motels within walking distance of downtown should render unnecessary the seedier, more distant, and expensive strip along Elvis Presley Blvd. and Brooks Rd. During the celebration of the earth-shattering days of Elvis' birth (early Jan.) and death (mid-Aug.), however, book way in advance. The visitor information center has a thorough listing of lodgings. Contact **Bed and Breakfast in Memphis,** P.O. Box 41621, Memphis 38174 (726-5920), for guest rooms in Memphis homes. French- and Spanish-speaking hosts available (singles/doubles $40-60).

India House II, 78 N. Main St. (529-9282), at Jefferson above Jack's Food Stores. Whether you're looking for action-packed nights on the town or a central location to sleep, eat, and play Nintendo, with no lock-out, no curfew, and hosts/social directors like Angus and Mark, this brand-new hostel is *the* place to stay in Memphis. Not for the uptight. Open 24 hrs. Free linen, common kitchen. Singles $10. Key deposit $5.

Lowenstein-Long House/Castle Hostelry, 1084 Poplar and 217 N. Waldran (527-7174). Take bus #50 from 3rd St. Beautiful grounds surround an elegant Victorian mansion. The hostel's institutionally tidy rooms are in a small red brick building out back. Laundry $2. Kitchens available in the hostel. Lockout 11am-5pm. Singles $10, nonmembers $13, private doubles $30. Key deposit $10.

Admiral Benbow Inn, 1220 Union (725-0630), at S. Bellevue. A monstrous tribute to 70s architecture, these rooms are clean and close to downtown. Rooms $27; just a few dollars more on weekends.

River Place Inn, 100 North Front St. (526-0583), overlooking the water. Pleasant hotel with very spacious rooms from $44. The visitors information center has a $35 coupon for 1-4 people. No meals or laundry. Reserve two weeks in advance during the summer.

Motel 6, 1360 Springbrook Rd. (346-0992), just east of intersection of Elvis and Brooks Rd. near Graceland. There is also a **Motel 6** at I-55 and Brooks Rd. (396-3620), but the neighborhood could be better. Both have pools and small, clean rooms with movies and unlimited local calls. No meals, no laundry, do not pass Go, do not collect $200. Singles $28, each additional person $6.

If you just have to camp in the middle of this accommodations haven, the campsites at **Memphis/Graceland KOA**, 3691 Elvis Presley Blvd. (396-7125), are right next to Graceland, so you can hear strains of Elvis all day long (full hookup $24, tent $15).

FOOD

When a smoky, spicy smell follows you almost everywhere, you are either extremely paranoid, malodorous, or in Memphis, where barbecue reigns. The city even hosts the World Championship Barbecue Cooking Contest in May. But don't fret if gnawing on ribs isn't your thing—Memphis has plenty of other Southern-style restaurants with down-home favorites like fried chicken, catfish, chitlins, grits, and fresh vegetables.

The Rendezvous (523-2746), Downtown Alley, in the alley across from the Peabody Hotel off Union St. between the Ramada and Days Inns. A Memphis legend, serving large portions of ribs ($6.50-10), and cheaper sandwiches ($3-4). Open Tues.-Thurs. 4:30pm-midnight, Fri.-Sat. noon-midnight.

Bluff City Grill and Brewery, 235 Union Ave. (526-BEER), at 4th. Huge and airy, this brewery serves everything from classic southern specialties like fried catfish ($6) to nouveau pizzas and veggie dishes ($4-8). Try it for lunch; the same food costs half the price. Open Sun.-Thurs. 11am-1am, Fri.-Sat. 11am-3am.

The North End, 346 N. Main St. (526-0319 or 527-3663), downtown. A happening place with an extensive menu specializing in tamales, wild rice, stuffed potatoes, and creole dishes ($3-8). Delicious vegetarian meals for under $6. Orgasmic hot fudge pie ($3.25). Happy Hour 5-7pm. Live music Wed.-Sun. starts at 10:30pm, with a small cover (around $2). Open 8 days/wk., 11am-3am. Next door, **Jake's Place** (527-2799) offers a similar menu, but with stir-fry specialties and breakfast.

Squash Blossom Market, 1720 Poplar Ave. (725-4823). This huge health food store/cafe is slightly out of place in a city dripping with sauces, grease, and above all, meat. Try the Sunday brunch where veggie delights run about $4. Open Mon.-Fri. 9am-9pm, Sat. 9am-8pm, Sun. 11am-6pm.

P and H Cafe, 1532 Madison Ave. (726-0906). The initials aptly stand for Poor and Hungry. This local favorite serves huge burgers, plate lunches, and grill food ($3-5); try the patty melt with grilled onions. The waitresses are a friendly Memphis institution—look at the wall murals. Local bands occasionally play Sat. night. Open Mon.-Fri. 11am-3am, Sat. 5pm-3am.

Front St. Delicatessen, 77 S. Front St. (522-8943). Lunchtime streetside deli in the heart of downtown with almost no room inside. Local yuppie hangout (how *80s!*). Patio dining in sunny weather. Hot lunch specials ($2-4). Open Mon.-Fri. 7am-3pm, Sat. 11am-3pm.

Corky's, 5259 Poplar Ave. (685-9744), about 25 min. from downtown. Very popular with the locals, and justifiably so. The BBQ dinner and ribs are served with baked beans, coleslaw, and homemade bread ($3-9) and are top notch, as are the pies and cobbler. Arrive early or expect a long wait. Open Mon.-Thurs. 11am-9:30pm, Fri.-Sat. 11am-10:30pm, Sun. noon-9:30pm.

ELVISSIGHTS AND MUSIC SIGHTS

Graceland, or rather "GRACE-lin" as the tour guides drawl, Elvis Presley's home, is a paradigm of American kitsch that every Memphis visitor must see. But any desire to learn about the man, to share his dream, or to feel his music may go unrealized even by those who venture to his monumental home; the complex has been built up to resemble an amusement park that shuffles visitors from one room to another. It seems that the employees adhere to the Elvismotto "Taking Care of Business in a Flash." Despite the monotony of the spiels, you'll never forget the mirrored ceilings, carpeted walls, and yellow and orange decor of Elvis' 1974 renovations. Elvis bought the mansion when he was only 22, and his baby Lisa Marie just inherited it this year at 25. The King and his family are buried next door in the **Meditation Gardens**, where you can seek the Buddha while reciting a mantra to the tune of "You're So Square." (Admission to amazing Graceland $8, children $5.)

Across the street, you can visit several Elvismuseums, and several more Elvissouvenir shops. The **Elvis Presley Automobile Museum** proves to be the most worthwhile Elvisoption. A huge hall houses a score of Elvismobiles, and an indoor drive-in movie theater shows clips from 31 Elvismovies ($4.50, seniors $4, kids $2.75). *If I Can Dream* is a free 20-min. film with performance footage which, unfortunately for Elvis, contrasts the early (otherwise known as slim) years with the later ones. **Elvis' Airplanes** features—yes, dear reader, yes—the two Elvisplanes: the *Lisa Marie* (named for the Elvisdaughter) and the tiny *Hound Dog II* Jetstar. The cost of visiting these planes is overpriced at $4.25 (seniors $3.80, kids $2.75), but the cost of seeing **Elvis' Tour Bus** is a bargain at $1. The **Elvis Up Close** exhibit gives you a glimpse of Elvis's private side by presenting some books he read, some shirts he wore, and his Social Security card ($1.75, free for Elvis when he finally comes out of hiding and admits he is *not* dead but merely roaming the countryside doing good deeds and spreading the Elvisgospel).

There are three different combination tickets available: (1) all attractions except the mansion for $10 (seniors $9, kids $7); (2) all attractions except the bus and planes for $13 (seniors $12, kids $8); (3) all the attractions for $16 (seniors $14.50, kids $11). Take Lauderdale/Elvis Presley bus #13 from 3rd and Union. (Open Memorial Day-Labor Day, 8am-7pm, last tour 5pm. Call 332-3322 or 800-238-2000.)

Long before Sam Phillips and the tiny **Sun Studio**, 706 Union Ave. (521-0664), first produced Elvis, Jerry Lee Lewis, U2, and Bonnie Raitt (animated and knowledgeable 30-min. tours every hr. on the ½ hr.; open daily 9am-8pm; $5, kids $3.25), historic **Beale St.** saw the invention of the blues. After a long period of neglect, the neighborhood has music literally pouring from almost every door once again. The **W.C. Handy Home and Museum,** 352 Beale (527-2583), exhibits the music and photographs of the man, the myth, the legend who so handily wrote down the first blues melody (open Mon.-Sat. 10am-6pm, Sun. 1-5pm; $2, kids 50¢; call for an appointment). Earphones that spew blues hits litter the **Memphis Music and Blues Museum** 97 S. 2nd St. (525-4007), as do photographs and TV footage of actual performances. If you like to sing, listen, or watch the blues, this is the place to go. (Open Sun.-Thurs. 10am-6pm, Fri.-Sat. 10am-9pm. $5, kids 1-12 $2.) **Center for Southern Folklore,** 130 Beale St. (525-3655), documents various aspects of music history, including a tribute to Memphis's WDIA—the nation's first all-black radio station where notables like B.B. King and Rufus Thomas began their musical careers as disc jockeys. (Open Mon.-Fri. 9:30am-7:30pm, Sat. 10am-7:30pm, Sun. 1-7:30pm; $2, seniors, students, and kids under 12 $1.)

SIGHTS BEYOND THE SOUNDS

A quick tram-ride over the picturesque Mississippi, **Mud Island** has it all: swimming pool and a museum, a great big sand box called "beach," and a scale model of the father of all waters you can stroll along (open May-Labor Day Tues.-Sun. 10am-5pm; entrance to the island $2). At the **Mississippi River Museum,** 125 N. Front St. (576-7241), you can experience history firsthand by strolling on the decks of an indoor steamboat, chilling to the blues in the Yellow Dog Cafe, or spying on a union ironclad gunboat from the lookout of a confederate bluff. Alongside the museum flow 1.2 million gallons of water through an amazing ½-mi.-long concrete sculpture of the river. In the summer, visitors can swim in the enormous pool that doubles as the Gulf of Mexico at the base of the sculpture. Also on **Mud Island** rests the renowned World War II B-17 **Memphis Belle.** Free tours of the Riverwalk and Memphis Belle Pavilion run several times daily.

Just as sturdy and tenacious as a WWII flight crew are the famed ducks of the **Peabody Hotel,** 149 Union St. (529-4000), in the heart of downtown. Folklore has it that this early 20th century social center was the birthplace of the Mississippi Delta. Try the French Strawberry Cheesecake while you're there ($4). Now that the hotel keeps ducks in its indoor fountain, every day at 11am and 5pm the management rolls out the red carpet and the ducks waddle to and from the elevator with piano accompaniment. Get there early; sometimes ducks are impatient.

Overseeing the waterfront, **The Great American Pyramid** (526-5177) is not the latest game show but the latest extravaganza in Memphis. You won't be able to miss the 32-story-high, six-acre-wide shining pyramid that holds the American Music Hall of Fame, the Memphis Music Experience, the College Football Hall of Fame, and a 20,000 seat arena. The whole experience includes daily music shows indoors and outdoor parks (admission $25).

A. Schwab, 163 Beale St. (523-9782), a five-and-dime store run by the same family since 1876, is still offering old-fashioned bargains. A "museum" of relics-never-sold gathers dust on the mezzanine floor, including an array of voodoo potions, elixirs, and powders. Elvis bought some of his flashier ensembles here. (Open Mon.-Sat. 9am-5pm. Free guided tours.) Next door on Beale St., the **Memphis Police Museum** (528-2370) summons visitors to gawk at 150 years of confiscated drugs, homemade weapons, and officer uniforms (open 24 hrs.; free).

In this city where travelers and natives alike agree that relations between races are unusually congenial, the **National Civil Rights Museum,** housed at the site of Martin Luther King Jr.'s assassination, the **Lorraine Motel,** 450 Mulberry St., at 2nd (521-9699), serves as a reminder of the suffering African Americans have endured and a tribute to their movement for change. A 10-min. movie, graphic photographs of lynching victims, live footage, and life-size exhibits vividly trace the progress of the Civil Rights Movement. Visitors can see rooms 306 and 307, where King's entourage stayed, preserved in their original condition. (Open Mon.-Sat. 10am-5pm, Sun. 1-5pm; $5, seniors and students with ID $4, kids 6-12 $3. Free Mon. 3-5pm.)

The people of Memphis are hardly only black and white; the Native American presence is culturally rich as well. The **C.H. Nash Museum-Chucalissa,** 1987 Indian Village Dr. (785-3160), take Winchester which becomes Mitchell which becomes Indian Village Dr. in T.O. Fuller State Park, recaptures the 16th century with its reconstructed Choctaw village and historical and archeological museum. Local Choctaw sell hand-made crafts at reasonable prices (Open Tues.-Sat. 9am-5pm, Sun. 1-5pm; $4, kids $3). Every mid-June, the **Native American Pow-Wow and Crafts Fair** draws people from across the country to celebrate Native American heritage with food, dance, and music. For information, call 789-9338.

The Pink Palace Museum and Planetarium, 3050 Central Ave. (320-6320), which is, by the way, gray, details the natural history of the mid-South and expounds upon the development of Memphis. Check out the sharp and sparkling crystal and mineral collection. (Open Mon.-Wed. and Fri.-Sat. 9am-10pm, Sun. 9am-8pm; $3, kids $2.) On the corner of Central Ave. and Hollywood mirthfully stands the **Children's Museum** as a wonderfully fun afternoon option for kids (open Tues.-Sat. 9am-5pm, Sun. at 1pm; $5, kids 1-12 $4).

Leaving from 3rd and Beale St. and other spots around the city, the **"Showboat" bus** (722-7192) runs to the big midtown sights (6:20am-6:15pm, all-day ticket $2). A major sight is the **Victorian Village,** which consists of 18 mansions in various stages of restoration and preservation. The **Mallory-Neeley House,** 652 Adams Ave. (523-1484), one of the village's two mansions open to the public, went up in the mid-19th century. Most of its original furniture remains intact and there for visitors to see. (Open Tues.-Sat. 10am-4pm, Sun. 1-4pm. $4, seniors and students $3.) For a look at a different lifestyle during the same era, visit the **Magevrney House,** 198 Adams Ave. (526-4464), that once held the clapboard cottage of Eugene Magevrney, who helped establish Memphis's first public schools (open Tues.-Sat. 10am-4pm; free; reservations required). French Victorian architecture and an extensive antique/textile collection live on in the **Woodruff-Fontaine House,** 680 Adams Ave. (open Mon.-Sat. 10am-4pm, Sun. 1-4pm; $4, students $2). The **Massey House,** 664 Adams Ave., stands as the oldest home on the block, with a doric-columned portico (open Mon.-Fri. noon-1pm; free).

In Overton Park, the **Memphis Brooks Museum of Art** (722-3500) houses a mid-sized collection of Impressionist painting and 19th-century U.S. art (open Tues.-Sat. 10am-5pm, Sun. 11:30am-5pm; $4, seniors, students, and kids $2; free Fri.). The **Memphis Zoo and Aquarium,** 2000 Galloway Ave. (726-4787) squawks next door (open daily 9am-5pm; $5, seniors and kids $3; free Mon. after 3:30pm).

Memphis has almost as many parks as museums, each offering a slightly different natural setting. Brilliant wildflowers in April and a marvelous Heinz of roses (57 varieties) bloom and grow forever at the **Memphis Botanical Garden,** 750 Cherry Rd. in Audubon Park off Park Ave. (685-1566; open Tues.-Sat. 9am-sunset, Sun. 11am-6pm; $2, kids 6-17 $1.) Across the street, the **Dixon Galleries and Garden,** 4339 Park Ave. (761-5250) flaunts its manicured landscape (open Mon.-Sat. 10am-5pm, Sun. 1pm-5pm; $4, students $3, kids 1-12 $1). The **Lichterman Nature Center,** 5992 Quince Rd. off Perkins (797-7322), is a wildscape with virgin forests and wild, wild wildlife. A picnic area is available. (Open Tues.-Sat. 9:30am-5pm, Sun. 1-5pm; $3, students $2, kids 1-3 free.)

ENTERTAINMENT AND NIGHTLIFE

The visitors center's *Key* magazine, the free *Memphis Flyer,* or the "Playbook" section of the Friday morning *Memphis Commercial Appeal* will give you an idea of what's goin' down 'round town. For more personalized social coordination, go to the **Sun Cafe,** 710 Union Ave. (521-9820), adjacent to the Sun Studios, for a tall, cool glass of lemonade ($1.75) and a talk with the young waiters and cashiers about what to do (open daily 9am-9pm, Sept.-May daily 10am-6pm).

The absolutely most happening place is **Beale Street.** Blues waft nightly throughout the street; you could save a few bucks by buying a drink at one of the many outdoor stands and just meandering from doorway to doorway, park to park. **B.B. King's Blues Club,** 147 Beale (527-5464; open daily from noon till the show stops), where the club's namesake still makes appearances, happily mixes young and old, tourist and native. While the clientele at the **Rum Boogie Cafe,** 182 Beale (528-0150; open daily 11:30am-2am) may be more transplanted, the music is certainly homegrown. For pool, **Peoples** (523-7627) on Beale is open from noon until at least 1am, and charges $7.35 ($8.40 on weekends) for a table. **Silky O'Sullivan's,** 183 Beale St. (522-9596), is an old Irish bar housed (or not, as the case may be) behind the facade of an almost completely razed historic landmark. Play "beach" volleyball and hear folk music outside, much on burgers ($4-6), and hear some Memphis blues inside next door. (Open daily 11-2:30am; $3-5 cover after 7pm.)

Off Beale St., the **Antenna Club,** 1588 Madison Ave. (725-9812), showcases hip progressive rock. **Captain Bilbo's,** 263 Wagner Pl. (526-1966), is the place to be for live rock and pop with a spectacular riverview, and the **Daily Planet,** 3439 Park (327-1270), throbulates with R&B. For a collegiate atmosphere, try the Highland St. strip near Memphis State University with hopping bars like **Newby's,** 539 S. Highland St. (452-8408), which hosts backgammon tournaments on Thursdays.

The majestic **Orpheum Theater,** 89 Beale St. (525-3000), is a dignified movie palace, complete with 15-ft.-high Czechoslovakian chandeliers and an organ. The theater shows classic movies on weekends along with an organ prelude and a cartoon, and occasionally live music. Call for info on the current summer film series. The **Memphis Chicks,** 800 Home Run Lane (272-1687), near Libertyland, are a big hit with fans of Southern League baseball ($4, box seats $5).

Visitors who hit this part of the world at the beginning of the summer may also join the festivities of **Memphis in May** (525-4611), a month long celebration with concerts, art exhibits, food contests and sports events. Book hotel reservations early during this season.

NASHVILLE

■■■ NASHVILLE

Long-forgotten Francis Nash was eponym to this city, one of only four Revolutionary War heroes so honored in U.S. city names (the others being Washington, Wayne and Knox). Nashville has been the capital of Tennessee since 1843. Despite its minor link with America's fight for independence, Nashville is better known for its country music than for its foothold in history. Banjo pickin' and foot stompin' have entrenched themselves securely in Tennessee's central pulse, providing Nashville with non-stop performances and the Country Music Hall of Fame. Behind this musical harmony resonates "the Wall Street of the South," a slick, choreographed financial hub. The city headquarters the Southern Baptists and higher morality alongside centers of the fine arts and higher learning at Fisk University and Vanderbilt. Nashville is a large, eclectic, unapologetically heterogeneous place.

PRACTICAL INFORMATION

Emergency: 911.

Visitor Information: Nashville Area Chamber of Commerce, 161 4th Ave. N. (259-4700), between Commerce and Church St. downtown. Ask for the *Hotel/Motel Guide,* the *Nashville Dining & Entertainment Guide,* and a *Calendar of Events.* Information booth in main lobby open Mon.-Fri. 8am-5pm. **Nashville Tourist Information Center,** I-65 at James Robertson Pkwy., exit 85 (259-4747), about ½ mi. east of the state capitol, just over the bridge. Take bus #3 ("Meridian") east on Broadway. Complete maps marked with all the attractions. Open daily 8am-8pm.

Traveler's Aid: 780-9471. Lost your wallet? Travelers checks? Plane ticket? This is the place to go. With characteristic Southern warmth, Traveler's Aid helps the stranded find their way home. Open Mon.-Fri. 8:30am-4pm.

Airport: Metropolitan Airport, (275-1675) 8 mi. south of downtown. Airport shuttle operating out of major downtown hotels, $8 one way, taxis $15-17, MTA buses at 75¢ are cheap but unreliable and infrequent.

Greyhound: 200 8th Ave. S. (256-6141), at Demonbreun St., 2 blocks south of Broadway downtown. Borders on a rough and rowdy neighborhood, but the station's benches, lockers, restaurant, and gift shop are clean, bright, and open 24 hours. To: Memphis (7 per day, 4 hr., $33); Washington, DC (5 per day, 16 hr., $94); Atlanta (7 per day, 7½ hr., $36); Louisville (8 per day, 4 hr., Mon.-Thurs. $25.50, Fri.-Sun. $38). One youth under 21 can travel free with each adult.

Public Transport: Metropolitan Transit Authority (MTA) (242-4433). Buses operate Mon.-Fri. 5am-midnight, less frequent service Sat.-Sun. Fare $1.15, zone crossing or transfers 10¢. The **Nashville Trolley** (242-4433) runs daily starting at 11am in the downtown area every 10 min. for 75¢.

Taxi: Nashville Cab, 242-7070. 90¢ first mi., $1.50 each additional mi.

Car Rental: Alamo Rent A Car, (800-327-9633). At the airport. $30 per day, weekends $20 per day. $6 per day extra for those under 25.

Help Lines: Crisis Line, 244-7444. **Rape Hotline,** 256-8526. Both open 24 hrs. **Gay and Lesbian Switchboard,** 297-0008, opens at 5pm.

Time Zone: Central (1 hr. behind Eastern).

Post Office: 901 Broadway (255-9447), across from the Park Plaza Hotel and next to Union Station. Open Mon.-Fri. 8am-6pm, Sat. 8am-noon. **ZIP code:** 37202.

Area Code: 615.

Nashville's streets are undeniably fickle: many are one-way; they are often interrupted by curving parkways and the names constantly change without you ever turning a corner. **Broadway,** the main east-west thoroughfare, spawns **West End Avenue** just outside downtown at Vanderbilt University and I-40, and later becomes **Hillsboro Pike.** Downtown, numbered avenues run north-south, parallel to the Cumberland River. The curve of **James Robertson Parkway** encloses the north end, becoming **Main Street** on the other side of the river (later **Gallatin Pike**), and

McGavock St. at the south end. The area south of Broadway between 2nd and 7th Ave., and the region north of James Robertson Parkway are both unsafe at night.

ACCOMMODATIONS AND CAMPING

Finding a room in Nashville is not difficult, just expensive. Most cheaper places are within 20 mi. of downtown. Make reservations well in advance, especially for weekend stays (which will also take a bigger toll on your budget). A dense concentration of budget motels line W. Trinity Lane and Brick Church Pike at I-65, north of downtown, off exit 87B. Even cheaper hotels inhabit the area around Dickerson Rd. and Murfreesboro, but the neighborhood is seedy at best. Closer to downtown (but still seedy) are several motels huddled on Interstate Dr. just over the Woodland St. Bridge. **Bed and Breakfast of Middle Tennessee** (331-5244) offers singles for $30, doubles for $50, kitchenettes and free continental breakfast.

The Cumberland Inn, I-65 North and Trinity Lane (226-1600), has cheerful, fragrant rooms with bright, modern furnishings, unlimited local calls for $1, laundry facilities, and a free continental breakfast. No pets, please. Singles $25. Doubles $35. Prices rise on weekends.

The Liberty Inn, 2400 Brick Church (228-2567), beckons with table and chairs in each room. Stall showers only. Singles $30. Doubles $38. $5 more on weekends.

Hallmark Inns (800-251-3294) is a local chain; its four inns in the Nashville area provide free continental breakfast and are generally cheaper than national chains. Singles $38, doubles $48 at 309 Trinity; prices may vary with location.

Motel 6, three locations. 311 W. Trinity Lane (227-9696), at exit 87B off I-24/I-65; 323 Cartwright St., Goodlettsville (859-9674), off Long Hollow Pike west from I-65; 95 Wallace Rd. (333-9933), off exit 56 from I-24. Tidy rooms with stall showers, and free local calls. Singles $27. $4 first additional person, $2 after that. 18 and under free with parents. The Wallace St. location is slightly more expensive.

Continental Inn, 303 Interstate Dr. (800-251-1856). Highlights are the view of the skyline and its guitar-shaped indoor pool. Singles $30. Double with two beds $40.

You can reach three campgrounds near Opryland USA via public transport from 5th St. For the **Fiddler's Inn North Campground** (885-1440, sites $19.50), the **Nashville Travel Park** (889-4225, $29 with A/C), and the **Two Rivers Campground** (883-8559, $17-21 for 2 people with full hookup), take the Briley Pkwy. north to McGavock Pike, and exit west onto Music Valley Dr. Ten min. north of Opryland is the **Nashville KOA,** 708 N. Dickerson Rd. (859-0075), I-65 in Goodlettsville, exit 98 (sites $22 with full hookup).

FOOD

In Nashville music even influences the local delicacies. Pick up a Goo-Goo cluster, (peanuts and pecans, chocolate, caramel, and marshmallow) sold at practically any store, and you'll bite into the initials of the Grand Ole Opry. Pecan pie is another favorite dessert, perfect after spicy barbecue or fried chicken. Nashville's food, however, is hardly parochial, and the finger-lickin' traditional joints are interspersed with varied and affordable international cuisines. Restaurants for collegiate tastes and budgets cram West End Avenue and the 2000 block of Elliston Place, near Vanderbilt. The **farmers market,** north of the capitol between 3rd and 7th Ave., sells fresh fruits and vegetables until sunset.

Loveless Motel Restaurant, 8400 Rte. 100 (646-9700). Accessible by car only; take 40W from downtown, left at exit 192, then left at Rte. 100; a 15-20 min. drive. True country-style cooking at its best and most stomach-fillin'. Famous for its preserves, fried chicken, and hickory-smoked ham ($3-8). Open Tues.-Sat. 8am-2pm and 5-9pm, Sun. 8am-9pm. Reservations on weekends recommended.

Calypso, 2424 Elliston, near Vanderbilt (321-3878) and 4910 Thoroughbred in Brentwood (370-8033). Lively, fresh, and easy on the pocket, Calypso serves up tasty Caribbean food like Jamaican chicken and boija muffins made with corn and coconut ($1.25), as well as some vegetarian entrees. Open Mon.-Thurs. 11am-9pm, Fri. 11am-10pm, Sat. 11am-9pm, Sun. noon-8pm.

Slice of Life, 1811 Division, next to music studios (329-2526). Yuppie hangout featuring fresh bread and wholesome Tex-Mex with a large vegetarian selection. Veggie chili ($4), veggie burger ($4), carrot and kale juice ($2). Try the bakery for giant cookies and muffins ($1). Some are even macrobiotic. Open Mon.-Sat. 7am-9:30pm, Sun. 8am-9:30pm. Favorable location for sighting country musicians.

Granite Falls, 2000 Broadway (327-9250). For a classier, if costlier, dining experience, Granite Falls is darkly lit and modishly decorated, offering herb-roasted chicken, grilled fish sandwiches, and other nouveau dishes ($6-12).

The World's End, 1713 Church St. (329-3480). Huge, airy gay restaurant which doubles as a mixed dance club (usually no cover) Fri.-Sat. nights. Standard burger and salad fare ($5-8). Open Sun.-Thurs. 4pm-12:30am, Fri.-Sat. 4pm-1:30am.

International Market, 2010-B Belmont Blvd.(297-4453). Asian grocery with a large Thai buffet ($4-6). Egg rolls ($1). Crowded at lunch. Open Mon.-Sat. 10:30am-9pm.

SIGHTS

Music Row, home of Nashville's signature industry, fiddles around Division and Demonbreun St. from 16th to 19th Ave. S., bounded on the south by Grand Ave. (take bus #3 to 17th Ave. and walk south). After surviving the mobs outside the **Country Music Hall of Fame,** 4 Music Sq. E. (256-1639) at Division St., you can marvel at classic memorabilia like Elvis' "solid gold" Cadillac, his 24-kt gold piano, as well as evocative photos from the early days of country music and aggressively colored outfits from more recent performances. Though Tennessee is the birthplace of bluegrass, the Hall of Fame shows off Cajun, cowboy, western-swing, and honky-tonk styles of country music as well. (Open Mon.-Thurs. 9am-5pm, Fri.-Sat. 8am-6pm.) Included in the admission is a tour of RCA's historic **Studio B,** where stars like Dolly Parton and Chet Atkins recorded their first hits. (Open daily 8am-7pm, Sept.-May 9am-5pm. $6.50, kids 6-11 $1.75, under 6 free.) When you want to record your own hit, the **Recording Studio of America,** 1510 Division St. (254-1282), underneath the **Barbara Mandrell Country Museum,** lets you do your own vocals on pre-recorded 24-track backgrounds to popular country and pop tunes. Choose a set and make a video, too. (Audio $13, video $20. Open daily 8am-8pm; Sept.-May daily 9am-5pm.) For a taste of southern extravagance, marvel at Webb Pierce's Silver Dollar car (adorned with 150 silver dollars and a pistol as a hood ornament) at **World Famous Car Collectors' Hall of Fame,** 1534 Demonbreun St. (255-6804; open Mon.-Thurs. 8am-8pm, Fri.-Sun. 8am-9pm; $5, kids 6-11 $3.25).

A 15-min. walk west from Music Row along West End Ave. to **Centennial Park** will bring you to Nashville's pride and joy. The "Athens of the South" boasts a full-scale replica of the **Parthenon,** complete with a towering Athena surrounded by her fellow Olympians (259-6358). Originally built as a temporary exhibit for the Tennessee Centennial in 1897, the Parthenon met with such olympian success that the model was rebuilt to last. The Nashville Parthenon also houses the **Cowan Collection of American Paintings** in the basement galleries, refreshing but erratic. Watch Greek theater and Shakespeare-in-the-park performed on the steps in mid-July and August. (Open Tues.-Sat. 9am-4:30pm, Sun. 1-5pm. $2.50, kids and seniors $1.25, under 4 free.) The park area also includes the **Upper Room Chapel Museum,** 1908 Grand St. off 21st Ave. S. (340-7200). The floor-to-ceiling stained glass window with over 9000 pieces of glass is spectacular. (Open Mon.-Sat. 8am-4:30pm.)

A walk through the downtown area reveals more of Nashville's eclectic architecture. The **Union Station Hotel,** at 1001 Broadway, next to the Post Office, displays a full stained glass arched ceiling and evokes the glamour of turn-of-the-century railroad travel with old time schedules and clocks. The **Ryman Auditorium,** 116 5th Ave. N. (254-1445), off Broadway at 5th, is better known as the "Mother Church of Country Music." In previous incarnations, it has housed a tabernacle and the Grand Ole Opry. (Guided tours daily 8:30am-4:30pm. $2.50, kids 6-12 $1.) Turn up 2nd

Ave. from Broadway to study the cast-iron and masonry facades of the handsome commercial buildings from the 1870s and 1880s. Now known as **Market Street,** the area has been gentrified into restaurants and nightspots.

The **Tennessee State Capitol,** Charlotte Ave. (741-0830) is the comely Greek Revival structure atop the hill next to downtown, offering free guided tours of, among other things, the tomb of James Knox Polk (open Mon.-Fri. 9am-4pm, Sat. 10am-5pm, Sun. 1-5pm). Across the street, the **Tennessee State Museum,** 505 Deaderick (741-2692) depicts the history of Tennessee from early Native Americans to "overlander" pioneers, Revolutionary War heroes to Civil War battles. Imaginative and interactive displays enhance this sometimes whitewashed version of Tennessee history. (Open Mon.-Sat. 10am-5pm, Sun. 1-5pm. Free.)

Although the state museum ranks corn and hogs as Tennessee's historically most important crops, tobacco's cultivation and use has proven one of its most tenacious, as it has across the world. The **Museum of Tobacco Art and History** 800 Harrison St. off 8th Ave. (271-2349), attests to this internationalism. From the dual-purpose Indian pipe/tomahawk (a slow and a quick way to death) to the giant glass-blown pipes, museum exhibits expound upon the unexpectedly captivating history of tobacco, pipes, and cigars. (Open Mon.-Sat. 9am-4pm. Free.)

While doing the museum thing you might want to check out Fisk University's **Van Vechten Gallery** (329-8543), corner of Jackson St. and D.B. Todd Blvd. off Jefferson St. (gallery entrance does not face street), which exhibits a distinguished collection of U.S. art. The gallery owns a portion of the Alfred Steiglitz Collection, donated to Fisk by Georgia O'Keeffe, Steiglitz's widow. Other exhibits feature O'Keeffe's work and a range of photography and African art. (Open Tues.-Fri. 10am-5pm, Sat.-Sun. 1-5pm. Donations accepted.)

If you tire of the downtown area, rest at the **Cheekwood Botanical Gardens and Fine Arts Center,** Forest Park Dr. (356-8000), 7 mi. southwest of town. The well-kept, leisurely, Japanese rose and English-style gardens are a welcome change from Nashville glitz. Take bus #3 ("West End/Belle Meade") from downtown to Belle Meade Blvd. and Page Rd. (Open Mon.-Sat. 9am-5pm, Sun. 1-5pm. $4, seniors and students $2, kids 7-17 $1). Dubbed "The Queen of Tennessee Plantations," the nearby **Belle Meade Mansion,** 5025 Harding Rd. (356-0501), travel down W. End, which becomes Harding Rd., provides a second respite. This 1853 plantation has the works: gorgeous grounds, smokehouse, dollhouse, and dairy (most buildings you can even see on the inside). Belle Meade was also the site of the nation's first thoroughbred and Tennessee walking horse breeding farm. (Two wonderful tours per hr. led by guides in period costumes; last tour at 4pm. Open Mon.-Sat. 9am-5pm, Sun. 1-5pm. $5.50, kids 13-18 $3.50, 6-12 $2.)

Thirteen mi. east of town is the **Hermitage,** 4580 Rachel's Lane (889-2941); take exit 221 off I-40. Andrew Jackson, the 7th U.S. president and a popular populist, built his beautiful manor house atop 625 gloriously shaded acres. The grounds make an ideal spot for a picnic. Beware the crowded summer months. (Open daily 9am-5pm. $7, seniors $6.50, kids 6-18 $3.50.)

ENTERTAINMENT

Nashville offers a dazzling array of inexpensive nightspots. Many feature the country tunes for which the town is known, while others cater to jazz, rock, bluegrass, or folk tastes. There are entertainment listings in the *Tennessean* Friday and Sunday, and in the *Nashville Banner* Thursday afternoon. The Nashville *Key,* available at the chamber of commerce, opens many entertainment doors. Comprehensive listings for all live music and events in the area abound in free copies of *Nashville Scene* or *Metro* around town. Muse over these publications plus many more at **Moskós,** 2204-B Elliston Place (327-2658), while stalling at their tasty muncheonette (open Mon.-Fri. 7am-midnight, Sat. 8am-midnight, Sun. 8:30am-midnight). Or stop in at the trendy **Botanical Cafe,** 124 2nd Ave. N. (244-3915), for listings of events and fresh muffins for $1 (open Mon.-Thurs. 7am-10pm, Fri. 7am-midnight, Sat. 8am-midnight, Sun. 8am-7pm).

Opryland USA (889-6611) cross-pollinates between Las Vegas schmaltz and Disneyland purity, or vice versa, with the best in country music thrown in. This amusement park contains all the requisite family attractions, from the Wabash Cannonball roller coaster to cotton candy, and it stages a dozen live music shows daily. Sometimes, a soundtrack of piped-in country music cascades through the park. Tune your radio to 580AM for more info. (Open late March-late April and early Oct.-early Nov. Sat.-Sun.; early May-late May and early Sept.-late Sept. Fri.-Sun.; late May-early Sept. daily. $25, 2 days $38; kids 11 and under $14, 2 days $21. Concert series $5.) The **Grand Ole Opry**, setting for America's longest-running radio show, moved here from the town center in 1976. *The* place to hear country music, the Opry howls every Friday and Saturday night ($14-16). Matinees are added on various days during peak tourist season (3pm April-Oct., $11-$14). Reserve tickets from Grand Ole Opry, 2808 Opryland Dr., Nashville 37214 (615-889-3060). General admission tickets can also be purchased at the box office, starting at 9am on Tuesday for weekend shows. Check the Friday morning *Tennessean* for a list of performers.

There's more to entertainment in Nashville than country music; just visit during the first weekend in June for the outdoor **Summer Lights** downtown, when top rock, jazz, reggae, classical, and, of course, country performers all jam simultaneously. (Open Mon.-Thurs. 4pm-12:30am.) For information on **Nashville Symphony** tickets and performances, call Ticketmaster at 741-2787.

NIGHTLIFE

For gay and lesbian hot spots, you might want try the **Warehouse**, 2529 Franklin Rd. (385-9689), at 8th Ave. S. (open daily 8pm-3am; cover $2-3), or **Chez Collette** (mostly women), 300 Hermitage Ave. (256-9134; open daily 4pm-3am; no cover). The **Pink Triangle Bookstore**, 2535 Franklin Rd. (386-0427), can fit you out with postcards, magazines, magnets, and leather—adults only (open daily 3pm-3am).

Tootsie's Orchid Lounge, 422 Broadway (726-3739). Many stars got their start here; it still has good C&W music and affordable drinks. For years owner Tootsie Bess lent money to struggling musicians until they could get on the Ole Opry. Women should think twice about going to this rather rowdy bar alone at night. Open Mon.-Sat. 9:30am-3am, Sun. noon-3am.

Blue Bird Cafe, 4104 Hillsboro Rd. (383-1461), in Green Hills. More genteel, this bird plays blues, folk, soft rock, and a smidgen of jazz. Women traveling solo probably will feel safer in this mellow, clean-cut establishment. Dinner, served until 11pm, consists of salads and sandwiches ($4-6.50). Music begins at 9:30pm. Open Mon.-Sat. 5:30pm-1am, Sun. 6pm-midnight. Cover $4-5.

Station Inn, 402 12th Ave. S. (255-3307), blues some serious grass. Open Tues.-Sat. 7pm-until. Music starts at 9pm. Cover $4-6. Free Sun. night jam session.

Bluegrass Inn, 1914 Broadway (244-8877), west of town, has beer, chips, and music with a cinderblock-and-cement motif. A good-natured place, the cover (around $3) depends on who's pickin'. Open Wed.-Thurs. 9pm-midnight, Fri.-Sat. 9pm-1am.

Ace of Clubs, 114 2nd S. (254-2237), in a huge downtown warehouse, packs 'em in for grand ol' rock n' roll. Open daily. Music around 9pm. Cover $4-7.

Ralph's Rutledge Hill Tavern, 515 2nd Ave. S. (256-9682), is so unassuming it is easily missed (there is no sign outside). But inside, this women's bar has pool tables, sandwiches and snacks ($2), and relaxed conversation. Open Sun.-Thurs. 5pm-midnight, Fri.-Sat. 5pm-3am. No cover charge.

■ Virginia

Virginians are usually *obviously* Virginians because they'll announce that fact long before you ask them. They're proud of their state. Throughout its history, "Old Dominion" has retained a deeply-rooted equilibrium and understated confidence. The permanent colonization of British North America began here with Jamestown colony in 1607. Thirteen years later, the New World's first African slaves set foot on Virginia's shores. Williamsburg burgeoned with the influx of plantation labor and made its fortune on tobacco. Nostalgia for this era swells in Colonial Williamsburg, where guides in costume show tourists around the restored 18th-century capital. Generations later, after slavery had become a political wedge between North and South, the Confederacy chose Richmond as its capital. Much of the state is rolling farmland, with tobacco still a major crop. But Virginia ain't just whistlin' *Dixie* these days. Charlottesville, Lexington, and Williamsburg are home to some of the finest schools in the nation. The world's most sophisticated military technology docks in Norfolk and checks in with the Pentagon in Arlington.

PRACTICAL INFORMATION

Capital: Richmond.
Visitor Information: Virginia Division of Tourism, Bell Tower, Capitol Sq., 101 N. 9th St., Richmond 23219 (800-847-4882 or 786-4484). **Division of State Parks,** 1201 Washington Bldg., Richmond 23219 (786-1712). For the free *Virginia Accommodations Directory,* write to Virginia Travel Council, 7415 Brook Rd., P.O. Box 15067, Richmond 23227.
Time Zone: Eastern. **Postal Abbreviation:** VA
Sales Tax: 4.5%.

■■■ CHARLOTTESVILLE

This college town in the Blue Ridge foothills proudly bears the stamp of its patron, Thomas Jefferson. The college he founded, the University of Virginia, dominates the town economically, geographically, and culturally, supporting a community of writers such as Peter Taylor and Pulitzer Prize-winning poet Rita Dove—not to mention a community of pubs. Visitors are steered to Monticello, the cleverly constructed classical mansion Jefferson designed. Even Charlottesville's friendly, hip, and down-to-earth populace seems to embody the third U.S. President's dream of a well-informed, culturally aware citizenry who choose to live close to the land.

PRACTICAL INFORMATION

Emergency: 911. **Campus Police:** dial 4-7166 on a UVA campus phone.
Visitor Information: Chamber of Commerce, 415 E. Market St. (295-3141), within walking distance of Amtrak, Greyhound, and historic downtown. Open Mon.-Fri. 9am-5pm. **Charlottesville/Albermarle Convention and Visitors Bureau,** P.O. Box 161 (977-1783), Rte. 20 near I-64. Take bus #8 ("Piedmont College") from 5th and Market St. Same info as Chamber of Commerce: brochures and maps. Combo tickets to Monticello, Michie Tavern, and Ash Lawn-Highland ($17; seniors $15.50, under 13 $7.50). Open daily 9:30am-5:30pm. **University of Virginia Info Center** (924-1019), at the rotunda in the center of campus. Some brochures, a university map, and info on tours. Open daily 9am-10pm. Students answer questions in **Newcomb Hall** (no phone). Open daily 9am-4:45pm. The larger **University Center** (924-7166) is off U.S. 250 west—follow the signs. Transport schedules, entertainment guides, and hints on budget accommodations. Answers phone "Campus Police." Campus maps. Open 24 hrs.
Amtrak: 810 W. Main St. (800-872-7245 or 296-4559), 7 blocks from downtown. To Washington, DC (8 per day, 3 hr., $22) and New York (8 per day, 7-8 hr., $81).

Greyhound: 310 W. Main St. (295-5131), within 3 blocks of historic downtown. To: Richmond (6 per day, 1½ hr., $12), Washington, DC (12 per day, 3 hr., $20.50), Norfolk (7 per day, 4 hr., $25).

Public Transport: Charlottesville Transit Service (296-7433). Bus service within city limits, including most hotels and UVA campus locations. Maps available at both info centers, Chamber of Commerce, and the UVA student center in Newcomb Hall. Buses operate Mon.-Sat. 6am-6:30pm. Fare 60¢, seniors and disabled 30¢, under 6 free. The more frequent blue University of Virginia buses require UVA ID or an expensive long-term pass to board.

Taxi: Yellow Cab, 295-4131. 90¢ first sixth mi., $1.50 each additional mile. To Monticello $12.

Help Lines: Region 10 Community Services Hotline, 972-1800. **Lesbian and Gay Hotline,** 971-4942. UVA-affiliated.

Post Office: 513 E. Main St. (978-7648). Open Mon.-Fri. 8am-5:30pm, Sat. 10am-noon. **ZIP code:** 22902.

Area Code: 804.

Charlottesville streets number east to west, using compass directions; 5th St. N.W. is 10 blocks from (and parallel to) 5th St. N.E. Streets running east-west across the numbered streets are neither parallel nor logically named. C-ville has two downtowns: one on the west side near the university called **The Corner,** and **Historic Downtown** about a mile east. The two are connected by **University Avenue,** running east-west, which becomes **Main Street** after the Corner ends at a bridge.

ACCOMMODATIONS AND CAMPING

Budget Inn, 140 Emmet St. (U.S. 29) (293-5141), near the university. 40 comfortable, hotel-quality rooms. TV, A/C, private baths. Senior discounts. Doubles $36 (1 bed) or $42 (2 beds). Each additional person $5.

Best Western, 105 Emmet St. (296-8111), offers clean, comfy rooms with A/C, TV, and a pool. Doubles $40.

Charlottesville KOA Kampground, P.O. Box 144, C-Ville, VA 22901 (296-9881 for info, 800-336-9881 for reservations). All campsites are shaded. Recreation hall with video games, a pavilion, and a pool (open Mon.-Sat. 10am-8pm). Fishing (not wading or swimming) allowed. Check-in after noon, check-out before noon. Sites $16, hook-up $22. Camping season is March 15-Nov. 15.

FOOD AND NIGHTLIFE

The Corner neighborhood near UVA has bookstores and countless cheap eats, with good Southern grub in C-ville's unpretentious diners. The town loves jazz, likes rock, and has quite a few pubs. Around the Downtown Mall, ubiquitous posters and the free *Charlottesville Review* can tell you who plays where and when.

The Hardware Store, 316 E. Main St. (977-1518), near the middle of the outdoor "mall." Bar atmosphere, but slightly off-beat: beers served in glass boots, appetizers in microcosmic basketball courts, and condiments in toolboxes. Collectors will drool over the 1898 building's antique collection. American grille and an eclectic set of entrees, from *ratatouille gratinée* ($5) to *crêpes* both sweet ($2-5) and savory ($6-7). Sandwiches ($5-7). Quality desserts. Open Mon.-Thurs. 11am-9:45pm, Fri.-Sat. 11am-10:30pm.

Garden Gourmet, 811 West Main St. (295-9991). Northern California circa 1967, with vegetarians, hippies, and "peacenluv." Homemade 7-grain bread, salad dressings, and creative veggie plates. Try the pasta primavera ($7). Wooden booths accompany artwork by the family and staff. Nightly folk music. Open Mon.-Fri. 11:30am-2:30pm; Sat. noon-3pm, Mon.-Thurs. 5:30-9pm, Fri.-Sat. 5:30-10pm.

Macado's, 1505 University Ave. (971-3558). Great sandwiches (around $4), homemade desserts, and long hours cure the late-night munchies. Pinball machine and candy store. Upstairs is a rockin' bar where Edgar Allen Poe once lived. Amontillado is the specialty of the house ($5). Listen for the throbulating beat of the tell-tale heart. Open Sun.-Thurs. 9am-12:30pm, Fri.-Sat. 9am-1:30am.

Sal's Caffé Italia, 221 E. Main St. (295-8484). Great pizza and sandwiches. Lunch or dinner ($4-7). Open Mon.-Sat. 10:30am-10pm.

The Tavern, 1140 Emmet St. (295-0404). A breakfast Eden; its banana-nut, bacon, or fruit-filled homemade pancakes ($3.50) are enormous. UVA jocks buy their kegs here. Open daily 7am-3pm.

SIGHTS AND ENTERTAINMENT

Most activity on the spacious **University of Virginia** campus clusters around the **Lawn** and fraternity-lined **Rugby Road.** Jefferson watched the University being built through his telescope at Monticello. You can return the gaze with a glimpse of Monticello from the Lawn, a terraced green carpet which unrolls down the middle of the university. Professors live in the Lawn's pavilions; Jefferson designed each one in a different architectural style. Lawn tours, led by students, leave on the hour at the Rotunda from 10am to 4pm; self-guided tour maps are provided for those who prefer to find their own way. **The Rotunda** is a target for pranks; students once adorned it with the inevitable cow. The **Old Cabell Building** across the Lawn from the Rotunda houses an auditorium with impressive acoustics. On its wall, a reproduction of Raphael's mural *The School of Athens* echoes Jefferson's vision of student-faculty harmony. The **Bayley Art Museum** (924-3592), Rugby Rd., features visiting exhibits and a small permanent collection including one of Rodin's castings of *The Kiss.* (Open Tues.-Sun. 1-5pm.)

The **Downtown Mall,** about 5 blocks off E. Main St., is a brick thoroughfare lined with restaurants and shops catering to a diverse crowd. A kiosk near the fountain in the center of the mall has posters with club schedules. At 110 E. Main, **The Movie Palace** shows current flicks for only $2. Other hip eateries, bars, and specialty stores provide places to treat your nose and tongue.

Jefferson's classical design for his home, **Monticello** (295-8181), derives from the 16th-century Italian architect Andrea Palladio. Jefferson oversaw every stage of design and construction, collecting gadgets for the inside on his travels, including a compass which registers wind direction through a weathervane on the roof. There's nary a non-picturesque spot on Monticello's landscape; from the west lawn, a roundabout floral walk leads to a magnificent hillside view. The garden lets you see **Montalto,** the "high mountain" on which Jefferson wanted to build an observation tower. Tours of Monticello begin every five minutes during the day, but the wait can be as long as 90 minutes during summer Saturdays. Because of the heat and lack of seating areas, come early. (Open daily 8am-5pm; Nov.-Feb. 9am-4:30pm; tickets $8, seniors $7, ages 6-11 $4, students $3 Mar.-Oct., $1 Nov.-Feb.)

Minutes away (take a right turn to Rte. 795) is **Ashlawn** (293-9539), the 500-acre former plantation home of James Monroe—one of those presidents who followed Jefferson. More quaint and less imposing than Monticello, Ashlawn has outdoor views to rival its domed neighbor's. The current owner, the College of William and Mary, has turned Ashlawn into a museum honoring its former owner. A colorful, dainty garden lines the pathway to the house, where a docent spews facts about President Monroe. Ashlawn's peacocks stroll the gardens and trees while making curious noises. (Open daily 9am-6pm; Nov.-Feb. daily 10am-5pm; tour $6, seniors $5.50, under 5 $2.)

In the **Box Gardens** behind Ashlawn, English-language opera highlights the **Summer Festival of the Arts** (box office 293-4500, open Tues.-Sun. 10am-5pm; tickets $14, seniors $13, students $10, plus $2 on Sat.). A 45-min. intermission allows for a picnic supper ($12), which you can order from **Festive Fare** (296-5496) or **Kortright Cafe** (979-9619). Ashlawn also hosts **Music at Twilight** ($10, seniors $9, students $6), including New Orleans jazz, Cajun music, blues, and swing. Combo tickets for the performance, house tour, and picnic supper are available ($22).

Down the road from Monticello on Rte. 53 is **Michie** (Mick-ee) **Tavern** (977-1234), with an operating grist mill, a general store, and a tour of the 200-year-old establishment (open daily 9am-5pm; $5, seniors $4.50, under 6 $1). Jefferson's daughter supposedly fled the tavern after improperly teaching a waltz to a man in the ballroom. **The Ordinary** (977-1235), located in the tavern, serves up a fixed buffet of fried chicken, beans, cornbread, and other dishes ($9, ages 6-11 $3.50). Eat outside in good weather. (Open 11:15am-3:30pm.) To see all of the above three sites at a discount price, purchase the President's Pass at the Charlottesville/Albemarle Convention and Visitors Bureau (see Practical Information above).

■■■ RICHMOND

The former capital of the Confederate States of America, Richmond proudly displays its Civil War past, with numerous museums and restored houses showing everything from troop movements to tablecloths belonging to Confederate President Jefferson Davis. But in districts like the sprawling, beautiful Fan and formerly industrial Shockoe Bottom, Richmond shows its development of the 20th century.

PRACTICAL INFORMATION

Emergency: 911.
Visitor Information: Richmond Visitors Center, 1700 Robin Hood Rd. (358-5511), exit 14 off I-95/64, in a converted train depot. Helpful 6-min. video introduces the city's attractions. Walking tours and quality maps. Open Memorial Day-Labor Day daily 9am-7pm; off-season 9am-5pm.
Traveler's Aid: 643-0279 or 648-1767.
Amtrak: far away at 7519 Staple Mills Rd. (264-9194 or 800-872-7245). To: Washington, DC (8 per day, 2 hr., $21), Williamsburg (1¼ hr., $9), Virginia Beach (3 hr., $18, the last third of the trip is on a shuttle), New York City (8 per day, 7 hr., $81), Baltimore (3 hr., $28), and Philadelphia (8 per day, 4¾ hr., $45). Taxi fare to downtown $12. Open 24 hrs.
Greyhound: 2910 N. Boulevard (353-8903). To get downtown, walk 2 blocks to the visitors center or take GRTC bus #24 north. To: Washington, DC (16 per day, 2½ hr., $18), Charlottesville (6 per day, 1½ hr., $12), Williamsburg (7 per day, 1 hr., $11.50), and Norfolk (7 per day, 3 hr., $19.50).
Public Transport: Greater Richmond Transit Co., 101 S. Davis St. (358-4782). Maps available in the basement of city hall, 900 E. Broad St., and in the Yellow Pages. Buses serve most of Richmond infrequently, downtown frequently; most leave from Broad St. downtown. Bus #24 goes south to Broad St. and downtown. Fare $1, transfers 10¢. Free trolleys provide dependable, if limited, service to downtown and Shockoe Slip 10am-4pm daily, with an extended Shockoe Slip schedule from 5pm-midnight.
Help Lines: Rape Crisis, 643-0888 or 648-9224. **Gay Information,** 353-3626.
Post Office: 10th and Main St. (783-0825). Open Mon.-Fri. 7:30am-5pm. **ZIP code:** 23219.
Area Code: 804.

Creative locals describe Richmond's urban area as a closed ladies' fan placed east to west: the center is the **state capitol,** the short handle to the east is **Court End** and **Shockoe Bottom,** and the long western blade begins downtown and cleverly becomes the **Fan** neighborhood. Streets form a grid, but are illogically named, save for First (west) through 14th (east) St. downtown. Both I-95, leading north to Washington, DC, and I-295 encircle the urban area.

ACCOMMODATIONS AND CAMPING

Budget motels in Richmond cluster on **Williamsburg Rd.,** on the edge of town, and along **Midlothian Turnpike,** south of the James River; public transport (see Practical Information) to these areas is infrequent at best. As usual, the farther away from downtown you stay, the less you pay. The visitors center (see Practical Information above) can reserve accommodations, sometimes at substantial ($10-20) discounts.

Massad House Hotel, 11 N. 4th St. (648-2893), 4 blocks from the capitol, near town. Shuttles guests via a 1940s elevator to clean, spacious rooms with shower and TV. The only inexpensive rooms downtown. Singles $32, doubles $37.

Executive Inn, 5215 W. Broad St. (288-4011 or 800-542-2801), 3 mi. from center of town; take Bus #6. Offers grand (by motel standards) but slightly faded rooms and a pool/health club. Free continental breakfast. Singles $37, doubles $44.

Motel 6, 5704 Williamsburg Rd. (222-7600), Sandston, about 6 mi. east on U.S. 60, across from the airport. Get there by Bus #7 ("Seven Pines"). Ah, Motel 6; there's one in every city in the nation. Singles $28, doubles $32.

The closest **campground, Pocahontas State Park,** 10300 Beach Rd. (796-4255), 10 mi. south on Rte. 10 and Rte. 655, offers showers, biking, boating, lakes, and a huge pool. (Sites $8.50. No hookups. Pool admission $2, ages 3-12 $1.50.) Reserving a site by phone through Ticketron (490-3939) costs an extra $8.

FOOD AND ENTERTAINMENT

Richmond's good budget restaurants hide among the shade trees and well-kept porches of the gentrified Fan district, formed by the bordering streets Monument Ave., Main St., Laurel St. and Boulevard.

The Commercial Cafe, 111 N. Robinson St. (353-7110), serves the best barbecue in this barbecue-rich town. Sandwiches start at $5, but real eaters will order the ribs—the "Taster" ($7) is quite filling, and the plates ($9-14) can be shared. Open daily 5-11pm; in summer Tues.-Sun. 5pm-11pm.

Texas-Wisconsin Border Cafe, 1501 W. Main St. (355-2907), features chili, potato pancakes, and *chalupas.* Sports indoor signs such as: "Dixie Inn," "Secede," and "Eat Cheese or Die." At night the cafe secedes to become a popular bar. Lunches $5-7. Dinners $6-11. Open daily 11am-2am.

Piccola's, 1100 W. Main St. (355-3111), at Harrison, serves piping-hot pizza, calzones ($3-4), and jumbo sandwiches ($3.50). Students rave about the cheap and delicious pizza. Open Mon.-Thurs. 11am-midnight, Fri.-Sat. 11am-2am, and Sun. 3pm-midnight.

The Ocean Restaurant, 414 E. Main St. (643-9485), serves excellent, filling breakfasts and lunches. Everything under $4. Open Mon.-Fri. 6:30am-3:30pm.

3rd St. Diner (788-4750), at the corner of 3rd and Main, has prices frozen from days of yore. The $2.25 meatless breakfast (two eggs, biscuit or toast, and home fries, grits, or Virginia fried apples) is served all day. The waitresses know all the regulars by name. Open 24 hrs.

The **Shockoe Slip** district from Main, Canal, and Cary St. between 10th and 14th St. features fancy shops in restored and newly painted warehouses, but few bargains. At the **farmers market,** outdoors at N. 17th and E. Main St., pick up fresh fruit, vegetables, meat, and maybe even a pot swine. Free concerts abound here in the summer; check *Style Weekly,* a free magazine available at the visitors center.

Nightlife crowds Shockoe Slip and sprinkles itself in a less hectic manner throughout the Fan. The **Tobacco Company Club,** 1201 E. Cary St. (782-9555), smokes with top 40 music and no cover charge. (Open Tues.-Sat. 8pm-2am.) **Matt's British Pub and Comedy Club,** 1045 12th St. (643-5653), next door, lives up to its name with stand-up comedy at 8 and 11pm. (Open Tues.-Sat. 8pm-2am.) **The Metro Cafe,** 727 W. Broad St. (649-4952), features local progressive bands most weekends 8pm-midnight. Usually $5 cover. **Flood Zone,** 11 S. 18th St. (643-6006), south of Shockoe Slip, offers a combination of big-name and off-beat rock bands. (Ticket office open Tues.-Fri. 10am-6pm. Tickets $6-20, depending upon the show.)

SIGHTS

Ever since Patrick Henry declared "Give me liberty or give me death" in Richmond's **St. John's Church,** 2401 E. Broad St. (648-5015), this river city has been quoting, memorializing, and bronzing its heroes. Sundays in summer at 2pm, an actor recreates the famous 1775 speech. You must take a tour to see the church. (Tours given Mon.-Sat. 10am-3:30pm, Sun. 1-3:30pm; $2, students $1.) Larger-than-life statues of George Washington and Thomas Jefferson grace the **State Capitol** grounds, 9th and Grace St. (786-4344). Jefferson modeled this masterpiece of neo-classical architecture after a Roman temple in France. (Open Apr.-Oct. daily 9am-5pm, Nov.-Mar. Mon.-Sat. 9am-5pm, Sun. 1-5pm.) For more sculpture, follow Franklin Ave. from the capitol until it becomes **Monument Avenue,** lined with trees, gracious old houses, and towering statues of Confederate heroes. Robert E. Lee, who survived the Civil War, faces his beloved South; Stonewall Jackson, who didn't, scowls at the Yankees.

The **Court End** district stretches north and east of the capitol to Clay and College Streets and guards Richmond's most distinctive historical sights. The **Museum of the Confederacy,** 1202 E. Clay St. (649-1861), is the world's largest Confederate artifact collection. The main floor leads visitors through the military history of the Great War of Northern Aggression; the basement displays guns and flags of the Confederacy; and the top floor houses temporary exhibits on such topics as slave life in the antebellum South. The museum also runs one-hour tours through the **White House of the Confederacy** next door (ask at the museum desk). Statues of Tragedy, Comedy, and Irony grace the White House's front door; decide for yourself which applies. (Museum open Mon.-Sat. 10am-5pm, Sun. 1-5pm; tours of the White House Mon., Wed., and Fri.-Sat. 10:30am-4:30pm, Tues. and Thurs. 11:30am-4:30pm, Sun. 1:15-4:30pm. Admission to museum or tour $4, students $2.50, under 13 $2.25; for both: $7, $5, $3.50.)

The **Valentine Museum,** 1015 E. Clay St. (649-0711), enamors visitors with exhibits on local and Southern social and cultural history. Tours through the museum are self-guided, but the admission price includes a tour of the recently renovated **Wickham-Valentine House** next door. (Both open Mon.-Sat. 10am-5pm, Sun. noon-5pm. $3.50, seniors $3, students $2.75, ages 7-12 $1.50.) Combination tickets to the Museum of the Confederacy, White House of the Confederacy, Valentine Museum, and **John Marshall House**—all within easy walking distance of each other—are $11, seniors and students $10, ages 7-12 $5.

East of the capitol, follow your tell-tale heart to the **Edgar Allan Poe Museum,** 1914 16 E. Main St. (648-5523). Poe memorabilia stuffs the five buildings, including the **Stone House,** the oldest standing structure within the original city boundaries. (Open Tues.-Sat. 10am-4pm, Sun.-Mon. 1:30-4pm. $5, students $2.)

Four blocks from the intersection of Monument Ave. and N. Boulevard reposes the Southeast's largest art museum, the **Virginia Museum of Fine Arts,** 2800 Grove Ave. (367-0844). An outstanding art gallery, the museum also holds a gorgeous collection of Fabergé jewelry and Easter eggs made for Russian czars (the largest outside the CIS—the former USSR), a fine showing of U.S. contemporary art (including a Jane Shaw piece), and what might just be the largest collection of horse sculpture and painting in North America (outside of Kentucky). (Open Tues.-Sat. 11am-5pm, Thurs. 11am-8pm in the North Wing Galleries, Sun. 1-5pm. Donation requested.)

The **Maggie L. Walker National Historic Site,** 110½ E. Leigh St. (780-1380), commemorates the life of an ex-slave's gifted daughter. Physically disabled, Walker advocated black women's rights and succeeded as founder and president of a bank. (Tours Thurs.-Sun. 9am-5pm. Free.) The **Black History Museum and Cultural Center of Virginia** (780-9093), on Clay St., opened in the summer of 1991. (Open Tues., Thurs.-Sat. 11am-4pm. Free.)

All of the above sites ("and much, much more!") can be seen from the **Cultural Link Trolley** (358-5511). The trolleys run 10am-5pm on Saturday and 12:30pm-5pm on Sunday ($5). Bus tours are organized by the Historic Richmond Foundation. There are three main tours: **Old Richmond Today** ($16, kids $13), **Civil War Battlefields** ($22, kids $11; only on Sun.), and the **Civil War City,** (April-Oct. Mon.-Sat.; $19, kids $15). Call 780-0107 for reservations and departure times.

Two architectural highlights are the opulent, art-deco **Jefferson Hotel** (788-8000), at Franklin and Adams St., and the **Byrd Theatre,** 2908 W. Cary St. (353-9911), where you can view Hollywood's latest in extraordinary style: marble balconies, enormous stained-glass windows, and a Wurlitzer Organ that rises from the floor to entertain before each show.

Civil War buffs should brave the trip to the city's boundaries and the **Richmond National Battlefield Park,** 3215 E. Broad St. (226-1981). The **Chimborazo Visitors Center,** located in a former Civil War hospital, contains an educational film and exhibits about the Civil War, as well as maps detailing the battlefields and fortifications surrounding the city. (Open daily 9am-5pm. Free.)

■■■ SHENANDOAH NATIONAL PARK

Before 1926, when Congress authorized the establishment of **Shenandoah National Park,** the area held a series of rocky, threadbare farms along the Blue Ridge Mountains. Congress ordered the planning of the park but (in true bureaucratic largesse) offered no monetary incentive. So, to pick up the government's fiscal slack, the state of Virginia appropriated over $1 million, and the citizens donated the rest. Thirteen years later, the farmers had been uprooted and the area was returned to its "natural state." Forests replaced fields, wild deer and bears supplanted cows and pigs, and a two-lane highway was paved over the dirt roads along the ridge.

Today, gawking comes naturally in Shenandoah; on clear days drivers and hikers can look out over miles of unspoiled ridges and treetops. In summer, the cool mountain air offers a respite from Virginia's typical heat and humidity. Go early in June to see mountain laurel blooming in the highlands. In fall, Skyline Drive and its lodges are choked with tourists who come to enjoy the magnificent fall foliage.

PRACTICAL INFORMATION

Emergency (in park): 800-732-0911, or contact the nearest ranger.

Visitor Information: 999-2243, 999-2266 for 24-hr. recorded message. Mailing address: Superintendent, Park Headquarters, Shenandoah National Park, Rte. 4, P.O. Box 348, Luray, VA 22835. **Dickey Ridge Visitors Center,** Mile 4.6 (635-3566), closest to the north entrance. Daily interpretative programs. Open April-Nov. daily 9am-5pm. **Byrd Visitors Center,** Mile 50 (999-3283), in the center of the park. Movie and museum explain the history of the Blue Ridge Range and its mountain culture. Open April-Oct. daily 9am-5pm, Nov.-March when weather permits. Both stations offer changing exhibits on the park, free pamphlets detailing short hikes, daily posted weather updates, and ranger-led nature hikes.

Area Code: 703.

Shenandoah's technicolor mountains—bluish and covered with deciduous flora in summer, smeared with reds, oranges, and yellows in the fall—can be ogled from overlooks along **Skyline Drive,** which runs 105 mi. south from Front Royal to Rockfish Gap (the mountains were colorized in 1973; black and white originals available on bootleg video only). The overlooks provide picnic areas for hikers; map boards also carry data about trail conditions. The drive closes during and after bad weather. Most facilities also hibernate in the winter. (Entrance $5 per vehicle, $3 per hiker, biker, or bus passenger; pass good for 7 days; seniors and disabled persons free.)

Miles along Skyline Dr. are measured north to south, beginning at Front Royal. **Greyhound** sends buses to Waynesboro, near the park's southern entrance, once each morning from Washington, DC ($39), but no bus or train serves Front Royal.

When planning to stay more than a day, purchase the *Park Guide* ($2), a booklet containing all the park regulations, trail lists, and a description of the area's geological history. Another good guide which doubles as a souvenir is *Exploring Shenandoah National Park* ($2). The *Guide to Shenandoah National Park and Skyline Drive* (the "Blue Bible" in Ranger parlance—$6.50) provides info on accommodations and activities. The free *Shenandoah Overlook* newspaper reports seasonal and weekly events. All four publications are available at the visitors centers.

ACCOMMODATIONS AND CAMPING

The **Bear's Den HI/AYH** (554-8708), located 35 mi. north of Shenandoah on Rte. 601 South, provides a woodsy stone lodge for travelers with two 10-bed dorm rooms. Drivers should exit from Rte. 7 onto Rte. 601 South and go about ½ mi., turn right at the stone-gate entrance, and proceed up the hostel driveway for another ½ mi. No bus or train service is available. The hostel has a dining room, kitchen, on-site parking, and a laundry room. Ask the friendly staff for activities info. (Check-in 5-9pm. Front gate locked and quiet hrs. begin at 10pm. Check-out by 9:30am. $9, non-members $12. Camping $4 per person. Reservations recommended; write Bear's Den HI/AYH, Postal Route 1, Box 288, Bluemont, VA 22012.)

The park maintains two lodges with motel-esque rooms in cabin-esque exteriors. **Skyland** (999-2211 or 800-999-4714), Mile 42 on Skyline Drive, closed Dec.-March, lands brown and green wood-furnished cabins ($41-70, $5 more in Oct.) and slightly more upscale motel rooms. **Big Meadows** (999-2221 or 800-999-4714), Mile 51, closed Nov.-April, raises similar cabins and motel rooms in a smaller complex. Both locations charge an extra $2 or more Fri.-Sat. Reservations are necessary, up to six months in advance for the fall season.

The park service maintains three major campgrounds: **Big Meadows** (Mile 51); **Lewis Mountain** (Mile 58); and **Loft Mountain** (Mile 80). All have stores, laundry facilities, and showers (no hookups). Heavily wooded and uncluttered by mobile homes, Lewis Mountain makes for the happiest tenters. All sites cost $10 except those reserved at Big Meadows (reservation line 800-365-2267; $12). Call a visitors center (see Practical Information above) to check availability.

Back-country camping is free, but you must obtain a permit at a park entrance, visitors center, ranger station, or the **park headquarters** (see Practical Information above) halfway between Thornton Gap and Luray on U.S. 211. Back-country camp-ers must set up 25 yd. from a water supply and out of sight of any trail, road, over-look, cabin or other campsite. Since open fires are prohibited, bring cold food or a stove; boil water or bring your own because some creeks are oozing with micro-scopic beasties. Illegal camping carries a hefty fine. Hikers on the **Appalachian Trail** can make use of primitive open shelters, three-sided structures with stone fire-places, which are strewn along the trail at approximately 7-mi. intervals. At full shel-ters, campers often will move over to make room for a new arrival. These shelters are reserved for hikers with three or more nights in different locations stamped on their camping permits; casual hikers are banned from them. The **Potomac Appala-chian Trail Club (PATC)** maintains six cabins in backcountry areas of the park. You must reserve in advance by writing to the club at 118 Park St., SE, Vienna, VA 22180 (242-0693), and bring lanterns and food. The cabins contain bunk beds, water, and stoves. (Sun.-Thurs. $3 per person, Fri.-Sat. $14 per group; one member in party must be 21.)

HIKES AND ACTIVITIES

The **Appalachian Trail** runs the length of the park. Trail maps and the PATC guide can be obtained at the visitors center (see Practical Information above). The PATC puts out three different topographical maps (each $5) of three different parts of the park. When purchased as a package, the maps come with a trail guide, descriptions, and suggestions for budgeting time ($16). Brochures that cover the popular hikes are available for free. Campers must avoid lighting fires and use stoves instead and leave *no* litter whatsoever. Overnight hikers should remember the unpredictability of mountain weather. Be sure to get the park service package of brochures and advice before a long hike.

Old Rag Mountain, 5 mi. from Mile 45, is 3291 ft.—not an intimidating summit—but the 7.2-mi. loop up the mountain is supremely difficult. The hike is steep, involves scrambling over and between granite, and at many points flaunts disappointing "false summits." Bring lots of water, energy food, and gumption. There are plenty of spots to camp around the summit area—avoid the main campground. The **Whiteoak Canyon Trail** beckons from its own parking lot at Mile 42.6. The trail to the canyon is easy; the waterfalls and trout-filled streams below them are spectacular. Visitors centers vend 5-day fishing licenses ($6), but hordes of regulations hem in the catch. From Whiteoak Canyon, the **Limberlost** trail slithers into a hemlock forest. At Mile 51.4, **Lewis Spring Falls** Trail takes only ¾-mi. to reach a gorgeous array of falls—the closest to Skyline Drive in the whole park. The trail descends further (about an hour's walk) to the base of the falls, where water drops 80 ft. over the crumbling stone of an ancient lava flow. **Hogback Overlook,** from Mile 20.8 to Mile 21, bristles with easy hikes and idyllic views of the smooth Shenandoah River and Valley; on a clear day, you can see 11 bends in the river.

Take a break from hiking or driving at one of Shenandoah's seven **picnic areas,** located at Dickey Ridge (Mile 5), Elkwallow (Mile 24), Pinnacles (Mile 37), Big Meadows (Mile 51), Lewis Mountain (Mile 58), South River (Mile 63) and Loft Mountain (Mile 80). All have tables, fireplaces, water fountains, and comfort stations. When you forget to pack a picnic basket, swing by the **Panorama Restaurant** (800-999-4714), at Mile 31.5, for a meal and a view. (Sandwiches $3-5, dinners $6-14. Open April-Nov. daily 9am-7pm.)

Outside the park, the **Shenandoah Caverns** (477-3115) tout an iridescent panoply of stalactites and stalagmites, with Rainbow Lake and amusing Capitol Dome among the mimetic underground formations prospering in the year-round 56°F air. Take U.S. 211 to Newmarket, get on I-81 North, go 4 mi. to the Shenandoah Caverns exit, and follow the signs for the caverns—not the town of the same name. (Accessible to disabled persons. $7, ages 8-14 $3.50, under 8 free.) **Skyline Caverns** (635-4545 or 800-635-4599) in Front Royal built a reputation on its anthodites, whose white spikes defy gravity and grow in all directions at the rate of an inch every seven thousand years. The caverns are 15 min. from the junction of Skyline Drive and U.S. 211. ($9, ages 6-12 $4, under 6 free.)

The **Downriver Canoe Co.,** P.O. Box 10, Rte. 1, Box 256-A, Bentonville (635-5526), is for the serious canoer. Canoe trips stretch from 3 mi. to 150-plus mi. From Skyline Drive Mile 20 follow U.S 211 west for 8 mi., then north onto U.S. 340, 14 mi. to Bentonville. Turn right onto Rte. 613 and go 1 mi. (Prices vary with length of trip. 3-mi. trips $29 per canoe; 33-mi. trips $122 per canoe.)

▪ Blue Ridge Parkway

If you don't believe that the best things in life are free, this ride could change your mind. The 469-mi. Blue Ridge Parkway, continuous with Skyline Drive, runs through Virginia and North Carolina, connecting the **Shenandoah** and **Great Smoky Mountains National Parks** (see Tennessee). Administered by the National Park Service, the parkway adjoins hiking trails, campsites, and picnic grounds. Every bit as scenic as Skyline Drive, the Parkway remains much wilder and less crowded. Don't expect to get anywhere fast on this Parkway, however—the speed limit is 45 mph. Also beware of fog during gloomy mornings and afternoons. From Shenandoah National Park, the road winds south through Virginia's **George Washington National Forest** from Waynesboro to Roanoke. The forest sprouts with spacious campgrounds, canoeing opportunities, and swimming in cold, clear mountain water at **Sherando Lake** (Mile 16).

Self-guided nature trails range from the **Mountain Farm Trail** (Mile 5.9), a 20-minute hike to a reconstructed homestead, to the **Rock Castle Gorge Trail** (Mile 167), a 3-hr. excursion. At **Mabry Mill** (Mile 176.1) or **Humpback Rocks** (Mile 5.8) you can visit mountain farms, and at **Crabtree Meadows** (Mile 339) you can purchase local crafts. Of course, real go-getters will venture onto the **Appalachian Trail,** which runs the length of the parkway. In addition to these trails, the Park Service hosts a variety of ranger-led interpretive activities. Information is available at the visitors centers (see below).

Practical Information For general info on the parkway, call **visitor information** in North Carolina (704-259-0779 or 704-259-0701). For additional details call the park service in Roanoke, VA (703-982-6458), or in Montebello, VA (703-377-2377). Write for info to **Blue Ridge Parkway Headquarters,** 200 BB&T Bldg., Asheville, NC 28801. Eleven **visitors centers** line the parkway at Miles 5.8, 63.8, 86, 169, 217.5, 294, 304.5, 316.4, 331, 364.6, and 382, and there are also seven stands where you can pick up brochures. Located at entry points where major highways intersect the Blue Ridge, the centers offer various exhibits, programs, and information facilities. Pick up a free copy of the helpful *Milepost* guide.

Greyhound provides access to the major towns around the Blue Ridge. Buses run to and from Richmond, Waynesboro, and Lexington; a bus serves Buchanan and Natural Bridge between Roanoke and Lexington once daily. For info, contact the station in Charlottesville (see Charlottesville Practical Information) or Greyhound, 26 Salem Ave. S.W. (703-342-6761; open 24 hrs.), in Roanoke.

In an **emergency** call 800-727-5928 anywhere in VA or NC. Be sure to give your location to the nearest mile. Use this number and not the emergency line.

Accommodations The **Blue Ridge Country HI/AYH Hostel,** Rte. 2, P.O. Box 449, Galax 24333 (236-4962), rests only 100 ft. from the parkway at Mile 214.5. (3-night max. stay. $10.50, nonmembers $13.50, which includes redeemable $3 stamp for membership. If they know in advance, they'll pick up visitors arriving by bus to Mont Airy, NC or Whytheville, VA. (For North Carolina hostels, see Asheville and Boone, NC.) There are nine **campgrounds** along the parkway, each with water and restrooms, located at Miles 61, 86, 120, 167, 239, 297, 316, 339, and 408. Fee $8, reservations not accepted. Contact the parkway for info on free backcountry and winter camping.

The cities and villages along the parkway offer a range of accommodations. For a complete listing, pick up a *Blue Ridge Parkway Directory* or the *Virginia Accommodations Directory* at one of the visitors centers. The communities listed have easy access to the parkway and many, such as Asheville, NC, Boone, NC, and Charlottesville, VA, have historic and cultural attractions of their own.

■■■ VIRGINIA BEACH

Aaah, the beach. Gaze upon endless miles of water, sand, and sky; inhale the perfume of the tide; listen to the insistent rhythm of the waves. Then turn around and face the boardwalk. Virginia Beach is unabashedly immersed in the present. Rows of hotels and motels, ice cream stands, surf shops, and fast-food joints flank the golden coastline, and swarms of cruising college students and servicemen descend upon the beach resort every summer.

PRACTICAL INFORMATION

Emergency: 911.

Visitor Information: Virginia Beach Visitors Center (425-7511 or 800-446-8038), 22nd and Parks Ave. Info on budget accommodations and area sights. Open daily 9am-8pm; Labor Day-Memorial Day daily 9am-5pm.

Greyhound: 1017 Laskin Rd. (422-2998), connects with Norfolk, Williamsburg, and Richmond, and with MD via the Bridge Tunnel. To: Washington, D.C. ($36, 6½ hr.); Richmond ($21, 3½ hrs.); Williamsburg ($12.50, 2½ hr.).

Amtrak: (245-3589 or 800-872-7245). The nearest station, in Newport News, provides free 45-min. bus service to and from the Radisson Hotel at 19th St. and Pavilion Drive in Virginia Beach, but you must have a train ticket to get on the bus. To: Washington, D.C. ($41, 5½ hr.); New York City ($79, 9 hr.); Philadelphia ($68, 8 hr.); Baltimore ($47, 7 hr.); Richmond ($18, 3 hr.); Williamsburg ($13, 2 hr.).

Public Transportation: Virginia Beach Transit/Trolley Information Center (428-3388) provides information on area transportation and tours, including trolleys, buses, and ferries. The **Atlantic Ave. Trolley** runs from Rudee Inlet to 42nd St. (Summer daily noon-midnight; 50¢, seniors and disabled 25¢.) Other trolleys run along the boardwalk, the North Seashore, and to Lynnhaven Mall.

Bike Rental: North End Cyclery, at Laskin Rd. and Arctic Ave. Bikes $3.50 per hr., $15 per day. Open 10am-7pm. **Moped Rentals, Inc.,** 21st St. and Pacific Ave. Open summer daily 9am-midnight. Mopeds $22.50 per 1½ hr.

Post Office: 24th and Atlantic Ave. (428-2821). Open Mon.-Fri. 8am-11am and noon-4:30pm. **ZIP code:** 23458.

Area Code: 804.

Virginia Beach is confusing to get to, but easy to get around in. Drivers from the north can take I-64 south from Richmond through the Bay Bridge Tunnel into Norfolk, then get onto Rte. 44 (the Virginia Beach-Norfolk Expwy.), which delivers them straight to 22nd St. and the beach. Virginia Beach's street grid pits east-west numbered streets against north-south avenues (Atlantic, Pacific, Arctic, and Baltic) parallel to the beach.

ACCOMMODATIONS

Atlantic Avenue and Pacific Avenue run parallel to the oceanfront, buzz with activity during the summer, and boast the most desirable hotels; reserve as far in advance as possible. If you're traveling in a group, shop around for "efficiency rate" apartments, which are sometimes rented cheaply by the week.

Angie's Guest Cottage-Bed and Breakfast and HI/AYH Hostel, 302 24th St. (428-4690), still ranks as the best place to stay on the entire Virginia Coast. Barbara Yates (who also answers to "Angie") and her team welcome guests with exceptional warmth. They'll pick you up from the train station (call before leaving with time of arrival for train or bus). (Open April 1-Oct. 1, March and Oct. with reservations. Memorial Day-Labor Day $10.50, non-members $13.50. off-season $8, non-members $11. Overflow camping at off-season rates. Linen $2. Kitchen and lockers available.) Iin the bed and breakfast, breakfast is (duh) included (doubles $48-68).

You can **camp** at the **Seashore State Park** (481-2131, reservations 490-3939), about 8 mi. north of town on U.S. 60, which has some juicy spots ($14). Because of its desirable location amid sand dunes and cypress trees, the park is very popular, so call two to three weeks ahead (during business hours) for reservations. (Park open 8am-dusk; take the North Seashore Trolley.) **KOA,** 1240 General Booth Blvd. (428-1444), runs a quiet campground with free bus service to the beach and boardwalk (sites $22, with hook-up $24; comfortable and spacious 1-room cabins $38).

FOOD AND NIGHTLIFE

Junk-food slughogs will love Virginia Beach, thanks to the jumble of fast-food joints along the boardwalk and the main drags. But don't let the neon glare blind you to restaurants with a more local flavor. **The Jewish Mother,** 3108 Pacific Ave. (422-5430), is one of the most popular eateries in town. The JM dotes on her customers with quiche, omelettes, crepes ($5-9), deli sandwiches ($4-6), and desserts ($2-4). At night it's a popular (and cheap) bar with live music. (Open daily 9am-3am.) **The Raven,** 1200 Atlantic Ave. (425-9556), lays out well-prepared seafood, steaks, and salad in a tinted-glass greenhouse. You can eat outdoors when it's warm. (Sandwiches and burgers $5-7, dinners $12-17. Open daily 11am-2pm.) **Giovanni's Pasta Pizza Palace,** 2006 Atlantic Ave. (425-1575), serves tasty Italian pastas, pizzas, and hot grinders. (Lunches and dinners $5-8. Open daily noon-11pm.)

Buy produce at **Virginia Beach Farmer's Market,** 1989 Landstown Rd. (427-4395; open daily 9am-6:30pm; in winter until dark). At 31st St. (Luskin Rd.) and Baltic Ave., the **Farm Fresh Supermarket** salad bar, stocked with fresh fruit, pastas, and frozen yogurt ($2.39 per lb.), is a cheap alternative (open 24 hrs.).

On summer nights, it's a good idea for women to avoid walking the boardwalk alone. In darkness the beach becomes a haunt for lovers, while singles hover around the bars and clubs between 17th and 23rd St. along Pacific and Atlantic Ave. Locals favor **Chicho's** (422-6011) and the **Edge,** along Atlantic Ave. between 20th and 21st Streets. (Dress code: T-shirts; short, tight dresses; tanned skin.) Bartenders shout to one another underneath videos of surfing competitions and bungee jumping, while hopeful patrons run their eyes up and down their neighbors' figures. (Chicho's open Mon.-Fri. 5pm-2am, Sat.-Sun. 1pm-2am; no cover charge. The Edge open daily 4pm-1:30am; no cover.) Cheap drinks, live bands, and graffiti-covered walls mingle and get mellow at the Jewish Mother (above). Clubs like **Peabody's,** at the corner of 21st St. and Pacific Ave., feature neon lighting and live bands playing a variety of music (open 7pm-2am; cover $5).

SIGHTS

Virginia Beach is biker-friendly, with **bike paths** along the boardwalk and some of the larger streets. Rent a bike at one of the many stands near the boardwalk (about $5 per hr.), then ask for the Virginia Beach Bikeway Map at the Visitors Center. If you're feeling athletic, bike south down the coast to **Sandbridge Beach,** where the locals hang out to avoid crowds of tourists; take the bike trail through the **Back Bay National Wildlife Refuge.** Or bike north to self-descriptive **Seashore State Park.** On the way back from Seashore State Park, test your psychic ability at the **Edgar Cayce Association for Research and Enlightenment** (428-3588), 67th St. and Atlantic Ave., dedicated to psychic potential and holistic health (open Mon.-Sat. 9am-10pm, Sun. 1-10pm; Sept.-May Mon.-Sat. 9am-5:30pm, Sun. 1-6pm).

■■■ WILLIAMSBURG

At the end of the 17th century, when English aristocrats wore brocades and wigs, Williamsburg was the capital of Virginia. During the Revolutionary War, the capital moved to Richmond, taking with it much of Williamsburg's grandeur. John D. Rockefeller, Jr., began pouring funds into the distressed city in 1926, restoring part of the town as a colonial village. His foundation still runs the restored section, a five-by-seven-block town-within-a-town called Colonial Williamsburg, where fife-and-drum corps parade and cobblers, bookbinders, blacksmiths, and clockmakers go about their tasks using 200-year-old methods.

Street-side Punch and Judy shows, evenings of 18th-century theater, and militia reviews are just part of everyday business in Williamsburg. Though the fascinating and beautiful ex-capital claims to be a faithfully restored version of its 18th-century self, don't look for dirt roads, open sewers, or African slaves. Williamsburg also prides itself on William and Mary, the second-oldest college in the United States.

PRACTICAL INFORMATION

Emergency: 911.

Visitor Information: Tourist Visitors Center, Rte. 132-132y (800-447-8679), 1 mi. northeast of the train station. Tickets and transportation to Colonial Williamsburg. Maps and guides to the historic district, including a guide for the disabled, available upstairs. Information on prices and discounts on Virginia sights, available downstairs. Open daily 8am-8pm.

Amtrak: 229-8750 or 800-872-7245, in the Transportation Center, at the end of N. Boundary St. To: New York ($79, 7 hr.); Washington, D.C. ($28, 3½ hr.); Baltimore ($33, 5 hr.); Richmond ($9, 1½ hr.); and Virginia Beach ($13, 2 hr.). Open Mon.-Tues. and Fri. 7am-9pm, Wed.-Thurs. and Sat. 7am-2:30pm, Sun. 1:30-9pm.

Greyhound: 229-1460, also in the Transportation Center. Ticket office open Mon.-Fri. 8am-6pm, Sat.-Sun. 8am-4pm. To: Richmond ($9.50, 1 hr.); Norfolk ($19.50, 2 hr.); Washington, D.C. ($19.50, 4 hr.).

Public Transport: James City County Transit (JCCT), 220-1621. Service along Rte. 60, from Merchants Sq. in the Historic District west to Williamsburg Pottery or east past Busch Gardens. No service to Yorktown or Jamestown. Operates Mon.-Sat. 6:15am-6:20pm. $1 plus 25¢ per zone-change; exact change required.

Bike Rentals: Bikes Unlimited, 759 Scotland St. (229-4620), rents for $10 per day, with $5 deposit. Open Mon.-Fri. 9am-7pm, Sat. 9am-5pm, Sun. noon-4pm.

Post Office, 425 N. Boundary St. (229-4668). Open Mon.-Fri. 9am-5pm, Sat. 10am-noon. **ZIP Code:** 23185.

Area Code: 804.

Williamsburg lies some 50 mi. southeast of Richmond between Jamestown (10 mi. away) and Yorktown (14 mi. away). The Colonial Parkway, which connects Williamsburg, Jamestown, and Yorktown, has no commercial buildings along its route, helping to preserve an unspoiled atmosphere. Travelers should visit in late fall or early spring to avoid the crowds, high temperature, and humidity of summer. Also, if you want to go to Colonial Williamsburg, don't follow the signs (they lead to the Visitors Center); instead take the Lafayette St. exit off Colonial Pkwy. You'll be surprised at how easy it is to park.

ACCOMMODATIONS AND CAMPING

The few bargains in the Williamsburg area lie along Rte. 60 west or Rte. 31 south toward Jamestown. From Memorial Day to Labor Day, rooms are scarce and prices higher, so try to call at least two weeks in advance. Centrally located, family-run guest houses are clean, comfortable, cheap, and friendly alternatives to hotels. For a complete listing of accommodations, pick up a free copy of the *Visitors Guide to Virginia's Historic Triangle* at the convention bureau.

The closest hostel, **Sangraal-by-the-Sea Youth Hostel (HI/AYH),** Rte. 626 (776-6500), near Urbanna, is 30 mi. away. It does provide rides to bus or train stations during business hours, but don't expect a daily ride to Williamsburg. (Singles $10, non-members more. Call ahead.) Closer to Williamsburg, guest houses are your best bet: some don't require reservations, but all expect you to call ahead and most expect customers to avoid rowdiness and behave like house guests.

Only five min. from the historic district, **Lewis Guest House,** 809 Lafayette St. (229-6116), frequently rents the upstairs unit with private entrance, kitchen, and bath ($25 for 1 or 2 people). The friendly proprietor keeps a very short dog. One block away is **Mrs. H.J. Carter,** 903 Lafayette St. (229-1117). Dust bunnies wouldn't dare hide under the beds in these airy singles ($25) and doubles ($28). Be forewarned: Mrs. Carter will not let unmarried men and women sleep in the same bed. **The Elms,** 708 Richmond Rd. (229-1551), offers elegant, colorful, antique-furnished rooms ($20 for 1 or 2 people). Both houses sleep eight. **Holland's Sleepy Lodge,** 211 Harrison Ave. (253-6476), rents one blue room at a time ($25). Hotels close to the historic district, especially chain-owned hotels, do not come cheap.

Several campsites blanket the area. **Anvil Campgrounds,** 5243 Moretown Rd. (526-2300), 3 mi. north of the Colonial Williamsburg Information Center on Rte. 60, boasts a swimming pool, bathhouse, recreational hall, and store. (Sites $14-15, with hookup $21.) **Brass Lantern Campsites,** 1782 Jamestown Rd. (229-4320 or 229-9089), charges $10, with full hookup $14.

FOOD AND NIGHTLIFE

Though Colonial Williamsburg proper contains several authentic-looking "taverns," few are cheap and most require reservations and forbid tank tops. For less pomp and more rustic circumstance, pack a picnic from one of the supermarkets clustered around the **Williamsburg Shopping Center,** at the intersection of Richmond Rd. and Lafayette St., or try the fast-food strip along Rte. 60. The **farmer's market** at Lafayette and North Henry St. sells cheap seafood or vegetables.

Chowning's Tavern, on Duke of Gloucester St. If you really have to eat in the historic district, you can wait in line for stew, sandwiches, or the misleading Welsh rarebit (pronounced "rabbit")—bread in cheese and beer sauce with ham (entrees from $6.25). Join in the gambols after 9pm: costumed waiters serve mixed drinks, sing 18th-century ballads, and teach patrons how to play out-dated dice and card games. Open daily 11:30am-3:30pm and 4pm-1am.

The Old Chickahominy House, 1211 Jamestown Rd. (229-4689), rests over a mile from the historic district. Share the antiques and dried-flowered decor with pewter-haired locals whose ancestors survived "Starvation Winter" in Jamestown. Miss Melinda's "complete luncheon" of Virginia ham served on hot biscuits, fruit salad, a slice of delectable homemade pie, and iced tea or coffee will fill you up for hours ($4.50). Expect a 20-30-min. wait for lunch. Open daily 8:30-10:15am and 11:30am-2:15pm.

Paul's Deli Restaurant and Pizza, 761 Scotland St. (229-8976), a summer hang-out for errant, leftover William & Mary students, sells crisp stromboli for 2 ($5.50-8.75) and filling subs ($3-5). The hot Italian subs are lipsmackers. Open daily 11am-2am.

Greenleafe Cafe (220-3405), next door to Paul's Deli, half-way upscale, serves sandwiches, salads, and the like ($5-10) and sways after 9pm on Tues. (cover $2) to the quiet sounds of live folk music. Locals and students eat at a 20% discount. Open daily 11am-2am.

SIGHTS

Unless you plan to apply to W&M, you've probably come to see the restored gardens and buildings, crafts, tours, and costumed actors in the historic district also known as **Colonial Williamsburg.** The Colonial Williamsburg Foundation (CWF) owns nearly everything in the historic district, from the **Governor's Palace** to the lemonade stands and even most of the houses marked "private home." A Patriot's Pass gains admission for one year to all the town's attractions (except Bassett Hall), including a 1-hr. guided tour ($29, kids 6-12 $17.50), and to nearby Carter's Grove Plantation. A Royal Governor's Pass lasts the length of your visit and covers all the attractions in the town itself, the Governor's Palace, and the **Wallace Decorative Arts Museum** ($26.50, kids 6-12 $15.75); a 1-day Basic Admission Ticket lets you into any of the historic-area exhibits but none of the museums ($24, kids 6-12 $14.25). Buy them at the CWF Visitors Center or from booths in town.

"Doing" the historic district without a ticket definitely saves money; for no charge you can walk the streets, ogle the buildings, march behind the fife-and-drum corps, lock yourself in the stocks, and even use the restrooms. Some old-time shops that actually sell goods—notably **McKenzie Apothecary,** by the Palace Green—are open to the public. Outdoor events, including a mid-day cannon-firing, are listed in the weekly *Visitor's Companion,* given away to ticket-holders—many of whom conveniently leave it where non-ticket-holders can pick it up.

Take one of the guided walking tours trampling Colonial Williamsburg night and day. The fascinating "Other Half" tour relates the experience of Africans and African-Americans (tours March-Sept.; separate ticket ostensibly required). The 2-hr. "Stepping into the Past" tour is designed especially for families (daily; $3).

Those willing to pay shouldn't miss the **Governor's Palace,** on the Palace Green. This mansion housed the appointed governors of the Virginia colony until the last one fled in 1775. Reconstructed Colonial sidearms and ceremonial sabers line the reconstructed walls, and the garden includes a hedge maze. (Open daily 9am-5pm. Separate admission $14.)

Spreading west from the corner of Richmond and Jamestown Rd., the other focal point of Williamsburg, **The College of William & Mary,** is the second-oldest college in the U.S. Chartered in 1693, the college educated Presidents Jefferson, Monroe, and Tyler. The **Sir Christopher Wren Building,** also restored with Rockefeller money, is the oldest classroom building in the country. The Wren building faces the old capitol, 1 mi. away, at the other end of Colonial Williamsburg's main drag, **Duke of Gloucester St.** Nearby, the shops at **Merchant Square** sprawl a hair's breadth from the historic district. Park here and walk straight into the restored town proper.

■ **Near Williamsburg**

Jamestown and Yorktown are both part of the U.S. colonial story. The National Park System provides free, well-administered visitors' guides to the two areas, which sport two attractions each: the feds run Jamestown National Historic Site and Yorktown Colonial Park, while Virginia operates the flashier Yorktown Victory Center and Jamestown Settlement.

Combination tickets to Yorktown Victory Center and to Jamestown Settlement are available at either site ($9, kids under 13 $4.40). Without a car, you won't find a cheap way to get to Jamestown or Yorktown; since the "towns" are tourist sights, guided tours provide the only transportation. With **Williamsburg Limousine** (877-0279), a group of at least four people can see both Jamestown attractions in the morning ($19.50 per person) or both Yorktown sights in the afternoon ($17.50 per person), or take the whole day and see it all ($35). Williamsburg Limousine also offers daily round-trip tours from Colonial Williamsburg to Carter's Grove Plantation ($8), but if you can, bike from South England Street in Colonial Williamsburg along the one-way, 7-mi., wooded **Carter's Grove Country Road.** The unlined **Colonial Parkway** makes a beautiful biking route.

At the **Jamestown National Historic Site** you'll see remains of the first permanent English settlement of 1607 as well as exhibits explaining Colonial life. At the visitors center (229-1733), skip the hokey film and catch a "living history" walking tour on which a guide portraying one of the colonists describes the Jamestown way of life. Call ahead for information since "living history" guides sometimes take the day off. (Open daily 8:30am-dark; off-season 9am-5:30pm. Entrance fee $8 per car, $3 per hiker or bicyclist.) Sniff around also at the nearby **Jamestown Settlement** (229-1607), a museum commemorating the settlement with changing exhibits, a reconstruction of James Fort, a Native American village, and full-scale replicas of the three ships that brought the original settlers to Jamestown in 1607. The 20-min. "dramatic film" lives up to its name and fills tourists in on the settlement's history, including an embarrassed treatment of settler relations with the indigenous Powhatan tribe. (Open daily 9am-5pm. Admission $7.50, kids under 13 $3.75.)

The British defeat at **Yorktown** signaled the end of the Revolutionary War. British General Charles Lord Coronaries and his men seized the town for use as a port in 1781, but were stranded when the French fleet blocked the sea approaches. Colonists and French troops soon surrounded and stormed it, so the British soldiers surrendered. Yorktown's **Colonial Park** (898-3400) vividly recreates this last significant battle of the war with an engaging film, dioramas, and a smart-looking electric map (behind the information center). The park also maintains the remnants of the original trenches built by the British; guided tours of the British defense line are given throughout the day. Take a 7-mi. automobile journey around the battlefield; rent a tape cassette and recorder for $2 at the visitors center to listen to while you drive (visitors center open daily 8:30am-6pm; last tape rented at 5pm). The **Yorktown Victory Center** (887-1776), one block from Rte. 17 on Rte. 238, offers a museum brimming with items from the Revolutionary War, as well as a film and an intriguing "living history" exhibit: in an encampment in front of the center, a troop of soldiers from the Continental Army of 1781 takes a well-deserved break from active combat. Feel free to ask them about tomorrow's march or last week's massacre. (Open daily 9am-5pm. $3.75, kids under 13 $1.75.)

James River Plantations Built near the water to facilitate the planters' commercial and social lives, these country houses buttressed the slave-holding Virginia aristocracy. Tour guides at **Carter's Grove Plantation,** 6 mi. east of Williamsburg on Rte. 60, show off the restored house and fields. The last owners doubled the size of the original 18th-century building while trying to keep its colonial "feel." The complex also includes reconstructed 18th-century slave quarters and, in front of the house, an archaeological dig. The brand-new **Winthrop Rockefeller Archaeological Museum,** built unobtrusively into a hillside, provides a fascinating case-study look at archaeology. (Plantation open daily 9am-5pm; Nov.-Dec. 9am-4pm. Museum and slave quarters open daily 9am-5pm. Country Road open daily 8:30am-4pm; Nov.-Dec. 8:30am-3pm. Admission $12, kids 6-12 $7, free with CWF Patriot's Pass.) **Berkeley Plantation** (829-6018), halfway between Richmond and Williamsburg on Rte. 5, saw the birth of President William Henry Harrison. Union Soldiers camped on the grounds here in 1862; one of them wrote the famous bugle tune *Taps*. Pause at the terraced box-wood gardens, which stretch from the original 1726 brick building to the river. (House open daily 9am-5pm; grounds open daily 8am-5pm. House and grounds $8, seniors $7.20, kids 6-16 $5. Grounds $4, seniors $3.60, kids 6-16 $2.)

West Virginia

History and geography have conspired to keep West Virginia among the poorest and most isolated states in the Union. The Appalachians are at their hightest and most rugged here; a fact which physically walls off the state. Historically, West Virginia mining was synonymous with the worst excesses of industrial capitalism, and the American labor movement underwent its most violent birth pangs here.

West Virginia formed from the Virginian counties that remained loyal to the Union (whether by choice or by presence of federal troops) during the Civil War. Plundered by Northern industrialists during the postwar era of "free market" capitalism, West Virginia has remained one of America's poorest and most isolated states, largely due to corrupt political machines controlled by unscrupulous profiteers. With the decline of heavy industry in the last 30 years, however, West Virginia has started cashing in on another resource—abundant natural beauty. Thanks to great skiing, hiking, fishing, and the best white-water rafting in the Eastern U.S., tourism has become one of the main sources of employment and revenue. West Virginians remain noticeably attached to traditional ways and despite the tourist onslaught, continue their long-standing penchant for hospitality and optimism.

PRACTICAL INFORMATION

Capital: Charleston.
Visitor Information: Travel Development Division, 1900 Washington St., State Capitol Complex, Bldg. 6, #B654, Charleston 25305 (348-2286 or 800-225-5982). **Division of Parks and Recreation,** 1900 Washington St., State Capitol Complex, Bldg. 6, #451, Charleston 25305. **U.S. Forest Service Supervisor's Office,** 200 Sycamore St., Elkins 26241 (636-1800).
Time Zone: Eastern. **Postal Abbreviation:** WV
Sales Tax: 6%.

■■■ HARPER'S FERRY NATIONAL HISTORICAL PARK

Strangely enough, the very thing that helped sink Harper's Ferry as a town—the October, 1859, raid on the U.S. armory by radical abolitionist John Brown and his 21-man "army of liberation"—has caused its rebirth as an historic attraction. Before the raid, Harper's Ferry thrived as a military and industrial town because of its prime location at the confluence of the Shenandoah and Potomac rivers. John Brown descended on the town to gather arms for a slave insurrection; federal troops under Col. Robert E. Lee foiled his plans and shot most of the raiders, including Brown's three sons. Brown himself was tried and hanged (for treason against Virginia) two months later. The insurrection (eulogized by Ralph Waldo Emerson) helped to spark the Civil War. The war, in turn, destroyed the town; retreating troops burned the armory down, and Harper's Ferry endured two years of siege before a series of floods finally did it in. The spectacular view from Harper's Ferry's many lookouts may be worth more than all the history exhibits combined.

Practical Information Make your first stop at the **visitors center** (535-6298), just inside the park entrance off Rte. 340, and get maps and info about the park. The center also shows a movie about John Brown. The visitors center also provides free 30- to 90-min. **tours** guided by park rangers (in summer daily 10am-3pm) and occasional summer evening programs. If you drive, park near the visitors center; you'll get ticketed any closer to town. A shuttle bus between the parking lot and Shenandoah St. in town runs every 15 min. (Park and visitors center open daily 8:30am-6pm; Sept.-May 8:30am-5pm. $5 per car, $3 per hiker or bicyclist; good for 7 consecutive days.) **Amtrak** (800-872-7245) goes to Harper's Ferry from D.C. once a day (call for reservations; $14). The closest **Greyhound** stations are ½-hr. drives away in Winchester, VA, and Frederick, MD. **Harper's Ferry's ZIP code** is 25425; the **area code** is 304. **Knoxville, MD's ZIP code** is 21758.

Accommodations and Food Hikers can try the **Harper's Ferry Hostel (HI/AYH),** 19123 Sandy Hook Rd. (301-834-7652), at Keep Tryst Rd. in Knoxville, MD, 2 mi. from Harper's Ferry, WV. This renovated auction house high above the Potomac, has 36 beds in 2 dormitory rooms. (Lockout 9am-5pm. Check-in 5-9pm. Limited parking. Oct. 16-Dec. members and ATC hikers $8; non-members $12, Feb.-April 14 $9. Linens provided. Camping $4 per member or ATC hiker, $7 per non-member. 3-night max. stay. 50% reservation deposit required.)

Camp along the C&O Canal, where sites are 5 mi. apart, or in one of the five Maryland state-park campgrounds lying within 30 mi. of Harper's Ferry. **Greenbrier State Park** (301-791-4767), a few mi. north of Boonsboro on Rte. 66 between exits 35 and 42 on I-70, has sites for $12 (open April-Nov.), but the commercial **Camp Resort,** Rte. 3, Box 1300 (535-6895), adjacent to the entrance to Harper's Ferry National Historical Park, is much closer (sites $18 for 2 people, with water and electricity $21; $4 per additional person, under 17 $2; registration fee $3 per person).

On High St. off Shenadoah St., you'll find a slew of antique stores, souvenir shops, cafes, and ice cream parlors, most serving standard fare. You'd do best to avoid them unless you're really hungry; then try the **Garden of Food** (535-2202), on High St., which serves salads and sandwiches ($4-7) indoors and outside on the patio (open Mon.-Fri. 11am-6pm, Sat.-Sun. 11am-7pm). The **Back Street Cafe** (725-8019) on Potomac St. has burgers and hot dogs for under $2.25 (open daily 10am-5pm).

Sights and Activities Recalling the days when the town flourished with a population of 3200 (today only 360), **Harper's Ferry National Historical Park** has restored many of the town's buildings to their original, 1850s style, including a renovated blacksmith's shop, ready-made clothing store, and general store. Wince as the blacksmith hammers at real iron fired in a furnace; the stores contain replicas of 19th-century goods. Guides in period costume discuss the effects of the Industrial Revolution. The Backstreet Cafe (see above) also doubles as an offbeat guide service; "Ghost Tours" of the town are offered weekend nights (tours May-Nov. 8 Fri.-Sun. 8pm; reservations recommended in Oct; $2).

The stairs on High St. lead uphill to the footpath to **Jefferson Rock,** where you look out on three states (Virginia, Maryland, and West Virginia) and two rivers (Shenandoah and Potomac) far below. Thomas Jefferson declared the experience "worth a voyage across the Atlantic." The old, abandoned campus of **Storer University,** one of America's first black colleges, moulders on Filmore St.

Those who prefer nature to history have several options, including hiking and boating. The **Maryland Heights Trail,** part of the Appalachian Trail, offers some of the best views in the Blue Ridge Mountains and winds past cliffs worthy of experienced rock climbers; climbers must register at the visitors center. The **Appalachian**

MONONGAHELA NATIONAL FOREST

Trail Conference Headquarters (535-6331), at Washington and Jackson St., offers members good deals on hiking books, as well as trail information and a maildrop for hikers. (Open Mon.-Fri. 9am-5pm, Sat.-Sun. 9am-4pm; Nov.-April Mon.-Fri. 9am-5pm. Membership $25, seniors and students $18. Write to P.O. Box 807 or call.) The less adventurous can walk along the **Chesapeake & Ohio Canal Towpath**.

Water fanatics should contact **River & Trail Outfitters,** 604 Valley Rd. at Rte. 340, (695-5177), at the blinking light, which rents canoes, inner tubes, and rafts, and organizes guided trips (canoes $40 per day person, raft trips $42 per person, tubing $22.50 per day). In winter it also runs cross-country skiing weekends ($199) and day trips ($60). Call ahead for reservations. A few 3-speed bikes are for rent near the Back Street Cafe ($3 per hr., $15 per day).

Near Harper's Ferry A few mi. north of Harper's Ferry is **Antietam National Battlefield,** where the bloodiest one-day battle of the Civil War was fought after skirmishing at Harper's Ferry. On September 17, 1862, 12,410 Union and 10,700 Confederate soldiers lost their lives as Confederate Gen. Robert E. Lee tried and failed to overcome the army of Union General George B. McClellan. The nominal Union victory provided President Abraham Lincoln with the opportunity to issue the Emancipation Proclamation, freeing all slaves in those states still in rebellion against the United States on January 1, 1863. The **visitors center** has a museum of artifacts used in the battle, free maps for self-guided tours of the battlefield, tapes for rent ($4) with a detailed account of the battle, and an introductory film on the battle (film 9am-5pm on the hr.; center open daily 8:30am-6pm; battlefield fee $1). To get to Antietam from Harper's Ferry, take Rte. 340 N. to Rte. 67 heading toward Boonsboro. Stay on Rte. 67 N. until you reach Rte. 65; follow 65 to Antietam.

■■■ MONONGAHELA NATIONAL FOREST

Mammoth **Monongahela National Forest,** popular with canoers and spelunkers, enshrouds deer, bear, wild turkeys, and magnificent limestone caverns. But camping is the main attraction here, with 600 mi. of prize hiking trails and over 500 campsites to lure the adventurer. The park is divided into six districts, each with its own campground and recreation area. A complete list of sites and fees can be obtained by contacting the park **Supervisor's Office,** Monongahela National Forest, 200 Sycamore St., Elkins, WV 26241-3962 (636-1800; open Mon.-Fri. 8am-4:45pm). Base prices for established campsites are $10 or less, but the bold can sleep in the backcountry for free. Sites with electricity or group facilities will cost $5-10 extra. Much of West Virginia's most scenic country is encompassed here, relatively unspoiled by noisy crowds. The forest's **Lake Sherwood Area** (536-3660), 25 mi. north of I-64 on Rte. 92, in the south of the Forest, offers fishing, hunting, swimming, hiking, and boating, as well as campgrounds, mostly undisturbed by roving Merry Men. The campsites fill only on major holidays. (2-week max. stay. Sites $8) **Cranberry Mountain** (846-2695), in the Gauley district approx. 6 mi. west of U.S. 219 on Rte. 39/55, has campgrounds (sites $5) and hiking trails through cranberry bogs.

THE GREAT LAKES

When the glaciers retreated from the northern border of the United States, they left behind a fertile, flat bed, filled with small pockets of water. The region is now covered with the five Great Lakes and thousands upon thousands of shallow pools. Northernmost Lake Superior, the largest freshwater lake in the world, has the least populated and most scenic coasts, and dances with one of the only significant wolf populations left in the contiguous United States. Lake Michigan, bordering on four states, is a sports-lover's paradise, offering deep-water fishing, swimming, sailing, and sugar-fine sand dunes. Lake Erie, connecting the east to the midwest, has suffered the most from industrial pollution, but thanks to vigilant citizens and strict regulations, the shallowest Great Lake is gradually reclaiming its former beauty. Lake Huron and Ontario provide splashing around and great fishing for both Americans and Canadians. The deep forests of the Great Lakes region were home to some of the earliest Native Americans, who blessed the fertile soil with its natural abundance. Since then much of the land has been taken, cultivated, and the once pristine splendor bears the scars of industrial boom and rust. In the 19th and early 20th centuries, millions of immigrants came here to search their fortune in the land of the region by farming the rich soil, mining the lodes of iron and copper, and logging the dense forests. Soon, natural resources were exhausted, and the economies of the region had to either change or collapse. Most areas weathered the shift by transporting and manufacturing rather than supplying raw materials. However, in the wake of modernization and adaptation, cities like Cleveland and Detroit were left behind, forced to retool their economic base and recapture a spirit of growth.

Today, the Great Lakes region has the strongest draw for the hostel-and-campground crowd, with its multitudinous water and wilderness opportunities in places where the talons of "progress" never reached. But the sophisticated urban traveler should not despair—Minneapolis/St. Paul has all the artsy panache of any coastal metropolis (minus the accompanying angst), and Chicago remains the focal point for Midwestern activity, with world-class music, architecture, and cuisine.

 Illinois

Once rolling prairies, Illinois has since been plowed and mined—it is now the largest producer of both soybeans and coal, giving the 21st state a diverse flavor. Bounded by water on three sides and an important railroad connection, if something is moving through the country chances are it goes through Illinois. And with 11½ million people, Illinois is as important for politics as for provisions. Most of the state is farmland; only Iowa produces more corn. The southern tip, known as Little Egypt for its resemblance to the fertile Nile Valley, is especially rich with cottonfields and a southern lifestyle. Lastly, Illinois contrasts the cornfields with the fast-moving, tough-minded Chicago, which pulses as the third-largest city in the U.S.

PRACTICAL INFORMATION

Capital: Springfield.
Office of Tourism, 620 E. Adams St., Springfield 62701 (217-782-7500).
Time Zone: Central (1 hr. behind Eastern). **Postal Abbreviation:** IL
Sales Tax: 6.25%.

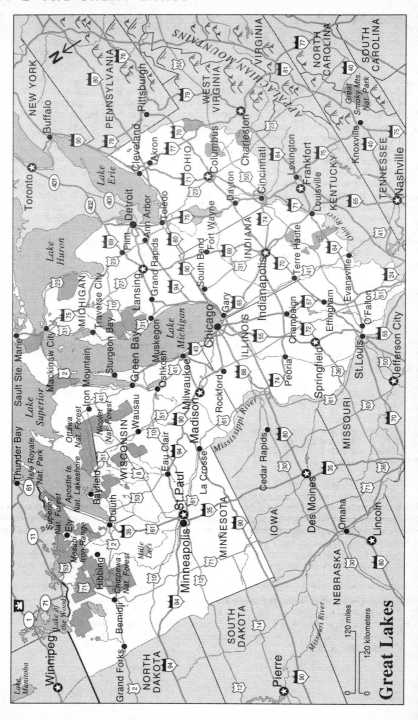

Great Lakes

■■■ CHICAGO

The Windy City is aptly named; its moniker is due not only to the sharp gusts that roll off Lake Michigan, but to the multitudes who have blown through the third largest city in the U.S. Since its founding in 1833, Chicago has been an urban center in a rural setting. With the advent of the railroad, Chicago became a transportation hub, moving large quantities of natural resources faster than anyone else. Chicago traders developed a system of commodity pricing, and industrialists developed assembly-line slaughterhouses, making meat a not-so-rare commodity. Chicago packers then developed refrigerated rail cars, which allowed meat to be moved during the summer. Unfortunately, de-industrialization has struck hard. The stockyards and freight depots which made the Armours and Pullmans rich have been closed for decades.

In a place where every building is a contrasting architectural statement, so too are the people and things the city has produced: Al Capone, Jesse Jackson, Jane Addams, Cracker Jack, deep dish pizza, Ebony magazine, and Playboy. Since minorities have now become the majority in Chicago, it has taken a tough breed of politician to find cohesion here. Chicago pulses as the financial center of the Midwest, captain of commodities and futures trading, and its cultural variety includes a score of major museums, and impressive collection of public sculpture, one of the world's finest symphony orchestras, excellent (and radical) small theaters, and the University of Chicago, which has employed more Nobel laureates than any other university in the world. Chicago was also the city where skyscrapers started. Modern highrise architecture owes its heritage to Louis Sullivan and Mies van der Rohe, and increases the value of Chicago as a tourist sight.

PRACTICAL INFORMATION

Emergency: 911.

Visitor Information: Chicago Visitor Information Center, 163 E. Pearson (280-5740 or 800-487-2446), in the Water Tower Pumping Station. Open daily 9:30am-5pm. Or at the **Chicago Cultural Center,** Randolph St. at Michigan Ave. Pick up a copy of the *Chicago Visitors Guide.* Open Mon.-Sat. 9am-5pm, Sun. 11am-5pm. Write or call the **Chicago Office of Tourism,** 806 N. Michigan Ave., Chicago, 60611 (280-5740).

Traveler's and Immigrant's Aid: Travelers should use the O'Hare Airport (686-7562; open Mon.-Fri. 8am-4:30pm) and Greyhound (435-4537, open Mon.-Fri. 8:30am-5pm) locations, which provide over 20 different programs.

Consulates: Australia, 321 N. Clark St. (645-9444); **Canada,** 180 N. Stetson Ave. (616-1860); **Ireland,** 400 N. Michigan Ave. (337-1868); **U.K.,** 33 N. Dearborn St. (346-1810). Hours vary, so call individual consulate to check.

Airport: O'Hare International Airport, (686-2200) off I-90. Inventor of the layover, holding pattern and headache. Depending on traffic, a trip between downtown and O'Hare can take up to 2 hrs. The **Rapid Train** runs between the Airport El station and downtown ($1.50). The ride takes 40 min.-1 hr. **Continental Air Transport** (454-7800) connects the airport to selected downtown and suburban locations including the Marriot Hotel at Michigan and Rush. Runs every 5-10 min. 6am-11:30pm from downstairs baggage terminals 1-3. Fare $14, 60-90 min. **Midway Airport** (767-0500), on the western edge of the South Side, often offers less expensive flights. To get downtown, take CTA bus #54B to Archer, then ride bus #62 to State St. For an extra 25¢, the 99M express runs from Midway downtown 6-8:15am and from downtown to Midway during the afternoon rush hour 3:55-6pm. Continental Air Transport costs $10.50 and runs every 15min, 7am-10pm. Airport baggage lockers $1 per day.

Amtrak: Union Station (558-1075 or 800-872-7245), Canal and Adams St. across the river, west of the Loop. Take the El to State and Adams, then walk west on Adams 7 blocks. Amtrak's main hub may look familiar; it was the backdrop for the final baby-buggy scene of *The Untouchables.* Destinations include: St. Louis ($39), Detroit ($29), and Milwaukee ($16). Station open 6am-11pm; tickets sold daily 6:15am-10pm. Baggage lockers $1 per day.

CHICAGO

Greyhound: 630 W. Harrison St. (781-2900), at Jefferson and Desplaines. Take the El to Linton. The hub of the central U.S. Also serves as home base for several smaller companies covering the Midwest. To: Milwaukee ($11), Detroit ($25), and St. Louis ($35). Station open 24 hrs., ticket office open 5am-2am.

Taxi: Yellow Cab, 829-4222; **Flash Cab,** 561-1444; **American United Cab,** 248-7600. Taxis average fare $1.20 for flag drop plus $1.20 per mile.

Car Rental: Dollar Rent-a-Car (800-800-4000), at O'Hare and Midway; P.O. Box 66181, Chicago, IL 60666. $39 per day, $144 per week; age 21-25, $5 surcharge per day. Must be 21 with major credit card. **Thrifty Car Rental** (800-367-2277), from O'Hare and Midway. Rates vary, $31 per day, $189 per week with unlimited mileage in state and bordering states. Must be 21 with major credit card.

Auto Transport Company: National U-Drive, 3626 Calumet Ave., Hammond, IN (219-852-0134). 20 min from the Loop. Call for rates.

Help Lines: Rape Crisis Line, 708-872-7799. 24 hrs. **Gay and Lesbian Hotline,** 871-2273. 24 hrs. **Police,** 744-4000 (non-emergency).

Medical Emergency: Cook County Hospital, 1835 W. Harrison (633-6000). Take the Congress A train to the Medical Center Stop.

Medical Walk-in Clinic: MedFirst, 3245 N. Halsted Ave. (528-5005). Non-emergency medical care. Open Mon.-Fri. 8am-8pm, Sat. 9am-3pm.

Post Office: 433 W. Van Buren St. (765-3210), 2 blocks from Union Station. Open Mon.-Fri. 7am-5:30pm, Sat. 8am-5:30pm, 24-hr. self-service available. **ZIP code:** 60607.

Area Code: 312 for numbers in Chicago, 708 for numbers outside Chicago's municipal boundaries. All numbers listed here without area code are for 312 area.

ORIENTATION

Chicago runs north-south along 29 mi. of southwest Lake Michigan lakefront. The city and its suburbs encompass the entire northeastern corner of Illinois. As a focal point of the Midwest, Chicago serves as a connection of the coasts; most cross-country road, rail, and airplane trips in the northern U.S. will pass through the city.

Chicago is a machine that accepts immigrants and produces Americans. Arriving with little or nothing but a foreign tongue, boatloads of newcomers have found jobs, apartments, and a new start here. To ease the transition, many remain in ethnic communities which sustain Old-World traditions in churches, social clubs, and local bars. The Chicago immigrant paradigm is a familiar one. Once established, immigrant children move to the suburbs to become middle class, and the neighborhood evaporates. Later, *their* children move back to the city as young professionals, gentrifying worn-out districts and rejoining the churn and bustle of this living city. This cycle continues today, and Chicago's neighborhoods are always in a state of flux. An area that illustrates the first step in this sequence is **Uptown,** whose new name is **New Chinatown;** it centers at Broadway and Argyle and is the center of the Southeast Asian influx into the city. It also has a strong Indian and Arab presence. The areas that were once **Greektown** (Halsted St. at Madison) and **Little Italy** (Taylor St. between Morgan and Racine) have reached middle-age; their residents have begun the exodus to the suburbs. Though it still exists, Greektown is fading; Little Italy is no more. In all, Chicago neighborhoods are neither discrete nor fixed; the city is constantly evolving.

The Chicago River on the north and west, Lake Michigan on the east, and the elevated train enclose the **Loop,** the downtown area and business hub which contains many of America's architectural treasures. Just south of the Loop and southwest of the natural history museum lies **Pilsen,** a center of Chicago's Latino community, and unfortunately *not* a safe place to venture at night. North of the Loop across the river are **Near North,** an area with more office buildings, and the glitzy shopping district known as the **Magnificent Mile:** Michigan Ave. between Grand Ave. and Division St. The north side of Chicago—a broad term subsuming all the territory north of the river—is generally safe during the day, with active commercial streets bounding residential areas. There are over a dozen neighborhoods with fairly ambiguous boundaries; the *Rand McNally Chicago Visitor's Guide and Map* labels them all. The

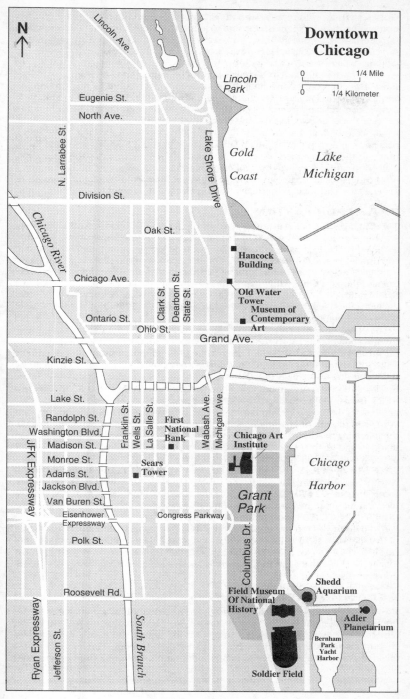

N

Downtown Chicago

0   1/4 Mile
0   1/4 Kilometer

Lincoln Ave.

Lincoln Park

Eugenie St.

North Ave.

N. Larrabee St.

Gold Coast

Lake Michigan

Chicago River

Division St.

Oak St.

Clark St.

Dearborn St.

State St.

Hancock Building

Chicago Ave.

Old Water Tower

Museum of Contemporary Art

Ontario St.

Ohio St.

Grand Ave.

Kinzie St.

Lake St.

Randolph St.

Washington Blvd.

Franklin St.

Wells St.

La Salle St.

First National Bank

Wabash Ave.

Michigan Ave.

JFK Expressway

Madison St.

Monroe St.

Sears Tower

Adams St.

Jackson Blvd.

Van Buren St.

Eisenhower Expressway

Congress Parkway

Chicago Art Institute

Chicago Harbor

Grant Park

Polk St.

Columbus Dr.

Roosevelt Rd.

Ryan Expressway

Jefferson St.

South Branch

Shedd Aquarium

Field Museum Of National History

Adler Planetarium

Bernham Park Yacht Harbor

Soldier Field

CHICAGO

Gold Coast, an elite residential area, glitters on North Lake Shore Drive. Further north along the lake sprawls **Lincoln Park,** a 19th-century English-style park which includes a zoo, a conservatory and beaches. South of the Loop, **Chinatown** preserves a sliver of China on Cermak Rd. at Wentworth; there are oodles of noodle restaurants, bakeries, and touristy shops. As it can be dangerous at night, it is wisest to go there for lunch. The city's sizable Polish community has an enclave near **Oak Park.** The city's most concentrated gay population, compared by many to equivalent areas in San Francisco, is in **Lakeview.** It's a fun area for anyone to visit, with many cheap restaurants and lots of vintage shops selling clothes, eclectic bunches of home furnishings, gewgaws, and decorative items. The streets surrounding Wrigley Field at Clark and Addison are known as **Wrigleyville,** a fun area full of sports bars and ethnic restaurants. Much farther south, at about 57th St., lies **Hyde Park,** home of the University of Chicago. Although Hyde Park is reasonably safe, especially during the day, avoid neighboring **Near South Side,** one of the country's most dangerous urban ghettos. Parts of the **West Side** are also extremely unsafe. In general, don't go south of Cermak or east of Halsted St. at night.

TRANSPORTATION

The **Chicago Transit Authority,** part of the **Regional Transit Authority** (836-7000 in the city, 800-972-7000 in the suburbs), runs rapid transit trains, subways, and buses. The El runs 24 hrs., but late-night service is infrequent and unsafe in some areas, especially the South Side. Some buses do not run all night. Call CTA for schedules. Maps are available at many stations, the Water Tower Information Center, and the RTA Office. It is worthwhile to get one of these maps and to spend a few minutes deciphering the system of bus routes and trains. Directions in *Let's Go* are generally given from the downtown area, but obviously there are usually several ways of getting to your destination.

The **elevated rapid transit train** system, called the **El,** bounds the major downtown section of the city, the **Loop.** Downtown some of the routes are underground, but are still referred to as the El. Trains marked "A," "B" or "all stops" may run on the same route, stopping only at stations designated as such. Also, different routes may run along the same tracks in some places. Because of Chicago's grid layout, many bus lines run for several miles along one straight road. Train fare is $1.50. Bus fare $1.25, from 6-10am and 3-7pm, $1.50; 10 tokens good for one train or bus ride each any time of day cost $2.50. Remember to get a transfer (30¢) from the driver when you board the bus or enter the El stop, which will get you up to two more rides in the following two hours. A $20.50 weekly pass (Sun.-Sat.) is available in many supermarkets and at the "Checks Cashed" storefronts with the yellow signs. A $78 monthly pass is available in many supermarkets.

METRA operates a vast commuter rail network with 11 rail lines and four downtown stations snaking far out to the suburbs to the north, west, and south. (For route info call 322-6700 Mon.-Fri. 8:30am-5pm or 800-972-7000 other times.) Schedules and maps are free at their office at 547 W. Jackson. Fare is based on distance ($1.75-5). **PACE** (708-364-7223) is the suburban bus system.

Avoid **driving** in the city as much as possible. Daytrippers can leave the car in one of the suburban subway lots for 24 hrs. ($1). There are a half-dozen such park-and-ride lots; call CTA (see above) for info. Parking downtown costs $6 per day for most lots; most residential areas in the north side have street parking for residents only (look for signs).

ACCOMMODATIONS

If you're in the mood for a "nap," Chicago has its share of hotels that charge by the hour. For a full night's sleep at a decent price, stop at one of the hostels, which are farther from downtown but social and worth the trek. If you have a car, there's a strip of moderately priced motels around 5600 N. Lincoln. The national motel chains have locations off the interstates, about an hour's drive from downtown;

they're inconvenient and expensive ($35 and up), but a reliable option for late night arrivals. **Chicago Bed and Breakfast,** P.O. Box 14088, Chicago 60614 (951-0085), is a referral service with over 150 rooms of varying prices throughout the city and outlying areas. None have parking, but the majority are near public transit; street parking is occasionally available. (Singles $55-75, doubles $65-85.)

Arlington House (AAIH), 616 Arlington Pl. (929-5380). Take the El to Fullerton, walk 2 blocks east to Orchard, turn left on Arlington Place; it's on the right. Parking is a hassle. Crowded rooms, most of them in a basement; shares a building with a senior citizens home. Laundry room, kitchenette. No curfew. In a wealthy residential yuppie neighborhood. Dorm-style rooms with 4, 6, or 10 beds each, $13, nonmembers $16. Singles $30. Doubles $34. Linens $2. Open 24 hrs.

Chicago International Hostel, 6318 N. Winthrop (262-1011). Take Howard St. northbound train to Loyola Station. Walk south 2 blocks on Sheridan Rd., then east 1 block on Sheridan Rd. (the road zigs) to Winthrop, then ½ block south. Clean rooms that are well worth the 30-min. ride from the Loop by train, 20 min. by #147 express bus. Free parking in the rear. 2-8 beds per room. Good place to meet traveling students. Kitchen, laundry room. Bike rentals ($8 per day). Check-in 7-10am, 4pm-midnight. Curfew winter weekdays midnight, winter weekends and summer, 2am. Reservations recommended.

International House (HI/AYH), 1414 E. 59th St. (753-2270), Hyde Park, off Lake Shore Dr. Take the Illinois Central Railroad to 59th St. and walk ½ block west. Part of the University of Chicago. Isolated from the rest of the city, the neighborhood can be dangerous at night. 200 comfortable dorm-style rooms; good price if you *need* privacy. Shared bath, linens provided, cheap cafeteria with nice outdoor cafe area. $15, nonmembers $29. Open mid-June-Aug., rooms occasionally available during school year. 1 week advance reservations necessary.

Hotel Wacker, 111 W. Huron (787-1386), Near North Side. Convenient to downtown, no parking. No reservations; often fills on summer weekends. Fill in your own joke here, you lecherous swine, you. Clean, good sized rooms. 24-hr. check-in. Singles $35. Doubles $40. Weekly: $80-85. Key and linen deposit $5.

Hotel Cass, 640 N. Wabash (787-4030), just north of the Loop. Take subway to Grand St. Convenient location, clean functional rooms. No parking. Singles $35, doubles $45, $5 extra with TV. A/C $5. Key deposit $5. International student ID card, $5 off. Reservations recommended.

Hotel Tokyo, 19 E. Ohio (787-4900), downtown, north of the Loop. Partly residential. There is a 24-hr. elevator operator who overlooks clean, conveniently located rooms, all with private bath. No parking, but decently priced lots nearby ($8). Single or double (one bed) $25, key deposit $2.

Leaning Tower YMCA, 6300 W. Touhy, Niles, 60714 (708-647-8222). From Jefferson Park El stop, take bus #85A; 1 hr. from the Loop. Look for an extraordinary ½-scale replica of the Leaning Tower of Pisa (it's a water tower, not the residence hall itself). Private baths, use of YMCA facilities, including swimming pool, gym, and other recreational facilities. Coed. Must be over 21. It's worth the commute if you want *more* than just a place to stay. Free parking. Singles $30, doubles $32. Key deposit $5. Off-season $4-5 less. Call ahead for summer reservations.

Acres Motel, 5600 N. Lincoln Ave. at Bryn Mawr Ave. (561-7777). Take the #11 bus from State St., about 50 min. from the Loop. Free parking. Classic and clean motel rooms. Private bath, 24-hr. check-in. Single or double $40, each extra person $5, key deposit $2. Made for a guest with a car, motel is near restaurants, supermarkets; there are about a dozen more motels with similar price and quality within ½ mi. in either direction on Lincoln Ave.

FOOD

Cooks of every nation stir the melting pot of Chicago. With new restaurants opening and closing almost daily, the city often seems ready to bubble over in this abundance and variety of victuals. Investigate this phenomenon on the blocks just south of Wrigley Field, especially on N. Clark St., where you can find chow that spans the globe from Ethiopia to Mexico to Mongolia. Those who are dexterous with chop-

CHICAGO

sticks should visit Chinatown at the Cermak El stop or, more conveniently, New Chinatown at Argyle and Sheridan at the Argyle El stop. Most of the original Greeks have left Greektown, on Halsted St. at Monroe, but their restaurants linger. Tourist brochures still call Taylor St. "Little Italy," but most of the Italian-Americans have said *ciao,* and their restaurants, except for three or four fairly expensive joints, have split as well. It's also worth noting that good, cheap Thai restaurants are opening up all over the city. Chicago is famous for its deep dish pan pizza, with thick crust slathered in melted cheese, whole fresh tomatoes, and a combination of any number of toppings. *Chicago* magazine includes an extensive restaurant guide which is cross-indexed by price, cuisine, and quality. All of the restaurants listed here can be reached in less than 30 min. by public transit from the Loop.

Pizza

Pizzeria Uno, 29 E. Ohio (321-1000), and **Due,** 619 N. Wabash (943-2400). As the hordes of tourists waiting for a table remind us, Uno is where it all began. In 1943, owner Ike Sewall introduced Chicago-style deep dish pizza, and though the graffiti-stained walls have been painted over and the restaurant is franchised across the nation, the pizza remains damn good. Due sits right up the street, with a terrace and more room than Uno's, but without the attendant legend. Pizzas $3.75-16. Uno open Mon.-Thurs. 11:30am-1am, Fri.-Sat. 11:30am-2am, Sun. 11:30am-11:30pm; Due open Mon.-Thurs. 11:30am-1:30am, Fri. 11:30am-2:30am, Sat. noon-2:30am, Sun. noon-11:30pm.

Gino's East, 160 E. Superior (943-1124). Wait 30-40 min. while they make your "pizza de résistance." Leave your mark on the graffiti-covered wall. Small pan pizza ($7.25) easily serves 2. Open Mon.-Thurs. 11am-11pm; Fri.-Sat. 11am-midnight, Sun. noon-10pm.

Loop

For a cheaper alternative to most Loop dining, try the surprisingly good fast-food pizza, fish, potato, and burger joints in the basement of the State of Illinois Building at Randolph and Clarke St., where entrees run $2.50-4.

The Berghoff, 17 W. Adams (427-3170). Moderately priced German and American fare. Wash down the corned beef ($3.90) with a home-brewed beer (stein $2.10). Open Mon.-Fri. 11am-9:30pm, Sat. 11am-10pm.

Morry's Old Fashioned Deli, 345 S. Dearborn St. (922-2932). Deli favorites sustain Loop-gawkers and the local lunch crowd. Homemade turkey breast $4.15. Open Mon.-Fri. 7am-8pm, Sat. 8am-5pm.

Near North

Billy Goat's Tavern, 430 N. Michigan (222-1525), underground on lower Michigan Ave. Descend through an apparent subway entrance in front of the Tribune building. The gruff service was the inspiration for *Saturday Night Live*'s legendary "Cheezborger, cheezborger—no Coke, Pepsi" greasy spoon. Cheezborgers $2.30. Butt in anytime Mon.-Fri. 7am-2am, Sat. 10am-2am, Sun. noon-2am.

Foodlife, 835 N. Michigan Ave. (335-3663), in Water Tower Place, mezzanine level. A funky upgraded fast-food court concept. Dine on anything from Asian to pizza to Mother Earth Pasta, and clean up with a recycled napkin. Outrageous strawberry shortcake $3.25. Huge portion entrees $3-6. Open daily 11am-10pm.

The Original A-1, 401 E. Illinois (644-0300), in North Pier. After a hard day on the trail, this Texas-style chuckwagon has good portions, an arcade, and is close to nightlife. Durango burger $5.95. Open Mon.-Thurs. 11:30am-10pm, Fri.-Sat. 11:30am-midnight, Sun. 11:30am-9pm.

Uptown (New Chinatown)

House of Thailand, 5120 N. Broadway (275-2684). El to Forster. Excellent Thai food at reasonable prices. Lunch special $4. Open Sat.-Sun., Tues.-Thurs. 5-10pm.

Mekong, 4953 N. Broadway (271-0206), at Argyle St. Busy, spotless Vietnamese restaurant. All you can eat lunch buffet, weekdays 11am-2:30pm, $4.95. Tasty soups $3.50-4. Open Sun.-Thurs. 10am-10pm, Fri.-Sat. 10am-11pm.

Gin Go Gae, 5433 N. Lincoln Ave. (334-3985). Korean place, popular with locals. *Be bim bob,* steamed rice with marinated beef, spinach, kim-chee, and an egg, $7.25. Lunch specials $5.50. Open Mon.-Tue., Thurs.-Sat. 11am-10:30pm, Sun. 11am-10pm.

Chinatown

Hong Min, 221 W. Cermak (842-5026). El to Cermak. Attention paid to the food, *not* the furnishings—unlike some Chinese restaurants nearby. Dinner entrees $6-12, excellent seafood. Open daily 10am-2am.

Three Happiness, 2130 S. Wentworth Ave. (791-1228). Reliable and predictable, a "far-east experience" (or so they promise). Entrees $4.50-9. Dim sum $1.70 Mon.-Fri. 10am-2pm, Sat.-Sun. 10am-3pm. Open Mon.-Thurs. 10am-midnight, Fri.-Sat. 10am-1am, Sun. 10am-10pm.

Little Italy

Al's Italian Beef, 1079 W. Taylor St. (226-4017), at Aberdeen near Little Italy. Take a number, please. There are no tables or chairs, so you'll have to eat standing at the long counter. Delicious Italian beef sandwich ($3.35); pass the napkins. Open Mon.-Sat. 9am-1am.

Mario's Italian Lemonade, 1074 W. Taylor St., across from Al's. Sensational Italian ices 60¢-$4.50 (tube size), every flavor you can think of in this classic neighborhood stand. Open mid-May-mid-Sept. 10am-midnight.

The Rosebud, 1500 W. Taylor (942-1117). This neighborhood staple serves huge portions of pasta ($9.95) that easily feed 3. Free parking, reservations recommended. Open for lunch Mon.-Fri. 11am-3pm; dinner Mon.-Thurs. 5-10:30pm, Fri.-Sat. 5:30-11:30pm.

Greektown

The Parthenon, 314 S. Halsted St. in Greektown (726-2407). Enjoy anything from gyros ($6) to *saganaki* (cheese flamed in brandy, $3.25). Try the combination dinner to sample *moussaka,* lamb, *pastitsio,* and *dolmades.* Dinners $4.25-13.50. Open daily 11am-1am.

Greek Islands, 200 S. Halsted (782-9855). Walk under the grape leaf awning and enter this native favorite. No reservations, so expect a wait on weekends. *Spanakopita* $5.50. Open Sun.-Thurs. 11am-midnight, Fri.-Sat. 11am-1am.

North Side

Café Phoenicia, 2814 N. Halsted St. (549-7088). El to Diversey, then 2 blocks along Diversey to Halsted. A tribute to the Phoenician alphabet and nautical tableaux spice up the walls of this little Lebanese outfit. Outstanding hummus $3, lamb kabob $8. Open Mon.-Thurs. 5-11pm, Fri.-Sat. 5pm-midnight, Sun. 4-10pm. Reservations required on weekends.

Addis Adeba, 3521 N. Clark, near Wrigley Field (929-9383). Ethiopian cuisine; it's not just food, it's an adventure. No utensils; scoop up dinner with a slap of spongy *injera* bread. Entrees $6-10. Open Mon.-Thurs. 5-10pm, Fri.-Sat. 5-11pm, Sun. 4-10pm.

Cafe Ba-Ba-Reeba! 2024 N. Halsted (935-5000). *Buena comida.* Hearty Spanish cuisine with subtle spices. Entrees $6-10. Outdoor terrace. Open Tues.-Sat. 11:30am-2:30pm, Mon.-Thurs. 5:30-11pm, Fri. 5:30pm-midnight, Sat. 5pm-midnight, Sun. 5:30-10:30pm.

Cafe Equinox, 2300 N. Lincoln (477-5126). House in the oldest ex-drugstore/apothecary in Chicago, this cafe features live jazz and a classical pianist, as well as local artists' work. Chocolate raspberry coffee $1.50. Open Sun.-Thurs. 8am-midnight, Sat. 10am-1am.

Downtown

Wishbone, 1001 W. Washington (850-2663). In this converted tire warehouse to southern cuisine extravaganza, they serve cornbread and banana bread on every table. Homemade pies $6.95. Cafeteria-style lunch Mon.-Fri. 11:30am-2pm and dinner Mon. 5-8pm; sit-down breakfast 7-11am and dinner 5-10:30pm. Sat.-Sun. brunch 8am-2:30pm.

SIGHTS

Chicago is truly massive, and its sights cannot be exhausted in a day, a week, or a lifetime. There is always another hole-in-the-wall restaurant, another architectural motif, another museum exhibit to discover. Chicago is a prime walking city, with lakefront, parks, residential neighborhoods and commercial districts all awaiting exploration. Use the public transportation system liberally, though, or you'll spend all your time walking. Avoid touristy and expensive bus tours which zip you past sights. For the price of one of these tours you can buy a pass and ride the city bus for a week.

Museums

Admission to each of Chicago's major museums is free at least one day a week. The "Big Five" allow exploration of everything from ocean to landscape to the stars; a handful of smaller collections represent diverse ethnic groups and professional interests. For more information, pick up the informative pamphlet *Chicago Museums* at the tourist information office (see Practical Information).

The Art Institute of Chicago, Michigan Ave. at Adams St. in Grant Park (443-3500). The city's premier art museum. Finest collection of French Impressionist paintings west of Paris which even the non-art lover can enjoy. Also works by El Greco, Chagall, Van Gogh, Picasso, and Rembrandt. Call for info on temporary exhibits. Open Mon. and Wed.-Fri. 10:30am-4:30pm, Tues. 10:30am-8pm, Sat. 10am-5pm, Sun. and holidays noon-5pm. Donation of any amount required (you can pay a nickel if you want to). Free Tues.

Museum of Science and Industry, 5700 S. Lake Shore Dr. (684-1414), housed in the only building left from the 1893 World's Columbian Exposition. In Hyde Park; take the Jeffrey Express, Bus #6 to 57th St. Hands-on exhibits ensure a crowd of grabby kids, overgrown and otherwise. Highlights include the Apollo 8 command module, a German submarine, a life-sized replica of a coal mine, and a new exhibit on learning disabilities. Omni-Max Theatre shows "Fires of Kuwait"; call for showtimes and prices. Open Memorial Day-Labor Day daily 9:30am-5:30pm; off-season Mon.-Fri. 9:30am-4pm, Sat.-Sun. 9:30am-5:30pm. $5, seniors $4, ages 5-12 $2. Free Thurs.

The Oriental Institute, 1155 E. 58th St. (702-9521), take Jeffrey Express, Bus #6, to the University of Chicago campus. Houses an extraordinary collection of ancient Near Eastern art and archeological treasures. You can't miss the massive statue of Tutankhamen. Open Tues. and Thurs.-Sat. 10am-4pm, Wed. 10am-8:30pm, Sun. noon-4pm. Free.

Field Museum of Natural History (922-9410), Roosevelt Rd. at Lake Shore Dr., in Grant Park. Take Bus #146 from State St. Geological, anthropological, botanical, and zoological exhibits. Don't miss the Egyptian mummies, the Native American Halls, the Hall of Gems, and the dinosaur display. Open daily 9am-5pm. Admission $4, seniors and students $2.50, families $13. Free Thurs.

The Adler Planetarium, 1300 S. Lake Shore Dr. (322-0300), in Grant Park. Astronomy exhibits, a sophisticated skyshow, and the $4-million Astro-Center. 5 skyshows per day in summer, less frequently in winter. Open daily 9:30am-5pm, Fri. until 9pm. Exhibits free. Skyshow daily at 11am and 1-4pm on the hour. $4, seniors and ages 6-17 $2.

Shedd Aquarium, 1200 S. Lake Shore Dr. in Grant Park (939-2438). The world's largest indoor aquarium with over 6600 species of fresh and saltwater fish in 206 exhibition tanks, including a Caribbean reef. The Oceanarium features small whales, dolphins, seals, and other marine mammals. Check out new exhibits on Asian rainforests and the Pacific Ocean, complete with simulated crashing waves. Parking available. Open March-Oct. daily 9am-6pm; Nov.-Feb. 10am-5pm. Feedings weekdays 11am and 2pm. Combined admission to Oceanarium and Aquarium $8, students and seniors $6; Thurs. admission $4; Thurs. free to Aquarium, but not Oceanarium. Buy weekend tickets in advance through Hot Tix.

Chicago Historical Society, N. Clark St. at North Ave. (642-4600). A research center for scholars with a good museum open to the public. The Society was founded in 1856, just 19 years after the city was incorporated, like a kid who keeps a diary for future biographers. Permanent exhibits on America in the age of Lincoln, plus changing exhibits. Open Mon.-Sat. 9:30am-4:30pm, Sun. noon-5pm. $3, students and seniors $2. Free Mon.

Terra Museum of American Art, 666 N. Michigan Ave. at Eric St. (664-3939). Excellent collection of American art from colonial times to the present, with a focus on 19th-century American Impressionism. Open Tues. noon-8pm, Wed.-Sat. 10am-5pm, Sun. noon-5pm. $3, seniors $2, teachers and students with ID free. Public tours noon and 2pm daily, free.

The Museum of Contemporary Art, 237 E. Ontario (280-5161), within walking distance of the Water Tower. Current exhibit on "Hand Painted Pop" included "Bathroom Sex Murder" by Peter Saul. However, exhibits change often. One gallery devoted to local artists. Open Tues.-Sat. 10am-5pm, Sun. noon-5pm. $4, seniors and students $2. Free Tues.

Museum of Broadcast Communications, at Michigan and Washington, in the Loop (629-6000). Celebrate couch-potato culture with these exhibits on America's favorite pastime: watching the tube. Open Mon.-Sat. 10am-4:30pm, Sun. noon-5pm. Free.

The Loop

When Mrs. O'Leary's cow kicked over a lantern and started the Great Fire of 1871, Chicago's downtown was turned into a pile of ashes. The city rebuilt with a vengeance, turning the functional into the fabulous and creating one of the most concentrated clusters of architectural treasures in the world.

The downtown area, the Loop, is hemmed in by the Chicago River and the lake, so its buildings spread up rather than out. Take a few hours to explore this street museum either by yourself or on a **walking tour** of the Loop by volunteers of the Chicago Architectural Foundation, starting from the foundation's bookstore/gift shop at 224 S. Michigan Ave. (922-3432). Learn to recognize Louis Sullivan's arch, the Chicago window, and Mies van der Rohe's glass and steel, geometrically rigorous boxes, which refashioned the concept of the skyscraper. Two tours are offered: one of early skyscrapers, one of modern. ($9 for one, $15 for both. Call for tour schedules. Weekdays one morning and one afternoon.)

Long ago, the city's traders developed the concept of a graded commodity, so that a real-life bag of wheat, once evaluated, could henceforth be treated as a unit akin to currency. Today, the three exchanges all coexist within a few blocks and are worth a visit. You can watch the frantic trading of Midwestern farm goods at the world's oldest and largest commodity, **Futures Exchange** (open Mon.-Fri. 9am-2pm, free) or the **Chicago Board of Options Exchange,** both located in **The Board of Trade Building,** 400 S. LaSalle (435-3455). The building has a huge monument to Ceres, Greek goddess of grain, standing 609 ft. above street level. The third, the **Chicago Mercantile Exchange** is at Wacker and Madison.

In the late 19th century, Sears, Roebuck, along with competitor Montgomery Ward, created the mail-order catalog business, undercutting many small general stores and permanently altering the face of American merchandising. Today, although the catalog business is over, the **Sears Tower,** 233 W. Walker, is more than just an office building; at 1707 ft., it stands as a monument to the insatiable lust of the American consumer. You can view the city from the top of this, the tallest building in the world. (Open daily 9am-11pm, Jan.-March 10am-10pm. $6, kids $3.25, seniors $4.50, family $16. Lines can be long.) **The First National Bank**

CHICAGO

Building and Plaza stands about two blocks northeast, at the corner of Clark and Monroe St. The world's largest bank building pulls your eye skyward with its diagonal slope. Marc Chagall's vivid mosaic, *The Four Seasons,* lines the block and sets off a public space often used for concerts and lunchtime entertainment.

State and Madison, the most famous block of "State Street that great street" and the focal point of the Chicago street grid, lies one street over. Louis Sullivan's **Carson Pirie Scott** store building is adorned with exquisite ironwork and the famous extra-large Chicago window (though the grid-like modular construction has been altered by additions). Also visit Sullivan's other masterpiece, the **Auditorium Building,** several blocks south at the corner of Congress and Michigan. Beautiful design and flawless acoustics highlight this Chicago landmark.

Chicago has one of the country's premier collections of outdoor sculpture. Many downtown corners are punctuated by large, abstract designs. The most famous of these is a Picasso at the foot of the **Daley Center Plaza,** Washington and Dearborn (346-3278), beside which there is often free entertainment in the summer. Across the street rests Joan Miró's *Chicago,* the sculptor's gift to the city. A great Debuffet sculpture is across the way in front of the **State of Illinois Building,** a post modern version of a town square designed by Helmut Jahn in 1985. Take the elevator all the way up, where there is a thrilling (and free) view of the sloping atrium, circular floors, and hundreds of employees at work. Definitely worth a look.

The city held a contest to design a building in honor of the late mayor, for only $144 million. The result is the **Harold Washington Library Center,** 400 S. State St. (747-4300), a researcher's dream and an architectural delight. (Tours Tues.-Sat. 11:30am, noon, 2pm; open Tues. and Thurs. 11am-7pm, Wed., Fri.-Sat. 9am-5pm.)

North Side

Extending north of Diversey Ave., the North Side offers an amalgam of ethnically diverse neighborhoods. Stroll the streets here and you'll find fresh-baked pita bread, vintage clothing stores, elite apartment buildings, and humble two-story abodes.

Elaborate tombs and monuments designed by Louis Sullivan and Lorado Taft make **Graceland Cemetery,** east of Clark St. between Irving Park Rd. and Montrose Ave., an interesting sight and a posthumous status symbol. Famous corpses here include Marshall Field, George Pullman, Daniel Burnham, and other Chicago luminaries. The cemetery office has guidebooks (75¢).

Though they finally lost their battle against night baseball in 1988, **Wrigleyville** residents remain, like much of the North Side, fiercely loyal to the Chicago Cubs. Just east of Graceland, at the corner of Clark and Addison, tiny, ivy-covered **Wrigley Field** at 1060 W. Addison is the North Side's most famous institution, well worth a pilgrimage for the serious or simply curious baseball fan, as well as for the *Blues Brothers* nuts who want to visit their falsified address. After a game, walk along Clark St. in one of the city's busiest nightlife districts, where restaurants, sportsbars, and music clubs abound. It's well worth the trip to explore the neighborhood, window shop in the hunk, junk, and 70's revival stores, or, if you prefer, people-watch.

Outdoors

A string of lakefront parks fringes the area between Chicago proper and Lake Michigan. On a sunny afternoon, a cavalcade of sunbathers, dog walkers, roller skaters, and skateboarders ply the shore, yet everyone still has room to stake out a private little piece of paradise. The two major parks, both close to downtown, are Lincoln and Grant, operated by the Recreation Department (294-2200). **Lincoln Park,** which extends over 5 mi. of lakefront on the north side of town, rolls in the style of the 19th-century English park: winding paths, natural groves of trees and asymmetrical open spaces. The **Lincoln Park Conservatory** encloses fauna from desert to jungle environments under its glass palace (249-4770). Great apes, snow leopards, a rhinoceros,33 and their neighbors call the **Lincoln Park Zoo,** 2200 N. Cannon

Drive (294-4600), home. (Both zoo and conservatory are free and open daily 9am-5pm.)

Grant Park, covering 14 blocks of lakefront east of Michigan Ave., follows the proper 19th-century French park style: symmetrical, ordered, with squared corners, a fountain in the center, and wide promenades. The **Petrillo Music Shell** hosts many free concerts here during the summer, great for mellowing under the stars with a bottle of wine, cheese, and a blanket; check the papers.

Kiss someone under the colored lights that illuminate **Buckingham Fountain** each night at 9-11pm. The **Field Museum of Natural History,** the **Shedd Aquarium,** and the **Adler Planetarium** beckon museum-hoppers to the southern end of the park (take the #146 bus, it's a 1-mi. walk from the park center), while the **Art Institute** calmly houses its collection on the northern side of the park, east of **Adams St.** Grant Park is also a good place to view the downtown skyline.

Lake Michigan lures swimmers to the **Lincoln Park Beach** and the **Oak Street Beach,** on the North Side. Both crowded, popular swimming spots soak in the sun. The beaches are patrolled 9am-9:30pm and are unsafe after dark. The rock ledges are restricted areas, and swimming from them is illegal. Call the Chicago Parks District for further information (294-2200).

Oak Park

Ten mi. west of downtown on the Eisenhower (I-290) sprouts **Oak Park.** Frank Lloyd Wright endowed the community with 25 of his spectacular homes and buildings. Wright pioneered a new type of home, the Prairie House, which sought to integrate the house with the environment, eliminating the discrete break between indoors and out. (The best example is the Robie House in Hyde Park.) The **Visitors center,** 158 Forest Ave. (708-848-1500), offers maps and guidebooks. (Open daily 10am-5pm.) Don't miss the **Frank Lloyd Wright House and Studio,** 951 Chicago Ave. (708-848-1500), with his beautiful 1898 workplace and original furniture. Two tours are offered: one of the exterior of the homes and one of the interior of the studio. (Tours Mon.-Fri. at 11am, 1pm, and 3pm, Sat.-Sun. every 15 min. 11am-4pm. Mon.-Fri. the exterior tour is self-guided only, with a tape recording. $6 each, $9 combined.) By car, exit north from the Eisenhower on Harlem Ave. and follow markers. By train, take the Lake St./Dan Ryan El to Harlem/Marion stop; it's 20 minutes from downtown. From the station, walk north to Lake St. and east to Forest Ave. to find the visitors center.

Hyde Park

Seven mi. south of the Loop along the lake, the **University of Chicago's** (702-1234) beautiful campus dominates the **Hyde Park** neighborhood. A former retreat for the city's artists and musicians, the park became the first U.S. community to undergo urban renewal in the 50s and is now an island of intellectualism in a sea of dangerous neighborhoods. Don't stray south of Midway Plaisance, west of Cottage Grove, or north of Hyde Park Blvd. Lakeside Burnham Park, to the east of campus, is relatively safe during the day but dangerous at night. On campus, U. Chicago's architecture ranges from knobby, gnarled, twisted Gothic to neo-streamlined high-octane Gothic. Check out Frank Lloyd Wright's famous **Robie House,** at the corner of Woodlawn Ave. and 58th St.; tours ($3, students and seniors $1 on Sun.) depart daily at noon. Representative of the Prairie school, this large house blends into the surrounding trees; its low horizontal lines now house university offices. From the Loop, take bus #6 ("Jefferson Express") or the Illinois Central Railroad from the Randolph St. Station south to 57th St. The Oriental Institute, Museum of Science and Industry, and DuSable Museum are all in or border on Hyde Park.

Near West Side

The **Near West Side,** bounded by the Chicago River to the east and Ogden Ave. to the west, is a fascinating assembly of tiny ethnic enclaves. Farther out, however,

CHICAGO

looms the West Side, one of the most dismal slums in the U.S. Dangerous neighborhoods lie alongside safe ones, so always be aware of where you stray. **Greektown** might not be as Greek now, but several blocks of authentic restaurants (north of the Eisenhower on Halsted) remain, and still draw people from all over the city.

A few blocks down Halsted (take the #8 Halsted bus), historic **Hull House** stands as a reminder of Chicago's role in turn-of-the-century reform movements. Here, Jane Addams devoted her life to her settlement house, garnering a reputation as a champion of social justice and welfare. The house itself was home to the settlement worker staff, *not* homeless locals, and was the focus of community activities ranging from kindergarten to night-time classes. Hull House has been relocated to 800 S. Halsted, but painstaking restoration, a slide show, and thoughtful exhibits about Near West Side history now make the **Hull House Museum** (413-5353) a fascinating part of a visit to Chicago. (Open Mon.-Fri. 10am-4pm, Sun. noon-5pm. Free.) **Ukrainian Village,** at Chicago and Western, is no longer dominated by ethnic Ukrainians, but now that the Ukraine has regained its independence, you may have even more reason to visit the **Ukrainian National Museum** at 2453 W. Chicago Ave. (276-6565), and the **Ukrainian Institute of Modern Art** at 2318 W. Chicago Ave. (227-5522) (donations suggested).

Near North

The city's ritziest district lies above the Loop along the lake, just past the Michigan Ave. Bridge. Overlooking this stretch is the **Tribune Tower,** 435 N. Michigan Ave., a Gothic skyscraper that resulted from a hotly-contested international design competition in the '20s. The building houses Chicago's largest newspaper; quotations exalting the freedom of the press emblazon the inside lobby. Roam the **Merchandise Mart** (entrances on N. Wells and Kinzie; 644-4664), the largest commercial building in the world, 25 stories high and two city blocks long. The first two floors are a mall open to the public; the rest of the building contains showrooms where design professionals converge from around the world to choose home and office furnishings, kitchen products, and everything else that goes into a building, including the "restroom" signs. (Public tours Mon., Wed., and Fri. 10am and 1:30pm. $7, seniors and students over 15 $5.50.)

Chicago's **Magnificent Mile,** along Michigan Ave. north of the Chicago River, is a conglomeration of chic shops and galleries. Some of these retail stores, including the recently opened Banana Republic and Crate & Barrel, were designed by the country's foremost architects. Hiding among them is the **Chicago Water Tower and Pumping Station** (467-7114), at the corner of Michigan and Pearson Ave. Built in 1867, these two structures were among the few to survive the Great Chicago Fire. The pumping station, which supplies water to nearly 400,000 people on the North Side, houses the glamorous *Here's Chicago.* Across the street is **Water Tower Place,** the first urban shopping mall in the U.S., where expensive and trendy stores meet.

Beautiful old mansions and apartment buildings fill the streets between the Water Tower and Lincoln Park. Known as the **Gold Coast,** the area has long been the elite residential enclave of the city. Early industrialists and city founders made their homes here and, lately, many families have moved back from the suburbs. Lake Michigan and the Oak St. Beach shimmer a few more blocks east.

Urban renewal has made **Lincoln Park,** a neighborhood just west of the park of the same name, a popular choice for upscale residents. Bounded by Armitage to the south and Diversey Ave. to the north, lakeside Lincoln Park is a center for recreation and nightlife, with beautiful harbors and parks and some of the liveliest clubs and restaurants along North Halsted and Lincoln Ave.

If you hear the bells of St. Michael's Church, you're in **Old Town,** a neighborhood where eclectic galleries, shops, and nightspots crowd gentrified streets. Absorb the architectural atmosphere while strolling the W. Menomonee and W. Eugenie St. area. In early June, the **Old Town Art Fair** attracts artists and craftsmen from across the country. Many residents open their restored homes to the public. (Take bus #151 to Lincoln Park and walk south down Clark or Wells St.)

Farther Out

The **Pullman Historic District** on the southeast side was once considered the nation's most ideal community. George Pullman, inventor of the sleeping car, hired British architect Solon S. Beman in 1885 to design a model working town so that his Palace Car Company employees would be "healthier, happier, and more productive." The **Hotel Florence**, 1111 S. Forrestville Ave. (785-8181) houses a museum and restaurant. Tours leave from the hotel the first Sun. of each month May-Oct. $3.50, seniors $3, students $2. By car, take I-94 to W. 111th St.; by train, take the Illinois Central Gulf Railroad to 111th St. and Pullman.

In **Wilmette**, the **Baha'i House of Worship** (708-256-4400), Shendan Rd. and Linden Ave., is an 11-sided Near Eastern-styled dome modeled on the House of Worship in Haifa, Israel. (Open daily 10am-10pm; Oct.-May 10am-5pm.)

Arlington International Racetrack (708-255-4300), Route 53 at Euclid, Arlington Heights, has thoroughbred racing at cheap—or not so cheap—prices. It's up to you to decide, at the betting windows. The **Brookfield Zoo** (708-485-0263), First Ave. and 31st St., Brookfield (about 20 mi. from the Loop), is a nationally renowned, superb zoo. **Great America** (708-249-1776), I-94 at Route 132 E., Gurnee, IL, is the largest amusement park in the Midwest. Check out the Screaming Eagle.

Chicago Botanical Gardens (708-835-5440), Lake Cook Rd. ½-mi. from I-94, Glencoe, IL, is a major plant show. Celebrate flora and fauna 25 mi. away from downtown.

ENTERTAINMENT

To stay on top of Chicago events, grab a copy of the free weekly *Chicago Reader,* published on Thursday and available in many bars and restaurants. *Chicago* magazine has exhaustive club listings. The Friday edition of the *Chicago Tribune* includes a thick section with full music, theater, and cultural listings.

Theater

Chicago is one of the foremost theater centers of North America, as well as the home of Improv and the Improvorgy. For an authentic local experience visit one of the intimate, smaller theaters that stage home-grown productions. At one point last summer, over 100 shows were running, ranging in respectability from *Julius Caesar* to *Coed Prison Sluts.* The "Off-Loop" theaters on the North Side specialize in original drama, with tickets in the $15 and under range.

Victory Gardens Theater, 2257 N. Lincoln Ave. (871-3000). 3 theater spaces. Drama by Chicago playwrights. Tickets $10-29.

Center Theatre, 1346 W. Devon Ave. (508-5422). Solid, mainstream work. Tickets vary show to show, $5-15.

Annoyance Theatre, 3153 N. Broadway (929-6200). Different show each night of the week, original works that play off pop culture; they launched *The Real-Life Brady Bunch.* In the center of an active gay neighborhood and currently showing gay/lesbian pride series.

Remains Theatre, 1800 N. Clybourn (335-9800). Off-beat works. Several members of the company are screen actors returning to the stage. Current performance art/dance piece "Animals." Walk-up tickets available. Tickets $10-20.

Bailiwick Repertory in the Theatre building, 1225 W. Belmont Ave. (327-5252). Original works including *Oh Holy Allen Ginsberg.* Tickets from $15.

Live Bait Theatre, 3914 N. Clark St. (871-1212). Shows with titles like *Late Night Catechism* and *Tango Eduardo.* Tickets $6-12.

Most theater tickets are expensive, although half-price tickets are available on the day of performance at **Hot Tix Booths,** 108 N. State St., downtown. Buy them in person only; show up 15-20 min. before booth opens to get first dibs. (Open Mon. noon-6pm, Tues.-Fri. 10am-6pm, Sat. 10am-5pm. Tickets for Sun. shows on sale Sat.) Phone **Curtain Call** (977-1755) for information on ticket availability, schedules and Hot Tix booths. **Ticket Master** (800-233-3123) supplies tickets for many theaters. Check with theaters for half-price student rush tickets 30 min. before showtime.

Two Chicago theaters are especially well-known, with prices to match their fame: the **Steppenwolf Theater,** 1650 N. Halsted (335-1650), where David fucking Mamet got his goddamn start, and the **Goodman Theatre,** 200 S. Columbus Dr. (443-3800); both present consistently good original works. (Tickets $20-30.) The big-name presentation house that hosts Broadway touring productions is the **Shubert Theater,** 22 W. Monroe St. (977-1700). The monthly *Chicago* and the weekly *Chicago Reader* give thumbnail reviews of all major shows, with times and ticket prices.

Comedy

Chicago boasts a giggle of comedy clubs, the most famous being **Second City,** 1616 N. Wells St. (337-3992), with its satirical spoofs of Chicago life and politics. Second City graduated John Candy, Bill Murray, and the late John Belushi and Gilda Radner, among others. (Shows Tues.-Thurs. 8:30pm, Fri.-Sat. at 8:30 and 11pm, Sun. at 8pm. Tickets $10-15. Reservations recommended; during the week you can often get in if you show up 1 hr. early.) Most nights a free improv session follows the show. **Second City ETC.** (642-8189) offers yet more comedy next door (same times and prices). The big names drop by and make it up as they go along at **The Improv,** 504 N. Wells (782-6387). (Shows Sun., Tues., Thurs. 8pm, Fri.-Sat. 7pm, 9:30pm, and midnight. Tickets $10-13.50 depending on day.)

Dance, Classical Music, and Opera

Chicago philanthropists have built the network of high-priced, high-art performance centers you've come to expect in a major metropolis. The **Chicago City Ballet** pirouettes under the direction of Maria Tallchief at the **Auditorium Theater,** 50 E. Congress Parkway (922-2110). From October to May, the **Chicago Symphony Orchestra,** conducted by Daniel Barenboim, crescendoes at **Orchestra Hall,** 220 S. Michigan Ave. (435-8111). The **Lyric Opera of Chicago** sings from September to February at the **Civic Opera House,** 20 N. Wacker Dr. (332-2244). The **Grant Park Music Festival** is more attractive to the budget traveler. From mid-June to early September, the acclaimed **Grant Park Symphony Orchestra** gives a few free evening concerts a week at the Grant Park Petrillo Music Shell. (Usually Wed.-Sun.; schedule varies. Call 819-0614 for details.) *Chicago* magazine has complete listings of music, dance, and opera performances throughout the city.

Seasonal Events

Like Chicago's architecture, the city's summer celebrations are executed on a grand scale. The **Taste of Chicago** festival cooks the ten days up to July Fourth, when over 70 restaurants set up booths with endless samples at Grant Park (free). Big name bands also come to perform. The last week in May, the **Blues Festival** celebrates the city's soulful, gritty music; the **Chicago Gospel Festival** hums and hollers in July, the Latin music festival Labor Day weekend, and the **Chicago Jazz Festival** swings in mid-September, all at the Grant Park Petrillo Music Shell. Call the Mayor's Office Special Events Hotline (800-487-2446) for info on all five free events.

Chicago also offers several free summer festivals on the lakeshore, including the **Air and Water Show** in mid-July, when Lake Shore Park, Lake Shore Dr., and Chicago Ave. are the scene of several days of boat races, parades, hang gliding, and stunt flying, as well as aerial acrobatics by the Blue Angels precision fliers.

The regionally famous **Ravinia Festival** (728-4642), in the northern suburb of Highland Park, runs from late June to late September. The Chicago Symphony Orchestra, ballet troupes, folk and jazz musicians, and comedians perform throughout the festival's 14-week season. (Shows Mon.-Sat. 8pm, Sun. 7pm. $15-40. $7 rents you a patch of ground for a blanket and picnic.) Round-trip on the train (METRA) about $7; the festival runs charter buses for $12. The bus ride is 1½ hrs. each way.

Sports

The **Cubs** play ball at gorgeous Wrigley Field, at Clark St. and Addison (831-2827), one of the few ballparks in America that has retained the early grace and intimate feel of the game; it's definitely worth a visit, especially for international visitors who haven't seen a baseball game. (Tickets $6-17.) The **White Sox** swing at the South Side at Comiskey Park, 333 W. 35th St. (924-1000). Da **Bears** play football at Soldier's Field Stadium, McFetridge Dr. and S. Lake Shore Dr. (663-1500). The **Blackhawks** hockey team skates and the **Bulls** basketball team slam-dunks at Chicago Stadium, 1800 W. Madison (Blackhawks 733-5300, Bulls 943-5800). The city is afire with Bulls-mania after having captured their third consecutive NBA National Championship. The **World Cup** will be hosted by Chicago in 1994 (923-1994 for info). Beware of scalpers who illegally sell tickets at inflated prices outside of sports events. For current sports events, call **Sports Information** (976-1313).

Nightlife

Chicago's frenetic nightlife is a grab bag of music, clubs, bars, and more music. "Sweet home Chicago" takes pride in the innumerable blues performers who have played here (a strip of 43rd St. was recently renamed Muddy Waters Drive). For other tastes, jazz, folk, reggae, and punk clubs throbulate all over the North Side. Aspiring pick-up artists swing over to Rush and Division, an intersection that has replaced the stockyards as one of the biggest meat markets of the world. To get away from the crowds, head to a little neighborhood spot for atmosphere. Lincoln Park is full of bars, cafes, and bistros, and is dominated by the gay scene, as well as singles and young married couples. Bucktown, west of Halsted St. in North Chicago, stays open late with bucking bars and dance clubs. For more raging, raving, and discoing, there are plenty of clubs in River N. and Riverwest, and on Fulton St.

Blues

B.L.U.E.S. etcetera, 1124 W. Belmont Ave. (525-8989), El to Belmont then 3 blocks west on Belmont. Cover $4 weekdays, $7 weekends. With the aid of a dance floor, it's a more energetic blues bar than its sibling location **B.L.U.E.S.,** 2519 N. Halsted St. (528-1012), El to Fullerton, then westbound Fullerton bus. Cramped, but the music is unbeatable. Music starts at both joints Mon.-Thurs. at 9pm, Fri.-Sun. at 9:30pm. Open Sun.-Fri. 8pm-2am, Sat. 8pm-3am. Cover Sun.-Thurs. $5, Fri.-Sat. $7.

Kingston Mines, 2548 N. Halsted St. (477-4646). Shows 6 nights per week. Watch for the "Blue Monday" jam session. Music starts at 9:30pm. Open Sun.-Fri. 8pm-4am, Sat. until 5am. Cover Sun.-Thurs. $8, Fri.-Sat. $10.

Other Nightlife

Butch McGuires, 20 W. Division St. (337-9080), at Rush St. Originator of the singles bar. Owner estimates that "over 2400 couples have met here and gotten married" since 1961—he's a little fuzzier on divorce statistics. Once on Rush St., check out the other area hang-outs. Drinks $2-5. Open Sun.-Thurs. 10:30am-2am, Fri. 10am-4am, Sat. 10am-5am.

The China Club, 616 W. Fulton (466-0812). A darker-side dance sensation; call about theme nights. There are discount passes floating around, so check off-beat stores. Cover varies.

Cabaret Metro, 3730 N. Clark (549-0203). Cutting-edge concerts from $6 and Wed. night "Rock Against Depression" extravaganzas ($4 for men, women free) entertain a hip, young crowd. Cool dance spot. Open Sun.-Fri. 9:30pm-4am, Sat. 9:30pm-5am. Cover $6-10.

Christopher Street, 3458 N. Halsted (975-9244). Lots of guppies swim in this attractive, upscale fishbowl with 3 bars, a huge dance floor, and aquarium wallpaper. Drinks $2-4. Open Sun.-Fri. 4pm-4am, Sat. 4pm-5am. Cover Fri.-Sat. $3 ($1 goes to AIDS research).

Jazz Showcase, 636 S. Michigan (427-4846), in the Blackstone Hotel downtown. #1 choice for serious jazz fans. During the jazz festival, big names heat up the elegant surroundings with impromptu jam sessions. No smoking allowed. Music Thurs. at 8 and 10pm, Fri.-Sat. at 9 and 11pm, Sun. at 4 and 8pm. Closing time varies; cover $5-10.

Wild Hare & Singing Armadillo Frog Sanctuary, 3350 N. Clark (327-0800), El to Addison. Near Wrigley Field. Live Rastafarian bands play nightly to a packed house. Open daily until 2-3am. Cover $3-5.

Tania's, 2659 N. Milwaukee Ave. (235-7120). Exotic dinner and dancing adventure with hot *salsa cumbia* and *merengue* bands. No jeans or sneakers. Live music Wed.-Sun. after 10:30pm. Open Sun.-Fri. 11am-4am, Sat. 11am-5am.

Refer to *Chicago* magazine for descriptions of many more clubs, a list of who is playing, current hip spots, and old-time favorites. *ChicagoLife* has a more selective, shorter list and will give you a good second opinion.

■■■ SPRINGFIELD

Springfield didn't even exist when Illinois became a state in 1818, but 15 years later the city was designated the state capitol. As the home of Abraham Lincoln from 1837 until he left for the Presidency, the whole city is geared towards re-living his memory with relish. Stephen Douglas is also revered, if only for his rivalry with Lincoln. Welcome to Lincolnsville, USA.

PRACTICAL INFORMATION

Emergency: 911.

Visitor Information: Springfield Convention and Visitors Bureau, 109 N. 7th St. (789-2360 or 800-545-7300). Open Mon.-Fri. 8am-5pm.

Amtrak: 3rd and Washington St. (800-872-7245), near downtown. To: Chicago (4 per day, 4 hr., $34) and St. Louis (3 per day, 2½ hr., $21). Lockers 50¢ 1st day, $1 subsequent days. Open daily 6am-9pm.

Greyhound: 2351 S. Dirksen Pkwy. (544-8466), on the eastern edge of town. Walk or take a cab ($3 flat rate) to the nearby shopping center, where you can catch the #10 bus. To: Chicago (Mon.-Thurs. $24, Fri.-Sun. $26); Indianapolis ($42); St. Louis ($16). Open Mon.-Fri. 7:30am-7pm, Sat. 7:30am-5pm. Lockers $1 per day.

Public Transport: Springfield Mass Transit District, 928 S. 9th St. (522-5531). Pick up maps at headquarters or at the tourist office on Adams. All 12 lines serve the downtown area on Capitol between 6th and 7th, or Monroe St., near the Old State Capitol Plaza. Fare 50¢, transfers free. Buses operate Mon.-Sat. 6am-6pm.

Taxi: Lincoln Yellow Cab, 523-4545 or 522-7766. $1.25 base, $1.50 each additional mile.

Post Office: 2105 E. Cook St. (788-7200), at Wheeler St. Open Mon.-Fri. 7:45am-5:30pm, Sat. 8am-noon. **ZIP code:** 62703.

Area Code: 217.

Numbered streets in Springfield run north-south, but only on the east side of the city. All other streets have names, with **Washington Street** dividing north-south addresses.

ACCOMMODATIONS AND CAMPING

Most inexpensive places ($24 and up) congregate in the eastern and southern parts of the city, off I-55 and U.S. 36 on Dirksen Parkway; bus service from downtown is limited. Downtown rooms cost $10-30 more. Make reservations on holiday weekends and during the State Fair in mid-Aug. Downtown hotels may be booked solid on weekdays when the legislature is in session. Check with the visitors bureau (see

Practical Information above) about finding reasonable weekend packages offered by slightly more upscale hotels. All accommodations listed have color TV and A/C.

The **Dirksen Inn Motel,** 900 N. Dirksen Pkwy. (522-4900; take #3 "Bergen Park" bus to Milton and Elm, then walk a few blocks east), has clean rooms in good condition (singles $24, doubles $27; office open 5am-1am). **Motel 6,** 3125 Wide Track Dr. (789-1063), near Dirksen Pkwy. at the intersection of I-90 and State Rte. 29, is, well, Motel 6, but with a nice pool (singles $23, doubles $29). **Mister Lincoln's Campground,** 3045 Stanton Ave. (529-8206), next to the car dealership 4 mi. southeast of downtown, has a large area for RVs, a field for tents, and showers. Take bus #10. (Tent sites $7 per person, with electricity $14, full hookup $16.)

FOOD

Horseshoe sandwiches are a Springfield original. Although they may look more like what ends up *on* horseshoes than horseshoes, these tasty concoctions consist of ham on prairie toast covered by cheese sauce and french fries. Depending on your personal taste, you may end up saying "neigh" to them. In and around the **Vinegar Hill Mall,** at 1st and Cook St., a number of moderately priced restaurants serve horseshoes, barbecued ribs, Mexican and Italian food, and seafood. Plan accordingly because Springfield tends to start shutting down between 3-5pm. **Bauer's,** 620 S. 1st St. (789-4311), has a moderately priced horseshoe for lunch. **The Feed Store,** 516 E. Adam S. St. (528-3355), across from the old state capitol, has inexpensive deli sandwiches ($2.75-4.50) and will decide what you eat if you can't with its no-choice special—sandwich, soup, and drink $4.65. (Open Mon.-Sat. 11am-3pm.) **Saputo's,** 801 E. Munroe at 8th St. (522-0105), two blocks from Lincoln's home, has been family-owned and operated for 40 years. Tasty southern Italian cuisine, red lighting, and red tomato sauce; try the baked lasagna ($4.75). (Open Mon.-Fri. 10:30am-midnight, Sat. 5pm-midnight, Sun. 5-10pm.)

SIGHTS

In Springfield, re-creating Lincoln's life is its business, and it goes about it zealously. The best way to see Lincoln is to park the car and walk from sight to sight—retracing the steps of the man himself (or so they keep telling you). Pleasing to most budget trekkers, all Lincoln sights are free. The **Lincoln Home Visitors Center,** 426 S. 8th St. at Jackson (523-0222), shows an 18-minute film on "Mr. Lincoln's Springfield" and doles out free tour tickets to see the **Lincoln Home** (492-4150), the only one Abe ever owned and *the* main Springfield attraction, which sits at 8th and Jackson, in a restored 19th-century neighborhood. (10-min. tours every 5-10 min. from the front of the house. Open daily 8:30am-5pm; bad weather may reduce winter hours. Arrive early to avoid the crowds. Free.)

A few blocks northwest, at 6th and Adams right before the Old State Capitol, the **Lincoln-Herndon Law Offices** (782-4836) let visitors experience where Abe honed his skills practicing law until he left for the Presidency. (Open for tours only daily 9am-5pm; last tour at 4:15pm. Free.) Around the corner to the left across from the Downtown Mall stands the magnificent limestone **Old State Capitol** (782-7691). It was here that, in 1858, Lincoln delivered his stirring and prophetic "House Divided" speech, warning that the nation's contradictory pro-slavery and abolitionist government risked dissolution. The manuscript copy of Lincoln's "Gettysburg Address" normally on display is on loan in California. The capitol is also the sight of the famous Lincoln-Douglas debates which bolstered Lincoln to national fame and acclaim. (Tours daily. Open daily 9am-5pm. Free.) The **New State Capitol,** four blocks away at 2nd and Capitol (782-2099), opened in 1877, is a beautiful example of the Midwestern State Capitol complete with murals of Illinois pioneer history and an intricately designed dome. (Tours Mon.-Fri. 8am-4pm, Sat.-Sun. 9am-3:30pm. Building open Mon.-Fri. 8am-5pm, Sat.-Sun. first floor only 9am-4pm.) The **Lincoln Tomb** (787-2717) at Oak Ridge Cemetery was his final resting place, as well as that of his wife and three sons (open daily 9am-5pm).

Springfield also contains the **Dana-Thomas House,** 301 E. Lawrence Ave. (782-6776), six blocks south of the Old State Capitol. This stunning and well-preserved 1902 home resulted from one of Frank Lloyd Wright's early experiments in design, providing a wonderful example of the Prairie School style. The furniture and fixtures are Wright originals as well. (Budget cuts threaten its accessibility; call for hours. Send a large donation to help keep it open. Tours $3, students $1, when available.) The **Illinois State Museum,** Spring and Edwards St. (782-7386), complements displays on the area's original Native American inhabitants with presentations of contemporary Illinois art. (Open Mon.-Sat. 8:30am-5pm, Sun. noon-5pm. Free.)

In June, the **Thomas Rees Carillon** in Washington Park hosts the world's only **International Carillon Festival.** Springfield's renowned Fourth of July shebang is called (of course) **Lincolnfest** and more than doubles the town's population with fireworks, patriotism, and, no doubt, quite a few references to the man himself.

Indiana

The contrast of two popular explanations for Indiana's nickname of "Hoosier" typifies the dichotomy between the state's rural and industrial traditions. The first explanation holds the name to be a corruption of the pioneer's call to visitors at the door, "Who's there?"; the second claims that it spread from Louisville, where labor contractor Samuel Hoosier employed Indiana workers. More than half a century later, visitors still encounter two Indianas: the heavily industrialized northern cities and the slower-paced agricultural southern counties.

Most tourists identify Indiana as either the state of Gary's smokestacks and the Indianapolis 500 or home of rolling hills thick with cornstalks. Don't try to choose between the farms and the factories; it is precisely this combination that makes Indiana interesting. Visit the athletic, urban mecca of Indianapolis, but don't miss the rural beauty downstate. The state that produced wholesome TV celebrities David Letterman and Jane Pauley, as well as basketball legend Larry Bird, also features beautiful scenery, especially when the fall foliage around Columbus explodes in a profusion of colors.

PRACTICAL INFORMATION

Capital: Indianapolis.
Indiana Division of Tourism, 1 N. Capitol #700, Indianapolis 46204 (232-8860; 800-289-6646 in IN). **Division of State Parks,** 402 W. Washington Room: W-298, Indianapolis 46204 (232-4124).
Time Zones: Eastern and Central. In summer, most of Indiana does not observe Daylight Saving Time.
Postal Abbreviation: IN
Sales Tax: 5%.

■■■ INDIANAPOLIS

On the seam of the Rust Belt and the Corn Belt, Indianapolis focuses more on the former, embracing the fuel-wasteful but All-American "sport" of automobile racing as its civic symbol. Its midwestern location produces a city that is All-American almost to the point of being nondescript, but like every good-sized U.S. city, Indianapolis has its points of interest: buildings, museums, ethnic festivals, the Nile-size nightlife area of Broad Ripple, a local celebrity (one-time meteorologist David Letterman, who was laughed out of town for warning of hail "the size of canned hams"), and, of course, a passion for sports. This reaches its apotheosis each Memorial Day weekend when the Indy 500 fuses exhaust and exhaustion in the largest single-day sporting event in the world.

PRACTICAL INFORMATION

Emergency: 911 or 632-7575.

Visitor Information: Indianapolis City Center, 201 S. Capital St. (237-5200), in the Pan Am Plaza across from the Hoosier Dome. Open Mon.-Fri. 10am-5:30pm, Sat. 10am-4pm. Also try 800-233-4639 (800-233-INDY).

Airport: Indianapolis International Airport (248-7243) 7 mi. southwest of downtown near I-465. To get to the city center, take bus #9 ("West Washington").

Amtrak: 350 S. Illinois (263-0550 or 800-872-7245), behind Union Station. In a somewhat deserted but relatively safe area. Trains travel east-west only, with almost all connecting in Chicago ($28) or Washington, DC ($95). Station hours are erratic and vary daily, so call to be sure.

Greyhound: 127 N. Capital Ave. (800-231-2222), downtown at E. Ohio St. 1 block from Monument Circle. Fairly safe area. To: Chicago ($29); Columbus, ($31); Louisville ($22); St. Louis ($22.50). Open 24 hrs. **Indiana Trailways** operates out of the same station and serves cities within the state.

Public Transport: Metro Bus, 36 N. Delaware St. (635-3344), across from City County building. Open Mon.-Fri. 7:30am-5:30pm. Fare 75¢, rush hour $1. Transfers 25¢. For disabled service call 632-3000.

Taxi: Yellow Cab, 637-5421; $2.45 first mi., $1.50 each additional mi.

Car Rental: Thrifty, 5860 Fortune Circle West (636-5622) at the airport. Daily $31 with 150 free mi., weekly $133 with 1050 free mi. Must be 21 with major credit card. $3 daily surcharge for under 25. Open Sun.-Fri. 8am-11pm, Sat. 8am-5pm.

Post Office: 125 W. South St. (464-6000), across from Amtrak. Open Mon.-Wed. and Fri. 7am-5:30pm, Thurs. 7am-6pm. **ZIP code:** 46206.

Area Code: 317.

I-465 laps the city and provides access to all points downtown. I-70 cuts through the city east-west and passes by the Speedway. The center of Indianapolis is located just south of **Monument Circle** at the intersection of **Washington Street** (U.S. 40) and **Meridian Street.** Washington divides the city north-south; Meridian east-west.

ACCOMMODATIONS AND CAMPING

Budget motels in Indianapolis cluster around the I-465 beltway, 5 mi. from downtown. They are particularly concentrated in the west near the Speedway; buses from downtown to this area cost an extra 25¢. Motels jack up their rates for the Indy 500 in May; make reservations a year in advance.

Fall Creek YMCA, 860 W. 10th St. (634-2478), just north of downtown. Small, clean rooms for both men and women include access to all recreational facilities and pool. Friendly staff. Singles $25, with private bath $35; weekly $66/$76; student weekly rate $52.

Motel 6, I-465 at Exit 16A (293-3220) 3 mi. from the Indy Speedway and 10 mi. from downtown, or take the #13 bus. Clean, bright rooms with a really nice outdoor pool which *isn't* in the parking lot. Singles $28, doubles $35.

Medical Tower Inn, 1633 N. Capitol Ave. (925-9831), in the tall building across from the Methodist Hospital. Luxurious 2-room suites with decor you wouldn't mind in your own home. Singles $43, doubles $53. With student ID $2 less.

Dollar Inn, I-465 at Harding St. (788-9561) or at Speedway (248-8500). Take #13 bus. Convenient to the Speedway and Eagle Creek Park. Clean rooms. Singles $22, doubles $27. Key deposit $2.

Indiana State Fairgrounds Campgrounds, 1202 E. 38th St. (927-7510). 170 nice sites $10.50, full hookup $12.60. Open year round. The State Fair is mid-Aug., so make reservations well in advance.

INDIANAPOLIS

FOOD AND NIGHTLIFE

Indianapolis greets visitors with a variety of restaurants that range from holes-in-the-wall to trendy hotspots. Tourists and residents alike head for **Union Station,** 39 Jackson Pl. (267-0700), near the Hoosier Dome four blocks south of Monument Circle. This 13-acre maze of restaurants, shops, dance clubs, bars, and hotels sells many edible substances in a beautiful, authentically refurbished rail depot. The second-level oval bustles with a moderately priced food court. Entrees average $2.50-5. (Open Mon.-Thurs. 10am-9pm, Fri.-Sat. 10am-10pm, Sun. 10am-6pm.) Another place to food-window-shop is **The City Market,** 222 E. Market St., 2 blocks east of Monument Circle, a renovated 19th-century building with produce stands and 15 ethnic markets. The City Market is open Mon.-Sat. 6am-6pm, but individual stall operators usually close earlier. The best time to go is on weekdays from 10am-3pm.

The Tug Boats Cafe, 1029 S. Virginia in Fountain Square is an old time luncheonette, welcoming one and all with "Get really stoned, drink wet cement." Open Mon.-Fri. 6am-7pm, Sat. 6am-3pm, Sun. 6am-1pm.

The Melano Inn, 231 S. College (264-3585), at Bates, has an excellent all-you-can-eat lunch buffet ($5) weekdays 11am-1:30pm in this pricey restaurant. Open Mon-Wed. 11am-10pm, Thurs. 11am-11pm, Fri.-Sat. 11am-midnight, Sun. 4-9pm.

Little Bit of Italy, 5604 Georgetown Rd. (293-6437). If Italian is your thing, you can't lose with the meatball sub or pizza. Lunch or dinner $3-5. Open Mon.-Wed. 10am-8pm, Thurs.-Sat. 10am-9pm.

Nightlife undulates and ululates 6 mi. north of the downtown area at **Broad Ripple,** at College Ave. and 62nd St., typically swamped with students and yuppies. The area has charming ethnic restaurants (many have lunch specials) and art studios in original frame houses, as well as some artsy bars and dance clubs. **Coffee ZON,** 137 E. Ohio St. (684-0432) downtown, offers excellent coffee concoctions (*latte* $1.75, mocha $2.25) and occasional live folk music. If you like your brew with hops, head for the **Broad Ripple Brew Pub,** 840 E. 65th St. (253-2739).

SIGHTS

The **State House** (232-3131), bounded by Capitol and Senate, looks like any other capitol from the outside, but enter and see an amazing marble palace with a majestic stained-glass dome. Self-guided tour brochures available inside. (Open daily 8am-5pm, on weekends tour main floor only.) "Please touch" is the motto of the **Children's Museum,** 3000 N. Meridian St. (924-5431), one of the largest in the country. Kids help run hands-on exhibits, which include a turn-of-the-century carousel, a huge train collection, petting zoos, and high-tech electronic wizardry. (Open Memorial Day-Labor Day Mon.-Sat. 10am-5pm, Sun. noon-5pm, off-season Tues.-Wed. and Fri.-Sat. 10am-5pm, Thurs. 10am-8pm, Sun. noon-5pm. $6, seniors $5, ages 2-17 $3. Admission free Thurs. 5-8pm.) The **Indianapolis Museum of Art,** 1200 W. 38th (923-1331), houses a large collection of Turner paintings and watercolors as well as Robert Indiana's *LOVE* sculpture. The museum sits among 154 acres of park, beautifully landscaped with gardens and nature trails. (Open Tues.-Wed. and Fri.-Sat. 10am-5pm, Thurs. 10am-8:30pm, Sun. noon-5pm. Free, except special exhibits, which are free only on Thurs.) Stunning African and Egyptian decor graces the **Walker Theatre,** 617 Indiana Ave. (236-2099). Erected in 1927, the theater commemorates Madame Walker, America's first self-made woman millionaire, as well as symbolizing Indianapolis' African-American community, hosting such jazz greats as Louis Armstrong and Dinah Washington. The complex also sponsors plays and dance performances. Upstairs in the ballroom, the **Jazz on the Avenue** series offers live music every Friday night. The **Indiana Film Society** (255-1178) has an annual fall film festival, with some movies shown in the Walker.

Indianapolis has a host of musical, theatrical, and cultural productions. The **Indiana Repertory Theater,** 140 W. Washington (635-5252), is Indiana's only full-season professional company, performing classical and modern plays. The **Pride of**

Indy Barbershop Harmony Chorus, 426 N. (897-0872), meets every Monday at 7:30pm at the Lawrence North Community Center, 5301 N. Franklin Rd., for a free open rehearsal.

THE INDIANAPOLIS 500: GENTLEMEN, START YOUR ENGINES

The **Indianapolis Motor Speedway,** 4790 W. 16th St. (481-8500), is clearly the quintessential Indianapolis tourist site. Take the Speedway exit off I-465 or bus #25 ("West 16th"). A shrine dedicated to worshipping the automobile, this 1909 behemoth encloses an entire 18-hole golf course. Except in May, you can take a bus ride around the 2½-mi. track for $1. The adjacent **Speedway Museum** (Indy Hall of Fame) houses a collection of Indy race cars and antique autos, as well as racing memorabilia and videotapes highlighting historic Indy moments. (Open daily 9am-5pm. $1, under 16 free.)

The country's passion for the automobile reaches a speeding frenzy during the **500 Festival** (636-4556), a month of parades, a mini-marathon, and lots of hoopla, leading up to the day when 33 aerodynamic, turbocharged race cars circle the track at speeds exceeding 225 mph. Beginning with the "time trials" (the two weekends in mid-May preceding the race), the party culminates with a big blowout on the Sun. of Memorial Day weekend (weather permitting). Book hotel reservations early and buy tickets in advance. For ticket info, call 481-8500 (open daily 9am-5pm). The 500 isn't the only race in town; call for information on other auto events at the **Indianapolis Raceway Park,** 9901 Crawfordsville Rd. (293-7223), near the intersection of I-74 and I-465. Another huge racing event is NASCAR's **Brickyard 400,** which sends stockcars zooming down the speedway in early Aug. Call 800-822-4639 for info.

Michigan

Ironically, the natural resources which first drew settlers to Michigan today provide the backbone of a growing tourist trade. Michigan's vast forests attracted furriers who set up trading posts along the Great Lakes' coasts. Eventually, the Astor Company dominated the trade from Mackinac. A century later Detroit would hold sway over another industry. Today fur is grown on ranches, and cars don't roll off the assembly line as often. But the land which started Michigan's economy is sustaining it. Vacationers travel the resort-lined west coast and the rustic Upper Peninsula. Ann Arbor draws scholars to the southeast. And despite popular belief, the area around Detroit still has plenty of things to see and do.

PRACTICAL INFORMATION

Capital: Lansing.

Michigan Travel Bureau, P.O. Box 30226, Lansing 48909 (800-543-2937). A listing of the week's events and festivals. **Department of Natural Resources,** Information Services Center, P.O. Box 30028, Lansing 48909 (517-373-1220). Information on state parks, forests, campsites and other public facilities.

Time Zones: Eastern and Central. **Postal Abbreviation:** MI

Sales tax: 4%.

■■■ DETROIT

An author recently proclaimed Detroit "America's first Third-World city," and indeed, the city has witnessed a quarter-century of hardship. In the 60s, as the coun-

DETROIT

try grooved to Motown's beat, the city erupted in some of the era's most violent race riots. Massive white flight to the suburbs has been the norm ever since; the population has more than halved since 1967, turning some neighborhoods into ghost towns. The decline of the auto industry in the late 70s exacerbated problems, and economic disempowerment has engendered frustration, violence, and hopelessness among the city's residents. Contrary to popular belief, downtown Detroit is not frightening because of roving things; it is frightening because there's no roving anything. Downtown is virtually empty—boarded up businesses line the streets. The *really* high crime areas are located in the suburbs, where there are people.

The five towers of the Renaissance Center symbolize the hope that a city-wide comeback is possible. However, without a growing job base and a shift in housing patterns, Detroit will remain in the doldrums.

PRACTICAL INFORMATION

Emergency: 911.

Visitor Information: Detroit Convention and Visitors Bureau, on Hart Plaza at 2 E. Jefferson St. (567-1170). Pick up the free *Detroit Visitors Guide.* Open daily 9am-5pm; phone after hours to hear a recorded list of entertainment events. Call 800-338-7648 to mail-order the slick *Metro Detroit Visitor's Guide.*

Traveler's Aid: 211 W. Congress at Shelby, 3rd floor (962-6740). Emergency assistance. Open Mon.-Thurs. 8:30am-5pm, Fri. 8:30am-4:30pm.

Airport: Detroit Metropolitan Airport (942-3550), 21 mi. west of downtown off I-94. **Commuter Transportation Company** (941-3252) runs shuttles downtown, stopping at major hotels (45 min.; $13 one way; 7am-midnight by reservation). Make reservations; taxi fare to downtown is a steep $25.

Trains: Amtrak, 2601 Rose St. (964-5335 or 800-872-7245), at 17th St., 1½ blocks south of Michigan Ave. Not in a good neighborhood, but okay in daytime. To: Chicago ($29); New York City ($107). Open daily 6am-11pm. For destinations in Canada, use the station across the river in Canada: **VIA Rail,** 298 Walker Rd., Windsor, Ont. (800-387-1144).

Greyhound: 1001 Howard St. (961-8011). To: Chicago ($26, $20 14 days in advance); Cleveland ($23/$18); Toronto ($44/37); New York ($87/$70). Open 24 hrs.; ticket office open daily 6:30am-1am.

Public Transport: Detroit Department of Transportation (DOT), 1301 E. Warren (833-7692). Carefully policed public transport system. Serves the downtown area, with limited service to the suburbs. Many buses now stop service at midnight. Fare $1, transfers 10¢. **People Mover,** Detroit Transportation Corporation, 150 Michigan Ave. (224-2160). Ultramodern elevated tramway facility circles the Central Business District with 13 stops on a 2.7-mi. loop. Worth a ride just for the view. Fare 50¢. **Southeastern Michigan Area Regional Transit (SMART),** 962-5515. Bus service to the suburbs. Fare $1-2.50, transfers 10¢. Pick up a free map of the SMART bus system at their office in the first floor of First National Bank at Woodward and Fort.

Taxi: Checker Cab, 963-7000. $1.10 base fare, $1.10 per mi.

Car Rental: Thrifty Rent-a-Car, 29111 Wick Rd. in Romulus (946-7830). Base rate $35. Must be 21 with credit card.

Help Lines: Crisis Hotline, 224-7000.

Time Zone: Eastern.

Post Office: Trolley branch office at 201 Michigan (965-0995) handles general delivery; **ZIP Code:** 48231. Open Mon.-Fri. 8am-5:30pm, Sat. 8am-noon.

Area Code: 313.

Detroit lies on the Detroit River, which connects Lake Erie and Lake St. Clair. Across the river (due south) lies Windsor, Ontario (pop. 200,000), reached by a tunnel (just west of the Ren Cen) or the Ambassador Bridge (2 mi. west). Detroit is a tough town—one t-shirt reads "I'm so bad I vacation in Detroit"—but if you stay inside the loop encompassed by the People Mover, you shouldn't have trouble. The suburbs begin at Eight Mile Road.

Metropolitan Detroit's streets form a grid; the major east-west arteries are the **Mile Roads**. **Eight Mile Road** is the northern boundary of the city. Three main surface streets cut diagonally across the grid. **Woodward Avenue** heads northwest from downtown, dividing city and suburbs into "east side" and "west side." **Gratiot Avenue** flares out to the northeast from downtown, and **Grand River Avenue** shoots west. Two main expressways pass through downtown; **I-94** heads west and north; **I-75** scoots north and south.

ACCOMMODATIONS AND CAMPING

Avoid hotels near the bus and train stations. Camping is only an attractive option if you don't mind a 45-min. commute to get into the city. The *Detroit Metro Visitor's Guide* has extensive listings for accommodations, including prices.

Park Avenue House, 2305 Park Ave. (961-8310), at Columbia, across from the Fox Theater and the police academy. Some rooms in this 1920s grand hotel were converted into a hostel after the manager's son returned from five years of world travel. Sparkling rooms, new wooden beds. Lounge, TV, laundry, parking in guarded lot ($1), and delicatessen on the 1st floor. Check-in 24 hrs., but preferred if before 11pm. Bring a lock for lockers. Bring or rent linen ($1). Beds $12 per night, private rooms for 1 or 2 persons $20. Full apartments $120 per week.

Shorecrest Motor Inn, 1316 E. Jefferson Ave. (800-992-9616). Unbeatable location 3 blocks east of the Renaissance Center. Singles $46. Doubles $64.

Algonac State Park (765-5605) sits on the shore of the Detroit River, 35 mi. from downtown. Take I-94 N., then Rte. 29 N., about 15 mi. Watch the big ships cruise the river at night, carrying cargo to and from Detroit, the fifth largest port in the U.S. (Sites $10, riverside sites $14.)

Sterling State Park, 2800 State Park Rd., Monroe, MI 48161 (289-2715), splashes on Lake Erie, 37 mi. south of Detroit, ½-mi. off I-75 just north of the city of Monroe. Swimming is available. (Open 24 hrs. Sites $10, including electricity.)

FOOD AND NIGHTLIFE

Most of the restaurants downtown have fled to the suburbs, leaving the budget traveler with limited dining options. **Greektown,** a block of eateries on Monroe, at the Greektown People Mover stop, has a dozen Greek restaurants and a handful of excellent dessert bakeries, all on one block of Monroe St. at Beaubien. **Trapper's Alley** (963-5445) in Greektown is an artsy and eclectic four-story mall of food and retail shops that veer from the norm (open Mon.-Thurs. 10am-9pm, Fri.-Sat. 10am-midnight, Sun. noon-7pm). **Mexican Town,** a lively neighborhood south of Tiger Stadium, has a number of terrific restaurants. The **Ren Cen** (local terminology for the Renaissance Center) has mall food targeting its captive lunch-crowd audience and business types. Though it has spread its grasp to Louisville and Cincinnati, the "Coney" was invented in Detroit. **American Coney Islands** and **Lafayette Coney Islands,** 114 and 118 W. Lafayette, just west of Cadillac Square, have the same basic menu of hamburger, fries, and, of course, the Coney: hot dog, chili, mustard and chopped onion ($1.40). They are packed at lunch and from 10pm to 4am with the post-bar crowd (open 24 hrs).

Oh—I drowned my blues at the **Soup Kitchen Saloon,** 1585 Franklin (259-2643). I say I drowned my blues in hearty, well-prepared entrees at that Soup Kitchen Saloon at Franklin and Orleans in Riverton. Sayin' now they got steak, chicken, or fish Cajun-style at that Soup Kitchen Saloon. I say entrees go fo' 'bout $8-14 at that So-oup Kitchen...So-oup Kitchen Saloo-ooon. (Live music Thurs.—Big Band Night—9:30pm-midnight, Fri.-Sat.—blues—9:30pm-2am; cover usually $5, but up to $15 for more prominent acts.)

SIGHTS

The colossal **Henry Ford Museum & Greenfield Village,** 20900 Oakwood Blvd., is off I-94 in nearby Dearborn; take SMART bus #200 or 250 (271-1620 or 271-1976; 24

DETROIT

hrs.). These exhibits alone justify a trip to Detroit. The museum—a 12-acre room—has a comprehensive exhibit on the importance of the automobile in America, with a 1960s Holiday Inn guest room and a 1946 diner rounding off its collection of over 100 cars. The museum is about more than just the auto; it covers the artifacts of industrialization, from 19th-century typewriters and paper copiers to farm machinery and underwater cables. Over 80 historic homes, workplaces, and community buildings from around the country have been moved to **Greenfield Village,** a 240-acre park next to the museum. Visit the workshop of the Wright Brothers or the invention factory where Thomas Edison used systematic research and development methods (98% perspiration, 1% inspiration and 1% deep-seated desire to best rival genius C.G. Steimetz). The "Stephen Foster House" is not Stephen Foster's house. (Open daily 9am-5pm. Museum or Village admission $11.50, seniors $10.50, ages 5-12 $5.75. Both sights, 2 days, $20, ages 5-12 $10.)

Compact downtown Detroit can be explored easily in one day. The city is in obvious decay—every other storefront is boarded up and the sidewalk is crumbling. The futuristic, gleaming steel-and-glass **Renaissance Center** provides a shocking contrast to this wasteland. A five-towered complex of office, hotel, and retail space, the Ren Cen encloses a maze of concrete walkways and spiraling stairs. Thrill to the **World of Ford** on level 2, or ride to the top of the 83-story **Westin Hotel,** the tallest hotel in North America, for a towering view of the city ($3; for general Ren Cen information call 568-5600; tour information 341-6810; lines open daily 9am-5pm).

Detroit's Cultural Center at Woodward and Warren St. (take bus #53), clusters public and private cultural institutions such as the **Detroit Institute of Arts (DIA)** (833-7900) and the **Museum of African-American History,** which has a continuing exhibit on the technical and social history of the Underground Railroad.

Although Berry Gordy's Motown Record Company has moved to Los Angeles, the **Motown Museum,** 2648 W. Grand Blvd. (867-0991), preserves its memories. Downstairs, shop around the primitive studio in which the Jackson Five, Marvin Gaye, Smokey Robinson and Diana Ross recorded the tunes that made them famous. (Open Mon.-Sat. 10am-5pm, Sun. 2-5pm. $3, under 12 $2.) The museum is east of Rosa Parks Blvd., about one mi. west of the Lodge Freeway (Rte. 10). Take the "Dexter Avenue" bus to the museum from downtown.

EVENTS

Jazz fans jet to Detroit during Labor Day weekend for the four-day **Montreux-Detroit Jazz Festival** (259-5400) at Hart Plaza. The festival is free, dig? The **Michigan State Fair,** the nation's oldest, gathers bake-offs, art exhibits and the heady whiff of livestock to the Michigan Exposition and State Fairgrounds at Eight Mile Rd. and Woodward (10 days long, late Aug.-early Sept.). Catch **Tiger** baseball while in town; the Stadium is a pain to get to, but tickets are cheap and plentiful; call 962-4000 for info. The **Lions** of the NFL roar at the Pontiac Silverdome (335-4151). Pick up a copy of the weekly arts mag *Metro Times* for complete listings of music, theater, art and freebies. Charge concert or sports tickets at **Ticketmaster,** 645-6666.

■ Near Detroit

Take exit 136 northbound or 144 southbound off I-75 between Flint and Saginaw to experience the incomparable **Frankenmuth.** The kitsch capital of Michigan is an uproarious Bavarian knock-off village which has become a gargantuan tourist draw. Squeaky-clean family fun awaits. Frankenmuth's claim to fame is the **Bavarian Inn Restaurant,** 713 South Main St. (652-9941), where all-you-can-eat chicken dinners ($11) have been wolfed down since 1888 (open daily 11am-9:30pm).

■■■ ISLE ROYALE NATIONAL PARK

Isle Royale's tourist literature reminds you that "more people visit Yellowstone National Park in one day than visit Isle Royale in the whole year"; this park offers the real backcountry seclusion which sometimes is lacking in the bumper-to-bumper traffic of other parks. Its relative desolation is not due to a lack of appeal but to natural barriers which filter out the Interstate-RV-with-TV and McDelibopper's-meal-style tourists and save the area for serious, quiet nature-lovers. Isle Royale (ROY-al, not roy-AL) is, as the name implies, an island. 45 mi. long and 10 mi. wide, it runs parallel to the northwestern coast of Lake Superior. The island itself is a car-, telephone-, and medical service-free wilderness zone, accessible only by boat (or by sea plane, for the thick of wallet); visitors to Isle Royale should plan ahead sensibly, hike, and take time to experience it as a living wilderness.

The island was home to quiet-living fisherfolk until it was made a national park in 1940. The inhabitants were allowed to remain on the island until they left or died, at which point their property reverted to the park, a process of eminent domain which is now nearly complete. Howard Sivertson's paintings, with exquisitely sensitive and varied treatments of sky and water, plus the annotations in his book *Once Upon an Isle,* document his childhood in this now-defunct community. Human history on the island has also left points of interest in lighthouses and 1000- to 2000-year-old Native American copper pit mines.

Practical Information Experienced seapersons can navigate to Isle Royale on their own (contact the park headquarters for advice in choosing a route and choosing whether to make the attempt; Lake Superior is big, cold, and treacherous), but the largest share of visitors come on the *Ranger III* (906-482-0984) boat from Houghton, which departs early June to mid-September Tuesday and Friday at 9am (return trip leaves Rock Harbor Wed. and Sat. 9am), and takes 6½ hours. (Round-trip mid-July-late Aug. $74-80, off-season $35; less for kids. Extra charge to transport a canoe, kayak, outboard motor, or boat under 20 ft. long.) The *Isle Royale Queen III* (operated by Isle Royale Ferry Service, The Dock, Copper Harbor, MI 49918, 906-289-4437; off-season 108 Center St., Hancock MI 49930) makes 4½-hour trips from Copper Harbor, MI, starting at 8am, and return trips the same afternoon. (Mid-May-mid-June and Labor Day-end of Sept. Mon. and Fri.; mid-June-end of June Mon.-Tues. and Thurs.-Sat., July Thurs.-Tues.; Aug.-Labor Day daily. Mid-May-mid-July $30, under 12 $15; mid-July-Sept. $34, kids $17. Extra charge for canoes, kayaks and suchlike; 10% discount for generally pointless same-day round-trips.) Both of these boats land at **Rock Harbor,** near the eastern end of the island, where the most services are available. **Grand Portage, MN,** near the northern end of the Minnesota Superior North Shore, originates two boats to the island, administered by **Sivertson Fishery** in Superior, WI (715-392-2100; $30-40, kids under 12 $15-20).

There are three **ranger stations: Windigo** on the western tip of the island; **Rock Harbor** on the eastern tip of the island; and near **Siskiwit Lake,** on the south shore, midway between Windigo and Rock Harbor. Despite its closer proximity to the Ontario and Minnesota mainland, the park is officially part of Michigan, and its headquarters are located in **Houghton,** on the Upper Peninsula (mailing address: Isle Royale National Park, Houghton, MI 49931; 906-482-0984).

Camping There are numerous **campgrounds** scattered around the island; permits, free and available at any ranger station, are required for camping. Some campgrounds have three-sided, screened-in shelters, but they're popular and can't be reserved; bring your own tent just in case. Nights are always cold (mid-40s°F in June); bring warm clothes and mosquito repellent. Use a 25-micron filter or boil water for at least two minutes, as it is infested with a nasty tapeworm; iodine tablets and charcoal purification are not sufficient. Wood fires are greatly restricted; bring a camp stove instead. Campers can buy supplies and groceries at Rock Harbor and in limited amounts at Windigo. Indoor accommodations are available at Rock Harbor; they tend to be nice but expensive. Housekeeping cottages at **Rock Harbor Lodge,** P.O. Box 405, Houghton (906-337-4993), start at $51 per day.

Activities Nature is what draws people to Isle Royale. Hiking most of the length of the island from Rock Harbor to Windigo on some of the 170 mi. of trails in the park is a two-day perambulation through forests recovered from 19th-century logging, with plenitudes of streams and lakes orders of magnitude smaller than Lake Superior. The **Greenstone Ridge Trail** follows the backbone of the island from Rock Harbor Lodge. **Ojibway Lookout,** on Mt. Franklin, affords a good view of the Canadian shore 15 mi. away. **Monument Rock,** 70 ft. tall, challenges even experienced climbers. **Lookout Louise,** also on the trail, offers one of the most beautiful views in the park. For a superlative time, go to **Ryan Island** in **Siskiwit Lake,** the largest island in the largest lake on the largest island in the largest freshwater lake in the world. Boat and canoe rentals are available at both Rock Harbor and Windigo, and the island's coast provides beautiful and surprising nooks (and crannies!) to explore by water. (Motor rentals $11 for ½-day, $18.50 full day. Boat and canoe rentals $9 for ½-day, $15 full day.)

LAKE MICHIGAN SHORE

The 350-mi. eastern shore of Lake Michigan stretches south from the Mackinaw Bridge to the Indiana border. It can be reached in less than two hours from downtown Chicago and has been a vacation spot for over a century with its dunes of sugary sand, superb fishing, abundant fruit harvests through October, and deep snow in winter. The region was one of Lake Michigan's shipping centers before the railroad to Chicago was completed, and though the harbors today welcome more pleasure boats than freighters, merchant vessels are still a common sight along the coast.

Many of the region's attractions are in small coastal towns with the highest concentration located around **Grand Traverse Bay** in the north. **Traverse City,** at the south tip of the bay, is famous as the "cherry capital of the world." Fishing is best in the **Au Sable** and **Manistee Rivers.** However, the rich **Mackinac Island Fudge,** sold in numerous specialty shops, seems to have the biggest pull on tourists, whom locals dub "fudgies." The **West Michigan Tourist Association,** 136 E. Fulton, Grand Rapids 49503 (616-456-8557), offers copious free literature on this area (open Mon.-Fri. 8:45am-5pm). The area's **time zone** is Eastern; the **area code** is 616.

■■■ SOUTHERN MICHIGAN SHORE

Grand Rapids The biggest city in the area, Grand Rapids is the hub of local bus routes. **Greyhound,** in the Grand Rapids Station, 190 Wealthy St. (456-1707) connects to Detroit, Chicago, Holland and Grand Haven. Motels line the junction of 28th St. and Rte. 96, but the cheapest room in town is at the **YMCA,** 33 Library St. N.E. (458-1141), for $10 a night (men only). There's plenty of camping in the area; your best guide to these is the *West Michigan Travel Planner.* Write or call the West Michigan Tourist Association (see above) for a copy. Also available is the *MARVAC RV and Campsite Guide,* listing both state and private sites.

In Grand Rapids one can tour the headquarters of the **Amway Corporation** (676-6000; call for free tours). Also, the stellar **Grand Rapids Public Museum,** 54 Jefferson S.E. (456-3977), will entertain young and old alike. By November 1994, the museum is scheduled to open a new complex at a riverside location next to the **Gerald Ford Museum.** Despite the inauspicious neighbor, the Public Museum will continue to dazzle with its indoor "Gaslight Village" restoration, a giant 1905 steam engine, a 50-animal 1928 carousel, and the world's largest whale skeleton. (Open Mon.-Fri. 10am-5pm, Sat.-Sun. 1-5pm. Admission $2.50, kids and seniors 75¢.)

Grand Haven 25 mi. west on I-95, Grand Haven has perhaps the best beach on Lake Michigan: several miles of fine sugary sand so pure that auto manufacturers use it to make cores and molds for engine parts. A cement "boardwalk" connects the beach to the small downtown, whose action centers on Washington St. The new **Smitty's Deli**, 200 S. Harbor Ave. (846-1550), has homemade pizza and meal-sized sandwiches for about $5 (open daily 9am-11pm). The **Bij De Zee Motel**, 1030 Harbor Ave. (846-7431), has rooms from $30, the cheapest near the beach.

Holland Just down the coast from Grand Haven, Holland was founded in 1847 by Dutch religious dissenters, and remained mostly Dutch until well into the 20th century. Today the town cashes in on its heritage with a wooden shoe factory, **Netherlands Museum** (392-9084), **Veldheer Tulip Gardens** (399-1900), and a recreated **Dutch Village** (396-1475). Explore these places (admission $1-4) or simply wander around downtown to get a sense of how this tightly-knit community has survived. The **Wooden Shoe Motel** (392-8521), U.S. 31 Bypass at 16th St., has singles starting at $30, doubles for $40, and a putt-putt course out back.

■■■ CENTRAL MICHIGAN SHORE

Traverse City In summer, vacationers head to Traverse City for its sandy beaches and annual **Cherry Festival,** held the first full week in July. The Traverse City area produces 50% of the nation's sweet and tart cherries, and they won't let you forget it—the cherry theme is emblazoned on everything. The surrounding landscape of the sparkling bay and ancient sand dunes makes this region a Great Lakes paradise, though a crowded and expensive one. In summer Grand Traverse Bay is the focal point for swimming, boating, and scuba diving. Free beaches and public access sites dot its shores. The Leeanau Peninsula pokes up between Grand Traverse Bay and Lake Michigan. Explore the coastline on scenic **M-22,** which will channel you to **Leland,** a charming one-time fishing village which now launches the Manitou Island ferries (see below). Five orchards near Traverse City let you pick your own cherries. One of them is **Amon Orchards** (938-9160), 10 mi. east on U.S. 31, which also bakes cherry products and contends that "cherries aren't just for dessert anymore."

There are many **campgrounds** around Traverse City—in state parks, the National Lakeshore (see below), and various local townships. The West Michigan Tourist Association's guide gives a comprehensive list of public and private sites. State parks usually charge $7-9. As usual, the national forests are the best deal ($4-7). The cheapest beds in Traverse City get made at **Northwestern Michigan Community College,** East Hall, 1701 E. Front St. (922-1406), offers dorms with shared bath. (Singles $20. Doubles $30. At least one-week advance reservation required. Open late June-Aug.) Look for great deals at the **Fox Haus Motor Lodge,** 704 Munson Ave. (947-4450), where frequent specials cut prices down from $89 (doubles) to $45.

Greyhound, 3233 Cass Rd. (946-5180), ties Traverse City to the Upper Peninsula and southern Michigan ($45 to Detroit; 2 per day; open Mon.-Fri. 8am-5pm). **Bay Area Transportation Authority,** at the same address (941-2324), runs buses once per hour on scheduled routes ($1.50 per ride) and can provide transportation for group outings (open Mon.-Fri. 6am-6pm, Sat. 9am-5pm).

For **visitor information,** contact the **Grand Traverse Chamber of Commerce,** corner of Grand View Ave. and Cass, P.O. Box 387, Traverse City 49685 (947-1120 or 800-872-8377; open Mon.-Fri. 9am-5pm). Ask for the *Traverse City Guide*. For a listing of local events and entertainment, pick up the weekly *Traverse City Record-Eagle Summer Magazine.*

LAKE MICHIGAN SHORE: CENTRAL

The **post office** is at 202 S. Union St. (946-9616; open Mon.-Fri. 8am-5pm). Traverse City's **ZIP code** is 49684.

Sleeping Bear Dunes According to legend, the mammoth sand dunes 20 mi. west of Traverse City on M-72 are a sleeping mother bear, waiting for her cubs—the **Manitou Islands**—to finish a swim across the lake. Local legend does *not* explain why the cubs didn't just take the ferry which serves the islands from Leland. (**Manitou Island Transit,** 256-9061. Daily trips to South Manitou, 4 per week to North Manitou, the larger and more wild of the pair. Check-in 9:30am. Round-trip $17, under 12 $12.) Free camping is available on both islands; no cars allowed.

The islands are just a part of the **Sleeping Bear Dunes National Lakeshore** (326-5134), which also includes 25 mi. of lakeshore on the mainland. The dunes are ancient glacial remains perilously hanging on steep cliffs. These mountains of fine sand rise to a precipitous 400 ft. above Lake Michigan. You can make the gritty climb to the top at the **Dune Climb,** five mi. north of Empire on M-109, or you can hike one of the two trails, 2.8 and 3.5 mi. long. The less adventurous can motor to an overlook along the **Pierce Stocking Scenic Drive,** off M-109 just north of Empire. Call the National Parks service **visitors center** (326-5134) on M-72 in Empire, for more info (open daily 9am-5pm). Two rivers which flow through the national lakeshore are suitable for canoeing: the Platte River at the southern end, and the Crystal River on the northern, near Glen Arbor. **Crystal River Canoes,** P.O. Box 133, Empire (334-3090), will equip you with a canoe and pick you up at the end of a three-hour paddle ($20). **Riverside Canoes** provides the same service for the same low price on the Platte River.

Sleeping Bear Dunes National Lakeshore has two campgrounds: **DH Day** (334-4634; $8, no showers), in Glen Arbor, and **Platte River** (325-5881; $10, $15 with hookup; has showers), in Honor. No reservations. For a roof over your head, stay on one of the 12 beds at the **Brookwood Home Hostel,** 538 Thomas Rd. (352-4296), in Frankfort near the Dunes, almost 50 mi. south of Traverse City on Rte. 31. ($7. Open mid-June-Sept. 20. Reservations required; call Marjorie Groenwald at 301-544-4514.)

The renowned **Interlochen Center for the Arts** (276-9221) aestheticizes between two lakes 17 mi. south of Traverse City on Rte. 137. Here, the high-powered **National Music Camp** instructs over 2000 young artists and musicians each summer in the visual arts, theater, dance, and music. Faculty and student concerts are free. Renowned performers command a modest $3-4 during the **International Arts Festival,** held late June-mid-August. Recent guest performers have included Dolly Parton, Yo-Yo Ma, and Shadowfax. The **Interlochen Arts Academy** at the center gives performances almost every weekend in winter (call 276-6230 for schedule). The 1200-acre wooded grounds are open year-round, and free tours leave the information center Tues.-Sat. at 10am. Across the road, the huge **Interlochen State Park** (276-9511) has camping facilities. (Primitive sites $6, with hookup $10, plus a $3.50 vehicle permit.) The **park store** (276-7074) rents row boats ($4 per hr., $18 per day; $20 deposit or driver's license required; open daily 9am-5pm).

Manistee, slightly to the south, beckons tourists with a Victorian shtick. At the **A.H. Lyman Store,** 425 River St., nothing is for sale except postcards: it's an exhibit of a turn-of-the-century store, with goods on the shelves as they were in 1900, including kitchen tools and quack medicines (admission $1). **Manistee National Forest** has copious camping (sites $5-7) with hookup or primitive sites. Call the **Manistee Ranger Station** (800-999-7677; open Mon.-Fri. 8am-5pm. Sat.-Sun. 8am-4:30pm) for more information. Boaters should visit the **Riverside Motel,** 520 Water St. (723-3554). Rooms range from $45-55. The motel backs right up to the river and has dock space available.

■■■ NORTHERN MICHIGAN SHORE

Charlevoix and Petoskey Hemingway set some of his Nick Adams stories on the stretch of coast near Charlevoix (SHAR-le-voy), north of Traverse City on U.S. 31. The town, which lies on a ½-mi.-wide ribbon of land between Lake Michigan and Lake Charlevoix, attracts more tourists than in Hemingway's time, as upscale downstaters triple Charlevoix's population in summer. **Sailing** is Charlevoix's specialty. Several companies offer cruises of Lake Charlevoix, some stopping on **Beaver Island.** Camping, RV stations, and cottages are available at **Uhrick's Lincoln Log** (547-4881) on U.S. 31. Prices vary, but clean, warm cottage rooms can start at $24. The **Petoskey Regional Chamber of Commerce,** 401 E. Mitchell (347-4150), in Petoskey, 18 mi. north of Charlevoix, has information on the area's attractions (open daily 8am-5pm). Petoskey is famed for its **Petoskey Stones,** fossilized coral from a long-gone sea, now found in heaps along the lakeshores. Petoskey's **Gaslight District,** one block from the Chamber of Commerce, has local crafts and foods in period shops. **Symon's General Store,** 401 E. Lake St. (347-2438), has a large wine selection. Vegetarians can head to **Grain Train Natural Foods Co-op,** 421 Howard St. (347-2381), for such delicacies as soy pizza ($3).

Straits of Mackinac Further north, **Fort Michilimackinac** (436-5563) guards the straits between Lake Michigan and Lake Superior, just as it did in the 18th century, though Mackinaw, the town that grew up around the fort, is out to trap tourists, not invading troops. (Tours of the fort daily 9am-5pm; $6, ages 6-12 $3.50.) **Mackinac Island** (which prohibits cars) has another fort, **Fort Mackinac** (906-847-3328), many Victorian homes, and the **Grand Hotel** (906-847-3331), an elegant, gracious summer resort with the world's longest porch. Horse-drawn **carriages** cart guests all over the island (906-847-3325; $10 per person; open daily 8:30am-5pm). Tourist-tempting fudge shops originated on the island. **Ferries** leave Mackinaw City and St. Ignace (June-Sept. every ½ hr., May and Sept.-Oct. every hr.; round-trip $10.50, ages 6-12 $6.50). **Greyhound** has a flag stop at the Standard gas station in downtown Mackinaw City. The Mackinaw **travel information center** (436-5566), off I-75, is loaded with brochures.

■■■ UPPER PENINSULA

A multimillion-acre forestland bordered by three of the world's largest lakes, Michigan's Upper Peninsula (U.P.) is one of the most scenic and unspoiled stretches of land in the Great Lakes region. One hundred years ago the region was almost completely deforested, its timber destined for houses and fences on the treeless Great Plains and for the fireplaces of voracious Chicago; these woodlands are only now returning to their former grandeur.

If you want to experience small-town America, *this* is the place. The largest town in the U.P. has a population of 25,000, and the region is a paradise for fishing, camping, hiking, snowmobiling, and getting away from it all. If you're looking for regional cuisine, stick to the Friday night fish-fry: a mess o' perch, walleye or whitefish, available everywhere for about $7-8. Try the local ethnic specialty, a meat pie imported by Cornish miners in the 19th century called a pastie (PASS-tee), and you'll taste why they haven't caught on in the rest of the country.

Half a dozen rivers in the U.P. beckon canoers. Those who heed the call of the rapids will be well-served by canoe livery services which outfit would-be explorers with equipment, launch them, and retrieve them at a specified destination. For a brochure listing the businesses along each river, write to **Michigan Recreational Canoeing Association,** P.O. Box 668, Indian River 49749. The area is a great place for campers; it's hard to get more than 15 mi. away from one of the peninsula's 200 **campgrounds,** including those at both national forests. Sleep with your dogs or bring extra blankets; temperatures in these parts can drop to a shivering 40°F even in July. **Welcome centers** operated by the Michigan Department of Transportation guard the U.P. at the five main entry points: **Ironwood, Iron Mountain, Menominee, St. Ignace, Sault Ste. Marie,** and **Marquette.** Their mission: to foist heaps of tourist info on all suspecting travelers. Pick up their handy-dandy *Upper Peninsula Travel Planner.* The **U.S. Forestry Service** has maps and advice to help you plan a trip into the wilderness; visit one of their info centers, or write to U.S. Forestry Service, Hiawatha National Forest, 2727 N. Lincoln Rd., Escanaba 49829 (786-4062). Contact **Upper Peninsula Travel and Recreation Association,** P.O. Box 400, Iron Mountain 49801 (774-5480), for general info.

The region's relative isolation and the distances between its cities make travel on the U.P. problematic. **Greyhound** (632-8643) has just three routes: Sault-Ste. Marie to St. Ignace and points south; St. Ignace to Rapid River, Iron Mountain, and Ironwood along U.S. 2; and Calumet south to Marquette, Rapid River, and on to Green Bay on U.S. 41. (All routes 1 per day.) Carless travelers should rent in one of the gateway cities: Green Bay from the west or Grand Rapids from the east, or bike the area.

The **area code** for the U.P. is 906.

■ Sault Ste. Marie

The water level of Lake Superior is 20 ft. higher than that of Lake Huron, and the first trading vessels to ply the Great Lakes faced a costly and arduous portage between the two. In 1855, entrepreneurs built the first lock at Sault Ste. Marie, and today the city's four locks are the busiest in the world, floating over 10,000 ships annually. For a sailor's-eye view of the operation, add your bodyweight to some of the 90 million tons of freight the locks handle each year and ride on the **Soo Locks Boat Tours** (632-6301), which leave from two docks (billboards with directions start 100 mi. away; open mid-May-mid-Oct.; $11, kids $7). The U.S. Army Corps of Engineers, which operates the locks, maintains a good **visitors center** with a working model of the locks, a free film, and an observation deck, at the nearby park. If you'd like to tour a freighter, head to the waterfront at the end of Johnston St., where the **Valley Camp** (632-3658), a 1917 steam-powered freighter, has been converted into a museum (open mid-May-mid-Oct. 10am-6pm, July-Aug. 9am-9pm; $6).

In Sault Ste. Marie, bed down at **Northern Lights Motel,** 722 E. Portage Ave. (635-1262; rooms from $32). On your way west, stay at **Tahquamenon Falls State Park,** 10 mi. east of Paradise (492-3415), on the river near the falls; hookup available at three of the four areas.

■ Middle of the Peninsula

The feds keep the trails clean here at one of the U.P.'s two huge **national forests,** the **Hiawatha,** which blankets central and eastern U.P. Campsites are available in all of the forest's five districts ($5-6; fee varies by district). For more information, contact the Supervisor's Office (786-4062; open Mon.-Fri. 7:30am-4:30pm). If you don't want to get into a pair of rubber waders and slog out into the wilderness, the best place to enjoy the wildlife and outdoors in the U.P. is the **Seney National Wildlife Refuge,** off M-77, 12 mi. north of U.S. 2. This 95,000-acre sanctuary was completely deforested and sold to unsuspecting farmers in the early 20th century. The state later took it over, and during the Depression, the Civilian Conservation Corps (CCC) reconstructed a natural environment here. Most tourists feed the Canada geese in the parking lot at the **visitors center** (open Mon.-Fri. 7:30am-4pm, Sat.-Sun. 9am-5pm) and, satisfied with their foray into nature, they leave. More adventurous readers can walk quietly around the ponds on the 1½-mi. walking trail through the forest, where they can view ducks, swans, woodpeckers, and beaver—over 200 different species have been sighted here. There are also 70 mi. of trails and a 7-mi. auto-tour. The refuge is open during daylight hours and is free. **Canoeing** and **fishing** are permitted, though overnight camping is not. A state **fishing permit** ($5.35 per day; available from any convenience store, grocery store, or tackle shop) is required if you want to dip your hook into these waters. The best time for viewing wildlife is in the early morning and the early evening. In **Shingleton**, 20 mi. west of the refuge, you can observe snowshoes being hand-made at the **Iverson Snowshoe Company's** "factory," actually a big garage (452-6370; open Mon.-Fri. 8am-3pm).

Drop a penny in and watch it sink all the way down to the bottom of the 45-ft. deep **Big Spring** (644-2517), on M-149, 10 mi. north of U.S. 2. This pellucid natural spring gushes 10,000 gallons per minute. Hop on the self-propelled raft, haul yourself to the center of the pool, and observe the billows of silt where the water streams in. Greet the two-ft. brown trout which school in the perpetually 49°F pool. ($3.50 per carload, open daily 9am-7pm.) According to folklore, Paul Bunyan, a fictional character who performed such herculean feats as creating a riverbed by dragging his axe, was born in **Manistique**. As you drive through on U.S. 2, you can't miss the 20-ft.-tall fiberglass statue of the legend himself. Camp at **Indian Lake State Park,** 5 mi. west of town; take U.S. 2 west, then M-149 north. (Sites $12, car permit $3.50. A state permit for unlimited car entry into all state parks for 1 yr. costs $18.) Contact the Park Office (341-2355; open daily 8am-noon, 1-5pm) for more information. You can rent canoes nearby at **Camper's Market** (341-5614), on Star Rte. (open daily 7am-10pm), for $17 per day or $10 per 6 hrs., with a $20 deposit.

The scenic beauty and recreational opportunities of the U.P. are concentrated at the **Pictured Rocks National Lakeshore,** which stretches for 40 mi. along Lake Superior between Munising and Grand Marais. The Pictured Rocks have been sculpted by wind, rain, and ice for millennia. The kaleidoscopic beauty of their arches and columns is hard to appreciate from land, but an overlook at **Miner's Castle** off Miner's Castle Rd. from H58, gives a decent perspective of the stone formations. The best way to see the carved cliffs is the **Pictured Rocks Boat Cruise** (387-2379) which leaves from Munising. (June-Oct.; 7 per day; $18, kids 5-12 $7, under 5 free.) The **Twelvemile Beach** and **Grand Sable Dunes** occupy the other half of the lakeshore. Enjoy the sand and rock beaches, but don't plan to swim unless you have a layer of blubber; Lake Superior is f-f-freezing year-round. The **North Country Trail,** which winds from Port Henry, NY to Lake Sakakawea, ND, passes through the lakeshore. You can hike through the lakeshore on the trail and sleep at primitive campsites along the way (free with use permit, available at Grand Marais, Manistique, or Munising visitors centers). The lakeshore is accessible from Munising and Grand Marais; in both towns you can find food, supplies, and lodging. For more info contact the **National Park Service** at P.O. Box 40, Munising 49862 (387-3700), or the **Grand Marais Chamber of Commerce,** P.O. Box 118, Grand Marais 49839 (494-2766). If you prefer to sleep with a roof above your head, the **Voyager Motel,** 312 E. Munising Ave., Munising 49862 (387-2127), is only three blocks from the Pictured Rocks Boat Cruise (from $20).

■ Keweenaw Peninsula

Before anybody even suspected that there was gold in California, the copper mines in the Keweenaw Peninsula were making some Boston speculators obscenely wealthy. The curved finger of land in the northwest corner of the U.P. sticks out into Lake Superior, beckoning travelers to tour its copper mines and stretches of wilderness. Between 1847 and 1887, prospectors came to the **Delaware Copper Mine** (289-4688), 11 mi. south of Copper Harbor on U.S. 41, and extracted 8 million pounds of copper from the earth. Now, tourists plunk down coppers to pay for the daily guided tours (June-Oct. 10am-5pm; $6, under 13 $3.50). The **Coppertown U.S.A. Mining Museum** (337-4364), west of U.S. 41, displays the tools and techniques of digging up the raw material for many a penny (open June-Oct. Mon.-Sat. 10am-6pm). **Estivant Pines,** the largest remaining stand of virgin pines in Michigan, has been preserved near Copper Harbor, 3 mi. out on Lake Manganese Rd. These trees *average* more than 500 years old.

The Keweenaw Peninsula offers more than memories of metal. Comb the agate beaches, see the Northern Lights, and in winter, ski, snowmobile, or snowshoe over the 250 inches of snow the region receives each year. The **Brockway Mountain Drive** between Eagle Harbor and Copper Harbor rises 1000 ft. above sea level and is one of the most scenic drives in the U.P. With 80 mi. of flash-marked trails, **Porcupine Mountain Wilderness State Park** (885-5275) is one of the best places in the U.P. to hike. The park is on the western side of the U.P., 16 mi. west of Ontonagon off M-107. The **Lake of the Clouds** glistens high in the mountains of this 58,000-acre preserve. Contact **Ontonagon County Chamber of Commerce**, P.O. Box 266, Ontonagon 49953 (884-4735), for more info.

Copper Harbor functions as the main gateway to **Isle Royale National Park** (see below). The *Isle Royale Queen* leaves daily at 8am (4½ hrs.; $34 round-trip, under 12 $17, canoes of any age $12.) The *Ranger III* makes two trips per week to Isle Royale from Houghton (Tues. and Fri. 9am, returns 9am Wed. and Sat.; 6½ hrs.; $43, kids $20, canoe $15.) The **Keweenaw Tourism Council** has offices at 326 Sheldon (482-2388 or 800-338-7982), in Houghton, and at 1197 Calumet Ave. (337-4579 or 800-338-7982), in Calumet. (Offices open Mon.-Fri. 8am-7pm, Sat.-Sun. 10am-6pm.

 # Minnesota

Minnesota is an orchestra of images, each one with its own unique muse. The Jolly Green Giant stands tall over the evergreen forests and the 20 million acres of farmland as the Pillsbury doughboy chuckles with the captains of industry and technology. Charles Schulz's Snoopy plays with the artists of the twin cities, while Bob Dylan, Prince, and Hüsker Dü provide a soundtrack. Loons and wolves fill Lake Superior's North Shore and inland forests with their own music while the spirit of the Native American resides over them. The Tonka truck drives slowly but surely over the Mesabi Iron Range. Together, the natural and cultural beauty creates a rhapsody that is Minnesota.

PRACTICAL INFORMATION

Capital: St. Paul.
Minnesota Office of Tourism, 100 Metro Sq., 121 7th Pl. E., St. Paul 55101-2112 (296-5029 or 800-657-3700, in Canada 800-766-8687). Open Mon.-Fri. 8am-5pm.
Time Zone: Central (1 hr. behind Eastern). **Postal Abbreviation:** MN
Sales Tax: 6.5%.

■■■ DULUTH

Duluth is still the largest port on the Great Lakes, but the area's population has declined more than a quarter during the past few decades. Many of the area mines are closed, and Duluth has instead become a tourist center of the northern wilderness. Minnesota's "refrigerated city," known for its oh-my-God-it's-so-fricking-cold weather and thick fog, is a great place to gear up for fishing, camping, or driving excursions into northwestern Minnesota. It retains an honest, raw, unpredictable quality born of its natural origins and harsh climate.

Practical Information The **Convention and Visitors Bureau,** at Endion Station, 100 Lake Place Dr. (722-4011; open Mon.-Fri. 9am-5pm), and the **Summer Visitors Center** (722-6024) on the waterfront at Harbor Dr. (open daily mid-May-mid-June and Labor Day-mid-Oct. Mon.-Fri. 10am-3pm, Sat.-Sun. 10am-5pm; mid-June-Labor Day 8:30am-8pm), have an ample supply of brochures and Duluth maps. **Greyhound,** 2212 W. Superior (722-5591), two mi. west of downtown, serves many locations in Minnesota, Wisconsin, and Michigan. To Minneapolis (3 per day,

3-4 hr., $16-21) and Chicago (3 per day, 12 hr., $67). Take #9 "Piedmont" bus from downtown. The **post office** is at 2800 W. Michigan St. (723-2590), six blocks west of the Greyhound station. (Open Mon.-Fri. 8am-5pm, Sat. 9am-noon.) Duluth's **ZIP code** is 55806; its **area code** is 218.

Accommodations and Camping Duluth **motels**, dependent for their livelihood on the summer migration of North Shore-bound tourists, raise their prices and are booked early during the warm months; call as far ahead as possible. The **College of St. Scholastica,** 1200 Kenwood Ave. (723-6483), has large, quiet dorm rooms with phones, kitchen access, and laundry, available for short stays early June-mid-August ($19). Group rates and week-long apartment rentals are available. Make reservations. Some relatively reasonable motels lie on **London Road,** west of downtown; the **Chalet Motel,** 1801 London Rd. (728-4238 or 800-235-2957), has singles for $29-39, doubles $38-57, depending on the season. **Jay Cooke State Park** (384-4610), southwest of Duluth off I-35, has 82 campsites (20 with electricity) in a pretty setting near the dramatic St. Louis River valley. (Open daily 8am-10pm. July-Sept. $12, with electricity $14.50; Oct.-June, $10 and $12.50. Vehicle permit $4.) **Spirit Mountain,** 9500 Spirit Mountain Pl. (628-2891), near the ski resort of the same name, is 10 mi. south on I-35, on the top of the hill. (Sites $10, with electricity $13, with electricity and water $15.) **Buffalo Valley** (624-9901), off I-35 N., provides new campgrounds with showers and bathrooms only 15 mi. from Duluth. (Open June-Aug. 11am-1am, off season 3pm-1am. Tent $8, electricity, water, and shower $14.)

Food The restored **Fitger's** brewery, 600 E. Superior St. (722-5624), and the **Canal Park** region south from downtown along **Lake Avenue** have a variety of pleasant eateries. **Sir Benedict's Tavern on the Lake,** 805 E. Superior St. (728-1192), occupies a cottage overlooking the lake, and serves soups and sandwiches ($3-4.50), desserts ($2-3), and a wide variety of beer ($3). Under 21 not admitted. (Live bluegrass Wed., Celtic music every 3rd Thurs. Open Mon.-Tues. and Thurs. 11am-11pm, Wed. 11am-midnight, Fri.-Sat. 11am-12:30am.) The **Blue Note Cafe,** 357 Canal Park Dr. (727-6549), has sandwiches ($2-3) and live music on Saturdays. (Open Mon.-Fri. 10am-8pm, Sat. 10am-10pm.) **Grandma's,** 522 Lake Avenue S. (727-4192), serves large portions in interestingly-wallpapered environs. Entrees $6-10, sandwiches $4-7. Under 21 accompanied by an adult. **Kegler's Bar & Grill,** 601 W. Superior St. (722-0671), in Incline Station, offers pizza and sandwiches ($3-16), and even a 24-lane bowling alley. (Open daily 9am-1am. Bowling $2, shoes $1, pool tables 75¢.)

Sights The best thing about Duluth is its proximity to majestic **Lake Superior.** Enjoy the Superior coast along Duluth's **Lakewalk,** a mile-long walkway stretching across the harbor. At **Hawk Ridge,** four mi. north of downtown off Skyline Blvd., perches a birdwatcher's paradise. In order to avoid flying over open water, hawks veer their migration over Duluth; in September and October they fly in flocks past this bluff. **Bayfront Park** hosts the **International Folk Festival** (722-7425) on the first Saturday in August.

For indoor entertainment, visit **The Depot,** 506 W. Michigan St. (727-8025), in the old Amtrak station, whose several museums include the **Lake Superior Museum of Transportation,** featuring antique locomotives restored to shining splendor by retired railway workers. (Open daily 10am-5pm. Admission $5, seniors $4, families $15, ages 6-17 $3.) **Glensheen,** 3300 London Rd. (724-8864), north towards the outskirts, is a 39-room neo-Jacobean mansion; one way to *really* annoy the tour guides is to ask where the double-murder, which apparently occurred in the house during the early 1970s, took place. (Open Feb.-Dec. Thurs.-Tues. 9am-4pm; Jan. Sat.-Sun. 1-3pm. Admission $6, seniors $5, under 12 $3. Make reservations for summer visits.)

■■■ MINNEAPOLIS AND ST. PAUL

The Twin Cities born of the Mississippi are more fraternal than identical. St. Paul, the slightly elder of the two, began as a settlement near Fort Snelling. With the influx of settlers, this sister grew to be an important steamboat port and Minnesota's capital. Minneapolis was born across a suspension bridge as the soldiers built lumber and flour mills. Together the twins have evolved into a metropolis complete with the culture of other large cities, but without as many of the problems. Both sisters share a family fondness for the arts, celebrating them with large scale sculptures and hole-in-the-wall galleries and cafes. Theater is especially enamored here, with off-beat and relatively cheap productions abounding. The 10,000 lakes within the metropolitan area and the nightly summertime music and events in all of the city's parks are enough to send anyone outdoors. Together progressive Minneapolis and traditional St. Paul join forces, creating a resourceful and dynamic duo.

PRACTICAL INFORMATION

Emergency: 911.

Visitor Information: Minneapolis Convention and Visitors Association, 1219 Marquette Ave. (348-4313). Open Mon.-Fri. 8am-5:30pm. Also in the City Center Shopping area, 2nd level skyway, open Mon.-Fri. 10am-8pm, Sat. 10am-6pm, Sun. noon-5pm. **St. Paul Convention and Visitors Bureau,** 101 Norwest Center, 55 E. 5th St. (297-6985 or 800-627-6101). Open Mon.-Fri. 8am-5pm. **Cityline** (645-6060) and **The Connection** (922-9000) are 24-hr. hotlines with information on local events, concerts, news, sports, weather, and much more.

Airport: Twin Cities International Airport, South of the cities, on I-494 in Bloomington (726-8100). **Northwest Airlines** has its headquarters here. **Airport Express** (726-6400) runs to downtown and suburban hotels, leaving from the lower level near baggage claim (5am-midnight; $6 to St. Paul, $8 to Minneapolis). Take bus #35 to Minneapolis ($1.60 peak, $1.35 off-peak; service available to the airport 6-8am and to downtown Minneapolis 3-4:45pm). Otherwise, take bus #7 to Washington Ave. in Minneapolis, or transfer at Fort Snelling for bus #9 to downtown St. Paul. Taxis are about $18 to Minneapolis, $15 to St. Paul.

Amtrak: 730 Transfer Rd. (800-872-7245), on the east bank off University Ave. S.E., between the Twin Cities. A nice station, but a fair distance from both downtowns. Take bus #7. Trains to Chicago (1 per day, 8½ hr., $72); Milwaukee (1 per day, $68). Open daily 6am-12:30am.

Greyhound: In **Minneapolis,** 29 9th St. at 1st Ave. N. (800-231-2222), 1 block northwest of Hennepin Ave. Very convenient. Open daily 24 hr. with security. In **St. Paul,** 7th St. at St. Peter (222-0509), 3 blocks east of the Civic Center in a somewhat unsafe area of town. Open daily 5:30am-8:10pm. To: Chicago (9 per day, $55, $44 with 14 day advance); New York (3 per day, $119/90); Seattle (3 per day, $99); Des Moines (3 per day, $52/39).

Public Transport: Metropolitan Transit Commission, 560 6th Ave. N. (827-7733). Call for information and directions Mon.-Fri. 6am-11pm, Sat.-Sun. 7am-11pm. Bus service for both cities. Some buses operate 4:30am-12:45am, others shut down earlier. Fare $1.10 peak hours of 6-9am and 3:30-6:30pm, 85¢ off-peak, ages under 18 25¢, off-peak express 25¢ extra. #16 bus connects the two downtowns (50 min.); the #94 freeway express bus is much faster (25-30 min.). **University of Minnesota Bus,** 625-9000. Buses run 7am-10pm. Free for students to campus locations and even into St. Paul. Off-campus routes 35-85¢, $1.10 peak.

Car Rental: Ugly Duckling Rent-A-Car, 6405 Cedar Ave. S. (861-7545), Minneapolis, near the airport. Used cars from $20 per day with 100 free mi., weekly from $119. Open Mon.-Fri. 9am-6pm, Sat. noon-4pm, or by appointment. Must be 23. Major credit card or a $300-500 deposit required. **Thrift Car Rental,** 160 E. 5th St. (227-7690). $38 with 200 mi. free, 20¢ each additional mi., $125 weekly with 2000 mi. free. Must be 21 with major credit card; $3 surcharge if under 25.

Taxi: Yellow Taxi (824-4444) in Minneapolis. **Yellow Cab** (222-4433) in St. Paul. Base rate $1.75, $1.30 per mi.

Help Lines: Contact, Twin Cities help line (341-2896); **Crime Victim Center,** 822 S. 3rd St., St. Paul (340-5400). Open 24 hrs. **Gay-Lesbian Helpline,** 822-8661. **Gay-Lesbian Information Line**: 822-0127.

Post Office: In **Minneapolis,** 1st St. and Marquette Ave. (349-4957), next to the Mississippi River. General Delivery open Mon.-Fri. 8:00am-5pm, Sat. 9am-noon. **ZIP code:** 55401. In **St. Paul,** 180 E. Kellogg Blvd. (293-3011). General Delivery open Mon.-Fri. 6am-6pm, Sat. 6am-1pm. **ZIP code:** 55101.

Area Code: 612.

In Minneapolis, the streets run east-west and Avenues run north-south. **Hennepin Avenue** is an important line which crosses the Mississippi and goes through downtown, curving south towards uptown. In St. Paul, the more residential and quieter city, navigation is more confusing. **Grand Avenue** (east-west) and **Snelling Avenue** (north-south) are major thoroughfares. **I-94** (east-west) and **I-35** (north-south) traverse both cities and can get you to your destination much faster than local roads. Many downtown streets in both cities parallel the curving Mississippi, so it is wise to acquire a good street map. A second-story tunnel system called **Skywalks** connects more than ten square blocks of buildings in each downtown area, protecting workers from the bitter winter cold and resembling more than slightly hamster habi-trails.

ACCOMMODATIONS AND CAMPING

While cheap airport hotels abound in the Twin Cities, most are of dubious cleanliness and safety. The convention and visitors bureaus have useful lists of **B&Bs.** The **University of Minnesota Housing Office** (624-2994; see Practical Information), has a list of rooms in different locations around the city that rent on a daily ($13-45) or weekly basis. The **Oakmere Home Hostel (HI/AYH),** 8212 Oakmere Rd. (944-1210), in Bloomington has beautiful rooms on wooded lakefront property and a friendly proprietor. Singles are $15. It's somewhat remote; the Minneapolis #44a bus comes to the area Mon.- Fri. three times per day ($1.60). The closest state park camping is in the **Hennepin Parks** system, 25 mi. outside the cities.

College of St. Catherine, Caecilian Hall (HI/AYH), 2004 Randolph Ave. (690-6604), St. Paul. Take St. Paul bus #7 or 14, or call for directions. 60 stark but quiet dorm rooms near the river in a nice neighborhood. Shared bath, kitchenette. Free local calls. No membership discount. Still worth the price for singles $14. Doubles $26. Triples $32. Max. stay 2 weeks. Open June-mid-Aug.

Kaz's Home Hostel (822-8286), in South Minneapolis. Call for directions. One room with 2 beds. Check-in 5-9pm. Curfew 11pm, checkout 9am. Max. stay 3 nights. $10. Reservations required.

Evelo's Bed and Breakfast, 2301 Bryant Ave. (374-9656), in South Minneapolis. A 15-min. walk from uptown; take bus #17 from downtown. 3 comfortable rooms with elegant wallpaper and furnishings in a beautiful house filled with Victorian artifacts. Friendly owners. Singles $40. Doubles $50. Reservations required.

Town and Country Campground, 12630 Boone Ave. S. (445-1756), 15 mi. south of downtown Minneapolis. From I-35 W., go west on Rte. 13 to Rte. 101 for ½ mi., then left onto Boone Ave. 60 sites. Well-maintained, with laundry and pool; quiet, but clearly close to an urban area. Sites $12 for 2, with electricity $15, full hookup $17. Each additional person $1.

Minneapolis Northwest I-94 KOA (420-2255), on Rte. 101 west of I-94 exit 213, 15 mi. north of Minneapolis. All the classic KOA amenities: pool, sauna, and showers. Sites $15.50, with water and electricity $17.50. Each additional person after 2, $2, $1.50 for kids.

FOOD

The Twin Cities' love of music and art carries over to their culinary choices—small cafes with nightly music and poetry readings are very popular—enjoy a thick slice of cake and any variation of mocha, or just sit and people watch. **Uptown** in Minneapolis has plenty of funky and eclectic restaurants and bars, without high prices.

The **Warehouse District**, near downtown Minneapolis, and **Victoria Crossing** (at Victoria and Grand St.) in St. Paul, serve the dessert crowd with pastries worthy of a meal. **Dinkytown** and the **West Bank** cater to student appetites with many low-end, dark, and intriguing places.

Minneapolis

The Loring Cafe, 1624 Harmon Pl. (332-1617), next to Loring Park and the Loring Theater. A truly beautiful cafe with extraordinary pasta and pizza ($8-11) and desserts ($3-5). A great place for dinner, or just for drinks or coffee. A good bar, too, with live music and no cover. Open Sun.-Thurs. 11am-11pm, Fri.-Sat. 11am-2am.

Lowry's, 1934 Hennepin Ave. S. (871-0806). Elegant pasta pizza, risotto, and polenta ($7-12). Open Mon.-Thurs. 7am-10pm, Fri. 7am-11pm, Sat. 10am-11pm, Sun. 10am-9pm.

It's Greek to Me, 626 Lake St. (825-9922), at Lyndale Ave. Take bus #4 south. Great Greek food that anybody can understand. Gyros $4. Dinners $8-13. Open daily 11am-11pm.

Annie's Parlor, 313 14th Ave. S.E. (379-0744), in Dinkytown, 406 Cedar Ave.; West Bank (339-6207), and 2916 Hennepin Ave. (825-4455), uptown. Classic malts that are a meal in themselves ($3.25) and great hamburgers ($3.25-5). Open Mon.-Thurs. 11am-11pm, Fri.-Sat. 11am-12:30am, Sun. 11am-10pm.

Mud Pie, 2549 Lyndale Ave. S. (872-9435), at 26th. Ask your waitron at this vegetarian/Mexican restaurant about their nationally renowned veggie burger ($4.75). Excellent black cherry kafir ($1). Open Mon.-Thurs. 11am-10pm, Fri. 11am-11pm, Sat. 8am-11pm, Sun. 8am-10pm. Breakfast served weekends only.

Blue Nile, 3008 Lyndale Ave. S. (823-8029), at Lake. Use your fingers to eat at this traditional Ethiopian restaurant. Entrees $5-10. Open Mon.-Thurs. 11am-10pm, Fri. 11am-11pm, Sat. 9am-11pm, Sun. 9am-10pm.

St. Paul

Café Latté, 850 Grand Ave. (224-5687), near Victoria Crossing. Cafeteria-style but elegant, with bi-level seating. Delicious, enormous chocolate cakes ($2.25). Try a steaming milk drink called Hot Moos ($1.65); the Swedish Hot Moo with cinnamon, cardamon, and maple syrup is especially good. Lines usually long. Open Mon.-Thurs. 10am-11pm, Fri. 10am-midnight, Sat. 9am-midnight, Sun. 9am-10pm.

Motor Oil Coffee Shop, 1166 Selby Ave. (647-1561). This small local hangout is an interesting slice of St. Paul's artsy life. Grease your wheels with a cup of coffee (65¢) and scrutinize the art in the adjoining **Speedboat Gallery.** Live music several times a month. Open Mon.-Fri. 11am-midnight, Sat. 2pm-midnight.

Table of Contents and **Hungry Mind Bookstore,** 1648 Grand Ave. (699-6595). An awesome bookstore attached to this classy cafe. Wafer crust pizza $4.50. Poetry readings often. Open Mon.-Thurs. 9am-10pm, Fri.-Sat. 9am-11:30pm, Sun. 10am-6pm.

St. Paul Farmers Market, 5th St. (227-6856), at Wall Market downtown. Fresh produce and baked goods. Get there before 10am on Sat. for the best quality and widest selection or after noon for the best bargains. Call to verify location and hours. Open Sat. 6am-1pm and May-Oct. Sun. 8am-1pm.

Mickey's Dining Car, 36 W. 7th St. (222-5633), kitty-corner to the Greyhound station. Small, cheap, and convenient; a great spot for wee-hour munchies runs. Steak and eggs from $4, lunch and dinner from $3. Open 24 hrs.

SIGHTS

Minneapolis

Situated in the land of 10,000 lakes, Minneapolis boasts a few of its own. Ringed by stately mansions, **Lake of the Isles,** off Franklin Ave., about 1½ mi. from downtown, is an excellent place to meet the local population of Canadian geese. Bikers, skaters, and joggers constantly round **Lake Calhoun,** on the west end of Lake St. south of Lake of Isles, making it a hectic social and recreational hotspot. Rent skates and roller blades at **Rolling Soles,** 1700 W. Lake St. (823-5711; skates $3 per hr.,

$7.50 per day; blades $5 per hr., $10 per day; open Mon.-Fri. 10am-9pm, Sat.-Sun. 9am-9pm, weather permitting). The **Minneapolis Park and Recreation Board** (348-2226) rents canoes ($4.50 per hr.) at the northeast corner of Lake Calhoun. Situated in a more residential neighborhood, **Lake Harriet** has a tiny paddleboat, a stage with occasional free concerts, and an endless marathon of joggers. The city provides 28 mi. of trails along these lakes for cycling, roller skating, roller blading, jogging, or strolling on a sunny afternoon; take bus #28 to all three lakes.

One of the top modern art museums in the country, the **Walker Art Center,** 725 Vineland Place (375-7622), a few blocks from downtown, draws thousands with daring exhibits and an impressive permanent collection, including works by Lichtenstein and Warhol. (Open Tues.-Sat. 10am-8pm, Sun. 11am-5pm. $3, seniors free, ages 12-18 and students with ID $2. Free on Thurs.) Inside is an excellent, not-too-expensive cafe (sandwiches $1.50-2.50; open Tues.-Sun. 11:30am-3pm), and adjacent is the Guthrie Theater (see Entertainment). Next to the Walker, the **Minneapolis Sculpture Garden** displays dozens of sculptures and a fountain in a maze of exquisitely landscaped trees and flowers. The **Minneapolis Institute of Arts,** 2400 3rd Ave. S. (870-3131), contains Egyptian, Chinese, American, and European art. Take bus #9. (Open Tues.-Sat. 10am-5pm, Thurs. 10am-9pm, Sun. noon-5pm. Free. Special exhibits $3, students, ages 12-18 and seniors $2; free to all Thurs. 5-9pm.)

St. Anthony Falls and Upper Locks, 1 Portland Ave. (333-5336), downtown, has a free observation deck that overlooks the Mississippi River (open April-Nov. daily 9am-10pm). Several miles downstream, Minnehaha Park provides a breathtaking view of **Minnehaha Falls,** immortalized in Longfellow's longwinded *Song of Hiawatha.* (Take bus #7 from Hennepin Ave. downtown.)

Just 10 mi. outside Minneapolis is the **Mall of America,** 60 E. Broadway, Bloomington (883-8850), the largest mall in the U.S. Normally malls are not considered tourist fare, but have ever seen one with an indoor roller coaster and carousel? Two mi. walks inside and more stores than you could shop in a weekend. A great rainy day excursion. Take I-35E South to I-494W to the 24th Ave. exit and follow signs. (Open daily Mon.-Sat. 10am-9:30pm, Sun. 11am-7pm.)

St. Paul

The capital city of Minnesota boasts some unique architectural sites. West of downtown, Summit Avenue stretches from the Mississippi to the capitol, displaying the nation's longest continuous stretch of Victorian homes, including the Governor's Mansion and the former homes of American novelist F. Scott Fitzgerald and railroad magnate James J. Hill. Most of these grand mansions were built in the 19th century with railroad money. Overlooking the capitol on Summit stands **St. Paul's Cathedral,** 239 Selby Ave. (228-1766), a scaled-down version of St. Peter's in Rome (open Thurs.-Tues. 7:30am-5:45pm). Battle school fieldtrips to see the golden horses atop the ornate **State Capitol** (296-3962 or 297-1503), at Cedar and Aurora St. (open Mon.-Fri. 9am-5pm, Sat. 10am-4pm, Sun. 1-4pm; tours on the hour Mon.-Fri. 9am-4pm, Sat. 10am-3pm, Sun 1-3pm). The nearby **Minnesota History Center,** 345 Kellogg Blvd. W. (296-1430), an organization older than the state itself, has moved to an impressive new building on Kellogg Blvd., where it houses a cafe and gift shop, as well as three exhibit galleries on (what else?) Minnesota history. The society also recreates life in the fur trapping era at **Fort Snelling,** Rte. 5 and 55 (725-2413). At the site of the original French settlement, this park teems with costumed role-playing artisans and guides (call for information and admission prices). Housing the **Minnesota Museum of Art** is the historic **Landmark Center,** 75 W. 5th St. (292-3225), a grandly restored 1894 Federal Court building replete with towers and turrets, a collection of pianos, art exhibits, a concert hall, and four restored courtrooms. (Open Mon.-Wed. and Fri. 8am-5pm, Thurs. 8am-8pm, Sat. 10am-5pm, Sun. 1-5pm. Free. Tours given Thurs. 11am and Sun. 2pm.) The Minnesota Museum of Art houses other collections in the **Jemne Building** at St. Peter and Kellogg Blvd.

A giant iguana sculpture basks outside the **Science Museum,** 30 E. 10th St. (221-9454), near the intersection of Exchange and Wabasha St. Aside from the mammoth reptile, the museum houses an array of informative exhibits, including an extensive anthropology section. The **McKnight-3M Omnitheater** (221-9400) inside presents a mind-swelling array of gigantic films. (Museum open Mon.-Fri. 9:30am-9pm, Sat. 9am-9pm, Sun. 10am-9pm. Exhibit-only tickets $5.50, seniors and under 13 $4.50; with theater $6.50, seniors and kids $5.50.)

Metro Connections (333-8687) gives tours of Minneapolis and St. Paul ($16, seniors $14, kids 6-14 $9). Also **Grayline** bus tours (591-9099; $15, seniors $13, ages 7-14 $7). Mississippi River paddle boat tours are also available (227-1100; $7.50, seniors $6.50, kids $5.50).

ENTERTAINMENT AND EVENTS

With more theaters per capita than any U.S. city outside of New York, the Twin Cities' theater scene can't be touched. The brightest star in this constellation is the **Guthrie Theater,** 725 Vineland Pl. (377-2224), just off Hennepin Ave. in Minneapolis, adjacent to the Walker Art Center. The Guthrie repertory company performs here from June to March. (Box office open Mon.-Fri. 9am-6pm, Sat. 10am-4pm, Sun. 11am-7pm. Tickets $9-38, rush tickets 10 min. before the show $6.)

The **Children's Theater Company,** 3rd Ave. at 24th S. (874-0400), by the Minneapolis Institute of Art, puts on classics and innovative productions for all ages Sept.-June. (Box office open Mon.-Sat. 9am-5pm, Sun. noon-5pm. Tickets $12-20, seniors, students, and kids $9-16. Student rush tickets 15 min. before performance $6.)

In July and early August, **Orchestra Hall,** 1111 Nicollet Mall (371-5656), in downtown Minneapolis, hosts the **Sommerfest,** a month-long celebration of Viennese music performed by the **Minnesota Orchestra.** (Box office open Mon.-Sat. 10am-6pm. Tickets $10-30. Student rush tickets 30 min. before show $6.50.) Don't miss the free coffee concerts and nighttime dance lessons at nearby **Peavey Plaza,** in Nicollet Mall, surrounding a spectacular fountain (no wading allowed).

St. Paul's glass-and-brick, accordion-fronted **Ordway Music Theater,** 345 Washington St. (224-4222), is one of the most beautiful public spaces for music in the country. The **St. Paul Chamber Orchestra,** the **Schubert Club,** and the **Minnesota Opera Company** perform here. (Box office open Mon.-Sat. 10am-9pm. Tickets $10-50.) Also notable is the **Theatre de la jeune lune,** (Theater of the young moon), which performs (in English) at the **Loring Playhouse,** 1645 Hennepin Ave. (333-6200; tickets $8-17), and the **Penumbra Theatre Company,** 270 N. Kent St., St. Paul (224-3180), Minnesota's only professional African-American theater company, which performed many of former St. Paul resident August Wilson's early plays.

The Twin Cities are filled with parks, and almost all of them feature free summertime evening concerts. For information on dates and locations, check at one of the visitors centers. The **Harriet Bandshell** (348-7275) hatches rock, blues, jazz, and high school bands and choirs throughout the summer (take bus #28). Also popular are **Loring Park's** Monday evening events (348-8226), featuring free local bands, followed by vintage films, on the hill toward the north edge. Take bus #1, 4, 6, or 28 going south. Also worth noting is the **Rooftop Cinema** (824-1240) at Calhoun Square, Lake, and Hennepin, where classic films are shown on the side of a building every Wed. night at dusk (free).

A giggle of comedy and improvisational clubs make the Twin Cities a downright hilarious place to visit. Dudley Riggs's **Brave New Workshop,** 2605 Hennepin Ave. (332-6620), stages consistently good musical comedy shows in an intimate club. (Box office open Tues.-Sat. 4-10pm. Performances Tues.-Sat. at 8pm. Tickets $12-15.) The **Comedy Gallery** (219 Main St., S.E., Minneapolis, and Galtier Plaza, 175 E. 5th St., St. Paul; 536-1923; tickets normally $5, high profile comedians $10-12) features individual comedians.

The Twin Cities have made extraordinary and far-ranging contributions to popular music in the last decade and a half. Minnesota-bred artists from all genres emerged from local-legend status to make their mark on national and international stages; as many others remain cult figures to this day. Prince still casts the greatest shadow; his state-of-the-art Paisley Park studio complex outside the city draws bands from all over to the Great White North. The post-punk scene thrives in the Land of 10,000 Aches: Soul Asylum, Bob Mould and the late, great Hüsker Dü, as well as the best bar band in the world, the ill-fated Replacements, rocked rafters here before it all went big (or bad). For great live music with high and low profile bands, try the **Uptown Bar and Cafe,** 3018 Hennepin (823-4719). (Open 8am-1am. Shows at 10:30pm. Weekend cover varies. For band information, call 823-5704.) The **400 Bar,** 4th St. (332-2903), at Cedar Ave. on the West Bank, is a great place, featuring live music nightly on a minuscule stage. (Open daily noon-1am. Occasional $2 cover.) Also, **First Avenue and 7th St. Entry,** 701 N. First Ave., Minneapolis (338-8388), Prince's old court where he still occasionally resides (open Mon.-Sat. 8pm-1am; cover $1-5, for concerts $7-18) or the Purple One's latest haunt, **Glam Slam,** 110 N. 5th St., Minneapolis (338-3383; live music Mon., cover $3-10; open Mon.-Sat. 8pm-1am). Note: At press time, Prince had apparently changed his name to ✳. This may change. **Mississippi Live** at Riverplace (331-3589), Hennepin and Main St., and **St. Anthony Main,** 1 Main St., are enclosed areas with multiple bars making bar hopping quite easy. Most importantly, these hangouts are country music places and hop at night. **The Gay 90s,** Hennepin Ave. (333-7755), at 4th St., is the popular gay nightspot (open daily 8pm-1am).

For general information on the local music scene and other events, pick up the free *City Pages* or *Twin Cities Reader,* or buy *Minneapolis-St. Paul* magazine ($2.50) available throughout the cities. In January, the 10-day **St. Paul Winter Carnival,** near the state capitol, cures cabin fever with ice sculptures, ice fishing, parades, and skating contests. On the Fourth of July, St. Paul celebrates **Taste of Minnesota** on the Capitol Mall. Following this, the nine-day **Minneapolis Aquatennial** begins, with concerts, parades, art exhibits, and kids dripping sno-cones on their shirts. (Call The Connection, 922-9000, for info on all these events.) During late August and early September, spend a day at the **Minnesota State Fair,** one of the largest in the nation, at Snelling and Como, or the **Renaissance Festival** (445-7361) in Shakopee. The **Minnesota Zoo** (432-9000), Rte. 32, houses a wide variety of well-maintained habitats accessible by path or monorail. (Open Mon.-Sat. 10am-6pm, Sun. 10am-8pm; off-season daily 10am-4pm. $6, seniors $4, ages 3-12 $2.50.)

The **Hubert H. Humphrey Metrodome,** 501 Chicago Ave. S. (332-0386), in downtown Minneapolis, houses the Minnesota Twins, the Twin Cities' baseball team, and the Minnesota Vikings, the resident football team. The Timberwolves kindle basketball hardwood at the **Target Center;** the North Stars light up the rink of the **Met Center** in Bloomington.

NORTHERN MINNESOTA

■■■ CHIPPEWA NATIONAL FOREST

The Norway pine forests, interspersed with lovely strands of birch, thicken as you move north into **Chippewa National Forest,** font of the Mississippi River, and nesting grounds to more eagles than anywhere else in the U.S. Nearly half of this "forest" is wetlands and lakes, making camping and canoeing the popular activities. Leech, Cass, and Winnibigoshish (win-nuh-buh-GAH-shish or simply "Winnie") are the largest of the lakes. The national forest shares territory with the **Leech Lake Indian Reservation,** home of 4560 members of the Minnesota Chippewa tribe, the fourth largest tribe in the U.S. The Chippewa migrated from the Atlantic coast, through the

424 ■ THE GREAT LAKES

Great Lakes, and into this area in the early 1700s, successfully pushing out the local Sioux. In the mid-1800s, the government seized most of the Chippewa's land, setting up reservations like Leech Lake.

■ The National Forest

Use the town of **Walker** on Leech Lake as a gateway to the Chippewa National Forest. Travelers, especially walkers, can find information on the tourist facilities at the **Leech Lake Area Chamber of Commerce** on Rte. 371 downtown (547-1313 or 800-833-1118; open Mon.-Fri. 8am-5pm, Sat. 9am-4pm, Sun. 12am-4pm). Material on abundant, cheap outdoor activities is available just east of the Chamber of Commerce, heading away from town, at the **Forest Office** (547-1044; open Mon.-Fri. 7:30am-5pm). **Greyhound** (722-5591), runs from Minneapolis to Walker (5½ hr., $21), stopping at the Lake View Laundromat, just east of the Chamber of Commerce. The **Deep Portage Conservation Reserve** (682-2325, call only on Sat.), 10 mi. south of Walker (take Rte. 371, left on Woman Lake Rd., right at Deep Portage Rd., follow the dirt road), runs naturalist workshops including bird hikes, morel (an edible mushroom) hunts, and discussions on water conservation ($3, Sat. 1:30pm).

The **area code** for the Chippewa National Forest Area is 218.

■ Lake Itasca State Park

The **Headwaters of the Mississippi** trickle out of **Lake Itasca,** 30 mi. west of Walker on Rte. 200, the only place where mere mortals can wade easily across the Mississippi. The comfortable **Mississippi Headwaters HI/AYH-Hostel** (266-3415), located in a newly-renovated log building, has 33 beds with some four-bed rooms for families. It's open in the winter to facilitate access to the park's excellent cross-country skiing ($10, nonmembers $13, kids $7). The park itself has **campgrounds** with showers (sites $12, with electricity $14.50. 2-day vehicle permit $4). The **Itasca State Park Office** (266-3654), through the north entrance and down County Rd. 38, has more information (open daily 8am-10pm, ranger on call after hours). **Bicycles** and **boats** are available from **Itasca Sports Rental** (266-3654 ext. 150) in the park. (Open May-Oct. daily 7am-9pm, single-speed bikes $2.50 per hr., $15 per day; canoes $3 first hr., $1.50 per hr. thereafter, $12 per day.)

For those who eventually come to crave the Great *Indoors*, there are alternatives to camping. **Park Rapids Inn** (732-9402) offers separated, wood-paneled rooms (singles $33, doubles $42, students 10% off). The **Dickson Viking Huss** (732-8089) in Park Rapids, south of Itasca, offers rooms ($22-$43) in a well-kept modern house; the **Dorset Schoolhouse** (732-1377) in nearby Dorset offers elegance and perhaps education—all notices are on small blackboards. (Summer Sun.-Thurs. singles $35, doubles $50, Fri.-Sat. $40 and $60; fall $35 and $50; winter-spring $30 and $40.)

■ Bemidji

Famous for its life-size statue of Paul Bunyan, Bemidji lumbers northeast of Lake Itasca. The town has a **Greyhound** station at 902½ Paul Bunyan Dr. (751-7600; open Mon.-Sat. 8am-1:30pm and 3-5pm, Sun. 8-8:30am and 12:30-1:30pm; Duluth to Bemidji, 3½ hr., $16), but there is no bus from the town to the park. In Bemidji, you can stay at **Taber's Log Cabin Court,** 2404 Bemidji Ave. (751-5781), a collection of 18 miniature cabins with kitchenettes near the shore of Lake Bemidji ($35-75; open May-Oct.). The motels across from the Greyhound station (see below) are fairly reasonable; try the **Lakeside Motel,** 809 Paul Bunyan Dr. N.E. (751-3266). (Singles $30, off-season $22; doubles $46, off-season $28.) The **post office** (751-5600) is open Mon.-Fri. 8:30am-5pm, Sat. 9:30am-2pm.

■■■ THE IRON RANGE

Inland from the North Shore lies the **Iron Range**, home to ore boom-towns and hills carved in a man-made parody of the Southwest. Adjacent to the Superior National Forest and Boundary Waters Canoe Area Wilderness, this region offers natural beauty as well as an interesting perspective on the history of technology.

■ Ely, Soudan, and Chisholm

Ely serves as a launching pad both into the BWCAW and the Iron Range. The **International Wolf Center**, 1396 Rte. 169 (365-4685), has informative displays on these creatures. (Open daily 8am-8pm; outer displays free, other displays $4, seniors and children $2.50.) **Kring's Kabins and Kampgrounds**, 60 W. Lakeview Pl., Ely (365-6637), has a loft full of bunks for $10 per night, including linen and showers (sites $7, RV $10, water and electricity $1.50).

The **Soudan Underground Mine** (753-2245), in Soudan west of Ely on Rte. 1, was retired in the middle of digging the 27th level, a full half-mile below the surface. Visitors take a 90-min. tour down the 11°-from-the-vertical mineshaft and are shown the principles and techniques of underground iron mining. unfortunately, the tour shies clear of the **Soudan Underground Research Site,** where an experiment to detect spontaneous conversion of nucleons to energy enjoys the protection of a half-mile-thick rock roof. ($5, ages 5-12 $3, plus state park vehicle fee. Tours Memorial Day-Labor Day every ½ hr., 9:30am-4pm, gates open until 6pm.) A little past the mine on the same road is **McKinley Park Campground** (753-5921), overlooking gorgeous Vermilion Lake (sites $7.50, electricity and water $9). **Chisholm,** to the southwest on U.S. 169, is home to **Ironworld USA** (254-3321 or 800-372-6437), a mining theme park which also contains displays on the area's ethnicity. (Admission $6.25, seniors $5.25, ages 7-17 $4; open Memorial Day-Labor Day daily 10am-7pm.) The **Chisholm KOA** (254-3635) kamps nearby. (Open May-early Oct. Tent sites $13, with water and electricity $15, with above and sewer $17, with cable TV $18, with personal manservant $230.)

■ Hibbing and Grand Rapids

Hometown to Bob Dylan, **Hibbing**, a few miles south of Chisholm, has made a park out of the open-pit **Hull Rust Mahoning Mine** (open mid-May-Sept. daily 9am-7pm). Carfree travelers in particular may wish to pay tribute at the **Greyhound Bus Origin Center,** 23rd St. and 5th Ave. E. (262-3895), which features model buses and more bus cartoons than you ever knew existed. Greyhound's puppyhood was spent here as a transport for miners in the Hibbing area. (Open mid-May-mid-Sept. Mon.-Sat. 9am-5pm. $1, ages 6-12 50¢.) **Grand Rapids**, a paper mill town of 8000, houses the **Forest History Center** (327-4482), with informative exhibits in the Interpretive Center and a recreated turn-of-the-century logging camp. ($3, ages 6-15 $1, family max. $10. Open mid-May-mid-Oct. Mon.-Sat. 10am-5pm, Sun. noon-5pm; interpretive center and trails also open mid-Oct.-mid-May daily noon-4pm.) Grand Rapids is the hometown of Judy Garland, and celebrates this with its own **Yellow Brick Road,** the world's largest collection of Garland memorabilia, in the **Central School,** 10 5th St. N.W., (326-6431; open Mon.-Fri. 9:30am-5pm, Sat. 9:30am-4pm, Sun. noon-4pm; $4, ages 6-12 $2), and a **Judy Garland Festival** (326-6431) every June around her birthday on the 10th.

The **Itascan Motel,** 610 Pokegama Ave. S. (326-3489 or 800-842-7733), has large new rooms with complimentary coffee (singles $30, with kitchenette $36). The **Prairie Lake Campground,** 400 Wabana Rd., 6½ mi. north of Grand Rapids on Rte. 38 (326-8486), has a nice, shady waterfront location. (Tent sites $8, RV with electricity $11, add $1 each for water and sewer, full hookup at 16 of 40 sites, $14.)

The **area code** for the Iron Range is 218.

■■■ THE SUPERIOR NORTH SHORE

The North Shore begins with the majestic **Sawtooth Mountains** just north of Duluth and extends 150 wild and woody miles to Canada. This stretch, defined by **Rte. 61 (North Shore Drive),** encompasses virtually all of Minnesota's Superior lakeshore and supports bear, moose, and the largest U.S. wolf range in the lower 48 states. Each break in the trees lets the driver catch glimpses of Lake Superior, inviting exclamations that the lake is aptly named. Summer brings a human tide to the area, as flocks of tourists drawn by the cool and breezy weather migrate north to fish, camp, hike, and canoe. Bring warm clothes, since even summer temperatures can drop into the low 40s°F at night, even lower in fog.

Practical Information The **Visitors Information Center** (387-2524), Broadway and 1st Ave., has a quiver of information about the area. (Open summer Mon.-Sat. 8am-8pm, Sun. 10am-6pm. Call for winter hours.) The **Gunflint Ranger Station** (387-2451;open summer daily 6am-6pm), ¼ mi. south of town, offers even more information, and issues permits for individual ports of entry into the **Boundary Waters Canoe Area Wilderness (BWCAW),** a unique area including over two million acres of forests and 1100 lakes. There are no roads, phones, electricity, or private dwellings here, and limited motorized vehicle access. Permits are required to enter the BWCAW from May to September. **Grand Marais** serves as the hub of North Shore activity. The 60 mi. **Gunflint Trail,** now widened into an auto road, begins in Grand Marais and continues northwest into the BWCAW.

Happy Trails runs one bus per day up the shore, leaving from the **Duluth Greyhound Station** (722-5591; Duluth-Grand Marais $17.50). The **area code** for the North Shore is 218.

Accommodations and Food Reward yourself at the end of the trail with a stay in the well-kept cabins at **"Spirit of the Land" Island HI/AYH Hostel** (388-2241), on an island in Seagull Lake. The hostel is run by **Wilderness Canoe Base,** which leads canoe trips and summer island camps for various groups. Call from Grand Marais to arrange a boat pick-up. ($10.50, nonmembers $13.50. $2 boat transport. Meals $4-6. Showers $2. Closed Nov. and April.) Although you wouldn't believe it from its elegance, the historic, brightly hand-painted **Naniboujou Lodge** (387-2688), 15 mi. east of Grand Marais on Rte. 61, has some rooms with shared baths for summer/fall family rates ($45, double occupancy $59).

The **South of the Border Cafe** (387-1505)—not a Mexican restaurant, the *other* border—is cheap and popular with fishermen. A big breakfast with 3 eggs, bacon, cheese omelette and toast $3.25. Grand Marais' specialty, the bluefin herring sandwich, is $2.75. (Open summer daily 4am-2pm, Sept.-mid-May 5am-2pm.) The **Angry Trout Cafe** (387-1265), right on the dock, serves up a mean fish and chips ($5.75).

Camping and Sights The North Shore teems with state parks, all beautiful, and most with camping facilities. **Gooseberry Falls** (834-3787) offers thundering cataracts and a popular swimming hole (sites $10, $4 vehicle fee). **Split Rock Lighthouse** shines a little way north of the falls. The lighthouse is situated next to an anomalous magnetic location which once fooled compasses and lured ships onto the rocky shore. Tour the lighthouse and visit the **History Center** (226-4372) to learn about the shipwrecks caused by the rocks' strange magnetic qualities. (Lighthouse and History Center open daily May 15-Oct. 15 9am-5pm; off-season History Center only, Fri.-Sun. noon-4pm. Admission $3 plus $4 vehicle fee.) **Split Rock Lighthouse State Park** (226-3065) has cart-in campsites: borrow a wheelbarrow to move your gear the ½ mi. from the central parking lot. Site #15 even has a split rock of its own (sites $8, $10 with showers). The **Grand Marais Recreation Area** (387-1712), off Rte. 61 in town, is crowded but offers a great view of Lake Superior, and has a pool. (Office open May-mid-Oct. daily 6am-10pm. 300 sites $12 each, with water and electricity $15.50, with full hookup $16.50.)

For the car-free or intrepid, the **North Shore Scenic Railroad** (722-1273) offers a scenic train ride ($16.50, kids 3-11 $8.25) from Duluth to **Two Harbors,** which hosts a **folk festival** (834-4898) the first weekend in July. Trains run less often to Lester River and Palmers along the same route.

Grand Portage, the furthest town north before the Canadian border, runs a ferry to **Isle Royale** (see Michigan). There is a campground adjacent to the marina. (Sites $10; RV hookups $15. Parking at marina $3 per day, $3.50 with trailer.) While waiting for the boat, visit the **Witch Tree,** an ancient, sacred cedar growing out of bare rock. (3 free tours per day; sign up at the **Grand Portage Lodge and Casino** near the marina.)

Outdoors The **Superior Hiking Trail,** presently being constructed in loops off Rte. 61 from Duluth to Canada along the Superior coast, offers excellent hiking opportunities for the carless. For more information write to the **Superior Trail Hiking Association,** P.O. Box 2175, Tofte 55615 (226-3539). **Wilderness Waters Outfitters** (387-2525), just south of Grand Marais on Rte. 61, rents canoes. ($14 per day, $13 per day for more than 4-days; deposit is first day rental. Paddles, life jackets, and car rack included. Open daily 7am-7pm; Nov.-April daily 9am-5pm.) Another equipment store is **Bear Track Outfitting Co.** (387-1162), which rents canoes ($15-32 per day, 7th day free) and kayaks ($32 per day) with free lodging the night before departure; also, winter cabins ($50 for 2 weekdays, $60 weekends) with cross-country skiing out the door. (Open May-Oct. daily 8am-8pm.)

Ohio

Ohio is best known for rust-belt industrial cities like Cincinnati and Cleveland, thought to combine the pollution of the East Coast with the cultural blandness of the Midwest. In reality, these cities have cleaned themselves up, Midwestern blandness is a misrepresentation, and the majority of the state lies outside metropoli in gentle, quintessentially middle-American farmland. Here rolling green wooded hills, verdant river valleys, the Great Lake shore, and enchanting small towns entice you to re-evaluate the mythos of the Midwest.

By the way—never, *ever* confuse Ohio with Iowa or Idaho, or the Tri-State Name Council will place you on their widely-distributed blacklist, and residents of all three otherwise friendly states will scorn and publicly humiliate you. Just a warning.

PRACTICAL INFORMATION

Capital: Columbus.
Tourist Information: State Office of Travel and Tourism, 77 S. High St., P.O. Box 1001, Columbus 43215 (614-466-8844). **Greater Columbus Convention and Visitors Bureau,** 1 Columbus Bldg., 10 W. Broad St. #1300, Columbus 43215 (614-221-6623 or 800-234-2657). Open Mon.-Fri. 8am-5pm.
Time Zone: Eastern. **Postal Abbreviation:** OH
Sales Tax: Does it matter? You've got to pay it no matter what, right?

■■■ CINCINNATI

Longfellow called it the "Queen City of the West." In the 1850s, more prosaic folk tagged it "Porkopolis," alluding to its position as the planet's premier pork-packer. Winged pigs guarding the entrance of downtown's Sawyer Point Park remind visi-

CINCINNATI

tors of the divine swine of yore. Today, pigs on the wing no longer snort through the streets, and the frontier has moved on to parts west; the city instead parades an excellent collection of museums, a renowned zoo, a pleasantly designed waterfront, and a blossom of parks. Hidden in a valley surrounded by seven rolling hills and the Ohio River, Cincinnati has always been surprisingly insulated despite its prosperity.

PRACTICAL INFORMATION

Emergency: 911.

Visitor Information: Cincinnati Convention and Visitors Bureau, 300 W. 6th St. (621-2142). Open Mon.-Fri. 9am-5pm. Pick up an *Official Visitors Guide.* **Information Booth** in Fountain Sq. Open Mon.-Sat. 8:30am-5:30pm. **Info Line,** 421-4636. Lists plays, opera, cruises and symphonies.

Airport: Greater Cincinnati International Airport, in Kentucky, 13 mi. south of Cincinnati. **Jetport Express** (606-283-3151) shuttles to downtown ($10).

Amtrak: (651-3337 or 800-872-7245). To Indianapolis ($30) and Chicago ($61). Open Mon.-Fri. 9:30am-5pm, Tues.-Sun. 11pm-6:30am. Avoid the neighborhood north of the station.

Greyhound: 1005 Gilbert Ave. (352-6000), just past the intersection of E. Court and Broadway. To: Indianapolis ($20.50); Louisville, KY ($19.50); Cleveland ($39); Columbus ($18.50). Open daily 7:30am-6:30am.

Public Transport: Queen City Metro, 122 W. Fifth St. (621-4455). Office has schedules and information. Telephone info Mon.-Fri. 6:30am-6pm, Sat.-Sun. 8am-5pm. Most buses run out of Government Sq. at 5th and Main, to outlying communities. Peak fare 65¢, other times 50¢, weekends 35¢, extra 30¢ to suburbs.

Taxi: Yellow Cab, 241-2100. Base fare $1.50, $1.20 per mi.

Weather Line: 241-1010.

Help Lines: Rape Crisis Center, 216 E. 9th St. (381-5610), downtown. **Gay/Lesbian Community Switchboard:** 221-7800.

Post Office: 122 W. 5th St. (684-5664), between Walnut and Vine St. Open Mon.-Fri. 8am-5pm, Sat. 8am-1pm. **ZIP code:** 45202.

Area Code: 513; Kentucky suburbs 606.

Fountain Square, E. 5th at Vine St., is the focal point of the downtown business community. Cross streets are numbered and designated East or West, with Vine Street as the divider. **Riverfront Stadium,** the **Serpentine Wall** and the **Riverwalk** are down by the river. The **University of Cincinnati** spreads out from Clifton, north of the city. Overlooking downtown from the east, **Mt. Adams,** adjoining Eden Park, harbors Cincinnati's most active nightlife.

ACCOMMODATIONS AND CAMPING

Cincinnati has many motels, but most cheap places and all the campgrounds are outside the heart of the city. Take a car and make reservations, especially on nights of Reds baseball games and on weekends.

Cincinnati Home Hostel (HI/AYH), 2200 Maplewood Ave. (651-2329), 1½ mi. north of downtown. Take bus #64 to Highland and Earnshaw; walking after dark is iffy, especially from the west. A 3-story house with large rooms. Singles $6.

College of Mount St. Joseph, 5701 Delhi Pike (244-4327), about 8 mi. west of downtown off U.S. 50. Take bus #32. Immaculate rooms in a quiet, remote location. Excellent facilities. Cafeteria lunch/dinner $3.50. Singles $15. Doubles $20.

Evendale Motel, 10165 Reading Rd. (563-1570). Take a ride on the Reading bus (not RR) #43 north to Reading and Columbia, then walk ½ hr. north on Reading. Do not pass Go. Do not collect $200. Dark but clean rooms. Singles/doubles $24.

Red Roof Inn, 5900 Pfeiffer Ave. (793-8811), off I-71 in Blue Ash, take exit 15. The reasonable rates of this chain (singles $32) and the location just outside of town make this a strong draw.

Yogi Bear's Camp Resort (398-2901), I-71 exit 25 at Mason. Pricey (basic $22, with water and electricity $29) but within a stone's throw of Kings Island. Sept.-April sites $15. Reservations recommended.

Rose Gardens Resort—KOA Campgrounds (606-428-2000), I-75 exit 166, 30 mi. south of Cincinnati. Tent sites $16. Cabins $25, with water and electricity.

FOOD

The city that gave us the first soap opera, the first baseball franchise (the Redlegs), and the Heimlich maneuver presents as its great culinary contribution **Cincinnati chili.** It's an all-pervasive ritual in local culture, though somehow no other city but Louisville, KY seems to have caught this gastronomical wave. Meat sauce, spaghetti and cheese are the basic ingredients. Chili is cheap; antacid tablets cost extra.

Skyline Chili, everywhere. This chain has over 16 locations, including 9254 Plainfield Rd. (793-3350). Better than other chains. Secret ingredient debated for years. Some say chocolate, but curry is more likely. Open Mon.-Fri. 11am-1am, Sat.-Sun. 11am-3am. 5-way jumbo chili $4.65, cheese coney (hot dog) $1.15.

Izzy's, 819 Elm St. (721-4241), also 610 Main St. A Cincinnati institution founded in 1901. Overstuffed sandwiches and potato pancake $3-4. Izzy's famous reuben $5. Open Mon.-Fri. 7am-5pm, Sat. 7am-4pm; Main St. site open Mon.-Sat. 7am-9pm.

Graeter's, 41 E. 4th St. (381-0653), downtown, and 10 other locations. Since 1870, Graeter's has been pleasing sweet-toothed locals with candy and ice cream made with giant chocolate chips. (Not very) small cone $1.50, $1.60 with chips; larger size 50¢ extra. Open Mon.-Sat. 11am-5:30pm.

Mulane's, 723 Race St. (381-1331). A street-side cafe and restaurant with terrific vegetarian food. Out-of-this world meatless entrees ($4-6), and hearty salads. Live music nightly. Chicken or ham can be added to entrees for $2. Not to be missed. (Open Mon.-Thurs. 11:30am-11pm, Fri. until midnight, Sat. 5pm-midnight.)

Findlay Market, 18th at Elm St., 1½ mi. north of downtown. Produce and picnic items $3-5. Open Wed. 7am-1:30pm, Fri.-Sat. 7am-6pm.

SIGHTS AND EVENTS

Downtown Cincinnati orbits around the **Tyler Davidson Fountain,** the ideal spot to people-watch while admiring this florid 19th-century masterpiece. If you squint your eyes, you can almost see Les Nesman rushing to WKRP to deliver the daily hog report. Check out the expansive gardens at **Proctor and Gamble Plaza,** just east of Fountain Square, or walk along **Fountain Square South,** a shopping and business complex connected by a series of second-floor skywalks. When the visual stimuli exhaust you, prick up your ears for a free concert in front of the fountain, produced by **Downtown Council,** Carew Tower (579-3191), open Mon.-Fri. 8:30am-5pm.

Close to Fountain Square, the **Contemporary Arts Center,** 115 E. 5th St., 2nd floor (721-0390), by Walnut, has earned a strong reputation among the national arts community. It continues to change its exhibits frequently, offering evening films, music, and multi-media performances. (Open Mon.-Sat. 10am-6pm, Sun. 1-5pm. Admission $2, seniors and students $1. Mon. free.) The **Taft Museum,** 316 Pike St. (241-0343), also downtown, has a beautiful collection of painted enamels, as well as pieces by Rembrandt and Whistler. (Open Mon.-Tues. and Thurs.-Sat. 10am-5pm, Sun. 2-5pm. $2, seniors and students $1, free on Sun.)

Cincinnati's answer to Paradise is **Eden Park,** northeast of downtown. Among the park's bounteous fruits is the **Cincinnati Art Museum** (721-5204), with a permanent collection spanning 5000 years, including musical instruments and Near Eastern artifacts. (Take bus #49 to Eden Park Dr. Open Tues.-Sat. 10am-5pm, Sun. noon-5pm. $5, seniors $4, students $2, under 18 free. Sat. free.) The **Krohn Conservatory** (352-4086), one of the largest public greenhouses in the world, illustrates an indoor Eden. (Open daily 10am-5pm. $2, seniors and under 15 $1.)

One mi. west of downtown, the **Union Terminal,** 1031 Western Ave. (241-7257), near the Ezzard Charles Dr. exit off I-75 (take bus #1), functions more as a

CINCINNATI

museum than as a bus terminal. The building itself is a fine example of Art Deco architecture and boasts the world's largest permanent half-dome. Cool down in the Ice-Age world of simulated glaciers inside the **Museum of Natural History** (287-7021), or inter yourself in the carefully constructed artificial cavern, featuring a colony of real live bats. On the other side of the dome, stroll about a model of a pre-1860 Cincinnati street at the **Cincinnati Historical Society** (287-7031), or dazzle your senses in the **Omnimax Theater** (shows Mon.-Thurs. hourly 11am-4pm and 7-8pm, Fri. 11am-4pm and 7-9pm, Sat. 11am-5pm and 7-9pm, Sun. 11am-5pm and 7-8pm). (Museums open Mon.-Sat. 9am-5pm, Sun. 11am-6pm; admission to either museum $5, ages 3-12 $3; to both $8/$4; to Omnimax $6/$4; combo ticket $12/$7.)

The **Cincinnati Zoo,** 3400 Vine St. (281-4700), at Forest Ave., can be reached by car (take Dana Ave. off I-75 or I-71), or by bus (#78 or 49 from Vine and 5th St.). *Newsweek* called it one of the world's "sexiest zoos" (this sort of thing presumably turns them on); the lush greenery and cageless habitats evidently encourage the zoo's gorillas and famous white Bengal tigers to reproduce like animals. (Open in summer daily 9am-dusk, usually 8pm; Labor Day-Memorial Day daily 9am-5pm. Children's Zoo open 10am-7pm. $6, seniors $4.25, and under 12 $3.50. Parking $4.)

Cincinnati is fanatical about sports. The **Reds** major league baseball team (421-7337) and the **Bengals** NFL football team (621-3550) both play in **Riverfront Stadium.** The **Riverfront Coliseum** (241-1818), a Cincinnati landmark, hosts other sports events and concerts year-round. In early July **Summerfair** (800-582-5804), an art extravaganza, is held at **Coney Island,** 6201 Kellogg Ave. (232-8230).

The city basks in its German heritage during **Oktoberfest-Zinzinnati,** held, as Oktoberfests are wont to be, in September (the 3rd weekend, to be precise). More diverse groups celebrate themselves during the **International Folk Festival** two months later. Labor Day's **Riverfest** and mid-October's **Tall Stacks** memorialize the roles of the river and steamboats in Cincinnati's history. For more info on festivals, contact the Convention and Visitors Bureau (see Practical Information).

ENTERTAINMENT AND NIGHTLIFE

The cliff-hanging communities that line the steep streets of Mt. Adams also support a vivacious arts and entertainment industry. Perched on its own wooded hill is the **Playhouse in the Park,** 962 Mt. Adams Circle (421-3888), a theater-in-the-round remarkably adaptable to many styles of drama. The regular season runs mid-Sept.-June, plus special summer programs. Performances daily Tues.-Sun. (Tickets $17-31, 15 min. before the show student and senior rush tickets $9.)

For a drink and a voyage back to the 19th century, try **Arnold's,** 210 E. 8th St. (421-6234), Cincinnati's oldest tavern, between Main St. and Sycamore downtown. After 9pm, Arnold's does that ragtime, traditional jazz, and swing thing while serving sandwiches ($4-5) and dinners ($6-10). (Open Mon.-Sat. 11am-1am.) Check out the antique toys inside or listen to jazz and blues in the courtyard at **Blind Lemon,** 936 Hatch St. (241-3885), at St. Gregory St. in Mt. Adams. (Open Mon.-Fri. 4pm-2:30am, Sat.-Sun. 3pm-2:30am. Music at 9:30pm.) The **City View Tavern,** also in Mt. Adams at 403 Oregon St. (241-8439), off Monastery St., is hard to find but worth the effort. This down-to-earth local favorite proudly displays an article heralding it as one of the best dives in Cincinnati. The deck in back offers a great view of the city's skyline and the Ohio River. Locally brewed draft beer 90¢. (Open Mon.-Fri. noon-1am, Sat. 1pm-1am, Sun. 2-11pm.)

The University of Cincinnati's **Conservatory of Music** (556-9430) often gives free classical recitals. A tad more upscale, the **Music Hall,** 1243 Elm St. (721-8222), hosts the **Cincinnati Symphony Orchestra** (381-3300) Sept.-May (tickets $9-48). A summer season is held at **Riverbend** on Old Coney Island in June and July (tickets $19-21). Other companies performing at the Music Hall are the **Cincinnati Ballet Company** (621-5219; Sept.-May, tickets $6-45) and **Cincinnati Opera** (241-2742; limited summer schedule). For updates, call **Dial the Arts** (751-2787).

■ Near Cincinnati

If you can't get to California's Napa or Sonoma Valleys, the next best thing may be
Meiers Wine Cellars, 6955 Plainfield Pike (891-2900). Take I-71 to exit 12 or I-75
to Galbraith Rd. Free tours of Ohio's oldest and largest winery allow you to observe
the entire wine-making operation and taste the fermented fruits of their labor. (Free
tours June-Oct. every hr. 10am-3pm; other times of the year by appointment.)

In the town of **Mason,** 24 mi. north of Cincinnati off I-71 at exit #24, the **Kings
Island** amusement park (241-5600) cages **The Beast,** the world's second-fastest
roller coaster. Admission entitles you to unlimited rides, attractions, and the opportunity to buy expensive food. Lines shrink after dark. (Open May 27-Sept. 2, Sun.-Fri.
10am-10pm, Sat. 10am-11pm. $23, seniors and ages 3-6 $11.50.)

■■■ CLEVELAND

"Just drive north until the sky and all the buildings turn gray. Then you're in Cleveland." One of Cleveland's many critics uttered this quote hoping to achieve the "city
cliche" honors normally reserved for Mark Twain. Alas, this witticism's author has
remained obscure, much as has any praise for poor, beleaguered Cleveland. These
days a visit to the city suggests that Cleveland may have an image adjustment on the
horizon. Business leaders are working to creatively convert its resources into new
and vital forms. Cleveland's old warehouses on the Cuyahoga River have been
reworked into rollicking nightclubs, and the much-anticipated Rock and Roll Hall of
Fame will soon open, drawing scads of youthful tourists. They will likely be
impressed with the city's arts scene and rapidly gentrifying downtown. With skillful
management, Cleveland could change from a popular joke to a pop culture haven.

PRACTICAL INFORMATION

Emergency: 911.
Visitor Information: Cleveland Convention and Visitors Bureau, 3100 Tower
City Ctr. (621-4110 or 800-321-1001), in Terminal Tower at Public Square. Free
maps and helpful staff. Publishes the mind-boggling *Greater Cleveland Travel
Planner* with phone numbers and addresses of every conceivable attraction;
write for a copy. Open Mon.-Fri. 9:30am-4:30pm, Sat.-Sun. 11am-4pm.
Cleveland Hopkins International Airport: (265-6030) in Brookpark, 10 mi. west
of downtown, but accessible on the RTA airport rapid line, which goes to the Terminal Tower on train #66X ("Red Line") for $1.25.
Amtrak: 200 Cleveland Memorial Shoreway N.E. (696-5115 or 800-872-7245),
across from Municipal Stadium, east of City Hall. To: New York ($94) and Chicago
($73). Open Mon.-Sat. 10:30am-4:30pm.
Greyhound: 1465 Chester Ave. (781-0520; schedules and fares 781-1400), at E.
14th St. near RTA bus lines and about 7 blocks east of Terminal Tower. To: Chicago ($39), New York City ($92); Pittsburgh ($21); Cincinnati ($41).
Regional Transit Authority (RTA): 315 Euclid Ave. (566-5074), across the street
from Woolworth's. Schedules for city buses and rapid transit lines. Bus lines, connecting with the Rapid stops, provide public transport to most of the metropolitan area. 24-hr. **rideline** (623-0180), accessible from touch-tone phones. Trains
$1.50, buses $1.25 ("local" service, free transfers—remember to ask), $1.50
express. Office open Mon.-Fri. 7am-6pm. Phone info Mon.-Sat. 6am-6pm (621-
9500). Service daily 4:30-12:30am.
Taxi: Yellow Cab, 623-1550; 24 hrs. **Americab,** 429-1111.
Help Line: Rape Crisis Line, 391-3912. 24 hrs.
Post Office: 2400 Orange Ave. (443-4199 or 443-4096). Open Mon.-Fri. 8am-7pm.
ZIP code: 44101.
Area Code: 216.

Terminal Tower in **Public Square** cleaves the land into east and west. North-south
streets are numbered and given an east-west prefix, e.g.: E. 18th St. is 18 blocks east

of the Terminal Tower. To reach Public Square from I-90 or I-71, follow the Ontario Ave./Broadway exit. From I-77, take the 9th St. exit to Euclid Ave., which runs into the Square. From the Amtrak station, follow Lakeside Ave. and turn onto Ontario, which leads to the tower. Almost all of the RTA trains and buses run downtown.

ACCOMMODATIONS AND CAMPING

For cheap lodgings, travelers are better off staying in the suburbs. Hotel taxes are a hefty 10%, not included in the prices listed below. If you know your plans well in advance, try **Cleveland Private Lodgings,** P.O. Box 18590, Cleveland 44118 (321-3213), which places people in homes around the city for as little as $30. All arrangements must be made through the office. Leave two to three weeks for a letter of confirmation. (Open Mon.-Tues. and Thurs.-Fri. 9am-noon and 3-5pm.)

Stanford House Hostel (HI/AYH), 6093 Stanford Rd. (467-8711), 22 mi. south of Cleveland in Peninsula. Exit 12 off I-80. Take bus #77F to Ridgefield Holiday Inn (the last stop) and call the hostel for a ride. Beautifully restored Greek Revival farmhouse in the Cuyahoga Valley National Recreation Area is on National Register of Historic Places. Excellent facilities; friendly houseparent. All hostelers encouraged to perform task (vacuuming, emptying trash, etc.). Check-in 5-10pm. Curfew 11pm. Office closed 9am-5pm. $10, sheets and pillow $2, sleep sack $1. Reservations recommended.

Lakewood Manor Motel, 12019 Lake Ave. (226-4800), about 3 mi. west of downtown in Lakewood. Take bus #55CX. Neat and clean. TV, central A/C. Complimentary coffee daily and donuts on weekends. Singles $27. Doubles $32.

Gateway Motel, 29865 Euclid Ave. (943-6777), 25 mi. east of Public Sq. in Wickliffe. Take Euclid Ave. exit off I-90 or bus #28X. Spacious, clean rooms with A/C and color TV. Singles $25. Doubles $30.

Two **campgrounds** are 40 minutes east of downtown, off I-480 in Streetsboro: **Woodside Lake Park,** 2256 Frost Rd. (626-4251; tent sites for 2 $16.50, with electricity $17.50; $2 per additional guest, ages 3-17 75¢); and **Valley View Lake Resort,** 8326 Ferguson (626-2041; tent sites $19, water and hookup available).

FOOD

You'll find Cleveland's culinary treats in tiny neighborhoods surrounding the downtown area. To satiate that lust for hot corned beef, step into one of the bakers' dozens of delis in the city center. Over 100 vendors sell produce, meat, cheese and other groceries at the indoor-outdoor **West Side Market** at W. 25th St. and Lorain Ave. (Open Mon. and Wed. 7am-4pm, Fri.-Sat. 7am-6pm.) For an extensive listing of restaurants, turn to the monthly magazine *Live* ($2).

Tommy's, 182 Coventry Rd. (321-7757), just up the hill from University Circle. Take bus #9X east to Mayfield and Coventry Rd. Did someone say hummus? Sample any of Tommy's delicious and creative Eastern-based dishes. Healthful pita bread sandwiches ($2.50-5.25). Try the Brownie Monster ($1.50) for dessert. Open Mon.-Sat. 7:30am-10pm, Sun. 9am-5pm.

Mama Santa's, 12305 Mayfield Rd. (421-2159), in Little Italy just east of University Circle. Authentic Sicilian food served beneath subdued lighting. Medium pizza $3.70, spaghetti $4.50. Open Mon.-Thurs. 11am-midnight, Fri.-Sat. 11am-1am. There are many other Italian cafes and restaurants nearby on Mayfield St.

Tony Roma's, several locations, including 7289 Mentor Ave. (953-0100). Chain of rib joints popular with locals. Entrees $7-12.

SIGHTS AND ENTERTAINMENT

Downtown Cleveland has escaped the hopeless blight which has struck other Great Lakes cities such as Detroit and Erie. Capital is moving *into* the town rather than out. The next two years will see the opening of Gateway Stadium and Gateway Arena for the Indians and the Cavs, the Rock and Roll Hall of Fame, a new theater in

Playhouse Square, and the Great Lakes Museum of Science; 1990 witnessed the opening of the long-awaited **Tower City Center** (771-6611), a three-story shopping complex in the Terminal Tower. Although essentially a luxury mall with prices to match, Tower Center is a notable emblem of the tremendous renovation and revitalization of downtown Cleveland. **Cleveland Lakefront State Park** (881-8141), two miles west of downtown and accessible from Lake Ave. or Cleveland Memorial Shoreway, is a mile-long beach with great swimming and picnicking areas.

Museums and The Arts

Playhouse Square Center, 1501 Euclid Ave. (771-4444), a 10-minute walk east of Terminal Tower, is the third-largest performing arts center in the nation. The **Cleveland Opera** (575-0900) and the famous **Cleveland Ballet** (621-2260) perform from September to May nearby at 1375 Euclid Ave. Four miles east of the city resides **University Circle,** a cluster of 75 cultural institutions. Check with the helpful visitors bureau (see Practical Information above) for details on museums, live music, and drama. The world-class **Cleveland Museum of Art,** 11150 East Blvd. (421-7340), in University Circle, contains a fine collection of 19th-century French and American Impressionist paintings, as well as a version of Rodin's ubiquitous "The Thinker." A beautiful plaza and pensive pond face the museum. (Open Tues. and Thurs.-Fri. 10am-5:45pm, Wed. 10am-9:45pm, Sat. 9am-4:45pm, Sun. 1-5:45pm. Free.) Nearby is the **Cleveland Museum of Natural History,** Wade Oval (231-4600), where you can see the only existing skull of the fearsome Pygmy Tyrant *(Nanatyrannus)*. (Open Mon.-Sat. 10am-5pm, Sun. 1-5pm. $5, seniors, students $4, children 5-17 $3. Free after 3pm Tues. and Thurs.) The renowned **Cleveland Orchestra,** one of the nation's best, blows, plucks and bows in University Circle at Severance Hall, 11001 Euclid Ave. (231-7300; tix $10-23). During the summer, the orchestra performs at **Blossom Music Center,** 1145 W. Steels Corners Rd., Cuyahoga Falls (920-8040), about 45 minutes south of the city (lawn seating $10). University Circle itself is safe, but some of the nearby neighborhoods can be rough, especially at night. East of University Circle, in a nice neighborhood, is the **Dobama Theatre,** 1846 Coventry Rd., Cleveland Hts. (932-6838). This little-known theater gives terrific, inexpensive ($6-9) performances in an intimate, living-room atmosphere. Peruse the monthly *Live* or the daily *Plain Dealer* for entertainment listings.

Sports and Nightlife

The **Cleveland Indians** whoop it up at the Municipal Stadium (861-1200, tickets $4-18), while the **Cavaliers** hoop it up at the Arena (659-9100, tickets $17 and up). In the fall, catch the orange-helmeted **Browns** in all their gridiron glory (891-5000, tickets $20 and up).

A great deal of Cleveland's nightlife is focused in the **Flats,** the former industrial core of the city along both banks of the Cuyahoga River. The northernmost section of the Flats, just west of Public Square, contains several nightclubs and restaurants. On weekend nights, expect large crowds and larger traffic jams. On the east side of the river, you can watch the sunset across the water through the steel frames of old railroad bridges from the deck at **Rumrunners,** 1124 Old River Rd. (696-6070). Live bands play (Thurs.-Sun.), and draft beer is $1.75. (Open daily 4pm-2am. $3 cover.) **Fagan's,** 996 Old River Rd. (241-6116), looks like a South Florida beachside resort, not a den of iniquity which trains hungry English waifs to pickpocket. "Please, sir. Can I have some $6-9 sandwiches or entrees starting at $11?" Yes, son, you can, but please tell your friends not to do dance numbers on the gorgeous riverside deck. On the west side of the river are several other clubs, including **Shooters,** 1148 Main Ave. (861-6900), a beautiful bar/restaurant with a great view of the river and Lake Erie. Prices are fairly high (dinners $7-10), but you can capture the flavor of Cleveland nightlife inexpensively by taking your drink to the in-deck pool. (Open Mon.-Sat. 11:30-1:30am, Sun. 11-1:30am.)

COLUMBUS

■ Near Cleveland

Within an hour's drive of Cleveland lie the Amish communities of bucolic **Holmes County.** Outsiders can visit the **Amish Farm** (893-2951) in **Berlin,** which offers a film presentation, demonstrations of non-electrical appliances, and a tour of the grounds. (Open April-Oct. Mon.-Sat. 10am-6pm. Tours $2.25, children $1. Buggy ride $2.75.) Unserved by public transportation, Berlin lies 70 mi. south of Cleveland on Rte. 39, 17 pastoral miles west of I-77. For demonstrations of electrical appliances which provoke raw fear, visit **Geauga Lake Amusement Park,** 1060 Aurora Rd. (800-THE-WAVE/843-9283), 30 mi. southeast of Cleveland in Aurora. Those over 55" tall can experience the brand new Texas Twister ride. Admission $16, kids under 42" free. Nearby **Sea World,** 1100 Sea World Drive, off Rte. 43 at Rte. 91 (800-63-SHAMU/637-4268), has just opened Shark Encounter, sequel to the less menacing Penguin Encounter. (Admission $21, children 3-11 $17.) Further south (60 mi. from town) is the **Pro Football Hall of Fame,** 2121 George Halas Dr. N.W. (456-8207), in Canton (take exit 107a at the junction of I-77 and U.S. 62). Memorabilia and films of American football. (Open 9am-8pm, Labor Day-Memorial Day 9am-5pm. Admission $5, over 62, $2.50, children 6-14 $2.)

■■■ COLUMBUS

State government, white collar business, and education are the mainstays of Columbus. Downtown is filled with towering office complexes and modern meeting facilities, of which the spacious but aesthetically disastrous Convention Center is the latest addition. In Columbus one can picnic on the Scioto River or stroll through Bexley, lawnscaped suburbia at its best.

PRACTICAL INFORMATION

Visitors to the city can contact the **Greater Columbus Visitors Center** (800-345-4FUN or 221-CITY), located in downtown's **Center City Mall** on the third floor. *The Other* is a free entertainment guide published weekly. Find it at many shops and restaurants. **Greyhound,** 111 E. Town St. (221-5311), offers the most frequent and complete service from downtown. To: Cincinnati ($15.50-18.50, varies by day); Cleveland ($15-23); Chicago ($60). Public transportation in the city is run by the **Central Ohio Transit Authority (COTA),** 177 S. High St. (228-1776; offices Mon.-Fri. 8:30am-5:30pm; fare $1, express $1.35). The **area code** for Columbus is 614; the **ZIP code** is 43216.

FOURTEEN NINETY-FOOD

The following are all located on Columbus' main drag, High St. **Bernie's Bagels and Deli,** 1896 N. High St. (291-3448), for a variety of sandwiches in a grunge rock cellar atmosphere ($3-6). Live shows nightly. (Opens Mon.-Fri. at 8:30am, Sat.-Sun. at 9:30 am. Closes Sun.-Tues. at 1am, Wed.-Sat. at 2am.) **Bermuda Onion Delicatessen,** 660 N. High St. (221-6296), specializes in hip sandwiches ($4-7) like grilled provolone on challah with herb mayo, sprouts, and tomato. Now putting the "funk" back into "food" with nightly table service. (Open Mon.-Thurs. 8:30am-10pm, Fri. 8:30am-11pm, Sat. 9am-11pm, Sun. 9am-10pm.) Downtown, **The Clock,** 161 N. High St. (221-2562), has mid-range entrees ($6-11) in a historic setting. This renovated 1920s pub is open for lunch Mon.-Fri. and for dinner Wed.-Sat. until 11pm. **Katzinger's Delicatessen** (228-3354), Third at Livingston, has excellent sandwiches, blintzes, and breads. Entrees $4-8. (Open Mon.-Thurs. 8:30am-8:30pm, Fri. 8:30am-9:30pm, Sat.-Sun. 9am-8:30pm.)

ACCOMMOD-OCEANS BLUE

The **Heart of Ohio Hostel (AYH),** 95 E. 12th Ave. (294-7157), one block from OSU, has outstanding facilities, and organizes bicycle trips in the area. ($8, $11 nonmembers. Check-in 5-9pm. Curfew 11pm.) Rooms in apartment houses near campus are cheap, abundant, and well advertised during the summer, when OSU students leave them vacant. The **Greater Columbus Bed and Breakfast Cooperative** (967-6060) includes some B&B's with rates around $35.

LAND HO!

Two mi. north of downtown Columbus looms gargantuan **Ohio State University**; its enrollment of over 58,000 students makes it the largest in the United States. **Visitor Information** is at the Ohio Union, 1839 N. High St. (292-0428 or 292-0418). The **Wexner Center for the Arts**, N. High St. (292-3535), at 15th Ave., displays avant-garde exhibits and films, and hosts progressive music, dance, and other performances. The Kronos Quartet plays here regularly. (Exhibits open Tues.-Wed. 10am-6pm, Thurs.-Sat. 10am-8pm, Sun. noon-5pm. Free. Ticket office open Mon.-Fri. 9am-5pm; call 292-2354 for prices.)

In 1991, the **Columbus Museum of Art**, 480 E. Broad St. (221-6801), acquired the **Sirak Collection** of Impressionist and European Modernist works. It is currently on tour but will be soon integrated into the permanent collection. (Open Tues. and Thurs.- Fri. 11am-4pm, Wed. 11am-9pm, Sat. 10am-5pm, Sun. 11am-5pm. Permanent collection free, traveling exhibits have a small fee.) Ohio's **Center of Science and Industry (COSI)**, 280 E. Broad St. (288-2674), will mesmerize kids with such hands-on exhibits as a mock coal mine. Located ½ mi. west of I-71 and Broad St. (Open Mon.-Sat. 10am-5pm, Sun. noon-5:30pm. $5, students and seniors $3.) Across the street is the first ever **Wendy's** restaurant. Just west is the light-hearted **Thurber House**, 77 Jefferson Ave. (464-1032), where rooms of James Thurber's childhood home are decorated with cartoons by the famous author and *New Yorker* cartoonist. Memorabilia from his life and times on display. (Open daily noon-4pm, free.)

Nature lovers can enjoy the **Columbus Zoo**, 9990 Riverside Dr. (645-3400) in Powell. (Open daily 9am-6pm, Wed. 9am-8pm; Labor Day-Memorial Day daily 9am-5pm. Admission $5, kids 2-11 $3, under 2 free. Parking $2.) Also appealing is the expansive **Franklin Park Conservatory**, 1777 E. Broad St. (645-8733). A mammoth collection of self-contained environments including rain forests, deserts, and Himalayan mountains.

Just south of Capitol Square is the **German Village**, first settled in 1843 and now the largest privately-funded historical restoration in the U.S. Visitors can tour stately brick homes and patronize old-style beer halls. At **Schmidt's Sausage Haus**, 240 E. Kossuth St. (444-6808), the oom-pah bands **Schnickelfritz** and **Schnapps** lead polkas Tues.-Sat. 8:30pm. (Open Sun.-Mon. 11am-10pm, Tues.-Thurs. 11am-11pm, Fri.-Sat. 11am-midnight.) For information, call or visit the helpful **German Village Society**, 634 S. 3rd St. (221-8888; open Mon.-Fri. 9am-4pm).

■ Near Columbus

Dense green forests swathe southeastern Ohio's narrow valleys, steep hills, and ragged rock formations, carved into the land by Pleistocene glaciers. The southern route of the Buckeye trail snakes through this jagged terrain, roughly tracked by **U.S. 50.** Along the highway, which runs east from Cincinnati to Parkersburg, lie spectacular Native American burial grounds, constructed by Adena, Hopewell, and Fort Ancient "Moundbuilders." Among the most interesting is the **Mound City Group National Monument** (774-1125), on Rte. 104, 3 mi. north of Chillicothe. Within a 13-acre area swell 24 still-enigmatic Hopewell burial mounds. The adjoining museum elucidates theories about Hopewell society based upon the mounds' configuration. (Museum open daily 8am-6pm. $1, max. $3 per vehicle, seniors and under 17 free.) Check with park officials for info on other nearby mounds. Visit **Chillicothe** to ogle the Greek Revival mansions that grace the northwest territory's first capital. Ten mi. south of Chillicothe off U.S. 23, you can camp at **Scioto Trail**

State Park (663-2125; 24-hr. self-registration; primitive camping free; designated sites $4, with electricity $8).

About 30 mi. east of Chillicothe, U.S. 50 passes near **Hocking Hills State Park,** accessible by Rte. 93 north or Rte. 56 west. Waterfalls, gorges, cliffs, and caves scar the rugged terrain within the park. **Ash Cave,** east of South Bloomingville on Rte. 56, gouges 80 acres out of a horseshoe-shaped rock. A trickling stream falls over the edge of this cliff to a pool at the cave entrance. **Cantwell Cliffs,** southwest of Rock-bridge on Rte. 374, is another horseshoe-shaped precipice. Camp at **Old Man's Cave** (385-6165), off State Rte. 664 (primitive camping $5; designated sites with pool $9, with electricity and pool $12).

Greyhound, 193 E. Main St. (775-2013), inside Parceland Post Express, at the corner of Hickory St., serves Chillicothe from both Cincinnati ($30) and Columbus ($18.50). The **area code** for these here parts is 614.

■■■ LAKE ERIE ISLANDS

Off the coast of northern Ohio are a group of islands which cater to the party mentality. Think of them as giant Carnival Cruise Ships, only standing still and with lots of trees. O.K., so that's a silly analogy—there's no shuffleboard. There are four major American islands and one Canadian island in the Lake Erie Islands region. North Bass Island and Middle Bass Island are closed to the public, except for a winery on Middle Bass. South Bass Island and Kelleys Island are both emphatically open to the public and share a relaxed atmosphere; cars are allowed but scarce, and the best way to get around is by bicycle. Both islands have a tram running between the dock, the sights and the campground ($1). Both islands also have some organized tourism activities, but the most enjoyable activity is a leisurely bike ride (both islands are about 3 mi. in diameter). The misnamed Catawba Island is actually a peninsula—don't be fooled.

■ South Bass Island

Two miles northeast of the South Bass ferry docks is the small town of **Put-in Bay.** Here's where you'll find the island's biggest attraction: the bars. The **Round House** (285-4595) in—you guessed it—a round house, attracts sippers and guzzlers with glasses and buckets of beer ($2.25 and $22.50, respectively). The bucket holds 13 glasses and is thus more economical, provided you don't spill any—plus you get to keep the nifty plastic bucket. Refills are $17.50, making it the best bulk beer bargain ever. Just a few steps down Lorain Ave., the **Beer Barrel Saloon** (285-BEER/285-2337) can probably find you elbow room at its bar, the longest in the world at 405 ft. 10 in. (glasses $2.50). (Both open noon-1am; music at both starts daily around 2pm.) Find fun for under-21sters at **Kimberly's Carousel** downtown, one of just 100 carousels with wooden horses left in America (75¢). On the eastern edge of Put-in Bay, **Perry's Victory and International Peace Memorial,** honoring both Commodore Oliver Hazard Perry's 1813 victory over the British in the Battle of Lake Erie and the 100 years of peace between the U.S. and Canada, rises 352 ft. above lake-level, the tallest Doric column in the world. (Elevator ride to the top $1.) In the center of the island, at the corner of Catawba Ave. and Thompson Rd., the **Heineman Winery** ferments a fun time. Tours of the wine-making equipment cost $3.50 and include a sampling. Their grape juice is made from the same recipe as the wine but not fermented; the heavenly nectar shames the store-bought variety. (Tours daily every hr. 11am-5pm; bottle of wine $5, of grape juice $2.25). While digging for a well, they discovered the **largest geode ever discovered;** a look at it is included in the winery tour. Keep in mind that the average geode is only baseball-sized.

Rooms on the island start at $55; the **South Bass Island State Park** on the western edge of the island charges $12 per night, children 6-11 $3 (showers, no hookup, no reservations). To get a site on weekends arrive before 8:30am on Friday. For more info on this park or the one on Kelleys Island, call the park office in Catawba (419-797-4530).

At the ferry dock, **Island Bike Rental** (285-2016) rents one-speeds ($2 per hr., $6 per day). Pick up a free map of the island a few yards away at **E's Golf Carts** (285-5553; carts $8 per hr., $45 per day). The **Miller Boat Line** (285-2421) ferries passengers and cars to South Bass Island from Catawba Point (June-Sept. 7:30am-7:30pm every ½-hr., less frequently in April, May, Oct. and Nov.; $4 one way, children 6-11 $1, bike $1.50, car $7). (Exit Rte. 2, follow Rte. 53 north to the end. Park at one of the ferry's free lots; be careful of the ones that charge $5 per day.) **Sonny S. Ferry** runs from Put-in Bay to **Lonz Winery** on Middle Bass Island. ($5 round-trip, winery tours $1.50.) Miller Boat Line also serves Middle Bass from Catawba Point ($4.50 one way).

■ Kelleys Island

Only one year ago, Kelleys Island had the reputation of being South Bass's sleepy-eyed little sister. No more. Though still less developed than South Bass, it is rapidly becoming the more popular of the two, thanks to the operation of a new ferry line, **Kelleys Island Ferry Boat Lines, Inc.,** 510 Main St., Marblehead (798-9763). The Kelleys Island Ferry runs year round, using a tug boat to break the winter ice. From late April-late September, the ferry departs every hour Mon.-Thurs., 7am-8pm, and Fri.-Sat., 7am-11pm. Adults $6, children 6-11 $3, automobiles $14. The **Neuman Boat Line,** Foot of Frances St., Marblehead (798-5800), charges $7.80, children 6-11 $4.50, and automobiles $14. Departure times vary depending on day and week from late April-late September, so calling ahead is recommended. Even on peak weekends, few Neuman boats leave past 9pm.

The new ferry has considerably opened Kelleys's nightlife and tourism. The island was once a large source of limestone; you can wander around abandoned, water-filled quarries, the best of which is **East Quarry** in the center of the island, a great place to watch birds in the air and carp in the water. A small section of ancient glacial grooves has been preserved on the northern side of the island. It looks like a 60-ft. section of dry streambed, but geologists and your dad will love it. The **Kelleys Island State Park** (419-797-4530), near the "grooves," charges a groovy $12 per night for sites. No reservations; arrive by early afternoon on Friday for weekend spots. (Has showers, toilets, a beach, and allows pets.) Accommodations on Kelleys include cottages, inns, and bed and breakfasts, but you're not likely to find anything below $60 a night. Plenty of restaurants await you, including the **West Bay Inn,** 1230 West Lakeshore Dr. (746-2207), all the way on the west side of the island. Burgers $3.25, famous chocolate peanut butter pie $2.50. Several rental shops supply bicycles ($8 and up) and golf carts.

■ Sandusky and the Coast

There are 40 motels and hotels on the mainland in nearby Sandusky; the **Visitors and Convention Bureau** (800-255-3743) has a directory. If you aren't camping, the best place to stay is the **Hotel Lakeside** (798-4461), on the lake in the heart of Lakeside, near Marblehead. Lakeside is one of the few remaining **Chautauqua Villages,** Methodist family resorts founded in the 19th century. Families still come here year after year, drawn by the activities available for children, nightly shows at the **Hoover Auditorium,** and good old-fashioned Christian fellowship. The hotel was built in 1875 and has recently undergone extensive renovation. This has bumped up the prices, but the price/quality ratio is still very high. Half bathrooms begin at $25 and full baths at $40. Antiques and period art decorate all the hotel's high-ceilinged rooms. The affiliated **Fountain Inn** is very modern and has comparable prices (same phone number). All-you-can-eat buffet meals ($5-8) are available at Hotel Lakeside's restaurant. Admission to **Lakeside** grounds includes all lectures, concerts, sport facilities, and other entertainment ($8 per day, plus $1 per day for cars).

Less than 10 mi. east of Lakeside is **Train-O-Rama,** 6732 E. Harbor Rd. (734-5856), a classic piece of American roadside kitsch. A diorama of a miniature landscape built with 1½ mi. of track, 1001 lights, 9,500 lbs. of plaster, and 200 miniature buildings (open Memorial Day-Labor Day, Mon.-Sat. 10am-6pm, Sun. 1-6pm. Admission $5).

Near Sandusky, experience **Cedar Point** (627-2350), the scenic playground's scenic amusement park off U.S. 6. Take the Ohio Turnpike (I-80) to exit 7 and follow signs north on U.S. 250 to the home of the **Magnum XL200,** the world's largest, fastest, longest, and steepest roller coaster. (Open mid-May-mid-Sept. Sun.-Thurs. 10am-10pm, Fri.-Sat. 10am-midnight. Admission $23, seniors $12.50, under 4 ft. $5, under 4 yrs. free. After 5pm, when lines diminish, admission drops to $12.50.)

Greyhound, 6513 Milan Rd., Sandusky (625-6907), on U.S. 250 south of Rte. 2, hurtles to: Cleveland ($9.50-14.50); Detroit ($22); Chicago ($39). **Taxis** to downtown Sandusky are $8; to Catawba Point $30-40. The region's **area code** is 419.

■ Wisconsin

Wisconsin is a home for cultivation, industrialization, and fermentation. Boasting its position as the nation's foremost producer of milk, cheese, and butter, "America's Dairyland" is also an outdoor thrill. In a land of almost 15,000 lakes, including Lake Superior to the north and Lake Michigan to the east, this Great Lakes state is a natural playland.

French fur trappers first explored the area in search of luctative, furry fauna. Later, hearty Norsemen lumbered to the logging and mining camps of this frontier. By the time the virgin forests had fallen and the mines had been exhausted, immigrant German farmers came to the fore. Discovering local barley, they perfected the art of brewing, making the state the beer capital of the nation. Wisconsin celebrates these ethnic roots in its food and drink. Fishboils—feasts fit for Thor—are a celebrated tradition dating back to the 19th century. This welcoming state for vacationers and residents alike explodes in the summer with ethnic fêtes, each with the local flavors of food, music, and (of course) oceans of beer.

PRACTICAL INFORMATION

Capital: Madison.
Division of Tourism, 123 W. Washington St., Madison 53707 (266-2161, 266-6797, or 800-372-2737).
Time Zone: Central (1 hr. behind Eastern). **Postal Abbreviation:** WI
Sales Tax: 5½%.

■■■ APOSTLE ISLANDS

The Apostle Islands float majestically off the northern coast of Wisconsin, some 90 mi. from Duluth. The rich cultural heritage and natural beauty of this former logging area are now protected as a National Lakeshore, encompassing 21 of the 22 islands and 11 mi. of its littoral. Summer tourists visit the wind- and wave-whipped caves by the thousands, camping on unspoiled sandstone bluffs and hunting for wild blueberries and raspberries.

■ Bayfield

Practical Information All Apostle Islands excursions begin in the sleepy mainland town of **Bayfield,** in the northwest part of Wisconsin on the Lake Superior coast. The nearest **Greyhound** station barks in **Ashland,** 101 2nd St. (682-4010), 22 mi. southeast of Bayfield on U.S. 2 (to Duluth, 2 hr., $7.50). The **Bay Area Rural Transit (BART)** (682-9664) offers a shuttle to Bayfield. (4 per day, Mon.-Fri., $1.80, seniors/disabled $1.10, students $1.50.) The **Bayfield Chamber of Commerce,** 42 S. Broad St. (779-3335), has helpful information on the area (open summer daily 9am-5pm). The **Apostle Islands National Lakeshore Headquarters Visitors Center,** 410 Washington Ave. (779-3397), dispenses information and free camping permits for the islands (open Mon.-Thurs. and Sat.-Sun. 9am-4pm, Fri. 9am-7pm). **Trek & Trail** (779-3320), on Rittenhouse Ave., rents sea kayaks with spray skirts ($15-35 for ½-day, $25-45 per day) and offers sailing tours of the ship wrecks (3½ hr., $40). The Bayfield **post office** is open Mon.-Fri. 9am-12:30pm and 1:30-4:30pm, and Sat. 10-11am. The **ZIP code** is 54814. The **area code** is 715.

Accommodations and Camping There are numerous campgrounds in the area. **Dalrymple Park** (779-5712), ¼-mi. north of town on Rte. 13, offers 30 sites under tall pines, right on the Lake, but has no showers ($7, $8 with electricity). **Red Cliff** (779-3743), a Chippewa settlement three mi. north on Rte. 13, offers tourists a campground with modern conveniences ($10, tents with electricity $11, trailers with electricity $12). Talk to the Native Americans for a different perspective on the area and its offerings. For those who prefer indoor accommodations, the **Frostman Home,** 24 N. 3rd St. (779-3239), has three spotless and comfortable rooms for $25 each. Down the street and around the corner, the **First Street Inn,** 17 Rittenhouse Ave. (779-5480), has pleasant, old-fashioned rooms $30-75.

Food In early summer, Bayfield's basket overflows with berry pies. **Maggie's,** 257 Manypenny Ave. (779-5641), also has sandwiches and burgers ($3-5). (Open May-Oct. 6am-10pm, Nov.-April 11:30am-10pm.) The **Bayfield Deli,** 201 Manypenny (779-5566), slices up huge sandwiches ($1.50-6) and spoons out the most creative ice cream names yet, like Ladybug and Elephant Tracks (scoop $1.25, sundaes $3).

■ Madeline Island

A few hundred years ago, the Chippewa came to **Madeline Island** from the Atlantic in search of the *megis shell,* a light in the sky that was purported to bring prosperity and health.

Practical Information The **Madeline Island Chamber of Commerce,** Main St. (747-2801), is especially helpful concerning accommodations (open summer daily 9am-5pm). Ferry service between Bayfield and **La Pointe,** on Madeline Island, is provided by **Madeline Island Ferry Line** (747-2051; summer ferries daily every 45 min. 7am-11pm; less frequently March-June and Sept.-Dec.; one way $3, ages 6-11 $1.75, bikes $1.50, cars $6.25, less off-season). Transport on Madeline Island is by foot, car, or bicycle. Rent a moped at **Motion to Go,** 102 Lake View Pl. (747-6585), about one block from the ferry. ($9-10 per hr., $35-45 per day. Open summer daily 9am-9pm.) The La Pointe **post office** (747-3712) lies just off the dock on Madeline Island. (Open Mon.-Fri. 9am-4:30pm, Sat. 9:30am-1pm.) The **ZIP code** is 54850.

Accommodations and Camping Madeline Island has two campgrounds. **Big Bay Town Park** (747-6913) is 6½ mi. from La Pointe, right next to beautiful Big Bay Lagoon (44 sites $9 each). Across the lagoon, **Big Bay State Park** (747-3346) has 55 sites for $8. Sites can be reserved by mail for an extra $3. Daily vehicle permit ($6, $4 for Wisconsinites) also required. The **Madeline Island Motel** (747-3000) lets clean rooms, each of which are named for a different personality in the island's history. (July-Labor Day singles $49, doubles $54; May-June and Labor Day-Nov. $41 and $45; Dec.-April all rooms $31.) On Colonel Woods Blvd., **Island Inn** (747-2450) has spacious rooms with walls of fresh-smelling pine (singles $55, off-season $45). Rooms in the area are scarce during the summer; call ahead for reservations.

Food Grandpa Tony's perky red-and-white decor houses tasty sandwiches $2.50-3.75 (open summer Mon.-Fri. 8am-9pm, Sat.-Sun. 8am-10pm). The **Beach Club,** just off the ferry in La Pointe, has a relaxed atmosphere, a view of the lake, superlative shortcake ($3.50), and a superb shrimp basket with fries ($7). (Open summer daily 11:30am-3:30pm and 5:30-9:30pm.) The **Island Cafe** serves up big breakfasts (ham and cheese omelette $4.25) and lunch ($4-6). Dinner selection changes daily, but always includes many vegetarian dishes.

Sights The **Madeline Island Historical Museum** (747-2415), right off the dock, accompanies the legend of Madeline with other historical info. (Open late May-Labor Day daily 9am-5pm; Labor Day-early Oct. daily 10am-4pm. $3, seniors $2.70, ages 5-12 $1.25.) The **Indian Burial Ground** 1 mi. south of La Pointe has dirt paths that lead to the graves of early settlers and christianized Chippewa, including Chief Great Buffalo. Towards the end of the day, head to **Sunset Bay** on the island's north side. **Madeline Island Tours** (747-2051) offers two 2-hr. tours of the island (daily, late June-Labor Day, tickets $6.75, ages 6-11 $3.75).

■ The National Lakeshore

The other islands have subtle charms of their own. The sandstone quarries of Basswood and Hermit Island, as well as the abandoned logging and fishing camps on some of the others, are mute reminders of a more vigorous era. Museums in their own right, the restored **lighthouses** on Sand, Raspberry, Michigan, Outer, and Devils Islands offer spectacular views of the surrounding country. An easy way to visit all of these sights is on one of three narrated 3-hr. cruises provided by the **Apostle Islands Cruise Service** (779-3925; tickets $20, kids $9). From late June-late Aug., the cruise service runs other trips ($19) from which passengers can disembark to camp on the islands and then be picked up the next time the cruise schedule brings the boat to that island. At other times, you can charter a **Water Taxi** (779-5153) to take you and five friends to the nearest (round trip $56) or farthest ($272) island. Some of the sea caves on Devils Island are large enough to accommodate a small boat; after June 26 it is possible to take a taxi to explore them and return by 10pm.

Legend has it that the islands were named in the 18th century when a band of pirates called the Twelve Apostles hid out on Oak Island. Today you don't have to hide to stay there, as long as you get a free camper's permit, available at the **National Lakeshore Headquarters Visitors Center,** 410 Washington Ave., Bayfield (779-3397). The permit allows you to camp on 19 of the 22 islands. The Headquarters will also tell you which islands allow camping only at designated sites, and which are more generally open.

■■■ DOOR COUNTY

The beautiful 40-mi. peninsula of Door County evokes in most a passionate response. A serene home to the locals, a retreat for the seasoned vacationer, and a treat to the first time visitor, the peninsula boasts 250 mi. of shoreline, five state parks, eight lakes, and backroad bicycle routes with over 100 mi. of scenic riding pleasure. In summer, boaters, fishers, and campers descend, and in the winter the county becomes a cross-country skiing fest. The diverse scenery includes sand beaches, rocky shores, woodlands, apple and cherry orchards, and foliage that in the fall is incomparable. Ever since the area was settled by Scandinavians, fishboils—fabulous feasts of fish—topped with homemade cherry pie have been *the* food. Given the tourist onslaught, Door County swings open to visitors, providing stores, restaurants, and parks, and yet still manages to shut out reckless developers.

PRACTICAL INFORMATION
Emergency: 911.

Visitor Information: Door County Chamber of Commerce, 6443 Green Bay Rd. (743-4456), on Rte. 42/57 entering Sturgeon Bay. Free brochures for every village on the peninsula and biking maps. Mailing address P.O. Box 406, Station A. Open June-Oct. Mon.-Fri. 8am-5pm, Sat. 10am-4pm; off-season Mon.-Fri. 8:30am-4:30pm. Each village has its own visitors center. **Triphone,** a free service located outside the Chamber of Commerce, allows you to call many hotels on the peninsula, as well as restaurant, police, weather, and fishing hotlines.

Greyhound: 800 Cedar, Green Bay (414-432-4883). The closest station to Door County, about 50 mi. from Sturgeon Bay. To: Milwaukee (5 per day, $16), Chicago (5 per day, $28), and Minneapolis (3 per day, $39). Open Mon.-Fri. 6am-6pm, Sat. 6am-12:30pm and 4-6pm, Sun. 9am-12:30pm and 4-6pm.

Car Rental: Advantage, 1629 Velp, Green Bay (414-497-2152), 50 mi. from Sturgeon Bay, 3 mi. from the Greyhound station. $14 per day, $89 per week, 10¢ per mi., extra $5 insurance. Must be 25 years old with credit card. Open Mon.-Fri. 8:30am-6pm, Sat. 8am-3pm.

Other Rentals: Nor Door Sport and Cyclery, Fish Creek (868-2275), at the entrance to Peninsula State Park. Mountain bikes $7 per hr., $25 per day; 18- and 21-speeds $5 per hr., $15 per day, $30 for 3 days. **Kurtz Corral,** 5712 Howard Lane, Sturgeon Bay (743-6742), 3 mi. east of Carlsville on C.R. "I." Horseback riding on 300 acres. $19 per hr., kids' rides $9; instruction included. Open daily 9am-4pm. No reservations necessary.

Police: 123 S. 5th Ave. (746-2450; non-emergency), in Sturgeon Bay.

Post Office: 359 Louisiana (743-2681), at 4th St. in Sturgeon Bay. Open Mon.-Fri. 8:30am-5pm. **ZIP code:** 54235

Area Code: 414.

The real Door County begins north of **Sturgeon Bay** where Rtes. 42 and 57 converge and then split again—Rte. 57 running up the eastern coast of the peninsula, Rte. 42 up the western side. The peninsula is 200 mi. northeast of Madison and 150 mi. north of Milwaukee; there is no land access except via Sturgeon Bay. Summer is high season in Door's twelve villages, the biggest of which are **Fish Creek** (rhymes with "fish stick"), **Sister Bay,** and **Ephraim.** There is no public transportation on the peninsula. The eastern side is less commercial than the western; the county is less developed and more traditional the farther north you go. Wherever in the area you are, dress warmly; temperatures can dip to 40°F at night in July, and strong bay winds make it even cooler.

ACCOMMODATIONS AND CAMPING

There is an abundance of hotels, motels, lodges, and inns up and down Door County. Most places cater to the family-with-boat crowd who have the money to get away from it all for $60 and up per night. Fortunately, motels for $40 and under do exist, but they are often smaller, shoddier, and without a view. Some of the best deals are cultivated at the **Century Farm Motel** (854-4069), on Rte. 57, 3 mi. south of Sister Bay. A really nifty place located on a farm complete with cows, chickens, and a crowing rooster, the individual cottages have pine walls, showers, and cozy bedspreads and curtains. The friendly owner lives in a log cabin built by his great-grandfather a century ago. (Cottage for 2 $40, for 5 $55. Open May-Oct. Reserve one week ahead, more for holiday weekends.) At the **Liberty Park Lodge** (854-2025), in Sister Bay north of downtown on Rte. 42, you can sit on a huge porch and watch the sun set over the lake or warm by a fire in the activity-filled (ping-pong and pool table) house. (Lodge rooms May-Oct. $42-56, Nov.-April $36-46.) The **Chal-A Motel,** 3910 Rte. 42/57 (743-6788), rests three mi. north of the bridge in Sturgeon Bay. Worth viewing is the proprietress' collection of several thousand dolls, including 700 Barbies. In the same barn her husband shows off his 24 vintage automobiles, ranging from a 1924 Model T to a 1983 DeLorean. Large rooms in a serene setting. (July-Oct. singles $39, doubles $44; Nov.-June $19/$24.)

Camping is the way to go in Door County, and four out of the five **state parks** (all except Whitefish Dunes State Park) have sites. Wisconsin state parks are divided into three **classes:** A ($10 per site per night), B ($9), and C ($8). Parks also require a $6 entrance fee for any motorized vehicle (good for 24 hr.). An annual admission sticker for motorized vehicles is $24 and permits access to all state parks. **Peninsula State Park** (Class A), P.O. Box 218, Fish Creek 54212 (868-3258), by Fish Creek village on Rte. 42, is the largest, with 472 sites. Make reservations *way* ahead of time (i.e. 6 months), or come in person and put your name on the waiting list for one of the 127 sites reserved for walk-ins. Peninsula has showers and flush toilets, 20 mi. of shoreline, a spectacular view from Eagle Tower, and 17 mi. of hiking. **Potawatomi State Park** (Class A), 3740 Park Dr., Sturgeon Bay 54235 (746-2890), just outside Sturgeon Bay off Rte. 42/57, has 125 campsites, half of which are open to walk-ins. Write for reservations. **Newport State Park** (Class A), a wildlife preserve at the tip of the peninsula, 7 mi. from Ellison Bay off Rte. 42, has only 16 sites; vehicles are allowed, but sites are accessible only by hiking. To get to **Rock Island State Park** (Class C), take the ferry from Gill's Rock to Washington Island (see Sights and Activities below) and then another ferry (847-2252; total price $12 round-trip) to Rock Island. (40 sites, open May-Dec.)

The best private campground is **Path of Pines** (868-3332), in Fish Creek, which has scenic sites and a truly hospitable staff. It's 1 mi. east of the perennially packed Peninsula, on County Rd. "F" off Rte. 42. (91 sites; tenting $13.50, motorhomes $16.50, free showers. $2.50 per additional adult, 3 or more.)

FOOD AND DRINK

Many people come to Door County just for **fishboils,** not a trout with blemishes but a Scandinavian tradition dating back to 19th-century lumberjacks. Fifty meals are cooked at a time in a steaming cauldron over a wood fire. To remove the fish oil from the top of the water, the boilmaster throws a can of kerosene into the fire, producing a massive fireball; this causes the cauldron to boil over and signals chowtime. The best fishboils are at: **White Gull Inn** (868-3517), in Fish Creek (all-you-can-eat $13.75, children $7.75, at 5:45, 7, and 8:15pm May-Oct. Wed. and Fri.-Sun.; Nov.-April Wed. and Sat.; reservations required); the **Edgewater Restaurant** (854-4034), in Ephraim ($12, June-mid-Oct. Mon.-Sat. at 5:30 and 6:45pm; reservations best); and **The Viking** (854-2998), in Ellison Bay ($11, mid-May-Nov. 4:30-8pm about every ½-hr.). Cherries are another county tradition, and each fishboil concludes with a big slice of cherry pie.

For groceries, locals shop at **Piggly Wiggly** (854-2391), on Country Walk Rd. off Rte. 42 at the Amoco station, in Sister Bay (open summer Mon.-Sat. 8am-8pm, Sun. 8am-6pm; winter Mon.-Sat. 8am-7pm, Sun. 8am-5pm). **Hy-Line Orchards** (868-3067), on Rte. 42 between Juddville and Egg Harbor, is a huge barn full of produce and a few old Model T's. Try the cherry cider. (Open daily 8am-7pm.)

> **Al Johnson's Swedish Restaurant** (854-2626), in Sister Bay on Rte. 42, down the hill and 2 blocks past the information center on the right. Enjoy excellent Swedish food along with 4 goats who dine daily on the thick sod roof. Eat what you want, but don't ask why the goats don't fall off. Entrees $7-16. Open in summer daily 6am-9pm, in winter Mon.-Sat. 6am-8pm, Sun. 7am-8pm.
>
> **Kirkegaard's Yum-Yum Tree** (839-2993), in Bailey's Harbor. Quite possibly the funniest name for any restaurant, anywhere. A sweets haven that serves everything but cherry pie. Floats $2.35, sundaes $1.95-3.35, cones $1.25, deli sandwiches $2.50-4.50. Open mid-May-Oct. daily 10am-10pm.
>
> **Pudgy Seagull,** 113 N. Third Ave. (743-5000), in Sturgeon Bay. A local patronage enjoys the cheap food that uses fresh fish and fruit from nearby orchards. Perch sandwich $3, cherry pie $1.75. Open Mon.-Sat. 5:30am-10pm, Sun. 6am-10pm.
>
> **Bayside Tavern** (868-3441), Fish Creek on Rte. 42. Serves serious burgers ($2.50-4) and a delicious Friday perch fry ($8). Also a hip bar. Beer 90¢. After 10pm, minors should be accompanied by an adult. Open daily 11am-2am.

SIGHTS AND ACTIVITIES

Door County is best seen by bike; ask for free bike maps at the tourist offices. **Cave Point County Park** offers the most stunning views on the peninsula. The park is on Cave Point Rd. off Rte. 57, just south of Jacksonport (open daily 6am-10pm; free). Next door is **Whitefish Dunes State Park,** with hikin' a-plenty through a well-kept wildlife preserve (open daily 8am-8pm; $6). Visit the small public beaches along Door's 250-mi. shoreline; one of the nicest is **Lakeside Park** at **Jacksonport.** The beach is wide and sandy, backed by a shady park and playground (open daily 6am-10pm; free). You can go windsurfing off the public beach at **Ephraim,** in front of the Edgewater Restaurant and Motel. **Windsurf Door County** (854-4071), across from the public beach at South Shore Pier, rents boards ($13 per hr., $33 per ½-day; major credit card required). **Peninsula State Park,** a few miles south of Ephraim in Fish Creek, has 3763 acres of forested land (open daily 6am-11pm; $6 per motorized vehicle). Ride a moped or bicycle along the 20 mi. of shoreline road, or mix, mingle, and sunbathe at **Nicolet Beach** in the park. From the immense Eagle Tower 1 mi. east of the beach, 110 steps up, you can see clear across the lake to Michigan.

Kangaroo Lake, the largest of the eight inland lakes on this thin peninsula, offers warmer swimming and a less intimidating stretch of water than Lake Michigan. Kangaroo Lake Road, south of Bailey's Harbor off Rte. 57, provides lake access; follow the county roads around the lake to find your own secluded swimming spot. The **Ridges Sanctuary** (839-2802), north of Bailey's Harbor off County Rte. Q, has an appealing nature trail that leads to an abandoned lighthouse (open Mon.-Sat. 9am-4pm, Sun. 1-4pm; free). **Newport State Park,** six mi. east of Ellison Bay on Newport Dr. off Rte. 42, provides more satisfying hiking than Peninsula (no vehicles). Newport has an expansive 3000-ft. swimming beach and 13 mi. of shoreline on Lake Michigan and on inland Europe Lake.

For more scenic seclusion, seek out **Washington Island,** off the tip of the Door Peninsula; ferries run by **Washington Island Ferry Line** (847-2546; round-trip for cars $15, adults $6.50, kids $3) and Island Clipper (854-2972; round-trip for adults $6.50, kids $3). Both leave Gills Rock and Northport Pier several times daily.

■ Near Door County: Green Bay

The largest city near Door County, Green Bay has facilities that the returning vacationer may have missed: pollution, noise, and lots of industry. A shipping and packing town, home of the aptly named (and oldest) NFL team, the Green Bay Packers, this city has plenty of bars and even a little gambling. **The Oneida Bingo and Casino,** County Rte. GG (414-497-8118), southwest of downtown is on a Native American reservation. Watch Native Americans call the shots (for a change); interesting for the non-gambler as well (free; 18 and older only). The **National Railroad Museum,** 2285 S. Broadway, Green Bay (414-435-7245), has exhibits on everything from Pullman cars to modern sleepers, Eisenhower's WWII staff train, and more. (Open May-Oct. daily 9am-5pm; $5.50, kids $2.75.)

■■■ MILWAUKEE

Milwaukee is a festive town, full of good food, drink, and celebrations. The influx of immigrants, especially German and Irish, gave the city its reputation for *gemütlichkeit*—hospitality, and are responsible for the outstanding number of churches dotting the city. The ethnic communities take turns throwing city-wide parties each summer weekend. This self-proclaimed "City of Fabulous Festivals" has top-notch museums, quality arts organizations, *baklava*, and bagpipes. And since Jacob Best, a German emigré, introduced lager, added to the large supply of Wisconsin's barley, there's been beer. As the nation's largest per capita producer and with over 1500 bars and taverns, there is *lots* of beer.

MILWAUKEE

PRACTICAL INFORMATION

Emergency: 911

Greater Milwaukee Convention and Visitors Bureau, 510 W. Kilbourne (273-7222, 273-3950, or 800-231-0903), downtown. Open Mon.-Fri. 8am-5pm, during the summer also open Sat. 9am-4pm, Sun. 9am-3pm. Also at Grand Avenue Mall at 3rd St. (open Mon.-Fri. 10am-8pm, Sat. 10am-6pm, Sun. noon-5pm). Pick up a copy of *Greater Milwaukee Official Visitor's Guide.*

Airport: General Mitchell International Airport, 5300 S. Howell Ave. (747-5300). Take bus #80 from downtown (30 min.).

Amtrak: 433 W. St. Paul Ave. (800-872-7245), at 5th St. 3 blocks from the bus terminal. To: Chicago ($16); Minneapolis ($70). Ticket office open daily 5:30am-9pm. Fairly safe during the day, less so at night.

Buses: Greyhound, 606 N. 7th St. (272-8900), off W. Michigan St. downtown. Ticket office open daily 2-3:30am and 6am-11:30pm; station open 24 hrs. To: Chicago (17 per day, $21); Madison (6 per day, $8); Minneapolis (7 per day, $52). **Wisconsin Coach,** in the Greyhound terminal (542-8861) has service to southeast Wisconsin. **Badger Bus** (276-7490) is across the street. To: Madison (6 per day; $8). Stations are not very safe at night.

Public Transport: Milwaukee Cty. Transit System, 1942 N. 17th St. (344-6711). Efficient service in the metro area. Most lines run 4am-1:30am. $1.10, weekly pass $8.75, seniors 50¢ with Medicare card. Pick up free map at the library or the info center at the Grand Ave. Mall. Call for schedules and information.

Taxi: City Veteran Taxi, 291-8080. Base rate $1.50, plus $1.25 per mi., 50¢ each additional passenger.

Car Rental: Payless Car Rental, 4939 S. Howell (482-0300), take bus #80 south to airport. $28 per day with unlimited mileage. $11 collision insurance. Must be 21 with liability insurance and major credit card; ages 21-25 $8 surcharge. Open daily 6am-11pm.

Auto Transport Company: Auto Driveaway Co., 9039 W. National Ave. (962-0008 or 327-5252), in West Alice. Must be 21 with good driving record. $250 deposit refunded at destination; driver pays for gas. Call in advance for availability. Open Mon.-Fri. 9am-5pm, Sat. 9am-noon.

Help Lines: Crisis Intervention, 257-7222. Open 24 hrs. **Rape Crisis Line,** 547-4600 or 542-3828. **Gay People's Union Hotline,** 562-7010. Open 7-10pm.

Traveler's Aid: At the airport, upper level (747-5245). Open daily 9am-9pm.

Post Office: 345 W. St. Paul Ave. (291-2544), south along 4th Ave. from downtown, next to the Amtrak station. Open Mon.-Fri. 7:30am-8pm. **ZIP code:** 53203.

Area Code: 414.

Milwaukee is constructed in an organized grid pattern, with address numbers increasing as you get farther away from **Second Street** and **Wisconsin Ave.** Downtown Milwaukee starts at **Lake Michigan** and runs west to about 10th St.

ACCOMMODATIONS

Sleeping rarely comes cheap in downtown Milwaukee, but there are two attractive hostels nearby, as well as the convenient University of Wisconsin dorms. **Bed and Breakfast of Milwaukee** (571-0780) is a reservation service; the closest B&B is 8 mi. south of downtown, 823 N. 2nd St. ($50 for 2 people). Avoid staying downtown at night, as it can be dangerous.

University of Wisconsin at Milwaukee (UWM): Sandburg Halls, 3400 N. Maryland Ave. (229-4065). Take bus #30 north to Hartford St. Nice rooms. Laundry, cafeteria, free local calls available, no kitchen. Convenient to nightlife and east side restaurants. Private singles with shared bath $21, doubles $28. Open May 31-Aug. 15. 2-day advance reservations required.

Hotel Wisconsin, 720 N. 3rd St. (271-4900), across from the Grand Avenue Mall. 250 very nice rooms at a convenient downtown location with free parking, private bath, and free cable TV. Singles $49, with 2 persons $59, $8 each extra adult. Key deposit $5. Availabilitiy varies, so make reservations early.

LET'S GO BY TRAIN

Eurail Passes

Convenient way to travel Europe.
Save up to
70% over
cost of
individual
tickets.

EURAILPASS
FIRST CLASS

15 days	$498
21 days	$648
1 month	$798
2 months	$1098
3 months	$1398

EURAIL FLEXIPASS
FIRST CLASS

Any 5 days in 2 months	$348
Any 10 days in 2 months	$560
Any 15 days in 2 months	$740

EURAIL SAVERPASS**
FIRST CLASS

15 days	$430
21 days	$550
1 month	$678

**Price per person for 2 or more people
travelling together. 3 people required
between April 1 - September 3.

EURAIL YOUTHPASS*
SECOND CLASS

15 days	$398
1 month	$578
2 months	$768

*Valid only if passenger is under 26 on first
date of travel.

EURAIL YOUTH FLEXIPASS*
SECOND CLASS

Any 5 days in 2 months	$255
Any 10 days in 2 months	$398
Any 15 days in 2 months	$540

*Valid only if passenger is under 26 on first
date of travel.

LET'S GO BY PLANE

Discounted Flights

Over 150 destinations including:

LONDON

MADRID

PARIS

ATHENS

ROME

Domestic fares too!
For prices & reservations
call 1-800-5-LETS-GO

EURAIL COUNTRY PASSES

**POLAND HUNGARY
AUSTRIA FRANCE
SCANDINAVIA
FINLAND
LUXEMBOURG
GREECE SPAIN
CZECHOSLOVAKIA
GERMANY PORTUGAL
NETHERLANDS
BRITAIN SPAIN**

Call for prices, rail n' drive
or rail n' fly options.
Flexotel passes too!

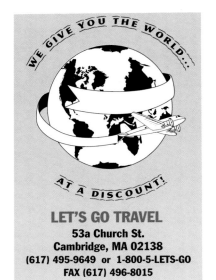

WE GIVE YOU THE WORLD...

AT A DISCOUNT!

LET'S GO TRAVEL
**53a Church St.
Cambridge, MA 02138
(617) 495-9649 or 1-800-5-LETS-GO
FAX (617) 496-8015**

LET'S GO HOSTELING
1994-95 Youth Hostel Card
Required by most international hostels.
Must be a U.S. resident.

F1 Adult (ages 18-55) $25

F2 Youth (under 18) $10

Sleepsack
Required at all hostels. Washable durable
poly/cotton. 18" pillow pocket. Folds into
pouch size.

G $13.95

1993-94 Youth Hostel Guide (IYHG)
Essential information about 4000 hostels in
Europe and the Mediterranean.

H $10.95

LET'S GET STARTED
Please print or type. Incomplete applications will be returned

Last Name	First Name	Date of Birth

Street	*We do not ship to P.O. Boxes. U.S. addresses only.*	

City	State	Zip Code

Phone	Date Trip Begins	

Item Code	Description, Size & Color	Quantity	Unit Price	Total Price

Shipping & Handling		
	Total Merchandise Price	
If order totals: · · · · · Add	Shipping & Handling (See box at left)	
Up to $30.00 · · · · · · $4.00	For Rush Handling Add $10 for continental U.S., $12 for AK & HI	
30.01-100.00 · · · · · · $6.00	MA Residents (Add 5% sales tax on gear & books)	
Over 100.00 · · · · · · $7.00	**Total**	

Mastercard/Visa Order

Cardholder name_____

Card number_____

Expiration date_____

Allow 2-3 weeks for delivery. Rush
orders delivered within one week •
our receipt.

Enclose check or money order
payable to:
Harvard Student Agencies, Inc.
53a Church St. Cambridge, MA 02

Prices subject to change without notice

LET'S GO® Travel

1994 CATALOG

We give you the world
at a discount!

•Discount Flights •Eurails •Travel Gear

LET'S PACK IT UP

Let's Go Supreme

Innovative hideaway suspension with parallel stay internal frame turns backpack into carry-on suitcase. Includes lumbar support pad, torso and waist adjustment, leather trim, and detachable daypack. Waterproof Cordura nylon, lifetime guarantee, 4400 cu. in. Navy, Green or Black.

A $175

Let's Go Backpack/Suitcase

Hideaway suspension with internal frame turns backpack into carry-on suitcase. Detachable daypack makes it 3 bags in 1. Waterproof Cordura nylon, lifetime guarantee, 3750 cu. in. Navy, Green or Black.

B $130

Let's Go Backcountry

Full size, slim profile expedition pack designed for the serious trekker. New Airflex suspension. X-frame pack with advanced composite tube suspension. Velcro height adjustment, side compression straps. Detachable hood converts into a fanny pack. Waterproof Cordura nylon, lifetime guarantee. Main compartment 6530 cu. in. extends to 7130 cu. in.

C $210

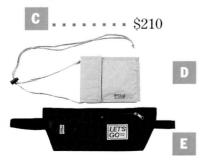

Undercover NeckPouch

Ripstop nylon with soft Cambrelle back. 3 pockets. 6 x 7". Lifetime guarantee. Black or Tan.

D $9.95

Undercover WaistPouch

Ripstop nylon with soft Cambrelle back. 2 pockets. 12 x 5" with adjustable waistband. Lifetime guarantee. Black or Tan.

E $9.95

Red Barn Hostel (HI/AYH), 6750 W. Loomis Rd. (529-3299), 13 mi. southwest of downtown via Rte. 894, exit Loomis. Take bus #10 or 30 west on Wisconsin Ave., get off at 35th St. and transfer to the #35 south to the Loomis and Ramsey intersection; then walk 3/4 mi. south on Loomis. A trek, almost not worth it without a car, but the price is right ($8). Musty, dark rooms in an enormous, red barn; bathroom is campground-quality. Full kitchen. The bus ride out is not very safe at night, Check-in 5-10pm. Members only, $8. Open May-Oct.

Belmont Hotel, 751 N. 4th St. (271-5880), at Wells downtown. 4-5 single rooms to rent in a mainly residential hotel. Moderate rooms in an excellent location. Not as safe at night. Some private baths, some share, $25.50. Key deposit $3.

FOOD

Milwaukee is a premier town of food and drink. German brewery masterminds took a gold liquid which has been around since 4000BC and industrialized it with refrigeration, glass bottles, cans and lots of PR, making beer available to all. In this dairy state, French ice cream, better known as frozen custard, is a renowned treat. There are stands all over the city with specialties like Snow Job and Grand Marnier Blueberry Crisp. To top it off, Milwaukeeans take advantage of their proximity to Lake Michigan with the Friday night fish fry, a local favorite.

Brady Street has many Italian restaurants, and the **South Side** is heavily Polish. The **Grand Avenue Mall's** third floor, a huge *Speisegarten* ("meal garden") on Wisconsin Ave. between 2nd and 4th St., cultivates reasonable ethnic and fast-food places. **East Side** eateries are a little more cosmopolitan, and good Mexican food sambas at S. 16th St. and National.

Taquería Jalisco, 2207 E. North Ave. (291-0645), on the East side. Authentic Mexican food, huge portions, at low prices. Burrito $2.50, tacos $1.25. Sit-down or take-out, 24 hrs.

Abu's Jerusalem of the Gold, 1978 N. Farwell (277-0485), at Lafayette on the East Side. Exotic tapestries, and plenty of trinkets adorn this tiny corner restaurant. Try the rosewater lemonade, 85¢. Plenty of veggie entrees, including felafel sandwich ($2.50). In case you want to try it at home, next door is Abu's Academy of Arabian Bites (277-0485). Open Mon.-Thurs. 11:30am-9pm, Fri.-Sat. 11:30am-11pm, Sun. noon-9pm.

Webster's Books and Café, 1932 E. Kenilworth Pl. (765-1221). Pour over the latest bestseller with a good cup of coffee and a delectable pastry ($1-2). Near North Ave. and other nightlife. Open Mon.-Thurs. 7:30am-11pm, Fri. 7:30am-midnight, Sat. 8am-11pm, Sun. 8am-11pm.

Three Brothers, 2414 St. Clair St. (481-7530), #15 bus to Conway and walk 4 blocks east. One of the best known of Milwaukee's famed Serbian restaurants, this family-owned business serves dishes such as *burek,* a strudel puff pastry filled with beef or chicken ($10). Open Tues.-Thurs. 5-10pm, Fri.-Sat. 4-11pm, Sun. 4-10pm. Reservations recommended.

Balisterer's (475-1414), 68 and Wells, a delectable-smelling Italian fare restaurant with excellent (and huge) pizza ($6.95 junior). Open Mon.-Thurs. 11am-1am, Fri.-Sat. 3pm-2am, Sun. 3pm-midnight.

SIGHTS

Although many of Milwaukee's breweries have left, the city's name still conjures up thoughts of a cold one. No visit to the city would be complete without a look at the yeast in action. **The Miller Brewery,** 4251 W. State St. (931-2337), offers free one-hour tours with free samples. (2 tours per hr. Mon.-Sat. 10am-3:30pm. 18 and under accompanied by adult.) "Heineken? Fuck that shit." **Pabst Brewing Company,** 915 W. Juneau Ave. (223-3709), offers free tours (Mon.-Fri. 10am-3pm, Sat. 10am-2pm on the hr., Sept.-May closed Sat.). The micro-brewery **Sprecher Brewing Co.,** 730 W. Oregon St. (272-2337), has 1, 2 and 3pm $2 tours on Saturday only. Make reservations 2 days in advance.

You've seen the t-shirts and the bikers, now see the factory. **Harley-Davidson Inc.,** 11700 W. Capitol Dr. (342-4680), assembles their engines in Milwaukee. (Tours vary; call to confirm times. No children under 12. Free.)

Milwaukee is graced with several excellent museums. The **Milwaukee Public Museum,** 800 W. Wells St. (278-2702), at N. 8th St., allows visitors to walk through exhibits of the streets of Old Milwaukee and a European village, complete with cobblestones and two-story shops. Other exhibits focus on Native American settlements and North American wildlife. (Parking available. Open daily 9am-5pm. $4.50, students $3, kids $2.50.) The lakefront **Milwaukee Art Museum,** in the War Memorial Building, 750 N. Lincoln Memorial Dr., houses Haitian art, 19th-century German art, and U.S. sculpture and paintings, including two of Warhol's soup cans. (Open Tue.-Wed. and Fri.-Sat. 10am-9pm, Thurs. noon-9pm, Sun. noon-5pm. $4, seniors, students, and persons with disabilities $2.) The **Charles Allis Art Museum,** 1801 N. Prospect Ave. (278-8295), at Royall Ave., is an English Tudor mansion with a fine collection of Chinese, Japanese, Korean, Persian, Greek, and Roman artifacts, as well as U.S. and European furniture. (Open Wed. 1-5pm and 7-9pm, Thurs.-Sun. 1-5pm. $2. Take bus #30 or 31.) The stone and ivy **Milwaukee County Historical Center,** 910 N. Old World 3rd St. (273-8288), details the early years of the city with many artifacts, photographs, documents, and displays. (Open Mon.-Fri. 9:30am-5pm, Sat. 10am-5pm, Sun. 1-5pm. Free.)

The **Mitchell Park Horticultural Conservatory,** 524 S. Layton Blvd. (649-9800), at 27th St., better known as "The Domes," recreates a desert, a rain forest, and seasonal displays in a series of three seven-story conical glass domes. (Open daily 9am-5pm. $2.50, seniors, kids, and persons with disabilities $1.25. Take bus #27.) Four mi. west, you'll find the **Milwaukee County Zoo,** 10001 W. Bluemound Rd. (771-3040), where zebras and cheetahs eye each other across a moat in the only predator-prey exhibit in the U.S. Also look for the elegant, misunderstood black rhinos and the trumpeter swans. (Open Mon.-Sat. 9am-5pm, Sun. 9am-6pm; shorter hours in winter. $6, children 3-12 $4. Parking $4. Take bus #10.)

Historic Milwaukee, Inc., P.O. Box 2132 (277-7795), offers tours focusing on ethnic heritage, original settlements, and architecture ($2-3). Ask about Milwaukee's many beautiful churches, including **St. Josaphat's Basilica,** 2333 S. 6th St. (645-5623), a turn-of-the-century landmark with a dome larger than the Taj Mahal's. Make phone arrangements to see the church, since it's usually locked. The **Milwaukee County Transit System** runs a 45-min. trolley tour of downtown that leaves from Grand Ave. at 2nd St. ($3; 11:15am and 12:15pm daily), and four-hr. **bus tours** that include a stop at a brewery and the domes. ($10, children and seniors $8; call 344-6711 for details.)

EVENTS AND ENTERTAINMENT

Milwaukee is festival-happy, throwing a different city-wide party almost every summer weekend. The tourist's office is overflowing with pamphlets and brochures on every kind of event. **Summerfest** (273-3378, outside Milwaukee 800-837-3378), the largest and most lavish, lasts over 11 days in late June and early July. Daily life is put on hold as a potpourri of musical acts, culinary specialities, and an arts and crafts bazaar take over. Kids will enjoy the circus show and children's theater. The **Rainbow Summer** (273-2787) is a series of free lunchtime concerts throughout the summer running the spectrum from jazz and bluegrass to country music. Concerts are held weekdays from noon-1:15pm in the Peck Pavilion at the Performing Arts Center (see below). Milwaukeeans line the streets for **The Great Circus Parade** (276-1234) in mid-July, an authentic re-creation of turn-of-the-century processions, with trained animals, daredevils, costumed performers, and 75 original wagons. (Call their office for information on special weekend packages at local hotels and motels during the parade.) In early August the **Wisconsin State Fair** (266-7000) rolls into the fairgrounds, toting big-name entertainment, 12 stages, exhibits, contests, rides, fireworks, and, of course, a pie-baking contest. ($5, under 11 free.) Pick up a copy of the free weekly entertainment mag, *Downtown Edition,* for the full scoop on festivals. There are ethnic festivals every weekend; the most popular are **Polishfest** (529-2140) in mid-June, **Festa Italiana** (223-2193) in mid-July, **Bastille Days** (223-7500) near Bastille Day (July 14), and **German Fest** (464-9444) in late July (tickets $6, children under 12 free).

For quality arts performances, visit the modern white stone **Performing Art Center (PAC),** 929 N. Water St. (800-472-4458), across the river from Père Marquette Park. The PAC hosts the Milwaukee Symphony Orchestra, First Stage Milwaukee, a Ballet Company, and the Florentine Opera Company. (Tickets $10-46, ½-price student and senior tix available day of show.) For information about events in the Milwaukee area, call **Milwaukee Tix** (271-3335, Mon.-Sat. noon-3pm). They also have ½-price tickets on the day of some shows.

The **Milwaukee Brewers** baseball team plays at County Stadium, 201 S. 46th St. and the interchange of I-94 and Rte. 41 (933-9000), as do the **Green Bay Packers** for half of their home games. The **Milwaukee Bucks** (227-0500), the local basketball team, lock horns with opponents at Bradley Center, 1001 N. 4th St. (227-0700); the **Milwaukee Admirals** (227-0550) also skate there.

NIGHTLIFE

In this land of over 15,000 lakes, it just about seems there's more beer flowing than water. With a bar almost always in sight, Milwaukee doesn't lack for *something* to do after sundown. Downtown gets a little seedy at night; the best nightlife district is on North Ave. on the East side, near the UW campus.

Downtown, come in from the cold to **Safehouse,** 779 N. Front St. (271-2007). Step through a bookcase passage and enter a bizarre world of spy hideouts, James Bond music, and a phone booth with 90 sound effects. A brass plate labeled "International Exports, Ltd." marks the entrance. Draft beer (code name: "liquid gold") costs $1.50, simple dinners $6-12. (Open Mon.-Sat. 11:30am-2am, Sun. 4pm-midnight. Cover $1-2.) For British-style drinking fun, dip into **John Hawk's Pub,** 607 N. Broadway (964-9729), on the National Register of Historic Places. (Beer $1.75. Open daily 11am-2am, live jazz Fri.-Sat. at 9:30pm.)

On North Ave. on the East Side, there are a slew of bars and clubs. **Von Trier's,** 2235 N. Farwell (272-1775), at North, is very cool and definitely the nicest. Authentic German-American artifacts adorn the walls; check out the ceiling painting of the town of Trier. There are no pitchers—strictly bottled imports (average $3.50 per bottle) in the lavish German interior or on the large outdoor patio. (Open Sun.-Thurs. 4pm-2am, Fri.-Sat. 4pm-3am.) **Hooligan's,** a block or so south at 2017 North Ave. (273-5230), is smaller, louder, and—as the name might suggest—rowdier. (Open daily 11am-2:30am. Pitchers $5. Live music Sept.-June on Mon. at 9:30pm. Cover $2-4.) For good food and drink and a widely renowned comedy show, try **Comedy Sportz,** 126 N. Jefferson (272-8888), in 3rd Ward, a restaurant, bar, and great entertainment. (Shows Thurs.-Sun. at 7:30pm, additional show Fri.-Sat. at 10pm. Bar open Sun.-Thurs. 4pm-midnight, Fri.-Sat. 4pm-2am.)

THE HEARTLAND

The Heartland (commonly called the "flyover region" by critical East- and West-Coasters) has been much maligned by big-city snobs and freeway travelers who don't take the time to figure out what this region is all about. Nearly 200 years ago, a newborn nation stretched westward across the Mississippi into what was then the Louisiana Territory, bought from the French at just 2¢ an acre. Here was forged the character of America. This is the stomping ground of Huckleberry Finn, Buffalo Bill, Laura Ingalls Wilder, and Chief Crazy Horse—the legend, the cowboy, the pioneer farmer, and the native.

Before the Homestead Act of 1862, the Great Plains—the states west of Missouri and Iowa—were simply a huge, flat barrier to be crossed en route to the fertile valleys of the West Coast. The new law and the new transcontinental railroad began an economic boom that did not bust until the Great Depression of the 1930s, when the emerging "Bread Basket" region became a devastated Dust Bowl. Modern farming techniques have since tamed the soil, and the region now produces most of the nation's grain and livestock; cities such as Des Moines and Dodge City thrive once more on the trading of farm commodities.

The land still rules here; some of the most staggering sights in the region, and the country, are those created without the touch of a human hand—from the Badlands of the Dakotas to the vast caverns of Missouri. Others overwhelm the visitor with the combined effort of earth and man—Mount Rushmore and the insanely gigantic Crazy Horse National Monument. And in the south the "amber waves of grain" quietly reign as perhaps the greatest of all symbols of America.

> Severe floods inundated the states bordering on the Mississippi and Missouri rivers in Summer 1993; Iowa and Missouri were especially hard-hit. The information in this book was researched prior to the worst of the damage. Some facilities and services may have been disrupted, so call ahead.

 **Iowa**

Depending on your perspective, the name "Iowa" evokes images of patchwork corn and soybean farmland, idyllic "fields of dreams," the sandman, or Hicksville, U.S.A. To see Iowa's real beauty, exit the freeway and meander along the old country roads. Here, far from the beaten and pummeled concrete path, you can cast your line into one of the state's innumerable fishing streams, bike 52 mi. along the Cedar Valley Nature Trail, see the dust-created Loess Hills in the west, or travel back in time at one of the many traditional communities dotting the area.

PRACTICAL INFORMATION

Capital: Des Moines.
Tourist Information: Iowa Department of Economic Development, 200 E. Grand Ave., Des Moines 50309 (515-281-3100 or 800-345-4692). **Conservation Commission,** Wallace Bldg., Des Moines 50319 (515-281-5145).
Time Zone: Central (1 hr. behind Eastern). **Postal Abbreviation:** IA
Sales Tax: 5%.

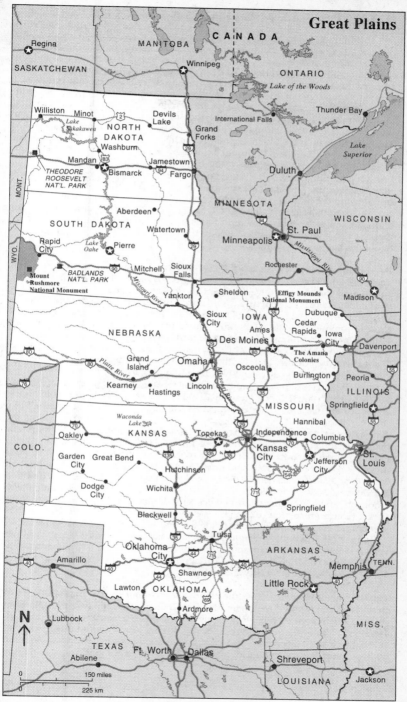

Great Plains

AMANA COLONIES

■■■ THE AMANA COLONIES

In 1714, German fundamentalists disillusioned with the established church formed the Community of True Inspiration. Facing persecution, they fled to the U.S. in 1843. Settling near Buffalo, NY, their community grew too large, so they migrated—this time to the rich promised land of Iowa. In 1855, along the Iowa River they founded the Amana Colonies ("Amana" means "to remain true"), living a communal lifestyle where everyone was equal and everything (yes, *everything*) shared. Eventually, the people became tired of the sacrifices required for such living and in 1932 they went capitalist. Some joined to form the Amana Society, Inc., which now owns most of the area's land and mills; another member started the hugely successful Amana Refrigeration Co. Unlike the Amish, the Inspirationists were not anti-technology; they believe God can be reached through personal piety. Today, the Amana Church still provides the colonies with a cultural and spiritual center.

In keeping with Old-World village custom, there are no addresses in the colonies, only place names. Anything that isn't on the road leading into town is easily found by following the profusion of signs that point to attractions off the main thoroughfare, the **Amana Trail,** which runs off U.S. 151 and goes through all seven colonies. **Main Amana** is the largest and most touristy of the seven Amana villages. The farther out you go into the smaller villages, the easier it is to imagine what life must have been like for the colonists.

Practical Information and Orientation The Amana Colonies lie 10 mi. north of I-80, clustered around the intersection of U.S. 6, Rte. 220, and U.S. 151. From Iowa City, take U.S. 6 west to U.S. 151; from Des Moines, take exit 225 off I-80 to U.S. 151. There is no public transportation to the Colonies. The **Amana Colonies Visitors Center** (622-6262 or 800-245-5465), just west of Amana on Rte. 220, shows promotional films (open Mon.-Thurs. 9am-5pm, Fri.-Sat. 9am-10pm, Sun. 10am-5pm). A private car caravan tour (622-6178) is given every Sat. at 10am, leaving from the visitors center (3 hr., $7, 12 and under $3.50; covers 6 villages). Throughout the colonies look for the *Visitors Guide*; it has maps and detailed listings including hours for all establishments, and most info is up to date.

There are four post offices in the Colonies, the largest in Main Amana at 101 2nd St. (622-3019), off I-51 (open Mon.-Fri. 7:30-11am, noon-4:30pm). Others in Middle and South Amana, and Homestead. Amana's **ZIP code** is 52203; **area code** is 319.

Accommodations and Camping Most lodging options consist of pricey but personal B&Bs, including **Noehouse Inn** (622-6350) on Main Street in Amana ($55-75), **Lucille's Bett und Breakfast** (668-1185), off I-80 7 mi. south of Main Amana (single or double $60), and **Loy's Bed and Breakfast** (624-7787), I-80 exit 216N near Main Amana (singles $44, doubles $55). The **Dusk to Dawn Bed and Breakfast** (622-3029) in Middle Amana offers beautiful rooms, a lovely garden with a hot tub, and a great breakfast (singles $35, doubles $42). An exception is the **Guest House Motor Inn** (622-3599) in downtown Main Amana, a converted 125 year-old communal kitchen house, with 38 rooms (singles $35, doubles $41).

Camp at the **Amana Community Park** in Middle Amana (622-3732, sites $3 per vehicle, $4.50 with electricity and water, no showers) or at the new **Amana Colonies RV Park** (622-6262), a grassy field right across from the visitors center. (Sites $8, $2 extra each for electricity and water.)

Food Numerous restaurants throughout the colonies serve huge portions of heavy food family-style. One of the best deals is the **Colony Inn** (622-6270) in Main Amana, which serves up hefty portions of delicious German and American food. Dinners ($10-14.50) and lunches ($5.50-7.50) are served with cottage cheese, bread, diced ham, sauerkraut, fruit salad, and mashed potatoes. Breakfast ($6) is an all-you-can-eat orgy of fruit salad, huge pancakes, fried eggs, thick sausage patties, bacon, and a bowl piled high with hash browns. (Open Mon.-Sat. 7am-10:30pm, Sun. 11am-7:30pm.) Middle Amana's **Hahn's Hearth Oven Bakery** (622-3439) sells the scrumptious products of the colonies' only functional open-hearth oven. (Open April-Oct. Tues.-Sat. 7am to sell-out (around 4:30pm); Nov.-Dec. and March Wed. and Sat. only.) **Heritage Wine and Cheese Haus** (622-3379) in Main Amana has delicious local goods, and free samples galore. Sample some rhubarb or dandelion wine here (open Mon.-Wed. 9am-6pm, Thurs.-Sat. 9am-7pm, Sun. 10am-5pm) or at any of the wineries scattered throughout the colonies.

Sights The **Museum of Amana History** (622-3567) has an informative (and sentimental) slide show, a friendly director, and exhibits to help imagine what it was like (including the neighborhood doctor's chair). (Open April 15-Nov. 15 Mon.-Sat. 10am-5pm, Sun. noon-5pm; $2.50, ages 6-17 $1.) At the **Woolen Mill** (622-3051), visitors can watch the machinery run on weekdays. Buy your famous Amana blankets, sweaters, and clothes here. (Open Mon.-Sat. 8am-6pm, Sun. 11am-5pm.) Down the street, watch artisans plane, carve, and sand wooden creations in the open workshop at the **Amana Furniture and Clock Shop** (622-3291; open Mon.-Sat. 9am-5pm, Sun. noon-5pm, visitors' workshop gallery open Mon.-Fri. 9-11:30am and noon-3pm). Beyond the **Amana Refrigeration Plant,** in Middle Amana, tour the **Communal Kitchen Museum** (622-3567), the former site of all local food preparation. (Open April-Nov. daily 9am-5pm. $1.50, kids 75¢.) **Miniature Americana** in South Amana on 220 trail (622-3058) has a fantastic exhibit depicting American history in miniature, including life on the prairie and the farm. The entire museum was built by Henry Moore and is run by his daughter. (Open daily April-Nov. 9am-5pm. $2.50, under 12 50¢.) For antique lovers, the **High Amana Store** of High Amana (622-3797), on Rte. 220, is the oldest store in the colonies, built in 1858, with an exceptional molded tin ceiling. (Usually open Mon.-Sat. 9:30am-5pm.) Although the colonies have become a large tourist attraction, it is important to realize that most of the stores are run by descendents of the colonists (and some former commune members themselves), and many are still active in the Church, proving that there is living history behind the chintz. For further spirit searching, take some time to gaze at the lotus lilies on **Amana Lily Lake** if you can catch them in bloom.

■■■ CEDAR RAPIDS

The second largest city in Iowa is much like Des Moines—it has a tidy downtown, excellent museums, a successful agricultural industry, and a friendly, relaxed pace. In the same city where Grant Wood modeled his famous painting "American Gothic," there is a unique population of Czech immigrants who add foreign spice among the corn rows.

Practical Information Cedar Rapids is a grid with streets divided into N., S., E., and W.; the Cedar River divides north and south, and U.S. 151 cleaves east and west. Stop at the **Cedar Rapids Area Convention and Visitors Bureau,** 119 1st Ave. S.E. (398-5009), for free maps, brochures, and helpful information. (Open Mon.-Fri. 8:30am-5pm, Sat. 9am-4pm.) Or, call the **Visitor Info Line** (398-9660).

Cedar Rapids lies at the junction of I-380 and U.S. 30 and 151, 19 mi. northeast of the Amana Colonies. **Greyhound,** 145 Transit Way S.E. (364-4167), races to Des Moines (3 per day, 3 hr., $10.50 Mon.-Thurs., $14.50 Fri.-Sun.) and Chicago (3 per day, 6½ hr., $31 Mon.-Thurs., $33 Fri.-Sun.). Get around town in **Easyride** buses. (Daily 5:20am-5:55pm; 50¢, seniors 25¢, students 30¢, transfers 10¢.) All routes stop at the **Ground Transportation Center,** 200 4th Ave. S.E. (398-5335), across from the Greyhound station. For taxis, try **Yellow Cab** (365-1444). A trolley runs downtown (50¢) 6:30-8:40am and 3-5:45pm. Pick up a schedule at the Visitors Bureau.

The **post office** is at 615 6th Ave. S.E. (399-2908). Open Mon.-Fri. 8:30am-5pm, Sat. 9am-noon. Cedar Rapids' **ZIP code** is 52401; the **area code** is 319.

Accommodations and Camping There are some budget motels on 16th Ave. S.W. The **Shady Acres Motel**, 1791 16th Ave. (362-3111), is a row of cottage-like, spotlessly clean rooms near a beautiful wooded area. Rooms have A/C, showers, and TV, but no phone. (Singles and doubles $22. Take bus #10 to the K-Mart 5 blocks away.) The **Red Cedar Campground** (398-5190) in the Seminole Valley Park is fairly far out, but also very pretty, with primitive and electric sites on shady riverbanks ($5). Take 380N to 42nd St. exit, left on 42nd St. and follow it all the way. There is a cluster of the big motel chains on 33rd Ave. S.W. off I-80 ($35 and up) that are worth it if you want more than a place to sleep.

Food Downtown Cedar Rapids is filled with moderately priced restaurants and delis, many of which cater to the lunchbreak market and close early. At **Gringo's**, 207 1st Ave. S.E. (363-1000), the artifacts from a historic building and thick cushioned booths give this Mexican restaurant an exotic feel, unlike the Hardees nearby. Certain nights feature all-you-can-eat buffets. (Entrees $5-8.50. Open Mon.-Thurs. 11am-10:30pm, Fri.-Sat. 11am-11pm, Sun. 11am-10pm.) For the car owner, a Cedar Rapids museum and restaurant in one is **Huckleberry's**, 4810 1st Ave. N.E. (373-1234), also buffet style ($6), with senior and children's discounts. (Open Mon.-Fri. 11am-9pm, Sat. 8am-9pm, Sun. 8am-8pm.) In the Czech Village, try the *houskas* (braided raisin bread) or *kolace* (fruit-filled sweet rolls) at family-owned **Sykora's Bakery**, 73 16th Ave. S.W. (364-5271). (Open daily 6am-5pm.) Try more substantial Czech meals at **Konecny's**, 72 16th Ave. S.W. (364-9492), a local favorite. Sandwiches cost $2-3, and goulash is only $1.25; fortunate travelers may catch the sausage & sauerkraut special for $3.75. (Open daily 6-10am and 11am-2pm.)

Sights and Entertainment Although a large part of Cedar Rapids' population has blond hair, the city has interesting ethnic roots. From 1870 to 1910, thousands of Czech immigrants settled in Cedar Rapids. Take bus #7 to 16th Ave. and C St. to visit the **Czech Village**, on 16th Ave. between 1st St. and C St. S.W., where the meat markets and harness shop have a charming Old-World feeling. At the end of the block Czech out the **National Czech and Slovak Museum and Library**, 10 16th Ave. S.W. (362-8500), which houses one of the largest collections of traditional costumes outside now-dissolved Czechoslovakia, and which just broke ground for a new museum five times as large. (Open Tues.-Sat. 9:30am-4pm; Dec.-Jan. Sat. 9:30am-4pm. $2.50, ages 8-13 $1.) In addition, Cedar Rapids is home to the oldest mosque in the U.S.

There's a row of bars and nightclubs from 3rd St. S.E. along 16 Ave. S.W. to C St. S.W. **Little Bohemia**, 1317 3rd St. S.E. (364-9396; open Mon.-Thurs. 10am-midnight, Fri.-Sat. 10am-2am) and **Al's Red Frog**, 88 16th Ave. S.W. (369-3940; open Mon.-Sat. 11am-2am, Sun. 11am-midnight) are popular bars, while live music shows occur on weekends at **Bruceski's**, 64 16th Ave. S.W. (362-1314; cover $2-3, open Tues.-Thurs. 4pm-midnight, Fri. 4pm-2am, Sat. 11am-2am). There's fun for the whole family at the **Freedom Festival** (365-8313), the ten days up to and including July 4th, featuring **gurney races** (the carts used to transport hospital patients).

■■■ DES MOINES

French explorers originally named the Des Moines river the "Rivière des Moingouenas," for a local Native American tribe, but then shortened the name to "Rivière des Moings." Because of its identical pronunciation (mwan), later French settlers called their river and city by a name much more familiar to them: Des Moines (of the monks). Today, Des Moines (pronounced "da moyne" like "da loin") shows neither Native American nor monastic influence, but rather the imprint of the agricultural state that spawned it. The price of soybeans is as hotly discussed here as stock prices are in New York. The World Pork Expo is a red letter event on the Iowan calendar and the city goes hog-wild for the Iowa State Fair every August. If Iowa's capital city is a meat market, it's a very cosmopolitan one; it's the third-largest insurance center in the world, after London and Hartford. Des Moines also boasts an excellent art museum and hosts numerous local festivals and events.

PRACTICAL INFORMATION

Emergency: 911.

Des Moines Convention and Visitors Bureau, 2 Ruan Center, Suite 222 (near the Kaleidoscope and Locust Malls downtown; 286-4960 or 800-451-2625). Open Mon.-Fri. 8:30am-5pm.

Airport: Des Moines International Airport (256-5857), Fleur Dr. at Army Post Rd., about 5 mi. southwest of downtown; take bus #8 ("Havens").

Greyhound: 1107 Keosauqua Way (800-231-2222), at 12th St. just northwest of downtown. To: Kansas City (3 per day, 4 hr., $43); St. Louis (5 per day, 10½ hr., $78); Chicago (10 per day, 7-10 hr., $50). Open 24 hrs.

Public Transport: Metropolitan Transit Authority (MTA), 1100 MTA Lane (283-8100), just south of the 9th St. viaduct. Open Mon.-Fri. 8am-5pm. Get maps at the MTA office or any Dahl's market. Routes converge at 6th and Walnut St. Buses run Mon.-Fri. 6:20am-6:15pm, Sat. 6:45am-5:50pm. Fare 75¢, transfers 5¢.

Taxi: Capitol Cab, 282-8111. **Yellow Cab,** 243-1111. $1.40 base rate, $1.20 per mi. Airport to downtown $8-9.

Car Rental: Budget (287-2612), at the airport. $33 first day, $36 per day thereafter, 100 free mi. per day, 25¢ per additional mi. Open Sun.-Fri. 6am-11:30pm, Sat. 6am-10pm. Must be 21 with major credit card. Under 25 add $5 per day.

Help Lines: Gay/Lesbian Resource Center, Info line 277-1454. Open Mon.-Thurs. 4-10pm, Sun. 4-8pm. **Rape/Sexual Assault Line,** 288-1750. Open 24 hrs.

Post Office: 1165 2nd Ave. (283-7500), just north of I-235, downtown. Open Mon.-Fri. 8:30am-5:30pm. **ZIP code:** 50318.

Area Code: 515.

Des Moines idles on the northwest side at the junction of I-35 and I-80. Numbered streets run north-south, named streets east-west. Numbering begins at the **Des Moines River** and increases east or west, starting at **South Union** where the river twists east. **Grand Avenue** divides addresses north-south along the numbered streets. Other east-west thoroughfares are **Locust Street, Park Avenue, Douglas Avenue, University Avenue,** and **Hickman Road.**

ACCOMMODATIONS AND CAMPING

Finding cheap accommodation in Des Moines is usually no problem, though you should make reservations for visits in March (high school sports tournament season) and in August, when the State Fair comes to town. Several cheap motels cluster around I-80 and Merle Hay Rd., 5 mi. northwest of downtown. Take bus #4 ("Urbandale") or #6 ("West 9th") from downtown.

Econo Lodge, 5626 Douglas Ave. (278-1601), across from Merle Hay Mall. Bus stop in front. Large, newly furnished rooms with cable TV, free coffee, juice, rolls, and newspaper. Spa and sauna available. Singles $36, doubles $40.

Royal Motel, 3718 Douglas Ave. (274-0459), 1 mi. from Merle Hay Mall. Take bus #6. 11 clean, comfortable, cottage-like rooms. Singles $27, doubles $32; $35 for 3.

YMCA, 101 Locust St. (288-2424), at 1st St. downtown on the west bank of the river. Small rooms, convenient downtown location. Lounge, laundry, athletic facilities, including pool. Men only. Key deposit $5. Singles $19.50, $61 per week.

YWCA, 717 Grand Ave. (244-8961), across from the Marriott Hotel downtown. In a fairly safe area. Women only. Clean dorm-style rooms with access to lounge, kitchen, and laundry, and pool. All rooms shared; its main purpose is to provide social services and emergency shelter. $8 per day, $44 per week.

Iowa State Fairgrounds Campgrounds, E. 30th St. (262-3111), at Grand Ave. Take bus #1 or 2 to the Grand Ave. gate. 2000 (yes, *2000*) sites with water and electricity; at fairtime, 2500 additional primitive sites are squeezed in. No fires. Open mid-May-mid-Oct. $8 per vehicle; fee collected in the morning.

Walnut Woods State Park, S.W. 52 Ave. (285-4502), 4 mi. south of the city on Rte. 5. Secluded campground with horse and hiking trails nearby; not accessible by public transportation. Floods occasionally; if the front gate is locked, it's for a good reason. Primitive sites $5, with electricity $7.

FOOD

Cheap, clean fast-food places are located on the lower level of the **Locust Mall** downtown on 8th and Locust St. (244-1005). **Kaleidoscope Skywalk** (244-3205), just east of the Locust Mall, at 6th and Walnut St. in the Hub Tower, also has quick eats. Both food courts close at 5:30pm; sup here early. You'll think that you saw it on **Mulberry Street,** but in reality **Court Avenue** (the continuation of Mulberry), two blocks south of Locust around 3rd St., has reasonable Mexican and Italian restaurants in renovated warehouses and is also the nightlife place to be, with bars and young people everywhere. A popular **farmers market** (245-3880) peddles its produce at 4th and Court Ave. every Sat. 7am-1pm in the summer.

Spaghetti Works, 310 Court Ave. (243-2195). A huge converted warehouse with portions to match. Unlimited spaghetti and salad bar and free soda refills $4-7. Open Mon.-Thurs. 11:15am-2pm, 5-10pm, Fri.-Sat. 11:15-11pm, Sun. noon-9pm.

A Taste of Thailand, 215 E. Walnut St. (243-9521), east of downtown. Authentic Thai food in American setting, and seventy-one zillion different kinds of beer. Dinners around $7. Mon.-Sat. 11am-2pm and 5-9pm.

Juke Box Saturday Night, 206-208 3rd St. (284-0901). Hot spot for fun and drink. Decorative '57 Chevy motif. Aid your (in-)digestion by participating in the frequent hula-hoop, twist, and jitterbug contests. Drinks average $2.50. Thurs. pay $3 and beers are 5¢. Summer Fri.-Sat. 7-11pm, cover $3 for all the beer you can drink and live music. Open daily 4:30pm-2am.

SIGHTS

The copper- and gold-domed **state capitol** (281-5591), on E. 9th St. across the river and up Grand Ave., is a beautiful building with an excellent view of the city. It's worth a look to see Iowa at its proudest. Note the "please walk in" sign on the Secretary of State's door. (Free tours Mon.-Sat., call in the morning for schedule. Building open Mon.-Fri. 8am-4:30pm, Sat.-Sun. 8am-4pm.) Take bus #5 ("E. 6th and 9th St."), #1 ("Fairgrounds"), #2, 4 or 7. Further downhill collects the **Iowa State Historical Museum and Archives,** at Pennsylvania and Grand Ave. (281-5111), a modern building with three floors exhibiting Iowa's natural, industrial, and social history, including an exhibit addressing the environmental overdevelopment of Iowa (once the state had three million acres of prairie, now just a few thousand). (Open Tues.-Sat. 9am-4:30pm, Sun. noon-4:30pm. Free. Take any bus that goes to the capitol.) Also vaguely related to Iowan government is the grandiose Victorian mansion **Terrace Hill,** 2800 Grand Ave. (281-3604), built in 1869 and currently the gubernatorial mansion. (Tours Feb.-Dec. Tues.-Sat. 10am-1:30pm, Sun. 1-4:30pm every 30 min. Tickets $2, kids 50¢.) The geodesic greenhouse dome of the **Botanical Center,** 909 E. River Dr. (238-4148), next to I-235 and not far from the capitol, encompasses a wide array of exotic flora. (Mon.-Thurs. 10am-6pm, Fri. 10am-9pm, Sat.-Sun. 10am-5pm. Admission $1.50, ages 6-18 25¢, under 6 free.)

Most cultural sights cluster west of downtown. The **Des Moines Art Center,** 4700 Grand Ave. (277-4405), is acclaimed for its wing of stark white porcelain tile designed by I.M. Pei. Impressive modern works include George Segal's *To All Gates,* with which every wayworn traveler can identify; also a small but high-quality American art collection. (Open Tues.-Wed. and Fri.-Sat. 11am-5pm, Thurs. 11am-9pm, Sun. noon-5pm. $2, seniors and students $1. Free all day Thurs. and until 1pm Fri.-Wed. Take bus #1.) Flapper-era cosmetics manufacturer Carl Weeks realized his aristocratic aspirations after he had salvaged enough ceilings, staircases, and artifacts from English Tudor mansions to complete **Salisbury House,** 4025 Tonawanda Dr. (279-9711), Grand Ave. to 42 St. (public tours Mon.-Thurs. at 2pm, Fri. 10am, or by appointment; $3, kids $1).

One way to see Iowa which will convince you once and for all that it isn't completely flat is to participate in **RAGBRAI,** the Des Moines **Register's Annual Great Bicycle Ride Across Iowa.** Contact the *Register* (515-284-8000) for more info.

The **Iowa State Fair,** one of the largest in the nation, captivates Des Moines for 10 days during the middle of August. Come see prize cows (and crafts and cakes and ears of corn) and enjoy rides and shows and more soybean recipes than you ever knew existed. For information contact the 24-hr. info line at the Administration Building, Iowa State Fair Grounds, Des Moines 50306 (262-3111). For lots of free event listings, pick up a copy of **Cityview,** the free local weekly paper.

■ Near Des Moines

Located only 5 mi. west on Grand Ave. in West Des Moines is **Valley Junction,** a restored railroad town with low brick buildings and an antique lover's paradise (lots and lots of antiques). A farmer's market chugs every Thurs. 4:30-8pm. The **Des Moines Metro Opera** (961-6221) produces three full-scale operas every summer in the Blank Performing Arts Center at Simpson college in **Indianola,** 12 mi. south of Des Moines on U.S. 69. Tickets $22-47. The nearby **National Balloon Museum,** 1601 N. Jefferson, (961-3714) is rumored to derive its hot air from the operatic performers, and holds balloon regattas. (Open Mon.-Fri. 9am–4pm, Sat. 10am-4pm, Sun. 1-4pm.) **Pella,** 25 mi. east of Des Moines on Rte. 163, hosts a famous Iowa festival, **Tulip Time** (628-4311), the second weekend in May. At other times the town maintains a tangible Dutch presence and several excellent Dutch bakeries.

■■■ IOWA CITY

Iowa City is a classic college town; housing the main University of Iowa campus, it's complete with bars, frozen yogurt, street musicians, and hordes of students. But more importantly, Iowa City is a mecca of liberalism in a conservative state. Each weekend, whole communes of Iowans make a pilgrimage to the city in order to burn incense, bar-hop, and cheer-on the Hawkeyes, the University's football team.

Practical Information The **Convention and Visitors Bureau,** 325 E. Washington St. (337-6592 or 800-283-6592), 2nd floor, has helpful self-guided walking tour brochures and friendly staff. From there you can walk to the main downtown area, which is bounded by **Madison** and **Gilbert** (east-west) and **Burlington** and **Market** (north-south). Burlington St. is an especially important thoroughfare since it intersects most north-south streets and crosses the Iowa River. Most people in Iowa City either ride a bike or take the bus. **Iowa City Transit** (356-5151), running Mon.-Fri. 6am-10:30pm and Sat. 6am-6:30pm, 50¢, seniors 25¢, monthly pass $18, or the free, University-sponsored **Cambus,** which connects the campus to downtown. **Greyhound** and **Burlington Trailways** are both located at 404 E. College St. (337-2127), at Gilbert. To: Minneapolis (3 per day, $42); Des Moines (6 per day, $16.50); Chicago (6 per day, $28-31); St. Louis (1 per day, $41). (Open Mon.-Sat. 6am-8pm, Sun. 10:30am-3pm, 5-8pm.) The **post office,** 400 S. Clinton St. (354-1560), is open 8:30am-5pm, Sat. 9:30am-1pm. The **ZIP code** is 52240, and the **area code** is 319.

Food and Accommodations The downtown is loaded with good, cheap restaurants and bars. At **The Kitchen,** 215 E. Washington (358-9524), you can devise your own pasta concoction ($5.25 and up). (Open Mon.-Sat. 11am-2:30pm, 5-9:30pm.) **Vito's,** 118 E. College (338-1393), is a restaurant and bar with cajun chicken fettucine ($6.50). (Open daily 11am-1:30am.) **Bushnell's Turtle,** 127 E. College (351-5536), serves the lunch crowd sandwiches ($3-5). (Open Mon.-Sat.

11am-7pm.) There are bars and nightspots all over downtown. Iowa City is an artsy place with **Hancher Auditorium,** North Riverside Dr. (800-426-2437 or 335-1130) as host to top-notch performances. At the **Pedestrian Mall,** an open area in downtown, you will often see a passerby whip out a guitar and serenade the shoppers.

For cheap and fast dining, try the **Iowa Memorial Union** (335-3055), the huge U of I student center at Madison and Jefferson. It also has a Ticketmaster, a mini-post office, an excellent bookstore, and many other services (open Mon.-Thurs. 7am-11pm, Fri.-Sat. 7am-midnight). Off one wing is **Iowa House** (335-3513), a pricey but classy hotel with large rooms at an excellent location close to downtown, the museums, and multiple parks. (Free parking. Singles $47, doubles $55. Reservations recommended, especially for U of I football and parents weekends.) Less expensive, but very much a hole-in-the-wall is **Wesley House Hostel (HI/AYH),** 120 N. Dubuque St. (338-1179), at Jefferson. (Check in 7-9pm only, and must be out again by 9am. Curfew is 10pm, and they mean it. 7 beds in one musty room. Members only, $10.) There are a bunch of cheap chain motels in Coralville, 2 mi. west of downtown on I-80. Get off at exit 242 and take your pick. For camping try **Kent Park Campgrounds,** 9 mi. west on 6W, a very pretty area with meadows and 86 nice sites. $4, with electricity, $8. No phone; first come, first serve.

Sights Iowa City was the state's capital until 1857, and the **Old Capitol** building (335-0548), at Union and Iowa St., which has been restored almost beyond recognition, is still the main attraction (open Mon.-Sat. 10am-3pm, Sun. noon-4pm; free, including tours). The capitol is also the focal point of the **Pentacrest,** at Clinton and Iowa, a five building formation with a center green perfect for hanging out. Also, one of the five is the **Museum of Natural History** (335-0480), which has interesting exhibits on the Native Americans of Iowa (open Mon.-Sat. 9:30am-4:30pm, Sun. 12:30-4:30pm; free). Five blocks west is the **Museum of Art,** 150 N. Riverside Drive (335-1727), housing an internationally acclaimed collection of African art (open Tues.-Sat. 10am-5pm, Sun. noon-5pm; free). **Coralville Lake** (338-3543), 5 mi. north on Dubuque St., has a beautiful view of the Iowa River and is an excellent place to sponge. Almost the entire city performs somehow in the **Iowa Festival,** for two weeks in mid-June, with all the cultural events the city could think of.

Kansas

The geographic center of the contiguous U.S., Kansas has been a major link in the nation's chain since the 1840s. Decades ago the roads of Kansas were smokey from the dust of hordes of cowboys herding cattle along the Chisholm, Santa Fe, and Oregon Trails. The influx of cowboys and their infrastructure unsettled the Native Americans in fierce battles. Additional grueling feuds over Kansas' slavery status (Kansas joined the Union as a free state in 1861) gave this heartland state the nickname "Bleeding Kansas." The wound has clotted, and today the smokey roads are due to the shipping trucks that rumble through on I-35 and I-70. Kansas is a major food producer, growing more wheat than any other state. Highway signs subtly remind travelers that "every Kansas farmer feeds 75 people—and *you.*"

PRACTICAL INFORMATION

Capital: Topeka.
Visitor Information: Department of Commerce and Housing, 700 SW Harrison Suite #1300, Topeka, 66603-3712 (800-2KANSAS/252-6727). **Kansas Wildlife and Parks,** 900 Jackson Ave., Suite #502N, Topeka 66612 (296-2281).
Time Zone: Central (1 hr. behind Eastern). **Postal Abbreviation:** KS
Sales Tax: 6.25%.

■■■ TOPEKA

Topeka has been a decisive battle ground throughout its history. It was founded in 1854 by abolitionist settlers willing to use their votes and bodies to keep Kansas a free state. When Kansas was admitted to the Union as a free state on January 29, 1861, Topeka became its capital with only 200 residents. In 1954, the famous anti-segregation case *Brown v. Topeka Board of Education* went before the supreme court, launching the Civil Rights movement.

Practical Information The schools—Sumner and Monroe Elementary—can still be visited by calling the **Topeka Convention and Visitors Bureau,** 120 E. 6th St. (234-1030 or 800-235-1030; open Mon.-Fri. 8am-5pm). The **Amtrak** station is at 5th and Holiday (357-5362 or 800-872-7245). One train goes west, one east daily to Lawrence (½ hr., $10), Kansas City (1½ hr., $19), and St. Louis (8 hr., $59). Open 24 hrs. **Greyhound** (233-2301) is at 200 S.E. 3rd, at Quincy a few blocks northeast of the capitol. Buses race to: Kansas City (6 per day, 1½ hr., $16.50), Lawrence (6 per day, 35 min., $6.75), Denver (3 per day, 13 hr., $16), Wichita (3 per day, 3 hr.; $27), and Dodge City (1 per day, 8 hr., $46). (Open Mon.-Fri. 7am-10pm, Sat.-Sun. 7-11:15am, 3-4pm, and 8-10pm.) **Topeka Transit** (354-9571) provides local bus transportation (Mon.-Fri. 6am-6pm, fare 75¢, seniors 35¢). Every 20 minutes from 11am-1:30pm, a 10¢ trolley runs along Kansas Ave. The Topeka **post office,** 424 South Kansas (295-9108), is open Mon.-Fri. 7:30am-5pm, Sat. 9:30am-noon. Topeka's **ZIP code** is 66601; the **area code** is 913.

Accommodations and Food There are no cheap places to stay in town—only on the outskirts are there motels. **Motel 6,** 709 Fairlawn (272-8283), off I-70, has functional rooms and free HBO (singles $26, doubles $32). Another standard is **Super 8 Motel,** 5966 SW 10th St. (273-5100), off I-70 (singles $36, doubles $47).

For something to eat, one block east of the state capitol is **Pore Richard's Cafe,** 705 S. Kansas Ave. (233-4276). Besides burgers and delicious shakes, you can have breakfast all day in booths with personal jukeboxes. (Open Mon.-Thurs. 11am-2am, Fri.-Sat. 11-3am, live Fri.-Sat. 9pm-1am.) Down the block is **Byrd's Nest,** 921 Kansas Ave. (232-6239), with a huge selection of sandwiches ($2.60-8.60) and dinners ($4-15). (Open Mon.-Sat. 11am-9pm.)

Sights Today the **state capitol building** (296-3966), between 10th and 8th Ave. at Harrison St., boasts a beautiful dome and murals of John Brown and the settling of the plains. Free tours let you ride the Willy Wonka-esque great glass elevator and then climb into the dome. (Tours Mon.-Fri. 9-11am and 1-3pm on the hr., Sat. every 2 hrs. 9am-3pm.) Try the cheap sandwiches downstairs. (Building open Mon.-Fri. 8am-6pm, Sat.-Sun. 8am-5pm.)

Adjoined by a tunnel is the **Docking State Office Building,** 915 Harrison (296-3429). Ask for the free key at the security desk and check out the 14th floor observation tower (often used to spot tornadoes; open Mon.-Fri. 9am-3pm). **Gage Park** at 6th St. and Gage Blvd. houses both the **Topeka Zoological Park,** 635 SW Gage Blvd. (272-5821), which bred the first bald eagles in captivity (open daily 9am-4:30pm; $3, seniors and kids $1.50) and the **Reinisch Rose Garden** (272-6150) with over 7000 beautiful bushes (open dawn to dusk as long as roses bloom, usually June-Oct.; free). The **Kansas Museum of History,** 6425 SW 6th St. (272-8681), at Wanamaker, has a tremendous collection of prairie memorabilia (open Mon.-Sat. 9am-4:30pm, Sun. 12:30-4:30pm; free).

■■■ WICHITA

When Coronado came to Wichita's present-day site in 1541 in search of the mythical gold-laden city Quivira, he was so disappointed that he had his guide strangled

W I C H I T A

for misleading him. 123 years later, the traders James Mead and Jesse Chisholm opened a trading post there. They inadvertently began the Chisholm Trail, over which millions of cattle from Texas were to travel on their way east. Soon the First and Last Chance Saloon was built, which gave refreshment to weary Texas cowboys. From these humble pioneer beginnings grew the "Peerless Princess of the Plains." Today, Wichita is one of the largest aircraft manufacturing centers and home to a symphony, museums, and plenty of barbecue.

Practical Information Wichita sits on I-35, 170 mi. north of Oklahoma City and about 200 mi. southwest of Kansas City. **Main Street** is the major north-south thoroughfare. **Douglas Avenue** lies between numbered east-west streets to the north and named east-west streets to the south. **Kellogg Avenue** is a main drag, turning into U.S. 54 on the outskirts of town. The **Convention and Visitors Bureau,** 100 S. Main St. (265-2800), has a "Quarterly Calendar" of local events. (Open Mon.-Fri. 8am-5pm.) Don't miss the **Winfield Bluegrass Festival** (316-221-3230), drawing big name artists for a long weekend of folk fun in mid-Sept.

The closest **Amtrak** station (283-7533) is in Newton, 25 mi. north of Wichita (tickets sold Wed.-Fri. 7:30am-4pm). **Greyhound,** 312 S. Broadway (265-7711), barks two blocks east of Main St. Buses serve: Kansas City (4 per day, 4 hr., $30); Denver (2 per day, 14 hr., $78); Dodge City (1 per day, 3 hr., $24); Dallas (3 per day, 9 hr., $75). (Open daily 2am-7pm.) **Hutch Shuttle** (800-288-3342) inside the station, provides transport daily Mon.-Fri. at 1pm to Newton Amtrak Station $12. The public transport, **WMTA,** 214 S. Topeka (265-7221; call for schedules), runs buses Mon.-Fri. 6am-6:30pm, Sat. 7am-5:30pm, 85¢ with 20¢ transfer, seniors 45¢, ages 7-17 55¢. (Station open Mon.-Fri. 6am-6:30pm, Sat. 7am-5:30pm.) **Thrifty Rent-A-Car,** 8619 W. Kellogg (721-9552), has cars for $26 per day, 250 free mi. or $140 per week, 2000 free mi. (Must be 21 with major credit card. Open daily 6:30am-10pm.) The **post office,** 7117 W. Harry (946-4511), at Airport Rd. is open daily 4-7am, 8:30am-noon, and 2:30-7pm. Wichita's **ZIP code** is 67276; the **area code** is 316.

Accommodations Wichita presents a bounty of cheap hotels. South Broadway has plenty, but be wary of the neighborhood. The **Mark 8 Inn,** 1130 N. Broadway (265-4679), is right on the mark, with well-kept, clean rooms, free local calls, and fridges (singles $34, doubles $41). Closer to downtown and the bus station is the **Royal Lodge,** 320 E. Kellogg (263-8877), with a clean interior and cable TV (singles $30, doubles $32; key deposit $5). Several other cheap, palatable motels line East and West Kellogg 5-8 mi. from downtown. The **Wichita KOA Kampground,** 15520 Maple Ave. (722-1154), has private showers, a laundromat, game room, pool, and convenience store. (Office open daily 8am-noon, and 3:30-8pm. Tent sites $13 per 2 people, with full hookup $17. Adults $3, ages 3-17 $2.)

Chow Time In Wichita they spell their meals "m-e-a-t;" if you have only one slab of meat in Wichita, go to **Doc's Steakhouse,** 1515 N. Broadway (264-4735), where the most expensive entree is the 17-oz. T-bone at $8.75. (Open Mon.-Thurs. 11:30am-9:30pm, Fri. 11:30am-10pm, Sat. 4-10pm.) For downtown home mesquite BBQ, stop by an outdoor lunch at **Gino's Mesquite Grill,** 828 W. 11th St. (265-7959), at Bitting. Beef or buffalo burger $2.50. Only outside dining, so it's closed in the harsh winter weather (call to be sure; open Mon. 5-9pm, Tues.-Fri. 11am-2pm and 5-9pm, Sat. 11am-8pm). The area around 800 E. Douglas has been renovated and is now a restaurant and a nightspot center. For vegetarians, **The Pasta Mill,** 808 E. Douglas (269-3858), has inexpensive homemade pasta and an adjoining bar. Free live jazz Sundays 7-10pm. (Open Mon.-Thurs. 11am-10pm, Fri.-Sun. 11am-11pm.)

Sights Museums-on-the-River hosts a series of different museums within a few miles of each other. The **Old Cowtown Historic Village Museum,** 1871 Sim Park Dr. (264-8894), takes you through the rough and tumble cattle days of the 1870s with a fantastic open air living history exhibit with 30 buildings on 17 acres. Certain days, period-dressed Girl Scouts run around, really making you feel like an old cow-poke. (Open Mon.-Sat. 10am-5pm, Sun. noon-5pm. $3.50, seniors $3, ages 6-12 $2, under 6 free.) Across the way is **Botanica,** 701 Amidon (264-0448), an interesting and colorful series of gardens. (Open Mon.-Sat. 10am-5pm, Sun. 1-5pm, Jan.-March Mon.-Fri. 10am-5pm. $3, students $2; 50% AAA discount. Free Jan.-March.) Just down the road is the **Mid-American Indian Center and Museum,** 650 N. Seneca (262-5221), which showcases traditional and modern works by Native American art-ists. The late Blackbear Bosin's monolithic sculpture, *Keeper of the Plains,* stands guard over the grounds. (Open Mon.-Sat. 10am-5pm, Sun. 1-5pm. $2, ages 6-12 $1, under 6 free.) Also home to the **Mid-America All-Indian Intertribal Powwow** the last weekend in July. In the **Wichita-Sedgwick County Historical Museum,** 204 S. Main (265-9314), posh antique furniture and heirlooms sit beside historical oddities, such as the hatchet used by crusading prohibitionist Carry A. Nation when she demolished the bar of the Eaton Hotel. (Open Tues.-Fri. 11am-4pm, Sat.-Sun. 1-5pm. $2, ages 6-16 $1, under 6 free.)

The **Wichita State University** campus, at N. Hillside and 17th St., contains an outdoor sculpture collection comprised of 53 works scattered across the campus, including pieces by Rodin, Moore, Nevelson, and Hepworth. Get free sculpture maps or free acoustic guides at the **Edwin A. Ulrich Museum of Art** office, 204 McKnight (689-3664), also on campus (open Mon.-Fri. 8am-3:30pm). One side of this striking building contains a gigantic glass mosaic mural by Joan Miró. (Open Sept.-June Wed. 9:30am-8pm, Thurs.-Fri. 9:30am-5pm, Sat.-Sun. 1-5pm. Free.) Take "East 17th" or "East 13th" bus from Century II.

▓ Missouri

Missouri's license plates read, rather cryptically, "Show Me State." This is *not* a state that encourages exhibitionists; rather, it is the home of some gruff, incredulous farmers who don't believe a damn thing until they see it with their own two eyes. Appropriately enough, it was the birthplace of quintessential skeptic Mark Twain.

Missouri's troubled entry into the Union and its Civil War-era status as border state were harbingers of a future of perpetual ambiguity. Missouri is smack dab in the middle of the United States, but a stranger to every region. Ohioans think Missouri is too far west to be Midwest, while Kansans feel it is too far east to be Great Plains. In Minneapolis, at the head of the Mississippi River, they think Missouri, with its river boat jazz and French settlements, is somehow connected to New Orleans; in New Orleans, if they think of Missouri at all it's as that stodgy place up north near Chi-cago. Missouri resists all attempts at pigeonholing because none applies.

And so it goes—to those in the know, Missouri is a patchwork quilt of a state. In the north, near Iowa, amber waves of grain undulate. Along the Mississippi, tower-ing bluffs inscribed with Native American pictographs evoke western canyonlands. In central Missouri descendants of German immigrants have created an ersatz Rhine with vintages to match. Towards the Mississippi spelunk the world's largest lime-stone caves—made famous by Tom Sawyer and Becky Thatcher. Further south, rip-pling into Arkansas, are the ancient and underrated Ozarks. To be sure, Missouri has MO exciting stuff than you'd ever realize. And besides, Missouri loves company.

PRACTICAL INFORMATION
Capital: Jefferson City.

Missouri Division of Tourism, Department MT-90, P.O. Box 1055, Jefferson City 65102 (751-4133; 869-7110 in St. Louis). **Missouri Department of Natural Resources,** 205 Jefferson St., Jefferson City 65102 (751-3443 or 800-334-6946).
Time Zone: Central (1 hr. behind Eastern). **Postal Abbreviation:** MO
Sales Tax: 4.225%.

■■■ KANSAS CITY

Originally a trading post and outfitter for the Santa Fe and Oregon Trail-goers and the gold rushers, Kansas City has grown into a large metropolis. Sprawled over seven counties, there are actually two KC's—the more residential in Kansas (KCKS) and the quicker-paced commercial one in Missouri (KCMO)—the two are really one, separated by State Line Road. Regarded as one of America's best planned cities, Kansas City even has architecturally pleasing shopping centers. A major home of "agribusiness," KC is a main cattle-trader and grain distributor. Immortalized in the song from *Oklahoma!,* "Ev'rythin's up to date in Kansas City," this burg has business, blues, and barbecue galore.

PRACTICAL INFORMATION

Emergency: 911.
Visitors Center, 1100 Main St. #2550 (221-5242 or 800-767-7700), in the City Center Square Bldg. downtown. Pick up *A Visitor's Guide to Kansas City.* Open Mon.-Fri. 8:30am-5pm. Also at 4010 Blue Ridge Cutoff (861-8800), just off I-70 next to the stadium.
Airport: Kansas City International Airport (243-5237) 18 mi. northwest of KC off I-29. The **KCI Shuttle** (243-5000) departs every 30-45 min., servicing downtown, Westport, Overland Park, Mission, and Lenexa ($10-15 one-way).
Amtrak: 2200 Main St. (421-3622 or 800-872-7245), directly across from Crown Center. Check bus schedules for correct number bus. To: St. Louis (2 per day, 5½ hr., $40-60) and Chicago (2 per day, 8-12 hr., $79). Open 24 hrs.
Greyhound: 1101 N. Troost (800-231-2222 or 221-2885). To: St. Louis (6 per day, 4-5 hr., $33); Chicago (5 per day, 12-13 hr., $51, $38 with 3-day advance purchase); Des Moines (3 per day, 3-4 hr., $43); Omaha (3 per day, 4-5 hr., $31); Lawrence (8 per day, 1 hr., $12.50). Tickets open daily 5:30am-1:30am.
Kansas City Area Transportation Authority (Metro): 1350 E. 17th St. (221-0660; open Mon.-Fri. 8am-4:45pm), at Brooklyn. Excellent downtown coverage. Fare 90¢, plus 10¢ for crossing zones, seniors 45¢, for KCKS, $1. Free transfers; free return receipt available downtown. Pick up maps and schedules at headquarters, airport gate #62, or buses.
Taxi: Checker Cab, 474-8294. **Yellow Cab,** 471-5000. Base $1.30 plus $1.10 per mi. Fare about $25-30 from airport to downtown; determine fare before trip.
Car Rental: Thrifty Car Rental, 2001 Baltimore (842-8550 or 800-367-2277), 1 block west of 20th and Main St.; also at KCI airport (464-5670). Mon.-Thurs. $30 per day, 250 mi. free, 29¢ per mi. thereafter. Drivers under 25 add $5. Must be 21 with major credit card. Open daily 5:30am-midnight.
Post Office: 315 W. Pershing Rd. (374-9275), near the train station. Open Mon.-Fri. 8am-6:30pm, Sat. 8am-2:30pm. **ZIP code:** 64108.
Area Codes: 816 in Missouri, 913 in Kansas.

Most sights worth visiting in KC lie south of the Missouri River on the Missouri side of town; KCMO is organized like a grid with numbered streets running east-west and named streets running north-south. **Main Street,** the central artery, divides the city east-west. The KC metropolitan area sprawls across two states, and travel may take a while, particularly without a car. Most sights are *not* located downtown. All listings are for Kansas City, MO, unless otherwise indicated.

ACCOMMODATIONS

Kansas City is a big convention center and can usually accommodate everyone who needs a room. The least expensive lodgings are near the interstate highways, especially those leading from Kansas City to Independence, MO. Downtown, most hotels are either expensive, uninhabitable, or unsafe—sometimes all three. Most on the Kansas side require a car. The Westport area is lively, but prices can be steep. **Bed and Breakfast Kansas City** (888-3636) has over 40 listings at inns and homes throughout the city ($40 and up).

White Haven Motor Lodge, 8039 Metcalf (649-8200 or 800-752-2892), 4 mi. west of state line. Amusing, 1950s-style family motor lodge with cold-war-era prices to match. Great place to stay in KCKS. Pool, restaurant, HBO. Free coffee, 5¢ morning doughnuts. Singles $32, doubles $37, triples $41, quads $43.

American Inn (373-8300), at I-70 and Noland Rd. Quick service, clean rooms with phones, cable TV, pool, and lounge. No pets. Singles from $28, doubles from $32. Also at I-70 and 78th St. (299-2999). Ask for the rate quoted on the billboard.

Red Roof Inn, 13712 E. 42nd Terrace (800-843-7663), also off I-70 and Noland Rd. Bright rooms with coffee and newspaper weekdays. Singles $35, doubles $41.

FOOD

Kansas City rustles up a herd of meaty, juicy barbecue restaurants that serve unusually tangy ribs. For fresh produce year-round, visit the large and exceptional **farmers market,** in the River Quay area, at 5th and Walnut St. Arrive in the morning, especially on Saturday.

Strouds, 1015 E. 85th St. (333-2132), off Troost. Sign proclaims "We choke our own chickens." Don't choke on the incredible fried chicken with cinnamon rolls, biscuits, and honey. Enormous dinners ($7-15) in a weathered wooden hut. Open Mon.-Thurs. 4-10pm, Fri. 11am-11pm, Sat. 2-11pm, Sun. 11am-10pm. Also at 5410 N. Oak Ridge Blvd. (454-9600). Open Mon.-Thurs. 5-9:30pm, Fri. 11am-10:30pm, Sat. 2-10:30pm, Sun. 11am-9:30pm.

Stephenson's Old Apple Farm Restaurant, 16401 E. U.S. 40 (373-5345), right off I-70, exit 14, several mi. from downtown. The hickory-smoked specialties are definitely worth the trip and the prices. The accompanying side dishes (fruit salad, apple fritters, corn relish) are as delicious as the entrees. ($6 lunch, $12-18 dinner, Sunday brunch $11, kids 6-10 $6.) Open Mon.-Thurs. 11:30am-10pm, Fri.-Sat. 11:30am-11pm, Sun. 11am-9pm.

The Pumpernickel Deli, 319 E. 11th St. (421-5766), 4 blocks from downtown. Friendly, busy place with simple, no-frills decor. Often sells cheap, fresh veggies outside. Sandwiches $1-2.50, jumbo hoagie tops the menu ($2.65). Sunrise special of bagels, ham, egg, and cheese $1.50. Open Mon.-Fri. 7am-5:30pm.

Gates & Sons Bar-B-Q, 1411 Swope Pkwy. (921-0409). Best ribs in town. Barbecue beef sandwiches ($4) and titanic short-end ribs ($8). Open Mon.-Sat. 10am-2am, Sun. 10am-midnight. Also at 12th and Brooklyn St. (483-3880). Open Sun.-Wed. 10am-midnight, Thurs.-Sat. 10am-2am.

SIGHTS

Located at 45th Terrace and Rockhill, 3 blocks east of Country Club Plaza, the **Nelson-Atkins Museum of Fine Art** (751-1278 or 561-4000) contains one of the best East Asian art collections worldwide. A Chinese temple room, Japanese screens, and a huge bronze Buddha are particularly impressive. A Henry Moore sculpture garden and interior display, plus a small, intriguing collection devoted to Thomas Hart Benton, make this museum a must-see. (Open Tues.-Thurs. 10am-4pm, Fri. 10am-9pm, Sat. 10am-5pm, Sun. 1-5pm. $4, students and kids 6-18 $1. Sat. free, also free tours Tues.-Sat. 10:30am, 11am, 1pm, and 2pm; Sun. 1:30 and 2:30pm.)

Black Archives of Mid-America, 2033 Vine (483-1300), is a large and fine collection of paintings and sculpture by African-American artists. Open Mon.-Fri. 9am-

4:30pm. For a taste of KC history, visit the **Kansas City Museum,** 3218 Gladstone Blvd. (221-3466), which even has a working soda fountain. Open Tues.-Sat. 9:30am-4:30pm, Sun. noon-4:30pm.

A few blocks to the west, the **Country Club Plaza** (known as "the plaza") is the oldest and perhaps most picturesque U.S. shopping center. Built in 1922 by architect J.C. Nichols, the plaza is modeled after buildings in Seville, Spain, replete with fountains, sculptures, hand-painted tiles, and the reliefs of grinning gargoyles. A Country Club Plaza bus runs downtown until 11pm. Just south of the plaza is the luxurious **Mission Hill** district.

Two mi. north of the plaza is **Crown Center,** 2450 Grand Ave. (274-8444), at Pershing. The headquarters of Hallmark Cards, it houses a maze of restaurants and shops alongside a hotel with a five-story indoor waterfall. Also in the Crown Center are the **Coterie Children's Theatre** (474-6552) and the **Ice Terrace** (274-8411), KC's only public ice skating rink. (Open mid-Nov. to mid-March. Take bus #40, 56, or 57, or any trolley from downtown; $4, ages 6-12 $3.) The Crown Center has **Free Concerts in the Park** (274-8411) every Fri. at 9pm (preshow at 8pm) during the summer. Performers have included Don McLean, the Guess Who, and the Grateful Dead. Run through a huge fountain designed for exactly that purpose; you can't have more fun on a hot summer night with your clothes on (uh, you *do* have to keep your clothes on). To the west stands the **Liberty Memorial,** 100 W. 26th St. (221-1918), a tribute to those who died in World War I. Pay to ride the elevator to the top for a fantastic view, then visit the free museum. (Open Wed.-Sun. 9:30am-4:30pm. $2, under 12 free, or just the elevator $1, ages 6-11 25¢.)

ENTERTAINMENT

Formerly the crossroads of the Santa Fe, Oregon, and California Trails, and an outfitting post for travelers to the West, the restored **Westport** area (931-3586), located near Broadway and Westport Rd. ½-mi. north of the plaza, is now packed only by nightspots. **Blayney's,** 415 Westport Rd. (561-3747), in a small basement, hosts live bands six nights a week, offering reggae, rock, or jazz. (Open Mon.-Sat. 8pm-3am. Max. cover $2-3 on weekends.)

In the '20s, Kansas City was a jazz hot spot. Count Basie and his "Kansas City Sound" reigned at the River City bars, while Charlie "Yardbird" Parker spread his wings and soared in the open environment. Stop by the **Grand Emporium,** 3832 Main St. (531-7557), voted best live jazz club in KC for the last seven years and twice voted the #1 blues night club in the U.S., to hear live jazz Fri.-Sat.; weekdays feature rock, blues, and reggae bands. (Open Mon.-Sat. 8am-3am.) **City Lights,** 7425 Broadway (444-6969), is dependable and fun with live bands Tues.-Sat. 9pm-1am. (Open Mon.-Sat. 4pm-1:30am. Cover $4.) **The Hurricane,** 4048 Broadway, Westport (753-0884), has live music nightly at 9:30pm and an outdoor area to get down in. (Open Mon.-Sat. 3pm-3am, cover $3.) **Kiki's Bon-Ton Maison,** 1515 Westport Rd. (931-9417), features KC's best in-house soul band, the Bon-Ton Soul Accordion Band Wed. 9-11pm and Sat. at 10:30pm. Kiki's serves up cajun food with zydeco and hosts the annual Crawfish Festival (complete with a "Crawfish Look-Alike Contest") the last weekend in May. (Open Mon.-Thurs. 11am-10pm, Fri. 11am-midnight, Sat. 11am-11pm. Food until 10pm.) Be a Huck Finn wanna-be and cruise on the **Missouri River Queen** (281-5300 or 800-373-0027; $6, seniors $5.40, ages 3-13 $3).

Sports fans will be bowled over by the massive **Harry S. Truman Sports Complex;** even Howard Cosell could not muster enough inscrutable superlatives to describe **Arrowhead Stadium,** 1 Arrowhead Dr. (924-3333), home of the Chiefs football team (924-9400). Next door, the water-fountained, artificial turf-clad wonder of **Royals Stadium,** 1 Royal Way (921-8000), houses the Royals baseball team. The stadium express bus runs from downtown on game days.

■■■ ST. LOUIS

French fur trader Pierre Laclede chose a spot directly below the junction of the mighty Mississippi, Missouri, and Illinois rivers to establish his trading post. From this vantage point he had easy access to New Orleans, as well as to the growing towns north on the Mississippi. Out of these beginnings grew St. Louis, one of the largest inland trading ports (competing with Pittsburgh for that title), starting point for the Lewis and Clark Expedition, and gateway to the West. Into the 20th century, the city thrived, hosting the 1904 World's Fair, which produced the first ice cream cone, hot dog, and iced tea.

As immigrants floated in, St. Louis diversified and divided into distinct neighborhoods, giving the city ethnic flavor. The Hill in South St. Louis is largely Italian, a pasta paradise. The historic Soulard District, bounded by I-55, I-40, and Broadway houses a farmers market, beautiful architecture, and nightly jazz and blues. As one of the largest transportation centers since it opened in 1894, St. Louis Union Station, a National Historic Landmark, is a festive shopping plaza. Farther west lie the charming Central West End and the attractions of Forest Park, the largest urban park in the country. At the Riverfront and Laclede's Landing, riverboats rest along the banks of the Mississippi. And above it all towers Eero Saarinen's magnificent Gateway Arch, both welcoming new visitors and commemorating America's westward expansion.

PRACTICAL INFORMATION

Emergency: 911.

Visitor Information: St. Louis Visitors Center, 308 Washington Ave. (241-1764). Pick up the *Quickguide,* maps, brochures, and friendly advice. Open daily 9am-4:30pm. Other visitors information locations at the airport and at Kiener Plaza (Mon.-Fri. 10am-2pm).

Airport: Lambert St. Louis International Airport (426-8000), 12 mi. northwest of the city on I-70. Hub for **TWA.** Served by Bi-State bus #4 "Natural Bridge," running hourly 5:50am-5:45pm from 9th and Locust St., and Greyhound (see below).

Amtrak: 550 S. 16th St. (331-3301 or 800-872-7245), follow Market St. downtown. To: Chicago (3 per day, 6 hr., $39); Dallas (1 per day, 14½ hr., $131); New Orleans (2 per day, 16 hr., $103); Denver (1 per day, 24 hr., $178); Kansas City (3 per day, 3½ hr., $40). Open daily 6am-midnight. Additional station in Kirkwood (966-6475), 116 W. Argonne Dr., at Kirkwood Rd. (Lindbergh Blvd.)

Greyhound: 13th and Cass (800-231-2222). Bus #30 takes less than 10 min. from downtown. To: Kansas City (6 per day, 5 hr., $32); Chicago (6 per day, 7 hr., $35); Indianapolis (8 per day, 4½ hr., $26); Memphis (4 per day, 6 hr., $48). Most are cheaper with 7 day advance purchase. Open 24 hrs.

Public Transport: Bi-State, (231-2345 in St. Louis; 271-2345 in E. St. Louis). Extensive daily service, but buses infrequent during off-peak hours. Maps, schedules available at the Bi-State Development Agency, 707 N. 1st St., on Laclede's Landing, or at the reference desk of the public library's main branch, 13th and Olive St. Fare $1, transfers 20¢; seniors 50¢, transfers 10¢. Free in the downtown area (bordered by I-40, Broadway, Jefferson, and Cole). **MetroLink,** the newly opened light-rail system, runs from 5th and Missouri in East St. Louis to North Hanley daily 5am-12:30am. Same fares as buses. Call for schedule information. The **Levee Line** to and around downtown offers free service to points of interest between Union Station and the Riverfront.

Taxi: County Cab, 991-5300. Base fare $1, $1.10 each additional mile. **Yellow Cab,** 991-1200. $2.45, $1 each additional mile.

Help Lines: Rape Crisis, 531-2003. Open 24 hrs. **Gay and Lesbian Hotline,** 367-0084. Open 6-10pm daily.

Post Office: 1720 Market St. (436-4458). Open Mon.-Fri. 7am-8:30pm, Sat. 7am-3pm. **ZIP code:** 63155.

Area Code: 314 (in Missouri); 618 (in Illinois)

The city of St. Louis hugs the Mississippi River in a crescent. University City, home to Washington University, lies west of downtown. Other suburbs (the "county") fan out in all directions. I-44, I-55, I-64, and I-70 meet in St. Louis. **U.S. 40/I-64** is the main drag running east-west through the entire metropolitan area. Downtown, **Market Street** divides the city north-south. Numbered streets begin at and run parallel to the river. The city's most dangerous sections include East St. Louis (across the river in Illinois), the Near South Side and most of the North Side.

ACCOMMODATIONS

The motels and universities that offer budget accommodations are generally located several mi. from downtown: try **Lindbergh Blvd.** near the airport or the area north of the junction of I-70 and I-270 in **Bridgeton,** 5 mi. beyond the airport. Also, **Watson Rd.,** old Rte. 66 in South County, is littered with cheap motels. **Bed and Breakfast of St. Louis/River County,** 11005 Manchester (965-9452), has moderately priced listings all over the city.

Huckleberry Finn Youth Hostel (HI/AYH), 1904-1906 S. 12th St. (241-0076), 2 blocks north of Russell St. in the Soulard District just off Rte. 66. From downtown, take bus #73 ("Carondelet"), or walk south on Broadway to Russell and over (30-40 min.); don't walk on Tucker, as the hostel is just past an unsafe neighborhood. Excellent location to downtown, friendly staff who insist you enjoy your stay, unbeatable for price. Full kitchen, free parking. 5-9 beds per dorm-style room. No curfew. Check-out 9:30am. $12, nonmembers $15. Linen $2 for stay. Office open 8-10am and 6-10pm.

Washington University, Eliot Hall (935-4637), at the corner of Big Bend Blvd. and Forsyth. Buses #91 and 93 take 40 min. from downtown. Pleasant dorm rooms with A/C, free local calls, laundry, and near Mallinckrodt student center cafeterias. Singles $18, doubles $32. Reservations recommended. Open May 25-Aug. 7.

Lewis and Clark Hostel (HI/AYH), 1500 S. 5th in St. Charles, MO (946-1000 ext. 119), 6 mi. from Lambert Airport and 1 mi. from Greyhound. Will arrange pick-up from airport and downtown St. Louis. Drivers should take I-70 about 15 mi. west of St. Louis to the 5th St. exit. The hostel is located in Noah's Ark Motor Inn. Full kitchen and common room. Use of pool. Near the head of the Katy Bicycle Trail. 24-hr. check-in. $10, nonmembers $13. Private rooms with 2 double beds $25.

Coral Court Motel, 7755 Watson Rd. (962-3000). An architectural landmark once famed for lunchtime liaisons. Yellow-orange tile units with lots of space and your own garage. Single $32, double $37.

Willow Motel, 10130 Natural Bridge (427-9432), across from the airport and I-70 on the service road. No frills, what-you-see-is-what-you-get rooms with one double bed and private bath for $17. No phone in room, cash or traveler's checks only. Check in 7am-10pm.

Horseshoe Lake Campgrounds, 3321 Kingshighway (Rte. 111), off I-70 in Granite City, IL. Tent sites $7 in woodsy area near lake. No electricity or water. Near Cahokia Mounds.

FOOD

Because of St. Louis' many historical and ethnic districts, you can cross a few blocks and find different culinary treats. The young and affluent gravitate to **Laclede's Landing** and the **Central West End.** Downtown on the riverfront, Laclede's Landing (241-5875) has experienced an amazing transformation from industrial wasteland to popular nightspot; the area is closed to minors from midnight-6am. Bars and dance clubs in this area occupy restored 19th-century buildings; most have no cover charge. Walk north along the river from the Gateway Arch or towards the river along Washington St. The Central West End caters to a slightly older crowd. Just north of Lindell Blvd., along Euclid Ave., a slew of restaurants has won the urban professional seal of approval. Take bus #93 from Broadway and Locust downtown.

Farther west, **Clayton** offers a pleasant setting for window-shopping and dining. Historic **South St. Louis** (the Italian "Hill") has plenty of pasta in inexpensive and

St. Louis Downtown and Region

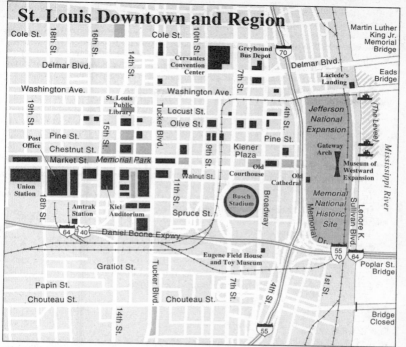

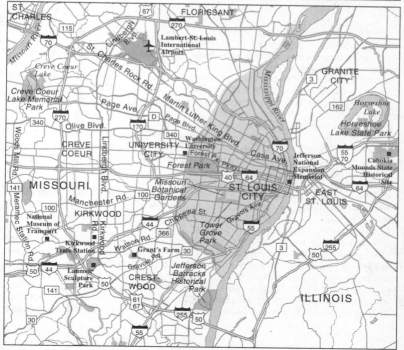

ST. LOUIS

atmospheric places and the **University City Loop** (Delmar Blvd. west of Skinker) features coffee houses and a mixed-bag of American and international restaurants.

Blueberry Hill, 6504 Delmar (727-0880), near Washington University. *The* college hangout. Collection of record covers, Howdy-Doody toys, and a world-class jukebox with over 2000 selections charm the premises. Live bands Fri.-Sat. nights. Sandwiches and specials $4-6. After 6pm, you must be 21 to enter. Open Mon.-Sat. 11am-1:30am, Sun. 11am-midnight.

Cunnetto's, 5453 Magnolia (781-1135) on the hill. 30 kinds of pasta, veal, chicken, and steak in this famous Italian favorite. *The Editor's Pick.* Entrees $6.50-11.75. Open Mon.-Thurs. 11am-2pm, 5-10:30pm, Fri.-Sat. 11am-2pm, 5pm-midnight.

Rigazzi's, 4945 Daggett Ave. (772-4900), at Boardman on the Hill. Family style Italian palace with all-you-can-eat spaghetti $6. Open Mon.-Thurs. 7am-11pm, Fri.-Sat. 7am-midnight.

Ted Drewe's Frozen Custard, 6726 Chippewa (352-7376), on old Rte. 66, and 4224 S. Grand. The place for the summertime St. Louis experience. Stand in line to order chocolate-chip banana concrete. Toppings blended, as in a concrete mixer, but the ice cream stays hard enough to hang in an overturned cup. Open March-Dec. Sun.-Thurs. 11am-midnight, Fri.-Sat. 11am-1am.

The Old Spaghetti Factory, 727 N. 1st St. (621-0276), on Laclede's Landing. A link in the chain, sure, but here it's an institution. Menus feature the history of the building and the funky artifacts contained therein. Dinners $4.25-6. Open Mon.-Thurs. 5-10pm, Fri. 5-11pm, Sat. 4-11pm, Sun. 3:30-10pm.

1860's Hard Shell Cafe, 1860 S. Ninth St. (231-1860), in historic Soulard, a cajun fest. $5-11. Live music Wed.-Sun., cover on weekends $2. Open Mon.-Thurs. 11am-10pm, Fri.-Sat. 11am-midnight, Sun. 11am-10pm.

SIGHTS

Downtown

Within the **Jefferson National Expansion National Memorial** is the **Gateway Arch** (425-4465), on Memorial Dr. by the Mississippi River, which can be seen from almost anywhere in the city (or southern Illinois for that matter). Eero Saarinen's arch is the nation's tallest monument at 630 ft. and the ultimate symbol of westward expansion. Take advantage of your only chance to ride an elevator whose path is an inverted catenary curve, the shape assumed by a chain hanging freely between two points (open 8am-10pm, winter 9am-6pm; $2.50, kids 3-12 50¢). Spend your one- to two-hour wait at the **Museum of Westward Expansion,** beneath the arch. Don't miss Thomas Jefferson's sexy pose and the *Monument to the Dream,* a half-hour documentary chronicling the sculpture's construction (17 showings per day in summer; $1), or *To Fly,* the new aviation film on a 4-story screen (shown every hr. on the ½-hr.; $4, ages 3-12 $3). (Museum hours same as arch's.)

Within walking distance, across the highway from the arch is the **Old Court-house,** 11 N. 4th St. (425-4468). As a slave, Dred Scott first sued for his freedom here in 1847. (Open daily 8am-4:30pm. Tour hours vary. Free.) The **Old Cathedral,** 209 Walnut St. (231-3250), is St. Louis' oldest church at 155 years. Museum is around the corner, 25¢. Masses daily; call for schedule.

Sightseers can also view St. Louis from the water with **Gateway Riverboat Cruises** (621-4040), one hr. cruises leaving from docks on the river right in front of the arch. (Daily summer departures every 1½ hr. beginning at 10:15am; spring and fall every 1½ hr. beginning 11am. Cruise $7, kids $3.50.)

North of the arch, on the riverfront, is historic **Laclede's Landing,** the birthplace of St. Louis in 1764. The cobblestone streets of this district are bordered by restaurants, bars, and two museums. The **Wax Museum,** 720 N. Second St. (241-1155), features heroes and anti-heroes of all kinds; be sure to see the Chamber of Horrors. ($4, ages 6-12 $3. Open Mon.-Sat. 10am-10pm, Sun. noon-8pm.) The **National Video Game and Coin-Op Museum,** 801 N. Second St. (621-2900), charts the development of video games and pinball machines (you can play the exhibits!);

you'll feel really old when you see Space Invaders, Pac-Man, and Donkey Kong treated as historic artifacts. Admission includes four game tokens. (Open Mon.-Sat. 10am-10pm, Sun. noon-8pm. $3, ages 12 and under $2.) There are other unique museums in St. Louis. **The Dog Museum,** 1721 S. Mason Rd. (821-DOGS/3647), between Manchester and Clayton, depicts the history of the canine. (Open Mon.-Sat. 9am-5pm, Sun. 1-4pm. $3, seniors $1.50, kids $1). Stroll down the lane at the **National Bowling Hall of Fame and Museum,** 111 Stadium Plaza (231-6340), across from Busch Stadium. (Open Mon.-Sat. 9am-5pm, Sun. noon-5pm; on ballgame days open until 7pm. $4, seniors $3, kids under 13 $1.50. Free after 4pm and on Sun.) The **Mercantile Money Museum,** Mercantile Tower (421-1819), 7th and Washington, caters to numismatists and the business school crowd. (Open daily 9am-4pm. Admission, oddly enough, is free.) Travelers should transport themselves to the **National Museum of Transport,** 3015 Barrett Station Rd. (965-7998), full of trains, planes, ferries, and more, which nonetheless seems to remain in one place. (Open daily 9am-5pm, $4, seniors and kids 5-12 $2.)

South St. Louis

Walk south of downtown down Broadway or 7th St. or take bus #73 ("Carondelet") to **South St. Louis.** The city proclaimed this area a historic district in the early 70s; it once housed German and East European immigrants, great numbers of whom worked in the breweries. Young couples and families are revitalizing South St. Louis but have not displaced an older generation of immigrants. The historic Soulard district surrounds the **Soulard Farmers Market,** 1601 S. 7th St. (622-4180), which claims a 200-plus-year tradition, but the produce is *still* fresh. (Open Tues.-Fri. 8am-5:30pm, Sat. 6:30am-6pm.) The end of 12th St. in the historic district features the **Anheuser-Busch Brewery,** 1127 Pestalozzi St. (577-2626), at 13th and Lynch, the largest brewery in the world. Take bus #40 ("Broadway") or 73 from downtown. Watch the beer-making process from barley to bottling and meet the famous Clydesdale horses. The 70-min. tour stops in the hospitality room, where guests can sample each beer Anheuser-Busch produces. Don't get too excited about the free brew, bucko—you'll get booted after 15 min. (Summer tours Mon.-Sat. 9am-5pm; off-season 9am-4pm. Pick up tickets at the office. Free.) Between downtown and south St. Louis, the **Eugene Field House and Toy Museum,** 634 S. Broadway (421-4689), explores the life of Eugene Field, the author of "Little Boy Blue" and "Wynken, Blynken, and Nod." Eugene's childhood home served as a house of ill repute in the 1920s before it was preserved as a museum with period furnishings and an abundance of toys, only a few of them Eugene's. (Open Wed.-Sat. 10am-4pm, Sun. noon-4pm. Admission $3, ages 12-18 $2, under 12 50¢.)

Also in South St. Louis, built on grounds left by botanist Henry Shaw, thrive the internationally acclaimed **Missouri Botanical Gardens,** 4344 Shaw (577-5100), north of Tower Grove Park. From downtown, take bus #99 ("Lafayette") from 4th and Locust St. going west, or take I-44 by car; get off at Shaw and Tower Grove. The gardens display plants and flowers from all over the globe; the Japanese Garden truly soothes the weary budget traveler. (Open Memorial Day-Labor Day daily 9am-8pm; off-season 9am-5pm. $3, seniors $1.50, under 12 free. Free Wed. and Sat. mornings and after 5pm Wed.) The second largest of its kind in the U.S., **Laumeier Sculpture Park,** 12580 Rott Rd. (821-1209), cultivates over 50 contemporary works on 96 acres. (Open daily 8am to ½-hr. past sunset. Gallery open Tues.-Sat. 10am-5pm, Sun. noon-5pm. Free.) The **Magic House,** 516 S. Kirkwood Rd. (822-8900), exposes kids to scientific principles made fun. (Call for hours. Free.) About 1 mi. west of downtown, visit magnificent old **Union Station,** easily accessible by the free and frequent Levee Line bus. At 18th and Market, this modern shopping mall retains the structure of the old railroad station and is a National Historical Landmark.

Forest Park Area

West of downtown, and worth as much of your time as the rest of St. Louis, is **Forest Park,** home of the 1904 World's Fair and St. Louis Exposition. Take bus #93 ("Lindell") from downtown. The park contains two museums, a zoo, a planetarium, a 12,000-seat amphitheater, a grand canal, countless picnic areas, pathways, and flying golf balls. All are connected by a $1 shuttle on the Metrolink. The **St. Louis Science Center-Forest Park** (289-4444) is newly expanded and renovated; learn how a laser printer works, watch on old Star Trek episode, or practice surgery. Lots of hands-on exhibits, an OmniMax and planetarium. (Exhibits free; call for show schedules and prices. Museum open Sun.-Tues. 9:30am-5pm, Wed.-Sat. 9:30am-9pm.) Marlin Perkins, the late great host of the TV show *Wild Kingdom,* turned the **St. Louis Zoo** (781-0900; at the southern edge of the park) into a world-class institution. At the "Living World" exhibit, view computer-generated images of future human evolutionary stages. (Open Memorial Day-Labor Day Sun. 9am-5:30pm, Mon. and Wed.-Sat. 9am-5pm, Tues. 9am-8pm, off-season daily 9am-5pm. Free.) The **Missouri Historical Society** (746-4599), at the corner of Lindell and DeBaliviere on the north side of the park, is filled with U.S. memorabilia including an exhibit devoted to Charles Lindbergh's flight across the Atlantic in the *Spirit of St. Louis.* (Open Tues.-Sun. 9:30am-5pm. Free.) Atop **Art Hill,** just to the southwest, stands an equestrian statue of France's Louis IX, the city's namesake and the only Louis of France to achieve sainthood. The king beckons with his raised sword toward the **St. Louis Art Museum** (721-0067), which contains masterpieces of Asian, Renaissance, and Impressionist art. (Open Tues. 1:30-8:30pm, Wed.-Sun. 10am-5pm. Free except for special exhibits.) From Forest Park, head north a few blocks to gawk at the residential sections of the Central West End, where every house is actually a turn-of-the-century version of a French château or Tudor mansion or baronial estate, all rubbing shoulders next to each other.

Near Forest Park, **Washington University** livens things up with a vibrant campus. The **Washington University Gallery of Art,** in Steinberg Hall at the corner of Skinker and Lindell (935-5490), has a diverse collection including a Pollack, a few Warhols and Conrad Atkinson's *Critical Mats,* which proffers an inviting welcome to "the seductiveness of the end of the world." (Open summer Tues.-Fri. 10am-5pm, Sat.-Sun. 1-5pm, in winter Mon.-Fri. 10am-5pm, Sat.-Sun. 1-5pm; free.) The **Cathedral of St. Louis,** 4431 Lindell Ave. (533-2824), just north of Forest Park at Newstead, strangely combines Romanesque, Byzantine, Gothic, and Baroque styles. Gold-flecked mosaics depict 19th-century church history in Missouri. (Free tour Sun. at 1pm. Open daily 7am-6pm. Take "Lindell" bus #93 from downtown.)

ENTERTAINMENT

In the early 1900s, showboats carrying ragtime and brassy Dixieland jazz regularly traveled to and from Chicago and New Orleans. St. Louis, a natural stopover, fell head over heels in love with the music and continues to nurture it happily. Float down the Mississippi while listening to jazz on **Gateway Riverboat Cruises'** (621-4040) old-fashioned paddle-boats. (1-2½ hr. cruises Tues.-Sun. 11am and 7pm. $7, kids $3.50; rates higher at night. Open June-Oct.) For other seasonal events, check *St. Louis Magazine,* published annually, or the comprehensive calendar of events put out by the Convention and Visitors Bureau (see Practical Information).

For year-round musical entertainment, head to Laclede's Landing. Bars and restaurants featuring jazz, blues, and reggae fill "the landing." Try **Kennedy's Second Street Co.,** 612 N. Second St. (421-3655), for cheap food (burgers $3.25-4.75) and varied bands (shows for all ages 8pm; the 11:15pm show is for 21-plus only). (Open Mon.-Fri. 11:30am-3am, Sat.-Sun. 1pm-3am.) **Muddy Waters,** 724 N. 1st (421-5335), has live music nightly and no cover. (Food until 2pm, no minors after 8pm. Open Mon.-Thurs. 11am-2pm, 8pm-3am, Fri.-Sat. 11am-3am.) Or take your pick of one of the dozens of clubs and bars lining the narrow streets. **Metropol,** 118 Morgan (621-1160), features funky neo-classical decor and late-night dancing. (Open Mon.-Sat.

9pm-3am.) Historic Soulard is also a groovy nightspot, where bars and pubs abound. **McGurk's** (776-8309), 12th and Russell, has live Irish music nightly and, cheerfully, no cover. (Open Mon.-Fri. 11am-1:30am, Sat. 11:30am-1:30am, Sun. 1pm-midnight.)

Founded in 1880, the **St. Louis Symphony Orchestra** is one of the finest in the country. **Powell Hall,** 718 N. Grand (534-1700), which houses the 101-member orchestra, is acoustically and visually magnificent. (Performances Sept.-May Thurs. 8pm, Fri.-Sat. 8:30pm, Sun. 3pm and 7:30pm. Box office open Mon.-Sat. 9am-5pm and before performances. Tickets $14-54. Sometimes half-price student rush tickets are available the day of the show. Take bus #97 to Grand Ave.)

St. Louis offers theater-goers many choices. The outdoor **Municipal Opera** (361-1900), the "Muny," performs hit touring musicals in Forest Park during the summer. The back rows provided 1400 free seats on a first-come-first serve basis; the gates open at 7pm. Otherwise, tickets cost $5-32. Bring a picnic (no bottles). Hot dogs and beer are also sold at moderate prices. Other regular productions are staged by the **St. Louis Black Repertory,** 2240 St. Louis Ave. (534-3807), and the **Repertory Theatre of St. Louis,** 130 Edgar Rd. (968-4925). Call for current show information. Tour the Fabulous **Fox Theatre** (534-1678; $2.50, under 12 $1.50; Tues., Thurs., and Sat. at 10:30am; call for reservations), or pay a little more for Broadway shows, classic films, Las Vegas, country, and rock stars. Renovated and reopened in 1982, the Fox was originally a 1930s movie palace.

St. Louis Cardinals baseball games (421-3060; tickets $4-12) chirp at Busch Stadium, downtown. **Blues** hockey games (781-5300; tickets $17-45, limited view $13) scat at the Arena.

■ Near St. Louis: Cahokia Mounds State Historic Sight and the KATY Trail

The Cahokia Mounds (618-346-5160), in Collinsville, IL, 8 mi. east of downtown on I-55/70 East to Kingshighway (Rte. 111). Only 15 min. from the city, these earthen mounds are the amazing remains of the extremely advanced city of Cahokia inhabited by early Mississippian Native Americans from 700-1500 AD. They built over 120 mounds of, well, dirt as foundations and protection for important buildings. You can climb the largest, Monk's Mound, which took 300 years to complete. Interestingly, they encountered the same problems of pollution, overcrowding (at one time housing 20,000 people), and depletion of resources that we do today, which might help explain their mysterious Roanokian disappearance. The **Interpretive Center** has an incredible 15 min. slide show illustrating this "City of the Sun" which runs every hr. 10am-4pm. The mounds site is open 8am-dusk. The Interpretive Center is open daily 9am-5pm. All free and definitely worth the trip.

The KATY Trail State Park (800-334-6946) is an old 1890's railroad route that has been converted into a hiking and biking trail. The 200 mi. include towering bluffs, wetlands, and lots of wildlife, which even Lewis and Clark stopped to admire. The route begins in St. Charles and ends in Kansas City. Call for more info.

■ Nebraska

The heart of the Great Plains, Nebraska has been a major stopover for a lot of Westward movement. From 1840-66, over 350,000 settlers followed the Oregon and Mormon trails throughout the state. In 1863, the westward flow was given steam power when the Union Pacific Railroad Co. broke ground and laid track in Omaha. Hungry gold seekers swept through on their way west, making Omaha a very prosperous pit-stop. Many of the gold rushers noticed the rich soil of Nebraska and settled, much to the distress of the famous Sioux and Pawnee war chiefs Crazy Horse and Red Cloud. But the cry of expansion was louder, and in 1867 Nebraska become the Cornhusker State. Almost all of the prairie is now plowed, but the 619 acres of the Willa Cather Memorial prairie, just south of Red Cloud, leave just enough for a fertile imagination.

PRACTICAL INFORMATION

Capital: Lincoln.
Tourist Information: Nebraska Department of Economic Development, P.O. Box 94666, Lincoln 68509 (471-3796 or 800-228-4307). **Nebraska Game and Parks Commission,** 2200 N. 33rd St., Lincoln 68503 (471-0641). Permits for campgrounds and park areas ($10). Open Mon.-Fri. 8am-5pm.
Time Zone: Central (1 hr. behind Eastern). **Postal Abbreviation:** NE
Sales Tax: 5-6.5%. **Hotel tax:** 11.5%.

■■■ LINCOLN

Lincoln, named in 1867 after the martyred president, is both the state's capital and a large college town. As home to the only unicameral (one-house) state legislature, the city is a unique government model; as residence of the Cornhuskers and the University, there are a number of museums, galleries, and nightspots.

PRACTICAL INFORMATION

Emergency: 911.
Lincoln Convention and Visitors Bureau, 1221 N. St., Suite #320 (434-5335 or 800-423-8212). Open Mon.-Fri. 8am-4:45pm.
Amtrak: 201 N. 7th St. (476-1295 or 800-872-7245). One train daily to: Omaha (1 hr., $14); Denver (7½ hr., $104); Chicago (10½ hr., $108); Kansas City (7 hr., $46). Open Mon.-Wed. 11:30pm-11am, 12:30-4pm, Thurs.-Sun. 11:30pm-7am.
Greyhound: 940 P St. (474-1071), close to downtown and city campus. To: Omaha (5 per day, 1 hr., $12.50); Chicago (5 per day, 12-14 hr., $75); Kansas City (3 per day, 6½ hr., $40); Denver (2 per day, 9-11 hr., $73). Open Mon.-Fri. 8am-5:30pm, Sat. 8:30am-5:15pm, Sun. 9am-11:30am.
Public Transport: Star Tran, 710 J St. (476-1234). Schedules are available on the bus at many downtown locations or at the office. Buses run Mon.-Sat. 5am-7pm. 75¢, ages 5-11 40¢.
Car Rental: U-Save Auto Rental, 2240 Q St. (477-5236), at 23rd St. Used cars starting at $18 per day, 25 free mi., or $110 per week, 150 free mi.; 15¢ each additional mile. Must be 21 yrs. old. $100 deposit.
Post Office: 700 R St. (473-1695). Open Mon.-Fri. 7:30am-5pm, Sat. 9am-noon. **ZIP code:** 68501.
Area Code: 402.

O Street is the main east-west drag, splitting the town north-south. Alphabetized streets increase northwards. **Cornhusker Highway (U.S. 6)** sheers the northwest edge of Lincoln.

ACCOMMODATIONS AND FOOD

There are few relatively inexpensive places to stay in downtown Lincoln. The small, ministry-run **Cornerstone Hostel (HI/AYH),** 640 N. 16th St. (476-0355 or 476-0926), is the city's only hostel, located on the university's downtown campus. The two rooms are single-sex, three female beds, five male. Bring a sleeping bag or blankets and pillow. (Showers, full kitchen, laundry facilities. Free parking. Curfew 10pm. $8 members, $10 nonmembers.) The **Town House Motel,** 1744 M at 18th St. (800-279-1744), has spacious suites with full kitchen, bath and cable TV. (Silverware and parking included. Single $36, double $41.) **The Great Plains Motel,** 2732

O St. (800-288-8499), has large rooms with small fridge. (Free parking. Singles $30, doubles $37.) Camping is possible at the **Nebraska State Fair Park Campground,** 2402 North 14th St. (473-4287), just south of the overpass at 14th and Cornhusker Hwy. Open mid-April-mid-Oct., these sites are cramped but functional, $8, with electricity $10, all services $12. Cheap motels abound on Cornhusker Hwy. around the 5600 block (east of downtown).

There are two main areas to chow in Lincoln, but go early because most places are closed by 10pm. **Historic Haymarket,** 7th to 9th and O to R St., is a newly renovated old warehouse district, with several restaurants and a **farmers market** (Sat. 8am-12:30pm mid-May to mid-Oct.). There's an excellent mural of the coming of the railroad at 7th and O St. **Lazlo's Brewery and Grill,** 710 N. P St. (474-2337), is the oldest brewery in Nebraska, founded, believe it or not, in 1991. Brewing occurs inside the restaurant. Entrees $5-9. (Open Mon.-Sat. 11am-1am, Sun. 11am-10pm.) Downtown between N and P and 12th to 15th St., there are some cheap bars and eateries. For roller-skating waitresses, foot-long chili cheese dogs ($4.25), and your ultimate diner experience, bop on into the **Rock 'n' Roll Runza,** 210 W. 14th St. (474-2030; open Mon.-Wed. 7am-11pm, Thurs.-Fri. 7am-12:30pm, Sat. 8am-12:30pm, Sun. 8am-10pm). **The Zoo Bar,** 136 N. 14th St. (435-8754), is the place to go for nightly live bands. (Open Mon.-Fri. 3pm-1am, Sat. noon-1am, some Sundays 6pm-1am. Cover $2-5, big shows $8-10.)

SIGHTS

The "Tower on the Plains," the **Nebraska State Capitol Building** (471-2311), 14th at K St., remarkable for its streamlined exterior and detailed interior, is an appropriate centerpiece for Lincoln, itself an oasis of learning, legislation, and culture on the prairie. Visible from nearly 20 mi. away, it soars far above the city and surrounding farmlands and maintains all the pomp and majesty of an art deco museum. Its floor, reminiscent of a Native American blanket in design, is an incredible mosaic of inlaid Belgian and Italian marble. Each pattern represents some facet of the land and peoples of Nebraska. Take the elevator to the 14th floor for a terrific view of the entire city. (Open Mon.-Fri. 8am-5pm, Sat. 10am-5pm and Sun. 1-5pm. Excellent tours June-Aug. Mon.-Fri. 9-11am, noon-4pm every ½-hr., Sat. 10am-4pm every hr. except noon, Sun. 1-4pm every hr. Sept.-May Mon.-Fri. 9am-4pm every hr. Free.)

The **Museum of Nebraska History** (471-4754), 15th and P St., has a phenomenal, moving exhibit on the history of the Plains Indians, as well as good Nebraska trivia (open Mon.-Sat. 9am-5pm, Sun. 1:30-5pm; free). The **University of Nebraska State Museum** at **Morrill Mall** (472-2642), 14th and U St., has an amazing fossil collection including the largest mounted mammoth in any American museum. Find the *Glypotodont*—it's worth the search. (Open Mon.-Sat. 9:30am-4:30pm, Sun. 1:30-4:30pm.) In the same building is **Muelles Planetarium** (472-2641) which has several shows daily and laser shows Fri.-Sat. Call for schedules and admission fees. For the art lovers, The **Sheldon Memorial Art Gallery** (472-2461), 12th and R St., has several excellent collections which document the development of American art.

■■■ OMAHA

Omaha, an old railroad town on the Missouri River, is the crossroads for many of the nation's calories. Early prosperity hit in the 1860s when the promise of gold and Western homesteads brought rushes of people here to be outfitted. In 1872, the Union Pacific bridge spanned the Missouri River, opening Omaha to eastern markets. Since, the city has embraced the Industrial Revolution, becoming a large smelting, and packing town. A great influx of immigrants from Germany and Russia, freed slaves, and more recently, Mexican migrant workers have come to Omaha for jobs. The lost history of the Native Americans is not as easily apparent; their influences surfaces most tangibly in museum galleries and in the region's place names.

PRACTICAL INFORMATION

Emergency: 911.

Greater Omaha Convention and Visitors Bureau, 1819 Farnam St. #1200 (444-4660 and 800-332-1819), in the Civic Center. Bus schedules in the basement, behind the cafeteria. Open Mon.-Fri. 8:30am-4:30pm. **Events Hotline,** 444-6800.

Amtrak: 1003 S. 9th St. (342-1501 or 800-872-7245). One train per day to: Chicago (9 hr., $100); Denver (9 hr., $105); Lincoln (1 hr., $14); and a van to Kansas City (4 hr., $48). Open Mon.-Fri. 10:30pm-3:30pm, Sat.-Sun. 10:30pm-8am.

Greyhound: 1601 Jackson (800-231-2222). Schedule changes monthly; call to confirm. To: Lincoln (6 per day, 1 hr., $12); Kansas City (4 per day, 4½ hr., $37); Chicago (6 per day, 12 hr., $72); Denver (4 per day, 10½-12 hr., $89). Open 24 hrs.

Public Transport: Metro Area Transit (MAT), 2222 Cuming St. (341-0800). Schedules available at the Park Fair Mall, 16th and Douglas near the Greyhound station. Open Mon.-Fri. 8am-4:30pm. **Buses** have thorough service downtown, but don't reach as far as M St. and 107th, where several budget hotels are located. Fare 90¢, transfers 5¢. Bus numbers change occasionally; check the schedule.

Taxi: Happy Cab, 339-0110. $1.80 first mi., $1.05 each additional mi. Fare to airport $7.

Car Rental: Cheepers Rent-a-Car, 7700 L St. (331-8586). $17 per day with 50 free mi., 15¢ per additional mi. or $22 per day with unlimited mileage. Must be 21 and have a major credit card. Open Mon.-Fri. 7:30am-6pm, Sat. 9am-3pm.

Help Lines: Rape Crisis, 345-7273, 24 hrs.

Post Office: 1124 Pacific St. (348-2895). Open Mon.-Fri. 7:30am-5pm, Sat. 7:30am-noon. **ZIP code:** 68108.

Area Code: 402.

Numbered north-south streets begin at the river; named roads run east-west. **Dodge Street** divides the city north-south. When night falls, it probably makes good sense to avoid 24th St., and to stay within a stone's throw of Creighton University at 25th and California.

ACCOMMODATIONS AND CAMPING

Many budget motels are off the L or 84th St. exits from I-80, 6½ mi. southwest of downtown. Buses #11, 21, and 55 service the area.

YMCA, 430 S. 20th St. at Howard (341-1600), both long-term and overnight stay in plain, basic rooms. Co-ed by floor. Women's singles $10.50, daily, $62 weekly. Men $9.50. $10 key deposit. Microwave, linen provided. $2.50 extra to use athletic facilities.

Excel Inn, 2211 Douglas St. (345-9565). Ideal for the car-less. In a slightly frayed neighborhood. Singles $25, with cable TV and VCR $29. Doubles with kitchenettes $34 and up. Stay 4 nights and 3 more nights are free.

Motel 6, 10708 M St. (331-3161), adjacent to the Budgetel Inn. Outdoor pool, phone, basic brown-bed-and-Bible rooms. Singles $24, doubles $30.

Bellevue Campground, Haworth Park (291-3379), on the Missouri River 10 mi. south of downtown at Rte. 370. Take the infrequent bus ("Bellevue") from 17th and Dodge to Mission and Franklin, and walk down Mission. Right next to the Missouri, it is a beautiful oasis in an industrial area. Showers, toilets, shelters. Sites $5, with hookup $9. Free water. Open daily 6am-10pm; quiet stragglers sometimes enter after hours. Boat tours nearby (see Sights).

FOOD

Once a warehouse district, the **Old Market,** on Howard St. between 10th and 13th, has been converted into cobblestone streets with hopping shops, restaurants, and bars. The police even ride bicycles here. **Coyote's Bar and Grill,** 1217 Howard St. (345-2047), howls with fun Tex-Mex appetizers like the "holy avocado" ($4), salads, chili, and staggeringly large burgers ($4-5) in hip wood and beveled glass surroundings. (Open Mon.-Thurs. 11am-11pm, Fri.-Sat. 11am-midnight, Sun. noon-11pm.)

Trini's, 1020 Howard St. (346-8400), marinates, sautées, and serves profoundly authentic Mexican and vegetarian food in an elegant, candlelit grotto—open the building's door and step into this ancient brick cavern, which is very cool, especially in the summer. Try the "Big Juan." Dinner $2.50-7. (Open Mon.-Thurs. 11:30am-10pm, Fri.-Sat. 11:30am-11pm, Sun. 1-8pm.) **The Diner** (341-9870), 12th and Harney, is cheap greasy-spoon at its best, with round, cushioned booths and a jukebox. An entire chicken-fried steak dinner $4.75. Open for breakfast and lunch Mon.-Sat. 6am-4pm. The **Bohemian Cafe**, 1406 S. 13th St. (342-9838), in South Omaha's old Slavic neighborhood, sells meaty fare accompanied by onions and potatoes for under $6.50 (open daily 11am-10pm). **Joe Tess' Place**, 5424 S. 24th St. (731-7278), at U St. in South Omaha (take bus from Farnam and 16th), is renowned for its fresh, fried carp and catfish served with thin-sliced potatoes and rye bread. (Entrees $4-8. Open Mon.-Thurs. 10:30am-10pm, Fri.-Sat. 10:30am-11pm, Sun. 11am-10pm.)

SIGHTS

Omaha's **Joslyn Art Museum**, 2200 Dodge St. (342-3300), is a three-story art deco masterpiece with an exterior made of Georgian Pink marble and an interior of over 30 different marble types. It contains an excellent collection of less prominent 19th- and 20th-century European and American art. In the summer, they host "Jazz on the Green" each Thurs. from 10am-9pm. (Open Tues.-Sat. 10am-5pm, Sun. 1-5pm. $3, seniors and kids under 12 $1.50. Free Sat. 10am-noon.)

The **Western Heritage Museum**, 801 S. 10th St. (444-5071), has a huge exhibit on life in Nebraska. Enter ignorant and leave a historian. The old **Union Pacific Railroad Station** from 1929-1973, the museum is nearly outshone by the grandeur of the building itself. (Open Mon.-Sat. 10am-5pm, Sun. 11am-5pm. $3, seniors $2.50, ages under 12 $2.) Housed in the historic Nebraska Telephone Building, the **Great Plains Black Museum**, 2213 Lake St. (345-2212), presents the history of black migration to the Great Plains in photographs, documents, dolls, and quilts. Especially compelling are the portraits and biographies of the first black women to settle in Nebraska, and the exhibit commemorating Malcolm X, born Malcolm Little in Omaha in 1925. (Open Mon.-Fri. 9am-5pm. $2. Take bus from 19th and Farnam.)

The **Henry Doorly Zoo**, 3701 S. 10th St. (733-8401), at Deer Park Blvd. or 13th St. off I-80, is home to white Siberian tigers and the largest free-flight aviary in the world. (Open Mon.-Fri. 9:30am-5pm, Sat.-Sun. 9:30am-6pm; in winter daily 9:30am-4pm. $6.25, seniors $4.75, kids 5-11 $3.)

Next to the Bellevue Campground in Haworth Park is the boat **Bell and Spirit**, which tolls out sight-seeing tours ($5.50) and moonlight cruises ($19, dinner included). Call 292-2628 for schedule info. **South Omaha**, "The Magic City" and the former bootleg and red-light district, has an interesting main street on 24th.

NIGHTLIFE

Omaha caters to several area universities, so punk and progressive folk have found a niche. Check the window of the **Antiquarium Bookstore**, 1215 Harney, in the Old Market, for information on shows. For tickets, call Tix-Ticket Clearinghouse at 342-7107. In the Old Market area, head to the **Howard St. Tavern**, 1112 Howard St. (341-0433). The local crowds and good music create a pleasant atmosphere. Live music downstairs ranges nightly from blues to reggae to alternative rock. (Open Mon.-Sat. 3pm-1am, Sun. 7pm-1am. Cover $2-3.50.) **Downtown Grounds**, 1117 Jackson St. (342-1654), also in the Old Market, has almost daily live music in a colorful coffeehouse and juice bar. Double mocha $3. No cover. **Omaha's Magic Theater**, 1417 Farnam St. (346-1227; call Mon.-Fri. 9am-5:30pm), is devoted to the development of new American musicals. (Evening performances Fri.-Mon. Tickets $10, seniors, students and kids $5.) There is a string of gay bars within a block of 16th and Leavenworth. One of the most popular is **The Max**, 1417 Jackson (346-4110), which caters to gay men, has five bars, a disco dance floor, DJ, patio, and fountains. (Open daily 4pm-1am. Cover $2 on weekends.)

North Dakota

Though a state (the 39th) since 1889, North Dakota and most of its windswept terrain remains a mystery to both foreign and domestic travelers. Those who do visit often pass like wildfire through the eastern prairie to the more sensational "badlands," the infertile, pock-marked buttes that dominate the western half of the state. Blessed solitude, however, is the reward for those who savor the tranquil expanses of farmland before moving on to a high time in tourist-filled western towns. But whether in the east or west of North Dakota, locals will extend an eager welcome. People here are about as sparse as snow in June (there are fewer than 10 per square mi.), but they are twice as amiable.

PRACTICAL INFORMATION

Capital: Bismarck.
Tourism Promotion Division, Liberty Memorial Bldg., Capitol Grounds, Bismarck 58505 (224-2525; 800-437-2077 outside ND). **Parks and Recreation Department,** 1424 W. Century Ave. #202, Bismarck 58502 (224-4887).
Time Zones: Central and Mountain. **Postal Abbreviation:** ND
Sales tax: 5-7%.

■■■ BISMARCK

Bismarck takes every opportunity to flout its 20-story art deco **State Capitol,** at 900 East Blvd. (224-2000). Built during the early 1930s art deco rage, the building showcases the very short history of flamboyant architecture in North Dakota. Walk across the wide green lawn in front of the capitol to reach the **North Dakota Heritage Center** (224-2666) and its sophisticated exhibits on the Plains tribes, buffalo, and the history of white settlement in the region (open Mon.-Fri. 8am-5pm, Sat. 9am-5pm, Sun. 11am-5pm; free).

Practical Information Most of Bismarck is lassoed in an oval formed by I-94 and its corollary Business 94, otherwise known as **Main Street.** Bismarck's small downtown shopping district coalesces in the southwest curve of this oval, bounded by Washington St. and 9th St. on the west and east, and Rosser Ave. and Business 94 on the north and south.

The **Bismarck-Mandan Convention and Visitors Bureau** dispenses pamphlets aplenty at 523 N. 4th St. (222-4308; open Mon.-Fri. 8am-5pm). The largely defense-oriented **Bismarck Municipal Airport,** 2½ mi. south of Bismarck, lies near the intersection of University Dr. (Rte. 1804) and Airport Rd. **Greyhound,** 1237 W. Divide (223-6576), three inconvenient mi. west of downtown off I-94, provides service to Minneapolis (10 hr., $64) and Seattle (1½ days, $118). (Open Mon.-Fri. 8am-8:30pm, Sat.-Sun. 9am-1pm and 6:30-8:30pm.) Bismarck's **time zone** is Central (1 hr. behind Eastern), except for Fort Lincoln, which is Mountain (2 hrs. behind Eastern). The **post office** (221-6517) is at 220 E. Rosser Ave. (open Mon.-Fri. 8am-5:30pm, Sat. 10am-noon); the **ZIP code** is 58501. Bismarck's **area code** is 701.

Accommodations, Camping, and Food The **Highway Motel,** 6319 E. Main St. (223-0506), 2 mi. east on Rte. 10, rents rooms to local workers by the month but often has space for those staying only a night or two (singles $22, doubles $26). **Motel 6,** 2433 State St. (255-6878), offers clean, small rooms, and a pool (singles $28, doubles $32; under 18 free). Your best bet close to town is the **Bismarck Motor Hotel,** 2301 E. Main Ave. (223-2474; singles $21, doubles $24).

The **Hillcrest Campground** (255-4334), 1½ mi. out of town on E. Main St., provides showers and scenery April-Sept. (tent $6, full $9). The sylvan **General Sibley**

Park (222-1844), 4 mi. south of Bismarck on S. Washington St., merits a visit even if you don't stay the night. Those who do decide to stay should call ahead for reservations, and then set up camp in a glen of huge, shady trees on the banks of the Missouri River. The park has showers. (Sites $6, with full hookup $11.) **Fort Lincoln State Park** (663-9571), 5 mi. south of Mandan on Rte. 1806, has a quiet campground on the east bank of the Missouri (sites $9, with water and electricity $13; daily pass to park and showers included).

Bismarck has several local diners that serve tasty, inexpensive meals. The **Little Cottage Cafe,** 2513 E. Main St. (223-4949), brings in droves of workers at the lunch whistle and families at dinnertime. Fantastic muffins ($1.25), or an 8-oz. sirloin steak ($8). (Open daily 6am-10pm.) A local favorite, the **Drumstick Cafe,** 307 N. 3rd St. (223-8449), serves breakfast all day. The home-baked desserts (fresh strawberry pie $1) and fresh-ground coffee are superb. Sandwiches ($2-4). (Open Mon.-Sat. 24 hrs.)

Sights and Activities Below **Mandan,** on the opposite bank of the Missouri, lies **Fort Lincoln.** General Custer's march towards his fatal encounter with Sitting Bull at Little Big Horn (see Little Big Horn National Monument, MT) began here. The fort is part of the worthwhile **Fort Lincoln State Park** (663-9571), which also features a reconstructed Mandan village on its original site, renovated army blockhouses, and a small collection of artifacts and memorabilia from Native Americans and early settlers. (Open daily 9am-sunset; Sept.-May Mon.-Fri. 9am-sunset. Museum open daily 9am-9pm; Sept.-May Mon.-Fri. 9am-5pm. $3 vehicle admission fee.)

In the first week of August, watch for the **Art Fair,** held on the Capitol Mall lawn. Call ahead (255-3285) for information on the **United Tribes Pow Wow,** held in mid-Sept., one of the largest gatherings of Native Americans in the nation; the festival includes dancing, singing, food, and crafts of many tribes. For more info about local entertainment, drop by or call the new **Bismarck Civic Center** (222-6487) at the terminus of Sweet Ave. E., for a schedule of events. The **Cross Ranch State Park and Nature Trail** has 150 archeological sites in its 6000 acres along the Missouri River. Pick up the trail off Rte. 1806, 15 mi. north of Mandan ($3 per vehicle).

■■■ THEODORE ROOSEVELT NATIONAL MEMORIAL PARK

President Theodore Roosevelt appreciated the beauty of the Badlands' red- and brown-hued lunar formations so much that he bought a ranch here. After his mother and his wife died on the same day, he came here seeking "physical and spiritual renewal"; today's visitor can find the same rejuvenation among the quiet canyons and dramatic rocky outcroppings which, along with Teddy's presence, earned the park the nickname "rough-rider country."

Pay the park entrance fee ($3 per vehicle, $1 per pedestrian) at the **visitors center** (623-4466), in Medora. The center serves as a mini-museum, displaying a few of Teddy's guns, spurs and old letters, and showing a beautiful film of winter Badlands scenes. Copies of *Frontier Fragments,* the park newspaper, with listings of ranger-led talks, walks, and demonstrations, are available here. (Open daily 8am-8pm; Sept.-May daily 8am-4:30pm. Inquire at desk for film times.) A 36-mi. scenic automobile loop ambles through the park; many hiking trails start from the loop and penetrate into the wilderness. The world's 3rd-largest **petrified forest** lies 14 mi. into the park. **Painted Canyon Overlook,** 7 mi. east of Medora, has its own **visitors center** (575-4020; open daily 8am-8pm), picnic tables, and a breathtaking view of the Badlands.

The park is split into southern and northern units, and bisected by the border between Mountain and Central time zones. The **north unit** of the park (time zone: Central) is 75 mi. from the south unit on U.S. 85. Most of the land is wilderness; very few people visit, and fewer stay overnight. This combination results in virtually unlimited backcountry hiking possibilities. Check in at the ranger station (623-4466 or 842-2333; open daily 8am-4:30pm) for information and a free overnight camping permit. As a compromise between the wilderness and Medora, the park maintains **Squaw Creek Campground,** 5 mi. west of the north unit entrance (sites $8). For more info, write to Theodore Roosevelt National Memorial Park, Medora 58645.

■ Medora

The entrance to the better-developed **south unit** (time zone: Mountain) is just north of I-94 in the historic frontier town of **Medora.** Restored with tourist dollars in mind, Medora is a place to hold tight to your purse strings. **Joe Ferris' General Store** (623-4447), is spotless and still inexpensive (open daily 8am-8pm). For more immediate nourishment, stop by the **Badlands Bake Shoppe,** four doors to the left of Ferris, for a midday snack. Large muffins cost $1, and a loaf of Dakota bread—perfect hiking food—is $2.50 (open May-Sept. daily 8am-4pm). In pleasant weather, indulge at the **Chuckwagon Restaurant** (623-4820), an outdoor buffet ($9.50, kids $4.25) with ribs and chicken (open daily 4:30-7pm). Budget motels are even harder to find than budget food, but the **Sully Inn,** 401 Broadway (623-4455), offers clean basement rooms at the lowest rates in town (singles from $20, doubles from $25).

Medora's only sight is the **Museum of the Badlands,** on Main St. (623-4451; open daily 9am-8pm; admission $2, kids $1). Except for the **Medora Musical** (623-4444) in the Burning Hills Amphitheatre in downtown, sponsoring different productions every summer, all dedicated to Teddy (June 10-Sept. 5 at 8:30pm Mountain time), that's all you need to know about the town. **Greyhound** serves Medora from the Sully Inn, with three buses daily to Bismarck ($20.25).

Oklahoma

Between 1831 and 1835, President Andrew Jackson ordered the forced relocation of "The Five Civilized Tribes" from Florida and Georgia to the designated Oklahoma Indian Territory. Tens of thousands of Native Americans died of hunger and disease on the brutal, tragic march that came to be known as the "Trail of Tears." The survivors rebuilt their decimated tribes in Oklahoma, only to be moved again in 1889 to make way for whites rushing to stake claims on newly-opened settlement lands. Those who slipped in and claimed plots before the first official land run were called "sooners"—what Oklahomans have been dubbed ever since. Ironically, when the territory was admitted to the union in 1907, it did so with a Choctaw name; Oklahoma means "land of the red man" and despite the serious mistreatment of the Native Americans, many street names carry Indian names, and cultural life seems to center around Native American heritage and experiences. There are reenactments and interpretations of the Trail of Tears throughout Oklahoma, and the world's largest collection of American art in Tulsa features 250,000 Native American artifacts.

PRACTICAL INFORMATION

Capital: Oklahoma City.
Oklahoma Tourism and Recreation Department, 500 Will Rogers Building, Oklahoma City 73105 (521-2409 or 800-652-6552 out of state), in the capitol.
Time Zone: Central (1 hr. behind Eastern). **Postal Abbreviation:** OK
Sales Tax: 4.5% and up, depending on city.

■■■ OKLAHOMA CITY

At noon on April 22, 1889, a gunshot sent settlers scrambling into Oklahoma Territory to claim land. By sundown, Oklahoma City, set strategically on the tracks of the Santa Fe Railroad, had a population of over 10,000 homesteaders. The city became the state capital in 1910. The 1928 discovery of oil modernized the city; elegant homes rose with the oil derricks. As the wells dried up and the oil business slumped, Oklahoma City fell on hard times. The **OKC National Stockyards** still thrive with activity, and the **National Cowboy Hall of Fame** pays homage to the city's rugged past.

PRACTICAL INFORMATION

Emergency: 911.

Visitor Information: Chamber of Commerce Tourist Information, 4 Santa Fe Plaza (278-8912), at the corner of Gaylord. Open Mon.-Fri. 8am-4:30pm.

Airport: Will Rogers Memorial Airport (681-5311), southwest of downtown. **Airport Limousine, Inc.,** 3805 S. Meridian (685-2638), has van service to downtown ($9 for 1 person; $3 per additional person).

Greyhound: 427 W. Sheridan Ave. (235-6425), at Walker. In a rough part of town. Take city bus #4, 5, 6, 8, or 10. To: Tulsa (7 per day, 2 hr., $16); Dallas (4 per day, 5 hr., $29); and Kansas City (6 per day, 10 hr., $65). Open 24 hrs.

Public Transport: Oklahoma Metro Area Transit, main terminal at 20 E. Greenham (235-7433). Bus service Mon.-Sat. 6am-6pm. All routes radiate from the station at Reno and Gaylord, where maps are available for 50¢. Route numbers vary depending on the direction of travel. Fare 75¢, seniors and kids 35¢.

Taxi: Yellow Cab, 232-6161. $1.25 base, $1.25 per mi. To airport, $12.50.

Car Rental: Rent-a-Wreck, 2930 N.W. 39th Expressway (946-9288). Used cars $28 per day with 150 free mi., 25¢ each additional mi. Open Mon.-Fri. 8am-6pm, Sat. 8am-noon. Must be 25 with major credit card. The state of Oklahoma does *not* honor the International Driver's License.

Bike Rental: Miller's Bicycle Distribution, 215 W. Boyd. (321-8296). Ten-speeds and mountain bikes $5 per day for first 3 days, $3 per day thereafter. Open Mon.-Sat. 9am-6pm. They may ask for a credit card deposit.

Help Lines: Contact, 848-2273 or 840-9396 for referrals and crisis intervention. **Rape Crisis,** 943-7273. Open 24 hrs.

Post Office: 320 S.W. 5th St. (278-6300). Open Mon.-Fri. 8:30am-5:30pm. Emergency window open 24 hrs. **ZIP code:** 73125.

Area Code: 405.

Main Street divides the town east-west. Traveling by car is the best way to go; almost all of the city's attractions are outside the city center, but are accessible by the all-encompassing Metro Transit.

ACCOMMODATIONS, CAMPING, AND FOOD

The **YMCA,** 125 N.W. 5th St. (232-6101), has rooms with shared bath for men only. Pool, gym, TV lounge. (Singles $13, $52.50 per week. Key deposit $5.) Nearby, the **Kirkpatrick Hotel,** 620 N. Robinson Ave. (236-4033), offers the cheapest motel-type rooms only 3 blocks from downtown. The aging building has nice clean rooms in a youthful neighborhood. Laundry service. (Singles $14, $58 per week; doubles $85 per week.) **Travel Inn,** 501 N.W. 5th Ave. (235-7455), beats it all. Unmatched in price and service, an easy 5 blocks from the Greyhound station, the Inn has large well-furnished rooms with A/C, heat, free local calls, cable and HBO. (Singles $25, doubles $30.) **Motel 6** also has 7 locations in the OKC area; call 946-6662 for info. (Singles range $21-28, doubles $27-35.) I-35 near Oklahoma City is lined with inexpensive hotels that offer singles for under $25.

Oklahoma City has two readily accessible campgrounds. **RCA,** 12115 Northeast Expwy. (478-0278), next to Frontier City Amusement Park 10 mi. north of the city on I-35, has a pool, laundry room, showers, and lots of fast-food restaurants nearby.

(sites $16; open 8am-9pm). The nearest state-run campground roosts on Lake Thunderbird, 30 mi. south of OKC at **Little River State Park** (360-3572 or 364-7634). Take I-40 East to Choctaw Rd., then south until the road ends, and make a left. Set up a tent, and a collector will come around for your money. (Tent sites $6, $7 in area with gate attendant; showers included. RV sites $10, $11 in area with gate attendant. Seniors and people with disabilities pay ½-price. Open 8am-5pm.)

Since Oklahoma City contains the largest feeder cattle market in the U.S., beef tops most menus. Established in 1926, **Cattleman's Steak House,** 1309 S. Agnew (236-0416), is a classic diner a block away from the stockyards. Try the chopped sirloin dinner ($6) or the navy bean soup with cornbread ($1.50). (Open Sun.-Thurs. 6am-10pm, Fri.-Sat. 6am-midnight.) **Sweeney's Deli,** 900 N. Broadway (232-2510), serves up tasty dishes in a friendly atmosphere; play pool or watch the big-screen TV. The restaurant received the 1988 "good country cooking" award. Sandwiches $3-4, burgers $2.20, hot plates $4. (Open daily 11am-11pm.) **Pump's Bar and Grill,** 5700 N. Western (840-4369), is a renovated gas station serving innovative fuel, like "Oklahoma crepes" (chicken, cream cheese, and jack cheese enchiladas topped with sour cream), burgers, and sandwiches ($3.50-7). (Open Sun.-Thurs. 11am-11pm, Fri.-Sat. 11am-midnight.) Downtown, the **Century Center Plaza,** 100 Main St., oozes with cheap lunch spots (open Mon.-Sat. 11am-3pm).

SIGHTS AND ENTERTAINMENT

The **Oklahoma City Stockyards,** 2500 Exchange Ave. (235-8675), are the busiest in the world. Cattle auctions, held here Mon.-Wed., begin at 7-8am and sometimes last into the night. Mon.-Tues. are the busiest days; Monday morning is the best time to visit. An auctioneer fires bids in a rapid monotone as cowhands chase the cattle through a maze of gates and passages into the auction building. Visitors enter free of charge via a calfwalk over the pens, leading from the parking lot east of the auction house. Take bus #12 from the bus terminal to Agnon and Exchange.

The plight of Native Americans along the "Trail of Tears" is commemorated by James Earle Fraser's *The End of the Trail.* Ironically, his sculpture of a man slumped over an exhausted pony is on display at the **National Cowboy Hall of Fame and Western Heritage Center,** 1700 N.E. 63rd St. (478-2250). The Hall commemorates such pistol-packin' frontiersmen as Barry "Buck" Goldwater and Ronald "Brawny Ronny" Reagan. Along with Frederic Remington sculptures and cowboy memorabilia, you'll find John Wayne's collection of Pueblo kachina dolls (and you thought *real* men didn't play with dolls!). Every summer, the museum showcases 150 works of the National Academy of Western Art. Take bus #22 from downtown. (Open daily 8:30am-6pm; Labor Day-Memorial Day daily 9am-5pm. $6, seniors $5, ages 6-12 $3.) The **State Capitol,** 2300 N. Lincoln Blvd. (521-3356), is the world's only capitol building surrounded by working oil wells. Completed in 1917, the Greco-Roman structure was inadvertently but appropriately built atop a large reserve of crude oil. (Open daily 8am-7pm. Guided tours 8am-3pm. Free.)

The **Kirkpatrick Center Museum Complex,** 2100 N.E. 52nd St. (427-5461), is a sort of educational amusement park. It looks like a mall but it's actually a pastiche of eight separate colorful and entertaining museums. Highlights are the **Air and Space Museum** and the **International Photography Hall of Fame.** Take bus #22. (Open Mon.-Sat. 9am-6pm, Sun. noon-6pm; Labor Day-Memorial Day Mon.-Fri. 9:30am-5pm, Sat. 9am-6pm, Sun. noon-6pm. Admission to all 8 museums $6, seniors, $4, ages 3-12 $3.50, under 3 free.)

Nightlife in Oklahoma City is as rare as the elusive jackelope. For ideas, pick up a copy of the *Oklahoma Gazette.* City slickers beware: the **First National Bar,** 4315 N. Western (525-9400), ain't no sushi place. Live bands, pool tables and a raucous crowd make this bar a local favorite. (Open Mon.-Sat. 10am-2am.) The **Oklahoma Opry,** 404 W. Commerce (632-8322), is home to a posse of country music stars (regular performances Sat. at 8pm; tickets $6, seniors $5, kids $2).

■ Near Oklahoma City

Prudent travelers will skip OKC's nightlife, wake up early, and drive to **Anadarko,** a short 60-mi. drive through the Great Plains. Anadarko is home to **Indian City USA** (247-5661), a museum which has reconstructed villages of seven Native American tribes. During the summer, each tour begins with a performance of Native American dances by prize-winning dancers. Talk to the dancers or one of the guides; the conversation will tell more about the tragedy of Native Americans than any Oscar-winning Kevin Costner movie ever can. Drive 40 mi. south from Oklahoma City on I-44 to exit #83, take a right on 9 West, go about 20 mi. to Anadarko, take a left on 8 South, and go 2 mi. to the museum entrance. (Open daily 9am-6pm, off-season 9am-5pm. First tour at 9:30am, last tour at 4:15pm. $7, kids 6-11 $4, under 6 free.)

For those in search of a home where the buffalo roam and the deer and the antelope play, check out the **Wichita Mountain Wildlife Refuge** (429-3222), an hour south of Anadarko. Created in 1905 by Teddy Roosevelt, the National Park is home to 625 buffalo, thousands of deer and Texas longhorns, and various other wildlife, all of which cavort freely in the park. **Mount Scott** is only 2464 ft. high, but because it rises over a plain, it offers a stupendous vista those who drive or hike to the top. Camping is permitted in certain areas of the park; stop at a refuge office for maps. Take exit #49 off I-44. (Open daily; some areas close at dusk.)

■■■ TULSA

First settled by Creeks arriving from the "Trail of Tears," Tulsa's location on the banks of the Arkansas River made it a logical trading outpost for Europeans and Native Americans. The advent of railroads and the discovery of huge oil deposits catapulted the city into an oil capital by the 1920s. The city's varied heritage is visible today in its art deco skyscrapers, French villas, and Georgian mansions, as well as its Native American community, the second largest among U.S. metropolitan areas.

PRACTICAL INFORMATION

Emergency: 911.
Visitor Information: Convention and Visitors Division, Metropolitan Tulsa Chamber of Commerce, 616 S. Boston (585-1201 or 800-558-3311).
Greyhound: 317 S. Detroit (800-231-2222). To: Oklahoma City (8 per day, 2 hr., $16); St. Louis (9 per day, 7½-9½ hr., $68); Kansas City (4 per day, 6-8 hr., $50); Dallas (5 per day, 7 hr., $46). Lockers $1. Open 24 hrs.
Public Transport: Metropolitan Tulsa Transit Authority, 510 S. Rockford (582-2100). Buses start running 5-6am and stop 6-7pm. Fare 75¢, transfers 5¢, seniors and disabled (disabled card available at bus offices) 35¢, ages 5-18 60¢, under 5 free with adult. Maps and schedules are widely available and at the main office (open Mon.-Fri. 8am-4:45pm), but are not always reliable.
Taxi: Yellow Cab, 582-6161. $1.25 base fare, $1 per mi., $1 per passenger.
Car Rental: Thrifty, 1506 N. Memorial Dr. $27 per day, $132 per week. Unlimited mileage. Must be 21 with major credit card.
Bike Rental: River Trail Sports Center, 6861 S. Peoria (743-5898). Five-speeds $4 per hr., $12 per day. Rollerblades $5 per hr., $10 per day. Open Mon.-Sat. 10am-7pm, Sun. 11am-6pm. Credit card deposit.
Help Lines: 583-4357, for information, referral, crisis intervention. Open 24 hrs.
Gay Information Line, 743-4297. Open daily 8am-10pm.
Post Office: 333 W. 4th St. (599-6800). Mon.-Fri. 8:30am-5pm. **ZIP code:** 74101.
Area Code: 918.

Tulsa is divided into blocks of one square mile. Downtown lies at the intersection of **Main Street** and **Admiral Boulevard.** Admiral divides addresses north and south; numbered streets lie in increasing order as you move away from Admiral. Named streets stretch north to south in alphabetical order. Those named after western cit-

T
U
L
S
A

ies are on the west side of Main St.; after eastern cities on the east side of it. Every time the alphabetical order reaches the end, the cycle begins again.

ACCOMMODATIONS AND CAMPING

Most cheap accommodations in Tulsa are outside of the city center. An exception is the **YMCA,** 515 S. Denver (583-6201), for men only. Ask for a room on the third floor. Guests have access to a TV lounge, pool and gym; the office is open 24 hrs. (Singles $11; key deposit $10.) The cheapest downtown motel is the **Darby Lane Inn,** 416 W. 6th St. (584-4461). Clean, spacious rooms have cable TV. (Singles $34, doubles $40. Suites with two queen-size beds and kitchen $40. Call for reservations.) Budget motels are plentiful along I-44 and I-244. To reach the **Gateway Motor Inn,** 5600 W. Skelly Dr. (446-6611), take bus #17 and get off at Rensor's Grocery. Clean rooms replete with large beds, HBO, and cable. (Singles $21, doubles $25.) Trusty **Motel 6** also has two locations, identical to every other Motel 6 in America: I-40 at exit 235 (234-6200) and I-44 at exit 222a (445-0223). (Singles $22, doubles $26.)

The **KOA Kampground,** 193 East Ave. (266-4227), ½ mi. west of the Will Rogers Turnpike Gate off I-44, has a pool, laundry, showers, and game room (sites $15 for 2 people, with hookup $17). **Keystone State Park** (865-4991) offers three campgrounds along the shores of Lake Keystone, 20 mi. west of Tulsa on the Cimarron Turnpike (U.S. 64). The wooded park offers hiking, swimming, boating, and excellent catfish and bass fishing. (Sites $10, with hookup $14. Tent camping $6.) Four-person cabins with kitchenettes available ($43); call 800-522-8565 for reservations.

FOOD

Nelson's Buffeteria, 514 S. Boston (584-9969), takes you on a sentimental journey through Tulsa's past. Operating since 1929 and now run by Nelson Jr., this old-style diner's walls are blanketed with Mid-American memorabilia. Try a blue plate special (two scrambled eggs, hash browns, toast and jam, $2) or the famous chicken-fried steak ($4.50). Remember to ask for extra gravy. (Open Mon.-Fri. 6am-2:30pm.) Only 3 blocks from the YMCA is the **Little Ancient Denver Grill,** 112 S. Denver (582-3790). Frequented by rough-hewn locals. Lunch specials ($4) include a salad, fresh rolls, and a choice of vegetables. (Open Mon.-Sat. 6am-8pm, Sun. 8am-4pm.) **Casa Bonita,** 2120 S. Sheridan Rd. (836-6464), dishes out Mexican feasts ($5-7) and all-you-can-eat dinners ($8) in a highly entertaining atmosphere. The dining areas range in decor from rustic candle-lit caves to south-of-the-border villages. (Open Sun.-Thurs. 11am-9:30pm, Fri.-Sat. 11am-10pm). Restaurants on Rte. 66 (between Main and Lewis) welcome hungry budget travelers. Inconspicuous but unrivaled among them is the **Route 66 Diner,** 2639 E. 11th St. (592-6666). Run by a couple with old Tulsa blood and a long culinary tradition, the diner is a great bargain for lunch ($3-6). Meatloaf ($4), the are-you-sure-you're-*that*-hungry double burger ($5.50), daily special ($4.75). Menu varies but will never leave you hungry. (Open Tues.-Sun. 7am-2pm.) Many downtown restaurants close at 3pm weekdays and 1pm Sat.

SIGHTS AND ENTERTAINMENT

Perched atop an Osage foothill 2 mi. northwest of downtown, the **Thomas Gilcrease Museum,** 1400 Gilcrease Museum Rd. (596-2700), houses one of the world's largest collections of American art. Designed as an anthropological study of North America from pre-history to the present, the museum contains 250,000 Native American artifacts and more than 10,000 paintings and sculptures by artists such as Remington and Russell. Take bus #7 ("Gilcrease") from downtown. (Open Mon.-Sat. 9am-5pm, Sun. 1-5pm. Donation requested. Disabled accessible.) The **Philbrook Art Center,** 2727 S. Rockford Rd. (749-7941), in the former Renaissance villa of an oil baron, houses a collection of Native American pottery and artifacts alongside Renaissance paintings and sculptures. Picnic by the lovely pond on the grounds. Take bus #16 ("S. Peoria") from downtown. (Open Tues.-Sat. 10am-5pm,

Thurs. 10am-8pm, Sun. 1-5pm. $3, seniors and students $1.50, ages 12 and under free.) The **Fenster Museum of Jewish Art,** 1223 E. 17th Pl. (582-3732), housed in B'nai Emunah Synagogue, contains an impressive if oddly located collection of Judaica dating from 2000 BC to the present (open Sun.-Thurs. 10am-4pm; free).

The most frequented tourist attraction in Tulsa, **Oral Roberts University,** 7777 S. Lewis (495-6161), was founded in 1964 when Oral had a dream in which God commanded him to "Build Me a university." The heavenly edict inspired a divine design so radiant it puts any secular campus to shame. Walking onto the campus is like entering the twilight zone. The ultra-modern, gold-mirrored architecture rising out of an Oklahoma plain, the 80-ft.-high praying hands sculpture guarding the campus, and the hordes of believers flocking to visit make this eerie and kitschy experience a must. The **Prayer Tower** (495-6807) takes visitors through an exhibition honoring the university's founder (open Mon.-Sat. 10:30am-4:30pm, Sun. 1-5pm; free). You might remember this as Oral's retreat when, a few years back, he threatened to have God "take him home" if he didn't get a giant wad of cash from his followers. Choirs sing in the background, spotlights illuminate mementos from the Roberts' childhood, and doors open and close automatically as if by divine command. The **ORU Healing Outreach** (496-7700) hosts a "Journey Through the Bible" tour, where Old Testament scenes are re-created in life-like, three-dimensional exhibits. (Open Mon.-Sat. 10:30am-4:30pm, Sun. 1-5pm. Tours every 15-20 min. Free.) The rest of the non-drinkin', non-smokin', and non-dancin' campus is (alas! alack!) closed to the public. The university is about 6 mi. south of downtown Tulsa between Lewis and Harvard Ave. Take bus #9. (Visitors center open Mon.-Sat. 10:30am-4:30pm, Sun. 1-4:30pm.)

During the oil boom years of the 1920s, art deco architecture was all the rage in Tulsa. The best example of this style is the **Boston Avenue United Methodist Church,** 1301 S. Boston (583-5181). Built in 1929, the house of worship is vaguely suggestive of the witch's palace in *The Wizard of Oz.* Climb the 14-story tower to the pea-green worship room with a skyline view of Tulsa. (Tours given Mon.-Fri. 9am-noon and 1-4pm, Sat. by appointment, Sun. 12:15pm. Free)

Rodgers and Hammerstein's *Oklahoma!* continues its run under the stars at the **Discoveryland Amphitheater** (245-0242), 10 mi. west of Tulsa on 41st St., accessible only by car. It features what is now the state song and commemorates the suffering of the Okie farmers in the 19th century. (Shows June-Aug. Mon.-Sat. at 8pm. Mon.-Thurs. $12, seniors $11, kids under 12 $7; Fri.-Sat. $14, seniors $13, kids under 12 $5.) Arrive early for the pre-show barbecue, starting at 5:30pm. ($7, seniors $6.50, kids $4.50.) A short western review precedes the show. A moving commemoration of Native American heritage is the **Trail of Tears Drama,** a show reenacting the Cherokees' tragic march, performed in Tahlequah, 66 mi. east of Tulsa on Rte. 51. (Performances June-Sept. 2 Mon.-Sat. 8pm. For tickets, call 456-6007, or write P.O. Box 515, Tahlequah 74465; reservations recommended. $9, under 13 $4.50.) For more cultural enlightenment, the **Tulsa Philharmonic** (747-7445) and **Tulsa Opera** (582-4035) perform year-round. The **Tulsa Ballet** (585-2573), acclaimed as one of America's finest regional troupes performs at the **Performing Arts Center** (596-7111), at the corner of 3rd St. and Cincinnati.

At night, head to the bars along 15th St. east of Peoria, or in the 30s along S. Peoria. Down at the **Sunset Grill,** 3410 S. Peoria (744-5550), catch nightly rowdy rock bands (open daily 4pm-2am; must be 21; no cover). Keep up to date on Tulsa's nightlife with a free copy of *Urban Tulsa,* available at newsstands, bookstores, and the chamber of commerce, or by calling 585-2787.

The best times to visit Tulsa are during annual special events like the **International Mayfest** (582-6435) in mid-May. This outdoor food, arts, and performance festival takes place in downtown Tulsa over a ten-day period. The **Pow-Wow** (835-8699), held the first weekend in June at the Tulsa Fairground Pavilion, attracts Native Americans from dozens of different tribes. The three-day festival features

Native American food, arts and crafts exhibits, and nightly dancing contests which visitors may attend. (Admission $1, kids under 10 free.)

■ South Dakota

From the forested granite crags of the Black Hills to the glacial lakes of the northeast, the Coyote State has more to offer than casual passers-by might expect. WALL DRUG. In fact, the state has the highest ratio of sights-to-people in all of the Great Plains. Stunning natural spectacles like the Black Hills, the Badlands, and the Wind and Jewel Caves, as well as colossal man-made attractions such as Mt. Rushmore and the Crazy Horse Monument, have made tourism the state's largest industry after agriculture. WALL DRUG. Cartographically speaking, South Dakota is the most average state in the Union, home to the geographic center of the United States (approximately 35 mi. north of Spearfish). Climatically, however, South Dakota is a land of extremes. Temperatures during the year oscillate between Arctic frigidity and Saharan heat. YOU ARE NOW ONLY A HALF-PAGE FROM WALL DRUG.

PRACTICAL INFORMATION

Capital: Pierre.
Division of Tourism, 221 S. Central, in Capitol Lake Plaza, P.O. Box 1000, Pierre 57051 (773-3301 or 800-952-2217; 800-843-1930 outside SD). Open Mon.-Fri. 8am-5pm. **U.S. Forest Service,** Custer 57730 (673-4853). Provides camping stamps for the national forest, Golden Eagle passes for those over 62, and Black Hills National Forest maps ($3). Open Mon.-Fri. 8am-7pm. **Division of Parks and Recreation,** Capitol Bldg., Pierre 57501 (773-3371). Information on state parks and campgrounds. Open Mon.-Fri. 8am-6pm.
Time Zones: Central and Mountain. **Postal Abbreviation:** SD
Sales Tax: 4%.

■■■ BADLANDS NATIONAL PARK

Some 60 million years ago, when much of the Great Plains was under water, tectonic shifts thrust up the Rockies and the Black Hills. Mountain streams deposited silt from these nascent highlands into what is now known as the Badlands, fossilizing in layer after pink layer the remains of wildlife that once wandered these flood plains. Erosion has carved spires and steep gullies into the land of this area, creating a landscape that contrasts sharply with the prairies of eastern South Dakota. The Sioux called these arid and treacherous formations "Mako Sica," or "bad land"; Gen. Alfred Sully—the opposition—simply called them "hell with the fires out."

The Badlands still smolder about 50 mi. east of Rapid City on I-90. Highway 240 winds through the wilderness in a 32-mi. detour off I-90 (take exit 131 or 110). There is almost no way to visit the park by highway without being importuned by employees from **Wall Drug,** 510 Main St. (279-2175), in Wall; the store is a towering monument to the success of saturation advertising. After seeing billboards for Wall Drug from as far as 500 mi. away, travelers feel obligated to make a stop in Wall to see what all the ruckus is about, much as they must have done 60 years ago when Wall enticed travelers on the parched Plains by offering free water. The "drug store" itself is quite a disappointment, mostly hawking overpriced souvenirs and other assorted kitsch. (Open daily 6:30am-9pm; Dec.-April Mon.-Sat. 8am-5pm.) Except for **The Flavor Creator,** across from THE store (ice cream $1.75), all of the other cafes and shops on Main St. are just as overpriced (a chunk of fudge at The Country

Store, located in the Wall Drug Mall, costs 71¢). All in all the town is just another brick in the...well, forget it.

From Wall, take Rte. 240, which loops through the park and returns to I-90 30 mi. east of Wall in Cactus Flat. From Rapid City, take Rte. 44 and turn northeast at Scenic, where it leads to Sage Creek and Rte. 240. There are ranger stations at both entrances off I-90, although the western portion of the park is much less developed. **Jack Rabbit Buses** (348-3300) makes two stops daily at Wall from Rapid City ($19). You can probably ask around for a ride into the park from Wall. Entrance to the park costs $1 per person, $5 per carload ($1.50 for a carload of Arikara Sioux).

The **Ben Reifel Visitors Center** (433-5361), 5 mi. inside the park's eastern entrance, is more convenient than **White River Visitors Center** (455-2878), 55 mi. southwest, off Rte. 27 in the park's less-visited southern section. Both centers sell trail guides and stock the *Prairie Preamble*, a free paper detailing park programs. (Ben Reifel open June-Aug. daily 7am-8pm; Sept.-May hours vary. White River open May 31-Aug. 7am-8pm.) Stock up on gas, food, and bug repellent before entering the park. Both of the visitors centers spout potable water. The Badlands experience extreme temperatures in midsummer and winter, but in late spring and fall offer pleasant weather and few insects. Always watch (and listen) for rattlesnakes.

ACCOMMODATIONS, CAMPING, AND FOOD

Two campgrounds lie within the park. **Ben Reifel Campground,** near the visitors center, has shaded picnic tables and a bathroom with running water, but no showers (sites $8). The **Sage Creek Campground,** 11 mi. from the Pinnacles entrance south of Wall, is free. It is merely an open field with pit toilets, no water, and it does *not* allow fires. What did you expect for nothing? Try backcountry camping for a more intimate introduction to this austere landscape. Bring at least one gallon of water per person per day and set up camp at least ½ mi. from a road. Go ahead and share the stars with local wildlife, but don't cozy up to the bison, especially in spring when nervous mothers become, shall we say, overprotective.

For tenderfoot tourists, the **Cedar Pass Lodge,** P.O. Box 5, Interior 57750 (433-5460), next to the visitors center, has air-conditioned cabins. (Singles with showers $37, doubles $41. Each additional person $4. Open mid-April-mid-Oct. Try to make reservations; leave a 50% deposit.) Try a buffalo burger ($3.25) at the lodge's mid-priced restaurant (the only one in the park). (Open June-Aug. daily 7am-8pm.)

SIGHTS AND ACTIVITIES

The park protects large tracts of prairie along with the stark rock formations. The Cedar Pass Visitors Center has an **audio-visual program** on the Badlands, and the park rangers lead **nature hikes,** all of which leave from the Cedar Pass amphitheater. The free hikes (at 6am, 8am, and 6pm, 1½ hr.) provide an easy way to appreciate the Badlands—you may find Oligocene fossils right at your feet. In the evening, the amphitheater slide program narrates Badlands history (cover up—the mosquitoes can be ravenous). A 1-hr. night-prowl or sky-trek (stargazing) follows the program. Check the *Prairie Preamble* for details on daily events.

You can also hike through the Badlands on your own. Pick up a trail guide at one of the visitors centers. If you're planning an overnight hike, be certain to ask for their **backcountry camping** information. Try the short but steep **Saddle Pass Trail** or the less hilly **Castle Trail** (10 mi. round-trip). If you'd rather drive than hike, follow **Loop Road** and pull over at the spectacular overlooks. Highlights of Loop Road are **Robert's Prairie Dog Town** and the **Yellow Mounds Overlook,** where brilliant red and yellow formations relieve the ubiquitous Badland bleached rose. Keep your eyes shucked along Sage Creek Rd. for the park's herd of about 400 bison. Respect the intense midday sun, and at all times be wary of crumbly footholds, prickly cacti, and the occasional rattlesnake. It is easy to lose your bearings in this convoluted territory, so consult with a ranger or tote a map.

BLACK HILLS

The Black Hills, named for the dark hue that distance lends the green pines covering the hills, have long been considered sacred by the Sioux. The Treaty of 1868 gave the Black Hills and the rest of South Dakota west of the Missouri River to the Sioux, but the U.S. government broke it during the gold rush of 1877-79. In 1980, the Supreme Court awarded the Sioux a "just compensation" of $200 million, which the tribe did not accept; the Sioux want the government to return their land to them. Today, white residents dominate the area, which contains a trove of treasures, including Mount Rushmore, Crazy Horse Monument, Custer State Park, Wind Cave National Park, Jewel Cave National Monument, and the Black Hills National Forest.

I-90 skirts the northern border of the Black Hills from Spearfish in the west to Rapid City in the east. The interconnecting road system through the hills is difficult to navigate without a good map; pick up one for free at the Rapid City Chamber of Commerce. The road that meanders through the hills is full of unexpected delights prefaced by turn-offs (waterfalls and historic markers).

Take advantage of the excellent and informative **Grayline** tours (342-4461). Tickets can be purchased at Rapid City motels, hotels, and campgrounds. Make reservations, or call 1 hr. before departure; they will pick you up at your motel. Tour #1 is the most complete Black Hills tour, going to Mt. Rushmore, Black Hills National Forest, Custer State Park, Needles Highway, and the Crazy Horse Monument (mid-May-mid-Oct. daily, 8 hrs., $34). Tour #4 heads to Spearfish for the Black Hills Passion Play, which has been "Praised by Press, Acclaimed by Clergy, Endorsed by Educators, and Lauded by Laymen" (June-Aug. Sun., Tues., and Thurs., 5 hrs., $19).

Hiking in the hills is quite enjoyable—there is little underbrush beneath the conifer canopy. The abandoned mines and strange rock outcroppings may beckon you to explore, but stay on the marked trails. Rainy, cool weather is common as late as July. Dress accordingly.

■■■ BLACK HILLS NATIONAL FOREST

Black Hills, like other national forests, adheres to the principle of "multiple use"; mining, logging, ranching, and tourism all take place in close proximity. "Don't miss" attractions like reptile farms and Flintstone Campgrounds lurk around every bend in the Black Hills' narrow, sinuous roads. Visit the forest outside of the peak tourist season (July-mid-Sept.), during which heathen hordes of cars and campers descend on the area in a rush for the modern-day gold of glow-in-the-dark souvenirs.

Practical Information The most convenient information centers are the **Pactola Ranger District**, 803 Soo San Dr., Rapid City (343-1567; open Mon.-Fri. 8am-5pm), and the **Spearfish Ranger District**, 2041 North Main St., Spearfish (642-4622; open Mon.-Fri. 8am-5pm). The main information office and visitors center at Pactola Reservoir, 17 mi. west of Rapid City on U.S. 385, has forestry exhibits in the summer in addition to the usual tourist literature. You can buy supplies before you head off to the hinterland at small grocery stores in Keystone and Custer, or at the not-so-cheap KOA campground 5 mi. west of Mt. Rushmore on Rte. 244.

Accommodations and Food Spearfish, located directly off I-90 at the northern end of the Black Hills National Forest, is an excellent access point for the hills. Comfortable accommodations can be found at the **Canyon Gateway Motel** on Route 14A (642-3402) at the edge of the famed **Spearfish Canyon** (singles $32, doubles $42). Also stop in at the **Valley Cafe**, 608 Main St. (642-2423), for pleasant conversation and great pancakes (3 enormo-flapjacks for $2.15) before heading into the woods. If you're feeling vigorous, climb or bike the 5.7 mi. of aspen and pine-lined

Rim Rock Trail to an altitude of 6,280 ft. The trailhead is approximately 18 mi. south-west of Spearfish on Highway 14A.

Camping Camping in the national forest is free. To save money the adventurous way, disappear down one of the many dirt roads (make sure it isn't someone's drive-way) and set up camp. There are a few rules to follow: you can't park on the side of the road, your campsite must be at least 1 mi. away from any campground or visitors center, and you can't build a campfire. Watch for poison ivy and afternoon thunder-showers. The most popular established campgrounds include **Bear Gulch** and **Pac-tola** (343-4283), on the Pactola Reservoir just south of the junction of Rte. 44 and U.S. 385 (sites \$10-12). You must register for sites at the Pactola campground (on 385 South, 1 mi. past the visitors center; turn right at sign for the Black Forest Inn). They fill quickly, so call for reservations up to 10 days in advance. Other favorites include **Sheridan Lake Campground** (574-2873 or 800-283-2267), east of Hill City on U.S. 385 (sites \$10-12), which provides picnic tables, pit toilets, water hydrants, and movies and talks on Saturday at 8pm. For more info, contact the Pactola or Spearfish Ranger District (see above). The Black Hills National Forest extends into Wyoming as well, with a ranger station (307-283-1361; open daily 8am-5pm, winter Mon.-Fri. 8am-5pm) in Sundance. The Wyoming side is sparsely visited, horses are permitted in more places, and campfires are allowed. Maps are \$3. Contact the **Black Hills Forest Service Visitors Center** (343-8755) on I-385 S., at Pactola Lake.

■■■ MT. RUSHMORE NATIONAL MONUMENT

South Dakota historian Doane Robinson originally conceived this "shrine of democ-racy" in 1923 as a memorial for local Western heroes like Kit Carson. By its comple-tion in 1941, the monument portrayed the 60-ft.-tall faces of George Washington, Thomas Jefferson, Abraham Lincoln, and Theodore Roosevelt. Think about it: these heads have nostrils large enough to snort a man! Millions have stared in awe at the four stony-faced patriarchs, designed and sculpted by chiseler extraordinaire Gut-zon Borglum. The monument proves that Americans do take great men for granite.

From Rapid City, take U.S. 16 to Keystone and Rte. 16A up to the mountain. The **visitors center** (574-2523) has multi-media exhibitions as well as braille brochures and wheelchairs. Programs for the disabled are held daily at 9pm. (Visitors center open daily 7am-10pm; Sept. 18-May 14 daily 8am-5pm.) Borglum's Studio, in the vis-itors center, holds the plaster model of the carving, as well as his tools and plans. (Ranger talks in summer hourly 10am-6:30pm; studio open daily 9am-6pm.) Also in the visitors center is **Mt. Rushmore Memorial Amphitheater,** the location of the evening monument-lighting programs. (May 14-Sept. 4 program at 9pm, monument lit 9:30-10:30pm; trail lights off at 11pm.) For close accommodations, try the **Hill City-Mt. Rushmore KOA** (574-2525), 5 mi. west of Mt. Rushmore on Rte. 244. With kabins (\$54) come use of showers, stove, heated pool, laundry facilities, and free shuttle service to Mt. Rushmore. (Office open daily 7am-11pm, Oct.-April 8am-10pm. Kampsites \$16 for 2 people, \$20 with water and electricity, \$22 with full hookup.) For a more remote and scenic sleeping place, try **Kemp's Kamp** (666-4654; kampsites \$14, kabins \$36, full hookups, showers, laundry facilities, and pool available; ½-mi. west of Keystone off Rte. 16A). Tours of Mt. Rushmore and Crazy Horse are provided by **Stagecoach West Tours** (605-343-3113) from June to mid-October (departs daily 8:30am, 8½ hr., \$29, under 12 \$14.50).

■■■ CRAZY HORSE NATIONAL MONUMENT

If you thought Mount Rushmore was big, think again. This monument is a wonder-of-the-world-in-progress; an entire mountain is being transformed into a 500-ft.-high memorial sculpture of the great Lacota chief Crazy Horse. When finished, this will relegate the denizens of Rushmore to the status of smurfs. The project began in 1947 and receives no government funding of any kind; the sculptor, Korczak Ziolkowski, believed in the American spirit of free enterprise, and twice refused $10 million in federal funding. Crazy Horse himself was a resolute Native American war chief who fought against the U.S. government to protect his people's land, rights, and pride. He was stabbed in the back (literally) by an American soldier in 1877, while at Fort Robinson, NE, under a flag of truce. The Monument, on Rte. 16/385 14 mi. south of Mt. Rushmore, includes the **Indian Museum of North America** as well as the mountain statue, and will one day become the site of the **University and Medical Training Center for the North American Indian.** (Open daily 7am-10pm, Sept.-May 8am-5pm. Admission $6, students $1.75, under 6 free, $10 per carload. Special rates for groups and AAA members. For information or to give a tax-deductible donation, write: Crazy Horse Memorial, Crazy Horse, SD, 57730-9506, or call 673-4681.)

■■■ CUSTER STATE PARK

Peter Norbeck, governor of South Dakota during the late 1910s, loved to hike among the thin, towering rock formations that haunt the area south of Sylvan Lake and Mt. Rushmore. Norbeck not only created Custer State Park, but spectacular Needles Highway as well, which follows his favorite hiking route. He purposely kept the highway narrow and winding so that newcomers could experience the pleasures of discovery. Watch for mountain goats and bighorn sheep among the rocky spires. For information, contact HC 83, P.O. Box 70, Custer 57730 (255-4515; open Mon.-Fri. 7:30am-5pm). There is a daily entrance fee ($3 per person, $8 per carload). At the entrance, ask for a copy of *Tatanka* (meaning "buffalo"), the informative Custer State Park newspaper. The **Peter Norbeck Welcome Center** (255-4464), on U.S. 16A 1 mi. west of the State Game Lodge, is the park's info center (open May-Sept. daily 8am-8pm). All six **campgrounds** charge $8-10 per night; some have showers and restrooms. Restaurants and concessions are available at all four park lodges, but you can save money by shopping at the local general stores in Custer, Hermosa, or Keystone.

Sylvan Lake, on Needles Hwy. (Rte. 87), is as lovely as its name, with hiking trails, fishing, horse concessions, paddle boats, and canoes. Horse rides are available at Blue Bell Lodge (255-4531, stable 255-4571; rides $13.50 per hr., under 12 $11.50; $21.50 per 2 hr., under 12 $19.50; hayride with steak dinner $22). Paddle and row boat rentals are available at Legion Lake Lodge (255-4521; paddleboats $2.50 per person for ½-hr.; $25 for 3 people to fish in row boat for 6 hrs.). All lakes and streams permit fishing, with a $6 daily license. Five-day nonresident licenses are $14.50. There is a limit of eight trout per day, six times per summer. Summer fishing is the best, especially around the first of the month when officials stock the waters. Rental equipment is available at the four area lodges.

■■■ WIND CAVE AND JEWEL CAVE

In the cavern-riddled Black Hills, the subterranean scenery often rivals what lies above-ground. Private concessionaires will attempt to lure you into the holes in their backyards, but the government owns the area's prime real estate. **Wind Cave National Park** (745-4600), adjacent to Custer State Park on Rte. 87, and **Jewel Cave**

National Monument (673-2288), 14 mi. west of Custer on U.S. 16A, are in the southern hills. There is no public transportation to the caves.

In the summer, both Wind and Jewel Cave visitors centers offer excursions daily, including short candlelight tours and strenuous but exhilarating spelunking tours, during which tourists crawl on the floor of the cave just like real explorers. Guides provide knee pads, helmets with lanterns, and instruction. Wear well-soled shoes, preferably ankle-high laced boots, and expendable clothing. Bring a sweater on all tours—Jewel Cave remains a constant 47°F, Wind Cave 53°F.

Wind Cave Though discovered in 1881, most of Wind Cave was not explored until 1890 when 17-year-old Alvin McDonald probed its depths. You can still see his name burned on the walls of some of the deeper chambers. The cave lies 12 mi. north of Hot Springs on U.S. 385. Besides several short walks, Wind Cave Park offers five **tours.** The easy **Garden of Eden Tour** gives a quick overview of the cave's interior (6 per day 8:40am-5:30pm; $2, seniors and under 15 $1). The one-hour **Natural Entrance Tour** leaves on the hour, 9am-6pm, and covers ½-mi. of the cave. ($4, ages 6-15 $2.) The more strenuous, 1½-hr. **Fairgrounds Tour** snakes ½ mi. through two levels of the cave (9:40am-4:20pm, $5, ages 6-15 $2.50). The four-hour **Spelunking Tour,** limited to 10 people ages 16 and over, leaves at 1pm ($8, reservations required). Finally, the **Candlelight Tour** ($5, minimum age 8). To make reservations for these tours, contact Wind Cave National Park, Hot Springs 57747 (745-4600; open daily 8am-7pm; Aug. 24-June 4 daily 8am-5pm). **Self-guided surface tours** begin at the Elk Mountain Campground Amphitheater (see below).

Jewel Cave Sprawling underground in one of the largest unexplored labyrinths in the world, Jewel Cave is formed of the same limestone as Wind Cave, but the similarities end there. Grayish calcite crystal walls are the highlight of the tours. Guides sponsor three kinds of tours during the summer. The ½-mi. **Scenic Tour** takes you over 700 stairs (every 20 min., 1 hr., $4, ages 6-15 $2). Make reservations for the **Spelunking Tour,** limited to 10 people ages 16 and over, and be sure to wear sturdy foot gear (Sun., Tues., Thurs., and Sat., $8). Contact Jewel Cave National Monument, Custer 57730 (673-2288; open June 12-Aug. 27 daily 8am-6pm). **Elk Mountain Campground** offers primitive sites with toilets for $8. There are no overnight accommodations at the Jewel Cave Monument, but you can camp at the national forest's facility 6 mi. east on Rte. 16A.

■■■ LEAD AND DEADWOOD

Many interesting small towns glitter like gold dust amidst the Black Hills, but Lead and Deadwood are truly 24-carat. During the 1877 gold rush, these towns attained legendary status for their idiosyncratic prospectors and boom-town exploits.

■ Lead

In **Lead** (LEED), almost everybody works for Homestake, the locally prominent gold-mining corporation. Here, after the hills "panned out" in 1878, hardrock mining began in earnest. Homestake still owns much of the northern Black Hills and continues to operate the largest gold mine in the Western Hemisphere. The **Open Cut,** a yawning chasm where a mountain once stood, is a monument to Homestake's handiwork. You'll see huge vats of tailings, conveyor belts loaded with ore, and contraptions that lower the miners down almost a mile into the belly of the earth. Operations there ceased some time ago—long enough for a Piggly-Wiggly store and many miners to make their homes in its path. The **Lead Civic Association** (584-3110) gives surface tours of the mine. (Tours June-Aug. daily 8am-5pm every ½-hr.; May and Sept.-Oct. Mon.-Fri. 8am-4pm every ½-hr. $3.50, seniors and students $2.50.) To get a more *in-depth* feeling for the mines, check out the **Black**

Hills Mining Museum, 323 W. Main St. (584-1605), where you can tour fake mines (every 20 min.) and try your hand at panning for gold (open May 20-Oct. 10 daily 9am-5pm; $3.50, students $2.50, under 6 free.)

The **post office** (584-2110) in Lead is at 329 W. Main St. (open Mon.-Fri. 8:30am-4:30pm, Sat. 10am-noon); the **ZIP code** is 57754. The **area code** for Lead is 605.

■ Deadwood

Gunslinging hero/outlaws Wild Bill Hickok and Calamity Jane sauntered into **Dead-wood** at the height of the Gold Rush. Bill stayed just long enough—two months—to spend eternity here. Legend has it he was shot while playing poker, and since he fell while holding eights and aces, this full house became known as "the dead man's hand." Visit **Mt. Moriah Cemetery** on Boot Hill, where Bill and Jane are buried beside each other in a plot overlooking the city (on Rte. 14A, just outside Deadwood; open daily 7am-8pm, admission $1) or take the one-hour **Alkali Iki Bus Tour** (578-3147) of historic Main St., Saloon #10, the Franklin Hotel, and Mt. Moriah Cemetery (10am-5pm; call for meeting place; $4.50, students $2.50).

In 1989 Deadwood voted to reinstate small-stakes gambling to recapture some of the town's less murderous Wild West atmosphere in order to lure tourists. As a result, **Main Street** sometimes resembles a smaller version of Las Vegas or Atlantic City. Parking in the narrow canyon has also grown inconvenient and expensive; check with your motel to see if it can arrange a guaranteed space for your car. Otherwise, take the 50¢ trolley which comes every 20 min. and passes all the motels. Some motels have a personal free trolley; ask.

The Deadwood **post office** (578-1505) is in the Deadwood Federal Building (open Mon.-Fri. 9am-4:30pm, Sat. 10am-noon); the **ZIP code** is 57732; the **area code** 605.

Food and Accommodations The **Nugget Cafe,** 815 W. Main St. (584-3337), in Lead, is almost a museum in its own right, decorated with photos documenting the town's history. Try the nugget burger ($3.75) or the tasty omelettes ($2.75-3.75). (Open Mon.-Sat. 6am-7pm.) For huge portions at a not-so-large price, try **Mama Leon's,** 638 Main (578-2440), in the Lucky Wrangler Casino, where all the yummy Italian food is under $8, combos $10-12 (open Sun.-Fri. noon-9pm, Sat. noon-10pm). Jack McCall, Wild Bill's assassin, was captured at **Goldberg Gaming,** 672 Main St. (578-1515), in Deadwood, where you can down an old-fashioned phosphate for 50¢ or a huge "Goldburger" for $1.50-3.50 (open June-Sept. 2 Mon.-Sat. 6:30am-6pm). The **#10 Saloon,** 657 Main St. (578-3346), claims to own Wild Bill's "death chair," and has live rock bands every night at 8:30pm (open daily 8am-2am).

There ain't no budget lodging in Lead or Deadwood. Your best bet is to stay at **Wild Bill's Campground** (578-2800), on Rte. 385 about 3 mi. south of Lead and Deadwood. It's a scenic spot with a swimming pool, showers, hookups, and cozy cabins among the mountain pines, and boasts a free shuttlebus to Deadwood (sites $12.50, $14.50 with water and hookup, cabins $40). Or try the **Jackpot Inn,** ½-mi. south of Rte. 85 on U.S. 385, outside Deadwood and Lead (singles $52, Sept.-May $25 negotiable, with shower, HBO, phone, and use of hot tub) which is on the trolley route (see above). If you'd rather commute, the **Deadwood Express** (343-5044) comes from Rapid City twice per day (1 hr., $2).

■■■ PIERRE

Pierre, South Dakota's capital, sits smack dab in the middle of the state. Situated on the Missouri River, it lies near the **Oahe Dam,** the 2nd-largest rolled-earth dam in the world. Forever a bustlin' cow town, Pierre still serves as a commercial center for farmers and ranchers. The newly restored copper-domed **capitol building** (773-3765) offers free 40-min. tours Mon.-Fri. at 1, 2, and 3pm (open daily 8am-10pm).

Behind the capitol, an unusual fountain dedicated to Korean and Vietnam War veterans spouts flame from a natural gas deposit. In the event of a sudden thermonuclear war, head for the brand-new, bunkerlike **Cultural Heritage Center,** 900 Governors Dr. (773-3458). Built into the side of a hill above the capitol, the museum gives an interesting and detailed history of both the Native American and white inhabitants of South Dakota (open Mon.-Fri. 9am-4:30pm, Sat.-Sun. 1-9:30pm; free).

Practical Information To reach Pierre from I-90, go 30 mi. north on U.S. 83. Visit the **Chamber of Commerce,** 108 E. Missouri St. (224-7361 or 800-962-2034; open Mon.-Fri.8am-5pm). **Greyhound/Jack Rabbit,** in the Phillips 66 station at 621 W. Sioux Ave. (224-7651), runs buses to: Omaha ($86); Rapid City ($44); Minneapolis ($98). Pierre is in the **Central time zone** (1 hr. behind Eastern). The **post office** is at 225 S. Pierre St. (224-2912; open Mon.-Fri. 8am-5:30pm, Sat. 10am-noon). Pierre's **ZIP code** is 57501; the **area code** is 605.

Accommodations and Food Sleep cheap four blocks from the capitol at the **Iron Horse Inn,** 205 W. Pleasant Dr. (224-5981 or 800-742-8612). Multiple rooms, and fairly big (singles $27, doubles $36). Conveniently located across the street from the bus station, the **Days Inn,** 520 W. Sioux Ave. (224-0411), serves free doughnuts, coffee, and milk every morning and popcorn upon arrival (singles $35, doubles $40). The popular **Farm Island State Park** (224-5605), 3 mi. east on Rte. 34, has campsites and showers ($7, $10 with hookup) and **Griffen Park,** along Oahe Lake at the end of Missouri Ave., serves as a free campsite with bathrooms.

Find cheap eats at the **D & E Cafe,** 115 W. Dakota Ave. (224-7200), where a burger is 90¢, and the priciest item on the menu, a T-bone steak, is $4.95. (Open Mon.-Sat. 24 hrs.) Grab a kup of koffee at the **Kozy Korner Restaurant,** 217 E. Dakota Ave. (224-9547), a family place with generous dinners ($3-9). (Open daily 5am-10pm.)

■■■ RAPID CITY

Rapid City's location, approximately 40 mi. east of Wyoming, makes it an ideal base from which to explore the Black Hills and the Badlands. Every summer the area welcomes about 2.2 million tourists, over 40 times the city's permanent population.

PRACTICAL INFORMATION

Emergency: 911.

Rapid City Chamber of Commerce, Visitors Bureau, 444 Mt. Rushmore Rd. N. (343-1744), in the Civic Center. Visitors Bureau (343-8221) open May 16-Oct 15 daily 7:30am-6pm; Chamber of Commerce open year-round Mon.-Fri. 8am-5pm, racks in lobby during other times, but no one working; call ahead.

Buses: Milo Barber Transportation Center, 333 6th St. (348-3300), downtown. **Jack Rabbit Lines** runs east from Rapid City. To: Pierre (1 per day, 3 hr., $44); Sioux Falls (1 per day, 8 hr., $75). **Powder River Lines** services Wyoming and Montana. To: Billings (5pm, 9 hr., $65); Cheyenne (5pm, 8½ hr., $75). Both honor the Greyhound Ameripass. Station open Mon.-Fri. 7:30am-5:30pm, Sat.-Sun. 10am-5:30pm, Sun. 10am-noon and 4-5:30pm.

Public Transport: Milo Barber Transportation Center, 394-6631. City bus transportation available by reservation for disabled travelers $2. Call 24 hrs. in advance. One way trip $1, seniors 50¢. Office open Mon.-Fri. 8am-4pm.

Taxi: Rapid Taxi, 348-8080. Base fare $2.20, $1 per mi.

Time Zone: Mountain (2 hr. behind Eastern).

Post Office: 500 East Blvd. (394-8600), several blocks east of downtown. Open Mon.-Fri. 8am-5pm, Sat. 9:30am-12:30pm. **ZIP code:** 57701.

Area Code: 605.

RAPID CITY

Orienting yourself may be difficult at first, since Rapid City sprawls across 27 flat sq. mi., and few of the buildings in town stand taller than four stories. The center of the downtown area is bordered on the east and west by 6th and 9th St., and on the north and south by Omaha and Kansas City St.

ACCOMMODATIONS, CAMPING, AND FOOD

The **HI/AYH hostel,** 815 Kansas City St. (342-8538), downtown in the YMCA, consists of 14 cots, with no separation between men and women. Access to YMCA facilities (pool, gym, game room) is free, but no bedding or kitchen facilities are available. A cot for the night costs $10. Rapid City accommodations are considerably more expensive during the summer. Make reservations, since budget motels often fill up weeks in advance. The **Big Sky Motel,** 4080 Tower Rd. (348-3200), looms large on a hill just south of town, affording a spectacular view of the city and the surrounding farmland (spotless but phoneless singles $33, doubles $38). **Motel 6** (343-3687) is less conveniently located northeast of town, off I-90 at exit 59, about a $4 cab trip from downtown. Some rooms have disabled access. There is a pool. Swim. (Singles $39, doubles $45.) The **Berry Patch Campground,** 1860 E. North St. (341-5588), one mi. east of I-90 off exit 60, has 15 berry nice grass campsites, a gameroom, playground, showers, and swimming. (Tent sites $16.50 for 2, with hookup $18 from end of May-Labor Day. Each additional person $1.50.)

Sixth St. Bakery and Delicatessen, 516 6th St. (342-6660), will cut up fresh sandwiches ($3-5) and cookies and muffins (50-75¢). **Tally's,** 530 6th St. (342-7621), downtown under the orange awning, serves family-style country meals such as chicken-fried steak for under $7 (open daily 7am-8pm; Sept. 2-May 27 daily 7am-7pm). The **Flying T** (342-1905), 6 mi. south on U.S. 16 next to the Reptile Gardens, serves a chuckwagon meal on a tin plate ($11.50, under 11 $5); singing cowboys included, but no tipping. Dinner (7:30pm sharp) and a Western musical show (8:15pm) are offered every night late May-mid-Sept.

SIGHTS AND ENTERTAINMENT

Tourism rears its flashing neon head in Rapid City. If you got dem *walkin' blues,* take the **Rapid City Walking Tour** of the historic and well-preserved downtown area; pick up a guidebook at the visitors center. The **Sioux Indian Museum** and the **Pioneer Museum** (both 348-0557) cohabitate at 515 West Blvd., between Main and St. Joseph St. in Halley Park. The two museums present interesting but limited exhibits. (Open Mon.-Sat. 9am-5pm, Sun. 1-5pm; Oct.-May Tues.-Sat. 10am-5pm, Sun. 1-5pm. Free.) The **Museum of Geology,** 501 E. St. Joseph St. (394-2467), in the administration building of the School of Mines and Technology, just east of Main St., exhibits the beautiful minerals and textbook fossils of the Badlands. (Open Mon.-Sat. 8am-6pm, Sun. noon-6pm; Labor Day-Memorial Day Mon.-Fri. 8am-5pm, Sat. 9am-2pm, Sun. 1-4pm. Free.) The **Dahl Fine Arts Center** (394-4101), 7th and Quincy St., houses rotating exhibits of local and Native American art. (Open Mon.-Fri. 9am-9:30pm, Sat. 9am-5pm, Sun. 1-5pm. Free.)

For nightlife, try Main St. between 9th and Mt. Rushmore St. **The Uptown Grill,** 615 Main St. (343-1942), is no piano man but serves food $2-7 and beer. Live bands Fri.-Sat. (open daily 11am-1:30am, cover $2, big shows $7). For boot-stompin', knee-slappin' country-western music and dancing, head to **Boot Hill,** 26 Main St. (343-1931), where live bands perform nightly (open Mon.-Sat. 3pm-2am, Sun. 5-11:30pm; cover Tues.-Sat. $2). Get sloshed at the **Firehouse Brewing Co.,** 610 Main (348-1915), which has different beers on tap daily, plus lunch sandwiches ($4-6) and dinner entrees ($5-6). (Open Mon.-Fri. 10am-10pm, Sat.-Sun. 10am-11pm.)

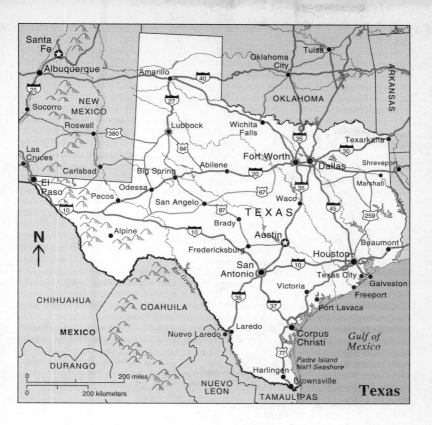

Texas

Texas

The stereotypical image of Texas as a land of tumbleweed, cowboy hats, and patriotic braggarts accurately describes the Texas of the past. Today, Texas provides its tourists with an environment of cosmopolitan cities, industries, and businesses in an incredibly diverse setting. Even more diverse is the state's physical landscape; whether it be Texas' mountains, seashore, woodlands, prairie-land or lake country, the state provides the adventurous traveler with a vast array of explorative options. Though cotton, cattle, and oil are the natural resources that built Texans' fortunes, it is the state's high-technology and growing tourism industries that will serve as the building blocks of its future.

Regional cuisine, like most of Texan culture, is enriched by the state's Mexican heritage. "Tex-Mex" is a variation of the dishes served across the border: chefs throw jalapeño peppers into chili as casually as a McDonald's crew chief shakes salt on french fries. Mexican pastries and genuine longhorn beef are staples, but also indispensable is chicken-fried steak—originally created to disguise bad meat at roadside dives, today a delicacy. And of course, get some BBQ with plenty of sauce.

PRACTICAL INFORMATION

Capital: Austin.

AUSTIN

Visitor Information: Texas Division of Tourism, P.O. Box 12728, Austin 78711 (512-463-8586). **U.S. Forest Service,** P.O. Box 130, Lufkin 75901 (409-831-2246). **State Parks and Recreation Areas,** Austin Headquarters Complex, 4200 Smith School Rd., Austin 78744 (512-463-4630).
Time Zones: Central and Mountain. **Postal Abbreviation:** TX
Sales Tax: 6-8%.

■■■ AUSTIN

Austin just doesn't seem like Texas. With a highly cosmopolitan flavor in an otherwise provincial area of the country, the city is both an expanding, bustling state capital and a haven for intellectuals. The University of Texas serves as a cultural oasis amid the ruggedness and conservatism of the country's second largest state.

PRACTICAL INFORMATION

Emergency: 911.

Visitor Information: Austin Convention Center/Visitor Information, 500 E. 1st St. (467-5561). Open Mon.-Fri. 8:30am-5pm, Sat. 9am-5pm, Sun. 1-5pm. **University of Texas Information Center,** 471-3151. **Texas Parks and Wildlife,** 389-4800 or 800-792-1112 in TX. Open Mon.-Fri. 8am-5pm. Call for info on camping outside Austin. Or contact **Texas Parks and Wildlife Dept.,** 4200 Smith School Rd., Austin 78744.

Airport: Robert Mueller Municipal Airport, 4600 Manor Rd. (480-9091), 5 mi. northeast of downtown. Cab fare to downtown runs about $7.

Amtrak: 250 N. Lamar Blvd. (800-872-7245). To: Dallas (7 per week, 6 hr., $35), San Antonio (7 per week, 3 hr., $15, continues to Houston), and El Paso (4 per week, 10 hr., $122).

Greyhound: 916 E. Koenig (800-231-2222), several mi. north of downtown off I-35. Easily accessible by public transportation. Buses #15 and 7 to downtown stop across the street. To: San Antonio (11 per day, 2-3 hr., $11); Houston (11 per day, 4 hr., $18); Dallas (11 per day, 5 hr., $20); San Antonio (11 per day, 13 hr., $11); El Paso (5 per day, 14 hr. $80). Open 24 hrs.

Public Transport: Capitol Metro, 504 Congress (474-1200; line open daily 8:30am-5:30pm). Maps and schedules available Mon.-Fri. 7am-6pm, Sat. 9am-1pm, or at the Visitor Information at the Convention Center. Fare 50¢, seniors, kids, students, and disabled 25¢. Downtown, the **Armadillo Express** connects major downtown points and runs every 10-15 min. in green trolley cars Mon.-Fri. 6:30am-10pm, Sat. 11am-7pm. Free. The **University of Texas Shuttle Bus** serves the campus area. Map and schedule at the UT Information Center (471-3151) or at any library, including the Main Library, 8th and Guadalupe St. Officially only for UT affiliates, but drivers rarely ask for ID.

Taxi: Yellow Cab, 472-1111. Base fare $1.25, $1.25 per mi.

Car Rental: Rent-A-Wreck, 6820 Guadalupe (454-8621). $20-40 per day, 50 free mi. with cash deposit; 100 free mi. with credit card deposit, 25¢ per additional mi. Open Mon.-Fri. 8am-7pm, Sat. 9am-5pm, Sun. 10am-3pm. Those under 21 get smacked with a $10 surcharge per day.

Bike Rental: Bicycle Sports Shop, 1426 Toomey St. (477-3472), at Jesse. Up to 2 hrs. $8, 3-5 hrs. $14, full day $20 (overnight $9 extra), 24 hrs. $26, 48 hrs. $48, 3 or more days $16 per day, 1 week $80. $100 deposit or credit card required. And they don't accept American Express. Open Mon.-Fri. 10am-8pm, Sat. 9am-6pm, Sun. 11am-5pm.

Help Lines: Crisis Intervention Hotline, 472-4357. **Austin Rape Crisis Center,** 440-7273. Both 24 hrs.

Time Zone: Central (1 hr. behind Eastern).

Post Office: 8225 Crosspark Dr. Open Mon.-Fri. 8am-5pm. **ZIP code:** 78710.

Area Code: 512.

Highway signs lead to the **capitol area** near Congress Ave. and 11th St., in the center of the city. Dividing the city into east and west addresses, **Congress Avenue** runs about 20 blocks south of the from the **Colorado River** and 12 blocks north to the capitol. Seven blocks north of the capitol starts the main campus of the **University of Texas (UT).** The university splits numbered streets into east and west and includes most tourist spots in this stretch. Austin is a cyclist's paradise, with roller-coaster hills and clearly marked bikeways.

ACCOMMODATIONS AND CAMPING

Cheap accommodations abound in Austin. **I-35,** running north and south of Austin, features a string of inexpensive hotels well outside downtown. Additionally, three co-ops run by **College Houses** (476-5678) at UT rent rooms to hostelers, including three meals per day. Those who are interested in staying at these co-ops should call College Houses, not the individual co-ops, to get info. Particularly ideal for young travelers, the co-ops welcome everyone. Patrons have access to all their facilities including a fully-stocked kitchen.

Austin International Youth Hostel (HI/AYH), 2200 S. Lakeshore Blvd. (444-2294), farther from center of town but still conveniently located. From Greyhound station take bus #7 ("Duval") to Lakeshore Blvd. and walk about ½ mi. From I-35 east, exit at Riverside, head east, and turn left at Lakeshore Blvd. About 3 mi. from downtown on Town Lake. Kitchen, A/C; located near grocery store and noisy power plant. Members $10, non-members $15. Linen $2. No curfew.

Motel 6, 9420 N. I-35 (339-6161), at the Rundberg exit, 12 mi. north of the capitol off N. Lamar and E. Rundberg Lane. Take bus #7 or 25 to Fawnridge and walk four blocks. Clean, air-conditioned rooms. Pool, color TV, HBO, free local calls. Singles $26, $6 per additional adult.

21st St. Co-op, 707 W. 21st St. (476-1857), has large and comfortable but unfurnished rooms and fills rapidly in summer. To get here from the bus station, take bus #15 to 7th and Congress St., walk down 7th to Colorado, and take #3 to 21st and Nueces St. $10 per person, plus $5 for three meals and kitchen access.

Pearl Street Co-op, 2000 Pearl St. (476-9478). Large, clean, sparsely furnished rooms. Laundry, kitchen, and a beautiful courtyard pool. Open and friendly atmosphere. Rooms, including 3 meals, $10, $20 for two.

Taos Hall, 2612 Guadalupe (474-6905), 6 blocks down Guadalupe, across the UT campus. Same deal as the other co-ops. Latest check-in time 9pm. You're most likely to get a private room here, and when you stay for dinner, the friendly residents will give you a welcoming round of applause. 3 meals and a bed $15.

Goodall Wooten Dorm, 2112 Guadalupe (472-1343). The "Woo" has private rooms with a small fridge, plus access to a TV room and basketball courts. Call ahead. Singles $20. Doubles $25.

Camping is a 15-45-min. drive away. The **Austin Capitol KOA** (444-6322), 6 mi. south of the city along I-35, offers a pool, game room, laundry, grocery, and playground. Some cabins are available. (Sites $20 for 2, cabins $30, $40 for 2.) **Emma Long Metropolitan Park,** 1600 City Park Rd. (346-1831), is a large preserve in the bend of the Colorado River. Take I-35 north, and 2222 Junction to Park Rd. The park is 6½ mi. south. Hookup, tent sites, boat ramp, and a concession stand. (Open 7am-10pm. Park entry fee $3, $5 on weekends. Tent sites $6. Full hookups $10.)

FOOD

Two main districts compete for Austin's restaurant trade. Along the west side of the UT campus, **Guadalupe Street** ("the drag") has scores of fast-food joints and convenience stores, including the **Party Barn,** replete with drive-through beer. Those who disdain the $3 all-you-can-eat pizza buffets and sub shops that line the drag can eat in the UT Union ($2-5). The second district clusters around **Sixth Street,** south of the capitol. Here the battle for happy hour business rages with unique intensity;

three-for-one drink specials and free hors d'oeuvres are common. You might also want to try the area along **Barton Springs Rd.,** which is a bit removed from downtown, but offers a diverse selection of restaurants, including Mexican, Italian, and Texas-style barbecue joints. Most are inexpensive and worth checking out. Though famous for its Texan specialties, Austin offers more cosmopolitan fare to its student population and visitors.

Trudy's Texas Star, 409 W. 30th St. (477-2935). Fine Tex-Mex dinner entrees $7-9, and a fantastic array of margaritas. Famous for *migas,* a corn tortilla souffle ($4). Open Mon.-Thurs. 7am-midnight, Fri.-Sat. 7am-2am, Sun. 8am-2am.

Sholz Garden, 1607 San Jacinto (477-4171), near the capitol. An Austin landmark recognized by the legislature for "epitomizing the finest traditions of the German heritage of our state." German only in name, though. Great chicken-fried steaks and Tex-Mex meals $5-6. Live country-rock music. Open Mon.-Thurs. 11am-midnight, Fri.-Sat. 11am-2am.

Katz's, 618 6th St. (472-2037). Offers delicious deli-style sandwiches in a high-class setting. Entrees tend to be a bit more expensive but are worth the dough. Great kosher sandwiches. A nice change of pace from the many Tex-Mex joints. Try homemade blintz with sour cream ($5.50, $3.50 for a half-order). Open 24 hrs.

Quackenbush's, 2120 Guadalupe (472-4477). Cafe/deli popular with students. Plowman sandwiches $2.50-4. Meet UT students over a cup of espresso or other stylish drink ($1-2.50). Try the chocolate eclair. Open daily 7am-9pm.

Sam's Bar-B-Que, 2000 E. 12th St. Take bus #12 or 6 eastbound. Tiny, dive-like interior thick with locals on weekends. Very popular, but in a seedy neighborhood. BBQ plates (with beans and potato salad) $4. Open Mon.-Thurs. 10am-3:30am, Fri.-Sat. 10am-5am, Sun. 10am-3am.

SIGHTS

In 1882, not to be outdone by Washington, D.C., Texans built their **state capitol,** Congress Ave. (463-0063), 7 ft. higher than the national one. This colossal building with colorful inlaid marble floors has "Texas" inscribed on everything from door hinges to hallway benches. (Open during legislative session 24 hrs.; off-season 6am-11pm. Free tours every 15 min. Mon.-Sat. 8:30am-4:30pm.) A **Tourist Information Center** (463-8586; open daily 8am-5pm) is in the south foyer. Across the street from the capitol, at 11th and Colorado St., sleeps the **Governor's Mansion** (463-5516), built in 1856. The bottom level stores the furniture of the past 10 governors. (Free tours Mon.-Fri. every 20 min. 10-11:40am.)

The **University of Texas at Austin,** the wealthiest public university in the country, forms the backbone of cultural life in Austin. With a 50,000 plus student enrollment, UT is the second largest university in the country. There are two **Visitors Information Centers** (471-1420), one in Sid Richardson Hall at 2313 Red River and the other in the Nowotny building at the corner of I-35 and Martin Luther King, Jr. Blvd. Campus tours leave from the admissions office, adjacent to the Nowotny building, Mon.-Sat. at 11am and 2pm. Campus highlights include the **Lyndon B. Johnson Library and Museum,** 2313 Red River St. (482-5279), which houses 35 million documents (open daily 9am-5pm; free), and the **Harry Ransom Center,** (471-8944) where a copy of the Gutenberg Bible rests. The center also hoards a vast collection of Aleister Crowley's manuscripts and correspondence as well as his personal library, perhaps the most complete Evelyn Waugh collection around, and the complete personal libraries of both Virginia Woolf and James Joyce. (Open Mon.-Sat. 9am-5pm, Sun. 1-5pm. Free.)

The **Laguna Gloria Art Museum,** 3809 W. 35th St. (458-8191), 8 mi. from the capitol in a Mediterranean villa-lookalike, is an exemplary blend of art, architecture, and nature in Austin. With rolling, spacious grounds that overlook **Lake Austin,** the Laguna displays 20th-century artwork and hosts **Fiesta Laguna Gloria,** a May arts and crafts festival, as well as inexpensive evening concerts and plays. Take bus #21.

(Tours Sun. at 2pm. Open Tues.-Sat. 10am-5pm, Thurs. 10am-9pm, Sun. 1-5pm. $2, seniors and students $1, under 16 free. Free to all Thurs.)

On hot afternoons, many zip to riverside **Zilker Park,** 2201 Barton Springs Rd., just south of the Colorado River. **Barton Springs Pool** (476-9044), in the park, is a popular swimming hole flanked by walnut and pecan trees. The spring-fed pool is 1000 ft. long and 200 ft. wide. Beware: the pool's temperature rarely rises above 60°F. Get away from the crowd and avoid paying by walking upstream (take an inner tube) and swimming at any spot that looks nice. ($1.75, Sat.-Sun. $2, ages 12-18 50¢, under 12 25¢. Swimming is free and at your own risk Nov.-Jan. Open daily 10am-7:30pm.) Zilker Park also has a botanical garden (477-8672), rentable canoes ($6), a train tour of the grounds and surrounding waters ($1.25), playgrounds, playing fields, and picnic areas. Parking inside the grounds costs $2 but is free on the roads near the entrance. For more fun and sun, drive to the **Windy Point,** a picturesque sandy park on **Lake Travis,** and try your hand (and body) at windsurfing or scuba-diving. The park is on Comanche Rd., 3 mi. west off the I-620 intersection.

ENTERTAINMENT

Austin draws all sorts of musicians from all over the country and has boosted many to lone-stardom. On weekends fans from around the city and nearby towns converge to swing to a wide range of music. Austin's version of Broadway is **Sixth Street,** a stretch of seven blocks east of Congress, dotted with warehouse nightclubs, fancy bars, a tattoo workshop, and an Oriental massage parlor. The *Weekly Austin Chronicle*, available at libraries and stores, provides detailed listings of current music performances, shows, and movies.

For great rock n' roll, try **Emo's,** 603 Red River (477-3667), just off 6th St. Local bands rock this former garage Thurs.-Sat. nights. On other days try your hand at the pool tables and play tunes of your choice on their jukebox. (Open daily, 3pm-2am. No cover. Happy Hour 2-11pm.) The **Chicago House,** 607 Trinity, also off 6th St. (473-2542), plays a different tune on weekends as well as hosting the occasional poetry reading. (Open Mon.-Sat. 5pm-2am, Thurs. 8pm-2am. $7, students and seniors $6.) Stumble safely along 6th St. (the street is closed to traffic after 7pm daily), especially on weeknights when there are neither crowds nor cover charges, to sample the bands from the sidewalk. For raunchy Texas-style rock n' roll and cheap beer, try **Joe's Generic Bar.** (No phone, no cover. Open daily 11am-until the last patron files out.) On campus, the **Cactus Cafe** (471-8228), 24th and Guadalupe, hosts different musicians almost every night. (Hours vary; usually 8am-1am. Cover $2-12.) Next door, the **Texas Tavern** (471-5651) favors country music and fast food. (Hours vary; usually 11:30am-1:45am. Cover $2-5.) Those journeying out to Lake Travis should seek out the **Oasis Cantina De Lago,** 6550 Comanche Trail (266-2441), a restaurant and bar bathed in a gorgeous sunset. (Open Sun.-Thurs. 11am-9pm, Fri.-Sat. 11am-10pm. No cover.)

■■■ CORPUS CHRISTI

After you've taken in all of Corpus Christi's sights—in other words, after half an hour—you may begin to wonder what you're doing in the "body of Christ." Look eastward into Corpus Christi Bay and the Gulf of Mexico, and you'll find the same answer as thousands before you. The sun and the sea are the city's religion; its piers and beaches are the temples on which devotees prostrate themselves. The popularity of Galveston and South Padre Island have left Corpus Christi unencumbered by unruly spring-break throngs and have allowed the city to retain its relatively peaceful seaside charm. This charm is augmented by the city's abundance of absolutely superior Tex-Mex restaurants. You may not be enlightened when you leave Corpus Christi, but after a while—about three days—you may feel divinely resurrected.

PRACTICAL INFORMATION

Emergency: 911

Visitor Information: Convention and Visitors Bureau, 1201 N. Shoreline (882-5603), where I-37 meets the water. Piles of pamphlets, bus schedules, and local maps. Open Mon.-Fri. 9am-5pm. Info also available at the **Corpus Christi Museum,** 1900 N. Chaparral (883-2862). Open Mon.-Sat. 10am-5pm, Sun. 1-5pm.

Airport: Corpus Christi International Airport, 1000 International Dr. (289-0171), 15 min. west of downtown, bordered by Rte. 44 (Agnes St.) and Joe Mireur Rd. Cabs to downtown about $8. Served by major airlines.

Greyhound: 702 N. Chaparral (882-2516), at Starr downtown. To: Dallas (5 per day, 8 hr., $41); Houston (12 per day, 5 hr., $19); Austin (5 per day, 6 hr., $27). Open daily 6am-2:30am. Lockers $1.

Public Transport: Regional Transit Authority (The "B"), 289-2600. Pick up route maps and schedules at the visitors bureau (see above). Central transfer points are at City Hall and Six Points. Buses run Mon.-Fri. 5:30am-10:30pm, Sat. 6:30am-10pm, Sun. 10:30am-6:30pm. Fare 50¢, seniors, disabled, students, and kids 25¢, 10¢ during off-peak hours. All buses 25¢ on Sat. **The Tide,** an old-fashioned trolley, runs along the shoreline and to the aquarium. Same fares as buses.

Taxi: American Cab Co., 835-6691. Base fare $1.35, $1.35 each additional mi. Major credit cards accepted. Airport-downtown $12.

Car Rental: Thrifty, 1928 N. Padre Island Dr. (289-0041), at Leopard St. Weekdays $27 per day, 150 free mi. per day. 20¢ each additional mi. with 4 days advance notice. Standard $38 per day, unlimited mi., no advance notice. Weekends $20 per day, 150 free mi. per day. Open Mon.-Fri. 6am-11pm, Sat.-Sun. 7am-11pm. Must be 25 with a major credit card.

Help Lines: 24-Hour Crisis Hotline, 853-9881. **Crisis Services,** 853-9883. **Women's Shelter,** 881-8888. Open 24 hrs.

Post Office: 809 Nueces Bay Blvd. (886-2200). Open Mon.-Fri. 7:30am-5:30pm, Sat. 8am-noon. **ZIP code:** 78469.

Area Code: 512.

The tourist district of Corpus Christi (pop. 225,000) follows **Shoreline Drive,** which borders the Gulf coast. The downtown business district lies 1 mi. west. Unfortunately, the streets don't quite follow a grid pattern, and the largely one-way roads downtown may frustrate drivers, sending them in circles up and down the bluff. **Agnes Street** and **Leopard Street** are the easiest routes to follow when approaching downtown from the west. Agnes St. goes directly downtown from the airport; Leopard follows a parallel path from most of the cheaper motels. Both streets end within one block of Shoreline Dr.

ACCOMMODATIONS AND FOOD

Cheap accommodations are a scarce commodity in the downtown area. Much of the scenic and convenient shoreline is gilded with posh hotels and expensive motels. Overshadowed by the plethora of expensive lodgings, the **Sand and Sea Budget Inn,** 1013 N. Shoreline Dr. (882-6518), surfs five blocks from the Greyhound station, across the street from the visitors bureau. Rooms have color TV, plush carpeting, and free local calls. On weekends and holidays, it's a good idea to make your reservations in advance, and expect a busy management. (Singles $24. Doubles $30, with a view of the bay $40.)

For the best motel bargains, drive several mi. south on Leopard St. (served by bus #27) or I-37 (served by #27 Express). Conserve sleep at the **Ecomotel,** 6033 Leopard St. (289-1116). Exit I-37 north at Corn Products Rd., turn left and go to the second light (at Leopard St.), and take another left. Comfortable, generic rooms with cable TV and pool. (Singles $33. Doubles $39.) Campers should head to **Padre Island National Seashore** or **Mustang State Park** (see Padre Island National Seashore below). Also, **Nueces River City Park** (241-1464), north on I-37 (exit 16 at Nueces River), has free tent sites and 3-day RV permits.

The mixed population of Corpus Christi and its seaside locale have resulted in a wide range of cuisine. The downtown area transubstantiates into many inexpensive and tasty eating establishments. **Bahía,** 224 Chaparral, serves simple but rib-sticking Mexican breakfasts and lunches. The authentic food compensates for the tacky decor. Try *nopalitos* (cactus and egg on a tortilla $1.25) or a taco and two enchiladas with rice, beans, tea, and dessert ($3.75). Live entertainment rocks the *casa* on Friday (7-9pm). (Open Mon.-Thurs. 7am-6pm, Fri. 7am-9pm, Sat. 7am-3pm.) Four blocks west, **Top Hat,** 601 N. Chaparral (887-0117), serves juicy steak and standard U.S. cuisine in a trendy setting. Entrees $4.25-7.75; all-you-can-eat Wed.-Thurs. nights $6 (open Mon. 9:30am-3pm, Tues.-Thurs. 9:30am-midnight, Fri. 9:30am-2am, Sat. 5pm-2am). The barbecue specialist in town is **Papaw's Bar-be-cue,** 200 N. Staples (882-0312), near the city hall. A former saloon, the diner has been broilin' and burnin' beef for over 30 years. Entrees $2.75-5.75. The restaurant has an impressive collection of piggy banks from the 1930s. (Open Mon.-Fri. 11am-5:30pm.)

SIGHTS

Corpus Christi's most significant sight is the shoreline, which is bordered for miles by wide sidewalks with graduated steps down to the water. Recently built lighthouses along the shoreline make the night view spectacular. The piers are filled with overpriced seaside restaurants, sail and shrimp boats, and hungry seagulls. Feeding these birds will produce a Hitchcockian swarm; wear a hat and prepare to run for your life. Almost all of the beaches on North Shoreline Dr. are open for swimming; just follow the signs.

The **Texas State Aquarium,** P.O. Box 331307 (881-1200), focuses on marine life in the Gulf of Mexico and the Caribbean Sea. It is located in the **Corpus Christi Beach,** a 5-min. walk from downtown. This undersea adventureland is worth the time and money to visit. (Open 9am-6pm. $7, seniors $5, kids $3.75.) The Tide (see Practical Information) runs between downtown and the aquarium. Just offshore floats the aircraft carrier **U.S.S. Lexington,** a World War II relic now open to the public. A new gem in Corpus Christi's treasure chest, the carrier is a world of amazement to the curious visitor. Walk on the runways and check out the machine that destroyed hundreds of enemy aircraft. (Open Mon.-Sat. 9am-5pm, Sun. 11am-5pm. $7, children $3.75, seniors and active military personnel $5.) For those determined to eke out a little culture after a day in the sun, your only option is on the north end of Shoreline Dr., at the **Art Museum of South Texas,** 1902 N. Shoreline (884-3844), whose small but impressive collection includes works by Monet, Matisse, Picasso, Rembrandt, Goya, and Ansel Adams. (Open Tues.-Sat. 10am-5pm, Sun. 1-5pm. Suggested donation $2, kids 12 and under 50¢. Wheelchair accessible.) The **Texas Jazz Festival** (883-4500) jams for its 32nd annual concert under the stars. The three-day performance in early July draws hundreds of musicians and thousand of fans from around the country (most performances free).

■■■ DALLAS

Denizens of Dallas like to brag about the number of contrasting elements in their city: a little bit of country, a little bit of rock n' roll, too many businessmen in Stetsons, and a stampede of cowgirls sporting short mini-skirts all tossed in together in a cosmopolitan mishmash of skyscrapers, neon lights and modern shopping malls. The dreams of founding father John Neely Bryan seem to have come true. In 1841 Bryan, an ambitious Tennessee lawyer, built a tiny little loghouse outpost in the hopes that one day it would grow into a bustling metropolis. Grow it did. Dallas rose to prominence in the 1870s when a major north-south railroad crossed a transcontinental east-west line just south of the town; converging waves of settlers lured by prospects of black gold caused the population to swell.

The eighth-largest city in America, Dallas today is a major business and cultural center. Its reputation as the "City of Dreams" has attracted immigrants from the Far

DALLAS

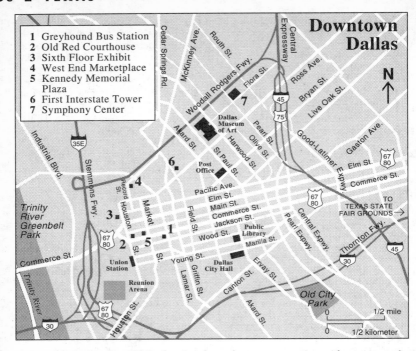

Downtown Dallas

1 Greyhound Bus Station
2 Old Red Courthouse
3 Sixth Floor Exhibit
4 West End Marketplace
5 Kennedy Memorial Plaza
6 First Interstate Tower
7 Symphony Center

East and Latin America. While the city's legendary preoccupation with commerce is evident, recent massive campaigns for historic preservation have restored many run-down urban areas to their pre-petro glory, and nurtured Texan culture.

PRACTICAL INFORMATION

Emergency: 911

Visitor Information: Dallas Convention and Visitors Bureau, 1201 Elm St., #24 (746-6677). **Dallas Visitors Center,** 1303 Commerce (746-6603). Both open Mon.-Thurs. 8am-5:30pm, Fri. 8am-5pm. **Special Events Info Line,** 746-6679.

Airport: Dallas-Ft. Worth International Airport (574-8888), 17 mi. northwest of downtown. **Love Field** (670-6080; take bus #39) has mostly intra-Texas flights. To get downtown from either airport, take the **Super Shuttle,** 729 E. Dallas Rd. (817-329-2001; in terminal, dial 02 on phone at ground transport services). 24-hr. service. DFW airport to downtown $10.50, Love Field to downtown $8.50.

Amtrak: 400 S. Houston Ave. (653-1101 or 800-872-7245), in Union Station. One train per day to Houston (6 hr., $32) and St. Louis (16 hr., $131).

Greyhound: 205 S. Lamar (800-231-2222), 3 blocks east of Union Station. To: Houston (6 per day, 6 hr., $26); San Antonio (15 per day, 6 hr., $31); El Paso (6 per day, 12½ hr., $67); New Orleans (10 per day, 12½ hr., $72). Open 24 hrs.

Public Transport: Dallas Area Rapid Transit (DART), 601 Pacific Ave. (979-1111). Serves most suburbs; routes radiate from downtown. Service 5am-midnight, to suburbs 5am-8pm. Base fare 75¢. Info desk open Mon.-Fri. 8:30am-4:45pm. Maps available at Main and Akard St. (open Mon.-Fri. 8am-5pm), or at Elm and Ervay St. (Mon.-Fri. 7am-6pm). **Hop-a-Bus** (979-1111) is DART's downtown Dallas service, with a park-and-ride system. Three routes (style blue, red, and green) run about every 10 min. Fare 25¢, transfers free. Look for buses with a blue bunny, a red kangaroo, or a green frog. No Hop-A-Bus service on weekends.

Taxi: Yellow Checker Cab Co., 426-6262. $2.70 first mi., $1.20 each additional mi. DFW Airport to downtown $25.

Car Rental: All-State Rent-a-Car, 3206 Live Oak (741-3118). $23 per day with 100 free mi., 16¢ per additional mi. Open Mon.-Sat. 7:30am-6pm. Must be 21 with major credit card.

Bike Rental: Bicycle Exchange, 11716 Ferguson Rd. (270-9269). Rates from $60 per week. Open Mon.-Fri. 9am-7pm, Sat. 9am-5pm. Must have a credit card.

Help Lines: Dallas Gay and Lesbian Community Center, 2701 Reagan (528-4233), open Mon.-Fri. 9am-9pm, Sat. 10am-6pm, Sun. noon-6pm.

Time Zone: Central (1 hr. behind Eastern).

Post Office: 400 N. Ervay St. (953-3045), on Thanksgiving Sq. downtown. Open Mon.-Fri. 8am-6pm. **ZIP code:** 75201; General Delivery, 75221.

Area Code: 214.

ACCOMMODATIONS AND CAMPING

Cheap accommodations of the non-chain motel type are hard to come by; big events like the Cotton Bowl (Jan. 1) and the State Fair in Oct. exacerbate the problem. If you can afford it, your most luxurious option undoubtedly is **Bed and Breakfast Texas Style,** 4224 W. Red Bird Ln. (298-5433 or 298-8586). They'll place you at a nice home, usually near town, with friendly residents who are anxious to make y'all as comfortable as possible. Just give them a call when you arrive in town and they'll direct you to your host. Good deal for two. (Singles $45. Doubles from $50.)

The best deal around is the **Delux Inn,** 3111 Stemmons Hwy. (637-0060). Accessible by bus (#49), the inn has beautifully furnished rooms with balconies, a pool, free morning coffee, free local calls, cable and HBO. Fast food restaurants and banks are only blocks away. (Singles $25. Doubles $30.) Major credit cards accepted. **U.S. 75 (Central Expressway), I-635 (LBJ Freeway),** and the suburbs of **Irving** and **Arlington** also have many inexpensive motels. Try **Motel 6** (505-891-6161), with 11 locations in the Dallas area, or **Exel Inns** (800-356-8013; singles $31-35).

If you have a car and camping gear, and are sleepy, grumpy, dopey, bashful, doc, sneezy, or happy try the **Hi-Ho Campground,** 200 W. Bear Creek Rd. (223-8574), south of town. Take I-35 14½ mi. to exit 412, turn right, and go 2 mi. (Tent sites $12 for 2 people, with hookup $16.50, $1 per additional person.)

FOOD

Pick up a copy of the Friday weekend guide of the *Dallas Morning News* for an overview of what's available. The **West End Historic District,** popular with family vacationers, supplies vittles, libations, and entertainment in the heart of downtown. For fast Tex-Mex food and a variety of small shops, explore the **West End Marketplace,** 603 Munger St. (954-4350). The **Farmers Produce Market,** 1010 S. Pearl Expressway (748-2082), between Pearl and Central Expressway near I-30 (open daily sunrise-sunset), can satisfy all of your picnicking fantasies. For gourmet restaurants and low-priced authentic barbecue joints, mosey down **Greenville Ave.**

Snuffer's, 3625 Greenville (826-6850). Has the best burgers ($3.50) in town. Nice all-wooden interior with friendly service and fun crowd. Don't miss the fried mushrooms ($3.25). Snuffer's has recently built an adjacent wooden patio. Cash bar. Other dishes range from $5-7. Open daily 11am-2am.

Herrera's Cafe, 4001 Maple Ave. (528-9644). Take bus #29. Informality doesn't daunt business people who partake of the excellent Tex-Mex dinners. Filling meals $4-6. Bring your own beer, and expect to wait on weekends. Open Mon. and Wed.-Thurs. 10am-9pm, Fri. 10am-10pm, Sat. 9am-10pm, Sun. 9am-9pm.

Bubba's, 6617 Hillcrest Ave. (373-6527). A remodeled, 50s-style diner near the heart of SMU. Serves the best chicken and chicken-fried steak dinners in town ($4-5.40). Entrees $5-7. Open daily 6:30am-10pm.

Sonny Bryan's Smokehouse, 302 N. Market St. (744-1610). Located at the threshold of the historic West End, this landmark is the ultimate Dallas experience. Eat where Queen Elizabeth II of England ate when she was in Dallas. The barbecue combination ($8) comes with your choice of vegetables, relish tray, and Sonny's own barbecue sauce. You don't need to worry about tipping. Open Mon.-Thurs. 11am-10pm, Fri.-Sat. 11am-11pm, Sun. noon-9pm.

Aw Shucks, 3601 Greenville Ave. (821-9449). A casual seafood bar with an unbeatable outdoor patio for slurping raw oysters ($3-7) in the summer. Open Mon.-Thurs. 11am-11pm, Fri.-Sat. 11am-mid., Sun. 11:30am-10pm.

Two Pesos, 1827 Greenville Ave. (823-2092). Fast-food style, but "Dos Pesos" is a late-night Dallas tradition. Serves tasty Mex dishes at prices slightly higher than two pesos. ($3-4 for a la carte items and great tacos and fajitas $1-2). Take bus #1 from downtown; get off at Greenville and Ross. Open 24 horas.

SIGHTS

Historically, Dallas has been a static city. Most of historic Dallas remains in present-day downtown. The 1841 log cabin of **John Neely Bryant,** the City's founder, still stands in the heart of Dallas (at Elm and Market St.). The city's layout can be viewed from 50 stories up, atop **Reunion Tower,** 300 Reunion Blvd. (651-1234). This is a good place to start a walking tour and to get acquainted with the city. (Open Mon.-Fri. 10am-10pm, Sat.-Sun. 9am-midnight; $2, seniors and kids $1.)

On your way out of Reunion Tower, take the underground walkway to the adjoining **Union Station,** 400 S. Houston Ave., and explore one of the city's few grand old buildings. Upon exiting the building, walk north along Houston, and you'll come upon the **West End Historic District,** an impressive example of urban gentrification. Two blocks down and six flights up on Elm is the **Sixth Floor** of the former **Texas School Book Depository** (653-6666), from where Lee Harvey Oswald allegedly fired the fatal shot at President John F. Kennedy on November 22, 1963. This floor, now a museum devoted to the Kennedy legacy, traces the dramatic and macabre moments of the assassination in various media. (Open Sun.-Fri. 10am-6pm, Sat. 10am-7pm. Last ticket sold one hour before closing. Self-guided tour $4, seniors and kids 6-18 $2. Audio tour with cassette $2.) Philip Johnson's illuminating **Memorial to Kennedy** looms nearby, at Market and Main St. At the corner of Houston and Main St. is the old **Dallas County Courthouse,** nicknamed "Old Red" for its unique red sandstone composition. Built in 1892, the Romanesque structure is one of Dallas's most revered landmarks.

Continue north on Houston as it curves east and becomes Ross Ave. in the heart of the commercial area of the West End. The streets of red brick warehouses converted to restaurants and bars end in the **West End Marketplace,** 603 Munger Ave., a passel of fast-food eateries, bars, shops, and tourists (open Tues.-Thurs. 11am-10pm, Fri.-Sat. and Mon. 11am-midnight, Sun. noon-8pm). Just east on the corner of Ross Ave. and Field St. stands Dallas's most impressive skyscraper, **The First Interstate Tower,** a multi-sided prism towering above a glistening water garden.

Walking farther east along Ross Ave. leads you to the new **Arts District,** the centerpiece of which is the **Dallas Museum of Art,** 1717 N. Harwood St. (922-1200). The museum offers Indonesian, impressionist, modern, and U.S. decorative art. The outdoor sculpture garden and art room will delight the children. (Open Tues.-Wed. 11am-4pm, Thurs.-Fri. 11am-9pm, Sat.-Sun. 11am-5pm. Free.)

Walking south from the museum on St. Paul, toward the downtown area, turn right on Bryan St. and walk one block to **Thanksgiving Square** (969-1977), a tiny park beneath massive towers. While viewing this monument to Thanksgiving in all religions, you too will give thanks for the respite from the busy streets the park's sunken gardens and waterfalls provide. (Open Mon.-Fri. 9am-5pm, Sat.-Sun. and holidays 1-5pm.) Continue south from Thanksgiving Square along Ervay St. to the imposing **Dallas City Hall,** 100 Marilla St. (670-3957), designed by the ubiquitous I.M. "Everywhere" Pei.

About nine blocks south of City Hall on Ervay St. is **Old City Park,** at Gano St. (421-5141). The park is both the oldest and the most popular recreation area and lunch spot in the city. Open spaces and picnic facilities are scattered among restored buildings, which include a railroad depot and a church. (Park open daily

9am-6pm. Exhibit buildings open Tues.-Sat. 10am-4pm, Sun. noon-4pm. Admission $5, seniors $4, kids $2, families $12. Free on Mon., when exhibits are closed.)

Fair Park (670-8400), southeast of downtown on 2nd Ave., has been home to the state fair since 1886, although most of the structures there today remain from the 1936 State Fair celebrating the Texas Centennial. The park is home to the Cotton Bowl, numerous museums, and a Texas-sized ferris wheel, all within walking distance of each other. A standout is the **Museum of Natural History** (670-8457), which has a small permanent display on prehistoric life (open daily 9am-5pm; free). Other buildings include the **Aquarium** (670-8441; open daily 10am-4:30pm; 50¢); the **Age of Railroad Steam Museum** (428-0101; open Thurs.-Fri. 10am-3pm, Sat.-Sun. 11am-5pm; $2, under 17 $1); the **Science Place** (428-5555; open daily 9:30am-5:30pm; $5.50, seniors and kids 4-16 $2.50, under 4 free); and the **Dallas Garden Center** (428-7476; open Tues.-Sat. 10am-5pm, Sun. 1-5pm).

Nearby **White Rock Lake** is good for walking, biking or rollerblading. On the eastern shore of the lake is the **Dallas Arboretum,** 8525 Garland Rd. (327-8263), a 66-acre botanical heaven on earth with resplendent flowers and trees. It's only a 15-min. bus ride from downtown. To gaze upon Dallas's mansions, drive up the **Swiss Avenue Historic District** or through the streets of **Highland Park,** a town within Dallas whose high school boasts a million-dollar astroturf football stadium.

ENTERTAINMENT

Dallas' culture and nightlife exploded out of nowhere in the late 1970s and continue to gush. The free weekly *Dallas Observer* (out Thursdays) will help you to sort your entertainment options. Enjoy free summer theater July-Aug. at the **Shakespeare in the Park** festival (599-2778), at Samuel-Grand Park just northeast of State Fair Park. Two plays are performed annually; each runs about two weeks. The **Music Hall** (565-1116) in Fair Park houses the **Dallas Civic Opera** (443-1043) Nov.-Feb. (tickets $7-75) and **Dallas Summer Musicals** June-Oct. (Performances nightly, $4-37; call 565-1116 for info, 787-2000 for tickets, 696-4253 for ½-price tickets on performance days.) The **Dallas Symphony Orchestra** (692-0203) orchestrates at the newly completed **Morton H. Meyerson Symphony Center,** at Pearl and Flora St. in the arts district. The I.M. Pei-designed structure is renowned for its acoustics. (Tickets $10-40.)

Downtown nightlife centers on the oft-visited **West End,** unless you have them **Deep Ellum** blues. The West End offers **Dallas Alley,** 2019 N. Lamar (988-0581), an ensemble of clubs with a single ($3-5) cover charge. The **Outback Pub** (761-9355) and **Dick's Last Resort** (747-0001), both at 1701 N. Market, are locally popular bars with no cover, good beer selections, and raucous crowds. (Both open Sun.-Thurs. 11am-midnight, Fri.-Sat. 11am-2am.) On weekends and occasionally during the week, various bands perform concerts out on the red brick marketplace.

Deep Ellum, on the east side of downtown, was known as the "Harlem of Dallas" in the 1930s, when it was home to blues greats like Blind Lemon Jefferson. By the early 1980s, however, the area had become an urban wasteland. A renaissance of sorts began with clandestine late-night parties thrown by artists and musicians in Deep Ellum's empty warehouses. Today, the area has become downright commercialized, but is still enjoyable. **Club Dada,** 2720 Elm (744-3232), former haunt of Edie Brickell, has scaled up with art on the walls, an outdoor patio, and live local acts. (Open daily 8pm-2am; cover $3-5, drinks $2-4.) **Tree's,** 2709 Elm (748-5009), hosts an eclectic range of local and national acts in a vast warehouse with pool tables in the loft. (Open daily 8pm-2am. Cover $2-10, drinks $1.50-4. 18 and over.)

The areas around SMU and Greenville Ave. rollick with nightlife. **Poor David's Pub,** 1924 Greenville (821-9891), stages live music for an older crowd that leans towards folk and blues. (Open Mon.-Sat. 8pm-2am. No cover charge, but you'll need to purchase a ticket, either at the door or from Ticketmaster.) The **Greenville Bar and Grill,** 2821 Greenville (823-6691), a Dallas classic, is an old-fashioned R&B bar with cheap beer ($1) and a cheeky attitude (open daily 11am-2am; pianist Fri. 5-8pm). Popular nightspots conveniently line **Yale Blvd.,** home of SMU's fraternity row. The current bar of choice is **Green Elephant,** 5612 Yale (750-6625), a pseudo-60s extravaganza complete with lava lamps and tapestries (open daily 11pm-2am).

Six Flags Over Texas (817-640-8900), 15 mi. from downtown off I-30 in Arlington, is the original link in the nationwide amusement park chain. The name alludes to the six different ruling states that have flown their flags over Texas. This is a thrill-lover's paradise, replete with an array of vomitous rides, restaurants, shops, and entertainment venues. The hefty admission charge itself is enough to induce nausea. ($25, over 55 years or under 4 ft. $19—includes unlimited access to all rides and attractions. Open June-Aug. Sun.-Thurs. 10am-10pm, Fri.-Sat. 10am-midnight; March-May and Sept.-Oct. Sat.-Sun. 10am-8pm. Parking $5.)

■ Near Dallas: Fort Worth

Lost but not forgotten alongside the cosmopolitan pretensions of Dallas, **Fort Worth** is a 30-min. drive west on I-30. You can't say you've visited Dallas if you haven't visited the Fort. If Dallas is the last Eastern city, Fort Worth is undoubtedly the first Western one; a daytrip here is worth your while if only for the **Stockyards District** (625-9715), at the corner of N. Main and E. Exchange Ave., which hosts weekly rodeos (April-Sept. Sat. 8pm) and cattle auctions (Mon. at 10am). The **Tarantula** steam train that connects downtown with the stockyards also takes the rider on a nostalgic journey through the Old West and on a comprehensive tour of downtown. The stockyards host such seasonal festivities as the **Chisholm Round-Up.** The Round-Up is a three-day jamboree during the second weekend of June commemorating the heroism of cowhands who led the long cattle drive to Kansas during the Civil War. Also check out the **Armadillo Races** in which grandfather and grandson work together to blow the beast to move. For info call 625-7005. The district's frontier feeling is accessorized by numerous Western bookstores, restaurants, and saloons. For more on the stockyards, go to the **visitor information center** kiosk (624-4741) 130 Exchange Ave. (open Mon.-Sat. 10am-5pm; Sun. noon-6pm). A far cry from the rugged stockyards is the **Kimbell Art Museum,** 3333 Camp Bowie Blvd. (332-8451), a beautiful building designed by Louis Kahn. Inside is one of the best collections of pre-20th-century European painting and sculpture in the Southwest. (Open Tues.-Fri. 10am-5pm, Sat. noon-8pm, Sun. noon-5pm. Free.)

Fort Worth's **area code** is 817.

■■■ HOUSTON

Houston (pop. 3,232,000) arose in the wake of Texas' battle for independence from Mexico when two New York speculators bought 2000 acres of land on Buffalo Bayou in 1906. An energy center since the discovery of nearby oil deposits, the settlement emerged as a major cotton shipping port with the 1915 completion of the Houston Ship Channel. Not surprisingly, Houston's geographical expansion parallels its history of quick economic growth; in all, the city sprawls over almost 500 sq. mi. The absence of zoning laws, combined with a recklessly swift building boom in the 70s and early 80s, has resulted in a peculiar architectural mix: a museum, an historic home, a 7-Eleven, and a mini-mall may share the same city block, while the downtown area showcases an oil-sprouted array of modern skyscrapers.

PRACTICAL INFORMATION

Emergency: 911.

Visitor Information: Greater Houston Convention and Visitors Bureau, 3300 Main St. (227-3100), at Stuart. Approximately 1 mi. off I-45. Take any bus serving the southern portion of Main St. (#7, 8, 14, 25, 65, 70, or 78). Open Mon.-Fri. 8:30am-5pm.

Traveler's Aid: 2630 Westbridge (526-8300). Open Mon.-Fri. 8am-4:30pm. Take bus #15 from Main St. Staffed by caring people who will find you a place to stay.

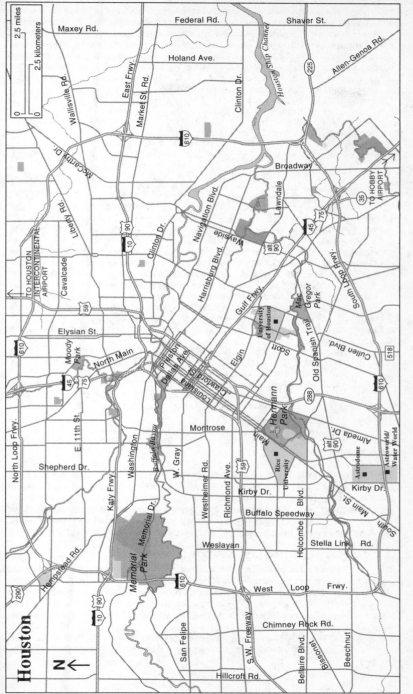

Airport: Houston Intercontinental Airport (230-3000), 25 mi. north of downtown. Get to the city center via the **Airport Express** (523-8888). Buses depart every 30 min. beginning at 7am; last bus leaves airport Sun.-Fri. at 11:50pm, Sat. at 11:10pm (fare $12.50, kids $6.50). **Hobby Airport** is 9 mi. south of downtown, just west of I-45. Take bus #73 to Texas Medical Center and then catch any bus to downtown. **Hobby Airport Limousine Service** (644-8359) leaves for downtown every 30 min. 7:30am-midnight (fare $5, under 13 free). Flights from Hobby to San Antonio, Dallas, and Austin (as low as $44).

Amtrak: 902 Washington Ave. (224-1577 or 800-872-7245), in a rough and tumble neighborhood. During the day, catch a bus by walking west on Washington (away from downtown) to its intersection with Houston Ave. At night, call a cab. To: San Antonio (3 per week, 4 hr., $44); New Orleans (3 per week, 9 hr., $72); Dallas (one per day, 6 hr., $32); El Paso (3 per week, 16 hr., $139).

Greyhound: 2121 S. Main St. (800-231-2222), on or near several local bus routes. All late-night arrivals should call a cab—this is an unsafe area. To: San Antonio (7 per day, 4 hr., $22); Dallas (6 per day, 5 hr., $26); El Paso (8 per day, 4 via San Antonio—the shorter route—and 4 via Dallas, $106); Corpus Christi (13 per day, 5 hr., $19); Galveston (6 per day, 1½ hr., $9). Open 24 hrs. Lockers $1.

Public Transport: Metropolitan Transit Authority (METRO Bus System), (658-0854; for route and schedule info call 635-4000). Mon.-Fri. 6am-8pm, Sat.-Sun. 8am-5pm. Buses usually operate 6am-midnight; less frequently on weekends. An all-encompassing system that can take you from NASA (15 mi. southeast of town) to Katy (25 mi. west of town). Get system maps at the Customer Services Center, 813 Dallas St. (658-0854; open Mon.-Fri. 9:30am-5:30pm) and individual route maps from Metro headquarters, 1201 Louisiana; the Houston Public Library, 500 McKinney at Bagby (236-1313; open Mon.-Fri. 9am-9pm, Sat. 9am-6pm; Sun. 2-6pm); or from the Metro RideStore at 813 Dallas and 405 Main, where packs of 10 tokens ($6.80) are available. Fare 85¢; students, seniors, and persons with disabilities with an ID ½ fare; express service $1.25; transfers free.

Taxi: Yellow Cab, 236-1111. Base rate $3.05; $1.35 per mi. Be *sure* to ask for a flat rate in advance.

Car Rental: Cash Plus Car Rental, 5819 Star Lane (977-7771). $24-35 per day with 200 free mi., 25¢ each additional mi. Open Mon.-Fri. 9am-5pm, Sat.-Sun. 10am-2pm. Must be 21; $350-400 cash deposit.

Help Lines: Crisis Center Hotline, 228-1505. Open 24 hrs. **Rape Crisis,** 528-7273. Open 24 hrs. **Gay Switchboard of Houston,** 529-3211. Counseling, medical and legal referrals, and entertainment info. Open daily 3pm-midnight.

Time Zone: Central (1 hr. behind Eastern).

Post Office: 401 Franklin St. (227-1474). Open Mon.-Fri. 6am-7pm, Sat 8am-noon. **ZIP code:** 77052.

Area Code: 713.

The flat Texan terrain supports several mini-downtowns. True downtown Houston, a squarish grid of interlocking one-way streets, borders the Buffalo Bayou at the intersection of I-10 and I-45. **The Loop** (I-610) lassoes the city center with a radius of 6 mi. Anything inside The Loop is easily accessible by car or bus. Find rooms on the southern side of the city—near Montrose Ave., the museums, Hermann Park, Rice University, and Perry House—for easy access to bus lines and points of interest.

ACCOMMODATIONS AND CAMPING

It is not a surprise that a city the size of Houston would have plenty of motels. The cheaper motels are concentrated southwest of downtown along the **Katy Freeway** (I-10 west), but for better and more convenient rooms, drive along **South Main Street.** Singles are as low as $20, doubles dip to $24. The rooms may be decent once you get inside, but these parts of town can be quite dangerous at night. (Buses #8 and 9 go down S. Main; #19, 31, and 39 go out along the Katy Freeway.) Ask around about **The Mayflower/Space City Hostel (HI/AYH)** at 2242 West Bay Area Blvd., Friendswood, TX (996-0323 or 482-2432; $10.50 per night) which opened in the late summer of 1992. Situated between Galveston and Houston, it is accessible by bus from downtown Houston.

Perry House, Houston International Hostel (HI/AYH), 5302 Crawford (523-1009), at Oakdale. From Greyhound station, take bus #8 or 9 south to Southmore St. (Bank of Houston) stop. Walk 5 blocks east to Crawford and 1 block south to Oakdale. Friendly management, nice rooms, and in a quiet neighborhood near Hermann park. Owners will sometimes offer makeshift city tours; ask about night-time version. Closed 10am-5pm; you can show up during lock-out and hang out in TV room. Curfew 11pm. Members $10.25, non-members $13.25. Linen $1.50.

Houston Youth Hostel, 5530 Hillman #2 (926-3444). Take bus #36 to Lawndale at Dismuke. Farther from downtown than Perry House with fewer beds, but more laid-back. No curfew. Co-ed dorm room, $7 per bunk. Linen $1.

YMCA, 1600 Louisiana Ave. (659-8501), between Pease and Leeland St. One of the better YMCAs in the Southwest. Men only. Good downtown location only blocks from Greyhound. Clean rooms with daily maid service. TV, selected movies upon request, wake-up calls, pool and gym, common baths. Rooms $16.35, key deposit $5. Another branch at 7903 South Loop (643-4396) is farther out but less expensive. Take Bus #50 at Broadway. $13, plus key deposit $10.

The Roadrunner, 8500 S. Main. (666-4971). One of 2 locations in Houston. Friendly and helpful management. Cable TV, mini pool, free coffee, and local calls. Large, well-furnished rooms. Singles $28. Doubles $35. Meep! Meep!

Grant Motor Inn, 8200 S. Main St. (668-8000), near the Astrodome. Clean and relatively safe. Satellite TV, swing-set, and pool. Maid service and continental breakfast. Luxurious rooms near the palm-tree-covered, sand-banked pool that adds a tropical flavor. Singles $32, $35 for 2 people. Doubles $43.

Two campgrounds grace the Houston area, but both are out in the boondocks, inaccessible by METRO Bus. **KOA Houston North,** 1620 Peachleaf (442-3700), about 20 mi. north on I-45, has a pool, showers, playground, and 24-hr. security (tent sites for 2 $16, with electricity $18, full hookup $22; $2 per additional adult). **Houston Campground,** 710 State Hwy. 6 S. (493-2391), charges $13 per 2-person tent site, $15 with water and electricity, and $17 for full hookup; $3 per additional adult.

FOOD

A port town, Houston has witnessed the arrival of many immigrants (today its Indochinese population is the second largest in the nation), and its range of restaurants reflects this diversity. Houston's cuisine mingles Mexican and Vietnamese food, and the state specialty, BBQ. Look for reasonably priced restaurants among the shops and boutiques along **Westheimer St.,** especially near the intersection with Montrose. This area, referred to as "Montrose," is Houston's answer to Greenwich Village, and is also popular with gay men. Bus #82 follows Westheimer from downtown to well past The Loop. For great Vietnamese cuisine, go to **Milam St.,** where it intersects Elgin St., just south of downtown.

Hobbit Hole, 1715 S. Shepherd Dr. (528-3418). A reddish, 2-story, dimly-lit diner with a nice backyard patio. A few blocks off Westheimer. Take bus #82 and get off at Shepard Drive intersection. For the herbivorous adventurer. Entrees ($4-8) named after Tolkien characters. Ramble on to Misty Mountain Strawberry ($3). Open Mon.-Thurs. 11am-10:30pm, Fri.-Sat. 11am-11:30pm, Sun. 11:30am-10pm.

On The Border, 4608 Westheimer Rd. (961-4494), near the Galleria. Take bus #82. Standard Tex-Mex fare with a twist (mesquite-grilled vegetable platter $6). Try the combo platter served with rice, beans, soft taco and enchilada ($5.75). Nice bar, loud crowd. Open Sun.-Thurs. 11am-11pm, Fri.-Sat. 11am-midnight.

Van Loc, 3010 Milam St. (528-6441). Yummy Vietnamese and Chinese food (entrees $5-8). Great all-you-can-eat luncheon buffet ($3.65) includes unlimited iced tea. Open Sun.-Thurs. 9:30am-11:30pm, Fri.-Sat. 9:30am-12:30am. Downtown location, 825 Travis, has a similar buffet but charges a bit more. Same hrs.

Good Company, 5109 Kirby Dr. (522-2530). Might be the best BBQ (and the most popular) in Texas, with honky-tonk atmosphere to match. Sandwiches $3, dinner $5-6. Open daily 11am-10pm. Expect a line.

Cadillac Bar, 1802 N. Shepherd Dr. (862-2020), at the Katy Freeway (I-10), northwest of downtown. Take bus #75, change to #26 at Shepherd Dr. and Allen Pkwy. Wild fun and authentic Mexican food. Tacos and enchiladas $5-7; heartier entrees more expensive. Open Sun.-Thurs. 11am-10:30pm, Fri.-Sat. 11am-midnight.

Luther's Bar-B-Q, 8777 S. Main St. (432-1107). One of 12 locations in the Houston area. Good Texas barbecue entrees ($5-7) and free refills on iced tea. Open Sun.-Thurs. 11am-10pm, Fri.-Sat. 11am-11pm.

SIGHTS

Amid Houston's sprawling sauna of oil refineries and food chains are a few worthwhile sights. Focus on the **downtown,** the nexus of virtually all the city's bus routes.

In the southwest corner of the downtown area is **Sam Houston Park,** just west of Bagby St. between Lamar and McKinney St. **Saint John's Lutheran Church,** built in 1891 by German farmers, contains the original pulpit and pews. Catch the one-hour tour to see four buildings in the park. (Tours on the hr. Mon.-Sat. 10am-3pm, Sun. 1-4pm. Tickets $4, students and seniors $2.)

Central downtown is a shopper's subterranean paradise. Hundreds of shops and restaurants line the **Houston Tunnel System,** which connects all the major buildings in downtown Houston, extending from the Civic Center to the Tenneco Building and the Hyatt Regency. On hot days, duck into the air-conditioned passageways via any major building or hotel. To navigate the tunnels, pick up a map at the Public Library, Pennzoil Place, Texas Commerce Bank, or call Tunnel Walks at 840-9255.

Antique-lovers will want to see the collection of 17th- to 19th-century American decorative art at **Bayou Bend Museum of Americana,** 1010 Milam (526-2600), in **Memorial Park.** The collection is housed in the palatial mansion of millionaire Ima Hogg (we *swear*), daughter of turn-of-the-century Texas governor Jim "Boss" Hogg. The museum houses some of the more obscure Remington paintings. (Open Tues.-Sat. 10am-4:30pm. $3, 12 and under free; free 2nd Sun. of each month. Tours of the house available Tues.-Fri 9am-4pm, Sat. 10am-12:45pm. Prices vary.)

On Main Street, 3½ mi. south of downtown, lies the beautifully landscaped **Hermann Park,** near all of Houston's major museums. The **Houston Museum of Natural Science** (639-4600) offers a splendid display of gems and minerals, permanent exhibits on petroleum, a hands-on gallery geared toward grabby children, and a planetarium and IMAX theater to boot (open Tues.-Sat. 9am-6pm, Sun. noon-6pm; $2.50, over 62 and under 12 $2; combined museum and IMAX admission $6, over 62 and under 12 $4.50). The **Houston Zoological Gardens** (525-3300) feature small mammals, alligators, and hippopotami eating spicy hippoplankton food (open daily 10am-6pm; $2.50, seniors $2, ages 3-12 50¢). The **Museum of Fine Arts,** 1001 Bissonet (639-7300), adjoins the north side of Hermann Park. Designed by Mies van der Rohe, the museum boasts a collection of Impressionist and post-Impressionist art, as well as a slew of Remingtons. (Open Tues.-Sat. 10am-5pm, Thurs. 10am-9pm, Sun. 12:15-6pm. $3, seniors and college students $1.50, under 18 free. Free Thurs. 10am-9pm.) Across the street, the **Contemporary Arts Museum,** 5216 Montrose St. (526-0773), has multi-media exhibits (open Tues.-Fri. 10am-5pm, Sat.-Sun. noon-5pm; free, but admission to Gallery 1 costs $3, seniors and students $2, under 12 free). Also on the park grounds are sports facilities, a zoo, a kiddie train, a Japanese garden and the Miller Outdoor Theater (see Entertainment below). The **University of Houston, Texas Southern University,** and **Rice University** all study in this part of town.

The **Astrodome,** Loop 610 at Kirby Dr. (799-9555), a mammoth indoor arena, is the home of the **Oilers** football team and the **Astros** baseball team (tours daily 11am, 1pm, 3pm, and 5pm; off-season 11am, 1pm, and 3pm; $4, seniors and students $3, under 7 free; parking $4). At these prices, you're better off paying admission to a game. Football tickets are hard to get, but seats for the Astros are usually available for as low as $4 (call 526-1709 for tickets).

Wander down Space Age memory lane at NASA's **Lyndon B. Johnson Space Center** (483-4321), where models of Gemini, Apollo, Skylab, and the space shuttle are displayed in a free walk-through museum. This NASA is the home of Mission Control, which is still HQ for modern-day Major Toms; when astronauts ask, "Do you read me, Houston?" the folks here answer. (Control center open daily 9am-7pm. $10, kids $6.) Arrive early to secure a *space* in mission control and allow 3-4 hrs. to orbit the complex. For launch info call 483-8600. The center has handicap facilities, and cameras are allowed. By car, drive 25 mi. south on I-45. The car-less should take the Park and Ride Shuttle #246 from downtown.

Terminus of the gruesomely polluted Houston Ship Channel, the **Port of Houston** leads the nation in foreign trade. Free 90-min. guided harbor tours are offered on the inspection boat *Sam Houston* (tours Tues.-Wed. and Fri.-Sat. at 10am and 2:30pm, Thurs. and Sun. at 2:30pm). Reservations for these deservedly popular tours should be made in advance, but you can join one if the boat doesn't reach its 90-person capacity. Call to make last-minute reservations between 8:30am and noon. To reach the port, drive 5 mi. east from downtown on Clinton Dr., or take bus #30 "Clinton/Clinton Drive" at Capital and San Jacinto to the Port Authority gate. For more info or reservations, write or call Port of Houston Authority, P.O. Box 2562, Houston 77252 (670-2146; open Mon.-Fri. 8am-5pm).

Check out a chunk of Texas history at the **San Jacinto Battleground State Historical Park**, 21 mi. east on Rte. 225, then 3 mi. north on Rte. 134. The battle which ultimately brought Texas independence from Mexico was fought here on April 21, 1836. The view from the top of the 50 story-high **San Jacinto Monument and Museum of Natural History** (497-2421) is amazing (open daily 9am-6pm; elevator $2, under 12 50¢; slide show $3.50, under 12 $2).

Back toward downtown, just east of Montrose, are two of the city's more highly acclaimed museums. The **Menil Collection**, 1515 Sul Ross (525-9400), is an eclectic collection of African and Asian artifacts and 20th-century European and American paintings and sculpture. Be sure to see Magritte's hilarious *Madame Récamier.* (Open Wed.-Sun. 11am-7pm. Free.) One block away, the **Rothko Chapel**, 3900 Yupon (524-9839), houses some of the artist's paintings. Fans of modern art will delight in Rothko's sanctified simplicity; others will wonder where the actual paintings are. (Open daily 10am-6pm.)

ENTERTAINMENT

Anyone with cable TV sorely remembers the period-piece *Urban Cowboy,* in which John Travolta proves his love for Debra Winger by riding a mechanical bull. Sexy, wasn't it? Gilley's has long since closed, but rip-roaring nightlife is still bullish here.

The **Westheimer** strip offers the largest variety of places for no cover. Rub elbows with venture capitalists and post-punks alike at **The Ale House**, 2425 W. Alabama (521-2333), at Kirby. The bi-level bar and beer garden offers over 100 brands of beer served with a British accent. Upstairs you'll find mostly New Wave music and dancing. (Open Mon.-Sat. 11am-2am, Sun. noon-2am.) A similar mix can be found at the more exclusive **Cody's Restaurant and Club,** penthouse of 3400 Montrose St. (522-9747). Sit inside or out on the balcony, and listen to live jazz. (Open Tues.-Fri. 4pm-2am, Sat. 6pm-2am. Informal dress.) **Sam's Place,** 5710 Richmond Ave. (781-1605), is your typical spring-break-style Texas hangout. On Sunday afternoons a band plays outdoors (5-10pm), and various booths proffer different beers. An indoor band continues 7pm-1am. (Happy Hour Mon. 2pm-closing, Tues. 2-8pm, Wed.-Fri. 2-9pm, Sat. 11am-5pm. Open Mon.-Sat. 11am-2am, Sun. noon-2am. Clothes required.) **The Red Lion,** 7315 Main St. (795-5000), features cheap beer and nightly entertainment that ranges from bluegrass to heavy metal. (Hours vary.)

Houston offers ballet, opera, and symphony at **Jones Hall,** 615 Louisiana Blvd. Tickets for the **Houston Symphony Orchestra** (224-4240) cost $8-30. The season runs Sept.-May. During July, the symphony gives free concerts Tuesday, Thursday, and Saturday at noon in the Tenneco Building Plaza. The **Houston Grand Opera**

(546-0200) produces seven operas each season, with performances Oct.-May (tickets $5-25, 50% student discount ½ hr. before performance). Call 227-2787 for info on the ballet, opera, or symphony. If you're visiting Houston in the summer, take advantage of the **Miller Outdoor Theater** (520-3290), in Hermann Park. The symphony, opera, and ballet companies and various professional theaters stage free concerts here on the hillside most evenings April-Oct., and the annual **Shakespeare Festival** struts and frets its hour upon the stage from late July to early August. For an event update call 520-3292. Sneak your Sally into the downtown **Alley Theater,** 615 Texas Ave. (228-8421), which stages Broadway-caliber productions at moderate prices (tickets $18-40, student rush seats 15 min. before curtain $10). For last-minute, ½-price tickets to many of Houston's sporting events, musical and theatrical productions, and nightclubs, try **Showtix** discount ticket center, at 11140 Westheimer St. (785-2787; open Mon.-Fri. 11am-5pm, Sat. 10am-noon).

■ Near Houston: Galveston Island

The narrow, sandy island of **Galveston** (pop. 65,000), 50 mi. southeast of Houston on I-45, offers not only a beach resort's requisite t-shirt shops, ice cream stands, and video arcades, but also beautiful vintage homes, oak-lined streets, and even a few deserted beaches. In the 19th century, Galveston was Texas' most prominent port and wealthiest city, earning the nickname "Queen of the Gulf." The advent of the 20th century dealt the city's economy two blows from which it could never recover. In September, 1900, a devastating hurricane struck the island, killing 6,000 people. The survivors were determined to rebuild the decimated city and built a 17-ft. seawall as protection. But the crippled shipping industry could not be protected from the refocus of commerce along the Houston Ship Channel, completed in 1914. Wealthy residents debarked for greener pastures, leaving the former port and their austere mansions behind.

Practical Information The **Strand Visitors Center,** 2016 Strand (765-7834; open daily 9:30am-6pm) provides information about island activities. Galveston's streets follow a grid that appears elementary. Lettered streets (A to U) run north-south, numbered streets run east-west, with **Seawall** following the southern coastline. Some confusion may arise from the fact that most streets have two names; Avenue J and Broadway, for example, are the same thoroughfare.

Texas Bus Lines, a **Greyhound** affiliate, operates out of the station at 613 University (765-7731), providing service to Houston (5 per day, 1½ hr., $9). **Emergency** is 911. The main **post office** is at 601 25th St. (763-1527; open Mon.-Fri. 9:30am-5pm, Sat. 9am-12:30pm). Galveston's **ZIP code** is 77550; the **area code** is 409.

Accommodations and Food Money-minded travelers will avoid lodging in Galveston. Accommodation prices fluctuate by season and can rise to exorbitant heights during holidays and weekends. The least expensive option is to make Galveston a daytrip from Houston. RVs can rest at any of several parks on the island. The **Bayou Haven Travel Park,** 6310 Heards Lane (744-2837), on Offatts Bayou, is nicely located on a peaceful waterfront. Laundry facilities and showers. (Full hookup $14 for 2 people, waterfront sites $17 for 2, each additional person $3.) You can pitch a tent at **Galveston Island State Park** (737-1222), on 13 Mile Rd. about 10 mi. southwest of the trolley-stop visitors center (sites $12). There are a few cheap motels along Seawall, but many of these are correspondingly shabby. Perhaps the best in the bunch is **Treasure Isle Inn,** 1002 Seawall (763-8561), with TV, pool, and A/C. (Singles $30. Doubles $40. Seniors receive a 10% discount.)

Seafood abounds in Galveston, along with traditional Texas barbecue. Plenty of eateries line Seawall and the Strand. For seafood, go to **Benno's on the Beach,** 1200 Seawall (762-4621), and try a big bowl of the shrimp gumbo ($3.75) or one of their crab variations (open Sun.-Thurs. 11am-10pm, Fri.-Sat. 11am-11pm). **El Nopalito,** 614 42nd St. (763-9815), sports cheap Mexican breakfast and lunch. Menu changes daily, but the favorites are always available. Entrees $3.75-5. (Open Tues.-Fri. 6:30am-2pm, Sat.-Sun 6:30am-4pm.) After a day at the beach, indulge yourself with a delectable root-beer malt ($2.30) at **LaKing's Confectionery,** 2323 Strand (762-6100), a large, old-fashioned ice cream and candy parlor (open Mon.-Fri. 10am-9pm, Sat. 10am-10pm, Sun. 10am-9pm).

Sights and Activities Finding your favorite beach is not difficult in tiny Galveston. Just stroll along the seawall and choose a spot. Immerse yourself in partying teenagers and high-spirited volleyball games at **Stewart Beach,** near 4th and Seawall. For a kinder, gentler student crowd, try **Pirates Beach,** about 3 mi. west of 95th and Seawall. There are two **Beach Pocket Parks** on the west end of the island, just east of Pirates Beach, with bathrooms, showers, playgrounds, and a concession stand (parking $3). **Apfel Park,** on the far eastern edge of the island, is a quiet, clean beach with a good view of ships entering and leaving the port (entry $5).

The historic **Strand,** near the northern coastline, between 20th and 25th St., is a national landmark with over 50 Victorian buildings; today the preserved district houses a range of cafes, restaurants, gift shops and clothing stores. The **Galveston Island Trolley** takes visitors to the seawall area and all the beaches (trains leave every 30 min., hourly Oct.-April.; $2, seniors and kids $1.) You can take the trolley from the Strand Visitors Center or the Visitors Bureau (see Practical Information), or take a 2-hr. cruise in Galveston harbor aboard the **Colonel** (763-4900), a Victorian paddlewheel boat, from Pier 22 at the far east end of 22nd St.

■■■ PADRE ISLAND NATIONAL SEASHORE

Bounded on the north by North Padre Island's string of condos and tourists and on the south by the Mansfield ship channel, which separates the national seashore from South Padre Island (a haven for hundreds of thousands of rowdy spring breakers every year), the Padre Island National Seashore (PINS) is an untainted gem, with over 60 mi. of perfectly preserved beaches, dunes, and a wildlife refuge. The seashore is an excellent place for windsurfing, swimming, or even surf-fishing—an 850-lb. shark was once caught at the southern, more deserted end of the island.

Practical Information Motorists enter the PINS via the JFK Causeway, which runs through the Flour Bluff area of Corpus Christi. PINS is difficult to reach by public transportation. Corpus Christi bus #8 (2 trips per day Mon.-Fri.) takes you to the tip of the Padre Isles (get off at Padre Isles Park-n-Ride near the HEB. This bus also stops at the Visitors Center). To reach the national seashore, call the **American Cab Shuttle** (949-8850; fare $1 per mi.). Round-trip distance from the bus stop to the Visitors Center is over 26 mi. The PINS **ZIP code** is 78418. The **area code** is 512.

Entry into PINS costs $4. For just a daytrip to the beach, venture toward the beautiful and uncrowded **North Beach** (24 mi. from Corpus Christi), which lies just before the $4 checkpoint. The **PINS Visitors Center,** 9405 S. Padre Island Dr. (937-2621; open Mon.-Sat. 8:30am-4:30pm), provides info on sight-seeing opportunities in nearby **Mustang State Park** and **Port Aransas.** Ask here about the **Padre Island International Hostel** (749-5937) in Port Aransas, just opened in 1993. Within the national seashore, the **Malaquite Visitors Center** (949-8068), about 14 mi. south of the JFK Causeway turn-off, supplies similar info plus exhibits and wildlife guidebooks (open daily 9am-6pm; Sept.-May daily 9am-4pm).

Camping and Activities Nothing beats camping on the beach at PINS, where crashing waves will lull you to sleep. Bring insect repellent, or you will end up awakening to the slurping noise of thousands of mosquitoes sucking you dry. The **PINS Campground** (949-8173) consists of an asphalt area for RVs, restrooms, and cold-rinse showers (RV and tent sites $5), but 5 mi. of beach is devoted to primitive camping. Free camping is permitted wherever vehicle driving is allowed. Near the national seashore is the **Balli County Park** (949-8121), on Park Rd. 22 3½ mi. from the JFK Causeway. Running water, electricity, and hot showers are available. (3-day max. stay. Full hookup $10. Key deposit $5.) Those who value creature comforts should head a few miles farther north to the **Mustang State Park Campground** (749-5246), on Park Rd. 53, 6 mi. from the JFK Causeway, for electricity, running water, dump stations, restrooms, hot showers, shelters, trailer sites, and picnic tables. Make reservations; there's often a waiting list. (Entry fee $2. Camping fee $9. Overnight camping on the beach $4.)

Hiking and driving are also popular activities at PINS. Those with four-wheel-drive vehicles can make the 60-mi. trek to the **Mansfield Cut,** the most remote and untraveled area of the seashore. Loose sands prevent vehicles without four-wheel drive from venturing far on the beach. Although the seashore has no hiking trails, the **Malaquite** (MAL-a-kee) **Ranger Station** (949-8173), 3½ mi. south of the park entrance, conducts hikes and programs throughout the year (call 949-8060 for info on group programs). They also provide first aid and emergency assistance.

■■■ SAN ANTONIO

Fabulous Tex-Mex, a late-night stroll by the river, a tour of the Alamo—what more could you ask for? These are just a few of the attractions San Antonio offers its tourists. Since most of downtown San Antonio was built before 1930, the architectural mixture is as varied as periods and materials allowed. Red-tiled roofs coupled with more modern commercial buildings line San Antonio's downtown avenues. Though Native Americans and Germans alike once claimed the city as their own, today the Spanish-speaking community outnumbers any other group. When visiting San Antonio make sure you have enough time to appreciate the city's vast array of sights; the Missions, the Riverwalk, the Tower of the Americas, and one of the country's most impressive zoos await you.

PRACTICAL INFORMATION

Emergency: 911.

Visitor Information Center, 317 Alamo Plaza (299-8155), downtown across from the Alamo. Open Mon.-Fri. 8:30am-6pm, Sat.-Sun. 8:30am-5pm.

Airport: San Antonio International Airport (821-3411), north of town. Served by I-410 and U.S. 281. Cabs to downtown $7-11. **Super Van Shuttle** (344-7433) departs for downtown every 15 min. 6am-6:45pm, every 45 min. 6:45pm-midnight. Fare $7, kids $4. By bus, take Rte. #12 at Commerce and Navarro or Market and Alamo.

Amtrak: 1174 E. Commerce St. (223-3226 or 800-872-7245), off the I-37 E. Commerce St. exit. To: Dallas (7 per week, 8 hr., $43); Austin (7 per week, 2½ hr., $15); Houston (3 per week, 4 hr., $44); and El Paso (3 per week, 11½ hr., $112).

Greyhound: 500 N. Saint Mary's St. (800-231-2222). To: Houston (8 per day, 4 hr., $22); Dallas (11 per day, 6 hr., $31); Austin (11 per day, 2½ hr., $14.50); and El Paso (6 per day, 11 hr., $81). Lockers $1. Terminal open 24 hrs.

Public Transport: VIA Metropolitan Transit, 112 Soledad (227-2020), between Commerce and Houston. Buses operate 5am-10pm, but many routes stop at 5pm. Inconvenient service to outlying areas. Fare 40¢ (more with zone changes), express 75¢. Cheap (10¢), dependable, and frequent old-fashioned **streetcars** operate downtown Mon.-Fri. 7am-9pm, Sat. 9am-9pm, Sun. 9:30am-6:30pm. Office open Mon.-Sat. 5:30am-8pm.

Taxi: Yellow Cab, 226-4242. $2.70 for first mi., $1.10 each additional mi.

Car Rental: Chuck's Rent-A-Clunker, 3249 SW Military Dr. (922-9464). Lives up to its name! $14-25 per day with 100 free mi., vans $25-45 per day. Must be 19 with a major credit card or cash deposit with reference check. Open Mon.-Fri. 8am-7pm, Sat. 9am-6pm, Sun. 10am-6pm.

Help Lines: Rape Crisis Center, 349-7273. 24 hrs. **Presa Community Service Center,** 532-5295. Referrals and transport for elderly and disabled. Open Mon.-Fri. 8:30am-noon and 1-4pm. **Gay/Lesbian Switchboard,** 733-7300 for referral and entertainment info 24 hrs.

Time Zone: Central (1 hr. behind Eastern).

Post Office: 615 E. Houston (227-3399), 1 block from the Alamo. Open Mon.-Fri. 8:30am-5:30pm. General Delivery: 10410 Perrin-Beitel Rd. (650-1630); really in the boondocks—about 15 mi. northeast of town. **ZIP code:** 78205-9998.

Area Code: 210.

ACCOMMODATIONS AND CAMPING

Since San Antonio is a popular city, downtown hotel managers have no reason to keep prices low to meet the needs of budget travelers. Furthermore, San Antonio's dearth of rivers and lakes makes for few good campsites. But cheap motels are bountiful along Roosevelt Ave., an extension of St. Mary's, only 2 mi. from downtown, accessible by the VIA bus (see Practical Information), and near the missions. Inexpensive motels also clutter Broadway between downtown and Breckenridge Park. Drivers should follow I-35 north to find cheaper and often safer accommodations within 15 mi. of town. The best value in public camping is about 30 mi. north of town at Canyon Lake in **Guadalupe River State Park** (512-438-2656; sites $4).

Bullis House Inn San Antonio International Hostel (HI/AYH), 621 Pierce St. (223-9426), 2 mi. northeast of the Alamo, across the street from Fort Sam Houston. From downtown take bus #11 at Market and St. Mary's to Grayson St. and get off at Grayson and Palmetto. Friendly hostel in a quiet neighborhood. Pool, kitchen. $13.50, nonmembers $16.50. Private rooms for 1-2 people $27, nonmembers from $30. Sheets $2. Fills rapidly in summer.

Elmira Motor Inn, 1126 E. Elmira (222-9463), about 3 blocks east of St. Mary's, a little over 1 mi. north of downtown—take bus #8 and get off at Elmira St. Very large and well-furnished rooms; more luxurious than any other place at this price. However, it is not in a safe area of town. TV, laundry service and free local calls. Caring management. Singles $29. Doubles $32. Key deposit $2.

Navarro Hotel, 116 Navarro St. (223-8453). A bit shabby but near the heart of town. A/C, color TV, daily maid service, laundry facilities, and free parking. Refreshments in the lobby. Singles $25 and up. Doubles $27 and up.

El Tejas Motel, 2727 Roosevelt Ave. (533-7123), at E. Southcross, 3 mi. south of downtown near the missions. Take bus #42. Family-run, with some waterbeds, color TV, and a pool. Rooms have thin walls. Singles start at $35, doubles at $40. In winter, singles start at $27, doubles at $36.

Alamo KOA, 602 Gembler Rd. (224-9296), 6 mi. from downtown. Take bus #24 ("Industrial Park") from the corner of Houston and Alamo downtown. Showers, laundry, A/C, pool, playground, movies, fishing pond. Full hookup $19.75 for 2 people, $2 for per additional person over age 3. Open daily 7:30am-10:30pm. A bit far from downtown, but lots of shade and a BBQ on premises.

Traveler's World RV Park, 2617 Roosevelt Ave. (532-8310 or 800-755-8310), 3 mi. south of downtown. Sites are large and have tables and benches. Showers, laundry, pool, spa, playground. Next to golf course and restaurants. Open Mon.-Sat. 8am-6pm, Sun. 9am-6pm. Tent sites $10 for 2; RV sites $18 for 2, $16 in winter. Each additional person $1, $2 in winter.

FOOD

Explore the area east of S. Alamo and S. Saint Mary's St. for the best Mexican food and BBQ. The **Riverwalk** abounds with expensive cafes and restaurants. Breakfast alone could clean you out, if you don't settle for just a muffin and coffee. **Pig Stand** diners offer decent, cheap food from all over this part of Texas; the branch at 801 S. Presa, off S. Alamo, is open 24 hrs. North of town, many Asian restaurants line Broadway across from Brackenridge. The best fast-food-style Mexican diner is **Casa Cabana,** with many locations across downtown.

Josephine St. Steaks/Whiskey, Josephine St. (224-6169), at McAllister. Off the beaten track—away from the more touristy spots along the riverwalk. A bit pricey; entrees range from $5-11. Josephine's specializes in Texan steaks, but offers an assortment of chicken, seafood, and pork entrees. Great desserts; try the carrot cake or tollhouse cookie pie ($2.50).

Casa Río, 430 E. Commerce (225-6718). Best deal on the riverwalk. *Cantando* mariachis, tasty Mexican cuisine, and a bargain to boot. Entrees $3-9. A la carte items $1.50-3. Open Mon.-Sat. 11:30am-10:30pm, Sun. noon-10:30pm. Frozen margaritas $2.50. Ask for dessert on the boat. Large parties need reservations.

Sulema's Mexican Kitchen, 319 E. Houston (222-9807). A standard Mexican diner serving cheap lunch and breakfast entrees. Lunch plates $4-6 with free iced tea or coffee. Breakfast specials under $2. Open Mon.-Sat. 7am-8pm.

Hung Fong Chinese and American Restaurant, 3624 Broadway (822-9211), 2 mi. north of downtown. Take bus #14. The oldest Chinese restaurant in San Antonio. Consistently good and crowded. Big portions. Try the egg rolls and lemon chicken. Meals $3-5. Open Mon.-Thurs. 11am-10:45pm, Fri. 11am-11:45pm, Sun. 11:30am-10:45pm.

SIGHTS

Much of historic San Antonio lies in present-day downtown and surrounding areas. The city may seem diffuse, but almost every major site and park is within a few miles of downtown and accessible by public transportation.

The Missions

The five missions along the San Antonio River once formed the soul of San Antonio; the city still preserves their remains in the **San Antonio Missions National Historical Park.** To reach the missions, follow the blue-and-white "Mission Trail" signs beginning on S. Saint Mary's St. downtown. **San Antonio City Tours** (520-8687), in front of the Alamo, offers a 2-hr. tour of the missions and the Alamo for $10, while **Tours for Kids,** 15411 Aviole Way (496-6030), offers what you might guess (9am-3pm). Bus #42 stops right in front of Mission San José, within walking distance of Mission Concepción. (Missions are open daily 9am-6pm; Sept.-May 8am-5pm. For general info on the missions, call 229-5701.)

Mission Concepción, 807 Mission Rd. (533-7109), 4 mi. south of the Alamo off E. Mitchell St. Oldest unrestored church in North America (1731). Traces of the once-colorful frescoes still visible. Active parish sanctuary. Open daily 9am-6pm.

Mission San José, 701 E. Pyron (922-0543). The "Queen of the Missions" (1720), with its own irrigation system, a church with a gorgeous sculpted rose window, and numerous restored buildings. The largest of San Antonio's missions, it provides the best sense of the self-sufficiency of these institutions. Catholic services (including a noon "Mariachi Mass") are held 4 times Sun.

Espada Aqueduct, 10040 Espada Rd., about 4 mi. south of Mission San José. Features a tiny chapel and a functioning mile-long aqueduct, built 1731-1745.

Mission San Juan Capistrano (534-3161) and **Mission San Francisco de la Espada** (627-2064), both off Roosevelt Ave., 10 mi. south of downtown as the swallow flies. Smaller and simpler than the other missions, these two are best at evoking the isolation such outposts once knew.

Downtown Tourist District

"Be silent, friend, here heroes died to blaze a trail for other men." Disobeying orders to retreat with their cannons, the defenders of the Alamo, outnumbered 20 to one, held off the Mexican army for 12 days. Then, on the morning of the 13th day, Mexican buglers commenced the infamous *degüello* (throat-cutting). Forty-six days later General Sam Houston's small army defeated the Mexicans at San Jacinto amidst cries of "Remember the Alamo!" Now phalanxes of tourists attack the **Alamo** (225-1391), at the center of Alamo Plaza by the junction of Houston and Alamo St., and sno-cone vendors are the only defenders. A single chapel and barracks preserved by the state are all that remain of the former Spanish mission. (Open Mon.-Sat. 9am-5:30pm, Sun. 10am-5:30pm. Free.) The **Long Barracks Museum and Library,** 315 Alamo Plaza (224-1836), houses Alamo memorabilia. (Open Mon.-Sat. 9am-5:30pm.) Next door, the **Clara Driscoll Theater** shows an historical documentary titled "The Battle of the Alamo." (Shows run every 20 min. Mon.-Sat. 9am-5:30pm.)

Heading southwest from the Alamo, black signs indicate access points to the **Paseo del Río (Riverwalk),** with shaded stone pathways following a winding canal built in the 1930s by the WPA. Lined with picturesque gardens, shops, and cafes, and connecting most of the major downtown sights, the Riverwalk is well-patrolled, safe, and especially beautiful at night, when it becomes the hub of San Antonio's nightlife. Ride the entire length of the Riverwalk by taking a boat ($2.50, kids $1) from the front of the Hilton Hotel. The **Alamo IMAX Theater** (225-4629), in River-center Mall, shows "The Price of Freedom," a 45-min. docudrama Alamo film, on its 6-story screen. (7 shows 10am-7pm. $6, seniors and military $5.50, kids $4.) A few blocks south, a cluster of 27 restored buildings called **La Villita,** 418 Villita (299-8610), houses restaurants, crafts shops, and art studios. (Open daily 10am-6pm.)

To take a self-guided tour of downtown, hop on an **old-fashioned street car** (10¢; see Practical Information), and spend at least an hour tooting by the sites. The pur-ple-line street car has the more extensive route, stretching from the Alamo to the Spanish Governor's Mansion to La Villita. The streetcar runs 7am-9pm.

Hemisfair Plaza (229-8570), on S. Alamo, the site of the 1968 World's Fair, is another top tourist spot. The city often uses the plaza, surrounded by restaurants, museums, and historic houses, for special events. The **Tower of the Americas,** 200 S. Alamo (299-8615), rises 750 ft. above the dusty plains, dominating the meager skyline. Get a view of the city from the observation deck on top (open daily 8am-11pm; $2, seniors $1.25, ages 4-11 $1). Stroll through the free museums in the plaza, including the **Institute of Texan Cultures** (226-7651; open Tues.-Fri. 9am-5:30pm, Sat.-Sun. 11am-5pm; parking $2), and the **Mexican Cultural Institute** (227-0123), filled with modern Mexican art (open Mon.-Fri. 9am-5pm, Sat. 11am-5pm).

On a spot near Hemisfair on Commerce St., across from the San Antonio Conven-tion Center, German immigrants erected **St. Joseph's Church** in 1868. Since this beautiful old church refused to move, a local store chain built their establishment around it. (Sun. Mass 8am and 11am in English, 9:30am and 12:30pm in Spanish.)

Walk west to the **Main Plaza** and **City Hall,** between Commerce and Dolorosa St. at Laredo. Directly behind the City Hall lies the **Spanish Governor's Palace,** 105 Plaza de Armas (225-4629). Built in Colonial Spanish style in 1772, the house has carved doors and an enclosed, shaded patio and garden. (Open Mon.-Sat. 9am-5pm, Sun. 10am-5pm. $1, kids 50¢.)

Market Square, 514 W. Commerce (229-8600), is a center for the sale of both schlocky souvenirs and handmade local crafts. The walkway **El Mercado** continues the block-long retail stretch. At the nearby **Farmers Market,** you can buy produce, Mexican chiles, candy, and spices. Come late in the day, when prices are lower and vendors more willing to haggle. (Open daily 10am-8pm; Sept.-May daily 10am-6pm.)

San Antonio North and South

Head to **Brackenridge Park,** main entrance 3900 N. Broadway (735-8641), 5 mi. north of the Alamo, for a day of unusual sight-seeing. From downtown, take bus #8. The 343-acre showground includes a Japanese garden, playgrounds, a miniature train, and an aerial tramway ($2.17). Directly across the street is the **San Antonio Zoo,** 3903 N. Saint Mary's St. (734-7183). The zoo is one of the country's largest, housing over 3,500 animals from 800 species in reproductions of their natural set-tings, including an extensive African mammal exhibit. (Open daily 9:30am-6:30pm; Nov.-March daily 9:30am-5pm. $5, seniors $4, kids 3-11 $4.) Nearby **Pioneer Hall,** 3805 N. Broadway (822-9011), contains a splendid collection of artifacts, docu-ments, portraits, cowboy and household accessories related to early Texas history. Three exhibit rooms are separately devoted to the Pioneers, the Texas Rangers and the Trail Drivers. Open Tues.-Sun. 10am-5pm, Oct. Wed.-Sun. 11am-4pm. $1, kids 25¢. Next door, at the **Witte Museum** (rhymes with city), 3801 Broadway (226-5544), permanent exhibits focus on Texas wildlife. (Open Mon. and Wed.-Sat. 10am-6pm, Tues. 10am-9pm, Sun. noon-6pm; off-season closes at 5pm. $4, seniors $2, ages 4-11 $1.75. Free Thurs. 3-9pm. Ticket receipt grants you ½-price admission to the Museum of Art.) The 38-acre **Botanical Center,** 555 Funston Pl. (821-5115), 1 mi. east of Brackenridge Park, includes the largest conservatory in the Southwest. (Open Tues.-Sun. 9am-6pm. $2.50.)

The **San Antonio Museum of Art,** 200 W. Jones Ave. (978-8100), just north of the city center, inhabits the restored Lone Star Brewery building. Towers, turrets, and spacious rooms decorated with ornate columns house Texan furniture and pre-Columbian, Native American, Spanish Colonial, and Mexican folk art. (Open Mon. and Wed.-Sat. 10am-5pm, Tues. 10am-9pm, Sun. noon-5pm. $4, seniors $3, ages 6-12 $1.75. Free Tues. 10am-9pm. Free parking.) The former estate of Marion Koogler McNay, the **McNay Art Institute,** 6000 N. New Braunfels (824-5368), displays a collection of mostly post-Impressionist European art. It also has a charming inner courtyard with sculpture fountains and meticulous landscaping. (Open Tues.-Sat. 9am-5pm, Sun. 2-5pm. Free.)

The **Lone Star Brewing Company,** 600 Lone Star Blvd. (226-8301), is about 2 mi. south of the city. Trigger-happy Albert Friedrich had managed to accumulate a collection of 3,500 animal heads, horns, and antlers when he opened the Buckhorn in 1887. What better place to put them than in his bar? Now you can pity his prey on tours which leave every 30 minutes and provide beer samples. (Open daily 9:30am-5pm. $3.50, seniors $3, ages 6-12 $1.50.) For a day of unusual and thrilling experience, drive 40 mi. to the **Natural Bridge Caverns** (651-6101), off I-35 N. The Caverns, only discovered in 1960, contain some of the most awe-inspiring caves and rock formations in the U.S. (Open daily 9am-6pm. Tours $6, seniors $5, kids $3.)

ENTERTAINMENT

Every April, the 10-day **Fiesta San Antonio** ushers in spring with concerts, parades, and plenty of Tex-Mex to commemorate the victory at San Jacinto and honor the heroes at the Alamo. However, San Antonio offers entertainment more often than just once a year. For fun after dark any time, any season, stroll down the Riverwalk. Peruse the Friday *Express* or the weekly *Current* which will guide you to concerts and entertainment. **Floore's Country Store,** 14464 Old Bandera Rd. (695-8827), toward the northwestern outskirts, is an old hangout of scruffy but lovable country music star Willie Nelson. Dancing takes place outside on a large cement platform. (Cover varies.) Some of the best Mexicali blues in the city play at **Jim Cullen's Landing,** 123 Losoya (222-1234), in the Hyatt downtown. The music inside starts at 9pm and goes until around 2am. A jazz quartet performs on Sunday nights. The riverside cafe outside opens at 11:30am (cover $3). For rowdy rock n' roll beat, stroll along **North Mary's Street** about 15 blocks from downtown.

WEST TEXAS

On the far side of the Río Pecos lies a region whose extremely stereotypical Texan character verges on self-parody. This is the stomping ground of Pecos Bill—a mythical cowpoke raised by coyotes whose exploits included lassoing a tornado. The land here was colonized in the days of the Texan Republic, during an era when the "law west of the Pecos" meant a rough mix of vigilante violence and frontier gunslinger machismo. Today, this desolate region does not lack urban attractions (although it *does* lack attractive urban areas). The border city of El Paso, and its Chihuahuan neighbor, Ciudad Juárez, beckon way, *wayyyy* out west—700 mi. from the Louisiana border.

■■■ BIG BEND NATIONAL PARK

Roadrunners, coyotes, wild pigs, mountain lions, and 350 species of birds make their home in Big Bend National Park, a 700,000-acre tract that lies within the great curve of the Río Grande. The spectacular canyons of this river, the vast **Chihuahuan Desert,** and the cool **Chisos Mountains** have all witnessed the 100 million years necessary to mold the park's natural attractions. Although the desert covers most of the park, colorful wildflowers and plants abound.

Practical Information The **park headquarters** (915-477-2291) is at **Panther Junction,** about 20 mi. inside the park. (Open daily 8am-6pm. Vehicle pass $5 per week.) For info, write Superintendent, Big Bend National Park 79834. The **Texas National Park Services** (800-452-9292) provides info on the park and will help you plan your excursion. Other **ranger stations** are at Río Grande Village, Persimmon Gap, Chisos Basin (open daily 8am-4pm), and Castolon (open daily 8am-6pm). In case of **emergency,** call 477-2251 until 6pm. Afterwards, call 477-2267 or any of the other numbers listed at each ranger station.

Big Bend may be the most isolated spot you'll ever encounter. The park is only accessible by car via Rte. 118 or U.S. 385. There are few gas stations along the way; be sure to gas up before you leave urban areas. **Amtrak** (800-872-7245) serves the town of Alpine, 70 mi. north of Big Bend (3 per week from San Antonio and Tucson).

Accommodations and Food The only motel-style lodging within the park is the expensive **Chisos Mountain Lodge** (915-477-2291). This lodge offers an older motel with two-bed rooms (singles $56, doubles $61, $10 per additional person); lodge units equipped with shower and baths but no A/C (singles $50, doubles $58, $10 per additional person); and stone cottages with three double beds ($66, $10 per additional person). Reservations are a must, since the lodge is often booked up a year in advance. The lodge also runs a restaurant and coffee shop, where entrees run $5-12 (open daily 7am-9pm). The entire complex is located in the **Chisos Basin,** 10 mi. southwest of the park's visitors center. Cheaper motels line Rte. 118 and Rte. 170 near Terlingua and Lajitas, 21 and 28 mi. respectively from park headquarters.

Groceries are available in Panther Junction, Río Grande Village, and the Chisos Basin at Castolon, but stock up before leaving urban areas for better prices. The park's only public **shower** (75¢ per 5 min.) is at the Río Grande Village Store.

Hiking and Camping You must get a free **wilderness permit** at the park headquarters to take an overnight hike. The park rangers will suggest hikes and places to visit. Most roads are well-paved, but many of the most scenic places are only accessible by foot or four-wheel-drive vehicle. The **Lost Mine Peaks Trail,** an easy 3-hr. hike up a peak in the Chisos, leads to an amazing summit view of the desert and the Sierra de Carmen in Mexico. Another easy walk leads up the **Santa Elena Canyon** along the Río Grande. The canyon walls rise up as much as 1000 ft. over the banks of the river. Three companies offer river trips down the 133-mi. stretch of the Río Grande owned by the park. Info on rafting and canoeing is available at the park headquarters (see above).

Designated **campsites** within the park are allotted on a first-come, first-served basis. **Chisos Basin** and **Río Grande Village** have sites with running water ($5), while **Cottonwood** has toilets but no water ($3). Free primitive sites pop up along the hiking trails, available with a required permit from any ranger station. Make sure you have the proper camping gear and plenty of water. Because of the relatively high temperatures at the river, you won't have to worry about getting a site at Río Grande Village, though you may have to quarrel with the resident buzzards. The best (and coolest) campsites by far are those in Chisos Basin. Get here early, as the basin sites fill up fast, especially those near the perimeter.

■■■ EL PASO

Hispanic culture undoubtably defines the regional flavor of El Paso—El Paso, along with the bordering Mexican city of Juárez, forms a bi-national metropolis unlike any of Texas' other urban centers. In the extremely dry western part of the state, El Paso is a choice destination of many northern sun-lovers. Just across the Río Grande is Juárez, Mexico's fourth largest city, whose roadside shops and markets offer tourists a variety of native products, from specially crafted Native American pottery to locally grown fruits. Juárez is so closely associated with El Paso that English is as widely spoken as Spanish.

Besides its cultural heritage, El Paso also provides its visitors with a collegiate atmosphere thanks to the University of Texas-El Paso (UTEP). Coupled with El Paso's growing student population is the city's decidedly modern flavor—downtown El Paso features an array of high-rise bank buildings and impressive skyscrapers that enables the city to rise majestically from Texas' barren desert.

PRACTICAL INFORMATION

Emergency: 911. **Juárez Police,** 248-35.

Visitor Information: El Paso Tourist Information Center, 1 Civic Center Plaza (544-0062), downtown across from Greyhound station. Open daily 8:30am-5pm.

Amtrak: 700 San Francisco Ave. (545-2247, 800-872-7245 for reservations), on the western side of the Civic Center, near Greyhound. Office open daily 11am-7pm. To: San Antonio ($112), Tuscon ($73), Phoenix ($85). Reservations required.

Greyhound: 111 San Francisco Ave. (800-231-2222), at Santa Fe across from the Civic Center. To: Albuquerque (4 per day, 6 hr. $36); Dallas (8 per day, 13 hr. $62); San Antonio (4 per day, 11 hr. $81); and Phoenix ($39). For info on buses into Mexico, call 533-3837. Office open 24 hrs. Lockers $1.

El Paso-Los Angeles Limousine Service, 72 S. Oregon (530-4061). Offers cheaper service to Albuquerque and Tucson en route to Los Angeles. To: Albuquerque $20, Tucson $25, Los Angeles $25.

Public Transport: Sun City Area Transit (SCAT), 533-3333. All routes begin downtown at San Jacinto Plaza (Main at Mesa). Fewer routes in the northwest. Connects with Juárez system. Maps and schedules posted in the Civic Center Park and at public libraries. Most buses stop around 5pm; limited service on Sun. Fare 75¢, seniors 15¢, students with ID 35¢.

Taxi: Yellow Cab, 533-3433. Base fare $1.20, $1.30 per mi.

Car Rental: Dollar-Rent-A-Car, 778-5445. $34 per day, $143 per week with unlimited free mileage. Cars are permitted 10 mi. into Mexico (Juárez); $11 extra charge. Open 24 hrs. They will deliver. Major credit card required; $5 per day extra if you're under 25.

Help Lines: Crisis Hotline, 779-1800. Open 24 hrs.

Post Office: 219 Mills St. (775-7500), open Mon.-Fri. 8:30am-5pm, Sat. 8:30am-noon. **ZIP code:** 79910.

Area Codes: El Paso, 915. To direct dial Ciudad Juárez, dial 011-52-16, followed by the local number.

The geographical intrusion of the Río Grande and the Franklin Mountains makes El Paso one of the more confusing cities you'll come across in Texas. Split by the Franklins, the city roughly forms a letter "Y," angling northwest to southeast along the river. Get yourself and a map and get oriented quickly.

ACCOMMODATIONS, CAMPING, AND FOOD

The cheapest hotel rooms land across the border, but downtown El Paso has several good budget offerings within easy walking distance of downtown. The **Gardner Hotel,** 311 E. Franklin (532-3661), at Stanton, is only six blocks from the Greyhound station and the visitors center. (Singles with bath $30, doubles $30-40.) The Gardiner is also home to the **El Paso International Hostel (HI/AYH).** The hostel has a pool table, laundry, and kitchen in the basement and pay phones in the lobby.

(Members $12; non-U.S. citizen nonmembers $18, U.S. citizen nonmembers $25.) Most other downtown motels are either very expensive or very shabby. The **Mesa Inn,** 4151 N. Mesa (532-7911), is a large, luxurious exception to this rule. Rooms are clean; local calls cost 50¢. ($23 for 2 people. Key deposit $10. Weekends $5 less.)

There are a few small RV campgrounds near downtown but the nicest outdoor lodgings lie miles outside El Paso and are not very accessible by public transportation. The **Hueco Tanks State Park** (857-1135), a 32-mi. hike east of El Paso on U.S. 62/180, is a great place for hiking and rockclimbing but offers meager service. (Sites $8, with electricity $11. Showers and restrooms.)

A great place to experience local culture and eat spicy Mexican food is **The Tap,** 500 San Antonio (532-4456), at Stanton downtown. Loud bar, cheap food. Mexican plate $3.25. Other entrees $2-5. (Open daily 7am-1am.) **Arnold's Mexican Restaurant,** 315 Mills Ave. (532-3147), at Kansas downtown (open Mon.-Fri. 7am-3pm), just a few blocks south of the hostel, serves excellent authentic Mexican dishes ($2.50-5), and a big breakfast special ($1.75). Also downtown, a block from the hostel, is **Big Bun Burger,** 501 Stanton (546-9359), at Franklin, which serves your standard diner fare at 1950s prices. Burgers ($1), fountain drinks (60¢), and tacos (70¢). (Open Mon.-Sat. 8am-8pm, Sun. 10am-4pm.)

SIGHTS AND ENTERTAINMENT

The majority of visitors to El Paso are either stopping off on the long drive through the desert or headed across the border for a taste of Mexico. Two pedestrian and motor roads cross the Río Grande: **El Paso,** an overcrowded one-way street, and **Santa Fe,** a parallel road lined with Western wear stores, clothing shops, and decent restaurants. Entry to Mexico is 25¢, and the trip back into the U.S. costs 50¢. Check out the **Border Jumper Trolleys** (544-0062), which depart every hour 9am-4pm (Mon.-Fri. $8, Sat.-Sun.$10, kids 5-12 $8, under 5 free). Day trippers, including foreign travelers with a multi-entry visa, need only flash their documents of citizenship in order to pass in and out. A walk across the border is worth your while but try to make it to downtown Juárez and avoid the border area tourist businesses

Volatile downtown El Paso has more to offer than just a cross-border trip. Historic **San Jacinto Plaza** swarms daily with men and women, young and old. Catch the true flavor of local culture and listen to street musicians perform here where Spanish *conquistadores,* Fort Bliss cavalry men, and *señoritas* once rested. South of the square, **El Paso Street** is another place you don't want to miss. Hundreds of locals hurry along the street and dash into stores trying to grab the best bargain. You can buy a pair of Wranglers for as little as $10. To take in a complete picture of the Río Grande Valley, head northeast of downtown on Rim Rd. (which becomes Scenic Dr.) to **Murchison Park,** at the base of the mountains; the park offers a fine view of El Paso, Juárez, and the Sierra Madre.

Strategic timing can make your visit to El Paso more entertaining. The town hosts the **Southwestern Livestock Show & Rodeo** (532-1401) in February, the **World Championship Finals Rodeo** (544-2582) in November, and a **Jazz Festival** (534-6277) in October at the Chamizal Memorial.

> For more information on Ciudad Juárez, see *Let's Go: Mexico.*

∎∎∎ GUADALUPE MOUNTAINS NATIONAL PARK

The existence of the Guadalupes in the vast Texas desert land is a miracle; extending from southern New Mexico, the range peaks at nearly 9000 ft. The Guadalupes carry with them a legacy of unexplored grandeur. Early westbound pioneers avoided the area, fearful of the climate and the Mescalero Apaches who controlled the range. By the 1800s, when the Apaches had been driven out, only a few homesteaders and *guano* miners inhabited this rugged region. Today the national park encompasses 86,000 acres of desert, canyons, and highlands. With over 70 mi. of trails, the mountains ensure challenging hikes in a mostly desert environment for those willing to journey to this remote part of the state. The passing tourist who hopes to catch only the most established sights should stop to see **El Capitán,** a 2000-ft. limestone cliff, and **Guadalupe Peak,** at 8749 ft. the highest point in Texas. Less hurried travelers should hike to **McKittrick Canyon,** with its spring-fed stream and amazing variety of vegetation. Lush maples grow next to desert yuccas, and thorny agaves circle stately pines. Mule deer and whiptail lizards sometimes greet visitors on the trails. **The Bowl,** a stunning high-country forest of Douglas fir and ponderosa pine, is an easy hike.

Practical Information Guadalupe Park is less than 40 mi. west of Carlsbad Caverns in New Mexico and 115 mi. east of El Paso. **TNM&O Coaches,** (808-765-6641) an affiliate of **Greyhound,** runs along U.S. 62/180 between Carlsbad, NM and El Paso, passing Carlsbad Caverns National Park and Guadalupe National Park en route. This line makes flag stops at the park three times per day in each direction ($25, $47.50 round-trip). Ask the driver to let you off at the entrance. The headquarters is 200 yds. away. Make sure you know the daily schedule so you that don't miss the bus. Guadalupe Mountains National Park is in the Mountain time zone (2 hr. behind Eastern). For further info, write: Guadalupe Mountains National Park, HC60, P.O. Box 400, Salt Flat, TX 79847-9400 (828-3251). The **area code** is 915.

Hiking and Camping Most major trails begin at the **Headquarters Visitors Center** (828-3215), right off U.S. 62/180 where the bus drops you. Guadalupe Peak is an easy 3-5-hr. hike, depending on your mountaineering ability, while the McKittrick Canyon and the Bowl can be hiked in a full day. At the headquarters, you can pick up topographical maps, hiking guides, backcountry permits, etc. (Open daily 7am-6pm; Sept.-May daily 8am-4:30pm. After-hours info is posted on the bulletin board outside.) The trail leading to the historic Pratt Cabin in the Canyon begins at the **McKittrick Visitors Center,** off U.S. 62/180. Here the Guadalupe Mountains Park Service conducts half- and full-day hikes June-Aug., as well as evening programs. The center is staffed during the fall and sporadically throughout the year. Visit the park in the fall for fabulous foliage free of summer heat or spring winds.

The **Pine Springs Campgrounds** (828-3251), just past the headquarters directly on the highway, has water and restrooms but no hookups. No fires allowed. (Sites $6, Golden Age and Golden Access Passport holders receive a 50% discount.) **Dog Canyon Campground** (505-981-2418), just south of the New Mexico state line at the north end of the park, can be reached only by a 70-mi. drive from Carlsbad, NM, on Rte. 137. Dog Canyon also lacks hookups but provides water and restrooms (sites $6). There are 10 backcountry campgrounds in the park, almost at every major site. There is no charge for the necessary permit that can be obtained at the headquarters. When convenience takes priority over proximity to the trails, you should use **Carlsbad, NM** as a base. The town, 55 mi. northeast of the park, has several cheap motels, campgrounds, and restaurants.

Food Guadalupe National Park's lack of development may be a bonus for backpackers, but it makes daily existence tough. All water in the backcountry is reserved for wildlife—you'll find no food available nearby. Bring water for even the shortest, most casual hike. **Pine Springs** (828-3338), ½-mi. east of the headquarters visitors center, sells ready-made but reasonably priced sandwiches, sodas, and beer. You can get ice cream and hamburgers at **Nickel Creek Cafe** (828-3348), 5 mi. east or fill up on a pancake and coffee breakfast ($3-6) before visiting McKittrick Canyon, 3 mi. farther east. (Both restaurants open daily 7am-6pm, Sept.-May daily 8am-4:40pm.)

ROCKY MOUNTAINS

These "purple mountain majesties" soar unexpectedly out of the Midwestern plain. Sagebrush, ponderosa, and mountain lupine replace corn and wheat as grasslands yield to open pine forest, and then, at the timberline, the forest gives way to the sharp-edged, alpine peaks of the Rocky Mountains. This continental divider stretches from northern Canada to central Utah, all the while blushing with pristine alpine meadows, forbidding rocky gorges and unpolluted streams. The beauty of the Rockies overwhelms the senses and renders even the most eloquent observer respectfully silent.

The states which frame these mountains are appropriately square and spacious. The whole Rocky Mountains area supports less than five percent of the population of the United States, and much of the land belongs to the public, preserved in national parks, forests, and wilderness areas. The stunning Waterton-Glacier International Peace Park straddles Montana's border with Alberta; Idaho encompasses two impressive back-country regions, as well as acre upon thrilling acre of state and national forest; Wyoming and Colorado are the proud landlords of Yellowstone and Rocky Mountain National Parks. The area boasts stunningly scenic trails for car, foot, or bike—there's a way for everyone to experience the Rockies.

Not surprisingly, most residents of the Mountain states live close to the land; even in Colorado, agriculture is still bigger business than tourism. The people of Denver, the only major metropolis in the region, combine big-city sophistication with an abiding appreciation for the area's rich natural endowment. Most other cities are oil towns, ski villages, university seats, or mining towns—commercial centers are in short supply in the Mountains.

 # Colorado

Southwestern Colorado's cliff dwellings around Mesa Verde suggest that Native Americans took their architectural inspiration from the state's rivers, with the Gunnison carving Black Canyon and the Colorado chiseling methodically away at the monoliths of Colorado National Monument. Europeans dug a lot faster for more pecuniary purposes—silver and gold attracted many of the state's first white immigrants. Even the U.S. military has dug enormous "intelligence" installations into the mountains around Colorado Springs, constructed to survive a nuclear holocaust. There is something for everybody to dig in Colorado.

Back on the surface, skiers worship Colorado's slopes, giving rise to the omnipresent, oh-so-chic condos of Aspen, Vail, and Crested Butte. As the hub of the state and the entire Rocky Mountain region, Denver provides both an ideal resting place for cross-country travelers and a "culture fix" for people heading to the mountains; Boulder is the crunchy alternative.

Bus transportation readily connects the Denver-Boulder area and most of the north, but driving is the way to see the more remote south. Luckily, finding accommodations proves easier; Colorado contains 23 youth hostels and a majority of the Rockies' B&Bs, and offers camping in 13 national forests and eight national parks.

PRACTICAL INFORMATION
Capital: Denver.

Colorado Board of Tourism, 1625 Broadway #1700, Denver 80202 (592-5510 or 800-265-6723). Open Mon.-Fri. 8am-5pm. **U.S. Forest Service,** Rocky Mountain Region, 11177 W. 8th Ave., Lakewood 80225 (236-9431). Tour maps free, forest maps $3. Open Mon.-Fri. 7:30am-4:30pm. **Ski Country USA,** 1540 Broadway #1300, Denver 80203 (837-0793, open Mon.-Fri. 8am-5:30pm; recorded message 831-7669). **National Park Service,** 12795 W. Alameda Pkwy., P.O. Box 25287, Denver 80255 (969-2000). For reservations for Rocky Mountain National Park, call (800-365-2267). Open Mon.-Fri. 8:30am-4pm. **Colorado State Parks and Recreation,** 1313 Sherman St. #618, Denver 80203 (866-3437). Guide to state parks and metro area trail guide. Open Mon.-Fri. 8am-5pm.

Time Zone: Mountain (2 hr. behind Eastern). **Postal Abbreviation:** CO
Sales Tax: 7.3%

■■■ ASPEN AND GLENWOOD SPRINGS

A world-renowned asylum for dedicated musicians and elite skiers, Aspen looms as the budget traveler's worst nightmare. Aspen was settled first by venturesome miners seeking a Colorado Eldorado. When the veins of silver began drying up in the 1940s, the shanty settlement went into a 20-year decline. But the Aspen of the 1990s shows no traces of its past hardships. A community of high-browed connoisseurs and wine lovers, Aspen has become too exclusive in the minds of many. In this upper-class playground, low-budget living will probably remain as much a thing of the past as the forsaken mining industry.

Practical Information The **Visitors Center,** at the Wheeler Opera House, is at 320 E. Hyman Ave. Pick up the free *What to Do in Aspen and Snowmass.* (Open daily 9am-7pm; winter 9am-5pm.) **Aspen District of the White River National Forest Ranger Station,** 806 W. Hallam (925-3445), at N. 7th St. (open daily 8am-5pm; winter Mon.-Fri. 8am-5pm), has info for hikers and a map of the whole forest ($3). **Aspen/Glenwood Bus** offers 4 buses between Aspen and Glenwood, Mon.-Fri. (last bus leaves Glenwood at 3:15pm; Aspen at 5:15pm), and 5 buses Sat.-Sun. $5 one way, children and seniors $4, 50¢ within Glenwood. The **area code** is 303.

Accommodations, Camping, and Food Budget accommodations don't come easy in Aspen, but surrounding national forests offer inexpensive summer camping, and some reasonably priced skiers' dorms double as guest houses in summer. The largest crowds and highest rates arrive during winter. Consider lodging in **Glenwood Springs,** 70 mi. north of Aspen, where inexpensive accommodations are plentiful (see below). If you plan to stay at least one week in Aspen, the **Little Red Ski Haus,** 118 E. Cooper (925-3333), 2 blocks west of downtown, is the place, with clean, bright, wood-paneled rooms. Rates vary drastically by season and privacy of bath and accommodations; winter rates are highest, ranging from $42 for a quad with shared bath to $62 for double with private bath; summer rates vary from $23 for a quad with a shared bath to $45 for a single. Breakfast included.

Unless 6 ft. of snow cover the ground, try **camping** in the mountains nearby. Hike well into the forest and camp for free, or use one of the ten **National Forest Campgrounds** within 15 mi. of Aspen. **Maroon Lake, Silver Bar, Silver Bell,** and **Silver Queen** are on Maroon Creek Rd. just west of Aspen. (3-5 day max. stay. Sites fill well before noon. Open July-early Sept.) Southeast of Aspen on Rte. 82 toward Independence Pass are six campgrounds: **Difficult, Lincoln Gulch, Lincoln Creek Dispersed Sites, Weller, Lost Man,** and **Portal.** For reservations at Silver Bar, Silver Bell, Silver Queen, and Difficult, contact MISTIX (800-283-2267), which handles both reservations and camping fees. (Open Mon.-Fri. 8am-5pm, Sat.-Sun. 8am-3pm PST. MC, Visa, checks, and money orders accepted.)

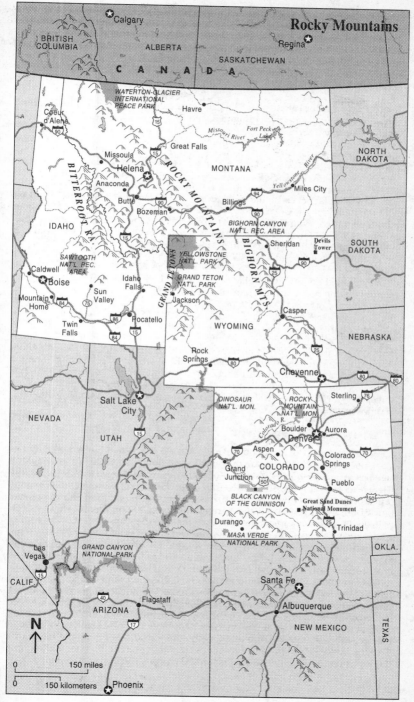

Rocky Mountains

Some relatively affordable eateries in Aspen make their meals on Main St. **The Main Street Bakery,** 201 E. Main St. (925-6446), offers sweets, gourmet soups ($3.50), homemade granola ($3.85), 3-grain pancakes ($4), and a reprieve from pretension. (Open Mon.-Sat. 7am-5:30pm, Sun. 7am-4pm.) The **In and Out House,** 233 E. Main St. (925-6647) is just that—a virtual revolving door of customers in an outhouse-sized space. Huge sandwiches on fresh-baked bread ($2-5) which barely git through the door. (Open Mon.-Fri. 8am-7pm, Sat.-Sun. 8am-4pm.)

Skiing and Entertainment The hills surrounding town contain four ski areas: **Aspen Mountain, Buttermilk Mountain,** and **Snowmass Ski Area** (925-1220) sell interchangeable lift tickets ($43, ages over 70 free, kids $26, under 6 free; daily hours: Aspen Mtn. 9:30am-3:30pm, Buttermilk Mtn. 9am-4pm, Snowmass 8:30am-3:30pm). **Aspen Highlands** (925-5300) does *not* provide interchangeable tickets ($33, seniors with ID and kids 13 and under $15; open daily 9am-4pm). Favorite slopes include **Sheer Rock Face** at Aspen, **Nipple** at Buttermilk, and **Catholic School** at Snowmass. You can enjoy the beauty of the mountains without going into debt paying for lift tickets. In the summer, ride the **Silver Queen Gondola** ($11, kids 3-12 $6) to the top of Aspen mountains. Hiking in the Maroon Bells and Elk Mountains is permitted when the snow isn't too deep. Undoubtedly Aspen's most famous event, the **Aspen Music Festival** (925-9042) holds sway over the town from late June-Aug. Free bus transportation goes from Rubey Park downtown to "the Tent," south of town, before and after all concerts. (Concerts June-late Aug. Free concert held almost every day. Tickets $16-40; Sun. rehearsals $2.)

The *après*-ski hours and nightlife of Aspen may be forbidden to the budget traveler (or anyone not worth millions of dollars). Of course, for voyeurs, Aspen is a great place to just sit and watch. A popular local hangout for the beautiful people is the **Cooper Street Pier,** 500 Cooper Ave. (925-7758; restaurant open daily 11:30am-10pm, bar until 1am). The **Flying Dog Brew Pub,** 424 E. Cooper Ave. (925-7464), just a few blocks down, is a mini-brewery serving American food. Try a 4-beer sampler for $3 (open Mon.-Sun. 11:30am-10pm). Off Rte. 82 towards Glenwood Springs, you'll find **Woody Creek Tavern,** 2 Woody Creek Pl. (923-4285), a reality check after the surreal experience of a resort town. Hefty burgers ($6), and great Mexican specialties. Sip a fresh lime margarita ($4.50) and munch on chips and salsa ($2.75) while you wait to catch a glimpse of gonzo journalist Hunter S. Thompson, a regular here. (Open daily 11:30am-10pm.)

■ Glenwood Springs

Forty mi. northwest of Aspen on Colorado Rte. 82, **Glenwood Springs** is neither as glitzy nor as overpriced as its larger-than-life neighbor to the south. This tranquil village has managed to take advantage of its natural resource—hot springs. Nearby **Glenwood Hot Springs,** 401 N. River Rd. (945-6571), provides most of its income (open daily 7:30am-10pm; day pass $6, after 9pm $3.75, ages 3-12 $3.75). Just one block from the large pools is the **Yampah Spa and Vapor Caves,** 709 E. 6th St. (945-0667), where hot mineral waters flow through the walls of the caves, creating a relaxing 125°F heat ($6.75, $3.75 for hostelers; open daily 9am-9pm). Ski 10 mi. west of town at **Sunlight,** 10901 County Rd. 117 (945-7491 or 800-445-7931). (4-5 lifts. Ski passes $26 per day for hostelers, including access to the hot springs. A cross-country skiing basic trail pass costs $4. Downhill rentals $10 for hostelers.)

Within walking distance of the springs you'll find the **Glenwood Springs Hostel (HI/AYH),** 1021 Grand Ave. (945-8545), a former Victorian home with spacious dorm and communal areas as well as a full kitchen. Ask Gary to play one of his collection of 1100 records. At night, groups go to the hot springs, the local pool halls, or the nearby coffee house. You can also rent mountain bikes for $9 per day and receive a free ride (by car) from train and bus stations. Hostelers can ski at Sunlight Ski Area for $16 Mon.-Fri., $21 Sat.-Sun., or go white-water rafting for $22, or visit the vapor caves for $3.75. (Hostel closed 10am-4pm. $9.50. Linen included. Free pasta, rice, potatoes.) The Victorian B&B next door is **Aducci's Inn,** 1023 Grand Ave. (945-9341). Private rooms cost $28-65 for a single, $38-65 for a double; $10 per additional person. Prices are negotiable according to room availability. Includes breakfast every morning and wine in the evenings. Hot tub. Call for free pick-up from bus and train stations. Cheap motels line the main drag, 6th St.

The **Amtrak** station thinks it can at 413 7th St. (800-872-7245). One daily train chugs west to Denver (6 hr., $53) and one east to Salt Lake City (8 hrs. 40 min., $83). (Station open daily 9am-5pm.) **Greyhound** serves Glenwood Springs from 118 W. 6th St. (945-8501). Four buses run daily to Denver (4 hr., $18) and Grand Junction (2 hr., $8). (Open Mon.-Fri. 7am-5pm, Sat. 8am-1pm.) For further information on the town, contact **Glenwood Springs Chamber Resort Association,** 1102 Grand Ave. (945-6589; open Mon.-Fri. 8:30am-5pm).

The **Strawberry Days** festival begins in mid-June and includes concerts, races, performances, and art shows. The parade that marks the start of the festival is followed by free strawberries and ice cream.

■■■ BOULDER

Boulder lends itself to the pursuit of both higher knowledge and better karma. It is home to the central branch of the University of Colorado (CU) and the only accredited Buddhist university in the U.S., the Naropa Institute. Only *here* can you take summer poetry and mantra workshops lead by Beat guru Allen Ginsberg at the Jack Kerouac School of Disembodied Poets. Boulder's universities also attract a range of musical performers, from bands with more of an edge, like the Dead Milkmen, to more traditional folk heroes, such as Tracy Chapman and the Indigo Girls. Top performers often appear in the Pearl Street cafes, surrounded by iced cappuccino.

Boulder is both an aesthetic and athletic mecca. The nearby Flatiron Mountains, rising up in big charcoal-colored slabs on the western horizon, beckon rock climbers, while an admirable system of paths make Boulder one of the most bike- and pedestrian-friendly areas around. For those motorists seeking a retreat into nature, Boulder is *On the Road* (Colorado Rte. 36) to Rocky Mountain National Park, Estes Park, and Grand Lake.

PRACTICAL INFORMATION

Emergency: 911.

Boulder Chamber of Commerce/Visitors Service, 2440 Pearl St. (442-1044 or 800-444-0447), at Folsom about 10 blocks from downtown. Take bus #200. Well-equipped, with comprehensive seasonal guides. Open Mon. 9am-5pm, Tues.-Fri. 8:30am-5pm. **University of Colorado Information** (492-6161), 2nd floor of UMC student union. Campus maps. Open Mon.-Thurs. 7am-11pm, Fri.-Sat. 7am-midnight, Sun. 11am-11pm. **CU Ride Board,** UMC, Broadway at 16th. Lots of rides, lots of riders—even in the summer.

Public Transport: Boulder Transit Center (299-6000), 14th and Walnut St.. Routes to Denver and Longmont as well as intra-city routes. Buses run Mon.-Fri. 6am-8pm, Sat.-Sun. 8am-8pm. Fare 50¢, $1 Mon.-Fri. 6-9am and 4-6pm. $1.50 to Nederland ("N" bus) and Lyons ("Y" bus); $2.50 to Golden ("G" bus) and to Boulder Foothills or Denver ("H" bus). Several other lines link up with the Denver system (see Denver Practical Information). Get a bus map ($1) at the terminal.

Taxi: Boulder Yellow Cab, 442-2277. $1.50 base fare, $1.20 per mi.

Car Rental: Budget Rent-a-Car, 1545 28th St. (444-9054), near the Clarion Harvest House. $30 per day; $150 per week. Must be at least 25. Open Mon.-Thurs. 7am-6pm, Sat. 8am-4pm, Sun. 9am-4pm.

Bike Rental: University Bicycles, 839 Pearl St. (444-4196), downtown. 12- and 14-speeds and mountain bikes $14 per 4 hr., $18 per 8 hr., $22 overnight, with helmet and lock. Open Mon.-Sat. 9am-7pm, Sun. 10am-6pm.

Help Lines: Rape Crisis, 443-7300. 24 hrs. **Crisis Line,** 447-1665. 24 hrs. **Gays, Lesbians, and Friends of Boulder,** 492-8567.

Post Office: 1905 15th St. (938-1100), at Walnut across from the RTD terminal. Open Mon.-Fri. 7:30am-5:30pm, Sat. 10am-2pm. **ZIP code:** 80302.
Area Code: 303.

Boulder (pop. 83,000) is a small, manageable city. The most developed part of Boulder lies between **Broadway** (Rte. 93) and **28th Street** (Rte. 36), two busy streets running parallel to each other north-south through the city. **Baseline Road,** which connects the Flatirons with the eastern plains, and **Canyon Boulevard** (Rte. 7), which follows the scenic Boulder Canyon up into the mountains, border the main part of the **University of Colorado** campus (CU). The school's surroundings are known locally as the **"Hill."** The pedestrian-only **Pearl Street Mall,** between 11th and 15th St. centers hip life in Boulder. Most east-west roads have names, while north-south streets have numbers; Broadway is a conspicuous exception.

ACCOMMODATIONS AND CAMPING

After spending your money at the Pearl St. Mall on tofu and yogurt, you may find yourself a little strapped for cash and without a roof under which to sleep—Boulder doesn't offer many inexpensive places to spend the night. In summer, you can rely on the **Boulder International Youth Hostel (RNA),** 1107 12th St. (442-9304 7-10am and 5pm-1am; 442-0522 10am-5pm), two blocks west of the CU campus and 15 min. south of the RTD station. The wonderfully friendly atmosphere and laid-back management more than make up for the slight scruffiness of these frat-house style rooms. Bring or rent sheets, a towel, and a pillow. (Curfew midnight in private rooms. Dorm beds $11; private singles $25 per night, $110 per week; doubles $30 per night, $130 per week. Towels and linen $2. Key deposit $5.) Reservations are recommended at the **Chautauqua Association** (442-3282), 9th St. and Baseline Rd., which offers rooms big enough for two in their lodge ($40 for two people) and highly popular cottages ($43 per night, room enough for 4 people; $80 for 10-person cottage; 4-night minimum stay). Guests at this cultural institution can take in films for free. Take bus #203. **The Boulder Mountain Lodge,** 91 Four Mile Canyon Rd. (444-0882), is a 2-mi. drive west on Canyon Rd., near creek-side bike and foot trails. Facilities include phone and TV; hot tub and pool are a nice plus. (Check-in after 10pm for campsites. Sites with/without hookup $14 per night for up to 3 people, each additional person $2; $80 per week. 2-week max. stay.)

You'll have an easy time finding camping spots elsewhere. Info on campsites in **Roosevelt National Forest** is available from the **Forest Service Station** at 2995 Baseline Rd. #16, Boulder 80303 (444-6600; open Mon.-Fri. 8am-5pm, and in the summer, Sat. 8am-5pm). Maps $2. A site at **Kelly Dahl** (reservations: 800-283-CAMP), 3 mi. south of Nederland on Rte. 119, costs $8. **Rainbow Lakes,** 6 mi. north of Nederland on Rte. 72, and 5 mi. west on Arapahoe Glacier Rd., is free, but no water is available (campgrounds open late May to mid-Sept.). **Peaceful Valley** and **Camp Dick** (north on Rte. 72; $8 per site) have cross-country skiing in the winter and first-come, first-served sites.

FOOD AND HANGOUTS

The streets on the "Hill" and those along the Pearl St. Mall burst with good eateries, natural foods markets, cafes, and colorful bars. Many more restaurants and bars line Baseline Rd. As one might expect, given the peace-love-nature-touchy-feely climate, Boulder has more restaurants for vegetarians than for carnivores. For an abundance of fresh produce, homemade breads, and pies, head for the **Boulder County Farmer's Market** at 13th and Canyon, which operates May-Oct. (Wed. 2-6pm, Sat. 8am-2pm). Get there early.

The Sink, 1165 13th St. (444-7465). When the word went out in 1989 that the Sink had reopened, throngs of former "Sink Rats" commenced their pilgrimage back to Boulder; the restaurant still awaits the return of its former janitor, Robert Redford, who quit his job and headed out to California back in the late 1950s. Individual pizza $2.75, burgers $3.25, vegetarian and Mexican specialties. Open Mon.-Sun. 11am-2am. Happy Hours Tues.-Fri. 4-6pm and 8-10pm, all day Mon. Call for info on live music nights (Tues. & Fri.). Food served until 10pm.

Hanna's Kitchen, 1122 Pearl St. Mall (443-0755), in the health food store, **New Age Foods**. Some of the cheapest meals in town, featuring healthful and veggie fare. Cafeteria-style restaurant offers soups ($1.75) and sandwiches ($3.50). Open Mon.-Fri. 9am-5:30pm, Sat. 9am-4pm. Restaurant open Mon.-Fri. 11:30am-3pm.

The Walrus Cafe, 1911 11th St. (443-9902). Universally popular night spot. Alas, Paul McCartney is nowhere to be found. Beer $1.50. Open Mon.-Fri. 4pm-1:30am, Sat.-Sun. 2pm-1:30am. Free pool until 6pm daily. Coo coo ka choo.

Harvest Restaurant and Bakery, 1738 Pearl St. (449-6223), at 18th St. inside a little mall. A fine example of mellow, "back-to-nature" Boulder. Very popular among CU students. Try the "Swiss Granola," with frozen yogurt and a pumpkin muffin ($4.50). You can sit at the community table to make friends. Open Sun.-Thurs. 7am-10pm, Fri.-Sat. 7am-11pm.

Espresso Roma, 1110 13th St. (442-5011), on the Hill near the youth hostel. Students head here for jumps of caffeine (85¢), almond biscotti (37¢), and fluffy, golden croissants (90¢). When the Cabaret Voltaire gets too grating, head for the more peaceful back room. Open daily 7am-midnight.

Sushi Zanmai, 1221 Spruce (440-0733), next to the Hotel Boulderado. Best Japanese food in Boulder served by wacky knife-throwing chefs. Chicken teriyaki lunch special $4.80. Happy Hour (sushi $1.25) Mon.-Fri 11:30am-2pm, 5-6:30pm, Sun. 5-10pm. Karaoke Sat.10pm-midnight. Lunch Mon.-Fri. 11:30am-2pm, dinner daily 5-10pm. Visa, MC, AmEx.

CU Student Cafeteria, 16th and Broadway, downstairs in the student union (UMC). Favorite restaurant of Mork and Mindy. The large **Alfred Packer Grill** (named after the West's celebrated cannibal) serves burgers ($1.79) and sizeable burritos ($3). Open Mon.-Fri. 7am-6pm, Sat. 9am-4pm, Sun. 11am-4pm.

SIGHTS AND ACTIVITIES

University of Colorado's intellectuals collaborate with wayward poets and back-to-nature granolas to find innovative things to do. Check out the perennially outrageous street scene on the Mall and the Hill and watch the university's kiosks for the scoop on downtown happenings.

The university's **Cultural Events Board** (492-8409) has the latest word on all CU-sponsored activities. The most massive of these undertakings is the annual **Arts Fest** in mid-July. Phone for tickets or stop by the ticket office in the **University Memorial Center** (492-2736; open Mon.-Sat. 10am-6pm). As part of Arts Fest, the **Colorado Shakespeare Festival** (492-0554) takes place from late June to mid-August. (Previews $9, tickets $10-30, student discounts available.) Concurrently, the **Chautauqua Institute** (442-3282) hosts the **Colorado Music Festival** (449-2413; performances June 12-July 30; tickets $10-22). The **Boulder Blues Festival** (443-5858; for tickets 444-3601, $10-15) is held the second week of July. The Parks and Recreation Department (441-3400; open Mon.-Fri. 8am-5pm) sponsors free summer performances in local parks; dance, classical and modern music, and children's theater are staples. **The Boulder Center for the Visual Arts,** 1750 13th St. (443-2122), focuses on contemporary regional art and has more wide-ranging exhibits as well. (Open Tues.-Fri. 11am-5pm, Sat. 9am-3pm, Sun. noon-4pm. Free.)

Boulder Public Library, 1000 Canyon Rd. (441-3197), and CU's **Muenzinger Auditorium,** near Folsom and Colorado Ave. (492-1531), both screen international films. Call for times and price. Museums in Boulder don't quite compare with the vitality and spectacle of Pearl St. and the Hill. When the need to see a more formal exhibit overtakes you, the intimate and impressive **Leanin' Tree Museum,** 6055 Longbow Dr. (530-1442), presents an interesting array of Western art and sculpture. (Open Mon.-Fri. 8am-4:30pm, Sat. 10am-4pm. Free.) The small **Naropa Institute** is located at 2130 Arapahoe Ave. (444-0202). Drop by and drop off at one of their many free meditation sessions with Tibetan monks. (Open daily 9am-5pm.)

The **Flatiron Mountains,** acting as a backdrop to this bright and vibrant town, offer countless variations on walking, hiking, and biking. Take a stroll or cycle along **Boulder Creek Path,** a beautiful strip of park that lines the creek for 15 mi. Farther back in the mountains lie treacherous, less accessible rocky outcroppings. Trails weave through the 6000-acre **Boulder Mountain Park,** beginning from several sites on the western side of town. **Flagstaff Road** winds its way to the top of the mountains from the far western end of Baseline Rd. The **Boulder Creek Canyon,** accessible from Rte. 119, emits splendid rocky scenery. Nearby **Eldorado Canyon,** as well as the Flatirons themselves, has some of the best **rock climbing** in the world.

Well-attended **running** and **biking** competitions far outnumber any other sports events in the Boulder area. The biggest foot race by far is the 10km Memorial Day challenge known as the "Bolder Boulder," which brings in 30,000 international athletes. The winner takes home $4000. For information on any running event, call the Boulder Roadrunners (499-2061; open daily 9am-6pm).

The **Rockies Brewing Company,** 2880 Wilderness Place (444-8448), offers tours for those who prefer sedentary pleasures to exercise. Yes, they feed you free beer at the end. (25-min. tours Mon.-Sat. at 2pm; open Mon.-Sat. 11am-10pm.)

■■■ COLORADO SPRINGS

On July 22nd, 1893, Katherine Lee Bates and several fellow teachers from Colorado College reached the top of Pikes Peak on a prairie wagon. It was the view from the summit that inspired her to write the poem "America the Beautiful." Today you can still view the purple mountain majesties from Pikes Peak, but the once-tiny city of Colorado Springs has become a resort town and tourist attraction. 300 million years ago the earth's inner turmoil resulted in the formation of Pikes Peak and the surrounding mountain ranges to the west, while uplifting the floor of an inland ocean basin made out of red rocks, now called the Garden of the Gods. The Ute Indians, who came to Colorado and Manitou Springs for their healing mineral waters, believed these rocks were the bodies of their enemies thrown down by gods. Colorado Springs bubbles with more than water. Home to the United States Olympic Team (the high altitude builds hemoglobin levels), the Springs churn out champion lugers and synchronized swimmers. While tourists pour millions into the Colorado Springs economy during the summer, the U.S. government pours in even more: North American Air Defense Command Headquarters (NORAD) lurks beneath nearby Cheyenne Mountain.

PRACTICAL INFORMATION

Emergency: 911.

Visitor Information: Colorado Springs Convention and Visitors Bureau, 104 S. Cascade #104, 80903 (635-7506 or 800-368-4748), at Colorado Ave. Check out the *Colorado Springs Pikes Peak Park Region Official Visitors Guide* and the city bus map. Open Mon.-Sat. 8:30am-5pm, Sun. 9am-3pm; Nov.-March Mon.-Fri. 8:30am-5pm.

Greyhound: 327 S. Weber St. (635-1505). To: Denver (8 per day, 2 hr., $9); Pueblo (5 per day, 50 min., $5.75); Albuquerque (5 per day, 7-9 hr., $60); Kansas City (4 per day, 16-17 hr., $89). Tickets sold daily 5am-midnight.

Public Transport: Colorado Springs City Bus Service, 125 E. Kiowa at Nevada (475-9733), 5 blocks from the Greyhound station. Serves the city, Widefield, Manitou Springs, Fort Carson, Garden of the Gods, and Peterson AFB. Service Mon.-Sat. 5:45am-6:15pm every ½ hr., 6:45-10pm every hr. Fare 75¢, seniors and kids 35¢, ages 5 and under free; long trips 15¢ extra. Exact change required.

Tours: Gray Line Tours, 3704 Colorado Ave. (633-11810 or 800-345-8197), at the Garden of the Gods Campgrounds. Trips to the U.S. Air Force Academy and Garden of the Gods (4 hrs. $15, kids $7.50), Pikes Peak (4 hrs. $20, kids $10). Also offers 10 mi. whitewater rafting trip (7 hrs., includes lunch, $50). Office open daily 7am-10pm.

Taxi: Yellow Cab, 634-5000. $3 first mi., $1.35 each additional mi.
Car Rental: Ugly Duckling, 2128 E. Bijou (634-1914). $18 per day, $108 per week. Open Mon.-Fri. 9am-5:30pm, Sat. 9am-1pm. Must stay in-state and be 21 with major credit card or $200 deposit.
Help Lines: Crisis Emergency Services, 635-7000. 24 hrs.
Post Office: 201 Pikes Peak Ave. (570-5336), at Nevada Ave. Open Mon.-Fri. 7:30am-5:30pm, Sat. 8am-1pm. **ZIP code:** 80903.
Area Code: 719.

Colorado Springs is laid out in a fairly coherent grid of broad, manicured thoroughfares. The mountains are to the west. **Nevada Ave.** is the main north-south strip, known for its many bars and restaurants. **Pikes Peak Ave.** serves as the east-west axis, running parallel to **Colorado Ave.,** which connects with **U.S. 24** on the city's west side. **U.S. 25** from Denver plows through the downtown area. East of Nevada Ave. there are basically only residential homes and large shopping centers. The streets west of Nevada are numbered, with the numbers increasing as you move west. A word of warning: the city's attractions are diffused over a wide area.

ACCOMMODATIONS

Avoid the mostly shabby motels along Nevada Ave. If the youth hostel fails you, head for a nearby campground or the establishments along W. Pikes Peak Ave.

Garden of the Gods Youth Hostel (HI/AYH), 3704 W. Colorado Ave. (475-9450 or 800-345-8197). Take bus #1 west to 37th St. 4-bunk shanties. Showers and bathrooms shared with campground. Immaculate facilities. Bunkrooms are not heated; bring your sleeping bag! Swimming pool, jacuzzi, laundry. $11; members only. Linen included. Open April-Oct.
Apache Court Motel, 3401 W. Pikes Peak Ave. (471-9440). Take bus #1 West down Colorado Ave. to 34th St., walk 1 block north. Very spiffy pink adobe rooms. Doubles have kitchens. A/C and TV, hot tub. Seasonal rates: singles $33 for one person, $37 for two; doubles $36, $50 for two, $5 each additional person; Sept. 15-April $26/$29/$36/$41. No pets. MC, Visa.
Amarillo Motel, 2801 W. Colorado Ave. (635-8539). Take bus #1 West down Colorado Ave. to 28th St. Ask for rooms in the older National Historic Register section. Bunker-like rooms lack windows, but all have kitchens, TV, and phones. Laundry available. Singles $24. Doubles $28-30. Off-season: from $20. MC, Visa.
Motel 6, 3228 N. Chestnut St. (520-5400), at Fillmore St. just west of I-25 exit 145. Take bus #8 west. TV, pool, A/C. Some rooms with unobstructed view of Pikes Peak. Some rooms with unobstructed view of parking lot. Singles $35, doubles $42. Oct.-May roughly $10 less.

CAMPING

Located in the city itself is the four-star **Garden of the Gods Campground,** 3704 W. Colorado Ave. (475-9450 or 800-345-8197). Enjoy flapjack breakfasts Sundays and coffee and doughnuts (only 25¢ each). Large pool and recreation area. (Sites $17, with electricity and water $20, full hookup $22.) Several popular **Pike National Forest** campgrounds lie in the mountains flanking Pikes Peak (generally open May-Sept.). No local transportation serves this area. Some campgrounds clutter around Rte. 67, 5-10 mi. north of **Woodland Park,** which is itself 18 mi. northwest of the Springs on U.S. 24. Others fringe U.S. 24 near the town of Lake George. (Sites at all, $6.) You can always camp off the road on national forest property for free if you are at least 100 yds. from road or stream. The **Forest Service Office,** 601 S. Weber (636-1602), has maps ($3) of the campgrounds and wilderness areas (open Mon.-Fri. 7:30am-4:30pm, summer Mon.-Fri. 7am-6pm). Farther afield, you can camp in the **Eleven Mile State Recreation Area** (748-3401 or 800-678-2267), off a spur road from U.S. 24 near Lake George. (Sites $6.75. Entrance fee $3. Reserve on weekends, but no reservations accepted after July 4.) Last resorts include the **Peak View**

Campground, 4954 N. Nevada Ave. (598-1545; sites $14; with water and electric $15; full hookup $16-18).

FOOD

You can get basic fare or fast food downtown, or try any of the restaurants and small cafes lining W. Colorado Ave.

Poor Richard's Restaurant, 324½ North Tejon (632-7721). The local coffee-house/college hangout. Pizza ($1.75 per slice; $8.75 per pie) and veggie food. Open Sun.-Thurs. 11am-10pm, Fri.-Sat. 11am-midnight. **Poor Richard's Espresso and Dessert Bar** is right next door (577-4291). Bagels and sinful desserts. Espresso 90¢, bagel $1. Sun.-Thurs. 7am-midnight, Fri.-Sat. 7am-1:30am.

Meadow Muffins, 2432 W. Colorado Ave. (633-0583), in a converted warehouse. Bright neon lights, smoke, beer and the "Mighty burger" ($4.50). Visa, MC, AmEx. Open daily 11am-2am.

Henri's, 2427 W. Colorado Ave. (634-9031). Genuine, excellent Mexican food. Popular with locals for 40 years. Fantastic margaritas. Meat, chicken, and cheese enchiladas ($2.25), and great free chips and salsa. Visa, MC, AmEx. Open Tues.-Sat. 11:30am-10pm, Sun. noon-10pm.

SIGHTS AND ENTERTAINMENT

From any part of the town, one can't help noticing the 14,110-ft. summit of **Pikes Peak** on the western horizon. You can climb the peak via the 13-mi. **Barr Burro Trail.** The trailhead is in Manitou Springs by the "Manitou Incline" sign. Catch bus #1 to Ruxton. Don't despair if you don't reach the top—explorer Zebulon Pike never reached it either, and they still named the whole mountain after him. Otherwise, pay the fee to drive up the **Pikes Peak Highway** (684-9383), administered by the Colorado Department of Public Works. (Open May-June 10 daily 9am-3pm, June 11-Sept. 2 7am-6:30pm; hours dependent on weather. $5, kids 6-11 $2.) You can also reserve a seat on the **Pikes Peak Cog Railway,** 515 Ruxton Ave. (685-5401; open May-Oct. 8 daily; round-trip $21, seniors $18 ages 5-11 $9, under 5 free if held on lap). At the summit, you'll see Kansas, the Sangre de Cristo Mountains, and the ranges along the Continental Divide. Expect cold weather; even when the temperature is in the 80s in Colorado Springs; the temperature at the acme only reaches the mid-30s. Roads often remain icy through the summer.

Pikes Peak is not Colorado Springs' only outdoor attraction. Eat amid the *other* Olympians in 300-million-year-old **Garden of the Gods City Park,** 1401 Recreation Way (578-6640). Take Colorado Ave. to 30th St. and then north on Gateway Rd. The park, composed of red rock monuments that Native Americans believed were the bodies of their enemies thrown down by gods, contains many secluded picnic and hiking areas. (Visitors center open daily 9am-5pm; Sept.-June 10am-4pm. Free.) The oft-photographed "balanced rock" is at the park's south entrance. The best vantage point for pictures is from Mesa Rd., off 30th St. on the opposite side of the park. For more strenuous hiking, head for the fantastically contorted caverns of the **Cave of the Winds** (685-5444), 6 mi. west of exit 141 off I-25 on Rte. 24 (guided tours daily every 15 min. 9am-9pm; off-season 10am-5pm). Just above Manitou Springs on Rte. 24 lies the **Manitou Cliff Dwellings Museum** (685-5242), U.S. 24 bypass, where you can wander through a pueblo of ancient Anasazi buildings dating from 1100-1300 (open daily May-Sept. 9am-5pm; $4, kids 7-11 $2, under 6 free).

Buried in a hollowed-out cave 1800 ft. below Cheyenne Mountain, the **North American Air Defense Command Headquarters (NORAD)** (554-7321) was designed to survive even a direct nuclear hit. A 3-mi. tunnel leads to this telecommunication center, which monitors every single plane in the sky. The **Peterson Air Force Base,** on the far east side of the city has a **visitors center** and the **Edward J. Peterson Space Command Museum** (554-4915; open Tues.-Fri. 8:30am-4:30pm, Sat. 9:30am-4:30pm; free).

The **United States Air Force Academy,** a college for future officers, marches 12 mi. north of town on I-25 and is the most popular attraction of the area, with over 1 million visitors each year. Its chapel is made of aluminum, steel, and other materials used in airplanes. On weekdays during the school year, uniformed cadets gather at 12:10pm near the chapel for the cadet lunch formation—a big production just to chow down. The **visitors center** (472-2555) has self-guided tour maps, info on the many special events, and a 12-min. movie every ½ hr. (open daily 9am-5pm).

The **Pioneers' Museum,** downtown at 215 S. Tejon St. (578-6650), covers the settling of Colorado Springs, including a display on the techniques and instruments of a pioneer doctor (open Mon.-Sat. 10am-5pm, Sun. 1-5pm; free). Everything you ever wanted to know about mining awaits at the **Western Museum of Mining and Industry,** 025 N. Gate Rd. (488-0880). Learn how to pan for gold. (Open Mon.-Sat. 9am-4pm, Sun. noon-4pm. $4, students $3.50, seniors and kids under 13 $3.50; closed Dec.-Feb.) Take exit 156-A off I-25 and all your questions about those famous Olympians will be answered at the **U.S. Olympic Complex,** 750 E. Boulder St. (632-5551; tour hotline 578-4444), which offers informative 1-hr. tours every ½ hr. with a tear-jerking film. Watch Olympic hopefuls practice in the afternoons. (Open Mon.-Sat. 9am-5pm, Sun. 10am-noon.) Take bus #1 east to Farragut.

A fun, hokey way to spend an evening is at the **Flying W Ranch,** 3330 Chuck-wagon Rd. (598-4000 or 800-232-3599). Grab a tin plate and chow down at the huge chuckwagon supper ($12) while you watch a Wild West show. Every evening a blacksmith shoes a horse—now that's entertainment!

At night, Colorado College's literati find comfortable reading at **Poor Richard's Espresso Bar** (577-4291), adjacent to the bookstore (see Food above). The bar occasionally hosts comedy, acoustic performances, and readings. (Open Mon.-Thurs. 7am-midnight, Fri.-Sat. 7am-1:30am.) A theater next door (through the coffee shop) usually plays artsy films. The **Dublin House,** 1850 Dominion Way at Academy St. (528-1704), is a popular sports bar, with Sunday night blues downstairs (open daily 4pm-2am; no cover). Call Funfare for current events (see Practical Information)."

■■■ DENVER

In 1858 the discovery of a small amount of gold at the base of the Rocky Mountains brought a premature rush of eager miners to northern Colorado. The town prospered with the patronage of desperadoes who searched the mountains for the mother-lode. The Denver of today was actually made up of three separate towns which fought over the right to name the city until peace was restored with the purchase of this right for a barrel of whiskey. Denver's economy is no longer based on saloons, nor will one get very far with a barrel of whiskey. Literally.

Today, Colorado's capital is the Rockies' largest and fastest growing metropolis. Centrally located between Colorado's eastern plains and western ski resorts, Denver today serves as the industrial, commercial, and cultural nexus of the region and has recently gone to the show with the newest major league baseball team, the Colorado Rockies. The gold mines may be depleted, but Denver retains its best assets—a rich cultural past and clear, sunny weather. The city has doubled in population since 1960 and continues to attract a diverse assortment of people—ski bums, sophisticated city-slickers from the coasts, and, of course, the old-time cowpokes.

PRACTICAL INFORMATION

Emergency: 911

Visitor Information: Denver Metro Convention and Visitors Bureau, 225 West Colfax Ave. (892-1112 or 892-1505), near Civic Center Park just south of the capitol. Open Mon.-Sat. 8am-5pm, Sun. 10am-2pm; winter Mon.-Fri. 8am-5pm, Sat. 9am-1pm. Pick up a free copy of the comprehensive *Denver and Colorado Official Visitors Guide.* **Big John's Information Center,** 1055 19th St. (800-767-4454), at the Greyhound station. Big John, an ex-professional basketball player, offers enthusiastic information on hosteling and activities in Colorado. Stop by for information on tours around Denver and day trips to the mountains. Open Mon.-Sat. 6:15am-noon. **16th St. Ticket Bus,** in the 16th St. Mall at Curtis St. Double-decker bus with visitor information, half-price tickets to local theater performances, and RTD bus info. Open Mon.-Fri. 10am-6pm, Sat. 11am-3pm.

Airports: Stapleton International Airport (398-3844 or 800-247-2336), in northeast Denver. Easily accessible from downtown. RTD bus lines #28, 32, 38 serve the airport. For buses to Denver, take a right out of Gate 12 (E concourse); wait at sign #2. Buses A and B go to Boulder. Cab fare to downtown $8-12. **Ground Transportation Information** on the 1st floor can arrange transport to surrounding areas such as Estes Park, Vail, and other nearby resorts. Open daily 7am-11pm. **Denver International Airport,** in northeast Denver, will be the largest airport in the world (53 sq. mi.) when it opens in Dec. 1993. Thirty min. from downtown, it will be accessible by both taxi and bus, and a high-speed "Air Train" is planned to run between downtown Denver and DIA.

Amtrak: Union Station (534-2812 or 800-872-7245), at 17th St. and Wynkoop, in the northwest corner of downtown. Ticket office open 7am-9pm. One train per day to: Salt Lake City (14 hr., $107); Omaha (9 hr., $105); Chicago (18 hr., $157); Kansas City (12 hr., $137).

Buses: Greyhound, 1055 19th St. (292-6111), downtown. Ticket office open 6:10am-10pm. Four per day to: Cheyenne (3 hr., $18, $14 if purchased 14 days in advance); Albuquerque (12 hr., $68/$59); Kansas City (15 hr., $89/$68); Salt Lake City (12 hr., $59). Also comprehensive service within CO. The **Ski Train-Budweiser Eagle Line,** 555 17th St. (296-4754). Leaves from Amtrak Union Station and treks through the Rockies, stopping in Winter Park (Dec.-April only). Departs Denver at 7:15am, Winter Park at 4:15pm; 2 hr.; $30 round-trip.

Public Transport: Regional Transportation District (RTD), 1600 Blake St. (299-6000). Service within Denver and to Longmont, Evergreen, Conifer, Golden, and the suburbs. Many routes shut down by 9pm or earlier. Fare Mon.-Fri. 6-9am and 4-6pm $1; all other times 50¢; over 65 15¢. Have exact fare. Free 16th Street Mall Shuttle covers 14 blocks downtown. Over 20 buses per day to Boulder (45 min.; $2.50). Call Mon.-Fri. 6am-8pm, Sat.-Sun. 8am-8pm. Bus maps $1.

Gray Line Tours: At the bus station, 19th and Curtis St. (289-2841). In the summer, daily to Rocky Mountain National Park (10 hr.; $36, under 12 $20) and to Pike's Peak and the U.S. Air Force Academy (10 hr.; $45, under 12 $23). Year-round tours of Denver Mountain Parks (3½ hr.; $19, under 12 $10) and of Denver City (2½ hr.; $16, under 12 $8), twice daily in summer.

Taxi: Metro Taxi, 333-3333. **Yellow Cab,** 777-7777. **Zone Cab,** 444-8888. All $1.40 base fare, $1.40 per mi. Ah, the magic of repetitive phone numbers.

Car Rental: Be wary of renting clunkers in the mountains; check out the car before accepting it. More expensive car rentals like Hertz and Avis may be worth it you are going to remote areas. **Rent-a-Heap,** 940 S. Jason St. (698-0345) $18 per day, $108 per week, unlimited free mi., but you must remain in the metro area. Open Mon.-Fri. 8am-5pm, Sat. 8am-1pm. Must have $50 deposit and proof of liability insurance. **Cheap Heaps Rent-a-Car,** 6005 E. Colfax Ave. (393-0028). $15 per day, $110 weekly; 30 free mi. per day, 15¢ each additional mi., $15 surcharge if you're heading for the mountains. Open Mon.-Fri. 8am-6pm, Sat. 8am-2pm. Must have at least $100 deposit and proof of liability insurance or $7 additional insurance charge per day. For both, must be at least 21 and stay in CO.

Auto Transport Company: Auto Driveaway, 5777 E. Evans Ave. (757-1211); take bus #21 to Hollis and Evans. Open Mon.-Fri. 8:30am-5pm. Must have a $250 cash deposit and a valid drivers license, be at least 21, and have three local references (last requirement waived for foreigners). There is a $10 processing fee.

Help Lines: Contact Lifeline, 237-4537, open Mon.-Fri. 7am-11pm, Sat. 3-11pm. Sun. 7-11pm. **Rape Crisis,** 329-9922. 24 hrs. Office open Mon.-Fri. 9am-5pm; call **Comitus** 343-9890, for immediate crises.

Post Office: 951 20th St. Mon-Fri. 9am-5pm, Sat. 9am-noon. **ZIP code:** 80202.

Area Code: 303.

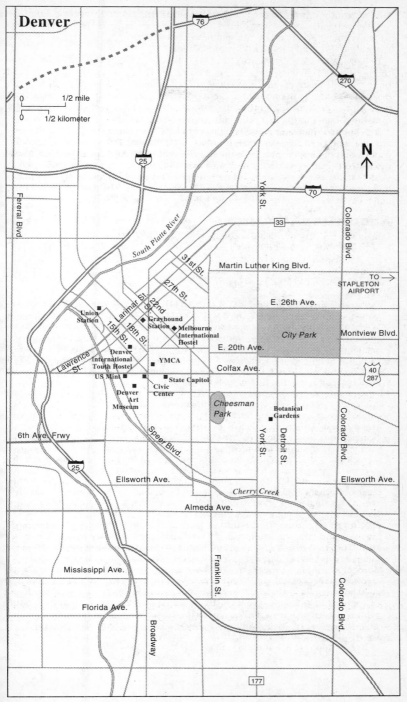

DENVER

Denver

0 | 1/2 mile
0 | 1/2 kilometer

N

Fereral Blvd.

South Platte River

York St.

Colorado Blvd.

TO →
STAPLETON
AIRPORT

Martin Luther King Blvd.

31 st St.

27th St.

22nd St.

Larimar St.

18th St.

15th St.

Lawrence St.

Union Station

Grayhound Station

Melbourne International Hostel

Denver International Touth Hostel

US Mint

Denver Art Museum

YMCA

State Capitol

Civic Center

E. 26th Ave.

City Park

Montview Blvd.

E. 20th Ave.

Colfax Ave.

Cheesman Park

Botanical Gardens

York St.

Detroit St.

Colorado Blvd.

6th Ave. Frwy

Speer Blvd.

Ellsworth Ave.

Ellsworth Ave.

Cherry Creek

Almeda Ave.

Mississippi Ave.

Franklin St.

Florida Ave.

Broadway

Colorado Blvd.

During rush hour, traffic sits at a virtual standstill between Denver and Colorado Springs. I-70 links Denver with Grand Junction (250 mi. west) and Kansas City (600 mi. east). Rte. 285 cuts south through the central Rockies, opening up the Saguache and Sangre de Cristo Ranges to easy exploration.

Broadway divides east Denver from west Denver and **Ellsworth Avenue** forms the north-south dividing line. Streets west of Broadway progress in alphabetical order, while the streets north of Ellsworth are numbered. Streets downtown run diagonal to those in the rest of the metropolis. Keep in mind that many of the avenues on the eastern side of the city become numbered *streets* downtown. Most even-numbered thoroughfares downtown run only east-west.

The hub of downtown is the **16th Street Mall.** Few crimes occur in the immediate area, but avoid the west end of Colfax Ave., the east side of town beyond the capitol, and the upper reaches of the *Barrio* (25th-34th St.) at night. **Lower downtown** ("Lo Do" to locals), a 22-block area from 20th St. to Speer, and from Wynkoop St., S.E. to Market St., is on the northern edge of downtown Denver. The Victorian buildings reflect the architecture of the silver boom era at the turn of the century, and today house trendy restaurants, art galleries, offices, and shops.

ACCOMMODATIONS

Denver offers many affordable accommodations within easy reach of downtown by foot or bus. Hostelers with specific interests (or no ideas at all) can see "Big John" Schrant at the Greyhound bus station for information and directions. The hotels in the downtown area are fairly expensive, but for discount packages that include events and tours, call **Mile High Lights** (800-489-4888; open Mon.-Fri. 8am-5pm).

Melbourne International Hostel (HI/AYH), 607 22nd St. (292-6386), downtown at Welton St. Owned by WWII pilot Leonard Schmitt and run by his son Gary, the Melbourne is a clean, well-run hostel, just 6 blocks from the 16th St. Mall. Ask Gary (the office is in the laundromat downstairs) about the great local restaurants and music clubs. Members: dorms $8, private rooms $15, couples $20; for nonmembers: $9 dorms, $18 private, $20 doubles. Sheet rental $2. $10 key deposit. MC, Visa. Call ahead. Women and lone travelers should be aware that this hostel is not in the best neighborhood.

Denver International Youth Hostel, 630 E. 16th Ave. (832-9996), 10 blocks east of the bus station, 4 blocks north of downtown. Take bus #15 to Washington St., 1 block away or take free 16th St. shuttle to Broadway and walk east on 16th Ave. for 6 blocks. Office open daily 8am-10am, 5pm-10:30pm. Dorm-style rooms with kitchen and laundry facilities. Free meal-fixings in the fridge. $7 with chore, $10 without. $1 discount with a copy of this guide. Sheet rental $1. Call to arrange arrival plans during office hours. "Professor K's" full-day tour of Denver and the surrounding mountains leave from the hostel Mon.-Sat. at 9:15am ($12).

Franklin House B&B, 1620 Franklin St. (331-9106). European-style inn within walking distance of downtown. Clean and spacious rooms, friendly hosts, free breakfast. Singles $20. Doubles $32, with private bath $42. $5 for each additional person. MC, Visa, and travelers checks welcome.

YMCA, 25 E. 16th St. (861-8300) at Lincoln St. Divided into 3 parts for men, women and families. Laundry and TV rooms. Single $20 per day, $81 weekly. With a shared bath $22.50, private bath $27. Doubles with bath $40.25, with shared bath $38 per day, $125 weekly. $12 key deposit. MC, Visa.

Motel 6, 8 locations in the greater Denver area, all with A/C, pool, and color TV. All are accessible by local bus. North: 6 W. 83rd Pl. (429-1550); Northwest: 10300 S. I-70 Frontage Rd. (467-3172), 9920 W. 49th Ave. (455-8888); East (near Stapleton Airport): 12020 E. 39th Ave. (371-1980), 12033 E. 38th Ave. (371-0740); South: 480 S. Wadsworth Blvd. (232-4924), 9201 E. Arapahoe Rd. (790-8220). Singles $20-30, second adult $6, additional adults $3. All major credit cards accepted.

Big Al's International Hostel, 1840 E. 18th Ave. (393-7165). Right across from #20 bus stop. Big Al's hosts a young crowd, and if you don't mind clutter, cobwebs, a rambunctious puppy, and long waits for the single shower, you'll feel like part of the family in no time. Breakfast included. Dorms $10, singles $20.

CAMPING

There are plenty of places to camp in the Denver area. Contact the Metro-Regional office of the **Colorado Division of Parks and Recreation** (791-1957; open Mon.-Fri. 9am-5pm) for more info on campgrounds, or **Denver Mountain Parks Reservations** (331-4029).

Cherry Creek Lake Recreation Area (699-3860 or 800-678-2267). Take I-25 to exit 200, then west on Rte. 225 for about 3 mi. and south on Parker Rd.—follow the signs. Take the "Parker Road" bus. The 102 sites fill only on summer weekends. Sites $7. Entrance fee $4. $6.75 reservation fee. Max. 90 days advance for reservations. Min. 14 days if reserving by check; 3 days for MC or Visa.

Chatfield Reservoir (791-7275 or 800-470-1144). Take Rte. 75 or 85 4 mi. past the center of Littleton to 153 well-developed sites. Sites $7, with electricity $10. Open mid-May to mid-Oct. Make reservations for weekends.

Aspen Meadows Campground (470-1144), 19 mi. south of Nederland (open Mon.-Fri. 9am-5pm). 35 tent sites on rugged terrain. Sites $7. Entrance fee $3.

National Forest Campgrounds are plentiful in the mountains 25 mi. west of Denver near Idaho Springs, Rte. 103 and 40, and in the region around Deckers, 30 mi. southwest of downtown on Rte. 67. 18 marked sites, but difficult to find. **Painted Rocks Campground** (719-636-1602), on Rte. 67, in the Pikes Peak Ranger District. Sites $7. **Top of the World** (236-7386), off Pine Junction on Rte. 126. Look down on creation. Free but no water. 7 units. Most sites open May-Sept. Call ahead or pick up maps at the National Forest's Rocky Mountain Regional Headquarters, 11177 W. 8th Ave., Lakewood (236-9431; open Mon.-Fri. 8am-5pm).

FOOD

Downtown Denver is great for inexpensive restaurants, many specializing in Mexican and Southwestern dishes. Eat al fresco and people-watch at the cafes along the 16th St. Mall. Or, follow the opera music to **Tristan's Hot Dogs** at the corner of Champa and 16th St. (Hot dogs, sodas, and chips, each 50¢; open Mon.-Fri. 9:30am-2:30pm.) The Food Court on the third floor of the **Tabor Center**, at the north end of the Mall, houses a variety of small fast food restaurants from Chinese to barbecue (open Mon.-Fri. 10am-9pm, Sat. 10am-6pm, Sun. noon-5pm). **Sakura Square,** at 19th St. and Larimer, offers authentic Japanese food in its restaurants and markets.

Colorado's distance from the ocean may make you wonder about *Rocky Mountain oysters*. This delicacy of fried bull testicles, and other buffalo-meat specialties can be found at the **Denver Buffalo Company,** 1109 Lincoln St. (832-0080). Expensive, but it may be worth a visit so you can tell the folks about it back home.

The Market, 1445 Larimer Sq. (534-5140), downtown. Popular with a young artsy crowd that people-watches from behind salads, pastry, and oversized magazines. Bring your sunglasses and your attitude so they won't know you're a tourist. Cappuccino $2, sandwiches $4-5. Open Mon.-Tues. 6:45am-6pm, Wed.-Thurs. 6:45am-10pm, Fri. 6:45am-midnight, Sat. 8am-midnight, Sun. 8:30am-6pm.

The Old Spaghetti Factory (295-1864), 18th and Lawrence, 1 block from Larimer St. Part of a national chain. Located in a gorgeously renovated old tramway building. Large, delicious spaghetti dinner with salad, bread, coffee, and ice cream, only $4.25. Open for lunch Mon.-Fri. 11:30am-2pm; for dinner Mon.-Thurs. 5-10pm, Fri.-Sat. 5-11pm, Sun. 4-10pm. MC, Visa. Don't miss this great deal!

City Spirit Cafe, 1434 Blake St. (575-0022), a few blocks from the north end of the 16th St. Mall. Check out the funky decor with waitstaff to match. Serving delicious salads ($6), vegetarian dishes (try the City Smart Burrita $5.50), and homemade desserts. Live music on Fri. and Sat. after 9pm coupled with $5 minimum; must be 21 with ID. Mon.-Thurs. 11-1am, Fri.-Sat. 11-2am. MC, Visa.

DENVER

Wynkoop Brewery (297-2700), at 18th St. and Wynkoop across from Union Station. An American pub in a renovated warehouse that serves beer on tap ($2.75 per pint), an Alfalfa mead, and a homemade rootbeer. Try one of their favorites ($4.25-6.50) for lunch or dinner and then head upstairs to the **Jazz Works** for live entertainment. (Cover $2 weekdays, $5 weekends.) Brewery open Mon.-Sat. 11am-2am, Sun. 11am-midnight. Free brewery tours Sat. 1-5pm.

Mercury Cafe, 2199 California (294-9281). Just across from the Melbourne Hostel. A wonderful surprise awaits you inside—decorated like an old tea parlor. Home-baked wheat bread and reasonably priced lunch and dinner items. Sandwiches $5, 10-oz. sirloin with bread, potato, and vegetable $7.50. Tues.-Thurs. 7am-2:30pm, 5:30-10pm (11pm in summer), Fri. 5:30-11pm, Sat. 8am-3pm, 5:30-11pm, Sun. 9am-3pm, 5:30-10pm. Nightclub open until 2am every night. Nightly events include live bands, open stage, and poetry readings.

Goldie's Deli, 511 16th St. (623-6007), at the Glenarm on the Mall. Great for pic-nic-fixings—or eat at outside tables. Sandwiches and salads $4, with low fat, low cholesterol options. Open Mon.-Sat. 11am-4pm.

The Eggshell, 1520 Blake St. (623-7555). Huge breakfast specials $2. Sandwiches $4-6. Open Mon.-Fri. 6:30am-2pm, Sat 7am-2pm., Sun. 7:30am-2pm.

SIGHTS

Denver's mild, dry climate and 300 days of sunshine (sorry, no money-back guarantees) promises pleasant days. The **Denver Metro Visitors Bureau,** across from the **U.S. Mint,** is a good place to plan tours in the city or to the mountains. A great deal is the **Cultural Connection Trolley** (299-6000), where $1 takes you to over 20 of the city's main attractions. The 1-hr. tour runs daily every 20 min. from 9:20am to 5:50pm; buy your tickets from the driver. The tour begins at the **Denver Performing Arts Complex** (follow the arches to the end of Curtis, at 14th St.), but can be picked up near any of the attractions. Look for the green and red sign. The fare entitles you to a full day of transportation, so feel free to get off at any or all of the sights.

Don't be surprised if the 15th step on the west side of the **State Capitol Building** is crowded—it is exactly 5280 ft. (1 mi.) above sea level. The gallery under the 24-karat-gold-covered dome gives a great view of the Rocky Mountains. Free tours include visits to the Senate and House of Representatives chambers (every 30 min., Mon.-Fri. 9:30am-3:30pm, Sat. (in summer only) 9:30am-3pm.

Just a few blocks from the capitol and the U.S. Mint stands the **Denver Art Museum,** 100 W. 14th Ave. (640-2793). Architect Gio Ponti designed this six-story "vertical" museum in order to accommodate totem poles and period architecture. The museum's collection of Native American art rivals any in the world. The fabulous third floor of pre-Columbian art of the Americas resembles an archeological excavation site, with temples, huts, and idols. Call for info on special exhibits. (Open Tues.-Sat. 10am-5pm, Sun. noon-5pm. $3, seniors and students $1.50, Sat. free for everyone.) Housed in the Navarre Building, the **Museum of Western Art,** 1727 Tremont Place (296-1880), holds a stellar collection of Russell, Benton, O'Keeffe, and Grant Wood paintings and drawings. You can still see the tunnel which connects this one-time brothel to the **Brown Palace,** across the street at 321 17th St. (297-3111), an historic grand hotel that once hosted presidents, generals, and movie stars. Step in to see the beautiful atrium lobby and watch the rich and famous sip tea. **The Black American West Museum and Heritage Center,** 91 California St. (292-2566), will show you a side of frontier history left unexplored by John Wayne movies. Come here to learn that one-third of all cowboys were African-American, and discover other details left out of textbooks. (Open Wed.-Fri. 10am-2pm, Sat. noon-5pm, Sun. 2-5pm. $2, seniors $1.50, ages 12-16 75¢, under 12 50¢.)

The **Natural History Museum,** 2001 Colorado Blvd. (322-7009), in City Park, presents amazingly lifelike wildlife sculptures and dioramas (open daily 9am-5pm; $4.50, ages 4-12 and seniors $2.50). The Natural History Museum complex includes the **Gates Planetarium** with its popular "Laserdrive" show and an **IMAX theater** (370-6300; call for shows, times and current prices). Across the park roars the **Den-**

ver **Zoo** (331-4100), at E. 23rd St. and Steele, where you can view the live versions of the museum specimens (open daily 9am-6pm; $6, seniors and kids 4-12 $3).

A modern reminder of Colorado's old silver mining days, the **U.S. Mint,** 320 W. Colfax (844-3582), issues U.S. coins with a small "D" for Denver embossed beneath the date. Free 20-min. tours, every 20 min. in summer and every 30 min. in winter, will lead you past a million-dollar pile of gold bars and expose you to the deafening roar of money-making machines that churn out a total of 20 million shiny coins per day. And, no, they do not give free samples. Arrive early; summer lines often reach around the block. (Open Mon.-Tues., Thurs.-Fri. 8am-3pm, Wed. 9am-3pm.)

The dramatic **Red Rocks Amphitheater and Park,** 12 mi. southwest of Denver on I-70, is carved into red sandstone. As the sun sets over the city, even the most well-known of performers must compete with the natural spectacle behind them. (For tickets call 694-1234, Mon.-Fri. 8am-5pm. Park admission free. Shows $15-40.) West of Denver in nearby Golden is the **Coors Brewery** (277-2337), 3rd and Ford St., founded by brewer Adolf Coors. (Free tours Mon.-Sat. 10am-4pm.)

For outdoor enthusiasts Denver has many public parks for bicycling, walking, or lolling about in the sun. **Cheesman Park** (take bus #6 or #10), one of the 205 parks in Denver, offers a view of the snow-capped peaks of the Rockies. For Denver Parks info, call 698-4900. For a wilder park experience from June-Sept., take I-70 from Golden to Idaho Springs, and then pick up Rte. 103 south over the summit (14,260 ft.) of **Mt. Evans.** Check with **Colorado Division of Parks and Outdoor Recreation** (866-3437) about road conditions in fall and winter (open Mon.-Fri. 8am-5pm).

A newly paved bike and foot trail runs along Cherry Creek for 20 mi. and offers a good workout. If you grow tired of these wimpy sports on land, **Bungee Jumping Colorado** (322-5867) will let you fling yourself off the highest bungee jumping tower in North America (130 ft.) for a sizeable fee ($45 for the first jump, $40 for each additional jump; you must be at least 18; MC & Visa accepted).

ENTERTAINMENT AND NIGHTLIFE

Denver's local restaurants and bars cater to young, college-age singles. Pick up a copy of *Westwood* for details on the downtown club scene and local events. At **Muddy's Java Cafe,** 2200 Champa St. (298-1631), you can spend nights reading a novel from their bookstore while you make your way through the all-you-can-eat Beggar's Banquet ($5; 6-8pm) or listening to live music (Fri.-Sat. 9pm-1am; cover $1). Muddy's will even serve you an early breakfast after a long night of partying. (Open daily 6pm-4am.) The "Hill of the Grasshopper," **El Chapultepec** (295-9126), 20th and Market St., is an authentic hole-in-the-wall bar with live music every night (open daily 7-2am; one drink min. per set). At **Bangles,** 4501 E. Virginia (377-2702), live bands blare in the evening, and the afternoon volleyball matches often become jubilant free-for-alls after a few pitchers of beer ($4). (Open daily 8pm-2am. Volley-ball games Tues.-Fri. at 5:30pm. Cover $1-5.)

From April to Sept. Denver's new Major League Baseball team, the **Colorado Rockies** (292-0200), rock Mile High Stadium. It doesn't matter if they win or lose (they lose)—the local enthusiasm is infectious. (Tickets $4-10, $1 on game day to sit in the Rock Pile.) In the fall the **Denver Broncos** (433-7466) reclaim the stadium and football fever spreads throughout the state.

Every January, Denver hosts the world's largest rodeo, the **National Western Stock Show** (297-1166). Cowfolk compete for prize money while over 10,000 head of cattle compete for "Best of Breed." **A Taste of Colorado** takes place during the last weekend in August, featuring a large outdoor celebration at Civic Center Park, near the capitol, with food vendors and open-air concerts from Colorado's own.

■ Mountain Resorts Near Denver

Summit County Skiers, hikers, and mountain bikers will find a sportman's par-adise in the sit towns of Summit County, about 55 mi. west of Denver on I-70. All six towns fall under the jurisdiction of the **Summit County Chamber of Commerce,**

DENVER

110 Summit Blvd., P.O. Box 214, Frisco 80443 (668-5800), which provides information on current area events (open daily 9am-5pm). Breckenridge, Dillon, Copper Mountain, Keystone, Frisco, and Silverthorne are extremely popular with skiers and outdoorsmen from in-state, but provide somewhat of a respite from the expensive and adulterated resorts of Aspen and Vail. Even if you aren't a sportsman, stay at the fantastic, incredible, amazing, perfect **Alpen Hütte (HI/AYH)**, 471 Rainbow Dr. (468-6336), in Silverthorne. The Greyhound bus from Denver stops just outside the door, as does the **Summit Stage** shuttle bus, which provides free transportation to and from any on the Summit County towns. This immaculate and delightful hostel is a bargain of unsurpassed quality. (Office open 7am-noon, 4-11pm. Guest rooms closed 9:30am-3:30pm. Curfew midnight. Rates vary seasonally; summer rates are lowest ($10, non-members $12), while winter rates are highest, peaking at $23. Discounts for groups. On-site parking, TV, wheelchair accessible. Lockers $5 deposit. Free sheets and towels. Reservations recommended.) **Breckenridge**, only 15 min. away by car, is a more fashionable town than Silverthorne. Despite the many expensive restaurants and stores, you can still find reasonable accommodations at the **Fireside Inn**, 114 N. French St. (453-6456), one block east of Main St. Located at the base of the mountain, this B&B is convenient for those skiers who want to be in the center of the action. This burg gets pretty hectic during ski season. (Closed in May. Rates vary seasonally; dormitory $15, private rooms $40-60 in summer, up to $27/$80-130.) Reservation deposit fee (first two nights lodging) due within 10 days of reservation; balance is due 30 days before arrival.

Winter Park Sixty-eight mi. northwest of Denver on U.S. 40, Winter Park slaloms among delicious-smelling mountain pines, surrounded by 600 mi. of skiing, hiking, and biking trails. The **Winter Park-Fraser Valley Chamber of Commerce**, 50 Vasquez Rd. (726-4118; from Denver 800-422-0666), provides information about skiing at the Winter Park Mary Jane Ski Area (open daily 8am-7pm; winter 9am-5pm). The chamber also serves as the Greyhound depot (2 buses per day from Denver, 2 hr., $11). **Home James Transportation Services** (726-5060 or 800-451-4844), runs door-to-door shuttles to and from Denver (6 per day Nov. 18-Dec. 23 and April 5-April 18; 10 per day Dec. 24-April 4; $24 one-way, $46 round-trip). Call ahead for reservations. From December to April, the **Ski Train-Budweiser Eagle Line**, (296-4754) leaves from Denver's Union Station Sat.-Sun. at 7:15am, arriving in Winter Park at 9:30am, and departing Winter Park at 4:15pm ($30 round-trip).

On the town's southern boundary, Polly and Bill run the **Winter Park Hostel (HI/AYH)** (726-5356), one block from the Greyhound stop and 2 mi. from Amtrak (free shuttle). The hostel is made up of roomy mobile units, each with its own kitchen, bathroom, and living area (32 beds including 2-, 4-, and 6- person bunkrooms and 3 double-bed rooms). Free shuttles run to the ski area and supermarket. Hosteler's discounts save you money on bike and ski rentals, raft trips, and restaurants. (Nov.-April $11, non-members $14; May-Oct. $7.50, non-members $9.50. Private room $3 more, $1 per extra person. Linen fee $2 for the sleep-sackless. Check-in 8-11:30am, 4-7pm. Closed April 15-June15.) Call for reservations during ski season or if you need a lift from Amtrak or late arrival. **Le Ski Lab**, 7894 U.S. 40 (726-9841), conveniently next door, offers discounts for hostelers (mountain bikes $9 per day; ski rentals $8). **Timber Rafting** offers an all-day rafting trip ($35 for hostelers, includes transportation and lunch). The **Alpine Slide**, at 1½ mi., is Colorado's longest. (Open daily June 5-Sept. 6, weekends through Sept. 9:30am-5pm; June 26-Aug. 15 until 7pm; $4, seniors and kids $3.) You and your bike can ride the **Zephyr Express** chairlift to access some challenging trails. (Open June 19-Sept. 6 9:30am-4:30pm; June 26-Aug. 15 until 6:30pm; $4 per day.) Every Saturday night at 6pm in July and August, get trampled underfoot at the **High Country Stampede Rodeo** at the John Work Arena, west of Fraser on County Rd. 73 ($6, children $3).

■■■ GRAND JUNCTION

Grand Junction gets its hyperbolic name from its location at the confluence of the Colorado and Gunnison Rivers and the conjunction-junction of the Río Grande and Denver Railroads. As western Colorado's trade and agricultural center, this unassuming city serves as a fantastic base from which to explore Colorado National Monument, the Gunnison Valley, the Grand Mesa, and the western San Juans.

Practical Information Grand Junction lies at the present juncture of U.S. 50 and U.S. 6 in northwestern Colorado. Denver is 228 mi. to the east; Salt Lake City 240 mi. to the west. For literature on the area, visit the **Tourist Information Center,** 759 Horizon Dr., Suite F (243-1001; open daily 9am-8pm). The **bus station,** 230 S. 5th St. (242-6012), has service to: Denver (3 per day, 7 hr., $24); Durango (1 per day, 4 hr., $32); Salt Lake City (1 per day, $37); Los Angeles (3 per day, $95). (Open Mon.-Fri. 3:30am-6pm and 8:30-9:30pm, Sun. 3:30-8am and 1:30-3:30pm.) **Amtrak,** 337 S. 1st St. (241-2733 or 800-872-7245), chugs once a day to Denver ($67) and Salt Lake City ($67). (Open daily 10am-5pm.)

Many of the sites are difficult to get to without a car, but the tours from the Melrose Hostel are fantastic. If you've got a wad to blow, you can get a rental car. **Avis Rent-A-Car** (244-9170), on Walker Field, rents economy cars for $36 per day, $138 per week with unlimited mi. You must be 25 with a major credit card. For the under-25 set, **Thrifty Car Rental** (243-7556 or 800-367-2277), on 752 Horizon Dr., rents compact cars for $32 per day, $150 per week with unlimited mi. You'll also get a discount here if you're staying at the Melrose.

Grand Junction's **post office** is at 241 N. 4th St. (244-3401; open Mon.-Fri. 8:30am-5pm, Sat. 9am-12:45pm). Its **ZIP code** is 81502; the **area code** is 303.

Accommodations and Food One reason to go to Grand Junction is the **Melrose Hotel (HI/AYH),** 337 Colorado Ave. (242-9636 or 800-430-4555), between 3rd and 4th St.. The hotel is old-fashioned with spacious, spotless rooms. Owners Marcus and Sabrina will make you feel at home and direct you to the best deals in town, including specials on movie tickets and all-you-can-eat specials. Marcus' tours to Arches National Park, Colorado National Monument, and Grand Mesa are a must-see, taking you off tourist paths for some serious sight-seeing. By now, he has probably been banned from ranger-guided tours because of his wisecracks (and because he is more informed than the rangers). A super-value package ($85) includes four nights at the hostel and three tours. (Dorms $10, including tax, breakfast, and kitchen facilities. Singles $18, with private bath $25. Doubles $23.50, with TV and private bath $30. Call for special winter rates. Visa & MC.) **Lo Master Motel,** 2858 North Ave. (243-3230), has singles as low as $17, doubles $21. Camp in **Highline State Park** (858-7208), 22 mi. from town and 7 mi. north of exit 15 on I-70 with fishing access and restrooms, or **Island Acres State Park** (464-0548), 15 mi. east on the banks of the Colorado River (both $6 per site plus $3 day pass to enter the park).

Some affordable restaurants conjoin grandly here. **Dos Hombres Restaurant,** 421 Branch Dr. (242-8861), just south of Broadway (Rte. 340) on the southern bank of the Colorado River, serves great Mexican food in a casual, family-style setting. (Combination dinners $3.75-6. Open daily 11am-10pm.) **Pufferbelly Station Restaurant,** 337 S. 1st St. (242-1600), by the Amtrak station, has a wide selection of sandwiches, salads, and entrees. Gotta love those generous portions with that homestyle touch. Try the pancake special (6 pancakes, 2 strips of bacon, and an egg—$3). Sunday buffet breakfast ($5) is served from 8am to noon. (Open daily 6am-2pm). **City Market,** 1909 N. 1st St. (243-0842), is open 24 hrs. and has everything you could ever want.

Sights Grand Junction also offers wineries and a variety of a few small but interesting museums. The **Museum of Western Colorado,** 248 S. 4th St. (242-0971), traces the history of western Colorado and includes an extensive collection of historical documents. ($2, ages 2-17 $1; open Mon.-Sat. 10am-4:45pm; closed Mon. during winter.) **Dinosaur Valley,** an extension of the museum, is located two blocks away at 362 Main St. Moving and growling dinosaurs entertain children, while displays of serious paleontological research cater to adults. ($4, ages 2-12 $2.50. Open daily 9am-5:30pm; Sept.-May 10am-4:30pm.)

■ Near Grand Junction: Colorado National Monument

European settlers once dismissed the arid, red, fearsome canyons and striated sand-stone of the **Colorado National Monument** as unusable land. If not for the efforts of intrepid trapper and hunter John Otto, who helped petition in 1911 for the land to become a national monument, the area's natural beauty might very well have been dismissed as a stony wasteland. Facilitate your explorations by renting a mountain bike in nearby Grand Junction at **Cycle Center,** 141 N. 7th St. (242-2541; $8 per ½-day, $15 per day. Open Mon.-Fri. 9:30am-6pm; Sat. 9:30am-5pm.)

Saddlehorn Campground offers campsites in the monument on a first come, first served basis, with picnic tables, grills, and restrooms (sites $7; free in winter). The **Bureau of Land Management** (244-3000; open Mon.-Fri. 7:30am-5pm) maintains three free, less-developed, "campgrounds" near **Glade Park** at Mud Springs. Bring your own water. **Little Dolores Fall,** 10½ mi. west of Glade Park, has fishing and swimming. The monument charges an additional admission fee of $4 per vehicle, $2 per cyclist or hiker, and is free for the disabled and those 62 and over. Check in at the monument **headquarters and visitors center** (858-3617), near the camp-ground on the Fruita side of the monument, and see the slightly spiritual 12-min. slideshow (every ½ hr., 8am-7:30pm). No permit is required. (Open daily 8am-8pm; off-season Mon.-Fri. 8am-4:30pm.)

■■■ GRAND MESA

Fifty mi. east of Grand Junction plops Grand Mesa ("Large Table"), the world's larg-est flat-top mountain. An ancient Native American story tells how an enormous eagle who lived on the rim of Grand Mesa captured a human child in its beak and flew away. The child's vengeful father found the eagle's nest and tossed out the baby eagles, who then became lunch for a serpent sunning at the base of the Mesa. In turn, the mother eagle snatched up the viper, flew to a dizzying height, and tore it to pieces, sending snake segments careening to the earth to make deep impres-sions in Grand Mesa; this explains the area's many lakes. Stodgy geologists claim that some 600 million years ago, a 300-ft.-thick flow of lava covered the area where the mesa now stands. Since then, wind and rain has eroded the surrounding land by over 5000 ft., leaving only the pitted, rocky eagle perch.

Whatever the Mesa's origin, this area, as you would expect, offers numerous out-door attractions, including fine **backcountry hiking**. To reach Grand Mesa from Grand Junction, take I-70 eastbound to Plateau Creek, where Rte. 65 cuts off into the long climb through the spruce trees to the top of the mesa. Near the top is the Land's End turn-off leading to the very edge of Grand Mesa, some 12 mi. down a well-maintained dirt road (closed in winter). On a clear day, you can see halfway across Utah. The higher areas of the Mesa remain cool into summer, so be sure to bring a sweater and long pants if you plan to venture from the car.

The mesa not only has an excellent view, but excellent camping as well. The Grand Mesa National Forest Service maintains a dozen **campsites** on the mesa; **Carp Lake, Island Lake,** and **Ward Lake** charge $7 each, and the rest are free. The district **forest service,** 764 Horizon Dr. (242-8211), in Grand Junction, disseminates truck-loads of info (open Mon.-Fri. 8am-5pm). Buy a map of the mesa's trails, campsites, and trout ponds ($2.50) here. **Vega State Park** (487-3407), 12 mi. east of Colbrain off Rte. 330, also offers camping in the high country. (Park entrance fee $3 per vehicle; campsites $6 per night.)

The **Alexander Lake Lodge** (856-6700), off scenic Rte. 65, is a good place to stop if you're cold, tired, or hungry. This old hunting lodge serves up burgers ($5), pasta dinners with salad and bread ($8), hot cocoa to warm you up ($1), and more (open 8am-8pm). The Lodge also runs a general store and rents out 6 cabins (3 with kitchenettes) for $40 ($15 per additional person). Mountain bikes are available at $5 per hr., $25 per day. There are over 200 lakes full of rainbow trout on the Mesa.

■■■ GREAT SAND DUNES NATIONAL MONUMENT

After Colorado's splendid mountains begin to look the same to you, make a path to the unique waves of grainy sand at the northwest edge of the **San Luis Valley.** The 700-ft. dunes lap the base of the **Sangre de Cristo Range,** representing thousands of years of wind-blown accumulation. The progress of the dunes at passes in the range is checked by the shallow but persistent **Medano Creek.** Visitors can wade across the creek from April to mid-July. For a short hike, head out on **Mosca Trail,** a ½-mi. jaunt into the desert sands. Try to avoid the intense afternoon heat.

Rangers preside over daily naturalist activities, hikes, and other programs. Full schedules are available at the **visitors center** (719-378-2312), ½-mi. past the entrance gate, where you can also view a 15-minute film on the dunes, shown every ½-hour. (Open daily 8am-7pm; Memorial Day-Labor Day 8am-5pm. Entrance fee for vehicles $4, pedestrians and bikers $2.) For more info contact the Superintendent, Great Sand Dunes National Monument, Mosca, CO 81146 (378-2312).

For those who thirst for more than just the first wave of dunes, the **Oasis** complex (378-2222) on the southern boundary also provides four-wheel-drive tours of the backcountry. The three-hour tour takes the rugged Medano Pass Primitive Road into the nether regions of the monument. (2 tours daily; 2 hr.; $14, kids 5-11 $8.)

Pinyon Flats, the monument's primitive campground, fills quickly in summer. Camping here among the prickly pear cacti is on a first-come, first-served basis. Bring mosquito repellent in June. (Sites $8.) If the park's sites are full, you can camp at Oasis. (Sites $9 for 2 people, with hookup $13.50. Each additional person $2.50. Showers included. Cabins and tepees $20 for 2 people.) **Backcountry camping** requires a free permit. For information on nearby National Forest Campgrounds, contact the Río Grande National Forest Service Office, 1803 W. U.S. 160, Monte Vista, CO 81144 (852-5941). All developed sites are $8.

Great Sand Dunes National Monument blows 32 mi. northeast of Alamosa and 112 mi. west of Pueblo, on Rte. 150 off U.S. 160. **Greyhound** sends one bus per day out of Denver to Alamosa (5 hr.; $40; see Denver: Practical Information), with a depot at 8480 Stockton St. (589-4948; open Mon.-Fri. 10am-4:30pm, Sat. 3-4:30pm). The country road from Mosca on Rte. 17 is strictly for four-wheel-drive vehicles. In case of an **emergency** within the park, call 911.

■■■ ROCKY MOUNTAIN NATIONAL PARK

Try to visualize every rustic and rugged Grape Nuts and Coors commercial you have ever seen on television. Cool glacier-fed brooks babble. Deer graze in an alpine meadow. A deep azure lake mirrors the scene, its tranquility disturbed only by a leaping fish. All around, snow-streaked crags pierce a clear summer sky. Hawks describe lazy circles overhead. Ahhh, *this* is Colorado. *This* is Rocky Mountain National Park. Although purists disparage its overpopularity, this remarkable sanctuary makes even the slickest city dweller don a flannel shirt and take in some of the best scenery in the Rockies. The lack of mineral resources may have been a disap-

ROCKY MOUNTAIN NATIONAL PARK

pointment to the hopeful miners who attacked the mountains with a vengeance in the 1880s, but it is only because the land was so profitless that today we are able to appreciate the park's preserved beauty. Because of the park's great size and diversity, visitors often find that they need a week or more to fully explore its offerings.

The mountain wilds are made accessible by tourist towns on the park's borders and by **Trail Ridge Rd. (U.S. 34),** the highest continuously paved road in the U.S., which runs 45 mi. through the park from the town of **Grand Lake** to the town of **Estes Park.** The Ute shied away from **Grand Lake,** believing that mists rising from its surface were the spirits of rafters who drowned in a storm. Today, this glacial lake and its eponymous town squat in the west end of the park. At the road's peak of over 2 vertical mi., oxygen is rare and an eerie silence prevails among the low vegetation of the tundra. Closed in winter for obvious reasons (like lots of snow).

PRACTICAL INFORMATION

Emergency: 911. Estes Park police 586-4465; Grand Lake police 627-3322.
Visitor Information: Estes Park Chamber of Commerce, P.O. Box 3050, Estes Park 80517, at 500 Big Thompson Hwy. (586-4431 or 800-443-7837). Slightly east of downtown. Open Mon.-Sat. 8am-7:30pm, Sun. 9am-5:30pm; Sept.-May Mon.-Sat. 9am-5pm, Sun. 10am-4pm. **Grand Lake Area Chamber of Commerce,** 14700 U.S. 34 (800-531-1019), just outside of the park's west entrance. Open daily 9am-5pm; off-season Mon.-Fri. 10am-5pm.
Park Entrance Fees: $5 per vehicle, $3 per biker or pedestrian, under 16 free, and over 61 ½-price. Valid for 7 days.
Park Visitor and Ranger Stations: Park Headquarters and Visitors Center, on Rte. 36 2½ mi. west of Estes Park, at the Beaver Meadows entrance to the park. Call 586-2371 for park info, or to make sure the Trail Ridge Rd. is open. Headquarters and visitors center open daily 8am-9pm; off-season 8am-5pm. **Kawuneeche Visitors Center** (627-3471), just outside the park's western entrance, 1¼ mi. north of Grand Lake. Open daily 8am-5pm; July 2-Labor Day 7am-7pm. **Moraine Park Visitors Center and Museum** (586-3777), on the Bear Lake Rd. Open daily 8am-5pm. Closed Nov.-April. **Alpine Visitors Center** (586-4927), at the crest of Trail Ridge Rd. Check out the view of the tundra from the back window. Open Memorial Day-closing day of Trail Ridge Rd. (mid-Oct.) daily 9am-5pm. **Lily Lake,** open Memorial Day-Labor Day, daily 9am-5pm.
Horse Rental: Sombrero Ranch, 1895 Big Thompson Rd. (586-4577), in Estes Park 2 mi. from downtown on U.S. 34 E., and on Grand Ave. in Grand Lake (627-3514). $15 for 1 hr., $25 for 2. The breakfast ride (at 7am, $25) includes a 2-hr. ride and a huge breakfast. Call ahead. Hostelers get 10% discount; special rates for those staying at the H Bar G Ranch. Both open daily 7am-5:30pm.
Help Lines: Roads and Weather 586-2385.
Post Office: Grand Lake, 520 Center Dr. (627-3340). Open Mon.-Fri. 8:30am-5pm. **ZIP code:** 80517.
Area Code: 303.

You can reach the National Park most easily from Boulder via U.S. 36 or from Loveland up the Big Thompson Canyon via U.S. 34. Busy during the summer, both routes lead to Estes Park and are easy biking trails. From Denver, take the RTD bus (20 per day, 45 min., $2.50) to its last stop in Boulder, and transfer (free) to bus #202 or 204 which will drop you off on U.S. 36 W. From there, you'll have to hike 30 mi. Some travelers hitch a ride in order to get into the park. In Boulder you can find the entrance to U.S. 36 at 28th and Baseline Rd.

Estes Park parks 65 mi. from Denver, 39 mi. from Boulder, and 31 mi. from Loveland. With a car, "loop" from Boulder by catching U.S. 36 through Estes Park, pick up Trail Ridge Rd. (U.S. 34), go through Rocky Mountain National Park (45 mi.), stop in Grand Lake, and take U.S. 40 to Winter Park and I-70 back to Denver.

Reach the western side of the park from Granby (50 mi. from I-70/U.S. 40). One of the most scenic entrances, CO Rte. 7 approaches the park from the southeast out of Lyons or Nederland, accessing the **Wild Basin Trailhead,** the starting point for

If you're going to
SAN FRANCISCO

Forget wearing flowers in your hair!! (This is the 90's.)

Just bring the incredible coupon on the other side of this page!

The right Eurail for me is:

Description	Name (Should appear as on passport)	Price

Free Shipping and Handling with this card! | Total

Bill my:

❑ Mastercard ❑ Visa ❑ AmEx ❑ Check or Money Order

Card #_____ Name on Card_____

Ship my Eurail to: Exp. Date:_____

_____
Name | Birthdate | Date trip begin

_____
Street address | City | ST | ZIP | Phone Number

some glorious hikes. When Trail Ridge Rd. (open May-Oct.) closes, you can drive around the park from Walden and Fort Collins, via CO Rte. 125 out of Granby and then CO Rte. 14 to Fort Collins. Or take the more traveled U.S. 40 over spectacular **Berthoud Pass** to I-70, then CO Rtes. 119 and 72 north to the park. Note: when Trail Ridge Rd. is closed, the drive jumps from 48 to 140 mi.

ACCOMMODATIONS

Although Estes Park and Grand Lake have an overabundance of expensive lodges and motels, there are few good deals on indoor beds near the national park, especially in winter when the hostels close down.

Estes Park

H Bar G Ranch Hostel (HI/AYH), 3500 H Bar G Rd., P.O. Box 1260, 80517 (586-3688). Hillside cabins, tennis courts, kitchen, and a spectacular view of the front range. Proprietor Lou drives you to the park entrance or into town every morning at 7:30am, and picks you up again at the Chamber of Commerce. Members only, $7.50. Rent a car for $26 per day. Open late May to mid-Sept. Call ahead.

YMCA of the Rockies, 2515 Tunnel Rd., Estes Park Center 80511 (586-3341), 2 mi. south of the park headquarters on Rte. 66 and 5 mi. from the Chamber of Commerce. Caters largely to clan gatherings and conventions. Extensive facilities on the 1400-acre complex, as well as daily hikes and other events. 4 people can get a cabin from $46, kitchen and bath included. Lodge with bunk beds that sleep up to 5 $38. Guest membership $3. Families $5. This large resort has plenty of room for recreation; great for kids. Call ahead; very busy in summer.

The Colorado Mountain School, 351 Moraine Ave. (586-5758). Dorm-style accommodations open to travelers unless already booked by mountain-climbing students. Wood bunks with comfortable mattresses and shower $16. Shower only $2. Reservations are recommended at least one week in advance. (Open in summer 8am-5pm daily. Check out 10am.)

Grand Lake

Shadowcliff Hostel (HI/AYH), P.O. Box 658, 80447 (627-9220). Near the western entrance to the park. Entering Grand Lake, take the left fork after the visitors center on West Portal Rd.; their sign is ¾-mi. down the road on the left. Beautiful, hand-built pine lodge on a cliff overlooking the lake. Offers easy access to the trails on the western side of the park and to the lakes of Arapahoe National Recreation Area. Kitchen. Large hall showers. $7.50, nonmembers $9. Private rooms $21-30. Cabins all have fireplaces, stoves, refrigerators, and private bath. 6-day min. stay. Two cabins sleep up to 8 ($50); one sleeps up to 20 ($60); good for large groups. Rates are for 5 people—$4 per additional person. Open June-Oct.

Sunset Motel, 505 Grand Ave., (627-3318). Friendly owners and gorgeous, cozy singles and doubles will warm your stay in Grand Lake. (1 or 2 people $36; 3 or 4 people $44.)

CAMPING

Sites fill up right quick in summer; call ahead or arrive early.

National Park Campgrounds: Moraine Park (5½ mi. from Estes) and **Glacier Basin** (9 mi. from Estes) require reservations in summer (sites at both $9). **Aspenglen** (5 mi. west of Estes Park near the Fall River entrance), **Longs Peak** (11 mi. south of Estes Park and 1 mi. off Rte. 7), and **Timber Creek** (10 mi. north of Grand Lake—the only campground on the western side of the park) all operate on a first-come, first-served basis (sites $7). Longs Peak and Timber Creek are open all year (in winter, there is no water and no charge); Aspenglen is open May 8- Sept. 30; Moraine Park and Glacier Basin are open May 29-Sept. 6. Three-day limit at Longs Peak, one-week limit elsewhere. Reservations through MISTIX (P.O. Box 85705, San Diego, CA., 92138-5705; 800-365-2267). Make reservations eight weeks in advance for family/individual; 12 weeks advance for groups.

Spring Lake Handicamp: (586-4459 for information; 586-2371, ext. 242 for reservations.) The park's free backcountry campsite for the disabled; 7 mi. from Estes Park Headquarters at Sprague Lake Picnic Area. Open summer daily 7am-7pm.

Backcountry camping: Offices at Park Headquarters (586-2371) and Kawuneeche Visitors Center (627-3471) on the western side of the park at Grand Lake. Open daily 7am-7pm. Get reservations and free permits at these offices or write the **Backcountry office,** Rocky Mountain National Park, Estes Park 80517 (586-0526). No charge for backcountry camping, but many areas are in no-fire zones; you may want to bring along a campstove.

Olive Ridge Campground, 15 mi. south of Estes Park on CO Rte. 7, in Roosevelt National Forest. Call 800-283-2267 for reservations. First-come, first-served sites $8. Contact the **Roosevelt-Arapaho National Forest Service Headquarters,** 161 2nd St., Estes Park (586-3440). Open June-July daily 9am-noon and 1-5pm; Aug.-May Mon.-Fri. 9am-noon and 1-4pm.

Indian Peaks Wilderness, just south of the park, jointly administered by Roosevelt and Arapaho National Forests. Permit required for backcountry camping during the summer. On the east slope, contact the Boulder Ranger District, 2915 Baseline Rd. (444-6003). Open Mon.-Fri. 8am-5pm. Last chance permits ($4) are available in Nederland at Coast to Coast Hardware (take Rte. 7 to 72 south). Open Mon.-Sat. 9am-9pm. On the west slope, contact the Hot Sulphur Ranger District, 100 U.S. 34, in Granby (887-3331). Open May 27-Sept. 2 daily 8am-5pm.

FOOD

Both towns near the park have several grocery stores where you can stock up on trail snacks. Look out for the "bulk foods" at **Safeway** in Estes—they are ideal. If you are aiming to get away from the kitchen on your vacation, the following establishments offer inexpensive and tasty food so you don't have to cook.

Johnson's Cafe (586-6624), 2 buildings to the right of Safeway, across from the Chamber of Commerce. Must try Milt's waffles (from $2.95) made from scratch and served all day long. Also, homemade "Arizona" hashbrowns, chili, crepes, and luscious pies at a great price. Open Mon.-Sat. 7am-2:30pm.

Poppy's, 342 E. Elkhorn Ave. (586-8282), in Barlow Plaza shopping area. A variety of your basic popular items. 18" pizza $10, sandwiches $4-6, all-you-can-eat salad bar $5. Open daily 11am-8pm.

Ed's Cantina, 362 E. Elkhorn Ave. (586-2919). Fastest Mexican food in the park area—your food comes before you can say "Speedy Gonzalez." Combination plate (cheese enchilada, bean burrito, and bean tostada) $6.75. Open daily 7am-10pm.

The Terrace Inn, 813 Grand Ave. (627-3079), in Grand Lake. Homemade, home-made, homemade! Breakfast, lunch, dinner, or just a piece of pie, you can be sure it's fresh. Debby's special Italian sauce and huge fluffy pancakes ($3.50) are definite favorites. Open summer 7am-10pm; call for winter hours.

SIGHTS AND ACTIVITIES

The star of this park is **Trail Ridge Road**. At its highest point, this 50-mi.-long stretch reaches 12,183 ft. above sea level; much of the road rises above timberline. The round-trip drive takes three hours by car, 12 hours by bicycle (if you have legs of titanium and the lungs of an Olympic marathoner). For a closer look at the fragile tundra environment, walk from roadside to the **Forest Canyon Overlook,** or take the half-hour **Tundra Trail** round-trip. **Fall River Road,** a one-way dirt road going from east to west merging with Trail Ridge Rd. at the alpine center, basks in even more impressive scenery, but also sharp cliffs and tight switchbacks along the road.

Rangers can help plan a **hike** to suit your interests and abilities. Since the trailheads in the park are already high, just a few hours of hiking will bring you into unbeatable alpine scenery along the Continental Divide. Be aware that the 12,000- to 14,000-ft. altitudes can make your lungs feel as if they're constricted by rubber bands; give your brain enough time to adjust to the reduced oxygen levels before starting up the higher trails. Some easy trails include the 3.6-mi. round-trip from Wild Basin Ranger Station to **Calypso Cascades** and the 2.8-mi. round-trip from the Long Peaks Ranger Station to **Eugenia Mine.** From the nearby **Glacier Gorge Junction** trailhead, take a short hike to **Mills Lake** or up to the **Loch.**

From Grand Lake, a trek into the scenic and remote **North** or **East Inlets** should leave camera-toting tourists behind. Both of these wooded valleys swim with excellent trout fishing. The park's gem is prominent **Longs Peak** (14,255 ft.), dominating the eastern slope. The peak's monumental east face, a 2000-ft. vertical wall known simply as the **Diamond,** is the most challenging rock-climbing spot in Colorado.

You can traverse the park on a mountain bike as a fun and challenging (!!!) alternative to hiking. **Colorado Bicycling Adventures,** 184 E. Elkhorn (586-4241), Estes Park, rents bikes ($5 per hr., $9 for 2 hr., $14 per ½-day, $19 per day; discounts for hostelers; helmets included). Guided mountain bike tours are also offered (2 hr. $20, 4 hr. $35, ½-day $40-60; open daily 10am-9pm; off-season 10am-5pm).

During the summer, the three major campgrounds have good nightly amphitheater programs that examine the park's ecology. The visitors centers have information on these and on many enjoyable ranger-led interpretive activities, including nature walks, birding expeditions, and artists' forays.

Of the two towns, Grand Lake draws fewer crowds in the summer. Though inaccessible without a car in the winter, the town offers hair-raising snowmobile and cross-country routes. Ask at the visitors center about seasonal events. Camp on the shores of adjacent **Shadow Mountain Lake** and **Lake Granby.**

SAN JUAN MOUNTAINS

Ask Coloradans about their favorite mountain retreats, and they'll most likely name a peak, lake, stream or town in the San Juan Range of southwestern Colorado. Four **national forests**—the **Uncompahgre** (pronounced un-cum-PAH-gray), the **Gunnison,** the **San Juan,** and the **Río Grande**—encircling this sprawling range.

Durango is an ideal base camp for forays into these mountains. In particular, the **Weminuche Wilderness,** northeast of Durango, tempts the hardy backpacker with a particularly large expanse of hilly terrain. You can hike for miles where wild, sweeping vistas are the rule. Get maps and info on hiking in the San Juans from **Pine Needle Mountaineering,** Main Mall, Durango 81301 (247-8728; open Mon.-Sat. 9am-9pm, Sun. 11am-4pm; maps $2.50).

The San Juan area is easily accessible on U.S. 50, traveled by hundreds of thousands of tourists each summer. **Greyhound** serves the area, but very poorly. Car travel is the best option in this region. On a happier note, the San Juans are loaded with HI/AYH hostels and campgrounds, making them one of the most economical places to visit in Colorado. Overall, the San Juans are a paradise for hikers, bikers, and just outdoorsy people who appreciate scenic America.

■■■ BLACK CANYON OF THE GUNNISON NATIONAL MONUMENT

The 53-mi. Black Canyon is the result of the 2-million-year erosion process of the Gunnison River carving through this 2500-ft. deep gorge. Dark shadows and rays of sunlight fall upon the walls of the canyon and the river at the bottom, inviting many tourists to take in the awesome view, and a few hardy souls to explore below. Those who stay on the beaten track will not be disappointed—along with a variety of tremendous views, there is plenty of wildlife to see along the road.

There is only one 12-mi. dirt road to the **North Rim,** the most remote area of the canyon. This route is closed in winter. From Montrose, take U.S. 50 west and Rte. 92 west through Curecanti National Recreation Area to Crawford. From the west side of the monument, take U.S. 50 west and Rte. 92 east through Delta to Crawford. From Crawford, a graveled county road takes you to the North Rim. The better-developed, more-populated **South Rim** is reached from U.S. 50, via Rte. 347 just outside of Montrose. There are seven "overlooks" along the rim, and a self-guiding nature trail starts from the campground. The 8-mi. scenic drive along this rim boasts spectacular **Chasm View,** where you can peer 2000 ft. down a sheer vertical drop. Although this view may seem like enough, don't miss the view of the **Painted Wall** (56 yds. away), the highest cliff in Colorado, and over a billion years old.

Practical Information The closest town to the Gunnison National Monument is **Montrose,** with administrative offices for the monument located at 2233 E. Main St. (249-7036; open daily 8am-7:30pm, shorter hours in the off-season). **Greyhound** serves Montrose, 132 N. 1st St. (249-6673), and Gunnison, 303 Tomichi Ave. (641-0060), in the Changing Hands building. Gunnison lies about 55 mi. east of Montrose on U.S. 50. Fare between Gunnison and Montrose is $10. The bus will drop you off at the junction of U.S. 50 and Rte. 347, 6 mi. from the canyon. **Western Express Taxi** (249-8880) will drive you in from Montrose for about $30.

The town's **visitors center** assists at 2490 S. Townsend Ave. (249-1726; open May-Oct. daily 9am-7pm). Montrose's **ZIP code** is 81401. The **area code** is 303.

Accommodations and Food The **Black Canyon Motel,** 1605 Main St. (U.S. 50), is at the end of Montrose (towards the Monument) and offers clean rooms with A/C, cable, and pool for a reasonable price (singles $30, doubles $32 and up; all major credit cards accepted). Many inexpensive motels line Main St. and have competitive prices without the amenities. The **Stockmen's Cafe and Bar,** 320 E. Main St. (249-9946), serves no-nonsense Mexican and western food (open Thurs.-Tues. 7am-midnight). Despite its name, **Starvin' Arvin's,** 1320 S. Townsend Ave. (249-7787; open 6am-10pm), serves generous portions and a variety of healthy items. You can't go wrong at a place that serves breakfast all day long. Feast on burgers ($3-5), or 3-egg omelettes with delicious hashbrowns and hotcakes ($4).

Hiking and Camping Inspired hikers can descend to the bottom of the canyon; the least difficult trail (more like a controlled fall) drops 1800 ft. over a distance of 1 mi. The hike up is a *tad* more difficult. At certain points you must hoist yourself up on a chain in order to gain ground. Suffice it to say, this hike is *not* to be undertaken lightly. A backcountry permit and advice from a ranger are required before any descent. But don't let this daunt your spirit of adventure—rangers are helpful, and the wild beauty of this canyon climb awaits the brave. Hiking permits are distributed on a first come, first serve basis at the **North Rim Ranger Station** (249-7086) and at the **South Rim Visitor Center** (249-1915). The visitors center also offers 40-min. guided nature walks at 11am and 2pm; meet at the visitors center. Free narrated evening programs are given at the park's entrance daily in summer at 8:45pm. (Visitors center open daily 8am-7:30pm, less Labor Day-Memorial Day. Park entrance fee $4 per car; if one of the passengers is 62 or over, everyone goes free, so be sure to bring grandma along.) A short walk down from the visitors center affords a view startling enough in its steepness to require chest-high rails to protect the vertiginous from falling.

Camp in either rim's beautiful desert **campgrounds.** Each has pit toilets and charcoal grills; the one in the **South Rim** has an amphitheater with summer programs at 8:45pm. Water is available, but use it sparingly. Both campgrounds are open May-Nov. (sites $6). Since wood gathering is not allowed, bring your own wood/charcoal or pick up some at the Information/Gift Shop at the turn off to the park on U.S. 50. (Open May-mid-Nov.) Backcountry camping and driftwood fires in the canyon bottom are permitted; beware the abundant poison ivy. Call the National Park Service at 249-7036 or the **South Rim Visitor Info Center** at 249-1915 for details.

If you begin to feel overcome with vertigo or hunger, head down to the **Crystal Dam** via the E. Portal Rd. off S. Rim Rd. before South Rim Campground. The road is long, steep, and winding, but the picnic tables and the beautiful setting of the Gunnison River will make you forget your swearing on the way down at whoever wrote this part of *Let's Go: USA and Canada.*

A few miles south of Montrose on U.S. 550, the **Ute Indian Museum,** 17253 Chipeta Dr. (249-3098), displays exhibits from the Bear Dance and the bilingual letters of chief Ouray (leader of the Southern Ute tribe). (Open mid-May-Sept. Mon.-Sat. 10am-5pm, Sun. 1-5pm. $2, 65 and over and ages 6-16 $1.)

■■■ DURANGO

As Will Rogers once put it, Durango is "out of the way and glad of it." Despite its increasing popularity as a tourist destination, Durango retains an almost insidiously relaxed small-town atmosphere. Come here to see nearby Mesa Verde and to raft down the Animas River, but don't be surprised if you end up staying longer than you expected.

Practical Information Durango parks at the intersection of U.S. 160 and U.S. 550. Streets run perpendicular to avenues, but everyone calls Main Avenue "Main Street." The **Durango Lift** (259-5438) provides hourly bus service beginning at Main Ave. and Earl St. from 8am-6:30pm (75¢). **Greyhound,** 275 E. 8th Ave. (259-2755), serves Grand Junction ($31), Denver ($51), and Albuquerque ($35). (Open Mon.-Fri. 7:30am-noon and 3:30-5pm, Sat. 7:30am-noon, holidays 7:30-10am.)

If, by chance, you run out of things to do or want to ask questions or make reservations (for accommodations or tours), the **Durango Area Chamber Resort Association,** 111 S. Camino del Rio, across from Gateway Dr. (247-0312 or 800-525-8855), is extremely helpful. They can also answer questions about camping. (Open Mon.-Fri. 8am-5pm, Sat.-Sun. 11am-5pm; winter Mon.-Fri. 8am-5pm.)

Pick up care packages at the **post office,** 228 8th St. (247-3434; open Mon.-Fri. 8:30am-5:30pm, Sat. 9am-1pm); the **ZIP code** is 81301. Durango's **area code** is 303.

Accommodations, Food, and Nightlife Durango Youth Hostel, 543 E. 2nd Ave. (247-9905), has very simple bunks and kitchen facilities in an old house. Bare-bones, but only one block from downtown and the only reasonable accommodations in the area. David, the host, will help orient you to the area. (Check-in 7-10am and 5-10pm. Check-out 7-10am. Bunks $10.) The **Budget Inn** has clean, spacious rooms and a nice pool and hot tub (singles $30, doubles $34; less during off-season). The **Cottonwood Camper Park,** on U.S. 160 (247-1977), ½ mi. west of town, has tent sites (with shower $16, full hookup $19.50).

You may decide to stay in the quieter and cheaper town of Silverton. Though less popular as a destination, this small mining town is situated at the base of some of the most beautiful mountains and hiking trails. The **Teller House Hotel,** 1250 Greene St. (387-5423 or 800-342-4338), right next to the French Bakery (which provides the hotel's complementary breakfast), has comfortable rooms in a well-maintained 1896 hotel. (Singles $23, with private bath $34. Doubles $29/$45, $8 per additional person.) Silverton is at the end of the Durango & Silverton RR (see below).

For fixin's, head to **City Market,** on U.S. 550 one block down 9th St., or at 3130 Main St. (Both open 24 hrs.) Or breakfast with locals at **Carver's Bakery and Brewpub,** 1022 Main Ave. (259-2545), which has good bread, breakfast specials ($2-4.50), veggie burritos ($5), and other vegetarian dishes. Brew-Jitas (beef fajitas sauteed in tequila) are $6.50. (Fri.-Sat. pitchers of beer $5. Open Mon.-Sat. 6:30am-10pm, Sun. 6am-1pm.) The **Durango Diner,** 957 Main St. (247-9889), serves up mongo cheeseburgers ($2.75) and scrumptious, plate-sized pancakes cooked by a singing chef. (Open Mon.-Sat. 6am-2pm, Sun. 7am-1pm.) Race over to **Pronto,** 150 E. 2nd Ave. (247-1510), for their Tuesday night spaghetti dinner ($4.25), all-you-can-eat specials ($4) or mozzarella burger ($4). Or don't race over—they have free pizza delivery. **Farquhart's,** 725 Main Ave. (247-9861), serves up delicious burritos for $5.75. They also have the best live music in town; keep an eye open for Walt Richardson and Morningstar. (Sun.-Tues. free bluegrass; Sun.-Mon. rock n' roll, $3-5 cover. Open daily 11am-2am.)

Activities Winter is Durango's busiest season, when nearby **Purgatory Resort** (247-9000), 20 mi. north on U.S. 550, hosts skiers of all levels. (Lift tickets $35, kids $17, one free child per adult.) When the heat is on, trade in your skis for a sled and test out the **Alpine Slide,** (Tickets $4, under 6 must ride with an adult. Open summer daily 9:30am-6pm.) or take the **Scenic Chairlift Ride** ($6).

Durango is best known for the **Durango and Silverton Narrow Gauge Train,** 479 Main St. (247-2733), which runs along the Animas River Valley to the glistening tourist town of **Silverton.** Old-fashioned, 100% coal-fed locomotives wheeze and cough through the San Juans, making a 2-hr. stop in Silverton before heading back to Durango (4 per day, at 7:30, 8:30, 9:15, and 10:15am, and 4:40pm; 6 hr., $37; ages 5-10 $19). If the prospect of sitting all day doesn't sound that great, consider buying a one-way train ticket ($24.75), and taking a bus back from Silverton along U.S. 550. **Buses** wait at the Silverton train station to service the weary (1½-hr.).

To backpack into the scenic **Chicago Basin,** purchase a round-trip ticket to Needleton ($34, ages 5-11 $17). To get into the **New York Basin,** you'll need $36 and a ticket to Elk Park. The train will drop you off here on its trip to Silverton. When you decide to leave the high country, return to Needleton and flag the train, but you must have either a return pass or $24 in cash to board. The train chugs through at 4:43pm. For more info on the train and its services for backpackers, contact the Durango & Silverton Narrow Gauge RR, 479 Main St., Durango 81301. (Offices open daily 6am-9pm; Aug.-Oct. 7am-7pm; Nov.-May 8am-5pm.)

For river rafting, **Rivers West,** 520 Main St. (259-5077), has good rates (1-hr. $12, 2-hr. $19; kids 20% discount; open daily 8am-9pm). **Durango Rivertrippers,** 720 Main St. (259-0289), organizes trips (2-hr. $19, ½-day $29, under 15 $15; open daily 8:30am-8:30pm). Biking gear is available from **Hassle Free Sports,** 2615 Main St. (259-3874 or 800-835-3800; bikes $8 per hr., $25 per day; open Mon.-Sat. 8:30am-6pm, Sun. 10:30am-5pm; must have driver's license and major credit card).

■■■ MESA VERDE NATIONAL PARK

Fourteen centuries ago, Native American tribes settled and cultivated the desert mesas of southwestern Colorado. In the year 1200, they constructed and settled the cliff dwellings which they mysteriously abandoned in 1275. Navajo tribes arriving in the area in 1450 named the previous inhabitants the Anasazi, or the "ancient ones." Today only five of the 1000 archeological sites are open to touring, because the fragile sandstone wears quickly under human feet. Such caution results in crowding within the park; it is best to arrive early.

Practical Information The park's main entrance is off U.S. 160, 36 mi. from Durango and 10 mi. from Cortez. Durango Transportation's **Mesa Verde Tours** (259-4818 in Durango; 565-1278 in Cortez) will pick you up in Durango or Cortez and take you on a 9-hr. tour of the park, leaving at 8:30am ($28, under 12 $14); bring a lunch. Make reservations the night before as tours fill up. Since sights lie up to 40 mi. apart, a car is helpful. Van transportation is also available at the Far View Lodge (see above) for self-guided tours (provide 24-hr. notice). Mesa Verde's **ZIP code** is 81330; nearby Mancos is 81328. The **area code** is 303.

Accommodations and Camping Mesa Verde's only lodging, **Far View Motor Lodge** (529-4421), is extremely expensive, but a few nearby motels can put you up for under $30. Try the **Ute Mountain Motel**, 531 S. Broadway (565-8507), in Cortez, CO. (Singles from $35; in winter from $27. Doubles from $42; in winter from $30.) However, your best bet is to stay at the nearby **Durango Hostel** (see Durango). The only camping in Mesa Verde is 4 mi. inside the park at **Morfield Campground** (529-4400; off-season 533-7731), which boasts some beautiful, secluded sites. In summer, go early to beat the crowds. (Sites $8, full hookup $16. Showers 75¢ for 5 min. Senior discount with Golden Age Pass.)

Activities Entrance fees to the park are $5 per car, $2 per hiker or biker. The southern portion of the park divides into the **Chapin Mesa** and the **Wetherill Mesa**. The **Far View Visitors Center** (529-4593), near the north rim, offers info on the park (open summer 8am-5pm). In the winter, you can obtain park info at the **Colorado Welcome Center/Cortez Chamber of Commerce,** 959 S. Broadway (800-253-1616 or 565-3414; open daily 8am-6pm; winter 8am-5pm), in Cortez. On Wetherill Mesa, tours leave from Far View Lodge (June-Sept. 3-hr. tours at 9:30am and 1:30pm, $12, under 12 $5; 5-hr. tours at 9:30am, $15, under 12 $5.) You may take guided tours up ladders and through the passageways of Anasazi dwellings. **Spruce Tree House** is one of the better-preserved ruins. To get an overview of the Anasazi lifestyle, visit the **Chapin Mesa Museum** (529-4475), at the south end of the park (open daily 8am-6:30pm; winter 8am-5pm). Ranger-led tours are given at the balcony house ruins (every ½ hr., daily 9am-6pm).

■ ■ ■ TELLURIDE

Site of the first bank Butch Cassidy ever robbed (the San Miguel), Telluride has a history right out of a 1930s black-and-white film. Prizefighter Jack Dempsey used to wash dishes in the Athenian Senate, a popular saloon/brothel that frequently required Dempsey to double as bouncer between plates. Now it simply serves delicious Greek food (see below). The **Sheridan Theatre** (see below) hosted actresses Sarah Bernhardt and Lillian Gish on cross-country theater tours. Presidential candidate William Jennings Bryan delivered his "Cross of Gold" speech in silver-scooping Telluride from the front balcony of the Sheridan Hotel. More recently, in his autobiography *Speak, Memory,* Vladimir Nabokov relates his pursuit of a particularly rare type of butterfly through Telluride. Not so rare (especially after its devaluation) was the silver that attracted all the less aesthetically inclined hoodlums to Telluride in the first place, beginning in 1875.

Skiers, hikers, and vacationers now come to Telluride to put gold and silver *into* these mountains; Telluride is becoming increasingly more popular with the glamorous ski set, and continues to grow, suggesting the Aspen of the future. However, with limited public access to the town (some say Telluride means "to hell you ride"), it still retains most of its innocence as a wild west mining town.

Practical Information The **Visitors Center** is upstairs at **Rose's,** near the entrance to town at the demonic address of 666 West Colorado Ave. (728-6621 or 800-446-3192; open 24 hrs.). You can only get to Telluride by car, on U.S. 550 or Rte. 145. The **post office** stamps and sorts at 101 E. Colorado Ave. (728-3900; open Mon.-Fri. 9am-5pm, Sat. 10am-noon). The **ZIP code** is 81435; the **area code** is 303.

Accommodations and Food The **Oak Street Inn,** 134 N. Oak St. (728-3383), offers dorm-style lodging complete with a sauna. (Singles with shared bath $27, doubles $40, 3 people $54, 4 people $68. Showers $3. More expensive during festivals.) When Oak Street is out of beds, head for the **New Sheridan Hotel,** 231 W. Colorado (728-4351; $35, off-season $25, $8 for each additional person). You can **camp** in the east end of town in a town-operated facility with water, restrooms, and showers

(728-3071; 2-week max. stay. Sites $8, except during the festivals.) If visiting Telluride for a festival, bring a sleeping bag; the cost of a bed—if you can find one—is outrageous. **Sunshine,** 4 mi. southwest on Rte. 145 toward Cortez, and **Matterhorn** (800-283-2267), 10 mi. farther on Rte. 145, are well-developed national forest campgrounds; the latter can accommodate trailers with hookup. (2-week max. stay. Sites $7.) Accessible by jeep roads, several free primitive campgrounds huddle nearby. During festival times, you can crash just about anywhere in town, and hot showers are mercifully available at the high school ($2 during festivals).

Baked in Telluride, 127 S. Fir St. (728-4775), has enough rich coffee and delicious pastry, pizza, salad and 50¢-bagels to get you through a festival weekend without sleeping, even if you *are* baked in Telluride. (Open daily 6am-2am; winter 10pm.) The **Athenian Senate,** 123 S. Spruce (728-3018), the only place to eat after dark, serves locally praised Greek and Italian food from $5. (Open daily 11am-2:30am; winter daily 5pm-2:30am.) For delicious Italian fare, head to **Eddie's Cafe,** 300 W. Colorado (728-5335), for eight-inch pizzas ($5) and hefty pasta entrees under $10. (Open Tues.-Sun. 11:30am-10pm.)

Festivals and Activities Neither rockslide nor snowmelt signals the end of the festivities in Telluride. The quality and number of summer arts festivals seem staggering when you consider that only 1500 people call the town home. While get-togethers occur just about every weekend in summer and fall, the most renowned is the **Bluegrass Festival** (800-624-2422) in late June—in recent years the likes of James Taylor and the Indigo Girls have attracted crowds of 16,000. Area music stores sell tickets for about $35 per night. Some people have managed to sneak in. On the weekend of the festivals, you can easily find dishwashing or food-serving jobs in exchange for tickets to the show. Telluride also hosts a **Talking Gourds** poetry fest (early June; call 728-4767 for info), a **Composer to Composer** festival (mid-July), and a **Jazz Festival** (early Aug.; 800-525-3455), among others. You can often hear the music festivals all over town, all day, and deep into the night as you try to sleep. Above all, the **Telluride International Film Festival** (Labor Day weekend), now in its 19th year, draws famous actors and directors from all over the globe. Guests in years past have included Daniel Day Lewis, Clint Eastwood, and twinly-piqued director David Lynch. For ticket info call 800-525-3455.

Two blocks from the visitors center lies the **Coonskin Chairlift,** which will haul you up 10,000 ft. for an excellent view of Pikes Peak and the La Sal Mountains. (Open June 11-Sept. 14 Thurs.-Mon. 10am-2pm. $7, seniors and kids 7-12 $4.) Biking, hiking, and backpacking opportunities around Telluride are endless; ghost towns and alpine lakes tucked behind stern mountain crags fill the wild terrain. For an enjoyable day hike, trek up the San Miguel River Canyon to **Bridal Veil Falls.** Drive to the end of Rte. 145 and hike the steep, misty dirt road to the spectacular waterfall. In winter, self-proclaimed atheists can be spied crossing themselves before tipping their planks down "Spiral Stairs" and the "Plunge," two of the Rockies' most gut-wrenching slopes. For more information, contact the **Telluride Ski Resort,** P.O. Box 307, 81435 (728-3856). For a copy of the *Skier Services Brochure,* call 728-4424. A free shuttle connects the mountain village with the rest of the town. Pick up a current schedule at the visitors center (see above). **Paragon Ski and Sport,** 213 W. Colorado Ave. (728-4525), has camping supplies, bikes, skis and roller blades. (Open Mon.-Thurs. 9am-7pm, Fri.-Sun. 9am-8pm; winter daily 8am-9pm.) Stop at the local sportshop or **Between the Covers** bookstore, 224 W. Colorado Ave. (728-4504), for trail guides and maps. (Open daily 9am-9pm.)

■ Idaho

Although most of the U.S. associates Idaho with "Famous Potatoes" (until recently its motto), Idaho ain't just tubers. The wild western scenery north of southern Idaho's potato farms ranges from the 12,000-ft. mountains and rippling estuaries of the Salmon River in the center to the spectacular, dense pine forests in the northern panhandle. Coeur d'Alene's beaches, lakes, and scenic overlooks complement the bustle of downtown Boise and the snow-capped mountains and fish-filled, freezing lakes of southern Idaho. The U.S. government quietly guards Idaho's most spectacular parts in the Selway-Bitterroot Wilderness and the Idaho Primitive Area, through which rushes the meandering Salmon. The Snake River's serpentine waters have carved out Hell's Canyon, the deepest gorge in North America. Idaho gets mixed reviews literarily: it is the native state of Ernest Hemingway and poet-cum-Nazi Ezra Pound.

PRACTICAL INFORMATION

Capital: Boise.

Visitor Information: Idaho Information Line, 800-635-7820. **Boise Convention and Visitors Bureau** (344-7777), corner of 9th and Idaho, 2nd floor. Open daily 8:30am-5pm. **Parks and Recreation Department,** 7800 Fairview Ave., Boise 83720 (327-7444). Open Mon.-Fri. 8am-5pm. **Idaho Outfitters and Guide Association:** P.O. Box 95, Boise 83701 (342-1438). Info on companies leading whitewater, packhorse, and backpacking expeditions in the state. Free vacation directories.

Time Zones: Mountain and Pacific. The dividing line runs east-west at about the middle of the state; if you straddle it, you'll break the bonds of time.

Postal Abbreviation: ID

Sales tax: 5%.

■■■ BOISE

While not exactly a tourist haven, Idaho's capital contains numerous grassy parks, making this small city both a verdant residential bulwark amid the state's dry southern plateau and a relaxing way-station on a cross-country jaunt. Most of the city's sights lie between the capitol and I-84 a few miles south; you can manage pretty well on foot. **Boise Urban Stages** (336-1010) also runs several routes through the city, with maps available from any bus driver and displayed at each stop. (Buses operate Mon.-Fri. 6:45am-6:15pm, Sat. 9am-6pm. Fare 50¢, seniors 25¢.)

Practical Information To get around in Boise, rent at **McU's Sports,** 822 W. Jefferson (342-7734). Rollerblades ($4 per hour, $12 per day, $15 overnight), and mountain bikes ($12 per ½-day, $18 per day), as well as equipment for sports of all seasons. **Amtrak** (800-872-7245) serves Boise from the beautiful Spanish-mission-style **Union Pacific Depot,** 1701 Eastover Terr. (336-5992), easily visible from Capitol Blvd. One train per day goes south to Salt Lake City (7¾ hr., $70); one goes west to Portland (10½ hr., $83) and Seattle (15½ hr., $111). **Greyhound** has I-84 schedules from its terminal at 1212 W. Bannock (343-3681), a few blocks west of downtown. Three buses per day head to Portland (8-10 hr., $54) and Seattle (11 hr., $97). Boise's main **post office** is on 770 S. 13th St. (383-4211; open Mon.-Fri. 7:30am-5:30pm, Sat. 10am-2pm). The **ZIP code** is 83707; the **area code** is 208.

Accommodations and Camping Finding lodging in Boise is harsh; neither the YMCA nor the YWCA provide rooms, and even the cheapest hotels charge more than $20 per night. The more reasonable places tend to fill quickly, so make reserva-

COEUR D'ALENE

tions. One of the most spacious is the **Capri Motel,** 2600 Fairview Ave. (344-8617), where air-conditioned rooms come with coffee and queen-sized beds. (Singles $25, doubles $30.) Farther out of town, the **Boisean,** 1300 S. Capitol Ave. (343-3645 or 800-365-3645), has smaller rooms but a more personable staff. (Singles $32, doubles $36.) The **Forest Service Campground** lies 3 mi. north of town. Contact **Boise National Forest,** 1715 Front St. (364-4100), for a map, or for mushroom permits to really get into nature (3 days, $10). (Open Mon.-Fri. 7:30am-4:30pm.) Other camp-grounds include **Boise KOA Kampground,** 7300 S. Federal Way (345-7673; sites $16, full hook-up $20); **Americana Kampground,** 3600 American Terrace Blvd. (344-5733; 90 sites, prices vary often); and **Fiesta Park,** 11101 Fairview Ave. (375-8207; sites $15, hookup without water and electricity $17.50, full hookup $18.50).

Food Food in Boise is more than just potatoes. Look to the downtown area, cen-tered around 6th and Main St., where the Basque specialties of northern Spain lend spice to the region's cuisine. For the unadventurous palate, a good measure of down-home burgers and fries is also available here. Try **Moon's Kitchen,** 815 W. Bannock St. (385-0472), in the rear portion of Criner's Tackle and Cutlery (soup, sandwich, drink special $5, huge breakfast $2.75; open Mon.-Fri. 7am-3pm, Sat. 8am-3pm). You can contemplate the rifles and shotguns mounted behind the counter while enjoying your meal. For instant cooking, try Boise's own fast food, **Big Bun Drive-In** (375-5361), at the corner of S. Curtis and Overland, where cheeseburgers are 60¢ and cokes are still 50¢ (open Mon.-Sat. 11am-11pm). For nighttime entertainment, head for **Old Boise,** the area between S. 1st and S. 6th St., where the town's bars fire up. Most have live music on weekends. The **Flying Pie Pizzeria,** 4320 State St. (345-8585), serves rare and imported beers (Chimay, almost ½-liter, $8.50). Pizza, too ($7). (Open daily 4-11pm.) Finally, watch a movie while you eat at **The Flicks,** 646 Fulton St. (342-4222). Huge portions $6-13. (Kitchen open 5-9:30pm, movies daily 7 and 9:45pm and Sun. 1:30pm.)

Sights The **Boise Tour Train** (342-4796) shows you 75 sites around the city in one hour. Tours start and end in the parking lot of **Julia Davis Park,** departing every 75 min. (Summer 3 tours per day, Mon.-Sat. 10am-3pm, Sun. noon-5pm, evening tour Fri.-Sat. 7pm; off-season Wed.-Sun. afternoons only. $5.50, seniors $5, ages 3-12 $3. Arrive 15 min. early.) To learn about Idaho and the Old West at your own pace, walk through the **Historical Museum** (334-2120), in Julia Davis Park. (Open Mon.-Sat. 9am-5pm, Sun. 1-5pm. Free, donations encouraged.) Also in the park, the **Boise Art Museum,** 670 Julia Davis Dr. (345-8330), displays international and local works. (Open Tues.-Fri. 10am-5pm, Sat.-Sun. noon-5pm. $2, students and seniors $1, under 18 free. Free in early July.) Take a self-guided tour through the country's only **state capitol** to be heated with natural geothermal hot water. (Open Mon.-Fri. 8am-5pm, Sat. 9am-5pm.) The tiny and crowded **Boise Zoo** (384-4260) roars and howls beyond these two buildings. (Open Mon.-Wed. and Fri.-Sun. 10am-5pm, Thurs. 10am-9pm. $3, seniors and ages 4-12 $1.25, under 4 free, Thurs. ½-price.) Taloned avians perch and dive at **World Center for Birds of Prey** (362-3716), 6 mi. south of I-84 on Cole Rd. You must call ahead to arrange a tour (donations of $4, seniors and kids $2, requested). For more back-to-nature fun, try the 22-mi. **Boise River Green-belt,** a pleasant, tree-lined path ideal for a leisurely walk or picnic.

Bask in the region's cultural history at the **Basque Museum and Cultural Center** (343-2671), at 6th and Grove St. in downtown Boise, where you'll find out about the surprisingly rich Basque heritage in the Great Basin and the Western Rockies. (Open Tues.-Fri. 10am-3pm, Sat. 11am-2pm.)

■■■ COEUR D'ALENE

The gaggles of tourists—one may also use the term "pride" or "annoyance" to denote such a group—can do little to mar the rustic beauty of this spot. No matter how many people clutter its beaches, the deep blue water of Lake Coeur d'Alene offers a serene escape from whichever urban jungle you call home. Sandpoint, to the north, is less touristy and equally spectacular.

PRACTICAL INFORMATION

Emergency: 911.

Visitor Information: Chamber of Commerce, 161 N. 3rd St. (664-3194), at Spruce. Open Mon.-Fri. 8am-8pm. **Visitors Center** (664-0587), corner of First and Sheridan St. Open Mon.-Fri. 9am-5pm, Sat.-Sun. 10am-3pm. **Toll-free Visitors Info:** 800-232-4068.

Bus Station: 1923½ N. 4th St. (664-3343), 1 mi. north of the lake. **Greyhound** serves Boise (12 hr., $46), Spokane (1 hr., $6.50), Lewiston (1 per day, $26) and Missoula (5 hr., $32). **Empire Lines** connects to Sandpoint at 5th and Cedar St. (1 per day, $8.30). Open Mon.-Sat. 8-10am and 4-8pm, Sun. 8-10am.

Car Rental: Auto Mart Used Car Rental, 120 Anton Ave. (667-4905), 3 blocks north of the bus station. $29 per day, $180 per week; 100 free mi. per day, 25¢ per extra mi. Open Mon.-Sat. 8am-6pm. Must be 21. Credit card or $100 cash deposit required. **U-Save Auto Rental,** 302 Northwest Blvd. (664-1712). Compact $22 per day with 150 free mi. Open Mon.-Fri. 8am-6pm, Sat. 8am-3pm, Sun. 10am-4pm.

Help Line: Crisis Services, 664-1443. 24 hrs.

Time Zone: Pacific (3 hrs. behind Eastern).

Post Office: 111 N. 7th St. (664-8126), 5 blocks east of the Chamber of Commerce off Sherman. Open Mon.-Fri. 8:30am-5pm. **ZIP code:** 83814.

Area Code: 208.

ACCOMMODATIONS, CAMPING, AND FOOD

Cheap lodgings are hard to find in this booming resort town. You'll have your best luck in the eastern outskirts of the city. In town, the **Star Motel,** 1516 Sherman Ave. (667-5035), has large, furnished rooms with TV, free HBO, phones, and fridges (singles $62, doubles $74; off-season all rooms $40-60; per week $160 single, $180 double). In Sandpoint, by all means stay at the elegant lakefront **Whitaker House,** 410 Railroad Ave. (263-0816). Rooms cost $32-48 and include breakfast. Near Silver Mt., about 35 mi. east of Coeur d'Alene, is a new **Youth Hostel,** 834 W. McKinley Ave., Kellogg, ID (783-4171); it has laundry, TV, VCR, and 40 beds. (April-Oct. $10, Nov.-March $12.) **Cricket on the Hearth,** 1521 Lakeside Ave. (664-6926), downtown, chirps up a bed and breakfast with rooms $45-75. Each room has a unique theme.

There are five **public campgrounds** within 20 mi. of Coeur d'Alene. The closest is **Robin Hood RV Park,** 703 Lincoln Way (664-2306); it has showers, laundry and hookups, no evil sheriffs, and is within walking distance of downtown. (Sites $15.50.) **Beauty Creek,** a forest service site 10 mi. south along the lake, is the next closest. Camp alongside a lovely stream trickling down the side of a mountain. Drinking water and pit toilets. (Sites $12. Open May 5-Oct. 15.) **Honeysuckle Campground,** 25 mi. northeast, has nine sites with drinking water and toilets ($8; open May 15-Oct. 15). **Bell Bay,** on Lake Coeur d'Alene (off U.S. 95 south, then 14 mi. to Forest Service Rd. 545) offers 26 sites, a boat launch, and good fishing (sites $5; open May 5-Oct. 15). Call the Fernan Ranger District Office, 2502 E. Sherman Ave. (765-7381), for info on these and other campgrounds. (Open Mon.-Fri. 7:30am-4:30pm, Sat. 8:30am-3pm.) **Farragut State Park** (683-2425), 20 mi. north on U.S. 95, is an extremely popular 4000-acre park dotted with hiking trails and beaches along Lake Pend Oreille (pronounced pon-do-RAY). (Sites $8, with hookup $11. $2 day-use fee for motor vehicles not camping in the park. Open May 27-Sept. 2.)

There are oysters aplenty in Coeur d'Alene, but if you like your snacks to come without shells, sit at the sidewalk tables at the **Coeur d'Alene Coffee Roastery,** 511 Sherman Ave. (664-0752). Sip their gourmet coffee (free refills) and indulge in hot cinnamon rolls. (Open Mon.-Fri. 7am-6pm, Sat.-Sun. 8am-6pm.) Create your own sandwich d'Alene at **Spooner's,** 215 Sherman Ave. (667-7666), for $4.25. Ice cream

$1-2 (open daily 9:30am-5:30pm). Not necessarily cheesy is **Tito Macaroni,** 210 Sherman Ave. (667-2782) which oven bakes pizza ($4-14); especially a BBQ chicken pizza ($8) (open Sun.-Thurs. 11am-10pm, Fri.-Sat. 11am-11pm). Breakfast at **Jimmy D's,** 320 Sherman Ave. (664-9774), sets you back $1-4, lunch $4-7, dinner $5-13 (open daily 9am-11pm, winter 9am-10pm).

SIGHTS AND ACTIVITIES

The lake is Coeur d'Alene's *raison d'être.* Hike 2 mi. up **Tubbs Hill** to a scenic vantage point, or head for the **Coeur d'Alene Resort** and walk along the **world's longest floating boardwalk** (3300 ft.). You can tour the lake on a **Lake Coeur d'Alene Cruise** (765-4000), departing from the downtown dock every afternoon June-Sept. (1:30, 4 and 6:30pm; 90 min.; $9.50, seniors $8.50, kids $5.50). Rent a canoe from **Eagle Enterprises** (664-1175) at the city dock to explore the lake yourself ($5 per hr., $15 per ½-day, $25 first whole day, $10 per day thereafter). A 3-mi. bike/foot path circles the lake. **Four Seasons Outfitting,** 105 Sherman Ave. (765-2863) organizes rafting (½-day $45, full day $89), equestrian rides ($12 1st hr., $20 2 hr., $30 3 hr.), and fly fishing (½-day walk $125, full day float trip $225). Call well in advance.

Twenty mi. east of town on I-90 is the **Old Mission at Cataldo** (682-3814), now contained in a day-use state park. Built in 1853 by Native Americans, the mission is the oldest extant building in Idaho. (Free tours daily. Open June-July daily 8am-6pm; Aug.-May 9am-7pm. Vehicle entry fee $2.) Near Sandpoint, about 50 mi. north of Coeur d'Alene, the **Roosevelt Grove of Ancient Cedars** nurtures trees of up to 12 ft. in diameter.

Continue another 35 mi. east on I-90 through mining country to the town of **Wallace,** for retail shops shaped like mining helmets and the **Wallace Mining Museum,** 509 Bank St. (753-7151), which features turn-of-the-century mining equipment. (Open Mon.-Fri. 8am-7pm, Sat.-Sun. 9am-5pm; off-season Mon.-Sat. 9am-6pm. $1, seniors and kids 50¢.) Next door, take the **Sierra Silver Mine Tour** (752-5151; leaves from museum) through a recently closed mine. (Tours May-Sept. daily every 20 min. 9am-4pm; July 9am-6pm. 1 hr. $6, seniors and ages under 12 $5.) Mining, mining, mining. Twenty mi. north on U.S. 95, ride the **world's largest gondola** up Silver Mountain. Mountain bikes can be transported in the gondola. (Call 783-1111 for info on hiking, biking, or eating on the mountain; $9, students and seniors $7, kids under 6 $1; chairlift rides $2.) "Rise and dine" packages (gondola ride and dinner) available Fri.-Sun. evenings, $26 per person. (Open mid-May-early Oct. Mon.-Thurs. 10am-6pm, Fri.-Sat. 10am-10pm, Sun. 10am-9pm.) In early August, on the campus of Northern Idaho University, **Art on the Green** is an outdoor celebration of local artists.

■■■ CRATERS OF THE MOON NATIONAL MONUMENT

Sixty mi. south of Sun Valley on U.S. 20/26/93, the black lava plateau of the **Craters of the Moon** rises from the surrounding fertile plains. Windswept and remarkably quiet, the stark, twisted lava formations are speckled with sparse, low vegetation. Volcanic eruptions occurred here as recently as 2000 years ago.

Park admission is $4 per car, $2 per tour bus, and the bizarre black campsites cost $8 (52 sites without hookup). Wood fires are prohibited but charcoal fires are permitted. You can also camp for free in the adjacent **Bureau of Land Management** properties. The park's sites often fill by 4pm on summer nights. Unmarked sites in the monument are free with free backcountry permits, but even with the topographical map ($4), it may be hard to find a comfortable spot: the first explorers couldn't sleep in the lava fields for lack of bearable places to bed down. You can camp in only one designated area, after a 4 mi. hike.

The **visitors center** (527-3257), just off U.S. 20/26/93, has displays and videotapes on the process of lava formation, and printed guides for hikes to all points of interest within the park. They also distribute backcountry camping permits and sell the maps mentioned above. Rangers lead evening strolls and programs at the campground amphitheater (daily mid-June to mid-Sept.). (Open daily 8am-6pm; off-season 8am-4:30pm.) Explore nearby **lava tubes,** caves formed when a surface layer of lava hardened and the rest of the molten rock drained out, creating a tunnel. If a ranger does not escort you, bring a flashlight. From nearby Arco, Blackfoot, or Pocatello you can connect with **Greyhound**. There is, however, neither public transportation to the national monument nor food available when you get there.

■■■ KETCHUM AND SUN VALLEY

In 1935, Union Pacific heir Averill Harriman sent Austrian Count Felix Schaffgotsch to scour the U.S. for a site to develop into a ski resort area rivaling Europe's best. The Count settled on the small mining and sheep-herding town of Ketchum in Idaho's Wood River Valley, which has since become Sun Valley, a ski resort for the American rich and famous. The budget traveler should avoid the Valley and head for the hills, where the surrounding Pioneer and Sawtooth Mountains provide endless warm-weather opportunities for camping, hiking, biking, and fishing.

Practical Information The best time to visit the area is during "slack" (late Oct.-Thanksgiving and May-early June), when the tourists magically vanish. For local info, visit the **Sun Valley/Ketchum Chamber of Commerce** (800-634-3347), at 4th and Main St., Ketchum, P.O. Box 2420, Sun Valley 83353, where a well-informed, helpful staff shines. (Open daily 9am-5pm, less when slacking.) The **Ketchum Ranger Station,** 206 Sun Valley Rd., Ketchum (622-5371), three blocks east of Rte. 75, is the place to go for information on national forest land around Ketchum, and tapes and maps on the Sawtooth Recreation Area. (Open Mon.-Fri. 8am-5pm.) The **post office** in Ketchum is at 301 1st Ave. (726-5161; open Mon.-Fri. 8:30am-5:30pm, Sat. 11am-1pm). The **ZIP code** is 83340. The **area code** is 208.

Food Though it's a small town, Ketchum has plenty of inexpensive, enjoyable restaurants (check out **Irving's,** the legendary local hot-dog stand, open 11:30am-3pm). Have this guidebook and eat it too at the **Main St. Bookcafe,** 211 Main St. (726-3700), which we grudgingly admit sells other books, as well as standard cafe fare (espresso $1.25, hummus plate $4.50, veggie burger $6). (Open Mon.-Tues. 7am-6pm, Wed.-Fri. 7am-10pm, Sat.-Sun. 7am-midnight.) Find HUGE! food at **Mama Inez** (726-4231), at 7th and Warm Springs, including bean burritos ($2.30) and beef enchiladas ($6). The nachos ($6.85) require dextrous utensil skill to eat.

Accommodations and Camping The food may be cheap; the same cannot be said for indoor accommodations. From early June to mid-October, **camping** is the best option for cheap sleep. The **Sawtooth National Forest** surrounds Ketchum—drive or hike along the forest service road and camp for free. The **North Fork** and **Wood River** campgrounds lie 7 and 10 mi. north of Ketchum, respectively, and cost $3 per site. Wood River has an amphitheater and flush toilets. You must bring your own water to the three **North Fork Canyon** campgrounds 7 mi. north of Ketchum (free). Call the Ketchum Ranger Station for information.

Hot Springs The hills of Ketchum have more natural **hot springs** than any spot in the Rockies except Yellowstone; bathing is free and uncrowded in most of the springs. Like the ghost towns of the surrounding mountains, many springs can be reached only by foot; for maps, inquire at **Chapter One Bookstore** (726-5425) on Main St. across from Pedro's Market, or **Elephant's Perch,** on Sun Valley Rd. (726-3497). "The Perch" is also the best source for mountain bike rentals and trail information. (Bikes $12 per ½-day, $18 per day; rollerblades $10 per ½-day, $15 per day.)

More accessible, non-commercial springs include **Warfield Hot Springs** on Warm Springs Creek, 11 mi. west of Ketchum on Warm Springs Rd., and **Russian John Hot Springs,** eight mi. north of the SNRA headquarters on Rte. 75, just west of the highway. For the best information on fishing conditions and licenses, as well as equipment rentals, stop by **Silver Creek Outfitters,** 507 N. Main St. (726-5282; open daily 8am-6pm). The fly-fishing bible *Curtis Creek Manifesto* is available here ($7).

■■■ SAWTOOTH NATIONAL RECREATION AREA

Rough mountains pack the 756,000 acres of wilderness in this recreation area. Home to the **Sawtooth** and **White Cloud Mountains** in the north and the **Smokey** and **Boulder** ranges in the south, the **Sawtooth National Recreation Area (SNRA)** is surrounded by four national forests, encompassing the headwaters of five of Idaho's major rivers.

If you have a car, getting to the heart of the SNRA is easy. Make sure to pause at the **Galena Summit,** 25 mi. north of Ketchum on Rte. 75. The 8701-ft. peak provides an excellent introductory view of the range. If you don't have a car, take the bus to Missoula (250 mi. north on U.S. 93) or Twin Falls (120 mi. south on Rte. 75); from there, rent a car with at least six cylinders or plan for a long and beautiful hike.

Practical Information Information centers in the SNRA are almost as plentiful as the peaks themselves. Stop by the **Stanley Chamber of Commerce** (774-3411), on Rte. 21 about three-quarters of the way through town. (Open daily 10am-6pm, winter hours vary.) Topographical maps ($2.50) and various trail books are available at McCoy's Tackle (see below) and at the **Stanley Ranger Station** (774-3681), 3 mi. south on Rte. 75 (open Mon.-Fri. 8am-5pm, Sat.-Sun. 8:30am-5pm). The **Redfish Visitors Center** (774-3376) lies 8 mi. south and 2 mi. west of Stanley at the **Redfish Lake Lodge.** (Open June 19-Sept. 2 daily 9am-6pm). Whatever you can't find at these three places awaits at **SNRA Headquarters** (726-7672), 53 mi. south of Stanley off Rte. 75. The headquarters building itself mimics the peaks of the Sawtooths. (Open daily 8am-5:30pm; fall and spring Wed.-Sun. 8am-5:30pm, winter Mon.-Fri. 8am-4:30pm, Sat.-Sun. 9am-4:30pm.) All the info centers provide maps of the Sawtooths ($3) and free taped auto tours of the impressive Ketchum-Stanley trip on Rte. 75. The **post office** (774-2230) is on Ace of Diamonds St. (open Mon.-Fri. 8am-5pm); the **ZIP code** is 83278.

Food and Camping In the heart of Stanley, on Ace of Diamonds St., the **Sawtooth Hotel and Cafe** (774-9947) is a perfect place to stay after a wilderness sojourn (singles $24, with private bath $40; doubles $27, with private bath $45). More scenic is **McGowan's Resort** (800-447-8141), 1 mi. down Rte. 75 in Lower Stanley. Hand-built cabins here sit directly on the banks of the Salmon River, house up to six people each, and usually contain kitchenettes. The resort's tackle shop rents kayaks and rafts (rafts $15 per day, single kayaks $25 per day, doubles $35). They also offer a terrific view of the Sawtooths and unmatched hospitality. ($50-85; Sept.-early June $40-75.) Campgrounds line Rte. 75; clusters are at **Redfish Lake** at the base of the Sawtooths and **Alturas Lake** in the Smokies. At Redfish, the catch of the day is the small campground at the Point, which has its own beach. The two campgrounds on nearby Little Redfish Lake are the best spots for trailers. Other free sites are **Redfish Overflow,** just off Rte. 75, and **Decker Flats,** just north of 4th of July Rd. on Rte. 75. Sites in the SNRA cost $6; primitive camping (no water) is free anywhere you find it.

Activities and Sights Places for **hiking, boating,** and **fishing** in all four of the SNRA's little-known ranges are unbeatable and innumerable. 2 mi. northwest of Stanley on Rte. 21, take the 3-mi. Iron Creek Rd. which leads to the trailhead of the **Sawtooth Lake Hike.** This 5½-mi. trail is steep but well-worn, and not overly difficult if you stop to rest. Bolder hikers who want to survey the White Cloud Range from above should head southeast of Stanley to the **Casino Lakes** trailhead. This trek terminates at **Lookout Mountain**, 3000 ft. higher than far-away Stanley itself. (Groups of 10-20 need to acquire free wilderness permits. If you want a big bonfire, get a burning permit, and always check with a ranger where you can light fires.) The long and gentle loop around **Yellow Belly, Toxaway,** and **Petit Lakes** is recommended for novice hikers or any tourists desiring a leisurely overnight trip. For additional hiking information, consult the detailed topographic maps in any of Margaret Fuller's *Trail Guides* ($13 for the Sawtooths and White Cloud guides), available at McCoy's Tackle Shop (see below). Stock up on food at the **Mountain Village Grocery Store** (774-3392) before venturing into the mountains.

In the heat of summer, the cold rivers beg for **fishing, canoeing,** or **whitewater rafting**. **McCoy's Tackle Shop** (774-3377), on Ace of Diamonds St. in Stanley, rents gear and sells a full house of outdoor equipment and has a gift shop (fly rod $10 per day, $42 per 6 days; spinning rod $6 per day, $27 per 6 days; open daily 8am-8pm). The **Redfish Lake Lodge Marina** (774-3536) rents paddleboats ($4-5 per ½-hr.), canoes ($5 per hr., $15 per ½-day, $25 per day), and more powerful boats for higher prices (open in summer daily 7am-9pm). **The River Company** (774-2244), based in Ketchum (726-8890) with an office in Stanley, arranges whitewater rafting and float trips. (Ketchum office open daily 8am-6pm. Stanley office open in summer daily 8:30am-6pm, unless a trip is in progress.)

The most inexpensive way to enjoy the SNRA waters is to visit the **hot springs** just east of Stanley. Watch for the rising steam on the roadside, often a sign of hot water. **Sunbeam Hot Springs,** 13 mi. from town, is the best of the batch. Be sure to bring a bucket or cooler to the stone bathhouse; you'll need to add about 20 gallons of cold Salmon River water before you can get into these hot pools. For evening entertainment, try to get in on the regionally famous **Stanley Stomp,** when fiddlers in **Casanova Jack's Rod and Gun Club** (774-9920) keep the foot-stomping going all through the night. (Open daily to 2am; live music Thurs.-Sat. evenings.)

■ Montana

Despite the recent acquisition of large amounts of acreage by such Eastern celebrities as Ted Turner, Tom Brokaw, and Liz Claiborne, Montana remains true to its image as Big Sky country. Prairies rise gently from the Great Plains grasslands occupying the eastern two-thirds of the state. The Rocky Mountains punctuate the western third of the state with wilderness, glaciers, and grizzlies, in a state with 25 million wild and wooly acres of national forests and public lands. This is a state where the populations of elk, deer, and pronghorn antelope outnumber its citizens. Copious fishing lakes, 500 species of wildlife (not including billions of insect types), and thousands of ski trails; Montana is where to go to get away from it all.

PRACTICAL INFORMATION

Capital: Helena.
Visitor Information: Montana Promotion Division, Dept. of Commerce, Helena 59620 (444-2654 or 800-541-1447). Write for a free *Montana Travel Planner*. **National Forest Information,** Northern Region, Federal Bldg., 5115 U.S. 93, Missoula 59801 (329-3511). Gay and lesbian tourists can write **Lambda Alliance,** P.O. Box 7611, Missoula, MT 59807, for information on gay community activities in Montana.
Time Zone: Mountain (2 hrs. behind Eastern). **Postal Abbreviation:** MT
Sales Tax: None.

■■■ BILLINGS

The city of Billings began in the spring of 1882 with a few buildings around a railroad station. Only five months later the area had grown into a typical western city with hundreds of buildings and thousands of inhabitants. Today, Billings is the largest city in Montana, and an excellent base from which to explore the southern part of the state; in any direction five minutes away from town you'll find mountains and rivers galore.

Practical Information The **visitors center** at the Chamber of Commerce, 815 S. 27th St. (252-4016), has an electronic map which highlights areas of good hiking and fishing. (Open daily 8:30am-7:30pm, off season Mon.-Fri. 8:30am-5pm.) **Rent-a-Wreck** (252-0219) has the cheap cars, from $28 per day ($28.50 winter), or $130 per week (winter $160), with 100 free mi./day, 19¢ (17¢ in winter) per additional mi. (Open Mon.-Fri. 8am-6pm, Sat. 9am-3pm, Sun. by appt. Must be 21 with credit card and have liability insurance.) Billings's **area code** is 406.

Accommodations and Food Rooms in Billings don't come cheap. Most have easy access to downtown, however. **Motel 6** has two locations, one at 5400 Midland (252-0093; singles $30, doubles $36), another at 5353 Midland (248-7551; same prices). Lounge on great porches at the base of the **Rainbow Motel,** 421 St. Johns (259-5222; singles $28, doubles $30, pot of gold not included). **Picture Court,** 5146 Laurel Rd. (252-8478), lets their hardy singles ($26) and doubles ($31).

There are a number of casino/fast-food joints (hamburgers and pizza with slot machines) downtown. For authentic Mexican food, try **Dos Machos** (652-2020), 4th St. West, where you can munch on cajun steak sandwich ($6.50), or tacos, enchiladas, and burritos ($1.50-9.50). (Open Mon.-Sat. 11am-10pm, Sun. 9am-9pm.) For "the best Chinese in Montana," the **Great Wall,** 1309 Grand Ave. (245-8601), has lunch dishes ($4-8) and dinner ($7-11). (Open Sun.-Thurs. 11am-10pm, Fri.-Sat. 11am-10:30pm) "Nearly world-famous wings," fantastic service, and atmosphere can be had at **Snuffy's,** 1301 Grand Ave. (256-9450). Split your sides eating 50 ribs ($18) or a smaller rib-dinner ($6.50). Snuffy's gourmet dipp'n sauce can come with you for $3.25 a pint.

Sights, of which there are very few in Billings The **Billings Night Rodeo** (248-1080), at the Four Cross Arena next to the Ramada. (June-Aug. daily 8pm. $7, seniors $5, and youth $4.) **Eastern Montana College** (657-2882), on Rimrock Rd., on the way to the airport, offers canoeing classes and other outdoor activities. Continue along this road, up the hill for a fantastic view of Billings and the surrounding valley. Look for the **Billings Summer Fair** the 3rd weekend in July.

■■■ BOZEMAN

Bozeman keeps on growing in Montana's broad Gallatin River Valley, wedged between the Bridger and Madison Mountains. The valley, originally settled by farmers who sold food to Northern Pacific Railroad employees living in the neighboring town of Elliston, is still chock full of fertile farmlands and still supplies food to a large portion of southern Montana. Bozeman's rapid expansion and the presence of Montana State University elicit a cosmopolitan air, but visitors can still find plenty of Western hospitality in both urban bars and farmhouse kitchens.

Practical Information **Greyhound** and **RimRock Stages** serve Bozeman from 625 N. 7th St. (587-3110). Greyhound runs to Butte (3 per day, $12) and Billings (3 per day, $14). RimRock runs two buses per day to Helena ($16.50) and Missoula ($24). (Open Mon.-Sat. 7:30am-5:30pm and 8:30-10pm, Sun. 12:30-5:30pm and 8:30-10pm.) **Rent-a-Wreck,** 112 N. Tracey St. (587-4551), rents well-worn autos from $29 per day, with 100 free mi., 18¢ each additional mi. You must be 21 with a major credit card. (Open Mon.-Fri. 8am-6pm, Sat. 8am-5pm, Sun. by appointment.) The **Bozeman Area Chamber of Commerce**, 1205 E. Main St. (586-5421), provides ample information concerning geography and local events (open Mon.-Fri. 8am-5pm). Next year Bozeman will host the **19th Annual Liver Eatin' Johnson Spring Rendezvous** (587-3212) in the first week of May, so be there.

The Bozeman **post office** is at 32 E. Babcock St. (586-1508; open Mon.-Fri. 9am-5pm). Bozeman's **ZIP code** is 59715; the **area code** is 406.

Accommodations Summer travelers in Bozeman support a number of budget motels. The **Alpine Lodge**, 1017 E. Main St. (586-0356), has fairly clean but rather small rooms. (Singles $26, doubles $33. Cabins with kitchen summer $55, winter $45.) The **Ranch House Motel**, 1201 E. Main St. (587-4278), has larger rooms with free cable TV and A/C (singles $22, doubles $24). At the **Rainbow Motel**, 510 N. 7th Ave. (587-4201), the friendly owners disburse good travel advice and offer large, pleasant rooms (singles $32, doubles $42, $36 in winter.) The **Sacajawea International Backpackers Hostel**, 405 West Olive St. (586-4659), services latter-day transcontinental trekkers with showers, laundry, full kitchen facilities, and transport to trailheads ($8, kids $5).

Food In Bozeman, eat cheaply and well at the **Western Cafe**, 443 E. Main St. (587-0436), which boasts the best chicken-fried steak in the West ($7.25). (Open Mon.-Fri. 5am-7:30pm, Sat. 5am-2pm.) In the **Baxter Hotel**, 105 W. Main St. (586-1314), the **Rocky Mountain Pasta Company** serves an Italian spaghetti dinner with bread and salad for $8.50. In the same building, the **Bacchus Pub** provides cocktails, ample soup, and salad plates for Bozeman's intellectual and yuppie crowds. (Both open daily 7am-10pm. Reservations advised.) The **Pickle Barrel**, 809 W. College (587-2411), across from the MSU campus, serves delicious, filling sandwiches on freshly baked sourdough bread. At about a cubit, even half a sandwich ($4) is hard to finish. (Open daily 11am-10:30pm; off-season daily 11am-10pm.)

Fishing Livingston, a small town about 20 mi. east of Bozeman off I-90, is an angler's heaven; the town is near the Yellowstone, Madison, and Gardiner rivers, all of which are known for their abundance of trout. The **Yellowstone Angler**, P.O. Box 660, U.S. 89 S. (222-7130), will equip you with fishing gear and outdoor wear, and can answer questions about fishing conditions (open Mon.-Sat. 7am-6pm, Sun. 8am-5pm; Oct.-March Mon.-Sat. 7am-5pm). After a day of flyfishing, cast a line to **Livingston's Bar and Grill**, 130 N. Main St. (222-7909), where the vast quantities of imported and domestic beer will hook you (open Mon.-Sat. 11:30am-11pm).

■■■ LITTLE BIG HORN NATIONAL MONUMENT

Little Big Horn National Monument, until recently known as the Custer Battlefield National Monument, marks the site where Sioux and Cheyenne warriors, fighting June 25, 1876, to protect land ceded to them by the Laramie Treaty, wiped out Lt. Col. George Armstrong Custer and five companies, over 210 men, from the Seventh Cavalry. Ironically, the monument is located on what is now a Native American reservation, 60 mi. southeast of Billings off I-90. A 5-mi. self-guided car tour through the Crow Reservation takes you past the area where Custer made his "last stand." You can also see the park on a 45-min. bus tour ($4). The **visitors center** (638-2621) has a small museum that includes 100-year-old eyewitness drawings depicting the Native American warriors' view of the battle. (Museum and visitors center open daily 8am-8pm; fall daily 8am-6pm, winter daily 8am-4:30pm. Free. Monument open daily 8am-8pm. Entrance $4 per car, $2 per person.)

■■■ MISSOULA

People visit Missoula less for the city itself than for the Great Outdoors. Many of the locals, including students of the **University of Montana,** moonlight as nature enthusiasts; you'll be hard-pressed to resist their pastime.

Practical Information Traveling within Missoula is easy thanks to reliable city **buses** (721-3333; buses operate Mon.-Fri. 6am-7pm, Sat. 9:30am-6pm; fare 50¢). The **Missoula Chamber of Commerce,** 825 E. Front St. (543-6623), provides bus schedules. (Open daily 8:30am-7pm, winter 8:30am-5pm.) The **Greyhound terminal** pants at 1660 W. Broadway (549-2339). To Bozeman (3 per day, $24) or Spokane (3 per day, $35). **Intermountain Transportation** serves Whitefish (2 per day, $28) and **RimRock Stages** serves Helena (1 per day, $15) and Bozeman (1 per day, $22) from the same terminal. **Rent-a-Wreck,** 2401 W. Broadway (721-3838), offers humble autos ($33 per day, $198 per week, 150 free mi. per day, 25¢ each additional mi.; local cars $20 per day in winter, $25 in summer with 50 free mi. per day, 25¢ each additional mi. Must be 21; credit card deposit required.)

Missoula's **post office** is at 1100 W. Kent (329-2200), near the intersection of Brooks, Russell, and South St. (open Mon.-Fri. 8am-6pm, Sat. 9am-1pm). The **ZIP code** is 59801; the **area code** is 406.

Food, Accommodations, and Camping Missoula's dining scene offers much more than the West's usual steak and potato greasefest. The **Mustard Seed,** the mustard-colored building at 419 W. Front St. (728-7825), serves wonderful midsummer night's dishes from a variety of Asian cuisines. Full dinners (soup, vegetables, and a main course) go for $5-9. (Open Mon.-Sat. 11am-2:30pm, Mon.-Thurs. 5-9:30pm, Fri.-Sat. 5-10pm, Sun. noon-9:30pm.) **Torrey's** restaurant and natural food store, 1916 Brooks St. (721-2510), serves health food at absurdly low prices. Seafood stir-fry costs $3.50. (Restaurant open Mon.-Sat. 11:30am-8:30pm; store open Mon.-Sat. 10am-8:30pm.) If you'd rather be happy than healthy, slurp up creamy, refreshing smoothies at **Goldsmith's Premium Ice Cream Shop,** 809 E. Front St. (721-6732), near the Chamber of Commerce. ($1.50-$2.75; open Sun.-Thurs. 7am-10:30pm, Fri.-Sat. 7am-11pm.) Shop at the **Farmer's Market** for fresh produce at the north end of Higgens Ave. (May 15-Oct. 16 Sat. 9am-dusk, June 29-Sept. 14 Tues. 6pm-7:30pm).

Spend the night in Missoula at the **Birchwood Hostel (HI),** 600 S. Orange St. (728-9799), 13 blocks east of the bus station on Broadway, then eight blocks south on Orange. The spacious, immaculate dormitory room sleeps 22. Laundry, kitchen, and bike storage facilities are available, and the owner is friendly and knows the area. ($7 for members and cyclists, $9 otherwise. Open daily 5-10pm. Closed for 2 weeks in late Dec.) The **Canyon Motel,** 1015 E. Broadway (543-4069 or 543-7251), has newly renovated rooms at prices that won't gouge your wallet. (Singles $20-25. Doubles $25-30.) Closer to the bus station, the **Sleepy Inn,** 1427 W. Broadway (549-6484), has soporific singles for $28 and doubles for $33. The **Outpost Campground** (two mi. north of I-90 on U.S. 93; 549-2016), has showers, laundry and scattered shade from its young trees (sites $7, full hookup $10; open year-round).

Outdoor Activities Cycling enthusiasts have put the town on the map with the rigorous **Bikecentennial Route.** The Bikecentennial Organization Headquarters, 150 E. Pine St. (721-1776), provides information about the route. To participate in Missoula's most popular sport, visit the **Braxton Bike Shop,** 2100 South Ave. W. (549-2513), and procure a bike for a day ($12), overnight ($15), or a week ($75). (Open Mon.-Sat. 10am-6pm; leave credit card deposit.)

Ski trips, raft trips, backpacking, and day hikes are other popular Missoula diversions. The **University of Montana Recreation Annex,** University Center #164 (243-5172), posts sign-up sheets for all these activities and proves a good source of information on guided hikes (open Mon.-Thurs. 7am-5pm, Fri. 7am-4pm, Sat. 9am-1pm), while the **Department of Recreation** (243-2802) organizes day hikes and overnight trips. (Open Mon.-Fri. 7:30am-5pm. $12 per day, $38 3 day weekend.) The **Rattlesnake Wilderness National Recreation Area** hisses a few miles northwest of town off the Van Buren St. exit from I-90 and makes for a great day of hiking. Wilderness maps ($2.20) are available from the **U.S. Forest Service Information Office,** 340 N. Pattee St. (329-3511; open Mon.-Fri. 7:30am-4pm). The Clark Fork, Blackfoot, and Bitterroot Rivers provide gushing opportunities for float trips. For float maps ($3.50), visit the **Montana State Regional Parks and Wildlife Office,** 3201 Spurgin Rd. (542-5500; open Mon.-Fri. 8am-5pm). For rafting trips, visit **Pancaea Expeditions,** 180 S. 3rd (721-7719; $15 for 2 hr., $25 ½-day, $45 per day).

The hottest sight in town is the **Aerial Fire Depot Visitors Center** (329-4934), 7 mi. west of town on Broadway (I-90/U.S. 93), where you'll learn to appreciate the courage and folly aerial firefighters need when jumping into flaming, roadless forests. (Open daily 8:30am-5pm; Oct.-April by appointment for large groups. Free tours every hr. in summer, except noon-1pm.)

For a touch of culture in Missoula, on the first Friday of every month, all of the local museums and galleries (15 total) have open houses. Artists are present at some. The **Historical Museum at Fort Missoula** has exhibits and lectures on forestry, agriculture, mining, and community life. (Open Memorial Day-Labor Day Tues.-Sat. 10am-5pm, Sun. noon-5pm. Winter hours vary.)

■ ■ ■ WATERTON-GLACIER INTERNATIONAL PEACE PARK

Waterton-Glacier transcends international boundaries to unite two of the most pristine but relatively accessible wilderness areas on the continent. Symbolizing the peace between the United States and Canada, the park provides sanctuary for many endangered bears (the parks' prize possessions), bighorn sheep, moose, mountain goats, and now the grey wolf—and for tourists weary of the more crowded parks farther south and north.

Technically one park, Waterton-Glacier is, for all practical purposes, two distinct areas: the small Waterton Lakes National Park in Alberta, and the enormous Glacier National Park in Montana. Each park charges its own admission fee (in Glacier, $5 per week; in Waterton Lakes, CN$5 per day, CN$10 per 4 days), and you must go through customs to pass from one to the other. Several **border crossings** pepper the park: **Chief Mountain** (open mid-May daily 9am-6pm, June-mid-Sept. daily 7am-10pm, closed in winter); **Piegan/Carway** (in U.S., year-round daily 7am-11pm; in Canada open March-Oct. 7am-11pm, off-season 9am-6pm); **Trail Creek** (open June-Oct. daily 9am-5pm); and **Roosville** (open year round 24 hrs.).

Since snow melt is an unpredictable process, the parks are usually in full operation only from late May to early September. To find the areas of the park, hotels and campsites that will be open when you visit, contact the headquarters of either Waterton or Glacier (888-5441). Also, there is the newspaper *Waterton Glacier Guide* published at the beginning of the summer. This has dates and times of trail, campground, and border crossing openings.

■ Glacier National Park, Montana

Practical Information Glacier's layout is simple: one road enters through West Glacier on the west side, and three roads enter from the east—at Many Glacier, St. Mary and Two Medicine. West Glacier and St. Mary provide the two main points of entry into the park, connected by **Going-to-the-Sun Road** ("The Sun"), the only road traversing the park. **U.S. 2** runs between West and East Glacier along

WATERTON-GLACIER INTERNATIONAL PEACE PARK

82 mi. of the southern park border. Look for the "Goat Lick" signs off Rte. 2 near **Walton.** Mountain goats often descend to the lick for a salt fix in June and July.

Stop in at the **visitors centers** at **St. Mary,** at the east entrance to the park (732-4424; open daily in early June 8am-5pm, late June-early Sept. 8am-9pm), or at **Apgar,** at the west park entrance (open daily early June 8am-5pm, late June-early Sept. 8am-8pm). A third visitors center graces **Logan Pass** on Going-to-the-Sun Rd. (Open daily mid-June 9am-5pm, late June-early Sept. 9am-6pm.) An **info center** (888-5743) for Alberta is in West Glacier; ask any questions there before hiking. (Open daily 8am-7pm.)

Amtrak (226-4452 locally, or 800-872-7245) traces a dramatic route along the southern edge of the park. Daily trains huff and puff to West Glacier from Whitefish ($7), Seattle ($123), and Spokane ($61); Amtrak also runs from East Glacier to Chicago ($208) and Minneapolis ($179). **Intermountain Bus Lines** (862-6700) is the only line that comes near the park (Kalispell). To Missoula (1 per day, 3 hr., $24.75). As with most parts of the Rockies, a car is the most convenient mode of transport, particularly within the park. **Rent-a-Wreck** rents used cars from Kalispell, 1194 U.S. 2 E. (755-4555; $35 per day), and East Glacier, at the Sears Motel (226-9293; $50 per day). You must be over 21; major credit card required, 125 mi. free per day, 25¢ each additional mi.

The Glacier **post office** is at Lake McDonald Lodge, in the park. (Open Mon.-Fri. 9am-3:45pm.) General Delivery **ZIP code** is 59921. The **area code** is 406.

Accommodations and Camping Staying indoors within Glacier is absurd and expensive. **Glacier Park, Inc.** handles all lodging within the park and offers only the **Swiftcurrent Motor Inn** for budget travelers. Cabins without bathrooms at the Swiftcurrent are $20, $29 for two bedrooms (each additional person $2; open late June-early Sept.). The Swiftcurrent has a motel, but rooms cost twice as much. Reservations can be made through Glacier Park, Inc. From mid-September to mid-May, contact them at 925 Dial Tower Mail Station, Phoenix, AZ 85077 (602-207-2600); from early May to late September at East Glacier Park, 59434 (406-226-5551). Other than the Swiftcurrent, the company operates seven pricier lodges which open and close on a staggered schedule. Apgar opens first, in mid-May.

Excellent, affordable lodging can be found just across the park border in **East Glacier,** which sits on U.S. 2, 30 mi. south of the St. Mary entrance, and about five mi. south of the Two Medicine entrance. East Glacier boasts the **Backpackers Inn,** 29 Dawson Ave. (226-9392), a home-away-from-home behind Soranno's restaurant. The owners of the Inn and restaurant, Pat and Renée Schur, offer excellent advice about trails and activities. The Mexican food is reasonably priced ($4-11), spicy, and extremely tasty. The young adults who work at the restaurant will befriend travelers and are also knowledgable about the park. The Inn offers clean beds and hot showers for only $8 per night (bring a sleeping bag or rent one for $1). There is also a hostel at **Brownies Grocery (HI/AYH),** 1020 Rte. 49 (226-4426), in East Glacier. It offers comfortable accommodations in its dorm which is rumored to have once been a brothel. Offers a great view from the porch. ($10 members, $13 nonmembers), private rooms (singles $15 members, $18 nonmembers; doubles $20/23), and a family room ($30, 4-6 people). The **Kalispell/Whitefish Home Hostel,** 2155 Whitefish Stage Rd., Kalispell 59901, beckons 25 mi. from Glacier's west entrance, between U.S. 93 and U.S. 2 (756-1908). The home has comfortable beds (bring a sleeping bag), kitchen utensils, a stereo, and rents mountain bikes ($10).

Camping offers a cheaper and more scenic alternative to indoor accommodations. All developed campsites are available on a first-come, first-camped basis ($8-10); the most popular sites fill by noon. However, "Campground Full" signs sometimes stay up for days on end; look carefully for empty sites. All 11 campgrounds accessible by car are easy to find. Just follow the map distributed as you enter the park. **Sprague Creek** on Lake McDonald has many peaceful sites near the lake, but arrive early to avoid those near the road; there are only 25 sites total. Some sites at

Sprague, Apgar, and Avalanche remain reserved for bicyclists; towed units are prohibited. Campgrounds without running water in the surrounding national forests
offer sites for $5. Check at the Apgar or St. Mary visitors centers for up-to-date infor-
mation on conditions and vacancies at established campgrounds. Weather and the
grizzlies can adjust the operating dates as they desire.

The Outdoors Backcountry trips are the best way to appreciate the pristine
mountain scenery and the wildlife which make Glacier famous. The **Highline Trail**
from Logan Pass is a good day hike through prime bighorn sheep and mountain goat
territory, although locals consider it too crowded. The visitors center's free *Nature
with a Naturalist* pamphlet has a hiking map marked with distances and backcountry campsites. All travelers who camp overnight must obtain a free wilderness permit from a visitors center or ranger station 24 hrs. in advance, in person;
backcountry camping is allowed only at designated campgrounds. The **Two Medicine** area in the southeast corner of the park is well traveled, while the trek to **Kintla
Lake** rewards you with fantastic views of nearby peaks. It's easy to find your own
backcountry trails. Before embarking on any hike, familiarize yourself with the pre-
cautions necessary to avoid a run-in with a bear (see Bear Necessities in the Essentials above). Rangers at any visitors center or ranger station will instruct you on the
finer points of noise-making and food storage to keep bears away.

   Going-to-the-Sun Rd., the only road traversing the park, may be the most beautiful 52-mi. stretch of road in the world. Even on cloudy days when there's no sun to
go to, the constantly changing views of Alpine peaks will have you struggling to
keep your eyes on the road. Snow keeps the road closed until late June, so check
with rangers for exact dates. There are vehicle restrictions; all vehicles must be
under 24 ft. long and under 8 ft. (including mirrors) wide.

   Although The Sun Rd. is a popular **bike route,** only experienced cyclists with
appropriate gear and legs of titanium should attempt this grueling stint. The sometimes nonexistent shoulder of the road creates a hazardous situation for cyclists: in
the summer (June 15-Sept. 2), bike traffic is prohibited from the Apgar turn-off at the
west end of Lake McDonald to Sprague Creek, and from Logan Creek to Logan Pass,
11am-4pm. The east side of the park has no such restrictions. Bikes are not permitted on any hiking trails. **Equestrian** explorers should check to make sure trails are
open; fines for riding on closed trails are steep.

   While in Glacier, don't overlook the interpretive programs offered by the rangers.
Ask about "jammers," the red buses that snake around the park. Inquire at any visitors center for the day's menu of guided hikes, lectures, bird-watching walks, and
children's programs. At the Backpacker's Inn, ask about **Sun Tours,** guides through
the park with the Native American interpretation of events. The tour guide is
extremely knowledgable about wildlife and vegetation.

Water Activities Boat tours explore all of Glacier's large lakes. At Lake
McDonald and Two Medicine Lake, 1-hr. tours leave throughout the day. (Tours at
Lake McDonald $6.50, ages 4-12 $3.25; at Two Medicine $6 and $3.) The tours from
St. Mary (90 min.) and Many Glacier (75 min.) provide access to Glacier's backcountry. (From St. Mary $8, ages 4-12 $4; from Many Glacier $7.50 and $3.75.) The $7
sunset cruise proves a great way to see this quotidian phenomenon which doesn't
commence until about 10pm in the middle of the summer. **Glacier Raft Co.,** in
West Glacier (800-332-9995 or 888-5454) hawks full- and half-day trips down the
middle fork of the Flathead River. A full-day trip (lunch included) costs $57, under
13 $28; ½-day trips ($29, under 13 $18) leave in both the morning and the after-
noon. Call for reservations.

   Rent **rowboats** ($5 per hr., $25 per 10 hr.) at Lake McDonald, Many Glacier and
Two Medicine; **canoes** ($5 per hr.) at Two Medicine and Many Glacier; and **out-
boards** ($10 per hr., $50 per 10 hr.) at Lake McDonald. All require a $50 deposit.
Fishing is excellent in the park—cutthroat trout, lake trout, and even the rare Arctic

Grayling challenge the angler's skill and patience. No permit is required—just be familiar with the fishing regulations of the park, as explained by the pamphlet *Fishing Regulations,* available at all visitors centers. Right outside the park, however, on Blackfoot Indian land, you need a special permit. Anywhere else in Montana you need a Montana permit.

■ Waterton Lakes National Park, Alberta

The Canadian section of Waterton-Glacier is only a fraction of the size of its U.S. neighbor, but it nonetheless offers much of the same scenery and many similar activities. While a trip north is not essential, Waterton is generally less crowded than Glacier during the peak tourist months of July and August.

Practical Information The only road from Waterton's park entrance leads 5 mi. south to **Waterton townsite.** On the way, grab a copy of the *Waterton-Glacier Guide* at the **Waterton Information Office,** 215 Mountain View Rd. (859-2224), 5 mi. south of the park entrance (open Mon.-Fri. 8am-4pm). Drive either the **Akamina Parkway** or the less-traveled **Red Rock Canyon Road;** both leave the main road near the townsite and end at the heads of popular backcountry trails. You can rent a bike from **Pat's Texaco and Cycle Rental,** Mount View Rd., Waterton townsite (859-2266; mountain bikes $5.50 per hr. plus $20 damage deposit).

In an **emergency,** call the ambulance (859-2636). Waterton's **post office** is on Fountain Ave. at Windflower, in Waterton townsite (open Mon.-Fri. 8:30am-4:30pm). The **Postal Code** is T0K 2M0. The **area code** is 403.

Accommodations, Camping, and Food As you enter the park, marvel at the enormous **Prince of Wales Hotel** (859-2231), where you can have tea while maintaining a proper distance from the common townsite. Don't spend the night, though, unless the Prince is treating. Instead, pitch a tent at one of the park's three campgrounds. RV drivers flock to the hot showers of the **Townsite** campground, at the south end of town (sites $13; full hookup $17.50). **Crandell** (sites $10.50), on Red Rock Canyon Rd., and **Belly River** (sites $7.25), on Chief Mountain Hwy., are cheaper and farther removed from the hustle and bustle characteristic of townsite life. **Backcountry camping** is free with a permit from the Information Office or from **Park Headquarters and Information,** Waterton Lakes National Park, Waterton AB T0K 2M0 (859-2224; open Mon.-Fri. 8am-4pm). To stay indoors, drop by **Dill's General Store** (859-2345), on Waterton Ave., and ask to sleep in one of the nine rooms of the **Stanley Hotel.** (Singles and doubles $45 with shared bath.)

Waterton is sorely lacking in budget restaurants; your best bet is the **Zum Burger Haus,** 116 B Waterton Ave. (859-2388), which serves decent cheeseburgers for $4 on a pleasant patio. (Open daily 7:30am-9pm.)

Outdoors If you've brought only hiking boots to Waterton, set out on the **Crypt Lake Hike,** which stretches 4 mi. from Waterton townsite; you'll feel entombed as you pass through a natural tunnel bored through the mountainside. Those fleeing the Royal Canadian Mounted Police should scurry down the **International Hike,** which delivers you to Montana some 4 mi. after leaving the Townsite.

Anglers will appreciate Waterton's **fishing;** a **license** is required ($5 per 7 days), available from the Park offices, campgrounds, wardens, and service stations in the area. A boat tour of Upper Waterton Lake leaves from the **Emerald Bay Marina** (859-2362), in the townsite (5 per day mid-May to mid-Sept.; 2 hr.; $14, ages 4-12 $7). You can also rent a rowboat at Cameron Lake ($10 per hr.)

In the evening, take in an **interpretive program** at the **Falls** or **Crandell Theatre.** "The Fall of the Roamin' Empire" examines the annihilation of the great buffalo herds; "Salamander Suicides and Other My-newt Tragedies" exposes the soft white underbellies of the park's tiniest residents. (Programs in summer daily at 8:30pm; contact the Information Office for schedule information. Free.)

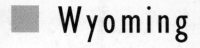

Wyoming

America's least-populated state, Wyoming is a natural Western wonderland, replete with expansive vistas and inexpensive adventure. A place where men wear cowboy hats and boots for *real,* and pick-up trucks are *de rigeur.* From a visitor's standpoint, Wyoming has everything you'd ever want to see in a state in the Mountain Time Zone: seasonal festivals (such as Frontier Days); national parks (Yellowstone and Grand Teton); spectacular mountain ranges (the Bighorns and the Winds); breathtaking panoramas; and, of course, plenty of beer. And cattle. Lots of cattle.

PRACTICAL INFORMATION

Capital: Cheyenne.
Visitor Information: Wyoming Travel Commission, I-25 and College Dr. at Etcheparc Circle, Cheyenne 82002 (777-7777 or 800-225-5996). Write for their free *Wyoming Vacation Guide.* **Wyoming Recreation Commission,** Cheyenne 82002 (777-7695). Information on Wyoming's 10 state parks. Open Mon.-Fri. 8am-5pm. **Game and Fish Department,** 5400 Bishop Blvd., Cheyenne 82002 (777-4600; license assistant 777-4599). Open Mon.-Fri. 8am-5pm.
Time Zone: Mountain (2 hr. behind Eastern). **Postal Abbreviation:** WY
Sales Tax: 5%.

■■■ BIGHORN MOUNTAINS

Bighorn Canyon and the blue ribbon trout stream, the Bighorn River, are just two hours from Billings. The Bighorns erupt from the hilly pastureland of northern Wyoming, a dramatic backdrop to the grazing cattle and sprawling ranch houses at their feet. In the 1860s, violent clashes occurred here between the Sioux, defending their traditional hunting grounds, and incoming settlers. Cavalry posts such as **Fort Phil Kearny,** on U.S. 87 between Buffalo and Sheridan, could do little to protect the settlers. The war reached a climax at the **Fetterman Massacre,** in which several hundred Sioux warriors wiped out Lt. Col. Fetterman's patrol. The massacre temporarily forced settlers out of the Bighorns, but within 20 years they were back, forging the Bighorns into permanent cattle country.

Hiking and Camping For sheer solitude, you can't beat the Bighorns' **Cloud Peak Wilderness Area,** in the **Bighorn National Forest.** To get to **Cloud Peak,** a 13,175-ft. summit in the range, most hikers enter at **Painted Rock Creek,** accessible from the town of **Tensleep,** 70 mi. west of Buffalo on the western slope, so named because it took the Sioux ten sleeps to travel from there to their main winter camps. The most convenient access to the wilderness area, though, is from the trailheads near U.S. 16, 25 mi. west of Buffalo. From the **Hunter Corrals** trailhead, move to beautiful **Mistymoon Lake,** an ideal base for forays into the high peaks beyond. You can also enter the wilderness area from U.S. 14 out of Sheridan in the north.

Campgrounds fill the forest, and all sites cost $6 per night. Near the Buffalo entrance, **Lost Cabin Middle Fork** (water and toilets; 28 mi. southwest of Buffalo on U.S. 16; open mid-May-Nov.; 4-day limit; for reservations call 800-284-2267; altitude 8,200 ft.) and **Crazy Woman** (6 sites; 25 mi. from Buffalo on U.S. 16; open mid-May-Oct.; altitude 7,600 ft.) boast magnificent scenery, as do **Cabin Creek** and **Porcupine** campgrounds near Sheridan. If you choose not to venture into the mountains, you can spend one night only free just off Coffeen St. in Sheridan's grassy **Washington Park.** Also, you can camp along the Bighorn River at Afterbay, Two Leggins, Bighorn, and Mallards Landing.

■ Buffalo and Sheridan

Most travelers will want to use either Buffalo or Sheridan as a base town from which to explore the mountains. At the junction of I-90 (east to the Black Hills area and north to Billings, MT) and I-25 (south to Casper, Cheyenne, and Denver), **Buffalo** is easy to reach. **Sheridan** is just 30 mi. to the north of Buffalo

Practical Information The **Buffalo Chamber of Commerce** is at 55 N. Main St. (684-5544 or 800-227-5122), 1 mi. west of the bus station (open Mon.-Sat. 8am-6pm; Sept.-June Mon.-Fri. 9am-5pm). The **U.S. Forest Service Offices,** 300 Spruce St. (684-7981), will answer questions about the Buffalo District in the Bighorns and sell you a road/trail map of the area for two greenbacks (open Mon.-Fri. 8am-5pm, Sat.-Sun. 9am-6pm). At **Alabam's,** 421 Fort St. (684-7452), you can buy topographical maps ($3.50), hunting, fishing, and camping supplies, and fishing licenses (1 day $5, 5 days $20). (Open daily 6am-9:30pm; off-season daily 6am-8pm.) Sheridan's **U.S. Forest Service Office,** 1969 S. Sheridan Ave. (672-0751), offers maps of the Bighorns ($3), along with numerous pamphlets on how to navigate them safely (open daily 8am-5pm). The **Sheridan Chamber of Commerce** (672-2485), 5th St. at I-90, can also provide info on the national forest (open May 15-Oct. 15 daily 8am-8pm).

Powder River Transportation serves Buffalo from a terminal at **Big Horn Travel Plaza,** 207 South By-Pass (684-5246), where twice daily you can catch a bus north to Sheridan ($8.50) and Billings ($35), or south to Cheyenne ($43). Buffalo, as the crossroads of north-central Wyoming, remains a popular place for hitchhikers to catch rides to the southern cities of Casper and Cheyenne; getting a lift on the freeway in Sheridan is more difficult. But never fear—**Powder River buses** run from the depot at the **Energy Inn Motel,** 580 East 5th St. (674-6188), to Billings (2 per day, $27), Buffalo (2 per day, $8), and Cheyenne (2 per day, $44). The **time zone** for both Sheridan and Buffalo is Mountain (2 hr. behind Eastern). The **ZIP code** for Buffalo is 82834, and for Sheridan 82801. The **area code** for the Bighorns is 307.

Accommodations and Food Motels, many with budget rates, line the town's two main drags, Coffeen Ave. and Main St. The **Mountain View Motel** (684-2881) is by far the most appealing of Buffalo's cheap lodgings. Pine cabins with TV, A/C, and/or heating complement the assiduous service and thematic sheets. (Singles $30, doubles $34; winter $20/24.) Also try the **Z-Bar Motel** next door (684-5535), with HBO, refrigerator or kitchen, and A/C. (Singles $32, doubles $36; winter $24/28; for kitchen add $5; reservations necessary.)

Heist away at the **Stagecoach Inn,** 845 Fort St. (684-2507), at the Singer sewing machine tables, bandanna napkins, and cowboy table cloths. Huge portions, specials with soup or salad, potato, pie, and amazing bread $9-12, lunch $3-9. (Open Mon.-Sat. 11:30am-2pm, 5pm-9pm.) Stock up on sandwiches at the **Breadboard,** 190 E. Hart (684-2318), where an eight-in.-long "Freight Train" (roast beef and turkey with all the toppings) knows it can for $3.50. (Open Mon.-Sat. 11am-10pm.) Or **Dash Inn,** 610 E. Hart St. (684-7930), for scrumptious fried chicken (2 pieces $3.75). (Open summer daily 11am-10pm, winter 11am-8:30pm.)

Sights If you have become jaded by postcard-perfect scenery and are hankerin' after a bit o' frontier history, visit the **Jim Gatchell Museum of the West,** 10 Fort St. (684-9331; $2, under 16 free), or the museum and outdoor exhibits at the former site of **Fort Phil Kearny** (684-7629), on U.S. 87 between Buffalo and Sheridan (open daily 8am-6pm; Oct. 16-May 14 Wed.-Sun. noon-4pm; $2, $1 students). If that doesn't sate you, become an occidental tourist at the historic **Occidental Hotel,** 10 N. Main St. (684-2788), the town hall/polling place/hospital since 1880 (open daily 10:30am-4:30pm and 6:30-8:30pm; free).

Sheridan escaped most of the military activity of the 1860s, but has its own claim to fame: Buffalo Bill Cody used to sit on the porch of the once luxurious **Sheridan Inn,** at 5th and Broadway, as he interviewed cowboy hopefuls for his *Wild West*

Show. The Inn has recently hit hard times, and may soon close; they no longer provide accommodations but do give tours.

■■■ CASPER AND ENVIRONS

Built primarily as a stop for the Union Pacific Railroad, Casper has a history characteristic of hundreds of other similar railroad towns. Casperites are proud of their city's *raison d'être* and their chief claim to fame: nine of the pioneer trails leading west, including the Oregon and Bozeman trails, intersected at a point not far from what is today the city's southern limit. Mountain men, fur trappers, Mormons, Shoshone, and Sioux all lived in the Casper area during the mid-1880s. The convergence of those famous paths lives in the minds of those who call Casper by its nicknames, "the Hub" and "the Heart of Big Wyoming," who also seem to have forgotten that most of those pioneers *kept moving on*.

Practical Information The friendly and helpful **Casper Area Convention and Visitors Bureau** convenes at 500 N. Center St. (234-5311 or 800-852-1889, fax 265-2643; open Mon.-Fri. 8am-7pm, Sat.-Sun. 10am-7pm; off-season Mon.-Fri. 8am-5pm.) They will help you find your way in Casper, Wyoming, and even provide suggestions for trips to neighboring states. **Powder River Transportation Services,** 596 N. Poplar (266-1904; 800-433-2093 outside WY), sends one bus per day to: Buffalo ($21), Sheridan ($26), Cheyenne ($30.45); and two per day to Billings ($55), Rapid City ($52.50). **Casper Affordable Used Car Rental,** 131 E. 5th St. (237-1733), rents cars for $22 per day, 50 free mi., 15¢ per additional mi.; $149 per week, 350 free mi., 15¢ per additional mi. (Open Mon.-Fri. 8am-5:30pm. Must be 22 to rent; $200 or credit card deposit required.) Casper's main **post office** is at 150 E. B St. (266-4000; open Mon.-Fri. 7:30am-5:30pm). The **ZIP code** is 82601; the **area code** is 307.

Accommodations, Camping, and Food Unforgiven high plains drifters can bunk down in the **Travelier Motel,** 500 E. 1st St. (237-9343), which offers spotless rooms near the center of town for only a fistful of dollars. (Singles $17.50. Doubles $20.) For a few dollars more, the good, the bad, *and* the ugly can enjoy regal treatment at **The Royal Inn,** 440 E. A St. (234-3501). Folks from the inn will pick pale riders up at the bus station for free. All rooms have showers and baths, cable, and phones. Friendly owners are eager to please. Outdoor heated pool. Pets allowed; Sister Sara keeps her two mules here. (Singles $19, with fridge and remote control TV $25. Doubles $27, with fridge and remote control TV $29. Extra person $5.) Just up the street, step out of the high noon sun into **The Virginian Motel,** 830 E. A St. (266-9731), which has been renovated in Victorian style but has not been repriced. (Singles $17, $64 per week. Doubles $22, $80 per week. Key deposit $2).

Campers can settle down at the **Ft. Caspar Campground,** 4205 W. 13th St. (234-3260; tents $10; full hookup $13.50). The **Natrona County Parks Office,** 182 Casper Mt. Park (234-6821), provides information about camping in the greater Casper area (open Mon.-Fri. 8am-5pm). The parks office presides over several campgrounds, including **Casper Mountain** (472-0452), 12 mi. south of Casper on Rte. 251, near Ponderosa Park and **Alcova Lake Campground,** 35 mi. southwest of Casper on Country Rd. 407 off Rte. 220, a popular recreation area with beaches, boats, and private cabins. (All park tent sites $5; RV hookups at Alcova $12.) The **Hell's Half Acre Campground** (472-0018), 45 mi. west on U.S. 20-26, proves more inviting than its name implies, offering more amenities than the primitive park sites, including showers and hookups (tent sites $2 per person; full hookup $11).

When you've kicked up enough dust for one day and are "hankerin' for a hunk of cheese," mosey on into the **Cheese Barrel,** 544 S. Center St. (235-5202), for a hearty and affordable breakfast or lunch. Try the pita veghead ($3.95) and be sure to have to at least one order of cheese bread (85¢ for two gooey slices). (Open Mon.-Sat. 6:30am-2:30pm.) **Anthony's,** 241 S. Center St. (234-3071), serves huge portions of

Italian food by candlelight (spaghetti $5.50; open daily 5-10pm, Mon.-Fri. 11:30am-2pm, Sun. "off-the-menu" brunch 9am-2pm and dinner 5-10pm). The best Chinese food in town is at **The Peking Restaurant,** 333 E. A St. (266-2207). Lunch specials (Mon.-Fri. 11am-2pm) from $3.75. A lot of dishes to chose from in a refreshing non-Western setting. (Open Mon.-Fri.11am-2pm, Sun.-Thurs. 5-8pm, Fri.-Sat. 5-9pm.)

Sights and Activities Casper's pride and joy, **Fort Caspar,** 4205 W. 13th St. (235-8462), is a reconstruction of an old army fort on the western side of town. There is an informative museum on the site. (Open mid-May to mid-Sept. Mon.-Fri. 9am-6pm, Sat. 9am-5pm, Sun. noon-5pm; winter Mon.-Fri. 9am-5pm, Sun. 1-4pm. Free.) From Ft. Caspar you can hike to **Muddy Mountain** or **Lookout Point** to survey the rugged terrain that hosted some of the last, bloody conflicts between the Native Americans and the white pioneers.

Forty-five mi. northwest of Casper on U.S. 20-26, you can see **Devil's Kitchen** (also called Hell's Half-Acre), a 320-acre bowl serving up hundreds of crazy colorful spires and caves. **Independence Rock,** 55 mi. southwest on Rte. 220, still welcomes travelers to the entrance of a hellish stretch of the voyage across Wyoming. In 1840, Father Peter DeSmet nicknamed it the "Great Registry of the Desert," honoring the godless renegades and Mormon pioneers who etched their name into the rock as they passed by. Explore the abandoned prospecting town on Casper Mountain or follow the **Lee McCune Braile Trail** through Casper Mountain's Skunk Hollow. If you are here in early August, check out the week-long **Central Wyoming Fair and Rodeo,** 1700 Fairgrounds Rd. (235-5775), which keeps the town in an extended state of Western hoopla replete with parades, demolition derbies, livestock shows, and, of course, rodeos.

If you are passing through Casper in the winter, consider surrendering to the snowy slopes nearby mountains have to offer. Casper Mountain, 11 mi. south of Casper, hosts the **Hogadon Ski Area** (235-8499), with 60 acres of downhill, cross-country, and snowmobile trails and runs rising 8000 ft. above sea level. For equipment, stop in at **Mountain Sports,** 543 S. Center St. (266-1136). Cross-country skis are $14 per day, $10 for children 12 and under, $5 for children under 5. (Open in the winter Mon.-Sat. 9am-6pm, Sun. noon-5pm; in summer Mon.-Sat. 9am-6pm.) Credit card deposit or cost of equipment in cash required. The location at Hogadon also rents downhill skis. For information on ski conditions, contact **Community Recreation, Inc.,** (235-8383; open Mon.-Fri. 8am-5pm).

■■■ CHEYENNE

What's in a name? Cheyenne, named for the Native American tribe that once roamed the wilderness surrounding the city, has had a nomenclatorial history worthy of note. For a period in the mid-19th century, Cheyenne was considered a prime candidate for the name of the Wyoming Territory. This moniker was struck down by vigilant Senator Sherman, who pointed out that the pronunciation of Cheyenne closely resembled that of the French word *chienne* meaning, shall we say, female dog. Residents of the city were not as bothered by such esoteric linguistic quibbles so they kept the name. By the 1860s the Union Pacific Railroad reached the end of the line in Cheyenne and Wyoming's capital became known as "Hell on Wheels." The red dust and general diabolism of the Wild West today lays dormant in Cheyenne most of the year, lending it a "Heck on Wheels" ambience. However, come during Frontier Days when throngs of visitors kick up the dust and come creaking through the doors of its few remaining weathered wood saloons and you'll call the place anything but dull.

PRACTICAL INFORMATION
Emergency: 911.

Visitor Information: Cheyenne Area Convention and Visitors Bureau, 309 W. 16th St. (778-3133; 800-426-5009 outside WY), just west of Capitol Ave. Extensive accommodations and restaurant listings. Open daily 8am-6pm, in winter Mon.-Fri. 8am-5pm. **Wyoming Information and Division of Tourism,** I-25 and College drive (777-7777; 800-225-5996 outside WY). Open daily 8am-5pm.

Tours: Cheyenne Street Trolley: 778-3133. Mid-May-mid-Sept., trolleys depart from 16th St. and Capitol St. Tours of downtown, Warren Air Force Base, and Old West Museum. Mon.-Sat. 10am, 1:30, and 4pm, Sun. at 1:30 and 4pm. Purchase tickets at Visitors Bureau on weekdays; Wrangler Department Store (16th and Capitol) on Sundays and Holidays. $6; kids 2-13 $3, under 2 free.

Amtrak: 102 W. Lincolnway (778-3912), in the lobby of Plains Hotel. Trains daily to: Denver ($21); Salt Lake City ($84); San Francisco ($157); Chicago ($178). Open daily 9:30am-5:30pm.

Buses: Greyhound, 1503 Capitol Ave. (634-7744), at 15th St. Three buses daily to: Salt Lake City (9 hrs., $73); Chicago ($110); Laramie ($9); Rock Springs ($33); Denver ($18). **Powder River Transportation,** in the Greyhound terminal (635-1327). Buses south to Rapid City twice daily ($69); north to Casper ($30.45) and Billings ($73) twice daily. Greyhound passes honored.

Taxi: Yellow Cab 638-3333. $1.30 base fare; $1.50 per mi. thereafter

Car Rental: Enterprise Rent-a-Car, 1700 W. Lincolnway (632-1907). $30 per day, unlimited mileage. Must be 21 with major credit card. Mon.-Fri. 7:30am-6pm, Sat. 8:30am-noon.

Help Line: Rape Crisis, 637-7233. 24 hrs.

Post Office: 2120 Capitol Ave. (772-6580), 6 blocks north of the bus station. Open Mon.-Fri. 7:30am-5:30pm, Sat. 7:30am-noon. General Delivery open Mon.-Sat. from 7:30am. **ZIP code:** 82001.

Area Code: 307.

Cheyenne's downtown area is small and manageable. Central, Capitol, and Carey Avenues form a grid with 16th-19th Streets, which encompasses most of the old sights and accommodations. 16th St. is part of I-80; it intersects I-25/84 on the western edge of town. Denver lies 90 mi. south on I-25.

ACCOMMODATIONS, CAMPING, AND FOOD

It's not hard to land a cheap room here among the lariats, plains, and pioneers, unless your visit coincides with **Frontier Days**, the last full week of July (see Sights and Entertainment). In days approaching this week, beware of doubling rates.

Many budget motels line **Lincolnway** (U.S. 30). Just a few blocks from the bus station, the old **Plains Hotel,** 1600 Central Ave. (638-3311), offers very attractive, oversized rooms with marble sinks, HBO, and phones in a grand-lobbied, Western setting. In addition to the great rooms and large beds, the motel boasts a 24-hr. coffee shop and saloon that are convenient and affordable. (Singles $26. Doubles $37. Extra person $5.) The **Guest Ranch Motel,** 1100 W. 16th St. (634-2137), is a short hike west from the bus stop. Large, tidy rooms with cable and phones, shower and bath. Leave the pets at home. (Singles with one queen bed $26. Doubles $32.) **Downtown Motor Inn,** 1719 Central Ave. (638-5433), at 18th St., has cable TV, pool, exercise room, and a 24-hr. coffee shop. (Singles $25. Doubles $32.)

For campers, spots are plentiful (except during Frontier Days) at the **Restway Travel Park,** 4212 Whitney Rd. (634-3811), 1½ mi. east of town. (Sites $12.50 for up to four people, with electricity and water $14.50, full hookup $15.50; prices rise slightly in July. Laundry, heated pool, free mini-golf.) You might also try **Curt Gowdy State Park,** 1319 Hynds Lodge Rd. (632-7946), 23 mi. west of Cheyenne on Rte. 210. This year-round park has shade, scenery, fishing, hiking, and an archery range, as well as land for horseback riding—BYO horse. (Entrance fee $2; sites $4 per night; annual camping permit $25.)

Cheyenne is basically a meat n' potatoes place, but there are also a few good ethnic eateries sprinkled around downtown. Here, the price difference between the humble cafe and posh restaurant can be a mere $4-6. For a taste of some home cookin', float into the **Driftwood Cafe,** 200 E. 18th St. (634-5304), and try the pies and specials ($4.25 and under) concocted daily in the diner's small kitchen (open Mon.-Fri. 7am-4pm). **Ruthie's Sub Shoppe,** 1651 Carey Ave. (635-4896), a few doors down from the Pioneer Hotel, has the best tuna salad around ($2.50), and morning donuts (open Mon.-Fri. 7am-5pm, Sat. 7am-3pm). **Los Amigos,** 620 Central Ave. (638-8591), serves burritos ($2-4) and humongous, friendly dinners (from $7.25). You might want to go with a half-order (60% of the price), or swing by for the $4 lunch specials. (Open Mon.-Thurs. 11am-8:30pm, Fri.-Sat. 11am-9pm.) Lunch buffets at the **Twin Dragon Chinese Restaurant,** 1809 Carey Ave. (637-6622), weekdays 11am-2pm ($5); kids under 11, $2.75. Vegetarian egg rolls just $1.80; regular dinners from $5.50. Lunch specials Sat.-Sun., dinner specials daily. (Open Mon.-Sat. 11am-10pm, Sun. noon-9pm.) **Lexie's Cafe,** 216 E. 17th (638-8712), serves breakfast and lunch, including Mexican and Italian specialties and salads. Towering stack of pancakes ($2.75), huge burger ($3.75). (Open Mon.-Sat. 7am-3pm.)

When the urge to guzzle consumes you, **D.T.'s Liquor and Lounge,** 2121 Lincolnway, will help you get the DTs. Look for a pink elephant above the sign; if you're already seeing two, move on. (Open Mon.-Sat. 7am-2am, Sun. noon-10pm.) The **Cheyenne Club,** 1617 Capitol Ave. (635-7777), is a spacious good-time country nightspot, hosting live bands nightly at 9pm. Every Wednesday and Thursday night from 7:30-9pm you can learn to swing your partner for free. You must be 21. (Open Mon.-Thurs. and Sat. 8:30pm-2am, Fri. 5pm-2am. Cover $1.)

SIGHTS AND ENTERTAINMENT

If you're within 500 mi. of Cheyenne during the last week in July, make every possible effort to attend the **Cheyenne Frontier Days,** nine days of non-stop Western hoopla. The town doubles in size as anyone worth a grain of Western salt comes to see the world's oldest and largest rodeo competition and partake of the free pancake breakfasts (every other day in the parking lot across from the chamber of commerce), parades, and square dances. Most remain inebriated for the better part of the week. Reserve accommodations in advance or camp nearby. For information, contact Cheyenne Frontier Days, P.O. Box 2477, Cheyenne 82003 (800-227-6336; fax 778-7213; open Mon.-Fri. 9am-5pm).

If you miss Frontier Days, don't despair; Old West entertainment abounds in "The Magic City of the Plains." Throughout June and July the **Cheyenne Gunslingers** perform a mock gunfight at W. 16th and Carey St. (Shows Mon.-Fri. at 6pm, Sat. at noon. Free. For info call the Cheyenne Area Convention and Visitors Bureau at 773-3133.) The **Cheyenne Frontier Days Old West Museum** (778-7290), in Frontier Park at 8th and Carey St., is a half-hour walk north down Carey St. The museum chronicles the rodeo's history from 1897 to the present, housing an "Old West" saloon, an extensive collection of Oglala Sioux clothing artifacts, and one of the nation's best covered wagon collections. (Open Mon.-Fri. 8am-6pm, Sat.-Sun. 10am-5pm. Admission $3, seniors $2, under 12 free, families $6.)

The **Wyoming State Museum,** 2301 Central Ave. (777-7024), at 24th St., presents an especially digestible history of Wyoming's cowboys, sheepherders, and suffragettes, along with exhibits on the Oglala, Cheyenne, and Shoshone who preceded them. (Open Mon.-Fri. 8:30am-5pm, Sat. 9am-4pm, Sun. noon-4pm; off-season closed Sun. Free.) The **Wyoming State Capitol Building** (777-7220), at the base of Capitol Ave. on 24th St., shows off its stained glass windows and yellowed photographs to tour groups trekking through (open Mon.-Fri. 8:30am-4:30pm; summer tours every 15 min.).

This oversized cowtown rolls up the streets at night; except for a few bars, the downtown goes to sleep at 5pm. One delightful exception is the **Old Fashioned Melodrama** (638-6543 mornings, 635-0199 afternoons and evenings), playing at the Old Atlas Theater, an old vaudeville house at 211 W. 16th St., between Capitol and Carey Ave. (Shows July-late Aug. Wed.-Thurs. 7pm, Fri.-Sat. 7 and 9:15pm. Tickets $7, 65+ and under 12 $5. Wed. $1 off.) To find out about beauty pageants and other events in the Atlas Theatre contact the **Cheyenne Civic Center,** 510 W. 20th St. (637-6363; box office open Mon.-Thurs. 11am-5:30pm, Sat. 10:30am-12:30pm).

■■■ DEVIL'S TOWER NATIONAL MONUMENT

We are not alone. 60 million years ago, in northeastern Wyoming, fiery magma forced its way through a layer of sedimentary rocks and cooled without breaking the surface. Centuries of wind, rain, and snow eroded the surrounding sandstone, leaving a stunning spire that was named the first National Monument in the U.S. in 1906. If looking at this obelisk of stone inspires you to play with mashed potatoes or gives you an eerie feeling of déjà vu, you will be comforted to know that Devils Tower was the cinematic landing strip for extra-terrestrials in *Close Encounters of the Third Kind.* The Mothership is not the only mode of transportation to the top. More than 5000 people climb it each year; there are more than 80 possible routes. Those interested in making the climb must register ($4) with a ranger at the **visitors center** (307-467-5377), 3 mi. from the entrance, before you set out and when you return (open daily 8am-8pm). There is also a **nature trail** around the tower and a **campground** (sites $7, water, bathrooms, fireplaces, picnic tables, no showers, open May 15-Nov.), but watch out for rattlesnakes and don't feed the prairie dogs. From I-90 take U.S. 14 25 mi. north to Rte. 24.

■■■ GRAND TETON NATIONAL PARK

When French fur trappers first peered into Wyoming's wilderness from the eastern border of Idaho, they found themselves face to face with three craggy peaks, each topping 12,000 ft. In an attempt to make the rugged landscape seem more trapper-friendly, they dubbed the mutant mountains "Les Trois Tetons," French for "the three tits." When they found that these triple nipples had numerous smaller companions, they named the entire range "Les Grands Tetons." Today the snowy heights of Grand Teton National Park delight modern hikers and cyclists with miles of strenuous trails. The less adventurous will appreciate the rugged appearance of the Tetons; the craggy pinnacles and glistening glaciers possess stunning beauty. Visitors will relish the park's relative lack of crowds in comparison with Yellowstone, its sometimes zoo-like neighbor to the north.

PRACTICAL INFORMATION

Emergency: 911. Also 733-2880 or 543-2581; **sheriff's office** 733-2331.
Park Headquarters: Superintendent, Grand Teton National Park, P.O. Drawer 170, Moose 83012 (733-2880). Office at the Moose Visitors Center (see below). Open daily 8am-7pm.
Park Entrance Fee: $10 per car, $4 per pedestrian or bicycle, $5 per family (non-motorized), under 16 (non-motorized) free. Good for 7 days in both the Tetons and Yellowstone.
Visitors Centers: Moose (733-2880), Rockefeller Pkwy. at the southern tip of the park. Open early June-early Aug. daily 8am-7pm; Sept.-May daily 8am-5pm. **Jenny Lake,** next to the Jenny Lake Campground. Open June-Aug. daily 8am-6pm. **Colter Bay** (543-2467), on Jackson Lake in the northern part of the park. Open early June-early Sept. daily 8am-8pm; May and late Sept.-early Oct. daily 8am-5pm. Park information brochures available in Braille, French, German, Japanese, Spanish, Elamite, Old High Persian, and Hebrew. Topographical maps ($2.50). Pick up the *Teewinot* newspaper (free) at any entrance or at the visitors center for a complete list of park activities, lodgings, and facilities.
Park Information and Road and Weather Conditions: 733-2220; 24-hr. recording. **Wyoming Highway Info Center,** 733-3316.

Bike Rental: Mountain Bike Outfitters, Inc. (733-3314), at Dornan's in Moose. Adult mountain bikes $6 per hr., $24 per day; kids $3.50 per hr., $14 per day; includes helmet. Open summer daily 9am-6pm. Credit card or deposit required.

Medical Care: Grand Teton Medical Clinic, Jackson Lake Lodge (543-2514 or 733-8002 after hours), near the Chevron station. Open June-mid-Sept. daily 10am-6pm. In a dire emergency, contact **St. John's Hospital** (733-3636), in Jackson.

Post Office: in **Colter Bay General Store** (733-2811). Open Mon.-Fri. 8:30am-1pm and 1:30pm-5pm, Sat. 9-10:30am. **ZIP code:** 83001.

Area Code: 307.

The national park occupies most of the space between Jackson to the south and Yellowstone National Park to the north. **Rockefeller Parkway** connects the two parks and is open year-round. The park is directly accessible from all directions except the west, as those lonely French trappers found out centuries ago.

ACCOMMODATIONS

If you want to stay indoors, grit your teeth and pry open your wallet. **The Grand Teton Lodge Co.** has a monopoly on lodging within the park. Make reservations for any Grand Teton Lodge establishment by writing the Reservations Manager, Grand Teton Lodge Co., P.O. Box 240, Moran 83013 (543-2855 or 800-628-9988 outside Wyoming). Accommodations are available late May through early October and are most expensive late June-early August. Reservations are recommended and can be made up to a year in advance. (See Jackson for accommodations outside the park.)

Colter Bay Tent Cabins: (543-2855). Cheapest accommodations in the park, but not the place to stay in extremely cold weather. Canvas shelters with wood-burning stoves, table, and 4-person bunks. Sleeping bags, wood, cooking utensils, and ice chests available for rent. Office open June-early Sept. daily 7am-10pm, or call Maintenance, 543-2811. Cabins $20 for 2, each additional person $2.50, cots $4. Restrooms and showers ($1.50) nearby.

Colter Bay Log Cabins: (543-2855). Quaint, well-maintained log cabins near Jackson Lake. Room with semi-private bath $25, with private bath $49-71. 2-room cabins with bath $72-94. Open mid-May-early Oct.

Flagg Ranch Village: P.O. Box 187, Moran 83013 (733-8761), on the Snake River near the park's northern entrance. Simple cabins for 2 with private bath $62.

CAMPING

Camping is the way to see the Tetons without emptying your savings account. The park service maintains five campgrounds, all on a first come, first served basis (sites $8). In addition, there are two trailer parks and some designated backcountry open to visitors whenever the snow's not too deep. RVs are welcome in all but Jenny Lake, but hookups are unavailable. Information is available at any visitors center.

Park Campgrounds: All campgrounds have rest rooms, cold water, fire rings, and picnic tables. Large groups can go to Colter Bay and Gros Ventre; all others allow a maximum of 6 people and 2 vehicles per site. **Jenny Lake:** 49 highly coveted sites; *arrive early.* No RVs. **Signal Mountain:** A few miles south of Colter Bay. 86 spots, usually full by noon. **Colter Bay:** 310 sites, shower, grocery store, and laundromat. Usually full by 2pm. **Snake River:** Northern campgrounds, with 60 sites, convenient to Yellowstone. Fills in late afternoon. **Gros Ventre:** On the park's southern border. 360 sites. A good bet if you arrive late. Max. stay in Jenny Lake 7 days, all others 14 days. Reservations required for large groups.

Colter Bay RV Park: 112 sites, electrical hookups. Reserved through Grand Teton Lodge Co. (733-2811 or 543-2855). Grocery store and eateries. Sites $21.40; May 15-June 7 and Sept.-Oct. 4 $17. Showers $1.50, towel rental $1.25.

Flagg Ranch Village Camping: Operated by Flagg Ranch Village (543-2861 or 800-443-2311). Right next to Yellowstone, so fills quickly. Grocery and eateries. Sites $15 for 2, $20 with hookup. Make reservations.

For **backcountry camping,** reserve a spot in a camping zone in a mountain canyon or on the shores of a lake by submitting an itinerary to the permit office at **Moose Ranger Station** (733-2880) from January 1 to June 1. Pick up the permit on the morning of the first day of your hike. You can make reservations by mail, but two-thirds of all spots are left open for reservation on a first come, first served basis; get a permit up to 24 hrs. before setting out at the Moose, Colter Bay, or Jenny Lake Ranger Stations. (Moose and Colter Bay open daily 8am-7pm, Jenny Lake mid-May-late Sept. daily 8am-6pm.) Camping is unrestricted in some off-trail backcountry areas (though you must have a permit). Wood fires are not permitted above 7000 ft.; check with rangers about fires in the lower regions. As the weather can be severe, even in the summer, backcountry campers should be experienced before venturing too far from civilization and help.

FOOD

The best way to eat in the Tetons is to bring your own grub. If this isn't possible, stick to what non-perishables you can pick up at the **Flagg Ranch Grocery Store** (543-2861 or 800-443-2311, open daily 7am-10pm; reduced winter hours), or **Dornan's Grocery** in Moose (733-2415, open daily 9am-6pm; reduced hours in winter). In Jackson, you can stock up on provisions at **Albertson's** supermarket (733-5950).

SIGHTS AND ACTIVITIES

The youngest mountain range in North America, the Tetons provide hikers, climbers, rafters, and sightseers with challenges and vistas not found in more weathered peaks. The Grandest Teton rises to 13,700 ft. above sea level, virtually without foothills. While Yellowstone wows visitors with its geysers and mudpots, Grand Teton's geology boasts some of the most scenic mountains in the U.S., if not the world.

Cascade Canyon Trail, one of the least arduous (and therefore most popular) hikes, originates at Jenny Lake. To start, take a boat trip (operated by monopolistic Grand Teton Lodge Co.) across Jenny Lake ($2, round-trip $4; children $1.50/2), or hike the 2-mi. trail around the lake. Trail guides (25¢) are available at the trailhead, at the west boatdock. The **Hidden Falls Waterfall** plunges ½-mi. from the trail entrance; only the lonely can trek 6¾ mi. further to **Lake Solitude.** Another pleasant day hike, popular for its scope of wildlife, is the 4-mi. walk from Colter Bay to **Hermitage Point.** The **Amphitheater Lake Trail,** which begins just south of Jenny Lake at the Lupine Meadows parking lot, will take you 4.6 breathtaking miles to one of the park's many glacial lakes. Those who were bighorn sheep in past lives can take the challenge of **Static Peak Divide,** a 15-mi. steep trail that climbs 4020 ft. from the Death Canyon trailhead (4½ mi. south of Moose Visitors Center) and offers some of the best lookouts in the park. All information centers (see Practical Information above) provide pamphlets about the day hikes and sell the *Teton Trails* guide ($2). Call **National Park Tours** (733-4325) for tours as well (open 9am-4pm, reservations required, prices vary greatly depending on where you want to start).

For a leisurely afternoon on Jackson Lake, rent boats at the **Signal Mountain Marina** (543-2831; late May-mid-Sept.). (Rowboats and canoes $8 per hr. Motorboats $15 per hr. Water-ski boats and pontoons $28 per hr. Open daily 7am-6pm.) **Colter Bay Marina** has a somewhat smaller variety of boats at similar prices. (Open daily 7am-8pm, rentals stop at 6pm.) **Grand Teton Lodge Company** (733-3471 or 543-2811) can also take you on scenic Snake River float trips within the park. (10½-mi. ½-day trip $29, under 12 $18. 20½-mi. luncheon or supper trips $31, under 17 $20.) **Triangle X Float Trips** (733-5500) can float you on a 5-mi. river trip for less ($19, under 13 $13). **Fishing** in the park's lakes, rivers and streams is excellent. A Wyoming license ($5) is required; get one in Jackson, at Moose General Store, at Signal Mt., at Colter Bay, in Flagg Ranch, or at Dornan's. **Horseback riding** is available through the Grand Teton Lodge Company (1-4 hr. rides, $16-34 per person).

The **American Indian Art Museum** (543-2467), next to the Colter Bay Visitors Center, offers an extensive private collection of Native American artwork, artifacts, movies, and workshops. (Open June-Sept. daily 8am-7pm; late May and late Sept. daily 8am-5pm. Free.) During July and August you can see Cheyenne, Cherokee, Apache, and Sioux dances at Jackson Lake Lodge (Fri. at 8:30pm). At the **Moose** and **Colter Bay Visitors Centers,** June through September, rangers lead a variety of activities aimed at educating visitors about such subjects as the ecology, geology, wildlife, and history of the Tetons. Check the *Teewinot* for exact times.

In the winter, all hiking trails and the unplowed sections of Teton Park Road are open to cross-country skiers. Pick up the trail map *Winter in the Tetons* or *Teewinot* at the Moose Visitors Center. From January through March, naturalists lead **snowshoe hikes** from Moose Visitors Center (733-2880; snowshoes distributed free). Call for reservations. **Snowmobiling** along the park's well-powdered trails and up into Yellowstone is a noisy but popular winter activity. Grab a map and guide at the Jackson Chamber of Commerce, 10 mi. south of Moose. For a steep fee you can rent snowmobiles at **Signal Mt. Lodge, Flagg Ranch Village,** or down in **Jackson;** an additional $10 registration fee is required for all snowmobile use in the park. Recently, millions of dollars were donated to develop snowmobile trails, which should be completed early 1994. All campgrounds close during the winter. The Colter Bay and Moose parking lots are available for RVs and cars, and backcountry snow camping (only for those who know what they're doing) is allowed with a free permit from Moose. Check with a ranger station for current weather conditions—many early trappers froze to death in the 10-ft. drifts—and avalanche danger.

■■■ JACKSON (JACKSON HOLE)

Colorado has Aspen, Idaho has Sun Valley, and Wyoming has Jackson—an expensive refuge for transplanted Eastern "outdoorsy" types. Mixing with tanned, svelte mountain bikers and rock climbers, you'll find busloads of camera-snapping tourists rushing to the Ralph Lauren and J. Crew outlets. If you head away from downtown, you may catch a glimpse of some real cowboys, of the type that established Jackson long before climbing mountains became fashionable (they're easily spotted on their fantastic ranches which line the mountains in and around Jackson).

PRACTICAL INFORMATION

Emergency: 911.

Visitor Information: Jackson Hole Area Chamber of Commerce, 32 N. Cache St. (733-3316), in a modern wooden split-level with grass on the roof. A crucial information stop. Open mid-June-mid-Sept. daily 8am-8pm; off-season daily 8am-5pm. **Bridger-Teton National Forest Headquarters,** 340 N. Cache St. (739-5500), 2 blocks south of the chamber of commerce. Maps $3 paper, $5 waterproof. Open Mon.-Fri. 8am-5:30pm, Sat. 8am-4:30pm.

Bus Tours: Grayline Tours, 330 N. Glenwood St. (733-4325), in front of Dirty Jack's Theatre. Full-day tours of Grand Teton National Park and Yellowstone National Park lower loop ($36). Call for reservations. **Wild West Jeep Tours,** P.O. Box 7506, Jackson 83001 (733-9036). In summer only, half-day tours of the Tetons and other areas ($30, seniors $27, under 12 $18). Call for reservations.

Public Transportation: Jackson START (733-4521), $1 per ride in town, $2 out. **Grand Teton Lodge Co.** (733-2811) runs a shuttle twice daily in summer to Jackson Lake Lodge ($14).

Car Rental: Rent-A-Wreck, 1050 U.S. 89 (733-5014). Compact $23 per day, $128 per week; mid-size $34 per day, $188 per week; 150 free mi., 20¢ each additional mi. Must be 21 with credit card, or if over 25, credit card or $300 cash deposit. Must stay within 500 mi. of Jackson. Open daily 8am-5pm.

Ski and Bike Rental: Hoback Sports, 40 S. Millward (733-5335). 10-speeds $7 per 2 hr., $16 per day; mountain bikes $11 per 2 hr., $22 per day; lower rates for longer rentals. Skis, boots, and poles $13 per ½-day, $16 per day. Open peak summer 9am-8pm, peak winter 7:30am-9pm, off-season daily 9am-7pm. Must have credit card. **Skinny Skis**, 65 W. Deloney St. (733-6094). Skis $6 per day; rollerblades $8 per ½-day, $12 per day; camping equipment also available. Major credit card or deposit for value of equipment required. Open daily 9am-8pm.

Help Lines: Rape Crisis Line, 733-5162. **Road Information,** 733-9966, outside WY 800-442-7850. **Weather Line,** 733-1731. 24-hr. recording.

Post Office: 220 W. Pearl St. (733-3650), 2 blocks east of Cache St. Open Mon.-Fri. 8:30am-5pm. **ZIP code:** 83001.

Area Code: 307.

Although most services in Jackson are prohibitively expensive, the town makes an ideal base for trips into the Tetons, 10 mi. north, or the Wind River Range, 70 mi. southeast. U.S. 191, the usual southern entry to town, ties Jackson to I-80 at Rock Springs (180 mi. south). This road continues north into Grand Teton Park and eventually reaches Yellowstone, 70 mi. to the north. The streets of Jackson are centered around **Town Square,** a small park on Broadway and Cache St. Teton Village refers to the skiing area directly towards the mountains from downtown, by Teton Village Road off Rte. 22.

ACCOMMODATIONS, CAMPING, AND FOOD

Jackson's constant influx of tourists ensures that if you don't book ahead, rooms will be small and expensive at best and non-existent at worst. Fortunately you can sleep affordably in one of two local hostels. **The Bunkhouse,** 215 N. Cache St. (733-3668), in the basement of the Anvil Motel, has a lounge, kitchenette, laundromat, ski storage, and, as the name implies, one large but quiet sleeping room with comfortable bunks. ($18. Linens included.) **The Hostel X (HI/AYH),** P.O. Box 546, Teton Village 83025 (733-3415), near the ski slopes, 12 mi. northwest of Jackson, is a budgetary oasis among the wallet-parching condos and lodges of Teton Village, and a favorite of skiers because of its location. It also has a game room, TV room, ski waxing room, and movies nightly in winter. Accommodations range from dorm-style rooms ($15 members, $25 for two members, $18 nonmember) to private suites ($34 for 2 people, $44 for 3 or 4). All are clean and well-maintained. If you prefer to stay in a Jackson motel, **The Pioneer,** 325 N. Cache St. (733-3673), offers lovely rooms with lazy teddy bears and stupendous quilts during the summer. (Singles $60, doubles $70, off-peak $36/$40.) The light will always be on at **Motel 6,** 1370 W. Broadway (733-1620), even though their rates rise steadily as the peak season approaches. (Singles from $39. Each additional person $6.)

While it doesn't offer amazing scenery, Jackson's RV/tent campground, the **Wagon Wheel Village,** 435 N. Cache St. (733-4588), doesn't charge an arm and a leg either. Call for reservations. (Sites from $16.50.) Cheaper sites and more pleasant surroundings are available in the **Bridger-Teton National Forest** surrounding Jackson. Drive toward Alpine Junction on U.S. 26/89 to find spots. Check the map at the chamber of commerce for a complete list of campgrounds. (Sites $6, no showers.)

The Bunnery, 130 N. Cache St. (733-5474), in the "Hole-in-the-Wall" mall, has the best breakfast in town—two eggs, homefries, chilis, cheese, and sprouts $5.25. Sandwiches $4-6. (Open daily 7am-9:30pm.) Chow down on barbecued chicken and spare ribs ($7) at **Bubba's,** 515 W. Broadway (733-2288). No reservations. (Open daily 7am-9pm.) Have a grand visit at **Vista Grande,** 320 Teton Village Dr. (733-6964), where all items, including veggie burritos, enchiladas *magnifico,* and corn tacos are $3-11. (Open daily 5pm-10pm.) For a cheap, light meal away from the cache on Cache St., head to **Pearl St. Bagels,** 145 Pearl St. (739-1218), where myriad bagel sandwiches are under $4.25 each. (Open Mon.-Fri. 6:30am-6pm, Sat.-Sun. 7:30am-3pm.) Another good option for cheap, quality food and excellent coffee is **Sugarfoot Cafe,** 145 N. Glenwood (733-9148), with sandwiches around $5 and Chocolate Oblivion at $3.75.

NIGHTLIFE AND ACTIVITIES

Western saddles serve as bar stools at the **Million Dollar Cowboy Bar,** 25 N. Cache St. (733-2207), Town Square. This Jackson institution is mostly for tourists, but attracts some rodeoers and local cowboys. (Open Mon.-Sat. 10am-2am, Sun. noon-10pm. Live music Mon.-Sat. 9pm-2am. Cover $2-5 after 8pm.) The **Mangy Moose,** Teton Village (733-4913), is a great place for live moosic, food, and general rambunctiousness. (Dinner daily 5:30-10:30pm, bar open 10pm-2am. 21 and over.)

Cultural activities in Jackson fall into two camps—the rowdy foot-stomping Western celebrations and the more formal, sedate presentations of music and art. Every summer evening except Sunday, the Town Square hosts a kitschy episode of the 37-year-old **Longest-Running Shoot-Out in the World.** For $2.50 on Friday evenings at 6:30pm, you can join in at the **Teton Twirlers Square Dance,** in the fair building on the rodeo grounds (733-5269 or 543-2825). Each June, the town celebrates the opening of the **Jackson Hole Rodeo** (733-2805; open June-Aug. Wed. and Sat. 8pm; tickets $6:50, ages 4-12 $4.50, under 4 free, family rate $21). Eat and watch at the **Bar J Chuckwagon** suppers and western show (733-3370) on Teton Village Rd. Show, steak or grilled chicken, and foil-wrapped potatoes $12, under 8 $4.50, lapsize free. The **Grand Teton Music Festival** (733-1128) blows and bows in Teton Village from mid-July through August. (Performances weeknights at 8pm, Sat.-Sun. 8:30pm; student tickets $3-5. Fri. and Sat. symphony at 8:30pm; $20, student tickets $9. Reserve in advance.) On Memorial Day, the town bursts its britches as tourists, locals, and nearby Native American tribes pour in for the dances and parades of **Old West Days.** Throughout September, the **Jackson Hole Fall Arts Festival** attracts painters, dancers, actors, and musicians to Jackson's four main theaters.

Between May 15 and Labor Day over 100,000 city slickers and backwoods folk go whitewater rafting out of Jackson. **Mad River Boat Trips,** 1060 S. Hwy. 89 (U.S. 89), 25 mi. from Jackson (733-6203 or 800-458-7238), offers the cheapest white-water and scenic raft trips ($20 for 2 hr., $22 for 3 hr.). **Lone Eagle Expeditions** (377-1090) gives you a meal on your 8-mi. raft trip (breakfast and lunch trips $21 per person; afternoon and evening dinner trips $29 per person). Ride the real thing with tours from **Black Diamond Llamas,** Star Route Box 11-G (733-2877; $50 day hike with meals, $125 per day overnight). Cheaper thrills include a lift 10,452 ft. up Rendez-Vous Mountain on the **Jackson Hole Aerial Tram** (733-2292; $14, seniors $12, teens $7, ages 6-12 $2, brochure has coupons). In winter, the **Jackson Hole Ski Resort** (733-2292) at Teton Village offers some of the steepest, most challenging skiing in the country.

■■■ YELLOWSTONE NATIONAL PARK

Had legendary mountain man John Colter been religious, he probably would have compared his 1807 trek into the Yellowstone area with a descent into the nether world. In any case, his graphic descriptions of boiling, sulfuric pits, spouting geysers, and smelly mudpots inspired a half-century of popular stories about "Colter's Hell." In 1870 the first official survey party, the Washburn Expedition, reached the area. As they crested a ridge, the explorers were greeted by a fountain of boiling water and steam spurting 130 ft. into the air. Members of the expedition watched it erupt nine times and named it "Old Faithful" before leaving the Upper Geyser Basin. A year later, President Grant declared Yellowstone a national park, the world's first.

Visitors in Grant's time might have encountered a handful of other adventurers amidst Yellowstone's 3472 sq. mi. Today's visitors will find the park cluttered with the cars, RVs, and detritus of some 50,000-odd tourists. The park's main attractions are huge, tranquil Yellowstone Lake, the 2100-ft.-deep Yellowstone River Canyon, and the world's largest collection of reeking, sputtering geysers, mudpots, hot springs, and fumaroles (steam-spewing holes in the ground). In the backcountry, you can escape the madding crowd and observe the park's abundant bear, elk, moose, bison, and bighorn sheep.

In 1988 Yellowstone was ravaged by a blaze that charred almost half the park. Crowds in Yellowstone doubled in 1989 in an extraordinary example of rubberneck tourism, with people pouring in to see "what really happened." While the fire damage is depressing and frightening, it does give a chance to visualize just how dense the forest once was. Peering through the rows of trees allows travelers to imagine how thick the other unravaged areas are. The toasted forests do make for interesting, if somewhat bleak, viewing; rangers have erected exhibits throughout the park to better explain the fire's effects.

PRACTICAL INFORMATION

Emergency: 911.

Park Information and Headquarters: Superintendent, Mammoth Hot Springs, Yellowstone National Park 82190 (344-7381). General information, campground availability, and emergencies. Headquarters open off-season Mon.-Fri. 9am-5pm.

Park Admission: $10 for non-commercial vehicles, $4 for pedestrians and bikers. Good for 1 week and also valid at Grand Teton National Park.

Visitors Centers and Ranger Stations: Most regions in this vast park have their own center/station. The district rangers have a good deal of autonomy in making regulations for hiking and camping, so check in at each area. All visitors centers have guides for the disabled and give backcountry permits, or have a partner ranger station that does. Each visitors center's display focuses on the attributes of its region of the park. All centers open daily. **Albright Visitors Center** at **Mammoth Hot Springs** (344-2263): natural and human history. Open late May-June 6 9am-5pm, June 7-Labor Day 8am-7pm, Labor Day-mid-May 9am-5pm. **Grant Village** (242-2650): wilderness. Open mid-June-mid-Aug. 8am-6pm, late May-mid-June and late Aug.-Labor Day 9am-5pm. **Old Faithful/Madison** (545-2750): geysers. Open early June-mid-Aug. 8am-8pm, mid-April-early June 9am-4:30pm, call for hrs. after late Aug. **Fishing Bridge** (242-2450): wildlife and Yellowstone Lake. Open 8am-6pm; off-season 9am-5pm. **Canyon** (242-2550): natural history and history of canyon area. Open mid-June-late Aug. 8am-6pm, late Aug.-Labor Day and late May-mid-June 9am-5pm. **Norris** (344-2812): park museum. Open mid-May-early June 9am-5pm, early June-Oct. 8am-9pm. **Tower/Roosevelt Ranger Station** (344-7746): temporary exhibits. Open 8am-5pm. *Yellowstone Today,* the park's activities guide, has a thorough listing of tours and programs.

Radio Information: Tune to 1610AM for service information.

West Yellowstone Chamber of Commerce: 100 Yellowstone Ave., West Yellowstone, MT 59758 (406-646-7701). Located 2 blocks west of the park entrance. Open daily at 8am-6pm.

Greyhound: 127 Yellowstone Ave., W. Yellowstone, MT (406-646-7666). To: Bozeman (1 per day, 2 hr., $12); Salt Lake City (1 per day, 9 hr., $60.50). Open summer only, daily 8am-6:30pm.

TW Services, Inc. (344-7311). Monopolizes concessions within the park. 9-hr. bus tours of the lower portion of the park leave daily from all lodges ($24, ages under 12 $12). Similar tours of the northern region leave Gardiner, MT and the lodges at Mammoth Lake and Fishing Bridge ($15-22). Individual legs of this extensive network of tour loops can get you as far as the Grand Tetons or Jackson, but the system is inefficient and costs much more than it's worth.

Gray Line Tours: 211 W. Yellowstone Ave., West Yellowstone, MT (406-646-9374). Offers full-day tours from West Yellowstone around the lower loop ($30, under 12 $15), upper loop ($30, under 12 $15), and Grand Tetons and Jackson ($40, under 12 $20). Open daily 7:30am-6:30pm.

Car Rental: Big Sky Car Rental, 429 Yellowstone Ave., West Yellowstone, MT (406-646-9564 or 800-426-7669). $32 per day, 100 free mi., 25¢ each additional mi. Must be 21 with a credit card, $100 deposit, or passport.

Bike Rental: Yellowstone Bicycles, 132 Madison Ave., West Yellowstone, MT (406-646-7815). 10-speeds $16.50 per day, mountain bikes $10.50 per ½-day, $3.50 per hr. Open daily 9am-8pm.

YELLOWSTONE NATIONAL PARK

Horse Rides: Mammoth Hot Springs Hotel, Roosevelt Lodge, and **Canyon Lodge,** late May-early Sept. $11.85 per hr., $22 for 2 hrs. Call TW Services (344-7311) for more information.

Medical Facilities: Lake Clinic, Pharmacy, and **Hospital** at Lake Hotel (242-7241). Clinic open late May-mid-Sept. daily 8:30am-8:30pm. Emergency Room open May-Sept. 24 hrs. **Old Faithful Clinic,** at Old Faithful Inn (545-7325), open mid-May-mid-Oct. daily 8:30am-5pm. **Mammoth Hot Springs Clinic** (344-7965), open year-round Mon.-Fri. 8:30am-5pm. Can always contact a ranger at 344-7381.

Post Offices: Old Faithful Station (545-7572), in the park behind the visitors center. Open Mon.-Fri. 8:30-11am and 1-5pm. **ZIP** code: 82190. Also at **West Yellowstone, MT,** 7 Madison Ave. (646-7704). Open Mon.-Fri. 8:30am-5pm. **ZIP** code: 59758.

Area Codes: 307 (in the park), 406 (in West Yellowstone and Gardiner). Unless otherwise listed, phone numbers have a 307 area code.

The bulk of Yellowstone National Park lies in the northwest corner of Wyoming with slivers slicing into Montana and Idaho. **West Yellowstone, MT,** at the park's western entrance, and **Gardiner, MT,** at the northern entrance, are the most built-up and expensive towns along the edge of the park. The southern entry to the park is through Grand Teton National Park. The northeast entrance to the park leads to U.S. 212, a gorgeous stretch of road known as **Beartooth Highway,** which climbs to **Beartooth Pass** at 11,000 ft. and descends to **Red Lodge,** a former mining town. (Road open summer only because of heavy snowfall; ask at the chamber of commerce for exact dates.)

Yellowstone's extensive system of roads circulates its millions of visitors. Side roads branch off to park entrances and some of the lesser-known sights. It's unwise to bike or walk around the deserted roads at night since you may risk startling large wild animals. The best time to see the animals is at dawn or dusk. You'll know when they're out when traffic stops and cars pull over. Approaching any wild beast at any time is illegal and extremely unsafe, and those who don't remain at least 100 ft. from bison, bear, or moose risk being mauled, gored to death, or made the victim of a *Far Side* cartoon. One unwise tourist tried to take a picture of his three-year-old son astride a buffalo; father and son were both killed when the buffalo objected to being photographed. Another danger is falling trees; dead trees can fall into a campsite or road with little or no warning. Near thermal areas, stay on marked trails, because "scalding water can ruin your vacation."

The park's high season extends from about June 15 to September 15. If you visit during this period expect large crowds, clogged roads and motels, and campsites filled to capacity. A better option is to visit in either late spring or early fall, when it is still fairly warm (except, for example, in July 1993 when a blizzard hit) and the Winnebagos and the tame animals they transport are safely home.

ACCOMMODATIONS

Cabin-seekers will find many options within the park. Standard hotel and motel rooms for the nature-weary also abound, but if you plan to keep your budget in line, stick to the towns near the park's entry-points.

In The Park

TW Services (344-7311) controls all of the accommodations within the park, and uses a special set of classifications for budget cabins: "Roughrider" means no bath, no facilities; "Western Frontier" means with bath, somewhat furnished. All cabins or rooms should be reserved well in advance of the June to September tourist season.

Old Faithful Inn and Lodge, near the west Yellowstone entrance. Offers pleasant Roughrider cabins ($19) and Western Frontier cabins ($32). Well-appointed hotel rooms from $37, with private bath $56.

Roosevelt Lodge, in the northwest corner. A favorite campsite of Roughrider Teddy Roosevelt. Provides the cheapest and most scenic indoor accommodations around. Rustic shelters $19, each with a wood-burning stove (bring your own bedding and towel). Also Roughrider cabins ($23, bring your own towel) and more spacious "family" cabins with toilet ($36).

Mammoth Hot Springs, 18 mi. west of Roosevelt area, near the north entrance. Unremarkable budget cabins $25. Frontier cabins from $52.

Lake Yellowstone Hotel and Cabins, near the south entrance. Overpriced, but with a nice view of the lake. Frontier cabins identical to Old Faithful's ($40) and Western cabins with a little more space ($74).

Canyon Village. Less authentic and more expensive than Roosevelt Lodge's cabins, but slightly closer to the popular Old Faithful area. Roughrider cabins $44, Frontier cabins $72.

West Yellowstone, MT

West Yellowstone International Hostel, at the Madison Hotel and Motel, 139 Yellowstone Ave. (406-646-7745). Friendly manager presides over old but clean, wood-adorned hotel. Singles $23, with bath $33; doubles with bath $40. Rooms $2 cheaper in the spring. Hostelers stay in more crowded rooms for members $14, nonmembers $15, no bedding, no kitchen. Open May 27-mid-Oct.

Alpine Motel, 120 Madison (406-646-7544). Plastic but clean rooms with cable TV and A/C. Singles $38, doubles $52. $3 less in off-season.

Traveler's Lodge, 225 Yellowstone Ave. (406-646-9561). Comfortable, large rooms; ask for one away from the hot tub. Singles $50, off-season $40; doubles $60, off-season $45. $5 discount if you rent a car from them (see Practical Information above).

Ho-Hum Motel, 126 Canyon Rd. (646-7746). Small, dark, ho-hum, but clean rooms. Open the windows. Singles $36, doubles $40.

Gardiner, MT

Located about 90 minutes northeast of West Yellowstone, Gardiner served as the original entrance to the park and is smaller and less tacky than its neighbor.

The Town Motel, Lounge, and Gift Shop (848-7322), on Park St. across from the park's northern entrance. Pleasant, wood-paneled, carpeted rooms. Phones and baths but no showers. Singles $33, doubles $37.

Wilson's Yellowstone River Motel (406-848-7303), E. Park St., ½-block east of U.S. 89. Large, well-decorated rooms overseen by friendly manager. Singles $47, doubles $47-51. Off-season singles $37, doubles $39.

Hillcrest Cottages (848-7353), on U.S. 89 near where it crosses the Yellowstone River. Small but clean singles $30, doubles $38. $6 each additional adult, $3 each additional kid under 12. 7 nights for the price of 6.

CAMPING

All developed campsites are available on a first come, first served basis except for the **Bridge Bay Campground,** which reserves sites up to eight weeks in advance through MISTIX (800-365-2267). During summer months, most campgrounds fill by 2pm. All regular sites cost $6-8. Arrive very early, especially on weekends and holidays. If all sites are full, try the free campgrounds outside the park in the surrounding National Forest land. Bring a stove or plan to search for or buy firewood. Except for **Mammoth Campground,** all camping areas close for the winter.

Two of the most beautiful and tranquil areas are **Slough Creek Campground,** 10 mi. northeast of Tower Junction (no RVs, open late May-Oct.), and **Pebble Creek Campground,** 15 mi. farther down the same road (no RVs, open mid-June-early Sept.). Both relatively uncrowded spots have good fishing. You can also try **Canyon Village.** Because of bear trouble, **Fishing Bridge Campgrounds** (344-7311) is for non-tenting travelers only (RV hookup $18; open late May-early Sept.). The popular and scenic campgrounds at **Norris** (open May-Sept.) and **Madison** (May-Oct.) fill early (by 1pm), while others, such as **Canyon** and **Pebble Creek,** sometimes have sites until 6pm. **Bridge Bay** (open late May-mid-Sept.), **Indian Creek** (open June-Sept.), and **Mammoth** (open year-round) campgrounds are treeless and non-scenic. You'd be better off camping in the **Gallatin National Forest** to the northwest. Good sites line U.S. 20, 287, 191, and 89. Call the Park Headquarters (344-7381) for information on any of Yellowstone's campgrounds.

More than 95% (almost two million acres) of the park is backcountry. To venture overnight into the wilds of Yellowstone, you must obtain a free **wilderness permit** from a ranger station or visitors center. It is always best to consult a ranger before any hike. Be sure you understand the most recent instructions regarding the closure of campgrounds and trails due to bears and other wildlife. Other backcountry regulations include: sanitation rules, pet and firearms restrictions, campfire permits, and firewood rules. The more popular areas fill up in high season, but you can reserve a permit up to 48 hr. in advance, in person; campfire permits are not required, but ask if fires at your site are allowed.

The campgrounds at Grant, Village Lake, Fishing Bridge, and Canyon all have coin-operated laundries and pay showers ($1.50 plus 25¢ for towel or soap). The lodges at Mammoth and Old Faithful have no laundry facilities but will let you use their showers for $1.50.

To discourage bears, campers should keep clean camps and store food in a locked car or suspended 10 ft. above ground, four ft. horizontally from a post or tree trunk.

FOOD

Be very choosy when buying food in the park, as the restaurants, snack bars, and cafeterias are quite expensive. If possible, stick to the **general stores** at each lodging location (open daily 7:30am-10pm). Harvest from the vast amounts of inexpensive food at **Food Farm,** corner of Park and 2nd St., Gardiner, MT (406-848-7524), or lasso some chow at the **Food Round-Up Grocery Store,** 107 Dunraven St., W. Yellowstone, MT (406-646-7501).

SIGHTS AND ACTIVITIES

TW Services, for unbelievable amounts of money, will sell you tours, horseback rides, and chuckwagon dinners until the cows come home. But given enough time, your eyes and feet will do an even better job than TW's tours, and won't bankrupt you. Hiking to the main attractions is much easier if you make reservations at the cabins closest to the sights you most want to see.

The **geysers** that made Yellowstone famous are clustered on the western side of the park, near the West Yellowstone entrance. Geysers are holes in the earth's crust into which water slowly trickles, then turns to steam; when the pressure reaches a certain point, the steam bursts out to the surface. The duration of the explosion depends on how much water has leaked into the hole and how hot the steam is. **Old Faithful,** while neither the largest, the highest, nor the most regular geyser, is certainly the most popular; it gushes in the **Upper Geyser Basin,** 16 mi. south of **Madison Junction** where the entry road splits north-south. Since its discovery in 1870, the granddaddy of geysers has consistently erupted with a whoosh of spray and steam (5000-8000 gallons worth) every 45 to 70 minutes. Avoiding crowds in summer is nearly impossible unless you come for the blasts at dusk or dawn. Enjoy other geysers as well as elk in the surrounding **Firehole Valley.** Swimming in any hot springs or geysers is prohibited, but you can swim in the **Firehole River,** three-quarters of the way up Firehole Canyon Drive (turn south just after Madison Jct.), or in the **Boiling River,** 2½ mi. north of Mammoth, which is not really hot enough to cook pasta. Still, do not swim alone, and beware of strong currents.

From Old Faithful, take the easy 1½-mi. walk to **Morning Glory Pool,** a park favorite, or head 8 mi. north to the **Lower Geyser Basin,** where examples of all four types of geothermal activity (geysers, mudpots, hot springs, and fumaroles) steam, bubble, and spray together in a cacophonous symphony. The regular star here is

Echinus, which erupts about every hour from a large basin of water. If you are lucky enough to witness it, the biggest show on earth is put on by **Steamboat,** the largest geyser in the world. Eruptions can last 20 minutes and top 400 ft. The last such enormous eruption occurred on Oct. 2, 1991; they used to occur about once a year. Don't hold your breath waiting for another one, but you might get lucky.

Whether you're waiting for geysers to erupt or watching them shoot skyward, don't go too close, as the crust of earth around a geyser is only two ft. thick, and the Surgeon General has determined that falling into a boiling sulfuric pit *could* be hazardous to your health. Pets are not allowed in the basin. Check out the squirrel-type animals roaming around without much fur to understand why.

Mammoth Hot Springs has famous hot springs terraces, built of multicolored striated limestone deposits which enlarge 6 in. every year. Wildlife is quite abundant in the northern part of the park, both along the road from Mammoth to Roosevelt—perhaps on the road itself—and past Roosevelt in the Lamar Valley.

The pride of the park's western side is the **Grand Canyon of the Yellowstone,** carved through glacial deposits and volcanic bedrock. For the best views, hike or drive to the 308-ft. Lower Falls at Artist Point, on the southern rim, or Lookout Point on the northern rim. All along the canyon's 19-mi. rim, keep an eye out for bighorn sheep; at dawn or dusk the bear-viewing area (at the intersection of Northern Rim and Tower roads) should be loaded with opportunities to use your binoculars.

Yellowstone Lake, 16 mi. south of the Canyon's rim at the southeastern corner of the park, contains tons o' trout; after procuring a free Yellowstone fishing permit, catch a few and have the chef fry them for you in the Yellowstone Hotel Dining Room. Most other lakes and streams allow catch-and-release fishing only. The aptly yellow **Lake Yellowstone Hotel,** originally built in 1891 and renovated in 1989, merits a visit, although its room rates place it well out of the range of budget travelers. The bright, airy lobby with large windows provides a magnificent view of the lake. Walks around the main body of the lake, as well as those that take you around one of the lake's three fingers, are scenic and serene rather than strenuous. Nearby **Mud Volcano,** close to Yellowstone Lake, features boiling sulfuric earth and the **Dragon's Mouth,** a vociferous steaming hole that early explorers reportedly heard all the way from the lake. You'll smell it that far away for sure.

Although most of the spectacular sights in the park are accessible by car, a hiking trip through the backcountry will remove you from the masses. The multilayered petrified forest of **Specimen Ridge** and the geyser basins at **Shoshone** and **Heart Lakes** are only accessible by well-kept trails. **Cascade Corner,** in the southwest, is a lovely area accessible by trails from Belcher. Over 1200 mi. of trails crisscross the park, but many are poorly marked. If you plan to hike, pick up a topographical trail map ($7) at any visitors center and ask a ranger to describe all forks in the trail and the wording of trail markings. Even after annoying the ranger, allow yourself extra time (at least 1 hr. per day) in case you lose the trail.

THE SOUTHWEST

Every fall, enormous flocks of Winnebagos migrate from the cold northern lands of the North to the sun-baked Southwest. These "snowbirds" come in search of warmer weather and an arid clime, but the states of the Southwest have much more to offer than sun-tan-perfect weather. Here clusters some of the world's most awe-inspiring scenery, including the Grand Canyon and Carlsbad Caverns, as well as a rich history of cultural intermingling unmatched in the rest of the U.S.

The Anasazi of the 10th and 11th centuries were the first to discover that the arid lands of the Southwest—with proper management—could support an advanced agrarian civilization. With the addition of a little water, the desert in areas like Chaco Canyon bloomed like a freeze-dried Eden. The Navajo, Apache, and Pueblo nations later migrated into the region, sharing the land with the Hopi , descendents of the Anasazi. Spanish conquest came early in the 17th century, bringing European colonists to modern-day Texas and New Mexico. Mexican independence in 1821 was followed by American conquest of the region. The Texan War of Independence in 1836 began as a revolt by U.S. settlers against Santa Anna's dictatorship, and culminated in the Mexican-American War. Santa Fe, Nuevo Mexico, became the first foreign capital ever to fall to the U.S. In 1853, Mexico's defeated government agreed to sell a tract of land south of the Gila River—vital to completion of the Southern Pacific Railway—that today forms a large part of Arizona and New Mexico.

The legacy of this bloody history is evident everywhere in the Southwest. Here live the largest Hispanic and Native American populations in the country; many Spanish and tribal place-names remain, as do several of the historical sites in the region. But much of the land retains the tranquility of nature unsullied by human hands. The austere, lonely beauty of the desert stretches for hundreds of miles, and the water- and wind-scored landscape stands in silent testimony to millennia of incessant battles waged by erosion. The cliffs of the Guadalupe Mountains, the gorges of the Colorado and Río Grande, the redstone arches and twisted spires of southern Utah and northern Arizona all await exploration and meditation.

 # Arizona

Arizona's diversity is perhaps its greatest asset. Almost one-seventh of the Native American population of the U.S. lives in Arizona. One-quarter of the state's land is occupied by reservations—the Navajo Nation of northeastern Arizona is the largest and most influential.

Providing a marked contrast to this way of life is the modern metropolis of Phoenix—gone are the canyons and uniquely shaped rock formations of the north—and in their place exist shopping malls and the state's most valuable asset: an excellent air-conditioning system. When the bustle of Phoenix and Tuscon become tiresome, a land of beauty and enchantment await. Whether it be the red rock of Sedona or the Painted Desert's magnificent display of color, Arizona offers more than enough for the curious traveler.

PRACTICAL INFORMATION
Capital: Phoenix.
Visitor Information: Arizona Tourism, 1100 W. Washington, Phoenix 85007 (602-542-8687). **Arizona State Parks,** 1688 W. Adams St., Phoenix 85007.

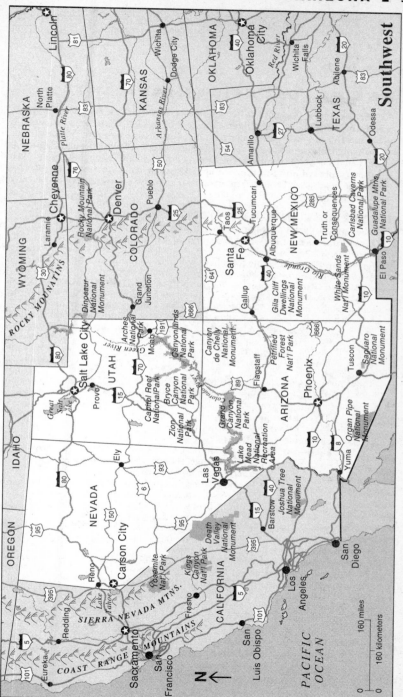

Time Zone: Mountain (2 hrs. behind Eastern). Arizona (with the exception of the reservations) does not follow Daylight Savings Time; in summer it is 1 hr. behind the rest of the Mountain Time Zone.

Postal Abbreviation: AZ

Sales Tax: 5%.

■■■ FLAGSTAFF AND VICINITY

For over a century, Flagstaff has been a symbol of Western expansion and exploration. Early pioneers celebrated their settlement by flying the American flag on Independence Day in 1876, thus naming their outpost. Today this sprawling, dusty town offers more than appears at first glance. If your schedule allows, consider Flagstaff as more than just a point of entry to the Grand Canyon. Some of the most spectacular natural treasures of northern Arizona lie in the immediate vicinity of the town. A hike in the nearby San Francisco mountains or a slide at the rocky creeks will leave an indelible memory.

PRACTICAL INFORMATION

Emergency: 911. **Police/Medical Assistance,** 774-1414.

Visitor Information: Flagstaff Chamber of Commerce, 101 W. Rte. 66 (800-842-7293 or 774-9541), across from the Amtrak station. Free city map, national forest map $2. The friendly folks here will help you plan your trip anywhere in Arizona. Open Mon.-Sat. 8am-9pm, Sun. and holidays 9am-5pm.

Tours: Blue Goose Backpacker Tours and Travels, 774-6731 or in Arizona 800-332-1944. Run by the Motel DuBeau International Hostel. Full-day guided tours and trips to: the Grand Canyon ($32); Walnut Canyon and Sunset Crater ($17); Sedona and Oak Creek ($15). All tours run daily. Leave from Motel Du Beau at 19 W. Phoenix Ave. (See Accommodations below.) **Gray Line/Nava-Hopi,** 774-5003; 800-892-8687 outside AZ. One-day sight-seeing tours year-round to: the Grand Canyon ($36); Sedona, Oak Creek Canyon, and Montezuma Castle ($34); the Museum of N. Arizona, Sunset Crater, Wupatki, and Walnut Canyon ($32). Tours April 4-Act. 30 to: Monument Valley and the Navajo Reservation ($74); the Hopi and Navajo Reservations and Painted Desert ($62). Kids 5-15 ride ½-price on all tours. Reservations required. Get tickets at the Amtrak or Greyhound station.

Amtrak: 1 E. Santa Fe Ave. (774-8679 or 800-872-7245). 1 train daily to Los Angeles (11 hr., $87) and Albuquerque (6 hr., $82). 1 connecting shuttle bus to the Grand Canyon ($12). Open daily 5:45-10am, 11am-2pm, 2:30-6pm, and 7-10:30pm.

Buses: Greyhound, 399 S. Malpais Lane (774-4573), across from NAU campus, 5 blocks southwest of the train station on U.S. 89A. To: Phoenix (5 per day; $18); Albuquerque (6 per day; $46); Los Angeles (5 per day; $76); Las Vegas (3 per day via Kingman, AZ; $43). Terminal open 24 hrs. **Gray Line/Nava-Hopi,** 774-5003. Shuttle buses to the Grand Canyon (2 per day; $25 round-trip, $13 with Greyhound Ameripass). First bus leaves Flagstaff at 8:20am, last one at 5:30pm.

Public Transport: Pine Country Transit, 970 W. Rte. 66 (779-6635). 3 routes covering most of town. Fare 75¢. Runs once per hr.

Camping Equipment Rental: Peace Surplus, 14 W. Rte. 66 (779-4521), 1 block from the hostel. Daily rental of dome tents ($5-8), packs ($5), stoves ($3), plus a good stock of cheap outdoor gear. 3-day min. rental on all equipment. Credit card or cash deposit required. Open Mon.-Fri. 8am-9pm, Sat. 8am-7pm, Sun. 9am-6pm.

Bike Rental: Cosmic Cycles, 113 S. San Francisco St. (779-1092), downtown. Mountain bikes $20 per day. City bikes with wide tires $8 per day. Open Mon.-Sat. 9am-6pm, Sun. 11am-4pm.

Taxi: Dream Taxi, (774-2934). Open 24 hrs.; airport to downtown $9.50.

Car Rental: Budget Rent-A-Car, 100 N. Humphreys St. (774-2763), within walking distance of the hostels. Guarantees the lowest rates in the competitive Flagstaff car rental market. Economy cars from $33 per day, with 100 free mi., 25¢ per additional mi. $145 weekly with 1050 free mi. Open daily 7am-9pm. Must be 21

or older with a major credit card or at least $200 cash deposit. $5 surcharge per day on the under 25 set. Ask for Tom about *Let's Go* discount rates.
Post Office: 2400 N. Postal Blvd. (527-2400), for general delivery. Open Mon.-Fri. 9am-5pm, Sat. 9am-noon. **ZIP Code** 86001.
Area Code: 602.

Flagstaff is easily accessible by U.S. 89A from the north and the south. Downtown lies at the intersection of **Beaver Street** and **Route 66** (formerly Santa Fe Ave.). Within ½-mi. of this spot are both bus stations, the three youth hostels, the chamber of commerce, and several inexpensive restaurants. Other commercial establishments lie on **South Sitgreaves Street** (U.S. 89A), near the NAU campus.

Because Flagstaff is a mountain town, it stays cooler than much of the rest of the state and receives frequent afternoon thundershowers. You can walk around most of downtown, but to get anywhere worth seeing, rent a car or take a tour bus.

ACCOMMODATIONS AND CAMPING

When buzzing swarms of tourists descend upon Flagstaff in the summer, accommodation prices shoot up. However, the town is blessed with three rival youth hostels, all of which offer good services in order to lure *Let's Go*-toting budget travelers. For cheap motels cruise historic Rte. 66. Camping in **Coconino National Forest** surrounding the city is a pleasant and inexpensive alternative.

Motel Du Beau, 19 W. Phoenix (774-6731 or 800-332-1944), just behind the train station. A registered National Landmark which once hosted L.A. film stars and Chicago gangsters. Now a top-rated hostel in the Southwest, offering superlative service to hostelers. Free ride to and from airport, bus and train stations. Free breakfast and coffee all day. Kitchen, library, and nightly videos. Dorm beds $11, private rooms $25, camp on the lawn for $6 per person. Open 24 hrs.
Downtowner Independent Youth Hostel, 19 S. San Francisco (774-8461). Flexible management will send a Mercedes to shuttle between hostel and bus stations. Decent rooms with wooden floors and comfortable beds. Kitchen, lounge, free bikes and free coffee. Dorm beds $9, semi-private rooms $11 per person. Linen included. Open mid-May to mid-Aug. Reception open 7:30am-noon, 1-9:30pm.
The Weatherford Hotel (HI/AYH), 23 N. Leroux (774-2731). Friendly management and convenient location. Dorm rooms, baths in rooms and halls, kitchen, and a cozy common area; ride board in lobby. Curfew midnight. $10. Required sleepsheet $1. Private singles $22. Doubles $24. Open daily 7-10am, 5-10pm. Guests enjoy ½ cover charge at **Charley's,** downstairs, which has live music.
KOA, 5803 N. U.S. 89 (526-9926), 6 mi. northeast of Flagstaff. Municipal bus routes stop near this beautiful campground. Showers, restrooms and free nightly movies. Sites $20 for 2 people; $21 for full hookup. Each additional person $4.

You'll probably need a car to reach the **public campgrounds** that ring the city. Campgrounds at higher elevations close during the winter; many are small and fill up quickly during the summer, particularly on weekends when Phoenicians flock to the mountains. If you stake out your site by 3pm you shouldn't encounter problems. National forest sites are usually $2-3 per night. Pick up a **Coconino National Forest** map ($2) in Flagstaff at the Chamber of Commerce (see Practical Information above). **Lake View** (527-3650), 13 mi. southeast on Forest Hwy. 3 (U.S. 89A), has 30 sites ($7). **Bonito** (527-3630), 2 mi. east at Forest Rd. 545, off U.S. 89, has 44 sites at Sunset Crater ($7). All have running water and flush toilets. Those who can live without amenities can camp for free on any national forest land outside the designated campsites, unless you see signs to the contrary. For more info, call the Coconino Forest Service (527-3600; Mon.-Fri. 7:30am-4:30pm).

FLAGSTAFF & VICINITY

FOOD AND ENTERTAINMENT

To suit every European taste, Flagstaff offers an odd blend of cafes and diners. Downtown eateries serve great sandwiches for as low as $4, but to get a real meal in a real restaurant be prepared to foot a fat bill.

Macy's, 14 S. Beaver St. (774-2243), behind Motel DuBeau. This tourist and college student hangout serves fresh pasta ($3.25-5.25), plus a wide variety of vegetarian entrees, pastries, and espresso-based drinks. Open daily 6am-8pm, Thurs. and Sat. until 10pm; food served until 7pm.

Café Espresso, 16 N. San Francisco, near the Weatherford. Fine danishes ($1.50), plus various sandwiches and coffees ($1). The artsy staff makes a cult of healthy food and dimmed lighting. Open Mon.-Fri. 7am-10pm, Sat.-Sun. 7am-11pm.

Alpine Pizza, 7 Leroux St. (779-4109) and 2400 E. Santa Fe Ave. (779-4138). A popular spot for beer, pool, and (oh, yeah) pizza. Excellent, huge *calzones* ($6) and *strombolis* ($6.75). Alpine with whole wheat crusts and multitudinous toppings. Open Mon.-Sat. 11am-11pm, Sun. noon-11pm.

Main St. Bar and Grill, 4 S. San Francisco (774-1519), across from the Downtowner. When the vegetarian meals and non-alcoholic drinks of the cafes get too healthy, try the delicious barbecued red meat ($2-11), the Buttery Texas Toast, and the calorie-laden but excellent selection of beers. Live music Tues.-Sat. at 8pm. No cover. Open Mon.-Sat. 11am-midnight, Sun. noon-10pm.

While there isn't much to see within Flagstaff proper, the one or two nights you spend here could be full of lively entertainment. Party animals with a taste for the wild West will enjoy the **Museum Club,** 3404 E. Rte. 66 (526-9434). Known locally as the **Zoo,** it rocks with live country-western and cowboys and cowgirls. The cover charge is $3 but you can call **Dream VIP Taxi** (774-2934) for your free round-trip ride. Below the Weatherford HI/AYH, **Charley's,** 23 N. Leroux (779-1919) plays great blues on weekends. Hostelers pay half the cover.

■ North and East of Flagstaff

Because most of Flagstaff's legions of tourists are Grand Canyon-bound, they miss the many other (uncrowded) natural wonders surrounding the city. **Sunset Crater Volcano National Monument** (556-7042) lies 17 mi. north on U.S. 89. This volcanic crater erupted in 1065, and formed cinder cones and lava beds; oxidized iron in the cinder gives the pre-nuclear crater its dramatic dusky color. (Visitors center open daily 8am-6pm; in winter 8am-5pm. $4 per car or $2 per person.) A self-guided tour wanders ½ mi. through the plain's surreal lava formations, 1½ mi. east of the visitors center. All interpretive materials along the trail are also available in Spanish, French, and German. Once-popular lava tube tours have temporarily been halted.

Eighteen mi. north and several hundred feet down from Sunset Crater on a scenic loop road rests **Wupatki National Monument.** The ancestors of the Hopi moved here over a thousand years ago when they found the black-and-red soil ideal for agriculture. After 300 years, however, droughts and over-farming precipitated the abandonment of the pueblos. Some of the Southwest's most scenic ruins, these stone houses are perched on the sides of *arroyos* in view of Monument Valley and the San Francisco Peaks just for your vacation pleasure. Five major abandoned pueblos stretch along the 14-mi. road from U.S. 89 to the visitors center. The largest and most accessible, **Wupatki Ruin,** rises three stories high. Below the ruin, you can see one of Arizona's two stone ballcourts, the sites of ancient games employing a rubber ball and a stone hoop in a circular court. Get info at the **Wupatki Ruin Visitors Center** (556-7040; open daily 8am-6pm; off-season 8am-5pm). When visiting Wupatki or Sunset Crater you can camp at the **Bonito Campground** (see Accommodations above).

In the 13th century, the Sinagua people built more than 300 rooms under hanging ledges in the walls of a 400-ft.-deep canyon. The remaining structures form the **Wal-**

nut Canyon National Monument (526-3367), 7 mi. east of Flagstaff off I-40. From a glassed-in observation deck in the visitors center you can survey the whole canyon; a stunning variety of plants sprout out of its striated grey walls. A trail snakes down from the visitors center past 25 cliff dwellings; markers along the trail describe aspects of Sinagua life and identify the plants they used for food, dyes, medicine and hunting. Rangers lead hikes down a rugged trail to the original Ranger Cabin and many remote cliff dwellings. These strenuous 2½-hr. hikes leave daily from the visitors center at 10am. Hiking boots and long pants are required. A walk along the main trail takes about 45 min. (Monument open daily 7am-6pm; Labor Day-Memorial Day 8am-5pm. Admission $4 per car, $2 per biker or hiker.)

The **San Francisco Peaks** are the huge, snow-capped mountains visible to the north of Flagstaff. **Humphrey's Peak**—the highest point in Arizona at 12,670 ft.—is sacred to the Hopi, who believe that the Kachina spirits live there. Nearby **Mt. Agassiz** has the area's best skiing. The **Arizona Snow Bowl** operates four lifts from mid-Dec. to mid-April; its 32 trails receive an average of 8½ ft. of powder each winter. Lift tickets cost $29. Call the switchboard (779-1951; 24 hrs.) for information on ski conditions, transportation, and accommodations.

During the summer, the peaks are perfect for hiking. You can see the North Rim of the Grand Canyon, the Painted Desert, and countless square miles of Arizona and Utah from the top of Humphrey's Peak when the air is clear. Those not up to the hike should take the **chairlift** (20-30 min.) up the mountain (779-1951; runs daily 10am-4pm, Labor Day-June 18 Sat.-Sun. 10am-4pm; $8, seniors $6, kids 6-12 $4.50). The vista from the top of the lift proves almost as stunning. Picnic facilities and a cafeteria are open from May-Oct. Since the mountains occupy national forest land, camping is free, but no organized campsites are available. To reach the peaks, take U.S. 180 about 7 mi. north to the Fairfield Snow Bowl turnoff. **Gray Line/Nava-Hopi** offers a tour of the Museum of Northern Arizona, Walnut Canyon, Sunset Crater, and Wupatki National Monument (see Flagstaff: Practical Information), but no other public transportation is available to these sights, or, during the summer, to the San Francisco Peaks.

■ South of Flagstaff

The main thoroughfare south of Flagstaff is **I-17.** A more circuitous path from Flagstaff to Phoenix, **U.S. 89A** nonetheless makes up for the longer travel time with awesome scenery—the 27-mi. segment from Flagstaff to Sedona affords a spectacular view of the green shady mountains of the **Oak Creek Canyon.** Once in Sedona, if you have four wheels, take **Schnebley Hill Road,** a 13-mi. dirt road that winds through the rugged backcountry with the speed of a tortoise and the charm of a snake. A few mi. south of Flagstaff, U.S. 89A descends into Oak Creek Canyon, a trout-stocked creek bordered by trees and reddish canyon cliffs. You can pull over to swim or fish at several points along the route; look for **Slide Rock,** an algae-covered natural water chute. National forest **campsites** are scattered along 12 mi. of Oak Creek Canyon on the highway. Arrive early; sites fill quickly. Most campgrounds are open from April-Oct. Call the forest service (282-4119) for info. **Manzanita, Cave Spring,** and **Pine Flat** have 7-day limits. All have running water and toilets. (Sites $8.)

The walls of Oak Creek Canyon open up 27 mi. south of Flagstaff, revealing the striking red rock formations surrounding **Sedona,** the setting for many western movies. The town itself is an incongruous blend of wealthy retirees and organic trend-followers. For info on trails, hiking, and accommodations, contact the **Oak Creek Canyon Chamber of Commerce** at 282-7722.

Twenty mi. southwest of Sedona (take U.S. 89A to Rte. 279 and continue through the town of Cottonwood) lies **Tuzigoot National Monument** (634-5564), which consists of a dramatic Sinaguan ruin overlooking the Verde Valley. (Open daily 8am-7pm. $2, 62 and over (and the rest of the car free), under 17 free.)

From Sedona, Rte. 179 leads south to I-17. An amazing five-story cliff dwelling sits 10 mi. south back on I-17. **Montezuma Castle National Monument** (567-3322) is a 20-room adobe abode. The dwellings were constructed around 1100, when over-population in the Flagstaff area forced the Sinagua south into the Verde Valley along Beaver Creek. Visitors can view the "castle" from a path below. (Open daily 8am-7pm. $2, 62 and over (and the rest of the car) free, under 16 free.) The **Montezuma Well,** 11 mi. from the Castle, is a beautiful lake formed by the collapse of an under-ground cavern; at one time, it served as a source of water for the Sinagua who lived here (open daily 7am-7pm; free).

If you're familiar with the stereotypes about so-called "New Agers" but have never met or seen them in action, have we got the place for you. From Montezuma Castle, follow I-17; from the turnoff at Cordes Junction, 28 mi. south, a 3-mi. dirt road leads to **Arcosanti.** When completed around the turn of the century, Arcosanti will be a self-sufficient community embodying Italian architect Paolo Soleri's concept of "arcology," defined as "architecture and ecology working together as one integral process." Budgetarians will appreciate the architect's vision of a city where personal cars are obsolete. The complete city, with its subterranean parks, will surprise even the most imaginative Legoland architect. (Tours daily every hr. 10am-4pm. Open to the public daily 9am-5pm. $5 donation.) For more info, contact Arcosanti, HC 74, P.O. Box 4136, Mayer 86333 (632-7135). **Arizona Central** buses (see Phoenix: Practical Information) can drop you off in **Cordez Junction,** 1½ mi. away from Arcosanti, but no tours go there.

■■■ GRAND CANYON

One of the greatest natural wonders in the United States, if not the world, the Grand Canyon is a breath-taking 277 mi. long, 10 mi. wide, and over 1 mi. deep. It is diffi-cult to believe that the Colorado River which trickles along the canyon floor could have created the looming walls and slashing valleys of limestone, sandstone, and shale, even over a period of millions of years. The dramatic landscapes of the can-yon are home to equally spectacular wildlife, including mountain lions, eagles, deer, and falcons. Don't just peer over the edge—hike down into the gorge to get a genu-ine feeling for the immensity of and beauty of this natural phenomenon.

The **Grand Canyon National Park** consists of three areas: **South Rim,** including Grand Canyon Village; **North Rim;** and the canyon gorge itself. The slightly lower, slightly more accessible South Rim draws 10 times more visitors than higher, more heavily forested North Rim.

The 13-mi. trail that traverses the canyon floor makes a two-day adventure for sturdy hikers, while the 214 mi. of perimeter road prove a good five-hr. drive for those who would rather explore from above. Despite commercial exploitation, the Grand Canyon is still untamed; every year several careless hikers take what locals morbidly refer to as "the 12-second tour." Please remember to observe all safety pre-cautions and the rules of common sense.

■ South Rim

In summer, everything on two legs or four wheels converges from miles around on this side of the Grand Canyon. If you plan to visit during this mobfest, make reserva-tions for lodging or campsites, and mules if you want them—and prepare to battle crowds. During the winter there are fewer tourists; however, the weather is brisk and many of the canyon's hotels and facilities are closed.

PRACTICAL INFORMATION
Emergency: 911.

Visitor Information: Park Headquarters: 638-7888. Open daily 8:30am-8:30pm. Information on programs 24 hrs. **Tourist Center:** 638-2626. Further information about tours, taxis, trips, etc. Ask for their *Trip Planner*. Open 8am-8pm.
Lodging Reservations: Reservations Dept., Grand Canyon National Park Lodges, Grand Canyon 86023 (638-2401).
Nava-Hopi Bus Lines: 774-5003. Leaves Flagstaff Greyhound station for Grand Canyon daily at 8:20am and 3:15pm; departs from Bright Angel Lodge at Grand Canyon for Flagstaff daily at 10:20am and 5:30pm. $12.50 each way, children $6.50; $2 entrance fee for Canyon not included.
Transportation Information Desk: In **Bright Angel Lodge** (638-2631). Reservations for mule rides, bus tours, Phantom Ranch, and taxi. Open daily 6am-6pm.
Equipment Rental: Babbit's General Store, in Mather Center Grand Canyon Village (638-2262 or 638-2234), near Yavapai Lodge. Rents comfortable hiking boots ($8 for the first day, $5 each additional day), sleeping bags ($7-9, $5 each additional day), tents ($15-16, $9 each additional day), and other camping gear. Hefty deposit required on all items. Open daily 8am-8pm.
Post Office: next to Babbit's (638-2512). Open Mon.-Fri. 9am-4:30pm, Sat. 11am-1pm. Lobby open Mon.-Sat. 5am-10pm. **ZIP code:** 86023.
Area Code: 602.

From Las Vegas, the fastest route to the Canyon is U.S. 93 south to I-40 east, and then Rte. 64 north. From Flagstaff, I-40 east to U.S. 89 north is the most scenic; from there, Rte. 64 north takes you to the Desert View entrance in the eastern part of the park. The **entrance fee** to the Grand Canyon is $10 per car and $4 for travelers using other modes of transportation—even bus passengers must pay. Upon arriving in the South Rim, grab a copy of *The Guide*, a small but comprehensive reference guide available at the entrance gate and the visitors center (free).

The National Park Service operates two free **shuttle buses.** The **West Rim Loop** runs between West Rim Junction and Hermit's Rest, with stops at all the scenic vistas along the way (Memorial Day-Labor Day every 15 min. 7:30am-sunset). The **Village Loop** covers Bright Angel Lodge, West Rim Junction, the visitors center, Grand Canyon Village, and Yavapai Point (year-round every 15 min. 6:30am-9:30pm).

Thanks to the efforts of the park service, much of the South Rim is wheelchair-accessible; pick up the free pamphlet *Accessibility Guide* at the visitors center. Pets are allowed in the park, provided they are on a leash. Pets may not go below the rim. There is a **kennel** on the South Rim; call 638-2631, ext. 6039.

ACCOMMODATIONS AND CAMPING

Compared with the 6 million years it took the Colorado River to cut the Grand Canyon, the 6 months it takes to get a room on the South Rim is a blink of an eye. Since the youth hostel closed in 1990, it is now nearly impossible to sleep indoors anywhere near the South Rim without reservations or a wad of cash; if you arrive unprepared, check at the visitors center (see Practical Information above) for vacancies.

Most accommodations on the South Rim other than those listed below are very expensive. The campsites listed usually fill by 10am in summer. Campground overflow usually winds up in the **Kaibab National Forest,** adjacent to the park along the southern border, where you can pull off a dirt road and camp for free. Sleeping in cars is *not* permitted within the park, but is allowed in the Kaibab Forest. The Nava-Hopi bus pauses at Bright Angel Lodge, where you can check your luggage for 50¢ per day. Reservations for **Bright Angel Lodge, Maswik Lodge, Trailer Village,** and **Phantom Ranch** can be made through Grand Canyon National Park Lodges, P.O. Box 699, Grand Canyon 86023 (638-2401). All rooms should be reserved 6 months in advance for the summer, 6 weeks for the winter.

Bright Angel Lodge, Grand Canyon Village. Rustic cabins with plumbing but no heat. Very convenient to Bright Angel Trail and both shuttle buses. Singles from $35, depending on how much plumbing you want. $9 per additional person.

GRAND CANYON

Maswik Lodge, Grand Canyon Village. Small, clean cabins with shower $49 (singles or doubles). $7 per additional person. Reservations required.

Mather Campground, Grand Canyon Village, ½-mi. from the visitors center. Shady, relatively isolated sites without hookups $10. Make reservations through Ticketron outlets 8 weeks in advance.

Trailer Village, next to Mather Campground. Clearly designed with the RV in mind. Campsites resemble driveways and lack seclusion. Sites with hookup $17 for 2 people. $1.50 per additional person.

Desert View Campsite, 25 mi. east of Grand Canyon Village. No hookups. Sites $8. Open May 15-Oct. 30. No reservations accepted (no telephone); arrive early.

Ten-X Campground in the Kaibab National Forest, (638-2443), 10 mi. south of Grand Canyon Village on Rte. 64. Chemical toilets, water. Sites $10. Open April-Nov. No reservations, no hookups.

Phantom Ranch, on the canyon floor, a 4-hr. hike down the Kaibab Trail. Reservations required 6 months in advance for April-Oct., but check at the Bright Angel Transportation Desk (see above) for last-minute cancellations. Don't show up without reservations made well in advance—they'll send you back up the trail, on foot. Dorm beds $21. Cabins for 1 or 2 people $55, $11 per additional person.

FOOD

Fast food has not sunk its greasy talons into the rim of the Canyon. While you might find meals for fast-food prices, uniformly bland cuisine is harder to locate. **Babbit's General Store** (638-2262), in Maswik Lodge, is more than just a restaurant—it's a supermarket, in fact, its a superdupermarket. Stock up on trail mix, water, and gear. (Open daily 8am-8pm; deli open 8am-7pm.) **The Maswik Cafeteria,** also in Maswik Lodge, has a variety of inexpensive options grill-made and served in a swish cafeteria atmosphere. (Open daily 6am-10pm.) **Bright Angel Restaurant** (638-2631), in Bright Angel Lodge, has hot sandwiches ($4-6; open daily 6:30am-10pm). The soda fountain at Bright Angel Lodge offers 16 flavors of ice cream (1 scoop $1) to hikers emerging from the Bright Angel Trail (open daily 11am-9pm).

ACTIVITIES

At your first glimpse of the canyon, you will realize that the best way to see it is to hike down into it, an enterprise that is much harder than it looks. Much sorrow has come to the plaid-clad, would-be hiker armed with a telephoto lens and an unopened can of Diet Coke—park rangers average over three rescues per day in this National Park with the highest fatality rate in the country. Even the young at heart must remember that what seems to be an easy hike downhill can become a nightmarish 100° incline on the return journey. Heat exhaustion, the second greatest threat after slipping, is marked by a monstrous headache and termination of sweating. You *must* take two quarts of water along; it's absolutely necessary. A list of hiking safety tips can be found in the *Grand Canyon Guide,* available at the entrance gate and the visitors center, and should be read thoroughly, underlined, and annotated before hitting the trail. Overestimating your limits is a common mistake; parents should think twice about bringing children more than a mile down the trails—kids have good memories and might exact revenge when they get bigger.

The two most accessible trails into the Canyon are the **Bright Angel Trail,** which begins at the Bright Angel Lodge, and **South Kaibab Trail,** originating at Yaki Point. Bright Angel is outfitted to accommodate the average tourist, with rest houses stationed strategically 1½ mi. and 3 mi. from the rim. **Indian Gardens,** 4½ mi. down, offers the tired hiker restrooms, picnic tables, and blessed shade; all three rest stops usually have water in the summer. Kaibab is trickier, steeper, and lacks shade or water, but it rewards the intrepid with a better view of the canyon's hypnotic contours. Remember that hiking back up is much, *much* more arduous and takes twice as long as the hike down.

If you've made arrangements to spend the night on the canyon floor, the best route is to hike down the **Kaibab Trail** (3-4 hr., depending on conditions) and back up the Bright Angel (7-8 hr.) the following day. The hikes down Bright Angel Trail to Indian Gardens and **Plateau Point,** 6 mi. out, where you can look down 1360 ft. to the river, make excellent daytrips. But start early (around 7am) to avoid the worst heat. One local rule: if you meet a mule train, stand quietly by the side of the trail and obey the wrangler's instructions so as not to spook the animals. Backcountry permits are required for any overnight stay.

If you're not up to descending into the canyon, follow the **Rim Trail** east to Grandeur Point and the **Yavapai Geological Museum,** or west to **Hermit's Rest,** using the shuttles as desired. There are no fences or railings between you and certain death—watch your footing. The Eastern Rim Trail swarms at dusk with sunset-watchers, and the Yavapai Museum at the end of the trail has a sweeping view of the canyon during the day from a glassed-in observation deck. The Western Rim Trail leads to several incredible vistas, notably **Hopi Point,** a favorite for sunsets, and the **Abyss,** where the canyon wall drops almost vertically to the Tonto Plateau 3000 ft. below. To watch a sunset, show up at your chosen spot 45 minutes beforehand and watch the earth-tones and pastels melt into darkness.

The park service rangers present a variety of free informative talks and hikes. Listings of each day's events are available at the visitors center or in the *Grand Canyon Guide* (10¢), available everywhere in the village. A free presentation at 8:30pm (7:30pm in winter) in **Mather Amphitheater,** behind the visitors center, highlights the Grand Canyon.

In addition to the freebies offered by the National Park Service, a variety of **commercial tours** cover the South Rim. Prices for tours by helicopter, airplane, inflatable raft, and mule soar beyond the reach of most budget travelers. You can book plane and chopper tours at **Tusayan,** 7 mi. south of the Grand Canyon Village. Of the three bus tours, the Sunset and West Rim tours cover places mostly accessible by free shuttle buses. You may decide to take the tour to **West Desert View** (2 per day, 1 per day in winter, 4 hr.; tickets $17, kids $8.50), which provides the only non-automobile access to Desert View—26 mi. east of the village—as well as to the Painted Desert to the east. Contact the Bright Angel Transportation Desk (638-2401) for information on all commercial tours.

■ North Rim

If you are coming from Utah or Nevada, or if you simply want a more solitary Grand Canyon experience, consider the North Rim. Here the canyon experience is a bit wilder, a bit cooler, and much more serene—with a view as groovy as that from the South Rim. Unfortunately, because it is less frequented, it's tough to get to the North Rim by public transportation. The only rim-to-rim transportation is available from **Transcanyon,** P.O. Box 348, Grand Canyon, AZ 86023 (638-2820), from late May to October. ($60, round-trip $100. Buses depart South Rim 1:30pm, arrive at North Rim at 6pm, and depart North Rim 7am, arriving at South Rim 11:30am. Call for reservations.) Canyon visitors are wary of those on foot, making hitching a non-option. From the South Rim, the North Rim is a 200-plus-mi., stunningly scenic drive away. Take Rte. 64 east to U.S. 89 north, which runs into Alt. 89; off Alt. 89, take Rte. 67 south to the edge. Between the first snows at the end of October and May 15, Rte. 67 is closed to traffic. Then, only a snowmobile can get you to the North Rim. The **National Park Service Information** desk is in the lobby of **Grand Canyon Lodge** (638-2611; open 8am-5pm). The solitary but comfortable lodge dangles at the very end of Rte. 67, offering you free, comfortable chairs overlooking the canyon, and informative ranger lectures throughout the day. In an **emergency** call 911.

ACCOMMODATIONS, CAMPING, AND FOOD

Since camping within the confines of the Grand Canyon National Park is limited to designated campgrounds, only a lucky minority of North Rim visitors get to spend the night "right there." If you can't get in-park lodgings, visit the **Kaibab National Forest,** which runs from north of Jacob Lake to the park entrance. Camp in an established site, or pull off the main road onto any forest road and camp for free. Campsite reservations can be made through MISTIX (800-365-2267). If you don't have reservations, mark your territory by 10am.

Canyonlands International Youth Hostel, 143 E. South, Kanab, UT 84741 (801-644-5554), 1½ hr. north of the Grand Canyon on U.S. 89, an equal distance south of Bryce Canyon. Errol fixes you up with a private room and bath, plus a do-it-yourself breakfast, all for the amazingly low price of $9. Office open daily 8-10am and 5-10pm. Reservations recommended.

Premium Motel, 94 S. 100 E. (644-9281), right around the corner from the hostel; head for this motel if the hostel is full. A/C, phones, color TV. Singles $22, doubles $26, triples $28.

Grand Canyon Lodge, on the edge of the rim. Call TW Recreational Services (801-586-7686). Cabins (some can accommodate up to 5 persons) and a motel. Doubles from $50. Front desk open 24 hrs. Open in summer daily 8am-7pm, off-season Mon.-Fri. 8am-5pm.

Jacob Lake Inn (643-7232), 44 mi. north of the North Rim at Jacob Lake. Cabins $50 for 2, $61 for 4, $69 for 6. Pricier motel units. Also offers 50 campsites at $10 per vehicle. Half the sites available first-come, first-served; others can be reserved through MISTIX (800-283-2267; $7 fee) or call Jacob Lake RV Park (643-7804). Has dining room and coffee shop. Campground open May-Oct. 15.

North Rim Campground, 82 sites on Rte. 67 near the rim. You really cannot see into the canyon from the pine-covered site, but you know it's there. Near food store; has laundry facilities, recreation room and showers. Sites $10. Reserve by calling MISTIX, 800-365-2267. Closes Oct. 27.

Kaibab National Forest Sites: DeMotte Park Campground, 5 mi. north of the park entrance. 25 sites ($10). First-come, first-served. Open camping also permitted in the National Forest surrounding the Grand Canyon; you must be ½ mi. from official campgrounds and ½ mi. from the road.

Both of the eating options on the North Rim are placed strategically at the **Grand Canyon Lodge.** The restaurant slaps together dinners for $4.50-12 and breakfast for $3.50. A skimpy sandwich at the "buffeteria" extorts $2.50. North Rim-ers are better off eating in Kanab or stopping at the Jacob Lake Inn for snacks and great shakes.

ACTIVITIES

A ½-mi. paved trail takes you from the Grand Canyon Lodge to **Bright Angel Point,** which commands a seraphic view of the Canyon. **Point Imperial,** an 11-mi. drive from the lodge, overlooks Marble Canyon and the Painted Desert.

The North Rim offers nature walks and evening programs, both at the North Rim Campground and at Grand Canyon Lodge (see Accommodations). Check at the info desk or campground bulletin boards for schedules. Half-day **mule trips** ($30) descend into the canyon from Grand Canyon Lodge (638-2292; open daily 7am-8pm). If you'd prefer to tour the Canyon wet, pick up a *Grand Canyon River Trip Operators* brochure and select among the 20 companies which offer trips.

On warm evenings, the Grand Canyon Lodge fills with an eclectic group of international travelers, U.S. families, and rugged adventurers. Some frequent the **Lodge Saloon** for drinks, jukebox disco, and the enthusiasm of a young crowd. Others look to the warm air rising from the canyon, a full moon, and the occasional shooting stars for their intoxication at day's end.

NORTHEASTERN ARIZONA

■■■ CANYON DE CHELLY NATIONAL MONUMENT

While not matching the Grand Canyon's awesome dimensions, Canyon de Chelly more than makes up in beauty what it lacks in size. In the aptly-named Beautiful Valley, the canyon's 30- to 1000-ft. sandstone cliffs tower over the sandy, fertile valley created by the Chelly River. The oldest ruins in the eroded walls of the Canyon date back to the Anasazi civilization of the 12th century. In the 1800s, the Navajo sought refuge here during hostilities with white settlers. In what was to become a sickening pattern, dozens of Native American women and children were shot by the Spanish in 1805; the site of the executions is now called Massacre Cave. Kit Carson starved the Navajo out of the Canyon in the 1860s. Today, Navajo farmers once again inhabit the canyon, cultivating the lush soil and living in traditional Navajo dwellings, *hogans*.

It's impossible to take an ugly approach to the park. The most common route is from Chambers, 75 mi. south, at the intersection of I-40 and U.S. 191, but you can also come from the north via U.S. 191. There is no public transportation to the park.

Camp for free in the park's **Cottonwood Campground,** ½ mi. from the visitors center. This giant campground in a pretty cottonwood grove rumbles at night with the din of a hungry army, and stray dogs tend to wander the site. Don't expect to find any budget accommodations in Chinle or anywhere else in Navajo territory. Farmington, NM, and Cortez, CO, are the closest major cities with cheap lodging.

The land constituting Canyon de Chelly National Monument is owned by the Navajo Nation and is administered by the National Park Service. All but one of the park trails are closed to public travel unless hikers are escorted by Navajo representatives. Although the park service offers free short tours into the canyon, the only way to get far into the canyon or close to the Anasazi ruins is to hire a Navajo guide. Check with the **visitors center** (674-5436), 2 mi. east of Chinle on Navajo Rte. 64, off U.S. 191, which houses a small museum. The staff can arrange for guides and tours at any time of day, although guides usually arrive at the visitors center at about 9am. Guides generally charge $10 per hr. to walk or drive into the canyon. Advance reservations are helpful, but you can try dropping in. (Open daily 8am-6pm; off-season 8am-5pm.) To drive into the canyon with a guide, you must provide your own four-wheel-drive vehicle. Horseback tours can be arranged through **Justin's Horse Rental** (674-5678), on South Rim Dr., at the mouth of the canyon. (Open daily approximately 8am-6pm. Horses "rented" at $8 per hr.; mandatory guide "hired" at $8 per hr. If you have a philosophical bent, notice that the horse's time is worth as much as the human guide's, and consider the social implications—or at least give a generous tip.) **Twin Trail Tours** (674-3466) also rents horses.

The 1-mi. trail to **White House Ruin,** 7 mi. from the visitors center off South Canyon Rd., winds down a 400-ft. face, past a Navajo farm and traditional *hogan,* through an orchard, and across the stream wash. The only one you can walk without a guide, this trail is best in the spring when you can hike in the canyon heat with the cool stream swirling about your ankles. Take one of the paved **Rim Drives** (North Rim 44 mi., South Rim 36 mi.), which skirt the edge of the 300- to 700-ft. cliffs; the South Rim is more dramatic. Try to make it all the way to the **Spider Rock Overlook,** 20 mi. from the visitors center, a narrow sandstone monolith towering hundreds of feet above the canyon floor. Native American lore says that the whitish rock at the top of Spider Rock contains bleached bones of victims of the *kachina* spirit Spider Woman (or her husband Peter Parker). Written guides to the White House Ruins and the North or South Rim Drives cost 50¢ at the visitors center.

■■■ MONUMENT VALLEY AND NAVAJO NATIONAL MONUMENT

You may have seen the red rock towers of **Monument Valley Navajo Tribal Park** (801-727-3287) in one of numerous westerns filmed here. Rather ironically, the 1000-ft. monoliths helped boost "injun"-killer John Wayne to heights of movie slaughter. The best and cheapest way to see the valley is via the Park's looping 17-mi. **Valley Drive.** This dirt road winds in and out of the most dramatic monuments, including the famous paired **Mittens** and the slender **Totem Pole.** The gaping ditches, large rocks, and mudholes on this road will do horrible things to your car: drive at your own risk, and hold your breath. Much of the valley can be reached only in a sturdy four-wheel-drive vehicle or by a long hike. In winter, snow laces the rocky towers, and almost all the tourists flee. Inquire about snow and road conditions at the Flagstaff Chamber of Commerce (800-842-7293).

The park entrance is 24 mi. north on U.S. 163 from the town of Kayenta and the intersection with U.S. 160 (park open daily 7am-8pm; Oct.-April 8am-5pm; entrance fee $2.50, seniors $1, kids 7 and under free).

The Navajo maintain a small campground with water and restrooms next to the Visitors Center (sites $10). The site at the National Monument has no showers or hookups, but it's free and has the added advantage of nightly ranger talks.

From the park entrance, Rte. 564 takes you 9 mi. to **Navajo National Monument.** This stunning site consists of three Anasazi cliff-dwellings, including **Keet Seel,** the best-preserved site in the Southwest. Inscription House has closed, and entrance into Keet Seel and **Betatakin,** a 135-room complex, is limited to 25 people per day in ranger-led groups. (Tours daily at 9am, noon, and 2pm; try to make reservations at least two months in advance. Write Navajo National Monument, Tanalea 86044.) For $50, Navajo guides put you on a horse, lead you down the 8-mi. trail, and leave you with a ranger to explore the 400-year-old Anasazi ruins. Allow a full day for the ride and the strenuous hike. Rangers also lead 5-mi. hikes. You can hike on your own, but you must obtain a permit. The **visitors center** (672-2366) has a craft shop as well as pottery and artifacts displays (open daily 8am-6pm; off-season 8am-5pm).

■■■ PETRIFIED FOREST NATIONAL PARK AND METEOR CRATER

Don't expect to see a forest here; that's the *last* thing the Petrified Forest Resembles. Color postcards may make it appear impressive, but the park consists of 60,000 acres of monotonous Arizona desert sparsely dotted with tree logs that turned into rock some 225 million years ago. Petrification involves an unlikely set of circumstances: logs must fall into a swamp, be cut off from air and water rapidly, then have each cell replaced by crystal—all in all, about as likely as seeing Tipper Gore at a Mötley Crüe concert. The park is 107 mi. from Flagstaff on I-40. The sunset view at its **Painted Desert** (named for the magnificent multicolored bands of rock inlaid with quartz and amethyst crystals that scatter across the desert floor) is spectacular—creating a sparkling kaleidoscope of color.

Entrances are off I-40 to the north and U.S. 180 to the south (entrance fee $5 per vehicle). The **Painted Desert Visitors Center,** near the north entrance, shows a film explaining petrification every ½ hr. A 27-mi. park road connects the two entrances, winding past piles of petrified logs and Native American ruins. Stop to look at oddly-named **Newspaper Rock,** covered not with newsprint but Native American petroglyphs; the headlines are a bit out-of-date but still cool to see. At **Blue Mesa,** a hiking trail winds through the desert. **Long Logs Crystal** and **Jasper Forest** contain some of the most exquisite fragments of petrified wood. Picking up fragments of petrified wood in the park is illegal and traditionally unlucky (a result of ancient curses cast by capitalist shamans); if the demons don't getcha then the district attorney will. Those who *must* take a piece home should buy one at a store along I-40, since the storekeepers are immune to both curses. To camp overnight, make arrangements at the visitors center in the **Rainbow Forest Museum** (524-6822), at the park's southern entrance (open daily 7am-7pm, in spring, fall, and winter 8am-5pm). Public transport does not feed the Petrified Forest; several bus lines do stop in Holbrook, on I-40, 27 mi. away.

Between Flagstaff and the Petrified Forest off I-40 is the privately-owned **Meteor Crater** (602-774-8350), located 35 mi. east of Flagstaff off the Meteor Crater Rd. exit. This meteor crater, one of the world's largest, was originally believed to be just another ancient volcanic cone. However, geologic tests in the crater and on rock fragments from the surrounding desert proved the hypothesis, once scoffed at, that about 50,000 years ago a huge nickel-iron meteorite plummeted through the atmosphere and onto the desert to create the 570-ft. deep pothole. The site was used to train the Apollo astronauts in the 1960s. (Open daily 6am-6pm, in winter daily 8am-5pm. $7, seniors $6, students $4, kids 13-17 $2, kids 6-10 $1.)

■■■ PHOENIX

Forget genetics—Phoenix is a product of its environment. Rising out of the aptly-named Valley of the Sun, it is a winter haven for frostbitten tourists and sun-loving students. During these balmy months, golf, spring-training baseball, and the Fiesta Bowl flourish. Phoenix's beautiful weather and proximity to the natural sights of the area make it an excellent point of entry to the Southwest. However, weather only goes so far. The city's urban sprawl and relative dearth of cultural activities also makes it a good place to leave after intercepting a few rays.

During the summer, the city crawls into its air-conditioned shell. Visitors at this time should be certain to carry a bottle of water with them if they plan on walking for *any* length of time. Although summer highs almost always top 100°F, the abundance and sophistication of cooling systems (some of them outdoors) make occasional jaunts outside tolerable. In addition, the drier air and lower prices of the summer make the asphalt-melting weather slightly more bearable.

PRACTICAL INFORMATION

Emergency: 911.
Visitor Information: Phoenix and Valley of the Sun Convention and Visitors Center, 400 E. Van Buren St. (254-6500) at 1 Arizona Center. Ask for a Valley Pass to save up to 50% at the more expensive resorts, hotels and attractions. Open Mon.-Fri. 8am-5pm. **Weekly Events Hotline,** 252-5588. 24-hr. recording.
Amtrak: 401 W. Harrison (253-0121 or 800-872-7245), 2 blocks south of Jefferson St. NOT safe at night. To: Los Angeles (3 per week, 8½ hr., $85); El Paso (9 hr., $85). Station open Sun.-Wed. 5:45am-11:30pm, Thurs. and Sat. 3-9:30pm.
Greyhound: 5th and Washington St. (800-231-2222). To: Flagstaff (5 per day, 2½ hr., $18); Tucson (10 per day, 2½ hr., $12); Los Angeles (11 per day, 7 hr., $32). Open 24 hrs. Lockers $1.
Public Transport: Phoenix Transit, 253-5000. Most lines run to and from the **City Bus Terminal,** Central and Washington. Most routes operate Mon.-Fri. 5am-9:30pm; severely reduced service on Sat. Fare $1; disabled persons, seniors, and kids 50¢. 10-ride pass $10, all-day $2.50; disabled persons and seniors ½-price. Pick up free time tables, maps of the bus system, and bus passes at the terminal. City bus #13 runs to the **Sky Harbor International Airport,** only minutes southeast of downtown.
Car Rental: Rent-a-Wreck, 2422 E. Washington St. (254-1000). Economy cars from $21 a day; unlimited mi.; 150-mi. radius. Open Mon.-Fri. 7am-6:30pm, Sat.-Sun. 9am-5pm. Must be 21 with credit card or cash deposit. **Admirals,** 427 N.

44th St. (275-6992). $20 per day with 200 free mi., 30¢ each additional mi. Open Mon.-Fri. 8am-5pm, Sat.-Sun. 9am-4pm. Must be 21 with credit card.

Auto Transport Company: Auto Driveaway, 3530 E. Indian School Rd. (952-0339). First tank of gas free. Open Mon.-Fri. 9am-4:30pm. Must be 21 with $250 deposit.

Taxi: Ace Taxi, 254-1999. $2.45 base fare, $1.10 per mi. **Yellow Cab,** 252-5252. $2.05 base fare, $1.30 per mi.

Help Lines: Center Against Sexual Assault, 241-9010. Open 24 hrs. **Gay and Lesbian Hotline,** 234-2752. **Community Switchboard,** 234-2752.

Post Office: 522 N. Central (407-2051), downtown. General Delivery at 4949 E. Van Buren St. Open Mon.-Fri. 8am-5pm. **ZIP code:** 85026.

Area Code: 602.

The **city bus terminal** at Central Ave. and Washington St. idles in the heart of downtown Phoenix. **Central Avenue** runs north-south; "avenues" are numbered west from Central and "streets" are numbered east. **Washington Street** divides streets north-south.

ACCOMMODATIONS AND CAMPING

Summer is the best season for the budget traveler to visit Phoenix. Almost all motels near downtown have vacancies and slash their rates by up to 70%. In the winter, however, when temperatures and vacancy signs go down, prices go up; be sure to make reservations if possible. Those without reservations cruise the row of motels on the occasionally decrepit and slightly dangerous East and West **Van Buren Street** or on **Main Street** (Apache Trail) in Tempe and Mesa. The strip is full of 50s ranch-style motels with names like "Kon-Tiki" and "Deserama," as well as the requisite modern chains. In the summer almost all lower their rates and offer gimmicks, making accommodations very cheap. **Bed and Breakfast in Arizona,** Gallery 3 Plaza, 3819 N. 3rd St. 85012 (265-9511), can help you find accommodations in homes in Phoenix and throughout Arizona. (Preferred 2-night min. stay. Singles from $25; doubles $35. Reservations recommended.)

Metcalf House (HI/AYH), 1026 N. 9th St. (254-9803), a few blocks northeast of downtown. From the city bus terminal, take bus #7 down 7th St. to Roosevelt St., then walk 2 blocks east to 9th St. and turn left—the hostel is ½ block north. About a 20-min. walk from downtown. Dorm-style rooms, wooden bunks, and common showers. Kitchen, porch and common room, laundry. Sleep sack required. Check-in 7-10am and 5-11pm. $9, nonmembers $12. Linen $1. Bike rental $3 per day.

Motel 6, many locations, including 6848 E. Camelback (946-2280), and I-17 exit 202/West Indian School Rd. (248-8881). Clean, sparsely decorated rooms. Singles $26-29. $6 each additional person.

Budget Lodge Motels, 402 W. Van Buren St. (254-7247), near downtown. Large, clean, rooms with A/C, TV, and free local calls, plus a small pool in the parking lot. Singles $20, doubles $27, weekly $100 in summer, but prices vary by season. Reserve a few weeks ahead in winter.

KOA, 2550 W. Louise (869-8189), 3 mi. north of Bell Rd. on I-17 at Black Canyon City. Showers, pool, spa, laundry, playground. AAA discount. Sites $15 for 2 people, $18 with hookup. Each additional adult $2.

FOOD

Rarely will you find several restaurants together amid Phoenix's sprawl. Downtown is fed mainly by small coffeeshops, most of which close on weekends. An exception to this rule is **The Mercado,** a faux-Mexican mall on E. Van Buren between 5th and 7th St., which contains several inexpensive eateries, most open on weekends. For more variety, drive down McDowell St.

Tacos de Juárez, 1017 N. 7th St. (258-1744), near the hostel. Standard Mexican fare at rock-bottom prices. Specializes in tacos. A la carte items all under $3. Open Mon.-Thurs. 11am-9pm, Fri. 11am-10:30pm, Sat. 8am-10:30pm, Sun. 8am-8pm.

The Matador, 125 E. Adams St. (254-7563), downtown. Standard Mexican dinners $5-8. The deep-fried ice cream is a novelty. Live music Fri. and Sat. nights. Open daily 7am-11pm. Lounge open until 1am.

The Purple Cow Deli, 200 N. Central (253-0861), in the San Carlos Hotel; also in the Park Central Mall. I've never met a purple cow, I never hope to meet one; but I can tell you anyhow, I'd rather eat than be one. Great sandwiches ($4) and frozen yogurt. Kosher food available. Open Mon.-Fri. 6am-6pm, Sat.-Sun. 8am-2pm.

Tee Pee's, 4144 E. Indian School Rd. (956-0178). Great Mexican food at low prices. Try the beef or chicken burros ($4.50) or the many combination plates ($4-6). Open daily 11am-whenever.

Bill Johnson's Big Apple, 3757 E. Van Buren (275-2107), 1 of 4 locations. A down-south delight with sawdust on the floor. Sandwiches ($4-6), hearty soups ($2-3). Open Mon.-Sat. 6am-11pm.

SIGHTS

If you're a connoisseur of the arts, stick around downtown for Phoenix's many museums and beautiful buildings. The **Heard Museum,** 22 E. Monte Vista (252-8848 or 252-8840), 1 block east of Central Ave. near the hostel, has outstanding collections of Navajo handicrafts and promotes the work of contemporary Native American artists, many of whom give free demonstrations. The museum also sponsors occasional lectures and Native American dances. (Guided tours daily. Open Mon.-Tues. and Thurs.-Sat. 9:30am-5pm, Wed. 9:30am-9pm, Sun. noon-5pm. $5, seniors and students $4, kids 3-12 $2.) The **Phoenix Art Museum,** 1625 N. Central Ave. (257-1222), 3 blocks south, has excellent exhibits of European, modern, and U.S. folk art (open Tues. and Thurs.-Sat. 10am-5pm, Wed. 10am-9pm, Sun. noon-5pm; $4, seniors $3, students $1.50, kids under 6 free; free Wed.).

The **Desert Botanical Gardens,** 1201 N. Galvin Pkwy. (941-1225), in Papago Park 5 mi. east of the downtown area, grows a beautiful and colorful collection of cacti and other desert plants. Visit in the morning or late afternoon to avoid the midday heat. (Open daily 7am-10pm; winter 8am-sunset. $5, seniors $4, kids 5-12 $1. Take bus #3 east to Papago Park.) Also within the confines of Papago Park is the **Phoenix Zoo,** at 62nd and E. Van Buren, boasting outstanding exhibits and a children's zoo. Walk around or take a guided tour via tram. (Open 9am-5pm; $6, kids $4.)

South of Phoenix across the dry Salt River lies Tempe's **Arizona State University (ASU)** and its exuberant college atmosphere. Cafes and art galleries abound in this area. The **Gammage Memorial Auditorium** (965-3434), at Mill Ave. and Apache Trail, is one of the last major buildings designed by omnipresent Frank Lloyd Wright. Painted in pink and beige to match the surrounding desert, the eccentric edifice's coloration is sure to either astound or nauseate you. (20-min. tours daily in winter. Take bus #60, or #22 on weekends.)

ENTERTAINMENT

Phoenix is the progressive rock and country capital of the Southwest, with an active (though awfully fashion-conscious) nightclub scene. **Phoenix Live** at Arizona Center, 455 N. 3rd St. (252-2112), quakes the complex with four bars and clubs. For the hefty $5 cover you'll have access to the entire building. On Fri.-Sat. **LTL Ditty's** plays piano and encourages sing-alongs and wild fans. **Char's Has the Blues,** 4631 N. 7th Ave. (230-0205), is self-explanatory. Dozens of junior John Lee Hookers rip it up nightly. (Music nightly at 9pm. Cover from $4.) Headbangers find their black leather, big guitar Eldorado in the bottom of the **Mäson Jar,** 2303 E. Indian School (956-6271). (*Heavy* jams nightly at 9. Cover $3 weekdays, $5 weekends.) The free *New Times Weekly* (271-0040), on local magazine racks, lists club schedules. Pick up a copy of the *Cultural Calendar of Events,* a concise guide covering three months of area entertainment activities.

Phoenix also has plenty for the sports-lover in you. Catch NBA action with the World Champion runner-up **Phoenix Suns** at the America West Arena (tickets at the box office or through Dilliard's Box Office), or root for the NFL's **Phoenix Cardinals** (379-0101), who have had slightly less playoff success recently. Phoenix also plays host to professional indoor tennis tournaments and a professional baseball team. For the truly dedicated, there is even a hockey team. For more information, check with the visitors center (see Practical Information).

■ Near Phoenix

The drive along the **Apache Trail** to Tonto National Monument makes a great day-trip from Phoenix. Take U.S. 60-89 to Apache Junction, about 30 mi. east of Phoenix, then turn right onto Rte. 88, which follows the Apache Trail through the **Superstition Mountains.** The good-humored town of **Tortilla Flat,** a way station for hot and dusty travelers, lies 3 mi. after Canyon Lake, the first of three artificial lakes along the trail; a spectacular stretch of scenery begins 5 mi. east of Tortilla Flat. A dangerous dirt road winds its way through 22 mi. of mountains and canyons to **Roosevelt Dam,** an enormous arc of masonry wedged between two huge red cliffs. The turn-off for **Tonto National Monument** (467-2241), where preserved dwellings of the Saledo tribe are tucked into sheltered caves in the cliffs, is 4 mi. beyond the dam. A 1-hr. self-guided hike up the mountainside, through the apartments and back, affords a lovely view of Roosevelt Lake. (Visitors center open daily 8am-5pm; trail open 8am-4pm. $4 per car or $2 per person.)

■■■ TUCSON AREA

Immortalized in song by Little Feat ("I've been from Tucson to Tucumcari, Tehachapi to Tonopah") as a western outpost for those willin' to be movin', Tucson at first glance appears indeed to be little more than a glorified truck stop. Dig deeper, though, and you'll find a lot more here than I-10. Settled by the Hohokam and Pima tribes, the region witnessed the arrival of the Spanish in 1776, who built a collection of forts and missions in this dry valley. What gives modern Tucson most of its zip and zing is the University of Arizona (UA). If modern Tucson gets you down, head to the outskirts of town and cavort with the cacti at Saguaro National Monument.

PRACTICAL INFORMATION

Emergency: 911.
Visitor Information: Metropolitan Tucson Convention and Visitors Bureau, 130 S. Scott Ave. (624-1817). Ask for a city bus map, the *Official Visitor's Guide,* and Arizona campground directory. Open Mon.-Fri. 8am-5pm, Sat.-Sun. 9am-4pm.
Traveler's Aid: 622-8900. Referrals and crisis intervention.
Airport: Tucson International Airport 573-8000, on Valencia Rd., south of downtown. Bus #25 runs every hr. to the Laos Transit Center, where bus #16 goes downtown. Last bus daily at 7:17pm. **Arizona Stagecoach** (889-1000) has a booth at the airport and will take you downtown for about $11. Open 24 hrs.
Amtrak: 400 E. Toole (623-4442 or 800-872-7245), at 5th Ave., next to the Greyhound station. Open Sun.-Wed. 7:45am-8:30pm, Thurs. 1:15-8:30pm, Sat. 7:45am-3pm. 3 trains per week to: Phoenix ($27); Los Angeles ($102); El Paso ($73).
Greyhound: 2 S. 4th Ave. (800-231-2222), downtown between Congress St. and Broadway. To: Phoenix (11 per day, 2 hr., $12); Los Angeles (7 per day, 10 hr., $45); Albuquerque (6 per day, $78); El Paso (7 per day, $53). Open 24 hrs.
Taxi: Yellow Cab, 624-6611. 24 hrs.
Sun-Tran: 792-9222. Buses leave from the Ronstadt terminal in downtown at Congress and 6th. Approximate times of operation are Mon.-Fri. 5:30am-10pm, Sat.-Sun. 8am-7pm. Fare 75¢, students 18 and under 50¢(student ID required), seniors 25¢. The "4th Avenue Trolley" (an eco-friendly, natural-gas burning, trolley-shaped van) runs from downtown, along 4th Ave., and to the university (25¢).

Car Rental: Care Free, 1760 S. Craycroft Rd., (790-2655). For the car free. $18 per day with 100 free mi. per day; within Tucson only. Open Mon.-Fri. 9am-5pm, Sat. 9am-3pm. Must be 21 with major credit card.

Bike Rental: The Bike Shack, 835 Park Ave. (624-3663), across from UA campus. $20 for 1 day, $30 for 2 days, $40 for 3 days. Open Mon.-Fri. 9am-7pm, Sat. 10am-5pm, Sun. noon-5pm.

Help Lines: Rape Crisis, 623-7273.

Post Office: 141 S. 6th St. (622-8454). Open Mon.-Fri. 8:30am-5pm, Sat. 9am-noon. General Delivery at 1501 Cherry Bell (620-5157). **ZIP code:** 85726.

Area Code: 602.

Tucson's downtown area is just east of I-10, around the intersection of Broadway (running east-west) and Stone Ave., and includes the train and bus terminals. The **University of Arizona** studies 1 mi. northeast of downtown at the intersection of Park and Speedway Blvd.

Although surrounded by mountains, Tucson is flat as an armadillo on I-10, making most major streets (the downtown area a notable exception) perfectly straight. Streets are marked north, south, east or west relative to Stone Ave. and Broadway. Avenues run north-south, streets east-west; because some of each are numbered, intersections such as "6th and 6th" are possible—and probable.

ACCOMMODATIONS AND CAMPING

When summer arrives, Tucson opens its arms to budget travelers. For motel bargains, browse through the stack of accommodation leaflets at the visitors center (see Practical Information above). Motel row lies along **South Freeway,** the frontage road along I-10, just north of the junction with I-19.

Hotel Congress, 311 E. Çongress (622-8848), is conveniently located across from the Greyhound and Amtrak stations. The hotel doubles as an RNA hostel, offering bunk beds in a clean room. Prices are higher in winter and for a renovated room. A cafe, a bar, and a club swing downstairs. Hostel $12, nonmembers $13. Singles $32. Doubles $36. Students receive 20% discount on hotel rooms.

The Tucson Desert Inn (624-8151), I-10 at Congress, has the largest pool in Tucson. Large, clean rooms have good furnishings and plenty of sun. Singles $24. Doubles $33. Seniors receive 10% discount. Light breakfast included.

Old Pueblo Homestays Bed and Breakfast, P.O. Box 13603, Tucson 85732 (800-333-9776; open daily 8am-8pm), arranges overnight stays in private homes. (Singles from $35. Doubles $45. Winter reservations usually required 2 weeks in advance.)

The best place to camp is the **Mount Lemmon Recreation Area** in the **Coronado National Forest,** that offers unofficial but legal camping in the wilderness. Campgrounds and picnic areas are two minutes to two hours outside Tucson via the Catalina Hwy. The best unofficial camping in the forest is in **Sabino Canyon,** on the northeastern outskirts of Tucson. **Rose Canyon,** at 7000 ft., is heavily wooded, comfortably cool, and has a small lake. Sites at the higher elevations fill quickly on summer weekends. (Sites $7 at Rose and Spencer Canyons; General Hitchcock Campground free, but no water available.) For more info, contact the **National Forest Service,** 300 W. Congress Ave. (670-4552), at Granada, 7 blocks west of Greyhound (open Mon.-Fri. 7:45am-4:30pm). Among the commercial campgrounds near Tucson, try **Cactus Country RV Park** (574-3000), 10 mi. southeast of Tucson on I-10 off the Houghton Rd. exit. It has showers, restrooms, and a pool. (Sites $12 for 1 or 2 people, with full hookup $18.50. Each additional person $2.50.)

FOOD

The downtown business district and the area farther east around the University feature—would you believe it?—excellent Tex-Mex cuisine. Those homesick for institutional food can get their fill at any of the eateries at UA's student union (open 7am-5pm in summer).

Big Ray's Cafe, 6372 S. Nogales Rd. (889-8294). Welcome to the real deal. Big Ray's not only has some of the most friendly service in town, but the BBQ sandwiches ($2.50-4) and homemade sauce are...well, they're just damn good. Open Mon.-Fri. 5am-2pm, Sat. 5am-1pm, Sun. 6am-5pm.

El Charro, 311 N. Court Ave. (622-5465), 4 blocks north of the Civic Center. The oldest Mexican restaurant in Tucson. Flavorful but not fiery sun-dried *carne seca* in various forms (enchilada $4.75). Chips, HOT salsa, and a pitcher of water (to douse the fire in your mouth) free with every order. Open Sun.-Thurs. 11am-9pm, Fri.-Sat. 11am-10pm.

El Minuto, 354 S. Main Ave. (882-4145), just south of the community center. Colorful atmosphere and impeccable quality. Tucson's best late-night restaurant. Usually packed with locals. Open daily 11am-11pm.

El Adobe, 40 W. Broadway (791-7458) in the heart of downtown. Beautiful atmosphere coupled with excellent, inexpensive Mexican cuisine. Many health-conscious items on the menu. Try the chicken burro ($4) or flautas (2 for $5). Open Mon.-Thurs. 11am-9pm, Fri.-Sat. 11am-10pm, June-Sept., Sat. 5-10pm.

El Dorado, 1949 S. 4th Ave. Mexican fare at terrific prices. The chimichangas ($5.25) are huge and the enchiladas ($4.25) are incredibly tasty. American and Mexican beer. Take-out service to boot.

ENTERTAINMENT

In Tucson, musical tastes are as varied as Arizona's climate. While UA students rock and roll on Speedway Blvd., more subdued folks do the two-step in several country music clubs on North Oracle. Pick up a copy of the free *Tucson Weekly* at any restaurant for current entertainment listings.

Berkey's, 5769 E. Speedway (296-1981). A smoke-filled blues and rock club. Open daily noon-1am. Live music nightly. Cover Fri.-Sat. $3.

Hotel Congress Historic Tap Room, 311 E. Congress (622-8848). Frozen in its 1938 incarnation. Eclectic—perhaps even weird—crowd, but very friendly. Open daily 11am-1am. Across the hall, a DJ plays "Mod/New-Age/Alternative" dance music Thurs.-Sat. at **Club Congress.** Occasional live music. Drink specials $1.25. Club opens 8pm.

Wild Wild West, 4385 W. Ina Rd. (744-7744), not accessible by public transportation. The most authentic manifestation of the Old West saloon with continuous country-western music and the largest dance floor in Arizona. An acre of dancin' and romancin'. *Don't* come in shorts. Buffet ($2) 5-7:30pm. Cover Fri.-Sat $2 for women, $3 for men. Open daily 4pm-1am.

SIGHTS

Most of Tucson's attractions lie some distance outside of town and are accessible by car or tour bus only. The city itself offers few diversions. The downtown is not "historic" by East Coast or European standards; few buildings date from before the Civil War. Tucson lays a better claim to being "artsy," with galleries and the **Tucson Museum of Art,** 140 N. Main Ave. (624-2333), downtown, whose impressive collection focuses on the pre-Columbian (open Mon.-Sat. 10am-4pm, Sun. noon-4pm; $2, seniors and students $1; free Tues.)

The **University of Arizona,** whose "mall" sits where E. 3rd St. should be, parades another main concentration of in-town attractions. The mall itself is lovely, less for the architecture than for the varied—and elaborately irrigated—vegetation. The **UA Visitors Center** (621-3621), at Cherry and the Mall, offers tours of campus. (Tours fall-spring, Mon.-Fri. 10am-2pm, Sat. 10am; summer Mon.-Sat. 10am.) Across the Mall, the **Flandrau Planetarium** (621-7827) has a museum and a public telescope, plus planetarium shows. (Eccentric hours for museum and shows; call ahead. Museum free; shows $4.50, seniors and students $4, kids 3-12 $2.50.) At the west end of campus, **University Blvd.** is jammed with shops catering to student needs—with clothing, records, and photocopies. **The Wild Cat Den,** 9111 E. University Blvd., prices its fully flavored sodas as low as 15¢, perhaps out of pure philanthropy (open Mon.-Fri. 7:30am-9pm, Sat. 9am-7pm, Sun. 10am-6pm).

A vibrant local event, the **mariachi mass,** thrills at **St. Augustine Church,** 192 S. Stone Ave., downtown. The singing and dancing, which are not intended as tourist attractions, take place in Tucson's old white Spanish cathedral. (Sun. 8am mass in Spanish.) The **Tucson Parks and Recreation Department** (791-4873) sponsors free concerts periodically throughout the summer. Call for info or check the Thursday evening *Citizen.*

■ Near Tucson

The natural and man-made attractions which surround Tucson are the city's saving grace for tourists. To the north, a **tram** whisks visitors from the visitors center through **Sabino Canyon** (749-2861), where cliffs and waterfalls make an ideal spot for picnics and day hikes. (Tram daily every ½ hr. 9am-4:30pm.) From Tucson, take I-10 and turn at exit 270. **Sabino Canyon Tours,** 5900 N. Sabino Canyon Rd. (749-2327), runs a shuttle bus ($5, kids $2; in summer Mon.-Fri. 9am-4pm, every hr. on the hr., Sat.-Sun. 9am-4:30pm every ½ hr.).

If you've ever wondered where to find those tall, gangly cacti you always see in Westerns and on the Arizona license plate, go to the **Saguaro National Monument** (296-8576), a park devoted to preserving the Saguaro cacti, which can live up to 200 years and grow over 40 ft. tall. Tucson divides this monument into two parts. To the west of the city, the **Tucson Mountain Unit** (883-6366), on N. Kinney Rd. at Rte. 9, has limited hiking trails for day use only and an auto loop. (Visitors center open daily 8am-5pm. Park open 24 hrs. Free.) Just south of this unit is the **Arizona-Sonora Desert Museum,** 2021 N. Kinney Rd. (883-2702), a naturalist's dream, which gives an up-close look at the flora and fauna of the Sonoran desert, including an excellent walk-though aviary, an underwater look at otters, and a beaver the size of a small cow. Take at least two hours to see the museum; the best time to visit during is the cool morning hours when the animals have not begun their afternoon siesta. (Open daily 7:30am-6pm; winter 8:30am-5pm. $8, kids 6-12 $1.50.) The way to and from the Tucson Mountain Unit and the Desert Museum goes through **Gates Pass,** whose vistas make it a favorite spot for watching sunrises and sunsets. To the east of the city, the **Rincon Mountain Unit** (296-8576), on the Old Spanish Trail east of Tucson, offers the same services as the Tucson Unit as well as overnight hikes. (Visitors center open daily 8am-5pm. $4 per vehicle.)

Pima's **Titan II Missile Museum,** 1580 W. Duvall Mine Rd. (791-2929), in Green Valley, 25 mi. south of Tucson, is a chilling monument built around a deactivated missile silo. (Open Wed.-Sun. 9am-4pm, Nov.-April daily 9am-5pm. $5, seniors and active military $4, ages 10-17 $3. Reservations advised.) The Southwest is the desert graveyard for many an outmoded aircraft; low humidity and sparse rainfall combine to preserve the relics. Over 20,000 warplanes, from WWII fighters to Vietnam War jets, are parked in ominous, silent rows on the **Davis-Monthan Air Force Base** (750-4570), 15 mi. southeast of Tucson. Take the Houghton exit off I-10, then travel west on Irvington to Wilmont. (Free tours Mon. and Wed. at 9am. Call ahead for reservations.) You can also view the 2-mi. long graveyard through the airfield fence.

Just next to the Desert Museum lies **Old Tucson,** a movie set attempting to convey the feel of the Old West. Since 1939, over 200 motion pictures were filmed here. More authentic is the small desert town of **Tombstone,** 70 mi. southeast of Tucson. This aptly named mining town will live forever in Western lore as the sight of the legendary **Shoot-out at the O.K. Corral** between the Earp brothers and the Clanton gang, as well as the home of such renowned Western figures as Wyatt Earp, Bat Masterson, and Doc Holiday. The **O.K. Corral** (457-3456), on Allen St. next to City Park, is open to visitors and doubles as a general tourist info center. (Open daily 8:30am-5pm. Admission $1.50. Tickets $3—includes a movie screening and a copy of the *Epitaph.*) Tombstone's sheriffs and outlaws, very few of whom died of natural causes, were laid to rot in the **Boothill Cemetery** northeast of downtown. Try to catch the mock gunfights staged every Sunday at 2pm, alternating between the O.K. Corral and the town streets. Come prepared to open your wallet; "the town too tough to die" touts an almost irresistible assortment of kitschy curios in several shops. For more info on Tombstone's sights, contact the O.K. Corral or the **Tombstone Tourism Association,** at 5th and Allen St. (457-2211; open Mon.-Fri. 9am-5pm, Sat.-Sun. 10am-5pm).

 Nevada

Nevada once walked the straight and narrow. Explored by Spanish missionaries and settled by Mormons, the Nevada Territory's arid land and searing climate seemed a perfect place for ascetics to strive for moral uplift. But the discovery of gold in 1850 and silver in 1859 won the state over permanently to the worship of filthy lucre. When the precious metal boom-bust ferris wheel finally stalled during the Great Depression, Nevadans responded by shirking the last vestiges of traditional virtue, and gambling and marriage-licensing became the state industries. In a final break with the rest of the country, Silver Staters legalized prostitution and began paying Wayne Newton enormous amounts of cash. Nevada's unique convergence of vice and chance have combined to make the state the tackiest in the Union.

But a different Nevada exists outside the gambling towns. The forested slopes of Lake Tahoe, shared with California, offer serenity in little resorts a far cry away from the casinos of the south shore. The rest of a mostly expansive and bone-dry Nevada is countryside, where the true West lingers in its barren glory.

PRACTICAL INFORMATION

Capital: Carson City.
Visitor Information: Carson City Visitors Authority, 1900 South Carson St. Suite #200, Carson City 89701 (883-7442). **Nevada Division of State Parks,** Nye Bldg., 201 S. Fall, Carson City 89701 (885-4384). Open Mon.-Fri. 8am-5pm.
Time Zone: Pacific (3 hrs. behind Eastern). **Postal Abbreviation:** NV
Sales Tax: 5.75-6%.

■■■ LAS VEGAS

Since Bugsy Segal built his dream of a then-extravagant casino-hotel, the Flamingo Hilton, in the 1930s, Las Vegas has only continued to outdo itself year after year. You will be impressed, if only by contemplating the electric bills generated by a town which runs non-stop 24 hours a day, 365 days a year. Even when you think you've seen it all, there's more! Whether you're there to gamble away the house, wife, and kids, or just drop nickles in the slot machine, every casino is vying for your business. What this means for the budget traveler is a dream come true: all-you-can-eat buffets and luxurious hotel rooms for unbelievable prices. Most of the entertainment is free, as each casino is a self-contained amusement park with its own theme—circus, medieval, Roman Empire. For an education in tacky American culture, Las Vegas is crash course 101.

PRACTICAL INFORMATION

Emergency: 911.

Visitor Information: Las Vegas Convention and Visitors Authority, 3150 Paradise Rd. (892-7575), at the Convention Center, 4 blocks from the Strip, by the Hilton. Up-to-date info on hotel bargains and buffets. Open daily 8am-5pm.

Tours: Gray Line Tours, 1550 S. Industrial Rd. (384-1234). Bus tours: Hoover Dam/Lake Mead Express (4½ hr., $18); the Grand Canyon (2 days; single $140, double $108, triple $95; March-Oct. Mon., Wed. and Fri. 7am).; Mini City Tours (1 per day, ½-day, $17.50). **Ray and Ross Tours,** 300 W. Owens St. (646-4661 or 800-338-8111). Bus tours to Hoover Dam (6 hr., $17) and Hoover Dam/Lake Mead (7 hr., $25).

Airport: McCarran International Airport (798-5410), at the southeast end of the Strip. Main terminal on Paradise Rd. Within walking distance of the University of Nevada campus and the southern casinos. Buses and taxis ($8) to downtown.

Amtrak: 1 N. Main St. (386-6896), in Union Plaza Hotel. To: Los Angeles ($68); San Francisco ($116); Salt Lake City ($89). Ticket office open daily 6am-3am.

Greyhound: 200 Main St. (800-752-4841), at Carson Ave. downtown. To: L.A. ($35; 14 days in advance $27); Reno ($56); Salt Lake City ($46-49); Denver ($85, 14 days ahead $64). Ticket office open daily 6am-3am; terminal open 24 hrs.

Public Transportation: CAT, 228-7433. Serves the Strip from the Downtown Transportation Center near Stewart Ave. to Hacienda Ave. #17 Express runs every 20 min. 5:30am-1:30am, making limited stops along the Strip from Tropicana Ave. to the Downtown Transportation Center. Adults $1, kids and seniors 50¢.

Car Rental: Rebel Rent-a-Car, 5466 Paradise Rd. (597-0427 or 800-372-1981), $20 per day; unlimited mi. within Clark County. Must be 21 with major credit card; $7 per day surcharge if you're under 25. $100 deposit. Like accommodations and restaurants, car rental agencies offer discounts in tourist publications.

Help Lines: Crisis Line, 876-4357. **Gamblers Anonymous,** 385-7732. 24 hrs.

Post Office: 301 E. Stewart (385-8944). Open Mon.-Fri. 9am-5pm, Sat. 9am-1pm. General delivery open Mon.-Fri. 10am-3pm. **ZIP code:** 89114.

Area Code: 702.

Gambler's specials number among the cheapest and most popular ways to reach Las Vegas. These bus tours leave early in the morning and return at night or the next day; ask in L.A., San Francisco, or San Diego tourist offices. You can also call casinos for info. Prices include everything except food and gambling, and although you are expected to stay with your group, "getting lost" shouldn't be a problem.

Vegas has two major casino areas. The **downtown** area, around Fremont and 2nd St., is foot-friendly; casinos cluster close together, and some of the sidewalks are even carpeted (man, oh man). The other main area, known as the **Strip,** is a collection of mammoth casinos on both sides of intimidatingly busy **Las Vegas Blvd. South.** Except for the neighborhoods just north and west of downtown, Vegas is generally a safe place for late-night strolling. Security guards and lights reproduce in amoeba-like fashion, and there is almost always pedestrian traffic.

ACCOMMODATIONS AND CAMPING

You can easily find cheap food and lodging in Vegas. Watch the travel and entertainment sections of local newspapers for ever-changing specials. Prices rise on weekends and holidays, but with over 73,000 hotel rooms, you can probably find some place to rest that slot-machine arm. If you are traveling in a group of two or more, it will be worth the couple of extra dollars to stay at one of the larger hotels with a more centralized Strip location and a pool. Don't let the glitz intimidate you—weekday rates (Sun.-Thurs.) are truly bargains.

Las Vegas Hostel, 1208 Las Vegas Blvd. S. (385-9955). Spartan, airy rooms with foam mattresses. Free breakfast; ride board in kitchen. Check-out 7-11am. Tours to Zion, Bryce, and the Grand Canyon ($115). Office open daily 7am-11pm, Nov.-March 8-10am and 5-11pm. Shared room and bath $9, $56 per week; private room and shared bath $20. Winter rates lower. Key deposit $5.

LAS VEGAS

Casablanca Inn, 1801 Las Vegas Blvd. S. (735-4050). The new hostel on the block (or rather Strip). Friendly staff, common room with pool table, TV, and kitchen. Try to catch the free chicken and beer dinner, served erratically three nights per week (no one knows when). Captain Louis Renault would be shocked to discover gambling in the back. Dorm rooms with A/C and private bath $12, $75 per week; Double with TV and A/C $27.50. Free breakfast, laundry, and pool.

Circus Circus, 500 Circus Circus Dr. (734-0410 or 800-634-3450). A major casino with 2800 rooms but some of the best prices, maybe because of the circus theme (it soon becomes exhausting). All rooms have color TV, and rates are for 1-4 people. Sun.-Thurs. $21-39, Fri.-Sat. $28-50; holidays higher. Roll-away bed $6.

Aztec Inn, 2200 Las Vegas Blvd. S. (385-4566). Pool, phone, A/C. Singles and doubles $32 with second night free, except on weekends and holidays.

You'll need a car to reach any of the noncommercial campsites around Vegas. 20 mi. west of the city on Rte. 159 rolls **Red Rock Canyon** (363-1921), where you can see an earthquake fault-line and other geological marvels. Camp for free in **Oak Creek Park.** 25 mi. east, **Lake Mead National Recreation Area** (293-4041) has several campgrounds. 55 mi. northeast via I-15 and Rte. 169, **Valley of Fire State Park** (875-4191) has sites ($4, off-season $2) amidst spectacular sandstone formations.

FOOD

Astonishingly cheap prime rib dinners, all-you-can-eat buffets, and champagne brunches beckon high- and low-rollers alike into the casinos. In most cafeterias, buffet food is served nonstop 11am-10pm. Cruise the Strip or roam downtown for advertised specials. The Convention Center keeps a reasonably up-to-date list of buffets (or just grab one of the free publications from any casino or hotel), the best of which may be the one at **Circus Circus,** 500 Circus Circus Dr. (794-3767); breakfast $3 (6-11:30am), lunch $3 (noon-4pm), dinner $4, including pasta and sundae bar, (4:30-11pm). **Hacienda,** 3950 Las Vegas Blvd. S. (739-8911), lies a cut above comparably priced buffets, with a champagne brunch, 12 entrees at lunch, and a prime rib and wine dinner (breakfast Mon.-Sat. 7-11am, $4; brunch Sun. 8am-3pm, $7; lunch 11:30am-3pm, $5; dinner 4-10pm, $7). **Caesar's Palace,** 3570 Las Vegas Blvd. S. (731-7731), is considerably more expensive than most; yet its comfortable chairs, friendly service, and especially appetizing display of fresh foodstuffs make it *the* place for a gastronomic orgy. Go for breakfast to get the most for your money. (Breakfast Mon.-Fri. 8:30-11am, $6.25. Lunch 11:30am-2:30pm, $7.75.)

Like inexpensive food, liquid meals come easy, operating on the same principle: casino operators figure that a tourist drawn in by cheap drinks will stay to spend tons more playing the slots or losing at cards. Drinks in most casinos cost 75¢-$1, but are free to those who look like they're playing.

CASINO-HOPPING AND NIGHTLIFE

Casinos and their restaurants, nightclubs, and even wedding chapels stay open 24 hrs. You'll almost never see clocks or windows in a casino—the owners are afraid that players might realize it's past midnight, turn into pumpkins, and neglect to lose a nickel more. You'll quickly discern which games are suited for novices and which require more expertise, from penny slots in laundromats to baccarat games in which the stakes can soar into the tens of thousands of dollars. Hotels and most casinos give first-timers "funbooks," with alluring gambling coupons that can stretch your puny $5 into $50 worth of wagering. But always remember: *in the long run, chances are you're going to lose money.* Don't bring more than you're prepared to lose cheerfully. Keep your wallet in your front pocket, and beware of the thieves who prowl casinos to nab big winnings from unwary jubilants. Some casinos offer free lessons on how to play the games (Circus Circus and Caesar's); more patient dealers may offer a tip or two (in exchange for one from you).

For best results, put on your favorite loud outfit, bust out the cigar and pinky rings, and begin. Remember, though: gambling is illegal for those under 21. The atmosphere, decor, and clientele differ from casino to casino, so gambol as you gamble. **Caesar's Palace,** 3570 Las Vegas Blvd. (731-7110), has taken the "theme" aspect of Vegas to the extreme; whereas other casinos have miniature, mechanized horse racing, Caesar's has chariot racing. Go see the surprising Festival Fountain Show at the entrance to the Forum Shops (every ½ hr. 10am-11pm). Next door, **Mirage,** 3400 Las Vegas Blvd. S. (791-7111), includes among its attractions Siberian white tigers and a "volcano" that erupts in fountains and flames every ¼ hr. from 8pm-1am, barring bad weather. **Circus Circus,** 2880 Las Vegas Blvd. S. (734-0410), attempts to cultivate a (dysfunctional) family atmosphere, embodied by the huge clown on its marquee. While parents run to the card tables and slot machines downstairs, their children can spend 50¢ tokens upstairs on the souped-up carnival midway and enjoy the titanic, futuristic video game arcade. Two stories above the casino floor, tightrope-walkers, fire-eaters, and rather impressive acrobats perform 1am-midnight. **Excalibur,** 3850 Las Vegas Blvd. S. (800-937-7777), has a medieval England theme that may make you nostalgic for the Black Plague. In the works for '94 is the completion of the **MGM Grand,** with over 5000 rooms and a giant amusement/theme park, and Treasure Island, with real, live pirates.

Aside from gambling, every major casino has nightly shows. Extra bucks will buy you a seat at a made-in-the-U.S.A. phenomenon—the Vegas spectacular. The overdone but stunning twice-nightly productions feature marvels such as waterfalls, explosions, fireworks, and casts of thousands (including animals). You can also see Broadway plays and musicals, ice revues, and individual entertainers in concert. Some "production shows" are topless; most are tasteless. To see a show by the musical stars who haunt the city, such as Diana Ross or Frank Sinatra, you may have to fork over $35 or more. Far more reasonable are the many "revues" featuring imitations of (generally deceased) performers. In Vegas you can't turn around without bumping into an aspiring Elvis clone, or perhaps the real Elvis, pursuing anonymity in the brilliant disguise of an Elvis impersonator.

Nightlife in Vegas gets rolling around midnight and keeps going until everyone drops or runs out of money. The casino lounge at the **Las Vegas Hilton,** 3000 Paradise Rd. (732-5111), has a disco every night (no cover, 2-drink min.). A popular disco, **Gipsy,** 4605 Paradise Rd. (731-1919), southeast of the Strip, may look deserted at 11pm, but by 1am the medium-sized dance floor packs in a gay, lesbian, and straight crowd. **Carrow's,** 1290 E. Flamingo Rd. (796-1314), has three outdoor patios, plus plenty of people and plants. During happy hour (4-7pm), the filling hors d'oeuvres are free. Laughter may be the best medicine for a painful losing streak. The **Comedy Stop at the Trop,** in the Tropicana, 3101 Las Vegas Blvd. (739-2714 or 800-634-4000), offers three comedians for $13 (includes 2 drinks); two shows every night (8 and 10:30pm).

Fans of klassical music and kitsch will be delighted by the **Liberace Museum,** 1775 E. Tropicana Ave. (798-5595), devoted to the flamboyant late "Mr. Showmanship." There's fur, velvet and rhinestone in combinations that boggle the rational mind. Though $6.50 might be a bit much for the privilege of sharing the experience, the proceeds go to the Liberace Foundation for the Performing and Creative Arts. (Open Mon.-Sat. 10am-5pm, Sun. 1-5pm. $6.50, seniors $4.50, ages 6-12 $2.)

■ ■ ■ RENO

Reno, the so-called "biggest little city in the world," is not much more than a branch outlet of Las Vegas. With the same artificial, non-stop environment (the casinos are immune to the rhythm of the sun), Reno feeds on gambling and not much else.

Practical Information Contact the **Reno-Sparks Convention and Visitors Center,** 4590 Virginia St. (800-367-RENO/7366), at Kitsky (open Mon.-Sat. 7am-8pm, Sun. 9am-6pm). **Amtrak** gambles on your business at E. Commercial Row and Lake St. (329-8638 or 800-872-7245; open 8:45am-noon and 2-4:45pm). Trains to:

San Francisco (1 per day, $58); Salt Lake City (1 per day, $111); Chicago (1 per day, $211). **Greyhound** bets on the dogs at 155 Stevenson St. (322-2970; open 24 hrs.), ½ block from W. 2nd St. Buses to: San Francisco (14 per day, $36); Salt Lake City (4 per day, $61); L.A. (10 per day, $47). **Arrow Trans** (786-2376) and **Reno-Tahoe Connection** (825-3900) both offer bus service to S. Lake Tahoe ($18 per person, 4-person min., or $72 base fare). The **post office** stork delivers your bundles at 50 S. Virginia St. (786-5523), at Mill (open Mon.-Fri. 9am-5pm, Sat. 10am-2pm; general delivery Mon.-Sat. 10am-2pm). Reno's **ZIP code** is 89501; the **area code** is 702.

Accommodations and Camping **El Cortez**, 239 W. 2nd St. (322-9161), 1 block east of Greyhound station, is run by pleasant management and offers terrific bargains. Rarely are city block hotels so clean. (Rooms $27; off-season $24. Add $3 on weekends and holidays.) The hall showers and rooms at **Windsor Hotel**, 214 West St. (323-6171), 1½ blocks from the Greyhound Station toward Virginia St., are wonderfully clean. Fans turn lazily overhead in compensation for the lack of A/C. (Singles $19, with bath $23; Fri.-Sat. $26/$28. Doubles $27; Fri.-Sat. $31.) Some of the best deals in town can be found in the major casinos, where all sorts of hidden discounts exist on rooms which ordinarily run $100 per night. Be nosy and ask enough questions and you just may find yourself paying $35 for a room on the 20th floor of the Hilton. Thursday night specials abound. Usually there is a welcome center in the casino which can give advice on discounts and specials.

You can park your RV overnight at the **Reno Hilton**, 2500 E. 2nd St. (789-2000), full hookup $18.53. But the **Toiyabe National Forest** begins only a few miles southwest of Reno, and if you're equipped to camp, you might make the drive to the woodland sites of **Davis Creek Park** (849-0684), 17 mi. south on U.S. 395 then ½ mi. west (follow the signs). (Full service, including showers, but no hookups. Sites $9, each extra vehicle $3. Picnic area open 8am-9pm.) **Boca Basin**, a beautiful Forest Service campground is located on the **Boca Basin Lake**, just over the California line, 23 mi. west on I-80. No hookups, and a two-week maximum stay (free). Pyramid Lake has undeveloped camping (see below).

Food At **Fitzgeralds**, 255 N. Virginia St. (786-3663), the 3rd floor feels a bit like the bridge of the *U.S.S. Enterprise* with its domed roof, but the setting is pleasant, the buffet cheap, and the service superb. Breakfast (7-11am, $3), lunch (noon-4pm, $4.50), and dinner (4-10pm, $4.90), with beverages included. Calories abound at **Cal Neva**, 38 E. 2nd St. (323-1046). 2-egg breakfast with ham, toast, and jelly (99¢). 1-lb. prime rib dinner (5-11pm, $6), as well as all-you-can-eat spaghetti ($3.75). With only 8 seats, salmon-colored counters, and turquoise walls, **Landrum's**, #3, 6770 S. Virginia St. (852-5464), is the quintessential diner serving dinners ($4-5) with thick shakes ($2.30). (Open Sun.-Thurs. 6am-3am, Fri.-Sat. 24 hrs.)

Gambling Those new to the gambling scene might try the **Behind the Scenes gaming tour** (348-7788), which takes you to the other side of the one-way mirrors, and instructs you in the rudiments of the games, teaching you exactly how they take your money. The 2-hr. tours show the surveillance at Calvera, and the tourists get a chance to play a few practice games. ($6. Tours leave from Ticket Station, 135 N. Sierra, daily 12:30pm.) Don't forget: gambling is illegal for persons under 21 years of age; if you win the jackpot at age 20, it'll be the casino's lucky day, not yours. Many casinos offer free gaming lessons and minimum bets vary between establishments—the best gamblers shop around before plunking down. Beer is usually free if you look as if you're gambling. Most casinos charge heftily for admission to their live shows, but **Circus Circus**, 500 N. Sierra (329-0711), has free 15-min. "big-top" performances (daily 11:15am-4:45pm and 6:10-11:40pm every ½-hr.).

- ▲ Hostel **$15** +Tax
  Only 4 Persons Per Room
  Passport Required
- ▲ Private Rooms **$50** +Tax
- ▲ Open 24 Hours
- ▲ Midtown Location
- ▲ Free Linen
- ▲ Free Coffee
- ▲ Bar, Rooftop Terrace
- ▲ Multilingual Staff

INTERCLUB

GERSHWIN HOTEL

7 East 27th Street, New York, NY 10016 Tel (212) 545 8000
Fax (212) 684 5546

YES! I WANT TO JOIN THE CLUB.

With my Hostelling International card I can stay at 6,000 hostels in 70 countries and enjoy great discounts around the world. Please sign me on as a: ❑ youth (under 18) $10, ❑ adult $25, ❑ family $35, ❑ senior (over 54) $15, or ❑ Life $250, member and send me my 12-month membership and **FREE** directory of all the hostels in North America.

Name _____

Address _____

City _____ State _____ Zip _____

Phone _____ Birth Date (m/d/y)_____

Departure Date_____ Destination _____

Or call 202-783-6161 for the office nearest you.

HOSTELLING INTERNATIONAL
The new seal of approval of the International Youth Hostel Federation.

HOSTELLING
INTERNATIONAL®

PLACE
STAMP
HERE

HOSTELLING INTERNATIONAL

American Youth Hostels
Membership Services Department
P.O. Box 37613
Washington, D.C. 20013-7613

‖₁‖₁‖‖₁‖₁‖₁₁₁₁₁₁‖₁‖‖₁‖₁₁₁₁‖₁₁‖₁‖₁₁₁‖

■ New Mexico

New Mexico appears at first to be a rolling plain strewn with isolated mountain ranges. A closer look shatters this myth. This state is actually one of the most diverse geographically; it sits at the pivotal meeting place of the Great Plains, the southern Rockies, and the Range and Basin Province of the four corners area.

Recreationally, New Mexico serves as a haven for hikers, backpackers, and mountain-climbers alike. Six national forests lying within the state provide miles and miles of beautiful and challenging opportunities for the outdoorsman at heart, while Sandia, Mogollon, and Sangre de Cristo are all exciting locales for mountain-climbers.

PRACTICAL INFORMATION

Capital: Santa Fe.
Visitor Information: New Mexico Dept. of Tourism, 491 Old Santa Fe Trail, Santa Fe 87501 (800-545-2040). Open Mon.-Fri. 8am-5pm. **Park and Recreation Division,** Villagra Bldg., P.O. Box 1147, Santa Fe 87504 (827-7465). **U.S. Forest Service,** 517 Gold Ave. SW, Albuquerque 87102 (842-3292).
Time Zone: Mountain (2 hr. behind Eastern). **Postal Abbreviation:** NM
Sales Tax: 5.75-7.25%, depending on the city.

■■■ ALBUQUERQUE

Don't forget to make that left turn at Albuquerque, Doc. While Santa Fe and Taos are more artsy and laid-back, Albuquerque's youthful flavor (the average age here is 29) and size lend it a cosmopolitan air. Approximately one-third of New Mexico's population thrives amidst the energy of the state's only "real" city. Against the dramatic backdrop of the Sandía Mountains, Albuquerque sprawls across a desert plateau. Although the town's Spanish past gave rise to touristy Old Town, the roadside architecture lining Rte. 66 and the city's high-tech industry speak to Albuquerque's modern image; the adobe campus of the University of New Mexico accentuates the town's bright-eyed vigor.

PRACTICAL INFORMATION

Emergency: 911.
Visitor Information: Albuquerque Convention and Visitors Bureau, 121 Tijeras N.E. 87102 (243-3696 or 800-284-2282). Free maps and the useful *Albuquerque Visitors Guide.* Open Mon.-Fri. 8am-5pm. After hours, call for recorded events info. **Old Town Visitors Center,** 303 Romero St. (243-3215), at N. Plaza. Open Mon.-Sat. 10am-5pm, Sun. 11am-5pm. They also have an information booth at the airport. Open Mon.-Sat. 9:30am-8pm.
Airport: Albuquerque International Airport, 2200 Sunport Blvd. S.E. (842-4366), south of downtown. Take bus #50 from Yale and Central downtown Mon.-Sat. 6:47am-6:05pm. Cab fare to downtown $6.
Amtrak: 214 1st St. S.W. (842-9650 or 800-872-7245). Open daily 9:30am-5:45pm. 1 train per day to: Los Angeles (13 hr., $91); Kansas City (17 hr., $153); Santa Fe (1 hr., $22); Flagstaff (5 hr., $82). Reservations required.
Buses: 300 2nd St. S.W., 3 blocks south of Central Ave. **Greyhound** (800-231-2222) and **TNM&O Coaches** (243-4435) go to: Santa Fe (4 per day, 1½ hr., $10.50); Flagstaff (4 per day, 6 hr., $54) Oklahoma City (4 per day, $87); Denver (5 per day, $76); Phoenix (4 per day, $41); Los Angeles (4 per day, $69).
Public Transport: Sun-Tran Transit, 601 Yale Blvd. S.E. (843-9200 for info; open Mon.-Fri. 7am-5pm). Most buses run Mon.-Sat. 6am-6pm. Pick up system maps at the transit office or the main library. Fare 75¢, ages 5-18 and seniors 25¢.
Taxi: Albuquerque Cab, 883-4888. $2.90 the first mi., $1.40 per additional mi.

ALBUQUERQUE

Car Rental: **Rent-a-Wreck,** 501 Yale Blvd. S.E. (242-9556 or 800-247-9556). Cars with A/C from $25 per day. 150 free mi., 20¢ each additional mi. $130 per week. Open Mon.-Fri. 7:30am-6pm, Sat. 8am-5pm, Sun. 10am-4pm. Must be 21 with credit card; $3 extra per day if you're under 25.

Help Lines: **Rape Crisis Center,** 1025 Hermosa S.E. (266-7711). Center open Mon.-Fri. 8am-noon and 1-5pm; hotline open 24 hrs. **Gay and Lesbian Information Line,** 266-8041. Open daily 7am-10pm.

Post Office: 1135 Broadway N.E. (247-2725). Open Mon.-Fri. 8am-6pm. **ZIP code:** 87101. **Area Code:** 505.

Central Avenue and the **Santa Fe railroad tracks** create four quadrants used in city addresses: Northeast Heights (N.E.), Southeast Heights (S.E.), North Valley (N.W.), and South Valley (S.W.). The all-adobe campus of the **University of New Mexico (UNM)** stretches along Central Ave. N.E. from University Ave. to Carlisle St.

ACCOMMODATIONS AND CAMPING

Along Central Ave., even near downtown, there are tons of cheap motels, but too many of them are too cheap to avoid the temptation of running at low maintenance. Hostelers usually head to the average, but well-located **Route 66 Youth Hostel (RNA),** 1012 W. Central Ave. (247-1813), at 10th St. (Office open daily 7-11am and 4-11pm. Check-out 11am. $10, nonmembers $12. Key deposit $5. Linen $1.) Most of Central Ave.'s cheap motels lie east of downtown around the university. The **De Anza Motor Lodge,** 4301 Central Ave. N.E. (255-1654), has bland decor but well-kept rooms, free Movie Channel, and continental breakfast to boot. (Singles $23-26. Doubles with 1 bed $27-30, with 2 beds $32-34.)

Named for the Spanish adventurer who burned some 250 Native Americans shortly after his arrival in 1540, **Coronado State Park Campground** (867-5589), 1 mi. west of Bernalillo on Rte. 44, about 20 mi. north of Albuquerque on I-25, offers unique camping. Adobe shelters on the sites provide respite from the heat. The Sandía Mountains are haunting, especially beneath a full moon. Sites have toilets, showers, and drinking water. (Open daily 7am-10pm. Sites $7, with hookup $11. 2-week max. stay. No reservations.) The nearby **Albuquerque West Campground,** 5739 Ouray Rd. N.W. (831-1912), has a swimming pool. Take I-40 west from downtown to the Coors Blvd. N. exit, or bus #15 from downtown. (Tent sites $13 per 2 people, each additional person $2.) Camping equipment and canoes ($35 per day) can be rented from the friendly folks at **Mountains & Rivers,** 2320 Central Ave. S.E. (268-4876), across from the university (deposit required; reservations recommended; open Mon.-Fri. 9:30am-6:30pm, Sat. 9am-5pm).

FOOD AND NIGHTLIFE

Downtown Albuquerque offers a myriad of excellent New Mexican restaurants. The best is the **M and J Sanitary Tortilla Factory,** 403 2nd St. S.W. (242-4890), at Lead St. in the hot-pink and blue building. (Free jug of water and chips with salsa. Crowds materialize at lunchtime. Entrees $4-6. Open Mon.-Sat. 9am-4pm.)

Tasty, inexpensive eateries border the University of New Mexico, which stretches along Central Ave. N.E. **Nunzio's Pizza,** 107 Cornell Dr. S.E. (262-1555), has great, inexpensive pizza at $1.50 per huge slice (open Sun.-Thurs. 11am-10pm, Fri.-Sat. 11am-11pm). "Feed your Body with Love, Light, and high VIBRATIONAL Food," advises **Twenty Carrots,** 2110 Central Ave. S.E. (242-1320). Wheatgrass smoothies ($2.25) and bulk organic food are, apparently, quite vibratory (open Mon.-Sat. 10am-6:30pm, Fri. until 9pm). The homemade ice cream (one scoop $1.10) and pastries at the nearby **Hippo Ice Cream,** 120 Harvard Dr. S.E. (266-1997), could turn you into one (open Mon.-Thurs. 7:30am-10:30pm, Fri.-Sat. 7:30am-11:30pm, Sun. 9am-9pm).

You can also dig in your spurs at **Caravan East,** 7605 Central Ave. N.E. (265-7877; continuous live music every night 4:30pm-2am; cover weekends $3). Less rurally-inclined music lovers can hear rock, blues, and reggae bands over cheap beer

($1.50) at **El Ray,** 622 Central Ave. S.W. (242-9300), a spacious old theater transformed into a bar and nightclub (open 8am-2am; music daily at 8:30pm; cover $3).

SIGHTS

Old Town, on the western end of downtown, consists of Albuquerque's Spanish plaza surrounded by restaurants and Native American art galleries. Located at the northeast corner of the intersection of Central Ave. and Rio Grande Blvd., 1 mi. south of I-40, Old Town provides the best place to hang out and watch tourists.

The **National Atomic Museum,** 20358 Wyoming Blvd. (845-6670), Kirkland Air Force Base, tells the story of the development of the atomic bombs "Little Boy" and "Fat Man," and of the obliteration of Hiroshima and Nagasaki. *Ten Seconds that Shook the World,* a 1-hr. documentary on the development of the atomic bomb, is shown four times daily at 10:30 and 11:30am, and 2 and 3:30pm. Access is controlled; ask at the Visitor Control Gate on Wyoming Blvd. for a visitors' museum pass. Be prepared to show *several* forms of ID. The Air Force base is several miles southeast of downtown, just east of I-25. (Open daily 9am-5pm. Free.)

For a different feel, the **Indian Pueblo Cultural Center,** 2401 12th St. N.W. (843-7270), just north of I-40 (take bus #36 from downtown), provides a sensitive introduction to the nearby Pueblo reservations. The cafeteria serves authentic Pueblo food (fry-bread $1.75; open 7:30am-3:30pm) and hosts colorful Pueblo dance performances on weekends year-round at 11am and 2pm. (Open daily 9am-5:30pm. $2.50, seniors $1.50, students $1.)

■ Near Albuquerque

Located at the edge of suburbia on Albuquerque's west side, **Indian Petroglyphs National Park** (897-8814) includes a trail leading through lava rocks written on by Native Americans. Take the Coors exit on I-40 north to Atrisco Rd. to reach this free attraction, or take bus #15 to Coors and transfer to bus #93. (Open daily 9am-6pm; off-season 8am-5pm. Parking $1, weekends and holidays $2.)

Just a short drive from the east side of the city, **Sandía Crest** rises 10,678 ft., providing a pleasant escape from Albuquerque's heat and noise. The Sandía Peaks, from the Spanish for "watermelon," are *not* named for their taste, but rather for the color they turn at sunset. Take Tramway Rd. from either I-25 or I-40 to the **Sandía Peak Aerial Tramway** (296-9585; 298-8518 for recorded info), a thrilling ride to the top of Sandía Crest, which allows you to ascend the west face of Sandía Peak and gaze out over Albuquerque, the Río Grande Valley, and western New Mexico. The ascent is most striking at sunset. (Operates daily 9am-10pm; Sept. 2-May 25 Mon.-Tues., Thurs., and Sun. 9am-9pm, Wed. 5-9pm, Fri.-Sat. 9am-10pm. Fare $12, seniors and students $9. Departs every 20-30 min., lasts 1½ hrs. Combination chairlift and tram ticket $13.50, seniors and kids $11.)

A trip through the **Sandía Ski Area** makes for a beautiful 58-mi., day-long driving loop. Take I-40 east up Tijeras Canyon 17 mi. and turn north onto Rte. 44, which winds through lovely piñon pine, oak, ponderosa pine, and spruce forests. Rte. 44 descends 18 mi. to Bernalillo, through a gorgeous canyon. A 7-mi. toll-road (Rte. 536) leads to the summit of **Sandía Crest** (call 281-3304 for info) and a dazzling ridge hike covers the 1½ mi. separating the crest and **Sandía Peak.** Rangers offer guided hikes on Saturdays in both summer and winter. Make reservations for the challenging winter snowshoe hikes (242-9052). In the summer, hiking and mountain-biking trails are open to the public during specific hours; call for complete hours, prices, and costs for lifts up the mountain to the trails.

■■■ CHACO CANYON

West of Albuquerque lies a vast land of forests, lava beds, and desert mesas populated by Native Americans and boomtown coal and uranium miners. Though difficult to explore without a car, the region can prove very rewarding for the dedicated adventurer.

Sun-scorched and water-poor, **Chaco Canyon** seems an improbable setting for the first great flowering of the Anasazi. At a time when most farmers relied on risky dry farming, Chacoans created an oasis of irrigated fields. They also constructed sturdy five-story rock apartment buildings while Europeans still lived in squalid wooden hovels. By the 11th century, the canyon residents had set up a major trade network with dozens of small satellite towns in the surrounding desert. Around 1150 AD, however, the whole system collapsed; with no food and little water, the Chacoans simply abandoned the canyon for greener pastures.

Chaco Canyon, a 160-mi., 3½-hour drive northwest from Albuquerque, lies 90 mi. south of Durango, CO. When the first official archaeologist left for the canyon at the turn of the century, it took him almost a year to get here from Washington, DC. Today's visitor faces unpaved **Rte. 57,** which reaches the park from paved Rte. 44 (turn off at the tiny town of **Nageezi**) on the north (29 mi.), and from I-40 on the south (about 60 mi., 20 mi. of it unpaved). **Greyhound's** I-40 run from Albuquerque to Gallup serves **Thoreau,** at the intersection of Rte. 57, five times per day (see Albuquerque: Practical Information).

Chaco Canyon is now part of the **Chaco Culture National Historical Park.** The **visitors center** (988-6727 or 786-7014; open 24 hrs.), at the eastern end of the canyon, houses an excellent museum that includes exhibits on Anasazi art and architecture, as well as a description of the sophisticated economic network by which the Chacoan Anasazi traded with smaller Anasazi tribes of modern Colorado and northern Mexico. (Museum open daily 8am-6pm; Sept. 2-May 27 daily 8am-5pm. Entrance fee $1 per person or $4 per carload.) **Camping** in Chaco costs $5; arrive by 3pm since space is limited to 46 sites. Registration is required. You can also make Chaco a daytrip from **Gallup,** where cheap accommodations are plentiful.

Only ruins remain, but these are the best-preserved sites in the Southwest. **Pueblo Bonito,** the canyon's largest town, demonstrates the skill of Anasazi masons. Among many other structures, one four-story wall still stands. Nearby **Chetro Ketl** houses one of the canyon's largest *kivas*, used in Chacoan religious rituals. Bring water, since even the visitors center occasionally runs dry.

Just west of the Continental Divide on Rte. 53, 4 mi. southeast of the Navajo town of **Ramah,** sits **Inscription Rock** (505-783-4226), where Native Americans, Spanish *conquistadores,* and later pioneers made their mark while traveling through the scenic valley. Today, self-guided trails allow access to the rock as well as to ruins farther into the park. (Open daily 8am-6:30pm.) The **visitors center** (open daily 8am-7pm; in winter 8am-5pm) includes a small museum as well as several dire warnings against emulating the graffiti artists of old and marking the rocks. For those unable to resist the urge to inscribe, an alternate boulder is provided.

■■■ GILA CLIFF DWELLINGS NATIONAL MONUMENT

While most of the civilized world flocks to the Grand Canyon or Yellowstone, the discerning tourist always searches for that rare place with great hiking and profound scenery devoid of family tenderfoots. The Gila Cliff Dwellings (505-536-9461) are just the place. Accessible only by a 44-mi. drive on Rte. 15 from Silver City in the southwest part of the state, the drive to the park winds up and down mountains to the canyon of the Gila River; deer cavort along the scenic drive. As if the drive weren't grand enough, at the end of the trail are the Gila Cliff Dwellings, named not for their creators (Pueblos), but the river which flows nearby. Built over 700 years ago, the remarkably well-preserved dwellings have been protected from erosion by overhanging caves. The 1-mi. round-trip hike to the dwellings moves quickly and provides plenty of photograph opportunities. The surrounding **Gila National Forest** beckons with excellent hiking and backcountry camping; for maps or info head to the **visitors center** (505-536-9461), at the end of Rte. 15, 1 mi. from the dwellings, or write to the district ranger at Rte. 11, Box 100, Silver City 88601. **Camping** throughout the national forest is free. (Visitors center open daily 8am-5pm; cliff dwellings daily 8am-6pm, off-season 8am-5pm.)

When you tire of camping, **Silver City** provides a nice, more urban stop. The city grew in the late 1800s as (surprise, surprise) a mining town; several large open pits still surround the city. Silver City was also home to fabled outlaw and Emilio Estevez look-alike Billy the Kid. The nearby ghost town of **Shakespeare** was less fortunate than Silver City; the town's only modern residents are deer and birds. For information on tours, contact **Shakespeare Ghost Town,** P.O. Box 253, Lordsburg, NM 88045 (505-542-9034). In Silver City, stay at the excellent **Carter House (HI/AYH),** 101 North Cooper St. (505-388-5485). Owners Lucy and Jim Nolan make it a point of pride to ensure that your stay is enjoyable. The hostel has separate dorm-style rooms, a kitchen, and laundry facilities; upstairs is a B&B. Check-in is officially 5-9pm; if you're going to be later than 9pm, call ahead. ($11, nonmembers $15. B&B doubles from $54.) **Copper Manor,** 710 Silver Heights Blvd. (505-538-5392), is also a clean and perfectly adequate place to stay (singles $34; doubles $40-44). The usual fast food chains line Silver Heights Blvd., but if you're all Mc'ed out, the **Red Barn,** 708 Silver Heights Blvd. (505-538-5666), offers a great selection of sandwiches and a terrific all-you-can-eat salad bar ($5-5.50).

■■■ SANTA FE

Santa Fe is more of a *mood* than a city. Coming to New Mexico's capital and visiting its museums and historic town plaza will tell you much less about the town than will a casual *paseo* down Camon Road, the local artists' turf. Santa Fe's multi-cultural population and its laws demanding all downtown buildings be in 17th-century adobe-style (and painted in one of 23 approved shades of brown) provide the perfect backdrop for the city's laid-back *zeitgeist.* This legendary spirit has attracted scores of artists to work and live amongst the city's earth-toned beauty and its mountainous backdrop. In the summer, when the town is besieged by tourists, the locals can adopt an attitude, but most visitors will only encounter a wealth of beauty and enlightenment.

PRACTICAL INFORMATION

Emergency: 911.

Visitor Information: Chamber of Commerce, 510 N. Guadalupe (800-777-2489). Open Mon.-Fri. 8am-5pm.

Gray Line Tours: 983-6565. Free pickup from downtown hotels. Tours Mon.-Sat. to: Taos and Taos Pueblo (at 9am, $50); Bandelier and Los Alamos (at 1pm, $35); around Santa Fe (Mon.-Sat. 9:30am, 3 hr., $15), Puye and Santa Clara (at 1pm, $40). Also operates the Roadrunner, a sight-seeing trolley around Old Santa Fe leaving from the La Fonda Hotel on the plaza downtown (5 per day, 1½ hr., $6, under 12 $3).

Greyhound: 858 St. Michael's Dr. (471-0008). To: Denver (via Raton, NM; 4 per day; $66); Taos (2 per day, 1½ hr., $15); Albuquerque (4 per day, 1½ hr., $10.50).

Public Transport: Shuttlejack, 982-4311 or 800-452-2665. Runs from the Albuquerque ($20) and Santa Fe airports; also goes to the opera ($6 round-trip).

Car Rental: Budget Rent-a-Car, 1946 Cerrillos Rd. (984-8028). $28 per day, $129 per week. Must be 25 with major credit card.

Taxi: Capital City Taxi, 438-0000. $1.85 first mi., $1 per additional mi.

New Age Referral Service: 474-0066. Info clearinghouse for holistic healing services and alternative modes of thought.

Post Office: in the Montoya Office Bldg. S. Federal Pl., (988-6351), next to the Courthouse. Open Mon.-Fri. 7:30am-6:30pm, Sat. 9am-noon. **ZIP code:** 87501.

Area Code: 505.

Except for a cluster of museums southeast of the city center, most restaurants and important sights in Santa Fe cluster within a few blocks of the downtown plaza and inside the loop formed by the **Paseo de Peralta.** Because the narrow streets make driving troublesome, park your car and pad the pavement. You'll find brown adobe parking lots behind Santa Fe Village, near Sena Plaza, and one block east of the Federal Courthouse near the plaza. Parking is available at 2-hr. meters on some streets.

ACCOMMODATIONS AND CAMPING

Besides hostel accommodations, hotels in Santa Fe tend to be very expensive. Hotels become swamped with requests as early as May for **Fiesta de Santa Fe** week in early September and **Indian Market** the third week of August; make reservations if you're coming then or plan on sleeping in the street. At other times, look around the **Cerrillos Road** area for the best prices. At many of the less expensive adobe motels, bargaining is acceptable. The beautiful adobe **Santa Fe Hostel (RNA),** 1412 Cerrillos Rd. (988-1153), 1 mi. from the adobe bus station, and 2 mi. from the adobe plaza, has a kitchen, library, and very large dorm-style adobe beds ($11, nonmembers $15; linen $2; B&B rooms $25-30).

To camp around Santa Fe, you'll need a car. The **Santa Fe National Forest** (988-6940) has numerous campsites as well as free backcountry camping in the beautiful Sangre de Cristo Mountains. **New Mexico Parks and Recreation** (800-283-2267 for site reservation) operates the **Black Canyon Campground** (8 mi. away; sites $5) on Rte. 475 northeast of Santa Fe. You can also find free camping on Rte. 475, 12 mi. out at **Big Tesuque,** and 15 mi. out at **Aspen Basin** (no reservations). (All three campgrounds open May-Oct.; call 988-6940 for info.)

FOOD

About the only thing Santa Fe doesn't do with adobe is eat it. Instead, spicy Mexican food served on blue corn tortillas is the staple. The few vegetarian restaurants here are expensive, catering to an upscale crowd. The better restaurants near the plaza dish up their chilis to a mixture of government employees, well-heeled tourists, and local artistic types. Because many serve only breakfast and lunch, you also should look for inexpensive meals along **Cerrillos Road** and **St. Michael's Drive** south of downtown. One little-known fact: the **Woolworth's** on the plaza actually serves a mean bowl of chili ($2.75).

San Francisco Street Bar & Grill, 114 W. San Francisco St. (982-2044), 1 block from the plaza. Excellent sandwiches and the best pasta salad ($6) in town. Open daily 11am-11pm.

Tomasita's Santa Fe Station, 500 S. Guadalupe (983-5721), near downtown. Locals and tourists line up for their blue corn tortillas and fiery green chili dishes ($4.50-5). Indoor and outdoor seating. Open Mon.-Sat. 11am-10pm.

Josie's, 225 E. Marcy St. (983-5311), in a converted house. Pronounce the "J" in the name like an "H." Family-run for 26 years. Incredible Mexican-style lunches and multifarious mouthwatering desserts worth the 20-min. wait. Specials $4-6. Open Mon.-Fri. 11am-4pm.

The Burrito Company, 111 Washington Ave. (982-4453). Excellent Mexican food at reasonable prices. Burrito plates $2-4.25. Open Mon.-Sat. 7:30am-7pm, Sun. 11am-5pm.

Tortilla Flats, 3139 Cerrillos Rd. (471-8685). Frighteningly bland family atmosphere belies Mexican masterpieces ($4-8). Breakfasts ($3-7), *huevos rancheros* ($4.75). Open daily 7am-10pm; winter Sun.-Thurs. 7am-9pm, Fri.-Sat. 7am-10pm.

SIGHTS

Since 1609, **Plaza de Santa Fe** has held religious ceremonies, military gatherings, markets, cockfights, and public punishments. The city also provided a pit-stop on two important trails: the **Santa Fe Trail** from Independence, MO and **El Camino Real** from Mexico City. The plaza is a good starting point for exploring the city's museums, sanctuaries, and galleries. **Santa Fe Detours** (983-6565) offers 2½-hr. walking tours and open-air bus tours of the city (daily at 9:30am and 1:30pm, $15) that leave from the La Fonda Hotel, on the corner of the plaza.

Since the following four museums are commonly owned, their hours are identical and a 2-day pass bought at one admits you to all. (Open daily 10am-5pm; Jan.-Feb. Tues.-Sun. 10am-5pm. $4, under 16 free, 3-day pass $5, kids $2.50. New Mexican seniors $1 on Wed.) The **Palace of the Governors** (827-6483), the oldest public building in the U.S., on the north side of the plaza, was the seat of seven successive governments after its construction in 1610. The *haciendas* palace is now a museum with exhibits on Native American, Southwestern, and New Mexican history. To buy Native American crafts or jewelry, check out the displays spread out in front of the Governor's Palace each day by artists from the surrounding pueblos; their wares are often cheaper and better quality than those in the "Indian Crafts" stores around town. Across Lincoln St., on the northwest corner of the plaza, lies the **Museum of Fine Arts** (827-4455), a large, undulating, adobe building with thick, cool walls illuminated by sudden shafts of sunlight. Exhibits include works by major Southwestern artists, including Georgia O'Keeffe and Edward Weston, and an amazing collection of 20th-century Native American art. Two other museums lie southeast of town on **Camino Lejo,** just off Old Santa Fe Trail. The **Museum of International Folk Art,** 706 Camino Lejo (827-6350), 2 mi. south of the plaza, houses the Girard Collection of over 100,000 works of folk art from around the world. Amazingly vibrant but unbelievably jumbled, the collection is incomprehensible without the gallery guide handout. In the nearby **Museum of American Indian Arts and Culture,** photographs and artifacts unveil a multifaceted Native American tradition.

About 5 blocks southeast of the Plaza lies the **San Miguel Mission** (983-3974), on the corner of DeVargas and the Old Santa Fe Trail. Built in 1710, the adobe mission is the oldest functioning church in the U.S. Inside, glass windows at the altar look down upon the original "altar" built by Native Americans. (Open Mon.-Sat. 9am-4:30pm, Sun. 1-4:30pm, Nov.-April Mon.-Sat. 10am-4pm, Sun. 1-4:30pm. Free.) Just down DeVargas St. is the adobe **Oldest House** in the U.S. (983-8206), dating from about 1200 AD. Built by the Pueblos, the house contains the remains of a certain Spaniard named Hidalgo, who allegedly bought some love potion from a woman who resided here. Apparently he started kissing everything in sight and was beheaded several days later. (Open Mon.-Sat. Love Potion Number 9am-5pm. $1.)

ENTERTAINMENT AND EVENTS

With numerous musical and theatrical productions, arts and crafts shows, and Native American ceremonies, Santa Fe offers rich entertainment year-round. Fairs, rodeos, and tennis tournaments complement the active theater scene and the world-famous musicians who often play in Santa Fe's clubs. For info, check *Pasatiempo* magazine, a supplement to the Friday issue of the *Santa Fe New Mexican.*

Don Diego De Vargas's peaceful reconquest of New Mexico in 1692 marked the end of the 12-year Pueblo Rebellion, now celebrated in the traditional three-day **Fiesta de Santa Fe** (988-7575). Held in early September, the celebration reaches its height with the burning of the 40-ft. *papier-mâché* **Zozobra** (Old Man Gloom). Festivities include street dancing, processions, and political satires. Most events are free. The *New Mexican* publishes a guide and schedule for the fiesta's events.

The **Santa Fe Chamber Music Festival** (983-2075) celebrates the works of great baroque, classical, and 20th-century composers. Tickets are not readily available. (Performances July-mid-Aug. Sun.-Mon. and Thurs.-Fri. in the St. Francis Auditorium of the Museum of Fine Arts. Tickets $20-32.) The **Santa Fe Opera,** P.O. Box 2408, Santa Fe 87504-2408 (982-3855), 7 mi. north of Santa Fe on Rte. 84, performs in the open, so bring a blanket. The downtown box office is in the gift and news shop of the El Dorado Hotel, 309 W. San Francisco St. (986-5900). Standing-room only tickets can be purchased for $6. (Performances July-Aug. at 9pm.) **Shuttlejack** (982-

4311; see Practical Information) runs a bus from downtown Santa Fe to the opera before each performance.

In August, the nation's largest and most impressive **Indian Market** floods the plaza. Native American tribes from all over the U.S. participate in dancing as well as over 500 exhibits of fine arts and crafts. The **Southwestern Association on Indian Affairs** (983-5220) has more info.

At night subdued revelers relax at the **El Farol**, 808 Canyon Rd. (983-9912), which features excellent up-and-coming rock and R&B musicians (shows nightly 9:30pm; cover $5).

■ Near Santa Fe

Pecos National Historical Park, located in the hill country 25 mi. southeast of Santa Fe on I-25 and Rte. 63, features ruins of a pueblo and Spanish mission church. The small monument includes an easy 1-mi. hike through various archaeological sites. Especially notable are Pecos's renovated *kivas*—underground ceremonial chambers used in Pueblo rituals—built after the Rebellion of 1680. Off-limits at other ruins, these *kivas* are open to the public. (Open daily 8am-dusk; Labor Day-Memorial Day 8am-5pm; entrance fee $1 per person, $3 per car.) The monument's **visitors center** (757-6414 or 757-6032) has a small, informative museum and a 10-min. film shown every ½-hr. (Open daily 8am-6pm; Labor Day-Memorial Day 8am-5pm. Free.) **Greyhound** sends early-morning and late-evening buses daily from Santa Fe to the town of Pecos, 2 mi. north of the monument (see Santa Fe: Practical Information). Use the campsites, or simply pitch a tent in the backcountry of the **Santa Fe National Forest,** 6 mi. north on Rte. 63 (see Santa Fe: Accommodations above).

Bandelier National Monument, 40 mi. northwest of Santa Fe (take U.S. 285 to Rte. 4), features some of the most amazing pueblo and cliff dwellings in the state (accessible by 50 mi. of hiking trails), as well as 50 sq. mi. of dramatic mesas and tumbling canyons. The most accessible of these is **Frijoles Canyon,** site of the **visitors center** (672-3861; open daily 8am-6pm, winter 9am-5:30pm). A 5-mi. hike from the parking lot to the Río Grande descends 600 ft. to the mouth of the canyon, past two waterfalls and fascinating mountain scenery. The **Stone Lions Shrine** (12-mi., 8-hr. round-trip from the visitors center), sacred to the Anasazi, features two stone statues of crouching mountain lions. The trail also leads past the unexcavated Yapashi Pueblo. A 2-day, 20-mi. hike leads from the visitors center past the stone lions to **Painted Cave,** decorated with over 50 Anasazi pictographs, and to the Río Grande. Both hikes are quite strenuous. Free permits are required for backcountry hiking and camping; pick up a topographical map ($6) of the monument area at the visitors center. A less taxing self-guided 1-hr. tour takes you through a pueblo and past some cliff dwellings near the visitors center. You can camp at **Juniper Campground,** ¼ mi. off Rte. 4 at the entrance to the monument (sites $6). Park rangers conduct evening campfire programs at 8:45pm. (Park entrance fee $5 per vehicle.)

Los Alamos, 10 mi. north of Bandelier on NM Loop 4, stands in stark contrast to nearby towns such as Santa Fe or Taos. The U.S. government selected Los Alamos, a small mountain village at the outset of World War II, as the site of a top-secret nuclear weapons development program; today, nuclear research continues at the **Los Alamos Scientific Laboratory.** The facility perches eerily atop several mesas connected by highway bridges over deep gorges, supporting a community with more Ph.D.s per capita than any other city in the U.S. The public may visit the **Bradbury Museum of Science** (667-4444), Diamond Dr., for exhibits on the Manhattan Project, the strategic nuclear balance, and the technical processes of nuclear weapons testing and verification (open Tues.-Fri. 9am-5pm, Sat.-Mon. 1-5pm; free). The **Los Alamos County Historical Museum,** 1921 Juniper St. (662-6272 or 662-4493), off Central, details life in the 1940s, when Los Alamos was a government-created "secret city" (open Mon.-Sat. 9:30am-4:30pm, Sun. 1-5pm; Oct.-April Mon.-Sat. 10am-4pm, Sun. 1-4pm).

SOUTHERN NEW MEXICO

■■■ CARLSBAD CAVERNS NATIONAL PARK

Imagine the surprise of the first Europeans wandering through southeastern New Mexico when tens of thousands of bats began swarming from out of nowhere at dusk. The legendary bat population of Carlsbad Caverns (a staggering 250,000) is responsible not only for its discovery at the turn of the century, when curious frontiersmen tracked the bats to their home, but also for its exploration. Miners first began mapping the cave in search of bat *guano*, an excellent fertilizer found in 100-ft. deposits in the cave. By 1923, the caverns had been designated a national park, and herds of tourists began flocking to this desolate region. The caverns are one of the world's largest and oldest cave systems. Beneath the surface rests a world of unusual creation that would make even the most jaded spelunker stand in awe. Gaping visitors can only whisper their appreciation. The unusual rock formations (with odd but descriptive names such as the Temple of the Sun and the King's Palace), the dripping waterfalls, and the enormity of this natural museum are absolutely breathtaking. There are 75 caves in the park, but only two are regularly open to the public.

Practical Information **White's City,** a tiny, rather tacky town on U.S. 62/180 20 mi. southeast of Carlsbad, and 7 mi. from the caverns along steep, winding mountain roads, serves as the access point to the caverns. Because flash floods occasionally close roads, call ahead. El Paso, TX is the closest major city, just 150 mi. to the west, past Guadalupe Mountains National Park, which is 35 mi. southwest of White's City. **Greyhound,** in cooperation with **TNM&O Coaches** (887-1108), runs three buses a day from El Paso ($25, $47.50 round-trip) or Carlsbad ($5.75 round-trip) to White's City. Two of these routes use White's City only as a flag stop. From White's City, you can take the overpriced **Carlsbad Cavern Coaches** to the visitors center ($15 round-trip for 1-3 people); buy tickets in the White's City Gift Shop where Greyhound drops you off. The **post office,** is located next to the Best Western Visitors Center (open Mon.-Fri. 8am-noon and 1-5pm) and its **ZIP code** is 88268-0218. The **area code** is 505.

Accommodations Since no camping is allowed in the park, the closest accommodations and the only viable option for an overnight stay in the area is White's City. Much of the town's business is owned by capitalist Jack White. Although many motels are criminally expensive, there are some reasonable places to bed down for the night. The **Carlsbad Caverns International Hostel** (785-2291) has six-bed rooms that include a TV, pool, and spa. Membership required. ($10. Open 24 hrs.) The **Shady Park Entrance Campground** (785-2291), is just outside the park entrance. The campground provides water, showers, restrooms, and pool. (Full hookups $15.) For cheap motels, drive 20 mi. north to Carlsbad's **Motel 6,** 3824 National Parks Hwy. (885-0011). Make reservations in summer. (Singles $30. Doubles $36.) More inexpensive motels lie farther down the road. Additional campsites are available at nearby **Guadalupe Mountains National Park** in Texas.

Sights Today, the **Carlsbad Visitors Center** (505-785-2232 or 885-8884; for a 24-hr. recording, call 785-2107) has replaced dung-mining with a restaurant, gift shop, nursery, and kennel. For 50¢ you can rent a small radio that transmits a guided tour. (Open daily 8am-7pm; Labor Day-Memorial Day daily 8am-5:30pm.) There are two ways to see the caverns. Those with strong knees and solid shoes can take the "blue tour," traveling by foot on a steep (but paved) 3-mi. trail that winds dramatically 750 ft., giving the best sense of the depth and extent of the caverns. The "red tour" follows an easier, shorter route, descending from the visitors center by elevator. Most of the trail is wheelchair-accessible. There are no guided tours, but explanatory plaques are posted along the paths, and small radios which transmit a guided tour are available both at the visitors center and down in the Big Room. Almost all visitors return to the surface by elevator, the last of which leaves a half-hour before the visitors center closes. Tourists should give thanks for the elevators; your 1920s counterparts either had to walk back up or ride in a bucket otherwise reserved for bat *guano*. ("Red tours" 8:30am-5pm; Sept.-May 8:30am-3:30pm; "blue tours" 8:30am-3:30pm; Sept.-May 8:30am-2pm. Tours cost $5, over 62 and ages 6-15 $2.50.)

Plan your visit to the caves for the late afternoon so as not to miss the magnificent nightly **bat flights**. An army of hungry bats pour out of the cave at the incredible rate of 6000 per minute. (Daily just before sunset from May to Oct.) A ranger talk precedes this amazing ritual. (Free *guano* samples.) The pre-dawn return can also be viewed. Talk to a ranger for details.

For a rugged and genuine caving experience, visit the undeveloped **Slaughter Canyon Cave** (formerly **New Cave**). Two-hour, 1¼-mi. flashlight tours traverse difficult and slippery terrain; there are no paved trails or handrails. Even getting to the cave takes some energy, or better yet, a car; the parking lot is 23 mi. down a dirt road off U.S. 62/180 south (there is no transportation from the visitors center or from White's City), and the cave entrance is still a steep, strenuous ½-mi. from the lot. Call 785-2232 at least two days in advance for reservations; the park limits the number of persons allowed inside each day. Bring a flashlight. (Tours daily 9am-12:30pm; Labor Day-Memorial Day weekends only. $6, kids 6-15 $3) Backcountry hiking is allowed in the Carlsbad Caverns National Park; potential hikers are advised to talk to rangers.

■■■ TRUTH OR CONSEQUENCES

The important thing about T or C for the average traveler isn't *what* it is so much as *where* it is. Smack dab in the middle of Billy the Kid country, T or C provides a launching pad for exploring the diverse attractions of this "wild West" area. T or C draws budget travelers with the **Riverbend Hot Springs Hostel**, 100 Austin St. (894-6183; call for directions). Located on the banks of the Río Grande, with hot outdoor mineral baths, Apache tepee sleep quarters (tepees $9; dorm beds $11), nearby Turtleback Mountain, and sportsperson's paradise Elephant Butte Lake—a stay at Riverbend is a fulfilling vacation all by itself. They also offer innertube rides for $5 per person. Ask Sylvia, the hostel's friendly and concerned proprietor, about discounts for local movies, museums, bowling, food, and bike rentals. Many cheap hotels perfect for the budget traveler also line Date St., such as the **Oasis Motel**, 819 N. Date (894-6629), with friendly owner Ada Brown—clean and quiet. with free HBO and local calls (singles $21.50; doubles $27.25). Another locally owned motel is the **Red Haven Motel**, 605 Date St. (894-2964), with proprietors Velma and Gerald Casey. Free cable TV. (Single $17, each additional person $4.) If you'd rather absorb the beauty of nature, **Elephant Butte Park**, 7 mi. from T or C has campsites available. (Park entrance fee $3 per car, tent sites $7, hookups $11.) For info, call 744-5421. If your stomach is growling, you can quiet it down at **TRC's "Big-A" Burger**, 719 Main St. (894-3099), with the best burgers in town. Try the Tex-Mex burger ($3.15) or the famous Big-A burger ($2.45). (Open 11am-9pm daily.) For Southern diner atmosphere, the **Hill-Top Cafe**, 1301 N. Date St. (894-3407), is the place. Standard diner fare, but the menu features a variety of foods. Mexican dinner plates ($4-6), chicken fried steak ($5.50), reasonably priced sandwiches. Try the apple pie a la mode ($1.25). (Open 9am-6pm daily.)

You'll have to drive a long way for most of the "nearby" attractions, but the **Geronimo Springs Museum**, 325 Main St. (894-6600), is right in T or C (open Mon.-Sat. 9am-5pm; $1.50, students 75¢). East of T or C on Rte. 70 in the town of Mescalero is the **Mescalero Apache Reservation**. For info on ceremonies and the area's recreational facilities, ask at the **community center** in town (671-4491).

The **area code** for T or C is 505.

■■■ WHITE SANDS NATIONAL MONUMENT

Do you remember walking in the sand? Located on Rte. 70, 15 mi. southeast of Alamogordo and 52 mi. northeast of Las Cruces, White Sands (505-479-6124) is the world's largest gypsum sand dune, composed of 300 sq. mi. of beach without ocean. Located in the Tularosa Basin between the Sacramento and San Andres mountains, the dunes were formed when rainwater dissolved gypsum in a nearby mountain and then collected in the basin's Lake Lucero. As the desert weather evaporated the lake, the gypsum crystals were left behind and eventually formed the continually growing sand dunes. Walking, rolling, or hiking through the dunes can provide hours of mindless fun; the brilliant white sand is especially awe-inspiring at sunset. Tragically, the basin is also home to a missile test range, as well as the **Trinity Site,** where the first atomic bomb was exploded in July 1945. Although a visit today won't make your hair fall out, the road to the park is subject to closures, usually no more than two hours, while missiles are tested; call ahead to make sure, and run like hell if you see a mushroom cloud. (Visitors center open 8am-7pm; Labor Day-Memorial Day 8am-4:30pm. Dunes drive open 7am-10pm; off-season 7am-sunset. $4 per vehicle. Disabled access.) To use the park's backcountry **campsites,** you must register and get clearance at the park headquarters. While you're at it, pick up maps at the visitors center. The nearest public camping facilities are in **Lincoln National Forest,** 35 mi. to the east and **Aguirre Springs,** 30 mi. to the west. For information, contact **Forest Supervisor,** Lincoln National Forest, Alamogordo 88310. There is also a campground in **Oliver Lee Memorial State Park;** go 10 mi. south of Alamogordo on U.S. 54, then 5 mi. east on Dog Canyon Rd. The campground is at the mouth of the canyon in the western face of the Sacramento Mountains (505-437-8284). (Park open daily 7:30am-8pm; **visitor center** open daily 9am-4pm. Admission $3 per vehicle.) If you're not camping, make nearby **Alamogordo** your base. The city is home to several motels and restaurants along White Sands Blvd., including ol' faithful: **Motel 6,** Panorama Dr. (505-434-5970), off Rte. 70, with clean, sparse rooms, TV, a pool, HBO, free local calls, and a view (singles $23; doubles $29), and the **All American Inn,** 508 S. White Sands Blvd. (505-437-1850), with clean rooms at a reasonable prices, A/C, pool, and adjacent restaurant. (Singles $26, each additional person $2; doubles $32.) While you're at it, you might as well check out the **Alameda Park and Zoo,** downtown on U.S. 54 (505-437-8430), a great place for a picnic. (Open daily 9am-5pm. $1, over 62 and under 12 50¢.) Or, "reach for the stars" at the **Space Center,** 2 mi. northeast of U.S. 54 in Alamogordo (505-437-2840 or 800-545-4021). (Open June-Aug. daily 9am-6pm, Sept.-May 9am-5pm. $2.25, seniors and kids 6-12 $1.75, family rate $7.)

For more information on White Sands, contact the **park superintendent,** P.O. Box 458, Alamogordo 88310 (505-437-1058).

■■■ TAOS

Lodged between the Sangre de Cristo mountains and the canyon gouged by the Río Grande, Taos first attracted Native American tribes; still-vital pueblos are scattered throughout the valley. Spanish missionaries came later in a vain attempt to convert the indigenous populace to Christianity. The 20th century saw the town invaded by dozens of artists, such as Georgia O'Keeffe and Ernest Blumenschein, captivated by Taos's untainted beauty. Aspiring artists still flock to the city, accompanied by athletes anxious to ski or hike the nearby mountains or brave the whitewaters of the Río Grande.

PRACTICAL INFORMATION

Emergency: Police, 758-2216. **Ambulance,** 911.

Visitor Information: Chamber of Commerce, Paseo del Pueblo Sur (758-3873 or 800-732-8267), just south of McDonald's. Open daily 9am-5pm, Sat.-Sun. 9am-5pm. **Information booth** (no phone) in the center of the plaza. Hours vary by number of volunteers available. Pick up maps and tourist literature from either.

Greyhound: Paseo del Pueblo Sur (758-1144), about 1 mi. south of Taos at Rtes. 68 and 64 E. To: Albuquerque (2 per day, $20); Santa Fe (2 per day, $15); Denver (2 per day, $61). Open Mon.-Fri. 9am-1pm and 3-7pm, Sat.-Sun. and holidays 9-11am and 5-7pm.

Public Transport: Pride of Taos Trolley, 758-8340. Serves several hotels and motels as well as the town plaza and Taos Pueblo. Schedules available in the plaza, the chamber of commerce, and most lodgings. Operates daily 10am-3pm. Variable fare depending on destination.

Taxi: Faust's Transportation, 758-3410. Operates daily 7am-10pm. If you sell your soul, he'll take you to hell (or Albuquerque for $25).

Post Office: 318 Paseo Del Pueblo Norte (758-2081), ¼ mi. north of the plaza. Open Mon.-Fri. 8:30am-5pm. **ZIP code:** 87571.

Area Code: 505.

Drivers should park on **Placitas Road,** one block west of the plaza, or at the Park-and-Ride lots along Rte. 68 at Safeway and Fox Photo. In town, Rte. 68 becomes Paseo del Pueblo.

ACCOMMODATIONS AND CAMPING

The **Plum Tree Hostel,** on Rte. 68, 15 mi. south of Taos in Pilar (758-0090 or 800-999-PLUM), hunkers down next to the Río Grande. This hostel, now under new management, is a flag stop on the Greyhound and airport shuttle routes between Santa Fe and Taos, so getting in and out of town isn't a problem. There are kitchen facilities and refrigerator for guests to use, and a summer arts programs and Río Grande rafting trips are available next door; call ahead to reserve a spot. (Office open daily 7:30am-10pm. Dorm beds $11, AYH members get $1 discount. Private rooms with bath $35 for 2 people, $40 for 3. Also has 2 bungalows available, $15 for 1 person, $24 for 2; must use shared bath in hostel. If you're planning a longer stay, you may want to talk to manager Eva Bahrens to negotiate a work-exchange. Breakfast $3.) Named for its proximity to Taos Ski Valley, the **Abominable Snowmansion Hostel (HI/AYH)** (776-8298) has been spotted in **Arroyo Seco,** a tiny town 10 mi. northeast of Taos on Rte. 150. The friendly, young hosts keep an exotic menagerie including a llama and a parrot. Guests may sleep in dorm rooms, bunk houses, or even a teepee. (Office open daily 8-10am and 4-9pm. $12.50, nonmembers $14.50; in winter $20 and $22. Private rooms $30-35, nonmembers $45. If you stay 2 nights or more, non-members $20. Tepees $8.50-10.50. Breakfast included.) Another option is the recently opened **New Buffalo Bed and Breakfast Retreat Center,** P.O. Box 247, Arroyo Hondo 87513 (776-2015), near Taos (call for directions). This former hippie commune, like many children of the 60s, has been reborn as a yuppie B&B (rooms $40-60). For the more budget-minded traveler, there are also teepees ($10) and tent sites ($12.50). No drugs or alcohol permitted in these rooms where Timothy Leary and Janis Joplin once slept. Hotel rooms are expensive in Taos. The cheapest rooms are at the **Taos Motel** (758-2524 or 800-323-6009), on Rte. 68, 3 mi. south of the plaza. (Singles $39. Doubles $45.)

Camping around Taos is easy for those with a car. Up in the mountains on wooded Rte. 64, 20 mi. east of Taos, the **Kit Carson National Forest** operates three campgrounds. Two are free but have no hookups or running water; look for campers and tents and pull off the road at a designated site. **La Sombra,** also on this road, has running water (sites $5). An additional six free campgrounds line the road to Taos Ski Valley. No permit is required for backcountry camping in the national forest. For more info, including maps of area campgrounds, contact the **forest service**

office (758-6200; open Mon.-Fri. 8am-4:30pm). On Rte. 64 west of town, next to the awesome **Río Grande Gorge Bridge** (758-8851), is a campground operated by the Bureau of Land Management. (Sites with water and porta-potty $7. Porta-visitors center open daily 9am-4:30pm.)

FOOD

The **Apple Tree Restaurant,** 123 Bent St. (758-1900), 2 blocks north of the plaza, serves up some of the best New Mexican and vegetarian food in the state. Dinner ($10-18) includes a huge entree (swimming in melted cheese and liberally garnished with chilis), homemade bread, and soup or salad. (Open Mon.-Sat. 11:30am-3pm and 5:30-9pm, Sun. 10am-3pm and 5:30-9pm.) **Michael's Kitchen,** 84 N. Pueblo Rd. (758-4178), makes mainstream munchies such as donuts, sandwiches ($4.50), and great apple pie ($1.25). (Open daily 7am-8:30pm.) Local sheriff's deputies and late night snackers frequent the **El Pueblo Cafe,** 2053 N. Pueblo (758-2053), on the east side of the road about ½ mi. north of the plaza. The cafe serves standard Tex-Mex fare ($4-6) and cheap breakfasts ($3.25-5.25). (Open Sun.-Thurs. 6am-midnight, Fri.-Sat. 6am-3am.) In the rear of **Amigo's Natural Foods,** 326 Pueblo Rd. (758-8493), across from Jack Donner's, sits a small but holistic deli serving such politically and nutritionally correct dishes as a not-so-spicy tofu on polygranulated bread ($3.25). (Open Mon.-Sat. 9am-7pm, Sun. 11am-5pm.)

SIGHTS AND ACTIVITIES

The spectacle of the Taos area has inspired artists since the days when the Pueblo exclusively inhabited this land. Many "early" Taos paintings hang at the **Harwood Foundation's Museum,** 238 Ledoux St. (758-9826), off Placitas Rd. (open Mon.-Fri. noon-5pm, Sat. 10am-4pm; free). The plaza features other galleries with works by notable locals such as R.C. Gorman, as do **Kit Carson Road, Ledoux Street,** and **El Prado,** a village just north of Taos. Taos' galleries range from high-quality operations of international renown to upscale curio shops. In early October of each year, the **Taos Arts Festival** celebrates local art.

Taos artists love rendering the **Mission of St. Francis of Assisi,** Ranchos De Taos Plaza (758-2754), patron saint of New Mexico. The mission has a "miraculous" painting that changes into a shadowy figure of Christ when the lights go out. (Open Mon.-Sat. 9am-4pm. $1 donation.) Exhibits of Native American art, including a collection of beautiful black-on-black pottery, grace the **Millicent Rogers Museum** (758-2462), north of El Prado St., 4 mi. north of Taos off Rte. 522 (open daily 9am-5pm; Nov.-April Tues.-Sun. 9am-4pm; $4, seniors $3, kids $2, families $8).

Remarkable for its five-story adobes, pink-and-white mission church, and striking silhouette, the vibrant community of **Taos Pueblo** (758-9593) unfortunately charges dearly to look around. Much of the pueblo also remains off-limits to visitors; if this is the only one you will see, make the trip—otherwise, skip it. (Open daily 8:30am-4:30pm. $5 per car, $2 per pedestrian. Camera permit $5, sketch permit $10, painting permit $15.) Feast days highlight beautiful tribal dances; **San Gerónimo's Feast Days** (Sept. 29-30) also feature a fair and races. Contact the **tribal office** (758-9593) for schedules of dances and other info. The less-visited **Picuris Pueblo** lies 20 mi. south of Taos on Rte. 75, near Peñasco. Smaller and somewhat friendlier to visitors, Picuris is best known for its sparkling pottery, molded from mica and clay.

The state's premier ski resort, **Taos Ski Valley** (776-2291), about 5 mi. north of town on Rte. 150, has powder conditions on bowl sections and "short but steep" downhill runs rivaling Colorado's. Reserve a room well in advance if you plan to come during the winter holiday season. (Lift tickets $35, equipment rental $10 per day. For info and ski conditions, call the Taos Valley Resort Association at 776-2233 or 800-776-1111.) In summer, the ski-valley area offers great hikes.

After a day of strenuous sight-seeing, soak your weary bones in one of the natural **hot springs** near Taos. One of the most accessible bubbles 9 mi. north on Rte. 522 near Arroyo Hondo; turn left onto a dirt road immediately after you cross the river.

Following the dirt road for about 3 mi., turn left when it forks just after crossing the Río Grande—the hot spring is just off the road at the first switchback. Though not very private, the spring's dramatic location part way up the Río Grande Gorge more than compensates. Located 10 mi. west of Taos, the **U.S. 64 Bridge** over the Río Grande Gorge is the nation's second-highest span, affording a spectacular view of the canyon and the New Mexico sunset.

 Utah

Once home to dinosaurs, Utah now beckons bipedal mammals to its variegated landscape, which ranges from a vast lake of salt water to a multitude of bizarre rock formations. Southern Utah is an otherworldly amalgam of redstone canyons, deep river gorges, arches, spires, and columns carved out of the terrain by wind and water. Northeastern and central Utah feature the Uinta Mountains, dotted with lakes and speckled with aspens and ponderosa pine; and the dinosaurs are still with us at Dinosaur National Monument, on the border with Colorado.

Driven westward by religious persecution, the Mormons began settling Utah— which they called *Deseret*—in 1848; today Mormons make up over 70% of the state population. Mormon culture is characterized by intensely family-oriented values, abstinence from alcohol and caffeine, and a history of polygamy. Mormon culture is ubiquitous in the state, making a trip to Utah a journey outside the "mainstream" U.S—unless, like the skiers who flock to Alta, you only come for the snow.

PRACTICAL INFORMATION

Capital: Salt Lake City.

Visitor Information: Utah Travel Council, 300 N. State St., Salt Lake City 84114 (538-1030), across the street from the capitol building. Information on national and state parks, campgrounds, and accommodations. Open summer Mon.-Fri. 8am-5pm. Pick up a free copy of the *Utah Travel Guide,* with a complete listing of motels, national parks, and campgrounds. **Utah Parks and Recreation,** 1636 W. North Temple, Salt Lake City 86116 (538-7220). Open Mon.-Fri. 8am-5pm.

Time Zone: Mountain (2 hrs. behind Eastern). **Postal Abbreviation:** UT

Sales Tax: 6.25%.

■■■ PROVO

Untouched by the tourist and convention business, Provo seems right out of the 1950s—religious conservatism maintains a quiet, peaceful college town. Too quiet. The students at Brigham Young University are dedicated to their religious studies and seem to promise a continuation of past traditions for years to come. The spirit of Provo really comes to the fore during the week-long 4th of July Freedom Festival, when the town celebrates wildly and children dress in red, white, and blue sequined jumpsuits to perform patriotic skits on the Tabernacle lawn. If you're here to see how Mormons live, you're in the right place; for touristy fun, take the freeway back to Salt Lake City.

Practical Information The **Visitor Center,** 51 S. University Ave. (370-8393 or 800-222-UTAH), in the Historic County Courthouse, is full of brochures on Provo and the surrounding area, as well as discount coupons for area attractions (open Mon.-Fri. 8am-8pm, Sat.-Sun. 10am-6pm). **Brigham Young University Information** (378-4636) can also help you find your way in the tourism desert (open Mon.-Fri. 8am-5pm). **Greyhound** dashes out of town from 294 N. 1st West (373-4211), heading for Salt Lake City (3 per day; 1 hr.; $8) and Las Vegas (2 per day; 8 hr.; $49). (Open Mon.-Fri. 8am-noon, 12:30-5pm, Sat. 8am-noon.). **Amtrak** chugs from 200 E. 600 S. St. (800-872-7245) to Salt Lake City (1 per day; $15) and Las Vegas (1 per day; 10 hr.; $96); tickets are available from travel agencies in town, including **Tockes Tours and Travel,** 480 N. 200 West (377-4110; open Mon.-Fri. 8:30am-5pm). Service to downtown (Center St.) and BYU (fare 65¢) is provided by **Utah Transit Authority** (375-4636), which also makes frequent trips to Salt Lake City (1½ hr.) and nearby Orem (fare $1.50). (Operates Mon.-Sat. 6am-10pm, Sun. 6am-6pm.) If you'd prefer more travel freedom, **Budget Car Rental,** 1333 N. State St. (800-237-7251), can provide you with wheels for $30 per day, with unlimited mileage. You must be at least 21 with a major credit card; if under 25, $5 extra per day. (Open Mon.-Sun. 8am-9pm.) The **Crisis Line** (374-6400) and the **Rape Hotline** (377-5500) both operate 24 hrs. In an **emergency** call 911. Look for Provo's lovely **post office** at 95 W. 100 South (374-2000), Mon.-Fri. 8:45am-5:30pm, Sat. 8:45am-12:45pm. It probably will be there at other times, but it won't do you much good. The **ZIP code** is 84601; the **area code** is 801.

Accommodations and Food The **Hotel Roberts,** 192 S. University Ave. (373-3400), is the best deal in town. Only one block south of the city center, this charming old hotel has large, clean rooms with cable TV and private baths which keep a loyal, older clientele coming back. (Singles $17-19. Doubles $19-20, $3 each additional person.) If the Hotel Roberts is full, there are also newer, more spartan motels nearby. **City Center Motel,** 150 W. 300 South (373-8489), offers rooms with color TV, HBO, kitchenettes, and pool. (Singles and doubles from $24.) **Friendship Uptown Motel,** 4679 W. Center (373-8248), is a little farther away from the center of town, 5 long blocks to be exact, but it does have HBO and a pool. (Singles $28. Doubles $32. $4 each additional person.) If you would rather be near the party at the University, **Motel 6** has a cookie-cutter room for you at 1600 S. University Ave. (375-5064). (Singles $29. Doubles $36.)

As always, the most budget of all budget options is camping. There are several campgrounds in the national forest and state parks near Provo. Follow the loop from U.S. 189 into the mountains, then go north on Rte. 92 to Highland, and you'll find a dozen campgrounds en route, most with drinking water, in **Uinta National Forest,** which encompasses the mountains to the east and north of Provo and comes down to the city limits. On the ridge directly over the city is the **Rock Canyon Campground,** closest to downtown Provo (sites $7). For information on camping (or hiking in the National Forest, contact the Federal Building, 88 W. 100 North (377-5780). **Deer Creek State Park,** with 31 sites, is also up the Provo River Canyon on U.S. 189, about 18 mi. from downtown Provo (sites $9). If it's all full, head 12 mi. north to **Wasatch Mountain State Park,** open year round (some sites with hookups; $11-13). There are also a number of private campgrounds in the area, including **Silver Fox Resort,** 101 W. 1500 South (377-0033; $10 per night for 2 people); **Lakeside Campground,** 4000 W. Center St. (373-5267), near Utah Lake (sites $13); and **KOA,** 320 N. 2050 West (375-2994; $14 per night for 2 people).

Should you forget, Provo is a college town, as proven by the obligatory number of fast-food chains and pizza parlors lining University Ave. In addition, some good cheap ethnic eateries have snuck in around **Center St.** and **University Ave.** downtown. **Los Hermanos,** 16 W. Center (375-5732), draws a large crowd for lunch and dinner with its comfortable wicker setting and huge portions. Combination dinners ($4-7) fill you up; make sure to save room for fried ice cream ($2.25). (Open Mon.-Sat. 11am-1am.) Nearer to the University (and those wild, crazy kids) is the extremely popular **Brick Oven,** 150 E. 800 North (374-8800), where everyone convenes for pizza feasts and conversation. Ten-inch pizzas go for $4.45, 16-inchers for $13. Get a fruity buzz off the homemade apple, cherry, and root beer. (Open Mon.-Thurs. 11am-11pm, Fri.-Sat. 11am-12:30am.) A pleasant surprise is the **Bamboo**

Hut, 1161 N. Canyon Rd. (375-6842). It doesn't look like much, but the big portions of tasty Tahitian specials ($3-4) are truly delicacies (open Mon.-Fri. 11am-2pm).

Sights and Entertainment 27,000 students who have taken an oath to abstain from alcohol, tobacco, tea, and coffee, and the last straw for most of us: pre-marital sex. What sight could be more wondrous? **Brigham Young University** (main entrance at 1230 N. on Canyon Rd.) is the largest church-related, privately-owned university in the U.S., sponsored by the Mormons, and believes that its code of honor helps in the higher education of the entire student body. If you're planning to infiltrate the campus incognito, clean yourself up (no grubby T-shirts)—hippies beware of the fashion police; a clean shave is also required. The University gives tours in open-air carts at 11am and 2pm. For more information, call **BYU Hosting Services** (378-4678).

The area around Provo is filled with natural wonders as well. Like Salt Lake City, Provo has the advantages of two mountain ranges and a lake to draw on. The view of the **Uintas** is one of the more exciting things about Provo. **Utah Lake** is popular with water-skiers and small craft sailboaters, but pollution has spoiled much of the lake's natural setting. Like the Great Salt Lake, it has fought back, flooding out Utah State Park and imperiling waterfront property.

Timpanogos Cave National Monument (756-5238), about 15 mi. from Provo off I-15, is made up of three interconnecting caves—Hansen, Middle, and Timpanogos. the subterranean limestone chambers are full of stalactites, stalagmites, and other crystal wonders. There are also small, clear cave pools, like Hidden Lake in Timpanogos Cave. (Open mid-May-mid-Oct. $5, kids 6-15 $4, seniors $2.50.)

Despite the restraint exercised by BYU students, you can still let loose with the looser locals at the casual bars along West Center St. Although most require you to be 21, some establishments feature college nights. **A. Beuford Gifford's** has live bands every Fri. and Sat. night. (Open Mon.-Sat. 10am-1am. Nearer to the rowdiness of University life is the **Star Palace,** 501 N. 900 East (373-2623), one of the nation's largest dance halls. (Open Wed.-Sat. 9am-1am; $4 cover.) **The Silver Spur,** 210 W. Center (373-9014), serves beer (SIN!) and live music Thurs.-Sat. (cover $2).

■■■ SALT LAKE CITY

On July 24, 1847, Brigham Young led a group of Mormon pioneers to find a place where they could practice their religion, based on the teachings of the *Bible* and the *Book of Mormon,* free of the persecution they faced in the East. When Young first saw the valley of the Great Salt Lake, he said, "This is the right place;" today, "This is the Place" monument commemorates the famous utterance. Salt Lake City is the spiritual center of the Church of Latter Day Saints, and the home of the ever-looming Mormon Temple and the Tabernacle Choir. Despite its commitment to preserving the Temple and traditions, Salt Lake is a booming modern city whose proximity to the mountains makes it a favorite base town for skiers and outdoorsmen.

PRACTICAL INFORMATION

Emergency: 911.

Visitor Information: Salt Lake Valley Convention and Visitors Bureau, 180 S. West Temple (521-2868 or 800-831-4332), 2 blocks south of Temple Sq. Open Mon.-Fri. 8am-6pm, Sat. 9am-4pm; off-season Mon.-Fri. 8am-5:30pm, Sat. 9am-4pm. The free *Salt Lake Visitors Guide* details a good self-guided tour.

Airport: Salt Lake City International Airport, 776 N. Terminal Dr. (539-2205), 4 mi. west of Temple Sq. UTA buses provide the best means of transport to and from the airport. Bus #50 serves the terminal directly to and from downtown.

Amtrak: 325 S. Rio Grande (364-8562 or 800-872-7245). Trains once daily to: Denver (13½ hr.; $107); Las Vegas (8 hr.; $89); Los Angeles (15 hr.; $111); San Francisco (17 hr.; $111). Ticket office open Mon.-Sat. 4am-9:30am, 10am-12:30pm and 4:15pm-1am; Sun. 4pm-1am.

Greyhound: 160 W. South Temple (800-231-2222), 1 block west of Temple Sq. To: Cheyenne (3 per day; 9 hr.; $61, $46 14 days in advance); Las Vegas (2 per day; 10 hr.; $51, $47 in advance); San Francisco (3 per day; 15 hr.; $82 and $61); Boise (3 per day; 7 hr.; $41 and $31); Denver (4 per day; 12 hr.; $61 and $58). Ticket counter open daily 5am-10pm. Terminal open 24 hrs.

Public Transport: Utah Transit Authority, 600 S. 700 West (287-4636 until 7pm). Frequent service to the University of Utah campus; buses to Ogden (#70/72 express), suburbs, airport, and east to the mountain canyons and Provo (#4 local or #1 express; fare $1.50). Buses every ½ hr. or more 6:30am-11pm. Fare 65¢, seniors 30¢ under 5 free. Get maps at libraries or the visitors bureau.

Taxi: City Cab, 363-5014. **Ute Cab,** 359-7788. **Yellow Cab,** 521-2100. 95¢ base fare, $1.40 per mi., about $12 from the airport to Temple Sq.

Car Rental: Payless Car Rental, 1974 W. North Temple (596-2596). $25 per day with 200 free mi., $120 per week with 1200 free mi.; 14¢ per additional mi. Open Sun.-Fri. 6am-10pm, Sat. 8am-6pm. Must be 21 with a major credit card.

Bike Rental: Wasatch Touring, 702 E. 100 South (359-9361). 21-speed mountain bikes $15 per day. Open Mon.-Sat. 9am-7pm.

Help Lines: Rape Crisis, 467-7273. 24-hr. hotline.

Post Office: 230 W. 200 South (530-5902), 1 block west of the visitors bureau. Open Mon.-Fri. 8am-5:30pm, Sat. 9am-2pm. **ZIP code:** 84101.

Area Code: 801.

Salt Lake's grid system makes navigation simple. Brigham Young, the city's founder, designated **Temple Square,** in the heart of today's downtown, as the center. Street names indicate how many blocks east, west, north or south they lie from Temple Square. **Main Street,** running north-south, and **Temple Street,** running east-west, are the "0" points. Smaller streets and streets that do not fit the grid pattern often have non-numeric names. Occasionally, a numbered street reaches a dead end, only to resume a few blocks farther on. The downtown is equipped with audible traffic lights for the convenience of blind pedestrians. A "cuckoo" is a green light for east-west travel while "chirps" indicate a green light for north-south travel.

ACCOMMODATIONS AND CAMPING

Conventions make hotels and accommodations numerous but expensive; luckily, the two hostels are some of the best around.

The Avenues (HI/AYH), 107 F St. (363-8137), 7 blocks east of Temple Sq. Bright rooms with 4 bunks each or private singles and doubles. Popular with British and German students. Blankets and linens provided. Kitchen and laundry available. Check-in 8am-10pm. Dorm rooms with shared bath $11, nonmembers $15. Singles with private bath $22. Doubles $25. Hostel closed noon-6pm daily.

Kendell Motel, 667 N. 300 West (355-0293), 10 blocks northwest of Temple Sq. From airport take #50 bus to N. Temple, then #70 bus. From Greyhound or downtown, take #70. You and your friends will have your own apartment in Salt Lake. Well-kept rooms with kitchens, color TV, and A/C $25, doubles $30. Huge dorm-style rooms with kitchen and nice bath for $15 per person.

Motel 6, 3 locations: 176 W. 600 South (531-1252); 1990 W. North Temple (364-1053), 2½ mi. from the airport (take bus #50); and 496 N. Catalpa (561-0058), just off I-15. Tom Bodett's favorite chain, rooms fill quickly. Singles $32. Doubles $39.

Dean's Motor Lodge, 1821 S. Main (486-7495). Basic rooms with A/C and heat, color TV with HBO. Check out the cute lobby. Singles and doubles $29-40.

Camping is available outside the city. The **Wasatch-Cache National Forest** (524-5030) skirts Salt Lake City on the east, proffering many established sites. Make reservations through MISTIX (800-283-CAMP). The terrain by the city is quite steep, making the best sites those on the far side of the mountains. Three of the closest campgrounds lie near I-215, which fronts the mountain off of I-80. Between Miles 11 and 18 out of Salt Lake City on I-80, there are four campgrounds with more than

100 sites altogether (no hookups). Go early on weekends to ensure a space (sites $7-8; take "Fort Douglas" bus #4). The **Utah Travel Council** (538-1030) has detailed information on all campsites in the area, including the three near the ski areas off Rtes. 152 and 210 to the south of Salt Lake. **East Canyon State Park,** 30 mi. from Salt Lake, near the junction of Rtes. 65 and 66, has sites by East Canyon Reservoir—a good place to go boating and fishing (sites $9). If you need a hookup, the **KOA,** 1400 W. North Temple (355-1192; sites $18, with water and electricity $21, full hookup $23) and other private campgrounds are your only options.

FOOD

Affordable food abounds in Salt Lake City. Fill up on **scones,** adopted from the British and made into a Utah specialty. Otherwise stick to ethnic food downtown or the cheap, slightly greasy eateries on the outer fringe. The two (literally) opposing main shopping malls, ZCMI Mall, and Crossroads Mall on Main St., have food courts with a variety of fast and ethnic eateries to appeal to almost every conceivable tastebud.

> **Rio Grande Cafe,** 270 Rio Grande (364-3302), in the Rio Grande Railroad depot, 4 blocks west of the Temple by Amtrak and the Historical Society. Take bus #16 or 17. Stylish, fun Mexican restaurant with neon-and-glass decor. Huge combination plates $6. Open for lunch Mon.-Sat. 11:30am-2:30pm and for dinner Mon.-Thurs. 5-10pm, Fri-Sat. 5-11pm, Sun. 5-10pm.
>
> **Bill and Nada's Cafe,** 479 S. 6th St. (354-6984), right by Trolley Sq. One of Salt Lake's most revered cafes. Patsy Cline on the jukebox and paper placemats with U.S. presidents on the tables. Two eggs, hash browns, toast $3. Roast leg of lamb, salad, soup, vegetable, roll, and potatoes $5.35. Open 24 hrs.
>
> **Salt Lake Roasting Company,** 249 E. 400 South (363-7572). Funky jazz and classical music amidst burlap bags of coffee beans. Caters to the twentysomething set. Coffee (85¢); quiche ($3); soup ($1.50). Open Mon.-Sat. 6:45am-midnight.
>
> **Cafe Rude,** 38 E. 13th South (467-6660), belches out breakfast all day long ($2.50-4.50) and creative veggie meals for lunch and dinner (around $5). Their slogan: "Yeah...so what's it to ya?!" How can you not love it! Breakfast anytime ($2.50-4.50), pasta, mexican, and veggie dishes. If you're not fully satisfied—go home, who cares?! Open Mon.-Thurs. 7am-10pm, Fri.-Sat. 7am-11pm, Sun. 8am-3pm.
>
> **The Sconecutter,** 2040 S. State St. (485-9981). The Elvis of sconemakers. Your favorite flavor of fluffy, stuffing scone ($1). Try the cinnamon and butter. Restaurant open Sun.-Thurs. 7am-midnight, Fri.-Sat. 7am-3am. Drive-thru open 24 hrs.

MORMON SIGHTS

What the Vatican is to Roman Catholics, Salt Lake City is to the **Church of Jesus Christ of Latter Day Saints,** whose followers hold both the *Book of Mormon* and the *Bible* to be the word of God. The highest Mormon authority and the central temple reside here. **Temple Square** (240-2534) is the symbolic center of the Mormon religion. Feel free to wander around the flowery and pleasant 10-acre square, but the sacred temple is off-limits to non-Mormons. Alighting on the highest of the building's three towers, a golden statue of the angel Moroni watches over the city. The square has two **Visitors Centers** (north and south), each of which stocks information and armies of smiling guides. A 45-min. **Historical Tour** leaves from the flagpole every 10 min. If you're interested in knowing more, 25-min. **Book of Mormon Tours** and **Purpose of Temple Tours** leave alternately every 30 min. and explain the religious meaning behind Temple Square. (Visitors centers open daily 8am-10pm; off-season 9am-9pm.)

Visitors on any tour in Temple Square will visit the **Mormon Tabernacle,** which houses the famed Choir. Built in 1867, the structure is so acoustically sensitive that a pin dropped at one end can be heard 175 ft. away at the other end. Rehearsals on Thursday evening (8pm) and Sunday morning broadcasts from the tabernacle are open to the public (9:30-10am; doors close at 9:15am). Though supremely impressive, the Choir can't match the size and sound of the 11,623-pipe organ that accompanies it. (Recitals Mon.-Sat. at noon; summer Sun. 2pm as well.) **Assembly Hall,** next door, also hosts various concerts almost every summer evening.

Around the perimeter of Temple Sq. stand several other buildings commemorating Mormon history in Utah. The **Genealogical Library,** 35 N. West Temple (240-2331), provides the resources for Mormons and others to research their lineage, in accordance with Mormon belief that ancestors must be baptized by proxy to seal them into an eternal family. If you've ever wanted to research your roots, this may be the place to do it; the library houses the largest collection of genealogical documents in the world. An orientation film is available. (Open Mon. 7:30am-6pm, Tues.-Fri. 7:30am-10pm, Sat. 7:30am-5pm. Free.)

The **Museum of Church History and Art,** 45 N. West Temple (240-3310), houses Mormon memorabilia from 1820 to the present. (Open Mon.-Fri. 9am-9pm, Sat.-Sun. and holidays 10am-7pm. Free.) Once the official residence of Brigham Young while he served as "governor" of the Deseret Territory (unrecognized by the U.S. government) and president of the Church, the **Beehive House,** N. Temple (240-2671), at State St., two blocks east of Temple Sq., gives half-hour guided tours every 10-15 min. (Open Mon.-Fri. 9:30am-6:30pm, Sat. 9:30am-4:30pm, Sun. 10am-1pm, Sept.-May Mon.-Sat. 9:30am-4:30pm, Sun. 10am-1pm. Closes 1pm on all holidays. Free.)

The city of Salt Lake encompasses the **Pioneer Trail State Park,** 2601 Sunnyside Ave. (584-8391), in Emigration Canyon on the eastern end of town. Take bus #4 or follow 8th South St. until it becomes Sunnyside Ave., then take Monument Rd. The **"This is the Place" Monument** commemorates Brigham Young's decision to settle in Salt Lake; a **visitors center** will tell you all about the Mormons' long march through Ohio, Illinois, and Nebraska. Tour **Brigham Young's forest farmhouse** (open daily 11am-5pm), where the dynamic leader held court with his numerous wives. (Park grounds open in summer daily 8am-8pm, but visit 9am-7:30pm for the best reception. Entrance fee $1.50 adults and $1 ages 6-15.)

SECULAR SIGHTS AND ACTIVITIES

The grey-domed **capitol** lies behind the spires of Temple Square. Tours (521-2822) are offered daily from 9am to 3:30pm. For more info, contact the **Council Hall Visitors Center** (538-1030), across from the main entrance. (Open Mon.-Fri. 8am-5pm, Sat.-Sun. and holidays 10am-5pm.) While in the capitol area, hike up City Creek Canyon to **Memory Grove,** savoring the shade as you gaze out over the city, or stroll down to the **Church of Jesus Christ of Latter Day Saints Office Building,** 50 E. North Temple, and take the elevator to the 26th-floor **observation deck** (240-3789; open Mon.-Fri. 9am-5pm, Sat. 9am-1pm) from which you can see the Great Salt Lake to the west, and the Wasatch Mountain Range to the east. Also on capitol hill is the **Hansen Planetarium,** 15 S. State St. (538-2098 or 538-2104). Even if you don't pay for a show, enjoy the fabulous free exhibits. (Open daily 10am-8pm.) Head for the **Children's Museum,** 840 N. 300 West (328-3383), to pilot a 727 jet or implant a Jarvik artificial heart in a life-sized "patient." (Open Mon. 9:30am-9pm, Tues.-Sat. 9:30am-5pm, Sun. noon-5pm. $3, ages 2-14 $2.50. Adult $1.50, kids $1 after 5pm Mon. Take bus #61.) You also can walk through the University of Utah campus to the **Utah Museum of Natural History,** 215 South and 1350 East (581-4303), which catalogues the variety of flora and fauna that has lived on the Salt Lake plain. (Open Mon.-Sat. 9:30am-5:30pm, Sun. and holidays noon-5pm. $2, ages under 14 $1.) Next door is the yard-sale-like collection at the **Utah Museum of Fine Arts** (581-7332; open Mon.-Fri. 10am-5pm, Sat.-Sun. 2-5pm; free). For information on university happenings contact the **Information Desk** in the U. of Utah Park Administration Building (581-6515; open Mon.-Fri. 8am-8pm), **general information** (581-7200), or the **Olpin Student Center** (581-5888; open Mon.-Sat. 8am-9pm).

Pioneer Memorial Museum, 300 North Main St. (538-1050), next to the state capitol has relics of the earliest settlers in the valley (guns, books, clothing) and gives insight into the two most prominent Mormon leaders: Brigham Young and his first counselor, Heber C. Kimball. (Open Mon.-Sat. 9am-5pm, Sun. 1-5pm, Sept.-May

Mon.-Sat. 9am-5pm. Free.) Next to the Amtrak station, the **Utah State Historical Society,** 300 Rio Grande (533-5755), hosts an interesting series of exhibits, including pre-Mormon photographs and quilts. (Open Mon.-Fri. 8am-5pm. Free.)

The **Utah Symphony Orchestra** (533-6407) performs in **Symphony Hall,** Salt Palace Center, 100 S. West Temple, one of the most spectacular auditoriums in the country. (Free tours Fri. at 1:30pm. Concert tickets $12-18 in summer, $14-$30 in winter; student rush $5.) Dance and opera performances occur at the neighboring **Salt Lake Art Center** (328-4201; open Mon.-Sat. 10am-5pm; donation).

ALCOHOL AND NIGHTLIFE

The Mormon Church's prohibitions against alcohol consumption among its members have led to a number of state restrictions. Utah law requires that all liquor sales be made through state-licensed stores; don't be surprised if you can't get more than a beer at most restaurants or bars. The drinking age of 21 is well-enforced. (State liquor stores open Mon.-Sat. 11am-7pm. There are 6 within 3 mi. of downtown Salt Lake City.) A number of hotels and restaurants have licenses to sell mini-bottles and splits of wine, but consumers must make drinks themselves. Public bars serve only beer. Only private clubs requiring membership fees are allowed to serve mixed drinks. Some clubs have two-week trial memberships for $5; others will give a free, temporary membership to visitors in town for a night or two.

Despite the alcohol restrictions, there are several fun downtown bars and clubs, which collegians keep fairly crowded, and popular bands, such as Bon Jovi and the Lollapalooza tour, do make their rounds. Pick up a free copy of *Private Eye Weekly* or *The Event,* both available at bars and restaurants, for local club listings and events. The **Dead Goat Saloon,** 165 S. West Temple (328-4628), attracts Anglo-Saxon tourists as well as locals. (Open Mon.-Fri. 11:30am-1am, Sat. 6pm-1am, Sun. 7pm-1am. Beer served until 1am. No BYOB. Cover $2-4, Fri.-Sun. $5.) Head over to the **X Wife's Place,** 465 S. 700 East (532-2353), to shoot stick with the boys. (Open Mon.-Fri. 11:30am-1am, Sat. 5pm-1am. Beer and mixed drinks served.) No cover, but you'll need a club membership ($12 per year) or get a member to sponsor you.

Club DV8, 115 S. West Temple (539-8400), deviates from the straight and narrow. Friday is college night. (Open Thurs.-Sat. 9pm-2am; ½-price drafts from 9-10pm; Thurs. is modern music night. Cover $1.) **The Zephyr,** 79 W. 300 South (355-2582), blows with live rock and reggae nightly. (Open daily 7pm-2am; off-season daily 7pm-1am. Cover $5-10.) **Junior's Tavern,** 202 E. 500 South (322-0318), is the favorite local watering hole for jazz and blues aficionados. (Open daily noon-1am. Music starts at 9pm. No cover.)

■ Near Salt Lake City

The **Great Salt Lake,** 17 mi. west of town on I-80 (exit 104), a remnant of primordial Lake Bonneville, is a bowl of salt water in which only blue-green algae and brine shrimp can survive. The salt content varies from 5-15% and provides such buoyancy that it is almost impossible for the human body to sink; only the Dead Sea has a higher salt content. Unfortunately, flooding sometimes closes the state parks and beaches on the lakeshore, but you can still try **Saltair Beach,** 17 mi. to the west, or head north 40 min. to fresh-water **Willard Bay.** Bus #37 ("Magna") will take you within 4 mi. of the lake. Be warned that the aroma around the lake ain't rosy. Contact the visitors center (see Practical Information) or the state parks (538-7220) for current information on lake access, as it is fairly difficult to reach without a car.

In the summer, escape the heat with a drive or hike to the cool breezes and icy streams of the nearby mountains. One of the prettiest roads over the Wasatch Range is **Route 210.** Heading east from Sandy, 12 mi. southeast of the city, this road goes up **Little Cottonwood Canyon** to the Alta ski resort. The **Lone Peak Wilderness Area** stretches away southward from the road, around which the range's highest peaks tower, at over 11,000 ft. **City Creek, Millcreek,** and **Big Cottonwood** also make good spots for a picnic or hike.

Of the seven **ski resorts** within 40 min. of Salt Lake City, **Snowbird** (521-6040; lift tickets $38) and **Park City** (649-8111; lift tickets $40) are two of the classiest. For a more affordable alternative, try nearby **Alta** (742-3333; lift tickets $23). The **Alta Peruvian Lodge** (328-8589) is a great place to pass the night. (Bunks $12.50.) You can ski Snowbird, Deer Valley, and Alta from the **Alpine Prospectors Lodge,** 151 Main St. (649-3483 or 800-457-3591), in Park City. (Rooms with shared bath: singles $25-49, doubles $35-59, depending on season; more for private bath. Also offers packages including 3 lift tickets and 4 nights for $198 per person; breakfast included.) **UTA** (see Practical Information above) runs buses from Salt Lake City to the resorts in winter, with pick-ups at downtown motels; **Lewis Bros. Stages** (800-826-5844) is one of many shuttle services providing transport to Park City, departing the airport every 30 min. in winter and 5 times per day in summer. ($18 one-way, $36 round-trip.) You can rent equipment from **Breeze Ski Rentals** (800-525-0314), at Snowbird and Park City ($15; 10% discount if reserved; lower rates for rentals over 3 days). Call or write the Utah Travel Council (see Utah: Practical Information above). Ask for the free *Ski Utah* for listings of ski packages and lodgings.

Some resorts offer summer attractions as well. You can rent mountain bikes at **Snowbird** (see above) for $16 per day or $9 per half-day. Snowbird's **aerial tram** climbs to 11,000 ft., offering a spectacular view of the Wasatch Mountains and the Salt Lake Valley below. (Open daily 11am-8pm. $8, seniors and 5-16 $6, under 5 free.) During the summer, **Park City** offers a comparable **gondola ride** (649-8111; open Fri.-Mon. noon-6pm. $5, under 12 $4). Their **alpine slide** provides the fastest transport down the mountain. (Open daily 10am-10pm. $3.75, seniors and kids $2.75. Take I-80 east 30 mi. from Salt Lake.)

NORTHEASTERN UTAH

■■■ DINOSAUR NATIONAL MONUMENT

Dinosaur National Monument is more than just a heap of bones. The Green and Yampa Rivers have here created vast, colorful gorges and canyons, and the harsh terrain evokes eerie visions of its reptilian past. Pick up the monument visitors guide *Echoes* for more detailed information.

Practical Information The park **entrance fee** is $5 per car, $2 for bikers, pedestrians, and those in tour buses. The more interesting western side lies along Rte. 149 off U.S. 40 just outside of **Jensen**, 30 mi. east of Vernal. The eastern side of the park is accessible only from a road off U.S. 40, outside **Dinosaur, CO.** The **Dinosaur National Monument Headquarters,** on U.S. 40 in Dinosaur, CO (303-374-2216), at the intersection with the park road, provides orientation for exploring the canyonlands of the park and information on nearby river rafting. (Open daily 8am-4:30pm; Sept.-May Mon.-Fri. 8am-4:30pm.) For more information on the eastern side of the park, write to the **Monument Superintendent,** P.O. Box 210, Dinosaur, CO 81610. For additional info and maps, call 800-845-3466.

Greyhound makes daily runs east and west along U.S. 40, fortunately *not* through the courtesy of Flintstone feet (2 per day each way), stopping in Vernal (see Vernal) and Dinosaur en route from Denver and Salt Lake City. Jensen is a flag stop, as is the monument headquarters, 2 mi. west of Dinosaur. There is no depot in Dinosaur—to catch the bus here, you'll have to flag it down. In an **emergency,** call 789-2115 (Utah) or 374-2216 (Colorado). Dino's **post office** is at 198 Stegosaurus Dr. (303-374-2353; open Mon.-Fri. 8:30am-12:30pm and 1-5pm). The **ZIP code** is 81610.

Camping and Accommodations A few mi. beyond the Quarry Center on Rte. 149 you'll find the shady **Green River Campground** with flush toilets, drinking water, and tent and RV sites. (Open late spring-early fall. Sites $8.) There are also several free primitive campsites in and around the park; call the visitors center for info. A rugged 13 mi. east of Harper's Corner, in the park's eastern half, is **Echo Campground,** the perfect location for a crystalline evening under the stars. Watch for signs near Harper's Corner leading to a dirt road that snakes its way past cattle and sheep into the valley below (free). For backcountry camping, obtain a free permit from the headquarters or from Quarry Center.

The **Park Motel**, 105 E. Brontosaurus Blvd. (303-374-2267), offers singles for $18, doubles for $22, and 2 beds for $24 (closed Nov.-April).

Sights and Activities Seven mi. from the intersection with U.S. 40 on the western side of the park is the **Dinosaur Quarry Visitors Center** (789-2115), accessible from the road by free shuttle bus or a fairly strenuous ½-mi. walk (cars prohibited in summer). A hill inside the center has been partially excavated to reveal the hulking remains of dinosaurs. (Center open daily 8am-4:30pm, in summer until 7pm. You can drive your car in after closing.) Winter finds the park lonely, cold, and fossilized with neither shuttle service nor the possibility of self-guided tours.

Past the campgrounds on Rte. 149, just beyond the end of the road, you can see one of the best examples of the monument's many Native American **petroglyphs.** The most accessible rock art is at **Club Creek** (a few mi. east of Quarry Visitors Center), but the finest petroglyph panels are at **McKee Spring.** You can also see relics of ancient cultures, such as pot sherds at **Jones Hole Trail,** and remains of granaries and other storage structures at **Yampa Canyon.**

The 25-mi. road (closed in winter) to majestic **Harper's Corner,** at the junction of the Green and Yampa River gorges, begins 2 mi. east of Dinosaur. From the road's terminus, a 2-mi. round-trip nature hike leaves for the corner itself. It's worth the sweat; the view is one of the most spectacular in all of Utah.

■■■ FLAMING GORGE NATIONAL RECREATION AREA

Wild horses roam the Flaming Gorge country, a reminder of mountain pioneers who once settled here on the western frontier. A combination of the Uinta Mountains and the Wyoming deserts, Flaming Gorge offers recreational activities from hiking to fishing to climbing. The Flaming Gorge National Recreation Area is part of the Ashley National Forest, which expands across southwest Wyoming and northeast Utah. The center of the area is marked by the Flaming Gorge Reservoir, a 91-mi.-long lake created by a towering army dam built on the Green River in the 1960s.

Practical Information From Wyoming, the most scenic route to the gorge is the amazing U.S. 191 south from I-80 (exit between Rock Springs and Green River). Rte. 530 closely parallels the reservoir's western shore, but the scenery is not as compelling—an occasional pronghorn antelope. Take this route only if you want to camp on the flat beaches of the lake's Wyoming section. To reach Flaming Gorge from the south, take U.S. 191 north from Vernal, over the gorgeous flanks of the Uinta Mountains (see below), to **Dutch John, UT.** Much of the recreation area is in Wyoming, but Utah has the most scenic and best-developed area of the park, at the base of the Uinta Range. The **Flaming Gorge Visitors Center** (885-3135), off U.S. 191, just outside of the government building complex in Dutch John, offers guided tours of the dam area along with maps of the area ($1; open daily 8am-6pm; off-season 9am-5pm). The **Red Canyon Visitors Center** (889-3713), a few mi. off U.S. 191 on Rte. 44 to Manila, perches a breath-taking 1360 ft. above Red Canyon and Flaming Gorge Lake. (Open daily 10am-5pm; closed winter.)

Camping and Accommodations Simple, inexpensive **campgrounds** abound in the Flaming Gorge area; reservations for large groups can be made by calling MISTIX (800-283-2267). You can camp next to the Red Canyon Visitors Center in **Red Canyon Campground** ($7), or in one of the numerous national forest campgrounds along U.S. 191 and Rte. 44 in the Utah portion of the park (sites $7-10; 2-week max. stay). **Buckboard Crossing** (307-875-6927; sites $8) and **Lucerne Valley** (801-784-3293; sites $10), located further north, tend to be drier and unshaded, but are close to the marinas on the reservoir. Either visitors center can offer you heaps of information on camping.

If you'd rather sleep indoors, **Red Canyon Lodge** (889-3759), west on Rte. 44, 2 mi. before the visitors center, offers reasonably priced rustic cabins. Frontier Cabins share bath facilities (singles $26, doubles $36), Deluxe Cabins have a private bath (single $38, doubles $48; $5 per additional person). **Flaming Gorge Lodge,** near the dam in Dutch John (889-3788), offers upscale rooms, with A/C and cable TV, for upscale prices (singles $49, doubles $55; Nov.-Feb., singles $33, doubles $39).

Sights and Activities The diversity of activities in the recreation area parallels the diversity of the terrain. Try your hand at **fishing** along the Green River Gorge below the dam. More than ½ million trout are stocked annually in Flaming Gorge Lake. The fish don't have much of a chance, but it does make the amateur fisherman look like a pro. For Green River fishing you must obtain a **permit** (available at Flaming Gorge Lodge and at several stores in Manila). For more information, call the **Utah Department of Wildlife Resources,** 152 E. North (789-3103; open Mon.-Fri. 8am-5pm). You can rent fishing rods and boats at **Cedar Springs Marina** (889-3795), 3 mi. before the dam in Dutch John, and at **Lucerne Valley Marina** (784-3483) in Manila. (Boats $8-23 per hr., 8 hr. and full day rates available. Rod rentals $15 per day. Open April-Aug. daily 7am-10pm.) **Dan River Hatch Expeditions,** 55 E. Main (789-4316 or 800-342-8243), in Vernal, offers a wide variety of summer rafting trips (1-day voyage $55, under 12 $45).

For a hide-out from tourists, the large valley of **Brown's Park,** 23 mi. east of Flaming Gorge, is the answer. The road is not kind to most vehicles; a four-wheel drive is recommended. The valley's incredible isolation was a magnet for 19th century western outlaws—Butch Cassidy and his Wild Bunch found it ideally located near 3 state lines for evading the local arm of the law. Free, primitive campsites (no water) are located within ¼ mi. of the park in either direction: **Indian Crossing,** just up the Green River, and **Indian Hollow,** just downstream. The river's shore is an idyllic place to camp or just stop for a while. To get to Brown's Park from Dutch John, head north about 10 mi. on U.S. 191 until you reach Minnie's Gap, from here follow the signs to Clay Basin (13 mi.) and to the park (23 mi.).

■■■ VERNAL

Vernal, 16 mi. west of Dinosaur National Monument on U.S. 40, is a popular base for exploring the attractions Flaming Gorge and the Uinta Mountains.

Practical Information Stop in at the **Visitors Center** at the Utah Fieldhouse of Natural History and Dinosaur Garden, 235 W. Main St. (789-3799), which offers brochures and helpful advice on day trips in the area (open Mon.-Sun. 8am-9pm). The **Chamber of Commerce,** 134 W. Main St. (789-1352), can also provide you with brochures and suggestions (open Mon.-Fri. 8am-5pm). The **Ashley National Forest Service,** 355 N. Vernal Ave. (789-1181), has jurisdiction over much of this area, including most public campgrounds.

Accommodations, Camping, and Food The **Sage Motel,** 54 W. Main St. (789-1442), one block from the Greyhound station, has big, clean rooms and cable TV. (Singles $32. Doubles $39.) **Dine-A-Ville Motel,** 801 W. Main St. (789-9571), at the far west end of town, is less centrally located, but the cheapest in town. Nice rooms with color TV and kitchenettes. (Singles $20. Doubles $25.)

Camping might be a better alternative for those on a tight budget. **Vernal KOA,** 1800 W. Sheraton Ave. (789-8935), off U.S. 40 south of town, has a store, laundry, pool, and all the amenities of the typical KOA. (Tent sites $12, with water and electricity $13.) **Campground Dina RV Park,** 930 N. Vernal Ave., about 1 mi. north of Main St. on U.S. 191 (789-2148), is more basic. (Tent sites about $6 per person, with water and electricity $15.50, full hookup $16.50.)

Make sure to stop by the **Open Hearth Donut Shop,** 360 E. Main St. (789-0274), for a homemade donut (37¢ each, $3.70 per dozen) or a large sub sandwich ($2.75). (Open Mon.-Fri. 5:30am-6pm, Sat. 5:30am-1pm.) The **7-11 Ranch Restaurant,** 77 E. Main St. (789-1170), serves good food in a western setting, including a big breakfast consisting of 2 eggs, hashbrowns, and toast ($2.50) and entrees with salad, vegetable, and bread from $6.

Sights and Activities In town, the **Utah Fieldhouse of Natural History and Dinosaur Garden,** 235 Main St. (789-3799), offers excellent displays on the state's geological and natural history. The dinosaur garden features life-size models. Check out the geological displays where fluorescent minerals make your shoelaces glow in the dark. (Open daily 8am-9pm; off season daily 9am-5pm. $1.50, ages 6-15 $1.)

SOUTHERN UTAH

The region of Utah east of I-15 and south of the Tavaputs Plateau (between U.S. 40 and I-70) is known to geologists as the Colorado Plateau Province, a fantastic terrain of sandstone arches, abyssal canyons, spiny, mountainous ridges, and mesas. Hot and dry for the most part, this infernal landscape inspired early settlers to place names such as Dead Horse Point, Desolation Canyon, and Phipps Death Hollow. Modern travelers should not be put off by these ominous appellations; the raw natural beauty of southern Utah cannot be missed.

■■■ ARCHES NATIONAL PARK

In Arches National Park, nature has experimented with modern sculpture for eons. Three hundred million years ago, a constantly moving primordial sea deposited an uneven, unstable salt bed on the Colorado Plateau. The sea evaporated, but periodic washes, along with the tireless winds, deposited layer after layer of debris upon the new salt crust. This detritus compacted into extremely heavy rock, and the salt twisted and crumbled under the weight. Through buckling and caving below and erosion above, the sandstone layers were shaped into fantastic spires, pinnacles, and, of course, arches. Arches National Park has more than 200 arches; because of their nearly perfect form, explorers first thought the huge arches were the works of some lost civilization.

Practical Information The entrance to the park is a paved road that winds for 25 mi. into its interior. This road is accessible from U.S. 191 at the junction 5 mi. north of Moab. There is no public transportation to Arches, but buses run along I-70, stopping in Crescent Junction. The park **visitors center,** 27 mi. on U.S. 191 south of I-70, 3½ mi. north of Moab, provides $2 self-guided car tours (open daily 8am-7pm; off-season daily 8am-4:30pm). An **entrance pass** ($4 per carload) remains valid for seven days; pedestrians and bikers pay only $2. Water is available in the park. For more information, write to **Superintendent,** Arches National Park, P.O. Box 907, Moab, UT 84532 (801-259-8161).

Camping The park's only campground, **Devil's Garden,** has 53 sites; get there early since sites are often snatched up by noon. The campground is 18 mi. from the visitors center and has running water April-Oct. (No wood-gathering allowed. 2-week max. stay. Sites $7. No reservations.) **Dead Horse Point State Park** ($3), perched on the rim of the Colorado Gorge south of Arches and 14 mi. south of U.S. 191, is accessible from Rte. 313. The campground has modern restrooms, water, electric hookups, and covered picnic tables. (Sites $8. Open April-Oct.) Winter camping is allowed on Dead Horse Point itself. For more info, contact the Park Superintendent, Dead Horse Point State Park, P.O. Box 609, Moab 84532 (259-2614 or 800-322-3770; Mon.-Fri. 8am-5pm).

Backcountry camping in Arches is a free adventure. Register at the National Park Service office in Moab (2 blocks west of the Ramada Inn on Main St.) first, and pick up a USGS map to avoid getting lost. Bring plenty of water and bug spray, and avoid hiking on summer afternoons. In the summer, escape the heat, crowds, and biting gnats at the **Manti-La Sal National Forest**. Campgrounds here are about 4000 ft. higher up and 20-25 mi. southeast of Moab off U.S. 191. All cost $6-8, except **Oowah,** which is free. Three mi. down a dirt road is **Oowah Lake,** a rainbow trout heaven, at least from an angler's point of view (fishing permit $5 per day). For more information on the forest, contact the Manti-La Sal National Forest Service office in Moab, 125 W. 200 South (259-7155; open Mon.-Fri. 8am-4:30pm).

Sights and Activities Plenty of scenic wonders embellish the 25-mi. road between the visitors center and Devil's Garden. No matter how short your stay, be sure to see the **Windows** section at **Panorama Point,** about halfway along the road. Cyclists will enjoy this ride in spring or fall, but the steep inclines make the trip almost unbearable in the summer heat. **Rim Cyclery,** 94 W. 100 North (259-5333), offers rimming bikes for $20 per day, including helmet and water bottle (open daily 9am-6pm). At the end of the paved road, **Devil's Garden** boasts an astounding 64 arches. A challenging hike from the **Landscape Arch** leads across harrowing exposures to the secluded **Double O Arch.** The climax of your visit should be **Delicate Arch,** the symbol of the monument. Take the Delicate Arch turn-off from the main road, 2 mi. down a graded unpaved road (impassable after rainstorms). Once you reach Wolfe Ranch, go down a 1½-mi. foot trail to the free-standing Delicate Arch. Beyond, you can get a glimpse of the Colorado River gorge and the La Sal Mountains. If you're lucky, you may come across petroglyphs on the stone walls left by the Anasazi and Ute who wandered the area 1000 to 100 years ago.

Of course, arches aren't the only natural wonders here. Two of the most popular trails, the 1-mi. **Park Avenue** and the moderately strenuous 2-mi. **Fiery Furnace Trail,** lead downward into the canyon bottoms, providing views of the cliffs and monoliths above. Only experienced hikers should attempt the Fiery Furnace Trail alone; a ranger leads group tours into this labyrinth at both 10am and 4pm daily. Make reservations 48 hrs. in advance.

■■■ BRYCE CANYON NATIONAL PARK

The fragile, slender spires of pink and red limestone that rise gracefully out of Bryce's canyons often seem more like the subjects of a surrealist painting than the result of whimsical wind and water currents. Beautiful as they may be, these barren canyons etched by millennia of erosion made life extremely difficult for both the Paiute and the white settlers who had to navigate the area. Ebenezer Bryce, the first white man to glimpse the canyon, called it "one hell of a place to lose a cow."

Practical Information Bryce Canyon lies 45 minutes east of Cedar City on U.S. 89 in southwestern Utah. From U.S. 89 at Bryce Junction (7 mi. south of Panguitch), turn east on Rte. 12 and drive 17 mi. to the park entrance (entrance fee $5 per car, $2 per pedestrian). There is no public transportation within the park or from Cedar City; this is *not* the place to get stranded. Bryce has a **post office** at Ruby's Inn (open Mon.-Fri. 8:15am-2:15pm, Sat. 8:15am-12:15pm). The **ZIP code** is 84764. The 24-hr. park **emergency** number is 801-676-2411. You can call collect.

The park's **visitors center** (801-834-5322) is the place to begin any tour. Pick up a copy of the free Bryce Canyon *HooDoo,* listing all park services, events, suggested hikes, and sight-seeing drives. (Open daily 8am-8pm; off-season daily 8am-4:30pm.)

Hiking and Camping, etc. Many designated hikes let you explore Bryce without guessing. The most popular scenery is concentrated within 2 mi. of the visitors center. Three spectacular lookouts—**Sunrise Point, Sunset Point,** and **Inspiration Point**—invigorate even the weariest traveler. Sunrises here are particularly rewarding. The section between Sunrise and Sunset Points is wheelchair-accessible. The 3-mi. loop of the **Navajo** and **Queen's Garden** trails wind you into the canyon itself. If you are up to the challenge, branch off onto the **Peek-A-Boo Trail,** a 4-mi. round-trip. Escape the crowds by conquering the **Trail to the Hat Shop,** a strenuous 4-mi. journey on an extremely steep descent. And if you think climbing *down* is tough...

If you don't want to hike, drive the 15 mi. from the visitors center to **Rainbow Point** and stop at the various lookouts along the way. Or take the **1938 Limousine Tour** that departs from Bryce Lodge. If you prefer organic transportation, arrange a horseback tour through **Bryce-Zion-Grand Trail Rides,** Box 58, Tropic, UT 84776 (801-834-5219, off-season 801-679-8665).

Bryce has two campgrounds planted among the tall ponderosa pines: **North Campground** and **Sunset Campground.** Both have toilets, picnic tables, and drinking water. (Sites at both $7.) **Sunrise Point** (834-5361), west of both campgrounds, has public showers and a small grocery store. (Open May-Oct. 7am-9pm. Showers $1.75 per 10 min., available 7am-10pm.) **Bryce Lodge,** open April-Oct., is very expensive ($65 for singles and doubles—heck, might as well get a double), but may be a good deal for a group of 4 ($75) or 5 ($80). **Backcountry camping** at designated sites is a lovely way to get intimate with the canyon's changing moods and wildlife. A free permit is required and available at the **Nature Center** by **Sunrise Point** (open 9am-5pm). Of the six **Dixie National Forest** campgrounds, most roughly an hour away off Rte. 14, the best are **TE-AH Campground, Spruces Campground,** and **Navajo Lake Campground.** All except Navajo Lake have toilets; all have running water, swimming, boating, and fishing. (All $7 per night; no showers.) The nearest forest service office is in **Panguitch,** 225 E. Center St. (676-8815; open Mon.-Fri. 8am-4:30pm).

From Memorial Day to Labor Day, **Ruby's Inn Rodeo** (834-5341) pits human against beast every night except Sunday at 7:30pm ($6, kids $3). Another popular annual event, the **Fiddler's Association Contest,** tunes up in early July.

■ Near Bryce

East of Bryce To hike into the desert environment of the ominously named **Phipps Death Hollow Outstanding Natural Area,** part of a network of sandstone canyons just north of **Escalante,** contact the **Bureau of Land Management,** Escalante Ranger District, Escalante 84726 (826-4291), on Rte. 12, about 1 mi. west of town (open Mon.-Fri. 7:45am-4:30pm, Sat. 8am-noon; off-season Mon.-Fri. 8am-4:30pm). Fifteen mi. east of Escalante on Rte. 12 is the popular **Calf Creek** camping grounds, with a great hike near a cascading waterfall. (Sites $5, including drinking water and fresh toilets.) **Boulder** has the **Anasazi Museum** off Rte. 12 (335-7308), which displays a reconstructed Anasazi village dating from about 1100 (open daily 8am-6pm). The Anasazi ("ancient ones") disappeared almost completely around 1250. The style of basket-weaving among present-day Hopis indicates a connection to the Anasazi, whom anthropologists think mostly left the area to assimilate with other tribes during a 23-year drought around 1200. If you don't mind dodging cows and driving on dirt roads, head out 3 mi. to **Lower Bowns Reservoir Lake** (826-4221; no drinking water, pit toilets).

West of Bryce Wandering out of Bryce in the opposite direction, on Rte. 14 to Cedar City, you'll come across the refreshing and surprisingly green **Cedar Breaks National Monument** ($4 per car, $2 per pedestrian). The rim of this giant amphitheater is a lofty 10,350 ft. above sea level; 2000 ft. of flowered slopes separate the rim from the chiseled depths. At **Point Supreme** you'll find a 30-site **campground** (sites $6) and the **visitors center** (586-9451; open summer Mon.-Thurs. 8am-6pm, Fri.-Sat. 8am-7pm). For more information, contact the Superintendent, Cedar Breaks National Monument, P.O. Box 749, Cedar City 84720.

Cedar City's **Iron Mission State Park,** 585 N. Main St. (586-9290), has an amazing horse-drawn vehicle collection which merits a visit (open daily 9am-7pm; off-season daily 9am-5pm; $1.50, ages 5-10 $1). The **Economy Motel,** 443 S. Main St. (586-4461), has very basic rooms; try to get one with a book-sized window. (Singles $30. Doubles $35.) For more information, contact the **Cedar City Visitors Center,** 100 E. Center St. (586-4484; open Mon.-Fri. 8am-5pm).

■■■ CANYONLANDS NATIONAL PARK

The grooved and gnarled landscape of Utah is largely indebted to the constant chiseling of the Green and Colorado Rivers. It is at Canyonlands National Park that these two arch-landscapers combine forces. The merging rivers here have gouged out rifts and gorges that sink into the desert's crust with a dizzying declivity. Harsh desert prevails in the rest of the park, producing a unique desert environment. Largely neglected by the family-with-a-Winnebago tourist throngs, this area is a diamond in the rough.

Practical Information Outside the park, there are two visitors centers. Monticello's **Interagency Visitors Center,** 32 S. 1st E. (587-3235), sells area maps ($3-6). (Open Mon.-Fri. 8am-4:30pm) In **Moab,** the **Park Service** resides at 125 W. 200 S. (259-7164) and has the same business hours. Both can provide information in French, Spanish, German, and Italian. The park entrance fee is $4 per car, $2 per hiker or cyclist. There is neither gas nor water available within the park.

The park contains three distinct areas. **Needles** (259-2652) lies in the park's southeast corner. To get there, take Rte. 211 west from U.S. 191, about 40 mi. south of Moab. Farther north, **Island in the Sky** (259-4351) sits deep within the "Y" formed by the two rivers. Take Rte. 313 west from U.S. 191 about 10 mi. north of Moab. The most remote district of the park is the rugged **Maze** area (visitors center 259-2652; open daily 8am-4:30pm), to the west of the canyons, accessible only by four-wheel drive. Once you've entered a section of the park, you're committed to it—unless you're flying a helicopter, transferring from one area to another involves retracing your steps and re-entering the park, a tedious trip lasting from several hours to a full day.

There are no food services in the park. Just outside the boundary in the Needles district, however, the **Needles Outpost** houses a limited, expensive grocery store and gas pumps. Hauling groceries, water, and first-aid supplies in from Moab or Monticello is the best budget alternative.

Hiking and Camping Each visitors center has a booklet of possible hikes (including photos), so you can pick your own. Hiking options from the Needles area are probably the best, though Island in the Sky offers some spectacular views. Cyclists should check at the visitors centers for lists of trails. If hiking in desert heat doesn't appeal to you, you can rent jeeps and mountain bikes in Moab, or take a one-hr. airplane flight from **Red Tail Aviation** (259-7421) that can cost as little as $45 per person for a group of four.

Each region has its own official **campground.** In the Needles district, **Squaw Flat** is situated in a sandy plain surrounded by giant sandstone towers, 35 mi. west of U.S. 191 on Rte. 211. Avoid this area in June, when insects swarm. Bring fuel and water, although the latter is usually available from April-Sept. A $7 fee is charged year-round. **Willow Flat Campground,** in the Island in the Sky unit, sits high atop the mesa, on Rte. 313, 41 mi. west off U.S. 191. You must bring your own water; sites are free. Willow Flat and Squaw Flat both have picnic tables, grills, and pit toilets; they operate on a first-come, first-served basis. The campground at the **Maze Overlook** has no amenities at all. Dead Horse Point State Park (adjacent to Island in the Sky) and Manti-la-Sal National Forest (adjacent to the Needles) provide alternative campsites. (See Arches National Park for information on these campgrounds.) Before **backcountry camping,** get a free permit from the visitors center in the proper district and take along bug spray and plenty of water (at least 1 gallon per person per day). Summer temperatures regularly climb to over 100°F.

■■■ CAPITOL REEF NATIONAL PARK

Spiny and forbidding, like the backbone of an immense prehistoric sea creature, Capitol Reef's Waterpocket Fold dominates the terrain of south-central Utah. This 100-mi. line of sheer cliffs bisects the state's southern region and was originally called a "reef" not for its oceanic origins, but because it posed a barrier to travel. To the west lie Zion and Bryce Canyon; to the east lie Arches and Canyonlands. Major bus lines don't serve the park itself.

You'll want to make at least a brief stop at the park's **visitors center** (801-425-3791), on Rte. 24, for info on the Capitol Reef and daily activities (open daily 8am-7pm, Sept.-May daily 8am-4:30pm). The center sells waterproof topographic maps ($8), regular maps ($2.50-8), and guides to specific trails (prices vary). The 25-mi. round-trip **scenic drive** is the best way to see the park by car; the 90-min. jaunt takes you out along the reef itself. Nearby **Capitol Dome,** which resembles the U.S. Capitol, explains the other half of the park's unusual name. If you have a few days to spare, explore the park's desert backcountry. Foot trails and rough roads crisscross the region, giving access to the area's most inspiring, remote scenery. Keep in mind that summer temperatures average 95° F, and most water found in seep springs and rain-holding water pockets is brackish and contaminated. The entrance fee for the park is $3 per vehicle, $1 per hiker, $5 for overnight camping. For more information on the park, contact the **Superintendent,** Capitol Reef National Park, Torrey, UT 84775 (801-425-3791).

For **backcountry camping,** register at the visitors center or at the campsites. There are three campgrounds available on a first-come, first-served basis. The main campground in **Fruita** has drinking water and toilets. Its 73 sites are located 1.3 mi. south off Rte. 24 ($6). **Cedar Mesa Campground** in the north end of the park and **Cathedral Valley** in the south both have only five sites and neither has water or a paved road, but they *are* free. In Fruita, for a market-based fee, you can pick your own fruit from the nearby orchards (cherries, apples, apricots, peaches, and pears).

For accommodations in the region, try: **Torrey,** 11 mi. west of the visitors center on Rte. 24; **Escalante,** 65 mi. south of the visitors center on Rte. 12; or **Hanksville,** 37 mi. from the visitors center on Rte. 24. The **Redrock Restaurant and Campground** (542-3235), in Hanksville, is the main tourist service in the region. Cheeseburgers are $2.15, the daily special $4.75. (Open daily 7am-10pm.) Tent sites at the campground are $8 with electricity and water, with full hookup $12. For couples, there's **Joy's Bed and Breakfast,** 296 South Center (801-542-3252 or 542-3235), in Hanksville. Room and bath begin at $35 for two.

■■■ MOAB

Dubbed "the mountain bike capital of the Known Universe," Moab's tongue-in-cheek sobriquet nevertheless evokes its dual populace—the hippie, Birkenstocked group whose universe is forever groovy, and the die-hard athletes who've hardly let the snow melt from their ski boots before they go white-water rafting or mountain biking. With its proximity to Arches and Canyonlands, and its youthful, crunchy character, the town of Moab provides a great base for exploring the region, either by car, mountain bike, or raft on the Green River.

Practical Information Moab is 50 mi. southeast of I-70 on U.S. 191, 15 mi. south of Arches. There is no public transportation to Moab, although buses will stop along I-70, in Crescent Junction. The **Moab Visitors Center,** 805 N. Main St. (259-8825 or 800-635-6622; open Mon.-Sat. 8am-5pm, Sun. 10am-7pm), can provide information on lodging and dining in Moab. The post office is at 39 S. Main St. (644-2760; open Mon.-Fri. 8:30am-4pm, Sat. 9am-noon); the **ZIP code** is 84532.

Accommodations, Camping, and Activities In summer, Moab fills up fast, especially on weekends; call ahead to guarantee your reservations. The owners of the **Lazy Lizard International Hostel,** 1213 S. U.S. 191 (259-6057), go out of the way to be helpful and will route your trip through Arches or elsewhere. The kitchen, VCR, laundry, and hot tub are at your beck and call. (Bunks $7.75. Singles and doubles $21.80, 3-person room $27. Tepee $5 per person. Showers included for guests; $12 for non-guests.) **The Prospector Lodge,** 186 N. 1st West (259-5145), one block west of Main Street, offers cool, comfy rooms across the street from the local hippie co-op. (Singles $30. Doubles $33.)

Private campgrounds speckle the area around Moab. The **Holiday Haven Mobile Home and RV Park,** 400 West (259-8526), charges $12 per site, $11 with water, $14 with electricity and water, and $16 with full hookup (open March-Oct.). The **Canyonlands Campark,** 555 S. Main St. (259-6848), asks $11.50 per site, $15 for electricity and water, $17 for a full hookup, and $2 per extra person, and has a pool.

Adrift Adventures, 378 N. Main (259-8594 or 800-874-4483), will show you the territory via raft, jeep, mountain bike, or horseback. Any way you choose will cost a pretty penny, but a ½-day rafting trip does the least damage ($28).

■■■ ZION NATIONAL PARK

Some 13 million years ago, the cliffs and canyons of Zion made up the sea floor. That sea has been reduced to the lone, powerful Virgin River, which today carves fingers through the Navajo sandstone. Cut into the Kolob Terrace, the walls of Zion now tower 2400 ft. above the river. In the 1860s, Mormon settlers came to this area and enthusiastically proclaimed they had found the promised land. But Brigham Young thought otherwise and declared to his followers that the place was awfully nice, but "not Zion." The name "not Zion" stuck for years until a new wave of entranced explorers dropped the "not," giving the park its present name.

Practical Information Zion National Park can be reached from I-15, via Rte. 17 (Toqueville exit) or from U.S. 89, via Rte. 9 (at Mount Carmel Junction). The main entrance to the park is in **Springdale,** on Rte. 9, which bounds the park to the south along the Virgin River. **Greyhound** runs along I-15, to the west of the park; ask to be let off, since the park is not a scheduled stop. In St. George (43 mi. southwest of the park on I-15), the bus station is located on 70 W. St. George Blvd. (673-2933), next to the Travelodge. Buses run to: Salt Lake City (2 per day, 6 hr., $54); Provo (5 hr., $45); Los Angeles (6 per day, 15 hr., $57); Las Vegas (4 per day, 2 hr., $22).

The main visitors center in the park, **Zion Canyons Visitors Center** (722-3256), takes up the southeast corner of the park, ½ mi. off Rte. 9. It has an introductory slide program and a small but interesting museum. The **Kolob Canyons Visitors Center** (586-9548) lies in the northwest corner of the park, off I-15. (Both open daily 8am-5pm; off-season daily 8am-4:30pm.) The **park entrance** fee is $5 per car, $2 per pedestrian. Carry water wherever you go in the park. For **emergency assistance,** call 772-3256 during the day, 772-3322 after hours.

Camping and Accommodations The park maintains two campgrounds at the south gate, **South Campground** and **Watchman Campground.** Bathrooms and drinking water are available. (Sites $7; 2-week max. stay. Always open.) **Zion Canyon Campground** (772-3237) has a supermarket, showers and laundry facilities for the weary, hungry and filthy. (Sites $13 for 2 people, full hookup $15. Extra adult $3.50, ages 4-15 50¢. Open 8am-9pm.) The visitors center rangers present campfire programs nightly at 9pm. Conveniences include a grocery store (772-3402; open 8am-8pm) and coin-op laundry just outside the south entrance, about a 10-min. walk from the campgrounds. The park's only other campground is a primitive area at **Lava Point,** accessible from a hiking trail in the mid-section of the park or from the gravel road that turns off Rte. 9 in **Virgin.** You must obtain a free permit from a visitors center for **backcountry camping,** but don't camp within the canyon. Check the backcountry shuttle board in the Zion Canyon Visitors Center for rides into and out of the canyon's rough. Observation Point provides one of the only canyon rim spots where you can pitch a tent. Many backpackers spend a few nights on the 27-mi. **West Rim Trail** (too long for a day hike) or in the Kolob Canyons, where crowds never converge. Zion Campground doesn't take reservations and often fills on holiday and summer weekends; if you don't get in, try one of the six campgrounds in Dixie National Forest (see Bryce Canyon).

If you don't plan to spend the night under the stars, spend it at **O'Toole's,** 980 Zion Park Blvd. (772-3457), in Springdale. Make reservations early; these gorgeous rooms, featuring four-poster beds and stained glass windows, go quickly. Perfect for couples and small families; pluses include a hot tub and a full breakfast. (Rooms for 2 people from $35, $10 per additional person.)

Forty mi. south of Zion in the town of **Kanab** is the **Canyonlands International Youth Hostel,** 143 E. 100th S. (801-644-5554). The hostel offers roomy bunks, and manager Errol offers free coffee and friendly conversation. Feels like home. (Room with private bath and breakfast $9.)

Sights Even if you wisely plan to visit **Kolob Canyon's** backcountry, be sure to make the pilgrimage to **Zion Canyon.** Drive along the 7-mi. dead-end road that follows the floor of the canyon or take the upper canyon tour (summer only; $2.75, kids $1.75). You'll ride through the giant formations of **Sentinel, Mountain of the Sun,** and the overwhelming symbol of Zion, the **Great White Throne.** Short hikes to the base of the cliffs may be made by wheelchair as well as on foot. A challenging trail takes you to **Observation Point,** where steep switchbacks let you explore an impossibly gouged canyon. Another difficult trail (5 mi.) ascends to **Angel's Landing,** a monolith that offers a heart-stopping path along the ridge and an amazing view of the canyon. A great two-mi. hike runs to the Upper Emerald Pool, passing the less spectacular lower and middle pools on the way. For fun without the sweat, rent an inner tube ($3) from the shop across from the Canyon Supermarket, and float down the **Virgin River** near the campgrounds at the southern entrance.

THE PACIFIC NORTHWEST

The drive of "manifest destiny" brought 19th-century pioneers to the Pacific Northwest, some of the most beautiful and awe-inspiring territory in the United States. Lush rainforests, snow-capped peaks, and the deepest lake on the continent all reside in this corner of the country. Oregon's Dunes, Washington's Cascade Mountains, miles and miles of the Pacific Crest Trail, and a long, stormy coast inhabited by sea lions and giant redwoods draw the rugged individualist and the novelty-seeking city-slicker alike.

Settled like jewels amidst the wet and wild lands of the Pacific Northwest, the cities of this region sparkle with all the urban flair of their Northeastern counterparts. But unlike New York, Washington, D.C., or Boston, the cosmopolitan communitiesof Seattle and Portland have spectacular mountain ranges in their backyards. The Northwestern traveler can hike the Cascade Range by day and club-hop by night, ride Seattle's monorail or raft down southern Oregon's wild river rapids.

> For more comprehensive coverage of the Pacific Northwest than can be provided here, please consult *Let's Go: Alaska & The Pacific Northwest.*

 # Oregon

Famed for its fir forests, Oregon and its tall trees have been the wellspring of intrastate conflict in recent years. Rising exports of unmilled logs have deprived the state's lumber mills of business, and the federal government's June 1990 decision to protect the endangered spotted owl—thus prohibiting logging on a full one-third of the state's timberland—has resulted in heavy job loss in the timber industry and much rancor between loggers and the environmentalists who lobbied for the change.

Things were a little more peaceful in Oregon nearly two centuries ago, when the intrepid duo of Meriwether Lewis and William Clark slipped quietly down the Columbia River on the last leg of their transcontinental trek. Later in the 19th century, waves of westward-moving settlers thronged the Oregon Trail. Most modern-day visitors head straight for the Pacific to gape at waves and cliffs which rival California's Big Sur in scenic beauty.

The coastal route is handsome, but you should also venture inland to see some of Oregon's greatest attractions—fabulous Mt. Hood, the volcanic cinder-cones near Crater Lake, and the world-renowned Shakespeare festival in Ashland. To escape the anomie of the countryside, head for Portland, an easy-going metropolis known for its public art, championship-contending basketball team, and tolerance of off-beat lifestyles.

PRACTICAL INFORMATION

Capital: Salem.
Visitor Information: State Tourist Office, 775 Summer St. NE, Salem 97310 (800-547-7842). **Oregon State Parks,** 525 Trade St. SE, Salem 97310 (378-6305). **Department of Fish and Wildlife,** P.O. Box 59, Portland 97207 (229-5403). **Oregon State Marine Board,** 3000 Market St. NE, Salem 97310 (378-8587).
Time Zone: Pacific and Mountain. **Postal Abbreviation:** OR
Sales Tax: None.

■■■ ASHLAND

Before their expropriation by the guardians of high-brow culture, Shakespeare's plays were popular entertainment for 19th-century Americans. Ashland's rural setting on the California border returns the plays to their lost candor each summer with its world-famous Shakespeare festival. Throughout its nine-month season, the festival offers an astonishing number of plays, neatly incorporated into the town itself—Ashland's balmy climate allows for nightly summertime performances in the outdoor Elizabethan theater and a money-back guarantee in case of rain.

The brainchild of local teacher Angus Bowmer, the **Shakespeare Festival** began with plays performed by schoolchildren during a boxing match intermission. Today, professional actors perform four Shakespeare plays and other dramas Feb.-Oct. on the three Ashland stages—the **Agnus Bowmer,** the **Elizabethan Stage,** and the **Black Swan.** Any boxing today is over the scarce tickets.

Due to the tremendous popularity of the productions, buy your tickets one or two months in advance ($7.50-21; for complete ticket information, write Oregon Shakespeare Festival, P.O. Box 158, Ashland 97520, or call 482-4331). From March–May, ½-price rush tickets are often available an hour before every performance that is not sold out. In the summer, almost everything is sold out, and obtaining tickets can be very difficult; arrive at the box office by 9:30am on the day of a show, when any unsold tickets for the day's performances are released. Locals occasionally leave their shoes to hold their place in line; you should respect this tradition.

The **backstage tours,** which leave from the Black Swan at 10am, provide a wonderful glimpse of the festival from behind the curtain. Tour guides divulge all kinds of anecdotes—from bird songs during an outdoor *Hamlet* to the ghastly events which take place when they do "that Scottish play"(2 hrs; $7, kids under 12 $3.50). One of the highlights of the Festival is the **Feast of Will** in mid-June, a celebration honoring the opening of the Elizabethan Theatre. Dinner and merrie madness are held in Lithia Park from 6-6:45pm (tickets $14; call 482-4331 for exact date).

After the show, sleep, perchance to dream, at the **Ashland Hostel (HI/AYH),** 150 N. Main St. (482-9217). The wonderful owner-managers will help you any way they can, from tracking down theater tickets to suggesting activities on days when tickets aren't available. ($11, non-members $13. Check-in 5pm-midnight. Lock-out 10am-5pm. Reservations advised.) Or enjoy a mid-summer night's dream under the stars at **Jackson Hot Springs,** 2253 Rte. 99 N (482-3776), off exit 19 from I-5, down Valley View Rd. to Rte. 99 N about ½ mi., the campground nearest to downtown, with laundry facilities, hot showers, and mineral baths (sites $10, with hookups $14; baths $4 per hr.).

■■■ CRATER LAKE NATIONAL PARK

Mirror-blue Crater Lake, Oregon's only national park, was regarded as sacred by Indian shamans who forbade their people to view it. The placid surface of the lake rests at an frigid and translumined 6000 ft. above sea level. Iceless in winter and flawlessly circular, it plunges to a depth of nearly 2000 ft., making it the nation's deepest lake.

Practical Information The **William G. Steel Center,** on Rim Drive next to the Park Headquarters, provides information and free backcountry camping permits (open June 1-July 1 and Labor Day-Sept. 30 10am-6pm, July 1-Labor Day 8am-7pm).

To get to the park from Portland, take I-5 to Eugene, then Rte. 58 east to U.S. 97 south. Travel south on 97 for 18 mi. and then head west on Rte. 138. **Rte. 62** cuts through Crater Lake National Park's southwest corner and then heads southwest to **Medford** or southeast to **Klamath Falls.** Klamath Falls, the nearest town of any size, lies 24 mi. south of the Rte. 62/U.S. 97 intersection. Call the Steel Center for road

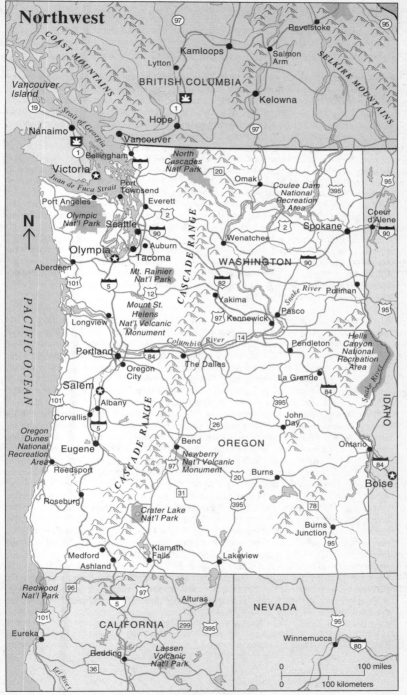

Northwest

conditions during winter, as Crater Lake averages several feet of snow per year. **Greyhound** trucks out of Klamath from 1200 Klamath Ave. (882-4616; open Mon.-Fri. 6am-5pm, Sat. 6am-4pm), with one bus daily north to Bend, OR and two daily south to Redding, CA. Park admission is charged only in summer ($5 per car, $3 for hikers and bikers, seniors free).

Accommodations and Food Klamath Falls sports several affordable camp-sites. Some of the best free sites are National Forest Service primitive campgrounds on the **Rogue River** off Rte. 62. (Pit toilets, fire pits, no water—fetch it from the river.) There are *no* campsites on the lake itself. Those who wish to camp within the park can either pick up free **backcountry camping** permits at the Steel Center, or stake out a tent-space at the small **Lost Creek Campground** (594-2111), with 16 sites for tents only, drinking water and pit toilets (sites $5, open mid-July-Sept.; no reservations) or the **Mazama Campground** (594-2111) with 200 sites (toilets, pay laundry and showers, and plenty of RVs but no hookups; sites $11). In Klamath Falls, try the **Value 20 Motel**, 124 N. 2nd St. (882-7741), which has very clean, spa-cious rooms equipped with kitchenettes, HBO, and A/C—and allows pets (singles $31, doubles $33). The **Fort Klamath Lodge Motel** (381-2234), on Rte. 62, is 6 mi. from the Park. The closest motel to the lake, it offers cozy rooms with knotted-pine walls, a friendly manager, and TV. (Singles $30. Doubles $35.)

Eating inexpensively in the Crater Lake area is difficult. Buying food—for instance, at the **Old Fort Store** (381-2345; open summer 8am-9pm) in **Fort Kla-math**—and cooking it yourself is the best option. In Klamath Falls you can purchase foodstuffs at the 24-hr. **Safeway**, at Pine and 8th St. (882-2660), or try **Hobo Junction,** 636 Main St. (882-8013) at 7th St., for good deli fare with hearty bowls of chili ($1.65) and 22 varieties of hot dogs.

Sights As you approach **Crater Lake,** you won't see anything remarkable. It's just a lake; it could be any lake. The sky and mountains are initially what capture your attention. As you ascend, however, the lake's reflected blue becomes almost unreal in its placidity. The fantastic depth (1932 ft.) of the lake, combined with the fact that it is a closed system, creates its amazingly serene, and intensely blue, effect. 7700 years ago, Mt. Mazama birthed this pacificity by means of one of the Earth's most destructive cataclysms. A massive eruption buried thousands of square miles under a deep layer of ash and left the massive crater now filled with still waters.

Rim Drive, open only in summer, is a 33-mi. route high above the lake. Points along the drive offer views and trailheads for hiking. Among the most spectacular are **Discovery Point Trail,** from which the first pioneer saw the lake in 1853 (1¼ mi. one way), **Garfield Peak Trail** (1¾ mi. one way), and **Watchman Lookout** (¾ mi. one way). The hike up **Mt. Scott,** the park's highest peak (just a tad under 9000 ft.), begins from the drive near the lake's eastern edge. Although steep, the 2½-mi. trail to the top gives the persevering hiker a unique view of the lake that justifies the sweaty ascent. Steep **Cleetwood Trail,** a 1-mi. switchback, is the only route to the lake's edge. From here, the **Lodge Company** (594-2511) offers boat tours on the lake (July-Sept. 9 tours per day 10am-4:30pm; $10, under 12 $5.50). Both **Wizard Island,** a cinder cone 760 ft. above lake level, and **Phantom Ship Rock** are fragile, tiny specks when viewed from above, yet they are surprisingly large when viewed from the surface of the water. Picnics and fishing are allowed, as is swimming—but surface temperature reaches a maximum of only 50°F. Park rangers lead free walk-ing tours daily in the summer and periodically during the winter (on snowshoes). Call the visitors center (524-2211) at Rim Village for schedules. If pressed for time, walk the easy 100 yd. from the visitors center down to the **Sinnott Memorial Overlook**—the view is the area's most panoramic and accessible. Rangers give short lectures on the area's history and geology at Rim Village.

OREGON COAST

The dark waves of the Pacific pound Oregon's rocky western coast with all the stubbornness of a miner picking for gold. Whatever treasures the ocean may horde are kept well-guarded, since the icy-cold and often dangerous coastal waters invite only the most intrepid for a snorkel or a swim. Most visitors are satisfied to wander along the huge stretches of unspoiled beach and observe the ocean's more comfortable inhabitants—the seals, sea lions, and waterfowl which reside just offshore.

The renowned coastal highway **U.S. 101** hangs close to the shore, from time to time gaining altitude and opening up to a number of lofty viewpoints. From Astoria in the north to Brookings in the south, the highway laces together the resorts and fishing villages that cluster around the mouths of rivers feeding into the Pacific. Its most breathtaking stretch lies between the coastal towns, where hundreds of miles of state and national parks allow direct access to the beach. Wherever the highway leaves the coast, look for a beach loop road—these quiet byways afford some of the finest scenery on the western seaboard.

For the most rewarding encounter with the coast, travel by car or bike. For those without, transportation becomes a bit tricky. **Greyhound** offers only two coastal runs from Portland per day; one of those takes place under cover of night, when the coast's beautiful scenery is hidden. Gasoline and grocery prices on the coast are about 20% higher than in the inland cities. Motorists should try to stock up and fill up before reaching the coastal highways.

■■■ REEDSPORT AND THE DUNES

For 50 mi. between Florence and Coos Bay, the beach widens to form the **Oregon Dunes National Recreation Area.** Shifting hills of sand rise to 500 ft. and extend up to 3 mi. inland (often to the shoulder of U.S. 101), clogging mountain streams and forming numerous small lakes. The dunes, created by glaciation 15,000 years ago, are maintained by a constant, unidirectional wind from the sea. Hiking trails wind around the lakes, through the coastal forests, and up the dunes themselves. In many places, no grasses or shrubs grow, and the vista holds only bare sand and sky.

Practical Information The dunes' shifting grip of the coastline is broken only once along the expanse when the Umpqua and Smith Rivers empty into Winchester Bay about 20 mi. south of Florence. **Reedsport** (pop. 5000) is a typical highway town of motels, banks, and fast food places, neatly subdivided by U.S. 101 and Rte. 38, which connects with I-5 60 mi. to the east. You can also avoid the huge stretches of pavement in Reedsport by passing through and heading for **Winchester Bay,** just 4 mi. south of Reedsport.

Campgrounds fill up early with dune buggy and motorcycle junkies, especially on summer weekends. The **National Recreation Area Headquarters,** 855 U.S. 101 (271-3611), Reedsport, just south of the Umpqua River Bridge, in Reedsport can tell you just how many decibels a dune-buggy engine puts out (too many). They will also provide trail maps needed for serene escape. (Open Mon.-Fri. 9:30am-6pm, Sat. 9am-5pm, Sun. noon-4pm. Labor Day-Memorial Day Mon.-Fri. 8am-4:30pm. Memorial Day-June 15 Mon.-Fri. 8am-4:30pm, Sat. 9am-5pm, Sun. noon-4pm.) **Greyhound** idles at 2207 Winchester Ave., Reedsport (271-5223; open Mon.-Fri. 5am-10pm, Sat.-Sun. 7am-10pm), at the 22nd St. Market. To: Portland (2 per day, $22.50); San Francisco (2 per day, $117). Call 911 in an **emergency.** The **post office** mails at 301 Fir St. (271-2521; open Mon.-Fri. 8:30am-5pm); the **ZIP code** is 97467.

Accommodations, Camping, and Food The more secluded motels in Winchester Bay are no more expensive than those in Reedsport and all are within a few blocks of the water. The **Harbor View Motel** (271-3352), Beach Blvd., has clean, comfortable rooms that are popular with anglers (singles $25; doubles $29; $4 less in off-season). Despite being on the highway, the **Salmon Harbor Motel** (271-2732), on U.S. 101 at the northernmost point of Winchester Bay, is quite pleasant (singles from $30; doubles from $33.50, with kitchens $37.50).

The Forest Service's pamphlet *Campgrounds in the Siuslaw National Forest* covers campgrounds in the dunes and in the National Forest. The sites closest to Reedsport are in Winchester Bay. The campgrounds that allow dune buggy access—**Spinreel, Lagoon, Waxmyrtle, Driftwood II, Horsfall,** and **Bluebill**—are generally loud and rowdy in the summer. Call 800-283-2267 for more information. **Umpqua Lighthouse State Park** (271-3546), 5 mi. south of Reedsport on U.S. 101, with hot showers, boat launch, hiker/biker sites ($2). Nearby **Lake Marie** is cold but swimmable with a beach to boot (sites $12, with hookup $14). A National Forest Service campground with no luxuries and no trace of commercialism, **Noel Ranch,** 8 mi. down Rte. 38 at Noel Creek off U.S. 101, just north of Reedsport, offers free respite from screaming children and dune buggies. **Windy Cove Campground** (271-5634), adjacent to Salmon Harbor in Winchester Bay, is a county park with a foghorn that will keep you company all night long—and its 75 sites are accompanied by drinking water, hot showers, flush toilets, and beach access (sites $8.40, with hookup $10.50).

Winchester Bay wins the contest with Reedsport for culinary charm and originality. Restauranteurs pride themselves on their seafood, especially salmon. Try the **Seven Seas Cafe** (271-4381), Dock A, Winchester Bay at the end of Broadway at 4th St., a small diner crowded with marine memorabilia and navigational charts. The seafood comes in huge helpings at low prices. (Open daily 7am-9pm.)

Outdoors Romp in the dunes—why else are you here? Those with little time or low sand-tolerance should at least stop at the **Oregon Dunes Overlook,** off of U.S. 101 about halfway between Reedsport and Florence. Steep wooden ramps lead to the gold and blue swells of the dunes and the Pacific. Trails wander off from the overlook, as they do at several other points on U.S. 101.

For dune encounters of a closer kind, venture out on wheels. **Oregon Dunes Tours** (759-4777) on Wildwood Dr., 10 mi. south of Reedsport off U.S. 101, gives dune-buggy rides (½ hr. $18, 1 hr. $30; open daily 9am-6pm). The buggy rides are more fun than the tacky base camp would suggest, and the drivers have lots of good stories. If you really want to tear up the dunes, shell out $30 for an hour on your own dune buggy. Rent from **Dunes Odyssey,** on U.S. 101 in Winchester Bay (271-4011; open Mon.-Sat. 8am-5:30pm, Sun. 9am-5:30pm), or **Spinreel Park,** Wildwood Dr., 8 mi. south on U.S. 101 (759-3313; open daily 9am-6pm).

Inside **Umpqua Lighthouse State Park,** 6 mi. south of Reedsport, the Douglas County Park Department operates the **Coastal Visitor Center** (271-4631), in the old Coast Guard administration building, which has exhibits on the shipping and timber industries at the turn of the century (open May-Sept. Wed.-Sat. 10am-5pm, Sun. 1-5pm; free). **Bird watching** and **whale watching** are also popular diversions.

■■■ PORTLAND

Back in the 1970s, local tavern-owner "Bud" Clark posed for a popular poster entitled "Expose Yourself to Art," depicting a man in a trenchcoat flashing a public sculpture. Shortly thereafter, he was elected mayor of Portland. Casual and idiosyncratic, Portland is the quietest big city on a crowded West Coast. Its name was decided by the toss of a coin—one more turn and Oregon's largest metropolis would have been called "Boston, Oregon."

Funded by a one-percent tax on new construction, Portland has fostered a growing body of outdoor sculpture and outdoor jazz concerts. Any number of improvisational theaters are in constant production, and the Center for the Performing Arts now lures actors from the renowned Shakespeare Festival in Ashland. This varied artistic scene is anchored by Portland's venerable Symphony Orchestra—the oldest in the U.S. And, knowing that good beverages are essential to the full enjoyment of any highbrow affair, the city's fine flock of small breweries pump out barrels of some of the nation's finest ale.

PRACTICAL INFORMATION

Visitors Information: Portland/Oregon Visitors Association, 26 SW Salmon St. (222-2223 or 275-9750), at Front St. Distributes extensive information on the city and surrounding area. The free *Portland Book* contains maps, general information, and historical trivia. Open Mon.-Fri. 9am-5pm, Sat. 9am-3pm. Detailed city road maps are free at **Hertz,** 1009 SW 6th (249-5727), at Salmon. Open Mon.-Fri. 7am-6:30pm, Sat. 8am-4pm.

Airport: Portland International Airport, north of the city on the banks of the Columbia. To get downtown, take Tri-Met bus #12, which will arrive on SW 5th Ave. (fare 90¢). **Raz Tranz** (recorded info 246-4676) provides a shuttle ($6) that leaves every 30 min. to major downtown hotels and the Greyhound station.

Amtrak: 800 NW 6th Ave. (800-872-7245 or 273-4865), at Hoyt St. To: Seattle (3 per day, $23); Eugene (1 per day, $24). Not in the best neighborhood. Open daily 7:30am-6pm.

Buses: Greyhound, 550 NW 6th Ave. (800-231-2222). Buses every 1½ hr. to Seattle ($18). To: Eugene (8 per day, $16). Ticket window open daily 5:30am-12:30am. Station open 24 hrs. **Green Tortoise** (for reservations call 225-0310). Pick-up point 616 SW College Ave. at 6th Ave. To: Seattle (3 per week; Sept.-June 2 per week; $15) and San Francisco (4 per week; Sept.-June 2 per week; $59).

Public Transportation: Tri-Met, Customer Service Center, #1 Pioneer Courthouse Sq., 701 SW 6th Ave. (238-7433; open Mon.-Fri. 7:30am-5:30pm). 24-hr. recorded information numbers for: fare information (231-3198); updates and changes (231-3197); special needs transportation (238-3511, Mon.-Fri. 7:30am-5:30pm). Service generally 5am-midnight, reduced Sat.-Sun. Fare 95¢-$1.25, ages 7-18 70¢. **MAX** is Tri-Met's "light rail." It only serves one line (from downtown east to Gresham, near Mt. Hood) but uses the same fare system as the buses. Buses and MAX are free within **"Fareless Square,"** a 300-square-block region downtown bounded by the Willamette River, NW Hoyt, and I-405.

Taxi: Broadway Cab, 227-1234. **New Rose City Cab Co.,** 282-7707. From airport to downtown $21-24. From airport to hostel $17. Both 24 hrs.

Car Rental: Practical Rent-A-Car, 1315 NE Sandy Blvd. (224-8110). $24 per day, 100 free mi., 15¢ per additional mi. Must be 21 with credit card or $300 deposit.

Help Lines: Crisis Line (223-6161). **General/Rape Hotline** (235-5333). Both 24 hrs. **Phoenix Rising,** 620 SW 5th #710 (223-8299). Counseling and referral for gay men and lesbians. Open Mon.-Fri. 9am-5pm.

Post Office: 715 NW Hoyt St. (294-2300). Open Mon.-Sat. 8:30am-5pm. **ZIP code:** 97208.

Portland is tucked into the Northwest corner of Oregon, just south of the Columbia River and about 75 mi. inland from the coast. The city is 637 mi. north of San Francisco and 172 mi. south of Seattle. East of the city, I-84 (U.S. 30) follows the route of the Oregon Trail through the Columbia River Gorge. West of Portland, U.S. 30 follows the Columbia downstream to Astoria. I-405 curves around the west side of the business district to link I-5 with U.S. 30.

Portland can be divided into five districts. **Burnside Street** divides the city into north and south, while east and west are separated by the Willamette River. **Williams Avenue** cuts off a corner of the northeast sector, which is called simply "North." All street signs are labeled by their districts—N, NE, NW, SE, and SW. **Southwest** district is the city's hub, encompassing the downtown area, the southern end of historic Old Town, and a slice of West Hills. The heart of the hub is the downtown mall area between SW 5th and 6th Ave., where car traffic is prohibited. The **Northwest** district contains the northern end of **Old Town** and a residential area culminating in the swanky Northwestern Hills. The **Southeast** district is a less-

PORTLAND

well-to-do residential neighborhood, but it is the hippest part of the city. The city's best ethnic restaurants line **Hawthorne Boulevard,** along with small cafes and theaters catering to the hippie-artist crowd, mostly supported by nearby Reed College's student population. The **North** and **Northeast** districts are chiefly residential, punctuated by a few quiet, small parks.

ACCOMMODATIONS AND CAMPING

As Portland moves toward gentrification, cheap lodgings dwindle. **Northwest Bed and Breakfast,** 610 SW Broadway (243-7616), has an extensive listing of member homes in the Portland area and throughout the Northwest. They promise singles from $35-60 and doubles from $50-80.

Portland International HI/AYH Hostel, 3031 SE Hawthorne Blvd. (236-3380), at 31st Ave. Take bus #5 (brown beaver). Cheerful, clean, and crowded. Sleep inside or on the back porch when it's warm. Kitchen facilities; laundromat across the street. Fills up early in the summer (particularly the women's rooms), so make reservations ahead (credit card required) or arrive at 5pm to get one of the beds saved for walk-ins. Daytrips available to Mt. St. Helens or the Columbia River Gorge and Mt. Hood ($24). All-you-can-eat pancakes every morning (a paltry 50¢). Open daily 7:30-10am and 5-11pm. Curfew midnight. $12, nonmembers $15.

Aladdin Motor Inn, 8905 SW 30th St. (246-8241 or 800-292-4466), at Barbur Blvd., a 10-min. ride from downtown. Take bus #12 (yellow rose) from 5th Ave. Big rooms, big beds, and cable. A/C and kitchens available. Mention *Let's Go* and get discounts. Singles $32 (with kitchen $37). Doubles $37.

YWCA, 1111 SW 10th St. (223-6281). *Women only.* Situated on the park blocks, close to major sights. Clean and safe. Small rooms. Singles $21, with semi-private bath $25. Shared doubles $16. Hostel with bunk beds $7.

Midtown Motel, 1415 NE Sandy Blvd. (234-0316). Take bus #12, 19, or 20 from 6th Ave. Standard rooms with TV and A/C. Singles from $22. Doubles from $26.

Milo McIver State Park, 25 mi. southeast of Portland, off Rte. 211, 5 mi. west of the town of Estacada. Fish, boat, and bicycle along the nearby Clackamas River. Hot showers, flush toilets. Sites with electricity $12.

FOOD

Mummy's, 622 SW Columbia St. (224-7465), across from the *Oregonian* newspaper building. This inconspicuous Egyptian restaurant is underground, and was built to resemble the interior of a pharaoh's tomb. All lunch items under $7. The Kutta Kebab (lamb & beef) is especially yummy ($5). Tap bar.

Western Culinary Institute Chef's Center, 1235 SW Jefferson (242-2433). The testing ground for the cooking school's creative adventures; you'll know you're there when you see the people in tall white hats hanging out in front. All the lunches are under $6. Breakfast is also delicious and cheap—try the hashbrowns. Good assorted breads ($1 a loaf). Open Mon. 8am-2:30pm, Tues.-Fri. 8am-6pm.

Fong Chong, 301 NW 4th Ave. (220-0235), in Chinatown. Portland's best dim sum. The ginger chicken is fabulous. Dim sum (*the* real reason to go here) served daily 11am-3pm—expect to spend about $7. Open daily 10:30am-10pm.

Kornblatt's, 628 NW 23rd Ave. (242-0055). Take bus #15 (red salmon). A delicatessen haven for homesick New Yorkers serving Matzoh ball soup ($3), knishes ($2.25), *latkes* ($3.50). Crowded, but the wait is worth it. Open Mon.-Tues. 7am-10pm, Wed.-Fri. 7am-11pm, Sat. 7:30am-11pm, Sun. 7:30am-10pm.

Blah-Blah, 300 NW 10th Ave. (223-9160). When the infamous Quality Pie closed, Portland's dining queens and anarchic youth were suddenly homeless—until this year. A late-night nook where almost anything goes, Blah-Blah boasts Portland's most eclectic jukebox and standard diner fare. Try the home-fries ($1.75) or the Soylent Green (spinach) omelette ($4.50). Open 24 hrs.

Cafe Lena, 2239 SE Hawthorne St. (238-7087). Take bus #5 (brown beaver). The Portland intelligentsia reverently frequent this cafe, known for its open-mike poetry every Tues. 7:30pm. Readings and music nightly accentuate an appetizing menu—try the Birkenstock Submarine ($5). Breakfast served until 4pm. Open Tues.-Fri. 7am-midnight, Sat. 8am-midnight, Sun. 8am-2pm.

Rimsky-Korsakoffee House, 707 SE 12th Ave. (232-2640). Take bus #15 (brown beaver) to 12th, then walk 2 blocks north. A cozy salon offering a bacchanalian frenzy of desserts and the inevitable array of espresso drinks. Live classical music nightly. Open Sun.-Thurs. 7pm-midnight, Fri.-Sat. 7pm-1am.

SIGHTS AND ACTIVITIES

Shaded parks, magnificent gardens, innumerable museums and galleries, and bustling open-air markets beckon the city's tourists and residents alike. Catch the best of Portland's dramatic and visual arts scene on the **"First Thursday"** (of each month), when many small galleries in the Southwest and Northwest all stay open until 9pm. For info contact **The Metropolitan Center for Public Art,** 1120 SW 5th Ave. (823-5111), or latch onto one of their **Public Art Walking Tours** (226-2811; museum open Tues.-Sat. 11am-5pm, Sun. 1-5pm). Historic and modern architecture mingle throughout the city, providing the backdrop to the outdoor sculpture and well-tended greenery that give Portland its colorful, progressive flavor.

Portland's downtown area is centered on the **mall,** bounded by 5th and 6th Ave. to the east and west and by W. Burnside St. and SW Madison St. to the north and south, and closed to all traffic except city buses. At 5th Ave. and Morrison St. sits the **Pioneer Courthouse,** the forefather of downtown landmarks. The monument is now the centerpiece for **Pioneer Courthouse Square,** 701 SW 6th Ave. (223-1613), which opened in 1983. Forty-eight thousand Portland citizens purchased personalized bricks to support the construction of an amphitheater in the square for live jazz, folk, and ethnic music. During the summer, the **Peanut Butter and Jam Sessions** often seem to draw all 48,000 back to bask in their gift and enjoy the music (Tues. and Thurs. noon-1pm).

Certainly the most controversial building in the downtown area is Michael Graves' postmodern **Portland Building** (823-4000), located on the mall. The building's 1984 opening was attended by King Kong (full-sized and inflatable), perched on the roof. Since then, this amazing confection of pastel tile and concrete has been both praised to the stars and condemned as an overgrown jukebox. You may find it hard to judge for yourself, however, as the building is surrounded by narrow streets and tall buildings, it can be difficult to get a good look at the exterior.

There is room for romping just west of the mall on the **South Park Blocks,** a series of cool, shaded parks down the middle of Park Ave., surrounded by **Portland State University.** Facing the parks is the **Oregon Art Institute,** 1219 SW Park Ave. (226-2811), at Jefferson St., which houses the **Portland Art Museum, The Pacific Northwest College of Art,** and the **Northwest Film and Video Center** (221-1156), which shows classics and off-beat flicks and has workshops with (and for) local filmmakers. Tickets are available at the box office, 921 SW Morrison. The Art Museum has a fine exhibit of Pacific Northwest Native American art, while the Asian galleries hold a collection of Chinese furniture. International exhibits and local artists' works are interspersed. (Open Tues.-Wed. and Fri.-Sat. 11am-5pm, Thurs. 11am-9pm, Sun. 1-5pm. $4.50, seniors and students $2.50, under 12 $1.50. Seniors free Thurs.)

Old Town, to the north of the mall, resounded a century ago with the clamor of sailors whose ships filled the ports. The district has been revived by the large-scale refurbishing of store fronts, new "old brick," polished iron and brass, and a bevy of recently opened shops and restaurants. Old Town also marks the start of **Waterfront Park,** a 20-block-long swath of grass and flowers along the Willamette River which is an excellent place to picnic, fish, stroll, and enjoy major community events. At **Where's the Art!!!,** 219 SW Ankeny (226-3671), for just 25¢ you can pray at the church of Elvis, view the world's first 24-hr. coin-operated art gallery, or get marriage counseling.

The festive **Saturday Market,** 108 W. Burnside St. (222-6072), under the Burnside Bridge between 1st and Front St., is overrun with street musicians, artists, craftspeople, chefs, and greengrocers clogging the largest open-air crafts market in the country (March-Christmas Sat. 10am-5pm, Sun. 11am-4:30pm).

Less than 2 mi. west of downtown, in the mowed **West Hills,** looping trails for day hiking, running, and picnic-laden expeditions crisscross **Washington Park.** The **Hoyt Arboretum,** 4000 SW Fairview Blvd. (228-8733 or 823-3655), at the crest of the hill above the other gardens, features "200 acres of trees and trails" (trails open daily 6am-10pm; visitors center open daily 9am-3pm; free 60-90 min. nature walks April-Nov. Sat.-Sun. at 2pm). The 5-acre **Japanese Garden** (223-4070) holds a formal arrangement of idyllic ponds and bridges. Cherry blossoms ornament the park in summer, thanks to Portland's sibling city of Sapporo, Japan. (Tours April-Oct. at 10:45am and 2:30pm. Open 9am-8pm; April-May and Sept. daily 10am-6pm; Oct.-March 10am-4pm. $5, seniors and students $2.50.) Roses galore and spectacular views of the city await a few steps away at the **International Rose Test Garden,** 400 SW Kingston St. (823-3636; open dawn-dusk).

Below the Hoyt Arboretum stands Portland's favorite tourist-attracting triad. The **Washington Park Zoo,** 4001 SW Canyon Rd. (226-1561 for operator; 226-7627 for recording), is renowned for its elephant-breeding. A miniature **choo-choo** connects the Washington Park Rose Gardens to the zoo (fare $2.50, seniors and students $1.75). Beginning in late June, the zoo sponsors **Your Zoo and All That Jazz,** a nine-week series of open-air jazz concerts (Wed. 7-9pm), and **Zoograss Concerts,** a 10-week series of bluegrass concerts (Thurs. 7-9pm), both free with zoo admission. (Open daily 9:30am-7pm, gates close at 6pm; in winter 9:30am-6pm; $5, seniors $3.50, kids $3, free 2nd Tues. of each month.) The **World Forestry Center,** 4033 SW Canyon Rd. (228-1367), specializes in exhibits of Northwestern forestry and logging (open daily 9am-5pm, Labor Day-Memorial Day 10am-5pm; $3, seniors and kids $2), while the **Oregon Museum of Science and Industry (OMSI),** 4015 SW Canyon Rd. (222-2828), occupies kids and adults with do-it-yourself science, computer, and medical exhibits (open Sat.-Wed. 9:30am-7pm, Thurs.-Fri. 9:30am-9pm; $6.50, seniors $5.50, kids 3-17 $4). "Zoo Bus" #63 connects many points in the park with the mall. The new **Vietnam Memorial** rests a few steps up the hill. From Washington Park, you have easy access to sprawling **Forest Park,** packed with hiking trails and picnic areas affording spectacular views of Portland.

The funky clientele in the cafes, theaters, and restaurants on Hawthorne Blvd. are artists and students from **Reed College,** SE 28th and Woodstock. A small liberal arts school founded in 1909, Reed sponsors numerous cultural events. The ivy-draped grounds, encompassing a lake and a state wildlife refuge, make up one of the most attractive campuses in the country. In 1968, this transplendent enclave of progressive politics became the first undergraduate college to open a nuclear reactor. Campus tours leave Eliot Hall (2 per day during the school year; call 771-7511 for hrs.).

Farther southeast sleeps **Mt. Tabor Park,** one of two city parks in the world on the site of an extinct volcano. Take bus #15 from downtown, or drive down Hawthorne to SE 60th Ave.

ENTERTAINMENT

Once an uncouth and rowdy port town, Portland manages to maintain an irreverent attitude. Many waterfront pubs have evolved into upscale bistros and French bakeries, but plenty of local taverns still hide away throughout the city. Nightclubs cater to everyone from the casual college student to the hard-core rocker. The best entertainment listings are in the Friday edition of the *Oregonian* and in a number of free handouts: *Willamette Week* (put out each evening and catering to students), the *Main Event,* and the *Downtowner* (friend of the upwardly mobile). All are available in restaurants downtown and in boxes on street corners.

Portland has its share of good, formally presented concerts, but why bother with admission fees? You'll find the most exciting talent playing for free in various public facilities around the city. Call the Park Bureau (796-5193) for info, and check the *Oregonian* (see above) for **Brown Bag Concerts,** free public concerts given around the city in a six-week summer series (Mon-Fri. at noon and Tues. evenings). The **Oregon Symphony Orchestra** plays in Arlene Schnitzer Concert Hall, 719 SW Alder (228-1353; Sept.-April; tickets $15, "Symphony Sunday" afternoon concerts $12), while **Chamber Music Northwest** performs summer concerts at Reed College Commons, 3203 SE Woodstock Ave. (223-3202; performances Mon., Thurs., and Sat. at 8pm; tickets $16, kids 7-14 $9).

Portland's many fine theaters produce everything from off-Broadway shows to experimental drama. At **Portland Civic Theatre,** 1530 SW Yamhill St. (226-4026), the mainstage often presents musical comedy, while the smaller theater-in-the-round puts on less traditional shows. (Tickets $12-20.) **Oregon Shakespeare Festival/Portland** (274-6588), at the Intermediate Theatre of PCPA, corner of SW Broadway and SW Main St., has a five-play season (Nov.-Feb.; tickets $9-30).

The best clubs in Portland are the hardest ones to find. Neighborhood taverns and pubs may be tucked away on back roads, but they also have the most character and best music. The most accessible clubs from downtown are in the Northwest.

Lotus Card Room and Cafe, 932 SW 3rd Ave. (227-6185), at SW Salmon. Everything from techno, house, and hip-hop to disco. Quite possibly *the* best (and certainly the grooviest) dance experience in the entire city. Well drinks $2.50, beer on tap $2.25-3. Open Mon.-Fri. 9am-2:30am, Sat.-Sun. 8am-2:30am.

Red Sea, 318 SW 3rd Ave. (241-5450). Harry Belafonte's happy hunting ground. Calypso galore. Live reggae on Thurs. Cover $2-3. Well drinks $2.50, Henry Weinhard's $2.25. Open Thurs. 9pm-1:30am, Fri.-Sat. 9pm-2:30am.

Gypsy, 625 NW 21st Ave. (796-1859). Take bus #17 (red salmon). Fabulous David Lynch-ian decor wasted on unmistakably American crowd. Bring your cool friends for moral support. Groovy hour Mon.-Fri. 4-7pm features beer for $1.50 and appetizers at ½ price. Pool tables and darts abound. Open Mon.-Fri. 9am-11pm, Sat.-Sun. 8am-11pm.

La Luna, 215 SE 9th Ave. (241-LUNA). Take bus #20 (purple raindrops), to 9th, walk 2 blocks south. Live concerts, 2 bars, 1 coffee room, and an anything-goes Generation X crowd. All ages admitted (except to the bars). Call for concert info. Bar open Thurs.-Sat. 8pm-2:30am, concerts and special events on other nights.

East Side, 3701 SE Division St. (236-5550). Take bus #4 (brown beaver). The city's only real bar-offering to the lesbian community is this country-western hideaway *à la* "Desert Hearts." Dancing Tues.-Sat., with lessons on Tues. and Thurs. On Thurs., draft beers 50¢. Open Sun.-Mon. 4pm-2am, Tues.-Sat. 11:30am-2am.

■ Washington

Geographically, politically, and culturally, Washington is divided by the spine of the Cascade Mountains. The personality difference between the state's eastern and western halves is pervasive, long-standing, and polarized. To "wet-siders" who live near Washington's coast, the term "dry-siders" conjures images of rednecks tearing through the eastern deserts in their Chevy trucks, slurring the endangered spotted-owl and avidly hooting for its destruction. In the minds of dry-siders, the residents of Seattle and the rest of western Washington are yuppified, liberal freaks too wealthy to respect rural livelihoods as much as wildlife. What does unify Washingtonians—whether from the wet or dry side—is an independent frame of mind. Like its ideological spectrum, Washington's terrain is all-encompassing: deserts, volcanoes, Pacific beaches, and the world's only non-tropical rain forest all lie within state boundaries. You can raft on Washington's rivers, sea kayak around the San Juan Islands, and build sand castles on the Strait of Juan de Fuca. Mount Rainier has fantastic hiking, while the Cascades boast perfect conditions for nearly every winter recreational activity. Seattle and Spokane drape themselves over handsome green landscapes, proving that natural beauty can be its own selling point.

PRACTICAL INFORMATION

Capital: Olympia.
Visitor Information: State Tourist Office, Tourism Development Division, 101 General Administration Bldg., Olympia 98504-0613 (206-586-2088 or 206-586-2102; 800-544-1800 for vacation planning guide). Open Mon.-Fri. 9am-5pm. **Washington State Parks and Recreation Commission,** 7150 Cleanwater Lane, KY-11, Olympia 98504 (206-753-5755, May-Aug. in WA 800-562-0990).
Time Zone: Pacific (3 hr. behind Eastern). **Postal Abbreviation:** WA
Sales Tax: 6.5%

CASCADE RANGE

The Northwestern Native Americans summed up their admiration succinctly, dubbing the Cascades "The Home of the Gods." Intercepting the moist Pacific air, the Cascades have divided the eastern and western parts of Oregon and Washington into the lush green of the west and the low, dry plains of the east.

The tallest of these mountains—the white-domed peaks of Baker, Vernon, Glacier, Rainier, Hood, Adams, and Mt. St. Helens—have been made accessible by four major roads offering good trailheads and impressive scenery. **U.S. 12** through White Pass approaches Mt. Rainier most closely; **I-90** sends four lanes past the major ski resorts of Snoqualmie Pass; scenic **U.S. 2** leaves Everett for Stevens Pass and descends the Wenatchee River, a favorite of whitewater rafters**; Route 20,** the **North Cascades Hwy.,** provides access to North Cascades National Park. These last two roads are often traveled in sequence as the **Cascade Loop.**

Greyhound covers the routes over Stevens and Snoqualmie Passes to and from Seattle (3 hr. round-trip), while **Amtrak** cuts between Ellensburg and Puget Sound. Rainstorms and evening traffic can slow hitchhiking; locals warn against thumbing across Hwy. 20, as a few hitchers apparently have vanished over the last few years. *Let's Go* **does not recommend hitching here.** This corner of the world can only be explored properly with a car. The mountains are most accessible in July, August, and September; many high mountain passes are snowed-in the rest of the year. The best source of information on the Cascades is the joint **National Park/National Forest Information Service,** 915 2nd Ave., Seattle 98174 (206-220-7450).

■■■ MOUNT RAINIER NATIONAL PARK

Rising 2 mi. above the surrounding foothills, 14,411-ft. Mt. Rainier presides regally over the Cascade Range. Though Native Americans once called it "Tahoma," meaning "mountain of God," Rainier is simply "The Mountain" to most modern-day Washingtonians. Rainier even creates its own weather, jutting up into the warm ocean air and pulling down vast amounts of snow and rain. Clouds mask the mountain up to 200 days per year. Some 76 glaciers patch the slopes and combine with sharp ridges and steep gullies to make Rainier an inhospitable place for the 3000 determined climbers who clamber to its summit each year. Even those who don't feel up to scaling The Mountain can find many places to play in the old-growth forests and alpine meadows. With over 305 mi. of trails, solitude is just a step away.

Practical Information Mt. Rainier is 65 mi. from Tacoma and 60 mi. from Seattle. To reach the park from the west, drive south from Seattle on I-5 to Tacoma, then go east on Rte. 512, south on Rte. 7, and east on Rte. 706. **Rte. 706** is the only access road open throughout the year; snow usually closes all other park roads Nov.-May. The park **entrance fee** is $5 per car, $3 per hiker; the gates are open 24 hrs. For **visitor information,** stop in at the **Longmire Hiker Information Center,** which distributes backcountry permits (open Sun.-Thurs. 8am-6pm, Fri.-Sat. 7am-7pm; fall-spring Sun.-Thurs. 8am-6pm); **Paradise Visitors Center** (open daily 9am-7pm; late Sept.-mid-Oct. 9:30am-6pm; mid-Oct.-winter daily 10am-5pm); **Sunrise Visitors Center** (open summer-mid-Sept. daily 9am-6pm); or **Ohanapecosh Visitors Center** (open summer-mid-Oct. daily 9am-6pm). All centers can be contacted by writing c/o Superintendent, Mt. Rainier National Park, Ashford 98304, or by telephoning the park's **central operator** (569-2211).

If you don't own all the specialized equipment needed for climbing, you can rent ice axes ($7), crampons ($7.25), boots ($15), packs ($15), and helmets ($5) by the day from **RMI** (569-2227), in Paradise. Their expert guides also lead summit climbs, seminars, and special schools and programs. (Open May-Oct. daily 9am-5pm. Winter office: 535 Dock St. #209, Tacoma 98402; 627-6242.) In an **emergency** in the park, call 569-2211. The park **area code** is 206.

Accommodations and Camping

Longmire, Paradise, and **Sunrise** offer accommodations and food out of reach to the budget traveler. Stock up and stay in **Ashford** or **Packwood** if you must have a roof over your head. Otherwise, camp. **Hotel Packwood,** 104 Main St. (494-5431), Packwood (singles from $20; doubles $30) and **Gateway Inn Motel,** 38820 Rte. 706 E (569-2506), Ashford (singles $30; doubles $35; cabins from $50) are both reasonable.

Camping at the auto-accessible campsites from June-Sept. requires a permit ($5-8), available at campsites. Each auto campground has its own personality. Go to **Ohanapecosh** for the gorgeous and serene high ceiling of old-growth trees, to **Cougar Rock** for the strictly maintained quiet hours, and to **White River** or **Sunshine Point** for the panoramas. Open on a first-come, first-camped basis, the grounds fill only on the busiest summer weekends. Sunshine Point is the only auto campground open year-round.

Alpine and **cross-country camping** require free permits year-round and are subject to restrictions. Be sure to pick up a copy of the *Wilderness Trip Planner* pamphlet at any ranger station before you set off. Alpine and cross-country access is strictly controlled to prevent forest damage. With a **backcountry permit,** cross-country hikers can use any of the free, well-established **trailside camps** scattered throughout the park's backcountry. Most camps have toilet facilities and a nearby water source, and some have shelters as well. *Fires are prohibited,* and the size of a party is limited. **Glacier climbers** and **mountain climbers** intending to go above 10,000 ft. must register in person at ranger stations in order to be granted permits.

Outdoors

Mother Nature beckons most visitors to Mt. Rainier. Each **visitors center** has a wealth of literature on everything from hiking to natural history, postings on trail and road conditions, and rangers to help point you in the right direction. Guided trips and talks, campfire programs, and slide presentations are given at the visitors centers and vehicle campgrounds. Pick up a copy of the free activity and program guide *Tahoma* for details.

A car tour is a good introduction to the park. All major roads offer scenic views of the mountain and have numerous roadside sites for camera-clicking and general gawking. The roads to Paradise and Sunrise are especially picturesque. **Stevens Canyon Road** connects the southeast corner of the national park with Paradise, Longmire, and the Nisqually entrance, unfolding spectacular vistas of Rainier and the rugged Tatoosh Range. The accessible roadside attractions of **Box Canyon, Bench Lake,** and **Grove of the Patriarchs** line the route.

Mt. Adams and Mt. St. Helens, not visible from the road, can be seen clearly from such **mountain trails** as **Paradise** (1½ mi.), **Pinnacle Peak** (2½ mi.), **Eagle Peak**

(7 mi.), and **Van Trump Peak** (5½ mi.). For more information on these trails, pick up *Viewing Mount St. Helens* at one of the visitors centers.

A segment of the **Pacific Crest Trail (PCT)**, running between the Columbia River and the Canadian border, crosses through the southeast corner of the park. The PCT is maintained by the U.S. Forest Service. Primitive **campsites** and **shelters** line the trail, which offers glimpses of snow-covered peaks as it snakes through delightful wilderness areas.

A trip to the **summit** of Mt. Rainier requires special preparation and substantial expense. The ascent is a vertical rise of more than 9000 ft. over a distance of 8 or more mi.—usually taking two days. Experienced climbers may form their own expeditions upon satisfactory completion of a detailed application; novices can sign up for a **summit climb** with **Rainier Mountaineering, Inc. (RMI),** which offers a one-day basic-climbing course followed by a two-day guided climb for $320. You must bring your own climbing gear and carry four meals. For more information, contact **Park Headquarters** or **RMI** (see Practical Information).

Hardcore hikers will also be thrilled by the 95-mi. **Wonderland Trail,** which circumscribes Rainier. The entire circuit takes 10-14 days and includes several brutal ascents and descents. Beware of early snowstorms in September, snow-blocked passes in June, and muddy trails in July—all of which can force hikers to turn back. Rangers can provide information on weather and trail conditions; they also can store food caches for you at ranger stations along the trail.

Less ambitious, ranger-led **interpretive hikes** interpret everything from area history to local wildflowers. Each visitors center conducts its own hikes on its own schedule. These free hikes complement evening campfire programs, also conducted by each visitors center. If you are llooking to spend an unusual day in a llovely llocation, **Llama Wilderness Pack Trips** (491-LAMA), Tatoosh Motel, Packwood offers a llunch with the llamas in the park (4-5-hr., $25 per person).

■■■ MOUNT SAINT HELENS

On the morning of May 18, 1980, Mt. St. Helens erupted violently, shaking the entire state of Washington out of bed. In the three days that followed, a hole 2 mi. long and 1 mi. wide opened in the mountain. Ash blackened the sky for hundreds of miles and blanketed the streets of nearby towns with inches of soot. Debris from the volcano flooded Spirit Lake, choked rivers with mud, and sent house-sized boulders tumbling down the mountainside. The blast leveled entire forests, leaving a stubble of trunks on the hills and millions of trees pointing arrow-like away from the crater.

Once the jewel of the Cascades, **Mt. St. Helens National Volcanic Monument** is slowly but steadily recovering from that explosion. Fourteen years later, the devastated grey landscape is brightened by signs of returning life—saplings press past their fallen brethren, insects flourish near newly formed waterfalls, and many small rodents scurry between burrows. Nature's power of destruction, it seems, is matched only by her power of regeneration.

Practical Information Start any trip to the mountain at the **Mount St. Helens National Volcanic Monument Visitors Center** (274-6644; 274-4038 for 24-hr. recording), on Rte. 504, 5 mi. east of Castle Rock (exit 49 off of I-5). Interpretive talks and displays recount the mountain's eruption and subsequent regeneration and are augmented by a 22-min. film, a 10-min. slide show, and many hands-on activities. The center also provides camping and mountain access information. (Open 9am-6pm; Oct.-March 9am-5pm.) If time permits, plan to spend the whole day in the monument and visit either the **Pine Creek Information Center** in the south or the **Woods Creek Information Center** in the north. While not as large as the main center near Castle Rock, these two are each within 1 mi. of excellent viewpoints and offer displays, maps, and brochures on the area. Pick up free copies of the *Volcano Review* and the *Tourist Guide to Volcano Country,* sources of local information, at any of these centers. (Open May-Oct. 9am-5pm, depending on funding and environmental conditions.) These centers are also the places to head in case of an **emergency** in the park.

To get here from the north, get on U.S. 12 and turn south on Forest Road 25 at the town of Randle. From the south, take Rte. 503, which becomes Forest Road 90 at Yale; follow 90 to Pine Creek. All drivers should fill up their gas tanks before starting the journey, as fuel is not sold within the park. Drivers of trailers or RVs should avoid Road 26, which turns off to the east from Road 25; it's a one-lane road, often steep and very curvy. Roads 25 and 26 intersect Road 99; at the junction of Roads 25 and 99, **Wakepish Sno-Park** serves as a trailer drop during the summer, and guests can make their trip along Road 99 to **Windy Ridge** without the additional weight of a trailer. **Gray Line,** 400 N.W. Broadway, Portland, OR (503-226-6755 or 800-426-7532) runs buses from Seattle to Mt. St. Helens (round-trip $37).

Mount St. Helens' **area code** is 206.

Camping For those who want an early start touring the mountain, there are two primitive **campgrounds** relatively near the crater. **Iron Creek Campground,** just south of the Woods Creek Information Center on Forest Road 25, has 98 sites ($8 each, call 800-283-2267 for reservations), and **Swift Campground,** just west of the Pine Creek Information Center on Forest Road 90, has 93 sites ($6 each, no reservations). Just west of Swift Campground on Yale Reservoir lie **Beaver Bay** and **Cougar Campgrounds,** both of which have flush toilets and showers and are run by Pacific Power & Light (sites $6; for reservations call 503-464-5035). There is also **free dispersed camping** in the monument—if you stumble across a site on an old Forest Service road, you can camp there. Contact a ranger for more info. The **Gifford Pinchot National Forest Headquarters,** 6926 E. Fourth Plain Blvd., P.O. Box 894, Vancouver, WA (696-7500), also has camping and hiking info.

Sights The newly paved, two-lane Road 99 leads visitors along 17 mi. of curves, clouds of ash, and precipices, past **Spirit Lake,** to a point just 3½ mi. from the crater. Without stops it takes nearly an hour to travel out and back, but the numerous interpretive talks and walks, and the spectacular views along the way are definitely worth exploring. Check with one of the visitors centers or in the free newsletters for times and meeting places of these interpretive activities. Continue 25 mi. south on Road 25, 12 mi. west on Road 90, then 2 mi. north on Road 83 to **Ape Cave,** a broken 2½-mi.-long lava tube formed in an ancient eruption, which is now open for visitors to explore. Be sure to wear a jacket and sturdy shoes; you can rent a lantern for $3. Interpreters lead cave walks daily; check at the center there for times.

For a direct view of the crater, visit the new **Coldwater Ridge Visitor Services Center.** Rte. 504 provides access to the area, opening up the spectacular western view of the crater, dome, Toutle River Valley, and new lakes formed by the 1980 eruption. The Coldwater Center plans include interpretive exhibits, trails, picnic and restaurant facilities, and a boat launch. A shuttle bus will run from the lake to Johnson Ridge, allowing a glimpse into the crater.

■■■ NORTH CASCADES

A favorite stomping ground for deer, mountain goats, and bears, the North Cascades—an aggregation of dramatic peaks in the northern part of the state—remain one of the last great expanses of untouched land in the continental U.S. The **North Cascades Hwy. (Rte. 20),** provides the major access to the area, as well as astounding views awaiting each twist in the road. Use the information below to follow the road eastward from Burlington (exit 230 on I-5) along the Skagit River to the Skagit Dams (whose hydroelectric energy powers Seattle), then across the Cascade Crest at Rainy Pass (4860 ft.) and Washington Pass (5477 ft.), finally descending to the Methow River and the dry Okanogan rangeland of eastern Washington. **Rte. 9** branches off of Rte. 20 and leads north through the rich farmland of **Skagit Valley,** offering roundabout access to **Mt. Baker** via forks at the Nooksack River and Rte. 542. Mt. Baker (10,778 ft.) has been belching since 1975, and in winter jets of steam often snort from its dome.

Practical Information Greyhound stops in Burlington once per day, and **Empire Lines** (affiliated with Greyhound), serves Okanogan, Pateros, and Chelan on the eastern slope. No public transportation lines run within the North Cascades National Park or along the North Cascades Highway. Avoid hitching in this area. Information on **North Cascades National Park** (surrounding Rte. 20 and the Ross Lake Recreation Area between Marblemount and Ross Dam) is available at 2105 Rte. 20, Sedro Wooley 98284 (206-856-5700; open Sun.-Thurs. 8am-4:30pm, Fri.-Sat. 8am-6pm). The info office for the **Okanogan National Forest** (surrounding Rte. 20 east of Ross Dam) is at 1240 2nd Ave. S., P.O. Box 950, Okanogan 98840 (509-422-2704); for **Wenatchee National Forest** (south of Okanogan National Forest and north of U.S. 2) it's at 301 Yakima St., P.O. Box 811, Wenatchee 98801 (509-662-4335). For **snow avalanche info** on all these jurisdictions call 206-526-6677.

■ Concrete to Marblemount

You would only have to sneeze three times in succession to miss the town of **Concrete** and its two neighbors, Rockport and Marblemount—and you may want to do so. The road off Rte. 20 from Concrete to Mt. Baker runs past the lakes created by the Upper and Lower Baker Dams. Concrete facts are available from the surprisingly large **Concrete Chamber of Commerce** (853-8400), tucked between Main St. and Rte. 20—follow the railroad tracks upon entering town (open Mon.-Fri. 8am-4pm, Sat. 9am-4pm). If you drive through Concrete at lunchtime, stop at the **Mount Baker Cafe,** 119 E. Main St. (853-8200; open Mon.-Thurs. 5am-9pm, Fri.-Sat. 5am-10pm, Sun. 8am-4pm).

Neighboring **Rockport** borders **Rockport State Park** (853-8461), which features magnificent Douglas firs, a trail that accommodates wheelchairs, and 62 campsites that rank among the largest in the state ($8, full hookup $12). The surrounding **Mt. Baker National Forest** permits free camping closer to the high peaks.

Marblemount is the next town east and the nearest one to the **Cascade Pass.** From Rte. 20 take Cascade River Rd. across the Skagit River; the trailhead for a 9-mi. hike to the pass is 22 mi. up the road. Replenish your energy in Marblemount at the **Mountain Song Restaurant,** 5860 Rte. 20 (873-2461; open daily 8am-9pm), which serves hearty and healthy meals—try the summit sandwich for 2 ($8.50). Pitch your tent at the free sites in the **Cascade Islands Campground,** on the south side of the Cascade River (ask for directions in town). Bring heavy-duty insect repellent.

■ Newhalem to Washington Pass

Newhalem is the next major town on Rte. 20, and the first town in the **Ross Lake National Recreation Area,** a buffer zone between the highway and the North Cascades National Park. A small grocery store and hiking trails to the dams and lakes nearby are the highlights of the town. Info emanates from the **visitors center,** on Rte. 20 (open late June-early Sept. Thurs.-Mon. 8am-4pm). At other times, stop at the **general store** (open Mon.-Fri. 9:30am-7pm; 206-386-4489).

Plugged up by Ross Dam, the artificial expanse of **Ross Lake** penetrates into the mountains as far as the Canadian border. Fifteen **campgrounds** gird the lake, some accessible by boat only, others by trail. The trail along Big Beaver Creek, a few mi. north of Rte. 20, leads from Ross Lake into the Picket Range and eventually to Mt. Baker and the **Northern Unit** of North Cascades National Park. The **Sourdough Mountain** and **Desolation Peak** lookout towers near Ross Lake have eagle's-eye views of the range.

Diablo Lake fumes directly to the west of Ross Lake, the foot of Ross Dam acting as its eastern shore and the top of the Diablo Dam stopping it up on the west. The town of **Diablo Lake** on the northeastern shore is the main trailhead for hikes into the southern part of the North Cascades National Park. The **Thunder Creek Trail** traverses Park Creek Pass to the Stehekin River Rd. in **Lake Chelan National Recreation Area.** Diablo Lake has a boathouse and a lodge that sells groceries and gas.

Thirty mi. farther on Rte. 20, the **Pacific Coast Trail** traverses **Rainy Pass** (alt. 4860 ft.) on one of the most scenic and challenging legs of its 2500-mi. Canada-to-Mexico span. The trail leads up to **Pasayten Wilderness** in the north and down to **Glacier Peak** (10,541 ft.), which dominates the central portion of the range. Glacier Peak can also be approached from the secondary roads extending northward from the Lake Wenatchee area near Coles Corner on U.S. 2, or from Rte. 530 to Darrington. **Washington Pass,** at Mile 163 of Rte. 20, has short, wheelchair-accessible trails leading to a flabbergasting view of the **Early Winters Creek's Copper Basin.**

■ Winthrop and Twisp

The town of **Winthrop** (25 mi. east of Rainy Pass as the crow flies, farther as Rte. 20 runs) is imbued with a kitschy wild-West theme. Rent real horses at the **Rocking Horse Ranch** (996-2768), 9 mi. north of Winthrop on the North Cascade Hwy. ($20 per 1½hr.), and mountain bikes at **The Virginian Hotel** just east of town on Rte. 20 ($5 for the 1st hr., then $3.50 per hr., full day $25).

The great billows of hickory-scented smoke draw customers to the **Riverside Rib Co. Bar B-Q,** 207 Riverside (996-2001), which serves tasty ribs in a converted prairie schooner; satisfying vegetarian dinners ($9) are also available (open Mon.-Fri. 11am-9pm). Across the street chats the **Winthrop Information Station** (996-2125), on the corner of Rte. 20 and Riverside (open Memorial Day-Labor Day daily 9am-5pm). The **Winthrop Ranger Station,** 24 W. Chewuch Rd., P.O. Box 579 (996-2266), up a marked road west of town, has info on camping in the surrounding National Forest (open Mon.-Fri. 7:45am-5pm, Sat. 8:30am-5pm).

North of Winthrop, the **Early Winters Visitors Center** (996-2534), outside Mazama (open daily 9am-5pm; in winter weekends only), stocks info about the **Pasayten Wilderness,** an area whose relatively gentle terrain and mild climate endear it to hikers and equestrians. **Early Winters** has 13 simple campsites ($6) 14 mi. west of Winthrop on Rte. 20, and **Klipchuk,** one mi. farther west, has 46 better developed sites ($6). Cool off at **Pearrygin Lake State Park** beach. From Riverside west of town, take Pearrygin Lake Rd. for 4 mi. Sites ($11) by the lake have flush toilets and pay showers. Arrive early, since the campground fills up by early afternoon.

Leave Winthrop's prohibitively expensive hotel scene and travel 9 mi. south of Winthrop on Rte. 20 to stay in **Twisp,** the town that should have been a breakfast cereal, which offers low prices and few tourists. **The Sportsman Motel,** 1010 E. Rte. 20 (997-2911), tries to hide its tasteful rooms and kitchens behind a gruff, barracks-like exterior (singles $29, doubles $34; Nov.-April $24/$29). The **Twisp Ranger Station,** 502 Glover St. (997-2131), has an extremely helpful staff ready to load you down with trail and campground guides (open Mon.-Sat. 7:45am-4:30pm; closed on Sat. in winter). The **Methow Valley Tourist Information Office,** at the corner of Rte. 20 and 3rd St., slings brochures (open Mon.-Fri. 8am-noon and 1-5pm). The **Methow Valley Farmers Market** sells produce in front of the community center (April-Oct. Sat. 9am-noon).

Five mi. east of Twisp stands a training station for **Smoke Jumpers,** folks who get their kicks by parachuting into the middle of blazing forest fires for strategic firefighting. Occasionally they give tours or have training sessions for public viewing. Call the base (997-2031) for details.

OLYMPIC PENINSULA

In the fishing villages and logging towns of the Olympic Peninsula, locals joke about having webbed feet and using Rustoleum instead of suntan oil. The Olympic Mountains wring the area's moisture (up to 200 in. of rain per year fall on Mt. Olympus) out of the heavy Pacific air. While this torrent supports bona fide rain forests in the peninsula's western river valleys, towns such as Sequim in the range's eastern rain shadow are the driest in all of Washington, with as little as 17 in. of rain per year.

Extremes of climate are matched by extremes of geography. The beaches along the Pacific strip are a hiker's paradise—isolated, windy, and wildly sublime. The seaports of the peninsula's northern edge crowd against the Strait of Juan de Fuca, hemmed in by the glaciated peaks of the Olympic range. Most visitors, however, come here for one reason: the spectacularly rugged scenery of Olympic National Park, which sits solidly at the Peninsula's center. Though the park's network of trails now covers an area the size of Rhode Island, these rough and wooded mountains resisted exploration until well into the 20th century.

■■■ OLYMPIC NATIONAL PARK

Lodged amidst the august Olympic Mountains, Olympic National Park unites 900,000 acres of velvet-green rainforest, jagged snow-covered peaks, and dense evergreen woodlands. This enormous region at the center of the peninsula allows limited access to four-wheeled traffic. No scenic loop roads cross the park, and only a handful of secondary roads attempt to penetrate the interior. The roads that do exist serve as trailheads for over 600 mi. of hiking. The only people who seem not to enjoy this diverse and wet wilderness are those who come unprepared; a parka, good boots, and a waterproof tent are essential here.

Practical Information The **Olympic Visitors Center,** 3002 Mt. Angeles Rd. (452-0330), Port Angeles, off Race St., fields questions about the whole park—camping, backcountry hiking, and fishing—and displays a map of the locations of other park ranger stations. This is the only reason to visit Port Angeles, a cheerless industrial complex dominated by paper and plywood mills. The park charges a **fee** of $3 per car, $1 per hiker or biker, at the more built-up entrances, such as the Hoh, Heart o' the Hills, and Elwha—all of which have paved roads and toilet facilities. Entrance permit good for 7 days. In an **emergency,** call 911.

The Park Service runs **interpretive programs** such as guided forest walks, tidal pool walks, and campfire programs out of its various ranger stations (all free). For a full schedule of events obtain a copy of the park newspaper from ranger stations or the visitors center. The **map** distributed at the park's gates is wonderfully detailed and extremely helpful.

July, August, and September are the best months to visit Olympic National Park, since much of the backcountry often remains snowed-in until late June, and only the summer provides rainless days with any regularity. Be prepared for a potpourri of weather conditions at any time. Make sure hiking boots are waterproof and have good traction, because trails can transform into rivers of slippery mud. **Backcountry camping** requires a free **wilderness permit,** available at ranger stations. The Park Service's backcountry shelters are for emergencies only.

Never, ever drink even one mouthful of untreated **water** in the park. *Giardia,* a *very* nasty microscopic parasite, lives in all these waters and causes severe diarrhea, gas, and abdominal cramps. Carry your own water supply, or boil local water for five minutes before drinking it. You can also buy water purification tablets at the visitors center (see above) or at most camping supply stores. **Dogs** are not allowed in the backcountry and must be leashed at all times within the park.

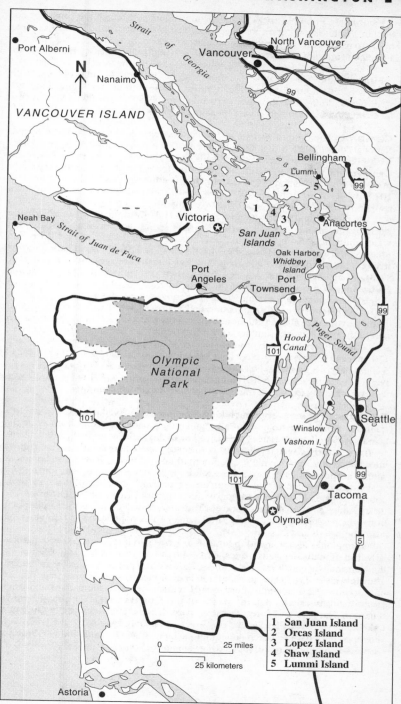

1 San Juan Island
2 Orcas Island
3 Lopez Island
4 Shaw Island
5 Lummi Island

0   25 miles
0   25 kilometers

Mountain climbing is tricky in the Olympic Range. Although the peaks are not high in absolute terms, they are steep, and their proximity to the sea makes them prone to nasty weather. Climbers are required to check in at a ranger station before any summit attempt. The rangers urge novices to buddy up with experienced climbers who are "wise in the ways of Northwest mountaineering."

Fishing within park boundaries requires no permit, but you must obtain a state game department punch card for salmon and steelhead trout at outfitting and hardware stores locally, or at the game department in Olympia. The Elwha River is best for **trout,** and the Hoh is excellent for **salmon.**

Camping The eastern section of the Park is accessible through the Olympic National Forest from U.S. 101 along Hood Canal. The auto campgrounds are popular with hikers, who use them as trailheads to the interior of the park. **Staircase Campground** (877-5569), 16 mi. northwest of Hoodsport at the head of Lake Cushman, has a ranger station (59 sites, $8). **Dosewallips** (doh-see-WALL-ups), off U.S. 101 3 mi. north of Brinnon, has 32 less well-developed sites for cars (free). The **ranger station** (open June-Sept.), has no electricity or telephones.

In the North Rim of the park, **Heart o' the Hills Campground** (452-2713; 105 sites), 5½ mi. from Port Angeles inside the park, has idyllic campsites with drinking water and toilets. Go up Race Rd. past the visitors center and toward Hurricane Ridge. Both Heart o' the Hills and **Elwha Valley** (452-9191; 41 sites) have interpretive programs and ranger stations, as does **Fairholm Campground** (928-3380; 87 sites), 30 mi. west of Port Angeles. (All 3 open year-round; sites $8.) **Soleduck Hotsprings Campground** (327-3534), to the southeast of Lake Crescent, 13 mi. off U.S. 101, is adjacent to the commercial hot springs resort (sites $8).

The **Hoh Rain Forest Campground and Visitors Center** (374-6925) is located 19 mi. down the Hoh River Rd. from the junction with U.S. 101 in the northeastern part of the park (open in summer daily 9am-4:30pm). To find shelter from the rains, seek out the **Rain Forest Home Hostel** (374-2270), between mileposts 169 and 170 on U.S. 101; the fireplace is a cozy place to chat on a cold, wet night. (Check-in 5-10pm daily. $8. Linen $1. Full kitchen facilities and showers.) **Forks,** 57 mi. southwest of Port Angeles on U.S. 101, is the last stop south on U.S. 101 to pick up groceries if you're going to cook in the hostel kitchen or over the campfire.

Outdoors For some inspiring **hiking,** head south on Soleduck Road 14 mi. to a trailhead. From there, **Soleduck Falls** and **Lover's Lane** are scenic trails along the Soleduck River. Lover's Lane is the easier hike of the two. For more secluded hiking, try **Aurora Ridge,** which goes mostly through forested areas instead. For further information and free overnight camping permits, get in touch with the **Soleduck ranger station** (327-3583) on Soleduck Rd. (open June-Aug. daily 8am-5pm).

The main attraction of the northern area, especially for those not planning backcountry trips, is **Hurricane Ridge,** with its splendid views of Mt. Olympus, the Bailey Range, and Canada on clear days. The often-crowded ridge is the easiest point from which to grab a hiker's view of the range. Thick populations of bear and deer roam the woods and meadows.

Washington is also home to the only temperate rain forest in the world. Particularly lush growths of gigantic trees, ferns, and mosses canopy the rain forest along the Hoh and Queets Rivers. You'll find several worthwhile hikes into the rainforest. The **Hoh River Trail** is for pros, but the **Hall of Mosses** and **Spruce** trails require only an hour. Farther south, after U.S. 101 rejoins the coast, the park's boundaries extend southwest to edge the banks of the **Queets River.** The road here is unpaved. The Park and Forest Services share the land surrounding the **Quinault Lake** and **River.** The Park Service land is accessible only by foot, but the Forest Service operates a day-use beach and an info center in the **Quinault Ranger Station** (288-2444), South Shore Rd. (open daily 9am-5pm; in winter Mon.-Fri. 9am-5pm).

■■■ PORT TOWNSEND

From Port Townsend on Puget Sound to Cape Flattery on the Pacific Ocean, the northern rim of the Olympic Peninsula defines the U.S. side of the **Strait of Juan de Fuca.** This sapphire passage was named for the legendary explorer, allegedly the first European to enter the ocean inlet. The Victorian splendor of Port Townsend's buildings has survived the progression of time and weather, though the bustling salmon industry has not. Although the Port itself has been artificially restored to its former grandeur, sailors and amateur boat-builders alike still congregate in town bars and cafes. Home to a thriving art and music community, Port Townsend stands as a cultural oasis on an otherwise untamed peninsula.

Practical Information The **Chamber of Commerce,** 2437 Sims Way, Port Townsend 98368 (385-2722), lies about 10 blocks from the center of town on Rte. 20 (open Mon.-Fri. 9am-5pm, Sat. 10am-4pm, Sun. 11am-4pm). By land, Port Townsend can be reached either from **U.S. 101** or from the **Kitsap Peninsula** across the Hood Canal Bridge. By water, get to Port Townsend via the **Washington State Ferry** (800-843-3779), which lands and departs from the dock at Water St., west of downtown. (7am-10pm every 45 min. Mid-Oct. to mid-May service reduced. Call for fares.) In an **emergency,** dial 911.

Port Townsend's **post office** is at 1322 Washington St. (385-1600; open Mon.-Fri. 9am-5pm); the **ZIP code** is 98368. The **area code** is 206.

Accommodations and Food Fort **Worden Youth Hostel (HI/AYH)** (385-0655), Fort Worden State Park, 2 mi. from downtown, has bulletin boards and trekkers' log which are good, if somewhat dated, sources of information on budget travel around the Olympics. Also kitchen facilities. (Open Feb.-Dec. 21. Call ahead for Nov.-Feb. Check in 5-10pm; check-out 9:30am; curfew 11pm. $8.50, nonmembers $11.50. Cyclists $6. Family rates available.) Campers should try nearby **Fort Worden State Park** (385-4730; $15 per night).

Strap on your Birkenstocks and grab your organic essentials at **Abundant Life Seed,** 1029 Lawrence (385-5660), at Polk. **Burrito Depot,** 609 Washington St. (385-5856), at Madison—the cacti in their garden may be small, but their servings are *muy grande.* Big big burritos from just $2.65. (Open Mon.-Sat. 10am-9pm, Sun.11am-4pm.) Port Townsend's first and finest pizza fills the tiny **Waterfront Pizza,** 951 Water St. (385-6629); 16" pies start at $10 (open daily 11am-11pm).

Sights Port Townsend's early pioneer settlers built sturdy maritime-style houses, but their wealthier successors preferred huge Queen Anne and Victorian mansions. Of the over 200 restored homes in the area, some have been converted into cozy, but costly, bed and breakfasts; others are open for tours. The 1868 **Rothschild House** (355-2722), at Franklin and Taylor St., has period furnishings and herbal and flower gardens. (Open daily 10am-5pm; mid-Sept. to mid-May Sat.-Sun. 11am-4pm. Requested donation $2.) Or peek into the **Heritage House** at Pierce and Washington (open daily 12:30-3pm; $1.50).

Fort **Norden** (385-4730), a strategic military post dating from the turn of the century, guards the mouth of Puget Sound and commands fine views of the sound and the Cascades. The fort was pressed back into service in 1981 as a set for the movie *An Officer and a Gentleman.* The **Marine Science Center** (385-5582), on the Fort Worden Dock, keeps live sea critters to touch and observe; this is your big chance to see a live sand dollar. (Open mid-June to mid-Sept. Tues.-Sun. noon-6pm; fall and spring weekends only. Admission $1 by donation, kids 50¢.)

■■■ SAN JUAN ISLANDS

The San Juan Islands are an accessible treasure. Bald eagles spiral above haggard hillsides, pods of killer whales spout offshore, and despite the lush vegetation it never seems to rain. An excellent guide to the area is *The San Juan Islands Afoot and Afloat* by Marge Mueller ($10), available on the islands and in Seattle.

Ferries depart Anacortes on the mainland about nine times per day on a route that stops at **Lopez, Shaw, Orcas,** and **San Juan Islands.** Purchase ferry tickets in Anacortes. You pay only on westbound trips to or between the islands; no charge is levied on eastbound traffic. Save money by traveling directly to the westernmost island on your itinerary and then make your way back to the mainland island by island. Foot passengers travel in either direction between the islands free of charge. For specific departure times and rates, call **Washington State Ferries** (206-464-6400; in WA 800-542-0810). On peak travel days, arrive with your vehicle at least 1 hr. prior to scheduled departure. The ferry authorities accept only cash.

The **area code** for the islands is 206.

■ San Juan Island

Because the 1846 Treaty of Oregon failed to assign the San Juans to either Canada or the U.S., a dispute over ownership of the islands arose in the 1850s. Although the Canadian Hudson's Bay Company had established facilities on the island, the Territorial Congress of Oregon declared the islands its own. By 1859, 25 Americans and many more animals lived on San Juan Island. The cold-blooded shooting of a British pig found in an American farmer's potato patch left both countries with no choice but to send in troops, thus initiating "The Pig War." For 12 years, two thoroughly bored garrisons yawned across the island at each other. According to local historians, 16 Americans died in the conflict, mostly of disease.

Practical Information With bicycle, car, and boat rentals all within a few blocks of the ferry terminal, Friday Harbor proves a convenient berth for exploring the islands. Roads are poorly marked; be sure to get a map. Both the **Chamber of Commerce** (378-5240), on Front St. at the Ferry Terminal, and the **National Park Service Information Center** (378-2240; open Mon.-Fri. 8am-4:30pm, Sat.-Sun. 9am-4:30pm; closed on weekends in winter), northeast corner of 1st and Spring, answer questions about San Juan and Friday Harbor. Get two-wheeled transportation at **Island Bicycles,** 380 Argyle St. (378-4941), in Friday Harbor. (5-speeds $15 per day, 10-speeds $20 per day, mountain bikes $25 per day. Credit card required. Open daily 10am-5:30pm; Labor Day-Memorial Day Thurs.-Sat. 10am-5:30pm.)

San Juan's post office (378-4511; open Mon.-Fri. 8:30am-4:30pm) stamps its feet at Blair and Reed St.; its **ZIP code** is 98250.

Camping and Food San Juan's campgrounds have become wildly popular of late; show up early in the afternoon to make sure you get a spot at either **San Juan County Park,** 380 Westside Rd. (378-2992), 10 mi. west of Friday Harbor on Smallpox and Andrews Bays, which has cold water and flush toilets (no hookups; sites for vehicles $14; biker/hiker sites $4.50), or **Lakedale Campgrounds,** 2627 Roche Harbor Rd. (378-2350), 4 mi. from Friday Harbor, where you can shower for $1 (sites with vehicle access for 1-2 people $15, July-Aug. $18, $3.50 per additional person; biker/hiker sites $5, Sept.-July-Aug. $6.50; open April 1-Oct. 15).

Stock up on bread and cheese at **King's Market,** 160 Spring St. (378-4505; open daily 8am-10pm) or drift in to **Vic's Driftwood Drive-In** (378-8427), at 2nd and Court, for great burgers ($1.60) and shakes ($1.50) so thick you'll get dimples trying to drink them (open Mon.-Fri. 6am-7pm, Sat. 6am-2pm).

Sights and Activities Friday Harbor is less than charming when the tourists are out in full force, but quite appealing at other times, especially in winter. Take the time to poke around the galleries, craft shops, and bookstores. The **Whale Museum,** 62 1st St. (378-4710), features skeletons, sculptures, and information on new research. The museum even has a toll-free **whale hotline** (800-562-8832) to report sightings and strandings. (Open daily 10am-5pm; in winter daily 11am-4pm. $3, seniors and students $2.50, under 12 $1.50.)

Head south out of Friday Harbor on Mullis Rd., which merges into Cattle Point Rd., to **American Camp** (378-2907), 5 mi. south of Friday Harbor, which dates to the Pig War of 1859. Two of the camp's buildings still stand. An interpretive shelter near the entrance to the park explains the history of the conflict. The **British Camp,** the second half of **San Juan Island National Historical Park,** lies on West Valley Rd. on **Garrison Bay.** Here, four original buildings have been preserved, including the barracks, now used as an **interpretive center.** The center chronicles the "War" and shows a 13-min. slide show on the epic struggle. (Park open year-round; buildings open Memorial Day-Labor Day daily 8am-4:30pm. Free.)

Returning north on Cattle Point Rd., consider taking the gravel **False Bay Rd.,** which will guide you down the straight and narrow to **False Bay,** a true bay that is home to a large number of nesting **bald eagles. Whale-watching** at **Lime Kiln Point State Park,** a few mi. north, is best during salmon runs in the summer.

If you're eager to **fish** or **clam,** pick up a copy of the Department of Fisheries pamphlet, *Salmon, Shellfish, Marine Fish Sport Fishing Guide,* for details on regulations and limits, available free at **Friday Harbor Hardware and Marine,** 270 Spring St. (378-4622). Fishing licenses are required on the islands; get one from the hardware store (open Mon.-Sat. 8am-6pm, Sun. 10am-4pm). Check with the **red tide hotline** (800-562-5632) if you'll be gathering shellfish; the nasty bacteria can wreak deadly havoc on your intestines.

■ Orcas Island

Mount Constitution overlooks much of Puget Sound from its 2409-ft. summit atop Orcas Island, the largest island of the San Juan chain. In the mountain's shadow dwells a small population of retirees, artists, and farmers, tending understated homes surrounded by the red bark of madrona trees and greenery.

Practical Information An **unstaffed shack** at North Beach Rd., ½ block north of Horseshoe Hwy., provides **visitor info** through the medium of pamphlets. The best way to see the island is by bike; rent one at **Wildlife Cycle** (376-4708), A St. and North Beach Rd., in Eastsound (21-speeds $5 per hr., $20 per day; open Mon.-Sat. 10:30am-5pm). Receive care packages at the **post office** (376-4121), A St. in Eastsound Market Place (open Mon.-Fri. 9am-4:30pm). The **ZIP code** is 98245.

Accommodations, Camping, Food, and Activities Avoid the expensive B&Bs and stay at the funky **Doe Bay Village Resort,** Star Rte. 86, Olga 98279 (376-2291 or 376-4755), off Horseshoe Hwy. on Pt. Lawrence Rd., 8 mi. out of Moran State Park on a secluded bay. The resort comes with co-ed dorms, kitchen facilities, a health food store, and an organic cafe. The crowning attraction is the steam sauna and mineral bath ($3 per day; bathing suits optional). ($12.50, non-members $14.50. Camping $8.50. Cottages from $32.50. Flexible work-trade program. Reservations recommended.) If the hostel is full, camp at **Moran State Park,** Star Rte. 22, Eastsound 98245 (376-2326), for all the best of San Juan fun—swimming, fishing, and hiking. (Sites with hot showers $11. Hiker or biker sites $5. Park open daily 6:30am-dusk; Sept.-March 8am-dusk. Reservations strongly recommended May-Labor Day. Send $11 per site plus a $5 reservation fee.)

For good Mexican cooking and *great* salsa, bounce to **Bilbos Festivo** (376-4728), Prune Alley and A St. You can try the peppy Christmas burrito year-round ($7), and the chocolate desserts ($3-4) are homemade. (Open Mon.-Fri. noon-2:30pm and 5-9:30pm, Sat.-Sun. 5-9:30pm.)

Trippers on Orcas Island don't need to travel with a destination in mind. At least half the fun lies in simply tramping about—pick a side road, select a particularly moving vista, and meditate on llife, llove, and llamas.

Moran State Park is unquestionably Orcas's greatest attraction. Pick up a copy of the trail guide from the **rangers station** (376-2837). From the summit of **Mt. Constitution,** the highest peak on the islands, you can see other islands in the group, as well as the Olympic and Cascade Ranges, Vancouver Island, and Mt. Rainier. The stone tower at the top serves as an observation tower for tourists and a fire lookout. You can also swim in two freshwater lakes easily accessible from the highway or rent rowboats ($8 per hr.) and paddleboats ($9 per hr.) from the park.

■ Whidbey Island

Whidbey Island, the longest island in the continental U.S., sits in the rain shadow of the Olympic Mountains. The clouds, wrung dry by the time they finally pass over Whidbey, release a scant 20 in. of precipitation on Whidbey each year, endowing the island with one of America's highest amounts of average sunshine.

Practical Information Get tourism info from the Chambers of Commerce in **Oak Harbor,** 5506 Rte. 20 (675-3535; open Mon.-Fri. 9am-5pm, Sat. 9am-6pm, Sun. 10am-4pm; Sept.-May open Mon.-Fri. 9am-5pm), **Coupeville,** 504 N. Main St. (678-5434; open Mon.-Fri. 9am-noon and 2-5pm), and **Langley,** 124½ 2nd St. (321-6765; open Mon.-Fri. 10am-3pm). The **ferry** to Clinton, at the southern end of the island, leaves from **Mukilteo,** just south of Everett (every 30 min. 6am-11pm, 20 min.). **Ferries** also travel between Port Townsend and Keystone, on the west side of the island (8 per day 7am-10pm, 35 min.). Call Washington State Ferries at 800-542-7052 for schedules and fares. **Evergreen Trailways** runs a bus to Whidbey from Seattle (3 per week). **The Pedaler,** 5603½ S. Bayview Rd., Freeland (321-5040), 7 mi. from Clinton, rents bicycles for $4 an hour, $18 a day, and $49 per week.

Post postcards to your friends from **Oak Harbor Post Office,** 7035 70th St. NW (675-6621; open Mon.-Fri. 8:30am-5pm), **ZIP code** 98277. The **area code** is 206.

Accommodations, Food, and Activities Inexpensive motels are few and far between on Whidbey, and those that do exist are often run-down. The **Tyee Motel and Cafe,** 405 S. Main St., Coupeville (678-6616), has clean, standard motel rooms, with showers, but no tubs. (Cafe open Mon.-Sat. 6:30am-8:30pm. Singles and doubles from $43.) You can also check in at the lounge (open 11:30am-2am) if the cafe is closed. A cheaper alternative is camping at **Fort Ebey State Park,** 395 N. Fort Ebey Rd. (678-4636), north of Fort Casey and just west of Coupeville. Miles of hiking trails and easy access to a pebbly beach make this Whidbey's best campground (RV sites $8; Oct.-April $6; hiker/biker sites $4; pay showers). Smoked salmon is the dish of choice on Whidbey. In Oak Harbor, your best bet is the **Safeway** grocery store on Rte. 20. In Langley, try the **Doghouse Tavern,** 230 1st St. (321-9996), a local hangout that serves 10¢ 6-oz. beers with lunch (limit 2) and $5 sandwiches (open Mon.-Fri. 11am-9:30pm. Sat.-Sun. 11am-10pm).

Rocky beaches lead back to bluffs crawling with wild roses and blackberry brambles; keep an eye out for loganberries and Penn Cove mussels as you explore. In general, the interior is uninspiring; Whidbey's real beauty lies in its beaches.

■■■ SEATTLE

Seattle's mid-19th-century pioneers originally named their city New York Alki, meaning "New York By and By," but nowadays, the mere mention of the big Big Apple is enough to make a native skittish. Nonetheless, Seattle has integrated its population into a cohesive and successful, modern city where no single culture dominates. Even Seattle's former Chinatown is now known as the "International

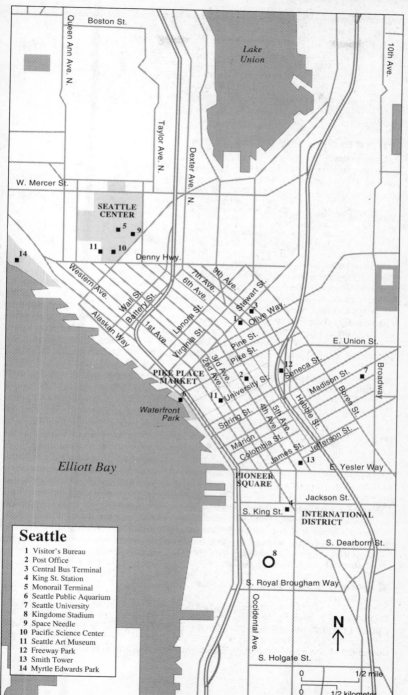

SEATTLE

Seattle

1 Visitor's Bureau
2 Post Office
3 Central Bus Terminal
4 King St. Station
5 Monorail Terminal
6 Seattle Public Aquarium
7 Seattle University
8 Kingdome Stadium
9 Space Needle
10 Pacific Science Center
11 Seattle Art Museum
12 Freeway Park
13 Smith Tower
14 Myrtle Edwards Park

District." Given its diversity, Seattle has been a prolific and creative cradle. The city has spawned musicians such as Jimi Hendrix, Heart, and Mudhoney, and even the Big Apple has been caught smelling the teen spirit of this corner of the country. The roar of the grungy "Seattle Sound"—best exemplified by groups like Nirvana, Pearl Jam, Soundgärden, and Screaming Trees—has outshined all other recent developments in rock and roll. The theater community supports Broadway shows and alternative vaudeville, while the opera consistently sells out. In relative size, the repertory theater community ranks second only to New York among U.S. cities. Seattle supports a dynamic palette of large-scale museums and parks, small galleries, and personable bistros throughout the downtown.

PRACTICAL INFORMATION

Emergency: 911.

Visitor Information: Seattle-King County Visitors Bureau, 666 Stewart St. (461-5840), on the Galleria level of the Convention Center. Well-stocked with maps, brochures, newspapers, and transit schedules. Helpful staff. Open Mon.-Fri. 8:30am-5pm, Sat.-Sun. 10am-4pm. Weekend hours summer only. **National Park Service, Pacific Northwest Region,** 915 2nd Ave. #442 (220-7450). Open Mon.-Fri. 8am-4:30pm.

Airport: Seattle-Tacoma International (Sea-Tac) (433-5217), on Federal Way, south of Seattle proper. **Gray Line** coaches (626-5208; $7 each way, $12 roundtrip) and **Greyhound** (2 per day, $3.50 one-way) both will whisk you to downtown. Metro buses #174 and 194 are cheaper and run daily every ½ hr. 6am-1am. A taxi from the airport to downtown costs about $22.

Amtrak: King Street Station, 3rd and Jackson St. (800-872-7245). To: Portland (3 per day, $23); Tacoma (3 per day, $8); Spokane (1 per day, $65); San Francisco (1 per day, $153). Station open daily 6am-10pm; ticket office open 6:30am-4:30pm.

Buses: Greyhound, 8th Ave. and Stewart St. (800-231-2222 or 628-5526). To: Sea-Tac Airport (2 per day, $3.50); Spokane (4 per day, $35); Vancouver, BC (4 per day, $22); Portland (8 per day, $19). Ticket office open daily 5am-9pm and midnight-1:30am. **Green Tortoise,** 9th Ave. and Stewart (324-7433 or 800-227-4766). Three per week to: Portland ($15); Eugene ($25); San Francisco ($69). Reservations are required and should be made 5 days in advance.

Public Transportation: Metro Transit, 821 2nd Ave. (24-hr. info 553-3000), in the Exchange Building downtown. Open Mon.-Fri. 8am-5pm. Buses run daily 6am-1am; a few buses offer night-owl service 1:30-4:30am. Fares based on a 2-zone system. Zone 1 is everything within the city limits ($1.10 during peak hours, 85¢ off-peak); Zone 2 is anything outside the city limits ($1.60 peak, $1.10 off-peak, kids 5-18 75¢). Seniors and disabled persons 25¢ with reduced fare permit ($1). Peak hours weekdays 6-9am and 3-6pm. Exact fare required. Weekend all-day passes $1.70. Between 4am-9pm, ride free within the "Magic Carpet" area bordered by Jackson St. on the south, 6th Ave. and I-5 on the east, Battery St. on the north, and the waterfront on the west. Transfers valid for 2 hrs. and for Waterfront Streetcars as well.

Ferries: Washington State Ferries, Colman Dock, Pier 52 (464-2000 for recording, ext. 4 for schedule and fare info; in WA 800-542-0810 or 800-542-7052). Service to Bremerton (on Kitsap Peninsula), Winslow (on Bainbridge Island), and Vashon Island (passenger ferry only). Ferries leave daily (and frequently) 6am-2am. Fares from $3.30; car and driver $6.65 ($5.65 in winter).

Car Rental: A-19.95-Rent-A-Car, 804 N. 145th St. (365-1995). $20 per day ($25 if under 21), with 100 free mi., 15¢ per additional mi. Drivers under 21 must have verifiable auto insurance. Credit card required.

Bike Rental: The Bicycle Center, 4529 Sand Point Way (523-8300). $3 per hr. (2-hr. min.), $15 per day. Credit card or license required as deposit. Open Mon.-Thurs. 10am-8pm, Fri.-Sat. 10am-6pm, Sun. noon-5pm.

Help Lines: Crisis Clinic, 461-3222. **Seattle Rape Relief,** 1905 S. Jackson St., #102 (632-RAPE). Both 24 hrs.

Post Office: (442-6340), Union St. and 3rd Ave. downtown. Open Mon.-Fri. 8am-5:30pm. **ZIP code:** 98101.

SEATTLE

Area Code: 206.

Seattle is a long, skinny city stretched out north to south between long, skinny **Puget Sound** on the west and long, skinny **Lake Washington** on the east. The head of the city is cut from its torso by Lake Union and a string of locks, canals, and bays. These link the saltwater of Puget Sound with the freshwater of Lake Washington. In the downtown area, avenues run northwest to southeast and streets southwest to northeast. After Western Ave., the avenues run numerically up the hill to 6th Ave. Downtown streets run south to north in pairs. Outside the downtown area, avenues run north to south and streets east to west, with only a few exceptions. The city is split into **quadrants:** 1000 1st Ave. NW is a long hike from 1000 1st Ave. S.

ACCOMMODATIONS

The **Seattle International Hostel** is the best option for the budget traveler staying downtown.

Seattle International Hostel (HI/AYH), 84 Union St. (622-5443), at Western Ave. Take Metro #174, 184, or 194 from the airport. 139 beds, common kitchen which never closes, immaculate facilities, plenty of modern amenities, and a friendly, knowledgeable staff. Convenient location and alluring crowd. Always full in summer, so make reservations (participates in international reservations system). During the summer, there is a supplemental hostel for overflow. Discount tickets for Aquarium and Omnidome. Sleep sacks required (linen rental $2). 5-day max. stay in summer. Front desk open 7am-midnight. Check-out 10:30am. $14, nonmembers $17. Members get priority in the summer.

YMCA, 909 4th Ave. (382-5000), near the Madison St. intersection. Men and women; must be over 18. Small but well-kept rooms. Good location; tight security, with a staffed security desk. TV lounge on each floor, laundry facilities, and use of swimming pool and fitness facilities. Bring your own bedding for the bunk-room and your own lock for lockers. Check-out by noon. No curfew. HI/AYH members: bunk-room $18, singles $33, doubles $36. Nonmembers: singles $39, with TV and bath $53; doubles $43.50, with TV and bath $57. Weekly rates for all visitors: singles $167; doubles $190.

Moore Motel, 1926 2nd Ave. (448-4851), at 2nd and Virginia. Next to the historic Moore Theater. Big rooms with 2 beds, bath, and TV. Singles $34. Doubles $39. Those with HI\AYH membership turned away from the full hostel, get singles for $20 and doubles for $25.

Commodore Hotel, 2013 2nd Ave. (448-8868), at Virginia. Clean and in a relatively safe area. The rates are worth sacrificing a private bath. Singles $33, with bath $42, with 2 beds and bath $49. One shared double with shared bath $37.

Vincent's Guest House, 527 Malden Ave. E (323-7849). This hostel-like guest house in Capitol Hill is a bit removed from downtown proper, but a friendly and funky alternative if the Seattle Hostel is full. Kitchen facilities and fresh herbs from the garden (but no, not *that* herb). No curfew. Checkout 11am. Private rooms available. Shared rooms $12.

Park Plaza Motel, 4401 Aurora Ave. N. (632-2101). Just north of the Aurora bridge; take Metro #6 to 46th Ave. or #5 to 43rd and Fremont. Friendly and surprisingly quiet. Bare rooms and halls. Singles $30. Doubles from $35.

FOOD

As the principal marketplace for Washington's famous fishing industries and orchards, Seattle is aswarm with salmon and apples. Seattle restauranteurs, however, seem equally inclined to stick their heads in ovens: bakeries proliferate alongside endless espresso stands. The best fish, produce, and baked goods can be purchased from various vendors in **Pike Place Market,** established in 1907, when angry Seattle citizens demanded the elimination of the middle-merchant (open Mon.-Sat. 6:30am-6pm, Sun. 6:30am-5pm).

For excellent ethnic food, head for the International District, along King and Jackson St., between 5th and 8th Ave., which crowds together immigrants—some of them excellent chefs—from China, Japan, the Philippines, and Southeast Asia. Fierce competition keeps prices low and quality high.

Soundview Cafe (623-5700), on the mezzanine level in the Main Arcade just to the left of the largest fish stall. This wholesome self-serve sandwich-and-salad bar offers fresh food, a spectacular view of the Sound (naturally), and occasional poetry readings. Get a View Special (eggs and potatoes) for $2.70, try the West African nut stew ($2.15), or bring a brown-bag lunch—the cafe offers public seating. Open Mon.-Sat. 7am-5:30pm, Sun. 9am-3:30pm.

Three Girls Bakery (622-1045), at Post and Pike Pl. Order to go or sit in the cafe. The rows of bread and pastry in the display alone will make you drool, not to mention the aroma. Mammoth apple fritters (95¢). Open Mon.-Sat. 7am-6pm.

Tai Tung, 655 S. King St. (622-7372). The busiest hours at Tai Tung are 1-3am, when the munchies take hold of university students. Waiters here rise to the occasion—they're likely to learn your name by the second night you're in. 10-page menu taped up around the dining room, with entrees $7-8. Open Mon.-Sat. 10am-3:30am, Sun. 10am-1:30am.

Phnom Penh Noodle Soup House, 414 Maynard Ave. S. (682-5690). Phnomenal Cambodian cuisine. Head to the tiny upstairs dining room for a good view of the park and a large bowl of noodles. Try the Phnom Penh Noodle Special ($3.70); some people come here weekly and never order anything else. Open Mon.-Tues. and Thurs.-Sun. 8:30am-6pm.

Hamburger Mary's, 401 Broadway E (325-6565), in the ritzy Broadway Market. Rockin' and racin' with the Broadway Ave. step, this branch outlet of Portland's famous H.M. is a hot-spot for the gay community. Nightly specials offer less meaty options than the obvious fare. Hamburgers around $5. Entrees under $12. Open Mon.-Fri. 10am-2am, Sat.-Sun. 9am-2am.

Cafe Paradiso, 1005 E. Pike (322-6960). A bit off the geographical beaten-path, this proud-to-be-alternative cafe gives you your RDA of both caffeine and counterculture. Open Mon.-Thurs. 6am-1am, Fri. 6am-4am, Sat. 8am-4am, Sun. 8am-1am.

The Cause Célèbre, 524 15th Ave. E (323-1888), at Mercer St. The special province of Seattle's well-fed left. Stay away if you don't like alternative music or discussions of Serbian atrocities. *Al fresco* dining on the spacious porch. Extensive vegetarian selection; try the eggplant parmigiana ($5). Great Sun. brunch ($4-6). Lunch sandwiches ($4-5). Open Mon.-Sat. 9am-9pm, Sun. 9am-5pm.

Asia Deli, 4235 University Way NE (632-2364). No corned beef here—this atypical deli offers quick service and generous portions of delicious Vietnamese and Thai food (mostly of the noodle persuasion). Try the sauteed chicken and onions ($3.75). Almost all the dishes are under $4 and all are prepared without MSG. Open Mon.-Sat. 11am-10pm, Sun. noon-9pm.

SIGHTS AND ACTIVITIES

If you have only a day to spare in Seattle, despair not. The best way to take in the city and its skyline is from one of the **ferries** that leave the waterfront at frequent intervals (see Practical Information above). You can get a closer look at most of the city sights in one day—most are walking distance from each other, within the Metro's free zone. You can easily explore Pike Place, waterfront, Pioneer Square and the International District in one easy excursion. Or skip the downtown thing altogether and take a rowboat out onto Lake Union, bike along Lake Washington, or hike through Discovery Park.

At the south end of Pike Place Market (see Food) begins the **Pike Place Hillclimb,** a set of staircases leading down past chic shops and ethnic restaurants to Alaskan Way and the **waterfront.** (An elevator is also available.) The waterfront docks once accepted shiploads of gold from the 1897 Klondike gold rush. Now, on a pier full of shops and restaurants, the credit card is standard currency. On Pier 59 at the base of the hillclimb, the **Seattle Aquarium** (386-4320) explains the history of marine life in Puget Sound and the effects of tidal action (open daily 10am-5pm; $6.50, seniors $5, kids 6-18 $4, kids 3-5 $1.50).

Westlake Park, on Pike St. between 5th and 4th Ave., with its Art Deco brick patterns and Wall of Water, is a good place to kick back and listen to steel drums. This small park is bordered by the original **Nordstrom's** and the gleaming new **Westlake Center.** Take the **monorail** (75¢) from the third floor of the Westlake Center to **Seattle Center,** a 74-acre park originally constructed for the 1962 World's Fair. Located between Denny Way, W. Mercer St., 1st, and 5th Ave., the Center has eight gates, each equipped with a model of the Center and a map of its facilities. The **Pacific Science Center** (443-2001), within the park, houses a laserium and IMAX theater (open daily 10am-6pm; Labor Day-June Mon.-Fri. 10am-5pm, Sat.-Sun. 10am-6pm. $5.50, seniors and ages 6-13 $4.50, ages 2-5 $3.50; laser shows $1 extra). The **Space Needle** (443-2100), a.k.a. the world's tackiest monument, has an observation tower and restaurant. On clear days, you can see a lot of **stuff.** (Observation Deck open daily 8am-midnight. $6, seniors $5, kids 5-12 $4.)

Two blocks from the waterfront bustles historic **Pioneer Square,** where 19th-century warehouses and office buildings were restored in a spasm of prosperity during the 70s. The *Complete Browser's Guide to Pioneer Square,* available in area bookstores, provides a short history and walking tour.

When Seattle nearly burned to the ground in 1889, an ordinance was passed to raise the city 35 ft. At first, shops below the elevated streets remained open for business and were moored to the upper city by an elaborate network of stairs. In 1907 the city moved upstairs permanently, and the underground city was sealed off. The vast **Bill Speidel's Underground Tours** (682-4646) does exactly what its name suggests. Speidel spearheaded the movement to save Pioneer Square from the apocalypse of renewal. The tours offer informative glimpses at Seattle's beginnings; just ignore the rats that infest the tunnels. Tours (1½ hr.) leave from Doc Maynard's Pub at 610 1st Ave. (March-Sept. 6-8 per day 10am-6pm. Make reservations. $4.75, seniors and students $3.50, kids 6-12 $2.75.) Once back above ground, learn about eating boots at the **Klondike Gold Rush National Historical Park,** 117 S. Main St. (442-7220). The "interpretive center" depicts the lives and fortunes of the miners. The park screens Charlie Chaplin's 1925 classic, *The Gold Rush,* on the first Sunday of each month at 3pm. (Open daily 9am-5pm. Free.)

Three blocks east of Pioneer Square, up Jackson on King St., is Seattle's **International District.** Though sometimes still called Chinatown by Seattleites, this area has peoples from all over Asia. Behold the **Tsutakawa Sculpture** at the corner of S. Jackson and Maynard St. and the gigantic dragon mural in **Hing Hay Park** at S. King and Maynard St. Peep in or duck into the **Wing Luke Memorial Museum,** 414 8th St. (623-5124), which houses a permanent exhibit on the different Asian groups that have settled in Seattle as well as temporary exhibits by local Asian artists. There are occasional free demonstrations of traditional crafts. (Open Tues.-Fri. 11am-4:30pm, Sat.-Sun. noon-4pm. $2.50, students and seniors $1.50, kids 5-12 75¢. Thurs. free.)

Capitol Hill inspires extreme reactions from both its residents and neighbors. The district's leftist and gay communities set the tone for its nightspots, while the retail outlets include a large number of collectives and radical bookstores. Saunter down Broadway or its cross-streets to window-shop, or walk a few blocks east and north for a stroll down the hill's lovely residential streets, lined with beautiful Victorian homes. Bus #10 runs along 15th St. and #7 along Broadway.

With 35,000 students, the **University of Washington** is the state's cultural and educational center of gravity. The **"U district"** swarms with bookstores, shops, taverns, and restaurants. Stop by the friendly and helpful **visitors center,** 4014 University Way NE (543-9198), to pick up a map of the campus and to obtain university info (open Mon.-Fri. 8am-5pm).

On campus, visit the **Thomas Burke Memorial Washington State Museum** (543-5590), 45th St. and 17th Ave. NE, in the northwest corner of the grounds. The museum houses artifacts of the Pacific Northwest Native American tribes. The scrimshaw display will remain engraved in your memory. (Open daily 10am-5pm, Thurs. until 8pm. Donation of $2.50, seniors and students $1.50 requested.) The **Henry Art Gallery** (543-2256), 15th Ave. and 41st St. NE, houses a collection of 18th- to 20th-century European and American art. (Open Tues.-Wed. and Fri.-Sun. 10am-5pm, Thurs. 10am-9pm. $3, students and seniors $1.50.) The **UW Arts Ticket Office,** 4001 University Way NE, has info and tickets for all events. (Open Mon.-Fri. 10:30am-6pm.) To reach the U district, take buses #71-74 from downtown, #7 or 43 from Capitol Hill.

Waterways and Parks

A string of attractions stud the waterways linking Lake Washington and Puget Sound. Houseboats and sailboats fill **Lake Union.** Here, the **Center for Wooden Boats,** 1010 Valley St. (382-2628), maintains a moored flotilla of new and restored small craft for rental (rowboats $8-12 per hr., sailboats $10-15 per hr.; open daily 11am-6pm). **Kelly's Landing,** 1401 Boat St. NE (547-9909), below the UW campus, rents canoes for outings on Lake Union (sailboats $10-20 per hr.; hours determined by weather, but normally Mon.-Fri. 10am-dusk, Sat.-Sun. 9am-dusk).

Mock and ridicule trout and salmon as they flop and flounder up 21 concrete steps at the **fish ladder** (783-7059) on the south side of the locks. Take bus #43 from the U District or #17 from downtown. On the northwestern shore of the city lies the **Golden Gardens Park** in Loyal Heights, between 80th and 95th NW, with a frigid beach. Several expensive restaurants line the piers to the south; the unobstructed views of the Olympics almost make their uniformly excellent seafood worth the price on salmon chanted evening.

Directly north of Lake Union, "Beautiful People" run, roller skate, and skateboard around **Green Lake.** Take bus #16 from downtown. The lake also draws windsurfers, but woe to those who lose balance. Whoever named Green Lake wasn't kidding; even a quick dunk results in gobs of green algae lodged in every pore and follicle. Next door grows Woodland Park and the **Woodland Park Zoo,** 5500 Phinney Ave. N. (684-4034), best reached from Rte. 99 or N. 50th St. Take bus #5 from downtown. The park looks shaggy, but the zoo is one of only three in the U.S. to receive the Humane Society's highest standard of approval. (Open daily 9:30am-6pm; in winter, closing time depends on day length. $6, seniors, disable persons, and kids 6-17 $3.50, kids 3-5 $1.50.)

ENTERTAINMENT AND NIGHTLIFE

The **Seattle Opera** (443-4700) performs in the Opera House in the Seattle Center throughout the winter. The popularity of the program requires that you order tickets well in advance, although rush tickets are sometimes available 15 min. before curtain time ($8 and up). During lunch hours in the summertime, the free, city-sponsored **"Out to Lunch"** series (623-0340) brings everything from reggae to folk dancing to the parks and squares of Seattle.

Boasting the second-largest number of professional companies in the U.S., Seattle hosts an exciting array of first-run plays and alternative works. You can often get **rush tickets** at nearly half price on the day of the show (cash only) from **Ticket/ Ticket** (324-2744). The **Seattle Repertory Theater,** 155 Mercer (443-2222), performs in the **Bagley Wright Theater** in Seattle Center. Artistic director Daniel Sullivan and the repertory company won the 1990 Tony for Regional Excellence. (Tickets for weekends and opening nights $16-32. Other nights and Sun. matinee $14-30. Student and seniors rush tickets available for $7 10 min. before each show with ID.) Other theaters worth checking out are **A Contemporary Theater (ACT),** 100 W. Roy (285-5110), at the base of Queen Anne Hill, the **Annex Theatre,** 1916 4th Ave. (728-0933), and **The Empty Space Theatre,** 3509 Fremont Ave. N. (547-7500). (Tickets $7-23.)

Seattle is also a *Cinema Paradiso.* Most of the theaters that screen non-Hollywood films are on Capitol Hill and in the University District. Most matinee shows (before 6pm) cost $4—after 6pm, expect to pay $6.50. **The Egyptian,** 801 E. Pine St. (323-4978), on Capitol Hill, is a handsome Art Deco theater best known for hosting the **Seattle Film Festival.** Half the fun of seeing a movie at **The Harvard Exit,** 807 E. Roy (323-8986), on Capitol Hill, is the theater itself, a converted residence—the lobby was once someone's living room. Arrive early for complimentary cheese and crackers over a game of chess, checkers, or backgammon. (Tickets at both $6.50, seniors and kids $4, first matinee $4.)

The best spot for guaranteed good beer, live music, and big crowds is **Pioneer Square.** Most of the bars around the Square participate in a **joint cover** ($10) that will let you wander from bar to bar and sample the bands you like. **Fenix Cafe and Fenix Underground** (343-7740), **Central Tavern** (622-0209), and the **Swan Cafe** (343-5288) all rock and roll consistently, while **Larry's** (624-5288) and **New Orleans** (622-2563) feature great jazz and blues nightly. All the Pioneer Square clubs close at 2am Fridays and Saturdays, and at around midnight during the week.

The Trolleyman Pub, 3400 Phinney N (548-8000). In the back of the Red Hook Ale Brewery. A mellow spot to listen to good acoustic music and contemplate the newly-made bubbles in a fresh pint, especially if it is a pint of Nut Brown Ale. Open Mon.-Fri. 8am-11pm, Sat. 11am-11pm, Sun. noon-6pm.

Off Ramp, 109 Eastlake Ave. E (628-0232). A popular venue for the local music scene. Always loud and sometimes wild. Open 5pm-2am daily. Varied cover.

OK Hotel, 212 Alaskan Way (621-7903), just below Pioneer Square towards the waterfront. Lots of wood, lots of coffee. No liquor, but great live bands with hot alternative sound. Open Sun.-Thurs. 6am-3am, Fri. and Sat. 8am-4am. Occasional cover up to $6.

RKCNDY, 1812 Yale Ave. (623-0470). Shares the spotlight with the Off Ramp as the venue of choice for bands peddling the now-classic "Seattle sound." Open 9pm-2am Wed.-Sun.

Weathered Wall, 1921 5th Ave. (448-5688). An audience as diverse and artistic as its offerings (poetry readings to punk). The Weathered Wall is always interesting. Open Tues.-Sun. 9pm-2am. Cover $3-7.

Re-Bar, 1144 Howell (233-9873). A gay bar for those who like dancing on the wild side, depending on the night. Open daily 8pm-2am.

■ Near Seattle: Vashon Island

About 75% of Vashon Island is undeveloped—green forests of Douglas firs, rolling cherry orchards, strawberry fields, and wildflowers cover it during the summer. The rest of the island is just a tiny town and several unimposing factories.

Ferries leave from Fauntleroy (in Seattle) for the northern end of Vashon. Contact **Washington State Ferries** (800-84-FERRY in WA, or 464-6400) for schedules and fares. The Seattle ferry carries passengers only.

The **Vashon Island Ranch/Hostel (HI/AYH)** (sometimes called **"Seattle B"**) is really the island's only accommodation, and it is in itself one of the main reasons to come here. The hostel is located at 12119 SW Cove Rd. (463-2592). Judy will come pick you up if the hour is reasonable, and she has never turned a hosteler away. "Seattle B" has all the comforts of home—free pancakes for breakfast, free use of old bikes, free fire wood, free volleyball games in the afternoon, and a caring manager. When all beds are full, you can pitch a tent (open year-round; tents and beds $8, nonmembers $11). Most hostelers get creative in the kitchen with supplies from **Thriftaway,** downtown (open Mon.-Sat. 8am-9pm, Sun. 8am-7pm).

The island is wonderful for **biking,** and **Point Robinson Park** is a gorgeous spot for a picnic (from Vashon Hwy. take Ellisburg to Dockton to Pt. Robinson Rd.). More than 500 acres of hiking trails weave their way through the woods in the middle of the island, and several lovely walks start from the hostel.

■ California

California is the most populous state in the U.S., and in terms of diversity and size, it is practically a nation unto itself. Indeed, its citizens often come across as blithely ignorant of the existence of the 49 other states. Californians have an understated pride, which comes across not as the bragging of Texans, the snobbery of New Yorkers, or the insecurity of Floridians, but rather as the quiet confidence of a people who firmly believe that they have found the best living space on the planet.

California residents should know; they hail from all corners of the globe, each looking to fulfill his own California dream. People are attracted to the state not solely for its natural beauty, nor for its seemingly limitless opportunities for economic success, nor for its toleration of different lifestyles. The California spirit is even more than a potent mixture of these hopes. There is a strong streak of narcissism infused in the dream—California almost demands it with its relentless celebration of individuality. Only here could self-realization be an industry.

Don't come to the Golden State looking for America. You won't find it. You will, however, find a culture and lifestyle that is peculiarly Californian, from sprawling Los Angeles, with its many suburbs in search of a city, to compact San Francisco, which combines the cultural flair of the East Coast with the laid-back, liberal attitudes of the Left Coast. The small towns and countryside in the hinterland of the two megalopoli have characters of their own, from the quiet beach settlements on the coast, to the agribusiness centers of the Central Valley, to the boom-and-bust towns of the Sierra Nevada. You will find low, sweltering deserts and cool alpine ski country. You will find towering redwoods and drifting sands. And in the end, you will perhaps understand how Californians can still exhibit vestiges of provincialism in the age of the global village—with a whole world right in their backyard, why would they look any further?

PRACTICAL INFORMATION

Capital: Sacramento.
Visitors Information: California Office of Tourism, 801 K St. #1600, Sacramento 95814 (call 800-862-2543 ext. A1003 to have a package of tourism materials sent to you). **National Park Information:** 415-556-0560.
Time Zone: Pacific (3 hrs. behind Eastern). **Postal Abbreviation**: CA
Sales Tax: 7.5%

> Dude! For a way radical trip, like, you should totally get *Let's Go: California & Hawaii*. It's a boss book! Get it at the mall. Like, in the bookstore, you know?

CENTRAL COAST

Although the popular image of the California dream is dominated by San Francisco and Los Angeles, it is the stretch of coast between these two cities that embodies everything that is uniquely Californian: rolling surf replete with surfers, sandy white beaches filled with tall palms, self-actuating New Agers, and dramatic cliffs topped with towering redwoods.

San Simeon anchors the southern end of Big Sur, a 90-mi. strip of sparsely inhabited coastline where the **Pacific Coast Highway** (Rte. 1), inches motorists right to the edge of jutting cliffs overhanging the ocean. Winding its way through this stunning wilderness, Rte. 1 reaches north to the Monterey Peninsula, where golf courses and the shopping mall lifestyle of Carmel announce a return to civilization. Just

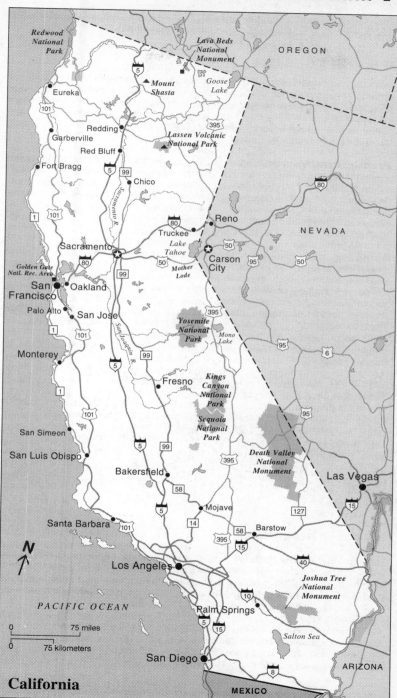

California

above Monterey, 79 mi. south of San Francisco, Santa Cruz fuses Southern Californian surfer culture with San Francisco's off-beat quirkiness.

■■■ BIG SUR

In 1542 Cabrillo sailed off the coast of Big Sur and wrote that here "there are mountains which seem to reach the heavens, and the sea beats on them." The imposing geography of the region—rugged mountains, towering redwoods, frothing surf, and glistening beaches—still defines Big Sur today. If you come here, it is to enjoy nature, be it by hiking, boating, fishing, or even driving. This 90-mi. stretch of coast has no golf, no bowling, no movies.

Practical Information Monterey's Spanish settlers simply called the entire region below their town "El Sur Grande"—the Vast South. Today, "Big Sur" signifies a more exact coastal region bordered on the south by San Simeon and on the north by Carmel. For a guide to Big Sur, send a self-addressed, stamped envelope to **Big Sur Chamber of Commerce,** P.O. Box 87, Big Sur 93920 (667-2100). The **post office** (667-2305) stirs on Rte. 1, next to the Center Deli in Big Sur Center (open Mon.-Fri. 8:30am-5pm). The **ZIP Code** is 93920; the **area code** is 408.

Camping Places to camp are abundant and beautiful. If you neglect to bring camping equipment, you've made a big mistake. The cheapest way to stay in Big Sur is to camp out in the free Ventana Wilderness (you must pick up a free permit at Big Sur Station). **Andrew Molera State Park** (667-2315) is 5 mi. north of Pfeiffer Big Sur, where the Big Sur River pours into the ocean. (Tents only. Beach, pit toilets, no showers. Sites $3 per person, dogs $1.) Though an inland park, **Pfeiffer Big Sur State Park** (667-2315), just south of Fernwood, 26 mi. south of Carmel, is no less popular than those on the beach. Reserve through MISTIX (800-365-2267). (218 developed campsites, no hookups. Hot showers. Sites $16. Day-use fee $6.) **Los Padres National Forest** shelters two USFS Campgrounds: **Plaskett Creek** (667-2315), south of Limekiln, near Jade Cove (43 sites), and **Kirk Creek,** 5 mi. north of Jade Cove, close to the highway (33 sites). (No showers or hot water. Open 24 hrs. Check-out 2pm. Sites $15, hikers and bikers $3. No reservations.)

Food Grocery stores are located at River Inn, Ripplewood, Fernwood, Big Sur Lodge, Pacific Valley Center, and Gorda, but it's better to arrive prepared; prices are high. Breakfast on the deck under the redwoods at **Big Sur River Inn** (667-2700), 24 mi. south of Carmel (3 pancakes with 2 eggs $5.25), or have the speciality, pan-fried trout ($14), anytime (open daily 8am-10pm, live music Sat. night and Sun. day). A local favorite, **Nepenthe Restaurant** (667-2345), Rte. 1, serves a hamburger—excuse us—a *ground steak sandwich* for $10 (yes, $10). Fire pit at night. Outdoor seating provides a spectacular view of water, mountains, and mist. Bring your camera. (Open daily 11:30am-4:30pm, 5-10pm.)

Sights and Activities The **state parks** and **wilderness areas** are exquisite settings for dozens of outdoor activities. **Hiking** on Big Sur is a dream: the state parks and **Los Padres National Forest** all have trails that penetrate redwood forests and cross low chaparral, offering even grander views of Big Sur than those available from Rte. 1. The northern end of Los Padres National Forest has been designated the **Ventana Wilderness** and contains the popular **Pine Ridge Trail.** Grab a map and a required permit at the USFS ranger station (see Practical Information above).

Within **Pfeiffer Big Sur State Park** are 8 trails of varying lengths (50¢ map available at park entrance). Try the **Valley View Trail,** a short, steep path overlooking the valley below. **Buzzard's Roost Trail,** on the other hand, is a rugged two-hour hike up tortuous switchbacks; if you can make it to the top, you'll be treated to a panorama of the Santa Lucia Mountains, the Big Sur Valley, and the Pacific Ocean.

Big Sur's most jealously guarded treasure is USFS-operated **Pfeiffer Beach,** 1 mi. south of Pfeiffer State Park. Turn off at the stop sign and the "Narrow Road not suitable for trailers" sign and follow the road 2 mi. to the parking area. Replete with sea caves and sea gulls, the small cove is partially protected from the Pacific by a massive offshore rock formation.

■ Near Big Sur: Hearst Castle

Commonly known as Hearst Castle, the **Hearst San Simeon Historic Monument** (927-2010) lies 5 mi. east of Rte. 1 near San Simeon. William Randolph Hearst, infamous magnate *cum* yellow journalist and instigator of the Spanish-American War, began building this Hispano-Moorish indulgence in 1919. Much of the castle's "art" is actually fake: concrete statuary, plaster pilasters, artificially aged tiles. Yet many genuine treasures remain tucked away: the world's largest private collection of Greek vases lines the shelves of the library; medieval tapestries hang in the halls; and ancient Chinese ceramics perch on the mantel pieces of Gothic fireplaces.

Visitors have a choice of five **tours,** each 2 hr. long. It's possible to take them all in one day, but each costs $14, ages 6-12 $8, under 6 free. Groups are taken up the hill in buses, shepherded around, then taken back down. Tours at least every hour 8am-3pm. If you really want to see the Castle in summer, advance reservations are a must (800-444-4445). Tickets go on sale daily at 8am.

■■■ MONTEREY

In the 1940s, John Steinbeck's Monterey docked as a coastal town geared to sardine fishing and canning. When Steinbeck revisited his beloved Cannery Row around 1960, he scornfully wrote that the area had mutated into a tourist trap. Where packing plants once stood, espresso bars and fudge shops now rule. But residents do treat with dignity some of the area's history, both as a canning town and former capital of Spanish and Mexican Alta California; visitors should forgive Monterey its crasser side.

Practical Information The town of Monterey is on the northern side of the Monterey Peninsula 115 mi. south of San Francisco. Pacific Grove, a quiet community frequented by fewer tourists, and Pebble Beach, an exclusive nest of mansions, occupy the peninsula proper. Carmel, lying southwest of Monterey, stands where the peninsula ends on its southern side. The **Monterey Peninsula Chamber of Commerce,** 380 Alvarado St., P.O. Box 1770, Monterey 93942 (649-1770), downtown, provides a 112-page *Visitor's Guide* ($2.50) with area restaurant, accommodation, and tourist info (open Mon.-Fri. 8:30am-5pm). **Greyhound** (800-231-2222) has no office but only a stop for wayward buses at 351 Del Monte Ave., site of the old office, with a schedule posted on the door. Tickets may be purchased from the driver or at another station (like Salinas or Santa Cruz). The **post office** stamps to a god unknown at 565 Hartnell (372-5803; open Mon.-Fri. 8:45am-5:10pm). The **ZIP code** is 93940; the **area code** is 408.

Accommodations and Camping Prices for Monterey lodgings often vary by day, month, and proximity to an important event, such as the Jazz Festival. As a general rule, reasonably priced hotels are found in the 2000 block of Fremont St. in Monterey (bus #9 or 10) and Lighthouse Ave. in Pacific Grove (bus #2 or some #1 buses). The **Monterey Peninsula Youth Hostel (HI/AYH)** (649-0375) theoretically has no location, but the hostel has been in the Monterey High School for the past few summers. Mattresses are put directly on the floor in a long line along the gymnasium walls, but the staff tries to make up for the deficiencies by providing inexpensive food and lots of information. To reach the high school, take Pacific away from the water, make a right on Madison and a left on Larkin St. (Lockout 9am-6pm. Curfew 11pm. Members $6, nonmembers $9. Under 18 50% off. Open daily mid-June to mid-Aug.) The **Paramount Motel,** 3298 Del Monte Blvd. (384-8674), in Marina, 8 mi. north of Monterey, and its decor date from the '50s. It's clean and well-run. (Check-out 11am. Singles $25-30, doubles $30-35, with kitchenette $40-50. No reservations, so arrive at noon to get a room.) **Veterans Memorial Park Campground** (646-3865), Via Del Rey, 1½ mi. from the town center, has a great view of the bay. (40 sites, hot showers. First-come, first-camped. Arrive before 3pm in summer and on weekends in winter. Sites $15, hikers $3.) **Laguna Seca Recreational Area** (422-6138), Rte. 68 10 mi. east of Monterey, is a lovely park with oak-strewn verdant hills overlooking valleys and a race track. (178 campsites, 103 with hookup. Showers, restrooms, barbecue pits, tables, and a dump station. Sites $15, with hookup $20.)

Food The whales may be gone and the sardines with them, but the unpolluted Monterey Bay still teems with squid, crab, rock cod, sand dab, red snapper, and salmon. Although the seafood is bountiful, it is often expensive—harvest gypsies should opt for an early bird special (4-6:30pm or so). The patio of this 1841 structure, with weathered wooden tables, Mexican wrought-iron chairs, and Mexican newspapers as placemats will delight you at **Casa de Gutiérrez,** 590 Calle Principal (375-0095). Get your tortilla flat here. Have two tacos ($2.75) or a combination plate ($6-10). (Open Mon.-Sweet Thursday 11am-9pm, Fri.-Sun. 10am-10pm.) **Tutto Buono Gastronomic Specialties,** 469 Alvarado (372-1880), serves fresh brick-oven pizzas (from $6), hearty pastas ($8-10), and specials tending toward seafood (open Mon.-Sat. 11am-3pm, dinner starting at 5pm daily, when the moon is down).

Sights and Entertainment The **Monterey Bay Aquarium,** 866 Cannery Row (648-4800), pumps in raw, unfiltered seawater, making the tanks an almost exact duplicate of the environment in the bay—right down to the dozens of species of algae and the simulated waves. In addition to enormous octopi and docile starfish, the aquarium contains 30-ft. kelps and diving birds; 1994's exhibit "Mating Games" deals with reproduction and survival in the aquatic world. The aquarium is sardined with tourists mornings and holidays, but after 3pm things ebb. You won't find the red pony at play in the pastures of heaven here. (Open daily 10am-6pm. Admission $11.25, seniors and students $8.25, ages 3-12 $5.)

On the waterfront, southeast of the aquarium and just east of eden, lies Steinbeck's **Cannery Row.** Once lined with languishing sardine-packing plants—homes of mice and men—this 1-mi. street has been transformed into a long valley of glitzy mini-malls, bars, and discos in dubious battle. To overcome the grapes of wrath here, take flight at one of the wine tasting rooms for a free sample of California's Lethe, a spirit for America and Americans.

At the south end of the row floats yet another **Fisherman's Wharf,** built in 1846. The fishermen have left for the Sea of Cortez, and the wharf now lures tourists with expensive restaurants and shops vending seashells and Steinbeck novels. The pearl of the wharf, and maybe even all of Monterey, is the smoked salmon sandwiches sold by local vendors, made with fresh sourdough bread, cream cheese, and plenty of the local salmon from the outer shores (smoked right on the pier).

Most of the town's historical buildings downtown now belong to the **Monterey State Historic Park.** Each is clearly marked by a sign out in front and can provide information and free maps of suggested walking tours. One such historic adobe is the **Stevenson House,** 530 Houston St., with Robert Louis Stevenson memorabilia. (Tours Tues.-Sun. 2-4pm, on the hour.) If you plan to visit more than one of the houses which charge admission, purchase a $5 pass which gets you into all the historic park buildings and allows you to participate in any or all of the walking tours. Buy your ticket at the **Visitors Center** (649-7118) inside the Park Headquarters in the Custom's House Plaza (open daily 10am-5pm, in winter 10am-4pm). The center sells the *Path of History* walking tour book ($2), and offers the Monterey Historic Park **House and Garden Tour** for hardcore history fans (daily 10:30am, 12:30, 2:30pm). The 1½-hour tour features 10 historic buildings and five gardens ($2, under 18 $1.50). In the same neighborhood as the adobes lies the **Monterey Peninsula Museum of Art,** 559 Pacific St. (372-7591), with a downstairs exhibit of European and American monochrome works from across the centuries, an upstairs collection of Western art including works by Charlie Russell, and another gallery for temporary shows. (Open Tues.-Sat. 10am-4pm, Sun. 1-4pm. Donation $2.)

The annual **Monterey Jazz Festival,** a series of concerts over three days in the third week of September, features the great names of jazz burning bright (closer to Buddy Rich than Alex Ross for the most part) and attracts crowds from all over California. Season tickets sell out by May 31 ($111-150). Call 373-3366 for information.

■ Near Monterey: Pinnacles National Monument

South of Salinas, U.S. 101 runs through the Salinas Valley, the self-styled "salad bowl of the nation." But if the Salinas Valley is a salad bowl, then the stunning, mysterious peaks of **Pinnacles National Monument** are the baco-bits. Gonzales, Soledad, Greenfield, and King City are the four towns in the Salinas Valley. While each is accessible by Greyhound bus service four or five times per day (from north or south), the Pinnacles cannot be accessed without a car. On the whole, fast food reigns supreme in these small towns, but try **Moody's Pizza,** 721 Broadway (385-3213), in King City, for great prices and service that's right on the Mark. Two (yes, two) 10-inch pizzas for $9.75, or a generous slice of pepperoni with 20-oz. drink for $2.50. (Open Mon.-Sat. 11am-9:30pm, Sun. 11am-8pm.)

The Outdoors Towering dramatically over the chaparral east of Soledad, **Pinnacles National Monument** contains the spectacular remnants of an ancient volcano. Set aside as a National Park by Teddy Roosevelt in 1908, the park preserves the erratic and unique spires and crags that millions of years of weathering carved out of the prehistoric lava flows. Thirty mi. of hiking trails wind through the park, meandering through low chapparal, boulder-strewn caves, and up among the pinnacles of rock that give the park its name. The **High Peaks Trail** runs a strenuous 5.3 mi. across the park between the east and west entrances, and offers amazing views of the surrounding rock formations. For a less exhausting trek, try the **Balconies Trail,** a 1½-mi. promenade from the west entrance up to the Balconies Caves. If you visit during the work week, you will have the park nearly to yourself. Wildflowers bloom in the spring, and Pinnacles offers excellent bird watching all year long. The park also has the widest range of wildlife of any park in California, including a number of rare predator mammals: mountain lions, bobcats, coyote, gold eagles, and peregrine falcons (park admission $4). The park headquarters (389-4485) is located at the East side entrance (Rte. 25 to Rte. 146), but there is also a ranger station on the west side (U.S. 101 to Rte. 146). **Camping** is to be found only at the monument. The campground is walk-in, but some of the sites are just 50 yds. from the parking lot. Reservations are not accepted, and with only 23 sites, it's best to show up early if you're trying to camp on a weekend. The campground has firepits, restrooms, and picnic tables, so you'll also have to fight off the daytripping picnickers. (Sites $10.)

■■■ SANTA CRUZ

Santa Cruz sports the kind of uncalculated hipness of which other coastal towns can only dream. The city was born as one of Father Junipero Serra's missions in 1791 (the name means "holy cross"), but today Santa Cruz is nothing if not liberal. One of the few places where the old 60s catch-phrase "do your own thing" still applies, it simultaneously embraces macho surfers and a large lesbian community. In Santa Cruz, the spirit of the 60s has not died or been slicked up, remade, and crassly exploited. The city continues to go its own way, with its own distinctive style.

The epicenter of the California earthquake of Oct. 1989 was only 10 mi. from Santa Cruz. The city was by no means reduced to rubble, but it did lose a bridge, the popular Pacific Garden Mall, and several retail shops. While some of the shops are still temporarily located in tents (euphemistically called "Pavilions"), a statewide tax increase sped the restoration efforts, and the city has recovered almost entirely.

Practical Information   Santa Cruz lies about 1 hr. south of San Francisco on the northern lip of Monterey Bay, along U.S. 101 and Rte. 1. **Greyhound/Peerless Stages,** 425 Front St. (423-1800 or 800-231-2222), cruzes to San Francisco (3 per day, $10) and L.A. (4 per day, $47). (Open Mon.-Fri. 7:45-11am and 2-7:45pm; call for weekend hours.) **Santa Cruz Metro District Transit (SCMDT),** 920 Pacific Ave. (425-8600), serves the city and environs. Pick up a free copy of *Headways* for route info. (Open Mon.-Fri. 8am-5pm.) The **Santa Cruz Visitor's Council** (425-1234 or 800-833-3494) santas at 701 Front St. (open Mon.-Sat. 9am-5pm, Sun. 10am-4pm). The **post office** (426-5200) dates at 850 Front St. (open Mon.-Fri. 8:30am-5pm, Sat. 9am-noon); the **ZIP code** is 95060. The **area code** is 408.

Accommodations and Camping   Santa Cruz innkeepers metamorphose winter bargains into summer wallet-drainers. The **Santa Cruz HI/AYH Hostel,** 511 Broadway (423-8304), is a 10-min. walk from the beach. From the bus depot, turn left on Laurel, veer left over the bridge, and you're on Broadway. Reservations are essential during summer ($12, members only). Also try the **Harbor Inn,** 645 7th Ave. (479-9731), a few blocks north of Eaton St. A small and beautiful hotel well off the main drag. One queen bed per room (1 or 2 people). Rooms $30, with bath $45. Weekends $45/70. A bargain during the week—rooms even come with coupons for a free breakfast at the **Yacht Harbor Cafe,** two blocks south on 7th St. RV sites with a full hookup in back for $18. A 10-min. walk north of the Boardwalk is **Inn California,** 370 Ocean St. (458-9220), at Broadway. A touch more tasteful that the average budget motel. Telephone, A/C, color TV, and pretty quilts. Coin-operated laundry room. (Rooms with double beds: Sun.-Thurs. $31, Fri.-Sat. $55, $5.50 per additional person. No reservations are accepted; show up between 11am and 2pm to maximize your chances of finding a vacancy.)

Reservations for **state campgrounds** can be made by calling MISTIX (800-283-CAMP/2267) at least two weeks in advance. The **New Brighton State Beach** (475-4850), 4 mi. south of Santa Cruz off Rte. 1 near Capitola, offers 112 lovely campsites on a high bluff overlooking the beach. (1-week max. stay. No hookups. Check-out noon. Sites $16, $14 in winter. Reservations highly recommended. Take SCMDT "Aptos" bus #54.) The **Henry Cowell Redwoods State Park** (335-9548), off Rte. 9, communes with 113 sites (35 in winter) 3 mi. south of Felton. Take Graham Hill Rd., or SCMDT buses #30, 34, or 35. (1-week max. stay. Sites $16, $14 in the winter.) **Big Basin Redwoods State Park** (338-6132), north of Boulder Creek, merits the 45-min. trip from downtown. Take Rte. 9 north to Rte. 236 north, or on weekends take the #35 bus to Big Basin. This spectacular park has 188 sites surrounded by dark red trees. **Mountain bikes** are available for rental (338-7313), and **horseback tours** can be arranged. (Showers. 15-day max. stay. Sites $14, tent cabins $32. Backpackers $7 at special backcountry campsites. Security parking $5 per night. Reservations recommended May-Oct. Open year-round.)

Food and Entertainment   For a city on the California coast, Santa Cruz sports an amazing number of restaurants in the budget range. For the fast-food junkie, there's a normal spread of chain burger joints, but much better food (served just as fast) is available at **Food Pavilion,** at the Pacific Mall Food Court, at Lincoln and Cedar (open daily 8am-9pm). If it's a sit-down meal you want, there's lovingly hand-rolled pita bread, steaming curry, or any of a dozen other mouth-watering options at **Royal Taj,** 270 Soquel Ave. (427-2400). Exquisite and exotic Indian dishes in a comfortable setting. (Open daily 11:30am-2:30pm and 5:30-10pm.) **Zoccoli's Delicatessen,** 1334 Pacific Ave. (423-1717), has hearty and zesty helpings of pasta. The lunch special of lasagna, salad, garlic bread, salami, cheese slices, and an Italian cookie goes for $5. (Open Mon.-Sat. 9am-6pm.) **The Crêpe Place,** 1134 Soquel (429-6994), between Ocean and Seabright St., is a casual but classy restaurant putting Santa Cruz's former courthouse to good use. Try "the Whole Thing": chocolate, bananas, walnuts, and ice cream in a crêpe ($3.50). (Open Mon.-Thurs. 11am-midnight, Fri. 11am-1am, Sat. 9am-1am, Sun. 9am-midnight.)

Santa Cruz fashions itself a classy operation, and most bars frown on backpacks and sleeping bags. Carding is stringent. The restored ballroom at the boardwalk makes a lovely spot for a drink in the evening, and the boardwalk bandstand also offers free Friday night concerts. The **Kuumbwa Jazz Center,** 320-322 E. Cedar St. (427-2227), has regionally renowned jazz, and welcomes music lovers under 21. (Tickets $5-17. Most shows at 8pm.) **The Catalyst,** 1011 Pacific Garden Mall (423-1336), is a 700-seat concert hall which draws second-string national acts and college favorites with local bands. A boisterous, beachy bar. Serves pizza ($1.70) and sandwiches ($4-5). (Open daily 9am-2am. Shows 9:30pm.) **Blue Lagoon,** 923 Pacific Ave. (423-7117), a relaxed gay bar, swims with a giant aquarium in back, taped music, videos, and dancing. ($1 cover. Drinks about $1.50. Open daily 4pm-2am.)

Sights A three-block arcade of ice cream, caramel apples, games, rides, and tacos, the **Boardwalk** (426-7433) dominates Santa Cruz's beach area. The classiest rides are two grizzled warhorses: the 1929 **Giant Dipper,** one of the largest wooden roller coasters in the country (rides $3), and the 1911 **Looff Carousel,** accompanied by an 1894 organ ($1.50). (Unlimited rides $17. Boardwalk open Memorial Day-Labor Day daily; weekends the rest of the year. Call for hours.)

Broad **Santa Cruz Beach** generally jams with high school students from San Jose during summer weekends. When seeking solitude, try the banks of the San Lorenzo River immediately east of the boardwalk. Nude sunbathers should flop on over to the **Red White and Blue Beach;** take Rte. 1 north to just before Davenport and look for the line of cars to your right. Women should not go alone. ($7 per car.) Those who prefer tan lines should try the **Bonny Doon Beach,** 11 mi. north of Santa Cruz on Bonny Doon Rd. off Rte. 1, a free but mostly untamed surfer hangout.

A pleasant 10-min. walk along the beach to the southwest will take you to two madcap and mayhem-filled Santa Cruz museums. The first is the unintentionally amusing **Shroud of Turin Museum,** 1902 Ocean St. Extension (426-1601), at St. Joseph's shrine. Earnest curators shepherd you through many exhibits, including one of only two replicas of Jesus' alleged burial shroud, "casting doubt" on recent carbon-14 tests that suggest the shroud isn't old enough to have graced anyone's corpse in Biblical times. The Geraldo Rivera video is particularly telling. (Open Sat.-Sun. 1-4pm. Call to visit weekdays. Donations requested.) Just south lies Lighthouse Point, home to the **Santa Cruz Surfing Museum** (429-3429). The cheerful, one-room museum features vintage boards and surfing videos which show little sign of the tragedy that inspired its creation; the lighthouse and gallery were given in memory of a surfer who drowned in a 1965 accident. (Open Wed.-Sun. noon-4pm. Donation $1.) You can still watch people challenge the sea right below the museum's cliff. The stretch of Pacific along the eastern side of the point offers famous **Steamer Lane,** a hotspot for local surfers for over 100 years.

The 2000-acre **University of California at Santa Cruz (UCSC)** campus tunes in and turns on 5 mi. northwest of downtown. Take bus #1 or ride your bike along the scenic paths. Then-governor Ronald Reagan's plan to make UCSC a "riot-proof campus" (without a central point where radicals could spark a crowd) when it was built in the late '60s resulted in a stunning, sprawling campus. University buildings appear intermittently amid spectacular rolling hills and redwood groves. Guided tours start from the **visitors center** at the base of campus. Fire trails behind the campus are perfect for day hikes, but don't go alone. (Maps available at the **police station,** 429-2231.) The UCSC **Arboretum** is one of the finest in the state (open daily 9am-5pm; free). Directly south of UCSC, **Natural Bridges State Beach** (423-4609), at the end of W. Cliff Dr., offers a nice beach, tidepools, and tours twice daily during Monarch butterfly season (Oct.-March). **Welcome Back Monarch Day** flutters on October 9 of each year, but it's best to visit in Nov.-Dec., when thousands of the little buggers swarm along the shore. (Open daily 8am-sunset. Parking $6.)

Whale-watching is best Jan.-April; boats depart from the Santa Cruz Municipal Wharf (425-1234). A different kind of mammal is on view during the **National Nude Weekend** in mid-July, held at the **Lupin Naturalist Club** (393-2250); admission is free, but reservations are required. (You may, of course, already have reservations about this type of thing.) August brings the **Cabrillo Music Festival** (662-2701), an eclectic celebration of music from Beethoven to the Kronos Quartet.

THE DESERT

Mystics, misanthropes, and hallucinogenophiles have long been fascinated by the desert's vast spaces, austere scenery, and often brutal heat. California's desert region has worked its spell on generations of passersby: from the Native Americans and pioneering fortune hunters of yesterday to modern city slickers disenchanted with smoggy L.A. The fascination stems from the desert's cyclical metamorphosis from a pleasantly warm refuge in winter into a technicolored floral landscape in spring, and then into a blistering wasteland in summer. A place of overwhelming simplicity, the desert's beauty lies not so much in what it contains, but in what it lacks.

ORIENTATION

California's desert divides roughly into two regions. The **Sonoran,** or **Low Desert,** occupies southeastern California from the Mexican border north to Needles; the **Mojave,** or **High Desert** spans the south central part of the state, bounded by the Sonoran Desert to the south, San Bernardino and the San Joaquin Valleys to the west, the Sierra Nevada to the north, and Death Valley to the east.

The **Low Desert** is flat, dry, and barren. The oases in this area are essential to the existence of human, animal, and plant life, with the largest of them supporting the super-resort of Palm Springs. Despite the arid climate, much of this region has become agriculturally important as water from the Colorado River irrigates the Imperial and Coachella Valleys. **Anza-Borrego Desert State Park** and the **Salton Sea** are other points of interest here.

In contrast, the **High Desert** consists of foothills and plains nestled within mountain ranges approaching 5000 ft. Consequently, it is cooler (by about 10°F in summer) and wetter. **Joshua Tree National Monument** is a popular destination for campers. **Barstow** is the central city of the High Desert and an important rest station on the way from L.A. to Las Vegas or the Sierras.

Death Valley represents the eastern boundary of the Mojave but could be considered a region unto itself, since it has both high and low desert areas. Major highways cross the desert east-west: I-8 hugs the California-Mexico border, I-10 goes through Blythe and Indio on its way to Los Angeles, and I-40 crosses Needles to Barstow, where it joins I-15, running from Las Vegas and other points west to L.A.

For special health and safety precautions in the desert, see Desert Survival in the Health section of the General Introduction to this book.

■■■ BARSTOW

Barstow is an adequate place to prepare for forays into the desert. Once a booming mining town, this desert oasis (pop. 60,000) now thrives on business from local military bases, tourists, and truckers. Stop in at the **California Desert Information Center,** 831 Barstow Rd., Barstow 92311 (256-8313), for free maps and information on hiking, camping, exploring, and nearby ghost towns, such as the commercialized **Calico Ghost Town,** Ghost Town Rd. (254-2122), 10 mi. northeast of town on I-15. (Center open daily 9am-5pm.) Barstow, the western terminus of I-40, orders drinks midway between Los Angeles and Las Vegas on I-15. At the **Amtrak** station, N. 1st St. (800-872-7245), you can get on or off a train—that's all. Two trains per day go to L.A. ($34) and San Diego ($54); one per day ventures to Las Vegas ($45). **Greyhound,** 681 N. 1st St. (256-8757), goes to L.A. (12 per day, $19) and Las Vegas (11 per day, $30). (Open daily 8am-2pm, 3-6pm, and 8-11:30pm.) **Police** are at 256-2211. The **post office** hops at 425 S. 2nd Ave. (256-8494; open Mon.-Fri. 9am-5pm, Sat. 10am-noon). The **ZIP code** is 92312, the **area code** 619.

What Barstow lacks in charm (and it truly lacks) is made up for by its abundant supply of inexpensive motels and eateries. To prevent a Big Mac attack, head for the **Barstow Station McDonald's,** on E. Main St. Constructed from old railway cars, this Mickey D's serves more burgers per annum than any other U.S. outfit (open daily 5:30am-10pm, Fri.-Sat. until 11pm). **Carlo's and Toto's,** 901 W. Main. St. (256-7513) offers huge platters of Mexican specialties for south-of-the-border prices (entrees $4-7). (Open daily 11am-10pm, Fri.-Sat. until 11pm.)

Motel 6, 150 N. Yucca Ave. (256-1752), relatively close to Greyhound and Amtrak, offers standard rooms with cable TV, free local calls, and a pool (singles $23, doubles $29). The **Economy Motels of America,** 1590 Coolwater Lane (256-1737), off I-40, has singles for $22 and doubles for $29. The **Barstow/Calico KOA** (254-2311), I-15 and Ghost Town Rd., is overpopulated with Ghost Town devotees (sites for 2 $17, with electricity $19, full hookup $21; each additional person $2.50.)

■■■ DEATH VALLEY NATIONAL MONUMENT

Dante, Blake, and Sartre would have been inspired. Nowhere on and few places beneath this planet can touch the daily summer temperatures here. The *average* high temperature in July is 116°F, with a nighttime low of 88°. Ground temperatures hover near an egg-frying 200°. Much of the landscape resembles *Viking* photographs of the surface of Mars, with its reddish crags and canyons, immobile and stark. The strangeness of the landscape lends to it a certain beauty. The earth-hues of the sands and rocks change hourly in the variable sunlight. The region features pure white salt flats on the valley floor, impassable mountain slopes, and huge, shifting sand dunes; elevation ranges from 11,049-ft. at Telescope Peak to Badwater, the lowest point in the hemisphere at 282 ft. below sea level. Nature appears to have focused all of its extremes and varieties here at a single location.

The region sustains a surprisingly intricate web of desert life. Observant tourists will discover a tremendous variety of desert dwellers, including the great horned owl, roadrunner (Meep! Meep!), coyote, kit fox, gecko, raven, and chuckwalla.

Late Nov.-Feb. is the coolest time of year (40-70° in the valley, freezing temperatures and snow in the mountains) and also the wettest period, with infrequent but violent rainstorms that can flood the canyons. Desert wildflowers bloom in March and April, accompanied by moderate temperatures and tempestuous winds that can whip sand and dust into an obscuring mess for hours or even days. Over 50,000 people vie for Death Valley's facilities and sights during the **'49ers Encampment Festival,** held the last week of October and the first two weeks of November. Other times that bring traffic jams include three-day winter holiday weekends, Thanksgiving, Christmas-New Year's Day, and Easter.

PRACTICAL INFORMATION

Emergency: 911.

Visitors Information: Furnace Creek Visitor Center (786-2331), on Rte. 190 in the east-central section of the valley. Simple and informative museum dispels some myths. Slide show every ½-hr. and nightly lecture during the winter. Purchase guides and topographic map. Activities schedule, weather conditions, and cold water. Open summer daily 8am-6pm, winter daily 8am-7pm. For info by mail, write the Superintendent, Death Valley National Monument, Death Valley 92328.

Ranger Stations: Grapevine, junction of Rte. 190 and 267 near Scotty's Castle; **Stovepipe Wells,** on Rte. 190; **Wildrose,** Rte. 178, 20 mi. south of Emigrant via Emigrant Canyon Dr.; and **Shoshone,** outside the southeast border of the valley at the junction of Rte. 178 and 127. Weather report, weekly naturalist program, and park information posted at each station. Emergency help. All closed during most of the summer.

Gasoline: Tank up outside Death Valley at Olancha, Shoshone, or Beatty, NV. Otherwise, you'll pay about 20¢ per gallon more at the stations across from the Furnace Creek Visitors Center, in Stove Pipe Wells Village, and at Scotty's Castle Don't play chicken with the fuel gauge: Fortuna does not smile on the foolish and Death Valley takes no prisoners. **AAA towing service** and **propane gas** are available at the Furnace Creek Chevron (786-2232); **white gas** at the Furnace Creek Ranch and Stove Pipe Wells Village stores; **diesel fuel** in Las Vegas, Pahrump, and Beatty, NV, and in Lone Pine, Olancha, Ridgecrest, Stateline, and Trona, CA.

Groceries and Supplies: Furnace Creek Ranch Store is well-stocked and expensive. Open daily 7am-9pm. **Stove Pipe Wells Village Store** is smaller and in the same price range. Open daily 7am-8pm. Both stores sell charcoal, firewood and ice. Ice also available at the Furnace Creek Chevron

Post Office: Furnace Creek Ranch (786-2223). Open Mon.-Fri. 8:30am-5pm, June-Sept. Mon.-Fri. 8:30am-3pm. **ZIP Code:** 92328.

Area Code: 619.

Death Valley spans over two million isolated acres (1½ times the size of Delaware). Visitors from the south can reach it with a small detour on the road to Sierra Nevada's eastern slope; those from the north will find it reasonably close to Las Vegas.

There is no regularly scheduled public transportation into Death Valley; only charter buses make the run. Bus tours within Death Valley are monopolized by **Fred Harvey's Death Valley Tours** (786-2345, ext. 22), the same organization that runs Grand Canyon tours. Excursions begin at Furnace Creek Ranch, which also handles reservations ($20-30, children $12-20). The best way to get into and around Death Valley is by car. The nearest agencies rent in Las Vegas, Barstow, and Bishop. Be sure to rent a reliable car: this is emphatically *not* the place to cut corners; it's worth the money not to get stuck with an overheated car in the middle of Death Valley. The $5 per vehicle entrance fee is collected only at the visitors center in the middle of the park. Resist the temptation not to pay: the Park Service needs all the money it can get (besides, it's a nice map). Year-long pass, $15.

Of the 13 **monument entrances,** most visitors choose Rte. 190 from the east. The road is well-maintained, the pass less steep, and more convenient to the visitors center. However, since most of the major sights adjoin the north/south road, a daytripper at the helm of a trusty vehicle should enter from the southeast (Rte. 178 west from Rte. 127 at Shoshone) or the north (direct to Scotty's Castle via NV Rte. 267 from U.S. 95) in order to see more of the monument. Unskilled mountain drivers should not attempt to enter via the smaller roads Titus Canyon or Emigrant Canyon Dr., since no guard rails prevent cars from emigrating over the canyon's cliffs.

Eighteen-wheelers have replaced 18-mule teams, but transportation around Death Valley still takes stubborn determination. Radiator water (*not* for drinking) is available at critical points on Rte. 178 and 190 and NV Rte. 374, but not on any unpaved roads. Obey the signs that advise "four-wheel-drive only." Those who do bound along the backcountry trails by four-wheel-drive should carry chains, extra tires, gas, oil, water (both to drink and for that radiator), and spare parts; also leave an itinerary with the visitors center. Be sure to check which roads are closed—especially in summer. Never drive on wet backcountry roads.

Check the weather forecasts before setting out—all roads and trails can disappear during a winter rainstorm. The dryness of the area, plus the lack of any root and soil system to retain moisture, transforms canyon and valley floors into riverbeds for deadly torrents during heavy rains. For other important tips, see Desert Survival, under Health in Essentials.

ACCOMMODATIONS

Fred Harvey's Amfac Consortium retains its vise-like grip on the trendy, resort-style, incredibly overpriced facilities in Death Valley. Look for cheaper accommodations in the towns near Death Valley: **Olancha** (west), **Shoshone** (southwest), **Tecopa** (south), and **Beatty, NV** (northwest).

The National Park Service maintains nine **campgrounds,** none of which accepts reservations. Call the visitors center to check availability and prepare for a battle if you come during peak periods. The Park Service campground fees range from free to $8, but camping fees are not pursued with vigor in the summer. All campsites have toilets; all except Sunset and Stove Pipe Wells have tables; all except Thorndike and Mahogany Flat have water. Be warned that water availability is not completely reliable, especially in winter, and supplies can at times be unsafe. Always pack your own. Bring a stove, since even where open fires are not prohibited, collecting wood, alive or dead, is prohibited everywhere in the monument. **Backcountry camping** is free, as long as you check in at the visitors center and pitch tents at least 1 mi. from main roads and 5 mi. from any established campsite.

SIGHTS

Death Valley has **hiking** trails to challenge the mountain lover, desert rat, or back-country camper. Ask a ranger for advice. Backpackers and dayhikers alike should inform the visitors center of their route, and take appropriate topographic maps. During the summer the National Park Service recommends that valley-floor hikers spend several days prior to the hike getting acclimated to the heat and low humidity, plan a route along roads where assistance is readily available, and outfit a hiking party of at least two people with another person following in a vehicle to monitor the hikers' progress. Wearing thick socks and carrying salve to treat feet parched by the nearly 200°F earth also makes good sense.

The **visitors center and museum** (see Practical Information) offers info on tours, hikes, and special programs. If you're interested in astronomy, speak to one of the rangers; some set up telescopes at Zabriskie Point and offer spontaneous shows. In **wildflower season** (Feb.-April), tours are lead to some of the best places for viewing the display. **Hells Gate** and **Jubilee Pass** are especially beautiful, **Hidden Valley** even more so, though it is accessible only by a difficult, 7-mi. four-wheel-drive route from Teakettle Junction (25 mi. south of Ubehebe Crater). Both the **Harmony Borax Works** and the **Borax Museum** are a short drive from the visitors center.

Artist's Drive is a one-way loop off Rte. 178, beginning 10 mi. south of the visitors center. The road twists and winds through rock and dirt canyons on the way to **Artist's Palette,** a rainbow of green, yellow, and red mineral deposits in the hillside. Several miles south you'll find **Devil's Golf Course,** a huge plane of spiny salt crust left from the evaporation of ancient Lake Manly. Amble across the gigantic links; the salt underfoot sounds like crunching snow.

Zabriskie Point is a marvelous place from which to view Death Valley's corrugated badlands, particularly at sunrise (the rock group Pink Floyd certainly thought so). The trip up to **Dante's View,** 15 mi. by paved road south off Rte. 190 (take the turn-off beyond Twenty Mule Team Canyon exit), will reward you with views of Badwater, Furnace Creek Ranch, the Panamint Range, and the Sierra Nevadas. Faintly visible on the valley floor are ruts from 20-mule-team wagons. Snows are common here in mid-winter, as are low temperatures anytime but mid-summer.

■■■ JOSHUA TREE NATIONAL MONUMENT

The low, scorching Sonoran Desert and the higher, cooler Mojave Desert mingle here, precipitating more than a half-million acres of extraordinarily jumbled scenery. The monument stars the Joshua Tree, a member of the lily family whose erratic limbs sometimes reach as high as 50 ft. The Mormons who came through here in the 19th century thought the crooked branches resembled the arms of the prophet Joshua leading them to the promised land. Sparse forests of gangly Joshuas extend for miles in the high central and eastern portions of the monument, punctuated by great piles of quartz monzonite boulders, some over 100 ft. high. This bizarre landscape emerged over millenia as shoots of hot magma pushed to the surface and erosion wore away the supporting sandstone. Together, the two forces have created fantastic textures, shapes, and rock albums. Alongside the natural environment appear vestiges of human existence: ancient rock pictographs, dams built in the 19th century in order to catch the meager rainfall for livestock, and the ruins of gold mines that operated as late as the 1940s.

Practical Information Joshua Tree National Monument occupies a vast area northeast of Palm Springs, about 160 mi. (3-3½ hr. by car) from west L.A. From I-10, the best approaches are via Rte. 62 from the west, leading to the towns of Joshua Tree and **Twentynine Palms** on the northern side of the monument, and via an unnumbered road that exits the interstate about 25 mi. east of Indio. The monument's **Visitors Center,** 74485 National Monument Dr., Twentynine Palms 92277 (367-7511), ¼ mi. off Rte. 62, offers displays, lectures, and maps (open daily 8am-5pm). Another visitors center sits at the southern gateway approximately 7 mi. north of I-10 (exit 4 mi. west of Chiriaco Summit); an info kiosk adjoins the west entrance on Park Blvd., several mi. southeast of the town of Joshua Tree. Entrance to the monument is $2 per person or $5 per vehicle. **Desert Stage Lines** (251-6162), based in Palm Springs, stops in Twentynine Palms (1 per day, $10; call before planning a trip). For **emergencies,** call 911; call 367-3523 for a ranger, 714-383-5651 collect for the 24-hr. dispatch center. The **area code** is 619.

Campgrounds Monument campgrounds accept no reservations, except for group sites at **Cottonwood, Sheep Pass,** and **Indian Cove,** for which MISTIX (800-365-2267) handles mandatory reservations. Sites are also available at **White Tank** (closed in summer), **Belle, Black Rock Canyon, Hidden Valley, Ryan,** and **Jumbo Rocks.** All sites have tables, fireplaces, and pit toilets; all are free except Cottonwood ($8) and Black Rock Canyon ($10), which have the only available water. You must bring your own firewood. If your trip to Joshua Tree is an educational endeavor contributing to a degree, you can secure a fee waiver; write to the monument on your best official stationery and explain your "bona fide educational" purposes. **Backcountry camping** is unlimited. Pitch your tent more than 500 ft. from a trail, 1 mi. from a road. (14-day max. stay Oct.-May; 30 days in summer.)

Sights Over 80% of the monument is designated wilderness area; for those experienced in backcountry desert hiking and camping, Joshua Tree provides some truly remote territory. Hikers should go to one of the visitors centers for the rules and advice on use of isolated areas of the monument, and to pick up a topographic map ($2.50). The wilderness lacks water except for the occasional flash flood; even these evaporate rapidly. Carry at least a gallon of water per person per day—two during the summer months. You must register at roadside boxes before setting out (see maps) to let the monument staff know your location, and to prevent your car from being towed from a roadside parking lot.

 Less hardy desert fans can enjoy Joshua Tree for a day or a weekend in relative comfort. The most popular time, as with other desert parks, is **wildflower season** (mid-March to mid-May), when the floor of the desert explodes in yucca, verbena, cottonwood, mesquite, and dozens of other floral variations. Summer is the hottest and slowest season. Bear in mind that no off-road driving is permitted.

A drive along the winding road from **Twentynine Palms** to the town of **Joshua Tree** (34 mi.) passes by the **Wonderland of Rocks,** a spectacular concentration of rock formations. The slightly longer drive between Twentynine Palms and I-10 through the monument offers both high and low desert landscapes. Along the way on both of these tours, explore as many of the side roads as time allows. Signs indicate whether turnoffs are paved, dirt, or only suitable for four-wheel-drive vehicles. One site not to miss, **Key's View,** off the park road just west of Ryan Campground, offers a stupendous vista. You can see as far as Palm Springs and the Salton Sea on a clear day. Also of note are the **palm oases** (Twentynine Palms, Forty-nine Palms, Cottonwood Spring, Lost Palms) and the **Cholla Cactus Garden** off Pinto Basin Rd.

A number of **hiking trails** lead to the most interesting features of Joshua Tree: oases, mine ruins, and fine vantage points. Short trails run near picnic areas and campsites. Visitors center brochures describe these trails, which range from a mere 200 yd. (the Cholla Cactus Garden) to 35 mi. (a section of the California Riding and Hiking Trail). The degree of difficulty varies almost as widely; the visitors center staff can help you choose. Plan on at least one hour per mi. on even relatively easy trails.

■■■ PALM SPRINGS

Former Mayor Sonny Bono having led by example from next to his swimming pool, Palm Springs continues to be a playground for the nouveau-riche. The beautiful San Jacinto Mountains grind to a halt only blocks from **Palm Canyon Drive,** the city's main drag. Medicinal waters bubbling from the town's hot springs have preserved not only the health of the area's opulent residents, but also the town's resort status. And cheap thrills are available for the budget-minded, not the least of which is the vantage of jaw-dropping opulence.

Practical Information Palm Springs lies off I-10, 120 mi. east of L.A., just beyond a low pass that marks the edge of the Colorado Desert. The **Chamber of Commerce** (325-1577) is at 190 W. Amado. Ask for a map ($1) and a free copy of *The Desert Guide.* (Open Mon.-Fri. 8:30am-4:30pm.) **Amtrak** (800-872-7245), on Jackson St. in Indio, 25 mi. southeast of Palm Springs (connect to Greyhound in Indio), sends three trains per week to and from L.A. ($29) with frequent stops along the way. **Greyhound,** 311 N. Indian Ave. (325-2053), is much more convenient (8 per day to L.A., $15). **Desert Stage Lines** (251-6162; buy tickets at the Greyhound terminal) serves Twentynine Palms and Joshua Tree National Monument (1 per day, $8.80), with Friday service to L.A. ($20-21) and San Diego ($23.50). **Sun Bus** (343-3451) is the local bus system, serving all Coachella Valley cities daily 6am-6pm (75¢; seniors and disabled 25¢). Rent a car at **Rent-a-Wreck,** 67555 E. Palm Canyon (324-1766), for $20 per day, or $120 per week; 700 free mi., 19¢ each additional mi. (must be 21 with major credit card). **Desert Cab** is at 325-2868.

Emergency is 911. The **post office** (325-9631) posts at 333 E. Amado Rd. (open Mon.-Fri. 9am-5pm, Sat. 9am-1pm). The **ZIP code** is 92262; the **area code** is 619.

Accommodations and Food Palm Springs' cheapest lodgings are at nearby state parks and national forest campgrounds. If you need a room with a roof, put your money on either **Motel 6** location: 595 E. Palm Canyon Dr. (325-6129), or the more convenient 660 S. Palm Canyon Dr. (327-4200). Both locations have a big pool and A/C, and both fill quickly, up to six months in advance in winter. Some on-the-spot rooms are available as no-shows are frequent. (Singles $30, doubles $34.)

For those who want to picnic—an excellent idea, given the surroundings—chain supermarkets abound in Palm Springs. **Ralph's,** 1555 S. Palm Canyon Dr. (323-8446), and **Vons** (322-2192), in the Palm Springs Mall on Tahquitz-McCallum, are both reliably low-priced. The best *comida mexicana* in the area is at **El Gallito Cafe,** 68820 Grove St., Cathedral City (328-7794). The velvet paintings on the wall and the trinkets adorning the booths suggest a just-south-of-the-border ambience. *Combinaciones* (2 entrees, beans, rice, and tortillas) fit for a glutton start at a mere $6, beef burritos go for $3.25. (Open daily 10am-9:30pm.)

Sights Rising nearly 6000 ft., the **Palm Springs Aerial Tramway** works its dramatic way up the side of Mt. San Jacinto to an observation deck that affords excellent views of L.A.'s distant smog. Stairs from the deck lead to a 360° viewing platform, usually covered by snow drifts. The base station is located on Tramway Dr., which intersects Rte. 111 just north of Palm Springs. (Tram operates at least every ½-hr. Mon.-Fri. 10am-9pm, Sat.-Sun. 8am-9pm; Nov.-April only to 8pm. Round-trip tram $15, seniors $12, ages under 12 $10. Ride and dine service $4 extra.)

The **Desert Museum,** 101 Museum Dr. (325-0189), behind the Desert Fashion Plaza on Palm Canyon Dr., offers an impressive collection of Native American art, talking desert dioramas, and live animals. The gorgeously posh museum sponsors curator-led field trips ($3) into the canyons. (Museum open late Sept.-early June Tues.-Fri. 10am-4pm, Sat.-Sun. 10am-5pm. $4, seniors $3, students $2, under 6 free. Free first Tues. of each month.) The **Indian Canyons** (325-5673) are oases that contain both a wide variety of desert life and remnants of the communities they once supported. Of the four canyons just outside Palm Springs, only Tahquitz requires a permit to gain entrance ($10), and can be grabbed at the front gate. All four can be accessed at the end of S. Palm Canyon Dr., 5 mi. from the center of town.

The **Living Desert Reserve,** 47900 Portola Ave. (346-5694), in Palm Desert, located 1½ mi. south of Rte. 111, contains displays recreating various desert environments with rare and exotic desert animals, such as Arabian oryces, iguanas, desert unicorns, and Grery's zebras. (Open Sept.-mid-June daily 9am-5pm. Admission $6, seniors $5.25, under 15 $3. Wheelchair access.) Bizarre **Moorten's Desertland Botanical Gardens,** 1701 S. Palm Canyon Dr. (327-6555), is a botanist's heaven—advertised as the world's first "cactarium": ocotillo, yucca, prickly pear, and beavertail cacti you can touch (open Mon.-Sat. 9am-4:30pm, Sun. 10am-4pm; admission $1.50, ages 5-16 50¢). For those travelers who saw more than enough desert simply getting to Palm Springs, a tour of **celebrity homes** offers an alternative view of mutant desert life forms. The budget method for this sight-seeing tour is to buy a map downtown and guide oneself.

Of course, most visitors to Palm Springs have no intention of studying the desert or taking in high culture. Palm Springs means sunning, with no activity more demanding than drinking a gallon of iced tea each day to keep from dehydrating. For complete info about other recreational activities (including tennis, golf, and hot-air ballooning), call the **Leisure Center** at 323-8272. **Oasis Water Park** (325-7873), off I-10 S. on Gene Autry Trail, is awash with a wave pool and seven water slides, including the seven-story-tall near-free-fall Scorpion. (Open daily 11am-6pm, Sat. until 7pm. Admission $16.50, seniors and ages 4-11 $12, under 4 free.) The **Palm Springs International Film Festival** (323-8274) bubbles each year during the second week of January.

■■■ LOS ANGELES

Los Angeles is perhaps the most American of cities. It embodies much of what is wrong with the U.S., yet millions of people would never live anywhere else. Substance lost out to style long ago; while out-of-towners scorn the idea that "image is everything," Angelenos accept that in their town, perception is reality. But the gilded body of Los Angeles is tarnishing—beyond the Mercedes and Porsches on the freeways, the mammoth billboards of the Sunset Strip, and the living theater of the Venice boardwalk lies a list of urban woes that are eating away at the soul of the city.

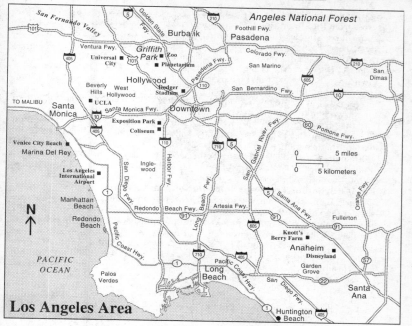

Los Angeles Area

Most of the issues confronting Los Angeles as the sprawling megalopolis speeds toward the 21st century arise from the tension between the demands of excess and limitations of reality. The city's freeways are overcrowded to the point that rush hour has ceased to be a meaningful concept. Too late it seems, Los Angeles has embarked upon construction of a light-rail system that will cost billions and will not be completed until well into the next century. Environmental apocalypse looms in the thick smog that Angelenos breathe and the scarce water they pour into their swimming pools, depleting natural resources in the rest of the state.

The most telling demonstration of reality asserting itself through layers of L.A. fantasy was the riots in April, 1992. The acquittal of four white police officers who were accused of beating African-American L.A. resident Rodney King sparked days of bloody protests ending in millions of dollars in damage and hundreds of arrests.

Despite it all, L.A. keeps growing. A drive into the far reaches of the L.A. Basin, to Simi Valley, to San Bernardino, or up Route 14 toward Palmdale and the Mojave Desert, reveals the wooden skeletons of new tract houses and the creeping tendrils of outer suburbia. Even Bakersfield, over 100 mi. to the northwest, plans to build a light-rail connection to L.A. and anticipates the day when it forms just another of the proverbial "suburbs in search of a city."

PRACTICAL INFORMATION

Visitors Information: Los Angeles Convention and Visitors Bureau, 685 S. Figueroa St., 90017 (213-689-8822), between Wilshire and 7th St. in the heart of the Financial District. Staff speaks Spanish, Filipino, Japanese, French, and German. Good maps for downtown streets, sights, and buses. Publishes *Destination Los Angeles,* a free booklet that includes tourist information, a lodging guide, and a shopping directory. Open Mon.-Fri. 8am-5pm, Sat. 8:30am-5pm. In **Hollywood** at 6541 Hollywood Blvd. (213-461-4213). Open Mon.-Sat. 9am-5pm. In **Santa Monica** at 1400 Ocean Ave. (310-393-7593), in Palisades Park. Open daily 10am-

5pm; in winter 10am-4pm. In **Pasadena** at 171 S. Los Robles Ave. (818-795-9311), across from the Hilton Hotel. Open Mon.-Fri. 8am-5pm, Sat. 10am-4pm.

Airport: Los Angeles International Airport (LAX) (310-646-5252; 24-hr. security 310-646-4268), in Westchester, about 15 mi. southwest of downtown. **Travelers Aid,** for major emergencies, is available in all terminals. Open daily 7am-10pm. **RTD** stops at the **transfer terminal** at Sepulveda and 96th St. and runs to: downtown (bus #439 Mon.-Fri. rush hr.; #42 from LAX daily 5:30am-11:15pm, from downtown daily 5:30am-12:10am); Westwood/UCLA (express #560); Long Beach (#232); West Hollywood and Beverly Hills (#220). **Cabs** are costly; fare to downtown is about $24, Hollywood $28. **Shuttle vans** offer door-to-door service from the terminal to different parts of L.A. for a flat rate. Typically to downtown ($12), Santa Monica ($14), San Fernando Valley ($30). In-flight haircuts $200.

Amtrak: Union Station, 800 N. Alameda (213-624-0171), at the northwestern edge of downtown Los Angeles. To: San Francisco (1 per day, 12 hr., $75); San Diego (9 per day, 3 hr., $24). Buses travel out of the station to Pasadena and Long Beach; get information upon arrival.

Buses: Greyhound-Trailways Information Center, 716 E. 7th St. (800-231-2222), at Alameda, downtown near Skid Row. Continuing to other area stations is far safer than disembarking downtown, especially if you arrive after dark. It is possible, though not recommended, to reach these other destinations by public bus. Can catch RTD buses #320 and #20, and nearby, #1. Greyhound runs to: San Diego (10 per day, 2½-3½ hr., $12); Santa Barbara (12 per day, 2-3½ hr., $12); San Francisco (20 per day, 8½-12½ hr., $39). Lockers $1 per day. In **Santa Monica** at 645 E. Walnut (818-792-5116). Open Mon.-Fri. 8:30am-5:30pm, Sat. 8:30am-3pm. To: Santa Barbara (1 per day, 4 hr., $14.50); San Diego (1 per day, 4 hr., $16.50); San Francisco (1 per day, 11 hr., $42). In **Pasadena** at 1433 5th St. (310-395-1708), between Broadway and Santa Monica Blvd. Open Mon.-Sat. 9:30am-5pm. To: Santa Barbara (2 per day, 2½ hr., $11); San Diego (2 per day, 3½ hr., $19); San Francisco (2 per day, 11 hr., $47). No lockers. **Green Tortoise** (310-392-1990) leaves L.A. each Sunday night with stops in Venice, Hollywood, and downtown.

RTD Bus Information Line: 213-626-4455. **Customer Service Center,** 5301 Wilshire Blvd. Open Mon.-Fri. 8:30am-5pm. See Public Transportation below.

Santa Monica Municipal (Big Blue) Bus Lines: 1660 7th St. (310-451-5445), at Olympic. Open Mon.-Fri. 8am-5pm. Faster and cheaper than the RTD. Fare 50¢ for most routes, and 25¢ transfer tickets for RTD buses. Transfers to other Big Blue buses are free. **Important buses:** #1 and #2 connect Santa Monica and Venice; #4 connects Santa Monica to Hollywood. Bus #10 provides express service from downtown Santa Monica (at 7th and Grand) to downtown L.A.

Taxi: Checker Cab (213-482-3456), **Independent** (213-385-8294), **United Independent** (213-653-5050). If you need a cab, it's best to call—cabbies don't search for fares on the streets. Approximate fare from LAX to downtown is $24.

Car Rentals: Avon Rent-A-Car, 8459 Sunset Blvd. (213-654-5533). Compacts as low as $15 per day with 100 free mi., 20¢ per mi. thereafter. $90 per week. Ages 18-20 $15 per day surcharge, $5 per day for 21-24. Open Mon.-Fri. 7:30am-9:30pm, Sat.-Sun. 8am-8pm. **Alamo Rentals,** at LAX (800-327-9633). Prices vary with availability from $21 per day, $120 per week, unlimited mi. Must be over 21 with major credit card. Under 25 pay $15 per day surcharge. Open 24 hrs. **Penny Rent-A-Car,** 12425 Victory Blvd., N. Hollywood (818-786-1733). $25 per day with 75 free mi., 15¢ per additional mi. $150 per week with 500 free mi. Must be 25 with major credit card or international driver's license. Open Mon.-Fri. 8am-6pm, Sat. 8am-2pm, Sun. 10am-noon.

Auto Transport Services: Dependable Car Travel Service, Inc., 18037 S. Broadway (310-659-2922). Must be 18. Four references and a valid driver's license required. Most cars go to the northeast, especially to New York, but also to Florida and Chicago. $150 deposit. Call 1-2 days ahead. Open Mon.-Fri. 8:30am-5:30pm. **Auto Driveaway,** 3407 W. 6th St. (213-666-6100). Must be 21 and have references in both L.A. and your destination city. Foreign travelers don't need references, but must have a passport, visa, and an international driver's license. Most cars go to metropolitan areas nationwide. $300 deposit.

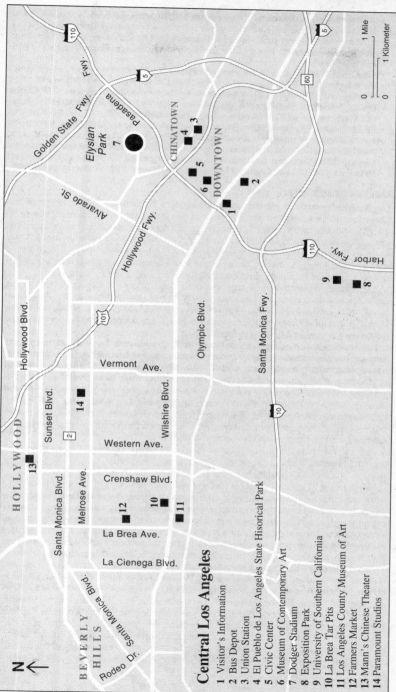

LOS ANGELES

Central Los Angeles

1 Visitor's Information
2 Bus Depot
3 Union Station
4 El Pueblo de Los Angeles State Hisorical Park
5 Civic Center
6 Museum of Contemporary Art
7 Dodger Stadium
8 Exposition Park
9 University of Southern California
10 La Brea Tar Pits
11 Los Angeles County Museum of Art
12 Farmers Market
13 Mann's Chinese Theater
14 Paramount Studios

Surfboard Rental: Natural Progression Surfboards, 22935½ W. Pacific Hwy., Malibu (310-456-6302). Boards $20 per day, plus $5 insurance. Wetsuits $8. Windsurfer rental ($30 per day, plus $5 insurance), and lessons. Open daily 9am-6pm.

Hotlines: Emergency: Dial 911 for fire, police, ambulance. **Rape Crisis:** 310-392-8381. 24 hrs.

Post Offices: Main office at **Florence Station,** 7001 S. Central Ave. (213-586-1467 for information on rates and schedules). **ZIP Code:** 90086. In **Hollywood,** 1615 Wilcox Ave. (213-464-2194). Open Mon.-Fri. 8am-5pm, Sat. 8am-1pm. **ZIP Code:** 90028. In **Santa Monica,** 5th and Arizona (310-576-2626). Open Mon.-Fri. 9am-6pm, Sat. 9am-1pm. **ZIP Code:** 90406. In **Pasadena,** 600 N. Lincoln (818-304-7122), at Orange. Open Mon.-Fri. 8am-7pm, Sat. 9am-5pm. **ZIP Code:** 91109.

Area Codes: Downtown, Hollywood, Huntington Park, Vernon, Montebello **213.** Malibu, Pacific Coast Highway, Westside, southern and eastern Los Angeles County **310.** Northern Los Angeles County, including San Fernando Valley and Pasadena **818.** Orange County **714.** San Diego County **619.** Ventura County **805.**

ORIENTATION

Los Angeles sprawls along the coast of Southern California, 127 mi. north of San Diego and 403 mi. south of San Francisco. You can still be "in" L.A. even if you're 50 mi. from downtown. Greater L.A. encompasses the urbanized areas of Orange, Riverside, San Bernadino, and Ventura counties. General approaches to Greater L.A. are I-5 from the south, Rte. 1, U.S. 101, or I-5 from the north, and I-10 or I-15 from the east. Driving into L.A. can be unnerving if you've never before run the gauntlet of ramps, exits, and four-story directional signs.

A legitimate **downtown** Los Angeles does exist, but only to explain where all the "suburbs in search of a city" lie. Immediately east of downtown are the vibrant Latino districts of **Boyle Heights, Montebello,** and **El Monte;** to the south is **Exposition Park,** and **Watts;** farther south on Rte. 11 is **Long Beach.** The heart of downtown is reasonably safe on weekdays.

Los Angeles is a city of distinctive boulevards; its shopping areas and business centers are distributed along these broad arteries. Streets throughout L.A. are designated east, west, north, and south from First and Main St. at the center of downtown. L.A.'s **east-west thoroughfares** are the most prominent; use them to get your bearings. Beginning with the northernmost, they are Melrose Avenue and Beverly, Wilshire, Olympic, Pico, Venice, and Washington Boulevards. The important **north-south streets** of this huge grid, from downtown westward, are Vermont, Normandie, and Western Avenues, Vine Street, Highland, La Brea, and Fairfax Avenues, and La Cienega and Robertson Boulevards.

The area west of downtown is known as the **Wilshire District** after its main boulevard. **Hancock Park,** a green and affluent residential area, covers the northeast portion of the district and harbors the Los Angeles County Museum of Art.

North of the Wilshire District is **Hollywood.** The next major east-west boulevard north of Melrose is Santa Monica, and north of that is **Sunset Boulevard.** This street, which runs from the ocean to downtown, presents a cross-section of virtually everything L.A. has to offer: beach communities, lavish wealth, famous nightclubs, sleazy motels, the old elegance of Silver Lake, and Chicano murals. Farther north is **Hollywood Boulevard,** running beneath the Hollywood Hills, where split-level buildings perched on hillsides house screenwriters, actors, and producers.

Regal **Beverly Hills,** an independent city geographically swallowed by L.A., lies west of the Wilshire District and east of **Westwood,** home to UCLA and its lively college village. Farther west, across the San Diego Freeway, **Santa Monica** strings its crowded beaches along the ocean. Just south is the beach community of **Venice.**

North of the Hollywood Hills and the Santa Monica Mountains stretches the **San Fernando Valley.** Over a million people inhabit the quiet suburbs of this basin.

Eighty mi. of beach line L.A.'s coast. **Zuma** is northernmost, followed by **Malibu,** 15 mi. up the coast from Santa Monica. The beach towns south of Santa Monica and Venice, comprising the area called the **South Bay,** are Marina del Rey, El Segundo, and Manhattan, Hermosa, and Redondo Beaches. South across the Palos Verdes Peninsula is **Long Beach,** a port city of a half-million people. Finally, farthest south are the **Orange County** beach cities: Seal Beach, Sunset Beach, Huntington Beach, Newport Beach, and Laguna Beach. Confused yet?

Before you even think about navigating Los Angeles's 6500 mi. of streets and 40,000 intersections, get yourself a good map—center-less Los Angeles defies all human comprehension otherwise. The best investment you can make is the *Thomas Guide Los Angeles County Street Guide and Directory.* It's worth the $15 price tag for those planning to stay longer than a week.

Once the sun sets, those on foot anywhere, especially outside West L.A. and off well-lit main drags, should exercise caution. Women should not walk alone *anywhere* after dark. Hollywood and the downtown area, east of Western Ave., are considered particularly crime-ridden, but remain alert in any area.

TRAVELING IN LOS ANGELES

Nowhere in America is the great god of Automobile held in greater reverence than in L.A. In the 1930s and 40s, General Motors, Firestone, and Standard Oil colluded to buy up the street car companies and run them into the ground, later ripping up the rails. This increased dependence on buses and, once they were largely phased out, on cars. In 1949 GM was convicted in federal court of criminal conspiracy—but it didn't bring back the trolleys or make public transportation any easier.

Public Transportation Most Angelenos will insist that it's impossible to live in or visit Los Angeles without a car, but the **Southern California Rapid Transit District (RTD)** does work—sort of. Using the RTD to sightsee in L.A. can be frustrating simply because attractions tend to be spread out. Those determined to see *everything* in L.A. should somehow get behind the wheel of a car. Bus service is dismal in the outer reaches of the city, and 2-hr. journeys are not unusual.

To familiarize yourself with the RTD write for a **Rider's Kit,** RTD, Los Angeles 90001, or stop by one of the 10 **customer service centers.** There are three downtown: in ARCO Plaza, 505 S. Flower St., Level B; at 419 S. Main St.; and at 1016 S. Main St. The RTD prints **route maps** for the different sections of the city. A brochure called *RTD Self-Guided Tours* details how to reach the most important sights from downtown. Call 800-2LA-RIDE (800-252-7433; daily 5:30am-11:30pm) for transit information and schedules. RTD's **basic fare** is $1.10, passengers with disabilities 45¢; transfers 25¢, 10¢ for seniors and disabled; exact change required. Transfers operate from one RTD line to another or to another transit authority, such as Santa Monica Municipal Bus Lines, Culver City Municipal Bus Lines, Long Beach Transit, or Orange County Transit District.

Bus service is best downtown and along the major thoroughfares west of downtown. (There is 24-hr. service, for instance, on Wilshire Blvd.) The downtown **DASH shuttle** is only 25¢ and serves Chinatown, Union Station, Olvera Street, City Hall, Little Tokyo, the Music Center, ARCO Plaza, and more, including Sunset Blvd. in Hollywood, Pacific Palisades, Fairfax, Venice Beach, and Watts. (Downtown DASH operates Mon.-Fri. 6:30am-6:30pm, Sat. 10am-5pm; other DASH shuttles do not run on Sat.) **All route numbers given are RTD unless otherwise designated.**

Gray Line Tours, 6541 Hollywood Blvd., Hollywood (213-856-5900), is a more expensive but easier way to reach distant attractions. Costs include transportation and admission: Disneyland ($62 for the day, $69 for day and evening); Magic Mountain ($53); Universal Studios ($56); San Diego Zoo ($55); Sea World ($59). Tours leave from the Gray Line office for 200 different locations in summertime. Some larger hostels offer bus trips to area beaches and attractions for reasonable fees.

In a desperate, expensive, last-ditch effort to alleviate the congestion that threatens to choke the city, L.A. has finally started building a **subway.** The first leg of L.A.'s 300-mi. Metro Rail Plan, the Blue Line, presently runs from 7th St. in Downtown to

Long Beach (call 213-626-4455 for information). The Red Line currently runs from McArthur Park Station in Westlake to Union Station downtown (5 stops, 7 min.).

Freeways and Their Users The freeway is perhaps the most enduring of L.A.'s images. When uncongested, these 10- and 12-lane concrete behemoths offer speed and convenience; the trip from downtown to Santa Monica can take as little as 20 min. No matter how crowded the freeway is, it's almost always quicker and safer than taking surface streets to your destination. To help them "get in touch with their freeway," Californians refer to the highways by names rather than by numbers. For freeway information, call **CalTrans** (213-897-3693). The main freeways are the **San Diego Freeway (I-405)**, the **Santa Monica Freeway (I-10; San Bernardino Freeway** east of downtown), the **Golden State Freeway (I-5; Santa Ana** south of downtown), the **Ventura Freeway (U.S. 101; Hollywood Freeway** in Hollywood), and the $2 billion **Glen Anderson Freeway (I-105)**.

ACCOMMODATIONS

If you arrive at LAX, do *not* accept an offer of free transportation to an unknown hostel. Airport solicitation is illegal and is a good indicator that a potential hostel is operating illegally as well. *Let's Go* lists a number of legitimate hostels, many of which *will* provide transportation assistance if you call from the airport or bus stations. Public transportation directions are also given if applicable.

Many inexpensive lodgings in Los Angeles bear a frightening resemblance to Poe's House of Usher. Dozens of flophouses around the Greyhound station charge $13-20 per night, but those who are concerned about personal safety or unnerved by skid-row street life should look elsewhere. Tolerable lodgings fall roughly into four categories: hostels, run-down but safe hotels, residential hotels offering weekly rates (these can save you a bundle), and budget motels located well off the beaten track but reasonably close by car.

In general, the downtown area offers the best transportation, but if you don't anticipate touring much by public bus it's best to move on. The Hollywood area also has convenient bus connections, and vies with Venice as the most intriguing part of town. Offering lots of sights, cheap victuals, and most of L.A.'s nightlife, West L.A. is the safest, quietest, and cleanest area, but you'll pay for it. Venice is, well, Venice, and given the kooky lifestyle and thriving international hostel culture, it's probably the best place to stay in L.A. Prices listed are without L.A.'s 12½% hotel tax.

Downtown

Though busy and relatively safe by day, the downtown area empties and becomes dangerous when the workday ends and on weekends. Both men and women should travel in groups after dark, especially in the area between Broadway and Main. Don't be afraid to haggle, especially during the off-season. Ask about weekly rates, which can be significantly cheaper.

Hotel Stillwell, 828 S. Grand St. (213-627-1151). This ultra-clean hotel is one of the most sensible downtown options. Bright and pleasantly decorated rooms. Indian restaurant and American grill in hotel. A/C, color TV. Singles $35, doubles $45.

Orchid Hotel, 819 S. Flower St. (213-624-5855). Central downtown location and cleanliness make up for the orchid-sized rooms. A/C, color TV. Singles $30, doubles $35. Reservations recommended.

Milner Hotel, 813 S. Flower St. (213-627-6981), next door to the Orchid. Like its neighbor, location and good upkeep compensate for the dinginess of the decor. Pub and grill in lobby. A/C, color TV. Singles $35, doubles $45. No reservations.

Royal Host Olympic Motel, 901 W. Olympic Blvd. (213-626-6255). A ritzy budget hotel—beautiful rooms, with bathtubs, balconies, telephone, radio, and color TV with cable. Some rooms have kitchens. Singles $36, doubles $40, with kitchenettes $45. Students can get a double room for as low as $32.

Park Plaza Hotel, 607 S. Park View St. (213-384-5281), on the west corner of 6th St. across from MacArthur Park. Built in 1927, this eerily grandiose Art Deco giant has a 3-story marble-floored lobby and a monumental staircase. Caters mainly to semi-permanent residents. A/C (in some rooms) and color TV in the clean but small and newly renovated rooms. Olympic pool. Singles from $50, doubles $55.

Motel de Ville, 1123 W. 7th St. (213-624-8474), 2 blocks west of the Hilton. Multi-lingual staff (Japanese, Chinese, English) welcomes international travelers. Pool, clean rooms with free HBO. Singles $35, doubles $40. Group discounts.

Hollywood

Jam-packed with exciting activities and blessed with excellent bus service to other areas of Los Angeles, Hollywood is a convenient, if a little run-down, base for tourists. Hollywood Blvd., east of the main strip area, is lined with budget motels, as is Sunset Blvd. The area gets creepy at night and side streets can be dangerous.

Banana Bungalow Hollywood, 2775 Cahuenga Blvd. (213-851-1129 or 800-446-7835), in West Hollywood, just past the Hollywood Bowl on Highland Ave. The hostel runs free shuttle service from the airport, as well as to area beaches and attractions (including Disneyland, Magic Mountain, and Universal Studios). Free nightly movies, arcade, and frequent parties. Pool, basketball court, weight-room, and store on premises. Standard bunks in rooms for 6, with bathroom and color TV. Rooms are mostly mixed-sex, although some are women-only. Linen included. $15 per night. Doubles $42. Full restaurant serving breakfast ($1-3), lunch, and dinner ($3-4) daily.

Hollywood International Guest House and Hostel, 6561 Franklin Ave. (213-850-6287), 2 blocks north of Hollywood Blvd., corner of Whittey. A beautiful house somewhat hidden (look for a street number). Extremely close to Hollywood attractions. Full kitchen, living room with books, and free coffee. Shared rooms for 2-4 people are each decorated with colorful carpets and partitions. Linen included. No curfew. $12 per night. Check-in 9am-8pm. Call for a ride.

Hollywood Wilshire YMCA International Hostel, 1553 N. Hudson Ave. (213-467-4161). Located 1½ blocks south of Hollywood Blvd., the dorm-style rooms are clean and light. Common room with cable TV, full kitchen, pool table, laundry facilities, storage lockers. Use of gym and pool. Free linen and breakfast. Must be over 18. No curfew. $10 per night.

Hollywood International Hostel, 7038½ Hollywood Blvd. (213-850-67287), across the street from the Hollywood Galaxy Shopping Center. A small, 2nd-floor hostel in the heart of Hollywood Blvd. Clean and new, though facilities limited. Small common room with TV and a stove-less kitchen. Free ride from the airport. $12 per night. Doubles $30.

Hollywood Downtowner Motel, 5601 Hollywood Blvd. (213-464-7191). Pleasant, clean rooms. Swimming pool, helpful staff. A/C, telephone, TV. Full kitchen units $2-3 extra (min. 4-night stay for kitchen rooms). Singles $38, doubles $40-46, cheaper rates in winter. Free parking.

Beverly Hills, Westside, Wilshire District

The Westside is an attractive and much safer part of town, but for the most part, room rates are out of sight. Call the **UCLA Off-Campus Housing Office** (310-825-4491), 100 Sproul Hall, and see if they can put you in touch with students who have a spare room through their "roommate share board."

Century City-Westwood Motel, 10604 Santa Monica Blvd. (310-475-4422). Very attractive rooms with refrigerators, color TVs, A/C. They make the whole bathroom *sparkle*. Singles $35-50, each additional person $5, up to 4 in a room.

Bevonshire Lodge Motel, 7575 Beverly Blvd. (213-936-6154). Near Farmers Market and Beverly Center. A popular choice for families. A/C, color TV, telephones, pool. Singles $38.50, doubles $42.50. Kitchen in room $48.50.

Hotel Del Flores, 409 N. Crescent Dr., Beverly Hills (310-274-5115), only 3 blocks east of chic Rodeo Dr. You *can* stay in Beverly Hills this cheaply. Communal microwaves and refrigerators. Some rooms with color TV and ceiling fans. Singles $40, with bath $45, weekly from $175; doubles $45, weekly from $175.

Wilshire Orange Hotel, 6060 W. 8th St. (213-931-9533), in West L.A. near Wilshire Blvd. and Fairfax Ave. Buses #20, 21, 22 serve Wilshire Blvd. from downtown. One of L.A.'s best-located budget accommodations. Near many major sights, in a residential neighborhood. Most rooms have refrigerators, color TV; all but 2 have their own bath or share with one other room. Weekly housekeeping. Many semi-permanent residents. 2-day min. stay. Singles $45, doubles $48.

Santa Monica and Venice

The hostels at Venice Beach are havens for budget travelers. They are just about the cheapest way to stay and may be the most enjoyable way to gaily play away your day in L.A. You'll find dazzling beaches, kinky architecture, and a mellow and unpretentious community devoted to worshiping the sun and cultivating its own eccentricities. The hostels are a popular destination among foreign students, who are lured by Venice's lively blend of indulgent beach culture (beaches *are not* safe at night) and relentless nightlife, centered around the 3rd St. Promenade.

Santa Monica International HI/AYH Hostel, 1436 2nd St., Santa Monica (310-393-9913), in a relatively unsafe area, although the hostel itself is relatively safe. Take RTD bus #33 from downtown to 2nd and Broadway, take Blue Bus #3 from the airport to 4th and Broadway, or Blue Bus #10 from downtown. New dorm areas contribute comfort; restored historical common room lends charm. Colossal kitchen, laundry facilities, and weekend BBQs. TV room, movies every night, storage room and lockers. Two blocks from the beach. Bunk in a dorm-style room $16 per night, doubles $43; nonmembers $3 more. $2 linen rental.

Jim's at The Beach, 17 Brooks Ave., Venice (310-399-4018). Outstanding location ½ block off the boardwalk. Passport required. No more than 6 beds per room. Both the rooms and the staff are clean and sunny. Kitchen. No curfew. Linen included. Free Breakfast, and BBQs on weekends. $15 per night, $90 per week.

Share-Tel International Hostel, 20 Brooks Ave., Venice (310-392-0325), ½ block off the boardwalk, across the street from Jim's. Student ID or passport required. Family-style atmosphere; clean, pleasant rooms with kitchen facilities and bathroom each sleep 6-8. Kitchen, continental breakfast, dinner, safe, linen service, and 2 BBQs per week. $15-17 per night, $100 per week. Open 24 hrs.

Venice Beach Cotel, 25 Windward Ave., Venice (310-399-7649), on the boardwalk, between Zephyr Court and 17th Ave. Located 1½ blocks from the beach. Good security. Shuttle from LAX ($5). Passport required; don't ask about the name. A friendly, lively hostel. 3-6 people share each of the tidy, functional rooms. No food allowed. Bar and social area loud and animated 7pm-1am. No curfew. $12 per night, with bath $15. Private rooms $30-44.

Airport Interclub Hostel, 2221 Lincoln Blvd., Venice (310-305-0250), near Venice Blvd. Take RTD #33 from downtown to Lincoln. Farther from the beach than most others listed. Passport required. Festive after-hours common-room atmosphere. Free airport pick-up, bike and skate rental, pool table, and TV. Rooms sleep 6, and a 25-bed dorm. Mixed- or single-sex accommodations. Kitchen with stove and fridge. Linen. Laundry room. $12-14 per person. $5 deposit.

Cadillac Hotel, 401 Ocean Front Walk, Venice (310-399-8876). A beautiful art-deco landmark directly on the beachfront. Airport shuttle service. Limited parking. Sundeck available for private sunning. No curfew. Shared accommodations $18 per night. Private ocean-view rooms from $49.

FOOD

The range of culinary options in L.A. is directly proportional to the city's ethnic diversity—keep in mind that Angelenos speak 116 different languages. There is Jewish and Eastern European food in the **Fairfax** area; Mexican in **East L.A.;** Japanese, Chinese, Vietnamese, and Thai around **Little Tokyo** and **Chinatown;** seafood along the coast; and Hawaiian, Indian, and Ethiopian restaurants scattered throughout. Sadly, the only cuisine truly indigenous to the area is fast food. For the optimal

Southern Californian fast food experience, try **In 'n' Out Burger** (various locations; call 818-287-4377 for the one nearest you), a family-owned and operated chain that has refused to expand beyond the L.A. area. The rewards of such stubbornness are the In 'n' Out's burgers and fries, which are arguably the best in the business.

Downtown

Lunch specials are easy to find in the financial district as restaurants contend for the businessperson's lunchtime dollar. However, finding a reasonably priced dinner that won't send you rushing to the Department of Health can be a challenge. Delis in **Chinatown** are generally inexpensive; **Weller Court** by the New Otani Hotel and Garden encases several Japanese restaurants, a few in the budget range.

Philippe's, The Original, 1001 N. Alameda (213-628-3781), 2 blocks north of Union Station. The sheer variety of food combined with sizeable portions and low, low prices make this a great place for lunch. Philippe's claims to have originated the French-dipped sandwich; varieties include beef, pork, ham, turkey, or lamb ($3-4). Brace yourself for their own hot mustard; ketchup is *verboten*. Top it off with a large slice of pie ($1.90) and a cup o' joe 10¢. Open daily 6am-10pm.

The Pantry, 877 S. Figueroa St. (213-972-9279). You may have to share a table with a complete stranger, and the waiter is as likely to insult you as to talk your ear off, and the patrons like it that way. The owners recently opened a deli/bakery next door (roast beef sandwich $4.25). Enormous breakfast specials ($6). Sun. brunch at the Pantry is an L.A. tradition. Open 24 hrs.

La Luz Del Dia, 1 W. Olvera St. (213-628-7495) an authentic and inexpensive Mexican restaurant hidden amidst the many tourist-trap Mexican joints along Olvera St. Tortillas are handmade on the premises, and the salsa is sharp. Combination plates around $4. Open Tues.-Sun. 11am-10pm.

Cafe China, 1123 W. 7th St. (213-689-9898). Filling combination plates like spicy shrimp and almond chicken served with soup, egg roll, and rice ($4.50). American breakfasts. Open Mon.-Fri. 9am-7pm. Sat 9am-2am.

Sarashina, 345 E. 2nd St. (213-680-0344), in Little Tokyo. This attractive Japanese restaurant serves hot and cold noodle specials ($4-8). $6 will get you 2 fried rice balls, wheat noodles, salad, and boiled vegetables. Open daily 11:30am-10pm.

Country Life Vegetarian Buffet, 888 S. Figueroa St. (213-489-4118), across the street from the Pantry. Sumptuous international cuisine, classical music, and reasonable prices. Tofu "eggs" for breakfast, all-you-can-eat soups with breads and spreads ($4) for lunch, or reasonably priced "wheat meat" and soy cheese entrees for dinner. Open Mon.-Thurs. 11am-3:30pm, Fri. 11am-2:30pm.

Hollywood and West Hollywood

Forget those rumors about outrageously priced celebrity hangouts—they're here, but you can ignore them. Hollywood offers the best budget dining in L.A. Hollywood and Sunset Boulevards offer a number of excellent, diverse cuisines, while Fairfax (the traditionally Jewish area of town) has Mediterranean-style restaurants and delis. Melrose is full of chic cafes and eateries, which provide outdoor seating so you can see and be seen by the extraordinary stylized and beautiful Melrosians.

Seafood Bay, 3916 Sunset Blvd. (213-664-3902), at Sanborn in Silver Lake, east of Hollywood. Skimps on decor to support a wide variety of seafood at great prices. "Light meals" such as fettucine with clam sauce run around $6. The fish is fantastic, and the accompaniments—garlicky sourdough, pungent rice pilaf—receive the same loving attention. Open Mon.-Fri. 11:30am-9:30pm, Sat.-Sun. 4-9:30pm.

Chayka Restaurant, 4953 Hollywood Blvd. (213-660-3739). Authentic and tantalizing Armenian restaurant. Various kebabs ($5) include pita bread, rice pilaf, and curried vegetables. First-time diners get a free salad. Open daily 9am-10pm.

Johnny Rocket's, 7507 Melrose Ave. (213-651-3361), away from the center of Hollywood in the trendy section of Melrose Ave. near Beverly Hills. The 30s Moderne architecture returns you to a lost era of American diners. Excellent hamburgers (from $3.35) and shakes ($3) and "real" flavored sodas, with syrup and everything ($1.35). Open Sun.-Thurs. 11am-midnight, Fri.-Sat. 11am-2am.

Duke's, 8909 Sunset Blvd. (310-652-3100), at San Vicente. In a neighborhood of trendy boutiques and rock clubs. Hangout for L.A.'s music industry bigwigs; its walls are a kaleidoscope of posters and autographed album covers. Entrees $4-7, 3-egg omelettes $4-6. Open Mon.-Fri. 7:30am-9pm, Sat.-Sun. 8am-4pm.

Pink's Famous Chili Dogs, 711 N. La Brea Ave. (213-931-4223). The chili dogs are good and cheap ($2.10) and that's why Pink's has been around since 1939. Open Sun.-Thurs. 8am-2am, Fri.-Sat. 8am-3am.

Beverly Hills, Westside, Wilshire District

Few restaurants in these upscale neighborhoods are in the budget range. Beverly Hills and the Wilshire District offer some of the finest dining in the country; don't expect any bargains here. La Brea Ave. and Pico Blvd., however, both offer a wide variety of restaurants.

Ed Debevic's, 134 N. La Cienoga Blvd. (310-659-1952), in Beverly Hills. Far and away the most mirthful of the phony 50s diners ("famous since 1984"). All dishes under $7—and served by dancing waitpeople on weekend nights. Full bar. Open Sun.-Thurs. 11:30am-11pm, Fri.-Sat. 11:30am-1am.

Trattoria Angeli, 11651 Santa Monica Blvd. (310-478-1191). Rustic and comfy interior. Regional Italian specialties, but come for the pizza. Spicy Pizza Puttanesca with olives, capers, and red hot peppers ($7.25). Other specialty pizzas around $8. Open Sun.-Thurs. 6am-10:30pm, Fri. and Sat. 6am-11pm.

El Nopal, 10426 National Blvd. (310-559-4732), in West L.A., between Motor and Overland. Known as the "home of the pregnant burrito." The famed *embarrasado* ($6.25), stuffed with chicken and avocado, lives up to its name. Tasty tacos and tangy salsa ($2). Open Mon.-Fri. 11am-9pm, Sat.-Sun. 11am-10pm.

Tommy's Original Hamburgers, 2575 W. Beverly Blvd. (213-389-9060), Wilshire District. Ignore the multitude of Tommy's knock-offs and head to the winner of the sloppiest chili dog contest—the paper towel dispensers every 2 ft. along the counters aren't there just for looks. Chili dog $1.50, chili burger $1.40, double cheeseburger (for those with galvanized stomachs) $2.20. Open 24 hrs.

Westwood

Westwood is filled with chic and convenient eateries perfect before a movie or while shopping, and you'll find everything from falafel to *gelato* in corner shops.

Sak's Teriyaki, 1121 Glendon Ave. (310-208-2002), in Westwood. Excellent, low-priced Japanese plates including chicken and beef teriyaki ($3.70-5). Popular with students. Happy Hour special from 3-6pm ($2.75). Open Mon.-Wed. 10am-10pm, Thurs.-Fri. 10am-11pm, Sat. 11am-11pm, Sun. 11am-10pm.

Tacos Tacos, 1084 Glendon Ave. (310-208-2038), Westwood Village. Trendy "Southwestern Cafe" with blue corn chicken tacos ($2). Try the *horchata* (cinnamon-flavored rice water, $1.25). Open Mon.-Sat. 11am-10:30pm, Sun. 11am-9pm.

Fatburger, 10955 Kinross (310-208-7365). Order a Double King chili-cheese-egg-burger, roll up your sleeves, and open wide your mouth and your arteries. Fat'n'-juicy burgers from $2.50. Open Sun.-Wed. 10am-3am, Thurs.-Sat. 10am-4am.

Sphinx, 1779 A Westwood Blvd. (310-477-2358), ½ block north of Santa Monica Blvd. The falafel ($2.75) is tasty, and the BBQ chicken kebab ($3.50) is delectable. Open Mon.-Fri. 10am-10pm, Sat. 11am-10pm.

Santa Monica and Venice

Unfortunately, most of Santa Monica's eateries are overpriced, and most of Venice's eateries are overgreased. The new **EATZ Cafe** in Santa Monica Place, at the end of the 3rd St. Promenade on Broadway, offers 17 different types of mall food to choose from, a number of which are tasty and reasonably priced.

Skorpio's, 109 Santa Monica Blvd. (310-393-9020), ½-block from Ocean Ave. Standard and solid Greek fare for under $6. Giant Gyro sandwich ($3.50) and great Spanakopita ($5.50). Beer, wine, and cappuccino. Open daily 11am-11pm.

Tito's Tacos, 11222 Washington Place (310-391-5780), in Culver City at Sepulveda, 1 block north of Washington Blvd. The name should have been Tito's Burritos, since the burrito, with its huge hunks of shredded beef, is the star attraction (at $2.10, it's also the most expensive thing on the menu). Tostadas and enchiladas $1.25, tacos 95¢. Plenty of parking. Open daily 9am-11:30pm.

Benita's Frites, 1437 3rd St. Promenade (310-458-2889), in Santa Monica. Fries are the sole option on this menu. French fries served the Belgian way, in a paper cone with any of the 20 hot and cold sauces—try the Andoulause. Small order with one sauce $1, each additional sauce 50¢. Open Sun. noon-8pm, Mon. 11:30am-4pm, Tues.-Thurs. 11:30am-10pm, Fri.-Sat. 11:30am-10:30pm.

San Fernando Valley

The entirety of Ventura Blvd. is chock full of a wide variety of restaurants. Eating lunch near the studios in **Studio City** is your best stargazing opportunity. The famous are willing to dine outside the studios because of Studio City's unwritten law—stare all you want, but don't bother them, *and don't ask for autographs.* The chili recipe at **Chili John's,** 2018 W. Burbank Blvd., Burbank (818-846-3611), hasn't changed since 1900 (bowl $4.25). As your mouth burns contemplate the mountain landscape painted on one wall; the former owner/chef took over 20 years to paint it—while serving customers. (Open Tues.-Fri. 11am-7pm, Sat. 11am-4pm.)

SIGHTS

Museums

Los Angeles County Museum of Art (LACMA), 5905 Wilshire Blvd. (213-857-6000), at the west end of Hancock Park. A distinguished, comprehensive collection that should rebut those who argue that L.A.'s only culture is in its yogurt. Opened in 1965, the LACMA is the largest museum in the West and still growing. Upcoming exhibits include "Picasso and the Weeping Women" (Feb. 13-May, 1994), and "Korean Arts of the 18th Century" (June 16-Aug. 21, 1994). Open Tues.-Thurs. 10am-5pm, Fri. 10am-9pm, Sat.-Sun. 11am-6pm. $6, seniors and students $4, ages 6-17 $1. Free 2nd Wed. of each month.

J. Paul Getty Museum, 17985 PCH (310-458-2003), set back on a cliff above the ocean. A re-creation of the first-century Villa dei Papiri in Herculaneum. Appropriately, the collection of Greek and Roman sculpture is given center stage—it includes a bronze athlete that is the only surviving work of Lysippos, a sculptor contemporaneous with Alexander the Great. The museum recently acquired one of Van Gogh's Iris paintings. Reservations are needed a day (weeks in summer) in advance. Bikers admitted without reservations. Take RTD #434 and mind that you ask for a free **museum pass** from the driver. Open Tues.-Sun. 10am-5pm. Free.

Museum of Contemporary Art (MOCA), California Plaza, 250 S. Grand Ave. (213-626-6222), downtown. The most striking and chic museum around, showcasing art from 1940 to the present. Focuses on abstract expressionism; works by Pollock, Calder, Miró, and Giacometti. Open Tues.-Wed. and Fri.-Sun. 11am-5pm, Thurs. 11am-8pm. $4, seniors and students $2, under 12 free. Free Thurs. 5-8pm.

L.A. Children's Museum, 310 N. Main St. (213-687-8800), downtown across from City Hall East; where everything can be handled. Children are invited to create their own MOCA pieces. Open Tues.-Fri. 11:30am-5pm, Sat.-Sun. 10am-5pm. $5.

California Museum of Science and Industry, 700 State Dr. (213-744-7400), in Exposition Park. Entrance next to the United DC-8 parked out front. Many of the exhibits are either corporate or governmental propaganda; those left to the MSI's own devices are rather amateurish. The **Aerospace Building** exhibits $8 million worth of aircraft, including the Gemini 11 space capsule. Lovers will enjoy the expansive, formal **rose garden** in the courtyard, with its 16,000 specimens of 190 sweet-smelling varieties of roses. Open daily 10am-5pm. Free. Parking $3.

Hollywood Studio Museum, 2100 N. Highland Ave. (213-874-2276), across from the Hollywood Bowl, provides a refreshing look at the history of early Hollywood film-making. Antique cameras, costumes, props, and other memorabilia clutter the museum along with vintage film clips. Open Sat.-Sun. 10am-4pm. $4, seniors and students $3, children $2. Ample free parking.

Gene Autry Western Heritage Museum, 4700 Zoo Dr. (213-667-2000), in Griffith Park at Golden State and Ventura Fwy. Collection covers fact and fiction of the Old West, with exhibits on pioneer life and on the history of Westerns, including costumes donated by Robert Redford, Gary Cooper, and Clint Eastwood. Open Tues.-Sun. 10am-5pm. $6, seniors and students $4.50, children $2.50.

Beit HaShoa Museum of Tolerance, 9786 W. Pico Blvd. (310-553-9036), corner of Roxbury just outside of Beverly Hills. Previously known as the **Simon Wiesenthal Center,** the museum received $5 million from former Governor Deukmeijian on the condition that the museum include displays on the Armenian and Native American genocides. The new museum holds displays on the Holocaust, anti-Semitism, prejudice in the U.S., and the U.S. civil rights movement. Mandatory tours leave at 10-min. intervals and last 2½ hr. Tickets cannot be reserved and often sell out on Fri. and Sun. Last tours leave 2½ hr. before closing. Open Mon.-Wed. 10am-7:30pm, Thurs. 10am-10:30pm, Fri. 10am-5pm, Sun. 10:30am-8:30pm. $7.50, seniors $5.50, students $4.50, ages 3-12 $2.50.

Norton Simon Museum of Art, 411 W. Colorado Blvd., Pasadena (213-681-2484), at Orange Grove Blvd. Pasadena's answer to LACMA and the Getty. Numerous Rodin and Brancusi bronzes; masterpieces by Rembrandt, Raphael, and Picasso. The flawlessly presented collection of art from ancient Southeast Asia is one of the world's best. Changing exhibits have included sculpture from India and etchings by Goya. From downtown L.A. take bus #483 from Olive St. to Colorado Blvd. and Fair Oaks Ave. in Pasadena. Then take #180 or 181. Museum is 4 blocks west. Open Thurs.-Sun. noon-6pm. $4, seniors and students $2, under 12 free.

Southwest Museum, 234 Museum Dr., Pasadena (213-221-2163). The best resource on the history and culture of Native Americans and the Southwest. Includes contemporary Native American art. Take bus #83 along Broadway to Museum Dr. and trek up the hill. Drivers should take the Pasadena Fwy. (Rte. 110) to Ave. 43 and follow the signs. Open Tues.-Sun. 11am-5pm. Admission $5, seniors and students $3, ages 7-18 $2. Library open Wed.-Sat. 11am-5pm.

Downtown

Providing a theoretical centerpoint for Los Angeles's fragmented communities, the downtown area alone is larger than most cities. Residents of the different neighborhoods, financiers who flee to valley domiciles come evening, and a substantial population that retires and rises on the street, coexist here by an accident of geography. The **Museum of Contemporary Art (MOCA)** is a sleek and geometric architectural marvel. Downtown is also home to the children's museum and the Museum of African-American Art. (See museums, above.) Visitors should be cautious. Secure valuables on your person or at home; leave nothing in your car should you want to see it again. Pay to park your car in a secure lot, rather than on the street. The best reason to spend time downtown is to see L.A.'s cultural attractions.

Financial District

A jungle of glass and steel, the gigantic corporate offices of such companies as ARCO, the Bank of America, Wells Fargo, and AT&T crowd the busy downtown center, an area bounded roughly by 3rd and 6th St., Figueroa St., and Grand Ave. The I.M. Pei-designed **First Interstate World Center,** 633 W. 5th St., conspicuously perched atop Bunker Hill, dominates the skyline; at 73 stories and 1017 ft., it's the tallest building west of the Mississippi River.

The financial district's skyline has been made famous by the TV show *L.A. Law,* and includes some of L.A.'s most impressive buildings. The **Times-Mirror Building** at 220 W. 1st, with the exception of the 1970s addition, is a classic example of Cal Moderne, as well as the area's most impressive building. The five cylindrical fingers of the **Westin Bonaventure Hotel,** 4045 Figueroa St., snatch at the smog. The **Civic Center,** a solid wall of bureaucratic architecture bounded by the Hollywood Fwy. (U.S. 101), Grand, 1st, and San Pedro St., runs east from the Music Center. It ends at **City Hall,** 200 N. Spring St. Another famous building in the Southland, the hall was cast as the home of the *Daily Planet* in the *Superman* TV series.

Broadway

South of 1st St., Broadway is predominantly Mexican. All billboards and store signs are in Spanish, and the **Grand Central Public Market** takes a center seat. Across the street, the **Bradbury Building,** 304 S. Broadway, stands as a relic of L.A.'s Victorian past. Its ornate staircases and elevators (wrought in iron, wood, and marble) are often bathed in sunlight, which pours in through the glass roof. Crews film period scenes here regularly (open Mon.-Fri. 9am-5pm, Sat. 9am-4pm).

El Pueblo

Farther north lies the historic birthplace of Los Angeles, bounded by Spring, Arcadia, and Macy. In the place where the original city center once stood, **El Pueblo de Los Angeles State Historic Park** (213-680-2525; open Tues.-Sat. 10am-3pm) preserves a number of historically important buildings from the Spanish and Mexican eras. Start out at the visitors center, 622 N. Main (213-628-1274). The center offers free walking tours (Tues.-Sat. 10am-1pm on the hr., but call to check). The **Old Plaza,** with its century-old Moreton Bay fig trees and huge bandstand, sprawls at the center of the pueblo. Tours start here and wind their way past the **Avila Adobe** (1818), 10 E. Olvera St., the oldest house in the city. Most tours also include the **catacombs** that formerly held gambling and opium dens. **Olvera Street,** one of L.A.'s original roads, is now called Tijuana North by the locals, and one tawdry stand after another sells schlocky Mexican handicrafts. Here L.A.'s large Chicano community celebrates Mexican Independence Day (Cinco de Mayo, May 5).

Chinatown

North of this area, Chinatown is roughly bordered by Yale, Spring, Ord, and Bernard St. From downtown, take the DASH shuttle. It was in this once vice-ridden neighborhood that Roman Polanski's Jake Giddis (played by Mr. L.A. himself, Jack Nicholson) in *Chinatown* learned just what a tough old world is out there. **Little Tokyo** is centered on 2nd and San Pedro St. on the eastern edge of downtown. The **New Otani Hotel,** 120 S. Los Angeles St., 1 block south of the Civic Center between 1st and 2nd, rents its lavish Meiji-style rooms for up to $700 per night. The **Japanese-American Cultural and Community Center** was designed by Buckminster Fuller and Isamu Noguchi, who crafted a monumental sculpture for the courtyard. (Administrative offices open Mon.-Fri. 9am-5pm.)

Exposition Park

Among the most notable sights near downtown is **Exposition Park.** At the turn of the century, this area was an upscale suburb of downtown; it deteriorated in the 20s but was renewed when the Olympiad first came to town in 1932, and revitalized yet again by the 1984 Olympics. Today, it is one of the few parts of L.A. where a number of important attractions are clustered together. The park is southwest of downtown, just off the Harbor Fwy., and is bounded by Exposition Blvd., Figueroa St., Vermont Ave., and Santa Barbara Ave. From downtown, take bus #40 or 42 (from Broadway between 5th and 6th St.) to the park's southern edge. From Hollywood, take #204 down Vermont. From Santa Monica, take bus #20, 22, 320, or 322 on Wilshire, and transfer to #204 at Vermont. The park is dominated by several major museums, including the **California Museum of Science and Industry** and the **Los Angeles County Natural History Museum.** (See Museums, above.)

Watts Towers

Watts was made notorious by riots in 1965. Los Angeles exploded once more in 1992, following the acquittal of the LAPD officers who beat African-American motorist Rodney King. This is an area where meandering tourists will probably feel unwelcome or unsafe. The only draw to the neighborhood are the **Watts Towers,** 1765 E. 107th St. (213-569-8181). These remarkable pieces of folk art were built single-handedly over 33 years by Simon Rodia. The delicate towers of glistening fretwork, decorated with mosaics of broken glass, ceramic tile, and sea shells, are an inspiring testament to the power of one man's extraordinary vision and dedication. (On-the-spot tours $2, children $1.50 during regular hours, Sat.-Sun. 10am-4pm. During the week appointments must be made in advance.) The Towers are a good 7-mi. drive from the nearest tourist attractions at Exposition Park. The safest parking is in the Arts Center lot. To reach the center by bus, take RTD #56 downtown to Wilmington and 108th St. Walk one block west on 108th to Graham, then one block north. Or, from downtown take the Metro Blue Line and get off at 103 St. station. Walk on 104th east to Beach, and then south to the corner of 106th and 107th. Pedestrians will remain safer in groups and during the day.

Wilshire District and Hancock Park

Wilshire Boulevard, especially the "Miracle Mile" between Highland and Fairfax Ave., played a starring role in Los Angeles's westward suburban expansion. On what was then the end of the boulevard, the Bullocks Corporation gambled on attracting shoppers from downtown and in 1929 erected one of L.A.'s few architecturally significant buildings, the massive, bronze-colored **Bullocks Wilshire** at 3050 Wilshire Blvd., near Vermont Ave., now called the **I. Magnin BW Wilshire.** The nearby residential neighborhoods and their 20s architecture are also worth touring by car. The streets south of Wilshire opposite Hancock Park are lined with Spanish-style bungalows and the occasional modernist manse. The **Los Angeles Conservancy** (213-623-2489) offers tours of downtown Art Deco sights.

La Brea Tar Pits

A few mi. farther down Wilshire, in **Hancock Park,** the acrid smell of tar pervades the vicinity of the **La Brea Tar Pits,** one of the most popular hangouts in the world for fossilized early mammals. Most of the million bones recovered from the pits between 1913 and 1915 have found a new home in the **George C. Page Museum of La Brea Discoveries,** 5801 Wilshire Blvd. (recording 213-936-2230, operator 213-857-6311), at Curson. Wilshire buses stop in front of the museum. The museum includes reconstructed Ice Age animals, a laboratory where paleontologists work behind plate-glass windows, and a display where you can feel what it's like to stick around in the tar. (Open Tues.-Sun. 10am-5pm. $5, seniors and students $2.50, children 1¢. Tours Wed.-Sun. 2:15pm. Tours of grounds 1pm.)

Hollywood

It's hard to believe that for decades, this tiny chunk of a massive city defined glamour on the West Coast. A grown-up's Disneyland, Hollywood symbolized the American desire to "make it," to forget one's past and fabricate an instant persona of sophistication and wealth. For years, this urban fantasy world succeeded, generating the image and style associated with California, and with America itself.

Visitors won't see a trace of the sunny farm community that first lured the movie men who brought glamour to its groves. Hollywood today has lost much of its sparkle. The major studios have moved over the mountains into the San Fernando Valley, and blockbusters are increasingly shot "on location" elsewhere in the U.S. or overseas. **Hollywood Boulevard** and other thoroughfares, once glittering and glamorous, are now rated X. At night, prostitutes abound. Hollywood is still a fascinating place, but a far cry from the Emerald City it was once thought to be.

HOLLYWOOD sign

Those 50-ft.-high, slightly erratic letters perched on Mt. Cahuenga north of Hollywood stand with New York's Statue of Liberty and Paris's Eiffel Tower as the universally recognized symbol of their city. The original 1923 sign, which read HOLLYWOODLAND, was an advertisement for a new subdivision in the Hollywood Hills (a caretaker lived behind one of the "L"s). By 1978 the city had acquired the sign and restored the crumbling letters, leaving off the last syllable. For a closer look at the site, follow Beachwood Dr. up into the hills (bus #208; off Franklin Ave. between Vine St. and Western Ave.). Drive along the narrow twisting streets of the Hollywood Hills for glimpses of the bizarre homes and lifestyles of the Rich and Famous. Once you've made the climb, kick back with a picnic and ponder the wondrous clutter stretching panoramically before you.

Hollywood Boulevard

Lined with souvenir shops, porno houses, clubs, and theaters, the Boulevard is busy both day and night. Most sights in this area now focus around the intersection of Highland Ave. and Hollywood Blvd., and then west down Hollywood. To the east, things turn seedier. The facade of **Mann's Chinese Theater** (formerly Grauman's), 6925 Hollywood Blvd. (213-464-8111), between Highland and La Brea, is an odd tropical interpretation of a Chinese temple. Hollywood hype at its finest, there's always a crowd of tourists in the courtyard, worshiping cement impressions of various parts of the stars' anatomies and trademark possessions (Al Jolson's knees, Trigger's hooves, R2D2's wheels, Jimmy Durante's nose, George Burns's cigar, etc.). Just across the street from Mann's is the newly-renovated **El Capitan Theatre**, 6838 Hollywood Blvd. (213-467-9545), which held the 1941 Hollywood premier of *Citizen Kane,* and now shows only Disney films.

If you want to stroll among stars, have a look at the **Walk of Fame** along Hollywood Blvd. and Vine St. More than 2500 bronze-inlaid stars are embedded in the sidewalk, inscribed with names and feats. Film, television, and radio celebrities are commemorated, but many names will be meaningless to the under-40 generation.

At the **Hollywood Wax Museum**, 6767 Hollywood Blvd. (213-462-5991), you'll meet 200 figures, from Jesus to Elvis. (Open Sun.-Thurs. 10am-midnight, Fri.-Sat. 10am-2am. $9, children $7.) Across the street from the Wax Museum you'll find two touristy "Odd-itoriums": the original **Frederick's of Hollywood** (with tasteful lingerie museum) and the **Max Factor Museum** (open Mon.-Sat. 10am-4pm; free).

Film is just one of the industries that grease Hollywood's cash-register wheels. Music is another. The pre-eminent monument of the modern record industry is the 1954 **Capitol Records Tower,** 1750 Vine St., just north of Hollywood Blvd. The building, which was designed to look like a stack of records, is cylindrical with fins sticking out at each floor (the "records") and a needle on top.

Adjacent to **Barnsdall Park,** 4800 Hollywood Blvd., on top of the hill, the **Hollyhock House,** 4808 Hollywood Blvd. (213-662-7272), commands a 360° view of Los Angeles and the mountains. Completed in 1922 for eccentric oil heiress Aline Barnsdall, the house remains one of Frank Lloyd Wright's most important works. It is the first building by Wright to reflect the influence of pre-Colombian Mayan temples. (Tours Tues.-Sun. on the hr. from noon-3pm. Admission $1.50, seniors $1, under 13 free. Buy tickets at the Municipal Art Gallery, 213-485-4581.)

Griffith Park

Sprawling over 4500 acres of hilly terrain is **Griffith Park.** The L.A. Zoo, the Greek Theater, Griffith Observatory and Planetarium, a bird sanctuary, tennis courts, two golf courses, campgrounds, and various hiking trails blanket the dry hills and mountains. Pick up a map at any of the entrance points. Several of the mountain roads through the park, especially Vista Del Valle Dr., offer stunning panoramic (though often smog-obscured) views of Los Angeles, looking south over downtown, Hollywood, and the Westside. For info, stop by the **Visitors Center and Ranger Head-quarters,** 4730 Crystal Spring Dr. (213-665-5188; open daily 7am-5pm).

The white stucco and copper domes of the Art Deco **Observatory and Planetarium** (213-664-1181, for a recording 213-664-1191) are visible from around the park. You might remember the planetarium from the climactic last scene of the James Dean film, *Rebel Without a Cause.* A 12-in. **telescope** opens the public eye to the sky (clear nights dusk-9:45pm; in winter clear nights Tues.-Sun. 7-10pm; sky report and information 213-663-8171). (Observatory open daily 12:30-10pm; winter Tues.-Sun. 2-10pm. Planetarium show Mon.-Fri. at 3 and 7:30pm, Sat.-Sun. also at 4:30pm; in winter Tues.-Fri. 3 and 8pm, Sat.-Sun. also at 4:30 pm. Admission $4, seniors $3, under 12 $2, under 5 not admitted.)

A large **bird sanctuary** at the bottom of the observatory hill serves its function well, but if you crave the sight of warm-blooded animals, you might go to the **L.A. Zoo,** 5332 Zoo Dr. (213-666-4090), at the park's northern end. The zoo's 113 acres accommodate 2000 crazy critters, and the facility is consistently ranked among the nation's best. (Open daily 10am-5pm. Admission $8, seniors $5, ages 2-12 $3.)

On the southern side of the park, below the observatory, the 4500-seat **Greek Theater** (213-665-5857) hosts a number of concerts in its outdoor amphitheater virtually year-round. Check advertisements in the *Sunday Times* "Calendar" section for coming attractions. To get to the Observatory and Greek Theater, take bus #203 from Hollywood. To reach the Zoo, take bus #97 from downtown. There is no bus service between the northern and southern parts of Griffith Park.

West Hollywood

Once considered a no-man's land between Beverly Hills and Hollywood, West Hollywood was incorporated in 1985 and was one of the first cities in the country to be governed by openly gay officials. There's always a lot going on here, and a list of each week's events can be found in the *L.A. Weekly.*

In the years before incorporation, lax zoning and other liberal laws gave rise to the **Sunset Strip.** Long the center of L.A. nightlife, the Strip was originally lined with posh nightclubs frequented by stars and now plays host to several rock clubs (see Clubs). Many world-famous bands from The Doors to Guns 'n' Roses got their start here. These days, most of the music on this stretch is heavy metal and hard rock, and weekend nights draw tremendous crowds and traffic jams. The **billboards** on the Strip are vividly hand-painted, many heralding the latest films.

Melrose Avenue, south of West Hollywood, is lined with swish restaurants, ultra-trendy boutiques, and art galleries. Punk clothing pits like **Retail Slut** and functional novelty shops like **Condom Mania** outfit clubbies for the evening. The choicest stretch is between La Brea and Fairfax, but all between Highland and Doheny is packed with frumpy people watchers and the stylized organisms they're staring at.

At the corner of Beverly and San Vicente Blvd. is the Los Angeles **Hard Rock Cafe** (310-276-7605), emblematic of all that is right and wrong in Los Angeles. Indiana Jones's leather jacket, one of Pete Townshend's guitars, and a 6-foot martini glass adorn the interior. The Hard Rock is all image, no substance. But, hey, the food's good and it's fun. (Open Sun.-Thurs. 11:30am-11:30pm, Fri.-Sat. 11:30am-midnight.)

North of the Beverly Center, at Melrose and San Vicente, is the **Pacific Design Center,** 8687 Melrose Ave. (310-657-0800), a huge, blue-and-green glass complex with a wave-like profile (nicknamed **The Blue Whale).** The building is no doubt destined for architectural history texts. In addition to some design showrooms, the PDC houses a public plaza with a 350-seat amphitheater, used to stage free summer concerts on Sundays. Call or inquire at the information desk in the entryway.

Beverly Hills

Though placed in the midst of Greater Los Angeles, between downtown L.A. and the coast, Beverly Hills remains a steadfast enclave of wealth. Beverly Hills seceded from L.A. in 1914 and has remained distinct from the city ever since. This is grossly apparent along Robertson Ave., at the eastern edge of the city, where only the western, Beverly Hills side of the street is lined with large, shady trees.

There is nothing understated about the city's wealth; stand on Rodeo Dr. for 15 minutes and count how many BMWs, Porsches, and Rolls-Royces purr past you; the Beverly Hills Post Office (on Beverly Dr.) must be the only one in the country with valet parking. The heart of the city rests in the **Golden Triangle,** a wedge formed by Wilshire and Santa Monica Blvd. centering on **Rodeo Drive,** known for its many opulent clothing boutiques and jewelry shops. On this famous street you might feel underdressed simply window-shopping. Across the way is the venerable **Beverly Wilshire Hotel** (310-275-5200), whose old and new wings are connected by **El Camino Real,** a cobbled street with Louis XIV gates. Inside, hall mirrors reflect the glitter of crystal chandeliers and marble floors.

The new **Beverly Hills City Hall** stands, looking a bit out of place, on Crescent Dr. just below Santa Monica. This beautiful Spanish Renaissance building was erected during the heart of the Great Depression, and is now engulfed in Beverly Hills's new **Civic Center.** The **Beverly Hills Library,** 444 N. Rexford Dr. (213-228-2220), is a case study in the city's overriding concerns—the interior is adorned with marble imported from Thailand, but contains a paltry collection of books.

Westwood and UCLA

UCLA

The gargantuan **University of California at Los Angeles** campus and the dearth of parking spaces make both UCLA and Westwood look like motorbike versions of Disneyland's *Autopia*. UCLA is not the uni-dimensional, hedonistic colony of blond, deep-tanned party animals it was once thought to be. The school is directly north of Westwood Village and west of Beverly Hills. Drivers can find free parking behind the Federal Building. Campus information kiosks sell a $4 day permit to park in student garages. Start your tour at the **visitors center,** 10945 Le Conte Ave., #147 (310-206-8147), in the Ueberroth Olympic Office Building. (Free 1½-hr. tours Mon.-Fri. 10:30am and 1:30pm. Maps available at kiosks.)

The **Dickson Art Center** (310-825-1462) houses the **Wight Art Gallery,** home to frequent internationally recognized exhibitions. (Open Sept.-June Tues. 11am-8pm, Wed.-Fri. 11am-5pm, Sat.-Sun. 1-5pm. Free.) The **Murphy Sculpture Garden,** scattered over five acres, includes works by Rodin, Matisse, and Miró. An innovation in the exciting field of fountain design, the **Inverted Fountain** spouts from the fountain's perimeter and rushes down into the gaping hole in the middle. The **Botanical Gardens** (310-825-3620) encompasses the Zen Buddhist-inspired Japanese Garden, which can be viewed only by appointment. (Open Tues. 10am-1pm, Wed. noon-3pm. Reserve 2 weeks in advance. Call 310-825-4574 to arrange for a tour.) **Ackerman Union,** 308 Westwood Plaza (310-825-7711), is the campus information bank. A calendar lists the month's lengthy line-up of movies (first-runs often free), lectures, and campus activities.

Westwood Village

Just south of the campus, this village, with its myriad movie theaters, trendy boutiques, and upscale bistros, is geared more toward the residents of L.A.'s Westside than collegians. Like most college towns, however, Westwood is humming on weekends when everyone (students, tourists, gang members, and police) shows up to do their thing. Off the main drag at 1218 Glendon Ave. is the **Westwood Memorial Cemetery.** Flowers, teddy bears, and even sprouted Chia Pets are left by family and fans who make pilgrimages to the graves of Marilyn Monroe, Natalie Wood, and young Heather O'Rourke (the late star of *Poltergeist*).

At 14523 Sunset Blvd., hike around **Will Rogers State Historical Park** (310-454-8212) and take in the panoramic views of the city and the distant Pacific. Follow Chatauqua Blvd. inland from PCH to Sunset Blvd., or take bus #2 which runs along Sunset. (Park open daily 8am-7pm; Rogers's house open daily 10am-5pm.)

Santa Monica

To a resident of turn-of-the-century L.A., a trip to the beach resort of Santa Monica meant a long ride over poor-quality roads. Today, it takes about half an hour (with no traffic) on express bus #10 or on the Santa Monica Fwy. from downtown. Though no longer far away, Santa Monica is still pretty far-out.

The beach is the closest to L.A. proper and is thus crowded and dirty. Still, the magical lure of sun, surf, and sand causes nightmarish summer traffic jams on I-10 and I-405; there are prettier and cleaner beaches to visit to the north and south. The colorful **Santa Monica Pier** is still nostalgic and popular, if a bit sleazy. The gem of the pier is the magnificent turn-of-the-century carousel, featured in *The Sting*.

With the creation of the **Third Street Promenade** in 1989, and the recent remodeling of **Santa Monica Place,** Santa Monica has recently become one of L.A.'s major walking, movie-seeing, and yuppie-spoor areas. The 3rd Street Promenade sports some cool cafes, a couple of L.A.'s better bookshops, overpriced bars and restaurants, and a number of fine, fresh street artists (not to mention some water-spouting, ivy-lined, mesh dinosaur sculptures).

Venice

The most unique part of a unique city, Venice is Los Angeles's saving grace for budget travelers. A perennial favorite among foreigners, Venice is wacky on weekdays, wild on weekends. A typical Sunday includes trapeze artists, spontaneous Rollerblade dancing competitions, and your run-of-the-mill clowns, jugglers, comedians, glass-eaters, hemp advocates, bikini-clad skaters, and choirs of gaping Angelenos.

Originally intended by Abbot Kinney to be canal-ridden like its namesake in Italy, Venice instead ran with dirt and oil until the canals were filled and buried around the turn of the century. For a sense of the Venice that Kinney envisioned, head for the traffic circle at Main St. and Windward Ave. This was once a circular canal, the hub of the whole network. Along Pacific Ave., columns and tiled awnings are all that remain of the grandiose hotels that once housed vacationers from L.A.

Venice finally came into its own in the 70s, when the sexual revolution spawned a swinging beach community. Although the revolution may have been defeated, Venice's peculiar beach renaissance lives on, a testament to the ongoing allure of the credo "do your own thing."

Ocean Front Walk

Venice's main beachfront drag is a drastic demographic departure from Santa Monica's promenade. Street people converge on shaded clusters of benches, yelping evangelists drown out off-color comedians, and bodybuilders of both sexes pump iron in skimpy outfits at the original **Muscle Beach** (1800 Ocean Front Walk, closest to 18th and Pacific Ave.). This is where the roller-skating craze began, and where ice-dancing has been brought to asphalt with the advent of in-line skates ("Rollerblades"). Fire-juggling cyclists, overdressed joggers, groovy elders (such as the "skateboard grandma"), and bards in Birkenstocks make up the balance of this playground population. If your feet don't move you through the crowds fast enough, rent skates or a bike. **Skatey's Sports,** 102 Washington (310-823-7971), rents in-line skates ($5 per hr., $10 per day) and bikes ($7.50 per hr., $15 per day). (Open Mon.-Fri. 9am-7pm, Sat.-Sun. 9am-6pm.)

Venice's **street murals** are another free show. Don't miss the brilliant, graffiti-disfigured homage to Botticelli's *Birth of Venus* on the beach pavilion at the end of Windward Ave.: an angelically beautiful woman, wearing short shorts, a Band-aid top, and roller skates, boogies out of her seashell. The side wall of a Japanese restaurant on Windward is covered with a perfect imitation of a Hokusai print of a turbulent sea. Insect sculptures loom in the rafters of many of the city's posh restaurants.

To get to Venice from downtown L.A., take bus #33 or 333 (or #436 during rush hour). From downtown Santa Monica, take Santa Monica bus #1 or 2. Drivers can avoid hourly meter-feedings by parking in the $5 per day lot at Pacific and Venice.

Pacific Coast Highway

From Santa Monica, where it briefly merges with I-10, the **Pacific Coast Highway (PCH)** runs northward along the spectacular California coast. Several of L.A. County's best beaches line the PCH between Santa Monica and the Ventura County line.

The celebrity colony of **Malibu** stretches along the low 20000 blocks of PCH. With their multi-million-dollar homes and neighbors, Malibu residents can afford to be hostile to non-locals, especially those from the Valley. The beach lies along the 23200 block of the PCH. Walk onto the beach via the **Zonker Harris** access way at 22700 PCH, named after the quintessential Californian of Trudeau's *Doonesbury.*

Visitors with cars should not miss **Mulholland Drive,** nature's answer to the roller coaster. Twisting and turning for 15 spectacular miles along the crest of the Santa Monica Mountains, Mulholland stretches from PCH, near the Ventura County line, east to the Hollywood Fwy. and San Fernando Valley. Numerous points along the way, especially between Coldwater Canyon and the San Diego Fwy., have compelling views of the entire Los Angeles basin.

Beaches

The uncrowded, windsurfing, swimming, and scuba-diving **Corral State Beach** lies on the 26000 block of PCH, followed by **Point Dume State Beach,** which is small and also generally uncrowded. North of Point Dume, along the 30000 block of PCH, lies **Zuma,** L.A. County's northernmost, largest, and most popular county-owned sandbox, with lifeguards, restrooms, and a $5 parking fee. The beach is frequented by a mixed bag of sun-worshippers. If you don't want to bring food, pick something up at **Trancas Market** (PCH and Trancas Canyon, around Station 12). There are fewer footprints at **Westward Beach,** just southeast of Zuma. Cliffs shelter the beach from the highway and provide a vantage point for watching the boogie-boarders and surfers who frequent the beach.

San Fernando Valley

At the end of the Ventura Freeway lies the spiritual center of American suburbia—a seemingly infinite series of communities with tree-lined streets, cookie-cutter homes, lawns, and shopping malls. A third of L.A.'s population resides here, where the portion of the valley incorporated into the City of Los Angeles alone covers 140 million acres. The area was settled after city engineer William Mulholland brought water to this desert valley in 1913. Mulholland watched the first torrents pour out of the Aqueduct and proclaimed, "There it is! Take it!" The city rushed to obey, and Northern California's lakes and streams have been continually violated ever since.

Ventura Boulevard, the main commercial thoroughfare, today combines business and recreation with its office buildings, restaurants, and shops. The sprawling valley viewed from the foothills at night, particularly from Mulholland Drive, is spectacular. The valley's biggest pull is its infamous stereotypical images of valley girls and dudes. In reality, they've paved paradise and put in a putting green.

Consider driving another hour out of your way on the San Fernando Freeway to **Simi Valley.** 1980s preservationists can find comfort in the **Ronald Reagan Presidential Library,** 40 Presidential Dr. (805-522-8444). (Open Mon.-Sat. 10am-5pm, Sun. noon-5pm. Admission $4, seniors $2, children under 15 free.)

Pasadena

Pasadena, a city-sized suburb about 10 mi. northeast of downtown Los Angeles, offers some respite from the frenetic pace of Greater L.A. Pasadena is quiet and placid, with pleasant tree-lined streets and greenery along with outstanding cultural facilities. Even the trip there, along the Pasadena Fwy., is interesting; the freeway, one of the nation's oldest, was built as a WPA project between 1934 and 1941. However, WPA engineers failed to anticipate the needs of the modern motorist; now, drivers at a dead stop must merge almost instantaneously with 55mph traffic.

Rose Bowl

In the gorge that forms the city's western boundary stands Pasadena's most famous landmark, the **Rose Bowl,** 991 Rosemont Blvd. (818-577-3106). Home to the "granddaddy" of the college-football bowl games, the annual confrontation between the champions of the Big Ten and Pac 10 conferences, the Rose Bowl is also regular-season home to the UCLA Bruins football team. The **New Year's Day Rose Bowl** game follows the **Tournament of Roses Parade** which runs along Colorado Blvd. through downtown Pasadena (818-449-4100 for more information). Thousands line the Pasadena streets (having staked out choice viewing spots days in advance) to watch the flower-covered floats go by. During the off-season, the Rose Bowl hosts a flea market on the second Sunday of each month.

Huntington Sights

The **Huntington Library, Art Gallery,** and **Botanical Gardens,** 1151 Oxford Rd., San Marino 91108 (818-405-2100, ticket information 818-405-2273), are a treat. The stunning botanical gardens nurture 207 acres of rare plants. The library houses one of the world's most important collections of rare books and manuscripts, including a Gutenberg Bible, Benjamin Franklin's handwritten autobiography, and a 1410 manuscript of Chaucer's *Canterbury Tales.* The gallery is also known for its 18th- and 19th-century British paintings. (Open Tues.-Fri. 1-4:30pm, Sat.-Sun. 10:30am-4:30pm; donation expected.) The museum sits between Huntington Dr. and California Blvd. in San Marino, south of Pasadena. From downtown, bus #79 runs from Union Station straight to the library (45 min.).

Near Pasadena

If you don't find any celebrities on the street, you can find many in their graves at the renowned **Forest Lawn** cemetery, 1712 Glendale Ave., Glendale (818-241-4151). Analyzed as the showy emblem of the "American Way of Death," its grounds include reproductions of many Michelangelo works, the "largest religious painting on earth" (the famous 195-ft. version of the *Crucifixion),* a stained-glass *Last Supper,* and innumerable other works of "art." (Grounds open daily 8am-6pm, mausoleum until 4:30.) From downtown, take bus #90 or 91 and disembark just after the bus leaves San Fernando Rd. Forest Lawn is easily approached from this side of paradise via the Golden State or Glendale Fwy.

ENTERTAINMENT

Its reputation as a "vast wasteland" notwithstanding, L.A.'s cultural scene is active and diverse. Nightlife is everything you'd expect, and if you're staying in Hollywood or have a car, you can spend all your time in L.A. enjoying Vampire-like revelry.

Film and Television Studios

All of the major TV studios offer free tickets to show tapings. Some are available on a first come, first served basis from the **Visitors Information Center** of the Greater L.A. Visitor and Convention Bureau, or by mail. Some networks won't send tickets to out-of-state addresses but will send a guest card or letter that can be redeemed for tickets. Be sure to enclose a self-addressed, stamped envelope. Write: Tickets, Capital City/**ABC** Inc., 4151 Prospect, Hollywood 90027 (213-557-4396); **CBS** Tickets, 7800 Beverly Blvd., Los Angeles 90036 (310-840-3537); **NBC**-TV Tickets, 3000 W. Alameda Ave., Burbank 91523 (818-840-3537); **FOX** Tickets, Audiences Unlimited at 100 Universal City Plaza, Bldg. 153, Universal City 91608 (818-506-0067). Tickets are also available to shows produced by **Paramount Television,** 860 N. Gower St., Hollywood 90038 (213-956-5575). Tickets don't guarantee admittance; arrive a couple of hours early, as seating is also first come, first served. The minimum age for many tapings is 16.

Universal Studios, Universal City (818-508-9600). Hollywood Fwy. to Lankershim, or take bus #424 to Lankershim Blvd. For a hefty fee, the studio will take you for a ride; visit the Bates Hotel, watch Conan the Barbarian flex his pecs, be attacked by Jaws, get caught in a flash flood, and experience an 8.3 earthquake. Reservations not accepted; arrive early to secure a ticket—despite the price, the tour is quite popular. Tours in Spanish daily. Open summer and holidays daily 8am-8pm (last tram leaves at 5pm); Sept.-June 9am-6:30pm. $29, international students with ID $25, ages 3-11 and over 60 $23. Parking $5.

NBC Television Studios Tour, 3000 W. Alameda Ave. (818-840-3572), at Olive Ave. in Burbank, 2 mi. from Universal. Hollywood Fwy. N., exit east on Barham Blvd. which becomes Olive Ave. Take bus #96 or #97 on Olive going northbound. Open Mon.-Fri. 9am-3pm, Sat. 10am-4pm. $6, ages 12 and under $3.75.

Warner Bros. VIP Tour, 4000 Warner Blvd., Burbank (818-954-1744). Personalized, unstaged tours (max. 12 people) through the Warner Bros. studios. These are technical 2-hr. treks which chronicle the detailed reality of the movie-making craft. No children under 10. Tours Mon.-Fri. 9am and 4pm, additional tours in summer. Reservations required in advance. $25 per person.

Cinema

In the technicolor heaven of Los Angeles, you'd expect to find as many movie theaters as stars on the Walk of Fame. You won't be disappointed. Some theaters show films the way they were meant to be seen: in a big space, on a big screen. Devotees of second-run, foreign-language, and experimental films are rewarded by the Santa Monica theaters, away from the Promenade. Foreign films play consistently at the six **Laemmle Theaters** in Beverly Hills, West L.A., Santa Monica, Pasadena, Encino, and downtown. For film-screening information, dial 213-777-FILM (777-3456). Tickets at all theaters listed below are $7.50, seniors and children $4, discounts as noted.

Cineplex Odeon Universal City Cinemas, atop the hill at Universal Studios (818-508-0588). Take the Universal Center Dr. exit off the Hollywood Fwy. (U.S. 101). Opened in 1987 as the world's largest cinema complex. The 18 wide-screen theaters, 2 *parisienne*-style cafés, and opulent decoration put all others to shame. Hooray for Hollywood. ¼-price before 6pm. Ask for $5 parking refund.

Mann's Chinese, 6925 Hollywood Blvd. (213-464-8111). Hollywood hype to the hilt. For more details, see Hollywood Sights. Students with ID $5.

Beverly Cineplex (310-652-7760), atop the Beverly Center, on Beverly Dr. at La Cienega. Unlike most first-run cinemas, the Cineplex screens movies in auditoriums hardly bigger than your living room. But it shows 14 of them every night, an assortment of recent artsy discoveries. Matinee $4.

Silent Movie, 611 N. Fairfax Ave. (213-653-2389), in L.A. near 3rd St. 250 seats creak to the live musical accompaniment to these silent film screenings. Largest private collection of pre-talkie gems. Wed. and Fri.-Sat. 8pm. $6, children $3.

Concerts

The commonly used concert venues range from small to massive. **The Wiltern Theater** (213-380-5005) has presented such artists as Suzanne Vega and The Church. **The Hollywood Palladium** (213-962-7200) is of comparable size. Mid-size acts head for the **Universal Amphitheater** (818-777-3931) and the **Greek Theater** (213-665-1927). Huge indoor sports arenas, such as the **Sports Arena** (213-748-6131) or the **Forum** (310-419-3182), double as concert halls for large shows. Few dare to play at the 100,000-plus-seat **L.A. Coliseum.** Only U2, Bruce Springsteen, the Rolling Stones, and Guns 'n' Roses have filled the stands in recent years.

Clubs

The club scene is what makes L.A.'s nightlife. With the highest number of bands per capita in the world, most clubs are able to book top-notch acts night after night. The distinction between music clubs and dance clubs fades in L.A. Underground clubs are generally cheaper, more fun, and more elite (of course, you'll have to find these roving parties yourself by befriending knowledgeable clubbies). Coupons in *L.A.*

LOS ANGELES

Weekly can save you a bundle, and many are handed out in bushels inside the clubs. To enter the club scene it's best to be 21—the next-best option is to look it.

Gazzari's, 9039 Sunset Blvd., West Hollywood (310-273-6606). Hardcore and scrungy, this is the best-known metal club on the strip. The Doors, Van Halen, and Guns 'n' Roses all fledged from this stage. Cover $6-10. No age restrictions.

Kingston 12, 814 Broadway, Santa Monica (310-451-4423). L.A.'s only full-time reggae club presents both local and foreign acts. Dredlocks and fragrant smoke flow freely. Jamaican food. Open Thurs.-Sun. 8:30pm-2am. Cover varies. Must be 21.

Club Lingerie, 6507 Sunset Blvd., Hollywood (213-466-8557). The favored music club of all kinds of people. Rock, reggae, ska, and funk. They've got it. 2 full bars. Must be 21. Open 9pm-2am.

Roxbury, 8225 W. Sunset, Hollywood (213-656-1750). L.A. pretense at its fullest. One of the most hotsy-totsy places in the city. You probably won't get in, but it's fun trying. Jazz room downstairs, huge bar and dancing upstairs. VIP room admits only the wealthy, famous, or startlingly beautiful. Open Tues.-Sat. 7pm-2am.

Roxy, 9009 Sunset Blvd. (310-276-2222). One of the best known of L.A.'s Sunset Strip clubs, the Roxy is filled with record-company types and rockers waiting to be discovered. Many big acts at the height of their popularity play here. Cover varies. No age restrictions.

Whisky A Go-Go, 8901 Sunset Blvd. (310-652-4202). Another venerable spot on the Strip, part of L.A.'s music history. The Whisky played host to many progressive bands in the late 70s and early 80s, and was a major part of the punk explosion. Mostly metal nowadays. Full bar; cover varies. No age restrictions.

Anti-Club, 4658 Melrose Ave. (213-661-3913), in East Hollywood. Appropriately named. The difference between clubs and Anti-Club: the graffiti on the walls here wasn't coordinated by the management; more tattoos per capita than any other place in L.A. David Lynch would love it here—a family-style Western bar featuring hardcore bands and a vicious pit. Full bar. Cover varies. No age restrictions.

Shark Club, 1024 S. Grand Ave. (213-747-0999), downtown. Popular dance club for L.A. young and trendy. Huge dance floor, laser lighting, monstrous bar, and a 40,000-watt sound system. Yikes! Latin American music Thurs. night, House/techno/pop Fri.-Sat. Restaurant takes reservations. Open Thurs.-Sun. 9pm-2am.

The Palms, 8572 Santa Monica Blvd. (310-652-6188), West Hollywood's oldest women's bar. Always top-40 dancing. Full bar. Low cover, if any. 21 and over.

Rage, 8911 Santa Monica Blvd., West Hollywood (310-652-7055). Dance and R&B sounds for a mainly gay crowd. Full bar. Cover varies. Must be 21.

Bars

L.A. isn't known for its bar scene, but bars do exist and generally hold a slightly older and more subdued crowd than the clubs. Bars on Santa Monica Promenade are currently some of the most popular in L.A.

Molly Malone's, 575 S. Fairfax (213-935-1579). Not your typical Irish pub—showcases some of L.A.'s big up-and-coming bands. Cover varies. Open 10am-2am.

Al's Bar, 305 S. Hewitt St. (213-625-9703), in downtown. One of L.A. nightlife's best-hidden secrets. Wide range of nightly entertainment: traditional rock 'n' roll, poetry, experimental bands, performance art, and more. Open daily 6pm-2am.

Stratton's, 1037 Broxton Ave. (310-208-0488). Hot spot with UCLA students (they all look like Santa Monica yuppie barhoppers in training). Open daily 11am-2am.

Comedy

The talent may be imported from New York and other parts of the country, but that doesn't change the fact that L.A.'s comedy clubs are usually the best in the world. Quality makes prices steep, of course, but it's worth the setback. Call ahead to check age restrictions. Cover charges are cheaper during the week.

Comedy Store, 8433 Sunset Blvd. (213-656-6225), in West Hollywood. The shopping mall of comedy clubs, with 3 different rooms. The Main Room: the big-name stuff and the most expensive cover charges (around $14). The Original Room: mid-range comics for $7-10. The Belly Room: the real grab-bag material, often with no cover charge. Over 21 only. 2-drink min. Reservations taken Sat.-Sun.

The Improvisation, 8162 Melrose Ave. (213-651-2583), in West Hollywood. Offers L.A.'s best talent, including, on occasion, Robin Williams and Robert Klein. Restaurant serves Italian fare. Open nightly; check *L.A. Weekly* for times. Cover $8-10, 2-drink min. Reservations recommended.

Improvisation in Santa Monica, 321 Santa Monica Blvd. (310-394-8664). The beach version of its Hollywood cousin is more laid-back, and brand new. Nightly improv and dancing, occasional special guests. N.Y.-style Italian food in the restaurant. Cover $8-10, 2-drink min.

Sports

L.A. sports, even those on ice, benefit from the warm climate of the region; there are solid professional teams in every sport, as well as numerous collegiate programs through USC and UCLA. In 1932 and 1984, L.A. hosted the Summer Olympic Games at the **Coliseum,** which seats over 100,000. For tickets to events at the **Great Western Forum** (310-673-1300) in Inglewood, call the box office (310-419-3182; open daily 10am-6pm) or **Ticketmaster** (213-480-3232).

Football: The **Los Angeles Raiders** and the **USC Trojans** rumble and fumble at the Los Angeles Memorial Coliseum, 2601 S. Figueroa St.

Basketball: The worthy **L.A. Lakers** careen at the Forum. The Forum has become a symbol of the city. Even Jack Nicholson's got courtside seats.

Baseball: The **L.A. Dodgers** evade tags at Dodger Stadium (213-224-1400) in Elysian Park, 3 mi. northeast of downtown. Tickets nominally $6-11.

Hockey: The **Los Angeles Kings** largesse at the Forum (310-673-1300).

NORTHERN CALIFORNIA

■■■ NAPA VALLEY AND WINE COUNTRY

Transplanted Europeans recognized the Dionysian virtues of this area when California was still a part of Mexico. Prohibition, however, turned the vineyards into fig plantations; only in the last 20 years have local vintners resurrected Bacchus. Today, the wine-tasting carnival lasts from sunup to sundown, dominating the life of small towns in Napa, Sonoma, Dry Creek, Alexander, and Russian River Valleys. **Napa Valley** holds the best-known U.S. vineyards.

Sonoma offers slightly less-crowded wineries than Napa, as well as more exciting local history. The Sonoma Mission, General Vallejo's home, and Jack London's Beauty Ranch may interest the wine-sodden traveler. Farther north, the **Russian River** flows lazily between small towns and smaller wineries.

Practical Information Pick up a copy of *California Visitors Review* (free) for maps, complete winery listings, and a weekly events guide, at the **Napa Visitor Center,** 1310 Town Center (226-7459), on 1st St. (open daily 9am-5pm). **Greyhound** sprints through the valley, stopping in front of Napa State Hospital, 2100 Napa-Vallejo Hwy., Napa (2 per day). Also stops in Yountville, St. Helena, and Calistoga. The closest bus station is in Vallejo (643-7661). For local transport, hop the **Napa City Bus** ("VINE" or Valley Intercity Neighborhood Express—the things people will do just to get a cute acronym), 1151 Peal St. (255-7631), providing transport throughout the valley and to Vallejo. Buses run 5:30am-6:15pm. (Fare varies: Napa to Calistoga is $2, to Yountville $1, to Vallejo $1.50.) To get around the old-fashioned way, rent a bike at **Napa Valley Cyclery,** 4080 Byway East (255-3377), in Napa. (Bicycles $6 per hr., $20 per day, $70 per week. Major credit card required for deposit. Open Mon.-Sat. 9am-6pm, Sun. 10am-5pm.) The **post office** tastes stamps at 1625 Trancas St. (255-1621; open Mon.-Fri. 8:30am-5pm). Napa's **ZIP Code** is 94558; the **area code** is 707.

Route 29 runs through the middle of the valley from **Napa** at its southern end, to **Calistoga** in the north, passing **St. Helena** and **Yountville** in between. The best way to see the area is by bicycle since the valley is dead level and only 30 mi. long. The **Silverado Trail,** parallel to Rte. 29, is a more scenic and less crowded route than the highway. Napa is 25 min. from Sonoma on Rte. 12, which passes through the Valley of the Moon and Sonoma Valley. If you're planning a weekend trip from San Francisco, the 60-mi. trip may take up to 1½ hours on Saturday mornings or Sunday afternoons. If at all possible, try to visit the valley on weekdays and avoid the bus tours with plastic glasses and frantic wine pouring in overcrowded tasting rooms.

Accommodations, Camping, and Food B&Bs and most hotels are an ulcer-inducing $55-225 per night. If you do have a car, it's better to stay in Sonoma or Santa Rosa, where budget accommodations are more plentiful. Without a reservation or a car, plan on camping. Probably the best deal in the valley is at the **Triple S Ranch,** 4600 Mountain Home Ranch Rd. (942-6730), in Calistoga. Take Rte. 29 toward Calistoga, and turn left past downtown, onto Petrified Forest Rd. Light, woodsy cabins. Probably the best deal in the valley. (SSSingles $35, doubles $45. Call in advance to ensure a room. Open April-Oct.) Camp at **Bothe-Napa Valley State Park,** 3601 St. Helena Hwy. (942-4575, for reservations 800-444-7275), north of St. Helena on Rte. 29. Often full, so call ahead to avoid a long, unnecessary ride. (Park open 8am-sunset. Sites with hot showers $14. Call for reservations.)

Sit-down meals are expensive here, but Napa and its neighboring communities support numerous delis where you can buy inexpensive picnic supplies. The **Jefferson Food Mart,** 1704 Jefferson (224-7112), is open daily from 7am to 11pm. Behind the Citibank building cooks **Villa Corona Panaderia-Tortilleña,** 3614 Bel Aire Plaza, Napa (257-8685), a tiny restaurant in an alley, with *piñata*-ed ceiling. Serves selection of Mexican beers, drinks, and spices. Large burritos with rice and beans ($4.35). (Open daily 9am-8:30pm, winter daily 9am-7:30pm.) Put a picnic together at **Guigni's,** 1227 Main St., St. Helena (963-3421), an unpretentious, friendly grocery store with sandwiches ($3). (Open Mon.-Fri. 9am-5pm, Sat.-Sun. 9am-5:30pm.)

Wine Napa Valley is home to the wine country's heavyweights; vineyards include national names such as Inglenook, Christian Brothers, and Mondavi. The large vineyards are better for neophytes since tours are well-organized, and there's no pressure to say anything intelligent-sounding at the tastings. Almost all give free tours and tastings, though the majority require that visitors phone ahead to ensure that someone is around to pour the wine. To reach the smaller places, pick up a list of vineyards from the Napa Chamber of Commerce or look for signs along the roadside. Visitors unfamiliar with U.S. drinking laws should be forewarned: you must be 21 or older to purchase or drink alcohol. And, yes, vineyards do card. The annual **Napa Valley Wine Festival** (252-0872) takes place in November.

Robert Mondavi Winery, 7801 St. Helena Hwy., Oakville (963-9611), 8 mi. north of Napa. Spirited tour through marvelous catacombs and past towering stacks of oaken barrels filled with mellowing wine. The best free tour for the unknowledgeable. Tours every 15 min. fill fast in the summer; call ahead. Reservations required. Open daily 9am-5pm; Oct.-April daily 10am-4:30pm.

Domaine Chandon, California Dr., Yountville (944-2280), next to the Veteran's Home. One of the finest tours in the valley (available in French). Owned by Moët Chandon of France (the makers of *Dom Perignon*), this is the place to learn the secrets of making sparkling wine. Tastings by the glass ($3-5) or by the bottle in the winery's restaurant. Open daily 11am-6pm; Nov.-April Wed.-Sun. 11am-6pm.

Clos Du Val Wine Company, Ltd., 5330 Silverado Trail, Napa (252-6711). Take Oak Knoll Rd. to Silverado Trail. Tours by appointment at 10am and 2pm; tasting room open all day. $3 charge. Open daily 10am-5pm.

Newlan, 5225 Solano Ave. (257-2399). A small premium winery, with the best in *Pinot Noir* and dessert wines. Tastings daily 10am-4pm, by appointment. Open daily 11am-5pm.

Hakusan Sake Gardens, One Executive Way (258-6160), off Rte. 29 S. A pleasant self-guided tour through the Japanese gardens provides a delightful respite from the power-chugging at the vineyards. Generous pourings of *Hakusan Sake,* known as *Haki Sake* to locals. Open daily 9am-6pm, Nov.-March daily 9am-5pm.

■■■ REDWOOD NATIONAL PARK

Although Redwood National Park encompasses only 2% of the Coastal Redwood's natural (pre-lumberjack) range, it holds many of the state's most impressive trees. The coastal redwoods, which can live for over 2000 years (the oldest known specimen was not recognized until after it had been chopped down in the 1930s), grow in a 500-mi. belt from Monterey County into Oregon, up to 30 mi. inland. A visitor cannot help but be awed by the towering giants and the astounding biodiversity they help to support. Elk and black bears roam the Prairie Creek area as whales float by the coast, and birds are everywhere. The park begins just south of the Oregon border and extends down the coast for almost 40 mi., encompassing three state parks while avoiding the tiny coastal towns which cling to U.S. 101.

The park divides into five segments (Orick, Prairie Creek, Klamath, Crescent City, and Hiouchi) ranging north to south along U.S. 101. The towns of **Orick** in the south and **Klamath** in the middle provide very basic services and hold a few motels, while **Crescent City** in the north lays, of the three, the least unconvincing claim to "urban" status.

Practical Information The national park is free, but Prairie Creek State Park costs $5 per car per day—hikers and bikers are charged as well. The **Redwood National Park Headquarters and Information Center,** 1111 2nd St., Crescent City 95531 (464-6101), offers one- to three-day field seminars ($10-75, register in advance) from the spotted owl to scenic photography (open daily 8am-5pm). **Greyhound** sniffs the trees at 1125 Northcrest Dr. (464-2807), in Crescent City. Or, flag buses down at three places within the park: at the Shoreline Deli (488-5761), 1 mi. south of Orick on U.S. 101; at Paul's Cannery in Klamath on U.S. 101; and in front of the Redwood Hostel. Call the Greyhound station directly preceding your stop, and ask the attendant to make the driver aware of your presence. **Fishing licenses** are required for fresh and saltwater fishing (1-day licenses $5-8). Call the ranger station or the License and Revenue Office at (916) 739-3380 for more info.

For road conditions, call 800-427-7623; **Emergency** at 911. **Post offices** are in Crescent City, 751 2nd St. (464-2151; open Mon.-Fri. 8:30am-5pm) and in Orick, 121147 U.S. 101 (open Mon.-Fri. 8:30am-noon, 1-5pm). **ZIP Codes:** Crescent City, 95531; Orick, 95555. The **area code** is 707.

Accommodations The most pleasant roost, if you're not camping, is the **Redwood Youth Hostel (AYH),** 14480 U.S. 101, Klamath 95548 (482-8265), at Wilson Creek Rd. This hostel, in the historic Victorian DeMartin House, combines ultramodern facilities with a certain ruggedness. Thirty beds, kitchen, dining room, and laundry facilities ($1.25 per load, free for passing cyclists). All wheelchair-accessible. Affording a spectacular view of the ocean, the hostel simply asks that you take your shoes off when you're inside the building. (Reservations are recommended, and must be made by mail 3 weeks in advance. $9; under 18 with parent $4.50. Linen $1. Check-in 4:30-9:30pm. Curfew 11pm. Closed 9:30am-4:30pm.)

Campsites are numerous and range from well-equipped (flush toilets and free hot showers; sites $14, hikers/bikers $3) to primitive (outhouses at best; free). Peak sea-

NORTHERN CALIFORNIA: REDWOOD NAT'L PARK

son coincides with the California school system's summer vacation, which runs mid-June-early Sept. The ideal time to visit is from mid-April to mid-June or Sept.-mid-Oct. The park is less crowded during these months and is free of summer fog. Call MISTIX (800-444-7275) for campsite reservations, essential in the summer season. See below for information about campgrounds in specific areas.

Orick Area This region covers the southernmost section of the park. Its **visitors center** lies 1 mi. south of Orick on U.S. 101 and ½ mi. south of the Shoreline Deli (the Greyhound bus stop). The main attraction is the **tall trees grove**, a 2½-mi. trail which begins 6 mi. from the ranger station. This grove includes the tallest redwoods in the park and the tallest known tree in the world (367.8 ft.—1/3 the height of the World Trade Center). Backpackers may camp anywhere along the way after obtaining a permit at the ranger station, but should be certain to consult a ranger before attempting the trek in winter, as adverse weather conditions sometimes render the trail impassable.

In Orick, grab grub at the reasonably priced **Orick Market** (488-3225). The market delivers groceries to Prairie Creek Campground at 7:30pm daily. Phone in your order of at least $10 before 6pm (market open daily 8am-7pm). **Rolf's Prairie Creek Motel** (488-3841) offers somewhat worn rooms (singles $23, doubles $35). Rolf's lies just after the turn-off to Davison Road; this dirt path runs through redwoods and then drops down to the ocean along Gold Bluffs Beach, passing the favorite grazing spots of some of the park's 500 elk. Watch for antlers sticking out of the grass, as the elk often snooze at mid-day.

Prairie Creek and Klamath Areas The **Prairie Creek Area** is perfect for hikers, who can experience 75 mi. of trails in the park's 14,000 acres. Starting at the Visitor's Center, the **James Irvine Trail** winds through magnificent redwoods, around clear and cold creeks, through **Fern Canyon** (famed for its 50-ft. fern walls and crystalline creek), and by a stretch of the Pacific Ocean. After hiking, you can elk-watch, as elk love to graze on the meadow in front of the ranger station.

To the north, the **Klamath Area** comprises a thin stretch of park land connecting Prairie Creek with Del Norte State Park. The main attraction here is the rugged and beautiful coastline. The **Klamath Overlook**, where Requa Rd. meets the Coastal Trail, is an excellent whale-watching site, but at **Patrick's Point,** 25 mi. south, the whale views are spectacular (southern migration Oct.-Dec.; northward March-May).

The **Klamath River** is a popular fishing spot (permit required; see Practical Information) during the fall and spring when salmon spawn and during the winter when steelhead trout do the same. **Nickel Creek Camp,** on U.S. 101 at the end of Enderts Beach Rd., has a walk-in, non-amenitized camp (5 sites) above the beach in a brushy creek canyon. From here, it is a short walk to the Enderts Beach Tidepool.

Crescent City and Hiouchi Areas Crescent City, the largest Californian polis north of Eureka, calls itself the city "where the Redwoods meet the Sea." In 1964, it met the sea for real, when a *tsunami* caused by oceanic quakes brought 500 mph winds and leveled the city. Today the rebuilt city offers an outstanding location from which to explore the National Park. The **Visitors Center,** 1001 Front St. (464-3174), has lots o' brochures (open Mon.-Fri. 9am-5pm; in summer, also open Sat.-Sun. 10am-6pm). Seven mi. south of the city lies **Del Norte Coast Redwoods State Park** (464-9533), a state-level extension of the Redwood Forest. The park's magnificent ocean views—along with picnic areas, hiking trails, and nearby fishing—lure enough campers to fill the sites at its **Mill Creek Campground** in summer. (Sites $14, hikers/bikers $3, day use $5.)

Food and lodgings in the city are depressingly overpriced. For the best deals, head to 9th St., the pre-*tsunami* location of U.S. 101. The surviving motels are cleaner and less expensive than those more centrally located. For a sit-down meal, **Los**

Compadres (464-7871) on U.S. 101 South, cooks up spicy Mexican food in *grande* portions (super burritos $4.55). (Open daily 11am-9pm, in winter 11am-8pm.)

The **Battery Point Lighthouse** (464-3089) houses a museum open only during low tide. Don't get caught once the sea starts coming in, and don't mistake the islands of kelp bobbing offshore for seals coming up for air. (Open May-Oct. Wed.-Sun. 10am-4pm, tide permitting. Admission $2, children 50¢.) From June-Aug., the National Park offers two-hour **tidepool walks** (464-6101) at the end of Endert's Beach Rd. (turn off 4 mi. south of Crescent City).

The **Hiouchi** region sits in the northern part of the park along Rte. 199 and contains several excellent hiking trails. The **Stout Grove Trail** is an easy ½-mi. walk, passing the park's widest redwood, 18 ft. in diameter. The path is also accessible to people with disabilities; call 458-3310 for arrangements.

■■■ ORANGE COUNTY

Orange County, Los Angeles' neighbor to the south, was part of Los Angeles County until 1861, when "O.C." seceded over a tax dispute. The two have become sibling rivals. Many O.C. residents live in "planned communities," neighborhoods designed by strict codes governing exactly where schools, shopping centers, and gas stations must be placed. Drive through inland Orange County and you'll be plagued by the eerie feeling that you are under a giant developer's model-community bubble. If regimented living isn't to your taste, head for the coast, where Orange County's fine surf and string of clean, uncrowded beaches have produced the truest approximation of stereotypical Southern California beach life.

PRACTICAL INFORMATION

Emergency: 911.

Visitors Information: 800 W. Katella Ave., Anaheim 92802 (999-8999), in the Anaheim Convention Center. Free brochures. Open Mon.-Fri. 8:30am-5pm.

Airport: John Wayne Orange County, Campus Dr. (recorded information 755-6500, terminal info. 252-5006). Flights to and from many major U.S. cities.

Amtrak: (800-872-7245 for reservations) 5 stops: 120 E. Santa Fe Ave., Fullerton (992-0530), at Harbor Blvd.; 1000 E. Santa Ana, Santa Ana (547-8389); Santa Fe Depot, San Juan Capistrano (661-8835); 2150 E. Katella, Anaheim (385-1448), by the stadium; unattended stop in San Clemente, off I-5 by the municipal pier.

Greyhound: 2080 S. Harbor, Anaheim (635-5060), 3 blocks south of Disneyland (open Mon.-Thurs. 7am-7:30pm, Fri.-Sun. 7am-9:30pm); 1000 E. Santa Ana Blvd., Santa Ana (542-2215; open daily 7am-8pm); and 510 Avenida de la Estrella, San Clemente (492-1187; open Mon.-Thurs. 7:45am-6:30pm, Fri. 7:45am-8pm).

Orange County Transit District (OCTD): 11222 Acacia Parkway, Garden Grove (636-7433). Thorough service, useful for getting from Santa Ana and Fullerton Amtrak stations to Disneyland, or for beach-hopping along the coast. Long Beach, in L.A. County, serves as the terminus for several OCTD lines. Bus #1 travels the coast from Long Beach down to San Clemente, with service 2 times per hr. early morning-8pm. Fare $1, transfers 5¢. Most buses accept dollar bills. Information center open Mon.-Fri. 6am-7pm, Sat.-Sun. 8am-5pm.

Local RTD Information: 800-2-LA-RIDE (252-7433). Lines open daily 5:30am-midnight. RTD buses run from L.A. to Disneyland and Knott's Berry Farm.

Rape Crisis Hotline: 831-9110. 24-hr. service of the O.C. Sexual Assault Network.

Post Office: 701 N. Loara, Anaheim (520-2609), 1 block north of Anaheim Plaza. Open Mon.-Fri. 8:30am-5pm, Sat. 8:30am-2pm. **ZIP Code:** 92803.

Area Code: 714; in Seal Beach 310.

ACCOMMODATIONS, CAMPING, AND FOOD

Disneyland singlehandedly grants **Anaheim** a thriving tourist trade. Because it's fairly remote from L.A.'s other sights, there is no reason to stay here unless you plan to linger in the Magic Kingdom. Start with the Anaheim Visitors Center, a travel industry dating service, which matches people with rooms they can afford. The road to Disneyland along Harbor Blvd. is lined with economy motels. The county's coastline is the other big attraction, and bargain rates can be found at motels scattered along Pacific Coast Hwy. and Newport Beach's Newport Blvd. There are state beaches in Orange County with campgrounds, listed below from north to south. All will probably fall well short of your beach camping fantasies. Reservations are required for all sites except the Echo Arch Area in San Onofre, made through MISTIX (800-365-2267) a maximum of eight weeks in advance. There is a $6.75 *non-refundable* fee for every reservation made.

Fullerton Hacienda Hostel (HI/AYH), 1700 N. Harbor Blvd., Fullerton (738-3721), 15-min. drive north of Disneyland. OCTD bus #43 runs up and down Harbor Blvd. to Disneyland, and the hostel managers can arrange car rentals for groups. This big, comfortable, Spanish-style house complete with porch swing is set back from the road on a quiet hill and maintains an intriguing international clientele. Modern kitchen, clean communal bathrooms, and spiffy single- and mixed-sex accommodations. 3-day max. stay. No curfew. Registration daily 7:30-10:30am and 5-11pm. $12. Reservations accepted.

Huntington Beach Colonial Inn Youth Hostel, 421 8th St., Huntington Beach (536-3315), 4 blocks inland at Pecan. Staff fosters a sense of family at this large Victorian house shaded by palm trees. Common showers, bathroom, kitchen. Reading/TV room. Lockout 9:30am-4:30pm. Check-in 7am-11pm. Curfew 11pm. Late night key rental $1 ($20 deposit). Multi-person dorms $12 per person, doubles $14, must have picture ID. Call 2 days in advance for summer weekends.

Motel 6, no fewer than **6 Anaheim locations,** including those at 921 S. Beach Blvd. (220-2866), and 7450 Katella Ave. (891-0717), both within a 10-min. drive of Disneyland. Both have pools and are filled with couples and their rambunctious, Mickey Mouse-eared children. The S. Beach Blvd. location, the best deal for groups, is not too worse for wear ($32 for 1-4 persons). The Katella Ave. motel is in better shape and a steal for singles ($27, doubles $33).

Doheny (496-6172), Rte. 1 at the south end of Dana Point. Beachside location turns this place into a zoo. TVs, lounge furniture, play pens, aquariums, and more. Does, however, offer the only sites in the area with real beach sand (and yes, they go very fast!). Beachfront sites $21, otherwise $16.

San Clemente (492-3156), I-5, get off on Avenida del Presidente and follow the state beach signs (there are no signs for the campground itself). Heavy on sites (a total of 157, 85 with hookups) and RVs, a little short on trees. Great vistas of ocean, and, unfortunately, of the adjacent neighborhoods as well. Sites $16.

San Onofre (492-0802), I-5, 3 mi. south of San Clemente. 221 campsites along an abandoned stretch of Pacific Coast Hwy.; about 90 are suitable for tents. The waves of hwy. traffic drown out those of the more distant surf. The **Echo Arch Area** has 34 primitive hike-in sites beneath the bluffs and the beach. Sites $16.

There is little dining to be done in the Anaheim area; eating, however, is possible thanks to a dizzying array of representatives from America's finest restaurant chains. Hungry campers in the San Clemente area should consider the **Sea Breeze Cafe,** 1640 N. El Camino Real, San Clemente (498-4771), where each morning the friendly and accommodating waitresses rattle off a list of 10 specials, all under $5 (open Mon.-Sat. 6am-2pm, Sun. 7am-2pm).

SIGHTS AND BEACHES

Among the architectural attractions in Orange County not blessed by Disney is the **Crystal Cathedral,** 12141 Lewis St., Garden Grove (971-4000). Opinions are split on this shining all-glass structure completed in 1980 by Phillip Johnson and John Burgee; some find it inspiring, most call it garish. From the pulpit of this church, Dr. Robert Schuller preaches his weekly TV show, *Hour of Power.* With 7000 people moving in and out every Sunday, the Cathedral is also a model of efficiency. (Free tours Mon.-Sat. 9am-3:30pm, Sun. noon-3:30pm.) Inland Orange County is graced with a number of attractions, the newest of which is a tribute to the foreign policy-guru president—the tan, rested, and ready Richard Nixon ⑧. At **The Richard Nixon Library and Birthplace,** 18001 Yorba Linda Blvd., Yorba Linda (993-3393), you can relax in Pat Nixon's rose garden and engage in a video conversation with the man himself ($5, seniors $3, open Mon.-Sat. 10am-5pm, Sun. 11am-5pm).

Despite inland fun, recreation for residents and visitors revolves primarily around the ocean. Visitors should not be lulled off guard by swishing coastal waters. Pedestrians should take extreme care in the cities, and vacationers should not be tempted to crash on the wide beaches. Transients make unsafe what is already illegal.

Huntington Beach (area code 714 for all subsequent beaches) served as a port of entry for the surfing craze, which transformed California coast life after being imported from Hawaii by Duke Kahanamoku in the early 1900s. Still popular, the sport culminates each year in the **OP Pro Surfing Championships** (580-1888) held in late July. The newly remodeled pier provides a perfect vantage point for oglers.

Newport Beach and the surrounding cities inland are the jewels of Orange County, with stunning multi-million-dollar homes lining Newport Harbor, the largest leisure craft harbor in the world. The beach itself displays few signs of ostentatious wealth; it is crowded with young, frequently rowdy hedonists in neon-colored bikinis and trunks. The area around Newport Pier is a haven for families; the streets from 30th to 56th give way to teenagers and college students sunning, surfing, and playing volleyball. The boardwalk is always a scene in the summer, with beach house renters partying wildly on their porches.

The sands of Newport Beach run south onto the **Balboa Peninsula,** separated from the mainland by Newport Bay. The peninsula is only two to four blocks wide and can be reached from PCH by Balboa Blvd. The Victorian **Balboa Pavilion,** once a sounding board for Big Band great Benny Goodman, is now a hub for harbor tours and winter whale-watching. At the end of the peninsula, **The Wedge,** seasonally pounded by waves up to 20 ft. tall, is a bodysurfing mecca. Bodysurfers (ostensibly furloughed from mental institutions) risk a watery grave for this monster ride. Melt into the crowds on Newport Beach and the Balboa Peninsula by hopping on a bicycle or strapping on a pair of rollerblades. Expensive **rental shops** cluster around the Newport Beach pier and at the end of the peninsula, letting bikes ($4-5 per hr., $18-20 per day), skates ($3-6 per hr., $15-18 per day), and boogie boards ($6-7 per day).

North of Newport Beach is **Costa Mesa,** home of the new and dazzling **Orange County Performing Arts Center,** 600 Town Center Dr. (556-2121), on Bristol St. off I-405. The opulent, 3000-seat structure was constructed in 1986 at a cost of $70 million and has enlivened Orange County arts by hosting the American Ballet Theatre and the Kirov Ballet, among other troupes.

More tourists than swallows return every year to **Mission San Juan Capistrano** (493-1424), ½-hour south of Anaheim on I-5; take Ortega Hwy. to Camino Capistrano. This "jewel of the missions" offers a peek at California's origins as a Spanish colony. Established in 1776 as one of 21 California missions of the Catholic church, it is somewhat run-down today due to an 1812 earthquake. Father Junípero Serra, the mission's founder, officiated from inside the beautiful **Serra Chapel,** the oldest building in the state. The chapel is dark and womby, warmed by a 17th-century Spanish cherrywood altar and Native American designs painted on walls and ceiling. It's still used by the Catholic Church, so enter quietly and inhale the scent of candles lit by worshipers. (Open daily 8:30am-7pm; Oct. 1-May 14 8:30am-5pm. Admission $3, ages 3-11 $1.) The mission is perhaps best known as a home to the thousands of swallows who return here from their annual winter migration to nest in mid-March. They are scheduled to return to Capistrano on St. Joseph's Day, March 19, but the birds aren't all that religious, and have a tendency to show up whenever you're not around. The swallows leave in mid-October. The best time to see the birds is when they feed in the early morning or early evening.

The marine base of **Camp Pendleton** stands at attention next door, lending this part of the coast a less than happy-go-lucky feel. Nevertheless, **San Onofre State**

ORANGE COUNTY

Beach is a prime surfing zone (particularly the world famous "Trestles" area). The southern end of the beach is frequented by nudists (drive down as far as you can go, and walk left on the trail for ½ mi.; beach contains both a gay and a straight area). Nude bathing is illegal, and you'll be fined if you're caught with your pants down.

DISNEYLAND

Stunningly animated Oscar nominee *Aladdin* and EuroDisney are among the recent additions to Mike Eisner's ever-evolving and seemingly unbounded Disney empire. Walt's original theme park among the orange groves of Anaheim has hardly been left to stagnate while the shadow of The Mouse's ears grows ever-larger. New attractions are added almost yearly. "The Happiest Place on Earth" has delighted hundreds of millions over the last 39 years. Soviet premier Nikita Kruschev was livid when Walt himself barred him from the park at the height of the Cold War.

All this otherworldliness can get disturbing at times, especially with crowds of 75,000 per day jamming into the park. Admission to the gleaming fantasy world is gained through the **Unlimited Use Passport** (1 day $28.75, ages 3-11 $23). (Park open daily 8am-1am; fall-spring, Mon.-Fri. 10am-6pm, Sat.-Sun. 9am-midnight. Extended hours around major holidays; call 719-999-4565 for more information.)

Getting There The park is located at 1313 Harbor Blvd., in Anaheim, bounded by Katella Ave., Harbor Blvd., Ball Rd., and West St. From L.A. take bus #460 from 6th and Flower St. downtown, about 1½ hours to the Disneyland Hotel. (Service to the hotel begins at 4:53am, service back to L.A. until 1:20am.) From the hotel take the free shuttle to Disneyland's portals (or go in style via the Disneyland monorail). Also served by Airport Service, OCTD, Long Beach Transit, and Gray Line (see Practical Information). If you're driving, take the Santa Ana Fwy. (I-5) to the Katella Ave. exit. Be forewarned, however: while parking in the morning should be painless, leaving in the evening often will not be. In addition, when the park closes early, Disneygoers must contend with the tail-end of L.A.'s maddening, rush-hour traffic.

In the Park Visitors enter the Magic Kingdom by way of **Main Street, U.S.A.,** a collection of shops, arcades, and even a movie theater designed to recreate Walt's maudlin turn-of-the-century childhood memories. Main Street, a broad avenue leading to a replica of Sleeping Beauty's castle at the center of the park, includes a bank, an info booth, lockers, and a first aid station. The **Main Street Electrical Parade** makes its way each summer night at 8:50 and 10:25pm (with the earlier parade followed by fireworks). Floats and even people are adorned with thousands of multicolored lights. This is one of Disneyland's most popular events and people begin lining the sidewalks on Main Street by 7pm. The new **Fantasmic!** laser show projects fiery villains and whirling heroes into the night sky.

Four "lands" branch off Main Street. **Tomorrowland,** to your immediate right at the top of Main Street, contains the park's best thrill rides, **Space Mountain** and the George Lucas-produced **Star Tours.** Moving counter-clockwise around the park, next is **Fantasyland,** with the **Matterhorn** rollercoaster, some excellent kids' rides, and the ever-popular **It's A Small World** (a hint: unless you want the cute, but annoying, theme song running through your head for the rest of the day, you may want to save this one for the after-life). Next is **Frontierland,** with the **Thunder Mountain Railroad** coaster and **Tom Sawyer Island.** Last, but not least, is **Adventureland,** with the **Jungle Cruise** and the **Swiss Family Robinson Treehouse.** In addition, tucked between Frontierland and Adventureland are two more areas that aren't official "lands." One is **New Orleans Square,** with **Pirates of the Caribbean,** the **Haunted Mansion,** and some excellent dining. The other is **Critter Country,** with Disneyland's latest super-attraction, **Splash Mountain,** a log ride that climaxes in a wet, five-story drop.

Food services in the park range from sit-down establishments to fast-food eateries such as the **Lunch Pad**. Save much time and money by packing a picnic lunch and eating a big breakfast before you leave home. Food in the park is mediocre and generally overpriced. If you're looking for a martini, you'll be left high and dry: alcohol doesn't exist in the Magic Kingdom. Fall months and weekdays are generally less crowded than summer days and weekends. Arrive shortly before the park opens to beat ticket queues. Lines for the most popular attractions are shorter just after opening and late at night; try midday and you'll see why some call it "Disneyline."

KNOTT JUST DISNEYLAND

Knott's Berry Farm, 8039 Beach Blvd. (714-220-5200 for a recording), resides at La Palma Ave. in Buena Park just 5 mi. northeast of Disneyland. (Take the Santa Ana Fwy. south, exit west on La Palma Ave. Bus #460 stops here on its way to Disneyland.) A berry farm in its early days, Knott's now cultivates a country fair atmosphere with a re-created ghost town, Fiesta Village, Roaring Twenties Park, rides, and a replica of Independence Hall. Thrill-seekers may find Knott's roller-coasters substantially more suited to their needs than those in the Magic Kingdom. (Open Sun.-Thurs. 9am-11pm, Fri.-Sat. 9am-midnight; winter Mon.-Fri. 10am-6pm, Sat. 10am-10pm, Sun. 10am-7pm. $23, seniors 60 and over $15, ages 3-11 $10.)

■ ■ ■ SAN DIEGO

First inhabited by the Yuman people, San Diego was not permanently settled by the Spanish until 1769, more than two centuries after its initial discovery by the Portuguese explorer, Cabrillo. Throughout the Spanish and Mexican periods, it remained a small town, and even after the boom of the 1880s, the city remained a little-known outpost bypassed by the railroads and ignored by immigrants from the East. After two international expositions (in 1915 and 1935), the landing of the Navy, and economic booms in the 1940s and 50s, San Diego matured into the metropolis that now sprawls for miles over the once-dry, rolling hills of chaparral.

San Diego has ample tourist attractions—a world-famous zoo, Sea World, and Old Town—but the most enjoyable destination might simply be a patch of sand at one of its superb beaches. The city proper of San Diego does not merit all your attention; explore the nearby mountains and deserts and the surrounding residential communities such as Hillcrest, La Jolla, and Ocean Beach, or head for Mexico, next door.

PRACTICAL INFORMATION

Emergency: 911.

International Visitors Information Center: 11 Horton Plaza (236-1212), downtown at 1st Ave. and F St. Like an old-fashioned hardware store, they don't display much, but they have whatever you need under the counter. Multilingual staff. Open Mon.-Sat. 8:30am-5pm, Sun. 11am-5pm.

Airport: San Diego International Airport lies at the northwestern edge of downtown, across from Harbor Island. San Diego Transit bus #2 goes downtown where visitors can transfer to other routes. Buses ($1.50) run Mon.-Fri. 4:30am-1:10am, Sat.-Sun. 5am-1am. Cab fare to downtown is around $7.

Amtrak: Santa Fe Depot, 1050 Kettner Blvd. (239-9021 or 800-872-7245), at Broadway. To L.A. (Mon.-Fri. 8 per day, $24). Information on bus, trolley, car, and boat transportation available at the station. Office open 4:45am-9:15pm.

Greyhound: 120 W. Broadway (239-9171), at 1st Ave. To: L.A. (every 45 min., 2:30am-11:45pm, $12). Terminal open for ticket sales 2am-midnight.

Public Transport: regional transit systems cover the area from Oceanside in the north to Tijuana in Mexico, and inland to Escondido, Julian, and other towns. Call for **public transit information** (233-3004; daily 5:30am-8:25pm) or stop by the **Transit Store** (234-1060), 5th and Broadway. Pick up the *Transit Rider's Guide,* which includes listings of which routes lead to popular destinations around town. Exact change required. Discounts for seniors and disabled persons. **Day Tripper passes** allow unlimited travel on buses, trolleys, and even the Bay Ferry ($4 for 1 day, $12 for 4 days).

Aztec Rent-A-Car, 2401 Pacific Hwy. (232-6117 or 800-231-0400). $22-50 per day with unlimited mi. (in California only). Must be 21 with major credit card. With purchase of Mexican insurance ($16.23 per day), cars may venture as far as Ensenada, Mexico (80 mi.). Open Mon.-Fri. 6am-8pm, Sat.-Sun. 8am-5pm.

Rent-A-Bike (232-4700), at 1st and Harbor Dr. Bikes $8 per hr., $28 per day, $75 per week. Free helmets and locks. Open Mon.-Fri. 8am-6pm, Sat.-Sun. 7am-6pm.

Rape Crisis Hotline: 233-3088. Open 24 hrs.

Post Office: Main Branch, 2535 Midway Dr. (627-0915), between downtown and Mission Beach. Open Mon.-Fri. 7am-1am, Sat. 8am-4pm. **ZIP Code:** 92138.

Area Code: 619.

San Diego rests in the extreme southwestern corner of California, 127 mi. south of L.A. and only 15 mi. north of the Mexican border. **I-5** runs south from Los Angeles and skirts the eastern edge of downtown. **I-15** runs northeast to Nevada. **I-8** runs east-west along downtown's northern boundary, connecting the desert to the east with Ocean Beach in the west. The major downtown thoroughfare, **Broadway,** also runs east-west. A group of skyscrapers in the blocks between Broadway and I-5 defines **downtown** San Diego. On the northeastern corner of downtown, **Balboa Park,** larger than the city center, is bounded by 6th Ave., I-5 and Russ Blvd., 28th St., and Upas St. To the north and east of Balboa Park are the main residential areas. **Hill-crest,** San Diego's most cosmopolitan district and a center for the gay community, lies at the park's northwestern corner. West of downtown is the bay, 17 mi. long and formed by the Coronado Peninsula (jutting northward from Imperial Beach) and Point Loma (dangling down from Ocean Beach). North of Ocean Beach are Mission Beach (with neighboring Mission Bay), Pacific Beach, and La Jolla.

ACCOMMODATIONS AND CAMPING

Lodging rates skyrocket in summer, particularly on weekends. If you have a car, consider camping. All **state campgrounds** are open to bikers for $3 per night. State law requires that no cyclist be turned away no matter how crowded the site. Camping reservations are handled by MISTIX (800-365-2267). Most parks are completely full in summer; weekend reservations are often made 8 weeks in advance.

Jim's San Diego, 1425 C St. (235-0234), south of the park, 2 blocks from "City College" trolley. Spruce, clean, hostel-type rooms for four with wooden bunks and free linen. Kitchen, sun deck, common room, laundry. $11 per night, $77-80 per week. Breakfast and Sunday BBQ included. A true "Backpacker's" haven.

Hostel on Broadway (HI/AYH), 500 W. Broadway (232-1133), in the core of downtown, close to train and bus stations, as well as Horton Plaza and the Gaslamp District. Singles, doubles, dorms, communal bathrooms, common room with TV. Not quite as clean as Jim's. Laundry and game room downstairs. Security guards and cameras. Parking underneath ($3). Front desk open until 11pm. No curfew. Checkout 10am. Members $11, non-members $14. $1 linen.

Imperial Beach Hostel (HI/AYH), 170 Palm Ave. (423-8039). In a converted fire-house 2 blocks from the beach, 5 mi. from Mexico and 10 mi. from downtown San Diego. Quiet, remote dormitory with bunkbeds for 36. Kitchen, common room with TV. Reserve by sending a check to cover the first night's lodging, or call ahead. Registration 4:30-11pm. Lockout 10am-4:30pm. Curfew 11pm. Late keys available ($2). Checkout 8-10am. Members $10, nonmembers $13.

Elliot-Point Loma Hostel (HI/AYH), 3790 Udall St., Point Loma (223-4778). The airy 2-story building is 1½ mi. from Ocean Beach. Wooden bunks for 60, common room, large kitchen, and patio. Check-out 10am. Office open 8-10am and 5:30-10pm. Lockout 11am-5:30pm. Curfew 2am. 3-night max. stay; reserve 48 hrs. in advance. Members $12, nonmembers $15.

San Elijo Beach State Park (753-5091), Rte. 21 south of Cardiff-by-the-Sea. 271 sites (150 for tents) in a setting similar to that at South Carlsbad to the north. Strategic landscaping gives a very secluded feel. Hiker/biker campsites for those traveling on their own steam. Make reservations for summer. Sites $21, in winter $16.

FOOD

San Diego has over 70 Jack in the Boxes and hundreds of other fast-food joints, an achievement befitting the birthplace of the genre. The good news is that the lunch-time business crowd has nurtured multitudinous restaurants specializing in well-made, inexpensive meals. Purchase high-quality fruits and vegetables at the **Farm-er's Market,** 1 Horton Plaza (696-7766), downtown, to complete the feast (open daily 8am-9pm).

Anthony's Fishette, 555 Harbor Ln. (232-2933), at the foot of Market St. on the bay. A downscale version of **Anthony's** posh seafood restaurants. A great catch, offering a grand bay view and bargain prices. Not a tourist trap; this is where the locals chow on $5-8 dinners. Open Sun.-Thurs. 11am-8pm, Fri.-Sat. 11am-8:30pm.

Dick's Last Resort, 345 4th Ave. (231-9100), in the Gaslamp Quarter. Visitors and natives alike turn out in droves for buckets o' Southern chow and a wildly irrever-ent atmosphere. Dick's stocks beers from around the globe, from Africa to Trin-idad, on top of native brews like Dixieland Blackened Voodoo Lager and Pete's Wicked Ale. No cover for the nightly rock, blues, or Dixie bands, but "you'd bet-ter be buyin'!" Burgers under $4, other dinners $10-15. Open daily 11am-1:30am.

El Indio, 3695 India St. (299-0333), in India St. Colony. When El Indio opened its doors in 1940, the owners probably never dreamed folks would line up along the block for a taste of their cooking. But a half-century later they're still lining up. Service is speedy and quality remains high. Sizeable portions; combination plates around $4, a la carte tacos and burritos from $2.25. Open daily 6am-9pm.

Casa de Bandini, 2660 Calhoun St. (297-8211), in the most beautiful spot in Old Town. Eat in the lush and festive courtyard, the first floor of which is an original 1829 adobe mansion, complete with rose trellises, *mariachis,* and fountains. Enormous chicken and avocado salad, around $7. Monstrous margaritas. Open Mon.-Sat. 11am-9:30pm, Sun. 10am-9:30pm.

SIGHTS

San Diego's buildings form a tangible record of the city's history. Examples include the early 19th-century adobes of **Old Town.** Just up Juan St. from Old Town, **Heri-tage Park** displays old Victorian homes, carefully trimmed and painted like ginger-bread houses. Extending south from Broadway to the railroad tracks and bounded by 4th and 6th Ave., the **Gaslamp Quarter** is home to a notable concentration of pre-1910 commercial buildings now being resurrected as upscale shops and restau-rants. For more relaxing pleasures, head toward the beaches, San Diego's biggest draw. Surfers catch tubular waves, sun-worshippers catch rays, and everybody gets caught up in sun-stimulated serenity. Or heatstroke.

Downtown

The **Embarcadero** (a fancy Spanish name for a dock) sits at the foot of Broadway on the west side of downtown. From Harbor Drive, the **Coronado Bridge** stretches westward from Barrio Logan to the Coronado Peninsula. High enough to allow the Navy's biggest ships to pass underneath, the sleek, sky-blue arc executes a graceful, swooping turn over the waters of San Diego Bay before touching down in Coro-nado. (Bridge toll $1. Bus #901 and other routes also cross.) When the bridge was built in 1969, its eastern end cut a swath through San Diego's largest Chicano com-munity, which created **Chicano Park** in response, painting splendid murals on the piers. The murals are heroic in scale and theme, drawing on Spanish, Mayan, and Aztec imagery. Take bus #11 or the San Ysidro trolley to Barrio Logan station.

Balboa Park

Balboa Park was begun in 1889, when San Diego was a small town. The population is now over a million, but the 1000-plus acre park remains relatively unmaimed by city expansion, drawing huge crowds with its concerts, theater, Spanish architec-ture, entertainers, lush vegetation, and a zoo. Bus #7 runs through the park and near the museum and zoo entrances. Drivers should take Laurel St. east from downtown to one of the park's many parking lots.

With over 100 acres of exquisitely designed habitats, the **San Diego Zoo** (234-3153) is one of the finest in the world, with flora as exciting as the fauna. They have recently moved to a system of "bioclimatic" areas, in which animals and plants are grouped together by habitat, rather than by taxonomy. Joining the stunning **Tiger River** and **Sun Bear Forest** is the new **Gorilla Tropics** enclosure, housing lowland gorillas and plant species imported from Africa. In addition to the usual elephants and zebras, the zoo houses such unusual creatures as Malay tapirs and everybody's favorite, the koala. **Pygymy Chimps,** known for their comic acrobatics, are the current celebrities of the park. The **Wings of Australasia Aviaries,** completed in 1993, is another popular attraction. Arrive as early as possible, sit on the left, and take the 40-minute open-air **double-decker bus tour,** which covers 70% of the park and avoids long lines ($3, ages 3-15 $2.50). The **children's zoo** squawks up a barnyard storm (free with admission). The **"skyfari" aerial tram** will make you feel like you're suspended over a box of animal crackers. (Main zoo entrance open daily 9am-5pm, must exit by 7pm; Labor Day-Memorial Day daily 9am-4pm, exit by 6pm. $12, ages 3-15 $4. Group rates available. Free on Founder's Day, Oct. 1.)

Balboa Park has the greatest concentration of museums in the U.S. outside of Washington DC. The park focuses at **Plaza de Panama,** on El Prado St., where the Panama-Pacific International Exposition took place in 1915 and 1916.

Before exploring El Prado on your own, stop in the House of Hospitality's **information center** (239-0512) which sells simple maps (65¢), more elaborate guides ($1.50), and the **Passport to Balboa Park** ($13), which contains nine coupons to gain entrance to the park's museums. (Passports also available at participating museums. Open daily 9:30am-4pm.) The western axis of the plaza stars Goodhue's California State Building, now the **Museum of Man** (239-2001). The museum recaps millions of years of human evolution with permanent exhibits on primates and the Mayan, Hopi, and other Native American societies. Behind the museum, the **Old Globe Theater** (239-2255), the oldest pro theater in California, plays Shakespeare and others nightly (Tues.-Sun., weekend matinees). Ranging from ancient Asian to contemporary Cal, the **San Diego Museum of Art** (232-7931), across the plaza, gathers an eclectic range of art. Other museums include the **Sculpture Court, The Museum of Photographic Arts,** and the **San Diego Model Railroad Museum.**

South of El Prado is the **Reuben H. Fleet Space Theater and Science Center** (238-1233), where two Omnimax projectors, 153 speakers, and a hemispheric planetarium whisk viewers inside the human body, up to the stars with the space shuttle, or 20,000 leagues under the sea. The world's largest motion pictures play here about 10 times per day ($6, ages 5-15 $3.50, seniors $4.50, military and students $4.80). Tickets to the space theater also valid for the **Science Center,** where visitors can play with a cloud chamber, telegraph, light-mixing booth, and other gadgets. (Open Sun.-Tues. 9:30am-9:30pm, Sat. 9:30am-10:30pm.)

Sea World, Old Town, and Mission Hills

Although the prices and number of gift shops at **Sea World** (226-3901) won't let you forget that it's a commercial venture, the Mission Park attraction is far more educational than your average amusement park. Its famous animal shows range from educational to exploitative, but once inside don't miss seeing five-ton killer whales breach high above water. Sea World also encompasses impressive, well-lit state-of-the-art aquaria, and open pools where you can touch and feed various wet critters. (Open daily 10am-dusk, ticket sales end 1½ hr. before closing time. Extended summer and holiday hours. Admission including shows $26, ages 3-11 $20.)

The site of the original settlement of San Diego, **Old Town** remained the center of San Diego until the late 19th century. Take bus #5 from downtown. The Spanish *Presidio,* or military post, started here in 1769. Before becoming a museum, Old Town held the county courthouse, the town gallows, and a busy commercial district. Now the partially enclosed pedestrian mall is an overcrowded, overpriced tourist trap. The state park people offer free walking tours daily at 2pm, starting at their office at San Diego Ave. and Wallace St. (237-6770). To appreciate Old Town's buildings on your own, pick up the indispensable visitors center's walking tour ($2). **La Panaderia** serves coffee and Mexican pastries (75¢).

Mission Basilica San Diego de Alcalá (281-8449) was moved in 1774 to its present location in the hills north of the Presidio, in order to be closer to the Native American villages. Take I-8 east to Mission Gorge Rd. and follow the signs, or take bus #43. The mission has a chapel, a garden courtyard, a small museum of artifacts, and a reconstruction of the living quarters of mission-builder-cum-would-be-saint Junípero Serra. (Mass held daily at 7am and 5:30pm.)

ENTERTAINMENT

Definitive pockets of action are to be found throughout the city after dark. The Gaslamp Quarter is home to numerous upscale restaurants and bars that feature live music nightly. Hillcrest draws a young, largely gay, crowd to its clubs and restaurants once the sun has set. The beach areas (especially Garnet Ave. at Pacific Beach) are host to dozens of dance clubs, bars, and inexpensive eateries, which attract droves of college-age revelers.

Viva Diego's, 860 Garnet Ave., Pacific Beach (272-1241). At the top of San Diego's popular dance clubs, Diego's attracts the young and unattached en masse with blaring hip-hop, house, techno, and top 40 hits. Outdoor restaurant serves dinner until 10pm on weekdays and until 11pm on weekends. Open Tues.-Sat. (21 and up) until 2am, Sun. (18 and up) until 2 am. Cover charge Thurs.-Sun. $3-7.

Croce's Top Hat Bar and Grille and **Croce's Jazz Bar,** 802 Fifth Ave. (233-6945), at F St. in Gaslamp District. Ingrid Croce, wife of the late singer Jim Croce, created a rock/blues and a classy jazz bar side by side in the historic Keating building. Live music nightly, up to $5 cover. Open daily 11am-2am.

Chillers, 3105 Ocean Front, Mission Beach (488-2077). Like an over-21 "7-11," this club offers intoxicating "slurpees." Sample your slush before you invest the $3.75 (small) or $5.75 (large). Live bands 3-4 times weekly. Open noon-2am daily.

■ Near San Diego

There are 70 mi. of beaches around this city. The waves regurgitate an endless stream of surfers and boogie-boarders, while the sand from Imperial Beach in the south to La Jolla in the north is choked with sun-worshippers (it may take a little ingenuity to find room to bask). Come prime sunning time on summer weekends, chic places like Mission Beach and La Jolla are likely to be as packed as funky Ocean Beach. The coastal communities do have more to offer than waves and white sand; wander inland a few blocks and explore.

Coronado Coronado's most famed site is its Victorian-style **Hotel del Coronado,** Orange Ave. (435-6611). The long, white verandas and the red, circular towers of the "Del" were built in 1898 as a resort getaway. One of the world's great hotels, it has hosted 12 presidents and was featured in the 1959 classic *Some Like It Hot.* Wander onto the white, seaweed-free beach in back, one of the prettiest in San Diego. Its uncrowded shore invites shell-gathering and shoes-in-hand strolling.

Point Loma Walking a fine line between residential community and naval outpost, the Navy as yet remains contained near the base of the point. The **Cabrillo National Monument** (557-5450), at the tip of Point Loma, is dedicated to Portuguese explorer João Rodriguez Cabrillo (the first European to land in California), but is best known for its views of San Diego and the herds of migrating California Gray Whales that pass beyond the offshore kelp beds from Dec.-Feb. on their way to breed in the warm Baja waters.

La Jolla Situated on a small rocky promontory, La Jolla (pronounced la HOY-a) in the 1930s and 40s was a hideaway for wealthy Easterners who built luxurious houses and gardens atop the bluffs over the ocean. The coastline buckles against **Prospect St.'s** lavish hideaways. La Jolla claims some of the finest beaches in the city. Grassy knolls run right down to the sea at **La Jolla Cove,** and surfers are especially fond of the waves at **Tourmaline Beach** and **Windansea Beach.** At **Black's Beach,** people run, sun, and play volleyball. It is a public beach, not *officially* a nude beach, but you wouldn't know it from the sun-kissed hue of most beachcombers' buns. The northern part of the beach generally attracts gay patrons. Take I-5 to Genesee Ave., go west and turn left on N. Torrey Pines Rd. until you reach the **Torrey Pines Glider Port** (where clothed hang gliders leap into the breeze and the young and unafraid "cliff dive" into the high tide).

SAN FRANCISCO BAY AREA

■■■ SAN FRANCISCO

San Francisco—a city whose name evokes cable cars, LSD, gay liberation, and Rice-A-Roni—began its life in 1776 as the Spanish mission of *San Francisco de Asís*. In 1848, just two years after the U.S. took possession of California, gold was discovered in dem dar hills up the Sacramento River delta. "Frisco's" 800 residents looked around and realized not *only* did they live just a short river-trip from the gold fields, but they were also sitting on one of the greatest natural ports in the world. That year, 10,000 people passed through the Golden Gate, and a city was born.

The city's history, like its geology, has moved in abrupt fits and starts. The city dug itself out of the massive earthquake of 1906 shaken but not stirred—though it didn't completely recover until the 1930s, when the openings of the Oakland and Golden Gate Bridges ended its isolation from the rest of the Bay Area. Moving to San Fran has often meant joining the cultural vanguard—the Beat Generation arrived here in the 1950s, and the 60s saw Haight-Ashbury blossom into the hippie capital of the universe. In the 70s, the gay population emerged as one of the most powerful and visible groups in the city; the 80s once again saw San Francisco leading the nation, this time teaching the United States to fight AIDS, not people with AIDS. But the land continues to buck San Francisco's progress—the city's latest tragedy came on October 17, 1989, when the biggest quake since 1906 killed 62 people, knocked out the Bay Bridge, and cracked Candlestick Park during a World Series game.

San Francisco is less a city and more a confederation of neighborhoods; most San Franciscans think in terms of the Mission, Chinatown, Nob Hill, etc. A few blocks will take you from affluent Pacific Heights to the impoverished Western Addition; the Italian community of North Beach borders the largest concentration of Chinese people outside of China. Despite its seeming disorder, such tightly packed diversity lends the city a cosmopolitan character unknown outside of world capitals. Today, San Francisco's community spirit continues to rest on mutual tolerance and appreciation of differences among the groups of people who call the city home.

PRACTICAL INFORMATION

Visitors Information: Visitor Information Center, Hallidie Plaza (391-2000), Market at Powell St., beneath street level in Benjamin Swig Pavillion. A great many pamphlets on display, but even more hidden from view behind counter. Ask staff for specific information. Open Mon.-Fri. 9am-5:30pm, Sat. 9am-3pm, Sun. 10am-2pm. Event and information recordings in English (391-2001), French (391-2003), German (391-2004), and Spanish (391-2122). **Travelers Aid Society,** 225-2252.
Airport: San Francisco International Airport (SFO) (761-0800), located on a small nub of land in San Francisco Bay about 15 mi. south of the city center on

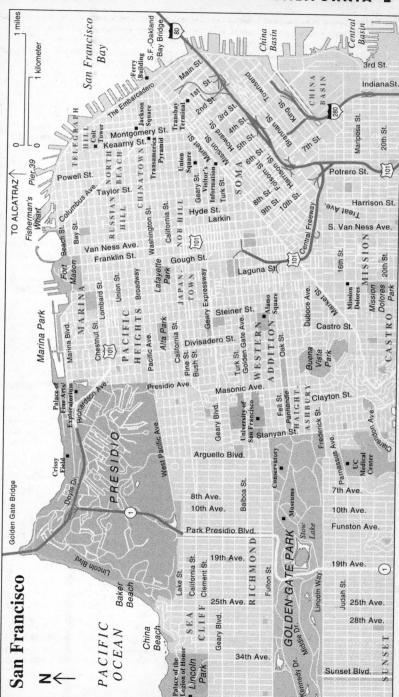

San Francisco

PACIFIC OCEAN

SAN FRANCISCO BAY AREA: SAN FRANCISCO

1 miles
1 kilometer
0

TO ALCATRAZ

Fisherman's Wharf
Pier 39

San Francisco Bay

China Basin

Central Basin

S.F.-Oakland Bay Bridge

80

Ferry Building
The Embarcadero
Jackson Square
Main St.
1st St.
2nd St.
3rd St.
4th St.
5th St.
6th St.
7th St.

3rd St.

Indiana St.

China Basin

280

Mariposa St.
20th St.

TELEGRAPH HILL
Coit Tower
Montgomery St.
Kearny St.
Powell St.
Columbus Ave.
Beach St.
Taylor St.
Transamerica Pyramid
California St.
Washington St.

NORTH BEACH
RUSSIAN HILL
CHINATOWN
NOB HILL

Transbay Terminal
Union Square
Geary St.
Visitor's Information
Turk St.
Hyde St.
Larkin

Market St.
Mission St.
Howard St.
Folsom St.
Harrison St.
Bryant St.
Brannan St.
Townsend St.
King St.

SOMA

7th St.

Potrero St.

101

Harrison St.

Teal Ave.

S. Van Ness Ave.

16th St.

MISSION

20th St.

Van Ness Ave.
Franklin St.
Gough St.
Union St.
Lombard St.
Broadway
Chestnut St.

MARINA
PACIFIC HEIGHTS
JAPAN TOWN

Lafayette Park
Gough St.
Laguna St.
Geary Expressway
Steiner St.
Divisadero St.
Pine St.
Bush St.

Alamo Square
WESTERN ADDITION
Oak St.

Duboce Ave.
Castro St.

Mission Dolores
Mission Dolores Park

CASTRO

Marina Park
Fort Mason
Marina Blvd.
Palace of Fine Arts / Exploratorium
Richardson Ave.

101

Alta Park
California St.
Pacific Ave.

Turk St.
Golden Gate Ave.
Masonic Ave.

Fell St.
Panhandle
HAIGHT

Clayton St.
ASHBURY
Frederick St.

Clarendon Ave.

UC Medical Center

Golden Gate Bridge

PRESIDIO

Crissy Field
Doyle Dr.

West Pacific Ave.

Geary Blvd.
University of San Francisco
Stanyan St.

Buena Vista Park

Parnassus Ave.

7th Ave.

Lincoln Blvd.

1

Arguello Blvd.

Conservatory

Museums

Stow Lake

GOLDEN GATE PARK

10th Ave.

Baker Beach
China Beach

8th Ave.
10th Ave.
Park Presidio Blvd.
Balboa St.

Funston Ave.

SEA CLIFF
Lake St.
California St.
Clement St.
19th Ave.
25th Ave.

RICHMOND
Fulton St.

Kennedy Dr.
Middle Dr.
Lincoln Way
Judah St.

10th Ave.
19th Ave.
25th Ave.
28th Ave.

SUNSET

Palace of the Legion of Honor
Lincoln Park
Geary Blvd.
34th Ave.

Sunset Blvd.

N

U.S. 101. Lockers $1 first day, $2 per day thereafter. **SamTrans** (800-660-4287) runs two buses to downtown, #7F (carry-on baggage only; 6-9am and 4-6pm every 30-60 min., 9am-4pm less frequently; 35 min.; $1.75, off-peak 85¢, under 18 85¢, seniors 60¢) and #7B (any baggage; same frequency; 55 min.; 85¢, under 18 35¢, seniors 25¢). **Airporter** (495-8404) buses between all 3 terminals and downtown at 301 Ellis St. (5:45am-10:50pm every ¼ hr.; $6). Cabs to downtown about $25.

Trains: Amtrak (800-872-7245), at 16th St. in Oakland. To: L.A. ($75). Free shuttles to Transbay Terminal, where Amtrak also has a desk. Open daily 6:45am-10:45pm. **CalTrain** (800-660-4287), at 4th and Townsend St., runs to: Palo Alto ($3, seniors and disabled $1.50); San Jose ($3.50, seniors and disabled $1.75).

Buses: Transbay Terminal, 425 Mission St. (495-1551), between Fremont and 1st St. downtown, houses **Greyhound** (800-231-2222; to L.A. $39), **Golden Gate Transit** (Marin County), **AC Transit** (East Bay), and **SamTrans** (San Mateo County). Free shuttles to Amtrak. Maps and free phones to each company on 2nd floor. Open daily 5am-12:35am. **Green Tortoise** (285-2441; 1667 Jerrold Ave.; open daily 8am-8pm) picks up at 1st and Natoma St. To: L.A. (Fri. night, $30); Seattle (Mon., Wed., Fri., and Sat., $69). Reserve 1 week in advance.

Public Transportation: See Traveling in San Francisco, below.

Taxi: Yellow Cab, 626-2345. **Luxor Cabs,** 282-4141. **DeSoto Cab,** 673-1414. For each, $1.70 plus $1.80 per additional mi. Each runs 24 hrs.

Car Rental: Bob Leech's Auto Rental, 435 S. Airport Blvd. (583-3844 or 800-635-1240), South San Francisco. Toyota Camry $30 per day, Corolla $20 per day. 150 free mi., 10¢ per additional mi. Must be 23 with major credit card. Travelers flying into SFO can ask for pickup. Open Mon.-Fri. 8am-9pm, Sat.-Sun. 9am-5pm.

Bike Rental: Lincoln Cyclery, 772 Stanyan St. (221-2415), on the east edge of Golden Gate Park, offers mountain bikes $5 per hr., $20 all day. Driver's license or major credit card and $15 deposit. Open Mon. and Wed.-Sat. 9am-5pm, Sun. 11:30am-5pm. **Presidio Bicycle Shop,** 5335 Geary (752-2453), between 17th and 18th Ave., rents 10-speeds or mountain bikes $7 per hr., $25 per day. Open Mon.-Sat. 10am-6pm, Sun. 11am-4pm.

24-Hour Emergency Hotlines: Drug Crisis Line, 752-3400; **Rape Crisis Center,** 647-RAPE (647-7273), operated by San Francisco Women Against Rape.

Post Office: 101 Hyde St., at Golden Gate Ave. Open Mon.-Fri. 7am-5:30pm, Sat. 7am-3pm. **ZIP Code:** 94142. General Delivery open Mon.-Sat. 10am-2pm.

Area Code: 415.

ORIENTATION

San Francisco is 548 mi. north of San Diego, 403 mi. north of Los Angeles, and 6174 mi. north of San Francisco, Argentina. The city proper lies at the northern tip of a peninsula that sets off San Francisco Bay from the Pacific Ocean.

San Francisco radiates outward from its docks, on the northeast edge of the peninsula just inside the lip of the bay. Most visitors' attention still gravitates to this area. Here, within a wedge formed by **Van Ness Avenue** running north-south, **Market Street** running northeast-southwest, and the **Embarcadero** (waterfront road) curving along the coast, many of San Francisco's shining attractions are found. Taking a diagonal course, Market Street disrupts the regular grid of streets and accounts for an exceptionally confusing street-numbering system. The streets aiming north from Market and west from Market and the Embarcadero are numbered beginning at those thoroughfares. Parallel streets do not bear the same block numbers.

At the top of this wedge lies **Fisherman's Wharf** and slightly below, around **Columbus Avenue,** is **North Beach,** a district shared by Italian-Americans, artists, and professionals. The focal point of North Beach is **Telegraph Hill,** topped by Coit Tower. Across Columbus Ave. begin the **Nob Hill** and **Russian Hill** areas, home of the city's old money. Below Nob Hill and North Beach, and still north of Market, **Chinatown** covers around 24 sq. blocks between Broadway, Bush, Powell, and Kearny St. The heavily developed **Financial District** lies between Washington St. in the north and Market in the south, east of Chinatown and south of North Beach and is home to the skyscrapers which define the city's skyline. Down Market from the

Financial District, toward the bottom of the wedge, you pass through the core downtown area centered on **Union Square** and then, beyond Jones St., the **Civic Center,** an impressive collection of municipal buildings including City Hall, the Opera House, and Symphony Hall.

Also within this wedge is the **Tenderloin,** where drugs and homelessness prevail among the sprouting high-rises, making the area unsafe at night. Below Market St. lies the **South-of-Market-Area (SoMa),** largely deserted during the day although it is home to much of the city's nightlife. The best of San Francisco's nightclubs, though, are separated by darkened office buildings and warehouses. Decide beforehand exactly where you're going and share a cab with friends on the way there and back; it will be tremendously worthwhile. The SoMa extends inland from the bay to 10th St., at which point the Latino **Mission District** begins and spreads south. The **Castro,** center of the gay community, adjoins the Mission District at 17th and also extends south, radiating from Castro St.

West of Van Ness Ave., the city extends all the way to the ocean side of the peninsula. At the top of Van Ness, the commercially developed **Marina** area embraces a yacht harbor and Fort Mason. **Fisherman's Wharf** lies immediately to its east. Below the Marina rise the wealthy hills of **Pacific Heights.** South of Pacific Heights and across Van Ness from the Civic Center is the **Western Addition,** extending west to Masonic Ave. This district is the site of many of the city's public housing projects and can be dangerous, especially near Hayes St. It is not a good place for tourists to hang out. **Japantown** is located within the Western Addition. Farther west is the rectangular **Golden Gate Park,** extending to the Pacific and bounded by Fulton Street in the north and Lincoln Street in the south. At its eastern end juts a skinny panhandle bordered by the **Haight-Ashbury** district. North of **Golden Gate Park** is the **Richmond District,** with a large Asian-American population. South of the park is the **Sunset District,** home to the UCSF Medical Center.

TRAVELING IN SAN FRANCISCO

Public Transportation

San Francisco Municipal Railway (MUNI) (673-6864) operates **buses,** cable cars, and a combined subway/trolley system. (Fares for buses and trolleys $1, ages 5-17 25¢, seniors and disabled 15¢. Exact change in coins is required. MUNI passes: 1 day, $6; 3 days, $10.) Ask for a free transfer, valid in any direction for several hours, when boarding. Most operate 6am-midnight; some 24 hrs. Purchase the minus *San Francisco Street and Transit Map* ($1.50), which contains information on frequency, accessibility, and late-night service, as well as a complete street index allowing it to double as a general street map.

Cable cars have been transporting San Franciscans since 1873. The cars are noisy, slow (9.5mph, to be precise), and so often full as to be a totally unreliable method of getting from point A to point B (you won't be the first person to think of taking one from Union Square to Fisherman's Wharf). Of the three lines, the California (C) line is by far the least crowded; it runs from the Financial District up Nob Hill. The Powell-Hyde (PH) line has the steepest hills and the sharpest turns. (Runs daily 7am-1am. $2, ages 5-17 75¢, seniors 15¢. 3-hr. unlimited transfers.)

Bay Area Rapid Transit (BART) (778-2278) does not really serve the entire Bay Area, but it does operate modern, beautifully carpeted trains along four lines connecting San Francisco with the East Bay, including Oakland, Berkeley, Concord, and Fremont. Use MUNI for transport within San Francisco. (BART trains run Mon.-Sat. 6am-midnight, Sun. 9am-midnight. One-way fares 80¢-$3.) Maps and schedules are available at all stations. All stations and trains are wheelchair-accessible.

Driving in San Fran

A car here is not the necessity it is in Los Angeles. Furthermore, parking in the city is *hell* and very expensive. In San Francisco, contending with the hills is the first task; if you've arrived in a standard transmission, you'll need to develop a fast clutch foot, since all hills have stop signs at the crests. If you're renting, get an automatic. The street signs admonishing you to "PREVENT RUNAWAYS" refer not to wayward youths but to cars improperly parked on hills. When parking facing uphill, turn the wheels toward the center of the street and leave car in 1st gear (if you're driving a standard); when facing downhill, turn the wheels toward the curb and leave the car in reverse (in a standard); and always set the emergency brake. And remember: in San Francisco, cable cars have the right of way.

ACCOMMODATIONS

There are a tremendous number of reasonably priced and conveniently located places to stay in San Francisco. Hostels and many cheap hotels dot the city.

Many of the hotels listed here are in areas where caution is advised both on the streets and within the buildings, particularly at night. The Tenderloin and the Mission District can be particularly unsafe. Women especially should go elsewhere and pay more if unsure about a given neighborhood or establishment.

Hostels

Pacific Tradewinds Guest House, 680 Sacramento St. (433-7970), in the Financial District between Montgomery and Kearny. Home to an extremely friendly and knowledgeable staff. Fax machine, guest telephone (10¢ per local call), laundry ($2), equipped kitchen, free tea and coffee. Open 24 hrs. No curfew. $12 per night. Discounts for VIP Backpacker and FIYTO cardholders.

San Francisco International Hostel (HI/AYH), Bldg. 240, Fort Mason (771-7277), in the Marina. Entrance at Bay and Franklin St. Clean, well-run, and efficient. The chore-a-day rule is enforced. One of the only hostels with sightseeing (or bar-hopping) tours. No curfew. Wheelchair accessibility, equipped kitchen, and clean rooms. $13 per night. Registration 7am-2pm and 3pm-midnight. Lines start at 6am. MC, Visa, JCB.

Interclub Globe Hostel, 10 Hallam Place (431-0540), in South-of-Market off Folsom St., between 7th and 8th. The funkiest of the bunch. The Globe itself is far from Establishment. Pool table, a snack bar, and some pretty wild parties. In a better neighborhood than some, but it seems that people can walk in and out without being questioned. Safety deposit, free coffee at night. $15. Key deposit $5.

San Francisco International Guest House, 2976 23rd St. (641-1411), in the Mission District at Harrison. If it were any more laid-back, it would be lying flat. A genuinely warm atmosphere in a beautiful Victorian house. Free sheets, free coffee, private doubles, and 2 spacious kitchens. Clean. 5-day min. stay. International passport required. $13 per night.

San Francisco International Student Center, 1188 Folsom St. (621-5464), in South of Market. Almost across the street from the Globe. Newly opened in the summer of 1993. The bay windows and brick walls scream "COZY!" Registration 8am-noon and 7-11pm. Open 24 hrs. $12 per night.

Hostel at Union Square (HI/AYH), 312 Mason St. (788-5604), 1 block from Union Square. The neighborhood is not the best. This mammoth has room for 220, and with its increased size comes decreased warmth. The management, does, however, emphasize safety. Big, clean common areas, TV room, equipped kitchen, vending machines. $14 per night, non-members $17. Sheet rental $2. ID photo $1.50 for a photograph. $5 key deposit.

Hotels

The most important fact to consider is that accommodations costing more than $20 (i.e., all of the hotels and none of the hostels) must charge an 11% bed tax which is not included in the prices listed below. Furthermore, most budget-range hotels in San Francisco are in unsafe areas, and in terms of cleanliness and helpfulness, you usually get what you pay for. Hostels generally offer a better package.

Downtown

Olympic Hotel, 140 Mason St. (982-5010), at Ellis St., a few blocks from Union Sq., snuggled up against the snazzy Parc Fifty-Five. Caters mostly to Japanese students and Europeans. Clean and comfortable. Atrocious wall-paper. Tends to fill up during the summer months. Olympic Deli next door has cappuccino ($1.20) and sandwiches ($3.10). Singles $30, singles and doubles with bath $40.

Herbert Hotel, 161 Powell St. (362-1600), at O'Farrell St., very close to Union Sq. Near cable car turnaround. Caters to an older crowd, but prime location. Singles $30, with bath $35, per week $90. Doubles with bath $40, per week $200.

Pensione International, 875 Post St. (775-3344), east of Hyde St., 4½ blocks west of Union Square. Very attractive rooms with interesting art. Singles $30, with bath $55. Doubles $50, with bath $75. Breakfast included.

Adelaide Inn, #5 Isadora Duncan (441-2261), off Taylor near Post St., 2 blocks west of Union Square. Perhaps the most charming of San Francisco's many "European-style" hotels. Does not answer door after 11pm. Steep stairs, no elevator. Kitchenette and microwave available. 18 rooms. Hall baths. Singles $38, twin bed or doubles $48. Continental breakfast included. Reservations accepted.

Chinatown

YMCA Chinatown, 855 Sacramento St. (982-4412), between Stockton St. and Grant Ave. Convenient location for those wanting to be near the center of the city in general and Chinatown in particular. Men over 18 only. Friendly young staff, pool, and gym. Rooms are not exactly fancy. Registration Mon.-Fri. 6:30am-10pm, Sat. 9am-5pm, Sun. 9am-1pm. Check-out 1pm. No curfew. Singles $26.50, doubles $34.75. 7th day free. Call 2 weeks in advance for reservations.

Gum Moon Women's Residence, 940 Washington (421-8827), at Stockton in Chinatown's center. Women only. Bright, spacious rooms with shared bath. Kitchen and laundry facilities. Primarily a boarding house, so call ahead to make sure there are rooms available. Registration 9am-5:30pm. Check-out noon. Singles $24, per week $100. Doubles $40, per week $164. Reserve 1 week in advance.

Grant Plaza, 465 Grant Ave. (434-3883 or 800-472-6899, within CA 800-472-6805), at Pine St. near the Chinatown gate. Excellent location. Renovated to look like a chain motel, but more colorful. Rooms with bath, phones, and color TV. Parking validated. Check-in after 2:30pm. Check-out noon. Singles $39, doubles $49. Reservations advised 2-3 weeks in advance.

Near the Civic Center

Harcourt Residence Club, 1105 Larkin (673-7720). One of the city's most popular residence clubs offers rooms by the week or by the month. Price includes maid service, TV room, 2 meals a day, and Sunday brunch. Filled by a younger set of traveling students and local residents. Occasional barbecues are organized by Harcourt. Weekly rates *per person:* $130-200.

YMCA Hotel, 220 Golden Gate Ave. (885-0460), at Leavenworth St., 2 blocks north of Market St. Men and women. One of the largest hotels in the city, but rooms don't quite measure up to the postmodern facade. Double locks on all doors. Pool, gym, and racketball court. Register any time. No curfew. Singles $26, with TV and private bathrooms $38. Doubles $36/$43. Hostel beds $16 for members only. Breakfast included. $5 key deposit.

Western Hotel, 335 Leavenworth St. (673-8317). From Transbay Terminal walk south to Market and turn left; walk northwest on Market past 7th St. to Leavenworth St. and turn left. Questionable neighborhood, but the hotel has a locked gate and is clean. Showers and toilets in the hall. 24-hr. counter. No visitors after 9pm. Check-out 11am. Singles $27, per week $110. Doubles $28/$150.

Haight-Ashbury

The Red Victorian Bed and Breakfast Inn, 1665 Haight St. (864-1978), 3 blocks west of Masonic Ave., 2 blocks east of Golden Gate Park in Haight-Ashbury. 3 mi. from downtown, but close to buses and the MUNI Metro "N" trolley. Barely describable, the Red Vic is more a state of mind than a hotel. 18 individually and lovingly decorated rooms honor butterflies, the nearby Golden Gate Park, and the equally proximate 1960s, among other subjects. Even the 4 hall baths, shared by some of the rooms, have their own names and motifs. Tête-à-tête with the hotel cat, Charlotte. The Red Victorian is a non-smoking, angst-free living environment that you won't want to miss if your pocketbook is up for the experience. Even if it isn't, at least stop by for a tour. Check-in 3-6pm. Check-out 11am. Breakfast of freshly baked bread, pastry, and (of course) granola included. Complimentary tea, coffee, popcorn, and cheese in the afternoons. Among the owners and staff members are speakers of Korean, Portuguese, Spanish, German, Italian, French, and English. 2-night stay usually required on weekends. Weekly discounts available. Doubles $65-135, in winter $55-120. Singles deduct $5. Extra futon $15. Make reservations well in advance for the summer months.

FOOD

The city of San Francisco is home to almost 4000 restaurants. Do not let this daunting number scare you, however, for the ones listed below are outstanding. The neighborhoods are listed in an order which reflects their potential to those seeking an inexpensive, satisfying meal. Your odds are best in the Mission.

Mission District and Castro Street

The Mission is the best place in the city to find excellent, satisfying cheap food. The only frustrating thing is choosing between all the inexpensive *taquerías* and other internationally flavored eateries. Those with substantial appetites should take a walk down 24th Street (east of Mission St.) and choose from the Mexican, Salvadoran, and other Latin American restaurants.

La Cumbre, 515 Valencia St. (863-8205). As you stand in line, your mouth-watering, raw steak is brought in from the back kitchen, dripping in marinade. It is then grilled to perfection, quickly chopped, combined with rice and beans, and deftly folded into a flour tortilla to make a superlative burrito. ($2.50 for a regular, which is ample; $4 for a "super," sure to fill any *gordito)*. A standout among *taquerías*. Open Mon.-Sat. 11am-10pm, Sun. noon-9pm.

Taquería San Jose, 2830 Mission St. (282-0203), at 24th. Don't be put off by the fast-food style menu; loving care goes into the cooking. Soft tacos with your choice of meat, from magnificent spicy pork to brains or tongue ($1.70), 5 for $3.50. Free chips and guacamole. Open daily 8am-1am.

Café Macondo, 3159 16th St. (863-6517). Appetizing Central American food and coffee in a homey yet artfully designed café. Hardwood floors with Oriental rugs, wicker furniture, couches, and native art. Bring a book and sip cappuccino ($1.50). Sandwiches $3. Open Mon.-Thurs. 11am-10pm, Fri.-Sun. 11am-11pm.

Manora, 3226 Mission (550-0856). This attractive Thai restaurant serves delicious cuisine at reasonable prices. Manora prepares sauces with a refreshingly light hand, so the food isn't smothered in peanut. The red beef curry garners high praise ($5.75). Most dishes under $10. Open Tues.-Sun. 5-10pm.

New Dawn Café, 3174 16th St. (553-8888), at Guerrero. An intense sensory experience. Absolutely anything is considered "art" at this hip restaurant, from the doll body parts and eggbeaters hanging on the walls to the music blasting through the restaurant. The menu, consisting mainly of breakfast food and burgers, is written around the room on mirrors. Enormous servings prepared with care by a 55-year-old drag queen. Vegetable home fries (made with fresh vegetables) $5.25, burgers $4.25. Open Mon.-Fri. 8am-2pm, Sat.-Sun. 8am-4pm.

Chinatown

Chinatown abounds with downright cheap restaurants; in fact, their multitude and incredible similarity can make a choice nearly impossible.

House of Nanking, 919 Kearney St. (421-1429). Outstanding Chinese food in a pleasant atmosphere. This small restaurant which prepares its food within the dining area always has lines out the door. People walk here all the way from the

Financial District on their lunch breaks. *Mu-shu* vegetables $5, onion cakes $1.75. Tsing Tao beer sauce is essential. Open Mon.-Sat. 11am-10pm, Sun. 4-10pm.

Sam Wo, 813 Washington (982-0596). The late hours and BYOB policy, not to mention the exceptionally cheap prices, make this restaurant a favorite among students from all over the Bay Area. Customers must pass by the chefs as they prepare the food in the kitchen. Most dishes $2-5. Fish soup *(jook)* $4.50, chicken chow mein $3.60. Open Mon.-Sat. 11am-3am, Sun. 12:30-9:30pm.

Yuet Lee, 1300 Stockton (982-6020), at Broadway. Not much for atmosphere, but the seafood makes up for that. Steamed fresh oysters in black bean sauce $8. Many exotic seasonal specialties for adventurous diners, such as sauteed pork stomach with boneless duck feet. Open daily 11am-3am.

Dol Ho, 808 Pacific Ave. (392-2828). A relaxing atmosphere perfect for afternoon tea and *dim sum*, traditionally served as brunch. 4 steamed shrimp dumplings, sweet doughy sesame balls, or pork buns $1.50. Open daily 8am-4pm.

North Beach

North Beach isn't cheap, but prices can be reasonable in this Italian neighborhood. Avoid eating at Fisherman's Wharf on the northern rim of North Beach, where food is frequently tasteless, overpriced, or both. A walk down Columbus Ave. will take you to a group of suitable cafes and an occasional inexpensive restaurant.

Ricos, 943 Columbus Ave. (928-5404), near Lombard. Monstrous burritos. Exceptional enchiladas. No fuss. ISIC discounts. Open daily 10am-10pm.

Tommaso's, 1042 Kearny St. (398-9696), between Pacific and Broadway just below Van Ness Ave. The super deluxe, piled high with mushrooms, peppers, ham, and Italian sausage is enough for two ($18). The *pizza Neapolitan* is simple and fulfilling ($14). Francis Ford Coppola tosses pizza dough every once in a while here. Open Tues.-Sat. 5-10:45pm, Sun. 4-9:45pm.

The Richmond District

The quiet Richmond District contains multi-ethnic neighborhoods and restaurants for exploration. The area east of Park Presidio Blvd. is populated by Chinese, earning it the nickname "New Chinatown," and some locals justly claim the Chinese restaurants here are better than the ones in old Chinatown. In addition, the area contains many fine Thai, Burmese, and Cambodian restaurants.

Ernesto's, 2311 Clement St. (386-1446), at 24th Ave. A well-kept San Francisco culinary secret. Dinners at this family-run Italian restaurant are reasonably priced (entrees $8-11, pizza $7.25-15.50) and are as authentic as anything in North Beach, if not Italy. Try the filling linguine with red clam sauce ($8.75). Wine is often served free to guests waiting outside the door. Open Tues.-Sun. 4-10pm.

The Golden Turtle, 308 5th Ave. (221-5285), at Clement. Prices at this small Vietnamese restaurant are reasonable, and the food is delicious. Service makes you feel like royalty. Entrees starting at $7. Open daily 11am-3pm and 5-11pm.

Civic Center

Hayes Street offers a terrific selection of cafes, and petite restaurants dot the entire Civic Center area. In the summer, load up on produce at the **Farmers Market** in the U.N. Plaza (every Wed. and Sun.). Use caution in this area at night.

Nyala Ethiopian Restaurant, 39A Grove St. (861-0788), east of Larkin St. Nyala's combination of Ethiopian and Italian cuisine is probably the only positive result of Mussolini's occupation. Newcomers should try *doro wet*, a traditional Ethiopian dish of slowly simmered chicken in a rich garlic and ginger sauce ($6.75 at lunch). Or, for variety, try the vegetarian all-you-can-eat buffet, Mon.-Sat. 11am-3pm ($5) and 4pm-closing ($7). Open Mon.-Sat. 11am-10pm.

Tommy's Joynt, 1101 Geary Blvd. (775-4216), at Van Ness Ave. Outrageously painted establishment with a stunning selection of beers brewed everywhere from Finland to Peru. Their thick pastrami sandwich is known throughout the city ($4). With two types of mustard and horseradish on every table, they clearly know what they're doing. Open daily 10am-1:50am.

Pendragon Bakery, 450 Hayes St. (552-7017), at Gough St. Excellent, imaginative pastries. A big, fluffy blueberry scone $1.85. Sandwiches $3.75-5.75. Open Mon.-Fri. 7am-4pm, Sat. 8am-4pm, Sun. 8am-2pm.

Swan Oyster Depot, 1517 Polk St. (673-1101), near the California St. cable car. Avoid the elbow-to-elbow lunch-time squeeze by coming at an off hour for some of the best, freshest seafood in the city. Pull up a stool to the marble counter (they don't have tables) and consume what might be the city's finest chowder ($3.25). Clam cocktail with Swan's zesty red sauce $5. Open Mon.-Fri. 7:30am-10:30pm.

Stars Cafe, 555 Golden Gate (861-4344), between Van Ness and Polk. Though you might not know it from the $10 entrees, this is actually a sort of discount outlet for the famous Stars Restaurant which is located next door. The $8 sandwiches or chicken salad are the cheapest way to sample one of super-chef Jeremiah Tower's creations. Both restaurants have the same desserts. Menu changes daily. Open Sun.-Thurs. 11:30am-10pm, Fri.-Sat. 11:30am-11pm.

Haight-Ashbury

Although the Haight boasts a terrific selection of bakeries, it offers little in the way of cheap victuals. There are a few interesting places worth checking out, but the often expensive food is uneven at some restaurants and downright bad at others.

Cha Cha Cha, 1801 Haight St. (386-5758). Love-children fighting against the stream of late capitalist society join hands with upwardly mobile professionals and line up for a chance to eat at this trendy Latin restaurant, thought to be the best in the Haight. Try the *tapas* ($4-6). Fried bananas in black bean sauce are a specialty ($5.75). Entrees $5-8. Be prepared to wait up to 2 hr. Open Mon.-Fri. 11:30am-3pm and 5-11:30pm, Sat.-Sun. 9am-3pm and 5:30-11:30pm.

Ganges, 775 Frederick St. (661-7290), not exactly in the Haight, but close enough. Between 9 and 13 curries prepared every day. Traditional, low Indian seating in back. Dinners $8.50-12.50. Live music Fri.-Sat. starting at 7:15pm. Reservations a good idea. Open Tues.-Sat. 5-10pm.

Marina and Pacific Heights

Pacific Heights and the Marina abound in high-quality, high-priced restaurants.

Bepple's Pies, 1934 Union St. (931-6225). The pies are divine creations, combining succulent fruit filling with a miraculous crust that is moist yet flaky, absorbing the flavor of the fruit. Slices of pie are $3, another $1.10 for a solid slab of excellent vanilla ice cream. $4.50-6 for dinner pies with soup and cole slaw. Whole fruit pies to go, $12. Open Sun.-Thurs. 9am-11pm, Fri.-Sat. 9am-2am.

Perry's, 1944 Union St. (922-9022). When asked what was special about Perry's Bar—one of the best-known places on Union St.—the host answered, "the drinks are a little stronger and the philosophy a little deeper." Small Caesar salad $5, fettuccine alfredo $8.25, and 9 beers on tap ($3.75). Open Sun.-Thurs. 9am-11pm, Fri.-Sat. 9am-midnight.

Jackson Fillmore Trattoria, 2506 Fillmore St. (346-5288). There's almost always a line at this hip *trattoria*. Great southern Italian cuisine and a lively atmosphere. Check out the Fillmore scene while you wait. The portions are large; if you're careful you can sneak out for less than $10 per person. Eat lots of tasty breadsticks to fill up. Reservations required for more than 3 people. Open Mon. 5:30-10pm, Tues.-Thurs. 5:30-10:30pm, Fri.-Sat. 5:30-11pm, Sun. 5-10pm.

SIGHTS

Mark Twain called San Francisco "the liveliest, heartiest community on our continent," and any resident will tell you that this city is not made by landmarks or "sights," but by neighborhoods. If you rush from the Golden Gate Bridge to Coit Tower to Mission Dolores, you'll be missing the point—the city itself. Off-beat bookstores, Japanese folk festivals, Chinese *dim sum,* architecture in Pacific Heights,

SoMa's nightlife, Strawberry Hill in Golden Gate Park, the Club Fugazi in North Beach, and the Haight for being the Haight...together, these are San Francisco.

Museums

San Francisco Museum of Modern Art, 401 Van Ness Ave. (252-4000), at McAllister St. in the Veterans Building, Civic Center. Though planning a 1995 move, the current site displays an impressive collection of both European and American 20th-century works. Open Tues.-Wed. and Fri. 10am-5pm, Thurs. 10am-9pm, Sat.-Sun. 11am-5pm. $4, seniors and students $2, under 13 free. Tues. seniors and students free. Thurs. 5-9pm $3, seniors and students $1. 1st Tues. of month free.

California Academy of Sciences (221-5100, 750-7145 for a recording), in Golden Gate Park. Houses several smaller museums that specialize in different branches of science. The **Steinhart Aquarium** (home to over 14,000 aquatic species) is more lively than the natural history exhibits. See the dungeness crab before it's been steamed and hear the plaintive song of the croakerfish. Unique **Fish Roundabout,** a tank shaped like a doughnut where the fish swim around you. The **Far Side of Science** gallery shows over 150 of Gary Larson's zaniest cartoons. The Academy's **Morrison Planetarium** (750-7141) re-creates the heavens above with an impressive show ($2.50, seniors and students $1.25). Academy open daily 10am-7pm; Sept.-June 10am-5pm. $6, with MUNI Fast Pass or transfer $3, seniors and ages 12-17 $2, ages 6-11 $1. Free 1st Wed. of month until 8:45pm.

Cable Car Powerhouse and Museum, 1201 Mason St. (474-1887), at Washington in Russian Hill. The building is the working center of the cable-car system. You can look down on the operation from a gallery or view displays to learn more than you ever cared to about the picturesque cars, some of which date back to 1873. Open daily 10am-6pm; Nov.-March 10am-5pm. Free.

Exploratorium, 3601 Lyon St. (561-0360), in the Marina district. Hundreds of interactive exhibits may teach even poets a thing or two about the sciences. Open Tues. and Thurs.-Sun. 10am-5pm, Wed. 10am-9:30pm. $8, students and seniors $6, ages 6-17 $4. Free on the first Wed. of every month. Within dwells the **Tactile Dome** (561-0362), a pitch-dark maze of tunnels, slides, nooks, and crannies designed to help refine your sense of touch; claustrophobes and those afraid of the dark should stay away ($7, reservations helpful).

Wells Fargo History Museum, 420 Montgomery St. (396-2619), in the Financial District. An impressive display of Gold Rush exhibits, including gold nuggets, maps, and a 19th-century stagecoach. Open Mon.-Fri. 9am-5pm.

Ansel Adams Center, 250 4th St. (495-7000), at Howard and Folsom in Tenderloin. Houses a permanent collection of the master's photographs and other, temporary, shows. Open Tues.-Sun. 11am-6pm. $4, students $3, seniors $2.

M. H. de Young Memorial Museum (750-3600), in Golden Gate Park. 21-room survey of American painting, from the Colonial period to the early 20th century and a gallery of late 19th-century *trompe l'oeil* paintings. Also noteworthy is the museum's glass collection, which features ancient, European, Tiffany, and Steuben pieces. Free tours; call for details. Open Wed.-Sun. 10am-5pm. Admission $4, with MUNI Fast Pass or transfer $3, seniors and ages 12-17 $2, under 12 free; free 1st Wed. of month. Admission fee covers the de Young, Asian, and Palace of the Legion of Honor (see Richmond) museums for one day, so save your receipt.

Asian Art Museum (668-8921), in Golden Gate Park. The largest museum outside Asia dedicated entirely to Asian artwork. This beautiful collection includes rare pieces of jade and porcelain, in addition to works of bronze over 3000 years old. Free tours; call for details. Same hours and fees as the de Young Museum.

Tattoo Art Museum, 841 Columbus (775-4991), North Beach. Fantastic collection of tattoo memorabilia, including hundreds of designs and exhibits on different tattoo techniques. Collection is the largest of its kind; works are exhibited on a rotating basis. A modern, clean tattoo studio is run by the eminent professional Lyle Tuttle, himself covered in tattoos from head to foot (the museum is his personal collection). $50 will buy a quick, glowing rose on the hip.

Downtown

Union Square

Now an established shopping area at the center of San Francisco, Union Square has a rich and somewhat checkered history. During the Civil War, a large public meeting was held here to decide whether San Francisco should secede. The square became the rallying ground of the Unionists, who bore placards reading "The Union, the whole Union, and nothing but the Union."

Even when the Barbary Coast (now the Financial District) was down and dirty, Union Square was cheaper and dirtier. **Morton Alley,** in particular, offered off-brand alternatives to the high-priced prostitutes and stiff drinks of the coast. At the turn of the century, murders on Morton Alley averaged one per week, and prostitutes with unbuttoned shirts waved to their favorite customers from second-story windows. After the 1906 earthquake and fire destroyed most of the flophouses, a group of merchants moved in and renamed the area **Maiden Lane** in hopes of changing the street's image. Surprisingly enough, the switch worked. Today Maiden Lane—extending 2 blocks from Union Square's eastern side—is home to smart shops and classy boutiques.

Views of the City

The best free ride in town is on the outside elevators of the St. Francis Hotel. As you glide up the building, the entire Bay Area stretches out before you. The "elevator tours" offer an unparalleled view of Coit Tower and the Golden Gate Bridge. The Powell St. cable cars grant an excellent view of the square. Or go up to the 30th floor of the **Holiday Inn,** 480 Sutter St. (398-8900; take MUNI bus #2, 3, or 4), where you can put down a potable in the **Sherlock Holmes Esquire Public House** (398-8900), which has been decorated to the specifications of 221B Baker St.

Golden Gate Ferries (332-6600) floats boats to Larkspur and Sausalito (see Marin County). Ferries depart frequently from the Ferry Building at the terminus of Market St. on the Embarcadero. This is an easy way to enjoy San Francisco's skyline and bay. (Fare to Sausalito is $3.50, ages 6-12 $2.60; to Larkspur $2.20, ages 6-12 $1.65. Seniors and people with disabilities travel at ½-price. Family rates available.)

Financial District

North of Market and east of Kearny, snug against the bay, beats the West's financial heart, or at least one of its ventricles. Montgomery Street, the Wall Street of the West, is only of passing interest to the visitor and is best seen before the workday ends. After 7:30pm, the heart stops, only to be resuscitated the next morning. The **Pacific Stock Exchange,** 301 Pine St., is a picayune and much more relaxed version of its counterpart in New York (free 45-min. tours by appointment; call 393-7969).

The Financial District also offers some inside attractions in the form of free museums, such as the Wells Fargo Museum (see museums), most of them sponsored by the public relations departments of large banks. The **Chinese Historical Society,** 650 Commercial St. (391-1188), tells the tale of the Chinese who came to California. In addition to the richly informative texts, the museum has some remarkable artifacts, including a 1909 parade dragon head. (Open Wed.-Sun. noon-4pm.)

Parking is next to impossible during business hours. If you must drive, park your car in SoMa and walk from there. To reach the Financial District take any MUNI Metro line (J, K, L, M, or N) or BART to the Montgomery or Embarcadero station.

Transamerica Pyramid

San Francisco's tallest and most distinctive structure, totally out of scale with the surrounding buildings, is the Transamerica Pyramid at Montgomery St. between Clay and Washington St. (take MUNI bus #15). The Montgomery Block, a four-story, fireproof brick building, once stood in its place. Nicknamed the Monkey Block, the Montgomery's in-house bar lured the likes of Mark Twain, Robert Louis Stevenson, Bret Harte, and Jack London. In the basement a man named Tom Sawyer operated sauna baths that Twain frequented, and in 1856, in one of the city's most notorious murders, newspaper editor James King of William was shot on the building's doorstep over one of his controversial editorials. The Chinese revolutionary Sun Yat-Sen plotted the overthrow of the Manchu Dynasty and wrote the 1911 Chinese constitution in an apartment here.

Nob Hill and Russian Hill

Before the earthquake and fire of 1906, Nob Hill was home to the mansions of the great railroad magnates. Today, Nob Hill remains one of the nation's most prestigious addresses. The streets are lined with many fine buildings, and the aura is that of idle and settled wealth. Sitting atop a hill and peering down upon the *hoi polloi* can be a pleasant afternoon diversion. Nearby Russian Hill is named after Russian sailors who expired during an expedition in the early 1800s and were buried on the southeast crest. At the top of Russian Hill, the notorious **Lombard Street curves,** on Lombard (the crookedest street in the world) between Hyde and Leavenworth St. afford a fantastic view of the city and harbor—that is, if you dare to allow your eyes to stray from the road down this plunge.

Grace Cathedral, 1051 Taylor St. (776-6611), the most immense Gothic edifice in the West, crowns Nob Hill. The castings for its portals are such exact imitations of Ghiberti's on the Baptistry in Florence that they were used to restore the originals. Inside, modern murals mix San Franciscan and national historical events with scenes from the lives of the saints. Visitors should respect the fact that Grace is still used as a house of worship.

Chinatown

The largest Chinese community outside of Asia (over 100,000 people), Chinatown is also the most densely populated of San Francisco's neighborhoods. Chinatown was founded in the 1880s when, after the gold had been dug and the tracks laid, bigotry fueled by unemployment engendered a racist outbreak against what was then termed the "Yellow Peril." In response, Chinese-Americans banded together to protect themselves in a small section of the downtown area. As the city grew, speculators tried to take over the increasingly valuable land, especially after the area was leveled by the 1906 earthquake, but the Chinese were not to be expelled, and Chinatown, which has gradually expanded, remains almost exclusively Chinese. **Grant Avenue** is the most picturesque part of Chinatown.

Although most visitors to Chinatown come for the food, there are other attractions. Watch fortune cookies being shaped by hand in the **Golden Gate Cookie Company,** 56 Ross Alley (781-3956), between Washington and Jackson St., just west of Grant Ave. Nearby **Portsmouth Square,** at Kearny and Washington St., made history in 1848 when Sam Brennan brought the news of the gold strike at Sutter's Mill. Now the square is filled with Chinese men playing lively card games. A stone bridge leads from this square to the **Chinese Culture Center,** 750 Kearny St., 3rd floor (986-1822), which houses exhibits of Chinese-American art and sponsors two walking tours of Chinatown. The Heritage Walk surveys various aspects of life in Chinatown (Sat. 2pm; $12, under 18 $2). The Culinary Walk discusses the preparation of Chinese food. (Wed. 10:30am; $25, under 12 $10. Includes a *dim sum* lunch at Four Seas of Grant Ave.) Both require advance reservations.

At Grant and Bush stands the ornate, dragon-crested **Gateway to Chinatown,** given as a gift by Taiwan in 1969. The dragon motif is continued on the lamp posts that line Chinatown's streets. The founder of the 1st Chinese republic, Dr. Sun Yat-Sen, is immortalized in a 12-ft.-tall statue that stands in St. Mary's Square (at Kearny St., between California and Pine). Some of Chinatown's noteworthy buildings include **Buddha's Universal Church** (at 720 Washington), the **Kong Chow Temple** (at 855 Stockton), and **Old St. Mary's,** behind the statue of Dr. Sun, which was built in 1854 of granite cut in China and which was San Francisco's only cathedral for almost four decades.

North Beach

Proceeding north along Stockton St. or Columbus Ave., there is a gradual transition from supermarkets displaying ginseng to those selling provolone, and from restaurants luring customers with roast ducks in the window to those using *biscotti*. Lying north of Broadway and east of Columbus, North Beach is split in character between the legacy of the bohemian Beatniks who made it their home—Jack Kerouac, Allen Ginsberg, and Lawrence Ferlinghetti among others—and the residents of the traditional Italian neighborhood. Drawn to the area by low rents and cheap bars, the Beats came to national attention when Ferlinghetti's **City Lights Bookstore** published Allen Ginsberg's anguished and ecstatic dream poem *Howl*. Banned in 1956, the book was found "not obscene" after an extended trial, but the resultant publicity turned North Beach into a must-see for curious tourists. City Lights still waxes poetic, though the Beat presence is waning. Through the middle of North Beach runs Broadway, the neon netherworld of pornography purveyors. North Beach is in its most flattering light at night, as the after-dinner, after-show crowd flocks to the area's numerous cafes for a relaxing cappuccino.

Washington Square and Coit Tower

Lying between Stockton and Powell is **Washington Square** (North Beach's *piazza),* a lush lawn edged by trees and watched over by a statue of Benjamin Franklin. Across Filbert to the north of the square is the **Church of St. Peter and St. Paul,** beckoning tired sightseers to an island of quiet in its dark, wooden nave. The fathers present mass in Italian, English, and Cantonese. Mrs. Lillie Hitchcock Coit's most famous gift to the city, **Coit Tower** (274-0203) sits on **Telegraph Hill,** the steep mount from which a semaphore signaled the arrival of ships in Gold Rush days. From the fire-nozzle-shaped top, the spectacular 360° view makes it one of the most romantic spots in the city. (Open daily 10am-5pm; Oct.-May 9am-4pm. Elevator fare $3, seniors $2, ages 6-12 $1, under 6 free. Last ticket sold ½ hr. before closing.) At night, you can watch the city light up for the night from the tower's base.

Fisherman's Wharf

Continuing northward, toward the water, one leaves San Francisco proper and enters tourist limbo. Stretching from Pier 39 in the east to Ghirardelli Square in the west is Fisherman's Wharf, ¾ mi. of porcelain figurines, gifts for lefties, and enough t-shirts to have kept Washington's army snug at Valley Forge. This area is very crowded, very expensive, and despite its blandness there is something to offend almost anyone. The best way go about this is to wake up at 4am, put on a warm sweater, and go down to the piers to see why it's called a fisherman's wharf. You can take in the loading and outfitting of small ships, the animated conversation, the blanket of the morning mist, and the incredible views.

   Tour boats and **ferries** dock just west of Pier 39. The two main tour fleets, the Blue and Gold Fleet and the Red and White Fleet—named after the colors of UC Berkeley and Stanford University respectively—symbolize the long-running rivalry between the two schools. The **Blue and Gold Fleet's** (781-7877) 1¼-hour tours cruise under both the Golden Gate and Bay Bridges, past the Marin hills; past Angel, Alcatraz, and Treasure Islands and the San Francisco skyline on 400-passenger sightseeing boats (begins at 10am; $14, seniors and ages 5-18 $7, military free). The **Red and White Fleet** (546-2700 for reservations, 546-2628 for recorded information within CA; also 800-BAY-CRUISE or 800-229-2784) at Pier 41 offers both tours and ferry rides. The 45-min. Bay Cruise leaves from Piers 41 and 43½ and goes under the Golden Gate Bridge and past Alcatraz ($15, seniors and ages 12-18 $12, ages 5-11 $8; ask about the multi-lingual narratives). In the summer, another 45-min. tour circumnavigates the island; the tour is narrated by a former prison guard ($7.50, over 55 $7, ages 5-11 $4). Ferries from Pier 43½ run to Sausalito ($4.50, ages 5-11 $2.25). Red and White boats also discharge passengers at Alcatraz. For a really great escape, try one of the **sailboat charters.** The *Ruby* (861-2165) departs from the China Basin

Bldg. ($25, under 10 $12.50, with sandwiches; May-Oct. daily, call for times). Tours leave from the Ramp Restaurant on Miraposa St., and reservations are required for sailboat charters. Mind you bring a heavy sweater in summer and a jacket in winter.

Alcatraz

Alcatraz Island is easily visible not only from boats and the waterfront but also from Powell St. Named in 1775 for the *alcatraces* (pelicans) that flocked to it, this former federal prison looms over the San Francisco Bay, 1½ mi. from Fisherman's Wharf. In 1934, Alacatraz was brought under federal purview and used to hold those who had wreaked too much havoc in other prisons. Of the 23 men who attempted to escape, all were recaptured or killed, except for the five "presumed drowned." In 1962, the prison was closed. Alcatraz is currently a part of the **Golden Gate National Recreation Area,** the largest park in an urban area in the United States, administered by the National Park Service. The Red and White Fleet (546-2896) runs boats to Alcatraz from Pier 41. Once on Alcatraz, you can wander by yourself or take a worthwhile audiotape-guided tour, full of clanging chains and the ghosts of prisoners past. (2 hr.; departs every ½ hr. from Pier 41, 9:15am-4:15pm in summer, 9:45am-2:45pm in winter. Fare $5, over 55 $4.50, ages 5-11 $3; tours cost $3 extra, ages 5-11 $1 extra.) Reserve tickets in advance through Ticketron (392-7469) for $1 extra or confront long lines and risk not getting a ride.

Vessels and Chocolate

At the Hyde Street Pier within the **Maritime National Historical Park** floats the *Balclutha* (929-0202), a swift trading vessel that plied the Cape Horn route in the 1880s and 90s and was featured in the first Hollywood version of *Mutiny on the Bounty.* (Open daily 10am-6pm. Admission $3, seniors and under 16 $1.) At Pier 45 you can also board a World War II submarine—the *U.S.S. Pampanito.* (Open daily 9am-9pm; in winter Sun.-Thurs. 9am-6pm, Fri.-Sat. 9am-9pm. $3, seniors and ages 6-12 $1, ages 13-18 $2, under 6 free.)

Finally, the left flank of the wharf area is anchored by shopping malls, the most famous of which is **Ghirardelli Square** (pronounced GEAR-a-deli), 900 N. Point St. (Information booth 775-5500. Open daily 10am-9pm.) The only remains of Ghirardelli's original **chocolate factory** (transformed from a uniform factory in the 1890s by Domingo Ghirardelli's family) now lie in the Clock Tower Basement (771-4903; open daily 10am-midnight). Pricey boutiques now fill the rest of the old factory's red brick buildings, and local musicians and magicians entertain the huddled masses. (Stores open Mon.-Sat. 10am-9pm, Sun. 10am-6pm.)

Marina, Pacific Heights, and Presidio Heights

The Heights

The Marina, Pacific Heights, and the adjoining Presidio Heights are the most sought-after addresses in San Francisco. Centered around Union and Sacramento St., Pacific Heights boasts the greatest number of Victorian buildings in the city. The 1906 earthquake and fire left the Heights area west of Van Ness Ave. unscathed; in 1989 the Heights area was not as lucky, and sustained serious damage. Victorian restoration has become a full-fledged enterprise; consultants determine the original form of fretwork, friezes, fans, columns, corbels, cartouches, pediments, stained glass, rosettes, etc. The **Octagon House,** 2645 Gough St. (441-7512), is currently the headquarters of the National Society of Colonial Dames. The house was built in 1861 with the belief that such architecture would bring good luck to its inhabitants; apparently, they had the good luck to build it. (Free sedate tours 1st Sun. and 2nd and 4th Thurs. of the month 1-4pm.) The **Haas-Lilienthal House,** 2007 Franklin St. (441-3004), is another grand example of Victorian architecture run rampant. (Open Wed. noon-3:15pm, Sun. 11am-4pm. $4, seniors and under 18 $2.) If you prefer shopping to architecture, **Union Street** is the place to be. Between Scott and Webster St., it's chocked with upscale shops, bars, restaurants, and bakeries.

Marina

Down from Pacific Heights toward the bay is the **Marina** district, whose Safeway hosted one of the first (if not *the* first) **supermarket singles' nights** in the country. By the water, **Marina Green** seethes with joggers and walkers and is well-known for spectacularly flown two-line kites. Wear a college sweatshirt. To the west lies the **Palace of Fine Arts,** on Baker St. between Jefferson and Bay St. The strange, domed structure and the two curving colonnades are reconstructed remnants of the 1915 Panama Pacific Exposition, which commemorated the opening of the Panama Canal and signalled San Francisco's recovery from the great earthquake. On summer days performances of Shakespeare are sometimes given in the colonnade section. The domed building houses the **Exploratorium,** 3601 Lyon St. (561-0360; see museums above). The **Wave Organ** is a short walk along the bay from the Exploratorium's main entrance. The organ is activated by the motion of waves and is an inviting place to sit or even meditate to the water's natural *om.*

Near the overdeveloped Fisherman's Wharf lies the commercially restrained **Fort Mason,** at Laguna and Marina. The army's former embarkation facility has been converted into a center for non-profit organizations, and houses many small museums, including those celebrating modern art, folk art, African-American history, Italian and Mexican art, and Sam Shepard.

The Presidio, Golden Gate, and Richmond District

Established in 1776, The **Presidio,** a sprawling army-owned preserve that extends all the way from the Marina in the east to the wealthy Sea Cliff area in the west, provides endless opportunities for perambulating through the trees or on the beach (MUNI bus #28, 29, or 76). Aficionados of military regalia and Presidio history may want to stop at the **Presidio Army Museum** (561-4115), Lincoln Blvd. at Funston Ave. The collection is heavy on guns, old uniforms, and sepia-toned photographs. (Open Tues.-Sun. 10am-4pm. Free.)

Golden Gate Bridge

The Golden Gate Bridge, the rust-colored symbol of the West's bounding confidence, sways above the entrance to San Francisco Bay. Built in 1937 under the direction of chief engineer Joseph Strauss, the bridge is almost indescribably beautiful from any angle on or around it. The bridge's overall length is 8981 ft., the main span 4200 ft. long, and the stolid towers 745 ft. high. Built to swing, the bridge was undamaged by the '89 quake. Just across the bridge, a Vista Point is just that, providing an incredible view of the city.

Lincoln Park

At the northwest extreme of the city, Lincoln Park is the biggest attraction in the **Richmond District.** To reach Lincoln Park, follow Clement St. west to 34th Ave., or Geary Blvd. to Point Lobos Ave. (MUNI bus #1 or 38). The park's newly renovated **California Palace of the Legion of Honor** (750-3659) is modeled after the Colonnade Hôtel de Salm in Paris and houses the city's best collection of European art. The gallery is particularly strong on French art; it includes one of the country's finest Rodin collections, both in plaster and bronze, plus many Impressionist works and two unusual Davids. The grounds also offer a romantic view of the Golden Gate Bridge. Take the **Land's End Path,** running northwest of the cliff edge, for an even better look. A **visitors center** dispenses information on the whiskered wildlife of the cliffs area, as well as on the history of the Cliff House series. (Open Mon.-Tues. and Thurs.-Fri. 11am-5pm, Sat.-Sun. 10am-5pm. Free.)

Golden Gate Park

No visit to San Francisco is complete without an encounter with Golden Gate Park. Frederick Law Olmsted—designer of New York's Central Park—said it couldn't be done when San Francisco's 19th-century elders asked him to build a park to rival

Paris's Bois de Boulogne on their city's western side. But engineer William Hammond Hall and Scottish gardener John McLaren proved him wrong. Hall designed the 1000-acre park—gardens and all—when the land was still just shifting sand dunes, and then constructed a mammoth breakwater along the oceanfront to protect the seedling trees and bushes from the sea's burning spray.

To get to the park from downtown, hop on bus #5 or 21. Bus #44 passes right by the major attractions and serves 6th Ave. to California Ave. to the north and the MUNI Metro to the south. Most of the park is bounded by Fulton St. to the north, Stanyan St. to the east, Lincoln Way to the south, and the Pacific Ocean to the west. The major north-south route through the park is named Park Presidio By-Pass Dr. in the north and Cross-Over Dr. in the south. The **Panhandle,** a thin strip of land bordered by Fell and Oak St. on the north and south respectively, is the oldest part of the park. Originally the "carriage entrance," it contains the most elderly trees and shoots some greenery into the veins of Haight-Ashbury. **Park Headquarters** (556-2920), where you can procure information and maps, is in McLaren Lodge at Fell and Stanyan St., on the eastern edge of the park (open Mon.-Fri. 8am-5pm).

There are three magnificent **museums,** the California Academy of Sciences, the M. H. de Young and Asian Art Museums, in the park, all in one large complex on the eastern side between South and John F. Kennedy Dr., where 9th Ave. meets the park (see museums above).

Gardens

Despite its sandy past, flowers bloom all around, particularly in spring and summer. The **Conservatory of Flowers** (666-7200), erected in 1879, is the oldest building in the park, allegedly constructed in Ireland and shipped from Dublin via Cape Horn. The delicate and luminescent structure houses scintillating displays of tropical plants, including the very rare Masdevallia and Dracula orchids. (Open daily 9am-6pm; Nov.-April daily 9am-5pm. $1.50, seniors and ages 6-12 75¢, under 6 free. Free daily 9:30-10am and 5:30-6pm, 1st Wed. of month and holidays.) The **Strybing Arboretum** (661-1316), on Lincoln Way at 9th Ave., southwest of the academy, is home to 5000 varieties of plants. The **Garden of Fragrance** is designed especially for the visually impaired; the labels are in Braille and the plants are chosen specifically for their texture and scent. (Open Mon.-Fri. 9am-4:30pm, Sat.-Sun. 10am-5pm. Tours daily 1:30pm, and Thurs.-Sun. 10:30am. Free.) Near the Music Concourse on a path off South Dr., the **Shakespeare Garden** contains almost every flower and plant ever mentioned by the herbalist of Avon. Plaques with the relevant quotations are hung on the back wall, and there's a map to help you find your favorite hyacinths and cowslips (open daily 9am-dusk, in winter closed Mon.; free).

Created for the 1894 Mid-Winter Exposition, the elegant **Japanese Tea Garden** is a serene collection of dark wooden buildings, small pools, graceful footbridges, carefully pruned trees, and plants. Watch the giant carp circle the central pond. (Open daily 9am-6:30pm; Oct.-Feb. 8:30am-5:30pm. Admission $2, seniors and ages 6-12 $1, under 6 free. Free 1st and last ½ hr. and on holidays.)

At the extreme northwestern corner of the park, the **Dutch Windmill** turns and turns again. The powerhouse, built in 1905 to pump irrigation water for the nascent park, measures 114 ft. from sail to sail. Rounding out the days of yore is the **carousel** (c. 1912), which is accompanied by a $50,000 Gebruder band organ. (Open daily 10am-5pm; Oct.-May Wed.-Sun. 10am-4pm. Admission $1, ages 6-12 25¢.)

Herd of **buffalo?** A dozen of the shaggy beasts roam a spacious paddock at the western end of John F. Kennedy Dr., near 39th Ave.

Haight-Ashbury

The 60s live in Haight-Ashbury. The Haight willfully preserves an era that many seek to experience, others desire to forget, and some can't remember. Originally a quiet lower-middle-class neighborhood, the Haight's large Victorian houses—perfect for communal living—and the district's proximity to the University of San Francisco drew a massive hippie population in the mid- and late 1960s. LSD—possession of which was not yet a felony—pervaded the neighborhood. The hippie voyage reached its apogee in 1966-67 when Janis Joplin, the Grateful Dead, and Jefferson Airplane all lived and made music in the neighborhood. During the 1967 "Summer of Love," young people from across the country converged on the grassy Panhandle of Golden Gate Park for the celebrated "be-ins." Despite recent gentrification, Haight-Ashbury remains exciting. Many of the bars and restaurants are remnants of that past era, with faded auras, games in the back rooms, and live-in regulars.

Haight Street

Walk down Haight St. and poke your head into the stores. With all the vintage clothing shops, you're likely to think you've landed in your grandparents' attic. **Aardvark's Odd Ark,** 1501 Haight St. (621-3141), at Ashbury, has an immense selection of used new wave jackets, music in the background, and prices that will take you back in time. (Open Sat.-Mon. and Thurs. 11am-9pm, Wed. 11am-7pm, Fri. 11am-8pm.) **Wasteland,** 1660 Haight St. (863-3150), is another used clothing store and is deserving of notice, if only for its wonderful facade and window displays. (Open Mon.-Fri. 11am-6pm, Sat. 11am-7pm, Sun. noon-6pm.) The **Global Family Networking Center,** 1665 Haight St. (864-1978), contains a cafe, market, and global awareness. The rooms at the **Red Victorian Inn** (or just "Red Vic") could be a museum but for the lack of velvet ropes and "Do Not Touch" signs (see Accommodations). Resembling a dense green mountain in the middle of the Haight, **Buena Vista Park** has a predictably bad reputation. Enter at your own risk, and once inside, be prepared for those doing their own thing.

Mission District and Castro Street

Castro Street and the Mission District enjoy the city's best weather, often while fog blankets nearby Twin Peaks. The area is home to two thriving cultures: the gay community around Castro St. and the Hispanic community to the east.

Castro Street

As AIDS has taken its toll, the scene has mellowed considerably from the wild days of the 70s, but **Castro Street** remains a proud and assertive emblem of gay liberation, where men display affection for each other publicly and without fear. In the Mission District, the colorful murals along 24th St. reflect the rich cultural influence of Latin America. The best way to see Castro Street is to wander, peering into shops or stepping into bars. Two popular hangouts are **Café Flor,** 2298 Market St. (621-8579), and **Café San Marco,** 2367 Market St. (861-3846).

Down the street, the **Names Project,** 2362 Market St. (863-1966), sounds a more somber note. This is the headquarters of an organization that has accumulated over 12,000 3 ft. x 6 ft. panels for the AIDS Memorial Quilt, including ones from 30 other countries. Each panel is a memorial to a person who has died of AIDS. In addition to housing the project's administration, the building contains a workshop where victims' friends and relatives create panels. Several panels are always on display. (Open Mon.-Fri. 10am-10pm, Sat.-Sun. noon-8pm.)

Mission Dolores

Celebrating its 201st birthday this year, Mission Dolores, at 16th and Dolores St. in the old heart of San Francisco, is reputed to be the oldest building in the city. The mission was founded in 1776 by Father Junípero Serra and, like San Francisco itself, was named in honor of St. Francis of Assisi. The mission, however, sat close to a marsh known as *Laguna de Nuestra Señora de los Dolores* (Laguna of Our Lady of Sorrows) and despite Serra's wishes, gradually became known as *Misión de los Dolores*. Exotic bougainvillae, poppies, and birds-of-paradise bloom in the cemetery, which was featured in Hitchcock's *Vertigo*. (Open daily 9am-4:30pm; Nov.-April 9am-4pm; $1). Like the Castro, the Mission is best seen by daytime strolling.

West of Castro, the peninsula swells with several large hills. On rare fogless nights, you can get a breathtaking view of the city from **Twin Peaks,** between Portola Dr., Market St., and Clarendon Ave., with a three-masted radio tower that can be seen from all around town. The Spanish called Twin Peaks *"Los Pechos de la Choca"* (the Breasts of the Indian Maiden). West of the peaks is the **San Francisco Zoo** (753-7061), on Sloat Blvd. at the Pacific Ocean. The zoo is especially strong on the closest relatives of *Homo sapiens*; watch out, they're often *on the loose.* (Open daily 10am-5pm. Admission $6.50, seniors and ages 12-16 $3, under 12 free.)

Civic Center

The municipal heart of the city and a bureaucrat's wet dream, the vast Civic Center is a collection of massive buildings arranged around two expansive plazas. The largest gathering of *Beaux Arts* architecture in the U.S. is centered on the palatial **San Francisco City Hall,** which was modeled after St. Peter's Cathedral. At the eastern end is the United Nations Plaza and public library, at the western end the Opera House and Museum of Modern Art. Parking is relatively easy on streets around the Civic Center. To get there by public transportation, take MUNI Metro to the Civic Center/City Hall stop or MUNI bus #5, 16X, 19, 21, 26, 42, 47, or 49. Or take the J, K, L, M, or N lines to Van Ness station, or Golden Gate Transit bus #10, 20, 50, or 70.

There are two ways to see the Civic Center: by day, for the architecture and museums, and by night, for the performing arts. The day show is the **San Francisco Museum of Modern Art,** 401 Van Ness Ave. (see museums above). In the evenings, the **Louise M. Davies Symphony Hall,** 201 Van Ness Ave. (431-5400; box office open 9:30am-5:30pm), at Grove St., rings with the sounds of the San Francisco Symphony. Its acoustics are poor, and 10 years after its opening, baffled engineers still tinker with seating arrangements and baffles. (Seats in the chorus benches behind the orchestra cost $5 and are available 1 hr. before performances, except, of course, when a chorus is performing.) Next door, the **War Memorial Opera House,** 301 Van Ness Ave. (864-3330), at Grove St., hosts the well-regarded San Francisco Opera Company (864-3330; box office open Mon.-Fri. 10am-6pm) and the San Francisco Ballet. (621-3838 for info. Charge-by-Phone 762-BASS or 762-2277. Open Mon.-Sat. noon-6pm. Any $5 SRO tickets go on sale 2 hr. before the performance.) The Civic Center has two other theaters: the **Orpheum,** 1192 Market St. (474-3800), tends to draw flashy overblown shows, while the smaller **Herbst Auditorium,** 401 Van Ness Ave. (392-4400; open Mon.-Sat. noon-7:30pm), at McAllister St., hosts string quartets, solo singers, and ensembles. (Tours of the symphony hall, opera house, and Herbst Auditorium leave every ½-hr. from the Grove St. entrance to Davies Hall Mon. 10am-2:30pm. Tours of only Davies Hall Wed. 1:30 and 2:30pm, Sat. 12:30 and 1:30pm. $3, seniors and students $2. For information, call 552-8338.)

Nihonmachi (Japantown)

Centered around the aptly named **Japan Center,** Nihonmachi encompasses an area three blocks long by three blocks wide. The smallish neighborhood 1.1 mi. from downtown San Francisco is bounded on its east side by Fillmore St., on its west side by Laguna St., by Bush St. to the north, and by the Geary Expressway to the south. Similar to the Tokyo Ginza, the five-acre Japan Center at Post and Buchanan (MUNI buses #2, 3, and 4) includes Japanese *udon* houses, sushi bars, and a massage center and bathhouse. Japan gave the **Peace Pagoda,** a magnificent 100-ft. tall, five-tiered structure which graces the heart of Japantown, as a gift to the 12,000 Japanese-Americans of San Francisco .

ENTERTAINMENT

Recreation in San Francisco is often liberation, as it should be. Relaxed bars, wild clubs, serious cinema houses, and provocative bookstores assertively satisfy San Franciscans. For spiritual and physical rejuvenation before (and likely after) experiencing the city's nightlife, women should plunge into the waters at **Osento,** 955

Valencia St. (282-6333), between 20th and 21st St., a women's bathhouse in the Mission with wet and dry sauna, jacuzzi, and pool. (Sliding door fee $7-11, unlimited time. $1 towel rental, $1 locker deposit. Open daily 1pm-1am.)

Sports enthusiasts should check the San Francisco Giants and 49ers schedules at **Candlestick Park** (467-8000), located 8 mi. south of the city via the Bayshore Freeway (U.S. 101). The Sights section above also discusses many entertainment opportunities. (Sights: Civic Center has information on ballet, opera, and symphony.)

In late February America's largest Chinese community throws the **Chinese New Year Celebration** (982-3000) to celebrate the Year of the Dog (4692 on the lunar calendar) with cultural festivities, a parade, and the crowning of Miss Chinatown USA. In late June, people come from all over the country to join the **Lesbian-Gay Freedom Parade** (864-3733). The celebration culminates in a tremendous parade starting at Castro and ending at Market.

Call the **Entertainment Hotline** at 391-2001 or 391-2002. The *Bay Guardian* always has a thorough listing of dance clubs and live music.

Clubs

The Paradise Lounge, 1501 Folsom St. (861-6906). With 3 stages, 2 floors, 5 bars, and up to 5 different bands a night, this club is one of those unique places where you feel equally comfortable in spike heels or Birkenstocks. Pool tables upstairs. Open daily 3pm-2am. Must be 21.

DNA Lounge, 375 11th St. (626-1409), at Harrison. Both live music and dancing. The best night for dancing is Wed. Funk, house, and soul. Cover varies with the performer but usually doesn't exceed $10. Open daily until 3:30am. Must be 21.

Perry's, 1944 Union St. (922-9022). San Francisco's most famous pick-up junction is a comfortable, vaguely old-fashioned place: lackadaisical by day, hopping at night. Large draft beer $3.25. Food until midnight. Open daily 7:30am-1am.

Club DV8, 540 Howard St. (777-1419). 3 floors of sheer dance mania. One of those "in places to be." For the best dancing, stick to the 3rd floor "osmosis." Cover $10 on Sat. and Sun., $5 otherwise. Open Wed.-Sun. 8pm-4am.

The Holy Cow, 1531 Folsom (621-6087), between 11th and 12th. A life-size plastic cow marks the spot. Formerly the Stud's location, this bar/dance club tends to attract the trendy mainstream with music to match, but the crowded bar has an energetic atmosphere. No cover. Tough carding. Open Tues.-Sun. 9am-2am.

The Mad Dog in the Fog, 530 Haight St. (626-7279). Very relaxed. Guinness served. Bands on Sun. Open mike on Tues. Dancing (with DJ) to soul and funk on Wed. No cover. Open daily 11:30pm-2am.

Gay and Lesbian Clubs

Gay nightlife in San Francisco flourishes. Most of the popular bars can be found in the city's two traditionally gay areas—the Castro (around the intersection of Castro St. and Market St.; see Sights) and Polk St. (several blocks north of Geary St.). Most "straight" dance clubs feature at least one gay night a week. Also consult the *San Francisco Bay Guardian* or friendly staffers at the **Gay Switchboard** (841-6224).

The Stud, 399 9th St. (863-6623). A classic gay club with great dance music. Mon. night is funk night. Wed. night is oldies night featuring cheap beer. $1 cover Wed., $3 cover Thurs.-Sun. Open Sun.-Thurs. 5pm-2am, Fri.-Sat. after hours.

The Kennel Club, 628 Divisadero (931-1914). "The Box," on Thurs. night, offers funk and soul for gays. The clientele is mixed all week long. Tea Dance (a S.F. tradition) Sun. 6am-9pm. Open Sun.-Thurs. 9pm-2am.

The Quake, 1748 Haight St. (668-6006). Site of the International Gay Free Style Dance Competition in mid-July. Tea Dance every Sun., free 5-7pm, $5 afterwards. Every Sat. is Grateful Dead Day, 1-5pm. $2 MGD pints, $1.50 Schnapps. Cover $5-7. Open 8pm-2am. Must be 21.

End Up, 401 6th St. (543-7700), at Harrison. Tea Dance Sun. 9am-6pm. Fri. night is men's night. Sat. night is women's night. Cover $4 (except for Tea Dance). Open 9pm-2am, until 3:30am sometimes.

The Phoenix, 482 Castro St. (552-6827), at Market St. International Gay Dance Bar. Non-stop dancing. DJ Michael and DJ Bobby Keith play disco tunes and house music. No cover. Open 8pm-2:30am. Must be 21.

■■■ BERKELEY

Almost 30 years ago, Mario Savio climbed on top of a police car and launched Berkeley's free speech movement. Today, Berkeley is still a national symbol of political activism and social iconoclasm, and Telegraph Avenue—the Champs Elysées of the 60s—remains the home of street-corner soothsayers, funky bookstores, aging hippies, countless cafés, and itinerant street musicians. The site of the country's most renowned public university, Berkeley is as well known for its street people and chefs as for its political cadres and academics. Chez Panisse is believed to have originated the elusive concept of California cuisine. Northwest of campus, the shopping area around Chez Panisse has been termed the "Gourmet Ghetto" because of the abundance of voluptuous ingredients hawked there. The rest of the city is blanketed by stylish clothing boutiques and specialty stores.

PRACTICAL INFORMATION

Campus Emergency: 9-911 from campus phone. 642-3333 otherwise. 24 hrs.
Visitors Information: Chamber of Commerce, 1834 University Ave. (549-7000), at Martin Luther King Jr. Way. Open Mon.-Fri. 9am-noon and 1-4pm. **U.C. Berkeley Visitor Center,** 101 University Hall, 2200 University Ave. Campus Calendar (642-2294). Open Mon.-Fri. 8am-5pm.
Bay Area Rapid Transit (BART): 465-2278. The Berkeley station is at Shattuck Ave. and Center St., close to the western edge of the university, about 7 blocks from the Student Union. $1.80 to downtown San Francisco.
Alameda County Transit (AC Transit): 800-559-4636 or 839-2882. Buses #14, 40, 43, and 51 all run from the Berkeley BART stop to downtown Oakland, via M.L. King Jr. Way, Telegraph Ave., Shattuck Ave., and College Ave. respectively. City bus fare $1.10, ages 5-16 $1, seniors and disabled 40¢. Transfers 25¢. Bus F runs to San Francisco Transbay Terminal (5:50am-midnight every ½ hr.; $2.50, seniors $1.25, ages 5-16 $2).
Transportation Information: Berkeley TRiP, 2033 Center St. (643-7665). Information on public transport, biking, and carpooling. Mostly local transportation. Open Mon.-Wed. and Fri. 8:30am-5:30pm, Thurs. 9am-6pm.
Taxi: Yellow A I Cab (843-1111). 24 hrs.
Bike Rental: Backroads, 1516 5th St. (527-1555). Bicycles $17.50 per ½-day, $35 per full day. $20 per 2nd full day, $15 per 3rd full day, and $10 per day after the 7th full day. Bicycles come fully equipped with helmet, lock, water bottle holder, spare tube, and handlebar bag. Open Mon.-Sat. 9am-6pm, Sun. 11am-4pm.
Rape Hotline: 845-RAPE/845-7273. 24 hrs. **U.C. Berkeley Multicultural Bisexual Lesbian Gay Alliance:** 642-6942.
Post Office: 2000 Allston Way (649-3100). Open Mon.-Fri. 8:30am-5pm, Sat. 10am-2pm. **ZIP Code:** 94704.
Area Code: 510.

Berkeley is sandwiched between a series of ridges to the east and San Francisco Bay to the west. The **University of California** campus stretches into the hills, but most of its buildings are in the westernmost section, near the BART. **Telegraph Avenue,** which runs south from the Student Union, is the spiritual center of town. The **downtown** area contains several businesses as well as the public library and central post office. The **Gourmet Ghetto** encompasses the area along Shattuck Ave. and Walnut St. between Virginia and Rose St. West of campus and by the bay lies the **Fourth Street Center.** Avoid walking the streets of Berkeley alone at night.

Construction and congestion on the freeway combine to make driving from San Francisco a bad idea. Crossing the bay by **BART** is quick and easy, and both the university and Telegraph Ave. are short walks from the station. Alternatively, the free university **Humphrey-Go-BART shuttle** (642-5149) connects the BART station with the central and eastern portions of campus (Sept.-June Mon.-Fri. 7am-7pm every 12 min., except on university holidays).

ACCOMMODATIONS

It is surprisingly difficult to sleep cheaply in Berkeley. There are no hostels, and clean, cheap motels are disconcertingly lacking. Most of the city's hotels are flophouses; spaces suitable for safe crashing are few. The **Bed and Breakfast Network** (540-5123) coordinates 15 B&Bs in the East Bay; some offer reasonable rates.

YMCA, 2001 Allston Way (848-6800), at Milvia St. Men over 17 only. No membership required. Registration daily 8am-noon. Check-out 11:30am-noon. No curfew. 14-day max. stay. Small rooms $22, medium rooms $23. Key deposit $2. Prices include tax and use of the pool and basic fitness facilities.

University of California Housing Office, 2700 Hearst Ave. (642-5925), in Stern Hall. Fairly spacious and clean dorm rooms with large windows and phones available in summer to "university visitors" (i.e. everybody). Call ahead. Open daily 7am-11pm. Someone on duty 11pm-7am. Singles $34, doubles $44.

California Motel, 1461 University Ave. (848-3840), 2 blocks from the North Berkeley BART station, 7 blocks west of campus. Some rooms are nicer than others. Check-out noon. Singles and doubles $32, 2 beds $40. Key deposit $1.

FOOD

While most of Berkeley's highbrow eats cost about as much as the highbrow education, with a little imagination and timing budget travelers can fill their stomachs affordably. For information about local culinary delights, consult *Bayfood* (652-6115), available free in Berkeley's cafes and restaurants. For reasonably priced, tasty fare, head downtown to **Shattuck Avenue** or **Solano Avenue.**

Blondie's Pizza, 2340 Telegraph Ave. (548-1129). Even though the 'za is better at Zachary's, you must stop at this Berkeley institution. Employees wear "Make Pizza, Not War" t-shirts. Consume Dagwood-sized slices of greasy, cheesy pizza for only $1.25. Daily special $1.75. Open Mon.-Thurs. 10:30am-1am, Fri.-Sat. 10:30am-2am, Sun. noon-midnight.

Café Intermezzo (849-4592), Telegraph Ave. at Haste. The ENORMOUS helpings of salad served with fresh bread distinguish this café from the multitude of others along Telegraph. A combination sandwich and salad ($4.75) is enough to keep you busy all day. Sandwiches $4.25. Open Mon.-Fri. 10:30am-9pm.

Zachary's, 1853 Solano Ave. (525-5950). Some deem Zachary's Chicago-style pizza the best in the Bay Area. A small chicken pizza costs $12.50, but serves 2-3 people. Open Sun.-Thurs. 11am-10pm, Fri.-Sat. 11am-10:30pm.

Liu's Kitchen, 1593 Solano Ave. (525-8766). Ideal for vegetarians or omnivores on a budget. Lunch dishes ($4-5, 11:30am-2pm) include the soup of the day and fortune cookies. Open Mon.-Tues. and Thurs. 11:30am-9:30pm, Wed. 11:30am-9pm, Fri.-Sat. 11:30am-10pm, Sun. 3-9:30pm.

Long Life Vegi House, 2129 University Ave. (845-6072). Tasty and innovative Chinese cooking, generous portions. No red meat. Vegetarian plates $4.39, seafood plates $4.15. Brunch Sat.-Sun. 11:30am-3pm. Open daily 11:30am-9:30pm.

The Blue Nile, 2525 Telegraph Ave. (540-6777). Authentic Ethiopian food in a dark, rich setting. Beaded curtains separate the different booths. Waitresses wear traditional gowns. Wide variety of vegetarian dishes. Lunch around $5, dinner $6-7.50. Open Mon.-Sat. 11:30am-10pm, Sun. 4-10pm.

The Cheese Board Collective, 1504 Shattuck Ave. (549-3183). A pillar of the Gourmet Ghetto. Fantastic selection of a few hundred different cheeses; add a few to the excellent French bread for a great picnic. 10% discount for customers over 60, 15% for over 70, and so on. Open Tues.-Fri. 10am-6pm, Sat. 10am-5pm.

SIGHTS

In 1868, the private College of California and the public Agricultural, Mining, and Mechanical Arts College coupled to give birth to the **University of California.** Pass through **Sather Gate** (a site of celebrated student sit-ins) into **Sproul Plaza** (another such site) and enter the university's world of open minds, relaxed atmosphere, and rigorous intellectual pursuits. The campus is bounded on the south by Bancroft Way, the west by Oxford St., the north by Hearst Ave., and the east by a vast parkland. The staff at the **Visitor Information Center,** 101 University Hall, 2200 University Ave. (642-5215; open Mon.-Fri. 8am-5pm), provides free maps and information booklets. (Campus tours 2 hr. Mon., Wed., Fri. 10am and 1pm.)

The most dramatic campus attraction is **Sather Tower** (much better known as the **Campanile,** Italian for "bell tower"), a 1914 monument to Berkeley benefactor Jane Krom Sather. It was created by campus architect John Galen Howard, who designed it after the clock tower in Venice's St. Mark's Square. You can ride to the observation level of the 307-ft. tower for a stupendous view (50¢). The tower's 61-bell carillon is played most weekdays at 7:50am, noon, and 6pm.

The **University Art Museum (UAM),** 2626 Bancroft Way (642-0808), holds a diverse and enticing permanent collection. 1994 exhibits include "Faces of the Gods: Art and Altars of the Black Atlantic World" (with Brazilian and Cuban altars influenced by four African cultures) in the fall, and "Passionate Visions of the American South: Self-Taught Artists from 1940 to the Present" (very funky sculptures) in the spring. Within the museum, the **Pacific Film Archives (PFA)** (642-1124), with one of the nation's largest film libraries, is a uniquely rich museum of cinematic art. (Museum open Wed.-Sun. 11am-5pm. Admission $5; students, seniors, and ages 6-17 $4. Free Thurs. and Sat. 11am-noon. PFA shows films in the evening.)

The **Lawrence Hall of Science** (642-5132), a concrete octagon standing above the northeast corner of campus, is one of the finest science museums in the Bay Area. Exhibits stress learning science through the hands-on use of everyday objects. The courtyard offers a spectacular view of the Bay, a DNA molecule, a whale for children to climb on, and stargazing workshops on clear Saturday evenings. Take bus #8 from the Berkeley BART station. (Open Mon.-Fri. 10am-4:30pm, Sat.-Sun. 10am-5pm. Admission $5; seniors, students, and ages 7-18 $4, ages 3-6 $2.)

The exhibits at **Bancroft Library,** in the center of campus across from the *Campanile,* change frequently and range from California history to folio editions of Shakespeare's plays. A gold nugget—purported to be the first one plucked from Sutter's Mill, and therefore the catalyst for the 1849 Gold Rush—is displayed in the library, as is the corroded bronze plaque left by Sir Francis Drake in the 16th century, claiming California for England. The immense stacks (7 million volumes strong) are open to the public. (Open Mon.-Fri. 9am-5pm, Sat. 1-5pm. Free.)

The **Botanical Gardens** (642-3343) in Strawberry Canyon contain over 10,000 varieties of plant life. Berkeley's Mediterranean summer, moderated by coastal fog, provides an outstanding setting (open daily 9am-5pm; free). For a display of roses unlike any you've ever seen, visit the **Berkeley Rose Garden** on Euclid Ave. at Eunice St., north of campus. Laid out by the WPA during the Depression, the garden spills from one terrace to another in a vast semicircular amphitheater. You can see Marin County and the Golden Gate Bridge from the far end (May-Sept. dawn-dusk).

Noteworthy museums and architectural achievements also exist outside of Berkeley's campus. The **Judah Magnes Museum,** 2911 Russell St. (849-2710), displays one of the West Coast's leading collections of Judaica (open Sun.-Thurs. 10am-4pm; free). The **Julia Morgan Theater,** 2640 College Ave. (box office 845-8542), is housed in a beautiful former church designed by its namesake and constructed of dark redwood and Douglas fir. Notable for its graceful and unusual mix of materials, this is regarded by some as Morgan's *pièce de résistance.*

After visiting the ever-tumultuous **People's Park,** relax in the simulated Japanese interior of the **Takara Sake Tasting Room,** 708 Addison St. (540-8250), at 4th St.

You can request a sample of several varieties, all made with California rice. A promotional film on *sake* brewing is shown on request (open daily noon-6pm; free).

ENTERTAINMENT AND NIGHTLIFE

The university offers a number of entertainment options. Hang out with procrastinating students at the **Student Union** (642-4636). **The Underground,** comprised of a ticket office, an arcade, bowling alleys, and a pool table, is run from a central big blue desk (642-3825; open Mon.-Fri. 8am-6pm, Sat. 10am-6pm; in winter Mon.-Fri. 8am-10pm, Sat. 10am-6pm). The **Bear's Lair,** a student pub with live music on Thursday and Friday, is next door at 2425 Bancroft (843-0373; open Mon.-Thurs. noon-midnight, Fri. 11am-8pm; hours vary in summer, usually Sat.-Wed. 11am-6pm). The **CAL Performances Ticket Office,** at the north corner of Zellerbach Hall (642-9988; open Mon.-Fri. 10am-5:30pm, Sat. 10am-2pm), is Berkeley's place to get the lowdown on and purchase tickets for concerts, plays, and movies.

Bars

Blakes, 2367 Telegraph Ave. (848-0886), at Durant. Named "best bar in Berkeley" by the *Daily Californian,* Blake's has 3 stories, 2 happy hours (sometimes), and one classic-packed 100-CD jukebox. Dancing on Tues. and Wed. at "The Cartoon Club." Ice-cream drinks and potato skins. Beverages start at $2. Cover $3-6. Must be 21. Open Mon.-Sat. 11:30am-2am, Sun. 4pm-2am.

Jupiter, 2181 Shattuck Ave. (843-8277), across the street from the BART station. New, and popular among Berkelians. Table-bowling, beer garden, and pizza. International beers on tap including Anchor Porter ($2.75 per pint) and *Hubsch Brau* pilsner ($3.25 per pint). Open Mon.-Fri. 11:30am-1am, Sat. 3pm-1am.

Spats, 1974 Shattuck Ave. (841-7225), in the Gourmet Ghetto. Locals, students, and professors enjoy the warmth provided by the welcoming staff, the original drinks (e.g. Borneo Fog Cutter), and the exquisite surroundings. The stuffed deer and Roman soldier are joined by an autographed poster of Walt Disney, antique mirrors, Chinese parasols, and downy velvet furniture. Order (drinks $2) from the 8-page drink menu. Food $6-10. Open Mon.-Fri. 11:30am-2am, Sat.-Sun. 4pm-2am.

Café Bottega, 2311 Telegraph Ave. (845-9114), a block from the Berkeley campus. An alternative, punkish, liberated, open-minded place. Rumor has it that some Berkeley students are too intimidated by the rockin' local regulars to enter. Jazz is always playing. Fresh pastries ($1) and pasta salads ($3). Cappuccino $1.10 each. Open daily 7am-midnight.

■■■ MARIN COUNTY

Home to Jerry Garcia, Dana Carvey, and 560 acres of spectacular redwood forest, Marin County (ma-RIN) boasts a bizarre blend of outstanding natural beauty, trendiness, liberalism, and wealth. The richest county in the West has grown up since the 1979 movie *The Serial* mocked its directionless, pot-smoking, hot-tubbing pre-Yuppies; Marinites love their real estate values as much as they cherish their open space and organic food. Neighboring communities grumble about Marin's excesses—most notably the $350 million oil stock fund left to the county by the late Mrs. Beryl Buck, for which many say Marin has little use—but Marin residents will tell you there's no hypocrisy in their indulgent and eco-conscious habits. Life is just *better* in Marin. If you can afford to stay, you may never leave.

Practical Information Marin was not designed for the wheel-less. Get your own four wheels at **Budget,** 20 Bellam Blvd. (457-4282), in San Rafael. $27 per day, unlimited mi.; they'll even rent to those 21-25 at no extra charge. If you don't have a car, and even if you do, you'll want a bike on Pt. Reyes Seashore. Pick up your two wheels at **Wheel Escapes,** 1000 Magnolia Ave., Larkspur (461-6903); Mon.-Fri. bikes are $5 per hr., $21 per day. There is public transport here for those willing to wait. **Golden Gate Transit** (453-2100) has daily bus service between San Francisco and Marin County, as well as local service in Marin. Buses #10, 20, 30, and 50 provide service from San Francisco's Transbay Terminal. Buses #65 and 24 run out to Pt. Reyes and Samuel P. Taylor State Park ($2 into Sausalito, $4 to West Marin). Info on the County dispenses from **Marin County Chamber of Commerce,** 30 N. San Pedro Rd. #150 (472-7470), open Mon.-Fri. 9:30am-4:30pm. For outdoors info, contact the **Point Reyes National Seashore Headquarters** (663-1092), Bear Valley Rd., ½-mi. west of Olema, which has the dope on wilderness permits, maps, and campsite reservations. (Open Mon.-Fri. 9am-5pm, Sat.-Sun. 8am-5pm.) The Marin County **area code** is 415.

The Marin peninsula is an inverted triangle on the north end of San Francisco Bay, connected to the city via the Golden Gate Bridge. At the extreme southeastern tip of Marin lies **Sausalito.** Initially a fishing center, the city has lost its sea-dog days to a bevy of retail boutiques. The eastern, bay side of the county cradles the larger settlements **Larkspur, San Rafael, Terra Linda, Ignacio,** and **Novato.** West Marin is more rural, with rolling hills and fog-bound coastal valleys. **Rte. 1,** easily the nation's most beautiful highway, runs through **Bolinas, Olema, Inverness,** and **Pt. Reyes National Seashore** (from south to north). If you're traveling by car, fill up in town before you head out to west Marin, where gasoline can cost 30¢ per gallon more.

Accommodations and Camping An ideal escape from San Francisco, the **Golden Gate Youth Hostel (HI/AYH)** (331-2777), portals in the Marin Headlands 6 mi. south of Sausalito and 10 mi. from downtown. The fit among those without cars can take the bus (#2, 10, 20) to Alexander Ave., then make a 4½-mi. uphill hike to the hostel. The hostel is equipped with a game room, kitchen, and laundry facilities. (Check-in 7:30-9:30am and 4:30pm-12:30am. Curfew 12:30am. Members and non-members $9. Linen rental $1. Reservations suggested in summer—those without, show up early.) You're more likely to get a last-minute room at the **Point Reyes Hostel (HI/AYH)** (663-8811), off Limantour Rd. To get there, take the Seashore exit west from Rte. 1, then Bear Valley Rd. to Limantour Rd. and drive 6 mi. Hiking, wildlife, birdwatching, and Limantour Beach are all within walking distance, but the hostel itself, on a spectacular site, is a 6-mi. trek into the park. Buy groceries in Inverness or Pt. Reyes Station before dinner; the hostel has a kitchen. (Registration 4:30-9:30pm. Members and nonmembers $9. Sleep sheet and towel $1 each.)

Samuel P. Taylor State Park (488-9897), on Sir Francis Drake Blvd., 15 mi. west of San Rafael, is the best camping in Marin, with shady sites in a forested setting. The park has 60 sites ($14) with hot showers (25¢ for 5 min.). Hiker/Biker sites are also available for $2 per person. (7-day max stay. Reservations through MISTIX 800-444-7275 necessary Apr.-Oct.) There are also four campgrounds (accessible by foot) on the national seashore in the southern, inner cape portion of Pt. Reyes. All are fairly rough, with pit toilets, firepits, and tap water, and require permits from Seashore Headquarters. (Max. stay of 4 nights per visit. All sites are free.)

Sights and Activities The undeveloped, fog-shrouded hills just to the west of the Golden Gate Bridge comprise the **Marin Headlands,** oddly populated by abandoned machine gun nests, missile sites, and soldiers' quarters, now converted into picnic spots, a hostel (the Golden Gate Youth Hostel), and the **Marine Mammal Center** (open daily 10am-4pm), which offers a sobering look at the rehabilitation of beached marine mammals. Nearly all of the headlands are open to hikers, and camping is allowed in designated areas. The vista from the headlands back over the bridge to San Francisco is arguably the most spectacular in the Bay Area.

Muir Woods National Monument, a 560-acre stand of primeval coastal redwoods, is located about 5 mi. west along the Panoramic Hwy. off U.S. 101. The centuries-old massive redwoods are shrouded in soft slanting sunlight, and an eerie silence reigns. Wildlife in the ancient forest is shy, and much of the action occurs 150 ft. above your head in the forest canopy. (Open daily 8am-sunset.) The **visitors center** (388-2595) is near the entrance and keeps the same hours as the monument.

Adjacent to Muir Woods is the isolated, largely undiscovered, and utterly beautifu **Mount Tamalpais State Park** (pronounced tam-ull-PIE-us). This park is favored b locals, many of whom consider it much more interesting than Muir Woods. Th heavily forested park has a number of challenging trails that lead to the top of M **Tam,** the highest peak in the county, and to a natural stone amphitheater. Th mountain bike was invented in this park, and hence has a number of demandin trails. Also in the park is **Stinson Beach,** a local favorite for sunbathing (at Red Roc Beach, ½-mi. north, clothing is optional). The park opens ½ hr. before sunrise an closes ½ hr. after sunset. On weekends, bus #63 runs from Mt. Tam Ranger Statio (commonly called Partoll Ranger Station) to Stinson Beach and back.

Encompassing 100 mi. of coastline along most of the western side of Marin, th **Point Reyes National Seashore** juts audaciously into the Pacific from the easter end of the submerged Pacific Plate. Sir Francis Drake Blvd. runs from San Rafac through Olema, where it crosses Rte. 1, all the way to Pt. Reyes itself. Here the inf; mous San Andreas Fault comes to an end. The point's remote position brings heav fog and strong winds in winter; in summer an explosion of colorful wildflower attracts crowds of tourists to gawk at it all, but with hundreds of miles of trails it possible to escape the crowds and gawk in privacy. The visitors center has a pictur map describing where to see which wildflowers. To reach the dramatic **Poin Reyes Lighthouse** at the very tip of the point, follow Sir Francis Drake Blvd. to i end and head right along the stairway to Sea Lion Overlook. From Dec.-Feb., gra whales can occasionally be spotted from the overlook.

SIERRA NEVADA

Sierra Nevada is the highest, steepest, and most physically stunning mountain rang in the contiguous United States. The heart-stopping sheerness of Yosemite's roc walls, the craggy alpine scenery of Kings Canyon and Sequoia National Parks, an the abrupt drop from the eastern slope into Owens Valley conspire to inspire driv ers, hikers, and climbers alike. An enormous hunk of granite created by plate tecton ics and shaped by erosion, the Sierra Nevada (Spanish for "snowy mountains" stretches 450 miles north from the Mojave Desert to Lake Almanor. At 14,495 ft., M Whitney surmounts all other points in the U.S. outside Alaska.

The **Sequoia National Forest** encompasses the southern tip of the Sierras an embraces popular recreational areas and isolated wilderness. The **Forest Head quarters** in Porterville, 900 W. Grand Ave. (209-784-1500), 15 mi. east of Rte. 9 between Fresno and Bakersfield, sells a detailed map for $2.10 (open Mon.-Fri. 8an 4:30pm); you can also order it by mail from the Three Forest Interpretative Associ; tion (3FIA), 13098 E. Wire Grass Ln., Clovis 93612. **Sierra National Forest** fills th area between Yosemite, Sequoia, and Kings Canyon. The forest is not exactl "undiscovered"—droves of Californians jam the busier spots at lower elevation; and even the wilderness areas can be overpopulated in summer. The excellent mail **information office** is at the Supervisor's Office, located along Rte. 168 just outsid of Clovis (mailing address 1600 Tollhouse Rd., Clovis 93612; 209-487-5155; 24-hi recorded information 487-5456; fire and weather info. 487-5525). Maps here are $; **Inyo National Forest** runs along both sides of U.S. 395 from Lone Pine as far nort as Mono Lake, surrounding popular **Mammoth Lakes.**

Overnight temperatures can dip into the 20s°F year-round. Only U.S. 50 and I-8 are kept open during the snow season. Exact dates vary from year to year, so chec with a ranger station on local road and weather conditions. During all times of th year bring sunscreen—the ultra-violet rays at this high elevation are harsh.

■■■ KINGS CANYON AND SEQUOIA NATIONAL PARKS

If your impression of national parks has been formed by touristy Grand Canyon- and Yosemite-like parks, you'll love the twin parks of Kings Canyon and Sequoia that can go sight-for-jaw-dropping-sight with those more famous national parks. Kings Canyon and Sequoia offer visitors a chance to tailor their level of immersion in the wilderness. The terrain here has been alternately tortured and healed by ambivalent nature; cool waters knit scars left by glaciers while a snowy gauze bandages mountains that have broken the skin of the earth and thrust themselves heavenward. Meadow life buzzes, blooms, and breeds in expanses that were once cleared by fire. Uncertain Sequoia saplings cower beside the stumps and felled remains of their ancestors, suggesting that even the blight left by men may someday be erased.

Glacier-covered **Kings Canyon** displays a stunning array of imposing cliffs and sparkling waterfalls. Home to the deepest canyon walls in the country, turn-outs along the roads offer breathtaking vistas into gaping near-vertical declivities. In **Sequoia,** the Sierra Crest lifts itself to its greatest heights. Several 14,000-ft. peaks scrape the clouds along the park's eastern border, including **Mt. Whitney,** the tallest mountain in the contiguous U.S. (14,495 ft.). Both parks contain impressive groves of massive sequoia trees in addition to a large and cantankerous bear population. Visitors like to cluster around the largest sequoias, which tower near the entrances to the parks; the vast stretches of backcountry remain relatively empty. Developed areas like **Grant Cove** and **Giant Forest** offer interpretive trails, lodging amenities, and paved vehicle access. In contrast, the backcountry at **Road's End** in Kings Canyon or along the **High Sierra Trail** across Sequoia offer little but the guidance of cumulative footsteps of the trail trekkers before you. The "summer season" usually runs Memorial Day-Labor Day, "snow season" Nov.-March.

Seasonal changes are definitive and exaggerated in this area of the Sierras. Peak foliage on dogwood, aspen, and oak is Oct.-Nov. as the parks settle into a winter freeze, leaving trails and many roads impassable. Spring brings opportunities for skiing, late storms, low fogs, and flooding meltwater. Be prepared for marked temperature drops at night in these high elevations.

Practical Information Main services are provided by the **Kings Canyon and Sequoia Main Line** (565-3341), offering 24-hr. direct contact with a park ranger in addition to dispatch service to any office within the parks; recommended by many visitors centers as a preferred alternative to dialing direct. The **Parks General Information Line** is 565-3134. Kings Canyon's **Grant Grove Visitors Center** (335-2856), 2 mi. east of the Big Stump Entrance by Rte. 180, has books, maps, exhibits, nightly campfire programs, and daily hikes (open daily 8am-5pm, in winter 9am-5pm). Sequoia's **Ash Mountain Visitors Center,** Three Rivers 93271 (565-3341), on Rte. 198 out of Visalia, has info on both parks and provides books, maps, and wilderness permits (open May-Oct. daily 8am-5pm, Nov.-April daily 8am-4:30pm); the **Lodgepole Visitors Center** (565-3341, ext. 782), on Generals Hwy. 4 mi. east of the Giant Forest, climbs in the heart of Sequoia, near the big trees and the tourists (open May-Sept. daily 8am-5pm, Oct.-April daily 9am-5pm).

Accommodations and Food Sequoia Guest Services, Inc., P.O. Box 789, Three Rivers 93271 (561-3314), has a monopoly on indoor accommodations and food in the parks. Their rustic **cabins** cluster in a little village in Sequoia's Giant Forest, as well as at Grant Grove. (Cabins available May-Oct., $32 per person, $6.50 for wooden roof) Most park service **campgrounds** are open mid-May-Oct. (2-week limit). For info about campgrounds, contact a ranger station or call 565-3351 for a recording. Kings Canyon offers sites for $10 at **Sunset, Azalea,** and **Crystal Springs,** all within spitting distance of Grant Grove Village, and at **Sheep Creek, Sentinel, Canyon View,** and **Moraine,** at the Kings River near Cedar Grove. (All have restrooms and water. First three locations free in winter. Azalea open year-round; Moraine serves primarily as overflow and is open only on busiest weekends. Canyon View accepts reservations from organized groups only.) Sites without hook-ups are at **Lodgepole** (800-365-2267), 4 mi. northeast of Giant Forest Village in the heart of Sequoia National Park. (Sites $12; free in winter.) Reserve up to eight weeks in advance through MISTIX mid-May-mid-Sept. In Sequoia National Forest you will find the **Princess** (800-283-2267 for reservations), a few mi. outside of Kings Canyon on the road from Grants Grove to Cedar Grove. Princess offers evidence of the area's logging history; gigantic stumps dot the grounds (sites $8). Other options are **Buckeye Flat,** a few mi. into the park from the Ash Mountain entrance on Rte. 198, at a fabulous waterfall (sites $10; no RVs), and **Atwell Mill** and **Cold Springs,** about 20 mi. along Mineral King Rd., in the Mineral King area. (Sites $5; tents only.)

Park food, like lodging, is monopolized by Sequoia Guest Services. None of the offerings is very palatable; bring a stove and fuel or rent a cabin with kitchen accommodations and cook for yourself. Outside the park roar at **Noisy Water Cafe** (561-4517), along Rte. 180 in Three Rivers. "The Home of the Hummingbirds"—so named for the frequented feeders that hang outside the back window—is the overwhelming favorite among the townfolk. Unique, tasty sandwiches ($4-6), breakfasts ($4-7), and dinners ($7-12). (Open Sun.-Thurs. 6:30am-9pm, Fri.-Sat. 6:30am-10pm.)

Sights The two parks are accessible to vehicles from the west only. You can reach trailheads into the John Muir Wilderness and Inyo National Forest on the eastern side from spur roads off U.S. 395, but *no* roads traverse the Sierras here. From **Fresno** follow **Rte. 180** through the foothills; a 60-mi. sojourn takes you to the entrance of the Grant Grove section of Kings Canyon. Rte. 180 ends 30 mi. later in the Cedar Grove, an island of park land enveloped within Sequoia National Forest. The road into this region closes in winter. From **Visalia,** take **Rte. 198** to Sequoia National Park. **Generals Highway** (Rte. 198) connects the Ash Mountain entrance to Sequoia with the **Giant Forest,** and continues to Grant Grove in Kings Canyon.

In summer (June-Oct.), the treacherous road to **Mineral King** opens up the southern parts of Sequoia. From Visalia, take Rte. 198; the turnoff to Mineral King is three mi. past Three Rivers, and the **Lookout Point Ranger Station** lies 10 mi. along the Mineral King Rd. Take a break from driving here: Atwell Springs Campground and the nearby town of Silver City are 10 mi. (but 45 min.) farther along. **Cold Springs Campground, Mineral King Ranger Station,** and several **trailheads** lie near the end of Mineral King Rd. in a valley framed by 12,000-ft. peaks. The route to Mineral King includes stunning scenery—that is, if you can tear your eyes away from the tortuous road while making 698 turns between Rte. 198 and the Mineral King complex. Allow two hours for the trip from Three Rivers.

A car is indispensable, but roads don't touch the northern two-thirds of Kings Canyon and the eastern two-thirds of Sequoia; here the backpacker and packhorse have free rein. Check at a ranger station or visitors center for more detailed info. Bicycles are not permitted on hiking trails or in back country.

■■■ LAKE TAHOE

Lake Tahoe is neither one big casino nor an untamed paradise; careful planning here has balanced the natural and civilized worlds. The intrepid traveler's best bet is to eat cheap in **Stateline,** sleep cheap in **South Lake Tahoe,** and head to North Lake Tahoe to enjoy the splendor of the waves or woods.

Activity in **North Lake Tahoe** centers around **Tahoe City,** where Western families come season after season, year after year, to enjoy the lake's extraordinary recreational and natural resources. The area has a warm, familiar atmosphere; everyone is happy to escape the chaos and pollution of urban civilization. Tahoe City is not the most economical place to find a motel in Lake Tahoe, but it is rich with campsites and excellent trails. An active club and bar scene in the city offers an alternative to casino nightlife, with an energetic younger crowd and plenty of local entertainers.

Practical Information Emergency, of course, is 911. For a local map and coupons, get *101 Things to Do in Lake Tahoe* (free) at the **South Lake Tahoe Visitors Center**, 3066 U.S. 50 (541-5255), at Lion's Ave. (open Mon.-Fri. 8:30am-5pm, Sat. 9am-4pm). The **U.S. Forest Service**, 870 Emerald Bay Rd. (541-6564), S. Lake Tahoe, supervises campgrounds and publishes two useful guidebooks (open Mon.-Fri. 8am-4:30pm). On weekends, they provide wilderness permits at Taylor Creek (Rte. 89) from 8am-5:30pm **Greyhound**, 1098 Park Ave. (544-2241; open daily 8am-5pm), by Raley's in S. Lake Tahoe, rolls to San Francisco (5 per day, $33) and Sacramento (5 per day, $19). To get around in town, take the **South Tahoe Area Ground Express (STAGE)** (573-2080), with hourly service to the beach ($1.25; 10-ride pass $10). To get your own wheels, fork over at least $29 to **Tahoe Rent-a-Car** (544-4500), U.S. 50 at Tahoe Keys Blvd. in S. Lake Tahoe (must be 24). Or, rent mountain bikes ($6 per hr., ½ day $18, full day $22) at **Anderson's Bicycle Rental**, 645 Emerald Bay Rd. (541-0500); convenient to the well-maintained west shore bike trail (deposit required; open daily 8:30am-6:30pm). The **Post Office** meters at **Stateline Station**, 1085 Park Ave. (544-6162), next to Greyhound (open Mon.-Fri. 8:30am-5pm); the **ZIP code** is 95729. The **area codes** are 916 in CA, 702 in NV.

Lake Tahoe is located 118 mi. northeast of Sacramento and 35 mi. southwest of Reno. U.S. 50, Rte. 89, and Rte. 28 overlap to form a ring of asphalt around the lake. U.S. 395 from Carson City and the Owens Valley area or I-80 from San Francisco or Reno are the most-traveled roads to the lake. In winter, tire chains are required and four-wheel drive is highly recommended.

Accommodations, Camping, and Food Motel 6, 2375 Lake Tahoe Blvd. (542-1400), is, as usual, standard-issue but very popular, especially on weekends. Pool and TV. (Singles $36, $4 per additional adult. Reservations recommended.) Tired of Tom Bodett? Head to the **Lake Shore Lodge**, 3496 Lake Tahoe Blvd. (544-2834), with a pool (singles Mon.-Thurs. $17; call for superhigh weekend rate).

The Forest Service at the visitors bureau provides up-to-date information on camping (see Practical Information). **Bayview** is the only free campground for miles (544-5994; 2-night max.; open June-Sept.). Advance reservations for all sites are essential (MISTIX at 800-365-2267 for state campgrounds). **Nevada Beach** (573-2600), 1 mi. from Stateline on U.S. 50, has flush toilets and drinking water, but no showers. Sites are 100 yds. from the shore. **D.L. Bliss State Park,** Rte. 89 (525-7277), a few miles west of Emerald Bay, runs hot showers near a blissful beach. (14-day max. 168 sites. $14, near-beach sites $19. Open June-Labor Day.)

For tidbits in Tahoe, eat at **The Siam Restaurant**, 2180 U.S. 50 (544-0370), a Thai restaurant with large portions at low prices ($5). Spicy dishes are a fire hazard. (Open Mon.-Tues. and Thurs.-Sun. 11am-10pm.) If it's too early in the day for Thai, try **Red Hut Waffles**, 2749 U.S. 50 (541-9024), which whips up plate-size waffles with fruit and whipped cream ($3.50), and omelettes toast, and hash browns ($5). (Open daily 6am-2pm.) At **Firesign**, 1585 West Lake Blvd. (583-0871), the stone hearth, wood tables, and homey country-style feeling make for a popular restaurant. Out-of-the-ordinary cooking and outdoor seating. Dill and artichoke omelettes, with home fries, toast, and muffin $5.25. Sandwiches $4.75. (Open daily 7am-3pm.)

Sights and Activities Bikers without wheels are in luck in Tahoe; the region supports at least 30 bike rental shops (usually lined up used-car-lot-style along the major roads). Sharing roads with automobiles can be dangerous, especially at the west shore and around Emerald Bay, where visiting drivers gawk at the dizzying heights and tend to swerve. The forest service office at Taylor Creek (see Practical Information) as well as any bike rental store can give advice on safer and often more scenic paths. There is no bicycle riding allowed in wilderness areas. **Cascade Sta-**

bles (541-2055), off Rte. 89 on Cascade Rd. in South Lake Tahoe, offers horsies ($15 per hr.). There are a number of equestrian/hiking trails in the area, including the near-complete **Rim Trail** (577-0676), which skirts the highest elevations of the basin and allows RVs free views of the lake and surrounding area. The **Rubicon Trail,** which runs 7.2 mi. along the south shore with trailheads and **D.L. Bliss State Park** and **Vikingsholm,** is a popular one with hikers. Vikingsholm (541-3030) is a Scandinavian-style castle built in the 1920s (open for tours mid-June-Labor Day 10am-4pm; $2, under 18 $1). The **Eagle Falls Trail,** which leads into the Desolation Wilderness and to Eagle Lake, is accessible from the parking lot. **Mt. Tallac** (trailhead across from Baldwin Beach on Rte. 89) and **Mt. Rose** (trailhead on Rte. 431 north of Incline Village) are both challenging day hikes into the wilderness area.

Finally, when the winter comes, skiers have many options. The visitors center has a ski map and prices. **Alpine Meadows** (583-4232 or 800-824-6348) is an excellent, accessible family vacation spot. **North Star** (562-1010), on Rte. 267 and North Star Dr. in Truckee, 6 mi. northwest of Tahoe City, is another winning spot, with condominiums that are a bargain, provided there are 12 people paying. **Mt. Rose** (702-849-0747), 11 mi. from Incline Village on Rte. 431, is one of the cheapest slopes in Lake Tahoe. **Boreal Ridge** (426-3663), 10 mi. west of Truckee on I-80, has less challenging terrain than some of its neighbors, but offers night skiing for reduced rates.

For cross-country skiing, head to **Royal Gorge** (426-3871) on Old Hwy. 40, the nation's largest cross-county ski resort, with 70 different trails totalling 300km. **Incline** (702-832-1150), in North Lake Tahoe, and **Spooner Lake** (702-749-5349), in Nevada where Rte. 28 and 50 meet, offer 35km and 25km of trails respectively.

■■■ MAMMOTH LAKES

Home to one of the most popular ski resorts in California, the town of Mammoth Lakes is a year-round playground; mountain biking and hiking now complement the traditional snow-bound pursuits. Mammoth is an outdoorsman's fantasy—spectacular peaks overlook a community in which every establishment seems to exist solely for the excursionist's benefit. Yet for all its glitz, the town's residents keep it friendly. Surprisingly, none of the more than 100 lakes here is called "Mammoth Lake." **Lake Mary** is the largest, popular with boaters and fisherfolk.

Practical Information Mammoth Lakes reposes on U.S. 395 about 160 mi. south of Reno and 40 mi. southeast of the eastern entrance to Yosemite. Rte. 203 runs through the town as Main St., then veers off to the right as Minaret Summit Rd. The **Visitors Center and Chamber of Commerce** (934-2712) spiels inside Village Center Mall West (open Sat.-Thurs. 8am-6pm, Fri. 8am-8pm; in winter daily 8am-6pm). The **Inyo National Forest Visitors Center** (924-5500) is east off U.S. 395 and dishes out exhibits and walks (open daily 6am-5pm; Oct.-June Mon.-Sat. 8am-4:30pm). **Greyhound** (213-620-1200 for info) stops in front of the Main St. McDonalds and goes once a day to Reno (1:05am) and L.A. (12:30pm). Board here, and buy ticket at next station. For ski info, call **Mammoth Mountain Ski Area** (932-2571). The **post office** (934-2205) is across from the visitors center (open Mon.-Fri. 8:30am-5pm). The **ZIP code** is 93546; the **area code** 619.

Camping and Accommodations Call the Mammoth Ranger District (924-5500) for info on nearly 20 Inyo Forest public **campgrounds** in the area (sites $7-9). Otherwise, the **Hilton Creek International Hostel (HI/AYH)** (935-4989), on the outskirts of Lake Crowley, about 10 mi. south of town, is the best deal around—in a supreme location, complete with aspen grove, babbling brook, and mountain view. Skiing, backpacking, inner-tubing, biking, multilingual conversations, and local music. ($8.75, nonmembers $11.75. Seniors and ages under 18 with parents half-price. Add $2 in winter.) Another great bet is the **ULLR Lodge** (934-2454), on

Minaret Rd. just south of Main St. (Shared bathrooms. Winter dorms $15. Singles $35, $41 on weekends, $45 on holidays; doubles $38/44/47. Cheaper in summer.)

Food They don't serve ambrosia, but **Angel's** (934-7427), at Main St. and Sierra, is an almost unanimous recommendation among the locals. A tad expensive (dinner entrees $6-13), but after a day on the slopes, you could probably convince yourself that you earned it. Angel's specializes in BBQ, but also has a deliciously huge burrito with big chunks of beef for only $7. The bar features over 70 beers from 19 different countries. (Open Mon.-Fri. 11:30am-10pm, Sat.-Sun. 5-10pm. Arrive early.) Susie sells subs by the ski slopes at **Susie's Subs** (934-7033), Old Mammoth Rd. just before Chateau. Swing by Susie's and slyly snag a scrumptious sub before schussing skillfully down the shimmering slopes. Subs $3.25-4.25. (Open daily 8am-6pm.)

Sights and Activities There's plenty to see in Mammoth Lakes, but unfortunately most of it is accessible only by car. **Devil's Postpile National Monument,** an intriguing geological oddity, was formed when lava flows oozed through Mammoth Pass thousands of years ago and then cooled to form columns 40-60 ft. high. The column's cross-sections range from geometrically precise equilateral triangles to strange heptagons. Ancient glaciers exposed and polished the basalt posts to create the mammoth jewels that glitter today. A pleasant 3-mi. walk away from the center of the monument is **Rainbow Falls,** where the middle fork of the San Joaquin River drops 140 ft. past dark cliffs into a glistening green pool. From U.S. 395, the monument and its nearby bubbling hot springs can be reached by a 15-mi. drive past Minaret Summit on paved Rte. 203. Three mi. south of Mammoth Junction on U.S. 395 bubbles **Hot Creek,** open to bathers. Ask locals about late-night skinny-dips. (Open sunrise-sunset.) You can ride the **Mammoth Mountain Gondola** (934-2571) during the summer for a spectacular view of the area. (Open daily 11am-3pm. Round-trip $6, children $3.) **Obsidian Dome** lies 14 mi. north of Mammoth Junction and 1 mi. west of U.S. 395 on Glass Flow Rd. (follow the sign to "Lava Flow"). The dark, glassy volcanic rock is a wobbly climb, so take sturdy shoes.

Adventurous travelers can enjoy hot-air balloons, snowmobiles, mountain bike paths, and dogsled trails. **Mammoth Adventure Connection** (800-228-4947) helps you evaluate your options. With 132 downhill runs, over 26 lifts, and oodles of nordic trails, Mammoth is also a skier's paradise. Lift tickets may be bought for several days at a time ($30 per day, $108 for 5-day pass). They can be purchased at the **Main Lodge** (934-2571) at the base of the mountain on Minaret Road (open Mon.-Fri. 8am-3pm, Sat.-Sun. 7:30am-3pm) or at **Warming Hut II** (934-0771) at the end of Canyon and Lakeview Blvd. (open Mon.-Fri. 8am-3pm, Sat.-Sun. 7:30am-3pm). A free shuttle bus transports skiers between lifts, town, and the Main Lodge.

■■■ MONO LAKE

As fresh water from streams and springs drains into the "inland sea" of Mono Lake (MOE-no) it evaporates, leaving behind a mineral-rich, 13-mi. wide expanse that Mark Twain called "the Dead Sea of the West." Although Mono supports no fish, brine flies, algae, and shrimp provide a buffet for migratory birds. The lake derives its lunar appearance from remarkable towers of calcium carbonate called *tufa,* which form when fresh-water springs well up in the carbonate-filled salt water.

Tourists and ecologists love Mono for its unique rock formations and varied bird population, but thirsty Los Angeles loves it for its water. The steady diversion of water to the south has lowered the lake's level nearly 50 ft. since 1941, endangering the delicate *tufa* and the birthplace of over 90% of California's shore gulls. Locals and lake lovers continue to fight for increased water flow to the lake, while Southern California's population continues to grow, sweat, bathe, and thirst at Northern California's expense. At over 700,000 years old, the extraordinary tub remains the Western Hemisphere's oldest enclosed body of water. For now.

Practical Information The two-block-long town of **Lee Vining** provides the best access to Mono Lake and the ghost town of **Bodie.** Lee Vining is located 70 mi. north of **Bishop** on U.S. 395 and 10 mi. west of the Tioga Pass entrance to **Yosemite.** In town, the first place to go is the **Mono Lake Visitors Center,** (647-6595) on Main St. The incredibly friendly staff are all part of the crusade to save Mono Lake from the clutches of that incarnation of Evil—the L.A. Dept. of Water and Power; the Visitors Center offers walking tours and canoe tours (see below). (Open daily 9am-9pm, Sept.-May 9am-5pm.) **Greyhound** sprints from the Lee Vining Market (647-6301) to L.A. and Reno once per day each. Buy your ticket at the next stop, because they don't sell them here. The **Lee Vining Ranger Station** of the U.S. Forest Service (647-6525), 2 mi. west of U.S. 395 on Rte. 120, disperses **backcountry camping permits** daily on a first-come, first-served basis, or reserved March-May (free). Lee Vining's **ZIP code** is 93541; the **area code** is 619.

Camping and Food Explore other food options (e.g. your clothing) before you decide to eat in Lee Vining. Spend your nights camping, since the town's hotels are small and often expensive. Besides, the terrain is beautiful. There are six Inyo National Forest **campgrounds** ($3-10) west of town on Rte. 120 within 15 mi. of Lee Vining and two north of town within 6 mi. **Sawmill Campground** and **Tioga Lake Campground** are 9000 ft. up, at the edge of Yosemite. **Ellery Lake Campground** has sites next to a bubbling creek ($10 with drinking water and chemical toilets; call 647-6525 for information). Dispersed camping is permitted in the scenic area above the shoreline. (Free permit required; make reservations well in advance with the Lee Vining District Ranger.)

Mono Lake In 1984, Congress set aside 57,000 acres of land surrounding Mono Lake and called it the **Mono Basin National Forest Scenic Area** (647-6525). **South Tufa Grove,** 10 mi. from Lee Vining, harbors an awe-inspiring collection of calcium carbonate formations. (Take U.S. 395 south to Rte. 120, then go 4 mi. east and take the Mono Lake Tufa Reserve turn-off 1 mi. south of Tufa Grove.) The *tufa* towers, which resemble giant drip sandcastles, startlingly poke through the smooth surface of what Twain called a "solemn, silent, sailless sea." 4 mi. north of Lee Vining on U.S. 395 is **Mono Lake County Park,** a public playground with bathrooms, picnic tables, swings, and a smaller *tufa* forest. The **Mono Lake Foundation** now offers guided **canoe tours** of the lake on weekends, an enlightening way to tour this enchanting body of water (tours at 8, 9:30, 11am; $10, ages 4-12 $5). Check at the visitors center for free guided **walking tours** of the lake, beginning daily at 6pm from the South Tufa parking lot. **Navy Beach,** ½ mi. from the South Tufa Grove, is one of the saltiest swimming holes in America. The Rangers at **Panum Crater,** a long-extinct volcano 4 mi. east of town on Rte. 120, offer excellent interpretive nature walks. Inquire at the Lee Vining Ranger Station for details.

Bodie You've seen Columbia, Placerville, Coloma, and Sonora, and you're probably thinking you'll never find an authentic, unexploited old ghost town. But wait—tucked away in the high, forsaken desert, **Bodie** is the real McCoy, even if it does charge admission ($5; self-guide booklet $1). Described as "a sea of sin, lashed by the tempests of lust and passion," in 1880 the town was home to 10,000 people, 65 saloons, 22 tumbleweeds, and one homicide per day. Today the streets and buildings are strewn with abandoned furniture, automobiles, wagons, and train engines, well-preserved by the dry climate and by the state of California. Bodie is accessible by a paved road off U.S. 395, 15 mi. north of Lee Vining (the last 10 mi. are a dusty delight), and by a dirt road all the way from Rte. 167 out of Mono Inn. (Open 9am-7pm; Sept.-May 9am-4pm. For information call Bodie State Historic Park at 647-6445 or write to P.O. Box 515, Bridgeport, CA 93517.)

■■■ YOSEMITE NATIONAL PARK

In 1868, when a young Scotsman named John Muir arrived by boat in San Francisco, he asked for directions to "anywhere that's wild," and was pointed toward the Sierra Nevadas. The wonders that awaited Muir at Yosemite inspired him to a lifetime of conservationism. Muir fought and lost many battles, but in 1880 he succeeded in securing national park status for Yosemite. Today, few of the park's 3.5 million annual visitors know of Muir's struggles, but most leave with an understanding of his love for Yosemite's natural treasures.

Hundreds of thousands of visitors make the pilgrimage to Yosemite each summer to gape at awe-inspiring granite cliffs, thunderous waterfalls, lush meadows, rock monoliths, and thick pine forests. While most travelers to the big ditch in Arizona stay for only the few hours it takes to absorb the colorful view from each scenic overlook, visitors to Yosemite tend to linger for a few days. The resulting pile-up makes for a congestion which more closely resembles an L.A. freeway than an Ansel Adams photograph.

PRACTICAL INFORMATION

Visitors Information: A map of the park and a copy of the informative *Yosemite Guide* are available for free at visitors centers. Wilderness **permits** are available at all visitors centers; it pays to write ahead and reserve in advance; call for information. All hours listed are valid **mid-May to mid-Sept.,** unless otherwise noted; call for off-season hours. **General Park Information,** 372-0265; 24-hr. recorded information 372-0200. Open Mon.-Fri. 9am-5pm. **Tuolumne Meadows Visitors Center,** Tioga Rd. (372-0263), 55 mi. from Yosemite Village. The headquarters of high-country activity, with trail information, maps, and special programs. Open daily 8am-8pm. **Wilderness Office,** P.O. Box 577, Yosemite National Park 95389 (372-0308; 24-hr. recorded information 372-0307), next to Yosemite Valley Visitors Center. **Backcountry** and trail information. Open daily 7:30am-7:30pm. **Campground information:** 372-0200 (recorded).

Park Admission: $3 by foot, bicycle, or bus. $5 for a 7-day vehicle pass.

Delaware North Co. Room Reservations, 5410 E. Home, Fresno 93727 (252-4848, TTY users 255-8345). Except for the campgrounds, DNCo has a monopoly on most tourist facilities within the park. Contact them for reservations.

Tour Information: Yosemite Lodge Tour Desk (372-1240), in Yosemite Lodge lobby. Open daily 7:30am-7pm, or contact any other lodge in the park.

Equipment Rental: Yosemite Mountaineering School, Rte. 120 (372-1224, open daily 8:30am-5pm), at Tuolumne Meadows. Sleeping bags $4 per day, backpacks $4 per day, snow shoes $6 per day. Driver's license or credit card required.

Bike Rentals: at **Yosemite Lodge** and **Curry Village** (372-1208 and 372-1200 respectively). $5 per hr., $16 per day. Both open 8am-6pm daily.

Post Office: Yosemite Village, next to the visitors center. Open Mon.-Fri. 8:30am-12:30pm and 1:30-5pm. **ZIP code:** 95389.

Area Code: 209.

ORIENTATION AND GETTING AROUND

Yosemite lies 200 mi. due east of San Francisco and 320 mi. northeast of Los Angeles. It can be reached by taking Rte. 140 from Merced, Rte. 41 north from Fresno, and Rte. 120 east from Manteca or west from Lee Vining.

The park covers 1189 sq. mi. of mountainous terrain. **El Capitán, Half Dome,** and **Yosemite Falls** lie in the Yosemite Valley, an area carved out by glaciers over thousands of years. Once you've seen these main attractions, though, head out to the other parts of the park. Little Yosemite Valley, accessible by hiking trails, offers two spectacular waterfalls: **Vernal** and **Nevada Falls. Tuolumne Meadows** (pronounced ta-WALL-um-ee) in the northeastern corner of the park is an Elysian expanse of alpine meadows surrounded by granite cliffs and rushing streams. **Mariposa Grove** is a forest of giant sequoia trees at the park's southern end.

Yosemite runs public buses that connect the park with Merced, Fresno, and Lee Vining. **Yosemite Gray Line (YGL),** P.O. Box 2472, Merced 95344 (383-1563), meets the morning train arriving in Merced from San Francisco and takes passengers to Yosemite. The bus returns to Merced in time to catch the return train to San Francisco. YGL also runs to and from Fresno ($19). From July-Sept., the **Yosemite Transportation System (YTS)** connects the park with Greyhound in Lee Vining (372-1240; one way $21). Reservations are required to buy a ticket. Greyhound does not sell tickets in Lee Vining, so be prepared when you board the bus.

The best bargain in Yosemite, aside from the price of admission, is the free **shuttle bus system.** Comfortable but often crowded, the buses have knowledgeable drivers and broad viewing windows. They run through the valley daily at 10-min. intervals from 7:30am-10pm. Call 372-1240 for information.

Although the inner valley is congested with traffic, the best way to see Yosemite is by **car.** Park at one of the lodging areas and ride the shuttle to see the valley sights, then hop back into your car to explore other places. Of the five major approaches to the park, Rte. 120 to the Big Oak Flat entrance is particularly tortuous. The easiest route from the west is Rte. 140 into Yosemite Valley. The eastern entrance, Tioga Pass, is closed during snow season. **Bicycling** is also an excellent way to see Yosemite Valley; bike paths abound, and most sights are within a 4-mi. diameter across the Valley center. (See Practical Information for rental information.)

ACCOMODATIONS, CAMPING, AND FOOD

Those who prefer some kind of roof over their heads must call 252-4848 for reservations and info. Clean, sparsely furnished cabins are available at **Yosemite Lodge** (singles/doubles $48, with bath $63). Southeast of Yosemite Village, **Curry Village** offers noisy but clean cabins (same prices). **Housekeeping Camp** has canvas and concrete units that accommodate up to six people. Bring your own utensils, warm clothes, and industrial-strength bug repellent ($37 for 1-4 people). **Tuolumne Meadows,** on Tioga Rd. in the northeast corner of the park, has canvas-sided tent cabins (2 people $37; each additional person $5, kids $2.50.) **White Wolf,** west of Tuolumne Meadows on Tioga Rd., has similar cabins ($32, with bath $56).

Most of the park's **campgrounds** are crowded with trailers and RVs. In Yosemite Valley's drive-in campgrounds, reservations are required April-Nov. and must be made through MISTIX (800-365-2267) up to eight weeks ahead. Sleeping in cars is emphatically prohibited. With the exception of major holidays, you should be able to camp in one of the first-come, first-served campgrounds provided you arrive at a reasonable hour. For info on **backcountry camping** (prohibited in the valley—you'll get slapped with a stiff fine if caught), see Beyond Yosemite Valley below.

Restaurants in Yosemite are expensive and dull. Buy your own groceries and supplies from the **Yosemite Lodge Store** or the **Village Store** (open daily 8am-10pm; Oct.-May 8am-9pm). Better yet, cart supplies in from outside the DNCo monopoly.

OUTDOORS IN YOSEMITE

By Car or Bike

You can see a large part of Yosemite from the bucket seat. The *Yosemite Road Guide* ($3.25 at every visitors center) is keyed to the roadside markers, and outlines a superb tour of the park—it's almost like having a ranger tied to the hood. The drive along **Tioga Road** (Rte. 120 E) presents one panorama after another and also includes views of burned forest remaining from the devastating fires which have plagued Yosemite. The road through Tioga Pass is the highest highway strip in the country; exiting the eastern side of the park, it winds down into the lunar landscape near Mono Lake. Driving west from the Pass brings you to **Tuolumne Meadows** and its open, alpine spaces, shimmering **Tenaya Lake,** and innumerable scenic views of granite slopes and canyons. The approach from the south passes through **Wawona Tunnel.** Dominating the spectacle on the other side of the tunnel are

7569-ft. **El Capitán** (the largest granite monolith in the world), misty **Bridalveil Falls,** and the **Three Brothers** (three adjacent granite peaks). A drive into the heart of the valley brings thunderous 2425-ft. **Yosemite Falls** (the highest in North America), **Sentinel Rock,** and **Half Dome** within view.

You'll think you've stumbled into Brobdingnag as you walk among the giant sequoias at **Mariposa Grove,** off Rte. 41. The short hiking trail begins at the **Fallen Monarch,** a massive trunk lying on its side, and continues to the 209-ft., 2700-year-old **Grizzly Giant,** and the fallen **Wawona Tunnel Tree.** Contemplate the fact that ancient Athens was in its glory when many of these trees were mere saplings.

Of course, when you drive through Yosemite you sacrifice intimacy with the land. One alternative is **cycling.** A brochure which indicates the safest roads is available at the visitors center. Roads are fairly flat near the villages, more arduous farther afield. Those near **Mirror Lake,** open only to hikers and bikers, guarantee a particularly good ride, and the valley roads, filled with traffic, are easily circumvented by the bike paths. For further information on bike routes, contact the bike rental stands at Yosemite Lodge (372-1208) or Curry Village (372-1200).

Day Hiking in the Valley

Many visitors to Yosemite find the Valley's motorized tourist culture a great distraction. The most splendid and peaceful experiences at Yosemite are had along the outer trails with just a backpack and canteen. A wealth of opportunities rewards anyone willing to lace up those hiking boots for a day trip.

Day-use trails are usually fairly busy, sometimes positively crowded, and occasionally (i.e. July 4th weekend) there are human traffic jams. A colorful trail map with difficulty ratings and average hiking times is available at the visitors center for 50¢ (see Practical Information). The easiest walks are to **Bridalveil Falls** and **Lower Yosemite Falls,** less than ¼ mi. from the shuttle bus stops. **The Mirror Lake Loop** is a level, 3-mi. walk to the glassy lake, which is slowly silting up to become a meadow. All three trails are accessible to hikers with disabilities.

Yosemite Falls Trail, a back-breaking trek to a windy summit, rewards the intrepid with an overview of the 2425-ft. drop. Leaving the marked trail is not a wise idea—every year someone wanders off and gets the ultimate tour of the Falls.

One of the most popular trails (and understandably so) begins at **Happy Isles.** From this point, one could reach Mt. Whitney via the John Muir Trail, but the 211-mi. trek is not for everyone. Most instead take the **Mist Trail** past Vernal Fall to the top of Nevada Fall, a steep and strenuous climb up hundreds of tiny stairs. The views of the falls from the trail are outstanding, and the proximity to the water shrouds the trail in a continuous drizzle that is welcome during the summer months. Take the **free shuttle** from the valley campgrounds to Happy Isles; there is no parking available. The Mist Trail continues to the base of **Half Dome,** a monolithic testament to the power of glaciation. Expert climbers tackle the its sheer front face; halfway up, a yard-wide ledge serves as a luxury resort on the otherwise smooth vertical wall. Look closely from below; the profile of an Ahwahnee princess is supposedly stained into the rock. For novices who don't dare dangle from the dome's face, there is a route up the back side which is itself challenging and requires the aid of climbing cables (summer only). You'll need all day to make it here and back in time for the last shuttle—this is considered the most difficult hike in the valley.

BEYOND YOSEMITE VALLEY: BACKCOUNTRY

Some folks never leave the valley, but a wilder, lonelier Yosemite awaits those who do. The visitors center has day-hike fliers for areas outside Yosemite valley, but there are many more marked trails than shown. Before venturing out, be sure to prepare yourself; obtain a **topographical map** of the region and plan your route.

Backcountry camping is generally unrestricted along the high-country trails with a free **wilderness permit** (call 372-0307 for general information). Each trailhead limits the number of permits available. Reserve by mail March-May (write Wilderness Office, P.O. Box 577, Yosemite National Park 95389), or take your chances with the 50% quota held on 24-hr. notice at the Yosemite Valley Visitors Center, the Wawona Ranger Station, or Big Oak Flat Station. Popular trails like **Little Yosemite Valley, Clouds Rest,** and **Half Dome** fill the quotas regularly. To receive a permit, you must show a planned itinerary, although you needn't follow it exactly. Many hikers stay at the undeveloped mountain campgrounds in the high country for the company and for the **bear lockers,** used for storing food. There are also five High Sierra walk-in campsites; contact the Wilderness Office for details.

A free shuttle bus to **Tuolumne Meadows** will deposit you at the heads of several trails. **Lembert Dome** has a trail to its peak which serves as a good warm-up for those eager to move on to more challenging terrain, while the **Pacific Crest Trail** follows a series of canyons that is likely to hurl you into a sublimity from which you may never return. South Yosemite is home to the **Giant Sequoia and Mariposa Grove,** the park's largest. Several trails of varying lengths wind through this stretch of mammoth trees, some of which began life over 3000 years ago. Some trails connect to other national park or forest trails that continue as far as Washington State.

Hawaii

No alien land in all the world has any deep, strong charm for me but that one, no other land could so longingly and beseechingly haunt me, sleeping and waking, through half a lifetime, as that one has done. Other things leave me, but it abides; other things change, but it remains the same....In my nostrils still lives the breath of flowers that perished twenty years ago.

—Mark Twain

Mark Twain's effusive recollections of his 1889 trip to what were then called the Sandwich Islands foreshadowed the exotic image that Hawaii conjures today. Dribbled across the ocean blue of the Pacific—2400 mi. off mainland America—the state is both physically and psychologically removed from the other United States. 132 islands comprise the Hawaiian chain, though only seven are inhabited.

Polynesian pioneers traveled in double-hulled canoes across thousands of miles of unbroken ocean as early as the 6th century AD and developed a high degree of civilization on the islands. By the time Captain Cook arrived in 1778, a rigidly hierarchical society and advanced irrigation techniques allowed the native Hawaiians to support a population estimated at 800,000—at a standard of living higher than most of Western Europe at that time. King Kamehameha I united the islands in a single kingdom early in the 19th century. But Western diseases decimated the Hawaiian population; 100 years after Cook's arrival, only 50,000 native Hawaiians remained. Hawaiian commerce developed uneventfully until the Japanese attack on Pearl Harbor on December 7, 1941. In 1959, Hawaii became the 50th state.

When in Hawaii, first enjoy the weather and the islands' natural environs. Witness lava ooze out of Kilauea and drift down to the sea, investigate offshore aquatic life with a snorkel, amble along the beach and into caves. Tourist-tailored traps will draw you of course, and you might well heed their call. All the while, attune your sixth sense to the mysteries of the islands. Above all, explore the indigenous culture of Hawaii. Take in exhibits of the native handicrafts on display in markets and museums or delve into a book about the region. With a little effort you can escape the islands' commercialism and get a true taste of Hawaii's unique flavor.

PRACTICAL INFORMATION

Capital: Honolulu.
Visitors Information: Hawaii Visitors Bureau, 2270 Kalakaua Ave., 8th floor, Honolulu 96815 (923-1811). Open Mon.-Fri. 8am-4:30pm. The ultimate source.
Time Zone: Hawaii (6 hr. behind Eastern in spring and summer; 5 hr. otherwise).
Postal Abbreviation: HI
Sales Tax: 4%

ISLAND HOPPING

When weighing which islands to visit, think carefully about what you like to do. Each offers its own atmosphere and range of activities. **Oahu** is heavily populated and revolves around tourism, making it the most accessible island in the chain, but as a consequence, there are few unexplored and unexploited places. The **Big Island (Hawaii)** has lots of open space and the added attraction of Volcanoes National Park, where you can see the goddess Pele spit hot lava from the bowels of the earth. **Maui's** strong winds have made it one of the premier windsurfing destinations in the world, and with the windsurfers comes a hopping nightlife. The major inter-island carriers, **Hawaiian Airlines** (537-5100) and **Aloha Airlines** (484-1111), can jet you quickly (about 40 min.) from Honolulu to any of the islands. Travel agents, such as **Pali Tour and Travel, Inc.** (533-3608), 1300 Pali Hwy. Ste. 1304, Honolulu, sell Hawaiian Air interisland coupon books that are extremely convenient for island-hopping (6 flights for $305). Hawaiian Airlines also sells 5-, 7-, and 14-day **passes** offering unlimited inter-island flights for $139, $159, and $239 respectively. **The Hotel Exchange,** 1946 Ala Moana Blvd., Hawaiian Colony (942-8544), sells Aloha Airlines tickets for $42.50 each. Check the miscellaneous section of the classified ads in the *Star-Bulletin* or *Advertiser* for individuals selling these coupons at cut-rate prices. Most carriers offer the same fare to each island they serve.

Aloha and Hawaiian Airlines often coordinate with resorts and/or car rental agencies to create economical packages. Ask a local travel or reservations agent about deals best suited to your needs, and keep an eye out for ads in pamphlets and newspapers. Many companies offer one-day **airplane** and **helicopter cruises** of the islands (kind of like on *Magnum, P.I.*). Consult a travel agent about current deals and specials or look in the Sunday paper travel section.

Perhaps the finest book ever written on the subject, *Let's Go: California & Hawaii* offers the budget traveler an even more in-depth look at Hawaii. Available in bookstores everywhere.

HAWAII (THE BIG ISLAND)

Pele, Polynesian goddess of the volcano, is believed to reside on Hawaii, the south-easternmost island in the Hawaiian chain. Hawaii possesses the archipelago's only two active volcanoes—Mauna Loa, the still-active Long Mountain (13,677 ft.), and Kilauea (4000 ft.), home of the hyperactive Halemaumau Crater. Kilauea is now in its 49th phase of eruption with no signs of relenting; Pele, it seems, is inexhaustible.

The Big Island is twice the size of all the other islands combined, but is home to scarcely a tenth of the state's population. But Hawaii certainly holds its own. The island's pastures support Hawaii's varied post-sugar economy and as well as experiments with many alternative energy sources; 13,000 ft. up Mauna Kea, Hawaii boasts the premier observatory in the world. The towns of Hilo and Kailua-Kona, on opposite sides of the island, are the main arrival points for tourists. The rest of the island is considered "country" by residents. The northwestern corner is the Kohala Peninsula, former sugar land and the northern border of the island's gigantic cattle range. The southern land mass is Kau, where the first Polynesian immigrants settled. You'll need a car to get to the countryside, but keep a careful eye on the fuel gauge, as distances between gas stations can be great. Coastal highways circle both volcanoes. In Volcanoes National Park, both the old Saddle Road (Rte. 200) and the Chain of Craters Road in Kilauea Crater permit closer views of the volcanoes. The Big Island does have a rudimentary bus system, and you should find most of the island's sights accessible.

■■■ HILO

After Honolulu, Hilo is the largest city in the state—a more relaxed and less tourist-ridden version of its big cousin. Moist tradewinds have made it the center of the Hawaiian orchid and anthurium industry. A primarily residential city, Hilo works well as a base from which to visit the island's other attractions: the rugged **Hamakua,** green **Waipio Valley** north of Hamakua, *paniolo* (cowboy) country above that, and, of course, **Volcanoes National Park.**

PRACTICAL INFORMATION
Emergency: 961-6022 or 911.
Visitors Information: The **Visitor Information Kiosk,** across the parking lot at 300 Kamehameha Ave., is a good source for bus schedules, maps, brochures, and

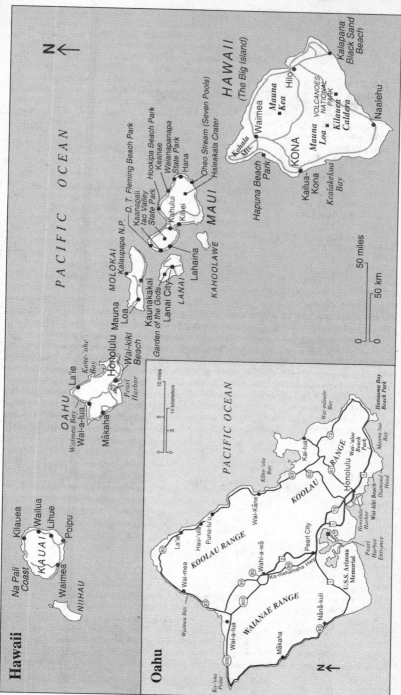

HAWAII ISLAND: HILO

Hawaii

PACIFIC OCEAN

KAUAI
Na Pali
Coast
Kilauea
Wailua
Lihue
Poipu
Waimea
NIIHAU

OAHU
Waimea Bay
Kane-ohe
Bay
La-ie
Wai-a-lua
Honolulu
Mauna
Loa
Wai-kiki
Beach
Pearl
Harbor
Mākaha

MOLOKAI
Kalaupapa N.P.
Kaunakakai
Garden of the Gods
Lanai City
LANAI

D. T. Fleming Beach Park
Hookipa Beach Park
Keanae
Kaanapali
Iao Valley
State Park
Waianapanapa
State Park
Hana
Kahului
Kihei
MAUI
Lahaina
Oheo Stream (Seven Pools)
Haleakala Crater
KAHOOLAWE

HAWAII
(The Big Island)
Waimea
Mauna
Kea
Hilo
Kohala
Mts.
VOLCANOES
NATIONAL
PARK
Kilauea
Caldera
Kalapana
Black Sand
Beach
Mauna
Loa
KONA
Kailua-
Kona
Hapuna Beach
Park
Kealakekua
Bay
Naalehu

50 miles

50 km

0
0

N

Oahu

PACIFIC OCEAN

Ka-'ena
Point
Waimea Bay
Wai-mea
Hau-'ula
Puna-lu'u
La-ie
Kāne-'ohe
Bay
Wai-manalo
Bay
Wai-Kāne
72
**KOOLAU
RANGE**
Wai-'alae Beach
Park
Kai-lua
Hanauma Bay
Beach Park
Mauna-lua
Bay
Wai-a-wā
Wahi-a-wā
Pearl City
83
99
80
803
WAIANAE RANGE
Ka-mehameha Hwy
830
Mākaha
Nanā-kuli
93
92
**KOOLAU
RANGE**
Honolulu
U.S.S. Arizona
Memorial
Pearl
Harbor
Entrance
Honolulu
Harbor
Wai-kiki Beach
Diamond
Head
1
1
61
63
72
Wai-a-lua
Wai-a-lua

10 miles
5
10 kilometers
5

N

a self-guided walking tour of historic downtown Hilo. **Wailoa Center,** P.O. Box 936, Hilo 96720 (933-4360), on the *makai* (seawards) side of the State Building. Helpful in planning itineraries. Maps, displays. Open Mon.-Fri. 8am-4:30pm.

Buses: Hele-on-Bus, 25 Aupuni St. (935-8241). Information on bus schedules. Operates Mon.-Sat. 6:30am-6pm. Luggage and backpacks $1 per piece. Runs between Kona and Hilo (1 per day), making a circuit of the island ($5.25).

Car Rentals: All national and state chains are located at Hilo airport. Make reservations several days in advance or take advantage of fly/drive deals for cheaper rates. **Budget,** 935-7293, rents to those 18-25, but slaps on a $20 surcharge per day. Basic economy car rate is $34 per day. Look for specials that can knock the price down to about $20 per day. Rental cars are not permitted on Saddle Rd.

Crisis/Help Line: 969-9111.

Post Office: Airport Access Rd. (935-6685), by the airport. Open Mon.-Fri. 9am-4:30pm, Sat. 9am-12:30pm. **ZIP code:** 96720.

Area Code: 808.

Hilo rests at the mouth of the Wailuku River. Its airport, **General Lyman Field,** is accessed by interisland service and flights from the mainland. Stop at the airport's visitor information booth; their maps and information are great for directions.

ACCOMMODATIONS AND CAMPING

The hotels clustered on Banyan Dr. by the bay are quiet and often empty. A listing of B&Bs across the Big Island are at the airport information kiosk or can be obtained in advance by writing the **Hawaiian Island Bed and Breakfast Association,** P.O. Box 726, Volcano, HI 96788.

Arnott's Lodge, 98 Apapane Rd., Keokaha (969-7097 or from Hawaii 800-953-7973, from mainland 800-368-8752). Clean, brightly painted, spacious accommodations serviced by friendly and personable staff. Small beach 1-min. walk from hostel. Ultramodern laundry 75¢ wash, 50¢ dry, 50¢ detergent. TV/VCR, kitchens. Spectacular and affordable ($15-30) daytrips to lava flow, Mauna Kea, snorkeling, Waipio Valley, and others. Bunk $15, single $26, double $36, group discounts (in advance). ISIC holders and VIPs of Backpackers, Australia/New Zealand get a 20% discount. Weekly discounts.

Hilo Hotel, 142 Kinoole St., Hilo 96720 (961-3733), downtown across from Kalakaua Park. Old, but neat, clean, and uniquely charming. Most convenient hotel to Hilo activities. A/C, refrigerators, free coffee, and an occasional sweet roll in the morning. Cocktail lounge offers free *pupus* Tues.-Fri. 4-6pm. Singles and doubles $39-45.

Onekahakaha Beach Park and **Kealoha Beach Park** (both 961-8311) are within 3 mi. of Hilo, but visitors should be aware that these are known as local tough-guy hangouts. Tent camping, bathrooms, and shower facilities. $1 permit required from Parks and Recreation Office, 25 Aupuni St., #210 (961-8311).

FOOD

You'll find macadamia nut bread, cookies, cakes, and pies galore to accompany cups of steaming Kona coffee grown on the island. Free samples of the nuts are given out at the **Hawaiian Holiday Macadamia Nut Company** in Haina, off Rte. 19 near Honokaa. Downtown Hilo is loaded with small, inexpensive Chinese restaurants with excellent lunch plates, sushi counters, and *okazu-ya*. Follow the locals.

Pescatore, 235 Keawe St. (969-9090). Means "fisherman" in Italian. Take the cue: ask for the catch of the day, in a white sauce. Open Mon.-Sat. 11am-2pm, 5-9pm.

Suisan's Retail Fish Market (935-9349), at Lihiwai and Banyan. If you're not into white sauce, buy some just-caught ahi (tuna) steaks here ($4 per lb.), take them back to Arnott's (see Accommodations), and broil them lightly ($1 barbecue fee). Also sells whole fish, oysters, and ogo seaweed. Open Mon.-Sat. 8am-3:45pm.

Ken's Pancake House, 1730 Kamehameha Ave. (935-8711). Imagine a Hawaiian IHOP. Serves breakfast all day, as well as burgers, hot dogs, etc. ($3.50-$5). Macadamia nut, coconut, or fresh banana pancakes $4.25. Open 24 hrs.

SIGHTS AND ACTIVITIES

Upslope Hilo receives 300 in. of rain per year; the coast receives 50-100 in. This wet climate has created a setting of true tropical splendor. Hilo is carpeted with lush mountain greenery and studded with plunging waterfalls, a testament to the Big Island's stunning beauty. And if things get too wet for you, just head for the sunny Kona-Kohala coast (about a 2-hr. drive away).

To get the most out of Hilo, start your sight-seeing early in the day. Rte. 11 will take you directly from the Hilo airport to the national park, but it's more rewarding to explore the town first. Even a cup of Kona coffee cannot beat a morning stroll around **Liliuokalani Garden** (an elaborate Japanese-style garden named after one of the royal princesses). You'll get a great view of Mauna Kea before the clouds roll in. Hilo is the orchid capital of the world; enough botanical gardens and nurseries have sprung up around the city to supply every senior prom in the country. **Orchids of Hawaii,** 2801 Kilauea Ave. (959-3581), features beautiful *leis* and an exotic variety of orchids and anthuriums (open Mon.-Fri. 7:30am-4:30pm). The **Hilo Tropical Gardens,** 1477 Kalanianaole Ave. (935-4957 or 935-1146), are a saturated botanical experience deserving a look and smell (open daily 9am-4pm).

Recent lava flows have covered the once glistening shores of **Kaimu Black Sand Beach** and various parts of the highway as well, making Rte. 11 the only way to round South Point from Hilo. **Lava Tree State Park,** which blooms year-round with lava casts of trees formed during the 1790 eruption, is still accessible. From Hilo, take Rte. 11 south to Keaau, turn onto Rte. 130 to Pahoa, and then take Pahoa-Pohoiki Rd. (Rte. 132). Continue around the loop on Rte. 132 past the **Kapoho Lighthouse** and the gardens nearby. Here a 1960 lava flow covered Kapoho Village; only trees and the lighthouse remain.

■■■ KONA

Occupying the western side of Hawaii, Kona claims a disproportionate share of the Big Island's white sand beaches, resorts, and realtors. It is also home to the town of **Kailua** (officially hyphenated as **Kailua-Kona),** a booming resort center with shops, nightlife, and perfect weather. Hot and gorgeous, the white sand beaches at **Hapuna** and **Kawaihae,** and the coves of the major hotels (all hotels must have public access paths to the beach) are perfect for tanning. The calm deep waters along this coast of the Big Island offer splendid snorkeling, scuba diving, and big game fishing. Upland, the fertile slopes of Mauna Kea and Haulalai yield the nation's best and only domestic coffee harvest.

Accommodations and Food Staying overnight in Kailua-Kona can be expensive, since its hotels cater to the affluent traveler. It's cheaper and more fun to stay away from the resort area, and daytrip into Kailua to use the hotel beaches. For the nearest **camping,** see Kohala. The **Kona Hotel** (324-1155), in Holualoa on Rte. 180, southeast of Kona, lends antique, high-ceilinged, and musty rooms. Each has two beds and a latch—not a lock—for the door. (Communal bathrooms. Singles $15. Doubles $23.) The **Manago Hotel,** P.O. Box 145, Captain Cook, 96704 (323-2642) on Rte. 11, is austere, comfy, and clean, with a generally older clientele. Inexpensive restaurant is a lunchtime favorite for guests and townies alike (open Tues.-Sun. 7-9am and 11am-2pm; dinner Tues.-Thurs. 5-7:30pm, Fri.-Sun. 5-7pm). (Singles $22, with bath $35. Doubles from $25.)

If you're interested in **Kona coffee,** you can taste the real thing for free at the **Mauna Loa Coffee Roastery,** 160 Napoopoo Road, Na Poopoo (328-2511; open daily 9am-5pm). Informative displays describe the history and mechanics of Kona coffee making. Their price of $12 per pound for the whole bean is reasonable, though it can be found for as low as $8.50. The **Ocean View Inn,** 75-5683 Alii Dr. (329-9998), across from the boat dock, serves seafood, American, Chinese, and Hawaiian fare in a diner setting and price range. Breakfast $4, lunch $4-7, dinner $7-10. Try some *laulau* and *poi* for $3. (Open Tues.-Sun. 6:30am-2:45pm and 5:15-9pm.) At **Stan's,** 75-5646 Palani Rd. (329-2455), in the Kona Seaside, breakfast specials include all-you-can-eat hotcakes ($4.25). Complete dinners ($7.50). (Open daily 7-9:30am and 5:30-8pm.)

Sights and Activities Despite other attractions, the beaches remain the main drawing card in Kona. White, sandy stretches line the coast through Kailua and up Rte. 19 to prime **Hapuna Beach** and **Spencer Beach Parks,** 35 mi. north. Both parks are wheelchair accessible. There are hotel-owned coves where you can rent sailboards. **Magic Sands** (also called "Disappearing Sands" because the sands get washed away for a couple of weeks every winter and then mysteriously return) at the Kona Magic Sands Hotel, 77-6452 Alii Dr. (329-9177), is a good place to park your towel and wade, but be sure the sand isn't about to go on vacation. Farther south on Rte. 11 is **Kealakekua Bay.** From Rte. 11 turn right onto Napoopoo Dr.; this winding road leads down to the historic bay (about 15 min.) where in 1778 Captain Cook tried to restock his ship during the *Makahiki,* a holy season honoring the god Lono. The Hawaiians thought Cook's white sails and masts heralded the return of Lono, and they proclaimed Cook a god.

■ Kohala and the Hamakua Coast

Going north up Rte. 19, tropical paradise gives way to desolate lava fields, left intact since 1859. Of course, the road itself is a more recent development, as are the white stone writings (the Hawaiian equivalent of graffiti) and the artificial oases of resort hotels. If the juxtaposition of resort culture with ancient Hawaiiana seems too incongruous, then fly down the road to **Puukohola Heiau** (at the intersection of Rte. 19 and Rte. 270). Stop at the **visitors center** (882-7218) for a brief introduction and a guide (open 7:30am-4pm). The **Puukohoa Heiau** is the last major religious structure of the old culture. Kamehameha the Great built this *heiau* about 200 years ago in honor of Ku Kailimoku, before his conquest of the Big Island. In 1791, a prophet told him that constructing the temple would enable him to conquer the entire chain of Hawaiian islands. About four years and many human sacrifices later, the prophecy was realized.

Hop along down Rte. 24 to the edge of the lush **Waipio Valley,** 8 mi. away, for one of the most striking panoramas anywhere in the islands. This 2000-ft. gorge is the crowning point of a series of breathtaking canyons between Waipio and Pololu. Bountiful flora and fauna made Waipio (the islands' largest gorge) the center of ancient Hawaiian civilization. In 1780, King Kamehameha was singled out here by reigning chiefs to be the future ruler. The jaunt down into the valley takes one hour and is not for vindictive knees. The way up is along a paved road. Many trails lead back into the valley and along the beach.

■■■ THE VOLCANO AREA

The volcanoes of the Big Island are unique in their size, frequency of eruption, and accessibility. Resting above the geological hot spot that fashioned each of the Hawaiian islands in turn, the two mountains in **Volcanoes National Park** continue to spout and grow, adding acres of new land each year. **Kilauea Caldera,** with its steaming vents, sulfur fumes, and periodic "drive-in" eruptions, is the star of the park, although the less active **Mauna Loa** and its dormant northern neighbor, **Mauna Kea,** are in some respects more amazing. Each towers nearly 14,000 ft. above sea level and drops some 16,000 ft. to the ocean floor. Mauna Loa is the largest volcano in the world, while Mauna Kea, if measured from its base on the ocean floor, would be the tallest mountain on earth. Entrance to the park is $5 per car, and is valid for seven days.

Accommodations and Camping Staying in the volcano area is expensive because of the limited number of hotels, but it is possible to camp for free in the backcountry. Consider the **Holo Holo Inn,** 19-4036 Kalani Holua Rd., Volcano Village 96784 (967-7950), which has 15 beds in dormitory-style rooms with a communal kitchen. The perfect locale, but beware of Howard the Territorial Goose. (Bunk $15. Call after 4:30pm and reserve in advance.) **Volcanoes National Park** (967-7311) offers free campsites at **Kipuka Nene, Namakani Paio** (near Kilauea Crater), and **Kamoamoa** (on the coast)—each with shelters and fireplaces, but no wood (7-day max; no reservations).

Sights Hiking around **Volcanoes National Park** is an explosive experience. Drive down **The Chain of Craters Road** and walk along the lava fields. At the end of the road lies a black sand beach, which wasn't there a few years ago. Each smooth black grain testifies to the tenacity of the sea which destroys even as Pele creates. The **Volcanoes National Park Visitor Center,** Volcano, Hawaii 96785 (967-7311), on Rte. 11, 13 mi. from Hilo offers trail maps, free ranger-guided hikes and important safety information (open daily 8am-5pm). They'll also tell you where you might see Pele in action. The center also offers free tours, weather permitting, of the volcano area (times posted every morning by 8:30am).

The 11-mi. scenic drive around the Kilauea Caldera on **Crater Rim Drive** is a good way to see the volcano by car. The road is accessible via Rte. 11 from the east and west or via the Chain of Craters Rd. from the south. Well-marked trails and lookouts dot the way, so stop frequently to explore. You might also take the easy hike along the vista-filled **Crater Rim Trail,** which traverses *ohia* and giant fern forests, *aa* (rough) and *pahoehoe* (smooth) lava flows, and smoldering steam and sulfur vents. Walk through the **Thurston Lava Tube,** formed by lava that cooled around a hot core which continued to move, leaving the inside of the flow hollow. **Devastation Trail** is a mi.-long psychedelic trip though landscape out of Dalí's imagination. The cinder cones and dead *ohia* trees were blasted by Kilauea Iki ("little Kilauea," west of "big" Kilauea Crater) in 1959.

Four-mi. **Kilauea Iki Trail** starts at the Kilauea Iki overlook on Crater Rim Rd. It leads around the north rim of Kilauea Iki, through a forest of tree ferns, down the wall of the little crater, past the vent of the '59 eruption, over steaming lava, and back to Crater Rim Rd. (Whew!) On the way you'll pass *ohelo* bushes laden with red berries. Legend has it that you must offer some berries to Pele before eating any or you'll incur her wrath. The 3½-mi. **Mauna Iki Trail** begins 9 mi. southwest of park headquarters on Rte. 11. It leads to ashen footprints left in 1790. From here you can hike down into the coastal area.

MAUI

Long before college athletes proclaimed "We're Number One," Maui's warlike chieftains proudly announced their island's supremacy over the archipelago with the words, "Maui no ka oi." As if to prove the point, Kamehameha the Great relocated the capital of his dynasty from the Big Island to Lahaina in 1810, commemorating his unification of the entire Hawaiian chain. The capital moved to Honolulu from Lahaina in 1845, and now, Lahaina is strictly a tourist burg.

The island takes its name from Maui, the demigod of mischief. According to legend, Maui's schoolboyish disposition led him to pull the island up from the sea bottom with fishhooks carved from his living mother's jawbone (not that he didn't love

MAUI

his mother—it was for her that he made the sun move more slowly across the sky). These accomplishments, along with his renowned lovemaking, were Maui's ticket to deification—and his spirit rules the island today.

PRACTICAL INFORMATION

Emergency: 911.

Visitors Information: Hawaii Visitors Bureau, P.O. Box 1738, Kahului 96732 (871-8691). The original moving tourist center. Call for location. Friendly assistance with itinerary planning, activities, and accommodations, but they will not make reservations. Information on Molokai and Lanai. Open Mon.-Fri. 8am-4:30pm. **Haleakala National Park,** P.O. Box 369, Makawao 96768 (572-7749), provides recorded information on weather conditions, daily ranger-guided hikes, and special activities. For information on camping and cabins call 572-9177. Park Headquarters (572-9306) is open daily 7:30am-4pm. **Division of State Parks,** 54 High St., Wailuku (244-5354), at Main St. Maui and Molokai state parks information. Helpful, but tough to find; go downstairs by the parking area. Open Mon.-Fri. 8-11am and noon-4:15pm.

Boats: Ferries are an ideal mode of transport to Molokai and Lanai. Going by boat is more exciting and cheaper than flying. The **Maui Princess** (661-8397) runs between Lahaina, Maui and Kaunakakai, Molokai (1 per day each way, 1¾ hr., $25 one way). **Expeditions** (661-3756) sails to Lanai 4 times per day for $25.

Taxi: Kaanapali Taxi (661-5285). $9 ride into Kahului, Wailuku from the airport.

Car Rental: VIP, Haleakala Hwy. (877-2054), near Kahului Airport. 3-day special on used cars $13 the first day, $15 for the next 2. $80 per week. Call the hostels to see if they can get you better rates.

Bicycle Rental: Bicycle touring on West Maui, with its flat roads, is highly rewarding. The twisting and crowded Hana Hwy., on the other hand, is deadly. **The Island Biker,** Kahului Shopping Center (877-7744), rents 21-speed mountain bikes for $18 per day. 5% discount with student ID. Open Mon.-Fri. 9am-5pm, Sat. 9am-3pm. **A&B Rentals,** 3481 Lower Honoapilani Rd. (669-0027), near Kaanapali. $15 per day for Beachcruiser bikes, or $60 per week. Open daily 9am-5pm.

Help Lines: Sexual Assault Crisis, 242-4357. 24 hrs. **Coast Guard Rescue,** 800-331-6176. **Gay and Bisexual Info,** 572-1884 (serves Maui, Molokai, Lanai).

Post Office: Lahaina, Baldwin Ave. Mon.-Fri. 8:15am-4:15pm. **ZIP Code:** 96761.

Area Code: 808.

Kahului is the major **airport,** landing regular flights from the mainland and other islands. Planes also fly into **Kaanapali** and **Hana.** (Hawaiian Air flies from: Honolulu, 18 per day; Hilo, 2 per day; Kona, 3 per day; Molokai, 2 per day; Kauai, variable.)

Maui consists of two mountains joined at an isthmus. The highways follow the shape of the island in a broken figure-eight pattern. The **Kahului Airport** sits on the northern coast of the isthmus. To the west lie **Kahului** and **Wailuku,** business and residential communities offering less expensive food and supplies than the resort towns. From Kahului, **Route 30** will lead you clockwise around the smaller western loop of the figure-eight to hot and dry **Lahaina,** the former whaling village, and **Kaanapali,** the major resort area.

On the north side of the eastern loop, **Route 36** winds through rainy terrain, over **54 one-lane bridges,** to **Hana.** Most roads are well-marked but poorly lit. Heed the four-wheel-drive warnings—a passing rainstorm can quickly drain your funds, since most rental car contracts stipulate that dirt road driving is at the driver's own risk.

ACCOMMODATIONS AND CAMPING

One of the fringe benefits of increasing tourism on Maui is the rise in the number of vacation rentals and bed and breakfasts, many catering to windsurfers and offering space to store equipment. Some go for as little as $20 per night. Check the classified section of the *Maui News*. The classifieds also list house-swap opportunities.

Campsites and hostels provide economic alternatives to Maui's resort hotels. The Wailuku hostels cater to windsurfers and others aquatically inclined. During the winter season, and especially around windsurfing events, these hostels are packed—so make it your maxim to book a month in advance.

Northshore Inn, 2080 Vineyard St. (242-8999), Wailuku. A clean, well-run hostel with a strict set of rules to insure guest comfort. Comfy common with TV. Fan, fridge, art in each room. Kitchen, laundry. Airport pick-up. European and Australian tourists and windsurfers. Bunks in spacious rooms $15, singles $33, doubles $43. $10 key deposit. Sheet rental $1, towels 50¢. Laundry soap 50¢ per load.

Banana Bungalow Hotel and International Hostel, 310 N. Market St., Wailuku (244-5090 or 800-846-7835). An unremarkable hostel supercharged with youthful energy. Windsurfers and international guests will conspire to plug you in to the local tourist subculture. Airport pickup. More activities than 1 person could possibly do: daytrips, night trips to clubs, athletic games. TV room with A/C, VCR. Laundry. Bulletin board with housing and windsurfing info. Kitchen with microwave. Bunks $15, singles with double bed $32, doubles $39. $5 key deposit.

The Bungalow, 2044 Vineyard St. (244-3294), Wailuku. Primitive quarters with shared bath. Some rooms with picnic coolers or fridges. Singles $15, doubles $25. Check for openings at **Cabebe Apartments** (244-9077), at the same address.

Maui Palms Hotel, 170 Kaahumanu Ave. (877-0071), Kahului. Unpretentious hotel by the sea. TV. Singles $47, doubles $50, triples $65.

Renting a car and camping on the island may be the best and cheapest way to luxuriate in Maui's natural magnificence. Sadly, the increasing number of tourists has made Maui, like Oahu, less tolerant of campers. East Maui, with its safe and well-organized campgrounds, is perhaps the surest option. **For permit information contact the County Dept. of Parks and Recreation (243-7389; open Mon.-Fri. 8-11am and noon-4:15pm).** Excursions in Haleakala National Park require no permits but enforce a maximum stay of 3 nights.

H.P. Baldwin Beach Park, Rte. 36, ½ mi. west of Paia. One of the 2 county parks. Summer home of friendly migrant surfers following the good waves. Outdoor shower, port-a-johns, and drinking water. Tent and permit required but latter is not often enforced. $3 per person, under 18 50¢.

Rainbow Beach Park, Rte. 39, between Paia and Makawao. From Paia take Rte. 39 (Baldwin Ave.) toward Makawao. Park is on the right just past Makawao Union Church. A bit isolated without a car, and a bit too close to the road. Set on a pretty, grassy field. Covered eating pavilion, drinking water, and portable toilets. $3 per person, under 18 50¢. Permit required.

Wainapanapa State Wayside, Hana Hwy., on the Paia-side of Hana, offers the best state camping facilities on the island. The cabins require reservations up to a year in advance. But ask the caretaker if she has any available, as such advance planning often leads to advance bailout. All sites include restrooms, picnic tables, barbecue grills, and outdoor showers, and are convenient to a black sand beach, blow holes, a *heiau* (temple), and Waianapanapa Cave as well as abundant coconut, papaya, and mango trees. You can take advantage of the hiking trail to reach Hana. Apply for a permit with the Dept. of State Parks. Camping is free; cabins sleep 6: $10 for one person, $14 for two, $30 for 6.

Oheo, at mile marker 42 on Rte. 31, near Kipahulu. A flat, grassy campground sporting 2 portable toilets but no drinking water or firewood. Set up some catch-basins for the rain that always is falling. Great hikes, including one to the 7 Sacred Pools, another through a tropical rainforest. Part of Haleakala National Park.

Hosmer Grove, Rte. 378, 7000 ft. up Haleakala's slope. Small campground with drinking water, toilet, grills, firewood, and covered tables. Excellent self-guided nature trail (pick up pamphlet at start of trail). At that height, it can get a bit chilly, so bring a sleeping bag. Part of **Haleakala National Park.**

FOOD AND NIGHTLIFE

Locals claim it is possible to live on Maui without spending a penny on food. The waters around the coast teem with fish, and the trees drip breadfruit, mango, coconut, pine nuts, papaya, and guava. The ground bears its share of delicacies as well, including pineapple and the sweet Kula onion, world-famous and sold for up to $6 per pound at the local market. *Guri guri,* a locally made pineapple or strawberry sherbet, has lured generations of islanders to its main supply source **Tasaka Guri Guri,** in Kahului's Maui Mall (871-4512; open daily, tropical paradise time—i.e. whenever). The cheapest places to eat are away from the resorts. **Wailuku** and **Paia** support the largest concentration of inexpensive restaurants. To dine in style, however, visit the hotels' attractive restaurants.

Uptown Grinds, 2080 Vineyard St. A diner with funky bird-of-paradise table coverings. Ask for the Let's Go special: a piping hot chili-cheeseburger with chips ($2).

Tasty Crust, 1770 Mill St., Wailuku (244-0845). A bare-bones backpacker diner serving drinks in paper cups and hearty food at unbeatable prices. Giant hotcakes ($1). Open Mon. 5:30am-1:15pm, Tues.-Sun. 5:30am-1:15pm and 5-9pm.

Pic-Nics, 30 Baldwin Ave., Paia (579-8021). The tofu burger with sprouts ($4.60) pleases. Browse their free guide and great map to Hana—it names and translates all 54 bridges of the Hana Drive. Open daily 7:30am-7pm.

The Vegan, 115 Baldwin Ave., Paia (579-9144). A great place to eavesdrop on Maui's animal-free intelligentsia as they rhapsodize about their *chi.* No meat, no dairy. A carnivore's nightmare. Try the celebratory "Mexican fiesta" ($5.95) or a "Maui sprout salad" ($3.50). Open Tues.-Sun. 11am-8:30pm.

Tutu's (248-8224), Hana Bay. Take-out joint feeding hungry tourists and locals for over 20 years. Plate lunches, $5.25. Open daily 8:30am-3:30pm.

For nightlife, gravitate toward West Maui which hosts the island's hottest dance scene. **Spats,** in the Hyatt Regency Maui (661-1234), rocks until 2am with two bars, two dance floors, a dress code, and no cover. **The Wunderbar,** 89 Hana Hwy. (579-8808), brings back memories of *Deutschland.* A fine selection of German beer. (Open daily 7:30am-10pm, until 2am for drinks.)

SIGHTS AND ACTIVITIES

Haleakala Haleakala Crater, the "House of the Sun," dominates the eastern end of the island from its perch 10,000 ft. above the sea. According to Hawaiian legend, the demigod Maui ascended Haleakala to slow the sun's trip across the sky so that his mother would have more time to dry her *tapa* cloth. When the sun arose at the end of the sky, Maui lassoed him by his genitals, and the sun genteely agreed to cruise across the sky more slowly. The House of the Sun is still a spectacular place for watching the sun rise. **Haleakala National Park** is open 24 hrs. (admission $4 per car for 4-day pass). Be sure to stop at the **park headquarters** (572-9300; open daily 7:30am-4pm), about 1 mi. from the Rte. 378 entrance. **Haleakala Visitors Center** (572-9172), near the summit, has exhibits on the geology, archeology, and ecology of the region (free natural history talks are given at 9:30, 10:30, and 11:30am; open daily sunrise-3pm). The **Puulaula Center,** at Haleakala's summit, is where you'll probably have to stay if you forget a sweater or jacket (open 24 hrs). A 12-mi. descent into the crater via **Sliding Sands Trail** and out again via **Halemauu Trail** is well worth the trip; your feet may feel like lead the next day, but that's only because they will have taken you light years, not just 12 mi. The silence of this journey is as vast as the crater itself. Heed the park's advice about sturdy walking shoes, water, sun screen, and rain gear, however. **Kaluuokaoo Pit** is one of several exposed lava tubes in the crater. Early Hawaiians threw the umbilical cords of newborns into the pit to safeguard the sacred coils from the valley's evil rodents. Drive farther south on Rte. 37 to **Tedeschi Winery** (878-6058), and taste their free "Maui Blanc" pineapple wine (open daily 9am-5pm; free tours given 9:30am-2:30pm).

Hana Missing the **Hana Coast** would be like visiting China without seeing the Great Wall. The northern route (**Hana Hwy. 360**) through **Paia** and **Keanae** redefines beauty with each twist and turn. This road has the dubious honor of being the

O
A
H
U

most pitted road west of NYC, but behind each curve reveals yet another breathtaking valley. Visit **Blue Pond** for a secluded swim in a waterfall-fed pond at the end of Ulaino Rd., past the Kakano Gardens. Cross the river and walk along the beach. And don't miss **Oheo,** known as the Seven Sacred Pools, 10 mi. south of **Hana.** Start from Paia with a full tank of gas, and don't go if the road is wet. It's a long way down. Paia's **Hookipa Beach Park** is an international windsurfing paradise.

While near the saddle of the island in central Maui, be sure to step into the unspoiled **Iao Valley,** on the southern slope of Puu Kukui. The valley is especially beautiful in the moonlight. **Iao Valley State Park** (open daily 7am-7pm), at the end of Rte. 32, includes the **Iao Needle,** a 1200-ft. basalt spire. Tour buses arrive by 10am, and clouds by 2pm; both leave by 6pm. The name is onomatopoeic, the cry of an unfortunate god who sat on this pointed peak. Really.

The **Hale Kii** ("House of Images") served as a place of worship throughout the 18th century until destroyed by natural erosion in 1819. Reconstructed in 1958, the *heiau* is now a temple of love. High-school love bunnies make the pilgrimage uphill on Thursday evenings for the island's most idyllic views. Follow Main St. (Rte. 32) to the traffic light at Rte. 330. Make a left, pass the macadamia nut grove, and turn right on Rte. 340. Continue to Kuhio Place, following the nerve-racking route to the right.

Lahaina An old whaling port in west Maui, Lahaina was the capital of the islands during the time of Kamehameha the Great. It's a sunny, dry town that infects visitors with drowsy calm. When Mark Twain visited, he planned to stay one week and work; he stayed a month and never lifted a pen. The enormous tree in Lahaina's town square is a 114-year-old East Indian banyan tree, rivaling Kauai's for the title of the islands' largest. The island's only remaining **steam locomotive** still carries tourists, if not sugar, between Lahaina and Kaanapali (one way $5, round-trip $8, under 12 half-price). A new **OMNI Theater,** 824 Front St., Lahaina (661-8314), presents Hawaii's history on the big, big screen with *Hawaii: Island of the Gods!* (Daily every hr. 10am-10pm. Admission $7, under 12 $5; $1 discount coupons available at nearby tourist centers.) At the **14 mi. marker,** near Olowalu, you can enjoy some of the calmest and most spectacular snorkeling in Hawaii, although it is rivaled by **Honolua Bay**, north of Kapalua. Those seeking more strenuous exercise should try their hand (shoulder and back, too) at windsurfing.

OAHU

King Kamehameha's victory on Oahu in 1795 consolidated his rule over the lower six islands and made the island the launching pad for his planned invasion of the kingdom of Kauai. By the time the first missionaries arrived in 1820, the city had become the economic and cultural center of Hawaii, and the dredging of Pearl Harbor's mouthway in 1900 allowed Oahu to develop almost overnight into the headquarters of the U.S. Pacific fleet.

Oahu can be roughly divided into four sections. **Honolulu** and its suburbs constitute the metropolitan heart of the state. The **North Shore,** from Kahuku to Kaena Point, is the home of the winter swells that surfers around the world dream of at night. The **Windward Coast** (on the east), especially around Hanauma Bay, is rife with tropical fish and coral reefs (not to mention reefer). The **Leeward Coast** (on the west) is raw and rocky, strikingly beautiful, and a great escape for campers seeking solitude. The slopes of two now-extinct volcanic mountain ridges, **Waianae** in the west and **Kooiau** in the east, run parallel from northwest to southeast and make up the bulk of Oahu's 600 square miles.

■■■ HONOLULU

Honolulu is the cultural, commercial, and political locus of Hawaii. Its industrial-strength harbor and concrete-and-glass business district attest to its status as a capital city and major Pacific seaport. At the same time, acres of white sand beaches make it one of the world's premier tropical vacation getaways. Honolulu's temperate island setting influences the lifestyle of its residents. Motorists in rush-hour retain an amazingly friendly disposition toward their fellow road warriors. And at night, the city vibrates with transient revelers, on whom residents capitalize by selling everything from party cruises to the odd *por favor*. Neither are likely to be a bargain, but hell, you're on vacation; book 'em, Dano.

PRACTICAL INFORMATION

Emergency: 911.

Visitors Information: Hawaii Visitors Bureau, 2270 Kalakaua Ave., 7th Floor, Honolulu 96815 (923-1811). Information on Oahu and the rest of the state. Pick up the *Accommodation Guide* and *Restaurant Guide,* a map of points of interest, and a walking tour of downtown Honolulu. Most brochures contain information for the disabled traveler. Also publishes the *Aloha Guide to Accessibility* for persons with mobility impairments. Open Mon.-Fri. 8am-4:30pm. **Department of State Parks,** 1151 Punchbowl St. #310, Honolulu 96813 (587-0300), at corner of S. Beretania St. (building with relief art at top). Information, trail maps, and while-you-wait permits for camping in state parks. Open Mon.-Fri. 8am-4pm. **Department of Parks and Recreation,** 650 S. King, Honolulu 96817 (523-4525). Information and permits for Oahu's county parks. Open Mon.-Fri. 9am-4pm. Permits available no earlier than 2 weeks in advance.

Buses: 848-5555. Covers the entire island, but different lines start and stop running at different times. Call for schedules. Also, backpackers beware: they won't let you carry on big packs or luggage. Fare 60¢. Bus passes valid for 1 month are available for $15 at satellite city halls, at Foodland grocery store, or Bank of Hawaii branches. Free senior citizens pass takes 1 week to process. Free Honolulu/Waikiki route maps available at tourist pamphlet stands throughout Waikiki.

Taxi: All cabs charge 25¢ per one-seventh mi. Flag rates are about $1.75. Airport to Waikiki $19.

Car Rental: Budget is the only national company that will rent to drivers under 21, and they slap on a $20 surcharge for ages 18-21. Used cars are a good bet, if you can stand non-A/C and ominous rattling. **Discover Rent-a-Car,** 1920 Ala Moana Blvd. (949-4767). $12.50 first day, $17 per 2 days thereafter, 3-day min.

Moped and Bike Rentals: Mopeds run about 40 mi. on $1 worth of gas. Most rental agencies require credit cards and a minimum age of 18. **Aloha Funway Rentals,** 1778 Ala Moana (942-9696) and 2976 Koapakapaka St. (834-1016), near the airport. Mopeds $15 per half day, $20 per day, $100 per week; bikes $20 per day. Open daily 8am-5pm.

Water Equipment Rentals: Kuhio Beach Service, to the right of the Kuhio Beach park pavilion, offers surfboard rentals with lessons ($20 per hr.), outrigger canoe rides ($6), and boogie boards ($5 per day). **Ohana Rentals,** near the breakers at Queen's Beach, also rents boogie boards with fins ($15 per day). Open daily 8am-6pm.

Crisis Lines: Coast Guard Search/Rescue, 800-552-6458. **Suicide and Crisis Center,** 521-4555. **Gay and Lesbian 24-hour Infoline,** 926-1000. Information about services and community events on Oahu.

Post Office: Main Office, 3600 Aolele Ave. (423-3990). Near the airport. Open Mon.-Fri. 8am-7:30pm, Sat. 8am-2:30pm. **ZIP Code:** 96813.

Area Code: 808.

Honolulu International Airport is 20 minutes west of downtown, off the Lunalilo Freeway (H-1). The **H-1 Freeway** stretches the length of Honolulu. Downtown Honolulu is about six blocks long and four blocks wide, wedged between Honolulu Harbor and Punchbowl Street. In Waikiki, **Ala Wai Boulevard, Kuhio Avenue,** and

Kalakaua Avenue run parallel to the ocean and are the main routes of transit. Bike and running paths abound in the city.

ACCOMMODATIONS

Honolulu, and especially Waikiki, cater to an affluent tourist crowd, but there *are* bargains for those willing to search and do without the grass-skirted frills. Because Hawaii is a stop on many round-the-world tickets, hostels are great places to meet travelers bound for the West Coast, Australia, or Europe. They do fill up, so reserve early by telephone or by mail.

Interclub Waikiki, 2413 Kuhio Ave. (924-2636). Five flags in front emphasize this hostel's international clientele: Americans must be en route overseas to stay here. Mr. Lim runs a clean, friendly hostel with excellent security. Female or mixed dorms. Laundry but no kitchen facilities. Lounge and pool table. Safe/lockers. Smoking/drinking allowed. No curfew or lights out; reception open 24 hrs. Checkout at 10am. Bunks $15. Doubles $45. $10 key deposit.

Honolulu International (HI/AYH), 2323A Seaview Ave. (946-0591), 1½ mi. north of Waikiki, near University of Hawaii at Manoa. By bus, take #6 from Ala Moana Shopping Center, to Metcalf and University Ave. (near Burger King). A peaceful, clean, though somewhat remote, haven from Waikiki's tourist kitsch; a turnoff if you prefer a perpetual party. Kitchen, locker, and clean single-sex facilities. Recreation room with TV and free movies. Beds guaranteed for 3 nights. Reception open 7:30-10am and 5pm-midnight. Check-out 10am. Lights out at 11pm; rooms are locked noon-4:30pm, but kitchen and TV room stay open. Members $10, non-members $13. Sheet sack rental $1. Reservations recommended.

Hale Aloha (HI/AYH), 2417 Prince Edward St. (926-8313), in Waikiki, 2 blocks from the beach. Take Waikiki (#8) bus to Kuhio and Uluniu, walk beachward 1 block, turn right. Clean hostel for HI/AYH members only. Beds guaranteed for 3 nights; ask politely and you might be allowed to stay a week. Check-in 8am-noon, 4pm-midnight. Check-out by 10am. No lockout or curfew; lights out at 11pm. Dorm bunks $15 per night; doubles $35. Sleepsack rental $1. Key deposit $5. Parking $2. Reservations essential.

Polynesian Hostel, 174 Kapahulu Ave., in Waikiki Grand Hotel, Room #1001. This older but well-maintained hotel has sold some rooms to the hostel, one of which affords a beach view. TV, kitchenette; 6-7 people per converted hotel room. Access to hotel pool. No curfew. Bunks $15.

Royal Grove Hotel, 151 Uluniu Ave. (923-7691). Clean, simple, carpeted rooms close to Waikiki Beach. Economy rooms have a stirring view of Vivian's Bar-B-Q. Elderly clientele. Single or double room with bath, TV, and fridge, $38. With kitchenette, $42.50.

CAMPING

Free permits for camping are available (see Practical Information above); be sure to have one, or the police and rangers who patrol the campgrounds will send you packing. Four state parks (Sand Island, Keaiwa Heiau, Kahana Bay, and Malaekahana) allow camping. Numerous county parks do as well, but their safety is dubious. Near Honolulu is **Keaiwa Heiau State Park,** from Waikiki, follow H-1 to Moanalua Hwy. (Rte. 78). Take Aiea turnoff to second traffic light; turn right there and follow Aeia Heights Drive until it ends. Oahu's only inland state park boasts the remains of a Heiau (a healing temple and herb garden). Camping area #4 is flat, grassy, and sheltered from winds. Restrooms, cold showers, tables, and BBQ pits. Also, try the **Malaekahana State Recreation Area** (293-1736), north of Laie. Take the Kamehameha Hwy. up the windward coast and watch carefully for the sign. The queen of Oahu's state parks, Malaekahana is ranger-patrolled for safety. Wade across the bay to Mokuauia Island, a bird refuge with unspoiled virgin beaches. Showers, toilets, picnic tables, and BBQ pits. The leeward (west) side of the island is notorious for assaults and robberies. Bear in mind that state parks enforce a five-day limit and are all closed Wed.-Thurs.

FOOD

Eating in Honolulu is an international dining experience. There's little reason for eating in Waikiki; the surrounding neighborhoods support many inexpensive restaurants that avoid the corny tourist ambience. The **Kapahulu, Kaimuki, Moiliili,** and **downtown** districts are all within 10 minutes of Waikiki by bus; with a good map, you can walk from one district to the next quite easily. For truly local flavor, take a trip to the **farmers market** across from Kewalo Basin, just west of Ala Moana Park. They have wonderfully fresh seafood and the delicate Hawaiian *lau lau*—a taro leaf stuffed with fresh fish. Go early in the morning and bargain for the day's catch.

Travelers to Waikiki will be deluged with ads and flyers recommending *luaus*. These feasts with Polynesian dancing rake in the tourist bucks and are often pretty cheesy, but some can be fun and belly-filling (and a few are even reasonably priced). The **Queen Kapiolani,** 150 Kapahulu Ave. (922-1941), offers an $11 unlimited *luau* luncheon buffet with entertainment, Mon.-Wed. and Fri.-Sat. 11am-2pm.

Perry's Smorgy, 2380 Kuhio Ave. (926-0184). All-you-can-eat smorgasbord. Dine on mahi-mahi, roast beef, fresh fruit, and endless Kona coffee in the indoor/outdoor garden (beautiful after dark). Breakfast 7-11am, $4.45. Lunch 11:30am-2:30pm, $5.95. Dinner 5-9pm, $8.

Leonard's Bakery, 933 Kapahulu Ave. (737-5591). Virtually a landmark, this Hawaiian institution has served perfect, hot *malasadas* (a Portuguese dessert) for years (45¢). Open daily 6am-10pm.

Wo Fat, 115 N. Hotel St. (549-6888). Very Cantonese, very old (founded 1882), and very popular. Pleasantly uncrowded at lunchtime. Karaoke on Thurs. and Sat. nights, 9pm-2am. Entrees $7-9, with specials under $5. Open daily 10:30am-9pm.

Ono Hawaiian Food, 726 Kapahulu Ave., Waikiki (737-2275), next to the Ala Wai golf course. Family-style restaurant that lives up to its name (*ono* means good). Try the *poi* or *opihi* (limpets) if you're adventurous. Go early; the lines often extend out the front door. *Kalua* plate $5.75. Open Mon.-Sat. 11am-7:30pm.

SIGHTS AND ACTIVITIES

If you're looking for the Honolulu of *Magnum, P.I.*, you'll find it. The one-hour loop on the #14 bus cuts across a sampling of Honolulu's diverse neighborhoods. Waikiki is, of course, centered around Waikiki Beach; Kaimuki and Kahala are small, close-knit communities; Moliliili's lifeblood is the university; and downtown is the shipping and business district, along with Chinatown.

In the 1950s, the image of a ¾-mi. crescent of white sand beach set against the profile of Diamond Head lured platoons of vacationers and honeymooners, eager to spend their post-war boom bucks, to wonderful Waikiki. Today, more savvy visitors spend time on the less crowded isles. Nevertheless, despite its glitzy facade, Waikiki remains fascinating. **Waikiki Beach,** actually comprised of several smaller beaches, is lined with shops and hotels of all varieties and is generally crammed with tourists. Furthest to the east is the **Sans Souci Beach,** with no showers or public restrooms. The **Queen's Surf Beach,** closer to downtown, attracts swimmers and roller skaters. The area to the left of the snack bar is a popular tanning spot for gay travelers.

When you want a break from sun and surf, hike the one mi. into the **Diamond Head Crater.** To get there, take bus #58 from Waikiki. Bring a flashlight to guide you through the pitch-dark section of the tunnel. The view of Waikiki is spectacular. If the gods do not favor your excursion to Diamond Head try visiting the **Damien Museum,** 330 Ohua St. (923-2690), behind St. Augustine Church. With original documents and a one-hour video, the museum displays the history of Father Damien's Molokai leper colony. (Open Mon.-Fri. 9am-3pm, Sat. 9am-noon. Free.) For the animal inside you, the **Honolulu Zoo,** 151 Kapahulu Ave. (971-7175), across from Kapiolani Park, is located on the east end of Waikiki. Call for a recorded schedule of events. ($4, under 13 free. Open daily 8:30am-4pm.)

Across the street is the **Waikiki Shell,** home to the **Kodak Hula Show** (833-1661), which is Waikiki at its photogenic tackiest. This production packages *hula* dancing and palm tree climbing into bite-size tourist portions. You may have discombobulating Brady Bunch flashbacks, but it *is* a laugh. (Shows Tues.-Thurs. at 10am. Free.) For more authentic dancing performances, contact the **Hawaii Visitor's Bureau** and ask about upcoming performances or competitions among the hula halau (schools).

Several cultural and historic attractions are found around downtown. The **Iolani Palace,** at King and Richard St. (522-0832), was first the residence of King Kalakaua and his sister Queen Liliuokalani and later served as the nerve center in the TV show *Hawaii Five-0.* The deposed Liliuokalani spent nine months here as a prisoner. The stunning breakfast room was once used to entertain heads of state from all over the world. Now millions of dollars back the museum's search for the original palace furniture. The fabulous palace displays sumptuously carved *koa* furniture and elegant European decor. (Tours Wed.-Sat. every 15 min. 9am-2:15pm; 45-min. tours by reservation only at the barracks in the palace grounds. Tours $4, kids 5-12 $1, under 5 not admitted.) Nearby, the **Honolulu Academy of Arts,** 900 S. Beretania St. (538-1006), houses one of the finest collections of Asian art in the U.S. The 30 galleries and six garden courts also display 17th-century samurai armor, African art, and temporary exhibits. (Open Tues.-Sat. 10am-4:30pm, Sun. 1-5pm. Free.) The **Bishop Museum,** 1525 Bernice St. (848-4129), in Kalihi, houses a well-respected, albeit disorganized, collection of artifacts from the Indo-Pacific region. It is the best Hawaiiana museum in the world, and deserves a good portion of your day. Their **planetarium** features a show entitled "Journey by Starlight" (daily at 11am and 2pm, Fri.-Sat. at 8pm also) which projects the history of Polynesian celestial navigation. Take bus #2 ("School St.") from Waikiki. (Open daily 9am-2:30pm; call 848-4106 for further info. Museum open Mon.-Sat. 9am-5pm. $5, ages 6-16 $2.50.)

On December 7th, 1941, "a day which will live in infamy," a stunned nation listened to the reports of the Japanese obliteration of the U.S. Pacific Fleet in **Pearl Harbor.** The **U.S.S. Arizona National Memorial** (422-2771) is an austere, three-part structure built over the sunken battleship in which over a thousand servicemen perished. Count on long lines. (Free tours 7:45am-3pm. Launches out to the hull every 15 min. No children under six years of age are admitted on the launch. The **visitors center** is open Tues.-Sun. 7am-5pm. Take bus #20 from Waikiki or #50, 51, or 52 from Ala Moana, or the $2 shuttle (839-0911) from major Waikiki hotels.)

One of the best dayhikes on the island begins *mauka* at the end of Manoa Rd. and trails through 1 mi. of lush tropical greenery to **Manoa Falls**. Once there you can take a cold, fresh-water dip in the pool under the falls. Take bus #5 from Waikiki to the end of Manoa Rd. Disembark to catch the bird shows in **Paradise Park,** 3737 Manoa Rd. (988-0200), a natural Hawaiian rainforest sheltering hundreds of tropical birds, some of which perform their own musical compositions daily. (Open daily 9:30am-5pm. Call for shows. Admission $15, ages 8-13 $10, 3-7 $8.)

Parallel to the Manoa Valley, the **Pali Highway** (Rte. 61) winds its way through **Nuuanu Valley** and over into Kailua, on the windward side of the island. On the way, stop at the **Pali Lookout.** Here, Kamehameha the Great consolidated his kingdom by defeating Oahu's soldiers and driving them over the cliff. Although this observation point is always packed with tourists, the view overlooking the windward side is undoubtedly one of the finest in all of the islands. Hang onto your hat—the wind can gust hard.

ENTERTAINMENT

Bars, restaurants, and theaters abound in Waikiki, making nightlife as wild as your feet and liver will allow. The University of Hawaii's **Hemenway Theatre** (956-6468), in the Physical Sciences Building, shows second-run films for $3.50. Also peruse the *Honolulu Weekly,* distributed free of charge on Tues., for information on community shows, movies, and events, as well as witty restaurant reviews.

Seagull Bar and Restaurant, 2463 Kuhio Ave. (924-7911), in Waikiki. Drink up with a truly international crowd. A lot of young hostelers hang out here for the low drink prices; slam a beer for a mere $1.50. Open daily 7pm-2am.

Hula's Bar and Leis, 2103 Kuhio Ave. (923-0669), at Kalaamoku. Popular gay bar; dark and intimate. Popcorn maker in back. No cover. Open daily 10am-2am.

Pink Cadillac, 478 Ena (942-5282). One of the few dancing options for the 18-21 crowd, featuring neo-rave and neon lights. Hip-hop and progressive, too. Open 9pm-1:45am. Under 21 cover $15; 21 and over $5, $3 Fri.-Sat.

Rose and Crown, 131 Kaiulani Ave. (923-5833). A stately British public house smack in the middle of Waikiki. Pitcher of Bud, $9.

■■■ THE OTHER SIDE OF THE ISLAND

Everything on Oahu outside Honolulu is considered "the other side." Concrete and glass quickly give way to pineapple and sugarcane fields sprinkled with small villages. A tour of the island can be done in five hours, but it's best to set aside at least a day. Start on the Windward Coast and work your way around the island. To reach the southern **Windward Coast,** take bus #55 from Ala Moana. To see the **North Shore,** hop on bus #52 at Ala Moana. Both buses run every hour daily 7am-6pm.

■ Windward Oahu and Hanauma Bay

Miles of beaches and rural towns span the 40-mi. Windward Coast, running from **Laie** in the north to **Mokapu Point** in the south. This is one of the most scenic drives on the island, and good snorkeling abounds. From Waikiki, take **Kalanianaole Highway** (Rte. 72) east to **Koko Head Crater.** Some of the most colorful fish and best snorkeling in the Pacific reside in **Hanauma Bay.** A 10-minute walk to the left of the bay brings you to the less well-known **Toilet Bowl**—you supply the joke about the name. Climb in when it's full and get flushed up and down as waves fill and empty the chamber through natural lava plumbing. One mi. farther, similar plumbing drives the **Halona Blow Hole** to release its spray. **Secret Beach,** to the right of Halona Blow Hole, was the site of Burt Lancaster and Deborah Kerr's famous "kiss in the sand" in *From Here to Eternity.* If you want your life to imitate art, be our guest.

Accommodations, Camping, and Food The budget traveler's best lodging bet is the **Backpacker's Vacation Inn and Plantation Villas,** 59-788 Kamehameha Hwy. (638-7838), ¼-mi. north of Waimea Bay, with a young and rowdy crowd, weekend BBQs, and free snorkeling equipment. (Bunks $16, doubles $35-45. Summer rates $96 per week. $20 key deposit. 3-night min. stay.) However, the buses provide reliable enough transportation to make it a day trip. Your best camping option is **Malaekahana State Recreation Area** (293-1736), north of Laie, ranger-patrolled for safety (see Honolulu, Camping above). At low tide, wade across the water to **Mokauaia Island,** a bird refuge and great picnic spot. Bear in mind that escalating tension between locals and tourists may make some beach parks unsafe. Those on the Windward Coast are probably your best choice.

Fruit vendors and drive-in restaurants with plate lunches and shaved ice speckle the Windward Coast. **Kaaawa Country Kitchen,** 51-480 Kamehameha Hwy. (237-8484), Kaaawa, across from Swana Beach Park, has kept the locals of Kaaawa satisfied for more than 30 years. (Open Mon.-Fri. 6am-2:30pm, Sat.-Sun. 6am-3:30pm.) **Bueno Nalo,** 41-865 Kalanianaole Hwy. (259-7186), in Waimanalo, serves flavorful Mexican meals ($6.25-7.75). (Open daily 11:30am-9pm.)

Surfing and Sights **Sandy Beach,** just beyond Halona, is a prime spot for body-surfing and boogie-boarding, the center of the summer surf circuit, and a year-round hangout for locals. **Makapuu Beach,** 41-095 Kalanianaole Hwy., is another prime place to bodysurf, but when the lifeguards put up red flags, stay out of the water. For novices, the best bodysurfing can be found at **Sherwoods** and, on weekends, at **Bellows Air Force Base.** Both are on Kalanianaole on the road to Kailua. Be warned, however, that neither of these parks provides lifeguards. Kalanianaole ends by intersecting **Kailua Road.** Follow this road toward **Kailua Town** and **Kailua Beach Park.** This is prime sailboarding territory. The sandy beach and strong, steady onshore winds are perfect for learning watersports. **Windsurfing Hawaii** (261-6067) rents beginner boards in the parking lot for $30 per day (harness $5 extra) and shortboards for $40 per day. They also have boogie boards ($10 per day), wave skis ($25 per day) and two-person kayaks ($35 per day). Sailboarding lessons run $35 per person for a three-hour group clinic. If you can bear the airborne grit, this is a great place to swim. Nearby **Lanikai Beach's** (on Mokulua Dr.) white sand and deep green waters make it the best place on Oahu to savor the sunrise. Kailua Rd. in the other direction takes you to **Kaneohe** via Kamehameha Hwy. Lanikai's beauty defies description. Grab your snorkel gear and swim or wade out into the bay; better yet, use an innertube and float around effortlessly.

Dig the **Valley of the Temples,** 47-200 Kahekili Hwy., a burial ground matching the Punchbowl for beauty. The serene **Byodo-In Temple,** with tropical gardens and a three-ton brass bell, can be found on the grounds. (Open daily sunrise to sunset. Admission to the valley $2 per person.) Right around the bend from **Punaluu** is the entrance to **Sacred Falls Park.** The falls and the pool underneath make the two-mi. hike from the parking lot worthwhile. Farther up the coast, the city of **Laie** is home to the **Polynesian Cultural Center,** 55-370 Kamehameha Hwy. (293-3333), a carefully recreated village representing the indigenous cultures of New Zealand, Samoa, Tonga, Fiji, Hawaii, Tahiti, and the Marquesas. (Open Mon.-Sat. noon-6:30pm for daytime activities. Dinner served 4:30-7pm, followed by an evening spectacle 7:30-9pm. $25, with dinner and show $41.50.)

■ North Shore and Central Oahu

Home to the sugar cane fields and surfers, the **North Shore** and Central Oahu are different worlds from Honolulu (and most other parts of the world). The pace is slow and peaceful in the summer, with beautiful sunsets and plenty of empty beaches. Things heat up in the winter when the surfer crowd descends to shred the infamous waves along **Sunset Beach** and the **Banzai Pipeline,** and the North Shore hops with surfing competitions and their concomitant bikini contests.

The action on the North Shore centers on **Haleiwa,** the surfers' Graceland. Haleiwa once was a plantation town, but now is enlivened by surf shops and art galleries. **Hawaii Surf and Sail,** 66-214 Kamehameha Hwy. (637-5373), rents all kinds of watersport equipment and gives surfing and sailboarding lessons ($30 per 2-hr. lesson). To the North of Haleiwa is **Waimea Beach Park,** where locals jump off a high rock formation into the sea daily at 11am, 12:30, 2, 2:45, and 3:30pm.

On the way home, take a poke around the **Dole Pineapple Pavilion,** 64-1550 Kamehameha Hwy. (621-8468). Displays offer the visitor a crash course on the ins and outs of pineapple breeding. Inside you can buy classy pineapple memorabilia, from t-shirts to the puzzling non-dairy Dole Whip. Be sure to drink some of the free pineapple juice flowing from the plastic pineapple in the corner. Also drop by the **Coffee Gallery,** 66-250 Kamehameha Hwy. (637-5571), and try their vegetarian chili ($1.75-$3) or a thirst-quenching ice coffee ($1). (Open Mon.-Thurs. 6am-9pm, Fri. 6am-11pm, Sat.-Sun. 7am-11pm.) When you get hungry, park at **Meg's Country Drive-In,** 66-200 Kamehameha Hwy. (637-9122), in Haleiwa, which offers 20 varieties of plate lunches ($4-5), *shaka min,* and yummy smoothies. (Open 7am-6pm.) **The Sugar Bar and Restaurant,** 67-069 Kealohanui (637-6989), is a classic dive, with bikers, surfers, locals, and occasional area bands, and without a cover. Open 11pm-2am.

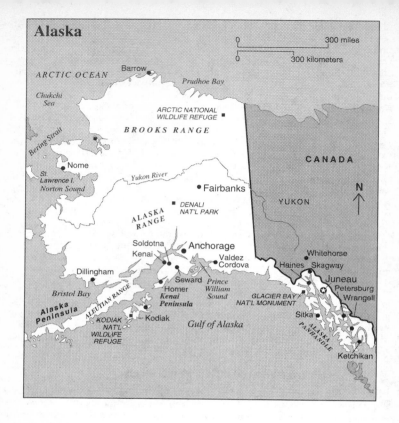

Alaska

Alaska

In a country given to hyperbole, Alaska is the ultimate land of extremes. By far the largest of the 50 states, it comprises fully one-fifth of America's land mass. It has the highest mountain in North America (20,320-ft.-tall Mt. McKinley/Denali), the largest American National Park (13 million acre Wrangell-St. Elias National Park), the hugest carnivore in North America (the Kodiak brown bear), and the greatest collection of bald eagles in the world. At the height of summer, Alaska becomes the "Land of the Midnight Sun," where you can start a pickup game of softball at 2am; in the depths of winter it is land of the noonday moon, where shimmering curtains of spectral color—the *aurora borealis*—dance like smoke in the darkened midday sky.

Alaska's history, like the state itself, is larger than life. The first humans to colonize North America crossed the Bering Strait into Alaska via a now-sunken land bridge. Russian-sponsored Danish navigator Vitus Bering was the first European visitor to arrive, bringing in his wake a wave of Russian fur traders who exhausted the fur supply within a century. Worldwide esteem for Alaska was at its nadir in 1867, when Secretary of State James Seward negotiated the United States' acquisition of the territory from Russia for a trifling $7,200,000 (about 2¢ per acre). The Secretary became the laughingstock of the nation—the purchase was called "Seward's Folly,"—but within 20 years Alaska showed its worth by revealing a mother lode of gold ore. In 1968, long after the gold rush had slowed to a trickle, the state's fortunes rebounded yet again, with the discovery of "black gold" (oil) on the shore of the Arctic Ocean. By 1981, $7,200,000 worth of crude oil flowed from the Arctic oil field every four-and-a-half hours.

PRACTICAL INFORMATION

Visitor Information: Alaska Division of Tourism, 33 Willoughby St. (465-2010); P.O. Box 11081, Juneau 99811. Open Mon.-Fri. 8am-5pm. **Alaska State Division of Parks,** Old Federal Building, Anchorage 99510 (762-2617). Open Mon.-Fri. 8am-4:30pm. **United States Forest Service,** 1675 C St., Anchorage 99501-5198 (271-4126). Info on national parks and reserves. Open Mon.-Fri. 8am-5pm.
Time Zones: Alaska (5 hrs. behind Eastern); Aleutian-Hawaii (6 hrs. behind).
Postal Abbreviation: AK
Sales Tax: None. Everything's already pretty damn expensive.

> Those contemplating a longer sojourn in Alaska should acquire a copy of *Let's Go: Alaska & The Pacific Northwest,* including invaluable information on the Aleutians, the Interior, the Alaskan West Coast, and Arctic Alaska.

CLIMATE

No single climatic zone covers the whole state; Prudhoe Bay differs from Ketchikan in climate as much as Minneapolis does from Atlanta. Fairbanks, Tok, and the Bush frequently enjoy 95°F hot spells, receiving less than eight in. of precipitation annually. The Interior freezes with -50°F temperatures in winter. Farther south, the climate is milder and rainier. Cordova rusts with 167 in. of precipitation annually. Anchorage and other coastal towns in the southcentral are blessed with the Japanese Current, which has a moderating effect on the climate. Average temperatures for Anchorage range from 13°F in January to 57°F in July.

TRAVEL

Driving in Alaska is not for the faint of heart. Roads reach only a quarter of the state's area, and many of the major ones remain in deplorable condition. Dust and flying rocks are a major hazard in the summer, as are miserable 10- to 30-mi. patches of gravel. "Frost heaves" from melting and contracting permafrost cause dips and surreal "twists" in the road. Radiators and headlights should be protected from flying rocks with wire screens, and a fully functioning spare tire and a good set of shocks are essential. Winter can actually offer a smoother ride. Active snow crews keep roads as clear as possible, and the packed surface and thinned traffic permit easier driving without summer's mechanical troubles. At the same time, the danger of avalanches and ice is cause for major concern. Anyone venturing onto Alaska's roads should own a copy of *The Milepost,* available for $10 from Vernon Publications, Inc., 300 Northrup Way, #200, Bellevue, WA 98004 (800-726-4707).

The **Alaska Marine Highway** consists of two completely unconnected ferry systems. The **southeast** system runs from Bellingham, WA up the coast to Skagway, stopping in Juneau, Ketchikan, Haines, and other towns. The **southcentral** network serves Kodiak Island, Seward, and Prince William Sound. Write ahead; for all schedules, rates, and information, contact Alaska Marine Highway, P.O. Box 25535, Juneau 99802-5535 (800-642-0666 from the U.S. except 800-585-8445 from WA state; 800-665-6444 from Canada; 907-465-3941; fax 907-277-4829).

■■■ THE ALASKA HIGHWAY

Built during World War II, the Alaska Highway maps out an astonishing 2647km route between Dawson Creek, BC, and Fairbanks, AK. After the Pearl Harbor attack in 1941, worried War Department officials were convinced that an overland route—far enough inland to be out of the range of carrier-based fighters—was necessary to supply the U.S. Army bases in Alaska. The U.S. Army Corps of Engineers completed the daunting task in just eight months and twelve days.

Travelers on the highway should be prepared for heavy-duty driving. For much of the route, pavement gives way to chip-seal, a layer of packed gravel held in place by hardened oil. In summer, dust and rocks fly freely, guaranteeing shattered headlights and a chipped windshield. Drivers should fit their headlights with plastic or wire-mesh covers. Most locals protect their radiators from bug splatter with large screens mounted in front of the grill. Travel with at least one spare tire and some spare gas; if you're crazy enough to drive the highway in winter, bring along a full set of arctic clothing and prepare your four-wheel-drive for subzero conditions.

Before setting out on your epic Alaskan journey, pick up the exhaustive listing of *Emergency Medical Services* and Canada Highway's *Driving the Alaska Highway* at a visitors bureau, or write the Department of Health and Social Services, P.O. Box H-06C, Juneau, AK 99811 (907-465-3027). The free pamphlet *Help Along the Way* lists emergency numbers along the road from Whitehorse to Fairbanks.

■■■ DENALI NATIONAL PARK

Established in 1917 to protect wildlife, Denali National Park is also the home of **Denali** (Athabaskan for "The Great One"), the highest mountain in North America. Anglicized as **Mt. McKinley,** Denali towers as the tallest mountain in North America and the greatest vertical relief in the world from base to summit. More than 18,000 ft. of rock scrapes upward toward the sky—even mighty Mt. Everest rises only 11,000 ft. from its base on the Tibetan Plateau. Denali is so big it manufactures its own weather (earning it the nickname "Weathermaker"). Denali's top is visible for only about 20% of the summer, but even if you can't see the peak, you can still experience the glories of the park's tundra, taiga, wildlife, and lesser mountains.

Practical Information Located 237 mi. north of Anchorage, the park is accessible by **Alaska Railroad** (683-2233) or by car from the George Parks Highway. For bus travel into Denali, try **Caribou Express** (278-5776), with daily departures to Fairbanks (3pm; $35), and Anchorage (11am; $54). **Denali Express** (800-327-7651), runs daily to Fairbanks (5:30pm; $25) and Anchorage (7:30pm; $75). All visitors must check in and pay the $3 entrance fee at the **Visitor Access Center** (683-1266, 24-hr. **emergency** number 683-9100), less than 1 mi. from Rte. 3 (open summer daily 9am-8pm). The **area code** in the park is 907.

Even those fully prepared for Denali should allow at least three days to get a space on the shuttle bus or in the campsite desired, and obtaining a backcountry permit usually requires an in-park wait as well. **Shuttle** and **camper buses,** both free with park admission, depart from the VAC and make their rounds on an 88-mi. access road. In order to ride the buses you need to obtain a coupon from the VAC—a same-day coupon, a next-day coupon, or a two-day advance coupon, all three of which are granted on a space-available basis. Same-day and next-day buses are almost always booked by mid-morning, so show up as early as possible.

Camping and Hiking There are six **campgrounds** within the park. Most have water and some form of toilet facilities (sites $12). The **Denali Hostel,** P.O. Box 801 Denali Park 99755 (683-1295), is 9.6 mi. north of the park entrance. Take a left on Otto Lake Rd.; it's the second house on the right. They offer bunks, showers, kitchen facilities, and morning shuttles into and out of the park ($22).

Backpackers waiting for a backcountry permit or a campsite within the park are assured a space in **Morino Campground** ($3), next to the hotel (with water and pit toilets). Permits are distributed on a first-come, first-served basis. Many people set up camp in Morino the first day while they take the shuttle bus in and preview potential campsites within the park. You may have to wait another day or two to get your first choices, so bring sufficient food—the nearby convenience store has necessary supplies, but is predictably pricey.

Denali National Park has no trails, and it is not a park that can be covered in one day. Although dayhiking theoretically is unlimited, in actuality, only 2-12 hikers can camp at one time in each of the park's 44 units. Select a few different areas in the park in case your first choice is booked. The first third of the park is varying degrees of taiga forest and tundra which is hellish to hike—imagine walking on old wet mattresses with bushes growing out of them. The last third of the park is infested with mosquitoes in July and biting "no-see-ums" in August. The prime hiking and back-country camping spots are in the middle third. Although rangers at the backcountry desk will not give recommendations for specific areas (they want to disperse hikers as widely as possible), especially good locations are along the **Toklat River, Marmot Rock,** and **Polychrome Pass.** You'll want to take the 10-hr. round-trip bus ride to Wonder Lake Campground for your best chance at a glimpse of Denali *sans* clouds, but if you're planning to camp there, reserve the last bus out to the campground and the first bus back in the morning, and bring protective netted head gear (available in the convenience store).

■■■ FAIRBANKS

If E.T. Barnette hadn't gotten stuck with his load of trade goods at the junction of the Tanana and Chena Rivers just when Felix Pedro, Italian immigrant-turned-prospector, unearthed a golden fortune nearby, and if territorial Judge James Wickersham hadn't been trying to woo political favors from an Indiana senator (Charles Warren Fairbanks by name), then this town might never even have existed—it certainly wouldn't have been named for somebody who never even set foot in Alaska.

Practical Information Fairbanks lies 358 mi. north of Anchorage via the **George Parks Hwy.,** and 480 mi. south of Prudhoe Bay on the gravelly **Dalton Highway.** Fairbanks's **Convention and Visitors Bureau** (456-5774 or 800-327-5774) is at 550 1st Ave. (open daily 8am-8pm; Oct.-April Mon.-Fri. 8am-5pm, Sat.-Sun. 10am-4pm). The **Alaska Public Lands Information Center (APLIC),** at 3rd and Cushman St. (451-7352), has exhibits and recreation information on different parks and protected areas of Alaska. The staff welcomes requests for information about hiking. (Open daily 9am-6pm; in winter Tues.-Sat. 10am-6pm.) Fairbanks is also home to the headquarters for nearby **Gates of the Arctic National Park,** 201 1st Ave. (456-0281; open Mon.-Fri. 8am-4:30pm) and the **Arctic National Wildlife Refuge,** 101 12th St., Room 266 (456-0250; open Mon.-Fri. 8am-4:30pm).

Fairbanks's **airport** is located 5 mi. from downtown on Airport Way, which doubles as the George Parks Hwy. **Alaska Air** (452-1661) flits to Anchorage ($184) and Juneau ($283); **Mark Air** (455-5104), to larger Bush towns, including Barrow ($235). The **Alaska Railroad,** 280 N. Cushman (456-4155), next to the *Daily News-Miner* building, is an excellent way to see the wilderness. May-Sept., there is one train daily to: Nenana ($18), Anchorage ($120), and Denali National Park ($45). Ages 2-11 ride ½-price. During the winter, a train leaves for Anchorage every Sunday ($70). (Depot open Mon.-Fri. 7am-9:45pm, Sat.-Sun. 6-10pm.) Take **Denali Express** (800-327-7651) daily to Denali ($25). **Alaskan Express** (800-544-2206) speeds daily to Anchorage ($105) and 4 times per week to Haines ($165; accommodations for overnight stay in Beaver Creek not included). Acquire a vehicle at **U-Save Auto Rental,** 3245 College Rd. (479-7060), for $35 per day, with 100 free mi.; 26¢ each additional mi. In an **emergency,** call 911. The **post office** licks at 315 Barnette St. (452-3203; open Mon.-Fri. 9am-6pm, Sat. 10am-2pm) and the general delivery **ZIP Code** is 99707. The **area code** is 907.

Accommodations, Camping, and Food The **Fairbanks Youth Hostel (HI/AYH),** 1641 Willow St. (456-4159), has moved around a lot in the past few years so call to check on availability of beds ($10), floor space ($8), or tent space ($6). Owner Paul Schmidt has a wealth of information about the area and is always willing to direct hostelers toward adventure (including Prudhoe Bay). No curfew, no lockout, free showers, laundry ($2.50 for wash and dry), and bike rental ($10 per day). Write P.O. Box 721196, Fairbanks for information. The closest campground is noisy **Tanana Valley,** 1800 College (456-7956), next to the Aurora Motel. It caters to RVs, but has no hookups available, although there are free showers and a laundromat (wash and dry $1). Sites are $10.

Fairbanks ferments with fast-food frieries; just about every fast-food chain in existence can be found along Airport Way and College Road. **The Whole Earth,** in College Corner Mall below Gulliver's Used Books (479-2052), is a health food store, deli, and restaurant all in one, with lots of plants, soft lighting, and funky wall murals. You can sit here all day over a cup of organic coffee and a Natchester Sandwich (beans, cheese, Greek peppers, and spices in a spread, $4). All sandwiches served on fresh homemade whole-wheat rolls. (Open Mon.-Fri. 10am-7pm, Sat. 10am-6pm, Sun. noon-5pm. Hot food served Mon.-Sat. 11am-3pm.) In Alaska on your birthday? Try **Denny's Farthest North,** Airport Way near Wilbur. Yes, it's Denny's *Farthest North,* and as always, it's an experience. And it's always open, 24 hrs. a day. Veggie cheese melt only $5; breakfast $5-7. **The Pumphouse Restaurant and Saloon,** Mile 1.3 Chena Pump Rd. (479-8452), is so cool that one of the city's bus lines goes out of its way to drop you here. This rave local spot features an out-of-this-world lunch buffet ($9.79) and dinner entrees for $10-15. (Open daily 11:30am-2pm and 5-10pm. Bar open weekends until 2am.)

Sights and Entertainment One of Fairbanks's proudest institutions is the **University of Alaska-Fairbanks,** at the top of a hill overlooking the flat cityscape. Both bus lines stop at the **Wood Campus Center** (474-7033). The **University of Alaska Museum,** a 10-min. walk up Yukon Dr. from the Campus Center (474-7505), houses a fascinating array of exhibits ranging from Russian Orthodox vestments to native baskets to a mummified prehistoric bison. The most popular exhibit is a seven-minute video of the *aurora borealis* (northern lights). (Open daily 9am-7pm; Oct.-April noon-5pm. $4, seniors and students $3. Oct.-April, free on Fri.)

View a technological wonder of the world, the **Trans-Alaska Pipeline,** at Mile 8 of the Hwy. heading out of Fairbanks. The pipeline was elevated on super-cooled posts to protect the tundra's frozen ecological system from the 108°F oil.

With nothing but black spruce to keep them company in the surrounding tundra, Fairbanksians turn to the bars at night. Come carouse with stiff drinks and boisterous, rugged types fresh from the North Slope oil fields. UAF students head for the **Howling Dog Saloon** (457-8780), 11½ mi. down Steese Hwy., for live rock-and-roll. Look for a colorful old wooden structure in the middle of nowhere encircled by pickup trucks. The local eye doctor and his wife, conservatively dressed, dance next to bikers, who dance next to field guides from Denali...get the picture? Volleyball and horseshoe games go on until 4am or so, as does the band. (Open Tues.-Fri. 5pm-5am, Sat.-Sun. noon-5am.)

SOUTHCENTRAL ALASKA

■■■ ANCHORAGE

Only 80 years ago cartographers wasted no ink on what is now Alaska's major metropolis. Not surprisingly, the city has an aroma of prefabrication—writer John McPhee called it "condensed, instant Albuquerque." Approximately half the state's population—some 250,000 people—live in "Los Anchorage," the moniker that some rural residents use to mock the city's urban pretensions. A decentralized jumble of fast-food joints and discount liquor stores, Anchorage also supports a full range of popular and high-brow culture: semi-pro baseball and basketball teams, frequent performances by internationally known orchestras and pop stars, dramatic theater, and opera. The Anchorage Daily News won a Pulitzer Prize in 1989 for its reporting on suicide and alcoholism among Native Americans in the region. Even though moose and bear frequently wander downtown and can actually be hunted legally within the municipality, this is as close to "big city" as Alaska gets.

PRACTICAL INFORMATION

Emergency: 911.

Visitor Information: Log Cabin Visitor Information Center (274-3531), W. 4th Ave. at F St. Open daily 7:30am-7pm; Sept. and May 8:30am-6pm; Oct.-April 9am-4pm. The Log Cabin is usually crammed with visitors and a staff of volunteers. Plenty of maps and brochures.

Airport: Alaska International Airport, P.O. Box 190649-VG, Anchorage 99519-0649 (266-2525). Serviced by 7 international carriers and 3 Alaskan carriers, including **Mark Air** (243-6275 or 800-426-6784), which has daily flights to: Kenai ($25); Homer ($40); Kodiak ($65). Nearly every airport in Alaska can be reached from Anchorage, either directly or through a connecting flight in Fairbanks.

Alaska Railroad: 411 W. 1st Ave., Anchorage 99510-7500 (265-2494; 800-544-0552 out of state), at the head of town. To: Denali ($85); Fairbanks ($120); Seward ($40). In winter, 1 per week to Fairbanks; no service to Seward. The train will make unscheduled stops anywhere along this route—just wave it down with a white cloth and wait to be acknowledged with a whistle. For more information write to Passenger Service, P.O. Box 107500, Anchorage. Office open daily 6am-11pm; ticket sales from 6:15am-5pm. May be closed if no trains are arriving.

Buses: Alaska Denali Transit, P.O. Box 2203, Anchorage (273-3331 24 hrs. for recorded message, or 733-2601 9am-5pm for reservations). Several trips per week to: Talkeetna ($25); Denali ($35); Fairbanks ($99). Schedules vary widely, so call ahead. **Caribou Express,** 501 L. St. (278-5776). To: Fairbanks (1 per day, $75); Valdez (1 per day, $75). **Moon Bay Express** (274-6454). To: Denali (1 per day, $35). Pickup at Anchorage Youth Hostel (see Accommodations) at 8am. **Homer and Seward Bus Lines** (800-478-8280). To: Seward (1 per day, $30); Homer (1 per day, $35).

Public Transportation: People Mover Bus (343-6543), in the Transit Center, on 6th Ave. between G and H St., just up the street from the Anchorage Youth Hostel. Buses leave from here to all points in the Anchorage Bowl (including a few per day to the airport) 6am-10pm; restricted schedule on weekends. Cash fare $1, tokens 90¢, day pass $2.50.

Help Lines: Crisis Line, 562-4048. Mon.-Fri. 8:30am-5pm.

Post Office (277-6568), W. 4th Ave. and C St. on the lower level in the mall. Open Mon.-Fri. 10am-5:30pm, Sat. 10am-4pm. **ZIP code:** 99510.

Area Code: 907.

From its seat 114 mi. north of Seward on the Seward Hwy., 304 mi. west of Valdez on the Glenn and Richardson Hwy., and 358 mi. south of Fairbanks on the George Parks Hwy., Anchorage is the hub of Southcentral Alaska. The **downtown area** of Anchorage is laid out in a grid. Numbered avenues run east-west, and addresses are designated East or West from **C Street.** North-south streets are lettered alphabetically west of **A Street,** and named alphabetically east of A Street. The rest of Anchorage spreads out—*way* out—along the major highways.

ACCOMMODATIONS AND CAMPING

There are several free campgrounds just outside the city; for info contact the **USDA Forest Service** (271-2500) or the **Alaska Parks and Recreation Dept.** (762-2617).

Anchorage Youth Hostel (HI/AYH), 700 H St. (276-3635), at 7th, 1 block south of the Transit Center downtown. A great gateway hostel in a convenient location. 3 kitchens and 2 balconies. Family and "couple rooms" available. Frequently filled to the rafters in summer; write ahead for reservations. The **Alaska Black Book,** in the 2nd floor reference room, is an invaluable compendium of previous travelers' (mis)adventures all over Alaska. Wheelchair accessible. Lockout noon-5pm. Curfew midnight. 4-day max. stay in summer. $12, non-members $15. Weekly and monthly rates during the off-season. Reservations recommended.

International Backpackers Inn, 324 Mumford (274-3870 or 272-0297), at Peterkin. Take bus #45 to Bragaw and Peterkin. As you watch the bus depart, turn left and walk 3 blocks. 25 dorm-style beds, common kitchens, bathrooms, and TVs. Free local phone and linen. Chore required. Key deposit $10. Beds $12-15 (go for the $15 building). Tent sites $10. Weekly and monthly rates available.

Midtown Lodge, 604 W. 26th (258-7778), off Arctic Blvd. Take bus #9. Simple, spotless rooms with shared bath. Free continental breakfast; free soup and sandwiches in the lobby for lunch. Singles $43. Doubles $48. Reservations essential up to 2 weeks ahead in summer.

Centennial Park, 8300 Glenn Hwy. (333-9711), north of town off Muldoon Rd.; look for the park sign. Take bus #3 or 75 from downtown. 72 sites for tents and RVs. Showers, dumpsters, fireplaces, pay phones, and water. 7-day max. stay. Check-in before 6pm in the summer peak-season. Sites $13.

Lions' Camper Park, 5800 Boniface Pkwy. (333-9711), south of the Glenn Hwy. In Russian Jack Springs Park across from the Municipal Greenhouse. Take bus #12 or 45 to the mall and walk. Overflow for Centennial Park. 10 primitive campsites with water station, fire rings, and showers. Self-contained vehicles only. 14-day max. stay. Sites $13. Open May-Sept. daily 10am-10pm.

FOOD AND NIGHTLIFE

With a diverse population and the advantage of an economy of scale, Anchorage presents budget travelers with the most affordable and varied culinary fare in Alaska. The closest grocery to downtown is **Save U More,** at 13th and I St., which carries many bulk foods and no-name brands (open Mon.-Sat. 10am-7pm, Sun. noon-6pm).

White Spot Cafe, 109 W. 4th Ave. (279-3954). An unrivaled cheeseburger with homecut fries ($3.50) has made this tiny establishment an Anchorage favorite since 1959. 2 eggs, potato, toast, and coffee ($2.75). Open daily 6:30am-7pm.

Kumagoro Restaurant, 533 4th St. (272-9905). The combination of Alaskan fish and Japanese expertise make this an excellent, reasonably priced sushi restaurant. Daily lunch specials (served 11:30am-2pm), such as halibut teriyaki with soup, rice, and vegetables ($6). Chicken teriyaki ($6.50). Bar open daily 10am-2am; restaurant open daily 11am-10pm, although food is available until 1am.

Twin Dragons, 612 E. 15th Ave. (276-7535). Heap a bowl from the fresh meat- and vegetable-buffet and watch the Mongolian barbecuer fry it with an amazing flourish. Soup and appetizer included with barbecue. Lunch buffet ($6), all-you-can-eat dinner ($9). Open for lunch Mon.-Sat. 11am-3:30pm, Sun. 2-3:30pm; open for dinner Mon.-Thurs. 3:30pm-1am, Fri.-Sat. 3:30-10:30pm, Sun. 3:30-9:30pm.

Alaska Flapjacks, 1230 W. 27th Ave. (274-2241). The best breakfast spot in town advertises itself as a family restaurant—possibly because you could almost feed a family with a single one of their breakfast specials. 3 eggs, 2 pancakes, bacon, gravy, and hashbrowns ($6). Superstack of 5 pancakes ($4). Open daily 6am-8pm.

Anchorageans from all of Uncle Sam's tax brackets party at **Chilkoot Charlie's,** 2435 Spenard Rd. (272-1010), at Fireweed. Take bus #7 or 60. Six bars, a rockin' dance floor, and a quiet lounge fill this highly commercial space. Ask about the nightly drink specials. Less crowded and more interesting is **Mr. Whitekey's Fly-by-Night Club,** 3300 Spenard Rd. (279-SPAM). Mr. Whitekey's is a "sleazy bar serving everything from the world's finest champagnes to a damn fine plate of Spam." The Monty Python-esque house special gives you anything with Spam at half-price when you order champagne. Try Spam nachos or Spam and cream cheese on a bagel ($3-7). Nightly music ranges from rock to jazz to blues. The *Whale Fat Follies*—an anti-tourist tourist attraction—plays nightly at 8pm (bar open 3pm-2:30am).

SIGHTS AND ACTIVITIES

Watching over Anchorage from Cook Inlet is **Mt. Susitna,** known to locals as the "Sleeping Lady." For a fabulous view of Susitna, as well as Denali (Mt. McKinley) on a clear day, head to **Point Warzenof,** on the western end of Northern Lights Blvd., about 4 mi. from downtown. **Earthquake Park** recalls the 1964 Good Friday earthquake, a day Alaskans refer to as "Black Friday." The quake was the strongest ever recorded in North America, registering 9.2 on the Richter scale.

A 4-hr. **walking tour** of downtown Anchorage begins at the visitors center (see Practical Information). The omnipresent **Grayline** (277-5581) also offers an Anchorage city tour (daily at 3pm, 3½ hr., $21, under 12 $10).

The public **Anchorage Museum of History and Art,** 121 W. 7th Ave. (343-4326), at A St., features permanent exhibits of Alaskan Native artifacts and art, as well as a Native dance series (open daily 9am-6pm; Sept. 16-May 14 Tues.-Sat. 10am-6pm, Sun. 1-5pm; $4, seniors $3.50, under 18 free). The **Imaginarium,** 725 5th Ave. (276-3179), recreates Arctic marine environments, glacier formation, and other scientific oddities of the North (open Mon.-Sat. 7am-6pm, Sun. noon-5pm; $4, under 12 $3). To see real Alaskan wildlife without the danger of being trampled or otherwise mauled, visit the **Alaska Zoo,** Mile 2 on O'Malley Rd. (346-2133; take bus #91; open daily 9am-6pm; $5, seniors $4, ages 13-18 $3, ages 3-12 $2).

If you're looking for authenticity, head to the non-profit gift shop at the **Alaska Native Medical Center** (257-1150), 3rd and Gampbell. Many Native Alaskans pay for medical services with their own arts and handicrafts. Walrus bone *ulus* (knives used by Natives, $17-60), fur moccasins, Eskimo parkas, and dolls highlight the selection (open Mon.-Fri. 10am-2pm, and occasionally Sat. 11am-2pm). Craftworks from Alaska's Bush are sold at the **Alaska Native Arts and Crafts Showroom,** 333 W. 4th Ave. (open Mon.-Fri. 10am-6pm, Sat. 10am-5pm, Sun. noon-5pm).

To counteract urban claustrophobia, head for the summit of **Flattop Mountain** in the "Glenn Alps" of the Chugach Range near Anchorage. The view from the top is well worth the hike. The trail is deceptively difficult due to its steepness and slippery shale, but even novices will find it manageable. To reach the trailhead, jump on bus #92 to the intersection of Hillside Rd. and Upper Huffman Rd. From there walk ¾ mi. along upper Huffman Rd. and take a right on Toilsome Hill Dr. Proceed for 2 mi. Trail signs at the park entrance point the way up.

Rabbit Lake is a beautiful alpine bowl which collects water in the shadow of 5,000-ft. Suicide Peak. Bus #92 is again your montane chariot; hop off at the corner of Hillside Dr. and De Armour Rd. Follow Upper De Armoun Rd. from here 1 mi. east, and then turn right onto Lower Canyon Rd. for 1.2 mi. The round-trip from where you debark the bus to the lake is 15.4 mi. Camping at the lake or along the way makes a pleasant two-day hike.

■■■ KODIAK ISLAND

Aptly nicknamed Alaska's "Emerald Isle," Kodiak Island is both astonishingly beautiful and the victim of amazingly hard luck. The island has in this century been rocked by earthquakes, washed over by *tsunamis,* hit by the oil of the Exxon *Valdez,* and blanketed in nearly 2 ft. of volcanic ash. Cursed as it may seem, Kodiak Island's present string of superlatives more than dwarfs such past misfortunes. The island is the largest in Alaska, and much of this vast acreage is preserved in the Kodiak National Wildlife Refuge, home to an estimated 2600 Kodiak bears and countless other furry creatures ranging from little brown bats to beavers. The rich waters around the island have made its fishing and crabbing fleet legendary, drawing flocks of young people each summer to work its canneries. The largest Coast Guard station in the U.S. is based less than 10 mi. from Kodiak City, patrolling against poachers. Islanders here take their seafood (and especially their crab) seriously.

■ Kodiak

Kodiak was the first capital of Russian Alaska, before Alexander Baranov moved the Russian-American Company headquarters to Sitka. It was here that the Russians committed their worst atrocities, importing Aleut slaves and using them to hunt the area's sea otters to near-extinction. The area also has been subject to the capricious whims of mother nature; in 1912, Mt. Katmai erupted, covering the island with 18 inches of ash and decimating the area's wildlife; in 1964 the biggest earthquake ever recorded in North America shook the area and created a tidal wave that destroyed much of downtown Kodiak, including 158 homes.

Practical Information For hunting and fishing information, charter arrangements, and a self-guided walking tour map, head to the **Information Center** (486-4070), at Center St. and Marine Way, right in front of the ferry dock (open Mon.-Fri. 8am-5pm and for most ferry arrivals). The **U.S. Fish and Wildlife Headquarters and Visitor Center,** just outside Buskin State Recreation Site, 4 mi. southwest of town, has wildlife displays, 150 films to choose from, and information on the Kodiak National Wildlife Refuge and its cabins. (Open Mon.-Fri. 8am-4:30pm, Sat.-Sun. noon-4:30pm.) Located 4 mi. southwest of town on Rezanof Dr., Kodiak's **airport** is served by **Mark Air** (487-9798), with flights to Anchorage ($65 with 21-day advance purchase). The **Alaska Marine Highway** terminal is next to the visitors center (800-526-6731 or 480-3800). Ferries come May-Sept. 1-3 times per week; in winter less frequently. To: Homer ($46); Seward ($52). In an **emergency,** call 911.

Kodiak's **post office** rests on Lower Mill Bay Rd. (open Mon.-Fri. 9am-5:30pm, Sat. 10am-4pm). The **ZIP code** is 99615; the **area code** is 907.

Accommodations, Camping, and Food Close to a dozen B&B's go for rates as low as $45 a night. Call the visitors center (see Practical Information) for a list and remember to reserve well in advance; finding a room becomes almost impossible when the airport shuts down due to bad weather (which is often). **Gibson Cove Campground (Tent City),** 2 mi. from the ferry terminal, a quiet transient worker community, has a friendly, on-site manager, raised gravel platforms for tents, hot showers, toilets, and drinking water. (Sites $2. No max. stay.) Designed for backpackers, **Fort Abercrombie State Park Campground,** 4 mi. northeast of town on Rezanof-Monashka Rd., has no RV hookups, but there are shelters, water, outhouses, WWII ruins, a lake, and spectacular sunsets (sites $6; 7-night max. stay).

Hobgoblins of conformity can always trudge to **McDonald's,** at Rezanof and Lower Mill Bay Rd., **Subway,** at 326 Center Ave., or **Pizza Hut,** on Mill Bay Rd. in front of Safeway. If service is what you want, try **El Chicano** (486-6116), in the nameless grey building across from the Orpheum Theater on Center St. Although this authentic Mexican restaurant presents no sign to passers-by in the street, it could advertise some of the best and biggest Mexican specialties north of the border. Try a bowl of black-bean soup with homemade Mexican bread ($4.75), or a filling burrito ($4.75-7.25). Complimentary corn chips and salsa. (Open Mon.-Sat. 11am-10pm, Sun. noon-9pm.)

Sights and the Outdoors Built in 1808 as a storehouse for sea otter pelts, the **Baranov Museum,** 101 Marine Way (486-5920), is the oldest Russian structure standing in Alaska—as well as the oldest wooden structure on the entire West Coast. The museum displays Russian and native artifacts, and a library shows period photos and literature from the Russian colony to the present. (Open Mon.-Fri. 10am-4pm, Sat.-Sun. noon-4pm; Labor Day-Memorial Day Mon.-Wed. and Fri. 11am-3pm, Sat. noon-3pm. $1, under 12 free.) The **Resurrection Russian Orthodox Church** (486-3854), not far from the museum, houses the oldest parish in Alaska. Built in 1794, its elaborate icons date back to the early 19th century, and its church bells are still rung by hand (call for tours by appointment; open Mon.-Fri. 1-3pm). Beautiful **Fort Abercrombie State Park,** 3½ mi. north of town, was the site of the first secret radar installation in Alaska (*shh!*). The fort is also the site of a WWII defense installation; after several islands in the Aleutian chain were attacked by the Japanese in 1942, American military minds assumed Kodiak would be next.

Home to one of the largest commercial fishing fleets in Alaska, the sheer number of fish in Kodiak Island's rivers and surrounding waters may have you reeling (and rodding). The 100-mi. road system permits access to a number of productive **salmon streams.** Right in Kodiak, surfcasting into Mill Bay around high tide often yields a pink or silver salmon.

On a clear day **hikers** can obtain a commanding view stretching from the Kenai Peninsula to the Aleutian Peninsula atop **Barometer Mountain.** To reach the trailhead, take the first right past the end of the airport runway on the way out of town. The trail up **Pyramid Mountain,** beginning from the parking lot at the pass on Anton Larsen Bay Rd., is another popular hike near town.

■ Kodiak National Wildlife Refuge

The Wildlife Refuge, on the western half of Kodiak Island, was inaugurated in 1941 and has grown to nearly two million acres. An estimated 2600 Kodiak bears live on the island along with a variety of other mammals and several hundred bald eagles. The bears are most commonly seen in July and Aug. during their fishing frenzy. They hibernate Dec.-April, bearing cubs Feb.-March. Though the bears are half-vegetarian and usually avoid contact with humans, be careful: Kodiaks are the largest and most powerful carnivores in North America, and they can—and do—kill humans.

Because it was established for the enjoyment of animals rather than humans, the refuge remains undeveloped and expensive to access. For the same reason, those intrepid (or monied) few who visit the refuge will be rewarded by one of the world's most pristine wilderness experiences. About the only affordable way to access the refuge is to join a scheduled **Mark Air** (487-9798) mail-run to any of the several small villages scattered throughout the wilderness. Although stopovers (possible for an extra fee) are brief, the aerial view of the island is stunning. The flights to Karluk and Larsen Bay or to Old Harbor are two of the best. Both routes are flown frequently and the passenger fare is $99. Call for schedules and information. For information about the park as well as reservations for the park's 10 **cabins,** contact the **Kodiak National Wildlife Refuge Managers,** 1390 Buskin River Rd., Kodiak 99615 (487-2600). If you're in Kodiak, drop by the **U.S. Fish and Wildlife Headquarters and Visitor Center** (see Kodiak: Practical Information).

■■■ SEWARD AND KENAI FJORDS NATIONAL PARK

Seward (SUE-urd) traces its origins to a nearby Russian shipyard built by the legendary Russian explorer Alexander Baranov in the 1830s. The town expanded to its present form in 1904 as the southern terminus of the Alaska railroad, and it is from here that the Iditarod Dogsled Trail led early gold prospectors into the Interior (even though the famous race now begins in Anchorage). The city itself offers little to attract outsiders other than fine hiking and halibut fishing, but Seward holds paramount importance as the gateway to the stupendous **Kenai Fjords National Park.**

Practical Information For the usual assortment of pamphlets, head for the **Chamber of Commerce,** Mile 2 on the Seward Hwy. (224-8051; open daily 9am-6pm; Labor Day-Memorial Day Mon.-Fri. 9am-5pm). They also operate a **railroad car** (224-3094), 3rd and Jefferson St., where you can pick up a self-guided walking tour and mark your home town on the world map (open in summer daily 11am-5pm). The **National Park Service Visitors Center,** 1212 4th Ave. (224-3175), at the small-boat harbor, can provide you with information and maps for the spectacular Kenai Fjords National Park. **Alaska Railroad** (224-3133, 278-0800 for reservations) choo-choos from their depot at the northern edge of town to Anchorage (1 per day, $40). **Homer and Seward Bus Lines,** 550 Railway Ave. (224-3608), speeds to Anchorage (1 per day, $30). **Alaska Marine Highway** (224-5485), dock at 4th and Railway Ave., on the southern edge of town, has about 1 ferry per week in summer (occasionally 1 every 2 weeks) to Kodiak ($52). In an **emergency,** call 911.

Seward's **post office** (224-3001) posts at 5th Ave. and Madison St. (open Mon.-Fri. 9:30am-4:30pm, Sat. 10am-2pm). The **ZIP code** is 99664; the **area code** is 907.

Accommodations, Camping, and Food The only hostel on the Kenai Peninsula lies 16 mi. outside Seward and lacks a telephone, but the hotel rates in town may give you the adrenaline you'll need to hike there. The **Snow River International Home Hostel (HI/AYH),** at Mile 16 of Seward Hwy., has no phone; call the central hosteling number in Anchorage (276-3635). This beautiful new house in a scenic location has 14 beds, showers, and laundry facilities. ($10, non-members $13.) A well-preserved site that could be the setting of any frontier Western, the **Van Gilder Hotel,** 308 Adams St. (224-3079), has beautiful rooms with TV and sink (singles and doubles $50, with bath $85; reservations necessary). Tent lawns and RV lots occupy some of Seward's choicest (and windiest) real estate, at the **Municipal Waterfront Campground.** Stretching along Ballaine Rd., the campground has a stunning view of the mountains across Resurrection Bay. Toilets are scattered throughout the campground, and restrooms with showers are located at the Harbormaster Bldg. 2-week max. stay. Check-out 4pm. (Open mid-May-Sept. Sites $5, parking spots $6; collected by strict honor code.)

Seward offers the usual spread of greasy diners and *très chic* tourist traps; stock up on groceries at the **Eagle Quality Center** at Mile 2 of the Seward Hwy. (open 24 hrs.). It's a bit of a walk from downtown, but you can reward yourself with a massive $1 ice cream cone from the in-store soda fountain. Breeze in to the **Breeze Inn** (224-5298), in the small-boat harbor, for the huge all-you-can-eat lunch buffet ($8). Slighter appetites should try the two-trips-to-the-soup-and-salad-bar ($4.25). (Open daily 6am-9pm.) Tasty Mexican dishes and pizza are served on an outdoor patio at the **Marina Restaurant** (224-3202), across from the small-boat harbor on 4th Ave. Have 3 eggs and hashbrowns for breakfast ($3.75), slice of pizza with soup or salad for lunch ($5), or a 15-in. cheese pizza for dinner ($14).

Outdoors Seward is the point of entry into the **Kenai Fjords National Park.** The **Park Service Visitors Center** sits near the small-boat harbor. The park protects a coastal mountain system packed with wildlife and glaciers. The best way to see this area is from boats in the bay; pick up the list of charters and prices at the Chamber of Commerce (see Practical Information). Most trips run $80-100 per day, $50-65 per ½-day, but prices are likely to change due to frequent price wars. For more information, contact **Alaska Renown Charters** (224-3806), **Mariah Charters** (243-1238), **Kenai Coastal Tours** (224-7114), and **Kenai Fjord Tours** (224-8030). These tours are worth every dime, gratifying visitors with incredible sights: glaciers larger than some eastern states, herds of orcas berthing and gliding under the boat, and sea lions cavorting in the sea.

Seward is a great base for **day hikes.** Nearby **Mt. Marathon** offers a great view of the city and ocean. Take Lowell St. to the very end to reach the trail. There is no final peak at the end of the trail, but the views out over Resurrection Bay are phenomenal. **Exit Glacier**—billed as Alaska's most accessible—is 9 mi. west on the road that starts at Mile 3.7 of Seward Hwy. If you're feeling energetic, take the steep and slippery 4-mi. trail from the ranger station to the magnificent **Harding Ice Field** above the glacier. The rangers will prevent you from getting within 50 ft. of the glacier's face, as several-ton chunks of ice are continually breaking off, or "calving."

■ ■ ■ WRANGELL-SAINT ELIAS NATIONAL PARK

Wrangell-St. Elias National Park and Preserve is Alaska's best-kept secret. The largest national park in the U.S., it could swallow more than 14 Yosemites. Four major mountain ranges converge within the park: the Wrangells, the Alaskas, the Chugach, and the St. Elias Mountains. Nine peaks tower at more than 14,000 ft. within the park, including the second highest mountain in the U.S. (18,008-ft. **Mt. St. Elias**). The heights are enveloped with eternal snow and ice; the Basley Icefield is the largest non-polar icefield in North America and the Malaspina Glacier, a piedmont glacier near the coast, is larger than Rhode Island. Mountain sheep populate the jagged slopes, and moose and bear are commonly sighted in the lowlands.

The park is located in the southeast corner of Alaska's mainland and is bounded by the Copper River to the west and the Alaskan boundary to the east. Kluane National Park in the Yukon lies adjacent to the east and the two parks together are designated a World Heritage Site. Park access is through two roads: the **McCarthy Road** which enters the heart of the park and the **Nabesna Road,** which enters from the northern park boundaries and is frequently washed out.

The **visitors center** (822-5234) lies 1 mi. off the Richardson Highway on the side road towards **Copper Center.** (Open daily 8am-6pm, in winter Mon.-Fri. 8am-5pm.) Informed rangers will give you the low-down on all the to-dos (and to-sees) in the park. There are also **ranger stations** in **Chitina** (823-2205, open Fri.-Sun. 9am-6pm) and in **Slana** on the northern park boundary (822-5238, open daily 8am-5pm).

■ From the Perimeter into McCarthy

Most visitors travel to **McCarthy,** a small town of fewer than 50 permanent residents smack-dab in the middle of the park. From Chitina, which is the last place to buy groceries (there's no store in the park), the **McCarthy Road** follows the old roadbed of the **Copper River and Northwestern Railway** for 58 mi. to the Kennicott River. This road is arguably the roughest state road in Alaska, and is a 2-3 hr. one-way trip (bring a spare tire). The road terminates on the western edge of the Kennicott River. There are two parking lots here; park in the upper lot as sudden glacial releases of water can submerge the lower lot (especially in July-Aug.). The only way across the river is by a hand-operated **tram** (a metal "cart" with two seats, running on a cable). **McCarthy** is an easy ½-mi. walk from the opposite bank.

In the early 1900s, the richest copper ore ever discovered was found in the nearby mountain ridge on the east side of the Kennicott Glacier. To transport the ore, the Copper River and Northwest Railway was constructed between 1908-1911. The CR&NW (jokingly called "Can't Run and Never Will") did run for 196 mi. from the Kennecott mines to the warm-water port of Cordova. A company town with a reputation for being very proper and maintaining strict conduct rules, **Kennicott** was home base for the mining operations until 1938, when falling copper prices forced the mine to shut down. Today, Kennicott remains remarkably intact, and has earned the name of "American's largest ghost town."

■ McCarthy

McCarthy, 5 mi. south of Kennicott, developed originally for miners' recreation. Both alcohol and women, prohibited in Kennicott by the company, made the town attractive to male miners. Today, McCarthy clusters along a few nameless streets.

Practical Information Walking from the river, the first building encountered houses the **McCarthy-Kennecott Historical Museum** (open daily 8am-6pm). This is a good place to get general info about the area and pick up a walking tour of Kennicott and McCarthy ($1 donation).

If you'd rather not drive to McCarthy, **Backcountry Connection** (822-5292) will take you aboard their vans. One-way fare from Glennallen is $55, from Chitina $35. Vans go every day of the week except Tuesday. **Wrangell Mountain Air** (see below in the Outdoors section) flies here daily from Chitina ($60 each way).

No **phones** in McCarthy—everybody is connected via the "bush phone" (a CB system) and most businesses have "phone bases" elsewhere. The McCarthy Lodge has **showers** for $5. There is no **post office.** (Local mail is flown in weekly.)

Accommodations, Camping and Food McCarthy **Lodge** (333-5402) in downtown McCarthy has rooms from $95 and the **Kennicott Glacier Lodge** (258-2350) in Kennicott has rooms from $109, but **camping** is free on the west side of the Kennicott River (pit toilets, no water). Because almost all of the land around McCarthy and Kennicott is privately owned and local drinking water comes from nearby creeks, camping is prohibited in all areas on the eastern side of the Kennicott River, with the exception of land north of Kennicott. Keep it clean!

A **cafe** adjacent to the Historical Museum (see above) purveys monster muffins for $1.25 (open daily 8am-6pm). The town has no general store, though the **Nugget Gift Shop** has some snacks and fruit (open daily 9am-12:30pm and 3-8pm). The **McCarthy Lodge** (see above) serves affordable breakfast ($5-8), and enormous "McCarthy burgers" for lunch ($9). Dinner is more expensive ($14-17). Rumor has it that a pizzeria is soon to open in town.

■ Outdoors in the Park

Because of the close proximity of 16,390-ft. Mt. Blackburn and the spectacular glaciers, a short 35-min. flight offers amazing views of even more incredible scenery. **Wrangell Mountain Air** (800-478-1160 for reservations), based in downtown McCarthy, offers the best deals. (35-min. flight up and over Kennicott and the icefalls of the Kennicott and Root Glaciers $40; 50-min. trip up the narrow Chitistone Canyon to the Chitistone Falls $55; 70-min. flight around Mt. Blackburn $70; 90-min. flight to Mt. St. Elias and Mt. Cogan $100. 3-person min. on all flights.) **McCarthy Air,** also in McCarthy, offers similar flights and rates.

St. Elias Alpine Guides (277-6867) organizes numerous day trips (a ½-day glacier walk costs $55). You can rent bikes here to explore some of the old, obscure roads that are everywhere around town ($25 per day, ½-day $15). **Copper Oar** (522-1670), located at the end of the McCarthy Rd., offers a two-hour whitewater trip down the Kennicott River for $40.

Most **hikers and trekkers** use the McCarthy Road or McCarthy as a diving board. The park maintains no trails, but miners and other travelers from decades past have established various routes and obscure roads that follow the more exciting pathways. The most common route, a hike out past Kennicott to the Root Glacier, takes from one to three days for the 16-mi. round-trip and follows road-bed and glacial moraine with three moderate stream crossings. **Dixie Pass** has the advantage of easy accessibility (it starts from Mile 13 of the McCarthy Road); hikers should allow three to four days for the 24-mi. round-trip. Those with a thirst for real adventure should try the **Goat Trail.** The trail is a 25-mi. one-way trek from Lower Skolai Lake to Glacier Creek traversing the ridge high above **Chitistone Canyon and Falls,** one of the park's more spectacular features. Access is only by air taxi. Wrangell Mountain Air (see above) offers the best service ($150-200 per person for drop-off and pick-up). Though only 25 mi., the extremely rugged terrain and numerous stream crossings make this a four- to eight-day trek for experienced hikers only. For any overnight trip, the park service requests a written itinerary. This is bear country, so be aware of the precautions necessary to reduce risk. (See Bear Necessities in the Essentials.) Make sure to have extra food, warm clothing, and know what you're doing (especially in stream crossings). And travel with someone, so you can make it back and share the memories.

THE PANHANDLE

■■■ JUNEAU

Confined within a tiny strip of land at the base of imposing Mt. Juneau, Alaska's capital city cannot accept its small size. Instead, Victorian mansions crowd up against log cabins, and hulking state buildings compete for space with simple frame houses. Juneau's jumbled architecture, nearly vertiginous streets, and a wharf-side tourist mecca have garnered it the nickname "Little San Francisco."

The only state capital in the nation inaccessible by road, Juneau was not founded for the convenience of its location but instead for the lucrative mining that once occurred here. In October, 1880, Tlingit Chief Kowee led Joe Juneau and Richard Harris to the gleaming "mother lode" in the hills up Gold Creek. By the next summer, boatloads of prospectors were at work in the already-claimed mines of Juneau. Twenty-five years later, the city replaced Sitka as capital of the territory of Alaska.

PRACTICAL INFORMATION

Emergency: 911.

Visitor Information: Davis Log Cabin, 134 3rd St., Juneau 99801 (586-2284 or 2201), at Seward St. Excellent source for pamphlets on walking tours, sights, and the natural wonders in the vicinity. Open Mon.-Fri. 8am-5pm, Sat.-Sun. 9am-5pm; Oct.-May Mon.-Fri. 8:30am-5pm. **U.S. Forest and National Park Services,** 101 Egan Dr. (586-8751), in Centennial Hall. Helpful staff and extensive pamphlets provide information on hiking and fishing in the Juneau area. Pick up a copy of the valuable *Juneau Trails* booklet ($3) listing numerous 5- to 12-mi. hikes. Open daily 8am-5pm, Mon.-Fri. 8am-5pm in winter.

Airport: Juneau International Airport, 9 mi. north of Juneau on Glacier Hwy. **Alaska Air** (789-0600 or 800-426-0333) flits to: Anchorage ($222; with 21-day advance purchase $125); Sitka ($87); Ketchikan ($124). Flights every morning and afternoon. Open Mon.-Fri. 10am-5pm. Closed holidays.

Alaska Marine Highway, P.O. Box R, Juneau 99811 (800-642-0066 or 465-3941). Ferries dock at the Auke Bay terminal, 14 mi. out of the city on the Glacier Hwy. To: Bellingham, WA ($216, vehicle up to 15 ft. $518); Ketchikan ($72/$177); Sitka ($24/$52); ($18/$39).

Post Office: 709 W. 9th St. (586-7138). Open Mon. 8:30am-5pm, Tues.-Fri. 9am-5pm. Pick up packages Mon.-Fri. 6am-5pm, Sat. 6am-3pm. **ZIP code:** 99801.

Area Code: 907.

ACCOMMODATIONS AND CAMPING

If you can't get into Juneau's hostel, the **Alaska Bed and Breakfast Association,** P.O. Box 3/6500 #169, Juneau 99802 (586-2959), will provide information on rooms in local homes year-round. Most Juneau B&Bs are uphill, beyond 6th St., and offer singles from $45 and doubles from $55. Reservations recommended.

Juneau Youth Hostel, 614 Harris St. (586-9559), at 6th, at the top of a steep hill. A spotless and highly efficient hostel that operates by a strict and structured set of rules. Kitchen facilities and common area. 48 beds. Will store packs during the day. Showers (5 min., 50¢), laundry (wash $1.25, dry 75¢), sheets (75¢). 3-day max. stay if beds are full. Lockout 9am-5pm. The 11pm curfew is not negotiable. $10. Make reservations by May for expected stays in July and Aug.

Alaskan Hotel, 167 Franklin St. (586-1000 or 800-327-9347 from the lower 48 states). A handsome hotel built of dark wood, right in the center of downtown. Has been meticulously restored to its original 1913 decor. Bar on the first floor features live jazz. Hot tubs noon-4pm $10 for 1 hr., after 4pm $21. Luggage storage at the desk $1.50. Singles $45, with bath $61. Doubles $55, with bath $72.

Mendenhall Lake Campground, Montana Creek Rd. Take Glacier Hwy. north 9 mi. to Mendenhall Loop Rd.; continue 3½ mi. and take the right fork. If asked, bus driver will let you off within 2 mi. walking distance of camp (7am-10:30pm only). A cool view of the glacier, with trails that can take you even closer. 61 sites. Fireplaces, water, pit toilets. 14-day max. stay. Sites $5.

Auke Village Campground, on Glacier Hwy., 15 mi. from Juneau. 11 sites. Fireplaces, water, pit toilets. 14 day max. stay. Sites $5.

FOOD AND ENTERTAINMENT

Juneau tries to accommodate those seeking everything from fresh salmon to filet-o'-fish sandwiches. The local grocery store is the **Foodland Supermarket,** 631 Willoughby Ave., near the Federal Building (open daily 7am-9pm). The recently-renovated **Federal Office Building Cafeteria** on the second floor above the post office is known for its good government cooking (open Mon.-Fri. 6am-4pm).

Armadillo Tex-Mex Cafe, 431 S. Franklin St. (586-1880). Fantastic food, and always packed with locals and tourists alike. Hunker down to a heaping plateful of T. Terry's nachos ($8). The *chalupa*—a corn tostada heaped with chicken, beans, guacamole, and cheese—goes for $7.50. Two enchiladas $6. Open Mon.-Thurs. 11am-9pm, Fri.-Sat. 11am-10pm.

Heritage Coffee Co., 1745 Franklin St. (586-1088), across from the Senate Bldg. A popular place to escape for an hour or two from Juneau's often wet and tourist-ridden streets. The jocular staff puts together large sandwiches ($5) and pours an excellent 16-oz. cup of coffee ($1.25). Open Mon.-Wed. and Fri. 6:30am-10pm, Thurs. 6:30am-6pm, Sat.-Sun. 8am-10pm. No sandwiches after 6:30pm.

Thane Ore House Salmon Bake, 4400 Thane Rd. (586-3442). A few miles outside of town, but "Mr. Ore" will pick you up at your hotel. All-you-can-eat salmon, ribs, and fixings ($17.50).

The doors swing and the cash registers ring at the **Red Dog Saloon,** 278 S. Franklin (463-3777), Juneau's most popular tourist trap (open daily 11:30am-12:30am). Locals hang out farther uptown. The **Triangle Club,** 251 Front St. (586-3140), attracts the more hard-drinking set, while the cruise ship crowd congregates at the **Penthouse** (463-4141), in the Senate Building (open 8pm-whenever).

SIGHTS

The **Alaska State Museum,** 395 Whittier St. (465-2910), leads you through the history, ecology, and cultures of "The Great Land" and its four main Native groups. It also houses the famous "First White Man" totem pole, on which the artist carved the likeness of Abraham Lincoln. (Open Mon.-Fri. 9am-6pm, Sat.-Sun. 10am-6pm; Sept. 16-May 14 Tues.-Sat. 10am-4pm. $2, seniors and students free.) Be sure to check out the **St. Nicholas Russian Orthodox Church** on 5th St. between N. Franklin and Gold St. Built in 1894, the church is the oldest of its kind in southeastern Alaska. Services are conducted in English, Slavonic (old Russian), and Tlingit. Open to the public ($1 donation requested). The **House of Wickersham,** 213 7th St. (586-9001), was home to one of Alaska's founding fathers, Judge James Wickersham. As a U.S. District Court Judge, Wickersham sailed around Alaska to oversee a region extending from Fort Yukon to the Aleutian Islands. (Open Sun.-Fri. noon-5pm. Free.)

OUTDOORS

Juneau is one of the best hiking centers in Southeast Alaska—within a half-hour hike from downtown one can easily forget the city ever existed. **Perseverance Trail,** which leads past the ruins of the historic **Silverbowl Basin Mine,** makes for a pleasant day trek. To reach this trailhead, follow Gold St. uphill until it turns into Basim Rd. The trail begins on the left side of this road just past a bridge. For more details on this and other area hikes, drop by the state museum bookstore, the Park Service Center, or any local bookstore to pick up *Juneau Trails,* published by the Alaska Natural History Association ($2.50). The rangers provide free copies of individual maps from this book at the Park Service Center.

During winter the slopes of the **Eaglecrest Ski Area** on Douglas Island (contact 155 S. Seward St., Juneau 99801, 586-5284 or 586-5330) offer decent alpine skiing. ($23 per day, kids grades 7-12 $16, up to 6th grade $11. Rental of skis, poles, and boots $20, for children $14.) The Eaglecrest Ski bus departs from the Baranof Hotel at 8:30am and returns at 5pm on winter weekends and holidays (round-trip to the slopes $5). In summer, the Eaglecrest "Alpine Summer" self-guided nature trail is a good way to soak in the mountain scenery of virtually untouched Douglas Island.

Three thousand years ago, the "Little Ice Age" froze over much of what is now Southeastern Alaska, creating thousands of giant ice cubes whose descendants spot the region today. The most visited of these is the **Mendenhall Glacier,** about 10 mi. north of downtown Juneau. Mendenhall is only one of 38 glaciers in the **Juneau Ice Field,** which covers an area of over 1500 sq. mi. At the **Glacier Visitors Center,** rangers will explain everything you could possibly want to know about the glacier (open daily 9am-6:30pm). The rangers also give an interesting walking tour Sunday through Friday at 9:30am, beginning from the flagpole. The best view of the glacier without a helicopter is from the 3½-mi. **West Glacier Trail.** Take the local public bus ($1.25) down Glacier Hwy. and up Mendenhall Loop Rd. until it connects with Glacier Spur Rd. From there it's less than a ½-hr. walk to the visitors center.

■■■ KETCHIKAN

"People don't tan in Ketchikan," according to a local proverb, "they rust." Fourteen feet of rain per year explain the ubiquitous awnings projecting over the streets of Alaska's southernmost and fourth-largest city. Cradled at the base of Deer Mountain, Ketchikan is also the first stopping point in Alaska for northbound cruise ships and ferries, which disgorge loads of tourists and dump hordes of students in search of the summer bucks offered at the canneries.

Practical Information Ketchikan sits on Revillagigedo island 235 mi. south of Juneau and 90 mi. north of Prince Rupert, BC. The **Ketchikan Visitors Bureau,** 131 Front St. (225-6166 or 800-770-3300), on the cruise ship docks downtown, offers a good map along with friendly advice and a cup of coffee (open Mon.-Fri. 8am-5pm, Sat.-Sun. depending on cruise ship arrival times). The **United States Forest Service,** Ranger District Office, Federal Building, 648 Mission St. (225-2148), can provide you with info on hiking and paddling in the Ketchikan area. They also sell a kayaker's map of nearby Misty Fjords ($3) and reserve cabins around Ketchikan. Ask for the guide to recreation facilities for complete cabin listings. (Open Mon.-Fri. 7:30am-4:30pm, and in summer Sat.-Sun. 8am-4:30pm.) Ketchikan's **airport** is located across from the city on Gravina island. A small ferry runs from the airport to just above the state ferry dock ($3). **Alaska Airlines** (225-2141 or 800-426-0333) provides flight information from Ketchikan. Daily flights to Juneau $124. (Open Mon.-Fri. 9:30am-5pm.) Rent a kayak at **Southeast Exposure,** 507 Stedman St. (225-8829). (Single fiberglass kayak rental, $35 per day; 4 or more days, $30 per day. Double kayak, $45 per day; 4 or more days $40 per day. $200 deposit. Required 1½-hr. orientation class $20. Open daily 8am-5pm.) In an **emergency,** call 225-6631. Ketchikan's **post office** (225-9601) is located next to the ferry terminal (open Mon.-Fri. 9am-5pm); the general delivery **ZIP Code** is 99901. The area code is 907.

Sleeping and Eating Except for the hostel, housing in town is relatively expensive. **Ketchikan Youth Hostel (HI/AYH),** P.O. Box 8515 (225-3319), rests at Main and Grant St. in the basement of the United Methodist Church. Although there are no beds, the 4-in.-thick foam mats on the floor are quite comfortable if you have a sleeping bag, and the hostel does have a clean kitchen, common area, and 2 showers. Houseparents change, and their management styles vary widely. ($7, nonmembers $10. Tea and coffee. Lockout 9am-6pm. Lights off at 10:30pm, on at 7:00am. Curfew 11pm. Call ahead if coming in on a late ferry. No reservations; 3- or 4-day limit subject to availability, and overflow sleeps in the sanctuary. Open June 1-Sept.

1.) If you plan well in advance, camping provides an escape from Ketchikan's high accommodation prices. There is no public transportation to the campgrounds, so plan on hiking, biking, or paying the exorbitant cab fare out there. **Ketchikan Ranger District** (225-2148) runs the **Signal Creek Campground** 6 mi. north on Tongass Hwy. from the ferry terminal, which has 25 units on the shores of Ward Lake with water and pit toilets (sites $5; open in summer), and **Three C's Campground,** ½ mi. north of Signal Creek, with four units for backpackers with water, pit toilets, and firewood (sites $5; 2-week limit).

The supermarket most convenient to downtown is **Tatsuda's,** 633 Stedman (225-4125), at Deermount St. just beyond the Thomas Basin (open daily 7am-midnight). If you'd rather eat someone else's cooking, try the **Diaz Cafe** on Stedman St. This long-standing Chinese, Filipina, and American eatery inspires fierce loyalty among many of Ketchikan's more frugal sons and daughters. The deluxe burger with a heap of sweet and sour rice ($4.75) explains why. (Open Mon.-Fri. 11:30am-2pm, 4-8:30pm, Sat. 11:30am-8:30pm, Sun. noon-8pm.)

Sights and Activities in the Great Outdoors Some of the finest ancient and contemporary totems inhabit Ketchikan and the surrounding area. Pick up the guided walking totem tour at the visitors bureau. World-renowned totem carver Nathan Jackson lives here; his work stands in front of the Federal Building. If you can see only one thing in Ketchikan, visit the best and largest totem park in the world—the **Saxman Native Village,** 2½ mi. southwest of Ketchikan on Tongass Hwy. ($8 by cab), including an open studio where artisans carve new totems. (Open daily 9am-5pm and on weekends when a cruise ship is in.) Also, 13½ mi. north of Ketchikan on Tongass Hwy. is **Totem Bight,** featuring 13 totems. Entry to both parks is free, and visitors are welcome during daylight hours.

Like most towns in the Alaskan Southeast, Ketchikan celebrates the Fourth of July with a vengeance. August brings crafts, food, and live music to the streets along with a fiercely contested **slug race.**

A good day-hike from Ketchikan is 3001-ft. **Deer Mountain.** Walk past the city park on Fair St. up the hill towards the town dump. The marked trail head branches off to the left just behind the dump. A steep but manageable ascent leads 2 mi. up the mountain, and continues above treeline along a sometimes steep-sided ridge where snow and ice may remain into the summer. **Blue Lake,** an alpine pond stocked with trout, lies at the middle of the ridge walk. The entire hike, manageable for well-shod, experienced hikers in one full day, is 10 mi. long.

Many of the boats and planes continually buzzing through Ketchikan's harbor travel to nearby **Misty Fjords National Monument.** Only 20 mi. from Ketchikan, this region of narrow waterways and old-growth forests, home to both whales and mountain goats, invites hikers and kayakers to play in a small state-sized wilderness.

■■■ SITKA

The only major Panhandle town with direct access to the Pacific, Sitka was settled by the Russians in 1799. The manager of the Russian-American Company, Alexander Baranov, made Sitka the capital of Russian Alaska. For the next 63 years, the city was the "Paris of the Pacific," with a larger population than either San Francisco or Seattle. After the Russian Tsar sold Alaska to America in 1867 (the transaction was officiated here), Sitka became the territory's capital from 1884 until 1906. Currently the fifth-largest city (population 8600) in Alaska, Sitka is still a center for the arts today.

Practical Information Sitka inhabits the western side of **Baranov Island,** 95 mi. southwest of Juneau. Although not as wet as other parts of the Panhandle, Sitka still receives a full fathom (6 ft.) of rain each year. Sitka's **Chamber of Commerce,** 330 Harbor Dr. (747-3225), is extremely organized (open Mon.-Sat. 8am-5pm, Sun. when cruise ships are in). Get info on the outdoors from the **U.S. Forest Service,** Sitka Ranger District, Tongass National Forest, 204 Siqinaka Way off Katlian St. (747-

6671; open Mon.-Fri. 8am-5pm). The **Alaska Marine Highway,** 7 Halibut Rd., 7 mi. from town (747-8737 or 800-642-0066), can take you to Ketchikan ($52), Petersburg ($24), and Juneau ($24). Mountain bikes at **J&B Bike Rental** (747-8279), on Lincoln St., near Southeast Diving & Sports, will cost you $4 per hr., $24 per day.

Sitka's **post office** sits far from downtown; go to the **Pioneer Station** at 201 Katlian (747-5525) for general delivery (open Mon.-Sat. 8:30am-5pm). The **ZIP Code** for general delivery is 99835. Sitka's **area code** is 907.

Accommodations, Camping, and Food

Sitka has 20 **bed and breakfasts** from $40 a night up, but the **Sitka Youth Hostel (HI/AYH),** 303 Kimshan St., (747-8356), in the United Methodist Church, is the best deal. Near the McDonald's 1 mi. out of town on Halibut Point Rd. (Kitchen facilities, free local calls, and a TV/VCR. Lockout 8:30am-6pm. Curfew 11pm. $7, nonmembers $10. Will store packs during the day.) Camping facilities are decent, but all are at least 5 mi. from town. **Sawmill Creek Campground,** 14 mi. SE of the ferry terminal, is an unmaintained 9-unit campground with spots for tents and RVs. To get here, take Halibut Point Rd. to Sawmill Creek Rd. junction in Sitka. Follow Sawmill Creek Rd. to pulp mill, then take left spur for 1.4 mi. (14-day max. stay. Free.) A USFS campground, **Starrigaven Creek Campground,** at the end of Halibut Point Rd., 8 mi. from town, has 30 tent and RV sites, with water and pit toilets. (14-day max. stay. Sites $5.)

Stock up at **Lakeside Grocery,** 705 Halibut Point Rd. (open Mon.-Sat. 9am-9pm, Sun. 11am-7pm). Pick up fresh seafood from fisherfolk along the docks or at **Alaskan Harvest,** a new store run by Sitka Sound Seafood (open Mon.-Sat. 8am-6pm). The best deal in Sitka, if not the state, **Sheldon Jackson College Cafeteria,** at the east end of Lincoln St., is a refuge in the Alaskan wilderness of overpriced, often under-nourishing eateries. All-you-can-eat breakfast ($4.50), lunch ($5.50), and dinner ($8). No breakfast on Sunday. (Open daily 6:45-8am, noon-1pm, 5-6pm.) The **Channel Club,** 2906 Halibut Point Rd. (747-9916), 3 mi. from downtown, is the restaurant every Sitkan will recommend, with a fantastic salad bar of over 35 individual salads ($12). (Open Sun.-Thurs. 5-10pm, Fri.-Sat. 5-11pm.)

Sights and Outdoor Activities

Sitka's lasting symbol of Slavic influence is the onion-domed **St. Michael's Cathedral,** built in 1848 by Bishop Veniaminov. The cathedral was such a success that Veniaminov was canonized as St. Innocent in 1977. The cathedral was entirely rebuilt after a fire in 1966, and haunting icons still gleam on its walls. Services are open to the public, conducted in English, Tlingit, and Old Church Slavonic. (Hours vary; generally open Mon.-Sat. 11am-3pm. $1 "donation" required.) It took the Park Service 15 years and $5 million to restore the **Russian Bishop's House** to its original 1842-3 condition, but the results are spectacular. The house is one of four remaining Russian colonial buildings in the Americas, adorned with beautiful gold and silver icons (which, unlike those in St. Michael's, may be photographed). (Open 8:30am-4:30pm, tours every ½ hr.)

Stroll down the enchanting, manicured trails of the **Sitka National Historical Park** (747-6281), at the end of Lincoln St., 1 mi. east of St. Michael's. Locals call it Totem Park. The trails pass by 15 masterfully replicated totems placed in a well-suited setting along the shoreline among old growth trees. At one end of the 1-mi. loop stands the site of the **Tlingit Fort** where the hammer-wielding chieftain Katlean almost held off the Russians in the battle for Sitka in 1804. The park **visitors center** offers an audio-visual presentation on the battle and the opportunity to watch native artists at work in the Native American Cultural Center. There is also a small museum dedicated entirely to the local Kiksadi Tlingits (open daily 8am-5pm).

The Sitka area offers excellent **hiking** opportunities—don't forget to bring rain gear, and make sure to pick up the thick booklet *Sitka Trails* at the USFS information booth or office. Outstanding trails include the **Indian River Trail,** a 5½-mi. riverside trek up to the base of Indian River Falls. A shorter, steeper hike leads from downtown up to the summit of **Gavan Hill,** a 2500 ft. ascent with excellent views of Sitka and the Sound.

■ CANADA

O Canada! Encompassing almost 10 million sq. km (3.85 million sq. mi.), Canada as of 1993 became the largest country in the world, but one of the most sparsely populated. Ten provinces and two territories sprawl over six time zones. But numbers don't tell Canada's story, geography does. Framed by the rugged Atlantic coastline to the east and the Rockies to the west, Canada spreads north from fertile farmland and urbanized lakeshores to barren, frozen tundra.

The name Canada derives from the Huron-Iroquois world "kanata," meaning "village" or "community." However, the Canadian community is anything but unified. Periodically, ethnic, linguistic, and cultural tensions flare into actual conflict. The division between Canada's two dominant cultures—the French and the English—is so strong that Canadian society has been described as "two solitudes." Although the grounds of the conflict shift from linguistic to philosophical, from religious to economic, it persists. Recently, the collapse of the Meech Lake Accord—which would have given French-speaking regions such as Québec and New Brunswick increased autonomy—has strengthened *québecois* separatist movements.

Another persistent schism divides the dominant Euro-colonist cultures and the aboriginal tribes. Treatment of Native Americans in Canada historically has not been much better than in the United States. A recent headline-grabbing conflict involved *québecois* Mohawks, who spent weeks under police siege after they armed themselves to prevent sacred burial grounds from being converted into a golf course.

The division between West and East also tears at the Canadian fabric. French monarchists and English tories settled the Eastern provinces; their intellectual descendants in the politically dominant provinces of Ontario and Québec are comfortable with Canada's active federal government. But the Western provinces probably have more in common with the America's libertarian West—from which came many of their settlers—than with the rest of Canada; here, opposition parties led by anti-government politicos such as Preston Manning are growing in popularity.

Finally, the blurring between the United States and Canada must be mentioned. The U.S./Canadian border is the largest undefended border in the world; it is also perhaps the most irrelevant border in the world. Canadian nationalists have become concerned that the ubiquity of American culture and mass communication in the provinces threatens the survival of indigenous attributes; steps have been taken to protect genuine Canadian media and cultural products from Americanization. At the same time, recent approval of a free trade pact between the United States and Canada has further eroded the distinctions between the two national identities.

Much crucial information concerning Canada can be found in the Essentials section at the front of the book. Only information specific to Canada is contained here.

■ Canadian Culture

Culturally, Canada is often overshadowed by its more flashy neighbor to the south. Canada actually is a mixture of many different cultures, including the Native cultures, English-Canadian culture, and a vibrant French-speaking culture, mainly in Québec. Québecois culture experienced a renaissance in the mid-60s, concurrent with the rise of Québecois nationalism. Today, Canada is officially bilingual, and this blend has created a unique and rich cultural heritage, in which most Canadians take vociferous pride.

HISTORY

The original settlement of Canada followed the same lines as that of the U.S. (read "In The Beginning" in the U.S. history section). And though Canada's history once Europeans arrived is substantially different from that of the U.S., the story is also essentially the same. Foreign empires give way to nationalistic movements, the economy alternatively slumps and soars, and people generally get offended by and upset with each other.

The French and British Empires

Jacques Cartier landed on the gulf of the St. Lawrence River in 1534, ostensibly founding Canada. But everyone has since claimed part of the pie; apparently England got to it earlier when John Cabot sighted Newfoundland, and of course, the Vikings had been along the coast centuries before. Not to mention the Native Americans and Inuit. In 1608 the explorer Champlain established Québec City. By the mid-1600s, colonization was well underway due to the fur-trade; the Company of New France was declared a colony of France in 1663. Meanwhile, Britain was gobbling up territory, too, forming the Hudson Bay Company in 1670. A rivalry for land persisted for a century until the French and Indian War, when the British captured Québec in 1759 and the rest of New France in 1763, giving the French the boot.

On the heels of this acquisition came the American Revolution, in which the British lost the southern colonies to the United States. Loyalists fled to the north and established New Brunswick in 1784. In 1791, Québec was divided into two colonies, Upper and Lower Canada; after an open rebellion by the French Canadians in 1837, Québec was reunited as a single colony called Canada in 1841. The drive for national sovereignty was accelerating. In 1847, the colonies were given the right to self-government under the watchful eye of the British monarchy. This only fueled the confederation movement which thrust Canada into the 1860s.

The Dominion of Canada

The desire for a unified country was in part sparked by first-hand witnessing of the U.S. Civil War. Other reasons might be the threat that the U.S. might turn its aggressions outwards (as it had in the War of 1812) and try to absorb British North America (including Canada). Regardless of the reason, the Colonial Secretary struggled to establish the Confederation, working quickly to oust reluctant colony heads. The first Confederation proposal (1865) was nixed by the two maritime colonies of Nova Scotia and New Brunswick, which feared they were too remote from the other colonies to gain equal representation. Over the next two years, though, sufficient support was swiftly herded (a Confederation resolution was passed through the Nova Scotia legislature in the *same month* that a pro-Confederation government replaced an anti-Confederation one). The appropriate legislation made its way to British Parliament, where, despite anti-Confederation lobbyists, the four colonies of Québec, Ontario, Nova Scotia, and New Brunswick were united as the Dominion of Canada. The British North America (BNA) Act, as it was called, was signed by Queen Victoria on March 29, 1867 and proclaimed on July 1, Canada Independence Day. Canada had its country, but was still a dominion of the throne.

Westward Ho!

With the BNA Act came a wave of conservatism in power; Sir John MacDonald in the English colonies and Sir George-Etienne Cartier in Québec. The destiny of the Dominion was not so manifest, and the government was dedicated to national expansion through three methods: pumping money into economic growth, encouraging mass settlement in the west, and creating high protectionist tariffs. As a result, Canada quickly grew to encompass most of the land it does today: Manitoba and the Northwest Territories were molded from Rupert's Land in 1870, a purchase from the Hudson Bay Company; British Columbia, fearing American expansionism, hopped on board in 1871, after receiving promise of a trans-Canada railway; and Prince Edward Island signed on in 1873. By 1885, B.C. had its railroad, and the economy boomed. Increased wheat production and immigration to the west sparked the addition of Alberta and Saskatchewan to the provincial list in 1905.

Just as in the U.S., all this westward growth necessarily displaced those who had been there before. In the Arctic, the Inuit were largely left alone, and their lands were tacitly incorporated into the growing Canadian territory. But in the west the Native Americans and the Metis (mixed-blood children of Native American women and French fur-traders who inhabited Manitoba) lost their way of life as the settlers moved in. The western land was gathered for the Dominion in return for treaty and reservation rights for the natives. Unlike the trouble south of the 49th parallel, the acquisition of the west was peaceful and largely unchallenged.

Turn of the Century Politics and WWI

The need for protection and power was dawning in the hearts of Canadians. A steadfast nationalism and a newfound imperialism drove Prime Minister Sir Wilfrid Laurier, leader of the Liberal Party and the first French-speaking Prime Minister, to send troops to aid Britain in the Boer War from 1899-1902 and to create a national navy in 1910. Laurier lost the election in 1911, however, because with the foresight and wisdom of a man 80 years ahead of his time, he proposed reciprocal trade agreements with the U.S. which would lower the high trading tariffs, similar to the accomplishments of the current North American Free Trade Agreement (NAFTA).

Though a new party ruled, the tinge of imperialism did not abate, and the Dominion sent hordes of troops to aid Britain in the World War. Canada split along entirely new, acultural lines—the question of the draft. The conservatives, a proconscription party, maintained their hold through the 1917 election. Even given the horrors of it all, the casualties, the returning vets, the country divided, Canada gained significantly from the Great War. The Dominion acquired new international status through signing the Treaty of Versailles and being a charter member of the League of Nations. Women made headway on account of their war efforts, receiving the right to vote in 1918, two years before the U.S.

The Inter-war Years

But hard times hit. Returning vets from the war and post-war slumps fueled high inflation and unemployment; protesting farmers ousted governments in the west and in Ontario, and the provincial economies collapsed. In 1919, with 3 million employed in the Dominion, over 4 million working days were lost due to strikes, the most famous of which was the Winnipeg General Strike. Almost the entire labor force responded to a call to aid the ailing metal-trades workers who had been denied wage increases; the entire town was on the picket line. The government stepped in with police and troops, and the strike collapsed. The strike was effective only in bringing the workers to political action; they have since been sending their own representatives to the federal Parliament.

Like many other countries, Canada experienced an economic and cultural boom in the 20s and 30s, and Prohibition was abolished. But wheat prices plummeted, and the Great Depression moved in. Unemployment skyrocketed to 20% in 1933. Provincial governments tried to assist the troubled farmers, but their relief was limited and washed up quickly due to drought, and the liberals gained power in 1935 with Mackenzie King. As in the U.S., the government initiated direct relief programs and regulated businesses; the government established both the Bank of Canada and the Canadian Wheat Board during the depression. King sponsored bills on family allowance and unemployment insurance, as well. Following in the footsteps of the U.S., the workers formed a multitude of unions, and Canada was able to drag itself out of the depression with the assistance of World War II.

Cold War Party-Hopping

Louis St. Laurent took the helm of the Liberal party in 1948, just after the war. The Liberals held the majority and held office from 1935 to 1957, largely due to their relief programs of the late 30s (again, akin to the U.S.) and later to their prosperity during the early Cold War years. Imperialistic acts which would have otherwise irked the populace were deemed permissible because of the Cold War; thus, Canada joined the United Nations in 1945, hopped into the North Atlantic Treaty Organization in August, 1949, and sent troops to Europe in 1951. With inspiring visions of a "new" Canada, the conservatives, led by John Diefenbaker, grabbed precarious control in June, 1957. A new party, the growing, left-wing National Democratic Party, introduced Medicare to Saskatchewan in 1962. This program quickly spread nationally and became the popular and successful national health care program Canada has today. Impaired by high unemployment rates (again) and record budget deficits (foreshadowing the U.S.'s similar problems), the Prime Ministership fell to Lester Pearson of the minority Liberal party in April, 1963.

Québec had always been a thorn in the side of the mainly British Dominion. In an attempt to unite Québec and the rest of the Dominion, Pierre Trudeau was selected to head the Liberal party in 1968. Trudeau espoused bilingualism and biculturalism, and brought many Québecois to his government. But the move toward biculturalism apparently threatened the English Canadians; Liberal victory in 1972 was slim, and the New Democratic Party held the deciding votes in Parliament. The Liberals bowed to the radicals and shifted left to acquire their support—this dramatically affected the party and its positions thereafter. The Liberals were dependent on Québec and urban Ontario for their support; the Conservatives on western Canada and Ontario. The NDP relied mainly on unskilled workers for its minor power.

In the late 70s came the drive for French separatism. Under the banner *Parti Québecois*, separartist René Lévesque gained power in Québec in 1976, stunning Canadians across the country. Under Bill 101, the Parti Québecois established French as the only official language seen and heard in Québec, forcing everyone there to use French. Trudeau rose to the occasion and took head-on the rising separatism movement by fighting for a united Canada. In 1979, Québec stood solidly behind Trudeau, but the rest of the Dominion backed the Conservative head, Joe Clark, who won the election in May. Clark floundered early, and with the defeat of his budget and a no-confidence motion in December, Trudeau and the liberals returned in early 1980. This election marked perhaps the greatest national division of the century; the liberals swept Québec but won no seats west of Manitoba, and only two there. Trudeau succeeded in preventing Québec from seceding in a 1980 referendum, and the country remained united if torn through early 1982.

The Canada Act of 1982

Finally, Britain let go. On March 25, 1982, Canada's constitution was ratified by British Parliament. Queen Elizabeth II gave her royal assent on March 29, exactly 115 years to the day after Queen Victoria assented to the BNA Act of 1867. The Canada Act was proclaimed by her majesty three weeks later, and the BNA Act was patriated to Canada, releasing Canada from the legal bonds of England. The act was a compromise between the vision of "one Canada with two official languages" and provincial concerns. Modeled in part on the U.S., the constitution includes an unusual Charter of Rights and Freedoms, akin to the Bill of Rights, without its extensive power—in order to preserve parliamentary supremacy, individual rights may be superseded by federal Parliament or provincial legislatures via "notwithstanding clauses" for periods of up to five years. True to form, Québec tried to claim veto power over the constitution, but such claims were rejected by courts at every level, including the Supreme Court of Canada, on December 6, 1982.

Mulroney, Meech Lake, and NAFTA

In 1983 the conservatives chose a new leader, the president of the Iron Ore Company of Canada, Brian Mulroney, an amiable Montréal lawyer. Conservative support rose as Mulroney pronounced social programs "a sacred trust" and supported an NDP attempt to provide bilingual support in Manitoba. When Trudeau resigned in 1984 and Turner took his place, the stage was set for a conservative comeback. Turner buckled under pressure to the charming Mulroney, and lost money and support. Mulroney flew to a landslide victory, claiming 211 of 281 seats in the Parliament, a clear mandate for conservative change. Mulroney and his conservatives supported privitazation of federal activities, increased armed forces, and reduction of the deficit. Government had not really changed, however, and Mulroney could do little to help the west, not as loud in the federal ear. By 1986, Mulroney was lagging last in the polls as elections approached. As a result, Mulroney's government entered two massive endeavors—the Meech Lake Accord and the North American Free Trade Agreement (NAFTA).

The Meech Lake Accord was, in the final analysis, an attempt to keep Québec in Canada and to gain Québecois support for the conservatives. The Accord would have provided constitutional protection for the French language and culture in Québec. English Canadians feared the Accord gave Québec too much power in relation to the Charter of Rights and Freedoms while not guaranteeing similar powers for other minority groups. The Accord was defeated in June 1990, when Newfoundland and Manitoba failed to approve it. Meech Lake had floundered.

NAFTA is, in most ways, a success. By finally lowering trade tariffs between the monsters of the western hemisphere, NAFTA promises to allow the economy to thrive in a free market system. After years of negotiations (the roots for NAFTA stretch back to 1987), the central agreement was signed in May, 1992, though the national governments still had to ratify the accord. Between Mexico, the U.S., and Canada, trade barriers would be largely abolished, along with previous foreign employment and business restrictions.

The State of Affairs As It Stands

Even the promise of the benefits of free trade along the longest peaceful open border in the world was not enough to prevent Mulroney's fall from popularity in 1992. Just as he was finishing up NAFTA, the country was finishing with him. In a cloud of alleged incompetence, scandal, and dislike, Mulroney was ousted from power in April, 1993, as Kim Campbell became the first woman Prime Minister of Canada. Another round of elections, scheduled for October 1993, could replace her.

LITERATURE

The very first expressions of the Canadian literary mind were poetry, descriptive verses composed by the first settlers in the early 17th century. Canadian fiction, however, did not come into its own until the early 19th century. Much of the work of this time detailed the difficulties of settling in a wild, new land or satirized the existence of life in the colonies. *The Literary Garland,* published in Montréal from 1838 to 1851 served as a forum for all sorts of fiction, including historical romances. As the 19th century progressed, Canadian literature reflected the first stirrings of a national conscience, with historical and political novels, and historical romances. The opening of the northwest and the Klondike Gold Rush led the way for the blossoming of the adventure story. Jack London penned stories of wolves and prospectors based on his experiences of the time, while the Bard of the Yukon, Robert Service, composed the ballad "The Cremation of Sam McGee." Back east, L.M. Montgomery authored the *Anne of Green Gables* series, which have delighted generations of young readers. The onset of the 20th century brought a shift in emphasis to the cities and led to works exposing the dark side of urban conditions. Authors became more aware of the man's relationship to society, and the work of the 20th century reflects a dehumanization of society and man's helplessness and lack of control over his destiny. Gwenthalyn Graham exposed subtle anti-Semitism in *Earth and High Heaven,* and A.M. Klein (also a prominent poet) explored Jewish heritage in *The Second Scroll.* Novelist and playwright Robert Davies satirized small town Canadian life in *Tempest-tost,* and Margaret Laurence detailed the difficult lives of prairie women in such novels as *A Jest of God* and *A Bird in the House.* Two of Canada's best authors, Malcolm Lowry and Hugh McLellan, also produced their most significant works, *Under the Volcano* and *Barometer Rising* (respectively), during this period. Prominent contemporary authors include Margaret Atwood, whose works include the landmark novel *Surfacing* and the futuristic bestseller *The Handmaid's Tale*, Alice Munro *(Lives of Girls and Women)*, and playwright/singer/songwriter Paul Gailiumas.

MOVIES AND TELEVISION

Canadian films have yet to achieve the commercial success of Canadian literature. Recently, however, Québecois filmmakers have captured the world's attention, producing Oscar-nominated movies like *Le declin de l'empire americain*, directed by Denys Arcand, who also directed the critically acclaimed *Jesus de Montréal*; recent art-flick *Léolo* was deemed a classic by critics. A high proportion of Canadian movies are projects of the National Film Board, which funds experimental projects.

Canada has also made some notable contributions to the American entertainment industry; there are many famous actors and comedians of Canadian origin, including Dan Aykroyd, Mike Myers of *Saturday Night Live* and *Wayne's World* fame, Michael J. Fox *(Family Ties, Back to the Future)*, newscasters Peter Jennings and Dan Rather, *Jeopardy* host Alex Trebek, and William Shatner (Captain James T. Kirk himself). The Canadian comedy troupe SCTV (catch the reruns on Nickelodeon if your motel has cable TV) spawned the careers of many famous comedians, such as Martin Short, John Candy, Rick Moranis, Eugene Levy, and more. Also, in an effort to hold down production costs, many American TV shows and movie companies shoot in Canadian cities, such as Toronto and Vancouver.

MUSIC

Canada has made a major contribution to popular music, lending the world's airwaves an eclectic range of artists such as Neil Young, Joni Mitchell, Bruce Cockburn, Rush, Cowboy Junkies, Bare Naked Ladies, k.d. lang, and the brilliant Crash Test Dummies. Today, Canadian popular music shows even stronger signs of life, as MuchMusic, the Canadian version of MTV, has been inspiring bands all over the country to capture the national identity on vinyl and on video. Canada is also home to a number of world-class orchestras, including the Montréal, Toronto, and Vancouver Symphonies. And if jazz is your thing, you'll be able to find excellent clubs in any of Canada's major cities.

Canada Essentials

■■■ CURRENCY AND EXCHANGE

US$1 = CDN$1.31	CDN$1 = US$0.76
UK£1 = CDN$1.99	CDN$1 = UK£0.50
IR£1 = CDN$1.83	CDN$1 = IR£0.55
AUS$1 = CDN$1.47	CDN$1 = AUS$1.13
NZ$1 = CDN$0.73	CDN$1 = NZ$1.37

The main unit of currency in Canada is the Canadian dollar, which is identical to the U.S. dollar in name only. You will need to exchange your currency when you go over the border. As in the U.S., Canadian currency uses a decimal system, with the dollar divided into 100 cents (¢); fractions are represented in the same way: 35¢. Paper money comes in denominations of $2, $5, $10, $20, $50, and $100, which are all the same size but color-coded by denomination. Several years ago, the Canadian government phased out the $1 bill and replaced it with a $1 coin, known as the loony for the loon which graces its reverse.

Many Canadian shops, as well as vending machines and parking meters, accept U.S. coins at face value (which is a small loss for you). Many stores will even convert the price of your purchase for you, but they are under no legal obligation to offer you a fair exchange. During the past several years, the Canadian dollar has been worth roughly 20% less than the U.S. dollar; the exchange rate hovers around 18%.

Prices in general tend to be higher in Canada than in the U.S., as are taxes; you'll quickly notice the 7% **goods and services tax (GST)** and an additional **sales tax** in some provinces. See the provincial introductions for information on local taxes. Oddly enough, you will often find yourself being taxed on taxes; in Québec, for example, provincial sales tax of 8% is computed on the price including GST, so that the total tax will be 15.56%. Visitors to Canada can claim a rebate of the GST they pay on accommodations of less than one month and on most goods they buy and take home, so be sure to save your receipts and pick up a GST rebate form while in Canada. The total claim must be at least CDN$7 of GST and must be made within one year of the date on which you purchased the goods and/or accommodations for which you are claiming your rebate. A brochure detailing numerous other restrictions is available from local tourist info booths or by contacting Revenue Canada, Customs and Excise Visitor's Rebate Program, Ottawa, Canada K1A 1J5 (800-668-4748 in Canada, 613-991-3346 outside Canada). Some provinces offer refunds of provincial sales tax as well; contact the Provincial Tourist Information Centres for details (see Practical Information listing of each province).

All prices in the Canada section of this book are listed in Canadian dollars unless otherwise noted.

■■■ GETTING AROUND CANADA

For information on traveling by plane or bus in Canada, or on driving, motorcycling, bicycling, or hitchhiking, see Getting There and Getting Around, in the Essentials section at the beginning of this book.

VIA Rail, Place Ville Marie, Lobby Level, Montréal, Québec H3B 2G6 (800-561-7860), is Amtrak's Canadian analogue, and makes all of the country's provinces accessible to travelers. Routes are as scenic as Amtrak's and the fares are often more affordable. If you'll be traveling by train a great deal or across great distances you may save money with the **Canrail Pass,** which allows travel on 12 days within a 30-day period; distance traveled is unlimited. Between early June and late September, passes cost $489, and, for senior citizens and youths under 24, $439. Off-season passes cost $329, and $299 for youths and senior citizens.

Remember in pricing tickets that round-trip tickets are simply double the price of a one-way fare, and that off-season rates are 40% off peak rates, which are in effect between mid-June and early-September. During the peak season, a one-way ticket from Montréal to Halifax sells for $143 in either direction; a one-way ticket between Toronto and Vancouver sells for $474 in either direction; a one-way ticket between Montréal and Toronto sells for $80; and a one-way ticket between Toronto and Québec City sells for $108.

A number of **discounts** apply on full-fare tickets: children ages two to 11 accompanied by an adult (half-fare); children under two (free on the lap of an adult); students and seniors (10% discount); passengers with disabilities and their companions together are charged a single fare, although a letter from a physician stating the companion is necessary for travel is required (see Specific Concerns in Essentials).

■■■ KEEPING IN TOUCH

■ Mail

In Canada, mailing a letter (or a postcard, which carries the same rate as a letter) to the U.S. costs 49¢ for the first 30 grams and $1.10 if the letter is between 31-100 grams. To every other foreign country, a 20-gram letter costs 86¢, a 21-50 gram letter $1.29, and a 51-100 gram letter $2.15. The domestic rate is 43¢ for a 30 gram letter, and 86¢ for a letter between 31-100 grams. Aerogrammes can be mailed only to other locations in Canada (86¢). Letters take from three to eight working days to reach the U.S. and a week or two to get to an overseas address. Guaranteed next-day delivery exists between any two Canadian cities and costs $8.10 within a single province and $11.50 between provinces; for the purposes of Priority Courier, Québec and Ontario represent one region, so that mail traveling between those provinces costs $8.10.

In Canada, postal codes are the equivalent of U.S. ZIP codes and contain letters as well as numbers (for example, H4P 1B8). The normal form of address is nearly identical to that in the U.S.; the only difference is that the apartment or suite number can *precede* the street address along with a dash. For example, 23-40 Sherbrooke St. refers to Room #23 at 40 Sherbrooke St.

General Delivery (Poste Restante) mail can be sent to any post office and will be held for 15 days; it can be held for longer at the discretion of the Postmaster if such a request is clearly indicated on the front of the envelope. General Delivery letters should be labeled like this:

Mr. Elroy Jessica <u>Sossenpheffer</u> (underline last name for accurate filing)
c/o General Delivery
Station C
354 Fletcher St.
St. John's, Newfoundland, A1C 5H1
CANADA

Alternatively, **American Express** offices throughout Canada will act as a mail service for cardholders, *if* you contact them in advance. Under this free "Client Letter Service," they will hold mail for 30 days, forward upon request, and accept telegrams. For a complete list of offices and instructions on how to use the service, call 800-528-4800.

■ Telephones And Telegrams

Telephones and telegrams in Canada work exactly as in the United States. See Keeping in Touch in the USA Essentials section.

Newfoundland

John Cabot, who sailed into St. John's harbor in 1497, has long been credited with "discovering" Newfoundland. However, excavations completed in L'Anse aux Meadows in the 1960s have conclusively proven that he was not the first European to set foot in Newfoundland. Rather, Norse Vikings seem to have settled, if only momentarily, in the island's Northern corner sometime around 1000 AD, and it is even possible that the Irish came here in the 6th century AD.

Having been a British Dominion since 1855, Newfoundland became Canada's tenth province in 1949 after a squeakingly close referendum. Containing the easternmost point in Canada and much of its eastern seaboard, Newfoundland Province is the Pacific Northwest of the Atlantic northeast. Like the territories and rural areas of Canada, the inhabitants are dwarfed by the sheer area of the countryside; in Labrador, each person could have his own private little piece of ice. But the sparse population is unified. With English as the mother tongue to more than 98% of its 568,349 people, Newfoundland is the most homogeneous province in Canada.

PRACTICAL INFORMATION

Capital: St. John's.
Visitor Information: Department of Tourism and Culture, P.O. Box 8730, St. John's, NF A1B 4K2 (729-2830 or 800-563-6353).
Time Zones: Atlantic (in Labrador; 1 hr. ahead of Eastern) and Newfoundland (on the island; 1½ hr. ahead of Eastern). **Postal Abbreviation:** NF
Provincial Sales Tax: 12%.

NEWFOUNDLAND ISLAND

The "rock," so called for its craggy profile, seems to soar out of the water, unwarranted and unexpected. A spectacular natural setting complements deep fjords and towering cliffs with quasi-lunar expanses at times, gentle forests at others. Newfoundland's breathtaking, if daunting, landscape is a natural wonder. Blessed with a population geographically, climatically, and politically locked into isolation for centuries, it is a cultural marvel. The central region, hardly accessible, combines lowlands, boggy forests, and rolling ranges of hills. Gros Morne National Park (designated a World Heritage Site by UNESCO) in the west and Terra Nova National Park in the east offer dazzling glimpses of Newfoundland's natural setting. The island's interior is virtually uninhabited and hardly paved.

The diversity of accents found throughout the land reveals the inhabitants' various origins, as well as the fact that Newfoundland evolved separately from the continent. "Newfies" may speak in a deep, often incomprehensible drawl which combines unique sounds and original idiom. Depending on the region, accents may take an Irish or western English (Dorset, Devon, Cornwall, to name a few) quality. Newfie food is equally unique. Fish is cooked imaginatively, and Screech, the locally made rum, is recognized Canada-wide for its, well, special punch. More than all, Newfies are characterized by a sense of humor and friendliness virtually unparalleled on the mainland.

Getting There and Getting Around There are two ways to reach Newfoundland: boat or plane. Taking the boat is the cheaper option. **Marine Atlantic** (800-341-7981 from Continental U.S.; 794-5700 from North Sydney, Nova Scotia; 695-7081 from Port-aux-Basques; 772-7701 from St. John's) ferries depart from North Sydney to Port-aux-Basques (1-3 per day, 5 hr., $16.50, ages 5-12 $8.25,

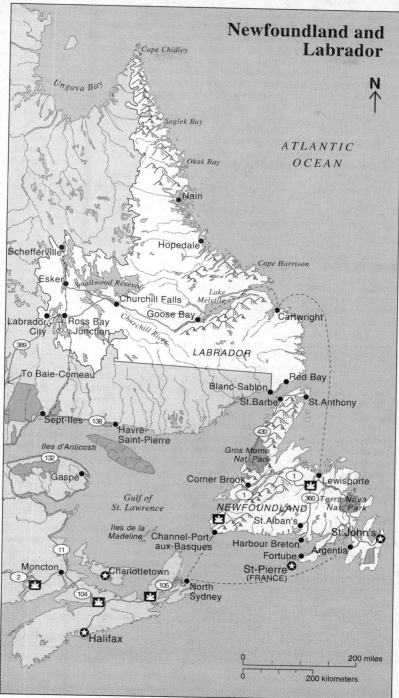

Newfoundland and Labrador

seniors $12.50, cars $51.50) and Argentia (2 per week, 14 hr., $46.25, ages 5-12 $23.25, seniors $34.75, cars $103). Reservations are required, especially for the Argentia Ferry. Carless travelers can usually get on without a reservation, but must be at the terminal at least 2 hr. in advance. **Marine Atlantic** also runs ferries to Labrador (see Getting to Labrador, page 800). **CN Roadcruiser** (737-5912 in St. John's) services the whole island, and goes from Port-aux-Basques to St. John's (1 per day, 14 hr., $80). The bus leaves early in the morning so try taking a night ferry if you don't want to be stranded overnight in barren Port-aux-Basques. Bus service to Argentia remains mysterious (see St. John's practical info). Considering its gargantuan distances and limited bus service, Newfoundland is best explored by car.

Accommodations For a comprehensive, town-by-town listing of Newfoundland's accommodations, pick up the *Newfoundland & Labrador Travel Guide* at any visitors center, including the one in the Marine Atlantic Ferry Terminal in North Sydney, NS (open before ferry departures). Rooms at hotels, motels, and B&Bs tend to go for $35-55, but are few and far between. Staying at one of the island's 74 campgrounds allows more flexibility and closer contact with the area's superb nature. Newfoundland has one hostel, **Woody Point (HI-C)** (453-2442 or 453-2470), offering a roof over your head and a prime location in Gros Morne National Park. Kitchen and laundry facilities ($10, nonmembers $13; open June-Sept.).

■ ■ ■ ST. JOHN'S

St. John's, an oasis of civilization amidst Newfoundland's picturesque expanses of caribou and conifers, is docked on the eastern coast of the island's southeastern corner, the Avalon Peninsula. Located almost halfway between Europe and Montréal, St. John's is typically "Newfie" for its distinct culture and character. With a population of nearly 162,000, it is visibly un-Newfie by virtue of its skyscrapers (admittedly small but undeniably there) and impressive pub and club collection.

Legend has it that John Cabot, sailing from Bristol in 1497, stumbled upon St. John's Harbor on St. John's Day. Despite Sir Humphrey Gilbert's 1583 claim that the newly found land was English, St. John's was periodically besieged by coveting European nations as well as freelancing pirates. Final victory went to the British in 1762, when they recaptured St. John's after the French had briefly occupied it during the Seven Years' War.

Most of St. John's claims to fame are related to its geographic location as the continent's easternmost point—it received the first transatlantic wireless signal in 1901 and saw the first successful nonstop transatlantic flight take off in 1919—and historical significance as one of North America's oldest European settlements. However, St. John's has more to offer than important dates and names. Exceedingly friendly locals, a unique culture and tradition, and an unexpected, rather impressive nightlife combine in St. John's for a memorable stay.

PRACTICAL INFORMATION
Emergency: 911.
Visitor Information: The City of St. John's Economic Development and Tourism Division (576-8106 or 576-8455), on New Gower St. across from City Hall, provides numerous pamphlets and free maps of the city and area, as well as the invaluable *St. John's Tourist Information Guide*. Open Mon.-Fri. 9am-4:30pm, early Sept.-May Mon.-Fri. 9am-5pm. The **Rail Car Tourist Chalet** (576-8514), on Harbor Drive (you can't miss it, it's the only rail car in town), and **Paddy's Pong Tourist Chalet** (368-5900) on Trans-Canada Hwy. (Rte. 1), 10 min. from downtown, offer the same services early June-early Sept. daily 9am-7pm.
Student Travel Agency: Travel CUTS (737-7926 or 737-7936; fax 737-4743), in the Thomson Student Center, Memorial University. Open Mon.-Thurs. 9am-4:30pm, Fri. 9am-4pm, Labor Day-late May Mon.-Fri. 9am-5pm.

Airport: St. John's International Airport, 10km from downtown off Portugal Cove Rd. (Rte. 40). No buses go there and **Bugdon's Taxi** (726-4400) will charge $11-13 for the ride. **Air Canada** (726-78800) has excellent stand-by rates for youths under 25 who are willing to take the chance on flights within Canada. ($145 to Montréal and $377 to Vancouver instead of $413/$1077.)

Buses: CN Roadcruiser, 495 Water St. (737-5912), serves the entire island. To: Port-aux-Basques (1 per day, 14 hr., $80); Lewisporte (3 per week, 6 hr., $45). Students get 15% discount. Open daily 7am-5:30pm. CN Roadcruiser does not serve Argentia, but rumor has it that a taxi service called Newhooks runs a shuttle. Newhooks remains elusive and mysterious. Try calling 227-2552 or 551-0865.

Taxi: Bugdon's Taxi, 726-4400. 24 hrs. $2 base fare, 90¢ per km.

Public Transportation: Metrobus, 245 Freshwater Rd. (722-9400), provides service 6:30am-11:30pm throughout the city. Fare: $1.25, kids 75¢. Office open daily 5:30am-12:30am.

Car Rental: Rent-a-Wreck, 43 Pippy Pl. (753-2277). $32 per day, 100km free, 10¢ per km thereafter. Insurance $9 per day, under 25 $11. Must be 21 with major credit card or major cash deposit. Open Mon.-Fri. 8am-5pm, Sat. 9am-1pm. Also try **Discount,** 350 Kenmount Rd. (722-6699).

Help Lines: Rape Crisis and Information Center, 726-1411; 24 hrs. **Crisis Line Telecare,** 579-1601; 24 hrs.

Post Office: Postal Station C, 354 Water St. (758-1003). Open Mon.-Fri. 9am-5pm. **Postal Code:** A1C 5H1.

Area Code: 709.

St. John's is located on a hill, the bottom of which is **St. John's Harbour. Harbour Drive** borders the water and is paralleled by downtown's two main streets, **Water Street** and **Duckworth Street. Freshwater Road** (further out, Kenmound Rd.) and **New Cove Road** (further out, Portugal Cove Rd.) extend up the hill towards Memorial University and the airport.

ACCOMMODATIONS AND CAMPING

Most of St. John's accommodations are expensive. B&Bs tend to be cheaper ($40-60 for a single) and more enjoyable than hotels and motels. However, cheap lodging does exist in a few select locations where clean, comfortable rooms virtually never run out. For a listing more complete than that offered in the provincial guide, consult *St. John's Tourist Information Guide* available in the city's visitors centers.

Memorial University Residences at Hatcher House (737-7590 or fax 737-3520), off Elizabeth Ave. From downtown take bus #3 or walk 45 min. Clean dorm rooms with basic student amenities. Definitely the best prices in town. Singles $16, student $13; doubles $25/$20. Open 24 hrs., but the phone rarely answers. Go directly to Hatcher house and find the on-guard proctor's phone number on the conference office booth. Call the proctor if necessary. Rooms reputedly never run out. Open June-Aug.

Catherine Booth House Traveler's Hostel, 18 Springdale St. (738-2804). Off Water St., 3 min. from downtown's heart. From bus station, walk down Water St. and turn left on Springdale. Run by the Salvation Army, this hostel functions like a B&B and offers 32 carefully cleaned and very comfortable rooms. Singles $30, doubles $35. Breakfast (7:30-9:30am) and late night snack (8:30-10pm) included. Open 24 hrs. After 12:30am, the phone and door might not answer for long spans of time as the night guard regularly leaves his desk.

Southcott Hall, 100 Forest Rd. (737-6495). 10 min. walk from downtown. 30 singles ($27.50) in 12-story high-rise with great view. Open 24 hrs.

Traveler's Home Hostel (754-5626), on Lemarchant Rd. Jerry and Donna can welcome up to 3 people, preferably "genuine travelers and backpackers," in their home. Call ahead (before 11pm) since drop-ins cannot be accommodated. Breakfast included. $25.

Pee Wee Park Resort (834-4634 or 229-7704), on Salmonier Line. 100 sites 7km west of Rte. 1. Numerous activities available, plus laundry and showers. Keep in mind that St. John's summers can be mighty chilly. Sites for 4 people $11, hookup $12. Each additional person $1.50, with hookup $2.50. Open May 15-Sept. 15.

FOOD AND ENTERTAINMENT

Newfoundlanders enjoy food and drink and St. John's shows it. The city, with a strange affinity for Chinese and Mexican food, can please every palate and every wallet. Don't leave before having sampled traditional Newfie foods, such as jigg's dinner or fish 'n' brewis (basically fish mixed with soaked and boiled hardbread; it's better than it sounds) and scrunchions. You'll probably never run into these again.

Cafe Duckworth, 190 Duckworth St. (722-1444), is where you'll find coffee-sipping long-haired musicians drawing long puffs from cigarettes you've never heard of before, blue-haired, body-pierced women reading *The New Yorker,* and sandwiches ($3.75-4.50), breakfast specials ($3-4.25), and coffees. Open Mon.-Sat. 8am-8pm, Sun. 10am-8pm; Sept.-mid July Mon.-Sat. 8am-6pm, Sun. 10am-6pm.

House of Hayne's, 207 Kenmount Rd. (754-4937), specializes in Newfie style home cookin'. Try the Fish 'n' Brewis ($6.30) or the Jiggs Dinner ($6). Open daily 6:15am-10pm.

Ches's, 9 Freshwater St. (722-4083), is where fish & chips ($5), superbly greased and fried, have become an art form. Don't be put off by the fast-food setting; the food is good and famous. Open Sun.-Thurs. 10am-2am, Fri.-Sat. 10am-3am.

Magic Wok Eatery, 402 Water St. (753-6907), offers Szechuan, Cantonese, and Peking dishes at friendly prices. Lunch specials ($5.50-7) dinner specials ($5-6), and entrees ($7-9). Open Mon.-Sat. noon-midnight, Sun. 3pm-midnight.

Classic Cafe, 364 Duckworth St. (579-4444), serves classic cafe foods and drinks. Sandwiches ($4.50-7), quiche ($4.50), and in case you're needing a complete refill, the "Big Hungry Human" ($10) will do it. Open 24 hrs.

St. John's seems to undergo a metamorphosis with the setting of the sun. Otherwise quiet streets come alive with the vibrancy and expectancy of a young partying crowd. George St. in particular becomes one continuous strip of clubs where loud music and over-drunk youths congregate. Most clubs and bars close at 2am and have cover charges. To avoid the long lines behind the clubs' closed doors (especially on weekends), show up before 10pm. **The Sundance Saloon,** 33 George St., has noteworthy food and drink specials and an active dance floor. Tues.-Wed. are wing nights (20¢ wings) and Karaoke nights (9pm-midnight). The line-up at the door can count more than 200 people so plan early. ($3 cover Fri.-Sat. 8pm-1am. Open Mon.-Sat. 11am-2am, Sun. 11am-midnight.) Across the street, **Jungle Jim's** (753-1774) features the same music in a more equatorial, somewhat cheesy setting. When dancing, beware of the palm trees. ($2 cover Fri.-Sat. 10pm-1am. Open Mon.-Sat. 11am-2am, Sun. 11am-midnight.) The **Duke of Duckworth,** 325 Duckworth St. in McMurdo's Lane, serves up traditional pub food and drink, including the best pint of Irish beer in town ($5.25) (open Mon.-Sat. midnight-2am; Sun. noon-midnight). **Nautical Nellies,** 201 Water St. (726-0460), is famous for its happy hours (daily 2:30-7:30pm), especially on Fri. when it's accompanied by free finger food (5-7:30pm). (Open Mon.-Wed. 11:30am-1am, Thurs.-Sat. 11:30am-2am, Sun. 11:30am-midnight.)

SIGHTS

One of the oldest cities in North America, St. John's is steeped in history. Downtown is cluttered with architectural landmarks, prominently **St. John the Baptist Anglican Cathedral** (726-5677), Gower St., one of the finest examples of ecclesiastical Gothic architecture in North America (tours available May-mid-Oct. 10:30am-4:30pm), and **Commissariat House** (729-6730), King's Bridge Rd., a late Georgian style building where guides show you around in period costumes (open June-mid-Sept. daily 10am-6pm).

Up and to the east from the waterfront are **Signal Hill** and the **Cabot Tower.** The French and English fought several times for control of the hill and Marconi received the first transatlantic cable transmission here in 1901. Today the Hill offers a great view of St. John's and features a **Military Tatoo** (July-Aug. Wed.-Sun. 3pm and 7pm). Look to the south from Signal Hill and see **Cape Spear,** the easternmost point of land in North America.

Museum junkies will not find nirvana in St. John's, but can get a fix at the **Newfoundland Museum,** 285 Duckworth St. (729-2329), where 900 years of Newfoundland history are explored, or at the **Murray Premises** (729-5044), Beck's Cove, off Water St., with permanent exhibits on local aquatic and military historical activities. (Both museums open Mon.-Fri. 9am-noon and 1-4:45pm, Sat.-Sun. 2-4:45pm. Both free.) Across from the Murray Premises, on the Waterfront, **Adventure tours** (726-5000) promises to show you whales and make you a certified Newfoundlander. The trip (2½ hr.; $20, under 12 $10) involves sighting whales, codjigging, drinking screech rum, kissing a cod, and receiving a screechers certificate. You'll also find Bosun, an enormous Newfoundland dog. (Open daily 10am-5pm.) The annual **St. John's Regatta** is North America's oldest continuing sporting event. Since 1825, on every first Wednesday of August (weather permitting), the city shuts down while all gather at the shore of Quidi Vidi Lake. The last weekend in July, St. John's gathers on Prince Edward Plaza for the **George Street Festival,** where contemporary and traditional local musicians strut their stuff.

■■■ THE REST OF THE ISLAND

Caribou rather than people roam Newfoundland's interior. Communities and roads tend to concentrate along the island's rugged coast and the Trans-Canada Highway's beautifully paved embankment. Newfie towns are, for the most part, grimly industrial. It isn't rare to see one devour truckload after truckload of lumber only to later dump out millions of metric tons of rather unnatural smoke. **Corner Brook** in the west and **Placentia** in the east are the island's main towns after St. John's. Visit them to get a taste of local folklore, but don't expect much more.

The Trans-Canada Highway conveniently paves its way by **Gros Morne National Park** and **Terra Nova National Park,** absolute must-sees. Both parks extract a car entrance fee ($5 per day, $10 for four days, $20 per season mid-June-Labor Day). For **park information,** contact the superintendents at Gros Morne National Park, P.O. Box 130, Rocky Harbour, NF A0K 4N0 (458-2066; fax 458-2059) and at Terra Nova National Park, Glovertown NF A0G 2L0 (533-2801; fax 533-2706).

■ Gros Morne National Park

Where receding glaciers once created spectacular fjords, UNESCO has now designated a World Heritage Site. Hiking opportunities there are both numerous and dazzling. In particular, the **James Callaghan Trail** which ascends **Gros Morne Mountain** offers a mind-boggling, word-exhausting panorama at the top. Keep in mind that the hike is very strenuous, very steep, and saturated with black furry spiders. Gros Morne is blessed with five **campgrounds** totaling 296 sites: Berry Hille, Green Point, Lomond, Shullon Bay, and Trout River. (Sites $7.25-11.25. Systematically stay 4 nights for the price of 3 and 7 for the price of 5. No electrical hookup available. Green Point is open year round.) **Berry Hill,** with 156 wooded, semi-services sites, is popular thanks to the three hiking trails within the campground, its proximity to Gros Morne Mountain, and its services (sites $11.25; showers, kitchen shelters, and fireplaces; open mid-May-Oct.).

■ Terra Nova National Park

About 400km from Gros Morne, on the other side of the island, this park shelters 400 sq. km of typical Newfie habitat: secluded bays, rugged shores and rolling forest hills. You might meet a lynx, a moose, or an *ursus americanus* here. Terra Nova numbers 16 hiking trails (45 min. to 6 hr. long) and one main campground at **New-**

man Sound (387 semi-serviced sites; showers, laundry, bike rental, convenience store; sites $10, $30 for 4 nights, $50 for 1 week; open year round). Primitive and free campgrounds are also located at Minchin Cove, South Broad Cove, Overs Island, and Dumphy's Pond. You must register at a visitors center before enjoying their isolated nature. Learn all you'll ever want to know on the area's fauna and flora at the **Twin Rivers Visitors Center,** at the southern entrance to the park (open mid-June-early Sept. daily 10am-6pm).

LABRADOR

The Alaska of the Atlantic Coast, Labrador in the winter is a snowy wonderland full of snow and caribou and snow and musk oxen and snow and 30,000 people, and *snow*. In summer, it beckons nature lovers with virgin forests and untouched wilderness. Unlike Alaska, however, Labrador has only three roads, a railway, and a few airports, and is not even as far north. Once you've been to Labrador, you'll understand why labrador retrievers are so loyal, strong, friendly, and warm.

Getting to Labrador **Marine Atlantic** runs ferries June-Sept. from Lewisporte, Newfoundland to Goose Bay, Labrador with an optional stop in Cartwright (2 per week, 35 hr., $80, ages 5-12 $40, seniors $60, cars $130). **CN Roadcruiser** stops in Lewisporte en route from St. John's to Port-aux-Basques (see page 794). Another ferry service, the **Puddister Trading Company,** with offices in St. John's (for information only, 726-0015 or 722-4000; 23 Springdale St., St. John's; open Mon.-Fri. 9am-5pm), Québec (418-461-2056), and Labrador (709-931-2309), provides ferry service from St. Barbe on the north coast of Newfoundland Island to Blanc Sablon, Québec (1-2 per day May and Sept.-Oct., 2-3 per day June-Aug., 1 per day Nov.-Jan; 1½ hr.; $8, seniors $6.25, ages 5-12 $4, under 5 free, cars $16.25, bicycles $2.75; reservations taken up to 48 hr. in advance). From Blanc Sablon, it's a quick drive along Hwy. 510 up to Red Bay, Labrador, where the paved roads end. Flying is another option, though hideously expensive. Adventurous souls should contact the **Québec North Shore and Labrador Railroad** (418-968-7803; 968-7805 for Labrador info), which runs trains from Sept-Iles, Québec, to Labrador City (Mon. 10am and Thurs. 8am; 10 hr.; $47, seniors $24) and Schefferville (Thurs. 8am; $65, seniors $33). Offices in Labrador City (709-944-8205) and Schefferville (418-585-3608). The truly hardy can always drive to Labrador City via Rte. 389, a partially-paved highway that begins in Baie Comeau, Québec. From Labrador City, Rte. 500 bumps and jolts for 530 gravel-covered km to Goose Bay. Road conditions are harsh, and services are few and far between; do not take this trip lightly.

If you thought our map had a lot of grey space, check out the *Newfoundland and Labrador Official Highway Map,* which provides inset town maps, campsite information, and practical information, as well as the three roads that grace Labrador's tundra. Contact local consulates or Labrador's **Department of Tourism and Culture,** P.O. Box 8730, St. John's A1B 4K2 (800-563-6353 or 729-2830), in the Confederation Bldg. west block, which provides basic information on Labrador (open Mon.-Fri. 8:30am-4pm; message center with basic facilities open 24 hrs.).

▓ New Brunswick

Two cultures dominate New Brunswick today. The Acadians, French pioneers who had originally settled in Nova Scotia in the 17th century, migrated to the northern

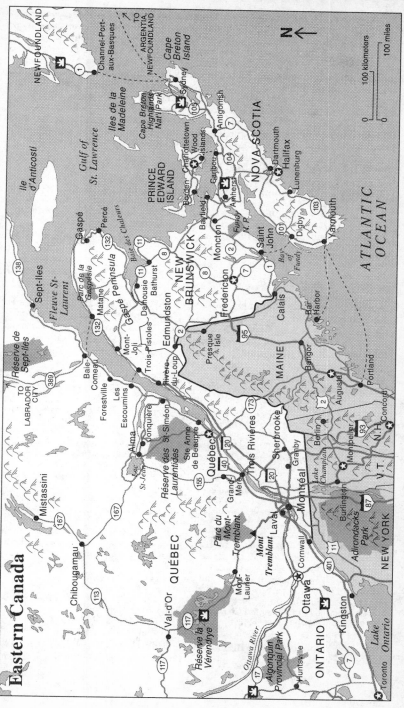

Eastern Canada

and eastern coasts and established the farming and fishing nation of *l'Acadie,* or Acadia. When the British took control of the area in 1755, they expelled many of these farmers who then drifted all the way down to the Gulf of Mexico to found Acadiana amidst their compatriots in Louisiana. The southern region of New Brunswick was settled by the Loyalists, British subjects who fled in the wake of the American Revolution. Although over a third of the province's population is French-speaking, it is rare to encounter someone in the larger cities who doesn't speak English.

New Brunswick naturally prides itself on its deep forests, vast spaces, and spectacular coast. The tremendous Bay of Fundy gives rise to the world's highest tides, at 30 feet. Other natural oddities include the Reversing Falls in St. John and Moncton's Magnetic Hill. Museums and cultural products may take a back seat here, but that's a tolerable loss for a province best seen when seats are left behind.

PRACTICAL INFORMATION

Capital: Fredericton.
Department of Economic Development and Tourism: P.O. Box 12345, Fredericton, NB E3B 5C3. Distributes free publications including the *Official Highway Map, Outdoor Adventure Guide, Craft Directory, Fish and Hunt Guide,* and *Travel Guide* (with accommodation and campground directory and prices).
Alcohol: Legal drinking age 19.
Time Zone: Atlantic (1 hr. ahead of Eastern). **Postal Abbreviation:** NB
Provincial Sales Tax: 11%.

■■■ FREDERICTON

In 1758 the American Revolution projected some 2000 British Loyalists up the St. John River Valley to Ste. Anne's Point. They renamed the settlement "Fredericstown," in honor of King George III's second son. It was selected provincial capital two years later because of its ready access to the Atlantic Ocean via the St. John River and its defensible location in the heart of New Brunswick.

Today, Fredericton maintains its importance as New Brunswick's governmental and administrative center. It has also earned renown as Canada's center of pewtersmithing and handcrafts. Quiet and genteel, the streets of the "City of Stately Elms" are lined with gracious old houses.

PRACTICAL INFORMATION

Emergency: 911.
Visitor Information: Visitor Information Centre (452-9500), City Hall, on the corner of Queen and York. The exceptionally courteous and ready-to-help staff provides tourists with the *Street Index Map/Transit Guide* and the invaluable *Fredericton Visitor Guide* with complete listings of area accommodations and attractions. Open daily 8am-8pm; early Sept.-mid-May daily 8:15am-4:30pm.
Student Travel Agency: Travel CUTS (453-4850), in the student Union Bldg. of the University of New Brunswick. Ride-showing board posted. Open Mon.-Fri. 9am-4pm, mid-Sept.-May Mon.-Fri. 9am-5pm.
Trains: VIA Rail (368-7818 or 800-561-3952), in Fredericton Junction, about 50 min. from Fredericton. A VIA Rail shuttle bus will pick you up in front of the **Lord Beaverbrook Hotel,** 659 Queen St. To: Montréal (Mon., Thurs., and Sat.), 12½ hr., $98, students $88; 7 days in advance $73/$63); Halifax (Tues., Fri., and Sun., 9 hr., $71/$63; 5 days in advance and traveling on Tues. $43/$35).
Bus: SMT, 101 Regent St. (458-6000). On-time service to: Saint John (2-3 per day, 2 hr., $15); Edmunston (2 per day, 5 hr., $35); Moncton (2 per day, 2½ hr., $25). Connections to Halifax and Charlottetown (P.E.I.) in Moncton.
Public Transport: Fredericton Transit, 470 St. Mary's (458-9522), circulates around town every hr. Mon.-Sat. 7am-10pm. Fare $1, kids 50¢. All buses stop downtown on King St. in front of King's Place. Office open Mon.-Fri. 8:30am-4:30pm.

Taxi: Budget, 450-1199. **Student,** 459-8294, driven by hired students. Both function 24 hrs. and average about $3 per trip.

Car Rental: Delta, 304 King St. (458-8899). Rents economy cars at $20 per day with 100km free, 12¢ per additional km. Insurance $10 per day. Must be 21 with major credit card. Open Mon.-Fri. 7:30am-8pm, Sat. 8am-5pm, Sun. 10am-5pm.

Bike Rental: Savage's, 449 King St. (458-8985), will provide you wheels for $3 per hr. or $15 per day. Must have some sort of ID. Open Mon.-Wed. 8:30am-6pm, Thurs.-Fri. 8:30am-9pm, Sat. 9am-5pm.

Help lines: Rape Crisis Center, 454-0437. 24 hrs.

Post Office: Station "A," 527 Queen St. (452-3345), next to Officer's Sq. Open Mon.-Fri. 8am-5:15pm. **Postal Code:** E3B 4Y1.

Area Code: 506.

Traffic congestion is rare downtown, and almost all areas of interest can easily be reached on foot. **Officer's Square,** a small park between Queen St. and the river, is the geographic heart of activity.

ACCOMMODATIONS AND CAMPING

Cheap housing, though rare, is generally not too competitive in the summer. Most motels and B&Bs run $35-50, and campgrounds are plentiful. A comprehensive listing of accommodations and prices is available in the *Fredericton Visitor Guide*.

York House Hostel (HI-C), 193 York St. (454-1233). Ideally positioned downtown. Zealous young staff makes sure you are tucked in at midnight and awake at 7:30am. 30 beds. Kitchen and lounge. Breakfast 7:30-8:30am ($1.50-3). Reception open 4pm-midnight. Check-out 9:30am. $9, nonmembers $12. Open June-Aug.

University of New Brunswick, Residential Administration Bldg. (453-4835) on campus. Take bus 16 South from downtown to the university. The **Student Hotel** is open to students, $12.50 per day, $68 per week. The **Tourist Hotel** is pricier but open to all. Singles $27.50, doubles $39.90. Open May-late Aug.

Norfolk Motel (472-3278), Trans-Canada Highway East on the north shore of the river, 3km east of downtown. Bus 15 North passes by the near end of the route. Singles $29, doubles $32.

Hartt Island Campground (the Bucket Club) (450-6057). Located off the Trans-Canada Highway, 5km west of town. Next to an amusement park along the river's shore. 125 sites, pool, laundry, showers. Sites $14, with hookup $17-19; $2 per person in groups larger than 4 people. Reservations highly recommended July-Aug. Open May-Oct.

FOOD AND ENTERTAINMENT

Decently-priced places to eat abound in Fredericton. **Mexicali Rosa's,** 546 King St. (451-0686), offers a $4-7 lunch special (Mon.-Sat. 11:30am-6pm) in a decor unabashedly strewn with cowboy figurines and fake cacti (open Mon.-Wed. 11:30am-11:30pm, Thurs. 11:30am-midnight, Fri.-Sat. 11:30am-1am, Sun. noon-11pm). At **Molly's Coffee House,** 422 Queen St. (457-9305), you can buy anything in the shop including gourmet coffees, antique chairs, and scrumptious breads baked on the premises. Perfect for breakfast or a light lunch (sandwiches $1.50-1.75, muffins 60¢, soup with home-made bread $2.25-2.75). (Open Mon.-Wed. 7:30am-6pm, Thurs.-Fri. 7:30am-9pm, Sat. 10am-5pm, Sun. noon-5pm.) **Trumpers,** 349 King St. (444-0819), serves a wide variety of vegetarian and vegan sandwiches ($2.75) as well as quiche ($2.25) and lasagne ($2.75). (Open Mon.-Fri. 7:30am-6pm, Sat. 8:20am-3:30pm.) The town boasts a number of supermarkets, but you may want to protest their artificial price-inflating packaging practices by shopping at the **Boyce Farmers Market** (451-1815), located behind the Old York County Gaol between Regent and St. John St. Over 140 stalls sell farm-fresh foods, crafts, and other goodies. (Open Sat. 6am-1pm.)

Much of Fredericton's nightlife is inspired by students of the University of New Brunswick, a majestic campus sprawling over a hill overlooking the city. The oldest

FREDERICTON

and largest dance club, **Club Cosmopolitan,** 546 King St. (458-8165), is where locals take worldly guests first ($2.75 cover; open Mon.-Fri. 4pm-2am, Sat. 7pm-2am, Sun. 7pm-1am). **The Hilltop Pub,** 152 Prospect St. (458-9057), serves heaping portions of steak ($8-14) by day and "I'm-going-to-get-wasted"-cheap drafts by night (95¢ draft on Twisted Tuesday 7-10pm, Fri. 4-6pm and 8-10pm, Sat. 8-10pm; 50¢ gets "ladies" a draft Thurs. 7-10pm). Local youth boogie to country music in this barn with lights but no hay. **The Lunar Rogue Pub,** 625 King St. (450-2065), serves up roguish nachos and an eclectic conglomeration of live Irish, contemporary, and folk music (Thurs.-Sat. 9pm-1am; open Mon.-Sat. 11am-1am, Sun. noon-1am).

SIGHTS

Just inside the entrance to the **Beaverbrook Art Gallery,** 703 Queen St. (458-85845), hangs Salvador Dalí's awe-inspiring, 13x10 ft. masterpiece, *Santiago el Grande.* A gift to local-boy Lord Beaverbrook, the gallery also houses a collection of Anglo paintings including works by Gainsborough, Turner, and Constable. (Open Sun.-Mon. noon-8pm, Tues.-Wed. 10am-8pm, Thurs.-Sat. 10am-5pm; Sept.-June Sun.-Mon. noon-5pm, Tues.-Sat. 10am-5pm. $3, seniors $2, students $1.) New Brunswick's provincial government meets in the **Legislative Assembly Building** (453-2527), a three-story sandstone building with mansard roof and corner towers. Tours of the building, including the Assembly Chamber when the Legislature isn't spending money, leave every half-hour. (Open daily 9am-8pm, Sept.-early June Mon.-Fri. 9am-4pm.) In July and August, pageantry-lovers can witness the **Changing of the Guard** (452-9500)—specifically the Royal New Brunswick Regiment—in Officers' Sq. (Tues.-Sat. at 11am and 7pm. Sentries change every hr. Inspection of the guard Thurs. at 11am.) Also catch Officers' Sq.'s open-air concerts in July and August on Tues. and Thurs. evenings, with everything from pipe bands to bluegrass. The quirky **York-Sunbury Historical Society Museum** (455-6041) operates within the Old Officers' Quarters in Officers' Square. Exhibits detail aspects of New Brunswick life from the Micmac natives to the recreation of a World War I trench. Also in residence is the famous 42-lb. Coleman Frog. Old Fred Coleman supposedly fed his pet croaker bran and ox blood, although it had a predilection for scotch, rum, and gin. To preserve the enigma of the frog, museum officials have forbidden scientific examination of the specimen. (Open daily 10am-6pm; mid-Oct.-April Mon., Wed., and Fri. 11am-3pm. $1, students 50¢.) The green which borders the river's banks over several km makes for a pleasant walk or bike ride. Those of more aquatic taste can rent a **canoe** from the **Small Craft Aquatic Center** (458-5513), off Woodstock Rd., on the river bank behind the Victoria Health Center. (Canoes, kayaks, and rowing shells for a beastly $6.66 per hr. A $5 registration fee per season is necessary. Open Mon.-Fri. 6-9am and 4:30-9pm, Sat.-Sun. 10am-6pm.) Paddle along the St. John, stopping at the **Fredericton Lighthouse** (459-2515 or 800-561-4000), where the public is allowed access all the way to the top. (Open daily 10am-9pm; June and Sept. Mon.-Fri. 9am-4pm, Sat.-Sun. noon-4pm, Oct.-May Mon.-Fri. 9am-4pm. $2, kids under 12 $1.) The walking tour presented in the *Fredericton Visitor Guide* hits all the attractions in central Fredericton.

Kings Landing Historical Settlement, Trans-Canada Highway (Hwy. 2) exit #259 (363-5805), lies 37km west of Fredericton. This superb re-creation of an early Loyalist township is a living, breathing museum, staffed by period actors whose daily chores from buttermaking to blacksmithing make it a completely self-sufficient village. The saw and grist mills particularly stand out in the 300-acre expanse of Kings Landing. Leave several hours for exploration. (Open July-Aug. daily 10am-6pm; June and Sept.-Oct. daily 10am-5pm. $7.50, seniors $6.50, under 12 $4.25, families $17.50.) The Settlement has an efficient **Reception Center** that offers guided tours of the community (Tues., Thurs., and Sat. at 6:30pm; open slightly longer than the Settlement; $2.50, families $5.50). There is no public transportation to the landing.

■■■ FUNDY NATIONAL PARK

Fundy is characteristically New Brunswickian in that its main attractions are its natural wonders. Here oscillate the world's largest tides. The size of the bay is such that it resonates at the same frequency as the tides—about once every 12 hr. The effect is similar to that of water sloshing around in a giant bathtub. In the park, you can hike through the wooded trails or slog out more than 1km onto the ocean floor at low tide. The park occupies a territory along the Bay of Fundy, about an hour's drive from Moncton. Hwy. 114 is the only major access road to and through the park, running northwest to the Trans-Canada Hwy., and east along the shore to Moncton.

Practical Information **Park Headquarters,** P.O. Box 40, Alma, NB, E0A 1B0 (887-2000), is made up of a group of buildings in the southeastern corner of the Park facing the Bay, across the Upper Salmon River from the town of Alma. The area includes the administration building, the assembly building, an amphitheater, and the **Visitors Reception Center,** which sits at the east entrance (open daily 8am-9pm; mid-Sept.-late May Mon.-Fri. 8:15am-4:30pm). **Wolfe Lake Information** (432-6026), the park's other visitors center, lurks at the northwest entrance, off Hwy. 114 (open mid-June-Sept. Sat.-Thurs. 10am-6pm, Fri. 9am-9pm). In the off-season, contact Park Headquarters (open Mon.-Fri. 8:15am-4:30pm). No public transport serves Fundy, and the nearest bus depots are in Moncton and Sussex. The park extracts a car entrance fee of $5 per day and $10 for four days from mid-June to Labor Day, but is free year-round for bicyclists and hikers. The free and invaluable park newspaper *Salt and Fir,* available at the park entrance stations, includes a map of all hiking trails and campgrounds as well as details on all of the interpretive programs and activities.

Camping The park operates four **campgrounds** totalling over 600 sites; getting a site is seldom a problem, although landing one at your campground of choice may be a little more difficult. Reservations are *not* accepted; all sites are first-come, first-grabbed. **Headquarters Campground** is in highest demand, often commanding a two-day wait in summer, because of its three-way hookups and proximity to facilities. When the campground is full, put your name on the waiting list, and sleep somewhere else for the night. Return the next day at noon when names from the list admitted for that night are read. Showers and washrooms available. (Open mid-May-mid-Oct. Sites $10, with hookup $15.50; $30/$46.50 for 4 nights; $50/$77.50 per week.) **Chignecto North Campground,** off Hwy. 114, 5km inland from the headquarters, is the other campground with electrical hookups. The forest and distance between campsites affords more privacy. Ten sites here offer three-way hookup, 42 offer electricity and water, 56 offer electricity only, and 212 have no hookup at all. (Open mid-June-mid-Sept. Sites $8, with varying degrees of hookup $11-15; $24/$33-45 for 4 nights; $40/$55-75 per week.) **Point Wolfe Campground,** scenically located along the coast west of Headquarters, stays cooler and more insect-free than the inland campgrounds. (Open late-June-early Sept. Sites $7.75, $23 for 4 nights, $39 per week.) The **Wolfe Lake Campground** offers primitive sites near the northwest park entrance. About a minute's walk from the lake; no showers or washrooms. (Open late May-early Oct. Sites $6, $18 for 4 nights, $30 per week.) Wilderness camping is also available, and those sites are located in some of the most scenic areas of the park, especially at **Goose River** along the coast. The campsites are open year-round, are free, and all have fireplaces, wood, and an outhouse. Reservations are accepted only during the summer, and should be made one or two weeks in advance (call 887-2000).

Accommodations and Food For those wishing a roof over their heads, the new **Fundy National Park Hostel** (887-2216) is near Devil's Half Acre in the general vicinity of the park headquarters buildings. It has a full kitchen and showers, although both are located in separate buildings from the bunkrooms. ($8.50, nonmembers $10; open June-Aug.) Other accommodations can be found in Alma, by the park's eastern entrance, as well as grocery stores, postal services, banks, and laundry facilities. For a cheap, home-cooked meal, try **Harbor View** (887-2450), on Main St. The breakfast special is two eggs, toast, bacon, and coffee ($3); after any and every meal get the fantastic strawberry shortcake ($2). (Open daily 7am-10pm; Sept.-May daily 7:30am-8pm.)

Activities About 120km of park trails are open year-round. Each trail, along with complete description, is detailed in *Salt and Fir*. Only a handful are open to mountain bikes. Look for such highlights as waterfalls, ocean views, and wild animals. Though declining in numbers, deer are still fairly common, and raccoons are thick as thieves around the campsites. Catching a glimpse of a moose or a peregrine falcon will require considerably more patience.

Most recreational facilities open only in the summer season (mid-May-early Oct.), including interpretive programs, boat rentals, the nine-hole golf course, lawn bowling, a heated salt-water swimming pool, tennis courts, campgrounds, and restaurants. The daily interpretive activities are free, friendly, and always fun. Try a **Beach Walk,** during which the guide takes you down to the beach during low tide to examine ocean-bottom critters, the **Evening Program** held in the Amphitheatre, or guided **nature walks** which are never cancelled due to inclement weather. Activities are organized for kids (ages 6-12), and **campfire programs** are held weekly. Visit the park in Sept.-Oct. to avoid the crush of vacationers and to catch the fall foliage. Those seeking quiet, pristine nature would be wise to visit in the chillier off-season.

Fundy weather can be unpleasant for the unprepared. Evenings are often chilly, even when days are warm. It's best to always bring a wool sweater or jacket, as well as a can of insect repellent for the warm, muggy days. **Weather** forecasts are available from the info centers by calling 887-2000.

A worthwhile excursion from Fundy National Park is **The Rocks Provincial Park,** located at Hopewell Cape, off Hwy. 114, 45km east of Alma and 34km south of Moncton. The Rocks are 50-ft.-high sandstone formations with trees on top. At high tide, they look like little islands off the coast. The best time to view the Rocks is during low tide, when they look like gigantic flowerpots rising from the ground. Tourists are free to explore the Rocks on foot. Call the nearby craft shop (734-2975) or Tourism New Brunswick for tide info.

■■■ MONCTON

Moncton is the unofficial capital city of the province's Acadian population. Its demographics accurately reflect New Brunswick's cultural schizophrenia; the francophone one-third and anglophone two-thirds of Moncton's population coexist without tension. English predominates except around the campus of the Université de Moncton, Canada's only French-language university outside of Québec. The city's inexpensive B&Bs and restaurants, and its central location to the Fundy and Kouchibouguac National Parks, the Rocks Provincial Park, the town of Shediac on the coast, and Halifax farther east in Nova Scotia, make it an excellent base for exploring the region.

PRACTICAL INFORMATION

Visitor Information: City Hall's Convention and Visitor Services, 774 Main St. (853-3590), handles tourists Sept.-mid-May Mon.-Fri. 9am-5pm and distributes the *Moncton Information* booklet which covers everything down to tide schedules.
Trains: VIA Rail, 1240 Main St. (857-9830), behind the mall. To: Halifax (6 per week, 4½ hr., $36, students $32; $18 for students if booked 5 days in advance, $22 for adults traveling any day except Fri., Sun., or holidays); Montréal (6 per week, 14 hr., $110/$99; $55 for students if booked 7 days in advance, $83 for adults). Open Mon.-Fri. 9:30am-7pm, Sat.-Sun. 10am-7pm.

Buses: SMT, 961 Main St. (859-2170), at Bonaccord St. downtown. To: Halifax (2 per day, 5 hr., $33); Saint John (2 per day, 2 hr., $20); Charlottetown, P.E.I. (2 per day, 4½ hr., $29); connecting service to Acadian Lines in Amherst. Open Mon.-Fri. 7:30am-6:30pm, Sat.-Sun. 10am-6:30pm.

Public Transport: Codia Transit, 280 Pacific Ave. (857-2008), provides service through Greater Moncton Mon.-Wed. and Sat. 7am-7pm, Thurs.-Fri. 7am-11pm. Buses all congregate at Highfield Square downtown. Fare $1, students and seniors 70¢; exact change only. Office open Mon.-Fri. 6:30am-4:30pm.

Car Rental: Econo, 740 Mountain Rd. (858-9100), rents for $23 per day, with 200km free, 10¢ per km thereafter. Insurance $10. Must be 25 with major credit card. Open Mon.-Fri. 8:30am-5:30pm, Sat. 9am-1pm.

Help line: Greater Moncton Crisis Line, 859-4357, a United Way agency. Lines open daily 4pm-8am. **Help-24-au secours** (24 hr.), 859-4357.

Post Office: 281 St. George St. (857-7240), near Highfield St. Open Mon.-Fri. 8am-5:30pm. **Postal code:** E1C 8K4.

Area Code: 506.

ACCOMMODATIONS, CAMPING, AND FOOD

Moncton's dozen or so B&Bs definitely offer the best prices (singles $25-40), as well as clean, comfortable rooms. Try to plan in advance as these are unlikely to be available without a reservation. Your second best bet for affordable lodging is, boringly enough, a motel. A number of these line up along the Trans-Canada Hwy., preying on those who drive through the area to experience Magnetic Hill.

The **McCarthy Bed and Breakfast,** 82 Peter St. (383-9152), is a jewel in the accommodations business. Gerry and Marge will welcome you with genuine warmth and unforgettable hospitality in the home where they raised their seven kids. Talk to Gerry about his philanthropic activities or simply look at his St. Patrick Card Collection, the largest in the world (singles $25, doubles $35. Full breakfast included.) Reservations very highly recommended. Gerry will pick you up at the bus or train station. (Open May-Sept.) The **Université de Moncton** (858-4008 or 858-4014) opens two dorms for summer lodging. The LaFrance building—the tallest on campus—provides spacious but Spartan dorm rooms with kitchen facilities (singles $40, students $35). The Lefebvre building is more low-key, more student-like, and more affordable (singles $20, students $18). Laundry facilities are available in both. From Queen St. downtown, follow Archibald St. all the way out (10 min. drive). From downtown, take bus #5 ("Elmwood A.") (Open May-Aug.) The **YWCA,** 35 Highfield St. (855-4349), one block from Main St. behind the bus station, also provides good-sized, clean rooms upstairs for women only (singles $20, doubles $30; kitchen and laundry; check-out 11am). A reservation is highly recommended as these tend to fill up fast. From May-Aug., the Y doubles as a hostel, renting cot-like bunks in a cellar-like basement for $8 (linen rental $4, so bring a sleeping-bag; check-in 11:30pm; check-out 9am). Breakfast is available for both ($3).

The area does have a campground: **Camper's City** (384-7867), located on Trans-Canada Hwy. at Mapleton, only 5km north of downtown. The campground has 193 sites, with showers, toilets, pool, grocery, and laundry, and mostly RVs. (Sites $14, with hookup $17.50. Office open daily 7:30am-11pm.)

Pubs are generally the cheapest place for a meal, short of fast food. **Alibi's Pub,** 841 Main St. (853-5966), serves inexpensive daily specials ($3-4) and cheap draughts, provided you can prove you're there. (Open Mon.-Sat. 9am-2am, Sun. noon-midnight.) **Fancy Pokket,** 589 Main St. (858-7898), is an elegant Lebanese restaurant, carrying a wide variety of pita pockets ($5-7) and brochettes ($7.50-10.25). (Open Mon.-Wed. and Sat. 11am-9pm, Thurs.-Fri. 11am-10pm.)

SIGHTS

Moncton is deservedly proud of its two natural wonders, the Tidal Bore and Magnetic Hill. Both are more impressive in person than on paper. The **Tidal Bore,** best viewed from Tidal Bore Park near the corner of Main St. and King St., is yet another product of the Bay of Fundy tides. Twice a day the incoming tide surges up the Petit-codiac River, a muddy river bottom along whose banks Moncton is situated, some-times with birds surfing on the Bore, and within an hour fills up to its 25-ft.-high banks. Then the flow of water reverses direction, and a mighty river starts flooding back into Chignecto Bay. It's best to arrive 15 min. before posted Tidal Bore times (consult the city guide) in case it hits early. Spring and fall are the best seasons to catch the phenomenon at full force, as well as at a full or new moon.

Magnetic Hill on Mountain Rd. just off the Trans-Canada Hwy. (Hwy. 2) north-west of central Moncton, is a phenomenon notorious among Canucks. Drive your car down to the bottom of the hill, put it in neutral, and feel your car inexplicably rolling back up to the top of the hill. (Feel free to supply your own explanation.) Best of all, it's never closed; you can try it as many times as you like; and it's always free (although the commercialized complex of theme parks built next to and upon the fame of Magnetic Hill is not).

■ Near Moncton

The Acadian town of **Shediac,** 30km north of Moncton on Hwy. 15, stakes its claim as the Lobster Capital of the World by holding their annual **Shediac Lobster Festival** in mid-July. More important to sun worshipers is the popular **Parlee Beach Provin-cial Park** (533-8813) in Shediac Bay near the warm salt waters of the Northumber-land Strait. For more info about scheduled events, write to **Shediac Information,** P.O. Box 969, Shediac E0A 3G0 (533-8800; open June-Aug. daily 9am-9pm).

Kouchibouguac, the "other" National Park in New Brunswick, suffers no inferi-ority complex from being the less popular sibling. In sharp contrast to Fundy's rug-ged forests and high tides along the Loyalist coast, Kouchibouguac (meaning "river of the long tides" in Micmac) proudly emphasizes its warm lagoon waters, salt marshes, peat bogs, and white sandy beaches along the Acadian coast. Swim or sun-bathe along the 25km stretch of barrier islands and sand dunes. Canoe waterways that were once highways for the Micmacs. You can rent canoes and bikes at **Ryans Rental Center** (876-2571) in the park between the South Kouchibouguac Camp-ground and Kellys Beach. The park operates two campgrounds in the summer (sites $8.50-11.75), neither with hookups. Several nearby commercial campgrounds just outside of the park are available for off-season campers. Kouchibouguac National Park charges a vehicle permit fee of $5 per day, $10 per four days, or $20 per year. The **Park Information Centre** is located at the Park Entrance on Hwy. 117 just off Hwy. 11, 90km north of Moncton. (Open mid-May-mid-June daily 8am-5pm, mid-June-early Sept. daily 10am-6pm, early Sept.-mid-Oct. daily 10am-6pm.) Park admin-istration (876-2443) open year-round Mon.-Fri. 8:15am-4:30pm.

Fort Beauséjour A stone's throw from the Nova Scotia border is the **Fort Beauséjour National Historical Park,** located on a hill off the Trans-Canada Hwy. (Hwy. 2) in Aulac, 40km southeast of Moncton (536-0720). One of the numerous forts built by the French and captured by the English, Fort Beauséjour (renamed Fort Cumberland under the Union Jack) is not much more than foundations and rubble these days. Some trinkets of the soldiers, including coins, weapons, and handiwork (check out the ship-in-a-bottle crafted by a French prisoner), have been excavated by archaeologists and put on display at the museum. The real reason to visit the site, though, is the panoramic view on a clear day. Looking southward to the Cumber-land Basin of the Chignecto Bay and northward toward the Tantramar River Valley, one is immediately struck by the aesthetic and strategic importance of this location, on a narrow strip of land connecting Nova Scotia to the continent. (Site always open. Museum open June-mid-Oct. daily 9am-5pm. Free.))

■■■ SAINT JOHN

The city of Saint John was founded literally overnight on May 18, 1783, by a band of about 10,000 American colonists (known as the United Empire Loyalists) loyal to the British crown. Saint John's long Loyalist tradition is apparent in its architecture, festivals, and institutions; the walkways of King and Queen Squares in central Saint John (never abbreviated so as to prevent confusion with St. John's, Newfoundland) were laid out to resemble the Union Jack. The city rose to prominence in the 19th century as a major commercial and shipbuilding port. Saint John's location on the Bay of Fundy ensures cool summers and mild winters, albeit foggy and wet; locals joke that Saint John is where you go to get your car, and yourself, washed for free.

PRACTICAL INFORMATION

Emergency: 911.

Visitor Information: Saint John Visitors and Convention Bureau (658-2990), on the 11th floor of City Hall at the foot of King St., operates year-round. Open Mon.-Fri. 8:30am-4:30pm. The **City Center** information center, alias **The Little Red Schoolhouse** (658-2555), offers info in Loyalist Plaza by the Market Slip uptown. Open mid-May-mid-June and mid-Sept.-mid-Oct. daily 9am-6pm; mid-June-mid-Sept. daily 9am-7pm.

Trains: VIA Rail, 125 Station St. (642-2916), next to Hwy. 1 north of Market Square. To: Halifax (Fri., Sun. and Tues.; $56, students $51; 5 days in advance, $34/$28); Montréal (Mon., Thurs., and Sat.; $104/$94; 7 days in advance $79/$68). Station open Tues., Fri., and Sun. 7:30am-1pm, Mon., Thurs., and Sat. 4-9pm.

Buses: SMT, 300 Union St. (648-3555), provides service to: Montréal (2 per day, 14 hr., $80); Moncton (2 per day, 2 hr., $20); Halifax (2 per day, 8 hr., $52). Station open daily 7:30am-9pm.

Public Transport: Saint John Transit (658-4700), runs daily 6am-11:30pm with frequent service through King Square. Fare: $1.25, under 14 $1. Also gives a 3-hr. guided tour of historic Saint John leaving from Loyalist Plaza and Reversing Falls June 15-Sept. Tour fare $15, ages 6-14 $5. Office open daily 5am-12:30am.

Ferry: Marine Atlantic (636-4048 or 800-341-7981 from the continental U.S.), on the Lancaster St. extension in West Saint John, near the mouth of Saint John Harbor. Crosses to Digby, Nova Scotia (1-3 per day, 2½ hr., $20, seniors $15, ages 5-12 $10, bike $10, car $45; Oct.-May $15/$12/$7.50/$5/$40). To get to the ferry, take the Saint John Transit West-Saint-John bus, then walk 10 min.

Taxi: Royal Taxi, 800-561-8294; **Diamond,** 648-8888. Both open 24 hrs.

Car Rental: Downey Ford, 10 Crown St. (632-6000). $22 per day, with 100km free, 10¢ per additional km. Ages 21-24 must have major credit card. No charge for insurance, but the deductible is a hefty $1500. All cars are automatics. (Open Mon.-Fri. 7am-6pm, Sat. 8am-5pm, Sun. 9am-5pm.)

Weather: 636-4939. **Dial-a-Tide:** 636-4429.

Post Office: Main Office, 125 Rothesay Ave. (800-565-0726). Open Mon.-Fri. 7:30am-5:15pm. **Postal Code:** E2L 3W9.

Area Code: 506.

Saint John is divided from West Saint John by the Fort Latour Harbor Bridge (toll 25¢), on Hwy. 1. Saint John's busy downtown (Saint John Centre) is bounded by Union St. to the north, Princess St. to the south, King Square on the east, and Market Square and the harbor on the west.

ACCOMMODATIONS AND CAMPING

Finding lodging for under $35 per night is difficult, especially in summer. A number of nearly identical motels cover the 1100 to 1300 blocks of Manawagonish Rd. in West Saint John (take the Fairville bus), usually charging $35-45 for a single.

Saint John YM/YWCA (HI-C), 19-25 Hazen Ave. (634-7720), from Market Square, 2 blocks up Union St. on left. Drab, bare, but clean rooms. Access to YMCA recreational facilities. Pool, work-out room. Reservations recommended in the summer. $22, nonmembers and nonstudents $28. Open daily 5:30am-11pm.

Tartan B&B, 968 Manawagonish Rd. (672-2592). No frills, but clean and well-decorated. Stay here in off-season; with the full breakfast included, it's a good deal. Shared baths. Singles $35, doubles $40. Off-season $30/$35. Open mid-May-mid-Oct.

Hillside Motel, 1131 Manawagonish Rd. (672-1273). Standard clean motel room with TV and private bath. Haggle with the owner over the room price, which ranges around $35 for singles, $45 for doubles; Sept.-April $28/$35.

Rockwood Park Campground (652-4050), at the southern end of Rockwood Park, off Hwy. 1, 2km north of uptown in a semi-wooded area. Sites $12, with electric hookup $14; 2 days $21/$26; weekly $50/$70. Take University bus to Park entrance, then walk 5 min. Open mid-May-Sept.

FOOD AND ENTERTAINMENT

Reggie's Restaurant, 26 Germain St. (657-6270), provides fresh, homestyle cooking of basic North American fare. Reggie's uses famous smoked meat from Ben's Deli in Montréal. From 6-11am, two eggs, sausage, homefries, toast, and coffee is $3.25. (Open daily 6am-9pm; Nov.-May Mon.-Wed. 6am-6pm, Thurs.-Fri. 6am-7pm, Sat. 6am-5pm, Sun. 7am-3pm.) For cheap, fresh produce and seafood, your best bet is the **City Market** (658-2820), between King and Brunswick Squares. The oldest building of its kind in Canada, City Market is opened and closed by the ringing of the 83-year-old Market Bell. It is also your best source for **dulse,** or sun-dried seaweed picked in the Bay of Fundy's waters, a local specialty not found outside New Brunswick, best described as "Ocean jerky." (Market open Mon.-Thurs. and Sat. 8:30am-5:30pm, Fri. 8:30am-9pm.) At **Slocum and Ferris** (652-2260), in the market, you can sample everything from Argentinian *empanadas* ($1.50) to Ukrainian *pierogis* ($1) to Indian *samosas* (65¢), and wash it down with a glass of fantastic peach juice. In 1994 the best time to be in Saint John will be July 17-23, when the unique **Loyalist Days** festival (634-8123) celebrates the long-ago arrival of Loyalists, complete with re-enactment, costumes, and street parade. The **Festival By the Sea** (632-0086), August 5-14, 1994, brings in a number of stage and musical productions.

SIGHTS

Saint John's main attraction is **Reversing Falls,** but before you start imagining 100-ft. walls of gravity-defying water, read on. The "falls" are actually beneath the surface of the water; what patient spectators will see is the flow of water at the nexus of the St. John River and Saint John Harbor slowly halting and changing direction due to the powerful Bay of Fundy tides. Most amazing may be the number of people amazed by the phenomenon. (24 hrs. Free.) You can learn more about the phenomenon by watching the 15-min. film offered at the **Reversing Falls Tourist Centre** (658-2937), located at the west end of the Hwy. 100 bridge crossing the river; unfortunately, the film does not show the Big Event. (Center open July-Aug. daily 8am-8pm; mid-May-June and Sept.-mid-Oct. daily 9am-6pm. Film $1.25; screenings every hr. on the hr. To reach the viewpoint and tourist center, take the west-bound East-West bus.)

Moosehead Breweries, 49 Main St. (635-7020), in West Saint John, offers free 1-hr. tours of the factory twice daily, June through August, leaving from the Country Store. Since tours are limited to 20 people, make reservations one or two days ahead. (The tours, of course, include samples.)

Three thematic **walking tours** are provided by the city, each lasting about 2 hr. **The Loyalist Trail** traces the places frequented by the Loyalist founders; the **Victorian Stroll** takes you past some of the old homes in Saint John; **Prince William's Walk** details commerce in the port city. All of the walking tours heavily emphasize history, architecture, and nostalgia. The walking tour brochures can be picked up at any tourist info center. **Trinity Church,** 115 Charlotte St. (693-8558), on the Loyalist

Trail tour, displays some amazing stained-glass windows, as well as the Royal Coat of Arms of the House of Hanover, stolen (residents here say "rescued") from the walls of the old Boston Council Chamber by fleeing Loyalists during the American Revolution (open Mon.-Fri. 8am-4pm).

Fort Howe Lookout affords a fine view of the city and its harbor. Originally erected to protect the harbor from American privateers, the landmark bristles with cannon. Shooting still occurs here—though predominantly with tripod-mounted cameras rather than with the huge, now-defunct guns. To visit the Lookout, walk a few blocks in from the north end of the harbor and up the hill; look for the wooden blockhouse atop the hill. (Open 24 hrs. Free.)

Nova Scotia

French colonists known as Acadians began sharing the Annapolis Valley and Cape Breton's shores with the indigenous Micmac Indians around 1605. The next wave of colonists added 50,000 Highland Scots in the 1800s. A strong Scottish identity has been preserved in Pictou and Antigonish Counties, where they primarily settled. Subsequent immigration of the English, Irish, and other Northern Europeans also added to the original population of Micmacs.

The early settlers had extremely strong trading ties with Massachusetts to the south. However, when the rebellious American colonies declared their sovereignty from the British throne, Nova Scotia declined the opportunity to become the 14th star in the emerging U.S. flag, instead serving as a refuge for fleeing British Loyalists. Fearing an American takeover, Nova Scotia joined three other provinces in 1867 to form the Dominion of Canada.

Four distinct geographies dominate the province: the rugged Atlantic coast, the agriculturally lush Annapolis Valley, the calm coast of the Northumberland Strait, and the magnificent highlands and lakes of Cape Breton Island.

PRACTICAL INFORMATION

Capitol: Halifax.

Nova Scotia Department of Tourism and Culture, Historic Properties, P.O. Box 456, Halifax, NS B3J 2R5. A dozen provincial info centers providing free comprehensive maps and the *Nova Scotia Travel Guide/Outdoors Guide* are scattered throughout Nova Scotia. Call 800-565-0000 (from Canada) or 800-341-6096 (from the continental U.S.) to make reservations with participating hostelries.

Time Zone: Atlantic (1 hr. ahead of Eastern time). **Postal abbreviation:** NS

Provincial Sales Tax: 10%.

■■■ ANNAPOLIS VALLEY

Green and fertile, the Annapolis Valley stretches along the **Bay of Fundy** between **Yarmouth** and the **Minas Basin.** Its calm, sunny weather draws harried city-folk seeking a relaxed lifestyle. The Annapolis River Valley runs slightly inland, but parallel to the coast flanked by the imaginatively named North and South Mountains. Charming towns scatter along the length of the Valley connected by scenic Hwy. 1. In spring, orchards covered with aromatic pink apple blossoms perfume the Valley.

French Acadian farmers settled this serene valley in the 17th century. Their expulsion from the Valley by the British in 1755 was commemorated by Henry Wadsworth Longfellow's tragic epic poem "Evangeline," and although Longfellow himself never actually visited this "forest primeval" the appellation "Land of Evangeline" has nevertheless stuck. Rushing from sight to sight is not the most satisfying method of exploring the Valley. Take it slowly and without worries; bicycling is an ideal means of transport.

Northern Coast **Digby,** home of the famous Digby scallops, harbors one of the world's largest scallop fleets as well as the annual August **Scallop Days** festival. About 104km up the coast from Yarmouth, Digby is connected by the **Marine Atlantic Ferry** (245-2116), to Saint John, New Brunswick, which lies across the Bay of Fundy. (1-2 trips daily, 2-3 daily in summer; $20, seniors $15, ages 5-12 $10, car $45; off-season $15/$11.25/$7.50/$40.)

Brier Island, the home of Joshua Slocum (the first person to sail around the world solo), prickles at the top of Digby Neck, a 90-min. drive south from Digby on Hwy. 217. The island's surrounding waters apparently provide a very attractive habitat for whales; sightings have been so numerous that **Brier Island Whale and Seabird Cruises** (839-2995) in **Westport** guarantees whale sightings or you go again free. The guides are scientific researchers from the **Brier Island Ocean Study** or from local universities. (Voyages, weather permitting, last 4 hr. Fare $33, ages 6-12 $16. Reserve at least 1 week in advance.)

Founded by French explorer Samuel de Champlain in 1605, the **Habitation Port-Royal** was the earliest permanent European settlement in North America north of Florida. It served as the capitol of French Acadia for nearly a century until its capitulation to the British in 1710, who renamed it Annapolis Royal in honor of Queen Anne. The original town later fell into ruin but has been restored faithfully in the form of the **National Historical Park** (532-2898) across the Annapolis Basin, 12km from modern-day Annapolis Royal. The restoration affords a rare glimpse of the wooden palisades and stone chimneys typical in early French fur-trading posts. To get to the Habitation, turn off Hwy. 1 at the Granville Ferry and go about 10km. (Open May 15-Oct. 15 daily 9am-6pm. Free.) **Kejimkujik National Park** (682-2772), Hwy. 8, about 60km inland from Annapolis Royal and 160km west of Halifax, lies relatively close by. Called "Keji," the park is remote, densely wooded, and liberally peppered with small lakes and unspoiled waterways best explored by canoe. Fees are charged for bringing vehicles into the park ($5 for 1 day, $10 for 4 days). The park also has a **campground** with hot showers and 329 sites ($10.50, no hookup).

For a less historical park experience, seek out the new amusement park, **Upper Clements Theme Park** (532-7557 or 800-565-7275 from Atlantic Canada), 6km west of Annapolis Royal on Hwy. 1. Yes, there are roller coasters, water rides, and a mini-golf course, but you'll also find petting farms, artisans, storytellers, and craftspeople plying their trade. (Open late June-early Sept. daily 10am-7pm, late May-late June and late Sept. Sat.-Sun. 10am-7pm. Park admission free, but pass for attractions $11, after 3pm $5.50. Tickets for rides also sold individually.) Of note to engineers and "tidophiles" is the **Annapolis Tidal Generating Station,** just off Hwy. 1 (532-5454), the first attempt to generate electrical energy by harnessing the powerful Bay of Fundy tides. (Open daily 9am-8pm, off-season daily 9am-5:30pm. Free.) The station is paired with a Provincial **visitors center** (same hours).

Eastern Annapolis Valley **Wolfville,** 55km north of Annapolis Royal, attracts students from all over Canada to Acadia University, with its serene valley campus. Wolfville was renamed in the 1800s at the urging of Judge de Wolf, whose daughter was ashamed of saying she was from the town of Mud Creek. The most panoramic view in the Valley is from **The Lookoff,** Hwy. 358, 20km north of Hwy. 1, perched on a mountain top within view of four counties.

Grand Pré, or **Great Meadow,** stands at the eastern head of Annapolis Valley, 100km northwest of Halifax. The highlight is the **Grand Pré National Historic Site** (542-3631), a memorial of the deportation of the Acadians in 1755. After refusing to take oaths of allegiance, the Acadians of Grand Pré were imprisoned in the Stone Church before their deportation from the British colonies. They were the first of 6000 Acadians to be deported that year. Deported Acadians resettled further south on the continent, establishing communities in modern-day Louisiana (where they became known as Cajuns, a bastardization of "Acadians"). (Grounds always open. Buildings open mid-May-mid-Oct. daily 9am-6pm. Free.) Canada's best wines ferment in the Annapolis Valley; the **Grand Pré Estate Vineyard** (542-1470) gives daily tours. (3 guided tours per day. Open May-Sept. daily 9am-5pm. Free.)

Yarmouth The port of **Yarmouth,** 339km from Halifax, is on the southwestern tip of Nova Scotia, a major ferry terminal with ships departing across the **Bay of Fundy** to Maine. **Marine Atlantic Ferry** (742-6800 or 800-341-7981 from continental U.S.) provides service to Bar Harbor (1 per day, off-season 3 per week; 6-7 hr.; $45, seniors $34, ages 5-12 $22.50, car $60; Oct.-May $30/$22.50/$15/$55). **Prince of Fundy Cruises** (800-341-7540 in USA and Canada), sail from Yarmouth's port to Portland, ME. (Departs only May 2-Oct. 20 at 10am, but still doesn't sail many days, so call ahead; 11 hr.; early May-mid-June and mid-Sept.-mid-Oct. US$55, age 5-14 US$27.50; mid-June-mid-Sept. US$75/US$37.50.) Renting a car upon arrival in Yarmouth is a very popular idea, so reserve ahead. **Avis,** 44 Starr's Rd. (742-3323), and **Budget,** 509 Main St. (742-9500), are the only rental agencies.

■■■ CAPE BRETON ISLAND

> *"I have travelled around the globe. I have seen the Canadian and American Rockies, the Andes and the Alps, and the Highlands of Scotland; but for simple beauty, Cape Breton out rivals them all."*
> —Alexander Graham Bell

Bell backed his boast by building Beinn Bhreagh, the estate where he spent the waning years of his life, in Cape Breton. Breathtaking coastline, loch-like finger-lakes, steep, dropping cliffs, and rolling green hills characterize Cape Breton, which has been called Scotland's missing west coast.

Practical Information Cape Breton Island, the northeastern portion of Nova Scotia, connects to the mainland by the **Trans-Canada Hwy.** across the **Canso Causeway,** 280km from Halifax. **Port Hastings** is the first town you'll encounter in Cape Breton; it supports a **Tourism Nova Scotia** center (625-1717), on the right-hand side of the road after crossing the causeway. Pick up the booklet *Vacation Planner to National Parks & Historic Sites on Cape Breton Island.* (Open July-Aug. 8:30am-8pm, May 15-June and Sept.-Oct. 15 9am-5pm.) Public transport serves only the major cities—New Glasgow, Antigonish, and Baddeck—bypassing Cape Breton's renowned scenery. The **Bras d'Or Lake,** an 80km-long inland sea, roughly divides Cape Breton in two. The larger western section includes the scenic Cape Breton Highlands and the Cabot Trail. The industrial eastern section has been developed with revenues mined from steel and coal. **Sydney** and **Glace Bay,** Cape Breton's two largest cities, are depressed industrial centers.

■ Cabot Trail and Cape Breton Highlands

The **Cabot Trail,** named after English explorer John Cabot who supposedly landed in the Highlands in 1497, is the most scenic marine drive in Canada—the Canadian answer to California's Rte. 1. The 300km-long loop winds precipitously around the perimeter of northern Cape Breton. A photographer's dream, the Trail takes 7-10 hours to enjoy (allowing for a lunch break, stops at overlooks, and slow traffic). Lodging is expensive along the Trail, generally $40-50 for a double (except the **Keltic Lodge** in Ingonish Beach, where it can range up to $240). There is one hostel on the island, the **Glenmore International Hostel** (258-3622; call for directions), in Twin Rock Valley west of Whycocomagh. Although dilapidated and miles from nowhere, it's the only reasonably priced way to put a roof over your head within

140km (Full kitchen, linen and sheets provided. $13, nonmembers $16; June-Sept. $10/$13.) Very few B&Bs line the Cabot Trail. However, **campgrounds** abound both on the Trail and within Cape Breton Highlands National Park. To prevent morbid thoughts about plunging off the edge, you should drive the trail clockwise, shying away from the sheer cliffs. Bicyclists, too, should go clockwise, to take full advantage of the predominantly westerly winds. For **bike rentals,** contact the nonprofit **Les Amis Du Plein Air,** P.O. Box 472, Cheticamp B0E 1H0 (224-3814).

The stretch of land extending across the northern tip of Cape Breton and wedged within the northern loop of the Cabot Trail belongs to the **Cape Breton Highlands National Park,** 950 sq. km of highlands and ocean wilderness. One **park info center** (224-2306), is located along the Cabot Trail in **Cheticamp,** 5km south of the southwest park entrance, and the other at the southeast entrance in **Ingonish Beach** (285-2535). (Both centers open daily 8am-8pm; mid-May-late June and early Sept.-late Oct. 9am-5pm; mid-Oct.-mid-May Mon.-Fri. 8am-4:30pm for phone inquiries only.) The park provides six **campgrounds** within its boundaries. (First come, first served basis; weekdays yield the best selection. Sites $8-11, with fireplace $13, hookup $17; if you pay for 3 days, you can camp for 4. Park motor vehicle admission $5 per day, $10 per 4 days. Camping in the winter is free. Open mid-May-mid-Oct.)

On the southern loop of the Cabot Trail, the resort village of **Baddeck** lies on the shore of Lake Bras d'Or. **The Alexander Graham Bell National Historic Site** (295-2069), Chebucto St. (Rte. 205) in the east end of Baddeck, provides a spectacular view of the lake from its roof gardens. Inside the building is an insidiously fascinating museum dedicated to the life and inventions of Bell. More than just the inventor of the telephone, Bell was a fountain of ideas, spewing forth such creations (some useful, some not) as medical tools, hydrofoils, and airplanes. Bell's humanitarian spirit also inspired his toils to allay problems of the deaf and sailors lost at sea. (Open daily 9am-9pm, Oct.-June 9am-5pm. Free.)

■ Glace Bay

Not all of Cape Breton is scenic. Innumerable immigrants once migrated to the grimy, industrial city of **Glace Bay** for hazardous jobs in the Sydney coalfields. Although coal mining has now ceased, the **Miners' Museum** (849-4522), Birkley St. off of South St. east of downtown, preserves its memory with exhibits on the techniques of coal mining and the plight of organized labor, as well as a reconstructed miners' village and films on life as a coal miner. The real highlight of the museum, though, is the ¼-mi. tour of an underground coal mine, guided by experienced miners who paint a bleak, unromanticized picture of the hard days' toil. Watching tourists knocking their heads on the five-ft.-high ceiling supports (safety hat and cape provided) is almost as much fun as navigating the dim, dank, narrow passages of coal. (Open daily 10am-6pm; Sept.-May 9am-4pm. $5, without tour $2.75; kids $3, without tour $1.75.)

■ Sydney

North Sydney, Sydney Mines, Sydney River, and Sydney all conglomerate within a 20km radius, 430km northeast of Halifax. **North Sydney** stands out as the starting point of the **Trans-Canada Highway** (you can actually watch the highway spring from nothingness to full-fledged-four-lane existence; 24 hrs., free) and as the departure point for ferries to **Newfoundland** (see Newfoundland: Getting There). The Marine Atlantic Ferry Terminal sits at the end of the Hwy.

The **North Sydney Tourist Bureau,** 230 Rear Commercial St. (794-7719), next to the Marine Atlantic Terminal, is a little house decorated with question marks where you can find a friendly staff and complete documentation on the area, including accommodations info (open July-early Sept. daily 8am-8pm). Lodging is expensive on Cape Breton Island, and the Sydney area is no exception. The best deal in North Sydney is the **Seaview Inn,** 30 Seaview Dr. (794-3066), 2km from the Ferry

Terminal. Clean singles with shared bath $22, doubles $26-32. B&Bs tend to be cheaper and more pleasant than hotels or motels. To circulate within North Sydney, use your feet or take a taxi (**Blue & White Taxi,** 794-4764, charges $3.25 from any point within town to the Ferry Terminal). Accommodation reservations are highly recommended, especially on those nights preceding the departure of the ferry to Argentia, when the whole area can be booked.

■ Louisbourg

The **Fortress of Louisbourg** (LOO-iss-burg; in French Loo-ee-BOORG) was the King of France's most ambitious military project in the Colonies, his "New World Gibraltar"—the launching pad from which France would regain the Americas. A small band of New Englanders laid siege to and quickly captured Louisbourg in 1745. A treaty soon returned it to France, but then the British took the fortress back again in 1758, with even greater ease. The $25 million rebuilding of Louisbourg, the largest historic reconstruction in North America, resulted in **Fortress of Louisbourg National Historic Park** (733-2280), 37km southeast of Sydney on Rte. 22, far more successful as a tourist attraction than it ever was as a military outpost. Every attempt has been made to recreate the atmosphere of 1744. Speaking French will help you get past the gate sentries, who don't take kindly to intruders wearing red coats. Most of the buildings feature period rooms, staffed by costumed actors doing their 1744 thing, or historical museums depicting fortress life. The scope is startling, the re-creation, well, almost convincing. (Open July-Aug. 9am-6pm, May-June and Sept.-Oct. 9:30am-5pm. $6.50, kids $3.25, families $16.)

The **Hôtel de la Marine** within the fortress prepares full-course meals ($8.50) from authentic 1744 French recipes—lots of fun, but be forewarned that the 18th century had no Cordon Bleu chefs. No red meat is served Fri.-Sat.—it was outlawed as a religious observance. Peek at the kitchen, if you can skirt the actors. The 80% whole wheat/20% rye bread from the **King's Bakery** ($2.50) looks like a cannonball and is almost as hard. From the visitors center, where tickets are purchased and cars parked, a shuttle bus takes you to the fortress gates. The fort offers 2-4 guided walking tours daily, in English and French. The modern town of **Louisbourg** also has 9 **B&Bs** (singles $32, doubles $44). Contact **Louisbourg Tourist Bureau** (733-2720), off Rte. 22 near the fortress, for info and reservations. (Open July-Aug. daily 9am-7pm, May-June and Sept.-Oct. daily 9am-5pm.)

■■■ HALIFAX

The Halifax Citadel was erected in 1749 as a British garrison to counter the French Fortress of Louisbourg on the northeastern shoulder of Cape Breton Island. Both fortresses still stand today, completely renovated and refurbished. Although the Halifax Citadel was never captured or even attacked in the days of the colonial empires, it is now engaged in a rather fierce battle with its Cape Breton cousin for the most sizeable portion of the tourist trade. From its perch on a hill overlooking one of the world's finest natural harbors, the Citadel has seen the surrounding city grow to become the largest in Atlantic Canada. Metropolitan Halifax, population 320,000, is an unexpectedly yet delightfully cosmopolitan magnet for the province's youth. With an active nightlife, it is all the more attractive as a base for provincial travel throughout beautiful, pacific, and un-self-conscious areas up and down the coast.

Halifax's placid history is marred by one event: the Halifax Explosion of 1917. Miscommunication between a Belgian relief ship and a French ship carrying picric acid and 400,000 tons of TNT resulted in a collision in Halifax Harbor, hurling sparks into the picric acid. One hour later, Halifax felt the brunt of the largest man-made explosion before the atomic bomb. Approximately 11,000 people were killed or injured, north Halifax was razed, and windows were shattered as far as 50 mi. away.

PRACTICAL INFORMATION

Emergency: 4105.

Visitor Information: Halifax Tourist Information, City Hall (421-8736), on the corner of Duke and Barrington. Open Sat.-Wed. 8:30am-6:30pm, Thurs.-Fri. 8:30am-7:30pm; Sept.-May Mon.-Fri. 9am-5pm. Another branch (421-2772) on the corner of Sackville and S. Park, across from the Public Garden. Open mid-June-Labor Day, same hours. **Tourism Nova Scotia** has locations on the downtown harbor boardwalk (424-4247; open daily 8:30am-7pm; mid-Oct.-early June Mon.-Fri. 8:30am-5:40pm).

Student Travel Agency: Travel CUTS, Dalhousie University Student Union Building 1st floor (494-2054). Open Mon.-Fri. 9am-4pm. **Rideboard** posted near Travel CUTS, near the cafeteria.

Airport: Halifax International Airport, 40km from the city on Hwy. 102. The **Aerocoach City Shuttle** (468-1258) runs to downtown (12-13 per day, 6am-10pm; $11, round-trip $18, under 10 free with adult). **Ace Y Share-a-cab** (429-4444) runs service to the airport 5am-9pm. Phone 3 hrs. ahead of pick-up time. Fare $18 ($30 for 2) from anywhere in Halifax.

Trains: VIA Rail, 1161 Hollis St. (429-8421), on the corner of South in the South End near the harbor. Service to: Montréal ($134, student or senior $121, under 11 $67; with 7 day advance purchase 25% discount). Open daily 9am-5:30pm.

Buses: Acadian Lines and **MacKenzie Bus Line** share the same terminal, 6040 Almon St. (454-9321), near Robie St. To get downtown from the bus terminal, take bus #7 or #80 on Robie St., or any of the 6 buses running on Gottingen St. 1 block east of the station. MacKenzie runs service along the Atlantic coast to: Yarmouth (1 per day, 6 hr., $26). Acadian covers most of the remainder of Nova Scotia, with connections to the rest of Canada: Annapolis Royal (2 per day, 5 hr., $23); Charlottetown (2 per day, 8½ hr., $37); North Sydney (3 per day, 6-8 hr., $42). Senior discount 25%. Station open daily 7am-7pm.

Public Transport: Metro Transit (421-6600; info line open Mon.-Fri. 7:30am-10pm, Sat.-Sun. 8am-10pm). Efficient and thorough. Pick up route map and schedules at any info center. Fare $1.20, seniors and ages 5-15 70¢. Buses run daily roughly 7am-midnight.

Dartmouth-Halifax Ferry (464-2639), on the harborfront. 15-min. harbor crossings depart both terminals every 15-30 min. Mon.-Fri. 6:30am-midnight; every 30 min. Sat. 6:30am-midnight and Sun. noon-5:30pm. Fare 85¢, kids 5-12 60¢. Call 464-2217 for parking info.

Taxi: Aircab, 456-0373; **Sunshine Cab,** 429-5555. Both open 24 hrs.; $2.40 base fee, $1.30 per km.

Car Rental: Rent-a-Wreck, 2823 Robie St. (454-2121), at Almon St. $30 per day, 200km free, 12¢ per extra km. Insurance $9 per day, ages 21-25 $11. Must be 21 with credit card. Open Mon.-Fri. 8am-5pm, Sat. 8am-noon.

Driver/Rider Services: Alternative Passage, 5945 Spring Garden Rd. (429-5169), promotes ecological rides. To: Montréal ($50); North Sydney ($21); Fredericton ($28); Cape Tourmentine ($16). $7 yearly membership required. Open Mon.-Wed. 9am-5:30pm, Thurs.-Fri. 9am-7:30pm, Sat.-Sun 10am-5pm. **Auto-Driveaway,** 752 Bedford Hwy. (457-7111). $25 application fee, $300 security deposit, and you only pay for the gas. Open Mon.-Fri. 9am-7pm.

Help Lines: Sexual Assault: 425-0122, 24 hrs. **Crisis Centre:** 421-1188, 24 hrs. **Gayline:** 423-7129, Thurs.-Sat. 7-10pm.

Post Office: Station "A," 6175 Almon St. (494-4712), in the North End 2.5km from downtown. **Postal Code:** B3K 5M9. Open Mon.-Fri. 8am-5:15pm.

Area Code: 902.

Barrington is the major north-south street. **Sackville Street,** approaching the Citadel and the Public Garden, runs east-west, parallel to **Spring Garden Road,** Halifax's shopping thoroughfare. Flanking downtown are the **North End,** considered unsavory by locals, and the **South End,** mostly quiet and arboreal on the ocean. Downtown traffic is bearable, but parking difficult. If you visit in the winter, do *not* park on the street; it's prohibited in case snowplows are needed. Heed this warning even if it is sunny and warm; if you park for any length of time you will be towed.

ACCOMMODATIONS

You will have no trouble finding affordable summer accommodations in Halifax, unless you happen upon a major event, such as the Tatoo Festival or the Moosehead Grand Prix. The impressive *Doer's and Dreamer's Complete Guide* lists over 300 pages of accommodations in all of Nova Scotia and is available for free at any tourism office. By calling **Check-In** (800-565-0000) you can reserve space in nearly 90% of the province's accommodations.

Halifax Heritage House Hostel (HI-C), 1253 Brunswick St. (422-3863), 1 block from the train station, 3 min. from the heart of downtown. Clean rooms. Lounge with TV. Kitchen and laundry. Ask for a room on the 1st floor where bathrooms are not shared by many, many people. No curfew. Check-in 8:30-11am and 4-10:30pm. $12.75, nonmembers $15.75. Linen $1.

Technical University of Nova Scotia, M. M. O'Brien Bldg., 5217 Morris St. (420-7780) at Barrington. Heart of downtown. Free laundry. Check-in daily 9am-midnight. Singles $23, doubles $38; students $20/$34. Reservations recommended July-Aug. Open May-Aug.

Dalhousie University (494-3401, after 8pm 494-2108), Howe Hall on Coburg Rd. at LaMarchant, 3km southwest of downtown. Usually packed, so arrive early. Laundry, access to Dal recreation facilities extra. Singles $29 (breakfast included), students $18 ($4.60 extra for breakfast). Under 11 free. Make July-Aug. reservations 1 week in advance. Open early May-late Aug., 24 hrs.

Saint Mary's University, 923 Robie St. (494-8840), in the Loyola building 2km from downtown in the South End. Take bus #9 from downtown, or bus #17 from Winsor St. Look for the big tower on campus. Serene neighborhood near Point Pleasant Park. Standard dorm rooms on an active campus. Singles $22, doubles $32; students $17/$29. Under 12 free. Open May 15-Aug. 15, 24 hrs.

Gerrard Hotel, 1234 Barrington St. (423-8614), between South and Morris St. Subdued. Kitchen and parking. Must check in Mon.-Fri. 8am-6pm, Sat. 10am-4pm. Singles $30, doubles $45. $5 per additional person.

FOOD AND ENTERTAINMENT

You needn't become a fast-food junkie to enjoy an inexpensive meal in Halifax. Downtown pubs provide cheap grub and vitality. Over 40 pubs are crammed into a few competitive city blocks, inciting draft wars and wonderfully low prices; at night, $1 draughts are common. Try the local mussels (about $3), served on generous platters. Pubs are generally open from 11am to midnight or 2am, although kitchens close a few hours earlier.

Granite Brewery, 1222 Barrington St. (423-5660). The best pub food in town and its own microbrewery, which produces three labels; the Old Peculiar is strangely good ($2.20 for 9 oz. glass). Try some with the shrimp and sausage *jambalaya* ($9.50). Open Mon.-Sat. 11:30am-11:30pm, Sun. noon-11pm.

Lawrence of Oregano, 1726 Argyle St. (425-8077). Called Larry O's by the regulars; you can grill your own bread at the eat-in bread-and-salad bar ($3). Satisfying Italian and seafood dishes around $5, daily specials $3-4. Open daily 11am-2am.

Mediterraneo, 1571 Barrington St. (423-6936), where long-haired, somber students engage in obviously profound conversation over Middle Eastern dishes. Tabouli with 2 huge pita pockets $2.50, felafel sandwich $3. Filling daily specials $3.25-4. Open daily 7am-8pm.

Different bars and pubs tend to be the favorite hang-outs of students from different local universities. One exception to this is the **Seahorse Pub,** 1665 Argyle St. (423-7200), a dark, heavily carved basement room where blue-haired student meets white-collar lawyer to discuss soccer (open Mon.-Wed. 11:30am-12:30am, Thurs.-

Sat. 11:30am-1am). **Peddler's Pub** (423-5033), in Barrington Place on Granville St., is huge and always packed; favored for good pub food, including wings ($3.75) and steamed mussels ($3.25), and 99¢ daily specials, from pizza to shrimp depending on the day (open Mon.-Sat. 11am-11pm, Sun. noon-10pm). **J.J. Rossy's,** 1883 Granville St. (422-4411), across the street from Peddler's, attracts nocturnal crowds with its dance floor and tremendous drink specials, prominently during the power hours (Wed.-Sat. 10-11pm and midnight-1am) when a draft falls to 50¢. Also, all-you-can eat lunch specials 11:30am-2pm $3. Dancing daily. (Cover charge after 8pm Thurs.-Sat. $2.50. Open Mon.-Sat. 11am-2am, kitchen closes 10pm.) The **Double Deuce,** 1560 Hollis St. (422-4033), proud to be the "hottest alternative rock bar east of Montréal" has live entertainment virtually every night and open stage Tuesday nights (cover charge $1-5; open Mon.-Sat. 11am-2am, Sun. noon-2am).

SIGHTS

The star-shaped **Halifax Citadel National Historic Park** (426-5080) in the heart of Halifax, with noonday cannon firings and the old **Town Clock** at the foot of Citadel Hill, has become a well-ensconced Halifax tradition. A walk along the walls affords a fine view of the city and harbor. Small exhibits and a 1-hr. film hide behind the fortifications. (Open April-June 15 daily 10am-5pm, June 15-Labor Day daily 9am-6pm, Labor Day-Oct. daily 9am-5pm. Grounds are open all year. Admission charged June 15-Labor Day only: $2, under 15 and students $1. Seniors always free.)

The **Halifax Public Gardens,** across from the Citadel near the intersection of South Park and Sackville St., provide a relaxing spot for a lunch break. Overfed loons on the pond, Roman statues, a Victorian bandstand, gaslamps, and exquisite horticulture are very properly British in style. From July to Sept., concerts are given Sundays at 2pm. (Gates open daily 8am-sunset.)

Point Pleasant Park, a car-free, wooded tract of land encompassing the southern tip of Halifax, boasts ownership of the **Prince of Wales Martello Tower,** an odd fort built by the British in 1797 that started leaking within 15 years of its construction. Perhaps Halifax's motive for preserving the structure is to subtly chortle at British engineering. To reach the park, take bus #9 from downtown Barrington St. Much farther south, overlooking the mouth of Halifax Harbor, is another example of British architecture, the **York Redoubt.** Built to defend British holdings against the French, this fort apparently has survived *sans* drainage problems; it was used until World War II. The tower commands a gorgeous view of the harbor. To get to the fort, take bus #15 to Purcell's Cove.

The **Historic Properties** district (429-0530), downtown on lower Water St., holds reconstructed early-19th-century architecture. The charming stone-and-wood facades, however, are only sheep's clothing disguising wolfishly overpriced boutiques and restaurants of tourist-trap commercialism. The real item of interest here is the summer docking of the *Bluenose II* (hint: look at a Canadian dime). The annual **International Town Crier's Championship** (*Oye! Oye! Oye!*) used to be held here, but has now gone truly international. However, the Town Crier, Peter Cox, is still busily around. Meet him at **Tea with the Mayor** (421-8736), Town Hall, where you can feel important in the company of, yes, the mayor, free tea, and free food (July-Aug. Mon.-Fri. 3:30-4:30pm; free). **Province House,** on the corner of Granville and George St., can be a show in itself during parliament. Inside the small, Georgian brownstone, the Assembly Speaker and Sergeant-at-Arms don elegant top hats and black cloaks for sometimes lively debate.

Museums in Halifax don't stack up to the competition within Nova Scotia. However, die-hard museum-goers might enjoy the **Maritime Museum of the Atlantic,** 1675 Lower Water St. (424-7490), which has an interesting display on the Halifax Explosion. (Open Mon. and Wed.-Sat. 9:30am-5:30pm, Tues. 9:30am-8pm, Sun. 1-5:30pm. Closed Mon. mid-Oct.-May. $2.25, under 17 50¢. Free Tues. 5:30-8pm and mid-Oct.-May.) The **Nova Scotia Museum,** 1747 Summer St. (424-7353), behind Citadel Hill, offers exhibits on the natural history, geology, and native cultures of the province. (Open June-mid-Oct. Mon.-Tues. and Thurs.-Sat. 9:30am-5:30pm, Wed. 9:30am-8pm, Sun. 1-5:30pm. Closed Mon. mid-Oct.-May. $2.25, under 16 50¢. Free Wed. 5:30-8pm and mid-Oct.-May.)

Festival 94 (421-2900) celebrates Halifax's birthday for one weekend in early August. The highlight is the **Natal Day** parade and fireworks. The **Buskerfest** (425-4329), held for 10 days in mid-August, showcases street performers from around the world in the streets. Also in Halifax is the **Nova Scotia International Tattoo** (420-1114 or 451-1221 for tickets), presented by the Province of Nova Scotia and the Canadian Maritime Armed Forces. In the first week of July, the festival is kicked off by a street parade of international musicians, bicyclists, dancers, acrobats, gymnasts, and military display groups. At noon, the Metro area spawns lots of free entertainment. Later, a two-hour show, featuring 1800 performers, is held in the Halifax Metro Centre. (Tickets for the show $15-18, seniors and kids $10.)

■ Prince Edward Island

Prince Edward Island, more commonly called "P.E.I." (not to be confused with the architect) or simply "the Island," is the smallest and most densely populated province in Canada. Referred to as "a million-acre farm," the Island is blanketed with soil brick-red from its high iron-oxide content. Prince Edward Island radiates an array of arresting hues in the spring and summer. The Island's red soil complements the green crops and shrubbery, azure skies and turquoise waters, and purple roadside lupin. Even some stretches of the endless beaches on the north and south coasts are layered with red sand. The relaxing countryside and slow pace of life are what attract "outsiders" from all over Canada. A P.E.I. city is an oxymoron; always small, towns on the Island seem to exist more for visitors than for residents and consist mainly of restaurants and attractive shopping areas. The largest "city" is Charlottetown, the provincial capital, with a whopping 15,000 residents. Effusively hospitable, the Island's population is 17% Acadian French and 80% British. Ancestral residents named the Island's three counties Kings, Queens, and Prince.

Public transportation is nearly non-existent on the Island, although SMT and Island Transit connect Charlottetown with the mainland. Fortunately, distances are minuscule—driving from Charlottetown on the south coast to the beaches on the north coast requires less than 20 minutes. The network of highways, actually country roads, is superb for bikers. You never have to worry about getting lost; just keep going and you'll eventually hit a major road, most of which are well-marked. Three scenic drives cover the Island for those who simply want to un-hurry themselves and breathe deeply the saliferous country air.

PRACTICAL INFORMATION

Capital: Charlottetown.
Time Zone: Atlantic (1 hr. ahead of Eastern time). **Postal Abbreviation:** P.E.I.
Area code: 902.
Provincial Sales Tax: 10%.
Emergency: 911.
Visitor Information: P.E.I. Visitor Information Centre, P.O. Box 940, C1A 7M5 (368-4444), on the corner of University Ave. and Summer St. in Charlottetown, distributes the *P.E.I. Visitor's Guide* (with map). Open daily 8am-10pm, Sept.-May daily 9am-5pm. The **Charlottetown Visitors Bureau,** 199 Queen St. (566-5548), inside City Hall, distributes free maps. Open Mon.-Sat. 8am-8pm, Sun. 10am-6pm.
Tours: Abegweit Tours, 157 Nassau St. (894-9966), offers sightseeing tours on a London double-decker bus. Tours of Charlottetown (7 per day, 1 hr., $5.50, kids

under 11 $1), the North Shore including Green Gables (1 per day, 7 hr., $27, kids $13), and the South Shore (1 per day, 5 hr., $27, kids $13). Tours run June-Sept.

Buses: SMT, 330 University Ave. (566-9744), provides service to: Moncton (2 per day, 5 hr., $29); Amherst (2 per day, 4 hr., $22); Halifax (1 per day, 8 hr., $47), via **Acadian Lines** connections in Amherst. Station open daily 9:30-10pm, and Mon.-Fri. 7am-5:30pm, Sat. 7am-1pm, Sun. 7-8am, 11:30am-1pm, and 4:30-5:30pm.

Island Transit: 308 Queen St. (566-9962 or 566-5664). Services Summerside and Surrey (1 per day, $29; reservations required) and New Glasgow, Nova Scotia (1 per day, 3¼ hr., $26). Buses run late May-mid-Oct. Station open daily 7am-5pm.

Beach Shuttles: Sherwood Beach Shuttle (566-3243) picks up at P.E.I. Visitor Information Centre (see above) and drops off in Cavendish (9:30am-3:30pm, 5 per day, $7, round-trip $12).

Ferries: Marine Atlantic (855-2030 or 800-341-7981 from continental U.S.), in Borden, 56km west of Charlottetown on Trans-Canada Hwy., makes runs to Cape Tormentine, New Brunswick (12-18 per day; 1 hr., round-trip $6.75, seniors $5, ages 5-12 $3.50, cars $17.50). **Northumberland Ferries** (962-2016, or 800-565-0201 from P.E.I. and Nova Scotia), in Wood Islands 61km east of Charlottetown on Trans-Canada Hwy., goes to Caribou, Nova Scotia (12-19 per day, 1½ hr., round-trip $8.50, seniors $6, ages 5-12 $4, cars $26.50). *For both ferries, fares are only round-trip and only collected leaving P.E.I. Thus, it is cheaper to leave from Borden than from Wood Islands, no matter how you come over.*

Taxi: City Cab, 892-6567. No credit cards accepted. **Star Cab,** 892-6581. Does accept credit cards. Both open daily 24 hrs.

Car Rental: Rent-a-Wreck, 114 St. Peter's Rd. (894-7039). $25 per day, with 200km free, 12¢ per additional km, damage waiver $9 per day, ages 21-25 $10.50. Must be 21 with credit card or $250 deposit. Open Mon.-Fri. 7am-10pm, Sat.-Sun. 8am-10pm. **Hillside Autohost,** 207 Mt. Edward Rd. (894-7037), rents for $25 per day, 200km free, 15¢ per additional km; insurance $9 per day; must be 21 with major credit card. Open Mon.-Fri. 7:30am-5pm, Sat.-Sun. 8am-3pm.

Bike Rental: MacQueens, 430 Queen St. (368-2453), rents road and mountain bikes, $20 per day, $80 per week. Must have credit card for deposit. Open Mon.-Sat. 8:30am-5pm.

Charlottetown Police: 566-5548. **Royal Canadian Mounted Police:** 566-7100.

Help lines: Crisis Centre, 566-8999. 24 hrs.

Post Office: 135 Kent St. (566-7070). Open Mon.-Fri. 8am-5:15pm. **Postal Code:** C1A 7N1.

Queen St. and University Ave. are Charlottetown's main thoroughfares, straddling Confederation Centre along the west and east, respectively. The most popular beaches lie on the north shore in the middle of the province, opposite but not far from Charlottetown. Hamlets (villages, not Danish princes) and fishing villages dot the Island landscape of **Kings County** on the east, as well as **Prince County** on the west. Acadian communities thrive on the south shore of Prince County. **Rte. I (TCH)** follows the southern shore, from ferry terminal to ferry terminal, passing through Charlottetown.

ACCOMMODATIONS

Almost a hundred **bed& breakfasts** and **country inns** litter every nook and cranny of the province; many are open year-round. Rates generally bobble around $25 for singles and $35 for doubles. **P.E.I. Visitor Information** (see Practical Information) distributes info about available B&Bs and will make reservations for you. In addition, 26 farms participate in a provincial **Farm Vacation** program, in which tourists spend some time with a farming family (no phone; ask at P.E.I. Visitor Information).

P.E.I. has one hostel, the **Charlottetown International Hostel (HI-C),** 153 Mt. Edward Rd. (894-9696), across the yard from University of P.E.I., one long block east of University Ave. and a 45-min. walk from the bus station, in a big, green barn with curious acoustics. The sociable staff attracts many international guests. (Bike rentals $5. Max. stay 3 nights. Check-in 7-10am and 4pm-midnight. Curfew midnight. $13, nonmembers $16. Blanket rental $1. Open June-Labor Day.) The **University of Prince Edward Island,** 550 University Ave. (566-0442), in Blanchard Hall in the southwestern end of campus overlooking Belvedere St., offers fully serviced and furnished two-bedroom apartments with kitchen, living room and hall laundry room—a great value for four people. (Check-in 8:30am-10pm. $52 plus tax for up to 4 people, extra cot $5. Weekly and monthly rates also available. Open May 20-Aug.) The University also runs a B&B in **Marion Hall,** with a full all-you-can-eat breakfast included. ($22 per person, open July-Aug.)

Prince Edward Island National Park (672-6350 or 963-2391) operates three campgrounds (sites $8.75-13.50, serviced $19), and 14 of the 30 provincial parks offer camping. Additionally, there are over 30 other private campgrounds scattered throughout the Island, ensuring that there will always be a campsite available. (Campgrounds are open at different dates, but one is always open mid-June-Sept.)

FOOD

Lobster suppers, sumptuous feasts originally thrown by churches and community centers, have become deeply ingrained in Island tradition. The "run-of-the-mill" lobster suppers supplement their crustacean guest of honor with a host of all-you-can-eat goodies such as clam chowder, salad bars, and desserts. The delicious suppers are quite expensive ($18-26, depending on the size of lobster), so fast all day before the feast. Fresh seafood, including the world famous **Malpeque oysters,** can be found for sale along the shores of the Island, especially in North Rustico on the north shore. See the back of the *P.E.I. Visitor's Guide* (see Practical Information) for a listing of fresh seafood outlets.

Fisherman's Wharf (963-2669), Rte. 6 in North Rustico, is the most famous lobster-supper house, featuring the world's largest lobster pound (holding tank, as in "dog pound") and a 60-ft.-long buffet bar. All-you-can-eat dinner, including lobster, mussels, chowder, salads, and desserts $20. Seating capacity 500. Open mid-May-mid-Oct. daily 4-10pm.

Bonnie Brae Restaurant (566-2241), Rte. 1 in Cornwall, 11km west of Charlottetown. The lobster smorgasbord ($32) promises all-you-can-eat lobster and more than 60 side-dishes. More simply, a complete lobster dinner is $17. Open mid-June-Labor Day daily 4-9pm.

Cedar's Eatery, 81 University Ave. (892-7377). A local favorite serving Lebanese and Canadian cuisine. Try their sizeable lunch specials 11:30am-2pm ($5). Open Mon.-Thurs. 11am-midnight, Fri.-Sat. 11am-1am, Sun. 4-10:30pm.

Peake's Quay (368-1330), Great George St. below Lower Water St., on the Charlottetown waterfront overlooking the Marina (pronounced PEEKS KEY). Seafood sandwich and salad $5-9. Scallops $7.50. Supper entrees $13-19. Open daily 11:30am-2am. Kitchen closes 10pm.

SIGHTS

Prince Edward Island National Park (672-2211 or 963-2391), a coastal strip of 32 sq. km, embraces some of Canada's finest beaches, over a fifth of P.E.I.'s northern coast. It is the most popular Canadian national park east of Banff (see Alberta). Along with the beaches, heap-big sand dunes and salt marshes rumple the park's terrain. The park is home to many of the Island's 300-odd species of birds, including the endangered **piping plover;** birdwatchers might want to pick up the *Field Check List of Birds* (free) from any National or Provincial Park office. Campgrounds, programs, and services in the park operate mid-June-Labor Day, with **Cavendish campground** staying open until late September. At the entrance kiosks, receive a copy of the park guide *Blue Heron.* (Vehicle permits $5 per day, $10 per 4 days.)

The National Park also runs **Green Gables House** (672-6350), located off Rte. 6 in Cavendish near Rte. 13. Popularized by Lucy Maud Montgomery's novel, *Anne of Green Gables,* this house is the mecca for adoring readers. Interestingly, Montgomery's series of books about the freckle-faced orphan of Cavendish have a cult following among Japanese schoolgirls, many of whom drag their families here to pay homage. The House and Haunted Woods are certain to be recognized by fans but will appear to be just a nice little estate for the uninitiated. Green Gables can get very crowded between late July and September, so it's best to arrive in the early morning or the evening. Tours available in English and French. (Open daily 9am-8pm, mid-Oct.-June Mon.-Fri. 9am-5pm. Free.)

Woodleigh (836-3401), just off Rte. 234 in Burlington midway between Cavendish and Summerside, will satisfy the monarchist in you. It contains miniature but still sizeable replicas of British architectural icons including St. Paul Cathedral, Tower of London, and Lord Nelson's statue in Trafalgar Square—all available for exploration. Yes, the Crown Jewels are inside the Tower. The craftsmanship is striking, but the cuteness of the whole concept can rankle after a while. (Open June and Sept. 9am-5pm, July-Aug. 9am-8pm. $5, seniors $4.50, kids $3, preschoolers free.)

Charlottetown prides itself on being the "Cradle of Confederation." The brownstone **Province House** (566-7626), on the corner of Great George and Richmond St., was where delegates from the British North American colonies met to discuss the union which would become, in 1867, the Dominion of Canada. Chambers of historical importance are open for viewing, as are exhibits and the modern-day legislative chambers. (Open daily 9am-8pm; mid-Oct.-June Mon.-Fri. 9am-5pm. Free.) Adjoining the Province House is the **Confederation Centre for the Arts** (628-1864), located on the corner of Queen and Grafton St., a modern performing-arts complex with theaters, displays, a library, and an art gallery. Free hour-long guided tours of the Centre are conducted July-Aug. (Open daily 9am-8pm, Sept.-June Mon.-Sat. 9am-5pm, Sun. 2-5pm.) Every summer, a musical production of **Anne of Green Gables** warbles in Mackenzie Theatre, as part of the Charlottetown Festival. (Performances mid-June-early Sept. Mon.-Sat. at 8pm. Tickets $20-30. For ticket info, call 566-1267 or 800-565-1267 in the Maritimes Mon.-Sat. 9am-9pm.)

Québec

Home to 90% of Canada's French-origin citizenry, Québec continues to fight for political and legal recognition of its separate cultural identity. All of the signs here are in French only, flouting a Supreme Court ruling. Canada's 1990 failure to ratify the Meech Lake Accord, which would have awarded recognition of Québec as a "distinct society," has reopened debate over the possibility of secession, formerly rejected in a 1980 referendum. Many now share the attitude of former Premier René Lévesque, who quipped, "If you can't sleep together, you might as well have separate beds." For all their pillowfighting, and despite the constantly looming threat of another referendum, the two bedmates seem reluctant to tamper with a healthy trading relationship. In a North American sea of English, the *Québecois* are fighting to keep their identity; 95% of Québec is French-speaking, but Québec is distinctively not French. The *québecois* provincial motto *Je me souviens* promises a prosperous future as well as a remembered past.

PRACTICAL INFORMATION

Capital: Québec City.

Tourisme Québec, c.p. 20,000, Québec G1K 7X2 (800-363-7777; 514-873-2015 in Montréal).

Time Zone: Eastern. **Postal abbreviation:** QU

Alcohol: Legal drinking age 18.

Sales Tax: 8%, plus a 7% GST.

Accommodation Information

For general assistance in locating accommodations, try the following organizations.

Bed and Breakfast: Vacances-Familles, 1291, boul. Charest Ouest, Québec G1N 2C9 (418-682-5464; in Montréal 514-251-8811). $40 yearly membership in club provides discounts of 10-15% on lodging throughout the province.

Camping: Association des terrains du camping du Québec, 2001, rue de la metropole, Bureau 70 Longueil, Québec J4G 1S9 (514-651-7396) and **Fédération québecoise du camping et de caravaning,** 4545, ave Pierre-de-Coubertin c.p. 1000, succursale "M," Montréal H1V 3R2 (514-252-3003).

Hostels: Regroupement Tourisme Jeunesse (HI), at the Fédération address (514-252-3117). For reservations in any Québec hotel call 800-461-8585 at least 24 hrs. in advance, with a credit card.

■■■ MONTRÉAL

In the 17th century the city of Montréal struggled with Iroquois tribes for control over the area's lucrative fur trade, and erected walls circling the settlement as a defensive measure. Today the remnants of those ramparts do no more than delineate the boundaries of Vieux Montréal (Old Montréal), and the most serious conflict Montréalers endure is a good bit of polyglottal bickering amongst themselves. As one of the world's largest bilingual cities, Montréal has had to work through a number of disputes between its Anglo- and Francophone inhabitants. The current French hegemony—all students learn French in Québec schools and all city signs read only in French—seems at the same time oppressive to English speakers and vital to those wishing to preserve their Francophone culture. For visitors, however, this tension imparts a dynamic, romantic atmosphere to this city on the Fleuve St-Laurent where cultures and tongues simultaneously mingle and chafe.

PRACTICAL INFORMATION

Emergency: 911.

Visitors Information: Infotouriste, 1001, rue du Square-Dorchester (873-2015; outside Montréal 800-363-7777), on Dorchester Sq. between rue Peel and rue Metcalfe. Métro: Peel. Free city maps and guides, and extensive food and housing listings. Open daily 8:30am-7:30pm; Labor Day-June daily 9am-6pm. A branch office in **Old Montréal** (174, rue Notre-Dame Est at Place Jacques Carhier) is open at the same hours and seasons as the main branch.

Tourisme Jeunesse (youth tourist info) **Boutique Temps Libre,** 3063, rue St-Denis (252-3117). Métro: Sherbrooke. Free maps; youth hostel info available. Travel gear and helpful suggestions from friendly staff. A non-profit organization that inspects and ranks all officially recognized youth hostels in Québec. Open Mon.-Wed. 10am-6pm, Thurs.-Fri. 10am-9pm, Sat. 10am-5pm, Sun. noon-5pm (summer only). Mailing address: c.p. 1000, Succursale "M," Montréal P.Q., H1V 3R2. **Travel CUTS,** a student travel agency at the McGill Student Union, 3480, rue McTavish (398-0647). Métro: McGill. They specialize in budget travel for college students. Open Mon.-Fri. 9am-5pm.

Language: The population of Montréal is 80% French-speaking. Many citizens are bilingual. If you know French, speak it; you're less likely to be dismissed as an English-speaking Canadian.

Consulates: U.S., 1155, rue St-Alexander (398-9695). Open Mon.-Fri 8:30am-1pm for passports; for visas Mon.-Fri. 8:30am-noon. **U.K.,** 1155, rue de l'Université, suite 901 (866-5863). Open for info Mon.-Fri. 9am-5pm. For consular help, open Mon.-Fri. 9am-12:30pm and 2-4:30pm.

Currency Exchange: Bank of America Canada, 1230, rue Peel (393-1855). Métro: Peel. Open Mon.-Fri. 8:30am-5:30pm, Sat. 9am-5pm. **Thomas Cook,** 625, boul. René-Lévesque Ouest (397-4029). Métro: Square-Victoria. Open Mon.-Sat. 9am-5pm. **National Commercial-Foreign Currency,** 1250, rue Peel (879-1300). Métro: Peel. Another office at 390, rue St-Jacques (844-3401). Métro:

Square-Victoria. Open Mon.-Fri. 8am-5pm, Sat. 8:30am-5pm. Although many cafés will take U.S. dollars, you'll get a better deal from a currency exchange store. The locations listed here exchange for free, but many don't—be sure to ask. Most **bank machines** are on the PLUS system.

Airports: Dorval (info service: 633-3105), 20-30 min. from downtown by car. From the Lionel Groulx Métro stop, take bus #211 to Dorval Shopping Center, then transfer to bus #204 (total fare $1.75). **Connoisseur Grayline** (934-1222) runs bus service daily to Dorval from the Queen Elizabeth Hotel at the corner of René-Lévesque and Mansfield. Other stops include the Château Champlain, the Sheraton Center, and the Voyageur Terminal. (Buses run Mon.-Fri. every ½-hr., 5:20-7:20am, every 20 min. 7:20am-11:20pm, Sat.-Sun. every ½ hr. 7am-2am. $8.50 one way, $16 round-trip; under age 5 free.) **Mirabel International Airport** (476-3040), 45 min. from downtown by car, handles all flights from outside North America. Greyline buses service Mirabel (daily 3-9am every 2 hr., 9am-noon every hr., noon-8pm every ½ hr., 8pm-midnight every hr., $13).

Trains: Central Station, 935, rue de la Gauchetière under the Queen Elizabeth Hotel. Métro: Bonaventure. Served by **VIA Rail** (871-1331) and **Amtrak** (800-872-7245). To: Québec City (2-4 per day, 3 hr., $45, students $41; book at least 5 days ahead except Fri. and Sun. $27/23); Toronto (5-7 per day, 5 hr., $85/77 and $51/43); Ottawa (3-4 per day, 2 hr., $35/32 and $21/18); Vancouver via Toronto (3 per week, $470/423). Amtrak service to: New York City (2 per day, 11 hr., US$76-101). VIA ticket counters open Mon.-Sat. 6:15am-9pm, Sun. 8am-9pm. Amtrak ticket counters open daily 7:30am-6:30pm.

Buses: Terminus Voyageur, 505, boul. de Maisonneuve Est (287-1580). Métro: Berri-UQAM. Voyageur offers 14-consecutive-day unlimited tour passes for $177 May-Oct., which will take you all over Québec and Ontario. Voyage to: Toronto (5 per day, 6½ hr., $60); Ottawa (17 per day, 2½ hr., $25); Québec City (17 per day, 3 hr., $35). The Ottawa Bus also leaves from **Dépanneur Beau-soir,** 2875, boul. St-Charles, (on the West Island). **Greyhound** serves New York City (6 per day, 8¾ hr., $80). **Vermont Transit** serves Boston (2 per day, 8½ hr., $72) and Burlington, VT (2 per day, 3 hr., $21).

Public Transport: STCUM Métro and Bus, (288-6287). A safe and efficient network, with Métro subway service. The 4 Métro lines and most buses operate daily 5:30am-12:30am; some have night schedules as well. Get network maps at the tourist office, or at any Métro station toll booth. Take a transfer ticket from the bus driver; it's good as a subway ticket. Fare for trains or bus $1.75, 6 tickets $7.

Car Rental: Via Route, 1255, rue MacKay at Ste-Catherine (871-1166; collect calls accepted). $29 per day; 200km free, 12¢ each additional km. Insurance for over age 25 $12 per day; ages 21-24 $13. Must be 21 with credit card. Open Mon.-Fri. 8am-7pm, Sat. 8am-5pm, Sun. 9am-5pm.

Driver/Rider Service: Allo Stop, 4317, rue St-Denis (985-3032). Will match you with a driver (a portion of the fee goes to the driver, who must be a member as well) heading for Québec City ($15), Ottawa ($10), Toronto ($26), Sherbrooke ($9), New York City ($50), or Boston ($42). Fees for Vancouver vary; riders and drivers fix their own fees for rides over 1000 mi. Membership required ($6). Open Mon.-Wed. 9am-5pm, Thurs.-Fri. 9am-7pm, Sat. 10am-5pm, Sun. 10am-7pm.

Bike Rental: Cycle Pop, 978, Rachel Est (524-7102). Métro: Mont-Royal. Rent a mountain bike or 18-speed; $25 per day, $35 on Sat. and Sun. Open Mon.-Wed. 9:30am-6pm, Thurs.-Fri. 9:30am-9pm, Sat.-Sun. 9:30am-5pm. Credit card or $250 deposit required.

Ticket Agencies: Ticketmaster (514-790-2222). Open Mon.-Sat. 9am-9pm, Sun. noon-6pm. Also try **Admission Ticket Network** (514-522-1245 or 800-361-4595). Credit card number required.

Help Lines: Tel-aide, 935-1101. 24 hrs. **Sexual Assault,** 934-4504. **Suicide-Action,** 522-5777. **Rape Crisis,** 934-4505. **Gay Info,** 768-0199. **Gay Line,** 931-8668. **Déprimés anonymes,** 842-7557.

Post Office: Succursale "A," 1025, St-Jacques Ouest (846-5390). Open Mon.-Fri. 8am-5:45pm. **Postal code:** H3C 1T1.

Area Code: 514.

MONTREAL

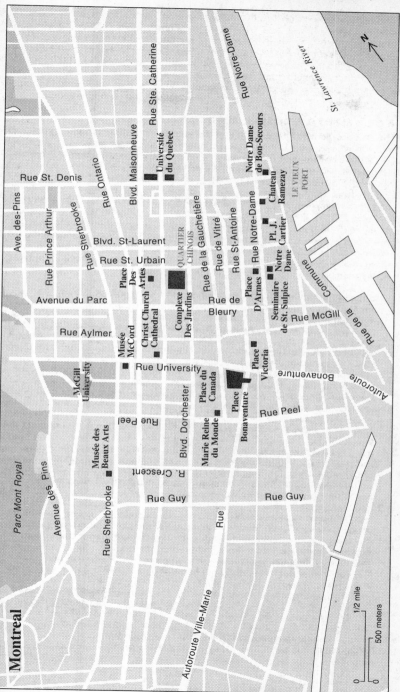

Montreal

St. Lawrence River

LE VIEUX PORT

Rue Notre-Dame

Notre Dame de Bon-Secours

Chateau Ramezay

Pl. J. Cartier

Notre Dame

Rue Notre-Dame

Séminaire de St. Sulpice

Rue McGill

Place D'Armes

Rue St-Antoine

Rue de Vitré

Rue de la Gauchetière

QUARTIER CHINOIS

Rue de Bleury

Complexe Des Jardins

Place Des Artes

Blvd. St-Laurent

Rue St. Urbain

Université du Quebec

Rue Ste. Catherine

Blvd. Maisonneuve

Rue Ontario

Rue St. Denis

Rue Sherbrooke

Rue Prince Arthur

Ave. des-Pins

Avenue du Parc

Rue Aylmer

Christ Church Cathedral

Musée McCord

Rue University

McGill University

Rue Peel

Blvd. Dorchester

Place du Canada

Place Victoria

Place Bonaventure

Rue Peel

Marie Reine du Monde

Rue McGill

Rue de la Commune

Autoroute Bonaventure

Musée des Beaux Arts

R. Crescent

Rue Guy

Rue Guy

Rue Sherbrooke

Avenue des Pins

Parc Mont Royal

Rue

Autoroute Ville-Marie

Rue Peel

0   1/2 mile
0   500 meters

Two major streets divide the city, making it convenient for orientation. The **boulevard St-Laurent** (also called "The Main") runs north-south, splitting the city and streets east-west. The Main also serves as the unofficial French/English divider: English **McGill University** lies to the west while St-Denis, the **French student quarter** (also called the *Quartier Latin*) is slightly east. **Rue Sherbrooke** which is paralleled by de Maisonneuve and Ste-Catherine downtown, runs east-west almost the entire length of Montréal. Parking is often difficult in the city, particularly in winter when snowbanks narrow the streets and slow traffic. Take the **Métro** instead.

ACCOMMODATIONS AND CAMPING

The **Québec Tourist Office** is the best resource for info about hostels, hotels, and *chambres touristiques* (rooms in private homes or small guest houses). B&B singles cost $25-40, doubles $35-75. The most extensive B&B network is **Bed & Breakfast à Montréal**, P.O. Box 575, Montréal H3X 3T8 (738-9410), which recommends that you reserve by mail ($15 per night deposit upon confirmation). (Singles from $35, doubles from $55. Leave a message on the answering machine if the owners are out.) The **Downtown Bed and Breakfast Network**, 3458, ave Laval, Montréal H2X 3C8 (289-9749 or 800-267-5180), at Sherbrooke, lists about 80 homes downtown. (Singles $25-40, doubles $35-55. Open spring and summer daily 8:30am-9pm; fall and winter 8:30am-7pm.) For cheaper B&B listings, check with the **Marbel Guest House**, 3507, boul. Décarie, H4A 3J4. Métro: Vendôme (486-0232; singles $20, with breakfast $25; doubles $30/$40). Make reservations by sending a check for the first night as deposit. Virtually all B&Bs have bilingual hosts.

Montréal Youth Hostel (HI), 3541, rue Aylmer, Montréal H2X 2B9 (843-3317), in the McGill campus area, 10 min. walk from downtown. Métro: McGill. Recent renovations and a great location make this a clean and comfortable place to stay. Carpeted rooms with 4-16 beds, huge kitchen and refrigerator, laundry facilities. Activities include free tours of the city, notice board listing downtown nightspots and their covers, extensive ride board. Continental breakfast special $2.25. Linen $1.75. Open 24 hrs., no curfew. Max stay 1 week. $15, Canadian nonmembers $17, non-Canadian nonmembers $19.45. Reservations by credit card accepted with 24 hr. notice. 102 beds are available year-round and a summer annex provides an additional 100 beds. Since the main building tends to fill up in the summer, you'd be better off calling early to know whether to go to the annex directly.

Collège Français, 5155, boul. de Gaspé, H2T 2A1 (495-2581 or 270-9260 after 5pm and on holidays). Métro: Laurier, then walk west and north to corner of Fairmount. Rooms year-round. Clean and well-located. Access to gym. Young clientele. Prices vary from $12.50 depending on the number of beds in the room (4-8) and whether the showers are in the room or down the hall. Free parking. Summer breakfast $3. Open July-Aug. 24 hrs., Sept.-June 7:30am-11pm. More beds inconveniently located at 1391, rue Beauregard Longueuil (Métro: Longueuil, then take Bus 71 up Taschereau and Ségin), open June-Aug.

McGill University, Bishop Mountain Hall, 3935, rue de l'Université, H3A 2B4 (398-6367). Métro: McGill. Follow Université through campus (bring your hiking boots; it's a long haul). Ideally located singles. Kitchenettes and payphones on each floor. Common room with TV, laundry. Ask for Gardner building, where the views are best. Desk open Mon.-Fri. 7am-10:30pm, Sat.-Sun. 8am-10pm; a guard will check you in late at night. $26.50, non-students $36.50. $48 per 2 nights. Weekly $115. Continental breakfast ($2.90) served Mon.-Fri. 7:30-9:30am. Open May 15-Aug. 15. Reservations by mail (1-night deposit) needed for July and Aug.

Université de Montréal, Residences, 2350, rue Edouard-Montpetit, H2X 2B9 off Côte-des-Neiges (343-6531). Métro: Edouard-Montpetit. Located on the edge of a beautiful campus; try East Tower for great views. Singles $31, $24 for students, alumni, and conferees (weekly $90). Laundry. Phone and sink in each room. Desk open 24 hrs. Cafeteria open Mon.-Fri. 7am-7pm. Open May 6-Aug. 19.

YWCA, 1355, rue René-Lévesque Ouest (866-9941). Métro: Lucien l'Allier. Clean, safe rooms in the heart of downtown. Women only. Newly-renovated. Access to

Y facilities. Kitchen, TV on every floor. Doors lock at 10pm but the desk will buzz you in all night. Singles $30, with shared bathroom $40, with private bath $45. Doubles $50, with semi-private bath $54. $5 deposit. Reservations accepted.

YMCA, 1450, rue Stanley (849-8393), downtown. Métro: Peel. 331 rooms. Co-ed. Singles: men $30, women $33. Doubles $48. Triples $57. Quads $66. Students and seniors $2 off. Cafeteria open Mon.-Fri. 7am-7pm, Sat.-Sun. 8am-2pm. Access to Y facilities. TV and phone in every room. Usually fills up June-Aug.

Many of the least expensive *maisons touristiques* (tourist homes) and hotels are around rue St-Denis, which ranges from quaint to seedy. The area flaunts lively nightclubs, a number of funky cafés and bistros, and abuts Vieux Montréal. Before choosing a place to stay, pick up a **Tourist Guide** at the Tourist Office; it maps the location of hundreds of accommodations.

Maison André Tourist Rooms, 3511, rue Université (849-4092). Métro: McGill. Mme. Zanko will rent you a room in her old, well-located house and spin great yarns, but only if you don't smoke. Guests have been returning to this bastion of German cleanliness and decor for over 30 years. Singles $26-35, doubles $38-45, $10 per extra person in room. Reservations recommended.

Hotel Le Breton, 1609, rue St-Hubert (524-7273). Around the corner from bus station. Métro: Berri-UQAM. Prides itself on international clientele. Lobby and some rooms recently renovated. Looks like the Huxtables' neighborhood from the *Cosby Show.* All 13 rooms have TV and A/C. Singles $30-55. Doubles $42-58. Fills up quickly—make reservations.

Those with a car and time can camp at **Camping Parc Paul Sauvé** (479-8365), 45 min. from downtown. Take Autoroutes 20 west to 13 north to 640 west and follow the signs to the park. There are 873 beautiful sites on the **Lac des Deux Montagnes** (Sites $15, with hookup $20). For private sites, try **KOA Montréal-South,** 130, boul. Monette, St-Phillipe J0L 2K0 (659-8626), a 15-min. drive from the city. Follow Autoroute 15 south, take exit 38, turn left at the stop sign, and go straight about 1 mi. (1.6km)—it's on your left. (Sites $17, with hookup $21. Both accommodate 2 people; $3 per each additional person up to six.) If these don't wet your camping whistle try **Camping Pointe-des-Cascades,** 2 ch. du Canal, Pte. des Cascades (455-9953). Take Autoroute 40 west, exit 41 at Ste. Anne de Bellevue, junction 20, direction west to Dorion. In Dorion, follow "Théâtre des Cascades" signs. (Sites $12, with hookup $17.)

FOOD

French-Canadian cuisine is unique but generally expensive. When on a tight budget, look for *tourtière,* a traditional meat pie with vegetables and a thick crust, or *québecois crêpes,* stuffed with everything from scrambled eggs to asparagus with *béchamel.* Wash it down with *cidre* (hard cider). Other Montréal specialties include French bread (the best on the continent), smoked meat, Matane salmon, Gaspé shrimp, lobster from the Iles de la Madelene, and *poutine,* a gooey concoction of French fries *(frites),* cheese curds, and gravy, which you can find everywhere.

Montréal's ethnic restaurants offer cuisine ranging from curry to *pierogis* at reasonable prices. Look for Greek *souvlaki* or Vietnamese asparagus and crab soup. A small **Chinatown** orients itself along rue de la Gauchetière, near Vieux Montréal's Place d'Armes. Between 11:30am-2:30pm, most of its restaurants offer mouth-watering Canton and Szechuan lunch specials ranging from $3.50-5. A couple of Jewish delis and bagel bakeries (vestiges of the Jewish neighborhood that once was) lie north of downtown around boul. St-Laurent. A trip to Montreal would not be complete without savoring a dozen or so bagels (35-50¢ each but just try to eat only 1)— baked before your eyes in brick ovens—at **La Maison de l'Original Fairmount Bagel,** 74, rue Fairmount Ouest (272-0667; Métro: Laurier), or the **Bagel Bakery,** 263, rue St-Viateur Ouest (276-8044; Métro: Place-des-Arts), both open 24 hrs.

For a quick sampling of Montréal's international cuisine, stop by **Le Faubourg,** 1616, rue Ste-Catherine Ouest at rue Guy (939-3663; Métro: Guy). The food here is diverse (crêpes, felafel, Szechuan) and fresh, despite the fast-food atmosphere. Markets here sell seafood, meats, bread, and produce. Before you leave Le Faubourg, stop by **Monsieur Félix and Mr. Norton Cookies** (939-3207). Aside from summing up the French-English duality in Montréal, they make the richest cookies in town. (Open Mon.-Thurs. 9am-10pm, Fri-Sat. 9-midnight; locations around the city.)

The drinking age in Montréal is 18. You can save money by buying your own wine at a *dépanneur* or at the **SAQ** (Sociéte des alcohols du Québec) and bringing it to one of the unlicensed restaurants, concentrated on the boul. St-Laurent, north of Sherbrooke, and on the pedestrian precincts of rue Prince Arthur and rue Duluth. When preparing your own grub, look for produce at the **Atwater Market** (Métro: Lionel-Groulx); the **Marché Maisonneuve,** 4375, rue Ontario Est (Métro: Pie-IX); the **Marché St-Jacques** (Métro: Berri UQAM, at the corner of Ontario and Amherst); or the **Marché Jean-Talon** (Métro: Jean Talon). (For info on any call 872-2491; all open Sat.-Wed. 8am-6pm, Thurs.-Fri. 8am-9pm.)

Rue St-Denis, the main thoroughfare in the French student quarter, has many small restaurants and cafés, most of which cater to student pocketbooks. **Da Giovanni,** 572, Ste-Catherine Est, Métro: Berri, serves generous portions of fine Italian food; don't be put off by the lines or the diner atmosphere. The sauce and noodles cook up right in the window. (842-8851; open Sun.-Tues. 7am-1am, Wed.-Thurs. 7am-2am, Fri.-Sat. 7am-3am.)

You'll be charged 15% tax for meals totaling more than $3.25. All restaurants are required by law to post their menus outside, so shop around. For more info, consult the free *Restaurant Guide,* published by the Greater Montréal Convention and Tourism Bureau (844-5400) which lists more than 130 restaurants by type of cuisine and is available at the tourist office.

Café Santropol, 3990, rue Duluth (842-3110), at St-Urbain. Métro: Sherbrooke, then walk north on St-Denis and west on Duluth. "Bienvenue à la planète Santropol!" Student hangout, complete with aquarium and outdoor terrace for schmoozing. Eclectic menu: huge veggie sandwiches with piles of fruit ($6-8). Cream cheese, cottage cheese, yogourt, and nuts are main staples. Open Mon.-Thurs. 11:30am-midnight, Fri.-Sat. noon-3am, Sun. noon-midnight.

Terasse Lafayette, 250, rue Villeneuve Ouest (288-3915), at rue Jeanne Mance, west of the Mont-Royal Métro. Pizzas, pastas, souvlaki, and salad $7.50-10; gyro plate $9.85. One of the better Greek restaurants, with a huge outdoor terrace. BYOB. 10% discount on pick-up. Open daily 11am-midnight. Free delivery.

Etoile des Indes, 1806, Ste-Catherine Ouest (932-8330), near St-Matthieu. Métro: Guy-Concordia. Split-level dining room with tapestries covering the walls. The best Indian fare in town. Dinner entrees $7-17, daily lunch specials $7 (11:30am-4:30pm). The brave should try their bang-up *bangalore phal* dishes. Open Mon.-Sat. 11:30am-11pm, Sun. noon-11pm.

Le Mazurka, 64, rue Prince Arthur (844-3539). Métro: Sherbrooke; cross St-Denis and dance through the park; Prince Arthur is on the other side. Classy décor belies great prices and fine Polish fare. *Pierogis* with soup, $4.50. Specials abound, especially Mon.-Thurs. after 9pm; it gets crowded. Dine on the terrace. Open daily 11:30am-midnight.

Wilensky's, 34, rue Fairmount Ouest (271-0247). Métro: Laurier. A great place for quick lunch. Pull out a book from Moe Wilensky's shelf, note the sign warning "We always put mustard on it," and linger. Hot dogs $1.60, sandwiches $1.85-2.35. Open Mon.-Fri. 9am-4pm.

Dunn's, 892, Ste-Catherine Ouest (866-3866). Arguably the best smoked meat in town, served in monstrous slabs tucked between bread and mustard (sandwiches $4, larger meat plates $7.10). Dunn's also reckons that it is famous for its strawberry cheesecake ($4). Open 24 hrs.

The Peel Pub, 1107, rue Ste-Catherine (844-6769). Métro: Peel. Other location: 1106, boul. de Maisonneuve (845-9002). At the main branch, students and suited folks sit side by side in a raucous, rollicking pub. TV screens and live bands nightly. Spaghetti every day $1.25. Daily specials make this an inexpensive and happening place to be. Have Sex on the Beach on Friday nights for 69¢. Open daily 6:30am-1:30am; de Maisonneuve open Mon.-Fri. 11am-3am, Sat.-Sun. 4:30pm-3am.

SIGHTS

An island city, Montréal has matured from a riverside settlement of French colonists into a major metropolis. The city's ethnic pockets and architectural diversity can captivate you for days on end. Museums, Vieux Montréal (Old Montréal), and the new downtown may be fascinating, but Montréal's greatest asset is its cosmopolitan flair. This is a hip place to be where people from all over have managed to coexist— and bilingually at that. Wander aimlessly and often—and *not* through the high-priced boutiques the tourist office touts. Many attractions between Mont Royal and the Fleuve St-Laurent are free: from parks (Mont Royal and Lafontaine) and universities (McGill, Montréal, Concordia, Québec at Montréal) to ethnic neighborhoods.

Walk or bike down **Boulevard St-Laurent** north of Sherbrooke. Originally settled by Jewish immigrants, this area now functions as a sort of multi-cultural welcome wagon, home to Greek, Slavic, Latin American, and Portuguese immigrants. **Rue St-Denis,** abode of the French language elite around the turn of the century, still serves as the mainline of Montréal's **Latin Quarter** (Métro: Berri-UQAM). Jazz fiends command the street the first 10 days of July during the annual **Montréal International Jazz Festival** (525-7732 HQ; info 871-1881) with over 200 outdoor shows. Headliners play many other concerts indoors. **Carré St-Louis** (Métro: Sherbrooke) with its fountain and sculptures, **Rue Prince-Arthur** (Métro: Sherbrooke) packed with street performers in the summer, and **Le Village,** a gay village in Montréal from rue St-Denis Est to Papineau along rue Ste-Catherine Est, are also worth visiting.

The **McGill University** campus (main gate at the corner of rue McGill and Sherbrooke; Métro: McGill) stretches up Mont Royal and boasts Victorian buildings and pleasant spots of green grass in the midst of downtown. More than any other sight in Montréal, the university illustrates the impact of British tradition in the city. The campus also contains the site of the 16th-century Native-American village of Hochelaga and the **Redpath Museum of Natural Science** (398-4086), with rare fossils and two genuine Egyptian mummies. (Open June-Sept. Mon.-Thurs. 9am-5pm; Sept.-June Mon.-Fri. 9am-5pm. Free.) Guided tours of the campus are available (June-Sept. Mon.-Fri. with 1 day advance notice; 398-6555).

The Underground City

Montréal residents aren't speaking cryptically of a sub-culture or a hideout for dissidents when they rave about their Underground City. They mean *under the ground:* 29km of tunnels link Métro stops and form a subterranean village of climate-controlled restaurants and shops. The ever-expanding network now connects railway stations, two bus terminals, restaurants, banks, cinemas, theaters, hotels, two universities, two department stores, 1700 businesses, 1615 housing units, and 1600 boutiques. Rather frighteningly hailed by the city as "the prototype of the city of the future," these burrows give the word "suburban" a whole new meaning. Enter the city from any Métro stop or start your adventure at the **Place Bonaventure,** 901, rue de la Gauchetière Ouest (397-2205; Métro: Bonaventure), Canada's largest commercial building. The **Viaduc** shopping center inside contains a diverse mélange of shops, each selling products of a different country. The tourist office supplies city guides that include treasure maps of the tunnels and underground attractions. (Shops open Mon.-Fri. 9:30am-6pm, Sat.-Sun. 9:30am-5pm.) Poke your head above ground long enough to see **Place Ville-Marie** (Métro: Bonaventure), a 1960s office-shopping complex. Revolutionary when first built, the structure triggered Montréal's architectural renaissance. **Cathédrale Marie Reine du Monde** (Mary Queen of the World Cathedral), corner of René-Lévesque and Mansfield (Métro: Bonaven-

MONTRÉAL

ture; 866-1661), is a scaled-down replica of St. Peter's in Rome. (Open daily 7am-7:30pm; off-season Sun.-Fri. 9:30am-7:30pm, Sat. 8am-8:30pm.)

Parks and Museums

The finest of Montréal's parks, **Parc du Mont-Royal,** Centre de la Montagne (844-4928; Métro: Mont-Royal), swirls in a vast green expanse up the mountain from which the city took its name. Visitors from New York may recognize the green hand of Frederick Law Olmsted, the architect who planned Central Park (and half the U.S.). From rue Peel, hardy hikers can take a foot path and stairs to the top. The lookouts on Camillien-Houde Parkway and the Mountain Chalet both offer phenomenal views of Montréal. In 1643, De Maisonneuve, founder of Montréal, promised to climb Mont Royal bearing a cross if the flood waters of the St-Laurent would recede. The existing 30-ft. cross (which, it's safe to assume, is not the same one) commemorates this climb. When illuminated at night, you can see the cross for miles. In winter, *Montréalais* congregate on "the Mountain" to ice-skate, toboggan, and cross-country ski. In summer, Mont Royal welcomes joggers, cyclists, picnickers, and amblers. (Officially open 6am-midnight.) **Parc Lafontaine** (872-2644; Métro: Sherbrooke), bordered by Sherbrooke, Rachel, Papineau, and ave Parc Lafontaine, has picnic facilities, an outdoor puppet theater, seven public tennis courts (hourly fee), ice-skating in the winter, and an international festival of public theater in June.

Musée des beaux-arts (Fine Arts Museum), 1379 and 1380, rue Sherbrooke Ouest (285-1600; Métro: Peel or Guy-Concordia), houses a small permanent collection that touches upon all major historical periods and includes Canadian and Inuit work (open Tues.-Sun. 11am-6pm, Wed. and Sat. closes at 9pm; $4.75, students $3, seniors and under 12 $1). It also hosts visiting exhibits. **Musée d'art contemporain** (Museum of Contemporary Art), 185, Ste-Catherine Ouest at Jeanne-Mance (847-6226; Métro: Place-des-Arts), has the latest by *québecois* artists, and textile, photography, and avant-garde exhibits (open Tues. and Thurs.-Sun. 11am-6pm, Wed. 11am-6pm; $4.75, seniors $3.75, students $2.75, under 12 free; free Wed. 6-9pm).

The newly renovated and expanded **McCord Museum of Canadian History,** 690, rue Sherbrooke Ouest (398-7100; Métro: McGill), saves and studies a collection of textiles, costumes, paintings, prints, and 700,000 pictures spanning 133 years in their photographic archives (archives by appointment only; contact Nora Hague). (Open Tues.-Wed. and Fri. 10am-6pm, Thurs. 10am-9pm, Sat.-Sun. 10am-5pm; $5, students $2, seniors $3. Free Thurs. 6-9pm.) Opened in May 1989, the **Centre Canadien d'Architecture,** 1920, ave Baile (939-7000; Métro: Guy-Concordia), houses one of the most important collections of architectural prints, drawings, photographs, and books in the world. (Open Tues.-Wed. and Fri.-Sun. 11am-6pm, Thurs. 11am-8pm; Oct.-May Wed. and Fri. 11am-6pm, Thurs. 11am-8pm, Sat.-Sun. 11am-5pm; $5, students and seniors $3, children under 12 free.) **Olympic Park,** 4141, ave Pierre-De-Coubertin (252-4737; Métro: Pie-IX or Viau), hosted the 1976 Summer Olympic Games. Its daring architecture, uncannily reminiscent of the *U.S.S. Enterprise,* includes the world's tallest inclined tower and a stadium with one of the world's only fully retractable roofs. Despite this, games *still* get rained out because the roof cannot be put in place with crowds in the building (small goof, really). (Guided tours daily at 12:40 and 3:40pm; more often May-Sept. $7, seniors $6, ages 5-17 $5.50, under 5 free.) Take the *funiculaire* to the top of the tower for a panoramic view of Montréal. (every 10 min., Mon.-Thurs. 10am-9pm, Fri.-Sun. 10am-11pm; off-season daily 10am-6pm; $7, seniors $6, kids $5.50.) The most recent addition to the attractions at the Olympic Park is the **Biodôme** (868-3000). Housed in the building which was once the Olympic Vélodrome, the Biodôme is a "living museum" in which four complete ecosystems have been reconstructed: the Tropical Forest, the Laurentian Forest, the St-Laurent marine ecosystem, and the Polar World. The goal is environmental awareness and conservation; the management stresses repeatedly that the Biodôme is *not* a zoo, rather a means for people to connect themselves with the natural world. (Open daily 9am-6pm. $8.50, seniors $6, ages 6-17 $4.25. Special packages available for viewing the Gardens and Biodôme together.) In the summer a train will take you across the park to the **Jardin Botanique** (Botanical Gardens), 4101, rue Sherbrooke Est (872-1400; Métro: Pie-IX), one of the most important gardens in the world. The Japanese and Chinese areas opened only recently, and house the largest *bonsai* and *penjing* collection outside of Asia. (Gardens open 8am-sunset; greenhouses 9am-7pm, Nov.-April 9am-4:30pm. $7, seniors $5, ages 6-17 $3.50, under 6 free. 30% less Nov.-April.)

Vieux Montréal (Old Montréal)

Montréal's first settlement dug itself in at Vieux Montréal, on the stretch of riverbank between rue McGill, Notre-Dame, and Berri. The fortified walls that once protected the quarter have crumbled, but the beautiful 17th- and 18th-century mansions of politicos and merchants retain their splendor. (Métro: Place d'Armes.)

The 19th-century church **Notre-Dame-de-Montréal,** 116, rue Notre-Dame Ouest (849-1070), towers above the Place d'Armes and the memorial to De Maisonneuve. A historic center for the city's Catholic population, the neo-Gothic church once hosted separatist rallies, and, more recently, a tradition-breaking ecumenical gathering; it seats 4000 and is one of the largest and most magnificent churches in North America. Concerts are held here throughout the year. After suffering major fire damage, the **Wedding Chapel** behind the altar re-opened in 1982 replete with an enormous bronze altar. (Open daily 7am-8pm; Labor-Day-June 24 7am-6pm. Guided tours offered.)

From Notre-Dame walk next door to the **Sulpician Seminary,** Montréal's oldest building (built in 1685) and still a functioning seminary. The clock over the façade is the oldest public timepiece in North America and has overseen the passage of over nine billion seconds since it was built in 1700. A stroll down rue St-Sulpice will bring you to **rue de la Commune** on the banks of the Fleuve St-Laurent. Here the city's old docks compete with the new. Proceed east along rue de la Commune to **rue Bonsecours.** At the corner of rue Bonsecours and the busy rue St-Paul stands the 18th-century **Notre-Dame-de-Bonsecours,** 400, rue St-Paul Est (845-9991; Métro: Champ-de-Mars), founded on the port as a sailors' refuge by Marguerite Bourgeoys, leader of the first congregation of non-cloistered nuns. Sailors thankful for their safe pilgrimages presented the nuns and priests with the wooden boat-shaped ceiling lamps in the chapel. The church also has a museum in the basement and a bell tower with a nice view of Vieux Montréal and the Fleuve St-Laurent. (Chapel open daily 9am-5pm; Nov.-April 10am-3pm. Tower and museum open daily 9am-4:30pm; Nov.-April Tues.-Sun. 10:30am-2:30pm. $2, under 12 50¢.)

Opening onto rue St-Paul is **Place Jacques Cartier,** site of Montréal's oldest market. Here the modern European character of Montréal is most evident; cafés line the square, and in the summer street artists strut their stuff. Visit the grand **Château Ramezay,** 280, rue Notre-Dame Est (861-3708; Métro: Champ-de-Mars), built in 1705 to house the French viceroy, and its museum of *Québecois,* British, and American 18th-century artifacts. (Open daily 10am-4:30pm; Sept.-May Tues.-Sun. 10am-4:30pm. $5, students and seniors $3.) Then check out the Vieux Palais de Justice, built in 1856 in Place Vaugeulin. Across from it stands City Hall. **Rue St-Jacques** in the Old City, established in 1687, is Montréal's answer to Wall Street.

There are many good reasons to venture out to **Ile Ste-Hélène,** an island in the Fleuve St-Laurent, just off the coast of Vieux Montréal. The best is **La Ronde** (872-6222), Montréal's popular amusement park: it's best to go in the afternoon and buy an unlimited pass. From late May to mid-June on Wed. and Sat., stick around La Ronde until 10pm to watch the **International Fireworks Competition** (872-8714). (Park open June-Labor Day Sun.-Thurs. 11am-11pm, Fri.-Sat. 11am-midnight. $17.30, under 12 $8.50.) If you don't want to pay admission to the park, watch the fireworks from people-packed Pont Jacques-Cartier.

To cool off after your frolics, slide over to **Aqua-Parc** (872-7326) and splash the day away. (Open mid-June-late Aug. daily 10am-5pm. $15.25, under 12 $8.50; after

MONTREAL

3pm $10.25/6.25.) **Le Vieux Fort** (The Old Fort, also known as the **David M. Stewart Museum; 861-6701**), was built in the 1820s to defend Canada's inland waterways. Now primarily a military museum, the fort displays artifacts and costumes detailing Canadian colonial history. (Open Wed.-Mon. 10am-6pm; Sept.-April Wed.-Mon. 10am-5pm. 3 military parades daily June-Aug. $5, seniors, students, and kids $3, under 6 free.) Take the Métro under the St-Laurent to the Ile Ste-Hélène stop.

Whether swollen with spring run-off or frozen over during the winter, the **Fleuve St-Laurent (St. Lawrence River)** can be one of Montréal's most thrilling attractions. The whirlpools and 15-ft. waves of the **Lachine Rapids** once precluded river travel. No longer—now St-Laurent and Montréal harbor cruises depart from Victoria Pier (842-3871) in Vieux Montréal (mid-May-mid-Oct., 4 per day, 2 hr., $18.75). Tours of the Lachine Rapids (284-9607) leave five times per day (May-Sept. 10am-6pm; ½-hr. cruise $45, seniors $40, ages 13-18 $35, ages 6-12 $25).

Explore the **West Island,** formerly the summer residence for affluent city dwellers, by bike (along the Lachine Canal) or by bus (#211 from Lionel Groulx). Walk along the boardwalk in Ste. Anne de Bellevue and watch the River locks in action. The local crowd rocks Ste. Anne's at night, at one of the many *brasseries,* or the renowned **Annie's** and **Quai Sera.**

NIGHTLIFE AND ENTERTAINMENT

Should you choose to ignore the massive neon lights flashing "films érotiques" and "Château du sexe," you can find true nightlife in Québec's largest city—either in **brasseries** (with food as well as beer, wine, and music) or in **pubs** (with more hanging out and less eating). Downstairs at 1107, rue Ste-Catherine Ouest, for example, is **Peel Pub** (844-6769; see listing in Food, above), providing live rock bands and good, cheap food nightly. Here waiters rush about with three pitchers of beer in each hand to keep up with the mötley crüe of Montréal's university students; this pub has another location on boul. de Maisonneuve as well.

For slightly older and more subdued drinking buddies, search the side streets of rue Ste-Catherine Ouest. Try the English strongholds around **rue Crescent** and **rue Bishop** (Métro: Guy), where bar-hopping is a must. **Déjà-Vu,** 1224, Bishop near Ste-Catherine (866-0512), has live bands each night. (Open daily 3pm-3am; happy hour 3-10pm. No cover.) Set aside Thursday for a night at **D.J.'s Pub,** 1443, Crescent (287-9354), when $12 gets you 12 mixed drinks. (Open 11:30am-3am.) **Sir Winston Churchill's** is another hotspot. (Open daily 11:30am-3am.) For an eclectic scene, head down to St-Laurent. The trendy and chic mingle at **DiSalvio's,** 3519 St-Laurent (if they are allowed in), **The Opera,** or **The Shed Café.** University students hang at **Angel's.** True beer drinkers/pool-players frequent either **Bar St-Laurent** or **Biftèque** farther down on St-Laurent. French nightlife parleys in the open air cafés on **rue St-Denis** (Métro: UQAM). Stop in for live jazz at **Le Grand Café,** 1720, rue St-Denis (849-6955; open daily 11am-3:30am; evening cover $5-10). While in the Latin Quarter, scout out energetic **rue Prince Arthur,** which vacuum-packs Greek, Polish, and Italian restaurants into its tiny volume. Here maître-d's stand in front of their restaurants and attempt to court you toward their cuisine. Street performers and colorful wall murals further enliven this ethnic neighborhood. The accent changes slightly at **avenue Duluth,** where Portuguese and Vietnamese establishments prevail. Vieux Montréal, too, is best seen at night. Street performers, artists, and *chansonniers* in various *brasseries* set the tone for lively summer evenings of clapping, stomping, and singing along; the real fun goes down on St-Paul, in the *brasseries* near the corner of St-Vincent. For a sweet Sunday in the park, saunter over to **Parc Jeanne-Mance** for bongos, dancing and handicrafts (May-Sept. noon-7pm).

The city bubbles with a wide variety of theatrical groups: the **Théâtre du Nouveau Monde,** 84, Ste-Catherine Ouest (861-0563; Métro: Place-des-Arts), and the **Théâtre du Rideau Vert,** 4664, rue St-Denis (844-1793), stage *québecois* works (all productions in French). For English language plays, try the **Centaur Theatre,** 453, rue St-François-Xavier (288-3161; Métro: Place-d'Armes), whose season runs mainly

Oct.-June. The city's exciting **Place des Arts,** 260, boul. de Maisonneuve Ouest (842-2112 for tickets), houses the **Opéra de Montréal** (985-2222), the **Montréal Symphony Orchestra** (842-3402), and **Les Grands Ballets Canadiens** (849-8681). **The National Theatre School of Canada,** 5030, rue St-Denis (842-7954), stages excellent student productions during the academic year. **Théâtre Saint-Denis,** 1594, rue St-Denis (849-4211), hosts traveling productions like *Cats* and *Les Misérables.* Check the *Calendar of Events* (available at the tourist office and reprinted in daily newspapers), or call **Ticketmaster** (790-2222) for tickets and further info.

Montréalais are rabid sports fans, and there's opportunity aplenty for like-minded visitors to foam at the mouth. During the second weekend in June, the **Circuit Gilles-Villeneuve** on the Ile Notre-Dame hosts the annual **Molson Grand Prix,** a Formula 1 race (392-0000), and this August, as in every other August, **Tennis Canada** will host the world's best tennis players at Jarry Park (Métro: De Castelnau; 273-1515 for info and tickets.) The **Expos,** Montréal's baseball team, swing in Olympic Stadium (see address in Sights above; for Expos info call 253-3434).

Montréalais don't just watch: their one-day **Tour de l'île** is the largest participatory cycling event in the world, with a 40,000-member fan club attending. (Call 847-8687 to see how you can attend, too.) A trip to Montréal between Oct.-April is incomplete without attending a **Montréal Canadiens** hockey game: the **Montréal Forum,** 2312, Ste-Catherine Ouest (Métro: Atwater), is the shrine to hockey and **Les Habitants** (nickname for the Canadiens) are its acolytes. In 1993 they roughed-up everyone and sailed home with the Stanley Cup. Games are usually sold out, so call for tickets as early as possible. (For more info, call 932-2582.)

■■■ QUEBEC CITY

Québec is Canada's oldest city, and its citizens gleefully steep themselves in their history; fully staffed, admission-charging, tour-giving historic sites rear their heads everywhere you look. Built on the rocky heights of Cape Diamond, where the Fleuve St-Laurent narrows and joins the St. Charles River in northeast Canada, the city has been called the "Gibraltar of America" because of the stone escarpments and military fortifications protecting the port. Steeping themselves so gleefully in their cultural history, it is surely cause for wonder—and for pleasure—that the *Québecois* and their city can retain such vitality, energy, and *joie de vivre.* The best times to sample this are during the summer arts festival in mid-July and February's winter carnival, a raucous French-Canadian Mardi Gras.

PRACTICAL INFORMATION

Emergency: Police, 691-6911 (city); 623-6262 (provincial). **Info-santé:** 648-2626, 24 hr. service with info from qualified nurses.

Visitor Information: Centre d'information de l'office du tourisme et des congrés de la communauté urbaine de Québec, 60, rue d'Auteuil (692-2471), in the Old City. Visit here for accommodation listings, brochures, free maps (look for the one with a black cover, on the wall with the brochures), and friendly bilingual advice. Free local calls. Open June-Labor Day daily 8:30am-8pm; April-May and Sept.-Oct. Mon.-Fri. 8:30am-5:30pm; off-season Mon.-Fri. 8:30am-5pm. **Maison du tourisme de Québec,** 12, rue Ste-Anne (800-363-7777), deals specifically with provincial tourism, distributing accommodation listings for the entire province and free road and city maps. Some bus tours and Budget (see Car Rental below) also have desks. Open 8:30am-7:30pm; Labor Day-mid-June 9am-5pm.

Youth Tourist Information: Boutique Temps-Libre of Regroupement tourisme jeunesse 2700, boul. Laurier, in Ste-Foy (651-7108), in the Place Laurier. Sells maps, travel guides and equipment, ISICs and HI-C memberships, and health insurance. Can also make reservations at any hostel in the province of Québec, or you can do it yourself by calling 800-461-8585 with a credit card. (Open Mon.-Wed. 9:30am-5:30pm, Thurs.-Fri. 9:30am-9pm, Sat. 9:30am-5pm, Sun. noon-5pm.)

Airlines: Air Canada (692-0770 or 800-361-7413) and **Inter-Canadian** (692-1031). Special deals available for youths under 21 (with ID) willing to go standby and fly only in Canada. The airport is way, way out of town with no quick way, if any, to get there by public transport. By car, turn right onto Rte. de l'aéroport and then take either boul. Wilfred-Hamel or, beyond it, Autoroute 440 to get into the city. **Maple Leaf Sightseeing Tours** (649-9226) runs a shuttle service between the airport and the city's major hotels (Mon.-Fri. 5 per day, 8am-5:30pm, Sat.-Sun. 3 per day, 10am-3pm; $7.50).

Trains: VIA Rail Canada, 450, rue de la Gare du Palais in Québec City (524-6452); 3255, ch. de la Gare in Ste-Foy (658-8792); 5995, St-Laurent Autoroute 20 Lévis (833-8056). Call 800-361-5390 anywhere in Canada or the U.S. for reservations and info. To: Montréal (3 per day; 3 hr.; $39, students $35; 50% discounts if booked at least 5 days in advance and not traveling on Fri., Sun., or a holiday).

Buses: Voyageur Bus, 225, boul. Charest Est (524-4692). Open daily 5:30am-1am. Outlying stations at 2700, ave Laurier, in Ste-Foy (651-7015; open daily 6am-midnight), and 63, Hwy. Trans-Canada Ouest (Hwy. 132), in Lévis (837-5805; open Mon.-Fri. 6:30am-11pm, Sat.-Sun. 7am-11pm). To Montréal (every hr. 6am-9pm and 11pm, 3 hr., $34.50) and Ste-Anne-de-Beaupré (2 per day, $5). Connections to U.S. cities via Montréal or Sherbrooke.

Public Transport: Commission de transport de la Communauté Urbaine de Québec (CTCUQ), 270, rue des Rocailles (627-2511 for route and schedule info; open Mon.-Fri. 7am-9:30pm, Sat.-Sun. 8:30am-9:30pm; for lost objects, call 622-7412). Buses operate daily 5:30am-12:30am although individual routes vary. Fare $1.80, seniors and children under 4 feet 6 inches $1.25.

Taxis: Coop Taxis Québec, 525-5191. $2.25 initial charge, $1 each additional km.

Driver/Rider Service: Allo-Stop, 467, rue St-Jean (522-0056) will match you with a driver heading for Montréal ($15) or Ottawa ($29). Must be a member ($6). Open Mon.-Wed. 9am-5pm, Thurs.-Fri. 9am-7pm, Sat. 10am-5pm, Sun. 10am-7pm.

Car Rental: Pelletier, 900, boul. Pierre Bertrand (681-0678). $33 per day; unlimited km, $15 insurance. Must be 25 with credit card deposit of $300. (Open Mon.-Fri. 7:30am-8pm, Sat.-Sun. 8am-5pm).

Help Lines: Tél-Aide, 683-2153. Open Sun.-Thurs. noon-midnight, Fri.-Sat. noon-2am. **Viol-Secours** (sexual assault line), 692-2252.

Post Office: 3, rue Buade (648-4686). Open Mon.-Fri. 8am-5:45pm. **Postal Code:** G1R 2J0. Another location at 300 rue St-Paul (648-3340). **Postal code:** G1K 3W0.

Area Code: 418.

Québec's main thoroughfares, both in the Old City (*Vieux Québec*) and outside it, all tend to run parallel to each other in a roughly east-west direction. Within **Vieux Québec,** the main streets are **St-Louis, Ste-Anne,** and **St-Jean.** Most streets in Vieux Québec are one way, the major exception being rue d'Auteuil, bordering the walls, which is the best bet for parking during the busy times of day. Outside the walls of Vieux Québec, both St-Jean and St-Louis continue (St-Louis becomes **Grande Allée**). **Boul. René-Lévesque,** the other major street outside the walls, runs between them. *La Basse-ville* (lower town) is separated from *la Haute-ville* (upper town) by an abrupt cliff which is roughly paralleled by rue St-Vallier Est.

ACCOMMODATIONS AND CAMPING

Québec City now has two B&B referral services. Contact Michelle Paquet-Rivière at **B&B Bonjour Québec,** 450, rue Champlain, Québec G1K 4J3 (524-0524) for lodgings throughout the city, city maps, and descriptions of houses. (Singles $42-52, doubles $55-85.) **Gîte Québec** offers similar services. Contact Thérèse Tellier, 3729, ave Le Corbusier, Ste-Foy, Québec G1W 4R8 (651-1860). (Singles $30-40, doubles $60-70; call 8am-1pm or after 6pm.) Hosts are usually bilingual, and the B&B services inspect the houses for cleanliness and convenience of location.

You can obtain a list of nearby campgrounds from the Maison du Tourisme de Québec (see Practical Information), or by writing Tourisme Québec, c.p. 20,000 Québec, Québec G1K 7X2 (800-363-7777, open daily 9am-5pm).

Centre international de séjour HI-C, 19, Ste-Ursule (694-0755), between rue St-Jean and Dauphine. Follow Côte d'Abraham uphill from the bus station until it joins Ave Dufferin. Turn left on St-Jean, pass through the walls, and walk uphill, to your right, on Ste-Ursule. If you're driving, follow St-Louis into the Old City, and take the second left past the walls onto Ste-Ursule. The rooms are cramped, but a friendly staff, youthful clientele, and fabulous location should make it your first choice. Laundry machines, microwave, TV, pool and ping-pong tables, living room, kitchen (open 7:30am-9:30pm), cafeteria in basement; breakfast served 7:30-10am ($3.50). Check-out 11am, new check-ins starting at noon. Doors lock at 11pm, but front desk will let you in if you flash your key. One bed in a 2-bed room $16, in a 4-to 8-person room $14, in an 8- to 16-person room $11; nonmembers pay $3 more, kids under 8 free; ages 8-13 $7. HI-C memberships sold. Usually full July-Aug.; make reservations or arrive early.

Auberge de la Paix, 31, rue Couillard (694-0735). Has neither the activity nor the facilities of the Centre; stay here when the Centre's full. Both offer great access to the restaurants and bars on rue St-Jean. Rooms a bit smaller and mattresses a bit better than the Centre; rooms are co-ed; 56 beds, 2-8 beds per room, most have 3-4. Curfew 2am. $15. Breakfast of toast, cereal, coffee, and juice included (8-10am). Kitchen open all day. Linen $2. Make reservations July-Aug.

Montmartre Canadien, 1675, ch. St-Louis, Sillery (681-7357), on the outskirts of the city, in the Maison du Pelerin; a small white house behind the main building at 1671. Take bus #25 or #1. Clean house in a religious sanctuary overlooking the Fleuve St-Laurent. Relaxed, almost ascetic, setting—don't expect to meet tons of exciting new people here. Mostly used by groups. Run by Assumptionist monks. Common showers. Dorm-style singles $15. Doubles $26. Triples $36. Bed in 7-person dormitory $11; groups of 20 or more, $13. Breakfast (eggs, cereal, bacon, and pancakes) $3.50. Reserve 2-3 weeks in advance.

Manoir La Salle, 18, rue Ste-Ursule (692-9953), opposite the youth hostel. Clean private rooms fill up quickly, especially in the summer. Reservations necessary. Cat-haters beware: felines stalk the halls. Singles $25-30; doubles $40-55 depending on bed-size and shower/toilet status.

Maison Demers, 68, rue Ste-Ursule GIR 4E6 (692-2487), up the road from the youth hostel. Clean, comfortable rooms with TV and live conversation with Jean-duc Demers; all rooms have a sink, some have a private bath. Singles $30-32, doubles with shower $42-65, 2-bed, 4-person room $70. Breakfast of coffee and fresh croissants included. Parking available. Reservations recommended.

Camping Canadien, rue Ancienne-Lorette (872-7801). Sites $16.50, with hookup $18.50. Showers, laundry. Open May 15-Oct. 15. Take Autoroute 73 out of the city to Boul. Wilfred-Hamel, and follow signs.

Municipal de Beauport, Beauport (666-2228). Take Autoroute 40 east, exit #321 at rue Labelle onto Hwy. 369, turn left, and follow signs marked "camping." Ask the tourist office about buses to Beauport and enjoy this campground overlooking the Montmorency River. Swimming pool, volleyball courts ($2), and canoes ($6 per hr.) are available. Showers, laundry. 128 sites. $14, with hookup $19; weekly $81 and $120, respectively. Open June-early Sept.

FOOD AND NIGHTLIFE

In general, rue Buade, St-Jean, and Cartier, as well as the **Place Royale** and **Petit Champlain** areas offer the widest selection of food and drink. The **Grande Allée,** a 2-km-long strip of nothing but restaurants on both sides, might seem like heaven to the hungry, but its steep prices (except for a few havens—see the Vieille Maison du Spaghetti below) make it a place to visit rather than to eat. Go here to stare at the funny people drinking beer out of glasses so tall they need a wooden support to stand up. One of the most filling yet inexpensive meals is a *croque monsieur,* a large, open-faced sandwich with ham and melted cheese (about $5), usually served with salad. Be sure to try *québecois* French onion soup, slathered with melted cheese, and generally served with bats of French bread. Also try *aux pois* (pea soup) and *tourtière,* a thick meat pie. Other specialties include the French *crêpe,* stuffed differently for either main course or dessert, and the French-Canadian "sugar pie," made with brown sugar and butter. Don't be fooled into thinking that your best bet for a simple and affordable meal is to line up behind one of the many fast-food joints which proliferate throughout the city. Instead experience culinary excellence at the **Pâtisserie au Palet d'Or**, 60, rue Garneau (692-2488), where $2.75 will get you a salmon sandwich and $1.50 a crisp, golden baguette. Open Mon.-Thurs. 7:30am-7pm, Fri.-Sun. 7:30am-8pm. Remember that some of these restaurants do *not* have non-smoking sections.

For those doing their own cooking, **J.A. Moisan**, 699, rue St-Jean (522-8268) sells groceries in an old country-style store. Open daily 9am-10pm. **Dépanneurs** are Québec's answer and challenge to the corner store. Besides milk, bread, and snack food, they'll also sell you booze.

Chez Temporel, 25, rue Couillard (694-1813). If you want to stay off the tourist path while staying on the budget course, try this genuine *café Québecois* discretely tucked in a side alley off rue St-Jean. Besides the usual café staples—coffee served in a bowl ($2), sandwiches ($2.50), and croissants ($1.50)—it offers exotic coffee and liquor drinks ($4.50). You can sip Irish coffee while listening to Edith Piaf. Open Sun.-Thurs. 7am-1:30am, Fri.-Sat. 7am-2:30am.

La Vieille Maison du Spaghetti, 625, Grande Allée Est or 40, rue Marché Champlain. Both in the Petit-Champlain quarter close to the Place Royale. Great, fresh Italian food in a perfect setting—red tablecloths and wine glasses at each table. Spaghetti with tangy sauces ($7-9.50) and pizzas with intricate toppings ($8-10) automatically come with a skimpy salad bar, bread, and tea or coffee. If you can't decide between the two, chose the combo "maison," a somewhat smaller pizza with a portion of spaghetti ($9). Open Sun.-Thurs. noon-10pm, Fri.-Sat. noon-11pm.

La Fleur de Lotus, 38, Côte de la Fabrique (692-4286), across from the Hôtel de Ville. Cheerful and unpretentious. Thai, Cambodian, Vietnamese, and Japanese dishes $7.75-14. Open Mon.-Wed. 11:30am-10:30pm, Thurs.-Fri. 11:30am-11pm, Sat. 5-11pm, Sun. 5-10:30pm.

Café Méditerranée, 64, boul. René Lévesque (648-1849 lunchtime; 648-0768 dinner). Take the #25 bus or walk for about 10 min. outside the walls. Elegant surroundings for a Mediterranean buffet. Enjoy vegetable platters, *couscous,* spicy chicken dishes—or all 3: the ideal, filling lunch. Soup, dessert, coffee, and as much as you want for a main meal for $7.50 (lunch) or $15 (dinner). Open Mon.-Thurs. 11:30am-2:30pm, Fri.-Sat. 6-10pm, Sun. 10am-2:30pm. The buffet depletes quickly, so arrive early. Reservations recommended.

Mille-Feuille, 32, rue Ste-Angèle (692-2147). Vegetarian meals ($5-7) served in a chic restaurant with an outdoor terrace to match. Try *tourtière* or vegetable quiche ($4). Open daily 9am-11pm.

Restaurant Liban, 23, rue d'Auteuil, off rue St-Jean (694-1888). Great café for lunch or a late-night bite. Tabouli and hummus plates $3.25, both with pita bread. Excellent felafel ($4) and a fantastic variety of baklava. Open for coffee at 10am, for meals 11am-4am.

Café Ste-Julie, 865, rue des Zouaves off St-Jean (647-9368). No frills lunch-counter joint with specials scrawled on the walls—breakfast (2 eggs, bacon, coffee, toast, beans) $3.50; lunch (2 cheeseburgers, fries, and a soft drink) $4.25. Open daily 8:30am-5am.

Les Couventines, 1124, rue St-Jean (692-4850). The upscale version of the Casse-Crêpe next door, serving genuine—yet ecological—French crêpes in a quiet, elegant dining room. Accompany a traditional *crêpe au beurre* ($1.80) or egg, ham, and cheese crêpe ($5.75) with a glass of imported Kerisac *cidre* ($2.25). Open Tues.-Sun. 11am-11pm.

Numerous boisterous nightspots line rue St-Jean. Duck into any of these establishments and linger over a glass of wine or listen to some *québecois* folk music. Most don't have cover charges and close around 3am. The Grande Allée's many restaurants are interspersed with a number of *Bar Discothèques,* the *Québecois'* equivalent of a dance club. **Chez Dagobert,** 600 Grande Allée (522-0393), saturates its two dance floors with mainstream dance music while the sedentary listen to a live orchestra downstairs (open daily 9pm-3am, no cover). **Vogue,** 1170, ave d'Artigany (647-2100), right off the Grande Allée, features slightly more alternative musical choices (open daily 9:30pm-3am, no cover). If you are looking for an evening more in tune with Québec's traditional culture, go to **Les Yeux Bleux,** 117½, rue St-Jean (694-9118), a local favorite where *chansonniers* perform nightly (open daily 8pm-3am, no cover). A more alternative approach to burning the midnight oil can be found at **La Fourmi Atomik,** 33, rue d'Autreuil (694-1463). La Fourmi features underground rock dating from 1960 to 1999 in a black-, white-, and grey-graffitied decor. Monday is reggae only and Wednesday is rap only (open 8:30am-3am, Oct.-May 2pm-3am, no cover). At **L'Ostradamus,** 29, rue Couillard (694-9560) you can listen to live jazz and intellectual conversations in a smoke-drenched pseudo-spiritual and artsy Thai decor (open daily 4pm-3am, $2-5 cover when band is playing).

SIGHTS

Confined within walls built by the English, *Vieux Québec* (Old City) holds most of the city's historic attractions. Though monuments are clearly marked and explained, you'll get more out of the town with the tourist office's *Greater Québec Area Tourist Guide* which contains a walking tour of the Old City. (Available from all 3 tourist offices listed in Practical Information above.) It takes one or two days to explore Vieux Québec on foot, but you'll learn more than on the many guided bus tours. Take the time to hang out with the corpses in **St-Mathieu Cemetery,** 755, rue St-Jean, and to stumble past monuments such as the one commemorating the first patent issued in Canada.

Begin your walking tour of Québec City by climbing uphill to the top of **Cap Diamant** (Cape Diamond), just south of the **Citadelle.** From here take Promenade des Gouverneurs downhill to **Terrasse Dufferin.** Built in 1838 by Lord Durham, this popular promenade offers excellent views of the Fleuve St-Laurent, the Côte de Beaupré (the "Avenue Royale" Highway), and Ile d'Orléans across the Channel. The promenade passes the landing spot of the European settlers, marked by the **Samuel de Champlain Monument,** where Champlain built Fort St-Louis in 1620, securing the new French settlement. Today, the promenade is a favorite location for performers of all flavors—clowns, bagpipers, and banjo and clarinette duos alike. A *funiculaire* (692-1132; operates June-Labor Day daily 8am-midnight; $1, under 6 free) connects Upper Town with the Lower Town and Place Royale.

At the bottom of the promenade, towering above the *terrasse* next to rue St-Louis, you'll find **le Château Frontenac,** built on the ruins of two previous *châteaux.* The immense, baroque Frontenac was built in 1893 by the Canadian Pacific Company and has developed into a world-renowned luxury hotel. Named for Comte Frontenac, governor of *Nouvelle-France,* the château was the site of two historic meetings between Churchill and Roosevelt during WWII. Although budget travelers must forego staying here, the hoi polloi can still enter the grand hall and browse in its small shopping mall.

Near Château Frontenac, between rue St-Louis and rue Ste-Anne, lies the **Place d'Armes.** The *calèches* (horse-drawn buggies) that congregate here in summer provide atmosphere, and especially strong scents in muggy weather; a carriage will give you a tour of the city for $56, but your feet will do the same for free, and hopefully without the smell. From the Place d'Armes, the pedestrian and artist-ridden rue du Trésor leads to rue Buade where stands the **Notre-Dame Basilica** (692-2533). The clock and outer walls date back to 1647; the rest of the church has been rebuilt twice (most recently after a fire in 1922). (Open daily 6:30am-6pm. Tours in multiple languages, mid-May-mid-Oct. daily 9am-4:30pm.) An ornate gold altar and a sky painted on the ceiling help worshippers reach their God (freely, but in mysterious ways). At night, three giant screens magically appear on the Basilica's walls for a 3D historical and cultural **sound and light show** (daily at 6:30, 7:45, and 9pm; Oct.-May twice a week; tickets $5, ages 12-17 $3, under 12 free.) Notre-Dame, with its odd mix of architectural styles, contrasts sharply with the adjacent **Seminary of Québec,** founded in 1663, which stands as an excellent example of 17th-century *québecois* architecture. At first a Jesuit boot camp, the seminary became the *Université de Laval* in 1852, later moving to Ste-Foy. The **Musée du Séminaire,** 9, rue de l'Université (692-2843), lurks nearby. (Open daily 10am-5:30pm; Oct.-May Tues.-Sun. 10am-5pm; $3, seniors $2, students $1.50, under 16 $1.)

The **Musée du Fort,** 10, rue Ste-Anne (692-2175), presents a sound and light show that narrates the history of Québec City and the series of six battles fought to control it. (Open daily 10am-6pm; $4.25, seniors and students $2.75.)

The **Post Office,** 3, rue Buade, now called **The Louis St-Laurent Building** (after Canada's second French Canadian Prime Minister) was built in the late 1890s and towers over a statue of Monseigneur de Laval, the first bishop of Québec. Across the Côte de la Montagne, a lookout park provides an impressive view of the Fleuve St-Laurent. A statue of Georges-Etienne Cartier, one of the key French-Canadian Fathers of Confederation, presides over the park.

Walk along rue St-Louis to see its 17th- and 18th-century homes. The surrender of Québec to the British occurred in 1759 at **Maison Kent,** 25, rue St-Louis, built in 1648. The Québec government now uses and operates the house. At the end of rue St-Louis is **Porte St-Louis,** one of the oldest entrances to the fortified city.

Walk down Côte de la Montagne and negotiate the *casse-cou* staircase ("breakneck"—but the stairs don't live up to the name), or take the *funiculaire* down to the oldest section of Québec. Either way leads to **rue Petit-Champlain,** the oldest road in North America. Many of the old buildings that line the street have been restored or renovated and now house cozy craft shops, boutiques, cafes, and restaurants. The **Café-Théâtre Le Petit Champlain,** 68, rue Petit-Champlain (692-2631), presents *québecois* music, singing, and theater.

From the bottom of the *funiculaire* you can also take rue Sous-le-Fort and then turn left to reach **Place Royale,** built in 1608, where you'll find the small but beautiful **l'Eglise Notre-Dame-des-Victoires** (692-1650), the oldest church in Canada, dating from the glorious year of 1688. (Open Mon.-Sat. 9am-4:30pm, closed on Sat. if a wedding is being held, Sun. 7:30am-4:30pm; Oct. 16-April Tues.-Sat. 9am-noon, Sun. 7:30am-1pm. Free.) The houses surrounding the square have undergone restoration to late 18th-century styles. Considered one of the birthplaces of French civilization in North America, the Place Royale now provides one of the best spots in the city to see outdoor summer theater and concerts. Also along the river stands the recently opened, ambitiously named **Musée de la Civilisation,** 85, rue Dalhousie (643-2158). A celebration of Québec's culture of past, present, and future, this thematic museum targets French Canadians, though English tours and exhibit notes are available. One permanent exhibit looks at communications, tingling the senses with giant phone booths, satellites, videos, and recreated moon landings. (Open late daily 10am-7pm; early Sept.-late June Tues.-Sun. 10am-5pm, Wed. 10am-9pm; $4.75, seniors $3.75, students $2.75.)

Outside The Walls

From the old city, the **promenade des Gouverneurs** and its 310 steps leads to the **Plains of Abraham** (otherwise known as the **Parc des Champs-de-Bataille**) and the **Citadelle** (648-3563). Hike or bike through the Plains of Abraham, site of the September, 1759 battle between General James Wolfe's British troops and General de Montcalm's French forces. Both leaders died during the decisive 15-min. confrontation, won by the British. A beautiful park, the Plains have since served as drill fields and the Royal Québec Golf Course. A **tourist reception center** (648-4071) at 390, ave des Berniéres, offers maps and pamphlets about the park (open Thurs.-Tues. 10am-5:45pm, except Wed. 10am-9:45pm). A magnificent complex, the **Citadelle** is the largest fortification still guarded by troops in North America, home to the Royal 22 Regiment (the "Van-Douze" in English parlance, from the French *vingt-deux-*

ième). Visitors can witness **the changing of the guard** (mid-June-Labor Day daily 10am) and the **beating of the retreat** (July-Aug. Tues. and Thurs., Sat.-Sun. 7pm). Tours are given every 55 min. (Citadelle open daily 9am-6pm; Labor-Day-Oct. and May-June 9am-4pm; mid-March-April 10am-3pm; Nov-mid-March open by reservation only. $4, ages 7-17 $2, disabled and under 7 free.)

At the far end of the Plains of Abraham you'll find the newly transformed **Musée du Québec**, 1, ave Wolfe-Montcalm, parc des Champs-de-Bataille (643-2150), which contains a collection of *québecois* paintings, sculptures, decorative arts, and prints. The Gérard Morisset pavilion, which greets you with the unlikely *mélange à trois* of Jacques Cartier, Neptune, and Gutenberg, houses a portion of the Musée's permanent collection, while the renovated old "prison of the plains," the Baillarce Pavilion, displays temporary exhibits. (Open Thurs.-Tues. 10am-6pm, Wed. 10am-10pm; Labor Day-mid May Tues. and Thurs.-Sun. 10am-6pm, Wed. 10am-10pm. Admission $4.75, seniors $3.75, students $2.75, disabled persons with companions $2.75, under 16 free. Free Wed.) At the corner of la Grande Allée and rue Georges VI, right outside Porte St-Louis, stands **l'Assemblée Nationale** (643-7239). Built in the style of French King Louis XIII's era and completed in 1886, the hall merits a visit. You can view debates from the visitors gallery; Anglophones and Francophones have recourse to simultaneous translation earphones. (Free 30-min. tours daily 9am-4:30pm; Labor-Day-late June Mon.-Fri. 9am-4:30pm. Call ahead to ensure a space.)

Locals follow the **Nordiques,** Québec's atrocious hockey team, with near-religious fanaticism; they play from Oct.-April in the Coliseum (For info, call 529-8441; for tickets, Nordtel 523-3333). The raucous **Winter Carnival** (626-3716), parties February 3-13, 1994. Québec's **Summer Festival** (692-4540; July 8-18, 1994) boasts a number of free outdoor concerts. The **Plein Art** (694-0260) exhibition of arts and crafts takes over the Pigeonnier on Grande-Allée in early August. **Les nuits Bleue** (849-7080), Québec's rapidly growing jazz festival, bebops the city for two weeks in late June. But the most festive day is June 24, **la Fête nationale du Québec** (Saint-Jean-Baptiste Day) (681-7011), a celebration of the *québecois* culture.

■ Near Québec City

Québec City's public transport system leaves the St-Laurent's **Ile-d'Orléans** untouched. The island's proximity to Québec (about 10km downstream), however, makes it an ideal short side trip by car or bicycle; take Autoroute 440 Est, and cross over at the only bridge leading to the island (Pont de l'Ile). A tour of the island covers 64km. Originally called *Ile de Bacchus* because of the plethora of wild grapes fermenting here, the Ile-d'Orléans still remains a sparsely populated retreat of several small villages, with strawberries its main crop. The **Manoir Mauvide-Genest**, 1451, ch. Royal (829-2630), dates from 1734. A private museum inside has a collection of crafts as well as traditional colonial furniture. (Open daily June 10am-5pm; July-Aug. 10am-8pm; Sept.-Oct. weekends; $3, ages 10-18 $1.50.)

Exiting Ile-d'Orléans, turn right (east) onto Hwy.138 (boul. Ste-Anne) to view the splendid **Chute Montmorency** (Montmorency Falls), which are substantially taller than Niagara Falls. In winter, the falls freeze completely and look, well, very frozen. About 20km (13 mi.) along 138 lies **Ste-Anne-de-Beaupré** (Voyageur buses link it to Québec City, $5). This small town's entire *raison d'être* seems to be the famous **Basilique Ste-Anne-de Beaupré,** 10018, ave Royale (827-3781). Since 1658, this double-spired basilica containing a Miraculous Statue and the alleged forearm bone of Saint Anne (the mother of the Virgin Mary) reportedly has pulled off miraculous cures. Every year, more than one million pious pilgrims trek here in the hopes that their prayers, gallstones, and mortgages will divinely be spirited away. (Open early May-mid-Sept. daily 8:30am-5pm.) Ask the tourist office about bike rentals in this scenic area. Go to Ste-Anne in the winter months (Nov.-April) for some of the best skiing in the province. (Lift tickets $38 per day.) Contact **Parc du Mont Ste-Anne,** P.O. Box 400, Beaupré, G0A IE0 (827-4561), which has a 625m/2050ft. vertical drop and night skiing to boot.

■ Ontario

First claimed by French explorer Samuel de Champlain in 1613, Ontario soon became the bastion of English influence within Canada. The British tentatively asserted control with a takeover of New France in 1763 during the French and Indian War; 20 years later, a flood of Loyalist emigrés from the newly-forged United States streamed into the province, fortifying its British character. To this day Ontario remains the standard bearer of English cultural hegemony within Canada, home to an ersatz Stratford and eminently Victorian Niagara-on-the-Lake.

Aside from being the most English, Ontario is also the most Americanized of the provinces. In the south you'll find world-class Toronto—American in that it is multi-cultural, enormous (3 million plus, by *far* the largest city in sparse Canada), and vibrant; un-American, perhaps, in that it is clean and safe as well. Surrounding this sprawling megalopolis are yuppified suburbs, the occasional beer-soaked college town, and farms. In the east, Ottawa sits on Ontario's frontier with Québec. Nowhere is the Canadian dichotomy more apparent than in this city where "Hi-Bonjour" is the most common greeting. Head further north, and the layers of cottage country and ski resorts will yield to true Canadian wilderness; land of national parks and beautiful lakes.

PRACTICAL INFORMATION

Capital: Toronto.
Ontario Ministry of Tourism and Recreation, 77 Bloor St. W., 9th floor, Toronto M7A 2R9 (800-668-2746; open daily 8am-6pm, Mon.-Fri. off-season). Free brochures, guides, maps, and info on upcoming special events.
Alcohol: Legal drinking age 19.
Time Zone: Eastern. **Postal Abbreviation:** ONT
Sales Tax: 8%, plus a 7% GST.

■■■ OTTAWA

Legend has it that Queen Victoria chose this capital of Canada by closing her eyes and poking her finger at a map. Whatever her real method, the choice of this once-remote logging settlement was an excellent compromise between French and English interests; moreover, the site's distance from the ever-expanding U.S. border added much-needed security. Today, Ottawa protects Canada not from the encroachments of the USA or from the harsh environs, but from the divisiveness of Canada itself: each of the provinces sends representatives to the capital with the increasingly tricky task of forging a national unity while preserving local identity.

The rough-hewn character of the city was not polished until the turn of the century, when Prime Minister Sir Wilfred Laurier, lamenting its appearance, called on urban planners to create a "Washington of the North." Nearly a century of conscientious grooming has left Ottawa with museums, cultural facilities, and parks which its counterpoint on the Potomac can seriously envy.

PRACTICAL INFORMATION

Emergency: (Police, Ambulance, Fire) 911. **Ontario Provincial Police:** 800-267-2677. **Ottawa Police:** infoline: 230-6211.
Visitor Information: National Capital Commission Information Center, 14 Metcalfe St. (239-5000, 800-465-1867 across Canada), at Wellington opposite Parliament Buildings. Open summer daily 8:30am-9pm; Sept. 3-May 5 Mon.-Sat. 9am-5pm, Sun. 10am-4pm. **Ottawa Tourism and Convention Authority Visitor Information Centre,** National Arts Centre, 65 Elgin St. (237-5158). Open summer daily 9am-9pm; Sept. 7-April 30 Mon.-Sat. 9am-5pm, Sun. 10am-4pm. Both

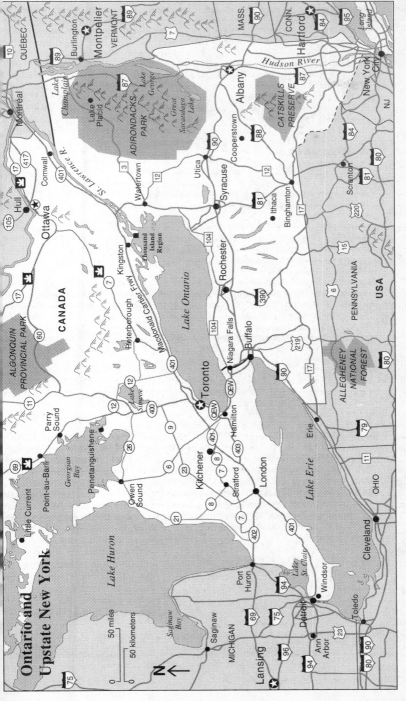

Ontario and Upstate New York

OTTAWA

provide free maps and a visitors guide to restaurants, hotels, and sights. Free 30-min. parking in the Arts Centre lot with ticket validation at the Visitor Centre. For info on the Hull region, turn to the **Association Touristique de l'Outaouais,** 25 rue Laurier, Hull, on the corner of rue Victoria (819-778-2222). Also has info on the entire province of Québec. Open mid-June-Sept. Mon.-Fri. 8:30am-8:30pm, Sat.-Sun. 9am-5pm; off-season Mon.-Fri. 8:30am-5pm.

Student Travel Agencies: Travel CUTS, 1 Stewart St., Suite #203 (238-8222) at Waller, just west of Nicholas or on the 1st level of the Unicentre, Carleton Univ. (238-5493). Experts in student travel: youth hostel cards, cheap flights, VIA Rail and Eurail passes. Open Mon.-Tues. and Thurs.-Fri. 9am-5pm, Wed. 9am-4:30pm. **Hostelling International-Canada (HI-C), Ontario East Region,** 18 Byward Market (230-1200). Eurail and youth hostel passes, travel info and equipment. Open Mon.-Fri. 9:30am-6pm, Sat. 9:30am-5pm.

Embassies: U.S., 100 Wellington St. (238-5335), directly across from Parliament. Open for info daily 9am-5pm. **U.K.,** 80 Elgin St. (237-1530), at the corner of Queen. Open for info Mon.-Fri. 8:30am-5pm. **Australia,** 50 O'Connor St. (236-0841), at Queen St., suite 710. Open Mon.-Fri. 9am-noon and 2-4pm for visas and info. **South Africa,** 15 Sussex Dr. (744-0330). Open Mon.-Fri. 8:30am-4:30pm for visas and info. **New Zealand,** 99 Bank St. (238-5991). Open for info Mon.-Fri. 8:30am-4:30pm.

American Express: 220 Laurier W. (563-0231), between Metcalfe and O'Connor in the heart of the business district. Open Mon.-Fri. 8:30am-5pm. In case of lost Traveler's Cheques, call 800-221-7282; for lost cards call 800-268-9805.

Airport: Ottawa International Airport (998-3151), 20 min. south of the city off Bronson Ave. Take bus #96 from Le Breton station, Albert St. at Booth, or Slater St. for regular fare. Tourist info available daily 8:30am-9:30pm in arrival area. Express airport **Pars Transport** buses (523-8880) from Lord Elgin Hotel, 100 Elgin Blvd. at Slater, and 10 other hotels including the Delta, the Westin and the Château Laurier. Pick-up from 14 other hotels can be arranged by phone. Fare $9, ages 7-12 $5, under 7 free. Daily every ½-hr. 5am-1am. Call for later pick-up and schedule specifics. Service from airport too. **Air Canada** (237-1380) has student standby rates for those under 21 with ID. **Delta** (236-0431) has youth fares for ages 12-21 on transatlantic flights.

VIA Rail Station: 200 Tremblay Rd. (244-8289 for reservations or recorded departure info), off Alta Vista Rd. To: Montréal (4 per day, 2 hr., $32, student $29); Toronto (4 per day, 4 hr., $69/$62). To Québec City, must travel via Montréal ($62/$56). There is a 40% discount for reservations 5 days in advance for students while tickets last, for adults traveling Sat. or Mon.-Thurs. Ticket office open Mon.-Fri. 5am-9pm, Sat. 6:30am-9pm, Sun. 8:30am-9pm.

Voyageur Bus: 265 Catherine St. (238-5900), between Kent and Lyon. Service throughout Canada. To: Montréal (18 per day, 2½ hr., $24), Toronto (7 per day, 4½ hr., $51), Québec City (13 per day, 6 hr., $57). For service to the U.S. must first go to Montréal or Toronto; connections made through Greyhound. Open daily 5:30am-midnight. Tickets can be purchased at station only.

Public Transport: OC Transport, 1500 St. Laurent (741-4390). Excellent bus system. Buses congregate on either side of Rideau Centre. Fare $1.30, rush hour (3-5:30pm) $2, express routes (green buses) rates $2.60. Seniors $1.30 at all times. **Minipass** for a day of unlimited travel after 9am $3, plus 70¢ during peak hrs., under 5 free.

Taxi: Blue Line Taxi, 238-1111. **A-1,** 746-1616. Rates fixed by law ($2 plus distance and waiting). 24 hrs.

Car Rental: Hertz, 30 York St. in Byward Market (238-7681). $29 per day with unlimited km. Insurance $12 per day. Must be 21 with credit card. (Open Mon. 7am-7pm, Tues.-Wed. 7:30am-7pm, Thurs.-Fri. 7:30am-8pm, Sat.-Sun. 8am-6pm.) **Budget,** 443 Somerset W. at Kent (232-1526). $29 per day. 200km free, 14¢ each additional km. Insurance $12 per day. Must be 21 with credit card. (Open Mon.-Fri. 7am-7pm, Sat.-Sun. 8am-6pm.)

Rider/Driver Matching Agency: Allostop, 246 Maisonneuve at Verdun St., Hull (778-8877). To: Toronto ($24), Québec City ($29), Montréal ($10), and New York

($50). Membership ($6 per yr.) required. Open Mon.-Wed. 9am-5pm, Thurs.-Fri. 9am-7pm, Sat.-Sun. 10am-5pm.
Bike Rental: Rent-A-Bike-Location Velo, 1 Rideau St. (233-0268), behind the Château Laurier Hotel. $6 per hr., $18 per day. Family deals. Escorted tours for a price. Maps, locks free. Tandems available. Open mid-May-mid-Oct. daily 9am-8pm. Credit card required.
Alcohol: Legal ages 19 (Ottawa) and 18 (Hull). Bars stay open later in Hull.
Help Line: Gayline-Telegai, 238-1717. Info on local bars, special events and meetings, as well as counseling. Open Mon.-Thurs. 7:30-10:30pm, Fri.-Sun. 6-9pm. **Ottawa Distress Centre,** 238-3311, English-speaking. **Tel-Aide,** 741-6433, French-speaking. **Rape Crisis Centre,** 729-8889. All 3 lines 24 hrs.
Post Office: Postal Station "B," 59 Sparks St. at Elgin St. (844-1545). Open Mon.-Fri. 8am-6pm. **Postal Code:** K1P 5A0.
Area Code: 613 (Ottawa); 819 (Hull).

The **Rideau Canal** divides Ottawa into eastern and western sections. West of the canal, Parliament buildings and government offices line **Wellington Street,** one of the main east-west arteries. **Laurier** is the only other east-west street which permits traffic from one side of the canal to the other. East of the canal, Wellington St. becomes Rideau St., surrounded by a fashionable new shopping district. To the north of Rideau St. lies the **Byward Market,** a recently renovated shopping area and the focus of Ottawa's nightlife. **Elgin Street,** a primary north-south artery, stretches from the **Queensway (Hwy. 417)** to the War Memorial in the heart of the city in front of **Parliament Hill. Bank Street,** another main street, runs parallel to Elgin and services the town's older shopping area. The canal itself is a major access route: in winter, thousands of Ottawans skate to work on the world's longest skating rink; in summer, power boats breeze by. Bike paths and pedestrian walkways border the canals, allowing a pleasant alternative to car or bus transit. Parking is painful downtown; meters cost 25¢ for 10 minutes with a one-hour limit. Residential neighborhoods east of the canal have one-hour and three-hour limits and the police ticket less often than on main streets.

Across the Ottawa River lies **Hull,** Québec, most notable for its proximity to Gatineau Provincial Park and the many bars and clubs that rock nightly until 3am. Hull is accessible by several bridges and the blue Hull buses from downtown Ottawa.

ACCOMMODATIONS AND CAMPING

Clean, inexpensive rooms and campsites are not difficult to find in Ottawa, except during May and early June, when large groups may monopolize a certain area, or during July and August when the tourism season is at its peak. The area also boasts a number of B&Bs for those who can afford the extra expense. An extensive listing can be found in the *Ottawa Visitor Guide,* available at the National Capital Commission Info Center (see above); the guide also lists two referral services. The **Olde Bytown Bed & Breakfast,** 459 Laurier E., K1N 6R4 (565-7939), in one of Ottawa's wealthiest neighborhoods, is a 20-minute walk from downtown; 18 airy rooms in two old Ottawa houses overlook the **Strathcona Park.** Full English breakfast; afternoon high tea; free pick- up at train or bus station or airport. Especially welcoming to graduate students and summer interns for longer stays. Reservations recommended. Parking available (singles $50, doubles $65).

Ottawa International Hostel (HI-C), 75 Nicholas St. K1N 7B9 (235-2595), in downtown Ottawa. The site of Canada's last public hanging, this trippy hostel now "incarcerates" travelers in the former Carleton County Jail. The jailor on duty will assign you to a cell with 3-7 other prisoners. Hot communal showers, kitchen, laundry, large and comfortable lounges, and friendly, personable wardens. Due to the centrality of location, a funky international crowd, and a plethora of organized activities (bike, canoe, tours), you'll want to serve time here. All-day access; doors locked 2-7am. 150 beds. $14, nonmembers, $18. Spend 12 hours locked on the 8th floor and you'll get one night free.

University of Ottawa Residences, 100 University St. (564-5400), in the center of campus directly across from the University Center. Take bus #1, 7, or 11 on Bank St. to the Rideau Centre from the bus station and walk up Nicholas to the U of O campus, bus #95 west from the train station or the easy walk from downtown. Clean dorm rooms. Shared hall showers. Free local phone in hall. Check-in 4:30pm but they'll store your luggage until then. Linen, towels free. Access to university student center (with bank machines). Continental breakfast $2. Singles $31. Doubles $40. Students with ID: $19/$34. Open early May-late Aug.

YM/YWCA, 180 Argyle St. (237-1320), at O'Connor. Close to the bus station; walk left on Bank and right on Argyle. Nice-sized rooms in a modern high-rise. Phones in every room. Kitchen with microwave available until midnight. Guests can use gym facilities. Singles with shared bath $38, with private bath $40. Doubles $49.30. Weekly and group rates available. Payment must be made in advance. Cafeteria (breakfast $2.75) open Mon.-Fri. 7am-7pm, Sat.-Sun. 8am-2:30pm.

Centre Town Guest House Ltd., 502 Kent St. (233-0681), just north of the bus station, a 10- to 15-min. walk from downtown. Impeccably clean rooms in a friendly, comfortable house. Free breakfast (eggs, cereal, bacon, toast) in a cozy dining room. Singles $30. Doubles $35. 2 twin beds $40. Monthly rates from $400. Reservations recommended.

Camp Le Breton (943-0467), in a field at the corner of Fleet and Booth. Urban tent-only camping within sight of Parliament, a 15-min. walk from downtown. More of a football field with trees than a campsite. Washrooms, showers, free wood. 5-day max. stay. Check-in 24 hrs. Sites $7.50 per person, seniors $3.75, under 12 free. Reservations unnecessary—they'll squeeze you in.

Gatineau Park (reservations 456-3494; info 827-2020), northwest of Hull. Map available at visitors center. Three rustic campgrounds within 45 min. of Ottawa: **Lac Philippe Campground,** with facilities for family camping, trailers, and campers; **Lac Taylor Campground,** with 34 "semi-wilderness" sites; and **Lac la Pêche,** with 36 campsites accessible only by canoe. All campgrounds off Hwy. 366 northwest of Hull—watch for signs. From Ottawa, take the Cartier-Mac-Donald Bridge, follow Autoroute 5 north to Scott Rd., turn right onto Hwy. 105 and follow it to 366. To reach La Pêche continue on 366 to Eardley Rd. on your left. Camping permits for Taylor and Philippe available at the entrance to the campground. Pay for a site at La Pêche on Eardley Rd. June 14-Sept. 2 all sites $12, seniors $7; Sept. 3-Oct. 8 and May 15-June 13 $11, $5.50; off-season (some sites open at Lac Philippe) $3.

FOOD AND NIGHTLIFE

Look for restaurant/bars in Ottawa serving dirt-cheap food to lure you into their dens of high-priced beer. **Tramps,** 53 William St. (238-5523), serves 20¢ chicken wings daily after 4pm (open Mon.-Fri. 11am-1am, Sat.-Sun. 9am-1am). **Heart & Crown,** 67 Clarence St. (562-0674) offers 10¢ wings Mon.-Fri. 2-7pm (open daily 11am-1am). If it's cheap beer and not cheap food that you want, head to **Grand Central,** 141 George St. (233-1435), where the $1.50 draft is the cheapest in the Byward Market area. (Bands Thurs.-Sat., $1 cover when bands play. Open Mon-Sat. 11:30am-1am, Sun. 10:30am-1am.) During the day, fresh fruit, vegetable, and flower stands as well as occasional street musicians cluster at **Byward Market** on Byward between York and Rideau (open daily 8am-6pm).

Sunset Grill, 47 Byward St. (594-9497), at Parent St.. Sit on the huge outdoor terrace and grapple with the oh-my-God-it's-so-big "sunset beach club sandwich" ($8). The less ambitious appetite and wallet can tackle the "in a hurry-on a diet-or just broke" meal ($6). Open Sun.-Tues. 11am-10pm, Thurs.-Sat. 11am-1am.

Blue Cactus, 2 Byward Mkt. (238-7061), at Clarence, specializes in Tex-Mex dishes with an exotic twist. For a new experience, try the brie and papaya quesadilla ($8, at lunch $6). Their bowl of soup ($2.50) comes with two slices of Mexican bread and constitutes a hearty meal. Open Mon.-Wed. 11:30am-midnight, Thurs.-Sat. 11:30am-1am, Sun. 11:30am-11pm.

Bagel Bagel, 92 Clarence St. (236-8998). Simply savor one of their "they're sooooo good" bagels for 40¢ or be more adventurous and try the cream cheese and pesto ($3.75). Open Sun.-Wed. 6:30am-midnight, Thurs. 6:30am-2am, Fri.-Sat. 24 hrs.

Boko Bakery, 87 George St. (230-1417), in the Byward Market Mall, is a local favorite. The Boko's menu displays a very British blurb from the management which promises to maintain "olde-fashioned" methods of baking bread. Sit down and enjoy a breakfast special (7:30-11am): 2 eggs, ham, coffee, and croissant ($2.75); or go to the take-out counter and melt at the delicious aroma which wafts from freshly baked goods. Open Sun.-Fri. 7:30am-5pm, Sat. 7:30am-6pm.

Peel Pub, 62 William St. (562-PEEL/562-7335). You just can't beat the 99¢ breakfast: 2 eggs, toast, and bottomless coffee or tea (Mon.-Fri. 6:30-11:30am, Sat.-Sun. 6:30am-4:30pm). Good cheap specials daily. Open daily 6:30am-1am.

The International Cheese and Deli, 40 Byward St. (234-0783). Deli and Middle Eastern sandwiches to go. Vegetable *samosa* $1.25. Turkey and cheese $4, falafel on pita $2.30. Open Sat.-Thurs. 7:30am-6pm, Fri. 7:30am-8pm.

Father and Sons, 112 Osgoode St. (233-6066), at the eastern edge of the U of O campus. Student favorite for tavern-style food with some Lebanese dishes thrown in. Try the falafel platter ($6.50) or a triple decker sandwich ($6.50). Drink-encouraging specials daily 8-11pm: Mon.-Sat., 8-11pm wings 15¢, Thurs. shooters $2.50. Open daily 8am-1am, kitchen until midnight.

The dedicated nightlifer should descend into Hull, where most establishments grind and gnash until 3am every day of the week and the legal drinking age is 18. In Ottawa, the Byward Market area contains most of the action. Ottawa clubs close at 1am (many at 11pm on Sun.) but most, in an effort to keep people from going to Hull, offer free admission. **Stoney Monday's,** 62 York St. (236-5548), just west of William, is a trendy bar for people in their early to mid-20s. **Château Lafayette,** 42 York St. (233-3403), the oldest tavern in Ottawa, lures the budgeteer with $3 pints. The regulars are hard-core beer drinkers who hold their mugs with both hands, pound a beer, slam the mug down on the bar, and say "Mr. Keeper, I'll hava 'nuther." The management steadfastly refuses to serve hard liquor, upholding the noble tavern tradition. **Houlihan's,** 110 York St. (234-0950), spreads over two decks with the game room upstairs and the dancing room downstairs (dancing only when avid sports fans aren't crowding the dance floor for a glimpse at the hockey on TV). On Thursday, Sunday, and Monday $3 cover charge, but all drinks are $2. On Monday and Wednesday, all drinks are $2.75. (Open Mon.-Fri. 4pm-1am, Sat.-Sun. noon-1am.) For a taste of life, the universe, and a bit of everything, head to **Zaphod Beeblebrox,** 27 York in Byward Market, (562-1010), a popular alternative club with live bands Tuesday and Thurs.-Sat. nights. Be advised of one small hitch: the cover is usually hiked up to $5 on nights with bands. Famous for their $7 Pangalactic Gargle Blasters. (Open noon-1am daily.) Over 20 popular nightspots pack the **Promenade du Portage** in Hull, just west of Place Portage, the huge government office complex. **Le Coquetier** (771-6560), is one of the more peaceful places on the promenade to treat a friend to a "brewski" (open daily 11:30am-3am).

SIGHTS

Although overshadowed by Toronto's size and Montréal's cosmopolitan color, Ottawa's status as capital of Canada is shored up by its cultural attractions. Since the national museums and political action are packed in tightly, most sights can be reached on foot. **Parliament Hill,** on Wellington St. at Metcalfe, towers over downtown as the city's focal point, while its Gothic architecture sets it apart. Roast a marshmallow over the **Centennial Flame** at the south gate, lit in 1967 to mark the 100th anniversary of the Dominion of Canada's inaugural session of Parliament. The central parliament structure, **Centre Block,** contains the House of Commons, the Senate and the Library of Parliament and is where the recently-elected (elections were in Oct. 1993) reigning rookie Prime Minister can occasionally be spotted. The Library was the only part of the original (1859-66) structure to survive the 1916 fire. On display behind the library is the original bell from Centre Block, which, according to legend, crashed to the ground after chiming midnight on the night of the fire. Free, worthwhile tours in English and French depart every 10 min. from the Infotent. (Group reservations year-round 996-0896. Public information 992-4793. Open mid-May-early Sept. Mon.-Fri. 9am-8:30pm, Sat.-Sun. 9am-5:30pm; off season daily 9am-4:30pm. Last tour begins ½-hr. before closing time.) Watch Canada's Prime Minister and her government squirm on the verbal hot seat during the official **Question Period** in the House of Commons chamber (call 992-4793 for info on days and times; free). Far less lively or politically meaningful, the sessions of the **Senate of Canada** (992-4791) also welcome spectators. See (while you can) the body of "sober second thought," on which some Canadians are ready to lock the doors and throw away the gavel. After the tour, look up the **Peace Tower** and wonder what it would be like to hoist your body up those 293 ft. (the tower will be closed in 1994). The white marble **Memorial Chamber** honors Canadian war dead. Those interested in trying to make a number of statuesque soldiers giggle should attend the **Changing of the Guard** (993-1811),on the broad lawns in front of Centre Block (June 25-Aug. 29 daily at 10am, weather permitting). At dusk, Centre Block and lawns transform into the set for *Sound and Light,* which relates the history of the Parliament Buildings and the development of the nation (early May-early June Wed.-Sat.; early June-early Sept. daily. May-July 9:30 and 10:30pm; Aug.-Sept. 9 at 10pm also). Catch the carillon concerts that chime most Tuesdays and Wednesdays in the summer from 8 to 9pm (992-4793; dates due to change). A 5-min. walk west along Wellington St. is the **Supreme Court of Canada** (995-5361), where nine justices preside. Worthwhile 30-minute tours of the Federal Court and the Supreme Court, both housed in this building, are offered. (Open daily 9am-5pm; off-season Mon.-Fri. 9am-5pm. Free.) One block south of Wellington, Sparks St. greets one of North America's first pedestrian malls, hailed as an innovative experiment in 1960. The **Sparks Street Mall** recently received a $5-million facelift, rejuvenating many of Ottawa's banks and upscale retail stores. The **Rideau Centre,** south of Rideau St. at Sussex Dr., is the city's primary shopping mall as well as one of the main OC Transport stations. The sidewalks in front of Rideau Street's numerous stores are enclosed by glass, making them bearable during the cold winter months.

East of the Parliament Buildings at the junction of Sparks, Wellington, and Elgin stands **Confederation Square,** its enormous **National War Memorial** dedicated by King George VI in 1939. The towering structure symbolizes the triumph of peace over war, an ironic message on the eve of WWII. **Nepean Point** (239-5000), several blocks northwest of Rideau Centre and the Byward Market behind the National Gallery of Canada, provides a panoramic view of the capital.

Parks and Museums

Ottawa is pleasantly unaffected by the traditionally urban vices of pollution and violent crime; a multitude of parks and recreational areas will make you forget you're in a city at all. **Gatineau Park** extends 350 sq. km into the northwest and is a favorite destination for Ottawans who want to cycle, hike, or fish. Half a league onward within stands a relic from the Crimean War, the **Noon Day Gun,** which fires Monday through Friday at (you guessed it) noon. **Dow's Lake** (232-1001), accessible by means of the Queen Elizabeth Parkway, is an artificial lake on the Rideau Canal, 15 minutes south of Ottawa. Pedal boats, canoes, and bikes are available at the Dow's Lake Pavilion, just off Queen Elizabeth Parkway.

The Governor-General, the Queen's representative in Canada, opens the grounds of **Rideau Hall,** his official residence, to the public. Tours leave from the main gate at One Sussex Dr. (Call 998-7113, 998-7114 or 800-465-6890 for tour info; free.) At nearby **24 Sussex Drive** you'll find the official residence of the Prime Minister.

Gawk from afar or use a scope; you can't get any closer to the building than the main gates.

Ottawa headquarters many of Canada's huge national museums. **The National Gallery,** 380 Sussex Dr. (990-1985), in a spectacular glass-towered building adjacent to Nepean Point, contains the world's most comprehensive collection of Canadian art, as well as outstanding European, American, and Asian works. The building's exterior is a postmodern parody of the facing neo-Gothic buttresses of the Library of Parliament. (Open daily 10am-6pm, Thurs. 10am-8pm; mid-Oct.-April Tues.-Sun. 10am-5pm, Thurs. until 8pm. $5, seniors and groups $4, under 18 and students free.) The gallery is free on Thursday and wheelchair-accessible, as are most of Ottawa's public museums and galleries. The **Canadian Museum of Contemporary Photography,** 1 Rideau Canal between the Chateau Laurier and the Ottawa Locks (990-8257), opened its doors for the first time in 1992. The museum allows a glimpse of life in modern Canada which might not otherwise be seen. (Open Fri.-Tues. 11am-5pm, Wed. 4-8pm, Thurs. 11am-8pm; mid-Oct.-April Wed.-Thurs. 11am-8pm, Fri.-Sun. 11am-5pm. $2.50, seniors $1.25, under 18 and full-time students free. Free Thurs.) A spaceship-like structure across the river in Hull houses the **Canadian Museum of Civilization** at 100 Laurier St. (776-7000). Admire the architecture but be wary of overly ambitious exhibits that attempt perspective on 1000 years of Canadian history. Don't miss breathtaking films screened in **CINEPLUS,** the first in the world capable of projecting both Imax and Omnimax. (Open May-June daily 9am-5pm, Thurs. 9am-8pm; July-early Sept. daily 9am-6pm, Thurs. 9am-8pm; winter Tues.-Sun. 9am-5pm, Thurs. 9am-8pm. Museum $4.50, seniors and students $3.50, under 15 free; Thurs. free from 5-8pm for museum only. CINEPLUS $7, seniors and students $5.) The **Canadian Museum of Nature,** at McLeod St. at Metcalfe (996-3102), explores the natural world, from dinosaur skeletons to minerals, through multi-media displays. Be sure to check out the Discovery Den. (Open Sun.-Mon. and Thurs. 9:30am-8pm, Tues.-Wed. and Fri.-Sat. 9:30am-5pm; Oct.-April daily 10am-5pm, Thurs. 10am-8pm. $4, students $3, ages 6-12 and seniors $2, under 6 free; Thurs. ½-price 10am-5pm, free 5-8pm.)

Canadian history buffs could easily lose themselves in the **National Library Archives,** 395 Wellington St. at Bay St. (995-5138), which houses oodles of Canadian publications, old maps, photographs and letters, as well as historical exhibits. (Library open daily 9am-9pm and will provide group tours for those with professional interest only. Exhibit area open daily 9am-9pm.) Anyone who enjoys an occasional guffaw at the government's expense (and who doesn't?) will double up with laughter at the new **Canadian Museum of Caricature,** 136 Patrick St. at Sussex (995-3145). (Open Sat.-Tues. 10am-6pm, Wed.-Fri. 10am-8pm. Free.) Walk to the elegant **Laurier House,** 335 Laurier Ave. E. (692-2581), from which Liberal Prime Minister William Lyon Mackenzie King governed Canada for most of his lengthy tenure. Admire at your leisure the antiques accumulated by King, as well as the crystal ball he used to consult his long-dead mother on matters of national importance. (Open Tues.-Sat. 9am-5pm, Sun. 2-5pm; Oct.-March Tues.-Sat. 10am-5pm, Sun. 2-5pm. Free.)

Further out of town, the **National Museum of Science and Technology,** 1867 St. Laurent Blvd. at Smyth (991-3044), lets visitors explore the developing world of mech, tech, and transport with touchy-feely exhibits. The museum entrance is on Lancaster, 200m east of St. Laurent. (Open daily 9am-5pm, Thurs. 9am-9pm; Sept.-April closed Mon.; $4.30, students and seniors $3.50, ages 6-15 $1.50, under 6 free. Free Thurs. 5-9pm.) The **National Aviation Museum** (993-2010), at the Rockcliffe Airport off St. Laurent Blvd. north of Montréal St., illustrates the history of flying, and displays more than 100 aircraft. (Open daily 9am-5pm, Thurs. 9am-9pm; Labor Day-April, closed Mon. $4.30, students and seniors $3.50, ages 6-15 $1.50; free on Thurs. after 5pm.)

ENTERTAINMENT

The **National Arts Centre,** 53 Elgin St. at Albert St. (tickets 755-1111; info 996-5051), home of an excellent small orchestra and theater company, frequently hosts international entertainers. **Odyssey Theatre** (232-8407) holds open-air comedy at **Strathcona Park,** at the intersection of Laurier Ave. and Range Rd. well east of the canal, on the Rideau River. (Shows late July-mid-Aug. Admission $10, students and seniors $8, under 12 $6.) In summer on Parliament Hill, roving acting troupes sporadically present historical vignettes (late June-Aug. Wed.-Sun. 10:45am-3:30pm is the general time frame). Don't be surprised if you're suddenly entangled in a wild political rally or an emotional legal case—you've merely stumbled through a dimension of time and mind into one of these intriguing skits.

Ottawans seem to have a celebration for just about everything, even the bitter Canadian cold. During early February, **Winterlude** (239-5000) lines the Rideau Canal with a number of ice sculptures which illustrate how it feels to be an Ottawan in the winter—frozen. In mid-May the **Tulip Festival** (567-5757) explodes around Dow's Lake in a colorful kaleidoscope of more than 100,000 blooming tulips. Labor Day weekend the politicians over on Parliament Hill farm out some of their bombast to the **Hot Air Balloon Festival** (243-2330), which sends aloft hundreds of beautiful balloons from Canada, the U.S., and Europe.

■■■ STRATFORD

If drama be the base of an economy, play on. Since 1953, the **Stratford Shakespeare Festival** has fostered the growth of this quaint...hamlet. Stratford-born scribe Tom Patterson founded the festival which opened its inaugural season with Sir Alec Guinness in the title role of *Richard III*. Today, the town and the festival are inextricably entwined.

Practical Information The **Tourism Stratford Information Booth,** 30 York St. (273-3352 or 800-561-7926), on the river, has extensive info on Stratford, the surrounding area, and much of Ontario. Call ahead and they will send you a 75-page visitor's guide, with a season calendar, accommodations, food, shopping, and maps of town. (Open Sun.-Mon. 9am-5pm, Tues.-Sat. 9am-8pm.)

You can get to Stratford by **train** on **VIA RAIL** (273-3234 or 800-361-1235 for reservations). The depot is on Shakespeare St. Trains also run to: Toronto ($22; 40% off 5-day advance purchase); Ottawa ($77); Chicago ($85, via Amtrak). **Chaco Trails** (271-7870), owned by Greyhound, operates buses to surrounding cities, including Kitchener (6 per day; $13) and Toronto (4 per day, 3hr., $22).

Stratford's **post office** is stationed in Blomes Stationary, 1 Wellington St. (271-5712; open Mon.-Fri. 8am-5pm). The **postal code** is N5A 7M3; the **area code** is 519.

Accommodations and Food The budget travelers' best bet for accommodations is the **Stratford General Hospital Residence,** 130 Youngs St. (271-5084), a 25-min. walk from the bus station. Space is usually available; large groups should call ahead. (Singles $29.) The info booth also has an album of photos, prices and info on over 60 B&Bs. The **Festival Accommodations Bureau** (273-1600) can book you into local B&Bs ($40-100) and hotels. Their office is also the only way to access Stratford guest homes, providing you with a room and possibly a continental breakfast in a private home whose owner wishes only to cater to Festival patrons. Be warned that the homes are not necessarily within walking distance of the theaters. (Single bed $28. Double bed $31. Twin beds $33.) The **Burnside Guest Home and Hostel,** 139 William St., Stratford, Ont. N5A 4X9 (271-7076), overlooks Lake Victoria from an Edenic perch. The horticulturist manager tends several gorgeous gardens and cooks a hearty breakfast (included in room charge). B&B rooms range from $35-60; hostel rooms are $20 ($2.50 for breakfast). The info booth (see above) publishes a guide to 50 local restaurants and has all of their menus.

Bard Events The Shakespeare Festival runs from late April, when previews begin, through early Nov. Several brilliant blasts from Shakespeare's canon form the vanguard of the season's program; musicals, comedies, and Canadian plays complete the revue. In high season there are six different shows per day. A matinee at 2pm and evening performance at 8pm run at each of the three theaters: the crown-shaped **Festival Theatre,** the **Avon Theatre,** once a vaudeville house, and the intimate **Tom Patterson Theatre.** Alas, tickets are expensive—you know the problem well. Complete info about casts, performances and other aspects of the Festival can be obtained by phone (273-1600) or by writing the Stratford Festival, P.O. Box 520, Stratford, Ont. N5A 6V2. Ticket prices vary from $18-$56 depending on show, day of week, and location. Some rush tickets are reserved for every performance and sold at 9am on the morning of the show at the Festival Theatre Box Office ($26-37). Student and senior tickets are available for some shows in May, Sept., and Oct. ($14.50-15.50). Between shows, you may fain jump in the Avon River or cast bread to the swans. Spend time browsing through bookstores, art galleries and taking in local daily events, ranging from a farmer's market to free jazz concerts.

■■■ TORONTO

The United Nations dubbed Toronto the world's most multi-cultural city in 1988. And in the late 70s, when the perceived threat of *québecois* nationalism caused a number of companies to move their head offices from Montréal to Toronto, the city donned the crown of Canada's financial capital. Today, the Toronto Stock Exchange handles over 70% of the country's stock trade.

Toronto is as big-city as Canada gets. With that honor come the obligatory superlatives: biggest "free-standing" structure (the CN tower) and biggest retractable roof (the Sky Dome). Most important to the visitor, however, is the diversity of cultures which Toronto manages to squeeze into its variegated ethnic neighborhoods—comparable only to New York and Chicago in this respect. What it *doesn't* come with are many of the urban problems that plague these American metropoli to the south.

Torontonians maintain an efficient and safe public transportation system, promote recycling virtually everywhere, and keep the city impeccably clean and safe. Two film crews learned this the hard way. One crew, after dirtying a Toronto street to make it look more like a typical "American" avenue, went on a coffee break and returned a short time later only to find their set spotless again, swept by the ever-vigilant city maintenance department. Another, filming an attack scene, was twice interrupted by Toronto residents hopping out of their cars to "rescue" the actress.

PRACTICAL INFORMATION

Emergency: 911.

Visitor Information: Travel Information Center, Eaton Centre, level 2, corner of Dundas and Yonge, has flyers and info. Open Mon.-Sat. 9am-7pm, Sun. 9:30am-6pm. Temporary booths line the streets, including one at the **Royal Ontario Museum,** Queen's Park Crescent. **Ontario Travel,** (800-668-2746). Enter Eatons at Dundas and Yonge, go down 2 flights, exit store; it's on the right. Info on all of Ontario. Open Mon.-Fri. 10am-9pm, Sat. 9:30am-6pm, Sun. 1-5pm.

Student Travel Agency: Travel CUTS, 187 College St. (979-2406), just west of University Ave. Subway: Queen's Park. Smaller office at 74 Gerrard St. E. (977-0441). Subway: College. Open Mon.-Fri. 9am-5pm.

Traveler's Aid: each terminal at Pearson Airport, and Union Station (366-7788). Mon.-Fri. 9am-9pm.

Consulates: U.S., 360 University Ave. (595-0228, 595-1700 for visa info). Subway: St. Patrick. Open Mon.-Fri. 8:30am-2pm for consular services. **Australia,** 175 Bloor St. E., suite #314-6 (323-1155). Subway: Bloor St. Open Mon.-Fri. 9am-1pm and 2-5pm for info; 9am-1pm for visas. **U.K.,** 777 Bay St. #1910 (593-1267). Subway: College. Open Mon.-Fri. 9:30am-3:30pm, 9am-4:50pm for telephone info.

Currency Exchange: Toronto Currency Exchange, 391 Yonge St. and 780 Yonge St. Gives the best rates around, and *doesn't charge a service fee.* Both open daily 9am-6pm. **Royal Bank of Canada** has exchange centers at Pearson Airport (676-3220). Open daily 6am-11pm.

Airport: Pearson International Airport (247-7678), about 20km west of Toronto via Hwy. 427, 401, or 409. Take Bus #58 west from Lawrence W. subway. **Pacific Western Airport Express** (351-3311) runs buses each day directly to downtown hotels every 20 min., 5am-10:45pm. Last bus from downtown at 11:10pm. $11, round-trip $18.50. Buses also serve the Yorkdale ($6.50), York Mills ($7.50), and Islington ($6) subway stations every 40 min. 6:20am-midnight. **Air Canada** (925-2311 or 800-422-6232) flits to: Montréal ($223); Calgary ($697); New York City ($243); Vancouver ($826). Student fares available to some cities depending on season (max. age 24).

Trains: All trains chug into **Union Station,** 61 Front St. at Bay (366-8411). Subway: Union. **VIA Rail** (366-8411) cannonballs to: Montréal (6 per day, $72); Windsor (4 per day; $55); Vancouver (3 per week; $443). Student and senior discounts available as well; 40% discount for 5-day pre-reservation on all trains except to Vancouver. **Amtrak** (800-426-8725) choo-choos to: New York City (1 per day, 12 hrs. US$101); Chicago (1 per day, 11 hr., US$137). Seniors 10% discount on all fares. Ticket office open Mon.-Sat. 7am-9pm, Sun. 8am-9pm.

Buses: Voyageur (393-7911) and **Greyhound** (367-8747), 610 Bay St., just north of Dundas. Subway: St. Patrick or Dundas. Voyageur has service to Montréal (5 per day, 7 hr., $58). Greyhound takes you west or south to: Calgary ($232); Vancouver ($272); New York City ($118). Ticket office open daily 5:30-1am.

Public Transport: Toronto Transit Commission (TTC) (393-4636). Network includes 2 subway lines and numerous bus and streetcar routes. Free pocket maps at all stations. Some routes 24 hrs. New policy requires buses running after dark to stop anywhere along the route at a female passenger's request. Free transfers among subway, buses, and streetcars, but only within stations. Fare $2, 5 tokens $6.50, seniors 50% off with ID, under 12 50¢, 8 for $2.50. Unlimited travel day pass, good for subway, bus and streetcar, $5. Monthly pass $67.

Toronto Island Ferry Service (392-8193, 392-8194 for recording). Numerous ferries to Centre Island, Wards Island and Hanlans Point leave daily from Bay St. Ferry Dock at the foot of Bay St. Service approximately every ½ hr., 8am-midnight. $3 round-trip; seniors, students, ages 15-19 $1.50, under 15 $1.

Taxi: Co-op Cabs, 364-7111. $2.20 plus distance and waiting.

Car Rental: Wrecks for Rent, 77 Nassau St. (585-7782). Subway: Spadina or Bathurst. $30 per day; first 200km free, 12¢ each additional km. Insurance $9.50 if over 25 with credit card, $15 without. Surcharge for ages 21-25. Open Mon.-Fri. 8am-6pm, Sat. 9am-4pm. **Hertz** (800-263-0600), **Tilden** (922-2000), **Budget** (673-3322), and **Discount** (961-8006) also serve Toronto.

Auto Transport: Allostop, 663 Yonge St., Suite 301 (323-0874), at Bloor. Matches riders and drivers to: Ottawa ($24); Montréal ($26); Québec City ($41); New York ($40). Open Mon. and Wed. 9am-5pm, Thurs.-Fri. 9am-7pm, Sat.-Sun. 10am-5pm.

Bike Rental: Brown's Sports and Bike Rental, 2447 Bloor St. W. (763-4176). $14 per day, $32 per weekend, $42 per week. $100 deposit or credit card required. Open Mon.-Wed. 9:30am-6pm, Thurs.-Fri. 9:30am-8pm, Sat. 9:30am-5:30pm.

Help Lines: Rape Crisis, 597-8808. 24 hrs. **Services for the Disabled,** Ontario Travel, 314-0944. **Toronto Area Gays (TAG),** 964-6600. Open Mon.-Fri. 7-10pm. **Distress Centre,** 367-2277.

Post Office: Toronto Dominion Centre (973-3120), at King and Bay St. General Delivery at Postal Station K, 2384 Yonge St. (483-1334). Subway: Eglington. Open Mon.-Fri. 8am-5:45pm. **Postal Code:** M4P 2E0.

Area Code: 416.

The city maps available at tourism booths are inadequate for getting around. At any drugstore or postcard shack, buy the indispensable *Downtown and Metro Toronto Visitor's Map Guide* in the yellowish-orange cover ($1.50). The pocket *Ride Guide*, free at all TTC stations and tourism info booths (see Practical Information), shows

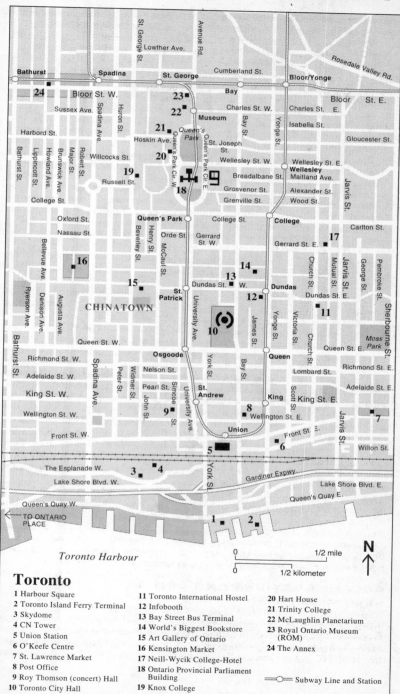

Toronto

1 Harbour Square
2 Toronto Island Ferry Terminal
3 Skydome
4 CN Tower
5 Union Station
6 O'Keefe Centre
7 St. Lawrence Market
8 Post Office
9 Roy Thomson (concert) Hall
10 Toronto City Hall

11 Toronto International Hostel
12 Infobooth
13 Bay Street Bus Terminal
14 World's Biggest Bookstore
15 Art Gallery of Ontario
16 Kensington Market
17 Neill-Wycik College-Hotel
18 Ontario Provincial Parliament
   Building
19 Knox College

20 Hart House
21 Trinity College
22 McLaughlin Planetarium
23 Royal Ontario Museum
   (ROM)
24 The Annex

═══○═══ Subway Line and Station

the subway and bus routes for the metro area; it only depicts major streets, but is vital for getting around once you know where you are and where you're going.

There is no one spot downtown that can be called the heart of the action. Instead, there are many decentralized neighborhoods; each has its own distinctive character. Zoning regulations require that Toronto developers include housing and retail space in commercial construction; this has kept downtown from becoming a barren canyon of glass boxes at night, since people actually live there.

The city streets lie in a grid pattern, running north-south or east-west. The addresses on north-south streets increase as you head north, away from Lake Ontario. **Yonge Street** is the main artery. East-west streets have the suffix East or West depending on which side of Yonge they are. Numbering for both sides starts at Yonge and increases as you move in either direction. Heading west from Yonge St., the main streets are **Bay Street, University Avenue, Spadina Avenue,** and **Bathurst.** Major east-west routes are **Queen Street, Dundas, College,** and **Bloor.**

Traffic is heavy in Toronto—avoid rush hour (4-7pm). Parking on the street is hard to find and usually limited to one hour, except on Sundays when street parking is free and abundant. Street parking is free at night, but your car must be gone by 7am. Day parking is free at outlying subway stations, the best bet for inbound daytrippers. Parking overnight at the subway stations is, however, prohibited.

Getting Around

There are many neighborhoods worth exploring. **Chinatown** is on Dundas St. W. between University Ave. and Spadina Ave. **Kensington Market** is found on Kensington Ave., Augusta Ave., and the western half of Baldwin St.—a largely Portuguese neighborhood with many good restaurants, vintage clothing shops, and an outdoor bazaar of produce, luggage, spices, nuts, clothing, and shoes. The **University of Toronto** campus occupies about 200 acres in the middle of downtown. The law-school cult-flick *The Paper Chase* was filmed here because the campus looked more Ivy League than Harvard, where the movie was set. The less-memorable Fox-TV series *Class of '96* was also shot here. **Queen Street West,** from University Ave. to Bathurst St., is a fun mix of shopping from upscale uptight boutiques to reasonable used book stores, restaurants, and cafes. Listen to street musicians or visit the store devoted exclusively to condoms. **The Annex** on Bloor St. W. starts at the Spadina subway and goes west. You'll find excellent budget restaurants serving a variety of ethnic cuisines (see Food) as well as some nightclubs. This is the best place to come at night when you're not sure exactly what you're hungry for. **Harborfront** is on Queen's Quay W. from York St. to Bathurst, on the lake. A paradigm for what a city can do with its waterfront with a little money and a lot of TLC: music, food, ferry rides, dance companies and art all dock here. Call 973-3000 for info. There are three main **Toronto Islands,** all accessible by ferry (see Practical Info above). The islands offer beaches, bike rental, and an amusement park.

Corso Italia is on St. Clair W. at Dufferin St.; take the subway to St. Clair W. and bus #512 west. **Little India** is on Gerrard St. E. at Coxwell. Subway: Coxwell; bus #22 south to 2nd Gerrard stop. **Greek Village** (better known as "**the Danforth**") is on Danforth Ave., at Pope Ave.; subway: Pope. These three ethnic enclaves are similar in form. Street signs are bilingual, and most businesses cater to locals, not tourists. All three take about 30-45 min. by public transit from downtown, not worth the ride just for the food, but okay if you want to explore specialty food shops.

ACCOMMODATIONS AND CAMPING

Budget travelers in Toronto have a staggering number of first-rate lodging choices in Toronto. The hostels and U. of Toronto dorms are remarkable for their towering quality-price ratio. Avoid the cheap hotels concentrated around Jarvis and Gerrard St. You can call the Visitors Bureau to obtain B&B registry numbers, but beware! Always visit a B&B before you commit, as it is difficult to regulate these registries.

Toronto International Hostel (HI), 223 Church St. (368-1848 or 368-0207); 5 min. from Eaton Centre. Subway: Dundas. 150 beds, no TV. Huge lounge, excellent kitchen, laundry facilities, tourist info, and an HI retail store stocked with *Let's Go* guides. Daily organized activities run the gamut from dart tournaments to bar-hopping. Check-out 10am. Quiet hours midnight-7am. Bed in 10-person dorm $15, in 4-bed dorm $22, in 2-bed dorm $24.50. $5 key deposit. No curfew. 24 hr. office. Reservations essential. Ask about discount coupons for local cafes.

Knox College, 59 St. George St. (978-2793). Subway: Queen's Park. Huge rooms with wood floors around an idyllic courtyard. Many rooms refinished by the crew from *Class of '96*. This gothic residence is U of T's most coveted. Common rooms and baths on each floor. Great location in the heart of U of T's campus. Singles $25. Doubles $39. Call for reservations Mon.-Fri. 10am-5pm. Open June-Aug.

Trinity College and St. Hilda's College Residences, 6 Hoskin Ave. (978-2523), up the street from Knox; bursar's office for check-in on Queen's Park Crescent on U of T campus. Subway: Museum. Prices start at $37. Office hours same as Knox.

Neill-Wycik College Hotel, 96 Gerrard St. E. (977-2320). Subway: College. Rooms impeccably clean, some with beautiful views of the city. Kitchen on every floor, but no utensils. Check-in after 1pm (locked storage room provided). Check-out 11am. Singles (including simple breakfast) $30, mini-twin $36, doubles $36. Family room $47. Dorm bunks for backpackers $18. 10% discount for 7-night stay if you pay up front; 20% discount for students and seniors. Will cancel reservations after 6:30pm unless arrangements made. Open early May-late Aug.

Leslieville Home Hostel, 185 Leslie St. M4M 3C6 (461-7258). Subway: Queen. Take any Queen streetcar from the subway stop and get off at Leslie; walk left to hostel. Inviting home setting at this hostel. Friendly owners will work hard to place all comers. Dorm style bed $15. Single $35. Double $45. Price includes linens, towels, soap, and breakfast. No curfew. No smoking. Also check in here for the **Merry Mattress Hostel** (same phone number). Dorm-style accommodations ($12), catering to the backpacker crowd. Linen and parking free. Managers will direct you from the Leslieville office.

Bed and Breakfast Accommodations, 223 Strathmore Blvd. (461-7095). Subway: Greenwood. Spacious, pristine rooms in a quiet neighborhood. Subway stop next door adds convenience, not noise. Private-use kitchens and bathrooms abound. Long-term and groups stays encouraged. Singles $35. Doubles $40

Karabanow Guest House and Tourist Home, 9 Spadina Rd. (phone and fax 923-4004), at Bloor St. 6 blocks west of Yonge. Subway: Spadina. Good location by subway stop. Small and intimate. 20 rooms with desks (mostly doubles) in a renovated Victorian house. TV, free parking. Check-in 9am-9pm, later by arrangement; check-out 11am. No curfew. Singles $40. Doubles $50. $10 key deposit. Oct.-April rooms $10 less. No kids under 12 please. Reservations recommended.

Hotel Selby, 592 Sherbourne St. (921-3142). Subway: Sherbourne. Hotel Selby has seen many changes but today is a registered historic spot and a thriving guest house. Completely refurbished, including cable TV, A/C, and phones in this Victorian marvel. Special period suites have been set up to capture the splendor of the 1920's Selby as Hemingway lived it (his desk is still there). Singles start at $49.

Indian Line Tourist Campground, 7625 Finch Ave. W. (678-1233), at Darcel Ave. Follow Hwy. 427 north to Finch and go west. Showers, laundry. Close to Pearson Airport. Sites $14, with hookup $18. Open May 10-early Oct.

FOOD

A burst of immigration from around the world has made Toronto a haven for good ethnic food rivalled in North America only by New York City. Over 5000 restaurants squeeze into metro Toronto; you could eat at a different place every night for the next 15 years. Best bets are Bloor St. W. and Chinatown. For fresh produce, go to Kensington Market (see Getting Around) or the St. Lawrence Market at King St. E. and Sherbourne, six blocks east of the King subway stop. The budget traveler staying in town for more than a few days will want *Toronto Dinners for $7.95 or Less,* by PBG Productions, a pocket guide to 100 restaurants ($6, available at **World's Largest Bookstore,** Edward and College St.; subway: Dundas; they also stock other

books listed here). "L.L.B.O" posted on the window of a restaurant means that it ha
a liquor license.

Real Peking Restaurant, 355 College St. (920-7952), at Augusta Ave. The effor
many Chinese restaurants put into decorations here goes into the food instead
Understanding server explains the menu. Entrees $6.50-8.50. Open Mon.-Fri
5pm-2am, Sat. 5-11pm, Sun. 5-10pm.

Shopsy's, 33 Yonge St. (365-3333), at Front St. 1 block from Union Station. Th
definitive Toronto deli. 300 seats, quick service. Sandwiches $4.25.

Hart House, cafeteria inside Hart House residential college on U of T campus (978
2444). Subway: Museum. The best lunch deal in the city. Dine on gourmet cuisin
in the vaulted dining hall or in the Gothic courtyard. Cold entrees such a
poached filet of salmon with watercress dressing, $3.75. Hot entrees $4.15. Sal
ads 25¢ per oz., bread 20¢, fresh fruit 65¢. Open lunch only, 11:30am-2pm.

Mr. Greek, 568 Danforth Ave. (461-5470) at Carlow. Subway: Pope. Shish kabobs
salads, steak, chicken, Greek music, and wine. Family atmosphere, fast service
Open Sun.-Thurs. 11-1am, Fri.-Sat. until 3am.

Renaissance Cafe, 509 Bloor St. W. (968-6639). Subway: Spadina. Fun for tofu-lov
ers and other hip health eccentrics. Moon burger (tofu, spices, and *tahini* sauce
$7. Lite bites (noon-4pm) $5. Luncheon specials $6. Open daily noon-midnight.

Country Style Hungarian Restaurant, 450 Bloor St. W. (537-1745). Heart
stews, soups, and casseroles. Entrees come in small and large portions; bette
terms would be "more than enough" and "stop, lest I burst." Entrees $3-8. Ope
daily 11am-10pm.

Viva, 459 Bloor St. W. (922-8482), at Major St. Latin music, colorful Latin-America
costumes on walls. Seafood, chicken, vegetables, beef, pork or sausage in corn o
flour tortillas ($5). BBQ plates with corn meal, sticky rice, and vegetable $7. Ope
daily 11:30am-1am.

Ariana, 255 College St. (599-2618), at Spadina Ave. Excellent Persian/Afghan food
Chicken, beef or lamb kabob, $4-6. Good felafel plate: 3 balls of fried chick pea
with parsley, onion, and spices; with salad and pita $4.

Vanipha, 193 Augusta Ave. (340-0491), across from playground. Curry, poultry
meat, vegetarian—the standard range of Thai food. Menu has good English expla
nations of dishes titled in Thai. Entrees $8-9. Open Tues.-Sun. noon-11pm.

Saigon Palace, Spadina Ave. (963-1623), at College St. Subway: Queen's Park. Pop
ular with locals. Great spring rolls. Variety of beef, chicken, or vegetable dishe
over rice or noodles ($7). Open daily 9am-10pm, Fri.-Sat. until 11pm.

SIGHTS

Exploring the **ethnic neighborhoods** on foot is one of the most enjoyable (an
cheapest) activities in Toronto. Life takes place on the streets here: watch locals hag
gling at outdoor produce markets, teenagers courting, and old men chatting on th
corner, all in a foreign tongue. For a more organized expedition, join one of the 1
free **walking tours** operated by the **Royal Ontario Museum** (Wed. and Sun. in sum
mer; 586-5514). Study the varied architecture of the downtown financial district o
a **Toronto Architecture Tour** ($10). Modern architecture aficionados should als
visit **City Hall** at the corner of Queen and Bay St. between the Osgoode and Quee
subway stops (392-9111), with its curved twin towers and a rotunda which wa
considered quite avant-garde when completed in 1965 (now the garde has passed)
(922-7606; open Tues.-Sun.) The **University of Toronto** has free guided tours of th
campus (978-5000). The Ontario government legislates in the **Provincial Parlia
ment Buildings** (325-7500), at Queen's Park in the city center. Subway: Queen'
Park. Free guided tours daily every ½ hr., 9am-3:30pm. Free visitors gallery passe
available at info desk in main lobby at 1:30pm. (Building open 8:30am-6:30pm
chambers close 4:30pm. Parliament in session Oct.-Dec. and March-June, Mon
Thurs. 1:30-6pm, and Thurs. 10am-noon.) At 553m, the **CN Tower** (360-8500; sub
way: Union, and follow the skywalk) does not quite pierce the ozone layer, but th
ride to the top, at a towering $12, will poke a big hole in your wallet and may spli

your eardrums. (Open Mon.-Sat. 9-1am, Sun. 10am-10pm. Seniors $8, kids 4-16 $6, under 4 free.) Another classic tourist attraction is the 98-room **Casa Loma** (923-1171), Davenport Rd. at 1 Austin Terrace, near Spadina a few blocks north of the Dupont subway stop. Although the outside of the only real turreted castle in North America belongs in a fairy tale, the inside's dusty old exhibits can be skipped. (Open daily 10am-4pm. $8, seniors and ages 5-16 $4.50, under 5 free with parent.) The **Royal Ontario Museum (ROM),** 100 Queen's Park (586-5551), is a royal success. Subway: Museum. It has artifacts from ancient civilizations (Greek, Chinese, Egyptian), a floor of life sciences (kids will love the stuffed animals and live bugs), plus more imaginative displays such as "Caravans and Clipper Ships—the story of trade" and a self-conscious one that shows how museum experts study new specimens. (Open in summer daily 10am-6pm, Tues. and Thurs. until 8pm; closed Mon. in winter. $7, seniors and kids $3.50. Free Tues. after 4:30pm; includes entry to the **George M. Gardiner Museum of Ceramic Art** across the street.) The **Art Gallery of Ontario (AGO),** 317 Dundas St. W. (979-6648; Subway: St. Patrick), three blocks west of University Ave. in the heart of Chinatown, houses an enormous collection of Western art spanning the Renaissance to the 1980s, with a particular concentration on Canadian artists. (Open mid-May to early Sept. daily 10:30am-5:30pm, Wed. to 9pm. $7.50, seniors and students $4, under 12 free, families $9. Free Wed. 5-9pm.) Toronto also has a range of smaller museums dedicated to subjects such as textiles, sugar, hockey, marine history, medicine, and the Holocaust, . Budget travelers who have spent all day on their feet may enjoy the **Bata Shoe Museum,** 131 Bloor St. W. (924-7463), 2nd floor, two blocks from the Museum subway stop. A fascinating collection of footwear from many cultures and ages: the moon boot worn by Buzz Aldrin, boots with nasty spikes on the soles, used to crush chestnuts, and two-inch slippers once worn by Chinese women with bound feet. (Open Tues.-Sun. 11am-6pm. $3, students and seniors $1, families $6.)

From April-Sept., the **Toronto Blue Jays** (info. 341-1111) swing for the hotel in the four-year-old **Sky Dome;** subway: Union and follow the signs. The dome is more of an entertainment center than a ballpark; it lacks the charm and chutzpah of a Fenway Park or Wrigley Field, but boasts a retractable roof, a 348-room hotel (some of its windows face the field), and retail outlets and offices. All games sell out, but before the game the box office usually has some obstructed view seats. (Tickets $4-17.50.) Scalpers sell tickets for far beyond face value; wait until the game starts and you can get tickets from them at face value. To get a behind-the-scenes look at the Sky Dome, take the tour (341-2770; daily 10am-5pm on the hr.; $8, seniors and under 16 $5.50). For info on concerts and other Sky Dome events, call 341-3663. Hockey fans should head for **Maple Leaf Gardens** (977-1641; Subway: College), at Carlton and Church St., to see the knuckle-crackin', puck-smackin' **Maple Leafs.** **Biking** and **hiking trails** wriggle through metropolitan Toronto. For a map of the trails, write the **Metro Parks and Property Department,** 365 Bay St., 8th floor, Toronto M5H 2V1. Serious hikers might want *Great Country Walks Around Toronto* by Elliot Katz ($4). For a relaxing afternoon, go to **High Park** (392-1111; Subway: High Park) for the free summer Shakespeare festival, the fishing pond, or the sports facilities. **Toronto Islands Park,** a 4-mi. strip of connected islands just opposite the downtown area (15-min. ferry trip; 392-8193 for ferry info), is a popular "vacationland," with a boardwalk, bathing beaches, canoe and bike rentals, a Frisbee golf course, and a children's farm and amusement park. Ferries leave from the Bay Street Ferry Dock at the foot of Bay St. (see Practical Information above). Further out from the city are **Canada's Wonderland** (832-7000), Canada's answer to Disneyland, the **Ontario Science Center** (429-4100), and the **Metro Toronto Zoo** (392-5900). All three are about 1 hr. from downtown and accessible by public transportation. For info on offbeat recreation near the metro area, check out *52 Weekend Activities for the Toronto Adventurer,* by Sue Lebrecht ($13). For info on everything else to do in Toronto, buy *The Toronto Guide,* by Margaret and Rod MacKenzie ($17), eh?

ENTERTAINMENT

Nightlife

Some of Toronto's clubs and pubs remain closed on Sundays because of liquor laws. Some of the more formal clubs uphold dress codes and the city still shuts down at 1am. To mingle with students try **The Brunswick House, Lee's Palace** (see below), and the **All-Star Eatery,** 277 Victoria (977-7619), at Dundas one block east of the Dundas subway stop. The most interesting new clubs are on trendy **Queen Street West.** The gay scene centers around Wellesley and Church, although there's also some gay activity on Queen and Yonge St. *Now* magazine, published every Thurs., is the city's comprehensive entertainment guide, available in restaurants and record stores all over Toronto. *Eye* magazine, also published on Thurs. and free, has similar info. *Where Toronto,* a monthly available free at tourism booths, gives a good arts and entertainment run-down.

Bamboo, 312 Queen St. W. (593-5771), 3 blocks west of the Osgoode subway stop. Popular with students. Live reggae, jazz, rock, and funk daily. Great dancing. Patio upstairs. Open Mon.-Sat. noon-1am. Hefty cover ($8-10) varies band to band.

Brunswick House, 481 Bloor St. W. (964-2242), between the Bathurst and Spadina subway stops. Reeling with students. Beer $2.95. Upstairs is **Albert's Hall,** famous for its blues. Open Mon.-Fri. 11:30-1am, Sat. noon-1am.

George's Spaghetti House, 290 Dundas St. E. (923-9887), at Sherbourne St.. Subway: Dundas; take the streetcar east to Sherbourne. The city's best jazz club attracts the nation's top ensembles. Don't forget your jacket and tie or you may feel out of place. Dinner entrees from $8.50. Restaurant open Mon.-Thurs. 11am-11pm, Fri. 11am-midnight, Sat. 5pm-midnight. Jazz Mon.-Sat. 6pm-1am. Cover Tues.-Thurs. $4, Fri.-Sat. $5; free on Mon. No cover at bar.

Lee's Palace, 529 Bloor St. W. (532-7383), just east of the Bathurst subway stop. Amazing crazy creature art depicting rock n' roll frenzy. Live music nightly. Pick up a calendar of bands. Dancing upstairs Thurs.-Sat. starting 10pm. Cover $2-5. Open daily noon-1am; club until 3am.

Second City (863-1111), in The Old Firehall, 110 Lombard St. at Jarvis, 2 blocks east and 2 short blocks south of Queen's Park subway stop. One of North America's wackiest and most creative comedy clubs. Spawned comics Dan Aykroyd, John Candy, Gilda Radner, Dave Thomas, Rick Moranis and Martin Short; a hit TV show (SCTV); and the legendary "Great White North." Dinner and theater $29-35. Theater without dinner $13-18, students $8 and dinner discount. Free improv sessions (Mon.-Thurs. at 10:15pm)—students welcome. Shows Mon.-Thurs. at 6 and 8:30pm, Fri.-Sat. at 8 and 11pm. Reservations required.

Festivals and Cultural Events

The city offers a few first-class freebies. **Ontario Place,** 955 Lakeshore Blvd. W. (314-9900; 314-9980 recording), features top-notch cheap entertainment in summer—the Toronto Symphony, National Ballet of Canada, Ontario Place Pops, and top pop artists perform here free with admission to the park. (Park open mid-May-early Sept. daily 10am-1am. $7.50, seniors and kids $2.) Spectacular IMAX movies can be seen at the **Six-Storey Cinesphere** ($4, seniors and kids $2; call for screening schedule). On five evenings in early July, watch the **Benson and Hedges Symphony of Fire** blaze in the Toronto skies. From mid-August through Labor Day, the **Canadian National Exhibition (CNE)** brings a country carnival atmosphere to Ontario Place. Enjoy superb performances of Shakespeare by **Canadian Stage** (367-8243) amid the greenery of High Park, Bloor St. W. at Parkside Dr. (Subway: High Park.) Bring something to sit on or wedge yourself on the 45° slope to the stage. ($5 donation requested. Call for performance schedules.) Now in its seventh year, the **du Maurier Ltd. Downtown Jazz Festival's** (363-5200) mix of old and new talents mesmerizes the city in late June. Budget travelers will appreciate the abundance of free, outdoor concerts at lunchtime and in the early evening.

Roy Thomson Hall, 60 Simcoe St. (872-4255), at King St. W., is the home of the Toronto Symphony Orchestra. Tickets are expensive ($10-75), but rush tickets ($8-10) go on sale at the box office the day of the concert (at 11am for concerts Mon.-Fri., 1pm Sat.) Or order by phone (592-4828; Mon.-Fri. 10am-6pm, Sat. noon-5pm; office opens 2 hrs. before Sun. performances). Ask about discounts. The same office serves **Massey Hall,** 178 Victoria St. (593-4828), near Eaton Centre (Subway: Dundas), a great hall for rock and folk concerts and musicals. The opera and ballet companies perform at **O'Keefe Centre,** 1 Front St. E. (872-2262; tickets from $30), at Yonge. Rush tickets (for the last row of orchestra seats) on sale at 11am ($9 ballet, $12 opera). Seniors and students can line up 1 hr. before performances for the best unsold seats ($10.75). (Box office open daily 11am-6pm or until 1 hr. after curtain.) Next door, **St. Lawrence Centre,** 27 Front St. E. (366-7723), presents excellent classic and Canadian drama and chamber music recitals in two different theaters. Special student and senior tickets may be available depending on the company performing. (Box office open Mon.-Sat. 10am-8pm.)

You can beat the high cost of culture by seeking out standby or student discount options. **Five Star Tickets** (596-8211) sells ½-price tickets for theater, music, dance, and opera on the day of performance: their booth at Dundas and Yonge in front of Eaton Centre opens at noon, so arrive before 11:45am for first dibs. (Subway: Dundas. Open Mon.-Sat. noon-7:30pm, Sun. 11am-3pm). **Ticketmaster** (870-8000) will supply you with tickets to many events.

■ "Near" Toronto: Algonquin Provincial Park

The wilder Canada of endless rushing rivers and shimmering lakes awaits in Algonquin Provincial Park, about 300km north of Toronto. Experience Algonquin through one of two venues: the Hwy. 60 Corridor, where tents and trailers crowd the roadside; or the park interior, the "essence of Algonquin." You can rent gear for a backcountry adventure at several outfitting stores around and inside the park. Try **Algonquin Outfitters,** RR#1-Oxtongue Lake, Dwight P0A 1H0 (705-635-2243), just off Hwy. 60 about 10km west of the park's west gate. They have two other locations in the park. To enter the park, you'll need an Interior Camping Permit ($5.75 per person each night), available at the main gate or from any outfitter.

▓ Manitoba

Manitoba marks the beginning of the Canadian West. While frontier prairie predominates, there are tens of thousands of lakes in this province of diverse terrain. To the north, tundra and the lush forests developed out of the wooded parkland of the central region. Farther west, the rolling mountains, replete with grain- and wheat-rich fields, belie the misconception that Manitoba is a flat prairie.

Manitoba lacks sophistication, but it has a peculiar midwestern quality all its own. Its largest city, **Winnipeg,** combines cosmopolitan elements with a local folksy atmosphere. Farther north are the prairie areas, still largely inhabited by Native Americans.

By taking the train up north you can reach **Churchill,** on **Hudson Bay,** itself quite an attraction and worth the trip. A summer seaport operates out of Churchill which becomes the "Polar Bear Capital of the World" in the winter. Beluga whales, seals, and caribou also live in and along Churchill's coast. The northern lights are spectacular here.

Around Winnipeg, **Lake Manitoba** offers excellent facilities, and **Riding Mountain National Park** displays forest, open grassland, meadows, prairies, and mountains. The fishing is superb and you are guaranteed to see bison, moose, and bears.

PRACTICAL INFORMATION

Capital: Winnipeg.
Time Zone: Central (1 hr. behind Eastern). **Postal Abbreviation:** MAN
Sales Tax: 7% plus a 7% General Service Tax.

■■■ RIDING MOUNTAIN NATIONAL PARK

Situated amidst a sea of farming and prairie land, the present-day configuration of the land that makes up Riding Mountain National Park (RMNP) was primarily determined over 10,000 years ago by the advances and retreats of glaciers. The irregularity of these movements account for the unpredictable pattern of hills, lakes, and ponds. This islanded preserve is home to a variety of wildlife including black bears, bison, elk, wolves, and coyotes. Because of its remote location, from 1943-1946 there was a German POW camp on the northeast short of Whitewater Lake.

The human history of this park begins with the three Native American tribes which inhabited the area: Assiniboine, Cree, and Ojibwa, who were all displaced by the fur traders that arrived in the 1730s-40s. In 1895, Riding Mountain was designated a timber reserve and in 1930 an order was passed establishing Riding Mountain as a National Park. A year later, the first naturalist ever to be employed by a National Park was hired at Riding Mountain. He left after only six months because a drought led to unsuitable conditions for his pet beavers Rawhide and Jelly Roll. Despite this setback, the park officially opened in July of 1933.

PRACTICAL INFORMATION, EH?

The park is easily accessible by car from any direction. Hwy. 10 runs from Brandon (95km south of RMNP) through Wasagaming (visitors center and commercial strip) and up to Dauphin (13km north of the northern border of RMNP). Hwy. 19 enters from Norgate, to the east of the park, and continues to Wasagaming where it connects with Hwy. 10.

Wasagaming Visitors Center (848-2811; open daily 8am-8pm). The informed, friendly staff gives hints about where the animals are and other goings-on. There is a small display about the wildlife of the park and in June rangers give nature lectures.

Lake Audy is 45 min. away from Wasagaming, off Lake Audy Rd. Along the way there are gorgeous ponds and a wishing well with big fish to sniff your coins. Out at Lake Audy the bison are enclosed in a field that runs parallel to the road. In the opposite direction, on Hwy. 19, Lake Katherine and Whirlpool Lake offer fantastic swimming and splendid picnic spots. North of Wasagaming on Hwy. 10 are entrances to most of the backcountry trails and excellent opportunities to view wildlife. All the trails and camping spots are well-marked and the animals could pop up anywhere. Get trail maps from the visitors center; they can also tell you which overnight backcountry hikes are open.

SHACKING UP, FOOD, AND ACTIVITIES

Camping sites change from season to season. The park never accepts reservations, and special rates are available from late August to the end of June. The largest campground, right downtown, never closes. **Wasagaming Campground** has 342 unserviced sites at $9.50 per day, 72 electrical sites at $12.50 per day, and 86 full service sites at $14 per day.

All of the hotels can be found along Wasagaming or directly behind the main road. **Manigaming Motel** (848-2459) provides motel units with kitchenettes (May-June $48 for up to 4 people, July-April $60-95). **Idylwyde Bungalows** (848-2383) has

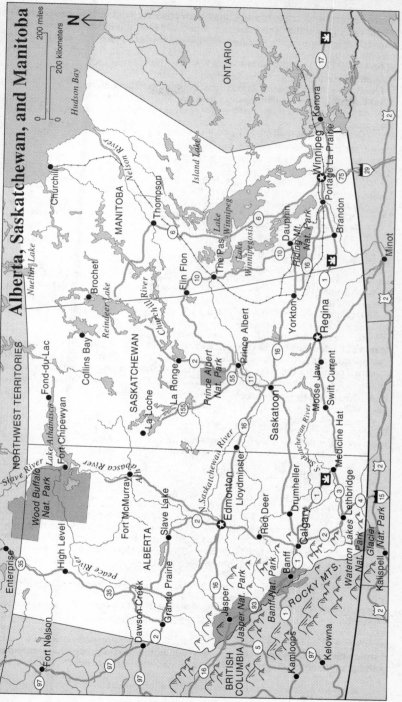

Alberta, Saskatchewan, and Manitoba

N

200 miles
0   200 kilometers

Hudson Bay

NORTHWEST TERRITORIES

Nueltin Lake

Churchill

MANITOBA

Nelson River

Thompson

Island Lake

ONTARIO

Kenora

Winnipeg

Portage La Prairie

Lake Winnipeg

Dauphin

Riding Mt. Nat. Park

Brandon

Minot

Brochet

Reindeer Lake

Flin Flon

The Pas

Lake Winnipegosis

Yorkton

Regina

Moose Jaw

Collins Bay

Fond-du-Lac

Churchill River

La Ronge

Prince Albert Nat. Park

Prince Albert

Saskatoon

Medicine Hat

Swift Current

SASKATCHEWAN

La Loche

Lake Athabasca

Fort Chipewyan

Wood Buffalo Nat. Park

Slave River

Athabasca River

Fort McMurray

N. Saskatchewan River

S. Saskatchewan River

Edmonton

Lloydminster

Red Deer

Drumheller

Calgary

Lethbridge

Waterton Lakes Nat. Park

Glacier Nat. Park

Kalispell

Enterprise

High Level

Peace River

Dawson Creek

Grande Prairie

Slave Lake

ALBERTA

Jasper Nat. Park

Jasper

Banff Nat. Park

Banff

ROCKY MTS.

BRITISH COLUMBIA

Kamloops

Kelowna

Fort Nelson

suites and cabins from $70 to $95. **McTavish's Motel** (848-7366) has rooms from $78-88 in season and $58-68 off-season. They also have a bookstore, video rental, and ice cream store on the premises. **The New Chalet** (848-2892) owned by the friendly husband-wife time of the Mitchells is $63 for up to 2 people in the summer ($69 with kitchen) and $53 in the winter ($57 with kitchen). They recently winterized the rooms in anticipation of heavy skiing traffic.

Food stores along Wasagaming are reasonably priced. Grocery stores have everything you need. Pizza and burgers can be found alongside numerous ice cream parlors. **Chicken Delight** (885-7570) delivers chicken and chips ($2.60) and fresh dough pizza ($6.25).

At the **Tempo Gas Station** (848-2535; open 8am-11pm) you can rent **bikes** (single $4 per hr., double $7 per hr., and mountain bike $5 per hr.). Many outfitters inside and outside the park will rent camping equipment and horses. **Agassiz Wilderness Trail Rides** in Kelwood (967-2550) offers day rides for $45 and overnight for $70 (up to 6 days, $70 for 2). The **Elkhorn Ranch** (848-2802) in Clear Lake rents horses by the hour at $14, children $10. Pack, fishing, and skiing trips can be organized by **Riding Mountain Nature Tours** (636-2968) in Erickson. These range from $100 to $775 depending on what you want. Another popular park activity is fishing; check with the rangers for regulations.

■■■ WINNIPEG

The transformation of Winnipeg from a "little village" into the greatest grain center in North America has not robbed it of its midwestern roots. This gateway to western Canada has many viable attractions of its own. Winnipeg offers variety and quality second to none and combines the excitement and adventure of a cosmopolitan center with a safe, friendly environment of prairie charm and flair.

As the capital of Manitoba, Winnipeg has an extremely diverse population, celebrated at **Focklorama**, an annual summer festival in early August. In February, the **Festival du Voyageur** commemorates the legacy of the *voyageurs*. Winnipeg is also a cultural center for the West. The Royal Winnipeg Ballet is one of the best in North America, and its museums and art galleries are celebrated nationally. Additionally, Winnipeg has produced some of Canada's most famous rock stars. Neil Young and the Guess Who both began their careers here.

PRACTICAL INFORMATION

Visitor Information: Tourism Winnipeg, 232-375 York Ave., R3C 3J3 (800-665-0204 or 943-1970). Also, **Travel Manitoba** (800-665-0040 ext. 36, or 945-3777) in the Legislative Bldg.

Trains: VIARAIL (U.S.: 800-561-3949, Canada: 800-561-8630), south of town on Main St. No U.S. service from Winnipeg. To: Toronto (Mon., Wed., Sat., 31 hr., $160); Churchill (Sun., Tues., Thurs., 34½ hr., $105).

Buses: Greyhound (783-8840) and **Greygoose** (786-8891), in the same station on Portage Ave. behind the Art Gallery. Greygoose is the best choice within Manitoba (Riding Mountain National Park, $24; Winnipeg Beach $7.80) and the only choice to the U.S. (Grand Forks, US$27.50; Fargo, US$38). Greyhound serves all of Canada (Calgary, 20 hr., $125; Regina, 8 hr., $53; Montréal, $142; Vancouver, $162; Toronto, 36 hr., $134). Special fares if purchased 7 days ahead.

Post Office: 266 Graham Ave. (987-5481). **Postal Code:** R3C 2E9.

Area Code: 204.

The streets of Winnipeg are all one-way, so it is vital to plan your routes well in advance.

ACCOMMODATIONS

Two youth hostels located only 10 blocks from downtown offer the least expensive lodging in Winnipeg. **Guest House International,** 168 Maryland St. (772-1272; $11), and **Ivey House International Hostel (HI/AYH),** 210 Maryland St. (772-3022; $12), 1 block farther down Maryland. **The University of Manitoba**, Pembina Highway (474-9981), has dorm rooms for $17 (June-Aug.).

Motels and hotels luxuriate downtown. Those right in the heart of things are more expensive while only blocks away more reasonable accommodations can be found. The **Balmoral Motor Hotel, Ltd.** (943-1544), at the corner of Notre Dame and Balmoral, has reasonable rooms (singles $33, doubles $40). Five blocks further down Notre Dame, at the corner with Maryland, is the **Maryland Motor Hotel** (786-5981; singles $29, doubles $31). For a real treat, go a bit outside the city; behind the Legislative Building in the middle of Osborne Village lies the **Osborne Village Motel,** 160 Osborne (452-9824), with large, clean rooms (singles $35, doubles $38).

FOOD

In addition to the numerous American fast food chains that have worked their way up north, Winnipeg has fine restaurants of its own for budget travelers. **Grapes on Main,** 180 Main St. (943-1570), has a large menu, popular bar, and is open until 2am. Their express lunch sandwiches ($5-7) come with soup or salad and a drink, and their chicken burgers ($6) are fantastic. Drink specialities include Grape Mocha and Grapes of Wrath. **Johnny G's,** 557 Osborne (942-6656), off Main, serves a full menu in 50s and 60s decor until 4am. Entrees ($5-9) and big burgers ($4-6). All beer is $2.75. In the large downtown shopping center, **Eaton's** is a true gem. **The Bombay Bicycle Club** (942-1199), at Hargrave and St. Mary's, has an inexpensive lunch menu ($5-11) and a more complete dinner offering. Their cheese and mushroom omelette ($6) is delicious anytime of day, and their shrimp and steak special ($17) is no small meal. With the big tomato in front, **East Side Mario's,** 155 Smith St. (942-8034; open until midnight), has entrees ($8-10) with unlimited soup or salad and bread. Their speciality pizzas are famous throughout town; try the *frutti di mare* with calamari, shrimp, and mussels ($11). (See also The Forks, below.)

MANITOBAN ATTRACTIONS

Winnipegers are most proud of their unique shopping attraction, **The Forks.** Originally the site of fur trades and other exchanges between natives and settlers, it was later home to the Canadian railways. Restored stables, where trains used to shack-up, have since been converted to a large market place with restaurants, stores, grocery stands, and crafts booths. **Fenton's Gourmet** has smoked chicken breast ($1.60) and imported cheese. For a touch of Americana, try orange juice at **Florida Citrus.** Hidden treasures at Forks include two sit-down restaurants. The fine cuisine at **Branigan's** ranges from veal ($13) to for shrimp ($7). **The Bridgeport Restaurant** has barbecue steak ($15) and seafood lasagna ($12), and a daily vegetarian special.

St. Boniface Cathedral (237-4500), on Cathedral Ave., was one of the largest cathedrals in the world until it blew up in 1968. The explosion blew the roof to the banks of the river, a few blocks away (open Mon.-Fri. 9am-5pm, Sat.-Sun. 10am-4pm; admission $2, children $1.50). **Assiniboia,** in the northwest of Winnipeg, has horse racing at **Assiniboia Downs,** 3975 Portage (885-3330), and horses (among other animals) grazing at **Assiniboine Park Zoo** (888-3634), on Portage. The zoo houses several endangered species (sika, leopard, and wallaby) and a children's petting zoo (open daily 10am-dusk).

For dancing or bar hopping in wintry Winnipeg, try the **Palomino Club,** 1133 Portage (country, with dancing lessons), the **Zaxx/Diamond Club,** 2100 McPhillips St. (pop), **Club Soda/Night Moves,** 1034 Elizabeth, at the Windsor Park Inn (pop and rock). Gay and lesbian establishments include **Club Zoo,** 190 Garry St. (rock and pop), and **Happening's Social Club,** 274 Sherbrook (rock and pop).

■ **Saskatchewan**

Saskatchewan (a Native term meaning "the river that flows swiftly") produces over 60% of Canada's wheat, thus earning its nickname, "Heartland of North America." It also houses Canada's only training academy for the Royal Canadian Mounted Police (in Regina). Saskatchewan is not composed solely of wheat fields, however, and its diverse terrain also is made up of southern highlands (Cypress Hills reach a higher elevation than Banff, Alberta), water-covered valley (the Qu'Appelle Valley with eight lakes and multiple gardens and parks), muddy Badlands (Butch Cassidy had a station here) and northern deserts. The north also boasts nearly 100,000 lakes and 80 million acres of forests.

PRACTICAL INFORMATION

Capital: Regina.
Time Zone: Mountain (2 hr. behind Eastern). **Postal Abbreviation:** SASK
Sales Tax: 7%, plus a 7% GST.

■■■ REGINA

Home to the training academy for the Canadian Mounties, Saskatchewan's capital city literally sprouts up out of the vast plains. Originally the site of great buffalo slaughters carried out by the Natives, in 1881 the Canadian Pacific Railway breathed life into the dusty tent settlement of Pile O' Bones, and it thrived despite its desolate location. Quickly the budding town became known as the Queen City of the plains, and in 1882 the city was rechristened Regina in tribute to Queen Victoria.

If you're interested in mixing with the inhabitants, remember that Ukrainian is Regina's second language, the French are a proud and assertive group, and that all Reginians are loyal subjects of the Queen. Around the university you may also find foreigners seeking a haven from the turmoil of their own country. In Regina they have certainly escaped that turmoil.

PRACTICAL INFORMATION

Emergency: 911.
Visitor Information: Tourism Regina, east of town on the Trans-Canadian Highway (TCH) (789-5099). Open May-Sept. Mon.-Fri. 8am-7pm, Sat.-Sun. 10am-6pm, Oct.-April Mon.-Fri. 8:30am-4:30pm.
Buses: Greyhound and **Saskatchewan Transport Company (STC)** share the same depot at 2041 Hamilton St. (787-3340). STC serves the cities of the province. To: Saskatoon (5 per day, 3 hr., $23.60), Yorkton (3 per day, 2½ hr., $17.20), and Prince Albert (5 per day, 5 hr., $36.40). Greyhound runs east and west along the TCH to Winnipeg (4 per day, 8 hr., $53) with connections to Toronto, and Calgary (5 per day, 10 hr., $79).
Public Transport: Regina Transit (777-7433), 11th. Ave. next to Eaton's Shopping, provides frequently changing inter-city routes. Call for info.
Kids Help Hotline: 800-668-6868. **Rape Crisis/Sexual Assault:** 352-0434.
Post Office: 2200 Saskatchewan Dr. (761-6307). Open Mon.-Fri. 8am-5pm. **Postal Code:** S4P 2Z4.
Area Code: 306.

ACCOMMODATIONS AND CAMPING

Turgeon International Hostel (IYHF/CHA), 2310 MacIntyre St. (791-8165), is in a beautifully restored old mansion. Kitchen, lockers. 50 beds. Members $10, nonmembers $13. Open after 5pm.

YMCA, 2400 13th Ave. (757-9622), has 12 rooms for $17 per day, $72 per week. The **YWCA** offers their 32 rooms for $27 per day and $105 per week. Appropriate sex only, please. Gender, that is.

The Inn Tower, 1009 Albert St. (525-3737), has large rooms for $40 single ($3 for another person). Contains a rare treat—full sized closets.

Regina's Victoria Inn, 1717 Victoria Ave. (757-0663), presents spacious rooms with coffee makers. In season, $50-64, off-season $44.

Plains Motor Home, 1965 Albert St. (757-8661), at the intersection of Albert and Victoria, right in the heart of downtown. Small but clean rooms with clean and well-lit hallways. Single $34, double $38.

Two campgrounds pitch close to downtown, both directly off the TCH, and well-marked from the highway. **Buffalo Lookout Campground** (525-1448), 5km east (entry by service road south off the TCH) sports clean showers and recreation facilities. (Sites $10 for 2, hook-up $14, each additional person $1. Open May-Sept.) More private and quieter, **King's Acres Campground** (522-1619), is only 1km east of downtown on the north service road. This campground also has recreation and they allow pets (open year-round; sites $9, hook-up $16).

FOOD AND NIGHTLIFE

Martini Brothers, 2305 Smith St. (545-7766)., parallel to Albert St., one block from Victoria. The secret find of Regina, offering huge portions for the weary traveler. Hot breakfasts run $5-7 or around $1.25 for a cold breakfast. Lunches from $4 (sandwich) to $6.50 (linguine with clam sauce and amazing garlic bread). Dinner ranges from salad ($4) to pasta carbonara ($6.60) to tortellini with seafood ($9.50). (Open 8am-10pm, midnight if the place is shaking or stirring.)

Simply Delicious, 826 Victoria Ave. (352-4929). Advertising only by word of mouth, in this diner the homemade food is better (and bigger) than mom's. Look carefully—the awning on this white building simply says "Rest." and the name is discretely placed on the window. Eggs $4-7, pancakes $4. Sandwiches are all under $6, entrees $6-11.

Saje, 2330 Albert (569-9726), an open room with a row of booth-like tables, invites friendly conversations between diners and future visits. The large, homemade dishes run from $4 to $25. The special is the seasonal salad ($4.75) with fresh veggies on a bed of lettuce. Bagel sandwiches are also popular ($4-7).

TOPS, 3847 Albert St. (584-5558), is both a restaurant and lounge. All dinners come with salad or soup, toast, and rice/pasta or potato. Try the $6 shrimp scampi or the $13 BBQ ribs (open 11am-1am).

New Canton Gardens, 1845 Victoria Ave. (565-3232). On weekends, the large all-you-can-eat Chinese buffet is $8. Regular entrees $6-14 (open daily 11am-11pm).

For an evening, try these nightclubs: **Channel One,** 1326 Hamilton (569-2123), live pop/rock; **Gerry Lee's,** 1047 Park (525-8828), best of 50s and 60s; **Brewster's Brew Pub and Bar,** 1832 Victoria Ave. E. (761-1500), Saskatchewan's first brew pub; **The Keg,** 1425 Mailton St. (352-9691), student hangout. Dance the night away at **Longbranch Saloon,** 1400 McIntyre St. (525-8336), country, ladies night Wed., and the **Manhattan Club,** 2300 Dewdrey Ave. (359-7771), with a large dance floor and ladies night Thurs.

SIGHTS AND ATTRACTIONS

The crown jewel of this royal city is **Wascana Centre;** at 2300 acres it is the largest urban park on the continent. The **Mackenzie Art Gallery,** 3475 Albert Street (522-4242), with over 1600 exhibits, many of them from western Canada (open Wed.-Thurs. 11am-10pm, Mon.-Tues. and Fri. 11am-6pm) is within the boundaries of the park, as are the **Saskatchewan Legislative Building** and the **University of Regina.** Hundreds of geese on Wascana Lake. Start a tour of the park with the **Saskatchewan Science Center** (522-4629 or 791-7900), at Winnipeg and Wascana St., where hands-on exhibits bring science to life. Also home of the huge IMAX theatre. (Open summer, Mon.-Fri. 10am-6pm, Sat.-Sun. noon-6pm, winter hours vary. Admission to museum and IMAX $9, seniors $6, ages 6-18 $6, under 6 $3.) Also visit the **Museum of Natural History** (787-2815) at Albert St. and College Ave., exhibiting Saskatchewan's geological and indigenous history. Home of Megamunch, Canada's first animated dinosaur. (Open daily 9am-8:30pm. Free.)

Your chance to find out how the famous Canadian Mounties, the austere, sharply uniformed soldiers on horseback, are molded comes at the **Royal Canadian Mounted Police Training Academy,** 11th Ave. (780-5900). The Academy houses a museum (open daily 8am-6:45pm), offers tours (daily 9-11am and 1:30-3:30pm hourly), and presents daily parades (12:45pm) and a sunset retreat ceremony (July-Aug. Tues. 6:45pm); come see the finest mounted fighting force in the western hemisphere learning to ride, free!

Regina has rich artistic and multicultural traditions. It is the home to Canada's oldest continuously operating symphony orchestra, as well as an annual outdoor summer Shakespeare festival in late July and early August. Other festivals include **Buffalo Days** (late July-Early August), a celebration of local art, fashion, and livestock. It's kicked off by the Pile O' Bones parade. The big festival of the winter is **Winterfest** (mid-February). This fireworks extravaganza and Christmas display always coincides with the Prince Albert Festival, and is full of outdoor athletic contests such as Dog Sled Races, trapping contests, and jigging contests.

Alberta

Alberta's glitter is concentrated in the west of the province; the icy peaks and turquoise lakes of Banff and Jasper National Parks reign as Alberta's most prominent landscapes. To the east, less sublime vistas of farmland, prairie, and oil fields fill the yawning expanses. Alberta boasts thousands of prime fishing holes, world-renowned fossil fields, and centers of Native American culture. Calgary caught the world's eye when it hosted the XV Winter Olympics in 1988, and is annual host to the wild and wooly Stampede.

PRACTICAL INFORMATION

Capital: Edmonton.
Visitor Information: Alberta Tourism, 3rd floor, 10155 102 St., Edmonton T5J 4L6 (800-661-8888, 427-4321 in Alberta). **Provincial Parks Information,** Standard Life Centre #1660, 10405 Jasper Ave., Edmonton T5J 3N4 (427-9429). **Canadian Parks Service,** Box 2989, Station M, Calgary T2P 3H8 (292-4401).
Time Zone: Mountain (2 hr. behind Eastern). **Postal Abbreviation:** AB
Drinking Age: 18.

> The province of Alberta receives even more complete coverage in our sister book, *Let's Go: Alaska & The Pacific Northwest.* Seek it out!

■■■ BANFF NATIONAL PARK

Banff is Canada's best-loved and best-known natural preserve. It offers peaks and canyons, white foaming rapids and brilliant turquoise lakes, dense forests and open meadows—and an abundance of unspoiled backcountry opportunities to novices and purists alike.

PRACTICAL INFORMATION

Emergency: Banff Warden Office (762-4506). **Lake Louise Warden Office** (522-3866). Both open 24 hrs.

Visitor Information: Banff Information Centre, 224 Banff Ave. (762-1550). Includes **Chamber of Commerce** (762-8421) and **Canadian Parks Service** (762-4256). Open daily 8am-8pm; Oct.-May 9am-5pm. **Lake Louise Information Centre** (522-3833). Open mid-May to mid-June daily 10am-6pm; mid-June-Aug. daily 8am-10pm; Sept.-Oct. daily 10am-6pm.

Buses: Greyhound, 100 Gopher St. (762-6767). To: Lake Louise (5 per day, $7); Calgary (5 per day, $15); Vancouver ($89).

Car Rental: Banff Used Car Rentals (762-3352), junction of Wolf and Lynx. $34 per day. 100 free km, 10¢ per additional km. Must be 18 with major credit card.

Bike Rental: Bactrax Rentals, 337 Banff Ave. (762-8177). Mountain bikes $5 per hr., $20 per day. Discounts for HI-C members. Open daily 8am-8pm.

Post Office: 204 Buffalo St. (762-2586). Open Mon.-Fri. 9am-5:30pm. **Postal Code:** T0L 0C0.

Area Code: 403.

Banff National Park hugs the Alberta-British Columbia border, 120km west of Calgary. The **Trans-Canada Hwy.** (Hwy. 1) runs east-west through the park; the **Icefields Parkway** (Hwy. 93) connects Banff to Jasper National Park in the north. Civilization in the park centers around the townsites of Banff and **Lake Louise,** 55km northwest of Banff on Hwy. 1.

ACCOMMODATIONS, CAMPING, AND FOOD

Although the budget traveler may have difficulty finding an affordable restaurant in town, inexpensive lodging is abundant. Fifteen residents of the townsite offer rooms in their own homes, most in the $20-40 range. Ask for the *Banff Private Home Accommodation* list at the Banff Information Centre (see Practical Information). A string of HI-C hostels runs from Banff to Lake Louise on to Jasper.

Banff International Hostel (HI-C), Box 1358, Banff T0L 0C0 (762-4122), 3km from Banff townsite on Tunnel Mountain Rd. BIH has the look and setting of a ski lodge. Clean rooms with 2 bunk beds. A hike from the center of the townsite, but the modern amenities and friendly staff make it worthwhile. Cafeteria, laundry facilities, TVs, hot showers. Wheelchair-accessible. Registration 6-10am and 4pm-midnight. $16, nonmembers $21. Linen $1.

Hilda Creek Hostel (HI-C), 8.5km south of the Icefield Centre on the Icefields Parkway. The most noteworthy feature is a primitive **sauna** that holds about 4 people. Full-service kitchen. Excellent hiking and skiing nearby at Parker's Ridge. $8, nonmembers $13. Call BIH for reservations.

Rampart Creek Hostel (HI-C), 34km south of the Icefield Centre. Rampart's proximity to several world-famous ice climbs makes it a favorite of winter mountaineers. Rustic cabins. Sauna, full-service kitchen, wood-heated bathtub. $8, nonmembers $13. Call BIH for reservations.

Lake Louise International Hostel (HI-C) (522-2200), Village Rd., 0.5km from Samson Mall in Lake Louise townsite. Brand-new super-hostel à la Banff International. Cafeteria, full-service kitchen, hot showers. Wheelchair-accessible. The adjacent Canadian Alpine Centre sponsors various programs and events for hikers and skiers. $15, nonmembers $22. Call BIH for reservations and information.

None of the park's popular camping sites accepts reservations, so arrive early. Many campgrounds reserve sites for bicyclists and hikers; inquire at the office. Rates range from $7.25-13. Park facilities include (listed from north to south): **Waterfowl** (116 sites), **Lake Louise** (220 sites), **Protection Mountain** (89 sites), **Johnston Canyon** (132 sites), **Two Jack Main** (381 sites) and **Tunnel Mountain Village** (620 sites). Each site holds a maximum of two tents and six people.

The restaurants in Banff generally charge high prices for mediocre food. Luckily, the Banff **(Cafe Aspenglow)** and Lake Louise **(Bill Deyto's Cafe)** International Hostels serve affordable, wholesome meals for $3-6. Your best option, however, is to pick up a propane grill and a 10-lb. bag of potatoes and head for the mountains (baked potatoes, potato skins, hash browns, french fries, potato salad...). Do your shopping at **Safeway** (762-5378), at Marten and Elk St. (open daily 8am-10pm).

OUTDOORS

Hike to the **backcountry** for privacy, beauty, and over 1600km of trails. The pamphlet *Drives and Walks,* available at the Information Centres (see Practical Information), describes day and overnight hikes in the Lake Louise and Banff areas. A free backcountry permit (also available at information centres and park warden offices) is required for overnight stays—bring a propane stove; no wood may be chopped in the parks. The Park Information Centre has the *Canadian Rockies Trail Guide,* with excellent information and maps.

Two easy but rewarding trails lie within walking distance of the townsite. **Fenland** winds 2km through an area creeping with beaver, muskrat, and waterfowl. Follow Mt. Norquay Rd. out of Banff and look for signs. About 25km out of Banff toward Lake Louise, **Johnston Canyon** offers a popular ½-day hike. The 1.1km hike to the canyon's lower falls and the 2.7km trip to the canyon's upper falls consist mostly of a catwalk along the edge of the canyon. Don't stop here, though; continue along the trail for another 3.1km to seven blue-green cold-water springs known as the **Inkpots.** Your car will find **Tunnel Mountain Drive** and **Vermillion Lakes** particularly scenic places to cough fumes into the clear air.

When Canada's first national park was established in 1885, it was called the Hot Springs Reserve and its featured attraction was the **Cave and Basin Hot Springs.** The **Cave and Basin Centennial Centre** (762-4900), on Cave Ave. southwest of the city, is a refurbished resort. Walk along the Discovery Trail to see the original spring discovered over 100 years ago by three Canadian Pacific Railway workers. (Open daily 10am-7pm; in winter 10am-5pm. Pool open early June-late Aug. only. Pool admission $3, seniors and kids $2.) If you find Cave and Basin's 32°C (90°F) water too chilly, try the **Upper Hot Springs pool** (762-2056), a 40°C (104°F) sulphurous cauldron up the hill on Mountain Ave. (Open Mon.-Thurs. 12:30-9pm, Fri.-Sun. 8:30am-11pm. $3, seniors and kids $2.)

The **Sulphur Mountain Gondola** (762-5438), next to the Upper Hot Springs pool, lifts you 700m to a view of the Rockies normally reserved for birds and mountain goats (open daily 8:30am-8pm; $8.50, kids 5-11 $3.75, under 5 free.) **Brewster Tours** (762-6767) offers an extensive array of bus tours with knowledgeable and entertaining guides. If you don't have a car, these tours may be the only way to see some of the main attractions, such as the Athabasca Glacier and the spiral railroad tunnel. (One way $60, 9½-hr. round-trip $83. Purchase tickets at the bus depot.)

Fishing is legal virtually anywhere you can find water, but you must hold a National Parks fishing permit, available at the Information Centre ($5 for a 7-day permit, $10 for an annual permit). Those who prefer more vigorous water sports can **raft** the white waters of the **Kootenay River.** A particularly good deal is offered by the Banff International Hostel—rafting on the Kicking Horse River (transportation included) for $44.

Bicycling is permitted on public roads and highways and on certain trails in the park. *Trail Bicycling in National Parks in Alberta and British Columbia,* available at the Information Centres in Banff and Lake Louise, lists appropriate trails. Horseback riding is available at the **Banff Springs Hotel,** Spray Ave. (daily 9am-5pm; $18 for 1 hr., $28 for 2 hr., $34 for 3 hr.; reservations recommended).

The spectacularly clear waters of Lake Louise often serve North American filmmakers' need for Swiss Alpine scenery. Renting a canoe from the **Chateau Lake Louise Boat House** (522-3511) will give you the closest look at the lake ($20 per hr.; open 9am-8pm). Several hiking trails also begin at the water. The **Friendly**

Giant Sight-seeing Lift (522-3555), which runs up Mt. Whitehorn, across the Trans-Canada Hwy. from Lake Louise, provides another chance to gape at the landscape. (Open mid-June to late Sept. daily 9am-6pm. $9, students $8, ages 5-12 $4.)

■■■ CALGARY

Calgary was founded in 1875 as the summer outpost of the Northwest Mounted Police. The discovery of oil in 1947 transformed this cowtown into a wealthy, cosmopolitan city, and in 1988, Calgary hosted the Winter Olympics. The oil may be crude, but the city is refined. Skyscrapers overshadow oil derricks, businesspeople scurry about, and a modern transport system threads soundlessly through immaculate downtown streets. Calgary hasn't forgotten its frontier roots; when the Stampede yahoos into town, cowboy hats and Western accents are *de rigueur.*

PRACTICAL INFORMATION

Emergency: 911.

Visitor Information: Calgary Convention and Visitors Bureau, 237 8th Ave. SE (263-8510). Call or write for help finding accommodations, especially around Stampede time. Open daily 8am-5pm.

Airport: Calgary International Airport (292-8477), about 5km northwest of the city center. Bus #57 provides sporadic service to the city. The **Airporter Bus** (291-3848) offers frequent and friendly service for $7.50. **Brewster Tours** (221-8242) operates buses to: Banff (3 per day, $26); Jasper (1 per day, $50).

Greyhound: 877 Greyhound Way SW (from outside Calgary 800-661-TRIP; from within Calgary 260-0846). Frequent service to: Edmonton ($26); Banff ($15).

Public Transport: Calgary Transit, 206 7th Ave. SW (262-1000). Bus schedules, passes and maps. Open Mon.-Fri. 8:30am-5pm. Buses run all over the city; Streetcars (C-Trains) cover less territory, but they're free downtown (along 7th Ave. S.; between 10th St. SW and City Hall). Fare $1.50, ages 6-14 90¢, under 6 free; exact change required. Day pass $4.50, kids $3. Book of 10 tickets $12, kids $8.50.

Taxi: Checker Cab, 299-9999; **Yellow Cab,** 250-8311.

Car Rental: Dollar (221-1888 at the airport, 269-3777 downtown). Cars start at $37 per day with unlimited km. Weekend special $33 per day. Must be 23 with a major credit card. $9 per day extra if under 25. Open daily 7am-midnight.

Bike Rental: Global Sports, 7218 McLeod Trail SW (252-2055). $17 per day.

Help Lines: Crisis Line: 266-1605. **Sexual Assault Centre:** 237-5888. Open daily 9:30am-5pm.

Post Office: 220 4th Ave. SE (292-5512). Open Mon.-Fri. 8am-5:45pm. **Postal Code:** T2P 1B0.

Area Code: 403

Calgary is divided into quadrants: **Centre Street** is the east-west divide, and the **Bow River** divides the north and south sections. The rest is fairly simple: avenues run east-west, streets run north-south. Pay careful attention to the quadrant distinctions (NE, NW, SE, SW) at the end of each address.

ACCOMMODATIONS AND FOOD

Cheap lodging in Calgary is rare only when packs of tourists Stampede into the city's hotels—reserve ahead for the month of July. The **Calgary International Hostel (HI-C),** 520 7th Ave. SE (269-8239), located several blocks south of downtown, has a snack bar, meeting rooms, cooking and barbecue facilities, laundry, and a cycle workshop. (Curfew 2am. Front desk closes at midnight. $13, nonmembers $18.) As luxurious as a "Y" can be, the **YWCA,** 320 5th Ave. SE (232-1599), is in a fine, quiet neighborhood. The trade-off for the security is somewhat lifeless lodging. (Cafeteria open daily. Women only; no male visitors permitted. Singles $25, with bath $30. Dorm beds $15. 10% senior discount.) **St. Regis Hotel,** 124 7th Ave. SE (262-4641), has friendly management and clean, comfortable rooms, with a tavern and snack bar downstairs (singles $37, with TV $40, with TV and bath $48).

Finding food is relatively easy in Calgary. Ethnic and cafe-style dining spots line the **Stephen Avenue Mall,** 8th Ave. S. between 1st St. SE and 3rd St. SW. **Hang Fung Foods Ltd.,** 119 3rd Ave. SE (269-5853), in the rear of a Chinese market with the same name, has combination dinners which include won ton soup, a spring roll, pork fried rice, and an entree for $8.50. (Open daily 9am-9pm.) California cool pervades **4th Street Rose,** 2116 4th St. SW (228-5377), a fashionable restaurant on the outskirts of town. The house specialty is the Caesar Salad ($4), served in a large Mason jar, but gourmet pizzas and homemade pastas run $4-9. (Open Mon.-Thurs. 11am-1am, Fri. 11am-2am, Sat. 10am-2am, Sun. 10am-midnight.)

SIGHTS

Don't just gaze at the **Calgary Tower,** 101 9th Ave. SW (266-7171); ride an elevator to the top for a spectacular view of the Rockies on clear days ($4.25, seniors, students, and HI members $3, kids $2; 7:30-10:30am $2.75). The **Glenbow Museum,** 130 9th Ave. SE (268-4100), is just across the street. The proximate placement of such unrelated artifacts as Indian bronzes, pre-Columbian pottery, and 19th-century firearms endows the museum with the feel of the world's most expensive garage sale. (Open Tues.-Sun. 10am-6pm. $4.50, seniors, students, and kids $3, under 7 free; free Sat.) Five blocks west on 8th Ave. are the **Devonian Gardens.** Located on the 4th floor of Toronto Dominion Sq. (8th Ave. between 2nd and 3rd St. SW), this 2.5-acre indoor garden contains fountains, waterfalls, bridges, and over 20,000 plants, representing 138 species. (Open daily 9am-9pm. Free.) A few blocks to the northwest, the **Energeum,** 640 5th Ave. SW (297-4293), in the lobby of the Energy Resources Building, is Calgary's shrine to "black gold." A short film re-creates the mania that followed Alberta's first oil find. (Open Sun.-Fri. 10:30am-4:30pm; Sept.-May except holidays Mon.-Fri. 10:30am-4:30pm. Free.)

The **Calgary Zoo** (232-9300), on **St. George's Island,** is accessible by the river walkway to the east. The Canadian Wilds exhibit, opened in July of 1992, re-creates the sights, the sounds, and, yes, the smells of Canada's wilderness. (Open 9am-6pm; 9am-4pm in winter. $7.50, seniors $4.75, kids $3.75. Tues. $5, seniors free.)

THE STAMPEDE

Even those who think that rodeo is grotesque and silly have trouble saying "Calgary" without letting a quick "Stampede" slip out. Indeed, Calgarians take great pride in their "Greatest Outdoor Show on Earth." Every year around Stampede time, locals in ten-gallon hats command tour groups to yell "yahoo" in the least likely of circumstances. Simply put, the entire city of Calgary flips out.

And why not? Any event that draws millions from across the province, the country, and the world deserves some gratuitous hype. Make the trip out to **Stampede Park,** southeast of downtown, for a glimpse of steer wrestling, bull riding, and the famous chuckwagon races. For information and ticket order forms, contact the **Calgary Exhibition and Stampede**, Box 1860, Station M, Calgary T2P 2L8 (800-661-1260; 261-0101 in Calgary; tickets $15-38 depending on event and seats; rush tickets $7.50, youth $6.75, seniors and kids $3.50). Take the C-Train to the Stampede stop.

■ Sort of near Calgary: Head-Smashed-In Buffalo Jump

Coveted as a source of fresh meat, sustenance, tools, and shelter, the buffalo was the victim of one of history's most innovative forms of mass slaughter: the buffalo jump. For over 5500 years, Native Americans in Southern Alberta created instant all-you-can-eat buffets by maneuvering a buffalo herd into a "gathering basin," and then spooking it into a stampede over a 10m-high cliff. No buffalo jump is as well-preserved as the **Head-Smashed-In Buffalo Jump,** located about 170km southeast of

Calgary on Secondary Rte. 785. Learn about buffalo jumps at the $10 million **Interpretive Centre** (553-2731), which shows reenactments of the fatal plunge, filmed with frozen buffalo (open daily 9am-8pm; Labor Day-Victoria Day 9am-5pm. $5, kids $2, under 6 free, Tues. free).

■■■ JASPER NATIONAL PARK

Before the Icefields Parkway was built, few travelers dared to venture north from Banff into the untamed wilderness of Jasper. But those bushwhackers who made it returned with rave reviews, and the completion of the Parkway in 1940 paved the way for everyone to appreciate Jasper's astounding beauty. Be sure to set aside a couple of days to explore the backcountry (a free permit, available at the Park Information Centre, is required).

PRACTICAL INFORMATION

Emergency: RCMP, 852-4848. **Ambulance and Fire,** 852-3100.
Visitor Information: Park Information Centre, 500 Connaught Dr. (852-6176). Trail maps and information on all aspects of the park. Open daily 8am-8pm; early Sept.-late Oct. and late Dec. to mid-May daily 9am-5pm; mid-May to mid-June daily 8am-5pm. For further info, write to **Park Headquarters,** Superintendent, Jasper National Park, 632 Patricia St., Box 10, Jasper T0E 1E0 (852-6161).
VIA Rail: 314 Connaught Dr. (800-852-3168). 3 per week to: Vancouver ($126); Edmonton ($73); Winnipeg ($200). 10% discount for senior citizens and students. Kids ½ price. Coin-operated lockers $1 for 24 hrs.
Buses: Greyhound, 314 Connaught Dr. (852-3926), in the VIA station. To: Edmonton (4 per day, $42); Kamloops ($45); Vancouver ($83). **Brewster Transportation and Tours** (852-3332), also in the VIA station. To: Banff (full-day tour $60, daily 4¼-hr. express $39); Calgary (daily, 8 hr., $47).
Taxi: Heritage Taxi, 611 Patricia (852-5558). Flat rate of $8 between town and Whistler's hostel, and a 30% discount from regular fares to HI members.
Car Rental: Tilden Car Rental, in the VIA depot (852-4972). $44 per day with 100 free km. Must be 21 with credit card. $2500 deductible for drivers under 25.
Bike Rental: Freewheel Cycle, 611 Patricia Ave. (852-5380). Mountain bikes $5 per hr., $13 per 5 hr., $20 per day. Open in summer daily 9am-8pm; in spring and fall Tues.-Sun. 10am-6pm.
Post Office: 502 Patricia St. (852-3041), across from the townsite green. Open Mon.-Fri. 9am-5pm. **Postal Code:** T0E 1E0.
Area Code: 403.

All of the above addresses are found in **Jasper townsite,** which is located near the center of the park, 362km southwest of Edmonton and 287km north of Banff. **Hwy. 16** transports travelers through the northern reaches of the park, while the **Icefields Parkway** (Hwy. 93) connects to Banff National Park in the south. Buses run to the townsite daily from Edmonton, Calgary, Vancouver, and Banff. Trains arrive from Edmonton and Vancouver. Renting a bike is the most practical option for short jaunts within the park.

ACCOMMODATIONS, CAMPING, AND FOOD

Hotels in Jasper townsite are too expensive to be viable budget options. You may, however, be able to stay cheaply at a **B&B** (singles $20-35, doubles $25-45). Ask for the *Private Homes Accommodations List* at the Park Information Centre. If you have some sort of transportation, head for one of Jasper's hostels (listed below from north to south). Reservations are channeled through the Edmonton-based **Northern Alberta Hostel Association** (439-3139; fax 403-433-7781).

Maligne Canyon Hostel (HI-C), 11km east of townsite on Maligne Canyon Rd. (852-3584). Small, recently renovated cabins on the bank of the Maligne River. An ideal place for viewing wildlife; the knowledgeable manager leads guided hikes through nearby Maligne Canyon. $8, nonmembers $12. Closed Wed. in winter.

Whistlers Mountain Hostel (HI-C), on Sky Tram Rd. (852-3215), 7km south of the townsite. Closest to the townsite and the park's most modern hostel. Usually full in summer. Bring your own food. Curfew midnight. $12, nonmembers $16.

Mt. Edith Cavell Hostel (HI-C), on Edith Cavell Rd., off Hwy. 93A. The road is closed in winter, but welcomes anyone willing to ski 11km from Hwy. 93A. Really. $8, nonmembers $12. Open mid-June-early Oct., key system in winter.

Athabasca Falls Hostel (HI-C), on Hwy. 93 (852-5959), 30km south of Jasper townsite, 500m from Athabasca Falls. Huge dining/recreation room with wood-burning stove. $9, nonmembers $14. Closed Tues. in winter.

Beauty Creek Hostel (HI-C), on Hwy. 93, 78km south of Jasper townsite. Next to the stunning Sunwapta River. Accessible through a key system in winter (groups only). $8, nonmembers $12. Open May-mid-Sept., closed Wed.

For campground updates, tune your radio to **1450 AM** near Jasper Townsite. The park maintains sites at 10 campgrounds, including (north to south): **Pocahontas** (140 sites), **Snaring River** (56 sites), **Whistlers** (781 sites), **Wapiti** (366 sites), **Wabasso** (238 sites), **Columbia Icefield** (33 sites), and **Wilcox Creek** (46 sites). Sites range from $7.25-17.50.

For cheap eats, stock up at a local market or bulk foods store before heading for the backcountry. For around-the-clock grocery supplies, stop at **Wink's Food Store,** 617 Patricia St. (852-4223). **Nutter's,** 622 Patricia St. (852-5844), offers grains, nuts, dried fruits and (if you're sick of healthful food) candy, all in bulk form. They also sell deli meats, canned goods and fresh-ground coffee. (Open Mon.-Sat. 9am-10pm, Sun. 10am-9pm.) For a sit-down meal, the Egyptian food at **Roony's,** 618 Connaught Dr. (852-5830; open daily noon-2am, in winter 2pm-2am), will make your mouth light up like a pinball machine. Try the *kofta*, spicy ground beef with parsley and onions on toasted bread ($7). Burgers are also cheap ($3.25-3.75).

OUTDOORS

An extensive network of trails connects most parts of Jasper; many paths start at the townsite itself. Information Centres (see Practical Information for locations) distribute *Day Hikes in Jasper National Park* (free) and a summary of longer hikes.

Mt. Edith Cavell, named after a German nurse who was executed during WWI for providing aid to the Allies, will shake you to the bone with the thunderous roar of avalanches off the Angel Glacier. Take the 1.6km loop trail Path of the Glacier to the top or the 8km hike through **Cavell Meadows.** Edith rears her enormous head 30km south of the townsite on Mt. Edith Cavell Rd.

Maligne Lake, the largest glacier-fed lake in the Canadian Rockies, is located 50km southeast of the townsite at the end of Maligne Lake Rd. Farther north in the valley and 30km east of the townsite, the Maligne River flows into **Medicine Lake**— but no river flows out. The trick? The water escapes underground through tunnels in the easily dissolved limestone, re-emerging 16km downstream in the **Maligne Canyon,** 11km east of the townsite on Maligne Canyon Rd. (This is the longest known underground river in North America. Pretty sneaky, eh?) **Whitewater Rafting (Jasper) Ltd.** (852-7238) offers several rafting trips (from $35; 2-hr. trip down the Maligne River $45). Register by phone or stop at the Esso station in the townsite.

Trout abound in Jasper's spectacular lakes during the month of May—but so do anglers. **Beaver Lake,** however, located about 1km from the main road at the tip of Medicine Lake, is never crowded and even novice fisherfolk can hook themselves a dinner. Rent equipment at **Currie's,** in the Sports Shop at 416 Connaught Dr. (852-5650; rod, reel, and line $10; one-day boat rental $25).

Let your steed do the sweating on a **guided horseback trail ride** at the Jasper Park Lodge (852-5794; 1½-hr. ride $25), Maligne Lake (3-hr. ride $45), or Pyramid Lake (852-3562; $17 per hr.). The saddle-sore can revive their numbed buns at **Miette Hot Springs** (866-3939), north of the Townsite off Hwy. 16 along the clearly marked, 15km Miette Hotsprings Rd. Free from nutrient-filled additives and the rotten-egg reek of sulfur, the pools are heated via external pipes through which the spring water is pumped from the smelly source. Unfortunately, the 40°C (102°F) water is off-limits in winter. (Open May 25-June 24 Mon.-Fri. 12:30-8pm, Sat.-Sun. 10:30am-9pm; June 25-Sept. 5 daily 8:30am-10:30pm. $2.50, children $1.50. Suit rental $1.25, towels $1, lockers 25¢.)

Not to be outdone by Banff, Jasper also has a gondola. The **Jasper Tramway** (852-3093), offers a panoramic view of the park as it rises 2.5km up the side of **Whistlers Mountain** ($9.65, ages 5-14 $4.85, under 5 free; open mid-April-early Sept. 8am-9:30pm; Sept.-mid-Oct. 9am-4:30pm). A steep 10km trail from the Whistlers Mountain Hostel also leads up the slope; you may want to take the tram ride down ($5).

British Columbia

Larger in area than California, Oregon, and Washington combined, British Columbia, Canada's westernmost province, attracts so many visitors that tourism has become the province's second largest industry after logging. Although skiing is excellent year-round, most tourists arrive in summer, flocking to the twin cities of Vancouver and Victoria and the pristine lakes and beaches of the Okanagan Valley.

As you head north, clouds begin to replace the crowds. Thick forests, low mountains, and occasional patches of high desert are interrupted only by such supply and transit centers as Prince George and Prince Rupert. Farther north, even these outposts of civilization defer to thick spruce forests. BC's extensive and accessible park system allows for an affordable escape from urbandom, and while the government may view such retreats in terms of pecuniary possibility, to most of those who take them (and take them again) they climb high onto the list of necessities.

PRACTICAL INFORMATION

Capital: Victoria.
Visitor Information: Call 800-663-6000 or write the **Ministry of Tourism and Provincial Secretary,** Parliament Bldgs., Victoria V8V 1X4 (604-387-1642). Ask for the *Accommodations* guide. **Canadian Parks Service,** 220 4th Ave. SE, P.O. Box 2989, Station M, Calgary, AB T2P 3H8.
Time Zone: Pacific and Mountain. **Postal Abbreviation:** BC
Drinking Age: 19.

For even more thorough coverage of British Columbia (as though that were possible), refer to *Let's Go: Alaska & The Pacific Northwest,* carried by reputable booksellers worldwide.

■■■ GLACIER NATIONAL PARK

For a $5000 salary bonus and immortality on the map, Major A.B. Rogers discovered a route through the Columbia Mountains which finally allowed East to meet West in Canada's first transcontinental railway. Completed in 1885, the railway was a dangerous enterprise; more than 200 lives were lost to avalanches during its first 30 years of operation. Today, **Rogers Pass** lies in the center of Glacier National Park, and 1350 sq. km commemorate the efforts of Rogers and other hardy explorers who united British Columbia with the rest of Canada.

Practical Information The Trans-Canada Highway (TCH) has numerous **scenic turn-offs** with picnic facilities, bathrooms, and historical plaques. For a detailed description of the park's 19 hiking trails, call the **Park Administration Office,** at 3rd and Boyle in Revelstoke, west of the park (837-7500; open Mon.-Fri. 8am-4:30pm), or pick up a copy of *Footloose in the Columbias* at the **Rogers Pass Information Centre,** located along the TCH in Glacier (open daily 8am-8pm; in winter 9am-6pm). **Park passes** are available at the Centre ($5 per day, $10 for four days, $30 per year). For more info, write the Superintendent, P.O. Box 350, Revelstoke V0E 2S0.

Glacier lies right in the path of the Trans-Canada Hwy., 262km west of Calgary and 723km east of Vancouver. **Greyhound** (837-5874) makes four trips daily from Revelstoke to Glacier ($6.15). In an emergency, call the **Park Warden Office** (837-6274; open daily 7am-11pm; in winter 24 hrs.). The **area code** is 604.

Accommodations, Camping, and Food The only beds in the park are at the **Best Western Glacier Park Lodge** (837-2126), on the TCH; prepare to cough up $90 for a single, $95 for a double (10% senior discount, kids under 12 free). There are two campgrounds in Glacier: **Illecillewaet** (ILL-uh-SILL-uh-watt) and **Loop Brook.** Both offer flush toilets, kitchen shelters with cook stoves, drinking water, and firewood (open mid-June-Sept; sites at both $10.50). Illecillewaet stays open in winter without plumbing; winter guests must register at the Park Administration Office at Rogers Pass. **Backcountry campers** must pitch their tents at least 3km from the highway and register with the Administration Office beforehand.

The only **restaurant** in the area is at the **Best Western** (see above), where prices are prohibitive and proper attire is required. You'd do well to drop by a supermarket in Golden or Revelstoke before you enter the park.

Outdoors in the Park A century after Rogers' discovery, Glacier National Park remains one of the few unspoiled wilderness areas in the interior of British Columbia. The jagged peaks and steep, narrow valleys of the Columbia Range prevent development within Glacier. Try to visit the park in late July or early August, when brilliant explosions of mountain wildflowers offset the deep green of the Columbia rainforests. Glacier receives measurable precipitation one out of every two days during the summer; avoid the park in winter, as near-daily snowfalls and the constant threat of avalanches often restrict travel to the Trans-Canada Hwy.

Eight popular **hiking trails** begin at the Illecillewaet campground, 3.4km west of Rogers Pass. The relaxing, 1km **Meeting of the Waters** trail leads to the confluence of the Illecillewaet and Asulkan Rivers. The 4.2km **Avalanche Crest** trail offers spectacular views of Rogers Pass, the Hermit Range, and the Illecillewaet River Valley; the treeless slopes below the crest testify to the destructive power of winter snowslides. From early June to late August, the Information Centre runs daily **interpretive hikes** through the park beginning at 9am. Come prepared for one of these 4-6 hour tours with a picnic lunch, a rain jacket, and a sturdy pair of walking shoes. Due to the steepness of the terrain, there is no biking on the trails in Glacier.

■■■ VANCOUVER

Canada's third largest city comes as a pleasant surprise to the jaded, metropolis-hopping traveler. Tune out the language, and Vancouver could be a North American Switzerland, with immaculate and efficient public transport and spotless sidewalks; even the seedy areas can be relatively safe. Mayor Gordon Campbell has vowed that his city will "not become like a city in the United States." With nature walks among 1000-year-old virgin timber stands, wind-surfing, and the most technologically advanced movie theater in the world all downtown, Vancouver is keeping that promise.

PRACTICAL INFORMATION
Emergency: 911.

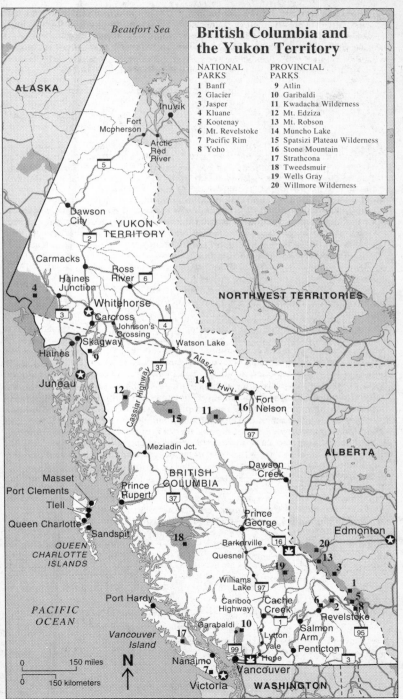

British Columbia and
the Yukon Territory

NATIONAL
PARKS
1 Banff
2 Glacier
3 Jasper
4 Kluane
5 Kootenay
6 Mt. Revelstoke
7 Pacific Rim
8 Yoho

PROVINCIAL
PARKS
9 Atlin
10 Garibaldi
11 Kwadacha Wilderness
12 Mt. Edziza
13 Mt. Robson
14 Muncho Lake
15 Spatsizi Plateau Wilderness
16 Stone Mountain
17 Strathcona
18 Tweedsmuir
19 Wells Gray
20 Willmore Wilderness

Visitor Information: Travel Infocentre, 1055 Dunsmuir St. (683-2000), in the West End. Racks of literature. Open daily 8am-6pm. **Parks and Recreation Board,** 2099 Beach Ave. (681-1141). Open Mon.-Fri. 8:30am-4:30pm.

Airport: Vancouver International Airport, on Sea Island 11km south of the city center. Connections to major cities. To reach downtown from the airport, take BC Transit bus #100 to Granville and 70th Ave.; transfer there to bus #20, which arrives downtown heading north on the Granville Mall. The private **Airport Express** (273-9023) leaves from airport level #2 and heads for downtown hotels and the Greyhound station every 15 min. 6:15am-12:30am, $8.25 per person.

VIA Rail, 1150 Station St. (800-561-8630 or 669-3050), at Main St. Sky Train stop. To: Jasper (3 per week, $116); Edmonton (3 per week, $161). Open Thurs.-Tues. 7:30am-9:30pm, Wed. 7:30am-2:30pm.

Buses: Greyhound, 1150 Station St. (662-3222), in the VIA Rail station. Service to the south and across Canada. To: Calgary (7 per day, $90); Banff (6 per day, $85); Jasper (4 per day, $83); Seattle (4 per day, $25). Open daily 5:30am-midnight. **Pacific Coach Lines,** 150 Dunsmuir St. (662-5074). Serves southern BC in conjunction with Greyhound. To: Victoria ($20, including ferry).

BC Ferries: (669-1211 general information, 685-1021 recorded information, Tsawwassen ferry terminal 943-9331). Ferries to Victoria, the Gulf Islands, Sunshine Coast, Mainland to Vancouver Island ($6, car and driver $27, motorcycle and driver $15.50, bicycle and rider $8; ages 5-11 ½-price). The terminal serving Victoria is actually located in Swartz Bay, north of Victoria.

Public Transport: BC Transit (Information Centre: 261-5100) covers most of the city and suburbs, including Tsawwassen, Horseshoe Bay and the airport. Central zone fare $1.50, seniors and ages 5-11 80¢. 2-zone peak-hr. (6:30-9:30am and 3-6:30pm) fare $2/$1; 3-zones $2.75; off-peak fares same as 1-zone price. Daypasses $4.50. Transfers free. Single fares, passes and transfers are good for the Sea-Bus and SkyTrain also. The **SeaBus** runs from the Waterfront Station, at the foot of Granville St. in downtown Vancouver, to the Lonsdale Quay at the foot of Lonsdale Ave. in North Vancouver. The **SkyTrain** runs from the Waterfront Station to Scott Rd. in New Westminster. Schedules available at Vancouver Travel.

Taxis: Yellow Cab, 681-3311. 24 hrs.

Car Rental: Rent-A-Wreck, 180 W. Georgia St. (688-0001), in the West End. From $45 per day; 150km free plus 15¢ per additional km. Must be 19 with credit card. Open Mon.-Fri. 7am-7pm, Sat. 9am-5pm, Sun. 10am-3pm.

Bike Rental: Bayshore, 745 Denman St. (688-2453). Convenient to Stanley Park. Practically new bikes $5.60 per hr., $20 per ½ day, $25 per day. Open May-Sept. daily 9am-9pm. Winter hours vary with the amount of sunlight.

Help Lines: Vancouver Crisis Center, 733-4111. **Rape Crisis Center,** 255-6344. Both 24 hrs. **Gay and Lesbian Switchboard,** 684-6869.

Post Office: Main branch, 349 W. Georgia St. (662-5725). Open Mon.-Fri. 8am-5:30pm. **Postal Code:** V6B 3P7.

Area Code: 604.

Rivers, inlets and bays divide Vancouver into regions and neighborhoods, and the profusion of waterways can confuse even the most diligent map-reader. Most of the city's attractions converge on the city-center peninsula and the larger rhino-snout-shaped peninsula to the south. The center peninsula's residential area, bounded by downtown to the east and Stanley Park to the west, is the **West End.** The western portion of the southern peninsula from around Alma Ave. to the University of BC campus is **Point Grey,** while the central area on the same peninsula, from the Granville Bridge roughly to Alma Ave., is the **Kitsilano** (the **"Kits"**).

ACCOMMODATIONS

Greater Vancouver is a rabbit warren of B&Bs. Rates average about $45-60 for singles and $55-75 for doubles. The visitors bureau (see Practical Information) has a list of B&Bs. Several private agencies also match travelers with B&Bs, usually for a fee; get in touch with **Town and Country Bed and Breakfast** (731-5942) or **Best Canadian** (738-7207).

Vancouver International Hostel (HI-C), 1515 Discovery St. (224-3208), in Jericho Beach Park. Semi-suburban location in a park. 285 beds in dorm rooms and 8 family rooms. Cooking facilities, TV room, laundry facilities, and a convenient cafeteria. 5-day limit in summer, but flexible during at other times. Registration open 7:30am-midnight. Bedding $1.50. $13.50, nonmembers $18.50. Reserve at least 2 weeks in advance during summer. Top-quality mountain bikes for $20 per day.

Globetrotter's Inn, 170 W. Esplanade (988-5141), in North Vancouver. As close to downtown as the hostel. Take the SeaBus to Lonsdale Quay, then walk 1 block east to W. Esplanade and Chesterfield. Kitchen facilities and shared baths. $13 per night. Private singles $27. Doubles $33, with bath $38.

Vincent's Backpackers Hostel, 927 Main St. (682-2441), next to the VIA Rail station, above a store called "The Source." Take bus #3 (Main St.) or #8 (Fraser). Narrow, dark hallways. Kitchen, fridge, TV, stereo. Washer and dryer. Mountain bikes for $5 per day. Office open 8am-midnight. Best to check in before noon. Shared rooms $10. Singles with shared bath $20. Doubles with shared bath $25. Weekly rates: shared rooms $60, singles $100, doubles $130. Pay before 10am after first night for 20% discount on all rates.

Paul's Guest House, 345 W. 14th Ave. (872-4753), at Alberta. Take bus #15. Nestled in a beautiful residential area. Shared baths. Complimentary full breakfast. Check in before 11pm. Call ahead for reservations. Tidy and cozy singles $36. Doubles $46. Rates $5 lower in winter.

Richmond RV Park, 6200 River Rd. (270-7878), near Holly Bridge in Richmond. Take Hwy. 99 to Westminster Hwy., then follow the signs. The best deal within 15km of downtown. Sites $15, with hookups $18-20. Open April-Oct.

Hazelmere RV Park and Campground, 18843 8th Ave. (538-1167), in Surrey. Quiet sites on the Campbell River with beach access. Showers 25¢. Sites for 1-2 people $14, with hookups $18; $2 per additional person.

FOOD

Steer clear of restaurants hawking "Canadian cuisine"—the phrase could be officially certified by the International Oxymoron Commission. The city's best eateries are the diverse ethnic and natural-foods culinaria. Vancouver's **Chinatown** is second in size only to San Francisco's, and the East Indian neighborhoods along Main, Fraser, and 49th St. serve up the spicy dishes of the subcontinent. Groceries, shops, and restaurants also cluster around E. Pender and Gore St.

The **Granville Island Market,** under the Granville Bridge, off W. 4th Ave. across False Creek from downtown, intersperses trendy shops, art galleries, and restaurants with countless produce stands. Take bus #50 from Granville St. downtown. (Open daily 9am-6pm; Labor Day-Victoria Day Tues.-Sun. 9am-6pm.)

Nirvana, 2313 Main St. (876-2911), at 7th. Take bus #8, 3, or 9. Smells like...authentic, savory, and possibly spiritual Indian cuisine. Find or lose yourself in the chicken curry ($6.50) or vegetable *biryani* ($8). Open Mon.-Fri. 11:30am-11pm, Sat.-Sun. noon-11pm.

The Green Door, 111 E. Pender St. (685-4194). Follow the alley off Columbia St. to find the hidden entrance. This legendary, wildly green establishment takes a prominent place in the annals of Vancouver hippie lore. Huge portions of slightly greasy Chinese seafood ($6-7). BYOB (no liquor license). Open Thurs.-Tues. noon-10pm; Oct.-May Wed.-Mon. noon-10pm.

The Souvlaki Place, 1181 Denman (689-3064). This Greek place pulsates with wailing Mediterranean music. *Spanikopita* ($3.25); *souvlaki* ($5). Open daily 11:30am-11pm.

Nuff-Nice-Ness, 1861 Commercial Dr. (255-4211), at 3rd. Still P. Hudson's home for Jamaican cuisine and located on a hip strip. Vegetable and meat patties ($1.80 each). Jerk chicken with salad and rice $7.50. Daily specials offered in the late afternoon for $5.50. Open Tues. 12:30-8pm, Wed.-Sat. 11am-8pm, Sun. 1-6pm.

Isadora's Cooperative Restaurant, 1540 Old Bridge Rd. (681-8816), 1 block to the right near the "Kids Only" complex. This socially conscious natural food restaurant sends its profits to community service organizations. Sandwiches $7, entrees $10-13. Open Mon.-Thurs. 7:30am-9pm, Fri.-Sun. 9am-9pm.

The Naam, 2724 W. 4th Ave. (738-7151), at Stephens. Take bus #4 or 7 from Granville. Vancouver's oldest natural-food restaurant. Truly a delight. Tofu-nut-beet burgers ($5), spinach enchiladas ($8.25), and salad bar ($1.25 per 100g). Live music nightly from 7-10pm. Open 24 hrs.

SIGHTS AND ACTIVITIES

The remaining landmark of the Expo '86 World's Fair is a 17-story, metallic, geodesic sphere which houses **Science World,** 1455 Québec St. (687-7832), at Terminal Ave. Science World features hands-on exhibits for kids and the **Omnimax Theatre** (875-6664), the most technologically advanced theater in the world. (Call for show times. Admission to both $11, seniors and kids $7; to Science World only $7, seniors and kids $4.50; to Omnimax alone after 4pm $9.) The Canada Pavilion, now called **Canada Place,** is about ½km away. You can reach it by SkyTrain from the main Expo site. Visitors who make this 4-min. journey can view Canadian arts and crafts as well as films in the **CN IMAX Theatre** (682-4629). The images on the flat, 5-story screen may not be as stunning as those on the domed Omnimax screen, but they have incredible clarity with no peripheral distortion. So there. (Open daily noon-9pm. Tickets $6.25-9.25, seniors and kids $5.25-8.25.)

Newly renovated, the **Lookout!** 555 W. Hastings St. (649-0421), offers a fantastic view of the city and surrounding areas. Though expensive! ($5.35!, seniors and students $3.75!), tickets last all day; you can leave and come back for the romantic night skyline! (Open daily 8:30am-10:30pm. 50% discount with HI membership or receipt from the Vancouver International Hostel.)

Gastown, named for "Gassy Jack" Deighton, the con man who opened Vancouver's first saloon, is a tourist snare disguised as a restored turn-of-the-century neighborhood. Listen for the continent's only steam-powered clock on the corner of Cambie and Water St.—it whistles every 15 min. Gastown is a fair walk from downtown or a short ride on bus #22 along Burrard St. to Carrall St. **Chinatown,** replete with restaurants and shops, also lies within walking distance of downtown, but you can take bus #22 on Burrard St. northbound to Pender St. at Carrall St. and return by bus #22 westbound along Pender St. The area is run-down and somewhat unsafe.

One of the city's most alluring sites is **Stanley Park,** on the western end of the city-center peninsula (take bus #19). Surrounded by a **seawall promenade,** this thickly wooded park is crisscrossed with cycling and hiking trails, a testament to far-sighted urban planning. Within the park's boundaries lie various restaurants, tennis courts, the **Malkin Bowl** (an outdoor theater), and equipped beaches. Nature walks are given May-Sept. Tues. at 10am and July-Aug. at 7pm. They start from the Lost Lagoon bus loop (in the morning in May, June, and Sept.) or from Lumberman's Arch Water Park (all other times). Cavort alongside beluga whales at the **Vancouver Aquarium** (682-1118), on the eastern side of the park near the entrance (open daily 9:30am-8pm; $9.50, seniors and students $8.25, under 12 $6.25).

Follow the western side of the seawall south to **Sunset Beach Park** (738-8535), a strip of grass and beach that extends all the way to the Burrard Bridge. At the southern end of Sunset Beach splashes the **Aquatic Centre,** 1050 Beach Ave. (665-3424), a public facility with a 50m indoor saltwater pool, sauna, gymnasium, and diving tank. (Open Mon.-Thurs. 7am-10pm, Sat. 8am-9pm, Sun. 11am-9pm. Pool opens Mon.-Thurs. at 7am. Gym use $3.20; pool use $2.85.) Vancouverites frequent Kitsilano Beach, known to locals as **"Kits,"** on the other side of English Bay from Sunset Beach. Its heated saltwater outdoor pool (731-0011) has changing rooms, lockers and a snack bar. (Pool open June-Sept. Mon.-Fri. 9am-8:30pm, Sat.-Sun. 10am-8:30pm. $3, seniors $1.50, kids $2.) **Jericho Beach,** to the west, tends to be less crowded than Kits Beach. (Lifeguards on duty at most Vancouver beaches Victoria Day-Labor Day daily 11:30am-9pm.) Scramble down the cliffs to the southwest of the UBC campus to **Wreck Beach,** an unofficial, unsanctioned, unlifeguarded beach for the unclothed. Any UBC student can point you toward one of the semi-hidden access paths.

Jericho Beach begins a border of beaches and park lands that lines Point Grey and the **University of British Columbia (UBC).** At the University, visit the terrific **Museum of Anthropology,** 6393 N.W. Marine Dr. (822-3825 for recording, 822-5087 for operator), where a dramatic glass and concrete building houses totems and other massive sculptures by Native Americans (open Tues. 11am-9pm, Wed.-Sun. 11am-5pm. $5, seniors and students $2.50, under 6 free. Free Tues. after 5pm).

ENTERTAINMENT

To keep abreast of the entertainment scene, pick up a copy of the weekly *Georgia Straight* (an allusion to the body of water between mainland BC and Vancouver Island) or the new monthly *AF Magazine,* both free. Music of all genres can be heard in Vancouver's pubs and clubs; *Georgia Straight* has the rundown. Unfortunately, most clubs and bars shut down at 2am.

The Fringe Cafe, 3124 W. Broadway (738-6977). Hip, working-class crowd mixes with UBC students to create one of the hottest bars in town. Open Sun.-Thurs. noon-midnight, Fri.-Sat. noon-2am.

Graceland, 1250 Richards St. (688-2648). Warehouse space pulses to house music on Fri. and Sat. nights, reggae on Wed., and Elvis—well, Elvis is dead. Open Mon.-Fri. 9pm-2am, Sat. 8:30pm-2am, Sun. 8pm-2am.

Basin St. Cabaret, 23 West Cordova St. (688-5351). Bluesy jazz nightly. Local talent who play "cause they love the music" jam til the small hours. This new club is one of the hippest in Vancouver. No cover. Open daily 9pm-2am.

Spats, 1222 Hamilton St. (684-7321), in the warehouse district. Enter on the side facing Pacific Blvd. Most innovative of the dozen gay and lesbian clubs in the city. Open Mon.-Sat. 9pm-2am.

The **Vancouver Symphony Orchestra (VSO)** plays in the refurbished **Orpheum Theater,** 884 Granville St. (280-4444). The VSO ticketline is 280-3311. **Robson Square Conference Centre,** 800 Robson St. (660-2487), sponsors concerts, theater productions, exhibits, and films (free or nearly free) almost daily in summer and weekly the rest of the year, either on the plaza at the square or in the Centre itself.

Vancouver has an active theater community. The **Arts Club Theatre** (687-1644) hosts big-name theater and musicals, and the **Theatre in the Park** program (687-0174 for ticket information), in Stanley Park's Malkin Bowl, puts on a summer season of musical comedy.

SEASONAL EVENTS

Attend one of Vancouver's annual fairs, festivals, or celebrations to confirm rumors of the city's cosmopolitan nature. The famed **Vancouver Folk Music Festival** is held in mid-July in Jericho Park. For three days the best acoustic performers in North America give concerts and workshops. Tickets can be purchased for each day or for the whole weekend. (Tickets $26 per evening, $37 for the whole day.) The annual **Vancouver Shakespeare Festival** (734-0194; June-Aug. in Vanier Park) often needs volunteer ticket-takers and program-sellers, who work in return for free admission to the critically acclaimed shows.

The annual **Du Maurier International Jazz Festival Vancouver** (682-0706) in the third week of June features over five hundred performers and bands like Randy Wanless's Fab Forty and Charles Eliot's Largely Cookie. The 10-day festival is hot. Call 682-0706 or write to 435 W. Hastings, Vancouver V6V 1L4 for details.

Vancouver also celebrates its relationship with the sea. The Vancouver Maritime Museum in Vanier Park hosts the annual **Captain Vancouver Day** (737-2211) in mid-June to commemorate the 1792 exploration of Canada's west coast by Captain George Vancouver. In mid-July, the **Vancouver Sea Festival** (684-3378) schedules four days of parades, concerts, sporting events, fireworks, and salmon barbecues,

VICTORIA

including the notorious **Nanaimo to Vancouver Bathtub Race,** a journey across the rough waters of the Strait of Georgia for Gilgameshes with rubber duckies.

■ Near Vancouver

To the east, the town of **Deep Cove** maintains the salty atmosphere of a fishing village. Sea otters and seals cavort on the pleasant Indian Arm beaches. Take bus #210 from Pender St. to the Phibbs Exchange on the north side of Second Narrows Bridge. From there, take bus #211 or 212. **Cates Park,** at the end of Dollarton Hwy. on the way to Deep Cove, has popular swimming and scuba waters and makes a good day bike trip out of Vancouver. Bus #211 also leads to **Mount Seymour Provincial Park.** Trails leave from Mt. Seymour Rd., and a paved road winds 8km to the top. One hundred campsites ($8 per site) are available, and the skiing is superb.

For an easy hike offering fantastic views of the city, head for **Lynn Canyon Park** in North Vancouver. The suspension bridge here is free and uncrowded, unlike its more publicized twin in Capilano Canyon. Take bus #228 from the North Vancouver SeaBus terminal and walk ½km to the bridge.

■■■ VICTORIA

The sun may have set on the British empire years ago, but like an aging, eccentric Redcoat, Victoria still dresses up and marches to the beat of a bygone era. Set among the rough-hewn logging and fishing towns of Vancouver Island, this jeweled capital city of British Columbia evinces enough reserve and propriety to chill even the Windsors. On warm summer days, Anglophilic residents sip their afternoon teas on the lawns of Tudor-style homes in the suburbs, while downtown, horse-drawn carriages clatter through the streets.

PRACTICAL INFORMATION

Emergency: 911.
Visitor Information: Tourism Victoria, 812 Wharf St., Victoria V8W 1T3 (382-2127), in the Inner Harbour. An unbelievable number of pamphlets on the area. Open daily 9am-9pm; in winter 9am-5pm.
Buses: Pacific Coast Lines (PCL) and its affiliate **Island Coach Lines,** 700 Douglas St. at Belleville (385-4411). Connects all major points and most minor ones, though fares can be steep. To: Nanaimo (7 per day, $14.70), Vancouver (8 per day,$21), Seattle (daily at 10am, $29). Lockers $2 per 24 hrs.
Ferries: BC Ferry (656-0757 for recording, 386-3431 for operator). Ferries run 5:30am-10pm to Vancouver ($6.50, bike $2.50, car $20). Take bus #70 to the terminal. **Washington State Ferries** (381-1551). From Sidney, BC to Anacortes, WA: 2 per day in summer, 1 per day in winter. Fares vary by season (call for rates and schedules). Take bus #70 to the terminal.
Public Transportation: Victoria Regional Transit (382-6161). Daily service throughout the city, with major bus connections at the corner of Douglas and Yates St. downtown. Single-zone travel $1.50, multi-zone (to Sidney and the Butchart Gardens) $2. Daily passes for unlimited single-zone travel available at the visitors center and 7-11 stores for $4 (seniors and under 12 $3).
Car Rental: Budget Discount Car Rentals, 727 Courtney St. (388-7874). (Not to be confused with the far more expensive Budget Rent-A-Car on the same block.) Must be 19 with a major credit card. Used cars from $22 per day plus 10¢ per km. Open daily 7:30am-5:30pm.
Bike Rental: Biker Bill's, 1007 Langley St. (361-0091). 18-speed mountain bikes $5 per hr., $20 for 24 hrs. Lock and helmet included. Deposit required. Open daily 8am-8pm.
Help Lines: Crisis Line, 386-6323. **Rape Crisis,** 383-3232. Both 24 hrs.
Post Office: Victoria CRO, 714 Yates (363-3887). Open Mon.-Fri. 8:30am-5pm.
  Postal Code: V8W 1L0.
Area Code: 604.

Ferries and buses connect Victoria to many cities in British Columbia and Washington. The city of Victoria enfolds the Inner Harbour; **Government Street** and **Douglas Street** are the main north-south thoroughfares.

ACCOMMODATIONS

Victoria Youth Hostel (HI-C), 516 Yates St. (385-4511), V8W 1K8, at Wharf St. downtown. 104 beds in the newly remodeled Victoria Heritage Building. Big, modern, and spotless. Kitchen and laundry facilities. Family rooms available. Open daily 7:30am-midnight. $13.50, nonmembers $18.50.

YWCA, 880 Courtney St. (386-7511), at Quadra, within easy walking distance of downtown. Women only. Heated pool and private rooms with shared baths. Check-in 8:30am-6pm. Check-out 6-11am. Singles $36.27. Doubles $53.82.

Victoria Backpackers Hostel, 1418 Fernwood Rd. (386-4471). Take bus #1, 10, 11, 14, 27, or 28 to Fernwood and Douglas. Shared rooms $10, private $25-30.

Battery Street Guest House, 670 Battery St. (385-4632), 1 block from the ocean near Government St. Non-smokers only. Singles $35-55. Doubles $55-75.

Fort Victoria Camping, 127 Burnett (479-8112), 7km NW of downtown, off the Trans-Canada Hwy. Free hot showers. Sites $15 for 2 people. Full hookup $18.

FOOD

Victoria's predilection for anachronisms surfaces in its culinary customs. Victorians actually doth take tea. No visit to the city would be complete without participating in the ceremony at least once.

Eugene's, 1280 Broad St. (381-5456). Vegetarian souvlaki $3, dinners $5-7.50. *Rizogalo* or *bougatsa* is a nice change for breakfast ($2). Open Mon.-Fri. 8am-8pm, Sat. 10am-8pm.

Goodies, 1005 Broad St., 2nd floor (382-2124), between Broughton and Fort. Build your own omelette for $4.45 plus 65¢ per ingredient, or choose from a list of sandwiches like the "Natural High" (mushroom, cheese, and avocado $5). Tex-Mex dinners $6-8. Breakfast served until 3:30pm. Open daily 7am-9pm.

Rising Star Bakery, 1320 Broad St. (386-2534). Giant cheese croissant, fresh out of the oven ($1). Open Mon.-Sat. 7:30am-5:30pm, Sun. 8:30am-2:30pm.

Ferris' Oyster and Burger Bar, 536 Yates St. (360-1824), next to the hostel. Almond tofu burger ($4.25) is a rare find. Open Mon. 11:30am-8pm, Tues.-Fri. 11:30am-10pm, Sat. 11:30am-11pm. HI members discount.

The Blethering Place, 2250 Oak Bay Ave. (598-1413), at Monterey St. in upright Oak Bay. Afternoon tea served with scones, Devonshire cream tarts, English trifle, muffins, and sandwiches all baked on the premises ($9). Open daily 8am-9pm.

SIGHTS AND ACTIVITIES

Most sights cluster together, except for the elegant residential neighborhoods and the parks and beaches, which are better accessed by car or bus. The first stop for every visitor should be the **Royal British Columbian Museum,** 675 Belleville St. (387-3014 for recording, 387-3701 for operator). Arguably the best museum in Canada, it chronicles the geological and cultural histories of the province. The extensive exhibits of Native American art, culture and history include full-scale replicas of various forms of shelter used centuries ago. (Open daily 9:30am-7pm; Oct.-April 10am-5:30pm. 2-day admission $5, seniors, disabled persons and students with ID or HI card $3, kids 6-18 $2. Free after 5:45pm and on Mon. Oct.-April.) Behind the museum, **Thunderbird Park** displays a striking bevy of totems and longhouses.

Across the street from the museum are the imposing **Parliament Buildings,** 501 Belleville St. (387-3046), home of the provincial government. The 10-story dome and Brunelleschi-esque vestibule are gilded with almost 50 oz. of gold (free tours from the main steps daily 9am-5pm; every 20 min. in summer, every hr. in winter).

South of the Inner Harbor, **Beacon Hill Park** (take bus #5) surveys the Strait of Juan de Fuca splendiferously. East of the Inner Harbor, **Craigdarroch Castle,** 1050 Joan Crescent (592-5323), embodies Victoria's wealth (take bus #10, 11 or 14). The house was built in 1890 by Robert Dunsmuir, a BC coal and railroad tycoon, in order to tempt his wife away from their native Scotland. (Open daily 9am-7pm, in winter 10am-5pm. $5, students $4.)

Almost worth the exorbitant entrance fee are the stunning **Butchart Gardens,** 800 Benvennto, 22km north of Victoria (652-4422 Mon.-Fri. 9am-5pm; 652-5256 for recording). Jennie Butchart began the rose, Japanese and Italian gardens in 1904 in an attempt to reclaim the wasteland that was her husband's quarry and cement plant. From mid-May through September, the whole area is lit at dusk, and the gardens host variety shows and cartoons; Saturday nights in July and August, the skies shimmer with fireworks displays. Take bus #75. Motorists should consider taking the **Scenic Marine Drive,** which follows the coastline for 45 min. (Gardens open daily 9am; call for closing times. Summer admission $10.50, ages 13-17 $7.50, ages 5-12 $3; in winter $7, $5, and $2. Readmission within 24 hrs. $1.)

ENTERTAINMENT AND NIGHTLIFE

You can get an exhaustive listing of what's where in the free weekly *Monday Magazine,* available throughout the city. For an eclectic mix of jazz, blues, folk, and whatever else is in town, check out **Harpo's Cabaret,** 15 Bastion Sq. (385-5333), at Wharf St. (open Mon.-Sat. 9pm-2am, Sun. 8pm-midnight; cover around $5). **Rumors,** 1325 Government St. (385-0566), has a gay and lesbian clientele for drinking and dancing (open Mon.-Sat. 9pm-3am).

The **Victoria Symphony Society,** 846 Broughton St. (385-6515), performs under conductor Peter McCoppin, and the **University of Victoria Auditorium,** Finnerty Rd. (721-8480), is home to a variety of student productions. The **Pacific Opera** performs at the McPherson Playhouse, 3 Centennial Sq. (386-6121), at the corner of Pandora and Government St. The **Folkfest** in late June and early July celebrates Canada's birthday (July 1) and the country's "unity in diversity" with performances by "P.C." and "C.D." (Culturally Diverse) musicians. Occurring at the same time, the **JazzFest** is sponsored by the Victoria Jazz Society (388-4423 or 386-2441).

▓ Yukon Territory

Native Americans recognized the majesty of this land when they dubbed the Yukon River "Yuchoo," or Big River. Gold-hungry white settlers streamed in at the end of the 19th century, interested in more metallic aspects of the land, and left almost as quickly. Although the Yukon and Northern British Columbia were the first regions of North America to be settled some 20,000 years ago, today they remain largely untouched and inaccessible. With an average of only one person per 15 sq. km, the loneliness of the area is overwhelming—as is its sheer physical beauty, a reward for those willing to put up with nasty, often frigid weather and poor road conditions.

For a golden description of the Yukon, consult *Let's Go: Alaska & The Pacific Northwest,* a book riddled with nuggets of wisdom.

■■■ KLUANE NATIONAL PARK

On July 16, 1741—St. Elias Day—Captain Vitus Bering, on board a sealer out of Russia, sighted the mountains of what is now the southwest Yukon. The pristine St. Elias Mountains have remained almost completely undeveloped. A brief gold rush in the early 1900s and the later construction of the Alaska Highway in 1942 have led to what limited development there is around the perimeter of the mountains. In 1976, the Canadian government gazetted the entire southwest corner of the Yukon and proclaimed it **Kluane** (Kloo-AH-nee) **National Park.** ("Kluane" is a southern Tutch-one word, meaning "the place of many fish.") Kluane is Canadian wilderness at its most rugged, unspoiled, and beautiful.

The "Green Belt" along the eastern park boundary, at the feet of the mountains' Kluane Range, supports the greatest diversity of plant and animal species in northern Canada. Beyond the Kluane loom the glaciers of the Icefield Range—home to Canada's highest peaks, including the tallest of all, 19,850-foot Mt. Logan.

Practical Information Kluane's 22,015 sq. km are bounded by Kluane Game Sanctuary and the Alaska Hwy. to the north, and Haines Rd. to the east. The town of Haines Junction is located at the eastern park boundary, 158km west of Whitehorse. Pick up free info at the **Haines Junction Visitor Centre,** on Logan St. in Haines Junction (Canadian Park Service 634-2251; Tourism Yukon 634-2345; open mid-May-mid-Sept. daily 9am-9pm), which also sponsors a number of guided hikes and campfire talks from mid-June-Aug. **Alaska Direct** (800-770-6652) runs three buses per week from Haines Jct. to: Anchorage, AK (US$125); Fairbanks, AK (US$100); Haines, AK (US$30); Whitehorse (US$20). In a **medical emergency,** call 634-2213; in case of **fire,** 634-2222; the **police station** is at the junction of Haines Rd. and the Alaska Hwy. (635-5555; if no answer, call 1-667-5555). The **Postal Code** is Y0B 1L0; the **area code** is 403.

Camping, Accommodations, and Food Stay outdoors and fall victim to bloodthirsty mosquitoes; head for shelter and fall victim to exorbitant hotel rates (solution: get some bug spray, bite the bullet, and pitch a tent). If you're allergic to bug spray, try **Kathleen Lake Lodge,** Mile 142 Haines Rd., 25km south of Haines Junction (634-2319), and stay two to a cabin with private bathtubs but no shower. The restaurant is a bit pricey, but the watchdog is free. (Single $37, double $47.) If you're a stoic, hit the **Pine Lake Campground,** about 7km east of Haines Junction on the Alaska Hwy. (634-2345), with 40 sites, seven of which are tent only, with pit toilets, hand-pumped cold water, nearby hiking, and a boat launch (sites $8).

Outdoors in the Park Kluane National Park offers an opportunity to explore wild wilderness. There are few actual trails in the park; the major ones are the 4km **Dezadeash River Loop** which begins at the Haines Junction Visitor Centre, the 15km **Auriol Trail** which starts from Haines Rd. Km 248 and is an excellent overnight hike, and the 85km **Cottonwood Trail,** a 4-6-day trek beginning either 27 or 55km south of Haines Junction on Haines Rd. Cottonwood is a loop trail which offers 25km of trail above tree-line and a short detour up an adjacent ridge which provides a view of the Ice Field Ranges and Mount Logan on clear days.

■ ■ ■ WHITEHORSE

Named for the once perilous Whitehorse Rapids (now tamed by a dam), once said to resemble an entourage of galloping pale mares, Whitehorse marks the first navigable point on the Yukon River. Capital of the Yukon since 1953, Whitehorse now boasts a population of more than 20,000 and is as cosmopolitan as one might expect a city of its size to be—yet it still maintains much of its century-old gold rush architecture, and it serves as a gateway to the surrounding country.

Practical Information The **Whitehorse Visitor Reception Centre,** on the Alaska Hwy. next to the airport (667-2915), has an entire forest's worth of free brochures and maps. The Centre's state-of-the-art bathroom is one of the great unsung pleasures of the Canadian North. (Open mid-May-mid-Sept. daily 8am-8pm.) Or, get info by writing **Tourism Yukon,** P.O. Box 2703, Whitehorse, YT Y1A C26.

Canadian Airlines (668-4466, for reservations 668-3535) soars to: Calgary (2-3 per day, $519); Edmonton (3 per day, $448); Vancouver (3 per day, $448). **Grey-**

hound labors out of town from 2191 2nd Ave. (667-2223). All buses run Tues., Thurs., and Sat. at noon. To: Vancouver ($281); Edmonton ($222); Dawson Creek ($155). (Open Mon.-Fri. 8:30am-5:30pm, Sat. 8am-noon, Sun. 5-9am.) **Alaskan Express** also operates from the Greyhound depot (667-2223). Buses run late May-mid-Sept. to: Anchorage (4 per week, US$179); Haines (4 per week, US$76); Fairbanks (4 per week, US$149); Skagway (daily, US$52).

There is no main **post office** in Whitehorse. For general services, go to 211 Main St. (668-5847; open Mon.-Fri. 8am-6pm, Sat. 9am-5pm). For general delivery, head for 3rd and Wood, in the Yukon News Bldg. (668-3824; open Mon.-Sat. 7am-7pm). General Delivery **Postal Code** for last names beginning with the letters A-L is Y1A 3S7; for M-Z it's Y1A 3S8. Whitehorse's **area code** is 403.

Accommodations and Food The **Fourth Avenue Residence (HI-C),** 4051 4th Ave. (667-4471), boasts cooking and laundry facilities, good security, and free use of the city pool next door. (Hostel beds in a shared triple $16, nonmembers $18. Private singles $38. Doubles $50.) The **Fort Yukon Hotel,** 2163 2nd Ave. (667-2594), near shopping malls and Greyhound, has old but untarnished rooms (singles from $40; doubles from $45). Camping in Whitehorse is sparse. Tenters praying for a hot shower should wend their way to the group of campgrounds clustered 10-20km south of town on the Alaska Highway. **Robert Service Campground,** 1km out on South Access Rd., is covenient, with firewood, drinking water, toilets, metered showers. (Open late May-early Sept. Gate closed midnight-6am. Sites $13.)

Don't be discouraged by the dilapidated exteriors of many Whitehorse gastro-centers; the insides are usually well-worn but cozy. Prices are reasonable by Yukon standards (which still means expensive to outsiders). The **No Pop Sandwich Shop,** 312 Steele (668-3227), is an artsy alcove very popular with Whitehorse's small suit-and-tie crowd. You can order a Beltch (BLT and cheese, $4.50), but not a coke here—it's strictly fruit juice and milk. (Open Mon.-Thurs. 8am-9pm, Fri. 8am-10pm, Sat. 10am-8pm, Sun. 10am-3pm.) **Mom's Kitchen,** 2157 2nd Ave. (668-6620), at Alexander, whips up pretty good omelettes ($6-9) and a three-course Chinese special for $7.50 (open Mon.-Fri. 6:30am-8pm, Sat. 6:30am-5pm, Sun. 7am-3pm).

Sights and Activities The restored *S.S. Klondike* (667-4511), on S. Access Rd., is a dry-docked sternwheeler that recalls the days when the Yukon River was the city's sole artery of survival. Pick up a ticket for a free tour at the information booth at the parking lot entrance (open May-Sept. daily 9am-6pm). **Miles Canyon** whispers 2km south of town off South Access Rd. Once the location of the feared Whitehorse rapids, this dammed stretch of the Yukon now swirls silently under the first bridge to span the river's banks. The oddly placed speaking podium nearby is perfect for souls who wish to address an apostrophe to the mighty river.

The **MacBride Museum** (667-2709), 1st Ave. and Wood St., features memorabilia from the early days of the Yukon, including photographs of Whitehorse as a tent city. The log cabin in the museum courtyard, built by Sam McGee in 1899, has thus far managed to avoid the flames that consumed its occupant. (Open daily May-Aug., hours vary. $3.25, seniors and students $2.25, families $7.50.)

Two-hour river tours are available on two different lines. From June-Sept., the **Youcon Kat** (668-2927) will take you on a jaunt downstream from the hydroelectric dam. Boats leave daily at 1, 4, and 7pm from the ramshackle pier at 1st and Steele. ($14, children $7.) **Schwatka Tours** (668-4716) runs upstream from the dam through what's left of the rapids (the dam raised the water level almost 10m). Tours leave daily at 2 and 7pm from the boat dock on S. Access Rd. ($14, kids $7.)

Canada USA Alaska
ADVENTURES
Mexico Guatemala Belize

62 ADVENTURE TOURS
Camping/Hotel Treks
3 Days–13 Weeks
Small International Groups
(13 People Maximum)
GUARANTEED DEPARTURES

RIVER RAFTING
In Colorado
5 Days

CAR PURCHASE
With Guaranteed Repurchase
(Minimum Age 18)
Camping Equipment
(Minimum Age 18)

DISCOVER SUNTREK

For your free catalog see your travel agent or contact SUNTREK:

USA/Canada:
Sun Plaza
77 West Third Street
Santa Rosa, CA 95401
Phone (707) 523-1800
Fax: (707) 523-1911
Reservations Toll-Free:
1 (800) 292-9696

Australia:
The Trek House
62 Mary Street
Surry Hills, Sydney
NSW 2010
Phone: 02 281 8000
Fax: 02 281 2722
Reservations Toll-Free:
008 80 5454

Germany:
Sedanstr. 21
D-8000 Munich 80
Phone: 089 480 28 31
Fax: 089 480 24 11

Switzerland:
Birmensdorferstr. 187
CH-8003 Zurich
Phone: 01 462 61 61
Fax: 01 462 65 45

"SPECIALIZING IN ADVENTURE TRAVEL SINCE 1974"

■ INDEX

Downtown Washington, D.C.

Central Washington, D.C.

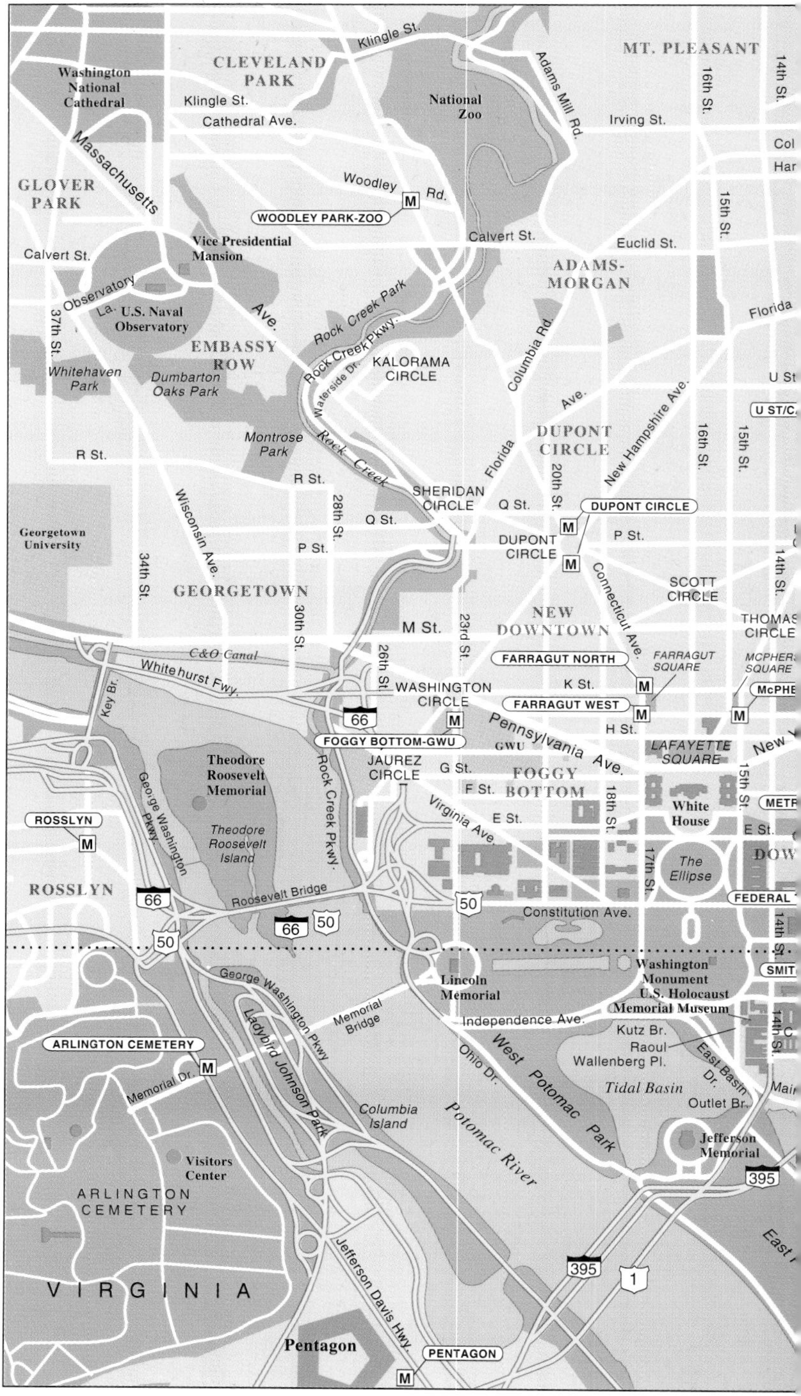

Central Washington, D.C.

BROOKLAND-CUA Ⓜ Lawrence St.

Catholic University

Michigan Ave.

Trinity College

7th St. 9th St. 13th St.

Franklin St.

McMillan Reservoir

Rhode Island Ave.

Howard University

Georgia Ave.

Ⓜ RHODE ISLAND AVE

N ↑

5th St. 4th St.

LE DROIT PARK

Rhode Island Ave.

7th St.

Lincoln Rd.

9th St.

1

Ⓜ SHAW/HOWARD UNIV.

Florida Ave.

Brentwood Park

New Jersey Ave.

P St.

Mount Olivet Rd.

Gallaudet University

U.S. National Arboretum

West Virginia Ave.

Ⓜ MT VERNON SQ-UDC

New York Ave.

50

North Capitol St.

1st St.

K St.

Florida Ave.

Bladensburg Ave.

15th St.

NON RE

TOWN seum can tl.

H St.

4th St.

H St.

Ⓜ GALLERY PLACE

2nd St.

Ⓜ UNION STATION

Union Station

COLUMBUS CIRCLE

6th St. 7th St.

Maryland Ave.

11th St.

Tennessee Ave.

7th St. F St.

Ⓜ JUDICIARY SQ

3rd St. E St.

Stanton Park

395

Louisiana Ave.

Delaware Ave.

1st St.

4th St.

Massachusetts Ave.

C St.

S Ⓜ

Pennsylvania Ave.

Constitution Ave.

ian Museums

U.S. Capitol

CAPITOL HILL

E. Capitol St.

Capitol Plaza

Folger Shakespeare Library

Lincoln Park

E. Capitol St.

MALL

dence Ave.

E. Capitol St.

D.C. Armory

Maryland Ave.

Seward Park

North Carolina Ave.

Independence Ave.

Ⓜ FEDERAL CENTER SW

2nd St.

South Carolina Ave.

Ⓜ STADIUM ARMORY Ⓜ

Ⓜ FANT PLAZA

4th St.

South Capitol St.

New Jersey Ave.

Ⓜ CAPITOL SOUTH

Ⓜ Pennsylvania Ave.

19th St.

395

F St.

Ⓜ EASTERN MARKET

Ⓜ POTOMAC AVENUE

Southwest Fwy.

G St.

11th St.

Ⓜ

SW

SE

Southeast Fwy.

Potomac Ave.

M St. Ⓜ

Ⓜ NAVY YARD

Ⓜ

Anacostia River

Sousa Bridge

Ⓜ WATERFRONT

Washington Navy Yard

11th St. Bridge

Anacostia Bridge

Anacostia Park

n Channel

0 — 1500 feet

0 — 500 meters

The Mall Area, Washington, D.C.

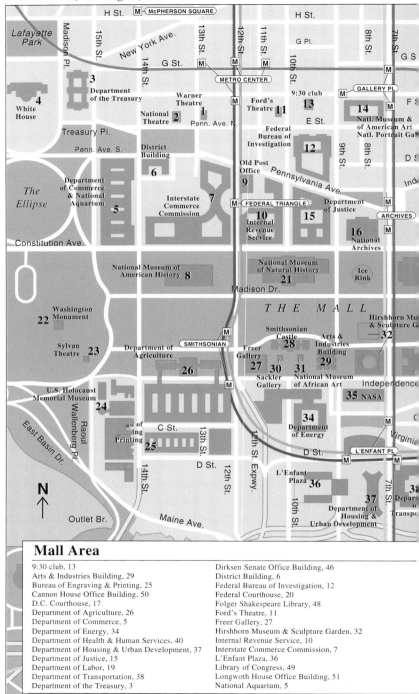

Mall Area

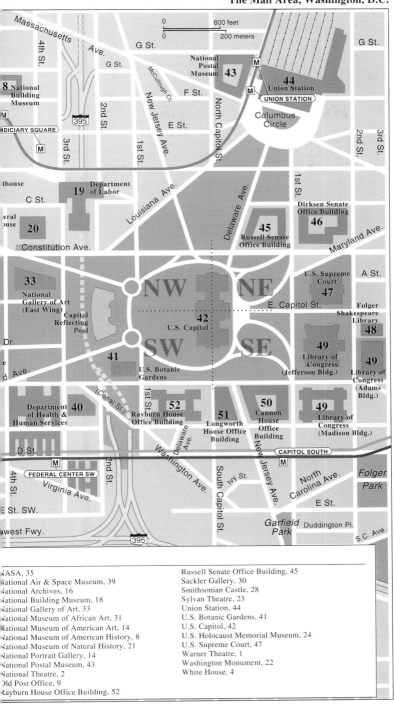

The Mall Area, Washington, D.C.

Massachusetts
4th St.
Ave.
G St.
G St.
G St.

0
600 feet
0
200 meters

National
Postal
Museum **43**

McCullough Ct.

New Jersey Ave.

M

44
Union Station

M

UNION STATION

8 National
Building
Museum

2nd St.

F St.

E St.

North Capitol St.

Columbus
Circle

3rd St.

2nd St.

M

DICIARY SQUARE

395

3rd St.

1st St.

1st St.

thouse

C St.

19 Department
of Labor

Louisiana Ave.

Delaware Ave.

Dirksen Senate
Office Building
46

eral
ouse

20

Constitution Ave.

45
Russell Senate
Office Building

U.S. Supreme
Court
47

Maryland Ave.

A St.

Folger
Shakespeare
Library
48

33
National
Gallery of Art
(East Wing)

Capitol
Reflecting
Pool

NW

NE

E. Capitol St.

Dr.

e
d Ave.

41

SW

SE

42
U.S. Capitol

U.S. Botanic
Gardens

49
Library of
Congress
(Jefferson Bldg.)

49
Library of
Congress
(Adams
Bldg.)

(Canal St.)

1st St.

Department
of Health &
Human Services
40

52
Rayburn House
Office Building

Delaware Ave.

51
Longworth
House Office
Building

New Jersey Ave.

50
Cannon
House
Office
Building

49
Library of
Congress
(Madison Bldg.)

D St.

M

FEDERAL CENTER SW

2nd St.

Washington Ave.

South Capitol St.

Ivy St.

CAPITOL SOUTH

M

North
Carolina Ave.

Folger
Park

4th St.

Virginia Ave.

E St. SW.

west Fwy.

395

Garfield
Park

Duddington Pl.

E St.

S.C. Ave.

White House Area, Foggy Bottom, and Nearby Arlington

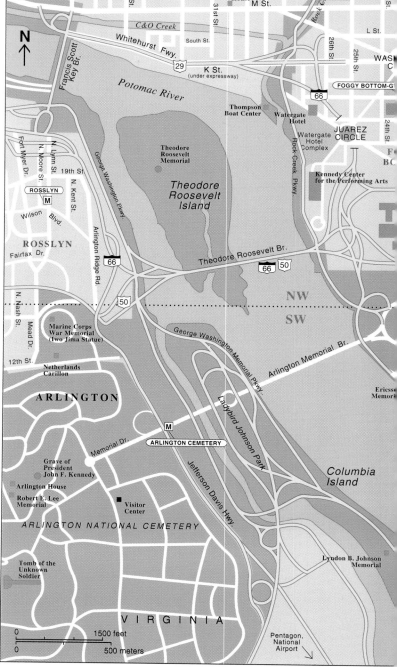

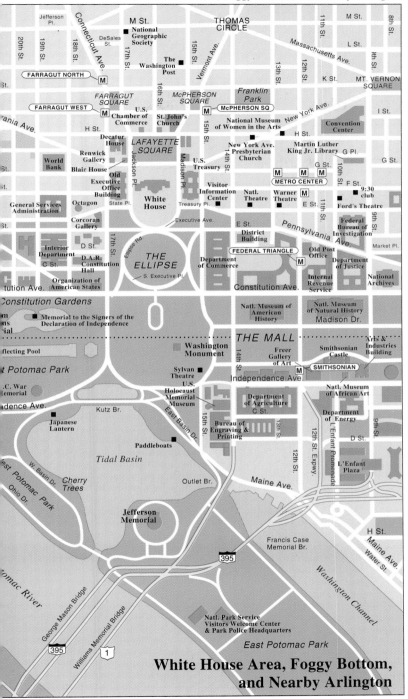

White House Area, Foggy Bottom, and Nearby Arlington

Metrorail System, Washington, D.C.

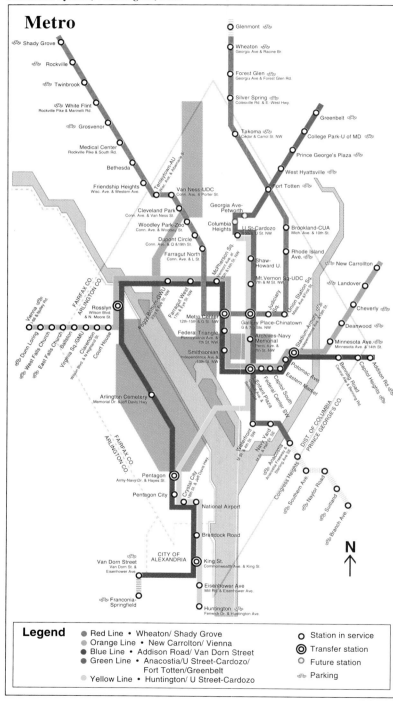

Metro

Glenmont ⟨P⟩

Shady Grove ⟨P⟩

Wheaton
Georgia Ave. & Racine Br.

Rockville ⟨P⟩

Forest Glen ⟨P⟩
Georgia Ave. & Forest Glen Rd.

Twinbrook ⟨P⟩

Silver Spring ⟨P⟩
Colesville Rd. & E.-West Hwy.

White Flint ⟨P⟩
Rockville Pike & Marinelli Rd.

Greenbelt ⟨P⟩

Grosvenor ⟨P⟩

Takoma ⟨P⟩
Cedar & Carrol St. NW

College Park-U of MD ⟨P⟩

Medical Center
Rockville Pike & South Rd.

Prince George's Plaza ⟨P⟩

Bethesda

West Hyattsville ⟨P⟩

Tenleytown-AU
Wisc. Ave. & Albemarle St.

Fort Totten ⟨P⟩

Friendship Heights
Wisc. Ave. & Western Ave.

Van Ness-UDC
Conn. Ave. & Porter St.

Georgia Ave-
Petworth

Cleveland Park
Conn. Ave. & Van Ness St.

Columbia
Heights

U St-Cardozo
13th & U St. NW

Brookland-CUA
Mich. Ave. & 10th St.

Woodley Park-Zoo
Conn. Ave. & Woodley St.

Dupont Circle
Conn. Ave. & Q &19th St.

Shaw-
Howard U.

Rhode Island
Ave. ⟨P⟩

New Carrollton ⟨P⟩

Farragut North
Conn. Ave. & L St.

Mt.Vernon Sq-UDC
7th & M St. NW

Landover ⟨P⟩

Vienna ⟨P⟩
Saintsbury & Nutley Rd.

McPherson Sq.
Vermont at 14th & I St. NW

Union Station ⟨P⟩
Mass. Ave.& First St.

Cheverly ⟨P⟩

FAIRFAX CO.
ARLINGTON CO.

Rosslyn
Wilson Blvd.
& N. Moore St.

Farragut West
17th & Eye St. NW

Judiciary

Deanwood ⟨P⟩

Foggy Bottom-GWU
23rd & Eye St. NW

Gallery Place-Chinatown
G & 7th Sts. NW

Stadium-Armory
Independence Ave. & 19th St.

Minnesota Ave. ⟨P⟩
Minnesota Ave. & 14th St.

Dunn Loring ⟨P⟩

West Falls Church ⟨P⟩

East Falls Church ⟨P⟩

Virginia Sq. (GMU)
Wilson Blvd. & Highland St.

Clarendon

Court House

Metro Center
12th-15th & G St. NW

Federal Triangle
Pennsylvania Ave. &
7th St.

Archives-Navy
Memorial
Penn. Ave. &
7th St. NW

Potomac Ave.

Benning Road ⟨P⟩
Central Ave. & Benning Rd.

Capitol Heights ⟨P⟩

Addison Rd. ⟨P⟩

Smithsonian
Independence Ave. &
13th St. NW

Eastern Market

Arlington Cemetery
Memorial Dr.& Jeff Davis Hwy.

Capitol South

Federal Center SW

FAIRFAX CO.
ARLINGTON CO.

Waterfront
4th & M St. SW

Navy Yard
M & New Jersey Ave. SE

DIST. OF COLUMBIA
PRINCE GEORGE'S CO.

Anacostia
Anacostia Freeway &
Sterling Ave.

Congress Heights

Southern Ave. ⟨P⟩

Naylor Road

Suitland ⟨P⟩

Pentagon
Army-Navy Dr. & Hayes St.

Crystal City
18th & Jeff Davis Hwy.

Pentagon City

Branch Ave. ⟨P⟩

National Airport

N
↑

Braddock Road

CITY OF
ALEXANDRIA

Van Dorn Street ⟨P⟩
Van Dorn St. &
Eisenhower Ave.

King St. ⟨P⟩
Commonwealth Ave. & King St.

Eisenhower Ave
Mill Rd. & Eisenhower Ave.

Franconia-
Springfield ⟨P⟩

Huntington ⟨P⟩
Fenwick Dr. & Huntington Ave.

Legend

- ● Red Line • Wheaton/ Shady Grove
- ● Orange Line • New Carrolton/ Vienna
- ● Blue Line • Addison Road/ Van Dorn Street
- ● Green Line • Anacostia/U Street-Cardozo/
  Fort Totten/Greenbelt
- ● Yellow Line • Huntington/ U Street-Cardozo

- ○ Station in service
- ◎ Transfer station
- ○ Future station
- ⟨P⟩ Parking

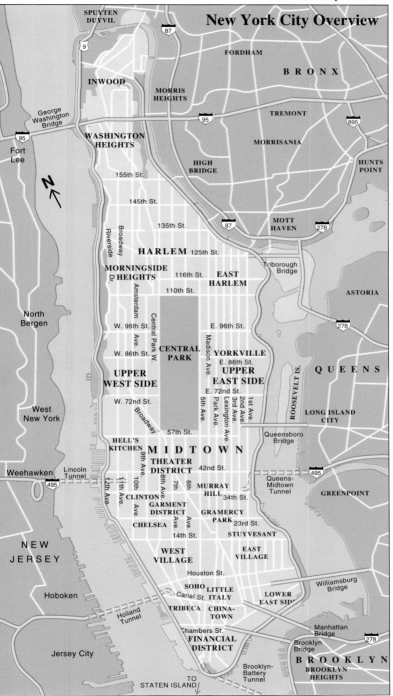

New York City Overview

New York City Subways

Subways

Stops are not served by all trains at all times.
Refer to Transit Authority map for descriptions
of express, local, and limited service.

LEGEND

K,B Line
168 St Terminal

179 St/ Jamaica F,R
Jamaica Center E,J,Z
169 St
Parsons Blvd
Sutphin Blvd
Van Wyck
Jamaica Van Wyck
121 St
111 St
102 St
Woodhaven Blvd
Forest Pkwy
Elderts La
Cypress Hills
Crescent St
Rockaway Blvd
A Lefferts Blvd
111 St
104 St
88 St/Boyd Av
80 St/Hudson St
Grant Av
Euclid Av
Shepherd Av
Van Siclen Av
Liberty Av
Aqueduct Racetrack
Aqueduct/ N Conduit Av
Howard Beach/ JFK Airport
Broad Channel
Far Rockaway/ Mott Av A,H
Beach 25 St/ Wavecrest
Beach 36 St/ Edgemere
Beach 44 St/ Frank Av
Beach 60 St/ Straiton Av
Beach 67 St/ Gaston
Beach 90 St/ Holland
Beach 98 St/ Playland
Beach 105 St/ Seaside
C,H Rockaway Pk/ Beach 116 St
M Metropolitan Av
Fresh Pond Rd
Forest Av
Myrtle Av/Wycoff Av
Seneca Av
Halsey St.
Knickerbocker
Norwood Av
Cleveland St
Van Siclen Av
Alabama Av
Bushwick/ Aberdeen
Wilson Av
Central
Chauncey St
Halsey St
Ralph Av
Gates Av
Kosciusko St
Utica Av
Kingston Av
Rockaway Av
Broadway/ Eastern Pkwy
Atlantic Av
Sutter Av
3 New Lots Av
Van Siclen Av
Pennsylvania Av
Livonia Av
New Lots Av
E 105 St
Rockaway Pkwy L
Junius Av
Rockaway Av
Saratoga Av
Sutter Av/ Rutland Rd
Montrose Av
Morgan Av
Jefferson St
DeKalb Av
Graham Av
Grand St
Lorimer St
Flushing Av
Myrtle Av
Broadway
Marcy Av
Hewes St
Flushing Av
Myrtle Av/Willoughby Av
Bedford Av/Nostrand Av
Classon Av
Clinton Av
Fulton
Lafayette Av
Clinton Av
S Franklin Av
Nostrand Av
Kingston Av
Franklin Av
Nostrand Av
President St
Sterling St
Winthrop St
Church Av
Beverley Rd
Newkirk Av
Flatbush Av/ Brooklyn College 2,5
Essex St/ Delancey St
E Broadway
York St
High St/ Bklyn Br
Jay St/Borough Hall
Court St/Borough Hall
Hoyt St
Hoyt St/Schermerhorn St
4 Av/ 9 St
Bergen St
Grand Army Pl
Eastern Pkwy/ Bklyn Mus
7 Av
7 Av/ Park Slope
S Prospect Pk
Park-side
Church Av
Beverley Rd
Cortelyou Rd
Newkirk Av
Av H/Brooklyn College
Av J
Av M
Kings Hwy
Av U
Neck Rd
Sheepshead Bay
Q Brighton Beach
Ocean Pkwy
W 8th St/ Aquarium
Church Av
Ditmas Av
18 Av
Av I
22 Av/ Bay Pkwy
Av N
Av P
Kings Hwy
Av X
15 St/ Prospect Pk
Ft Hamilton Pkwy
Stillwell Av/ Coney Island B,D,F,N
South Ferry 1,9
SEE DETAIL ABOVE RIGHT
Smith St/9 St G
Union St
4 Av/9 St
Prospect Av
25 St
36 St
45 St
53 St
59 St
Bay Ridge Av
77 St
86 St
95 St/ Fort Hamilton R
9 Av
Ft Hamilton Pkwy
55 St
8 Av
Fort Hamilton Pkwy
62 St/ New Utrecht Av
71 St
79 St
18 Av
20 Av
Bay Pkwy
18 Av
20 Av
22 Av/ Bay Pkwy
M
25 Av
Bay 50 Av

Downtown Manhattan

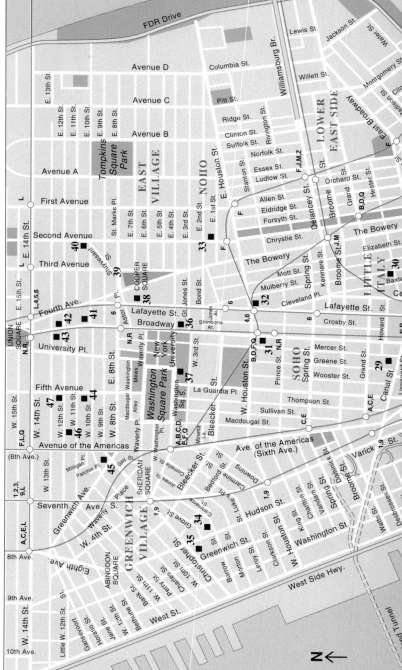

Downtown Manhattan

Midtown Manhattan

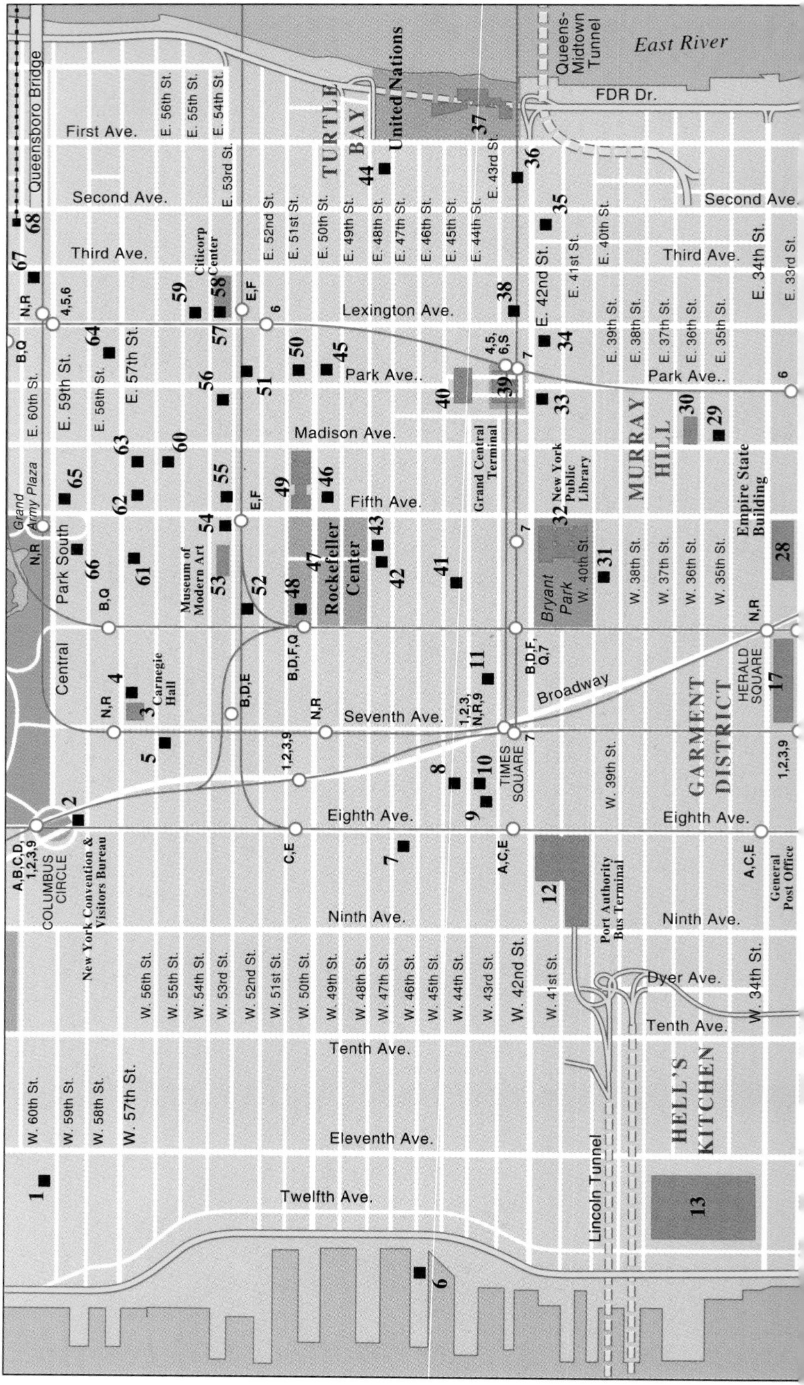

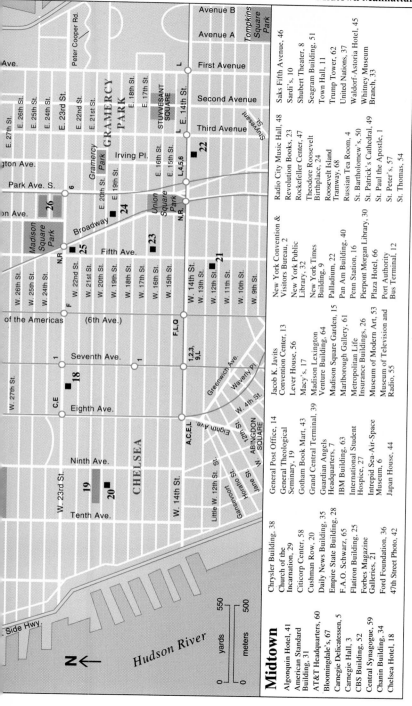

Uptown

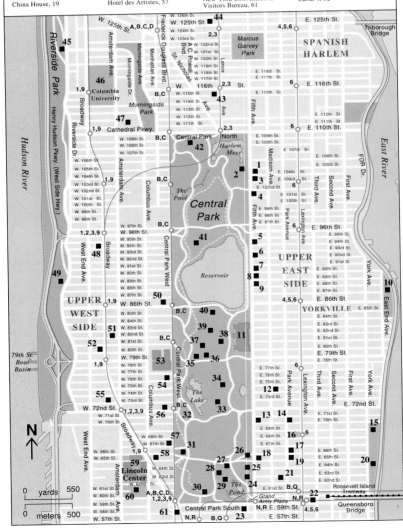